Tolley's Capital Gains Tax 2017-18

CW01597778

by

Philippa Cave MEng FCA CTA

Tolley®

Members of the LexisNexis Group worldwide

United Kingdom	RELX (UK) Limited trading as LexisNexis, 1–3 Strand, London WC2N 5JR
Australia	Reed International Books Australia Pty Ltd trading as LexisNexis, Chatswood, New South Wales
Austria	LexisNexis Verlag ARD Orac GmbH & Co KG, Vienna
Benelux	LexisNexis Benelux, Amsterdam
Canada	LexisNexis Canada, Markham, Ontario
China	LexisNexis China, Beijing and Shanghai
France	LexisNexis SA, Paris
Germany	LexisNexis GmbH, Dusseldorf
Hong Kong	LexisNexis Hong Kong, Hong Kong
India	LexisNexis India, New Delhi
Italy	Giuffrè Editore, Milan
Japan	LexisNexis Japan, Tokyo
Malaysia	Malayan Law Journal Sdn Bhd, Kuala Lumpur
New Zealand	LexisNexis NZ Ltd, Wellington
Singapore	LexisNexis Singapore, Singapore
South Africa	LexisNexis Butterworths, Durban
USA	LexisNexis, Dayton, Ohio

© 2017 RELX (UK) Limited

Published by LexisNexis
This is a Tolley Title

All rights reserved. No part of this publication may be reproduced in any material form (including photocopying or storing it in any medium by electronic means and whether or not transiently or incidentally to some other use of this publication) without the written permission of the copyright owner except in accordance with the provisions of the Copyright, Designs and Patents Act 1988 or under the terms of a licence issued by the Copyright Licensing Agency Ltd, Saffron House, 6–10 Kirby Street, London EC1N 8TS. Applications for the copyright owner's written permission to reproduce any part of this publication should be addressed to the publisher.
Warning: The doing of an unauthorised act in relation to a copyright work may result in both a civil claim for damages and criminal prosecution.

Crown copyright material is reproduced with the permission of the Controller of HMSO and the Queen's Printer for Scotland. Parliamentary copyright material is reproduced with the permission of the Controller of Her Majesty's Stationery Office on behalf of Parliament. Any European material in this work which has been reproduced from EUR-lex, the official European Communities legislation website, is European Communities copyright.
A CIP Catalogue record for this book is available from the British Library.

ISBN for this volume: 9780754553694

Printed and bound by CPI Group (UK) Ltd, Croydon, CR0 4YY

Visit LexisNexis at www.lexisnexis.co.uk

About This Book

The text of this work includes full coverage of Finance Act 2017 and Finance (No 2) Act 2017, including the new deemed domicile status for capital gains tax, changes to the substantial shareholding exemption and employee shareholder share rules and all other relevant material to 15 September 2017 e.g. statutes, statutory instruments, court cases, Tribunal decisions, press releases, concessions, Statements of Practice, HMRC Briefs, and other publications.

The date of Royal Assent to F(No 2)A 2017 is not yet known at time of going to press. It is expected to be in November 2017. Once Royal Assent has been given, the date should be available at https://services.parliament.uk/bills/2017-19/finance.html.

We welcome all comments and suggestions for improvement to this work. You can contact us in this respect by e-mailing the Editor, Gemma Murray at gemma.murray@lexisnexis.co.uk. Any technical queries will be passed on to the author.

Tolley's Capital Gains Tax

Whilst care has been taken to ensure the accuracy of the contents of this book, no responsibility for loss occasioned to any person acting or refraining from action as a result of any statement in it can be accepted by the author or the publisher. Readers should take specialist professional advice before entering into any specific transaction.

This edition gives the position for the tax year 2017–18 and covers all legislation, HMRC's published guidance and other relevant sources of information including the provisions of Finance Act 2017 and Finance (No 2) Act 2017.

The date of Royal Assent to F(No 2)A 2017 is not yet known at time of going to press. It is expected to be in November 2017. Once Royal Assent has been given, the date should be available at https://services.parliament.uk/bills/2017-19/finance.html.

Consolidation of Tax Enactments

With effect generally for 1992/93 and subsequent years of assessment (and for companies' accounting periods beginning after 5 April 1992) the *Taxes Acts* provisions relating to the taxation of chargeable gains are consolidated in the *Taxation of Chargeable Gains Act 1992 (TCGA 1992)*.

Tolley's Capital Gains Tax 2017/18 sets out the position for the four years prior to 2017/18, i.e. for 2013/14 to 2016/17, but occasional references are still required to earlier years.

The approach which has been adopted to statutory references in this work is as follows.

(i) References to current legislation invariably quote the *TCGA 1992* reference in the familiar form, i.e. '*TCGA 1992, s XXX*' to identify a section and '*TCGA 1992, Sch XX*' to identify a Schedule. Where there has been no change in the legislation in the last six years, no statutory reference other than the current legislation is quoted.

(ii) Where the legislation has changed during the last four years, the earlier provisions continue to be described in the text, and the appropriate earlier statutory reference is quoted. Legislation current during those four years but now repealed is similarly dealt with. Where any part of the current legislation was introduced during those four years, the commencement date is quoted.

Contents

About This Book		v
Consolidation of Tax Enactments		vii
Abbreviations and References		xiii
1	Introduction to capital gains tax	
2	Annual Rates and Exemptions	
3	Alternative Finance Arrangements	
4	Anti-Avoidance	
5	Appeals	
6	Assessments	
7	Assets	
8	Assets held on 6 April 1965	
9	Assets held on 31 March 1982	
10	Capital Sums Derived from Assets	
11	Charities	
12	Children	
13	Claims	
14	Companies	
15	Companies — Corporate Finance and Intangibles	
16	Computation of Gains and Losses	
17	Connected Persons	
18	Corporate Venturing Scheme	
19	Death	
20	Disclosure of Tax Avoidance Schemes	
21	Double Tax Relief	
22	Employee Share Schemes	
23	Enterprise Investment Scheme	
24	Entrepreneurs' Relief	
25	Exemptions and Reliefs	
26	Furnished Holiday Accommodation	
27	Gifts	
28	Government Securities	
29	Groups of Companies	

30 HMRC — Administration
31 HMRC — Confidentiality of Information
32 HMRC Explanatory Publications
33 HMRC Extra-Statutory Concessions
34 HMRC Investigatory Powers
35 HMRC Statements of Practice
36 Hold-Over Reliefs
37 Incorporation and Disincorporation Reliefs
38 Indexation
39 Interaction with Other Taxes
40 Investors' Relief
41 Land
42 Late Payment Interest and Penalties
43 Life Insurance Policies and Deferred Annuities
44 Losses
45 Market Value
46 Married Persons and Civil Partners
47 Mineral Royalties
48 Offshore Settlements
49 Overseas Matters
50 Partnerships
51 Payment of Tax
52 Penalties
53 Private Residences
54 Qualifying Corporate Bonds
55 Remittance Basis
56 Repayment Interest
57 Residence and Domicile
58 Returns
59 Rollover Relief — Replacement of Business Assets
60 Seed Enterprise Investment Scheme
61 Self-Assessment
62 Settlements
63 Shares and Securities
64 Shares and Securities — Identification Rules
65 Social Investment Relief
66 Substantial Shareholdings of Companies

67 **Time Limits — Fixed Dates**

68 **Time Limits — Miscellaneous**

69 **Underwriters at Lloyd's**

70 **Unit Trusts and Other Investment Vehicles**

71 **Venture Capital Trusts**

72 **Wasting Assets**

73 **Finance Acts 2017 — Summary of CGT Provisions**

74 **Tax Case Digest**

75 **Table of Statutes**

76 **Table of Statutory Instruments**

77 **Table of Cases**

78 **Index**

Abbreviations and References

Abbreviations

A-G	Attorney-General.
Art	Article.
BES	Business Expansion Scheme.
CA	Court of Appeal.
CAA	Capital Allowances Act.
CCA	Court of Criminal Appeal.
CCAB	Consultative Committee of Accountancy Bodies.
CES	Court of Exchequer (Scotland).
Cf.	compare.
CGT	Capital Gains Tax.
CGTA	Capital Gains Tax Act.
CJEC	Court of Justice of the European Communities.
Ch D	Chancery Division.
CIR	Commissioners of Inland Revenue ('the Board' or 'the Revenue').
CRCA	Commissioners for Revenue and Customs Act.
CTA	Corporation Tax Act.
DC	Divisional Court.
EC	European Community.
ECHR	European Court of Human Rights.
EIS	Enterprise Investment Scheme.
ESC	Inland Revenue Extra-Statutory Concession.
EU	European Union.
Ex D	Exchequer Division (now part of Chancery Division).
FA	Finance Act.
Fam D	Family Division.

FTT	First-tier Tribunal.
HC	House of Commons.
HL	House of Lords.
HMRC	Her Majesty's Revenue and Customs.
I	Ireland.
ICAEW	Institute of Chartered Accountants in England and Wales.
ICTA	Income and Corporation Taxes Act.
IHT	Inheritance Tax.
IHTA	Inheritance Tax Act.
ISA	Individual Savings Account.
ITA	Income Tax Act.
ITEPA	Income Tax (Earnings and Pensions) Act.
ITTOIA	Income Tax (Trading and Other Income) Act.
KB	King's Bench Division.
LLP	Limited Liability Partnership.
LLPA	Limited Liability Partnership Act.
NI	Northern Ireland.
OEIC	Open-ended Investment Company
PC	Privy Council.
PDA	Probate, Divorce and Admiralty Division (now Family Division).
PEP	Personal Equity Plan.
QB	Queen's Bench Division.
QIS	Qualified Investor Scheme
R	Regina or Rex (i.e. The Crown).
Reg	Regulation.
RPI	Retail Prices Index.
s	Section.
SC(I)	Supreme Court (Ireland).
SCS	Scottish Court of Session.
Sch	Schedule.
SE	*Societas Europaea* (European Company)
SI	Statutory Instrument.

SP	Inland Revenue Statement of Practice.
Sp C	Special Commissioners.
TCEA	Tribunals, Courts and Enforcement Act.
TCGA	Taxation of Chargeable Gains Act.
TIOPA	Taxation (International and Other Provisions) Act.
TMA	Taxes Management Act.
UT	Upper Tribunal.

References

(*denotes a series accredited for citation in court).

All ER	*All England Law Reports (LexisNexis).
All ER(D)	All England Reporter Direct (LexisNexis).
AC	*Law Reports, Appeal Cases (Incorporated Council of Law Reporting for England and Wales, Megarry House, 119 Chancery Lane, London WC2A 1PP).
ATC	*Annotated Tax Cases (publication discontinued).
Ch	*Law Reports, Chancery Division.
CMLR	Common Market Law Reports.
Ex D	Law Reports, Exchequer Division (1875–1880; see also below).
Fam D	*Law Reports, Family Division.
KB	*Law Reports, King's Bench Division (1900–1952).
IR	*Irish Reports (Incorporated Council of Law Reporting for Ireland, First Floor, Áras Uí Dhálaigh, Inns Quay, Dublin 7).
ITC	*Irish Tax Cases (Government Publications, 1 and 3 G.P.O. Arcade, Dublin 1).
LR Ex	*Law Reports, Exchequer Division (1865–1875; see also above).
NILR	Northern Ireland Law Reports.
QB	*Law Reports, Queen's Bench Division (1891–1901 and 1952 onwards).
QBD	Law Reports, Queen's Bench Division (1875–1890).

SFTD	*Simon's First-tier Tax Decisions (LexisNexis).
SLT	Scots Law Times.
Sp C	Special Commissioner's Decisions.
SSCD	Simon's Tax Cases—Special Commissioners' Decisions (LexisNexis).
STC	*Simon's Tax Cases (LexisNexis).
STI	Simon's Tax Intelligence (LexisNexis).
TC	*Official Reports of Tax Cases (The Stationery Office, P.O. Box 29, Norwich, NR3 1GN).
TR	Taxation Reports (publication discontinued).
WLR	*Weekly Law Reports (Incorporated Council of Law Reporting).

The first number in the citation refers to the volume, and the second to the page, so that [1978] 2 WLR 10 means that the report is to be found on page ten of the second volume of the Weekly Law Reports for 1978. Where no volume number is given, only one volume was produced in that year. Some series have continuous volume numbers.

Where legal decisions are very recent and in the lower courts, it must be remembered that they may be reversed on appeal. However, references to the official Tax Cases ('*TC*'), and to the Appeal Cases ('*AC*') may be taken as final.

In English cases, Scottish and Northern Irish decisions (unless there is a difference of law between the countries) are generally followed but are not binding, and Republic of Ireland decisions are considered (and vice versa).

1

Introduction to capital gains tax

Basic principles of capital gains tax	**1.1**
The charge to tax	**1.2**
Key points	**1.3**

Basic principles of capital gains tax

[1.1] Capital gains tax is charged on chargeable gains made by individuals, personal representatives and trustees on the disposal of ASSETS (7.2). The tax is chargeable on the total gains on disposals in a 'year of assessment', after deductions, including LOSSES (44) and the annual exempt amount (see **2** ANNUAL RATES AND EXEMPTIONS). Every gain is a chargeable gain unless expressly excluded (see **25** EXEMPTIONS AND RELIEFS). For this purpose, a '*year of assessment*', otherwise known as a '*tax year*', is a year ending on 5 April. Thus '2017/18' indicates the year of assessment ending on 5 April 2018 (and so on). [*TCGA 1992, s 288(1)(1ZA)*].

Companies and other corporate bodies within the scope of corporation tax do not pay capital gains tax as such but instead are chargeable to corporation tax on their chargeable gains. The computation of their gains is now significantly different from the computation principles applying for capital gains tax (see **14.2** COMPANIES). Companies pay corporation tax by reference to accounting periods rather than years of assessment.

For both capital gains tax and corporation tax purposes, a gain is computed by reference to the excess of the disposal consideration over the acquisition consideration, received and given, for an asset. In certain circumstances the legislation deems a disposal or acquisition to take place where there is no actual disposal or acquisition. Certain types of expenditure are deductible in computing the gain. See **16** COMPUTATION OF GAINS AND LOSSES. Companies are given an allowance, known as the indexation allowance (see **38** INDEXATION), which for each gain adjusts for the effects of inflation. For CGT purposes, gains on certain business disposals may, subject to a lifetime limit, qualify for ENTREPRENEURS' RELIEF (24). Similarly, gains on certain disposals by individuals of shares in unlisted trading companies may, subject to a lifetime limit, qualify for INVESTORS' RELIEF (40). Entrepreneurs' relief and investors' relief do not apply for the purposes of corporation tax on chargeable gains.

Capital gains tax (CGT) was introduced by *FA 1965* and commenced on 6 April 1965. The legislation was consolidated by *CGTA 1979* and subsequently by *TCGA 1992*. Assets acquired before 7 April 1965 are within the charge if they are disposed of on or after that date, but there are special provisions dealing with the computation of gains on the disposal of such assets (see **8** ASSETS HELD ON 6 APRIL **1965**). *FA 1988* replaced the 1965 base date with 31 March 1982, subject to the detailed provisions of ASSETS HELD ON 31 MARCH 1982 (**9**). For CGT purposes, re-basing to 31 March 1982 applies to all assets held on that date without exception. Exceptions continue to apply for corporation tax purposes.

Both CGT and corporation tax are administered and paid under SELF-ASSESSMENT (**61**). For individuals, gains are treated as if they were the top slice of the taxpayer's income. For 2017/18 and 2016/17, to the extent that gains fall within the basic rate band they are taxable at 10% unless the gains are on disposals of residential property or carried interest, in which case they are taxable at 18%. Where they exceed the basic rate band limit, gains are taxable at 20% or, for gains on disposals of residential property or carried interest, 28%. For 2015/16 and earlier years, to the extent that gains fall within the basic rate band they are taxable at 18%. Where they exceed the basic rate band limit they are taxable at 28%. Trustees of settlements and personal representatives are chargeable to CGT for 2017/18 and 2016/17 at 20% or, for gains on disposals of residential property or carried interest, 28%. For 2015/16 and earlier years they are chargeable to CGT at 28%. See **2** ANNUAL RATES AND EXEMPTIONS. For companies, chargeable gains form part of the taxable total profits and are accordingly taxable at the appropriate corporation tax rate. See **14** COMPANIES.

The charge to tax

[1.2] Subject to exceptions and special provisions, a person is chargeable to capital gains tax in respect of chargeable gains accruing to him in 2013/14 or a later year of assessment if he meets the *'residence condition'* that:

- in the case of an individual, he is resident in the UK for the year;
- in the case of personal representatives of a deceased person, the deemed single and continuing body (see **19.9** DEATH) is resident in the UK;
- in the case of the trustees of a settlement, the deemed single person (see **48.1** OFFSHORE SETTLEMENTS) is resident in the UK during any part of the year; or
- in any other case, the person is resident in the UK when the gain accrues.

For disposals on or after 6 April 2015, a person who does not meet the residence condition is chargeable to capital gains tax on certain disposals of UK residential property interests (see **41.25** LAND). This applies also to such disposals made by individuals in the overseas part of a split tax year (see below).

If the year of assessment is a split year for an individual under the statutory residence test (see **57.18** RESIDENCE AND DOMICILE), he is not chargeable to capital gains tax on any gains accruing in the overseas part of the year. This rule does not apply to gains on which the individual would have been chargeable to capital gains tax under *TCGA 1992, s 10* (trading in the UK through a branch or agency — see **49.3** OVERSEAS MATTERS) had he been non-resident for the year or to gains on UK residential property interests (as above). The rule is also subject to the charge on temporary non-residents (see **49.5** OVERSEAS MATTERS).

[*TCGA 1992, ss 1(1), 2(1)–(1C), 14B, 14D(1); FA 2013, Sch 45 paras 93, 153(2), Sch 46 paras 75, 112; FA 2015, Sch 7 paras 2, 11, 60*].

Subject to two exceptions, companies are chargeable to corporation tax in respect of their chargeable gains. [*TCGA 1992, s 1(2)*]. Although *TCGA 1992, s 2(1)* refers to a 'person' (i.e. including a company), the key factor in charging companies is residence in the UK. The exceptions to the rule are for the capital gains tax charges on high value disposals of dwellings (see **14.10** COMPANIES) and non-resident disposals of UK residential property interests (see **41.25** LAND).

See **14** COMPANIES, **49.9** OVERSEAS MATTERS, and **57.33** RESIDENCE AND DOMICILE.

Special rules apply to persons not resident or individuals not domiciled in the UK, to temporary visitors to the UK and to persons becoming temporarily non-UK resident. See **49** OVERSEAS MATTERS, **50** PARTNERSHIPS, **56** REPAYMENT INTEREST and **57** RESIDENCE AND DOMICILE.

Married persons and civil partners are taxed independently. Transfers between spouses or civil partners living together are made on a 'no gain, no loss' basis. See **46** MARRIED PERSONS AND CIVIL PARTNERS.

Persons may be assessed in a representative capacity. See **6** ASSESSMENTS, **12** CHILDREN, **19** DEATH, **61** SELF-ASSESSMENT and **62** SETTLEMENTS.

There are special rules for UK resident shareholders of certain overseas resident companies. See **49.7** OVERSEAS MATTERS. See **49** OVERSEAS MATTERS for the provisions applying to trustees, settlors and beneficiaries of settlements which are or become overseas resident.

For unit and investment trusts, real estate investment trusts, open-ended investment companies and qualifying investor schemes, see **70** UNIT TRUSTS AND OTHER INVESTMENT VEHICLES. For venture capital trusts, see **71.10** VENTURE CAPITAL TRUSTS.

See Tolley's Corporation Tax under Friendly Societies for provisions of *TCGA 1992* (and related provisions) which are integral with the corporation tax regime applicable to life assurance business carried on by such entities.

TCGA 1992, ss 194–198I, which deal with matters relating to oil exploration taxed under the *Oil Taxation Act 1975* and in practice apply mainly to companies, are not dealt with in this book.

Key points on the charge to capital gains tax

[1.3] The simplest tax planning ideas can be very effective. Whenever advising on capital gains tax consider whether a potential gain can be:

- split over two tax years to utilise two annual exempt amounts/the remainder of the basic rate band/the small profits rate;
- delayed in whole or part until after 6 April/next accounting period to provide a cash flow advantage in terms of payment of tax;
- split between spouses or civil partners to utilise two annual exempt amounts and the remainder of basic rate bands;
- offset by capital losses brought forward; always ask new clients and old accountants about any brought forward capital losses as they are often missed;
- offset by current year capital losses; consider any potential unrealised losses including assets held by any spouse (civil partner) or connected companies;
- offset by any trade tax losses;
- made to qualify for entrepreneurs' relief or substantial shareholdings exemption;
- made to qualify in whole or part for deferral by reinvestment;
- potentially qualify for any other capital gains deduction or relief such as private residence relief, EIS, SEIS, double tax relief and indexation allowance.

Other tax planning can centre on whether 'income' can be converted to a capital gain (taxable at 0%, 10%, 18%, 20% or 28%). For example, profits are rolled up in a limited company until the end of a venture when the company is sold or wound up realising a capital gain. Assuming the gain qualifies for entrepreneurs' relief, it will be taxed at 10% compared to profits being extracted via dividends liable to higher rates of income tax.

2

Annual Rates and Exemptions

Rates of tax	**2.1**
Individuals — 2016/17 and 2017/18	**2.1**
Individuals — 2011/12 to 2015/16	**2.2**
Personal representatives	**2.3**
Settlements	**2.4**
Companies	**2.5**
Annual exempt amount	**2.6**
Key points	**2.7**

Rates of tax

Individuals — 2016/17 and 2017/18

[2.1] There are four rates of capital gains tax which may apply to gains arising in 2016/17 and 2017/18: 10%, 18%, 20% and 28%.

Where gains qualify for entrepreneurs' relief and a claim is made for relief, the rate of tax is **10%**. See **24.8** ENTREPRENEURS' RELIEF. In other cases the rate depends on the type of asset disposed of and on the level of the individual's taxable income for the year.

Upper rate gains

The following applies where the taxpayer's gains for the tax year consist entirely of 'upper rate gains' or entirely of such gains and gains to which entrepreneurs' relief applies. Where the taxpayer's taxable income exceeds the basic rate limit (so that part of his income is taxable at the higher rate or dividend upper rate — but see below for application to Scottish and Welsh taxpayers), the rate of capital gains tax on the upper rate gains is 28%. In other cases, the rate is 18% on any part of the upper rate gains that does not exceed the 'unused part of the basic rate band' for the year, and the 28% rate applies to any excess. The unused part of the basic rate band is set first against gains which are charged to tax at 10% as a result of an entrepreneurs' relief claim.

An individual's '*unused part of the basic rate band*' for this purpose is the amount by which basic rate limit (£32,000 for 2016/17; £33,500 for 2017/18) exceeds the 'Step 3 income' for the year. The '*Step 3 income*' is the net income less allowances deducted at Step 3 of the calculation in *ITA 2007, s 23* (calculation of income tax liability).

'*Upper rate gains*' are:

- 'residential property gains' (see below);
- NRCGT gains (i.e. gains by non-residents on disposals of interests in UK residential property — see **41.25** LAND); and
- 'carried interest gains'.

'*Carried interest gains*' are:

- gains accruing under *TCGA 1992, s 103KA(2)(3)* (carried interest — see **50.20** PARTNERSHIPS); and
- gains accruing to an individual as a result of carried interest arising to him where he performs investment management services directly or indirectly in respect of an investment scheme under arrangements not involving a partnership and the carried interest arises under the arrangements and does not constitute a 'co-investment' repayment or return (see **50.20** PARTNERSHIPS).

Other gains

The following applies where the taxpayer's gains for the tax year consist entirely of gains other than upper rate gains or entirely of such gains and gains to which entrepreneurs' relief applies. Where the taxpayer's taxable income exceeds the basic rate limit, the rate of capital gains tax is 20%. In other cases, the rate is 10% on any part of the gains that does not exceed the unused part of the basic rate band for the year, and the 20% rate applies to any excess. The unused part of the basic rate band is set first against gains which are charged to tax at 10% as a result of an entrepreneurs' relief claim.

Upper rate gains and other gains accrued in same tax year

Where an individual makes both upper rate gains and other gains in the same tax year and his taxable income exceeds the basic rate limit, the rate of tax is 28% or 20% as appropriate. In other cases, the rate is 10% or 18% on any part of the gains that does not exceed the unused part of the basic rate band for the year, and the 20% or 28% rate applies to any excess. The taxpayer may choose which gains are to be allocated to the unused part of the basic rate band (and therefore charged at the 10% or 18% rates), but only after allocating any gains charged to tax at 10% as a result of an entrepreneurs' relief claim.

[*TCGA 1992, ss 4, 4BA; FA 2016, ss 2, 83(1)–(12)(14)(17)*].

Devolution of income tax

For 2017/18 onwards, for the purposes of the above provisions, an individual who is a Scottish taxpayer is treated as if he were not a Scottish taxpayer i.e. the basic rate band for the rest of the UK (£33,500 for 2017/18) is used above when calculating capital gains tax and *not* the Scottish basic rate band (£31,500 for 2017/18). This means, for example, that a Scottish taxpayer paying Scottish higher rate income tax on his non-savings income exceeding the Scottish basic rate band, could still pay some capital gains tax at lower rates if within the basic rate band for the rest of the UK. In respect of 2016/17, higher rates of capital gains tax (i.e. 28% for upper rate gains and 18% for other gains) apply if any income is charged to income tax at the Scottish higher rate (or at the higher rate or dividend upper rate as above) but as there is a single basic rate band for UK taxpayers in 2016/17, a Scottish taxpayer is effectively treated no differently to a UK taxpayer who is not Scottish. See Tolley's Income Tax for details of the devolution of income tax. [*TCGA 1992, s 4(10)(11); Scotland Act 2016, s 15(4); FA 2016, s 83(11)(19); SI 2016 No 1161*].

From a date to be fixed, the higher rates of capital gains tax apply where part of the income is taxable at the higher rate, Welsh higher rate or dividend upper rate. Until then, the rules outlined above for other UK taxpayers apply. [*Wales Act 2014, s 9(13)(14); FA 2016, s 83(18)*].

Special cases

Where:

(a) under *ITTOIA 2005, s 539* (gains from contracts for life insurance etc.), a person is entitled to relief by reference to the amount of a deficiency, or

(b) under *ITTOIA 2005, s 669(1)(2)* (reduction in residuary income: inheritance tax on accrued income) the residuary income of an estate is treated as reduced so as to reduce a person's income by any amount for the purposes of extra liability,

the person's Step 3 income for the year is treated (for the purpose only of computing the unused part of the basic rate band) as reduced by the amount of the deficiency or, as the case may be, the amount in (b) above.

Where under *ITTOIA 2005, s 465* (gains from contracts for life insurance etc.) a person's total income for the year is deemed to include any amount(s):

(i) in determining the unused part of the basic rate band, his Step 3 income is treated as including not the whole of the amount(s) concerned but only the annual equivalent within the meaning of *ITTOIA 2005, s 536(1)* or (as the case may be) the total annual equivalent within the meaning of *ITTOIA 2005, s 537*, and

(ii) if relief is given under *ITTOIA 2005, s 535* and the calculation under *s 536(1)* or *s 537* does not involve the higher rate of income tax, the capital gains tax rate is determined as if the person's taxable income does not exceed the basic rate limit as described above.

[*TCGA 1992, s 4A; FA 2016, s 83(13)*].

Deduction of losses and annual exempt amount

Where it is necessary to determine from which chargeable gains a loss may be deducted or which losses are to be deducted from a chargeable gain, the losses may be used in the most beneficial way. If gains for a year are chargeable at different rates, the taxpayer can deduct the annual exempt amount (see **2.6** below) in the most beneficial way. This rule is, however, subject to any provision limiting the way in which losses can be deducted (for example where a loss is made on a disposal to a connected person — see **44.6** LOSSES).

It will be most beneficial to set losses and the annual exempt amount against gains chargeable at 28% before those chargeable at 20%, against those chargeable at 20% before those chargeable at 18% and so on.

[*TCGA 1992, s 4B*].

Residential property gain

A '*residential property gain*' or loss is a gain or loss (computed as below) on the disposal of a residential property interest, being either a 'disposal of a UK residential property interest' or a 'disposal of a non-UK residential property interest' but excluding a gain or loss on a non-resident CGT disposal (see **41.25** LAND). A '*disposal of a UK residential property interest*' is defined as at **41.29** LAND but the reference there to 6 April 2015 is replaced for this purpose by a reference to 31 March 1982.

A '*disposal of a non-UK residential property interest*' is a disposal of an 'interest in non-UK land' which has, at any time in the period from acquisition or, if later, 31 March 1982 to the day before the date of disposal (the '*relevant period of ownership*'), consisted of or included a 'dwelling', or which subsists for the benefit of land that has consisted of or included a dwelling at any time in that period. Alternatively it is a disposal of an interest in non-UK land which subsists under a contract for an off-plan purchase, i.e. a contract for acquisition of land consisting of, or including, a building or part of a building that is to be constructed or adapted as a dwelling. In determining the period of ownership, where the interest disposed of results from interests which have been acquired at different times, the date of acquisition of the first interest is taken as the date on which all the interests were acquired. The grant of an option (defined as at **7.7** ASSETS) binding the grantor to sell an interest in non-UK land is treated for these purposes as the disposal of an interest in non-UK land.

An '*interest in non-UK land*' is an estate, interest, right or power in or over land outside the UK, or the benefit of an obligation, restriction or condition affecting the value of such, but not including:

(a) any interest or right held to secure payment of money or performance of any other obligation; or
(b) a licence to use or occupy land.

A '*dwelling*' is a building (including a part of a building) which is used or suitable for use as a dwelling or is in the process of being constructed or adapted for such use. It includes gardens and grounds (and any building or structure in a garden or grounds). The following are excluded from being a dwelling:

(i) school residential accommodation;
(ii) residential accommodation for members of the armed forces;
(iii) homes or institutions providing residential accommodation for children;
(iv) homes or institutions providing residential accommodation with personal care for the elderly, the disabled, persons with drug or alcohol dependency or a mental disorder;

(v) hospitals and hospices;
(vi) prisons and similar establishments;
(vii) hotels, inns and similar establishments; and
(viii) any other institution which is the sole or main residence of its residents.

In addition, a building which includes at least 15 bedrooms, is purpose-built or converted for occupation by students other than school pupils and is occupied by them for at least 165 days in a tax year is not a dwelling for that year.

Buildings which become temporarily unsuitable for use as a dwelling are generally treated as continuing to be such, but there are some exceptions. A building is not considered suitable for use as a dwelling if the temporary unsuitability resulted from damage to the building which was accidental, or otherwise outside the control of the person making the disposal and the period of temporary unsuitability was at least 90 days (whether or not within the relevant period of ownership but ending before the disposal). If this is the case any work done within that period is not treated as construction or adaption of the building for use as a dwelling. Any damage occurring during alterations to, or partial demolition of, a building which involved, or could be expected to involve, the building being unsuitable for use as a dwelling for at least 30 days is not considered accidental or otherwise outside the control of the person making the disposal for these purposes.

A building which has been demolished either to ground level or, in accordance with planning permission or development consent, to a single façade (double if on a corner) is regarded as having ceased to exist. Where a person disposes of an interest in non-UK land which contains or contained a building which has been suitable for use as a dwelling at any time in the relevant period of ownership, and that building has undergone complete or partial demolition or other works which result in it ceasing to exist or becoming unsuitable as a dwelling before the 'completion' of disposal then, provided the conditions below are met, the building is treated as being unsuitable as a dwelling throughout the period when the works were in progress, and any period ending immediately before that during which the building was, for reasons connected with the works, not used as a dwelling. The conditions are that:

- the works result in the building ceasing to exist or becoming unsuitable as a dwelling before the completion of the disposal; and
- any planning permission or development consent has been issued (even if retrospectively after completion of the disposal) and the works were carried out in accordance with it.

If planning permission or development consent for the works was required but not granted (unless given subsequently), or it was contravened, the building is not treated as being unsuitable as a dwelling.

'*Completion*' occurs either at the time of disposal or when the interest is conveyed where the contract is completed by conveyance.

The Treasury may by regulations exclude any other interest or right from being treated as an interest in non-UK land and amend the definition of 'dwelling'.

[*TCGA 1992, Sch BA1; FA 2016, Sch 11 para 5*].

Computation of residential property gain

The following rules apply to determine how much of a gain on a disposal of a residential property interest (an '*RPI disposal*') is a residential property gain and therefore is taxable as an upper rate gain. The rules apply equally to losses but do not apply to non-resident CGT disposals (for which see **41.30, 41.31** LAND).They apply to the disposal of contracts for off-plan purchases (see above) as if the interest consisted of (or included) a dwelling throughout the period in which the taxpayer owned it.

Default method

This method applies if the RPI disposal is not, and does not involve, a high value disposal of dwellings within **14.10** COMPANIES. The gain or loss is calculated in the normal way and is then apportioned by the fraction:

$$\frac{RD}{TD}$$

where RD is the number of days in the relevant period of ownership on which the disposed of interest consisted wholly or partly of a dwelling (defined as above for non-UK interests and as at **41.29** LAND for UK interests); and
TD is the number of days in that period.

The resulting gain or loss is the residential property gain or loss.

Where there are any days in the relevant period of ownership on which the land disposed of consists partly but not exclusively of one or more dwellings (i.e. there is '*mixed use*') a just and reasonable apportionment must be made to calculate the residential property gain or loss.

Any remaining part of the actual gain or loss on the RPI disposal after deducting the residential property gain or loss is not a residential property gain or loss.

Method where disposal involves a high value disposal

Where an RPI disposal by a company is, or involves, one or more high value disposals of dwellings within **14.10** COMPANIES the residential property gain or loss is the sum of the residential property gains or losses accruing on each such high value disposal calculated as described below. Where part only of the land disposed of is such a high value disposal, the remaining part of the land is treated for these purposes in the same way as if it formed part of the high value disposal. Where there are any days in the ownership period in question on which the land disposed of consists partly but not exclusively of one or more dwellings (i.e. there is '*mixed use*') a just and reasonable apportionment must be made to calculate the residential property gain or loss on the non-high value disposal. The balancing gain or loss on the RPI disposal is the sum of the balancing gains or losses for each high value disposal.

(1) **High value disposal not within Cases 1–3 or where an election is made.** Where the high value disposal does not fall within any of Cases 1–3 or an election for the retrospective basis of computation is made (see **14.10**

COMPANIES), the residential property gain or loss arising on the high value disposal is the fraction of the actual gain or loss on that disposal found by applying:

$$\frac{SD}{TD}$$

where SD is the number of days in the relevant period of ownership on which the interest disposed of consisted wholly or partly of a dwelling but which was not an ATED chargeable day (see **14.10** COMPANIES); and TD is the total number of days in that period.

The amount of the gain or loss which is neither ATED-related nor a residential property gain or loss in these circumstances is the balancing gain or loss. It is found by applying the fraction:

$$\frac{BD}{TD}$$

where BD is the number of days in the relevant period of ownership which are neither days on which the interest disposed of consisted wholly or partly of a dwelling but was not an ATED chargeable day nor ATED chargeable days, and

TD is the number of days in that period.

(2) **High value disposal within Cases 1–3 and no election made.** Where the high value disposal falls within any of Cases 1–3 at **14.10** COMPANIES and no election for the retrospective basis of computation is made (see **14.10** COMPANIES), the residential property gain or loss is the sum of a proportion of the 'notional post-ATED gain' and a proportion of the 'notional pre-ATED gain or loss'. The proportion of the notional post-ATED gain or loss is that given by the fraction:

$$\frac{SD}{TD}$$

where SD is the number of days in the period from 6 April in the 'relevant year' to the day before the date of disposal on which the interest disposed of consisted wholly or partly of a dwelling but which was not an ATED chargeable day, and

TD is the total number of days in that period.

The proportion of the notional pre-ATED gain or loss is that given by the fraction:

$$\frac{SD}{TD}$$

where SD is the number of days in the period from the date of acquisition, or 31 March 1982 if later, to 5 in the relevant year, on which the interest disposed of consisted wholly or partly of a dwelling but which was not an ATED chargeable day, andTD is the total number of days in that period.

The '*notional post-ATED gain or loss*' is the notional gain or loss on the disposal of the disposed of interest had the company acquired it at market value on 5 April in the relevant year. In calculating the notional post-ATED gain or loss the assumption that the interest was acquired on 5 April of the relevant year is ignored when determining whether the interest is a WASTING ASSET (72).*TCGA 1992, s 41* (restriction of losses by reference to capital allowances: see **16.13** COMPUTATION OF GAINS AND LOSSES) and *TCGA 1992, s 47* (wasting assets qualifying for capital allowances: see **72.2** WASTING ASSETS) apply in relation to any capital or renewals allowance made in respect of the expenditure actually incurred in acquiring or providing the asset as if that allowance were made in respect of the expenditure treated as incurred on the deemed acquisition date.

The '*notional pre-ATED gain or loss*' is that which would have accrued on 5 April of the relevant year if the interest had been disposed of at market value on that date.

The '*relevant year*' is 2013 where Case 1 applies, 2015 where Case 2 applies or 2016 where Case 3 applies.

The amount of the gain or loss which is neither ATED-related nor a residential property gain or loss in these circumstances is the balancing gain or loss. This is the sum of the balancing gain or loss belonging to the notional post-ATED gain or loss and the balancing gain or loss belonging to the notional pre-ATED gain or loss. These are the fraction of the gains or losses relating to the days in the appropriate period which are neither days on which the interest disposed of consisted wholly or partly of a dwelling but were not an ATED chargeable day nor ATED chargeable days.

[*TCGA 1992, s 57C, Sch 4ZZC; FA 2016, Sch 12 paras 3, 5*].

Example 1

Erica owns an established business and has taxable profits of £38,000 for her accounting year ended 5 April 2018. She has no other income for 2017/18 but she makes a chargeable gain (before deduction of the annual exempt amount) of £30,000. The gain is not an upper rate gain and does not qualify for entrepreneurs' relief. Her capital gains tax liability for 2017/18 is computed as follows.

	£
Trade profits	38,000
Deduct Personal allowance	11,500
Step 3 income	£26,500
Unused part of the basic rate band (£33,500 – £26,500)	£7,000
Chargeable gain	30,000

		£
Deduct Annual exempt amount (see **2.6** below)		11,300
Taxable gain		£18,700
£		
7,000	@ 10%	700
11,700	@ 20%	2,340
£18,700		£3,040

Example 2

Felix owns an established business and has taxable profits of £42,000 for his accounting year ended 31 March 2018. He has no other income for 2017/18 but he makes two chargeable gains (before deducting the annual exempt amount) of £17,000 each. Neither gain is an upper rate gain but one of them qualifies for entrepreneurs' relief. His capital gains tax liability for 2017/18 is computed as follows.

	£
Disposal qualifying for entrepreneurs' relief	
Capital gains tax £17,000 × 10%	£1,700
Disposal not qualifying for entrepreneurs' relief	
Chargeable gain	17,000
Deduct Annual exempt amount (see **2.6** below)	11,300
Taxable gain	£5,700
Capital gains tax £5,700 × 20%	£1,140
Total capital gains tax for 2017/18 (£1,700 + £1,140)	£2,840

Notes to the example

(a) Gains qualifying for entrepreneurs' relief are treated as the lowest part of the gains for the year. The unused part of the basic rate band (£3,000) is set against the gain qualifying for entrepreneurs' relief even though it does not affect the rate of tax for that gain. The whole of the gain not qualifying for entrepreneurs' relief is therefore chargeable to tax at 20%.

(b) It is assumed that Felix sets his annual exempt amount against the gain chargeable at 20% as this achieves the greater tax saving.

Example 3

Marley owns an established business and has taxable profits of £42,000 for her accounting year ended 31 March 2018. She has no other income for 2017/18 but she makes two chargeable gains (before deducting the annual exempt amount) of £17,000 each. Neither gain qualifies for entrepreneurs' relief but one of them is an upper rate gain. Her capital gains tax liability for 2017/18 is computed as follows.

	£
Trade profits	42,000
Deduct Personal allowance	11,500
Step 3 income	£30,500
Unused part of the basic rate band (£33,500 – £30,500)	£3,000

Standard rate gain

£		£
3,000	@ 10%	300
14,000	@ 20%	2,800
£17,000		£3,100

Upper rate gain

Chargeable gain	17,000
Deduct Annual exempt amount (see **2.6** below)	11,300
Taxable gain	£5,700
Capital gains tax £5,700 × 28%	£1,596
Total capital gains tax for 2017/18 (£3,100 + £1,596)	£4,696

Notes to the example

(a) The taxpayer can choose to set the unused part of the basic rate band (£3,000) against either the upper rate gain or the other gain. In practice the effect is the same as there is a 10% reduction in the rate of CGT applicable to the gain falling within the unused part of the band. In this example the unused part is set against the standard rate gain for illustration purposes.

(b) It is assumed that Marley sets her annual exempt amount against the gain chargeable at 28% as this achieves the greater tax saving.

Individuals — 2011/12 to 2015/16

[2.2] There are three rates of capital gains tax which may apply to gains arising in 2011/12 to 2015/16: 10%, 18% and 28%.

Where gains qualify for entrepreneurs' relief and a claim is made for relief, the rate of tax is **10%**. See **24.8** ENTREPRENEURS' RELIEF. In other cases the rate is either **18%** or **28%** depending on the level of the individual's taxable income for the year.

Where the taxpayer's taxable income exceeds the basic rate limit so that part of his income is taxable at the higher rate or dividend upper rate, the rate of capital gains tax is 28%. In other cases, the rate is 18% on any part of the gains that does not exceed the 'unused part of the basic rate band' for the year, and the 28% rate applies to any excess. Any gains which are charged to tax at 10% are treated for this purpose as the lowest part of the overall gains (so that the unused part of the basic rate band is set first against such gains).

An individual's '*unused part of the basic rate band*' for this purpose is the amount by which basic rate limit (£31,785 for 2015/16) exceeds the 'Step 3 income' for the year. The '*Step 3 income*' is the net income less allowances deducted at Step 3 of the calculation in *ITA 2007, s 23* (calculation of income tax liability). For earlier years the basic rate limit was as follows.

2014/15	£31,865
2013/14	£32,010
2012/13	£34,370

See Tolley's Income Tax under Allowances and Tax Rates.

[*TCGA 1992, s 4(1)(2)(4)–(9); FA 2014, Sch 38 para 15; FA 2015, s 4; F(No 2)A 2015, s 6*].

Special cases

Where:

(a) under *ITTOIA 2005, s 539* (gains from contracts for life insurance etc.), a person is entitled to relief by reference to the amount of a deficiency, or
(b) under *ITTOIA 2005, s 669(1)(2)* (reduction in residuary income: inheritance tax on accrued income) the residuary income of an estate is treated as reduced so as to reduce a person's income by any amount for the purposes of extra liability,

the person's Step 3 income for the year is treated (for the purpose only of computing the unused part of the basic rate band) as reduced by the amount of the deficiency or, as the case may be, the amount in (b) above.

Where under *ITTOIA 2005, s 465* (gains from contracts for life insurance etc.) a person's total income for the year is deemed to include any amount(s):

(i) in determining the unused part of the basic rate band, his Step 3 income is treated as including not the whole of the amount(s) concerned but only the annual equivalent within the meaning of *ITTOIA 2005, s 536(1)* or (as the case may be) the total annual equivalent within the meaning of *ITTOIA 2005, s 537*, and
(ii) if relief is given under *ITTOIA 2005, s 535* and the calculation under *s 536(1)* or *s 537* does not involve the higher rate of income tax, the capital gains tax rate is determined as if no income tax were chargeable at the higher rate (or the dividend upper rate or Scottish higher rate) in respect of his income.

[*TCGA 1992, s 4A; FA 2014, Sch 38 para 15*].

Deduction of losses and annual exempt amount

Where it is necessary to determine from which chargeable gains a loss may be deducted or which losses are to be deducted from a chargeable gain, the losses may be used in the most beneficial way. If gains for a year are chargeable at different rates, the taxpayer can deduct the annual exempt amount (see **2.6** below) in the most beneficial way. This rule is, however, subject to any provision limiting the way in which losses can be deducted (for example where a loss is made on a disposal to a connected person — see **44.6 LOSSES**).

It will be most beneficial to set losses and the annual exempt amount against gains chargeable at 28% before those chargeable at 18%, and against those chargeable at 18% before those chargeable at 10%.

[*TCGA 1992, s 4B; FA 2015, Sch 7 para 7; SI 2013 No 662*].

Example 1

Patsy, who is under 65, owns an established business and has taxable profits of £37,600 for her accounting year ended 5 April 2016. She has no other income for 2015/16 but she makes a chargeable gain (before deduction of the annual exempt amount) of £30,000. The gain does not qualify for entrepreneurs' relief. Her capital gains tax liability for 2015/16 is computed as follows.

		£
Trade profits		37,600
Deduct Personal allowance		10,600
Step 3 income		£27,000
Unused part of the basic rate band (£31,785 – £27,000)		£4,785
Chargeable gain		30,000
Deduct Annual exempt amount (see **2.6** below)		11,100
Taxable gain		£18,900
£		
4,785	@ 18%	861
14,115	@ 28%	3,952
£18,900		£4,813

Example 2

Bradley, who is under 65, owns an established business and has taxable profits of £40,000 for his accounting year ended 31 March 2016. He has no other income for 2015/16 but he makes two chargeable gains (before deducting the annual exemption) of £17,000 each. One of the gains qualifies for entrepreneurs' relief. His capital gains tax liability for 2015/16 is computed as follows.

	£
Disposal qualifying for entrepreneurs' relief	
Capital gains tax £17,000 × 10%	£1,700
Disposal not qualifying for entrepreneurs' relief	
Chargeable gain	17,000
Deduct Annual exempt amount (see **2.6** below)	11,100
Taxable gain	£5,900
Capital gains tax £5,900 × 28%	£1,652

Total capital gains tax for 2015/16 (£1,700 + £1,652)	£3,352

Notes to the example

(a) Gains qualifying for entrepreneurs' relief are treated as the lowest part of the gains for the year. The unused part of the basic rate band (£2,385) is set against the gain qualifying for entrepreneurs' relief even though it does not affect the rate of tax for that gain. The whole of the gain not qualifying for entrepreneurs' relief is therefore chargeable to tax at 28%.

(b) It is assumed that Bradley sets his annual exempt amount against the gain chargeable at 28% as this achieves the greater tax saving.

Personal representatives

[2.3] For 2016/17 and 2017/18 the rate of tax is 28% for upper rate gains (see **2.1** above) and 20% for other gains. For 2011/12 to 2015/16, the rate of tax is 28%. [*TCGA 1992, s 4(3); FA 2016, s 83(5)*]. Where it is necessary to determine from which chargeable gains a loss may be deducted or which losses are to be deducted from a chargeable gain, the losses may be used in the most beneficial way. [*TCGA 1992, s 4B; FA 2015, Sch 7 para 7*].

Settlements

[2.4] See SETTLEMENTS (62.7).

Companies

[2.5] With two exceptions, companies and other corporate bodies within the charge to corporation tax do not pay capital gains tax as such. Instead they are chargeable to corporation tax on their chargeable gains. The whole of a company's gains for an accounting period (net of allowable losses) are included in the profits chargeable to corporation tax, and the rate of tax will therefore depend on the level of those profits. The exceptions to the rule are for the capital gains tax charges on high value disposals of dwellings (see **14.10** COMPANIES) and non-resident disposals of UK residential property interests (see **41.25** LAND). See **14.3** COMPANIES.

Annual exempt amount

[2.6] For 2017/18 an individual is exempt from capital gains tax on the first £11,300 of his 'taxable amount'. This amount is known as the 'annual exempt amount' or sometimes, the 'annual exemption'. The annual exempt amounts for earlier years were as follows:

2016/17	£11,100
2015/16	£11,100
2014/15	£11,000
2013/14	£10,900

2012/13	£10,600

Where an individual makes a claim under *ITA 2007, s 809B* (see **55.2** REMITTANCE BASIS) for the remittance basis to apply for a tax year, however, he is not entitled to the annual exempt amount for that year.

The '*taxable amount*' is the amount on which the individual is chargeable to capital gains tax (including any gains treated under *Taxation of Chargeable Gains Act 1992 (TCGA 1992), s 86* as accruing to him as settlor from a non-UK resident settlement in which he has an interest (see **48.5** OFFSHORE SETTLEMENTS)) after deducting allowable losses for the year or UK part and brought-forward allowable losses, plus any gains treated under *TCGA 1992, s 87* or *s 89(2)* as accruing to him as a beneficiary of a non-UK resident settlement (an offshore trust) (see **48.14–48.20** OFFSHORE SETTLEMENTS).

Where an individual's 'adjusted net gains' are equal to or less than the annual exempt amount, any allowable losses brought forward from a previous year or carried back from the year of death (see **19.7** DEATH) need not be deducted and are thus preserved for further carry-forward (or, if possible, carry-back). Where the 'adjusted net gains' exceed the annual exempt amount, such losses are deducted only to the extent necessary to wipe out the excess.

The '*adjusted net gains*' are:

(i) where the residence condition at **1.2** INTRODUCTION is met and the tax year is not a split year under the statutory residence test (see **57.18** RESIDENCE AND DOMICILE), the chargeable gains for the year (including gains attributed under *TCGA 1992, s 86*) *less* any current year allowable losses. Where *TCGA 1992, s 16ZB* applies (gains charged on REMITTANCE BASIS (**55.2**)), the 'relevant gains' within that section are deducted from the chargeable gains for the year before deducting current year losses. Where gains are attributed under *TCGA 1992, s 87* or *89(2)*, such gains are also included in the adjusted net gains to the extent that they do not exceed the annual exempt amount (and will thus be covered by that amount);

(ii) where the residence condition is not met, the gains realised for the year on UK residential property falling within the non-resident CGT regime that applies for disposals made on or after 6 April 2015, reduced by losses realised under the same regime for that year (not including losses brought forward) (see **41.25** LAND);

(iii) where the residence condition is met and the year is a split year, the total amount of the gains in (i) and (ii) above.

These provisions also apply to personal representatives for the year of death and the following two years (see **19.9** DEATH).

[*TCGA 1992, ss 2(2), 3(1)(2)(5)–(5D)(7); FA 2012, s 34(2)(5)(6); FA 2013, Sch 45 para 93(3); FA 2014, ss 8, 9; FA 2015, Sch 7 para 5; SI 2010 No 923*].

Where a taxpayer is chargeable to capital gains tax at more than one rate, he may allocate the annual exempt amount (and any allowable losses) against gains in the most tax-efficient way. See **2.2** above.

The exempt amount for the year, unless Parliament determines otherwise, is the previous year's exempt amount as increased by a percentage which is the same as the percentage increase in the consumer prices index (for 2013/14 and earlier years, the retail prices index) for the September preceding the year of assessment over the index for the previous September. The resulting figure is rounded up to the nearest £100 and is announced before the relevant year of assessment in a Treasury statutory instrument (see list of references above). For 2013/14 onwards, if there is no such increase in the relevant index, the previous year's exempt amount is used for the next year without the need for a statutory instrument (unless Parliament determines otherwise). [*ITA 2007, s 989; TCGA 1992, ss 3(2A)–(4), 288(2); FA 2011, s 8(3)(6); FA 2012, s 34(3)(4)(7)*].

See **62.8** and **62.9** SETTLEMENTS for further applications of the above rules.

The annual exempt amount is available regardless of the residence status of the individual and is available separately to each spouse or civil partner. See above for the loss of the annual exempt amount where a claim for the remittance basis has been made by a non-UK domiciled individual.

Examples

For 2017/18, Paul, who is resident in the UK, has chargeable gains of £13,800 and allowable losses of £1,200. He also has allowable losses of £13,000 brought forward.

	£
Adjusted net gains (£13,800 – £1,200)	12,600
Losses brought forward (part)	1,300
	11,300
Annual exempt amount	11,300
Taxable gains	Nil
Losses brought forward	13,000
Less utilised in 2017/18	1,300
Losses carried forward	£11,700

For 2017/18, Mary (who is also UK-resident) has the same gains and losses (including brought-forward losses) as Paul above, but is also a beneficiary of an offshore trust. Trust gains of £12,000 are attributed to her for 2017/18 under *TCGA 1992, s 87*.

	£
Adjusted net gains (£13,800 – £1,200 + £11,300*)	23,900
Losses brought forward (part)	12,600
	11,300
Annual exempt amount	11,300
	Nil
Add: TCGA 1992, s 87 gains not brought in above	700
Taxable gains	£700

Losses brought forward	13,000
Less utilised in 2017/18	12,600
Losses carried forward	£400

* Gains attributed under *TCGA 1992, s 87* are included in adjusted net gains only to the extent that they do not exceed the annual exempt amount. Such gains cannot be covered by personal losses.

For 2017/18, Peter is in the same position as Mary except that his attributed gains are only £6,100.

	£
Adjusted net gains (£13,800 – £1,200 + £6,100)	18,700
Losses brought forward (part)	7,400
	11,300
Annual exempt amount	11,300
Taxable gains	Nil
Losses brought forward	13,000
Less utilised in 2017/18	7,400
Losses carried forward	£5,600

In Peter's case, £6,100 of the annual exempt amount is set against the attributed gains. Losses brought forward are used only to the extent necessary to reduce the personal gains to the balance of the annual exempt amount (£5,200).

Key points on annual rates and exemptions

[2.7] Points to consider are as follows:

- At its lowest level the annual exempt amount is worth £1,130 (11,300 × 10%); at its highest it is worth £3,164 (11,300 × 28%). Significant tax planning therefore revolves around trying to crystallise gains that will be covered by this relief (or multiple annual exempt amounts). For example, the overall tax rate may be reduced where a gain can be split between spouses or civil partners or over two tax years. Also, popular is partially breaking the terms for a relief so a small gain arises (covered by the exemption) whilst the majority of the gain is rolled/held over. For example, adjust the consideration for the transfer such that a gain arises equal to the amount of the annual exempt amount. No tax is payable on the cash proceeds whilst the base cost is increased, reducing the potential gain on a future disposal.
- Entrepreneurs' relief reduces the rate of capital gains tax to 10% for gains on qualifying disposals of business assets. See **24** ENTREPRENEURS' RELIEF. See also **40** INVESTORS' RELIEF.

- Taxpayers can choose how the annual exempt amount and any allowable losses are allocated against gains if they are liable to capital gains tax at two or more different rates. It is normally beneficial to offset these amounts against the gains taxable at the highest rates.
- A taxpayer's basic rate band is expanded by qualifying pension contributions and gift aid donations (gross amounts). Certain gift aid donations can be carried back.
- If a taxpayer does not use the annual exempt amount for a tax year, it is wasted: the amount cannot be carried forward or transferred to a spouse or civil partner. Consideration should therefore be given to realising sufficient gains to maximise use of the exemption.
- Spouses and civil partners may consider transferring an asset to the other spouse or partner before disposal in order to benefit from a lower rate of capital gains tax or to utilise their annual exempt amount. However care is required where the asset potentially qualifies for entrepreneurs' relief; will the other party also qualify?
- An individual who claims the remittance basis is not entitled to the annual exempt amount for that year.

3

Alternative Finance Arrangements

Introduction	3.1
Capital gains tax consequences of alternative finance arrangement	3.2
Further consequences for diminishing shared ownership arrangements	3.3
Further consequences for investment bond arrangements	3.4
Investment bond arrangements where the underlying asset is land	3.5

Simon's Taxes. See A1.3.

Introduction to alternative finance arrangements

[3.1] Certain types of finance arrangements (known as '*alternative finance arrangements*') which are broadly equivalent to loans, deposits etc. but which do not involve the receipt or payment of interest are subject to special tax provisions designed to ensure that they are taxed no more nor less favourably than equivalent products which do involve interest. Such arrangements are usually aimed at those wishing to adhere to Shari'a law, which prohibits the receipt or payment of interest. The tax rules are not, however, restricted to Shari'a-compliant products, but apply to any arrangements falling within their terms.

This chapter describes the tax rules for alternative finance arrangements only to the extent of their effect on capital gains tax. See Tolley's Income Tax and Tolley's Corporation Tax for the detailed provisions.

For corporation tax purposes, the arrangements are loan relationships so that all profits and losses are dealt with as income: see **15.5** COMPANIES — CORPORATE FINANCE AND INTANGIBLES. For capital gains tax purposes, the return on the arrangement that is broadly equivalent to interest is excluded from the consideration for the purchase and sale of the asset purchased under the arrangements.

A further chargeable gains relief applies to certain investment bond arrangements involving land which are equivalent to a securitisation of the land.

The Treasury has the power by statutory instrument to amend the existing provisions, and to introduce new provisions, relating to alternative finance arrangements. [*CTA 2009, s 521; TIOPA 2010, s 366*].

Capital gains tax consequences of alternative finance arrangement

[3.2] Where, under any of three types of alternative finance arrangements, an asset is sold by one party to the arrangements to the other party, the 'alternative finance return' is excluded in determining for capital gains tax purposes the consideration for the sale and purchase of the asset. This does not affect the operation of any provision providing for the consideration to be treated as an amount other than the actual consideration.

This provision applies to the following types of arrangements: 'purchase and resale arrangements', 'diminishing shared ownership arrangements' and 'investment bond arrangements'. For each type of arrangement there is a particular definition of 'alternative finance return'.

Arrangements which are not at arm's length are not alternative finance arrangements for these purposes if the transfer pricing rules of *TIOPA 2010, s 147(3)(5)* require the alternative finance return to be recomputed on an arm's length basis and the party receiving the return is not subject to income tax, corporation tax or a corresponding foreign tax on the return.

[*TCGA 1992, ss 151O, 151X*].

Purchase and resale arrangements

For this purpose, '*purchase and resale arrangements*' are, broadly, arrangements entered into between two persons (A and B), at least one of whom is a 'financial institution' (as defined), under which:

(a) A purchases an asset and sells it to B;
(b) the amount payable by B in respect of the sale (the '*sale price*') is greater than the amount paid by A in respect of the purchase (the 'purchase price');
(c) all or part of the sale price does not have to be paid until a time after the sale; and
(d) the difference between the sale price and the purchase price equates, in substance, to the return on an investment of money at interest.

The sale of the asset in (a) above must take place immediately after the purchase unless A is a financial institution and the asset was purchased by A for the purpose of entering into the arrangements.

The '*alternative finance return*' is so much of the sale price as exceeds the purchase price. If, however, the purchase price is paid by instalments, the alternative finance return in each instalment is the amount of interest which would have been included in the instalment if the purchase price were a loan from A to B, the instalment were a part repayment of principal with interest and the loan were made on arm's length terms and accounted for under generally accepted accounting practice. If the alternative finance return is paid in a currency other than sterling, then if either A or B is not a company and the payment is not made for the purposes of a trade, profession, vocation or property business, the amount of the return is calculated in that currency and then translated into sterling at a spot rate for the day of payment.

[*TCGA 1992, ss 151J, 151P, 151Q*].

Diminishing shared ownership arrangements

'*Diminishing shared ownership arrangements*' are, broadly, arrangements under which a financial institution acquires a beneficial interest in an asset and another person (the '*eventual owner*'):

(i) also acquires a beneficial interest in the asset;
(ii) is to make payments to the financial institution amounting in aggregate to the consideration paid for the acquisition of its beneficial interest;
(iii) is to acquire (whether or not in stages) the financial institution's beneficial interest as a result of those payments;
(iv) is to make other payments to the financial institution (whether under a lease forming part of the arrangements or otherwise);
(v) has the exclusive right to occupy or otherwise use the asset; and
(vi) is exclusively entitled to any income, profit or gain attributable to the asset (including any increase in its value).

The '*alternative finance return*' is equal to the payments made by the eventual owner under the arrangements other than payments within (ii) above and payments in respect of any arrangement fee or legal or other costs or expenses which the eventual owner is required to pay under the arrangements.

[*TCGA 1992, ss 151K, 151R*].

Investment bond arrangements

'*Investment bond arrangements*' are, broadly, arrangements which:

- provide for one person (the '*bond holder*') to pay a sum of money (the '*capital*') to another (the '*bond issuer*');
- identify assets or a class of assets which the bond issuer will acquire for the purpose of generating income or gains;
- specify a term at the end of which they cease to apply;
- include an undertaking by the bond issuer to dispose of any bond assets still in his possession at the end of the bond term;
- include an undertaking by the bond issuer to make a repayment of the capital to the bond holder during or at the end of the bond term (whether or not in instalments);
- include an undertaking by the bond issuer to make additional payments not exceeding a reasonable commercial return on a loan of the capital during or at the end of the bond term;
- include an undertaking by the bond issuer to arrange for the management of the bond assets with a view to generating sufficient income to pay the redemption payment and the additional payments;
- allow the bond holder to transfer the rights under the arrangements;
- are a listed security on a recognised stock exchange (see **63.30** SHARES AND SECURITIES); and
- are wholly or partly treated in accordance with international accounting standards as a financial liability of the bond issuer (or would be if he applied them).

The '*alternative finance return*' is equal to the additional payments.

[*TCGA 1992, ss 151N, 151S(3)*].

Further consequences for diminishing shared ownership arrangements

[3.3] HMRC have published their view of the chargeable gains consequences arising where a person acquires an asset under a diminishing shared ownership arrangement. In their view, unless there are any special features leading to a different conclusion, the buyer is treated as acquiring each successive tranche of beneficial interest at the time they entered into the unconditional contracts with the seller and the financial institution. Where this is the case it follows that the date of acquisition of the asset for the purposes of indexation allowance (where available) is the date the diminishing shared ownership arrangements were entered into. (HMRC Brief 26/07).

A diminishing shared ownership arrangement is not a partnership for capital gains tax purposes. [*TCGA 1992, s 151Y*].

Further consequences for investment bond arrangements

[3.4] An alternative finance arrangement which is an investment bond arrangement is a security, but is neither an offshore fund nor a unit trust scheme, for capital gains purposes. [*TCGA 1992, ss 151V, 151W*].

Such an arrangement is also a qualifying corporate bond if certain conditions are met — see **54.3** QUALIFYING CORPORATE BONDS.

The bond holder is not treated as having a legal or beneficial interest in the bond assets and the bond issuer is not treated as a trustee of the assets. Gains accruing to the bond issuer in connection with the bond assets are gains of the bond issuer and not of the bond holder. Such gains do not accrue to the bond issuer in a fiduciary or representative capacity. Payments made by the bond issuer are not made in such a capacity. The bond holder is not entitled to relief for capital expenditure incurred in connection with the bond assets. [*TCGA 1992, s 151U*].

Investment bond arrangements where the underlying asset is land

[3.5] The following provisions (together with equivalent provisions relating to stamp duty land tax and capital allowances) are intended to ensure that the tax consequences of an alternative finance investment bond are the same as those for a conventional securitisation of land. The '*effective date*' of a land transaction is that date for the purposes of stamp duty land tax. Where a transaction is to be completed by conveyance, the effective date will in most cases be the date of completion. Where, however, 'substantial performance' of the contract takes place at an earlier date, that earlier date is the effective date. '*Substantial performance*' of a contract occurs when either the purchaser (or connected person) takes possession of substantially the whole of the interest or a substantial amount of the consideration is paid or provided. [*FA 2003, s 44; FA 2009, Sch 61 para 1(2)*]. See Tolley's Stamp Taxes for further details.

Relief for first transaction

Relief applies where:

(a) two persons ('P' and 'Q') enter into arrangements under which P transfers to Q a 'qualifying interest' in land (the '*first transaction*') and P and Q agree that when Q ceases to hold the interest as a 'bond asset' (see (b) below), Q will transfer the interest to P;

(b) Q, as 'bond issuer', enters into an alternative finance investment bond (see **3.2** above), either before or after making the arrangements in (a) above, and holds the interest in land as a bond asset; and
(c) to generate income or gains for the bond, Q and P enter into a leaseback agreement (i.e. Q grants a lease or sub-lease to P out of the interest transferred to Q by the first transaction).

For this purpose, '*bond asset*' and '*bond issuer*' have the same meaning as at **3.2** above. A '*qualifying interest*' in land is a major interest in land (within *FA 2003, s 117*), but leases with a term or period of less than 21 years are excluded. The Treasury can make regulations specifying an alternative to condition (c) above.

[*FA 2009, Sch 61 paras 1(1), 5(1)–(5); TIOPA 2010, Sch 8 para 229*].

If all of the above conditions are met within 30 days beginning with the effective date of the first transaction, that transaction is treated for chargeable gains purposes as being neither an acquisition by Q nor a disposal by Q. The granting of the lease or sub-lease under the leaseback agreement in (c) above is treated as neither an acquisition by P nor a disposal by Q. [*FA 2009, Sch 61 para 10*].

Withdrawal of relief

This relief is, however, withdrawn in certain circumstances. For this purpose, the following conditions are relevant.

(i) Within 120 days beginning with the effective date of the first transaction, Q must provide HMRC with evidence prescribed by HMRC in regulations that a satisfactory legal charge has been entered in the register of title kept under *Land Registration Act 2002, s 1* (or Scottish or NI equivalent). For this purpose, a charge is satisfactory if it is a first charge in favour of HMRC over the interest transferred by the first transaction for the amount of stamp duty land tax which would have been chargeable on the first transaction if it had been carried out at market value, together with any interest and penalties.
(ii) The total payments of 'capital' (see **3.2** above) made to Q before the termination of the bond must be not less than 60% of the value of the interest in land at the time of the first transaction.
(iii) (Subject to the substitution of asset rules below) Q must hold the interest in land as a bond asset until the termination of the bond.
(iv) Within 30 days beginning with the date on which the interest in land ceases to be held as a bond asset, it must be transferred by Q back to P (the '*second transaction*').
(v) The second transaction must be effected within ten years after the first transaction (or within a period specified by Treasury regulations).

The relief is withdrawn if:

(A) where the interest is in land in the UK, condition (i) above is not met;
(B) the interest in land is transferred by Q back to P without conditions (ii) and (iii) above having been met;
(C) the ten-year period in condition (v) above expires without conditions (ii) and (iii) above having been met; or

(D) it becomes apparent for any other reason at any time that any of conditions (ii) to (v) above cannot or will not be met.

If a chargeable gain or allowable loss arises as a result of the withdrawal of relief, it is treated as accruing:

- where (A) above applies, at the end of the 120-day period;
- where (B) above applies, immediately before the transfer from Q to P;
- where (C) above applies, at the end of the 10-year period; and
- where (D) above applies, at the time it becomes apparent that the conditions cannot or will not be met.

[*FA 2009, Sch 61 paras 5(6)–(12), 10, 11*].

Relief for second transaction

The second transaction (see (iv) above) is treated for chargeable gains purposes as being neither an acquisition by P nor a disposal by Q if (a) to (c) and (ii) to (v) above are satisfied and, where the land is in the UK, (i) above is satisfied. [*FA 2009, Sch 61 para 12*].

Substitution of asset

If the interest in land is transferred by Q back to P before the termination of the investment bond (so that condition (iii) above is not met), the above reliefs nevertheless continue to apply if conditions (iv) and (v) above are met and P and Q enter into further arrangements within (a) above relating to another interest in land. The value of the interest in the replacement land at the time it is transferred from P to Q must be equal to or greater than the value of the interest in the original land at the time of the first transaction.

In such circumstances, the reliefs in respect of the original land apply despite the fact that condition (iii) above has not been met, provided that (a)–(c) above and conditions (iii)–(v) above are met in relation to the replacement land.

In relation to the replacement land, condition (ii) above operates by reference to the value or the interest in the original land, and the ten-year limit in (v) above runs from the date of the first transaction relating to the original land.

These provisions also apply, with any necessary modifications where replacement land is itself replaced.

[*FA 2009, Sch 61 para 18*].

Anti-avoidance

The above reliefs are not available where control of the underlying asset is acquired by a bond holder (see **3.3** above) or a group of connected bond holders. This occurs where the rights of bond holders under a bond include the right of management and control of the bond assets and a bond holder or group acquires sufficient such rights to enable them to exercise that right to the exclusion of any other bond holders.

If the bond holder or group acquire such control before the end of the 30 days beginning with the effective date of the first transaction, no relief is available. If control is acquired at a later date, any relief already given is withdrawn as above.

This provision does not, however, prevent relief being given if either:

- at the time the rights were acquired, the bond holder or holders did not know and had no reason to suspect that the acquisition enabled the exercise of the right of management and control to the exclusion of other bond holders and as soon as reasonably practicable after becoming so aware they transfer sufficient rights for such management and control no longer to be possible; or
- the bond holder underwrites a public offer of rights under the bond and does not exercise the right of management and control of the bond assets.

For this purpose, a person underwrites an offer of rights if he agrees to make payments of capital under the bond in the event that others do not make the payments.

The above reliefs are also not available if the arrangements within (a) above are not made for genuine commercial reasons or form part of arrangements a main purpose of which is the avoidance of liability to income tax, corporation tax, capital gains tax, stamp duty or stamp duty land tax.

[*FA 2009, Sch 61 paras 20–22*].

4

Anti-Avoidance

Introduction	4.1
Approach of the Courts	4.2
General anti-abuse rule	4.3
Procedure	4.4
Provisional counteraction notices	4.5
Counteraction of equivalent arrangements	4.6
Specific legislation	4.7
Value shifting	4.8
Value shifting to give tax-free benefit	4.10
Certain disposals of shares by companies	4.11
Connected persons	4.12
Assets disposed of in a series of transactions	4.13
Close company transferring asset at undervalue	4.14
Restrictions on company reconstructions	4.15
Schemes involving the transfer of a business owned by companies	4.16
Depreciatory transactions within groups of companies	4.17
Dividend stripping	4.18
Abuse of concessions	4.19
Tax arbitrage	4.20
Factoring of income receipts	4.21
Transfer of income stream	4.22
Disposal of income stream through partnership	4.23
Disposal of asset through partnership	4.24
Follower notices	4.25
Giving of follower notice	4.26
Action required following giving of follower notice	4.27
Late appeal against a judicial ruling	4.28
Accelerated payment notices	4.29
Giving of accelerated payment notice	4.30
Effects of accelerated payment notice	4.31
Serial avoiders regime	4.32
Warning notices	4.33
Meaning of 'relevant defeat'	4.34
Requirement of annual information notices	4.35
Restriction of reliefs	4.36
Partnerships	4.37
Groups of companies	4.38
Penalties	4.39
Publishing taxpayer's details	4.40
Key points	4.41

Cross-references. See **14.6** COMPANIES for provisions relating to corporate losses; **17** CONNECTED PERSONS; **20** DISCLOSURE OF TAX AVOIDANCE SCHEMES; **21.9** DOUBLE TAX RELIEF for schemes and arrangements designed to increase such relief; **49**

OVERSEAS MATTERS for provisions relating to overseas resident settlements; **49.9**, **49.10** OVERSEAS MATTERS for interests in controlled foreign companies and in offshore funds respectively; **50.17** PARTNERSHIPS; **62.16** SETTLEMENTS for restrictions on transfer of settlement losses to beneficiary becoming absolutely entitled to settled property; **62.20–62.23** SETTLEMENTS for further anti-avoidance provisions.

Introduction to anti-avoidance

[4.1] Anyone attempting to structure a transaction so as to avoid a liability to tax on chargeable gains arising or to mitigate such a liability must consider:

(a) whether the line of cases often referred to as the 'Ramsay principle' will operate to make the arrangements ineffective;
(b) whether the tax advantage under the arrangements is counteracted by the general anti-abuse rule;
(c) whether the arrangements give rise to a duty to disclose the details to HMRC under the provisions for DISCLOSURE OF TAX AVOIDANCE SCHEMES (**20**); and
(d) whether the arrangements fall foul of one of the many pieces of specific anti-avoidance legislation.

This chapter covers three of these considerations. For (c) above see **20** DISCLOSURE OF TAX AVOIDANCE SCHEMES.

The approach of the courts to avoidance cases is dealt with at **4.2** below, and the rules for the disclosure of tax avoidance schemes are at **20.2–20.5** below. The general anti-abuse rule is described at **4.3** and **4.4** below. The next part of the chapter describes specific anti-avoidance provisions, many of which, it should be noted, apply where the particular conditions are satisfied whether or not there is any intention to avoid tax. Note that there are many anti-avoidance provisions which are dealt with outside this chapter where they relate to legislation described elsewhere in this work. See the list of provisions at **4.7** below and the cross references at the head of the chapter.

HMRC has powers, by way of a 'follower notice' to require a person using an avoidance scheme which is defeated in the courts in relation to another taxpayer to concede their position to reflect the court's decision. See **4.25** onwards below. Powers to enable HMRC to issue an 'accelerated payment notice' which requires a user of an avoidance scheme to pay tax upfront before the success or failure of the scheme has been finally determined have also been introduced. See **4.29** onwards below.

FA 2016 has introduced a regime of warnings and escalating sanctions for taxpayers ('serial avoiders') who persistently engage in tax avoidance schemes that are defeated by HMRC. See **4.32–4.40** below.

Repayment claims in avoidance cases

HMRC have published their policy on withholding repayment claims in avoidance cases where they are challenging or considering challenging the claim by enquiry. See HMRC Brief 28/2013.

Approach of the Courts

[4.2] For the general approach of the Courts to transactions entered into solely to avoid or reduce tax liability, leading cases are *Duke of Westminster v CIR HL 1935*, 19 TC 490; *W T Ramsay Ltd v CIR; Eilbeck v Rawling* HL 1981, 54 TC 101; *CIR v Burmah Oil Co Ltd* HL 1981, 54 TC 200; *Furniss v Dawson (and related appeals)* HL 1984, 55 TC 324. See also *Coates v Arndale Properties Ltd* HL 1984, 59 TC 516; *Reed v Nova Securities Ltd* HL 1985, 59 TC 516; *Magnavox Electronics Co Ltd (in liquidation) v Hall* CA 1986, 59 TC 610; *Commissioner of Inland Revenue v Challenge Corporation Ltd* PC, [1986] STC 548; *Craven v White; CIR v Bowater Property Developments Ltd; Baylis v Gregory* HL 1988, 62 TC 1; *Dunstan v Young Austen Young Ltd* CA 1988, 61 TC 448; *Shepherd v Lyntress Ltd; News International plc v Shepherd* Ch D 1989, 62 TC 495; *Ensign Tankers (Leasing) Ltd v Stokes* HL 1992, 64 TC 617; *Moodie v CIR and another (and related appeals)* HL 1993, 65 TC 610; *Countess Fitzwilliam and others v CIR (and related appeals)* HL 1993, 67 TC 614; *Pigott v Staines Investments Co Ltd* Ch D 1995, 68 TC 342; *CIR v McGuckian* HL 1997, 69 TC 1; *MacNiven v Westmoreland Investments Ltd* HL 2001, 73 TC 1; *CIR v Scottish Provident Institution* HL 2004, [2005] STC 15; *Mawson v Barclays Mercantile Business Finance Ltd* HL 2004, [2005] STC 1 and *HMRC v Tower Mcashback LLP1* SC, [2011] UKSC 19.

See also *DR Collins v HMRC* (Sp C 675), [2008] SSCD 718, *Trustees of the Eyretel Unapproved Pension Scheme v HMRC*, (Sp C 718), [2009] SSCD 17, *Mayes v HMRC* CA [2011] EWCA Civ 407; 2011 STI 1444, *Berry v HMRC* UT, [2011] STC 1057 and *Explainaway Ltd v HMRC* UT, [2012] STC 2525.

Classical interpretation

The classical interpretation of the constraints upon the Courts in deciding cases involving tax avoidance schemes is summed up in Lord Tomlin's statement in the *Duke of Westminster* case that 'every man is entitled if he can to order his affairs so that the tax attaching . . . is less than it otherwise would be'. The judgment was concerned with the tax consequences of a single transaction, but in *Ramsay*, and subsequently in *Furniss v Dawson*, the House of Lords has set bounds on the ambit within which this principle can be applied in relation to modern sophisticated and increasingly artificial arrangements to avoid tax. In *CIR v McGuckian*, it was observed that while Lord Tomlin's words in the *Duke of Westminster* case 'still point to a material consideration, namely the general liberty of the citizen to arrange his financial affairs as he thinks fit, they have ceased to be canonical as to the tax consequences of a tax avoidance scheme'. It was further observed that the *Ramsay* principle was 'more natural and less extreme' than the majority decision in *Duke of Westminster*.

The 'Ramsay' principle

Ramsay concerned a complex 'circular' avoidance scheme at the end of which the financial position of the parties was little changed but it was claimed that a large capital gains tax loss had been created. It was held that where a preconceived series of transactions is entered into to avoid tax and with the clear intention to proceed through all stages to completion, once set in motion, the Duke of Westminster principle does not compel a consideration of the individual transactions and of the fiscal consequences of such transactions in isolation. The opinions of the House of Lords in *Furniss v Dawson* are of outstanding importance, and establish, *inter alia*, that the *Ramsay* principle is not confined to 'circular' devices, and that if a series of transactions is 'preordained', a particular transaction within the series, accepted as genuine, may nevertheless be ignored if it was entered into solely for fiscal reasons and without any commercial purpose other than tax avoidance, even if the series of transactions as a whole has a legitimate commercial purpose.

However, in *Craven v White* the House of Lords indicated that for the *Ramsay* principle to apply all the transactions in a series have to be preordained with such a degree of certainty that, at the time of the earlier transactions, there is no practical likelihood that the transactions would not take place. It is not sufficient that the ultimate transaction is simply of a kind that was envisaged at the time of the earlier transactions. See, however, *CIR v Scottish Provident Institution* below. In the unanimous decision of the House of Lords in *Ensign Tankers (Leasing) Ltd v Stokes*, the lead judgment drew a clear distinction between 'tax avoidance' and 'tax mitigation', it being said that the *Duke of Westminster* principle is accurate as far as the latter is concerned but does not apply to the former.

Fitzwilliam involved five transactions entered into over a short period of time to avoid capital transfer tax on appointments from a will trust, the last four transactions being determined by the Revenue to form a preordained series of transactions subject to the *Ramsay* principle but which the taxpayers claimed should be viewed separately with the result that by reason of a number of available reliefs no liability to capital transfer tax arose. The House of Lords stated that the correct approach to a consideration of steps 2 to 5 was to ask whether realistically they constituted a single and indivisible whole in which one or more of the steps was simply an element without independent effect and whether it was intellectually possible so to treat them. It was held that both questions should be answered in the negative. The case put by the Revenue did not depend on disregarding for fiscal purposes any one or more of steps 2 to 5 as having been introduced for fiscal purposes only and as having no independent effect, nor on treating the whole of steps 2 to 5 as having no such effect. Each of the four steps had a fiscal effect of giving rise to an income tax charge on two of the taxpayers for a period of time, and there was a potential capital transfer tax charge should either have died whilst in enjoyment of the income associated with the transactions. Although steps 2 to 5 were 'preordained', in the sense that they formed part of a pre-planned tax avoidance scheme and that there was no reasonable possibility that they would not all be carried out, the fact of preordainment in that sense was not sufficient in itself to negative the application of an exemption from liability to tax which the series of transactions was intended to create, unless the series was capable of being construed in a manner inconsistent with the application of the exemption. In the particular circumstances of the case, the series of transactions could not be so construed. Two or more transactions in the series could not be run together, as in *Furniss v Dawson*, nor could any one or more of them be disregarded. There was no rational basis on which the four separate steps could be treated as effective for the purposes of one provision which created a charge to tax on a termination of an interest in possession but ineffective for the purposes of two other provisions which gave exemptions from that charge where the interest was disposed of for a consideration and where the interest reverted to the settlor. Accordingly, the case was one to which the *Ramsay* principle, as extended by *Furniss v Dawson*, did not apply.

In *MacNiven v Westmoreland Investments Ltd*, where the HL held that the *Ramsay* principle did not apply to a payment of interest, Lord Nicholls held that 'the very phrase "the *Ramsay* principle" is potentially misleading. In *Ramsay* the House did not enunciate any new legal principle. What the House did was to highlight that, confronted with new and sophisticated tax avoidance devices, the courts' duty is to determine the legal nature of the transactions in question and then relate them to the fiscal legislation'. Lord Hoffmann held that 'what Lord Wilberforce was doing in the *Ramsay* case was no more . . . than to treat the statutory words "loss" and "disposal" as referring to commercial concepts to which a juristic analysis of the transaction, treating each step as autonomous and independent, might not be determinative'. Lord Hutton held that 'an essential element of a transaction to which the *Ramsay* principle is applicable is that it should be artificial'.

In *Mawson v Barclays Mercantile Business Finance Ltd* the HL held that Lord Hoffman's distinction in *Westmoreland* between 'legal' and 'commercial' concepts was not 'intended to provide a substitute for a close analysis of what the statute means'. It 'does not justify the assumption that an answer can be obtained by classifying all concepts a priori as either "commercial" or "legal"'. Instead, in applying any statutory provision, it is necessary 'first, to decide, on a purposive construction, exactly what transaction will answer to the statutory description and secondly, whether the transaction in question does so'.

In *CIR v Scottish Provident Institution* the issue was whether the decision in *Craven v White* meant that a series of transactions could not be treated as a composite transaction under the *Ramsay* principle because there was a real commercial risk that the transactions would not take place. The HL held that 'it would destroy the value of the *Ramsay* principle . . . as referring to the effect of composite transactions if their composite effect had to be disregarded simply because the parties had deliberately included a commercially irrelevant contingency, creating an acceptable risk that the scheme might not work as planned'. Such a 'commercially irrelevant contingency' was found to be present in a purchased tax scheme involving options in *Schofield v HMRC* CA, [2012] STC 2019.

See also *Exors of Connell v HMRC* FTT, [2016] UKFTT 154 (TC); 2016 STI 1802 (market value of loan notes) and *Trustees of the Morrison 2002 Maintenance Trust v HMRC* UT, [2017] UKUT 300 (TCC) (disposal of shares by trustees involving intermediate sale to non-resident trust).

Sham

In *Hitch and Others v Stone* CA, [2001] STC 214, the Revenue mounted a successful challenge to a complex and artificial tax avoidance scheme on the grounds that agreements on which it was based were shams. It was noted that 'sham' meant acts done or documents executed by the parties thereto which were intended by them to give to third parties or to the court the appearance of creating between the parties legal rights and obligations different from the actual legal rights and obligations (if any) which the parties intended to create. The law did not require that in every situation every party to the act or document should be a party to the sham, although a case where a document was properly held to be only in part a sham would be the exception rather than the rule and would occur only where the document reflected a transaction divisible into several parts.

Simon's Taxes. See **A2.115–A2.123**.

General anti-abuse rule

[4.3] *FA 2013* introduced a new general anti-abuse rule ('GAAR') which is intended to counteract the 'tax advantages' arising from 'tax arrangements' which are 'abusive'. Before HMRC can take action under the GAAR, they must generally first refer the case to an independent GAAR Advisory Panel established by the Commissioners for HMRC. With effect from 15 September 2016, HMRC can, however, make a provisional counteraction under the GAAR before referral to the Panel where, for example, assessing time limits are about to expire. Also with effect from that date, a GAAR Advisory Panel opinion allows HMRC to apply the GAAR to equivalent arrangements used by other taxpayers without further referral.

The GAAR applies to a range of taxes including income tax, corporation tax and capital gains tax.

The rule applies to tax arrangements entered into on or after 17 July 2013. Where tax arrangements entered into on or after that date form part of any other arrangements entered into before that date, those other arrangements are ignored for the purposes of the GAAR unless the effect of taking them into account would be to determine that the later arrangements were not abusive.

[*FA 2013, ss 206, 215*].

HMRC do not give formal or informal clearances that the GAAR does not apply. As part of their engagement with large businesses and wealthy individuals, however, HMRC do discuss commercial arrangements and confirm where appropriate that they don't regard particular arrangements as tax avoidance. See www.gov.uk/government/collections/seeking-clearance-or-approval-for-a-transaction.

Definitions

Arrangements are '*tax arrangements*' if, having regard to all the circumstances, it would be reasonable to conclude that the obtaining of a tax advantage was the main purpose, or one of the main purposes, of the arrangements. For this purpose, '*arrangements*' include any agreement, understanding, scheme, transaction or series of transactions, whether or not legally enforceable.

Tax arrangements are '*abusive*' if entering into them or carrying them out cannot reasonably be regarded as a reasonable course of action in relation to the relevant tax provisions, having regard to all the circumstances. Those circumstances include:

- whether the substantive results of the arrangements are consistent with any express or implied principles on which the provisions are based and their policy objectives;
- whether the means of achieving the results of the arrangements involve one or more contrived or abnormal steps; and
- whether the arrangements are intended to exploit any shortcomings in the provisions.

Where the tax arrangements form part of other arrangements, regard must be had to those other arrangements (but see the commencement rules above where the other arrangements were entered into before 17 July 2013).

The legislation gives the following non-exhaustive examples of what might indicate that tax arrangements are abusive.

- The arrangements result in taxable income, profits or gains significantly less than the economic amount.
- The arrangements result in a tax deduction or loss significantly greater than the economic amount.
- The arrangements result in a claim for repayment or crediting of tax, including foreign tax, that has not been, and is unlikely to be, paid.

The legislation also gives an example of what might indicate that arrangements are not abusive: the arrangements accord with established practice accepted by HMRC.

A '*tax advantage*' includes relief or increased relief from tax, repayment or increased repayment of tax, avoidance or reduction of a charge or assessment to tax, avoidance of a possible assessment to tax or of an obligation to deduct or account for tax, deferral of a payment of tax, and advancement of a repayment of tax.

[*FA 2013, ss 207, 208, 214(1); FA 2016, s 157(8)*].

Effect of the GAAR

The GAAR operates by counteracting the tax advantage under the tax arrangements by HMRC or the taxpayer making adjustments that are just and reasonable. Adjustments can be made by assessment, modification of an assessment, amendment or disallowance of a claim or otherwise. An adjustment can impose a tax liability where there would not otherwise be one or can increase an existing liability. Adjustments may be made in respect of the tax in question or any other tax to which the GAAR applies. Adjustments have effect for all tax purposes. The normal time limits for making assessments etc apply to the making of GAAR adjustments.

HMRC must follow the appropriate procedures at **4.4–4.6** below before making an adjustment under the GAAR.

For arrangements entered into on or after 15 September 2016, where a matter is referred to the GAAR Advisory Panel (see **4.4**(4) or (6) below), the taxpayer cannot make any adjustments to counteract the tax advantage himself in the '*closed period*' beginning with the thirty-first day after the end of the 45-day period for making representations (see **4.4**(2) below) and ending immediately before the day on which the person is given notice of HMRC's final decision after considering the opinion of the Panel. Similarly a person cannot make any such adjustments in the closed period following the issue of a pooling notice or notice of binding (see **4.5** below). For this purpose, the 'closed period' is as defined at **4.5** below.

[*FA 2013, s 209; FA 2016, ss 157(4), 158(4)(15)*]

Consequential adjustments

Where the counteraction of a tax advantage is final and, if the counteraction was not made as a result of an HMRC final counteraction notice, the taxpayer has notified HMRC of it, a person (not necessarily the taxpayer) has twelve months, beginning with the day the counteraction becomes final, to make a claim for one or more consequential adjustments to be made in respect of any tax to which the GAAR applies. For this purpose, counteraction of a tax advantage is final when the adjustments made and any amounts resulting from them can no longer be varied, on appeal or otherwise.

Consequential adjustments can be made for any period and may affect any person, whether or not a party to the tax arrangements. Adjustments are made on a just and reasonable basis but cannot increase a person's liability to any tax. HMRC must notify the person who made the claim of any adjustments made in writing. Consequential adjustments can be made by assessment, modification of an assessment, amendment of a claim or otherwise. There are no time limits for making such an adjustment.

The procedure for claims made outside a return in *TMA 1970, Sch 1A* (see **13.3** CLAIMS) applies to claims for consequential adjustments for income tax, capital gains tax and corporation tax purposes. See *FA 2013, s 210(6)* for the procedure rules for other taxes.

[*FA 2013, s 210; FA 2016, s 157(5)*]

See **52.11** PENALTIES for the 60% penalty which applies to arrangements entered into on or after 15 September 2016 which are counteracted by the GAAR.

Court and tribunal proceedings

In any court or tribunal proceedings in connection with the GAAR, HMRC must show both that the tax arrangements are abusive and that the adjustments made to counteract the tax advantage are just and reasonable.

In making a decision in connection with the GAAR a court or tribunal must take into account any HMRC guidance on the GAAR which was approved by the GAAR Advisory Panel at the time the tax arrangements were entered into and also any relevant opinion of the sub-panel (see **4.4**(9) and **4.6** below) .

[*FA 2013, s 211; FA 2016, s 157(6)*].

Priority rules

The GAAR can override any priority rule in tax legislation, i.e. any rule to the effect that particular provisions have effect to the exclusion of, or otherwise in priority to, anything else. [*FA 2013, s 212*].

Procedure

[4.4] Except where a provisional counteraction notice is issued, the following procedure must be followed before HMRC can make an adjustment under the GAAR.

(1) An HMRC officer designated by the Commissioners for HMRC for the purpose of the GAAR must give the taxpayer a written notice specifying:
- the arrangements and the tax advantage;
- why the officer considers that a tax advantage has arisen from abusive tax arrangements;
- the counteraction which the officer considers should be taken;
- the period within which the taxpayer can make representations (see (2) below); and
- the effect of the rules in (3)–(5) below and of the PENALTIES (**52.11**) which may apply if the proposed counteraction takes effect.

The notice may set out steps that the taxpayer may take to avoid the application of the GAAR.

(2) The taxpayer has 45 days starting with the day on which HMRC's notice is given to send written representations in response to the notice to the designated HMRC officer. The designated officer may extend the period if the taxpayer makes a written request.

(3) For arrangements entered into on or after 15 September 2016, where a person who has been given a notice under (1) takes 'corrective action' before the beginning of the closed period (see **4.3** above under 'Effect of the GAAR'), the matter is not referred to the GAAR Advisory Panel under (4) or (6) below. A person takes '*corrective action*' for this purpose only if he amends a return or claim to counteract the tax advantage or relinquishes the tax advantage by entering into a written agreement with HMRC to determine an appeal. A person can amend a return or claim for this purpose during an enquiry even if the normal time limits have expired. No appeal may then be made against any enquiry closure notice (see **58.12** RETURNS) to the extent that it takes into account an amendment made as corrective action. The person must notify HMRC of the action taken and the additional tax amount which has or will become due. Where a person takes corrective action in this way no penalty can be charged under the provisions at **52.11** PENALTIES.

(4) If the taxpayer makes no representations and, where relevant, does not take corrective action, a designated HMRC officer must refer the matter to the GAAR Advisory Panel.

The officer must at the same time notify the taxpayer that the matter is being referred. The notice must inform the taxpayer of the period for making representations under (7) below and of the requirement to send any such representations to the officer. The officer must provide the Panel with a copy of the notice given to the taxpayer at step (1) above and the notice informing the taxpayer that the matter has been referred to the Panel.

(5) If the taxpayer does make representations but, where relevant, does not take corrective action, the representations must be considered by a designated HMRC officer.

(6) If the designated HMRC officer in (5) above still considers that the GAAR should apply, he must refer the matter to the GAAR Advisory Panel, together with a copy of the taxpayer's representations and any comments he has on those representations. With effect from 15 September 2016, the officer must notify the taxpayer of his decision on whether or not to refer the matter to the GAAR Advisory Panel as soon as is reasonably practicable.

The same requirements for the officer to notify the taxpayer and to provide information to the Panel apply as at step (4) above. The notice to the taxpayer must, however, also include a copy of any comments on the taxpayer's representations sent by the officer to the Panel.

(7) The taxpayer has 21 days to send written representations to the Panel and the designated HMRC officer about the notice given at step (1) above and any comments made by HMRC on the taxpayer's original representations. The Panel may extend the period for making representations if the taxpayer makes a written request.

(8) If the taxpayer makes representations at step (7) above but did not make representations at step (2) above, the designated HMRC officer may provide the Panel and the taxpayer with comments on the step (7) representations.

(9) A sub-panel of three members of the Panel will consider the matter in question. The sub-panel may invite the taxpayer or the designated HMRC officer to supply further information within a specified period. Information supplied to the sub-panel must also be sent to the other party.

The sub-panel must produce an opinion notice stating its collective opinion as to whether or not the entering into and carrying out of the tax arrangements was a reasonable course of action in relation to the relevant tax provisions, having regard to the circumstances outlined at **4.3** above. An opinion notice may indicate that the sub-panel considers that it is not possible to reach a view on the information available. Alternatively, the sub-panel may produce two or three opinion notices which, taken together, state the opinions of all the members. An opinion notice must include the reasons for the opinion and is given to both the designated HMRC officer and the taxpayer.

See www.gov.uk/government/publications/gaar-advisory-panel-opinion-employee-rewards-using-gold-bullion for the GAAR Advisory Panel's first published opinion notices.

(10) The designated HMRC officer must, having considered the sub-panel's opinion or opinions, give the taxpayer a written notice setting out whether or not the tax advantage under the arrangements is to be counteracted under the GAAR. It should be noted that HMRC are not bound by the decision of the sub-panel and may proceed with the application of the GAAR even if the sub-panel's opinion is that the GAAR ought not to apply.

If the GAAR is to apply, the counteraction notice must specify the adjustments required and any steps that the taxpayer must take to give effect to them.

HMRC are not required to know for certain that a tax advantage has arisen before they embark on this procedure. A designated HMRC officer may carry out the above steps where he considers that a tax advantage might have arisen to the taxpayer. Any notice he gives may be expressed to be given on the assumption that a tax advantage arises.

[*FA 2013, Sch 43; FA 2016, s 157(11)(30), s 158(8)(9)(15)*].

Provisional counteraction notices

[4.5] With effect from 15 September 2016, regardless of when the tax arrangements were entered into, an HMRC officer may issue a provisional counteraction notice under the GAAR. Such a notice will, for example, be issued to protect against loss of tax where an assessing time limit is about to expire. A notice must:

- specify adjustments (as in **4.3** above) which the HMRC officer reasonably believes may be required to counteract a tax advantage that would (apart from the GAAR) arise to the recipient from tax arrangements;
- detail the arrangements and tax advantage concerned; and
- explain the appeals procedure and the circumstances in which the notice may be cancelled.

Adjustments specified in a notice which are made by HMRC are treated as effecting a valid counteraction of the tax advantage under the GAAR. The taxpayer may appeal against adjustments, stating the grounds of appeal, within the 30 days beginning with the date he receives the notice. If the taxpayer appeals the adjustments are treated as cancelled after 12 months from the date on which the provisional counteraction notice is given, unless, before that time (and whether before or after the issue of the provisional counteraction notice), an HMRC officer gives a notice to the taxpayer:

(1) cancelling the adjustments or withdrawing the notice (without cancelling the adjustments);
(2) issuing a notice within **4.4**(1) above in respect of the same arrangements and tax advantage and specifying the same or lesser adjustments as the counteraction which should be taken;
(3) issuing a pooling notice or a notice of binding (see **4.6** below) in respect of the same arrangements and tax advantage and specifying the same or lesser adjustments as the counteraction which should be taken; or
(4) issuing a generic referral notice (see **4.6** below) in respect of the same arrangements and tax advantage and specifying the same or lesser adjustments as the counteraction which should be taken.

Where a notice within (2)–(4) above specifies lesser adjustments, the provisional counteraction notice must be amended accordingly (unless it was issued after the notice in (2)–(4) above).

If a notice within (2) above is given and the matter is not referred to the GAAR Advisory Panel or if a notice within (2)–(4) above is given and subsequently the taxpayer is given a notice stating that the tax advantage is not to be counteracted under the GAAR, the adjustments in the provisional counteraction notice are treated as cancelled unless HMRC has the power to make the adjustments under provisions other than the GAAR and they state that the adjustments are therefore not cancelled. If a notice within (4) above is withdrawn, the adjustments in the provisional counteraction notice are likewise treated as cancelled, subject to the same exception.

Where a notice within (2)–(4) above is given and subsequently the taxpayer is given a notice stating that the tax advantage is to be counteracted, the adjustments in the provisional counteraction notice are confirmed so far as specified in the notice as adjustments required to give effect to the counteraction and are otherwise treated as cancelled.

[*FA 2013, ss 209A–209F; FA 2016, s 156*].

Counteraction of equivalent arrangements

[4.6] With effect from 15 September 2016, regardless of when the tax arrangements were entered into, there are provisions to enable the counteraction of 'equivalent' arrangements entered into by other taxpayers. The provisions enable HMRC to issue a 'pooling notice'

A designated HMRC officer may issue a '*pooling notice*' to a taxpayer (R), where:

(a) a person (P) has been given a notice under **4.4**(1) above in relation to tax arrangements ('*lead arrangements*');
(b) the 45-day period for representations in **4.4**(2) above has expired but no final counteraction notice under **4.4**(10) above or the generic referral provisions below has been given in respect of the matter;
(c) the officer considers that a tax advantage has arisen, or may have arisen, to R from tax arrangements which are abusive;
(d) the officer considers that those arrangements are equivalent to the lead arrangements; and
(e) the officer considers that the advantage should be counteracted.

The notice places R's arrangements in a pool with the lead arrangements. There can be only one pool for any lead arrangements. Arrangements placed in a pool remain in the pool except as indicated below, even if the lead arrangements or any other arrangements cease to be in it. A pooling notice may not be given if R has already been given a notice under **4.4**(1) above.

A designated HMRC officer may issue a '*notice of binding*' to a taxpayer (R), where:

(i) a person has been given a final counteraction notice under **4.4**(10) above or the generic referral provisions below in relation to tax arrangements ('*counteracted arrangements*') which are in a pool;
(ii) the officer considers that a tax advantage has arisen, or may have arisen, to R from tax arrangements which are abusive;
(iii) the officer considers that those arrangements are equivalent to the counteracted arrangements; and
(iv) the officer considers that the advantage should be counteracted.

A notice of binding may not be given if R has already been given a pooling notice or a notice under **4.4**(1) above.

A pooling notice or notice of binding must be given as soon as is reasonably practicable after HMRC become aware of the relevant facts. The notice must specify the tax arrangements and tax advantage concerned; explain why the officer considers them to be equivalent to the lead arrangements or the counteracted arrangements and why a tax advantage is considered to have arisen from abusive arrangements; set out the counteraction that the officer considers should be taken; and the effects of the notice. It may, but is not required to, set out steps R could take to avoid the proposed counteraction.

Arrangements are '*equivalent*' if they are substantially the same as one another, having regard to their results, the means of achieving those results, and the characteristics on the basis of which it could reasonably be argued in each case that the arrangements are abusive tax arrangements under which a tax advantage has arisen.

Where a person who has been given a pooling notice or a notice of binding takes 'corrective action' before the beginning of the 'closed period', he is treated as not having been given the notice and the arrangements are accordingly no longer in the pool. A person takes '*corrective action*' for this purpose only if he amends a return or claim to counteract the tax advantage or relinquishes the tax advantage by entering into an agreement with HMRC to determine an appeal. A person can amend a return or claim for this purpose during an enquiry even if the normal time limits have expired. No appeal may then be made against any enquiry closure notice (see **58.12** RETURNS) to the extent that it takes into account an amendment made as corrective action. The person must notify HMRC of the action taken and the additional tax amount which has or will become due. The '*closed period*' begins on the thirty-first day after the day on which the pooling notice or notice of binding was given. In the case of a pooling notice, the closed period ends immediately before the day on which the person is given notice of HMRC's final decision after considering the opinion of the GAAR Advisory Panel (see below). In the case of a notice of binding, the period is treated as ending at the same time as it begins. Where a person takes corrective action in this way no penalty can be charged under the provisions at **52.11** PENALTIES.

If P in (a) above takes corrective action within the 75-day period beginning with the day on which the notice under **4.4**(1) above was given, the lead arrangements are treated as ceasing to be in the pool.

Where, after a pooling notice has been issued to a person, the GAAR Advisory Panel issue an opinion notice (see **4.4**(9) above) in respect of another set of arrangements in the pool (the '*referred arrangements*'), the HMRC officer must give the person a '*pooled arrangements opinion notice*' setting out a report of the opinion and the person's right to make representations. Only one such notice may be given to a person about the same arrangements. The taxpayer has 30 days from the date of the notice to make representations that no tax advantage has arisen to him or that his arrangements are materially different from the referred arrangements.

The HMRC officer must consider any opinion of the GAAR Advisory Panel about the referred arrangements, together with any representations made, and issue a written notice with his decision as to whether the tax arrangements under consideration are to be counteracted under the GAAR. If so, the notice must set out the adjustments required to give effect to the counteraction and any steps that the taxpayer must take to give effect to it.

Where an HMRC officer gives a notice of binding, he must at the same time give a '*bound arrangements opinion notice*' setting out a report of any opinion of the GAAR Advisory Panel about the counteracted arrangements and the person's right to make representations. The taxpayer has 30 days from the date of the notice to make representations that no tax advantage has arisen to him or that his arrangements are materially different from the counteracted arrangements.

The HMRC officer must then consider any opinion of the GAAR Advisory Panel about the counteracted arrangements, together with any representations made, and issue a written notice with his decision as to whether the tax arrangements under consideration are to counteracted under the GAAR. If so, the notice must set out the adjustments required to give effect to the counteraction and any steps that the taxpayer must take to give effect to it.

The Treasury may amend these provisions by regulations.

[*FA 2013, s 209(9), Sch 43A; FA 2016, ss 157(2)(30), 158(4)*].

Generic referral of equivalent arrangements to the GAAR Advisory Panel

With effect from 15 September 2016, regardless of when the tax arrangements were entered into, there are provisions for HMRC to make a generic referral to the GAAR Advisory Panel of arrangements in a pool.

Where pooling notices have placed one or more sets of arrangements in a pool with lead arrangements, the lead arrangements have ceased to be in the pool and none of the arrangements have been referred to the GAAR Advisory Panel (see **4.4** (4), (6) above) a designated HMRC officer may give to each of the taxpayers whose arrangements are in the pool a notice of a proposal to make a generic referral to the Panel in respect of the arrangements in the pool. The notices must specify the arrangements and the tax advantage and the period within which the taxpayer can make a proposal (see below).

A person who has been given a notice has 30 days beginning with the day the notice was given to propose to HMRC that it should give him a notice under **4.4**(1) above and should not proceed with the generic referral.

If none of the notified taxpayers makes such a proposal within the 30-day period, the HMRC officer must make a referral (a '*generic referral*') to the GAAR Advisory Panel. If at least one of the recipients makes a proposal within the 30-day period, the officer must, after that period ends, decide whether to give one of the taxpayers a notice under **4.4**(1) above or to make a generic referral.

Where HMRC make a generic referral to the GAAR Advisory Panel, the designated HMRC officer must provide the Panel with a general statement of the material characteristics of the arrangements together with a declaration that this is applicable to *all* the arrangements and that nothing material to the panel's consideration has been omitted. The general statement must contain a factual description as well as HMRC's opinion, and a copy must be provided to the taxpayers.

A sub-panel of three members of the Panel will consider the referral. The sub-panel must produce an opinion notice stating its collective opinion as to whether or not the entering into and carrying out of the tax arrangements described in the general statement was a reasonable course of action in relation to the relevant tax provisions. An opinion notice may indicate that the sub-panel considers that it is not possible to reach a view on the information available. Alternatively, the sub-panel may produce two or three opinion notices which, taken together, state the opinions of all the members. An opinion notice must include the reasons for the opinion and is given to the designated HMRC officer.

The HMRC officer must then provide a copy of the opinion notice (or notices) to each taxpayer, any one of whom may then, within 30 days, make representations that:

- no tax advantage has arisen to him;
- he has already been given a bound arrangements opinion notice in relation to the arrangements concerned (see above); or
- a matter set out in HMRC's general statement is materially incorrect.

The officer must then, for each taxpayer, consider any opinion of the GAAR Advisory Panel, together with any representations made, and send a written notice with his decision as to whether the tax arrangements under consideration are to counteracted under the GAAR. If so, the notice must set out the adjustments required to give effect to the counteraction and the steps that the taxpayer must take to give effect to it.

The Treasury may amend these provisions by regulations.

[*FA 2013, s 214(3), Sch 43B; FA 2016, s 157(3)(10)(30)*].

Specific legislation

[4.7] Specific anti-avoidance legislation is intended to counteract transactions designed to avoid tax, but genuine transactions may also sometimes be caught. The anti-avoidance provisions relating to capital gains tax and corporation tax on chargeable gains and described in this work are summarised in the table below and dealt with in detail in the paragraph indicated. Provisions which are targeted at a specific area of legislation or a relief are included in the relevant chapter; the remaining provisions are dealt with in this chapter.

Provision	Description	Para
Investment bond arrangements where the underlying asset is land. [*FA 2009, Sch 61 paras 20–22*].	Relief is not available where: (a) control of the underlying asset is acquired by a bond holder or a group of connected bond holders; or (b) the arrangements are not made for genuine commercial reasons or form part of arrangements for the avoidance of tax.	3.5 ALTERNATIVE FINANCE ARRANGEMENTS

Provision	Description	Para
Value shifting. [*TCGA 1992, s 29*].	A disposal of an asset is deemed to arise: (i) where a person exercises control of a company so that value passes out of shares or rights owned by him and passes into other shares or rights; (ii) where a property owner becomes the lessee of the property and there is a subsequent adjustment of the rights and liabilities under the lease favourable to the lessor; or (iii) on the abrogation or extinction of a right or restriction to which an asset is subject by the person entitled to enforce it. The consideration is the arm's length value received by the transferee.	**4.8**
Value shifting to give tax-free benefit. [*TCGA 1992, ss 30, 31*].	Applies to the disposal of an asset if a scheme or arrangements have been made whereby the asset's value has been materially reduced and a tax-free benefit arises to the person making the disposal, a connected person or, except where tax avoidance was not a main purpose, any other person. The consideration for the disposal is increased by a just and reasonable amount. Separate provisions apply to the disposal by a company of shares or securities of another company. See **4.11** below.	**4.10, 4.11**
Connected persons. [*TCGA 1992, s 18*].	A transaction between CONNECTED PERSONS (17) is treated as having been made by way of a non-arm's length bargain so that acquisition and disposal are treated as being made at market value in most cases. There are restrictions on losses in such circumstances.	**4.12**
Assets disposed of in a series of transactions. [*TCGA 1992, ss 19, 20*].	Applies where a person disposes of assets to a connected person or persons by way of two or more gifts or other transactions within a period of six years ending on the date of the last transaction and the items singly are worth much less than their appropriate portion of the value of all of them together. The consideration for each disposal is deemed to be that appropriate proportion.	**4.13**
Close company transferring asset at undervalue. [*TCGA 1992, s 125*].	Where a close company transfers an asset to any person otherwise than at arm's length and for a consideration of an amount or value less than the market value of the asset, an amount equal to the difference is apportioned among the issued shares of the company. On a disposal of the shares by the person who owned them at the date of transfer, an amount equal to the amount so apportioned is not treated as allowable expenditure.	**4.14**

Provision	Description	Para
Restrictions on company reconstructions. [*TCGA 1992, ss 137, 138*].	Subject to certain exceptions, *TCGA 1992, ss 135, 136* (see **63.5, 63.7** SHARES AND SECURITIES) do not apply unless the exchange of securities or scheme of reconstruction is for bona fide commercial reasons and not part of a scheme or arrangement for the purpose of avoiding tax.	**4.15**
Depreciatory transactions within groups of companies. [*TCGA 1992, s 176*].	Where two or more members of a group of companies are parties to a disposal of assets at other than market value which has the effect of materially reducing the value of the shares or securities of one of those companies ('a depreciatory transaction'), any loss arising on the ultimate disposal of those shares or securities within six years by a member or a former member of the group is allowable only so far as is 'just and reasonable'.	**4.17**
Dividend stripping. [*TCGA 1992, s 177*].	Where a company holds 10% or more of a class of shares in another company otherwise than as a dealing company, and a distribution is or has been made to the first company which materially reduces or has reduced the value of the holding, the distribution is to be treated as a depreciatory transaction in relation to any disposal of the shares.	**4.18**
Abuse of concessions. [*TCGA 1992, ss 284A, 284B*].	A statutory charge applies where a person has at any time obtained the benefit of a capital gains relief in reliance on a concession published before 9 March 1999 and circumstances arise in a subsequent chargeable which, if that benefit had been obtained under a statutory relief, would have resulted in the whole (or part) of the benefit falling to be recouped. A chargeable gain equal to the full amount of that benefit is deemed to accrue to the person from whom the benefit would have been recouped for the chargeable period in which the circumstances arise.	**4.19**
Tax arbitrage. [*TIOPA 2010, ss 232–257*].	Applies to prevent the exploitation by companies of differences between or within national tax codes using hybrid entities or instruments (known as tax arbitrage). The provisions operate by reducing or disallowing deductions or by bringing receipts into charge, but apply only where HMRC issue a notice to the company.	**4.20**
Factoring of income receipts. [*ITA 2007, ss 809BZA–809BZS; CTA 2010, ss 758–776*].	Applies to schemes (any of three types of structured finance arrangement) involving the factoring of income receipts. Broadly, the provisions operate by deeming the intended effects of the arrangements not to have effect for tax purposes.	**4.21**

Provision	Description	Para
Transfer of income stream. [*ITA 2007, ss 809AZA–809AZF; CTA 2010, ss 752–757*].	Applies to ensure that where a person sells or otherwise disposes of a right to receive income and does not sell the underlying asset from which the income derives, the lump sum obtained is taxed as income and not as a chargeable gain.	4.22
Disposal of income stream through partnership. [*ITA 2007, ss 809AAZA, 809AAZB; CTA 2010, ss 757A, 757B*].	Applies to ensure that where a person sells or otherwise disposes of a right to receive income by or through a partnership, the consideration obtained is taxed as income and not as a chargeable gain.	4.23
Disposal of asset through partnership. [*ITA 2007, ss 809DZA, 809DZB; CTA 2010, ss 779A, 779B*].	Applies to ensure that where a person disposes of an asset by or through a partnership and the consideration would have been chargeable to tax as income had the disposal been made directly to the transferee, the consideration is taxed as income and not as a chargeable gain.	4.24
Options and futures — transactions with guaranteed returns. [*TCGA 1992, ss 148A–148C; ITTOIA 2005, ss 551–569*].	Applies to a disposal of futures or options or an exercise of an option if it is one of two or more related transactions intended to produce a guaranteed return. Broadly, any profits arising are treated as income rather than as capital. Does not apply for corporation tax purposes.	7.7, 7.8 ASSETS
Corporation tax — avoidance utilising losses. [*TCGA 1992, ss 184D–184H*].	Applies where, in connection with arrangements intended to achieve a tax advantage, an income receipt is turned into capital or a deduction from income is generated as part of a scheme to crystallise a capital gain. The effect of the provision is to restrict the use of capital losses. It applies only where HMRC issue a notice to the company concerned.	14.7–14.9 COMPANIES
Reconstructions involving transfer of business. [*TCGA 1992, s 139(5)*].	Relief under *TCGA 1992, s 139* will not apply to any transfer unless the scheme is for bona fide commercial reasons and not to avoid corporation tax, capital gains tax or income tax.	14.11 COMPANIES

Provision	Description	Para
Shares treated as creditor relationships. [*CTA 2009, ss 521A–521F*].	Certain shares held by a company which would be accounted for under GAAP by the issuing company as a liability and which produce a return to the investing company which is economically equivalent to interest are treated as rights under a creditor relationship of the investing company. The company must hold the share for the purpose of obtaining a tax advantage in relation to the return (or may elect for the provision to apply).	**15.6** COMPANIES — CORPORATE FINANCE AND INTANGIBLES
Schemes and arrangements to increase double tax relief. [*TIOPA 2010, ss 81–95*].	Applies to prevent the use of specified arrangements intended to increase credit relief for foreign tax. The provision applies only where HMRC issue a counteraction notice.	**21.9** DOUBLE TAX RELIEF
Enterprise investment scheme. [*ITA 2007, ss 165, 178; TCGA 1992, Sch 5B para 1*].	EIS reliefs (income tax and CGT) are not available unless the shares concerned are issued by the company and subscribed for by the investor for genuine commercial reasons and not as part of a scheme or arrangement a main purpose of which is the avoidance of tax.	**23.3, 23.4, 23.15** ENTERPRISE INVESTMENT SCHEME
Companies buying gains or losses. [*TCGA 1992, ss 184A–184F, Sch 7A*].	Applies where there is a change in ownership of a company in connection with arrangements with a main purpose of securing a tax advantage from either the deduction from any chargeable gains of a loss accruing to the company on a disposal of a pre-change asset or the deduction of a loss from a gain accruing to the company or any other company on a disposal of a pre-change asset. The effect is to restrict the gains against which the purchased losses can be set or the losses which can be set against the purchased gains. Where the above does not apply, restrictions are placed on the use, by a company joining a group, of pre-entry losses realised before it enters the group.	**29.15–29.23** GROUPS OF COMPANIES
Transactions in land. [*ITA 2007, ss 752–772; CTA 2010, ss 815–833*].	Where land in the UK is acquired or developed with the sole or main object of realising a gain from disposing of it or is held as trading stock, any capital gain from 'disposal' of the land is, subject to certain exemptions, treated as income of the person realising the gain (or the person who transmitted to him the opportunity of making that gain).	**41.4** LAND

Provision	Description	Para
New lease of land after assignment or surrender. [*ITA 2007, ss 681B–681BM; CTA 2010, ss 849–862*].	As regards certain arrangements for the surrender (or assignment) and lease-back of land, part of the consideration received by the lessee for giving up the original lease (or undertaking to pay an increased rent) is treated as an income receipt and not a capital one.	**41.22** LAND
Losses — arrangements to secure tax advantage. [*TCGA 1992, s 16A*].	A loss accruing on a disposal directly or indirectly in consequence of, or otherwise in connection with, any arrangements the main purpose of which, or one of the main purposes of which, is to secure a tax advantage is not an allowable loss.	**44.7** LOSSES
Individuals temporarily non-resident in the UK. [*TCGA 1992, s 10A*].	Where an individual leaves the UK for a period of temporary residence outside the UK, and the period of non-residence is five years or less, the individual is chargeable to CGT as if gains and losses accruing in the non-resident years were gains or losses of the year of return. Four out of the seven tax years immediately preceding the year of departure must have been either years when the individual was UK resident or split years (see **57.18** RESIDENCE AND DOMICILE).	**49.5** OVERSEAS MATTERS
UK participator in overseas resident company. [*TCGA 1992, s 13*].	Subject to de minimis limits, a participator in an overseas resident company which would be a close company if it were resident in the UK is chargeable on a part of any chargeable gain made by the company provided that at the time the gain accrues the person is resident or ordinarily resident in the UK and, if an individual, is domiciled in the UK.	**49.7** OVERSEAS MATTERS
European cross-border mergers. [*TCGA 1992, ss 140E(8), 140F(5)*].	The reliefs do not apply if the merger is not effected for genuine commercial reasons or if it forms part of a scheme or arrangements of which a main purpose is avoiding liability to UK tax.	**49.15** OVERSEAS MATTERS
Rollover relief. [*TCGA 1992, s 152(5)*].	Relief is denied if the acquisition of the new assets was made wholly or partly for the purpose of realising a gain from their subsequent disposal.	**59.2** ROLLOVER RELIEF
Seed enterprise investment scheme. [*ITA 2007, ss 257BE, 257CE*].	SEIS reliefs (income tax and CGT) are not available unless the shares concerned are issued by the company and subscribed for by the investor for genuine commercial reasons and not as part of a scheme or arrangement a main purpose of which is the avoidance of tax.	**60.9, 60.16** SEED ENTERPRISE INVESTMENT SCHEME

Provision	Description	Para
Settlements — deemed disposal of underlying assets on disposal of interest in settled property. [*TCGA 1992, Sch 4A*].	Where a disposal of an interest in settled property is made, or is effectively completed for consideration and specified conditions are present (as to UK residence of trustees and settlor and as to settlor interest in the settlement), the trustees of the settlement are deemed for all CGT purposes to have disposed of and immediately reacquired the underlying assets at market value.	62.20 SETTLEMENTS
Settlements — transfer of value by trustees linked with trustee borrowing. [*TCGA 1992, Schs 4B, 4C*].	Where the trustees of a settlement make a transfer of value which is treated as linked with trustee borrowing and the transfer takes place in a tax year in which the settlement is within *TCGA 1992, s 86* or *s 87*, the trustees are deemed for all CGT purposes to have disposed of and immediately reacquired the whole or a proportion of each of the chargeable assets that continue to form part of the settled property immediately after the transfer. Where applicable, gains (less losses) on the deemed disposals are then chargeable on the settlor or on beneficiaries receiving capital payments.	48.22–48.28 OFFSHORE SETTLEMENTS; 62.21 SETTLEMENTS
Restriction on set-off of settlement losses. [*TCGA 1992, s 79A*].	Applies where, in computing a gain accruing to the trustees of a settlement, the allowable expenditure would be greater if it were not for a claim having been made for gifts hold-over in respect of an earlier disposal (not necessarily of the same asset) to the trustees, and the person who made that earlier disposal, or a person connected with him, has at any time acquired an interest in the settled property, or entered into an arrangement to acquire such an interest, as a result of which any person has at any time received (or become entitled to receive) any consideration. No allowable loss may be set against any part of the trustees' gain.	62.22 SETTLEMENTS
Attribution to trustees of gains of non-resident companies. [*TCGA 1992, s 79B*].	Applies where the trustees of a settlement are participators in a close company or in a non-UK resident company which would otherwise be a close company. Where, by reason of such participation by the trustees, any part of a chargeable gain accruing to a non-UK resident company falls to be attributed to them under *TCGA 1992, s 13* (see above), nothing in any double tax agreement is to be taken as averting the tax charge otherwise arising.	62.23 SETTLEMENTS

Provision	Description	Para
Substantial shareholdings exemption. [*TCGA 1992, Sch 7AC para 5*].	Applies where there are arrangements from which the sole or main benefit that could be expected is that the gain would be exempt. The exemptions are not available if an untaxed gain accrues to an investing company (Company A) on a disposal of shares, or an asset related to shares, in another company (Company B) and before the accrual of that gain, either Company A acquired control of Company B, or the same person(s) acquired control of both companies, or there was a significant change of trading activities affecting Company B at a time when it was controlled by Company A or both companies were controlled by the same person(s).	66.7 SUBSTANTIAL SHAREHOLDINGS OF COMPANIES
Venture capital trusts. [*TCGA 1992, s 151A(2); ITA 2007, s 261(3)*].	VCT reliefs (income tax and CGT) are not available unless the shares concerned are issued by the VCT and subscribed for by the investor for genuine commercial reasons and not as part of a scheme or arrangement a main purpose of which is the avoidance of tax.	71.6, 71.11 VENTURE CAPITAL TRUSTS

Value shifting

[4.8] Without prejudice to the generality of *TCGA 1992*, any of the following transactions are to be treated as giving rise to a disposal of an asset for capital gains tax purposes and, if made gratuitously or at an undervalue, the consideration (or additional consideration) for the disposal which could have been obtained in an arm's length transaction is treated as having been actually received. The same disposal value is treated as the cost of acquisition to the person or persons acquiring value as a result of the transaction. [*TCGA 1992, s 29(1)*].

(a) If a person having control of a company exercises his control so that value passes out of shares in the company owned by him (or by CONNECTED PERSONS (17)) or out of rights over the company exercisable by him (or by connected persons) and passes into other shares in or rights over the company, a disposal is deemed to have been made out of those shares or rights. Losses arising from such a deemed disposal are not allowable. [*TCGA 1992, s 29(2)(3)*]. An omission to act may be treated as an exercise of control and 'person' includes the plural i.e. the provisions apply where two or more persons have control (*Floor v Davis* HL 1979, 52 TC 609).

(b) Where an owner of property enters into a transaction whereby he becomes the lessee of that property (e.g. a sale and lease-back) and there is a subsequent adjustment of the rights and liabilities under the lease (whether or not including the grant of a new lease) which is as a whole favourable to the lessor, such an adjustment is a disposal by the lessee of an interest in the property. [*TCGA 1992, s 29(4)*].

(c) If an asset is subject to any right or restriction, the extinction or abrogation, in whole or part, of that right etc. by the person entitled to enforce it is treated as a disposal thereof. [*TCGA 1992, s 29(5)*].

The aim of the legislation is to tax the amount of value passing *into* the transferee holdings, not (if different) the amount passing from the transferor. The disposal value is thus the value received by the transferee(s). (HMRC Capital Gains Manual CG58855). This will be of relevance where value passes from a majority shareholding into one or more minority holdings — see the *Example* at **4.9** below.

Example

[4.9]

Jak owns all the 1,000 £1 ordinary shares of K Ltd. The shares were acquired on subscription in 1978 and had a value of £65,250 on 31 March 1982. In December 2017, the trustees of Jak's family settlement subscribed at par for 250 £1 ordinary shares in K Ltd, thereby acquiring 20% of the voting power in the company. It is agreed that the value per share of Jak's holding immediately before the December 2017 share issue was £175 and immediately afterwards was £150. The value per share of the trust's holding, on issue, was £97 per share.

The proceeds of the deemed disposal are computed as follows

Value passing out of Jak's 1,000 shares is £25,000 (1,000 × £25 per share (£175 – £150)).

Value passing into the trust's 250 shares is £24,250 (250 × £97 per share) *less* the subscription price paid of £250 (250 × £1 per share) = £24,000.

The proceeds of the deemed disposal are equal to the value passing into the new shares, i.e. £24,000. (The trust's acquisition cost is £24,250, i.e. actual plus deemed consideration given).

The disposal is a part disposal (see **16.5** COMPUTATION OF GAINS AND LOSSES), the value of the part retained being £150,000 (1,000 × £150 per share).

Jak will have a capital gain for 2017/18 as follows:

	£
Proceeds of deemed disposal	24,000
Allowable cost $\frac{24,000}{24,000 + 150,000} \times £65,250$	9,000
Chargeable gain	£15,000

Simon's Taxes. See C1.335, C2.115.

Value shifting to give tax-free benefit

[4.10] The following provisions apply to the disposal of an asset (the *s 30* disposal) if a scheme has been effected or arrangements have been made (whether before or after the disposal) whereby the value of the asset has been materially reduced and a 'tax-free benefit' is conferred at any time on:

(a) the person making the disposal or a person connected with him (see **17** CONNECTED PERSONS); or

(b) any other person, except in a case where tax avoidance was not a main purpose of the scheme or arrangements.

Where the disposal of an asset precedes its acquisition, references to a reduction include references to an increase. See *Land Securities plc v Revenue and Customs Comrs* [2011] UKFTT 599 (TC), 81 TC 843, [2012] SFTD 215 and *Adrian Kerrison v Revenue and Cutoms Comrs* (TC05800) [2017] UKFTT 322 (TC) for the application of this rule to shares etc. treated as acquired following disposal (see **64** SHARES AND SECURITIES — IDENTIFICATION RULES).

The provisions do not apply if the disposal of the asset is a disposal by a company of shares in, or securities (within *TCGA 1992, s 132* as in **25.5** EXEMPTIONS AND RELIEFS) of another company. Instead the provisions at **4.11** below apply.

Any allowable loss or chargeable gain accruing on the *s 30* disposal is to be calculated as if the consideration were increased by such amount as is 'just and reasonable' having regard to the scheme or arrangements and the tax-free benefit. Where such an increase of consideration has been made for one asset and the tax-free benefit was an increase in value of another asset, the consideration for the first subsequent disposal of that other asset is to be reduced by such amount as is 'just and reasonable' in the circumstances. (There is no provision for the acquirer's cost of the asset to be correspondingly increased or reduced.)

These provisions do not apply to disposals by personal representatives to legatees (see **19.14** DEATH), or between spouses living together (see **46.5** MARRIED PERSONS AND CIVIL PARTNERS) or between companies in a group (see **29.3** GROUPS OF COMPANIES).

[*TCGA 1992, s 30(1)(2)(4)–(7)(9)*].

A '*tax-free benefit*' arises to a person if he becomes entitled to money or money's worth or his interest in the value of any asset is increased or he is wholly or partly relieved from any liability to which he is subject *and* none of the foregoing benefits when conferred is otherwise liable to income tax, capital gains tax or corporation tax. [*TCGA 1992, s 30(3)*].

HMRC do not regard ordinary commercial group relief transactions (e.g. the purchase of group relief) as falling within *TCGA 1992, s 30*.

A lease of a farm at a rack-rent by a retiring farmer to his son, followed by a sale of the reversion at market value to an outside investor, would likewise be outside it (HMRC Statement of Practice D18).

Where a disposal within *TCGA 1992, s 30* would otherwise form the basis for a claim for loss relief against income under *ITA 2007, Pt 4 Ch 6* or *CTA 2010, Pt 4 Ch 5* these provisions apply if *any* benefit is conferred, whether tax-free or not. [*TCGA 1992, s 125A*]. See also **44.15** and **44.18** LOSSES.

The Revenue confirmed that where a person was caught by the value shifting provisions before 14 March 1989, the deemed gain could be held over under the then applicable provisions of *FA 1980, s 79* (provided that the other conditions were satisfied). This may also apply to the other reliefs mentioned in **36** HOLD-OVER RELIEFS which are still current.

Simon's Taxes. See C2.116.

Certain disposals of shares by companies

[4.11] The following provision applies (and those at **4.10** above do not apply) for corporation tax purposes to the disposal by a company of shares in, or securities (within *TCGA 1992, s 132* as in **25.5** EXEMPTIONS AND RELIEFS) of, another company if:

(a) 'arrangements' have been made under which the value of the shares or securities, or any 'relevant asset' is materially reduced (or, where the disposal precedes the acquisition of the shares or securities, is materially increased);
(b) the main purpose, or one of the main purposes, of the arrangements is to avoid a liability to corporation tax on chargeable gains (of the disposing company or any other person); and
(c) the arrangements do not consist solely of the making of an 'exempt distribution'.

In calculating the chargeable gain or allowable loss on the disposal, the consideration is increased by an amount which is just and reasonable having regard to the arrangements and any charge to or relief from corporation tax that would have arisen from the disposal or arrangements but for this provision.

In (a) above, '*arrangements*' include any agreement, understanding, scheme, transaction or series of transactions, whether or not legally enforceable. An asset is a '*relevant asset*' if it is owned by a member of the disposing company's group (within *TCGA 1992, s 170* — see **29.2** GROUPS OF COMPANIES) at the time of the disposal. In (c) above, an '*exempt distribution*' is one within the exempt class under *CTA 2009, s 931H* or which would be within that class but for the recipient being a small company (within *CTA 2009, s 931S*).

The following applies where there are arrangements (as above) under which the value of shares or securities is materially reduced and the main purpose, or one of the main purposes of the arrangements is to avoid a liability to corporation tax on chargeable gains (of the company carrying out the transaction concerned or any other person). If, but for the arrangements, a transaction would be treated as a disposal of shares by a company under *TCGA 1992, s 29(2)* (value passing out of shares in company — see **4.9**(a) above), the transaction is to be treated as such a disposal.

[*TCGA 1992, s 31*].

Connected persons

[4.12] Simon's Taxes. See C2.110, C2.113.

A transaction between CONNECTED PERSONS (**17**) is treated as having been made by way of a non-arm's length bargain so that acquisition and disposal are treated as being made at market value in most cases (see **45.1** MARKET VALUE). [*TCGA 1992, s 18(1)(2)*].

There are restrictions on losses in such circumstances. See **44.6** LOSSES.

Where the asset disposed of is subject to a right or restriction enforceable by the person making the disposal or a person connected with him, then if the acquisition consideration is treated as being the market value of the asset, that value is ascertained by deducting from the market value of the unencumbered asset either the market value of the right or restriction or, if less, the amount by which its extinction would enhance the value of the asset to its owner. Rights or restrictions the enforcement of which might effectively destroy or substantially impair the value of the asset without bringing any countervailing advantage either to the person making the disposal or to a person connected with him are disregarded, e.g. rights to extinguish incorporeal assets by way of forfeiture or merger (but see below). Options and other rights to acquire assets are also disregarded.

The valuation provisions outlined above do not apply to rights of forfeiture etc. exercisable on the breach of a covenant in a lease, nor to any right or restriction under a mortgage or other charge.

[*TCGA 1992, s 18(6)–(8)*].

Assets disposed of in a series of transactions

[4.13] Simon's Taxes. See C2.114.

Where by way of two or more 'material transactions' which are 'linked' (a '*series of linked transactions*')

(a) a person disposes of assets to another person with whom he is connected (or to two or more other persons with each of whom he is connected) (see **17** CONNECTED PERSONS); and
(b) the 'original market value' of the assets disposed of by any of the transactions in the series is less than the appropriate portion of the 'aggregate market value' of the assets disposed of by all the transactions in the series,

the disposal effected by the linked transaction in (b) is deemed to be for a consideration equal to the appropriate portion referred to in that paragraph. The above is not, however, to affect the consideration for any disposals between married persons (see **46** MARRIED PERSONS AND CIVIL PARTNERS) living together.

A '*material transaction*' is any transaction, whether by gift or otherwise (subject to the exception below as regards intra-group transfers). Two or more such transactions are '*linked*' if they occur within the period of **six years** ending on the date of the last of them.

The provisions apply *both* when a second material transaction causes a series of linked transactions to come into being *and* when an existing series is extended by a further material transaction (whether or not an earlier transaction ceases to form part of the series). Assessments and adjustments are made accordingly.

Original market value

If a transaction is the most recent in the series, the original market value of the assets disposed of by it is the market value which would otherwise be deemed to be the consideration for it under the general capital gains tax rules (e.g. MARKET VALUE (**45**)). In the case of any other transaction in the series, the original market value of the assets disposed of by it is the value which, prior to the occurrence of the most recent transaction in the series, was or would have been deemed to be the consideration, whether under the general capital gains tax rules or by the previous operation of these provisions.

Aggregate market value

Subject to further provisions below, aggregate market value is the amount which would have been the market value of all the transactions in the series under the general capital gains tax rules if, 'considering all the assets together', they had been disposed of by one disposal occurring at the time of the transaction concerned. The appropriate portion of the aggregate market value is that portion which it is reasonable to apportion to those of the assets which were actually disposed of by the transaction concerned.

'*Considering all the assets together*' refers not only to considering them as a group or holding or collection of assets retaining their separate identities but also (if it gives a higher market value) to considering them as brought together, physically or in law, so as to constitute either a single asset or a number of assets which are distinct from those which were comprised in each of the transactions concerned.

Groups of companies

Intra-group transfers of assets which are treated as taking place on a no gain/no loss basis (see **29.3** GROUPS OF COMPANIES) are not material transactions. In a case where:

(a) a company ('company A') disposes of an asset by way of a material transaction; and
(b) company A acquired the asset (after 19 March 1985) by way of an intra-group transfer as above; and
(c) the disposal by company A is to a person who is connected with another company ('company B') which at some time disposed of the asset by way of an intra-group transfer as above; and
(d) either the disposal by way of intra-group transfer which is referred to in (c) above was the occasion of the acquisition in (b) above or, between that disposal and acquisition, there has been no disposal of the asset which was not an intra-group transfer as above,

then, in determining whether the above provisions apply in relation to a series of linked transactions, the disposal by company A is treated as having been made by company B; but any increase in the consideration for that disposal resulting from the application of the new provisions has effect with respect to company A.

Disposal preceding acquisition

If any of the assets disposed of by all the transactions in a series of linked transactions were acquired after the time of the first of those transactions, then, in considering aggregate market value in relation to each of the transactions in the series, no account is taken of any assets which were acquired after the time of that transaction (unless they were acquired by way of an intra-group transfer). Further, the number of assets taken into account is limited to the maximum number held at any time in the period beginning immediately before the first transaction and ending immediately before the last; and in arriving at this figure any intra-group transfers prior to the first transaction are treated as taking place after that transaction. For identification purposes, fungible assets are treated as disposed of on a 'first in/first out' basis. [*TCGA 1992, ss 19, 20*].

For further commentary and examples, see HMRC Capital Gains Manual CG14650–14740.

Example

L purchased a set of 6 antique chairs in June 1992 at a cost of £12,000. He gave 2 chairs to his daughter in February 2012, another pair to his son in November 2013, and sold the final pair to his brother for their market value in August 2017.

The market value of the chairs at the relevant dates were:

	2 chairs	4 chairs	6 chairs
	£	£	£
February 2012	6,000	14,000	26,000
November 2013	7,800	18,000	34,200
August 2017	10,400	24,000	46,200

The capital gains tax computations are as follows:

February 2012

Disposal to daughter

Deemed consideration	£6,000

As the consideration does not exceed £6,000, the disposal is covered by the chattel exemption (see note (a)).

November 2013

(i) *2011/12 disposal to daughter recomputed*

Original market value (deemed disposal consideration at February 2012)	£6,000

Reasonable proportion of aggregate market value as at February 2012 of all assets disposed of to date: £14,000 × 2/4	£7,000
	£
Deemed consideration (greater of £6,000 and £7,000)	7,000
$\text{Cost}\ \frac{7{,}000}{7{,}000 + 14{,}000} \times £12{,}000$	4,000
Chargeable gain 2011/12	£3,000
(ii) *2013/14 disposal to son*	
Original market value (deemed disposal consideration)	£7,800
Reasonable proportion of aggregate market value as at November 2013 of all assets disposed of to date: £18,000 × 2/4	£9,000
	£
Deemed consideration (greater of £7,800 and £9,000)	9,000
$\text{Cost}\ \frac{9{,}000}{9{,}000 + 7{,}800} \times (£12{,}000 - £4{,}000)$	4,286
Chargeable gain 2013/14	£4,714
August 2017	
(i) *Gain on 2011/12 disposal to daughter recomputed*	
Original market value (deemed consideration in recomputation at November 2013)	£7,000
Reasonable proportion of aggregate market value as at February 2012 of all assets disposed of to date: £26,000 × 2/6	£8,667
	£
Deemed consideration (greater of £7,000 and £8,667)	8,667
$\text{Cost}\ \frac{8{,}667}{8{,}667 + 14{,}000} \times £12{,}000$	4,588
Revised chargeable gain 2011/12	£4,079
(ii) *Gain on 2013/14 disposal to son recomputed*	
Original market value (deemed consideration in computation at November 2013)	£9,000
Reasonable proportion of aggregate market value as at November 2013 of all assets disposed of to date:	£11,400
£34,200 × 2/6	

	£
Deemed consideration (greater of £9,000 and £11,400)	11,400
Cost $\frac{11,400}{11,400+7,800} \times (12,000-4,588)$	4,401
Revised chargeable gain 2013/14	£6,999
(iii) *Gain on 2017/18 disposal to brother*	£
Original market value (actual consideration)	£10,400
Reasonable proportion of aggregate market value as at August 2017 of all assets disposed of to date:	
£46,200 × $^2/_6$	£15,400
	£
Deemed consideration (greater of £10,400 and £15,400)	15,400
Cost (£12,000 – £4,588 – £4,401)	3,011
Chargeable gain 2017/18	£12,389

Notes to the example

(a) The disposal in February 2012 is at first covered by the chattel exemption (£6,000). As the second disposal in November 2013 is to a person connected with the recipient of the first disposal, the two must then be looked at together for the purposes of the chattel exemption, and, as the combined proceeds exceed the chattel exemption limit, the exemption is not available. [*TCGA 1992, s 262*].

(b) The three disposals are linked transactions within *TCGA 1992, s 19* as they are made by the same transferor to persons with whom he is connected, and take place within a six-year period.

(c) It is assumed in the above example that it is 'reasonable' to apportion the aggregate market value in proportion to the number of items. In other instances a different basis may be needed to give the 'reasonable' apportionment required by *TCGA 1992, s 20(4)*.

Close company transferring asset at undervalue

[4.14] Where, on or after 31 March 1982, a close company (within *CTA 2010, ss 439–454*) transfers (other than within a group of companies under *TCGA 1992, s 171(1)*, see **29.3** GROUPS OF COMPANIES) an asset to any person otherwise than at arm's length and for a consideration of an amount or value less than the market value of the asset, an amount equal to the difference is apportioned among the issued shares of the company. On a disposal of the shares by the person who owned them at the date of transfer, an amount equal to the amount so apportioned is not treated as allowable expenditure.

Where the owner of such shares is itself a close company, an amount equal to the amount apportioned to those shares is apportioned among the issued shares of that close company, the owners thereof being treated as above, and so on through any number of close companies.

Where the gain or loss on disposal of shares held at 31 March 1982 falls to be computed *other than* by reference to their value at that date (see **9.2** ASSETS HELD ON 31 MARCH **1982**), any transfers of assets as above which were made before that date (but not before 6 April 1965) are also taken into account.

Where the asset is transferred to a settlement for the benefit of employees, etc. (see **25.91** EXEMPTIONS AND RELIEFS), the amount apportioned is the difference between the market value of the asset or the amount of the allowable expenditure attributable to the asset, whichever is the less, and the consideration. [*TCGA 1992, s 239(3)*].

The above provisions do not apply in two sets of circumstances. The first is where the transferee is a participator or an associate of a participator in the company and the undervalue amount is treated as an income distribution within *ICTA 1988, s 209(2)(b)* or *(4)* or as a capital distribution within *TCGA 1992, s 122* (see **63.11** SHARES AND SECURITIES). The second is where the transferee is an employee of the company and the undervalue amount is charged to income tax as employment income (and is not exempt income).

[*TCGA 1992, s 125*].

Restrictions on company reconstructions

[4.15] *TCGA 1992, s 135* applies to the takeover of one company by another wholly or partly for shares or debentures and provides that the original holding and the new holding are to be treated as the same asset. See **63.5** SHARES AND SECURITIES. *TCGA 1992, s 136* deals with company reconstructions where a company issues shares or debentures to another company's shareholders whose original holdings are either retained or cancelled. The original and new holdings are likewise treated as the same asset. See **63.7** SHARES AND SECURITIES.

Neither of these provisions applies, however, unless the exchange of securities or scheme of reconstruction is for 'bona fide commercial reasons', and not part of a scheme or arrangement for the main or only purpose of avoiding capital gains tax or corporation tax. This restriction does not apply where a recipient of the shares, etc. holds 5% or less of, or of any class of, the relevant shares, etc. (including holdings by connected persons) in the company being acquired etc., or where the Commissioners for HMRC, on written application by either company, have given clearance before the issue is made. In determining whether a recipient holds 5% or less of the shares concerned for this purpose, any of its own shares that the company holds as treasury shares (see **63.19** SHARES AND SECURITIES) do not count (HMRC Capital Gains Manual CG52620).

See *Snell v HMRC* Ch D, [2007] STC 1279 in which the above provisions were held to apply where the taxpayer became non-resident after exchanging his shareholding in a company for loan notes and before selling the loan notes. A similar decision was reached in *Coll and another v HMRC* UT, [2010] STC 1849.

The above provisions also apply to interests in a company without share capital (where relevant — see **63.5, 63.7** SHARES AND SECURITIES) and certain quoted options.

Tax assessed on a person (the '*chargeable person*') by virtue of the above provisions and not paid within six months of the date when it is payable may be recovered, in whole or in part, from certain third parties, in the name of the chargeable person, within two years of that date. There is a right of recourse to the chargeable person for the tax so paid together with, in the case of corporation tax, interest paid in respect of that tax. The third parties are restricted to persons holding the shares, etc. issued to the chargeable person who acquired them as a result of one or more disposals within *TCGA 1992, s 58(1)* (spouses or civil partners living together) or *s 171(1)* (companies within same group) without any intervening disposals not within those provisions.

Seeking to retain family control of a company may be a 'bona fide commercial reason', see *CIR v Brebner* HL 1967, 43 TC 705; *Clark v CIR* Ch D 1978, 52 TC 482 and *CIR v Goodwin* HL 1976, 50 TC 583, which dealt with the similar phrase in *ICTA 1988, s 703(1)*.

[*TCGA 1992, ss 137, 138*].

Clearance applications

Application for clearance must contain particulars of operations contemplated and the Commissioners may, within 30 days of receipt, call for further particulars (to be supplied within 30 days, or longer if the Commissioners allow). If the particulars are not supplied, the application lapses. Subject to this, the Commissioners must indicate their decision within a further 30 days. If not so notified, or if dissatisfied with the decision, the applicants may within a further 30 days require the Commissioners to refer the particulars to the Tribunal for its decision. All material facts and considerations must be disclosed, otherwise any decision is void.

Applications for clearance should be directed to HMRC, CTIS Clearance SO483, Newcastle NE98 1ZZ (if market-sensitive information is included, for the attention of the team leader). Applications may be emailed to reconstructions@hmrc.gsi.gov.uk. A hard copy need not then be sent. Only a single application need be made as above for clearances under any one or more of: *CTA 2010, ss 1091, 1092* (demergers), *CTA 2010, ss 1044, 1045* (purchase of own shares), *ITA 2007, s 701* or *CTA 2010, s 748* (transactions in securities), *TCGA 1992, s 138(1)* (as above), *TCGA 1992, s 139(5)* (reconstructions involving the transfer of a business — see **14.11** COMPANIES), *TCGA 1992, s 140B* (transfer or division of a UK business between EU member states — **49.13** OVERSEAS MATTERS), *TCGA 1992, s 140D* (transfer or division of a non-UK business between EU member states — **49.14** OVERSEAS MATTERS) and *CTA 2009, s 831* (clearances under the corporation tax intangible assets regime). (Revenue Internet Statement 23 October 2002).

For the Revenue's response to a number of concerns regarding aspects of clearances under *TCGA 1992, s 138*, see ICAEW Guidance Note TR 657, 10 April 1987.

Schemes involving the transfer of a business owned by companies

[4.16] See **14.11** COMPANIES where a scheme of reconstruction involves the transfer of a UK resident company's business to another UK resident company for no consideration other than the assumption of liabilities of the business. [*TCGA 1992, s 139*].

Depreciatory transactions within groups of companies

[4.17] Simon's Taxes. See D2.350, D2.351.

Where two or more members of a group of companies are parties to a 'disposal of assets' at other than market value which has the effect of materially reducing the value of the shares or 'securities' of one of those companies ('a depreciatory transaction'), any loss arising on the ultimate disposal of those shares or securities by a member or a former member of the group (having been a member when the transaction took place) is to be allowable only so far as is 'just and reasonable'. Account may be taken of any other post-30 March 1982 transaction which has:

(i) enhanced the value of the assets of the company the shares in which are being disposed of; and
(ii) depreciated the assets of any other group member.

Where the ultimate disposal of the shares or securities takes place on or after 19 July 2011, only depreciatory transactions occurring in the six-years ending with that disposal are taken into account. Previously any such transaction occurring on or after 31 March 1982 were taken into account and where the loss on the ultimate disposal of an asset held at 31 March 1982 fell to be computed *other than* by reference to its value at that date (see **9.2** ASSETS HELD ON 31 MARCH **1982**), depreciatory (and other) transactions before that date (but not before 6 April 1965) were also taken into account.

Where a loss has been wholly or partly disallowed as above, any chargeable gain accruing within six years of the depreciatory transaction on the disposal of shares or securities of another company which was a party to it is reduced as is just and reasonable (but not so as to exceed the reduction in the allowable loss). Regard is to be had to the effect of the depreciatory transaction on the value of the shares at the date of disposal. All adjustments, by discharge or repayment of tax, or otherwise, as are required to give effect to these provisions may be made at any time.

A '*depreciatory transaction*' also includes any other transaction where:

(a) the company, the shares or securities in which are the subject of the ultimate disposal, or any 75% subsidiary of that company, was party to that transaction; and
(b) the parties to the transaction were, or included, two or more companies which, when the transaction occurred, were in the same group.

A transaction is not depreciatory to the extent that it is a payment which is required to be, or has been, brought into account in computing a chargeable gain or allowable loss of the company making the ultimate disposal. Cancellation within *Companies Act 2006, s 641* (previously *Companies Act 1985, s 135*) of shares or securities of one member of a group which are owned by another is deemed to be a depreciatory transaction unless it falls within this exemption. The deemed disposal arising under a claim that shares or securities have become of negligible value under *TCGA 1992, s 24(2)* (see **44.11** LOSSES) may constitute a depreciatory transaction.

References to '*disposal of assets*' include appropriation by one member of a group of the goodwill of another member.

'*Securities*' includes loan stock or similar securities whether secured or unsecured.

A group of companies, and related expressions, are construed for these purposes in accordance with **29.2** GROUPS OF COMPANIES.

[*TCGA 1992, s 176*].

Where a subsidiary company pays dividends to its parent out of post-acquisition profits, HMRC do not regard the payment as being a depreciatory transaction (HMRC Capital Gains Manual CG46540).

For consideration of these provisions, see HMRC Capital Gains Manual CG46500–46580.

Dividend stripping

[4.18] Simon's Taxes. See D2.352.

Where a company (the 'first company') holds 10% or more of a class of shares in another company (the 'second company') otherwise than as a dealing company, and a distribution is or has been made to the first company which materially reduces or has reduced the value of the holding, the distribution is to be treated as a depreciatory transaction under *TCGA 1992, s 176* (see **4.17** above) in relation to any disposal of the shares. This applies whether the disposal is by the first company or any other company to which the holding has been transferred under the provisions of *TCGA 1992, s 140A* (transfer or division of UK business between companies in different EC member states, see **49.13** OVERSEAS MATTERS), *s 171* (transfers within a group, see **29.3** GROUPS OF COMPANIES) or *s 172* (now repealed). If the first and second companies are not members of the same group, they are deemed to be so.

For these purposes, a company's holding of different classes in another company are treated as separate holdings and holdings of the same class which differ in the entitlements or obligations they confer are treated as holdings of different classes. Subject to this, all of a company's holdings of the same class in another company must be treated as a single holding and other holdings of the same class held by connected persons are aggregated in determining whether the 10% test is satisfied. For the meaning of connected persons, see **17** CONNECTED PERSONS. For the above provisions only, the persons mentioned in **41.28** specifically include persons acting together to secure or acquire a holding in a company (and not just control).

A distribution need not be treated as a depreciatory transaction under these provisions to the extent that it consists of a payment which is required to be, or has been, brought into account in calculating a chargeable gain or allowable loss by the person making the ultimate disposal.

[*TCGA 1992, s 177*].

Abuse of concessions

[4.19] A statutory charge applies where a person (the '*original taxpayer*') has at any time obtained the benefit of a capital gains relief in reliance on a 'concession' and circumstances arise in a subsequent chargeable period which, if that benefit had been obtained under a statutory relief, would have resulted in the whole (or part) of the benefit falling to be recouped from any person (whether or not the original taxpayer). A chargeable gain equal to the full amount of that benefit is deemed to accrue to the latter person for the chargeable period in which the circumstances arise. The chargeable gain is not eligible for ROLLOVER RELIEF (**59**) (see HMRC Capital Gains Manual CG13659). The total recouped under these provisions cannot exceed the original benefit (which might otherwise have been the case where there are part disposals, such that the said circumstances arise in more than one chargeable period — see HMRC Capital Gains Manual CG13655).

The above provision does not, however, apply where the person to whom the deemed chargeable gain would otherwise accrue indicates in writing to HMRC that he accepts that the benefit obtained by the original taxpayer may be recouped from him. Such acceptance may be indicated simply by the making or amending of a self-assessment to include the deferred gain. Where, *following* an assessment under this provision:

- such indication of acceptance is given on or before the latest of the deadlines listed below; or
- it transpires that the original taxpayer did not, or was not entitled to, rely on the concession and *his* tax position for the earlier period is finally determined on that basis,

such adjustments are to be made to ensure that the chargeable person's liability is no greater than would have been the case had such an event occurred earlier such that no assessment would have been necessary. The above-mentioned deadlines are:

- twelve months after an assessment is made under the above provision;
- the latest date for amending the self-assessment tax return or company tax return for the period in which the gain accrues (see **58.7**, **58.19** RETURNS); and
- where a claim for further relief (for example, rollover relief) is possible against the gain and is made, the latest possible date for making that claim.

For the purpose of the above provision, '*concession*' means any concession which:

- was first published by the Revenue before 9 March 1999 or replaces a concession so published and having similar effect;
- was available generally to any person falling within its terms at the time it was relied upon by the original taxpayer,

and which has the effect of:

- applying (with or without modifications) the provisions of any enactment to a case to which they would not otherwise have applied; or
- treating, without applying a specific enactment:
  - (i) any asset as the same as any other asset and acquired as the other asset was acquired;
  - (ii) any two or more assets as a single asset; or

(iii) any disposal as having been a disposal on which neither a gain nor a loss accrued.

For these purposes, the term 'concession' is not restricted to those listed as HMRC EXTRA-STATUTORY CONCESSIONS (**33**) but includes any practice, interpretation or other statement in the nature of a concession and within the above definition.

[*TCGA 1992, ss 284A, 284B*].

The following extra-statutory concessions are *examples* of concessions at which the above provisions are aimed.

- D15 (which extends rollover relief on business assets to cover gains on assets of a company which is 90% owned by an unincorporated association (now superseded by statutory provision for disposals after 5 April 2009) — see **59.5** ROLLOVER RELIEF).
- D16 (which extends rollover relief on business assets where the proceeds from the disposal of an asset are reinvested in the repurchase of the same asset — see **59.2** ROLLOVER RELIEF).
- D22 (which extends rollover relief on business assets where the proceeds from the disposal of an asset are used to enhance the value of another asset — see **59.2** ROLLOVER RELIEF).
- D39 (which treats a lease of property which is surrendered before its expiry date as the same asset as a new lease to replace it — see **41.15** LAND).

(Treasury Explanatory Notes to the Finance Bill 1999). For further commentary and examples, see HMRC Capital Gains Manual CG13650–13659.

Tax arbitrage

[4.20] There are anti-avoidance provisions to prevent the exploitation by companies of differences between or within national tax codes using hybrid entities or instruments (known as tax arbitrage). *FA 2016* introduced revised provisions to comply with the outcome of the OECD's Base Erosion and Profit Shifting project. Those provisions do not apply to corporation tax on chargeable gains — see Tolley's Corporation Tax under Anti-Avoidance for details of the provisions. The new provisions effectively replace those described below which are accordingly repealed for accounting periods beginning on or after 1 January 2017 (treating, for this purpose, accounting periods straddling that date as two separate accounting periods, the second of which starts on 1 January 2017). [*FA 2016, Sch 10 paras 15, 22, 24*].

Subject to the above, the pre-*FA 2016* provisions operate by reducing or disallowing deductions or by bringing receipts into charge, but apply only where HMRC issued a notice to the company. Separate provisions apply in relation to deductions cases and receipts cases.

The following apply for the purposes of the provisions. A '*scheme*' is any scheme, arrangements or understanding of any kind, whether or not legally enforceable, involving a single transaction or two or more transactions. The circumstances in which any two or more transactions are to be taken as forming part of a series of transactions or a scheme include any case in which it would be reasonable to assume that one or more of them would not have been entered into independently of the others or if entered into independently would not have taken the same form or been on the same terms. It is immaterial in determining whether any transactions form part of a series of transactions that the parties to any of the transactions are different from the parties to another of the transactions. A scheme achieves a '*UK tax advantage*' for a person if in consequence of the scheme that person is in a position to obtain, or has obtained:

- a relief (including a tax credit) or increased relief from;
- a repayment or increased repayment of; or
- the avoidance or reduction of a charge to,

corporation tax. In particular, avoidance or reduction of a charge to tax may be effected by receipts accruing in such a way that the recipient does not pay or bear tax on them or by a deduction in computing profits or gains. [*TIOPA 2010, ss 234, 258*].

Deductions cases

The following provisions apply to a company which is resident in the UK, or a non-resident company which is within the charge to corporation tax, if the following conditions are satisfied in relation to a transaction to which the company is a party.

(a) The transaction forms part of a scheme which is a 'deduction scheme' (see below).
(b) The scheme is such that for corporation tax purposes the company is in a position to claim, or has claimed, an amount by way of deduction in respect of the transaction or is in a position to set off, or has set off, against profits in an accounting period an amount relating to the transaction.
(c) The main purpose, or one of the main purposes, of the scheme is to achieve a UK tax advantage for the company.
(d) The amount of the UK tax advantage is more than minimal.

If HMRC consider, on reasonable grounds, that the above conditions are or may be satisfied they may give the company a notice specifying the transaction involved, the accounting period in respect of which condition (b) above is or may be satisfied and informing the company that as a consequence the provisions apply. HMRC may issue such a notice to a company in respect of two or more transactions.

If a company receives a notice and conditions (a)–(d) above are in fact satisfied at the time it is given, the company must compute (or recompute) its income or chargeable gains for corporation tax purposes or its liability to corporation tax for the specified accounting period and any subsequent accounting period in accordance with the following two rules.

The first rule is that no deduction is allowable in respect of the transaction specified in the notice to the extent that an amount in relation to the expense in question may be otherwise deducted or allowed in computing the income, profits or losses of any person for the purposes of any tax (including non-UK tax (within the meaning of *CTA 2010, s 187*) but excluding petroleum revenue tax and tax chargeable under *CTA 2010, s 330(1)* in respect of ring fence trades), or would be so deductible or allowable but for a rule (whether a UK or non-UK tax provision) that has the same effect as this provision.

The second rule applies where a transaction or series of transactions forming part of the scheme involves a payment which creates a deduction or allowance for tax purposes (including non-UK tax purposes) for the payer or another party to the scheme but the payee is not liable to tax on the receipt or has his tax liability reduced as a result of the scheme. For this purpose, the circumstances in which a payee is treated as having his liability to tax reduced as a result of the scheme include where he can set off against his income an expense or relief arising out of the scheme. A payee is not treated as not liable to tax on the receipt if he is not liable to tax on any income or gains under the tax law of any territory or if he is not liable to tax on the receipt because of a statutory exemption which exempts him from tax in respect of income or gains without providing that those income or gains are to be treated as those of another person. Where the rule applies, the aggregate of the amounts allowable as a deduction in computing profits for corporation tax purposes arising from the transaction specified in the notice and any other transactions forming part of the scheme and to which the company is party must be reduced. If the payee is not liable to tax on the receipt (as above), the aggregate is reduced to nil. If the payee is liable to tax on part of the receipt or his liability to tax is reduced as above, the aggregate is reduced proportionately to correspond to the payee's liability (treating the amount by which the payee's liability is reduced as an amount on which the payee is not liable to tax).

Instead of applying the above two rules, the company may choose to incorporate in its tax return for the specified accounting period any adjustments that are necessary to counteract the effects of the scheme that are referable to the purpose mentioned in (c) above. The adjustments to be made are to treat all or part of a deduction as not being allowable, or all or part of an amount which may be set off against profits as not falling to be set off. If the adjustments fully counteract the effects of the scheme the company is treated as having complied with the provisions.

See below for further provisions governing the effects of a notice under the above provisions.

[*TIOPA 2010, ss 232, 233, 235, 243–248; FA 2016, Sch 10 paras 15, 22, 25*].

Deduction schemes

A scheme is a '*deduction scheme*' for the purposes of the above provisions if it is one of the following types.

(1) A scheme in which a party to a transaction forming part of it is a 'hybrid entity', i.e. if under the tax law of any territory it is regarded as a person but its profits or gains are, for the purposes of a '*relevant tax*' (i.e. income tax, corporation tax or similar non-UK tax) under the law of any territory, treated as the profits or gains of a different person or

persons. An entity is not so treated by reason only of its profits or gains being subject to a non-UK tax rule similar to that in *ICTA 1988, s 747(3)* (imputation of profits of controlled foreign company — see **49.9** OVERSEAS MATTERS).

(2) A scheme one of the parties to which is party to an instrument of which, under the law of a particular territory, a 'tax characteristic' may be altered on the election of any party to it. A characteristic of an instrument is a '*tax characteristic*' if, under the law of a particular territory, altering it has the effect of determining whether or not, for that territory's tax purposes, the instrument is taken into account as giving rise to income or capital. For this purpose, an instrument is taken into account as giving rise to capital if a gain on disposal would be a chargeable gain, or would be if the person making the disposal were UK-resident.

(3) A scheme which includes the issuing by a company of shares subject to conversion or the amendment of rights attaching to shares issued by a company such that the shares become shares subject to conversion. Shares of a company are subject to conversion for this purpose if the rights attaching to them include provision by virtue of which a holder is entitled, on the occurrence of an event, to acquire shares in that or another company by conversion or exchange and the occurrence of that event is within the reasonable expectation of the company either at the time when the shares are issued or at the time the rights attaching to the shares are amended.

(4) A scheme which includes the issuing by a company of securities subject to conversion or the amendment of rights attaching to securities issued by a company such that the securities become securities subject to conversion. Securities of a company are subject to conversion for this purpose if the rights attaching to them include provision by virtue of which a holder is entitled, on the occurrence of an event, to acquire shares in that or another company by conversion or exchange and the occurrence of that event is within the reasonable expectation of the company either at the time when the securities are issued or at the time the rights attaching to the securities are amended.

(5) A scheme which includes a 'debt instrument' issued by a company that is treated as equity in the company under generally accepted accounting practice. A '*debt instrument*' for this purpose is an instrument issued by a company that represents a loan relationship (see **15.5** COMPANIES — CORPORATE FINANCE AND INTANGIBLES), or would do if the company were UK-resident.

(6) A scheme which includes the issue by a company to a connected person (within *CTA 2010, s 1122*) of shares other than shares which, on their issue, are ordinary shares that are fully paid-up, which confer a 'beneficial entitlement' at all times in the accounting period in which they are issued and in respect of which there is no arrangement or understanding at the time of issue under which the rights attaching to the shares may be amended. A share in a company confers a '*beneficial entitlement*' if it confers a beneficial entitlement to the same proportion of any profits available for distribution to equity holders of the company and of any assets available for distribution to equity holders

on a winding-up as the proportion of the issued share capital represented by that share. *CTA 2010, Pt 5 Ch 6* (equity holders and profits or assets available for distribution) applies for this purpose as it applies for the purposes of group relief.

(7) A scheme which includes a transaction or series of transactions under which a person transfers rights to receive a payment under a security to one or more other persons or otherwise secures that one or more other persons are similarly benefited (i.e. that they receive a payment which would, but for the transaction or series of transactions, have arisen to the transferor) and:

- the transferor and at least one of the persons to whom a transfer of rights is made or similar benefit is secured are connected (within **17** CONNECTED PERSONS), and
- following the transfer of rights or securing of the similar benefit, two or more persons either hold rights to receive a payment under the security or enjoy a similar benefit and the rights held and benefits enjoyed by such of those persons as are connected have, taken together, a market value equal to or greater than the market value of all other such rights and benefits, taken together.

For this purpose, a '*security*' includes any agreement under which a person receives an annuity or other annual payment (whether payable annually or at shorter or longer intervals) for a term which is not contingent on the duration of a human life or lives.

[*TIOPA 2010, ss 236–242, 259(2); FA 2016, Sch 10 paras 15, 22, 25*].

Receipts cases

The following provisions apply to a company resident in the UK if the following conditions are satisfied.

(i) A scheme makes or imposes provision (the '*actual provision*') as between the company and another person (the '*paying party*') by means of a transaction or series of transactions.

(ii) The actual provision includes the making by the paying party, by means of a transaction or series of transactions, of a 'qualifying payment'. For this purpose, a '*qualifying payment*' is a contribution to the capital of the company.

(iii) As regards the qualifying payment there is an amount that is available for deduction for UK tax purposes or that may be deducted or otherwise allowable under the tax law of a territory outside the UK. (Such an amount is, however, disregarded for this purpose if or to the extent that it is set for tax purposes against any income arising to the paying party from the transaction or transactions forming part of the scheme.) This condition is not treated as satisfied if the paying party is a dealer (as defined) who incurs losses in the ordinary course of his business in respect of the transaction or transactions and the amount by reference to which this condition would otherwise be satisfied is an amount in respect of those losses.

(iv) At least part of the qualifying payment is not:

(A) income or gains arising to the company in the accounting period in which the qualifying payment was made;

(B) income arising to any other company resident in the UK in a 'corresponding' accounting period (i.e. an accounting period with at least one day in common with the accounting period in (A) above); or

(C) brought into account under the loan relationship provisions of *CTA 2009, ss 486A–486E* or *ss 521A–521F* (disguised interest and shares treated as loan relationships — see **15.3** and **15.6** COMPANIES — CORPORATE FINANCE AND INTANGIBLES) (or before 22 April 2009, taken into account in determining the loan relationship credits or debits to be brought into account by a company as respects a share in another company under *CTA 2009, s 523* (shares treated as loan relationships — see **15.6** COMPANIES — CORPORATE FINANCE AND INTANGIBLES)).

(v) The company and the paying party expected on entering into the scheme that a benefit would arise as a result of (iv) above being satisfied (whether by reference to all or part of the qualifying payment).

If HMRC consider, on reasonable grounds, that the above conditions are or may be satisfied they may give the company a notice specifying the qualifying payment involved, the accounting period in which the payment is made and informing the company that as a consequence the following provisions apply.

If a company receives a notice and conditions (i)–(v) above are in fact satisfied at the time it is given, the company must compute (or recompute) its income or chargeable gains for corporation tax purposes or its liability to corporation tax for the specified accounting period as if the part of the qualifying payment by reference to which (iii) and (iv) above are satisfied were an amount of income arising to the company in that period and chargeable to corporation tax. If (iii) and (iv) above are satisfied in relation to the whole of the qualifying payment, the whole of the payment is so chargeable.

See below for further provisions governing the effects of a notice under the above provisions.

[*TIOPA 2010, ss 249–254; FA 2016, Sch 10 paras 15, 22, 25*].

Effects of a notice

If a notice under either of the above provisions is given before the company has made its return for the specified accounting period then, if the return is made in the period of 90 days beginning with the day on which the notice is given, it may disregard the notice, and at any time before the end of the 90 days the company may amend the return in order to comply with the notice.

If no notice has been given before the company's return has been made, a notice may only be given if the company has been given a notice of enquiry (see **58.19** RETURNS) in respect of the return. After an enquiry has been completed (or, completed in relation to any matters, for enquiries commenced on or after the date of Royal Assent to *F(No 2)A 2017*), a notice may only be given if:

- at the time the enquiry was completed HMRC could not have reasonably been expected, on the basis of the information made available (within *FA 1998, Sch 18 para 44(2)(3)* — see **6.10** ASSESSMENTS) to them before that time, to have been aware that the circumstances were such that a notice could have been given; and

- the company was requested to provide information during the enquiry (relating to the matters in question, for enquiries commenced on or after the date of Royal Assent to *F(No 2)A 2017* or in progress on that date) and, if it had been so provided, HMRC could reasonably have been expected to give the company a notice.

If the notice is given after the company has made its return, it may amend the return to comply with the notice within 90 days beginning with the day on which the notice is given. If the notice is given after an enquiry into the return has started, a closure notice (see **58.12** RETURNS) may not be issued until the end of the period of 90 days beginning with the issue of the notice or, if earlier, an amendment is made to the return complying with the notice. For enquiries commenced on or after the date of Royal Assent to *F(No 2)A 2017* or in progress on that date, this does not apply to a partial closure notice which does not relate to any matter to which the notice here relates. If the notice is given after the completion of an enquiry (or, for enquiries commenced on or after the date of Royal Assent to *F(No 2)A 2017*, after completion of any enquiries so far as relating to the matters to which the notice relates), a discovery assessment (see **6.10** ASSESSMENTS) in relation to the income or chargeable gain to which it relates may not be made until the end of the period of 90 days beginning with the issue of the notice or, if earlier, an amendment is made to the return complying with the notice.

Where a notice is issued and no amendment is made to the return for the purpose of complying with it, the above provisions do not prevent a return becoming incorrect if such an amendment should have been made.

[*TIOPA 2010, ss 255–257; FA 2016, Sch 10 paras 15, 22, 25; F(No 2)A 2017, Sch 15 paras 41, 42, 44*].

Clearance

HMRC operate an advance clearance scheme for the above provisions and will give a decision wherever possible as to whether a notice will be issued in respect of proposed transactions. Sufficient information must be provided to enable HMRC to reach a view as to whether the provisions apply HMRC will consider themselves bound by any clearance given in accordance with those procedures. See HMRC International Manual INTM596550.

Factoring of income receipts

[4.21] Anti-avoidance provisions apply to counter schemes (defined in the legislation as any of three types of structured finance arrangement) involving the factoring of income receipts. The schemes involve the transfer of an asset on which there is a predictable income stream or a transfer of the right to such an income stream, in return for a lump sum. The income stream acquired by the transferee is then sufficient to repay both the lump sum and interest. The transferor then claims that the income or receipts arising during the period of the arrangement are not taxable on him and that the lump sum is either a capital receipt giving rise to a chargeable gain only or is not taxable at all.

Broadly, the provisions operate by deeming the intended effects of the arrangements not to have effect for tax purposes. See *ITA 2007, ss 809BZA–809BZS, CTA 2010, ss 758–776* and Tolley's Income Tax and Corporation Tax for full details.

For capital gains purposes, where:

(a) *ITA 2007, ss 809BZB* or *809BZC* or *CTA 2010, ss 759* or *760* apply to a 'type 1 finance arrangement';
(b) the 'borrower' or a person connected with him (other than the 'lender') makes a disposal at any time of any 'security' under the arrangement to or for the benefit of the lender or a person connected with him (other than the borrower); and
(c) either:
    – the person making the disposal, and no-one else, has the right or obligation under the arrangement (whether or not subject to conditions) to acquire the asset disposed of at any subsequent time; or
    – the asset will subsequently cease to exist and it is intended that the asset will be held by the lender or connected person from the time of the disposal until it ceases to exist,

then the disposal of the security in (b) above and (except where there has been a deemed disposal as below) any subsequent re-acquisition of the asset are disregarded.

If it becomes apparent at any time after the disposal that the person making the disposal will not subsequently acquire the asset disposed of or that the asset will not be held by the lender or connected person from the time of the disposal until it ceases to exist, then the person making the disposal is treated as disposing of the asset at that time at market value.

An 'arrangement' is a '*type 1 finance arrangement*' in relation to a person (the '*borrower*') for these purposes if:

(i) under the arrangement the borrower receives from another person (the '*lender*') any money or other asset (the '*advance*') in any period;
(ii) the accounts of the borrower for that period record a financial liability in respect of the advance in accordance with generally accepted accounting practice (or would so record a financial liability if accounts were drawn up in accordance with generally accepted accounting practice);
(iii) the borrower or a person connected with him (other than the lender) makes a disposal (including anything which would constitute a disposal for capital gains purposes) under the arrangement of an asset (the '*security*') to or for the benefit of the lender or a person connected with him (other than the borrower);
(iv) the lender or a person connected with him (other than the borrower) is entitled to 'payments' in respect of the security under the arrangements; and

(v) those payments reduce the amount of the financial liability in respect of the advance recorded in the accounts of the borrower in accordance with generally accepted accounting practice (or would so reduce the amount if accounts were drawn up in accordance with generally accepted accounting practice).

The circumstances in which the borrower is treated for the purposes of (i) above as receiving an asset include the borrower's obtaining directly or indirectly the value of the asset or otherwise deriving directly or indirectly any benefit from it and the discharge, in whole or part, of any liability of the borrower. Similarly, the circumstances in which the lender or other person is treated as entitled to payments in respect of the security for the purposes of (iv) above include the person's obtaining directly or indirectly the value of the security or otherwise deriving directly or indirectly any benefit from it and payments in respect of any other asset substituted for the security under the arrangement. Where the borrower is a partnership, references above to the accounts of the borrower include the accounts of any member of the partnership.

For the purposes of (iv) above it does not matter if the entitlement to payments is subject to any condition. Although this rule applies to arrangements whenever made, where the arrangements were made before 21 March 2012, an amount can be charged to tax or brought into account in calculating income, or deducted from income, for tax purposes only if it arises on or after that date.

Where the borrower is a company, references to the accounts of the borrower include the consolidated group accounts of any group of companies of which it is a member. An '*arrangement*' includes any agreement or understanding, whether or not legally enforceable.

[*TCGA 1992, s 263E; ITA 2007, ss 809BZA, 809BZQ–809BZS; CTA 2010, ss 758, 774–776FA 2012, Sch 13 paras 33, 38, 42, 43*].

Transfer of income stream

[4.22] *FA 2008* introduced anti-avoidance provisions to ensure that where a person sells or otherwise disposes of a right to receive income and does not sell the underlaying asset from which the income derives, the lump sum obtained is taxed as income and not as a chargeable gain.

The provisions apply where a taxpayer 'transfers' a right to any income which would otherwise be chargeable to income tax or corporation tax as income of the taxpayer or brought into account in calculating the taxpayer's profits for tax purposes. The transfer must not be a consequence of the transfer of an asset (other than a transfer under a sale and repurchase agreement) from which the right to the income arises. This condition does not apply if the transfer of the right is a consequence of a transfer of all rights under an agreement for annual payments.

A transfer consisting of the reduction of the transferor's share in the profits or losses of a partnership is regarded for this purpose as a consequence of the transfer of an asset from which the right to income arose. For transfers before

6 April 2014 (1 April 2014 for corporation tax purposes), there must be a proportionate reduction in the transferor's share in the partnership property and securing that the income not be chargeable to tax as income of a partner must not be a main purpose of the transfer. The grant or surrender of a lease of land is regarded for the purposes of the above provisions, as a transfer of the land, and the disposal of an interest in an oil licence is treated as a transfer of the licence. Where the transferor is a company, the grant or disposal of an interest in intellectual property excluded from the intangible fixed assets regime by its commencement provisions (see **15.14** COMPANIES — CORPORATE FINANCE AND INTANGIBLES) is treated as a transfer of that property. The Treasury can, by order, added other transactions which are to be treated as the transfer of an asset.

The provisions do not apply to the extent that the income is charged to tax as income of the transferor, or brought into account as income in calculating the transferor's profits, under other provisions. They also do not apply if the income is brought into account for capital allowances purposes, if the consideration for the transfer is the advance under a structured finance arrangement within the provisions mentioned at **4.21** above or if the right is to annual payments under certain annuities.

A '*transfer*' includes a sale, exchange, gift, assignment or any other arrangement equating in substance to a transfer. Also included are transfers to or by a partnership of which the transferor or transferee is a member and transfers to the trustees of a trust of which the transferee is a beneficiary.

Effect of provisions

Where the provisions apply, the consideration for the transfer of the right to income is treated as income of the transferor chargeable to income tax or corporation tax in the same way and to the same extent as the income would have been chargeable but for the transfer. Where there is no consideration or the consideration is less than the market value of the right, the market value of the right is so treated as income of the transferor. If the transferee is a company, the consideration for the transfer is treated as a loan relationship.

[*ITA 2007, ss 809AZA–809AZF; CTA 2009, ss 486F, 486G; CTA 2010, ss 752–757; FA 2014, Sch 17 paras 23, 27*].

Disposal of income stream through partnership

[4.23] *FA 2014* introduced anti-avoidance legislation to ensure that where a person sells or otherwise disposes of a right to receive income by or through a partnership, the consideration obtained is taxed as income and not as a chargeable gain.

The provisions apply where, directly or indirectly in consequence of, or otherwise in connection with, 'arrangements' made on or after 6 April 2014 (1 April 2014 for corporation tax purposes) and involving a person within the charge to income tax or corporation tax (the 'transferor') and another person (the 'transferee'):

(a) there is, or is in substance, a disposal of a right to receive any income which would otherwise be chargeable to income tax or corporation tax as income of the transferor (directly or as a partner) or brought into account in calculating the taxpayer's profits (directly or as a partner) for tax purposes;
(b) the disposal is effected wholly or partly by or through a partnership, including a limited liability partnership;
(c) at any time the transferor is a member of the partnership or an associated partnership and the transferee is a member of the partnership or an associated partnership (and for this purpose it does not matter if the transferor and transferee are not members of such a partnership at the same time); and
(d) the main purpose, or one of the main purposes, of one or more steps taken in effecting the disposal is the obtaining of a tax advantage (within *CTA 2010, s 1139*) for any person.

The provisions do not apply if the transferor is the spouse or civil partner of the transferee and they are living together or if the transferor is a brother, sister, ancestor or lineal descendant of the transferee.

In (a) above, 'disposal' of a right includes anything constituting a disposal of such a right for capital gains purposes. For the purposes of (b) above, it is specifically stated that the disposal might, in particular, be effected by an acquisition or disposal of, or an increase or decrease in, an interest in the partnership (including a share of the profits or assets of the partnership or an interest in such a share). In (c) above, the references to the transferor and transferor include a connected person. A partnership is associated with the partnership through which the disposal is effected if it is a member of that partnership or it is a member of a partnership which is itself a member of that associated partnership (and so on). '*Arrangements*' include any agreement, understanding, scheme, transaction or series of transactions (whether or not legally enforceable).

Effect of provisions

Where the provisions apply, the consideration for the disposal of the right to income is treated as income of the transferor chargeable to income tax or corporation tax in the same way and to the same extent as the income would have been chargeable but for the disposal. Where there is no consideration or the consideration is less than the market value of the right, the market value of the right is so treated as income of the transferor.

Priority rule

Where these provisions and those at **4.24** below would otherwise both apply to a disposal, only the provisions which give the greater amount of income chargeable to tax apply.

[*ITA 2007, ss 809AAZA, 809AAZB; CTA 2010, ss 757A, 757B; FA 2014, Sch 17 paras 24, 28*].

Disposal of asset through partnership

[4.24] *FA 2014* introduced anti-avoidance legislation to ensure that where a person disposes of an asset by or through a partnership and the consideration would have been chargeable to tax as income had the disposal been made directly to the transferee, the consideration is taxed as income and not as a chargeable gain. The provisions apply where both condition A and condition B below are met.

Condition A is that directly or indirectly in consequence of, or otherwise in connection with, 'arrangements' made on or after 6 April 2014 (1 April 2014 for corporation tax purposes) and involving a person within the charge to income tax or corporation tax (the 'transferor') and another person (the 'transferee'):

(a) there is, or is in substance, a disposal of an asset by the transferor to the transferee;
(b) the disposal is effected wholly or partly by or through a partnership, including a limited liability partnership;
(c) at any time the transferor is a member of the partnership or an associated partnership and the transferee is a member of the partnership or an associated partnership (and for this purpose it does not matter if the transferor and transferee are not members of such a partnership at the same time); and
(d) the main purpose, or one of the main purposes, of one or more steps taken in effecting the disposal is the obtaining of a tax advantage (within *CTA 2010, s 1139*) for any person.

Condition A is not met if the transferor is the spouse or civil partner of the transferee and they are living together or if the transferor is a brother, sister, ancestor or lineal descendant of the transferee.

In (a) above, 'disposal' of a right includes anything constituting a disposal of such a right for capital gains purposes. For the purposes of (b) above, it is specifically stated that the disposal might, in particular, be effected by an acquisition or disposal of, or an increase or decrease in, an interest in the partnership (including a share of the profits or assets of the partnership or an interest in such a share). In (c) above, the references to the transferor and transferor include a connected person. A partnership is associated with the partnership through which the disposal is effected if it is a member of that partnership or it is a member of a partnership which is itself a member of that associated partnership (and so on). '*Arrangements*' include any agreement, understanding, scheme, transaction or series of transactions (whether or not legally enforceable).

Condition B is that it is reasonable to assume that, had the transferred asset been disposed of directly by the transferor to the transferee, the consideration received by the transferor would have been chargeable to income tax or corporation tax as income or would have been brought into account as income in calculating profits for income tax or corporation tax purposes. If the transferor receives no consideration or consideration which is substantially less than the asset's market value he is treated for this purpose as receiving consideration equal to the market value.

Effect of provisions

Where the provisions apply, the consideration received by the transferor for the disposal of the asset (or its market value) is treated as income of the transferor chargeable to income tax or corporation tax in the same way and to the same extent as it would have been chargeable had the asset been transferred directly from the transferor to the transferee.

Priority rule

Where these provisions and those at **4.23** above would otherwise both apply to a disposal, only the provisions which give the greater amount of income chargeable to tax apply.

[*ITA 2007, ss 809DZA, 809DZB; CTA 2010, ss 779A, 779B; FA 2014, Sch 17 paras 25, 29*].

Follower notices

[4.25] With effect from 17 July 2014, users of avoidance schemes which have been defeated in a Tribunal or court hearing in another taxpayer's case can be required to concede their position to reflect the Tribunal's or court's decision. HMRC can issue a follower notice requiring such users for whom there is an open enquiry or appeal to amend their tax return or agree to resolve their appeal in accordance with the decision.

The taxes covered by the provisions are income tax, capital gains tax, corporation tax (including amounts chargeable as if they were corporation tax or treated as if they were corporation tax), inheritance tax, stamp duty land tax and annual tax on enveloped dwellings. The Treasury may extend the provisions to other taxes by order. [*FA 2014, ss 200, 232*]. The provisions are described below only to the extent that they relate to income tax, capital gains tax and corporation tax.

For HMRC guidance see www.gov.uk/government/publications/follower-notices-and-accelerated-payments/follower-notices-and-accelerated-payments.

Definitions

Arrangements are '*tax arrangements*' if, having regard to all the circumstances, it would be reasonable to conclude that the obtaining of a 'tax advantage' was their main purpose or one of the main purposes of them. '*Arrangements*' include any agreement, understanding, scheme, transaction or series of transactions, whether or not legally enforceable.

A '*tax advantage*' includes relief or increased relief from tax, repayment or increased repayment of tax, avoidance or reduction of a charge or assessment to tax, avoidance of a possible assessment to tax, deferral of a payment, or advancement of a repayment, of tax and avoidance of an obligation to deduct or account for tax.

An '*enquiry*' means an enquiry under *TMA 1970, ss 9A* or *12AC* (see **58.9**, **58.18** RETURNS), *TMA 1970, Sch 1A para 5* (see **13.3** CLAIMS) or *FA 1998, Sch 18 para 24* (see **58.19** RETURNS). An enquiry is '*in progress*' in the period beginning with the day on which the notice of enquiry is given and ending on the day on which the enquiry is completed.

An '*appeal*' means an appeal or further appeal against an assessment, amendment of a self-assessment, closure notice, amendment of a partnership return or a counteraction notice under *ITA 2007, s 705* or *CTA 2010, s 750* (transactions in securities).

A '*judicial ruling*' means a ruling of a court or tribunal on one or more issues. Such a ruling is relevant to particular tax arrangements if it relates to tax arrangements, it is a 'final ruling' and the principles laid down, or reasoning given, in it would, if applied to the arrangements in question, deny the asserted tax advantage or part of it. A judicial ruling is a '*final ruling*' if it is a decision of the Supreme Court, if no further appeal can be made (including where a time limit for further action by the appellant has expired) or if a further appeal was abandoned or otherwise disposed of before it was determined. If a ruling becomes final because of the passing of a time limit or because a further appeal is abandoned or otherwise disposed of before being determined, the ruling is treated as made at the time when the time limit expired or the appeal was abandoned or disposed of.

[*FA 2014, ss 201–203, 205*].

Giving of follower notices

[4.26] HMRC may give a follower notice to a person if:

(a) an enquiry into a return or claim made by that person is in progress or that person has made an appeal which has not been finally determined, abandoned or otherwise disposed of;
(b) the return, claim or appeal is made on the basis that a particular tax advantage results from particular tax arrangements;
(c) HMRC are of the opinion that there is a judicial ruling which is relevant to those arrangements; and
(d) no previous follower notice has been given to the same person (and not withdrawn) by reference to the same tax advantage, tax arrangements, judicial ruling and tax year or accounting period.

A follower notice must identify the judicial ruling, explain why HMRC consider that the ruling is relevant to the tax arrangements and explain the effects of the notice. A notice may not be given after the end of the twelve-month period beginning with the later of the date of the judicial ruling and the date the return or claim was received by HMRC or the appeal was made. Where the judicial ruling is made before 17 July 2014, the notice may not be given after the later of 16 July 2016 and the end of the twelve months beginning with the date the return or claim was received by HMRC or the appeal was made.

The recipient of a follower notice has 90 days beginning with the date the notice is given to send written representations to HMRC objecting to the notice on the grounds that any of (a), (b) or (d) above are not satisfied, that the judicial ruling is not relevant to the arrangements or that the notice was not given within the time limit. Having considered the representations HMRC will notify the recipient of whether they have decided to confirm the notice or withdraw it.

Partnerships

A follower notice may be given to a partnership in respect of a partnership return (see **58.16** RETURNS) or an appeal relating to such a return. The notice is given to the representative partner (i.e. the partner responsible for dealing with the return) or to the successor of that partner (see **58.16** RETURNS). For the purposes of (b) above, a return or appeal is made on the basis that a particular tax advantage results from particular tax arrangements if the arrangements increase or reduce any of the items required to be included in the return and they result in a tax advantage for at least one of the partners. Where a partnership follower notice is given to a person as representative partner or to the successor of that partner, (d) above does not prevent a follower notice from being given to that person in another capacity. All notices given to the representative partner and any successor, in that capacity, are treated as given to the same person for the purposes of (d) above.

[*FA 2014, ss 204, 206, 207, 217, Sch 31 paras 2, 3*].

Action required following giving of follower notice

[4.27] Where a person is given a follower notice and it is not withdrawn, he (or, in the case of a partnership notice given to a representative partner who is no longer available, his successor) must take the following corrective action before the time specified below. Where an enquiry is in progress, the person must amend the return or claim to counteract the tax advantage denied by principles laid down, or reasoning given, in the judicial ruling. If an appeal is open, the person must take all necessary action to enter into a written agreement with HMRC for the purpose of relinquishing the denied advantage. After carrying out the necessary action the person must, before the specified time, notify HMRC that he has done so, including details of the denied advantage and (except in the case of a partnership follower notice) any additional amount of tax that has or will become due and payable.

If no representations were made following the giving of the notice, the specified time is the end of the period of 90 days beginning with the day on which the notice was given. If representations were made and the notice confirmed, the specified time is the later of the end of that 90-day period and the end of the period of 30 days beginning with the day on which the person is notified of HMRC's decision to confirm the notice.

No appeal may be brought against an amendment made by an enquiry closure notice to the extent that it takes into account an amendment to a return or claim resulting from corrective action under the above provision. Where the corrective action requires an amendment to a return or claim, such an amendment is not prevented by any time limit.

Where a person fails to take the necessary corrective action before the specified time, a penalty arises. See **52.26** PENALTIES.

[*FA 2014, s 208, Sch 31 para 4*].

Late appeal against a judicial ruling

[4.28] Where a final judicial ruling is reopened because a court or Tribunal grants leave to appeal out of time, and a follower notice has been given based on that ruling, the notice is suspended until HMRC notify the taxpayer that the appeal has resulted in a final judicial ruling or has been abandoned or otherwise disposed of. HMRC must notify the taxpayer that the follower notice has been suspended. No new follower notice may be issued in respect of the original ruling unless the new appeal is abandoned or disposed of without being determined by a court or Tribunal, but this does not prevent a follower notice from being issued in respect of a new final ruling resulting from the appeal. Where the appeal is abandoned or so disposed of, the period beginning when leave to appeal out of time was granted and ending when the appeal is disposed of does not count towards the twelve-month time limit for issuing follower notices in respect of the original ruling (see **4.26** above).

If a new final ruling results from the appeal and it is not relevant to the tax arrangements in question, a suspended follower notice ceases to have effect. In any other case it continues to have effect after the suspension ends and, if there is a new final ruling, the notice is treated as if it were in respect of that ruling. HMRC's notification to the taxpayer that the suspension has ended must indicate which of these outcomes applies. If there is a new final ruling, the notification must also make any amendments to the follower notice needed to reflect the new ruling.

The period during which a follower notice is suspended does not count in determining the specified time by which corrective action must be taken (see **4.27** above).

[*FA 2014, s 216*].

Accelerated payment notices

[4.29] With effect from 17 July 2014, users of avoidance schemes may be required to pay tax upfront before the success or failure of the scheme has been finally determined. HMRC may issue an 'accelerated payment notice' in certain cases which may override any postponement of tax pending an appeal or, where there is no appeal, require the payment of disputed tax within a specified time. There are special provisions for partnerships. With effect from 26 March 2015, the provisions are extended to prevent the surrender as group relief of corporation tax losses etc. arising from an avoidance scheme. The extension applies to surrenders of, and claims to, group relief made before, on or after that date (see *FA 2015, Sch 18, para 12*). For details of the extension see Tolley's Corporation Tax.

The taxes covered by the provisions are income tax, capital gains tax, corporation tax (including amounts chargeable as if they were corporation tax or treated as if they were corporation tax), inheritance tax, stamp duty land tax and annual tax on enveloped dwellings. The Treasury may extend the provisions to other taxes by order. [*FA 2014, ss 200, 232*]. The provisions are described below only to the extent that they relate to income tax, capital gains tax and corporation tax (except that the extension of the provisions to surrenders of group relief are not covered).

Where relevant, the definitions at **4.25** above apply for the purposes of these provisions.

HMRC have published a list of disclosed avoidance schemes likely to be subject to accelerated payment notices. See gov.uk/government/publications/tax-avoidance-schemes-on-which-accelerated-payments-may-be-charged-by-hmrc.

For HMRC guidance generally see www.gov.uk/government/publications/follower-notices-and-accelerated-payments/follower-notices-and-accelerated-payments.

Attempts to have the giving of an accelerated payment notice declared unlawful were unsuccessful in *R (on the application of Walapu) v Revenue and Customs Commissioners* [2016] EWHC 658 (Admin), [2016] 4 All ER 955, [2016] STC 1682 and *R (oao Graham) v HMRC* QB, [2017] STC 1. A judicial review application was unsuccessful in *Sword Services Ltd v HMRC* QB, [2016] EWHC 1473 (Admin); 2016 STI 1799.

Giving of accelerated payment notice

[4.30] HMRC may give an accelerated payment notice to a person if:

(a) an enquiry into a return or claim made by that person is in progress or that person has made an appeal which has not been finally determined, abandoned or otherwise disposed of;
(b) the return, claim or appeal is made on the basis that a particular tax advantage results from particular arrangements;
(c) either HMRC has given a follower notice (see **4.25** above) in relation to the same return, claim or appeal by reason of the same tax advantage and the arrangements, the arrangements are 'DOTAS arrangements' or a final counteraction notice under the general anti-abuse rule (see **4.4** and **4.6** above) has been given for the tax advantage (or part of it) and the arrangements in circumstances in which at least two members of the sub-panel of the GAAR Advisory Panel which considered the case concluded that entering into the tax arrangements (or the equivalent arrangements the Panel considered) was not a reasonable course of action (see **4.4**(9) and **4.6** above).

In (c) above, '*DOTAS arrangements*' are notifiable arrangements under the provisions for DISCLOSURE OF TAX AVOIDANCE SCHEMES (see **20.2** onwards) to which HMRC has allocated a reference number, notifiable arrangements implementing a notifiable proposal where HMRC has allocated a reference number to the proposed notifiable arrangements or arrangements in respect of which the promoter must provide prescribed information by reason of the arrangements being substantially the same as notifiable arrangements. Notifiable arrangements are excluded if HMRC have given notice that promoters need not notify the reference number to clients.

A notice must specify which of the requirements in (c) above applies and must explain its effects. If the notice is given whilst an enquiry is in progress, it must specify the accelerated payment required; if an appeal is open it must state the amount of the disputed tax (see **4.31** below).

The recipient of an accelerated payment notice has 90 days beginning with the date the notice is given to send written representations to HMRC objecting to the notice on the grounds that any of (a)–(c) above are not satisfied or objecting to the amount specified. Having considered the representations HMRC will notify the recipient of whether they have decided to confirm the notice, to withdraw it or to amend the amount specified in it.

[*FA 2014, ss 219, 220(2), 221(2), 222; FA 2016, s 157(18)–(20)*].

Partnerships

Where a partnership return (see **58.16** RETURNS) has been made, no accelerated payment notice may be given to the representative partner (i.e. the partner responsible for dealing with the return) or to the successor of that partner (see **58.16** RETURNS) if an enquiry is in progress into that return or an appeal has been made against an amendment of that return or, following an enquiry into that return, a conclusion stated in a closure notice. Instead, a '*partner payment notice*' may be given to each person who was a partner at any time in the period to which the return relates if:

(1) the return or appeal is made on the basis that a particular advantage results from particular tax arrangements;

(2) either HMRC has given a follower notice (see **4.25** above) to the representative partner or successor in relation to the same return or appeal by reason of the same tax advantage and the arrangements, the tax arrangements are DOTAS arrangements or the partner in question has been given a final counteraction notice under the general anti-abuse rule (see **4.4** and **4.6** above) for the tax advantage (or part of it) and the arrangements in circumstances in which at least two members of the sub-panel of the GAAR Advisory Panel which considered the case concluded that entering into the tax arrangements (or the equivalent arrangements the Panel considered) was not a reasonable course of action (see **4.4**(8) above).

For the purposes of (1) above, a return or appeal is made on the basis that a particular tax advantage results from particular tax arrangements if the arrangements increase or reduce any of the items required to be included in the return and they result in a tax advantage for at least one of the partners.

There are provisions as to the contents of a notice and as to representations by the recipient which are similar to those applicable to accelerated payment notices (see above).

[*FA 2014, Sch 32 paras 1–3, 4(1), 5; FA 2016, s 157(26)–(28)*].

Withdrawal, modification or suspension

HMRC may withdraw a notice at any time and if they do so the notice is treated as never having had effect and any accelerated payments (and penalties) paid must be repaid. If a notice is given as a result of more than one of the requirements in (c) or (2) above, they may at any time withdraw it to the extent that it is given by one of those requirements (leaving it effective to the extent it was given by virtue of the remaining requirements). HMRC may also reduce the amount of the accelerated or partner payment required or the disputed tax specified in the notice (and, where an accelerated payment has already been made in excess of the reduced amount, that excess must be repaid).

An accelerated or partner payment notice given by virtue of a follower notice must be withdrawn if the follower notice is withdrawn (to the extent that it is given by virtue of the follower notice). If a follower notice is suspended following a late appeal against a judicial ruling (see **4.28** above), the accelerated or partner payment notice is similarly suspended and the period of suspension does not count towards the 30-day and 90-day periods in **4.31** below. A notice is not so suspended if it was also given (and not withdrawn) by virtue of either of the other requirements in (c) or (2) above. If a follower notice is amended following such a late appeal, HMRC may by notice make consequential amendments to the accelerated payment notice.

HMRC must withdraw a notice to the extent that it is given by virtue of DOTAS arrangements if they give notice under *FA 2004, s 312(6)* with the result that promoters are no longer required to notify clients of the reference number (see **20.4** DISCLOSURE OF TAX AVOIDANCE SCHEMES).

Where a notice is given by virtue of more than one of the requirements in (c) or (2) above and is withdrawn to the extent that it was given by virtue of one of those requirements and that requirement was the one stated in the notice to apply to determine the accelerated payment required or disputed tax (see **4.31** below), HMRC must modify the notice to specify one of the remaining requirements as the one which applies for that purpose (and to reduce the payment or tax where necessary). This rule also applies where a a follower notice by virtue of which the accelerated payment notice was given is suspended as if the follower notice were withdrawn, but any change made only applies during the period of suspension.

[*FA 2014, s 227, Sch 32 para 8*].

Effects of accelerated payment notice

[4.31] If an accelerated payment notice is given whilst an enquiry is in progress or a partner payment notice is given, the recipient of the notice must make the payment specified in it. If no representations were made following the giving of the notice, the payment must be made within the period of 90 days beginning with the day on which the notice was given. If representations were made and the notice confirmed or amended, the payment must be made by the later of the end of that 90-day period and the end of the period of 30 days beginning with the day on which the person is notified of HMRC's decision to confirm or amend the notice.

The amount of the payment required is (subject to any representations) the amount which a designated HMRC officer determines, to the best of his information and belief as the 'understated tax'.

(1) Where the notice is given as a result of a follower notice, the '*understated tax*' is the additional amount that would be due and payable if the necessary corrective action under the follower notice were taken in respect of what the designated HMRC officer determines, to the best of his information and belief, as the tax advantage denied by the judicial ruling (see **4.27** above).
(2) Where the notice is given because the tax arrangements are DOTAS arrangements, the '*understated tax*' is the additional amount that would be due and payable if adjustments were made to counteract what

the designated HMRC officer determines, to the best of his information and belief, as so much of the asserted tax advantage as is not a tax advantage which results from the arrangements or otherwise.

(3) Where the notice is given as a result of a GAAR counteraction notice, the '*understated tax*' is the additional amount that would be due and payable if the adjustments set out in that notice which counteract the asserted tax advantage were made.

Where more than one of (1)–(3) above would apply, the notice must stipulate which of them applies and the payment required must be determined accordingly. Where any of the tax included in the accelerated payment required under the notice has already been paid, the payment required is treated as having been paid at the time of the earlier payment. HMRC's recovery powers apply to the required payment as they apply to payments of tax (see **51** PAYMENT OF TAX).

If an accelerated payment notice is given (and not withdrawn) whilst an appeal is open, the understated tax or understated partner tax or the disputed tax (see below) cannot be postponed (see **51.17** PAYMENT OF TAX) pending the outcome of the appeal. If an amount of disputed tax is postponed immediately before the giving of an accelerated payment notice, it ceases to be postponed at that time and becomes due and payable on or before the last day of the 90-day period beginning with the day the notice is given. If representations are made against the notice (see **4.30** above), the tax becomes due and payable on or before the later of the end of that 90-day period and the last day of the 30-day period beginning on the day on which HMRC notify their decision about the representations.

The '*disputed tax*' is so much of the tax which is the subject of the appeal as the designated HMRC officer determines, to the best of his information and belief, as the amount required to counteract what that officer so determines to be the tax advantage in dispute (calculated in the same way as the understated tax in (1)–(3) above). Where more than one of (1)–(3) above would apply, the notice must stipulate which of them applies and the tax advantage in dispute must be determined accordingly.

Where an accelerated payment notice is in force in relation to an open appeal and a court or Tribunal decides against HMRC but they seek permission to appeal against the decision, they may apply to the court or Tribunal from which they are seeking permission to appeal to disapply the rule requiring repayment of tax in accordance with the decision (see **51.18** PAYMENT OF TAX). If the court or Tribunal considers it necessary for the protection of the revenue, it may give permission to withhold the affected repayment or to require the provision of adequate security before repayment is made.

[*TMA 1970, ss 55(8B)–(8D), 56(4)–(6); FA 2014, ss 220(3)–(7), 214(3)–(5), 223, 224(1), 225(1), Sch 32 paras 4(2)–(5), 6; FA 2016, s 157(21)*].

See **52.27** PENALTIES for the penalties chargeable for failure to make an accelerated payment.

Serial avoiders regime

[4.32] *FA 2016* introduces a regime of warnings and escalating sanctions for taxpayers who persistently engage in tax avoidance schemes that are successfully counteracted ('*defeated*') by HMRC. Following the first defeat of a scheme, HMRC will place the taxpayer on a warning (see **4.33**, **4.34** below). The taxpayer has to annually provide HMRC with information during a five-year warning period (see **4.35** below). If the taxpayer uses any such avoidance scheme while under warning, penalties of up to 60% of the understated tax will be charged (see **52.29** PENALTIES) if the scheme is defeated. If three avoidance schemes which exploit reliefs are used while under warning and are defeated, the taxpayer is denied further benefit of reliefs until the warning period expires (see **4.36**). If HMRC defeat three avoidance schemes while the taxpayer is on warning, the taxpayer's details can be published (see **4.40**). See **4.37** for the application of the regime to partnerships.

The regime applies to a number of direct and indirect taxes and also national insurance contributions (see *FA 2016, Sch 18 para 4* for the full list). It is described below in terms of its application to capital gains tax and corporation tax on chargeable gains, but it should be noted that the regime does not operate independently for each type of tax but embraces all avoidance schemes that a person uses which cover any tax on the list.

In relation to taxes other than VAT, '*tax advantage*' is defined widely by *FA 2016, Sch 18 para 7* for the purposes of these provisions.

For HMRC guidance see www.gov.uk/guidance/serial-tax-avoidance.

Commencement

The serial avoiders regime has effect in relation to 'relevant defeats' (see **4.34** below) incurred after 15 September 2016, except for defeats incurred before 6 April 2017 in relation to arrangements entered into before 15 September 2016. A relevant defeat incurred on or after 6 April 2017 in relation to any such pre-15 September 2016 arrangements is outside the regime if, before 6 April 2017, the person incurring the defeat makes a full disclosure of the arrangements or both gives HMRC notice of a firm intention to do so and makes the disclosure within any time limit HMRC may set.

A warning notice given to any person is to be disregarded for the purposes of **4.36** below (restriction of reliefs) and **4.40** below (publishing taxpayer's details) if the defeat specified in the notice relates to arrangements entered into before 15 September 2016. As regards any such pre-15 September 2016 arrangements, a relevant defeat incurred in relation to the arrangements and any warning notice specifying such a defeat are disregarded for the purposes of the penalty at **52.29** PENALTIES.

[*FA 2016, Sch 18 paras 63–65*].

Warning notices

[4.33] Where a person has incurred a 'relevant defeat' (see **4.34** below) in relation to any arrangements (as widely defined), HMRC must give that person a written notice (a '*warning notice*') within the 90 days beginning with the day on which the defeat is incurred. The warning notice must specify the defeat in question, state when the 'warning period' begins and ends and explain the statutory consequences of the notice. The '*warning period*' is the five years following the day on which the warning notice is given. If a person incurs a relevant defeat during a warning period, that period is extended to the end of the five years following the day on which the defeat occurs. [*FA 2016, Sch 18 paras 2, 3*].

Associated persons

Where a person (P) incurs a relevant defeat in relation to any arrangements, any person who is 'associated' with P at the time when P is given the warning notice is also treated for the above purposes as having incurred that relevant defeat, unless both persons are companies in the same group. However, a warning notice thus given to an associated person is disregarded for the purposes of **4.36** below (restriction of relief notices) and see **52.29** PENALTIES. For these purposes, two persons are '*associated*' with one another only if one of them is a body corporate which is controlled (as defined) by the other or if they are bodies corporate under common control (as defined). [*FA 2016, Sch 18 paras 47, 48*].

Meaning of 'relevant defeat'

[4.34] For the purposes of taxes other than VAT, a person (P) incurs a '*relevant defeat*' in relation to arrangements if any of conditions A to C below is met in relation to P and the arrangements. The relevant defeat is incurred when the condition in question is first met.

- Condition A is that a tax advantage has arisen to P from the arrangements and this has been counteracted as in **4.3** above (the GAAR), with the counteraction having become final.
- Condition B is that (in a case not falling within Condition A) a follower notice (see **4.25** above) has been given to P by reference to the arrangements (and not withdrawn) and either the necessary corrective action has been taken (see **4.27** above) or the denied tax advantage has been otherwise counteracted, with the counteraction having become final (determined in the same manner as under **4.3** above).
- Condition C is that (in a case not falling within Condition A or B) the arrangements are 'DOTAS arrangements' (see below) on which P has relied, and the arrangements have been counteracted, with the counteraction having become final. The time at which it falls to be determined whether or not the arrangements are DOTAS arrangements is when the counteraction becomes final.

Condition B applies also where the follower notice is a partnership follower notice in connection with a partnership return and is given to a partnership in which P was a partner in the period covered by the return.

For the purposes of Condition C, P relies on the arrangements if he makes a return, claim or election, or a partnership return is made, on the basis that a 'relevant tax advantage' arises, or if P fails to discharge a 'relevant obligation' and there is reason to believe that the failure is connected with the arrangements. A '*relevant tax advantage*' is one which the arrangements might be expected to enable P to obtain. An obligation is a '*relevant obligation*' if the arrangements might be expected to have the result that the obligation does not arise.

Arrangements are counteracted for the purposes of Condition C if P's tax position is adjusted (other than at his own behest), or an HMRC assessment is made on P, or any other action is taken by HMRC, on the basis that the whole or part of the relevant tax advantage does not arise or that the relevant obligation does arise. Contract settlements (see **6.8** ASSESSMENTS) are treated as assessments for this purpose. P's tax position is adjusted at his own behest if he makes the adjustment at a time when he had no reason to believe that an HMRC enquiry was in the offing (regarding the tax in question) or if HMRC make the adjustment as a result of a full and explicit disclosure by P which is made at such a time.

A counteraction is final for the purposes of Condition C when the assessment, adjustments or action in question, and any amounts thereby arising, can no longer be varied on appeal or otherwise.

[*FA 2016, Sch 18 paras 11–14, 54*].

Meaning of 'DOTAS arrangements'

For the purposes of the serial avoiders regime, arrangements are '*DOTAS arrangements*' at any time if they are 'notifiable arrangements' at that time and a person has provided information in relation to them under *FA 2004, s 308(3)* (obligation of promoter in relation to notifiable arrangements), *s 309* (obligation of person dealing with non-UK promoter) or *s 310* (obligation of parties to notifiable arrangements not involving a promoter) or has failed to comply with any of those provisions in relation to the arrangements. They do not include arrangements in respect of which HMRC has given notice that promoters are not under a duty to notify clients of the reference number. However, they do include arrangements which are excepted from the notification requirement for the reason only that they either had been notified as proposed arrangements or are substantially the same as arrangements already notified.

For the meaning of 'notifiable arrangements' and more on the above-mentioned *FA 2004* provisions, see **20.3** DISCLOSURE OF TAX AVOIDANCE SCHEMES. For the above purposes, a person fails to comply with any of those provisions if (and only if) the Tribunal has determined this to be the case (or has determined against a reasonable excuse), and their determination can no longer be appealed, or the person has made a written admission of such failure to HMRC.

[*FA 2016, Sch 18 paras 8, 10*].

Requirement of annual information notices

[4.35] A person (P) who has been given a warning notice (as in **4.33** above) must give HMRC a written notice (an '*information notice*') in respect of each 'reporting period' within the warning period. The information notice must be given within 30 days after the end of the reporting period to which it relates. Groups of companies may give a combined information notice. The first '*reporting period*' begins with the first day of the warning period and ends with a day specified by HMRC. The remainder of the warning period is divided into further reporting periods of 12 months duration, though the final reporting period ends at the same time as the warning period, even if that results in a reporting period of less than 12 months.

An information notice must state whether, in the reporting period, P:

(a) has made a return, claim or election on the basis that a 'relevant tax advantage' arises (and this includes a return made on that basis since the reporting period ended if the return was due in the reporting period); or
(b) has failed to take action which he would be required to take under, or by virtue of, any tax enactment if it were not for particular DOTAS arrangements (see **4.34** above) or 'disclosable VAT arrangements' (within *FA 2016, Sch 18 para 9*) to which he is a party; or
(c) has become a party to arrangements relating to a supplier's VAT position which might be expected to enable P to obtain a relevant tax advantage in connection with the supplies,

and whether or not P has failed to make any return that he was required to make by a date falling in the reporting period.

A '*relevant tax advantage*' is a tax advantage which particular DOTAS arrangements or disclosable VAT arrangements enable, or might be expected to enable, P to obtain. If (a) above is in point, P must include in the information notice an explanation of how the tax advantage arises and its amount. If (b) is in point, P must similarly explain how the arrangements result in there being no requirement to take the action in question and state the amount of any resulting tax advantage. If (c) is in point, P must state whether it is his view that the relevant tax advantage arises to him and, if so, he must explain how the arrangements enable him to obtain the advantage and state its amount.

If the due date for a return falls within the reporting period and P fails to make the return in that period, HMRC may require from P a supplementary information notice setting out any matters which he would have been required to include in the original information notice if it had not been for that failure. Any such HMRC requirement must be notified in writing and must state the period allowed for compliance.

If P fails to provide a notice (whether an information notice or a supplementary information notice) or provides a notice that is defective, HMRC may by written notice extend the warning period to the end of the five years beginning with the day by which the notice should have been given, or the day on which the defective notice was given. The warning period cannot thus be extended by more than five years from what would otherwise have been its expiry date.

[*FA 2016, Sch 18 para 17*].

Restriction of reliefs

[4.36] HMRC must give a person a written notice (a '*restriction of relief notice*') if:

- the person incurs a relevant defeat (see **4.34** above) in relation to arrangements which he has used whilst in a warning period (see **4.33** above);
- he has been given at least two warning notices in respect of other relevant defeats of arrangements used in that same warning period;
- all the relevant defeats are by virtue of Condition A, B or C in **4.34** (as opposed to conditions relating to VAT that are not reproduced here);
- all the relevant defeats relate to the misuse of a relief; and
- in the case of each of the relevant defeats, either the counteraction was made on the basis that a particular 'avoidance-related rule' applied in relation to a person's affairs or the misused relief in question was a relief for losses under *ITA 2007, Pt 4* or *CTA 2010, Pts 4, 5*.

If a person has been given a single warning notice in relation to two or more relevant defeats, he is treated for the above purposes as having been given a separate warning notice in relation to each defeat. The time at which, for the purposes of the serial avoiders regime, a person has 'used' arrangements is determined by *FA 2016, Sch 18 para 55* in terms of the filing date for returns (meaning the earlier of the actual filing date and the due date), the dates on which claims and elections are made and the date of any failure to comply with an obligation (meaning the date on which the person is first in breach of the obligation).

A relevant defeat relates to the misuse of a relief if the tax advantage in question (or part of it), results from a relief (or an increased relief) or it is reasonable to conclude that the making of a particular claim for relief, or the use of a particular relief, is a significant component of the arrangements in question. A relief means any relief from tax (however described) which must be claimed; management expenses of a company's investment business; any relief for losses under *ITA 2007, Pt 4* or *CTA 2010, Pts 4, 5*; or any other relief listed in *ITA 2007, s 24* (reliefs deductible at Step 2 of the calculation of income tax liability).

'*Avoidance-related rule*' is defined by *FA 2016, Sch 18 para 25*, which also includes an example of such a rule. A statutory rule to the effect that the avoidance of tax must not be a main object or an expected benefit of a transaction or arrangements, or that an action must be carried out for commercial reasons, would be an avoidance-related rule.

The restricted period

A restriction of relief notice must explain its effect (see below) and state when the 'restricted period' begins and ends. The '*restricted period*' is the three years beginning with the day on which the restriction of relief notice is given. If during the restricted period the person to whom a restriction of relief notice has been given incurs a further relevant defeat, HMRC must give him a written notice (a '*restricted period extension notice*'); this extends the restricted period to the end of the three years beginning with the day on which the further defeat occurs. A further defeat is taken into account for this purpose only if it is incurred by virtue of Condition A, B or C in relation to arrangements which the person used in the warning period and relates to the misuse of a relief. If a person to whom a restriction of relief notice has been given incurs a further defeat after the restricted period has ended but during a warning period which at some time ran concurrently with the restricted period, HMRC must give that person a restriction of relief notice.

Effect of restriction of relief notice

A person to whom a restriction of relief notice has been given may not, in the restricted period, make any claim for relief. (For the purposes of the serial avoiders regime, 'claim for relief' includes any election or similar action which is in substance a claim for relief.) Reliefs for charitable giving and contributions to a registered pension scheme are excluded from this restriction, as are claims for relief under a double tax treaty. No losses may be deducted in calculating the total amount of chargeable gains, or the total amount of ATED-related gains or NRCGT gains, for any tax year the first day of which is in the restricted period. Further restrictions are listed in *FA 2016, Sch 18 para 20*.

Mitigation, reasonable excuse and appeals

The Commissioners for HMRC may mitigate, in any way they think appropriate, the effect of a restriction of relief notice insofar as it appears to them that there are exceptional circumstances such that it would otherwise have an unduly serious impact with respect to the tax affairs of the taxpayer concerned or another person.

If a person (P) who has incurred a relevant defeat satisfies HMRC or, on appeal, the Tribunal that he had a reasonable excuse for the matters to which the defeat relates, he is treated for the purposes of the restriction of relief provisions as not having incurred that defeat, and any warning notice given to him in relation to that defeat is treated as not having been given. Reasonable excuse does not include insufficiency of funds (unless attributable to events outside P's control), reliance on another person to do anything (unless P took reasonable care to avoid the failure or inaccuracy in question) or reliance on advice if that advice is addressed to, or was given to, a person other than P or takes no account of P's individual circumstances. A person with a reasonable excuse is treated as having continued to have it if the failure or inaccuracy in question was remedied without unreasonable delay after the excuse ceased.

A person may appeal against a restriction of relief notice or a restricted period extension notice within 30 days beginning with the day on which the notice is given. The appeal is to be treated in the same way as an appeal against an income tax assessment. The Tribunal, on an appeal brought before it, may cancel or affirm HMRC's decision to issue the notice. It may also mitigate the effect of a notice to the same extent as HMRC (see above) or to a different extent, but in the latter case only if the Tribunal regards HMRC's decision on mitigation as flawed.

[*FA 2016, Sch 18 paras 19–29, 55*].

Partnerships

[4.37] The consequences described below apply in relation to a partnership tax return under *TMA 1970, s 12AA* if:

- the return has been made on the basis that a tax advantage arises to a partner from any arrangements and that partner has incurred, in relation to that tax advantage and those arrangements, a relevant defeat by virtue of Condition A or Condition C in **4.34** above; or
- a person has incurred a relevant defeat by virtue of Condition B in **4.34** above and the follower notice in question is a partnership follower notice.

A partnership return is regarded as made on the basis that a particular tax advantage arises to a partner from particular arrangements if it is made on the basis that an increase or reduction in any of the items to be included in the partnership statement (see **58.17** RETURNS) results from those arrangements and that increase or reduction results in that tax advantage for the partner. Limited liability partnerships are within these rules in the same way as other partnerships. For the above purposes a relevant defeat does not include one which an associated person is treated as having incurred (see **4.33** above).

Each 'relevant partner' is treated for the purposes of the serial avoiders regime as having also incurred the relevant defeat in question. A '*relevant partner*' is any person who was a member of the partnership at any time during the period covered by the partnership return.

The appropriate partner (meaning a partner nominated by HMRC for this purpose) must give HMRC a written notice (a '*partnership information notice*') in respect of each sub-period in the 'information period'. The '*information period*' is the five years following the day of the relevant defeat. If a new information period (relating to another partnership return) begins during an existing information period, those periods are treated as a single period. An information period ends if the partnership ceases. The partnership information notice must be given within 30 days after the end of the sub-period to which it relates. The first sub-period begins with the first day of the information period and ends with a day specified by HMRC. The remainder of the information period is divided into further sub-periods of 12 months duration, though the final sub-period ends at the same time as the information period, even if that results in a sub-period of less than 12 months. A partnership information notice must state (i) whether or not any partnership return which was, or was required to be, delivered in the sub-period has been made on the basis that a 'relevant tax advantage' arises; and (ii) whether or not there has been a failure to deliver a partnership return in the sub-period. A '*relevant tax advantage*' is a tax advantage which particular DOTAS arrangements (see **4.34** above) enable, or might be expected to enable, a member of the partnership to obtain. Where relevant, the information notice must go on to explain how the DOTAS arrangements enable the tax advantage to be obtained and describe any variation in the amounts required to be stated in the partnership statement included in the return. There is similar provision to require supplementary information notices as in **4.35** above, and similar consequences for failure to provide an accurate information notice.

There is provision to the effect that if a partnership return is amended, whether by the partnership itself or by HMRC following an unprompted disclosure, then, for the purpose of applying Condition C in **4.34** above, each affected partner is treated as having simultaneously amended his own return so as to give effect to the amendment of the partnership return.

[*FA 2016, Sch 18 paras 49–53, 58(1)(4)*].

Groups of companies

[4.38] Where HMRC have a duty to give a warning notice (see **4.33** above) to a company (C) which is a member of a 'group', that duty has effect as a duty to give such a notice to every other company which is then a member of the group. HMRC may fulfil that duty by delivering the notice to C (and if it does so may combine warning notices in a single notice). Any warning notice previously given to a current group member is treated as having been given to each current group member.

Where a group company incurs a relevant defeat, however, the provisions for restriction of relief notices (see **4.36** above) and penalties (see **4.39** below) apply by reference only to warning periods of the company which would be warning periods if the above provisions did not apply.

Any warning notice which applies to a company only as a result of the above provisions ceases to apply to it when it leaves the group.

Two companies are members of the same group for this purpose if one is a 75% subsidiary (within *CTA 2010, s 1154*) of the other or both are 75% subsidiaries of a third company.

The warning period rules at **4.34** above apply as if successive representative members of a VAT group were a single person, but the serial avoiders regime applies in general to any company as if the company acting in its capacity as representative member were a different person from the company acting in any other capacity.

[*FA 2016, Sch 18 paras 45, 46*].

Penalties

[4.39] See **52.29** PENALTIES which apply where a person incurs a relevant defeat in relation to any arrangements used during a warning period.

Publishing taxpayer's details

[4.40] The Commissioners for HMRC may publish information about a person if he incurs a relevant defeat (see **4.34** above) in relation to arrangements which he has used in a warning period and has been given at least two warning notices (see **4.33** above) in respect of other defeats of arrangements which were used in the same warning period. If a person has been given a single warning notice in relation to two or more relevant defeats, he is treated for these purposes as having been given a separate warning notice in relation to each of those defeats.

The Commissioners can publish the person's name (including trading name, previous name or pseudonym), address or registered office, the nature of any business carried on, information about the fiscal effect of relevant defeated arrangements (had they not been defeated), e.g. the amount of tax understated, the amount of any penalty, the periods in which or times when relevant defeated arrangements were used, and any other information which they consider appropriate in order to make the person's identity clear. In the case of a person carrying on a trade or business in partnership, the information which may be published includes any trading name of the partnership and the names and addresses of the partners. In the case of a company which is a member of a group, the information which may be published includes any trading name of the group and the name, address or registered office and nature of business of any other group member. Defeated arrangements are relevant if the person used them in the said warning period and has been given a warning notice in respect of them. The information may be published in any manner the Commissioners consider appropriate. It can only be first published in the period of one year beginning with the giving of the most recent of the warning notices in question, and information cannot continue to be published for more than a year. Before publishing the information, the Commissioners must inform the person that they are doing so and provide a reasonable opportunity to make representations about whether it should be published.

[*FA 2016, Sch 18 para 18*].

Key points of anti-avoidance

[4.41] Points to consider are as follows.

- If you are considering a complex tax mitigation scheme, be sure that the intended result at each stage reflects the documentation. If the intention is to do something different, and the scheme is found to be a sham, then you have not only failed in your objective but you have almost certainly wasted a great deal of time and money along the way.
- Correct implementation is also crucial. Many schemes have failed because the documents were not signed in the right order, directors were not in the country when board meeting purportedly took place, etc. These practical issues matter — HMRC will happily negate the effect of a piece of tax planning because it was not correctly implemented.
- In cases of incorrect implementation, HMRC also believes that it can charge penalties for the submission of incorrect returns.
- The experience of recent years suggests that the Tribunals and courts are more likely to find for the taxpayer where there is some commercial motivation behind the transactions carried out. So it is important to consider commercial reasons in advance and to keep a record of them. HMRC enquiries can last a long time and, by the time evidence of a commercial rationale is required, the people who know why things were done may no longer be with the organisation.

- For similar reasons, a full set of all documents and supporting evidence should be collected together immediately after the transactions are complete. If one set is kept by the client and another by the adviser, there is a good chance that at least one will be accessible when HMRC's enquiries commence.
- *TCGA 1992, s 13* applies to attribute gains to corporate shareholders as well as individuals. This point is often forgotten by advisers. See **4.7**.
- It is not clear whether there is an implicit motive test in *TCGA 1992, s 29*; this may depend on the meaning attributed to the words 'so that'. But a subscription by a third party on arm's length terms should not give rise to a value shifting charge, if the subscription turns out on later analysis as having been at less than market value. See **4.8**.
- A transfer of assets (or cash) by a close company, on less than arm's-length terms, may also be a chargeable transfer for the purposes of inheritance tax (*IHTA 1984, s 94*). See **4.14**.
- It is important to note that an HMRC clearance only states that HMRC is satisfied that the transactions are being entered into for bona fide commercial reasons and not for the avoidance of corporation tax. The clearance does not confirm that HMRC agrees that the transaction amounts to a reorganisation or a scheme of reconstruction.
- The depreciatory transactions rules will not generally be applied to dividend strips where the dividends were paid out of post-acquisition profits, i.e. profits that arose after the shares were acquired by the shareholder. The rationale is that it would not be just or reasonable to apply an adjustment when a shareholder is merely exercising their rights to access profits that accrued during their period of ownership. See **4.18**.
- Although capital gains tax planners are used to specific and targeted anti-avoidance rules, future plans should also consider the general anti-abuse rule.

5

Appeals

Introduction	5.1
Right of appeal	5.2
Making an appeal	5.3
Special regulations for capital gains tax appeals	5.4
The appeal process	5.5
HMRC review	5.6
Conduct of the review	5.7
Appeal to the Tribunal	5.8
Settlement by agreement	5.9
Alternative dispute resolution	5.10
The Tribunal	5.11
First-tier Tribunal procedure	5.12
Failure to comply with rules	5.13
Categorisation of cases	5.14
Default paper cases	5.15
Basic cases	5.16
Standard cases	5.17
Complex cases	5.18
The hearing	5.19
The Tribunal's decision	5.20
Appeal against the Tribunal's decision	5.22
Payment of tax pending further appeal	5.23
Award of costs	5.24
Upper Tribunal procedure	5.25
Failure to comply with rules	5.26
Appeal against decisions of the First-tier Tribunal	5.27
Notice of appeal	5.28
Other cases before the Upper Tribunal	5.29
The hearing	5.30
The Upper Tribunal's decision	5.31
Appeal against the Tribunal's decision	5.32
Award of costs	5.33
Appeal to the Court of Appeal	5.34
Judicial Review	5.35
Costs	5.36
Key points	5.37

Cross-references. See **6** ASSESSMENTS; **13.3** CLAIMS for appeals in connection with claims and elections made outside the annual tax return; **34** HMRC INVESTIGATORY POWERS; **42.2, 42.5** LATE PAYMENT INTEREST AND PENALTIES as regards interest on tax becoming due where an appeal is made or determined; **51.18, 51.18** PAYMENT OF TAX for postponement provisions; **52.27, 52.34** PENALTIES; **57.35** RESIDENCE AND DOMICILE.

Simon's Taxes. See **A3.7**, **A5.3**, **A5.5**, **A5.6**.

Introduction to appeals

[5.1] A taxpayer who disagrees with an assessment or other decision made by HMRC can appeal against it. This is done by giving notice in writing to HMRC, stating the grounds of appeal. The notice must normally be given within 30 days after the date of issue of the assessment or decision, although late appeals can be made in some circumstances (see **5.3** below).

The appeal process has been dramatically changed with effect from 1 April 2009. Appeals made, but not concluded, before that date are generally dealt with under the new process, but there are some transitional rules, for which see previous editions of this work.

After a taxpayer appeals there are three main options:

- a different HMRC officer can carry out a review of the decision;
- the taxpayer can ask the Tribunal to decide the matter in dispute;
- the appeal can be settled by agreement at any time.

Reviews are not compulsory, and where HMRC carry out a review but the taxpayer still disagrees with the decision, he can ask the Tribunal to decide the issue (or continue negotiations with HMRC in order to settle the appeal by agreement).

For HMRC reviews, see **5.6** below and for settlement by agreement, see **5.9** below.

Where the taxpayer asks the Tribunal to decide the appeal, the case is usually dealt with by the First-tier Tribunal. The appeal is allocated to one of four categories, default paper, basic, standard or complex, and the process differs according to the category. Basic, standard and complex cases are normally decided at a hearing at which the taxpayer (or his representative) and HMRC are able to present their cases.

Default paper cases can also be decided at a hearing where one of the parties requests a hearing. Complex cases may be transferred for hearing by the Upper Tribunal.

For the First-tier Tribunal process, see **5.12–5.24** below.

If either the taxpayer or HMRC disagree with a decision of the First-tier Tribunal, there is a further right of appeal to the Upper Tribunal, but only on a point of law. Permission to appeal must be obtained from the First-tier Tribunal, or where it refuses permission, from the Upper Tribunal.

For the Upper Tribunal process, see **5.25–5.33** below. Where either party disagrees with an Upper Tribunal decision, there is a similar right of appeal to the Court of Appeal. See **5.34** below.

Where there is no right of appeal or a taxpayer is dissatisfied with the exercise by HMRC or the Tribunal of administrative powers, he may in certain circumstances seek a remedy by way of application for judicial review. See **5.35** below.

Costs can be awarded to or against a taxpayer in cases dealt with by either tribunal or by the courts. See **5.24, 5.33** and **5.36** below.

See generally HMRC Appeals, Reviews and Tribunals Guide.

Right of appeal

[5.2] A taxpayer can appeal against:

(a) any assessment other than a self-assessment;
(b) any conclusion stated, or amendment made, by a final or partial closure notice on completion or part completion of an enquiry into a personal, trustees' or partnership tax return (see **58.12** RETURNS);
(c) any HMRC amendment made by a final or partial closure notice on completion or part completion of an enquiry into a company tax return;
(d) any HMRC amendment (of a self-assessment) made, during an enquiry, to prevent potential loss of tax (see **58.13** RETURNS);
(e) any amendment of a partnership return where loss of tax is 'discovered' (see **6.11** ASSESSMENTS);
(f) any discovery determination (i.e. a determination by HMRC of an amount included in a company tax return which affects the tax payable for another accounting period or by another company).

The right of appeal in (a) above includes a right of appeal against a 'simple assessment', but an appeal can be made only after the person assessed has raised a query about the assessment and has been given a final response to that query. See **6.9** ASSESSMENTS.

An appeal within (d) above while an enquiry is in progress in relation to any matter affected by the amendment cannot be taken forward until a partial closure notice is issued in relation to the matter or, if no such notice is issued, a final closure notice is issued (see **58.12** RETURNS).

[*TMA 1970, s 31(1)(2)(3A); FA 1998, Sch 18 paras 30(3), 34(3), 48(1), 49; FA 2016, s 167, Sch 23 para 4; F(No 2)A 2017, Sch 15 paras 18, 30, 44*].

An appeal against an assessment to corporation tax is an appeal against the total amount of profits charged to tax in the assessment (*Owton Fens Properties Ltd v Redden* Ch D 1984, 58 TC 218).

In partnership cases, the right of appeal is not restricted to the nominated partner (*Phillips v HMRC* FTT, [2010] SFTD 332).See, however, **52.34** PENALTIES for the restriction of the right of appeal against a penalty under *Finance Act 2009, Sch 55* to the nominated partner (which restriction was upheld in *Dyson v HMRC* FTT [2015] SFTD 529, despite the Tribunal holding that the provision contravened the European Convention on Human Rights).

Specific rights of appeal against HMRC decisions, notices or determinations are also included in a number of other provisions and, where relevant, such rights are referred to at the appropriate place in this work. Appeals in connection with claims and elections, where made outside the tax return, are dealt with at **13.3** CLAIMS.

There is no right of appeal against a determination of liability made by HMRC in the event of non-submission of a tax return (see **58.15** RETURNS).

Unless otherwise stated or required by context, the remainder of this chapter applies to all appeals and all matters treated as appeals, and not only to appeals within (a)–(f) above. [*TMA 1970, s 48; TIOPA 2010, Sch 7 para 31; SI 2009 No 56, Sch 1 para 28*].

Making an appeal

[5.3] An appeal is made by giving notice in writing to the officer of Revenue and Customs concerned and specifying the grounds of appeal. Notice must normally be given within 30 days after the date of issue of the assessment or determination, the closure notice or the notice of amendment. In the case of a 'simple assessment' (see **6.9** ASSESSMENTS) notice of appeal must be given within 30 days after the date on which the person assessed is given notice by HMRC of their final response to his query about the assessment. [*TMA 1970, s 31A(1)–(5); FA 1998, Sch 18 paras 30(3)(4), 34(3)(4), 48(2), 92(2); FA 2016, s 167, Sch 23 para 5*].

Late appeals

If a taxpayer fails to make an appeal within the normal time limit, an appeal can still be made if HMRC agree or, where HMRC do not agree, the Tribunal gives permission.

HMRC must agree to a written request for a late appeal if they are satisfied that there was a reasonable excuse for not making the appeal within the time limit and that the request was made without unreasonable delay after the reasonable excuse ceased.

Before 1 April 2009, HMRC could accept a late appeal only if satisfied that there was such a reasonable excuse and no unreasonable delay. Otherwise, HMRC had to refer the application to the Commissioners (normally the General Commissioners) for their decision.

[*TMA 1970, s 49; SI 2009 No 56, Sch 1 para 29*].

In the event of refusal to accept a late appeal, the decision is not subject to further appeal (*R v Special Commrs (ex p. Magill)* QB (NI) 1979, 53 TC 135), but is subject to judicial review (see *R v Hastings and Bexhill General Commrs and CIR (ex p. Goodacre)* QB 1994, 67 TC 126, in which a refusal was quashed and the matter remitted to a different body of Commissioners). In *R (oao Browallia Cal Ltd) v General Commissioners of Income Tax* QB 2003, [2004] STC 296, it was held that the Appeal Commissioners had a wider discretion than HMRC in considering a late appeal. The court held that the Commissioners in that case had misunderstood their powers and that the lack of any reasonable excuse was 'potentially relevant' but was 'not conclusive'. The decision was followed in *R (oao Cook) v General Commissioners of Income Tax* QB, [2007] STC 499 in which the General Commissioners' refusal of a late appeal application was quashed because they had only considered the lack of a reasonable excuse and did not consider the possible merits of the appeal itself. (When the case was remitted to the General Commissioners, however, they again refused the late appeal, and the court upheld their decision — see *R (oao Cook) v General Commissioners of Income Tax (No. 2)* QB, [2009] STC 1212.)

Withdrawing an appeal

An appeal once made cannot, strictly, be withdrawn unilaterally (see *R v Special Commissioners (ex p. Elmhirst)* CA 1935, 20 TC 381 and *Beach v Willesden General Commissioners* Ch D 1981, 55 TC 663). If, however, a taxpayer or his agent gives HMRC oral or written notice of his desire not to proceed with an appeal, the appeal is treated as if settled by agreement, so that the provisions at **5.9** below apply (and the appeal is settled without any variation). Agreement is effective from the date of the taxpayer's notification. This does not apply if HMRC give written notice of objection within 30 days of the taxpayer's notice. [*TMA 1970, s 54(4)(5)*].

Payment of tax

For postponement of tax pending appeal and for payment of tax on determination of the appeal, see respectively **51.18, 51.18** PAYMENT OF TAX.

Special regulations for capital gains tax appeals

[5.4] *The Capital Gains Tax Regulations 1967 (SI 1967 No 149)* make special provisions in relation to CGT appeals and are summarised below. In particular, they lay down procedures under which a question of market value or apportionment which affects the liability of two or more persons (e.g. a donor and donee, or a vendor and purchaser in a transaction not at arm's length) can be settled.

Joinder of third parties in appeals

Where the market value of an asset on a particular date or the apportionment of any amount or value is a material question in an appeal, any person whose liability to CGT for any period may be affected by that market value may apply to be joined in the appeal. Application is in writing to HMRC and should state, *inter alia*, how the applicant's liability may be affected and his contention in relation to the matters under appeal. A copy of the application is sent by HMRC to the appellant and any other party to the appeal. If the application is received before the appeal has been notified to the tribunal (or, before 1 April 2009, more than 30 days before the date of the appeal hearing, or before that date is set), then if HMRC are satisfied with the propriety of the applicant's case, the applicant will be joined as a third party and appropriate notice given to the other parties. Otherwise, HMRC will refer the application to the Tribunal (before 1 April 2009, the Commissioners) who may allow or refuse the application at its discretion. Insofar as his interest is being considered, the third party has the same rights as the appellant. [*SI 1967 No 149, Reg 8; SI 2009 No 56, Sch 2 para 3*].

Applications for determination of market value

Where the market value of an asset or the apportionment of any amount or value may affect the liability to CGT of two or more persons, either or any of them may apply to the Tribunal (before 1 April 2009, the Commissioners (General or Special)) for a ruling if the point is not, nor has been, a material question in an appeal brought by any of them. HMRC are a party to such proceedings. [*SI 1967 No 149, Reg 9; SI 2009 No 56, Sch 2 para 4*].

Conclusive effect of determination on appeal

The values as determined are conclusive between HMRC, the parties to the appeal and any third party who was given notice of the appeal in reasonable time unless that person's application (made without undue delay) to be joined as a party to the appeal was refused. [*SI 1967 No 149, Reg 11*].

Agreements in writing

There can be no binding agreement on the value of an asset between HMRC and the taxpayer unless the agreement is joined by any proper third party to the appeal. A written agreement will be effective against the taxpayer's personal representatives, trustee in bankruptcy etc. An agreement conclusive against trustees of a settlement will be effective against any person becoming absolutely entitled to the settled property. [*SI 1967 No 149, Regs 12, 13; SI 2009 No 56, Sch 2 para 5*].

The appeal process after 31 March 2009

[5.5] When an appeal to HMRC is made, there are four options for the appeal to proceed:

(a) the appellant can require HMRC to review the matter in question;
(b) HMRC can offer to review the matter in question;
(c) the appellant can notify the appeal to the Tribunal for it to decide the matter in question; or
(d) the appeal can be settled by agreement between HMRC and the appellant (including by way of alternative dispute resolution).

Where the appellant requires an HMRC review, he can still notify the appeal to the tribunal if he disagrees with the review's conclusions or HMRC fail to complete a review within the required time. If HMRC offer a review and the appellant does not accept the offer, he can likewise notify the appeal to the tribunal. Taking any of options (a) to (c) above does not prevent the appeal from being settled by agreement at any time.

[*TMA 1970, s 49A; SI 2009 No 56, Sch 1 para 30*].

For details of the review process, see **5.6** below; for notifying an appeal to the tribunal, see **5.8** below; and for settlement of appeals by agreement, see **5.9** below.

Notices

All notices given under the appeal provisions must be made in writing. Notifications by the appellant can be made by a person acting on his behalf, but all HMRC notifications must be made directly to the appellant (although copies can be sent to his agent). [*TMA 1970, s 49I; SI 2009 No 56, Sch 1 para 30*].

HMRC review

[5.6] Where an appellant notifies HMRC that he requires them to review the matter in question, HMRC must first notify him of their view of the matter. They must do this within the 30 days beginning with the day on which they receive the notification from the appellant, or within such longer period as is reasonable. They must then carry out a review of the matter in question, as described at 5.7 below.

The appellant cannot request a second review of the matter in question and neither can he request a review if he has already notified the appeal to the tribunal.

If it is HMRC who offer to review the matter in question, they must, when they notify the appellant of the offer, also notify the appellant of their view of the matter. The appellant then has 30 days beginning with the date of the document notifying him of the offer to notify HMRC of acceptance of it. If the appellant does so, HMRC must then carry out a review of the matter in question, as described at 5.7 below. Alternatively, the appellant can, within the same 30-day period, notify the appeal to the tribunal for it to decide the matter in question.

If the appellant does not either accept the offer of review or notify the appeal to the tribunal within the 30-day period, then HMRC's view of the matter in question is treated as if it were contained in a written agreement for the settlement of the appeal, so that the provisions at 5.9 below apply (and the appeal is settled on the basis of HMRC's view). The appellant's normal right to withdraw from such agreements does not apply to the deemed agreement. The tribunal may, however, give permission for the appellant to notify the appeal to it after the 30-day period has ended.

HMRC cannot make a second offer of a review or make an offer if the appellant has already required a review or has notified the appeal to the tribunal.

[*TMA 1970, ss 49B, 49C, 49H; SI 2009 No 56, Sch 1 para 30*].

Conduct of the review

[5.7] The nature and extent of HMRC's review will be determined by them as seems appropriate in the circumstances, but they must take into account the steps taken before the start of the review both by them in deciding the matter in question and by anyone else seeking to resolve the disagreement. They must also take into account representations made by the appellant, provided that these are made at a stage which gives HMRC a reasonable opportunity to consider them.

The review must be completed and HMRC's conclusions notified to the appellant in writing within 45 days beginning with:

- where the appellant required the review, the day HMRC notified him of their view of the matter in question; or
- where HMRC offered the review, the day HMRC received notification of the appellant's acceptance of the offer.

HMRC and the appellant can, however, agree any other period for completion of the review.

If HMRC fail to notify the appellant of their conclusions within the required period, the review is treated as if the conclusion was that HMRC's original view of the matter in question were upheld. HMRC must notify the appellant in writing accordingly.

[*TMA 1970, s 49E; SI 2009 No 56, Sch 1 para 30*].

Effect of conclusions

HMRC's notice stating the conclusions to the review is treated as a written agreement for the settlement of the appeal, so that the provisions at **5.9** below apply (and the appeal is settled on the basis of those conclusions). The appellant's normal right to withdraw from such agreements does not apply to the deemed agreement.

The appellant does, however, have a further opportunity to notify the appeal to the tribunal for them to determine the matter in question. This must normally be done within the period of 30 days beginning with the date of the document notifying the conclusions of the review. Where, however, HMRC have failed to notify the conclusions within the required period, the time limit is extended to 30 days after the date of the document notifying the appellant that the review is to be treated as if concluded on the basis of HMRC's original opinion. The tribunal may give permission for an appeal to be notified to them after the time limits have expired.

[*TMA 1970, ss 49F, 49G; SI 2009 No 56, Sch 1 para 30*].

HMRC practice

Reviews are carried out by HMRC officers who have experience of the subject matter of the appeal but are independent of the decision maker and the decision maker's line management (HMRC Appeals, Reviews and Tribunals Guide, ARTG4310).

The review officer will consider whether the case is one which HMRC would want to defend before the tribunal, and in particular will consider:

- whether the facts have been established, and whether there is disagreement about the facts;
- the technical and legal merits of the case;
- whether it would be an efficient or desirable use of resources to proceed with an appeal that will cost more than the sum in dispute;
- the likelihood of success; and
- whether the appeal raises unusual questions of law or general policy or may in some other way potentially have an effect on future decisions.

(HMRC Appeals, Reviews and Tribunals Guide, ARTG4080).

Review officers are instructed generally to avoid discussing the case with the caseworker during the review in order to ensure that the review remains independent. If exceptionally it is necessary to discuss a case with the caseworker in any depth during the review the review officer will tell the appellant and offer equivalent telephone or face to face contact with him or his agent, so the appellant has an equal opportunity to make representations. (HMRC Appeals, Reviews and Tribunals Guide, ARTG4620).

See further HMRC Appeals, Reviews and Tribunals Guide, ARTG4000–4860.

Appeal to the Tribunal

[5.8] A taxpayer who has appealed to HMRC can notify the appeal to the Tribunal without requesting an HMRC review first. If he does so, HMRC cannot then make an offer of a review. [*TMA 1970, s 49D; SI 2009 No 56, Sch 1 para 30*].

An appellant can also notify an appeal to the tribunal if he does not wish to accept an HMRC offer of a review or if he disagrees with the conclusions of a review. In both cases there are short time limits within which notification must be made, although the tribunal can give permission for notification to be made outside those limits: see **5.6** and **5.7** above.

There is no provision for HMRC to notify an appeal to the tribunal (unlike under the appeals system before 1 April 2009 where HMRC was responsible in most cases for listing appeals for hearing by the Commissioners — see **5.36** below).

Notice of appeal must include the appellant's details, details of the decision etc. appealed against, the result the appellant is seeking and the grounds of appeal. The notice must be accompanied by a copy of any written record of the decision and the reasons for it that the appellant has or can reasonably obtain. If the notice is made late it must also include a request for extension of time and the reason for lateness. [*SI 2009 No 273, Rule 20*].

Appeals should be notified to the tribunal by e-mail to taxappeals@tribunals.gsi.gov.uk or by post to the HM Courts and Tribunals Service, First-tier Tribunal (Tax), 3rd Floor, Temple Court, 35 Bull Street, Birmingham B4 6EQ. A Notice of Appeal form can be obtained from the Tribunals Service website (www.tribunals.gov.uk) or by phoning 0300 123 1024.

See **5.11** onwards below for the process by which an appeal notified to the tribunal is decided.

Settlement by agreement

[5.9] At any time before an appeal is determined by the tribunal, it may be settled by agreement between HMRC and the appellant or his agent. Where such an agreement is reached, in writing or otherwise, the assessment or decision as upheld, varied, discharged, or cancelled by that agreement, is treated as if it had been determined on appeal. Oral agreements are, however, effective only if confirmed in writing by either side (the date of such confirmation then being the effective date of agreement).

The taxpayer may withdraw from the agreement by giving written notice within 30 days of making it.

[*TMA 1970, s 54(1)–(3)(5); SI 2009 No 56, Sch 1 para 33*].

The agreement must specify the figure for assessment or a precise formula for ascertaining it (*Delbourgo v Field* CA 1978, 52 TC 225).

The agreement only covers the assessments (or decisions) which are the subject of the appeal, and does not bind HMRC for subsequent years, for example where relievable amounts are purported to be carried forward from the year in question (*MacNiven v Westmoreland Investments Ltd* HL 2001, 73 TC 1 and see also *Tod v South Essex Motors (Basildon)* Ltd Ch D 1987, 60 TC 598).

The issue of an amended notice of assessment cannot in itself constitute an offer for the purposes of a *s 54* agreement; nor can a lack of response by the taxpayer constitute acceptance of an offer (*Schuldenfrei v Hilton* CA 1999, 72 TC 167).

An agreement based on a mutual mistake of fact was as a result invalid, so that the taxpayer could proceed with his appeal (*Fox v Rothwell* (Sp C 50), [1995] SSCD 336).

See *Gibson v General Commissioners for Stroud* Ch D 1989, 61 TC 645 for a case where there was held not to have been a determination and *R v Inspector of Taxes, ex p. Bass Holdings Ltd; Richart v Bass Holdings Ltd* QB 1992, 65 TC 495 for one where rectification of an agreement was ordered where a relief had been deducted twice contrary to the intention of Revenue and taxpayer.

See *CIR v West* CA 1991, 64 TC 196 for a case where the taxpayer was unsuccessful in seeking leave to defend a Crown action for payment of tax on the ground that the accountant who had entered into an agreement had no authority to do so given him by the taxpayer.

In *Foulser v HMRC* FTT, [2014] UKFTT 483 (TC); 2014 STI 2764 the taxpayer argued that he had sent a cheque to HMRC with a covering letter indicating that it was 'in full and final settlement' of his liability, and that since HMRC had cashed the cheque, this should be treated as a settlement by agreement of the appeal. The FTT rejected this contention.

Alternative dispute resolution

[5.10] Small and medium-sized enterprises and individuals can, with effect from 2 September 2013, apply to HMRC to use alternative dispute resolution (ADR) to seek to settle tax disputes, whether or not an appealable tax decision or assessment has been made by HMRC. The ADR process was introduced nationwide following a two year trial under which certain taxpayers had been invited by HMRC to use it. Entering into the ADR process does not affect the taxpayer's existing review and appeal rights. ADR is open to all taxpayers whose tax affairs are handled by HMRC's Local Compliance SME and Local Compliance Individuals and Public Bodies business units.

ADR involves an independent person from HMRC (known as a 'facilitator'), who has not previously been involved in the dispute, working with both the taxpayer and the HMRC case owner to try to broker an agreement between them. The process does not guarantee resolution of the dispute. Entering into the ADR process does not affect the taxpayer's existing review and appeal rights. See www.gov.uk/guidance/tax-disputes-alternative-dispute-resolution-adr.

Taxpayers can apply to use ADR by following the link from the above web page and completing the online form.

The Tribunal

[5.11] Under the unified tribunal system established by the *Tribunals, Courts and Enforcement Act 2007*, there are two tribunals; the First-tier Tribunal and the Upper Tribunal. The Tribunals are presided over by a Senior President of Tribunals. [*TCEA 2007, s 3*].

The First-tier Tribunal

Tax appeals notified to the Tribunal are in most cases initially heard and decided by the First-tier Tribunal. [*TMA 1970, s 47C; SI 2009 No 56, Sch 1 para 27*].

The First-tier Tribunal is organised into separate chambers each with responsibility for different areas of the law and with its own Chamber President. With certain exceptions, the Tax Chamber is responsible for all appeals, applications, references or other proceedings in respect of the functions of HMRC. It is also responsible for appeals etc. in respect of the exercise of Revenue functions by the Serious Organised Crime Agency (see **30.9** HMRC — ADMINISTRATION) and for appeals relating to certain other non-tax matters. The exceptions relate to certain tax credit and national insurance matters and to matters for which the Upper Tribunal is responsible. [*TCEA 2007, s 7; SI 2008 No 2684, Arts 2, 5A; SI 2009 No 196, Arts 3, 5; SI 2010 No 2655, Art 2*].

The Upper Tribunal

The Upper Tribunal is a superior court of record, so that its decisions create legally binding precedents. [*TCEA 2007, s 3(5)*].

It is similarly divided into chambers, including the Tax and Chancery Chamber. In relation to tax matters, the Chamber is responsible for:

(a) further appeals against decisions by the First-tier Tribunal Tax Chamber (see **5.27** below);
(b) applications by HMRC for a tax-related penalty under *FA 2008, Sch 36 para 50* in respect of failure to comply with an information notice or obstruction of an inspection (see **52.16** PENALTIES);
(c) complex appeals, applications or references transferred from the First-tier Tribunal (see **5.29** below); and
(d) matters referred to the Upper Tribunal following a decision by the First-tier Tribunal Tax Chamber to set aside its own original decision (see **5.29** below); and
(e) applications for judicial review (see **5.35** below).

[*SI 2008 No 2684, Arts 6, 8; SI 2009 No 196, Arts 6, 8; SI 2009 No 1590, Art 8; SI 2010 No 2655, Arts 9, 13*].

Overriding objective

The Tribunal Procedure Rules which govern the operation of the Tribunals include an explicit statement of their overriding objective, which is to deal with cases fairly and justly. The Tribunals are required to deal with each case in ways proportionate to its importance, its complexity and the anticipated costs and resources of the parties to the appeal etc. They must avoid unnecessary formality and delay and seek flexibility in the proceedings. They must ensure that the parties are able to participate fully in the proceedings.

The parties to the appeal etc. are in turn required to help the Tribunal to further the overriding objective and to co-operate with the Tribunal generally.

[*SI 2008 No 2698, Rule 2; SI 2009 No 273, Rule* 2].

Alternative dispute resolution

The Tribunals also have an explicit duty to point out to the parties the availability of any alternative procedure for resolving the dispute and to facilitate the use of the procedure if the parties wish. [*SI 2008 No 2698, Rule 3; SI 2009 No 273, Rule* 3]. See **5.10** above for HMRC's alternative dispute resolution process.

Composition of tribunals

Both the First-tier and Upper Tribunal consist of judges who have particular legal qualifications or experience, and other members who are not legally qualified but meet specified selection criteria. Judges of the Upper Tribunal are appointed by the Crown on the recommendation of the Lord Chancellor. Judges and members of the First-tier Tribunal, and members of the Upper Tribunal, are appointed by the Lord Chancellor. See *TCEA 2007, ss 4, 5, Schs 2, 3*.

First-tier Tribunal procedure

Case management

[5.12] The Tribunal has wide powers to regulate its own procedures and to give directions about the conduct or disposal of cases. In particular it can, by direction:

- consolidate or hear two or more cases together or treat a case as a lead case (see *SI 2009 No 273, Rule 18*);
- permit or require a party to the case or another person to provide documents, information or submissions to the tribunal or another party;
- hold a hearing to consider any matter, including a case management hearing;
- decide the form of any hearing;
- require a party to produce a bundle of documents for a hearing.

The Tribunal can also substitute a party to a case where necessary or add a person to the case as a respondent. A person who is not a party to the case can apply to the Tribunal to be added as a party.

Either party to a case can apply for the Tribunal to make a direction, either in writing or orally at a hearing, or the Tribunal can make a direction on its own initiative. Applications for a direction must include the reason for making it. Directions can be challenged by applying for a further direction.

Any action required to be done in relation to a case on or by a particular day must be done before 5pm on that day (or, if that day is not a working day, by 5pm on the next working day).

[*SI 2009 No 273, Rules 5, 6, 9, 12*].

Administration of cases referred to the Tribunal, including the categorisation of cases (see **5.14** below), is carried out by the Tribunals Service.

Starting proceedings

See **5.8** above for how to notify an appeal to the Tribunal. There are also rules for proceedings to be determined without notice to a respondent (*Rule 19*), and for proceedings started by originating application or reference (*Rule 21*).

Representation

A party to a case can appoint a representative to represent him in the proceedings. The representative does not need to be a lawyer. The party has to notify the Tribunal and the other parties of the appointment of a representative and they will then treat the representative as authorised until notified otherwise.

Where no such person has been appointed, a party can, with the Tribunal's permission, nevertheless be accompanied at a hearing by another person who can act as a representative or assist in presenting the case.

[*SI 2009 No 273, Rule 11; SI 2010 No 40, Rule 16*].

Withdrawal from a case

Subject to any legislation relating to withdrawal from or settlement of particular proceedings, a party can notify the Tribunal of the withdrawal of its case, or part of it. This can be done in writing before a hearing or orally at a hearing. If the case is to be settled without a hearing, written notice must be given before the Tribunal disposes of the case.

A party who has withdrawn its case can, however, apply (in writing) to the Tribunal to reinstate it. The application must be received by the Tribunal within 28 days after it received the withdrawal notice or the date of the hearing.

[*SI 2009 No 273, Rule 17; SI 2013 No 477, Rules 1, 39*].

Failure to comply with rules

[5.13] An irregularity resulting from any failure to comply with the Tribunal Procedure Rules, a practice direction or a direction by the Tribunal does not in itself make the proceedings void.

Where a party fails to comply with the Rules etc. the Tribunal can take such action as it considers just. This could be to require compliance or waive the requirement, to strike the case out (see below) or, in certain cases, to refer the failure to the Upper Tribunal.

The Tribunal can refer to the Upper Tribunal any failure to:

- attend a hearing, or otherwise be available, to give evidence;
- to swear an oath in connection with giving evidence;
- to give evidence as a witness;
- to produce a document; or
- to facilitate the inspection of a document or other thing (including premises).

The Upper Tribunal then has the same powers as the High Court to deal with the failure (which may include financial penalties).

[*TCEA 2007, s 25; SI 2009 No 273, Rule 7*].

Striking out a case

A case will automatically be struck out if the appellant fails to comply with a direction which states that failure to comply will lead to striking out.

The Tribunal can also strike out a case if the appellant fails to comply with a direction which states that failure to comply may lead to striking out, if the appellant has failed to co-operate with the Tribunal to such an extent that the case cannot be dealt with fairly and justly, or if the Tribunal considers that there is no reasonable prospect of the appellant's case succeeding. In the last two cases, however, the Tribunal must first give the appellant an opportunity to make representations.

If the case is struck out because of the appellant's failure to comply with a direction, the appellant can apply for the case to be reinstated. This must be done in writing within 28 days after the date the Tribunal sent the notification of the striking out.

The above rules also apply to respondents except that, instead of the case being struck out, the respondent is barred from taking any further part in the case.

[*SI 2009 No 273, Rule 8*].

An attempt to have HMRC barred from taking any part in a case was unsuccessful in *Foulser and another v HMRC* FTT 2011, [2012] SFTD 94. On appeal to the Upper Tribunal, however, the case was remitted for rehearing by the FTT ([2013] STC 917). An attempt to have HMRC barred also failed in *Ritchie v HMRC* FTT, [2016] UKFTT 509 (TC), [2016] STI 2753.

Categorisation of cases

[5.14] When an appeal, application or reference is notified to the Tribunal, the Tribunals Service allocate it to one of four categories of case:

(a) default paper;

(b) basic;
(c) standard; or
(d) complex.

Cases may be re-categorised by the Tribunal at any time either on the application of one of the parties or on the Tribunal's own initiative.

[*SI 2009 No 273, Rule 23(1)–(3); SI 2013 No 477, Rules 1, 34, 41*].

The process by which the appeal etc. will be decided varies according to the category to which the case is allocated as described below.

Default paper cases

[5.15] The following types of cases must normally be categorised as default paper cases:

(a) appeals against penalties for late self-assessment tax returns (see **52.4–52.6** PENALTIES) and certain other late returns or notifications;
(b) appeals against surcharges for late payment of tax under *TMA 1970, s 59C* (see **42.6** LATE PAYMENT INTEREST AND PENALTIES); and
(c) applications for a daily penalty for a late personal self-assessment tax return (see **52.4** PENALTIES).

Cases can be allocated to a different category if the Tribunal considers it appropriate to do so.

(Tribunals Practice Direction, 10 March 2009).

In a default paper case, the respondent (i.e., in an appeal, HMRC) must provide a statement of case to the Tribunal, the appellant and any other respondents to be received within 42 days after the Tribunal sends it notice of the proceedings (or by such time as the Tribunal directs). The statement must state the legislation under which the decision in question was made and set out the respondent's position. If the statement is late it must also include a request for a time extension and give the reason for lateness.

The statement can also contain a request for the case to be dealt with either at or without a hearing.

Once such a statement has been given to the appellant, he may send a written reply to the Tribunal. The reply must be received within 30 days after the date on which the respondent sent its statement to the appellant and must be sent also to each respondent. The reply may include the appellant's response to the respondent's statement of case, provide any further relevant information and contain a request for the case to be dealt with at a hearing. If the reply is late it must also include a request for a time extension and give the reason for lateness.

The Tribunal must hold a hearing before determining a case if any party has requested one in writing. Otherwise, on receipt of the appellant's reply or the expiry of the time limit for such a reply, the Tribunal will determine the case without a hearing, unless it directs otherwise.

[*SI 2009 No 273, Rules 25, 26*].

Default paper cases are decided by one judge or other member of the First-tier Tribunal. (Tribunals Practice Statement, 10 March 2009).

Basic cases

[5.16] The following types of cases must normally be allocated as basic cases (unless they must be allocated as default paper cases):

(a) appeals against penalties for late filing and late payment, including daily penalties;
(b) appeals against penalties under *FA 2007, Sch 24* (errors in documents and failure to notify HMRC of errors in assessments — see **52.8–52.10** PENALTIES);
(c) appeals against indirect tax penalties on the basis of reasonable excuse and certain construction industry scheme decisions;
(d) appeals against information notices (including those at **34.4** and **34.11**(d) HMRC INVESTIGATORY POWERS and **58.11** RETURNS);
(e) applications for permission to make a late appeal (see **5.3** above);
(f) applications for the postponement of tax pending an appeal (see **51.17** PAYMENT OF TAX); and
(g) applications for a direction that HMRC close an enquiry (see **58.12** RETURNS).

Appeals against penalties for deliberate action or where an appeal is also brought against the assessment to which the penalty relates are excluded from (b) above (as are indirect tax cases).

Cases can be allocated to a different category if the Tribunal considers it appropriate to do so.

(Tribunals Practice Direction, 10 March 2009).

Basic cases normally proceed directly to a hearing, without the need for the respondent to produce a statement of case. Where, however, the respondent intends to raise grounds at the hearing of which the appellant has not been informed, the appellant must be notified of those grounds as soon as is reasonably practicable. The respondent must include sufficient detail to enable the appellant to respond to the grounds at the hearing. [*SI 2009 No 273, Rule 24*].

A decision in a basic case that disposes of proceedings or determines a preliminary issue made at, or following, a hearing must be made by either one, two or, where the Chamber President so decides, three members. The members can be judges or other members as the Chamber President decides, and he will choose one of them to be the presiding member. Any other decision will be made by one judge or other member. (Tribunals Practice Statement, 10 March 2009).

Standard cases

[5.17] In a standard case, the respondent (i.e., in an appeal, HMRC) must provide a statement of case to the tribunal, the appellant and any other respondents to be received within 60 days after the Tribunal sends it notice of the proceedings (or by such time as the Tribunal directs). The statement must state the legislation under which the decision in question was made and set out the respondent's position. If the statement is late it must also include a request for a time extension and give the reason for lateness.

The statement can also contain a request for the case to be dealt with either at or without a hearing.

Within 42 days after the date on which the respondent sent the statement of case, each party to the case must send to the Tribunal and each other party a list of documents of which that party has possession (or the right to take possession or make copies) and on which the party intends to rely or to produce in the proceedings. The other parties must then be allowed to inspect or copy those documents, except for any which are privileged.

The case will then normally proceed to a hearing (see **5.19** below).

[*SI 2009 No 273, Rules 25, 27*].

A decision in a standard case that disposes of proceedings or determines a preliminary issue made at, or following, a hearing must be made by one judge or by one judge and one or two members as determined by the Chamber President. The judge will be the presiding member, unless one or more of the other members is also a judge, in which case the Chamber President will choose the presiding member. Any other decision will be made by one judge. (Tribunals Practice Statement, 10 March 2009).

Complex cases

[5.18] A case can be classified as a complex case only if the Tribunal considers that it will require lengthy or complex evidence or a lengthy hearing, involves a complex or important principle or issue, or involves a large financial sum. [*SI 2009 No 273, Rule 23(4)*].

The criteria for categorising a case as complex are considered in *Capital Air Services Ltd v HMRC* UT, [2010] STC 2726.

The procedures in a complex case are the same as those described at **5.17** above for standard cases. The same rules regarding the membership of the Tribunal also apply.

Transfer to Upper Tribunal

The Tribunal can, with the consent of the parties, refer a complex case or a preliminary issue to the Chamber President with a request for transfer to the Upper Tribunal. The Chamber President can then, with the agreement of the President of the Tax and Chancery Chamber of the Upper Tribunal, direct that the case be so transferred. [*SI 2009 No 273, Rule 28*].

Costs

See **5.24** below for the taxpayer's option to request that a complex case be excluded from potential liability for costs.

The hearing

[5.19] Basic, standard and complex cases normally require a hearing before they are decided (and see **5.15** above for hearings in default paper cases).

This does not apply, however, if all of the parties consent to a decision without a hearing and the Tribunal considers that it is able to make a decision without a hearing. Hearings are also not required for the correction, setting aside, review or appeal of a tribunal decision (see **5.20–5.22** below) or where the Tribunal strikes out a party's case (see **5.13** above).

Each party to the proceedings is normally entitled to attend the hearing and the Tribunal must give reasonable notice of its time and place. Where the hearing is to consider disposal of the proceedings, at least 14 days' notice must be given except in urgent or exceptional circumstances or with the consent of the parties.

Hearings are normally held in public. The public interest generally requires the precise facts relevant to the decision to be a matter of public record, and not to be veiled by a process of anonymisation or redaction (*Revenue and Customs Comrs v Banerjee* [2009] EWHC 1229 (Ch), [2009] 3 All ER 930n, [2009] STC 1930), and see *TC05575: MR D v Revenue and Customs Comrs* [2017] UKFTT 850 (TC). The Tribunal may, however, direct that a hearing should be private if it considers that restricting access is justified in the interests of public order or national security, to protect a person's right to respect for their private and family life, to maintain the confidentiality of sensitive information, to avoid serious harm to the public interest or because not to do so would prejudice the interest of justice. An application for an appeal by a well-known broadcaster to be heard in private, and for any published decision to be anonymised, was refused in *A v HMRC* FTT, [2012] SFTD 1257. The Tribunal ruled that the fact that a taxpayer was rich, or that he was in the public eye, did not dictate a different approach to other cases. The hearing of the appeal of such a person in private would give rise to the suspicion that riches or fame could buy anonymity and protection from scrutiny which others could not avoid. It would not be in the public interest to release a decision which, by concealing the appellant's personal characteristics, made it impossible for the reader to reach a full understanding of why the appeal had been determined as it had (*Clunes v HMRC* FTT (TC 5692), [2017] UKFTT 204 (TC)).

[*SI 2009 No 273, Rules 29–32*].

Failure to attend hearing

If a party fails to attend a hearing, the Tribunal can nevertheless proceed with the hearing if it considers that it is in the interests of justice to do so. The Tribunal must be satisfied that the party was notified of the hearing or that reasonable steps were taken to notify the party. [*SI 2009 No 273, Rule 33*].

The following cases were decided under the rather different provisions applicable before 1 April 2009 to failure to attend a hearing of the General Commissioners, but may be relevant to the above provision. Determinations in the absence of the taxpayer or his agent were upheld where notice of the meeting was received by the appellant (*R v Tavistock Commrs (ex p. Adams) (No 1)* QB 1969, 46 TC 154; *R v Special Commr (ex p. Moschi)* CA, [1981] STC 465 and see *Fletcher & Fletcher v Harvey* CA 1990, 63 TC 539), but Commissioners were held to have acted unreasonably in refusing to re-open proceedings when the taxpayer's agent was temporarily absent when the appeal was called (*R & D McKerron Ltd v CIR* CS 1979, 52 TC 28). Where the taxpayer was absent through illness, a determination was quashed because the Commissioners, in refusing an adjournment, had failed to consider whether injustice would thereby arise to the taxpayer (*R v Sevenoaks Commrs (ex p. Thorne)* QB 1989, 62 TC 341 and see *Rose v Humbles* CA 1971, 48 TC 103). See also *R v O'Brien (ex p. Lissner)* QB, [1984] STI 710 where the determination was quashed when the appellant had been informed by the inspector that the hearing was to be adjourned.

Evidence and submissions

The Tribunal has wide powers to make directions as to issues on which it requires evidence or submissions, including the nature of such evidence or submissions, the way in which and time at which it must be provided and the need for expert evidence. It may also limit the number of witnesses whose evidence a party can put forward.

The Tribunal can accept evidence whether or not it would be admissible in a civil trial and can exclude evidence provided late or not in accordance with a direction.

[*SI 2009 No 273, Rule 15(1)(2)*].

The following cases relate to evidence given at hearings of the General Commissioners before 1 April 2009, but may be relevant to the above provision. A party to the proceedings could not insist on being examined on oath (*R v Special Commrs (in re Fletcher)* CA 1894, 3 TC 289). False evidence under oath would be perjury under criminal law (*R v Hood Barrs* CA, [1943] 1 All ER 665). A taxpayer was held to be bound by an affidavit he had made in other proceedings (*Wicker v Fraser* Ch D 1982, 55 TC 641). A remission to Commissioners to hear evidence directed at the credit of a witness was refused in *Potts v CIR* Ch D 1982, 56 TC 25. Rules of the Supreme Court under which evidence can be obtained from a witness abroad could not be used in proceedings before the Commissioners (*Leiserach v CIR* CA 1963, 42 TC 1). As to hearsay evidence under *Civil Evidence Act 1968*, see *Forth Investments Ltd v CIR* Ch D 1976, 50 TC 617 and *Khan v Edwards* Ch D 1977, 53 TC 597.

The Commissioners were under no obligation to adjourn an appeal for the production of further evidence (*Hamilton v CIR* CS 1930, 16 TC 28; *Noble v Wilkinson* Ch D 1958, 38 TC 135), and were held not to have erred in law in determining assessments in the absence abroad of the taxpayer (*Hawkins v Fuller* Ch D 1982, 56 TC 49).

In *HMRC v Tower MCashback LLP1* SC, [2011] UKSC 19 it was held that HMRC were entitled to rely on grounds to defend an enquiry closure notice other than the grounds which had been stated in that notice.

HMRC were prohibited by the First-tier Tribunal from citing an unpublished Special Commissioners' decision in *Ardmore Construction Ltd v HMRC* FTT, [2014] UKFTT 453 (TC); 2014 STI 2585.

Witnesses

The Tribunal, on the application of any party to the proceedings or its own initiative, can issue a summons (in Scotland, a citation) requiring any person either to attend the hearing of those proceedings to give evidence or to produce any relevant document in his possession or control. A witness required to attend a hearing must be given 14 days' notice or a shorter period if the Tribunal so directs and, if the witness is not a party, the summons or citations must make provision for necessary expenses of attendance and state who is to pay them. If, before the summons or citation was issued, the witness did not have an opportunity to object, he may apply to the Tribunal for the summons to be varied or set aside. The application must be made as soon as reasonably practicable after the summons or citation is received.

A witness cannot be compelled to give evidence or produce documents which he could not be compelled to give or produce in an action in a court of law.

[*SI 2009 No 273, Rule 16*].

The Tribunal's decision

[5.20] In an appeal case, if the Tribunal decides:

(a) that the appellant is overcharged or undercharged by a self-assessment;
(b) that any amounts in a partnership statement (see **58.17** RETURNS) are excessive or insufficient; or
(c) that the appellant is overcharged or undercharged by an assessment other than a self-assessment,

the assessment or amounts are reduced or increased accordingly, but otherwise the assessment or statement stands good. The Tribunal is given the power to vary the extent to which a claim or election included in a tax return is disallowed following an enquiry. (Separate rules apply to claims and elections made outside returns, for which see **13.3** CLAIMS.) In a case within (c) above, the Tribunal can normally only reduce or increase the amount assessed, and this determines the appeal; the Tribunal is not obliged to determine the revised tax payable. In a case within (b) above, HMRC must amend the partners' own tax returns to give effect to the reductions or increases made.

The Tribunal's decision is final and conclusive, subject to:

(i) the correction of clerical mistakes etc. (see **5.21** below);
(ii) the setting aside of a decision (see **5.21** below); and
(iii) a further appeal against the decision (see **5.22** below).

[*TMA 1970, s 50(6)–(11); SI 2009 No 56, Art 31*].

See **42.6** LATE PAYMENT INTEREST AND PENALTIES and **52.4** PENALTIES for the Tribunal's options in an appeal against a surcharge or a late filing penalty, which turns on the question of whether the appellant had a 'reasonable excuse' for his non-compliance.

The Tribunal can give its decision orally at a hearing or in writing. In either case it will give each party a decision notice in writing within 28 days after making a decision which finally disposes of all the issues in the case or as soon as practicable. The notice will also inform the party of any further right of appeal.

Unless each party agrees otherwise the notice should also include a summary of the findings of fact and the reason for the decision. If it does not, any party to the case can apply for full written findings and reasons, and must do so before applying for permission to appeal (see **5.22** below). The application must be made in writing so that the Tribunal receives it within 28 days after the date it sent the decision notice.

[*SI 2009 No 273, Rule 35; SI 2013 No 477, Rules 1, 42*].

Case law

The following cases relate to decisions of the General Commissioners before 1 April 2009, but may be relevant to the above provisions.

In reaching their decision, the Commissioners could not take into account matters appropriate for application for judicial review (*Aspin v Estill* CA 1987, 60 TC 549). They did not generally have the power to review on appeal the exercise of a discretion conferred on HMRC by statute (see *Slater v Richardson & Bottoms Ltd* Ch D 1979, 53 TC 155; *Kelsall v Investment Chartwork Ltd* Ch D 1993, 65 TC 750).

Onus of proof

The onus is on the appellant to displace an assessment. See *Brady v Group Lotus Car Companies plc* CA 1987, 60 TC 359 where the onus of proof remained with the taxpayer where the amount of normal time limit assessment indicated contention of fraud. The general principle emerges in appeals against estimated assessments in 'delay cases', which, before self-assessment, made up the bulk of appeals heard by the General Commissioners. For examples of cases in which the Commissioners have confirmed estimated assessments in the absence of evidence that they were excessive, see *T Haythornthwaite & Sons Ltd v Kelly* CA 1927, 11 TC 657; *Stoneleigh Products Ltd v Dodd* CA 1948, 30 TC 1; *Rosette Franks (King St) Ltd v Dick* Ch D 1955, 36 TC 100; *Pierson v Belcher* Ch D 1959, 38 TC 387. In a number of cases, the courts have supported the Commissioners' action in rejecting unsatisfactory accounts (e.g. *Cain v Schofield* Ch D 1953, 34 TC 362; *Moll v CIR* CS 1955, 36 TC 384; *Cutmore v Leach* Ch D 1981, 55 TC 602; *Coy v Kime* Ch D 1986, 59 TC 447) or calling for certified accounts (e.g. *Stephenson v Waller* KB 1927, 13 TC 318; *Hunt & Co v Joly* KB 1928, 14 TC 165; *Wall v Cooper* CA 1929, 14 TC 552). In *Anderson v CIR* CS 1933, 18 TC 320, the case was remitted where there was no evidence to support the figure arrived at by the Commissioners (which was between the accounts figure and the estimated figure assessed), but contrast *Bookey v Edwards* Ch D 1981, 55 TC 486. The Commissioners were entitled to look at each year separately, accepting the appellant's figures for some years but not all (*Donnelly v Platten* CA(NI) 1980, [1981] STC 504). Similarly, the onus is on the taxpayer to substantiate his claims to relief (see *Eke v Knight* CA 1977, 51 TC 121; *Talib v Waterson* Ch D, [1980] STC 563).

For the standard of proof required in evidence, see *Les Croupiers Casino Club v Pattinson* CA 1987, 60 TC 196.

Consent orders

The case can also be settled by the Tribunal making a consent order where the parties have reached agreement. Such an order is made at the request of the parties but only if the Tribunal considers it appropriate to do so. No hearing is necessary if such an order is made. [*SI 2009 No 273, Rule 34*].

Correction of mistakes in a decision

[5.21] The Tribunal can correct any clerical mistake or other accidental slip or omission in a decision at any time by notifying the parties of the amended decision. This rule applies also to directions and any other document produced by the Tribunal. [*SI 2009 No 273, Rule 37*].

Setting aside a decision

The Tribunal can set aside a decision disposing of a case and re-make the decision if it considers that to do is in the interests of justice and one of the following applies:

- a relevant document was not sent to, or was not received at an appropriate time by, a party or his representative;
- a relevant document was not sent to the Tribunal at a relevant time;
- there was some other procedural irregularity; or
- a party or representative was not present at a hearing.

A party to a case can apply for a decision to be set aside. The application must be in writing and must be received by the Tribunal within 28 days after the date on which the Tribunal sent the decision notice.

[*SI 2009 No 273, Rule 38*].

An application for a decision to be set aside was successful in *Wright v HMRC (No 3)* FTT, [2009] UKFTT 227 (TC); 2009 STI 2813. In *SRI International v HMRC* FTT, [2010] SFTD 873 the taxpayer's application was unsuccessful as it sought to introduce new evidence which had been available to it before the appeal was heard and could have been brought forward even before the hearing.

Appeal against the Tribunal's decision

[5.22] A further appeal to the Upper Tribunal can be made against the First-tier Tribunal's decision. The appeal can be made only on a point of law. No appeal can be made against a decision on whether or not to review a decision (see below), to set aside a decision (see **5.21** above) or to refer a matter to the Upper Tribunal.

A person wishing to appeal must make a written application to the First-tier Tribunal for permission to appeal. Such an application must be received by the Tribunal no later than 56-days after the date the Tribunal sent full reasons for the decision to that person. Where a decision has been amended or corrected following a review (see below) or an application (other than a late application) for a decision to be struck out has been unsuccessful (see **5.21** above), the 56 day limit runs from the date on which the Tribunal sent the notification of amended reasons or correction of the decision or of the failure of the striking out application. On and after 1 April 2013, the Tribunal can direct that the 56 days within which a party may apply for permission to appeal against a decision that disposes of a preliminary issue shall run from the date of the decision that disposes of all issues in the proceedings.

The application must identify the alleged errors in the decision and state the result sought. Late applications must include a request for extension of time and the reason for lateness.

On receiving an application, the Tribunal will first consider whether to review the decision. It can do so only if satisfied that there was an error in law in the decision. Unless it decides to take no action following the review, the Tribunal will notify the parties of the outcome and must give them an opportunity to make representations before taking any action.

If the Tribunal decides not to review the decision or, following a review, decides to take no action, it will then consider whether to give permission to appeal to the Upper Tribunal. It will send a record of its decision to the parties as soon as practicable together with, where it decides not to give permission, a statements of its reasons for refusal and details of the right to apply directly to the Upper Tribunal for permission to appeal (see **5.27** below). The Tribunal's permission can be in respect of part only of the decision or on limited grounds.

[*TCEA 2007, s 11; SI 2009 No 273, Rules 39–41; SI 2013 No 477, Rules 1, 43*].

Payment of tax pending further appeal

[5.23] Tax is payable or repayable in accordance with the decision of the Tribunal even if a party appeals to the Upper Tribunal. If the amount charged in the assessment concerned is subsequently altered by the Upper Tribunal, any amount undercharged is due and payable at the end of the 30 days beginning with the date on which HMRC issue the appellant a notice of the amount payable in accordance with the Upper Tribunal's decision. Any amount overpaid will be refunded along with such interest as may be allowed by the decision. See **4.31** ANTI-AVOIDANCE for applications to the court or Tribunal by HMRC to disapply the requirement to repay tax where an accelerated payment notice is in force.

This provision applies equally to any further appeal from a decision of the Upper Tribunal to the Courts.

[*TMA 1970, s 56; FA 2014, s 225(1); SI 2009 No 56, Sch 1 para 35*].

Award of costs

[5.24] The Tribunal can make an order awarding costs (or, in Scotland, expenses):

(a) under *TCEA 2007, s 29(4)* ('wasted costs') and, on and after 1 April 2013, costs incurred in applying for such costs;
(b) where it considers that a party or representative has acted unreasonably in bringing, defending or conducting the case; and
(c) in a complex case (see **5.18** above), where the taxpayer has not sent a written request that the case be excluded from potential liability for costs or expenses.

A request within (c) above must be sent within 28 days of the taxpayer receiving notice that the case has been allocated as a complex case.

'*Wasted costs*' are any costs incurred by a party because of an improper, unreasonable or negligent act or omission by any representative or employee of a representative, which the Tribunal considers it unreasonable for the party to pay.

Before making an order for costs, the Tribunal must give the person who will have to pay them the chance to make representations. If the payer is an individual, it must consider his financial means.

The Tribunal can make an order on its own initiative or on an application from one of the parties. Such an application must be sent both to the Tribunal and to the person from whom costs are sought, together with a schedule of the costs claimed. An application must be made no later than 28 days after the date on which the Tribunal sends a notice recording the decision which finally disposes of all the issues or notice of a withdrawal which ends the case.

The amount of costs will be decided either by agreement of the parties, by summary assessment by the Tribunal or, if not agreed, by assessment. Where the amount is to be decided by assessment, either the payer or the person to whom the costs are to be paid can apply to a county court, the High Court or the Costs Office of the Supreme Court for a detailed assessment of the costs on the standard basis or, where the tribunal's order so specifies, the indemnity basis. On and after 1 April 2013, upon making an order for the assessment of costs, the Tribunal may order an amount to be paid on account before the costs are assessed.

[*TCEA 2007, s 29(4); SI 2009 No 273, Rule 10; SI 2013 No 477, Rules 1, 35–38*].

For the award of costs where HMRC successfully applied to admit late evidence see *Earthshine Ltd v HMRC* FTT, [2010] UKFTT 314 (TC); 2010 STI 2621. An application for costs arising from an application to have a case recategorised as complex was unsuccessful in *Capital Air Services Ltd v HMRC* UT, [2011] STC 617. Partially successful appellants were ordered to pay two-thirds of HMRC's costs in *Bastionspark LLP v HMRC* UT, [2016] STC 2549.

The power of the Tribunal to award costs does not include a power to direct, before the conclusion of an appeal, that the costs of complying with a direction should be borne by one party rather than the other, or by both (*Eclipse Film Partners No. 35 LLP v HMRC* SC, [6] STC 1385).

Upper Tribunal procedure

Case management

[5.25] The powers of the Upper Tribunal to regulate its own proceedings are broadly the same as the powers of the First-tier Tribunal. See *SI 2008 No 2698, Rules 5, 6, 9, 12* and **5.12** above.

Representation

The same rights to representation in a case before the Upper Tribunal apply as in a case before the First-tier Tribunal. See *SI 2008 No 2698, Rule 11* and **5.12** above.

Withdrawal from a case

A party can notify the Upper Tribunal of the withdrawal of its case, or part of it. This can be done in writing before a hearing or orally at a hearing. If the case is to be settled without a hearing, written notice must be given before the Tribunal disposes of the case.

The withdrawal only takes effect, however, if the Tribunal consents (but this requirement does not apply to the withdrawal of an application for permission to appeal).

A party who has withdrawn its case can, however, apply (in writing) to the Tribunal to reinstate it. The application must be received by the Tribunal within one month after it received the withdrawal notice or the date of the hearing.

[*SI 2008 No 2698, Rule 17; SI 2013 No 477, Rules 1, 54*].

Failure to comply with rules

[5.26] An irregularity resulting from any failure to comply with the Tribunal Procedure Rules, a practice direction or a direction by the Upper Tribunal does not in itself make the proceedings void.

Where a party fails to comply with the Rules etc. the Upper Tribunal can take such action as it considers just. This could be to require compliance or waive the requirement, to strike the case out (see below) or to restrict a party's participation in the case.

The Upper Tribunal has the same powers as the High Court to deal with the failure (which may include financial penalties).

[*TCEA 2007, s 25; SI 2008 No 2698, Rule 7*].

Striking out a case

The Upper Tribunal has similar powers to strike out a case as the First-tier Tribunal. See *SI 2008 No 2698, Rule 8* and **5.13** above. Note, however, that the Upper Tribunal cannot strike out an appeal from the decision of another tribunal or judicial review proceedings on the grounds that there is no reasonable prospect of the appellant's case succeeding.

Appeal against decisions of the First-tier Tribunal

Application for permission to appeal

[5.27] A party to a case who disagrees with a decision of the First-tier Tribunal can apply for permission to appeal against it. Applications must first be made to the First-tier Tribunal (see 5.22 above), but if that Tribunal refuses permission a further application can be made to the Upper Tribunal.

Applications to the Upper Tribunal must be in writing and must be received no later than one month after the date on which the First-tier Tribunal sent the notice refusing permission to appeal. An application must include the grounds for appeal and state whether the appellant wants the application to be dealt with at a hearing. It must be accompanied by copies of any written record of the decision being challenged, any statement of reasons for that decision, and the notice of the First-tier Tribunal's refusal of permission to appeal. Late applications must include a request for extension of time and the reason for lateness.

If the application to the First-tier Tribunal for permission to appeal was refused because it was made out of time, the application to the Upper Tribunal must include the reason for the lateness of the first application. The Upper Tribunal can then admit the application only if it considers that it is in the interests of justice to do so.

If the Tribunal refuses permission to appeal it will notify the appellant of its decision and its reasons. If the refusal is made without a hearing the appellant can apply in writing for the decision to be reconsidered at a hearing. The application must be received by the Tribunal within 14 days after the date that written notice of its decision was sent. This rule applies also where the Tribunal gives permission on limited grounds or subject to conditions without a hearing.

If the Tribunal grants permission, the application for permission is then normally treated as a notice of appeal, and the case will proceed accordingly. If all the parties agree, the appeal can be determined without obtaining any further response.

[*SI 2008 No 2698, Rules 21, 22; SI 2009 No 274, Rule 14; SI 2009 No 1975, Rules 15, 16*].

See the Tribunals Service leaflet 'Appealing to the Upper Tribunal (Tax and Chancery Chamber)'.

Notice of appeal

[5.28] If the First-tier Tribunal gives permission to appeal to the Upper Tribunal (or the Upper Tribunal gives permission but directs that the application for permission should not be treated as a notice of appeal) an appellant can appeal to the Upper Tribunal by providing a notice of appeal. This must be received by the tribunal within one month after the notice giving permission to appeal was sent.

The notice must include the grounds for appeal and state whether the appellant wants the application to be dealt with at a hearing. If, the First-tier Tribunal gave permission to appeal, the notice must be accompanied by copies of any written record of the decision being challenged, any statement of reasons for that decision, and the notice of permission to appeal. Late applications must include a request for extension of time and the reason for lateness.

A copy of the notice and the documents provided will then be sent by the Upper Tribunal to the respondents who can provide a written response. The response must be received by the Tribunal not later than one month after the copy of the notice of appeal was sent. (Where an application for permission to appeal stands as the notice of appeal (see **5.27** above), the response must be received not later than one month after the Tribunal sent to the respondent notice that it had granted permission to appeal.)

The response must indicate whether the respondent opposes the appeal, and if so, the grounds for opposition (which can include grounds which were unsuccessful before the First-tier Tribunal) and whether the respondent wants the case to be dealt with at a hearing. Late responses must include a request for extension of time and the reason for lateness.

A copy of the response and any documents provided will then be sent by the Tribunal to the appellant and any other parties to the case who can, in turn, provide a written reply. The reply must be received by the Tribunal within one month of the date the tribunal sent the copy of the respondent's response.

[*SI 2008 No 2698, Rules 23–25; SI 2009 No 1975, Rules 17, 18*].

An application by HMRC for the Tribunal to accept a late notice of appeal was rejected in *HMRC v McCarthy and Stone (Developments) Ltd* UT, [2014] STC 973.

Other cases before the Upper Tribunal

[5.29] Where a case has been transferred or referred to the Upper Tribunal from the First-tier Tribunal (see **5.18** above) or where a case is started by direct application to the Upper Tribunal, the Upper Tribunal will determine by direction the procedure for considering and disposing of the case. [*SI 2008 No 2698, Rule 26A; SI 2009 No 274, Rule 16; SI 2009 No 1975, Rule 19*].

The hearing

[5.30] The Upper Tribunal can make any decision with or without a hearing, but in deciding whether to hold a hearing, it must have regard to any view expressed by any party to the case.

Each party is normally entitled to attend the hearing and the Upper Tribunal must give reasonable notice of its time and place. At least 14 days' notice must normally be given except in urgent or exceptional circumstances or with the consent of the parties. In application for permission to bring judicial review cases, the notice period must normally be at least two days.

Hearings are normally held in public, but the Tribunal can direct that a hearing, or part of it, should be held in private.

[*SI 2008 No 2698, Rules 34–37; SI 2009 No 274, Rule 19; SI 2009 No 1975, Rule 29*].

Failure to attend hearing

If a party fails to attend a hearing, the Upper Tribunal can nevertheless proceed with the hearing if it considers that it is in the interests of justice to do so. The Tribunal must be satisfied that the party was notified of the hearing or that reasonable steps were taken to notify the party. [*SI 2008 No 2698, Rule 38*].

Evidence and witnesses

Similar rules apply in relation to evidence, submission and witnesses as apply to the First-tier Tribunal. See *SI 2008 No 2698, Rules 15, 16* and **5.19** above.

The Upper Tribunal's decision

[5.31] If the Upper Tribunal decides that the First-tier Tribunal's decision involved an error on a point of law it can set aside that decision and either remit the case back to the First-tier Tribunal or remake the decision itself.

If it remits the case to the First-tier Tribunal, the Upper Tribunal can direct that the case is reheard by different members.

If it decides to remake the decision itself, the Upper Tribunal is free to make any decision that the First-tier Tribunal could make if it were rehearing the case (see **5.20** above) and can make such findings of fact as it considers appropriate.

[*TCEA 2007, s 12*].

The Upper Tribunal can give its decision orally at a hearing or in writing. In either case it will give each party a decision notice in writing as soon as practicable. The notice will include written reasons for the decision unless the decision was made with the consent of the parties or the parties have consented to the tribunal not giving written reasons. The notice will also inform the party of any further right of appeal. [*SI 2008 No 2698, Rule 40; SI 2009 No 274, Rule 21; SI 2009 No 1975, Rule 21; SI 2013 No 477, Rules 1, 56*].

Consent orders

The case can also be settled by the Upper Tribunal making a consent order where the parties have reached agreement. Such an order is made at the request of the parties but only if the Tribunal considers it appropriate to do so. No hearing is necessary if such an order is made. [*SI 2008 No 2698, Rule 39; SI 2009 No 274, Rule 20*].

Correction of mistakes in a decision

Identical provisions to those applicable to decisions by the First-tier Tribunal apply to decisions of the Upper Tribunal. See *SI 2008 No 2698, Rule 42* and **5.21** above.

Setting aside a decision

Virtually identical provisions to those applicable to decisions by the First-tier Tribunal apply to decisions of the Upper Tribunal. An application for a decision to be set aside must be received by the Upper Tribunal no later than one month after the date on which the Tribunal sent the decision notice. See *SI 2008 No 2698, Rule 43* and **5.21** above.

Appeal against the Tribunal's decision

[5.32] A further appeal to the Court of Appeal (in Scotland, the Court of Session) can be made against the Upper Tribunal's decision. The appeal can be made only on a point of law and the Tribunal will give permission to appeal only if the appeal would raise some important point of principle or practice or there is some other compelling reason for the Court to hear it.

A person wishing to appeal must make a written application to the Tribunal for permission to appeal. Such an application must be received by the Tribunal within one-month after the date the Tribunal sent written reasons for the decision to that person. Where a decision has been amended or corrected following a review (see below) or an application (other than a late application) for a decision to be struck out has been unsuccessful (see **5.26** above), the one month limit runs from the date on which the tribunal sent the notification of amended reasons or correction of the decision or of the failure of the striking out application.

The application must identify the alleged errors of law in the decision and state the result sought. Late applications must include a request for extension of time and the reason for lateness.

On receiving an application, the Upper Tribunal will first consider whether to review the decision. It can do so only if either it overlooked a legislative provision or binding authority which could have affected the decision or if a court has subsequently made a decision which is binding on the Upper Tribunal and could have affected the decision.

The Tribunal will notify the parties of the outcome of a review. If it decides to take any action following a review without first giving every party an opportunity to make representations, the notice must state that any party not given such an opportunity can apply for the action to be set aside and for the decision to be reviewed again.

If the Tribunal decides not to review the decision or, following a review, decides to take no action, it will then consider whether to give permission to appeal. It will send a record of its decision to the parties as soon as practicable together with, where it decides not to give permission, a statements of its reasons for refusal and details of the right to apply directly to the court for permission to appeal (see **5.34** below). The Tribunal's permission can be in respect of part only of the decision or on limited grounds.

[*TCEA 2007, s 13; SI 2008 No 2698, Rules 44–46; SI 2008 No 2834*].

See **5.23** above for the payment of tax pending an appeal from a decision of the Upper Tribunal.

Award of costs

[5.33] The Upper Tribunal can make an order awarding costs (or, in Scotland, expenses):

(a) in proceedings on appeal from the Tax Chamber of the First-tier Tribunal;

(b) in judicial review cases (see **5.35** below);
(c) in cases transferred from the Tax Chamber of the First-tier Tribunal;
(d) under *TCEA 2007, s 29(4)* (wasted costs — see **5.24** above) and, on and after 1 April 2013, costs incurred in applying for such costs; or
(e) where the Tribunal considers that a party or representative has acted unreasonably in bringing, defending or conducting the case.

Before making an order for costs, the Tribunal must give the person who will have to pay them the chance to make representations. If the payer is an individual, it must consider his financial means.

The Tribunal can make an order on its own initiative or on an application from one of the parties. Such an application must be sent both to the tribunal and to the person from whom costs are sought, together with a schedule of the costs claimed. An application must be made no later than one month after the date on which the Tribunal sends the notice recording the decision which finally disposes of all the issues in the case.

The amount of costs will be decided either by agreement of the parties, by summary assessment by the Tribunal or, if not agreed, by assessment. Where the amount is to be decided by assessment, either the payer or the person to whom the costs are to be paid can apply to a county court, the High Court or the Costs Office of the Supreme Court for a detailed assessment of the costs on the standard basis or, where the Tribunal's order so specifies, the indemnity basis. On and after 1 April 2013, upon making an order for the assessment of costs, the Tribunal may order an amount to be paid on account before the costs are assessed.

[*SI 2008 No 2698, Rule 1; SI 2009 No 274, Rule 7; SI 2013 No 477, Rules 1, 50–53*].

Appeal to the Court of Appeal

[5.34] As noted at 5.32 above a party who disagrees with a decision of the Upper Tribunal can ask the Tribunal for permission to appeal to the Court of Appeal (in Scotland, the Court of Session). The appeal can be made only on a point of law.

If the Tribunal refuses permission, the party can seek permission to appeal directly from the Court. The Court will give permission only if the appeal would raise some important point of principle or practice or there is some other compelling reason for the Court to hear it.

[*TCEA 2007, s 13; SI 2008 No 2834*].

There are no tax-specific rules governing the making of applications for permission to appeal or for notifying appeals where permission has been given by the Court or Upper Tribunal. The *Civil Procedure Rules 1998, SI 1998 No 3132* therefore apply.

The Court's decision

If the Court finds that the decision of the Upper Tribunal involved an error on a point of law it can set aside the decision. It must then either remake the decision itself or remit the case back to either the Upper Tribunal or the First-tier Tribunal, with directions for its reconsideration. Those directions can include a direction that the case is to be re-heard by different tribunal members.

Where the case is remitted to the Upper Tribunal, it can itself decide to remit the case to the First-tier Tribunal.

If the Court decides to remake the decision itself, it can make any decision that the Upper Tribunal or first-tier Tribunal could have made, and can make such findings of fact as it considers appropriate.

[*TCEA 2007, s 14*].

Case law

The following cases relate to the pre-1 April 2009 appeal process (which involved initial appeal to the High Court rather than the Court of Appeal) but remain relevant to the new process.

Withdrawal etc.

Once set down for hearing, a case cannot be declared a nullity (*Way v Underdown* CA 1974, 49 TC 215) or struck out under *Order 18, Rule 19 of the Rules of the Supreme Court* (*Petch v Gurney* CA 1994, 66 TC 473), but the appellant may withdraw (*Hood Barrs v CIR (No 3)* CA 1960, 39 TC 209, but see *Bradshaw v Blunden (No 2)* Ch D 1960, 39 TC 73). Where the appellant was the inspector and the taxpayer did not wish to proceed, the Court refused to make an order on terms agreed between the parties (*Slaney v Kean* Ch D 1969, 45 TC 415).

Remission of cases to tribunal

In *Consolidated Goldfields plc v CIR* Ch D 1990, 63 TC 333, the taxpayer company's request that the High Court remit a case to the Commissioners for further findings of fact was refused. Although the remedy was properly sought, it would only be granted if it could be shown that the desired findings were:

(a) material to some tenable argument;
(b) reasonably open on the evidence adduced; and
(c) not inconsistent with the findings already made.

However, in *Fitzpatrick v CIR* CS 1990, [1991] STC 34, a case was remitted where the facts found proved or admitted, and the contentions of the parties, were not clearly set out, despite the taxpayer's request for various amendments and insertions to the case, and in *Whittles v Uniholdings Ltd (No 1)* Ch D, [1993] STC 671, remission was appropriate in view of the widely differing interpretations which the parties sought to place on the Commissioners' decision (and the case was remitted a second time (see [1993] STC 767) to resolve misunderstandings as to the nature of a concession made by the Crown at the original hearing and apparent inconsistencies in the Commissioners' findings of fact). If a case is remitted, the taxpayer had the right to attend any further hearing by the Commissioners (*Lack v Doggett* CA 1970, 46 TC 497) but the Commissioners could not, in the absence of special circumstances, admit further evidence (*Archer-Shee v Baker* CA 1928, 15 TC 1; *Watson v Samson Bros* Ch D 1959, 38 TC 346; *Bradshaw v Blunden (No 2)* Ch D 1960, 39 TC 73), but see *Brady v Group Lotus Car Companies plc* CA 1987, 60 TC 359 where the Court directed the Commissioners to admit further evidence where new facts had come to light suggesting the taxpayers had deliberately misled the Commissioners. Errors of fact in the case may be amended by agreement of the parties prior to hearing of the case (*Moore v Austin* Ch D 1985, 59 TC 110). See *Jeffries v Stevens* Ch D 1982, 56 TC 134 as regards delay between statement of case and motion for remission.

Appeal restricted to point of law

Many court decisions turn on whether the Commissioners' decision was one of fact supported by the evidence, and hence final. The courts will not disturb a finding of fact if there was reasonable evidence for it, notwithstanding that the evidence might support a different conclusion of fact. The leading case is *Edwards v Bairstow & Harrison* HL 1955, 36 TC 207, in which the issue was whether there had been an adventure in the nature of trade. The Commissioners' decision was reversed on the ground that the only reasonable conclusion from the evidence was that there had been such an adventure. For a recent discussion of the application of this principle, see *Milnes v J Beam Group Ltd* Ch D 1975, 50 TC 675.

A new question of law may be raised in the courts on giving due notice to the other parties (*Muir v CIR* CA 1966, 43 TC 367) but the courts will neither admit evidence not in the stated case (*Watson v Samson Bros* Ch D 1959, 38 TC 346; *Cannon Industries Ltd v Edwards* Ch D 1965, 42 TC 625; *Frowd v Whalley* Ch D 1965, 42 TC 599, and see *R v Great Yarmouth Commrs (ex p. Amis)* QB 1960, 39 TC 143) nor consider contentions of which evidence in support was not produced before the Commissioners (*Denekamp v Pearce* Ch D 1998, 71 TC 213).

Use of Parliamentary material

Following the decision in *Pepper v Hart* HL 1992, 65 TC 421, the courts are prepared to consider the parliamentary history of legislation, or the official reports of debates in Hansard, where all of the following conditions are met.

- Legislation is ambiguous or obscure, or leads to an absurdity.
- The material relied upon consists of one or more statements by a Minister or other promoter of the Bill together if necessary with such other parliamentary material as is necessary to understand such statements and their effect.
- The statements relied upon are clear.

Any party intending to refer to an extract from Hansard in support of any argument must, unless otherwise directed, serve copies of the extract and a brief summary of the argument intended to be based upon the extract upon all parties and the court not less than five clear working days before the first day of the hearing (Supreme Court Practice Note, 20 December 1994) (1995 STI 98).

Status of decision

A court decision is a binding precedent for itself or an inferior court except that the House of Lords, while treating its former decisions as normally binding, may depart from a previous decision should it appear right to do so. For this see *Fitzleet Estates Ltd v Cherry* HL 1977, 51 TC 708. Scottish decisions are not binding on the High Court but are normally followed. Decisions of the Privy Council and of the Irish Courts turning on comparable legislation are treated with respect. A court decision does not affect other assessments already final and conclusive (see **6.5** ASSESSMENTS) but may be followed, if relevant, in the determination of any open appeals against assessments and in assessments made subsequently irrespective of the years of assessment or taxpayers concerned (*Re Waring decd* Ch D, [1948] 1 All ER 257; *Gwyther v Boslymon Quarries Ltd* KB 1950, 29 ATC 1; *Bolands Ltd v CIR* SC(I) 1925, 4 ATC 526). Further, a court decision does not prevent the Crown from proceeding on a different basis for other years (*Hood Barrs v CIR (No 3)* CA 1960, 39 TC 209). A general change of practice consequent on a court decision may affect error or mistake relief (see **13.8** claims).

For joinder of CIR in non-tax disputes, see In *re Vandervell's Trusts* HL 1970, 46 TC 341.

Judicial review

[5.35] A taxpayer who is dissatisfied with the exercise of administrative powers may in certain circumstances (e.g. where HMRC has exceeded or abused its powers or acted contrary to the rules of natural justice, or where the Tribunal has acted unfairly or improperly) seek a remedy in a mandatory or prohibiting order or a quashing order. This is done by way of application for judicial review to the High Court under *Supreme Court Act 1981, s 31* and *Part 54 of the Civil Procedure Rules*. With effect from 1 April 2009, the High Court can in certain cases transfer an application for judicial review or for leave to apply for judicial review to the Upper Tribunal (see *Supreme Court Act 1981, s 31A*).

Application for leave to apply for judicial review is made ex parte to a single judge who will usually determine the application without a hearing. The Court will not grant leave unless the applicant has a sufficient interest in the matter to which the application relates. See *CIR v National Federation of Self-Employed and Small Businesses Ltd* HL 1981, 55 TC 133 for what is meant by 'sufficient interest' and for discussion of availability of judicial review generally.

The issue on an application for leave to apply for judicial review is whether there is an arguable case (*R v CIR (ex p. Howmet Corporation and another)* QB, [1994] STC 413). The procedure is generally used where no other, adequate, remedy, such as a right of appeal, is available. See *R v Special Commr (ex p. Stipplechoice Ltd) (No 1)* CA, [1985] STC 248 and *(No 3)*

QB 1988, 61 TC 391, *R v HMIT (ex p. Kissane and Another)* QB, [1986] STC 152, *R v CIR (ex p. Goldberg)* QB 1988, 61 TC 403 and *R v Dickinson (ex p. McGuckian)* CA(NI) 1999, 72 TC 343.

There is a very long line of cases in which the courts have consistently refused applications where a matter should have been pursued through the ordinary channels as described earlier in this chapter. See, for example, *R v Special Commrs (ex p. Morey)* CA 1972, 49 TC 71; *R v Special Commrs (ex p. Emery)* QB 1980, 53 TC 555; *R v Walton General Commrs (ex p. Wilson)* CA, [1983] STC 464; *R v Special Commrs (ex p. Esslemont)* CA, 1984 STI 312; *R v Brentford General Commrs (ex p. Chan and Others)* QB 1985, 57 TC 651; *R v Special Commr (ex p. Napier)* CA 1988, 61 TC 206; *R v North London General Commrs (ex p. Nii-Amaa)* QB 1999, 72 TC 634; *R (oao Derrin Brothers Properties Ltd) v HMRC (and related applications)* CA, [2016] STC 1081.

See, however, *R v HMIT and Others (ex p. Lansing Bagnall Ltd)* CA 1986, 61 TC 112 for a successful application where the inspector issued a notice under a discretionary power on the footing that there was an obligation to do so, and *R v CIR (ex p. J Rothschild Holdings plc)* CA 1987, 61 TC 178 where the Revenue were required to produce internal documents of a general character relating to their practice in applying a statutory provision. See also *R v CIR (ex p. Taylor) (No 1)* CA 1988, 62 TC 562 where an application for discovery of a document was held to be premature, and *R v Inspector of Taxes, Hull, ex p. Brumfield and others* QB 1988, 61 TC 589, where the court was held to have jurisdiction to entertain an application for judicial review of a failure by the Revenue to apply an established practice not embodied in an extra-statutory concession (cf. *R v CIR (ex p. Fulford-Dobson)* QB 1987, 60 TC 168 at **30.2** HMRC — ADMINISTRATION, which see for 'care and management' powers of the Revenue). It was held that there had been no unfairness by the Revenue when it refused to assess on the basis of transactions that would have been entered into by the applicants had a Revenue Statement of Practice been published earlier (*R v CIR, ex p. Kaye* QB 1992, 65 TC 82). A similar view was taken in *R v CIR (ex p. S G Warburg & Co Ltd)* QB 1994, 68 TC 300 where the Revenue declined to apply a previously published practice because not only was it not clear that the taxpayer's circumstances fell within its terms but also the normal appeal procedures were available. The underlying facts in *Carvill v CIR (No 2); R (oao Carvill) v CIR* Ch D, [2002] STC 1167 were that in two separate appeals relating to different tax years, income from an identical source had been held liable to tax for some years (the earlier years) but not others; an application for judicial review of the Revenue's refusal to refund tax, and interest on tax, paid for the earlier years was rejected; the assessments for those years were valid assessments which the Sp C in question had had jurisdiction to determine, and the taxpayer the right to challenge, and those assessments had not been set aside. See also *Davies and another v HMRC CA,* [2008] STC 2813, in which an application for judicial review was to be heard before any appeal to the Special Commissioners as it related to whether the taxpayers had a legitimate expectation that they would be treated in accordance with HMRC's published guidance.

Time limit

Applications must be made **within three months** of the date when the grounds for application arose. The Court has discretion to extend this time limit where there is good reason, subject to conditions, but is generally very reluctant to do so. Grant of leave for review does not amount to a ruling that application is made in good time (*R v Tavistock Commrs (ex p. Worth)* QB 1985, 59 TC 116).

Costs of appeals

[5.36] Costs may be awarded by the courts in the usual way. In suitable cases, e.g. 'test cases', HMRC may undertake to pay the taxpayer's costs. See **5.24** and **5.33** for the award of costs by the First-tier and Upper Tribunals. See above as regards costs awarded by the Special Commissioners. Costs awarded by the courts may include expenses connected with the drafting of the case stated (*Manchester Corporation v Sugden* CA 1903, 4 TC 595). Costs of a discontinued application for judicial review were refused where the Revenue were not informed of the application (*R v CIR (ex p. Opman International UK)* QB 1985, 59 TC 352).

Law costs of appeals are not allowable for tax purposes generally (*Allen v Farquharson* KB 1932, 17 TC 59; *Smith's Potato Estates Ltd v Bolland* HL 1948, 30 TC 267; *Rushden Heel Co v Keene* HL 1948, 30 TC 298; *Spofforth & Prince v Golder* KB 1945, 26 TC 310); and see **16.11** COMPUTATION OF GAINS AND LOSSES.

Key points on appeals

[5.37] Points to consider are as follows.

- HMRC provide the option of internally reviewing decisions made by its officers. A finite timeframe is given for providing the independent review decision. The benefits of an internal review are that an independent officer reviews the decision and how it was made, the quantum (where appropriate) and the risk to HMRC of losing the appeal. There is no material cost to the client in the majority of cases in opting for internal review.
- Any appeal or referral for internal review must accurately and clearly state the grounds for the appeal, as these are normally the points considered by the Tribunal. To avoid disputes over 'not at arms length' transactions it is essential a professional valuation is obtained at the time of the transfer.
- Data released by HMRC of internal reviews under taken in 2010/11 shows that 80% of all internal reviews related to penalties and taxpayers had the most success in connection with VAT penalties where 75% of cases were cancelled or varied. The data also indicates that 79% of appeals to the first-tier tribunal were decided wholly or partially in HMRC's favour.

- HMRC also operate a new way to resolve disputes between small businesses and HMRC called the alternative dispute resolution process. This allows a facilitator (from HMRC) to mediate between the two parties. See **5.10** above.
- The Tribunals Service manages the appeal and the system is formal and structured so it is essential that the adviser is disciplined and organised to avoid damaging their client's case. If you are not happy with the categorisation of the appeal you can ask for the appeal to be moved to another category, if you believe this will be beneficial.
- HMRC will appoint Counsel to represent them so the adviser needs to consider seriously whether to appoint Counsel where a hearing is scheduled.
- In the majority of cases the burden of proof rests with the taxpayer. However in cases where HMRC suspects that the taxpayer deliberately omitted or failed to report income or gains the burden of proof is on HMRC.
- Use the additional information 'white space' in the tax return to explain and provide information on transactions, estimated or provisional figures and other relevant information. If HMRC is made aware of these issues it restricts the chances HMRC can make a 'discovery' assessment.
- HMRC is guided by its Litigation and Settlement Strategy. If the dispute is over a point of law then it is not normally possible to negotiate a settlement for a proportion of the disputed figure.
- Taking matters before the Tribunal is costly in terms of time and money so the client needs to be made fully aware of these two factors when deciding whether to take an appeal before the Tribunal. What are the chances of success? Is the client prepared to pay the tax on top of the professional costs and to suffer the disruption the process will cause?

6

Assessments

Introduction	6.1
Assessments in general	6.2
Construction of references to assessments etc.	6.3
Double assessment	6.4
Finality of assessments	6.5
Trustees and personal representatives	6.6
Non-corporate bodies, personal representatives and receivers	6.7
Contract settlements	6.8
Simple assessments	6.9
Discovery assessments	6.10
Amendment of partnership return on discovery	6.11
Non-resident CGT disposals: discovery determinations	6.12
Time limits	6.13
Extended time limits	6.14

Cross-references. See **5** APPEALS; **12.3** CHILDREN as regards assessments on trustees, guardians etc. where tax due from a child or other 'incapacitated person'; **13.5** CLAIMS; **49.3** OVERSEAS MATTERS as regards UK representatives of non-residents; **50.2** PARTNERSHIPS; **58.15** RETURNS for HMRC determinations of tax liability in the event of the non-filing of a self-assessment tax return; **61** SELF-SSESSMENT.

Introduction to assessments

[6.1] Although both capital gains tax and corporation tax operate under a system of SELF-ASSESSMENT (**61**) so that the taxpayer must self-assess his own tax liability, HMRC retain the power to make assessments where necessary. In particular, HMRC can make a 'discovery' assessment where they discover that any income or gains which ought to have been assessed have not been assessed, that an existing assessment is insufficient or that any relief already given is excessive. The power to make an assessment is separate from HMRC's power to make a determination of tax liability in the event of the non-filing of a self-assessment tax return — see **58.15** RETURNS.

The power to make an assessment is, however, restricted by the operation of time limits within which it must be made. Normally an assessment for a tax year or accounting period must be made not more than four years after the end of the year or period. This time limit is extended in certain circumstances and in particular where a loss of tax has been brought about carelessly or deliberately by the taxpayer. In the case of a loss brought about carelessly the time limit is six years after the end of the year or period; for a loss brought about deliberately the time limit is twenty years.

HMRC can make a 'simple assessment' of an individual's or trustee's income tax or capital gains tax liability for **2016/17** or a subsequent year without the taxpayer first being required to complete a self-assessment tax return. The simple assessment will be made on the basis of information already held by HMRC. See **6.9** below.

Assessments in general

[6.2] Income tax assessments and CGT assessments on individuals (including individual members of partnerships), trustees and personal representatives are made for years of assessment (tax years). Corporation tax assessments on companies are made for accounting periods.

An assessment is made by an officer of Revenue and Customs by the giving of a notice of assessment. The notice must be served on the person assessed (normally by post) and must state its date of issue and the time limit for giving notice of appeal (**5.3** APPEALS). All income tax falling to be charged by such an assessment, even if chargeable under more than one Part or Chapter of *ITTOIA 2005*, may be included in one assessment, but there is no provision for income tax and CGT to be charged in the same assessment.

Where any statutory provision gives the Commissioners for HMRC the power to make an assessment, the assessment is nevertheless to be made by an officer as described above.

[*TMA 1970, s 30A(1)–(3)(5); FA 1998, Sch 18 para 47(1); CRCA 2005, ss 5, 7, Sch 4 para 68*].

An assessment must include a statement of the tax actually payable (*Hallamshire Industrial Finance Trust Ltd v CIR* Ch D 1978, 53 TC 631). An assessment defective in form or containing errors may be validated by *Taxes Management Act 1970 (TMA 1970), s 114(1)*. However, *s 114(1)* does *not* extend to integral fundamental parts of the assessment such as an error in the year of assessment for which it is made (*Baylis v Gregory* HL 1988, 62 TC 1).

A taxpayer may authorise HMRC (on form 64-8) to automatically provide his agent with a copy of any assessment made on him. If an assessment is not dealt with promptly, interest (or additional interest) may arise on unpaid tax, and any appeal may be out of time.

See **58.15** RETURNS for HMRC's power to make a determination of the tax liability in a case where an annual self-assessment tax return has been issued but not filed. Tax is payable as if the determination were a self-assessment, with no right of appeal, and the determination can only be displaced by the filing of a return and the making of a self-assessment based on it.

See **14.15** COMPANIES regarding the application of the corporation tax provisions where a company ceases to be UK-resident in the course of the formation of an SE or where an SE becomes non-UK resident.

Construction of references to assessments etc.

[6.3] References to a person being assessed to tax, or being charged to tax by an assessment, are to be construed as including a reference to his being so assessed, or being so charged, by a self-assessment or by a determination under *TMA 1970, s 28C* or *FA 1998, Sch 18 paras 36, 37* (see **58.15**, **58.19** RETURNS) which has not been superseded by a self-assessment. [*FA 1994, s 197; FA 1998, Sch 18 para 97*].

Double assessment

[6.4] Where there has been 'double assessment' for the same cause and for the same chargeable period, a claim may be made to the Commissioners for HMRC for the assessment reflecting the overcharge to be vacated. An appeal against a refusal of a claim may be made by giving notice to the HMRC officer concerned in writing within 30 days after the day on which notice of the refusal is given. [*TMA 1970, s 32; CRCA 2005, s 5; SI 2009 No 56, Sch 1 para 22*]. See **13.8** CLAIMS for error or mistake relief and **39.1** INTERACTION WITH OTHER TAXES as regards alternative income tax and CGT assessments.

Finality of assessments

[6.5] An assessment cannot be altered after the notice has been served except in accordance with the express provisions of the *Taxes Acts* (for example where the taxpayer appeals — see **5** APPEALS). [*TMA 1970, s 30A(4); FA 1998, Sch 18 para 47(2)*]. See **13.8** CLAIMS for claims for the recovery of tax charged in an assessment which the taxpayer believes not to be due. An assessment as determined on appeal, or not appealed against, is final and conclusive (but see **51.30** PAYMENT OF TAX for HMRC 'equitable liability' treatment (now withdrawn)).

Trustees and personal representatives

[6.6] CGT due from trustees or personal representatives may be assessed and charged on and in the name of any one or more of the 'relevant trustees' or, as the case may be, 'relevant personal representatives'. In relation to chargeable gains, the '*relevant trustees*' means the trustees in the tax year in which the gains accrue and any subsequent trustees of the settlement, and '*relevant personal representatives*' has a corresponding meaning. See **48.2** OFFSHORE SETTLEMENTS for the modification of this rule in relation to the 'exit charge' under *TCGA 1992, s 80* on trustees ceasing to be resident in the UK.

Unless the assets are held by the trustees or personal representatives as nominees or bare trustees for another person absolutely (see **62.3** SETTLEMENTS), chargeable gains accruing to, and CGT chargeable on, the trustees or personal representatives are not to be regarded as accruing to, or chargeable on, any other person. No trustee or personal representative is to be regarded as an individual for the purposes of *TCGA 1992*.

[*TCGA 1992, s 65(1)(2)(4)*].

See also 62.6, 62.11 SETTLEMENTS.

Non-corporate bodies, personal representatives and receivers

[6.7] Assessments may be made on the treasurer etc. of bodies which are not corporations; on personal representatives in respect of disposals made *by the deceased person*; and receivers appointed by a court. [*TMA 1970, ss 71, 74, 75, 77*]. As regards receivers, however, see *CIR v Piacentini and others* QB 2003, 75 TC 288.

Simon's Taxes. See C1.102.

Contract settlements

[6.8] In cases where penalties are chargeable, the taxpayer may be invited to offer a sum in settlement of liability of tax, interest and penalties (a 'contract settlement') and such offers are often accepted by HMRC without assessment of all the tax. A binding agreement so made cannot be repudiated afterwards by the taxpayer or his executors. Where the liability is agreed and the tax etc. paid, this cannot afterwards be set aside, notwithstanding any alleged over-charge and no formal assessment (see cases at 52.31 PENALTIES and *CIR v Nuttall* CA 1989, 63 TC 148 and *CIR v Woollen* CA 1992, 65 TC 229). See, however, *R (oao HMRC) v Berkshire General Commissioners* Ch D 2007, [2008] STC 1494, in which a contract settlement included a provision allowing HMRC to make further inquiries in relation to a partnership in which certain of the parties to the settlement were partners.

Simple assessments

[6.9] HMRC can make a 'simple assessment' of an individual's or trustee's income tax or capital gains tax liability for **2016/17** or a subsequent year without the taxpayer first being required to complete a self-assessment tax return. The simple assessment will be made on the basis of information already held by HMRC, whether it was received from the taxpayer or a third party. HMRC can withdraw a simple assessment by notice to the taxpayer, and it is then taken as never having had any effect.

The notice of assessment must include particulars of the income and gains, and any relief or allowance, taken into account in the assessment, and must state the amount payable, net of any income tax deducted at source, and the due date for payment (see 51.2 PAYMENT OF TAX). In the case of a trust, the notice of assessment can be given to any one or more of the relevant trustees (see 62.11 SETTLEMENTS). HMRC can make more than one simple assessment on a person for any tax year. A simple assessment cannot be made if the taxpayer has already made a return or if he has been given notice to do so and that notice has not been withdrawn.

[*TMA 1970, ss 28H–28J; FA 2016, s 167, Sch 23 para 3*].

Querying a simple assessment

An appeal can be made against a simple assessment (see 5.2 APPEALS) but only after the person assessed has raised a query about the assessment and has been given a final response to that query. The person may query the simple assessment by notifying HMRC of his belief that the assessment is, or may be, incorrect, and stating the reasons for that belief. He must do so within 60 days after the date the notice of assessment was issued or such longer period as HMRC may allow in a particular case. He can withdraw his query at any time.

HMRC must consider a query and give a final response. If they need more time or information, they can postpone the simple assessment in whole or part (according to how much of it is being queried) and notify the taxpayer accordingly. If the simple assessment is postponed in part, HMRC must state the amount that remains payable. The taxpayer is under no obligation to pay a postponed amount. After considering the query, HMRC's final response must be to confirm, amend or withdraw the assessment, and in each case to notify the taxpayer in writing. An amended simple assessment given as a final response to a query cannot itself be queried.

[*TMA 1970, s 31AA; FA 2016, s 167, Sch 23 para 6*].

Discovery assessments

[6.10] If HMRC 'discover', as regards any person (the taxpayer) and a chargeable period (i.e. for income tax and CGT purposes, a year of assessment or for corporation tax, an accounting period), that:

(a) any profits (i.e. income or chargeable gains) which ought to have been assessed to tax have not been assessed, or
(b) an assessment is or has become insufficient, or
(c) any relief given is or has become excessive,

then with the exceptions below, an assessment (a discovery assessment) may be made to make good to the Crown the apparent loss of tax.

In a case where a return under *TMA 1970, s 8* or *s 8A* (see **58.3** RETURNS), or a company tax return (see **58.19** RETURNS), has been filed in respect of a chargeable period,

(1) no discovery assessment may be made in respect of that chargeable period if it would be attributable to an error or mistake in the return as to the basis on which the liability ought to have been computed and the return was, in fact, made on the basis, or in accordance with the practice, generally prevailing at the time when it was made;
(2) no discovery assessment may be made in respect of that chargeable period unless either:
    (i) the loss of tax is brought about carelessly or deliberately by the taxpayer or a person acting on his behalf, or
    (ii) at the time when an HMRC officer either ceased to be entitled to enquire (see **58.9** RETURNS) into the return or, where an enquiry has been opened, has issued a closure notice, he could not have been reasonably expected, on the basis of the information so far made available to him, to be aware of the loss of tax. After the date of Royal Assent to *F(No 2)A 2017*, the reference here to a closure notice is to a final closure notice or to a partial closure notice in respect of a matter to which the discovery relates (see **58.12** RETURNS).

See below for the meaning of 'carelessly' and 'deliberately'.

For the purposes of (2)(ii) above, information is regarded as having been made available to HMRC if it has been included in:

(A) the return (or accompanying accounts, statements or documents) for the chargeable period concerned or for either of the two immediately preceding it, or
(B) a partnership return (see **58.16** RETURNS), where applicable, in respect of the chargeable period concerned or either of the two immediately preceding it, or
(C) an NRCGT return containing an advance self-assessment (see **58.20** RETURNS) in respect of the tax year concerned or either of the two chargeable periods immediately preceding it, or
(D) any claim or any application under *ICTA 1988, s 751A* (reduction in profits of controlled foreign company for certain activities of EEA business establishments — see **49.9** OVERSEAS MATTERS) for the chargeable period concerned, or
(E) documents, etc. produced for the purposes of any enquiries into such a return or claim,

or is information the existence and relevance of which could reasonably be expected to be inferred from the above-mentioned information or are notified in writing to HMRC. See also below.

The requirement for either of the conditions in (i) or (ii) in (2) above to be met does not apply in respect of chargeable gains (and income) in relation to which the taxpayer has been given, after the completion of any enquiries, a notice under *TIOPA 2010, s 81(2)* (schemes and arrangements designed to increase DOUBLE TAX RELIEF (**21.9**)), *TCGA 1992, s 184G* or *s 184H* (avoidance utilising losses — see **14.7** COMPANIES) or, for accounting periods beginning before 1 January 2017, *TIOPA 2010, ss 232* or *249* (tax arbitrage — see **4.20** ANTI-AVOIDANCE).

An objection to a discovery assessment on the grounds that neither (i) nor (ii) in (2) above applies can be made only on an appeal against the assessment. (See **5.2** APPEALS for right of appeal.)

[*TMA 1970, s 29; FA 1998, s 117, Sch 18 paras 41–45; FA 2008, s 118, Sch 36 para 71; TIOPA 2010, Sch 8 paras 5, 321; FA 2015, Sch 7 para 46; FA 2016, Sch 10 paras 2, 4; F(No 2)A 2017, Sch 15 paras 14, 31, 32, 44; SI 2009 No 403*].

See **51.2** PAYMENT OF TAX as regards due date of payment of income tax and CGT under these provisions. For time limits for making assessments, see **6.13** onwards below.

A change of HMRC opinion on information previously made available to them is not grounds for a discovery assessment. See **58.4** RETURNS for the use of discovery assessments in amending provisional figures in a self-assessment.

Particularly in large or complex cases, the standard accounts information details and other information included in the personal tax return may not provide a means of disclosure adequate to avoid falling within (2)(ii) above.

The submission of further information, including perhaps accounts, may be considered appropriate but will not necessarily provide protection against a discovery assessment beyond that arising from submission of the return alone. The reasonable expectation test (see (2)(ii) above) must be satisfied. Where voluminous information beyond the accounts and computations is sent with the return, HMRC do not accept that the test is satisfied if the information is so extensive that an officer could not reasonably be expected to be aware of the significance of particular information and the officer's attention has not been drawn to it by the taxpayer. HMRC will accept that for *TMA 1970, s 29* purposes documents submitted within a month of the return 'accompany' it (see (A) above) provided the return indicates that such documents have been or will be submitted. They will consider sympathetically a request that this condition be treated as satisfied where the time lag is longer than a month. (Revenue Tax Bulletin June 1996 pp 313–315; HMRC Statement of Practice 1/06).

In *Veltema v Langham* CA, [2004] STC 544 a company director (V) was liable to income tax on the value of a house, and in his tax return he submitted a valuation of £100,000. After the deadline for making an enquiry into the return (see **58.9** RETURNS) had passed, the Revenue formed the opinion that the value of the house had been more than £100,000, and they subsequently issued a further assessment on the basis that the true value had been £145,000. V appealed, contending that the issue of a further assessment was not authorised by *TMA 1970, s 29*. The CA rejected this contention and upheld the assessment, holding that the assessment was not prohibited by *TMA 1970, s 29(5)* (i.e. (2)(ii) above). Prior to the enquiry deadline, the Revenue 'could not have been reasonably expected' to be aware that the valuation was inadequate. The CA observed that 'it would frustrate the aims of the self-assessment scheme, namely simplicity and early finality of assessment to tax, to interpret *s 29(5)* so as to introduce an obligation on tax inspectors to conduct an immediate and possibly time consuming scrutiny of self-assessment returns . . . when they do not disclose insufficiency, but only circumstances further investigation of which might or might not show it'. Furthermore, the definition of 'information made available' to the Revenue given above was exhaustive for the purpose of (2)(ii) above. The key to the scheme was that the inspector was precluded from making a discovery assessment under *s 29* only when the taxpayer or his representatives, in making an honest and accurate return, had clearly alerted him to the insufficiency of the assessment. He was not precluded from making an assessment where he might be able to obtain some other information, not normally part of his checks, that might put the sufficiency of the assessment in question.

Following the decision in this case the Revenue issued guidance on the amount of information which taxpayers need to provide to reduce or remove the risk of a discovery assessment in certain circumstances. That guidance has subsequently been formalised as HMRC Statement of Practice 1/06.

Where an entry in a return depends on the valuation of an asset, HMRC consider that most taxpayers who state in the additional information space at the end of the return that a valuation has been used, by whom it has been carried out, and that it was carried out by a named independent and suitably qualified valuer if that was the case, on the appropriate basis, will be able to rely on protection from a later discovery assessment after the enquiry period, provided those statements are true. Alternatively, in capital gains cases, completion of the entry in the capital gains pages indicating that a valuation has been made and inclusion of a copy of the valuation with the return will be sufficient to provide protection if the copy of the valuation includes all the information mentioned above. In some circumstances provision of the above information will not protect against a discovery assessment, particularly where other parties to the same transaction subsequently include a (different) valuation of the asset in their return.

Where a properly advised taxpayer adopts a different view of the law from that published as HMRC's view, to protect against a discovery assessment after the enquiry period HMRC consider that the return would have to indicate that a different view had been adopted. This might be done by an entry in the additional information space to the effect that HMRC guidance has not been followed on the issue or that no adjustment has been made to take account of it. In HMRC's view it is not necessary for the taxpayer to provide with the return enough information for the HMRC officer to be able to quantify any resulting under assessment of tax.

(Revenue Internet Statement 23 December 2004; HMRC Statement of Practice 1/06).

In *Corbally-Stourton v HMRC* (Sp C 692), [2008] SSCD 907 the taxpayer (C) entered into a marketed scheme as a result of which on her tax return she declared that she had made a substantial capital loss. The return included a description of the scheme in the 'white space'. HMRC subsequently reached the conclusion that the scheme did not work and that the loss was not allowable and made a discovery assessment under *TMA 1970, s 29*. C appealed, contending that the assessment was prohibited by *s 29(5)*. The Special Commissioner rejected this contention and dismissed the appeal The fact that C had claimed a large 'round sum' loss in her tax return meant that 'an inspector could have been expected to have been aware that it was possible that there was an insufficiency but could not have been reasonably expected to conclude that it was probable that there was an insufficiency'. Accordingly the conditions of *s 29(5)* were satisfied and the assessment was not prohibited. This decision was followed in *R (oao Pattullo) v HMRC* CS, [2010] STC 107 and a similar decision was reached in *Sanderson v HMRC* CA, [2016] STC 638.

In *Hancock v CIR* (Sp C 213), [1999] SSCD 287, it was held that a taxpayer who had made errors in his tax return had exhibited standards of competence beneath those to be reasonably expected, that his conduct thus amounted to negligence (under the legislation then applicable — see now (2)(i) above), and that the Revenue did therefore have the power to make a discovery assessment.

In *McEwan v Martin* Ch D, [2005] STC 993, a capital gains tax computation prepared by a professional adviser was held to constitute negligent conduct on the taxpayer's behalf, so that a discovery assessment could be made. The Revenue were entitled to assume that a professionally prepared tax computation was prepared properly, and the fact that they accepted a negligent computation at face value did not mean that it somehow ceased to be prepared negligently.

In *Anderson and another v HMRC* FTT, [2009] UKFTT 258 (TC); 2009 STI 2938, the taxpayer incorrectly treated a chargeable event gain on an offshore investment bond as if it were from an onshore gain and claimed a tax credit to which she was not entitled. The provision to HMRC of a chargeable event certificate by the insurance company which issued the bond was disregarded in determining whether HMRC could make a discovery assessment to disallow the tax credit. Similarly, information in a trust return was disregarded in determining whether HMRC could make a discovery assessment in respect of income from the trust omitted from an individual's return in *Trustees of the Bessie Taube Discretionary Settlement Trust and others v HMRC* FTT 2010, [2011] SFTD 153.

In *Landsdowne Partners Ltd Partnership v HMRC* CA 2011, [2011] EWCA Civ 1578; 2012 STI 36, the taxpayer's appeal against a discovery assessment succeeded on the grounds that when HMRC ceased to be entitled to enquire into the return, an officer would have been reasonably expected, on the basis of information already made available to him, to have been aware of an insufficiency in the return (i.e. condition (2)(ii) above applied).

See also *Hankinson v HMRC* CA 2011; [2012] STC 485 in which the conditions in (2) above were held to be objective tests which, once an assessment had been made, could be tested on appeal. The conditions were not concerned with the subjective view of the assessing officer.

In *Charlton v HMRC* UT, [2013] STC 866 it was held that the information provided with the taxpayer's return was sufficient to show that 'no officer could have missed the point that an artificial tax avoidance scheme had been implemented' and that 'on the basis of the information made available to him before the closure of the enquiry window, an officer would have been reasonably expected to have been aware of the insufficiency of tax such as to justify an assessment'; therefore, no discovery assessment was possible. It was not necessary that a hypothetical officer should have been able to comprehend all the workings of the scheme, or the legal and factual arguments that might arise, or be able to form a reasoned view of those matters. Discovery assessments in cases involving avoidance schemes were, however, upheld in *Smith v HMRC* FTT, [2013] UKFTT 368 (TC) and *Pattullo v HMRC (No 2)* UT, [2016] STC 2043.

In *Easinghall Ltd v HMRC* UT, [2016] STC 1476, an additional discovery assessment made following an agreement under *TMA 1970, s 54* (see **5.9** appeals) was held to be invalid. Such an assessment could only be made if it was founded on a point other than the particular matter which had been the subject of the agreement.

In *Anderson v HMRC* FTT, [2017] SFTD 100 the appellant had relied on a valuation of shares by the corporate finance department of a leading firm of accountants. The Tribunal held that he had not been careless in doing so. His appeal against a discovery assessment charging CGT on the disposal of the shares was therefore upheld.

There is nothing to stop HMRC raising a discovery assessment (or recognising the potential for doing so in setting the amount of a contract settlement — see **6.8** above) where an enquiry window is still open (see **58.9** RETURNS). See Revenue Tax Bulletin August 2001 pp 875, 876 for a note of the circumstances in which they would do so.

See **13.5** CLAIMS for extended time limits for claims where a discovery assessment is made in a case where no fraudulent or negligent conduct is involved.

Amendment of partnership return on discovery

[6.11] Provisions broadly similar to those in **6.10** above apply to an understatement of profits or excessive claim for relief or allowances in a partnership statement (see **58.17** RETURNS), although HMRC's remedy in this case is to amend the partnership return, with consequent amendment of partners' own returns. [*TMA 1970, s 30B; F(No 2)A 2017, Sch 15 paras 17, 44; SI 2009 No 403*].

Non-resident CGT disposals: discovery determinations

[6.12] If HMRC discover, as regards a non-resident CGT disposal (see **41.25** LAND) made by any person (the taxpayer) and a tax year, that:

(a) an amount that ought to have been assessed as the amount notionally chargeable in an advance self-assessment has not been so assessed by the filing date for the NRCGT return (see **58.20** RETURNS for the definitions of all expressions), or
(b) an assessment of the amount notionally chargeable contained in an NRCGT return has become insufficient,

then with the exceptions below, HMRC may determine that the amount which in their opinion ought to be assessed to remedy the failure or insufficiency is to be treated as if it were assessed in an NRCGT return.

In a case where an NRCGT return containing an advance self-assessment has been filed in respect of a disposal, no discovery determination may be made in respect of that disposal unless either:

(i) the situation in (a) or (b) above is brought about carelessly or deliberately by the taxpayer or a person acting on his behalf, or
(ii) at the time when an HMRC officer either ceased to be entitled to enquire (see **58.21** RETURNS) into the return or, where an enquiry has been opened, has issued a closure notice, he could not have been reasonably expected, on the basis of the information so far made available to him, to be aware of the situation in (a) or (b) above. After

the date of Royal Assent to *F(No 2)A 2017*, the reference here to a closure notice is to a final closure notice or to a partial closure notice in respect of a matter to which the discovery relates (see **58.21** RETURNS).

For the purposes of (ii) above, information is regarded as having been made available to HMRC if it has been included in:

(A) an NRCGT return for the tax year concerned or for either of the two immediately preceding it, or
(B) a self-assessment return under *TMA 1970, s 8* or *s 8A* (see **58.3** RETURNS) in respect of the two immediately preceding tax years, or
(C) any claim relating to the taxpayer's CGT position for the tax year concerned or for either of the two immediately preceding it, or
(D) accounts, statements or documents accompanying such a return or claim;
(E) documents, etc. produced for the purposes of any enquiries into such a return or claim,

or is information the existence and relevance of which could reasonably be expected to be inferred from the above-mentioned information or are notified in writing to HMRC. The reference to a return in (B) above includes, where the taxpayer carries on a trade, profession or business in partnership, any partnership return made by the taxpayer or by a person acting on his behalf.

An objection to a determination on the ground that neither (i) nor (ii) can only be made by way of appeal against the assessment.

[*TMA 1970, s 29A; FA 2015, Sch 7 para 47; F(No 2)A 2017, Sch 15 paras 15, 44*].

Time limits

[6.13] For assessments made on or after 1 April 2010, the normal time limit for the making of an assessment to income tax, capital gains tax and corporation tax is four years after the end of the tax year or accounting period in question. For assessments made before 1 April 2010, the normal time limit for the making of an assessment to income tax and capital gains tax was five years after 31 January following the tax year in question. For companies, the equivalent time limit was six years after the end of the corporation tax accounting period. An 'assessment' for this purpose includes a determination under *TMA 1970, s 29A* (see **6.12** above). [*TMA 1970, s 34(1)(1A); FA 1998, s 117, Sch 18 para 46(1); FA 2015, Sch 7 para 48*].

The latest time for assessing the personal representatives of a deceased person in respect of gains accruing before his death is four years after the end of the tax year in which he died (for assessments made before 1 April 2010, the third anniversary of 31 January following the tax year in which he died). [*TMA 1970, s 40(1)(3)*].

For capital gains tax purposes (but not for corporation tax purposes), the above changes in assessing time limits apply by reference to assessments made before, or on or after, 1 April 2012 where the assessment concerned relates to a tax year for which the taxpayer has not been given notice to make a return under *TMA 1970, s 8* or *s 8A* (see **58.3** RETURNS) or *s 12AA* (see **58.16** RETURNS) within one year of the end of the tax year (in effect, where the taxpayer is outside self-assessment). This rule does not, however, apply if for that year any gains which ought to have been assessed have not been assessed, or an assessment has become insufficient, or any relief given has become excessive. [*SI 2009 No 403, Art 10*].

In certain cases, specific provisions extend the normal time limits (see, for example, **13.5** CLAIMS, **51.31, 51.24** PAYMENT OF TAX; **69.2** UNDERWRITERS AT LLOYD'S). For extended time limits in cases of a loss of tax brought about carelessly or deliberately, see below.

An objection to the making of any assessment on the grounds that it is out of time can only be made on an appeal against the assessment. [*TMA 1970, s 34(2); FA 1998, s 117, Sch 18 para 46(3)*].

An assessment is made on the date on which the officer authorised to make it signs a certificate in the appropriate assessments volume that he made certain assessments including the assessment in question (*Honig v Sarsfield*) CA 1986, 59 TC 337.

Self-assessments

The above time limits do not apply to self-assessments (see *R (oao Higgs) v HMRC* UT, [2015] STC 1600). [*TMA 1970, s 34(3); FA 2016, s 168(2)*]. See **58.6** RETURNS for the time limits which apply to the making of a self-assessment contained in a return for 2012/13 or later years.

Extended time limits

[6.14] An assessment made on or after 1 April 2010 in a case involving a loss of income tax, capital gains tax or corporation tax brought about carelessly by the taxpayer (or by a person acting on his behalf or, where the taxpayer is a company, a partner of the company) may be made at any time not more than six years after the end of the tax year or accounting period to which it relates.

Where the loss of tax is brought about deliberately (by the taxpayer, a person acting on his behalf or a partner of a company), an assessment may be made at any time not more than 20 years after the end of the tax year or accounting period to which it relates. This time limit applies also where a loss of tax is attributable to:

- a failure to notify chargeability under *TMA 1970, s 7* or *FA 1998, Sch 18 para 2* (see **52.3** PENALTIES);
- avoidance arrangements in respect of which the taxpayer failed to make a disclosure under *FA 2004, ss 309, 310* or *313* (see **20.2** DISCLOSURE OF TAX AVOIDANCE SCHEMES); or
- arrangements which were expected to result in a tax advantage in respect of which the taxpayer was under an obligation to notify HMRC of a monitored promoter's reference number under the high-risk promoters of avoidance schemes provisions (see **20.13** DISCLOSURE OF TAX AVOIDANCE SCHEMES) but failed to do so,

but, where the tax year involved is 2008/09 or an earlier year, only where the assessment is for the purposes of making good to the Crown a loss of tax attributable to the taxpayer's negligent conduct or such conduct by a person acting on his behalf.

If the taxpayer so requires, the assessment may give effect to reliefs or allowances to which he would have been entitled had he made the necessary claims within the relevant time limits (with some exceptions for income tax).

[*TMA 1970, s 36(1)–(1B)(3)(3A); FA 1998, Sch 18 paras 46(2)–(2B), 65; FA 2014, s 277(1)(3); SI 2009 No 403*].

For the purposes of the above provisions, a loss of tax is brought about carelessly by a person if he fails to take reasonable care to avoid bringing about that loss. Where information is given to HMRC and the person providing it (or on whose behalf it is given) later discovers it was inaccurate and fails to take reasonable steps to inform HMRC, any loss of tax brought about by the inaccuracy is treated as having been brought about carelessly. A loss of tax brought about deliberately includes a loss brought about as a result of a deliberate inaccuracy in a document given to HMRC. [*TMA 1970, s 118(5)*]. For HMRC's view of what constitutes 'reasonable care' see **52.8** PENALTIES.

An objection to the making of any assessment on the grounds that it is out of time can only be made on an appeal against the assessment. [*TMA 1970, s 34(2); FA 1998, s 117, Sch 18 para 46(3)*].

Deceased persons

[6.15] In the case of a loss of tax brought about carelessly or deliberately by a deceased person (or by a person acting on the deceased's behalf before his death), assessments on his chargeable gains accrued before death must be made on the personal representatives no later than four years after the end of the tax year in which death occurred, for any year of assessment ending *not earlier* than six years before the death. For assessments made before 1 April 2010, this provision applied where there was a loss of tax attributable to the deceased's fraudulent or negligent conduct, and the time limit for making the assessment was the third anniversary of 31 January following the tax year of death. [*TMA 1970, s 40(2)(3); SI 2009 No 403*].

7

Assets

Introduction	7.1
Meaning of 'assets'	7.2
Location of assets ('situs')	7.3
Treatment of particular assets	7.4
Know-how	7.4
Patents	7.5
Plant or machinery used for long funding lease	7.6
Options	7.7
Futures contracts	7.8
Milk quota	7.9
Bookmakers' pitches	7.10
Domain names	7.11
Bitcoin and other cryptocurrencies	7.12
Image rights	7.13
Single payment scheme payment entitlement	7.14

Cross-references. See 8 ASSETS HELD ON 6 APRIL 1965; 9 ASSETS HELD ON 31 MARCH 1982; 25 EXEMPTIONS AND RELIEFS for assets exempt from capital gains tax; 26 FURNISHED HOLIDAY ACCOMMODATION; 28 GOVERNMENT SECURITIES; 43 LAND; 44.11 LOSSES for assets of negligible value; 53 PRIVATE RESIDENCES; 54 QUALIFYING CORPORATE BONDS; 63 SHARES AND SECURITIES; 70 UNIT TRUSTS AND OTHER INVESTMENT VEHICLES; 72 WASTING ASSETS.

Introduction to assets

[7.1] Capital gains tax is charged in respect of chargeable gains accruing to a person on the disposal of 'assets'. [*TCGA 1992, s 1(1)*]. By implication, this applies also to corporation tax on chargeable gains. The definition of 'assets' is very widely drawn to include almost all forms of property and is discussed further at 7.2 below.

Specific provisions apply to particular types of assets and these are described in this chapter and in dedicated chapters throughout this work as follows.

Type of asset	Location
Assets held under alternative finance arrangements	3 ALTERNATIVE FINANCE ARRANGEMENTS
Derivative contracts of companies	15.8–15.13 COMPANIES — CORPORATE FINANCE AND INTANGIBLES
Bitcoin and other cryptocurrencies	7.12
Bookmakers' pitches	7.10

Type of asset	Location
Business assets	36.2 HOLD-OVER RELIEFS; 59 ROLLOVER RELIEF
Domain names	7.11
Exempt assets	25.2–25.17 EXEMPTIONS AND RELIEFS
Furnished holiday accommodation	26 FURNISHED HOLIDAY ACCOMMODATION
Futures contracts	7.8
Government securities	28 GOVERNMENT SECURITIES
Image rights	7.13
Intangible fixed assets of companies	15.14, 15.15 COMPANIES — CORPORATE FINANCE AND INTANGIBLES
Know-how	7.4
Life insurance policies etc.	43 LIFE INSURANCE POLICIES AND DEFERRED ANNUITIES
Land	41 LAND
Loan relationships of companies	15.2–15.7 COMPANIES — CORPORATE FINANCE AND INTANGIBLES
Options	7.7
Patents	7.5
Plant or machinery used for long funding lease	7.6
Private residences	53 PRIVATE RESIDENCES
Qualifying corporate bonds	54 QUALIFYING CORPORATE BONDS
Shares and securities	22 EMPLOYEE SHARE SCHEMES; 63 SHARES AND SECURITIES; 64 SHARES AND SECURITIES — IDENTIFICATION RULES; 66 SUBSTANTIAL SHAREHOLDINGS OF COMPANIES
Single payment scheme payment entitlement	7.14
Wasting assets	72 WASTING ASSETS

Meaning of 'assets'

[7.2] '*Assets*' comprise all forms of property, wherever situated, including incorporeal property (goodwill, options, debts, etc.), currency other than sterling, and any form of property created by the disposer, or otherwise coming to be owned without being acquired. [*TCGA 1992, s 21(1)*]. Sovereigns minted after 1837 are still sterling currency and as such are not within this definition.

The restating in euros of a holding of a participating EU currency on or after 1 January 1999 is not treated as involving the disposal of the original currency or the acquisition of a new holding of euros. The original currency and the new holding are treated as the same asset, acquired as the original currency was acquired. [*SI 1998 No 3177, Reg 36*].

For the treatment of currency other than sterling when disposed of by a 'qualifying company' in certain circumstances, see **25.5** and **25.8** EXEMPTIONS AND RELIEFS.

There is no general principle that assets must have a market value or that they must be transferable or assignable (*O'Brien v Benson's Hosiery (Holdings) Ltd* HL 1979, 53 TC 241). A right to share in a statutory fund for compensation to owners of expropriated foreign property is a form of property and therefore an asset (*Davenport v Chilver* Ch D 1983, 57 TC 661). (To a great extent this decision was superseded by ESC D50 announced in Revenue Press Release 19 December 1994 (see **10.2** CAPITAL SUMS DERIVED FROM ASSETS)). Tax is only chargeable in relation to an asset which existed at the time of disposal and not to an asset coming into existence only on a disposal which created it. 'Property' has the meaning of that which is capable of being owned in a normal legal sense and thus does not extend to include the right of freedom to trade and compete in the market place, but such a right must be distinguished from the goodwill in respect of the trade in question and which is an asset for capital gains tax purposes (*Kirby v Thorn EMI plc* CA 1987, 60 TC 519). The right to unquantified and contingent future consideration on the disposal of an asset is itself an asset (*Marren v Ingles* HL 1980, 54 TC 76).

The right to bring an action to enforce a genuine claim, and which can be turned to account by negotiating a compromise yielding a capital sum, constitutes an asset. Such a right is acquired otherwise than by way of a bargain made at arm's length and at the time when the cause of action arises. Any capital sum received derives only from the right and not from other assets which may have been associated with the existence of the right (*Zim Properties Ltd v Proctor* Ch D 1984, 58 TC 371). However, in similar cases not involving contractual or statutory rights of action (see HMRC Capital Gains Manual CG13010) by concession HMRC now treat damages and compensation payments as derived from any underlying asset (and therefore exempt or taxable like that asset). If there is no underlying asset, HMRC treat damages and compensation as exempt up to a limit of £500,000 for any amount awarded in a single set of legal proceedings. This exemption was unlimited before 27 January 2014. Where compensation exceeds the limit HMRC will consider a claim for further relief on a case-by-case basis. Entitlement to other reliefs is also determined on the same basis, and HMRC are prepared to consider extending time limits for claims where there has been a delay in obtaining compensation. (HMRC Extra-Statutory Concession D33; HMRC Notice 27 January 2014). For notes and examples on the effect of ESC D33 on computations of ROLLOVER RELIEF (**59**) and PRIVATE RESIDENCES (**53**), see Revenue Tax Bulletin October 2002 pp 967–970.

See also **10.2** CAPITAL SUMS DERIVED FROM ASSETS.

Location of assets ('situs')

[7.3] Where liability depends on where the assets are actually situated (e.g. a non-resident trading in the UK or individuals not domiciled here, see **49** OVERSEAS MATTERS) the following provisions apply to determine the location of assets.

(a) The situation of rights or interests (otherwise than by way of security) in or over *immovable property* is that of the immovable property.

(b) Subject to the following provisions, the situation of rights or interests (otherwise than by way of security) in or over *tangible movable property* is that of the tangible movable property.

(c) Subject to the following provisions, *a debt*, secured or unsecured, is situated in the UK if, and only if, the creditor is resident in the UK.

(d) *Shares or debentures issued by any municipal or governmental authority*, or by any body created by such an authority, are situated in the country of that authority.

(e) Subject to paragraph (d) above, *shares in or debentures of a company incorporated in the UK* are situated in the UK.

(f) Subject to paragraphs (d) and (e) above, *registered shares or debentures* are situated where they are registered and, if registered in more than one register, where the principal register is situated.

(g) A *ship or aircraft* is situated in the UK if, and only if, the owner is then resident in the UK, and an interest or right in or over a ship or aircraft is situated in the UK if, and only if, the person entitled to the interest or right is resident in the UK.

(h) The situation of *goodwill* as a trade, business or professional asset is at the place where the trade, business or profession is carried on.

(i) *Patents, trade-marks and registered designs* are situated where they are registered, and if registered in more than one register, where each register is situated, and rights and licences in respect of a patent, trade-mark or registered design are situated in the UK if they, or any rights derived from them, are exercisable in the UK. This provision applies equally to rights under the law of a country or territory outside the UK which correspond or are similar to rights under patents, trade-marks or registered designs.

(j) *Copyright, design right and franchises*, and rights or licences in respect of any copyright work or design in which design right subsists, are situated in the UK if they or any right derived from them are exercisable in the UK. This provision applies equally to rights under the law of a country or territory outside the UK which correspond or are similar to copyright, design right or franchises.

(k) A *judgment debt* is situated where the judgment is recorded.

(l) A *non-sterling debt owed by a bank* and represented by a sum standing to the credit of an individual not domiciled (nor, from 6 April 2017, deemed domiciled) in the UK is situated in the UK if, and only if, that individual is resident in the UK and the branch or other place of business of the bank where the account is maintained is itself situated in the UK.

In relation to a company that has no share capital, references in paragraphs (d), (e) and (f) above to shares or debentures include any interests in the company possessed by members of the company. References to 'debentures' in (d) and (f) above include, in relation to a person other than a company, securities.

[*TCGA 1992, s 275; Trade Marks Act 1994, Sch 5; F(No 2)A 2017, Sch 8 para 8*].

Under the general law, *bearer shares and securities* transferable by delivery are situated where the certificate, etc. is kept (*Winans v A-G (No 2)* HL, [1910] AC 27).

See also *Standard Chartered Bank Ltd v CIR* Ch D, [1978] STC 272 where share certificates lodged in the UK by a person who was resident and domiciled abroad were held to be situated abroad, being registered in South Africa and effectively transferable only in that country. Renounceable letters of allotment of registered shares in a company are documents evidencing rights against the company and are only enforceable (and thus situated) where the register is kept (*Young and Another v Phillips* Ch D 1984, 58 TC 232).

Securities issued by designated European Communities or international organisations (e.g. The Asian Development Bank, The African Development Bank and The European and International Banks for Reconstruction and Development) or the European Investment Bank are taken for capital gains purposes to be situated outside the UK. Organisations are designated by Treasury order. [*TCGA 1992, s 265; F(No 2)A 2005, Sch 4 para 3*]. A similar treatment applies to securities issued by the Inter-American Development Bank [*TCGA 1992, s 266*] and by the OECD Support Fund [*OECD Support Fund Act 1975, s 4*].

Other intangible assets

Where the situation of an 'intangible asset' is not '*otherwise determined*' (under the above provisions or any other provision of *TCGA 1992*), the asset is taken at all times to be situated in the UK if it is 'subject to UK law' at the time it is created. For this purpose, an '*intangible asset*' is intangible or incorporeal property including a thing in action or anything which corresponds to or is similar to intangible or incorporeal property or a thing in action under the law of a country or territory outside the UK. An asset is '*subject to UK law*' at a particular time if any right or interest which comprises or forms part of it is at that time governed by or otherwise subject to, or enforceable under, the law of any part of the UK.

Non-UK futures and options

Special rules apply in the case of an intangible asset ('*asset A*') which is a 'future' or 'option' which is not subject to UK law at the time it is created. Broadly, whether asset A is treated as situated in the UK will depend on its 'underlying subject matter' (as defined). If the underlying subject matter consists of or includes a future or option, asset A is treated as situated in the UK at all times if that future or option is subject to UK law at the time it is created and, on the assumption that there were no rights in or over that contract, its situation would not be otherwise determined. Where there is a nested sequence of futures or options, in which the underlying subject matter of each contract in the sequence consists of or includes the next contract in the sequence, asset A is taken to be situated in the UK at all times if any contract in the sequence meets those conditions. Asset A is also treated as situated in the UK at any time at which its underlying subject matter either consists of or includes shares or debentures of a company incorporated in the UK which had not been issued at the time the contract was created or is otherwise treated for capital gains purposes as being situated in the UK. Again, where there is a nested sequence of futures or options, asset A is taken to be situated in the UK if any contract in the sequence meets those conditions. For these purposes, '*future*' and '*option*' have the same meaning as for the derivative contract provisions (see **15.9** COMPANIES — CORPORATE FINANCE AND INTANGIBLES).

[*TCGA 1992, ss 275A, 275B*].

Interests of co-owners

In determining the situation of any asset, the situation of an 'interest' in an asset is taken to be the same as the situation of the asset, determined on the assumption that the asset is wholly-owned by the person holding the interest in it. An '*interest*' in an asset for this purpose means an interest as a co-owner of the asset, whether the asset is owned jointly or in common, and whether or not the interests of the co-owners are equal. [*TCGA 1992, s 275C*].

Simon's Taxes. See **C1.604–C1.604B**.

Treatment of particular assets

Know-how

[7.4] For corporation tax purposes, 'know-how' is generally within the definition of an intangible fixed asset for the purposes of the intangible assets regime (see **15.14** COMPANIES — CORPORATE FINANCE AND INTANGIBLES). Broadly, know-how created after 31 March 2002 or acquired by a company from an unrelated party after that date falls within that regime (and see **15.14** COMPANIES — CORPORATE FINANCE AND INTANGIBLES for the detailed transitional provisions).

The following provisions apply for capital gains tax purposes and for corporation tax purposes where know-how does not fall within that regime.

Consideration for a disposal of know-how used in a trade which continues to be carried on by the disposer after the disposal is treated, for all purposes, as a trading receipt unless:

- (i) the consideration is brought into account as a disposal value for the purposes of *CAA 2001, s 462* or is otherwise chargeable as a revenue or income receipt; or
- (ii) the buyer is a body of persons (this term, here and in (iii) and (iv) below, includes a partnership), exercising control over the seller; or
- (iii) the seller is a body of persons exercising control over the buyer; or
- (iv) the buyer and seller are bodies of persons together controlled by a third person.

Where a person disposes of know-how in connection with the disposal of part or the whole of the trade in which it was used, any consideration for the know-how is treated as a capital payment for goodwill. This provision does not apply to:

- (a) both parties where a written joint election is made within two years of the disposal; or

(b) the acquirer only where the trade concerned was, before the acquisition, carried on wholly outside the UK.

If the consideration is, under (a) or (b), not regarded as a payment for goodwill, the acquirer is treated, for the purpose of claiming writing-down allowances, as if he had acquired the know-how for use in a trade previously carried on by him. However, the exclusion at (a) or (b) does not apply where any of (ii)–(iv) above applies.

Where consideration for the disposal of know-how is not taxed as a deemed trading receipt, or otherwise as an income or revenue receipt, or as a payment for goodwill, it is charged to income tax under *ITTOIA 2005, s 583* or to corporation tax under *CTA 2009, s 908* unless any one of (ii)–(iv) above applies. The consideration received is subject to the deduction of expenditure wholly and exclusively incurred in the acquisition or disposal of the know-how concerned.

For the above purposes, '*know-how*' is defined as any industrial information and techniques likely to assist in the manufacture or processing of goods or materials, in the working of a mine, oil-well or other source of mineral deposits (including the searching for, discovery or testing of deposits or the winning of access thereto), or in the carrying out of any agricultural, forestry or fishing operations.

[*TCGA 1992, s 261A; ITTOIA 2005, ss 192–195, 583–586; CTA 2009, ss 176–179, 908–910*].

Patents

[7.5] Except where the corporation tax intangible assets regime applies (see **15.14** COMPANIES — CORPORATE FINANCE AND INTANGIBLES and Tolley's Corporation Tax under Intangible Assets), capital sums received from the sale of patent rights are specifically taxable as income (see Tolley's Income Tax under Intellectual Property). In either case, the consideration for the sale is not therefore taxable as a chargeable gain.

Plant or machinery used for long funding lease

[7.6] Where plant or machinery is used for the purpose of leasing under a 'long funding lease', the 'lessor' is treated for chargeable gains purposes as disposing of and immediately reacquiring the plant or machinery at the 'commencement' of the 'term' of the lease for an amount equal to:

(a) where the lease is a 'long funding finance lease' whose inception is after 21 April 2009, the greater of the market value of the plant or machinery at the commencement of the term of the lease or the 'qualifying lease payments';
(b) where the lease is a long funding finance lease whose inception is before 22 April 2009, the amount that would fall to be recognised as the lessor's investment in the lease if accounts were prepared in accordance with generally accepted accounting practice on the date (the '*relevant date*') on which the lessor's net investment in the lease is first recognised in the books or other financial records of the lessor; or

(c) where the lease is a 'long funding operating lease', the market value of the plant or machinery at the commencement of the term of the lease.

In (a) above, the '*qualifying lease payments*' are the minimum payments under the lease, including any initial payment, but excluding any amount which would fall under generally accepted accounting practice to be treated as the gross return on investment in the lease, any amount representing charges for services and any amount representing UK or foreign tax (other than income tax, corporation tax or foreign equivalent) to be paid by the lessor. For leases granted on or after 13 December 2007, for the purposes of (b) above, rentals under the lease made or due on or before the relevant date are treated as made and due after that date. For leases granted on or after 12 March 2008, the lessor is treated for those purposes as having no 'liabilities' of any kind at any time on the relevant date (but only if this would increase the amount under (a) above). Where the lessor is a company, liabilities for this purpose include any share capital issued by the company which falls to be treated as a liability for accounting purposes.

On 'termination' of the lease, the lessor is treated as having disposed of and immediately reacquired the asset for a consideration equal to the 'termination amount'.

For the purposes of these provisions, a '*long funding lease*' is, broadly (and subject to further exclusions), a lease of plant or machinery with a term of more than five years (seven years in certain cases) which at its inception meets one or more of the following tests:

- the lease would fall, under generally accepted accounting practice, to be treated as a finance lease or a loan;
- the present value of the minimum lease payments equals 80% or more of the fair value of the leased plant or machinery; or
- the term of the lease is more than 65% of the remaining useful economic life of the leased plant or machinery.

The expressions '*lessor*', '*commencement*', '*term*', '*long funding finance lease*', '*long funding operating lease*', '*termination*' and '*termination amount*' are defined as in *CAA 2001, Pt 2 Ch 6A*. See Tolley's Income Tax or Tolley's Corporation Tax.

These provisions apply where the commencement of the term of the lease is on or after 1 April 2006.

[*TCGA 1992, s 25A; CAA 2001, ss 70G–70U, 70YI(2)*].

For the restriction of a loss arising on the disposal of an asset which includes plant or machinery which is a fixture and which has been used for leasing under a long funding lease, see **16.13** COMPUTATION OF GAINS AND LOSSES.

Options

[7.7] The tax treatment of an option is different for companies and capital gains tax payers.

Companies

As regards companies, see **15.8–15.13** COMPANIES — CORPORATE FINANCE AND INTANGIBLES for a summary of the special rules on **derivative contracts.** An option is a derivative contract unless falling within one of the exclusions. See Tolley's Corporation Tax for full details.

Employee share options

See **22** EMPLOYEE SHARE SCHEMES.

Grant of option

The grant of an option is the disposal of an asset (i.e. the option). This applies in particular to the grant of an option under which the grantor binds himself to sell what he does not own, and because the option is abandoned, never has occasion to own, and the grant of an option under which the grantor binds himself to buy that which he does not acquire because the option is abandoned. This treatment is without prejudice to *TCGA 1992, s 21* (see **7.2** ASSETS and **16.5** COMPUTATION OF GAINS AND LOSSES) and is subject to the provisions below as to treating the grant of an option as part of a larger transaction. [*TCGA 1992, s 144(1)*]. A grant of an option is not a part disposal of an asset that was the subject of the option even though the grantor possessed that asset at the time of the grant (*Strange v Openshaw* Ch D 1983, 57 TC 544).

Any reference to an 'option' includes a reference to an option binding the grantor to grant a lease for a premium, or enter into any other transaction that is not a sale, so that references to 'buying' and 'selling' under an option are construed accordingly. [*TCGA 1992, s 144(6)*].

Exercise of option

Subject to the treatment of cash-settled options below, if an option is exercised, the grant of the option and the transaction entered into by the grantor in fulfilment of his obligations under the option are treated as a single transaction, so if a sale by the grantor can be called for under the option, the option consideration is part of the consideration for the sale, and if the grantor can be called on to buy, the option consideration is deducted from the acquisition cost incurred by him in buying in accordance with his option obligations. The exercise of an option by the grantee is not a disposal, but on that event the acquisition of the option (whether directly from the grantor or not) and the transaction entered into by the grantee (or his assignee etc.) on the exercise are treated as a single transaction. Therefore if a sale by the grantor can be called for under the option, the option cost is part of the cost of acquiring what is sold, and if the grantor can be called on to buy, the option cost is treated as an incidental cost of disposal of what is bought by the grantor. [*TCGA 1992, s 144(2)(3)*]. The time of the 'single transaction' is taken to be the time the option is exercised. [*TCGA 1992, s 28(2)*].

As a consequence of the option being exercised, any tax paid on the gain arising on the grant of the option should be set off or repaid (and, for years before self-assessment, any assessment should be discharged) (HMRC Capital Gains Manual CG12317).

Options binding buyer to sell and buy

If an option binds the grantor both to sell and to buy, it is treated for the purposes of the above provisions (and for the purposes of *TCGA 1992, ss 144ZA–144ZD* below) as two separate options with half the consideration attributable to each. [*TCGA 1992, s 144(5)*]. Any reference to an 'option' includes a reference to an option binding the grantor to grant a lease for a premium, or enter into any other transaction that is not a sale, so that references to 'buying' and 'selling' under an option are construed accordingly. [*TCGA 1992, s 144(6)*].

Application of market value rule

Subject to the exclusion below, the following provisions apply to options exercised after 9 April 2003 to which the above 'single transaction' treatment applies where the market value rule in *TCGA 1992, s 17(1)* (see **45.1** MARKET VALUE) applies (or would apply but for these provisions) in relation to the grant of the option, the acquisition of the option by the person exercising it (whether or not the acquisition was directly from the grantor) or the transaction resulting from its exercise.

Where the option binds the grantor to sell, the market value rule does not apply for determining the consideration for the sale, except to the extent (if any) that it applies for determining the option consideration (which forms part of the sale consideration as indicated above). Likewise, the rule does not apply for determining the acquisition cost of the person exercising the option, except to the extent (if any) that it applies for determining the cost of acquiring the option.

Where the option binds the grantor to buy, the market value rule does not apply for determining the acquisition cost of the grantor, except to the extent (if any) that it applies for determining the option consideration. Likewise, it does not apply for determining the disposal consideration, but without prejudice to its application for determining the cost of the option.

To the extent that the market value rule is disapplied in determining an amount or value by the above provisions, the amount or value to be taken into account is:

- where the option is exercised on or after 2 December 2004, the 'exercise price' (subject to the inclusion of any amount by virtue of *TCGA 1992, s 119A* — see **22.6, 22.8, 22.13, 22.15** and **22.22** EMPLOYEE SHARE SCHEMES); or
- where the option is exercised before that date, the *actual* amount or value (subject to the inclusion of any amount by virtue of *TCGA 1992, s 120* — see **22.6, 22.8** and **22.14** EMPLOYEE SHARE SCHEMES).

The '*exercise price*' for this purpose is the amount of value of the consideration which, under the terms of the option, is receivable (where the option binds the grantor to buy) or payable (if it binds the grantor to sell) as a result of the exercise of the option, but does not include the amount or value of any consideration for the acquisition of the option.

[*TCGA 1992, s 144ZA*].

An attempt to exploit *TCGA 1992, s 144ZA* as part of an avoidance scheme failed in *Trustees of the Morrison 2002 Maintenance Trust v HMRC* UT, [2017] UKUT 300 (TCC).

Exclusion

For options to which the above provision would otherwise apply which are exercised 'non-commercially', the provision does not apply, and *TCGA 1992, s 144(2)(3)* above applies in modified form. The 'single transaction' rule continues to apply, but, if the option binds the grantor to buy, his cost of acquisition in buying in pursuance of his obligations, and the disposal consideration for what he buys are deemed for chargeable gains purposes to be the market value of what is bought at the time of exercise. If the option binds the grantor to sell, the consideration for the sale and the cost to the person exercising the option are deemed to be the market value of what is sold at the time of exercise. If the whole or any part of the 'underlying subject matter' of the option is subject to any right or restriction which is enforceable by the person disposing of it or a connected person, the market value of the underlying subject matter is determined for the purposes of these provisions as if the right or restriction did not exist and *TCGA 1992, s 18(6)(7)* (disposal to connected person of asset subject to right or restriction — see **4.12** ANTI-AVOIDANCE) is disapplied.

For this purpose, the '*underlying subject matter*' of an option is, if the option binds the grantor to sell, what falls to be sold on exercise, and, if the option binds the grantor to buy, what falls to be bought on exercise.

This provision does not apply if the option is a 'share option' to which the income tax provisions at **22.6** EMPLOYEE SHARE SCHEMES apply (or, for 2013/14 and earlier years, would apply but for *ITEPA 2003, s 474*). It also does not apply if:

- at the time the option is exercised the 'open market price' of the underlying subject matter differs from its open market price at the time the option was granted;
- some or all of that change in open market value results, directly or indirectly, from 'relevant arrangements';
- the exercise of the option would not be non-commercial if there were to be disregarded so much of that change in open market value as results to any extent, directly or indirectly, from the relevant arrangements; and
- the grantor and the person exercising the option would otherwise obtain, or might be expected to obtain, a tax advantage (as defined) directly or indirectly in consequence of, or otherwise in connection with, the exercise of the option.

For these purposes, the '*open market price*' of the underlying subject matter of an option is the price which that subject matter might reasonably be expected to fetch on a sale in the open market at the time of exercise, with no allowance made for any reduction arising out of the whole of the assets being placed on the market at one and the same time. Where the underlying subject matter includes unquoted shares or securities, the open market price is determined on the assumption that all information is available which a prudent prospective purchaser might reasonably require before purchase by private treaty at arm's length from a willing vendor. If any part of the underlying subject matter is subject to a right or restriction enforceable by the person disposing of it or a connected person, the open market price is determined as if the right or restriction did not exist.

'*Relevant arrangements*' are arrangements (including any agreement, understanding, scheme, transaction or series of transactions, whether or not legally enforceable) to which, or which include one or more transactions to which, a '*relevant person*' (i.e. the grantor, any person holding the option at any time, or any person connected with either of them) is or has been a party.

An option is exercised '*non-commercially*' if, in the case of an option which binds the grantor to buy, the exercise price (as above) is less than the open market price of what is bought. In the case of an option binding the grantor to sell, the option is exercised non-commercially if the exercise price is greater than the open market price of what is sold.

[*TCGA 1992, ss 144ZB–144ZD; FA 2014, Sch 9 paras 25, 47–50*].

TCGA 1992, s 144ZA above was introduced to reverse the effect of the decision in *Mansworth v Jelley* CA 2002, 75 TC 1. In that case, an employee (J) was granted options to acquire shares in his employer's parent company. He was not resident in the UK at the time he was granted these options, but subsequently became UK-resident, exercised the options, and then sold the shares. The Revenue issued CGT assessments on the basis that the acquisition cost of the shares was the sum of the price paid for the shares on the exercise of the options and the market value of the options when they were originally granted (which was treated as nil). However, in the CA, Chadwick LJ held that the acquisition of the shares was clearly 'an incident of the taxpayer's employment', and was therefore within *TCGA 1992, s 17(1)(b)* (see **45.1** MARKET VALUE). In the CGT computation, the cost of acquisition of the shares was 'the market value of the underlying asset' at the time when the options were exercised.

Following this case, HMRC accept that where an asset is acquired via an option exercised before 10 April 2003 and granted otherwise than by way of a bargain at arm's length or by reason of employment (so that the market value rule applies in respect of the grant (or would apply but for *TCGA 1992, s 149A* — see **22.3** EMPLOYEE SHARE SCHEMES)), the acquisition cost of the asset is equal to the market value of the asset at the time the option is exercised (and for the treatment of any amount charged to income tax on the exercise, see **22.6** and **22.22** EMPLOYEE SHARE SCHEMES). Any corresponding disposal proceeds are also equal to the market value at that time, but HMRC have indicated that they will implement this only in the case of returns made on or after 12 December 2002 (Revenue Internet Statement, 8 January 2003).

Cash-settled options

Alternative provisions to those in *TCGA 1992, s 144(2)(3)* above apply to a 'cash-settled' option, i.e. an option which is exercised where the nature of the option (or its exercise) is such that the grantor is liable to make, and the grantee is entitled to receive, a payment in full settlement (for partial settlement, see below) of all obligations under the option. [*TCGA 1992, s 144A(1)*].

Under the alternative provisions, the grantor of a cash-settled option is treated as having disposed of an asset consisting of the liability to make the payment and the payment is treated as an incidental cost of making the disposal. Here, the grant of the option and the disposal are treated as a single transaction and the consideration for the option is treated as the consideration for the disposal. Whereas, the grantee of the cash-settled option is treated as having disposed of an asset consisting of the entitlement to receive the payment and the payment received is treated as the consideration for the disposal. In this case the acquisition of the option and the disposal are treated as a single transaction and the cost of acquiring the option and related expenses is treated as allowable expenditure deductible under *TCGA 1992, s 38(1)(a)* (acquisition and incidental costs; see **16.11** COMPUTATION OF GAINS AND LOSSES). [*TCGA 1992, s 144A(2)(3)(a)(b)*].

Where a payment is only in partial settlement of all obligations under a cash-settled option, *TCGA 1992, s 144(2)(3)* and *s 144A(2)(3)* above both apply subject to the modification that, in those provisions, any reference to the grant or acquisition of an option is replaced by a reference to the grant or acquisition of so much of the option as relates to the making and receipt of the payment or, as the case may be, the sale or purchase by the grantor, and any reference to the consideration for, or the cost of or of acquiring, the option is replaced by a reference to a just and reasonable proportion of that consideration or cost. [*TCGA 1992, s 144A(4)(5)*].

Other matters

The above provisions apply generally but the further treatment of options depends on the circumstances as follows.

(a) **Options to acquire assets for trading use.** An option to acquire an asset exercisable by a person intending to use it, if acquired, for the purpose of a trade carried on by him, is not a wasting asset, and abandonment of such an option constitutes a disposal of it (such that an allowable loss may accrue). [*TCGA 1992, ss 144(4)(c), 146(1)(c)*].

(b) **Traded options.** A 'traded option', i.e. an option listed on a 'recognised stock exchange', or on a 'recognised futures exchange', is not a wasting asset, and an abandonment of such an option constitutes a disposal of it (such that an allowable loss may accrue). [*TCGA 1992, ss 144(4)(b), (8)(b), 146(1)(b), (4)(a)*].

    '*Recognised stock exchange*' has the meaning given at **63.30** SHARES AND SECURITIES.

    '*Recognised futures exchange*' means the London International Financial Futures and Options Exchange and any other UK or non-UK futures exchange designated by order. [*TCGA 1992, s 288(6)(7)*]. A list of recognised futures exchanges appears in **Simon's Taxes.**

    Gains arising in the course of dealing in traded options, which, but for the exemption in *CTA 2009, s 981* or *ITTOIA 2005, s 779*, would have been chargeable to tax as income under *CTA 2009, Pt 10 Ch 8* or under

ITTOIA 2005, Pt 5 Ch 8 are instead within the scope of capital gains tax. Losses are treated similarly. [*TCGA 1992, s 143(1)(2)(b); SI 2006 No 959, Art 3(2)*]. See also **7.8** below.

Where a person ('the grantor') who has granted a traded option ('the original option') closes it out by acquiring a traded option of the same description ('the second option'), any disposal by the grantor involved in closing out the original option is disregarded for the purposes of capital gains tax. The allowable expenditure attributable to the incidental costs to the grantor of making the disposal constituted by the original option is treated as increased by the aggregate of the amount or value of the consideration, in money or money's worth, given by him or on his behalf wholly and exclusively for the acquisition of the second option and the incidental costs of that acquisition. [*TCGA 1992, s 148*].

(c) **Quoted options to subscribe for shares.** An option to *subscribe* for shares in a company, which option is itself listed on a recognised stock exchange (see (b) above), is not a wasting asset and an abandonment of such an option constitutes a disposal of it (such that an allowable loss may accrue). [*TCGA 1992, ss 144(4)(a), (8)(a), 146(1)(a), (4)(a)*]. (The term 'quoted option' is understood to have become virtually otiose following the introduction of the term 'traded option'; the technical differences between the definitions, which have changed from time to time, are believed to have few, if any, practical consequences.)

(d) **Financial options.** 'Financial options' are treated in the same way as traded options in (b) above, except that *TCGA 1992, s 148* does not apply to financial options. A '*financial option*' is an option, other than a traded option, which:

  (i) relates to currency, shares, securities or an interest rate and is granted (otherwise than as agent) by a member of a recognised stock exchange, an 'authorised person' (defined by reference to *Financial Services and Markets Act 2000, s 31* and *SI 2001 No 544*); or
  (ii) relates to shares or securities which are quoted on a recognised stock exchange (see (b) above) and is granted by a member of such an exchange, acting as agent; or
  (iii) relates to currency, shares, securities or an interest rate and is granted to an authorised person and concurrently and in association with an option falling within (i) above which is granted by the authorised person concerned to the grantor of the first-mentioned option; or
  (iv) relates to shares or securities which are quoted on a recognised stock exchange and is granted to a member of such an exchange, including such a member acting as agent; or
  (v) is of a description specified in a Treasury order.

[*TCGA 1992, ss 144(4)(b), (8)(c), (9), 146(1)(b), (4)(a)*].

Two options, purchased by the taxpayer company from the same fellow group company, intended to have effect together, and undoubtedly financial options within (i) above when considered separately, could not be re-characterised as a loan (*Griffin v Citibank Investments Ltd* Ch D 2000, 73 TC 352).

(e) **Options to acquire or dispose of gilt-edged securities and qualifying corporate bonds.** Disposals of any such options are exempt. [*TCGA 1992, s 115(1)(b)*].

(f) **Options not within (a)–(e) above.** Such options are WASTING ASSETS (**72**) and the abandonment of such an option is not a disposal. Options (other than those in (b), (c) or (d) above) to buy or sell quoted shares and securities (being shares or securities which are listed on a recognised stock exchange in the UK or elsewhere — see **63.30** SHARES AND SECURITIES) are regarded as wasting assets, the life of which end when the right to exercise the option ends, or when the option becomes valueless, whichever is the earlier. [*TCGA 1992, ss 144(4), 146(2)(3)(4)(b)*].

Example

On 1 February 2014 F granted an option to G for £10,000 to acquire freehold land bought by F for £50,000 in September 2000. The option is for a period of five years, and the option price is £100,000 plus 1% thereof for each month since the option was granted. On 1 February 2016, G sold the option to H for £20,000. On 30 June 2017, H exercises the option and pays F £141,000 for the land. Neither G nor H intended to use the land for the purposes of a trade.

2014 Grant of option by F

	£
Disposal proceeds	10,000
Allowable cost	—
Chargeable gain	£10,000

2016 Disposal of option by G

	£	£
Disposal proceeds		20,000
Allowable cost	10,000	
Less: Wasted — ²/₅ × £10,000	4,000	
		6,000
Chargeable gain		£14,000

2017 Exercise of option

	£
(i) Earlier assessment on F vacated	
(ii) Aggregate disposal proceeds (£10,000 + £141,000)	151,000
Allowable cost of land	50,000
Chargeable gain (on F)	£101,000

H's allowable expenditure is

	£
Cost of option	20,000
Cost of land	141,000
	£161,000

A sum paid to a person to relinquish his rights to call on another person to buy property from him (a put option) is a capital sum derived from an asset (the option) and can bring about a chargeable event as regards gains although such a transaction is not able to give rise to an allowable loss. Properly construed, the provision above that an abandonment of an option is not to be treated as a disposal is a specific exception to the general rule that the extinction of an asset constitutes a disposal of it (see **10.2** CAPITAL SUMS DERIVED FROM ASSETS) for the purpose of allowable losses. However, the provision does not exempt a gain made from such a transaction (*Golding v Kaufman* Ch D 1984, 58 TC 296; *Powlson v Welbeck Securities Ltd* CA 1987, 60 TC 269). The consideration to be taken into account in respect of the receipt of a contingently repayable sum in return for the grant of an option to purchase land is valued subject to the contingency, provided the contingency is not within **16.13**(f) and (g) COMPUTATION OF GAINS AND LOSSES (*Randall v Plumb* Ch D 1974, 50 TC 392). If, however, a contingency is related to matters which do not directly bear upon the value of the consideration, it does not necessarily have to be taken into account (*Garner v Pounds Shipowners & Shipbreakers Ltd (and related appeal)* HL 2000, 72 TC 561).

If, under *Building Societies Act 1986*, the whole of a building society's business is transferred to a successor company, and in connection therewith rights are conferred on members to acquire shares in priority to other persons, at a discount or for no payment, the rights are treated as options within *TCGA 1992, s 144* having no value and granted for no consideration. [*TCGA 1992, ss 216(1), 217(1)(6)*]. See also **63.27** SHARES AND SECURITIES. Similar provisions apply where a building society confers on its members or former members (or any class of them) similar acquisition rights after 24 July 1991 over 'qualifying shares' in the society (meaning, generally, permanent interest bearing shares (PIBS) — see **54.3** QUALIFYING CORPORATE BONDS for full definition). [*TCGA 1992, s 149*].

HMRC have set out in a Statement of Practice their views, with examples, on the tax treatment of transactions in financial futures and options otherwise within *TCGA 1992, s 143* (see (b) and (d) above and **7.8** below) and relating to shares, securities, foreign currency or other financial instruments, with particular reference to whether or not such transactions are to be regarded as profits or losses of a trade (in which case *section 143* is of no application) or taxed under the chargeable gains rules. The principles they set out are of relevance to:

- UK residents such as unauthorised unit trusts, charities and others (including companies but not approved pension schemes), and
- non-UK resident collective investment vehicles, pension funds and others (including companies),

which either do not trade or whose principal trade is outside the financial area. As regards companies, principles do not apply to derivative contracts within **15.8–15.12** COMPANIES — CORPORATE FINANCE AND INTANGIBLES. Whilst each case must be judged on its merits, HMRC consider that an *individual* is unlikely to be regarded as trading as a result of purely speculative transactions in financial futures or options, whereas transactions in financial futures or options by a company may be either trading or capital in nature. In *all* cases where the transaction is clearly ancillary to another transaction, the question of whether it is trading or capital will depend on the nature of the other transaction. The Statement lists factors to be considered in determining whether an ancillary relationship exists between the financial futures or options transaction and another transaction. In particular, such a relationship exists if the intention is to eliminate or reduce risk, or to reduce transaction costs, in respect of the other transaction, and the financial futures or options transaction is 'economically appropriate' (as defined) to such elimination or reduction. Even if the other transaction is abandoned, these principles will normally be applied, although it is politic to close out the financial futures or options transaction as soon thereafter as is practicable.

(HMRC Statement of Practice 3/02, replacing SP 14/91).

See **25.60** EXEMPTIONS AND RELIEFS for options contracts entered into by pension schemes.

See **63.9** SHARES AND SECURITIES and **22** EMPLOYEE SHARE SCHEMES for quoted options granted following a reorganisation and options granted to employees respectively.

See **38.8** INDEXATION for indexation allowance provisions relating to options generally.

Derivatives over assets which are the subject of euroconversion

The following applies where: (A) a 'derivative' represents rights or obligations in respect of an asset, liability or other amount; (B) there is a 'euroconversion' of the underlying asset; (C) a transaction is entered into that would otherwise result in a disposal of the original derivative and the acquisition of a new derivative; (D) the terms of the new derivative differ from those of the original only to the extent necessary to reflect the euroconversion; *and* (E) no party to the transaction receives any consideration other than the new derivative. The transaction is not treated as involving a disposal or acquisition for CGT purposes. Instead, the original derivative and the new derivative are treated as the same asset, acquired as the original derivative was acquired. '*Derivative*' means any commodity or financial futures or an option. A '*euroconversion*', in relation to an asset, liability, contract or instrument, is the redenomination into euros of that asset etc. where it was previously expressed in the currency of an EU member state participating in the European single currency. [*SI 1998 No 3177, Regs 2, 3, 38*].

Futures contracts

[7.8] The tax treatment of a futures contract differs for companies and capital gains tax payers.

Companies

See **15.8–15.12** COMPANIES — CORPORATE FINANCE AND INTANGIBLES for a summary of the special rules on **derivative contracts.** A future (as defined) is a derivative contract unless falling within one of the exclusions. See Tolley's Corporation Tax for full details.

Commodity and financial futures

Gains arising in the course of dealing in '*commodity or financial futures*' (which here means commodity futures or financial futures which are for the time being dealt in on a 'recognised futures exchange' (as in 7.7(b) above)) which would otherwise (apart from *CTA 2009, s 981* (corresponding treatment for corporation tax on income) or *ITTOIA 2005, s 779* (corresponding treatment for income tax)) have been chargeable to tax as income under *CTA 2009, Pt 10 Ch 8* or under *ITTOIA 2005, Pt 5 Ch 8*, are instead brought within the scope of tax on chargeable gains. Losses are treated similarly. In addition, the following transactions, not being entered into in the course of dealing on a recognised futures exchange and except in so far as any gain or loss arising to any person from any such transaction arises in the course of a trade, are regarded as being so dealt in.

(a) A transaction under which an 'authorised person' (defined by reference to *Financial Services and Markets Act 2000, s 31* and *SI 2001 No 544*) enters into a commodity or financial futures contract with another person.
(b) A transaction under which the outstanding obligations under a commodity or financial futures contract to which an authorised person is a party are brought to an end by a further contract between the parties to the futures contract.

[*TCGA 1992, s 143(1)(2)(a), (3)(4)(8); SI 2006 No 959, Art 3(2)*].

For the purposes of *TCGA 1992*, where, in the course of dealing in commodity or financial futures (whether or not, it seems, ones dealt in on a recognised futures exchange) a person who has entered into a futures contract closes out that contract by entering into another futures contract with reciprocal obligations to those of the first contract, the transaction is regarded as the disposal of an asset consisting of the outstanding obligations under the first contract. Any money received or paid on the transaction is treated, respectively, as consideration for the disposal or as incidental costs of the disposal. [*TCGA 1992, s 143(5)*].

In any case where, in the course of dealing in commodity or financial futures (whether or not, it seems, ones dealt in on a recognised futures exchange) a person has entered into a futures contract and has not closed out that contract as above, and he becomes entitled to receive, or liable to make, a payment, whether under the contract or otherwise, in full or partial settlement of any obligations under the contract, he is treated for the purposes of *TCGA 1992* as having disposed of an asset consisting of that entitlement or liability. The payment received or made is treated, respectively, as consideration for, or as incidental costs of, the disposal. [*TCGA 1992, s 143(6)*].

TCGA 1992, s 46 (**72** WASTING ASSETS) does not apply to obligations under a commodity or financial futures contract which is entered into by a person in the course of dealing in such futures on a recognised futures exchange, or a commodity or financial futures contract to which an authorised person is a party. [*TCGA 1992, s 143(7)(8)*].

See **7.7** above as regards SP 3/02 setting out HMRC's views on whether isolated transactions in financial futures are to be regarded as trading or taxed under the chargeable gains rules.

See **25.60** EXEMPTIONS AND RELIEFS for futures contracts entered into by pension schemes.

Gilt-edged securities and qualifying corporate bonds

The disposal of the outstanding obligation under any contract to acquire or dispose of such securities and bonds is exempt. Without prejudice to the provisions within *TCGA 1992, s 143(5)* above regarding the closing out of futures contracts generally, where a person closes out a contract for gilts or bonds as above by entering into another, reciprocal, contract, that transaction is treated as a disposal of the outstanding obligation under the first-mentioned contract. [*TCGA 1992, s 115(1)(b), (2)(3)*].

Derivatives over assets which are the subject of euroconversion

See 7.7 above.

Milk quota

[7.9] The milk quota system was introduced by the European Community in 1984 in order to regulate overall milk production (EC Council Regulation 856/84). Under the scheme, each member state was allocated a production quota. The national quota was then divided between all of the country's milk producers. If total UK production for any year exceeds the national quota then a levy is payable to the European Union by the Intervention Board (previously the Milk Marketing Board). This levy is then charged on to individual producers who have exceeded their own quota. Milk quota is abolished on 31 March 2015 (see further below).

Quota was originally allocated to milk producers in the UK by reference to levels of production for 1983 and was attached both to the producer and to the producer's land in use for milk production at 1 April 1984 (his 'holding'). Originally it was only possible to transfer milk quota permanently to another producer as part of a disposal of all or part of the holding to which it was attached (*SI 1984 No 1047*). This could be by outright sale of the land or by use of a scheme by which a permanent transfer of the quota is achieved by granting a short lease of the land. From 1 April 1994, it is possible in limited circumstances to sell milk quota without selling the land (*SI 1994 No 160*).

HMRC consider that milk quota is an asset separate from the land to which it is attached, and does not constitute an interest in or right over land. The decision in *Cottle v Coldicott* (Sp C 40), [1995] SSCD 239 supports this view.

The taxpayer sold part of his quota using the scheme involving a short lease of land referred to above. The Special Commissioners held that the sale of milk quota amounted to the disposal of a separate asset. It was not a part disposal of the taxpayer's land, as he had contended, and neither were the proceeds a capital sum derived from the land within *TCGA 1992, s 22(1)* (see **10.2** CAPITAL SUMS DERIVED FROM ASSETS). Since the quota was a separate asset which had been allocated without cost in 1984, it followed that the allowable cost of acquisition was nil. The decision was followed in *Foxton v HMRC* (Sp C 485), [2005] SSCD 661.

For HMRC's view of the treatment of milk quota as a separate asset, see HMRC Capital Gains Manual CG77820. See also Revenue Tax Bulletin February 1993 pp 49–51 and December 1995 p 265. Where land and milk quota are acquired in a single transaction and the consideration is not allocated separately to each, an apportionment is required on a just and reasonable basis under *TCGA 1992, s 52(4)*.

For corporation tax purposes, milk quota is generally within the definition of an intangible fixed asset for the purposes of the intangible assets regime (see **15.14** COMPANIES — CORPORATE FINANCE AND INTANGIBLES). Broadly, milk quota acquired by a company from an unrelated party after 31 March 2002 is therefore outside the scope of corporation tax on chargeable gains (but see **15.14** COMPANIES — CORPORATE FINANCE AND INTANGIBLES for the detailed transitional provisions). A gain on disposal of milk quota not falling within that regime remains within the charge to corporation tax on chargeable gains (but see below as regards rollover relief).

Milk quota is a *fungible* asset, i.e. one which grows or diminishes as parts are acquired or disposed of but the individual parts of which cannot be separately identified. Acquisitions and disposals of quota are expressed in terms of a specific number of litres. Quota acquired in stages before 6 April 1998 formed a single asset for the purposes of both capital gains tax and corporation tax on chargeable gains. For the latter purposes, this treatment continues on and after that date (for acquisitions not falling within the corporation tax intangible assets regime — see above). Any quota allocated without cost on 1 April 1984 forms part of that asset but without contributing to its overall acquisition cost. Expenditure is allocated to a part disposal of the single asset in accordance with the formula in *TCGA 1992, s 42* (see **16.5** COMPUTATION OF GAINS AND LOSSES). For acquisitions and disposals on or after 6 April 2008, single asset treatment is reintroduced and the identification rules at **64.2** SHARES AND SECURITIES — IDENTIFICATION RULES apply. (HMRC Capital Gains Manual CG77901).

Abolition of milk quota

Milk quota is abolished with effect after 31 March 2015. Where a pool of milk quota is of negligible value, a negligible value claim (see **44.11** LOSSES) may be made to HMRC on or before that date. If no such claim is made there is a deemed disposal on the extinguishment of the asset resulting in an allowable loss equivalent to the amount incurred on acquiring the quota. See HMRC Brief 48/2014.

Tenant farmers

On the termination of a tenancy, the milk quota reverts to the landlord. The tenant and the landlord may agree compensation for the tenant's loss of milk quota. If not, the tenant is entitled to statutory compensation under *Agriculture Act 1986, s 13*. Where the compensation is paid under a contract, the time of the disposal is the time the contract is made. If the contract is conditional, it is the time the condition is satisfied. Where the compensation is statutory or is paid under a contractual agreement which does not provide for the reversion of the quota, the date of the disposal is the date of receipt of the compensation.

Tenant farmers require the consent of the landlord before selling milk quota. If the tenant makes a payment to the landlord in consideration of such consent the expenditure qualifies as a deduction in computing the chargeable gain on disposal of the milk quota. The landlord will have received a capital sum derived from an asset, taxable under *TCGA 1992, s 22(1)* (see **10.2** CAPITAL SUMS DERIVED FROM ASSETS).

(HMRC Capital Gains Manual CG77885, 77940).

Rollover relief etc.

For capital gains tax purposes, milk quota is a qualifying asset for rollover relief purposes (see **59.4** ROLLOVER RELIEF).

Milk quota is not regarded as a **72** WASTING ASSET (HMRC Capital Gains Manual CG77940). The rollover relief available for the exchange of joint interests in land also includes the parallel exchange of joint interests in milk quota (see **41.13** LAND).

Compensation payments

Compensation in respect of the temporary suspension of a proportion of quota is treated as a receipt of the farming trade, taxable as income. (HMRC Capital Gains Manual CG77920).

Compensation paid for a permanent reduction in milk quota is a capital sum derived from an asset, chargeable to capital gains tax under *TCGA 1992, s 22(1)* (see **10.2** CAPITAL SUMS DERIVED FROM ASSETS). (HMRC Capital Gains Manual CG77920 and Revenue Tax Bulletins May 1994 p 128, October 1997 p 474).

Bonus issue of Milk Marque shares to dairy farmers

In October 1998, milk producers who supplied Milk Marque Ltd in the year to 31 March 1998 were awarded a bonus consisting of preference shares (or in some cases loan stock) in the company. HMRC consider that the cost of acquisition of the shares or loan stock for capital gains tax purposes is equal to their nominal value. (Revenue Tax Bulletin August 1999 p 685).

Bookmakers' pitches

[7.10] A bookmaker's pitch is a specified position at a racecourse on which the bookmaker may erect a stand and take bets. HMRC take the view that the right to occupy a particular pitch at a particular racecourse is an asset for capital gains tax purposes. A disposal of such a right by way of auction, which is permitted with effect from 8 October 1998, is therefore a disposal of a chargeable asset. The date of disposal is the date on which the purchaser's bid is accepted. Where a pitch has not previously changed hands by way of auction, it will normally have no acquisition cost and no 31 March 1982 value. The exception is where the pitch was acquired by inheritance on or after 8 October 1998, in which case its acquisition cost to the legatee will be its market value at date of death, under the general rule at **19.2** DEATH.

A pitch does not fall within any of the classes of asset qualifying for ROLLOVER RELIEF (**59.4**).

(Revenue Tax Bulletin October 1999 pp 699, 700).

Domain names

[7.11] The sale of an internet domain name is a disposal of an asset for the purposes of capital gains tax and corporation tax on chargeable gains. The exception is where a business deals in domain names as, or as part of, its trade, in which case such sales contribute to its trading profits for income tax or corporation tax purposes. (Revenue Technical Note: Guide to the Tax Consequences of Trading over the Internet, November 2000).

Bitcoin and other cryptocurrencies

[7.12] Bitcoin is the world's first decentralised digital currency, otherwise known as a 'cryptocurrency'. HMRC consider that no special rules are required in relation to Bitcoin for tax purposes, and whether any profit or gain is chargeable or any loss is allowable will be looked at on a case-by-case basis taking into account the specific facts. If a profit or loss on a currency contract involving Bitcoin is not within trading profits or otherwise within the loan relationship rules, it would normally be taxable as a chargeable gain or allowable as a loss for corporation tax or capital gains tax purposes. (HMRC Brief 9/2014).

Image rights

[7.13] For a discussion of the legal status and capital gains tax treatment of 'image rights' see HMRC Capital Gains Manual CG68405-68440.

Single payment scheme payment entitlement

[7.14] The EU single payment scheme for farmers ceased on 31 December 2014 and is replaced by a new basic payment scheme. The CGT treatment of single payment scheme payment entitlement is as follows.

Scotland, Wales and Northern Ireland

All single payment scheme payment entitlement ceased to exist on 31 December 2014. HMRC accept that payment entitlement became of negligible value on 16 May 2014 because 15 May 2014 was the last day that the entitlement must have been held in order for a person to establish that they were eligible for a payment under the scheme. Accordingly, a negligible value claim (see **44.11** LOSSES) may be made to HMRC on or before 31 December 2014. If no such claim is made, a deemed disposal occurs on the entitlement ceasing to exist (and an allowable loss may arise equal to the acquisition cost). HMRC do not accept that payment entitlement was of negligible value before 16 May 2014.

England

In England the choice was made to continue to use single payment scheme payment entitlement in the basic payment scheme. As a result, such entitlement has not become of negligible value and did not cease to exist on 31 December 2014.

(HMRC Brief 48/2014).

See also **59.4** ROLLOVER RELIEF.

8

Assets held on 6 April 1965

Introduction	8.1
Quoted securities	8.2
Elections	8.3
Identification rules	8.4
Reorganisation, exchange etc. following partial election	8.5
Land reflecting development value	8.6
Other assets — time apportionment	8.7
Election	8.8
Identification rules for unquoted securities, commodities etc. where no election under **8.8** above	8.9
Time apportionment restrictions	8.10
Miscellaneous aspects	8.11
Capital allowances	8.11
Assets transferred to close companies	8.12
Key points	8.13

Cross-reference. See **9** ASSETS HELD ON 31 MARCH **1982** for the restricted circumstances in which disposals after 5 April 1988 of such assets will be assessed by reference to the provisions of this chapter.

Simon's Taxes. See **C2.610–C2.614**.

Introduction to assets held on 6 April 1965

[8.1] For the purposes of corporation tax on chargeable gains, assets held on 6 April 1965 (the original base date for the purposes of capital gains tax) are subject to special provisions contained in *TCGA 1992, Sch 2* and described in this chapter.

For capital gains tax purposes, the special provisions do not apply. The general re-basing rule for assets held on 31 March 1982 applies automatically without exception for capital gains tax purposes, so that special rules for assets held on 6 April 1965 are not required. The special rules in this chapter did, however, apply for capital gains tax purposes in relation to disposals before 6 April 2008. [*TCGA 1992, s 35(9)*].

For the purposes of the special provisions, assets may be divided into three categories.

(i) Quoted securities (see **8.2–8.5** below).
(ii) Land subsequently disposed of at a price including development value (see **8.6** below).
(iii) Other assets and miscellaneous aspects (see **8.7–8.12** below).

Groups of companies

The special provisions apply to the disposal of an asset by a company which is or has been a member of a group of companies (within **29.2** GROUPS OF COMPANIES), and which acquired the asset from another member of the group at a time when both were members of the group, as if all members of the group for the time being were the same person, and as if the acquisition or provision of the asset by the group, taken as a single person, had been the acquisition or provision of it by the member disposing of it. This does not apply where the disposing company is an investment trust or acquired the asset after 31 March 1980 from an investment trust. [*TCGA 1992, s 174(4)(5)*].

Quoted securities

[8.2] The following provisions apply only for the purposes of corporation tax on chargeable gains (see **8.1** above).

Subject to the election in **8.3** below, on a disposal of 'quoted securities' after 5 April 1965, computation of the gain or loss accruing is made:

(a) by reference to allowable expenditure computed according to the normal rules (i.e. cost/value at the *actual* date of acquisition and other allowable expenditure) (see **16.11** COMPUTATION OF GAINS AND LOSSES), *and*

(b) by reference to allowable expenditure, etc. calculated according to identical rules, except that market value at 6 April 1965 is treated as the acquisition cost. Market value at 6 April 1965 (except where special circumstances may affect the value, see *Hinchcliffe v Crabtree* HL 1971, 47 TC 419) is the greater of

   (i) a price half-way between the prices quoted in The Stock Exchange Daily Official List (or, for unit trusts, those published by the managers) and

   (ii) for shares and securities, the average of the highest and lowest prices for normal bargains, if any, on that day.

Of the computations under (a) and (b), the one which prevails is that which produces (after, if available, any indexation allowance) the smaller gain or the smaller loss. But if one computation produces a gain and the other a loss, the disposal is treated as giving rise to neither a chargeable gain nor an allowable loss.

[*TCGA 1992, Sch 2 para 2(1), Sch 11 para 6*].

Where the original cost of the shares is not known and no election (see **8.3** below) has been made, it is HMRC's practice to compute gains by reference to the value of the shares at 6 April 1965 and to disallow losses (computed on the same basis) altogether.

These provisions apply to '*quoted securities*', which are as follows.

(i) Shares and securities which on 6 April 1965, or at any time within six years prior to that date, had quoted market values on a 'recognised stock exchange' in the UK or elsewhere.

(ii) Interests in unit trusts (see **70** UNIT TRUSTS ETC.), the prices of which are published regularly by the scheme's managers.

Shares or securities issued to an employee on terms restricting his right to dispose of them are excluded.

[*TCGA 1992, Sch 2 para 1*].

'*Recognised stock exchange*' has its natural meaning. So far as the UK is concerned, it is understood that HMRC accept that all the stock exchanges in the UK during the six years ended on 6 April 1965 were within this meaning but that the Provincial Brokers Exchange was outside it.

Elections

[8.3] The taxpayer (or his personal representatives) may, however, elect (under *TCGA 1992, Sch 2 para 4*) that in respect of *all* disposals after 19 March 1968 (including those made before the election) of:

(a) fixed interest securities and preference shares, or
(b) other quoted securities etc., or
(c) both kinds of securities etc. under (a) and (b),

their actual cost be ignored and computations made by reference to their market value at 6 April 1965 only.

The election, which is irrevocable, must be made, by notice in writing to HMRC. An election for pooling may be made for the purposes of capital gains tax on or before the first anniversary of the 31st January next following the tax year in which the first relevant disposal is made. An election for the purposes of corporation tax may be made not later than two years after the end of the accounting period in which the first relevant disposal is made. In either case, HMRC may allow an extension. [*TCGA 1992, Sch 2 para 11*].

After 5 April 1985 (31 March 1985 for companies), another opportunity is available for an election to be made where the time limit given above has expired by reference to the first relevant disposal after 19 March 1968. The time limit is extended so as to apply by reference to the first relevant disposal after 5 April 1985 (31 March 1985 for companies).

'*Fixed interest security*' is as defined in **63.8** SHARES AND SECURITIES.

'*Preference share*' means any share the holder of which has a right to a dividend at a fixed rate but no other right to share in the profits of the company. Fixed rate dividends include those payable before 6 April 1973 and which varied at a rate fluctuating in accordance with the standard rate of income tax.

These provisions apply only for the purposes of corporation tax on chargeable gains (see **8.1** above).

Example

H Ltd acquired 3,000 U plc ordinary shares in 1962 for £15,000. Their market value was £10 per share on 6 April 1965 and £12 per share on 31 March 1982. In September 2017, H Ltd sells 2,000 of the shares for £40 per share. For the purpose only of this example, it is assumed that the indexation factor for March 1982 to September 2017 is 2.050.

	£	£	£
Sale proceeds	80,000	80,000	80,000
Cost	10,000		
6 April 1965 value		20,000	
31 March 1982 value			24,000
Unindexed gain	70,000	60,000	56,000
Indexation allowance			
£24,000 × 2.050	49,200	49,200	49,200
Indexed gain	£20,800	£10,800	£6,800
Chargeable gain			£6,800

Notes to the example

(1) The comparison is firstly between the gain arrived at by deducting cost and that arrived at by deducting 6 April 1965 value. The smaller of the two gains is taken. If, however, an election had been made under either *TCGA 1992, Sch 2 para 4* or *TCGA 1992, s 109(4)* for 6 April 1965 value to be used in computing all gains and losses on quoted shares held at that date, this comparison need not be made and the taxable gain, subject to (2) below, would be £10,800.

(2) The second comparison is between the figure arrived at in (1) above and the gain using 31 March 1982 value. As the latter is smaller, it is substituted for the figure in (1) above by virtue of *TCGA 1992, s 35(2)*. If, however, an election had been made under *TCGA 1992, s 35(5)* for 31 March 1982 value to be used in computing all gains and losses on assets held at that date, neither this comparison nor that in (1) above need be made and the taxable gain would still be £6,800.

(3) Indexation is based on 31 March 1982 value in all three calculations as this gives the greater allowance.

(4) All comparisons are between gains *after* indexation.

Groups of companies

An election does not cover quoted securities which a company acquired from another group company (see **29.2** GROUPS OF COMPANIES) on a disposal after 19 March 1968 (or, again, after 31 March 1985) but such securities continue to be covered by an election which the transferor company may have made. Where it is necessary to identify securities disposed of, earliest acquisitions are deemed to be disposed of first. An election by a company which is at the 'relevant time' the principal company of the group has effect as an election by any other company which at that time is a member of the group. No election may be made by any other company which is a member of the group at that time. The '*relevant time*' is the first occasion after 19 March 1968 (or, again, after 31 March 1985) when any company which is then a member of the group disposes of quoted securities of a kind covered by the election. These provisions apply notwithstanding that a company ceases to be a member of the group at any time after the relevant time. They do not apply to securities owned by a company which, after 19 March 1968 (or, again, after 31 March

1985) and before the relevant time, was not a member of the group and in relation to which either an election was made or no election was made within the time limit following a disposal.

[*TCGA 1992, s 109(4)(5), Sch 2 para 3, para 4(1)(2)(8)–(13), paras 5, 8*].

For the position as regards *partnerships*, see **50.16** PARTNERSHIPS.

Identification rules

[8.4] Where quoted securities of the same class are held on 6 April 1965, the identification rules for matching acquisitions with disposals depend on whether an election for 6 April 1965 market values under **8.3** above has been made or not. In addition, the rules are further governed by the general identification rules for securities etc. at **64** SHARES AND SECURITIES — IDENTIFICATION RULES. Consequently this paragraph should be read with those general rules. For the position where there has been a reorganisation or exchange etc. of quoted securities following an election under **8.3**(a) or (b) but not both, see **8.5** below. Where it is necessary to re-establish which shares remain following a disposal before the '1985 date' (see below), see the 2005/06 and earlier editions for the identification rules for disposals in the period before that date but on or after the '1982 date' (i.e. 6 April 1982 (1 April 1982 for companies)) and for the period before the '1982 date'. For disposals on or after 6 April 2008, these provisions do not apply for capital gains tax purposes (see **8.1** above), but they continue to apply for the purposes of corporation tax on chargeable gains.

After the '1985 date', the identification rules given in (a) or (b) below apply to quoted securities held on 6 April 1965 excluding any 'relevant securities' so held. The full definition of 'relevant securities' is given at **64.6** SHARES AND SECURITIES — IDENTIFICATION RULES as are the identification rules. So far as concerns quoted securities held on 6 April 1965, this definition is only relevant to securities within the accrued income scheme at **63.20** SHARES AND SECURITIES (broadly any government, public authority, or company loan stock). Government securities retain their own identification rules for disposals before 2 July 1986, being exempt from capital gains tax for disposals on or after that date.

(a) Where *no* election has been made, pre-7 April 1965 acquisitions are treated as disposed of on a 'last-in, first-out' basis and only identified with disposals after all post-6 April 1965 acquisitions have been identified under the general identification rules. See **64.3–63.6** SHARES AND SECURITIES — IDENTIFICATION RULES.
(b) Where an election *is* made, pre-7 April 1965 acquisitions (at 6 April 1965 market values) form part, or the whole, of the '1982 holding' which is treated as a single asset (but one which cannot grow by further acquisitions). See **64.5** SHARES AND SECURITIES — IDENTIFICATION RULES. Disposals are only identified with the '1982 holding' after any subsequent acquisitions have been identified.

The '*1985 date*' is 6 April 1985 (1 April 1985 for companies).

[*TCGA 1992, ss 104(3), 105, 106A, 107, 108, Sch 2 paras 2(2), 3, 4(3)–(7); TIOPA 2010, Sch 8 para 164*].

Reorganisation, exchange etc. following partial election

[8.5] Where an election has been made under 8.3(a) *or* under 8.3(b) above *but not both* and there is a disposal out of a 'new holding' (see definition below) following a reorganisation or exchange etc. of quoted securities held on 6 April 1965, the election applies according to the nature of the securities in the new holding, notwithstanding that it is to be treated as one with the 'original holding' and that the election would have applied differently to the original holding.

Where the election does cover the disposal out of the new holding, but does not cover quoted securities of the kind comprised in the original holding, the question of how much of the new holding derives from securities held on 6 April 1965, and how much derives from other quoted securities is decided on the assumption that an election does not apply.

Where the election does not cover a disposal out of the new holding, but does cover quoted securities of the kind comprised in the original holding, then, in computing the gain accruing on the disposal out of the new holding, the question of what remained undisposed of on any disposal out of the original holding is calculated on the footing that an election did not apply to that earlier disposal.

[*TCGA 1992, Sch 2 para 6*].

'*Original holding*' means securities held before and concerned in the reorganisation etc. and '*new holding*' means, in relation to any original holding, the shares in and debentures of the company which, following the reorganisation etc., represent the original holding, together with any remaining original holding. [*TCGA 1992, ss 126, 127*]. See **63.2** SHARES AND SECURITIES for full coverage of reorganisations etc. generally.

Note

Where (i) disposals are made on or after the '1982 date' (see **8.4** above) out of the new holding and (ii) there were disposals out of the original holding before the '1982 date', the legislation does not make clear whether the 'last-in, first-out' basis applying on or after the '1982 date' in respect of original shares held on 6 April 1965 (as under **8.4**(a) above) is the appropriate identification procedure for disposals in (ii) or if it is the 'first-in/first-out' basis applying before the 1982 date. In addition it should be noted that there is no provision to adjust the original *computation* of any gain arising on a disposal out of the original shares.

These provisions apply only for the purposes of corporation tax on chargeable gains (see **8.1** above).

Land reflecting development value

[8.6] If land in the UK held on 6 April 1965 is disposed of either:

(i) at a price exceeding 'current use value' (as defined and see *Morgan v Gibson* Ch D 1989, 61 TC 654) at the time of the disposal, or

(ii) if any 'material development' (as defined) has been carried out after 17 December 1973 by the disposer,

on the disposal, computations of the gain or loss accruing are made

(a) by reference to the original cost, or market value when acquired if appropriate — see **45** MARKET VALUE, and
(b) by reference to market value on 6 April 1965.

Of these two computations, the one which produces the smaller gain or the smaller loss prevails, but if one computation produces a gain and the other a loss, the result is treated as giving rise to neither gain nor loss. The provisions apply only if before 6 April 1965, expenditure was *incurred* which would otherwise have been deductible in computing the gain on the disposal. A deemed acquisition cost by virtue of *TCGA 1992, s 17* (or similar previous legislation) is 'expenditure incurred' for this purpose. See *Mashiter v Pearmain* CA 1984, 58 TC 334. [*TCGA 1992, Sch 2 paras 9–15*].

These provisions apply only for the purposes of corporation tax on chargeable gains (see **8.1** above).

Example

K Ltd sells a building plot, on which planning permission has just been obtained, in November 2017 for £200,000. The company acquired the plot in 1958 for £2,000. The market value was £5,000 at 6 April 1965 and £10,000 at 31 March 1982, and the current use value in November 2017 is £15,000. For the purpose only of this example, the indexation factor for March 1982 to November 2017 is taken to be 2.100.

	£	£	£
Sale proceeds	200,000	200,000	200,000
Cost	2,000		
Market value 6.4.65		5,000	
Market value 31.3.82			10,000
Unindexed gain	198,000	195,000	190,000
Indexation allowance			
£10,000 × 2.100	21,000	21,000	21,000
Gain after indexation	£177,000	£174,000	£169,000
Chargeable gain			£169,000

Notes to the example

(1) Time apportionment would have substantially reduced the gain of £177,000, using cost, such that re-basing to 31 March 1982 would have given a greater gain than that based on cost and would not therefore have applied. However, as the plot has been sold for a price in excess of its current use value, no time apportionment can be claimed.
(2) Gains are compared after applying the indexation allowance, which is based on 31 March 1982 value, this being greater than either cost or 6 April 1965 value.

(3) In this case, the gain is computed in accordance with the rules in **9 ASSETS HELD ON 31 MARCH 1982** as the gain by reference to 31 March 1982 value is lower than the lowest of the alternatives at (a) and (b) above.

See **41.8 LAND** for part disposals with development value of an estate of land acquired before 6 April 1965.

Other assets — time apportionment

[8.7] Special provisions apply to other assets not falling within **8.2–8.6** above (including unquoted shares and land not covered by **8.6** above) held on 6 April 1965. The provisions apply only for the purposes of corporation tax on chargeable gains (see **8.1** above).

Subject to **8.8** below, gains on disposals of such assets which are held on 6 April 1965 are apportioned (on the basis of relative costs) between the original asset and any additions to it, and are deemed to have arisen evenly over the period from acquisition (or addition), or from 6 April 1945 if later, to the date of disposal. Only the part of the gain or loss attributable, on this basis, to the period from 6 April 1965 to disposal is taxable or allowable. [*TCGA 1992, Sch 2 para 16*]. This basis is known as **time apportionment**.

According to HMRC Statement of Practice 3/82, indexation allowance, where available, is calculated and deducted before applying such apportionment, and the case of *Smith v Schofield* HL 1993, 65 TC 669 subsequently confirmed this practice.

Example

On 6 April 1953, A Ltd acquired 5,000 shares in C Ltd, an unquoted company, for £15,204. It sells these shares (its entire holding in the company) on 6 April 2017 for £75,000. The retail prices index for March 1982 is 79.44 and for April 2017 it is 270.6. No election for universal 31 March 1982 re-basing is made but the market value of the holding on that date is agreed at £17,000.

The chargeable gain is computed thus

Total period of ownership	64 years
Period after 6 April 1965	52 years
Unindexed gain	
£(75,000 – 15,204)	£59,796
Indexation allowance	
(270.6 – 79.44)/79.44 × £17,000	£40,908
Overall gain £(59,796 – 40,908)	£18,888
Chargeable gain	£18,888 × $^{52}/_{64}$ = £15,347
The gain by reference to 31 March 1982 value is	
£(75,000 – 17,000 – 40,908)	£17,092

31 March 1982 re-basing does not apply as a higher gain would thereby result. See also **8.8** below re election for 6 April 1965 value (not illustrated above).

Assume, however, that in April 1960, A Ltd, having discovered a defect in its title to the shares, incurred legal costs of £1,500 in order to correct it.

The gain would then be computed as follows

Overall gain (as revised)		
£75,000 – £(15,204 + 1,500 + 40,908)	£17,388	
Proportion of gain attributable to original expenditure (E(0))	£15,204/£16,704 × £17,388	£15,827
Proportion of gain attributable to enhancement expenditure (E(1))	£1,500/£16,704 × £17,388	£1,561

Period of ownership since 6 April 1965/Total period of ownership × E(0) = 52/64 × £15,827 = £12,859

Period of ownership since 6 April 1965/Total period of ownership since enhancement × E(1) = 52/57 × £1,561 = £1,424

Total chargeable gain £12,859 + £1,424 = £14,283

The gain by reference to 31 March 1982 value is again £17,092 so re-basing at that date does not apply.

The formulae for apportionment of gains are contained in *TCGA 1992, Sch 2 para 16* (whence the designations 'E(0)' and 'E(1)' are taken).

Where the original expenditure (compared with the enhancement expenditure) is disproportionately small having regard to the value of the asset immediately before the enhancement expenditure was incurred (or where there is no original expenditure) the *actual gain* attributable to the enhancement expenditure is substituted for the figure arrived at under the formula, and the balance is treated as attributable to original expenditure. This is done in practice by establishing as a fact what the proceeds for the asset would have been without any of the enhancement expenditure in question.

HMRC are prepared to accept a period of tenancy prior to a period of ownership as part of the time apportionment denominator e.g. where farm land was gifted by a father to his son in 1956 and subsequently sold by the son in 1980, if the son had been a tenant since 1945 a time apportionment factor of 15/(20+15) would apply rather than 15/(15+9). The existence of an ordinary tenancy is sufficient to allow the extended time apportionment formulae to apply even though no formal lease or tenancy agreement was in existence, provided sufficient rent was paid. Any sale of land, including buildings, follows the same pattern but any 'wasted cost' of a lease has to be added to the cost of the 'freehold reversion'. (CCAB Statement TR 500, 10 March 1983).

For the circumstances in which HMRC will require a valuation of the asset transferred where a claim for hold-over relief is made, see **36.2** HOLD-OVER RELIEFS.

Election

[8.8] Alternatively (except in the case of an asset which has been the subject of a previous part disposal after 5 April 1965; see **16.5** COMPUTATION OF GAINS AND LOSSES) the taxpayer may elect, by notice in writing that the gain should be computed by reference to the market value at 6 April 1965 of the asset disposed of. An election for the purposes of capital gains tax must be made on or before the first anniversary of 31st January following the tax year in which the disposal is made. In the case of corporation tax, it must be made within two years after the end of the accounting period in which the disposal is made.

HMRC have discretion to extend the time limit for instances of which see *Whitaker v Cameron* Ch D 1982, 56 TC 97, **4.13** ANTI-AVOIDANCE and **29.7** GROUPS OF COMPANIES. The election is irrevocable, and HMRC will not normally discuss a valuation before an election is made. On a part disposal, an election will affect all later such disposals, or the ultimate disposal, made by the same person.

[*TCGA 1992, Sch 2 para 17(1)(3)–(5)*].

If the election to use 6 April 1965 value results in a gain, it is valid irrespective of all other figures (and the election will thus be to the detriment of the taxpayer if the time apportionment basis would have produced a smaller gain or a loss). If the election results in a loss, that loss is allowable, unless:

(i) there is a smaller loss by reference to cost in which case that smaller loss is taken (and this means that the full loss by reference to cost is taken instead of the time apportionment loss, so that the election has been beneficial to the taxpayer), or
(ii) there is a gain by reference to cost, in which case the disposal will be treated as producing neither a gain nor a loss.

[*TCGA 1992, Sch 2 para 17(2)*].

Part disposals out of an estate of land may be able to be treated as disposals of separate assets and thus allow 6 April 1965 value to be used in relation only to parts. See **41.8** LAND.

Identification rules for unquoted securities, commodities etc. where no election under 8.8 above

[8.9] On the realisation of part of an unquoted shareholding or other fungible assets, any shares held on 6 April 1965 are not pooled but are identified with shares disposed of on a last-in, first-out basis. [*TCGA 1992, Sch 2 para 18*]. For disposals on or after 6 April 2008, these provisions do not apply for capital gains tax purposes (see **8.1** above and **64** SHARES AND SECURITIES — IDENTIFICATION RULES), but they continue to apply for the purposes of corporation tax on chargeable gains.

Post-6 April 1965 acquisitions are treated as in **64** SHARES AND SECURITIES — IDENTIFICATION RULES.

Time apportionment restrictions

[8.10] Where, after the date of acquisition and before 6 April 1965,

(a) there was a *reorganisation* of a company's share capital (see **63.2** SHARES AND SECURITIES), time apportionment is not available. In such a case, 6 April 1965 value must be used. [*TCGA 1992, Sch 2 para 19(1)*], or

(b) a *part disposal* was made, time apportionment is calculated from the date of that part disposal by reference to market value at that time. [*TCGA 1992, Sch 2 para 16(7)*].

Where, after 5 April 1965,

(i) there is a *reorganisation* of a company's share capital, the new holding is treated as having been sold and immediately re-acquired at that time by the owner at the then market value. The amount of any gain on the disposal of the new holding, or part thereof, is computed by time apportioning any gain or loss over the period ending at that time and bringing into account the full gain or loss from that time to the date of disposal, computed by reference to the ultimate disposal value and the aforesaid market value. [*TCGA 1992, Sch 2 para 19(2)*], or

(ii) there is a *part disposal*, the asset is treated as having been sold and immediately re-acquired at that time by the owner at the then market value. The amount of any gain on the disposal is calculated as under (i) above. [*TCGA 1992, Sch 2 para 16(8)*].

The provisions under (a) and (i) above do not apply (i.e. normal time apportionment applies) in relation to a reorganisation of a company's share capital if the new holding differs only from the original shares in being a different number of shares of the same class as the original shares. [*TCGA 1992, Sch 2 para 19(3)*]. Following the decision in *CIR v Beveridge* CS 1979, 53 TC 178, HMRC do not consider this provision to apply where the shares comprised in the new holding are in a different company from the old shares (HMRC Statement of Practice 14/79). In *Unilever (UK) Holdings Ltd v Smith CA*, 2002 STI 1806, in which a scheme of arrangement involved the cancellation of preference shares without altering the rights attaching to the ordinary shares, it was held that there had been no 'reorganisation' and that, consequently, (i) above could not apply.

Where (a) or (i) above has applied, gains chargeable on the disposal of the entire new holding are limited to the actual gains realised. Separate transactions in the year or accounting period are treated as a single disposal provided the entire holding is so disposed of. (HMRC Extra-Statutory Concession D10).

Where the provisions in (ii) above would normally apply to unquoted shares in a winding-up, the time apportionment fraction determined at the date of the first distribution may be able to be used to calculate the gain on each additional distribution without further adjustment (HMRC Statement of Practice D3). See also **63.12** SHARES AND SECURITIES.

Part disposals out of an estate of land may be able to be treated as disposals of separate assets and so prevent the operation of (b) and (ii) above. See **41.8** LAND.

Miscellaneous aspects

Capital allowances

[8.11] Where the gain on the disposal of an asset is calculated by reference to its value on 6 April 1965, the restriction of relief given for losses accruing on assets which have qualified for capital allowances (*TCGA 1992, s 41*, see

16.13(i) COMPUTATION OF GAINS AND LOSSES) and the provisions relating to wasting assets qualifying for capital allowances (*TCGA 1992, s 47*, see **72.2** WASTING ASSETS) apply as if the capital allowances for 1965/66 and subsequent years were allowances in respect of expenditure incurred on the asset on 6 April 1965. [*TCGA 1992, Sch 2 para 20*].

Assets transferred to close companies

[8.12] Where, at any time, a person who has 'control' of a 'close company', or a person 'connected' with him, transfers an asset to the company, and subsequently the first person (or any person with a 'substantial holding' of shares in the company) disposes of shares in circumstances such that the chargeable gain is to be determined by time apportionment, to the extent that the gain accruing on the disposal is attributable to a profit on the asset transferred, the shares are deemed to have been acquired at the date when the asset was transferred. The provisions do not apply where a loss accrues on the disposal. [*TCGA 1992, Sch 2 para 21*].

'*Control*' is as given by *CTA 2010, ss 450, 451*. '*Close company*' has the meaning given by *CTA 2010, ss 439–454*. '*Connected*' is as given at **17** CONNECTED PERSONS. '*Substantial holding*' is not defined.

Key points on assets held on 6 April 1965

[8.13] Points to consider are as follows.

- Special provisions apply in calculating a capital gain or loss of a company where an asset was held on 6 April 1965. These rules do not apply to non-corporates.
- The provisions apply to three categories of assets: (i) quoted securities; (ii) land reflecting development value; and (iii) other assets.
- For disposals or assets in categories (i) or (ii) generally the gain or loss is calculated taking into account the original costs as well as the 6 April 1965 value and the 31 March 1982 values. The lowest gain is brought into charge or the lowest loss is allowable.
- For other assets, the gain or loss is generally calculated either by reference to the 31 March 1982 value or by time apportionment between the periods up to and after 5 April 1965.
- There are provisions that allow for an election to just use the April 1965 market value. Such an election is irrevocable and binds a spouse or company where the assets were transferred under the no gain no loss provisions. Alternatively, an irrevocable election can be made to use the 31 March 1982 value of all assets held at that date.
- The tax computations may include a valuation. If the valuation is an estimate this should be explained on the corporation tax return and if this figure is to be replaced in the future an indication of

when it will be replaced should be given. Failure to disclose this could result in a penalty for the company.

9

Assets held on 31 March 1982

Introduction	**9.1**
General re-basing rule	**9.2**
Election for universal re-basing at 31 March 1982	**9.3**
Excluded disposals	**9.4**
Groups of companies	**9.5**
Previous no gain/no loss disposals	**9.6**
Supplementary provisions	**9.7**
Captial allowances	**9.7**
Part disposals etc.	**9.8**
Assets derived from other assets	**9.9**
Time apportionment of pre-6 April 1965 gains and losses	**9.10**
Deferred charges on gains before 31 March 1982	**9.11**
Key points	**9.12**

Cross-references. See **64.5** SHARES AND SECURITIES — IDENTIFICATION RULES for identification of certain share pools held by companies at 31 March 1982 and by others at 5 April 1982; **50.7, 50.16** PARTNERSHIPS for partnership transactions involving assets held on 31 March 1982.

Simon's Taxes. See C2.6.

Introduction to assets held on 31 March 1982

[9.1] Subject to certain exceptions, disposals of assets which were held on 31 March 1982 by the person making the disposal are 're-based' by reference to the market value of the assets on that date; see **9.2** below. Where indexation allowance is applicable (see below), re-basing applies to both the unindexed gain and the indexation allowance.

Capital gains tax

For capital gains tax purposes, re-basing applies automatically and with no exceptions. For disposals before 6 April 2008, the same exceptions applied as for corporation tax (see below) and the same irrevocable election for indexation to apply to all assets regardless of the exceptions could be made. The 50% reduction mentioned below for certain deferred gains also applied for disposals before 6 April 2008.

Corporation tax

For corporation tax purposes, rebasing applies subject to exceptions where its application would result in a larger gain or loss. The company may irrevocably elect (with one exception mentioned in **9.3** below), and subject to the modification in **9.2** below concerning certain disposals of 'oil industry assets', for such re-basing to apply to all assets held on 31 March 1982 regardless of the exceptions; see **9.3** below.

A 50% reduction is made in taxing certain deferred gains (except, in certain cases, where the deferred gain is never deemed to accrue at all) where such gains are wholly or partly attributable to an increase in value of an asset before 31 March 1982; see **9.11** below.

General re-basing rule

[9.2] The general re-basing rule is that on a disposal of an asset held on 31 March 1982 it is to be assumed that the asset was sold on the last-mentioned date by the person making the disposal and immediately reacquired by him at its market value on that date.

For capital gains tax purposes (i.e. in relation to disposals by individuals, trustees and personal representatives), the general rule applies without any exceptions (see **9.1** above). The exceptions below apply for the purposes of corporation tax on chargeable gains.

[*TCGA 1992, s 35(1)–(2A)*].

Indexation allowance

Indexation allowance on the disposal of an asset held on 31 March 1982 is calculated, without need for a claim, on the assumption that the asset was sold on the last-mentioned date by the person making the disposal and immediately reacquired by him at its market value on that date. [*TCGA 1992, s 55(1)*]. Except where an irrevocable election as in **9.3** below has effect and subject to the modification below concerning certain disposals of 'oil industry assets', neither this provision nor the general re-basing rule of *TCGA 1992, s 35(1)(2)* above is to apply for the purposes of calculating indexation allowance in a case where that allowance would be greater if they did not apply. [*TCGA 1992, s 55(2)*]. Note that indexation allowance is only available for the purposes of corporation tax on chargeable gains (having been abolished for capital gains tax purposes for disposals on or after 6 April 2008). See **38.1** INDEXATION.

Exceptions to general rule

For corporation tax purposes the following exceptions to the general rule apply. They are, however, subject to the irrevocable election in **9.3** below and to the modification below concerning certain disposals of 'oil industry assets'.

The exceptions (often referred to as the 'kink test') are where:

(a) a gain would accrue on the disposal if the general rule applied, and either a smaller gain or a loss would accrue if it did not, or
(b) a loss would accrue if the general rule applied, and either a smaller loss or a gain would accrue if it did not, or
(c) either on the facts of the case or by virtue of the provisions for assets held on 6 april 1965 (8) in *TCGA 1992, Sch 2*, neither a gain nor a loss would accrue if the general rule did not apply, or
(d) where, under *TCGA 1992, ss 195B, 195C* or *195E* (oil licence swaps) the disposal gives rise to neither a gain nor a loss, or
(e) the disposal is one within the 'no gain/no loss provisions' as in **9.6** below.

[*TCGA 1992, s 35(3)*].

Where the effect of the general re-basing rule would be to substitute a loss for a gain or a gain for a loss, but under (a)–(e) the application of that rule is excluded, it is to be assumed in relation to the disposal that the asset was acquired for a consideration such that, on the disposal, neither a gain nor a loss accrues. [*TCGA 1992, s 35(4)*].

Valuations

Shares etc.

Where, for the purposes of the re-basing and indexation provisions above, it is necessary to determine the market value of shares or securities of the same class in any company on 31 March 1982, all the shares or securities held at that date will be valued as a single holding whether they were acquired on or before 6 April 1965 or after that date. If the shares or securities in the disposal concerned represent some but not all of those valued at 31 March 1982 then the allowable cost or indexation allowance as appropriate will be based on the proportion that the shares or securities disposed of bears to the total holding at 31 March 1982 (HMRC Extra-Statutory Concession D34). See also **9.6** below for HMRC's practice as to the valuation of shares deemed held on 31 March 1982 by reason of 'no gain/no loss disposals' since that date.

Where a valuation at 31 March 1982 of unquoted shares is required for a number of shareholders, all of whom agree to be bound by the valuation, HMRC's Shares and Assets Valuation may initiate valuation procedures before receiving a formal request to do so from the tax office, provided that a full list of the company's shareholders and the size of their holdings, both at 31 March 1982 and at the date of disposal, is supplied, together with details of the tax offices involved, if available. (Revenue Press Release 18 November 1991).

Land and buildings

Companies and groups of companies may ask HMRC to agree the value of land and buildings held by them at 31 March 1982 in advance of a statutory need for such valuations (the 'Pre-disposal Portfolio Valuation Scheme'). The application should extend to the entire property portfolio of the company or group (but see below as regards part portfolios). The service is available only if the company or group have at least 30 properties held since 31 March 1982 or fewer such properties but with an aggregate current value greater than £20 million. Companies must provide values for checking, prepared by qualified valuers (whether independent or in-house). Companies may obtain further information on this service from HMRC, Land Portfolio Valuation Unit, 5th Floor, Sherbourne House, 1 Manor House Drive, Coventry, CV1 2TG. (Revenue News Release BN2G, 21 March 2000). Further details are given in Revenue Tax Bulletin October 2003 pp 1064, 1065. Part portfolios are admissible if they are clearly distinguishable from other property held and they meet the minimum size requirement; a portfolio which includes overseas as well as UK properties is admissible but only the values of the UK properties can be agreed. The information required on initial application is summarised in Revenue Tax Bulletin October 2003 pp 1064, 1065. Using the service does not prevent a company from agreeing individual valuations, either under normal procedures or using the pre-return valuation service (see **58.19** RETURNS), if it sells a property before the portfolio valuations have been agreed (Revenue Tax Bulletin February 2002 p 918).

A further scheme (the 'Multiple Land Valuation Scheme') is available to taxpayers (including companies) who dispose of 30 or more interests in land in a single tax year or company accounting period. (A group of companies is considered together to determine if the threshold has been reached.) The scheme involves a sampling process carried out by the Land Portfolio Valuation Unit of the HMRC Valuation Office Agency and designed to avoid, if possible, the need to agree individual valuations for all properties disposed of. Further information is available at Revenue Tax Bulletin February 2002 pp 917, 918 and by contacting Land Portfolio Valuation Unit, 5th Floor, Sherbourne House, 1 Manor House Drive, Coventry, CV1 2TG (Tel. 03000–503983).

Example 1

Robbie sells an asset on 25 April 2017 for £200,000. He had purchased the asset in 1979 for £50,000, and its value at 31 March 1982 was £42,000. The chargeable gain on the asset is computed as follows.

	£
Sale proceeds	200,000
31.3.1982 value	42,000
Chargeable gain	£158,000

Note

(a) As, for capital gains tax purposes, re-basing applies without any exceptions, the 31 March 1982 value is used in the computation even though it is less than the original cost.

Example 2

An asset (which is neither tangible movable property nor otherwise exempt) was acquired by a company for £900 in 1980 and, after having been held continuously by the same company, is disposed of in July 2017. For *illustration purposes*, the indexation factor is taken to be 200%. The disposal proceeds are £3,900. The corporation tax consequences, for differing 31 March 1982 values, are as follows. 'N/A' means that indexation allowance is not applicable and 'NGNL' means that the disposal is treated as giving rise to neither a gain nor a loss.

Example 2A

	(1)	(2)
	£	£
Sale proceeds	3,900	3,900
(1) Cost; (2) 31.3.1982 value	900	1,000

	(1)	(2)
	£	£
Unindexed gain	3,000	2,900
Indexation allowance		
at 200% of higher of (1) and (2)	2,000	2,000
Gain arising	£1,000	£900
Chargeable gain		£900

Example 2B

	(1)	(2)
	£	£
Sale proceeds	3,900	3,900
(1) Cost; (2) 31.3.1982 value	900	1,400
Unindexed gain	3,000	2,500
Indexation allowance		
at 200% of higher of (1) and (2)	2,800	N/A
Gain/NGNL arising	£200	£NGNL

The disposal is treated as giving rise to neither a gain nor a loss. The corresponding acquisition is unaffected by this treatment.

Example 2C

	(1)	(2)
	£	£
Sale proceeds	3,900	3,900
(1) Cost; (2) 31.3.1982 value	900	800
Unindexed gain	3,000	3,100
Indexation allowance		
at 80% of higher of (1) and (2)	1,800	1,800
Gain arising	£1,200	£1,300
Chargeable gain	£1,200	

Example 2D

	(1)	(2)
	£	£
Sale proceeds	3,900	3,900
(1) Cost; (2) 31.3.1982 value	900	5,000
Unindexed gain/(Loss)	3,000	(1,100)
Indexation allowance		
at 80% of higher of (1) and (2)	N/A	N/A
NGNL/(Loss) arising	NGNL	£(1,100)

The disposal is treated as giving rise to neither a gain nor a loss. The corresponding acquisition is unaffected by this treatment.

Example 3

An asset (which is neither tangible movable property, land with development value, quoted securities nor otherwise exempt) was acquired by a company in 1960 for £400. After having been held continuously by the company, the asset is completely destroyed in July 2017. For *illustration purposes*, the indexation factor is taken to be 200%. The asset was under-insured and, later in the month of disposal, £1,900 only was recovered from the insurers. The company elects for valuation at 6 April 1965, which value is later agreed with HMRC to be £4,000. The value at 31 March 1982 was similarly agreed at £1,700.

	(1)	(2)
	£	£
Insurance proceeds	3,900	3,900
(1) Cost; (2) 6.4.1965 value	400	4,000
	3,500	(100)
Indexation allowance		
at 200% of 31.3.1982 value (£1,700) for (1) only	3,400	N/A
Gain/(Loss) arising	£100	£(100)

Re-basing at 31 March 1982 does not apply since, under *TCGA 1992, Sch 2 para 17(2)* (see **8.8** ASSETS HELD ON 6 APRIL **1965**), the disposal is deemed to have given rise to neither a gain nor a loss. The corresponding acquisition is unaffected by this treatment.

Election for universal re-basing at 31 March 1982

[9.3] If a company so elects, disposals made by it (including any made by it before the election) after 5 April 1988 of assets which it held on 31 March 1982 will all have the general re-basing rule of *TCGA 1992, s 35(1)(2)* in **9.2** above applied to them regardless of the exclusion of that rule that might otherwise apply under *TCGA 1992, s 35(3)*.

Similarly in such a case, indexation allowance will always be calculated under the equivalent provision of *TCGA 1992, s 55(1)* as in **9.2** above regardless of the exclusion of that provision that might otherwise apply under *TCGA 1992, s 55(2)*.

[*TCGA 1992, s 35(5), s 55(2)*].

An election is irrevocable and must be made by notice in writing to HMRC at any time before 6 April 1990 or at any time during the period beginning with the time of the first disposal after 5 April 1988 of an asset held on 31 March 1982 or treated (see **9.6** below) as so held ('*the first relevant disposal*') and ending within two years after the end of the accounting period in which the disposal is made or such later period as HMRC may allow. An election made by a company in one capacity does not cover disposals made by it in another capacity. Adjustments as required may be made, whether by way of discharge or repayment of tax, the making of assessments or otherwise, to give effect to an election. [*TCGA 1992, s 35(6)–(8)*].

Time limit for elections — HMRC practice

HMRC will always exercise their discretion to extend the time limit for an election to at least the date on which the statutory time limit would expire if certain disposals did not count as a first relevant disposal. There are three such kinds of disposal, as follows.

(1) Disposals on which the gain would not be chargeable by virtue of a particular statutory provision. The main examples of these provisions are as follows.
  (a) Private cars (see **25.11** EXEMPTIONS AND RELIEFS).
  (b) Chattels, except commodity futures and foreign currency, worth less than the chattel exemption (see **25.4** EXEMPTIONS AND RELIEFS).
  (c) Chattels which are wasting assets, except plant and machinery used in business and commodity futures (see **25.4** EXEMPTIONS AND RELIEFS).
  (d) Non-marketable government securities (see **25.15** EXEMPTIONS AND RELIEFS).
  (e) Gilt-edged securities and qualifying corporate bonds, except ones received in exchange for shares or other securities (see **28** GOVERNMENT SECURITIES and **54** QUALIFYING CORPORATE BONDS).
  (f) Life assurance policies and deferred annuity contracts, unless purchased from a third party (see **43.1** LIFE ASSURANCE POLICIES AND DEFERRED ANNUITIES).
  (g) Foreign currency acquired for personal or family expenditure abroad (see **25.8** EXEMPTIONS AND RELIEFS).
  (h) Rights of compensation for a wrong or injury suffered by an individual in his person, profession or vocation (see **25.25** EXEMPTIONS AND RELIEFS).
  (i) Debts, not on a security, held by the original creditor, his personal representative or his legatee (see **25.5** EXEMPTIONS AND RELIEFS).
  (j) Business expansion scheme shares issued after 18 March 1986 for which relief has been given and not withdrawn (see **25.22** EXEMPTIONS AND RELIEFS).
  (k) Gifts of eligible property, including works of art, for the benefit of the public (see, **25.41** EXEMPTIONS AND RELIEFS).
  (l) Decorations for valour or gallantry (see **25.6** EXEMPTIONS AND RELIEFS).
  (m) Betting winnings (see **25.21** EXEMPTIONS AND RELIEFS).
  (n) A right to or to any part of an allowance, annuity or capital sum from a superannuation fund or any other annuity (but not under a deferred annuity policy) or annual payments received under a covenant which is not secured on property (see **25.3** EXEMPTIONS AND RELIEFS).

(2) Disposals which, in practice, do not give rise to a chargeable gain or allowable loss. The main examples of these disposals are as follows.
  (a) Withdrawals from building society accounts.
  (b) The disposal of an individual's private residence where the whole of the gain is exempt under *TCGA 1992, s 223(1)* (see **53.2** PRIVATE RESIDENCES).

(c) Disposals which give rise to neither a chargeable gain nor an allowable loss by virtue of the statutory 'no gain/no loss' provisions listed at *TCGA 1992, s 35(3)(d)* (see **9.6** below).

(3) Excluded disposals (see **9.4** below).

As sterling is not an asset for capital gains tax purposes (see **7.2** ASSETS), a disposal of it cannot be a first relevant disposal.

Where a company holds assets in more than one capacity (for example, as trustee, partner or member of a European Economic Interest Grouping), there will be a first relevant disposal and a separate time limit for each group of assets which the company holds in a different capacity. See also **50.16** PARTNERSHIPS.

Where a company which is non-UK resident on 6 April 1988 makes a disposal which would otherwise count as a first relevant disposal between that date and the date on which it first becomes UK resident, HMRC will give sympathetic consideration to extending the time limit to the end of the second accounting period after that in which the first disposal is made *after becoming UK resident*. In other words, the disposal made while non-resident may be disregarded at the discretion of HMRC.

There are a variety of other circumstances where, having regard to the facts of each case, HMRC will or may exercise their discretion to extend the statutory time limit.

(HMRC Statement of Practice 4/92).

In circumstances other than those covered by SP 4/92, HMRC may accept a late election by exercising its collection and management powers. In exercising those powers, HMRC adopt the same principles as they apply to late claims — see **67.1** TIME LIMITS — FIXED DATES. (HMRC Capital Gains Manual CG13800, 16780).

HMRC point out that in special cases elections need to be made by a person other than the person assessed. In the case of an assessment under *TCGA 1992, s 13* (charge on UK resident shareholder of an overseas resident company — see **49.7** OVERSEAS MATTERS), the election needs to be made by the company concerned. (HMRC Capital Gains Manual CG16760).

Excluded disposals

[9.4] An election does not cover a disposal of (or of an interest in):

- plant or machinery;
- an asset which the person making the disposal held at any time for the purposes of or in connection with a trade or part of a trade involving the working of a 'source of mineral deposits' (within *CAA 2001, s 394*);
- a licence under *Petroleum Act 1998, Pt I* (or earlier corresponding legislation) or *Petroleum (Production) Act (Northern Ireland) 1964*; or
- for disposals after 21 January 1990, 'shares' which, on 31 March 1982, were 'unquoted' and derived their value, or the greater part thereof, directly or indirectly from 'oil exploration or exploitation assets'

situated in the UK or a 'designated area' or from such assets and 'oil exploration or exploitation rights' taken together (the quoted terms having the meanings given by the legislation).

However, disposals within the first two of these four categories are not excluded unless a capital allowance in respect of any expenditure attributable to the asset has been made to the person making the disposal or would have been made to him had he made a claim. Where that person acquired the asset on a 'no gain/no loss disposal' (see **9.6** below), references in the foregoing to the person making the disposal are references to that person, the person who last acquired the asset other than on a no gain/no loss disposal or any person who subsequently acquired the asset on such a disposal.

[*TCGA 1992, Sch 3 para 7; Petroleum Act 1998, Sch 4 para 32*].

For capital gains tax purposes the general re-basing rule at **9.2** above applies to the above assets automatically and without exceptions.

Groups of companies

[9.5] Where a member of a group of companies disposes of an asset acquired by it from another group member after 5 April 1988 and the no gain/no loss basis of *TCGA 1992, s 171* applied to the acquisition (see **29.3** GROUPS OF COMPANIES and **9.6** below), an election made by the transferee company does not apply to the disposal, and, whether or not an election is made by that company, the making of such an election by the transferor company applies to the ultimate disposal made by the transferee company. Where the transferor company also acquired the asset after 5 April 1988 and *TCGA 1992, s 171* applied to that acquisition, an election made by it does not have effect on the ultimate disposal, but an election made by the last company by which the asset was acquired after 5 April 1988 otherwise than on an acquisition to which *TCGA 1992, s 171* applied or, if there is no such company, the company which held the asset on 5 April 1988, does have effect on the ultimate disposal. [*TCGA 1992, Sch 3 para 2*].

Election by principal company

Only a company which is the 'principal company' of a 'group' (for both of which see **29.2** GROUPS OF COMPANIES) may make an election unless the company did not become a group member until after the 'relevant time'. For this purpose the time limit for the making of an election (see **9.3** above) applies with the modification that a reference to 'the first relevant disposal' is a reference to the first disposal after 5 April 1988 of an asset held on 31 March 1982 by a company which is *either* a group member but not an 'outgoing company' in relation to the group *or* an 'incoming company' in relation to the group.

An election made by the principal company also has effect as one made by any other company which is a group member at the relevant time. This treatment does not, however, extend to a company which, in some period after 5 April 1988 and before the relevant time, is not a member of the group if during that period the company makes a disposal of an asset which it held on 31 March 1982 and the time limit for the making of an election expires without an election having been made. However, the effect of an election continues to extend to a company notwithstanding that it ceases to be a group member after the relevant time except where it is an outgoing company in relation to the group and the election relating to the group is made after it ceases to be a group member. [*TCGA 1992, Sch 3 para 8, para 9(3)*].

'*The relevant time*', in relation to a group, is the earliest of: the first time when any company which is then a group member, and is not an outgoing member in relation to the group, makes a disposal after 5 April 1988 of an asset which it held on 31 March 1982; the time immediately following the first occasion when a company which is an incoming company in relation to the group becomes a group member; and the time when an election is made by the principal company. [*TCGA 1992, Sch 3 para 9(1)*].

'*Incoming company*', in relation to a group, means a company which makes its first disposal after 5 April 1988 of an asset which it held on 31 March 1982 at a time when it is not a group member, and which becomes a group member before the expiry of the time limit for the making of an election which would apply to it and at a time when no such election has been made.

'*Outgoing company*', in relation to a group, means a company which ceases to be a group member before the expiry of the time limit for the making of an election which would apply to it and at a time when no such election has been made. [*TCGA 1992, Sch 3 para 9(2)*].

See HMRC Capital Gains Manual CG46330–46395 for consideration of the above provisions (including extension of time limits in certain cases).

Previous no gain/no loss disposals

[9.6] For corporation tax purposes, where:

(a) a person makes a disposal, other than one within the 'no gain/no loss provisions', of an asset which he acquired after 31 March 1982, and
(b) the disposal by which he acquired the asset and any previous disposal of the asset after 31 March 1982 was a no gain/no loss disposal,

he is treated for the purposes of the re-basing provisions of *TCGA 1992, s 35* and the equivalent provisions for indexation allowance of *TCGA 1992, s 55(1)* in **9.2** and **9.3** above as having held the asset on 31 March 1982. [*TCGA 1992, ss 52A, 55(5)(6)(a), Sch 3 para 1*].

HMRC have confirmed that where a person is treated as having held an asset on 31 March 1982 under these provisions, enhancement expenditure on the asset incurred after 31 March 1982 by a previous owner may be taken into account for indexation and re-basing purposes on a disposal by the current owner (HMRC Capital Gains Manual CG16880; Revenue Tax Bulletin, August 1992, p.32).

For capital gains tax purposes (but not corporation tax purposes), in relation to disposals on or after 6 April 2008, where:

- a person makes a disposal (including a no gain/no loss disposal) of an asset which he acquired after 31 March 1982 and before 6 April 2008,

- the disposal by which he acquired the asset and any previous disposal of the asset after 31 March 1982 was a disposal on which, under any enactment, neither a gain nor a loss accrued to the person making the disposal, and
- the re-basing provisions of *TCGA 1992, s 35* did not apply to the disposal by which he acquired the asset,

it is assumed that the re-basing provisions did apply to that disposal and that *TCGA 1992, s 56(2)* (deemed consideration on no gain/no loss disposal — see **38.4** INDEXATION) applied accordingly. [*TCGA 1992, s 35A*]. The effect of this provision is that, in computing the gain or loss on the post-5 April 2008 disposal, the allowable expenditure includes the value of the asset at 31 March 1982 and the indexation allowance due for the period from that date to the date on which the person making the post-5 April 2008 disposal acquired the asset (or April 1998 if earlier). The provision does not affect the position of the person from whom the person making the post-5 April 2008 disposal acquired the asset.

No gain/no loss provisions

The '*no gain/no loss provisions*' are the following enactments (being enactments by virtue of which neither a gain nor a loss accrues).

(i) *TCGA 1992, s 58* (transfers between spouses living together, see **46.5** MARRIED PERSONS AND CIVIL PARTNERS), *s 73* (reversion of settled property to settlor on death of person entitled to life interest, see **62.18** SETTLEMENTS), *s 139* (company reconstructions, see **14.11** COMPANIES), *s 140A* (transfer or division of UK business between companies in different EC member states, see **49.13** OVERSEAS MATTERS), *s 140E* (European cross-border merger: assets left within UK tax charge, see **49.15** OVERSEAS MATTERS), *s 171* (intra-group disposals of assets, see **29.3** GROUPS OF COMPANIES), *s 172* (transfer of UK branch or agency before 1 April 2000, see **49.3** OVERSEAS MATTERS), *s 211* (insurance business transfer schemes), *s 215* (amalgamation of building societies, see **14.11** COMPANIES), *s 216* (transfer of building society's business to company, see **14.11** COMPANIES), *s 217A* (transfer of assets on incorporation of registered friendly society, see **25.51** EXEMPTIONS AND RELIEFS), *s 271D* (disposal of assets on union, amalgamation or transfer of engagements of industrial and provident societies etc., see **14.11** COMPANIES), *ss 218–220* (housing associations, see **25.53** EXEMPTIONS AND RELIEFS), *s 221* (transfers before 1 April 2013 under harbour reorganisation schemes, see **25.77** EXEMPTIONS AND RELIEFS), *s 257(3)* (gifts to charities etc. out of settlements, see **11.8** CHARITIES), *s 258(4)* (gifts of national heritage property, see **25.85** EXEMPTIONS AND RELIEFS), *s 264* (transfers between constituency associations, see **25.70** EXEMPTIONS AND RELIEFS) and *s 267(2)* (sharing of transmission facilities, see **14.11** COMPANIES);

(ii) *CGTA 1979, s 148* (assets transferred to maintenance funds for historic buildings);

(iii) *FA 1982, s 148* (transfers by Hops Marketing Board, see **25.79** EXEMPTIONS AND RELIEFS);

(iv) *Trustee Savings Banks Act 1985, Sch 2 para 2* (see **14.11** COMPANIES);

(v) *Transport Act 1985, s 130(3)* (see **14.11** COMPANIES);

(vi) *ICTA 1988, s 486(8)* (amalgamation of industrial and provident societies before enactment of *CTA 2010*, see **14.11** COMPANIES);
(vii) *FA 1990, Sch 12 para 2(1)* (broadcasting undertakings, see **14.11** COMPANIES);
(viii) *F(No 2)A 1992, Sch 17 para 5(3)* (privatisation of Northern Ireland Electricity, see **14.11** COMPANIES);
(ix) *FA 1994, Sch 24 para 2(1), para 7(2), para 11(3)(4), para 25(2)* (provisions relating to *Railways Act 1993*, see **14.11** COMPANIES);
(x) *FA 1994, Sch 25 para 4(2)* (Northern Ireland Airports Ltd, see **14.11** COMPANIES);
(xi) *Coal Industry Act 1994, Sch 4 para 2(1)*;
(xii) *Broadcasting Act 1996, Sch 7 para 2(1)*;
(xiii) *Transport Act 2000, Sch 7 para 2(1);*
(xiv) *Transport Act 2000, Sch 26 paras 3, 9*;
(xv) *Energy Act 2004, Sch 9 paras 3, 18, 29, 32;*
(xvi) *Railways Act 2005, Sch 10 paras 5, 16*;
(xvii) *Consumers, Estate Agents and Redress Act 2007, Sch 9 para 4*;
(xviii) *Housing and Regeneration Act 2008, Sch 7*;
(xix) *SI 2009 No 3227, Reg 3(1)*;
(xx) *Localism Act 2011, Sch 24 para 6(1)*;
(xxi) *SI 2012 No 1709, Art 5(1)*; and
(xxii) *SI 2015 No 1540, Reg 6(1).*

[*TCGA 1992, ss 35(3)(d), 288(3A); Localism Act 2011, Sch 24 para 6(3); FA 2012, Sch 39 para 17; SI 2008 No 3002, Sch 1 para 43; SI 2009 No 3227, Reg 3; SI 2012 No 1709, Art 5; SI 2015 No 1540, Reg 6*].

Neither *TCGA 1992, s 257(2)* (gifts to charities etc., see **11.7** CHARITIES), nor *s 259(2)* (gifts to housing associations, see **25.53** EXEMPTIONS AND RELIEFS), is included as a no gain/no loss provision. They are, however, included for the equivalent provisions for indexation allowance under *TCGA 1992, s 55(1)*. However, both provisions deem (for the purposes of *TCGA 1992*) the original acquisition by the transferor making the disposal to which the provision concerned applies to be the acquisition of the transferee on the occasion of the transferee making a subsequent disposal. Consequently it seems that in practice both provisions are no gain/no loss provisions for the purposes of re-basing under *TCGA 1992, s 35*. Special rules apply to disposals giving rise to neither gain nor loss under *TCGA 1992, ss 195B, 195C* or *195E* (oil licence swaps).

Certain disposals of a share in partnership assets may be treated as if they were no gain/no loss disposals. See **50.7** PARTNERSHIPS.

Where a company to which an election under *CTA 2009, s 18A* exemption for foreign permanent establishments) applies makes a no gain/no loss disposal, the amount of the deemed consideration which results in that no gain/no loss, is to be arrived at after taking account of any adjustments under those provisions— see **49.8** OVERSEAS MATTERS.

Indexation allowance

Where *TCGA 1992, s 55(5)* (see above) applies on the disposal of an asset (so that, as stated above, the person making the disposal is treated for the purposes of computing the indexation allowance on the disposal as having held the asset on 31 March 1982 (*TCGA 1992, s 55(6)(a)*)), then for the purpose of determining any gain or loss on the disposal, the consideration which otherwise that person would be treated as having given for the asset is reduced by the amount of indexation allowance brought into account under *TCGA 1992, s 56(2)* (consideration on disposal treated as giving rise to neither a gain nor a loss to be computed on assumption that on the disposal an unindexed gain accrues equal to the indexation allowance on the disposal; see **38.4** INDEXATION) on any disposal falling within (b) above. [*TCGA 1992, s 55(6)(b)*].

Further rules as below apply (after the application of the computation of any indexation allowance under *TCGA 1992, s 53* (see **38.2** INDEXATION) but before the application of the provisions of *TCGA 1992, s 35(3)* or *(4)* (which disapply or amend the general re-basing rule of *TCGA 1992, s 35(1)(2)* in certain cases; see **9.2** above) in relation to disposals on or after 30 November 1993. The rules apply where *TCGA 1992, s 55(5)* above applies to the disposal ('*the disposal in question*') of an asset by any person ('*the transferor*') and, but for *TCGA 1992, s 55(6)(b)* above, the consideration the transferor would be treated as having given for the asset would include an amount or amounts of indexation allowance brought into account under *TCGA 1992, s 56(2)* on any disposal made before 30 November 1993. [*TCGA 1992, s 55(7)*]. The rules are that:

(A) where otherwise there would be a loss, an amount equal to the 'rolled-up indexation' is added to it so as to increase it,

(B) where otherwise the unindexed gain or loss would be nil, a loss is deemed to accrue equal to the rolled-up indexation, and

(C) where otherwise there would be an unindexed gain and the gain or loss would be nil but the amount of the indexation allowance used to extinguish the gain would be less than the rolled-up indexation, the difference is deemed to constitute a loss.

[*TCGA 1992, s 55(8)*].

For the purposes of the above, the '*rolled-up indexation*' means, subject to *TCGA 1992, s 55(10)* and *(11)* below (which provisions, as well as applying on the disposal in question, are also treated as having applied on any previous part disposal by the transferor), the amount or, as the case may be, the aggregate of the amounts of indexation allowance which, but for *TCGA 1992, s 55(6)(b)* above, would be brought into account under *TCGA 1992, s 56(2)* on any disposal made before 30 November 1993. [*TCGA 1992, s 55(9)*].

Where, for the purposes of any disposal of the asset made by the transferor on or after 30 November 1993, any amount, amounts or combination of amounts within *TCGA 1992, s 38(1)(a)–(c)* (acquisition consideration etc., enhancement expenditure etc. and incidental disposal costs respectively; see **16.11** COMPUTATION OF GAINS AND LOSSES) is required to be excluded, reduced or written down, the amount or amounts constituting the rolled-up indexation (or so much of it as remains after the application of this provision and *TCGA 1992,* *s 55(11)* below on a previous part disposal) are reduced in proportion to any reduction made in the amount falling within one or any combination of *TCGA 1992, s 38(1)(a)–(c)*. [*TCGA 1992, s 55(10)*].

Where the transferor makes a part disposal of the asset at any time on or after 30 November 1993, then, for the purposes of that and any subsequent part disposal, the amount or amounts constituting the rolled-up indexation (or so much of it as remains after the application of this provision and *TCGA 1992, s 55(10)* above on a previous part disposal by him or after the application of *TCGA 1992, s 55(10)* on the part disposal) is apportioned between the property disposed of and the property which remains in the same proportions as the amounts within *TCGA 1992, s 38(1)(a)* and *(b)*. [*TCGA 1992, s 55(11)*].

Note that indexation allowance is now available only for the purposes of corporation tax on chargeable gains. See **38.1** INDEXATION.

Example

X Ltd, Y Ltd and Z Ltd are all members of the same group within *TCGA 1992, s 170* (see **29.2** GROUPS OF COMPANIES), all three companies having joined the group before 1 April 1987 and making up annual accounts for calendar years. No election under *TCGA 1992, s 35(5)* (universal re-basing — see **9.3** and **9.5** above) is in force. An asset was acquired by X Ltd from outside the group for £90,000 in 1980 and at 31 March 1982 the value of the asset is £100,000. The asset was transferred to Y Ltd in October 1985 such that the no gain/no loss basis of *TCGA 1992, s 171* (see **29.3** GROUPS OF COMPANIES) applied. X Ltd made the appropriate election under *FA 1985, s 68(4)(5)* (indexation allowance to be calculated by reference to value at 31 March 1982 rather than original cost — see **9.12** below). In January 1995 Y Ltd transferred the asset to Z Ltd such that *TCGA 1992, s 171* again applied. Z Ltd sells the asset outside the group in March 2018 for £80,000. The relevant retail prices indices are

March 1982	79.44	January 1995	146.00
October 1985	95.59		

	£
Original cost of asset to X Ltd in 1980	90,000
Indexation allowance: March 1982–October 1985 on 31 March 1982 value under *FA 1985, s 68(4)(5)*	
$\frac{95.59 - 79.44}{79.44} \times £100,000$ (indexation factor 0.203)	20,300
Deemed consideration under *TCGA 1992, s 56(2)*	£110,300

	£
Deemed cost of asset to Y Ltd in October 1985	110,300
Indexation allowance: October 1985–January 1995	

$\frac{146.0 - 95.59}{95.59} \times$ £110,300 (indexation factor 0.527)	58,128
Deemed consideration under *TCGA 1992, s 56(2)*	£168,428

Under *TCGA 1992, ss 35(10), 55(6)(a), Sch 3 para 1*, Z Ltd is treated as having held the asset on 31 March 1982 for the purposes of re-basing under *TCGA 1992, s 35* and calculating indexation allowance.

	Cost	Re-base
	£	£
Proceeds received by Z Ltd	80,000	80,000
Deemed consideration under *TCGA 1992, s 55(6)(b)* (£168,428 – £58,128 – £20,300)	90,000	
Market value at 31 March 1982		100,000
Loss before *TCGA 1992, s 55(8)* adjustment	10,000	20,000
Rolled-up indexation under *TCGA 1992, s 55(9)*	20,300	20,300
Loss after *TCGA 1992, s 55(8)* adjustment	£30,300	£40,300

TCGA 1992, s 35(3) applies, so the allowable loss arising is £30,300.

Note to the example

(1) It should be noted that the effect of the legislation in force for disposals before 30 November 1993 meant that Z Ltd would not have been prejudiced on the ultimate disposal outside the group if X Ltd had not made a valid claim under *FA 1985, s 68(4)(5)* within the time limit in respect of the transfer of the asset to Y Ltd in October 1985. However, the legislation in force for disposals on or after 30 November 1993 means that, in the absence of such an election in respect of that disposal, the rolled-up indexation in the above example would have to be computed by reference to the original cost to X Ltd (i.e. 0.203 × £90,000 = £18,270). The allowable loss would then be £28,270 (i.e. £18,270 + £10,000).

Shares and securities

Shares or securities of the same class in any company which are *treated* as above as held on 31 March 1982 by a person will be treated as a single holding with any shares or securities of the same class in the same company *actually* held by that person in determining the market value for re-basing purposes of the shares or securities. If the shares or securities in the relevant disposal represent some but not all of those valued at 31 March 1982 then the allowable cost or indexation allowance as appropriate will be based on the proportion that the shares or securities disposed of bears to the total holding (HMRC Statement of Practice 5/89). See also **9.2** above regarding the concessional valuation of a holding of shares or securities at 31 March 1982 where part of the holding was held on 6 April 1965.

Valuation

The following treatment applies where a company disposes of shares or securities of the same class in a company and some or all of the shares or securities were held by another company on 31 March 1982 but are treated as above both as having been held by the company on 31 March 1982 and as constituting or forming part of a single holding held by the company on that date. Both the disposal by which the company acquired the shares or securities, and any previous disposal of them after 31 March 1982, must have been by way of no gain/no loss transfer under *TCGA 1992, s 171* (intra-group disposals). Where the company makes a claim, the market value at 31 March 1982 of the shares or securities disposed of is regarded as the appropriate proportion of the value of any larger holding of shares or securities of the same class which included some or all of those disposed of and which was held by the other company at that date. If some of the shares or securities disposed of in fact formed part of two or more larger holdings held by two different companies on 31 March 1982, the apportionment is made by reference to the largest such holding. A claim for this treatment must be made within two years (or such further time as HMRC may allow) of the end of the accounting period in which the disposal is made.

[TCGA 1992, s 55(6)(aa), Sch 3 para 1A; SI 2010 No 157, Art 7].

Note that, for disposals before 1 April 2010, this provision applied by concession only (HMRC Extra-Statutory Concession D44). For disposals before 6 April 2008, the concession applied also to inter-spouse transfers under *TCGA 1992, s 58*, but following the changes noted above with effect from that date, the concession could have no effect for CGT purposes. CCT claims had to be made within two years (or such further time as HMRC allowed) of the end of the tax year in which the disposal was made.

Supplementary provisions

Capital allowances

[9.7] If, under either the re-basing provisions of *TCGA 1992, s 35* or the equivalent provisions for indexation allowance of *TCGA 1992, s 55(1)* (see **9.2** and **9.3** above), it is to be assumed that any asset was on 31 March 1982 sold by the person making the disposal and immediately reacquired by him, *TCGA 1992, s 41* (restriction of losses by reference to capital allowances, see **16.13**(i) COMPUTATION OF GAINS AND LOSSES) and *s 47* (wasting assets qualifying for capital allowances, see **72.2** WASTING ASSETS) apply with suitable modifications on the assumed reacquisition at 31 March 1982. [*TCGA 1992, s 55(3), Sch 3 para 3*].

Part disposals etc.

[9.8] Where, on a disposal to which the general re-basing rule of *TCGA 1992, s 35(1)(2)* in **9.2** above applies, *TCGA 1992, s 42* (allowable expenditure on a part disposal, see **16.5** COMPUTATION OF GAINS AND LOSSES) has effect by reason of an earlier disposal made after 31 March 1982 and before 6 April 1988, the sums to be apportioned under that provision on the later disposal are to take the general re-basing rule into account. [*TCGA 1992, Sch 3 para 4(1)*].

If in relation to disposals after 5 April 1989 the general re-basing rule of *TCGA 1992, s 35(1)(2)* applies, and if that rule did not apply expenditure would under specified enactments not be allowable in computing a gain arising on the disposal, and the disallowance would be attributable to the reduction of the amount of the consideration for a disposal made after 31 March 1982 but before 6 April 1988, the amount otherwise allowable as a deduction on the disposal is reduced by the amount of the disallowance that would have been made if the general re-basing rule had not applied. The enactments specified are:

(i) *TCGA 1992, s 23(2)* (disallowance of allowable expenditure where allowance already given against receipts of compensation or insurance money, see **10.3** CAPITAL SUMS DERIVED FROM ASSETS);
(ii) *TCGA 1992, s 122(4)* (disallowance where allowance already given against capital distribution, see **63.11** SHARES AND SECURITIES);
(iii) *TCGA 1992, s 133(4)* (disallowance where allowance already given against premium on conversion of securities, see **63.8** SHARES AND SECURITIES); and
(iv) *TCGA 1992, s 244* (disallowance where allowance already given against gain from small part disposal of land, see **41.9** and **41.11** LAND).

[*TCGA 1992, Sch 3 para 4(2)*].

Assets derived from other assets

[9.9] The re-basing provisions of *TCGA 1992, s 35* in **9.2** and **9.3** above apply with the necessary modifications in relation to a disposal of an asset which was not held on 31 March 1982, if its value is derived from another asset which is taken into account under *TCGA 1992, s 43* (assets derived from other assets, see **16.5** COMPUTATION OF GAINS AND LOSSES). [*TCGA 1992, Sch 3 para 5*]. For indexation allowance purposes, where, after 31 March 1982, an asset which was held on that date has been merged or divided or has changed its nature or rights in or over the asset have been created, then *TCGA 1992, s 55(1)(2)* (re-basing for indexation allowance purposes) in **9.2** above has effect to determine for the purposes of *TCGA 1992, s 43* the amount of the consideration for the acquisition of the asset which was so held. [*TCGA 1992, s 55(4)*]. Note that indexation allowance is available only for the purposes of corporation tax on chargeable gains. See **38.1** INDEXATION.

Time apportionment of pre-6 April 1965 gains and losses

[9.10] If *TCGA 1992, Sch 2 para 16* (time apportionment of gains and losses accruing on ASSETS HELD ON 6 APRIL **1965**; see **8.7**) applies so that only part of a gain or loss is a chargeable gain or an allowable loss, the exclusion of the general re-basing rule of *TCGA 1992, s 35(1)(2)* under **9.2**(a) and (b) above has effect as if the amount of the gain or loss that would accrue if the general re-basing rule did not apply were equal to that part. [*TCGA 1992, Sch 3 para 6*]. (*Schedule 2 para 16* does not apply for capital gains tax purposes, as re-basing to 31 March 1982 applies without exceptions for such disposals.)

Deferred charges on gains before 31 March 1982

[9.11] The following relief applies for the purposes of corporation tax on chargeable gains (and, for disposals before 6 April 2008 only, capital gains tax). [*TCGA 1992, s 36, Sch 4 para A1*].

Subject to the above, the relief applies where, before 6 April 1988, a gain was deferred in respect of one or more disposals which related in whole or in part to an asset acquired before 31 March 1982, and the deferred gain is brought into charge on a disposal or other occasion after 5 April 1988. The deferred gain is, subject to conditions and on a claim, halved (except, in certain cases, where the deferred gain is never deemed to accrue at all) when the charge to tax is computed in respect of it.

The provisions under which a gain can be deferred effectively fall into two groups for this purpose. In the first group (*TCGA 1992, Sch 4 para 2*), which includes the hold-over provisions for gifts made before 14 March 1989 and rollover relief on the replacement of business assets, the deferred gain is deducted from the expenditure allowable in computing the gain on a later disposal. In the second group (*TCGA 1992, Sch 4 paras 3, 4*), the deferred gain is brought into charge on the occurrence of a subsequent event. For both groups, the deferred gain will be half of what it would otherwise be. [*TCGA 1992, s 36, Sch 4 para 1*].

Group 1

As regards the first group of provisions, both of the following circumstances must be fulfilled in order to bring about the halving of the deferred gain.

(a) There is a disposal, other than one within the 'no gain/no loss provisions' (see **9.6** above), after 5 April 1988 of an asset acquired after 31 March 1982 by the person making the disposal.
(b) A deduction from allowable expenditure falls to be made under any of the first group of provisions in computing the gain on that disposal and is attributable directly or indirectly, in whole or in part, to a chargeable gain accruing on the disposal before 6 April 1988 of an asset acquired before 31 March 1982 by the person making that disposal.

No relief is given under *TCGA 1992, Sch 4* where, by reason of the previous operation of it, the amount of the deduction in (b) is less than it otherwise would be. Where the disposal takes place after 18 March 1991, no relief under *TCGA 1992, Sch 4* is available if the amount of the deduction would have been less had relief by virtue of a previous application of it been duly claimed. (In effect, for disposals after 18 March 1991, the relief for the first group of provisions (*TCGA 1992, Sch 4 para 2*) cannot be claimed twice for the same gain and must be claimed in respect of the earliest possible occasion. For disposals after 5 April 1988 and before 19 March 1991, it was possible to claim other than on the earliest possible occasion. See below as regards time limits for claims affected by this change.) [*TCGA 1992, Sch 4 para 2(1)–(3)*].

Where the asset was acquired after 18 March 1991, the deduction is partly attributable to a claim under *TCGA 1992, s 154(4)* (rollover into non-depreciating asset instead of into depreciating asset, see **59.9** ROLLOVER RELIEF), and the claim applies to the asset, no relief under *TCGA 1992, Sch 4* is available by virtue of its application in respect of the first group of provisions below (*TCGA 1992, Sch 4 para 2*) (but see below as regards the relief available in respect of the second group of provisions). [*TCGA 1992, Sch 4 para 2(4)*].

In the case of rollover relief on the replacement of business assets and subject to the usual time limits, the disposal of the old asset may be before 31 March 1982, and the replacement asset may be acquired afterwards (Revenue Press Release 8 July 1988).

For the circumstances in which HMRC will require a valuation of the asset transferred where a hold-over relief claim is made, see **36.2** HOLD-OVER RELIEFS.

The first group of provisions mentioned above is as follows.

(i) *TCGA 1992, s 23(4)(5)* (rollover where replacement asset acquired after receipt of compensation or insurance money, see **10.4** CAPITAL SUMS DERIVED FROM ASSETS);
(ii) *TCGA 1992, s 152* (rollover where replacement asset acquired on disposal of business asset, see **59** ROLLOVER RELIEF);
(iii) (for disposals before 6 April 2008) *TCGA 1992, s 162* (hold-over where shares acquired on disposal of business to company, see **37.2** INCORPORATION AND DISINCORPORATION RELIEFS);
(iv) (for disposals before 6 April 2008) *TCGA 1992, s 165* (hold-over where business asset acquired by gift, see **36.2–36.9** HOLD-OVER RELIEFS);
(v) *TCGA 1992, s 247* (rollover where replacement land acquired on compulsory acquisition of other land, see **41.12** LAND);
(vi) (for disposals before 6 April 2008) *FA 1980, s 79* (hold-over where asset acquired by gift after 5 April 1980 and before 14 March 1989, see **36.12** HOLD-OVER RELIEFS).

[*TCGA 1992, Sch 4 para 2(5)*].

Where deferral has been claimed under one of the first group of provisions and there is a subsequent no gain/no loss disposal (or continuous series of such disposals) as in **9.6** above, relief is available (subject to the conditions in (a) and (b) above) in computing the gain on the first later disposal which is not within the no gain/no loss provisions. [*TCGA 1992, Sch 4 paras 6, 7*].

Group 2

As regards the second group of provisions and subject to the exception below, both of the following circumstances must be fulfilled in order to bring about the halving of the deferred gain.

(A) Under any of the second group of provisions a gain is treated as accruing in consequence of an event occurring after 5 April 1988.
(B) The gain is attributable directly or indirectly, in whole or in part, to the disposal before 6 April 1988 of an asset acquired before 31 March 1982 by the person making that disposal.

[*TCGA 1992, Sch 4 para 4(1)*].

Where a gain is treated as accruing in consequence of an event after 18 March 1991, relief under *TCGA 1992, Sch 4* does not apply if the gain is attributable directly or indirectly, in whole or in part, to the disposal of an asset after 5 April 1988, or the amount of the gain would have been less had relief by virtue of a previous application of *TCGA 1992, Sch 4* been duly claimed. [*TCGA 1992, Sch 4 para 4(4)*]. (In effect, for events after 18 March 1991, the relief for the second group of provisions (*TCGA 1992, Sch 4 paras 3, 4*, and see below as regards *TCGA 1992, Sch 4 para 3*) cannot be claimed twice for the same gain and must be claimed in respect of the earliest possible occasion. For events after 5 April 1988 and before 19 March 1991, it was possible to claim other than on the earliest possible occasion and more than once. See below as regards time limits for claims affected by this change.)

The second group of provisions mentioned above is as follows (and see also below).

(I) *TCGA 1992, s 116(10)(11)* (postponement of charge on reorganisation etc. involving acquisition of qualifying corporate bonds, see **54.4** QUALIFYING CORPORATE BONDS).

(II) *TCGA 1992, s 134* (postponement of charge where gilts acquired on compulsory acquisition of shares, see **63.8** SHARES AND SECURITIES);

(III) *TCGA 1992, s 140* (postponement of charge where securities acquired in exchange for business acquired by overseas resident company until transferor company disposes of securities as mentioned in *s 140(4)* or transferee company within six years of exchange disposes of assets acquired on exchange as mentioned in *s 140(5)*, see **49.12** OVERSEAS MATTERS);

(IV) *TCGA 1992, s 154(2)* (postponement of charge where depreciating asset acquired as replacement for business asset, see **59.9** ROLLOVER RELIEF) (and see below as regards *TCGA 1992, Sch 4 para 3*);

(V) (For disposals before 6 April 2008) *TCGA 1992, s 168* (as modified by *TCGA 1992, s 67(6)*) (activation of charge held over under *FA 1980, s 79* on emigration of donee in relation to a gift after 5 April 1981 and before 14 March 1989, see **36.12** HOLD-OVER RELIEFS);

(VI) *TCGA 1992, s 179(3)* (or earlier equivalent) (charge on company leaving group of companies in respect of asset acquired from another member of same group within previous six years, see **29.7** GROUPS OF COMPANIES, but only if the asset was acquired by the chargeable company before 6 April 1988, so no longer relevant);

(VII) *TCGA 1992, s 248(3)* (postponement of charge where depreciating asset acquired on compulsory acquisition of land, see **41.12** LAND).

[*TCGA 1992, Sch 4 para 4(2)(3)*].

Where relief under *TCGA 1992, Sch 4* would have applied on a disposal but for the effect of *TCGA 1992, Sch 4 para 2(4)* (exclusion of relief under *TCGA 1992, Sch 4 para 2* where deduction partly attributable to claim under *TCGA 1992, s 154(4)*) above, then such relief (on the same lines as for the second group of provisions above) is available (under *TCGA 1992, Sch 4 para 3*) if the relief for the second group of provisions (*TCGA 1992, Sch 4 para 4*) would have applied had *TCGA 1992, s 154(2)* (see (IV) above) continued to apply to the gain carried forward as a result of the claim under *TCGA 1992, s 154(4)*, and the time of disposal been the time when that gain was treated as accruing by virtue of *TCGA 1992, s 154(2)*. [*TCGA 1992, Sch 4 para 3*].

There is an exception to the bringing about of the halving of the deferred gain in respect of certain provisions contained in the second group. Neither *TCGA 1992, s 134, s 140(4), s 154(2)* nor *s 248(3)* (see (II)–(IV) and (VII) above) is to apply in consequence of an event occurring after 5 April 1988 if its application would be *directly* attributable to the disposal of an asset before 1 April 1982. [*TCGA 1992, Sch 4 para 4(5)*]. In effect the deferred gain is in such circumstances never deemed to accrue. See also below regarding views expressed by HMRC.

It is understood that HMRC accept that the crystallisation under *TCGA 1992, s 67(4)(5)* of a gain deferred by *FA 1980, s 79* (as extended by *FA 1981, s 78* and *FA 1982, s 82*) (clawback of deferred gain on death of life tenant, see **36.8** and **36.12** HOLD-OVER RELIEFS) can by concession be treated as if it were amongst the second group of provisions in (I)–(VII) above. In addition, a gain deferred on a transfer into settlement occurring before 1 April 1982 and which would otherwise crystallise on the death after 5 April 1988 of a life tenant will by concession be deemed never to accrue (and so treated in the same way as for the exception given by *TCGA 1992, Sch 4 para 4(5)* above).

Asset not held on 31 March 1982

Relief is available as regards both groups of provisions where a person makes a disposal of an asset which he acquired after 30 March 1982 where the disposal by which he acquired it and any previous disposal of it after that date was within the 'no gain/no loss provisions' (see **9.6** above). In such a case, the person is treated for the purposes of (b) and (B) above as having acquired the asset before 31 March 1982. [*TCGA 1992, Sch 4 paras 5, 7*].

Relief is available as regards both groups of provisions for an asset which was not acquired before 31 March 1982 if its value was derived from another asset which was so acquired and which is taken into account under *TCGA 1992, s 43* (see **16.5** COMPUTATION OF GAINS AND LOSSES). [*TCGA 1992, Sch 4 para 8*].

Claims

No relief is available under *TCGA 1992, Sch 4* unless a claim is made:

(a) in respect of gains accruing to a person chargeable to corporation tax within two years of the end of the accounting period, and
(b) on or before such later date as HMRC may allow,

in which, for the first group of provisions, the disposal to which the claim relates is made, or for the second group of provisions, the deferred gain is treated as accruing (except where (VI) above applied where the claim had to be made within two years of the end of the accounting period in which the chargeable company ceased to be a member of the group). A claim must be supported by any particulars the inspector may require for establishing the validity and quantum of any relief. [*TCGA 1992, Sch 4 para 9*]. HMRC may accept a late claim by exercising its collection and management powers — see

67.1 TIME LIMITS — FIXED DATES. (HMRC Capital Gains Manual CG13800, 17012).

Key points on assets held on 31 March 1982

[9.12] Points to consider are as follows.

- The general rule regarding the disposal of assets which were held on 31 March 1982 is that the market value at that date is substituted for cost. This is referred to as rebasing.
- For capital gains tax purposes there are no exceptions to the rule.
- For corporation tax purposes there is an exception where the rebasing would result in a larger gain or loss. The corporate could irrevocably elect for the rebasing to apply to all assets held on 31 March 1982 such that the exception does not apply.
- The use of the March 1982 value requires a valuation or estimate. For corporation tax and capital gains tax purposes this needs to be disclosed in the self assessment returns. It is advisable to have a professional valuation where the tax at stake is significant.
- The decision for companies to elect can be complex so a full review of all the facts should be undertaken before submitting an election.
- Indexation allowance, which applied from 31 March 1982, was abolished for capital gains tax purposes (but not for corporation tax purposes) for disposals from 6 April 2008. However a note should be kept of the amount of any indexation 'banked' on the acquisition of an asset on a no gain/no loss basis before that date, in case indexation is restricted on a disposal of the asset.

10

Capital Sums Derived from Assets

Introduction	**10.1**
General rule	**10.2**
Capital sums applied in restoring assets and small capital sums	**10.3**
Assets lost and replaced out of compensation	**10.4**

Cross-references. See 7 ASSETS; **39.1** INTERACTION WITH OTHER TAXES; **41.9** and **41.11** LAND for small part disposals of land.

Simon's Taxes. See C1.319, C1.501–C1.504.

Introduction to capital sums derived from assets

[10.1] There is a disposal of an asset by its owner where any capital sum is derived from it, even though an asset may not be acquired by the person paying the sum. Accordingly, a chargeable gain or allowable loss will normally result from the receipt of such a sum. Circumstances where this rule applies may include, for example, the receipt of compensation for damage or loss or payment for use of an asset. This rule can be disapplied in certain cases where the capital sum is applied in restoring the asset or where the sum is small as compared with the value of the asset. Where an asset has been lost or destroyed and the capital sum received in compensation is used to acquire a replacement asset, the deemed disposal under the above provisions can be treated as giving rise to neither a gain nor a loss (and the acquisition cost of the new asset reduced accordingly). Partial relief is also available.

General rule for capital sums derived from assets

[10.2] Subject to 10.3, 10.4 and the exception below, there is a disposal of assets by their owner where any 'capital sum' is *derived from* them, 'notwithstanding that no asset is acquired by the person paying the capital sum' (which means 'whether or not an asset is acquired', see *Marren v Ingles* HL 1980, 54 TC 76, and thus not following *CIR v Montgomery* Ch D 1974, 49 TC 679). See also *Zim Properties Ltd v Proctor* Ch D 1984, 58 TC 371 (which has been superseded by extra-statutory concession; see 7.2 ASSETS) and *Kirby v Thorn EMI plc* CA 1987, 60 TC 519.

For general consideration of what constitutes an 'asset' for tax purposes, see 7.2 ASSETS.

'*Capital sum*' means any money or money's worth which is not otherwise excluded from the computation of chargeable gains.

The provisions apply in particular to capital sums received as follows (other than those brought into charge to income tax — see Revenue Tax Bulletin December 1997 pp 490, 491 for the treatment of compensation received by a business).

(a) By way of compensation for any kind of damage or injury to assets or for the loss, destruction or dissipation of assets or for any depreciation or risk of depreciation of an asset.
Following *Stoke-on-Trent City Council v Wood Mitchell & Co Ltd* CA 1978, [1979] STC 197, any element of compensation paid for the acquisition of business property by an authority possessing powers of compulsory acquisition which relates to temporary loss of profits is treated as a trading receipt. Compensation for losses on trading stock and to reimburse revenue expenditure, such as removal expenses and interest, are similarly treated. (HMRC Statement of Practice 8/79). See also *Lang v Rice* CA (NI) 1983, 57 TC 80 and **39.1** INTERACTION WITH OTHER TAXES.
In *Pennine Raceway Ltd v Kirklees Metropolitan Borough Council* CA, 1988, [1989] STC 122, to which the Revenue was not a party, the company held a licence to conduct motor racing in accordance with existing planning permission. Compensation under *Town and Country Planning Act 1971* paid by the local authority for revoking the planning permission was held to be derived from the licence, the value of which had been depreciated.
See **7.9** ASSETS re compensation receivable in respect of milk quota.

(b) Under a policy of insurance of the risk of any kind of damage or injury to, or the loss or depreciation of, assets.

(c) In return for the forfeiture or surrender of rights or for refraining from exercising rights.
Statutory compensation payable to agricultural tenants under *Agricultural Holdings Act 1986, ss 60, 64* or under *Agricultural Tenancies Act 1995, s 16* and to business tenants under *Landlord and Tenant Act 1954, s 37* is not chargeable to capital gains tax. This follows the decision in (*Davis v Powell* Ch D 1976, 51 TC 492) where a tenant quit the holding in consequence of a notice to quit.
Following the decisions in *Davis v Henderson* (Sp C 46), [1995] SSCD 308 and *Pritchard v Purves* (Sp C 47), [1995] SSCD 316, where a tenant is issued with a notice to quit and quits before the expiry of the notice period in return for payments made by his landlord under a surrender agreement, HMRC does not consider that the part of the landlord's payment that represents statutory compensation is chargeable to capital gains tax. (Revenue Tax Bulletin April 1996 pp 303, 304). (Grants for giving up agricultural land may be specifically exempt. See **25.19** EXEMPTIONS AND RELIEFS.) Compensation under *Landlord and Tenant Act 1954, Pt II* to a tenant giving up possession is similarly excluded (*Drummond v Austin Brown* CA 1984, 58 TC 67).

(d) As consideration for use or exploitation of assets.

Time of disposal under (a) to (d) above is when the capital sum is received.

The above provision does not apply where a company receives, or becomes entitled to receive, a capital distribution (within *TCGA 1992, s 122* — see **63.11** SHARES AND SECURITIES) or a distribution to which a charge under *CTA 2009, Pt 9A* applies or would apply were the distribution not exempt.

[*TCGA 1992, s 22*].

HMRC consider that *TCGA 1992, s 22* does not change the normal meaning of the word 'owner' so all that the provision needs for it to apply is that the person receiving the capital sum has, or had, beneficial ownership of the asset, and the receipt of a capital sum derived from that ownership. They cite the case of an asset being damaged prior to its sale where a claim for compensation results in compensation being received after the time of sale. Unless the owner has assigned his rights to compensation, the receipt of compensation will be chargeable within the provision. (HMRC Capital Gains Manual CG12975).

See *British Telecommunications plc v HMRC* (Sp C 535), [2006] SSCD 347 where a payment received (in unusual circumstances) on the termination of a merger agreement was held not to constitute a capital sum derived from an asset.

A right to unquantified and contingent future consideration on the disposal of an asset is itself an asset and the future consideration, if received, is a capital sum derived from that asset (*Marren v Ingles* above and *Marson v Marriage* Ch D 1979, 54 TC 59), but see **63.6** SHARES AND SECURITIES for mitigation of this principle in the case of 'earn-outs'.

In HMRC's view, the receipt for a grant of indefeasible rights to use a telecommunications cable system, where falling to be treated as a capital (rather than a trading) receipt, falls within (d) above; the only allowable costs will be incidental costs such as those of drawing up the relevant contracts (Revenue Tax Bulletin December 2000 p 816).

Where under *Matrimonial Causes Act 1973, s 31* the court effectively replaces in whole or in part an order for periodic payments by an order for a lump sum payment, it is HMRC's view that the lump sum is not a capital sum derived from an asset and that the recipient is not liable to capital gains tax (Revenue Tax Bulletin April 2001 p 840).

Entire loss, destruction etc. of asset

The *entire* loss, destruction, dissipation or extinction of an asset (whether or not any capital sum is received as above) constitutes a disposal of that asset (with certain exceptions for options as in **7.7** ASSETS). (The fact that the asset may be a capital asset employed in a business makes no difference to this tax treatment — see Revenue Tax Bulletin December 1997 pp 490, 491.)

For this purpose, land and buildings may be regarded as separate assets so that where there is a deemed disposal of a building, the land comprising the site of the building (including any land occupied for purposes ancillary to the use of that building) is treated as if it were sold and immediately reacquired at its then market value.

[*TCGA 1992, s 24(1)(3)*].

See also the treatment under *TCGA 1992, s 23(4)(5)* in **10.3** below. For relief where the value of an asset becomes *negligible*, see **44.11** LOSSES.

Compensation for deprivation of foreign assets

Subject to the conditions below, a capital sum is not treated as giving rise to a chargeable gain on the person entitled to receive it, where it is received as compensation for the loss or deprivation of property then situated outside the UK. The payment of the compensation must be:

(i) under a statutory order under *Foreign Compensation Act 1950* or under equivalent arrangements set up by foreign governments; or
(ii) in consequence of a recommendation of the Spoliation Advisory Panel (set up by the Government to consider claims for the return of cultural items looted during the Nazi era (1933–1945)) or of any non-UK equivalent body; or
(iii) in settlement of legal claims to the effect that the deprivation was unlawful or in accordance with a judgment to that effect.

Deprivation of property includes its sale under duress for less than market value. Payment of a capital sum includes a payment as a result of the abandonment or extinguishment of rights in respect of the deprivation or the return of the asset itself.

The provision applies only where no form of legal redress was available to the owner at the time the property was confiscated, expropriated or destroyed and where a claim is made.

If the capital sum is paid to a person other than the person who owned the asset at the time of the deprivation, the provision can still apply provided that no consideration has been given (whether by that person or another) for the right to receive the compensation. Any consideration given for a no gain/no loss transfer of the right between spouses or group companies is, however, ignored for this purpose.

If an allowable capital loss has been established in consequence of the loss or deprivation, the provision does not apply to so much of the gain as is equal to the allowable loss claimed.

Where this provision applies to a capital sum paid by means of a transfer of an asset or the foreign asset is returned, that asset is treated as acquired for its market value at the time of the transfer or return.

This provision does not apply to a gain to which *TCGA 1992, s 268A* (exemption for gain on disposal of right to receive interest on deposit of victim of Nazi persecution — see **25.14** EXEMPTIONS AND RELIEFS) applies.

[*TCGA 1992, s 268B; SI 2010 No 157, Art 9*].

Capital sums applied in restoring assets and small capital sums

[10.3] Where a capital sum within **10.2**(a)–(d) above is derived from an asset which is not lost or destroyed, the recipient may claim under *TCGA 1992, s 23(1)* that the asset is not treated as disposed of, provided the capital sum is:

(a) wholly applied in restoring the asset; or
(b) (subject to the following) applied in restoring the asset (not being a wasting asset) except for a part which is not reasonably required for the purpose and which is 'small' compared with the whole capital sum; or
(c) (subject to the following) 'small' as compared with the value of the asset (not being a wasting asset).

'*Small*' for the purposes of (b) and (c) above is normally taken by HMRC to mean the greater of an amount not exceeding 5% and £3,000 (Revenue Tax Bulletin February 1997 p 397). Additionally, for small part disposals of land, see **41.9** and **41.11** LAND.

If the receipt is not treated as a disposal, the capital sum is deducted from the allowable expenditure on a subsequent disposal. [*TCGA 1992, s 23(1)(6)(8)(a)*].

Where the allowable expenditure relating to the asset (not being a wasting asset) immediately prior to the receipt of the capital sum (including the cost of any restoration work before receipt) is less than the capital sum (or is nil), (b) and (c) above do not apply, but the recipient may elect under *TCGA 1992, s 23(2)* to reduce the capital sum by the amount of any allowable expenditure. The balance of the capital sum is treated as a part disposal. The capital sum so utilised cannot be deducted again either on the part disposal or any subsequent disposal of the asset by the recipient. [*TCGA 1992, s 23(2)(6)(8)(a)*]. Where the capital sum received is subsequently wholly applied in restoring the asset, the recipient may alternatively make a claim as under (a) above for the asset not to be disposed of.

If part only of the capital sum within **10.2**(a) or (b) derived from an asset is applied in restoring the asset (but not sufficient so as to fall within (b) above) the recipient may claim under *TCGA 1992, s 23(3)* to have the part so applied deducted from any allowable expenditure on a subsequent disposal. The balance of the capital sum is treated as a part disposal of the asset. [*TCGA 1992, s 23(3)(6)(8)*]. In the part disposal computation, HMRC take the market value after any restoration work.

Where *TCGA 1992, s 23(1)* or *(3)* above applies in the case of a wasting asset, the amount of the allowable expenditure from which the appropriate deduction is made is the amount that would have been allowable if the asset had been disposed of immediately after the application of the capital sum. [*TCGA 1992, s 23(8)(b)*].

Examples

An Old Master painting belonging to X and worth £100,000 (in its undamaged state) is damaged in June 2017. Subsequently, X successfully claims £20,000 from his insurance company. The picture cost X £40,000 in 1996 and in its damaged state in 2017 is valued at £60,000. The following possibilities arise, the capital gains tax calculations being as shown.

(i) X retains the insurance moneys and does nothing to restore the picture. He is treated as having made a part disposal, and the gain is computed according to the formula for part-disposals (see **16.5** COMPUTATION OF GAINS AND LOSSES). The allowable expenditure apportioned to the disposal is thus £10,000.

(ii) X subsequently expends the whole of the sum on restoration of the picture, but *does not* make a claim under (a) above. He will be treated as having made a part disposal as in (i) above, and his allowable expenditure on a future disposal is computed as follows.

	£
Original allowable expenditure	40,000
Deduct: apportioned allowable expenditure	10,000
	30,000
Add: Expenditure on restoration	20,000
Revised allowable expenditure	£50,000

(iii) X expends the whole of the sum on restoration of the asset *and* makes a claim under (a) above. The position is as follows

	£
Original allowable expenditure	40,000
Deduct: compensation moneys received	20,000
	20,000
Add: Expenditure incurred on the asset after compensation received	20,000
Revised allowable expenditure	£40,000

(iv) X expends £19,000 on restoration of the asset and makes a claim under (b) above. The shortfall of £1,000 is small in relation to the compensation moneys received, and will effectively be treated as a deferred capital gain.

	£
Original allowable expenditure	40,000
Deduct: compensation	20,000
	20,000
Add: Expenditure out of compensation	19,000
Revised allowable expenditure	£39,000

(v) X manages to have the asset restored for £15,000. The shortfall is not small in relation to the compensation moneys received. X makes a claim under *TCGA 1992, s 23(3)*. The market value of the restored asset is £95,000.

	£
Consideration deemed to have been received for the part disposal (£20,000 – £15,000)	5,000
Deduct: Allowable expenditure on that disposal $\frac{5{,}000}{(5{,}000 + 95{,}000)} \times £(40{,}000 + 15{,}000)$	2,750
Gain	£2,250

The allowable expenditure on a future disposal is as follows

	£
Allowable expenditure after part disposal £(40,000 + 15,000 – 2,750)	52,250
Deduct: Compensation expended on asset	15,000
Revised allowable expenditure	£37,250

Assets lost and replaced out of compensation

[10.4] Where an asset is lost or destroyed and a capital sum is received in compensation, there is a disposal of the asset under *TCGA 1992, s 22(1)* as in **10.2** above. A form of rollover relief is available, however, where within one year of receipt (or such longer period as HMRC allow) the whole capital sum is applied in acquiring a replacement asset. HMRC officers are instructed to allow two years from receipt where the delay can reasonably be regarded as unavoidable (HMRC Capital Gains Manual CG15744).

In these circumstances, the owner may claim under *TCGA 1992, s 23(4)* to have the disposal of the old asset (if otherwise greater) treated as made at a consideration giving rise to neither a gain nor a loss. The consideration for the acquisition of the new asset is then reduced by the amount of the excess of the capital sum received plus any residual or scrap value of the old asset over the amount of the deemed consideration.

[*TCGA 1992, s 23(4)(6)(8)*].

Where all of the gain on the disposal of the old asset is not chargeable as it was acquired before 6 April 1965, the amount of the reduction in the acquisition cost of the new asset is the amount of the chargeable gain and not the whole amount of the gain. [*TCGA 1992, Sch 2 para 23*].

Partial relief

If part only of the capital sum received in respect of the old asset is applied in acquiring the new asset, the relief above cannot be claimed. However, provided that the amount not applied is less than the gain (whether chargeable or not) accruing on the disposal of the old asset, the owner can claim under *TCGA 1992, s 23(5)* to reduce the gain arising to the amount not applied (and if not all chargeable, with a proportionate reduction in the amount of the chargeable gain). The amount of the consideration for the acquisition of the new asset is reduced by the same amount as the original gain. [*TCGA 1992, s 23(5)(6)(8)*].

Where all of the gain on the disposal of the old asset is not chargeable as it was acquired before 6 April 1965, the amount of the reduction in acquisition cost is the amount by which the chargeable gain is reduced and not the amount by which the original gain is reduced. [*TCGA 1992, Sch 2 para 23*].

Buildings

If a building (including a structure in the nature of a building) is destroyed or irreparably damaged, and all or part of any capital sum received is applied by the recipient in constructing or otherwise acquiring a replacement building (but excluding the land on which the building stands) situated elsewhere, then for the purposes of a claim under *TCGA 1992, s 23(4)* or *(5)* above each of the old building and the new building are regarded as an asset separate from the land on which it was or is situated and the old building treated as lost or destroyed. Just and reasonable apportionments of expenditure, compensation or consideration are made for this purpose. [*TCGA 1992, s 23(6)(7)*]. Cf. the treatment under *TCGA 1992, s 24(1)(3)* in **16.6** COMPUTATION OF GAINS AND LOSSES.

Examples

(a) A Ltd bought an asset for £50,000 in September 2010. It is subsequently destroyed by fire in October 2017 and A Ltd receives £90,000 compensation later in that month. A Ltd buys a new asset six months later for £100,000 and makes a claim under *TCGA 1992, s 23(4)*. For the purpose of this example only, the indexation factor for the period September 2010 to October 2017 is assumed to be 0.193.

	£
Cost of destroyed asset	50,000
Indexation allowance £50,000 × 0.193	9,650
Deemed consideration	£59,650
Compensation received	90,000
Deemed consideration	59,650
Excess (i.e. the gain otherwise accruing)	£30,350
Consideration for acquisition of new asset	100,000
Excess as above	30,350
Reduced allowable expenditure on new asset	£69,650

(b) Facts as in *Example* (a) above except that A Ltd buys another asset to replace the old at a cost of £80,000 and makes a claim under *TCGA 1992, s 23(5)*.

	£	£
Gain on disposal (see above)		£30,350
Compensation moneys received	90,000	
Compensation moneys expended	80,000	
Excess (being less than the gain of £30,350)	£10,000	
The chargeable gain is treated as reduced to the balance arrived at as above and is		£10,000
Amount by which the gain otherwise chargeable is reduced (£30,350 – £10,000)		£20,350
The allowable expenditure on the new asset is reduced as follows		

	£
Actual expenditure	80,000
Amount by which chargeable gain is reduced	20,350
Total allowable expenditure	£59,650

11

Charities

Introduction	**11.1**
Definition of charity	**11.2**
Exemption from tax on chargeable gains	**11.3**
Restriction of exemption	**11.4**
Payments to substantial donors	**11.5**
Reliefs for donations to charities	**11.6**
Gifts of assets to charities	**11.7**
Gifts of assets out of settlements	**11.8**
Gifts of pre-eminent property to the nation	**11.9**
Gift aid donations by individuals	**11.10**
Anti-avoidance: tainted donations	**11.11**
Community amateur sports clubs	**11.12**

Simon's Taxes. See B1.440, C1.220, C1.415, C5.101–C5.117A, C5.124, E1.811.

Introduction to charities

[11.1] A gain made by a charity is exempt from tax on chargeable gains provided that the gain is 'applicable and applied for charitable purposes only'.

This exemption is, however, restricted, together with similar income tax and corporation tax exemptions, where a charity incurs non-charitable expenditure. The expression 'non-charitable expenditure' is widely defined to include losses in, and payments in connection with, non-exempt businesses carried on by the charity, as well as non-approved investments and loans. Certain payments to substantial donors (broadly, those giving £25,000 or more a year or £100,000 or more over six years) are also treated as non-charitable expenditure.

Relief from tax on chargeable gains is also available to donors. Where a person gives an asset to a charity (or sells it to the charity for no more than its cost) the disposal is treated as one giving rise to neither a gain nor a loss. Where an asset is sold to a charity for more than its acquisition cost but the sale is not at arm's length, the normal rule treating the disposal as made at market value is disapplied.

Relief for donations of money by individuals under Gift Aid is also covered in this chapter, as capital gains tax paid can be used to cover any liability for the income tax treated as deducted from such donations.

Anti-avoidance provisions apply to donations which are tainted by arrangements for the donor to obtain a financial advantage.

The definition of 'charity' for the purposes of this chapter is given at **11.2** below, and the treatment of sports clubs which are registered as community amateur sports clubs as charities for the purposes of the various reliefs is described at **11.12** below.

Charities are regulated in England and Wales by the Charity Commission and in Scotland by the Office of the Scottish Charities Regulator. Under *Charities Act 2011, ss 54–59*, HMRC may disclose information regarding charities to the Charity Commission.

Definition of charity

[11.2] For the purposes of most taxes, including capital gains tax and corporation tax, a '*charity*' is a body of persons or trust that meets the following conditions:

- the 'charitable purposes' condition;
- the jurisdiction condition;
- the registration condition; and
- the management condition.

HMRC are entitled to publish the names and addresses of any body or trust which appears to them to meet the definition.

A charity that is a body of persons is a '*charitable company*'; a charity which is a trust is a '*charitable trust*'.

The charitable purposes condition

The body or trust must be established for charitable purposes only. For this purpose, a 'charitable purpose' is one which is for the public benefit and which is within one of the following categories:

(a) the prevention or relief of poverty;
(b) the advancement of education;
(c) the advancement of religion;
(d) the advancement of health or the saving of lives;
(e) the advancement of citizenship or community development;
(f) the advancement of the arts, culture, heritage or science;
(g) the advancement of amateur sport;
(h) the advancement of human rights, conflict resolution or reconciliation or the promotion of religious or racial harmony or equality and diversity;
(i) the advancement of environmental protection or improvement;
(j) the relief of those in need by reason of youth, age, ill-health, disability, financial hardship or other disadvantage;
(k) the advancement of animal welfare;
(l) the promotion of the efficiency of the armed forces of the Crown, or of the efficiency of the police, fire and rescue services or ambulance services;
(m) any purposes not within (a) to (l) above but recognised as charitable purposes under existing charity law or under *Charities Act 2011, s 5* or under the law preceding *Charities Act 2011*;

(n) any purposes that may reasonably be regarded as analogous to, or within the spirit of, any purposes falling within (a) to (m) above; and

(o) any purposes that may reasonably be regarded as analogous to, or within the spirit of, any purposes which have been recognised under charity law as falling within (n) above or this category.

The jurisdiction condition

The body or trust must be subject to the control of the High Court, Court of Session or High Court in Northern Ireland in the exercise of those courts' jurisdiction with respect to charities or of any other court in the exercise of a corresponding jurisdiction under the law of an EU member State or a territory specified in HMRC regulations (currently Iceland, Norway and Liechtenstein).

The registration condition

If the body or trust is a charity within the meaning of *Charities Act 2011, s 10*, it must have complied with any requirement to be registered in the register of charities kept under *Charities Act 2011, s 29*. In any other case, the body or trust must have complied with any requirement under the law of a territory outside England and Wales to be registered in a corresponding register.

The management condition

The managers of the body or trust must be fit and proper persons to be such managers. For this purpose, the managers are the persons with the general control and management of the administration of the body or trust. If this condition is not met for a period of time it is nevertheless treated as met throughout that period if HMRC consider either that the failure has not prejudiced the charitable purposes of the body or trust or that it is just and reasonable for the condition to be treated as met.

The expression 'fit and proper' is not defined and so takes its natural meaning. HMRC have issued guidance on how this test is applied — see HMRC Guidance Note 9 July 2010.

[*Charities Act 2006, s 2; FA 2010, Sch 6 paras 1–7, 33, 34; Charities Act 2011, ss 2, 3, Sch 7 para 143; SI 2010 No 1904; SI 2012 No 736; SI 2014 No 1807*].

The Commonwealth War Graves Commission and the Imperial War Graves Endowment Fund Trustees are treated as charities. [*FA 2015, s 123*].

Exemption from tax on chargeable gains

[11.3] Subject to the restrictions in **11.4** and **11.5** below, a gain accruing to a charity is not a chargeable gain provided it is 'applicable and applied for charitable purposes only'. [*TCGA 1992, s 256(1)*]. For the scope of 'applicable and applied for charitable purposes only', see *Lawrence v CIR* KB 1940, 23 TC 333, *Slater (Helen) Charitable Trust Ltd* CA 1981, 55 TC 230 and *Guild and others v CIR* CS 1993, 66 TC 1.

Where a UK charity is a beneficiary of an offshore trust and receives a capital payment, such that a gain would otherwise be treated as accruing to the charity under *TCGA 1992, s 87* (see **48.14** OFFSHORE SETTLEMENTS), the above exemption is available to the extent that the capital payment is applicable and applied for charitable purposes. (Revenue Tax Bulletin August 1998 pp 573, 574).

Where property held on charitable trusts ceases to be subject to those trusts, the trustees are deemed to have disposed of, and immediately reacquired, the property at its market value at that time. Any gain arising is not treated as accruing to a charity. Furthermore, insofar as the property represents, directly or indirectly, the consideration for the disposal of assets by the trustees, any gain accruing on that earlier disposal (and previously exempt) is treated as not having accrued to a charity and capital gains tax is chargeable as if the exemption had never applied. A cumulative liability may therefore arise and an assessment may be made within three years of the end of the year of assessment in which the property ceases to be subject to charitable trusts. [*TCGA 1992, s 256(2)*]. Such an assessment seems to be able to be made even where the gain arising on an earlier disposal is outside the normal time limit for assessment.

Restriction of exemption

[**11.4**] If, in any 'chargeable period' (i.e. tax year or accounting period), a charity incurs (or is treated as incurring) 'non-charitable expenditure', the amount of relief given under the following exemptions is reduced by an amount equal to that expenditure (or, if less, the total otherwise exempt income and gains). The exemptions are those under:

- *TCGA 1992, s 256* (see **11.3** above);
- *ITA 2007, ss 524–537* (income tax exemptions for charitable trusts);
- *CTA 2010, ss 478–489* (corporation tax exemptions for charitable companies);
- *ICTA 1988, s 56(3)(c); CTA 2010, Sch 2 para 70* (exemption for certain income of charitable companies from certificates of deposit in existence before 1 April 1996); and
- *SI 2009 No 3001, Reg 31* (exemption for offshore income gains of charitable companies).

The charity may by notice in writing to HMRC specify against which items of income or gains the reduction is to be treated as made. If, within 30 days of a request to do so, the charity does not give such notice, HMRC determine the attribution.

If the charity's non-charitable expenditure for a chargeable period exceeds the aggregate for the period of:

- income and gains which, but for the application of these provisions, would qualify for any of the above exemptions;
- other income and gains chargeable to tax; and
- donations, legacies and other similar receipts that are not chargeable to tax,

the excess is treated as non-charitable expenditure of previous chargeable periods ending not more than six years before the end of the chargeable period in which the expenditure was actually incurred. Attributions are made to later periods in priority to earlier periods. Adjustments by way of assessment or otherwise are made in consequence of an attribution to a previous period.

Non-charitable expenditure

A charity's '*non-charitable expenditure*' for a tax year or accounting period is:

(a) any loss made in the year or period (i.e., for income tax purposes, any loss made in the basis period for the year) in a trade other than a trade within one of the charitable exemptions;

(b) (for charitable trusts only) any payment made in the year in connection with a trade where post-cessation expenditure relief within *ITA 2007, s 96* is available unless the trade was within one of the charitable exemptions at *ITA 2007, ss 526, 529* or *530* at cessation;

(c) any loss made in the year or period in a trade, UK or overseas property business where the loss relates to land and any profits generated from the land for the year would not have been within the exemption at *ITA 2007, s 531* or *CTA 2010, s 485*;

(d) (for charitable trusts only) any payment made in the year in connection with a trade or UK or overseas property business where post-cessation expenditure relief within *ITA 2007, ss 96* or *125* is available where the payment relates to land and any profits generated from the land immediately before cessation would not be within the exemption at *ITA 2007, s 531*;

(e) any loss made in the year or period in a 'miscellaneous transaction' entered into otherwise than in the course of carrying on a charitable purpose;

(f) any 'expenditure' incurred in the year or period not within (b) or (d) above which is not incurred solely for charitable purposes and is not required to be taken into account in calculating the profits or losses of any trade or property business or miscellaneous transaction;

(g) any amounts for the year or period treated as non-charitable expenditure under the substantial donor provisions at **11.5** below;

(h) the amount of any funds invested in the year in any investment which is not an 'approved charitable investment'; and

(i) any amount lent in the year by the trust, if the loan is neither an investment nor an 'approved charitable loan'.

Any amount falling within more than one of the above categories is treated as non-charitable expenditure only once.

For the purposes of (e) and (f) above, a '*miscellaneous transaction*' is a transaction any income or gains from which would have been chargeable to income tax or corporation tax under any of the provisions listed in *ITA 2007, s 1016* or *CTA 2010, s 1173* but for the miscellaneous income and gains exemption at *ITA 2007, s 527* and *CTA 2010, s 481*.

For the purposes of (f) above, '*expenditure*' includes capital expenditure but does not include the investment of any of the charity's funds, the making of a loan by the trust or the repayment by the charity of the whole or part of a loan. Expenditure which is referable to commitments (contractual or otherwise) entered into before or during a particular tax year or accounting period is treated as incurred in that year or period if, had accounts been drawn up in accordance with UK generally accepted accounting practice for the year or period, it would have had to be taken into account in preparing those accounts.

The further provisions at (i) and (iii) above apply also for the purposes of the above definition.

The following are '*approved charitable investments*'.

(A) An investment in securities (including shares, stocks and debentures (as defined)):
- issued or guaranteed by the government of an EU member state or the government or a governmental body of any territory or part of a territory;
- issued by an international entity listed in the Annex to Council Directive 2003/48/EC;
- issued by an entity meeting the four criteria set out at the end of that Annex;
- issued by a building society;
- issued by a credit institution operating on mutual principles which is authorised by an appropriate governmental body in the territory of issue;
- issued by an open-ended investment company (within *CTA 2010, ss 613, 615*);
- issued by a company and listed on a recognised stock exchange (within *ITA 2007, s 1005*); or
- issued by a company and not listed on a recognised stock exchange.

Further conditions (see *ITA 2007, s 560* and *CTA 2010, s 513*) must be met in the case of certain of the above securities.

(B) An investment in a common investment fund established under *Charities Act 1960, s 22* (or NI equivalent) or *Charities Act 1993, s 24*.

(C) An investment in a common deposit fund established under *Charities Act 1960, s 22A* or *Charities Act 1993, s 25*.

(D) An investment in a fund which is similar to those in (B) or (C) above which is established for the exclusive benefit of charities by or under legislation relating to any particular charities or class of charities.

(E) An interest in land other than an interest held as security for a debt.

(F) Any bills, certificates of tax deposit, savings certificates or tax reserve certificates issued in the UK by the Government.

(G) Northern Ireland Treasury bills.

(H) Units in a unit trust scheme within *Financial Services and Markets Act 2000, s 237(1)* or in a recognised scheme within *Financial Services and Markets Act 2000, s 237(3)*.

(I) A deposit with a bank (within *ITA 2007, s 991*) in respect of which interest is payable at a commercial rate, but excluding a deposit made as part of an arrangement under which the bank makes a loan to a third party.

(J) A deposit with the National Savings Bank, a building society or a credit institution operating on mutual principles which is authorised by an appropriate governmental body in the territory in which the deposit is taken.

(K) Certificates of deposit within *ITTOIA 2005, s 552(2)*, including uncertificated eligible debt security units as defined in *ITA 2007, s 986(3)*.

(L) Any loan or other investment as to which HMRC are satisfied, on a claim, that it is made for the benefit of the charity and not for the avoidance of tax (whether by the charity or any other person). Loans secured by mortgage etc. over land are within this heading.

As regards swap contracts, e.g. interest rate or currency swaps, see Revenue Tax Bulletin August 2003 p 1056.

The following are '*approved charitable loans*' if they are not made by way of investment.

(1) A loan made to another charity for charitable purposes only.
(2) A loan to a beneficiary of the charity which is made in the course of carrying out the purposes of the charity.
(3) Money placed on a current account with a bank (within *ITA 2007, s 991*), but excluding a loan made as part of an arrangement under which the bank makes a loan to a third party.
(4) A loan, not within (1)–(3) above, as to which HMRC are satisfied, on a claim, that the loan is made for the benefit of the charity and not for tax avoidance purposes (whether by the charity or by a third party).

[*ITA 2007, ss 539–548, 558–564; CTA 2010, ss 492–501, 511–517, Sch 2 para 77; TCGA 1992, ss 256(3)–(8), 256A–256D; TIOPA 2010, Sch 8 paras 81, 82; FA 2010, Sch 6 para 13, Sch 8 paras 2, 8(3); SI 1997 No 1154, Reg 16; SI 2006 No 964, Reg 94 (7); SI 2009 No 23, Art 3; SI 2009 No 3001, Reg 126*].

Payments to substantial donors

[11.5] Anti-avoidance provisions apply to restrict the transactions that can take place between a 'substantial donor' and a charity without loss of the tax exemptions listed above. The provisions operate by treating certain payments and deemed payments to be non-charitable expenditure for the purposes of the restriction of exemptions provisions at **11.4** above. The provisions are repealed for transactions occurring on or after 1 April 2013 other than transactions entered into under a contract made before that date (excluding such transactions entered into under a variation of the contract made on or after that date). In effect the provisions are replaced by those at **11.11** below and transitional rules apply with effect from 1 April 2011 — see below.

Subject to the transitional rule below, the following are treated as non-charitable expenditure under the current provisions:

(I) a payment made by a charity to a substantial donor in the course of, or for the purposes of, one of the transactions listed below;
(II) where the terms of such a transaction are less beneficial to the charity than terms which might be expected at arm's length, the amount that HMRC determine as the cost to the charity of the difference in terms (the deemed expenditure being treated as incurred at such time or times as HMRC determine); and
(III) a payment by a charity of remuneration to a substantial donor other than remuneration for services as a trustee which is approved by the Charity Commission or other body with responsibility for regulating

charities by virtue of legislation having effect in respect of any part of the UK, or a court. Where the remuneration is not paid in money, the cash equivalent under the employment benefits rules of *ITEPA 2003, Pt 3* is used to determine the amount of the non-charitable expenditure.

Payments and benefits arising to a donor are disregarded for these purposes to the extent that they relate to a donation by the donor and do not exceed the limits on donor benefits for the purposes of the gift aid provisions (see **11.10** below for donations by individuals and *CTA 2010, ss 191–198* for donations by companies).

Non-charitable expenditure may be deemed to be incurred in respect of a single transaction under both (I) and (II) above, but any amount treated as incurred under (I) above is deducted from any amount which the charity would otherwise be treated as incurring under (II) above. A transaction entered into in a chargeable period falls within the provisions even if it occurs before the donor first satisfied the definition of substantial donor in respect of that period.

Two or more charities which are connected in a matter relating to the structure, administration or control of a charity are treated as a single charity for the purposes of the provisions.

Subject to the exclusions below, (I) and (II) above apply to the following transactions:

- the sale or letting of property by a charity to a substantial donor or by a substantial donor to a charity;
- the provision of services by a charity to a substantial donor or by a substantial donor to a charity;
- an exchange of property between a charity and a substantial donor;
- the provision of financial assistance (including, in particular, the provision of a loan, guarantee or indemnity or entering into alternative financial arrangements within *ITA 2007, s 564A* or *CTA 2009, s 501* (see **3** ALTERNATIVE FINANCE ARRANGEMENTS)) by a charity to a substantial donor or by a substantial donor to a charity; and
- investment by a charity in the business of a substantial donor other than by purchase of shares or securities listed on a recognised stock exchange (see **63.30** SHARES AND SECURITIES).

The sale or letting of property, or the provision of services, to a charity by a substantial donor is excluded if HMRC determine that the transaction occurs in the course of the donor's business on terms which are no less beneficial to the charity than those to be expected at arm's length and that the transaction is not part of an arrangement for the avoidance of tax. The provision of services to a substantial donor is excluded if HMRC determine that the services are provided in the course of carrying out a primary purpose of the charity on terms which are no more beneficial to the donor than those on which services are provided to others. The provision of financial assistance to a charity by a substantial donor is excluded if HMRC determine that the assistance is on terms which are no less beneficial to the charity than those which might be expected at arm's length and is not part of an arrangement for the avoidance of tax.

A disposal at an undervalue to which *ITA 2007, s 431*, *CTA 2010, s 203* or *TCGA 1992, s 257(2)* (gifts of assets to charities — see **11.7** below) apply is not itself a transaction to which the above provisions apply, but it may be taken into account in determining whether a person is a substantial donor to the charity.

Transitional rule

Where a payment within (I) or (III) above made on or after 1 April 2011 would otherwise be treated as non-charitable expenditure, or non-charitable expenditure would otherwise be treated as incurred on or after that date under (II) above, that payment or expenditure is not treated as non-charitable expenditure if the transaction with the substantial donor (whether it took place before, on or after 1 April 2011) is not 'tainted'.

For this purpose, a transaction is 'tainted' if it is reasonable to assume from the likely effects of the gifts to the charity and the transaction, and the circumstances in which they were made and entered into, that the gifts would not have been made and the transaction would not have been entered into independently of one another.

Substantial donor

A person is a '*substantial donor*' to a charity for a chargeable period if the charity receives, before 1 April 2011, 'tax relievable' gifts (including non-monetary gifts) from him to a value of at least:

- £25,000 in a period of twelve months in which the chargeable period wholly or partly falls; or
- £150,000 (£100,000 before 23 April 2009) in a period of six years in which the chargeable period wholly or partly falls.

Gifts received by a charity on or after 1 April 2011 are disregarded for this purpose.

Where a person qualifies as a substantial donor for a chargeable period in this way, he continues to be treated as a substantial donor for the following five chargeable periods. The Treasury may by regulations vary these amounts or periods of time. A company that is wholly owned by a charity (within *CTA 2010, s 200*) is not treated as a substantial donor to that charity. A registered social landlord or housing association (as defined) is not treated as a substantial donor to a charity with which it is connected (i.e. where one owns or controls the other or both are under common ownership or control). Note that a person may be a substantial donor by reference to gifts made at any time.

References above to a substantial donor are to be taken to include any person connected (within *ITA 2007, s 993* — see **17** CONNECTED PERSONS) with him.

'*Tax relievable*' gifts are effectively gifts and donations on which the donor is entitled to some form of income tax, corporation tax or capital gains tax relief; full lists of the types of gifts covered are given (in terms of the legislation under which the tax relief is available) at *ITA 2007, s 550* and *CTA 2010, s 503* and are comprehensive.

[*ITA 2007, ss 549–557; CTA 2010, ss 502–510, Sch 2 paras 73–76; FA 2011, s 27, Sch 3 paras 13, 14, 24, 25, 27(2)(3), 29, 30; SI 2009 No 56, Sch 1 paras 147, 453, 703, 704; SI 2009 No 1029, Reg 2*].

Reliefs for donations to charities

[11.6] Relief from tax is available to donors to charities. Reliefs which are relevant to tax on chargeable gains are for gifts of assets and gifts by individuals of cash. Those reliefs are covered at **11.7** to **11.10** below. Anti-avoidance provisions apply to donations made on or after 1 April 2011 which are tainted by arrangements for the donor to obtain a financial advantage — see **11.11** below.

Gifts of assets to charities

[11.7] Where a disposal of an asset is made otherwise than under a bargain at arm's length to a charity, the normal MARKET VALUE (**45**) provisions (which deem the acquisition and disposal as being made at market value) do not apply. See **11.11** below for the anti-avoidance provision for tainted donations which disapplies this rule in certain cases.

If the disposal is by way of gift (including a gift into settlement) or for a consideration not exceeding the allowable expenditure which would be available on a disposal of the asset (see **16.11** COMPUTATION OF GAINS AND LOSSES) the transaction is treated as made for a consideration producing neither a gain nor a loss. Where the asset is subsequently disposed of by the charity, its acquisition by the person making the original disposal is treated as the acquisition of the asset by the charity. See **9.6** ASSETS HELD ON 31 MARCH **1982** and **38.4** INDEXATION for consequential re-basing and indexation provisions. Where the asset is a qualifying investment for the purposes of *ITA 2007, ss 431–446* or *CTA 2010, ss 203–217* (gifts of shares, securities and real property to charities) and the disposal qualifies for income tax or corporation tax relief under those sections (see Tolley's Income Tax and Tolley's Corporation Tax under Charities), the amount treated as the charity's acquisition cost is reduced by the amount on which income tax or corporation tax relief is given or, if this would otherwise produce a negative figure, is reduced to nil.

If the disposal to the charity is for a consideration exceeding the allowable expenditure, the market value is not substituted for the actual consideration.

These provisions apply also to gifts made to a registered community amateur sports club (see **11.12** below).

See **54.4** QUALIFYING CORPORATE BONDS as regards making a gift of such a bond received on a reorganisation of share capital.

These provisions do not apply to disposals in relation to which venture capital trust relief is available (see **71** VENTURE CAPITAL TRUSTS).

The above provisions do apply to disposals made otherwise than under a bargain at arm's length to any of the bodies mentioned in *IHTA 1984, Sch 3*.

[*TCGA 1992, s 257(1)(2)–(2C)(4)(5); SI 2009 No 3001, Reg 126*].

The bodies listed in *IHTA 1984, Sch 3* (as amended) comprise:

- The National Gallery.
- The British Museum.
- The National Museum of Scotland.
- The National Museum of Wales.
- The Ulster Museum.
- Any other similar national institution which exists wholly or mainly for the purpose of preserving for the public benefit a collection of scientific, historic or artistic interest and which is approved for this purpose by the Treasury (see list at HMRC Capital Gains Manual Appendix 4).
- Any museum or art gallery in the UK which exists wholly or mainly for that purpose and is maintained by a local authority or university in the UK.
- Any library the main function of which is to serve the needs of teaching and research at a university in the UK.
- The Historic Buildings and Monuments Commission for England.
- The National Trust for Places of Historic Interest or Natural Beauty.
- The National Trust for Scotland for Places of Historic Interest or Natural Beauty.
- The National Art Collections Fund.
- The Trustees of the National Heritage Memorial Fund.
- The National Endowment for Science, Technology and the Arts.
- The Friends of the National Libraries.
- The Historic Churches Preservation Trust.
- Nature Conservancy Council for England.
- Scottish National Heritage.
- Countryside Council for Wales.
- Any local authority.
- Any Government department (including the National Debt Commissioners).
- Any university or university college in the UK.
- A health service body within *CTA 2010, s 986*.

Gifts of assets out of settlements

[11.8] Where a charity becomes absolutely entitled to any assets (or part thereof) which were previously settled property and those assets are deemed to be disposed of and reacquired by the trustees on that occasion (under *TCGA 1992, s 71* — see **62.16** SETTLEMENTS) then, if no consideration is received by any person for or in connection with the transaction, the disposal is deemed to take place on a no gain, no loss basis. This does *not* apply where the charity becomes absolutely entitled to the assets on the termination of a life interest (within the meaning of *TCGA 1992, s 72*, see **62.4** SETTLEMENTS) by the death of the person entitled to it. These provisions also apply to a gift to a registered community amateur sports club (see **11.12** below) or any of the bodies mentioned in *IHTA 1984, Sch 3* (gifts for national purposes). See **11.7** above. See also **11.11** below for anti-avoidance provisions. [*TCGA 1992, s 257(3)*].

In *Prest v Bettinson* Ch D 1980, 53 TC 437, the residue of an estate was held on trust for five institutions, four of which were charities, subject to the payment of annuities to six individuals. No specific fund was set aside, but distributions of capital and income were made annually to the five institutions, the income of the residuary fund being more than sufficient to pay the annuities. The trustee failed in his claim that four-fifths of any capital gain arising was exempt as accruing for charitable purposes. Since no fund had been set aside to pay the annuities, the trustee retained full control of the trust property until the distribution of the proceeds of sale, and any gain from a disposal thereof had accrued to him as trustee and not to the charities.

Gifts of pre-eminent property to the nation

[11.9] With effect for tax years or accounting periods beginning on or after 1 April 2012, an individual or company making a 'qualifying gift' of 'pre-eminent property' to be held for the benefit of the public or the nation qualifies for a reduction in tax liability equal to a percentage of the value of the property. A gain accruing on a qualifying gift is not a chargeable gain (and a loss is not an allowable loss). [*TCGA 1992, s 258(1A); FA 2012, Sch 14 paras 34, 36*].

It is explicitly provided that nothing in the following provisions gives rise to any right or expectation that an offer to make a qualifying gift will be accepted. [*FA 2012, Sch 14 para 25*].

Qualifying gift

A person makes a '*qualifying gift*' if:

(a) he offers to give pre-eminent property to be held for the benefit of the public or nation;
(b) he is legally and beneficially entitled to the property and the property is not owned jointly or in common with others;
(c) the offer is in accordance with a scheme set up for this purpose by the Secretary of State;
(d) the offer is registered in accordance with the scheme;
(e) the offer, or part of it, is accepted in accordance with the scheme; and
(f) the gift is made pursuant to the offer, or part, accepted.

In the following paragraphs, the '*agreed terms*' means the terms on which acceptance of the offer is agreed, as recorded in the way required by the scheme, and the '*offer registration date*' means the date the offer was registered under (d) above.

[*FA 2012, Sch 14 para 1*].

Pre-eminent property

'*Pre-eminent property*' means:

(1) any picture, print, book, manuscript, work of art, scientific object or other thing that the relevant Minister (i.e. the Secretary of State and/or Scottish, Welsh or Northern Irish equivalent as applicable — see *FA 2012, Sch 14 para 23*) is satisfied is pre-eminent for its national, scientific, historic or artistic interest;

(2) any collection or group of pictures, prints, books, manuscripts, works of art, scientific objects or other things if the relevant Minister is satisfied that the collection or group taken as a whole is pre-eminent for its national, scientific, historic or artistic interest; or
(3) any object that is or has been kept in a significant building (within *IHTA 1984, s 230(3)(a)–(d)*) if it appears to the relevant Minister desirable for the object to remain associated with the building.

For this purpose, '*national interest*' includes interest within any part of the UK. In determining whether an object or collection or group of objects is pre-eminent, regard must be had to any significant association which they have with a particular place.

[*FA 2012, Sch 14 paras 22, 23*].

Relief for individuals

Relief is given by way of a total reduction of the individual's liability to income tax and capital gains tax equal to 30% of the value set out in the agreed terms as the agreed value of the property. The reduction can be spread across any or all of the tax year in which the offer registration date occurs and the four following tax years. The taxpayer is free to allocate the total reduction to those tax years as he wishes, but the allocations must form part of the agreed terms.

Where all or part of the total tax reduction is allocated to a tax year, a portion of the taxpayer's income tax and capital gains tax liability for that year is treated as satisfied, as if he had paid that portion when it became due (or on the offer registration date, if the portion became due before that date). The portion so treated as satisfied is the smaller of:

(i) the part of the tax reduction allocated to the tax year; and
(ii) the taxpayer's income tax and capital gains tax liability for the year, less any amount allocated to the year in respect of a previous qualifying gift.

Where the amount allocated to the year is less than the amount in (ii) above, the tax reduction is allocated between income tax and capital gains tax liabilities in the order specified in the agreed terms or, if no order is specified, against the income tax liability before the capital gains tax liability. If the taxpayer's tax liability is revised at any time, the relief given under these provisions must be recalculated (but revision of the agreed terms is not permitted).

Relief is not available to an individual in the capacity of trustee or personal representative.

[*FA 2012, Sch 14 paras 2–5, 7*].

If a qualifying gift is set aside or declared void, the tax reduction is withdrawn and the taxpayer is required to pay the portions of his liabilities no longer treated as satisfied under the above provisions, together with any late payment interest and penalties in respect of them by the later of the end of the period of 30 days beginning with the day on which the gift was set aside or declared void and the date by which he would have been required to pay those amounts but for the relief. [*FA 2012, Sch 14 para 8*].

Effect on interest and penalties

Any liability to pay late payment interest or late payment penalties (and interest on such penalties) arising in the period beginning with the offer registration date and ending with the date the qualifying gift is made ceases when the gift is made, and is treated as if it had never arisen, to the extent that the tax concerned is treated as satisfied under the above provisions. In determining whether or to what extent interest or a penalty is attributable to that tax, any attribution or apportionment is to be done so as to minimise the interest and penalties payable by the taxpayer. This provision does not affect any interest that accrued, or penalty to which the taxpayer became liable, before the offer registration date. [*FA 2012, Sch 14 para 6*].

The effect of this provision is negated if the qualifying gift is set aside or declared void. [*FA 2012, Sch 14 para 8(b)*].

Suspension of tax pending negotiations

Where an individual makes an offer within (a) above and:

(A) the offer is registered in accordance with the scheme;
(B) the offer includes a proposal of what should be the agreed terms;
(C) the individual will be required to pay an amount of, or on account of, income tax or capital gains tax for a tax year for which a tax reduction is proposed by a certain date; and
(D) the negotiation of the terms is not expected to conclude before that date,

he may make a request that the obligation to pay the amount by the due date be suspended until the negotiations conclude. Such a request must be made in writing to HMRC at least 45 days before the due date concerned, and must be accompanied by a copy of the donor's proposal within (B) above and such other information as HMRC may reasonably require. The running total of amounts for which suspension can be requested in respect of the same offer and the same tax year must not exceed the proposed tax reduction figure for that year. For these purposes, negotiations conclude when the qualifying gift is made or when the offer is withdrawn or rejected.

Suspension of an amount stops the donor from becoming liable to late payment penalties for failing to pay that amount but does not stop late payment interest from accruing.

In considering whether or to what extent to agree to a request, HMRC must have regard to all the circumstances of the case (including the creditworthiness of the potential donor, and they may impose conditions on their agreement to the suspension. HMRC may by notice in writing to the potential donor, withdraw its agreement to a suspension with effect from the date specified in the notice. If they do so, the potential donor must pay the suspended amount, together with any late payment interest, by the end of the period of 30 days beginning with the specified date. The last day of that period is then treated for the purposes of late payment penalties as the date on or before which the amount must be paid.

When the negotiations conclude, then, if the offer is withdrawn or rejected, the potential donor must pay the amount suspended, together with any late payment interest, within 30 days. The last day of the 30-day period is treated for the purposes of late payment penalties as the date on or before which the amount must be paid. If the negotiations conclude because a qualifying gift is made, the potential donor is only required to pay so much as is not treated as satisfied under the above provisions. If the negotiations conclude in relation only to part of the offer, these provisions take effect as far as reasonably practicable in relation to that part and, on receipt of a revised copy of the donor's proposal, HMRC may agree to a further suspension in relation to the part still under negotiation.

[*FA 2012, Sch 14 paras 9–11*].

Relief for companies

Relief is given by way of a reduction of the company's corporation tax liability for the accounting period in which the offer registration date falls. A portion of the liability is treated as satisfied, as if the company had paid that portion when it became due (or on the offer registration date, if the portion became due before that date). The portion so treated as satisfied is the smaller of:

- 20% of the value set out in the agreed terms as the agreed value of the property (or such lower figure as may be specified in the agreed terms); and
- the company's corporation tax liability for the accounting period, less any amount treated as satisfied in respect of a previous qualifying gift.

If the company's corporation tax liability is revised at any time, the relief given must be recalculated (but revision of the agreed terms is not permitted).

Provisions similar to those applying to individuals relating to a qualifying gift being set aside or declared void, interest and penalties and suspension of tax pending negotiations apply for corporation tax purposes.

[*FA 2012, Sch 14 paras 12–20*].

Treasury powers to amend provisions

The Treasury has the power by order made by statutory instrument to change the percentages specified for determining the amount of the tax reduction. [*FA 2012, Sch 14 paras 4(6), 14(4), 21*].

Gift aid donations by individuals

[11.10] Gifts of money made by individuals to charities which are 'qualifying donations' attract relief under the Gift Aid provisions described below. The provisions are subject to the anti-avoidance rules at **11.11** below. For the Gift Aid provisions applicable to companies, see the corresponding chapter of Tolley's Corporation Tax.

For the purposes of these provisions, '*charity*' has the same meaning as in **11.2** above, but also includes the Trustees of the National Heritage Memorial Fund, the historic Buildings and Monuments Commission for England and the

National Endowment for Science, Technology and the Arts. The provisions have effect as if a registered community amateur sports club (see **11.12** below) were a charity, but club membership fees are not gifts for the purposes of these provisions. [*ITA 2007, s 430*].

The donor

Where a qualifying donation is made by an individual ('*the donor*') in a tax year, then, for that year, he is treated for the purposes of income tax and CGT as if:

(a) the gift had been made after deduction of income tax at the basic rate; and

(b) the basic rate limit and the higher rate limit were increased by an amount equal to the 'grossed up amount of the gift' (i.e. the amount which, after deducting income tax at the basic rate for the tax year in which the gift is made, leaves the amount of the gift).

As the basic rate limit is used in determining the CGT liability of a higher rate taxpayer, the increase mentioned in (b) above gives potential CGT relief for those years in a case where *income* is insufficient to fully obtain higher rate relief on the amount of the gift. For this purpose, higher rate relief means relief for the excess of tax at the higher rate over tax at the basic rate for which relief is effectively given at source. The increase in the basic rate limit does not apply for the purposes of computing top-slicing relief on life assurance policy gains chargeable to income tax.

To the extent, if any, necessary to ensure that the amount of income tax and capital gains tax to which the donor is charged for a tax year in which one or more gifts is made is an amount at least equal to the tax treated under (a) above as deducted from the gift or gifts, the donor is *not* entitled to the following reliefs for that year:

- the personal allowance;
- the blind person's allowance;
- the married couple's allowance; and
- the miscellaneous life assurance-related reliefs at *ITA 2007, ss 457, 458* (payments to trade unions and police organisations) and *ITA 2007, s 459* (payments for benefit of family members).

The restriction does not adversely affect the donor's ability to transfer unused married couple's allowance to a spouse or civil partner.

Where the tax treated as deducted exceeds the amount of income tax and capital gains tax to which the donor is charged for the year (or, for capital gains tax, the amount to which the donor would be charged but for double tax relief) after taking into account the above restriction of reliefs, the donor is liable to an income tax charge for the year, the tax chargeable being equal to the excess.

The amount of income tax to which the donor is charged for a tax year for these purposes is calculated according to the steps at *ITA 2007, s 23* (see Tolley's Income Tax under Allowances and Tax Rates), but with the following modifications.

(i) At Step 6 (tax reductions), the following tax reductions are ignored:
- relief for qualifying maintenance payments within *ITA 2007, s 453*; and
- any double tax relief (whether given under a double tax agreement or unilaterally).

(ii) Step 7 is ignored.

(iii) The following amounts are then deducted:
- any notional tax treated as having been paid under *ITTOIA 2005, s 399* or *s 400* (distributions without a tax credit), *ITTOIA 2005, s 414* (stock dividends), *ITTOIA 2005, s 421* (release of loan to participator in close company), *ITTOIA 2005 s 530* (life assurance gains), or *ITTOIA 2005, s 685A* (payments from settlor-interested settlements); and
- any tax treated as deducted from estate income under *ITTOIA 2005, s 656(3) or s 657(4)*, to the extent that it is treated as paid out of sums within *ITTOIA 2005, s 680(3)(b)* or *(4)*.

[*ITA 2007, ss 414, 415, 423–425; SI 2009 No 2859, Art 4*].

Carry-back of relief

A person making a qualifying donation can elect for it to be treated, for the purposes of the above provisions, as if it were a qualifying donation made in the previous tax year, provided that the condition below is satisfied.

The condition is that the donor's 'charged amount' for that previous tax year must be at least equal to the 'increased total of gifts'. For this purpose, the donor's '*charged amount*' for a tax year is the sum of his 'modified net income' (as defined at *ITA 2007, s 1025*) and the amount on which he is chargeable to capital gains tax for the year. The '*increased total of gifts*' is the aggregate of the sum of the grossed up amounts of all the gifts made in the current year which are to be, or have already been (by an earlier election), carried back to the previous year and the sum of the grossed up amounts of any qualifying donations actually made in the previous year (and not themselves carried back). All the grossed up amounts are calculated for this purpose as if the gifts were made in the previous year.

The election must be made by notice in writing to an officer of HMRC on or before the date on which the donor delivers his tax return for the previous tax year, and not later than 31 January in the tax year in which the gift is actually made. An election cannot be made by way of amendment to a return (*Cameron v HMRC* FTT, [2010] UKFTT 104 (TC), 2010 STI 1726).

The carry-back facility is *not* available in respect of gifts made through the self-assessment return as below.

[*ITA 2007, ss 426, 427; FA 2012, s 50(2)*].

The charity

The receipt by a charity of a qualifying donation is treated as the receipt, under deduction of income tax at the basic rate for the tax year in which the gift is made, of an amount equal to the 'grossed up amount of the gift' (see (a) above). [*ITA 2007, s 520; CTA 2010, ss 471, 661D; FA 2012, Sch 15 para 6*]. An election by the donor to treat a qualifying donation as being made in the previous tax year does not affect the position of the charity; the donation is grossed up by reference to the basic rate for the tax year in which payment is *actually* made.

Qualifying donations

A '*qualifying donation*' is a gift to a charity by the donor which meets the following conditions:

(I) it takes the form of a payment of a sum of money;
(II) it is not subject to a condition as to repayment;
(III) it is not deductible under the payroll deduction scheme — see Tolley's Income Tax under Charities);
(IV) it is not deductible in calculating the donor's income from any source;
(V) it is not conditional on or associated with, or part of an arrangement involving, the acquisition of property by the charity, otherwise than by way of gift, from the donor or a person connected with him;
(VI) neither the donor nor any person connected with him (see **17** CONNECTED PERSONS) receives any benefit, in consequence of making it, in excess of specified limits (see below); and
(VII) the donor or, for donations made on or after 6 April 2017, an 'intermediary' representing the donor gives the charity or, for donations on or after the same date, an intermediary representing the charity, a 'gift aid declaration' in relation to it.

A gift to charity is also a '*qualifying donation*' if it meets the conditions above and the payment is by way of a waiver by the individual of entitlement to sums (whether principal or interest) due to him from the charity in respect of an amount advanced to the charity on which social investment income tax relief has been obtained (see **65** SOCIAL INVESTMENT RELIEF).

A '*gift aid declaration*' for the purposes of (VII) above is a declaration which is given in the manner prescribed by regulations. It may be made in writing, by fax, over the internet or orally (e.g. by telephone). It must contain the donor's name and address, the name of the charity, a description of the gift(s) to which it relates and a statement that the gift(s) is (are) to be treated as qualifying donations for these purposes. In order for the declaration to have effect, it must have been explained to the donor that he must pay sufficient income tax or capital gains tax to cover the tax deemed to be deducted at source from the donation. No signature is required. Charities and intermediaries must maintain a satisfactory auditable (by HMRC) record of declarations given to them. A donor may still cancel the donation of his own volition. An '*intermediary*' is a person authorised by the donor to give a declaration on his behalf to the charity; a person authorised by a charity to receive a declaration on its behalf; or a person authorised to perform both of those roles. Penalties may be imposed on charities and intermediaries who fail to comply with the regulations.

[*ITA 2007, ss 416, 417, 422, 428; FA 2012, s 50(3)(b); FA 2014, Sch 11 para 11; FA 2015, s 20; FA 2016, s 173; SI 2000 No 2074; SI 2005 No 2790; SI 2016 Nos 1010, 1195*].

As regards (VI) above, the benefit does not have to be received from the charity to be taken into account (see *St Dunstan's v Major* (Sp C 127), [1997] SSCD 212, in which the saving of inheritance tax by personal representatives as a result of the variation of a will to provide for a donation which would otherwise qualify under these provisions constituted a benefit).

The release of a loan not for consideration and not under seal cannot amount to a gift of money (see *Battle Baptist Church v CIR and Woodham* (Sp C 23), [1995] SSCD 176).

Limits on donor benefits

Where the donor or a person connected with him receives a benefit or benefits in consequence of making the gift, the gift will not be a qualifying donation if either:

(1) the aggregate value of the benefits received exceeds:
- where the gift is £100 or less, 25% of the amount of the gift;
- where the gift is greater than £100 but not more than £1,000, £25;
- where the gift is greater than £1,000, 5% of the amount of the gift; or

(2) the aggregate of the value of the benefits received in relation to the gift and the value of any benefits received in relation to any qualifying donations previously made to the charity by the donor in the same tax year exceeds £2,500.

The operation of (1) above is modified where a benefit:

(A) consists of the right to receive benefits at intervals over a period of less than twelve months;
(B) relates to a period of less than twelve months;
(C) is one of a series of benefits received at intervals in consequence of making a series of gifts at intervals of less than twelve months; or
(D) is not one of a series of benefits but the gift is one of a series of gifts made at intervals of less then twelve months.

Where (A), (B) or (C) above apply, the value of the benefit and the amount of the gift are 'annualised' for the purposes of (1) above. Where (4) above applies, the amount of the gift (but not the value of the benefit) is likewise annualised. For these purposes a gift or benefit is '*annualised*' by multiplying the amount or value by 365 and dividing the result by the number of days in the period of less than twelve months or the average number of days in the intervals of less than twelve months as appropriate.

In applying the above limits, the benefit of a 'right of admission' is disregarded provided that:

- the opportunity to make a gift and to receive the right of admission in consequence is available to the public;
- the right of admission is a right granted by the charity for the purpose of viewing property preserved, maintained, kept or created by a charity in pursuance of its charitable purposes, including buildings, grounds or other land, plants, animals, works of art (but not performances), artefacts and property of a scientific nature; and

- either:
  - a member of the public could purchase the same right of admission (i.e. a right relating to the same property, classes of person and period of time) and the amount of the gift is at least 10% greater than the amount payable for that right, or
  - the right of admission applies, for a period of at least one year, at all times at which the public can obtain admission other than certain days specified by the charity as an 'event day' (i.e. a day on which an event is to take place on the premises concerned). Where the right is for a period of one year, there must be no more than five specified days in the period. Where the right is for a period of more than one year, there must be no more than five specified days in each calendar year during all or part of which the right applies.

For this purpose, a '*right of admission*' is a right of free or reduced-price admission for the donor (or for the donor and one or more family members, whether or not the right must be exercised by all those persons at the same time) to premises or property to which the public are admitted on payment of an admission fee.

[*ITA 2007, ss 417–421*].

HMRC have published guidance on the right of free admission to charity property. See HMRC Guidance Note 22 September 2005 on HMRC's website.

Anti-avoidance: tainted donations

[11.11] There are anti-avoidance provisions which remove entitlement to tax reliefs and counteract tax advantages where a person makes a relievable charitable donation which is a 'tainted donation' (see below, but broadly a donation linked to arrangements for the donor to obtain a financial advantage). The provisions apply to donations made on or after 1 April 2011, including where the arrangements involved were made, or made and implemented, before that date. [*FA 2011, s 27, Sch 3 paras 27(1), 28*]. The provisions apply equally to donations to community amateur sports clubs (see **11.12** below).

The following reliefs can be denied under the provisions:

(a) gifts of chargeable assets (*TCGA 1992, s 257* — see **11.7**, **11.8** above);
(b) gifts of plant and machinery (*CAA 2001, s 63(2)*);
(c) payroll giving (*ITEPA 2003, Pt 12*);
(d) gifts of trading stock (*ITTOIA 2005, s 108; CTA 2009, s 105*);
(e) gift aid donations by individuals (*ITA 2007, Pt 8 Ch 2* — see **11.10** above);
(f) gifts of shares and real property (*ITA 2007, Pt 8 Ch 3; CTA 2010, Pt 6 Ch 3*);
(g) cash gifts by companies (*CTA 2010, Pt 6 Ch 2*); and
(h) any other gift or disposal in respect of which a charity is entitled to claim a repayment of tax.

An amount of income arising under a UK settlement (within *ITTOIA 2005, s 628*) to which a charity is entitled under the settlement's terms is treated for these purposes as an amount gifted to the charity by the trustees.

[*ITA 2007, ss 809ZH, 809ZI, 809ZR(1); CTA 2010, ss 939A, 939B, 939I(1); FA 2011, Sch 3 paras 1, 2*].

Tainted donations

A donation is a '*tainted donation*' if each of the following three conditions is satisfied.

(1) The donor or a person connected with him (a '*linked person*') enters into 'arrangements' (before or after the donation is made) and it is reasonable to assume from the likely effects of the donation and the arrangements or of the circumstances in which they are made that neither would have been made independently of one another. Where it is a connected person who enters into the arrangements, he must be connected (see below) with the donor at a time in the period beginning with the earliest, and ending with the latest, of the time the arrangements are made, the time the donation is made, and the time when the arrangements are first materially implemented.

(2) The main purpose, or one of the main purposes, of the linked person entering into the arrangements is to obtain a financial advantage directly or indirectly from the charity or a connected charity for one or more linked persons.

(3) The donor is neither a 'qualifying charity-owned company' nor a 'housing provider' linked with the charity. A housing provider is linked with a charity if one is wholly owned or subject to control by the other or both are wholly owned or subject to control by the same person.

For the above purposes, '*arrangements*' include any scheme, arrangement or understanding of any kind, whether or not legally enforceable, involving a transaction or transactions. *ITA 2007, s 993* and *CTA 2010, s 1122* apply to determine whether two persons are '*connected*', but in addition, a beneficiary is treated as connected with a person in the capacity as trustee and with the settlor. In applying those sections for the purposes of these provisions, persons living together as husband and wife or as if they were civil partners are treated as if they were in fact husband and wife or civil partners of each other and 'close company' includes a company which would be close if it were UK-resident. Two charities are connected for the purposes of (2) above if they are connected in a matter relating to the structure, administration or control of either of them.

A '*qualifying charity-owned company*' is a company which:

(i) is wholly owned by one or more charities (within *CTA 2010, s 200*), at least one of which is the charity to whom the donation is made or a connected charity; and

(ii) has not previously been under the control of, and does not carry on a trade previously carried on by, any of the linked persons potentially financially advantaged by the arrangements or any person (other than a charity) connected with such a linked person at any time in the four years ending on the day on which (i) above was first satisfied.

A '*housing provider*' is a body which is a non-profit provider of social housing or is entered on a register maintained under *Housing Act 1996, s 1, Housing (Scotland) Act 2001, s 57, Housing (Scotland) Act 2010, s 20* or NI equivalent.

[*ITA 2007, ss 809ZJ, 809ZP, 809ZQ, 809ZR(1); CTA 2010, ss 939C, 939G, 939H, 939I(1); FA 2011, Sch 3 paras 1, 2, 31*].

Financial advantage

The following applies where the arrangements involve a 'transaction' to which the linked person entering into them or any other linked person ('X') and another person ('Y') are parties. X is treated as obtaining a financial advantage within (2) above if the terms of the transaction are less beneficial to Y or more beneficial to X (or both) than those reasonably to be expected in a transaction at arm's length or if the transaction is not of a kind which a person acting at arm's length and in Y's place might reasonably be expected to make. This rule is not, however, intended to limit the circumstances in which a person is treated as obtaining a financial advantage. '*Transaction*' includes, for example, the sale, letting or exchange of property, the provision of services or of a loan, or other form of financial assistance, and investment in a business.

A financial advantage is ignored for the purposes of the above provisions in the following circumstances:

- where the advantage is applied by the person obtaining it for charitable purposes only;
- where the advantage is a benefit associated with a gift aid donation (within *ITA 2007, s 417* — see **11.10** above) or with a payment within (g) above;
- where the donation is within (f) above and the advantage is a benefit of value which would be taken into account in determining the relievable amount for the purposes of the reliefs in (f) above; and
- where the donation is within (d) above and the advantage would be brought into account under *ITTOIA 2005, s 109* or *CTA 2009, s 108* (receipt of benefits by donor or connected person).

[*ITA 2007, ss 809ZK, 809ZL; CTA 2010, ss 939D, 939E; FA 2011, Sch 3 paras 1, 2*].

Effect of provisions

Where the provisions apply, any relief that would otherwise have been available in respect of the tainted donation or an 'associated donation' under (a) to (h) above is not available. For the purposes of tax on chargeable gains, *TCGA 1992, s 257* (disapplication of market value rule for gifts of assets to charities — see **11.7** above) does not apply to the tainted donation or any associated donation.

An '*associated donation*' is an otherwise relievable donation made under the arrangements by a person other than a company which is a qualifying charity-owned company (see above) in relation to the donation or a housing provider (see above) linked with the charity to which the donation is made.

A gift aid donation for which relief is not available is nevertheless treated as a qualifying donation in the hands of the charity (see **11.10** above under 'The charity') and a similar rule applies where the donation is made under the payroll giving scheme.

[*TCGA 1992, s 257A; ITA 2007, s 809ZM; CTA 2010, s 939F; FA 2011, Sch 3 paras 1–3*].

Where a tainted donation is made and it or an associated donation would otherwise be a qualifying donation for gift aid purposes, an income tax charge will apply on an amount equal to the repayment which the charity is entitled to claim. The liability falls jointly and severally on the donor of the gift aid donation, the donor of the tainted donation (if different), any linked person potentially advantaged under the arrangement and the charity receiving the gift aid donation or the tainted donation (if different) and certain connected charities. See *ITA 2007, s 809ZN*. See also *ITA 2007, s 809ZO* for a similar provision applying to donations made through a settlement.

Community amateur sports clubs

[11.12] An exemption for certain gains can be claimed by sports clubs which are registered with HMRC as community amateur sports clubs ('*registered clubs*').

For a club to be eligible to register, it must, and its constitution must require it to:

- be 'open to the whole community';
- be 'organised on an amateur basis'; and
- have as its main purpose the provision of facilities for, and promotion of participation in, one or more 'eligible sports'.

The club must also meet the location condition, the management condition and the income condition.

For the above purposes, a club is '*open to the whole community*' if membership is open to all, and the club facilities are available to members, without discrimination (leaving aside necessary differentiation on grounds of age, gender or disability relative to a particular sport). Additionally, fees must be set at a level which does not pose a significant obstacle to membership, use of the facilities or full participation in club activities. Costs are deemed to represent a significant obstacle if the total of the membership fees and sporting activity costs exceed £520 per year and the club has not made arrangements to ensure that the costs do not represent an obstacle to membership. With effect from 1 April 2015, a club is not eligible to register if it receives membership fees exceeding £1,612 in respect of any member for any year. For the meaning of 'membership fees', 'sporting activity costs' and for the increase or decrease of the limits for periods of more than or less than a year see *SI 2015 No 725, Regs 7–9*.

A club is not prevented from being open to the whole community simply because it charges different fees for different descriptions of persons.

A club is '*organised on an amateur basis*' if it meets the following four conditions.

(a) The club must be non-profit making, i.e. its constitution must require surplus income or gains to be reinvested in the club and must not permit the distribution of club assets (whether in cash or in kind) to members or third parties. However, donations by a club to charities or other registered clubs are allowed.

(b) It must provide only the following benefits for members and their guests:
   - provision of sporting facilities and suitably qualified coaches;
   - reasonable provision and maintenance of club-owned sports equipment;
   - provision of, or reimbursement of the costs of, coaching courses;
   - provision of insurance cover and medical treatment;
   - reimbursement of reasonable and, with effect from 1 April 2015, necessary travel or subsistence expenses incurred by players, match officials and, with effect from 1 April 2015, coaches, first aiders and accompanying individuals travelling to away matches;
   - reasonable provision of post-match refreshments for players and match officials; and
   - sale or supply of food or drink as a social adjunct to the sporting purposes of the club.

(c) It does not exceed the limit on paid players. The limit is, broadly, £10,000 per year. For the detailed rules see *SI 2015 No 725, Regs 11–13*.

(d) The club's constitution must provide for any net assets on the dissolution of the club to be applied for the purposes of:
   - a charity;
   - another registered club; or
   - the governing body of an eligible sport for the purposes of which the club existed, for use in related community sport,

   as approved by the members of the club in general meeting or by its governing body.

An '*eligible sport*' is one designated as such by Treasury order for the purposes of these provisions. See now *SI 2002 No 1966* which designates for these purposes sports appearing on the National Sports Councils list of activities recognised by them.

A club is not regarded as a community amateur sports club if the number of social members within the club exceeds 50% of the total members. For these purposes a social member is defined as a member who either does not participate or only occasionally participates in the sports activities of the club. For the meaning of 'participation' and 'occasional participation' and for the method of calculating the percentage of social members see *SI 2015 No 725, Regs 16–19*.

A club meets the location condition if it is established in an EU member State or a territory specified in HMRC regulations and its facilities for eligible sports are all in one such State or territory.

A club meets the management condition if its managers are fit and proper persons. For this purpose, the managers are the persons with the general control and management of the administration of the club. If this condition is not met for a period of time it is nevertheless treated as met throughout that period if HMRC consider either that the failure has not prejudiced the purposes of the club or that it is just and reasonable for the condition to be treated as met. The expression 'fit and proper' is not defined and so takes its natural meaning. HMRC consider that the fit and proper person test is the same as that for charities (see **11.2** above).

A club meets the income condition if the total of its trading receipts and property receipts does not exceed £100,000 for an accounting period. The limit is reduced proportionately where the accounting period is less than 12 months. The receipts taken into account are those that would be included in computing the club's trading income and property income for corporation tax if the exemptions for such income did not apply.

[*CTA 2010, ss 658(1)–(1C), 659–661CA; FA 2012, s 52; FA 2013, Sch 21; SI 2010 No 1904; SI 2014 No 1807; SI 2015 Nos 674, 725*].

For HMRC guidance on eligibility conditions see www.gov.uk/government/publications/community-amateur-sports-clubs-detailed-guidance-notes/community-amateur-sports-clubs-detailed-guidance-notes.

Registration

Applications for registration are made to HMRC. Registration may be backdated (possibly to before the date of the application).

HMRC may terminate a club's registration (possibly with retrospective effect) if it appears to them that the club is not, or is no longer, entitled to be registered.

HMRC must notify a club of a decision to register it, to refuse its application or to terminate its registration. The club may appeal against any such decision by notice in writing to HMRC within 30 days of the date of the notification. The notice of appeal must specify the grounds of appeal. The provisions of *TMA 1970* relating to **5 APPEALS** apply to such an appeal. If not dismissing the appeal, the Tribunal may either remit the matter to HMRC for reconsideration, or, as applicable, direct that the club be registered from a particular date, rescind a termination of registration, or direct that a termination take effect on a particular date.

HMRC publishes the names and addresses of registered clubs. This enables potential donors to confirm that they are donating to a registered club (and, therefore, that the donation may qualify for gift aid relief — see below). For a list of the names of registered clubs see www.gov.uk/government/publications/community-amateur-sports-clubs-casc-registered-with-hmrc--2.

[*CTA 2010, ss 658(2)–(5), 670, 671*].

Tax exemptions

Subject to the restriction noted below, a gain accruing to a registered club is not a chargeable gain if it is wholly applied for 'qualifying purposes' and the club makes a claim to that effect. '*Qualifying purposes*' means purposes of providing facilities for, and promoting participation in, one or more eligible sports (and in the following paragraphs, '*non-qualifying purposes*' are to be construed accordingly). [*CTA 2010, ss 661(3), 665*].

In addition to the exemption for gains, registered clubs also enjoy tax exemptions relating to trading income, interest and gift aid income and property income. For full details, see Tolley's Corporation Tax under Voluntary Associations.

Restriction of exemption

The above exemptions are restricted where a registered club incurs any expenditure for non-qualifying purposes in an accounting period and any of the club's income or gains for that period are exempted from tax (or would be but for the restriction).

The restriction operates by comparing the amount of the expenditure incurred in the accounting period for non-qualifying purposes ('*the non-qualifying expenditure*') with the aggregate of the club's income (whether or not taxable, and before deducting expenses) and gains (whether chargeable gains or gains exempted as above) for the accounting period ('*the total income and gains*'), as follows.

(1) Where the non-qualifying expenditure is less than the total income and gains, the amount of exempt income and gains is restricted in the proportion that the non-qualifying expenditure bears to the total income and gains.

(2) Where the non-qualifying expenditure equals the total income and gains, the amount of exempt income and gains is reduced to nil.

(3) Where the non-qualifying expenditure exceeds the total income and gains, the amount of exempt income and gains is reduced to nil, and the 'surplus amount' is carried back to previous accounting periods (latest first) ending not more than six years before the end of the current period, and deducted from income and gains exempted for those periods. To the extent that the amount exempted for an accounting period has already been reduced under this provision or (1) or (2) above, it cannot be reduced again by reference to expenditure of a later accounting period. The '*surplus amount*' is the excess of:
    (i) an amount equal to the proportion of the originally exempt income and gains that the non-qualifying expenditure bears to the total income and gains, over;
    (ii) the amount of the originally exempt income and gains.

Where, as a consequence of this restriction, a registered club has an amount of income and gains for which exemption is not available, the club may, by notice to HMRC, specify which items of income and gains are, in whole or part, to be attributed to that amount. If no such notice is given by the club within 30 days of being required to do so by HMRC, it falls to HMRC to make the attribution.

[*CTA 2010, ss 666–668*].

Property ceasing to be held for qualifying purposes

Where a club holds property and, without disposing of it, ceases at any time to be a registered club or to hold the property for 'qualifying purposes' (see under 'Tax Exemptions' above), it is treated for the purposes of *TCGA 1992* as having disposed of, and immediately reacquired, the property at that time at its then market value. Any gain resulting from the deemed disposal does not attract the above exemption. Additionally, to the extent that any of the property represents, directly or indirectly, the consideration for the disposal of assets by the club, any gain that accrued on that disposal does not attract the exemption. Assessments in respect of resulting chargeable gains can be made at any time not later than three years after the end of the accounting period in which falls the event giving rise to this treatment. [*CTA 2010, s 669*].

Reliefs for donations

Gifts to registered clubs by individuals can qualify for relief under the gift aid provisions (see **11.10** above) and gifts of assets can qualify for relief under *TCGA 1992, s 257* (gifts of assets to charities — see **11.7**, **11.8** above).

12

Children

General	**12.1**
Nominees and bare trustees	**12.2**
Assessment of guardians etc	**12.3**
Default of infant	**12.4**

Cross-references. See 25.24 EXEMPTIONS AND RELIEFS for Child Trust Funds; 57.34 RESIDENCE AND DOMICILE for domicile of children.

General matters relating to children

[12.1] There is no general bar to the chargeable gains made by an infant (i.e. an individual under 18 years of age) being assessed and charged on him personally (see *R v Newmarket Commissioners (ex p. Huxley)* CA 1916, 7 TC 49 and *FA 2012, s 222(3)*). HMRC can, therefore, resort directly to the infant and, for 2012/13 onwards, must do so, subject to the general legal framework for appointing people to assist those who lack capacity. Previously, there were specific tax provisions which enabled HMRC to charge and assess tax due from an infant on a guardian etc. Whether or not, in practice, they did so depended on particular circumstances.

A child is entitled to the same capital gains tax reliefs and exemptions as an adult (subject to specific exclusions).

Nominees and bare trustees

[12.2] Where property is held by a person as nominee, or as trustee for any person who would be absolutely entitled against him but for being an infant, the provisions of *TCGA 1992* apply as if the acts of the nominee or trustee are the acts of the infant. Acquisitions from or to the trustee or nominee to or from the infant are accordingly disregarded. References in *TCGA 1992* to a person being absolutely entitled against the trustee mean that the person has the exclusive right (subject only to satisfying any outstanding charge, lien or other right of the trustee to resort to the relevant property for payment of duty, taxes, costs or other outgoings) to direct how the property shall be dealt with. [*TCGA 1992, s 60*]. For the wider implications of nominees and bare trustees generally, see 62.3 SETTLEMENTS.

Assessment of guardians etc.

[12.3] In practice, HMRC often makes use of the machinery of *TMA 1970*, which enables it, for 2011/12 and earlier years, to charge and assess the tax due from an 'incapacitated person' (this term includes an 'infant': see *TMA*

1970, s 118), on the trustee, guardian, tutor, curator or committee, having the direction, control or management of that person's property. Such machinery applies whether or not the incapacitated person resides in the UK. The person chargeable in this way is answerable for all matters required to be done under the capital gains tax provisions, for the purpose of assessment of that tax, but is given a right of retention and indemnity in respect of tax charges or payments made on the incapacitated person's behalf. The machinery is abolished for 2012/13 onwards (see further **12.1** above). [*TMA 1970, ss 72, 77; FA 2012, s 222(1)(5)*].

Default of infant

[12.4] For 2011/12 and earlier years, where the person chargeable to tax is an infant, then his parent, guardian, or tutor is liable for the tax in the event of the infant's default. On neglect or refusal of payment, the parent etc. may be proceeded against for sums due to HMRC. This provision is repealed for 2012/13 onwards. [*TMA 1970, ss 73, 77; FA 2012, s 222(1)(5)*].

13

Claims

Introduction	**13.1**
Capital gains tax claims and elections	**13.2**
Claims etc. not included in returns	**13.3**
Corporation tax claims	**13.4**
Time limits for claims	**13.5**
Appeals in respect of claims	**13.6**
Claim for recovery of tax overpaid	**13.7**
Claim for restitution of payment made under mistake of law	**13.8**
Key points	**13.9**

Cross-reference. See **44.4** LOSSES for requirement to notify capital losses.

Introduction to claims

[13.1] This chapter outlines the procedures and time limits for making claims and elections for reliefs, allowances and tax repayments for both capital gains tax and corporation tax purposes.

Claims are personal matters and (except in the case of trustees for persons under disability etc.) can be made only by the person entitled to the relief (cf. *Fulford v Hyslop* Ch D 1929, 8 ATC 588). See **58.4** RETURNS for the signing of claims by an attorney.

Also covered in this chapter are two specific types of claim:

(a) claims for recovery of overpaid tax (previously 'error or mistake' relief); and

(b) claims through the courts for the restitution of payments made under a mistake of law.

Capital gains tax claims and elections

[13.2] A formal procedure applies to the making of capital gains tax (and income tax) claims, elections and notices. A claim for a relief, allowance or tax repayment must be for an amount quantified at the time of the claim. Where notice has been given by HMRC requiring the delivery of a return (see **58.3**, **58.16** RETURNS), a claim etc. can only be made at any time by inclusion in such a return (or by virtue of an amendment to a return) *unless it could not be so included* either at that time or subsequently (but see below for claims involving two or more years). These provisions do not apply to claims to be given effect by a PAYE coding adjustment, to claims by charities for specified exemptions and repayments of income tax, or to claims for consequential adjustments after the counteraction of a tax advantage under the GAAR (see **4.3** ANTI-AVOIDANCE).

In the case of a partnership business, a claim under any of numerous provisions specified in *TMA 1970, s 42(7)* must be made by a partner nominated by the partnership if it cannot be included in a partnership return (or amendment to such a return). See **13.3** below for provisions applying where a claim etc. is made otherwise than by inclusion in a return.

Where a claimant discovers that an error or mistake has been made in a claim (whether or not made in a return), he may make a supplementary claim within the time allowed for making the original claim.

[*TMA 1970, s 42; FA 2012, s 222(1), Sch 15 paras 11, 17(6); FA 2013, s 213; FA 2015, Sch 7 para 49*].

Claims for relief involving two or more years

A claim for a loss incurred or payment made in one tax year to be carried back to an earlier year or years need not be made in a return, is treated as a claim for the year of loss or payment (the later year), must be for an amount equal to what would otherwise have been the tax saving for the earlier year, and is given effect *in relation to the later year* by repayment, set-off etc. or by treating the said amount as a tax payment made on account under SELF-ASSESSMENT (**61.2**). The tax position for the earlier year is not adjusted. [*TMA 1970, Sch 1B para 2*]. See Tolley's Income Tax for more details. The non-reopening of the earlier year's self-assessment does not prevent the making or revising of other claims for that earlier year that are consequential to the carry-back (Revenue Tax Bulletin August 2000 pp 774, 775). In relation to the carry-back claim, repayment interest or (before 31 October 2011) repayment supplement may be due as in **56.2**, **56.3** REPAYMENT INTEREST, though only from 31 January following the *later year* (as above). An example of a capital gains provision affected by these rules is the potential three-year carry-back of capital losses incurred by an individual in the tax year in which he dies — see **19.7** DEATH.

Claims etc. not included in returns

[13.3] Subject to any specific provision requiring a claim, etc. to be made to the Commissioners for HMRC, an income tax or capital gains tax claim or election made otherwise than in a return (see **13.2** above) must be made to an officer of Revenue and Customs. The claim, etc. must include a declaration by the claimant that all particulars are correctly stated to the best of his information or belief. No claim requiring a tax repayment can be made unless the claimant has documentary proof that the tax has been paid or deducted. The claim must be made in a form determined by HMRC and may require, inter alia, a statement of the amount of tax to be discharged or repaid and supporting information and documentation. In the case of a claim by or on behalf of a person who is not resident (or who claims to be not resident or not domiciled or, for 2012/13 and earlier years, not ordinarily resident) in the UK, HMRC may require a statement or declaration in support of the claim to be made by affidavit.

A person who may wish to make a claim must keep all such records as may be requisite for the purpose and must preserve them until such time as HMRC may no longer enquire into the claim (see below) or any such enquiry is completed. HMRC have the power to make regulations specifying records which are required to be kept. There is a maximum penalty of £3,000 for non-compliance in relation to any claim actually made. Similar provisions and exceptions apply as in **58.8** RETURNS as to the preservation of copies of documents instead of originals.

Provisions similar to those in **58.7** RETURNS (amendments of self-assessments) apply to enable a claimant (within twelve months of the claim) or HMRC officer (within nine months of the claim) to amend a claim etc. HMRC has power of enquiry into a claim, etc. (or amendment) similar to that in **58.9** RETURNS (enquiries into returns). Notice of intention to enquire must be given by the first anniversary of 31 January following the tax year (or where the claim relates to a period other than a tax year, the first anniversary of the end of that period) or, if later, the quarter day (meaning 31 January, 30 April, etc.) next following the first anniversary of the date of claim, etc. See also **34.3–34.10** HMRC INVESTIGATORY POWERS. Where an enquiry is in progress, an HMRC officer may give provisional effect to the claim, etc. (or amendment thereof) to such extent as he thinks fit. Provisions similar to those in **58.12**, **58.13** RETURNS apply as regards completion of enquiries and amendments of claims upon completion (except there is no provision for issuing *partial* closure notices). HMRC must give effect (by assessment, discharge or repayment) to an amendment arising out of an enquiry within 30 days after the date of issue of the closure notice. An appeal may be made against any conclusion stated, or amendment made, by a closure notice by giving written notice to the relevant officer within 30 days after the date of issue of the closure notice, extended to three months where certain specified issues concerning residence are involved. If an amendment is varied on appeal, HMRC must give effect to the variation within 30 days.

Where a claim etc. does not give rise to a discharge or repayment of tax, there are provisions for disallowance of the claim on completion of enquiry, with appeal procedures similar to those above.

[*TMA 1970, s 42(11), Sch 1A; SI 2009 No 402; SI 2009 No 56, Sch 1 paras 53–58; FA 2013, Sch 46 para 117; SI 2009 No 2035, Sch para 9*].

In *Cotter v HMRC* SC, [2013] STC 2480 a claim for loss relief which was included in a tax return form was held to be made outside the return and therefore subject to the enquiry provisions above. For the purposes of the enquiry provisions, a tax return referred to the information in the return form which was submitted for the purpose of establishing the amounts in which a person was chargeable to tax for the relevant tax year. In this case, the claim had no effect on the tax chargeable for the year concerned and so did not form part of the tax return.

Corporation tax claims

[13.4] Under corporation tax self-assessment, provisions having broadly similar effect as those in **13.2** above (other than those of *TMA 1970, Sch 1B*) apply to companies. Subject to any express provision to the contrary and certain exceptions for charitable companies, claims and elections made after notice has been given requiring the delivery of a company tax return must be made in the return, or by amendment of the return, if they can be so made (see **58.19** RETURNS) and must be quantified. A claim etc. made by a company which could have been made by amending the return is treated for this purpose as an amendment of the return. Otherwise, *TMA 1970, Sch 1A* (see **13.3** above) provides the procedure for claims etc. A supplementary claim (where there was an error or mistake in the original claim) may be made within the time limit for the original claim. A group relief or capital allowances claim *must* be made in a return or by amendment of a return. [*FA 1998, Sch 18 paras 9, 10, 54, 56–60; FA 2010, Sch 8 para 6; FA 2012, Sch 15 paras 14, 15, 17(6)*].

Time limits for claims

[13.5] See **67** TIME LIMITS — FIXED DATES and **68** TIME LIMITS — MISCELLANEOUS for check-lists of claims and elections.

The following general time limits apply where no specific time limit is prescribed. A claim made on or after 1 April 2010 must be made within **four years** of the end of the tax year or accounting period to which it relates. A capital gains tax (or income tax) claim made before 1 April 2010 had to be made within five years after 31 January following the tax year to which it related. For corporation tax purposes, the general time limit for claims made before 1 April 2010 was **six years** after the end of the accounting period to which the claim related.

For capital gains tax purposes (but not for corporation tax purposes), the above changes in time limits apply by reference to claims made before, or on or after, 1 April 2012 where the claim concerned relates to a tax year for which the taxpayer has not been given notice to make a return under *TMA 1970, s 8* or *s 8A* (see **58.3** RETURNS) or *s 12AA* (see **58.16** RETURNS) within one year of the end of the tax year (in effect, where the taxpayer is outside self-assessment). This rule does not, however, apply if for that year any gains which ought to have been assessed have not been assessed, or an assessment has become insufficient, or any relief given has become excessive.

In effect these changes mean that (except where the changes apply from 1 April 2012) the time limit for capital gains tax claims for 2004/05 is 31 March 2010 and that for 2005/06 is 5 April 2010.

[*TMA 1970, s 43(1); FA 1998, s 117, Sch 18 para 55; SI 2009 No 403*].

By concession, where an overpayment of tax arises because of an error by HMRC or another Government department and where there is no dispute as to the facts, claims to repayment of the tax overpaid made outside of the statutory period will be allowed (HMRC Extra-Statutory Concession B41).

A claim (including a supplementary claim) which could not have been allowed but for the making of an assessment to capital gains tax after the tax year to which it relates, may be made at any time before the end of the tax year following that in which the assessment was made. [*TMA 1970, s 43(2)*].

If an assessment is made under the extended time limits at **6.14** ASSESSMENTS, the person assessed can require effect to be given to reliefs or allowances to which he would have been entitled had he made the necessary claims within the relevant time limits. [*TMA 1970, s 36(3); FA 1998, s 117, Sch 18 para 65*].

Where HMRC issue an amendment to a return as part of an enquiry closure notice (see **58.12** RETURNS), the above extended time limits apply in relation to the amendment as they apply in relation to assessments. [*TMA 1970, s 43C(1)–(3)*].

Discovery etc.

In the case of a 'discovery' assessment (see **6.10** ASSESSMENTS), which is *not* for making good loss of tax brought about carelessly or deliberately,

(a) any 'relevant' claim, election, application or notice which could have been made or given within the normal time limits of the *Taxes Acts* may be made or given within a year of the end of the chargeable period in which the assessment is made, and

(b) any 'relevant' claim, etc. previously made or given, except an irrevocable one, can, with the consent of the person(s) by whom it was made or given (or their personal representatives), be revoked or varied in the manner in which it was made or given.

A claim, etc. is '*relevant*' to an assessment for a chargeable period if:

(i) it relates to, or to an event occurring in, the chargeable period, and

(ii) it, or its revocation or variation, reduces, or could reduce,

   (A) the increased tax liability resulting from the assessment, or

   (B) any other liability of the person for that chargeable period or a later one ending not more than one year after the period in which the assessment is made.

A claim in respect of overpaid tax within **13.7** below is also 'relevant' to an assessment for a tax year if it relates to that year.

These extended time limits cannot be used for the purpose of making an election for universal re-basing under *TCGA 1992, s 35(5)* (see **9.3** ASSETS HELD ON 31 MARCH **1982**).

The normal APPEALS (5) provisions apply, with any necessary modifications.

If the making, etc. of a claim, etc. would alter another person's tax liability, the consent of that person (or his personal representatives) is needed. If such alteration is an increase, the other person cannot make, etc. a claim, etc. under the foregoing provisions.

If the reduction in tax liability resulting from one or more claims etc. would exceed the additional tax assessed, relief is not available for the excess. If the reduction involves more than one period, or more than one person, HMRC will specify by notice in writing how it is to be apportioned; but within 30 days of the notice being given, or the last notice being given if there is more than one person, the person (or persons jointly) can specify the apportionment by notice in writing to HMRC.

[*TMA 1970, ss 43A, 43B*].

Where HMRC issue an amendment to a return as part of an enquiry closure notice (see **58.12** RETURNS), these provisions apply to the amendment as they apply to assessments. [*TMA 1970, s 43C(2)(3)*].

The provisions broadly apply to companies under corporation tax self-assessment. [*FA 1998, s 117, Sch 18 paras 61–64*].

Extended time limits for assessment

Where it is necessary to make an assessment on any person to give effect to, or as a result of allowing, a claim, supplementary claim, election, application or notice given or made under the extended time limits of *TMA 1970, ss 36(3), 43(3), 43A* or *43C* above, the assessment is not out of time if made within one year of the final determination of the claim etc. For this purpose a claim etc. is finally determined when it can no longer be varied, on appeal or otherwise. [*TMA 1970, s 43C(4)(5); TIOPA 2010, Sch 8 para* 6].

Appeals in respect of claims

[13.6] See **13.3** above and **5.2** APPEALS.

Claim for recovery of overpaid tax

[13.7] A claim under the following provisions can be made on or after 1 April 2010. The provisions replace the narrower error or mistake relief provisions, for which see the 2013/14 or earlier edition of this work. A claim to the special relief described below can be made on or after 1 April 2011; the relief replaces HMRC's concessional practice of 'equitable liability' — see **51.30** PAYMENT OF TAX.

Where a taxpayer has paid an amount of capital gains tax (or income tax) or corporation tax and believes that the tax is not due, he can make a claim to HMRC for repayment of the tax. Where a taxpayer has been assessed as liable to pay an amount of tax, or there has been a determination or direction to that effect, he can likewise make a claim for the amount to be discharged if he believes that the tax is not due. For these purposes, tax paid by one person on behalf of another is treated as paid by the other person.

HMRC will not give effect to such a claim in the following circumstances:

(a) the amount is excessive because of a mistake in a claim or a mistake consisting of making, or failing to make, an election claim or notice (or because of certain mistakes relating to capital allowances);
(b) the claimant can seek relief by taking other steps under tax legislation;
(c) the claimant could have sought relief by taking such steps within a period which has expired by the time the claim is made, if he knew, or ought reasonably to have known, before the end of that period that such relief was available;
(d) the claim is made on grounds that have been put to a court or tribunal in the course of an appeal relating to the amount or grounds that have been put to HMRC in the course of such an appeal settled by agreement;
(e) the claimant knew, or ought reasonably to have known, of the grounds for the claim before the latest of: the date an appeal relating to the amount was determined by a court or tribunal, the date on which such an appeal was withdrawn by the claimant, and the end of the period in which the claimant could have appealed;

(f) the amount was due as a result of proceedings by HMRC against the claimant, or under an agreement between the claimant and HMRC settling such proceedings; and

(g) the amount is excessive because of a mistake in calculating the claimant's liability where the liability was calculated in accordance with the practice generally prevailing at the time (and for this purpose special rules apply in relation to PAYE).

The exclusion in (g) above does not apply where a claim to relief relates to tax charged contrary to EU law. For this purpose, an amount is charged contrary to EU law if it is contrary to the provisions of the Treaty on the Functioning of the European Union relating to the free movement of goods, persons, services or capital (or replacement provisions under any subsequent treaty). This rule is made statutory for claims made on or after 17 January 2014 but was previously applied by HMRC in accordance with HMRC Brief 22/10.

[*TMA 1970, s 33, Sch 1AB paras 1, 2; FA 1998, Sch 18 paras 51, 51A; FA 2013, s 231(1)(3)(5)*].

Making a claim

For capital gains tax (and income tax) purposes, a claim must be made within four years after the end of the tax year concerned. Where the claim relates to tax overpaid, that year is the year in respect of which the payment was made or, where the amount paid is excessive due to a mistake in a tax return or returns, the year to which the return (or if more than one, the first return) relates. Where the claim relates to an assessment, determination or direction, the year concerned is the year to which that assessment etc. relates or, for claims made on or after 17 January 2014 where the amount due is excessive due to a mistake in a tax return or returns, the year to which the return (or if more than one, the first return) relates. The time limit is extended for claims relating to mistakes in returns made before 1 April 2012 by a person other than a company if the return was not issued within one year of the end of the tax year to which it relates. In such cases, the claim must be made within five years after the 31 January following the end of the tax year concerned.

For corporation tax purposes, a claim must be made within four years after the end of the accounting period concerned. Where the claim relates to tax overpaid, that accounting period is the period in respect of which the payment was made or, where the amount paid is excessive due to a mistake in a tax return or returns, the period to which the return (or if more than one, the first return) relates. Where the claim relates to an assessment, determination or direction, the accounting period concerned is that to which that assessment etc. relates or, for claims made on or after 17 January 2014 where the amount due is excessive due to a mistake in a tax return or returns, the period to which the return (or if more than one, the first return) relates.

In *Raftopoulou v HMRC* UT 2015, [2016] STC 656, the provisions of *TMA 1970, s 118(2)* (see **52.2** PENALTIES) were held to apply to a late claim under these provisions so that a late claim could be treated as made within the time limits if there was a reasonable excuse for the failure and, if the reasonable excuse ceased, if there was no unreasonable delay in making the claim after the excuse ceased.

A claim cannot be made in a tax return.

Where, under PAYE, the construction industry scheme or other tax legislation, one person (P) is accountable to HMRC for capital gains tax (or income tax) or corporation tax payable by another person or for any other amount that has been or is to be set off against another person's liability, a claim in respect of the amount can only be made by that other person. If, however, P has paid such an amount but was not in fact accountable to HMRC for it, P, and only P, can make a claim in respect of that amount. Effect will not be given to such a claim by P to the extent that the amount has been repaid to, or set against amounts payable by, the other person.

Partnerships

A claim in respect of an amount paid or due by one or more partners in accordance with a self-assessment which is excessive because of a mistake in a partnership return must be made by a nominated partner (or his personal representative). The partner must have been a partner at some time in the period for which the return was made.

[*TMA 1970, Sch 1AB paras 3–5; FA 1998, Sch 18 paras 51B–51D; FA 2013, s 232(1)(3)(4)*].

Discovery assessment etc. following claim

Where the grounds for a claim also provide grounds for HMRC to make a discovery assessment or determination (see **6.10** ASSESSMENTS) for any period and such an assessment or determination could not otherwise be made as a result of one of the restrictions noted below, those restrictions are disregarded and an assessment or determination is not out of time if made before the final determination of the claim (i.e. before the time at which the claim can no longer be varied). The restrictions concerned are those at **6.10**(2) ASSESSMENTS and the expiry of a time limit for making a discovery assessment or determination (see **6.13, 6.14** ASSESSMENTS).

Similar provisions apply in relation to amendments of partnership returns.

[*TMA 1970, Sch 1AB paras 6, 7; FA 1998, Sch 18 paras 51E, 51F*].

Contract settlements

The above provisions apply also to amounts paid under a contract settlement (see **6.8** ASSESSMENTS). If the person who paid the amounts due under the settlement (the '*payer*') was not the person from whom the tax concerned was due (the '*taxpayer*'), then the provisions are modified accordingly. If an amount is repayable to the payer as a result of a claim, HMRC can set the amount repayable against any amount payable by the taxpayer under any discovery assessment or determination made as a result of the claim.

[*TMA 1970, Sch 1AB para 8; FA 1998, Sch 18 para 51G*].

Special relief

A claim can be made for discharge or repayment of tax charged in an HMRC determination (under *TMA 1970, s 28C* or *FA 1998, Sch 18 paras 36, 37* — see **58.15, 58.19** RETURNS) on or after 1 April 2011 if the following apply:

(1) the claimant believes the tax is not due or, if already paid, was not due;
(2) relief under the above provisions would have been available but for (c) above or because the tax is due as a result of proceedings by HMRC against the claimant (see (f) above) or because more than four years have passed since the end of the tax year or accounting period; and
(3) where the claim would fail because the tax is due as a result of proceedings by HMRC, the claimant was neither present nor legally represented during the proceedings.

A claim can be made in relation to a determination made before 1 April 2011 but not if a claim to concessional relief under HMRC's practice of 'equitable liability' (see **51.30** PAYMENT OF TAX) has been refused before that date.

HMRC will not give effect to the claim unless:

(i) in HMRC's opinion it would be unconscionable to seek to recover the tax or withhold repayment of it;
(ii) the taxpayer's affairs (in matters concerning HMRC) are otherwise up to date or satisfactory arrangements have been put in place to bring them up to date as far as possible; and
(iii) either the taxpayer has not previously made a claim for relief or relief under HMRC's equitable liability practice or, where such a claim has been made, the exceptional circumstances of the case mean that the present claim should be allowed.

For the purposes of (iii) above, it does not matter whether the previous claim succeeded. A claim must include information and documentation which is reasonably required to determine whether (i)–(iii) above apply.

The jurisdiction of the Tribunal in determining whether (i) above applies is limited to deciding whether the opinion of HMRC was 'unreasonable' in the judicial review sense. The Tribunal cannot consider afresh whether it would be unconscionable to seek to recover the tax or withhold repayment. See *Currie v HMRC* FTT 2014, [2015] SFTD 51. An appeal against HMRC's refusal to allow relief was successful in *Clark v HMRC* FTT, [2015] UKFTT 324 (TC), [2015] STI 2660. HMRC had failed to take into account the taxpayer's learning difficulties and other personal problems. An appeal was also successful in *Scott v HMRC* FTT, [2015] UKFTT 420 (TC); HMRC had failed to consider the disparity between the tax due as per the determinations made by HMRC and the tax due as per the appellant's late self-assessments.

The above provisions replace HMRC's concessional practice of 'equitable liability' — see **51.30** PAYMENT OF TAX.

[*TMA 1970, Sch 1AB para 3A; FA 1998, Sch 18 para 51BA; SI 2011 No 1037, Arts 1–5*].

Claim for restitution of payment made under mistake of law

[13.8] It was confirmed in *R v CIR (ex p. Woolwich Equitable Building Society)*, HL 1990, 63 TC 589 that a claim can be made through the courts, under common law, for restitution of tax payments made to the Revenue under an unlawful statutory demand and that interest is payable from the dates of the payments. In *Deutsche Morgan Grenfell Group plc v CIR* HL 2006, [2007] STC 1 the company successfully sought to obtain this remedy in respect of tax paid under a mistake of law. In making its claim the company contended that under *Limitation Act 1980, s 32(1)(c)* it could make the claim for restitution within six years of the time it discovered the mistake (or could with reasonable diligence have discovered it), rather than within the normal time limit of six years from the time of payment under *Limitation Act 1980, s 5*. In upholding the company's claim, the House of Lords held that the effect of *Limitation Act 1980, s 32(1)(c)* was that the limitation period had not begun until 8 March 2001 (the date of the CJEC decision in *Metalgesellschaft Ltd & Others v CIR* CJEC 2001, [2001] STC 452).

Following the High Court decision in this case provisions were included in *FA 2004* to prevent the application of the extended time limit of *Limitation Act 1980, s 32(1)(c)* to taxation matters. Accordingly, *s 32(1)(c)* (and the NI equivalent) does not apply in relation to any action or claim for relief from the consequences of a mistake of law relating to a taxation matter under the care and management of HMRC brought after 7 September 2003, whether the action or claim is expressed to be brought on the grounds of mistake or on some other ground (such as unlawful demand or *ultra vires*). [*FA 2004, s 320(1)(6)*]. The effect of this provision is that court actions for restitution based on mistake of law must generally be brought within six years of the tax having been paid. *FA 2004, s 321* makes a similar change to Scottish law, so that claims for relief for tax paid under an error of law must generally be made within five years of the tax having been paid.

FA 2004, s 320 also includes provisions to prevent a claim to amend an existing action, seeking to introduce claims for a different payment, transaction, period or other matter, from being treated by the courts under *Limitation Act 1980, s 35* as being a separate action commenced on the same date as the original action (and thereby in some cases potentially circumventing the above provisions). This applies to amendment claims made after 19 November 2003, and for this purpose, such a claim is treated as made before 20 November 2003 if the Revenue consented to the making of it in writing before that date or if, immediately before that date, the Revenue's consent had been sought and not refused or an application to the court for permission to make the claim had been made and not refused. [*FA 2004, s 320(2)(5)*].

The above provisions take legal effect only on 22 July 2004 (the date of Royal Assent to *FA 2004*). *FA 2004, s 320(3)* therefore deems an action begun before that date but after 7 September 2003, or a claim to amend an existing action made before 22 July 2004 but after 19 November 2003 to be discontinued on 22 July 2004 and provides for the recovery (with interest) of any amount paid out by the Revenue in relation to such an action or amendment.

These provisions are extended by *FA 2007, s 107* to prevent the application of *Limitation Act 1980, s 32(1)(c)* in relation to actions brought before 8 September 2003 as well as those brought on or after that date. This is subject to the following exceptions:

(a) where the action, or cause of action, has been the subject of a House of Lords judgment or order before 6 December 2006 as to the application of *s 32(1)(c)*;
(b) where the parties to the action are bound, under a group litigation order, by a House of Lords judgment or order before 6 December 2006 in another action as to the application of *s 32(1)(c)*; and
(c) where the action, or cause of action, relates to the charging of tax contrary to European Union law.

The extended provisions take legal effect only on 19 July 2007 (the date of Royal Assent to *FA 2007*). Any court judgment or order given or made before that date but after 5 December 2006 is therefore deemed to have been what it would have been had the extended provisions been in force at all times since the action was brought and any available defence of limitation had been raised. Any payment made under the judgment that is accordingly taken not to have been imposed is repayable with interest.

In *Test Claimants in the FII Group Litigation v HMRC* CJEU, [2014] STC 638 *FA 2007, s 107* above was held to breach European Community law because it does not incorporate any transitional provisions. The exception in (c) above was introduced by *FA 2014, s 299* to amend *FA 2007, s 107* to comply with that decision. Although the exception takes legal effect on 17 July 2014 (the date of Royal Assent to *FA 2014*), it applies to actions brought, and causes of action arising, before, on or after that date. See also *United Kingdom v European Commission* CJEU, (C-640/13); 2015 STI 52, which confirmed that *FA 2007, s 107* breached EU law (but note that the decision did not consider the changes made by *FA 2014*).

In *Monro v HMRC* CA, [2008] STC 1815 it was held that a common law claim for restitution cannot be made where error or mistake relief cannot be claimed because of the exclusion for returns made on the basis or in accordance with the practice generally prevailing at the time (see **13.8** above).

Key points concerning claims

[13.9] Points to consider are as follows.

- For capital gains tax claims the time limit is four years after the end of a tax year (reduced from five years and ten months for claims made after 1 April 2010). Care needs to be taken, to ensure time limits are not missed. The same time limits also apply to the notification of a capital loss.
- Where the taxpayer has received notice to file a tax return the claim must be included in the tax return unless it could not be included or the claim involves two or more years.
- For a taxpayer who did not receive a notice to make a self-assessment return within 12 months of the end of the relevant tax year, the date on which the new time limits took effect, where tax has been overpaid, was 1 April 2012.

- Claims for recovery of overpaid tax replaced error and mistake claims with effect from 1 April 2010. This procedure cannot be used where there is a mistake in a claim or as a result of omitting to make a claim. Where there is an error in a claim this can only be revised within the time periods for making the claim.

14

Companies

Introduction	14.1
Liability of companies to corporation tax on their chargeable gains	14.2
Rate of corporation tax in respect of chargeable gains	14.3
Liquidation	14.4
Interest charged to capital	14.5
Capital losses	14.6
Avoidance utilising losses	14.7
Schemes converting income into capital	14.8
Schemes securing deductions	14.9
Capital gains tax charge on high value disposals of dwellings	14.10
Company reconstructions	14.11
Reconstructions involving transfer of business	14.11
Demergers	14.12
Overseas matters	14.13
Use of non-sterling currencies	14.14
European Company (Societas Europaea)	14.15
European Co-operative (Societas Co-operative Europaea)	14.16
Tax accounting arrangements of large companies	14.17
Publication of tax strategies by large businesses	14.18
Special measures regime for unco-operative large businesses	14.19
Key points	14.20

Cross-references. See **4.14** ANTI-AVOIDANCE where a close company transfers an asset otherwise than at arm's length for a consideration less than market value; **15** COMPANIES — CORPORATE FINANCE AND INTANGIBLES; **29** GROUPS OF COMPANIES; **57.33** RESIDENCE AND DOMICILE for company residence; **63** SHARES AND SECURITIES; **66** SUBSTANTIAL SHAREHOLDINGS OF COMPANIES; **70** UNIT TRUSTS ETC.; **71** VENTURE CAPITAL TRUSTS.

Simon's Taxes. See **D1.9**, **D6.450**.

Introduction to companies

[14.1] With two exceptions, companies do not pay capital gains tax. Instead they pay corporation tax on their chargeable gains. Gains are included in a company's profits liable to corporation tax and taxed at the applicable rate.

Chargeable gains and allowable losses are nevertheless computed according to capital gains tax principles, although there are now many important differences in the computational rules. The main differences are listed at **14.2** below.

The first exception is the capital gains tax charge on high value disposals of dwellings subject to the annual tax on enveloped dwellings: see **14.10** below. The second exception is the non-resident CGT charge on disposals of UK residential property interests: see **41.25** LAND.

This chapter also covers a number of additional issues specific to companies. Provisions relating to capital losses, including anti-avoidance provisions, are detailed at **14.6–14.9** below. Reliefs for reconstructions etc. of companies are at **14.12** below. Overseas matters are noted at **14.13–14.16** below, including provisions relating to the formation and residence of European Companies and European Co-operatives.

Senior accounting officers of certain large companies are required to take steps to ensure that the company maintains adequate tax accounting arrangements to enable the company's tax liabilities to be calculated accurately. See **14.17** below.

Following *FA 2016*, large companies (and partnerships) must publish an annual tax strategy online, outlining their approach to tax risk, tax planning and dealing with HMRC (see **14.18** below). If they have a history of unco-operative behaviour they may become subject to a special measures regime (see **14.19** below).

Liability of companies to corporation tax on their chargeable gains

[14.2] Companies resident in the UK (and non-resident companies in respect of UK permanent establishment assets, see **49.3** OVERSEAS MATTERS) are liable to corporation tax on their chargeable gains. These gains are included in their profits liable to corporation tax as described in **14.3** below. [*CTA 2009, ss 4, 19; TCGA 1992, s 10B; FA 2016, s 76(8)*].

Subject to the two exceptions noted at **14.1** above, companies accordingly do not pay 'capital gains tax' as such, but their chargeable gains less allowable losses are computed in accordance with provisions relating to capital gains tax, except that:

(i) computations are made by reference to accounting periods instead of tax years [*TCGA 1992, s 8(3)*];
(ii) provisions in the legislation confined to individuals do not apply to companies [*TCGA 1992, s 8(4)(5)*];
(iii) re-basing to market value at 31 March 1982 applies to individuals etc. automatically and without any exceptions for disposals on or after 6 April 2008, but the exceptions continue to apply to companies (see **9** ASSETS HELD ON 31 MARCH 1982);
(iv) special provisions apply to tax as income gains and losses in respect of loan relationships, derivative contracts and intangible assets (see **15** COMPANIES — CORPORATE FINANCE AND INTANGIBLES);
(v) ENTREPRENEURS' RELIEF (**34**) applies to qualifying business disposals by individuals, etc., but not by companies;
(vi) INVESTORS' RELIEF (**40**) applies to disposals of qualifying shares by individuals and trustees but not by companies;
(vii) indexation allowance is available to companies (see **38.1** INDEXATION);
(viii) the rules for matching shares and securities sold with those acquired are not the same for corporation tax as for capital gains tax (see **64.1** SHARES AND SECURITIES — IDENTIFICATION RULES);

(ix) certain provisions, as contained in this chapter, apply only to companies.

See also 6 ASSESSMENTS; 42 LATE PAYMENT INTEREST AND PENALTIES; 51 PAYMENT OF TAX; 52 PENALTIES; 56 REPAYMENT INTEREST; and 58 RETURNS for matters applicable to companies generally.

The definition of 'company' includes any body corporate or unincorporated association but does not include a partnership. [*TCGA 1992, s 288(1)*]. References to 'persons' in the capital gains tax legislation generally include unincorporated associations (*CIR v Worthing Rugby Football Club Trustees* CA 1987, 60 TC 482).

Rate of corporation tax in respect of chargeable gains

[14.3] The whole of the chargeable gains (net of allowable losses under **14.6** below) of a company is included in the taxable total profits, chargeable to corporation tax. For financial year 2015 onwards there is a single rate of corporation tax. For financial years 2015 and 2016 the rate is 20% and for financial year 2017 the rate is 19%. Previously, the rate of corporation tax applicable was dependent upon, inter alia, the residence position of the company, its status, the number of associated companies and the level of the chargeable profits and certain franked investment income but the rate so determined applied to both income and chargeable gains included in the chargeable profits. If the company's accounting period straddles different financial years, chargeable profits are apportioned on a time basis between the years. [*CTA 2009, s 8; TCGA 1992, s 8(1)*].

For financial years 2018 and 2019 the rate will be 19%; for financial year 2020 it will be 17%. [*F(No 2)A 2015, s 7; FA 2016, s 45*]. For the rates of corporation tax generally, see Tolley's Corporation Tax.

Alternative rules apply as in 70 UNIT TRUSTS AND OTHER INVESTMENT VEHICLES and 71 VENTURE CAPITAL TRUSTS.

Liquidation

[14.4] The vesting of a company's assets in a liquidator is disregarded for chargeable gains purposes (i.e. the assets are not treated as disposed of). All the acts of the liquidator in relation to such assets are treated as acts of the company. [*TCGA 1992, s 8(6)*].

All expenses properly incurred in a voluntary winding-up, including the remuneration of the liquidator, are payable out of the company's assets in priority to all other claims. [*Insolvency Act 1986, s 115*]. *Insolvency Rules 1986, Rule 4.218(3)* provides that expenses of a liquidation are to be paid out of the assets in the order of priority therein specified, subject to a discretionary power of the court under *Insolvency Act 1986, s 156* to vary the order where assets are insufficient to satisfy liabilities. [*SI 1986 No 1925, Rule 4.218(3), Rule 4.220*]. Included in the normal order of priority is the amount of any corporation tax on chargeable gains accruing on the realisation of any asset of the company (*Rule 4.218(3)(p)*).

Notwithstanding the specific inclusion of corporation tax on chargeable gains, corporation tax chargeable on a company's post-liquidation profits is to be treated as a 'necessary disbursement' of the liquidator (within *Insolvency Rules 1986, Rule 4.218(3)(m)*), and thus as an expense requiring priority as above (*Re Toshoku Finance UK plc; Kahn and another v CIR* HL, [2002] STC 368).

See also **63.11**, **63.12** and **63.13** SHARES AND SECURITIES.

Interest charged to capital

[14.5] For interest paid in accounting periods beginning after 31 March 1981, interest on money borrowed by a company for the construction of any building, structure or works, and referable to a time before disposal of it, may be added to the expenditure allowable as a deduction under *TCGA 1992, s 38* in computing the gain on the disposal of the building etc. by the company, provided the expenditure on the construction was itself so allowable. No such relief is given for interest referable to any accounting period ending after 31 March 1996 (in consequence of the loan relationship provisions at **15.2** COMPANIES — CORPORATE FINANCE AND INTANGIBLES) or for interest treated as a charge on income under *ICTA 1988, s 338*. This restriction also applies to any amount which is allowable as a deduction in computing income, profits, gains or losses for corporation tax purposes (or would be so but for an insufficiency of profits or gains) or which would be allowable if the building etc. was held as a fixed asset of a trade. The practical effect of these restrictions is that a payment of interest is unlikely to qualify as allowable expenditure in computing a chargeable gain.

For interest paid in accounting periods ending before 1 April 1981, the provisions and comment made in the last two sentences above do not apply. Instead, interest had to be charged to capital in order to qualify as allowable expenditure, which treatment prevented it being treated as a charge on income by virtue of *ICTA 1970, s 248(5)(a) as originally enacted.*

[*TCGA 1992, s 40*].

Capital losses

[14.6] The amount of chargeable gains to be taken into account for an accounting period is the amount of the chargeable gains accruing to the company in that period less the aggregate amount of the allowable losses in that period and allowable losses and allowable NRCGT losses (in respect of non-resident CGT disposals of UK residential property interests — see **41.25** LAND) brought forward from any previous period. Allowable losses include short-term losses accruing under *Schedule D, Case VII* for years before 1971/72 which remain unrelieved. [*TCGA 1992, s 8(1), Sch 11 para 12; FA 2015, Sch 7 para 8(2)*].

For corporation tax on chargeable gains purposes an allowable loss does not include any loss which, if it had been a gain, would have been exempt from corporation tax in the hands of the company (and see also the anti-avoidance provisions mentioned below). [*TCGA 1992, s 8(2)*].

Corporate allowable losses cannot normally be offset against trading profits or other income but see **44.18** LOSSES. Since chargeable gains are included in total profits which are liable to corporation tax as in **14.2** above, claims under *CTA 2010, s 37* to set trading losses against such profits mean that trading losses can be set against chargeable gains arising in the same accounting period and, to the extent permitted by that *section*, preceding accounting periods. Trading losses arising on or after 1 April 2017 may also be carried forward and set against the total profits (including gains) of future periods, subject to certain restrictions. See Tolley's Corporation Tax under Losses for the detailed provisions. [*CTA 2010, s 37; F(No 2)A 2017, s 18, Sch 4 para 11*].

Management expenses of a company with investment business may be offset against chargeable gains within the same or succeeding accounting periods. [*CTA 2009, ss 1219, 1223; F(No 2)A 2017, s 18, Sch 4 para 6*].

Anti-avoidance

There are a number of anti-avoidance provisions relating specifically to corporate capital losses. In particular, *FA 2006* introduced three targeted provisions attacking arrangements entered into which have as a main purpose the obtaining of a tax advantage. For details of the provisions, see **14.7–14.9** below (avoidance utilising losses), **29.16, 29.17** GROUPS OF COMPANIES (gain buying and loss buying) and **44.7** LOSSES (losses accruing from arrangements to secure tax advantage).

See also **29.18** GROUPS OF COMPANIES for the restriction, where the provisions at **29.16, 29.17** GROUPS OF COMPANIES do not apply, on set-off of pre-entry losses where a company joins a group.

Avoidance utilising losses

[14.7] The following provisions are intended to ensure that capital losses cannot be used against income profits. HMRC have indicated that the provisions are intended to affect only companies that deliberately and knowingly enter into arrangements to avoid tax (HMRC Guidance 'Avoidance through the creation and use of capital losses by companies', 22 March 2006).

Two strategies to utilise capital losses are targeted by the provisions. The first is to turn an income receipt into capital (see **14.8** below). The second is to generate a deduction from income as part of arrangements to crystallise a capital gain (see **14.9** below). The effect is to restrict the use of capital losses. In both cases, the provisions apply only where HMRC issue a notice to the company concerned (see below).

Both sets of provisions require that there be 'arrangements' the main purpose, or one of the main purposes, of which is to secure a 'tax advantage' (although each contains a qualification of the definition of tax advantage given below — see **14.8** and **14.9** below). [*TCGA 1992, ss 184G(2)(5), 184H(2)(4)*].

'*Arrangements*' for this purpose include any agreement, understanding, scheme, transaction or series of transactions, whether or not legally enforceable. A '*tax advantage*' means obtaining or increasing relief from, or repayment of, corporation tax, the avoidance or reduction of a corporation tax charge or assessment or the avoidance of a possible assessment to corporation tax. [*TCGA 1992, ss 184D, 184G(10), 184H(10)*].

For HMRC's view on the application of the terms 'arrangements', 'tax advantage' and 'main purpose', see **44.7** LOSSES and HMRC Capital Gains Manual CG44102–44106.

HMRC notices

As noted above, the application of the provisions is contingent upon the issue of a notice to the company by HMRC. Such a notice may be issued if HMRC have reasonable grounds for considering that the statutory conditions triggering the legislation are present. It must specify the arrangements in question, the accounting period (or periods) involved and the effect of the anti-avoidance provisions.

If the company has not yet made a return for the accounting period it may, if it makes a return within the 90-day period beginning with the day on which the notice is given, make the return disregarding the notice and make any necessary amendment later within the same 90-day period.

If the company has already made a return for the accounting period, HMRC may only issue a notice if a notice of enquiry (see **58.19** RETURNS) has been given in respect of that return. The company may amend its return in light of the notice at any time within the 90-day period beginning with the day on which the notice is given. A closure notice in respect of the enquiry may not be issued before the earlier of the company amending its return or the end of the 90-day period. This does not apply to a partial closure notice which does not relate to any matter to which the notice here relates, where enquiries commenced on or after the date of Royal Assent to *F(No 2)A 2017*, or were in progress on that date.

If enquiries into the return have been completed (and for enquiries commenced on or after the date of Royal Assent to *F(No 2)A 2017*, or in progress on that date, if enquiries have been completed in relation to any matters), the power enjoyed by HMRC to issue a notice relating to those matters is subject to two requirements, both of which must be met. The first is that at the time those enquiries were completed HMRC could not, on the basis of information made available to them (within *FA 1998, Sch 18 para 44(2)(3)* — see **6.10** ASSESSMENTS) before that time, reasonably have been aware of circumstances indicating that a notice could have been issued. The second is that a request for information was made during the enquiry relating to the matters in question which, if duly complied with, would have resulted in a reasonable expectation that HMRC would issue a notice. If a notice is issued in these circumstances no discovery assessment may be made before the earlier of the company amending its return or the end of the 90-day period beginning with the day on which the notice is given. However, the normal restrictions on making discovery assessments in *FA 1998, Sch 18 paras 43, 44* do not apply (see **6.10** ASSESSMENTS).

On receiving a notice containing HMRC's view of the position, it is up to the company to decide if it needs to amend its self-assessment. If it fails to make an amendment which ought to have been made its return will be incorrect (with all the resulting implications for penalties, etc.).

[*TCGA 1992, ss 184G(6)(8)(9), 184H(6)(8)(9), 184I; F(No 2)A 2017, Sch 15 paras 22, 44*].

Clearances

HMRC operate an informal clearance procedure and will give advice on actual or proposed transactions. Applications for clearance should be sent to HM Revenue & Customs, CTISA Clearance SO 528, PO Box 194. Bootle, L69 9AA. A clearance will state the terms on which it has been given and HMRC will regard itself bound by a clearance provided that all relevant facts are accurately given and (where the clearance is sought in advance) the transaction is executed in accordance with the proposals set out in the clearance application. Where a clearance cannot be given HMRC will state the reasons, but taxpayers are not bound by their decision. For details of the information required by HMRC in clearance applications, see HMRC Capital Gains Manual CG44156. (HMRC Capital Gains Manual CG44150–44156).

Schemes converting income into capital

[14.8] HMRC may issue a notice (see **14.7** above) invoking anti-avoidance measures where it has reasonable grounds for considering that the following four conditions are, or may be, satisfied:

(a) a receipt or other amount arises to a company directly or indirectly in consequence of, or otherwise in connection with, any arrangements (see **14.7** above);

(b) that amount is taken into account in calculating a chargeable gain (the '*relevant gain*') accruing to a company (the '*relevant company*') and losses arise (or have arisen) to that company, whether before or after or as part of the arrangements;

(c) but for the arrangements an amount would have been taken into account wholly or partly instead of the amount in (a) above as income of the relevant company (or as the income of a company in the same capital gains tax group (see **29.2** GROUPS OF COMPANIES) at any time in the period beginning with the time at which the arrangements were made and ending when the matters, other than the tax advantage, intended to be secured by the arrangements are secured); and

(d) the main purpose, or one of the main purposes, of the arrangements was the obtaining of a tax advantage (see **14.7** above) involving the deduction of the capital losses from the relevant gain.

If all these conditions are satisfied when the HMRC notice is given, the relevant company may not deduct any loss from the relevant gain.

The conditions as stated above apply to arrangements entered into on or after 30 January 2014 and to arrangements entered into before that date to the extent that a chargeable gain arises on a disposal occurring on or after that date. Previously, the condition at (a) above was that any receipt arises to a company (the '*relevant company*') on the disposal of an asset and that receipt arises directly or indirectly in consequence of, or otherwise in connection with, any arrangements, and the condition at (b) was that a chargeable gain (the '*relevant gain*') accrues to the relevant company on the disposal and that company has allowable losses available. In condition (c), the reference to the 'amount in (a) above' was to 'the receipt in (a) above'.

[*TCGA 1992, s 184G(1)–(5)(7)(10); FA 2014, s 63(1)(3)*].

Schemes securing deductions

[14.9] HMRC may issue a notice (see **14.7** above) invoking anti-avoidance measures where it has reasonable grounds for considering that the following four conditions are, or may be, satisfied:

(a) a chargeable gain (the '*relevant gain*') accrues to a company (the '*relevant company*') directly or indirectly in consequence of, or otherwise in connection with, any arrangements (see **14.7** above) and that company has capital losses available;
(b) the relevant company, or a company connected with it, becomes entitled to an 'income deduction' directly or indirectly in consequence of, or otherwise in connection with, the arrangements;
(c) the main purpose, or one of the main purposes, of the arrangements was the obtaining of a tax advantage (see **14.7** above) involving both the income deduction and the deduction of losses from the relevant gain; and
(d) the arrangements are not 'excluded arrangements' (see below).

It does not matter whether the tax advantage is secured for the relevant company or any other company.

'*Excluded arrangements*' are certain arm's length sale and leaseback transactions involving land where there is no connection between the lessor and the lessee. An '*income deduction*' means a deduction in calculating income for corporation tax purposes or a deduction from total profits.

If all the above conditions are satisfied when the HMRC notice is given, the relevant company may not deduct any loss from the relevant gain.

The conditions as stated above apply to arrangements entered into on or after 30 January 2014 and to arrangements entered into before that date to the extent that a chargeable gain arises on a disposal occurring on or after that date. Previously, condition (b) was that the relevant company, or a company connected with it, incurs expenditure in connection with the arrangements which is deductible in calculating total profits but not in calculating chargeable gains and condition (c) was that the main purpose, or one of the main purposes, of the arrangements was the obtaining of a tax advantage (see **14.7** above) involving both the deduction of the expenditure in calculating total profits and the deduction of losses from the relevant gain.

[*TCGA 1992, s 184H(1)–(5)(7)(10)(11); FA 2014, s 63(2)(3)*].

Capital gains tax charge on high value disposals of dwellings

[14.10] Companies are chargeable to capital gains tax on 'high value disposals' on or after 6 April 2013 of dwellings that are subject to the annual tax on enveloped dwellings ('ATED') in *FA 2013, ss 94–174*. The charge is the one of only two exceptions to the rule that companies are not subject to capital gains tax but pay corporation tax on their chargeable gains (see **14.1** above). It applies whether or not the company is resident in the UK. [*TCGA 1992, ss 2(7A), 2B(1); FA 2013, Sch 25 paras 3, 4, 20*].

An 'EEA UCITS' (within *Financial Services and Markets Act 2000, s 237*) which is neither a unit trust scheme nor an open-ended investment company is exempt from the charge. [*TCGA 1992, s 100A; FA 2013, Sch 25 para 10*].

The charge

A company is charged to capital gains tax on the total amount of 'ATED-related chargeable gains' accruing to it in a tax year on high value disposals, after deducting 'ATED-related allowable losses' accruing in the tax year on high value disposals and any such losses for previous tax years (2013/14 onwards) which have not been allowed as a deduction from gains of any previous tax year. No other deductions are allowable from ATED-related gains. The gains are chargeable to capital gains tax at a rate of 28%.

Losses cannot be carried back to be set against gains of an earlier tax year. Relief in respect of a loss may be given only once by deduction from ATED-related gains, and may not be given at all if relief has been or may be given under any other provision.

A disposal is a '*high value disposal*' if:

(a) the disposal is of the whole or part of a 'chargeable interest';
(b) the disposed of interest has, at any time in the 'ownership period' been or formed part of a 'single-dwelling interest';
(c) the company has been within the charge to annual tax on enveloped dwellings with respect to the single-dwelling interest on one or more days in the ownership period which are not 'relievable days' (or would have been so within the charge if ATED had commenced on 31 March 1982); and
(d) the consideration for the disposal exceeds the 'threshold amount'.

Where the disposed of interest is a partnership asset, it is the 'responsible partners' who must be within the charge to ATED for the purposes of (c) above. Where the disposed of interest was held for the purposes of certain collective investment schemes, the person with day-to-day control over the management of its property must be within the charge.

The expressions 'chargeable interest', 'dwelling', 'single-dwelling interest' and 'responsible partners' have the same meaning for these purposes as for the annual tax on enveloped dwellings. The '*ownership period*' is the period beginning with the date on which the company acquired the chargeable interest or, if later, 6 April in the relevant year, and ending on the day before the disposal. If the company has made an election under *TCGA 1992, Sch 4ZZA para 5*, the ownership period starts on the day on which the company acquired the chargeable interest or, if later, 31 March 1982. The relevant year depends on whether the property being sold was held on 5 April 2013, 2015 or 2016, and whether ATED was chargeable before the date in question. It is 2016 if the interest disposed of was held on 5 April 2016 and no single-dwelling interest within (b) above was within the charge to ATED on one or more days, or would have been in the charge but for the charge being relievable, in the period ending with 31 March 2016 during which P held the interest disposed of (Case 3). If it is not 2016, it is 2015 if the interest disposed of was held on 5 April 2015 and no single-dwelling interest within (b) above was within the charge to ATED, or would have been in the charge but for the charge being relievable, in the period ending with 31 March 2015 during which P held the interest disposed of (Case 2). If it is not 2015 or 2016, it is 2013 (Case 1).

A '*relievable day*' is one for which any of the ATED reliefs in *FA 2013, s 132* has been claimed (or, for days falling before 1 April in the relevant year (as above), would have been claimable if ATED had then been in force).

In (d) above, the '*threshold amount*' is, subject to the following, £1 million for disposals in 2015/16 (previously £2 million). For disposals in 2016/17 onwards, the threshold amount is £500,000. If the disposal is a part disposal or the company has made any 'related disposals', the threshold amount is:

TA × C/TMV

where TA is the unreduced threshold amount, C is the consideration for the disposal and TMV is what would be the market value of a notional asset consisting of the disposed of interest, any part of the chargeable interest not disposed of, any chargeable interest (or part) which was the subject of a related disposal and any chargeable interest (or part) held by the company at the time of the disposal which, if the company had disposed of it at that time, would have been the subject of a related disposal.

If the disposed of interest is a fractional share of the whole of a chargeable interest (or part), these rules apply by reducing the normal threshold amount by reference to the company's fractional share.

A disposal made by the company in the six years ending with the day of the disposal in question (but not before 6 April 2013) is a '*related disposal*' if it meets conditions (a)–(c) above and the single-dwelling interest in (c) above is either the same interest or another single-dwelling interest in the same dwelling.

[*TCGA 1992, ss 2B–2D, 4(3A), Sch 4ZZA para 2; FA 2013, Sch 25 paras 4, 5; FA 2015, Sch 7 para 4, Sch 8 paras 2–4, 8; FA 2016, s 90(1)(3)*].

Restriction of losses

A disposal which would not otherwise be a high value disposal only because it does not meet condition (d) above is treated as a high value disposal if:

- an ATED-related loss would accrue in a tax year on the disposal if it were a high value disposal; and

- the total allowable deductions under *TCGA 1992, s 38* (see **16.11** COMPUTATION OF GAINS AND LOSSES) exceeds the threshold amount.

In such a case, the ATED-related loss is restricted to the amount which would have been the loss if the consideration had been £1 greater than the threshold amount. This rule does not restrict the amount of any loss which is not ATED-related nor does it affect any gain arising on the disposal.

[*TCGA 1992, s 2E; FA 2013, Sch 25 para 4; FA 2015, Sch 8 para 5*].

Tapering of gains

The amount of an ATED-related gain is reduced where the capital gains tax chargeable would otherwise leave the company worse off than it would have been had it sold the interest for less than the threshold amount. The gain is reduced by so much of it as exceeds five thirds of the difference between the consideration and the threshold amount. Where only a part of the gain is an ATED-related gain, the amount excluded from charge in this way is reduced by the same proportion.

This rule does not restrict the amount of any gain which is not ATED-related nor does it affect any loss arising on the disposal.

[*TCGA 1992, s 2F; FA 2013, Sch 25 para 4*].

Computation of gains and losses

The calculation of an ATED-related gain or loss differs according to which of the categories below applies.

Interest held on 5 April 2013, 5 April 2015, or 5 April 2016 — ATED-related gain

The ATED-related gain or loss is an amount equal to the 'relevant fraction' of a notional post-commencement gain or loss.

The notional post-commencement gain or loss is the gain or loss, computed using capital gains tax rules, which (apart from the current provisions) would have accrued on the disposal if the company had acquired the interest on 5 April in the relevant year at market value. The relevant year is 2013, 2015 or 2016 depending on whether Case 1, Case 2 or Case 3 applies (see above). The '*relevant fraction*' is the number of days in the period beginning on 6 April in the relevant year and ending with the day before the disposal which are 'ATED chargeable days' divided by the total number of days in that period. '*ATED chargeable days*' are days by reference to which condition (c) above is met. If there is a change in the number of ATED chargeable days as a result of a claim under *FA 2013, s 105(3)* (adjustment of chargeable amount under ATED), any necessary adjustments can be made by assessment etc. to give effect to any resulting change to the capital gains tax liability.

If there is no ATED-related gain or loss after applying the above rules, the gain or loss on the disposal is calculated according to normal principles ignoring the current provisions unless there is a non-resident CGT disposal (see **41.25** LAND) which is or involves a high value disposal on or after 6 April 2015 to which the provisions of *TCGA 1992, Sch 4ZZB* apply, in which case the current provisions may also apply (see **41.31** LAND).

Interest held on 5 April 2013, 5 April 2015, or 5 April 2016 — Non-ATED-related gain

If there is an ATED-related gain or loss, a non-ATED-related gain or loss (which remains within the charge to corporation tax on chargeable gains) must be calculated using the following steps.

(1) Compute, using corporation tax rules, the gain or loss (the notional pre-commencement gain or loss) which would have accrued on 5 April in the relevant year if the company had disposed of the interest at market value;
(2) if there is a notional post—commencement gain, deduct the ATED-related gain and adjust the remaining gain by notional indexation allowance (see below);
(3) if there is a notional post-commencement loss, deduct the ATED-related loss;
(4) add the amount in (1) above to the amount in (2) or (3) above together (treating any amount which is a loss as a negative amount).

The notional indexation allowance in (2) above is a fraction of the difference between the indexation allowance which would, but for the current provisions, be due on the disposal and the indexation allowance given in computing the notional pre-commencement gain in (1) above. The fraction is the number of days in the period beginning on 6 April in the relevant year and ending with the day before the disposal which are not ATED chargeable days, divided by the total number of days in that period.

A company can make an irrevocable election to disapply the above rules for a particular interest. If it makes such an election, the ATED-related gain or loss is computed using the rules applicable where none of cases 1, 2 or 3 apply. The election must be made in a return (or amendment to a return).

Election for retrospective basis of computation

A company can make an irrevocable election to disapply the above rules for a particular interest. If it makes such an election, the ATED-related gain or loss is computed using the rules applicable where none of cases 1, 2 or 3 apply. The election must be made in a return (or amendment to a return). An election for the retrospective basis of computation based on entire period of ownership under *TCGA 1992, Sch 4ZZB para 2(1)(b)* (see **41.31** LAND) is treated as if it were also an election under these provisions.

Election made or Cases 1, 2 or 3 do not apply

The ATED-related gain or loss is computed using the following steps.

(i) Compute the gain or loss on the disposal using capital gains tax principles (and ignoring the current provisions).
(ii) The ATED-related gain or loss is the proportion of the gain or loss that the number of days in the period beginning on the day the company acquired the interest (or 31 March 1982 if later) and ending with the day before the disposal which are 'ATED chargeable days' bears to the total number of days in that period.

The gain or loss which is not ATED-related (and remains within the charge to corporation tax on chargeable gains) is computed as follows. Deduct the ATED-related gain from the gain in (i) above and adjust the remaining gain by notional indexation allowance. Where there is a loss in (i) above, deduct from it the ATED-related loss.

The notional indexation allowance for this purpose is a fraction of the indexation allowance which would, but for the current provisions, be due on the disposal. The fraction is the number of days in the period beginning on the day the company acquired the interest (or 31 March 1982 if later) and ending with the day before the disposal which are not ATED chargeble days, divided by the total number of days in that period.

Interaction with non-resident CGT disposals

The above rules for calculating the ATED-related gain or loss are replaced by the following rules where:

(A) the high value disposal is a non-resident CGT disposal (see **41.31** LAND), or is one of two or more disposals which are treated as comprised in a non-resident CGT disposal; and

(B) the interest disposed of by the relevant high value disposal was held by the company on 5 April 2015, neither Case 2 nor Case 3 applies (see above), and no election has been made for the retrospective basis of computation based on entire period of ownership under the above provisions or under *TCGA 1992, Sch 4ZZB para 2(1)(b)* (see **41.31** LAND).

The gain or loss is determined by applying the following steps.

(I) Determine the 'relevant fraction' of the gain or loss (using capital gains tax rules) which would have accrued on the high value disposal if the company acquired the interest on 5 April 2015 at its market value (the 'post-April 2015 ATED-related gain or loss'). The '*relevant fraction*' is the number of days in the period beginning on 6 April 2015 and ending with the day before the disposal which are ATED chargeable days divided by the total number of days in that period.

(II) Determine the relevant fraction of the notional pre-April 2015 gain or loss (see below), using capital gains tax rules. The '*relevant fraction*' is the number of days in the period beginning on the day the company acquired the interest, or 6 April 2013 if later, and ending with 5 April 2015 which are ATED chargeable days divided by the total number of days in that period.

(III) Add the results of (I) and (II) together, treating a loss as a negative amount. The result is either an ATED-related gain or loss.

If the company did not hold the interest disposed of on 5 April 2013 the 'notional pre-April 2015 gain or loss' is that which would have accrued on 5 April 2015 if the interest had been disposed of at market value on that date. Otherwise it is that which would have accrued on 5 April 2015 if the company had acquired it on 5 April 2013 at market value and disposed of it on 5 April 2015 at market value.

For the calculation of the non-ATED related gain or loss which accrues where a non-resident CGT disposal is, or involves, one or more relevant high value disposals, see **41.31** LAND.

Wasting assets

Any assumption for the above purposes that an interest was acquired on a particular 5 April 2015 is ignored when determining whether the interest is a WASTING ASSET (72).

Capital allowances

Where an assumption is to be made in a computation for determining a notional post-commencement gains or loss or a notional pre-April 2015 gain or loss that an interest was acquired on 5 April 2013 at market value, *TCGA 1992, s 41* (restriction of losses by reference to capital allowances: see **16.13** COMPUTATION OF GAINS AND LOSSES) and *TCGA 1992, s 47* (wasting assets qualifying for capital allowances: see **72.2** WASTING ASSETS) apply in relation to any capital or renewals allowance made in respect of the expenditure actually incurred in acquiring or providing the asset as if that allowance were made in respect of the expenditure treated as incurred on 5 April 2013.

[*TCGA 1992, s 57A, Sch 4ZZA; FA 2013, Sch 25 paras 9, 16, 20; FA 2015, Sch 7 paras 15, 38, Sch 8 paras 6–13; FA 2016, Sch 12 para 2*].

Company reconstructions

Reconstructions involving transfer of business

[14.11] See also **63.5** and **63.7** SHARES AND SECURITIES.

If the conditions below are satisfied, where a 'scheme of reconstruction' involves the transfer of a company's business to another company for no consideration (other than the assumption of liabilities of the business), capital assets (not used as trading stock by either company) are regarded as being transferred at a 'no gain/no loss' disposal value and the acquiring company takes over the disposing company's acquisition date for the purposes of ASSETS HELD ON 6 APRIL 1965 (8).

For this purpose, '*scheme of reconstruction*' is as defined by *TCGA 1992, s 136, Sch 5AA* (see **63.7** SHARES AND SECURITIES). For practical illustrations of schemes of reconstruction, see HMRC Capital Gains Manual CG52720–52728.

The conditions that must be satisfied are:

- that *either* the transferee company is UK-resident at the time of acquisition *or* the assets are 'chargeable assets' or 'NRCGT assets' in relation to that company immediately after that time; *and*
- that *either* the transferor company is UK-resident at that time *or* the assets are 'chargeable assets' or 'NRCGT assets' in relation to that company immediately before that time.

For these purposes, an asset is a '*chargeable asset*' in relation to a company at a particular time if, on a disposal by that company at that time, any gain would be a chargeable gain and would be within the charge to corporation tax by virtue of *TCGA 1992, s 10B* (non-UK resident company trading in the UK through a permanent establishment — see **49.3** OVERSEAS MATTERS). An asset is an '*NRCGT asset*' at a particular time if a disposal of the asset would be a non-resident CGT disposal (see **41.25** LAND) and the company would not be within one of the categories of persons not chargeable to non-resident CGT (see **41.27** LAND).

[*TCGA 1992, s 139(1)(1A)(1AA)(2)(9); FA 2015, Sch 7 para 21*].

Anti-avoidance, disapplication of relief and advance clearance

TCGA 1992, s 139 will not apply to any transfer unless either the scheme is for bona fide commercial reasons and not to avoid corporation tax, capital gains tax or income tax, or HMRC, on written application by the acquiring company, has notified its satisfaction with the scheme before the transfer is made. HMRC may, within 30 days of receipt, call for further particulars to be supplied within 30 days, or longer if HMRC allows; if the information is not supplied, the application lapses. Subject to this, HMRC must notify its decision within a further 30 days. If not so notified, or if dissatisfied with the decision, the applicant may within a further 30 days require HMRC to refer the application to the Tribunal for its decision. All material facts and considerations must be disclosed, otherwise any decision is void. [*TCGA 1992, ss 138(2)–(5), 139(5); SI 2009 No 56, Sch 1 para 179*].

Applications for clearance should be directed to HMRC, CTIS Clearance SO483, Newcastle, NE98 1ZZ (if market-sensitive information is included, for the attention of the team leader). Applications may be emailed to reconstruc tions@hmrc.gsi.gov.uk. A hard copy need not then be sent. Only a single application need be made for clearances under any one or more of: *CTA 2010, ss 1091, 1092* (demergers), *CTA 2010, ss 1044, 1045* (purchase of own shares), *ITA 2007, s 701* or *CTA 2010, s 748* (transactions in securities), *TCGA 1992, s 138(1)* (share exchanges — see **4.15** ANTI-AVOIDANCE), *TCGA 1992, s 139(5)* (as above), *TCGA 1992, s 140B* (transfer or division of a UK business between EU member states — **49.13** OVERSEAS MATTERS), *TCGA 1992, s 140D* (transfer or division of a non-UK business between EU member states — **49.14** OVERSEAS MATTERS) and *CTA 2009, s 831* (various clearances under the corporation tax intangible assets regime). (Revenue Internet Statement 23 October 2002).

Where, if the disposing company had not been wound up, tax could have been assessed on it because of the effect of *TCGA 1992, s 139(5)* above, that tax can be assessed and charged (in the name of the disposing company) on the acquiring company. Subject to this, tax assessed on either company which is unpaid six months after the date when it is payable, may be similarly assessed and charged on certain third parties. The third parties are restricted to any person holding all or any part of the assets in respect of which the tax is charged and who either is the acquiring company or subsequently acquired them as a result of one or more disposals within *TCGA 1992, s 139* or *s 171(1)* (companies within same group) without any intervening disposals not within those provisions. Tax assessed on the third party is restricted to the proportion held of the assets in respect of which the tax was originally charged and may be recovered from the company originally assessed, along with any interest which the third party has paid on the outstanding tax. The assessment on the third party must be made within two years after the later of the date the tax became due and payable by the company and the date the assessment was made on the company. [*TCGA 1992, s 139(6)–(8); SI 1992 No 3066*].

Unit, investment and venture capital trusts

The provisions of *TCGA 1992, s 139* do not apply in the case of a transfer of the whole or part of a company's business to a unit trust scheme (including an umbrella scheme), within *TCGA 1992, s 100(2)* or which is an authorised unit trust, to an investment trust or to a venture capital trust (see **70** UNIT TRUSTS AND OTHER INVESTMENT VEHICLES and **71** VENTURE CAPITAL TRUSTS). [*TCGA 1992, ss 99A(3), 139(4)*].

Where *TCGA 1992, s 139* has applied in relation to a transfer to a company which was not then an investment trust but which subsequently becomes one for an accounting period, then any assets transferred and still owned by the company at the beginning of that accounting period are deemed to have been sold and immediately reacquired by the transferee company, immediately after the transfer, at their market value at that time. The resulting chargeable gain or allowable loss arising is deemed to accrue to the transferee company not at the time of the deemed disposal but at the end of the accounting period preceding the accounting period in which the company becomes an investment trust. Notwithstanding normal time limits, a corporation tax assessment in respect of any resulting liability can be made within six years after the end of the last-mentioned accounting period.

Similar provisions apply where, after a transfer to which *TCGA 1992, s 139* applied and after 16 March 1998, the transferee company becomes a venture capital trust (see **71** VENTURE CAPITAL TRUSTS). They apply by reference to the time at which HMRC's approval of the company as a VCT comes into effect, and the resulting gain or loss is deemed to accrue immediately before that time rather than at the time of the deemed disposal. In a case in which HMRC's approval has effect as from the beginning of an accounting period, any consequential corporation tax assessment can be made, notwithstanding normal time limits, within six years after the end of that accounting period. These provisions do not apply if those above relating to investment trusts have already applied (in relation to the same transfer of assets) and *vice versa*.

[*TCGA 1992, ss 101, 101B*].

Life assurance business

The provisions of *TCGA 1992, s 139* are adapted for certain transfers of an insurance company's long-term business.

Privatisations etc.

In connection with privatisations, and reorganisations of public corporations, various specific provisions have been enacted, mainly to cause transfers of assets to be treated on a 'no gain/no loss' basis, and to preclude a liability from arising under *TCGA 1992, s 179* (see **29.7** GROUPS OF COMPANIES) when a company leaves a group. See, for example, *British Telecommunications Act*

1981, s 82; Telecommunications Act 1984, s 72; Trustee Savings Bank Act 1985, Sch 2 paras 2–6; Transport Act 1985, s 130(3)(4); Airports Act 1986, s 77; Gas Act 1986, s 60; ICTA 1988, s 513; Water Act 1989, s 95; Electricity Act 1989, Sch 11; FA 1990, Sch 12 (broadcasting undertakings); *TCGA 1992, s 267* (sharing of transmission facilities); *F(No 2)A 1992, Sch 17* (privatisation of Northern Ireland Electricity); *FA 1994, Sch 24* (provisions relating to *Railways Act 1993*); and *FA 1994, Sch 25* (Northern Ireland Airports Ltd).

London Crossrail

Similar provisions apply as for privatisations etc. above in relation to the building of the London Crossrail. See *Crossrail Act 2008, Sch 13 paras 11, 12, 22, 31, 39.*

Building society's business etc. transferred to a company or other building society

Similar provisions apply as for privatisations etc. above where there is a transfer of the whole of a building society's business to a successor company in accordance with the relevant provisions of *Building Societies Act 1986* [*TCGA 1992, s 216*] and where there is a disposal by one society to another as part of an amalgamation etc. of societies. [*TCGA 1992, s 215*]. With effect from 22 April 2009, similar provisions also apply to transfers of assets as part of the transfer by a building society of the whole of its business to a subsidiary of a mutual society. [*SI 2009 No 2971, Regs 3, 5–7*].

Provision has also been made to ensure that the transfer of part of the business of Northern Rock plc to a new company wholly owned by the Treasury takes place without adverse tax consequences: see *SI 2009 No 3227.*

Industrial and provident societies etc.

Similar provisions apply as for privatisations etc. above where there is a union or amalgamation of two or more registered societies within *Co-operative and Community Benefit Societies Act 2014* or NI equivalent (previously, registered industrial and provident societies) or a transfer of engagements from one society to another. This treatment also applies to certain co-operative associations established and resident in the UK, the primary purposes of which are to assist members in carrying on husbandry in the UK or fishery operations. [*TCGA 1992, s 217D; Co-operative and Community Benefit Societies Act 2014, Sch 4 para 52; FA 2014, Sch 39 para 1*]. With effect from 22 April 2009, similar provisions also apply where an industrial and provident society converts into a company, amalgamates with a company, or transfers the whole of its business to a company. [*SI 2009 No 2971, Regs 3, 16–18; SI 2011 No 37*].

Demergers

[14.12] The provisions of *CTA 2010, ss 1073–1099* have effect for facilitating certain transactions whereby trading activities carried on by a single company or 'group' are divided so as to be carried on by two or more companies not belonging to the same group or by two or more independent groups. '*Group*' means a company and all of its 75% subsidiaries (with the effect of direct and indirect ownership of shares held as trading stock being ignored in deciding whether one company is a 75% subsidiary of another).

An exempt distribution within *CTA 2010, s 1076* (transfer by company of shares in one or more 75% subsidiaries) is not a capital distribution within *TCGA 1992, s 122* (see **63.11** SHARES AND SECURITIES). *TCGA 1992, ss 126–130* (see generally **63.2** SHARES AND SECURITIES) are applied as if that company and the subsidiary whose shares are transferred were the same company and the distribution were a reorganisation of share capital.

A charge under *TCGA 1992, s 179* (see **29.7** GROUPS OF COMPANIES) on a company ceasing to be a member of a group does not apply where the cessation is by reason only of an exempt distribution. However, this exemption does not apply if there is a chargeable payment (within *CTA 2010, s 1088*: payment not made for genuine commercial reasons or made for tax avoidance purposes) within five years of the exempt distribution, and such a payment will result in the *TCGA 1992, s 179* charge being able to be the subject of an assessment made within three years of the chargeable payment.

[*TCGA 1992, s 192*].

For full details of the provisions see Tolley's Corporation Tax under Groups of Companies. For the treatment of distributions arising from demergers in the hands of trustees, see HMRC Capital Gains Manual CG33900–33936.

See also **49.13**, **49.14** OVERSEAS MATTERS for division of a business between companies in different EC member states.

Overseas matters

[14.13] Various provisions apply where a UK resident company has an interest in a controlled foreign company. See **49.9** OVERSEAS MATTERS.

Where a UK resident company transfers all or part of a trade carried on by it outside the UK to a company not resident in the UK in exchange, wholly or partly, for shares, see **49.12** OVERSEAS MATTERS. Where the transferee company is resident in an EC member state, see **49.14** OVERSEAS MATTERS. Where a UK company's business is carried on in the UK and is transferred to a company resident in another EC member state, see **49.13** OVERSEAS MATTERS. For European cross-border mergers, see **49.15** OVERSEAS MATTERS.

There are 'exit charges' and provisions for the recovery of unpaid tax where a company ceases to be UK resident etc., is a dual resident company or is not resident in the UK. See **49.17** and **49.18** OVERSEAS MATTERS.

See also **14.15** below as regards European Companies (SEs) and **14.16** below as regards European Co-operatives (SCEs).

Use of non-sterling currencies

[14.14] There are provisions (see now *CTA 2010, ss 5–17*) under which a currency other than sterling is used to determine profits and losses of a company for corporation tax purposes. For full details see Tolley's Corporation Tax.

Chargeable gains and allowable capital losses are generally excluded from the provisions (but see further below). Such gains and losses must be calculated and expressed in sterling. [*CTA 2010, s 5(1)*]. They are translated into sterling using the rules at **16.11**(a) COMPUTATION OF GAINS AND LOSSES, subject to the exception there noted.

Special rules apply where a company disposes of a ship, aircraft, stocks or shares or an interest in stocks or shares on or after 1 September 2013 if at any time in the company's period of ownership of the asset its 'relevant currency' is not sterling. If the company incurs allowable expenditure within **16.11** COMPUTATION OF GAINS AND LOSSES before it acquires the asset, the period of ownership is treated for this purpose as beginning at the time the first such expenditure was incurred.

For this purpose '*ship*' and '*aircraft*' include the benefit of a finance lease or hire purchase contract to which *CAA 2001, s 67* applies and which relates to plant or machinery which is a ship or aircraft.

A company's '*relevant currency*' at any time is its 'functional currency' at that time or, where the company is a UK resident investment company which has made an election under *CTA 2010, s 9A*, the currency designated in the election. A company's '*functional currency*' is the currency of the primary economic environment in which it operates.

If the company's relevant currency when it disposes of the ship etc. is not sterling, the gain or loss is calculated in the relevant currency at the time of the disposal and then translated into sterling by reference to the spot rate of exchange on the day of the disposal.

In all cases where the special rules apply (whether or not the relevant currency is sterling at the date of disposal), the following computational rules must be followed.

(a) Where any allowable expenditure within **16.11** COMPUTATION OF GAINS AND LOSSES is incurred in a currency other than the company's then relevant currency, it must be translated into the relevant currency using the spot rate of exchange for the day on which it is incurred.
(b) Where there is a change in the company's relevant currency before the asset is disposed of, allowable expenditure incurred before the change must be translated into the new relevant currency using the spot rate for the day of the change.
(c) Any disposal consideration given in a currency other than the company's relevant currency must be translated into the relevant currency using the spot rate for the day of the disposal.

Any translation of expenditure under (a) above must be done before any translation of the expenditure under (b) above. If there is more than one change in a company's relevant currency, (b) above must be applied to each change in order, earliest first. If the acquisition of the asset was treated either as a no gain/no loss transaction or was treated as made at market value, the deemed expenditure is treated for these purposes as incurred at the time of the acquisition.

[*CTA 2010, ss 9C, 17(4); FA 2013, s 66; F(No 2)A 2015, s 34(13); SI 2013 No 1815*].

European Company (Societas Europaea)

[14.15] *Council Regulation (EC) No 2157/2001* provided for the creation of a new type of company, the European Company or *Societas Europaea* ('SE'). The Regulation came into effect on 8 October 2004. It permits the formation of new SEs and also allows for the 'transformation' of existing companies into SEs and for the merger between two (or more) companies in different member states into an SE. For most tax purposes, an SE based in the UK is treated like a UK-resident plc, but special provisions are required to deal with, among other matters, the formation of SEs by cross-border merger. The provisions are intended to be broadly tax-neutral. (Revenue Technical Note, 'Implementation of the European Company Statute', January 2005).

Formation of SE by merger

See **49.15** OVERSEAS MATTERS.

Residence

For the residence for tax purposes of an SE transferring its registered office to the UK, see **57.33** RESIDENCE AND DOMICILE.

Continuity on ceasing to be UK resident

If at any time a company ceases to be resident in the UK in the course of the formation of an SE by merger (whether or not the company continues to exist following the merger), *FA 1998, Sch 18* (company RETURNS (**58.19**), ASSESSMENTS (**6**), APPEALS (**5**), etc.) applies after that time in relation to liabilities accruing and other matters arising before that time as if the company were still UK-resident and, if the company has ceased to exist, as if the SE were the company.

Where an SE transfers its registered office outside the UK and ceases to be UK-resident, *FA 1998, Sch 18* applies after that time in relation to liabilities accruing and other matters arising before that time as if the SE were still UK-resident.

[*FA 1998, Sch 18 paras 87A–87C; TIOPA 2010, Sch 7 para 108*].

Groups of companies

See **29.2** GROUPS OF COMPANIES.

European Co-operative (Societas Co-operative Europaea)

[14.16] *Council Regulation (EC) No 1435/2003* provided for the creation of a new type of co-operative, the European Co-operative or *Societas Co-operative Europaea* ('SCE'). The Regulation came into effect on 18 August 2006. It permits the formation of new SCEs and also allows for the 'transformation' of existing co-operatives into SEs and for the merger between two (or more) co-operatives in different member states into an SCE. For most tax purposes, an SCE based in the UK is treated like a registered society within *Co-operative and Community Benefit Societies Act 2014* (previously, a registered industrial and provident society), but special provisions are required to deal with, among other matters, the formation of SCEs by cross-border merger.

Formation of SCE by merger

See 49.15 OVERSEAS MATTERS.

Residence

For the residence for tax purposes of an SE transferring its registered office to the UK, see 57.33 RESIDENCE AND DOMICILE.

Tax accounting arrangements of large companies

[14.17] The 'senior accounting officer' of a 'qualifying company' has a statutory duty to take reasonable steps to ensure that the company establishes and maintains 'appropriate tax accounting arrangements'. In particular, the officer must take reasonable steps to monitor the accounting arrangements of the company and to identify any respects in which they are not appropriate tax accounting arrangements. Failure to comply with this obligation will result in the officer becoming liable to a penalty of £5,000 for each financial year involved.

For this purpose, '*appropriate tax accounting arrangements*' are accounting arrangements, including arrangements for keeping accounting records, which enable the company's relevant tax liabilities (including corporation tax on chargeable gains) to be calculated accurately in all material respects. Subject to the Treasury's power to make regulations excluding certain companies, a '*qualifying company*' is, broadly a company with a turnover of more than £200 million and/or a balance sheet total of more than £2 billion. Where the company is a member of a group, the requirements relate to the aggregate amounts for the group. A company's 'senior accounting officer' is the director or officer or group director or officer with overall responsibility for the company's financial accounting arrangements. A person can be the senior accounting officer of more than one company.

The officer must also provide HMRC with a certificate for every financial year, stating whether the company had appropriate arrangements throughout the year and, if not, explaining the ways in which the arrangements were deficient. The certificate must be given to HMRC not later than the end of the *Companies Act 2006, s 442* period for filing the accounts (or such later time as HMRC allow) and can relate to more than one qualifying company. If the officer fails to provide the certificate, or provides a certificate containing a careless or deliberate error, he will be liable to a penalty of £5,000. An error that is neither careless nor deliberate is treated for this purpose as careless if the officer later discovered it and did not take reasonable steps to inform HMRC. A penalty cannot be charged for a financial year if the officer has already been assessed to a penalty under this provision in respect of another company in the same group for a year ending in the same financial year.

To facilitate the operation of these provisions, a qualifying company must ensure HMRC are notified of the name of each person who was its senior accounting officer at any time during a financial year. Notification must be given not later than the end of the *Companies Act 2006, s 442* period for filing the accounts (or such later time as HMRC have allowed for providing the certificate for the year). A single notification can be made for more than one company. Failure to notify will result in the company being liable to a penalty of £5,000. A penalty cannot, however, be charged for a financial year if another company in the same group has already been assessed to a penalty under this provision for a year ending in the same financial year.

A company or officer can appeal against the above penalties within 30 days of the date of the HMRC notification of the penalty. No penalty will be due if HMRC or, on appeal, the Tribunal, are satisfied that there was a reasonable excuse for the failure. Insufficiency of funds or reliance on another person to do anything are not normally reasonable excuses, and where a reasonable excuse ceases, the failure must be rectified without unreasonable delay. A reasonable excuse for failure to comply includes any circumstance where the failure is attributable to any matter outside the person's control or any matter of which a person could not reasonably be expected to be aware. Where the identity of the senior accounting officer changes during a financial year, there are provisions to ensure that only one person is liable to any of the penalties (and to determine which of the officers it will be).

[*FA 2009, s 93, Sch 46*].

HMRC have published guidance on the above provisions in HMRC Guidance Note 17 August 2009.

Publication of tax strategies by large businesses

[14.18] For financial years beginning on or after 15 September 2016, certain large businesses must publish their tax strategy each year. The strategy must be published on the internet before the end of the financial year to which it relates. If the business was required to publish its tax strategy for the previous financial year, the current year's strategy must be published no more than 15 months after the previous strategy was published. The strategy must be freely available to public view free of charge and must remain so until the next year's strategy is published or, if no such strategy need be published, for at least one year. The strategy may be published either as a separate document or as a self-contained part of a wider document.

The requirement to publish a tax strategy applies to the following entities.

(1) The 'head' of a 'UK group' which is a 'qualifying group' for the financial year. A '*UK group*' is a 'group' whose head is a body corporate incorporated in the UK. A '*group*' is either an 'MNE group' (as defined in the OECD Model Legislation in the OECD Country-by-Country Reporting Implementation Package) or a 'group other than an MNE group' (as defined by reference to 51% subsidiaries and including at least two UK companies or UK permanent establishments). The '*head*' of a group is the member of the group which is not a 51% subsidiary of another member of the group.
A group other than an MNE group is a '*qualifying group*' for a financial year if either the aggregate turnover of its UK companies and UK permanent establishments for the preceding year was more than £200 million or the aggregate balance sheet total assets for those

companies and permanent establishments for that year exceeded £2 billion. An MNE group is a 'qualifying group' for a financial year if there was a mandatory country-by-country reporting requirement under *FA 2015, s 122* for the previous financial year or there would have been if the head of the group were UK-resident for tax purposes.

(2) The 'head' of a 'UK sub-group' of a 'foreign' group' where the foreign group is a qualifying group for the financial year. A '*foreign group*' is a group whose head is a body corporate incorporated outside the UK. A '*UK sub-group*' consists of two or more bodies corporate that would be a UK group but for the fact that they are members of a larger foreign group. The '*head*' of a UK sub-group is the member of the sub-group which is not a 51% subsidiary of another member of the sub-group.

(3) A UK company which is a 'qualifying company' for the financial year. A company is a '*qualifying company*' for a financial year if at the end of the previous financial year it was not a member of a UK group or a UK sub-group and for that year its turnover exceeded £200 million or its balance sheet total assets exceeded £2 billion. If the company was a member of a foreign group at the end of the previous year, the turnover and balance sheet thresholds apply as in (1) above. The requirement to publish the company's tax strategy for a financial year applies even if the company becomes a member of a group or UK sub-group during the year.

A UK permanent establishment of a foreign body corporate is treated as if it were a company for these purposes and, if the foreign body corporate is a member of a group or a UK sub-group, as a member of that group or sub-group.

(4) A 'UK partnership' which is a 'qualifying partnership' for the financial year. A '*UK partnership*' is a UK partnership, limited partnership or limited liability partnership which is carrying on a trade, business or profession with a view to profit. A UK partnership is a 'qualifying partnership' if, for the previous financial year, its turnover exceeded £200 million or its balance sheet total assets exceeded £2 billion.

In relation to a partnership, a '*financial year*' means any period of account for which its representative partner is required to provide a partnership statement in a return (see **58.17** RETURNS).

A tax strategy must set out the following:

- the approach of the group, sub-group, company, permanent establishment or partnership to risk management and governance in relation to UK taxation;
- the attitude of the group etc. towards tax planning affecting UK taxation;
- the level of risk in relation to UK taxation that the group etc. is prepared to accept; and
- the approach of the group etc. towards its dealings with HMRC.

It may include other information relating to taxation (UK or otherwise). In the case of a group or sub-group, the tax strategy may set out the required information by reference to the group or sub-group as a whole or to individual members (or both). Information about activities consisting of the provision of tax advice or related professional services to other persons does not have to be included in the tax strategy. The strategy must make it clear that the group etc. regards its publication as complying with the above requirements. The Treasury may be regulations require group tax strategies to include a country-by-country report (as defined).

For HMRC guidance see www.gov.uk/guidance/large-businesses-publish-your-tax-strategy.

Penalty for failure to comply

See **52.30** PENALTIES.

[*FA 2016, s 161(2), Sch 19 paras 1–17, 19, 20, 22, 23, 25*].

Special measures regime for unco-operative large businesses

[14.19] *FA 2016* introduced a special measures regime for large businesses which engage in what HMRC consider to be aggressive tax planning or which do not engage with HMRC in an 'open and collaborative manner' (see HM Treasury Explanatory Notes to the 2016 Finance Bill). The regime operates by HMRC first issuing a warning notice which provides the taxpayer with an opportunity to make representations about whether the regime should apply. A warning notice may be followed by a special measures notice, the effect of which is that any inaccuracies in a document given to HMRC are deemed to be at least careless (and therefore subject to a penalty). If a special measures notice is confirmed by a confirmation notice then HMRC may publicly identify the taxpayer as subject to the regime.

A warning notice may not be given to a taxpayer before the beginning of its first financial year beginning on or after 15 September 2016. [*FA 2016, s 161(3)*].

The regime is described in the following paragraphs as it applies to UK groups. See below for its application to other types of taxpayer.

Warning notice

An HMRC officer who has been designated for the purpose may give a notice (a '*warning notice*') to the 'head' of a 'UK group' if he considers that the group is a 'qualifying group' that meets the following conditions. The conditions are that:

(1) the group has 'persistently' engaged in 'unco-operative behaviour';
(2) some or all of that behaviour has caused or contributed to two or more 'significant tax issues' in respect of the group or members of it which are unresolved; and
(3) there is a reasonable likelihood of further instances of unco-operative behaviour causing or contributing to significant tax issues in respect of the group or its members.

For this purpose a UK group has engaged in '*unco-operative behaviour*' if a member of the group or two or more members taken together satisfy either or both of the behaviour condition or the arrangements condition. A group has '*persistently*' engaged in such behaviour if a member of the group or two or more members taken together have done so on a sufficient number of occasions for it to be clear that it represents a pattern of behaviour.

A group member, or two or more members taken together, satisfy the behaviour condition if they behave in a way which has delayed or otherwise hindered HMRC in the exercise of their functions in connection with determining the UK tax liability of the group or a member. The extent to which HMRC have used statutory powers to obtain information, the reasons why those powers have been used, the number and seriousness of inaccuracies in and omissions from documents given to HMRC and the extent to which group members (or their agents) have relief on interpretations of UK tax legislation which are 'speculative' are all actors indicative of such behaviour. An interpretation is '*speculative*' for this purpose if it is likely that a court or tribunal would disagree with it.

A member of a UK group satisfies the arrangements condition if it is a party to a '*tax avoidance scheme*': i.e. arrangements in respect of which a final counteraction notice under the general anti-abuse rule (see **4.3** ANTI-AVOIDANCE), arrangements which are notifiable arrangements under the provisions for DISCLOSURE OF TAX AVOIDANCE SCHEMES (**20.4**) other than any arrangements for which the promoter has been notified that clients need no longer be provided with the scheme number) or arrangements notifiable under equivalent VAT provisions.

There is a 'significant tax issue' in respect of a UK group or a group member if there is a disagreement (or reasonable likelihood of a disagreement) between HMRC and a group member about an issue affecting the amount of the UK tax liability of the group or member which has been, or could be, referred to a court or tribunal to determine. The tax at stake must be, or be likely to be, at least £2 million.

'UK group', 'qualifying group' and the 'head' of a UK group are all as defined at **14.18**(1) above. References above to things done by a group member include acts or omissions of former members when they were still members of the group but do not include acts or omissions of current members before they joined.

The warning notice must set out the reasons why the officer considers that the above conditions are met and may be withdrawn at any time by giving a further notice to that effect. If the notice has not been withdrawn it expires after 15 months. Once a warning notice has been given, the notice, and any subsequent special measures notice (see below), continue to have effect even if the group ceases to be a qualifying group, changes its membership or becomes a UK sub-group of a foreign group (see **14.18**(2) above).

If, while the warning notice is in effect, the head of the group becomes a member of a group headed by another body corporate (H), the warning notice is treated as having been given to H on the day it was actually given to the original head of the group. A notice deemed to be given in this way is valid even if H is not the head of a qualifying UK group to which the conditions at (1)–(3) above apply.

Special measures notice

A designated HMRC officer may give the head of a UK group a '*special measures notice*' if:

(a) a warning notice has been given to the head and not withdrawn;
(b) twelve months have passed since the day on which the warning notice was given;
(c) the 15 months beginning with the day on which the warning notice was given have not elapsed; and
(d) the officer considers that the UK group meets the conditions at (1)–(3) above. The officer may take into account any behaviour for this purpose, whether or not mentioned in the warning notice and must consider any representations made by any group member before the end of the twelve months beginning with the day the warning notice was given.

The special measures notice must set out the reasons why the officer considers that the above conditions are met and may be withdrawn at any time by giving a further notice to that effect. If the notice has not been withdrawn it expires after 27 months beginning with the later of the day it was given and the day on which it was last confirmed (see below).

A designated HMRC officer may also give the head of a UK group a special measures notice if:

(A) a warning notice or special measures notice has been given to the head and has expired;
(B) it appears to the officer that in the period of six months since the notice expired the group has engaged in unco-operative behaviour and there is a reasonable likelihood that, if the behaviour had occurred before the notice expired a special measures notice or confirmation notice could have been given;
(C) during the seven months beginning with the day on which the notice expired HMRC have notified the head of the group that a special measures notice may be given; and
(D) no more than nine months have elapsed since the notice expired.

In deciding whether to give such a notice the officer must consider any representations made by any group member within eight months from the day the original notice expired.

If, while a special measures notice is in effect, the head of the group becomes a member of a group headed by another body corporate (H), the notice is treated as having been given to H on the day it was actually given to the original head of the group. A notice deemed to be given in this way is valid even if H is not the head of a qualifying UK group to which the conditions at (1)–(3) above apply.

Confirmation notice

A designated HMRC officer may give the head of a UK group a notice (a '*confirmation notice*') confirming a special measures notice if:

(i) a special measures notice has been given to the head and not withdrawn;

(ii) 24 months have passed since the later of the day on which the special measures notice was given and the day on which it was last confirmed;

(iii) the 27 months beginning with the later of the day the notice was given and the day on which it was last confirmed have not elapsed; and

(iv) the officer considers that the UK group meets the conditions at (1)–(3) above. The officer may take into account any behaviour for this purpose, whether or not mentioned in the warning notice, special measures notice or a previous confirmation notice and must consider any representations made by any group member before the end of the period in (ii) above.

The confirmation notice must set out the reasons why the officer considers that the above conditions are met and may be withdrawn at any time by giving a further notice to that effect. If the notice has not been withdrawn it expires after 27 months beginning with the day on which it was given.

If, while a confirmation notice is in effect, the head of the group becomes a member of a group headed by another body corporate (H), the notice is treated as having been given to H on the day it was actually given to the original head of the group. A notice deemed to be given in this way is valid even if H is not the head of a qualifying UK group to which the conditions at (1)–(3) above apply.

Sanctions

Penalties

For the purposes of the penalty provisions at **52.8** PENALTIES, an inaccuracy in a document given to HMRC by or on behalf of a member of a group whilst the group is subject to a special measures notice is treated as being due to failure by the member to take reasonable care if either:

- the inaccuracy relates to a tax avoidance scheme which was entered into whilst the group member at a time when it was a member of a group and the group was subject to a special measures notice; or
- the inaccuracy is attributable, wholly or in part, to an interpretation of UK tax law which, at the time the document was given, was speculative.

This rule does not, however, apply to treat a deliberate inaccuracy as merely careless. It also does not apply where, during the currency of a special measures notice, the head of the group becomes a member of a group headed by another body corporate (H), and the inaccuracy is in a document given to HMRC by a member of H's group at a time before the head of the group to which the notice was originally given became a member of H's group.

Publication of information

The Commissioners for HMRC may publish certain information about a UK group if a special measures notice given to the head of the group is in force and the notice has been confirmed by a confirmation notice. They may also publish information if a special measures notice confirmed by a confirmation notice has expired but a further special measures notice has been given to the head of the group as a result of the conditions in (A)–(D) above and is in force.

The information which may be published is the name of the group and its address or registered office, the fact that it is subject to a confirmed special measures notice and any other information HMRC consider it appropriate to publish in order to identify the group. When the group ceases to be subject to a special measures notice HMRC must publish a notice stating that it is no longer subject to the notice within the 30 days beginning with that on which the notice is withdrawn or expires.

Before publishing information the Commissioners must inform the head of the group of their intention to do so and allow the head a reasonable opportunity to make representations about whether publication should go ahead.

Application of regime to UK sub-groups, companies and partnerships

The special measures regime applies to UK sub-groups of overseas groups which are qualifying groups (see **14.18**(2) above), qualifying companies (see **14.18**(3) above) and qualifying partnerships (see **14.18**(4) above), the above provisions being modified as necessary. In particular, in the case of a UK sub-group, once a warning notice has been given, the notice, and any subsequent special measures notice, continue to have effect even if the group ceases to be a qualifying group, the sub-group changes its membership or becomes a UK sub-group of another foreign group. In the case of a partnership, references to the head of a UK group should be read as references to the representative partner of the partnership, and references to a member of a group as references to a partner in a partnership acting in his capacity as partner.

[*FA 2016, Sch 19 paras 35–53*].

Key points concerning companies

[14.20] Points to consider are as follows.

- If a company enters administration or liquidation, an accounting period is ended and a new one begins. The timing of the process may therefore be crucial in deciding what rate of corporation tax is applicable to the pre- and post-insolvency periods. See **14.4**.
- Similarly, since the ranking of pre- and post-liquidation tax debts is different, it may be appropriate for creditors to give some thought to the timing of the appointment of a liquidator, to maximise the return to business creditors. See **14.4**.
- Capital losses are often carried forward for many years before they are used. It is therefore essential that companies have reliable long-term record keeping processes in place, so that the availability of an agreed loss can be demonstrated at the point of use. See **14.6**.
- One often overlooked impact of the substantial shareholdings exemption is that there is no relief for losses arising on qualifying shares, because the sale of those shares at a profit would have been exempt. See **14.6**.

- There is a targeted anti-avoidance rule at *TCGA 1992, s 16A* which denies companies the benefit of capital losses that arise in disqualifying circumstances, i.e. the loss arises from arrangements designed to generate a tax advantage. Losses arising in disqualifying circumstances are just lost and can never be used. See **14.7**.
- Where there are schemes to turn income into capital or to secure a deduction, the company should self-assess on the basis of the arrangements entered into. It is implicit in the fact that HMRC must issue a notice to counteract these schemes that there is no requirement to consider the anti-avoidance legislation when preparing the company's self-assessment. See **14.7–14.9**.
- Many people consider the UK residence requirement in *TCGA 1992, s 139* is contrary to the terms of the Treaty for the Functioning of the EU and that the provisions should apply to transfers to companies resident in any EU (or EEA) Member State. HMRC currently resists that interpretation.
- Further helpful guidance about clearances can be found on the gov.uk website at www.gov.uk/government/collections/seeking-clearance-or-approval-for-a-transaction. See **14.11**.
- It is important to note that an HMRC clearance under *TCGA 1992, s 138* or *s 139* only states that HMRC is satisfied that the transactions are being entered into for bona fide commercial reasons and not for the avoidance of corporation tax. The clearance does not confirm that HMRC agrees that the transaction amounts to a reorganisation or a scheme of reconstruction. See **14.11**.
- A clearance for a demerger will necessarily confirm that HMRC agrees that the detailed technical requirements of the legislation are satisfied. As such, these clearances are quite comprehensive, in comparison to clearances under *TCGA 1992, s 138* or *s 139* (see **4.15**, **14.11**). See **14.12**.
- HMRC have a toolkit 'chargeable gains for companies' that considers the perceived risk areas such as access to historical data, date of disposal, valuations, qualifying expenditure and reliefs. Using the toolkit or an alternative checklist may help show that reasonable care has been taken. Showing reasonable care is important if the computation of the gain is subsequently challenged and found to be incorrect as it affects the penalty that can be charged.
- Large companies (and partnerships) must publish an annual tax strategy online, outlining their approach to tax risk, tax planning and dealing with HMRC (see **14.18** above). If they have a history of unco-operative behaviour they may become subject to a special measures regime (see **14.19** above).

15

Companies — Corporate Finance and Intangibles

Introduction	**15.1**
Loan relationships	**15.2**
Summary of provisions	**15.3**
Loan relationships with embedded derivatives	**15.4**
Definition of 'loan relationship'	**15.5**
Shares treated as creditor relationships	**15.6**
Chargeable gains	**15.7**
Derivative contracts	**15.8**
Definition of 'derivative contract'	**15.9**
Derivative contracts taxed on a chargeable gains basis	**15.10**
Issuers of securities with embedded derivatives	**15.11**
Miscellaneous rules with potential chargeable gains consequences	**15.12**
Transitional provisions with potential chargeable gains consequences	**15.13**
Intangible fixed assets	**15.14**
Definition of 'intangible fixed asset'	**15.15**
Key points	**15.16**

Introduction to companies: corporate finance and intangibles

[15.1] There are three sets of special corporation tax rules which seek to apply accepted accounting principles to particular types of profits and gains. Broadly (and with certain exceptions), under each of the regimes all profits are treated for corporation tax purposes as income and all losses as income losses, including those which would ordinarily be capital. The regimes concerned are those which cover:

- loan relationships (see **15.2–15.7** below);
- derivative contracts (see **15.8–15.13** below); and
- intangible fixed assets (see **15.14**, **15.16** below).

This chapter describes these regimes in detail only insofar as they interact with chargeable gains provisions. For full coverage see Tolley's Corporation Tax.

See also **51.8** PAYMENT OF TAX for exit charge payment plans which companies may enter into with HMRC where they incur certain exit charges, including those under the three regimes discussed in this chapter.

Loan relationships

[15.2] The intention of the loan relationship provisions is for the corporate taxation of income and expenditure from corporate and government debt to equate with its accepted accounting treatment. This is brought about by first establishing the existence of a 'loan relationship' and secondly, by treating all company profits and losses from such relationships as income and not capital, regardless of whether the company is borrower or lender.

See also 28 GOVERNMENT SECURITIES, 54 QUALIFYING CORPORATE BONDS and HMRC Corporate Finance Manual CFM30000 onwards.

Summary of provisions

[15.3] As the underlying criteria is for the tax treatment of each loan relationship to follow generally accepted accounting practice, the terms *debit* and *credit* are used to describe the method of accounting for individual items of income and expenditure. The debits and credits will include all profits, gains and losses, including those of a capital nature, interest payments, charges and expenses appertaining to the company's loan relationship or its attributed rights and liabilities. Charges and expenses appertaining to loan relationships include only those incurred directly:

(i) in bringing any of the loan relationships into existence;
in entering into or giving effect to any of the related transactions;
in making payments under any of the relationships or in pursuance of any of the related transactions; or

(ii) in taking steps for ensuring the receipt of payments under any of the relationships or in accordance with any of the related transactions.

[*CTA 2009, ss 306A, 307; F(No 2)A 2015, Sch 7 paras 3, 4*].

Interest on money debts which are not themselves loan relationships is also brought into account as debits and credits under the provisions. Profits from disposals of interest and from discounts are also brought into account. [*CTA 2009, ss 478–486; TIOPA 2010, Sch 8 para 91; FA 2012, Sch 16 para 162*].

Return on arrangements which is 'economically equivalent to interest' (defined broadly as for the provisions treating shares as creditor relationships — see **15.6** below) is also treated as a profit from a loan relationship where the company becomes party to the arrangements on or after 22 April 2009. [*CTA 2009, ss 486A–486E; TIOPA 2010, Sch 8 para 139; FA 2012, Sch 20 paras 26, 27*].

For the calculation of credits and debits, see *CTA 2009, ss 306–327.*

Debits and credits arising from loan relationships to which a company is party are brought into account according to the purposes for which the company is party to it. Where the loan relationship is one to which the company is party for trading purposes, credits and debits are treated as receipts and expenses to be brought into account in computing the profits of the trade. Credits and debits in respect of non-trading loan relationships are aggregated and, where the aggregate credits exceed the aggregate debits, that excess is taxable as income. Relief is available for deficits. If only part of a loan relates to trading purposes the debits and credits should be apportioned accordingly. [*CTA 2009, ss 295–301; FA 2012, Sch 16 para 147*].

However, a general corporate interest restriction effective from 1 April 2017 places a limit on the amount of interest expense and certain other finance costs that companies with high interest costs can deduct when calculating profits subject to corporation tax. For details of the corporate interest restriction, see Tolley's Corporation Tax. [*F(No 2)A 2017, s 20, Sch 5*].

Foreign exchange gains and losses

The reference above to profits, gains and losses to be included in debits and credits includes, subject to certain exceptions, foreign exchange gains and losses arising to a company in relation to any asset or liability representing a loan relationship of the company.

Hedging instruments

Special rules apply where a loan relationship is a hedging instrument matched with another foreign currency asset. Broadly (and subject to anti-avoidance provisions), exchange gains or losses on such relationships are initially disregarded and are then brought back into charge when the matched asset is disposed of (otherwise than on a no gain/no loss disposal).

If the matched asset is itself a loan relationship, a ship or an aircraft the exchange gains and losses are brought back into charge as loan relationship debits and credits. In most other cases the exchange gains and losses are brought back into charge under the chargeable gains rules. Any net exchange gain (i.e. gains less losses) is added to the consideration for the disposal. Any net loss is deducted from the consideration and, where the loss exceeds the consideration, the excess is added to the acquisition cost. The exchange gains or losses are not brought back in to charge if the disposal of the asset is within the exemption for SUBSTANTIAL SHAREHOLDINGS OF COMPANIES (**66**) or if the asset is an asset of a foreign branch (other than shares not held on trading account).

[*TCGA 1992, s 151E; CTA 2009, ss 328–328H, 475A; F(No 2)A 2015, Sch 7 paras 20, 21, 54, 98; SI 2002 No 1970; SI 2004 No 3256; SI 2010 No 809; SI 2011 Nos 698, 2912; SI 2013 No 1843; SI 2014 Nos 3188, 3325; SI 2015 Nos 1960, 1961*].

Loan relationships with embedded derivatives

[15.4] Special provisions apply to loan relationships with 'embedded derivatives'. This is where a company in accordance with generally accepted accounting practice splits the rights and liabilities under the loan relationship into those under the loan relationship (the '*host contract*') and '*embedded derivatives*', which are those under one or more derivative financial instruments or equity instruments (as defined). In this case, the host contract will fall, for corporation tax purposes, within the loan relationship rules and the embedded derivative within the derivative contracts rules (see **15.8** below) which provide, in certain cases, for the embedded derivative to be taxed on a chargeable gains basis. The embedded derivative is treated as having the character (be it an option, a future or a contract for differences) which the rights and liabilities would have if contained in a separate contract. [*CTA 2009, s 415*].

Election for embedded derivatives provision to apply

A company which, for a period of account beginning on or after 1 January 2005, is subject to '*old UK GAAP*' (i.e. UK generally accepted accounting practice as it applied for periods of account beginning before that date) and holds assets ('*relevant assets*') which it is not permitted under old UK GAAP to split as above (so that the above provision does not apply), may make an election for the loan relationship and derivative contract rules to have effect as if the above provision did apply. The election can only be made if the company would have been permitted so to split the assets had it been subject to international accounting standards or '*new UK GAAP*' (i.e. UK generally accepted accounting practice as it applies for periods of account beginning on or after 1 January 2005).

An election has effect in relation to all relevant assets held by the company, including any acquired later. It must be made in writing to an officer of Revenue and Customs, generally on or before 31 December 2005. The deadline is extended if the company does not hold any relevant assets at the beginning of its first period of account beginning on or after 1 January 2005 but subsequently acquires one or more; in such a case the deadline is 90 days after the acquisition of the first relevant asset. The deadline is also extended if the company does not have a period of account beginning in 2005 and holds a relevant asset at the beginning of its first period of account beginning after the end of that year, in which case the election must be made no later than 90 days after the beginning of that period.

The election takes effect from the beginning of the company's first period of account beginning on or after 1 January 2005, unless it is made after 31 December 2005 as a result of the company acquiring its first relevant asset, in which case it takes effect from the beginning of the period of account in which that asset is acquired.

Where an election is made, the provisions of *CTA 2009, ss 315–318* and *CTA 2009, ss 613–615* (adjustments on change of accounting policy) apply as if there were a change of accounting policy consisting in the company splitting its relevant assets as above as from the date the election takes effect.

[*CTA 2009, ss 416, 417, Sch 2 para 64*].

Simon's Taxes. See **D1.723**.

Definition of 'loan relationship'

[15.5] A '*loan relationship*' exists whenever a company is in the position of debtor or creditor to a 'money debt' which arises from the lending of money. [*CTA 2009, s 302(1)*].

A '*money debt*' is defined as a debt which is, or at any time has been, one that falls (or that may at the option of the debtor or of the creditor fall) to be settled:

(a) by the payment of money;
(b) by the transfer of a right to settlement under a debt which is itself a money debt; or
(c) by the issue or transfer of shares in any company;

disregarding any other option exercisable by either party.

[*CTA 2009, s 303*].

The legislation does not define a *debtor* or *creditor* and therefore the accepted meaning is understood to apply. The meaning of 'money debt' and 'the lending of money' were considered in *HSBC Life (UK) Ltd v Stubbs (and related appeals)* (Sp C 295), [2002] SSCD 9 (although these appeals pre-dated the tightening of the statutory definition of 'money debt' for accounting periods beginning on or after 1 October 2002).

Examples of loan relationships are: bank overdrafts, bank borrowings and third party borrowings plus corporate bonds and gilt-edged securities (subject to special rules for 5½% Treasury Stock 2008–2012 held by non-financial traders).

However, normal debtor/creditor relationships are not included as these do not arise from the lending of money and a debt arising from shareholders' rights is specifically excluded. Thus, ordinary shares and preference shares are not loan relationships. However, all building society shares, including permanent interest bearing shares, are within the loan relationships rules.

[*CTA 2009, ss 303(4), 305*].

Alternative finance arrangements within *CTA 2009, ss 503–507* are also loan relationships. [*CTA 2009, s 501*].

For accounting periods beginning on or after 1 April 2008, certain 'investment life insurance contracts' (broadly, life insurance policies which have a surrender value, contracts for a purchased life annuity and capital redemption policies) held by a company which is not a life insurance company are treated as creditor relationships of the company. See *CTA 2009, ss 560–569*.

An advance under a repo or quasi-repo within the post-1 October 2007 regime for sale and repurchase of securities (see **63.26** SHARES AND SECURITIES) is treated as a money debt for the above purposes — see *CTA 2009, ss 546(2), 551(2)*.

A '*creditor relationship*', in relation to a company, is a loan relationship of that company where it stands in the position of a creditor as respects the debt in question. A '*debtor relationship*' has a corresponding meaning. '*Fair value*' has the meaning it has for accounting purposes (but for accounting periods beginning before 1 January 2016, the fair value of a loan relationship has a specific statutory definition: it is the amount which, at the time at which the value falls to be determined, the company would obtain from, or would have to pay to, an independent person for the transfer of all its rights and liabilities under the relationship). [*CTA 2009, ss 302(5)(6), 313(6), 476(1); F(No 2)A 2015, Sch 7 paras 7, 55*].

Corporate holdings in authorised unit trusts, open-ended insurance companies, and offshore funds

Holdings of rights under a unit trust scheme, shares in an open-ended investment company or interests in an offshore fund which fail to satisfy the 'qualifying investments test' at any time in an accounting period, are treated for that period as rights under creditor relationships, in relation to which a fair value basis of accounting must be used.

The '*qualifying investments test*' requires that not more than 60% of the market value of scheme or fund investments is represented by 'qualifying investments' (as defined, and including money placed at interest, securities, derivative contracts etc.).

Where the above provisions start or cease to apply to a holding without the company disposing of it, that event is treated as if it resulted from a reorganisation within *TCGA 1992, s 116* (see **54.4** QUALIFYING CORPORATE BONDS). The holding immediately before the end of the accounting period at the end of which the above provisions started or ceased to apply is the 'old asset' for the purposes of *section 116* and the holding immediately afterwards is the 'new asset'.

[*CTA 2009, ss 487–497; TCGA 1992, s 116A; TIOPA 2010, Sch 8 para 172; FA 2014, s 27; SI 2006 No 964, Regs 90, 95, 96A; SI 2006 No 981; SI 2009 No 3001, Reg 131; SI 2012 No 519, Reg 8*].

Simon's Taxes. See **D1.703, D1.788.**

Shares treated as creditor relationships

[15.6] There are provisions which treat certain shares held by companies as rights under creditor relationships. The original provisions were replaced with effect from 22 April 2009, subject to a transitional provision. The new provisions are described below, followed by the chargeable gains effects.

The provisions apply in relation to times in a company's accounting period when the company (the '*investing company*') holds a share in another company (the '*issuing company*') and:

(i) the share would, in accordance with generally accepted accounting practice, be accounted for by the issuing company as a liability;
(ii) the share produces for the investing company a return in relation to any amount which is 'economically equivalent to interest';
(iii) the issuing and investing companies are not connected companies (within *CTA 2009, s 466*);
(iv) the share is not treated as rights under a creditor relationship under *CTA 2009, s 490* (holdings in open-ended investment companies, unit trusts and offshore funds);
(v) the share is not an 'excepted share'; and
(vi) the investing company holds the share for an 'unallowable purpose'.

For this purpose, a return is '*economically equivalent to interest*' in relation to an amount only if it is reasonable to assume that it is a return by reference to the time value of the amount and it is at a rate reasonably comparable to a commercial rate of interest. At the time the company first holds the share (or, if later, when the share begins to produce a return) there must be no practical likelihood that the return will cease to be produced unless the payer is prevented from paying it.

A share is an '*excepted share*' if it was issued as part of an issue to persons not connected with the issuer provided that less than 10% of the shares in that issue are held by the investing company or persons connected with it. A share is also an excepted share if it mirrors a public issue (as defined).

A company holds a share for an '*unallowable purpose*' if one of the main purposes for which it holds the share is to obtain a tax advantage (as defined) in relation to the return on the share. Where the investing company is a controlled foreign company within the pre-*FA 2012* regime for such companies, shares held by it are not normally treated as held for an unallowable purpose.

Where these provisions would not otherwise apply because condition (vi) above is not satisfied, the investing company can make an election for them to apply. Such an election is irrevocable and must normally be made no later then the time the company first holds the share or, if later, when the share begins to produce a return. Where, however, a return begins to be produced before 1 August 2009, the election can be made at any time before that date (but applies only to return produced on or after the date it is made).

At any time at which the above conditions apply, the share is treated as if it were rights under a creditor relationship of the investing company. No debits are to be brought into account by the investing company (other than any debits in respect of exchange gains or losses). If a share begins or cease to be within the provisions the investing company is treated for loan relationship purposes as having disposed of it and immediately reacquired it for consideration equal to what would have been its tax-adjusted carrying value (as defined) if accounts had been drawn up at that time.

[*CTA 2009, ss 521A–521F; FA 2012, Sch 20 paras 28, 49, 50; F(No 2)A 2015, Sch 7 para 57*].

Chargeable gains

Where the above provisions begin to apply in the case of any shares, the investing company is deemed for chargeable gains purposes to have disposed of the share immediately before that time, and to have immediately reacquired it. The consideration for the deemed disposal and acquisition is the amount that would be the share's carrying value if accounts were drawn up on that date.

Where at any time, the above provisions cease to apply to a share, the investing company is deemed for chargeable gains purposes to have disposed of the share immediately before that time, and to have immediately reacquired it. The consideration for the deemed disposal and acquisition is the amount that would be the share's carrying value if accounts were drawn up on that date.

[*TCGA 1992, s 116B*].

Chargeable gains

[15.7] No chargeable gain will arise on the disposal of any loan relationship because every asset representing a loan relationship of a company is a QUALIFYING CORPORATE BOND (see **54.3**).

Derivative contracts

[15.8] Subject to the special rules below for certain contracts which are taxed on a chargeable gains basis, under the derivative contracts regime, all profits/and losses arising to a company from its derivative contracts are taxed as/(relieved against) income, using credits and debits under rules analogous to those for taxing loan relationships (see **15.3** above). Non-trading credits and debits are, in fact, taken into account under the loan relationships rules themselves. Such profits/(losses) are thus outside the charge to corporation tax on chargeable gains. [*CTA 2009, ss 571, 572, 574; SI 2005 No 2082, Art 9*]. The same treatment is applied to certain foreign exchange gains and losses arising to a company from its derivative contracts, and there are non-elective 'matching' rules similar to those referred to at **15.3** above. There are anti-avoidance and other special computational provisions (see *CTA 2009, ss 624–638, 674–698D*).

Special provisions apply to certain contracts whose value derives essentially from land or tangible movable property and certain 'embedded derivatives'. Non-trading profits, gains and losses on such derivative contracts are treated as capital gains and allowable losses (see **15.10** below). [*SI 2004 No 2201, Art 1*].

See Tolley's Corporation Tax under Financial Instruments and Derivative Contracts for detailed coverage.

Definition of 'derivative contract'

[15.9] For the purposes of **15.8** above, a company's '*derivative contracts*' are 'relevant contracts' entered into or acquired by it which are not excluded under the accounting conditions referred to below or by virtue of their underlying subject matter (see below). A '*relevant contract*' is any of the following:

- an option (including a warrant (as defined)); or
- a future, i.e. a contract for the sale of property under which delivery is to be made at a date and price agreed (as defined) when the contract is made; or
- a contract for differences, i.e. a contract the purpose or pretended purpose of which is to make a profit or avoid a loss by reference to fluctuations in the value or price of property described in the contract or fluctuations in an index or other factor designated in the contract. For accounting periods ending on or after 31 December 2013, a contract within *Energy Act 2013, s 6(2)* or *Sch 2 para 1(1)* is also a contract for differences. None of the following is a contract for differences: an option, a future, a contract of insurance, a capital redemption policy (as defined), a contract of indemnity, a guarantee, a warranty or a loan relationship.

A contract which can only be cash settled, and which does not provide for the delivery of any property, is excluded from being an option or a future but not from being a contract for differences. This does not apply if the underlying subject matter (see below) of the contract is currency.

Embedded and hybrid derivatives

A company is also treated as party to a relevant contract in the following circumstances.

(I) Where a company, in accordance with generally accepted accounting practice, treats rights and liabilities under a loan relationship to which it is party, as divided between rights and liabilities under a loan relationship and rights and liabilities under one or more derivative financial instruments or equity instruments ('embedded derivatives'). The company is treated for the purposes of these provisions as party to a relevant contract (or contracts) whose rights and liabilities consist only of those of the derivative or derivatives. The embedded derivative is treated as having the character (be it an option, a future or a contract for differences) which the rights and liabilities would have if contained in a separate contract. See also **15.4** above.

(II) Where a company, in accordance with generally accepted accounting practice, treats rights and liabilities under a contract to which it is party and which is neither a loan relationship nor within (III) below, as divided between rights and liabilities under one or more derivatives (for accounting periods ending before 30 December 2006, derivative financial instruments) and the remaining rights and liabilities (the 'host contract'). The company is treated for the purposes of these provisions as party to a relevant contract (or contracts) whose rights and liabilities consist only of those of the derivative or derivatives (referred to as 'embedded derivatives'). The embedded derivative is treated as having the character (be it an option, a future or a contract for differences) which the rights and liabilities would have if contained in a separate contract.

(III) Where a company, in accordance with generally accepted accounting practice, treats rights and liabilities under a relevant contract within (2), (3) or (4) below to which it is party as divided between rights and liabilities under one or more derivatives ('embedded derivatives') and the remaining rights and liabilities (the 'host contract') and a contract consisting only of those remaining rights and liabilities would be a relevant contract. The company is treated for the purposes of these provisions as party to a relevant contract (or contracts) whose rights and liabilities consist only of those of the embedded derivative or derivatives and to a relevant contract whose rights and liabilities are those of the host contract. Each relevant contract is treated as having the character (be it an option, a future or a contract for differences) which the rights and liabilities would have if contained in a separate contract.

A contract which is a relevant contract other than by virtue of (I) to (III) above is referred to as a '*plain vanilla contract*'.

[*CTA 2009, ss 576–578, 580–582, 584–586; SI 2006 No 3269, Arts 3, 4; SI 2013 No 3218*].

Accounting conditions

A relevant contract is *not* a derivative contract for the purposes of these provisions for an accounting period unless

(1) it is treated for accounting purposes as a derivative (for accounting periods ending before 30 December 2006, a derivative financial instrument) in accordance with the relevant accounting standard (as defined) used by the company (or would be so treated if the company applied a relevant accounting standard to the relevant contract); or
(2) it is not so treated solely because it does not meet the requirement in paragraph 9(b) of FRS 26 issued in December 2004 but for accounting purposes is, or forms part of, a financial asset or liability in accordance with the relevant accounting standard used by the company (or would be so treated if the company applied a relevant accounting standard to the relevant contract); or
(3) its 'underlying subject matter' (see below) is commodities; or
(4) it is a contract for differences (see above) and its underlying subject matter is:
   - land (wherever situated);
   - tangible movable property other than commodities which are tangible assets;
   - intangible fixed assets (see **15.14** below);
   - weather conditions; or
   - creditworthiness.

[*CTA 2009, s 579; SI 2006 No 3269, Art 5*].

Contracts excluded by virtue of their underlying subject matter

Subject to the qualifications below, a relevant contract is *not* a derivative contract for the purposes of these provisions if its underlying subject matter consists wholly of one or more types of 'excluded property'.

The following are '*excluded property*':

(A) intangible fixed assets (see **15.14** below) (but these are not excluded if the relevant contract is a contract for differences);
(B) shares in a company (as defined);
(C) rights of a unit holder under a unit trust scheme.

Exclusions (B) and (C) above apply only where certain further conditions are met, including where the contract is entered into for non-trading purposes or by a life assurance company or mutual trading company or where the contract is part of a hedging relationship or where the contract is designed to produce a return equating in substance to the return on an investment of money at a commercial rate of interest.

The underlying subject matter of a relevant contract is *treated* as consisting wholly of one or more of the above in certain circumstances if it consists partly of such property and partly of other property, where the latter is subordinate to the former or of small value compared with the whole. See also **15.12** below for the splitting of a contract into two notional contracts (applicable only to futures and options).

The '*underlying subject matter*' of a relevant contract is:

- (in the case of an option) the property which would fall to be delivered if the option were exercised; or, where such property is itself a derivative contract, the underlying subject matter of that contract;
- (in the case of a future) the property which, if the future were to run to delivery, would fall to be delivered at the date and price agreed when the contract is made; or, where such property is itself a derivative contract, the underlying subject matter of that contract;
- (in the case of a contract for differences), where the contract relates to fluctuations in the value or price of property described in the contract, the property so described; or, where the contract designates an index or factor, the matter by reference to which the index or factor is determined (and in particular, underlying subject matter may include interest rates, weather conditions or creditworthiness, but the use of interest rates to establish the amount of a payment whose due date may vary does not make those rates the underlying subject matter of the contract).

Where the underlying subject matter of a relevant contract consists of or includes income from shares in a company or rights of a unit trust holder or unit trust scheme, the underlying subject matter is not to be treated, by reason only of that income, as being such shares or right.

[*CTA 2009, ss 583, 589–592; FA 2012, Sch 16 para 167; SI 2006 No 3269, Arts 6, 8*].

Treasury power to vary definition of derivative contract

The above provisions may be amended by Treasury order so as to vary the above definition of a 'derivative contract'. This is so that account can be taken of developments in markets, the creation of new types of derivatives, and changes to applicable accounting standards (in which case the amendment may have effect for accounting periods current at the time the order comes into force). The Treasury may also so amend the provisions at **15.10** and **15.12** below. [*CTA 2009, s 701*].

Derivative contracts taxed on a chargeable gains basis

[15.10] Non-trading debits and credits in respect of certain types of derivative contract are not brought into account under the loan relationship rules as outlined at **15.8** above. Instead, where such credits of a company for an accounting period exceed the debits for that period, a chargeable gain is deemed to accrue to the company in that period. Where the debits exceed the credits an allowable loss arises. See below for the carry back of allowable losses arising under these provisions.

This treatment applies to the following types of contract where the contract is not one to which the company is party at any time in the accounting period concerned for the purposes of a trade carried on by it (other than life assurance business or mutual trading):

(a) contracts where the underlying subject matter relates to land (wherever situated) or tangible movable property other than commodities which are tangible assets;
(b) certain 'embedded derivatives' which are options or exactly tracking contracts for differences (see further below);
(c) contracts which are 'property-based total return swaps'.

In addition, for (a) and (c) above for accounting periods beginning on or after 5 December 2012 (treating accounting periods straddling that date as two accounting periods for this purpose, the second of which starts on that date), no two or more of the parties to the derivative contract can be connected parties.

Chargeable gains treatment does not apply where the company is an authorised unit trust, an investment trust, an open-ended investment company or a venture capital trust. As regards (a) above, where the underlying subject matter includes income, this is ignored in determining the underlying subject matter of the contract, where it is subordinate to the land or property in question, or small in value in comparison with the underlying subject matter of the contract as a whole.

[*CTA 2009, ss 639–641, 643–650; FA 2013, s 41; SI 2006 No 3269, Arts 12, 13, 15*].

Embedded derivatives

Chargeable gains treatment as above applies to two types of embedded derivative within **15.9**(I) above where the loan relationship in which the derivative is embedded is a creditor relationship of the company. Subject to further conditions and exclusions, these are:

(i) options whose underlying subject matter is 'qualifying ordinary shares' or 'mandatorily convertible preference shares' (both as defined); and
(ii) contracts for differences whose subject matter is land or qualifying ordinary shares and which are 'exactly tracking contracts' (as defined).

Chargeable gains treatment does not apply in the case of (i) above where the substantial shareholdings exemptions under *TCGA 1992, Sch 7AC para 2* (see **66.4** SUBSTANTIAL SHAREHOLDINGS OF COMPANIES) would apply to a gain arising on the disposal at the end of the accounting period in question of the option if it were contained in a separate contract.

Where chargeable gains treatment applies to embedded derivatives within (i) or (ii) above, the loan relationship in which they are embedded are not QUALIFYING CORPORATE BONDS (**54**).

[*CTA 2009, ss 642, 645–649; SI 2006 No 3269, Arts 13–15*].

See *CTA 2009, s 592* for the tax treatment of host contracts and embedded derivatives whose underlying subject matter is shares or rights of a unit trust holder in a unit trust scheme.

Property-based total return swaps

A '*property-based total return swap*' is a contract for differences in which one or more indices is designated where at least one of the indices is an index of changes in the value of land (wherever situated) and the underlying subject matter of the contract also includes interest rates. Special rules apply to determine the debits and credits to be taken into account in computing the chargeable gains and allowable losses under the above provisions. [*CTA 2009, ss 650, 659(3)–(6); FA 2013, s 41*].

Carry back of losses

Where there is a 'net loss' under the above provisions in an accounting period and, in a previous accounting period falling wholly or partly within 24 months immediately preceding the start of the loss period, there is a 'net gain' under the above provisions, a claim can be made for the loss to be wholly or partly carried back and set against part or all of the gain (but not so as to reduce either the loss or the gain below nil). The claim must be made within two years of the end of the period in which the net loss arose. Losses must be set against gains of a later period before those of an earlier period. Where a gain period falls partly before the 24-month period mentioned above, the loss can be only offset against the proportion of the gain falling within the 24-month period (time-apportioned based on the number of days).

A '*net loss*' in this case is the sum of any allowable losses arising under the above provisions ('*section 641 losses*') in a period less the sum of any chargeable gains arising under the above provisions ('*section 641 gains*') in the same period, in both cases in respect of the company's derivative contracts. A '*net gain*' is the excess of *section 641* gains over *section 641* losses, further reduced by any 'non-section 641 allowable losses' (i.e. allowable losses arising other than under the above provisions). Any non-*section 641* allowable losses must be set against any non-section 641 gains before the remainder is deducted from section 641 gains.

[*CTA 2009, ss 663, 664*].

Terminal exercise of options

There are provisions dealing with the chargeable gains consequences of the exercise or disposal of rights to acquire shares comprised in a derivative contract which is, or is treated as, an option.

Where the contract is an embedded derivative within (i) above, the following applies.

(A) In computing any chargeable gain accruing on a disposal of the asset representing the original creditor relationship associated with the embedded derivative, the acquisition cost is increased by the amount by which G (see below) exceeds L or, where L exceeds G, is reduced by the excess.

(B) In computing any chargeable gain accruing on a disposal of all the shares acquired in exercising the rights where the acquisition was in circumstances such that no disposal was deemed to arise by virtue of

TCGA 1992, s 127 (reorganisation of share capital — see **63.2** SHARES AND SECURITIES), the acquisition cost is increased by the amount by which G (see below) exceeds L or, where L exceeds G, is reduced by the excess. In the case of a part disposal of the shares, the part disposal apportionment rule at **16.5** COMPUTATION OF GAINS AND LOSSES applies accordingly.

In either case, where L exceeds G and the excess is greater than the acquisition cost, any remaining amount is added to the disposal consideration.

TCGA 1992, s 37 (exclusion from consideration of amounts charged to tax as income — see **39.1** INTERACTION WITH OTHER TAXES) and *TCGA 1992, s 39* (exclusion from allowable expenditure of amounts deductible in computing profits or losses for income tax purposes — see **39.1** INTERACTION WITH OTHER TAXES) do not apply to any of the disposals mentioned above.

For these purposes, G is the sum of CV and any chargeable gains accruing under the above provisions in respect of the contract for the accounting period in which the disposal is made and any previous accounting periods so far as they are referable, on a just and reasonable apportionment, to the shares. L is the sum of any allowable losses accruing for those accounting periods so far as they are so referable. CV is the amount by which the tax-adjusted carrying value of the host contract at the date on which the option is exercised exceeds the tax-adjusted carrying value of that contract at the date on which the company became party to the loan relationship or, if later, the date that the derivative contract came within (i) above.

[*CTA 2009, ss 670, 671; F(No 2)A 2015, Sch 7 para 85; SI 2006 No 3269, Art 17*].

Where the contract is a plain vanilla contract (i.e. it is not an embedded derivative), in computing any chargeable gain accruing on a disposal of all the shares acquired in exercising the rights, the acquisition cost is increased by the amount by which X (see below) exceeds Y or, where Y exceeds X, is reduced by the excess and, in the case of a part disposal of the shares, the part disposal apportionment rule at **16.5** COMPUTATION OF GAINS AND LOSSES applies accordingly. Where Y exceeds X and the excess is greater than the acquisition cost, any remaining amount is added to the disposal consideration.

For this purpose, X is the sum of any credits brought into account as trading receipts in respect of the derivative contract for the accounting period in which the disposal is made and any previous accounting periods so far as they are referable, on a just and reasonable apportionment, to the shares. Y is the sum of any debits so brought into account for those accounting periods so far as they are so referable.

This provision applies also where delivery is taken of shares in accordance with the terms of a plain vanilla contract which is a future.

[*CTA 2009, ss 667–669; SI 2006 No 3269, Art 19*].

Disposal of embedded exactly tracking contracts for differences

There are provisions dealing with the chargeable gains consequences of the disposal of an asset representing a creditor relationship in which a derivative contract within (ii) above is embedded.

In computing any chargeable gain accruing on the disposal, the acquisition cost is increased by the amount by which G exceeds L or, where L exceeds G, is reduced by the excess. Where L exceeds G and the excess is greater than the acquisition cost, any remaining amount is added to the disposal consideration. For these purposes, G is the sum of CV and any chargeable gains accruing under the above provisions in respect of the contract for the accounting period in which the disposal is made and any previous accounting periods. L is the sum of any allowable losses accruing for those accounting periods. CV is the amount by which the tax-adjusted carrying value of the host contract at the date of the disposal exceeds the tax-adjusted carrying value of that contract at the date on which the company became party to the loan relationship.

TCGA 1992, s 37 (exclusion from consideration of amounts charged to tax as income — see **39.1** INTERACTION WITH OTHER TAXES) and *TCGA 1992, s 39* (exclusion from allowable expenditure of amounts deductible in computing profits or losses for income tax purposes — see **39.1** INTERACTION WITH OTHER TAXES) do not apply to the disposal.

[*CTA 2009, ss 672, 673; F(No 2)A 2015, Sch 7 para 86; SI 2006 No 3269, Art 18*].

Issuers of securities with embedded derivatives

[15.11] There are also provisions dealing with certain embedded derivatives within **15.9**(I) above on a chargeable gains basis where the loan relationship in which the derivative is embedded is a *debtor* relationship of the company.

Deemed options

Subject to further conditions, the following provisions apply to embedded derivatives which are deemed to be options and whose underlying subject matter is shares.

Where the provisions apply, non-trading and trading debits and credits are not brought into account under the loan relationship rules as outlined at **15.8** above. Instead, the following applies.

(a) Where the option is exercised and shares are issued or transferred in fulfilment of the obligations under the option (the '*relevant disposal*'), *TCGA 1992, s 144(2)* (see **7.7** ASSETS) applies to the relevant disposal as if the tax-adjusted carrying value of the option at the time the company became party to the loan relationship was the consideration for the grant of the option. The market value rule at *TCGA 1992, s 17(1)* (see **45.1** MARKET VALUE) is disapplied.
(b) Where the option is exercised, there is no relevant disposal and an amount is paid in fulfilment of the obligations under the option, a chargeable gain is treated as accruing to the company equal to the amount by which E exceeds F. If F exceeds E, an allowable loss equal to the excess is treated as accruing. For this purpose, E is the tax-adjusted carrying value of the option at the time the company became party to the loan relationship. F is the amount paid by the debtor in fulfilment of the obligations under the debtor relationship reduced, but not below nil, by the fair value of the host contract at the date on which the option is exercised.

(c) Where the debtor relationship comes to an end without the option having been exercised, the company is treated for the purposes of corporation tax on chargeable gains as having disposed of an asset for an amount equal to the tax-adjusted carrying value of the option at the time the company became party to the loan relationship. The company is treated as having acquired the asset for a consideration equal, where the company ceases to be party to the relationship on the redemption or repayment of the liability, to the amount paid by the company or in any other case, the consideration given by the company on the relationship coming to an end less, in either case, the fair value of the host contract at the date the relationship comes to an end.

[*CTA 2009, ss 652–655; F(No 2)A 2015, Sch 7 paras 81, 82; SI 2006 No 3269, Art 21*].

Equity instruments

Subject to further conditions, the following applies where a debtor relationship is divided under the embedded derivatives provisions between the loan relationship and an equity instrument of the company, such that the equity instrument is a relevant contract treated as an option. For accounting periods ending before 30 December 2006, the relevant contract must not be a derivative contract. Where the company pays an amount to the person who is party to the loan relationship as creditor in discharge of any obligations under the relationship, an allowable loss is treated as accruing to the extent that RA exceeds E. RA is the amount so paid reduced (but not below nil) by the fair value of the host contract at the time the payment is made. E is the amount treated as the tax-adjusted carrying value of the relevant contract at the time the company became party to the loan relationship. [*CTA 2009, ss 665, 666; F(No 2)A 2015, Sch 7 para 84; SI 2006 No 3269, Art 22*].

Deemed contracts for difference

Subject to further conditions, the following applies where a debtor relationship is divided under the embedded derivatives provisions such that the relevant contract to which the company is treated as being party is a derivative contract whose underlying subject matter is shares or, for accounting periods ending before 30 December 2006, land and which is a contract for differences (other than one falling within *CTA 2009, s 652* above). The contract must be an exactly tracking contract (as defined).

Debits and credits are not brought into account under the loan relationship rules as outlined at **15.8** above. Where the debtor relationship comes to an end and an amount is paid to discharge all of the company's obligations (the '*discharge amount*'), a chargeable gain or allowable loss is treated as accruing, calculated on the assumption that the derivative contract is an asset of the company, that there is a disposal of that asset at the time the relationship comes to an end, and that the cost of the asset is the discharge amount. The consideration for the disposal is deemed to be equal to the amount of the proceeds of issue of the security representing the relationship, except where the company became party to the loan relationship after its creation, in which case the consideration is equal to the amount of the tax-adjusted carrying value of the host contract at the time of its creation.

[*CTA 2009, ss 656–658; F(No 2)A 2015, Sch 7 para 83; SI 2006 No 3269, Art 23*].

Miscellaneous rules with potential chargeable gains consequences

[15.12] The following provisions potentially give rise to chargeable gains consequences.

Contracts which become or cease to be derivative contracts

The following provision applies where a company is a party to a relevant contract which, having not been a derivative contract, becomes a derivative contract on or after 30 December 2006 if, immediately before the change, the contract was a chargeable asset (i.e. an asset on a disposal of which any gain would be a chargeable gain, including any obligation under a futures contract which would be regarded as a chargeable asset by virtue of *TCGA 1992, s 143* (see **7.8** ASSETS)). When the company ceases to be a party to the relevant contract it must bring into account (for the accounting period in which it so ceases) a chargeable gain or allowable loss calculated on the basis that the company had disposed of the contract immediately before the time it became a derivative contract for a consideration equal to the 'notional carrying value' at that time. For this purpose, the '*notional carrying value*' of a contract at any time is the amount which would have been the carrying value had an accounting period ended immediately before that time. [*CTA 2009, ss 622(4), 661, 703; SI 2006 No 3269, Art 10*].

Where a company is party to a relevant contract which ceases to be a derivative contract, the company is treated:

- for the purposes of the derivative contracts provisions, as if it had disposed of the contract at the time it ceased to be a derivative contract for consideration equal to the notional carrying value of the contract at that time, and
- for the purposes of *TCGA 1992*, as if it had acquired the contract immediately after that time for the same consideration.

[*CTA 2009, s 662; SI 2006 No 3269, Art 10*].

Contracts treated as two separate contracts

Where a relevant contract is an option or a future and its underlying subject matter consists partly of excluded property (as in **15.9** above) and partly of non-excluded property, it is treated, for all corporation tax purposes (including those of corporation tax on chargeable gains), as split (on a just and reasonable basis) into two separate notional contracts. This treatment does not apply if the contract is excluded under the accounting tests etc. referred to above or if the non-excluded property meets the 'subordinate' or 'small value' tests referred to immediately following **15.9**(f) above (in which case it is merely disregarded rather than dealt with separately). [*CTA 2009, s 593*].

Transitional provisions with potential chargeable gains consequences

[15.13] The following applies where:

- a company is party to a contract immediately before and on its commencement day, i.e. the first day of its first accounting period beginning on or after 1 October 2002;
- the contract was outside the financial instruments regime of *FA 1994* but is a derivative contract within the *FA 2002, Sch 26* regime; and
- the contract was, immediately before the company's commencement day, a chargeable asset, i.e. it was within the scope of corporation tax on chargeable gains.

When the company ceases to be a party to the contract, it is deemed to have made a chargeable gain or allowable loss equal to that which it would have made had it disposed of the asset immediately before its commencement day at the accounting value (if any) given to the contract at the end of the accounting period immediately preceding its first accounting period beginning on or after 1 October 2002. The gain or loss is to be brought into account in the accounting period in which the company ceases to be a party to the contract. In the case of an allowable loss, the company may elect, within two years after the end of that accounting period, that it be treated instead as a non-trading debit under the loan relationships rules.

[*FA 2002, Sch 28 paras 4, 5, 7*].

Intangible fixed assets

[15.14] *FA 2002, Sch 29* introduced a new corporation tax regime for the treatment of expenditure and receipts in respect of 'intangible fixed assets' (see **15.15** below). Such assets are therefore removed from the charge to corporation tax on chargeable gains, subject to the commencement provisions described below. For full details of the regime, see Tolley's Corporation Tax under Intangible Assets.

In summary, the regime encompasses expenditure on the creation, acquisition and enhancement of intangibles (including abortive expenditure) as well as on their preservation and maintenance, and also applies to payments for the use of such assets, e.g. royalties. Profits on disposal of such assets are taxed as income. Losses on disposal and payments are relievable against income. The tax treatment of amortisation normally follows the accounts treatment, but for assets with an indefinite or longer life, a company can elect for a fixed allowance of 4% per annum. The rules extend to agricultural and fishing quotas, payment entitlements under the single payment scheme and Lloyd's syndicate capacity. A form of rollover relief (similar to, but not to be confused with, capital gains tax rollover relief) is available where realisation proceeds of intangibles are reinvested in new intangibles. The relief is available even on the disposal (after 31 March 2002) of an intangible asset excluded from the regime by the commencement provisions, and in such a case may reduce or eliminate a chargeable gain (and reduce the tax-recognised cost of the new intangible asset for the purposes of the regime). See also **37.4** INCORPORATION AND DISINCORPORATION RELIEFS, **59.3**, **59.4** ROLLOVER RELIEF and **69.6** UNDERWRITERS AT LLOYD'S.

Commencement

The regime applies only to intangible fixed assets of a company that are:

(a) created by the company after 31 March 2002; or
(b) acquired by the company after 31 March 2002 from a person who is not a 'related party' (as defined at **45.2** MARKET VALUE; and see further below); or
(c) acquired by the company after 31 March 2002 from a related party in the following cases:
  (i) where the asset is acquired from a company in whose hands the asset fell within the intangible assets regime;
  (ii) where the asset is acquired from an intermediary who acquired the asset after 31 March 2002 from a third party which was not a related party of the intermediary (at the time of the intermediary's acquisition of the asset) or of the company (at the time of the company's acquisition); or
  (iii) where the asset was created by any person after 31 March 2002.

In (b) above, for accounting periods beginning on or after 25 November 2015, persons are treated as related parties where the transfer pricing 'participation condition' (see *TIOPA 2010, s 147*) is met between them. Accounting periods straddling 25 November 2015 are treated for this purpose as two accounting periods. the second of which begins on that date.

It should be noted, therefore, that an asset cannot be brought within the regime simply by means of a transfer between related parties, for example from a sole trader to a company in which he has a major interest. Anti-avoidance provisions apply, broadly, to treat an asset created after commencement and acquired by a company from a related party as excluded from the regime by the above provisions where either the asset is derived from assets themselves so excluded, or the acquisition is directly or indirectly in consequence of, or in connection with, the disposal of an excluded asset.

For the above purposes and subject to the exceptions below, an asset is treated as acquired or created after 31 March 2002 to the extent that expenditure on its acquisition or creation is incurred after that date. Where only part of such expenditure was incurred after that date, the asset is treated as two separate assets, one falling within the regime and one not; expenditure on the asset is apportioned between the two notional assets on a just and reasonable basis. In general, expenditure is regarded as incurred for this purpose when it is recognised for 'accounting purposes' (see **15.15** below). In certain cases, however, either the capital gains rule (see **16.4** COMPUTATION OF GAINS AND LOSSES), or the capital allowances rule governing the date expenditure is treated as incurred is applied.

Goodwill is treated as created before 1 April 2002 if the business in question was carried on at any time before that date by the company concerned or a 'related party' (as defined at **45.2** MARKET VALUE) and is treated as created on or after that date in any other case. There is therefore no division of goodwill created before 1 April 2002 into two notional assets, and on disposal it will remain within the charge to corporation tax on chargeable gains.

A similar rule applies in the case of an asset, other than goodwill, which represents expenditure which would not be qualifying expenditure for capital allowances purposes under the law applicable prior to the introduction of the intangible assets regime. Such an asset is treated as created before 1 April 2002 if it was held at any time before that date by the company concerned or a related party, and in any other case is treated as created on or after that date. Where part of the expenditure on such an asset would have qualified for capital allowances, the asset is treated as two separate assets, one qualifying for capital allowances and one not. The notional asset which would have qualified for capital allowances is then treated as created or acquired at the time given by the general provisions above (but using the capital allowances rule to determine the date the expenditure is deemed to have been incurred). Necessary apportionments are made for this purpose on a just and reasonable basis. This provision previously applied to internally-generated assets, subject to the same commencement provisions as apply to the goodwill provisions above.

Assets acquired by means of certain no gain/no loss transfers made after 27 June 2002 are excluded from the intangible assets regime in the hands of the transferee company if they fell outside the regime in the hands of the transferor company. The transfers in question are those within *TCGA 1992, s 139* (company reconstructions involving transfer of business — see **14.11** COMPANIES), *TCGA 1992, s 140A* (transfer of UK business between companies resident in different EC member states — see **49.13** OVERSEAS MATTERS) or *TCGA 1992, s 140E* (European cross-border merger: assets left within UK tax charge — see **49.15** OVERSEAS MATTERS).

Special commencement provisions apply in the case of assets consisting of licences or other rights within *FA 2000, Sch 23* (certain telecommunications rights) and Lloyd's syndicate capacity (see **69.6** UNDERWRITERS AT LLOYD'S). The intangible assets regime applies to such assets in respect of any amounts to be brought into account for tax purposes in accounting periods ending after 31 March 2002.

Special commencement provisions also apply in the case of fungible assets, such as milk quota (see **7.9** ASSETS). For the purpose of the intangible assets regime, fungible assets of the same kind held by the same person in the same capacity are generally pooled and treated as indistinguishable parts of a single asset. Where, however, only part of the single asset would fall within the intangible assets regime under the above commencement provisions, the single asset is divided into two assets, one falling within the regime (the '*new regime pool*') and the other not so falling (the '*existing asset pool*'). Realisations of assets are treated as diminishing the existing asset pool in priority to the new regime pool. Assets acquired are allocated to the existing asset pool (and therefore do not fall within the intangible assets regime) to the extent that they can be identified with assets realised by the company from the existing asset pool in accordance with the following rules. The rules are that acquisitions are to be identified with assets realised from the existing asset pool within the period beginning 30 days before and ending 30 days after the acquisition; assets realised earlier fall to be identified before those realised later, and acquisitions are considered in the date order in which they take place.

Royalties from intangible fixed assets which are recognised for accounting purposes after 31 March 2002 fall within the intangible assets regime regardless of whether or not the asset in respect of which they are payable does so. Transitional provisions apply to prevent royalties being taken into account for tax purposes more than once.

[*CTA 2009, ss 858, 880–900; FA 2013, Sch 46 para 138; FA 2016, s 52; SI 2007 No 3186, Sch 1 para 24*].

Definition of 'intangible fixed asset'

[15.15] The term '*intangible asset*' has the same meaning for the purposes of the intangible assets regime as it has for '*accounting purposes*' (i.e. for the purposes of accounts drawn up in accordance with generally accepted accounting practice). The definition includes also any '*intellectual property*', being:

- any patent, trade mark, registered design, copyright or design right, plant breeders' rights or rights under *Plant Varieties Act 1997, s 7*; or
- any corresponding non-UK right; or
- any information or technique not protected by any of the rights above but having industrial, commercial or other economic value; or
- any licence or other right in respect of any of the above rights, information or techniques.

An '*intangible fixed asset*' is an intangible asset acquired or created by a company for use on a continuing basis in the course of the company's activities, and includes options or other rights to acquire or dispose of an intangible fixed asset. An intangible asset is an intangible fixed asset if it falls within this definition, whether or not it is capitalised in the company's accounts.

'Goodwill' (defined as for accounting purposes — see above) is specifically included within the intangible assets regime (but see further below).

It is specifically enacted that intangible assets include internally-generated intangible assets, that goodwill includes internally-generated goodwill, and that goodwill is treated as created in the course of carrying on the business in question.

[*CTA 2009, ss 712, 713, 715; F(No 2)A 2015, s 33(2)*].

Assets excluded

The following types of intangible fixed asset (and options or other rights to acquire or dispose of such assets) are excluded from the intangible assets regime:

(a) assets representing rights enjoyed by virtue of an estate, interest or right in or over land;

(b) assets representing rights in relation to tangible movable property (see **25.4** EXEMPTIONS AND RELIEFS);

(c) an oil licence (as defined) or an interest in an oil licence (including all goodwill, and any other intangible asset, relating to, deriving from or connected with such a licence or interest);

(d) financial assets (as defined for accounting purposes (see above) and including loan relationships (see **15.2** above), derivative contracts (see **15.8** above), contracts or policies of insurance or capital redemption policies and assets derived from or referable to such policies, and rights under a collective investment scheme within the meaning of *Financial Services and Markets Act 2000*);

(e) an asset representing shares or other rights in relation to the profits, governance or winding up of a company;

(f) an asset representing rights under a trust (other than rights that for accounting purposes fall to be treated as representing an interest in trust property that is an intangible fixed asset within the regime);

(g) an asset representing the interest of a partner in a partnership (other than an interest that for accounting purposes falls to be treated as representing an interest in partnership property that is an intangible fixed asset within the regime);

(h) assets held for a purpose that is not a business or commercial purpose;

(i) assets held for the purpose of activities of a company in respect of which the company is outside the charge to corporation tax (otherwise than as a result of an election to exempt profits of a foreign permanent establishment — see **49.8** OVERSEAS MATTERS);

(j) an asset held by a film production company to the extent that it represents production expenditure on a film to which *FA 2006, Sch 4* (taxation of activities of film production company) applies;

(k) an asset held by an television production company to the extent that it represents production expenditure on a television programme treated as expenditure of a separate trade;

(l) an asset held by an video games development company to the extent that it represents core expenditure on a video game treated as expenditure of a separate trade;

(m) an asset held by an theatrical production company to the extent that it represents expenditure on a theatrical production treated as expenditure of a separate trade;

(n) an asset held by an orchestral concert production company to the extent that it represents expenditure on a concert or concert series treated as expenditure of a separate trade;

(o) (except in relation to royalties) an asset (other than computer software) held for the purposes of a life assurance business;

(p) (except in relation to royalties) an asset held for the purposes of a mutual trade or business;

(q) (except in relation to royalties) an asset representing expenditure on the production of, or on the acquisition before 31 March 2008 of, the original master version (as defined) of a film to which *FA 2006, Sch 4* does not apply;

(r) (except in relation to royalties) an asset representing expenditure on the production or acquisition of the master version of a sound recording;

(s) (except in relation to royalties) an asset which represents expenditure on computer software that is to be treated for accounting purposes as part of the cost of the related hardware; and

(t) assets previously treated as tangible assets in accounts of the company concerned and in respect of which capital allowances have been made to the company under *CAA 2001, Pt 2* (plant and machinery).

For the purpose only of applying the extension of category (c) above to goodwill and other intangible assets connected with an oil licence etc., accounting periods which straddle 23 March 2011 are treated as two separate accounting periods, the second of which begins on that date (so that the extended rules apply to that deemed period).

Category (t) above is intended specifically to exclude certain expenditure on websites treated as a tangible asset under UK generally accepted accounting practice, but treated as an intangible asset under international accounting standards (Treasury Explanatory Notes to the Finance Bill 2004).

Where an asset does not wholly fall within one of the above categories, it is treated as if it were two separate assets, one falling within the intangible assets regime and one not so falling; any necessary apportionment is to be made on a just and reasonable basis. Assets representing expenditure on research and development or (by election) computer software are excluded from the regime to a limited extent, but proceeds from a disposal of such an asset do fall within the regime to the extent that they are not brought into account for capital allowances purposes.

[*CTA 2009, ss 800–816; FA 2012, Sch 16 paras 174–177; FA 2013, Sch 18 para 9; FA 2014, Sch 4 para 10; FA 2016, Sch 8 para 9; SI 2006 No 3265; SI 2007 No 1050, Reg 8*].

After 14 August 2002, but subject to the commencement rules above (as modified for this purpose), the intangible assets regime is applied (with exceptions and modifications), in relation to corporate finance lessors, to any intangible asset that is the subject of a finance lease (notwithstanding that the asset may be accounted for by the finance lessor as a financial asset — see exclusions above). [*SI 2002 No 1967*].

Assets excluded from the intangible assets regime are not excluded from the charge to corporation tax on chargeable gains as a result of the introduction of the regime (although assets within a number of the above categories are not within the charge in any event).

Goodwill etc.

No debits may be brought into account under the regime in respect of any of the assets listed below which are acquired on or after 8 July 2015 (other than those acquired under a contract which was unconditional before that date) except for debits arising on realisation. Any such debits which are so brought into account are treated as non-trading debits. The assets are:

(1) goodwill;
(2) an asset consisting of information relating to customers or potential customers of a business;
(3) an asset consisting of a relationship (contractual or otherwise) between a person carrying on a business and one or more customers;
(4) an unregistered trade mark or other sign used in the course of a business; and

(5) a licence or other right in respect of an asset within (1)–(4) above.

[*CTA 2009, s 816A; F(No 2)A 2015, s 33*].

Key points concerning companies: corporate finance and intangibles

[15.16] Points to consider are as follows.

- Since a loan relationship can only arise from the lending of money, there is no loan relationship between the parties where an amount of consideration in a transaction is merely left outstanding for a period. But it is vital to properly document the position at the time. See **15.5**.
- An amount left outstanding can then be converted into a loan relationship by agreement between the parties. But, again, proper and contemporaneous documentation is essential. See **15.5**.
- Where pre-1 April 2002 intangibles are disposed of, the gain cannot be rolled over into chargeable assets under *TCGA 1992, s 152*, they can only be rolled over into the acquisition of new intangible fixed assets. See **15.14**.
- There is a further rollover relief where the acquisition is of a company holding chargeable intangible assets: the gain on the disposal of the old intangible fixed asset can be rolled over into those underlying chargeable intangible assets, reducing their tax cost in respect of any further realisation. See **15.14**.

16

Computation of Gains and Losses

Introduction	16.1
Basic computation	16.2
Disposal	16.3
Date of disposal	16.4
Part disposals	16.5
Forfeited deposit of purchase money	16.6
Transfer of dormant bank and building society accounts	16.7
Consideration	16.8
Appropriations to and from trading stock	16.9
Finance leases	16.10
Allowable and non-allowable expenditure	16.11
General provisions	16.11
Special cases	16.12
Non-allowable expenditure	16.13
Key points	16.14

Cross-references. See **2.6** ANNUAL RATES AND EXEMPTIONS; **7.7** ASSETS for options; **8** ASSETS HELD ON 6 APRIL 1965; **9** ASSETS HELD ON 31 MARCH 1982; **10** CAPITAL SUMS DERIVED FROM ASSETS; **38** INDEXATION; **39** INTERACTION WITH OTHER TAXES; **41** LAND for disposals of land and leases; **44** LOSSES; **45** MARKET VALUE; **64** SHARES AND SECURITIES — IDENTIFICATION RULES; **72** WASTING ASSETS.

Simon's Taxes. See **C1.105, Part C2.**

Introduction to computation of gains and losses

[16.1] Gains and losses on disposals of assets are initially computed by deducting allowable expenditure (broadly, the acquisition cost, incidental costs of acquisition and disposal and the costs of any improvements) from the amount realised on the disposal. There are, however, a number of issues which make this apparently straightforward exercise more complicated. Allowances, reliefs and special computational rules can all operate to affect the computation, often with different rules applying depending on whether the gain or loss is within the scope of capital gains tax or corporation tax on chargeable gains. These complexities are summarised at **16.2** below and covered in this chapter and throughout this work.

The circumstances in which there is a disposal of an asset include where it is sold or given away but there are also a number of situations in which a disposal is deemed to occur even though there is no actual disposal. Special computational provisions apply to apportion the acquisition cost where only part of the asset is disposed of.

In certain circumstances, the actual amount received for the disposal is not used in computing the gain or loss. Instead a deemed consideration is taken, which may be the amount which leads to there being neither a gain nor a loss or the market value of the asset. In some cases, certain amounts are excluded from the consideration.

Basic computation

[16.2] Gains and losses accruing on disposals (see **16.3** below) of assets are computed by deducting allowable expenditure (see **16.11–16.13** below) from the amount realised or deemed to be realised on the disposal (i.e. the actual or deemed consideration — see **16.8** below). [*TCGA 1992, ss 15, 38*].

There are special computational provisions in respect of certain types of assets. See the list at **7.1** ASSETS.

No deduction is allowable more than once from any sum or from more than one sum. [*TCGA 1992, s 52(1)*].

See **16.4** below for date of disposal. See **16.5** below for part disposals.

For the use by certain companies of foreign currencies in computing chargeable gains on ships, aircraft and shares see **14.14** COMPANIES.

Bundles of assets

Where a bundle of assets is sold together, it is necessary to consider each disposal separately, in the light of the rules which apply to that asset (*Aberdeen Construction Group Ltd v CIR* HL 1978, 52 TC 281). See also *Fullarton and ors v CIR* Sp C, [2004] SSCD 207. See also HMRC Guidance Note, 30 January 2009, which describes HMRC's approach to the apportionment of sale proceeds of a business as a going concern where the assets sold include a 'trade related property' such as a public house, hotel, petrol station, restaurant or care home.

Indexation

For corporation tax purposes the gain (if any) arrived at as above is termed the '*unindexed gain*' and indexation allowance (if due) is deducted from it to give the gain for the purposes of *TCGA 1992* unless otherwise provided. If the allowance equals or exceeds the unindexed gain, no gain or loss arises. If a loss arises as above, no indexation allowance is available. See **38.1, 38.2** INDEXATION.

Losses

See **44** LOSSES for the deduction of allowable losses from chargeable gains.

Entrepreneurs' relief

Entrepreneurs' relief applies (on a claim) to certain gains realised on business disposals by individuals and trustees. The relief is subject to a lifetime limit of gains, currently £10 million, and operates in different ways depending on whether or not the disposal is made before 23 June 2010. Where the disposal is before that date, the net gains are reduced by $^4/_9$ths so that they are effectively taxed at a rate of 10%. For subsequent disposals, the net gains are not reduced but are taxed at an actual rate of 10%. See **24** ENTREPRENEURS' RELIEF.

Investors' relief

Investors' relief applies (on a claim) to certain gains on disposals by individuals of shares in unlisted trading companies on or after 6 April 2019. The relief is subject to a lifetime limit of gains, currently £10 million, and operates by taxing the gains at a rate of 10%. See **40** INVESTORS' RELIEF.

Annual exempt amount

Individuals are exempt from capital gains tax in respect of so much of their taxable gains for a tax year as do not exceed the annual exempt amount. Where the gains exceed that amount, only the excess is taxable. Personal representatives (for a limited period) and trustees of settlements are also entitled to an annual exempt amount, but companies are not. See **2.6** ANNUAL RATES AND EXEMPTIONS.

Assets held on 6 April 1965

For corporation tax purposes, there are special computational provisions for assets held on 6 April 1965, the broad purpose of which is to exclude from tax that part of the eventual gain on disposal which accrued before that date. See **8** ASSETS HELD ON 6 APRIL **1965**. For most disposals on or after 6 April 1988 the provisions are displaced by the rebasing provisions for assets held on 31 March 1982 (see below), but they still apply in certain cases.

Assets held on 31 March 1982

Special provisions also apply to the disposal after 5 April 1988 of assets held on 31 March 1982. Broadly, on the disposal of such an asset, the acquisition cost for tax purposes is re-based to its market value on 31 March 1982. For corporation tax purposes this only applies where it results in a smaller gain or loss than would be the case using the actual acquisition cost (or applying the rules for assets held on 6 April 1965) in the computation. For capital gains tax purposes re-basing applies automatically to all assets held on 31 March 1982. Companies are able to make a universal rebasing election for re-basing to apply to all of their assets held on 31 March 1982 and so avoid the need for comparative computations on each disposal. See **9** ASSETS HELD ON 31 MARCH **1982**.

Assets held on 5 April 2017: deemed domicile

Special provisions apply to disposals of foreign assets held on 5 April 2017 by certain non-UK domiciled individuals, who are deemed domiciled in the UK from 2017/18 due to long-term residence (see **57.34** RESIDENCE AND DOMICILE). The acquisition cost of such an asset is re-based to its market value on 5 April 2017, provided qualifying conditions are met in respect of the individual and the asset (see **57.34** RESIDENCE AND DOMICILE).

Examples

(1) Ray acquired an asset in November 1986 for £28,000. He sells the asset on 11 June 2017 for £99,000. Ray incurs allowable sale costs of £5,000. Ray makes no other disposals in 2017/18 and his taxable gains for the year are as follows.

	£
Sale consideration	99,000
Less costs of sale	5,000
Cost of asset	28,000
Chargeable gain	66,000
Annual exempt amount	11,300
Taxable gain	£54,700

(2) The facts are as in (1) above except that the taxpayer is a company and its accounting date is 30 June. For the purposes only of this example, the indexation factor for the period November 1986 to June 2017 is assumed to be 1.805. The company's taxable gain for the accounting period ended 30 June 2017 is as follows.

	£
Sale consideration	99,000
Less costs of sale	5,000
Cost of asset	28,000
Unindexed gain	66,000
Less indexation allowance £28,000 × 1.805	50,540
Chargeable (and taxable) gain	£15,460

Disposal

[16.3] Simon's Taxes. See C1.104, C1.307.

'*Disposal*' is not defined in the legislation. The term includes a part disposal (see **16.5** below) and there are numerous circumstances in which the legislation deems there to be a disposal for tax purposes even though there has been no actual disposal. See in particular **10** CAPITAL SUMS DERIVED FROM ASSETS, **16.4** below for assets lost or destroyed and **44.11** LOSSES for assets becoming of negligible value.

A conveyance or transfer of an asset or of a right therein *by way of security* (e.g. a mortgage) is not a disposal, but if the creditor or any person appointed as receiver, manager, etc. deals with the asset in order to enforce the security, his activities are imputed to the giver of the security. The existence of a security is ignored for both acquisition and disposal of an asset save that the amount of liability assumed forms part of the acquisition and disposal consideration in addition to any other consideration. [*TCGA 1992, s 26*]. Relief is available if there has been a sale of an asset at arm's length in circumstances such that the vendor granted the purchaser a mortgage (in full or in part) in order for the purchaser to buy and where there has later been a default on the mortgage loan. If, as a result, the vendor regains beneficial ownership of the asset he has contracted to sell he may elect that the gain realised by him on that sale be taken as limited to the net proceeds (after incidental costs of disposal) retained by him and for the loan to be treated as never coming into existence (although interest on the loan would be subject to income tax in the usual way). On any subsequent disposal of the asset concerned, the computation will be by reference to the original date and costs of acquisition etc. (HMRC Extra-Statutory Concession D18).

In *Hardy v HMRC* UT, [2016] UKUT 349 (TCC), [2016] STI 2592, the rescinding of two contracts for the purchase of land was held not to constitute the disposal of assets. The loss of the deposits paid by the intended buyer was not a loss capable of being allowed against chargeable gains.

A taxpayer who, in consideration of a loan, promised his parents 60% of the net proceeds of any sale of his shares in his personal company, whilst retaining beneficial ownership of the shares in the meantime, was held liable to capital gains tax in respect of the total proceeds of the eventual sale (*Burca v Parkinson* Ch D 2001, 74 TC 125).

See also *Underwood v HMRC* CA 2008, [2009] STC 239.

Date of disposal

[16.4] Simon's Taxes. See **C1.322**.

Contracts

Where an asset is disposed of and acquired under a contract, the disposal and acquisition are made at the time the contract is made (and not, if different, the time at which the asset is conveyed or transferred, e.g. on a contract for the sale of land). This rule applies even if the contract is unenforceable, provided that the disposal is actually completed (*Thompson v Salah* Ch D 1971, 47 TC 559). (However, HMRC point out that the authority of this case is no longer valid where the general law provides that contracts entered into in respect of land must be made in writing (as is required under *Law of Property (Miscellaneous Provisions) Act 1989* and which applies in England and Wales although a similar requirement applies in Scotland (HMRC Capital Gains Manual CG18162, 70280)).) If the contract is conditional (and, in particular, if it is conditional on the exercise of an option), the disposal and acquisition are made at the time the condition is satisfied. [*TCGA 1992, s 28*].

See *Eastham v Leigh London & Provincial Properties Ltd* 1971, 46 TC 687; *Johnson v Edwards* Ch D 1981, 54 TC 488; *Burt v HMRC* (Sp C 684), [2008] SSCD 814.

In *Jerome v Kelly* HL, [2004] STC 887; [2004] All ER(D) 168(May), in which there was an intermediate disposal of part of the asset to a Bermudan trust between contract and completion, the taxpayer was held not to be liable to CGT on the original disposal of the part of the asset covered by the intermediate disposal. Lord Hoffmann observed that the draftsman responsible for what is now *TCGA 1992, s 28(1)* 'did not think about what should happen in the situation which has arisen in this case'. He held that it would be wrong 'to attribute to Parliament an intention to impose a liability to tax upon a person who would not be treated as having made a disposal under the carefully constructed scheme for taxing the disposals of assets held on trust'. *TCGA 1992, s 28(1)* should be treated as 'concerned solely with fixing the time of disposal by a person whose identity is to be ascertained by other means'.

A question of whether the buyer and seller under a conditional contract are connected (see, for example **44.6** LOSSES) is determined as of the time the contract becomes unconditional — see *Kellogg Brown and Root Holdings (UK) Ltd v HMRC* CA, [2010] EWCA Civ 118, 2010 STI 558.

See also under hire purchase below.

Gifts

A gift is treated as having been made when the donor has done everything within his power to transfer the property to the donee (*Re Rose, Rose and ors v CIR* CA, [1952] 1 All ER 1217).

Hire purchase

A transaction under which the assets may pass to the hirer at the end of the hire is treated as a disposal of the whole asset at the beginning of that period, with subsequent adjustments if the agreement terminates without the hirer acquiring the asset. [*TCGA 1992, s 27*]. For consideration of hire-purchase and conditional contracts (see above), see *Lyon v Pettigrew* Ch D 1985, 58 TC 452.

Capital sums

Deemed disposals covered by **10** CAPITAL SUMS DERIVED FROM ASSETS take place on the receipt of the capital sum. [*TCGA 1992, s 22(2)*]. See *Chaloner v Pellipar Investments Ltd* Ch D 1996, 68 TC 238 in which it was held, by reference to the particular facts of the case, that a capital sum received by the taxpayer in 'money's worth' fell outside *s 22* and that the date of disposal had thus to be determined by reference to the contract date as above.

Options

See **7.7** ASSETS.

Assets lost or destroyed

Such assets are deemed to be disposed of at the time of loss etc. [*TCGA 1992, s 24(1)*]. It seems that this provision does not override *TCGA 1992, s 22(2)* above where an actual capital sum is received subsequent to the loss etc. (see comments by Hoffmann J in the Ch D in *Powlson v Welbeck Securities Ltd* CA 1987, 60 TC 269).

Assets becoming of negligible value

See **44.11** LOSSES.

Land compulsorily acquired

See **41.10** LAND for acquisition of land by an authority possessing any power of compulsory purchase.

Rollover relief

See **59.1** ROLLOVER RELIEF.

Part disposals

[16.5] Simon's Taxes. See C2.4.

References to a disposal for the purposes of the chargeable gains legislation include, unless otherwise required, references to a part disposal. There is a part disposal of an asset where an interest or right in or over the asset is created by the disposal, as well as where it subsists before the disposal, and generally, there is a part disposal of an asset where, on a person making a disposal, any description of property derived from the asset remains undisposed of. [*TCGA 1992, s 21(2)*].

Where a disposal is partial, those deductions which are not wholly attributable either to the part retained or to the part disposed of are apportioned over the total value of the asset, including the part retained, and only the portion relative to the part disposed of is deductible from the consideration received for it. The apportioned allowable expenditure is calculated by reference to the formula:

$$\frac{A}{A+B}$$

where:

A is the consideration received or deemed to have been received; and

B is the market value of the part retained.

For corporation tax, this apportionment also applies for indexation allowance purposes.

Any such apportionment is to be made before applying the following provisions.

(a) *TCGA 1992, s 41* (restriction of losses by reference to capital allowances, see **16.13**(i) below). (If after the part disposal there is a subsequent disposal of the asset, the capital allowances to be taken into account on that subsequent disposal are those referable to the expenditure incurred under **16.11**(a)–(c) below whether before or after the part disposal, but those allowances are reduced by the amount, if any, by which the loss on the earlier disposal was restricted under *TCGA 1992, s 41*.)
(b) *TCGA 1992, s 58(1)* (transfers between spouses or civil partners, see **46.5** MARRIED PERSONS AND CIVIL PARTNERS).

(c) *TCGA 1992, ss 152–158* (replacement of business assets, see **59 ROLLOVER RELIEF**).
(d) *TCGA 1992, s 171(1)* (transfers within GROUPS OF COMPANIES (**29.3**)).
(e) Any other provision making an adjustment to secure that neither a gain nor a loss occurs on disposal.
(f) The computation of any indexation allowance. [*TCGA 1992, s 56(1)*].

[*TCGA 1992, s 42*].

Similar apportionments of allowable deductions are made where assets have been merged or divided, have changed their nature, or have had interests created out of them, etc. [*TCGA 1992, s 43*].

See **9** ASSETS HELD ON 31 MARCH **1982** for further applications of *TCGA 1992, s 42* and *s 43*.

Any other necessary apportionment is to be made as may be 'just and reasonable'. [*TCGA 1992, s 52(4), Sch 11 para 11*]. HMRC cite the case of *EV Booth (Holdings) Ltd v Buckwell* Ch D 1980, 53 TC 425 as authority for their view that it is not open to either of the parties to a contract to seek to alter an apportionment contained in the contract for capital gains tax purposes. HMRC also consider that they can apply *TCGA 1992, s 52(4)* only where no apportionment is provided or where the apportionment provided is unreasonable on the facts of the case (HMRC Capital Gains Manual CG14773).

Example

X buys a piece of land in 1989 for £182,000. He subsequently sells half of it to Y in May 2017 for £150,000. The remainder of the land, because of its better position, is estimated to be then worth £200,000.

X's chargeable gain is computed as follows

A = £150,000

B = £200,000

Allowable expenditure attributable to the part disposed of

$$\frac{150,000}{(150,000+200,000)} \times £182,000 = £78,000$$

Chargeable gain: £150,000 – £78,000 = £72,000

The allowable expenditure on a disposal of the remaining land will be £104,000, i.e. £182,000 less £78,000.

In *Anders Utkilens Rederi A/S v O/Y Lovisa Stevedoring Co A/B and anor* Ch D 1984, [1985] STC 301, a plaintiff had initially obtained judgment for a liquidated sum against a defendant, but the action was then compromised by an agreement for the defendant's property to be sold and the proceeds divided between the parties. It was held that there had been a part disposal of an interest in the property by the defendant to the plaintiff followed by a disposal by each party of his interest then held to the final purchaser.

A 1995 assignment, for a capital sum, of the right to receive rental income for a fixed period (a 'rent factoring' transaction) was held to be a *part* disposal of the property in question (*CIR v John Lewis Properties plc* CA 2002, [2003] STC 117), but note that, under subsequent legislation, rent factoring receipts are now chargeable as income (see Tolley's Corporation Tax under Property Income).

See **41.8** LAND for relief for certain part disposals of land and **41.17** where part of the premium received for a lease is liable to income tax.

Simon's Taxes. See **C2.4.**

Forfeited deposit of purchase money

[16.6] A forfeited deposit of purchase money or other consideration money for a prospective purchase or other transaction which is abandoned is treated in the same way as consideration given for an option to purchase which is not exercised. [*TCGA 1992, s 144(7)*]. There is no disposal for capital gains tax purposes by the person who abandons his deposit and no loss relief is available (except in the case of a forfeited deposit on an asset intended to be used, if acquired, for the purposes of a trade carried on by the forfeiter (see 7.7(a) ASSETS)). There is, however, a disposal of an asset to which no allowable expenditure attaches by the person receiving the forfeited deposit the amount of which is treated as the consideration received. See **7.7** ASSETS.

Transfer of dormant bank and building society accounts

[16.7] Under the *Dormant Bank and Building Society Accounts Act 2008*, a bank or building society can transfer the funds in a dormant account (broadly, an account in respect of which no transactions have been carried out for 15 years) to an authorised reclaim fund for use for the benefit of good causes. In the case of building societies and certain smaller banks, part of the balance can be transferred directly to a charity. Where such a transfer is carried out, the account holder ceases to have any rights against the bank or building society for payment of the balance, but acquires equivalent rights against the reclaim fund.

With effect from 1 February 2011, a transfer under the above provisions is not treated for capital gains purposes as involving any disposal or acquisition of an asset. The account holder's rights against the reclaim fund are treated as the same asset as the original rights against the bank or building society, acquired as those rights were acquired and having the same characteristics as those rights. [*TCGA 1992, s 26A; SI 2011 No 23*].

Consideration

[16.8] The consideration for the disposal or acquisition of an asset which is to be used in computing a gain or loss is in the most straightforward cases the agreed sale or purchase price. This applies regardless of how the price is to be applied (*Spectros International plc v Madden* Ch D 1996, 70 TC 349). See also *Crusader v HMRC* Sp C 2007 (Sp C 640), [2008] SSCD 281, where an amount paid to a charity by the purchaser of a company was held to form part of the consideration for the sale of the company. See also *Collins v HMRC* [2009] STC 1077, in which a payment to a company under the terms of an agreement for the sale by the taxpayer of the shares in the company was held to form part of the consideration for the sale of the shares.

Where a bundle of assets is sold together (see **16.2** above) it may be necessary to apportion the consideration between the assets. Any necessary apportionment is to be made as may be 'just and reasonable'. [*TCGA 1992, s 52(4), Sch 11 para 11*]. HMRC cite the case of *EV Booth (Holdings) Ltd v Buckwell* Ch D 1980, 53 TC 425 as authority for their view that it is not open to either of the parties to a contract to seek to alter an apportionment contained in the contract for capital gains tax purposes. HMRC also consider that they can apply *TCGA 1992, s 52(4)* only where no apportionment is provided or where the apportionment provided is unreasonable on the facts of the case (HMRC Capital Gains Manual CG14773).

In certain circumstances a disposal (and/or acquisition) may be deemed by the legislation to be made at MARKET VALUE (see **45.1**) or on a no gain/no loss basis (see, in particular, **29.3** GROUPS OF COMPANIES, **46.5** MARRIED PERSONS AND CIVIL PARTNERS and the list of no gain/no loss provisions at **9.6** ASSETS HELD ON 31 MARCH 1982).

There are also a number of circumstances where certain amounts are excluded from the consideration. See **39.1** INTERACTION WITH OTHER TAXES for the exclusion of amounts charged to income tax; **70.10** UNIT TRUSTS AND OTHER INVESTMENT VEHICLES for the deduction from consideration of the amount of an income gain under the FINROF rules; and **3** ALTERNATIVE FINANCE ARRANGEMENTS for the exclusion of the return on such arrangements that is broadly equivalent to interest from the consideration for the purchase and sale of the asset involved.

Appropriations to and from trading stock

[16.9] Where an asset acquired by a person otherwise than as trading stock is appropriated by him for the purposes of his trade as trading stock (whether on the commencement of the trade or otherwise) and a chargeable gain or allowable loss would have accrued to him if he had then sold the asset for its market value, he is treated as having then disposed of the asset at its then market value. Where the asset is appropriated for the purposes of a trade carried on wholly or partly in the UK and chargeable to income tax or corporation tax and a chargeable gain would otherwise arise, the person may alternatively elect (under *TCGA 1992, s 161(3)*) that, in computing the assessable profits of the trade, the market value of the asset is reduced by the amount of the chargeable gain that would otherwise arise (i.e. he may treat the gain as subject to tax as income rather than as a capital gain). For appropriations prior to 8 March 2017 only, the election could also be made where an allowable loss would otherwise arise, such that when computing trading profits, the market value of the asset was instead increased by the allowable loss which would otherwise arise. A partner must have the agreement of all his co-partners to make the election effective.

For CGT purposes the election must be made on or before the first anniversary of 31 January following the tax year in which ends the period of account in which the asset is appropriated. For corporation tax purposes it must be made within two years after the end of the accounting period in which the asset is appropriated.

[*TCGA 1992, ss 161(1)(3)(3A)(4), 288(1); SI 2006 No 959, Art 3(3); F(No 2)A 2017, s 26(2)(4)*].

If any gain (or loss) on a sale of the asset would have been exempt (or non-allowable) under the provisions of *TCGA 1992, Sch 7AC* (see **66** SUBSTANTIAL SHAREHOLDINGS OF COMPANIES), the appropriation is still treated as a disposal at market value. [*TCGA 1992, Sch 7AC para 36*].

Where an asset forming part of a person's trading stock is:

(a) appropriated by him for any other purpose, or
(b) retained by him on his ceasing to carry on the trade,

he is treated as having acquired it at the time for a consideration equal to the amount brought into the accounts of the trade for tax purposes. [*TCGA 1992, s 161(2)*]. For the valuation of trading stock in such circumstances, see Tolley's Income Tax under Trading Income.

See **29.4** GROUPS OF COMPANIES for intra-group transfers of assets which are trading stock of one of the companies but not of the other and for acquisition 'as trading stock' generally.

See **41.4, 41.6** LAND for deemed appropriation as trading stock on certain transactions in land.

Finance leases

[16.10] There are anti-avoidance provisions which apply to finance leases for both corporation tax and income tax purposes. The provisions are intended to ensure that the tax treatment of such leases are aligned with the commercial accounting treatment in two situations. The first situation is arrangements by finance lessors to turn some of the lease rental income into capital receipts and the provisions ensure that any part of the capital receipt which is recognised as return on investment under generally accepted accounting practice is brought into account for tax purposes as income. See now *ITA 2007, ss 614B–614BY* and *CTA 2010, ss 899–924*. The second situation is arrangements under which rentals are concentrated towards the end of the lease term: see now *ITA 2007, ss 614C–614CD* and *CTA 2010, ss 925–929*. See Tolley's Income Tax and Tolley's Corporation Tax for the detailed provisions.

Where a lessor under a lease within the provisions (or a connected person) disposes of his interest in the lease, the leased asset or an asset representing the leased asset, the consideration for the disposal is reduced by setting against it any 'cumulative accountancy rental excess' which relates to the lease for the period of account of the disposal.

Broadly, the '*cumulative accountancy rental excess*' represents the amount by which the taxable rental income of the lessor (or connected person) under the above provisions exceeds the actual rental income over the period for which he was the lessor. See *ITA 2007, s 614BH, CTA 2010, s 907* for the detailed definition.

Where the disposal concerned is a part disposal, the cumulative accountancy rental excess must be apportioned using the formula at **16.5** above. If two or more disposals which trigger an adjustment to the consideration take place at the same time, the cumulative accountancy rental excess must be apportioned between the disposals on a just and reasonable basis.

Where an adjustment to the disposal consideration is made under these provisions, no further adjustment is made under *TCGA 1992, s 37* (see **39.1** INTERACTION WITH OTHER TAXES).

[*TCGA 1992, s 37A*].

Allowable and non-allowable expenditure

General provisions

[16.11] Simon's Taxes. See C2.2.

Except as otherwise expressly provided, the sums allowable as a deduction from the consideration in the computation of any gain accruing to a person on the disposal of an asset are restricted to the following.

(a) **The amount or value of the consideration, in money or money's worth, given wholly and exclusively for the acquisition of the asset** (plus 'incidental costs') or expenditure incurred wholly and exclusively in providing the asset. [*TCGA 1992, s 38(1)(a)*].
See also *Cleveleys Investment Trust Co v CIR (No 2)* CS 1975, 51 TC 26; *Allison v Murray* Ch D 1975, 51 TC 57; *Garner v Pounds Shipowners & Shipbreakers Ltd (and related appeal)* HL 2000, 72 TC 561.
'*Incidental costs*' of acquisition are (strictly) limited to expenditure wholly and exclusively incurred for the purposes of the acquisition, being:
    (i) fees, commission or remuneration for the professional services of a surveyor, valuer, auctioneer, accountant, agent or legal adviser;
    (ii) transfer/conveyancing charges (including stamp duty); and
    (iii) advertising to find a seller.
[*TCGA 1992, s 38(2)*].
Where the purchaser is a company, and the purchase price is satisfied by the issue of fully paid-up shares in the company, the consideration is the shares and their value is normally that placed on them by the parties, i.e. the purchase price satisfied by the issue. 'Value' in *TCGA 1992, s 38(1)(a)* (see above) does not mean 'market value' (*Stanton v Drayton Commercial Investment Co Ltd* HL 1982, 55 TC 286). Disposals which are deemed to take place at market value will, generally speaking, give rise to an equivalent base cost in the acquir-

er's hands (but see **45.1** MARKET VALUE). **No allowance is given for notional costs of disposal or reacquisition, where there is a deemed disposal and reacquisition.** [*TCGA 1992, ss 17, 38(4)*].

See (b) below for capital contributions by shareholders.

A company with an annual turnover of not less than £5 million may round incidental costs of acquisition to the nearest £1,000 subject to certain conditions and exceptions (HMRC Statement of Practice 15/93).

Foreign currency. Where the cost (or deemed cost) of an asset is in foreign currency, it is converted into sterling at the exchange rate ruling at the time of acquisition. Similarly, consideration is converted at the date of disposal. (*Bentley v Pike* Ch D 1981, 53 TC 590; *Capcount Trading v Evans* CA 1992, 65 TC 545). **For the use by certain companies of foreign currencies in computing chargeable gains on ships, aircraft and shares see 14.14** COMPANIES.

See also **15.3** COMPANIES — CORPORATE FINANCE AND INTANGIBLES **for matching of exchange differences on chargeable assets generally with those on borrowings.**

(b) **Expenditure wholly and exclusively incurred for the purpose of enhancing the value of the asset being expenditure reflected in the state or nature of the asset at the time of disposal.** [*TCGA 1992, s 38(1)(b)*].

Expenditure on initial repairs (including decoration) to a property, undertaken to put it into a fit state for letting, and not allowable in computing taxable property business profits, is regarded as allowable expenditure under this heading (HMRC Statement of Practice D24).

HMRC consider that capital contributions made to a company by shareholders are not normally allowable expenditure under this heading, but that if made at the time of issue of the shares they might be treated as in the nature of a share premium (ICAEW Guidance Note TR 713, 23 August 1988 and HMRC Capital Gains Manual CG43500–43502). This view was upheld in *Trustees of the FD Fenston Will Trusts v HMRC*, (Sp C 589), [2007] SSCD 316. See also **16.13**(a) below.

In *Blackwell v HMRC* CA, [2017] EWCA Civ 232 it was held that this provision applied to the bundle of rights and obligations which would be acquired by the purchaser at the time of the disposal, not the asset as it operated in the vendor's hands.

'*Expenditure*' does not include the value of personal labour and skill (*Oram v Johnson* Ch D 1980, 53 TC 319). However, it may be in the form of providing money's worth and may be first reflected in the state or nature of the asset before completion even if this is after the time of disposal (*Chaney v Watkis* Ch D 1985, 58 TC 707).

(c) **Expenditure wholly and exclusively incurred in establishing, preserving or defending title to, or to a right over, the asset.** [*TCGA 1992, s 38(1)(b)*]. This includes resealing Scottish confirmation and other probate etc. expenses incurred to establish the title of the personal representatives (*Richards' Executors* HL 1971, 46 TC 626 and see **19.10** DEATH) and see **62.16** SETTLEMENTS.

In *Lee v Jewitt* (Sp C 257), [2000] SSCD 517, legal costs incurred by a partner in defending an action by fellow partners resulting in dissolution of the partnership were held to have been incurred under this heading.

(d) **Incidental costs of disposal.** [*TCGA 1992, s 38(1)(c)*]. Strictly, such costs are limited to expenditure wholly and exclusively incurred for the purposes of the disposal, being:
   (i) fees, commission or remuneration for the professional services of a surveyor, valuer, auctioneer, accountant, agent or legal adviser;
   (ii) transfer/conveyancing charges (including stamp duty);
   (iii) advertising to find a buyer; and
   (iv) any other costs reasonably incurred in making any valuation or apportionment for capital gains tax purposes, including, in particular, expenses reasonably incurred in ascertaining market value where this is required under *TCGA 1992*.

   [*TCGA 1992, s 38(2)*].

   Expenses of terminating a settlement incurred to bring about a chargeable occasion within *TCGA 1992, s 71* are allowable (*Chubb's Trustee* CS 1971, 47 TC 353).

   Costs within (iv) above extend only to costs reasonably incurred in making the valuation or apportionment, and not to any subsequent costs incurred in negotiating a value with HMRC or in litigation with them concerning the value (Revenue Tax Bulletin February 1994 p 116) and see *Caton's Administrators v Couch* CA 1997, 70 TC 10. The same principle applies where the costs are incurred in relation to a post-transaction valuation check (see **58.5** RETURNS) (HMRC Capital Gains Manual CG15260, 16615).

   In *O'Donnell v HMRC* FTT (TC 5821), [2017] UKFTT 347 (TC) O was unable to repay loans, secured on properties he owned, when called for immediate repayment by the bank. The properties were conveyed to O's uncle and charged to his lender. When calculating the gain realised by O on sale to his uncle, the First-tier Tribunal rejected mortgage broker fees incurred by O as 'incidental costs of disposal' as those fees had been incurred for the purpose of retaining rather than disposing of the properties. The First-tier Tribunal also rejected the notion that an allowable loss arose on the mortgage loan which should be offset against any gain as *TCGA 1992* is concerned with losses on assets, not liabilities.

   A company with an annual turnover of not less than £5 million may round incidental costs of disposal to the nearest £1,000 subject to certain conditions and exceptions (HMRC Statement of Practice 15/93).

Example

Mr Hopkins bought a second home in August 1978 for £15,000. Mr Hopkins' neighbour, Mr Douglas, claimed that part of the garden of the house belonged to him. Mr Hopkins won the court case resulting, but incurred legal fees of £5,000 in September 1985.

In 2001 Mr Hopkins had a tennis court built for £5,000, but this was demolished in 2008.

Mr Hopkins sold the house in November 2017 for £126,000. It was agreed that the value of the house at 31 March 1982 was £25,000. The house has never been treated as Mr Hopkins' main residence.

The chargeable gain is as follows.

	£
Sale consideration	126,000
Less 31 March 1982 value	25,000
Legal fees re boundary dispute	5,000
Chargeable gain	£96,000

Note to the example

(a) The expenditure on the tennis court in 2001 is not allowable as it is not reflected in the state or nature of the asset at the time of disposal in November 2017. The demolition of the tennis court is not within *TCGA 1992, s 24(1)* as it is not the 'entire loss, destruction, dissipation or extinction' of an asset because the court is not an 'asset': it is only part of an asset, the land (see HMRC Capital Gains Manual CG15190).

Special cases

[16.12] In addition to the general provisions relating to allowable expenditure in **16.11** above, specific items of expenditure are allowed as follows.

(a) **Interest in certain (now very rare) circumstances** on money borrowed by a *company* for financing allowable expenditure on the construction of a building, structure, or work. There is no such provision for individuals, trustees, etc. See **14.5** COMPANIES.

(b) **Income tax paid by a close company participator** on income which has been apportioned to him (broadly in relation only to accounting periods ending before 1 April 1989) but which remains undistributed is an allowable deduction. [*TCGA 1992, s 124*]. See also **4.14** ANTI-AVOIDANCE regarding *TCGA 1992, s 125* (close company transferring assets at undervalue).

(c) **Foreign tax** borne by the disposer on the disposal is deductible. See **21.5** DOUBLE TAX RELIEF.

(d) **Inheritance tax** is a deduction in some circumstances. See **39.2** INTERACTION WITH OTHER TAXES.

(e) **Acquisitions from persons neither resident nor ordinarily resident in the UK.** Where, *after 9 March 1981 and before 6 April 1983*:
   (i) a person acquired an asset for no valuable consideration, or for a consideration lower than the asset's market value, and no other amount or value was imputed to the consideration by operation of *CGTA 1979* (e.g. under the MARKET VALUE (**45**) rules); and
   (ii) there was a corresponding disposal of the asset by a person neither resident nor ordinarily resident in the UK; and

(iii) a charge to income tax, corporation tax or capital gains tax arose in respect of the acquisition in (i) above,

a deduction is given on the subsequent disposal of the asset by the acquirer, equal to the amount in respect of which the charge in (iii) above arises. The condition in (iii) above was taken to be satisfied where, under *FA 1981, s 80(3)* (see now *TCGA 1992, s 87* at **48.14** OFFSHORE SETTLEMENTS), in any year of assessment, gains were attributed to a beneficiary of a non-resident settlement, by reason of that beneficiary's acquisition of an asset in that or an earlier fiscal year. In such circumstances, the deduction is the amount of the gains attributed to the beneficiary because of the acquisition of the said asset.

After 5 April 1983, the market value rules were amended so that, subject to the election below, an acquisition under the circumstances in (i) to (iii) is treated as being made at market value and the above provisions do not apply. Where, however, the corresponding disposal under (ii) is made *after 5 April 1983 and before 6 April 1985* the persons acquiring and disposing of the asset could jointly elect that both the acquisition and disposal were excepted from the amended market value rules in which case the above provisions still apply. [*CGTA 1979, s 32(5)(6); FA 1981, s 90(2); FA 1984, s 66(3)*]. See **45.1** MARKET VALUE for further details.

(f) **Stock dividends.** The 'appropriate amount in cash' relating to a stock dividend is deductible. See **63.10** SHARES AND SECURITIES.

(g) **Offshore funds.** Certain sums charged to income tax on the disposal of interests in offshore funds. See **49.10–49.13** OVERSEAS MATTERS.

(h) **Shares acquired by employees.** See **22** EMPLOYEE SHARE SCHEMES.

(i) **Legatees and beneficiaries.** Where a person disposes of an asset held by a personal representative or trustee to which he became absolutely entitled as legatee or as against the trustee, any incidental expenditure incurred by that person, the personal representative or the trustee in relation to the transfer of the asset to him, is allowable. [*TCGA 1992, s 64(1)*]. See **19.14** DEATH and **62.16** SETTLEMENTS.

(j) **Devaluation of sterling in November 1967.** In computing gains on the disposal of foreign securities purchased out of foreign currency borrowed before 19 November 1967 for that purpose (by permission given, subject to specified conditions, under *Exchange Control Act 1947*) the deduction under **16.11**(a) above is increased by one-sixth. A similar increase applies to disposals after 18 November 1967 of foreign securities which at that date formed part of a trust fund established abroad by a Lloyd's underwriter, etc., or a company engaged in marine protection or indemnity assurance on a mutual basis, which consists of premiums received and used mainly for meeting business liabilities arising in the country in which the fund is set up. [*TCGA 1992, Sch 11 paras 13, 14*].

(k) **Betterment levy.** Betterment levy paid in respect of certain development land is deductible as expenditure wholly and exclusively incurred in enhancing the value of the asset in the CGT computation arising on the disposal or part disposal of that land. [*TCGA 1992, Sch 11 para 17*].

Non-allowable expenditure

[16.13] In no case is allowance given for the following.

(a) Expenditure which is deductible in computing profits or losses for income tax purposes [*TCGA 1992, s 39(1)*] or would be so deductible if the asset were held as a fixed asset of a trade [*TCGA 1992, s 39(2)*]. See *Emmerson v Computer Time International Ltd* CA 1977, 50 TC 628. However, when calculating a gain, deductions are allowable for expenditure on which capital allowances are made or, from 2017/18, for capital expenditure deducted when calculating profits under the cash basis for small businesses or unincorporated property businesses, but see (i) below in respect of losses. [*TCGA 1992, s 41(1)(4); F(No 2)A 2017, Sch 2 paras 45, 64(1)*].

(b) Premiums paid to cover the risk of damage to, or loss or depreciation of, the asset. [*TCGA 1992, s 205*].

(c) Any expenditure recoverable from any government or public or local authority in the UK or elsewhere. Where such a grant is subsequently repaid, the consideration on disposal of the asset may be treated, by concession, as reduced by the amount repaid. (HMRC Extra-Statutory Concession D53). [*TCGA 1992, s 50*]. (See Revenue Tax Bulletin April 1999 pp 642–645 (in particular, Example 2) re the application of this provision to land introduced by a public sector body into a Private Finance Initiative contract as a contribution to the private sector operator's construction costs.) This provision has no effect on the quantum of rollover relief available under *TCGA 1992, s 152* (see **59.1** ROLLOVER RELIEF) where the asset attracting the grant is the new asset for the purposes of that relief (*Wardhaugh v Penrith Rugby Union Football Club* Ch D 2002, 74 TC 499).

(d) Interest, except as under **16.12**(a) above. [*TCGA 1992, s 38(3)*].

(e) Income tax chargeable on shares acquired under certain employee schemes. See **22** EMPLOYEE SHARE SCHEMES.

(f) Liabilities remaining with, or assumed by, the disposer contingent upon the default of the assignee of a lease, or upon the breach of covenants in a conveyance or lease of land, or of warranties, or representations made on the sale or lease of other property. If the contingent liability subsequently becomes enforceable and is enforced, relief is given by way of discharge, repayment or other adjustment. [*TCGA 1992, s 49*]. An amount received under a warranty or indemnity is normally deductible from the purchaser's acquisition cost (HMRC Extra-Statutory Concession D33). See further **41.24** LAND. A payment made by the chairman of a company to settle legal proceedings alleging fraudulent misrepresentation in relation to the takeover of the company and associated legal costs were held to fall within *s 49* in *HMRC v Morrison* SCS, [2015] STC 659.

(g) Any discount for postponement of receipt of the consideration and, in the first instance, for any risk of non-recovery, or for any contingency in the right to receive any part of the consideration. If, however, any part of the consideration subsequently proves to be irrecoverable, on a claim to that effect the tax liability will be adjusted accordingly which may result in a discharge or repayment of tax. On or after 20 July 2005 this provision does not apply to so much of any consideration as consists of rights under a creditor relationship (see **15.5** COMPANIES — CORPORATE FINANCE AND INTANGIBLES) to which a company becomes a party as a result of the disposal. Instead, the amount to be brought into account in respect of that consideration is the 'fair value' (within *CTA 2009, s 313(6)*) of the creditor relationship. [*TCGA 1992, s 48*]. (See *Marson v Marriage* Ch D 1979, 54 TC 59.) See also **10.2** CAPITAL SUMS DERIVED FROM ASSETS and **51.5** PAYMENT OF TAX for the possibility of payment by instalments.

Where consideration for a disposal is fixed in a foreign currency, any subsequent loss on exchange is not irrecoverable consideration for the purposes of a claim under *TCGA 1992, s 48*. See *Goodbrand v Loffland Bros North Sea Inc* CA 1998, 71 TC 57.

A subsequent payment, by the vendor of an option to a third party, to release restrictive covenants did not alter the consideration received for the option and was not allowable expenditure in computing the gain (*Garner v Pounds Shipowners & Shipbreakers Ltd (and related appeal)* HL 2000, 72 TC 561).

(h) Notional expenses on deemed disposals and acquisitions. [*TCGA 1992, s 38(4)*].

(i) Where a 'loss' would otherwise be shown, expenditure otherwise allowable as a deduction is reduced to the extent that capital allowances have been made in respect of it. The capital allowances taken into account are those granted (less any balancing charge) to the disposer. Where the asset was treated for capital allowance purposes as acquired at written-down value, allowances granted to any former owner which were not taken into account in restricting his loss are also deducted from allowable expenditure.

From 2017/18 onwards, 'capital allowance' for the purpose of this restriction includes any deduction allowable for capital expenditure when calculating profits on the cash basis for small businesses or unincorporated property businesses.

Where the loss-making disposal is of plant or machinery in relation to expenditure on which allowances or charges have been made for capital allowance purposes (but not where this includes an allowable deduction under the cash basis) and which has been used solely for trade purposes and has not attracted partial depreciation subsidies which would deny capital allowances, the capital allowances (if any) are deemed to be the difference between the qualifying expenditure incurred (or treated as incurred) by the disposer, and the disposal value. Where the allowances *do* include an allowable deduction under the cash basis, the capital allowances to be taken into account are deemed to equal the total amount of expenditure which has qualified for capital allowances less any balancing charge to which the disposer is liable. [*TCGA 1992, ss 41(1)–(10), 53(3); FA 2016, s 73(3); F(No 2)A 2017, s 16, Sch 2 paras 45, 64(1)*]. See also **8.11** ASSETS HELD ON 6 APRIL **1965**, **9.7** and ASSETS HELD ON 31 MARCH **1982**.

In *HMRC v Smallwood* CA, [2007] STC 1237, *TCGA 1992, s 41* was held not to restrict a loss on units in an enterprise zone unit trust where the trustees of the unit trust had used the funds subscribed for the units to acquire land and buildings, in respect of which the taxpayer had been credited with capital allowances. The Court upheld the Special Commissioner's decision that capital allowances had not been made in respect of the taxpayer's expenditure in subscribing for the units. It was the trustees' expenditure that had resulted in capital allowances for the taxpayer.

(j) Where a loss would otherwise be shown on the disposal of an asset which includes plant or machinery which is a fixture for the purposes of *CAA 2001, Pt 2 Ch 6A* (long funding leases: interpretation) and which has been used by the person making the disposal for the purpose of leasing under one or more 'long funding leases', expenditure otherwise allowable as a deduction is reduced by an amount equal to the fall in value of the plant or machinery during the period of that lease (or, where there was more than one such lease, the periods of those leases). For this purpose, the fall in value of plant or machinery during the period of a lease is equal to the excess of the 'market value' of the plant or machinery at the 'commencement' of the 'term' of the lease over its market value at the 'termination' of the lease.

For the meaning of '*long funding lease*' see **7.6** ASSETS. '*Market value*' is determined on the assumption of a disposal by an absolute owner free from all leases and other encumbrances. The expressions '*commencement*', '*term*', and '*termination*' are defined as in *CAA 2001, Pt 2 Ch 6A*. See Tolley's Income Tax or Tolley's Corporation Tax.

[*TCGA 1992, s 41A*].

Key points concerning computation of gains and losses

[16.14] Points to consider are as follows.

- Where property is owned jointly between two (or more) persons, each person is able to set their annual exempt amount against their share of the gain. Consider whether each joint owner has the full annual exempt amount available in the tax year of disposal, or whether a delay in the disposal date may be beneficial.
- Transfers between spouses or civil partners are free from capital gains tax and it may be tax efficient to consider a transfer prior to disposal. Although watch entitlement to any reliefs such as entrepreneurs' relief and whether both parties will still qualify.
- Trustees are, in general, entitled to one half of the annual exempt amount. However, this amount is then divided by the number of trusts created by the same settlor (up to a maximum of five trusts).
- Consider the timing of the disposal and potentially spreading the disposal across two tax years where part disposals are a possibility. Two part disposals on either side of the tax year end will each be eligible for a full year's annual exempt amount (assuming that it is fully available), which may give a beneficial result in terms of tax payable.

- Remember to offset all deductible items against acquisition costs and costs of disposal, including accountancy fees for the transaction itself such as determining market value.
- Where the disposal is a gift, the market value is substituted for the sale proceeds — see 27 GIFTS.

17

Connected Persons

Meaning of 'connected'	**17.1**
Individuals	**17.1**
Trustees of a settlement	**17.2**
Partners	**17.3**
Companies	**17.4**
Person controlling company	**17.5**
Meaning of expressions used to define 'connected persons'	**17.6**

[*ITA 2007, s 993; CTA 2010, s 1122; TCGA 1992, s 286*].

Cross-references. See **4.12**, **4.13** ANTI-AVOIDANCE for certain disposals between connected persons; **44.6** LOSSES for losses on disposals to connected persons; **50.4** PARTNERSHIPS for transactions between partners; and **62.14** SETTLEMENTS for settlors and trustees being connected persons.

Meaning of 'connected'

Individuals

[17.1] An individual is connected with his spouse or civil partner, any 'relative' (see **41.28** below) of himself or of his spouse or civil partner, and with the spouse or civil partner of any such relative. It appears that a widow or widower is no longer a spouse (*Vestey's Exors and Vestey v CIR HL 1949, 31 TC 1*). Spouses divorced by decree nisi remain connected persons until the divorce is made absolute (*Aspden v Hildesley* Ch D 1981, 55 TC 609).

Trustees of a settlement

[17.2] A 'trustee' of a 'settlement', in his capacity as such, is connected with:

(a) the 'settlor' (if an individual) (see **41.28** below),
(b) any person connected with the settlor,
(c) a 'body corporate connected with the settlement' (see **41.28** below),
(d) if the settlement is the principal settlement in relation to one or more sub-fund settlements (see **62.12** SETTLEMENTS), the trustees of those settlements, and
(e) if the settlement is a sub-fund settlement, the trustees of any other sub-fund settlements of its principal settlement.

HMRC has confirmed (a) above applies as regards the time when a settlement is created and property first transferred to it. On the death of the settlor, neither (a) nor (b) apply (Revenue Tax Bulletin February 1993 p 56).

Partners

[17.3] Partners are connected with each other and with each other's spouses (see **17.1** above), civil partners and relatives (see **41.28** below), except in connection with acquisitions and disposals of partnership assets made pursuant to *bona fide* commercial arrangements. See also **17.5** below.

Companies

[17.4] A company is connected with another company if:

(a) the same person 'controls' both (see **41.28** below), or
(b) one is controlled by a person who has control of the other in conjunction with persons connected with him, or
(c) a person controls one company and persons connected with him control the other, or
(d) the same group of persons controls both, or
(e) the companies are controlled by separate groups which can be regarded as the same by interchanging connected persons.

For consideration of (d) above, see *Kellogg Brown and Root Holdings (UK) Ltd v HMRC* CA, [2010] STC 925.

Person controlling company

[17.5] A company is connected with another person who (either alone or with persons connected with him) has control of it.

Persons acting together to secure or exercise control of a company are treated in relation to that company as connected with each other and with any other person acting on the direction of any of them to secure or exercise such control (see *Steele v EVC International NV* CA 1996, 69 TC 88). Control may be 'exercised' passively. See *Floor v Davis* HL 1979, 52 TC 609. See **4.18** ANTI-AVOIDANCE for an extension of this provision in connection with dividend stripping.

Meaning of expressions used to define 'connected persons'

[17.6] '*Company*' includes any body corporate, unincorporated association or unit trust scheme but does not include a partnership.

'*Control*' is as defined in *CTA 2010, ss 450, 451*. [*TCGA 1992, s 288(1)*]. See Tolley's Corporation Tax under Close Companies.

'*Relative*' means brother, sister, ancestor or lineal descendant. [*TCGA 1992, s 286(8)*].

'*Settlement*' includes any disposition, trust, covenant, agreement, arrangement or transfer of assets. [*ITTOIA 2005, s 620(1)*]. It must contain an element of bounty. It does not include a transfer of assets for full consideration (*CIR v*

Plummer HL 1979, 54 TC 1). '*Trustee*' specifically includes, where otherwise a settlement would have no trustees, any person in whom the settled property or its management is vested. [*TCGA 1992, s 286(3ZA)*].

'*A body corporate connected with the settlement*' is a close company (or one which would be so if resident in the UK) the participators in which include the trustees of the settlement, or a company controlled by such a close company. Control for these purposes is as under *CTA 2010, s 1124*: namely, the power of a person by shareholding or voting power (whether directly or through another company), or under Articles of Association, to secure that the company's affairs are conducted according to his wishes.

'*Settlor*' is as at **62.5** SETTLEMENTS. [*ITTOIA 2005, s 620(2)(3); ICTA 1988, s 660G(1)(2)*]. See *Countess Fitzwilliam and ors v CIR (and related appeals)* HL 1993, 67 TC 614.

18

Corporate Venturing Scheme

Introduction	**18.1**
Investment relief	**18.2**
Form of relief	**18.3**
Claims for relief	**18.4**
Qualifying investing company	**18.5**
Qualifying issuing company	**18.6**
Qualifying trades	**18.7**
General requirements	**18.8**
Withdrawal or reduction of investment relief	**18.9**
Disposal	**18.10**
Value received by investing company	**18.11**
Meaning of, and amount of, value received	**18.12**
Replacement value	**18.13**
Value received by other persons	**18.14**
Put options and call options	**18.15**
Identification rules	**18.16**
Chargeable gains and allowable losses	**18.17**
Computation of allowable loss	**18.18**
Set-off of allowable loss against income	**18.19**
Deferral relief	**18.20**
Company restructuring	**18.21**
Reorganisations of share capital	**18.21**
Company reconstructions	**18.22**
Issuing company becoming wholly-owned subsidiary of new holding company	**18.23**
Key points	**18.24**

Introduction to corporate venturing scheme

[18.1] The corporate venturing scheme provides tax relief for shares issued on or after 1 April 2000 but **before 1 April 2010**. Under the scheme, most trading companies are able to obtain corporation tax relief at 20% ('*investment relief*') on corporate venturing investments, i.e. acquisitions (by cash subscription) of minority shareholdings in 'small higher risk' trading companies.

In addition, investing companies are able to postpone chargeable gains ('*deferral relief*') on disposals of corporate venturing investments where they reinvest in other shares attracting investment relief. Also, an allowable capital loss on the disposal of a corporate venturing investment, computed net of investment relief, can be relieved against *income* of the accounting period in which the loss arises and accounting periods ending in the previous 12 months (but may alternatively be relieved against chargeable gains in the normal way). [*FA 2000, s 63(1)(4), Sch 15 para 1*].

Companies in which corporate venturing investments can be made are limited to those with gross assets not exceeding £7 million immediately before the investment and £8 million immediately afterwards. Such companies must exist for the purpose of carrying on trading activities other than the kind of 'lower risk' activity excluded under the ENTERPRISE INVESTMENT SCHEME (23) or the provisions for VENTURE CAPITAL TRUSTS (71). Potential investee companies may request advance clearance from HMRC. The maximum investment qualifying for relief is 30% of the issued ordinary share capital of the investee company, and no minimum investment is stipulated. It is a further condition that at least 20% of the ordinary share capital of the investee company be held by individuals (other than directors and employees of the investing company). To qualify for the relief, the investing company must retain the shares acquired for at least three years. Investing companies carrying on financial trades (e.g. banking, share dealing etc.) are not eligible.

See generally HMRC Venture Capital Schemes Manual VCM2010–2070, 90000 onwards. See also **Simon's Taxes**. See **D8.3**.

Investment relief

[18.2] An investing company is eligible for investment relief (see **18.3** below) in respect of an amount subscribed by it for shares in an investee company (the '*issuing company*') if:

(a) the shares (the '*relevant shares*') are issued to the investing company;
(b) the investing company is a 'qualifying investing company' (see **18.5** below);
(c) the issuing company is a 'qualifying issuing company' (see **18.6** below) in relation to the relevant shares; and
(d) the general requirements at **18.8** below are met.

For advance clearance as regards (c) and (d) above, see **18.4** below.

Qualification period

In these provisions, the '*qualification period*' is normally the three-year period beginning with the date of issue of the relevant shares. If, however, the money raised by the issue is employed wholly or mainly for the purposes of a qualifying trade (or trades) (see **18.7** below) which, on the date of issue, was not being carried on by the issuing company or a qualifying 90% subsidiary (see **18.6** below), the qualification period begins on the date of issue and ends immediately before the third anniversary of the date of commencement of the trade (or the latest such date where there is more than one such trade). Any carrying on of a trade by a subsidiary before it became a qualifying 90% subsidiary is disregarded in determining when the trade commences for this purpose.

[*FA 2000, Sch 15 paras 2, 3, 102(8)*].

Form of relief

[18.3] Investment relief is given, on a claim (see **18.4** below), by reducing the investing company's corporation tax liability for the accounting period in which the shares are issued by the lesser of:

- 20% of the amount (or aggregate amount) subscribed, and
- the amount which reduces the liability to nil.

[*FA 2000, Sch 15 para 39*].

The reduction in corporation tax liability is made in priority to any reduction for community investment tax relief (see Tolley's Corporation Tax) but before any DOUBLE TAX RELIEF (**21**). [*FA 1998, Sch 18 para 8(1); TIOPA 2010, Sch 8 para 54(2)*].

Investment relief is said to be 'attributable to shares' if relief as above has been obtained in respect of those shares and has not been withdrawn (as opposed to reduced) — see **18.9** below. Where for any one accounting period relief has been obtained by reason of more than one issue of shares, the relief is attributed to those issues in proportion to the amounts subscribed. Relief attributable to any one issue of shares is attributed *pro rata* to each share in that issue, and any reduction of relief (see **18.9** below) is similarly apportioned between the shares in question. For these purposes, any bonus shares, issued in respect of the original shares and being shares in the same company, of the same class and carrying the same rights, are treated as if comprised in the original issue, and relief is apportioned to them accordingly. This applies only if the original shares have been held continuously since issue (as in **18.19**(a) below), and, where it does apply, the bonus shares are themselves treated as having been held continuously since the time of the original issue. [*FA 2000, Sch 15 para 45*].

Claims for relief

[18.4] No deadline is specified for making a claim, so the general four-year time limit applies as in **13.5** CLAIMS. A claim for relief cannot be made in respect of any investment until:

- the 'funded trade' has been carried on by no person other than the issuing company or a qualifying 90% subsidiary (see **18.6** below) of that company for at least four months disregarding
  - time spent *preparing* to carry on the trade), and
  - where the funded trade is carried on by a partnership or joint venture, the other partners or parties to the joint venture; and
- the investing company has received from the issuing company a 'compliance certificate' (see below).

No postponement of tax pending appeal (see **51.17** PAYMENT OF TAX) can be made on the grounds of eligibility for investment relief until a claim for that relief can be and has been made.

The '*funded trade*' is the trade or trades by reference to which the requirement at **18.8** below as to 'use of money raised' is met (or, where applicable, the notional trade of research and development therein mentioned). A claim *can* be made if the funded trade is carried on as above for less than four months by reason of the winding-up or dissolution of any company or its going into administration or receivership (both as defined), provided that this is for commercial reasons and not part of tax avoidance arrangements.

A '*compliance certificate*' is a certificate issued, with the authority of HMRC and in such form as they may direct, by the issuing company in respect of the relevant shares and confirming that, from the issuing company's point of view, the requirements for investment relief are for the time being met. To obtain authority for the issue of a certificate, the issuing company must provide HMRC with a 'compliance statement' in respect of the issue of shares which includes the relevant shares. Where notice of an event giving rise to withdrawal etc. is given to HMRC by or in relation to the issuing company (see **18.9** below), any authority already given is invalid unless renewed.

A '*compliance statement*' is a statement, in respect of an issue of shares, to the effect that, from the issuing company's point of view, the requirements for investment relief are for the time being met and have been met at all times since the shares were issued. The statement must be in required form and must contain any additional information as HMRC reasonably require, a declaration that it is correct to the best of the company's knowledge and belief, and such other declarations as HMRC reasonably require. A compliance statement cannot be made until such time as the funded trade has been carried on for at least four months (or such shorter time as is specified above). It *must* be made within two years after the end of the accounting period in which the shares were issued or, if later, two years after the minimum period of trading condition is satisfied.

The issuing company may give notice of appeal, within 30 days, against an HMRC refusal to authorise a compliance certificate (as if that refusal were the disallowance of a claim other than for discharge or repayment of tax — see **13.3** CLAIMS).

The issuing company is liable to a penalty of up to £3,000 for issuing a compliance certificate which is made fraudulently or negligently or without HMRC authority, or for making a compliance statement fraudulently or negligently.

[*FA 2000, Sch 15 paras 40–44, 102(4)*].

Qualifying investing company

[18.5] The investing company is a '*qualifying investing company*' (see **18.2**(b) above) in relation to the relevant shares if it meets all the requirements below as to absence of material interest, reciprocal arrangements, control and tax avoidance, the nature of its activities, and the relevant shares being a chargeable asset. [*FA 2000, Sch 15 para 4*].

'No material interest' requirement

At no time in the qualification period (see **18.2** above) must the investing company have a material interest in the issuing company. For this purpose, a person has a material interest in a company if he (alone or together with any person connected with him — within *CTA 2010, s 1122* — see **17** CONNECTED PERSONS) directly or indirectly possesses, or is entitled (or will in future be entitled) to acquire (at present or at a future date), more than **30%** of:

- the 'ordinary share capital' of, or

- the voting power in,

the company or any 51% subsidiary. In applying the test, there must be attributed to a person any rights or powers of any associate of his (as defined by *FA 2000, Sch 15 para 99*). For these purposes, a company's '*ordinary share capital*' comprises:

(a) all of its issued share capital other than 'relevant preference shares', and
(b) all of its loan capital (as widely defined but excluding a bank overdraft or an ordinary business debt) that carries a right to convert into, or to acquire, shares which would fall within (a) above.

'*Relevant preference shares*' are, broadly, non-voting, non-convertible shares issued for new consideration and carrying no right to dividends other than dividends which

- are of a fixed amount or at a rate which is fixed or which varies according to a standard published interest rate, a tax rate, a retail price index or an official share price index, and
- which are not dependent on the company's business results or asset values and do not represent more than a reasonable commercial return on the investment.

[*FA 2000, Sch 15 paras 5, 7, 9, 102(3)*].

'No reciprocal arrangements' requirement

The investing company's subscription for the relevant shares must not be part of any arrangements which provide for any other person to subscribe for shares in a 'related company'. A '*related company*' is a company in which the investing company, or any other person who is party to the arrangements, has a material interest (as defined immediately above). Arrangements are disregarded to the extent that they provide for the issuing company to subscribe for shares in any qualifying subsidiary (see **18.6** below). [*FA 2000, Sch 15 para 6*].

'No control' requirement

At no time in the qualification period must the investing company 'control' the issuing company. '*Control*' is determined in accordance with *CTA 2010, ss 450, 451* as modified for this purpose. [*FA 2000, Sch 15 para 8*].

'No tax avoidance' requirement

The relevant shares must be subscribed for by the investing company for commercial reasons and not as part of a tax avoidance scheme or arrangement. [*FA 2000, Sch 15 para 14*].

Non-financial activities requirement

Throughout the qualification period, the investing company,

- if a single company (i.e. a company which is not a parent company or a 51% subsidiary), must exist wholly for the purpose of carrying on one or more 'non-financial trades'; and

- if a group company, must be part of a 'non-financial trading group' and must either exist wholly for the purpose of carrying on one or more 'non-financial trades' or businesses other than trades or be the parent company of the group.

In determining the purpose for which a company exists, purposes having no significant effect (other than in relation to incidental matters) on the extent of the company's activities are disregarded. Purposes for which a company exists are also disregarded to the extent that they consist of:

- (as regards a single company) the holding and managing of property used by the company for one or more 'non-financial trades' carried on by it;
- (as regards a group company) any activities within (a) or (b) below; or
- (as regards any company) holding shares to which investment relief is attributable (see **18.3** above) unless the holding of such shares is a substantial part of the company's business.

A trade is a '*non-financial trade*' if:

- it is conducted on a commercial basis and with a view to profit, and
- it does not consist, wholly or as to a substantial part, in the carrying on of 'financial activities'.

'*Financial activities*' include for this purpose:

- banking, or money-lending, carried on by a bank, building society or other person;
- debt factoring, finance-leasing or hire-purchase financing;
- insurance;
- dealing in shares, securities, currency, debts or other assets of a financial nature; and
- dealing in commodity or financial futures or options.

A group is a '*non-financial trading group*' unless the business of the group (treating the activities of the group companies, taken together, as a single business) consists, wholly or as to a substantial part, in the carrying on of trades other than non-financial trades (as above) and/or businesses other than trades. Activities of a group company are disregarded to the extent that they consist of:

(a) holding shares in or securities of, or making loans to, another group company;

(b) holding and managing property used by a group company for the purposes of one or more non-financial trades carried on by a group company; or

(c) holding shares to which investment relief is attributable (see **18.3** above), unless the holding of such shares is a substantial part of the company's business.

Amendments to the non-financial activities requirement may be made in the future by Treasury Order.

[*FA 2000, Sch 15 paras 10–12, 101, 102(1)*].

Requirement as to shares being a chargeable asset

The relevant shares must be a chargeable asset of the investing company immediately after they are issued to it. For this purpose, an asset is a chargeable asset at a particular time if, on a disposal at that time, a gain would be a chargeable gain. [*FA 2000, Sch 15 para 13*].

Qualifying issuing company

[18.6] The issuing company is a '*qualifying issuing company*' (see **18.2**(c) above) in relation to the relevant shares if it meets all the requirements below as to unquoted status, independence, individual-owners, partnerships and joint ventures, qualifying subsidiaries, property managing subsidiaries, gross assets, number of employees and trading activities. [*FA 2000, Sch 15 para 15*].

Unquoted status requirement

At the time of issue of the relevant shares, none of the issuing company's shares, debentures or other securities must be listed on a recognised stock exchange (see **63.30** SHARES AND SECURITIES) or a 'designated' exchange outside the UK or be dealt in outside the UK by 'designated' means, and there must be no arrangements in existence for such a listing or such dealing. This applies whether or not the company is UK-resident. '*Designated*' means designated by order for the purposes of the ENTERPRISE INVESTMENT SCHEME (**23**) (see now *ITA 2007, s 184(3)*). The company does not fail to meet the requirement simply because a designation order is made, or a stock exchange obtains recognition, after the time of issue of the shares.

If, at the time of issue of the relevant shares, arrangements are in existence for the issuing company to become a wholly-owned subsidiary of a new holding company by means of a share exchange within **18.23** below, there must be no arrangements made for any of the new company's shares, debentures or other securities to be listed or dealt in as above.

[*FA 2000, Sch 15 para 16*].

Independence requirement

At no time in the qualification period (see **18.2** above) must the issuing company be a 51% subsidiary of another company or otherwise under the control (within *CTA 2010, s 1124*) of another company or of another company and persons connected with it (within *CTA 2010, s 1122* — see **17** CONNECTED PERSONS). No arrangements must exist at any time during that period whereby the company could become such a subsidiary or fall under such control (whether during that period or otherwise). Arrangements with a view to a company reconstruction within **18.23** below are disregarded for this purpose. [*FA 2000, Sch 15 paras 17, 102(3)*].

Individual-owners requirement

Throughout the qualification period, at least **20%** of the issued ordinary share capital of the issuing company must be beneficially owned by one or more 'independent individuals'. An '*independent individual*' is one who is not, at any time during the qualification period when he holds ordinary shares in the issuing company, a director or employee of the investing company or of any company connected with it (within *CTA 2010, s 1122* — see **17** CONNECTED PERSONS), or a relative (i.e. husband, wife, civil partner, forebear or issue) of such a director or employee. Where an independent individual owned shares immediately prior to his death, they are treated for these purposes as continuing to be owned by an independent individual until they cease to form part of the deceased's estate. [*FA 2000, Sch 15 paras 18, 102(3)*].

Partnerships and joint ventures requirement

At no time in the qualification period must the issuing company or any qualifying subsidiary (see below) be a member of a partnership or a party to a joint venture where:

- a trade by reference to which the trading activities requirement (see below) is met by the issuing company is being carried on, or is to be carried on, by the partners in partnership or, as the case may be, by the company or a qualifying subsidiary (see below) as a party to the joint venture;
- the other partners or parties to the joint venture include at least one other company; and
- the same person(s) is/are the beneficial owner(s) of more than 75% of the issued share capital or the ordinary share capital of both the issuing company and at least one of the other partners/parties.

For these purposes, there must be attributed to any person any share capital held by an associate of his (within *FA 2000, Sch 15 para 99*).

[*FA 2000, Sch 15 para 19*].

Qualifying subsidiaries requirement

At no time in the qualification period must the issuing company have a 'subsidiary' other than a 'qualifying subsidiary'. For this purpose, a '*subsidiary*' of a company is any company which it controls (within *CTA 2010, ss 450, 451*), with or without the aid of CONNECTED PERSONS (**17**). A subsidiary is a '*qualifying subsidiary*' of another company (the '*relevant company*') if the following conditions are met.

(a) The subsidiary is a 51% subsidiary (within *CTA 2010, Pt 24 Ch 3*) of the relevant company;
(b) No other person has control (within *CTA 2010, s 1124*) of the subsidiary; and
(c) No arrangements exist whereby (a) or (b) could cease to be satisfied (though see also below).

The fact that a subsidiary or another company is wound up or otherwise dissolved or goes into administration or receivership (both as defined) does not mean the subsidiary ceases to be a qualifying subsidiary, provided that the winding-up etc., and anything done as a consequence of administration or receivership, is for genuine commercial reasons and not part of a tax avoidance scheme or arrangements. Similarly, the fact that arrangements may exist to dispose of the entire interest held in the subsidiary does not prevent the subsidiary from being a qualifying subsidiary of the relevant company if the disposal is to be for commercial reasons and is not to be part of a tax avoidance scheme or arrangements.

[*FA 2000, Sch 15 paras 20, 21, 102(3)(4)*].

Property managing subsidiaries requirement

The issuing company must not have, at any time in the qualification period, a 'property managing subsidiary' other than one which is its 'qualifying 90% subsidiary'. For this purpose, a '*property managing subsidiary*' is a qualifying subsidiary (see above) whose business consists wholly or mainly in the holding or managing of land or any property deriving its value from land (and the terms 'land' and 'property deriving its value from land' have the same meaning as in **41.4** LAND).

A subsidiary is a '*qualifying 90% subsidiary*' of the issuing company if the following conditions are met.

(1) The issuing company possesses at least 90% of the issued share capital of, and the voting power in, the subsidiary, and is beneficially entitled to at least 90% of the assets available for distribution to shareholders on a winding-up etc. and of the profits available for distribution to shareholders;
(2) No other person has control (within *CTA 2010, s 1124*) of the subsidiary; and
(3) No arrangements exist whereby (1) or (2) could cease to be satisfied (though see also below).

The fact that a subsidiary or another company is wound up or otherwise dissolved or goes into administration or receivership (both as defined) does not mean the subsidiary ceases to be a qualifying 90% subsidiary of the issuing company, provided that the winding-up etc., and anything done as a consequence of administration or receivership, is for genuine commercial reasons and not part of a tax avoidance scheme or arrangements. Similarly, the fact that arrangements may exist to dispose of the entire interest held in the subsidiary does not prevent the subsidiary from being a qualifying 90% subsidiary of the issuing company if the disposal is to be for commercial reasons and is not to be part of a tax avoidance scheme or arrangements.

On or after 6 April 2007, a company (company A) is also a qualifying 90% subsidiary of the issuing company if:

- company A would be a qualifying 90% subsidiary of another company (company B) if company B were the issuing company, and company B is a 'qualifying 100% subsidiary' of the issuing company; or
- company A is a qualifying 100% subsidiary of company B and company B is a qualifying 90% subsidiary of the issuing company.

No account is taken for this purpose of any control the issuing company may have of company A. The definition of a qualifying 90% subsidiary is used to define a '*qualifying 100% subsidiary*', replacing the references in that definition to 'at least 90%' with references to '100%'.

[*FA 2000, Sch 15 paras 21A, 23(10)(11), 23A*].

Gross assets requirement

The value of the company's gross assets must not exceed £7 million immediately before the issue of the relevant shares or £8 million immediately afterwards. For shares issued before 6 April 2006 or subscribed for before 22 March 2006 the limits were £15 million immediately before the issue and £16 million immediately afterwards. If the company is the parent company of a group, those limits apply by reference to the aggregate value of the gross assets of the group (disregarding certain assets held by any member of the group which correspond to liabilities of another member). The limits may be amended in the future by Treasury Order. [*FA 2000, Sch 15 paras 22, 101*].

HMRC's approach to the gross assets requirement is the same as for the similar requirement under the EIS (for which see **23.5** ENTERPRISE INVESTMENT SCHEME) (HMRC Statement of Practice 2/06).

Number of employees requirement

The 'full-time equivalent employee number' for the company must be less than 50 at the time the shares are issued. If the company is a parent company, the sum of the full-time equivalent employee numbers for it and each of its qualifying subsidiaries must be less than 50 at that time.

This requirement must be satisfied only in relation to shares issued on or after 19 July 2007.

A company's '*full-time equivalent employee number*' is the number of its full-time employees plus, for each employee who is not full-time, a just and reasonable fraction. Directors count as employees for this purpose, but employees on maternity or paternity leave and students on vocational training are excluded.

[*FA 2000, Sch 15 para 22A*].

HMRC consider that a full-time employee is one whose standard working week (excluding lunch breaks and overtime) is at least 35 hours (HMRC Venture Capital Schemes Manual VCM13120).

Trading activities requirement

Throughout the qualification period, the issuing company must meet the trading activities requirement, which is as follows. If the company is a single company (i.e. neither the parent company of a group nor a subsidiary), it must exist wholly for the purpose of carrying on one or more qualifying trades (see **18.7** below) and must actually be carrying on such a trade or preparing to do so. Purposes having no significant effect (other than in relation to incidental matters) on the extent of the company's activities are disregarded.

If the company is a parent company, the business of the group (treating the activities of the group companies, taken together, as a single business) must not consist wholly or as to a substantial part in any 'non-qualifying activities', and at least one company in the group (which must be either the issuing company or a qualifying 90% subsidiary (see above) of the issuing company) must satisfy the above trading activity requirement for a single company. '*Non-qualifying activities*' means 'excluded activities' (as in **18.7** below, and with similar exceptions in relation to the letting of ships and the receiving of royalties or licence fees) and non-trading activities.

Where the trading activities requirement would otherwise be met by reason of a company *preparing* to carry on a qualifying trade, the requirement is treated as not having been met at any time if that trade does not commence within two years after the issue of the relevant shares. Any carrying on of a trade by a subsidiary before it became a qualifying 90% subsidiary is disregarded in determining when the trade commences for this purpose.

Purposes for which a company exists are disregarded to the extent that they consist of:

- (as regards a single company) the holding and managing of property used by the company for one or more qualifying trades carried on by it;
- (as regards a group company) any activities within (a), (b) or (d) below; or
- (as regards any company) holding shares to which investment relief is attributable (see **18.3** above), unless the holding of such shares is a substantial part of the company's business.

For the purposes of determining the business of a group, activities of a group company are disregarded to the extent that they consist of:

(a) holding shares in or securities of, or making loans to, another group company;

(b) holding and managing property used by a group company for the purposes of one or more qualifying trades carried on by a group company;

(c) holding shares to which investment relief is attributable (see **18.3** above), unless the holding of such shares is a substantial part of the company's business; or

(d) incidental activities of a company which meets the above trading activities requirement for a single company.

A company does not cease to meet the trading activities requirement purely by reason of it or a qualifying subsidiary (see above) being wound up or otherwise dissolved, provided that the winding-up or dissolution is for commercial reasons and not part of a tax avoidance scheme or arrangements. A similar let-out applies in relation to a company or its qualifying subsidiary going into administration or receivership (both as defined) and to anything done as a consequence thereof.

Amendments to the trading activities requirement (including the provisions at **18.7** below) may be made in the future by Treasury Order.

[*FA 2000, Sch 15 paras 23, 24, 101, 102(1)(4)(8)*].

Qualifying trades

[18.7] A trade is a qualifying trade (see the trading activities requirement at **18.6** above) if:

(i) it is carried on wholly or mainly in the UK;
(ii) it is conducted on a commercial basis and with a view to profit; and
(iii) it does not consist wholly or as to a 'substantial' part in the carrying on of any 'excluded activities' (see below).

In considering the requirement at (i) above, HMRC will take into account the totality of the activities of the trade; a company can satisfy the requirement if the major part of the trade, i.e. over half of the trading activity, taken as a whole, is carried on within the UK. See HMRC Statement of Practice 3/00. '*Substantial*' in (iii) above is not defined, but where, judged by any measure which is reasonable in the circumstances (for instance turnover or capital employed), excluded activities account for not more than 20% of the activities of the trade as a whole, HMRC do not regard them as amounting to a substantial part of the trade (HMRC Venture Capital Schemes Manual VCM3010).

Activities of research and development (within *CTA 2010, s 1138*) from which it is intended that a 'connected qualifying trade' will be derived or will benefit are treated as a notional qualifying trade, but preparing to carry on such activities is not treated as preparing to carry on a qualifying trade. A '*connected qualifying trade*' is a qualifying trade carried on either by the company carrying out the research and development or, where applicable, by another member of the group (which must be either the issuing company or a qualifying 90% subsidiary (see **18.6** above) of the issuing company).

'*Excluded activities*' are as follows:

(a) dealing in land, commodities or futures, or in shares, securities or other financial instruments;
(b) dealing in goods otherwise than in an ordinary trade of wholesale or retail distribution (for more detail, see the similar exclusion at **23.9** ENTERPRISE INVESTMENT SCHEME);
(c) banking, insurance, money-lending, debt-factoring, hire purchase financing or other financial activities;
(d) leasing or receiving royalties or licence fees (see further below);
(e) providing legal or accountancy services;
(f) property development (see further below);
(g) farming or market gardening;
(h) holding, managing or occupying woodlands, any other forestry activities or timber production;
(i) (for shares issued on or after 6 April 2008) shipbuilding within the meaning of the EU Framework on state aid to shipbuilding (2003/C 317/06 published in the Official Journal on 30 December 2003);
(j) (for shares issued on or after 6 April 2008) producing or extracting 'coal' (as defined in Council Regulation (EC) No 1407/2002, Article 2);
(k) (for shares issued on or after 6 April 2008) producing any of the steel products listed in Annex 1 to the EU Guidelines on national regional aid (2006/C 54/08 published in the Official Journal on 4 March 2006);
(l) operating or managing hotels or comparable establishments (including guest houses, hostels and other establishments whose main purpose is to offer overnight accommodation with or without catering) or property used as such (see further below);

(m) operating or managing nursing homes or residential care homes (both as defined) or property used as such (see further below);

(n) providing services or facilities for any business consisting to a substantial extent of activities within (a)–(m) above and carried on by another person, where a person has a controlling interest (see below) in both that business and the business of the provider company.

The term 'leasing' in (d) above includes the letting of ships on charter or other assets on hire. A trade will be not be excluded by reason only of its consisting of letting ships, other than pleasure craft (as defined) or offshore installations (within *CTA 2010, s 1132*), on charter, provided certain conditions are satisfied.

As regards the receiving of royalties or licence fees (see (d) above), a trade is not excluded from being a qualifying trade solely because at some time in the qualification period (see **18.2** above) it consists to a substantial extent in the receiving of royalties or licence fees substantially attributable (in terms of value) to the exploitation of intangible assets, such as intellectual property, which have been created by the issuing company or one of its qualifying subsidiaries (slightly different rules applying before 6 April 2007) — for more details, see the similar let-out at **23.9** ENTERPRISE INVESTMENT SCHEME.

As regards (f) above, see the comments at **23.9** ENTERPRISE INVESTMENT SCHEME, which apply equally here. The exclusions at (m) and (n) above apply only if the person carrying on the activity has an estate or interest (e.g. a lease) in the property concerned or occupies that property.

As regards (p) above, see the comparable exclusion at **23.9** ENTERPRISE INVESTMENT SCHEME as regards the meaning of 'controlling interest', which applies similarly here.

[*FA 2000, Sch 15 paras 25–33, 102(1)*].

As regards (e) above, the provision of accounting staff by a company to a firm of accountants was held in an EIS case to be synonymous with the provision of accountancy services, with the result that the company's trade was not a qualifying trade (*Castleton Management Service Ltd v Kirkwood* (Sp C 276), [2001] SSCD 95).

General requirements

[18.8] For investment relief to be available in respect of the relevant shares (see **18.2** above), the following requirements (see **18.2**(d) above) must be met as to the shares, the maximum amount raised annually through risk capital schemes, the use of money raised by the issue, the absence of pre-arranged exits and the absence of a tax avoidance motive. [*FA 2000, Sch 15 para 34*].

The shares

The relevant shares must be ordinary, fully paid up, shares and must be subscribed for wholly in cash. Shares are not fully paid up for this purpose if there is any undertaking to pay cash to any person at a future date in respect of the acquisition of the shares. At no time in the qualification period (see **18.2** above) must the shares carry any present or future preferential right to dividends or to assets on a winding-up, or any present or future right to be redeemed. [*FA 2000, Sch 15 para 35*].

The maximum amount raised annually through risk capital schemes

Subject to the commencement provisions below, the total amount of 'relevant investments' in the company and its subsidiaries in the year ending with the date of issue of the relevant shares must not exceed £2 million. Investments in subsidiaries count towards the limit if the company concerned was a subsidiary of the issuing company at any time in the year and whether or not it was a subsidiary at the time of the investment.

A '*relevant investment*' in a company is made if:

(i) an investment of any kind in the company is made by a VENTURE CAPITAL TRUST (**71**); or

(ii) the company issues shares (money having been subscribed for them) and provides HMRC with an ENTERPRISE INVESTMENT SCHEME (**23**) compliance statement under *ITA 2007, s 205* or a CVS compliance statement (see **18.4** above) in respect of the shares.

Investments within (ii) above are treated as made when the shares concerned are issued.

An investment made by a VCT is not a relevant investment within (i) above if it is made before 6 April 2007 or if it is an investment of money raised by the issue of shares or securities of the VCT before that date or of money derived from the investment of such money. An issue of shares before 19 July 2007 or to the 'managers of an approved fund' (see **23.2** ENTERPRISE INVESTMENT SCHEME) which closed before that date is not a relevant investment within (ii) above.

[*FA 2000, Sch 15 para 35A*].

Use of money raised

The money raised by the 'relevant issue of shares' must be employed wholly (disregarding any insignificant amount) for the purposes of a 'relevant trade' within two years after the issue, and, for shares issued before 22 April 2009, 80% of that money must be so employed within 12 months after the issue. These two-year and 12-month periods begin with the date of commencement of the relevant trade where this is later than the date of issue. This applies in relation to shares issued on or after 7 March 2001, and also applies on and after that date in relation to shares issued before then to which investment relief was attributable (see **18.3** above) immediately before that date. Previously, *all* the money had to be so employed within the said 12-month period. Any carrying on of the relevant trade by a subsidiary before it became a qualifying 90% subsidiary (see **18.6** above) is disregarded in determining the date of commencement of the relevant trade for this purpose.

For these purposes, employing money for the purposes of *preparing* to carry on a trade (other than a notional trade of research and development — see **18.7** above) is equivalent to employing it for the purposes of a trade.

The '*relevant issue of shares*' means the issue of shares which includes the relevant shares. A '*relevant trade*' is a trade by reference to which the issuing company meets the trading activities requirement in **18.6** above. Where the trade by reference to which the trading activities requirement is met is a notional trade of research and development (see **18.7** above), the term 'relevant trade' also refers to any qualifying trade which is derived or benefits from that notional trade and is carried on by the issuing company or a qualifying 90% subsidiary (see **18.6** above); in this case, all the money raised by the issue must be employed for the purposes of that trade before the third anniversary of the date of issue of the shares (notwithstanding that a later date may be given by the rules above), and the 80% requirement does not apply.

[*FA 2000, Sch 15 paras 36, 102(8)*].

No pre-arranged exits

The arrangements (as very broadly defined) under which the relevant shares are issued to the investing company (including arrangements preceding the issue but relating to it and, in certain cases, arrangements made on or after the issue and within the qualification period) must not:

(a) provide for the eventual disposal by the investing company of the relevant shares or other shares or securities of the issuing company;
(b) provide for the eventual cessation of a trade of the issuing company or a person connected with it;
(c) provide for the eventual disposal of all, or a substantial part of, the assets of the issuing company or of a person connected with it; or
(d) provide (by means of any insurance, indemnity, guarantee or otherwise) partial or complete protection for investors against the normal risks attaching to the investment (but excluding commercial arrangements which merely protect the issuing company and/or its subsidiaries against normal business risks).

Arrangements with a view to a company reconstruction within **18.23** below are excluded from (a) above. Arrangements applicable only on an unanticipated winding-up of the issuing company for commercial reasons are excluded from (b) and (c) above.

[*FA 2000, Sch 15 paras 37, 102(1)*].

No tax avoidance motive

The relevant shares must be issued for commercial reasons and not as part of a tax avoidance scheme or arrangement. [*FA 2000, Sch 15 para 38*].

Withdrawal or reduction of investment relief

[18.9] Investment relief falls to be withdrawn or reduced on a disposal of the relevant shares (see **18.10** below), if value is received in respect of the shares (see **18.11–18.14** below), or on the grant of certain options relating to the shares (see **18.15** below).

Where investment relief given falls to be withdrawn or reduced, and also where it is found not to have been due, the withdrawal etc. is achieved by means of an assessment for the accounting period of the investing company *in which the relief was given*. For relief to be withdrawn on the grounds that the issuing company is not a qualifying issuing company (see **18.6** above), or that the general requirements at **18.8** above are not met, or by virtue of value received by the investing company (see **18.11** below) or other persons (see **18.14** below), certain statutory notice procedures must be followed. The investing company may give notice of appeal, within 30 days, against an HMRC notice pending withdrawal of relief on such grounds (as if the giving of that notice were the disallowance of a claim other than for discharge or repayment of tax — see **13.3** CLAIMS).

(Subject to the extended time limits at **6.14** ASSESSMENTS) HMRC cannot make an assessment to withdraw (or reduce) investment relief, or give statutory notice pending withdrawal of relief on the above-mentioned grounds, more than six years after the end of whichever is the later of the following accounting periods:

- the accounting period in which falls the deadline for employing money raised by the issue of the shares (see **18.8** above);
- the accounting period in which occurs the event giving rise to withdrawal (or reduction) of relief.

In most cases, interest on overdue tax runs from the date of the event giving rise to withdrawal (or reduction) of relief, if this is later than the normal due date, or the latest such date, for payment of corporation tax for the accounting period for which the assessment is made (see **51.4** PAYMENT OF TAX).

[*FA 2000, Sch 15 paras 60–63*].

Information

Certain events giving rise to withdrawal or reduction of investment relief must be notified to HMRC, generally within 60 days, by the investing company or the issuing company (or any person connected with the issuing company and having knowledge of the matter), as the case may be. HMRC have power to require information from such persons where they have reason to believe that such notice should have been given or from a person whom they believe to have given or received value which would have triggered a requirement to give such notice but for the amount of value being insignificant (see **18.11** below). The penalty provisions of *TMA 1970, s 98* apply in the event of non-compliance with these information provisions. [*FA 2000, Sch 15 paras 64–66, Sch 16 para 1*].

Disposal

[18.10] Where, during the qualification period (see **18.2** above), the investing company disposes of any shares to which relief is attributable (see **18.3** above) and which it has held continuously since their issue (see **18.19**(a) below), relief is withdrawn or reduced as set out below. See **18.9** above re consequences of withdrawal etc.

If the disposal is either:

- by way of bargain at arm's length; or

- by way of a distribution on a dissolution or winding-up of the issuing company; or
- a disposal within *TCGA 1992, s 24(1)* (entire loss, destruction etc. of asset — see **10.2** CAPITAL SUMS DERIVED FROM ASSETS); or
- a deemed disposal under *TCGA 1992, s 24(2)* (assets of negligible value — see **44.11** LOSSES),

the relief attributable to the shares disposed of is withdrawn, or is reduced by 20% of the disposal consideration (if such reduction would not amount to full withdrawal). If the relief initially obtained was less than 20% of the amount subscribed for those shares (i.e. because the company's corporation tax liability was insufficient to fully absorb the available relief), the reduction is correspondingly restricted.

In the case of any other disposal, for example a transaction not at arm's length, the relief attributable to the shares disposed of is withdrawn.

[*FA 2000, Sch 15 para 46*].

For the above purposes, shares are regarded as being disposed of if they are so regarded for the purposes of corporation tax on chargeable gains, and see also **18.22** below (certain company reconstructions treated as disposals). [*FA 2000, Sch 15 para 96*]. In the case of a part disposal, see **18.16** below for the rules for identifying shares disposed of.

Value received by investing company

[18.11] Subject to **18.13** below (replacement value), where during the 'period of restriction' the investing company 'receives value' (see **18.12** below), other than an 'amount of insignificant value', from the issuing company, investment relief attributable to the relevant shares is withdrawn, or is reduced by 20% of the amount of value received (if such reduction would not amount to full withdrawal). If the relief initially obtained was less than 20% of the amount subscribed for those shares (i.e. because the company's corporation tax liability was insufficient to fully absorb the available relief), the reduction is correspondingly restricted. These provisions apply equally to receipts of value by and from persons connected (within *CTA 2010, s 1122* — see **17** CONNECTED PERSONS), at any time in the period of restriction, with the investing company or, as the case may be, the issuing company. See **18.12** below for the meaning of 'value received' and the determination of the amount of value received. See **18.9** above for consequences of withdrawal etc.

The '*period of restriction*' in relation to the relevant shares is the period beginning one year before their issue and ending at the end of the qualification period in **18.2** above.

Where two or more issues of shares have been made by the same issuing company to the same investing company, in relation to each of which investment relief is claimed, and value is received during a period of restriction relating to more than one such issue, the value received is apportioned between them by reference to the amounts subscribed for each of those issues.

An '*amount of insignificant value*' is an amount of value which:

- does not exceed £1,000, or
- in any other case is insignificant in relation to the amount subscribed by the investing company for the relevant shares.

If at any time in the period beginning one year before the date of issue of the relevant shares and ending with the date of issue, there are in existence arrangements (as very broadly defined) providing for the investing company to receive, or become entitled to receive, any value from the issuing company at any time in the period of restriction (see above), no amount of value received by the investing company is treated as an amount of insignificant value.

There are provisions to aggregate a receipt of value, whether insignificant or not, with amounts of insignificant value received previously, and treating that aggregate, if it is not itself an amount of insignificant value, as an amount of value received at the time of the latest actual receipt.

Where relief is withdrawn or reduced by reason of a disposal (see **18.10** above), the investing company is not treated as receiving value from the issuing company in respect of the disposal.

[*FA 2000, Sch 15 paras 47, 48, 51–53, 102(1)*].

Meaning of, and amount of, value received

[18.12] The investing company '*receives value*' from the issuing company if the latter (and see **18.11** above re connected persons):

(a) repays, redeems or repurchases any part of the investing company's holding of the issuing company's share capital or securities, or makes any payment to the investing company in respect of the cancellation of any of the issuing company's share capital or any security;

(b) repays, in pursuance of any arrangements for or in connection with the acquisition of the relevant shares, any debt owed to the investing company other than one incurred by the issuing company on or after the date of issue of the shares and otherwise than in consideration of the extinguishment of a debt incurred before that date;

(c) makes any payment to the investing company in respect of the cancellation of any debt owed to it;

(d) releases or waives any liability of the investing company to the issuing company (which it is deemed to have done if discharge of the liability is twelve months or more overdue) or discharges, or undertakes to discharge, any liability of the investing company to a third person;

(e) makes a loan or advance to the investing company which has not been repaid in full before the issue of the relevant shares; for this purpose a loan includes any debt incurred, other than an ordinary trade debt (as defined), and any debt due to a third person which is assigned to the issuing company;

(f) provides a benefit or facility for the directors or employees of the investing company or any of their associates (as defined), except in circumstances such that, if a *payment* had been made of equal value, it would have been a 'qualifying payment';

(g) disposes of an asset to the investing company for no consideration or for consideration less than market value (as defined), or acquires an asset from the investing company for consideration exceeding market value; or

(h) makes a payment to the investing company other than a 'qualifying payment'.

References above to a debt or liability do not include one which would be discharged by making a 'qualifying payment'. References to a payment or disposal include one made indirectly to, or to the order of, or for the benefit of, the person in question.

Each of the following is a '*qualifying payment*':

(i) a reasonable (in relation to their market value) payment for any goods, services or facilities provided by the investing company in the course of trade or otherwise;

(ii) the payment of interest at no more than a reasonable commercial rate on money lent;

(iii) the payment of a dividend or other distribution which represents no more than a normal return on investment;

(iv) a payment to acquire an asset at no more than its market value;

(v) a payment not exceeding a reasonable and commercial rent for property occupied;

(vi) a payment discharging an ordinary trade debt.

The *amount of value received* is:

- in a case within (a), (b) or (c) above, the amount received or, if greater, the market value of the shares, securities or debt in question;
- in a case within (d) above, the amount of the liability;
- in a case within (e) above, the amount of the loan etc. less any amount repaid before the issue of the relevant shares;
- in a case within (f) above, the cost (net of any consideration given for it by the recipient or his associate) of providing the benefit etc.;
- in a case within (g) above, the difference between market value and the consideration received (if any); and
- in a case within (h) above, the amount of the payment.

[*FA 2000, Sch 15 paras 49, 50, 99, 102(5)*].

Replacement value

[18.13] The provisions at **18.11** above are disapplied if the person from whom the value was received (the '*original supplier*') receives, by way of a 'qualifying receipt' and whether before or after the original receipt of value, at least equivalent replacement value from the original recipient. A receipt is a '*qualifying receipt*' if it arises by reason of:

(a) any one, or any combination, of the following:

   (i) a payment by the original recipient to the original supplier other than an 'excepted payment';

   (ii) the acquisition of an asset by the original recipient from the original supplier for consideration exceeding market value (as defined);

(iii) the disposal of an asset by the original recipient to the original supplier for no consideration or for consideration less than market value; or

(b) (where the original receipt of value falls within **18.12**(d) above) an event having the effect of reversing the original event.

The amount of replacement value is:

- in a case within (a) above, the amount of any such payment plus the difference between the market value of any such asset and the consideration received; and
- in a case within (b) above, the same as the amount of the original value.

The receipt of replacement value is disregarded if:

- it occurs before the start of the period of restriction (see **18.11** above);
- there was an unreasonable delay in its occurrence; or
- it occurs more than 60 days after the relief falling to be withdrawn (or reduced) has been determined on appeal.

Each of the following is an '*excepted payment*' for the purposes of (a)(i) above:

(1) a reasonable (in relation to their market value) payment for any goods, services or facilities provided (in the course of trade or otherwise) by the original supplier;
(2) a payment of interest at no more than a reasonable commercial rate on money lent to the original recipient;
(3) a payment not exceeding a reasonable and commercial rent for property occupied by the original recipient;
(4) a payment within **18.12**(iii)(iv) or (vi) above;
(5) a payment for any shares or securities in any company in circumstances not within (a)(ii) above.

Each reference in (1)–(3) above to the original supplier or recipient includes a reference to any person who at *any* time in the period of restriction is an associate (as defined) of his or connected with him (within *CTA 2010, s 1122* — see **17** CONNECTED PERSONS).

Where:

- the receipt of replacement value is a qualifying receipt (as above), and
- the event giving rise to the receipt is (or includes) a subscription for shares by the investing company or a person connected (as above) with it at any time in the period of restriction,

the subscriber is not eligible for investment relief, EIS income tax relief or EIS capital gains deferral relief in relation to those shares or any other shares in the same issue.

Any apportionment made as in **18.11** above (where there are two or more share issues) is taken not to reduce the original value for the above purposes.

[*FA 2000, Sch 15 paras 54, 55, 99, 102(3)(5)*].

Value received by other persons

[18.14] Investment relief is withdrawn (or reduced) in certain cases of value received by persons other than the investing company (see **18.9** above re consequences of withdrawal etc.). This applies where, during the period of restriction (as in **18.11** above), the issuing company or a 'subsidiary':

(a) repays, redeems or repurchases any part of its share capital belonging to a member (other than the investing company) who does not thereby suffer a withdrawal or reduction of any investment relief, EIS income tax relief or EIS capital gains deferral relief attributable to his shares; or
(b) makes any payment to any such member in respect of the cancellation of any of the share capital of the issuing company or subsidiary.

The fact that no withdrawal or reduction of the kind referred to in (a) above falls to be made is disregarded if this is due only to the insignificance of the value received (see, for example, **18.11** above).

The investment relief attributable to the relevant shares held by the investing company is withdrawn, or is reduced by 20% of the amount received by the member (if such reduction would not amount to full withdrawal). If the relief initially obtained was less than 20% of the amount subscribed for those shares (i.e. because the company's corporation tax liability was insufficient to fully absorb the available relief), the reduction is correspondingly restricted. The amount received is also apportioned between investing companies (by reference to amounts subscribed) where the receipt of value causes a withdrawal or reduction of more than one such company's investment relief. Where the receipt of value falls into overlapping periods of restriction in relation to more than one issue of shares which includes shares to which investment relief is attributable, the value received is similarly apportioned between issues.

If the amount received by the member in question is insignificant in relation to the remaining issued share capital of the issuing company or, as the case may be, subsidiary, it is disregarded. In applying this test, the market value, immediately before the event concerned, of the shares to which the event relates is substituted for the amount received if this would give a greater amount. The assumption is made that the shares in question are cancelled at the time of the event. This let-out does not apply if at any time in the period beginning one year before the date of issue of the relevant shares and ending with the date of issue, there are in existence arrangements (as very broadly defined) providing for a payment within these provisions to be made, or entitlement to such a payment to come into being, at any time in the period of restriction.

For the above purposes, a '*subsidiary*' is a company which is a 51% subsidiary of the issuing company at any time in the period of restriction, whether or not at the time of receipt of value.

The above provisions do not apply to the redemption, within twelve months of issue, of any share capital of nominal value equal to the authorised minimum issued to comply with *Companies Act 1985, s 117* (or NI equivalent).

[*FA 2000, Sch 15 paras 56–58, 102(1); SI 2008 No 954, Art 26*].

Put options and call options

[18.15] Where there is granted during the qualification period (see **18.2** above):

- an option, the exercise of which would bind the grantor to purchase any of the relevant shares from the investing company, or
- an option, the exercise of which would bind the grantor, in this case the investing company, to sell any of the relevant shares,

investment relief attributable (see **18.3** above) to those of the relevant shares which would (on given assumptions) be treated as disposed of on exercise of the option is withdrawn. See **18.9** above re consequences of withdrawal.

[*FA 2000, Sch 15 para 59*].

Identification rules

[18.16] The rules below apply, for the purpose of identifying shares disposed of, where a company makes a part disposal of a holding of shares of the same class in the same company, and the holding includes shares to which investment relief is attributable (see **18.3** above) and which have been held continuously (see **18.18**(a) below) since the time of issue. The rules apply for the purposes of the corporate venturing scheme and for the purposes of corporation tax on chargeable gains generally. The normal rules at **64.3** SHARES AND SECURITIES — IDENTIFICATION RULES are disapplied.

Where shares comprised in the holding have been acquired on different days, a disposal is identified with acquisitions on a first in/first out basis. In matching the shares disposed of with shares acquired on a particular day, shares to which investment relief is attributable and which have been held continuously since issue are treated as being disposed of *after* any other shares acquired on that day.

If, on a reorganisation of share capital (e.g. a scrip issue), a new holding falls, by virtue of *TCGA 1992, s 127* (or any other chargeable gains enactment which applies that *section* — see, for example, **63.2, 63.5, 63.7, 63.8** SHARES AND SECURITIES, and see also **18.21** below), to be equated with the original shares, shares comprised in the new holding are deemed for the above purposes to have been acquired when the original shares were acquired.

[*FA 2000, Sch 15 para 93*].

Chargeable gains and allowable losses

[18.17] A gain on the disposal at any time by the investing company of shares to which investment relief is attributable (see **18.3** above) is a chargeable gain, though see **18.20** below as regards possibility of deferral relief. A loss on such a disposal is an allowable loss — see **18.18** below as to the computation of the loss and **18.19** below as regards possibility of setting the loss against income rather than gains. For the rules for identifying disposals with acquisitions, see **18.16** above.

Computation of allowable loss

[18.18] If a loss would otherwise accrue on a disposal by the investing company of shares to which investment relief is attributable, and the investment relief does not fall to be withdrawn (as opposed to reduced) as a result of the disposal (see **18.9** above), the company's acquisition cost for the purposes of corporation tax on chargeable gains is reduced by the amount of investment relief attributable to the shares immediately after the disposal, but not so as to convert the loss into a chargeable gain. This applies only if the condition at **18.19**(a) below (shares held continuously) is met from issue to disposal. [*FA 2000, Sch 15 para 94*].

Set-off of allowable loss against income

[18.19] Subject to all the conditions at (a)–(c) below being satisfied and a claim being made, an allowable loss, on a disposal by the investing company of shares to which investment relief is attributable (see **18.3** above), may be set against *income* (as an alternative to setting it against chargeable gains in the normal way — see **14.6** COMPANIES). The loss is as computed after applying the reduction at **18.18** above. The conditions are as follows.

(a) The shares must have been held continuously by the company from time of issue to time of disposal. If, during any period,
   - the company was deemed under any provision of *TCGA 1992* to have disposed of and immediately reacquired the shares; or,
   - following a scheme of reconstruction within *TCGA 1992, s 136* — see **63.7** SHARES AND SECURITIES (or which would have been within that section but for the provisions at **4.15** ANTI-AVOIDANCE), the company was deemed by virtue of **18.22** below to have made a disposal of shares which it retained under the scheme;

   it is not treated for the purposes of the corporate venturing scheme provisions as having held the shares continuously throughout that period.
(b) The investment relief must not fall to be withdrawn (as opposed to reduced) as a result of the disposal.
(c) The disposal must be either:
   - by way of bargain at arm's length for full consideration; or
   - by way of a distribution on a dissolution or winding-up of the issuing company; or
   - a disposal within *TCGA 1992, s 24(1)* (entire loss, destruction etc. of asset — see **10.2** CAPITAL SUMS DERIVED FROM ASSETS); or
   - a deemed disposal under *TCGA 1992, s 24(2)* (assets of negligible value — see **44.11** LOSSES).

The set-off is against income of the accounting period in which the loss is incurred. As regards any unrelieved balance, the claim may be extended to income of accounting periods ending within the 12 months immediately preceding the accounting period in which the loss is incurred. Income of an accounting period beginning before, and ending within, that 12 months is apportioned on a time basis so as to exclude income thereby deemed to have accrued prior to that 12-month period. The income of each accounting period included in the claim is treated as reduced by the loss, or by so much of it as cannot be relieved in a later accounting period. Where claims are made to relieve two or more losses, they are relieved in the order in which they were incurred. Relief is given before any relief claimed under *CTA 2010, Pt 4 Ch 5* (loss incurred by investment company on disposal of unlisted shares — see **44.18** LOSSES) and before any deduction for charges on income or other deductible amounts. Once relief has been obtained under these provisions for an amount of loss, that amount cannot be relieved under *CTA 2010, s 70* or against chargeable gains.

Claims must be made within two years after the end of the accounting period in which the loss is incurred.

Where a claim is made under these provisions, *TCGA 1992, s 30* (value shifting to give tax-free benefit) has effect in relation to the disposal if *any* benefit is conferred, whether tax-free or not. No loss relief against income is available if the disposal is the result of a company reconstruction effected for tax avoidance rather than commercial reasons, such that it falls within the ambit of **4.15** ANTI-AVOIDANCE.

[*FA 2000, Sch 15 paras 67–72, 97*].

Example

X Ltd draws up accounts each year to 31 December. The company subscribes for 50,000 shares in Y Ltd for £50,000 in July 2006. Y Ltd commences to trade at that time. The investment qualifies for corporate venturing scheme investment relief of £10,000 which X Ltd is able to claim in full. It sells the shares in July 2011 for £20,000, having held the shares continuously since July 2006. X Ltd's trading profits for the year ended 31 December 2011 are £12,000, and those for the year ended 31 December 2010 are £6,000. The company has no other income or chargeable gains for either year.

X Ltd may claim relief for its loss on the Y Ltd shares as follows:

	£	£
Disposal proceeds		20,000
Deduct acquisition cost	50,000	
Less investment relief	10,000	40,000
Allowable loss		£20,000

£12,000 of the loss may be set off against the income of the year ended 31 December 2011, and £6,000 against the income of the year ended 31 December 2010. The balance of the loss (£2,000) is carried forward to the year ended 31 December 2012 as a capital loss, relievable against chargeable gains only.

Deferral relief

[18.20] Deferral relief is available where a chargeable gain would otherwise accrue to the investing company:

- on a disposal of shares to which investment relief was attributable (see **18.3** above) immediately before the disposal and which satisfy the condition at **18.19**(a) above (shares held continuously) from issue to disposal; or
- on the occurrence of a chargeable event under these provisions,

and the company makes a 'qualifying investment'. A '*qualifying investment*' is a subscription for shares ('*qualifying shares*') on which investment relief is obtained under the corporate venturing scheme, other than shares issued by a 'prohibited company'. The qualifying shares must be issued to the investing company within the one year immediately preceding or the three years immediately following the time the chargeable gain in question accrues. If the qualifying shares are issued *before* the gain accrues, they must have been held continuously (see **18.19**(a) above) by the investing company from issue until the time the gain accrues, and investment relief must still be attributable to them. A '*prohibited company*' means either:

(a) the company whose shares are disposed of or, or as the case may be, in relation to whose shares the chargeable event occurred; or
(b) a company which, when the gain accrues or when the qualifying shares are issued, is a member of the same group as the company in (a) above.

Deferral relief is said to be 'attributable to shares' if expenditure on those shares has been used to defer the whole or part of a chargeable gain and no chargeable event has occurred resulting in the deferred gain being brought back into charge.

The following themselves become qualifying shares:

- any bonus shares, issued in respect of the qualifying shares and being shares in the same company, of the same class and carrying the same rights;
- any shares issued on a company reconstruction within **18.23** below in exchange for qualifying shares.

Postponement of the original gain

On a claim by the investing company, the whole or part of the chargeable gain can be deferred. The amount to be deferred is the lower of:

- the amount of the gain (or the amount remaining in charge after any previous deferral relief claim);
- the amount subscribed for the qualifying shares (to the extent that it has not been used in previous deferral relief claims); and
- the amount specified by the company in the claim.

No time limit is specified for making a claim, so the general six-year time limit applies as in **13.5** CLAIMS.

Deferred gain becoming chargeable

The deferred gain will become chargeable on the occurrence of, *and at the time of*, one of the following chargeable events:

(i) a disposal of qualifying shares by the investing company; or

(ii) any other event giving rise to a withdrawal of, or reduction in, the investment relief attributable to qualifying shares (see **18.9** above).

If the qualifying investment is made before the gain accrues, any reduction made by reason of an event occurring before the gain accrues is disregarded for the purposes of (ii) above.

The chargeable gain accruing to the investing company at the time of the chargeable event is equal to so much of the deferred gain as is attributable to the shares in relation to which the chargeable event occurs. For these purposes, a proportionate part of the net deferred gain (i.e. the deferred gain less any amount brought into charge on an earlier chargeable event, e.g. a part disposal) is attributed to each of the qualifying shares held immediately before the chargeable event. Thus, a part disposal of qualifying shares brings into charge a proportionate part of the deferred gain.

Provision is made to ensure that a previously deferred gain accruing as above is brought into charge under *TCGA 1992, s 10B* (see **49.3** OVERSEAS MATTERS) in the case of a non-UK resident company carrying on a trade or vocation through a UK permanent establishment (previously a branch or agency).

[*FA 2000, Sch 15 paras 73–79*].

Example

Z Ltd, which makes up accounts to 31 March each year, sells its shares in F Ltd (to which CVS investment relief is attributable) in January 2007, realising a chargeable gain of £100,000. Z Ltd makes the following investments in shares, all of which qualify for CVS investment relief:

(i) 10,000 shares in K Ltd for £10,000 in July 2006;

(ii) 10,000 shares in L Ltd for £50,000 in February 2007;

(iii) 25,000 shares in M Ltd for £50,000 in January 2008;

(iv) 10,000 shares in S Ltd for £100,000 in January 2010.

Z Ltd can claim up to a total amount of £100,000 in deferral relief in respect of the gain on the F Ltd shares by setting corresponding amounts of expenditure on the share issues in (i), (ii) or (iii) against it. It need not defer the gain against the earliest acquisition, so it can claim to defer the full amount of the gain against (ii) and (iii) only if it wishes. The company cannot defer any of the gain against (iv) because the S Ltd shares are not issued in the period beginning one year before and ending three years after the chargeable gain accrued.

Z Ltd chooses to defer the gain against the shares in K Ltd (£10,000), L Ltd (£50,000) and M Ltd (£40,000), but sells half of the shares in M Ltd in March 2009 for £35,000. It makes no other disposals of assets in the year ended 31 March 2009.

Z Ltd's chargeable gains for the year ended 31 March 2009 are:

M Ltd shares

	£
Disposal proceeds	35,000
Less acquistion cost £50,000 × $^1/_2$	25,000
Unindexed gain	10,000
Less indexation £25,000 @ say 10%	2,500

Chargeable gain	£7,500
F Ltd shares	
Deferred gain revived £40,000 × 1/2	£20,000
Taxable gains y/e 31.3.09 (£7,500 + £20,000)	£27,500

Company restructuring

Reorganisations of share capital

[18.21] The following applies where a company holds shares in another company, being shares of the same class, held in the same capacity and forming part of the ordinary share capital of that other company, and there is a reorganisation within the meaning of *TCGA 1992, s 126* (see **63.2** SHARES AND SECURITIES). If the shares fall within two or more of the categories below, *TCGA 1992, s 127* (see **63.2** SHARES AND SECURITIES), or, where appropriate, *TCGA 1992, s 116* (reorganisations involving QUALIFYING CORPORATE BONDS (**54.4**)), applies separately to each category. (This is subject to the disapplication of those provisions in the circumstances set out below.) The categories are:

- shares to which deferral relief is attributable (see **18.20** above);
- shares to which investment relief, but not deferral relief, is attributable (see **18.3** above) and which have been held continuously (see **18.19**(a) above) by the company since they were issued; and
- shares in neither of the categories above.

[*FA 2000, Sch 15 para 80*].

Rights issues etc.

Where:

- a reorganisation (within *TCGA 1992, s 126* — see **63.2** SHARES AND SECURITIES) involves an allotment of shares or debentures in respect of and in proportion to an existing holding;
- investment relief is attributable (see **18.3** above) to the shares in the existing holding or to the allotted shares; and
- if investment relief is attributable to the shares in the existing holding, those shares have been held continuously (see **18.19**(a) above) by the company since they were issued,

the share reorganisation rules of *TCGA 1992, ss 127–130* (see **63.2** SHARES AND SECURITIES) are disapplied. The effect is that the allotted shares are treated as a separate holding acquired at the time of the reorganisation. This does not apply in the case of bonus shares where these are issued in respect of shares comprised in the existing holding and are of the same class and carry the same rights as those shares.

If, in a case otherwise within **54.4** QUALIFYING CORPORATE BONDS:

- the old asset consists of shares to which investment relief is attributable and which have been held continuously (see **18.19**(a) above) by the company since they were issued, and

- the new asset consists of a qualifying corporate bond,

the usual treatment is disapplied. The effect is that the investing company is deemed to have disposed of the shares at the time of the relevant transaction, and the resulting chargeable gain or allowable loss crystallises *at that time*.

[*FA 2000, Sch 15 para 81*].

Company reconstructions

[18.22] Subject to **18.23** below, *TCGA 1992, s 135* (exchange of securities for those in another company — see **63.5** SHARES AND SECURITIES) and *s 136* (schemes of reconstruction involving issue of securities — see **63.7** SHARES AND SECURITIES), which equate the new holding with the original shares, are disapplied in the following circumstances:

- a company holds shares in another company (Company A),
- investment relief is attributable (see **18.3** above) to those shares,
- those shares have been held continuously (see **18.19**(a) above) by the investing company since they were issued, and
- there is a reconstruction whereby a third company issues shares or debentures in exchange for, or in respect of, Company A shares or debentures.

The result is that the transaction is treated, both for the purposes of the corporate venturing scheme provisions and for the purposes of corporation tax on chargeable gains generally, as a disposal of the original shares (and an acquisition of a new holding).

[*FA 2000, Sch 15 paras 82, 96*].

Issuing company becoming wholly-owned subsidiary of new holding company

[18.23] Notwithstanding **18.22** above, *TCGA 1992, s 135* is not disapplied (and there is thus no disposal and acquisition) where, by means entirely of an exchange of shares, all the shares in one company (the '*old shares*') are acquired by another company, and the conditions below are satisfied. Following such a share exchange, the shares thereby issued by the acquiring company (the '*new shares*') stand in place of the old shares, so that:

- any investment relief or deferral relief attributable to the old shares (see, respectively, **16.4**, **18.20** above) is attributed to the new shares for which they were exchanged;
- the new shares are treated as having been issued at the time the old shares were issued and as having been held continuously (see **18.19**(a) above) by the investing company since that time (provided the old shares had been so held);
- generally speaking, anything done, or required to be done, by or in relation to the acquired company is treated as having been done etc. by or in relation to the acquiring company; and
- certain of the requirements of **18.5**, **18.6** above which were met to any extent in relation to the old shares are deemed to be met to the same extent in relation to the new shares.

The conditions to be satisfied are as follows.

(a) The consideration for the old shares consists entirely of the issue of the new shares.
(b) New shares are issued only at a time when the issued shares in the acquiring company consist entirely of subscriber shares (and any new shares already issued in consideration of old shares).
(c) The consideration for new shares of each description consists entirely of old shares of the 'corresponding description'.
(d) New shares of each description are issued to holders of old shares of the 'corresponding description' in respect of, and in proportion to, their holdings.
(e) Before any exchange of shares takes place, HMRC have given an 'approval notification'.

For the purposes of (c) and (d) above, old and new shares are of a '*corresponding description*' if, assuming they were shares in the same company, they would be of the same class and carry the same rights. All references above to 'shares' (other than to 'subscriber shares') include references to 'securities'. An '*approval notification*' (see (e) above) is given by HMRC, on an application by either company involved, if they are satisfied that the share exchange will be effected for commercial reasons and does not form part of a scheme or arrangements to avoid liability to corporation tax or capital gains tax.

The provisions of *FA 2000, Sch 15 para 80* (see **18.22** above) are applied to a reconstruction within the above provisions where a company's holding of 'old shares' falls within more than one of the categories there mentioned.

For interaction between these provisions and the exemptions relating to SUBSTANTIAL SHAREHOLDINGS OF COMPANIES, see **66.14**.

[*FA 2000, Sch 15 paras 83–87*].

Key points concerning corporate venturing scheme

[18.24] Points to consider are as follows.

- The scheme is closed for new investments.
- The main relief relevant to companies holding qualifying shares is loss relief. However, if the qualifying conditions for substantial shareholdings of companies (see chapter **66**) are met any gain or loss is ignored for corporation tax purposes.

19

Death

Introduction	19.1
General provisions applying on death of taxpayer	19.2
Scotland	19.3
Northern Ireland	19.4
Valuation	19.5
Donatio mortis causa	19.6
Carry-back of losses	19.7
Deeds of family arrangement etc	19.8
Personal representatives	19.9
Allowable expenditure	19.10
Personal representatives	19.11
Corporate trustees	19.12
Acquisitions and disposals, or deemed disposals, after 5 April 2004	19.13
Legatees	19.14
Key points	19.15

Cross-references. See **39.2** INTERACTION WITH OTHER TAXES for inheritance tax; **42.9** LATE PAYMENT INTEREST AND PENALTIES for relief given if probate is delayed; **45** MARKET VALUE; **58.3** RETURNS for simplified procedures for small deceased estates; **62.3** SETTLEMENTS for death of a bankrupt etc. and **62.16–62.18** for termination of a life interest by the death of the person entitled thereto; **63.20** SHARES AND SECURITIES.

Simon's Taxes. See **C1.206–C1.206C, C4.1.**

Introduction to death

[19.1] This chapter examines the capital gains tax consequences of a person's death from the perspective of the deceased, the personal representatives and the legatees. In summary, the consequences are as follows. No liability to capital gains tax arises on death. The personal representatives are treated as having acquired the deceased's assets at market value at the time of death and are liable to capital gains tax on disposals of assets made by them. They are entitled to the same annual exempt amount as individuals for the year of death and the following two years. No liability to capital gains tax arises on the transfer of assets from the personal representatives to a legatee. The legatee is then treated as having acquired the asset at market value at the time of death.

In addition, a special relief applies to allowable losses incurred by the deceased in the tax year of death (on disposals made before death). Where the losses exceed the deceased's chargeable gains for the tax year, the excess can be carried back and set off against chargeable gains in the three preceding tax years.

General provisions applying on death of taxpayer

[19.2] All 'assets of which a deceased person was competent to dispose' are deemed to have been acquired on his death by his personal representatives (or other person on whom they devolve) for a consideration equal to their market value at the date of death. However, they are not deemed to be disposed of by the deceased on his death (whether or not they were the subject of a testamentary disposition). The effect of these provisions is that no chargeable gain or allowable loss arises on death and any gain or loss arising on the disposal of the asset by the personal representatives, etc. after the death is calculated by reference to the market value of the asset at the date of death (subject to the further provisions in this chapter).

'*Assets of which the deceased was competent to dispose*' are those assets which (otherwise than in right of a power of appointment or of the testamentary power conferred by statute to dispose of entailed interests) he could, if of full age and capacity, have disposed of by his will, assuming that all the assets were situated in England and, if he was not domiciled in the United Kingdom, that he was domiciled in England, and include references to his severable share in any assets to which, immediately before his death, he was beneficially entitled as joint tenant.

[*TCGA 1992, s 62(1)(10)*].

Scotland

[19.3] So far as the provisions in *TCGA 1992* relate to the consequences of the death of a proper liferenter of any property, then, on the death of any such liferenter, the person (if any) who, on the death of the liferenter, becomes entitled to possession of the property as heir, is deemed to have acquired all the assets forming part of the property at the date of the deceased's death for a consideration equal to their market value at that date. [*TCGA 1992, s 63*].

Northern Ireland

[19.4] So far as the provisions in *TCGA 1992* relate to the consequences of the death of a person to whom property in Northern Ireland stands limited for life, a person who acquires property in fee simple absolute or fee tail in possession as a consequence of the deceased's death, is deemed to have acquired all the assets forming part of the property at the date of death for a consideration equal to their market value at that date. [*TCGA 1992, s 63A*].

Valuation

[19.5] Where on the death of any person, inheritance tax is chargeable on the value of his estate immediately before his death and the value of an asset forming part of his estate has been ascertained for the purposes of the application of that tax to the estate, that value is taken to be the market value at the date of death for capital gains tax purposes. [*TCGA 1992, s 274*]. See also Revenue Tax Bulletin April 1995 p 209.

Therefore, where the inheritance tax valuation for quoted shares and securities (see **45.3** MARKET VALUE) has been used to determine inheritance tax on death, those shares are valued in the same way for capital gains tax. In the case of land and quoted shares and securities, proceeds of certain post-death sales within a specified period may be substituted for values at date of death for inheritance tax purposes. The value of related property (as defined for inheritance tax purposes) may also be revised in the event of a post-death sale. If such substitutions/revisions are made for inheritance tax purposes, they must be made for CGT purposes also (but see *Stonor and Another (Executors of Dickinson deceased) v CIR* (Sp C 288), [2001] SSCD 199 in which the executors failed in an attempt to use this rule to upgrade values of freehold properties for CGT purposes where there was no inheritance tax liability). See Tolley's Inheritance Tax for details.

Where, in consequence of a death before 31 March 1971 (when death *was* an occasion of charge for CGT), capital gains tax was chargeable or an allowable loss accrued, then if the market value of any property on the date of death which was subject to charge has been depreciated *by reason of the death*, then any later estimate of the market value is to take that depreciation into account. [*TCGA 1992, Sch 11 para 8*]. This provision may still, therefore, be relevant in computing allowable expenditure on a first disposal subsequent to the date of death. The legislation now refers to deaths before 31 March 1973 but the reasoning for this is not clear; see *FA 1965, s 44(2) proviso* as repealed by *FA 1971, Sch 14 Pt V* for deaths occurring after 30 March 1971 and *CGTA 1979, Sch 6 para 2(2)*.

Following the decision in *Gray v CIR* CA, [1994] STC 360, HMRC's view is that two or more different assets comprised in an estate can be treated as a single unit of property if disposal as one unit was the course that a prudent hypothetical vendor would have adopted in order to obtain the most favourable price without undue expenditure of time and effort.

This principle will apply for capital gains tax purposes in the following cases:

(a) An acquisition by personal representatives or legatees under *TCGA 1992, s 62* of assets which a deceased person was competent to dispose.
(b) An acquisition of settled property under *TCGA 1992, s 71(1)* on the occasion of a person becoming absolutely entitled to that settled property.

There are certain situations when a single valuation will still apply, such as:

(i) the disposal of an asset for consideration deemed to be equal to its market value under *TCGA 1992, s 17*;
(ii) when a valuation of an asset is required for the purpose of re-basing to 31 March 1992 under *TCGA 1992, s 35*.

The single asset valuation for *TCGA 1992, s 17* is modified by *TCGA 1992, s 19* where there is a series of linked transactions between connected persons. Each disposal in the series may be treated as being made for consideration equal to a proportion of the aggregate value of all the assets in the series.

Donatio mortis causa

[19.6] No chargeable gain arises on the making of a disposal by way of '*donatio mortis causa*' i.e. a gift of personal property made in 'contemplation of the conceived approach of death' (see *Duffield v Elwes* Ch D 1827, 1 Bligh's Reports (New Series) 497), and the recipient is treated as a legatee acquiring the property at the date of death. [*TCGA 1992, ss 62(5), 64(2)*].

Carry-back of losses

[19.7] Allowable losses in excess of chargeable gains incurred by the deceased in the tax year in which death occurs can be carried back and set off against chargeable gains in the three preceding tax years. See **2.6** ANNUAL RATES AND EXEMPTIONS for the interaction between losses carried back and the annual exempt amount. Subject to this, chargeable gains accruing in a later year must be relieved before those of an earlier year. Losses carried back cannot be set against gains treated under *TCGA 1992, s 87* or *s 89(2)* as accruing to the individual as a beneficiary of a non-UK resident settlement (see **48.14–48.20** OFFSHORE SETTLEMENTS) or against NRCGT gains (i.e. gains on non-resident disposals of UK residential property interests (see **41.25** LAND)).

[*TCGA 1992, s 62(2)(2A); FA 2015, Sch 7 para 17(2)*].

Similarly, allowable NRCGT losses in excess of NRCGT gains incurred by the deceased in the tax year in which death occurs can be carried back and set off against NRCGT gains in the three preceding tax years (taking gains accruing in a later year first). [*TCGA 1992, s 62(2AA); FA 2015, Sch 7 para 17(3)*].

Any remaining unused losses *cannot* be carried forward and set off against gains made by the personal representatives or legatees.

A carry-back of a loss is within the scope of *TMA 1970, Sch 1B* (claims for relief involving two or more years). This provision is fully covered in Tolley's Income Tax (and see also **13.2** CLAIMS) and its effect is that whilst the resulting tax saving/repayment is computed by reference to the facts for the tax year(s) to which the loss is carried back (the earlier year), it is then treated as a reduction or repayment of tax for the tax year in which the loss is incurred (the later year). The tax position for the earlier year is not adjusted. The general requirement that claims be made in a self-assessment tax return (see **13.2** CLAIMS) does not apply to a carry-back under *section 62(2)*. [*TMA 1970, Sch 1B para* 2]. Repayment interest or (before 31 October 2011) repayment supplement may be due as in **56.2, 56.3** REPAYMENT INTEREST, though only from 31 January following the *later year* (as above).

Example

On 1 June 2017 Paul sells an asset, realising an allowable loss of £15,000. On 30 June 2017 he dies. Paul has no chargeable gains for 2017/18 but in 2016/17 and 2015/16 he made chargeable gains (before the annual exempt amount) of £14,100 and £22,100 respectively.

The 2017/18 allowable loss is carried back and set off against the gains for 2016/17 and 2015/16 as follows.

2016/17

	£
Adjusted net gains	14,100
Loss carried back (part)	3,000
	11,100
Annual exempt amount	11,100
Taxable gains	Nil
Losses brought back	15,000
Less utilised in 2016/17	3,000
Losses carried back	£12,000

2015/16

	£
Adjusted net gains	22,100
Loss carried back	11,000
	11,100
Annual exempt amount	11,100
Taxable gains	£nil
Losses brought back	12,000
Less utilised in 2015/16	11,000
Losses carried back	£1,000

Deeds of family arrangement etc.

[19.8] Variations or disclaimers of the dispositions (whether effected by will, under the intestacy rules or otherwise) of the 'property of which the deceased was competent to dispose' (see **19.2** above) which are made by deed of family arrangement (or similar instrument in writing) within two years of death do not constitute disposals but are related back to the date of death so that a variation is treated as having been effected by the deceased and a disclaimed benefit is treated as never having been conferred. Such treatment does not apply in respect of variations or disclaimers made for any consideration in money or money's worth other than consideration consisting of the making of a variation or disclaimer in respect of another of the dispositions.

In the case of a variation (as opposed to a disclaimer), the above treatment applies only if the instrument contains a statement by the persons making the instrument to the effect that they intend the treatment to apply. It is necessary to send HMRC a copy of the instrument only if it has immediate tax consequences or if it is requested as part of an enquiry (see Revenue Tax Bulletin August 2002 pp 957–959).

The above provisions apply whether or not the administration of the estate is complete or the property has been distributed in accordance with the original dispositions.

[*TCGA 1992, s 62(6)–(9)*].

In HMRC's view, the above provisions apply to a variation of the deceased's interest in jointly held assets, which pass on death to the surviving joint owner(s) (Revenue Tax Bulletin October 1995 p 254).

In a case based upon the original *FA 1965* legislation, it was held that the equivalent provisions to *TCGA 1992, s 62(6)* above and *s 62(4)* (see **19.14** below), although deeming provisions, were to be given their normal and natural meaning. But, where such construction would lead to an injustice or absurdity, the application of the statutory fiction should be limited to the extent needed to avoid such injustice or absurdity. Thus, nothing in *TCGA 1992, s 62(6)* requires one to assume something which is inconsistent with the legatee under an original will, who then varies dispositions under *TCGA 1992, s 62(6)* to a third party, as having been the actual settlor of the arrangement. The deeming provisions apply only to assets of which the testator was competent to dispose at his death. However, the property settled by the legatee comprised, not the assets in the deceased's estate which eventually came to be vested in the third party, but a separate chose in action, i.e. the right to due administration of the estate, and this could only have been settled by the legatee and not by the deceased. (*Marshall v Kerr* HL 1994, 67 TC 56). Where, in the rare event, the administration of an estate has been completed before a deed of variation is made, a different analysis may follow.

For HMRC's comments on the provisions affecting the variation of the devolution of a deceased estate, see HMRC Capital Gains Manual CG31400–32080. For cases bearing on the effectiveness of similar deeds used for inheritance tax purposes, see Tolley's Inheritance Tax under Deeds Varying Dispositions on Death.

Personal representatives

[19.9] Personal representatives are treated as a single and continuing body (distinct from persons who may from time to time be the personal representatives) which has the deceased's residence and domicile at the date of death. [*TCGA 1992, s 62(3)*].

They are liable to capital gains tax on disposals of assets made by them by reference to the disposal proceeds and the market value at the date of death (but see **19.10** below). They may be assessed in respect of disposals made by the deceased prior to death as well as in respect of their own disposals. See **6.6, 6.13** ASSESSMENTS.

For the tax year in which death occurs and the following two tax years, the personal representatives are entitled to the same annual exempt amount as individuals, with the same general provisions applying. [*TCGA 1992, s 3(7)(7A)*]. See **2.6** ANNUAL RATES AND EXEMPTIONS.

See **2.3** ANNUAL RATES AND EXEMPTIONS for the rate of capital gains tax applicable to personal representatives.

Losses made by personal representatives during the administration period cannot be passed on to the legatees. The position should be compared with that for losses made by trustees as in **62.16** SETTLEMENTS.

CGT due from personal representatives may be assessed and charged on and in the name of any one or more of the 'relevant personal representatives'. In relation to chargeable gains, the '*relevant personal representatives*' means the personal representatives in the tax year in which the gains accrue and any subsequent personal representatives of the deceased. [*TCGA 1992, s 65(1)((4)*].

Allowable expenditure

[19.10] The decision in *Richards' Executors* HL 1971, 46 TC 626 enables personal representatives, in computing chargeable gains on the disposal of assets, to add to the cost of acquiring the assets from the testator (i.e. the market value at the date of death) those legal and accountancy costs that are involved in preparing the inheritance tax or capital transfer tax account and obtaining the grant of probate etc. See also **16.11** COMPUTATION OF GAINS AND LOSSES.

Because of the practical difficulty of identifying the costs applicable to individual assets comprised in the estate, HMRC have agreed expenditure based on the following scales (HMRC Statement of Practice 2/04).

Personal representatives

[19.11]

Deaths after 5 April 2004

	Gross value of estate	*Allowable expenditure*
A	Up to £50,000	1.8% of the probate value of the assets sold by the personal representatives.
B	Between £50,001 and £90,000	A fixed amount of £900, to be divided between all the assets in the estate in proportion to the probate values, and allowed in those proportions on assets sold by the personal representatives.
C	Between £90,001 and £400,000	1% of the probate value of the assets sold.
D	Between £400,001 and £500,000	A fixed amount of £4,000, to be divided as at B above.
E	Between £500,001 and £1,000,000	0.8% of the probate value of the assets sold.
F	Between £1,000,001 and £5,000,000	A fixed amount of £8,000, to be divided as at B above
G	Over £5,000,000	0.16% of the probate value of the assets sold, subject to a maximum of £10,000

In practice, HMRC will accept computations based either on these scales or on the actual expenditure incurred.

Corporate trustees

[19.12] HMRC have also agreed the following scales of allowable expenditure for expenses incurred by corporate trustees in the administration of estates and trusts. They will accept computations based either on these scales or on the actual allowable expenditure incurred.

Acquisitions and disposals, or deemed disposals, after 5 April 2004

[19.13]

(a)	Transfers of assets to beneficiaries etc.	
(1)	Publicly marketed shares and securities	
	(A) One beneficiary	£25 per holding transferred.
	(B) More than one beneficiary between whom a holding must be divided	As (A), to be divided in equal shares between the beneficiaries.
(2)	Other shares and securities	As (1) above, with the addition of any exceptional expenditure.
(3)	Other assets	As (1) above, with the addition of any exceptional expenditure.
	Shares and securities are regarded as marketed to the general public for this purpose if buying and selling prices are regularly published in the financial pages of a national or regional newspaper, magazine or journal.	
(b)	Actual disposals and acquisitions	
(1)	Publicly marketed shares and securities	The investment fee as charged by the trustees.
(2)	Other shares and securities	As (1) above, plus actual valuation costs.
(3)	Other assets	The investment fee as charged by the trustees, subject to a maximum of £75, plus actual valuation costs.
	Where a comprehensive annual management fee is charged, covering both the cost of administering the trust and the expenses of actual disposals and acquisitions, the investment fee for (1)–(3) above will be taken to be £0.25 per £100 on the sale or purchase moneys.	
(c)	Deemed disposals by trustees	
(1)	Publicly marketed shares and securities	£8 per holding disposed of.
(2)	Other shares and securities	Actual valuation costs.
(3)	Other assets	Actual valuation costs.

Legatees

[19.14] A '*legatee*' includes any person taking under a testamentary disposition or an intestacy or partial intestacy, whether he takes beneficially or as trustee. [*TCGA 1992, s 64(2)*].

On a 'person acquiring any asset as legatee', no chargeable gain accrues to the personal representatives, and the legatee is treated as if the personal representatives' acquisition of the asset had been his acquisition of it. The Treasury may make regulations to apply in place of this rule in respect of assets formerly held in an individual savings account. [*TCGA 1992, s 62(4)(4A); FA 2016, s 27(3)*]. The consequences of this are that the asset is taken as acquired at either the market value at the date of death or, if the asset was acquired subsequent to death, the allowable expenditure incurred by the personal representatives in providing etc. the asset. See also **19.8** above.

For the purposes of the meaning of '*legatee*' and '*person acquiring an asset as legatee*', property taken under a testamentary disposition or on an intestacy or partial intestacy includes any asset appropriated by the personal representative in or towards satisfaction of a pecuniary legacy or any other interest or share in the property devolving. [*TCGA 1992, s 64(3)*].

Where a person disposes of an asset held by a personal representative to which he became absolutely entitled as legatee, any incidental expenditure incurred by that person or the personal representative in relation to the transfer of the asset to him is allowable as a deduction in the computation of the gain arising on the disposal. [*TCGA 1992, s 64(1)*]. The expenditure incurred by the person concerned, but not that incurred by the personal representative, may qualify for indexation allowance (HMRC Capital Gains Manual CG31192).

Key points concerning death

[19.15] Points to consider are as follows.

- Deeds of variation are deemed to take effect from the date of death for the purposes of capital gains tax and inheritance tax, but not for income tax purposes.
- Personal representatives do not need to claim for the capital gains tax free uplift on death — this is given automatically.
- When disposing of assets from the estate, the capital gain is calculated by subtracting the probate value of the asset from the sale proceeds. Note that, for inheritance tax purposes, the sale proceeds may be substituted for the probate value, which will have a knock on effect on the inheritance tax due.
- Where the personal representatives wish to sell property realising a gain it can be advantageous to transfer the assets to the legatees prior to the sale and use the legatees' annual exempt amounts and capital gains tax rates. Specific calculations are required to reflect the actual circumstances. In general a higher potential benefit may exist where:

  - there is a high number of legatees (more annual exempt amounts); and or
  - some legatees are not liable to UK CGT (eg non resident or UK charities); and or
  - legatees' personal incomes are low and hence the gain will be partly taxable at 10%/18%.
- Death cannot normally be predicted although it should always be considered in significant transactions where assets qualify for IHT business property relief. For example, Albert, 60 sells his shares in the family company to his sons for £1 million cash. Two days later he goes into hospital for planned major surgery and dies. His estate has a liability for capital gains tax on the sale (at 10%, assuming that entrepreneurs' relief applies) and includes the balance of the cash proceeds which are potentially liable to IHT (at 40%). If he had held the shares at death they would have qualified for IHT relief and received uplift to market value for capital gains tax; therefore avoiding both of the above tax liabilities.

20

Disclosure of Tax Avoidance Schemes

Introduction	**20.1**
Disclosure regime	**20.2**
Persons required to make disclosure	**20.3**
Reference numbers allocated to arrangements	**20.4**
Compliance	**20.5**
Publication of information by HMRC	**20.6**
High-risk promoters of avoidance schemes	**20.7**
Definitions	**20.8**
Threshold conditions	**20.9**
Relevant defeat	**20.10**
Conduct notices	**20.11**
Monitoring notices	**20.12**
Effects of a monitoring notice	**20.13**
Information powers: further provisions	**20.14**
Concealing, destroying or disposing of documents	**20.15**
Offences and penalties	**20.16**
Partnerships	**20.17**
Key points	**20.18**

Introduction to disclosure of tax avoidance schemes

[20.1] There are provisions requiring 'promoters' of, and, in some cases, taxpayers making use of, tax avoidance schemes to disclose details to HMRC. The provisions apply to schemes which have the features of one or more prescribed 'hallmarks'. See **20.2** onwards below.

With effect from 17 July 2014, a special compliance regime applies to promoters of tax avoidance schemes who satisfy one or more 'threshold conditions' relating to previous behaviour. The regime provides for the issuing of a 'conduct notice' requiring the person to whom it is given to comply with specified conditions as to the information they provide to clients, compliance with any disclosure requirements and not promoting schemes which rely on contrived or abnormal steps to produce a tax advantage. Promoters who fail to comply with a conduct notice may be issued with a monitoring notice. Names of promoters subject to such a notice may be published by HMRC, including details of how the conduct notice was breached, and promoters are required to notify their monitored status to clients. Information powers and penalties apply to promoters subject to a conduct notice and to promoters subject to a monitoring notice and their clients and intermediaries. See **20.7** onwards below.

Disclosure regime

[20.2] 'Promoters' of tax avoidance schemes and, in some cases, taxpayers making use of such schemes are required to disclose details to HMRC. The disclosure provisions cover a number of taxes including income tax, capital gains tax and corporation tax and are triggered where arrangements feature one of a number of hallmarks. There are compliance powers specific to the disclosure regime.

Disclosure can be made online via HMRC's Counter Avoidance Directorate website (www.gov.uk/dealing-with-hmrc/tax-avoidance), or alternatively, forms for making disclosures can be downloaded from the same location.

Legal professional privilege

The provisions do not require the disclosure of any information with respect to which a claim to legal professional privilege (or, in Scotland, to confidentiality of communications) could be maintained in legal proceedings. [*FA 2004, s 314*].

Note, however, that where a person who would otherwise be a promoter is not required to make a disclosure as a result of this provision, he is treated as not being a promoter, and the obligation to disclose the arrangements will (if there is no other person who is a promoter) fall on the taxpayer making use of the scheme (as the scheme will be one with no promoter). See further below.

Arrangements requiring disclosure

'*Notifiable arrangements*' requiring disclosure under the provisions are 'arrangements' which:

- fall within any description prescribed by Treasury regulations (see below);
- enable, or might be expected to enable, any person to obtain an 'advantage' in relation to any tax (which may include capital gains tax and corporation tax) that is so prescribed in relation to arrangements of that description; and
- are such that the main benefit, or one of the main benefits, that might be expected to arise from the arrangements is the obtaining of that advantage.

The provisions also require disclosure of '*notifiable proposals*', i.e. proposals for arrangements which would be notifiable arrangements if entered into, whether the proposal relates to a particular person or to any person who may seek to take advantage of it.

For these purposes, '*arrangements*' include any scheme, transaction or series of transactions. An '*advantage*', in relation to any tax, means:

- relief or increased relief from, or repayment or increased repayment of, that tax;
- the avoidance or reduction of a charge or assessment to that tax;

- the avoidance of a possible assessment to that tax;
- the deferral of any payment of tax;
- the advancement of any repayment of tax; or
- the avoidance of any obligation to deduct or account for any tax.

[*FA 2004, ss 306, 318(1)*].

Prescribed arrangements

Any arrangements which fall within any of the descriptions (or '*hallmarks*') listed below are prescribed by the Treasury for the purposes of these provisions. The taxes covered are income tax, capital gains tax and corporation tax. The hallmarks are as follows.

(1) **Confidentiality in cases involving a promoter.** Arrangements fall within this hallmark if it might be reasonably expected that a promoter would wish the way in which the arrangements secure a tax advantage (or might secure a tax advantage) to be kept confidential from any other promoter at any time following the event which triggers the disclosure. Arrangements also fall within this hallmark if:
   - with effect from 4 November 2013, it might reasonably be expected that a promoter would, but for these provisions, wish to keep the way in which the arrangements secure or might secure) a tax advantage confidential from HMRC for some or all of that period, and a reason for doing so is to facilitate repeated or continued use of the element of the arrangements which secure the advantage or of substantially the same element; or
   - before 4 November 2013, the promoter would, but for these provisions, wish to keep the way in which the arrangements secure or might secure a tax advantage confidential from HMRC for some or all of that period, and a reason for doing so is to facilitate repeated or continued use of the element of the arrangements which secure the advantage or of substantially the same element; or
   - with effect from 4 November 2013, where there is no promoter by virtue only of the provision relating to legal professional privilege in (C) below, or the promoter is not UK resident, it might reasonably be expected that the user of the arrangements would wish to keep confidential from HMRC the way that the arrangements secure a tax advantage for some or all of that period; or
   - before 4 November 2013, where there is no promoter by virtue only of the provision relating to legal professional privilege in (C) below, or the promoter is not UK resident, the user of the arrangements wishes to keep confidential from HMRC the way that the arrangements secure a tax advantage for some or all of that period.

(2) **Confidentiality in cases not involving a promoter.** Arrangements fall within this hallmark if there is no promoter and:
   (a) the intended user of the arrangements is a business (as defined) which is not a '*small or medium-sized enterprise*' (broadly, a micro, small or medium-sized enterprise as defined in the Commission Recommendation of 6 May 2003);

(b) it might reasonably be expected that the user would wish (before 4 November 2013, the user wishes) the way in which the arrangements secure a tax advantage to be kept confidential from HMRC at any time following the event triggering the disclosure (before 1 January 2011, for some or all of the period beginning with the date on which he enters into the first transaction forming part of the arrangements and ending with the latest date by which he must notify HMRC of the reference number); and

(c) a reason for doing so is to facilitate repeated or continued use of the element of the arrangements which secure the advantage or of substantially the same element or to reduce the risk of HMRC opening an enquiry into a return or account.

With effect from 4 November 2013, arrangements also fall within this hallmark if there is no promoter and (a) above applies and, if there had been a promoter, it might reasonably be expected that they would wish to have kept the way in which the arrangements secure a tax advantage to be kept confidential from HMRC at any time following the event triggering the disclosure and a reason for doing so would be to facilitate repeated or continued use of the element of the arrangements which secure the advantage or of substantially the same element.

(3) **Premium fee.** Arrangements fall within this hallmark if they are such that it might reasonably be expected that a promoter or a person connected with a promoter of arrangements that are the same as, or substantially similar to, the arrangements in question, would, but for these provisions, be able to obtain a 'premium fee' from a person experienced in receiving services of the type being provided. Arrangements where there is no promoter or where the tax advantage is intended to be obtained by an individual, or business that is a small or medium-sized enterprise, are excluded. A '*premium fee*' for this purpose is one chargeable by virtue of any element of the arrangements from which the tax advantage is expected to arise and which is to a significant extent attributable to, or to any extent contingent on the obtaining of, that advantage. The premium fee must be so attributable on the obtaining of the tax advantage as a matter of law (rather than upon other factors such as the take up of an employment scheme by a certain number of employees).

(4) **Standardised tax products.** Arrangements fall within this hallmark if they are made available by a promoter for implementation by more than one person and an informed observer who had studied the arrangements could reasonably be expected to conclude that:

- the arrangements have substantially standardised documentation to enable implementation, the form of that documentation is determined by the promoter and the substance of the documentation does not need to be tailored to any material extent;
- a person implementing the arrangements must enter into a specific transaction or series of transactions;
- the transaction or series of transactions are substantially standardised in form; and

- (with effect, broadly, from 23 February 2016) either the main purpose of the arrangements is to enable a person to obtain a tax advantage or the arrangements would be unlikely to be entered into but for the expectation of obtaining a tax advantage.

Arrangements which are the same, or substantially the same, as arrangements first made available for implementation before 1 August 2006 are excluded, as are arrangements consisting solely of one or more plant or machinery leases (see (6) below), an ENTERPRISE INVESTMENT SCHEME (**23**) or ISA, arrangements using the CORPORATE VENTURING SCHEME (**18**) or VENTURE CAPITAL TRUSTS (**71**), arrangements qualifying for community investment tax relief, specified EMPLOYEE SHARE SCHEMES (**22**), certain pension schemes; schemes to which *ITTOIA 2005, s 731* (periodical payments of personal injury damages) applies and arrangements which would fall within (8) below but for the exclusions from that hallmark.

(5) **Loss schemes.** Arrangements are within this hallmark if the promoter expects more than one individual to implement them or to implement arrangements which are substantially the same and an informed observer, having studied them, could reasonably be expected to conclude that:

   (a) the main benefit or one of the main benefits of the arrangements for some or all of the participants is the provision of losses;

   (b) (with effect, broadly, from 23 February 2016) the arrangements (including the way they are structured) contain an element or elements unlikely to have been entered into but for the provision of those losses; and

   (c) the participants would be expected to use the losses to reduce their liability to income tax or capital gains tax.

(6) **Leasing arrangements.** This hallmark covers certain arrangements which include high-value plant or machinery leases. See Tolley's Corporation Tax for further details.

(7) **Employment income provided through third parties.** This hallmark applies with effect from 4 November 2013. See Tolley's Income Tax for further details.

(8) **Financial products.** This hallmark applies, broadly, with effect from 23 February 2016. Arrangements are within the hallmark if they include at least one 'specified financial product' and it would be reasonable to expect an informed observer (having studied the arrangements and having regard to all relevant circumstances) to conclude that:

   (a) one of the main benefits of including a specified financial product in the arrangements is to give rise to a tax advantage; and

   (b) either:

      (i) a specified financial product included in the arrangements contains at least one term unlikely to have been entered into were it not for the tax advantage; or

      (ii) the arrangements involve one or more contrived or abnormal steps (other than certain specified steps which are deemed not to be contrived or abnormal) without which the tax advantage could not be obtained.

The condition at (b)(i) is treated as not met if it would otherwise be met only because the specified financial product includes a term requiring that it be held for a minimum period before it is redeemed and *TCGA 1992, s 135* (exchange of securities — see **63.5** SHARES AND SECURITIES) or *s 136* (schemes of reconstruction — see **63.7** SHARES AND SECURITIES) applies to it. The condition is also treated as not met if it would otherwise be met only because the specified financial product includes a term under which the issuing company can secure that the redemption date falls before the end of the 'permitted period' and but for that term, the specified financial product would be an 'equity note'. 'Permitted period' and 'equity note' are defined for this purpose by *CTA 2010, s 1016*. Both of the conditions at (b) above are treated as not met if they would otherwise both be met only because the specified financial product includes a term providing for conversion into, or redemption in, a currency other than sterling.

The '*specified financial products*' are loans, shares, derivative contracts, certain repos and quasi-repos, stock lending arrangements, alternative finance arrangements and contracts which, whether alone or in combination with other contracts, are required under generally accepted accounting practice to be treated as a loan, deposit or other financial asset or obligation or would be if the person entering into the arrangements were a company. Financial products held in an individual savings account are excluded.

Arrangements are excluded from the hallmark if a promoter is a participating entity or part of a participating group in the Code of Practice on Taxation for Banks and HMRC had confirmed or could reasonably be expected to confirm to the promoter that the arrangements are acceptable transactions under the Code.

For the purpose only of determining whether arrangements are prescribed by (1)–(3) or (6) above, **20.3**(C) below is disregarded.

[*SI 2006 No 1543; SI 2007 No 2484, Art 4; SI 2009 No 1890, Art 3(1); SI 2009 No 2033; SI 2010 No 2834; SI 2013 No 2595; SI 2016 No 99*].

See also HMRC's guidance published on their website on 16 June 2006.

Persons required to make disclosure

[20.3] The following persons are required to make disclosures of avoidance schemes in particular circumstances.

Disclosure by promoter

A 'promoter' must provide HMRC with specified information on any notifiable proposal within five business days of the '*relevant date*' (i.e. the earliest of: the date he first makes a firm approach to another person; the date on which he makes the proposal available for implementation by any person; and the date he first becomes aware of any transaction forming part of arrangements implementing the proposal). Before 1 September 2012, the time limit for disclosure was extended where the promoter reasonably expected to make a clearance application to HMRC under certain specified provisions (see *SI 2004 No 1864, Reg 5*).

There is a separate requirement for a promoter to provide HMRC with specified information relating to notifiable arrangements and to do so within five business days of the date on which he first becomes aware of any transaction forming part of those arrangements; but this does not apply if the arrangements implement a proposal which has been notified as above.

The disclosure under these provisions must provide sufficient information as might be reasonably expected to enable an HMRC officer to comprehend the manner in which the proposal or arrangements are intended to operate, including the details specified in *SI 2012 No 1836, Reg 4*.

Where a promoter has complied with the above requirements and another person is a promoter in relation to the same proposal or arrangements or to a proposal or arrangements that are substantially the same (whether they relate to the same or different parties), the notification obligation of that other promoter is discharged if:

- the promoter who made the disclosure has notified the identity and address of the other promoter to HMRC or the other promoter holds the reference number allocated to the arrangements; and
- the other promoter holds the information included in the disclosure.

If a promoter has discharged his obligations in relation to a proposal or arrangements, he is not required to notify proposals or arrangements which are substantially the same as those already notified (whether or not they relate to the same parties).

[*FA 2004, s 308; SI 2004 No 1864, Regs 3(1)(2), 4(1)–(3), 5; SI 2011 No 171; SI 2012 No 1836, Regs 4(1), 5(1)(4)(5)*].

Details of clients

A further disclosure requirement applies where a promoter of notifiable arrangements provides services to any client in connection with the arrangements and either the promoter is subject to the requirement to provide the client with specified information relating to the reference number of the arrangements (see **20.4** below) or would be subject to that requirement if he had not failed to make the necessary disclosure of the proposal or arrangements. Unless HMRC have withdrawn the obligation to notify the reference number to the client, the promoter must provide HMRC with specified information about the client within 30 days. The specified information is the scheme reference number (if there is one), the name and address of the client, the promoter's name and address and the end date of the quarter in relation to which the information is provided.

HMRC have a further power with effect from 17 July 2013 which applies where a promoter has provided HMRC with the specified information but HMRC suspect that a person other than the client to whom the information relates is or is likely to be a party to the arrangements. HMRC may by written notice require the promoter to provide specified information about any person the promoter might reasonably be expected to know is or is likely to be a party to the arrangements. The promoter must comply with the requirement within ten days of receiving the notice or such longer period as HMRC direct. The specified information is the name and address of, and any identification number allocated by HMRC to, any person other than the client who is or is likely to be a party to the arrangements (but only those who will, or are likely to, either sell the arrangements to another person or achieve a tax advantage by implementing the arrangements), together with sufficient information as might be reasonably expected to enable HMRC to comprehend how such a person is involved in the arrangements. Only information held by the promoter at the time of receipt of the notice can be required.

[*FA 2004, ss 313ZA, 313ZB; FA 2013, s 223(3); SI 2004 No 1864, Reg 8ZA; SI 2010 No 2928, Reg 3; SI 2012 No 1836, Regs 13, 13A, 18; SI 2013 No 2592, Reg 20*].

Duty to provide updated information

Where, in compliance with the main obligations above, information has been provided to HMRC about notifiable arrangements, or proposed notifiable arrangements, and a reference number has been allocated to the arrangements (see **20.4** below), the promoter must inform HMRC of:

(i) any change in the name by which the notifiable arrangements are known; and
(ii) any change in the name or address of any person who is a promoter in relation to the notifiable arrangements or the notifiable proposal.

This duty applies on and after 26 March 2015, but only where the original information is provided, *and* the reference number is allocated, on or after that date. Where it applies, the promoter must give HMRC the updated information (on the prescribed form) within 30 days after the change occurs. If there is more than one promoter, the obligation to inform HMRC of a change within (ii) above falls on the promoter whose details have changed. Once a promoter has informed HMRC of a change within (i) or (ii), the duty of any other promoter to inform HMRC of that change is discharged.

[*FA 2004, ss 310C, 316; FA 2015, Sch 17 paras 1, 2, 19*].

Meaning of promoter

A '*promoter*' is a person who conducts a 'relevant business' and who in the course of that business:

(a) in relation to a notifiable proposal:
    (i) is to any extent responsible for the design of the proposed arrangements; or
    (ii) makes a 'firm approach' to another person with a view to making the proposal available for implementation by that person or any other person; or
    (iii) makes a notifiable proposal available for implementation by another person; or
(b) in relation to notifiable arrangements:
    (i) is a promoter by virtue of (a)(ii) or (iii) above in relation to a notifiable proposal which is implemented by the arrangements;
    (ii) is to any extent responsible for the design of the arrangements; or

(iii) is to any extent responsible for the organisation or management of the arrangements.

A '*relevant business*' for this purpose is a trade, profession or business which involves the provision to other persons of services relating to taxation or which is carried on by a bank (within *CTA 2010, s 1120*) or securities house (within *CTA 2010, s 1009(3)*). Anything done by a company which is a member of the same 51% group (as defined) as a bank or securities house is taken to be done in the course of a relevant business if it is done for the purposes of the trade etc. of the bank or securities house.

For the purposes of (a)(ii) above, a person makes a '*firm approach*' to another person if he makes a 'marketing contact' with that person when the proposed arrangements have been 'substantially designed'. A promoter makes a '*marketing contact*' with another person if he provides information about the proposal, including an explanation of the tax advantage to be obtained, with a view to that person or any other person entering into transactions forming part of the proposed arrangements. Arrangements have been '*substantially designed*' when it would be reasonable to believe that a person wishing to obtain the tax advantage might use the scheme or a scheme which is not substantially different.

The following exclusions apply.

(A) A company providing services within (a) or (b) above to a company which is a member of the same group (as defined) is not a promoter.

(B) Neither is an employee of (or of a person connected (within **17** CONNECTED PERSONS) with) either a promoter or a person entering into any transaction forming part of the proposed arrangements. On and after 17 April 2015, the exclusion of employees is disapplied in cases where a non-UK resident promoter fails to disclose.

(C) A person is not treated as a promoter where his involvement in the proposal or arrangements is such that he is not required to provide all of the required information because of the legal professional privilege rules above.

(D) A person is not treated as a promoter by virtue of (a)(i) or (b)(ii) above where:
   - in the course of providing tax advice, he is not responsible for the design of any element of the proposed arrangements or arrangements from which the tax advantage expected to be obtained arises;
   - his relevant business is the provision of tax services but he does not provide tax advice in the course of carrying out his responsibilities in relation to the proposed arrangements or arrangements; or
   - he is not responsible for the design of all the elements of the proposed arrangements or arrangements from which the tax advantage is expected to be obtained arises and could not reasonably be expected to have sufficient information to comply with the disclosure requirements or to know whether a disclosure is required.

(E) Before 17 April 2015, a person is not treated as a promoter by virtue of (b)(iii) above if he is not connected (within *ICTA 1988, s 839*) with another person who is a promoter by virtue of (a)(i) or (b)(ii) above in relation to the arrangements or substantially similar arrangements.

[*FA 2004, s 307; SI 2004 No 1865; SI 2015 No 945*].

Disclosure by introducer

Where HMRC suspect that a person (P) is an 'introducer' of a proposal which may be notifiable, they can by notice require P to provide them with the name and address of each person who has provided him with information about the proposal (usually a promoter or another introducer). On and after 26 March 2015, HMRC may also, or alternatively, require P to provide them with specified information in relation to each person with whom P has made a 'marketing contact' (see above under 'Meaning of promoter') in relation to the proposal. The notice must be in writing and must specify the proposal concerned. P must comply with the notice within ten days or such longer time as HMRC direct.

A person is an '*introducer*' of a notifiable proposal if he makes a marketing contact with another person about the proposal. A person is not, however, an introducer by reason of anything done in circumstances prescribed in regulations.

[*FA 2004, ss 307, 313C; FA 2015, Sch 17 para 12; SI 2010 No 2928, Reg 5; SI 2010 No 3019; SI 2012 No 1836, Reg 15*].

Disclosure by person dealing with non-UK promoter

A person who enters into any transaction forming part of notifiable arrangements in relation to which there is a non-UK resident promoter (and no UK resident promoter) must himself provide HMRC with specified information relating to those arrangements. He must do so within five business days after entering into the first such transaction. The information to be supplied to HMRC is similar to that which promoters must provide (see above). This obligation is discharged if a promoter makes disclosure of the notifiable arrangements in question.

[*FA 2004, ss 309, 319(4); SI 2004 No 1864, Regs 1, 3(3), 4(4)(7), 6; SI 2011 No 171; SI 2012 No 1836, Regs 4(2)(4), 5(6)*].

Disclosure by parties to arrangements not involving a promoter

A person who enters into any transaction forming part of notifiable arrangements in respect of which neither he nor any other person in the UK has a disclosure obligation under the above provisions must himself provide HMRC with specified information relating to those arrangements. Such disclosure must normally be made within 30 days beginning with the day after the day in which he enters into the first transaction forming part of the arrangements. Where, however, there is no promoter only because the person who would otherwise be the promoter is not required to make a disclosure because of the legal professional privilege rules above, the disclosure by the client must be made within five days after the day on which he enters into the first transaction. The information to be supplied to HMRC is similar to that which promoters must provide (see above).

[*FA 2004, ss 310, 319(4); SI 2004 No 1864, Regs 1, 3(4), 4(5)(5A), 6; SI 2006 No 1544, Reg 4; SI 2011 No 171; SI 2012 No 1836, Regs 4(3)(4), 5(7)(8)*].

Further information requested by HMRC

Where, on or after 17 July 2014, a person has provided the required information about notifiable proposals or arrangements in accordance with *FA 2004, ss 308, 309* or *310* above or has provided information in purported compliance with *FA 2004, ss 309* or *310* but HMRC believe that not all of the required information has been provided, HMRC may require that person to provide further specified information about the proposals or arrangements (in addition to that required under *FA 2004, ss 308, 309* or *310*) and documents relating to the proposals or arrangements. The information or documents must be provided within the ten working days (as defined) beginning with the day on which HMRC imposed the requirement or within such longer period as HMRC direct. Where HMRC believe that a person has failed to provide the required information or documents they may apply to the Tribunal for an order requiring them to be provided. The Tribunal may make such an order only if satisfied that HMRC have reasonable grounds for suspecting that the information or documents will assist them in considering the proposals or arrangements. If the Tribunal make an order, the information or documents must be provided within the ten working days (as defined) beginning with the day on which the order is made or within such longer period as HMRC direct. [*FA 2004, ss 310A, 310B; FA 2014, s 284(2)(11)*].

Duty of client to provide employee details

The following applies on and after 26 March 2015 if a promoter of notifiable arrangements, or a notifiable proposal, provides services to any client in connection with the arrangements or proposal and the following conditions are met:

(I) the client receives from the promoter the reference number allocated to the arrangements (or proposed arrangements) as in **24.4** above; and

(II) the client is an employer, and, as a result of the notifiable arrangement (or proposed arrangement):

  (i) one or more of the client's employees receive, or might reasonably be expected to receive, in relation to their employment, an advantage in relation to any tax covered by the DOTAS regime; or

  (ii) the client receives, or might reasonably be expected to receive, any such advantage in relation to the employment of one or more of the client's employees.

Where an employee is within subsection (b)(i) above, or is an employee within (b)(ii), the client must provide HMRC with prescribed information relating to the employee within 14 days after the end of the final PAYE tax month or quarter of the tax year in which any person first enters into a transaction forming part of the notifiable arrangements and on the same date in each subsequent year until an advantage ceases to apply to either employee or employer. For this purpose, 'employee' includes an office holder and a former employee. Regulations may exempt a client from complying with this duty in prescribed circumstances.

The information to be provided as above must be provided in the prescribed form and manner or the duty will not be regarded as complied with. If, as in 20.4 below, HMRC have given notice, in relation to specified notifiable arrangements, that promoters no longer have to pass on reference numbers, or that parties do not have to report such numbers to HMRC, the client is discharged from the above obligation in relation to those arrangements.

[*FA 2004, ss 313ZC, 316; FA 2015, Sch 17 paras 9, 10; SI 2012 No 1836, Reg 13B; SI 2015 No 948, Regs 1, 11*].

Reference numbers allocated to arrangements

[20.4] Where a person has made a disclosure as above, HMRC may allocate a reference number to the arrangements in question within 90 days (previously, before 26 March 2015, 30 days) after the disclosure. HMRC may allocate a reference number even if the disclosure is incomplete or defective. The allocation of a reference number does not in itself indicate that HMRC accept that the arrangements could as a matter of law result in the obtaining by any person of a tax advantage. HMRC must then notify the number to the person making the disclosure and to any co-promoter whose identity and address has been notified to HMRC by that person. A promoter who is providing services to a client in connection with notifiable arrangements must pass on to the client the reference number for those arrangements or the number for arrangements which are substantially the same as those arrangements. He must do so within 30 days after the date he first becomes aware of any transaction forming part of the arrangements or, if later, the date on which the reference number is notified to him (by HMRC or a co-promoter).

The duty of a promoter to notify the reference number to the client is discharged where he has provided the client with prescribed information relating to the reference number allocated to a notifiable proposal for the arrangements, provided that the proposal and the arrangements are substantially the same. HMRC may, by notice, withdraw the obligation of a promoter to notify a reference number to a client. A client who has been notified of a reference number must notify the reference number (on form AAG6) to any other person that he might reasonably be expected to know, is or is likely to be, a party to the arrangements and who might reasonably be expected to gain a tax advantage under the arrangements. He must do so within 30 days beginning with the date he first becomes aware of any transaction forming part of the arrangements or, if later, the date on which the reference number is notified to him by the promoter.

Where client is an employer

On and after **26 March 2015**, where the client is an employer and receives, or might reasonably be expected to receive, by reason of the notifiable arrangements, a tax advantage covered by the regime in relation to the employment of any of the client's employees, the client must, within 30 days, provide (on the prescribed form) the reference number to each of the employees in question. For this purpose, 'employee' includes an office holder and a former employee. Regulations may exempt a client from complying with this duty in prescribed circumstances.

HMRC may give notice that, in relation to notifiable arrangements or a notifiable proposal specified in that notice, clients do not have to pass on reference numbers after the date specified in the notice. Any such notice given before 26 March 2015 is treated on and after that day as given also in relation to the duty imposed on employers.

Duty to report number to HMRC

A party to any notifiable arrangements giving rise to an income tax or capital gains tax advantage must quote the allocated reference number in his personal tax return for the year in which the person first enters into a transaction forming part of the arrangements and in all subsequent returns until the advantage ceases to apply to him. He must also quote the tax year in which, or the date on which, the advantage is expected to arise. Comparable provisions apply for corporation tax. For arrangements connected with employment, before 16 April 2015 the obligation fell on the employer to quote the reference number etc. on form AAG4, and see now **20.4** above. Persons not required to file a tax return must instead provide HMRC (on form AAG4) with specified information no later than what would have been the filing date for such a return. If the notifiable arrangements give rise to a claim (made outside a tax return) to relieve a trading loss, the claimant must provide HMRC (on form AAG4) with specified information at the time the claim is made. On and after 16 April 2015, these duties are disapplied for employees in cases where an employer has a duty under **20.4** above to provide HMRC with information relating to those employees.

HMRC may give notice that, in relation to notifiable arrangements specified in that notice, the above obligation does not apply after the date specified in the notice. To this end, a list of withdrawn scheme reference numbers is now published at www.gov.uk/dealing-with-hmrc/tax-avoidance. Clients and other parties who have received any of these reference numbers no longer have a duty to notify them to HMRC on their tax returns or on form AAG4 from the date shown on the list.

Duty to provide information to promoter

With effect from 17 July 2013, where a promoter has provided the reference number to a client under the above provisions, the client must provide the promoter with specified information. The client must provide the information within ten days of the later of the date the client receives the reference number and the date the client first enters into a transaction forming part of the notifiable arrangements. The information required is the client's unique tax reference number or national insurance number or confirmation that he does not have such a number.

Duty to provide additional information

Where, as above, a promoter is required to pass on to the client the reference number for arrangements, or a client is required to pass on the reference number to other parties, then on and after 26 March 2015 HMRC may specify additional information which must be simultaneously passed on in each case. This is confined to information supplied by HMRC relating to notifiable proposals or notifiable arrangements in general. HMRC may specify the form and manner in which such additional information is to be provided.

[*FA 2004, ss 311–313, 316, 316A; FA 2013, s 223(2); FA 2015, Sch 17 paras 4–7, 14, 20; SI 2004 No 1864, Reg 8; SI 2012 No 1836, Regs 8A–12; SI 2013 No 2592, Reg 16; SI 2015 No 948, Regs 1, 3–10*].

Compliance

[20.5] The following compliance powers apply.

Pre-disclosure enquiries

If HMRC suspects that a person is the introducer of a proposal, or the promoter of a proposal or arrangements, which may be notifiable under the above provisions, they may, by written notice, require that person to state whether in his opinion notification is required, and if not, the reasons for his opinion. In giving those reasons, it is not sufficient to indicate that a lawyer or other professional has given an opinion. The recipient of a notice must comply with it within the ten days beginning on the day after that on which the notice is issued. On and after **26 March 2015**, HMRC may also, or alternatively, require a person that they suspect is an introducer of a proposal to provide them with specified information in relation to each person with whom the person has made a marketing contact in relation to the proposal.

If HMRC receive a statement (whether or not in response to a notice) giving reasons why a proposal or arrangements are not notifiable, they may apply to the Tribunal for an order requiring specified further information or documents to be provided in support of the reasons. The information or documents must be provided within the 14 days beginning on the day after that on which the order is made.

[*FA 2004, ss 313A, 313B; SI 2004 No 1864, Reg 8A; SI 2007 No 2153, Reg 4; SI 2009 No 56, Sch 1 para 431; SI 2012 No 1836, Reg 14; SI 2015 No 945, Regs 1, 12*].

Order to disclose

HMRC can apply to the Tribunal for an order that a proposal or arrangements are notifiable under the above provisions. The application must specify both the proposal or arrangements concerned and the promoter. [*FA 2004, s 314A; SI 2009 No 56, Sch 1 para 432*].

They can also apply to the Tribunal for an order that a proposal or arrangements be treated as notifiable. Again, the application must specify both the proposal or arrangements concerned and the promoter. Before making such an order, the Tribunal must be satisfied that HMRC have taken all reasonable steps (which need not include making use of the pre-disclosure enquiry provisions above) to establish whether the proposal or arrangements are notifiable and have reasonable grounds for suspecting that they may be notifiable. Grounds for suspicion may include an attempt by the promoter to avoid or delay providing information or documents under the pre-disclosure enquiry provisions and failure to comply with a requirement under those provisions in relation to other proposals or arrangements. The disclosure required as a result of an order under this provision must be made within the ten days beginning on the day after that on which the order is made. [*FA 2004, s 306A; SI 2004 No 1864, Reg 4(1A); SI 2007 No 2153, Reg 3(4); SI 2009 No 56, Sch 1 para 429*].

Supplementary information

Where HMRC believe that a disclosure by a promoter has not included all the information required to be disclosed they can apply to the Tribunal for an order requiring the promoter to provide specified information or documents. Before making an order, the Tribunal must be satisfied that HMRC have reasonable grounds for suspecting that the information or documents form part of, or will support or explain, the required information. Information or documents required by an order under this provision must be provided within the ten days beginning on the day after that on which the order is made. [*FA 2004, s 308A; SI 2004 No 1864, Reg 4(3A); SI 2007 No 2153, Reg 3(5); SI 2009 No 56, Sch 1 para 429*].

Penalties

See **52.24** PENALTIES for the penalties applicable for failure to fulfil the above requirements.

Voluntary disclosure of information to HMRC

On and after 26 March 2015, no duty of confidentiality or other restriction on disclosure (however imposed) prevents the voluntary disclosure by any person to HMRC of information or documents which the person has reasonable grounds for suspecting will assist HMRC in determining whether there has been a breach of any requirement imposed as above under the DOTAS regime. [*FA 2004, s 316B; FA 2015, Sch 17 para 16*].

Publication of information by HMRC

[20.6] HMRC may publish specified information about notifiable arrangements (or proposed notifiable arrangements) to which a reference number is allocated (see **20.4** above) and any person who is a promoter in relation to them. This can include information identifying a person as a promoter, but in this case HMRC must first inform him that they are considering publishing that information and give him reasonable opportunity to make representations about whether it should be published. No information can be published that identifies a person who enters into a transaction forming part of the notifiable arrangements (unless he is identified as a promoter).

The above applies where a reference number is allocated to the arrangements on or after 26 March 2015, except where the original obligation to disclose (see **20.3** above) was met before that date.

Once any such information has been published about notifiable arrangements, HMRC must also publish information about any ruling of a court or tribunal that is made in relation to arrangements intended to secure a tax advantage if, in HMRC's opinion, the ruling is relevant to the notifiable arrangements in question. A ruling is relevant to the notifiable arrangements if it is final and if the principles laid down, or reasoning given, in the ruling would, if applied to the notifiable arrangements, allow the purported tax advantage arising from those arrangements.

[*FA 2004, ss 316C, 316D; FA 2015, Sch 17 paras 17, 21*].

High-risk promoters of avoidance schemes

[20.7] With effect from 17 July 2014, a special compliance regime applies to promoters of tax avoidance schemes who satisfy one or more 'threshold conditions' relating to previous behaviour or, with effect from 23 September 2016, who promote a series of avoidance schemes which are defeated. The regime provides for the issuing of a 'conduct notice' (see **20.11** below) requiring the person to whom it is given to comply with specified conditions as to the information they provide to clients, compliance with any disclosure requirements under the provisions at **20.2** onwards above and not promoting schemes which rely on contrived or abnormal steps to produce a tax advantage. Promoters who fail to comply with a conduct notice may be issued with a monitoring notice (see **20.12** below). Names of promoters subject to such a notice may be published by HMRC, including details of how the conduct notice was breached, and promoters are required to notify their monitored status to clients. Information powers and penalties apply to promoters subject to a conduct notice and to promoters subject to a monitoring notice and their clients and intermediaries. Clients who fail to comply with their duty to provide HMRC with a monitored promoter's reference number are subject to extended time limits for assessment (see **6.14** ASSESSMENTS). Special rules apply to partnerships — see **20.17** below.

The taxes covered by the provisions are income tax, capital gains tax, corporation tax, petroleum revenue tax, inheritance tax, stamp duty land tax, stamp duty reserve tax and annual tax on enveloped dwellings. The provisions applicable to promoters who promote a series of avoidance schemes which are defeated also apply to VAT. [*FA 2014, ss 281A, 283(1); FA 2016, s 160(7)(9)*].

For HMRC guidance on the provisions see www.gov.uk/government/uploads/system/uploads/attachment_data/file/403423/Promoters_of_Tax_Avoidance_Schemes_Guidance.pdf.

Definitions

[20.8] Arrangements are subject to the provisions if they enable, or might be expected to enable, any person to obtain a 'tax advantage' and the main benefit, or one of the main benefits, that might be expected to arise from the arrangements is the obtaining of that advantage. '*Arrangements*' include any agreement, scheme, arrangement or understanding of any kind, whether or not legally enforceable, involving one or more transactions.

A proposal is subject to the provisions if it is a proposal for arrangements which, if entered into, would be subject to the provisions (whether the proposal relates to a particular person or to any person who may seek to use it).

A '*tax advantage*' includes relief or increased relief from tax, repayment or increased repayment of tax, avoidance or reduction of a charge or assessment to tax, avoidance of a possible assessment to tax, deferral of a payment, or advancement of a repayment, of tax and avoidance of an obligation to deduct or account for tax.

A person carrying on a business in the course of which he is, or has been, a promoter in relation to a proposal or arrangements carries on that business 'as a promoter'. A person is a '*promoter*' in relation to a proposal if he:

(i) is to any extent responsible for the design of the proposed arrangements; or
(ii) makes a 'firm approach' to another person with a view to making the proposal available for implementation by that, or any other, person; or
(iii) makes the proposal available for implementation by other persons.

A person is a '*promoter*' in relation to arrangements if he:

(a) is a promoter by virtue of (ii) or (iii) above in relation to a proposal which is implemented by the arrangements; or
(b) is to any extent responsible for the design, organisation or management of the arrangements.

A company is not, however, a promoter if the only persons to whom it provides services in connection with a proposal or arrangements are companies in the same group, provided that it has not provided such services to any person other than a group member during the three previous years. If the company subsequently provides such services to a person other than a group member, this rule is deemed not to have applied during the previous three years. Companies are members of the same group for this purpose if one is a 51% subsidiary of the other or both are 51% subsidiaries of a third company.

A person is not a promoter on account of (i) above or by virtue of being responsible for the design of arrangements within (b) above, if either he does not provide any tax advice in connection with the arrangements or could not reasonably be expected to know that the arrangements or proposal are subject to the provisions.

Where a promoter (a '*monitored promoter*') of a proposal is subject to a monitoring notice (see **20.12** below), the proposal is a '*monitored proposal*' if the promoter, on or after the date the notice takes effect:

- first makes a firm approach to another person about the proposal;
- first makes the proposal available for implementation by another person; or
- first becomes aware of any transaction forming part of the proposed arrangements being entered into by any person.

Where a promoter of arrangements is a monitored promoter, the arrangements are '*monitored arrangements*' if:

- the promoter is a promoter of a proposal implemented by the arrangements by virtue of (ii) or (iii) above and, on or after the date the notice takes effect he:
  - first makes a firm approach to another person about the proposal;
  - first makes the proposal available for implementation by another person; or
  - first becomes aware of any transaction forming part of the proposed arrangements being entered into by any person; or

- the date on which the promoter first takes part in designing, organising or managing the arrangements is on or after the date on which the notice takes effect; or
- the arrangements enable, or are likely to enable, the person entering into the transactions forming them to obtain the tax advantage on or after the date the notice takes effect.

A person makes a '*firm approach*' to another person if he provides information about the proposal, including an explanation of the expected tax advantage, at a time when the proposed arrangements have been 'substantially designed', with a view to that, or any other, person entering into transactions forming part of the proposed arrangements. Arrangements have been '*substantially designed*' when it would be reasonable to believe that a person wishing to obtain the tax advantage might use the scheme or a scheme which is not substantially different.

A person is an '*intermediary*' in relation to a proposal if he is not a promoter of it but he communicates information about it to another person in the course of a business with a view to that, or any other, person entering into transactions forming part of the proposed arrangements.

'*Prescribed*' means prescribed, or of a description prescribed, in regulations made by HMRC by statutory instrument.

A person ('P') is a '*controlling member*' of a partnership (see **20.17** below) at any time when P has a right to a share of more than half the assets or income of the partnership. Any interests or rights of any individual who is connected with P (if P is an individual) and of any body corporate controlled by P are attributed to P for this purpose. The following are connected with P: P's spouse or civil partner; P's relatives (i.e. a brother, sister, ancestor or lineal descendant); the spouse or civil partner of P's relatives; relatives of P's spouse or civil partner; and the spouse or civil partner of a relative of P's spouse or civil partner. P controls a body corporate if P has power to secure that its affairs are conducted in accordance with P's wishes either by means of holding shares or voting power in a body corporate (whether or not the body corporate in question) or as a result of powers under the articles of association or other document regulating a body corporate.

A '*managing partner*' of a partnership is a member of the partnership who directs, or is on a day to day level in control of, the management of the partnership's business.

The Treasury may amend the definitions of 'controlling member' and 'managing partner' by statutory instrument.

An '*authorised HMRC officer*' is an HMRC officer who is, or is a member of a class of officers who are, authorised by the Commissioners for HMRC for the purposes of the high-risk promoter provisions.

[*FA 2014, ss 234–236, 254, 282, 283, Sch 36 paras 19–21; FA 2015, Sch 19 paras 5, 9; FA 2016, s 160(8)(9); SI 2015 No 130*].

Threshold conditions

[20.9] A person meets a threshold condition if:

(a) HMRC publish information about the person under the deliberate tax defaulter provisions in *FA 2009, s 94* (see **31.3** HMRC — CONFIDENTIALITY OF INFORMATION);
(b) the person is named in a report under *FA 2014, s 285* because HMRC have determined that the person has breached the Code of Practice on Taxation for Banks by promoting arrangements which they cannot reasonably have believed achieved a tax result intended by Parliament;
(c) the person has been given a conduct notice under the dishonest conduct of tax agents provisions in *FA 2012, Sch 38 para 4* (see **34.11** HMRC INVESTIGATORY POWERS) and either the time limit for making an appeal against the notice has expired or an appeal has been made and rejected by the Tribunal;
(d) the person fails to comply with disclosure requirements under *FA 2004, ss 308–310, 313ZA* (see **20.3** above), including where the person had a reasonable excuse for non-compliance (see also below);
(e) the person is charged with a specified criminal offence (but such a charge is disregarded for this purpose if it has been dismissed, if the proceedings have been discontinued or following final acquittal);
(f) arrangements of which the person is a promoter have been referred to the GAAR Advisory Panel (see **4.4** ANTI-AVOIDANCE and **52.21** PENALTIES) or are in a pool (see **4.6** ANTI-AVOIDANCE) in respect of which a referral has been made; the referral has been subject to one or more opinion notices of the sub-panel considering the case that the arrangements are not reasonable; and those notices, taken together, state the opinion of at least two of the members of the sub-panel;
(g) the person carries on a trade or profession that is regulated by a specified professional body, is found guilty of misconduct of a type prescribed for this purpose, has prescribed action taken against him, and has a prescribed penalty imposed on him (see below);
(h) the Financial Conduct Authority, Financial Services Authority or another prescribed regulatory body imposes a prescribed sanction for misconduct (including a fine or suspension of approval);
(i) the person fails to comply with an information notice under *FA 2008, Sch 36 paras 1, 2, 5* or *5A* (see **34.4** HMRC INVESTIGATORY POWERS);
(j) the person ('P') enters into an agreement with another person ('C') which relates to a proposal or arrangements of which P is the promoter on terms which impose certain contractual obligations on C (see further below); or
(k) the person has been given a 'stop notice' and, after the end of the period of 30 days beginning on the day the notice is given, makes a firm approach to another person with a view to making an 'affected proposal' (i.e. a proposal which is in substance the same as the proposal specified in the stop notice) available for implementation by that person or another or makes an affected proposal available for implementation by other persons.

As regards (d) above, with effect for the purposes of determining whether a person meets this threshold condition in a three-year period ending on or after 26 March 2015, it is clarified that a failure to comply with a said requirement occurs only at the time (if any) that:

- the 'appeal period' ends following a determination by the Appeal Tribunal that such a failure occurred, or that it would have occurred but for the person's having a reasonable excuse, and it has ended without the determination being overturned; or
- the person admits in writing to HMRC that he has failed to comply with the requirement in question.

The '*appeal period*' is the period during which an appeal could have been made or, where an appeal has been made, the period during which it has not yet been finally determined, withdrawn or otherwise disposed of.

For the purposes of (e) above, the following offences are specified:

- a common law offence of cheating the public revenue;
- in Scotland, an offence of fraud or uttering;
- an offence under *Theft Act 1968, s 17* (false accounting) or NI equivalent;
- an offence under *TMA 1970, s 106A* (fraudulent evasion of income tax);
- an offence under *TMA 1970, s 107* (false statements: Scotland);
- an offence under *Customs and Excise Management Act 1979, s 50(2)* (improper importation of goods with intent to defraud or evade duty), *s 167* (untrue declarations etc.), *s 168* (counterfeiting documents etc.), *s 170* (fraudulent evasion of duty) or *s 170B* (taking steps for the fraudulent evasion of duty);
- an offence under *VATA 1994, s 72(1)* (being knowingly concerned in the evasion of VAT), *s 72(3)* (false statement etc.), or *s 72(8)* (conduct involving commission of other offence);
- an offence under *Fraud Act 2006, s 1*;
- an offence under *CRCA 2005, s 30* (impersonating a Commissioner or officer of HMRC), *s 31* (obstruction of HMRC officer etc.) or *s 32* (assault of HMRC officer);
- an offence under *SI 2007 No 2157, Reg 45(1)* (money laundering); and
- an offence under *Criminal Justice and Licensing (Scotland) Act 2010, s 49(1)* (possession of articles for use in fraud).

For the purposes of (g) above, the type of misconduct prescribed, with effect on and after 2 March 2015, is conduct by a person which a professional body describes as misconduct or which is a breach of a rule or condition imposed by such a body and which is relevant to the provision of tax advice or tax-related services. Prescribed action means any action by a professional body which results in any claim of misconduct being referred to a disciplinary process or a conciliation, arbitration or similar settlement process. A prescribed penalty means a fine or financial penalty greater than £5,000 and/or a condition or restriction attached to, or the suspension, withdrawal or non-renewal of, a practicing certificate, or suspension, expulsion or exclusion from membership of the professional body, whether it be temporary or permanent. In (f) above, the specified professional bodies are the Institutes of Chartered Accountants in England and Wales and of Scotland, the General Council of the Bar, the Faculty of Advocates, the General Council of the Bar in Northern Ireland, the Law Society, the Law Societies of Scotland and Northern Ireland, the Association of Accounting Technicians, the Association of Chartered Certified

Accountants, the Association of Taxation Technicians, (with effect on and after 2 March 2015) the Chartered Institute of Taxation and (with similar effect) Chartered Accountants Ireland. With effect for the purposes of determining whether a person meets this threshold condition in a three-year period ending on or after 26 March 2015, the threshold condition is no longer confined to decisions and actions taken by the professional body itself and may thus take account of decisions and actions by independent bodies in matters of relevant forms of professional misconduct.

The threshold condition in (j) above is met if the contractual obligation prevents or restricts the disclosure by C to HMRC of information about the proposals or arrangements, whether or not by referring to a wider class of persons, or if the obligation requires C to impose a similar contractual obligation on any tax advisor to whom C discloses information. The condition is also met if contractual obligations require C:

- to meet the whole or part of the costs of, or contribute to a fund to meet the costs of, any 'proceedings' relating to arrangements promoted by C (whether or not implemented by C) or, where C implements the arrangements, to take out an insurance policy to insure against the risk of having to meet such costs; and
- to obtain P's consent before making any agreement with HMRC regarding arrangements promoted by P or withdrawing or discontinuing any appeal against a decision about such arrangements.

'*Proceedings*' for this purpose include any sort of proceedings for resolving disputes (i.e. not just court proceedings) which are commenced or contemplated.

Note that, where the threshold condition in question is within (i) above, it is treated as met when the time limit for compliance with the information notice expires without the promoter complying with it.

Stop notices

An authorised HMRC officer may give a person ('P') a '*stop notice*' (see (k) above) if:

- a person has been given a follower notice (see **4.25** ANTI-AVOIDANCE) relating to particular arrangements;
- P is a promoter of a proposal implemented by those arrangements; and
- 90 days have passed since the follower notice was given, the notice has not been withdrawn and, if representations objecting to the notice were made, HMRC have confirmed the notice.

A stop notice must specify the arrangements which are the subject of the follower notice, specify the court or tribunal ruling identified in that notice, specify the proposal implemented by those arrangements and explain the effect of the stop notice. An authorised HMRC officer may notify P in writing that a stop notice is to cease to have effect from a specified date (which may be before the notice is given).

[*FA 2014, Sch 34 paras 1–12, 14; FA 2015, Sch 19 paras 6–9; FA 2016, s 157(29); F(No 2)A 2017, Sch 16 para 61; SI 2015 No 131*].

Relevant defeat

[20.10] For the purposes of the high-risk promoter regime, and subject to the commencement rules below, a '*defeat*' of arrangements occurs in any of the following circumstances.

(A) A tax advantage arising from the arrangements is counteracted (partly or wholly) by HMRC under the general anti-abuse rule ('GAAR'; see **4.3** ANTI-AVOIDANCE) and the counteraction is 'final'.

(B) A follower notice (see **4.25** ANTI-AVOIDANCE) has been given by reference to the arrangements (and not withdrawn) and either the taxpayer takes corrective action or the denied tax advantage is counteracted (partly or wholly) and the counteraction is final.

(C) A tax advantage arising from 'DOTAS arrangements' is counteracted and the counteraction is final. '*DOTAS arrangements*' are arrangements which a person has disclosed to HMRC under *FA 2004, ss 308, 309* or *310* (see **20.3** above) or in respect of which a person has 'failed to comply' (as defined) with a requirement to do so. Arrangements which a person would be so required to disclose but for certain specified exceptions are treated for this purpose as having been disclosed. A tax advantage is counteracted if 'adjustments' are made to the taxpayer's position on the basis that the whole or part of the advantage does not arise. Arrangements in respect of which HMRC have given notice that the reference number need no longer be notified to clients (see **20.4** above) are excluded.

(D) A tax advantage arising from 'disclosable VAT arrangements' (as defined) is counteracted and the counteraction is final.

(E) A final judicial ruling holds that a particular 'avoidance-related rule' applies to counteract the whole or part of a tax advantage arising from the arrangements. An '*avoidance-related rule*' is a rule falling within category 1 or category 2. A rule falls within category 1 if it refers to the purpose or main purpose or purposes of a transaction, arrangements or other action or matter and to whether or not the purpose is or involves the avoidance of tax or obtaining an advantage in relation to tax. A rule is also in category 1 if it refers to expectations as to what are, or may be, the expected benefits (whether or not the sole or main benefits) of a transaction, arrangements or any other action or matter and to whether or not the avoidance of tax or obtaining an advantage in relation to tax is such a benefit. A rule falls within category 2 if it results in a person being treated differently for tax purposes depending on whether or not purposes referred to in the rule are commercial purposes.

A counteraction is '*final*' for these purposes when the assessment or adjustments made to effect it, and any amounts arising as a result, can no longer be varied, on appeal or otherwise. A judicial ruling is '*final*' if it is a Supreme Court ruling or a ruling of any other tribunal or court against which no further appeal can be made. *Adjustments*' are any adjustments, by assessment, modification of an assessment or return, amendment or disallowance of a claim, entering into a contract settlement or otherwise.

A defeat of arrangements entered into by any person which are 'promoted arrangements' of a promoter is a '*relevant defeat*' in relation to that promoter if either:

(i) the arrangements are not 'related' to any other promoted arrangements of the promoter; or
(ii) they are related to other promoted arrangements of the promoter and any of cases 1–3 below applies (in which case there is a relevant defeat of the arrangements in question and of each of the related arrangements).

If there has been a relevant defeat in relation to promoted arrangements of a promoter there can be no further relevant defeat of those arrangements or of any related arrangements.

For the purpose of (ii) above, case 1 applies if any of (A)–(D) above are met in relation to any of the arrangements and the decision to make the counteraction in question has been upheld by a judicial ruling which is final. Case 2 applies if (E) above is met in relation to any of the arrangements. Case 3 applies if at least 75% of the 'tested arrangements' have been defeated and no final judicial ruling has upheld a corresponding tax advantage under any of the arrangements. The '*tested arrangements*' are any of the arrangements in respect of which: there has been an enquiry or investigation by HMRC into a return, claim or election; HMRC has assessed a taxpayer on the basis that the tax advantage (or part of it) does not arise; a final counteraction notice under the GAAR (see **4.4–4.6** ANTI-AVOIDANCE) has been given in relation to the tax advantage (or part of it); or HMRC have taken any other action on the basis that a tax advantage does not arise under the arrangements.

Arrangements are '*promoted arrangements*' in relation to a promoter if they are arrangements to which the high-risk promoter regime applies or would apply if that regime applied generally to VAT. Separate arrangements are '*related*' to each other if they are substantially the same. For this purpose, arrangements which have been allocated the same reference number under **20.4** above or the equivalent VAT provisions are treated as substantially the same (if they would not otherwise be so treated). Arrangements which are subject to follower notices by reference to the same judicial ruling are likewise treated as substantially the same. Where a notice of binding under the GAAR has been given (see **4.5** ANTI-AVOIDANCE, the bound arrangements are treated as being substantially the same as the lead arrangements and any other arrangements otherwise treated as substantially the same as the lead arrangements.

Attribution of relevant defeat

A relevant defeat in relation to a person (Q) is treated as a relevant defeat in relation to another person (P), whether or not it is also treated as a relevant defeat of Q, if either:

(1) where P is not an individual:
 - at a time when the defeated arrangements were promoted arrangements in relation to Q either P was a body corporate or partnership controlled by Q or Q was a body corporate or partnership controlled by P; and

- at the time of the relevant defeat, P was a body corporate or partnership controlled by Q, Q was a body corporate or partnership controlled by P or both were bodies corporate or partnerships controlled by a third person; or

(2) where P and Q are both bodies corporate or partnerships, at a time when the defeated arrangements were promoted arrangements in relation to Q, a third person (C) controlled Q and C controls P at the time of the relevant defeat.

This rule applies even if Q has ceased to exist or if P did not exist at any time when the defeated arrangements were promoted arrangements in relation to Q. For the purposes of the rule, in determining whether arrangements are promoted arrangements in relation to Q, the definition of 'promoter' applies as if the word 'design' were omitted at **20.8**(b) above.

A person controls a body corporate if he has power to secure that the affairs of the body corporate are conducted in accordance with his wishes, whether by means of the holding of shares, the possession of voting power or the articles of association or other document or by means of his controlling a partnership. A person controls a partnership if he is a 'controlling member' or 'managing partner' of the partnership (see **20.8** above).

The Treasury may amend the above provisions by statutory instrument.

[*FA 2014, s 237D(6), Sch 34A paras 1–17, 19, 24–31; FA 2016, s 160(2)(5)*].

Defeat notices

Subject to the commencement rules below, an authorised HMRC officer (or an another officer acting with the approval of an authorised officer) may give a person carrying on a business as a promoter a '*defeat notice*' if:

(a) he becomes aware of one (and only one) relevant defeat in relation to the promoter in the previous three years (in which case the notice is a '*single defeat notice*'); or

(b) he becomes aware of two (but not more than two) relevant defeats in relation to the promoter in the previous three years (a '*double defeat notice*').

If, after a single defeat notice has ceased to have effect because of a judicial ruling (see below), the officer becomes aware of a further relevant defeat in relation to the promoter which occurred whilst the notice was in effect, he may issue a further single defeat notice (even if the further defeat did not occur in the three years preceding the issuing of the notice).

A defeat notice must be given before the end of the 90 days beginning with the date on which the defeat in question came to HMRC's attention. The notice must state the 'look-forward period', explain the effect of the notice (see **20.11** below) and include any further information which HMRC have specified must be included in such notices. A notice given to a partnership must state that it is a partnership defeat notice. A defeat notice has effect throughout the look-forward period unless it ceases to have effect because the relevant defeat is 'overturned'. The '*look-forward period*' is the five years beginning the day after the notice is given or, in the case of a further single defeat notice, the period beginning the day after the notice is given and ending five years from the day on which the further relevant defeat occurred.

A single defeat notice ceases to have effect if, and on and after the day that, the relevant defeat is overturned. If one (and only one) of the relevant defeats on which a double defeat notice is based is overturned, the notice is treated as if it had always been a single defeat notice based on the other relevant defeat. If both the relevant defeats on which a double defeat notice is based are overturned on the same date, the notice ceases to have effect on that date. HMRC must notify the promoter accordingly.

Only a relevant defeat to which case 3 above applies can be overturned. Such a defeat is '*overturned*' if, before the notice was given, less than 100% of the tested arrangements had been defeated and, at a time when the notice has effect, a court or tribunal upholds a tax advantage arising under any of the arrangements taken into account in determining the case 3 relevant defeat. The relevant defeat is overturned on the day on which the judicial ruling becomes final. For this purpose, a court or tribunal upholds a tax advantage if it makes a ruling that no part of the advantage is to be counteracted and that ruling is final.

Deemed defeat notices

Provision is made for a defeat notice to be deemed to have been given to a person (P) who is carrying on a business as a promoter when certain conditions are met in respect of 'third party defeats'. This applies where an authorised officer becomes aware at any time (the '*relevant time*') that a relevant defeat has occurred in relation to P and in the preceding three years there have been one or two third party defeats. A '*third party defeat*' is a relevant defeat which has occurred in relation to a person other than P.

Where there has been one such third party defeat, then if

- a conduct notice or single or double defeat notice has been given to the other person in respect of the third party defeat; at the time of that defeat, HMRC would have been able to give a defeat notice to P under the rules for attributing relevant defeats above if they had been aware that the defeat was also a relevant defeat in relation to P; and so far as the HMRC officer is aware, the conditions for giving P a defeat notice in respect of the defeat have never otherwise been met; and
- had a defeat notice in respect of the third party defeat been given to P at the time of that defeat, the defeat notice would still have effect at the relevant time,

the high-risk promoter provisions apply as if the officer had, with due authority, given P a single defeat notice at the time of the third party defeat.

Where there have been two third party defeats, then if:

- a conduct notice or single or double defeat notice has been given to the other person in respect of each, or both, of the third party defeats; at the time of the second defeat, HMRC would have been able to give a double defeat notice to P under the rules for attributing relevant defeats above if they had been aware that either of the defeats was also a relevant defeat in relation to P; and so far as the HMRC officer is aware, the conditions for giving P a defeat notice in respect of either or both of the defeats have never otherwise been met; and

- had a defeat notice in respect of the two third party defeats been given to P at the time of the second defeat, the defeat notice would still have effect at the relevant time,

the high-risk promoter provisions apply as if the officer had, with due authority, given P a single defeat notice at the time of the third party defeat.

Commencement

The above provisions, and those at **20.11** below under the headings 'Defeat of promoted arrangements' and 'Related companies and partnerships — defeat of promoted arrangements' apply with effect from 15 September 2016.

A defeat of arrangements is treated for the purposes of those provisions as not having occurred if there was a final judicial ruling before 15 September 2016 as a result of which the counteraction in (A)–(D) above is final or, where (E) above applies, if the judicial ruling in question became final on or before that date. This does not apply, however, if at any time on or after 17 July 2014 a promoter takes action as a result of which he or an associated person becomes a promoter in relation to the arrangements or related arrangements or would have become a promoter in relation to those arrangements had he not already been a promoter in relation to them. For this purpose two persons (P and Q) are associated if P is a body corporate or partnership and is controlled by Q, Q is a body corporate, P is not an individual and Q is controlled by P or if P and Q are bodies corporate or partnerships and a third person controls both of them. Control is defined as above.

A defeat of arrangements is also treated for the purposes of the provisions as not having occurred if it would otherwise occur on or before 15 September 2016 by virtue of (A)–(D) above otherwise than as a result of a final judicial ruling.

[*FA 2014, ss 241A, 241B, Sch 34A para 18, Sch 36 para 4A; FA 2016, s 160(3)(5)(11)(20)–(25)*].

Conduct notices

[20.11] A '*conduct notice*' is a notice requiring the person to whom it is given to comply with specified conditions. HMRC must issue such a notice in any of the four situations described below.

A conduct notice has effect from the date specified in it and may be amended at any time by an authorised HMRC officer. A notice ceases to have effect after two years or on an earlier date specified in the notice. It also ceases to have effect if a monitoring notice (see **20.12** below) takes effect. A notice may also be withdrawn by an authorised HMRC officer. A provisional notice may cease to have effect as a result of a judicial decision (see further below).

Threshold condition satisfied

An authorised HMRC officer must issue a conduct notice if he becomes aware at any time that a person carrying on a business as a promoter has, in the previous three years and at a time when he was carrying on such a business, met one or more of the threshold conditions (see **20.9** above) and the officer determines that the meeting of the condition or conditions should be regarded as significant in view of the purposes of the high-risk promoter regime. For this purpose, meeting any of the threshold conditions in **20.9**(a)–(c), (e) or (f) is automatically treated as significant. No conduct notice need be issued if the officer determines that it is inappropriate to do so, having regard to the extent of the impact that the promoter's activities are likely to have on the collection of tax. A conduct notice cannot be issued if the promoter is already subject to such a notice or to a monitoring notice (see **20.12** below). A conduct notice given to a partnership must state that it is a partnership conduct notice.

Related companies and partnerships — threshold conditions

The following applies where the 'relevant time' is on or after 26 March 2015. An authorised HMRC officer must also issue a conduct notice if he becomes aware at any time (the '*relevant time*') that:

(i) a person (P1) has, in the previous three years, met one or more of the threshold conditions;
(ii) at the relevant time another person (P2) is treated as meeting one or more of the threshold conditions by virtue of the 'control rules' described below;
(iii) P2 is, at the relevant time, carrying on a business as a promoter; and

the officer determines that the meeting of the condition(s) by both P1 and P2 should be regarded as significant in view of the purposes of the high-risk promoter regime.

The officer must issue the conduct notice to P2, unless he determines that it is inappropriate to do so, having regard to the extent of the impact that P2's activities are likely to have on the collection of tax. The giving of a conduct notice to P2 does not prevent the giving of such a notice to P1 in his own right.

The '*control rules*' referred to in (ii) above treat persons under another's control, persons in control of others and persons under common control as meeting a threshold condition at the relevant time as set out below. From 8 March 2017, persons with 'significant influence' over a body corporate or partnership fall within the control rules in the same way as if they controlled the body corporate or partnership.

For these purposes a person controls a body corporate if he has power to secure that the affairs of the body corporate are conducted in accordance with his wishes, whether by means of the holding of shares, the possession of voting power or the articles of association or other document or by means of his controlling a partnership. From 8 March 2017, two or more persons together control a body corporate if together they have the power to secure by any of those means that its affairs are conducted in accordance with their wishes.

From 8 March 2017, a person controls a partnership if he is a member of the partnership and either has the right to a share of more than half its assets or income or directs, or (on a day-to-day level) is in control of, the management of its business. Two or more persons together control a partnership if they are members of the partnership and together meet one of those conditions. For these purposes, the interests or rights of any individual who is connected with a person (if the person is an individual) and any body corporate controlled by the person are attributed to the person; see **20.8** above (under the definition of 'controlling member') for more details. Before 8 March 2017, a person controls a partnership if he is a 'controlling member' or 'managing partner' of the partnership (see **20.8** above).

A person has '*significant influence*' over a body corporate or partnership if, whilst not controlling it, he exercises, or is able to exercise, significant influence over it (whether or not as the result of a legal entitlement). Two or more persons together have significant influence over a body corporate or partnership if together they meet that condition.

The changes described here as applying from 8 March 2017 have effect for the purposes of determining whether a person meets a threshold condition in a period of three years ending on or after that date.

Persons under another's control

P2 is treated as meeting a threshold condition at the relevant time if it is controlled by P1 at that time and P1 met the threshold condition at a time when either P1 was carrying on a business as a promoter or P2 was carrying on a business as a promoter and P1 controlled P2. However, where P1 is an individual, this treatment applies only where the threshold condition in question is one within **20.9**(a) or (c) or any of (e)–(i) above. From 8 March 2017, the provisions are amended to allow for the possibility of a body corporate or partnership being controlled by two or more persons.

Persons in control of others

Where P2 is a person other than an individual, P2 is treated as meeting a threshold condition at the relevant time if P1 is a body corporate or partnership and met the threshold condition at a time (the 'earlier time') when it was carrying on a business as a promoter and was controlled by P2. This applies additionally if at the earlier time it was another body corporate or partnership controlled by P2 that was carrying on a business as a promoter. Before 8 March 2017, neither of these rules applied if P2 was an individual.

Persons under common control

Where P2 is a body corporate or partnership, P2 is treated as meeting a threshold condition at the relevant time if:

- P2 or another body corporate or partnership met the threshold condition at a time (the 'earlier time') when it was controlled by P1;
- at the earlier time there was a body corporate or partnership controlled by P1 which carried on a business as a promoter; and
- P2 is controlled by P1 at the relevant time.

From 8 March 2017, the provisions are amended to allow for the possibility of a body corporate or partnership being controlled by two or more persons.

Earlier legislation

If a threshold condition within **20.9**(a) or (c) or any of (e)–(i) above was met by a person at a time (the 'earlier time') when he had control of a body corporate and a determination as above was made by an authorised HMRC officer in relation to the body corporate at a later time, then, if the person had control of the body corporate at that later time, the body corporate was regarded as having met the threshold condition at the earlier time.

Where a threshold condition within **20.9**(a) or (c) or any of (e)–(i) above is met by a person who is a controlling member or managing partner of a partnership and HMRC subsequently make a determination as to whether a conduct notice should be given to the partnership, then, if the person is still a controlling member or managing partner of the partnership, the partnership is treated as meeting the threshold condition at the earlier time (whether or not the partnership was bound by the act or omission in question).

These earlier rules are replaced, where the relevant time is on or after 26 March 2015, by the more comprehensive rules above.

Defeat of promoted arrangements

The following applies subject to the commencement rules in **20.10** above. An authorised HMRC officer must issue a conduct notice if he becomes aware at any time (the '*relevant time*') that a person who is carrying on a business as a promoter meets any of the following conditions and the officer determines that the meeting of the condition(s) should be regarded as significant in view of the purposes of the high-risk promoter regime. The conditions are that:

(I) in the previous three years, at least three 'relevant defeats' have occurred in relation to the promoter; or

(II) at least two relevant defeats have occurred in relation to the promoter at times when he was subject to a single defeat notice (see **20.10** above); or

(III) at least one relevant defeat has occurred in relation to the promoter at a time when he was subject to a double defeat notice (see **20.10** above).

A determination that either of the conditions at (II) or (III) above is met can only be made while the relevant defeat notice is still in effect or on or before the 90th day after that on which it ceased to have effect. No conduct notice need be issued if the officer determines that it is inappropriate to do so, having regard to the extent of the impact that the promoter's activities are likely to have on the collection of tax.

A conduct notice cannot be issued in these circumstances if the promoter is already subject to a conduct notice or a monitoring notice. If an HMRC officer is considering at the same time whether or not a conduct notice must be made because of a threshold condition, the meeting of a condition in (I)–(III) above is treated as meeting a threshold condition and any conduct notice must be given on that basis.

An authorised HMRC officer must give a further conduct notice to a promoter if:

(1) a conduct notice has ceased to have effect otherwise than because of a judicial ruling or because it is withdrawn or a monitoring notice is given, and the notice was 'provisional';
(2) the officer determines that the promoter had failed to comply with one or more conditions in the conduct notice;
(3) the conduct notice relied on a case 3 relevant defeat (see **20.10** above) but less than 100% of the tested arrangements had been defeated before the notice was given;
(4) after the conduct notice ceased to have effect, one or more case 1 or 2 relevant defeats has occurred in relation to the promoter and any arrangements to which the case 3 relevant defeat also relates; and
(5) had that defeat or defeats occurred before the conduct notice ceased to have effect, HMRC would have had to notify the promoter that it was no longer provisional.

A further conduct notice cannot be issued in these circumstances if the promoter is already subject to a conduct notice or a monitoring notice and need not be issued if the HMRC officer determines that it is inappropriate to do so, having regard to the extent of the impact that the promoter's activities are likely to have on the collection of tax.

A conduct notice is '*provisional*' if (3) above applies to it, unless an authorised HMRC officer notifies the promoter that it is no longer provisional. A notice ceases to be provisional if:

(A) (i) two, or all three, of the relevant defeats by reference to which the notice is given would not have been relevant defeats if case 3 in **20.10** above had required 100% of the tested arrangements to have been defeated, and (ii) the same number of 'full relevant defeats' occur in relation to the promoter; or
(B) where (A)(i) above does not apply, a full relevant defeat occurs in relation to the promoter.

A '*full relevant defeat*' is either a relevant defeat other than one under case 3 or a case 3 relevant defeat where all of the tested arrangements are defeated. For this purpose, the rule that there can be only one relevant defeat of particular arrangements and any related arrangements (see **20.10** above) does not prevent a full relevant defeat from occurring in respect of arrangements in relation to which a relevant defeat under case 3 has previously occurred.

A provisional conduct notice ceases to have effect if a court or tribunal upholds a tax advantage arising under any of the arrangements taken into account in determining the case 3 relevant defeat. For this purpose, a court or tribunal upholds a tax advantage if it makes a ruling that no part of the advantage is to be counteracted and that ruling is final. HMRC must notify the promoter accordingly.

Related companies and partnerships — defeat of promoted arrangements

The following applies subject to the commencement rules in **20.10** above. An authorised HMRC officer must also issue a conduct notice if he becomes aware at any time (the '*relevant time*') that:

(a) a person (P1) meets any of conditions (I)–(III) above;
(b) at the relevant time another person (P2) meets that condition by virtue of the 'control rules' described below;
(c) P2 is, at the relevant time, carrying on a business as a promoter; and

the officer determines that the meeting of these conditions by both P1 and P2 should be regarded as significant in view of the purposes of the high-risk promoter regime.

The officer must issue the conduct notice to P2, unless he determines that it is inappropriate to do so, having regard to the extent of the impact that P2's activities are likely to have on the collection of tax. The giving of a conduct notice to P2 does not prevent the giving of such a notice to P1 in his own right.

A conduct notice cannot be issued in these circumstances if P2 is already subject to a conduct notice or a monitoring notice. If an HMRC officer is considering at the same time whether or not a conduct notice must be made because of a threshold condition, P2's meeting of the condition in (b) above is treated as P2 meeting a threshold condition and any conduct notice must be given on that basis.

The '*control rules*' referred to in (b) above treat persons under another's control, persons in control of others and persons under common control as meeting a condition within (I)–(III) above at the relevant time as set out below. From 8 March 2017, persons with significant influence over a body corporate or partnership fall within the control rules in the same way as if they controlled the body corporate or partnership. See above under Related companies and partnerships — threshold conditions for as to when a person controls, or has significant influence over, a body corporate or partnership.

The changes described here as applying from 8 March 2017, have effect for the purposes of determining whether a person meets a condition in (I)–(III) above in a period of three years ending on or after that date.

Persons under another's control

Where P2 is a body corporate or partnership, P2 is treated as meeting a condition at the relevant time if it is controlled by P1 at that time and P1 met the condition at a time when either P1 was carrying on a business as a promoter or P2 was carrying on a business as a promoter and P1 controlled P2. However, this rule does not apply where P1 is an individual. From 8 March 2017, the provisions are amended to allow for the possibility of a body corporate or partnership being controlled by two or more persons.

Persons in control of others

P2 is treated as meeting a condition at the relevant time if P1 is a body corporate or partnership and met the condition at a time (the 'earlier time') when it was carrying on a business as a promoter and was controlled by P2.

This applies additionally if at the earlier time it was another body corporate or partnership controlled by P2 that was carrying on a business as a promoter. Before 8 March 2017, neither of these rules applied if P2 was an individual.

Persons under common control

Where P2 is a body corporate or partnership, P2 is treated as meeting a condition at the relevant time if:

- another body corporate or partnership met the condition at a time ('time T') when it was controlled by P1;
- at time T there was a body corporate or partnership controlled by P1 which carried on a business as a promoter; and
- P2 is controlled by P1 at the relevant time.

From 8 March 2017, the provisions are amended to allow for the possibility of a body corporate or partnership being controlled by two or more persons.

Terms of a conduct notice

The terms of a conduct notice are determined by the officer giving it, but are limited to conditions that it is reasonable to impose to ensure that the promoter:

(a) provides adequate information (as defined, and including an assessment of the risk that the expected tax advantage will not be achieved) to clients (as defined) about proposals and arrangements of which he is a promoter;
(b) provides adequate information to intermediaries about proposals of which he is a promoter;
(c) does not fail to comply with any specified duties under the disclosure of tax avoidance schemes provisions (see **20.2** above) or under *FA 2008, Sch 36 paras 1–9* (see **34.4** HMRC INVESTIGATORY POWERS);
(d) does not discourage others from complying with any specified disclosure obligation;
(e) does not enter into an agreement which imposes on another person contractual obligations within **20.9**(j) above;
(f) does not promote proposals or arrangements which rely on, or involve a proposal to rely on, one or more contrived or abnormal steps to produce a tax advantage; and
(g) does not fail to comply with any stop notice (see **20.9** above).

In the case of a partnership conduct notice, conditions may be imposed relating to the persons who are partners when the notice is given and to persons who subsequently become partners.

Before deciding on the terms of a notice, the officer must provide an opportunity for the promoter to comment on the proposed terms.

[*FA 2014, ss 237–241, Sch 34 paras 13, 13A–13D, 14, Sch 34A paras 17–23, Sch 36 paras 4, 5, 20, 21; FA 2015, Sch 19 paras 2, 4, 5, 8, 9; FA 2016, s 160(2)(5)(6); FA 2017, s 24*].

Information

HMRC may (as often as is necessary) by notice in writing require a person subject to a conduct notice to provide information or produce a document which is reasonably required for the purpose of monitoring compliance with the notice. [*FA 2014, s 262*].

Monitoring notices

[20.12] If an authorised HMRC officer determines that a promoter has failed to comply with one or more conditions in a conduct notice, he must apply to the Tribunal for approval to give the promoter a 'monitoring notice', unless the conditions in question were imposed under **20.11**(a)–(c) above and the officer considers the failure to comply to be such a minor matter that it should be disregarded. An application for approval must include a draft notice and the officer must also notify the promoter of the application. The notice to the promoter must state which conditions have not been complied with and the officer's reasons for determining that there has been a failure to comply.

No application can be made to the Tribunal in respect of a conduct notice which is provisional. Any failure to comply with a condition in such a notice can, however, be taken into account in determining whether to make an application if the notice ceases to be provisional.

The Tribunal may approve the giving of a monitoring notice only if it is satisfied that the officer would be justified in giving it and that the promoter has been given a reasonable opportunity to make representations to the Tribunal. If the promoter's representations include a statement that it was not reasonable to include a particular condition in the conduct notice and the Tribunal is satisfied that it was not so reasonable, the Tribunal must assume that there was no failure to comply with the condition (and must refuse HMRC's application if this applies to all the conditions which HMRC consider have not been complied with). If the Tribunal gives approval it may amend the draft notice. A promoter may appeal against the decision of the Tribunal in the usual way (see **5** APPEALS).

A monitoring notice must explain its effect and specify the date from which it takes effect (which cannot be earlier than the date the notice is given). It must also inform the recipient of the right to request its withdrawal (see further below). The notice must state the conditions of the conduct notice which HMRC have determined that the promoter has failed to comply with and the reasons for that determination. A notice given to a partnership must state that it is a partnership monitoring notice. If the notice is a replacement notice given to a former partner of a partnership itself subject to a monitoring notice (see **20.17** below) it must also state the date of that notice and the name of the partnership.

Withdrawal of a monitoring notice

An authorised HMRC officer may withdraw a notice if he thinks it is no longer necessary, taking into account matters including the promoter's behaviour and compliance whilst the notice has had effect and likely future behaviour.

A person subject to a monitoring notice (a '*monitored promoter*') may make a request in writing to an authorised HMRC officer that the notice should cease to apply. Such a request can be made at any time after the twelve months beginning with the end of the period in which an appeal against the Tribunal's decision to approve the giving of the notice could have been made or, where such an appeal was made, the twelve months beginning with the date on which the appeal was finally determined, withdrawn or otherwise disposed of. If the notice is a replacement notice, the twelve-month period applies by reference to appeals against the Tribunal's decision about the original notice. HMRC must determine whether or not the notice should cease to apply within the 30 days beginning with the date on which the request is received and must notify the promoter of their determination specifying the date from which the notice is to cease to apply (and whether or not a follow-on conduct notice – see below – is to be given) or their reasons for refusal of the request.

A monitored promoter can appeal against a refusal by HMRC by notice in writing within 30 days beginning with the date on which the refusal notice was given, stating the grounds of appeal.

If HMRC decide to withdraw a notice or, following a request from the promoter, decide that a notice should cease to apply, they may issue a follow-on conduct notice to take effect immediately after the monitoring notice ceases to have effect.

[*FA 2014, ss 242–247, Sch 36 para 6; FA 2016, s 160(4)*].

Effects of a monitoring notice

[20.13] A monitoring notice has the following effects.

Publication by HMRC

HMRC may publish the name (including business name and any previous name or pseudonym) of a monitored promoter together with the business address or registered office, the nature of the business carried on, a statement of the conditions in a conduct notice with which the promoter has failed to comply and any other information which they consider appropriate to publish to make clear the promoter's identity. Where the monitored promoter is a partnership, it is the details of the partnership which may be published (and not those of particular partners). Publication may not take place before the end of the period in which an appeal against the Tribunal's decision to approve the giving of the notice can be made or, where such an appeal is made, before the appeal is finally determined, withdrawn or otherwise disposed of. If the notice is a replacement notice (see **20.17** below), the restriction applies by reference to appeals against the Tribunal's decision about the original notice. If HMRC publish details of a monitored promoter they must publish the fact of a withdrawal of the notice in the same way. [*FA 2014, s 248, Sch 36 para 14*].

Publication by monitored promoter

The monitored promoter must give a notice stating that he is a monitored promoter and which conduct notice conditions have not been complied with to anyone who is a client (as defined) at the time the monitoring notice takes effect and to anyone who becomes a client whilst the notice has effect. The notice must also identify the original monitoring notice if the monitoring notice in question is a replacement notice (see **20.17** below). The information in the notice must also be published in a prominent position on the promoter's website and any other websites promoting, or providing information on, the activities of the promoter. The requirement to give such notices does not apply until ten days after the end of the period in which an appeal against the Tribunal's decision to approve the giving of the notice can be made or, where such an appeal is made, ten days after the appeal is finally determined, withdrawn or otherwise disposed of. If the notice is a replacement notice (see **20.17** below), the requirement applies by reference to appeals against the Tribunal's decision about the original notice. In the case of someone becoming a client whilst the monitoring notice has effect, the promoter must give them the required notice within ten days of their first becoming a client.

The information, together with the promoter's reference number (see below), must also be included in certain publications and correspondence with clients and intermediaries and in correspondence with professional bodies and regulatory authorities.

[*FA 2014, s 249; SI 2015 No 549, Regs 2, 3*].

Reference number

Once all rights to appeal against the decision of the Tribunal to approve the giving of the monitoring notice (or original notice) are exhausted, HMRC will allocate a reference number to the monitored promoter. HMRC then notify the number to the promoter or, if the promoter is non-UK resident, to any person who HMRC know is an intermediary in relation to a proposal of the promoter. A promoter so notified must in turn notify the number to anyone who becomes a client while the monitoring notice has effect or who is an intermediary whilst the notice has effect. Unless the monitoring notice is a replacement notice, he must also notify the number to any person he can reasonably be expected to know has entered into arrangements, in the period in which the conduct notice preceding the monitoring notice had effect, which are likely to enable that person to obtain a tax advantage whilst the monitoring notice has effect if the monitored promoter is a promoter of those arrangements or of a proposal implemented by those arrangements. Notification must be given within 30 days of HMRC's notification of the number or later event triggering the requirement to notify.

An intermediary who is notified by HMRC of a reference number or a person so notified by a promoter must, within 30 days of being so notified, provide the number to any other person they might reasonably be expected to know has become, or is likely to have become, a client of the monitored promoter whilst the monitoring notice has had effect. An intermediary must also, within 30 days, provide the number to any person to whom he has communicated, in the course of a business and since the monitoring notice took effect, information about a proposal of the monitored promoter and to any person who he might reasonably be expected to know has, since the notice took effect, entered into, or is likely to enter into, transactions forming part of arrangements of which the monitored promoter is a promoter. An intermediary or other person notified of a reference number by the promoter does not have to provide the number to a person if he reasonably believes that that person has already been provided with the number.

A person who has been notified of a reference number under any of the above provisions must report it to HMRC if he expects to obtain a tax advantage from arrangements of which the promoter to whom the number relates is a promoter. The report must normally be made in each tax return for any period which includes a period for which the tax advantage is obtained (irrespective of whether the return relates to the tax affected). If no tax return has to be made for such periods or if a tax return is not submitted by the filing date, a separate report must be made by 31 January following the end of each tax year in which a tax advantage may arise (or, for corporation tax purposes, not later than twelve months from the end of each accounting period in which a tax advantage may arise) to HMRC, Counter Avoidance Directorate CA Intelligence SO528, PO Box 194 Bootle L69 9AA. If the arrangements give rise to a claim under *TCGA 1992, s 261B* (trade loss treated as CGT loss — see **44.21** LOSSES) and that claim is made outside of a tax return, the claim must include the reference number.

[*FA 2014, ss 250–253; SI 2015 No 549, Regs 5, 6, Sch* 2].

Information

The following information powers apply where a monitoring notice has effect.

Information and documents

HMRC may by notice in writing require a monitored promoter or a person who is an intermediary in relation to a monitored proposal (see **20.8** above) to provide information or produce a document which is reasonably required by HMRC for:

- considering the possible consequences of implementing a monitored proposal for the tax positions of those implementing it;
- checking the tax position of any person that HMRC believe has implemented a monitored proposal;
- checking the tax position of any person that HMRC believe has entered into transactions forming monitored arrangements.

A notice can be given to an intermediary only after he has been notified of the promoter's reference number. A notice given for the purpose of checking the tax position of a person cannot be given more than four years after that person's death. '*Checking*' and '*tax position*' are defined as for HMRC's general information powers (see **34.3** HMRC INVESTIGATORY POWERS) but a person's tax position also includes his position as regards deductions or repayments of tax, or sums representing tax, that he is required to make under PAYE regulations or other provisions and the withholding by him of another person's PAYE income (within *ITEPA 2003, s 683*).

Information or a document required under a notice must be provided or produced within ten days beginning with the day the notice is given or within such longer period as HMRC direct.

The giving of a notice under the above provisions must be approved by the Tribunal if it requires a promoter or intermediary to provide information or produce a document relating (wholly or partly) to a person who is not that promoter or intermediary and not an 'undertaking' of which the promoter or intermediary is the 'parent undertaking'. The promoter or intermediary must normally have been told that the information or documents are required and have been given a reasonable opportunity to make representations to HMRC, but is not entitled to be present at the hearing. The Tribunal must be given a summary of any representations made. Where the Tribunal is satisfied that informing the promoter or intermediary would prejudice the assessment or collection of tax, it can approve the giving of the notice without the taxpayer having been informed. There is no right of appeal against a decision of the Tribunal. '*Undertaking*' and '*parent undertaking*' are defined as in *Companies Act 2006, ss 1161, 1162, Sch 7*.

[*FA 2014, ss 255, 256*].

Ongoing duty to provide information

HMRC may give a notice to a monitored promoter requiring him to provide prescribed information and produce prescribed documents relating to all monitored proposals and monitored arrangements of which he is a promoter at the time of the notice or of which he becomes a promoter after that time but before the monitoring notice ceases to have effect. A notice must specify the time within which information must be provided or a document produced. [*FA 2014, s 257*]. See *SI 2015 No 549, Reg 7* for the prescribed information and documents.

Person dealing with non-resident monitored promoter

Where a non-UK resident monitored promoter fails to comply with a duty to provide information under either of the above powers, HMRC may issue a notice requiring the information from:

(1) a person who is an intermediary in relation to the monitored proposal concerned;
(2) a person to whom the promoter has made a firm approach with a view to making the proposal available for implementation by a third person;
(3) where HMRC are not aware of any person within (1) or (2) above to whom a notice could be given, a person who has implemented the proposal in question; or
(4) where the duty in question relates to monitored arrangements, a person who has entered into any transaction forming part of those arrangements.

The HMRC officer giving the notice must reasonably believe that the person to whom the notice is given is able to provide the information. Information required under a notice must be provided within ten days beginning with the day the notice is given or within such longer period as HMRC direct.

[*FA 2014, s 258*].

Duty to provide information about clients

HMRC may give notice to a monitored promoter under which the promoter must give HMRC, for each 'relevant period', the name, address and certain additional prescribed information (see *SI 2015 No 549, Reg 8*) for each client (as defined) for whom such information has not been given for a previous relevant period. Each of the following is a 'relevant period':

(a) the 'calendar quarter' in which the notice is given (but excluding any time before the monitoring notice takes effect);
(b) any period from the time the monitoring notice takes effect until the start of the period in (a) above; and
(c) each subsequent calendar quarter (excluding any time after the monitoring notice ceases to have effect).

A '*calendar quarter*' is a period of three months beginning on 1 January, 1 April, 1 July or 1 October.

Information must be provided within the 30 days beginning with the end of each relevant period or, for a relevant period within (b) above, within the 30 days beginning with the day on which the notice is given, if later.

A similar notice may be given to a person who is an intermediary in relation to a monitored proposal.

Where a promoter or intermediary has provided information under the above provisions in connection with a particular proposal or particular arrangements but an authorised HMRC officer suspects that a person for whom such information has not been provided has been, or is likely to be, a party to transactions implementing the proposal or is a party to a transaction forming the whole or part of the arrangements, the officer may by notice in writing require the promoter or intermediary to provide the information about any such person together with the reason why the information was not provided as required. Information required under a notice must be provided within ten days beginning with the day the notice is given or within such longer period as HMRC direct. A notice does not require information to be provided if it has already been provided under the above provisions.

[*FA 2014, ss 259–261, 283(1); SI 2015 No 549, Regs 8–10*].

Duty to notify HMRC of address

A monitored promoter must inform HMRC of its address within 30 days of the end of any calendar quarter at the end of which the monitoring notice applies. [*FA 2014, s 263*].

Duty of client or intermediary to provide information to promoter

An intermediary or client who is informed of a monitored promoter's reference number must within ten days notify the promoter of his national insurance number and unique taxpayer reference number. If he has neither of those numbers he must inform the promoter of that fact within ten days. There is no need to provide the information if the client or intermediary has previously provided it to the promoter. [*FA 2014, s 265*].

Information powers: further provisions

Failure to provide information

[20.14] Where a person has provided information or produced a document in purported compliance with any of the information powers at **20.11** or **20.13** above (other than those under *FA 2014, s 263* or *s 265*), HMRC may apply to the Tribunal for an order for the person to provide further specified information or produce further specified documents which they have reasonable grounds for suspecting are required by the information power in question or will support or explain information required by the power.

If the Tribunal grants such an order the information or documents must be provided or produced within ten days or such later date as HMRC direct. The duty to provide information or produce a document under such a notice is treated as part of the duty under the original information power (for the purposes of penalties etc.).

[*FA 2014, s 264*].

Appeals

A person given a notice under any of the information powers at **20.11** or **20.13** above (other than those under *FA 2014, s 263* or *s 265*) may appeal against the notice as a whole or against any particular requirement in the notice. There is, however, no right of appeal where the information or documents form part of the person's 'statutory records' or where the Tribunal has approved the giving of the notice (see **20.13** above under 'Information and documents').

Notice of appeal must be given in writing to the HMRC officer who gave the notice within the period of 30 days beginning with the date on which the notice was given and must state the grounds of appeal. A decision on an appeal by the Tribunal is final (so that there is no further right of appeal to the Upper Tribunal or Court of Appeal). Where the Tribunal confirms or varies the notice or a requirement in it, the person to whom the notice was given must comply with the notice or requirement within the period specified by the Tribunal. If the Tribunal does not specify such a period, compliance must be within such period as an HMRC officer reasonably specifies in writing.

Subject to the above, the appeal provisions of *TMA 1970, Pt 5* (see **5** APPEALS) apply to an appeal against a notice.

For this purpose, '*statutory records*' are information and documents which a taxpayer is required to keep and preserve under any enactments relating to any of the taxes to which the high-risk promoter provisions apply. Information and documents cease to be statutory records when the period for which they must be kept and preserved ends.

[*FA 2014, s 266*].

Compliance with a notice

HMRC may specify the form and manner in which information must be provided or documents produced. Documents must be produced for inspection either at a place agreed to by the recipient of the notice and an HMRC officer or at a place (other than one used solely as a dwelling) that an HMRC officer reasonably specifies. Copies of documents can be produced unless the notice requires the production of the original document or an HMRC officer in writing subsequently requests the original document. Where a copy is produced, it must be an exact copy of the original document, which must be retained and unaltered (except for the redaction of any privileged information). Where an officer makes a request for the original document, it must be produced within the period and at the time and by the means reasonably requested by the officer.

The production of a document under these provisions does not break any lien (i.e. any right) claimed on it.

[*FA 2014, ss 267, 268; SI 2015 No 549, Reg 11*].

Restrictions on information powers

The recipient of a notice under any of the information powers at **20.11** or **20.13** above is not required to:

(i) produce a document if it is not in his possession or power;
(ii) provide or produce information that relates to the conduct of a pending tax appeal or any part of a document containing such information;
(iii) provide journalistic material (within *Police and Criminal Evidence Act 1984, s 13*) or information contained in such material;
(iv) subject to the exceptions below, provide or produce 'personal records' (within *Police and Criminal Evidence Act 1984, s 12*); or
(v) produce a document the whole of which originates more than six years before the giving of the notice.

With regard to (iv) above, a notice may require a person to produce documents that are personal records, omitting any personal information (i.e. information whose inclusion in the documents makes them personal records) and to provide any information in personal records that is not personal information.

[*FA 2014, ss 269, 270*].

Legal professional privilege

A notice cannot require a person to provide information in respect of which a claim to legal professional privilege (or, in Scotland, a claim to confidentiality of communications) could be maintained in legal proceedings. [*FA 2014, s 271*].

Tax advisers

A notice under **20.13**(3) or (4) above does not require a 'tax adviser' to provide information about, or to produce documents which are his property and which consist of, communications between him and a person in relation to whose tax affairs he has been appointed or between him and any other tax advisor of such a person, the purpose of which is the giving or obtaining of advice about any of those tax affairs. For this purpose, a '*tax adviser*' is a person appointed (directly or by another tax adviser) to give advice about the tax affairs of another person.

This restriction does not apply to any information, or any document containing information, which explains any information or document which the tax adviser has, as tax accountant, assisted any client in preparing for, or delivering to, HMRC. The restriction is not disapplied if the information concerned, or a document containing the information, has already been provided or produced to an HMRC officer. [*FA 2014, s 272*].

Confidentiality

No duty of confidentiality or other restriction on disclosure (however imposed) prevents the voluntary disclosure to HMRC of information or documents about a monitored promoter of monitored proposals or arrangements by a client or intermediary. [*FA 2014, s 273*].

Concealing, destroying or disposing of documents

[20.15] A person must not conceal, destroy or otherwise dispose of, or arrange for the concealment, destruction or disposal of, a document that is subject to a requirement under the information powers in *FA 2014, s 263* (see **20.11** above) or *FA 2014, ss 255, 257* (see **20.13** above). This does not apply if he does so after the document has been produced to HMRC in accordance with the notice, unless an HMRC officer has notified him in writing that the document must continue to be available for inspection (and has not withdrawn the notification). It also does not apply if a copy of the document was produced in compliance with the notice and the destruction, etc. takes place after the end of the period of six months beginning with the day on which the copy was produced unless within that period, an HMRC officer makes a request for the original document.

Similarly, where a person has been informed that a document is, or is likely to be, the subject of such a notice addressed to him, he must not conceal, destroy or otherwise dispose of, or arrange for the concealment, destruction or disposal of, the document. This does not apply if he acts more than six months after he was so informed (or was last so informed).

A person who conceals, destroys or otherwise disposes of, or arranges for the concealment, destruction or disposal of, a document in breach of the above provisions is treated as having failed to comply with the duty to produce the document under the provision in question. If more than one provision is in question the person is treated as only having failed to comply with the duty under *FA 2014, s 248* or, if that section is not in question, with the duty under *FA 2014, s 257*.

[*FA 2014, Sch 35 paras 6, 7*].

Failure to comply with the above provisions may be a criminal offence. See **20.16** below.

Offences and penalties

[20.16] For penalties under the high-risk promoters provisions, see **52.25** PENALTIES.

It is an offence for a person required to produce a document by a notice under *FA 2014, s 255* (see **20.13** above) which has been approved by the Tribunal to conceal, destroy or otherwise dispose of the document or to arrange for its concealment, destruction or disposal. This does not apply if he does so after the document has been produced to HMRC in accordance with the notice, unless an HMRC officer has notified him in writing that the document must continue to be available for inspection (and has not withdrawn the notification). It also does not apply if a copy of the document was produced in compliance with the notice and the destruction, etc. takes place after the end of the period of six months beginning with the day on which the copy was produced unless within that period, an HMRC officer makes a request for the original document.

It is also an offence for a person to conceal, destroy or otherwise dispose of, or to arrange for the concealment, destruction or disposal of, a document after an HMRC officer has informed him in writing that the document is, or is likely to be, the subject of such a notice and approval for giving the notice is to be obtained from the Tribunal. This does not apply if the person so acts more than six months after he was so informed (or was last so informed).

On summary conviction of either of the above offences the offender is liable to a fine. On conviction on indictment the punishment is imprisonment for a maximum of two years and/or a fine.

[*FA 2014, ss 278–280*].

Partnerships

[20.17] Persons carrying on a business in partnership (within the meaning of *Partnership Act 1890*) are treated as a person for the purposes of the high-risk promoter provisions. A partnership is treated as continuing to be the same partnership (and the same person) regardless of a change in membership, provided that a person who was a member before the change remains a member after the change. Accordingly, a partnership is taken to have done any act which bound the members (restricted, in the case of a limited partnership, to the general partners) and to have failed to comply with any obligation of the firm (within the meaning of *Partnership Act 1890*) which the members failed to comply with. Where, however, a member has done, or failed to do, an act at any time, the partnership is not treated at any later time as having done or failed to do that act if at that later time neither that member nor any other person who was a member at the earlier time is still a member.

A 'partnership' does not include, for the purposes of the high-risk promoter provisions, a body of persons forming a legal person that is distinct from themselves.

Responsibility of partners

A notice under the high-risk promoter provisions given to a partnership has effect at any time in relation to the persons who are members of the partnership at that time (the '*responsible partners*'). This does not, however, affect any liability of a member who has left the partnership for anything that the responsible partners did or failed to do before he left. Anything which must be done by the responsible partners must be done by all of them (but see below regarding 'nominated partners'). References in the provisions to a right of a person (such as a right of appeal) must be interpreted accordingly.

The responsible partners are jointly and severally liable to any penalty under **52.25** PENALTIES and to any interest on such a penalty, but no amounts can be recovered from a person who did not become a responsible partner until after the act or omission which led to the penalty occurred or, in the case of a daily penalty or interest accruing for a particular day, until after the beginning of that day.

A notice given to a partnership by HMRC must be served either on all of the current partners or on a 'representative partner'. For this purpose a '*representative partner*' is a nominated partner or, if there is no nominated partner, a partner designated by an authorised HMRC officer as a representative partner and notified to the partnership as such.

Anything which must be done by the responsible partners can instead be done by a '*nominated partner*', i.e. a partner nominated by the majority of the partners to act as the partnership's representatives for the purposes of the high-risk promoter provisions. The partnership must notify HMRC of a nomination or its revocation.

Partnership changes

Where the business of a partnership subject to a defeat notice, conduct notice or monitoring notice starts to be carried on by one of the partners but not in partnership (i.e. where the other partners leave the partnership), the notice continues to apply to the continuing partner.

Where a controlling member of a partnership subject to a defeat notice leaves the partnership and carries on a business as a promoter, an authorised HMRC officer may give that person a replacement defeat notice. If the business is conducted by a partnership of which that person is a controlling member the replacement notice may be given to the partnership, but the notice will cease to have effect if that person leaves the partnership. Similar provisions apply to allow the giving of replacement conduct notices and monitoring notices.

Where a partner in a partnership which is subject to a defeat notice, conduct notice or monitoring notice ceases to carry on the partnership's business but continues to carry on a part (but not the whole) of the business, an authorised HMRC officer may give that partner a replacement notice. If the departing partner carries on the part of the business in partnership, a replacement notice may be given to that partnership, but the notice will cease to have effect if the partner leaves the partnership. These rules apply whether it is one, some or all of the partners in the original partnership who carry on a part of the business.

A replacement conduct notice ceases to have effect on the date on which the original notice would have ceased to have effect and must state that date as its expiry date. Such a notice may not be given after the expiry of the original notice. The look-forward period for a replacement defeat notice begins on the day after that on which the notice is given and ends at the end of the look-forward period of the original notice. Such a notice cannot be given after the end of the look-forward period of the original notice. A replacement conduct or monitoring notice may not be given to a person if a conduct or monitoring notice previously given to that person still has effect.

[*FA 2014, Sch 36 paras 1–3, 7–13, 15–18; FA 2016, s 160(12)–(16)*].

Key points on disclosure of tax avoidance schemes

[20.18] Points to consider are as follows.

- A key point about the disclosure of tax avoidance schemes rules is that it is the promoter that has ultimate responsibility for deciding whether to disclose a piece of planning. While counsel's opinion can be helpful, HMRC will not accept this as an excuse for a failure to disclose. That said, in the case of *HMRC v Mercury Tax Group* (Sp C 737), 2009 STI 628, the Special Commissioner decided that the fact that the company had gone 'to the trouble and expense of taking counsel's opinion' meant that no penalty should be charged for a failure to disclose. But another Tribunal judge on another day might take a different view.
- While lawyers are able to avoid disclosure on the basis of legal professional privilege, there is no such protection for accountants, even if the advice is given in contemplation of litigation (see *R (on the application of Prudential plc and another) v Special Commissioner of Income Tax and another* QB 2009, [2010] STC 161).
- It is important to remember that any one hallmark is sufficient to trigger a disclosure requirement. So, for example, even if a piece of planning is well known within the tax profession and even to HMRC, if a promoter is able to obtain a premium fee (as defined), a disclosure is required.
- The hallmark for standardised tax products does not apply just because a particular type of transaction always uses the same documents. For example, settling funds into a trust isn't necessarily disclosable tax planning, just because the lawyers always use a standard trust deed.
- You are not a promoter of a scheme if your client merely asks you to review it and say if it works. But you may become a promoter if you were to suggest improvements or to assist the promoter in fitting the scheme to your client's circumstances.

21

Double Tax Relief

Introduction	21.1
Relief under double tax agreements	21.2
Current agreements	21.3
Unilateral relief by UK	21.4
Relief by deduction	21.5
Credit relief — further provisions	21.6
Claims	21.7
HMRC practice	21.8
Anti-avoidance — schemes and arrangements designed to increase relief	21.9
Special withholding tax	21.10
Key points	21.11

(See also HMRC Pamphlet RDR1 and Capital Gains Manual CG14380.)

Cross-references. See 22.38 EMPLOYEE SHARE SCHEMES; 48 OFFSHORE SETTLEMENTS; 49 OVERSEAS MATTERS; 50.2 PARTNERSHIPS; 55 REMITTANCE BASIS; and 57 RESIDENCE AND DOMICILE.

Simon's Taxes. See C1.615–C1.618, E6.438.

Introduction to double tax relief

[21.1] Double tax relief operates to mitigate the effect of a single source of income, chargeable gain etc. being chargeable to tax in both the UK and another country. This chapter describes the reliefs available insofar as they apply to UK taxpayers in respect of UK capital gains tax and corporation tax on chargeable gains. Broadly, where the same gain is liable to be taxed in both the UK and another country, relief may be available as follows.

(a) Under the specific terms of a double tax agreement between the UK and that other country. In most cases, such agreements provide for credit against UK tax for foreign taxes on gains arising to UK residents. In some cases, however, agreements provide for exemption from taxes on gains in the country where they arise for UK residents.

(b) Under the unilateral double tax relief provisions contained in UK tax legislation. The provisions provide for credit against UK tax for foreign taxes on gains arising to UK residents.

(c) By deduction. Where no relief can be obtained under (a) or (b) above, relief may be given by deducting foreign tax paid in computing the chargeable gain for UK tax purposes.

There are anti-avoidance provisions which operate to defeat schemes designed to increase credit relief for foreign tax. Also covered in this chapter is the relief available for special withholding tax under the EU Savings Directive which is given by set-off against income tax and capital gains tax.

Relief under double tax agreements

[21.2] The UK has made, and continues to make, bilateral agreements, usually known as double tax agreements, with other countries for the avoidance of double taxation. Under these agreements, exemption from taxes in the country where they arise may be granted for gains realised by UK residents, whether individuals or companies. More usually, however, agreements provide for overseas tax to be allowed as a credit against UK tax on the gain in respect of which the overseas tax was computed. For the way in which such credit relief is given see **21.6** below. Reciprocal relief under agreements is given to overseas residents from UK capital gains tax and corporation tax. See **21.6** below as regards claims.

[*TIOPA 2010, ss 2–7, 26; TCGA 1992, s 277*].

The specific provisions of the particular agreement concerned must be examined carefully. For relevant court decisions, see Tolley's Tax Cases. Where tax on overseas gains is not relieved, or is only partly relieved, under an agreement, unilateral relief (see **21.4** below) will normally apply.

Where double tax relief by credit applies under an agreement, no deduction for foreign tax is allowed in computing the foreign gains. If a taxpayer chooses not to take relief by way of credit, any foreign tax paid is treated as allowable expenditure for the purposes of the UK assessment. See **21.5** below.

For further details of how relief by credit is given, see **21.6** below.

See also **49.22** OVERSEAS MATTERS for the tax collection agreement between the UK and Switzerland.

Current agreements

[21.3] A list is given below of the double tax agreements made by the UK which are currently operative. The agreements have effect to the extent, and as from the operative dates, specified therein (SI numbers in round brackets). Additional notes for certain agreements are given after the list, together with details of agreements made but not yet in force.

Albania (2013/3145), **Algeria** (2015/1888 — applies in the UK for financial years beginning on or after 1 April 2017 for corporation tax purposes and from 6 April 2017 for capital gains tax purposes), **Antigua and Barbuda** (1947/2865; 1968/1096), **Argentina** (1997/1777), **Armenia** (2011/2722), **Australia** (1968/305; 1980/707; 2003/3199), **Austria** (1970/1947; 1979/117; 1994/768; 2010/2688), **Azerbaijan** (1995/762),

Bahrain (2012/3075), **Bangladesh** (1980/708), **Barbados** (2012/3076), **Belarus** (1995/2706 — see notes below), **Belgium** (1987/2053; 2010/2979), **Belize** (1947/2866; 1968/573; 1973/2097), **Bolivia** (1995/2707), **Bosnia-**

Herzegovina (see note below), **Botswana** (2006/1925), **British Virgin Islands** (2009/3013), **Brunei** (1950/1977; 1968/306; 1973/2098; 2013/3146), **Bulgaria** (2015/1891; 1987/2054), **Burma** (see Myanmar below),

Canada (1980/709; 1980/1528; 1985/1996; 2003/2619; 2014/3274; 2015/2011), **Cayman Islands** (2010/2973), **Chile** (2003/3200), **China** (2011/2724; 2013/3142), **Croatia** (2015/2011), **Cyprus** (1975/425; 1980/1529), **Czech Republic** (see note below),

Denmark (1980/1960; 1991/2877; 1996/3165),

Egypt (1980/1091), **Estonia** (1994/3207), **Ethiopia** (2011/2725),

Falkland Islands (1997/2985), **Faroe Islands** (2007/3469; 1961/579; 1971/717; 1975/2190 until 6 April 1997), **Fiji** (1976/1342), **Finland** (1970/153; 1980/710; 1985/1997; 1991/2878; 1996/3166), **France** (2009/226),

Gambia (1980/1963), **Georgia** (2004/3325; 2010/2972), **Germany** (2010/2975; 1967/25; 1971/874; 2014/1874), **Ghana** (1993/1800), **Greece** (1954/142), **Grenada** (1949/361; 1968/1867), **Guernsey** (1952/1215; 1994/3209; 2015/2008; 2016/750), **Guyana** (1992/3207),

Hong Kong (2010/2974), **Hungary** (2011/2726),

Iceland (2014/1879; 1991/2879), **India** (1981/1120; 1993/1801; 2013/3147), **Indonesia** (1994/769), **Ireland** (1976/2151, 1976/2152; 1995/764; 1998/3151), **Isle of Man** (1955/1205; 1991/2880; 1994/3208; 2009/228; 2013/3148; 2016/749), **Israel** (1963/616; 1971/391), **Italy** (1990/2590), **Ivory Coast** (1987/169),

Jamaica (1973/1329), **Japan** (2006/1924; 2014/1881), **Jersey** (1952/1216; 1994/3210; 2015/2009; 2016/752), **Jordan** (2001/3924),

Kazakhstan (1994/3211; 1998/2567), **Kenya** (1977/1299), **Kiribati** (as per Tuvalu), **Korea, Republic of (South)** (1996/3168), **Kosovo** (2015/2007), **Kuwait** (1999/2036),

Latvia (1996/3167), **Lesotho** (1997/2986), **Libya** (2010/243), **Liechtenstein** (2012/3077), **Lithuania** (2001/3925; 2002/2847), **Luxembourg** (1968/1100; 1980/567; 1984/364; 2010/237),

Macedonia (2007/2127), **Malawi** (1956/619; 1964/1401; 1968/1101; 1979/302), **Malaysia** (1997/2987; 2010/2971), **Malta** (1995/763), **Mauritius** (1981/1121; 1987/467; 2003/2620; 2011/2442), **Mexico** (1994/3212; 2010/2686), **Moldova** (2008/1795), **Mongolia** (1996/2598), **Montserrat** (1947/2869; 1968/576; 2011/1083), **Morocco** (1991/2881), **Myanmar** (1952/751),

Namibia (1962/2352; 1962/2788; 1967/1490), **Netherlands** (2009/227; 1980/1961; 1983/1902; 1990/2152; 2013/3143), **New Zealand** (1984/365; 2004/1274; 2008/1793), **Nigeria** (1987/2057), **Norway** (2013/3144; 1985/1998; 2000/3247),

Oman (1998/2568; 2010/2687),

Pakistan (1987/2058), **Panama** (2013/3149), **Papua New Guinea** (1991/2882), **Philippines** (1978/184), **Poland** (2006/3323), **Portugal** (1969/599),

Qatar (2010/241; 2011/1684),

Romania (1977/57), **Russia** (1994/3213),

Saudi Arabia (2008/1770), **St. Christopher (St. Kitts) and Nevis** (1947/2872), **Senegal** (2015/1892 — applies in the UK from 1 April 2016 for corporation tax purposes and from 6 April 2016 for capital gains tax purposes), **Serbia and Montenegro** (see note below), **Sierra Leone** (1947/2873; 1968/1104), **Singapore** (1997/2988; 2010/2685; 2012/3078), **Slovak Republic (Slovakia)** (see note below), **Slovenia** (2008/1796), **Solomon Islands** (1950/748; 1968/574; 1974/1270), **South Africa** (1969/864; 2002/3138; 2011/2441), **Spain** (2013/3152), **Sri Lanka** (1980/713), **Sudan** (1977/1719), **Swaziland** (1969/380), **Sweden** (2015/1891; 1984/366), **Switzerland** (1978/1408; 1982/714; 1994/3215; 2007/3465; 2010/2689),

Taiwan (2002/3137), **Tajikistan** (2014/3275), **Thailand** (1981/1546), **Trinidad and Tobago** (1983/1903), **Tunisia** (1984/133), **Turkey** (1988/932), **Turkmenistan** (2016/1217 — applies in the UK for financial years beginning on or after 1 April 2017 for corporation tax purposes and from 6 April 2017 for capital gains tax purposes), **Tuvalu** (1950/750; 1968/309; 1974/1271),

Uganda (1952/1213; 1993/1802), **Ukraine** (1993/1803), **United Arab Emirates** (2016/754 — applies in the UK for financial years beginning on or after 1 January 2017 for corporation tax purposes and from 6 April 2017 for capital gains tax purposes), **Uruguay** (2016/753 — applies in the UK for financial years beginning on or after 1 January 2017 for corporation tax purposes and from 6 April 2017 for capital gains tax purposes), **U.S.A.** (1980/568; 2002/2848), **USSR** (see note below), **Uzbekistan** (1994/770),

Venezuela (1996/2599), **Vietnam** (1994/3216),

Yugoslavia (1981/1815 and see note below),

Zambia (2014/1876; 1972/1721; 1981/1816), **Zimbabwe** (1982/1842).

Shipping & Air Transport only—Algeria (Air Transport only, replaced with the more comprehensive agreement above) (1984/362), Brazil (1968/572), Cameroon (Air Transport only) (1982/1841), Ethiopia (Air Transport only) (1977/1297 — now replaced by comprehensive agreement above), Hong Kong (Air Transport) (1998/2566), Hong Kong (Shipping Transport) (2000/3248), Iran (Air Transport only) (1960/2419), Jordan (1979/300), Lebanon (1964/278), Saudi Arabia (Air Transport only) (1994/767), Zaire (1977/1298).

Czechoslovakia

The Agreement published as *SI 1991 No 2876* between the UK and Czechoslovakia is treated as remaining in force between the UK and, respectively, the Czech Republic and the Slovak Republic. (HMRC Statement of Practice 5/93).

USSR

The Agreement published as *SI 1986 No 224* (which also continued in force the Air Transport agreement published as *SI 1974 No 1269*) between the UK and the former Soviet Union was to be applied by the UK as if it were still in force between the UK and the former Soviet Republics until such time as new agreements took effect with particular countries. It later came to light that Armenia, Georgia, Kyrgyzstan (but see below), Lithuania and Moldova did not consider themselves bound by the UK/USSR convention and were not operating it in relation to UK residents. Accordingly, the UK ceased to apply it to residents of those countries from 1 April 2002 for corporation tax and from 6 April 2002 for income tax and capital gains tax. (The Agreement published as *SI 2001 No 3925* between the UK and Lithuania has effect from those dates.) A similar discovery has subsequently been made in relation to Tajikistan and the agreement ceased to be applied by the UK from 1 April 2014 for corporation tax and from 6 April 2014 for income tax and capital gains tax (see above for the current agreement with Tajikistan). The position for other former Republics (Belarus and Turkmenistan) with which new conventions are not yet in force remains as before. (HMRC Statement of Practice 4/01 (replacing SP 3/92) and Revenue Tax Bulletin June 2001 p 864).

Yugoslavia

The Agreement published as *SI 1981 No 1815* between the UK and Yugoslavia is regarded as remaining in force between the UK and, respectively, Bosnia-Herzegovina, and Serbia and Montenegro (and, prior to the implementation of new agreements, Croatia, Slovenia and Macedonia). (HMRC Statements of Practice 3/04, 3/07).

Copies of double tax agreements and other statutory instruments published from 1987 onwards are available on the Stationery Office website at www.hmso.gov.uk/stat.htm.

Agreements not yet in force

The Agreement with Belarus had not yet entered into force in August 2008 and was then considered unlikely to enter into force in the near future. (HMRC Double Taxation Relief Manual DT3300). A protocol to the agreement with Belgium was signed on 13 March 2014 (see *SI 2014 No 1875*). A comprehensive agreement with Colombia was signed on 2 November 2016. A new agreement with Lesotho was signed on 3 November 2016. A new agreement with Kyrgyzstan was signed on 13 June 2017.

Unilateral relief by UK

[21.4] Tax on chargeable gains payable under the law of any territory outside the UK and computed by reference to gains arising in that territory is allowed as a credit against UK tax paid on those gains by UK residents (and certain non-residents — see below).

The above relief (known as '*unilateral relief*') is not available where relief or credit for foreign tax is available under a double tax agreement.

The foreign taxes must be charged on gains and correspond to capital gains tax or corporation tax in the UK but may include similar taxes payable under the law of a province, state or part of a country, or a municipality or other local body. See *Yates v GCA International Ltd (and cross-appeal)* Ch D 1991, 64 TC 37. HMRC examine foreign taxes to determine whether, in their own legislative context, they serve the same function as UK taxes, and are thus eligible for unilateral relief. (HMRC Statement of Practice SP 7/91). The overseas taxes which the HMRC consider admissible or inadmissible for relief are listed country by country in the HMRC Double Taxation Relief Manual at DT2100 onwards.

The requirement for the claimant to be UK resident does not apply in the following cases.

(a) Unilateral relief is available for foreign tax paid in respect of the chargeable gains of a UK branch or agency of a non-UK resident person or UK permanent establishment of a non-UK resident company. The relief does not extend to taxes of the non-resident's home state, and it is limited to that which would have been available if the branch or agency or permanent establishment had been a UK-resident person to whom such gains had accrued.

(b) Credit for Channel Islands or Isle of Man tax if the claimant is resident for the particular year of assessment or accounting period either in the UK or the Channel Islands or Isle of Man. The restriction to tax on '*income arising in the territory*' does not apply in the case of the Channel Islands or the Isle of Man.

In relation to double tax agreements made after 20 March 2000, unilateral relief will not be given in particular circumstances if the agreement expressly precludes relief by credit under the agreement in those circumstances.

[*TIOPA 2010, ss 8, 9, 11, 26, 28, 30, Sch 9 para 13; TCGA 1992, s 277*].

For further details of how unilateral relief by credit is given, see **21.6** below.

Relief by deduction

[21.5] Foreign tax on the disposal of an asset which is borne by the disposer is an *allowable deduction* in computing UK chargeable gains, to the extent that no relief is to be allowed by way of credit under a double tax agreement or as unilateral relief.

Where the amount of any deduction allowed is rendered excessive or insufficient by an adjustment of any tax payable either in the UK or under the law of any other territory, the time limit for revising the UK liability accordingly is extended to six years after the time when all material determinations (i.e. assessments etc.) have been made to give effect to the adjustment.

In a case where a deduction is rendered excessive because of an adjustment of a foreign tax charge, the taxpayer must give HMRC written notification of the adjustment within one year of its being made. The maximum penalty for non-compliance is equal to the additional tax payable for the tax year or company accounting period in question.

[*TIOPA 2010, ss 31(2), 113–115; TCGA 1992, s 278*].

See HMRC Capital Gains Manual CG14410, 14425–14427.

Credit relief — further provisions

[21.6] Relief by way of credit under double tax arrangements or as unilateral relief must be claimed and is given effect by reducing the capital gains tax or corporation tax chargeable in respect of the gain by the amount of the credit. No credit is available for tax paid by a company in respect of profits subject to an election under *CTA 2009, s 18A* (exemption for company foreign permanent establishments — see **49.8** OVERSEAS MATTERS). [*TIOPA 2010, s 18; TCGA 1992, s 277(1); FA 2011, Sch 13 para 26*]. See *George Wimpey International Ltd v Rolfe* Ch D 1989, 62 TC 597 and *Yates v GCA International Ltd (and cross-appeal)* Ch D 1991, 64 TC 37.

Computation of gain where credit allowable

Remittance basis

Where credit for foreign tax is allowable in respect of a gain which is chargeable on the remittance basis, the amount received in the UK and so chargeable is treated as increased by the foreign tax on that gain. An increase may also be required in respect of special withholding tax: see **21.10** below. [*TIOPA 2010, s 32; TCGA 1992, s 277(1)–(1C)*].

Arising basis

Where the remittance basis does not apply and credit for foreign tax is to be allowed in respect of a gain, no deduction may be made in the computation of the gain for foreign tax, or special withholding tax in respect of which a claim under **21.10** below has been made, on that, or any other gain. [*TIOPA 2010, s 31; TCGA 1992, s 277(1)*].

Limits of relief

For capital gains tax purposes, credit relief is limited to the difference between the capital gains tax (before double tax relief) which would be payable by the claimant:

(i) if he were charged on his total capital gains, and
(ii) if he were charged on those gains excluding the gain in respect of which the credit is to be allowed.

Where double tax relief is due from more than one gain, this limitation is applied successively to each gain, but so that on each successive application, (i) above applies to the total capital gains exclusive of the capital gains to which the limitation has already been applied.

[*TIOPA 2010, s 40*].

Where the above provision applies to restrict the set-off of an amount of credit, the taxpayer's chargeable gains are treated as reduced by the amount of the disallowed credit. This applies only so far as the disallowed credit does not exceed any loss attributable to the gain in respect of which the foreign tax was paid. In calculating any such loss for this purpose, the payment of the foreign tax is taken into account. [*TIOPA 2010, s 35*].

In no case may a person's total credits in respect of income and chargeable gains exceed the total capital gains tax payable by the claimant for the tax year. [*TIOPA 2010, s 41*].

For corporation tax purposes, credit cannot exceed the amount of the gain multiplied by the company's tax rate (before deduction of any credit). [*TIOPA 2010, s 42; FA 2014, s 292(6)*].

Before 19 March 2010, HMRC took the view that if the UK chargeable gain (before deducting any losses) was less than the sterling equivalent of the gain chargeable in the overseas territory, the foreign tax eligible for relief had to be proportionately restricted. They were also of the view that where the gain chargeable abroad accrued over a longer period than the UK chargeable gain, the foreign tax had again to be proportionately restricted. Neither of these views appears to have any basis in either statute or case law, and HMRC have now withdrawn them with effect from 19 March 2010. From that date, HMRC accept that the whole of the foreign tax will be allowable up to the amount of the UK tax on the gain, provided that the gain charged in both countries relates to the same disposal. (HMRC Brief 17/10).

Minimisation of foreign tax

Credit relief is restricted to the foreign tax that would have been payable had all reasonable steps been taken, under the law of the territory concerned and under any double tax agreement, and on the assumption that no double tax relief were available, to minimise the liability. Such steps include the claiming of available reliefs and allowances and the making of available elections. [*TIOPA 2010, s 33*]. For a case in which HMRC sought unsuccessfully to include in these provisions steps which could have been taken before the transaction concerned, see *Hill Samuel Investments Ltd v HMRC* (Sp C 738), [2009] SSCD 315.

Payment received by reference to foreign tax

Where credit for foreign tax is to be allowed and a payment is made by a tax authority by reference to that foreign tax, either to the taxpayer or a person connected with him (within *CTA 2010, s 1122*) or, for payments made on or after 5 December 2013, to some other person directly or indirectly under a 'scheme' that has been entered into, the amount of the credit is reduced by the amount of the payment. A '*scheme*' includes any scheme, arrangement or understanding of any kind, whether or not legally enforceable, involving one or more transactions. [*TIOPA 2010, s 34; FA 2014, s 292(2)(3)(8)*].

Example

Lyra, a higher rate income tax payer, has the following chargeable gains for 2017/18.

UK gain	£30,300	
Foreign gain	16,000	(Foreign tax £6,400)

Neither of the gains are upper rate gains. Lyra claims credit relief for the foreign tax paid. Her capital gains tax liability for 2017/18 is as follows.

	UK gain	Foreign gain
	£	£
Chargeable gain	30,300	16,000
Less annual exempt amount	11,300	—
Gain chargeable to tax	19,000	16,000
Capital gains tax: £19,000/£16,000 × 20%	3,800	3,200
Less credit for foreign tax	—	3,200
Tax payable	£3,800	Nil

Notes to the example

(a) No relief is available for the excess of the foreign tax over the CGT liability in respect of the foreign gain (£6,400 – £3,200 = £3,200).

(b) The annual exempt amount is allocated against the UK gain as this maximises the double tax relief available.

Claims

[21.7] The normal time limit for claims for credit relief is not more than four years after the end of the tax year or accounting period for which the gain is chargeable. This time limit applies to claims made on or after 1 April 2010. Previously claims normally had to be made on or before the fifth anniversary of 31 January following the year of assessment for which the gain was chargeable to CGT; or within six years after the end of the company accounting period for which the gain was chargeable to corporation tax. For capital gains tax purposes (but not for corporation tax purposes), the changes in time limits apply by reference to claims made before, or on or after, 1 April 2012 where the claim concerned relates to a tax year for which the taxpayer has not been given notice to make a return under *TMA 1970, s 8* or *s 8A* (see **58.3** RETURNS) or *s 12AA* (see **58.16** RETURNS) within one year of the end of the tax year (in effect, where the taxpayer is outside self-assessment). This rule does not, however, apply if for that year any gains which ought to have been assessed have not been assessed, or an assessment has become insufficient, or any relief given has become excessive.

The claim deadline is extended to 31 January following the year of assessment in which the foreign tax is paid or one year after the end of the company accounting period in which the foreign tax is paid, where this is later than the deadline given above.

[*TIOPA 2010, s 19; TCGA 1992, s 277; SI 2009 No 403*].

Written notice must be given to HMRC where any credit allowed for foreign tax has become excessive by reason of a reduction in credit because of a payment in respect of the foreign tax (see **21.6** above) or an adjustment of the amount of any foreign tax payable (except in the case of UNDERWRITERS AT LLOYD'S (**69**) where the consequences of such a reduction or adjustment are dealt with under regulations). The notice must be given within one year after the making of the reduction or adjustment. The maximum penalty for failure to comply is the amount by which the credit was rendered excessive by the reduction or adjustment. [*TIOPA 2010, s 80*]. For what constitutes an adjustment and when an adjustment should be considered to have been made for these purposes, see Revenue Tax Bulletin June 1999 p 673.

HMRC practice

[21.8] The standard credit article in double tax agreements provides for overseas tax to be allowed as a credit against UK tax on the gain in respect of which the overseas tax was computed. Unilateral relief operates similarly. There is no requirement for the two liabilities to arise at the same time or on the same persons; and therefore HMRC consider that relief is available in the following situations.

(a) A capital gain is taxed overseas as income.
(b) Tax is charged overseas on a no gain/no loss transfer within a group of companies, and a UK liability arises on a subsequent disposal (see **29.3**, **29.7** GROUPS OF COMPANIES).
(c) An overseas trade carried on through a branch or agency is transferred to a local subsidiary, with an immediate overseas tax charge; and a UK tax charge arises on a subsequent disposal of the securities or on a disposal of the assets by the subsidiary within six years (see **49.12** OVERSEAS MATTERS).
(d) UK liability arises on a disposal of assets after overseas tax has become payable by reference to an increase in value without a disposal.

This relief is not available where a gain is rolled over in the UK (see **59** ROLLOVER RELIEF); but the overseas tax can be deducted from the gain (see **21.5** above).

(HMRC Statement of Practice 6/88).

Anti-avoidance — schemes and arrangements designed to increase relief

[21.9] *FA 2005* introduced anti-avoidance provisions intended to defeat schemes designed to increase credit relief for 'foreign tax'. The provisions apply where the following conditions are satisfied.

(a) In relation to any chargeable gains (or income) taken or to be taken into account for the purposes of determining a person's liability to tax in a chargeable period there is an amount of foreign tax for which, under any arrangements, credit is allowable against UK tax for that period.
(b) There is a scheme or arrangement the main purpose, or one of the main purposes, of which is to cause an amount of foreign tax to be taken into account in the case of that person for that chargeable period.

(c) The scheme or arrangement is a 'prescribed scheme or arrangement' within (1) to (6) below.
(d) The aggregate of the amount of the claims for credit made by the person for that chargeable period and the amount of claims for credit made by all the persons connected to that person for an overlapping chargeable period is more than a minimal amount. For this purpose, a chargeable period of one person overlaps with a chargeable period of another if they have at least one day in common.

If HMRC consider, on reasonable grounds, that the above conditions are or may be satisfied in relation to any person they may give that person a notice (a '*counteraction notice*') informing him of their view and that as a consequence he will be required, in his tax return for the period concerned, to make such adjustments as are necessary to counteract the effects of the scheme or arrangement that are referable to the purpose in (b) above. The notice may (but is not required to) specify the adjustments required.

Where a person receives a counteraction notice and the conditions at (a)–(d) above are in fact satisfied, that person must, in his tax return for the period concerned, make such adjustments as are necessary to counteract the effects of the scheme or arrangement that are referable to the purpose in (b) above.

If the counteraction notice is given before the person has made his return for the chargeable period concerned then, if the return is made in the period of 90 days beginning with the day on which the notice is given, it may disregard the notice, and at any time before the end of the 90 days the person may amend the return in order to comply with the notice.

If no counteraction notice has been given before the person's return has been made, a notice may only be given if the person has been given a notice of enquiry (see **58.9** RETURNS) in respect of the return. After an enquiry has been completed, a counteraction notice may only be given if:

- at the time the enquiry was completed HMRC could not have reasonably been expected, on the basis of the information made available (within *TMA 1970, s 29(6)(7)* — see **6.10** ASSESSMENTS) to them before that time, to have been aware that the circumstances were such that a notice could have been given; and
- the person was requested to provide information during the enquiry and, if it had been so provided, HMRC could reasonably have been expected to give the person a notice.

If the counteraction notice is given after the person has made his return, he may amend the return to comply with the notice within 90 days beginning with the day on which the notice is given. If the notice is given after an enquiry into the return has started, a final closure notice (see **58.12** RETURNS) may not be issued until the end of the period of 90 days beginning with the issue of the notice or, if earlier, an amendment is made to the return complying with the notice (though this does not prevent the issue of a partial closure notice that is unrelated to any matter to which the counteraction notice relates). If the notice is given after the completion of an enquiry, a discovery assessment (see **6.10**

ASSESSMENTS) in relation to the gains (or income) to which it relates may not be made until the end of the period of 90 days beginning with the issue of the notice or, if earlier, an amendment is made to the return complying with the notice.

Where a notice is issued and no amendment is made to the return for the purpose of complying with it, the above provisions do not prevent a return becoming incorrect if such an amendment should have been made.

'*Foreign tax*' includes any tax which is treated under *TIOPA 2010, s 63(5)* (dividends paid between related companies) as payable under the law of a territory outside the UK.

[*TIOPA 2010, ss 81, 82, 89–95; F(No 2)A 2017, Sch 15 paras 38, 39, 44*].

Prescribed scheme or arrangement

The above provisions apply to schemes or arrangements falling within one or more of the following types.

(1) A scheme or arrangement which enables a person who is party to it or concerned in it to pay, in respect of a chargeable gain (or source of income), an amount of foreign tax all or part of which is properly attributable to one or more other gains (or sources of income).

(2) A scheme or arrangement under which a person (the '*claimant*') has claimed, or is in a position to claim, for a chargeable period, any credit that under any double tax arrangements is allowable for the payment of an amount of foreign tax if, when the claimant entered into the scheme, it could reasonably be expected that the effect on the 'foreign tax total' of the amount being paid or payable would be to increase it by less than the amount allowable as a credit in respect of the payment.
For these purposes, the '*foreign tax total*' is the amount found by aggregating the amounts paid or payable in respect of the transactions forming part of the scheme or arrangement by persons party to it or concerned in it and taking into account any reliefs, deductions, reductions or allowances against or in respect of any tax that arise to those persons (including any such reliefs etc. arising as a consequence of the amount of foreign tax being paid or payable).

(3) A scheme or arrangement under which, in relation to a claimant, an amount ('*amount X*') is treated under the Tax Acts as if it were an amount of foreign tax paid or payable in respect of a source of income or a chargeable gain and it could reasonably be expected by the claimant, at the time he entered the scheme, either that no real foreign tax would be paid or payable by a participant or that such an amount would be paid or payable but would increase the foreign tax total (as in (2) above) by less than the amount allowable to the claimant for amount X.

(4) A scheme or arrangement where a step is taken by a person who is party to it or concerned in it or a step that could have been taken by such a person is not taken where that action or omission has the effect of increasing a claim made by such a person for an allowance by way of credit or of giving rise to such a claim. The steps concerned are those

that may be made under the law of any territory or under double tax arrangements made in relation to any territory and include claiming or otherwise securing the benefit of reliefs, deductions, reductions or allowances, and making elections for tax purposes. Steps taken or not taken before the scheme or arrangement was made are taken into account and the reason for taking or not taking a step is irrelevant if it has the requisite effect.

(5) A scheme or arrangement under which 'amount A' is less than 'amount B' in relation to a person who has claimed, or is in a position to claim, for a chargeable period an allowance by way of credit for foreign tax. For this purpose, '*amount A*' is the amount of UK tax payable in respect of income and chargeable gains arising in the chargeable period and '*amount B*' is the amount of UK tax that would be payable in respect of income and chargeable gains for the period if, in determining that amount, the transactions forming part of the scheme or arrangement were disregarded.

(6) A scheme or arrangement which includes the making by a person (A) of a 'relevant payment' or payments and the giving, for that payment or payments, of consideration, all or part of which consists of a payment or payments made to A, or a person connected (within *CTA 2010, s 1122*) with A, which is chargeable to tax under the law of a territory outside the UK. For this purpose, a '*relevant payment*' is a payment by A all or part of which may be brought into account in computing A's income for UK tax purposes. A '*payment*' includes the transfer of money's worth.

[*TIOPA 2010, ss 83–88*].

Special withholding tax

[21.10] The following provisions apply to give relief by way of set-off against UK income tax or capital gains tax liabilities for 'special withholding tax' levied on foreign 'savings income'. To the extent that the tax cannot be so set off, relief is given by repayment.

'*Special withholding tax*' is withholding tax (however described) levied under the law of a territory outside the UK which implements either Article 11 of the EU Savings Directive (Council Directive 2003/48/EC) or, in the case of a territory which is not a member state, any corresponding provisions of 'international arrangements'. The Directive came into effect on 1 July 2005 (HMRC Internet Statement, 1 July 2005) and was repealed with effect from 1 January 2016 (European Council Press Release 10 November 2015). '*International arrangements*' in relation to a particular territory are arrangements made to ensure the effective taxation of savings income under the law of the UK or under that law and the law of that territory. '*Savings income*' has the same meaning as the expression 'interest payment' has for the purposes of the Directive or, in relation to territories which are not member states, the same meaning as the corresponding expression has for the purposes of the international arrangements concerned.

[*TIOPA 2010, ss 135, 136*].

Under the terms of the Directive, three EU member states, Austria, Belgium and Luxembourg, imposed special withholding tax for a transitional period. The other member states will instead adopt the system of automatic exchange of information on cross-border payments for which the Directive provides. Certain non-EU states are also expected to apply special withholding tax during the transitional period, and agreements to this effect have been made between the UK and the British Virgin Islands (*SI 2005 No 1457*), Jersey (*SI 2005 No 1261*), Guernsey (*SI 2005 No 1262*), the Isle of Man (*SI 2005 No 1263*), the Netherlands Antilles (*SI 2005 No 1460*) and Gibraltar (*SI 2006 No 1453*) (HMRC Internet Statements, 2 February 2005, 17 May 2005, 21 December 2005). The rate of special withholding tax is 15% for the first three years, 20% for the next three years and 35% thereafter. Special withholding tax is to be withdrawn in the Isle of Man by July 2011 (HM Treasury News Release 61/09, 24 June 2009).

Income tax credit

Where a person is chargeable to income tax for a tax year in respect of a payment of savings income which has suffered special withholding tax (or would be so chargeable but for an exemption or relief), income tax of an amount equal to the special withholding tax is deemed for tax purposes to have been paid by or on behalf of that person and to have been deducted at source from the income. For this treatment to apply, the person concerned must be UK resident for the tax year in question and must make a claim. If the deemed tax exceeds the person's income tax liability for the year, the excess is first set against any capital gains tax liability for the year, with any remaining balance relieved by way of a repayment of income tax. [*TIOPA 2010, ss 137, 138*].

Capital gains tax credit

Where:

- a person disposes of assets in a tax year so that any chargeable gain accruing on the disposal would accrue to him and he would be chargeable to capital gains tax on it (if the annual exempt amount, any allowable losses and *TCGA 1992, s 77(1)* (charge, for 2007/08 and earlier years, on settlor with interest in settlement were disregarded), and
- the consideration for the disposal consists of or includes savings income which has suffered special withholding tax

capital gains tax of an amount equal to the special withholding tax is deemed for tax purposes to have been paid by or on behalf of that person for that year and to have been deducted at source. For the purposes of repayment supplement (see **56.3** REPAYMENT INTEREST), the deemed tax is, however, treated as paid on 31 January following that year. If the deemed tax exceeds the person's capital gains tax liability for the year, the excess is first set against any income tax liability for the year, with any remaining balance relieved by way of a repayment of tax. For this treatment to apply, the person concerned must be UK resident for the tax year in question and must make a claim. This treatment only applies to the extent that income tax credit relief as above is not available in respect of the special withholding tax concerned.

[*TIOPA 2010, ss 139, 140*].

Interaction with other double tax relief provisions

A person cannot obtain relief under the above provisions if double tax relief has been obtained in respect of the special withholding tax under the law of a territory outside the UK and the person was resident in that territory (or treated as so resident under any double tax arrangements) in the tax year in question. Similarly, a person cannot obtain double tax relief under the normal income tax double tax relief provisions for special withholding tax.

Credit for foreign tax due by agreement (see **21.2** above) or unilaterally (see **21.4** above) is given in priority to relief for special withholding tax. This enables overall relief to be maximised, as excess foreign tax other than special withholding tax is not repayable.

[*TIOPA 2010, ss 138(2), 140(2), 141*].

Computation of chargeable gains subject to special withholding tax

Where a chargeable gain accrues to a person on a disposal of assets in circumstances where the consideration consists of or includes an amount of savings income which has suffered special withholding tax in respect of which a claim has been made under the above provisions, and the REMITTANCE BASIS (**55**) does not apply, no deduction may be made in the computation of the gain for any special withholding tax in respect of that or any other gain.

Where the remittance basis applies, the amount of the gain received in the UK is treated as increased by the proportion of the special withholding tax suffered that the chargeable gain received in the UK bears to the total gain less the special withholding tax.

[*TIOPA 2010, ss 142, 143; TCGA 1992, s 277(1)–(1C)*].

Certificates to avoid levy of special withholding tax

On receipt of a valid application, HMRC will issue a certificate (valid for up to three years) which can be forwarded to a person's paying agent so that he will not levy special withholding tax on payments of savings income. An application for such a certificate must be in writing and must include certain required information listed in *FA 2004, s 113(3)*. There is a right of appeal against an HMRC decision not to issue such a certificate. The appeal must be in writing and must be given to HMRC within 30 days of the date of HMRC's notice refusing a certificate. [*TIOPA 2010, ss 144, 145; SI 2009 No 56, Sch 1 para 422*].

Key points concerning double tax relief

[21.11] Points to consider are as follows.

- Relief is available against UK tax where overseas tax is paid on a gain chargeable to tax in another country.
- Where there is no double tax treaty in place the relief is given in accordance with UK legislation (unilateral relief) which provides for a credit for overseas tax paid or where relief is not available as a credit it can be treated as an allowable deduction.
- If there is a double tax agreement in place the relief is available under the specific terms of the agreement. In some double tax agreements there may be an exemption from tax on gains in the overseas country where they arise to UK residents.
- The starting point in applying double tax relief is to look at what the domestic position is i.e. is there a taxable gain. If there is and overseas tax has been paid the next step is to check if there is a double tax agreement in place, if so it should be applied. If there is no double tax agreement in place the UK relieving provisions will apply.
- If relief is not available as a credit the foreign tax paid can be treated as a deductible expense in calculating the gain.
- New and amended treaties are regularly added to the list of treaties.
- See **49.8** OVERSEAS MATTERS for the exemption regime for profits of foreign permanent establishments of UK resident companies (which includes chargeable gains).

22

Employee Share Schemes

Introduction	**22.1**
Extended meaning of 'shares'	**22.2**
Consideration for grant of share option	**22.3**
Release and replacement of options	**22.4**
Employee share schemes which are not tax-advantaged	**22.5**
Exercise of share option which is not tax-advantaged	**22.6**
Other charges in respect of share options which are not tax-advantaged	**22.7**
Shares acquired for less than market value	**22.8**
Shares disposed of for more than market value	**22.9**
Anti-avoidance — shares with artificially depressed market value	**22.10**
Anti-avoidance — shares with artificially enhanced market value	**22.11**
Post-acquisition benefits	**22.12**
Restricted shares	**22.13**
Conditional interests in shares	**22.14**
Convertible shares	**22.15**
Research institution spin-out companies	**22.16**
Share Incentive Plans	**22.17**
Rollover relief on disposals of shares to a SIP — Requirements for relief	**22.18**
Form of relief	**22.19**
Special rules where replacement asset is a dwelling-house	**22.20**
Special rules where replacement asset is EIS shares	**22.21**
Enterprise Management Incentives	**22.22**
Other tax-advantaged share option schemes	**22.23**
Save as you earn (SAYE) share option schemes	**22.24**
Company share option plan (CSOP) schemes	**22.25**
Employee shareholder shares	**22.26**
Executive share option schemes	**22.27**
Approved profit sharing schemes	**22.28**
Employee Share Ownership Trusts	**22.29**
Rollover relief on disposals of shares to a trust	**22.30**
Chargeable event when replacement assets owned	**22.31**
Chargeable event when replacement property owned	**22.32**
Chargeable event when qualifying corporate bonds owned	**22.33**
Dwelling houses — special provisions	**22.34**
Shares qualifying for EIS relief — special provisions	**22.35**
Information powers	**22.36**
Priority allocations in public share offers	**22.37**
Double tax relief	**22.38**
Key points	**22.39**

Cross-reference. See **25.89** EXEMPTIONS AND RELIEFS re employee trusts.

Introduction to employee share schemes

[22.1] Income tax and capital gains tax (CGT) legislation applies where there are arrangements to allow employees (which term includes for these purposes directors) to acquire shares in their employing companies. Tax reliefs and exemptions apply where such arrangements take the form of one or more of the various statutory schemes and have been granted HMRC approval.

This chapter is concerned with the CGT consequences of both tax-advantaged schemes and other schemes (and for these purposes the term 'scheme' encompasses any such arrangements as mentioned above). The expression 'shares' is used in its broadest sense. For the application of the chapter to stocks and securities, as well as shares, see **22.2** below. For context, the coverage includes in most cases a brief note of the income tax position, but for the full provisions (and, as regards approved schemes, the conditions for approval) see Tolley's Income Tax under Share Related Employment Income and Exemptions. For the general income tax liability in respect of shares given to employees as part of their earnings see Tolley's Income Tax under Employment Income. See HMRC Capital Gains Manual CG56300–56550 for HMRC's own notes on the CGT provisions, and see generally **Simon's Taxes.** See **C1.430–C1.441, C2.810–C2.818, E4.5.**

See **64.2**, **64.4** SHARES AND SECURITIES — IDENTIFICATION RULES for special rule where shares are acquired as an employee and are subject to restricted disposal rights.

See also **7.7** ASSETS and **72** WASTING ASSETS for CGT treatment of options generally.

Extended meaning of 'shares'

[22.2] For the purposes of **22.6**, **22.8–22.15** (except **22.14**) below, the meaning of 'shares' is extended to embrace a broader range of financial products, including, for example, government and local authority stocks. All of the following are 'shares' for these purposes:

- shares (including stock) in any body corporate, wherever incorporated, or in any unincorporated body constituted under the law of a foreign country;
- rights under 'contracts of insurance' other than 'excluded contracts' (but see further below);
- debentures, debenture stock, loan stock, bonds, certificates of deposit and other instruments creating or acknowledging indebtedness (other than contracts of insurance);
- warrants and other instruments entitling the holders to subscribe for securities;
- certificates and other instruments conferring rights in respect of securities held by persons other than the persons on whom the rights are conferred and which may be transferred without the consent of those persons;
- units in a collective investment scheme (as defined by *ITEPA 2003, s 420(2)*);

- futures (as defined by *ITEPA 2003, s 420(3)*) and options (other than 'share options' — see below) acquired on or after 2 December 2004;
- rights under contracts for differences (or under similar contracts — as defined by *ITEPA 2003, s 420(4)*), other than contracts of insurance;
- alternative finance arrangements which are investment bond arrangements (see **3.3** ALTERNATIVE FINANCE ARRANGEMENTS).

However, none of the following are 'shares' for these purposes:

- cheques, bills of exchange, bankers' drafts and letters of credit (other than bills of exchange accepted by a banker);
- money and statements showing balances on a current, deposit or savings account;
- leases and other dispositions of property and heritable securities;
- options acquired before 2 December 2004; and
- share options (within the meaning given at **22.6** below) acquired on or after 2 December 2004.

The above lists can be amended by Treasury order.

Note that contracts of insurance are brought within the definition of shares on and after 2 December 2004. This applies to rights under contracts acquired before that date as well as those acquired on or after that date. Previously such contracts were not shares. A contract is an '*excluded contract*' if it is:

- a contract for an annuity which is, or will be, pension income within *ITEPA 2003, Pt 9*;
- a 'contract of long-term insurance', other than an annuity contract, which does not have, and cannot acquire (whether on conversion or otherwise), a surrender value; or
- a 'contract of general insurance' other than one falling in accordance with generally accepted accounting practice (as defined in *FA 2004, s 50*) to be accounted for as a financial asset or liability.

For the above purposes, 'contract of insurance', 'contract of long-term insurance' and 'contract of general insurance' all have the same meaning as in *Financial Services and Markets Act 2000 (Regulated Activities) Order 2001 SI 2001 No 544*.

It is important to note that the above extended meaning of 'shares' does *not* apply for the purposes of the HMRC-approved schemes at **22.17** *et seq*. below. For the purposes of **22.22** and **22.28** below, 'shares' includes stock but not securities, and there are specific rules restricting the types of shares eligible under the other schemes. For details see Tolley's Income Tax under Share-Related Employment Income and Exemptions.

An '*interest in shares*', for the purposes of **22.6, 22.8–22.15** (but not **22.14**) below, means an interest which is less than full beneficial ownership. It includes an interest in their sale proceeds but not a right to acquire them.

[*ITEPA 2003, ss 420, 434(1), 470(1), 487(1) as originally enacted, ss 516(4), 521(4), 548(1), Sch 5 para 58; TCGA 1992, ss 119A(7), 120(1)(7)(8); ITA 2007, s 564T; TIOPA 2010, Sch 2 para 21, Sch 8 para 204; SI 2007 No 2130*].

For the purposes of this chapter, '*employment-related shares*' are shares or an interest in shares (as above) acquired by a person by virtue of a right or opportunity made available by reason of the employment (past, present or prospective) of that or any other person. For this purpose, shares are deemed to be acquired when the beneficial entitlement to them is acquired and not, if different, at the time of conveyance or transfer. Any right or opportunity made available by a person's employer, or by a person connected (within *ITA 2007, s 993*) with a person's employer, is treated as made available by reason of the employment of that person, other than in the case of an individual conferring a right or opportunity in the normal course of his domestic, family or personal relationships. There are rules dealing with company reorganisations (such as conversions, scrip issues and rights issues); these treat replacement shares or additional shares acquired on such a reorganisation as acquired by virtue of the same right or opportunity as the original interest and treat any consequent reduction in the market value of the original shares as consideration given or a payment made for the replacement shares or additional shares. [*ITEPA 2003, ss 421B, 421D; FA 2014, Sch 9 para 35*].

Consideration for grant of share option

[22.3] Where a 'share option' to which the income tax provisions at **22.6** below apply (or, for 2013/14 and earlier years, would apply but for *ITEPA 2003, s 474*) is granted *TCGA 1992, s 17(1)* (see **45.1** MARKET VALUE) is disapplied (where it would otherwise apply), so that, for CGT purposes, the amount or value of the consideration for the grant, as regards both the company and employee, is the actual value or consideration passing (if any). However, in computing actual value for this purpose, any value put on the employee's services, past or present, is ignored. [*TCGA 1992, s 149A; FA 2013, Sch 9 paras 23, 43–46*].

Release and replacement of options

[22.4] The following applies where an option to acquire shares in a company ('*the old option*') which was obtained by an individual by reason of his office or employment as director or other employee of that or any other company is released in whole or in part for a consideration which consists of or includes the grant to him of another option ('*the new option*') to acquire shares in that or any other company. The new option is not regarded for CGT purposes as consideration received by him for the release of the old option. Any consideration given by him for the old option is taken to be the consideration given for the new option and any additional expenditure paid by him for the acquisition of the new option is treated as allowable expenditure. The release of the old option is disregarded in determining the consideration received for the new option by the grantor company. [*TCGA 1992, s 237A*].

Employee share schemes which are not tax-advantaged

[22.5] Where an employee (including a director) receives shares by reason of his employment and otherwise than under a tax-advantaged scheme (see **22.17–22.28** below), he is generally treated by virtue of *TCGA 1992, s 17* (see

45.1 MARKET VALUE) as acquiring them at their market value at the time of acquisition. Likewise, any disposal by the employer is treated as made at market value (but see Revenue Tax Bulletin December 1994 p 181 for concessional treatment applied in certain cases to pre-6 April 1995 transactions). As regards certain shares subject to risk of forfeiture, *s 17* is disapplied as regards the employee only (see **22.14** below).

See also, at **45.1** MARKET VALUE, the **exception to the market value rule** where an asset is acquired for nil consideration or at less than its market value *and* there is no corresponding disposal. This would apply, for example, where *new* shares are *issued* by a company to an employee (as opposed to existing shares being transferred), as an issue of shares is not a disposal by a company for the purposes of corporation tax on chargeable gains; in such a case, the employee's CGT acquisition cost of the shares is restricted to the actual consideration given (if any).

A transfer of shares to a director or other employee for nil consideration or at less than market value normally gives rise to a charge to income tax if regarded as part of his general earnings. The amount so charged does not form part of the acquisition cost of the shares for CGT purposes (see also **22.6** below re shares acquired on the exercise of an option).

See **22.37** below for disapplication of market value rules where employees receive priority allocations in public share offers.

See **22.6** below where shares are acquired as a result of the *exercise* of an option.

Exercise of share option which is not tax-advantaged

[22.6] An income tax charge may arise on the exercise of a share option which is not tax-advantaged. The provisions apply to a 'share option' (an '*employment-related share option*') acquired by a person where the right or opportunity to acquire it is available by reason of the employment (past, present or prospective) of that person or any other person.

A '*share option*' is a right to acquire 'shares'. A right to acquire shares which is acquired pursuant to a right or opportunity made available under arrangements the main purpose, or one of the main purposes, of which is the avoidance of tax or national insurance contributions is not a share option. See the extended meaning of '*shares*' in **22.2** above.

Subject to exclusions, the acquisition of shares on the exercise of the option by an employee results in the chargeable amount being taxed as employment income of the employee for the tax year in which the exercise occurs under *ITEPA 2003, s 476*. The chargeable amount is the difference between the open market value of the acquired shares at the time of exercise and the aggregate of the consideration given for the shares and any given for the option. Certain other amounts may be deducted in arriving at the chargeable amount, including any amount charged on *grant* of the option. Relief is given by deduction from the chargeable amount in respect of any liability to secondary Class 1 national insurance contributions (i.e. employer contributions) in respect of the exercise of the option borne by the employee under a voluntary agreement or a joint election under *Social Security Contributions and Benefits Act 1992, Sch 1 para 3A* or *para 3B* (or NI equivalent). Consideration given for an option does not include any value placed on the performance of duties in connection with the employment. (In specified circumstances, a person is likewise chargeable even though the gain in question is realised by another person.)

[*ITEPA 2003, ss 419, 420(8), 421–421B, 421D, 471–484, 485, 487 as originally enacted, ss 718, 721(1), Sch 7 paras 62–67; FA 2013, Sch 45 para 67; FA 2014, Sch 8 paras 133, 134, 194–197, Sch 9 paras 14, 15; SI 2003 No 1997*].

For shares in research institution spin-out companies, see **22.16** below.

Capital gains tax

Employment-related share options to which the above provisions apply (or would apply but for the exclusions in *ITEPA 2003, s 474*) are treated as options for capital gains tax purposes, whether or not they would ordinarily be regarded as such. The acquisition of shares pursuant to such an option is accordingly treated as the exercise of an option. [*TCGA 1992, s 288(1A)*].

The acquisition of an option and the transaction entered into by the grantee on the exercise of the option, being in this case an acquisition of shares, are treated for CGT purposes as a single transaction taking place at the time the option is exercised (see also **7.7** ASSETS).

Any sum charged to income tax as employment income under the above provisions forms part of the cost of acquisition of the shares for CGT purposes (within *TCGA 1992, s 38(1)(a)* — see **16.11**(a) COMPUTATION OF GAINS AND LOSSES). For this purpose only, however, any deduction made in arriving at the amount chargeable to income tax in respect of any tax charged on *grant* of the option (see above) is added back and no account is taken of any relief given for national insurance contributions met by the employee. Where the shares would otherwise have ceased to be 'employment-related shares' (see **22.2** above) by virtue of *ITEPA 2003, s 421B(6)* (death of employee) or *s 421B(7)* (shares ceasing to be employment-related shares seven years after employee leaves the employer, the company which issued the shares or connected person), they are treated as continuing to be employment-related shares until they are next disposed of (so that on that disposal, any amounts counting as employment income under the above provisions can be added to the acquisition cost).

For 2014/15 onwards, the amount counting as employment income for this purpose is reduced to the extent that it is unchargeable foreign securities income for the purposes of *ITEPA 2003, s 41F* (share income of internationally mobile employees; see *ITEPA 2003, s 41H*) or chargeable foreign securities income which has not been remitted to the UK by the end of the tax year in which the disposal occurs. For 2013/14 and earlier years, the amount counting as employment income is so reduced to the extent that it is foreign securities income within *ITEPA 2003, s 41A* (income charged on remittance basis) which has not been remitted to the UK by the end of the tax year in which the disposal occurs. Where, however, unremitted chargeable foreign securities income (for 2013/14 and earlier years, unremitted foreign securities income) is subsequently remitted to the UK, the taxpayer can make a claim for the remittance to be treated as having occurred in the tax year of disposal.

[*TCGA 1992, ss 119A, 119B, 120(2)(4)(9), 144(3); FA 2014, Sch 9 paras 23, 24, 47–50*].

In respect of options exercised after 9 April 2003, where *TCGA 1992, s 144ZA* (see **7.7** ASSETS) applies, the cost of acquisition will therefore consist of the aggregate of:

- the amount counting as employment income (with the adjustments indicated above),
- the consideration given for the shares acquired on the exercise of the option, and
- any consideration given for the option (for options granted before 28 November 1995, the market value of the option at the time it was granted — see **22.3** above).

This is the same aggregate that the Revenue took to make up the acquisition cost prior to the decision in *Mansworth v Jelley* CA 2002, 75 TC 1. Following that decision, the Revenue accepted that the market value rule at **22.5** above applied to shares acquired as a result of the exercise of an option. They therefore accepted that, in respect of options exercised before 10 April 2003 (i.e. where *TCGA 1992, s 144ZA*, which is intended to reverse the effect of the decision (see **7.7** ASSETS), does not apply), the cost of acquisition consisted of the aggregate of:

- the amount counting as employment income (with adjustments), and
- the market value of the shares at the time the option is exercised

(Revenue Internet Statement 8 January 2003).

In May 2009, however, HMRC published new guidance. Their revised view is that, for options exercised before 10 April 2003, the acquisition cost is not augmented by any amount counting as employment income, and that the full measure of the acquisition cost is the market value of the shares at the time the option was exercised. HMRC have indicated that they will apply their new approach to cases where there was an open enquiry or appeal on 13 May 2009. (HMRC Brief 30/09). See also HMRC Brief 60/09 for a series of questions and answers relating to HMRC's change of view. In a case in which HMRC sought to apply the 2009 guidance to a taxpayer who had relied on the 2003 guidance, however, the Court initially found that taxpayer had a legitimate expectation that HMRC would apply the 2003 guidance and his application for judicial review was upheld. However, HMRC appealed and the Court of Appeal found that HMRC has been entitled to change its policy. The Court also observed that taxpayers with losses as a result of *Mansworth v Jelley* were not in the same position if they were in open years as opposed to closed years. For the latter, HMRC had no power to reopen their affairs and to remove the ability to utilise the *Mansworth v Jelley* loss. Those whose years were open, including this taxpayer, were in a different position so that comparative unfairness was not established. Furthermore, balancing the public interest against the interest of taxpayers affected by the decision to withdraw the 2003 guidance, there was no conspicuous unfairness; the taxpayer was returned to the same position as he was in when he committed himself to the transaction which gave rise to the capital losses. See *Revenue and Customs Commissioners v Hutchinson* [2017] EWCA Civ 1075, [2017] STC 2048.

Where the cost of acquisition of shares acquired on the exercise of an option includes the market value of the shares at the time of exercise, the proceeds of any corresponding disposal are likewise treated as the market value at that time (see **45.1** MARKET VALUE). However, the Revenue implemented this provision only in the case of returns made on or after 12 December 2002, the date of the judgment in *Mansworth v Jelley* (Revenue Internet Statement 8 January 2003).

See **22.38** below for relief from double taxation where a tax charge also arises in a country other than the UK.

Other charges in respect of share options which are not tax-advantaged

[22.7] A charge to income tax under *ITEPA 2003, s 476* also arises on the happening of certain other events in relation to share options which are not tax-advantaged. The events are the assignment, release (including the cancellation or surrender) or abandonment of the option or the receipt of a benefit in connection with the option.

The assignment or release of an option is a CGT disposal, and the amount charged to income tax is excluded by *TCGA 1992, s 37* (see **39.1** INTERACTION WITH OTHER TAXES) from the proceeds to be taken into account for CGT purposes (HMRC Capital Gains Manual CG56384). See **22.4** above re the release of an option in return for a replacement option. By virtue of *TCGA 1992, s 144(4)* (see **7.7**(f) ASSETS), the abandonment (i.e. the lapse) of an employee share option is not a disposal for CGT purposes, so no capital loss may be claimed in respect of any consideration given for the option. Any amount charged to income tax in respect of a benefit in connection with an option is *not* added to the acquisition cost of the option or shares for CGT purposes.

Shares acquired for less than market value

[22.8] A charge to income tax may apply where an employee obtains shares for less than their market value. The provisions operate by creating the fiction of a notional interest-free loan on the amount of the under-value. See **22.2** above for the meaning of 'shares' for the purposes of these provisions.

Subject to the anti-avoidance provisions of *ITEPA 2003, s 446UA*, the provisions apply where, at the time of acquisition of the shares, either no payment is (or has been) made for them or a payment below market value is (or has been) made for them. The employee is regarded as having the benefit of an interest-free loan, which attracts a charge under the employment income benefits code. The amount of the notional loan is the market value less any payment made for the shares and any amounts treated as earnings (other than exempt income) or counting as employment income under other provisions (see in particular **22.5**, **22.6** above). The notional loan terminates on the happening of specified chargeable events, viz. (i) the making good of the loan by payments or further payments for the shares, (ii) any obligation to make further payment ceasing to bind the employee (or connected person), (iii) the disposal of the shares, (iv) the doing of something which affects the shares as part of a scheme or arrangement the main purpose, or one of the main purposes, of which is the avoidance of tax or National Insurance contributions, or (v) the death of the employee. Subject to further conditions, where the notional loan terminates as a result of any of (ii), (iii) or (iv), then the amount of the loan thus deemed to be written off is treated as employment income.

[*ITEPA 2003, ss 192–197, 419, 421, 421B–421D, 421E(2)–(5), 421F–421H, 446Q–446W, Sch 7 paras 28, 29; FA 2013, Sch 45 para 66; FA 2014, Sch 9 paras 8, 35, 37*].

These provisions are most likely to be applied where shares are issued partly-paid, where payment is due in instalments or on the exercise of an option where the employment is outside the scope of *ITEPA 2003, s 476* in **22.6** above. See Tolley's Income Tax under Employment Income for further detail.

For shares in research institution spin-out companies, see **22.16** below.

Capital gains tax

Where a chargeable event is also a disposal of the shares for CGT purposes, and in any other case on the first disposal after a chargeable event, the aggregate of any amount counting as employment income in respect of that chargeable event and any other chargeable events occurring after the last disposal to which this provision applied, is added to the cost of acquisition (within *TCGA 1992, s 38(1)(a)* — see **16.11**(a) COMPUTATION OF GAINS AND LOSSES) of the person making the disposal. Where shares acquired after 15 April 2003 would otherwise cease to be employment-related shares by virtue of *ITEPA 2003, s 421B(6)* (death of employee) or *s 421B(7)* (shares ceasing to be employment-related shares seven years after employee leaves the employer, the company which issued the shares or connected person), they are treated as continuing to be employment-related shares until they are next disposed of (so that on that disposal, any amounts counting as employment income in respect of chargeable events can be added to the acquisition cost). For 2014/15 onwards, the amount counting as employment income for this purpose is reduced to the extent that it is unchargeable foreign securities income for the purposes of *ITEPA 2003, s 41F* (share income of internationally mobile employees; see *ITEPA 2003, s 41H*) or chargeable foreign securities income which has not been remitted to the UK by the end of the tax year in which the disposal occurs. For 2013/14 and earlier years, the amount counting as employment income is so reduced to the extent that it is foreign securities income within *ITEPA 2003, s 41A* (income charged on remittance basis) which has not been remitted to the UK by the end of the tax year in which the disposal occurs. Where, however, unremitted chargeable foreign securities income (for 2013/14 and earlier years, unremitted foreign securities income) is subsequently remitted to the UK, the taxpayer can make a claim for the remittance to be treated as having occurred in the tax year of disposal. [*TCGA 1992, ss 119A, 119B, 120(2)(3); FA 2003, Sch 22 paras 50, 51; FA 2014, Sch 9 paras 23, 24, 47–50*].

Shares disposed of for more than market value

[22.9] A charge to income tax may apply where shares are disposed of for more than their market value. See **22.2** above for the meaning of 'shares' for the purposes of these provisions.

Where shares within these provisions are disposed of (such that no associated person any longer has a beneficial interest) at more than their market value at the time of disposal, the excess over market value is chargeable to income tax as employment income. Any expenses incurred in connection with the disposal are also deductible in arriving at the chargeable amount.

[*ITEPA 2003, ss 198–200, 419, 421, 421, 421A–421D, 421E(2)–(5), 421F–421H, 446X–446Z, Sch 7 paras 30, 31, 61A; FA 2013, Sch 45 para 66*].

The amount charged to income tax is excluded by *TCGA 1992, s 37* (see **39.1** INTERACTION WITH OTHER TAXES) from the proceeds to be taken into account for CGT purposes.

Anti-avoidance — shares with artificially depressed market value

[22.10] There are provisions 'designed to ensure that if the value of employment-related securities is depressed by means of non-commercial transaction(s), then that reduction in value is taxed on the employee.' (Treasury Explanatory Notes to Finance Bill 2003). Subject to exclusions, the provisions apply in certain cases where the market value of 'employment-related shares' (see **22.2** above) (or, where relevant, other shares or interests in shares) is reduced by things done otherwise than for genuine commercial purposes; this specifically includes anything done as part of a scheme or arrangement a main purpose of which is to avoid tax or national insurance contributions and any transaction (other than a payment for corporation tax group relief) between members of a 51% group of companies otherwise than on arm's length terms. See **22.2** above for the extended meaning of 'shares', in relation to these provisions.

If anything done otherwise than for genuine commercial purposes within the seven years ending with the acquisition reduces the market value of employment-related shares at acquisition by at least 10%, there is a charge to income tax on the employee for the tax year in which the acquisition occurs; the amount chargeable counts as employment income for tax purposes. The provisions may also modify the operation of those at **22.9** above and **22.12**, **22.13**, **22.14**, and **22.15** below, broadly with the effect of replacing, in computing various amounts, the artificially reduced market value with what would have been the market value if it were not for the reduction.

[*ITEPA 2003, ss 419, 421, 421A–421D, 421E(2)–(5), 421F–421I, 446A–446J; FA 2013, Sch 45 para 66; FA 2014, Sch 9 paras 8, 35*].

See Tolley's Income Tax under Share-Related Employment Income and Exemptions for the detailed provisions.

Amounts charged to income tax under these provisions on the acquisition of shares are *not* added to the acquisition cost of the shares for CGT purposes.

Anti-avoidance — shares with artificially enhanced market value

[22.11] There are provisions 'designed to ensure that if the value of employment-related securities is enhanced by means of non-commercial transaction(s) during any tax year, then that appreciation in value is taxed on the employee at the earlier of the disposal of the employment-related securities or 5 April.' (Treasury Explanatory Notes to Finance Bill 2003). Subject to exclusions, the provisions apply in certain cases where the market value of 'employment-related shares' (see **22.2** above) is increased by things done otherwise than for genuine commercial purposes (a '*non-commercial increase*'); this specifically includes anything done as part of a scheme or arrangement a main purpose of which is to avoid tax *or national insurance contributions* and any transaction (other than a payment for corporation tax group relief) between members of a 51% group of companies otherwise than on arm's length terms. See **22.2** above for the extended meaning of 'shares', in relation to these provisions.

Where, on the 'valuation date' for a 'relevant period', the market value of employment-related shares is at least 10% greater than it would be if any 'non-commercial increases' (see above) during the relevant period were disregarded, the whole of the excess is taxed as employment income of the employee for tax purposes for the tax year in which the valuation date falls. For these purposes:

- the '*valuation date*' is the last day of the 'relevant period'; and
- the '*relevant period*' means any tax year, except that the first such period runs from date of acquisition to the following 5 April and the last runs from 6 April to the date in the tax year on which the provisions cease to apply. If the provisions cease to apply to an interest in the shares, the relevant period ends at that time in relation to that interest, but these provisions apply separately to that interest and to what remains.

[*ITEPA 2003, ss 419, 421, 421B–421D, 421E(2)–(5), 421F–421H, 446K–446P; FA 2013, Sch 45 para 66; FA 2014, Sch 9 paras 8, 12*].

See Tolley's Income Tax under Share-Related Employment Income and Exemptions for the detailed provisions.

Amounts charged to income tax under these provisions are *not* added to the acquisition cost of the shares for CGT purposes.

For shares in research institution spin-out companies, see **22.16** below.

Post-acquisition benefits

[22.12] Subject to exclusions, the following provisions apply if an 'associated person' (as defined) receives a benefit in connection with 'employment-related shares' (see **22.2** above). The amount or market value (determined as for capital gains tax purposes) of the benefit is taxed as employment income of the employee for the tax year in which the benefit is received. [*ITEPA 2003, ss 421, 421B–421D, 421E(1)(1A)(1B)(3)–(5), 421F–421H, 447–450, Sch 7 para 54; FA 2013, Sch 45 para 66; FA 2014, Sch 9 paras 8, 35*].

For shares in research institution spin-out companies, see **22.16** below.

Capital gains tax

On a disposal of employment-related shares after 5 April 2005, where that disposal is the first following the receipt of a benefit within the above provisions which is an increase in the market value of the shares, the aggregate of any amount counting as employment income in respect of that benefit and any other such benefits occurring after the last disposal to which this provision applied, is added to the cost of acquisition of the person making the disposal. Where shares would otherwise cease to be employment-related shares by virtue of *ITEPA 2003, s 421B(6)* (death of employee) or *s 421B(7)* (shares ceasing to be employment-related shares seven years after employee leaves the employer, the company which issued the shares or connected person), they are treated as continuing to be employment-related shares until they are next disposed of (so that on that disposal, any amounts counting as employment income in respect of chargeable events can be added to the acquisition cost). For 2014/15 onwards, the amount counting as employment income for this purpose is reduced to the extent that it is unchargeable foreign securities income for the purposes of *ITEPA 2003, s 41F* (share income of internationally mobile employees; see *ITEPA 2003, s 41H*) or chargeable foreign securities income which has not been remitted to the UK by the end of the tax year in which the disposal occurs. For 2013/14 and earlier years, the amount counting as employment income is so reduced to the extent that it is foreign securities income within *ITEPA 2003, s 41A* (income charged on remittance basis) which has not been remitted to the UK by the end of the tax year in which the disposal occurs. Where, however, unremitted chargeable foreign securities income (for 2013/14 and earlier years, unremitted foreign securities income) is subsequently remitted to the UK, the taxpayer can make a claim for the remittance to be treated as having occurred in the tax year of disposal. [*TCGA 1992, ss 119A, 119B; FA 2014, Sch 9 paras 23, 24, 47–50*].

Where the above does not apply, amounts charged to income tax under these provisions are *not* added to the acquisition costs of the shares for CGT purposes.

Pre-FA 2003 provisions

The above income tax provisions replaced earlier provisions dealing with post-acquisition benefits (see *ITEPA 2003, ss 453–456* and *ICTA 1988, s 138*). Amounts charged under those earlier provisions form part of the CGT acquisition cost of the shares to the person making the first disposal of them after the income tax charge. [*TCGA 1992, s 120*].

Restricted shares

[22.13] The following provisions apply, subject to exclusions, to 'employment-related shares' (see **22.2** above) if, at the time of acquisition, they are 'restricted shares' (or a 'restricted interest in shares'). For the extended meaning of 'shares', in relation to these provisions, see **22.2** above. Employment-related shares are '*restricted shares*' (or a '*restricted interest in shares*') if there is a contract, agreement, arrangement or condition that imposes any of three types of restriction *and* the market value of the shares or interest (determined as for capital gains purposes) is less than it otherwise would have been. The types of restriction covered are any provision for the transfer, reversion or forfeiture of the shares, any restriction on the freedom of the holder to dispose of the shares (or to retain the proceeds if they are sold) or on his right to retain the shares or proceeds or on any right conferred by the shares themselves, and any provision whereby the disposal or retention of the shares, or the exercise of a right conferred by them, may result in a disadvantage to the holder or (if different) the employee or a connected person.

No liability to income tax under the general provisions at **22.5** above arises on the acquisition of employment-related shares if the shares are subject to transfer, reversion or forfeiture and will cease to be so within five years after the acquisition. If a 'chargeable event' occurs in relation to restricted shares, there is a charge to tax on the employee for the tax year in which it occurs, the amount chargeable (which is calculated by applying a complex formula) counting as employment income for tax purposes. Relief is given by deduction from the chargeable amount in respect of any liability to secondary Class 1 national insurance contributions (i.e. employer contributions) in respect of that amount which is borne by the employee under a voluntary agreement or a joint election under *Social Security Contributions and Benefits Act 1992, Sch 1 para 3A* or *para 3B* (or NI equivalent).

Broadly, a chargeable event occurs when the shares cease to be restricted shares or a restriction is varied or removed, or the shares are disposed of for consideration by an 'associated person' (as defined) at a time when they are still restricted shares. Various elections can be made jointly by the employer and employee to disapply or moderate these provisions.

[*ITEPA 2003, ss 419, 421, 421A–421D, 421E(1)(1A)(1B)(3)–(5), 421F–421I, 422–432, 721(1); FA 2013, Sch 45 para 66; FA 2014, Sch 8 paras 47, 132, Sch 9 paras 8–12, 35, 36; SI 2003 No 1997; SI 2004 No 1945*].

See Tolley's Income Tax under Share-Related Employment Income and Exemptions for full details of the provisions.

For shares in research institution spin-out companies, see **22.16** below.

Capital gains tax

Where an individual acquires, on or after 1 September 2003, employment-related shares which are restricted shares (or a restricted interest in shares), the consideration for the acquisition of the shares is taken as the aggregate of:

(i) the actual amount or value given for the restricted shares (or restricted interest in shares), and
(ii) any amount that constituted earnings for income tax purposes in relation to the acquisition.

This does not affect the calculation of the consideration received by the person from whom the acquisition is made.

For disposals on or after 12 March 2008, it is explicitly provided that amounts of exempt income (within *ITEPA 2003, s 8*) and, with effect from 6 April 2015, amounts which would have been exempt income if the taxpayer had been subject to income tax at the appropriate time are excluded from the amount in (ii) above.

On a disposal of employment-related shares where that disposal constitutes a chargeable event under the restricted share provisions or is the first disposal of the shares following a chargeable event not involving disposal, the aggregate of any amount counting as employment income in respect of that chargeable event and any other chargeable events occurring after the last disposal to which this provision applied, is added to the cost of acquisition of the person making the disposal. In determining amounts counting as employment income for this purpose, no account is taken of any relief given for national insurance contributions borne by the employee (see above). Where shares would otherwise cease to be employment-related shares by virtue of *ITEPA 2003, s 421B(6)* (death of employee) or *s 421B(7)* (shares ceasing to be employment-related shares seven years after employee leaves the employer, the company which issued the shares or connected person), they are treated as continuing to be employment-related shares until they are next disposed of (so that on that disposal, any amounts counting as employment income in respect of chargeable events can be added to the acquisition cost). For 2014/15 onwards, the amount counting as employment income for this purpose is reduced to the extent that it is unchargeable foreign securities income for the purposes of *ITEPA 2003, s 41F* (share income of internationally mobile employees; see *ITEPA 2003, s 41H*) or chargeable foreign securities income which has not been remitted to the UK by the end of the tax year in which the disposal occurs. For 2013/14 and earlier years, the amount counting as employment income is so reduced to the extent that it is foreign securities income within *ITEPA 2003, s 41A* (income charged on remittance basis) which has not been remitted to the UK by the end of the tax year in which the disposal occurs. Where, however, unremitted chargeable foreign securities income (for 2013/14 and earlier years, unremitted foreign securities income) is subsequently remitted to the UK, the taxpayer can make a claim for the remittance to be treated as having occurred in the tax year of disposal.

[*TCGA 1992, ss 119A, 119B, 149AA; FA 2014, Sch 9 paras 23, 24, 27, 47–50*].

Example 1

Nick is given some shares in Lowe Ltd, the company that he works for on 1 July 2017. Nick is not allowed to sell the shares for three years. The shares have an unrestricted market value of £10,000 when received, but a restricted value (taking account of the fact that they cannot be sold for three years) of only £8,000. The value of the shares on 1 July 2020 when the restriction is lifted is £14,000. No elections in relation to the shares are made by Nick and Lowe Ltd. Nick sells the shares on 2 July 2020 for £14,000.

Nick is chargeable to income tax and capital gains tax as follows.

Income tax

When Nick receives the shares in Lowe Ltd he will charged to income tax and NICs under the restricted shares provisions on the lower restricted value, i.e. £8,000. The uncharged proportion of the unrestricted original value is 20%. On 1 July 2020 when the restriction is lifted there is a chargeable event. Nick is charged to income tax and NICs on 20% of the market value on that date, i.e. 20% × £14,000 = £2,800. Overall, therefore Nick is charged to income tax on £10,800.

Capital gains tax

		£
Consideration for disposal of shares		14,000
Less	Acquisition cost	—
	Amount charged to income tax	10,800
Chargeable gain 2020/21		£3,200

Example 2

The facts are as in Example 1 above except that Nick and Lowe Ltd elect (before 15 July 2017) for the restriction on the shares to be disregarded. The tax consequences are as follows.

Income tax

When Nick receives the shares in Lowe Ltd he will be charged to income tax and NICs on the unrestricted market value, i.e. £10,000. No income tax charge arises on the lifting of the restriction on 1 July 2020. Overall, therefore Nick is charged to income tax on £10,000.

Capital gains tax

		£
Consideration for disposal of shares		14,000
Less	Acquisition cost	—
	Amount charged to income tax	10,000
Chargeable gain 2020/21		£4,000

Conditional interests in shares

[22.14] The following provisions are replaced by those at **22.13** above but still have effect in relation to shares (or interests in shares) acquired before 16 April 2003.

The provisions apply where, after 16 March 1998, a beneficial interest in shares in or securities of a company is acquired by an employee or director (of that or another company) on terms such that, subject to certain exclusions, his interest is only conditional, i.e. subject to the risk of forfeiture. Employment income chargeable to income tax may arise on the interest ceasing to be conditional or on an earlier disposal. As regards shares acquired after 16 March 1998 and before 27 July 1999, employment income could also arise under the provisions on the employee's acquisition of the shares if the terms were such that his interest might have remained conditional for more than five years. For shares acquired on or after 27 July 1999 on such terms, no charge arises under the provisions, but a charge may still arise under the general employment earnings provisions referred to at **22.5** above. There is no charge on acquisition, whether before, on or after 27 July 1999, if the terms are such that the interest will cease to be conditional within five years or less, except for any charge that may arise under *ITEPA 2003, s 476* (see **22.6** above) or *ss 192–197* (previously *ICTA 1988, s 162*) (see **22.8** above). [*ITEPA 2003, ss 422–434 as originally enacted, Sch 6 para 18, Sch 7 paras 44–48; ICTA 1988, ss 140A, 140C; FA 2003, Sch 22 para 46(6)–(9); SI 2003 No 1997*].

Capital gains tax

For CGT purposes, the consideration given for the interest (see below) is increased by any amount counting as employment income under the above provisions. [*TCGA 1992, s 120(2)(5A)(8); ITEPA 2003, Sch 6 para 210(5)(10)*].

TCGA 1992, s 17 (see **45.1** MARKET VALUE) is disapplied (where it would otherwise apply) so that, instead of his being deemed to have acquired the interest at market value, the consideration given by the individual for the interest is the actual amount or value of the consideration given as computed under *ITEPA 2003, s 429 as originally enacted* (previously *ICTA 1988, s 140B*) (which does not include the value of duties performed in the office or employment concerned). However, this does not apply in calculating the consideration received for the interest by the person from whom the individual acquired it. [*TCGA 1992, s 149B*].

As regards shares acquired before 17 March 1998 and subject to risk of forfeiture, it was originally the Revenue's view that an income tax charge arose when that risk was lifted and by reference to the value of the shares at that time. Following legal advice received on 26 May 1995, they now take the view that a charge arises at the time of acquisition and by reference to the then value of the shares taking into account the risk of forfeiture, with no charge arising on the risk being lifted. The CGT acquisition cost of the shares is whatever value has been taken into account for income tax purposes. See Revenue Tax Bulletin June 1998 pp 545–548.

The employee's acquisition date for CGT purposes of employee shares held in trust and subject to risk of forfeiture or other restrictions is the date the employee becomes absolutely entitled as against the trustees, normally the date the risk of forfeiture or other restrictions are removed. This applies regardless of when or whether an income tax charge arises as above. Where the employee makes a payment for the shares, the terms of the employee's agreement with the trustees establish when 'absolute entitlement' occurs. Separate rules apply as regards share incentive plans (see **22.17** below) and approved profit sharing schemes (see **22.28** below). (Revenue Tax Bulletin February 2001 pp 828, 829).

Convertible shares

[22.15] The following provisions apply, subject to exclusions, to 'employment-related shares' (see **22.2** above) if, at the time of acquisition, they are 'convertible shares' (or an interest in 'convertible shares'). For the extended meaning of 'shares', in relation to these provisions, see **22.2** above. Employment-related shares are '*convertible shares*' if they confer on the holder any entitlement (for shares acquired before 2 December 2004, an immediate or conditional entitlement) to convert them into shares of a different description, or a contract, agreement, arrangement or condition authorises or requires the grant of such an entitlement to the holder if certain circumstances arise, or do not arise, or makes provision for the conversion of the shares (otherwise than by the holder) into shares of a different description.

In relation to acquisitions on and after 1 September 2003, for the purposes of any liability to income tax in respect of the acquisition of shares (under the general charging rules at **22.5** above, under **22.6** above (unapproved share options) or under **22.8** above (acquisition for less than market value)), the market value of the employment-related shares is to be determined as if they were not convertible shares or an interest in convertible shares. For acquisitions on or after 2 December 2004, this does not apply if the shares are acquired as part of an arrangement to avoid tax or NICs. Instead, in such cases the market value is computed as if there were an immediate and unfettered right to convert (if this is greater than the value without the right to convert).

If a chargeable event occurs in relation to convertible shares, there is a charge to tax on the employee for the tax year in which it occurs, the amount chargeable counting as employment income for tax purposes. Broadly, the conversion of the employment-related shares (or the shares in which they are an interest) into shares of a different description, the disposal for consideration of the shares (or any interest in them), the release, for consideration, of the conversion right and the receipt by an 'associated person' (as defined) of a benefit in money or money's worth in connection with the conversion right are chargeable events. The chargeable amount is found by computing the gain (if any) realised on the occurrence of the chargeable event and deducting from it any consideration given for the conversion right and any expenses incurred by the shareholder in connection with the conversion, disposal, release or receipt (whichever is applicable). An adjustment is made where the market value on acquisition was computed under the alternative rules for avoidance cases above. Relief is given by deduction from the chargeable amount in respect of any liability to secondary Class 1 national insurance contributions (i.e. employer contributions) in respect of that amount which is borne by the employee under a voluntary agreement or a joint election under *Social Security Contributions and Benefits Act 1992, Sch 1 para 3A* or *para 3B* (or NI equivalent).

[*ITEPA 2003, ss 419, 421, 421A–421D, 421E(1)(3)–(5), 421F–421I, 435–444, 721(1); FA 2014, Sch 9 paras 8, 35; SI 2003 No 1997; SI 2004 No 1945*].

See Tolley's Income Tax under Share-Related Employment Income and Exemptions for full details of the provisions.

For shares in research institution spin-out companies, see **22.16** below.

Capital gains tax

Where an individual acquires, on or after 1 September 2003, employment-related shares which are convertible shares (or an interest in convertible shares), the consideration for the acquisition of the shares is taken as the aggregate of:

(i) the actual amount or value given for the convertible shares (or interest in convertible shares), and
(ii) any amount that constituted earnings for income tax purposes in relation to the acquisition.

This does not affect the calculation of the consideration received by the person from whom the acquisition is made.

It is explicitly provided that amounts of exempt income (within *ITEPA 2003, s 8*) and, with effect from 6 April 2015, amounts which would have been exempt income if the taxpayer had been subject to the charge to income tax at the appropriate time are excluded from the amount in (ii) above.

On a disposal of employment-related shares which constitutes a chargeable event under the convertible share provisions or is the first disposal of the shares following a chargeable event not involving disposal, the aggregate of any amount counting as employment income in respect of that chargeable event and any other chargeable events occurring after the last disposal to which this provision applied, is added to the cost of acquisition of the person making the disposal. In determining amounts counting as employment income for this purpose, no account is taken of any relief given for national insurance contributions borne by the employee (see above). Where shares would otherwise cease to be employment-related shares by virtue of *ITEPA 2003, s 421B(6)* (death of employee) or *s 421B(7)* (shares ceasing to be employment-related shares seven years after employee leaves the employer, the company which issued the shares or connected person), they are treated as continuing to be employment-related shares until they are next disposed of (so that on that disposal, any amounts counting as employment income in respect of chargeable events can be added to the acquisition cost). For 2014/15 onwards, the amount counting as employment income for this purpose is reduced to the extent that it is unchargeable foreign securities income for the purposes of *ITEPA 2003, s 41F* (share income of internationally mobile employees; see

ITEPA 2003, s 41H) or chargeable foreign securities income which has not been remitted to the UK by the end of the tax year in which the disposal occurs. For 2013/14 and earlier years, the amount counting as employment income is so reduced to the extent that it is foreign securities income within *ITEPA 2003, s 41A* (income charged on remittance basis) which has not been remitted to the UK by the end of the tax year in which the disposal occurs. Where, however, unremitted chargeable foreign securities income (for 2013/14 and earlier years, unremitted foreign securities income) is subsequently remitted to the UK, the taxpayer can make a claim for the remittance to be treated as having occurred in the tax year of disposal.

[*TCGA 1992, ss 119A, 119B, 149AA; FA 2014, Sch 9 paras 23, 24, 27, 47–50; SI 2003 No 1997*].

Pre-FA 2003 provisions

The above income tax provisions replaced earlier provisions dealing with convertible shares (see *ITEPA 2003, ss 435–446 as originally enacted* and *ICTA 1988, s 140D*). For CGT purposes, the cost of acquiring the shares is increased by the amount counting as employment income under those provisions. [*TCGA 1992, s 120*].

Research institution spin-out companies

[22.16] *FA 2005* introduced provisions to ensure, broadly, that no income tax charge arises on an increase in the value of academics' shares in 'spin-out companies' due to the transfer of intellectual property from a research institution or a company controlled by it. The provisions apply where:

- an agreement is made for one or more transfers of intellectual property from one or more research institutions to a company (a '*spin-out company*');
- a person acquires shares in the spin-out company either before the making of the agreement or within 183 days beginning with the date of the agreement;
- the right or opportunity to acquire the shares was available by reason of employment by any of the research institutions or the company; and
- the person is involved in research in relation to any of the intellectual property which is the subject of the agreement.

The provisions do not apply if the avoidance of tax or national insurance is one of the main purposes of the arrangements under which the shares are acquired.

Where the provisions apply, the following income tax consequences follow.

(a) On acquisition, the market value of the shares is calculated disregarding the effect of both the transfer agreement and the transfer itself.

(b) If the shares are acquired before the agreement is made or before any transfer, the taxable amount under the provisions at **22.12** above in respect of any benefit received by the employee deriving from the agreement or transfer in connection with the shares is treated as nil.

(c) If the shares are restricted shares, the employer and employee are (subject to a right to make an irrevocable agreement to the contrary) deemed to make an election disapplying the provisions at **22.13** above.

(d) For the purposes of **22.11** above, neither the transfer agreement nor any transfer pursuant to it are treated as things done otherwise than for genuine commercial purposes.

For the purposes of these provisions, the extended meaning of shares at **22.2** above does not apply, but '*shares*' includes stock and an interest in shares.

[*ITEPA 2003, ss 451–460; FA 2005, ss 20, 21*].

Capital gains tax

Where an individual acquires shares (or an interest in shares) in circumstances such that (a) above applies, the consideration for the acquisition is taken as the aggregate of:

- the actual amount or value given for the shares or interest, and
- any amount charged to income tax as earnings in relation to the acquisition.

This does not affect the calculation of the consideration received by the person from whom the acquisition is made.

On a disposal of employment-related shares which is the first disposal of the shares following a chargeable event fixed by an employee election under similar provisions for pre-2 December 2004 cases, the amount counting as employment income in respect of that chargeable event is added to the cost of acquisition of the person making the disposal. Where shares would otherwise cease to be employment-related shares by virtue of *ITEPA 2003, s 421B(6)* (death of employee) or *s 421B(7)* (shares ceasing to be employment-related shares seven years after employee leaves the employer, the company which issued the shares or connected person), they are treated as continuing to be employment-related shares until they are next disposed of (so that on that disposal, any amounts counting as employment income in respect of chargeable events can be added to the acquisition cost). For 2014/15 onwards, the amount counting as employment income for this purpose is reduced to the extent that it is unchargeable foreign securities income for the purposes of *ITEPA 2003, s 41F* (share income of internationally mobile employees; see *ITEPA 2003, s 41H*) or chargeable foreign securities income which has not been remitted to the UK by the end of the tax year in which the disposal occurs. For 2013/14 and earlier years, the amount counting as employment income is so reduced to the extent that it is foreign securities income within *ITEPA 2003, s 41A* (income charged on remittance basis) which has not been remitted to the UK by the end of the tax year in which the disposal occurs. Where, however, unremitted chargeable foreign securities income (for 2013/14 and earlier years, unremitted foreign securities income) is subsequently remitted to the UK, the taxpayer can make a claim for the remittance to be treated as having applied in the tax year of disposal.

[*TCGA 1992, ss 119A, 119B, 149AB; FA 2005, s 22; FA 2014, Sch 9 paras 23, 24, 47–50*].

HMRC have issued guidance on the operation of the above provisions (HMRC Internet Statement 28 April, 2005).

Share incentive plans

[22.17] A company may set up a Share Incentive Plan (SIP), which is a tax-advantaged all-employee share plan of which the main features are as follows.

- A company which establishes a SIP on or after 6 April 2014 must notify HMRC and make a declaration that the SIP meets the relevant conditions. Before 6 April 2014, SIPs had to be approved by HMRC. Annual returns are also required by companies operating SIPs (whenever established) for 2014/15 onwards.
- A plan is operated by trustees, who buy or subscribe for shares with funds provided by the company (or, in the case of partnership shares, the employees) and appropriate them to the participating employees.
- With limited exceptions, the plan must be open to all employees (other than those with a material interest where the company is a close company), but may incorporate performance-related awards within certain parameters.
- An employer can appropriate to an employee free shares in the company valued at up to £3,600 per tax year (£3,000 for 2013/14 and earlier years) without any charge to income tax at that time ('*free share plans*').
- An employee can buy shares in the company out of amounts deducted from his salary up to a limit of £1,800 in any tax year (£1,500 for 2013/14 and earlier years) or, if less, 10% of salary (or such lower limits as the employer's particular plan may specify), these being allowable deductions for income tax ('*partnership share plans*').
- In respect of each partnership share an employee buys, the employer may appropriate to him up to two free '*matching shares*', again without any charge to income tax at that time.
- Free and matching shares must normally be kept in the plan for a specified period which must be not less than three years nor more than five (the '*holding period*') — no such restriction applies to partnership shares. The employer's plan may provide that free and/or matching shares be forfeited in certain circumstances (see further below under Capital gains tax).
- An employee who keeps shares in the plan for at least five years after they are awarded to him receives them free of income tax. With some exceptions (e.g. on death, disability, normal retirement or redundancy), an employee who withdraws shares from the plan within three to five years pays income tax on the lower of their value at the time of award (or, for partnership shares, their cost) and their value at withdrawal. With similar exceptions, an employee who withdraws shares from the plan within three years of appropriation pays income tax on their value at withdrawal.
- An employer's plan may provide for reinvestment of up to £1,500 worth of dividends on plan shares per tax year, in which case such dividends are tax-free. Shares acquired by such reinvestment are known as '*dividend shares*'.

- The employer's costs of setting up and running the scheme are tax deductible as is the market value at acquisition of free and matching shares awarded to employees under the plan.

[*ITEPA 2003, ss 488–515, Sch 2; ITTOIA 2005, ss 392–396, 405–408, 770; CTA 2009, ss 983–998; FA 2012, Sch 16 para 185; FA 2013, Sch 2 paras 2–6, 33–38; FA 2014, ss 49, 50, Sch 8 paras 1–96, Sch 37 para 19*].

For detailed coverage of the above, see Tolley's Income Tax under Share Related Employment Income and Exemptions.

Capital gains tax

Notwithstanding anything in the plan or the trust instrument, an employee (a '*participant*') is treated for CGT purposes as absolutely entitled as against the plan trustees to any shares awarded to him under a SIP. [*TCGA 1992, s 238A, Sch 7D para 3; FA 2014, Sch 8 paras 35, 124, 184*]. Shares are awarded to a participant when free or matching shares are appropriated to him or when partnership shares are acquired on his behalf. [*ITEPA 2003, Sch 2 para 5(1)*]. For the purpose of applying **64.2** SHARES AND SECURITIES — IDENTIFICATION RULES, plan shares (including free, matching, partnership and dividend shares) are treated as of a different class from any shares (otherwise of the same class) held by the participant outside the plan. [*TCGA 1992, Sch 7D para 4(1)*]. A company reconstruction is not normally treated as a disposal of plan shares (see Tolley's Income Tax for details and for a note on rights issues).

Shares cease to be subject to a plan when either the shares are withdrawn from the plan, or the participant ceases to be in relevant employment, or in certain circumstances the trustees dispose of shares in order to meet PAYE obligations. See Tolley's Income Tax for full details. Shares are withdrawn from the plan when on the direction of the participant (or, after his death, of his personal representatives) the plan trustees either transfer them (whether to the participant etc. or to another person) or dispose of them and similarly account for the proceeds, or when the participant etc. assigns, charges or otherwise disposes of his beneficial interest in them. [*ITEPA 2003, Sch 2 para 96*]. Shares which cease to be subject to a plan at any time are deemed to have been disposed of and immediately reacquired by the participant at their then market value, but no chargeable gain (or allowable loss) arises on the deemed disposal. [*TCGA 1992, Sch 7D para 5*].

Shares (but not securities or other rights) which have ceased to be subject to the plan but remain in the participant's beneficial ownership may be transferred without CGT consequences to an Individual Savings Account (see **25.30** EXEMPTIONS AND RELIEFS), subject to the annual subscription limits for such an Account (applied by reference to market value transferred) and provided the transfer is made within 90 days after the shares ceased to be subject to the plan.

Plan trustees

A gain (or loss) accruing in respect of shares to the trustees of a SIP is not a chargeable gain (or an allowable loss) if the shares:

- satisfy the requirements of *ITEPA 2003, Sch 2 Pt 4* as to the type of share that may be used in a plan (see Tolley's Income Tax); and

- are awarded to employees (see above), or acquired on their behalf as dividend shares, in accordance with the plan within the 'relevant period'; for these purposes, shares of a particular class acquired by the trustees are deemed to be awarded on a first in/first out basis (subject to special rules for shares acquired by qualifying transfer from an employee share ownership trust).

The '*relevant period*' depends on whether or not any of the shares in the company are 'readily convertible assets' within *ITEPA 2003, ss 701, 702* — broadly, whether or not they are capable of being readily converted into cash (see Tolley's Income Tax under Pay As You Earn). In determining whether shares are readily convertible assets, one may disregard any market for the shares which is created by virtue of the trustees acquiring shares for the plan and exists solely for the purposes of the plan. If any of the shares in the company are readily convertible assets at the time of acquisition by the trustees, the relevant period is the two years beginning with that time. If none of them are, the relevant period is extended to five years, but if within that period any of the shares in the company become readily convertible assets the relevant period ends no later than two years beginning with the date on which they did so.

A payment made by the employer company to the trustees sufficient to enable them to acquire a significant block of shares (at least 10% of the company's ordinary share capital) attracts an 'up-front' corporation tax deduction under *CTA 2009, s 989* (i.e. the deduction will not, as normal, be deferred until the shares are awarded to employees). The deduction will, however, be clawed back unless at least 30% of those shares are awarded within five years of acquisition by the trustees and all of the shares are awarded within ten years. As a consequence, the 'relevant period' above is extended to ten years in relation to shares acquired by virtue of such a payment.

[*TCGA 1992, Sch 7D para 2; FA 2014, Sch 8 para 43*].

If the plan trustees acquire shares from the trustees of an approved profit sharing scheme (see **22.28** below), the disposal by the scheme trustees and acquisition by the plan trustees are deemed to be made for such consideration as to secure that neither a gain nor a loss accrues on the disposal. For the purpose *only* of determining the relevant period as above, the shares are deemed to have been acquired by the plan trustees at the time they were acquired by the trustees of the profit sharing scheme. [*ITEPA 2003, Sch 7 para 86*].

A SIP *may* provide for free or matching shares to be forfeited in certain circumstances, i.e. if, other than for a permitted reason, the participant leaves the relevant employment within a specified forfeiture period of up to three years or withdraws the shares, or any related partnership shares, from the plan within that period. [*ITEPA 2003, Sch 2 para 32*]. Forfeited shares are deemed to have been disposed of by the participant and acquired by the plan trustees at their market value at the date of forfeiture, but no chargeable gain (or allowable loss) arises on the deemed disposal. [*TCGA 1992, Sch 7D para 7*].

Subject to their duty to act in accordance with the participant's directions, the plan trustees may dispose of some of the rights under a rights issue in respect of a participant's plan shares in order to raise funds to take up other rights under the issue. [*ITEPA 2003, Sch 2 para 77*]. Provided similar rights are conferred in respect of all ordinary shares in the company, the gain (or loss) arising on such a disposal is not a chargeable gain (or an allowable loss). [*TCGA 1992, Sch 7D para 8*].

For the purpose of applying **64.2** SHARES AND SECURITIES — IDENTIFICATION RULES,

- any shares transferred to the plan trustees by way of qualifying transfer from an employee share ownership trust (see Tolley's Income Tax) are treated as of a different class from any other shares (otherwise of the same class) held by the trustees; and
- any shares acquired by the trustees by virtue of a payment by the employer attracting an up-front corporation tax deduction under *CTA 2009, s 989* are treated as of a different class from any other shares (otherwise of the same class) held by the trustees.

[*TCGA 1992, Sch 7D para 4(2)–(6)*].

Rollover relief on disposals of shares to a SIP

[22.18] A form of capital gains rollover relief is available, as described below, on a disposal of shares, or an interest in shares, to the trustees of an approved share incentive plan and the reinvestment of the proceeds into a chargeable asset. The relief is not available where the person making the disposal is a company. [*TCGA 1992, s 236A, Sch 7C; FA 2014, Sch 8 paras 34, 36–38*].

Requirements for relief

The relief (see **22.19** below) applies only where all the following requirements are met.

(a) The person making the disposal (the claimant) obtains consideration for the disposal and, at any time in the '*acquisition period*' (the period of 6 months beginning with the date of disposal or, if later, the date on which the requirement at (d) below is first met) or under an unconditional contract made within that period, he either
    (i) applies the whole of the consideration in acquiring 'replacement assets', or
    (ii) applies part of the consideration as in (i) above, and the part *not* so applied is less than the gain on the disposal (whether all chargeable gain or not).

    A '*replacement asset*' is one which, immediately after the acquisition, is a 'chargeable asset' in relation to the claimant. The term includes an interest in an asset but does not include shares in, or debentures of, the company whose shares are the subject of the disposal or a company which, at the time of the acquisition, is in the same CGT group (see **29.2** GROUPS OF COMPANIES, as amended by *FA 2000*) as that company. A '*chargeable asset*' is broadly an asset the immediate disposal of which would give rise to a chargeable gain which would not be outside the charge to CGT as a result of the claimant's residence status or the terms of a double tax agreement.

(b) The plan must be a SIP at the time of the disposal. Before 6 April 2014, this requirement was that the share incentive plan had to be HMRC-approved at the time of the disposal (though the relief was not withdrawn if the plan subsequently lost approval — HMRC Capital Gains Manual CG61970).

(c) The shares disposed of

- are not of a class listed on a recognised stock exchange (within *ITA 2007, s 1005* — see **63.30** SHARES AND SECURITIES),
- are not shares in a company which is under the control (within *ITA 2007, s 995*) of a company (other than a close company or non-resident equivalent) whose shares are so listed,

but otherwise meet the requirements of *ITEPA 2003, Sch 2 paras 25–33* (see Tolley's Income Tax) as to the types of share that may be awarded under a SIP. (This appears to be what the draftsman intended, and is confirmed by HMRC Capital Gains Manual CG61973, though the wording of the legislation is ambiguous.)

(d) At some time in the '*entitlement period*' (the period of 12 months beginning with the date of disposal), the plan trustees hold (for the beneficiaries) shares in the company concerned that constitute at least 10% of ordinary share capital and carry rights to at least 10% of distributable profits and of distributable assets on a winding-up. Shares appropriated under the plan, or acquired on a beneficiary's behalf, but still subject to the plan count towards this requirement.

(e) At no time in the '*proscribed period*' (the period beginning with the date of disposal and ending with the date of acquisition of the replacement asset or, if later, the date on which the requirement at (d) above is first met) are there any unauthorised arrangements under which the claimant (or a person connected with him — see **17** CONNECTED PERSONS) may be entitled to acquire (directly or indirectly) from the plan trustees any shares (or an interest in or right deriving from any shares). For this purpose, all arrangements are unauthorised unless they only allow shares to be appropriated to or acquired on behalf of an individual under the plan.

[*TCGA 1992, Sch 7C paras 1–4, 8; FA 2013, Sch 46 para 111; FA 2014, Sch 8 paras 38, 89*].

Form of relief

[22.19] Where the requirements at **22.18** are met, the person making the disposal may make a claim for rollover relief under these provisions, such claim to be made within the two years beginning with the acquisition.

Where the whole of the consideration was reinvested (as in **22.18**(a)(i) above), the effect of the claim is that for CGT purposes the disposal is deemed to have been made for such consideration (if it would otherwise be greater) as would result in no gain and no loss. The acquisition cost of the replacement asset is reduced by the excess of the actual consideration over the deemed consideration.

Where part only of the consideration was reinvested (as in 22.18(a)(ii) above), the effect of the claim is that for CGT purposes the gain on the disposal is reduced to the amount of consideration not reinvested. The acquisition cost of the replacement asset is reduced by the amount by which the gain is reduced.

The other parties to the disposal and acquisition are not affected by a claim for relief. Any provision of *TCGA 1992* fixing deemed consideration for a disposal or acquisition is applied before the above adjustments are made.

[*TCGA 1992, Sch 7C para 5*].

Where a claim relates to more than one replacement asset, the relief is to be allocated between them on a just and reasonable basis (HMRC Capital Gains Manual CG61979).

Special rules where replacement asset is a dwelling-house

[22.20] Special rules may apply where:

- a rollover relief claim is made under **22.19** above,
- any replacement asset (as in **22.18**(a) above) is a dwelling-house, part of a dwelling-house or land, and,
- as is required, that asset was a chargeable asset in relation to the claimant immediately after the acquisition.

The said rules apply where the property later comes within the private residence exemption (see **53** PRIVATE RESIDENCES) (or would do if it were disposed of) by reference to the claimant or the claimant's spouse or civil partner (whether as an individual taxpayer or as a person entitled to occupy the property under the terms of a settlement).

If there is a time after the acquisition and *before* the making of the rollover relief claim when the dwelling-house etc. would fall within the private residence exemption, it is treated as if it had not been a chargeable asset in relation to the claimant immediately after the acquisition, with the result that the rollover relief claim fails. If, instead, there is a time *after* the making of the rollover relief claim when the dwelling-house etc. would fall within the private residence exemption, it is similarly treated, but in this case the gain rolled over is treated as not having accrued until that time (or until the earliest of such times if there is more than one).

Similar rules apply where the replacement asset is an option to acquire (or to acquire an interest in) a dwelling-house etc., and the option is exercised.

[*TCGA 1992, Sch 7C para 6*].

Special rules where replacement asset is EIS shares

[22.21] Special rules apply where:

- a rollover relief claim is made under **22.19** above;
- any replacement asset (as in **22.18**(a) above) is shares;
- that asset was a chargeable asset in relation to the claimant immediately after the acquisition; and

- the claimant makes a claim for Enterprise Investment Scheme (EIS) income tax relief in respect of the shares (see **23.2** ENTERPRISE INVESTMENT SCHEME).

Regardless of whether the EIS relief claim is made before or after the rollover relief claim, the shares are treated if they had not been a chargeable asset in relation to the claimant immediately after the acquisition, with the result that the rollover relief claim fails (and any relief already given is treated as if never due).

[*TCGA 1992, Sch 7C para 7*].

Enterprise management incentives

[22.22] 'Small higher risk' trading companies are able to grant options over shares worth (at time of grant) up to £250,000 (£120,000 before 16 June 2012) to eligible employees without income tax consequences (except to the extent that the option is to acquire shares at less than their market value at time of grant). The total value of shares in respect of which unexercised options exist must not exceed £3 million. The company may be quoted or unquoted but must be an independent company trading or preparing to trade and whose gross assets do not exceed £30 million. The company must have a permanent establishment in the UK (or be the parent company of a company with such a permanent establishment). The company (or, where the company is a parent company, it and its subsidiaries) must have no more than the equivalent of 250 full-time employees. A company carrying on certain specified activities deemed to be lower risk activities does not qualify, such exclusions being similar to those at **18.7** CORPORATE VENTURING SCHEME.

Broadly, an employee is eligible if he is employed by the company for at least 25 hours per week or, if less, at least 75% of his total working time, and he controls no more than 30% of the company's ordinary share capital. Companies must give notification to HMRC within 92 days after an option is granted.

[*ITEPA 2003, ss 527–541, Sch 5; FA 2014, Sch 8 paras 51, 216–225, Sch 9 para 16, Sch 37 para 22; SI 2001 No 3799; SI 2008 No 706; SI 2012 No 1360; SI 2014 No 2461*]. For full details, see Tolley's Income Tax under Share-Related Employment Income and Exemptions.

Capital gains tax

On a disposal of shares acquired under an option satisfying the requirements of the enterprise management incentives (EMI) scheme (hereafter referred to as a '*qualifying option*'), where *TCGA 1992, s 144ZA* (see **7.7** ASSETS) applies, the cost of acquisition of the shares for CGT purposes (within *TCGA 1992, s 38(1)(a)* — see **16.11**(a) COMPUTATION OF GAINS AND LOSSES) consists of the aggregate of:

- (by virtue of *TCGA 1992, ss 119A, 120(2)(4)* — see **22.6** above) any amount counting as employment income under *ITEPA 2003, s 476* after the deductions mentioned at **22.6** above, which might be the case

if the option was to acquire shares at less than their market value at the time of grant or if a disqualifying event (see below) occurred while the option remained unexercised,
- the consideration given for the shares acquired on the exercise of the option, and
- any consideration given for the option.

This is the same aggregate that the Revenue took to make up the acquisition cost prior to the decision in *Mansworth v Jelley* CA 2002, 75 TC 1. For options exercised before 10 April 2003, the acquisition cost is determined as for unapproved share options — see **22.6** above. Note, in particular, HMRC's change of view in May 2009.

The provisions at **22.7** above (as regards release of options) and **22.9** above apply to options under an EMI scheme and to shares acquired under such options. Those at **22.8** above are disapplied (see Tolley's Income Tax).

Following *FA 2013*, chargeable gains arising on EMI shares are now eligible for entrepreneurs' relief – see **24.6**.

Rights issues

If there is a rights issue affecting qualifying shares, the share reorganisation rules of *TCGA 1992, ss 127–130* (see **63.2** SHARES AND SECURITIES) are disapplied, with the result that the rights shares are treated as a separate acquisition and are not qualifying shares.

[*TCGA 1992, Sch 7D paras 14, 16*].

Identification rules

For an election to modify the normal rules in a case where EMI scheme shares are acquired on the same day as other shares in the same company, see **64.2** SHARES AND SECURITIES — IDENTIFICATION RULES.

Other tax-advantaged share option schemes

[22.23] The following apply generally to other tax-advantaged share option schemes (see **22.24** onwards below).

Assignment, release or abandonment of tax-advantaged employee share option

The same comments apply as for unapproved options at **22.7** above.

Identification rules

For an election to modify the normal rules in a case where approved share option scheme shares are acquired on the same day as other shares in the same company, see **64.2** SHARES AND SECURITIES — IDENTIFICATION RULES.

Save as you earn (SAYE) share option schemes

[22.24] Under a SAYE share option scheme, a company grants to an employee of itself or its group an option to acquire ordinary shares in the company at a specified price (the option price) at a specified future date. No income tax charge arises on either the grant of the option or, on exercise of the option, on any excess of the then value of the shares over the option price. The option price must not be less than 80% of the market value of shares of the same class at the time the option is granted. The scheme is linked to an approved certified contractual savings (CCS) scheme with a bank, building society or other authorised provider, to which the employee makes regular contributions by deduction from salary and to which a tax-free bonus is added at maturity (the bonus date), the funds then being used to purchase the agreed number of shares at the option price (though the funds may alternatively be repaid to the employee if he so chooses, the option being allowed to lapse). Savings contracts of between three years and five years are available (the option of a seven year savings period was withdrawn from 23 July 2013, although not affecting existing contracts). Aggregate monthly contributions to all such schemes to which an employee contributes at any one time cannot exceed £500 from 2014/15 onwards (£250 for 2013/14 and earlier years), and the minimum monthly contribution set for any scheme must not exceed £10 (although monthly contributions as low as £5 are permitted).

Other than in specified circumstances, the option cannot be exercised before the bonus date, nor can it be exercised, except in the case of death (for which special rules apply), more than six months after that date. The circumstances under which early exercise may be permitted include *inter alia* (i) the takeover of the company whose shares are scheme shares, (ii) where the eligible employment is in a subsidiary company, the company which established the scheme ceasing to have control of that subsidiary, and (iii) the transfer (to a person other than a subsidiary or associated company) of the business (or part thereof) to which the employment relates. In each case, the option can be exercised within six months of the change but if, in any of these three instances, the option is thus exercised within three years of its being granted, the income tax exemption on exercise is lost and a charge may arise under *ITEPA 2003, s 476* (see **22.6** above); the income tax exemption on the *grant* of the option does, however, continue to apply.

The scheme *must* be available on similar terms (subject to any variations by reference to salary level, period of service etc.) to all employees and full-time directors within *ITEPA 2003, s 15* (for 2007/08 and earlier years, *ITEPA 2003, ss 15* or *21*) and with a stipulated minimum period of service, which cannot be more than five years. It *may* be made available to other employees and directors. Prior to 17 July 2013, where the company was a close company, those with material interests were excluded.

[*ITEPA 2003, ss 516–520, Sch 3; FA 2013, Sch 2 paras 7–13, 39–43; FA 2014, Sch 8 paras 97–157, Sch 37 para 20*].

See Tolley's Income Tax for the full provisions and conditions.

Capital gains tax

Other than where early exercise of the option results in the loss of the income tax exemption as mentioned above (in which case see **22.6** above), the provisions of *TCGA 1992, s 17* (see **45.1** MARKET VALUE) are specifically disapplied both in calculating the CGT acquisition cost of the shares to the employee and for the purposes of any corresponding disposal to him. Those provisions are likewise disapplied where an option is exercised following the death of the employee in accordance with a rule included in the scheme by virtue of *ITEPA 2003, Sch 3 para 32*. [*TCGA 1992, Sch 7D para 10; FA 2014, Sch 8 para 128*].

On a disposal of the shares by the employee, his allowable expenditure consists of the actual consideration given on the exercise of the option, i.e. the amount saved plus the tax-free bonus (plus, if applicable, any consideration given for the option itself — see **22.3** above). The date of acquisition of the shares for CGT purposes is the date the option is exercised.

Shares acquired through an approved SAYE share option scheme may be transferred without CGT consequences to an Individual Savings Account (see **25.30** EXEMPTIONS AND RELIEFS), subject to the annual subscription limits (applied by reference to market value transferred) and provided the transfer is made within 90 days after the option is exercised.

Company share option plan (CSOP) schemes

[22.25] CSOP schemes were introduced by *FA 1996* to replace executive share option schemes (see **22.27** below). Unlike SAYE share option schemes and profit sharing schemes, company share option plans and their predecessors are not required to be open to all employees, and are more likely to be used to reward directors and key employees. CSOP schemes are more restrictive than their predecessors in that they place a lower ceiling on the value of options an individual may hold at any one time and do not permit the option price to be discounted by reference to the current share price.

Under a CSOP scheme, a company grants to an employee of itself or its group an option to acquire ordinary shares in the company at a specified price (the option price) at a specified future date. The option price should not be less than the market value of the shares at the time of the grant. Normally, no income tax charge arises on either the grant of the option or, on exercise of the option, on any excess of the then value of the shares over the option price. In the exceptional case where the aggregate of the option price and any amount paid for the option itself is less than the market value of the shares at the time of the grant, the amount of the difference counts as employment income for the tax year in which the option is granted. The normal tax exemption on *exercise* of the option does not apply if the scheme is no longer a tax-advantaged scheme at the time of exercise or if the option is exercised less than three years or more than ten years after it was granted. There is an exception for options exercised within three years of grant but no later than six months after the individual ceases to be a qualifying employee of the scheme organiser (or of a constituent company in a group scheme) because of injury, disability, redundancy or retirement. Special rules apply in cases of death.

Only full-time directors (generally taken to mean those working at least 25 hours per week) are eligible. Part-time employees (other than directors) may be included. Where the company is a close company, employees and directors with material interests are excluded.

It is a condition of approval that the aggregate market value (at the time of grant) of shares over which an individual may hold unexercised rights under the scheme (and any other CSOP scheme established by the company or an associated company) must at no time exceed £30,000.

[*ITEPA 2003, ss 521–526, Sch 4; FA 2013, Sch 2 paras 14, 15, 44; FA 2014, Sch 8 paras 50, 158–215, Sch 37 para 21*].

See Tolley's Income Tax for the full provisions and conditions.

Capital gains tax

Where the income tax exemption on exercise of the option applies (see above), the provisions of *TCGA 1992, s 17* (see **45.1** MARKET VALUE) are specifically disapplied both in calculating the CGT acquisition cost of the shares to the employee and for the purposes of any corresponding disposal to him. Those provisions are likewise disapplied where an option is exercised following the death of the employee in accordance with a rule included in the scheme by virtue of *ITEPA 2003, Sch 4 para 25*. [*TCGA 1992, Sch 7D para 13; FA 2014, Sch 8 para 189*].

Where, exceptionally, an income tax liability arises on the grant of the option (due to the option price being discounted — see above), the amount counted as employment income is included in the cost of acquisition of the shares for CGT purposes. This applies whether or not the exercise is in accordance with the provisions of the scheme and whether or not the scheme is still tax-advantaged at the time of the exercise. [*TCGA 1992, s 120(2)(6)(c), Sch 7D para 12; FA 2014, Sch 8 para 188*].

Thus, on a disposal of the shares by the employee, his allowable expenditure within *TCGA 1992, s 38(1)(a)* (see **16.11**(a) COMPUTATION OF GAINS AND LOSSES) consists of:

- the actual consideration given on the exercise of the option,
- any consideration given for the option itself, and
- the amount, if any, counting as employment income.

The date of acquisition of the shares for CGT purposes is the date the option is exercised. Any deemed expenditure corresponding to an amount chargeable to income tax is also deemed to have been incurred on that date.

Employee shareholder shares

[22.26] A special employment status, known as 'employee shareholder' status, was introduced by *Growth and Infrastructure Act 2013, s 31*. Employee shareholders are issued or allotted at least £2,000 worth of shares in consideration of an employee shareholder agreement. Subject to conditions, an income tax relief and capital gains tax exemption apply to the shares, as described below, but only to shares received through the adoption of employee shareholder status on or after 1 September 2013 but before December 2016 (see below). [*FA 2013, Sch 23 para 38; SI 2013 No 1755; FA 2017, ss 12–14*]. Businesses wishing to award shares under an employee shareholder agreement may propose a share valuation to HMRC's Shares and Assets Valuation team in advance of the award (HMRC Employment-Related Shares & Securities Bulletin No. 10, September 2013). For official guidance on the beneficial CGT treatment of employee shareholder shares acquired prior to December 2016 see www.gov.uk/government/publications/guidance-on-the-capital-gains-tax-treatment-of-employee-shareholder-shares/guidance-on-the-capital-gains-tax-treatment-of-employee-shareholder-shares.

After only being in effect for just over three years, the income tax and capital gains tax reliefs in relation to employee shareholder status have been withdrawn, as a precursor to the whole concept of employee shareholder status being abolished at some future point. This is in response to HMRC's findings that these reliefs were primarily being used for tax-planning purposes by wealthier employees rather than fulfilling their original objective which was to enable small companies to recruit without committing to a permanent workforce with full employment rights.

Agreements entered into before 1 December 2016, or before 2 December 2016 where independent advice was received on 23 November 2016 before 1:30 pm, retain their tax benefits, which are described below.

The independent advice received by an individual before entering into an Employee Shareholder agreement continues to be tax-free.

These changes do not affect the reliefs available to the employer company.

See www.gov.uk/government/publications/income-tax-and-capital-gains-tax-employee-shareholder-status.

Charge to income tax — shares acquired prior to December 2016

The following income tax treatment applies to shares acquired before 1 December 2016 (or before 2 December 2016 where independent advice was received by the employee on 23 November 2016 before 1:30 pm). For employee shareholder shares issued after that date, an amount equal to the market value of shares is treated as earnings i.e. there is no deemed payment (see below).

When shares ('*employee shareholder shares*') with a market value of at least £2,000 are acquired by an employee in consideration of an 'employee shareholder agreement', an amount is treated as earnings from the employment, in respect of the acquisition of the shares, for the tax year in which they are acquired. The amount is found by applying a formula, MV – P where:

> MV = the market value of the shares (see below) on the day on which they are acquired; and
> P = the payment (if any) that the employee is treated as having made for the shares as set out below.

If P exceeds MV, the amount is nil.

Where the above applies, no other sums can constitute earnings from the employment in respect of the acquisition of the employee shareholder shares.

Market value is determined as for capital gains purposes.

An '*employee shareholder agreement*' means an agreement by virtue of which an employee is an employee shareholder (see *Employment Rights Act 1996, s 205A(1)(a)–(d)*). Shares are acquired by an employee for these purposes if the employee becomes beneficially entitled to them; they are acquired at the time when the employee becomes so entitled.

Deemed payment for the shares

Provided that, as above, shares with a market value of at least £2,000 are acquired by an employee in consideration of an employee shareholder agreement, the employee is treated, for income tax purposes, as having made a payment for those shares as follows. Where all the shares acquired in consideration of the agreement are acquired on the same day, the employee is treated as having made on that day a payment of £2,000 for those shares. Where shares are acquired by the employee in consideration of the agreement on more than one day, with shares with a market value of at least £2,000 acquired on the first of those days, the employee is treated as having made, on the first of those days, a payment of £2,000 for the shares acquired on that day. Where shares with a value in excess of £2,000 are acquired, the payment which the employee is treated as having made for each share is determined on a pro rata basis.

Except as provided above, the employee is to be treated for income tax purposes as having given no consideration for shares acquired in consideration of the employee shareholder agreement.

See Tolley's Income Tax for the full provisions and conditions.

[*ITEPA 2003, ss 226A–226D; FA 2013, Sch 23 paras 1–3; FA 2017, s 12*].

Capital gains tax — shares acquired prior to December 2016

The capital gains tax exemption described below applies only to shares acquired before 1 December 2016 (or before 2 December 2016 where independent advice was received by the employee on 23 November 2016 before 1:30 pm).

Subject to the lifetime limit below, gains on 'exempt' employee shareholder shares are not chargeable gains when the shares are disposed of by the person who acquired them under the employee shareholder agreement. An employee shareholder share acquired in consideration of an employee shareholder agreement is '*exempt*' if, immediately after its acquisition, the total value of employee shareholder shares, in the employer company or an 'associated company', which have been acquired by the employee does not exceed £50,000. For these purposes, the value of a share at any time is its unrestricted market value at the time when it was acquired by the employee. Where shares acquired on a particular day take an employee over the £50,000 limit, an apportionment is made to treat the appropriate proportion up to the limit (rounded down to the nearest share) as acquired before the remainder (and so as exempt shares).

For these purposes, a company is an associated company of another if one has control of the other or both are under the control of the same person(s). 'Control' is construed in accordance with *CTA 2010, ss 450, 451*. If a company controls another when an employee shareholder agreement is entered into with an employee, this is treated as continuing to be the case when any subsequent employee shareholder agreement is entered into with that same employee. However, this does not apply if:

- one of the two companies has been dissolved;
- two years have passed since the date of dissolution; and
- the employee has not, at any time in that two-year period, been engaged in any office or employment (including engagement under a contract for services) with any company which is an associated company of the dissolved company.

An employee shareholder share is not exempt if:

- on the date on which the share is acquired or at any time in the twelve months ending on that date, the employee has (or has had) a 'material interest' in the employer company or a parent undertaking (within *Companies Act 2006, s 1162*) of the employer company; or
- on the date on which the share is acquired, the employee is connected (within **17** CONNECTED PERSONS) with an individual who has a material interest in the employer company or a parent undertaking or who has had such an interest at any time in the twelve months ending on that date.

For these purposes, an individual (A) has a '*material interest*' in a company if at least 25% of the voting rights are exercisable by A, or by persons connected with A, or by A and persons connected with A together. If the company is a close company, or would be but for being a non-UK resident company or a quoted company, A has a material interest in it if A, or persons connected with A, or A and persons connected with A together, are entitled to at least 25% of the assets available for distribution among the participators in a winding-up or in any other circumstances. A is *treated* as having a material interest in a company at any time if A, or persons connected with A, or A and persons connected with A together, have an entitlement to acquire such rights as would (together with any existing rights) give A a material interest in the company. Any arrangements in place (as widely defined and to which the employer company or a parent undertaking is also party) to acquire such rights must also be taken into account.

Where an individual has acquired shares in consideration of entering into an employee shareholder agreement, he is not regarded as disposing of an asset by reason of ceasing to have, or not acquiring, the rights mentioned in *Employment Rights Act 1996, s 205A* as a result of entering into the agreement.

The above exemption does not apply to gains arising on or after 6 April 2016 where the proceeds of the disposal constitute a disguised investment management fee within *ITA 2007, s 809EZA(3)* or carried interest within *ITA 2007, s 809EZC* (see **50.21** PARTNERSHIPS).

Lifetime limit

A lifetime limit of gains of £100,000 applies to disposals of exempt employee shareholder shares acquired under employee shareholder agreements entered into on or after 17 March 2016. Gains falling partly within the limit are exempt to the extent that they do not exceed the unused balance of the limit. Gains on disposals of shares acquired under agreements entered into before that date do not count in applying the limit.

See **46.5** MARRIED PERSONS AND CIVIL PARTNERS for transfers of exempt employee shareholder shares between spouses or civil partners and the effect of the lifetime limit.

Identification rules

The normal identification rules (see **64.2** SHARES AND SECURITIES — IDENTIFICATION RULES) are each disapplied as regards exempt employee shareholder shares. Where an employee holds shares of the same class in a company and only some of those shares are exempt employee shareholder shares, on a disposal of a part of that holding the employee may choose what proportion of the shares disposed of are to be treated as exempt employee shareholder shares (up to the number of such shares in the holding) and the consideration received is apportioned accordingly.

Reorganisations etc.

TCGA 1992, s 127 (reorganisations — see **63.2** SHARES AND SECURITIES) does not apply to exempt employee shareholder shares (including that section as applied by *TCGA 1992, ss 135, 136* (share exchanges and reconstructions — see **63.5**, **63.7** SHARES AND SECURITIES)). Where, however, there is a disposal of exempt employee shareholder shares on a reorganisation on or after 17 March 2016, the taxpayer is treated as disposing of the shares for a consideration calculated as follows.

(1) If the whole of the '*notional gain*' (i.e. the gain that would arise on the disposal if the shares were disposed of at market value) would be a chargeable gain because the taxpayer's lifetime limit has been used against previous disposals, the deemed consideration is the amount that would give rise to neither a gain nor a loss.
(2) If part (but not all) of the notional gain would be a chargeable gain as a result of the lifetime limit, the deemed consideration is the maximum amount (not exceeding market value) that would secure that no chargeable gain arises.
(3) If none of the notional gain would be a chargeable gain, the deemed consideration is the market value.
(4) If there would be no notional gain, the deemed consideration is the amount that would give rise to neither a gain nor a loss.

[*TCGA 1992, ss 236B–236G; FA 2013, Sch 23 paras 20, 38; FA 2016, s 88(2)(3)–(6)(10), s 89; FA 2017, s 13; SI 2013 No 1755*].

Example

On 15 May 2016, Sarah acquires 1,000 shares with a market value of £5,000 by way of an Employee Shareholder Agreement. The shares qualify as employee shareholder shares.

An amount of £3,000 (£5,000 less £2,000 deemed payment) is treated as earnings on the day on which she acquires them.

Sarah disposes of the shares when the market value is £10,000. There is no chargeable gain arising on the shares.

If Sarah had another 1,000 shares in the company and she disposed of these shares together with her qualifying employee shareholder shares for £30,000, then the proceeds could reasonably be divided as £15,000 for each of the employee shareholder shares and Sarah's other non-qualifying shareholding.

Executive share option schemes

[22.27] Executive share option schemes were superseded by CSOP schemes in relation to (broadly) options granted on or after 17 July 1995. See **22.25** above.

Capital gains tax

The same comments apply as for CSOP schemes in **22.25** above. [*TCGA 1992, s 120(2)(6)(a)(b); ICTA 1988, s 185(7)*].

Approved profit sharing schemes

[22.28] Approved profit sharing schemes were phased out following the introduction of share incentive plans (see **22.17** above).

Under a profit sharing scheme approved by the Revenue, a company provided funds to trustees who used them to acquire ordinary shares in the company for appropriation free-of-charge to employees of the company or group. There was no income tax charge on the appropriation of shares to an eligible employee (the participant) nor on the transfer of shares to him after three years. On a disposal before the third anniversary of the date of appropriation (the release date), the 'locked-in value' (as defined) counted as employment income of the participant, chargeable to income tax for the tax year of disposal. The charge was reduced to 50% of the locked-in value if the disposal follows the cessation of employment due to injury, disability, redundancy or on reaching a specified retirement age of between 60 and 75. Where an appropriation of shares was made to a non-eligible employee or in excess of a permitted limit an income tax charge arose at the earlier of the date of disposal, the release date or the employee's death and was on the market value at that time.

There was also an income tax charge on any capital receipts (e.g. proceeds of a sale of rights) between date of appropriation and release date. The charge varied according to the length of time that has elapsed since appropriation.

[*ICTA 1988, ss 186, 187, Schs 9, 10*].

See Tolley's Income Tax for the full provisions and conditions for approval.

Capital gains tax

A participant who had shares appropriated to him under a scheme was treated as absolutely entitled as against the trustees for CGT purposes. [*TCGA 1992, s 238(1)(3)*]. The date of the participant's acquisition of the shares for CGT purposes is the date of appropriation. By virtue of *TCGA 1992, s 17* (see **45.1** MARKET VALUE), the participant's acquisition cost is the market value of the shares at the date of appropriation. On a disposal of the shares, neither this acquisition cost nor the proceeds are adjusted to take account of any amount chargeable to income tax in relation to the shares at that or any earlier time. [*TCGA 1992, s 238(2)(a)*].

The fact that a capital receipt may have been charged to income tax does not prevent its being a capital distribution within *TCGA 1992, s 122* (see **63.11** SHARES AND SECURITIES). [*TCGA 1992, s 238(2)(b)*].

Part disposals of scheme shares acquired at different times are subject to the normal IDENTIFICATION RULES (**64**) notwithstanding anything to the contrary in the income tax provisions. [*TCGA 1992, s 238(2)(c)*]. For as long as the shares remained subject to restrictions on their disposal, i.e. until the release date, they were regarded as a separate holding as compared to other shares of the same class in the same company held by the participant. [*TCGA 1992, s 104(4)*].

Employee share ownership trusts

[22.29] Under provisions contained in *FA 1989, ss 67–74, Sch 5*, payments made by a UK resident company in an accounting period beginning before 1 January 2003 to a 'qualifying employee share ownership trust' (broadly, a trust set up to acquire shares in a company and distribute them to employees of that company) were, subject to conditions, deductible for corporation tax purposes. The relief is abolished for payments in accounting periods beginning on or after 1 January 2003 by *FA 2003, s 142*, in consequence of the introduction of the general corporation tax relief for employee share acquisition in *CTA 2009, ss 1006–1038* (see Tolley's Corporation Tax). An employee share ownership trust and its beneficiaries did not qualify for any special income tax or CGT reliefs, but could be used in conjunction with an approved SAYE share option scheme (see **22.24** above) or an approved profit sharing scheme (see **22.28** above). See Tolley's Income Tax under Share-Related Employment Income and Exemptions for the detailed provisions.

Rollover relief on disposals of shares to a trust

[22.30] On a disposal of shares, or an interest in shares, **before 6 April 2001** to a qualifying employee share ownership trust, a relief in the form of a rollover of a chargeable gain applied subject to detailed conditions where the company applied the proceeds of the sale in acquiring other assets. The relief is abolished for disposals on or after that date by *FA 2000, s 54*.

The relief given under *TCGA 1992, s 229(1)* below is available where the following conditions are met.

(a) The claimant makes a disposal of, or of his interest in, shares to the trustees of a trust which is a 'qualifying employee share ownership trust' at the time of the disposal and which was established by a company (the 'founding company') which, immediately after the disposal, was a 'trading company' or the 'holding company' of a 'trading group'.

(b) The shares are fully paid up, not redeemable, form part of the 'ordinary share capital' of the founding company, and are not subject to any restrictions other than those which attach to all shares of the same class or are authorised by *FA 1989, Sch 5 para 7(2)*.

(c) At any time in the 'entitlement period', the trustees are beneficially entitled to at least 10% of the 'ordinary share capital' of the founding company and of any 'profits available for distribution to equity holders' therein, and would be beneficially entitled to at least 10% of any of the founding company's 'assets available for distribution to equity holders' on a winding-up.

(d) The claimant obtains consideration for the disposal and, at any time in the 'acquisition period', applies all (but see below under *TCGA 1992, s 229(2)(3)*) the consideration in acquiring assets ('replacement assets') (or an interest therein) which are, immediately thereafter, 'chargeable assets' in relation to the claimant and which are not shares in, or debentures issued by, the founding company or a company which, at the time of the acquisition, is in the same 'group' as the founding company. The requirement that the consideration be applied in the 'acquisition period' is satisfied if the acquisition is made pursuant to an unconditional contract entered into in that period.

(e) At all times in the 'proscribed period', there are no 'unauthorised arrangements' under which the claimant or a person connected with him may be entitled to acquire any of the shares, or an interest in or right deriving from any of the shares, which are the subject of the disposal by the claimant.

(f) No 'chargeable event' occurs in relation to the trustees in the chargeable period(s) in which the claimant makes the disposal and acquisition or in any other chargeable period between those of the disposal and the acquisition, 'chargeable period' meaning year of assessment or (if the claimant is a company) claimant company accounting period.

[*TCGA 1992, s 227*].

Where relief is available as above, the claimant may, within two years of the acquisition, claim that, for the purposes of *TCGA 1992*, the disposal be treated as made at a no gain/no loss consideration (if it otherwise would be greater), the consideration for the acquisition being treated as reduced by the excess of the actual consideration for the disposal over that no gain/no loss consideration. [*TCGA 1992, s 229(1)*].

Partial relief is available on a claim made within the same time limit where part only of the consideration for the disposal is applied as under (d) above and the amount of the consideration not so applied is less than the gain (whether all chargeable gain or not) accruing on the disposal. In such a case, the amount of the gain on the disposal is treated as reduced to the amount of the consideration not so applied, and the consideration for the acquisition is treated as reduced by the reduction so made to the amount of the gain. [*TCGA 1992, s 229(2)(3)*].

The other parties to the disposal and acquisition are not affected by such claims for relief. Any provision of *TCGA 1992* fixing deemed consideration for a disposal or acquisition is applied before the above adjustments are made. [*TCGA 1992, s 229(4)(5)*].

For the purposes of *TCGA 1992, s 227* above, the following applies.

(A) The '*entitlement period*' is the period beginning with the disposal and ending twelve months after the date of the disposal.

(B) The '*acquisition period*' is the period beginning with the disposal and ending six months after the date of the disposal or, if later, the date on which the condition at (*c*) above first becomes fulfilled.

(C) The '*proscribed period*' is the period beginning with the disposal and ending on the date of the acquisition or, if later, the date on which the condition at (*c*) above first becomes fulfilled.

(D) Arrangements are '*unauthorised arrangements*' unless either they arise wholly from a restriction authorised by *FA 1989, Sch 5 para 7(2)*, or they only allow, as regards shares, interests or rights, acquisition by a beneficiary under the trust and/or appropriation under an approved profit sharing scheme (within *ICTA 1988, Sch 9*).

(E) An asset is a '*chargeable asset*' at a particular time in relation to the claimant if:
   (i) he is at that time resident or ordinarily resident in the UK and, were the asset to be disposed of at that time, a gain accruing to him would be a chargeable gain; or
   (ii) were it to be disposed of at that time, any gain accruing to him would be a chargeable gain under *TCGA 1992, s 10(1)* or form part of his corporation tax profits under *TCGA 1992, s 10(3)* or *s 10B* (see **49.3** OVERSEAS MATTERS),

   but not if, were he to dispose of it at that time, double tax relief arrangements under *TIOPA 2010, s 2(1)* would render him not liable to UK tax on any gain accruing to him on the disposal.

(F) '*Qualifying employee share ownership trust*' has the same meaning as under *FA 1989, Sch 5*, and '*chargeable event*' in relation to the trustees has the same meaning as under *FA 1989, s 69*.

(G) '*Holding company*', '*trading company*' and '*trading group*' have the same meanings as in **36.2** HOLD-OVER RELIEFS; and '*group*' (except in the expression 'trading group') is construed in accordance with **29.2** GROUPS OF COMPANIES.

(H) '*Ordinary share capital*' means all issued share capital other than that carrying a right to a dividend at a fixed rate but with no other right to share in profits.

(I) As regards the condition at (c) above, the provisions of *CTA 2010, Pt 5 Ch 6* (group relief: equity holders etc.) apply with suitable adaptations as appropriate.

[*TCGA 1992, s 228, s 288(1); FA 2000, Sch 29 para 33; FA 2003, s 155, Sch 27 para 2(3); TIOPA 2010, Sch 8 para 47*].

Chargeable event when replacement assets owned

[22.31] Where:

(a) relief under *TCGA 1992, s 229(1)* or *(3)* is given as in **22.30** above;

(b) a 'chargeable event' in relation to the trustees (within *FA 1989, s 69* as amended) occurs on or after the date on which the disposal is made;

(c) the claimant was neither an individual who died before the occurrence of the chargeable event nor trustees of a settlement which ceased to exist before that occurrence; and
(d) at the time of the occurrence of the chargeable event, the claimant or a person connected with him (within *TCGA 1992, s 286*) is beneficially entitled to all the replacement assets acquired as under **22.30**(d) above,

the claimant or the connected person (as the case may be) is deemed, immediately before the occurrence of the chargeable event, to have disposed of, and immediately reacquired, all the replacement assets at the 'relevant value'.

The '*relevant value*' is such value as secures on the deemed disposal a chargeable gain equal to the amount of the gain carried forward by virtue of *TCGA 1992, s 229(1)* or *(3)*, i.e. the amount by which the consideration for the acquisition was treated as reduced as a result of a claim for that relief to apply.

Where only a part of the replacement assets falls within **22.30**(d) above, there is a deemed disposal and reacquisition of that part, the relevant value being reduced as is just and reasonable.

An adjustment may be made where there is a deemed disposal and reacquisition under these provisions, and before the occurrence of the chargeable event it can be said that, because of something which has happened as regards any of the replacement assets, a charge has accrued in respect of any gain carried forward as a result of relief having been given under *TCGA 1992, s 229(1)* or *(3)*. In these circumstances, the deemed disposal and reacquisition rules apply, if it is just and reasonable, as if the relevant value either were such value as secures that the deemed disposal produces neither gain nor loss (if that is just and reasonable), or, unless it produces a lower value, were reduced to whatever value is just and reasonable.

[*TCGA 1992, s 232*].

Where a charge can be said, on a just and reasonable basis, to accrue by virtue of a deemed disposal as above in respect of any of the gain carried forward by virtue of *TCGA 1992, s 229(1)* or *(3)*, so much of the gain charged is not to be capable of being carried forward for the purposes of ROLLOVER RELIEF (**59**) under *TCGA 1992, ss 152–158*. For the purposes of ROLLOVER RELIEF (**59.9**) under *TCGA 1992, s 154* (new assets which are depreciating assets), a charge will arise under that provision by reference to the earlier of the disposal of the replacement asset, the deemed disposal of it under the above and the expiration of ten years beginning with the acquisition of the replacement asset. [*TCGA 1992, ss 154(3), 236(1)(2)*].

Chargeable event when replacement property owned

[22.32] Where:

(a) the conditions described in **22.31**(a)–(c) above are fulfilled,

(b) before the time when the chargeable event occurs all the gain carried forward by virtue of *TCGA 1992, s 229(1)* or *(3)* (see **22.30** above) was in turn carried forward from all the replacement assets to other property by virtue of a claim for ROLLOVER RELIEF (**59**) to apply under *TCGA 1992, ss 152–158*, and

(c) at the time of the occurrence of the chargeable event, the claimant or a person then connected with him (as above) is beneficially entitled to all the property,

the claimant or the connected person (as the case may be) is deemed, immediately before the occurrence of the chargeable event, to have disposed of, and immediately reacquired, all the property at the 'relevant value'.

The '*relevant value*' is as defined for *TCGA 1992, s 232* in **22.31** above.

Where the conditions at (b) and (c) above were satisfied as regards only part of the gain carried forward, the replacement assets from which it was in turn carried forward or the beneficial entitlement to the property into which it was further carried forward, there is a deemed disposal and reacquisition of the property concerned, the relevant value being reduced as is just and reasonable.

An adjustment may be made where there is a deemed disposal and reacquisition under these provisions, and before the occurrence of the chargeable event it can be said that, because of something which has happened as regards any of the replacement assets or any other property, a charge has accrued in respect of any gain carried forward by virtue of *TCGA 1992, s 229(1)* or *(3)*. In these circumstances, the deemed disposal and reacquisition rules apply, if it is just and reasonable, as if the relevant value either were such value as secures that the deemed disposal produces neither gain nor loss (if that is just and reasonable), or, unless it produces a lower value, were reduced to whatever value is just and reasonable.

[*TCGA 1992, s 233*].

Where a charge can be said to accrue, on a just and reasonable basis, by virtue of a deemed disposal as above in respect of any of the gain carried forward by virtue of *TCGA 1992, s 229(1)* or *(3)*, so much of the gain charged is not to be capable of being carried forward for the purposes of ROLLOVER RELIEF (**59**) under *TCGA 1992, ss 152–158*. [*TCGA 1992, s 236(1)(2)*].

Chargeable event when qualifying corporate bonds owned

[22.33] Where:

(a) the conditions described in **22.31**(a)–(c) above are fulfilled,

(b) all the replacement assets were shares in a company or companies (referred to below as 'new shares'),

(c) there has been a transaction within *TCGA 1992, s 116(10)* (see **54.4** QUALIFYING CORPORATE BONDS) as regards which all the new shares constitute the 'old asset' and qualifying corporate bonds constitute the 'new asset', and

(d) at the time of the occurrence of the chargeable event, the claimant or a person then connected with him (as above) is beneficially entitled to all the bonds, a chargeable gain of the 'relevant amount' is deemed to have accrued to the claimant or the connected person (as the case may be) immediately before the time when the chargeable event occurs.

The '*relevant amount*' is the lesser of the 'first amount' and the 'second amount'.

The '*first amount*' is the amount of the chargeable gain that would be deemed to accrue under *TCGA 1992, s 116(10)(b)* if there were a disposal of all the bonds at the time the chargeable event occurs (or nil if an allowable loss would arise). The '*second amount*' is the relevant value as for *TCGA 1992, s 232* in **22.31** above.

Where the conditions at (b), (c) and (d) above were satisfied as regards only part of the replacement assets, the new shares constituting the old asset or the bonds to which there is beneficial entitlement, a chargeable gain is nevertheless deemed to arise as above, but the first amount is determined only by reference to the bonds concerned, the second amount is reduced as is just and reasonable, and the relevant amount is reduced accordingly.

An adjustment may be made where a chargeable gain arises as above, and before the occurrence of the chargeable event it can be said that, because of something which has happened as regards any of the new shares or any of the bonds, a charge has accrued in respect of any gain carried forward by virtue of *TCGA 1992, s 229(1)* or *(3)* (see **22.30** above). In these circumstances, the chargeable gain is, if it is just and reasonable, calculated as if the second amount were reduced as is just and reasonable (but not so as to reduce it below nil) and the relevant amount reduced (if appropriate) accordingly.

[*TCGA 1992, s 234*].

Where a charge arises as above in the case of qualifying corporate bonds and subsequently a chargeable gain accrues under *TCGA 1992, s 116(10)(b)* on a disposal of them (see above), the chargeable gain is reduced by the relevant amount or (if the amount exceeds the gain) reduced to nil. The relevant amount is apportioned for this purpose where the subsequent disposal is of only some of the bonds. [*TCGA 1992, s 236(3)(4)*].

Dwelling-houses: special provisions

[22.34] As regards **22.30**(d) above, a replacement asset which is a dwelling-house (or part thereof) or land is not treated (where it would otherwise be so treated) as being a chargeable asset in relation to the claimant immediately after the asset's acquisition if on a disposal of it (or an interest in it) at some time in the period from its acquisition to the time a claim is made under *TCGA 1992, s 229(1)* or *(3)* (see **22.30** above), the PRIVATE RESIDENCES (**53.2**) exemption of *TCGA 1992, s 222(1)* would apply to the asset (or interest in it) and the 'individual' (which includes references to a person entitled to occupy the dwelling-house etc. under the terms of a settlement; see **53.11** PRIVATE RESIDENCES) mentioned in *TCGA 1992, s 222(1)* would be the claimant or his spouse or civil partner.

A similar treatment applies retrospectively where the replacement asset is a dwelling-house etc. which would otherwise be a chargeable asset in relation to the claimant immediately after its acquisition and which becomes eligible for the private residences exemption at some time after a claim under *TCGA 1992, s 229(1)* or *(3)* is made. In such a case, any gain thereby treated as having accrued is deemed not to have accrued until the time (or the earliest time) on which a disposal of the dwelling-house would be within the private residences exemption.

Similar provisions apply in relation to a replacement asset which is an option to acquire (or to acquire an interest in) a dwelling-house and the application of the private residences exemption in the period from the exercise of the option and the time of claim, and subsequent to the time of claim, respectively.

[*TCGA 1992, s 230; SI 2005 No 3229, Reg 119*].

Shares qualifying for EIS relief — special provisions

[22.35] As regards 22.30(d) above, a replacement asset which consists of shares is not treated (where it would otherwise be so treated) as being a chargeable asset in relation to the claimant immediately after the asset's acquisition if at some time in the period from its acquisition to the time a claim is made under *TCGA 1992, s 229(1)* or *(3)* (see **22.30** above) Enterprise Investment Scheme (EIS) income tax relief (see **23.2** ENTERPRISE INVESTMENT SCHEME) is claimed in respect of it.

A similar treatment applies retrospectively where the replacement asset consists of shares which would otherwise be a chargeable asset in relation to the claimant immediately after their acquisition and EIS relief is claimed at some time after a claim under *TCGA 1992, s 229(1)* or *(3)* is made.

Similar provisions applied as regards relief under the Business Expansion Scheme for shares issued before 1 January 1994 (see **25.22** EXEMPTIONS AND RELIEFS).

[*TCGA 1992, s 231*].

Information powers

[22.36] Before 13 August 2009, the Inspector could, by notice in writing, require a return containing specified information by the trustees of an employee share ownership trust (within *FA 1989, Sch 5*) where a disposal of shares (or an interest therein) had been made to them and a claim was made under *TCGA 1992, s 229(1)* or *(3)* (see **22.30** above). The information specified had to be needed for the purposes of *TCGA 1992, ss 232–234* (see **22.31–22.33** above), and could include information about: expenditure incurred by the trustees (including the purpose of the expenditure and the recipients); assets acquired by them (including the persons from whom the assets were acquired and the consideration); and transfers of assets made by them (including the persons to whom they were transferred and the consideration). Penalties under *TMA 1970, s 98* applied for failure to comply with a notice. Where relief had been given by virtue of *TCGA 1992, s 229(1)* or *(3)*, the Inspector had to send to the trustees a certificate that it had been given, stating the effect on the consideration for the disposal or on the gain accruing on the disposal. [*TCGA 1992, s 235; SI 2009 No 2035, Sch para 32*].

Priority allocations in public share offers

[22.37] If a benefit derived by an employee from a priority allocation of shares in a public offer is exempted from income tax by *ITEPA 2003, ss 542* or *544* (see Tolley's Income Tax under Employment Income), the usual MARKET VALUE (**45**) rules do not apply and the allowable expenditure for CGT on a disposal of the shares is the consideration given. [*TCGA 1992, s 149C*].

Double tax relief

[22.38] Where an employee is internationally mobile, a tax charge may arise both in the UK and in another country when a share option is exercised, assigned or released. An article in the Revenue Tax Bulletin October 2001 pp 883–887 sets out the HMRC practice for dealing with possible double taxation in the most common scenarios. The article is concerned with options granted under unapproved schemes and those granted under one of the approved schemes where the circumstances are such that a UK income tax charge nevertheless arises.

The article is concerned primarily with the income tax aspects, but does consider the position of an employee who is not resident and not ordinarily resident in the UK when an option is granted, moves to the UK and exercises the option whilst performing the duties of the employment there, and then disposes of the shares. There would normally be no UK income tax charge in such a case but there may well be a CGT charge on the disposal, i.e. under general principles. Strictly, the exercise of the option and the disposal of the shares are distinct events and the UK is not obliged to grant relief against UK CGT for any foreign tax paid on the grant or exercise of, or otherwise in connection with, the option. However, where such foreign tax is that of a country with which the UK has a double tax agreement (see **21.2** DOUBLE TAX RELIEF), HMRC will by concession allow a proportion of the foreign tax as a credit against the UK CGT liability on all or part of the gain depending on the circumstances — see p 886 of the Tax Bulletin for more details.

Key points concerning employee share schemes

[22.39] Points to consider are as follows.

- Generally, where employees receive remuneration from employment by means of shares or share options the value received is taxable as income deriving from that employment and is usually subject to national insurance as well.
- The meaning of 'shares' is quite wide and includes securities.
- Where the receipt of shares has been subjected to income tax the amount taxed is taken into account in calculating the base cost for capital gains tax purposes.
- It should be noted that HMRC's previous view following *Mansworth v Jelley* has been revised. Whereas some share options exercised before 10 April 2003 had produced very large base costs

— in some cases double the market value — HMRC state this is not now the case. Practitioners should consider the ongoing treatment of losses that arose under the previous HMRC guidance which are being carried forward. See **22.6** above for the case of *Revenue and Customs Commissioners v Hutchinson* 2017] EWCA Civ 1075, [2017] STC 2048.

- There are a number of arrangements which have been approved by HMRC and which do not attract an income tax charge. As a result shares acquired under such arrangements will have a lower base cost.
- For capital gains tax purposes shares acquired on the same day are treated as a single acquisition, but, where some of the shares are acquired under an approved scheme and others are not, an election can be made to treat those shares as a separate acquisition. This enables shares disposed of to be identified first with those with a higher base cost.
- In some circumstances shares acquired by employees have restrictions attached to them which depress the market value and hence the income tax charge. If those restrictions are subsequently lifted and the value of the shares is increased, the proportionate increase in value can be applied to the gain on disposal and that proportion can be chargeable to income tax and national insurance rather than capital gains tax.
- However, it is possible to avoid this by making an election to be taxed on the unrestricted value when the shares are acquired. The election is made jointly with the employer and must be made within 14 days of acquiring the shares, although the election is not submitted to HMRC.

23

Enterprise Investment Scheme

Introduction	**23.1**
Conditions for income tax relief	**23.2**
General requirements	**23.3**
Qualifying investor	**23.4**
Qualifying company	**23.5**
Qualifying subsidiary	**23.6**
Qualifying 90% subsidiary	**23.7**
Qualifying business activity	**23.8**
Qualifying trade	**23.9**
Form of income tax relief	**23.10**
Claims for relief	**23.11**
Restriction or withdrawal of income tax relief	**23.12**
Capital gains tax	**23.13**
Capital gains deferral relief	**23.14**
Reinvestment into EIS shares issued after 5 April 1998	**23.15**
Reinvestment into EIS shares issued after 5 April 1998 — application to trustees	**23.16**
Reinvestment into EIS shares issued after 5 April 1998 — further provisions	**23.17**
Reinvestment into EIS shares issued before 6 April 1998	**23.18**
Key points	**23.19**

Cross-references. See **22.21**, **22.35** EMPLOYEE SHARE SCHEMES for restriction on rollover relief arising from disposal of shares to, respectively, an approved share incentive plan and, before 6 April 2001, an employee share ownership trust, where replacement asset is shares and a claim for EIS income tax relief is made; **60** SEED ENTERPRISE INVESTMENT SCHEME; **63** SHARES AND SECURITIES; **71** VENTURE CAPITAL TRUSTS.

Simon's Taxes. See C3.10.

Introduction to enterprise investment scheme

[23.1] The Enterprise Investment Scheme (EIS) offers income tax relief to a qualifying individual to whom shares in a qualifying company (see **23.5** below) have been issued by subscription. The company concerned must use the money raised within the specified time limit for a qualifying business activity (see **23.8** below).

For more detailed coverage of the income tax provisions, see Tolley's Income Tax under Enterprise Investment Scheme. As regards both income tax and CGT, see also HMRC Venture Capital Schemes Manual VCM10010 *et seq*.

Gains on disposal of shares on which EIS income tax relief has been given are not chargeable gains if the disposal is made after the end of a specified period. The capital gains tax exemption is described at **23.13** below. See **23.14** below re capital gains deferral relief.

All enquiries about whether a company newly raising money under the EIS meets the requirements should be made to HMRC's Small Company Enterprise Centre. This initial point of contact is supported by specialist HMRC units that also deal with the corporation tax affairs, and the monitoring, of such companies as well as companies raising money under other types of venture capital scheme or granting options under enterprise management incentives. (Revenue Press Release 25 September 2000).

State aid information

With effect from 15 September 2016, HMRC may give a company in respect of whose shares EIS income tax relief has been given, or may be given in future, a notice requiring it to provide specified information for the purpose of complying with EU state aid obligations. See *FA 2016, ss 180–182, Sch 24.*

Conditions for income tax relief

[23.2] An individual investor is eligible for EIS income tax relief in respect of an amount invested by him on his own behalf for an issue of shares in a company if:

(a) the shares are issued to the investor;
(b) the general requirements at **23.3** below are met in respect of the shares;
(c) the investor is a 'qualifying investor' (see **23.4** below) in relation to the shares; and
(d) the company issuing the shares is a 'qualifying company' (see **23.5** below) in relation to the shares.

The EIS applies to shares issued before 6 April 2025 but this date may be amended by the Treasury via statutory instrument.

[*ITA 2007, s 157(1)(1A); F(No 2)A 2015, Sch 5 para 2*].

Bare trustees and nominees

Relief is available where shares which satisfy the requirement at **23.3**(i) below are held on a bare trust for two or more beneficiaries as if each beneficiary had subscribed as an individual for all of those shares, and as if the amount subscribed by each was the total subscribed divided by the number of beneficiaries. [*ITA 2007, s 250(2)(3)*].

Relief is also available where shares are subscribed for by a nominee for the individual claiming relief, including the managers of an investment fund approved by HMRC for this purpose (an '*approved fund*'). With regard to an approved fund closed for the acceptance of further investments, the provisions at **23.10** below (dealing with the form and attribution of relief) apply as if the eligible shares were issued at the time at which the fund was closed, provided that the amount subscribed on behalf of the individual for eligible shares issued within twelve months (six months for funds closed before 7 October 2007) after the closure of the fund is not less than 90% of the individual's investment in the fund. [*ITA 2007, ss 250(1), 251(1)(2)*].

General requirements

[23.3] The general requirements mentioned at **23.2**(b) above are as follows.

The shares requirement

The shares must:

(i) be ordinary shares which do not, at any time during 'period B', carry (subject to below) any present or future preferential right to dividends or to assets on a winding-up or any present or future right to be redeemed; and
(ii) unless they are 'bonus shares', be subscribed for wholly in cash and be fully paid up at the time of issue.

Shares issued on or after 6 April 2012 are, however, permitted to carry a preferential right to dividends provided the amount and timing of the dividends do not depend on a decision of the company, the shareholder or any other person and provided the dividends are not cumulative.

For the purposes of (i) above, '*period B*' is the three years beginning with the date of issue. If the company satisfied the purpose of the issue requirement below by virtue of (a) or (c) below and the trade had not yet commenced on the issue date, period B is the period from date of issue to immediately before the third anniversary of commencement. (In determining for this purpose the time at which a qualifying trade begins to be carried on by any 'qualifying 90% subsidiary' (see **23.7** below) of a company, any carrying on of the trade etc. by it before it became such a subsidiary is disregarded.)

For the purposes of (ii) above, '*bonus shares*' are shares issued otherwise than for payment (whether in cash or otherwise). Shares are not fully paid up if there is any undertaking to pay cash to any person at a later date in respect of the acquisition.

[*ITA 2007, ss 159(3), 173, 256, 257(1); FA 2012, Sch 7 paras 6, 22(1)*].

In *Flix Innovations Ltd v HMRC* UT, [2016] STC 2206, ordinary shares which carried small preferential rights to a return of capital on a winding-up were held not to qualify for relief.

Shares are not issued until the company's register of members has been completed (*National Westminster Bank plc v CIR; Barclays Bank plc v CIR* HL 1994, 67 TC 1 and see Revenue Tax Bulletin June 1995 p 217).

The maximum amount raised annually through risk finance investments requirement

The total amount of 'relevant investments' in the company and its subsidiaries in 12 months ending with the date of issue of the shares must not exceed £5 million (£2 million in relation to shares issued before 6 April 2012). The following also count towards this limit:

(a) any relevant investment in a 51% subsidiary (within *CTA 2010, Pt 24 Ch 3*) of the issuing company (including any made before it became a 51% subsidiary but not any made after it last ceased to be one);
(b) any relevant investment made in any company to the extent that the money raised by the investment has been employed for the purposes of a trade (as widely defined) carried on by another company that has at any time in the said 12-month period been a 51% subsidiary of the issuing company (disregarding any money so employed after it last ceased to be such a subsidiary); and
(c) any other relevant investment made in any company to the extent that the money raised has been employed for the purposes of a trade (as widely defined), and within that 12-month period, but after the investment was made, the trade (or a part of it) was transferred to the issuing company, a 51% subsidiary or a partnership of which the issuing company or a 51% subsidiary is a member (but disregarding trades transferred after a 51% subsidiary in question last ceased to be such a subsidiary).

In relation to shares issued by the issuing company before 18 November 2015, (a)–(c) above did not apply but investments made in any company that was a subsidiary of that company at any time in the said 12-month period counted towards the limit (regardless of whether or not it was a subsidiary when the investment was made).

[*ITA 2007, s 173A(1)–(2B)(6)(7); FA 2012, Sch 7 paras 7, 22, 23; F(No 2)A 2015, Sch 5 paras 7, 23; SI 2012 No 1896*].

Relevant investment

For the purposes of the EIS requirements, '*relevant investments*' comprise:

(I) investments (of any kind) made by a VENTURE CAPITAL TRUST (VCT) (**71**);
(II) money subscribed for shares issued under the EIS or the SEED ENTERPRISE INVESTMENT SCHEME (SEIS) (**60**);
(III) (in relation to shares issued on or after 18 November 2015) investments made under the SOCIAL INVESTMENT RELIEF (**65**) scheme; and
(IV) (in relation to shares issued on or after 6 April 2012) any other investment made which is aid received by the company pursuant to a measure approved by the EC as compatible with Article 107 of the Treaty on the Functioning of the European Union in accordance with the principles laid down in the European Commission's Guidelines on State aid to promote risk finance investment (previously the Community Guidelines on Risk Capital Investments in Small and Medium-sized Enterprises).

As regards (II) above, shares are treated as having been issued under the EIS or SEIS if at any time the investee company provides an EIS compliance statement (see **23.11** below) or SEIS equivalent in respect of those shares; an investment is regarded as made when the shares are issued. As regards (III) above, an investment is treated as made under the social investment relief scheme if at any time the investee company provides a compliance statement as in **65.36** SOCIAL INVESTMENT RELIEF; *ITA 2007, s 257KB* (see **65.1** SOCIAL INVESTMENT RELIEF) applies in determining when such an investment is made.

[*ITA 2007, s 173A(3)–(5); FA 2012, Sch 6 paras 12, 24(1), Sch 7 paras 7, 22, 23; F(No 2)A 2015, Sch 5 paras 7, 23*].

The maximum risk finance investments at the issue date requirement

In relation to shares issued on or after 18 November 2015, the total amount of 'relevant investments' (see above) made in the issuing company on or before the date the EIS shares are issued must not exceed £12 million or, if the company is a 'knowledge-intensive company' (see below) at the time the shares are issued, £20 million. Relevant investments of the kind in (a)–(c) above also count towards these limits, but disregarding references there to a 12-month period and instead taking into account all times before the issue date. [*ITA 2007, s 173AA; F(No 2)A 2015, Sch 5 paras 8, 23*].

Knowledge-intensive companies

A '*knowledge-intensive company*' is broadly a company whose costs of research and development or innovation are at least 15% of its operating costs in at least one of the years comprising the 'relevant three-year period' or at least 10% of its operating costs in each of those years, and which meets at least one of the two conditions below. The '*relevant three-year period*' is normally the three years ending immediately before the beginning of the last accounts filing period. However, if the last accounts filing period ends more than 12 months before the issue date of the EIS shares in question, the relevant three-year period is the three years ending 12 months before the issue date. (In relation to shares issued on or after 18 November 2015 and before 6 April 2016, a company may make an election under *FA 2016, s 30* the effect of which is that the relevant three-year period is in any case the three years ending 12 months before the issue date.) A company's operating costs are defined by reference to the items recognised as expenses in its profit and loss account. The conditions to be met are that:

- the company has created, is creating or is intending to create, intellectual property (the '*innovation condition*'); or
- the company's full-time employees with a relevant Masters or higher degree who are engaged in research and development or innovation comprise at least 20% of the total of its full-time employees (the '*skilled employee condition*'). The skilled employee condition must continue to be met throughout period B (subject to a let-out for companies entering administration or receivership).

In order to meet the innovation condition, the issuing company must be engaged in intellectual property creation at the time the EIS shares are issued, and it must be reasonable to assume that, within ten years after the issue, the exploitation of its intellectual property, or business which results from new or improved products, processes or services utilising its intellectual property, will form the greater part of its business. A company is engaged in intellectual property creation if intellectual property is being created by the company, or has been created by it within the previous three years; or the company is taking (or preparing to take) steps in order that intellectual property will be created by it; or the company demonstrates via an independent expert's report that it is reasonable to assume it will create intellectual property in the foreseeable future. Intellectual property is taken into account only if the whole or greater part (in terms of value) of it is created by the company and it is created in circumstances in which the right to exploit it vests in the company (whether alone or jointly with others).

If the issuing company is a parent company, the above rules are appropriately modified to also take account of its 'qualifying subsidiaries' (see **23.6** below).

[*ITA 2007, s 252A; F(No 2)A 2015, Sch 5 para 19; FA 2016, s 29(2)(6), s 30*].

The 'maximum risk finance investments during period B' requirement

In relation to shares issued on or after 18 November 2015, there is a requirement which is tested only during period B and only if the issuing company effectively acquires a company or trade after it receives the EIS investment in question. The requirement is that at any time in period B the total of the relevant investments (see above) so far made must not exceed £12 million or, if the company is a 'knowledge-intensive company' (see above) at the time the EIS shares are issued, £20 million. Without this requirement, the investment limits above could be sidestepped where the acquired company or trade had already benefited from earlier relevant investments. Relevant investments of the kind in (a)–(c) above also count towards these limits, but disregarding references there to a 12-month period and instead taking into account all times before the time in period B when the requirement is being tested. The requirement applies where:

- a company becomes a 51% subsidiary of the issuing company at a time during period B (other than as a result of an exchange of shares within *ITA 2007, s 247*);
- all or part of the money raised by the issue of the EIS shares in question is employed for the purposes of a qualifying business activity (see **23.8** below) consisting (wholly or partly) of a trade (as widely defined) carried on by that company; and
- the trade (or a part of it) was carried on by that company before that time.

The requirement also applies where all or part of the money raised by the issue of the EIS shares is employed for the purposes of a qualifying business activity consisting (wholly or partly) of a trade (as widely defined) which, during period B, is transferred as in (c) above.

[*ITA 2007, ss 173AB, 247(3A); F(No 2)A 2015, Sch 5 paras 8, 17, 23*].

The spending of money raised by SEIS investment requirement

In relation to shares issued before 6 April 2015, if a SEIS investment had been made in the issuing company, at least 70% of the money raised by that investment had to have been spent as mentioned in **60.7** SEED ENTERPRISE INVESTMENT SCHEME before the EIS shares were issued. A SEIS investment is made if the company issues shares (for which money has been subscribed) and provides a compliance statement under *ITA 2007, s 257ED* in respect of them. [*ITA 2007, s 173B; FA 2012, Sch 6 paras 13, 23(1); F(No 2)A 2015, Sch 5 paras 9, 21*].

The purpose of the issue requirement

The shares, other than any which are bonus shares, must be issued to raise money (i.e. cash, see *Thompson v Hart* Ch D 2000, 72 TC 543) for the purpose of a 'qualifying business activity' (see **23.8** below). In relation to shares issued on or after 18 November 2015, it is made explicit, for EU State aid purposes, that the issuing company must use the money for this purpose so as to promote the growth and development of the company or, where the company is a parent company, the group. [*ITA 2007, s 174; F(No 2)A 2015, Sch 5 paras 10, 23(1)*].

This requirement may be satisfied where money is raised to acquire shares in a company carrying on a 'qualifying trade' (see **23.9** below), provided the target company has no non-trading assets and the hive up of the trade is not unnecessarily delayed. Money used to meet the expenses of issuing the shares should be regarded as employed in the same way as the remainder of the money raised. Where the company obtains a listing, for example on the Alternative Investment Market, at the same time as it issues the shares, the use of money to meet the expenses of flotation is normally acceptable. (HMRC Venture Capital Schemes Manual VCM12060).

The requirement was held to be satisfied where the money raised was loaned to overseas subsidiaries for the purpose of enabling them to supply information and analysis for the purposes of the issuing company's business (*4Cast Ltd v Mitchell* (Sp C 455), [2005] SSCD 287).

The requirement is *not* satisfied if the money raised by the issue is used partly to pay dividends to investors (*Forthright (Wales) Ltd v A L Davies* Ch D 2004, 76 TC 138). The requirement was not satisfied where a company issued convertible loan notes which it subsequently converted into shares; the issue of the shares was not then for the purpose of raising money (*Optos plc v HMRC* (Sp C 560), 2006 STI 2236).

The use of money raised requirement

The 'money raised' must be employed wholly (disregarding insignificant amounts) for the purpose of the qualifying business activity for which it was raised by the end of the two years following the issue or, if the only qualifying business activity falls within **23.8**(a) or (c) below, and if later, by the end of the two years starting when the company (or, where applicable, a subsidiary) began to carry on the qualifying trade. Additionally, for shares issued before 22 April 2009, 80% of that money must be so employed within twelve months after the issue/commencement of trade.

For this purpose, the '*money raised*' means the money raised by the issue of the shares in question (other than any of them which are bonus shares) and any other shares in the company of the same class (as defined) which are within (i) above and which are issued on the same day. In determining the time at which a qualifying trade begins to be carried on by a 'qualifying 90% subsidiary' of a company, any carrying on of the trade etc. by it before it became such a subsidiary is disregarded.

In relation to shares issued on or after 6 April 2012, employing money on the acquisition of shares in a company does not of itself amount to employing it for the purposes of a qualifying business activity. Additionally, in relation to shares issued on or after 18 November 2015, employing money on the acquisition of any of the following does not amount to employing it for the purposes of a qualifying business activity: an interest in another company such that a company becomes a 51% subsidiary of the issuing company; a further interest in a 51% subsidiary of the issuing company; a trade (as widely defined); and goodwill or other intangible assets employed for the purposes of a trade.

[*ITA 2007, ss 175, 257(5); FA 2012, Sch 7 paras 8, 22(1); F(No 2)A 2015, Sch 5 paras 11, 23(1)*].

See *Richards and another v HMRC* UT 2011, [2012] STC 174 in which money which was held to have been employed to supplement trading receipts in order to cover losses was held not to satisfy this requirement.

In *GC Trading Ltd v HMRC* Sp C 2007 (Sp C 630), [2008] SSCD 178, this condition was held to be satisfied even though the money raised was loaned to another company before being used to purchase a qualifying trade. On the evidence, the loans were the equivalent of a bank deposit and were simply the means used to preserve the money needed to acquire the trade.

In *Skye Inns Ltd v HMRC* FTT, [2009] UKFTT 266 (TC), 2010 STI 799 this requirement was held not to be satisfied where the company's purchase of a pub fell through at the last minute so that the funds raised were not used within the required period, even though the directors continued to look for new acquistions.

This requirement is *not* satisfied if the money raised by the issue is used partly to pay dividends to investors (*Forthright (Wales) Ltd v A L Davies* Ch D 2004, 76 TC 138).

The permitted maximum age requirement

In relation to shares issued on or after 18 November 2015, if the EIS shares in question are issued after the 'initial investing period', one of three conditions must be met. These are that:

(A) a 'relevant investment' (see above) was made in the issuing company before the end of the initial investing period, and some or all of the money raised by that investment was employed for the purposes of the same qualifying business activity (see **23.8** below) as that for which the money raised by the current issue is employed;

(B) the total amount of relevant investments made in the issuing company in a period of 30 consecutive days which includes the date of issue of the shares is at least 50% of the annual turnover of the company averaged over five years (see *ITA 2007, s 175A(7)–(8)*), and the money raised by those investments is employed for the purpose of 'entering a new product or geographical market' (as defined in the General Block Exemption Regulation (Commission Regulation (EU) No 651/2014); or

(C) the condition in (B) or the equivalent condition for VCT approval (see **71** VENTURE CAPITAL TRUSTS) was previously met in relation to one or more relevant investments in the issuing company, and some or all of the money raised by those investments was employed for the purposes of the same qualifying business activity as that for which the money raised by the current issue is employed.

The '*initial investing period*' is the seven years beginning with the 'relevant first commercial sale' (ten years where the issuing company is a 'knowledge-intensive company' (see above) when the EIS shares are issued). '*First commercial sale*' has the same meaning as in the EC's Guidelines on State aid to promote risk finance investments. The '*relevant first commercial sale*' is defined in *ITA 2007, s 175A(6)* by reference to the earliest date of any commercial sale made by (broadly) the company or a 51% subsidiary or any other person who has carried on any trade which is carried on by the company or a subsidiary.

[*ITA 2007, ss 175A, 247(3A); F(No 2)A 2015, Sch 5 paras 12, 17, 23; FA 2016, s 29(1)(6), s 30*].

The minimum period requirement

The trade or research and development within **23.8**(a), (b) below must have been carried on for a period of at least four months ending at or after the time of the share issue by no person other than the qualifying company or a 'qualifying 90% subsidiary' (see **23.7** below) of that company.

A period shorter than four months is permitted if this is by reason only of the winding-up or dissolution of any company or anything done as a consequence of a company being in administration or receivership, provided the winding-up etc. is for genuine commercial reasons and not part of a tax avoidance scheme or arrangements.

[*ITA 2007, s 176*].

The no pre-arranged exits requirement

The arrangements (as broadly defined) under which the shares are issued to the investor (or arrangements preceding the issue but in relation or in connection to it) must not:

- provide for the eventual disposal by the investor of the shares in question or other shares or securities of the company; or
- provide for the eventual cessation of a trade of the company or of a person connected with it; or
- provide for the eventual disposal of all, or a substantial amount (in terms of value) of, the assets of the company or of a person connected with it; or
- provide (by means of any insurance, indemnity, guarantee or otherwise) complete or partial protection for investors against the normal risks attaching to EIS investment (but excluding arrangements which merely protect the company and/or its subsidiaries against normal business risks).

Arrangements with a view to the company becoming a wholly-owned subsidiary of a new holding company within the terms of *ITA 2007, s 247(1)* (see **23.5** below) are excluded from (a) above. For shares issued on or after

5 December 2016, arrangements with a view to shares in the company being exchanged for, or converted into, shares of a different class in that company, are also excluded from (a) above. Arrangements applicable only on an unanticipated winding-up of the company for genuine commercial reasons are excluded from (b) and (c) above.

[*ITA 2007, ss 177, 257(1); FA 2012, Sch 7 paras 21, 25; F(No 2)A 2017, s 11(2)(4)*].

The no tax avoidance requirement

The shares must be issued for genuine commercial reasons and not as part of a scheme or arrangement a main purpose of which is the avoidance of tax.

[*ITA 2007, s 178*].

The no disqualifying arrangements requirement

This requirement has effect in relation to shares issued on or after 6 April 2012, regardless of when the disqualifying arrangements were entered into. The requirement is that the shares must not be issued, nor any money raised by the issue spent, in consequence or anticipation of, or otherwise in connection with, 'disqualifying arrangements'. Arrangements (as broadly defined) are '*disqualifying arrangements*' if they are entered into with the purpose of ensuring that any of the 'relevant tax reliefs' (see below) are available in respect of the issuing company's business and either or both of conditions A and B below are met. It is immaterial whether the issuing company is a party to the arrangements.

Condition A is that, as a result of the money raised by the issue of the shares being employed as required by the use of the money raised requirement above, an amount representing the whole or most of the amount raised is, in the course of the arrangements, paid to (or for the benefit of) one or more parties to the arrangements or a person or persons connected with such a party (within **17** CONNECTED PERSONS). Condition B is that, in the absence of the arrangements, it would have been reasonable to expect that the whole or greater part of the component activities (as defined) of the qualifying business activity for which the issue of the shares raised money would have been carried on as part of another business by one or more parties to the arrangements or a person or persons connected with such a party.

The '*relevant tax reliefs*' comprise:

- EIS income tax and CGT reliefs (as in **23.10**, **23.13** and **23.14** below);
- SEIS income tax and CGT reliefs (see **60.32**, **60.43** and **60.45** SEED ENTERPRISE INVESTMENT SCHEME);
- qualification as an investee company for VCT purposes (see **71.4** VENTURE CAPITAL TRUSTS);
- share loss relief (see **44.15** LOSSES) and
- (in relation to shares issued on or after 6 April 2017 but not so as to apply to arrangements involving transactions entered into before that date) SOCIAL INVESTMENT RELIEF (**65**).

[*ITA 2007, ss 178A, 257(1); FA 2012, Sch 7 paras 9, 21, 22, 25; F(No 2)A 2017, Sch 1 paras 11(2), 16*].

Qualifying investor

[23.4] An individual is a '*qualifying investor*' in relation to shares if the following requirements are met.

The no connection with the issuing company requirement

The investor must not (except as below) be at any time in the period specified below 'connected with' the issuing company (whether before or after its incorporation) (i.e. there must be no such connection at any time in that period, see *Wild v Cannavan* CA 1997, 70 TC 554). The specified period is the period beginning two years before the issue of the shares and ending immediately before the third anniversary of the issue date or, if later and where relevant, the third anniversary of the date of commencement of the intended trade referred to in **23.8**(a) below.

In determining the time at which a qualifying trade begins to be carried on by any 'qualifying 90% subsidiary' (see **23.7** below) of a company, any carrying on of the trade by it before it became such a subsidiary is disregarded.

[*ITA 2007, ss 163, 256*].

An investor is '*connected with*' the issuing company if he, or an 'associate' of his, is either:

(a) an employee, partner, or director of, or an employee or director of a partner of, the issuing company or any 'subsidiary'; or

(b) an individual who directly or indirectly possesses or is entitled to acquire (whether he is so entitled at a future date or will at a future date be so entitled):

  (I) more than 30% of the voting power, the ordinary share capital or the issued share capital of the issuing company or any 'subsidiary'; or

  (II) such rights as would entitle him to more than 30% of the assets of the issuing company or any 'subsidiary' available for distribution to the company's equity holders (as defined); or

(c) an individual who has control (as defined by *ITA 2007, s 995*) of the issuing company or any 'subsidiary'; or

(d) an individual who subscribes for shares in the issuing company as part of an arrangement providing for another person to subscribe for shares in another company with which, were that other company an issuing company, the individual (or any other individual party to the arrangement) would be connected as above.

Rights or powers of associates are taken into account as regards (b) and (c) above (see *Cook v Billings CA*, [2001] STC 16 on the similar wording under the earlier BES provisions). An '*associate*' of any person is any 'relative' (i.e. spouse, civil partner, ancestor or linear descendant) of that person, the trustee(s) of any settlement in relation to which that person or any relative (living or dead) is or was a settlor and, where that person has an interest in any shares of obligations of a company which are subject to any trust or are part of a deceased estate, the trustee(s) of the settlement or the personal representatives of the deceased. For this purpose, 'settlor' is defined as in *ITA 2007, ss 467–473*.

As regards (b)(I) above, an individual is not connected with the company by virtue only of the fact that he or an associate is a shareholder if at that time the company has issued no shares other than subscriber shares and has neither commenced business nor made preparations for doing so.

In relation to shares issued before 6 April 2012, the requirement in (b)(I) above is whether the individual possesses etc. more than 30% of the voting power, the ordinary share capital or the loan capital and issued share capital of the company or subsidiary. The test of possession etc. of 'more than 30% of the loan capital and issued share capital of the issuing company or any subsidiary' requires possession etc. of more than 30% of the loan capital and issued share capital combined (and not 30% of the loan capital and 30% of the issued share capital): see *Taylor v HMRC* UT, [2011] STC 126. Loan capital includes any debt incurred by the company for money borrowed, for capital assets acquired, for any right to income created in its favour, or for insufficient consideration, but excludes any debt incurred for overdrawing a bank account in the ordinary course of the bank's business.

A '*subsidiary*' for these purposes is a company more than 50% of whose ordinary share capital is at any time in 'period A' owned by the issuing company, regardless of whether or not that condition is fulfilled while the individual falls within (a)–(d) above in respect of it.

'*Period A*' for this purpose is the period beginning with the incorporation of the company or, if later, two years before the date of issue of the shares and ending immediately before the third anniversary of the issue date or, if later and where relevant, the third anniversary of the date of commencement of the intended trade referred to in **23.8**(a) below.

(In determining for this purpose the time at which a qualifying trade begins to be carried on by any 'qualifying 90% subsidiary' (see **23.7** below) of a company, any carrying on of the trade by it before it became such a subsidiary is disregarded.)

[*ITA 2007, ss 159(2), 166–167(1)(2), 170, 171, 253, 256; FA 2012, Sch 7 paras 4, 22(1); F(No 2)A 2015, Sch 5 para 5*].

As regards (a) above, directorships are taken into account only where the individual or an associate (or a partnership of which either of them is a member) receives or is entitled to receive, during the period specified at (i)–(iii) above, a payment (whether directly or indirectly or to his order or for his benefit) from the issuing company or a 'related person' other than by way of:

- (A) payment or reimbursement of allowable expenditure against employment income;
- (B) interest at no more than a commercial rate on money lent;
- (C) dividends etc. representing no more than a normal return on investment;
- (D) payment for supply of goods at no more than market value;
- (E) rent at no more than a reasonable and commercial rent for property occupied; or
- (F) any reasonable and necessary remuneration for services rendered (other than secretarial or managerial services, or those rendered by the payer) which is taken into account in computing the recipient's trading profits.

A '*related person*' is any company of which the individual or an associate is a director and which is a subsidiary or partner of the issuing company, or a partner of the issuing company or a subsidiary, or any person connected (within *ITA 2007, s 993* — see **17** CONNECTED PERSONS) with such a company; 'subsidiary' for this purpose requiring ownership of more than 50% of ordinary share capital at some time in the specified period.

For these purposes (and those below), in the case of a person who is both a director and an employee of a company, references to him in his capacity as a director include him in his capacity as an employee, but otherwise he is not treated as an employee.

An individual who is connected with the issuing company may nevertheless qualify for relief if he is so connected only by reason of his (or his associate's) being a director of (or a partner of) the issuing company or any subsidiary receiving, or entitled to receive, remuneration (including any benefit or facility) as such, provided that:

(I) the remuneration (leaving out any within (F) above) is reasonable remuneration for services rendered to the company as a director;

(II) he subscribed for shares in the company meeting the requirement at **23.2**(i) above at a time when he had never been either:
   - (i) connected with the issuing company; or
   - (ii) involved (as sole trader, employee, partner or director) in carrying on its (or its subsidiary's) trade, business or profession (or any part thereof).

Where these conditions are satisfied in relation to an issue of shares, subsequent issues are treated as fulfilling (II) where they would not otherwise do so, provided that they are made within three years of the date of the last issue which did fulfil (II). Where relevant, the said three-year period is replaced by a longer period beginning with the date of the last such issue and ending with the date of commencement of the intended trade referred to in **23.8**(a) below. (In determining for these purposes the time at which a qualifying trade begins to be carried on by any 'qualifying 90% subsidiary' (see **23.7** below) of a company, any carrying on of the trade by it before it became such a subsidiary is disregarded.)

[*ITA 2007, ss 167(3), 168, 169, 256; FA 2012, Sch 6 para 10*].

The no linked loans requirement

No loan may be made to the investor or to an associate (see above) at any time in period A (see above) if it would not have been made, or would not have been made on the same terms, if the investor had not subscribed, or had not been proposing to subscribe, for the shares. The giving of credit to, or the assignment of a debt due from, the investor or associate is counted as a loan for these purposes. [*ITA 2007, s 164*].

For HMRC's views on loan-linked investments, see HMRC Statement of Practice 6/98.

The 'existing shareholdings' requirement

Shares issued on or after 18 November 2015 and subscribed for by an individual in a company in which he already holds shares are not eligible for EIS relief unless those other shares are a 'risk-finance investment'. The same applies if the pre-existing shareholding is in a qualifying subsidiary of the company (see **23.6** below). There is a let-out in certain cases where the pre-existing shares are subscriber shares. Shares are a '*risk-finance investment*' if they were issued by the company to the individual under the EIS, SEED ENTERPRISE INVESTMENT SCHEME (60) or SOCIAL INVESTMENT RELIEF (65) scheme. [*ITA 2007, s 164A; F(No 2)A 2015, Sch 5 paras 4, 23(1)*].

The no tax avoidance requirement

The shares must be subscribed for by the investor for genuine commercial reasons and not as part of a scheme or arrangement a main purpose of which is the avoidance of tax. [*ITA 2007, s 165*].

Qualifying company

[23.5] The issuing company is a '*qualifying company*' in relation to the shares if the following requirements are met. The company may be resident in the UK or elsewhere.

The UK permanent establishment requirement

For shares issued on or after 6 April 2011, the issuing company must have a 'permanent establishment' in the UK throughout 'period B'.

For this purpose, a company has a '*permanent establishment*' in the UK if, and only if, either:

- it has a 'fixed place of business' there through which its business is wholly or partly carried on; or
- an agent (other than one of independent status acting in the ordinary course of his business) acting on its behalf has, and habitually exercises there, authority to enter into contracts on the company's behalf,

unless the activities carried on in the UK are of a 'preparatory or auxiliary character'. The Treasury can amend this definition by regulations.

A '*fixed place of business*' includes a place of management, a branch, office, factory or workshop, a mine, oil or gas well, quarry or other place of natural resource extraction and a building site, construction or installation project. Activities of a '*preparatory or auxiliary character*' include the use of facilities for the purpose of storage, display or delivery of goods or merchandise belonging to the company; the maintenance of a stock of goods or merchandise belonging to the company for the purpose of storage, display, delivery or processing by another person; or purchasing goods or merchandise, or collecting information, for the company.

A company is not treated as having a permanent establishment in the UK by reason of its controlling a company resident there or a company carrying on business there (whether or not through a permanent establishment).

'*Period B*' is the period beginning with the date of issue of the shares and ending either three years after that date or, where **23.8**(a) below applies and the company (or subsidiary) was not carrying on the qualifying trade on that date, three years after the date on which it begins to carry on the trade. In determining for these purposes the time at which a qualifying trade begins to be carried on by any 'qualifying 90% subsidiary' (see **23.7** below) of a company, any carrying on of the trade by it before it became such a subsidiary is disregarded.

[*ITA 2007, ss 159(3), 180A, 191A; F(No 3)A 2010, Sch 2 paras 1(4)(5), 7(1); SI 2011 No 662*].

This requirement replaces the previous, narrower requirement for the qualifying trade to be carried on wholly or mainly in the UK (see **23.8** below).

The financial health requirement

For shares issued on or after 6 April 2011, the company must not be 'in difficulty' at the beginning of period B (as above). For this purpose, a company is 'in difficulty' if it is reasonable to assume that it would be so regarded under the Community Guidelines on State Aid for Rescuing and Restructuring Firms in Difficulty (2004/C244/02).

[*ITA 2007, s 180B; F(No 3)A 2010, Sch 2 paras 1(4), 7(1); SI 2011 No 662*].

The trading requirement

The company must, throughout period B (as above), either:

(a) exist wholly for the purpose of carrying on one or more 'qualifying trades' (see **23.9** below) (disregarding purposes having no significant effect on the extent of its activities); or
(b) be a '*parent company*' (i.e. a company that has one or more 'qualifying subsidiaries' (see **23.6** below)) and the business of the '*group*' (i.e. the company and its qualifying subsidiaries) must not consist wholly or as to a substantial part (i.e. broadly 20% — see HMRC Venture Capital Schemes Manual VCM3010) in the carrying on of 'non-qualifying activities'.

Where the company intends that one or more other companies should become its qualifying subsidiaries with a view to their carrying on one or more qualifying trades, then, until any time after which the intention is abandoned, the company is treated as a parent company and those other companies are included in the group for the purposes of (b) above.

For the purpose of (b) above, the business of the group means what would be the business of the group if the activities of the group companies taken together were regarded as one business. Activities are for this purpose disregarded to the extent that they consist in:

(i) holding shares in or securities of any of the company's subsidiaries;
(ii) making loans to another group company;
(iii) holding and managing property used by a group company for the purposes of a qualifying trade or trades carried on by any group company; or

(iv) holding and managing property used by a group company for the purposes of research and development from which it is intended either that a qualifying trade to be carried on by a group company will be derived or a qualifying trade carried on or to be carried on by a group company will benefit.

References in (iv) above to a group company include references to any existing or future company which will be a group company at any future time.

Activities are similarly disregarded to the extent that they consist, in the case of a subsidiary whose main purpose is the carrying on of qualifying trade(s) and whose other purposes have no significant effect on the extent of its activities (other than in relation to incidental matters), in activities not in pursuance of its main purpose.

'*Non-qualifying activities*' are:

(I) excluded activities within **23.9** below; and
(II) non-trading activities (not including research and development (see **23.8** below)).

[*ITA 2007, ss 181, 257(1)*].

For the ascertainment of the purposes for which a company exists, see HMRC Venture Capital Schemes Manual VCM13050.

Although a winding-up or dissolution in period B generally prevents a company meeting the above conditions, they are deemed met if the winding-up or dissolution is for genuine commercial reasons and not part of a scheme a main purpose of which is tax avoidance. A company does not cease to meet the above conditions by reason of anything done as a consequence of its being in administration or receivership (both as defined by *ITA 2007, s 252*), provided everything so done and the making of the relevant order are for genuine commercial (and not tax avoidance) reasons. These provisions apply also to the winding-up, dissolution, administration or receivership of any of the company's subsidiaries. [*ITA 2007, s 182*].

The issuing company to carry on the qualifying business activity requirement

At no time in period B (as above) must any of the following be carried on by a person other than the 'issuing company' or a 'qualifying 90% subsidiary' (see **23.7** below) of that company:

- the '*relevant qualifying trade*', i.e. the 'qualifying trade' which is the subject of the 'qualifying business activity' referred to under the purpose of the issue requirement at **23.3** above;
- '*relevant preparation work*', i.e. preparations to carry on a 'qualifying trade' where such preparations are the subject of that qualifying business activity (see **23.8**(c) below);
- research and development which is the subject of that qualifying business activity (see **23.8**(d) below); and
- any other preparations for the carrying on of the qualifying trade.

Where relevant preparation work is carried on by the issuing company or a qualifying 90% subsidiary, the carrying on of the 'relevant qualifying trade' by a company other than the issuing company or one of its subsidiaries is disregarded for these purposes if it occurs before the issuing company or a qualifying 90% subsidiary carries on that trade.

This requirement is not regarded as failing to be met if, by reason only of a company being wound up or dissolved or being in administration or receivership (both as defined by *ITA 2007, s 252*), the relevant qualifying trade ceases to be carried on in period B by the issuing company or any qualifying 90% subsidiary and is subsequently carried on by a person who is not connected (within *ITA 2007, s 993* — see **17** CONNECTED PERSONS) with the company at any time in 'period C'. This let-out applies only if the winding-up, dissolution or entry into administration or receivership (and everything done as a consequence of the company being in administration or receivership) is for genuine commercial reasons and not part of a tax avoidance scheme or arrangements.

'*Period C*' is the period beginning one year before the issue of eligible shares and ending immediately before the third anniversary of the issue date or, if later and where relevant, the third anniversary of the date of commencement of the intended trade referred to in **23.8**(a) or (c) below. In determining for these purposes the time at which a qualifying trade begins to be carried on by any qualifying 90% subsidiary (see **23.7** below) of a company, any carrying on of the trade by it before it became such a subsidiary is disregarded.

HMRC consider that where the relevant trade, preparation work or research and development, is carried on by the company in partnership or by a limited liability partnership of which the company is a member the above requirement is not satisfied. This does, however, represent a change in view by HMRC, which they will apply to shares issued on or after 9 December 2009 and to shares issued before that date if the certificate of compliance was not issued before that date (unless they had given an advance assurance that a certificate would). (HMRC Brief 77/09). HMRC also consider that the above requirement is not satisfied in the case of a film or television co-production (HMRC Guidance Note 12 March 2014).

Although a winding-up or dissolution in period B generally prevents a company meeting this requirement, it is deemed to be met if the winding-up or dissolution is for *bona fide* commercial reasons and is not part of a scheme a main purpose of which is tax avoidance. A company does not cease to meet the requirement by reason of anything done as a consequence of its being in administration or receivership (both as defined by *ITA 2007, s 252*), provided everything so done and the making of the relevant order are for *bona fide* commercial (and not tax avoidance) reasons.

[*ITA 2007, ss 159(4), 183*].

The unquoted status requirement

The issuing company must be 'unquoted' when the shares are issued and no arrangements must then exist for it to cease to be unquoted. If, at the time of issue, arrangements exist for the company to become a wholly-owned subsidiary of a new holding company by means of a share exchange within *ITA 2007, ss 247–249* (see below), no arrangements must exist for the new company to cease to be unquoted. A company is '*unquoted*' if none of its shares etc. are listed on a recognised stock exchange or on a foreign exchange designated for the purpose, or dealt in outside the UK by such means as may be designated for the purpose. Securities on the Alternative Investment Market ('AIM') are treated as unquoted for these purposes. (Revenue Press Release 20 February 1995).

[*ITA 2007, s 184*].

The control and independence requirement

The issuing company must not at any time in period B either:

(1) control another company other than a qualifying subsidiary (see **23.6** below), 'control' being construed in accordance with *CTA 2010, ss 450, 451* and being considered with or without connected persons within *ITA 2007, s 993*, or
(2) be a 51% subsidiary of another company or otherwise under the control of another company, 'control' being construed in accordance with *ITA 2007, s 995* and again being considered with or without connected persons, or
(3) be capable of falling within (1) or (2) by virtue of any arrangements (as broadly defined).

[*ITA 2007, ss 185, 257(1)(3); FA 2012, Sch 7 paras 21, 25*].

The above is subject to provisions in *ITA 2007, ss 247–249* which enable an EIS company to become a wholly-owned subsidiary of a new holding company in certain circumstances. The investors receive shares in the new company in exchange for their original shares and the new shares then stand in the shoes of the old for the purposes of EIS income tax relief. See Tolley's Income Tax for details.

The gross assets requirement

The value of the issuing company's gross assets must not exceed £15 million immediately before the issue of EIS shares and must not exceed £16 million immediately afterwards. In relation to shares issued before 6 April 2012, these figures are £7 million and £8 million respectively.

If the issuing company is a parent company, the gross assets test applies by reference to the aggregate gross assets of the company and all its qualifying subsidiaries (disregarding certain assets held by any such company which correspond to liabilities of another). [*ITA 2007, s 186; FA 2012, Sch 7 paras 11, 23; SI 2012 No 1896*].

For HMRC's approach to the gross assets requirement see Statement of Practice 2/06.

The number of employees requirement

The 'full-time equivalent employee number' for the company must be less than 250 at the time the shares are issued. In relation to shares issued before 6 April 2012, the limit is 50. In relation to shares issued on or after 18 November

2015, the limit of 250 is doubled to 500 if the issuing company is a 'knowledge-intensive company' (see **23.3** above) at the time the shares are issued. If the company is a parent company, the sum of the full-time equivalent employee numbers for it and each of its qualifying subsidiaries must be less than 250 (or 50) at the time the shares are issued.

A company's '*full-time equivalent employee number*' is the number of its full-time employees plus, for each employee who is not full-time, a just and reasonable fraction. Directors count as employees for this purpose, but employees on maternity or paternity leave and students on vocational training are excluded.

[*ITA 2007, s 186A; FA 2012, Sch 7 paras 12, 23; F(No 2)A 2015, Sch 5 paras 13, 23(1); SI 2012 No 1896*].

HMRC consider that a full-time employee is one whose standard working week (excluding lunch breaks and overtime) is at least 35 hours (HMRC Venture Capital Schemes Manual VCM13120).

The qualifying subsidiaries requirement

At any time in period B (as above) any subsidiary of the issuing company must be a 'qualifying subsidiary' (see **23.6** below). [*ITA 2007, s 187*].

The property managing subsidiaries requirement

The company must not at any time in period B (as above) have a 'property managing subsidiary' which is not a 'qualifying 90% subsidiary' (see **23.7** below) of the company. A '*property managing subsidiary*' is a subsidiary whose business consists wholly or mainly in the holding or managing of land or any 'property deriving its value from land'. For this purpose, '*property deriving its value from land*' includes any shareholding in a company, any partnership interest or interest in settled property, which derives its value directly or indirectly from land and any option, consent or embargo affecting the disposition of land. [*ITA 2007, s 188*].

Informal clearance

Enquiries from companies as to whether they meet the conditions of the EIS should be directed to Small Company Enterprise Centre (Admin), Mid-size Business SO777, Newcastle NE98 1ZZ (Tel. 0300 1231083; e-mail: enterpri se.centre@hmrc.gsi.gov.uk).

Qualifying subsidiary

[23.6] The meaning of '*qualifying subsidiary*' is given below.

The subsidiary must be a '51% subsidiary' of the qualifying company (within *CTA 2010, Pt 24 Ch 3*) and no person other than the qualifying company or another of its subsidiaries may have control (within *ITA 2007, s 995*) of the subsidiary. Furthermore, no arrangements (as broadly defined) may exist by virtue of which either of these conditions would cease to be satisfied.

However, the above conditions are not regarded as ceasing to be satisfied by reason only of the subsidiary or any other company being wound up or dissolved or by reason only of anything done as a consequence of any such company being in administration or receivership (both as defined by *ITA 2007, s 252*), provided the winding-up, dissolution, entry into administration or receivership or anything done as a consequence of its being in administration or receivership is for genuine commercial reasons and is not part of a tax avoidance scheme or arrangements. Also, the above conditions are not regarded as ceasing to be satisfied by reason only of arrangements being in existence for the disposal of the interest in the subsidiary held by the qualifying company (or, as the case may be, by another of its subsidiaries) if the disposal is to be for genuine commercial reasons and is not to be part of a tax avoidance scheme or arrangements.

The above conditions must continue to be satisfied until the end of period B, except that the winding-up or dissolution, during that period, of the subsidiary or of the qualifying company does not prevent those conditions being satisfied, provided that the winding-up etc. meets the conditions applied in relation to qualifying companies (see the trading requirement at **23.5** above). The conditions are also not regarded as ceasing to be satisfied by reason only of the disposal of the interest in the subsidiary within the relevant period if it can be shown to be for genuine commercial reasons and not part of a tax avoidance scheme.

[*ITA 2007, ss 191, 257(1), 989; FA 2012, Sch 7 paras 21, 25; SI 2007 No 1820, Art 2*].

Qualifying 90% subsidiary

[23.7] A company (the subsidiary) is a '*qualifying 90% subsidiary*' of another company (the relevant company) if:

(a) the relevant company possesses at least 90% of both the issued share capital of, and the voting power in, the subsidiary;
(b) the relevant company would be beneficially entitled to at least 90% of the assets of the subsidiary available for distribution to equity holders on a winding-up or in any other circumstances;
(c) the relevant company is beneficially entitled to at least 90% of any profits of the subsidiary available for distribution to equity holders;
(d) no person other than the relevant company has control (within *ITA 2007, s 995* — see **17** CONNECTED PERSONS) of the subsidiary; and
(e) no arrangements (as broadly defined) exist by virtue of which any of the above conditions would cease to be met.

For the above purposes, *CTA 2010, Pt 5 Ch 6* applies, with appropriate modifications, to determine the persons who are equity holders and the percentage of assets available to them.

The above conditions are not regarded as ceasing to be satisfied by reason only of the subsidiary or any other company being wound up or dissolved or by reason only of anything done as a consequence of any such company being in administration or receivership (both as defined by *ITA 2007, s 252*), provided the winding-up, dissolution, entry into administration or receivership or anything done as a consequence of its being in administration or receivership is for genuine commercial reasons and is not part of a tax avoidance scheme or arrangements. Also, the above conditions are not regarded as ceasing to be satisfied by reason only of arrangements being in existence for the disposal of the relevant company's interest in the subsidiary if the disposal is to be for genuine commercial reasons and is not to be part of a tax avoidance scheme or arrangements.

A company (company A) is also a qualifying 90% subsidiary of another company (company C) if:

- company A is a qualifying 90% subsidiary of another company (company B) and company B is a 'qualifying 100% subsidiary' of company C; or
- company A is a qualifying 100% subsidiary of company B and company B is a qualifying 90% subsidiary of company C.

No account is taken for this purpose of any control company C may have of company A. The definition of a qualifying 90% subsidiary is used to define a '*qualifying 100% subsidiary*' by replacing the references in that definition to 'at least 90%' with references to '100%'.

[*ITA 2007, ss 190, 257(1); FA 2012, Sch 7 paras 21, 25; SI 2007 No 1820, Art 2*].

Qualifying business activity

[23.8] Either of the following is a '*qualifying business activity*' in relation to the issuing company.

(a) The issuing company or any 'qualifying 90% subsidiary' (see **23.7** above) (i) carrying on a 'qualifying trade' which, on the date of issue of the shares, the company or any such subsidiary is carrying on, or (ii) preparing to carry on such a trade which, on the date of issue of the shares, is intended to be carried on by the company or any such subsidiary and which is begun to be so carried on within two years after that date, or (iii) actually carrying on the trade mentioned in (ii) above. For shares issued before a date to be fixed, the intention in (ii) above must be to carry on the qualifying trade 'wholly or mainly in the UK', and at any time in period B when the trade is carried on as in (i) or (iii) above it must be carried on wholly or mainly in the UK.

(b) The issuing company or any 'qualifying 90% subsidiary' (see **23.7** above) carrying on research and development which, on the date of issue of the shares, the company or any such subsidiary is carrying on or which company or any such subsidiary begins to carry on immediately afterwards, and from which it is intended on that date that a 'qualifying trade' which the company or any such subsidiary will carry on 'wholly or mainly in the UK' will either be derived or benefit. For shares issued before a date to be fixed, the intention must be to carry on the qualifying trade 'wholly or mainly in the UK' and at any time in period B when the research and development or the qualifying trade derived or benefiting from it is carried on, it must be carried on wholly or mainly in the UK.

In determining for the purposes of (a) and (b) above the time at which a qualifying trade or research and development begins to be carried on by a qualifying 90% subsidiary of the issuing company, any carrying on of the trade etc. by it before it became such a subsidiary is disregarded. References to a qualifying 90% subsidiary include, in cases where the qualifying trade is not carried on at the time of issue of the shares, references to any existing or future company which will be such a subsidiary at any future time.

[*ITA 2007, ss 179, 257(1); FA 2012, Sch 7 paras 10, 21(1)*].

As regards (a) above, 'preparing' to carry on a trade covers both the setting up of a new trade and the acquisition of an existing trade from its present owner. It does not cover preliminary activities such as market research aimed at discovering whether a trade would be likely to succeed or raising capital or research and development. (HMRC Venture Capital Schemes Manual VCM12110).

For HMRC's views as to whether a trade is carried on '*wholly or mainly in the UK*', see Statement of Practice 3/00.

For the manner in which the scheme operates where a company wishes to raise money by a single issue of shares either partly for preparing to carry on a trade and partly for the subsequent carrying on of that trade, or for more than one qualifying business activity (e.g. for a trade carried on by one subsidiary and for research and development carried on by another), see Revenue Tax Bulletin April 1996 pp 305, 306.

Qualifying trade

[23.9] A trade is a '*qualifying trade*' if it is conducted on a commercial basis with a view to the realisation of profits and it does not, at any time in period B (as defined in **23.5** above), consist to a substantial extent in the carrying on of 'excluded activities'. For these purposes, 'trade' (except in relation to the trade mentioned in (t) below) does not include a venture in the nature of trade.

Excluded activities

'*Excluded activities*' are:

(a) dealing in land, commodities or futures, or in shares, securities or other financial instruments;
(b) dealing in goods otherwise than in an ordinary trade of wholesale or retail distribution (see below);
(c) banking, insurance or any other financial activities;
(d) leasing or letting or receiving royalties or licence fees;
(e) providing legal or accountancy services;
(f) 'property development';
(g) farming or market gardening;
(h) holding, managing or occupying woodlands, any other forestry activities or timber production;
(i) shipbuilding (defined by reference to relevant EU State aid rules);
(j) producing coal or steel (both defined by reference to relevant EU State aid rules and including the extraction of coal);

(k) operating or managing hotels or comparable establishments (i.e. guest houses, hostels and other establishments whose main purpose is to offer overnight accommodation with or without catering) or property used as such;

(l) operating or managing nursing homes or residential care homes (both as defined) or property used as such;

(m) (in relation to shares issued on or after 6 April 2016) generating or exporting electricity or making electricity generating capacity available;

(n) (in relation to shares issued on or after 6 April 2016) generating heat;

(o) (in relation to shares issued on or after 6 April 2016) generating any form of energy not within (m) or (n);

(p) (in relation to shares issued on or after 6 April 2016) producing gas or fuel;

(q) (in relation to shares issued before 6 April 2016) the subsidised generation or export of electricity;

(r) (in relation to shares issued before 6 April 2016) the subsidised generation of heat or subsidised production of gas or fuel;

(s) (in relation to shares issued on or after 30 November 2015 and before 6 April 2016) making reserve electricity generating capacity available (or using such capacity to generate electricity); and

(t) providing services or facilities for any business consisting of activities within any of (a) to (s) and carried on by another person (other than a parent company), where one person has a 'controlling interest' in both that business and the business carried on by the provider.

As regards (e) above, the provision of the services of accountancy personnel is the provision of accountancy services (*Castleton Management Services Ltd v Kirkwood* (Sp C 276), [2001] SSCD 95).

Exclusions (l) and (m) apply only if the person carrying on the activity in question has an estate or interest (e.g. a lease) in the property concerned or occupies that property.

HMRC regard as 'substantial' for the above purposes a part of a trade which consists of more than 20% of total activities, judged by any reasonable measure (for instance turnover or capital employed). (HMRC Venture Capital Schemes Manual VCM3010). As regards (a) above, dealing in land includes cases where steps are taken, before selling the land, to make it more attractive to a purchaser; such steps might include the refurbishment of existing buildings. (HMRC Venture Capital Schemes Manual VCM3020).

As regards (b) above, a trade of wholesale distribution is a trade consisting of the offer of goods for sale either to persons for resale (or processing and resale) (which resale must be to members of the general public for their use or consumption) by them. A trade of retail distribution is a trade in which goods are offered or exposed for sale and sold to members of the general public for their use or consumption. A trade is not an ordinary wholesale or retail trade if it consists to a substantial extent of dealing in goods collected or held as an investment (or of that and any other activity within (a)–(t) above), and a substantial proportion of such goods is held for a significantly longer period than would reasonably be expected for a vendor trying to dispose of them at market value. Whether such trades are 'ordinary' is to be judged having regard to the following features, those under (A) supporting the categorisation as 'ordinary', those under (B) being indicative to the contrary.

(i) The breaking of bulk.
(ii) The purchase and sale of goods in different markets.
(iii) The employment of staff and incurring of trade expenses other than the cost of goods or of remuneration of persons connected (within *ITA 2007, s 993*) with a company carrying on such a trade.
(i) The purchase or sale of goods from or to persons connected (within *ITA 2007, s 993*) with the trader.
(ii) The matching of purchases with sales.
(iii) The holding of goods for longer than would normally be expected.
(iv) The carrying on of the trade at a place not commonly used for wholesale or retail trading.
(v) The absence of physical possession of the goods by the trader.

As regards the application of (d) above, a trade is not excluded from being a qualifying trade solely because at some time in period B it consists to a substantial extent in the receiving of royalties or licence fees substantially attributable (in terms of value) to the exploitation of 'relevant intangible assets'.

A '*relevant intangible asset*' is an 'intangible asset' the whole or greater part of which (by value) has been created by the issuing company or by a company which was a qualifying subsidiary (within **23.6** above) of the issuing company throughout the period during which it created the whole or greater part (by value) of the asset. For this purpose only, '*issuing company*' includes a company all of whose shares were acquired by the issuing company at a time when the only shares issued in the issuing company were subscriber shares and the consideration for the acquisition consisted wholly in the issue of shares in the issuing company.

Where the asset is 'intellectual property', it is treated as created by a company only if the right to exploit it vests in that company (alone or with others). The term '*intellectual property*' incorporates patents, trade marks, copyrights, design rights etc. and foreign equivalents. An '*intangible asset*' is an asset falling to be treated as such under generally accepted accounting practice, including all intellectual property and also industrial information and techniques (see HMRC Venture Capital Schemes Manual VCM3060).

Also as regards (d) above, a trade will not be excluded by reason only of its consisting of letting ships, other than offshore installations (previously oil rigs) or pleasure craft (as defined), on charter, provided that:

(i) the company beneficially owns all the ships it so lets,
(ii) every ship beneficially owned by the company is UK-registered,
(iii) throughout period B, the company is solely responsible for arranging the marketing of the services of its ships, and

(iv) in relation to every letting on charter, certain conditions as to length and terms of charter, and the arm's length character of the transaction, are fulfilled,

and if any of (i)–(iv) above is not fulfilled in relation to certain lettings, the trade is not thereby excluded if those lettings and any other excluded activities taken together do not amount to a substantial part of the trade.

For HMRC's views on the scope of the exclusions in relation to (e) above, see Revenue Tax Bulletin August 2001 pp 877, 878.

'*Property development*' in (f) above means the development of land by a company, which has (or has had at any time) an 'interest in the land' (as defined), with the sole or main object of realising a gain from the disposal of an interest in the developed land.

The exclusion for farming in (g) above used to apply only to UK farming, but in relation to shares issued on or after 18 November 2015 it is extended to overseas farming also.

Exclusion (q) above referred to the generation or export of electricity in respect of which the company received a feed-in tariff under a UK Government scheme or a similar overseas scheme. The exclusion did not apply to trades carried on by community interest companies, co-operative societies, community benefit societies, NI industrial and provident societies or, in relation to shares issued on or after 17 July 2014, European Co-operative Societies. In relation to shares issued on or after 17 July 2014, exclusion (q) applied also to the generation of electricity in connection with which a renewables obligation certificate was issued (i.e. a certificate issued under *Electricity Act 1989, s 32B* or NI equivalent) or which was incentivised by a corresponding scheme established in an overseas territory. In relation to shares issued on or after 6 April 2015, the exclusion applied also where the generation of the electricity was carried on in connection with a contract for difference (within *Energy Act 2013, Pt 2, Ch 2*), a new Government subsidy due to replace renewables obligations certificates and renewable heat incentives (or with a corresponding overseas scheme). In relation to shares issued before 6 April 2015, the exclusion did not apply if the plant used for the generation of the electricity relied on anaerobic digestion or if the electricity was hydroelectric power.

Exclusion (r) above had effect in relation to shares issued on or after 17 July 2014. For this purpose, the generation of heat, or production of gas or fuel, was subsidised if a payment was made, or another incentive was given, under a scheme established by regulations under *Energy Act 2008, s 100* or *Energy Act 2011, s 113* (renewable heat incentives) or under a similar scheme established in an overseas territory, in respect of the heat generated or the gas or fuel produced. A let-out similar to that for exclusion (q) applied to trades carried on by particular entities. In relation to shares issued before 6 April 2015, exclusion (r) did not apply if the plant used for the generation of the heat, or the production of the gas or fuel, relied on anaerobic digestion.

As regards (t) above, a person has a '*controlling interest*' in a business carried on by a company if he controls (within *CTA 2010, ss 450, 451*) the company; or if the company is a close company and he or an 'associate' is a director of the company and the owner of, or able to control, more than 30% of its ordinary share capital; or if at least half of its ordinary share capital is directly or indirectly owned by him. In any other case it is obtained by his being entitled to at least half of the assets used for, or income arising from, the business. In either case, the rights and powers of a person's 'associates' are attributed to him. An '*associate*' of any person is any 'relative' (i.e. spouse, civil partner, ancestor or linear descendant) of that person, the trustee(s) of any settlement in relation to which that person or any relative (living or dead) is or was a settlor and, where that person has an interest in any shares or obligations of a company which are subject to any trust or are part of a deceased estate, the trustee(s) of the settlement or the personal representatives of the deceased and, if that person is a company, any other company which has an interest in those shares or obligations. For this purpose, 'settlor' is defined as in *ITA 2007, ss 467–473*.

[*ITA 2007, ss 189, 192–199, 253, 257(3), 996(7); FA 2012, Sch 7 paras 13–15, 24; FA 2014, s 56(2)–(4)(8); Co-operative and Community Benefit Societies Act 2014, Sch 4 para 106; FA 2015, Sch 6 paras 2–5, 10, 12, 14; F(No 2)A 2015, ss 27(1)(3), 28; FA 2016, s 28(1)(3)(5)*].

Form of income tax relief

[23.10] Relief is (except as below) given for the tax year in which the shares were issued, by a reduction in what would otherwise be the individual's income tax liability (a '*tax reduction*') equal to tax at the 'EIS rate' (30% for 2011/12 onwards; previously 20%) on the amount (or aggregate amounts) subscribed for shares in respect of which he is eligible for and claims EIS relief (subject to the minimum and maximum limits below). Investors may restrict a claim to EIS relief in respect of a single issue of shares so that relief is given only in respect of some of the shares.

For the order in which tax reductions are given against an individual's tax liability, see Tolley's Income Tax under Allowances and Tax Rates. A tax reduction must be restricted to the extent (if any) that it would otherwise exceed the individual's remaining income tax liability after making all prior reductions.

The individual may claim relief as if so many of the shares as he specifies had been issued in the preceding tax year.

[*ITA 2007, s 158; SI 2011 No 2459*].

Attribution of relief to shares

Subject to any reduction or withdrawal of relief (see **29.9** onwards), where an individual's income tax liability is reduced for a year of assessment as above by reason of an issue or issues of shares made (or treated as made) in that year, the tax reduction is attributed to that issue or those issues (being apportioned in the latter case according to the amounts claimed for each issue). Issues of shares of the same class by a company to an individual on the same day are treated as a single issue for this purpose. A proportionate amount of the reduction attributed to an issue is attributed to each share in the issue in respect of which the claim was made and is adjusted correspondingly for any subsequent bonus issue of shares of the same class and carrying the same rights.

An issue to an individual part of which is treated as having been made in the preceding tax year (as above) is treated as two separate issues, one made on a day in the previous year.

Where relief attributable to an issue of shares falls to be withdrawn or reduced, the relief attributable to each of the shares in question is reduced to nil (if relief is withdrawn) or proportionately reduced (where relief is reduced).

[*ITA 2007, ss 201, 255*].

Maximum and minimum amounts

There is in all cases an upper limit of £1 million for 2012/13 onwards (£500,000 for 2008/09 to 2011/12) on the amount in respect of which an individual may obtain relief for a tax year (regardless of whether the shares were issued in that year or in the following year).

In relation to shares issued before 6 April 2012, relief could not be obtained on investments of less than £500 in any company in any tax year. This restriction did not apply to investment through approved funds (see **23.2** above).

[*ITA 2007, ss 157(2)(3), 158(2), 251(3); FA 2012, Sch 7 paras 2, 3, 20, 22(1); SI 2008 No 3165*].

Example

W is a UK resident and not a Scottish taxpayer, and on 2 January 2018 subscribes £20,000 for 20,000 EIS shares in E Co Ltd. His pension income for the year ended 5 April 2018 amounts to £61,500. PAYE deducted amounts to £13,300. He has no other sources of income.

W's 2017/18 income tax liability is calculated as follows:

		£
Pension Income		61,500
Less Personal Allowance		11,500
Taxable ('Step 3') Income		£50,000
Tax Liability		£
£33,500	@ 20%	6,700.00
£16,500	@ 40%	6,600.00
£50,000		13,300.00
Less EIS relief £20,000 @ 30%		6,000.00
Income tax liability		7,300.00
Less PAYE deducted		13,300.00
Income tax repayment due		£6,000.00

Claims for relief

[23.11] A claim for relief must be made not earlier than the end of the four-month minimum period referred to at **23.3** above, and not later than the fifth anniversary of 31 January following the tax year for which relief is claimed. A claim cannot be made until, with the authority of HMRC, the company has furnished the individual with a compliance certificate to the effect that, from its point of view, the conditions for the relief are satisfied. [*ITA 2007, ss 202, 203*].

Restriction or withdrawal of income tax relief

[23.12] EIS income tax relief is restricted or withdrawn in the circumstances described below. References to a reduction of relief include its reduction to nil, and references to the withdrawal of relief in respect of any shares are to the withdrawal of the relief attributable to those shares (see **23.10** above). Where no relief has yet been given, a reduction applies to reduce the amount which apart from the provision in question would be the relief, and a withdrawal means ceasing to be eligible for relief in respect of the shares in question. [*ITA 2007, s 257(4)*]. For the purposes of the following provisions, the '*EIS original rate*' means the EIS rate for the tax year for which income tax relief was obtained. [*ITA 2007, s 256A*].

An assessment to income tax withdrawing or reducing relief is made for the tax year for which the relief was given.

Disposal of shares

Where the investor disposes of shares (or an interest or right in or over shares) to which relief is attributable (see **23.10** above) or grants an option the exercise of which would bind him to sell the shares before the end of 'period A' (see **23.4** above):

(a) if the disposal is at arm's length, relief attributable to those shares (see **23.10** above) is withdrawn or, if that relief exceeds an amount equal to tax at the EIS original rate (see above) on the disposal consideration, reduced by that amount;
(b) otherwise, the relief is withdrawn.

Where the relief attributable to the shares was less than the tax at the EIS original rate on the amount subscribed for the issue, the amount referred to in (a) above is correspondingly reduced. For this purpose, shares are treated as having been issued in an earlier year where relief was carried back as in **23.8** above. Where the relief attributable to the shares has been reduced (otherwise than as a result of an issue of bonus shares (see **23.10** above)) before the relief was obtained, in calculating the amount referred to in (a) above, the gross relief attributable to the shares before that reduction is used.

Relief is also withdrawn where, during period A, an option is granted to the investor, the exercise of which would bind the grantor to purchase shares. There are provisions for identifying the shares to which an option relates, where these form part of a larger holding.

These provisions do not apply on a transfer to the investor's spouse or civil partner made at a time they are living together; the transferee stands in the shoes of the transferor as regards any subsequent disposal. The provisions also do not apply to a disposal of shares occurring as a result of the investor's death.

Disposals are identified with shares of the same class issued earlier before shares issued later (i.e. first in/first out (FIFO)). Further rules apply as to the order in which shares acquired on the same day are deemed to be disposed of where only some of those shares have attracted income tax relief and/or CGT deferral relief (see **23.14** below). These rules are the same as those described at **23.13** below (under 'Identification rules') for CGT purposes. A share exchange is treated as a disposal for these purposes unless it is within *ITA 2007, ss 247–249* (see **23.5** above).

[*ITA 2007, ss 209–212, 245, 246, 254; FA 2012, Sch 7 para 17*].

Value received by investor

Where, during a specified period, an investor receives value (other than insignificant value) from the company, any EIS income tax relief attributable to those shares (see **23.10** above) and not previously reduced in respect of the value received is withdrawn or, if that relief exceeds an amount equal to tax at the EIS original rate (see above) on the 'value received' reduced by that amount.

The provisions apply equally to value received from a person who is connected (within *ITA 2007, s 993* — see **17** CONNECTED PERSONS) with the issuing company.

[*ITA 2007, ss 213–223*].

For full details of the provisions, see Tolley's Income Tax.

Value received other than by investor

Relief is similarly restricted or withdrawn where, within the same specified period, the company or any 51% subsidiary (as defined) of the company repays, redeems or repurchases any of its share capital belonging to a member other than:

- the individual; or
- another individual whose relief is thereby withdrawn or reduced (as above) or who thereby suffers a qualifying chargeable event under the capital gains deferral provisions (see **23.14** below); or
- (in relation to any repayment, redemption or repurchase of share capital, or payment to a member, on or after 6 April 2014) another individual whose relief under the SEED ENTERPRISE INVESTMENT SCHEME (**60**) is thereby withdrawn or reduced; or
- a company whose investment relief under the CORPORATE VENTURING SCHEME (**18**) is thereby withdrawn or reduced,

or makes any payment to any such member for giving up rights on the cancellation or extinguishment of any of the share capital of the company or subsidiary. There is an exception for insignificant repayments etc.

[*ITA 2007, ss 224–230; F(No 2)A 2015, Sch 5 paras 15, 22; SI 2008 No 954, Art 39*].

For full details of the provisions, see Tolley's Income Tax.

Acquisition of a trade or trading assets

Relief is withdrawn if, at any time in period A (see **23.4** above), the company or any qualifying subsidiary (see **23.6** above), begins to carry on as its trade, business or profession (or part) a trade etc. (or part) previously carried on at any time in that period otherwise than by the company or a qualifying subsidiary, or acquires the whole or the greater part of the assets used for a trade etc. previously so carried on, and the individual is a person who, or one of a group of persons who together, either:

- owned more than a half share in the trade etc. previously carried on (ownership and, if appropriate, respective shares being determined by applying *CTA 2010, s 941(6)* and by treating an interest in a trade belonging to a company in accordance with the options in *CTA 2010, s 942*) at any time in period A, and also own or owned at any such time such a share in the trade etc. carried on by the company; or
- control (within *CTA 2010, ss 450, 451*), or at any time in period A have controlled, the company, and also, at any such time, controlled another company which previously carried on the trade etc.

For these purposes, interests etc. of 'associates' (see **23.4** above) are taken into account. There are special rules relating to shares held by certain directors of, or of a partner of, the issuing company or any subsidiary.

[*ITA 2007, ss 232, 257(3)*].

Acquisition of share capital

Relief is also withdrawn if the company, at any time in period A (see **23.4** above), comes to acquire all the issued share capital of another company, and where the individual is a person who, or one of a group of persons who together, control (within *CTA 2010, ss 450, 451*) or have, at any such time, controlled the company and who also, at any such time, controlled the other company. There are special rules relating to shares held by certain directors of, or a partner of, the issuing company or any subsidiary. [*ITA 2007, s 233*].

Relief subsequently found not to have been due

Relief is withdrawn if it is subsequently found not to have been due. Relief can be withdrawn on the ground that the issuing company is not a qualifying company (see **23.5** above) or that the purpose of the issue or use of money raised requirements at **23.3** are not met only if:

- the issuing company has given notice to that effect under *ITA 2007, s 241* or *TCGA 1992, Sch 5B para 16*; or
- an HMRC officer has given notice to the issuing company of his opinion that the whole or part of the relief was not due because of the ground in question.

The issuing company may appeal against an HMRC notice as though it were refusal of a claim by the company. The determination of an appeal against an HMRC notice under the capital gains deferral provisions is conclusive for the purposes of any income tax relief appeal.

[*ITA 2007, ss 234, 236*].

Capital gains tax

[23.13] See also **23.14** below re EIS deferral relief.

Gains

Gains arising on the disposal by the investor, after the end of 'period A' (see below), of shares on which EIS income tax relief has been given are not chargeable gains. (There is no such exemption for shares disposed of before the end of period A, and any EIS income tax relief given will be withdrawn — see **23.12** above.)

Where EIS income tax relief was not given on the full amount subscribed for the shares (other than by reason of the income tax liability being insufficient to support the relief), the capital gains tax exemption is restricted to a proportion of the gain. Where this arises, it will usually be because the investor's EIS subscriptions exceeded the annual maximum on which relief is available (see **23.2** above). The exempt gain is the proportion of the gain (after any indexation allowance available) found by applying the multiple A/B where:

> A = the actual income tax relief given (expressed in terms of the reduction in the tax liability); and
> B = tax at the 'EIS original rate' (i.e. the EIS rate for the tax year for which income tax relief was obtained) on the amount subscribed for the issue.

'*Period A*' for these purposes is the period beginning with the incorporation of the company or, if later, two years before the date of issue of the shares and ending immediately before the third anniversary of the issue date or, if later and where relevant, the third anniversary of the date of commencement of the intended trade referred to in **23.8**(a) or (c) above.

(In determining for this purpose the time at which a qualifying trade begins to be carried on by any 'qualifying 90% subsidiary' (see **23.7** above) of a company, any carrying on of the trade by it before it became such a subsidiary is disregarded.)

[*TCGA 1992, s 150A(2)(3); ITA 2007, ss 159(2), 256; FA 2012, Sch 6 para 19, Sch 7 paras 27, 28, 34(1)*].

See *Example 1* below.

In *Ames v HMRC* FTT, [2015] UKFTT 337 (TC), 2015 STI 3041, it was held that the exemption did not apply in a case where the taxpayer had not claimed EIS income tax relief because he had had no taxable income in the year in which the shares were issued.

Losses

If a disposal of shares on which EIS income tax relief has been given results in a capital loss, the loss is allowable *regardless* of whether the disposal occurs within or without 'period A' (see above). However, in calculating the loss, or in ascertaining whether a loss has indeed arisen, the cost of the shares for CGT purposes is reduced by the amount of EIS income tax relief attributable to the shares disposed of (expressed in terms of the reduction in the tax liability) to the extent that this has not been, or does not fall to be, withdrawn. See *Examples 2 & 3* below. The loss qualifies for relief against income, if claimed, under the provisions for losses on shares in unlisted trading companies — see **44.15** LOSSES.

[*TCGA 1992, s 150A(1)(2A); FA 2012, Sch 6 para 19*].

Example 1

On 8 November 2017 P subscribes £1,350,000 for 900,000 shares in the EIS company, S Ltd, and obtains the maximum EIS income tax relief of £300,000 (£1,000,000 × 30%) for 2017/18. On 3 April 2022 he sells the entire holding for £2,790,000.

The chargeable gain arising is calculated as follows:

	£
Disposal proceeds	2,790,000
Cost	1,350,000
Gain	1,440,000
Less TCGA 1992, s 150A(3) exemption	
£1,440,000 × (£300,000(A)/£405,000(B))	1,066,666
Chargeable gain	£373,334
Note:	
A = relief given (£1,000,000 × 30%)	£300,000
B = £1,350,000 × 30%	£405,000

Example 2

Assuming the facts are as in *Example 1* above except that the shares are sold for £1,000,000 on 3 April 2022.

The allowable loss arising is calculated as follows:

	£	£
Disposal proceeds		1,000,000
Less Cost	1,350,000	
Less income tax relief given (and not withdrawn)	300,000	1,050,000
Allowable loss		£50,000

Example 3

Assuming the facts are as in *Example 1* above except that the shares are sold on 3 April 2018 for £1,100,000. Income tax relief of £1,100,000 × 30% × (300,000/405,000) = £244,444 is withdrawn (see below). The balance of £55,556 is not withdrawn and is attributable to the shares sold.

	£	£
Disposal proceeds		1,100,000
Less Cost	1,350,000	
Less income tax relief given (and not withdrawn)	55,556	1,294,444
Allowable loss		£194,444

In calculating the EIS withdrawal, as not all the subscriber shares qualified for EIS income tax relief, the consideration must be reduced by applying the formula A/B, to the amount of the consideration received. [*ITA 2007, s 210*]. For this purpose, A is the actual income tax reduction and B is the tax at the EIS rate on the amount subscribed for the issue, i.e. £1,100,000 × (300,000/405,000) = £814,814. The EIS relief withdrawn is then calculated on this result, i.e. £814,814 × 30% = £244,444.

See HMRC Venture Capital Schemes Manual VCM20120 for an example involving a part disposal.

Identification rules

The normal identification rules (see **64.2** SHARES AND SECURITIES — IDENTIFICATION RULES) are each disapplied as regards EIS shares. Instead, the rules described below apply to match disposals with acquisitions of shares of the same class in the same company, and they apply where at least some of those shares have attracted EIS income tax relief. Shares are not treated as being of the same class unless they would be so treated if dealt with on a recognised stock exchange.

Disposals are identified with acquisitions on different days on a first in/first out (FIFO) basis. Shares transferred between spouses or civil partners living together are treated as if they were acquired by the transferee on the day they were issued. Shares comprised in a 'new holding' following a reorganisation to which *TCGA 1992, s 127* applies (including a case where it applies by virtue of any other chargeable gains enactment — see, for example, **63.2**, **63.5**, **63.7**, **63.8** SHARES AND SECURITIES) are treated as having been acquired when the original shares were acquired. Where shares within two or more of the categories listed below were acquired on the same day, any of those shares disposed of (applying the FIFO basis) are treated as disposed of in the order in which they are listed, as follows:

- shares to which no EIS income tax relief, EIS capital gains deferral relief (see **23.14** below) or SEIS relief (see **60** SEED ENTERPRISE INVESTMENT SCHEME) is attributable;
- shares to which SEIS income tax relief is attributable;
- shares to which EIS deferral relief, but not EIS income tax relief, is attributable;
- shares to which EIS income tax relief, but not EIS deferral relief, is attributable;
- shares to which both EIS income tax relief and EIS deferral relief are attributable.

Any shares within either of the last two categories which are treated as issued on an earlier day by virtue of the carry-back provisions at **23.10** above are to be treated as disposed of before any other shares within the same category.

[*TCGA 1992, s 150A(4)(5); ITA 2007, ss 246, 257(5); FA 2012, Sch 6 paras 17, 19*].

The above rules are appropriately modified where an individual makes the election described at **64.2** SHARES AND SECURITIES — IDENTIFICATION RULES for alternative treatment of same-day acquisitions and the shares covered by the election include EIS shares. [*TCGA 1992, s 105A(4)(7)—(9)*].

Reorganisations of share capital

Where EIS income tax relief has been given on some shares in a particular company but not others and there is a reorganisation (including a bonus issue) within the meaning of *TCGA 1992, s 126*, then *TCGA 1992, s 127* (see **63.2** SHARES AND SECURITIES) applies separately as regards the shares attracting and not attracting relief so that, in each case, the new shares will stand in the place of the old shares. A distinction is also made, as regards shares attracting income tax relief, between those (if any) to which EIS deferral relief (see **23.14** below) is attributable and those to which it is not, and the separate treatment described above also applies to each of those two categories. A further distinction is made to provide for separate treatment as regards shares attracting SEIS income tax relief (see **60** SEED ENTERPRISE INVESTMENT SCHEME).

Rights issues

If, immediately following a rights issue, EIS relief is attributable either to the original holding or the rights shares, the share reorganisation rules of *TCGA 1992, ss 127–130* (see **63.2** SHARES AND SECURITIES) are disapplied, with the result that the rights shares are treated as a separate acquisition.

[*TCGA 1992, s 150A(6)(6A)(7); FA 2012, Sch 6 para 19*].

Company reconstructions

If as part of a reconstruction, shares or debentures in another company are issued to an EIS shareholder in exchange for EIS shares to which income tax relief remains attributable, then the shares in the new company are not generally deemed to stand in the place of shares in the old company under *TCGA 1992, s 135* or *s 136* (see **63.5**, **63.7** SHARES AND SECURITIES) and there is thus a disposal of the shares in the old company. However, *s 135* or *136* does apply in the normal way if:

- the new holding consists of new ordinary shares issued after the end of 'period A' (as defined above under Gains and applied by reference to the original shares and the company which issued them) and carrying no present or future preferential rights to dividends or assets or right to redemption; and
- the company issuing the new shares has previously issued shares under the EIS and has issued the appropriate compliance certificate (see **23.11** above) enabling investors to obtain relief on that earlier issue.

In addition, *TCGA 1992, s 135* is not disapplied in a case to which *ITA 2007, s 247* applies. That provision enables an EIS company to become a wholly-owned subsidiary of a new holding company in certain circumstances. The investors receive shares in the new company in exchange for their original shares, and the new shares then stand in the shoes of the old for the purposes of EIS income tax relief. This treatment is generally applied for CGT purposes also. See Tolley's Income Tax for details.

[*TCGA 1992, s 150A(8)(8A)–(8D); FA 2012, Sch 6 para 19*].

Reduction of relief where value received etc.

Where a gain on disposal of EIS shares would otherwise be exempt due to their having been held until after the end of the 'relevant period' (see above), a special rule applies if EIS income tax relief has been, or falls to be, reduced (though not fully withdrawn) as a result of either or both of the following events occurring before the disposal:

- the investor receives value from the company within the meaning of *ITA 2007, s 213* (see **23.12** above);
- there is a repayment, redemption, repurchase or payment in circumstances within *ITA 2007, s 224* (see **23.12** above).

The CGT exemption applies only to so much of the gain as remains after deducting so much of it as is represented by the fraction X/Y where

X = the reduction(s) made, as mentioned above, to the income tax relief given, and
Y = the income tax relief given before applying such reductions.

Where the CGT exemption has already been restricted because EIS income tax relief was not given on the full amount subscribed for the shares (see above), the fraction is applied to the part of the gain otherwise exempt and the deduction made from that part.

[*TCGA 1992, s 150B; FA 2012, Sch 6 para 20*].

Example 4

On 9 November 2017, Q subscribed for 20,000 EIS £1 shares at par in H Ltd. The EIS relief given was £6,000. On 2 January 2018 he received £2,000 from the company, as a result of which EIS relief of £2,000 @ 30% = £600 is withdrawn under *ITA 2007, s 213*. In June 2022, the shares were sold for £60,000.

The CGT computation is as follows:

	£
Disposal consideration	60,000
Less Cost	20,000
Gain	£40,000
Chargeable gain	
$£40{,}000 \times \frac{600}{6{,}000}$ (TCGA 1992, s150B)	£4,000

		£
Exempt gain (balance)		£36,000

If only £3,000 EIS relief were given (say because the investor was also given £297,000 EIS relief on another investment in 2017/18, the maximum relief for that year being £300,000) the relief withdrawn would be (3,000/6,000) × £2,000 × 30% = £300.

The chargeable gain restriction would be calculated in two stages:

	Exempt	Chargeable
Gain as above		£40,000
Stage 1 (*TCGA 1992, s 150A(3)* restriction)		
Gain exempt:		
$£40,000 \times \frac{3,000}{6,000}$		£20,000
Gain chargeable (balance)		£20,000
Stage 2 (*TCGA 1992, s 150B* restriction)		
	£	£
Gain chargeable as above		20,000
Gain otherwise exempt	20,000	
Reduced by value received		
$£20,000 \times \frac{300}{3,000}$	(2,000)	2,000
Total chargeable gain		£22,000
Exempt gain	£18,000	

Capital gains deferral relief

Introduction

[23.14] A specific deferral relief was introduced by *FA 1995, s 67, Sch 13 para 4(3)* whereby any chargeable gain accruing after 28 November 1994 could be deferred to the extent that it could be matched with an investment in EIS shares to which income tax relief (see **23.2** above) was attributable.

In relation to EIS shares issued after 5 April 1998, significant changes were made to the relief. In particular, it is not a requirement that the shares qualify for income tax relief nor that the individual be unconnected with the company. The provisions are also extended to trustees. There is no limit on the amount of the gain that can be deferred under the new provisions, but the gross assets test at **23.5** above does limit the amount that may be invested in any one EIS company (or group).

The main provisions of the revamped EIS deferral relief are described at **23.15** below, with further provisions at **23.17** below. Their application to trustees is covered at **23.16** below. The provisions as they related to shares issued before 6 April 1998 are described briefly at **23.18** below.

Deferral relief is attributable to any EIS shares if expenditure on them has been used to defer the whole or part of any gain and there has been no chargeable event (see **23.15** and **23.18** below) in relation to those shares resulting in the deferred gain being brought back into charge. [*TCGA 1992, Sch 5B para 19(2)*].

Reinvestment into EIS shares issued after 5 April 1998

[23.15] Deferral relief applies where:

- a chargeable gain would otherwise accrue to an individual:
  - on the disposal by him of any asset; or
  - on the occurrence of a chargeable event under these provisions or the provisions governing reinvestment into VCT shares (see **71.12** VENTURE CAPITAL TRUSTS); or
  - to give effect to a withdrawal under *TCGA 1992, s 164F* or *s 164FA* of general reinvestment relief (see **25.86** EXEMPTIONS AND RELIEFS);
- the individual makes a 'qualifying investment'; and
- the individual is UK resident (or, for 2012/13 and earlier years, ordinarily resident) both when the chargeable gain accrues to him and when he makes the qualifying investment, and is not, at the time he makes the investment, regarded as resident outside the UK for the purposes of any double taxation arrangements the effect of which would be that he would not be liable to tax on a gain arising on a disposal, immediately after their acquisition, of the shares comprising the qualifying investment, disregarding any exemption available under *TCGA 1992, s 150A* (see **23.13** above).

See **23.16** below re the application of these provisions to trustees.

Subject to the further conditions below, a '*qualifying investment*' is a subscription for eligible shares (i.e. shares meeting the requirement at **23.3**(i) above) in a company which are issued within the one year immediately preceding or the three years immediately following the time the chargeable gain in question accrues. These time limits may be extended by HMRC in individual cases. If the shares are issued *before* the gain accrues, they must still be held at the time it accrues. For these purposes, shares are not treated as issued merely by being comprised in a letter of allotment or similar instrument. The further conditions are as follows:

(a) the shares (other than any of them which are 'bonus shares') must be subscribed for wholly in cash;
(b) the company must be a qualifying company (within **23.5** above) in relation to the shares;
(c) the shares must be fully paid up (see below) at time of issue (other than any of them which are bonus shares);

(d) the shares must be subscribed for and issued for *bona fide* commercial purposes and not as part of tax avoidance arrangements;

(e) the total amount of the 'relevant investments' (defined as for the purposes of the maximum amount raised annually through risk capital schemes requirement at **23.3** above) in the company and its subsidiaries in the year ending with the issue of the shares must not exceed £5 million (£2 million in relation to shares issued before 6 April 2012);

(f) the issuing company to carry on the qualifying business activity requirement at **23.5** above must be satisfied in relation to the company;

(g) the shares (other than any of them which are bonus shares) must be issued to raise money for the purpose of a qualifying business activity (see **23.8** above); and

(h) the money raised by the issue of the shares and all other eligible shares in the company of the same class issued on the same day must be employed wholly (disregarding insignificant amounts) for that purpose by the end of the two years following the issue or, if the only qualifying business activity falls within **23.8**(a) above, and if later, by the end of the two years starting when the company (or subsidiary) began to carry on the qualifying trade (see **23.9** above).

These conditions draw on those applicable to income tax relief (see **23.2** onwards above). However, there is no requirement that any income tax relief be attributable to the shares, and, in contrast to the position for income tax relief, the individual does not have to be unconnected with the company. '*Bonus shares*' are shares issued otherwise than for payment, whether in cash or otherwise.

Shares are not fully paid up for the purposes of (c) above if there is any undertaking to pay cash to any person in respect of the acquisition of the shares at a future date.

Investments in subsidiaries count towards the limit in (e) above if the company concerned was a subsidiary of the issuing company at any time in the year and whether or not it was a subsidiary at the time of the investment. The increase from £2 million to £5 million in (e) above was subject to EU State aid approval (now granted), and will be brought into effect by statutory instrument.

In determining for the purposes of (h) above when a qualifying trade is begun to be carried on by a subsidiary, any carrying on of the trade by it before it became a qualifying 90% subsidiary (see **23.7** above) is disregarded.

In *R (oao Devine) v CIR* QB 2003, TL 3713, the taxpayer unsuccessfully applied for judicial review of the Revenue's decision not to extend the reinvestment time limits noted above.

In *GC Trading Ltd v HMRC* (Sp C 630), 2007 STI 2231, the condition in (h) above was held to be satisfied even though the money raised was loaned to another company before being used to purchase a qualifying trade. On the evidence, the loans were the equivalent of a bank deposit and were simply the means used to preserve the money needed to acquire the trade. In *Harvey's Jersey Cream Ltd v HMRC* FTT 2013, [2014] SFTD 599 the condition in (h) above was held not to be satisfied where a company which was a partner in a trading partnership raised money by issuing shares and increased its interest in the partnership (the money effectively being paid out to the other partners). Judge Hellier held that 'the monies raised were not employed in the activities of the qualifying trade', as 'there was no evidence that they were used for anything other than to pay for changing the partners' interests in the partnership'. Furthermore, 'there was no evidence that the monies were raised with the intention that the money would be employed in the activities of the trade' and 'all the evidence showed that the monies were intended to be employed in giving the money to the other partners'.

In *East Allenheads Estate Ltd v HMRC* FTT, [2015] SFTD 908, an investor was held to be ineligible for deferral relief because the company existed in part for the purpose of conferring a personal benefit on the investor.

See also *Blackburn and another v HMRC* CA 2009, [2009] STC 188 and *Domain Dynamics (Holdings) Ltd v HMRC* (Sp C 701), [2008] SSCD 1136.

Postponement of the original gain

Where a chargeable gain would otherwise accrue to an individual ('the investor'), and he acquires a qualifying investment, a claim can be made by him to defer the whole or part of that gain against his investment up to an amount specified in the claim (limited to the amount of the gain or, where applicable, the amount of the gain not already relieved under either these provisions or those at **60.45** SEED ENTERPRISE INVESTMENT SCHEME). The amount of investment available to be matched with gains in this way is limited to the amount of the qualifying investment (to the extent that it has not already been so matched). The gain eligible for deferral is the gain after any mandatory deductions and reliefs which have to be claimed (HMRC Venture Capital Schemes Manual VCM23010).

Claims

Subject to what is said at **13.2** CLAIMS re claims being included in a self-assessment tax return if possible, there is no statutory form in which a claim *must* be made (though the claim form attached to form EIS 3 – see below – *may* be used, with or without a tax return). The provisions for income tax relief claims (see **23.11** above) are applied, with modifications, to deferral relief claims. Thus, a deferral relief claim cannot be made earlier than the end of the four-month minimum period referred to at **23.3** above and cannot be made later than the fifth anniversary of 31 January following the tax year in which the shares were issued. A claim cannot be made until, with the authority of HMRC, the company has furnished the individual with a compliance certificate (on form EIS 3) to the effect that, from its point of view, the conditions for deferral relief are satisfied. For more details relating to the issue of the certificate, see Tolley's Income Tax.

Deferred gain becoming chargeable

The deferred gain will become chargeable upon the occurrence of, *and at the time of*, any of the chargeable events listed below. The amount of the gain accruing at the time of the chargeable event is equal to so much of the deferred gain as is attributable to the EIS shares in relation to which the chargeable event occurs. For these purposes, a proportionate part of the net deferred gain (i.e. the deferred gain less any amount brought into charge on an earlier part disposal) is attributed to each of the 'relevant shares' held, immediately before the chargeable event, by the investor or by a person who acquired them from the investor on a transfer between spouses or civil partners within *TCGA 1992, s 58*. The '*relevant shares*' are the shares acquired in making the qualifying investment and, in a case where the original gain accrued at a later time than the making of the qualifying investment, still held at that time. They also include any bonus shares issued in respect of the relevant shares and of the same class and carrying the same rights. The said chargeable events are as follows.

(i) The investor disposes of the EIS shares otherwise than by way of a transfer between spouses or civil partners to which *TCGA 1992, s 58* applies.

(ii) Subsequent to a transfer within *TCGA 1992, s 58*, the shares are disposed of by the investor's spouse or civil partner (otherwise than by way of transfer back to the investor).

(iii) Within the 'relevant period', the investor becomes not resident in the UK.

(iv) Within the relevant period, the investor's spouse or civil partner, having acquired the shares by way of transfer within *TCGA 1992, s 58*, becomes not resident in the UK.

(v) The shares cease to be eligible shares or are treated as so ceasing (see below).

For these purposes, the '*relevant period*' is the period ending immediately before the third anniversary of the date of issue of the shares or, if later and where relevant, the third anniversary of the date of commencement of the intended trade referred to in **23.8**(a) above.

In the case of (iii) or (iv) above (non-residence), the deferred gain does not become chargeable where the investor (or, where applicable, spouse or civil partner) becomes not resident through temporary working outside the UK and again becomes resident within three years of that event, without having disposed of any of the relevant shares in the meantime in circumstances such that a chargeable event would have occurred had he been UK resident. No assessment is to be made until it is clear that the person concerned will not regain UK resident status within the three-year period.

EIS shares are *treated* as ceasing to be eligible shares (in which case a chargeable event occurs under (v) above) in any of the following circumstances (and see also the further provisions in **23.17** below).

(1) The condition at (b) above (qualifying company) ceases to be satisfied in consequence of an event occurring after the issue of the shares: the shares cease to be eligible shares at the time of that event. HMRC have confirmed that the company is required to retain its qualifying status only for the duration of 'period B' (as defined in **23.5** above), so no chargeable event can occur under this heading by reason of anything happening beyond the end of that period (*Taxation 18 February 1999 p 486*).

(2) The condition at (e) above (relevant investments) ceases to be satisfied in consequence of an event occurring after the issue of the shares: the shares cease to be eligible shares at the time of that event.

(3) The condition at (f) above (compliance with the issuing company to carry on the qualifying business activity requirement) ceases to be satisfied in consequence of an event occurring after the issue of the shares: the shares cease to be eligible shares at the time of that event.

(4) The condition at (h) above (money raised to be used for purpose of qualifying business activity within a specified time period) is not satisfied and the deferral claim was made before the end of the time period of twelve months or two years (whichever is relevant): the shares cease to be eligible shares at the end of that time period. (If the deferral claim has not been made by then, or if the condition at (f) above is not satisfied at all, the shares are treated as never having been eligible shares.)

Death

The deferred gain does not become chargeable on the death of the investor (or, where applicable, spouse or civil partner) or on the occurrence after death of any event which would otherwise have been a chargeable event.

Identification rules

In determining whether any shares disposed of are shares to which deferral relief is attributable (see **23.14** above), the normal identification rules (see **64.2** SHARES AND SECURITIES — IDENTIFICATION RULES) are disapplied and, instead, the same rules as in **23.13** above apply (broadly, first in/first out but with special rules where shares acquired on the same day fall into different specified categories — see examples at HMRC Venture Capital Schemes Manual VCM23170).

Where at the time of the chargeable event, any of the relevant shares are regarded under capital gains tax legislation as represented by assets which consist of or include assets other than such shares, the deferred gain attributable to those shares is to be apportioned between those assets on a just and reasonable basis. As between different assets regarded as representing the same shares, the identification of those assets follows the same identification rules as for shares.

Persons chargeable

The chargeable gain is treated as accruing, depending on which type of chargeable event occurs, to:

- the individual who makes the disposal;
- the individual who becomes non-resident;
- the individual who holds the shares in question when they cease (or are treated as ceasing) to be eligible shares.

Where the last category applies and some of the shares are held by the investor and some by a person who acquired them from the investor by way of transfer between spouses or civil partners within *TCGA 1992, s 58*, the gain is computed separately as regards each individual without reference to the shares held by the other.

[*TCGA 1992, ss 105A(4)(7)–(9), 150C, Sch 5B paras 1–6, 19; FA 2012, Sch 6 para 21, Sch 7 paras 29, 33; FA 2013, Sch 46 para 110; SI 2012 No 1896*].

See the further provisions at **23.17** below.

Example

Frank realises a chargeable gain of £270,000 in May 2017 on the disposal of an asset he had acquired in August 2009. He makes no other disposals in 2017/18. On 1 March 2018, he subscribes £234,000 for 60% of the issued ordinary share capital in a new company, ABC Ltd. The investment is a qualifying investment for the purposes of EIS deferral relief. Frank makes a claim to defer the maximum £234,000 of the May 2017 gain against the qualifying investment.

The CGT position for 2017/18 is as follows.

	£
Gain	270,000
Less deferred under EIS provisions	234,000
	36,000
Less annual exempt amount	11,300
Taxable gain 2017/18	£24,700

On 1 August 2023, he sells 40% of his holding of ABC Ltd shares for £213,600. The disposal does not qualify for ENTREPRENEURS' RELIEF (**24**). He makes no other disposals in 2023/24. His CGT position for that year is as follows.

Gain on ABC Ltd shares	£
Disposal proceeds	213,600
Less cost (£234,000 × 40%)	93,600
Gain	£120,000
Deferred gain brought into charge	
Total gain deferred	£234,000
Clawback restricted to expenditure to which disposal relates	£93,600
Taxable gains 2023/24 (subject to annual exempt amount) (£120,000 + £93,600)	£213,600
Gain remaining deferred until any future chargeable event (£234,000 – £93,600)	£140,400

Notes to the example

(a) Frank's subscription for ABC Ltd shares cannot qualify for EIS income tax relief. He is connected with the company by virtue of his shareholding being greater than 30%. (In practice, the holdings of his associates, e.g. wife and children, need to be taken into account as well.) See **23.4** above.

(b) As the ABC Ltd shares do not qualify for income tax relief, there is no exemption as in **23.13** above for the gain arising on part disposal, despite the shares having been held for over three years.

Reinvestment into EIS shares issued after 5 April 1998 — application to trustees

[23.16] The deferral provisions for individuals at **23.15** above (and the further provisions at **23.17** below) also apply to trustees of a settlement where, in a case where the gain to be deferred accrues to them on the disposal of an asset, that asset (the '*trust asset*') is comprised in settled property of the kind mentioned in either (a) or (b) below.

(a) Settled property on discretionary trusts (i.e. settlements where the beneficiaries' interests are not interests in possession, an interest in possession for this purpose excluding an interest for a fixed term; and see generally **62.4** SETTLEMENTS) where all of the beneficiaries are either individuals or charities.
(b) Settled property on non-discretionary trusts (i.e. settlements where the beneficiaries' interests are interests in possession as in (a) above) where any of the beneficiaries is an individual or a charity.

Where there is at least one beneficiary holding a non-discretionary interest and at least one beneficiary holding a discretionary interest (i.e. a mixed settlement), all of the discretionary interests are treated for these purposes as if they were a single interest in possession, and as if that interest were held, where all the discretionary beneficiaries are individuals or charities, by an individual or charity, and, in any other case, by a person who is not an individual or charity.

If, at the time of the disposal of the trust asset, the settled property comprising that asset is within (b) above but not all of the beneficiaries are individuals or charities, then only the 'relevant proportion' of the gain on the disposal is taken into account for the purposes of deferral relief. The '*relevant proportion*' at any time is the proportion which the aggregate amount of the income of the settled property interests in which are held by individuals or charities bears to the total amount of all of the income of the settled property.

If the settled property qualifies under (a) above at the time of the disposal of the trust asset, deferral relief is available only if, immediately after the acquisition of the EIS shares, the settled property comprising the EIS shares also qualifies under (a) above. This also applies with necessary modifications to settled property qualifying under (b) above but, if not all the beneficiaries are individuals or charities, with the additional condition that the relevant proportion immediately after the acquisition of the EIS shares must be not less than the relevant proportion at the time of the disposal of the trust asset.

[*TCGA 1992, Sch 5B para 17*].

Note that neither EIS income tax relief nor the CGT disposal relief at **23.13** above applies to trustees.

Reinvestment into EIS shares issued after 5 April 1998 — further provisions

[23.17] Some further provisions are as follows:

(1) **Reorganisations.** Provisions identical to those of *TCGA 1992, s 150A(6)(6A)(7)* (see **23.13** above under 'Reorganisations of share capital') apply in relation to shares to which deferral relief is attributable (see **23.14** above).

Acquisition of share capital by new company. Provisions similar to those of *ITA 2007, ss 247–249* (which enables an EIS company to become a wholly-owned subsidiary of a new holding company in certain circumstances — see **23.13** above under 'Company reconstructions' and also Tolley's Income Tax) apply for the purposes of deferral relief. Provided all the conditions are satisfied, deferral relief attributable to shares in the original EIS company is regarded as being attributable to the shares in the new company for which the original shares are exchanged.

Other reconstructions. Where *TCGA 1992, s 135* (exchange of securities — see **63.5** SHARES AND SECURITIES) or *s 136* (scheme of reconstruction involving issue of securities — see **63.7** SHARES AND SECURITIES) apply to shares to which deferral relief, but not income tax relief, is attributable, those sections are treated as not applying for the purpose of the provisions at **23.15** above under which a deferred gain becomes chargeable. There will therefore be a disposal of the shares for the purpose only of those provisions, giving rise to a chargeable event (see **23.15**(i) above). This does not apply where the acquisition of share capital by a new company provisions above apply or where:

- the new holding consists of new ordinary shares issued after the end of 'period A' (as defined at **23.13** above under Gains and applied by reference to the original shares and the company which issued them) and carrying no present or future preferential rights to dividends or assets or right to redemption; and
- the company issuing the new shares has previously issued shares under the EIS and has issued the appropriate compliance certificate (see **23.11** above) enabling investors to obtain relief on that earlier issue.

This provision applies to an exchange within *s 135* where the new holding is issued after 21 April 2009 and to schemes of reconstruction within *s 136* entered into after that date. Previously, provisions similar to those of *TCGA 1992, s 150A(8)(8A)–(8D)* (see **23.13** above under 'Company reconstructions') applied in relation to shares to which deferral relief was attributable, to treat an exchange of shares as a disposal for all purposes, (subject to the same exceptions as above). [*TCGA 1992, Sch 5B paras 7–9, 19; SI 2005 No 3229, Reg 127*].

(2) **Anti-avoidance provisions.**

Reinvestment in same company etc. If an individual realises a gain on disposal of shares in or securities of a company (Company A), he cannot defer that gain by virtue of a subscription for shares in an EIS company which is either Company A itself or is, either at the time of the disposal or the time of the issue of the EIS shares, a member of the same 'group' as Company A. A '*group*' is defined for this purpose as consisting of a company which has one or more 51% subsidiaries (within *CTA 2010, Pt 24 Ch 3*) and those subsidiaries.

Further provisions apply where an individual defers a gain by subscribing for EIS shares, disposes of any of those shares and makes a further subscription for shares in the same company (or member of the same group); no deferral relief is allowed in respect of the second subscription. This also applies where there has been no disposal of the original EIS shares but the further subscription is for shares in a company a disposal of shares in which resulted in the initial deferral (or a member of the same group as that company). The definition of a group given above applies for these purposes.

Investment-linked loans. Provisions analogous to the no linked loans requirement at **23.4** above apply where an investment-linked loan etc. is made to the investor or his associate in 'period A' (as in **23.4** above). For deferral relief purposes, the EIS shares are treated as never having been eligible shares (with the result that no such relief is available) if the loan is made on or before the date of their issue and as otherwise ceasing to be eligible shares (with the result that a chargeable event occurs in respect of deferral relief claimed — see **23.15**(v) above) on the date the loan is made.

Where the shares are subscribed for by trustees, and relief claimed by virtue of **23.16** above, the above applies to loans made not only to the trustees but to any individual (or associate) or charity (or connected person) by virtue of whose interest (at the time the shares are issued and/or at the time the loan is made) deferral relief is available in respect of the settled property.

Pre-arranged exits. Provisions identical to the no pre-arranged exit requirement at **23.4** above apply to prevent EIS shares from being eligible shares for deferral relief purposes where certain exit arrangements are made in relation to their issue.

Disqualifying arrangements. Provisions identical to the no disqualifying arrangements requirement at **23.4** above apply (subject to the same commencement rule) to prevent EIS shares from being eligible shares for deferral relief purposes where such arrangements are made in relation to their issue.

Put and call options. The granting of a put option or call option prevents the EIS shares to which it relates from being eligible shares for deferral relief purposes if the option is granted on or before the date of issue of the shares, or otherwise causes them to be treated as ceasing to be eligible shares (with the result that a chargeable event occurs in respect of deferral relief claimed — see **23.15**(v) above) at the time the option is granted. The provisions apply where an individual subscribes for EIS shares (or acquires them on a no gain/no loss transfer from a subscriber spouse or civil partner) and, during 'period A' (defined as in **23.4** above), either:

– an option for the grantor to purchase such shares (a '*put option*') is granted to the individual, or
– an option for the individual to sell such shares (a '*call option*') is granted by the individual.

Comparable provisions apply for the purposes of EIS income tax relief.

Value received by the investor from the EIS company. Where the EIS investor (or his associate — within **23.4** above) receives any value from the company during the 'period of restriction' (see below), the shares are treated as never having been eligible shares for deferral relief purposes if the value is received on or before the date of the share issue or as otherwise ceasing to be eligible shares (with the result that a chargeable event occurs in respect of deferral relief claimed — see **23.15**(v) above) at the time value is received. Note that the full amount of the deferred gain falls to be clawed back even if the investor receives back only a proportion of the value of his investment (see *Segesta Ltd v HMRC* UT, [2012] STC 1847). The provisions of *TCGA 1992, Sch 5B para 13* which determine whether value is received from a company are based on the EIS income tax relief withdrawal provisions (now *ITA 2007, ss 213–223*). They are fairly widely drawn but *not* so as to catch, for example, reasonable remuneration (or reimbursement of expenses) to the individual as an officer or employee of the company, interest at a commercial rate on a loan made to the company or dividends which represent no more than a normal return on investment in that company. The provisions *do* include, for example, any repayment, redemption or repurchase by the company of any of its share capital or securities which belong to the individual, any loan or advance by the company to the individual which is not repaid before the EIS shares are issued, and the provision of a benefit or facility for the individual. Value received from a connected person of the company (within *TCGA 1992, s 286* — see **17** CONNECTED PERSONS) falls within the provisions if it would have done so had it been received from the EIS company itself.

Value received is disregarded if its amount is *insignificant*, i.e. if it does not exceed £1,000 or, in any other case, if it is insignificant in relation to that part of the amount expended on subscribing for the shares that has been used as in **23.15** above to defer chargeable gains. In applying this let-out, multiple receipts of value must be aggregated (see examples at HMRC Venture Capital Schemes Manual VCM23390), and the let-out is disapplied in certain cases where value received is pre-arranged. Value received is also disregarded if the person from whom the value was obtained receives at least equivalent *replacement value* from the original recipient, though certain types of payment are treated as not giving rise to a receipt of replacement value.

Where the shares are subscribed for by trustees, and relief claimed by virtue of **23.16** above, the above provisions apply to value received not only by the trustees but by any individual (or associate) or charity (or connected person) by virtue of whose interest (at the time the shares are issued and/or at the time the value is received) deferral relief is available in respect of the settled property.

For these purposes, the '*period of restriction*' is the period beginning one year before the issue of the shares and ending immediately before the third anniversary of the issue date or, if later and where relevant, the third anniversary of the date of commencement of the intended trade referred to in **23.8**(a) above.

Where the trade is begun to be carried on by a subsidiary after the date of issue of the shares, in determining when the trade commenced, any carrying on of the trade by the subsidiary before it became a 'qualifying 90% subsidiary' (see **23.7** above) is disregarded.

See the corresponding chapter of Tolley's Income Tax for detailed coverage of the broadly equivalent income tax provisions.

See also *Blackburn and another v HMRC* CA 2008, [2009] STC 188 and *Segesta Ltd v HMRC* FTT, [2010] SFTD 962.

Value received by other persons from the EIS company. Provisions based on the EIS income tax relief withdrawal provisions (now *ITA 2007, ss 224–231*) apply where, at any time in the period of restriction (as defined immediately above), the EIS company (or one which is a 51% subsidiary at some time in 'period A' — defined as in **23.4** above) repays, redeems or repurchases any of its share capital from a member (other than the EIS investor in question) who does not thereby lose EIS income tax relief or deferral relief or CORPORATE VENTURING SCHEME (**18**) investment relief. They apply equally where the company or such subsidiary makes any payment to any such member for the giving up of rights to share capital on its cancellation or extinguishment. The shares are treated as never having been eligible shares for deferral relief purposes if such an event occurs on or before the date of the share issue or as otherwise ceasing to be eligible shares (with the result that a chargeable event occurs in respect of deferral relief claimed — see **23.15**(v) above) at the time such event occurs.

The absence of any loss of EIS income tax relief etc., as referred to above, is disregarded if it is due only to the amount received being of insignificant value. A repayment etc. is itself disregarded if the amount received by the member in question is insignificant in relation to the market value immediately after the event of the remaining issued share capital of the company or, as the case may be, 51% subsidiary. The assumption is made that the shares in question are cancelled at the time of the event. In applying the test, the market value, immediately before the event, of the shares to which the event relates is substituted for the amount received if this would give a greater amount. This let-out is disapplied in certain cases where a repayment etc. is pre-arranged. 'Insignificant' is taken by HMRC to mean 'trifling or completely unimportant' (HMRC Venture Capital Schemes Manual VCM23460).

[*TCGA 1992, Sch 5B paras 10–15, 18, 19; FA 2012, Sch 7 paras 30, 32, 34, 35; SI 2008 No 954, Art 18*].

(3) **Information.** Certain chargeable events and failures of conditions must be notified to HMRC, generally within 60 days, by either the investor, the EIS company or any person connected with the EIS company having knowledge of the matter. HMRC may require such notice where they have reason to believe it should have been made, and are given broad powers to require information generally.

[*TCGA 1992, Sch 5B para 16; FA 2012, Sch 7 para 31*].

Reinvestment into EIS shares issued before 6 April 1998

[23.18] Deferral relief was available to an individual where:

(a) a chargeable gain would otherwise have accrued to him on the disposal by him of any asset (or on the occurrence of a chargeable event either under these provisions or the similar provisions governing reinvestment into VCT shares (see **71.12** VENTURE CAPITAL TRUSTS)); and

(b) he subscribed for shares to which any EIS income tax relief was attributable within the one year before ant the three years after the time the chargeable gain in (a) above accrued.

Deferred gain becoming chargeable

The deferred gain would become chargeable upon the occurrence of, and at the time of, any of a number of specified chargeable events. The only remaining circumstances in which a deferred gain can become chargeable are as follows.

(i) The investor disposes of the EIS shares otherwise than by way of a transfer to which *TCGA 1992, s 58* (see **46.5** MARRIED PERSONS AND CIVIL PARTNERS) applies. As regards part disposals, HMRC interpret the law as requiring a proportionate part of the deferred gain to be brought into account.

(ii) Subsequent to a transfer within *TCGA 1992, s 58*, the shares are disposed of by the investor's spouse (otherwise than by way of transfer back to the investor).

The deferred gain is treated as accruing to the individual making the disposal. See the 2009/10 or earlier edition for full details.

[*TCGA 1992, s 150C, Sch 5B as originally enacted*].

Key points concerning enterprise investment scheme

[23.19] Points to consider are as follows.

- An investment in shares under the EIS provides for three types of tax relief:
  - (a) income tax relief;
  - (b) exemption from capital gains tax for the shares acquired;
  - (c) the possibility to defer some other capital gain.
- Relief under (b) is linked to (a) and relief for one is not possible without the other and is not available if the investor is connected with the company.
- Relief under (c) can be obtained without (a) and (b).
- EIS relief should not be claimed until a form EIS 3 has been issued by the company to the investor. It can be claimed via the Self Assessment Tax Return or separately. If the EIS 3 is available early enough relief can be included in a PAYE code.
- There is a maximum of £1,000,000 per year and an investment in one year can be carried back to the previous year subject to the maximum in that earlier year.

- EIS relief is only available where funds are 'employed' by the EIS company within the qualifying period. Once an investment has been made there is a need to monitor that the company uses the correct portion of the funds raised for qualifying purposes within the time allowed. This can often cause problems, for example, when market conditions change or investments fall through following due diligence.
- EIS deferral relief operates by reducing the allowable cost of the shares. A claim should be restricted, if necessary in order to utilise the annual capital gains tax exempt amount.
- Where income tax relief is withdrawn or reduced it is done by means of an assessment issued by HMRC. It cannot be recovered through the Self Assessment Tax Return although the liability will be added to the Statement of Account.
- Where shares are disposed of or relief withdrawn any gain deferred, as a result of EIS deferral relief, will be revived as though it was a gain arising at the date of disposal of the EIS shares or the date of the event giving rise to the withdrawal of the relief.
- Where gains have been deferred in the past the rate of tax at the time (after taper relief) may have been less than the current rates. If a gain is to be revived, it may be worth checking whether it is still within the time limit to revoke the deferral relief claim as the tax at a lower rate plus interest may be less than the tax due at current rates.
- Where the shares are disposed of at a loss (including negligible value claims), the loss is allowable even though any gain would have been exempt. If income tax relief is not withdrawn then the cost of the shares is reduced by the income tax relief obtained when calculating the loss. It should be possible to claim relief for the loss against income.
- A deferred gain does not become chargeable on the death of the investor. However as stated at VCM12140, subscription must be made for genuine commercial reasons and deathbed investments are unlikely to qualify.

24

Entrepreneurs' Relief

Introduction	**24.1**
Qualifying business disposals	**24.2**
Material disposal of business assets	**24.3**
Disposal of trust business assets	**24.4**
Associated disposal	**24.5**
Claims for relief	**24.6**
Assets qualifying for relief	**24.7**
Amount of relief	**24.8**
Restriction on relief for certain trust disposals	**24.9**
Restriction on relief for certain associated disposals	**24.10**
Deferred gains	**24.11**
Reorganisations	**24.12**
Key points	**24.13**

Cross-references. See **16** COMPUTATION OF GAINS AND LOSSES; **40** INVESTORS' RELIEF.

Simon's Taxes. See C3.13.

Introduction to entrepreneurs' relief

[24.1] Entrepreneurs' relief can be claimed in respect of 'qualifying business disposals' made on or after 6 April 2008. The relief applies for capital gains tax purposes only and is not available to companies.

Disposals by individuals qualify for relief if they are the disposal of the whole or part of a business, the disposal of business assets when the business ceases, or the disposal of shares in a trading company of which the individual is an employee and meets a minimum shareholding requirement. For disposals on or after 6 April 2013, relief is extended to shares acquired by the exercise of an option under the enterprise management incentives scheme. A disposal by the trustees of a settlement qualifies for relief if it is a disposal of shares in a company and the company meets requirements in relation to a beneficiary which are similar to those for individuals or if it is a disposal of assets used in a business carried on by a beneficiary which has ceased. Individuals can also claim relief in respect of a disposal of an asset used by a partnership or company if the disposal is associated with a disposal of assets of the partnership or share in the company which itself qualifies for entrepreneurs' relief. See **24.2–24.5** below for the full conditions. For disposals on or after 3 December 2014, taxpayers no longer have to choose between entrepreneurs' relief and the ENTERPRISE INVESTMENT SCHEME (**23.14**) or SOCIAL INVESTMENT RELIEF (**65.46**) deferral reliefs. Where such a gain is deferred under either of those schemes and would otherwise have qualified for entrepreneurs' relief, it will qualify for relief when brought back into charge on the happening of a chargeable event.

The relief is given by deducting the aggregate losses arising on the disposal from the aggregate gains and treating the resulting amount as a single chargeable gain taxable at a rate of **10%**. For gains arising before 23 June 2010, the relief operated slightly differently. The amount resulting from deducting the aggregate losses from the aggregate gains was, if a positive amount, reduced by $^4/_9$ths. This meant that the net gains were effectively charged to capital gains tax at a rate of 10% ($^5/_9 \times 18\% = 10\%$). See **24.6** below.

The relief is subject to a lifetime limit of £10 million (£5 million for disposals before 6 April 2011; £2 million for disposals before 23 June 2010; £1 million for disposals before 6 April 2010) — see **24.6** below. Disposals before 6 April 2008 do not affect the limit except in the case of deferred gains on which entrepreneurs' relief is claimed under the transitional rules at **24.11, 24.12** below.

Further restrictions on the amount of relief available are described at **24.9** below, and for the application of the relief to deferred gains or where there is a reorganisation of share capital see **24.11, 24.12** below.

The rules for entrepreneurs' relief are broadly based on those for retirement relief (see **25.88** EXEMPTIONS AND RELIEFS), which was abolished in 2003. Where the legislation uses terms that also appeared in the retirement relief legislation, they are intended to have the same meaning (except where the entrepreneurs' relief legislation specifically provides a different meaning). (Treasury Explanatory Notes to the 2008 Finance Bill). Although retirement relief cases are not binding precedent for entrepreneurs' relief purposes, HMRC consider that the courts are likely to consider them persuasive. (HMRC Capital Gains Manual CG64010). Accordingly, reference is made at **24.3** below to retirement relief cases thought to be relevant to entrepreneurs' relief.

See also HMRC Capital Gains Manual CG63950–64170, and Chartered Institute of Taxation Notice 13 February 2012 for HMRC's responses to various technical questions concerning the relief.

The Government is considering extending entrepreneurs' relief to gains made by academics on disposals of shares in spin-out companies that use intellectual property to which the academics have contributed.

HMRC have identified an avoidance scheme which seeks to convert employment income into a capital gain eligible for entrepreneurs' relief. HMRC intend to challenge the scheme. See www.gov.uk/guidance/capital-gains-tax-entrepreneurs-relief-tax-avoidance-scheme.

Qualifying business disposals

[24.2] A '*qualifying business disposal*' is:

(a) a 'material disposal of business assets' (see **24.3** below);
(b) a 'disposal of trust business assets' (see **24.4** below); or
(c) a disposal associated with a material disposal (usually referred to as an 'associated disposal') (see **24.5** below).

For this purpose (and throughout this chapter), a '*business*' is a 'trade', profession or vocation which is conducted on a commercial basis and with a view to the realisation of profits. A '*trade*' includes a venture in the nature of trade, and any property business which consists of, or so far as it consists of, the commercial letting of FURNISHED HOLIDAY ACCOMMODATION (**26**) is treated as a trade.

[*TCGA 1992, ss 169H(2), 169S(1), 241(3)(3A)*].

Material disposal of business assets

[24.3] A '*material disposal of business assets*' is a disposal by an individual of one of the following.

(a) A disposal of the whole or part of a business owned by the individual throughout the one-year period ending with the date of disposal.
What constitutes the disposal of 'part of a business', was considered in a number of retirement relief cases, particularly relating to farming. (See the comments at **24.1** above about terms used in both the entrepreneurs' relief and the retirement relief legislation.) See *McGregor v Adcock* Ch D 1977, 51 TC 692 where a farmer sold part of his land for which outline planning permission had been obtained and was refused retirement relief. This decision was followed in *Atkinson v Dancer; Mannion v Johnston* Ch D 1988, 61 TC 598, and see also *Pepper v Daffurn* Ch D 1993, 66 TC 68 and *Wase v Bourke* Ch D 1995, 68 TC 109. In *Jarmin v Rawlings* Ch D 1994, 67 TC 130, in which retirement relief was allowed, it was held that the taxpayer had disposed of a dairy farming business, which was 'a separate and distinguishable part' of his business. In *Barrett v Powell* Ch D 1998, 70 TC 432, it was held that a disposal of a tenancy to farm land which the taxpayer then continued to farm under a temporary licence did not qualify for retirement relief; the taxpayer had continued to carry on exactly the same business as before, albeit more precariously; see also *Purves v Harrison* Ch D 2000, 73 TC 390.
In *M Gilbert v HMRC* FTT [2011] UKFTT 705 (TC) a trader had carried on a business of selling food on commission, representing nine different suppliers. He received £285,000 from one of the suppliers under an agreement whereby he agreed to have no further contact with the supplier's customers. He claimed entrepreneurs' relief on the gain. The First-Tier Tribunal concluded that the taxpayer had sold part of his business as a going concern. Judge Radford held that 'what characterises a sale as a going concern is a sale of goodwill where it exists'. The taxpayer had sold the goodwill and had 'also sold his customer database, a crucial asset in distinguishing a sale of a going concern from a mere sale of assets'.
A disposal of Lloyd's syndicate capacity was held not be the disposal of the whole or part of a business (and did not fall within (b) below) in *Carver v HMRC* FTT [2015] SFTD 573.
See also HMRC Capital Gains Manual CG64015–64035.

(b) A disposal of, or a disposal of an interest in, one or more assets in use, at the time at which a business ceases to be carried on, for the purposes of the business, where the business was owned by the individual throughout the one-year period ending with the cessation of the business. The disposal must be made within the three-year period beginning with the date of cessation.

HMRC consider that, where the effect of *TCGA 1992, s 28* (disposal deemed to occur on date contract made: see **16.4** COMPUTATION OF GAINS AND LOSSES) is that the disposal of an asset precedes the cessation of the business, entrepreneurs' relief will nevertheless be available, provided that there is a genuine business disposal linked to a genuine business cessation (Chartered Institute of Taxation Notice 13 February 2012).

(c) A disposal of, or a disposal of an interest in, shares or 'securities' of a company where the company is the individual's 'personal company' and is either a 'trading company' or the 'holding company of a trading group' and the individual is an officer or employee of the company or, where the company is a member of a trading group, of one or more companies which are members of the group. These conditions must be satisfied throughout either:

   (i) the one-year period ending with the date of disposal; or

   (ii) the one-year period ending with the date on which the company ceases to be a trading company without continuing to be or becoming a member of a trading group or ceases to be a member of a trading group without continuing to be or becoming a trading company.

   Where (ii) above applies, the disposal must be made within the three-year period beginning with the date of cessation.

   An individual's '*personal company*' is a company in which he holds at least 5% of the ordinary share capital (within *ITA 2007, s 989*) and in which he is able to exercise at least 5% of the voting rights by virtue of that holding. For this purpose, where an individual holds any shares in the company jointly or in common with one or more others, he is treated as the sole holder of so many of the shares as is proportionate to the value of his share. In *Castledine v HMRC* FTT, [2016] SFTD 484, deferred shares which carried voting or income rights were held to be ordinary share capital. In *HMRC v McQuillan* UT, [2017] UKUT 344 (TCC), the Upper Tribunal did not agree with the First Tribunal's view that redeemable shares which carried no right to a dividend were not part of ordinary share capital. The two taxpayers claiming entrepreneurs' relief each owned more than 5% of the voting shares but a debt had been converted to non-voting redeemable shares, reducing the taxpayers' shareholdings below 5%. The Upper Tribunal observed that the definition of ordinary share capital was not susceptible to analysis by reference to economic risk and reward and that the classification of the redeemable shares as debt, as opposed to equity, in the accounts did not prevent them from being ordinary shares for the purpose of *ITA 2007, s 989*. Entrepreneurs' relief was therefore denied as this was not the personal company of the two taxpayers.

   For the meaning of the expressions 'trading company' and 'trading group' see below. '*Holding company*' has the same meaning as for the purposes of hold-over relief for gifts of business assets (see **36.3** HOLD-OVER RELIEFS).

A disposal of an interest in shares includes a deemed disposal of an interest in shares under *TCGA 1992, s 122* (capital distributions — see **63.11** SHARES AND SECURITIES). '*Securities*' include debentures deemed to be securities under *TCGA 1992, s 251(6)* (see **25.5** EXEMPTIONS AND RELIEFS).

Where a company has genuine doubt or difficulty as to its trading status it can seek an opinion from HMRC using the non-statutory clearance service (see **30.3** HMRC — ADMINISTRATION). (HMRC Capital Gains Manual CG64100). The meanings of 'officer' and 'employee' were considered in *Hirst v HMRC* FTT, [2014] UKFTT 924 (TC), 2015 STI 135.

HMRC accept in principle that, where there has been a share exchange to which *TCGA 1992, s 127* applied, the one-year period requirement can be satisfied by reference to both the old and the new holding of shares. Both holdings must satisfy the other conditions for entrepreneurs' relief (and there must have been no election in relation to the exchange under the provisions at **24.12** below). (Chartered Institute of Taxation Technical Note, 27 May 2010). HMRC consider that the 5% of ordinary share capital test applies by reference to the nominal value of the shares and not by reference to the number of shares which have been issued (Chartered Institute of Taxation Notice 13 February 2012).

(d) A disposal of 'relevant EMI shares' on or after 6 April 2013 where the company concerned is either a trading company or the holding company of a trading group and the individual is an officer or employee of the company or, where the company is a member of a trading group, of one or more companies which are members of the group. These conditions must be satisfied throughout either:

(i) the one-year period ending with the date of disposal; or

(ii) the one-year period ending with the date on which the company ceases to be a trading company without continuing to be or becoming a member of a trading group or ceases to be a member of a trading group without continuing to be or becoming a trading company. If the shares disposed of (or, where there has been a reorganisation or share exchange (see below), the original shares) were acquired after a disqualifying event within *ITEPA 2003, s 534(1)(c)* occurred in relation to the option but the option was exercised within 90 days after the event occurred (40 days for disqualifying events before 17 July 2013), the one-year period is that ending with the first day of the 90–day (or (40–day) period if that day is later than the cessation date.

Where (ii) above applies, the disposal must be made within the three-year period beginning with the date of cessation and the shares must be acquired before that date.

It is a further condition that the 'option grant date' must be on or before the first day of the one-year period ending on the date of disposal (or where (ii) above applies, the cessation date). If the shares disposed of (or, where there has been a reorganisation or share exchange, the original shares) were acquired after a disqualifying event (within *ITEPA 2003, s 533*) occurred in relation to the option but the option was exercised within 90 days after the event occurred (40 days for disqualifying events before 17 July 2013), the option grant date must be on or before the first day of the one-year period ending on the date of the disqualifying event rather than the date of disposal.

Shares are '*relevant EMI shares*' if they are acquired by an individual on or after 6 April 2013 as a result of the exercise of an enterprise management incentives qualifying option (within *ITEPA 2003, s 527(4)* — see **22.22** EMPLOYEE SHARE SCHEMES) within ten years of its grant (or, where the option is a 'replacement option' (within *ITEPA 2003, Sch 5 para 41*), within ten years of the grant of the original qualifying option). Shares are excluded if a disqualifying event occurred before the exercise of the option and the option was not exercised within 90 days after the event occurred (40 days for disqualifying events before 17 July 2013).

Shares acquired in 2012/13 are also 'relevant EMI shares' if they would have met the above definition if they had been acquired on or after 6 April 2013 and the individual makes no disposals during 2012/13 of any shares of the same class. If the individual does dispose of any other shares of the same class in 2012/13 an election can be made before 1 February 2014 to treat the shares in question as relevant EMI shares.

Shares are also '*relevant EMI shares*' if they are the new holding following a reorganisation of share capital within *TCGA 1992, s 126* (see **63.2** SHARES AND SECURITIES) or a share exchange within *TCGA 1992, s 135* (see **63.5** SHARES AND SECURITIES) and the original shares were themselves relevant EMI shares. In the case of a share exchange there are additional conditions that the exchange must be a qualifying exchange of shares within *ITEPA 2003, Sch 5 para 40* and that, when the exchange occurs, the EMI independence and trading requirements (within *ITEPA 2003, Sch 5 paras 9, 13, 14*) are met by the new company. Where shares are relevant EMI shares under this rule, the trading company/group and employee/officer conditions above must be considered at any time by reference to the company in which the individual held the shares at that time. Where (ii) above applies, the question of whether the shares were acquired before the cessation date is determined by reference to the date of acquisition of the original relevant EMI shares.

The '*option grant date*' is the date on which the qualifying option was granted or, where the option is a replacement option, the date on which the old option was granted (or, where the old option was itself a replacement option, the date on which the earlier old option was granted, and so on). During the currency of an old option the trading company/group and employee/officer conditions above must be considered by reference to the company whose shares were subject to that option.

See for special identification rules for relevant EMI shares.

Partnerships

For the purposes of the above provisions, where an individual carrying on a business enters into a partnership which is to carry on the business and, on entering into the partnership, he disposes of, or disposes of an interest in, assets used for the purposes of his business, he is treated as disposing of part of a business.

A disposal by an individual of the whole or part of his interest in the assets of a partnership is treated as a disposal by him of the whole or part of the partnership business.

At any time when a business is carried on by a partnership, the business is treated as owned by each individual who is at that time a member of the partnership.

[*TCGA 1992, ss 169I, 169S(2)–(5); FA 2013, Sch 24 paras 1, 5, 6; FA 2015, s 43*].

Meaning of 'trading company' and 'trading group'

Times after 17 March 2015

The following definitions apply for disposals on or after 18 March 2015, but only for the purposes of determining what is a trading company or trading group at times on or after that date. References in (c) and (d) above to a company ceasing to be a trading company do not include a company so ceasing simply because of the introduction of the revised definition below. A similar rule applies to companies who are members of a trading group immediately before 18 March 2015.

For the purposes of (c) and (d) above and of **24.4**(i) below, '*trading company*' and '*trading group*' have the same meaning as for the purposes of hold-over relief for gifts of business assets (see **36.3** HOLD-OVER RELIEFS) subject to the following modifications.

Activities of a joint venture company are attributed to a company under *TCGA 1992, s 165A(7)(12)* only if the individual (P) making the disposal passes both the shareholding test and the voting rights test below in relation to the joint venture company. In the case of a disposal of trust business assets, the tests are applied to each of the 'relevant beneficiaries' and the resulting percentages are aggregated to determine whether the tests are passed by those beneficiaries, considered as a single body. References to P in the following paragraphs should be interpreted accordingly. The '*relevant beneficiaries*' are the qualifying beneficiary and any other beneficiaries with an interest in possession as in **24.9** below.

P passes the shareholding test if, throughout the 'relevant one-year period', the sum of the following percentages is at least 5%:

- the percentage of the ordinary share capital of the joint venture company owned directly by P; and

- the percentage of the ordinary share capital of the joint venture company owned indirectly by P through '*investing companies*' (i.e. the company whose shares are the subject of the entrepreneurs' relief claim and any other company of which P owns part of the ordinary share capital).

The percentage of the ordinary share capital of the joint venture company owned indirectly by P through a particular investing company is:

R×S×100

where R is the fraction of the investing company's ordinary share capital owned by P; and S is the fraction of the joint venture company's ordinary share capital owned by the investing company (whether directly, indirectly or both). The fraction of the joint venture company's ordinary share capital owned indirectly by the investing company is calculated by applying *CTA 2010, ss 1155–1157* using the following assumptions. Where the investing company directly owns more than 50% of the ordinary share capital of a company, it is taken to own the whole of the ordinary share capital. Where a company other than the investing company (company B) directly owns more than 50% of the ordinary share capital of another company (company C) which is a member of the same group as the investing company, company B is taken to own the whole of the ordinary share capital of company C.

The '*relevant one-year period*' is the one-year period ending with the date of disposal or with the date on which the company ceases to be a trading company without continuing to be or becoming a member of a trading group or ceases to be a member of a trading group without continuing to be or becoming a trading company, as appropriate. In the case of a disposal within **24.4** (a) below it is a one-year period ending no earlier than three years before the date of the disposal.

P passes the voting rights test if, throughout the relevant one-year period, the sum of the following percentages is at least 5%:

- the percentage of the voting rights of the joint venture company held directly by P; and
- the percentage of the voting rights of the joint venture company held indirectly by P through investing companies.

The percentage of the voting rights of the joint venture company held indirectly by P through a particular investing company is calculated in the same way as the percentage of ordinary share capital. A person who has the ability to control the exercise of voting rights by another person is treated for this purpose as holding those rights.

Activities carried on by a company as a member of a partnership are treated as not being trading activities of the company within *TCGA 1992, s 165A(4)(9)* if P (defined as above) fails either the profits and assets test or the voting rights test below. Activities are also treated as not being trading activities of the company if the company is not a member of the partnership throughout the relevant one-year period.

P passes the profits and assets test if, throughout the relevant one-year period, the sum of the following percentages is at least 5%:

(1) the percentage which is P's direct interest in the partnership's assets;
(2) the percentage which is P's share of the partnership through investing companies which are partnership members; and
(3) the percentage which is P's share of the partnership through investing companies and 'relevant corporate partners' in the partnership.

A company is a '*relevant corporate partner*' in relation to P and a partnership if an investing company owns some portion of its ordinary share capital directly or indirectly (or both), it is a member of the same group as the investing company and is a member of the partnership.

The percentage which is P's share of the partnership through a particular investing company which is a partnership member is:

R×V×100

where R is the fraction of the investing company's ordinary share capital owned by P; and V is the lower of the fraction of the partnership's profits or the fraction of the partnership's assets in which the investing company has an interest.

The percentage which is P's share of the partnership through a particular investing company and a particular relevant corporate partner is:

R×V×W×100

where R is the fraction of the investing company's ordinary share capital owned by P; V is the lower of the fraction of the partnership's profits or the fraction of the partnership's assets in which the relevant corporate partner has an interest; and W is the fraction of the relevant corporate partner's ordinary share capital that is owned by the investing company directly or indirectly (or both). The fraction of a company's ordinary share capital owned indirectly by the investing company is calculated by applying *CTA 2010, ss 1155–1157* using the following assumptions. Where the investing company directly owns more than 50% of the ordinary share capital of a company, it is taken to own the whole of the ordinary share capital. Where a company other than the investing company (company B) directly owns more than 50% of the ordinary share capital of another company (company C) which is a member of the same group as the investing company, company B is taken to own the whole of the ordinary share capital of company C.

P passes the voting rights test if, throughout the relevant one-year period, the sum of the following percentages is at least 5%:

- the sum of the percentages of voting rights held directly by P in investing companies which are members of the partnership; and
- the sum of the percentages which are P's indirect holdings of voting rights in relevant corporate partners in the partnership through investing companies.

The percentage which is P's indirect holding of voting rights in a particular relevant corporate partner in the partnership through a particular investing company is:

T×X×100

where T is the fraction of the voting rights in the investing company held by P; and X is the fraction of the voting rights in the relevant corporate partner that is held by the investing company directly or indirectly (or both). The fraction of a company's voting rights held indirectly by the investing company is calculated by applying *CTA 2010, ss 1155–1157* using the following assumptions. Where the investing company directly holds more than 50% of the voting rights in a company, it is taken to all the voting rights. Where a company other than the investing company (company B) directly holds more than 50% of the voting rights in another company (company C) which is a member of the same group as the investing company, company B is taken to hold all of the voting rights in company C. A person who has the ability to control the exercise of voting rights by another person is treated for this purpose as holding those rights.

Assets held by a Scottish partnership, or any other partnership under the law of another territory where assets of a partnership are treated as held by the partnership as such are treated for these purposes as held by the partners in the proportions in which they are entitled to share in the partnership's capital profits.

For all entrepreneurs' relief purposes other than those of (c) and (d) above and of **24.4**(i) below, '*trading company*' and '*trading group*' have the same meaning as for the purposes of hold-over relief for gifts of business assets (see **36.3** HOLD-OVER RELIEFS) except that the provisions relating to joint venture companies in *TCGA 1992, s 165A(7)(12)* do not apply.

Times before 18 March 2015

'*Trading company*' and '*trading group*' have the same meaning as for the purposes of hold-over relief for gifts of business assets.

[*TCGA 1992, ss 169S(5), 169SA, Sch 7ZA; FA 2016, Sch 13*].

Disposal of trust business assets

[24.4] A '*disposal of trust business assets*' is a disposal, by the trustees of a settlement, of settled property of one of the following types:

(a) shares in, or 'securities' of, a company, or an interest in such shares or securities; or
(b) assets or interests in assets used or previously used for the purposes of a business.

An individual (a '*qualifying beneficiary*') must, under the settlement, have an interest in possession (excluding one for a fixed term) in either the whole of the settled property or a part of it which includes the assets disposed of and the following conditions must be met.

(i) Where the disposal is of assets within (a) above, the company must be the qualifying beneficiary's 'personal company' and be either a 'trading company' or the 'holding company' of a 'trading group', and the qualifying beneficiary must be an officer or employee of the company or, where the company is a member of a group, of one or more

companies which are members of the trading group. This condition must be satisfied throughout a one-year period ending not earlier than three years before the date of the disposal.
For the meaning of 'personal company', 'trading company', 'holding company', 'trading group' and 'securities', see **24.3** above. A disposal of an interest in shares in (a) above includes a deemed disposal of an interest in shares under *TCGA 1992, s 122* (capital distributions — see **63.11** SHARES AND SECURITIES).

(ii) Where the disposal is of assets within (b) above, the assets must be used for the purposes of a business carried on by the qualifying beneficiary throughout a one-year period ending not earlier than three years before the date of the disposal, and the qualifying beneficiary must cease to carry on the business on the date of the disposal or within the three years before that date. Alternatively, the assets must be used for the purposes of a business carried on by a partnership of which the qualifying beneficiary is a member throughout a one-year period ending not earlier than three years before the date of the disposal, and the qualifying beneficiary must cease to be a member of the partnership, or the partnership must cease to carry on the business, on the date of the disposal or within the three years before that date.

[*TCGA 1992, ss 169J, 169S(2)–(5)*].

Associated disposal

[24.5] Subject to the additional requirements below, where an individual makes a material disposal of business assets (see **24.3** above) consisting of the disposal of either all or part of his interest in the assets of a partnership or shares in or securities of a company (or an interest in such shares or securities), he makes a '*disposal associated with a material disposal*' if:

(a) the disposal is made as part of his withdrawal from participation in the business of the partnership or company (or, where the company is a member of a trading group, the business of a member of the trading group); and
(b) the assets which are disposed of (or the assets an interest in which are disposed of) are in use for the purposes of the business throughout the one-year period ending with the earlier of the date of the material disposal of business assets and the cessation of the business of the partnership or company; and
(c) for disposals of assets acquired on or after 13 June 2016, the disposal is of an asset or assets which the individual has owned throughout the three years ending with the date of disposal.

The following further requirements apply for disposals on or after 18 March 2015.

(i) Where the material disposal of business assets consists of the disposal of all or part of the individual's interest in the assets of a partnership, either:
   - the disposed of interest must be at least a 5% interest in the partnership's assets and there must be no 'partnership purchase arrangements' at the date of the disposal; or

- if the disposed of interest is an interest of less than 5%, the individual must have held at least a 5% interest in the partnership's assets for a continuous period of at least three years in the eight years ending on the date of the disposal and there must be no partnership purchase arrangements at the date of the disposal.

For this purpose, '*partnership purchase arrangements*' are arrangements (other than the material disposal) under which the individual or a connected person is entitled to acquire an interest in, or an increased interest in, the partnership (including a share of its profits or assets or an interest in such a share). Arrangements are not, however, partnership purchase arrangements if they were made before both the material disposal and the associated disposal and without regard to either of them.

(ii) Where the material disposal of business assets consists of the disposal of shares in a company (or an interest in such shares), all or some of which are ordinary shares, the ordinary shares disposed of must constitute at least 5% of the company's ordinary share capital and at least 5% of the voting rights in the company and there must be no 'share purchase arrangements' at the date of the disposal. For this purpose, '*share purchase arrangements*' are arrangements (other than the material disposal) under which the individual or a connected person is entitled to acquire shares or securities in the company or a company which is a member of the same trading group. Arrangements are not, however, share purchase arrangements if they were made before both the material disposal and the associated disposal and without regard to either of them. Two companies are treated as members of the same trading group if, at the date of the disposal, arrangements exist which it is reasonable to assume will result in them becoming such members. This requirement is not met if the disposal of shares is a deemed disposal in consideration of a capital distribution within *TCGA 1992, s 122* (see **63.11** SHARES AND SECURITIES) other than one made in the course of dissolving or winding up the company.

(iii) Where the material disposal of business assets consists of the disposal of securities in a company (or an interest in such securities), the securities disposed of must constitute at least 5% of the value of the company's securities and there must be no share purchase arrangements (as above) at the date of the disposal.

For disposals on or after 18 March 2015, a disposal is not treated as part of an individual's withdrawal from participation within (a) above if there are any partnership purchase arrangements or, as appropriate, share purchase arrangements on the date of disposal. For this purpose only, partnership purchase arrangements do not include any arrangements made in connection with a material disposal to which (i) above applies and share purchase arrangements do not include any arrangements made in connection with a material disposal to which (ii) or (iii) above applies.

'*Arrangements*' include any agreement, understanding, scheme, transaction or series of transactions (whether or not legally enforceable). A person is treated as entitled to acquire anything which he is entitled to acquire at a future date or will at a future date be entitled to acquire. The assets of a Scottish partnership or a non-UK partnership the assets of which are regarded as held by the partnership as such are treated as held by the partners in the proportions in which they are entitled to share in the capital profits (or, for disposals before 18 March 2015, the profits).

[*TCGA 1992, s 169K; FA 2015, s 41; FA 2016, s 84*].

HMRC consider that it is not necessary that the individual reduce the amount of work that he does for the partnership or company; only that the disposal be related to the required reduction of his interest in the partnership or holding of shares in the company.

As the disposal must be associated with the material disposal, HMRC consider that there should normally be no significant interval between the disposals. They accept, however, that this will not always be the case, particularly where the business of the partnership or company ceases. They will therefore accept that a disposal of an asset is associated with the material disposal if it takes place:

- within one year of the cessation of a business;
- within three years of the cessation of a business if the asset has not been leased or used for any other purpose at any time after the business ceased; or
- where the business has not ceased, within three years of the material disposal provided the asset has not been used for any purpose other than that of the business.

Where these conditions are not met, the disposal will be considered on its particular facts. If the asset has been used for any other purpose for a significant period it is unlikely that HMRC will accept that the conditions for relief are satisfied.

(HMRC Capital Gains Manual CG63995).

Claims for relief

[24.6] Entrepreneurs' relief must be claimed on or before the first anniversary of the 31 January following the tax year in which the qualifying business disposal is made. In the case of a disposal of trust business assets (see **24.4** above), the claim must be made jointly by the trustees and the qualifying beneficiary. [*TCGA 1992, s 169M(1)–(3)*]. Where the taxpayer is temporarily non-resident or claims the remittance basis, so that it is not immediately clear whether or not a chargeable gain will arise in respect of the qualifying business disposal, a protective claim can be made within the time limit (Chartered Institute of Taxation Notice 13 February 2012).

Assets qualifying for relief

[24.7] Except where the qualifying business disposal is of shares or securities or an interest in shares or securities, entrepreneurs' relief is given only in respect of the disposal of the following assets, or of interests in the following assets, comprised in a qualifying business disposal.

(a) In the case of a material disposal of business assets (see **24.3** above); assets used for the purposes of a business carried on by the individual or a partnership of which the individual is a member.

(b) In the case of a disposal of trust business assets (see **24.4** above); assets used for the purposes of a business carried on by the qualifying beneficiary or a partnership of which he is a member.

(c) In the case of a disposal associated with a material disposal (see **24.5** above); assets used for the purposes of a business carried on by the partnership or company.

Shares and securities, and other assets held as investments, are excluded from (a)–(c) above.

Goodwill

Goodwill is included in the assets within (a)–(c) above except where, for disposals on or after 3 December 2014, a person (P) disposes of goodwill to a close company (or a non-UK resident company which would be a close company if it were UK-resident) and, immediately after the disposal, P and any 'relevant connected person' together own 5% or more of the ordinary share capital or voting rights of the company or of any company in the same group. The exclusion does not, however, apply if P and any relevant connected person dispose of the close company's share capital to another company (company A) so that neither P nor any relevant connected person own any of the ordinary share capital immediately before the end of the period of 28 days beginning with the date of the qualifying business disposal (or such longer period as HMRC allow). If company A is itself a close company (or a non-UK resident company which would be a close company if it were UK-resident), P and any relevant connected person must, immediately before the end of that period, together own less than 5% of the ordinary share capital or voting rights of company A or of any company in the same group. A '*relevant connected person*' means a company connected with P or trustees connected with P.

The exclusion of goodwill from (a)–(c) above also applies to a disposal of goodwill on or after 3 December 2014 if the person making the disposal is a party to arrangements one of the main purposes of which is to secure that the above exclusion does not apply to the goodwill.

'*Arrangements*' include any agreement, understanding, scheme, transaction or series of transactions (whether or not legally enforceable). '*Associate*', '*control*', '*major interest*' and '*participator*' are as defined at *CTA 2009, ss 836, 837* and *841*.

[*TCGA 1992, ss 169L, 169LA; FA 2015, s 42; FA 2016, s 85*].

Amount of relief

Basic computation

[24.8] Where a qualifying business disposal is made on or after 23 June 2010, then subject to the application of the lifetime limit and the restrictions on relief at **24.9** below, the amount to which entrepreneurs' relief applies is computed by deducting the aggregate 'relevant losses' from the aggregate 'relevant gains'. If the resulting amount is positive it is then treated as a single chargeable gain accruing at the time of the disposal to the individual or trustees by whom the claim is made, chargeable at a rate of **10%**. The relevant gains and losses taken into account in computing the relief are treated as not themselves being chargeable gains or allowable losses.

For this purpose, '*relevant gains*' are, where the qualifying business disposal is of shares or securities or of interests in shares or securities, the gains on the disposal (computed under normal capital gains tax principles). In any other case, the relevant gains are the gains on the disposal of any assets qualifying for relief (as above) comprised in the qualifying business disposal (again, computed under normal capital gains tax principles). '*Relevant losses*' are losses made in circumstances in which a gain would be a relevant gain, computed under normal capital gains tax principles on the assumption that notice has been given under *TCGA 1992, s 16(2A)* (notification of capital loss — see **44.4** LOSSES) in respect of them.

Disposals before 23 June 2010

For qualifying business disposals made before 23 June 2010, entrepreneurs' relief operated slightly differently. The amount to which relief applied was calculated as above for disposals on or after 23 June 2010 and relief applied subject to the application of the lifetime limit and the restrictions on relief at **24.9** below. Where the amount resulting after the deduction of relevant losses from relevant gains was positive, it was reduced by $^4/_9$ths.

The reduced amount was then treated as a chargeable gain accruing at the time of the disposal to the individual or trustees by whom the claim was made.

This means that the net gains were effectively charged to capital gains tax at a rate of 10% ($^5/_9$ × 18% = 10%).

Application of lifetime limit

Entrepreneurs' relief is subject to a lifetime limit of £10 million (£5 million for disposals before 6 April 2011; £2 million for disposals before 23 June 2010; £1 million for disposals before 6 April 2010), which applies as follows.

The amount to which relief would otherwise apply in respect of a qualifying business disposal is added to any amounts to which relief applied in respect of earlier qualifying business disposals. Where the total exceeds the limit, only so much (if any) of the amount to which relief would otherwise apply in respect of the current disposal as, together with the earlier amounts, does not exceed the limit qualifies for the 10% rate or $^4/_9$ths reduction. Any part of the deemed gain excluded by the application of this rule is chargeable at the normal rates of CGT.

Where one of the previous lower lifetime limits was exceeded on disposals made before the increases, no further relief can be obtained for those disposals following the increases. Relief can, however, be obtained for qualifying business disposals on or after the dates of increase up to the appropriate new limit.

The earlier qualifying business disposals to be taken into account are:

- where the current qualifying business disposal is made by an individual, earlier qualifying business disposals made by him and earlier disposals of trust business assets (see **24.4** above) in respect of which he is the qualifying beneficiary; and
- where the current qualifying business disposal is a disposal of trust business assets in respect of which an individual is the qualifying beneficiary, earlier disposals of trust business assets in respect of which that individual is the qualifying beneficiary and earlier qualifying business disposals made by that individual.

Where there is a disposal of trust business assets in respect of which an individual is the qualifying beneficiary and a qualifying business disposal by that individual on the same day, then, in applying the lifetime limit, the disposal of trust business assets is treated as the later event.

Disposals before 6 April 2008 do not affect the lifetime limit except in the case of deferred gains on which entrepreneurs' relief is claimed under the transitional rules at **24.11**, **24.12** below.

[*TCGA 1992, ss 169M(4), 169N*].

HMRC consider that, under self-assessment, it is the taxpayer's responsibility to keep records of entrepreneurs' relief claims to enable the application of the lifetime limit (HMRC Capital Gains Manual CG63960). Where entrepreneurs' relief is claimed by a remittance basis user, it is HMRC's view that the lifetime limit to apply in respect of remittance basis gains is the limit in force when the gains arise (Chartered Institute of Taxation Notice 13 February 2012).

Example 1

In May 2017, Mr Henry sells his business, Joe's Toys, which he has owned since 1998, to an unrelated party, realising the following chargeable gains and allowable loss.

	Gain/(loss)
	£
Goodwill	700,000
Freehold shop 1	200,000
Freehold shop 2	200,000
Freehold shop 3	(150,000)

Mr Henry claims entrepreneurs' relief in respect of the sale of the business. He has made no previous claim to entrepreneurs' relief. He makes no other disposals in 2017/18.

Mr Henry's capital gains tax liability for 2017/18 is calculated as follows.

	£
Gains qualifying for entrepreneurs' relief	
Goodwill	700,000

Freehold shop 1	200,000
Freehold shop 2	200,000
	1,100,000
Less Loss on freehold shop 3	150,000
Deemed chargeable gain qualifying for entrepreneurs' relief	950,000
Annual exempt amount	11,300
Gain chargeable to tax	£938,700
Capital gains tax payable (£938,700 × 10%)	£93,870

Example 2

In August 2017 Mr Robertson sells his entire shareholding in Robbie Ltd, realising a gain of £10,050,000, which qualifies for entrepreneurs' relief. Mr Robertson makes no other disposals in 2017/18 and has made no previous disposals qualifying for entrepreneurs' relief. He is an additional rate income tax payer for 2017/18.

Mr Robertson's capital gains tax liability for 2017/18 is calculated as follows.

	£
Deemed chargeable gain qualifying for entrepreneurs' relief (subject to lifetime limit £10,000,000)	10,050,000
Annual exempt amount	11,300
Gain chargeable to tax	£10,038,700
Capital gains tax payable	
£10,000,000 × 10%	1,000,000
£38,700 × 20%	7,740
	£1,007,740

Note to the example

(a) The annual exempt amount of £11,300 is allocated against the part of the gain chargeable to tax at 20% as this gives the greater tax saving.

Example 3

In May 2017, Mr Helm sells his entire shareholding in Levon Ltd for £400,000. He had acquired the shares in March 2001 for £150,000 and has been a director of the company since that time. Levon Ltd is a trading company and qualifies as Mr Helm's personal company. He makes no other disposals in 2017/18 and has made no previous claims to entrepreneurs' relief. He claims entrepreneurs' relief in respect of the gain on the shares. Mr Helm made another gain on the disposal of an investment asset during 2017/18 which used the annual exempt amount.

Mr Helm's capital gains tax liability for 2017/18 on the sale of the shares is calculated as follows.

	£
Sale proceeds	400,000
Cost	150,000
Chargeable gain qualifying for entrepreneurs' relief	250,000
Capital gains tax payable (£250,000 × 10%)	£25,000

Following the disposal of his shares in Levon Ltd, Mr Helm buys a 25% shareholding in Amy Ltd, another trading company, for £200,000, and starts work as a director of the company. He continues as a director of the company until May 2020 when he sells his entire shareholding for £10,100,000. He claims entrepreneurs' relief in respect of the disposal. He makes no other disposals in 2020/21, but pays income tax at the additional rate. It is assumed for the purpose of this example only that the annual exempt amount for 2020/21 is £12,000 and the rates of tax remain as for 2017/18.

Mr Helm's capital gains tax liability for 2020/21 is calculated as follows.

	£
Sale proceeds	10,100,000
Cost	200,000
Chargeable gain qualifying for entrepreneurs' relief (subject to lifetime limit £10,000,000)	9,900,000
Annual exempt amount	12,000
Gain chargeable to tax	£9,888,000
Capital gains tax payable	
£9,750,000 × 10%	975,000
£138,000 × 20%	27,600
	£1,002,600

Notes to the example

(a) The lifetime limit applies to restrict the amount of the gain in 2020/21 which qualifies for entrepreneurs' relief as follows. Of the limit of £10,000,000, £250,000 was used in 2017/18 leaving (£10,000,000 – £250,000 =) £9,750,000 unused. As the otherwise qualifying gain for 2020/21 is greater than the unused part of the limit, entrepreneurs' relief is restricted so that the 10% rate applies to £9,750,000.

(b) The annual exempt amount of £12,000 is allocated against the part of the gain chargeable to tax at 20% as this gives the greater tax saving.

Example 4

If, in *Example 3*, Mr Helm's initial gain had been in May 2010 and had been, say, £2,500,000, his entrepreneurs' relief would have been restricted to the then lifetime limit of £2 million. Following the increases in the lifetime limit to £5 million with effect for disposals on or after 23 June 2010 and to £10 million for disposals on or after 6 April 2011, no further relief would have been due in respect of the 2010/11 gain. On the disposal in 2020/21, however, his unused lifetime limit would be £8 million (i.e. the new limit of £10 million less the £2 million in respect of which relief had previously been given).

Restriction on relief for certain trust disposals

[24.9] Entrepreneurs' relief is restricted where, on a disposal of trust business assets (see 24.4 above), there is, in addition to the qualifying beneficiary, at least one other beneficiary who, at the 'material time', has an interest in possession in either the whole of the settled property or a part of it which includes the assets, or interests in the assets, disposed of.

In such circumstances, relief applies only to a proportion of the amount to which it would otherwise apply. The remainder of that amount is treated as a chargeable gain (with no $^4/_9$ths reduction where otherwise applicable) to which the normal rate of CGT applies. The proportion is the same as the proportion which, at the material time, the qualifying beneficiary's interest in the income of the part of the settled property comprising the assets, or interests in the assets, disposed of bears to the interests in that income of all the beneficiaries, including the qualifying beneficiary, who then have interests in possession in that part of the settled property.

For this purpose, the '*material time*' is the end of the latest one-year period ending not earlier than three years before the date of the disposal throughout which:

- in the case of a disposal of shares or securities or interests in shares or securities, the condition at 24.4(i) above is satisfied; or
- in the case of a disposal of assets, or interests in assets, used or previously used for the purposes of a business, the business is carried on by the qualifying beneficiary.

In calculating the proportion above, only the interest by virtue of which the qualifying beneficiary is the qualifying beneficiary is taken into account in calculating his interest in the income of the part of the settled property concerned (and not any other interest he may have).

[*TCGA 1992, s 169O*].

Restriction on relief for certain associated disposals

[24.10] Entrepreneurs' relief is also restricted in the case of a disposal associated with a material disposal (see 24.5 above) where:

(a) the assets which are disposed of (or interests in which are disposed of) are in use for the purposes of the business only for part of the period in which they are owned by the individual;
(b) only part of those assets are in use for the purposes of the business for that period;
(c) the individual is concerned in the carrying on of the business (personally, in partnership or as an officer or employee of his personal company) for only part of the period in which the assets are in use for the purposes of the business; or

(d) for any part of the period for which the assets are in use for the purposes of the business, their availability is dependent on the payment of rent (which term includes any form of consideration given for the use of an asset). Any part of the period falling before 6 April 2008 is ignored for this purpose.

Where any of the above apply, relief applies only to such part of the amount to which entrepreneurs' relief would otherwise apply as is just and reasonable. The remainder of that amount is treated as a chargeable gain (with no $^4/_9$ths reduction where appropriate) to which the normal CGT rates apply. In applying the 'just and reasonable' test, regard is to be had to the following:

(i) where (a) above applies, the length of the period for which the assets are in use for the purposes of the business;
(ii) where (b) above applies, the part of the assets that are in use for the purposes of the business;
(iii) where (c) above applies, the length of the period for which the individual is concerned in the carrying on of the business; and
(iv) where (d) above applies, the extent to which the rent paid is less than the rent which would be payable in the open market.

[*TCGA 1992, ss 169P, 169S(5)*].

Deferred gains

[24.11] Where a chargeable gain (the '*first eventual gain*') arises as result of a chargeable event under either of the ENTERPRISE INVESTMENT SCHEME (**23.14**) or SOCIAL INVESTMENT RELIEF (**65.46**) deferral reliefs, the gain will qualify for entrepreneurs' relief if:

(a) the original disposal took place on or after 3 December 2014;
(b) the original gain would, but for its deferral, have arisen from a material disposal of business assets (within **24.3** above) or a disposal associated with such a disposal (within **24.5** above); and
(c) the first eventual gain is the first gain brought into charge in respect of the deferred original gain (so that if a previous chargeable event had resulted in a gain in respect of part of the original gain becoming chargeable and no claim to entrepreneurs' relief was made, no such claim may be made on a subsequent chargeable event).

Where a gain has been deferred more than once, the conditions in (a) and (b) above must be satisfied by the first gain to be deferred. For the purposes of (b) above, whether a disposal would have been a material disposal of business assets or a disposal associated with such a disposal is determined according to the law applicable at the time of that disposal.

A claim for relief must be made on or before the first anniversary of 31 January following the tax year in which the first eventual gain arises. Where such a claim is made, the first eventual gain is treated as if it were an amount resulting from a basic computation within **24.8** above in respect of a qualifying business disposal made when that gain arose. The gain is then ignored for any other chargeable gains purposes. If the first eventual gain does not represent the whole of the deferred gain, any remaining part of the gain brought into charge on a subsequent chargeable event is treated in the same way (but the qualifying business disposal is treated as occurring at the time of the later gain). No further claim is required.

If the disposal in (b) above would have been a disposal associated with a material disposal, the relief for the deemed qualifying business disposal is subject to the restriction in **24.10** above (applied by reference to the disposal in (b) above).

[*TCGA 1992, ss 169T–169V; FA 2015, s 44*].

Before the above provisions took effect (but only for disposals on or after 23 June 2010), where a disposal would potentially qualify for both entrepreneurs' relief and a deferral relief the taxpayer had to choose between the reliefs. He would either pay tax immediately on the gain at 10% if he chose entrepreneurs' relief or would defer the gain and paying tax at 18% or 28% when it came back into charge. Where a gain exceeded the lifetime limit for entrepreneurs' relief it was possible to claim entrepreneurs' relief on the gain up to the limit and to defer the gain above the limit. (Treasury Explanatory Notes to the 2010 Finance Bill.) For disposals before 23 June 2010 it was possible to claim entrepreneurs' relief and then defer the gain as reduced by $^{4}/_{9}$ths.

Transitional relief for enterprise investment scheme and venture capital trust deferral reliefs

Entrepreneurs' relief can be claimed where a chargeable gain (the '*original gain*') which would have accrued before the introduction of entrepreneurs' relief (i.e. before 6 April 2008) has been deferred under either the enterprise investment scheme (see **23.14** ENTERPRISE INVESTMENT SCHEME) or venture capital trusts scheme (see **71.12** VENTURE CAPITAL TRUSTS) and there is a chargeable event on or after that date in relation to any of the 'relevant shares' still held by the original investor immediately before the first such chargeable event. For this purpose, the '*relevant shares*' are the shares acquired in making the investment by virtue of which EIS or VCT deferral relief applies to the original gain and, in a case where the original gain accrued at a time after the making of the investment, still held at that time.

For entrepreneurs' relief to apply in such circumstances, the 'relevant disposal' must have been such that, had the provisions of this chapter then applied, it would have been a material disposal of business assets (see **24.3** above). The '*relevant disposal*' is normally the disposal on which the original gain would have accrued but for the deferral. Where, however, the original gain itself arose on the occurrence of a chargeable event under the EIS or VCT deferral provisions or to give effect to a withdrawal under *TCGA 1992, s 164F* or *s 164FA* of general reinvestment relief (see **25.86** EXEMPTIONS AND RELIEFS), the relevant disposal is the disposal (not being a deemed disposal on the occurrence of a chargeable event) by virtue of which the deferral provisions first had effect.

Where entrepreneurs' relief is claimed, the amount treated under the EIS or VCT deferral relief provisions as accruing on the chargeable event in respect of the original gain is the amount that would be arrived at under the rules at **24.8** above if the chargeable event were a qualifying business disposal and the amount to which relief applies were the proportion of the postponed gain equal to the proportion of the relevant shares held by the investor immediately before the first chargeable event on or after 6 April 2008. Where the chargeable event in question is a chargeable event in relation only to a proportion of the relevant shares held by the investor immediately before the first chargeable event on or after 6 April 2008, however, only a corresponding proportion of that amount is taken to be the amount accruing under the deferral provisions.

A claim for entrepreneurs' relief to apply in the above circumstances must be made on or before the first anniversary of the 31 January following the tax year in which the first chargeable event on or after 6 April 2008 occurs.

[*FA 2008, Sch 3 para 8*].

Reorganisations

[24.12] Where a reorganisation of share capital (within *TCGA 1992, s 126* — see **63.2** SHARES AND SECURITIES) takes place and *TCGA 1992, s 127* would otherwise apply to treat the 'original shares' and the 'new holding' (as defined for the purposes of that section — see **63.2** SHARES AND SECURITIES) as the same asset, an election can be made to disapply that section so that entrepreneurs' relief can be claimed in respect of the disposal of the original shares. (Note that the disapplication of *s 127* takes effect only where a claim to entrepreneurs' relief is made; without such a claim, the election has no effect.)

The election must be made on or before the first anniversary of the 31 January following the tax year in which the reorganisation takes place (which date is also the time limit for making the claim for relief — see **24.6** above). If the reorganisation would, if treated as a disposal, involve a disposal of trust business assets (see **24.4** above), the election must be made jointly by the trustees and the qualifying beneficiary.

The above provision applies also to exchanges of securities within *TCGA 1992, s 135* (see **63.5** SHARES AND SECURITIES) and to schemes of reconstruction within *TCGA 1992, s 136* (see **63.7** SHARES AND SECURITIES) to which *TCGA 1992, s 127* applies.

[*TCGA 1992, s 169Q*].

Reorganisations involving acquisition of qualifying corporate bonds

Where there is a reorganisation of share capital involving the acquisition of qualifying corporate bonds and the calculation required as a result by *TCGA 1992, s 116(10)(a)* produces a (deferred) chargeable gain for an individual (see **54.4**(a) QUALIFYING CORPORATE BONDS), the provisions of this chapter apply as follows.

Reorganisations on or after 23 June 2010

An election can be made so that a claim for entrepreneurs' relief can in turn be made on the basis that the reorganisation involved a disposal of the 'old asset'. Where such a claim is made, *TCGA 1992, s 116(10)* is disapplied so that a gain on the old asset will arise at the time of the reorganisation and can qualify for entrepreneurs' relief (if all the conditions are satisfied).

The election must be made on or before the first anniversary of the 31 January following the tax year in which the reorganisation takes place (which date is also the time limit for making the claim for relief — see **24.6** above). If the reorganisation would, if treated as a disposal, involve a disposal of trust business assets (see **24.4** above), the election must be made jointly by the trustees and the qualifying beneficiary.

If no election is made and the gain on the old asset is therefore deferred, it is likely that in almost all cases the gain will not qualify for entrepreneurs' relief when it comes into charge at a later date.

Reorganisations before 23 June 2010

The entrepreneurs' relief provisions apply as if the reorganisation were a disposal by the individual of business assets consisting of the 'old asset'.

Where the deemed disposal would be a material disposal of business assets (see **24.3** above) and entrepreneurs' relief is claimed, the amount to which the relief applies is the chargeable gain calculated under *TCGA 1992, s 116(10)(a)*. On subsequent disposal of the whole or part of the 'new asset', that gain as reduced by entrepreneurs' relief (i.e. reduced, subject to the lifetime limit, by $^4/_9$ths), or a corresponding part of it, is deemed to accrue to the individual under *TCGA 1992, s 116(10)(b)* (see **54.4**(b) QUALIFYING CORPORATE BONDS).

This treatment applies without the need for an election.

The effect of these provisions is that, where the disposal of the new asset takes place on or after 23 June 2010, the deferred gain will be chargeable at an effective rate of 15.55% ($^5/_9 \times 28\%$) where the 28% rate of CGT applies.

Definitions

'Old asset' and 'new asset' are defined for this purpose as at **54.4** QUALIFYING CORPORATE BONDS.

[*TCGA 1992, s 169R*].

Transitional relief for reorganisations involving acquisition of qualifying corporate bonds before 6 April 2008

Relief can be available where a chargeable gain is deemed to accrue to an individual on a disposal after the introduction of entrepreneurs' relief (i.e. on or after 6 April 2008) (a '*relevant disposal*') under *TCGA 1992, s 116(10)(b)* (see **54.4**(b) QUALIFYING CORPORATE BONDS) by reason of a reorganisation to which that individual was a party and which took place before that date. In such circumstances, entrepreneurs' relief can be claimed (provided that the other conditions are satisfied) as if the reorganisation were a disposal of the 'old asset' by the individual, even though the deemed disposal was made before 6 April 2008.

The amount to which entrepreneurs' relief applies is (subject to the lifetime limit (see **24.6** above)) the amount of the deferred chargeable gain calculated under *TCGA 1992, s 116(10)(a)* (see **54.4**(a) QUALIFYING CORPORATE BONDS) less any part of it deemed to accrue before 6 April 2008. For gains deemed to accrue on a relevant disposal under *TCGA 1992, s 116(10)(b)* before 23 June 2010, the deemed gain is therefore that amount reduced by 4/9ths. If, however, the relevant disposal is not a disposal of the whole of the 'new asset' (or, where applicable, of that part of the new asset which was not disposed of before 6 April 2008), the deemed gain is only a proportion of the amount equivalent to the proportion of the new asset (or of so much of the new asset as was not disposed of before 6 April 2008) disposed of on the relevant disposal.

'Old asset' and 'new asset' are defined for this purpose as at **54.4** QUALIFYING CORPORATE BONDS.

Where the above provisions apply, a claim must be made on or before the first anniversary of the 31 January following the tax year in which the first disposal on or after 6 April 2008 of the whole or part of the new asset is made.

[*FA 2008, Sch 3 para 7*].

Key points concerning entrepreneurs' relief

[24.13] Points to consider are as follows.

- Entrepreneurs' relief was introduced as a replacement for business asset taper relief but with limited application in terms of the amount of relief available and the assets to which it relates. The rules are partly based on those for retirement relief which ceased in 2003.
- Entrepreneurs' relief is subject to a lifetime limit so it is necessary to obtain details of any previous qualifying disposals since its introduction in 2008/09. The lifetime limit has also changed three times since its introduction. The current limit is £10 million for disposals after 5 April 2011. Qualifying gains are taxed at 10%.
- The relief is aimed at gains arising on the disposal of a business (or part of a business) and can include gains arising on the disposal of shares in an individual's personal company (broadly a trading company where the individual owns at least 5%) and shares acquired under the enterprise management incentive scheme. The relief can be available to trustees in certain circumstances.
- Capital gains tax planning predominantly centres on maintaining this valuable relief. However, it is complex and easy to fall foul of the various conditions. Some common areas to watch:
  - Giving shares to a spouse or civil partner. This can originally occur for a number of reasons such as to utilise their basic rate bands. However, it is worth ensuring the spouse meets the requirements to potentially qualify for entrepreneurs' relief in their own right. For example, sufficient length of ownership (12 months), qualifies as personal company (5%) and officer or employee (role of company secretary often popular).

- Commercial property owned outside the company, e.g. business premises. When commercial property is owned outside a company it can still qualify for entrepreneurs' relief as an associated disposal (in relation to a material disposal) provided the asset was used for business purposes for the relevant period and has been owned for at least three years. However relief is restricted where rent is paid. This can create problems especially where the purchase of the property has been funded by a mortgage (the individual needs to fund the loan repayments). It may therefore be worth comparing individual ownership to corporate ownership and or, where possible, ownership by a self invested pension plan (SIPP).
- Does the company/group qualify as 'trading'? If investment activity is significant can the position be improved with corporate restructuring?
- Business property relief for IHT. Although a disposal may potentially qualify for entrepreneurs' relief, is it advantageous and possible for the taxpayer to retain assets qualifying for BPR as on death there may be no charge to IHT and uplift to market value for capital gains tax?
- Is the sale 'part of a business' or merely a disposal of business assets? The relief applies to the disposal of part of a business but not assets unless trading has ceased. HMRC believe the 'part' sold should be separately identifiable in its own right. This is a complex area giving rise to case law such as *M Gilbert v HMRC* FTT [2011] UKFTT 705 (TC).
- Shares and securities can qualify for entrepreneurs' relief even though they don't count towards the 'personal company' requirement. For example, non-voting shares can qualify provided the individual meets the 'personal company' condition via other shares they hold.
- A shareholder can in theory make several disposals of shares over a number of years in the same company and claim entrepreneurs' relief on all gains provided they can meet the personal company, trading, ownership period and employment tests.

The relief needs to be claimed — it is not automatic.

- Although specific circumstances are required, pension tax planning and entrepreneurs' relief can be used successfully together. For example, a company makes a £50,000 contribution to a SIPP. The company obtains tax relief on the contribution. The individual sells shares to the SIPP for their market value of £50,000. The individual realises a capital gain (assume no base cost) against which he can use his 2017/18 annual exempt amount of £11,300 and the remaining gain (assuming meet qualifying conditions) is taxed at 10% = £3,870. Cash has therefore been extracted at a low tax rate while obtaining corporation tax relief and the shares remain effectively under the same control.

25

Exemptions and Reliefs

Introduction 25.1
Exempt assets 25.2
- Annuities and annual payments 25.3
- Chattels 25.4
- Debts 25.5
- Decorations 25.6
- Dwelling-houses 25.7
- Foreign currency 25.8
- Government securities 25.9
- Insurance policies 25.10
- Motor cars etc. 25.11
- Qualifying corporate bonds 25.12
- Renewables obligation certificates 25.13
- Right to receive interest on deposit of victim of National-Socialist persecution 25.14
- Savings certificates, savings schemes and savings accounts etc. 25.15
- Settlements 25.16
- Ships and other assets within the tonnage tax regime 25.17

Exempt gains and transactions 25.18
- Agricultural grants 25.19
- Assets used for the purposes of a trade etc. taxed on the cash basis 25.20
- Betting, lottery etc. 25.21
- Business expansion scheme (BES) 25.22
- Cashbacks 25.23
- Child Trust Funds 25.24
- Damages and compensation 25.25
- Enterprise investment scheme (EIS) 25.26
- Compensation from foreign governments 25.27
- Exempt amount for the year 25.28
- Gains arising partly before 6.4.1965 or 31.3.1982 25.29
- Individual Savings Accounts (ISAs) 25.30
- Legatees 25.31
- Personal Equity Plans (PEPs) 25.32
- Recovery of assets under *Proceeds of Crime Act 2002, Pt 5* 25.33
- Seed enterprise investment scheme (SEIS) 25.34
- Settled property 25.35
- Social investment relief 25.36
- Special reserve funds of individual Lloyd's underwriters 25.37
- Substantial shareholdings of companies 25.38
- Venture capital trusts 25.39
- Woodlands 25.40
- Works of art etc. 25.41

Exempt organisations and individuals 25.42

Asbestos compensation settlements **25.43**
Bare trustees and nominees **25.44**
British and Natural History Museums **25.45**
Central banks **25.46**
Charities **25.47**
Community amateur sports clubs **25.48**
The Crown **25.49**
Diplomatic agents **25.50**
Friendly societies **25.51**
The Historic Buildings and Monuments Commission for England **25.52**
Housing associations **25.53**
International organisations **25.54**
Local authorities etc. **25.55**
London Olympic Games **25.56**
National Debt **25.57**
The National Heritage Memorial Fund **25.58**
The National Radiological Protection Board **25.59**
Pension schemes **25.60**
Scientific research associations **25.61**
Self-build society **25.62**
Trade unions **25.63**
Unit and investment trusts, open-ended investment companies and venture capital trusts **25.64**
Visiting forces etc. **25.65**
Reliefs and deferrals **25.66**
Capital distributions and sale of rights **25.67**
Companies **25.68**
Company reconstructions **25.69**
Constituency associations **25.70**
Corporate venturing scheme **25.71**
Disposals — capital sums received as compensation etc. **25.72**
Enterprise investment scheme (EIS) **25.73**
Entrepreneurs' relief **25.74**
Gifts of business assets and assets on which inheritance tax is chargeable etc. **25.75**
Gifts to charities etc. **25.76**
Harbour reorganisation schemes **25.77**
Hold-over — general relief for gifts **25.78**
Hops Marketing Board **25.79**
Investors' relief **25.80**
Land — compulsory acquisition **25.81**
Land — part disposals **25.82**
Localism Act 2011 transfers **25.83**
Married persons and civil partners **25.84**
National heritage property **25.85**
Reinvestment relief **25.86**
Reorganisation of share capital **25.87**
Retirement relief **25.88**
Rollover relief — replacement of business assets **25.89**
Seed enterprise investment scheme (SEIS) **25.90**
Settlements for the benefit of employees **25.91**

Social investment relief	**25.92**
Taper relief	**25.93**
Transfer of a business to a company — incorporation relief	**25.94**
Unremittable overseas gains	**25.95**
Venture capital trusts (VCTs)	**25.96**

Cross-references. See 8 ASSETS HELD ON 6 APRIL 1965; 9 ASSETS HELD ON 31 MARCH 1982; 11 CHARITIES; 18 CORPORATE VENTURING SCHEME; 19 DEATH; 21 DOUBLE TAX RELIEF; 23 ENTERPRISE INVESTMENT SCHEME; 24 ENTREPRENEURS' RELIEF; 28 GOVERNMENT SECURITIES; 36 HOLD-OVER RELIEFS; 38 INDEXATION; 44 LOSSES; 49 OVERSEAS MATTERS; 53 PRIVATE RESIDENCES; 54 QUALIFYING CORPORATE BONDS; 57 RESIDENCE AND DOMICILE; 59 ROLLOVER RELIEF — REPLACEMENT OF BUSINESS ASSETS; 63 SHARES AND SECURITIES; 66 SUBSTANTIAL SHAREHOLDINGS OF COMPANIES; 70 UNIT TRUSTS AND OTHER INVESTMENT VEHICLES; 71 VENTURE CAPITAL TRUSTS.

Introduction to exemptions and reliefs

[25.1] A person is chargeable to capital gains tax on chargeable gains accruing to him on the disposal of assets in any tax year during any part of which he is resident in the UK. All forms of property except sterling are regarded as assets for these purposes and every gain, except as otherwise expressly provided, is a chargeable gain. There are, however, a number of exemptions and reliefs. These may broadly be classified as follows.

(a) Exempt assets (see 25.2–25.17 below).
(b) Exempt gains and transactions (see 25.18–25.41 below).
(c) Exempt organisations and individuals (see 25.42–25.65 below).

In addition, a number of reliefs are available to reduce or defer the amount of capital gains tax payable. See 25.66–25.96 and certain provisions in 25.53 and 25.62 below.

Exempt assets

[25.2] Gains accruing on the disposal of certain assets are exempt from capital gains tax. The exemption (total or partial) of the various types of asset is examined in 25.3–25.17 below. Losses arising from such disposals are similarly not allowable unless expressly provided otherwise. [*TCGA 1992, s 16(2)*].

Annuities and annual payments

[25.3] A gain accruing on the disposal of a right to or to any part of an allowance, annuity, or capital sum from a *superannuation fund* or annual payments receivable under a 'covenant' not secured on property, is exempt. [*TCGA 1992, s 237(a)(c)*]. '*Covenant*' means a gratuitous promise enforceable solely due to the form in which it is evidenced (i.e., in England, in a document under seal). It does not include contracts enforceable as such (*Rank Xerox Ltd v Lane* HL 1979, 53 TC 185).

A gain accruing on the disposal of, or of an 'interest' in, rights under a contract for a 'non-deferred annuity' or an annuity granted (or deemed to be granted) under *Government Annuities Act 1929* is also exempt. For this purpose, a '*non-deferred annuity*' is an annuity (including an annuity which includes instalments of capital) which is not granted under a contract for a deferred annuity and which is granted in the ordinary course of a business granting annuities on the life of any person. An '*interest*' in rights means an interest as co-owner of the rights, and it is immaterial whether the rights are owned jointly or in common or whether or not the interests of the co-owners are equal. [*TCGA 1992, ss 204(5)(7)–(9), 237(b)*].

Chattels

[25.4] A tangible movable asset (other than a commodity disposed of by or through a dealer on a terminal market) is entirely exempt, provided that the asset is not 'currency of any description' and that the disposal is for a consideration of £6,000 or less.

If the consideration exceeds £6,000, the chargeable gain is limited to five-thirds of the excess.

[*TCGA 1992, s 262(1)(2)(6)*].

Examples

(i) A chattel which cost £5,000 in May 2000 is disposed of in May 2017 for £8,000. Assume expenses of disposal of £300. The chargeable gain is ascertained as follows.

Excess of consideration over £6,000	£2,000
£2,000 × $^5/_3$	£3,333
Actual gain is £2,700 which is less than £3,333	
Chargeable gain	£2,700

(ii) A chattel which cost £2,000 in May 2000 is disposed of in May 2017 for £8,000. Assume expenses of disposal of £280.

Excess of consideration over £6,000	£2,000
£2,000 × $^5/_3$	£3,333
Actual gain is £5,720 which is more than £3,333	
Chargeable gain	£3,333

Part disposal

Where the disposal is of a right or interest in or over a tangible movable asset, and the sum of the consideration received plus the value of what remains exceeds £6,000, a similar limitation of the chargeable gain applies but the excess for this purpose is computed as follows.

$$(\text{consideration received} + \text{value of remainder} - £6{,}000) \times \frac{\text{considerationreceived}}{\text{total value}}$$

[*TCGA 1992, s 262(5)*].

Losses

For the purposes of loss relief, a disposal of a tangible movable asset for a consideration of less than £6,000 is deemed to be made for a consideration of £6,000. In the case of a partial disposal of an asset the total value of which is less than £6,000, the deemed consideration for loss relief purposes is computed as follows.

$$(\text{£}6{,}000 - \text{total value}) \times \left(\frac{\text{consideration received}}{\text{total value}}\right) + \text{consideration received}$$

Simplified, this becomes (£6,000 × consideration/total value).

[*TCGA 1992, s 262(3)*].

Assets forming a set

Where these are owned by the same disposer they are to be treated as a single asset where they are disposed of, whether on the same or on different occasions, to the same person or to persons acting in concert, or to CONNECTED PERSONS (17). [*TCGA 1992, s 262(4)*]. For HMRC's views on the circumstances in which a number of bottles of wine may constitute a set, see Revenue Tax Bulletin August 1999 p 686. For an article on pairs of shotguns, see Revenue Tax Bulletin February 2000 pp 726, 727.

Wasting assets

Subject to the following exceptions, tangible movable assets which are WASTING ASSETS (72) are exempt whatever the consideration received. This exemption is restricted or eliminated to the extent that the asset, by reason of its having been used in trade or otherwise, has been or could have been the subject of a capital allowance.

For disposals on or after 6 April 2015 (1 April 2015 for corporation tax purposes), the exemption is also eliminated where the asset has become plant as a result of its use for the purposes of a trade, profession or vocation carried on by a person other than the owner and it would not otherwise have been a wasting asset. This does not, however, apply if the asset is plant under a long funding lease and the disposal takes place during the term of the lease or it is a deemed disposal on termination of the lease (see **7.6** ASSETS).

The exemption is also not applicable to a disposal of commodities on a terminal market.

[*TCGA 1992, s 45; FA 2015, s 40*].

Where capital allowances were initially granted in respect of qualifying expenditure on movable machinery but were later withdrawn because the machinery was sold without it having been brought into use by the taxpayer, it was held that the taxpayer should be treated as if the allowance had never been made, with the result that the disposal on sale was exempt (*Burman v Westminster Press Ltd* Ch D 1987, 60 TC 418). If a restriction by reference to capital allowances would otherwise arise, relief as under *TCGA 1992, s 262* above may be available.

HMRC accept that any of the following is machinery and is thus a tangible movable wasting asset (see **72.2** WASTING ASSETS) which will be exempt where owned privately and not used in a business: antique clocks and watches; motor vehicles which are not normal private passenger vehicles and are thus outside the exemption at **25.11** below, e.g. taxi cabs, vans, motor cycles etc.; trawlers, fishing vessels, tankers and other vessels propelled by engines (and see below re boats generally). (Revenue Tax Bulletin October 1994 pp 166, 167). They 'generally accept' that all types of gun are within the general description of machinery (Revenue Tax Bulletin February 2000 p 727).

For HMRC's views on the circumstances in which bottled wine may qualify as a wasting asset and thus an exempt chattel, see Revenue Tax Bulletin August 1999 p 686.

Boats

Boats 'will generally be tangible movable wasting assets' and thus exempt (except where qualifying for capital allowances). This will not always apply to yachts, barges or boats used as a residence, as these may have a longer useful life. A houseboat which is permanently located on a site and connected to all mains services may in some circumstances be regarded as a dwelling house. (HMRC Capital Gains Manual CG64328 and see also above).

Debts

[25.5] A debt, other than a 'debt on a security' (see below), disposed of by the original creditor or his personal representative or legatee is exempt. For disposals on or after 6 April 2012, the disposal of a debt includes, for this purpose, the disposal of an interest in a debt (and references below to the amount of a debt are, in such a case, references to the amount of the interest).

Where the trustees of a settlement are the original creditor (or, for debts created before 6 April 2006, where the original creditor is a trustee and the debt, when created, is settled property), a person becoming absolutely entitled to the debt is treated as a personal representative or legatee as is his own personal representative or legatee.

[*TCGA 1992, s 251(1)(5)(5A); FA 2012, s 35(3)(6)*].

A right possibly to receive an unidentifiable sum at an unascertainable date is not a 'debt' (*Marren v Ingles* HL 1980, 54 TC 76; *Marson v Marriage* Ch D 1979, 54 TC 59).

Subject to the above, the satisfaction of a debt (including a debt on a security) or part of it is treated as a disposal of the debt by the creditor made at the time when the debt is satisfied. Where a debt on a security is involved this rule is subject to the provisions in *TCGA 1992, ss 132, 135, 136* covering reorganisations of share capital (see **63.5**, **63.7** and **63.8** SHARES AND SECURITIES). [*TCGA 1992, s 251(2)*].

Where property is acquired by a creditor in satisfaction of a debt then, subject to any reorganisation of share capital as above, the property is not treated as disposed of by the debtor or acquired by the creditor for a consideration greater than its market value at the time of the creditor's acquisition of it. But if no chargeable gain accrues as regards the debt either because the creditor is the original creditor or under the share capital reorganisation rules *and* a chargeable gain accrues to the creditor on a disposal by him of the property, then any resulting chargeable gain is reduced so as not to exceed the chargeable gain that would have accrued if he had acquired the property for a consideration equal to the amount of the debt. [*TCGA 1992, s 251(3)*].

Loss relief

Where the original creditor and a subsequent creditor are CONNECTED PERSONS (**17**), a loss incurred by the subsequent creditor on the disposal of a debt is not an allowable loss. See **44.6** LOSSES.

Loss relief is available to the maker of a 'qualifying loan' or a guarantor of a qualifying loan. See **44.12** LOSSES. See **44.13** LOSSES for a corresponding relief where the borrower's debt is a debt on a security which is a qualifying corporate bond.

Foreign currency bank accounts

For disposals on or after 6 April 2012, the exemption does not apply to the disposal of a bank balance in a foreign currency unless it is made by an individual, the trustees of a settlement or the personal representatives of a deceased person. Previously, the exemption was disapplied in relation to all disposals of such balances (including disposals by individuals, trustees or personal representatives), except to the extent that the balance represented currency acquired by an individual for purposes similar to those in *TCGA 1992, s 269* (see **25.8** below). [*TCGA 1992, s 252; FA 2012, s 35(4)(6)*].

Where the exemption does not apply, a taxpayer may treat all bank accounts in his name containing a particular foreign currency as one account and so disregard direct transfers among such accounts which would otherwise constitute disposals (withdrawals) and acquisitions (deposits) under *s 252*. The practice, once adopted, must be applied to all future direct transfers among bank accounts in the taxpayer's name designated in that currency until such time as all debt represented in the accounts has been repaid to the taxpayer. Accounts held as in **7.3**(l) ASSETS (non-domiciled individuals) do not qualify for this treatment before 6 April 2008. (HMRC Statement of Practice 10/84; HMRC Guidance Note 28 January 2010). (See **4.19** ANTI-AVOIDANCE for the charge arising where concessions involving deferral of gains are abused.)

See **55.7** REMITTANCE BASIS for HMRC's concessionary practice for 2011/12 and earlier years allowing for a net figure for deposits into and withdrawals from a foreign currency bank account to be computed for each month within a tax year and for further HMRC guidance on the effect of using the remittance basis on foreign currency accounts. See also **55.6** REMITTANCE BASIS for the restriction of losses on disposals of amounts in foreign currency accounts where the remittance basis is used.

Simon's Taxes. See C1.608.

Redenomination into euros

The redenomination into euros of a debt, other than a debt on a security, from the currency of a State participating in the European single currency on or after 1 January 1999 is not treated as involving the disposal of that debt or the acquisition of a new debt. The original debt and the new debt are treated as the same asset, acquired as the original debt was acquired. [*SI 1998 No 3177, Reg 37*]. Accordingly the disposal of the new debt by the original creditor retains its exemption.

Meaning of 'debt on a security'

A '*debt on a security*' is defined by reference to *TCGA 1992, s 132(3)(b),* so that '*security*' includes any loan stock or similar security of any government or public or local authority in the UK or elsewhere, or of any company, and whether secured or unsecured. The existence of a document may be indicative of a 'debt on a security', but it cannot be concluded from the absence of a document that the debt is not 'on a security' (*Aberdeen Construction Group Ltd v CIR* HL 1978, 52 TC 281; *W T Ramsay Ltd v CIR* HL 1981, 54 TC 101; *Cleveleys Investment Trust Co v CIR (No 1)* CS 1971, 47 TC 300). An intra-group loan secured on a promissory note was held not to be a marketable security in any realistic sense and was not a 'debt on a security' (*Taylor Clark International Ltd v Lewis* CA 1998, 71 TC 226). For further discussion of the meaning of 'security' see the income tax case of *Williams v Singer and Others* HL 1920, 7 TC 387, and for 'debt on security' see *Tarmac Roadstone Holdings Ltd v Williams* (Sp C 95), [1996] SSCD 409.

HMRC's view, based principally on the HL judgments of Lords Wilberforce and Fraser in *Ramsay*, is set out in HMRC Capital Gains Manual CG53420–53436. This guidance states that for a debt to be a debt on a security it should be capable of being *both*:

- held as an investment, and
- realised at a profit.

The position is to be judged by reference to circumstances prevailing at the time the debt is created, though these may include anticipated changes in market interest rates. For a debt to be capable of being held as an investment it should carry a commercial rate of interest, or offer an equivalent return by virtue of its being repayable at a premium or issued at a discount. It should also be marketable. Whether it can be realised at a profit depends not only on the rate of interest, premium etc. but also on whether the debt will last long enough to cover the costs of acquisition and obtain a worthwhile return. HMRC will accept that any loan which cannot be terminated by the borrower within a year of commencement will be outstanding long enough to have the required 'structure of permanence'. But a debt will not have a structure of permanence merely because the borrower is not in a position to repay it in the foreseeable future. A debt can, however, be capable of being realised at a profit if the terms require the lender to be adequately compensated in the event of early repayment. Standard clauses requiring early repayment on the happening of events considered improbable, such as the default or liquidation of the borrower, should not be seen as displacing any stated terms for repayment. The existence of a formal document constituting or evidencing the debt is not an *essential* feature of a debt on a security. Neither realised, nor potential, foreign exchange gains or losses should be taken into account in deciding whether a debt is a debt on a security.

A debenture issued by any company after 15 March 1993 is deemed to be a security within *TCGA 1992, s 132(3)(b)* above if:

(1) it is issued on a reorganisation or reduction of a company's share capital or in pursuance of its allotment on any such reorganisation or reduction;

(2) it is issued in exchange for shares in or debentures of another company and in a case to which *TCGA 1992, s 135* (see **63.5** SHARES AND SECURITIES) applies and which is unaffected by *TCGA 1992, s 137(1)* (restriction on application of share reorganisation rules in *TCGA 1992, ss 135, 136* — see **4.15** ANTI-AVOIDANCE);

(3) it is issued under any such arrangements as are mentioned in *TCGA 1992, s 136(1)(a)* (arrangement between company and share or debenture holders in connection with a scheme of reconstruction) and in a case unaffected by *TCGA 1992, s 137* where *s 136* requires shares or debentures in another company to be treated as exchanged for, or for anything that includes, that debenture; or

(4) it is issued in pursuance of rights attached to any debenture issued after 15 March 1993 and falling within (1), (2) or (3) above.

Any debenture resulting from a conversion of securities (within *TCGA 1992, s 132* — see **63.8** SHARES AND SECURITIES — and whether occurring before or after that date), or which is issued in pursuance of rights attaching to such a debenture, is similarly deemed to be a security.

[*TCGA 1992, s 251(6)*].

For the purposes of the above definition, the following instruments are deemed to be 'securities' where this would not otherwise be the case, but this fiction does not apply for the purposes of determining what is or is not an allowable loss in any case.

(i) Any instrument falling to be treated as an asset representing a company loan relationship if it were not for the exclusions at **15.7** COMPANIES — CORPORATE FINANCE AND INTANGIBLES.

(ii) Any instrument which, even apart from the exclusions mentioned in (i) above, is not a loan relationship of a company but which would be a deeply discounted security if it were not an 'excluded indexed security' (see **63.21** SHARES AND SECURITIES).

[*TCGA 1992, s 251(7)(8)*].

See also **54.3** QUALIFYING CORPORATE BONDS for a provision corresponding to *TCGA 1992, s 251(6)* and regarding the definition of 'corporate bond', so that combined the two provisions prevent, in the circumstances stated, the issue of a debenture which neither represents a debt on a security nor is a qualifying corporate bond.

Decorations

[25.6] A decoration for valour or gallantry (unless acquired by the vendor for money or money's worth) is exempt. [*TCGA 1992, s 268*].

Dwelling-houses

[25.7] A gain accruing to an individual on the disposal of (or of an interest in) a dwelling-house which has been his only or main residence during his period of ownership is exempt (or partly exempt). See 53 PRIVATE RESIDENCES for this exemption which is also extended, in certain circumstances, to trustees and personal representatives.

Foreign currency

[25.8] Foreign currency acquired for an individual's (or his dependant's) personal expenditure outside the UK (including the provision or maintenance of his residence outside the UK) is exempt. [*TCGA 1992, s 269*].

Exchange gains and losses of companies (FOREX) are dealt with under the loan relationships regime — see 15.3 COMPANIES — CORPORATE FINANCE AND INTANGIBLES.

See also 25.5 above.

Government securities

[25.9] Disposals of specified government and public corporation securities are exempt from capital gains tax whatever the period of ownership. This also applies to options or contracts to acquire or dispose of such securities. See 28 GOVERNMENT SECURITIES, 15.2–15.7 COMPANIES — CORPORATE FINANCE AND INTANGIBLES, and also 7.7, 7.8 ASSETS as regards options and contracts.

Insurance policies

[25.10] A gain on the disposal of, or of an 'interest' in, the rights conferred by a 'non-life insurance policy' is exempt. Where the policy is for damage to, or loss or depreciation of, assets, the exemption applies only so far as the rights do not relate to assets which on disposal could give rise to a chargeable gain. (This does not prevent sums received under such policies for loss, damage, etc. to assets from being chargeable; see 10 CAPITAL SUMS DERIVED FROM ASSETS.)

For this purpose, a '*non-life insurance policy*' is a contract made in the course of a capital redemption business within *FA 2012, s 56(3)* (previously within *ICTA 1988, Pt 12 Ch 1*) (i.e. a capital redemption policy) or any policy of insurance which is not a policy of insurance on the life of any person. An '*interest*' in rights means an interest as co-owner of the rights, and it is immaterial whether the rights are owned jointly or in common or whether or not the interests of the co-owners are equal.

[*TCGA 1992, s 204(1)–(4)(7)(8)(10); FA 2012, Sch 16 para 79*].

See also 43 LIFE INSURANCE POLICIES AND DEFERRED ANNUITIES.

Motor cars etc.

[25.11] A mechanically propelled road vehicle constructed or adapted for the carriage of passengers, except for a vehicle of a type not commonly used as a private vehicle and unsuitable to be so used, is not a chargeable asset, and thus no chargeable gain or allowable loss accrues on its disposal. [*TCGA 1992, s 263*].

This exemption applies regardless of whether or not the vehicle was eligible for capital allowances (see 25.4 above). For the interpretation of 'commonly used as a private vehicle' in relation to capital allowances, see cases mentioned in Tolley's Capital Allowances. Vehicles outside this exemption include taxi cabs, racing cars, single seat sports cars, vans, lorries, other commercial vehicles, motor cycles, scooters and motor cycle/sidecar combinations (HMRC Capital Gains Manual CG76907).

Motor vehicles which are outside the above exemption, and which are privately owned and not used in a business, are exempt as tangible movable wasting assets (see 25.4 above and Revenue Tax Bulletin October 1994 p 166).

Personalised car number plates are not covered by either exemption. The value of the number plate itself is usually negligible, and the plate is regarded as part of the car when sold attached thereto. However, the disposal of the inherent intangible right to use a specific combination of letters or numbers when registering a vehicle is neither a disposal of a motor car as above nor of a chattel as in 25.4 above, and any gain arising will be a chargeable gain. (HMRC Capital Gains Manual CG76921–76928).

Qualifying corporate bonds

[25.12] Qualifying corporate bonds are exempt whatever the period of ownership. This also applies to options or contracts to acquire or dispose of such bonds. See 54 QUALIFYING CORPORATE BONDS, and see 7.7 and 7.8 ASSETS as regards options and contracts. For loans to traders evidenced by qualifying corporate bonds, see 44.13 LOSSES.

Renewables obligation certificates

[25.13] A gain on the disposal by an individual of a 'renewables obligation certificate' is exempt if:

- the individual acquired the certificate in connection with the generation of electricity by a microgeneration system within *Climate Change and Sustainable Energy Act 2006, s 4*;
- the system is installed at or near premises occupied by the individual and used wholly or mainly as a separate private dwelling; and
- the individual intends that the amount of electricity generated will not significantly exceed the amount of electricity consumed on those premises.

For this purpose, a '*renewables obligation certificate*' is a certificate issued under *Electricity Act 1989, s 32B* (or NI equivalent).

[*TCGA 1992, s 263AZA*].

Right to receive interest on deposit of victim of National-Socialist persecution

[25.14] A gain on the disposal of a right, or an 'interest' in a right, to receive the whole or any part of a payment of interest eligible for income tax exemption under *ITTOIA 2005, s 756A* is not a chargeable gain. That section provides, broadly, for income tax exemption for interest paid under certain compensation schemes for deposits made on or before 5 June 1945 by, or on behalf of, victims of National-Socialist persecution. See Tolley's Income Tax for further details.

An '*interest*' in a right is for this purpose an interest as a co-owner of the right and it is immaterial whether the right is owned jointly or in common, or whether or not the interests of the co-owners are equal.

This exemption was introduced in *FA 2006* and applies with retrospective effect to disposals on or after 6 April 1996. No loss accruing on a disposal before 6 April 2006 is, however, to cease to be an allowable loss as a consequence. All necessary adjustments, whether by assessment, discharge or repayment of tax or otherwise, can be made for 2005/06 or any earlier year to give effect to the exemption for those years, provided that the person entitled to it makes a claim on or before 31 January 2012.

[*TCGA 1992, s 268A; FA 2006, s 64(8)(10)–(12)*].

See also **25.27** below for compensation from foreign governments for assets confiscated, destroyed etc.

Savings certificates, savings schemes and savings accounts etc.

[25.15] Savings certificates, and non-marketable securities issued under the *National Loans Acts 1939* and *1968* and corresponding NI enactments are not 'chargeable assets' and accordingly no chargeable gain accrues on their disposal. Interest resulting from certified SAYE savings arrangements and tax-exempt special savings accounts are ignored for capital gains tax purposes. [*TCGA 1992, ss 121, 271(4)*].

Settlements

[25.16] With certain exceptions, no chargeable gain accrues on the disposal of an interest created by or arising under a settlement by the original beneficiary or any other person (other than one who acquired, or derives his title from one who acquired, his interest for money or money's worth). See **62.15** SETTLEMENTS.

Ships and other assets within the tonnage tax regime

[25.17] Under this ring-fenced regime, a shipping company or group may elect to have its taxable profits computed by reference to the net tonnage of each of the qualifying ships it operates. The initial period for making an election was the 12 months beginning with 28 July 2000, but a further period, 1 July 2005 to 31 December 2006 has been added. An election is normally expected to remain in force for at least 10 years, although a limited opportunity to withdraw from an election was provided in 2005 (and further such opportunities may be provided for by Treasury order). Qualifying ships must be seagoing, of at least 100 tons gross tonnage and be engaged in qualifying activities, e.g. the transportation of goods or passengers by sea. Certain vessels are excluded, e.g. fishing and factory support vessels, harbour and river ferries, oil rigs, pleasure craft, floating restaurants etc. The strategic and commercial management of ships within the regime must be undertaken from the UK. New ships entering tonnage tax are to be registered in the EU (but this rule is disapplied for certain financial years by the Treasury).

Capital gains accruing during the currency of the election are not chargeable gains (and losses are not allowable losses) to the extent that the assets disposed of were used exclusively for the qualifying shipping activity. In the event of a company leaving the regime for certain specified reasons, anti-avoidance provisions apply to bring into charge a previously exempt gain arising in the last six years.

[*FA 2000, s 82, Sch 22; TIOPA 2010, Sch 8 paras 56, 119; FA 2012, Sch 20 paras 18–20; SI 2005 No 1449; SI 2006 No 333; SI 2007 No 850*].

HMRC have published guidance on the practical operation of the regime (see HMRC Statement of Practice 4/00 — in particular, para 131 on exemptions from exit charges).

Exempt gains and transactions

[25.18] The gains or transactions detailed in 25.19–25.41 below do not give rise to a liability to capital gains tax.

Agricultural grants

[25.19] Grants made to an individual under *Agriculture Act 1967, s 27* (grants for relinquishing occupation of uncommercial agricultural units) are not treated as part of the consideration obtained, or otherwise accruing, on the disposal before 6 April 2013 of any asset. [*TCGA 1992, s 249; FA 2012, Sch 39 para 49*].

See also 10.2(c) CAPITAL SUMS DERIVED FROM ASSETS.

Assets used for the purposes of a trade etc. taxed on the cash basis

[25.20] There is an exemption from capital gains tax for disposals of certain assets used for the purposes of a trade charged to income tax on the cash basis for small businesses. From 2017/18 onwards, the exemption also applies to disposals of certain assets used in an unincorporated property business charged to income tax on the cash basis. No chargeable gain arises where the disposal of an asset or an interest in an asset meets certain conditions, which changed with effect from 2017/18 as detailed below.

Disposals in 2017/18 and subsequent years

From 2017/18 onwards, the exemption applies to certain disposals whether the disposer is using the cash basis at the time of the disposal or has previously used the cash basis, provided the three conditions below are met.

- The asset is not land.
- The asset has been used at any time during the period of ownership by the person making the disposal for the purposes of a trade, profession, vocation, or property business.
- Disposal proceeds (as defined) are brought into account as a receipt (whether or not on the cash basis) when calculating the profits of the trading etc. business or property business (under *ITTOIA 2005 s 96A(3)* or *ITTOIA 2005, s 307E(12)* respectively) under, or after leaving, the cash basis.

Where an asset has been used partly for the purposes of the trade etc. and partly for other purposes or has been used for the purposes of the trade etc. for only part of the period of ownership, or where only part of the expenditure on the asset has qualified for capital allowances, an apportionment must be made. The disposal consideration and any acquisition or enhancement expenditure must be apportioned by reference to the extent that the expenditure qualified for capital allowances. Separate gains are then calculated using the apportioned parts of the consideration and expenditure, and the exemption applied accordingly.

Disposals prior to 2017/18

Prior to 2017/18, there are four conditions for the exemption as follows:

(a) the asset is tangible moveable property and a wasting asset (see 72 WASTING ASSETS);

(b) the asset is used by the person making the disposal for the purposes of a trade, profession or vocation;

(c) an election under *ITTOIA 2005, s 25A* (cash basis for small businesses) has effect at the time of disposal; and

(d) any expenditure on the acquisition or enhancement of the asset or interest has been brought into account in calculating the profits of the trade, profession or vocation or would have been so brought into account if the election in (c) above had been made at the time of the expenditure.

Similarly to the rules from 2017/18, where an asset has been used partly for the purposes of the trade etc. and partly for other purposes or has been used for the purposes of the trade etc. for only part of the period of ownership, an apportionment must be made. However, for years prior to 2017/18, the disposal consideration and any acquisition or enhancement expenditure must be apportioned by reference to the extent that the expenditure was, or would have been, brought into account in calculating the profits of the trade etc. As above, separate gains are then calculated using the apportioned parts of the consideration and expenditure, and the exemption applied accordingly.

Prior to 2017/18, the exemption only applies to a disposal made when a cash basis election is in force (condition (c) above). Where expenditure on the acquisition or enhancement of an asset, or an interest in an asset, was incurred at a time when a cash basis election had effect and has been brought into account in calculating the profits of the trade etc. the following apply if the asset or interest is disposed of at a time when the election no longer has effect.

(i) *TCGA 1992, s 39* (exclusion of expenditure by reference to tax on income — see **39.1** INTERACTION WITH OTHER TAXES) does not apply.

(ii) The restriction of losses by reference to capital allowances under *TCGA 1992, s 41* has effect as if the expenditure was not incurred under the cash basis scheme. Accordingly, the reference in *section 41* to 'qualifying expenditure' applies as if it included expenditure which would have been qualifying expenditure but for the election.

(iii) The exemptions for wasting assets under *TCGA 1992, s 45* (see **25.5** EXEMPTIONS AND RELIEFS) and for wasting assets qualifying for capital allowances under *TCGA 1992, s 47* (see **72.2** WASTING ASSETS) apply as if the election for cash basis had not been made. Accordingly, the references in those provisions to expenditure qualifying for capital allowances apply as if they included expenditure which would have been qualifying expenditure but for the election.

[*TCGA 1992, ss 47A, 47B; FA 2013, Sch 4 paras 45, 56; F(No 2)A 2017, Sch 2 paras 46, 47, 64(1)*].

See Tolley's Income Tax for detailed commentary on the cash basis for small businesses and for unincorporated property businesses.

Betting, lottery etc.

[25.21] Winnings from betting, including pool betting, or lotteries or games with prizes are not chargeable gains, and no chargeable gain or allowable loss accrues on the disposal of rights to such winnings obtained by participating. [*TCGA 1992, s 51(1)*].

Where prize winnings take the form of an asset, the recipient is regarded as having acquired the asset at its market value at the time of acquisition (HMRC Capital Gains Manual CG12602).

Business expansion scheme (BES)

[25.22] Any gain accruing to an individual, to whom BES income tax relief has been given, on the disposal of eligible shares **issued after 18 March 1986** and before 1 January 1994 (when the scheme was abolished) is exempt from CGT provided the income tax relief has not been withdrawn. Similarly, any loss is not allowable. [*TCGA 1992, s 150(2)*].

If the BES shares have been disposed of to a spouse and the inter-spouse exemption applies under *TCGA 1992, s 58*, the BES exemption for capital gains will still apply to disposals by the recipient spouse to third parties (see **46.5** MARRIED PERSONS AND CIVIL PARTNERS).

Only a complete withdrawal of relief, and not a partial one, will affect the CGT position, i.e. exemption for a gain, no allowance for a loss (Tolley's Practical Tax Newsletter 1987, p 115). If relief is withdrawn completely, any allowable loss which results on a disposal of the shares may be eligible for relief under *ICTA 1988, s 574* — CGT loss accruing to individual in respect of unquoted shares in a trading company converted to an income tax loss — see **44.15** LOSSES.

Further rules dealing with identification and other matters apply as follows.

(a) The normal share identification rules (see **64** SHARES AND SECURITIES — IDENTIFICATION RULES) do not apply to BES shares. Each acquisition is treated as a separate acquisition and shares are matched on a first in/first out (FIFO) basis. Where a disposal is so matched with shares acquired on the same day as one another, only some of which still have BES income tax relief attributable to them, it is first matched with shares in respect of which no such relief is still attributable. For these purposes and that in (d) below shares are only treated as being of the same class if they would be so treated if dealt with on the Stock Exchange and the grant of an option the exercise of which would bind the grantor to sell shares is treated as a disposal of those shares.

(b) If there is a reorganisation within the meaning of *TCGA 1992, s 126* then the new ordinary shares will stand in the place of the old ordinary shares and each is treated as a new holding.

(c) If, as part of a reconstruction, shares or debentures in another company are issued to a BES shareholder in exchange for the BES shares, then, unless the income tax relief is withdrawn, the shares in the new company are not generally deemed to stand in the place of shares in the old company under *TCGA 1992, s 135* or *s 136* (see **63.5**, **63.7** SHARES AND SECURITIES) and there is thus a disposal of the shares in the old company. However, *s 135* or *136* does apply in the normal way if:
   - the new holding consists of new ordinary shares issued after 28 November 1994 and more than five years after the issue of the original shares and carrying no present or future preferential rights to dividends or assets or right to redemption (no preferential right to redemption where the new shares were issued before 6 April 1998); and
   - the company issuing the new shares has previously issued shares under the BES and has issued the appropriate certificate enabling investors to obtain relief on that earlier issue.

   In addition, *TCGA 1992, s 135* is not disapplied in a case to which *ICTA 1988, s 304A* (inserted by *FA 1998, Sch 13 para 41*) applies. That provision enables a BES company to become, after 5 April 1998, a wholly-owned subsidiary of a new holding company in certain circumstances. The investors receive shares in the new company in exchange for their original shares, and the new shares then stand in the shoes of the old for the purposes of BES income tax relief. This treatment is generally applied for CGT purposes also.

(d) Where an original holding has been subject to the relief, a disposal of the whole or part of a new holding, allotted other than for payment as a result of a reorganisation within *TCGA 1992, s 126(2)(a)* after 18 March 1986 (allotments in respect of, and in proportion to, existing holdings or of any class of shares, e.g. a bonus issue within **63.2** SHARES AND SECURITIES above), will be treated, for the purposes of deciding whether relief given is to be withdrawn, as a disposal of the whole or a corresponding part of the original holding with which, by reason of *TCGA 1992, s 127*, the new holding is identified. Any reallocated shares under *s 127* will be deemed to stand in the place of the original shares.

(e) The general share reorganisation provisions of *TCGA 1992, ss 127–130* (see **63.2–63.4** SHARES AND SECURITIES above) do not apply after 18 March 1986 to ordinary shares in respect of which relief has been given if:
  (i) there is, by virtue of an allotment for payment within *TCGA 1992, s 126(2)(a)* (see also (d) above), a reorganisation affecting those shares; and
  (ii) immediately following the reorganisation, the relief has not been withdrawn in respect of those shares or relief has been given in respect of the allotted shares and not withdrawn.

  On such reorganisations occurring before 29 November 1994 where immediately before it the relief has not been withdrawn, and where both the amount of relief (or the amount remaining where it has been reduced) and the market value of the shares immediately before the reorganisation exceed their market value immediately after the reorganisation, the relief is reduced by an amount equal to whichever is the smaller of those excesses. This reduction also applies *mutatis mutandis* where the individual sells his rights instead of taking up his allotment. Where the relief is so reduced an amount equal to the reduction is treated as additional expenditure for CGT purposes on a disposal of the allotted shares or debentures and such expenditure is apportioned between the allotted shares etc. in a just and reasonable manner. Where a disposal of the original holding of ordinary shares is not ultimately exempt (e.g. because all relief has been withdrawn), the allowable expenditure relating to such shares is reduced by an amount equal to the above reduction and is again apportioned in a just and reasonable manner.

In computing gains or losses arising on an individual's disposal of shares **issued before 19 March 1986** in respect of which BES relief has been given and not withdrawn, that relief is disregarded *except* to the extent that an unindexed loss would otherwise accrue, in which case the deductible expenditure is reduced by the smaller of the BES relief given (and not withdrawn) and the amount of the loss. [*TCGA 1992, s 150(3)*]. It was held in *Quinn v Cooper* Ch D 1998, 71 TC 44 that indexation allowance should be based on the reduced cost. *Section 150(3)* does not apply to disposals within *TCGA 1992, s 58(1)* (see **46.5** MARRIED PERSONS AND CIVIL PARTNERS) but will apply on a subsequent disposal to a third party by the transferee. In determining whether any sums are excluded under *TCGA 1992, s 39(1)(2)* (exclusion of expenditure allowable against income — see **16.13** COMPUTATION OF GAINS AND LOSSES), the existence of any relief given and not withdrawn is ignored.

The provisions in (a) (except in relation to a grant of an option etc.) and (b) above also apply to shares issued before 19 March 1986 as do those in (d) in respect of reorganisations before that date. The provisions in (c) do not apply to shares issued before 19 March 1986 and those in (e) do not apply to reorganisations before that date. (*Note.* A Revenue Press Release of 19 December 1989 announced that an unintended change in the law had been made by *ICTA 1988* so as to apply the provisions in (c) above to shares issued before 19 March 1986 where a reconstruction involving an exchange or cancellation of shares occurs after 5 April 1988 with the result that the exchange or cancellation would give rise to a disposal. *FA 1990* restored the position for exchanges etc. occurring after 5 April 1988 save that in respect of an exchange before 1 January 1990 the shareholder could irrevocably elect to have the exchange treated as a disposal by giving written notice at any time before 6 April 1991.)

Where an allowable loss still arose after the above reduction in consideration, the loss may have been eligible for relief under *ICTA 1988, s 574* (CGT loss accruing to individual in respect of unquoted shares in a trading company converted to an income tax loss — see **44.15** LOSSES).

[*TCGA 1992, ss 39(3), 150; ICTA 1988, ss 289, 299, 305*].

It should be noted that 'relief' refers to the deduction falling to be made from a person's income and not to any amount of income tax which is not chargeable due to such a deduction.

For consideration of the determination of the time shares are issued under the scheme, see *National Westminster Bank plc v CIR; Barclays Bank plc v CIR* HL 1994, 67 TC 1.

Cashbacks

[25.23] A cashback is a lump sum received by a customer as an inducement for entering into a transaction for the purchase of goods, investments or services and received as a direct consequence of having entered into that transaction. An example of such a transaction is the taking out of a mortgage. The payer may be either the provider of the goods etc. or an interested third party. The term 'cashback' does not include a cash payment by a building society to its members on a takeover or conversion (for which see **63.27** SHARES AND SECURITIES), or by other mutual organisations such as insurance companies or friendly societies to their policy holders on demutualisation.

A cashback does not derive from a chargeable asset for CGT purposes. No chargeable gain therefore arises on its receipt. (An ordinary retail customer purchasing goods etc. at arm's length will not be liable to income tax on a cashback either.)

(HMRC Statement of Practice 4/97).

Child Trust Funds

[25.24] The Child Trust Fund scheme is a government assisted savings scheme for any child born after 31 August 2002 and before 3 January 2011 where, broadly, there is an entitlement to child benefit (an '*eligible child*'). The scheme provides for HMRC to make an initial contribution in the form of a voucher (initially worth £250, or £500 for children in lower income families), which is then used to open an account. Anyone, including the child, may then pay money into the account up to a yearly limit of £4,128 (£4,080 before 6 April 2017; £4,000 before 6 April 2015; £3,840 before 1 July 2014; £3,600 before 6 April 2014 and £1,200 before 1 November 2011). For children born before 3 August 2010 HMRC make a further contribution when the child reaches the age of seven. For 2010/11 a further government contribution was made to the accounts of disabled children. Government contributions of all kinds have, however, been phased out. For children born in the period 4 August 2010 to 2 January 2011 the initial contribution was £50 or £100. Disabled contributions ceased for 2011/12 onwards. Children born from 3 January 2011 onwards do not qualify for a child trust fund. Existing funds, however, continue to maturity and non-government contributions continue to be permitted. With effect from 6 April 2015 it is possible to transfer a child trust fund to a junior ISA.

The account provider, acting on the instructions of a nominated responsible person (the '*registered contact*'), or the child if over 16, invests the funds in a limited range of qualifying investments. Normally no withdrawals are permitted before the fund matures when the child reaches 18. For further details see Tolley's Income Tax.

Tax treatment

No tax is chargeable in respect of interest, dividends, distributions, gains, alternative financial arrangement return or building society bonus on account investments. Capital losses on account investments are disregarded. Any income from account investments is not to be regarded as income for any income tax purposes. For capital gains tax purposes, any assets held as account investments are regarded as held by the child concerned in a separate capacity from that in which he holds any other assets of the same description. The child is treated as having sold all the account investments, and as having reacquired them in his personal capacity, for their market value immediately before attaining the age of 18.

It is up to the account provider to make tax claims, conduct appeals, and agree liabilities and reliefs on behalf of the child or registered contact. It is unlikely therefore that the child or registered contact will have to deal with any tax matters arising from the account. However, there is power for HMRC to make an assessment as an alternative to the account provider in order to withdraw relief or recover tax.

[*Child Trust Funds Act 2004, s 13; SI 2004 No 1450, Regs 24–38; SI 2005 No 3349; SI 2006 No 3195; SI 2010 No 1894; SI 2011 No 2447; SI 2012 No 1870; SI 2013 No 1744; SI 2014 Nos 649, 1453; SI 2015 Nos 876, 1371; SI 2017 No 185*].

Damages and compensation

[25.25] Sums received by way of compensation or damages for any wrong or injury suffered by an individual 'in his person' or in his profession or vocation are not chargeable gains. [*TCGA 1992, s 51(2)*].

The words 'in his person' are distinct from 'in his finances', but are construed widely (see HMRC Capital Gains Manual CG13030). The exemption given in relation to vocation is extended by concession to an individual's trade or employment. See HMRC Extra-Statutory Concession D33 (referred to at **7.2** ASSETS). If the compensation relates to an asset (e.g. insurance recoveries), payment does constitute a disposal; see **10** CAPITAL SUMS DERIVED FROM ASSETS.

Equitable Life payments

Payments authorised by the Treasury in respect of persons adversely affected by maladministration in the regulation before December 2001 of the Equitable Life Assurance Society are disregarded for capital gains tax purposes (and also for the purposes of income tax, corporation tax and inheritance tax). [*SI 2011 No 1502*]. See also HMRC Brief 26/2011, 27 July 2011.

Enterprise investment scheme (EIS)

[25.26] Any gain arising on a disposal of shares more than, broadly, three years after the issue of them, where an amount of EIS income tax relief is attributable to them, is wholly or partly exempt. If a loss would otherwise arise on a disposal of shares where an amount of such relief is attributable to them, a reduction is made in the amount of allowable expenditure equal to the amount of relief. See **23** ENTERPRISE INVESTMENT SCHEME.

Compensation from foreign governments

[25.27] Gains on sums received by individuals from foreign governments by way of compensation for assets confiscated, destroyed or expropriated are exempt provided certain conditions are met. See **10.2** CAPITAL SUMS DERIVED FROM ASSETS.

Exempt amount for the year

[25.28] A specified amount of the taxable amount of gains for a year of assessment is exempt. See **2.6** ANNUAL RATES AND EXEMPTIONS.

Gains arising partly before 6.4.1965 or 31.3.1982

[25.29] Assets held on, and gains arising partly before, these dates are subject to special provisions. See **8** ASSETS HELD ON 6 APRIL 1965 and **9** ASSETS HELD ON 31 MARCH 1982.

Individual Savings Accounts (ISAs)

[25.30] ISAs are available to individuals over 18 (though see below) who are resident in the UK. The accounts can be made up of cash, stocks and shares and, after 5 April 2016, innovative finance (i.e., broadly, peer-to-peer loans made through a regulated peer-to-peer lending platform). For 2017/18, investors can subscribe up to £20,000 to an ISA in the tax year. For 2015/16 and 2016/17, the annual limit is £15,240. For 2014/15, the annual limit is £15,000 (but note that, before 1 July 2014, the annual limit was £11,880 of which a maximum of £5,940 could be saved in cash with one provider). For 2013/14 the overall limit is £11,520 and the cash limit is £5,760; and for 2012/13 the limits are £11,289 and £5,640. See further details below. Cash ISAs can be opened by 16 and 17-year olds. There is no statutory lock-in, minimum subscription, minimum holding period or lifetime subscription limit. Withdrawals may be made at any time without loss of tax relief but not so as to allow further subscriptions in breach of the annual maximum.

Where an ISA investor dies on or after 3 December 2014, their surviving spouse or civil partner is given an additional ISA allowance equivalent to the value of the deceased spouse or partner's ISAs (other than junior ISAs). The deceased and the spouse or civil partner must have been living together at the time of death. The surviving spouse or civil partner can reinvest non-cash assets inherited by them which were included in the deceased's ISA. Non-cash assets must be reinvested within the period beginning with the distribution of the assets to the surviving spouse or civil partner or, if later, 6 April 2015 and ending 180 days later. Cash must be invested in the period beginning with the date of death or 6 April 2015 if later and ending three years later or, if later, 180 days after the administration of the estate is complete. With effect from 15 September 2016, the Treasury may make regulations to allow ISA-status for investments made before death to continue during the post-death administration period.

For 2016/17 onwards, the terms and conditions of an account may allow an investor to replace cash withdrawn from an ISA earlier in the year without the replacement counting towards the annual subscription limit for that year.

From 1 December 2015, the Government has introduced Help to Buy ISAs under which a bonus will be paid at the time savings are used to purchase a home. Lifetime ISAs have been introduced from 6 April 2017 for adults under the age of 40 under which a bonus will be paid at the time savings are used to purchase a home or on withdrawal of funds after age 60. Only one bonus from a Help to Buy or Lifetime ISA can be used to purchase a home.

Interest and dividends are free of income tax. With effect from 1 February 2016, where an amount is withdrawn from a Help to Buy ISA on the closure of that account, an equivalent amount may be invested in an ISA within 12 months without counting towards the annual limit if the house purchase falls through.

Gains arising from assets held within an ISA are not chargeable gains for CGT purposes (and losses are not allowable).

With effect from 1 November 2011 a 'junior ISA' is available for children who did not qualify for a child trust fund (see **25.24** above). Subscriptions of up to £4,128 (£4,080 before 6 April 2017; £3,840 before 1 July 2014; £3,720 before 6 April 2014; £3,600 before 6 April 2013) can be made in each tax year and can be saved in cash or stocks and shares. The funds are locked in until the child reaches adulthood. With effect from 6 April 2015, child trust funds can be transferred to junior ISAs without using up any of the annual limit for the year of transfer.

[*TCGA 1992, s 151; ITTOIA 2005, ss 694–701; FA 2011, s 40; FA 2016, s 27*].

The Individual Savings Account Regulations 1998 (*SI 1998 No 1870* as amended) provide for the setting up of ISAs by HMRC-approved accounts managers, for the conditions under which they may invest and under which the accounts are to operate, for relief from tax in respect of account investments, and for general administration. The regulations are summarised below.

Eligibility

An application to subscribe to an ISA may be made by an individual who is 18 or over (though see below as regards junior ISAs) and who is resident in the UK (or who is a non-UK resident Crown employee with general earnings subject to UK tax within *ITEPA 2003, s 28* or who is married to, or a civil partner of, such an employee). Joint accounts are not permitted. An investor who subsequently fails to meet the residence requirement may retain the account and the right to the accompanying tax exemptions but can make no further subscriptions to the account until he again comes to meet that requirement. An application made on behalf of an individual suffering from mental disorder, by a parent, guardian, spouse, civil partner, son or daughter of his, is treated as if made by that individual.

Rules for accounts

An individual can subscribe to one or more of a single cash account, a single stocks and shares account and, for 2016/17 onwards, a single innovative finance account in each tax year. Before 1 July 2014, only an amount up to the cash limit could be saved in the cash account. The remainder of the allowance could be invested in the stocks and shares account with the same or another accounts manager. A cash account consists of a single cash component, a stocks and shares account consists of a single stocks and shares component and an innovative finance account consists of a single innovative finance component. For details of investments qualifying for inclusion in each component, see Tolley's Income Tax. See above for the subscription limits.

A PEP in existence immediately before 6 April 2008 is treated on and after that date as a stocks and shares account.

Subscriptions

Subscriptions to an ISA must be made in cash (and must be allocated irrevocably to the agreed component or single component) except that:

(a) shares acquired by the investor under a savings-related (SAYE) share option scheme (see **22.24** EMPLOYEE SHARE SCHEMES); or
(b) plan shares (but not securities or other rights) of a tax-advantaged share incentive plan (see **22.17** EMPLOYEE SHARE SCHEMES) which have ceased to be subject to the plan but remain in his beneficial ownership,

may be transferred to a stocks and shares component. See above for the reinvestment of non-cash assets to an ISA following the death of a spouse or civil partner. Transfers within (a) or (b) above count towards the annual subscription limits, by reference to the market value of the shares at the date of transfer. No chargeable gain or allowable loss arises on the transfer. A transfer of SAYE scheme shares must be made within 90 days after the exercise of the option. A transfer of share incentive plan shares must be made within 90 days after the shares ceased to be subject to the plan. In all cases, 'shares' includes a reference to shares held in the form of depositary interests.

With effect from 8 August 2012, certain subscriptions do not count towards the annual investment limits where they are made within 180 days of a default or failure in relation to an exiting ISA.

Investments

ISA investments cannot be purchased otherwise than out of cash held by the account manager and allocated to the particular component concerned, and cannot be purchased from the investor or his spouse or civil partner.

The title to ISA investments (other than cash deposits, national savings products and certain insurance policies) is vested in the account manager (or his nominee) either alone or jointly with the investor, though all ISA investments are in the beneficial ownership of the investor. The investor may elect to receive annual reports and accounts etc. in respect of ISA investments and/or to attend and vote at shareholders' etc. meetings.

Applications to subscribe to an ISA

The statements and declarations to be made when applying to subscribe to an ISA are specified. The maximum penalty for an incorrect statement or declaration is the amount (if any) of income tax and/or capital gains tax underpaid as a result. Assessments to withdraw tax relief or otherwise recover tax underpaid may be made on the account manager or investor. HMRC have power to require information from, and to inspect records of, account managers and investors.

Withdrawal of funds and transfer of accounts

The terms and conditions of an ISA cannot prevent the investor from withdrawing funds or from transferring his account (or a part of it) to another HMRC-approved account manager (subject to the conditions governing such transfers). For 2008/09 onwards, it is possible to transfer both current year subscriptions and previous year subscriptions to a cash account into a stocks and shares account. Current year subscriptions so transferred do not then count towards the cash subscription limit for the year. Investors in Northern Rock ISAs who withdrew their funds in the period 13 to 19 September 2007 were able to reinvest those funds in another ISA either with Northern Rock or another provider before 6 April 2008 without the reinvestment counting towards the annual maximum subscription.

For 2016/17 onwards, an investor may replace cash withdrawn from an ISA earlier in the year without the replacement counting towards the annual subscription limit for that year. Such a replacement may be by way of shares within (a) or (b) above. If the withdrawn cash was initially invested in the same year, the replacement subscription may be made into any account. Otherwise the replacement subscription must be made into the account from which the withdrawal was made. For this purpose, any withdrawal in a tax year is deemed to be made first out of a subscription made in that year and any replacement subscription is deemed to be a replacement first of any withdrawal made out of a previous year's subscription. Replacement subscriptions can only be made into accounts if the terms and conditions allow for them.

With effect from 1 February 2016, where an amount is withdrawn from a Help to Buy ISA on the closure of that account, an equivalent amount may be invested in an ISA within 12 months without counting towards the annual limit if the house purchase falls through.

Help to Buy ISAs

Help to Buy ISAs are available from 1 December 2015. The scheme is intended to help first-time property buyers (for residential purposes, not buy-to-let) by adding a government bonus to savings at the point of purchase of a property costing up to £250,000 (£450,000 for London properties). The bonus is equal to 25% of the savings, including interest added, subject to a maximum of £3,000 and a minimum of £400. The bonus must be claimed by the conveyancers acting on behalf of the saver in connection with the property purchase. There is also a maximum amount of savings per month of £200, although up to £1,000 may be deposited on opening the account. An account may be opened before 1 December 2019 but can remain open indefinitely. Bonuses cannot be claimed after 1 December 2030 (or earlier date notified by the Treasury). An individual may only have one Help to Buy ISA in the lifetime of the scheme.

Help to Buy ISAs are subject to their own conditions, for which see www.helptobuy.gov.uk/documents/2015/12/scheme-rules.pdf, but are otherwise subject to the normal ISA rules.

Lifetime ISAs

Lifetime ISAs are available from 6 April 2017. Accounts can be opened by individuals aged 18 or over but under 40 who are either resident in the UK or a Crown Servant. The maximum annual investment is £4,000 and investments can be made until the individual reaches 50. A government bonus of 25% of the amount invested (maximum £1,000) is added each tax year. Amounts invested in a Lifetime ISA count towards the investor's overall annual investment limit. Lifetime ISAs can hold cash, qualifying stocks and shares or a combination of both.

With effect from 6 April 2018, investors withdrawing amounts from a Lifetime ISA are liable to a 25% withdrawal charge. The charge does not apply if the investor is aged 60 or over, if the funds are used towards the purchase of a first home (value up to £450,000) or if the investor is terminally ill with less than 12 months to live. The account ends on death, with no withdrawal charge applying. Funds in a Lifetime ISA can only be used to purchase a first home if the account has been open for at least 12 months.

Holders of a Help to Buy ISA can transfer the savings into a Lifetime ISA in 2017/18 (without any amount saved before 6 April 2017 counting towards the annual limit) or can continue to save into both. Only the government bonus from one of the accounts can be used in buying a first home.

Junior ISAs and children under 18

16 and 17-year olds who otherwise satisfy the general conditions above may subscribe to a cash account.

In addition, with effect from 1 November 2011, 'junior ISAs' can be opened on behalf of eligible children. The child must either have been born on or after 3 January 2011 or, if born before that date, must not have been eligible for a child trust fund (see **25.24** above) and must be resident in the UK (or be a non-UK resident Crown employee with general earnings subject to UK tax within *ITEPA 2003, s 28* or be married to, a civil partner of, or a dependant of, such an employee). An eligible child may hold only one cash account and one stocks and shares account (although provision is made for the transfer of accounts to a different account manager). An application for a junior ISA must normally be made by the person who has parental responsibility for the child but children over the age of 16 may apply on their own behalf. See above for the annual limit for subscriptions. No withdrawals can be made except where the child is terminally ill or dies. The child is treated as the beneficial owner of the funds in the junior ISA. When the child reaches the age of 18 the junior ISA ceases to be a junior ISA so that the normal ISA rules apply. Subscriptions and withdrawals can then be made accordingly.

Tax exemptions

Except as stated below, no income tax or capital gains tax is chargeable on the account manager or the investor in respect of interest, dividends, distributions, gains, alternative financial arrangement return or building society bonus on ISA investments. Capital losses are not allowable.

Before 1 July 2014, interest on a cash deposit held within a stocks and shares component was, however, taxable at the basic rate of income tax, such tax to be accounted for by the account manager (by set-off against tax repayments or otherwise). There was no further liability; the interest did not form part of the investor's total income and the tax paid could not be repaid to the investor.

As regards ISAs, other than junior ISAs, held by children under 18 (see above), the exemption for interest on a cash account does not prevent the application of the settlements legislation of *ITTOIA 2005, s 629* (see Tolley's Income Tax under Settlements) whereby (subject to a *de minimis* limit) the income of an unmarried minor on capital provided by a parent is taxable as if it were the parent's income. Such income arising in an ISA is therefore taxable. The Government has indicated that this rule does not apply to junior ISAs.

Exempt income and gains do not have to be reported in the investor's personal tax return.

Further capital gains matters

A transfer of ISA investments by an account manager to an investor is deemed to be made at market value, with no capital gain or allowable loss arising. An investor is treated as holding shares or securities in an ISA in a capacity other than that in which he holds any other shares etc. of the same class in the same company, so that share identification rules (see **64.1** SHARES AND SECURITIES — IDENTIFICATION RULES) are applied separately to ISA investments (and separately as between different ISAs held by the same investor). The normal share reorganisation rules are disapplied in respect of ISA investments in the event of a reorganisation of share capital involving an allotment for payment, e.g. a rights issue. Shares transferred to an ISA in the limited circumstances described above are deemed for these purposes to have been ISA investments from,

- in the case of SAYE option scheme shares, their acquisition by the investor; or
- in the case of share incentive plan shares, the date when they ceased to be subject to the plan.

Where the investor held shares eligible for transfer to an ISA and other shares of the same class but not so eligible, disposals are generally identified primarily with the latter, thus preserving to the greatest possible extent the eligibility of the remaining shares.

Repairing of invalid accounts

There are provisions for the 'repairing' of certain incompatible accounts and excess subscriptions to prevent loss of ISA status and tax exemptions.

Account managers

The regulations cover qualification as an account manager, HMRC approval and withdrawal thereof, appointment of UK tax representatives of non-UK account managers, account managers ceasing to act or to qualify, claims for tax relief and agreement of liabilities, annual returns of income and of information, annual and interim tax repayment claims, record-keeping, and information to be provided to investors.

[*Savings (Government Contributions) Act 2017, ss 1, 3, Sch 1; SI 1998 Nos 1870, 3174; SI 2006 No 3194; SI 2007 No 2119; SI 2008 Nos 704, 1934; SI 2009 No 1550; SI 2010 No 2957; SI 2011 No 1780; SI 2012 No 1871; SI 2014 Nos 654, 1450; SI 2015 Nos 869, 941, 1370; SI 2016 Nos 16, 364; SI 2017 No 186*].

Separate regulations modify existing tax legislation so far as it concerns individual savings account business of insurance companies. [*SI 1998 No 1871 as amended*].

Closure and death

Subject to the ISA terms and conditions, an investor may close an ISA at any time without affecting tax exemptions up to the date of closure. Where an investor dies, income and gains in respect of ISA investments which arise after the date of death but before the date of closure are not exempt.

Legatees

[25.31] No chargeable gain accrues to the personal representatives where a person acquires an asset from them as legatee, and the legatee is treated as if the personal representatives' acquisition of the asset had been his acquisition of it. See **19.14** DEATH.

Personal Equity Plans (PEPs)

[25.32] Before 6 April 1999, an individual could make, subject to conditions, investments under a plan and obtain exemption from capital gains tax (as well as income tax) in respect of transactions covered by the plan. No further subscriptions to PEPs could be made after 5 April 1999, but existing PEPs could continue, and independently of individual savings accounts (see **25.30** above) until 5 April 2008. With effect from 6 April 2008, continuing PEPs are brought within the ISA rules.

Recovery of assets under Proceeds of Crime Act 2002, Pt 5

[25.33] *Proceeds of Crime Act 2002, Pt 5 Ch 2* provides for the recovery, in civil proceedings before the High Court (or, in Scotland, the Court of Session), of property which is, or represents, property obtained through 'unlawful conduct' (as defined in the Act). If the Court is satisfied that any property is recoverable under the provisions, it will make a '*recovery order*', vesting the property in an appointed trustee for civil recovery. Alternatively, the Court may make an order under *s 276* of the Act staying (or, in Scotland, sisting) proceedings on terms agreed by the parties. [*Proceeds of Crime Act 2002, ss 240(1), 266(1)(2), 276, 316(1)*].

A gain which is attributable to the vesting of property in a trustee for civil recovery or any other person either under a recovery order or in pursuance of an order under *s 276* (a '*Pt 5 transfer*'), and which accrues to the person who held the property immediately before the transfer (the '*transferor*'), is not a chargeable gain, unless a 'compensating payment' is made to the transferor. In the latter event, the amount of the compensating payment is treated as the consideration for the transfer of the property. Where property belonged, immediately before the *Pt 5* transfer, to joint tenants, and a compensating payment is made to one or more (but not all) of them, these provisions apply separately to each joint tenant.

A '*compensating payment*' for these purposes is any amount paid in respect of a *Pt 5* transfer by the trustee for civil recovery or another to a person who held the property in question immediately before the transfer. If a recovery order, or the terms on which an order under *s 276* is made, provides for the creation of any interest in favour of such a person, that person is treated as receiving (in addition to any actual compensating payment) a compensating payment equal to the value of the interest.

[*Proceeds of Crime Act 2002, s 448, Sch 10 paras 2(1)(3)–(5), 3(1)(2)*].

Proceeds of Crime Act 2002, s 298 provides for the forfeiture of 'cash' (which term includes coins and notes in any currency, postal orders, cheques of any kind (including travellers' cheques), bankers' drafts, bearer bonds and bearer shares) in summary proceedings before a magistrates' court (or, in Scotland, the sheriff). A gain attributable to such a forfeiture is not a chargeable gain if it accrues to the person who held the property immediately before the forfeiture and is attributable to property consisting of notes or coins in any currency other than sterling, of postal orders, cheques or bankers' drafts if expressed in any currency other than sterling or of bearer bonds or bearer shares. [*Proceeds of Crime Act 2002, s 289(6), Sch 10 para 3(3)*].

Seed enterprise investment scheme (SEIS)

[25.34] Any gain arising on a disposal of shares more than, broadly, three years after the issue of them, where an amount of SEIS income tax relief is attributable to them, is wholly or partly exempt. If a loss would otherwise arise on a disposal of shares where an amount of such relief is attributable to them, a reduction is made in the amount of allowable expenditure equal to the amount of relief. See 60 SEED ENTERPRISE INVESTMENT SCHEME.

Settled property

[25.35] No charge to capital gains tax arises:

(a) where a person disposes of an interest in settled property provided the interest either was created for his benefit or was not acquired for money or money's worth (see **62.15** SETTLEMENTS); or
(b) when a person becomes absolutely entitled to settled property on the termination of a life interest by the death of the person entitled to it (see **62.16** and **62.18** SETTLEMENTS); or
(c) on the termination, on the death of the person entitled to it, of a life interest in possession in settled property where the property does not cease at that time to be settled property (see **62.17** SETTLEMENTS).

Social investment relief

[25.36] Any gain arising on a disposal of an asset more than three years after its acquisition, where an amount of income tax social investment relief is attributable to it, is wholly or partly exempt. If a loss would otherwise arise on a disposal of an asset where an amount of such relief is attributable to it, a reduction is made in the amount of allowable expenditure equal to the amount of relief. See 65 SOCIAL INVESTMENT RELIEF.

Special reserve funds of individual Lloyd's underwriters

[25.37] Disposals of assets held in an individual underwriter's special reserve fund set up in respect of the 1992 or a subsequent underwriting year of account are exempt. See **69.2** UNDERWRITERS AT LLOYD'S.

Substantial shareholdings of companies

[25.38] A gain on a disposal by a company of shares is exempt (and a loss is not allowable) where, throughout a continuous twelve-month period beginning not more than six years before the disposal (not more than two years before the disposals, for disposals prior to 1 April 2017), the company held a 'substantial shareholding' (broadly, at least a 10% interest) in the company whose shares are the subject of the disposal. The exemption extends to assets 'related to shares' (as defined). The investee company must be a trading company or the holding company of a trading group (or subgroup). For disposals prior to 1 April 2017, the investing company must be a trading company or a member of a trading group. A form of the exemption, with amended conditions, is available where the investee company is not a trading company but the investing company is owned by qualifying institutional investors. See **66** SUBSTANTIAL SHAREHOLDINGS OF COMPANIES.

Venture capital trusts

[25.39] In respect of shares issued after 5 April 1995, any gain arising on a disposal of them where an amount of income tax relief is attributable to them is wholly or partly exempt. A loss arising on a disposal of shares is not an allowable loss, except to the extent that a gain on the disposal would have been a chargeable gain. See **71.11** VENTURE CAPITAL TRUSTS.

Woodlands

[25.40] Where woodlands are managed by the occupier on a commercial basis and with a view to the realisation of profits:

(a) any consideration for the disposal of trees (whether standing, felled or cut thereon) and saleable underwood; and
(b) any capital sum received under an insurance policy in respect of the destruction of, or damage or injury to, trees or saleable underwood by fire or other hazard thereon,

is excluded from any capital gains tax computation on the disposal if the person making the disposal is the occupier.

In *any* capital gains tax computation on the sale of woodlands in the UK, there is excluded so much of the cost of the woodlands and/or consideration for the disposal as is attributable to trees, including saleable underwood, growing on the land. [*TCGA 1992, s 250*].

The cultivation of 'short rotation coppice' is regarded as farming for capital gains purposes and not as forestry, and any land on which such activity takes place is regarded as farm land or agricultural land, as the case may be, and not as woodlands. '*Short rotation coppice*' means a perennial crop of tree species at high density, the stems of which are harvested above ground level at intervals of less than ten years. [*FA 1995, s 154*].

HMRC regard the initial cultivation of the land including any spraying, ploughing, fencing and planting of the cuttings as capital costs against which any Woodland Grants received should be matched. The stools from planting form part of the land and as such will be allowable for capital gains purposes. The cost of the stools will not be allowable for capital gains if they are grubbed up before the land is sold. Revenue Tax Bulletin October 1995 p 253.

Works of art etc.

[25.41] A gain is not a chargeable gain if it accrues on the disposal of property which has been (or could be) designated by HMRC under *IHTA 1984, s 31* where the disposal is:

(a) by way of sale by private treaty to a body mentioned in *IHTA 1984, Sch 3* (see **11.7** CHARITIES); or

(b) to such a body as in (a) above otherwise than by sale; or
(c) to HMRC in satisfaction of the payment of inheritance tax or capital transfer tax.

[*TCGA 1992, s 258(2); SI 2009 No 730, Art 12*].

For disposals before 6 April 2009, the above provision strictly applied only to an asset with respect to which an undertaking within **25.85** below had been given. By concession, however, the relief was in effect extended to apply as above. See **25.85**(a)–(e) below for types of national heritage property which may be sold by private treaty within (a) above. See also **36.10** HOLD-OVER RELIEFS for relief for gifts of works of art etc.

The standard of objects which can be accepted under (c) above is very much higher. They have to satisfy a test of 'pre-eminence' either in the context of a national, local authority, or university collection, or through association with a particular building.

Exempt organisations and individuals

[25.42] The organisations and individuals detailed in **25.65** below are completely exempt from capital gains tax except where otherwise indicated.

Asbestos compensation settlements

[25.43] A gain on the disposal by the trustees of an 'asbestos compensation settlement' of any property comprised in the settlement is not a chargeable gain. Although enacted in 2010, this provision is treated as having come into force on 6 April 2006.

An '*asbestos compensation settlement*' is a settlement made before 24 March 2010 under certain insolvency arrangements where the sole or main purpose of the settlement is to make compensation payments to individuals suffering from an asbestos-related condition (or who suffered from such a condition before their death). The insolvency arrangements concerned are voluntary arrangements under *Insolvency Act 1986, Pt 1*, compromises or arrangements under *Companies Act 1985, s 425* or *Companies Act 2006, Pt 26*, or equivalent arrangements in Northern Ireland or under the law of a territory outside the UK.

[*TCGA 1992, s 271(1)(ea)(1ZA)(1ZB)*].

Bare trustees and nominees

[25.44] Where property is held by bare trustees or nominees for another person, capital gains tax is chargeable as if the property were held by that other person. Consequently, there is no liability where the property is transferred from the bare trustees etc. to that other person. [*TCGA 1992, s 60*]. See further **62.3** SETTLEMENTS.

British and Natural History Museums

[25.45] The British Museum and the Natural History Museum are entitled, on a claim, to exemption from tax on chargeable gains. [*TCGA 1992, s 271(6)(a)*].

Central banks

[25.46] Non-resident central banks as specified by Order in Council and the issue departments of the Reserve Bank of India and the State Bank of Pakistan are exempt from tax on chargeable gains. [*TCGA 1992, s 271(7A)–(8)*].

Charities

[25.47] Subject to restrictions, a gain is not a chargeable gain if it accrues to a charity and is applicable and applied for charitable purposes. See **11.3–11.5** CHARITIES.

Community amateur sports clubs

[25.48] On a claim, and subject to restrictions, a gain is not a chargeable gain if it accrues to a registered community amateur sports club and is wholly applied for qualifying purposes. See **11.12** CHARITIES.

The Crown

[25.49] The Crown is not liable to tax unless statute otherwise provides; see *Bank voor Handel v Administrator of Hungarian Property* HL 1954, 35 TC 311 and *Boarland v Madras Electric Supply Corporation* HL 1955, 35 TC 612. In addition, gains arising on the disposal of stock belonging to the Crown, or in the name of the Treasury or National Debt Commissioners under statutory schemes under which transfers are made in accounts at the Bank of England, are not chargeable gains. [*TCGA 1992, s 271(1)(a)*]. Property held under trusts contained in *Chevening Estate Act 1959* is exempt from capital gains tax. [*TCGA 1992, s 270*].

Diplomatic agents

[25.50] Diplomatic agents (i.e. heads of mission or members of the diplomatic staff) of foreign states are exempt from capital gains tax except on gains arising from private investments or immovable property in the UK. [*Diplomatic Privileges Act 1964*].

Similar exemption is given to official agents of Commonwealth countries or the Republic of Ireland. Consular officers and their personal staffs are exempt from gains arising out of disposals of assets which are situated outside the UK at the time of disposal. [*TCGA 1992, ss 11(2)–(4), 271(1)(f); ITA 2007, s 841*].

An order made under *Arms Control and Disarmament (Privileges and Immunities) Act 1988, s 1(2)* can extend a similar exemption to the above to persons designated by states other than the UK.

Friendly societies

[25.51] A friendly society registered under *Friendly Societies Act 1974* (a registered friendly society) is an unincorporated society of individuals. Under *Friendly Societies Act 1992*, societies are able to incorporate, take on new powers and form subsidiary companies. *TCGA 1992, ss 217A–217C* provide continuity of tax treatment between registered societies and incorporated societies and removes adverse tax consequences which would otherwise arise as a result of incorporation.

Friendly societies which are neither registered nor incorporated, the incomes of which do not exceed £160 per annum, are wholly exempt from corporation tax on chargeable gains, but a claim must be made. Exemption for other friendly societies is broadly restricted in respect of life or other long-term insurance business to the assurance of gross sums under contracts under which the total premiums payable in any period of twelve months do not exceed £270 or the granting of annuities not exceeding £156. Lower limits apply to contracts made before 1 May 1995.

There are provisions to enable friendly societies to transfer existing tax exempt business to an insurance company or another friendly society without loss of the tax exemption.

[*FA 2012, ss 150–179, Schs 18, 19; ICTA 1988, ss 459–466; TCGA 1992, ss 217A–217C; SI 2007 No 2134; SI 2008 No 1942; SI 2009 No 56, Sch 1 paras 144–146; SI 2012 No 3008*]. See also Tolley's Income Tax under Life Assurance Policies and Tolley's Corporation Tax under Friendly Societies.

The Historic Buildings and Monuments Commission for England

[25.52] The Historic Buildings and Monuments Commission for England is exempt from tax in respect of chargeable gains. [*TCGA 1992, s 271(7)*].

Housing associations

[25.53] Housing associations approved under *CTA 2010, ss 644–646* (see Tolley's Corporation Tax under Housing Associations Etc.) may make a claim (within two years of the end of the relevant accounting period) for exemption from corporation tax on chargeable gains arising from the sale of property which is, or has been, occupied by a tenant of the association. [*CTA 2010, s 643*].

Relief from corporation tax generally by specific grant made by the Secretary of State for the Environment may also be obtainable under *Housing Act 1988, s 54* for registered non-profit making housing associations which are approved as above. See Tolley's Corporation Tax under Housing Associations Etc.

Disposals of land and other assets by a housing association (as defined) to the Housing Corporation (or the Secretary of State (formerly Housing for Wales) or Scottish Homes) under certain statutory schemes, and subsequent disposals of those assets by the Corporation etc. to a single housing association, are treated as taking place on a no gain/no loss basis. The same applies to:

(a) transfers of land between the Housing Corporation etc. and registered housing associations (as defined and see **25.62** below regarding self-build societies);
(b) transfers of land between such associations; and

(c) transfers under a direction from the Corporation etc. of property other than land between such associations.

Similar relief applies to NI housing associations.

[*TCGA 1992, ss 218–220; Government of Wales Act 1998, Sch 16 paras 77–80; Housing (Scotland) Act 2001, Sch 10 paras 18, 19; SI 1996 No 2325; SI 1998 No 2244*].

The disposal and corresponding acquisition of an estate or interest in land in the UK otherwise than under a bargain at arm's length to a registered housing association (as defined) is treated as being made for a no gain/no loss consideration (or for the actual consideration if the latter exceeds the disposer's allowable expenditure; see **16.11** COMPUTATION OF GAINS AND LOSSES) if a joint claim for such relief is made. On a subsequent disposal of the land by the association after a no gain/no loss acquisition its acquisition by the original donor is treated as the acquisition of the association. [*TCGA 1992, s 259*]. See **9.6** ASSETS HELD ON 31 MARCH **1982** and **38.4** INDEXATION for the consequential re-basing and indexation provisions which apply.

International organisations

[25.54] International organisations (e.g. the United Nations) may be specified by Order in Council as exempt from certain taxes [*International Organisations Act 1968*], as may certain financial bodies under the *Bretton Woods Agreement Act 1945* (e.g. the International Monetary Fund). Also exempt are the International Development Association [*International Development Association Act 1960, s 3* and *SI 1960 No 1383*]; the International Finance Corporation [*International Finance Corporation Act 1955, s 3* and *SI 1955 No 1954*]; and signatories to the Convention on the International Maritime Satellite Organisation in respect of capital gains tax on any payment received by the signatory from the Organisation in accordance with the Convention. [*TCGA 1992, s 271(5)*]. Bodies may be specified by Order as exempt under *European Communities Act 1972, s 2(2)*.

Securities issued by designated international organisations are treated as situated outside the UK. See **7.3** ASSETS.

Local authorities etc.

[25.55] Local authorities, local authority associations and health service bodies (as defined) are exempt from capital gains tax. [*TCGA 1992, s 271(3)*].

London Olympic Games

[25.56] The London Organising Committee of the Olympic Games Ltd, the company established to organise, manage and promote the London Olympic Games in 2012, is exempt from corporation tax (including tax on chargeable gains). The Treasury has wide powers to restrict or remove the exemption by regulations and to extend it to wholly-owned subsidiaries of the company. [*FA 2006, ss 65, 66*].

The Treasury also has powers to make regulations providing for the International Olympic Committee, and certain persons owned or controlled by it, to be exempt from capital gains tax, and to provide for certain activities undertaken by non-UK resident athletes and others in connection with the London Games to be disregarded for corporation tax and capital gains tax purposes. [*FA 2006, ss 67, 68*].

National Debt

[25.57] Gains accruing to trustees of a settlement the property of which is for the reduction of the National Debt and which qualifies under statute are not chargeable. [*TCGA 1992, s 271(1)(e)*].

The National Heritage Memorial Fund

[25.58] The National Heritage Memorial Fund is exempt from tax on chargeable gains. [*TCGA 1992, s 271(7)*].

The National Radiological Protection Board

[25.59] The National Radiological Protection Board is exempt from tax on chargeable gains accruing before 2 April 2005. [*TCGA 1992, s 271(7); F(No 2)A 2005, s 46(3)(5)*]. The Board ceased to exist on that date.

Pension schemes

[25.60] Subject to the following, gains accruing to a person from investments forming part of the funds of certain pension schemes are not chargeable gains. For 2006/07 onwards, the schemes covered by this exemption are registered pension schemes within *FA 2004, s 150(2)*, the House of Commons Members' Fund and certain overseas pension funds. Futures contracts and options contracts are included as investments (notwithstanding that one party to the contract will not be involved with a transfer of assets other than money). See 7.7 ASSETS.

The above exemption does not prevent a scheme sanction charge to income tax arising in the case of an investment-regulated pension scheme (as defined) on a gain on the disposal of certain taxable property (broadly, and subject to exceptions, residential and tangible moveable property). See Tolley's Income Tax.

[*TCGA 1992, s 99A(3), ss 271(1)(b)(c)(d)(g)(h)(j), (1A)(1B)(10)(11), 288(1)*].

The above exemption does not apply to gains accruing to a person as a member of a property investment limited liability partnership (see **50.18** PARTNERSHIPS). [*TCGA 1992, s 271(12)*].

Deregistration or withdrawal of approval of pension schemes

Where the registration of a registered pension scheme (within *FA 2004, s 150(2)*) is withdrawn and accordingly there is a charge to income tax under *FA 2004, s 242*, for capital gains purposes, the assets held for the purposes of the scheme in question are deemed to have been acquired immediately before the date of withdrawal of approval or registration (without any corresponding disposal) by the person who would be chargeable if there had been a disposal at that time giving rise to a gain. The acquisition cost of the assets is deemed to be equal to the amount on which income tax is charged as above. In all cases, that amount is the market value of the assets in question immediately before the date of withdrawal of approval or registration. Accordingly, only the gain accruing on the assets since approval or registration was withdrawn will be brought into account on a subsequent disposal. [*TCGA 1992, ss 239A, 239B, 288(1)*].

Mis-sold pensions

Capital sums received by way of compensation for 'bad investment advice' received during the period beginning on 29 April 1988 and ending on 30 June 1994 in connection with a person's membership of certain occupational pension schemes and his entry into a personal pension scheme or retirement annuity contract is not regarded as the disposal of an asset for capital gains tax purposes. [*FA 1996, s 148(2)*]. The same applies, by concession, to capital sums received by way of compensation for mis-sold free standing additional voluntary contribution schemes (FSAVCS), where such compensation is paid as a result of the Financial Services Authority (FSA)/Personal Investment Authority Policy Statement issued on 28 February 2000 and is determined under the related FSA Guidance. The Policy Statement required a review of specified categories of FSAVCS sold during the period 28 April 1988 to 15 August 1999 inclusive. (HMRC Extra-Statutory Concession A99).

Pension Protection Fund

The Treasury may make regulations providing for the application of certain taxes, including capital gains tax and corporation tax, in relation to the Board of the Pension Protection Fund and the funds that it controls. The Regulations provide that any gain accruing to the Board from disposals of investments are not chargeable gains if, or to the extent that, they were held for the purposes of the Pension Protection Fund or Fraud Compensation Fund. Receipt of certain specified fraud compensation payments from the Board is not a disposal of an asset for tax purposes. [*FA 2005, s 102; SI 2005 No 1907; SI 2006 No 575*].

Scientific research associations

[25.61] Scientific research associations are exempt from tax on chargeable gains, provided that in each case:

(a) the association's object is the undertaking of 'research and development' (within the meaning of *CTA 2010, s 1138*) which may lead to or facilitate an extension of any class or classes of trade; and
(b) it is prohibited by its Memorandum or similar instrument from distributing its income or property to its members in any form other than that of reasonable payments for supplies, labour, power, services, interest and rent.

Treasury regulations (see *SI 2007 No 3426*) prescribe circumstances in which associations are deemed to comply, or not to comply, with the above conditions.

[*TCGA 1992, s 271(6)(b); CTA 2010, ss 469, 470; SI 2007 No 3426*].

Self-build society

[25.62] An approved self-build society (as defined) may claim relief from corporation tax on chargeable gains arising on the disposal of any land to a member, provided that none of its land is occupied by a non-member. Claims must be made within two years of the end of the accounting period. [*CTA 2010, ss 650–657*].

Disposals of land by unregistered self-build societies (as defined) to the Housing Corporation (or the Secretary of State (formerly Housing for Wales) or Scottish Homes) are treated as made at a no gain/no loss price. [*TCGA 1992, s 219; Government of Wales Act 1998, Sch 16 para 79; Housing (Scotland) Act 2001, Sch 10 para 19; SI 1996 No 2325; SI 1998 No 2244*]. See Tolley's Corporation Tax under Housing Associations Etc. and 25.53 above.

Trade unions

[25.63] Registered trade unions, provided that they are precluded from assuring more than £4,000 by way of gross sum or £825 by way of annuity (excluding annuities constituting or held in connection with a registered pension scheme) in respect of any one person. The Treasury has power to increase the limits by order. Exemption is granted in respect of chargeable gains which are applicable and are applied to 'provident benefits' i.e. sickness, injury and superannuation payments, payment for loss of tools, etc. HMRC Statement of Practice 1/84, considered obsolete by HMRC by 1 January 2014, also included as provident benefits legal expenses incurred in representing members at Industrial Tribunal hearings of cases alleging unfair dismissal, or incurred in connection with a member's claim in respect of accident or injury suffered, and general administrative expenses of providing provident benefits.

The above exemption also applies to employers' associations registered as trade unions and to the Police Federations for England and Wales, Scotland, and Northern Ireland and other police organisations with similar functions.

[*CTA 2010, ss 981–983*].

Unit and investment trusts, open-ended investment companies and venture capital trusts

[25.64] Authorised unit trusts, investment trusts, open-ended investment companies and venture capital trusts are exempt from corporation tax on their chargeable gains. See 70 UNIT TRUSTS ETC. and 71.10 VENTURE CAPITAL TRUSTS.

Visiting forces etc.

[25.65] A period during which a member of a visiting force or the EU civilian staff to whom *ITA 2007, s 833* applies is in the UK solely because of such membership is not treated either as a period of residence in the UK or as creating a change in his residence or domicile. [*TCGA 1992, s 11(1); ITA 2007, s 833; FA 2012, Sch 37 para 5*].

Reliefs and deferrals

[25.66] In addition to the exemption from capital gains tax detailed in 25.2–25.65 above, a number of reliefs are available to reduce or defer the amount of tax payable. The more common of these are outlined in 25.67–25.96 below as well as in certain provisions in **25.53** and **25.62** above.

Capital distributions and sale of rights

[25.67] If small as compared with the value of the shares in respect of which it is made, a capital distribution may be treated not as a disposal but the proceeds deducted from the acquisition cost of the shares on a subsequent disposal. See **63.11** SHARES AND SECURITIES. This treatment also applies to any consideration received for the disposal of rights. See **63.4** SHARES AND SECURITIES.

Companies

[25.68] Reliefs and deferrals for companies are treated as follows:

(a) *Intra-group transfers of capital assets* are treated as if made at a no gain, no loss consideration (with certain exceptions). See **29.3** GROUPS OF COMPANIES.

(b) *Transfers of assets to non-UK resident company.* Where a UK resident company carrying on a trade outside the UK through a permanent establishment transfers that trade and its assets to a non-UK resident company partly or wholly for shares in that company, a proportion of the net chargeable gains relating to those shares may be claimed by the transferor company as being deferred. See **49.12** OVERSEAS MATTERS.

(c) *Transfers or divisions of UK businesses between companies resident in different EC member states* are treated as if made at a no gain, no loss consideration. See **49.13** OVERSEAS MATTERS.

Company reconstructions

[25.69] These do not normally constitute disposals, the original holding and the new holding being treated as the same asset acquired at the same date as the original shares. See **63.5** and **63.7** SHARES AND SECURITIES and **14.11** COMPANIES.

Constituency associations

[25.70] Where, as a result of the redistribution of parliamentary constituencies, an existing constituency association in a former parliamentary constituency disposes of any land:

(a) to a new association which is its successor, or
(b) to a body which is an organ of the political party (within *IHTA 1984, s 24*) and which, as soon as practicable thereafter, disposes of the land to a new association which is a successor to the existing association,

the disposal is treated as being made for such consideration as would secure that neither a gain nor loss accrues on disposal.

If the asset was originally held on 6 April 1965, time apportionment will be available (see **8.7** ASSETS HELD ON 6 APRIL 1965) to the new association as if it had held the land from the original date of acquisition.

Where, as a result of the redistribution of parliamentary constituencies, an existing constituency association in a former parliamentary constituency disposes of any land used and occupied by it for the purposes of its functions and transfers the whole or part of the proceeds to a new association which is its successor, ROLLOVER RELIEF (**59**) may be claimed as if the land disposed of had been the property of the new association since its acquisition. Where only part of the proceeds is transferred, rollover relief may be claimed on a corresponding share. [*TCGA 1992, s 264*].

Corporate venturing scheme

[25.71] Before 1 April 2010, companies may defer all or part of a chargeable gain on a corporate venturing scheme investment against a further subscription for shares (other than those of the same company or a company in its group) on which investment relief is obtained under the corporate venturing scheme. The deferred gain becomes chargeable on a disposal of the shares and in certain other circumstances. See **18.20** CORPORATE VENTURING SCHEME.

Disposals — capital sums received as compensation etc.

[25.72] Where such a sum is received in respect of an asset which is damaged or, alternatively, lost or destroyed, a number of reliefs are available provided the capital sum is expended on restoration of, or a replacement for, the asset. See **10.3** and **10.4** CAPITAL SUMS DERIVED FROM ASSETS.

Enterprise investment scheme (EIS)

[25.73] Individuals and most trustees may defer all or part of a chargeable gain against a subscription for eligible shares under the EIS. The deferred gain becomes chargeable on a disposal of the EIS shares and in certain other circumstances. See **23.14** ENTERPRISE INVESTMENT SCHEME.

Entrepreneurs' relief

[25.74] Entrepreneurs' relief can be claimed in respect of 'qualifying business disposals' made on or after 6 April 2008. Qualifying gains are chargeable at a rate of only 10% (but note that, for disposals before 23 June 2010, the relief operated by reducing the gains by $^4/_9$ths). The relief applies for capital gains tax purposes only and is not available to companies. It is subject to a lifetime limit of net gains of, currently, £10 million. See **24** ENTREPRENEURS' RELIEF.

Gifts of business assets and assets on which inheritance tax is chargeable etc.

[25.75] A form of holdover relief applies to:

(a) gifts of business assets (see **36.2** HOLD-OVER RELIEFS); and
(b) gifts of assets on which inheritance tax is chargeable etc. (see **36.10** HOLD-OVER RELIEFS).

Gifts to charities etc.

[25.76] Disposals (otherwise than under a bargain at arm's length), by way of gift or at a consideration not exceeding the allowable expenditure, to charities or any of the bodies mentioned in *IHTA 1984, Sch 3* are deemed to have been made for a consideration giving neither a gain nor a loss. See **11.7** CHARITIES.

Harbour reorganisation schemes

[25.77] Where the trade of any body corporate, other than a limited company, is transferred to a harbour authority by or under a certified harbour reorganisation scheme which provides for the dissolution of the transferor, any assets transferred before 1 April 2013 on the transfer of trade are treated as giving rise to neither gain nor loss and, for the purposes of any assets acquired before 6 April 1965, the transferor's acquisition of the asset is treated as the transferee's acquisition of it. The transferee is also entitled to relief for any amount for which the transferor would have been entitled to claim relief in respect of allowable losses if it had continued to trade. This relief is abolished for transfers on or after 1 April 2013. [*TCGA 1992, s 221; CTA 2010, ss 991, 993; FA 2012, s 227, Sch 39 paras 15, 16, 18(2)*].

Hold-over — general relief for gifts

[25.78] After 5 April 1980 and before 14 March 1989, a general deferral relief for gifts applied to the disposal of an asset otherwise than at arm's length. See **36.12** HOLD-OVER RELIEFS.

Hops Marketing Board

[25.79] Certain transfers of assets by the Hops Marketing Board were deemed to be for a consideration which gives rise to neither a gain nor a loss and the Board's period of ownership is imputed to the transferee for the purposes of applying (where relevant) the provisions relating to **8** ASSETS HELD ON 6 APRIL 1965. [*FA 1982, s 148; TCGA 1992, Sch 12*].

Investors' relief

[25.80] Investors' relief can be claimed in respect of disposals of shares in unlisted trading companies made by individuals on or after 6 April 2019. Qualifying gains are chargeable at a rate of only 10%. The relief applies for capital gains tax purposes only and is not available to companies. It is subject to a lifetime limit of gains of, currently, £10 million. See **40** INVESTORS' RELIEF.

Land — compulsory acquisition

[25.81] Where *part* of a holding of land is transferred under a compulsory acquisition order, in certain circumstances the transferor may claim not to treat the transfer as a disposal and the consideration is then deducted from the allowable expenditure on a subsequent disposal. See **41.11** LAND for this and **41.12** for deferral of any gain arising on the compulsory purchase of land by means of a claim for rollover relief where the proceeds are re-invested in new land.

Land — part disposals

[25.82] Where the value of the consideration for a part disposal of a larger holding of land does not exceed £20,000, in certain circumstances the transferor may claim that the transfer is not treated as a disposal and the consideration is then deducted from the allowable expenditure on a subsequent disposal. See **41.8** LAND.

Localism Act 2011 transfers

[25.83] A transfer in accordance with a transfer scheme under *Localism Act 2011, s 190* of property, rights or liabilities of the Homes and Communities Agency where the transferee is a public body is regarded as made on a no gain, no loss basis. A transfer in accordance with a transfer scheme under *Localism Act 2011, s 191* is similarly regarded where the transferee is a public body. [*Localism Act 2011, Sch 24 para 6*].

Married persons and civil partners

[25.84] Transfers between married persons and between civil partners are regarded as made on a no gain, no loss basis where the spouses or partners are living together. See **46.5** MARRIED PERSONS AND CIVIL PARTNERS.

National heritage property

[25.85] The following types of property are within the term 'national heritage property' provided they are so designated by HMRC.

(a) Any picture, print, book, manuscript, work of art or scientific object, any collection or group of such items taken as a whole, and any other item not yielding income, which appears to HMRC to be pre-eminent for its national, scientific, historic or artistic interest (with regard being taken of any significant association of the item, collection or group with a particular place). '*National interest*' includes interest within any part of the UK.

(b) Land which in the opinion of HMRC is of outstanding scenic or historic or scientific interest.

(c) A building for the preservation of which special steps should in the opinion of HMRC be taken by reason of its outstanding historic or architectural interest.

(d) Any area of land which in the opinion of HMRC is essential for the protection of the character and amenities of such a building as is mentioned in (c) above.

(e) An object which in the opinion of HMRC is historically associated with such a building as is mentioned in (c) above.

[*IHTA 1984, s 31(1)(5)*].

Where any of the above assets, which have been (or could be) designated by HMRC under *IHTA 1984, s 31,* are disposed of by gift (including a gift into settlement) or deemed to be disposed of by trustees on a person becoming absolutely entitled to settled property (other than on the death of the life tenant), then the person making the disposal and the person acquiring the asset are treated for capital gains tax purposes as making the transaction for a consideration giving neither gain nor loss. [*TCGA 1992, s 258(3)(4)*].

Certain undertakings must be given by such persons as HMRC think appropriate in the circumstances of the case that, until the person beneficially entitled to the property dies or the property is disposed of, certain conditions regarding the property are kept, e.g. reasonable access to the public. [*TCGA 1992, s 258(9); IHTA 1984, ss 30(1), 31(2)(4)*]. An undertaking given on or after 31 July 1998 may be varied by agreement between HMRC and the person bound by the undertaking or, in the absence of such agreement, by the Tribunal (before 1 April 2009, by a Special Commissioner) at HMRC's behest. Earlier undertakings, where access to the asset is by public appointment only (disregarding special exhibitions), may be similarly varied so as to include an extended access requirement and/or a requirement that certain information be published. This does not apply to earlier undertakings in relation to which a chargeable event for inheritance tax purposes (see Tolley's Inheritance Tax) occurs before 31 July 1998. [*TCGA 1992, s 258(8A); IHTA 1984, s 35A; SI 2009 No 56, Sch 1 para 109*].

If the asset is sold and inheritance tax is chargeable under *IHTA 1984, s 32* (or would be chargeable if an undertaking under that provision had been given), the person selling the asset is treated as having sold the asset for its market value. Similarly, if HMRC are satisfied that at any time during the period for which any undertaking was given that it has not been observed in a material respect, the owner is treated as having sold and immediately reacquired the asset for its market value. An undertaking for the purposes of these provisions is given for the period until the person beneficially entitled to the asset dies or disposes of the asset (whether by sale, gift or otherwise). [*TCGA 1992, s 258(5)(6)*].

If the asset subject to the undertaking is disposed of otherwise than on sale and without a further undertaking being given, the asset is treated as having been sold to an individual for its market value. [*TCGA 1992, s 258(6)*].

Where a person is treated as having sold for market value any asset within (c), (d) or (e) above, he is also treated as having sold and immediately reacquired at market value any asset 'associated' with it (unless HMRC direct otherwise). '*Associated*' assets are a building within (c) above and land or objects which, in relation to that building, fall within (d) or (e) above. [*TCGA 1992, s 258(7)*].

Where a person is treated as having sold an asset under these provisions and inheritance tax becomes chargeable on the same occasion, any capital gains tax payable is deductible in determining the value of the asset for inheritance tax purposes. [*TCGA 1992, s 258(8)*].

An undertaking to grant access will not be regarded as breached where suspension of access is due to foot and mouth disease restrictions, and nor will missed visiting days have to be made up later in 2001 (Revenue Tax Bulletin, Special Foot and Mouth Disease Edition, May 2001 p 4).

See also **36.10** HOLD-OVER RELIEFS for relief for gifts of works of art etc.

Exceptions

The above provisions do not apply where the disposal is by way of gift or sale by private treaty to a body within *IHTA 1984, Sch 3* or if the disposal is to HMRC in satisfaction of inheritance tax (or capital transfer tax). Such disposals are exempt. See **25.41** above.

Reinvestment relief

[25.86] Reinvestment relief enabled individuals and trustees to claim to roll-over chargeable gains accruing on any assets if the disposal proceeds were reinvested in a 'qualifying investment' within the 'qualifying period' and **before 6 April 1998**. The relief was given effect by reducing the sale proceeds of the disposed assets and the acquisition cost of the newly acquired investment by the lowest of the following amounts:

- the otherwise chargeable gain (net of any amount deferred by virtue of a previous claim for reinvestment relief);
- the acquisition cost of the new asset;
- if the new asset is not acquired at arm's length, the market value at the time of its acquisition;
- the amount specified by the individual in the claim.

These adjustments only affected the reinvestor claiming the relief and there was no consequential effect for either the complementary purchaser or vendor.

A '*qualifying investment*' was an acquisition of any 'eligible shares' in a 'qualifying company' (both as defined) unless, where the asset disposed of consisted of shares in or securities of any company, the qualifying company is that company or a member of that company's group. Where the eligible shares were acquired by their being issued to the taxpayer, the company was required to have an intention to employ the money raised by the issue wholly for the purposes of a 'qualifying trade' carried on by it.

For subsequent deferral reliefs applying for reinvestment in EIS and VCT shares, see respectively **23.14** ENTERPRISE INVESTMENT SCHEME and **71.12** VENTURE CAPITAL TRUSTS.

Withdrawal of relief

An effective withdrawal of reinvestment relief applied where certain events occurred within three years of the reinvestment. The withdrawal was made by deeming a chargeable gain equal to the whole or a proportion of the held-over gain to arise at the time of the event. In such circumstances so much of the held-over gain as is treated as the deemed gain is diregarded in computing a subsequent gain on disposal of the qualifying investment.

[*TCGA 1992, ss 164A–164N; FA 1998, s 141(1)(2), Sch 27 Pt III(32)*].

Reorganisation of share capital

[25.87] Reorganisations do not normally constitute disposals, the original holding and the new holding being treated as the same asset acquired at the same date as the original shares. See **63.2** SHARES AND SECURITIES. See also **63.8** for conversion of securities into shares where the same principles apply.

Retirement relief

[25.88] Retirement relief applied, subject to certain conditions, to gains made **before 6 April 2003** by an individual who had attained the age of 50 (or at a lesser age through ill-health), on a 'material disposal of business assets'. The gains qualifying for relief were eliminated or reduced, depending on their amount and on the length of time for which the business had operated. The relief had no effect on the acquisition cost of the person acquiring the business assets from the retiree.

Rollover relief — replacement of business assets

[25.89] A person disposing of certain qualifying assets used exclusively for the purposes of a trade who used the proceeds to purchase other qualifying assets so used may claim to defer the capital gains tax payable by deducting the otherwise chargeable gain on the old asset from the cost of the newly acquired one. See **59** ROLLOVER RELIEF.

Seed enterprise investment scheme (SEIS)

[25.90] A chargeable gain arising to an individual is exempt to the extent that it is matched with a subscription for shares in respect of which SEIS income tax relief is granted. For 2012/13 only, 100% of such a subscription may be matched with a gain, but for 2013/14 onwards only 50% of a subscription may be so matched. See **60.45** ENTERPRISE INVESTMENT SCHEME.

Settlements for the benefit of employees

[25.91] Where the circumstances surrounding a disposal are as in one of (a)–(c) below, the MARKET VALUE (**45.1**) rules do not apply to it; and if made gratuitously or for a consideration of an amount not exceeding the allowable expenditure attributable to the asset, the disposal, and the corresponding acquisition by the trustees, is treated as taking place on a no gain/no loss basis and the transferor's acquisition of the asset is imputed to the trustees.

The circumstances mentioned above are as follows.

(a) A close company (as in *CTA 2010, ss 439–454* but additionally including a non-UK resident company which would be close as defined by those provisions) disposes of an asset to trustees in circumstances such that the disposition is not a transfer of value for IHT purposes by virtue of *IHTA 1984, s 13* (employee trusts).

(b) An individual disposes of an asset to trustees in circumstances such that the disposal is an exempt transfer for IHT purposes by virtue of *IHTA 1984, s 28* (employee trusts).

(c) A company other than a close company (as in (a) above) disposes of property to trustees otherwise than under a bargain at arm's length in circumstances such that, broadly, had the disposition been made by a close company it would not be a transfer of value by virtue of *IHTA 1984, s 13*.

[*TCGA 1992, s 239(1)(2)(4)–(8); SI 2009 No 1890, Art 4*].

For coverage of *IHTA 1984, s 13* and *s 28* (each of which refers to the provisions of *IHTA 1984, s 86*), see Tolley's Inheritance Tax under Trusts for Employees.

A gain accruing to the trustees of an 'employee trust' on the disposal of an asset of the trust to a 'beneficiary', or on a deemed disposal under *TCGA 1992, s 71* (person becoming absolutely entitled to settled property — see **62.16** SETTLEMENTS) is not a chargeable gain. This applies only if no actual consideration (as opposed to deemed consideration) is given for the asset, there is an income tax charge of the full market value of the asset and neither the beneficiary nor the person liable for the income tax (if different) is an 'excluded person'.

For this purpose, an '*employee trust*' is a trust within *IHTA 1984, s 86* but ignoring the restriction in *s 86(3)* (class defined by employment with a particular body to include all or most employees). An 'excluded person' is a participator (as defined) in a company of which shares or securities are comprised in the trust or a close company (as above) that has provided property comprised in the trust and any person who was a participator in such a company at any time during the ten years before the share, securities or property became comprised in the trust. Also excluded is any person 'connected' with any such participator. A '*beneficiary*' is a person within *IHTA 1984, s 86(1)(a)* or *(b)*. '*Connected*' has the same meaning as in **17 connected persons**, but as if 'relative' included uncle, aunt, nephew and niece.

[*TCGA 1992, s 239ZA; SI 2009 No 730, Art 11*].

Note that, for disposals before 6 April 2009, the above provision applies only by concession (HMRC Extra-Statutory Concession D35). For notes on the application of ESC D35 in given situations, see Revenue Tax Bulletin April 2000 p 738.

For the position of the shareholders in a close company transferor which makes a transfer within (a)–(c) above at less than market value, see **4.14** ANTI-AVOIDANCE.

See also **36** HOLD-OVER RELIEFS and **22.18**, **22.30** EMPLOYEE SHARE SCHEMES for alternative reliefs which may be available in respect of transfers to settlements for the benefit of employees.

Social investment relief

[25.92] Individuals may defer all or part of a chargeable gain against an investment in a social enterprise. The deferred gain becomes chargeable on a disposal of the investment and in certain other circumstances. See **65.46** SOCIAL INVESTMENT RELIEF.

Taper relief

[25.93] For 1998/99 to 2007/08 inclusive, chargeable gains realised by individuals, trustees and personal representatives (but not companies) were reduced (tapered) according to the length of time the asset had been held after 5 April 1998, with greater reductions for 'business assets' (as defined). Losses were not reduced as such, but were set against gains before applying taper relief to the net gain so that the losses were effectively tapered.

Taper relief is abolished for gains accruing, or treated as accruing, in 2008/09 and subsequent years.

The relief applied where a person had an excess of chargeable gains over the aggregate of allowable losses for the year and losses brought forward and the excess was or included the whole or a part of any chargeable gain that was eligible for the relief. It thus applied *after* the deduction of any INDEXATION (**38**) allowance available and after any other deductions due in arriving at the chargeable gain, except that the relief was deducted in priority to the annual exemption (see **2.6** ANNUAL RATES AND EXEMPTIONS).

A chargeable gain was eligible for taper relief if at the time of disposal the asset had been held for at least one year in the case of a business asset or at least three years otherwise. For these purposes, only so much of the period for which the asset was held as falls after 5 April 1998 (called the '*qualifying holding period*') was taken into account. If the time of acquisition (see below) of an asset fell before 17 March 1998 and either the asset was a non-business asset or it was a business asset disposed of before 6 April 2000, an additional one year (the 'bonus year') was added, in arriving at the qualifying holding period, to the actual period for which the asset was held after 5 April 1998.

Chargeable gains were tapered according to the Table below up to a maximum of 75% for business assets and 40% for non-business assets, the maximum reductions applying where the qualifying holding period was at least two years (for disposals after 5 April 2002) for business assets and ten years for non-business assets. There were rules to determine the amount of the reduction for assets which were business assets only for part of the qualifying holding period or which were used for both business and non-business purposes at the same time.

Gains on disposals of business assets after 5 April 2002

No. of whole years in qualifying holding period	Percentage reduction available	Percentage of gain chargeable
0	—	100.0

Gains on disposals of business assets after 5 April 2002

No. of whole years in qualifying holding period	Percentage reduction available	Percentage of gain chargeable
1	50.0	50.0
2 or more	75.0	25.0

Gains on disposals of business assets after 5 April 2000 and before 6 April 2002

No. of whole years in qualifying holding period	Percentage reduction available	Percentage of gain chargeable
0	—	100.0
1	12.5	87.5
2	25.0	75.0
3	50.0	50.0
4 or more	75.0	25.0

Gains on disposals of business assets after 5 April 1998 and before 6 April 2000

No. of whole years in qualifying holding period*	Percentage reduction available	Percentage of gain chargeable
0	—	100.0
1	7.5	92.5
2	15.0	85.0
3	22.5	77.5
4	30.0	70.0
5	37.5	62.5
6	45.0	55.0
7	52.5	47.5
8	60.0	40.0
9	67.5	32.5
10 or more	75.0	25.0

* Including bonus year added for assets held on 17 March 1998 (see main text)

Gains on disposals of non-business assets after 5 April 1998

No. of whole years in qualifying holding period*	Percentage reduction available	Percentage of gain chargeable
0	—	100
1	—	100

Gains on disposals of non-business assets after 5 April 1998

No. of whole years in qualifying holding period*	Percentage reduction available	Percentage of gain chargeable
2	—	100
3	5	95
4	10	90
5	15	85
6	20	80
7	25	75
8	30	70
9	35	65
10 or more	40	60

*Including bonus year added for assets held on 17 March 1998 (see main text)

[*TCGA 1992, s 2A, Sch A1*].

Transfer of a business to a company — incorporation relief

[25.94] Where a person transfers a business and its assets to a company in return for shares in that company, any chargeable gain on disposal of the assets is deferred by reducing the amount otherwise chargeable in the proportion of the value of the shares received to the value of the overall consideration received by the transferor in exchange for the business. An election is available for the relief not to apply. See **37** INCORPORATION AND DISINCORPORATION RELIEFS.

Unremittable overseas gains

[25.95] On a claim, such gains may be treated as gains of the year in which conditions preventing remittance cease to apply. See **49.6** OVERSEAS MATTERS. See also **42.8** LATE PAYMENT INTEREST AND PENALTIES.

Venture capital trusts (VCTs)

[25.96] For 2003/04 and earlier years, individuals may defer all or part of a chargeable gain against subscriptions of up to £100,000 per tax year for shares in VCT companies by reference to which income tax investment relief is obtained. The deferred gain becomes chargeable on a disposal of the VCT shares and in certain other circumstances. The relief is abolished for VCT shares issued on or after 6 April 2004. See **71.12** VENTURE CAPITAL TRUSTS.

26

Furnished Holiday Accommodation

Introduction	**26.1**
Capital gains tax treatment	**26.2**
Key points	**26.3**

Introduction to furnished holiday accommodation

[26.1] Special provisions apply to the treatment for the purposes of tax on chargeable gains of the commercial letting of furnished holiday accommodation in the UK or the European Economic Area (EEA).

Definitions

'*Commercial letting*' is letting (whether or not under a lease) on a commercial basis and with a view to the realisation of profits (see *Brown v Richardson* (Sp C 129), [1997] SSCD 233 and Revenue Tax Bulletin October 1997 p 472), and accommodation is let '*furnished*' if the tenant is entitled to the use of furniture.

'*Holiday accommodation*' is accommodation which:

(a) must be available for commercial letting to the public generally as holiday accommodation for at least 210 days in a twelve month period (see below) (140 days for 2011/12 and earlier years or accounting periods beginning before 1 April 2012 (see further below)); and
(b) is so let for at least 105 such days (70 days for 2011/12 and earlier years or accounting periods beginning before 1 April 2012 (see further below)).

It must, however, not normally be in the same occupation for more than 31 consecutive days at any time during a period (although not necessarily a continuous period) of seven months in that twelve month period which includes any months in which it is let as in (b) above.

In the case of an individual or partnership, these conditions must be satisfied in the tax year in which the profits or gains arise, unless:

(i) the accommodation was not let furnished in the preceding tax year but is so let in the following tax year, in which case they must be satisfied in the twelve months from the date such letting commenced in the tax year; or
(ii) the accommodation was let furnished in the preceding tax year but is not so let in the following tax year, in which case they must be satisfied in the twelve months ending with the date such letting ceased in the tax year.

The increase in the number of days required to meet the above conditions to 210 and 105 days does not apply for any twelve month period which does not coincide with the tax year and which begins before and ends on or after 6 April 2012.

In the case of a company, the conditions must be satisfied in the twelve months ending on the last day of the accounting period in which the profits or gains arise, with similar variations as in (i) and (ii) above where the accommodation was not let furnished in the twelve months preceding or following the period in question. The increase in the number of days required to meet the above conditions to 210 and 105 days does not apply for any twelve month period which begins before and ends on or after 1 April 2012.

In satisfying condition (b) above averaging may be applied to letting periods of holiday accommodation already treated as such ('*qualifying accommodation*') and letting periods of any or all of other accommodation let by the same person which would be holiday accommodation if it satisfied the 105/70 day test. Any such other accommodation is then treated as holiday accommodation if the average of the days let in the twelve month period is at least 105 (70). For persons other than companies, a claim for averaging must be made on or before the first anniversary of 31 January following the tax year for which it is to apply. For companies, the time limit is two years after the end of the accounting period for which the averaging claim is to apply. Only one such claim may be made in respect of qualifying accommodation in any tax year or accounting period. Separate averaging claims must be made for accommodation in the UK and accommodation in the EEA.

If accommodation qualifies as holiday accommodation during a tax year, either by meeting conditions (a) and (b) above or as a result of an averaging election, the taxpayer may elect for the property to continue to qualify for the following tax year or the following two tax years if it would otherwise fail to do so only because it does not meet condition (b) for that year or years. The property is not, however, treated as qualifying for the purposes of averaging (or for the further application of this provision). An election can only be made if the taxpayer had a genuine intention to meet the condition in the affected tax years. A separate election is required for each tax year involved, but if no election is made for the first affected tax year then an election cannot be made for the second. An election must be made on or before the first anniversary of 31 January following the tax year for which it is to apply. A similar provision applies to companies by reference to accounting periods rather than tax years. An election must be made within two years after the end of the accounting period for which it is to apply.

Where there is a letting of accommodation only part of which is holiday accommodation, apportionments are made as are just and reasonable.

[*ITTOIA 2005, ss 323–326A; CTA 2009, ss 265–268A; TCGA 1992, ss 241(1)(2)(7), 241A(1)–(3)(9)*].

Furnished holiday accommodation may include caravans (Revenue Press Release 17 May 1984).

See Tolley's Income Tax regarding income tax provisions in respect of furnished holiday accommodation.

Example

Mr B owns and lets out furnished holiday cottages. None is ever let to the same person for more than 31 consecutive days. Three cottages have been owned for many years but Rose Cottage was acquired on 1 June 2017 (and first let on that day) while Ivy Cottage was sold on 30 June 2017 (and last let on that day).

In 2017/18, days available for letting and days let are as follows.

	Days available	Days let
Honeysuckle Cottage	230	200
Primrose Cottage	180	110
Bluebell Cottage	220	95
Rose Cottage	220	90
Ivy Cottage	60	15

Additional information

Rose Cottage was let for 30 days between 6 April and 31 May 2018.

Ivy Cottage was let for 50 days in the period 1 July 2016 to 5 April 2017 but was available for letting for 150 days in that period.

Qualification as 'furnished holiday accommodation'

Honeysuckle Cottage qualifies as it meets both the 210-day availability test and the 105-day letting test.

Primrose Cottage does *not* qualify although it is let for more than 105 days as it fails to satisfy the 210-day test. Averaging (see below) is only possible where it is the 105-day test which is not satisfied.

Bluebell Cottage does not qualify by itself as it fails the 105-day test. However it may be included in an averaging election.

Rose Cottage qualifies as furnished holiday accommodation. It was acquired on 1 June 2017 so qualification in 2017/18 is determined by reference to the period of twelve months beginning on the day it was first let, in which it was let for a total of 120 days.

Ivy Cottage was sold on 30 June 2017 so qualification is determined by reference to the period from 1 July 2016 to 30 June 2017 (the last day of letting). It does not qualify by itself as it was let for only 65 days in this period but it may be included in an averaging election.

Averaging election for 2017/18

	Days let
Honeysuckle Cottage	200
Bluebell Cottage	95
Rose Cottage	120
Ivy Cottage	65

$$\frac{200 + 95 + 120 + 65}{4} = 120 \text{ days} \quad \text{note (a)}$$

Note

(a) All four cottages included in the averaging election now qualify as furnished holiday accommodation as each is deemed to have been let for 120 days in the year 2017/18. If the averaging calculation had not resulted in all four cottages qualifying, the two cottages which qualify in any case could have been included in an averaging election together with one of the non-qualifying cottages (leaving the other as non-qualifying). If averaging three cottages still did not improve the position, an average of just two could be tried.

Capital gains tax treatment

[26.2] For the purposes of the following provisions, any UK property business which consists of, or so far as it consists of, the commercial letting of furnished holiday accommodation in the UK is treated as a trade, and all such lettings made by a particular person, partnership or body of persons are treated as one trade. Similarly, any overseas property business which consists of, or so far as it consists of, the such letting in one or more EEA states is treated as a trade, and all such lettings made by a particular person, partnership or body of persons are treated as one trade. Note that a taxpayer who lets furnished holiday accommodation in both the UK and the EEA will be treated as carrying on two separate trades.

The provisions are as follows.

(a) ROLLOVER RELIEF (59).
(b) Relief for gifts of business assets (see **36.2–36.9** HOLD-OVER RELIEFS).
(c) Relief for loans to traders (see **44.12** LOSSES).
(d) The exemptions relating to SUBSTANTIAL SHAREHOLDINGS OF COMPANIES (66).
(e) ENTREPRENEURS' RELIEF (24).

A notable omission from (a)–(e) above, which may be of advantage to the taxpayer, are the provisions applying in respect of a non-UK resident trading in the UK through a branch or agency or permanent establishment (see **49.3** OVERSEAS MATTERS).

HMRC will accept, subject to the time limits for claims, that an asset used for the purposes of a furnished holiday lettings business in the EEA is a trade asset for the purposes of the above reliefs from the latest of: 1 January 1994; the date the property was first let as furnished holiday accommodation; and the date on which the country in which it is located joined the EEA. (HMRC Technical Note 23 April 2009).

Where, in any chargeable period, a person makes a commercial letting within these provisions, the let property is to be taken for the purposes of (a)–(e) above as being used throughout that period only for the purposes of the deemed trade of making such lettings except for any period when it is neither commercially let nor available to be so let (unless it is only works of construction or repair that make this the case).

For the purposes of (a) above, where the only or main residence exemption in *TCGA 1992, s 222* (see **53** PRIVATE RESIDENCES) is also available to any extent, the gain to which *TCGA 1992, s 222* applies is reduced by the amount of the rolled-over gain.

[*TCGA 1992, ss 241(3)–(6)(8), 241A(4)–(8)(10)(11); FA 2011, Sch 14 para 14*].

The Revenue indicated in 1984 that the relief at (a) is available if the holiday accommodation is sold within three years of its ceasing to be let so long as the owner does not occupy it or use it for some other non-qualifying purpose (CCAB Statement TR 551, June 1984).

Simon's Taxes. See **C3.319**.

Example

In May 2012, Isobel sells Heene Cottage for £120,000. The cottage had qualified as furnished holiday accommodation throughout Isobel's period of ownership and had originally cost £55,000. The whole proceeds are invested in the acquisition in June 2012 of Croft Cottage at a cost of £150,000 and Isobel claims rollover relief under *TCGA 1992, s 152*. The new property is used as furnished holiday accommodation until June 2016 when it becomes Isobel's only residence. Croft Cottage is sold in June 2018 for £290,000. The chargeable gain on disposal is computed as follows.

Disposal of Heene Cottage		
	£	£
Allowable cost		55,000
Actual disposal consideration		120,000
Chargeable gain rolled over		£65,000
Deemed allowable cost of Croft Cottage (£150,000 – £65,000)		£85,000
Disposal of Croft Cottage		
Disposal consideration		290,000
Allowable cost		85,000
Gain before main residence relief		£205,000
Main residence relief		
Gain before relief	205,000	
Less amount of rolled-over gain	65,000	65,000
Gain eligible for relief	140,000	
Less relief (2/6 × £140,000)	46,667	93,333
Chargeable gain 2018/19		£158,333

Key points concerning furnished holiday accommodation

[26.3] Points to consider are as follows.

- Where a furnished holiday accommodation business ceases, for example it no longer qualifies under the new tighter rules, entrepreneurs' relief can normally be claimed where the assets are disposed of up to three years after cessation. For sole traders, provided the properties were used for the business at cessation there should be no restriction on the relief. This may cover the properties being used for other purposes prior to sale, e.g. empty or let out but not qualifying as furnished holiday accommodations.
- Property can often be acquired in joint names e.g., husband and wife. Joint ownership does not necessarily indicate the existence of a partnership (PIM1030). However, where the owners provided significant additional services to customers a partnership may exist and the conditions for claiming entrepreneurs' relief are more restrictive. For a partnership, a gain on the disposal of a property used in the business may need to be time apportion for any period when the property was not used for furnished holiday accommodation.
- Where the furnished holiday accommodation business contains several let properties and only some are disposed of, it is necessary to satisfy the 'part of a business' condition. Otherwise no entrepreneurs' relief will be available. See **24.3** ENTREPRENEURS' RELIEF.

27

Gifts

Tax consequences of a gift	**27.1**
Exemptions	**27.2**
Reliefs	**27.3**
Recovery of tax from donee	**27.4**
Key points	**27.5**

Cross-references. See **39.2** INTERACTION WITH OTHER TAXES for inheritance tax interaction on lifetime gifts; and **51.5** PAYMENT OF TAX for payment by instalments on certain gifts etc.

Tax consequences of a gift

[27.1] The fact that no proceeds are received on a disposal of an asset does not mean that a chargeable gain will not arise. With certain exceptions, where a person acquires or disposes of an asset, otherwise than by way of a bargain made at arm's length *and in particular where he acquires or disposes of it by way of gift,* his acquisition or disposal of the asset is deemed to be for a consideration equal to the market value of the asset. [*TCGA 1992, s 17(1)(a)*]. Thus, the donor of an asset is normally treated as making a chargeable gain computed by reference to market value at the date of disposal.

The date of disposal where a person gifts property is the time when he has done everything within his power to transfer the property to the donee (see *Re Rose, Rose and Others v CIR* CA, [1952] 1 All ER 1217).

See **45** MARKET VALUE for the full market value rules and the exceptions where the provisions do not apply.

Exemptions

[27.2] Once the market value of a gift has been established, the ordinary capital gains tax provisions relating to exemptions apply to that gift. See **25** EXEMPTIONS AND RELIEFS. For example, the gift of a chattel with a market value of £6,000 or less is exempt. The following gifts are expressly exempt.

- Gifts for public benefit.
- Gifts of property to bodies mentioned in *IHTA 1984, Sch 3* for national purposes (see **25.41** EXEMPTIONS AND RELIEFS).
- Donatio mortis causa (see **19.5** DEATH).

Reliefs

[27.3] Reliefs are available for:

- gifts of business assets (see **36.2** HOLD-OVER RELIEFS);

- gifts to charities (see **11.7** CHARITIES);
- gifts of assets on which inheritance tax etc. is chargeable (see **36.10** HOLD-OVER RELIEFS);
- gifts to housing associations (see **25.53** EXEMPTIONS AND RELIEFS);
- gifts of national heritage property subject to certain undertakings (see **25.85** EXEMPTIONS AND RELIEFS); and
- gifts to settlements for the benefit of employees (see **25.91** EXEMPTIONS AND RELIEFS).

Recovery of tax from donee

[27.4] Where capital gains tax arising on a disposal made by way of gift (including any transaction otherwise than at arm's length) is not paid by the donor (or, if he being an individual has died, his personal representatives) within twelve months from the date it became payable, it may be recovered, subject to the coverage below, from the donee within two years after the date on which it became payable. The donee then has a right of recovery from the donor or his personal representatives. The recovery is done by assessment and the donee is assessed and charged (in the name of the donor) to capital gains tax on an amount not exceeding the amount of the chargeable gain arising on the disposal, and not exceeding the grossed-up amount of the capital gains tax unpaid at the time such assessment is made, grossing up at the marginal rate of tax (i.e. by taking capital gains tax on a chargeable gain at the amount which would not have been chargeable but for that chargeable gain).

These provisions apply in relation to a chargeable gain accruing to a transferor under *TCGA 1992, s 169C(7)* (clawback of relief under *TCGA 1992, s 165* or *s 260* if settlement becomes settlor-interested — see **36.8** HOLD-OVER RELIEFS) as they apply in relation to a gain accruing on the disposal of an asset by way of a gift. For this purpose, the transferor is taken to be the donor, and the trustees to whom the relevant disposal in question (see **36.8** HOLD-OVER RELIEFS) was made are taken to be the donee.

[*TCGA 1992, s 282*].

Key points concerning gifts

[27.5] Points to consider are as follows.

- Where a disposal is made by way of a gift, the market value of the assets is substituted for the sale proceeds in the capital gains tax calculation. The tax is then payable by the donor under the usual rules.
- As well as capital gains tax, gifts may also be chargeable to inheritance tax. Practitioners should consider the implications of both taxes in relation to any gift. In general terms, where a gift is

immediately chargeable to inheritance tax, capital gains tax hold-over relief can be claimed under *TCGA 1992, s 260*. See **36** HOLD-OVER RELIEFS for further details of hold-over relief.

28

Government Securities

Exemption rules	**28.1**
Exempt securities	**28.2**

Cross-reference. See also **15** COMPANIES — CORPORATE FINANCE AND INTANGIBLES.

Exemption rules

[28.1] Gains on disposals of any of the UK government and public corporation stocks ('gilts') specified in **28.2** below are not chargeable gains, and losses are not allowable. [*TCGA 1992, s 115(1)(a)*].

The same applies to disposals of options or contracts to acquire or dispose of such gilts. See **7.7** and **7.8** ASSETS.

Gains and losses on disposals by companies of such assets are within the company loan relationship provisions described in **15.2–15.7** COMPANIES — CORPORATE FINANCE AND INTANGIBLES. They are thus treated for corporation tax purposes as *income* (and not capital) gains and losses, and are chargeable/allowable accordingly.

See **63.8** SHARES AND SECURITIES regarding government stock issued as compensation for shares compulsorily acquired.

Exempt securities

[28.2] Government securities (and certain public corporation securities guaranteed by the Treasury) are specified as exempt, as described in **28.1** above, by the Treasury in the form of a statutory instrument. In practice, all UK government securities charged on the National Loans Fund are so specified.

Any security which is a strip (within *FA 1942, s 47*) of a security which is a gilt specified as exempt is also itself a gilt specified for the purposes of the exemption. The Treasury are given powers to amend the legislation by regulations in connection with the introduction of gilt strips. [*TCGA 1992, s 288(8), Sch 9 Pt I; FA 1996, s 202*].

Those securities specified as exempt are listed in *TCGA 1992, Sch 9 Pt II* as supplemented by *SI 1993 No 950, SI 1994 No 2656, SI 1996 No 1031, SI 2001 No 1122, SI 2002 No 2849, SI 2004 No 438, SI 2005 No 276, SI 2006 Nos 184, 3170, SI 2008 No 1588, SI 2010 No 416, SI 2011 No 1295, SI 2012 No 1843, SI 2013 No 2983, SI 2014 No 1120, SI 2015 No 1790* and *SI 2017 No 10*. A list of the exempt securities has been made available on the gov.uk website (www.gov.uk/gilt-edged-securities-exempt-from-capital-gains-tax).

29

Groups of Companies

Introduction	**29.1**
Definitions	**29.2**
Intra-group transfers	**29.3**
Assets which are trading stock of one of the companies but not of the other	**29.4**
Indexation allowance	**29.5**
Intra-group transfers — clawback of relief	**29.6**
Degrouping charge	**29.7**
Deferral of degrouping charge	**29.8**
Exemption for substantial shareholdings	**29.9**
Exemption for mergers	**29.10**
Company becoming an investment trust after acquiring asset intra-group	**29.11**
Company becoming a venture capital trust after acquiring asset intra-group	**29.12**
Election to transfer gain or loss within group	**29.13**
Anti-avoidance	**29.14**
Companies buying gains or losses	**29.15**
Restriction on buying gains and losses: tax avoidance schemes	**29.16**
Restriction on set-off of pre-entry losses where a company joins a group	**29.18**
Key points	**29.24**

Cross-references. See **8.1**, **8.3** ASSETS HELD ON 6 APRIL **1965** and **9.3**, **9.5** ASSETS HELD ON 31 MARCH **1982** for irrevocable election by principal company of a group; **14** COMPANIES.

Simon's Taxes. See **D2.3**, **D2.4**, **D2.5**.

Introduction

[29.1] For certain chargeable gains purposes, the members of a group of companies are treated, in effect, as if they were one entity. This is achieved through the following reliefs:

(a) transfers of assets between group members are treated as if made for a disposal value giving rise to neither a gain nor a loss;
(b) an allowable loss of one group member can be set against a chargeable gain of another member, if both members elect for either the gain or the loss to be transferred from one to the other; and
(c) for the purposes of ROLLOVER RELIEF (**59**) on the replacement of business assets all the trades carried on by the members of the group are treated as a single trade (so that a gain of one member can be rolled over into the acquisition of an asset by another member).

For the detailed provisions and restrictions see **29.3** onwards below for (a) above, **29.13** below for (b) above and **59.10** ROLLOVER RELIEF for (c) above.

The relief for intra-group transfers at (a) above is withdrawn in certain circumstances. In particular this applies where a company which acquired an asset by intra-group transfer subsequently leaves the group within six years of the transfer (the 'degrouping charge'). The degrouping charge can itself be transferred to another company (so that that company's losses can be set against it) or can be rolled over into the acquisition of business assets. See **29.7** onwards below.

There are a number of anti-avoidance provisions which apply specifically to groups of companies as well as further such provisions which are more general but can apply to groups. The provisions are listed at **29.14** below and are mostly described in detail at **4** ANTI-AVOIDANCE. See, however, **29.15** onwards for the provisions dealing with gain and loss buying. These are designed to prevent groups of companies buying and selling companies in order to make use of capital losses suffered by another company or group.

The definition of a 'group' and other terms for the purposes of this chapter is given at **29.2** below.

Definitions

[29.2] For the purposes of this chapter, the following definitions apply.

Company

'*Company*' means a company within the meaning of the *Companies Act 2006, s 1(1)* (previously within the meaning of *Companies Act 1985* or the corresponding enactment in Northern Ireland) or a company (other than a limited liability partnership — see **50.18** PARTNERSHIPS) which is constituted under any other Act, Royal Charter, or letters patent or under the law of a country outside the UK. It also includes a registered society within *Co-operative and Community Benefit Societies Act 2014* or NI equivalent (previously, a registered industrial and provident society), a European Co-operative (see **14.16** COMPANIES), a trustee savings bank, a building society and an incorporated friendly society within the meaning of *Friendly Societies Act 1992*. There is no requirement for the company to be resident in the UK.

[*TCGA 1992, s 170(9); CTA 2010, s 1119; Co-operative and Community Benefit Societies Act 2014, Sch 4 paras 50, 168; FA 2014, Sch 39 paras 6, 13; SI 2009 No 1890, Art 3*].

Group

A '*group*' comprises:

(a) a company ('*the principal company of the group*'); and
(b) that company's '75% subsidiaries' (as in *CTA 2010, s 1154(3)* i.e. where not less than 75% of the 'ordinary share capital' (see below under 'General') is beneficially owned directly or indirectly by the

principal company), and those subsidiaries' 75% subsidiaries (and so on), except that any 75% subsidiary which is not 'an effective 51% subsidiary' of the principal company is excluded.

This definition is subject to the following rules.

(1) A company ('the subsidiary') which is a 75% subsidiary of another company cannot be a principal company of a group, unless,
  (i) because of the exclusion in (b) above, the two companies are not in the same group,
  (ii) the requirements of the definition of a group in (a) and (b) are otherwise satisfied, and
  (iii) no further company could, under this provision, be the principal company of a group of which the subsidiary would be a member.

(2) If a company would otherwise belong to more than one group (the principal company of each of which is called the 'head of a group' below), it belongs only to the group which can first be determined under the following tests.
  (i) The group to which it would belong if the exclusion of a company which is not an effective 51% subsidiary in (b) above were applied without the inclusion of any amount to which the head of a group is entitled of any profits available for distribution to equity holders of a head of another group or would be entitled to any assets of a head of another group available for distribution to its equity holders on a winding up.
  (ii) The group the head of which is entitled to a greater percentage than any other head of a group of its profits available for distribution to equity holders.
  (iii) The group the head of which would be entitled to a greater percentage than any other head of a group of its assets available for distribution to equity holders on a winding-up.
  (iv) The group the head of which owns (as in *CTA 2010, s 1154(2)*) directly or indirectly more of its ordinary share capital than any other head of a group.

(3) If a group was regarded as reconstituted purely because of the removal of the requirement for group companies to be UK-resident by *FA 2000*, such that the principal company of the 'old' group is not the principal company of the 'new' group, a subsidiary which is not 'an effective 51% subsidiary' of the new principal company remains part of the group for as long as it remains 'an effective 51% subsidiary' of the company which was the principal company of the old group.

A company ('the subsidiary') is '*an effective 51% subsidiary*' of another company ('the parent') at any time if and only if:

(A) the parent is entitled to more than 50% of any profits available for distribution to equity holders of the subsidiary; and
(B) the parent would be entitled to more than 50% of any assets available for distribution to the equity holders on a winding up.

CTA 2010, Pt 5 Ch 6 (group relief: equity holders and profits or assets available for distribution) applies with suitable modifications for the purposes of (2) and (A) and (B) above. One modification for these purposes disapplies the requirement that certain arrangements for changes in profit or asset shares are assumed to take place in applying the 50% tests above.

[*TCGA 1992, s 170(2)(b)(3)–(8); SI 2010 No 2902*].

For consideration of beneficial ownership of a company's shares where they are subject to cross-options by shareholders, see *J Sainsbury plc v O'Connor* CA 1991, 64 TC 208. Although legislation overturning the *Sainsbury* decision in respect of arrangements entered into after 14 November 1991 was introduced by *F(No 2)A 1992* for group relief purposes, it does not apply for chargeable gains purposes.

A group remains the same group so long as the same company remains the principal company of the group, and if at any time the principal company of a group becomes a member of another group, the first group and the other group are regarded as the same, and the question whether or not a company has ceased to be a member of a group is determined accordingly. [*TCGA 1992, s 170(10)*].

Where the principal company of a group:

- becomes an SE (see **14.15** COMPANIES) on or after 1 April 2005 by reason of being the acquiring company in the formation of an SE by merger by acquisition (in accordance with *Council Regulations (EC) No 2157/2001, Arts 2(1), 17(2)* and *29(1)*);
- becomes a subsidiary of a holding SE (formed on or after 1 April 2005 in accordance with *Art 2(2)*); or
- is transformed on or after 1 April 2005 into an SE (in accordance with *Art 2(4)*),

the group and any group of which the SE is a member on formation are regarded as the same, and the question whether or not a company has ceased to be a member of a group is determined accordingly. [*TCGA 1992, s 170(10A)*].

The passing of a resolution, or the making of an order, or any other act for the winding-up of a member of a group is not treated as an occasion on which any company ceases to be a member of the group. [*TCGA 1992, s 170(11)*].

Example

A Ltd, which is not itself a subsidiary of another company, owns 100% of the ordinary share capital of B Ltd and C Ltd. A Ltd also owns 75% of the ordinary share capital of D Ltd. In turn D Ltd owns 75% of the ordinary share capital of E Ltd and E Ltd owns 75% of the ordinary share capital of F Ltd. B Ltd and C Ltd have no subsidiaries. Each company has only one class of shares so that its percentage ownership of ordinary share capital of another company equates to its percentage entitlement to that company's profits available for distribution and to its assets on a winding up.

For chargeable gains purposes, A Ltd is the principal company of a group of companies consisting of itself, B Ltd, C Ltd, D Ltd and E Ltd.

F Ltd is excluded from the group. Although it satisfies the '75% subsidiary' test it is not an effective 51% subsidiary of the principal company, A Ltd. A Ltd would be entitled to only 42.19%(75% × 75% × 75%) of the profits and assets of F Ltd within (A) and (B) above.

General

'*Ordinary share capital*' means all issued share capital of a company except that carrying a fixed rate of dividend only. Any share capital of a registered industrial and provident society is treated as ordinary share capital. For HMRC's interpretation of 'ordinary share capital', see HMRC Brief 87/2009.

'*Group*' and '*subsidiary*' are construed with any necessary modifications where applied to a company incorporated under the law of a country outside the UK.

'*Profits*' means income and gains. '*Trade*' includes a vocation, office or employment (including the occupation of UK woodlands before 6 April 1993).

[*TCGA 1992, s 170(1)(2)(c)(d); CTA 2010, s 1119*].

For HMRC's own notes on the capital gains definition of a group of companies, see HMRC Capital Gains Manual CG45100–45140.

HMRC have confirmed that it is possible for a Delaware Limited Liability Company that issues shares to be a member of a capital gains group (Revenue Tax Bulletin February 2001 p 827). With effect for disposals on or after 1 April 2006, it is specifically provided that an open-ended investment company (see **70.8** UNIT TRUSTS, ETC.) cannot be the principal company of a group [*TCGA 1992, s 170(4A) treated as inserted by SI 2006 No 964, Reg 107*] or a member of a group (see HMRC Capital Gains Manual, CG45110).

As regards nationalised industries, etc., see *TCGA 1992, s 170(12)–(14)*.

See also **49.7**, **49.12**, **49.19** OVERSEAS MATTERS.

Intra-group transfers

[29.3] Disposals of capital assets by one member of a group to another member (i.e. 'intra-group transfers') are treated as if made at a 'no gain/no loss' disposal value if:

(a) *either* the transferor company is UK-resident at the time of disposal *or* the asset is a 'chargeable asset' in relation to that company immediately before that time; *and*

(b) *either* the transferee company is UK-resident at the time of disposal *or* the asset is a 'chargeable asset' in relation to that company immediately after that time.

For these purposes, an asset is a '*chargeable asset*' in relation to a company at a particular time if, on a disposal by that company at that time, any gain would be a chargeable gain and would be within the charge to corporation tax by virtue of *TCGA 1992, s 10B* (non-UK resident company trading in the UK through a permanent establishment — see **49.3** OVERSEAS MATTERS).

HMRC accept that the no gain/no loss rule can apply to the grant or surrender of a lease by one group company to another (HMRC Capital Gains Manual CG45325).

Exceptions

This rule does not, however, apply to the following.

(i) Assumed (as opposed to actual) disposals.
(ii) A disposal of a debt due from a group member effected by satisfying it (or part of it).
(iii) A disposal on redemption of redeemable shares.
(iv) A disposal of an interest in shares in consideration of a capital distribution within *TCGA 1992, s 122* whether or not involving a reduction of capital.
(v) The receipt of compensation for destruction etc. of assets (in that the disposal is treated as being to the insurer or other person who ultimately bears the burden of furnishing the compensation).
(vi) A disposal by or to an investment trust within *CTA 2010, s 1158* (and see also **29.11** below).
(vii) A disposal by or to a venture capital trust within *ITA 2007, Pt 6* (and see **29.12** below).
(viii) A disposal by or to a qualifying friendly society, i.e. an incorporated friendly society within *FA 2012, s 165* (previously *ICTA 1988, s 461B*) which is entitled to income tax and corporation tax exemptions on certain profits.
(ix) A disposal to a 'dual resident investing company' within *ICTA 1988, s 404*.
(x) A disposal by or to a real estate investment trust (see **70.5** UNIT TRUSTS ETC.).
(xi) A disposal by one member of a group to another in fulfilment of its obligations under an option granted to that other member at a time when the two companies were not members of the same group.
(xii) An exchange of securities which is treated by *TCGA 1992, s 127* as it applies by virtue of *TCGA 1992, s 135* as not involving a disposal by the member of the group first mentioned above (see **63.2** and **63.5** SHARES AND SECURITIES).
For HMRC's views on this topic, see HMRC Capital Gains Manual CG45550–45573.

[*TCGA 1992, s 171; FA 2012, Sch 18 para 16*].

As regards (iv) above, the assets acquired in the capital distribution are nevertheless transferred at a 'no gain/no loss' price (see *Innocent v Whaddon Estates Ltd Ch D 1981, 55 TC 476*).

Assets held on 6 April 1965

Where a company which is or has been a group member disposes of an asset which it acquired from another group member as a result of a no gain/no loss disposal, the provisions relating to **8** ASSETS HELD ON 6 APRIL **1965** apply as if all group members were one person. [*TCGA 1992, s 174(4)*].

Assets which are trading stock of one of the companies but not of the other

[29.4] Where a company (Company A) acquires an asset as trading stock of a trade from another member of the group (Company B), and the asset did not form part of the trading stock of a trade carried on by Company B, Company A is treated for the purposes of *TCGA 1992, s 161* (see **16.9** COMPUTATION OF GAINS AND LOSSES) as acquiring the asset otherwise than as trading stock and immediately appropriating it to trading stock. The effect is that, subject to an election being made for the alternative treatment in **16.9** COMPUTATION OF GAINS AND LOSSES, a chargeable gain or allowable loss accrues to Company A based on the difference between market value and the no gain/no loss (see **29.3** above) transfer value.

Where a company (Company C) disposes of an asset forming part of the trading stock of a trade to another member of the group (Company D), and the asset is acquired by Company D otherwise than as trading stock of a trade carried on by it, Company C is treated for the purposes of *TCGA 1992, s 161* as appropriating the asset immediately before the disposal for a purpose other than use as trading stock. The effect is that Company C is deemed to have acquired the asset at that time at the amount brought into the accounts of the trade for tax purposes (see **16.9** COMPUTATION OF GAINS AND LOSSES).

References above to a trade do not include a trade carried on by a non-UK resident company other than in the UK through a permanent establishment.

[*TCGA 1992, s 173*].

Acquisition 'as trading stock' implies a commercial justification for the acquisition, see *Coates v Arndale Properties Ltd* HL 1984, 59 TC 516, *Reed v Nova Securities Ltd* HL 1985, 59 TC 516, *N Ltd v Inspector of Taxes* (Sp C 90), [1996] SSCD 346 and *New Angel Court Ltd v Adam* CA, [2004] STC 779; [2004] EWCA Civ 242.

Indexation allowance

[29.5] See **9.6** ASSETS HELD ON 31 MARCH 1982 and **38.4** INDEXATION for re-basing and indexation provisions on 'no gain/no loss' disposals.

Intra-group transfers — clawback of relief

[29.6] In the following circumstances the relief given by treating an intra-group transfer as made at no gain and no loss is effectively clawed back:

(a) where the company to which the asset was transferred leaves the group within six years after the transfer (the 'degrouping charge');
(b) where the company to which the asset was transferred becomes an investment trust within six years after the transfer; and
(c) where the company to which the asset was transferred becomes a venture capital trust within six years after the transfer.

Broadly, the company concerned must still own the asset transferred. The clawback is made by treating the company as if, immediately after its acquisition of the asset, it had sold, and immediately reacquired, the asset at its then market value (although the resulting gain is treated as accruing at a time determined by the triggering event) or, where a share disposal causes the company to leave the group, broadly on or after 19 July 2011 (or, where a commencement election is made, 1 April 2011), by adjusting the gain or loss on that disposal. There are, however, a number of reliefs and exemptions which apply to the degrouping charge in (a) above. See **29.7–29.12** for the detailed provisions.

Degrouping charge

[29.7] A degrouping charge applies where a company ceases to be a member of a group at a time when it owns an asset previously transferred to it by another group member.

Note that these provisions do not apply if, before the chargeable company leaves the group (or leaves a second group — see below), it has become an investment trust or a venture capital trust and triggered the provisions at **29.11** or **29.12** below. [*TCGA 1992, s 179(2C)(2D)*].

Post-*FA 2011* provisions

The provisions apply where a company (the transferee company) has acquired an asset from another company (the transferor company) at a time when both companies are members of the same group and the transferee company ceases to be a member of the group within six years after the time of the acquisition. It is also a requirement that the asset be within the charge to UK corporation tax both before and after the transfer, the precise conditions being similar to those for intra-group transfers at **29.3** above.

If, when the transferee leaves the group it, or an 'associated' company also leaving the group, owns (not as trading stock) the asset, replacement property to which a gain on the disposal of the original asset has been carried forward under **59** ROLLOVER RELIEF or an asset the value of which is wholly or partly derived from the original asset, the transferee is treated as if, immediately after its acquisition of the asset (subject to **29.9** below), it had sold, and immediately reacquired, the asset at its then market value. There will thus be a gain or loss by reference to the market value of the asset at that time and its 'no gain/no loss' acquisition consideration under **29.3** above. The gain or loss on the deemed sale is normally treated as accruing immediately after the beginning of the accounting period in which (or at the end of which, if that be the case) the company ceases to be a member of the group. This will apply in most cases but it is subject to the proviso that the time of accrual cannot be earlier than the time of transfer of the asset. Companies are '*associated*' for this purpose if one is a 75% subsidiary (as defined in **29.2** above) of the other or both are 75% subsidiaries of another company.

CTA 2010, ss 138–142 (limits on group relief — see Tolley's Corporation Tax) have effect as if the actual circumstances were as they are treated above as having been.

[*TCGA 1992, s 179(1)(1A)(3)(4)(10)(10A)*].

Companies leaving the group at the same time

There is an exception to the degrouping charge where both the transferee and the transferor companies leave the group at the same time and either:

- the companies are both 75% subsidiaries and effective 51% subsidiaries (as defined in **29.2** above) of another company on the date of acquisition of the asset and continue to be so until immediately after they cease to be members of the group; or
- one of the companies is both a 75% subsidiary and an effective 51% subsidiary of the other on the date of acquisition and continues to be so until immediately after the companies cease to be members of the group.

Where either condition is satisfied, the degrouping charge does not apply.

However, the charge will nevertheless apply in certain circumstances where a company in a group transfers an asset intra-group and both transferor and transferee then leave that group to form a second group which, at the time the transferee leaves the first group, is 'connected' with the first. If the transferee company leaves the second group, the charge will apply (in relation to the departure from the second group) if the intra-group transfer, which is deemed for this purpose to have taken place in the second group, occurred within the preceding six years. Where the two groups cease to be connected (without the transferee having left the second group), the transferee company and any associated company are treated as having left the second group at that time and the provision applies accordingly. Where the above exception would otherwise apply in relation to the departure from the second group it does not do so if the transferee leaving the first group was part of arrangements a main purpose of which was the avoidance of a corporation tax liability. The two groups are '*connected*' at a particular time for this purpose if, broadly, at that time the second group is under the control of the first group or both groups are under the common control of a person or persons who control or have controlled the first group at any time since the chargeable company left the first group. The general definitions of *CTA 2010, ss 450, 451* (meaning of 'control') apply for this purpose (except for banking businesses). See Tolley's Corporation Tax under Close Companies.

[*TCGA 1992, s 179(2)–(2B)(9A)*].

Company leaving group due to share disposal

Where the conditions listed below are satisfied, a degrouping gain or loss under the above provisions is not treated as a separate gain or loss, but instead the gain or loss accruing on a 'group disposal' (see below) is adjusted to take account of the degrouping gain or loss. The conditions are as follows:

(A) the transferee company ceases to be a member of the group as a result of one or more disposals ('*group disposals*') by a group member of the transferee's shares or those of another group member;

(B) either:

   (i) the company making the group disposal (or, if there is more than one such disposal, at least one of them) is UK resident at the time of disposal, the shares are within the charge to corporation tax (or would be but for the substantial shareholdings exemption — see **66** SUBSTANTIAL SHAREHOLDINGS OF COMPANIES), or any part of the gains or loss on the disposal (or at least one of them) is treated as accruing to a person under *TCGA 1992, s 13(2)* (attribution of gains to members of non-resident companies — see **49.7** OVERSEAS MATTERS), or

(ii) had (i) above applied to the group disposal or to each of them, any gain arising would not have been a chargeable gain as a result of the substantial shareholdings exemption; and

(C) *CTA 2010, s 535* (UK real estate investment trusts: exemption of gains — see **70.5** UNIT TRUSTS AND OTHER INVESTMENT VEHICLES) would not apply to the degrouping gain or loss.

For these purposes, *TCGA 1992, s 127* (share reorganisations etc. treated as not involving disposal — see **63.2** onwards SHARES AND SECURITIES) is ignored in determining whether there has been a disposal.

Where the conditions are satisfied, a chargeable gain or allowable loss on a single group disposal is calculated by adding any degrouping gain which would have arisen but for these provisions to the consideration for the group disposal. Any degrouping loss which would have been allowable but for these provisions is treated as an allowable deduction (see **16.11** COMPUTATION OF GAINS AND LOSSES) in computing the gain or loss on the group disposal.

Where the group disposal is within *TCGA 1992, s 127* so that there is no disposal for chargeable gains purposes, the adjustments in respect of the degrouping gain or loss are made to any gain or loss on a disposal of the 'new holding' (see **63.2** SHARES AND SECURITIES) or a part of it. Where there is a degrouping gain, the amount of the gain reduces the allowable expenditure and any excess over the amount of that expenditure is treated as an additional gain on the new holding disposal. If the disposal is of only part of the new holding, only that part of the excess of the degrouping gain over the allowable expenditure that corresponds to the part of the new holding disposed of is treated as an additional gain in this way. Where there is a degrouping loss, it is added to the allowable expenditure.

If there is more than one group disposal, the degrouping profit or loss is apportioned to the group disposals as the companies making them jointly elect or, if no election is made, by dividing it equally between the group disposals. An election must be made to HMRC no later than two years after the end of the accounting period in which the first group disposal is made.

If a group disposal consists of shares of more than one class, the company can apportion any increase or deduction to be made under these provisions between the classes as it considers appropriate.

[*TCGA 1992, s 179(3A)–(3H)*].

Company ceasing to be group member on principal company joining another group

Where the transferee company ceases to be a member of a group only because the principal company becomes a member of another, second, group (e.g. it is not an 'effective 51% subsidiary' of the principal company of the other group as in **29.2** above) the following provisions apply.

(I) The transferee company is not treated under the above provisions as selling the asset at that time.

(II) If:

(i) within six years of that time the company ceases at any time (‘*the relevant time*’) to satisfy the following conditions: namely that it is a ‘75% subsidiary’ (as defined in **29.2** above) of one or more members of the other group mentioned in (a) above and an ‘effective 51% subsidiary’ (as defined in **29.2** above) of one or more of those members; and

(ii) at the relevant time the company or a company in the same group, owns (otherwise than as trading stock) the asset, or property to which a chargeable gain has been rolled over from the asset, or an asset the value of which is wholly or partly derived from the original asset,

the transferee company is treated as if, immediately after acquiring the asset (subject to **29.9** below), it had sold and reacquired it at its market value at the time of acquisition.

(III) (II) above does not apply if:

(i) the transferee company ceases at the relevant time to the conditions in (II)(i) above as a result of one or more disposals by a member of the second group of the transferee's shares or those of another group member;

(ii) either:

– the company making the share disposal (or, if there is more than one such disposal, at least one of them) is UK resident at the time of disposal, the shares are within the charge to corporation tax (or would be but for the substantial shareholdings exemption — see **66**), or any part of the gains or loss on the disposal (or at least one of them) is treated as accruing to a person under *TCGA 1992, s 13(2)* (attribution of gains to members of non-resident companies — see **49.7** OVERSEAS MATTERS); or

– had those conditions applied to the share disposal or to each of them, any gain arising would not have been a chargeable gain as a result of the substantial shareholdings exemption; and

(iii) in the absence of this provision *CTA 2010, s 535* (UK real estate investment trusts: exemption of gains — see **70.5** UNIT TRUSTS AND OTHER INVESTMENT VEHICLES) would not apply to the gain or loss in (II) above.

Instead the provisions above applying to a company leaving a group as a result of a share disposal (i.e. *TCGA 1992, s 179(3C)–(3H)*) apply (with appropriate modifications).

(IV) Any gain or loss on the deemed sale in (II) above is treated as arising immediately before the relevant time.

[*TCGA 1992, s 179(5)–(8)*].

Supplementary provisions

Ceasing to be a member of a group

Where a company ceases to be a member of a group in consequence of another member of the group ceasing to exist the company is not treated as ceasing to be a group member for the purposes of the degrouping charge provisions. [*TCGA 1992, s 179(1)*]. HMRC consider that this let out only applies to the case of a parent company ceasing to be a member of a group on the occasion of its only subsidiary ceasing to exist on dissolution (or all its subsidiaries ceasing to exist simultaneously on dissolution). HMRC has confirmed it does not apply the deemed sale and reacquisition where the company receiving the asset ceases to be a group member as a result of its only subsidiary leaving the group (HMRC Capital Gains Manual CG45410 and see *Dunlop International AG v Pardoe* CA 1999, 72 TC 71).

Where, as part of a process of merger to which *TCGA 1992, s 140E* (European cross-border merger: assets left within UK tax charge — see **49.15** OVERSEAS MATTERS) applies, a company which is a member of a group ceases to exist and as a consequence assets, or shares in one or more companies which were also members of the group, are transferred to the transferee, the company which has ceased to exist and any company whose shares have been transferred to the transferee are, for the purposes of these provisions, not treated as having left the group. The transferee and the company which ceased to exist are treated as the same entity and, if the transferee is itself a member of a group following the merger, any company which was a member of the first group and became a member of the transferee's group as a result of the merger is treated as if the two groups were the same. [*TCGA 1992, s 179(1B)–(1D)*].

Where shares in a company are transferred as part of the process of the transfer of a business to which *TCGA 1992, s 140A* (see **49.13** OVERSEAS MATTERS) or *TCGA 1992, s 140C* (see **49.14** OVERSEAS MATTERS) applies, and as a result, the company ceases to be a member of a group, it is treated as not having left the group. If the company becomes a member of a second group, of which the transferee company is a member, as a result of the transfer, the company is treated as if the two groups were the same. [*TCGA 1992, s 179(1AA)*].

Value shifting

If under these provisions a deemed sale arises at any time, and if on an actual sale at market value at that time any loss or gain would, under the value shifting provisions (see **4.11** ANTI-AVOIDANCE), have been calculated as if the consideration were increased by an amount, the market value at the time of the deemed sale is treated as having been greater by that amount. [*TCGA 1992, s 179(9)*].

Assessments etc.

Any adjustment of tax or recomputation of liability on a disposal may be made by assessment or otherwise as a result of any deemed disposal and reacquisition mentioned above. [*TCGA 1992, s 179(13)*].

Example

C Ltd had the following transactions.

1.3.88	Purchased a freehold property £20,000.
1.12.11	Sold the freehold to D Ltd (a wholly-owned subsidiary) for £40,000 (market value £100,000).
31.7.17	Sold its interest in D Ltd (at which time D Ltd continued to own the freehold property).

Both C Ltd and D Ltd prepare accounts to 30 April.

The consideration for the sale of the shares is £1 million, and C Ltd purchased the shares in March 1986 for £120,000.

Relevant values of the RPI are: March 1986 96.73, March 1988 104.1, December 2011 239.4, July 2017 (assumed, for these purposes only) 269.4.

(i) C Ltd's disposal of the property to D Ltd is to be treated as one on which, after taking account of the indexation allowance, neither gain nor loss arises (see **29.3** above and **38.4** INDEXATION).

Indexation factor 239.4 – 104.1/104.1 = 1.300

	£
Cost to C Ltd	20,000
Indexation allowance £20,000 × 1.300	26,000
Deemed cost to D Ltd	£46,000

(ii) On the sale of C Ltd's shares in D Ltd on 31.7.17 (i.e. within six years after the transaction in (i) above), *C Ltd* will have a deemed disposal as follows.

Deemed disposal by D Ltd on 1.12.11	
	£
Market value at 1.12.11	100,000
Cost (as above)	46,000
Degrouping gain	£54,000
D Ltd's new base cost for future gains	£100,000

C Ltd's chargeable gain on disposal of D Ltd shares on 31.7.17	
	£
Consideration	1,000,000
Add degrouping gain	54,000
	1,054,000
Less acquisition cost	120,000
Unindexed gain	934,000
Indexation allowance (269.4 – 96.73/96.73) × £120,000	214,209
Chargeable gain subject to CT	£719,791

Deferral of degrouping charge

[29.8] Where a company is treated as making a gain under the post-*FA 2011* degrouping charge provisions in **29.7** above or such a gain is taken into account in calculating a gain on a disposal of shares under those provisions a claim can be made to defer part of the gain.

Where the degrouping gain is taken into account in calculating a gain on a disposal of shares, the claim can be made by the company making the share disposal or, if there is more than one such disposal, the companies making those disposals acting jointly. In any other case the claim is to be made by the company to whom the degrouping gain is deemed to accrue. The effect is to reduce the amount of the gain by the amount specified in the claim. The reduction must be just and reasonable with regard, in particular, to any transaction as a direct or indirect result of which the asset to which the gain relates was acquired.

Where a gain is reduced in this way, the consideration for the deemed reacquisition of the asset (see **29.7** above) is taken to be its market value less the amount of the adjustment to the gain. In effect the part of the gain excluded is deferred until final disposal of the asset.

[*TCGA 1992, s 179ZA*].

Exemption for substantial shareholdings

[29.9] Where a company ceases to be a member of a group and is deemed under *TCGA 1992, s 179* to have sold and immediately reacquired at market value an asset transferred to it by another group member, then normally the time of the deemed sale is immediately after the transfer (see **29.7** above). However, where:

- a degrouping charge (as in **29.7** above) arises in relation to an asset, and
- a gain on a disposal of that asset (by the company then owning it) immediately before the time of degrouping would have been exempt under the provisions at **66** SUBSTANTIAL SHAREHOLDINGS OF COMPANIES,

the deemed sale and reacquisition is instead treated as taking place immediately before the time of degrouping.

A comparable rule applies where the degrouping charge arises under *TCGA 1992, s 179(5)–(8)*. In this case, the rule applies by reference to the 'relevant time' (see **29.7** above) rather than the 'time of degrouping'.

[*TCGA 1992, Sch 7AC para 38*].

Exemption for mergers

[29.10] *TCGA 1992, s 179* in **29.7** above does not apply, subject to conditions, where, as part of a 'merger', a company (Company A) ceases to be a member of a group ('the A group'), and it is shown that the merger was carried out for bona fide reasons and that the avoidance of a liability to tax was not the main or one of the main purposes of the merger.

'*Merger*', in broad terms, means an arrangement whereby one or more companies ('the acquiring compan(y)(ies)') not in the A group acquire interests in the business previously carried on by Company A, and one or more members of the A group acquire interests in the business or businesses previously carried on either by the acquiring company or companies or by a company at least 90% of the ordinary share capital of which is owned by two or more of the acquiring companies. For this purpose a group member is treated as carrying on as one business the activities of that group. 25% of the value of the interests acquired must take the form of ordinary share capital, whilst the remainder of the interests acquired by the A group must consist of share capital or debentures or both. The value of the interests acquired must be substantially the same, and the consideration for the interests acquired by the acquiring companies must substantially consist of the interests acquired by the A group.

For these purposes, references to a company include a non-UK resident company.

[*TCGA 1992, s 181*].

See HMRC Capital Gains Manual CG45463 for examples on the operation of these provisions. See also **14.12** COMPANIES regarding demergers.

Company becoming an investment trust after acquiring asset intra-group

[29.11] Similar treatment as in **29.7** above (company leaving group) applies where a company (the '*acquiring company*') becomes an investment trust (within *CTA 2010, s 1158* — see **70.4** UNIT TRUSTS ETC.) not more than six years after the company acquired an asset from another company in its group, the disposal by which it acquired the asset (the corresponding disposal) having been treated by virtue of *TCGA 1992, s 171* (intra-group transfers — see **29.3** above) as a no gain/no loss disposal. The provisions apply where at the beginning of the said accounting period, the acquiring company owns, otherwise than as trading stock, either the asset itself or replacement property, i.e. property into which a chargeable gain on disposal of the asset has been rolled over as in **59** ROLLOVER RELIEF, whether directly (i.e. as a result of a single rollover relief claim) or indirectly (where two or more such claims have been made). For the purposes of these provisions, an asset acquired is deemed to be the same as an asset owned subsequently if the value of the latter asset is derived, wholly or partly, from the original asset (in particular where the original was a leasehold and the lessee has acquired the freehold reversion). The provisions do not apply if the acquiring company was an investment trust at the time of the corresponding disposal (in which case the no gain/no loss treatment would not have applied — see **29.3**(vi) above) nor if it has been an investment trust for any intervening accounting period.

The acquiring company is treated as if, immediately after the corresponding disposal, it had sold and immediately reacquired the asset at its market value at that time. The resulting chargeable gain or allowable loss is treated as accruing immediately before the end of the acquiring company's accounting period which immediately preceded that in which it became an investment trust. Notwithstanding normal time limits, any consequential corporation tax assessment may be made at any time within six years after the end of the accounting period in which the company became an investment trust. These provisions are disapplied if, prior to the company becoming an investment trust, the above treatment has already applied to the asset by virtue either of **29.7** above or **29.12** below (company becoming a venture capital trust).

[*TCGA 1992, s 101A*].

Company becoming a venture capital trust after acquiring asset intra-group

[29.12] The same treatment as in **29.11** above (company becoming an investment trust) applies where the acquiring company becomes a venture capital trust (VCT) (within *ITA 2006, Pt 6* — see **71** VENTURE CAPITAL TRUSTS) not more than six years after it acquired the asset intra-group by means of a no gain/no loss disposal under *TCGA 1992, s 171* (see **29.3** above). For this purpose, a company becomes a VCT at the time of the coming into effect of HMRC's approval (the time of approval). The provisions apply where, at the time of approval, the acquiring company owns, otherwise than as trading stock, either the asset itself (with the same rules as in **29.11** above as to derivation of assets) or replacement property (as in **29.11** above). The provisions do not apply if the acquiring company was a VCT at the time of the intra-group disposal (in which case the no gain/no loss treatment would have applied only if that disposal occurred before 17 March 1998 — see **29.3**(via) above) and do not apply if it has been a VCT at any time in the intervening period. Nor do they apply if, prior to the company becoming a VCT, the said treatment has already applied to the asset by virtue either of **29.11** above or **29.7** above (company leaving group).

The chargeable gain or allowable loss resulting from the deemed disposal at market value immediately after the intra-group transfer is treated as accruing to the acquiring company immediately before the time of approval. Notwithstanding normal time limits, any consequential corporation tax assessment may, in a case in which HMRC's approval has effect as from the beginning of an accounting period, be made at any time within six years after the end of that accounting period.

[*TCGA 1992, s 101C*].

Election to transfer gain or loss within group

[29.13] Where two companies, X and Y, are members of a group, and a chargeable gain or allowable loss accrues to X, X and Y may make a joint election to transfer the gain or loss, or a specified part of it, from X to Y. The effect of the election is that, for the purposes of corporation tax on chargeable gains:

- the gain or loss, or specified part, is treated as accruing to Y (and not to X) at the time that, but for the election, it would have accrued to X; and

- if Y is not resident in the UK, the transferred gain or loss is taken to accrue in respect of a chargeable asset (i.e. an asset a gain on the disposal of which would be a chargeable gain forming part of Y's chargeable profits under *TCGA 1992, s 10B* (UK permanent establishment of non-UK company — see **49.3** OVERSEAS MATTERS)).

An election will be disregarded if, taken together with any earlier elections, it would have the effect of transferring more than the total gain or loss. An election cannot be made in respect of a degrouping charge within **29.7** above (but see **29.9** above for the intra-group transfer of a degrouping charge).

The election must be made in writing to an HMRC officer on or before the second anniversary of the end of the accounting period of X in which the gain or loss accrued (or actual disposal was made). It can be made only if an actual transfer of the asset (or part) from X to Y would have been a no gain/no loss disposal within *TCGA 1992, s 171*. For this purpose, the condition at **29.3**(b) above is that, at the time of the deemed transfer, company Y is resident in the United Kingdom, or carrying on a trade in the United Kingdom through a permanent establishment.

This provision is intended to facilitate the bringing together of chargeable gains and allowable losses within one group company. Any payment made by X to Y, or vice versa, in connection with the election is not to be taken into account in computing profits or losses of either company or treated as a distribution, *provided* it does not exceed the chargeable gain or allowable loss deemed to accrue to Y on the disposal.

An election cannot be made to transfer a gain made on the disposal of an interest in an oil field within *TCGA 1992, s 197* (or treated as so made under *TCGA 1992, s 197(4)*) from a company carrying on a 'ring fence trade' (as defined) to a company not carrying on such a trade. This rule applies to gains accruing (or treated under *TCGA 1992, s 197(4)* as accruing) in accounting periods ending on or after 6 December 2011 (and where an accounting period straddles that date, it is treated as two separate periods for this purpose, the first ending immediately before 6 December 2011 and the second beginning on that date).

[*TCGA 1992, ss 171A, 171B; FA 2012, s 181*].

Example

A Ltd and B Ltd are members of the same group of companies, preparing accounts each year to 31 March. On 30 September 2017, A Ltd sold an asset (asset 1) to an unconnected third party for £100,000. The asset had been acquired in June 2010 for £40,000. On 29 April 2017 B Ltd sold an asset (asset 2), which had cost £70,000 in January 2008, for £50,000 to an unconnected third party. B Ltd incurred costs on the disposal of £2,000. Neither company disposes of any other assets in the year ended 31 March 2018.

A Ltd and B Ltd jointly elect before 31 March 2020 under *TCGA 1992, s 171A* for the loss on asset 2 to be transferred to A Ltd.

The chargeable gains computation for the year ended 31 March 2018 for A Ltd is as follows.

Disposal of asset 1

		£
Consideration		100,000
Cost		40,000
Indexation allowance £40,000 × say 10%		4,000
Chargeable gain		£56,000

Disposal of asset 2

	£	£
Consideration		50,000
Cost to B Ltd	70,000	
Less Cost of disposal incurred by B Ltd	2,000	(72,000)
Allowable loss transferred to A Ltd		£(22,000)

Net chargeable gains £56,000 – £22,000 = £34,000

Anti-avoidance

[29.14] There are a number of anti-avoidance provisions which apply specifically to groups of companies as well as further such provisions which are more general but can apply to groups. The provisions are covered in the paragraphs noted in the table below.

Value shifting to give a tax-free benefit. Specific provisions apply to disposals before 19 July 2011 of shares in group situations.	*TCGA 1992, ss 30–33*	**4.11** ANTI-AVOIDANCE
Depreciatory transactions within a group.	*TCGA 1992, s 176*	**4.17** ANTI-AVOIDANCE
Dividend stripping.	*TCGA 1992, s 177*	**4.18** ANTI-AVOIDANCE
Buying gains and losses: tax avoidance schemes.	*TCGA 1992, ss 184A–184F*	**29.16, 29.17**
Restriction on set-off of pre-entry losses where a company joins a group.	*TCGA 1992, Sch 7A*	**29.18–29.23**

Companies buying gains or losses

[29.15] Over the years, governments have introduced three sets of anti-avoidance provisions designed to prevent groups of companies buying and selling companies in order to make use of capital losses suffered by another company or group.

The first set of provisions, introduced in 1993 and described at **29.18–29.23** below, applies to prevent 'loss buying' where a group of companies with unrealised gains would acquire a company with realised or unrealised losses.

The assets in question would then be transferred to the new group company at no gain/no loss as in **29.3** above, and the gain would then be realised by that company, thus enabling the losses to be utilised against the gain. The provisions now operate by restricting the deduction of losses accruing to a company before the time it becomes a member of a group.

These provisions were supplemented in 1998 by provisions countering 'gain buying', where a group of companies with unrealised capital losses would acquire a company with a realised gain. The provisions were repealed on the introduction of the third set of provisions.

The third set of provisions was introduced in *FA 2006* as part of a package of anti-avoidance provisions relating to capital losses of companies (see **14.6** COMPANIES). The provisions restrict the use of losses in both loss buying and gain buying situations where there is a change of ownership of a company as a result of arrangements with a tax avoidance purpose and are described at **29.16**, **29.17** below. The provisions apply in priority to the original loss buying provisions and replace the repealed gain buying provisions. The provisions are wide in scope and can apply in certain cases where there is no group of companies involved (see **29.16**(c) below). The stated intention of the provisions is to ensure that relief for a company's capital losses should only be available against its own capital gains or those of companies that were under the same economic ownership both when the capital loss was realised and when the loss is used to reduce other gains. (Treasury Explanatory Notes to the Finance Bill 2006).

Restriction on buying gains and losses: tax avoidance schemes

[29.16] The loss buying and gain buying provisions described below apply where:

(A) there is a 'qualifying change of ownership' of a company (the '*relevant company*'), and

(B) the change occurs directly or indirectly in consequence of, or otherwise in connection with, any 'arrangements' the main purpose, or one of the main purposes, of which is to secure a 'tax advantage'.

For this purpose, there is a '*qualifying change of ownership*' of a company if any of the following occur.

(a) The company joins a group of companies. Whether a company is a member of a group is determined as in **29.2** above except that nothing in *TCGA 1992, s 170(10)* or *(10A)* is treated as preventing all the companies of one group from being regarded as joining another group when the principal company of the first group becomes a member of the other group at any time unless:
    (i) the same persons own the 'shares' of the principal company of the first group immediately before that time and the shares of the principal company of the other group immediately after that time;
    (ii) the principal company of the other group was not the principal company of any group immediately before that time; and

  (iii) immediately after that time the principal company of the other group had assets consisting entirely (or almost entirely) of shares of the principal company of the first group.

  References above to '*shares*' of a company are to the shares comprised in the company's issued share capital.

(b) The company ceases to be a member of a group.

(c) The company becomes subject to different control, i.e. one or more of the following occur:
  (I) a person who did not previously have control (within *CTA 2010, ss 450, 451*) of the company comes to have control (whether alone or together with one or more others);
  (II) a person who previously had control of the company alone comes to have control of the company together with one or more others; or
  (III) a person ceases to have control of the company (whether the person had control alone or together with one or more others).

  A company is not, however, treated as becoming subject to different control where it joins a group of companies in circumstances in which (a)(i)–(iii) above apply or where, although there is a change in the direct ownership of the company, it continues to be a 75% subsidiary of the same company.

'*Arrangements*' include any agreement, understanding, scheme, transaction or series of transactions, whether or not legally enforceable. '*Tax advantage*' means relief or increased relief from, or repayment or increased repayment of, corporation tax or the avoidance or reduction of a charge or assessment to corporation tax or the avoidance of a possible assessment to corporation tax.

[*TCGA 1992, ss 184A(1)(4), 184B(1)(4), 184C, 184D, 288(1)*].

For HMRC's views on the application of the terms 'arrangements', 'tax advantage' and 'main purpose', see **44.7** LOSSES and HMRC Capital Gains Manual CG47024–47029. For HMRC's views generally, see HMRC Capital Gains Manual CG47020–47338.

Loss buying

The loss buying provisions apply where conditions (A) and (B) above are met and the tax advantage under the arrangements involves the deduction from any chargeable gains of a loss (a '*qualifying loss*') accruing to the relevant company on a disposal of a 'pre-change asset' (see **29.17** below). In these circumstances, the qualifying loss is not deductible from a company's chargeable gains except where the gains arise on the disposal before 21 March 2007 of a pre-change asset. It is immaterial whether the loss accrues before, after or at the time of the qualifying change of ownership, whether the loss accrues at a time when there are no gains from which it could be deducted, whether the tax advantage also involves something other than the deduction of a qualifying loss or whether the advantage would be secured for the company to which the loss accrues or any other company. [*TCGA 1992, s 184A(1)(2)(5)*].

Gain buying

The gain buying provisions apply where conditions (A) and (B) above are met and the tax advantage under the arrangements involves the deduction of a loss from a gain (a '*qualifying gain*') accruing to the relevant company or any other company on a disposal of a pre-change asset. In these circumstances, only a loss arising on a disposal before 21 March 2007 of a pre-change asset can be deducted from a qualifying gain. It is immaterial whether the gain accrues before, after or at the time of the qualifying change of ownership, whether the gain accrues at a time when there are no losses which could be deducted from it, whether the tax advantage also involves something other than the deduction of a loss from a qualifying gain or whether the advantage would be secured for the company to which the gain accrues or any other company. [*TCGA 1992, s 184B(1)(2)(5)*].

For HMRC examples of the operation of the provisions see HMRC Guidance 'Avoidance through the creation and use of capital losses by companies', 27 July 2006, available in the HMRC Capital Gains Manual CG-APP8.

Pre-change assets

[29.17] For the purposes of the provisions at **29.16** above, a '*pre-change asset*' is an asset held by the relevant company before the qualifying change of ownership occurs.

An asset ceases to be a pre-change asset on disposal by a company other than the relevant company if, after the qualifying change of ownership, it has been disposed of otherwise than by an intra-group no gain/no loss transfer within **29.3** above. If the company making the latter disposal retains an interest in or over the asset, that interest continues to be a pre-change asset.

If the relevant company or any other company holds an asset at or after the time of the qualifying change of ownership the value of which derives in whole or in part from a pre-change asset, the new asset is also treated as a pre-change asset provided that the company concerned did not acquire the asset as a result of a transfer other than an intra-group no gain/no loss transfer. For this purpose, the cases in which the value of an asset is derived from another asset include cases where assets have been merged or divided or have changed their nature and cases where rights or interests in or over assets have been created or extinguished.

Where a pre-change asset is the 'old asset' for the purposes of *TCGA 1992, s 116*, (reorganisation of share capital involving QUALIFYING CORPORATE BONDS (**54.4**)) the 'new asset' under that section is also a pre-change asset. Where a pre-change asset is the 'original shares' for the purposes of *TCGA 1992, ss 127–131* (reorganisation of share capital — see **63.2** SHARES AND SECURITIES), the 'new holding' under those provisions is also a pre-change asset.

Where one of the deferral provisions listed below applies to defer a gain on the disposal of a pre-change asset, so much of any gain or loss accruing on a subsequent occasion as accrues in consequence of the application of the deferral provision is treated as a gain or loss on the disposal of a pre-change asset. The provisions are:

- *TCGA 1992, s 139* (reconstruction involving transfer of business — see **14.11** COMPANIES);
- *TCGA 1992, s 140* (transfer of assets to non-resident company — see **49.12** OVERSEAS MATTERS);
- *TCGA 1992, s 140A* (transfer or division of UK business between companies in different EC member states — see **49.13** OVERSEAS MATTERS);
- *TCGA 1992, s 140E* (European cross-border merger leaving assets within UK tax charge — see **14.15** COMPANIES);
- *TCGA 1992, ss 152, 153* (**59** ROLLOVER RELIEF — REPLACEMENT OF BUSINESS ASSETS); and
- *TCGA 1992, s 187* (postponement of charge on deemed disposal on company ceasing to be UK resident — see **49.17** OVERSEAS MATTERS).

If a pre-change asset is transferred by the relevant company to another company directly or indirectly in consequence of, or in connection with the arrangements in **29.16**(A), and any of *TCGA 1992, ss 139, 140A* or *140E* apply to the transfer, the asset is a pre-change asset in the hands of the transferee company. The above provisions for determining when an asset ceases to be a pre-change asset then apply as if the transferee company were the relevant company.

Pooled assets

Special identification rules apply where a pre-change asset (whether held by the relevant company or, as a consequence of an intra-group no gain/no loss transfer, by another company) consists of a 'section 104 holding' or '1982 holding' (see **64.3** SHARES AND SECURITIES — IDENTIFICATION RULES) of shares, securities or other assets dealt in without identifying the particular asset disposed of or acquired. Such a holding (a '*pre-change pooled asset*') cannot be added to as a result of any disposal or acquisition taking place after the qualifying change of ownership. Any shares etc. that would otherwise be added to the pre-change pooled asset instead form or are added to a separate *s 104* holding (the '*other pooled asset*').

Shares etc. of the same class as those comprised in the other pooled asset which are disposed of at or after the time of the qualifying change of ownership are identified:

- first with shares etc. forming part of the other pooled asset;
- next with shares etc. forming part of the pre-change pooled asset; and
- finally, in accordance with the normal identification rules described at **64.3** SHARES AND SECURITIES — IDENTIFICATION RULES).

These identification rules apply even if some or all of the assets disposed of are separately identified by the disposal or by a transfer or delivery giving effect to it.

Shares etc. disposed of by a company in one capacity are not identified with shares etc. which are held, or which can only be disposed of, in some other capacity. Shares or securities of a company are not treated as being of the same class unless they are so treated by the practice of a recognised stock exchange (see **63.30** SHARES AND SECURITIES) or would be if dealt with on such an exchange.

[*TCGA 1992, ss 184A(3), 184B(3), 184E, 184F*].

Restriction on set-off of pre-entry losses where a company joins a group

[29.18] Where the loss buying provisions at **29.16** above do not apply, *TCGA 1992, Sch 7A* restricts the deduction of allowable losses ('pre-entry losses') which accrue to a company before the time it becomes a member of a group of companies (the '*relevant group*'). The restriction is described in detail at **29.19–29.23** below. For HMRC comment on this legislation, see HMRC Capital Gains Manual CG47000–47011, 47520–47989.

The restriction does not apply where the loss buying provisions at **29.16** above apply.

[*TCGA 1992, s 177A, Sch 7A para 1(1)*].

Before 19 July 2011, the provisions also applied to losses accruing to a company after the time at which it became a member of a group on assets held by it at that time. The restrictions on the use of such losses were removed by *FA 2011* as they are now considered unnecessary because of *TCGA 1992, s 184A* (see **29.16** above). The restrictions do, however, continue to apply to such losses realised before 19 July 2011 as if they had accrued immediately before the company became a member of the group. See earlier editions of this work for details.

Definitions

[29.19] A '*pre-entry loss*', in relation to a company, means any allowable loss that accrued to it at a time before it became a member of the relevant group. [*TCGA 1992, Sch 7A para 1(2)*].

If:

(a) the principal company of a group of companies ('*the first group*') has at any time become a member of another group ('*the second group*') so that the two groups are treated as the same under *TCGA 1992, s 170(10)* or *(10A)* (see **29.2** above), and
(b) the second group, together in pursuance of *TCGA 1992, s 170(10)* or *(10A)* with the first group, is the relevant group,

then, except where the circumstances are as listed below, the members of the first group are treated for the purposes of *Sch 7A* as having become members of the relevant group at that time, and not by virtue of *TCGA 1992, s 170(10)* or *(10A)* at the times when they became members of the first group. The circumstances are where:

(1) the persons who immediately before the time when the principal company of the first group became a member of the second group owned the shares comprised in the issued share capital of the principal company of the first group are the same as the persons who, immediately after that time, owned the shares comprised in the issued share capital of the principal company of the relevant group; and

(2) the company which is the principal company of the relevant group immediately after that time
  (i) was not the principal company of any group immediately before that time; and
  (ii) immediately after that time had assets consisting entirely, or almost entirely, of shares comprised in the issued share capital of the principal company of the first group.

[*TCGA 1992, Sch 7A para 1(6)(7)*].

For discussion of *Sch 7A para 1(6)(7)* see *Five Oaks Properties Ltd v HMRC (and related appeals)* (Sp C 563), [2006] SSCD 769 and *HMRC v Prizedome Ltd; HMRC v Limitgood Ltd* CA, [2009] STC 980.

Where an allowable loss accrues to a company under *TCGA 1992, s 116(10)(b)* (gain or loss on shares exchanged on reorganisation, conversion or reconstruction for qualifying corporate bonds to crystallise when bonds sold; see **54.4** QUALIFYING CORPORATE BONDS), that loss is deemed to accrue at the time of the reorganisation etc. for the purposes of deciding whether a loss accrues before a company becomes a member of the relevant group. [*TCGA 1992, Sch 7A para 1(9)*]. Likewise, the annual deemed disposals of unit trust etc. holdings of a life assurance company's long-term insurance fund under *TCGA 1992, s 212* are deemed to occur for this purpose without regard to the 'spreading' provisions of *TCGA 1992, s 213*. [*TCGA 1992, Sch 7A para 1(10)*].

Restrictions on the deduction of pre-entry losses

[29.20] In the calculation of the amount to be included in respect of chargeable gains in any company's total profits for any accounting period:

(a) if in that period there is any chargeable gain from which the whole or any part of any pre-entry loss accruing in that period is deductible in accordance with the provisions in **29.21** below, the loss or, as the case may be, that part of it is deducted from that gain;
(b) if, after all the deductions in (a) above have been made, there is in that period any chargeable gain from which the whole or any part of any pre-entry loss carried forward from a previous accounting period is deductible in accordance with the provisions in **29.21**, the loss or, as the case may be, that part of it is deducted from that gain;
(c) the total of chargeable gains (if any) remaining after all the deductions in (a) or (b) above is subject to deductions in accordance with *TCGA 1992, s 8(1)* (chargeable gains less allowable losses of company to be included in chargeable profits; see **14.3** COMPANIES) in respect of any allowable losses that are not pre-entry losses; and
(d) any pre-entry loss which has not been the subject of a deduction under (a) or (b) above (as well as any other losses falling to be carried forward under *section 8(1)*) are carried forward to the following accounting period of that company.

[*TCGA 1992, Sch 7A para 6(1)*].

Subject to (a)–(d) above, any question as to which or what part of any pre-entry loss has been deducted from any particular chargeable gain is decided in accordance with such elections as may be made by the company to which the loss accrued. An election must be made by notice to HMRC before the end of the period of two years beginning with the end of the company's accounting period in which the gain in question accrued. [*TCGA 1992, Sch 7A para 6(2)(3)*].

For the purposes of *Sch 7A* where any matter falls to be determined under the above provisions by reference to an election but no election is made, it is assumed, so far as consistent with any elections that have been made that losses are set against gains in the order in which the losses accrued, and that the gains against which they are set are also determined according to the order in which they accrued with losses being set against earlier gains before they are set against later ones. [*TCGA 1992, Sch 7A para 6(4)*].

Gains from which pre-entry losses are to be deductible

[29.21] A pre-entry loss that accrued to a company before it became a member of the relevant group is deductible from a chargeable gain accruing to that company if the gain is one accruing:

(a) on a disposal made by that company before the date on which it became a member of the relevant group ('*the entry date*');
(b) on the disposal of an asset which was held by that company immediately before the entry date; or
(c) on the disposal of any asset which:
    (i) was acquired on or after the entry date by the company to whom the loss accrued ('company A') or a company which, at the time of the acquisition, was a group company of company A (i.e. a member of the same group as company A), from a person who was not a member of the relevant group at the time of the acquisition; and
    (ii) since its acquisition from that person has not been used or held for any purposes other than those of a trade or business which was being carried on by company A immediately before the entry date and which continued to be carried on by company A, or a company which, when it carried on the trade or business, was a group company of company A, until the disposal.

Where the company subsequently becomes a member of another group, the above provision continues to apply to any loss which accrued before the company joined the relevant group by reference to the date it joined the relevant group (and does not apply separately to the loss by reason of it being a pre-entry loss in relation to the company becoming a member of the second group).

[*TCGA 1992, Sch 7A para 7(1)–(1C)*].

Where two or more companies become members of the relevant group at the same time and those companies were all members of the same group of companies immediately before they became members of the relevant group, then:

(I) an asset is treated for the purposes of (b) above as held, immediately before it became a member of the relevant group, by the company to which the pre-entry loss in question accrued if that company is one of those companies and the asset was in fact so held by another of those companies; and

(II) the acquisition of an asset is treated for the purposes of (c) above as an acquisition by the company to which the pre-entry loss in question accrued if that company is one of those companies and the asset was in fact acquired (whether before or after they became members of the relevant group) by another of those companies.

[*TCGA 1992, Sch 7A para 7(3)*].

An asset is not treated as a '*pre-entry asset*' (i.e. as held by a company immediately before the entry date) if the company which held the asset on the entry date is not the company making the disposal and since the entry date the asset has been disposed of in circumstances in which *TCGA 1992, s 171* (intra-group transfers at no gain/no loss — see **29.3** above) does not apply, except where the company making the disposal retains an interest in or over the asset (when the interest is treated as a pre-entry asset).

An asset ('*the second asset*') which derives wholly or partly its value from another asset ('*the first asset*') acquired or held by a company at any time, is treated as the same asset if the second asset is held subsequently by the same company, or by any company which is or has been a member of the same group of companies as that company (e.g. a freehold derived from a leasehold where the lessee acquires the reversion). Where this treatment applies, whether under this provision or not (*TCGA 1992, s 43* is similar; see **16.5** COMPUTATION OF GAINS AND LOSSES), the second asset is treated as a pre-entry asset in relation to a company if the first asset would have been.

[*TCGA 1992, Sch 7A para 7(4)–(4C)*].

Subject to *Sch 7A para 7(6)* below, where a gain accrues on the disposal of the whole or any part of:

(1) any asset treated as a single asset but comprising assets only some of which were held at the time mentioned in (b) above; or

(2) an asset which is treated as held at that time by virtue of a provision requiring an asset which was not held at that time to be treated as the same as an asset which was so held (see **29.19** above),

a pre-entry loss is deductible under (b) above from the amount of that gain to the extent only of such proportion of that gain as is attributable to assets held at that time or, as the case may be, represents the gain that would have accrued on the asset so held. [*TCGA 1992, Sch 7A para 7(5)*].

Where:

(A) a chargeable gain accrues under *TCGA 1992, s 116(10)* on the disposal of a qualifying corporate bond which has been exchanged for shares etc. (see **54.4** QUALIFYING CORPORATE BONDS and **29.19** above);

(B) that bond was not held as required by (b) above at the time mentioned in (b); and

(C) the whole or any part of the asset which is the 'old asset' for the purposes of *TCGA 1992, s 116* was so held,

the question whether that gain is one accruing on the disposal of an asset, the whole or any part of which was held by a particular company at that time, is determined for the purposes of *Sch 7A para 7* as if the bond were deemed to have been so held to the same extent as the old asset. [*TCGA 1992, Sch 7A para 7(6)*].

Change of a company's nature

[29.22] If:

(a) within any period of three years, a company becomes a member of a group of companies and there is (either earlier or later in that period, or at the same time) 'a major change in the nature or conduct of a trade or business' carried on by that company immediately before it became a member of that group; or
(b) at any time the scale of the activities in a trade or business carried on by a company has become small or negligible, and before any considerable revival of the trade or business, that company becomes a member of a group of companies,

the trade or business carried on before that change, or which has become small or negligible, is disregarded for the purposes of **29.21**(c) above in relation to any time before the company became a member of the group in question.

'*A major change in the conduct of a trade or business*' includes a reference to a major change in services or facilities provided or a major change in customers or, in the case of a company with investment business, a major change in the nature of investments held. Regard will also be had to appropriate changes in other factors such as the location of the company's business premises, the identity of the company's suppliers, management or staff, the company's methods of manufacture, or the company's pricing or purchasing policies to the extent that these factors indicate that a major change has occurred. Efficiency changes and technological advancements would not in themselves indicate that a major change in the nature or conduct of a trade or business has occurred.

HMRC will compare any two points in three years which include the date of change of ownership of the company. This applies even if the change is the result of a gradual process which began outside the period of three years mentioned in (a) above. HMRC take note of both qualitative and quantitative issues as discussed in the cases *Willis v Peeters Picture Frames Ltd* CA (NI) 1982, 56 TC 436 and *Purchase v Tesco Stores Ltd* Ch D 1984, 58 TC 46 respectively (HMRC Statement of Practice 10/91).

Where the operation of the above provisions depends on circumstances or events at a time after the company becomes a member of any group of companies (but not more than three years after), an assessment to give effect to the provisions may be made within six years from that time or the latest such time.

[*TCGA 1992, Sch 7A para 8; FA 2016, s 55*].

Miscellaneous

[29.23] Where, but for an election under *TCGA 1992, s 161(3)* (appropriation of asset to trading stock; see **16.9** COMPUTATION OF GAINS AND LOSSES), there would be deemed to have been a disposal on an appropriation prior to 8 March 2017 by a company of an asset, the amount by which the market value of the asset may be treated as increased under the election does not include the amount of any pre-entry loss that would have accrued on that disposal, and *Sch 7A* has effect as if the pre-entry loss of the last mentioned amount had accrued to the company at that time. [*TCGA 1992, Sch 7A para 10; F(No 2)A 2017, s 26*].

The provisions of *Sch 7A* are prevented from applying where a loss arises, or a company joins a group, as a result of any enactment under which transfers of property etc. are made from a statutory body, a subsidiary of such a body or a company wholly owned by the Crown. [*TCGA 1992, Sch 7A para 11*].

For the purposes of *Sch 7A*, and without prejudice to the provisions in *Sch 7A para 11* above, where:

(a) a company which is a member of a group of companies becomes at any time a member of another group of companies as the result of a disposal of shares in or other securities of that company or any other company; and
(b) that disposal is one within the no gain/no loss provisions in **9.6** ASSETS HELD ON 31 MARCH **1982**,

Sch 7A has effect in relation to the losses that accrued to that company before that time and the assets held by that company at that time as if any time when it was a member of the first group were included in the period during which it is treated as having been a member of the second group. [*TCGA 1992, Sch 7A para 12*].

Key points

[29.24] Points to consider are as follows.

- The case of *Swift v HMRC* FTT, [2010] UKFTT 88(TC) has thrown doubt on whether some Delaware LLCs have issued ordinary share capital. See **29.2**.
- Many people consider the UK residence requirement in *TCGA 1992, s 171* is contrary to the terms of the Treaty for the Functioning of the EU and that the provisions should apply to transfers to companies resident in any EU (or EEA) Member State. HMRC currently resists that interpretation. See **29.3**.
- *TCGA 1992, s 181* is exceptionally useful in setting up joint ventures. It allows one or more groups to hive business assets down to a new subsidiary, which then leaves the group when the other member of the joint venture acquires more than 25% of its

issued share capital (so it ceases to be a 75% subsidiary of the parent). Without *s 181*, the degrouping charge would make the formation of commercial joint ventures much more difficult. See **29.10**.

- Any number of elections to transfer a gain can be made in respect of any given gain, so the gain can be split between several group companies (providing the total does not exceed the original gain). This means that part of the gain can be transferred to a company with some allowable losses, part to a company with current year trading losses, and so on.

30

HMRC — Administration

Introduction — the Commissioners for HMRC	**30.1**
'Care and management' powers	**30.2**
Non-statutory clearances	**30.3**
Use of electronic communications	**30.4**
Power to give statutory effect to concessions	**30.5**
Complaints etc.	**30.6**
Mistake or delay by HMRC	**30.6**
HMRC Charter	**30.7**
Adjudicator	**30.8**
Revenue functions carried out by the National Crime Agency	**30.9**

Introduction — the Commissioners for HMRC

[30.1] The collection and management of capital gains tax and corporation tax is administered by the **Commissioners for Her Majesty's Revenue and Customs**. [*TMA 1970, s 1; CRCA 2005, Sch 4 para 12*].

Under the Commissioners for HMRC are officers of Revenue and Customs who are civil servants. They are responsible for processing returns, making assessments, dealing with claims, allowances and appeals, carrying out enquiries and collection and recovery of tax.

Criminal prosecutions of tax offences in England and Wales are conducted by an independent Revenue and Customs Prosecutions Office (now part of the Crown Prosecution Service), whose director is appointed by the Attorney General. [*CRCA 2005, ss 34–42, Sch 3*].

In this publication, 'HMRC' is generally used to mean both Her Majesty's Revenue and Customs and their predecessors in relation to direct taxes, the Inland Revenue. Where the context requires, however, 'the Revenue' is used to refer to the Inland Revenue.

The remainder of this chapter looks at certain HMRC administrative powers and the rules for complaints about HMRC. Also included is the power for the National Crime Agency to take over HMRC's powers where a chargeable gain arises as a result of criminal conduct.

'Care and management' powers

[30.2] As noted at **30.1** above, the Commissioners for HMRC have responsibility for the 'collection and management' of taxes, including capital gains tax and corporation tax. Before 18 April 2005, the Board of Inland Revenue had responsibility for the 'care and management' of direct taxes. The extent and limits of these care and management powers were considered before the Courts on a number of occasions. These decisions may be relevant to the powers of HMRC.

For the validity of amnesties by the Board, see *R v CIR (ex p. National Federation of Self-Employed and Small Businesses Ltd)* HL 1981, 55 TC 133. HMRC EXTRA-STATUTORY CONCESSIONS (**33**) have been the subject of frequent judicial criticism but their validity has never been directly challenged in the Courts. In *R v CIR (ex p. Fulford-Dobson)* QB 1987, 60 TC 168, it was held that there had been no unfair treatment by the Revenue when it failed to apply a published extra-statutory concession because it was clear from the facts of the case that it was one of tax avoidance and this was a clearly stated general circumstance in which concessions would not be applied (cf. *R v Inspector of Taxes, Hull, ex p. Brumfield and others* QB 1988, 61 TC 589 at **5.35** APPEALS). For a general discussion of the Board's care and management powers and an example of a ruling by the Court that the Board had acted reasonably, see *R v CIR (ex p. Preston)* HL 1985, 59 TC 1. See also *R v Attorney-General (ex p. ICI plc)* CA 1986, 60 TC 1, *R v CIR (ex p. MFK Underwriting Agencies Ltd and others)* QB 1989, 62 TC 607 and *R v CIR (ex p. Matrix-Securities Ltd)* HL 1994, 66 TC 587. See also **5.35** APPEALS regarding judicial review of Revenue powers.

The Inland Revenue had a common law power to prosecute, which is ancillary to, supportive of and limited by their duty to collect taxes (*R v Criminal Cases Review Commission (ex p. Hunt)* QB 2000, 73 TC 406).

The Inland Revenue policy of selective prosecution for criminal offences (see **52.40** PENALTIES) in connection with tax evasion did not render a decision in a particular case unlawful or *ultra vires*, provided that the case was considered on its merits fairly and dispassionately to see whether the criteria for prosecution were satisfied, and that the decision to prosecute was then taken in good faith for the purpose of collecting taxes and not for some ulterior, extraneous or improper purpose (*R v CIR (ex p. Mead and Cook)* QB 1992, 65 TC 1).

The making of a 'forward tax agreement' with a non-UK domiciled individual (see **55.8** REMITTANCE BASIS) was held to be 'not a proper exercise' of the Inland Revenue's 'duties of care and management' (*Fayed and Others v Advocate-General for Scotland (representing CIR)* SCS, [2002] STC 910).

HMRC have published a 'Code of Governance for resolving tax disuptes' which is intended to provide transparency and consistency to the Department's settlements of such disputes.

Agreements to forgo corporation tax reliefs

With effect, broadly, from 22 April 2009, there are provisions which prevent a company which has entered into an agreement with the Government under which it agrees to forgo a corporation tax relief, from obtaining that relief through the normal operation of tax legislation. The provisions are aimed in particular at banks using the Asset Protection Scheme announced on 19 January 2009. See *FA 2009, s 25*.

Taxpayers affected by the 2014 floods

HMRC have set up a helpline and announced a number of relaxations to the normal tax obligations for anyone affected by the flooding in the UK in early 2014. The helpline is 0800 904 7800 and operates 8am to 8pm on weekdays and 8am to 4pm at weekends. HMRC will agree instalment arrangements for taxpayers unable to pay as a result of the floods; agree a practical approach when individuals and businesses have lost records to the floods; suspend debt collection proceedings; and cancel penalties for missed deadlines. (HMRC Press Release 12 February 2014).

Non-statutory clearances

[30.3] HMRC's non-statutory clearance regime is covered at www.gov.uk/guidance/non-statutory-clearance-service-guidance and www.gov.uk/seeking-clearance-or-approval-for-a-transaction. HMRC will provide written confirmation of their view of the application of tax law to a specific transaction or event where a taxpayer has fully considered HMRC's guidance and been unable to find the necessary information or where a taxpayer remains uncertain about HMRC's interpretation of recent tax legislation. In certain circumstances, HMRC will not give advice under the service; for example, if they do not think that there are genuine points of uncertainty or they consider that the transactions concerned are for the purposes of avoiding tax. HMRC will in most cases aim to respond to clearance applications within 28 days. Clearance applications should be made to HMRC Non-statutory Clearances Team, 5th Floor, Alexander House, 21 Victoria Avenue, Southend-on-Sea, Essex SS99 1AA. Large Business Service taxpayers should send clearance applications to their client relationship manager.

Use of electronic communications

[30.4] HMRC have broad powers to make regulations, by statutory instrument (see *SI 2003 No 282*), to facilitate two-way electronic communication in the delivery of information, e.g. tax returns and the making of tax payments. The regulations may allow or require the use of intermediaries such as Internet Service Providers. They will have effect notwithstanding any pre-existing legislation requiring delivery or payment in a manner which would otherwise preclude the use of electronic communications or intermediaries. [*FA 1999, ss 132, 133*].

HMRC have further regulatory powers (see now *SI 2001 No 56*) to provide tax-free incentives to use electronic communications as above or otherwise in connection with tax matters. These may, in particular, take the form of discounts, the allowing of additional time for compliance or for payment of tax, or the facility to deliver information or make payments at more convenient intervals. [*FA 2000, s 143, Sch 38; ITTOIA 2005, s 778; CTA 2009, s 1287*]. In this connection, for one year from April 2000, individual taxpayers who personally filed their self-assessment tax return via the internet and paid any tax due electronically received a discount of £10 (Revenue Press Release 16 February 2000).

Agents are authorised to file individual clients' personal tax returns over the internet, subject to conditions as to authorisation of the agent by the client, authentication of the information by the client and use of Revenue approved software (see now Revenue Directions under *SI 2003 No 282, Reg 3*, 4 April 2008). After 4 March 2003, agents are likewise authorised to file companies' tax returns over the internet, subject to similar conditions (Revenue Directions under *SI 2003 No 282, Reg 3*, 4 March 2003; HMRC Directions under *SI 2003 No 282, Regs 3* and *10*, 6 January 2010).

For notes on electronic filing and payment, see Revenue Tax Bulletin June 2000 pp 757, 758. For payment by debit card over the internet, see Revenue Press Release 10 January 2001. For internet filing of returns and the Internet Corporation Tax Service (which allows companies and authorised agents to view details of liabilities and payments online), see the gov.uk website.

Mandatory e-filing

HMRC have wide powers to make regulations requiring the use of electronic communication for the delivery of information required or authorised to be delivered under tax legislation. [*FA 2002, ss 135, 136*]. Companies are to be required to deliver tax returns electronically in a specified data format (known as iXBRL). This requirement applies to returns for accounting periods ending after 31 March 2010 which are delivered on or after 1 April 2011. See **58.2** RETURNS.

Power to give statutory effect to concessions

[30.5] The Treasury has the power, by order, to give statutory effect to any HMRC 'concession' made before 21 July 2008 which is in effect on that date.

For this purpose, a '*concession*' is a statement by HMRC, whether described as an extra-statutory concession, a statement of practice, an interpretation, a press release, or in any other way, that they will treat taxpayers as if they were entitled to a reduction in a tax liability or any other concession to which they are not, or may not be, entitled to by law.

[*FA 2008, s 160*].

For the first orders made under this provision, see *SI 2009 No 730* and *SI 2010 No 157*.

For lists of existing concessions and statements of practice, see **33** HMRC EXTRA-STATUTORY CONCESSIONS and **35** HMRC STATEMENTS OF PRACTICE.

Complaints etc.

Mistake or delay by HMRC

[30.6] Where the taxpayer complains, HMRC will reimburse any 'reasonable costs' incurred by him as a direct result of their mistake or 'unreasonable' delay. They may also pay non-taxable compensation of usually between £25 and £500 for worry and distress caused by the mistake or delay and/or for further delays or errors in handling the complaint itself. They will not compensate for time spent by the taxpayer sorting things out, unless he can show lost earnings as a direct result, nor for a difference of opinion where they are proved wrong but had not taken an unreasonable view of the law. These practices are embodied in HMRC's Code of Practice 1 (COP 1) 'Putting things right when we make mistakes'.

See also **42.9** LATE PAYMENT INTEREST AND PENALTIES and **51.29** PAYMENT OF TAX.

HMRC Charter

[30.7] HMRC published in November 2009 a Charter setting out standards of behaviour and values to which they aspire in dealing with taxpayers. The Charter, entitled 'Your Charter' was revised in January 2016 and now sets out what taxpayers can expect under seven headings: HMRC undertake to:

(a) respect taxpayers and treat them as honest;
(b) provide a helpful, efficient and effective service;
(c) be professional and act with integrity;
(d) protect taxpayers' information and respect their privacy;
(e) accept that someone else can represent taxpayers;
(f) deal with complaints quickly and fairly; and
(g) tackle people who bend or break the rules.

The Charter also sets out what HMRC expect from taxpayers: to be honest and respect HMRC staff; to work with HMRC to get things right; to find out what they need to do and keep HMRC informed; to keep accurate records and protect their information; to know what their representative does on their behalf; to respond in good time and to take reasonable care to avoid mistakes.

The Charter must be regularly reviewed by HMRC and they must publish an annual report detailing the extent to which they have demonstrated the standards and values set out in the Charter. [*CRCA 2005, s 16A*].

HMRC have published a series of codes of practice, available from local tax offices, setting out the standards of service people can expect in relation to specific aspects of HMRC's work (see **32** HMRC EXPLANATORY PUBLICATIONS). The codes are not meant to represent any change of practice although some practices mentioned in them were not previously publicly available.

Adjudicator

[30.8] A taxpayer who is not satisfied with the HMRC response to a complaint has the option of putting the case to an Adjudicator. The Adjudicator's office considers complaints about HMRC's handling of a taxpayer's affairs, e.g. excessive delays, errors, discourtesy or the exercise of HMRC discretion. Matters subject to existing rights of appeal are excluded.

Complaints will normally go to the Adjudicator only after they have been considered by the Director of the relevant HMRC office, and where the taxpayer is still not satisfied with the response received. The alternatives of pursuing the complaint to HMRC's Head Office, to an MP, or (through an MP) to the Parliamentary Ombudsman continue to be available. The Adjudicator will review all the facts, consider whether the complaint is justified, and, if so, make recommendations as to what should be done.

The Adjudicator publishes annual reports summarising the outcome of complaints made. Recent reports can be viewed on the Adjudicator's website (at www.adjudicatorsoffice.gov.uk). Contact should be made with the Adjudicator's Office, PO Box 10280, Nottingham, NG2 9PF. Tel: 0300–057 1111. Fax: 0300–057 1212. An explanatory leaflet is available from the Adjudicator which describes the actions a taxpayer should take and how the Adjudicator will respond to complaints.

Revenue functions carried out by the National Crime Agency

[30.9] Under *Proceeds of Crime Act 2002, Pt 6*, the National Crime Agency (NCA) (previously the Serious Organised Crime Agency) is empowered to carry out the functions vested in HMRC in relation to (amongst other matters) capital gains tax and corporation tax. The NCA must have reasonable grounds to suspect either that:

(a) a gain accruing to a person in respect of a chargeable period is a chargeable gain and accrues as a result (whether wholly or partly, directly or indirectly) of the 'criminal conduct' of that person or another, or
(b) a company is chargeable to corporation tax on its profits arising in a chargeable period and the profits arise as a result (whether wholly or partly, directly or indirectly) of the criminal conduct of the company or another person,

and must serve a notice on HMRC specifying the person or company, the period or periods concerned, and the functions which he intends to carry out. The periods involved may include periods beginning before the *Act* was passed.

The NCA may cease carrying out the functions specified in the notice at any time (by notifying HMRC), but *must* so cease where the conditions allowing the notice to be made are no longer satisfied.

For the above purposes, '*criminal conduct*' is conduct which constitutes an offence anywhere in the UK or which would do so if it occurred there, but does not include conduct constituting an offence relating to a matter under the care and management of HMRC.

It should be noted that the vesting of a function in the NCA under these provisions does not divest HMRC of the function (so that, for example, they can continue to carry out routine work). Certain functions, as listed in *Proceeds of Crime Act 2002, s 323(3)* cannot be carried out by the NCA.

[*Proceeds of Crime Act 2002, ss 317, 323(1)(3), 326(1)(2); Crime and Courts Act 2013, Sch 8 paras 108, 122; SI 2008 No 755*].

31

HMRC — Confidentiality of Information

Introduction	**31.1**
Organisations to which HMRC may disclose information	**31.2**
Publication of details of deliberate tax defaulters	**31.3**
Publication of details of persons failing to correct	**31.4**
Publication of details of tax agents engaging in dishonest conduct	**31.5**
Criminal offence of disclosure of tax information	**31.6**

Introduction

[31.1] Officials of HMRC may not generally disclose information held by HMRC. All Commissioners and officers of HMRC must make a declaration acknowledging their duty of confidentiality as soon as reasonably practicable following their appointment. [*CRCA 2005, ss 3, 18*]. The exceptions to this rule are covered in this chapter at **31.2–31.5** below. See **31.6** below for the criminal offence of disclosing tax information held in the exercise of tax functions.

HMRC *are* permitted to use information held or acquired in connection with one function in connection with any other function. [*CRCA 2005, s 17(1)*].

As to production in Court proceedings of documents in the possession of HMRC or copies of documents previously submitted to HMRC which are held by a party to the proceedings, see *Brown's Trustees v Hay* SCS 1897, 3 TC 598; *In re Joseph Hargreaves Ltd* CA 1900, 4 TC 173; *Shaw v Kay* SCS 1904, 5 TC 74; *Soul v Irving* CA 1963, 41 TC 517; *H v H* Fam D 1980, 52 TC 454; *R v CIR (ex p. J Rothschild Holdings plc)* CA 1987, 61 TC 178; *Lonrho plc v Fayed and Others (No 4)* CA 1993, 66 TC 220.

HMRC were held to have breached their duty of confidentiality in *R (oao Ingenious Media Holding plc) v HMRC* SC, [2016] STC 2306.

Organisations to which HMRC may disclose information

[31.2] HMRC are authorised to disclose information to the following.

(a) **Charity Commissioners for England and Wales.** HMRC are authorised to disclose certain information to the Charity Commissioners regarding bodies which are or have been charities. Similar provisions apply in Scotland as regards disclosure to the Lord Advocate. [*Charities Act 1993, s 10; Law Reform (Miscellaneous Provisions) (Scotland) Act 1990, s 1; SI 2010 No 588*].

(b) **Department of Trade and Industry, Department of Employment or Statistics Board.** HMRC are authorised to disclose, for the purposes of statistical surveys, the names and addresses of employers and information concerning the number of persons employed by individual concerns. [*FA 1969, s 58*].

(c) **Tax authorities of other countries.** HMRC are authorised to disclose information concerning individual taxpayers where it is necessary to the administration or enforcement of double taxation agreements and may be required to disclose information to an advisory commission set up under the Arbitration Convention (*90/436/EEC*). [*TIOPA 2010, ss 126–129; ICTA 1988, s 816(1)(2A)–(5); TCGA 1992, s 277(4)*].

Disclosure may also be made to the tax authorities of other member states of the EU which observe similar confidentiality and use the information only for taxation purposes. [*FA 2003, s 197(1)–(5)*].

The UK may enter into agreements with other countries for mutual assistance in the enforcement of taxes. Such agreements may include provision for the exchange of information foreseeably relevant to the administration, enforcement or recovery of any UK tax or foreign tax. HMRC may disclose information under such agreements only if satisfied that the confidentiality rules applied by the foreign authorities concerned with respect to the information are no less strict than the equivalent UK rules. [*FA 2006, s 173*]. This power has been exercised to enter into the joint Council of Europe/Organisation for Economic Co-operation and Development Convention on Mutual Administrative Assistance in Tax Matters, signed on behalf of the UK on 24 May 2007. [*SI 2007 No 2126; SI 2011 No 1079*]. In addition to tax enforcement agreements included as part of double tax treaties, the UK has also signed tax enforcement agreements with Jersey (see *SI 2013 No 3151*), Guernsey (*SI 2013 No 3154*) and the Marshall Islands (*SI 2013 No 3153*).

In addition to tax information agreements included as part of double tax treaties (see **21.2** DOUBLE TAX RELIEF), the UK has also signed tax information exchange agreements with Bermuda (*SI 2008 No 1789*), the Isle of Man, Guernsey (*SI 2009 No 3011*), Jersey (*SI 2009 No 3012*), the British Virgin Islands (*SI 2009 No 3013; SI 2014 No 1359*), Anguilla (*SI 2010 No 2677; SI 2014 No 1357*), the Turks and Caicos Islands (*SI 2010 No 2679; SI 2014 No 1360*), Liechtenstein (*SI 2010 No 2678*), Gibraltar (*SI 2010 No 2680; SI 2014 No 1356*), the Bahamas (*SI 2010 No 2684*), St Lucia (*SI 2011 No 1076*), St Vincent and the Grenadines (*SI 2011 No 1078*), Antigua and Barbuda (*SI 2011 No 1075*), St Christopher and Nevis (*SI 2011 No 1077*), Belize (*SI 2011 No 1685*), Grenada (*SI 2011 No 1687*), San Marino (*SI 2011 No 1688*), Dominica (*SI 2011 No 1686*), the Netherlands Antilles, Liberia (*SI 2011 No 2434*), Aruba (*SI 2011 No 2435*), Curacao, Sint Maarten and BES Islands (*SI 2011 No 2433*), the Marshall Islands, Brazil (*SI 2015 No 1887*), Uruguay (*SI 2014 No 1358*), Monaco (*SI 2015 No 804*) and Macao (*SI 2015 No 801*). For agreements in connection with the EU Savings Directive and special withholding tax, see **21.10** DOUBLE TAX RELIEF.

HMRC may also disclose information to the tax authority of Switzerland pursuant to a request under Article 36 of the UK/Switzerland tax collection agreement (see **49.22** OVERSEAS MATTERS). [*FA 2012, Sch 36 para 25*]. See also **51.32** PAYMENT OF TAX.

(d) **Occupational Pensions Board.** HMRC are authorised to disclose information about pension schemes. [*Social Security Act 1973, s 89(2)*].

(e) **Social Security Departments.** HMRC may disclose information obtained in connection with the assessment or collection of income tax but for self-employed persons they may only disclose the fact that a person has commenced or ceased self-employment together with the identity of that person and information relating to earners employed by that person. [*Social Security Administration Act 1992, s 122*].

HMRC may, and *must* if an authorised social security officer so requires, supply to the social security authorities information held for the purposes of tax credit functions and functions relating to child benefit or guardian's allowance for use by those authorities for the purposes of functions relating to social security benefits, child support, tax credits, war pensions or prescribed evaluation or statistical studies. [*Tax Credits Act 1999, Sch 5 para 2; Tax Credits Act 2002, Sch 5 para 4; SI 2002 Nos 1727, 3036*].

Social security authorities are in turn permitted to supply information to HMRC for investigative purposes. [*FA 1997, s 110*].

(f) **Criminal investigations etc.** HMRC may disclose information to organisations such as the police, the National Criminal Intelligence Service and the National Crime Squad, having a legitimate interest in, and capable of carrying out, criminal investigations and/or bringing proceedings for criminal offences and for the purposes of assisting criminal investigations or proceedings in the UK or elsewhere, including whether such investigations or proceedings should be initiated or brought to an end. Disclosures may also be made to the intelligence services for the purposes of facilitating the carrying out of their functions. [*Anti-terrorism, Crime and Security Act 2001, ss 19, 20*].

See also Revenue Press Release 11 February 2002 and related voluntary Code of Practice on the Disclosure of Information.

Also, HMRC can disclose information to the police to assist investigation into suspected murder or treason (*Royal Commission on Standards of Conduct in Public Life 1976, para 93*).

(g) **Non-UK resident entertainers and sportsmen.** In connection with the deduction of sums representing income tax from certain payments to such persons, HMRC may disclose relevant matters to any person who appears to HMRC to have an interest. [*ITA 2007, s 970(2)(3); ICTA 1988, s 558(4)*].

(h) **Local authorities and Health Departments etc.** As regards information held for the purposes of tax credit functions (see Tolley's Income Tax under Social Security) and functions relating to child benefit or guardian's allowance, HMRC may disclose information to a local authority (or authorised delegate) for use in the administration of housing benefit or council tax benefit. Information must also be provided in the opposite direction if the Board so require but only for use for purposes relating to tax credits etc. [*Tax Credits Act 2002, Sch 5 paras 7, 8*].

As regards information held for the above-mentioned purposes, HMRC may disclose information to Health Departments for use for purposes of prescribed functions relating to health, to relevant Government Departments for purposes of prescribed functions relating to employment or training (with provision also for certain information to pass in the opposite direction) and (as regards information held for child benefit and guardian's allowance functions only) to any civil servant or other person for purposes of prescribed functions relating to provision of specified services concerning participation by young persons in education and training. [*Tax Credits Act 2002, Sch 5 paras 5, 6, 9, 10*].

(i) **Financial Conduct Authority and Prudential Regulation Authority.** HMRC may authorise the disclosure of information to the Financial Conduct Authority or the Prudential Regulation Authority (previously the Financial Services Authority) for the purpose of assisting or enabling that regulator to discharge its functions or to the Secretary of State for the purposes of investigations under *Financial Services and Markets Act 2000, s 168*. [*Financial Services and Markets Act 2000, s 350; Financial Services Act 2012, Sch 12 para 20*]. Note that HMRC may only disclose information in this way if it was obtained or is held in the exercise of a function previously vested in the Inland Revenue. [*CRCA 2005, Sch 2 para 18*].

(j) **Proceeds of crime etc.** Before 1 April 2008, HMRC may disclose information to the Director of the Assets Recovery Agency for the purpose of the exercise of his functions. Following the dissolution of the Agency after 31 March 2008, HMRC may, after that date, disclose information to the Director of Public Prosecutions or the Director of the Serious Fraud Office for the purpose of the exercise of their functions under *Proceeds of Crime Act 2002, Pts 5 and 8*. [*Proceeds of Crime Act 2002, s 436; Serious Crime Act 2007, Sch 8 para 132; SI 2003 No 120; SI 2008 No 755*]. HMRC may also disclose information to the Lord Advocate and the Scottish Ministers in connection with the exercise of their functions in Scotland under *Proceeds of Crime Act 2002, Pt 3* and *Pt 5* respectively. [*Proceeds of Crime Act 2002, s 439*].

(k) **Financial Reporting Review Panel.** HMRC may disclose information to the Financial Reporting Review Panel for the purpose of facilitating the taking of steps by it to discover whether there are grounds for an application to the courts for a declaration that the annual accounts of a company do not comply with *Companies Acts* requirements or determining whether or not to make such an application. HMRC and the Financial Reporting Review Panel have entered into a memorandum of understanding governing the disclosure of information under these provisions. See HMRC Internet Statement, 28 June 2005 and 2005 STI 1197.

(l) **National Crime Agency.** HMRC may disclose information to the National Crime Agency (formerly the Serious Organised Crime Agency) for the purpose of the exercise of the Agency's functions. [*Serious Organised Crime and Police Act 2005, s 34; SI 2006 No 378*].

(m) **Certification of British films.** In relation to films commencing principal photography on or after 1 January 2007, HMRC may disclose information to the Secretary of State for the purposes of his functions under *Films Act 1985, Sch 1* (certification of films as British films for the purposes of film tax relief). Information so disclosed may be disclosed to the UK Film Council. [*CTA 2009, s 1206; FA 2006, Sch 5 para 24*].

(n) **Criminal Assets Bureau in Ireland.** From 15 February 2008, HMRC may disclose information to the Criminal Assets Bureau ('CAB') in Ireland for the purpose of enabling or assisting the CAB to exercise any of its functions in connection with the proceeds of crime. [*Serious Crime Act 2007, s 85*].

(o) **Prosecuting authorities.** HMRC are permitted to disclose information to the Director of Public Prosecutions (previously the Revenue and Customs Prosecutions Office) for the purpose of enabling the Director to consider whether to institute criminal proceedings in respect of a matter considered in the course of an investigation by HMRC or to give advice in connection with a criminal investigation. In relation to Scotland, HMRC are similarly authorised to disclose information to the Lord Advocate or a procurator fiscal. In Northern Ireland disclosures to the Director of Public Prosecutions for Northern Ireland are likewise permitted. [*CRCA 2005, s 21; SI 2014 No 834*].

Publication of details of deliberate tax defaulters

[31.3] The Commissioners for HMRC can publish certain information about any person if as a result of an investigation one or more specified penalties have been incurred by him, provided that the total potential lost revenue in respect of which the penalty or penalties were calculated is more than £25,000.

The Commissioners can publish the person's name, trading name, address or registered office, the nature of any business carried on, the amount of the penalties and the potential lost revenue, the period of time to which the offences relate and any other information which they consider appropriate in order to make the person's identity clear. The information can only be first published in the period of one year beginning with the last day on which any of the penalties becomes final. It cannot continue to be published for more than one year.

Before publishing the information the Commissioners must inform the taxpayer that they are doing so and provide a reasonable opportunity to make representations about whether it should be published. No information will be published if the penalty is reduced, by reason of disclosure, to the full extent possible.

The penalties concerned are those under *FA 2007, Sch 24 para 1* (see **52.8** PENALTIES) and *para 1A* (see **52.9** PENALTIES), *FA 2008, Sch 41 para 1* (see **52.3** PENALTIES) and certain VAT and duty penalties, where in each case the error, failure or other action was deliberate. See the relevant paragraph for the meaning of '*potential lost revenue*' in relation to each penalty.

With effect from 1 April 2017, the above applies also where a body corporate, a partnership or one or more of the trustees of a settlement has incurred a penalty under **52.8** PENALTIES in respect of a deliberate inaccuracy involving an offshore matter or an offshore transfer or a penalty under **52.3** PENALTIES in respect of a deliberate failure which involves an offshore matter or an offshore transfer. In this case the Commissioners may publish information in respect of any individual who controls the body corporate or partnership ('control' being construed as in *CTA 2010, s 1124*) or any individual who is a trustee of the settlement, where in either case the individual has obtained a tax advantage (as in *FA 2013, s 208* — see **4.3** ANTI-AVOIDANCE) as a result of the inaccuracy or failure. This applies regardless of the amount of potential lost revenue, and the let-out applies only if the penalty is reduced, by reason of *unprompted* disclosure, to the full extent permitted.

[*FA 2009, s 94; FA 2016, s 164; SI 2017 No 261*].

Publication of details of persons failing to correct

[31.4] The Commissioners for HMRC may publish information about a person (P) if in consequence of an investigation they consider that:

- P has been found to have incurred (and been assessed to or had included in a contract settlement) one or more penalties under **52.14** PENALTIES (failure to correct offshore tax non-compliance) in relation to which the offshore potential lost revenue (offshore PLR) totals more than £25,000 in aggregate; or
- P has been found to have incurred five or more penalties under **52.14** PENALTIES.

Penalties relating to failure to correct offshore tax non-compliance existing at the end of 2016/17 of which P was aware at any time during the RTC period (see **52.14** PENALTIES) are taken into account for the above purposes only if P was aware at any time during the RTC period (see **52.14** PENALTIES) of the existence at the end of 2016/17 of the offshore tax non-compliance in question.

The Commissioners can publish P's name (including previous name or pseudonym), trading name, address, the nature of any business carried on, the amount of the penalties, the amount of the offshore PLR, the periods or times to which the uncorrected offshore tax non-compliance relates, and any other information which they consider appropriate in order to make P's identity clear. The information can only be first published in the period of one year beginning with the last day on which the penalty (or the latest day on which any of the penalties involved) becomes final. It cannot continue to be published for more than one year. No information can be published if the amount of the penalty is reduced for disclosure to no more than 100% of the offshore PLR or is reduced or stayed because of special circumstances (see **52.14** PENALTIES).

Before publishing any information, the Commissioners must inform P that they are considering doing so and afford P an opportunity to make representations about whether it should be published.

[*F(No 2)A 2017, Sch 18 paras 30, 31*].

Publication of details of tax agents engaging in dishonest conduct

[31.5] With effect from 1 April 2013, the Commissioners for HMRC can publish certain information about any individual who incurs a penalty under *FA 2012, Sch 38 para 26* (penalty for dishonest conduct — see **52.19** PENALTIES) if the penalty is more than £5,000.

The Commissioners can publish the individual's name (including previous name or pseudonym), trading name, address, the nature of any business carried on, the amount of the penalty, the periods or times to which the dishonest conduct relates, any other information which they consider appropriate in order to make the individual's identity clear, and the link (if any) between the dishonest conduct and any inaccuracy, failure or action as a result of which information is published under the provisions at **31.3** above. The information can only be first published in the period of one year beginning with the last day on which the penalty becomes final. It cannot continue to be published for more than one year.

Before publishing the information the Commissioners must inform the taxpayer that they are doing so and provide a reasonable opportunity to make representations about whether it should be published.

[*FA 2012, Sch 38 para 28; SI 2013 No 279*].

Criminal offence of disclosure of tax information

[31.6] It is a criminal offence for a person to disclose tax information relating to an 'identifiable person' (as defined) held by him in the exercise of 'tax functions' or as a member of an advisory commission set up under the Arbitration Convention (*90/436/EEC*). '*Tax functions*' include functions relating to the First-tier and Upper Tribunals, HMRC, and the Board of Inland Revenue and its officers. This applies equally as regards HMRC's tax credit functions and social security functions. It does not apply if the person has (or believes he has) lawful authority or the information has lawfully been made available to the public, or if the person involved has consented. The maximum penalty for an offence is imprisonment for up to two years, a fine, or both. The above applies equally as regards national insurance contributions, statutory sick pay, statutory maternity pay and tax credits. [*FA 1989, ss 182, 182A; F(No 2)A 1992, s 51(3); CRCA 2005, s 19, Sch 4 para 39; TIOPA 2010, Sch 8 para 39*].

32

HMRC Explanatory Publications

HMRC explanatory leaflets	**32.1**
HMRC Guidance Manuals	**32.2**
HMRC Tax Bulletin	**32.3**
HMRC Brief	**32.4**
HMRC helpsheets	**32.5**
Gov.uk website	**32.6**

HMRC explanatory leaflets

[32.1] HMRC publish explanatory leaflets on direct taxes. Those having a bearing on capital gains tax and corporation tax on chargeable gains are listed below, with the date of the latest edition in brackets. Leaflets are obtainable free of charge (except where otherwise stated) from HMRC offices or from the internet (at www.gov.uk). HMRC have now withdrawn a substantial number of pamphlets and the information formerly contained in them is now available from their website.

SA/BK4	Self-Assessment — A General Guide to Keeping Records (June 2003).
SA/BK8	Self-Assessment — Your Guide (June 2004).
CTSA/ BK4	A General Guide to Corporation Tax Self-Assessment (October 2000).
COP 1	Putting things right when we make mistakes (June 2003).
COP 8	Specialist investigations (fraud and bespoke avoidance) (November 2016)
COP 9 (2014)	HMRC investigations where we suspect tax fraud (June 2014).
AO 1	The adjudicator's office for complaints about HMRC and Valuation Office Agency (August 2008)
C/FS	Complaints and putting things right (August 2014)
CC/FS1a	General information about compliance checks (November 2015)
CC/FS1b	General information about checks by Campaigns and Projects (January 2017)
CC/FS1c	General information about compliance checks into large businesses (November 2015)
CC/FS2	Compliance checks — checking a customer's tax position (April 2017)
CC/FS3	Compliance checks — visits by agreement or with advance notice (April 2017)

CC/FS4	Compliance checks — unannounced visits for inspections (April 2017)
CC/FS5	Compliance checks — unannounced visits for inspections approved by tribunal (April 2017)
CC/FS6	Compliance checks — what happens when we find something wrong (March 2009)
CC/FS7a	Compliance checks — penalties for inaccuracies in returns or documents (September 2017)
CC/FS7b	Compliance checks — penalties for not telling HMRC about an under-assessment (November 2015)
CC/FS9	Compliance checks — Human Rights Act and penalties (November 2015)
CC/FS10	Compliance checks — suspending penalties for careless inaccuracies in returns or documents (December 2016)
CC/FS11	Compliance checks — penalties for failure to notify (March 2017)
CC/FS13	Compliance checks — publishing details of deliberate defaulters (November 2015)
CC/FS14	Compliance checks — managing serious defaulters (October 2015)
CC/FS15	Compliance checks — self assessment and old penalty rules (October 2015)
CC/FS17	Compliance checks — higher penalties for offshore matters (October 2016)
CC/FS18(a)	Compliance checks — penalties if you don't file income tax, capital gains tax and annual tax on enveloped dwellings returns on time (March 2017)
CC/FS21	Compliance checks — alternative dispute resolution (October 2015)
CC/FS22	Compliance checks — sending HMRC electronic records (August 2016)
CC/FS23	Compliance checks — third party information notices (April 2017)
CC/FS24	Tax avoidance schemes — accelerated payments (March 2017)
CC/FS25a	Tax avoidance schemes — follower notices (June 2017)
CC/FS25b	Tax avoidance schemes — partnership follower notices (June 2017)
CC/FS30a	Compliance checks — tax avoidance schemes — penalties for follower notices (October 2016)
CC/FS30b	Compliance checks — tax avoidance schemes — penalties for partnership follower notices (March 2017)
CC/FS34	General anti-abuse rule and provisional counteraction notices (December 2016)
CC/FS38	Compliance checks — serial tax avoidance — warning notices (October 2016)
	Take care to avoid a penalty (July 2008)

HMRC 1	HMRC decisions — what to do if you disagree (January 2017)
Pride 1	Taxes and benefits — Information for our lesbian, gay, bi-sexual and transgender customers (September 2011)
RDR1	Residence, Domicile and the Remittance Basis (June 2016)
RDR3	Statutory Residence Test (August 2016)
TH/FS1	Keeping records for business — what you need to know (February 2011)

HMRC Guidance Manuals

[32.2] The HMRC Guidance Manuals provide guidance to HMRC staff on the operation and application of tax law and the tax system and are also available to the public on the internet (at www.gov.uk).

References to the Capital Gains Manual are made throughout this book.

HMRC Tax Bulletin

[32.3] From 1991 to 2006 HMRC published a bi-monthly Tax Bulletin aimed at tax practitioners and giving the views of HMRC technical specialists on various issues. Tax Bulletin is available on HMRC's website (free of charge). Tax Bulletin is replaced by HMRC Brief (see **32.4** below).

HMRC Brief

[32.4] From 2007, HMRC publishes on its website (see **32.6** below) HMRC Briefs aimed at tax practitioners and giving HMRC's views on various issues. Unlike its predecessor Tax Bulletin (see **32.3** above), HMRC Brief is only published as and when required.

HMRC helpsheets

[32.5] HMRC produce a number of free helpsheets designed to explain different aspects of the tax system and to assist in the completion of self-assessment tax returns. These can be downloaded from www.gov.uk/government/collections/self-assessment-helpsheets-capital-gains. Those concerned with capital gains tax are listed below.

HS 275	Entrepreneurs' relief.
HS 276	Incorporation relief.
HS 278	Temporary non-residents and capital gains tax.
HS 281	Husband and wife, civil partners, divorce, dissolution and separation.
HS 282	Death, personal representatives and legatees.
HS 283	Private residence relief.
HS 284	Shares and capital gains tax.

HS 285	Share reorganisations, company takeovers and capital gains tax.
HS 286	Negligible value claims and income tax losses for shares you have subscribed for in qualifying trading companies.
HS 287	Employee share schemes and capital gains tax.
HS 288	Partnerships and capital gains tax.
HS 290	Business asset rollover relief.
HS 292	Land and leases, the valuation of land and capital gains tax.
HS 293	Chattels and capital gains tax.
HS 294	Trusts and capital gains tax.
HS 295	Relief for gifts and similar transactions.
HS 296	Debts and capital gains tax.
HS 297	Enterprise Investment Scheme and capital gains tax.
HS 298	Venture Capital Trusts and capital gains tax.
HS 299	Non-resident trusts and capital gains tax.
HS 301	Beneficiaries receiving capital payments from non-resident trusts and the calculation of the increase in tax charge.
HS 390	Trusts and estates of deceased persons: foreign tax credit relief for capital gains.
HS 393	Seed enterprise investment scheme — income tax and capital gains tax.

Gov.uk website

[32.6] The gov.uk website (at www.gov.uk) has copies of, *inter alia*, recent press releases, extra-statutory concessions, statements of practice, consultative documents, HMRC Manuals, Tax Bulletins, explanatory pamphlets and helpsheets, as well as internet-only guidance.

Toolkits

HMRC are publishing online toolkits to help agents prepare tax returns. The toolkits include checklists, explanatory notes, examples of the most common errors and how to avoid them. Four toolkits dealing with capital gains tax have been published on land and buildings, shares, companies and trusts and estates.

33

HMRC Extra-Statutory Concessions

Introduction

[33.1] Below are summarised the concessions relating to tax on capital gains published by HMRC. The full text of current extra-statutory concessions is published in an internet-only document on the gov.uk website (www.gov.uk). Copies of recently announced concessions are also available (with the relevant press release) on the website. In HMRC's document it is stated: 'The concessions described within are of general application, but it should be borne in mind that in a particular case there may be special circumstances which will need to be taken into account in considering the application of the concession. A concession will not be given in any case where an attempt is made to use it for tax avoidance'. See also **30.2** HMRC — ADMINISTRATION. Fuller coverage in context is normally given in the appropriate chapter referred to below. Except where the context otherwise requires, each concession relates to both individuals and companies. The full text of all current Extra-Statutory Concessions is reproduced in Tolley's Yellow Tax Handbook. See **30.5** HMRC — ADMINISTRATION for the Treasury's power, by order, to legislate concessions.

See **4.19** ANTI-AVOIDANCE for the charge arising where concessions involving deferral of gains are abused.

The concessions

[33.2]

D2	**Residence in the UK: year of commencement or cessation of residence.** Subject to conditions based on previous residence status, split year treatment is available to an individual becoming or ceasing to be UK resident partway through a tax year. Superseded by the statutory residence test for 2013/14 onwards. See **57.29** RESIDENCE AND DOMICILE.
D3	**Private residence exemption: periods of absence (a).** Periods of absence are ignored where husband and wife are living together and the conditions are satisfied by the spouse who is not the owner. Superseded by statutory provision for disposals after 5 April 2009. See **53.7** PRIVATE RESIDENCES.
D4	**Private residence exemption: periods of absence (b).** Resumption of occupation after certain periods of absence will not be necessary if the terms of his employment require the taxpayer to work elsewhere. Superseded by statutory provision for disposals after 5 April 2009. See **53.7** PRIVATE RESIDENCES.

D6 **Private residence exemption: separated couples.** If, as the result of a breakdown of the marriage, one spouse ceases to occupy the matrimonial home and later transfers it (or part of it) as part of a financial settlement to the other spouse who has continued in occupation, no gain will be chargeable unless election has been made for some other house to be the main residence of the transferring spouse. Superseded by statutory provision for disposals after 5 April 2009. See **53.7** PRIVATE RESIDENCES.

D10 **Unquoted shares acquired before 6 April 1965: disposals following reorganisation of share capital.** Tax is not charged on a disposal of the entire new shareholding on more than the actual gains realised. See **8.10** ASSETS HELD ON 6 APRIL **1965**.

D15 **Rollover relief: unincorporated associations.** Where property is held via the medium of a company in which at least 90% of the shares are held by the association or its members, the relief is available provided the other conditions are satisfied. Superseded by statutory provision for disposals after 5 April 2009. See **59.5** ROLLOVER RELIEF.

D16 **Rollover relief: repurchase of the same asset.** An asset which is repurchased for purely commercial reasons after having been sold may be treated as the 'new asset' for the purposes of the relief. See **59.2** ROLLOVER RELIEF.

D18 **Mortgage granted by vendor: subsequent default by purchaser as mortgagor.** In such circumstances and where the vendor regains beneficial ownership of the asset and so elects, the original sale is ignored and the chargeable gain arising is limited to the net proceeds obtained from the transactions. See **16.3** COMPUTATION OF GAINS AND LOSSES.

D21 **Private residence exemption: late elections in dual residence cases.** The two-year time limit will be extended in cases where the capital value of each of the residential interests, or each of them except one, is negligible and the individual was unaware of the possibility of electing. See **53.10** PRIVATE RESIDENCES.

D22 **Rollover relief: expenditure on improvements to existing assets.** Such expenditure is treated as incurred in acquiring other assets provided certain conditions are met. See **59.2** ROLLOVER RELIEF.

D23 **Rollover relief: partition of land and other assets on the dissolution of a partnership.** Partitioned assets are treated as 'new assets' for the purposes of the relief provided that the partnership is dissolved immediately thereafter. See **59.3** ROLLOVER RELIEF.

D24 **Rollover relief: assets not brought immediately into trading use.** The 'new asset' will qualify for relief even if not immediately taken into use for the purposes of the trade provided certain conditions are met. Land to be used for the site of a qualifying building will also qualify as the 'new asset' for the purposes of this concession subject to conditions. See **59.2** ROLLOVER RELIEF.

D25 **Rollover relief: acquisition of a further interest in an existing asset.** The further interest is treated as a 'new asset' for the purposes of the relief. See **59.2** ROLLOVER RELIEF.

D26 **Exchange of joint interests in land: form of rollover relief.** A form of rollover relief as on the compulsory purchase of land (see **41.12** LAND) is allowed on a disposal caused by the exchange of interests in land which is in the joint beneficial ownership of two or more persons. This relief is not confined to traders. The relief applies also to certain exchanges of milk or potato quota associated with such land. Superseded by statutory provision for disposals after 5 April 2010. See **41.13** LAND.

D32 **Transfer of a business to a company.** For the purposes of *TCGA 1992, s 162*, liabilities taken over by a company on the transfer are not treated as consideration so that no gain arises. See **37.2** INCORPORATION AND DISINCORPORATION RELIEFS.

D33 **Compensation and damages.** These are treated as derived from any underlying asset, and exempt or taxable accordingly, and as exempt if there is no underlying asset. See **7.2** ASSETS and **25.25** EXEMPTIONS AND RELIEFS.

D34 **Rebasing and indexation: shares held on 31 March 1982.** A single holding treatment will apply even if the shares were acquired on or before 6 April 1965. See **9.2** ASSETS HELD ON 31 MARCH **1982.**

D35 **Employee trusts.** Concessional treatment will apply where an asset is transferred to a beneficiary who as a result suffers an income tax charge. Superseded by statutory provision for disposals after 5 April 2009. See **25.91** EXEMPTIONS AND RELIEFS.

D37 **Relocation of employees.** The exemption for a gain arising on the disposal of an employee's private residence is extended similarly to his right to share in any profits made by a relocation business or his employer to whom he sells property and which later sells it to a third party. Superseded by statutory provision for disposals after 5 April 2009. See **53.7** PRIVATE RESIDENCES.

D38 **Loans to traders evidenced by qualifying corporate bonds.** A further concessional relief will apply in certain circumstances where the bonds concerned only became qualifying corporate bonds because of a change in definition, even though they are not evidenced by a qualifying loan. Obsolete as regards loans made on or after 17 March 1998. See **44.14** LOSSES.

D39 **Extension of leases.** No capital gains tax is payable where a lessee surrenders an existing lease and is granted, in an arm's length transaction (or equivalent), a new, longer lease on the same property at a different rent, but otherwise on the same terms. See **41.15** LAND.

D40 **Non-resident trusts.** The definition of 'participator' in *ICTA 1988, s 417(1)* is concessionally restricted for the purposes of *TCGA 1992, s 96* and specified provisions of *TCGA 1992, Sch 5*. Superseded by statutory provision from 6 April 2017. See **48.9, 48.19** OFFSHORE SETTLEMENTS.

D42 **Mergers of leases.** Where a superior interest in leasehold land is acquired (being either a superior lease or the reversion of freehold), and the land is disposed of after 28 June 1992, indexation allowance on the expenditure incurred on the inferior lease will be calculated by reference to the date of its acquisition. See **41.14** LAND.

D44 **Re-basing and indexation: shares derived from larger holdings held at 31 March 1982.** In certain circumstances a valuation of a shareholding held or treated as having been held at 31 March 1982 can be calculated by reference to the size of the shareholding held by a spouse or group member at that date. Superseded by statutory provision for disposals after 31 March 2010. See **9.6** ASSETS HELD ON 31 MARCH **1982.**

D45 **Rollover into depreciating assets.** Where an asset employed in a trade carried on by a claimant to rollover relief ceases to be used due to the claimant's death, no charge to tax will arise under *TCGA 1992, s 154(2)(b)*. Withdrawn with effect from 6 April 2016. See **59.9** ROLLOVER RELIEF.

D47 **Temporary loss of charitable status due to reverter of school and other sites.** A temporary loss of charitable status will in general be ignored for tax purposes. Withdrawn with effect from 1 April 2010. See **11.3** CHARITIES.

D49 **Private residence exemption: short delay by owner occupier in taking up residence.** Restriction of relief is removed in certain circumstances where an individual acquires a property but does not immediately use it as his only or main residence. See **53.7** PRIVATE RESIDENCES. This replaces SP D4.

D50 **Compensation for loss or deprivation of property situated outside the UK** does not give rise to a chargeable gain in specified circumstances. Concession superseded by statutory provision for compensation received after 5 April 2010 (31 March 2010 for corporation tax purposes). See **10.2** CAPITAL SUMS DERIVED FROM ASSETS.

D51 **Close company transferring asset at undervalue.** An anti-avoidance provision is not applied in two sets of circumstances. Superseded by statutory provision for disposals after 5 April 2009. See **4.14** ANTI-AVOIDANCE.

D52 **Share exchanges and company reconstructions: incidental costs of acquisition and disposal and warranty payments in respect of contingent liabilities.** Any such costs or payments are treated as allowable expenditure referable to the new holding of shares. See **63.5** and **63.7** SHARES AND SECURITIES.

D53 *TCGA 1992, s 50;* **Grants repaid.** Where a grant is repaid, and acquisition cost has been restricted by the amount of the grant, the consideration on disposal may be reduced by the amount repaid. See **16.13**(c) COMPUTATION OF GAINS AND LOSSES.

The following income tax and corporation tax concessions are also relevant for the purposes of capital gains tax or corporation tax on chargeable gains.

A11 **Residence in the UK: year of commencement or cessation of residence.** Although there is no provision for splitting a tax year in relation to residence, liability to UK tax which is affected by residence is computed by reference to the period of actual residence in the UK during the year. See also D2 above. Superseded by the statutory residence test for 2013/14 onwards. See Tolley's Income Tax.

A17 **Death of taxpayer before due date for payment of tax.** Personal representatives unable to pay tax before obtaining probate may have concessional treatment so that interest on tax falling due after the date of death runs from the later of the expiration of thirty days after the grant of probate and the statutory date for interest to run. Superseded by statutory provision for interest accruing on or after 31 October 2011. See **42.9** LATE PAYMENT INTEREST AND PENALTIES.

A19 **Arrears of tax arising through HMRC delay.** Arrears of tax arising due to the HMRC's failure to make proper and timely use of information supplied will be waived in certain cases. See **51.29** PAYMENT OF TAX.

A78 **Residence in the UK: accompanying spouse.** Where an employee leaving the UK to work abroad satisfies the conditions of A11 above, the residence treatment of the employee may be extended to an accompanying spouse in certain circumstances. Superseded by the statutory residence test for 2013/14 onwards. See **57.29–57.31** RESIDENCE AND DOMICILE.

A94 **Profits and losses of theatre backers (angels).** Profits and losses of UK resident non-trading angels may be assessed and relieved as income. Withdrawn with effect for all new productions from 1 April 2017. Productions using the concession before that date may continue to do so until 31 March 2019. See **44.9** LOSSES.

A99 **Tax treatment of compensation for mis-sold free standing additional voluntary contribution schemes.** Certain capital sums received by way of compensation are not regarded for capital gains tax purposes as the disposal of an asset. See **25.60** EXEMPTIONS AND RELIEFS.

B41 **Claims to repayment of tax.** Where an overpayment of tax arises because of an error by HMRC or another Government Department and where there is no dispute or doubt as to the facts, late claims to repayment of the tax overpaid will be allowed. See **51.29** PAYMENT OF TAX.

34

HMRC Investigatory Powers

Introduction to HMRC investigatory powers	**34.1**
Self-assessment enquiries	**34.2**
Information and inspection powers under *FA 2008, Sch 36*	**34.3**
Information and documents	**34.4**
Restrictions on information notice powers	**34.5**
Appeals against information notices	**34.6**
Concealing, destroying or disposing of documents	**34.7**
Inspection of business premises	**34.8**
Inspection of other premises	**34.9**
Offences and penalties under *FA 2008, Sch 36*	**34.10**
Power to obtain files of tax agent	**34.11**
Power to call for papers of tax accountant before 1 April 2013	**34.12**
HMRC practice in cases of serious tax fraud	**34.13**
HMRC use of Police and Criminal Evidence Act 1984 powers	**34.14**
HMRC use of Proceeds of Crime Act 2002 powers	**34.15**
Order for delivery of documents in serious tax fraud cases	**34.16**
Data-gathering powers	**34.17**
Computer records etc	**34.18**
Key points on HMRC investigatory powers	**34.19**

Cross-references. See **20.7** DISCLOSURE OF TAX AVOIDANCE SCHEMES onwards for information powers relating to high-risk promoters of tax avoidance schemes; **52** PENALTIES; **58** RETURNS.

Simon's Taxes. See **A6.3**.

Introduction to HMRC investigatory powers

[34.1] HMRC have wide powers to enforce compliance with tax legislation. There is a common set of information and inspection powers covering income tax, capital gains tax, corporation tax and other taxes, including inheritance tax and stamp duty land tax and VAT, enabling HMRC to conduct a single 'compliance check' into a taxpayer's tax position across any or, as relevant, all of those taxes. Evidence can be obtained both directly from the taxpayer and from third parties. The powers are described at **34.3–34.10** below and operate in tandem with those for enquiries into self-assessment returns, for which see **34.2** below and **58.9–58.12** RETURNS.

For compliance checks generally, see HMRC Factsheets CC/FS1–CC/FS6 and CC/FS8T and HMRC Compliance Handbook. HMRC have published a statement of the principles governing their litigation and settlements strategy. The statement covers how HMRC enters into, handles and settles disputes about any of the taxes for which they are responsible. See HMRC Compliance Handbook CH40350. See also **34.13** below for HMRC's practice in cases of serious tax fraud.

In addition to the above powers, HMRC can obtain specialist and bulk information from specified 'data holders': see **34.17** below.

With effect from 1 April 2013, HMRC have a cross-tax power to obtain working papers from tax agents who engage in dishonest conduct. See **34.11** below. Previously, HMRC could require a tax accountant who has been convicted by or before any UK court of a tax offence or incurred a penalty under *TMA 1970, s 99* (see **52.21** PENALTIES) to deliver 'documents' in his possession or power relevant to any tax liability of any of his clients. See **34.12** below.

HMRC are able to exercise certain powers under the *Police and Criminal Evidence Act 1984* when conducting direct tax criminal investigations. See **34.14** below. As a result of the availability of those powers, the pre-existing power to seek judicial authority to require the delivery of documents at **34.16** below is restricted to circumstances where the equivalent police power cannot be used.

There are special provisions relating to computer records (see **34.18** below).

Self-assessment enquiries

[34.2] The self-assessment enquiry procedures are explained at 58.9–58.12 RETURNS; these operate in tandem with the provisions below. See in particular 34.5 below for restrictions on HMRC's power to issue an information notice where a tax return has been made.

Information and inspection powers under *FA 2008, Sch 36*

[34.3] *FA 2008, Sch 36* provides for a common set of information and inspection powers for HMRC covering income tax, capital gains tax, corporation tax, and other taxes, including inheritance tax, stamp duty land tax and VAT. The powers are covered at **34.4–34.10** below only to the extent that they apply for the purposes of capital gains tax and corporation tax on chargeable gains.

See also 52.20 PENALTIES for the application of the provisions, with modifications, for the purposes of the penalty for enablers of offshore tax evasion.

Definitions

For the purposes of the provisions at **34.4–34.10** below, the following definitions apply.

'*Checking*' includes carrying out an investigation or enquiry of any kind. '*Document*' includes a part of a document (unless the context requires otherwise).

An '*authorised HMRC officer*' is an HMRC officer who is, or who is a member of a class of officers, authorised by the Commissioners for HMRC for the particular purpose.

The carrying on of a business includes the letting of property and the activities of a charity, a government department, a local authority (within *ITA 2007, s 999*), a local authority association (within *ITA 2007, s 1000*) or any other public authority. HMRC can make regulations specifying activities as businesses.

'*Tax*' means any or all of income tax, capital gains tax, corporation tax and VAT. It also includes taxes of EU member states in respect of which information can be disclosed and taxes of territories to which a tax enforcement agreement apply (see **31.2**(c) HMRC — CONFIDENTIALITY OF INFORMATION). With effect from 1 April 2010, '*tax*' also includes insurance premium tax, inheritance tax, stamp duty land tax, stamp duty reserve tax, petroleum revenue tax, aggregates levy, climate change levy, and landfill tax.

A person's '*tax position*' is his position at any time and in relation to any period as regards any tax, including his position as to past, present and future liability to any tax, penalties and other amounts which have been paid or are, or may be, payable by or to him in connection with any tax, and any claims, elections, applications and notices that have or may be made or given in connection with his liability to pay any tax. References to a person's tax position also include the tax position of a company that has ceased to exist and an individual who has died.

'*Parent undertaking*', '*subsidiary undertaking*' and '*undertaking*' have the same meanings as in *Companies Act 2006, ss 1161, 1162, Sch 7.*

For capital gains tax and corporation tax purposes, an '*involved third party*' is a person registered as a managing agent at Lloyd's in relation to a syndicate of underwriting members, and '*relevant information*' and '*relevant documents*' in relation to such a party, are information and documents relating to, and to the activities of, the syndicate.

[*FA 2008, Sch 36 paras 35(7), 58–60, 63, 64; SI 2009 Nos 404, 3054*].

Responsibility of company officers

Everything to be done by a company under the provisions at **34.4–34.10** below must be done by it through the '*proper officer*' (i.e. the secretary of a corporate body, except where a liquidator or administrator has been appointed when the latter is the proper officer, or the treasurer of a non-corporate body) or, except where a liquidator has been appointed, any authorised officer. The service of a notice on a company may be effected by serving it on the proper officer. [*TMA 1970, s 108; FA 2008, Sch 36 para 56*].

Information and documents

[34.4] An HMRC officer may by notice in writing require a person to provide information or to produce a document if it is reasonably required by him:

(a) for the purpose of checking that person's tax position; or
(b) for the purpose of checking the tax position of another person whose identity is known to the officer; or
(c) for the purpose of checking the tax position of a person whose identity is not known to the officer or of a class of persons whose individual identities are not known to the officer; or

(d) with effect from 17 July 2012 (in relation to periods or tax liabilities arising before, on or after that date), for the purpose of checking the tax position of another person, or class of persons, whose identity or identities are not known by the officer but can be ascertained from information held by the officer.

Such a notice (an '*information notice*') may require either specified information or documents or information or documents described in the notice (so that a notice is not restricted to information or documents which HMRC can specifically identify). Where it is given with the approval of the Tribunal (see further below), the notice must say so.

The information or documents must be provided or produced within the time period and at the time, by the means and in the form (if any) reasonably specified in the notice. Documents must be produced for inspection either at a place agreed to by the recipient of the notice and an HMRC officer or at a place (other than one used solely as a dwelling) that an HMRC officer reasonably specifies. Subject to any conditions or exceptions set out in regulations made by HMRC, copies of documents can be produced unless the notice requires the production of the original document or an HMRC officer in writing subsequently requests the original document. Where an officer makes such a request, the document must be produced within the period and at the time and by the means reasonably requested by the officer.

An HMRC officer may take copies of, or make extracts from, a document (or copy) produced to him, and if it appears necessary to him, he may remove the document at a reasonable time and retain it for a reasonable period. The officer must, without charge, provide a receipt for a document which is removed where this is requested and must also provide, again without charge, a copy of the document, if the person producing it reasonably requires it for any purpose. Where a document which has been removed is lost or damaged, HMRC are liable to compensate the owner for expenses reasonably incurred in replacing or repairing it.

The production or removal of a document under these provisions does not break any lien (i.e. any right) claimed on it.

The taxpayer was held not to be able to rely on the right of a person not to self-incriminate in order to refuse to comply with a notice under these provisions in *Gold Nuts Ltd v HMRC* FTT, [2016] SFTD 371.

Taxpayer notice

An information notice under (a) above can be given without the approval of the Tribunal (see **5.11** APPEALS), but where such approval is obtained the taxpayer has no right of appeal against the decision of the Tribunal to grant approval or against the notice or a requirement in it.

Where approval is sought from the Tribunal, the application for approval must be made by, or with the agreement of, an authorised HMRC officer. The taxpayer must normally have been told that the information or documents are required and have been given a reasonable opportunity to make representations to HMRC, but is not entitled to be present at the hearing. The Tribunal must be given a summary of any representations made. Where the Tribunal is satisfied that informing the taxpayer would prejudice the assessment or collection of tax, it can approve the giving of the notice without the taxpayer having been informed.

Third party notice

A notice within (b) above cannot be given without either the agreement of the taxpayer (i.e. the person whose tax position is to be checked) or the approval of the Tribunal and must normally name the taxpayer. Where approval is obtained from the Tribunal, there is no right of appeal against the decision of the Tribunal to grant approval or against the notice or a requirement in it.

Where approval is sought from the Tribunal, the application for approval must be made by, or with the agreement of, an authorised HMRC officer. The taxpayer must normally have been given a summary of the reasons why an officer requires the information or documents, but is not entitled to be present at the hearing. The person to whom the notice is to be given must normally have been told that the information or documents are required and have been given a reasonable opportunity to make representations to HMRC and the Tribunal must be given a summary of any such representations. These requirements can, however, be disapplied where the Tribunal is satisfied that informing the recipient of the notice or giving a summary of reasons to the taxpayer would prejudice the assessment or collection of tax.

The Tribunal can also disapply the requirement to name the taxpayer in the notice if it is satisfied that the officer has reasonable grounds for believing that naming him might seriously prejudice the assessment or collection of tax.

A copy of the notice must normally be given to the taxpayer. The Tribunal can, however, disapply this requirement if an application for approval is made by, or with the agreement of, an authorised HMRC officer and the Tribunal is satisfied that the officer has reasonable grounds for believing that giving a copy of the notice to the taxpayer might prejudice the assessment or collection of tax.

Where a third-party notice is given for the purpose of checking the tax position of a parent undertaking and any of its subsidiary undertakings, the above provisions apply as if the parent undertaking were the taxpayer. The requirement for the notice to name the taxpayer is satisfied by stating in the notice that its purposes is checking the tax position of the parent and subsidiary undertakings and naming the parent undertaking. Where a notice is given to a parent undertaking for the purpose of checking the tax position of one or more subsidiary undertakings, neither the agreement of the parent undertaking nor the approval of the Tribunal is required and a copy does not have to be given to the parent undertaking.

Where a third party notice is given for the purpose of checking the tax position of more than one of the partners in a business carried on in partnership, in their capacity as such, the above provisions apply as if the taxpayer were at least one of the partners. The requirement for the notice to name the taxpayer is satisfied by stating in the notice that its purpose is checking the tax position of more than one of the partners and giving a name in which the partnership is registered for any purpose. Where a third party notice is given to one of the partners for the purpose of checking the tax position of any of the other partners, neither the agreement of any of the partners nor the approval of the Tribunal is required and a copy does not have to be given to any other partners.

Notice about persons whose identity is not known

The giving of a notice under (c) above requires the approval of the Tribunal. The Tribunal can approve the giving of the notice only if it is satisfied that:

- there are reasonable grounds for believing that the person or class of persons to whom the notice relates may have failed, or may fail, to comply with any law relating to tax (including the law of a territory outside the UK);
- any such failure is likely to have led, or to lead, to serious prejudice to the assessment or collection of tax; and
- the information or document is not readily available from another source.

There is no right of appeal against a decision of the Tribunal to grant approval.

The approval of the Tribunal is permitted but not required for a notice to be given to a parent undertaking for the purpose of checking the tax position of one or more subsidiary undertakings whose identities are not known to the HMRC officer giving the notice. Such approval is also permitted but not required for a notice to be given to a partner in a business carried on in partnership for the purpose of checking the tax position of partners whose identities are not known to the officer giving the notice.

Notice about person whose identity can be ascertained

A notice within (d) above must be given by an authorised HMRC officer and can only require the recipient to provide all or any of the name, last known address and date of birth of the taxpayer (or class of taxpayer) concerned. The officer must have reason to believe that the recipient of the notice will be able to ascertain the taxpayer's identity (or taxpayers' identities) from the information held by the officer and that the recipient obtained the information required in the course of carrying on a business. A notice cannot be given if the taxpayer's identity (or taxpayers' identities) can be readily ascertained by other means from the information held by the officer.

[*FA 2008, Sch 36 paras 1–9, 15, 16, 34A, 35, 37; SI 2009 No 56, Sch 1 para 471; SI 2009 Nos 404, 3054*].

For further restrictions on the above powers, see **34.5** below. For appeals against information notices, see **34.6** below.

Restrictions on information notice powers

[34.5] An information notice does not require a person to:

(i) produce a document if it is not in his possession or power;

(ii) provide or produce information that relates to the conduct of a pending tax appeal or any part of a document containing such information;
(iii) provide journalistic material (within *Police and Criminal Evidence Act 1984, s 13*) or information contained in such material;
(iv) subject to the exceptions below, provide or produce 'personal records' (within *Police and Criminal Evidence Act 1984, s 12*); or
(v) produce a document the whole of which originates more than six years before the giving of the notice, unless the notice is given by, or with the agreement of, an authorised officer.

With regard to (iv) above, an information notice may require a person to produce documents (or copies) that are personal records, omitting any personal information (i.e. information whose inclusion in the documents makes them personal records) and to provide any information in personal records that is not personal information.

[*FA 2008, Sch 36 paras 18–20*].

Notice where tax return made

Where a person has made a tax return under *TMA 1970, ss 8, 8A* or *12AA* or *FA 1998, Sch 18 para 3* (see **58.3**, **58.16** and **58.19** RETURNS) in respect of a tax year or accounting period, a taxpayer notice (see **34.4**(a) above) can be given for the purpose of checking his income tax, capital gains tax or corporation tax position for that year or period only if:

(a) an enquiry notice under *TMA 1970, ss 9A* or *12AC* or *FA 1998, Sch 18 para 24* (see **58.9**, **58.18** and **58.19** RETURNS) has been given in respect of either the return or a claim or election for the year or period to which the return relates and the enquiry has not been completed (or, on and after the date of Royal Assent to *F(No 2)A 2017*, the enquiry has not been completed so far as relating to the matters to which the taxpayer notice relates);
(b) an HMRC officer has reason to suspect that, in relation to that person, an amount that ought to have been assessed to tax may not have been assessed, that an assessment for the period may be or have become insufficient or relief from tax for the period may be or have become excessive;
(c) the notice is given for the purpose of obtaining information or a document that is also required to check the taxpayer's position for any other tax other than income tax, capital gains tax or corporation tax (before 1 April 2010, the taxpayer's VAT position); or
(d) the notice is given for the purpose of obtaining information or a document that is required to check the taxpayer's position as regards his obligation to make deductions or repayments under PAYE, the construction industry scheme or any other provision.

Similar provisions apply where a person has made an NRCGT return (see **58.20** RETURNS).

Where a third party notice (see **34.1** above) is given to a parent undertaking for the purpose of checking the tax position of one or more subsidiary undertakings, the above provisions apply as if the notice were a taxpayer notice (see **38.1**(a) above) or taxpayer notices given to the subsidiary undertaking or each of them.

Where a business is carried in partnership and a partnership return (see **58.19** RETURNS) or partnership claim or election (see **13.2** CLAIMS) has been made by one of the partners, the above provisions apply as if the return, claim or election had been made by each of the partners.

Where it appears to HMRC that there has been a change in ownership of a company (within *CTA 2010, Pt 14 Ch 7*) and, in connection with that change, a person (the '*seller*') may be or become liable to corporation tax under *CTA 2010, ss 710* or *713* (recovery of unpaid corporation tax from persons controlling company), the above restriction does not apply to a taxpayer notice given to the seller.

[*FA 2008, Sch 36 paras 21, 21ZA, 35(4), 36, 37(1)(2); FA 2015, Sch 7 para 57; F(No 2)A 2017, Sch 15 paras 36, 44; SI 2009 No 3054*].

Deceased persons

An information notice for the purpose of checking the tax position of a deceased person cannot be given more than four years after death. [*FA 2008, Sch 36 para 22*].

Legal professional privilege

An information notice cannot require a person to provide information, or to produce any part of a document, in respect of which a claim to legal professional privilege (or, in Scotland, a claim to confidentiality of communications) could be maintained in legal proceedings.

With effect from 7 August 2009 disputes as to whether information or a document is privileged are settled under the following procedures. If the information notice is given in the course of correspondence the procedure is as follows.

(A) The recipient of the notice, or a person acting on his behalf, must compile a list of the information or documents required under the notice which are in dispute by the date given in the notice for providing information or producing documents. The list must include a description of the nature and contents of each such item of information or document unless the description would itself give rise to a dispute over privilege.

(B) The list must then be served on HMRC within a reasonable time agreed between the parties but not later than 20 working days (i.e. days other than saturdays, sundays or public holidays) after the date given in the notice for providing information or documents. Proof of such service must be provided to HMRC.

(C) HMRC must then notify the person who provided the list of any documents on the list that they require to be produced and which they do not consider privileged.

(D) On receipt of HMRC's notification, the recipient of the information notice, or person acting on his behalf, must make an application to the First-tier Tribunal to consider and resolve the dispute. The application must include copies of the information or documents and must be made within a reasonable time agreed between the parties but not later than 20 working days of the date of HMRC's notification.

If the information notice is given in the course of an inspection of premises (see **34.8**, **34.9** below), the recipient, or a person acting on his behalf, must indicate to the HMRC officer conducting the inspection each item of information or document required under the notice which is in dispute. The recipient of the notice or person acting on his behalf must then place the documents etc. (or copies) in a container which prevents the contents being visible. The container is then sealed, labelled and signed by that person and countersigned by the HMRC officer. That officer must then deliver the container to the First-tier Tribunal with the seal intact within 42 working days of having taken custody of it, together with an application to the Tribunal to consider and resolve the dispute.

A dispute may also be resolved at any time by HMRC and the recipient of the information notice reaching an agreement, in writing or otherwise.

These provisions do not affect the requirement to produce information or documents which are not in dispute. See also HMRC Brief 54/09.

[*FA 2008, Sch 36 para 23; SI 2009 No 56, Sch 1 para 471(6); SI 2009 No 1916*].

Legal professional privilege does not cover legal advice given by those who are not qualified lawyers (*R (oao Prudential plc) v Special Commissioner for Income Tax* CA, [2010] STC 2802), but see below for protections for auditors and tax advisers. The question of the extent to which an engagement letter was covered by legal professional privilege was considered in *Behague v HMRC* FTT, [2013] UKFTT 596 (TC), 2013 STI 3577.

Auditors

An information notice does not require an auditor (i.e. a person appointed as an auditor for the purpose of an enactment) to provide information held in connection with the performance of his functions under that enactment or to produce documents which are his property and which were created by him, or on his behalf, for or in connection with the performance of those functions.

This restriction does not apply to any information, or any document containing information, which explains any information or document which an auditor has, as tax accountant, assisted any client in preparing for, or delivering to, HMRC. Where the notice is given under **34.4**(c) above, the restriction also does not apply to information giving the identity or address of a person to whom the notice relates or of a person who has acted on behalf of such a person or to a document containing such information. Where the restriction is so disapplied, only that part (or parts) of a document which contains the relevant information has to be produced. The restriction is not disapplied if the information concerned, or a document containing the information, has already been provided or produced to an HMRC officer.

[*FA 2008, Sch 36 paras 24, 26, 27*].

Tax advisers

An information notice does not require a 'tax adviser' to provide information about, or to produce documents which are his property and which consist of, communications between him and a person in relation to whose tax affairs he has been appointed or between him and any other tax advisor of such a person, the purpose of which is the giving or obtaining of advice about any of those tax affairs. For this purpose, a '*tax adviser*' is a person appointed (directly or by another tax adviser) to give advice about the tax affairs of another person.

This restriction is disapplied in the same circumstances as the restriction applying to auditors is disapplied.

[*FA 2008, Sch 36 paras 25–27*].

Appeals against information notices

[34.6] A taxpayer can appeal against a taxpayer notice (see **34.4**(a) above) or any requirement in such a notice unless the notice was given with the approval of the Tribunal. No appeal can be made against a requirement to provide information or to produce a document which forms part of his 'statutory records'.

A person given a third-party notice (see **34.4**(b) above) can appeal against the notice or any requirement in it on the ground that compliance would be unduly onerous. An appeal can be made on any grounds by a parent undertaking against such a notice given to it for the purpose of checking the tax position of one or more subsidiary undertakings, by a partner against a notice given for the purpose of checking the tax position of other partners, or by an involved third party against a notice given for the purpose of checking the capital gains tax or corporation tax position of another person where the notice refers only to relevant information or relevant documents. No appeal can be made, however, where the notice was given with the approval of the Tribunal or against a requirement to provide information or produce a document forming part of the taxpayer's or involved third party's statutory records.

Where a third-party notice is given for the purpose of checking the tax position of a parent undertaking and any of its subsidiary undertakings, no appeal can be made against a requirement to provide information or produce a document forming part of the statutory records of the parent undertaking or any of its subsidiaries. No appeal can be made against a requirement, in a third-party notice given to a parent undertaking for the purpose of checking the tax position of one or more subsidiary undertakings, to produce a document forming part of the statutory records of the parent undertaking or any of its subsidiary undertakings.

Where a third-party notice is given for the purpose of checking the tax position of more than one of the partners in a business carried on in partnership, no appeal can be made against a requirement to provide information or produce forming part of the statutory records of any of the partners. No appeal can be made against a requirement, in a notice given to a partner for the purpose of checking the tax position of other partners, to produce a document forming part of the statutory records of the partner receiving the notice.

A person given a notice about persons whose identity is not known (see **34.4**(c) above) or a notice about persons whose identity can be ascertained (see **34.4**(d) above) can appeal against the notice or any requirement in it on the ground that compliance would be unduly onerous (or on any grounds where the notice is given to a parent undertaking for the purpose of checking the tax position of one or more unknown subsidiary undertakings, to a partner for the purpose of checking the tax position of unknown partners, or to an involved third party where the notice given for the purpose of checking the capital gains tax or corporation tax position of other persons and the notice refers only to relevant information or relevant documents). No appeal can be made against a requirement, in a notice given to a parent undertaking for the purpose of checking the tax position of one or more subsidiary undertakings, to produce a document forming part of the statutory records of the parent undertaking or any of its subsidiary undertakings. Likewise, no appeal can be made against a requirement, in a notice given to a partner in a business carried on in partnership for the purpose of checking the tax position of other partners, to produce a document forming part of the statutory records of the partner receiving the notice. No appeal can be made against a requirement in a notice given to an involved third party to provide any information or produce any document forming part of the involved third party's statutory records.

For this purpose, '*statutory records*' are information and documents which a taxpayer is required to keep and preserve for direct tax purposes (see **58.8**, **58.19** RETURNS), VAT purposes and the other taxes included in the definition of 'tax' at **34.3** above. To the extent that information or documents do not relate to the carrying on of a business and are not required to be kept or preserved for VAT purposes, they only form part of a taxpayer's statutory documents to the extent that the tax year or accounting period to which they relate has ended. Information and documents cease to be statutory records when the period for which they are required to be preserved ends. Private bank statements for an account used for both business and personal expenditure were held to be statutory records in *Beckwith v HMRC* FTT, [2012] UKFTT 181 (TC); 2012 STI 1842.

Procedure

Notice of appeal under the above provisions must be given in writing to the HMRC officer who gave the information notice within the period of 30 days beginning with the date on which the information notice was given. A decision on an appeal by the Tribunal is final (so that there is no further right of appeal to the Upper Tribunal or Court of Appeal — see *Jordan v HMRC* UT, [2015] STC 2314). Where the Tribunal confirms the notice or a requirement in it, the person to whom the notice was given must comply with the notice or requirement within the period specified by the Tribunal. If the Tribunal does not specify such a period, compliance must be within such period as an HMRC officer reasonably specifies in writing.

Subject to the above, the appeal provisions of *TMA 1970, Pt 5* (see **5** APPEALS) apply to an appeal against an information notice as they apply to an appeal against an income tax assessment.

[*FA 2008, Sch 36 paras 29–33, 34A, 35, 37, 62; FA 2012, s 224(4); SI 2009 No 56, Sch 1 para 471(7)–(10); SI 2009 No 3054*].

Concealing, destroying or disposing of documents

[34.7] A person to whom an information notice is addressed must not conceal, destroy or otherwise dispose of, or arrange for the concealment, destruction or disposal of, a document that is the subject of the notice. This does not apply if he does so after the document has been produced to HMRC in accordance with the notice, unless an HMRC officer has notified him in writing that the document must continue to be available for inspection (and has not withdrawn the notification). It also does not apply if a copy of the document was produced in compliance with the notice and the destruction, etc. takes place after the end of the period of six months beginning with the day on which the copy was produced unless within that period, an HMRC officer makes a request for the original document.

Similarly, where a person has been informed that a document is, or is likely to be, the subject of an information notice addressed to him, he must not conceal, destroy or otherwise dispose of, or arrange for the concealment, destruction or disposal of, the document. This does not apply if he acts more than six months after he was so informed (or was last so informed).

[*FA 2008, Sch 36 paras 42, 43*].

Failure to comply with the above provisions may be a criminal offence or result in penalties. See **34.10** below.

Inspection of business premises

[34.8] An HMRC officer may enter a person's 'business premises' and inspect the premises and any 'business assets' and 'business documents' that are on the premises if the inspection is reasonably required for the purpose of checking that person's tax position. The officer may not enter or inspect any part of the premises used solely as a dwelling.

An HMRC officer may enter business premises of an involved third party (see **34.3** above) and inspect the premises and any business assets and relevant documents that are on the premises if the inspection is reasonably required for the purpose of checking the tax position of any person or class of persons. It is not necessary that the officer know the identity of the person or persons. The officer may not enter or inspect any part of the premises used solely as a dwelling.

The officer may mark business assets and anything containing business assets to indicate that they have been inspected and may obtain and record information (electronically or otherwise) relating to the premises, assets and documents inspected. He may take copies of, or make extracts from, a document (or copy) which he inspects, and if it appears necessary to him, he may remove the document at a reasonable time and retain it for a reasonable period. He must, without charge, provide a receipt for a document which is removed where this is requested and must also provide, again without charge, a copy of the document, if the person producing it reasonably requires it for any purpose. Where a document which has been removed is lost or damaged, HMRC are liable to compensate the owner for expenses reasonably incurred in replacing or repairing it.

An inspection must normally be carried out at a time agreed to by the occupier of the premises. It can, however, be carried out at any reasonable time if:

(i) the occupier has been given at least seven days' notice (in writing or otherwise) of the time of the inspection; or
(ii) the inspection is carried out by, or with the agreement of, an authorised HMRC officer.

Where (ii) above applies, the officer carrying out the inspection must provide a notice in writing stating the possible consequences of obstructing the officer in the exercise of the power. If the occupier is present when the inspection begins, the notice must be given to him. If he is not present, the notice must be given to the person who appears to be the officer in charge of the premises, but if no such person is present, the notice must be left in a prominent place on the premises. The giving of such a notice does not require the approval of the Tribunal, but such approval can be applied for by, or with the agreement of, an authorised HMRC officer. A penalty for deliberate obstruction of an officer in the course of an inspection can only be charged where such approval has been obtained (see **34.10** below). A decision of the Tribunal to approve an inspection is final and there is no right of appeal.

An officer may not inspect a document if or to the extent that an information notice (see **34.4** above) given at the time of the inspection to the occupier of the premises could not require him to produce the document (see **34.5** above).

For the above purposes, '*business premises*' are premises (including any land, building or structure or means of transport), or a part of premises, that an HMRC officer has reason to believe are used in connection with the carrying on of a business by or on behalf of the taxpayer concerned. '*Business assets*' are assets, other than documents which are neither trading stock nor plant, that an HMRC officer has reason to believe are owned, leased or used in connection with the carrying on of any business. '*Business documents*' are documents, or copies of documents, relating to the carrying on of any business that form part of any person's statutory records.

[*FA 2008, Sch 36 paras 10–17, 28, 58; SI 2009 No 56, Sch 1 para 471; SI 2009 Nos 404, 3054*].

Inspection of other premises

[34.9] An HMRC officer can enter premises and inspect them and any other property there for the purpose of valuing them, measuring them or determining their character. The valuation, measurement of determination must be reasonably required for the purpose of checking any person's tax position (in this case restricted to capital gains tax, corporation tax on chargeable gains, inheritance tax, stamp duty land tax and stamp duty reserve tax). The officer can be accompanied by a valuation etc. expert.

The inspection must normally be carried out at a time agreed to by the occupier of the premises and he must be given notice in writing of the agreed time. If the occupier cannot be identified, agreement can be obtained from, and notice given to, a person who controls the premises. Where, however, the inspection has been approved by the Tribunal (see below), the only requirement is the occupier or person controlling the premises be given at least seven days' notice in writing of the time of the inspection. Where such notice is given it must state that the inspection has been approved by the tribunal and indicate the possible consequences of obstructing the inspection (see below).

The giving of a notice does not require the approval of the Tribunal, but such approval can be applied for by, or with the agreement of, an authorised HMRC officer. A penalty for deliberate obstruction of an officer in the course of an inspection can only be charged where such approval has been obtained (see **34.10** below). A decision of the Tribunal to approve an inspection is final and there is no right of appeal. Both the person whose tax position is in question and the occupier of the premises (unless he cannot be identified) must be given a reasonable opportunity to make representations to the HMRC officer and a summary of any representations must be given to the Tribunal.

An officer carrying out an inspection under these powers must produce evidence of his authority to do so if asked by the occupier or any other person who appears to be in charge of the premises or property. He may obtain and record information (electronically or otherwise) relating to the premises and property inspected.

[*FA 2008, Sch 36 paras 12A–14, 17; SI 2009 No 3054*].

Offences and penalties under FA 2008, Sch 36

[34.10] For penalties for failure to comply with an information notice within **34.4** above, for deliberately obstructing an HMRC officer in the course of an inspection of premises under the powers at **34.8** and **34.9** above that has been approved by the Tribunal and for deliberate or careless inaccuracies in information or documents provided in compliance with an information notice, see **52.16** PENALTIES.

It is an offence for a person required to produce a document by an information notice within **34.4** above which has been approved by the Tribunal to conceal, destroy or otherwise dispose of the document or to arrange for its concealment, destruction or disposal. This does not apply if he does so after the document has been produced to HMRC in accordance with the notice, unless an HMRC officer has notified him in writing that the document must continue to be available for inspection (and has not withdrawn the notification). It also does not apply if a copy of the document was produced in compliance with the notice and the destruction, etc. takes place after the end of the period of six months beginning with the day on which the copy was produced unless within that period, an HMRC officer makes a request for the original document.

It is also an offence for a person to conceal, destroy or otherwise dispose of, or to arrange for the concealment, destruction or disposal of, a document after an HMRC officer has informed him in writing that the document is, or is likely to be, the subject of an information notice approval for which is to be obtained from the Tribunal. This does not apply if the person so acts more than six months after he was so informed (or was last so informed).

On summary conviction of either of the above offences the offender is liable to a fine not exceeding the statutory maximum. On conviction on indictment the punishment is imprisonment for a maximum of two years and/or a fine.

[*FA 2008, Sch 36 paras 53–55; SI 2009 No 56, Sch 1 para 471(2)*].

Power to obtain files of tax agent

[34.11] With effect from 1 April 2013, HMRC have a power to obtain 'working papers' from 'tax agents' who engage in 'dishonest conduct' (and to charge penalties on such agents— see **52.19** PENALTIES). The power applies across most of the taxes administered by HMRC, including capital gains tax and corporation tax. It replaces the pre-existing power to call for the papers of tax accountants described at **34.12** below. See also **31.5** HMRC — CONFIDENTIALITY OF INFORMATION for HMRC's power to disclose details of tax agents who engage in dishonest conduct.

Nothing in *FA 2012, Sch 38* limits any liability a person may have under any other enactment in respect of conduct in respect of which a person is liable to a penalty under *Sch 38* or limits any power a person may have under any other enactment to obtain documents. [*FA 2012, Sch 38 para 43; SI 2013 No 279*].

Meaning of 'tax agent'

A '*tax agent*' is an individual who, in the course of business, assists other persons ('*clients*') with their tax affairs. Individuals who work for or are partners in, or members of, an organisation, person or firm are included, even if it is the organisation that is appointed or engaged to give assistance. Individuals can be tax agents even if they, or the organisations for which they work, are appointed or engaged indirectly or at the request of someone other than the client. For this purpose, assistance with a client's tax affairs includes advising a client in relation to tax, acting or purporting to act as agent on behalf of a client in relation to tax and assistance with any document likely to be relied on by HMRC to determine a client's tax position. Assistance given for non-tax purposes counts as assistance with a client's tax affairs if given in the knowledge that it is likely to be used by a client in connection with his tax affairs. '*Tax*' means any of the taxes listed at *FA 2012, Sch 38 para 37(1)* and includes capital gains tax and corporation tax. [*FA 2012, s 223, Sch 38 paras 2, 37–39, 41*].

Dishonest conduct

An individual engages in '*dishonest conduct*' if, in the course of acting as a tax agent, he does something dishonest with a view to bringing about a loss of tax revenue. It does not matter whether or not an actual tax loss arises nor whether or not the agent is acting on clients' instructions. For this purpose, a loss of tax revenue would be brought about if clients were to account for less tax, or account for tax later, than required by law or if clients were to obtain more 'tax relief', or obtain tax relief earlier, than they were entitled to by law. '*Tax relief*' includes any exemption from or deduction or credit against or in respect of tax and any repayment of tax. Doing something dishonest includes dishonestly omitting to do something and advising or assisting a client to do something that the agent knows to be dishonest. A loss of tax revenue is taken to be (or to be capable of being) brought about by dishonest conduct despite the fact that it can be recovered or properly accounted for (following discovery of the conduct or otherwise). [*FA 2012, Sch 38 paras 3, 40*].

Conduct notice

On or after the appointed day (see above), where HMRC determine that a tax agent has engaged in dishonest conduct they may notify the agent of their determination, stating the grounds on which it was made. The consequences of such a notice are that HMRC may then assess a penalty for dishonest conduct on the tax agent (see **52.19** PENALTIES) and seek to issue a file access notice to obtain the agents' working papers (see below).

The tax agent can appeal against a conduct notice by notice in writing within 30 days beginning with the date on which the conduct notice was given. The notice of appeal must state the grounds of appeal. The usual APPEALS (5) provisions apply to an appeal against a conduct notice as they apply to an appeal against an income tax assessment. Where the appeal is notified to the Tribunal, the Tribunal may confirm or set aside the determination made in the conduct notice, but setting aside a determination does not prevent a further conduct notice being given for the same conduct if further evidence emerges.

Once a conduct notice has been given to a tax agent, or HMRC have informed a tax agent that a notice will be or is likely to be given to him, it is an offence for any person to conceal, destroy or otherwise dispose of (or to arrange for the concealment etc. of) a document that could be sought under a file access notice given to the agent as a result of the conduct notice. The penalty for such an offence is, on summary conviction, a fine not exceeding the statutory maximum or, on conviction on indictment, imprisonment for a term not exceeding two years or a fine, or both. If the concealment etc. takes place after the giving of the conduct notice, no offence is committed if the determination in the notice has been set aside, if more than four years have passed since the giving of the notice, or if the person concerned acts without knowledge of the making of the conduct notice. If the concealment etc. takes place before the giving of the notice but after HMRC have informed the agent that such a notice will be or is likely to be given, no offence is committed if the person concerned acts without knowledge of HMRC having so informed the tax agent or if more than two years have passed after the tax agent was, or was last, so informed. For this purpose, a person acts without knowledge of an event if he is not the tax agent subject to the notice given or likely to be given and does not know, and could not reasonably be expected to know, that the event has occurred.

[*FA 2012, Sch 38 paras 4–6*].

File access notice

On or after the appointed day (see above) and subject to the following, an HMRC officer may, by notice in writing (a '*file access notice*') require a tax agent or any other person that the officer believes may hold 'relevant documents' (a '*document holder*') to provide such documents. It is not necessary for the tax agent concerned still to be a tax agent when the notice is issued. A notice may require the provision of specified relevant documents or all such documents in the document-holder's possession or power. The notice does not need to identify the clients of the tax agent, but if it is addressed to anyone other than the tax agent, it must name him. The notice may require documents to be provided within such period, by such means and in such form, and to such person and at such place as are reasonably specified either in the notice or a document referred to in the notice. Unless otherwise specified in the notice, only copies of the relevant documents need be provided. A document-holder cannot be required to provide documents not in his possession or power.

'*Relevant documents*' means the tax agent's working papers (whenever acting as a tax agent) and any other documents received, created, prepared or used by him for the purposes, or in the course of, assisting clients (including former clients) with their tax affairs. It does not matter who owns the papers or documents concerned. The papers or documents which may be required by a notice are not restricted to those relating to clients with respect to whom the tax agent has engaged in dishonest conduct. 'Document' for this purpose includes a copy of a document.

HMRC can issue a file access notice only with the approval of the Tribunal and only if:

(a) a conduct notice has been given to the tax agent concerned and either the time allowed for appeal has expired without an appeal being made or, where an appeal has been made, it has been withdrawn or the determination in the conduct notice has been confirmed; or
(b) the tax agent has been convicted of an offence relating to tax that involves fraud or dishonesty; the offence was committed after he became a tax agent (whether or not he was still a tax agent when it was committed and regardless of the capacity in which it was committed); either the time allowed for appeal against the conviction has expired without an appeal being made or, where an appeal has been made, it has been withdrawn or the conviction upheld; and no more than twelve months have passed since the date on which the appeal time limit passed or the appeal was withdrawn or conviction upheld.

For this purpose, a determination or conviction that has been appealed is not considered to be confirmed or upheld until the time allowed for any further appeal has expired or, if a further appeal is brought within that time, that further appeal has been withdrawn or determined.

The Tribunal cannot approve the giving of a file access notice unless:

- the application is made by or with the agreement of an HMRC officer authorised for this purpose;

- the Tribunal is satisfied that the case falls within (a) or (b) above and that, in the circumstances, HMRC are justified in giving the notice;
- the document-holder and, if different, the tax agent, have been told that relevant documents are to be required and given a reasonable opportunity to make representations to HMRC; and
- the Tribunal has been given a summary of any such representations.

Any decision by the Tribunal to approve or refuse the giving of a notice is final. It is not necessary for the Tribunal to determine whether an individual has engaged in dishonest conduct.

An HMRC officer may take copies of, or make extracts from, a document (or copy) provided to him, and if he thinks it necessary, he may retain it for a reasonable period. The officer must, without charge, supply a copy of the document, if the document holder reasonably requires it for any purpose. Where a document which has been retained is lost or damaged, HMRC are liable to compensate the owner for expenses reasonably incurred in replacing or repairing it. The retention of a document under these provisions does not break any lien claimed on it.

Restrictions on powers

A file access notice does not require the document holder to provide:

(i) parts of a document containing information relating to the conduct of a pending tax appeal;
(ii) journalistic material (within *Police and Criminal Evidence Act 1984, s 13*);
(iii) subject to the exceptions below, personal records (within *Police and Criminal Evidence Act 1984, s 12*);
(iv) a document the whole of which originated more than 20 years before the giving of the notice, provided that no part of the document has a bearing on tax years or accounting periods ending within the 20-year period; or
(v) any part of a document in respect of which a claim to legal professional privilege (or, in Scotland, a claim to confidentiality of communications) could be maintained in legal proceedings.

With regard to (iii) above, a file access notice may require a person to produce documents that are personal records, omitting any information the inclusion of which (whether alone or with other information) makes the original documents personal records. With regard to (v) above, the procedure for resolving disputes as to whether information is privileged is the same as that used in relation to information notices (see **34.5** above).

Appeals against file access notices

If the document holder is not the tax agent, he may appeal against a file access notice or any requirement in it, on the grounds that it would be unduly onerous to comply. Notice of appeal must be given in writing to the HMRC officer who gave the notice within the 30 days beginning with the day the notice was given and must state the grounds of appeal. If the appeal is notified to the Tribunal, the Tribunal may confirm, vary or set aside the notice or a requirement in it. If the Tribunal confirms or varies the notice or a requirement, the document holder must comply with the notice or requirement within the period specified by the Tribunal or, if no such period is specified, within a period reasonably specified in writing by HMRC. A decision by the Tribunal is final, but otherwise the usual APPEALS (5) provisions apply to an appeal against a file access notice as they apply to an appeal against an income tax assessment.

Offences and penalties

For penalties for failure to comply with a file access notice see **52.19** PENALTIES.

It is an offence for any person to conceal, destroy or otherwise dispose of (or to arrange for the concealment etc. of) a document that he is required to provide by a file access notice if either the notice has not been complied with or, if it has been complied with, he has been notified in writing by HMRC that he must continue to preserve the document (and the notification has not been withdrawn). It is similarly an offence for any person to conceal, destroy or otherwise dispose of (or to arrange for the concealment etc. of) a document if at the time he acts HMRC have informed him that he will, or is likely to, be required to provide the document by a file access notice and no more than six months have passed since he was, or was last, so informed. The penalty for such an offence is, on summary conviction, a fine not exceeding the statutory maximum or, on conviction on indictment, imprisonment for a term not exceeding two years or a fine, or both.

[*FA 2012, Sch 38 paras 7–21, 38, 42*].

Responsibility of company officers

Everything to be done by a company under the above provisions must be done by it through the '*proper officer*' (i.e. the secretary of a corporate body, except where a liquidator or administrator has been appointed when the latter is the proper officer, or the treasurer of a non-corporate body) or, except where a liquidator has been appointed, any authorised officer. The service of a notice on a company may be effected by serving it on the proper officer. [*TMA 1970, s 108; FA 2012, Sch 38 para 36*].

Power to call for papers of tax accountant before 1 April 2013

[34.12] The following provisions are repealed with effect from 1 April 2013 (the day the provisions at **34.11** above came into effect). Subject to this, an HMRC officer may (with the authority of the Commissioners for HMRC and the consent of a Circuit judge in England and Wales, a sheriff in Scotland or a county court judge in Northern Ireland) by notice in writing require a '*tax accountant*' (i.e. a person who assists another in the preparation of returns, etc. for tax purposes) who has been convicted by or before any UK court of a tax offence or incurred a penalty under *TMA 1970, s 99* (see **52.21** PENALTIES) to deliver 'documents' in his possession or power relevant to any tax liability of any of his clients. The tax accountant must be given an opportunity to deliver the documents in question before a notice is issued.

The notice must be issued within twelve months of the final determination of the conviction or penalty award and must specify or describe the documents required and the time limit for production (generally not less than 30 days).

A '*document*' is anything in which information of any description is recorded, but does not include personal records or journalistic material (within *Police and Criminal Evidence Act 1984, ss 12, 13*). Photographic etc. facsimiles may be supplied provided the originals are produced if called for, and documents relating to any pending tax appeal need not be delivered.

A notice to a barrister, advocate or solicitor can be issued only by the Commissioners for HMRC, although they may nevertheless delegate their powers (see *R v CIR (ex p. Davis Frankel & Mead)* QB 2000, 73 TC 185). The barrister etc. cannot (without his client's consent) be required to deliver documents protected by professional privilege. [*TMA 1970, s 20B(3)(8)*].

The penalty for failure to comply with a notice is given by *TMA 1970, s 98* (see **52.23** PENALTIES). In addition there are severe penalties (in summary proceedings, a fine of the statutory maximum, and on indictment, imprisonment for two years and/or an unlimited fine) for the falsification, concealment, destruction or disposal of a document which is the subject of a notice, unless strict conditions and time limits are observed.

[*TMA 1970, ss 20A, 20B(1)(2)–(4)(8), 20BB, 20D; FA 2008, Sch 36 paras 68–70; FA 2012, s 223, Sch 38 paras 45–47; SI 2009 No 56, Sch 1 para 11*].

HMRC practice in cases of serious tax fraud

[34.13] The policy of the Commissioners for HMRC in cases of suspected tax fraud, as set out in Code of Practice COP 9, is as follows:

- The Commissioners reserve complete discretion to pursue a criminal investigation with a view to prosecution where they consider it necessary and appropriate.
- Where a criminal investigation is not commenced the Commissioners may decide to investigate using the COP 9 procedure.
- The recipient of COP 9 will be given the opportunity to make a complete and accurate disclosure of all his deliberate and non-deliberate conduct that has led to irregularities in his tax affairs.
- Where HMRC suspect that the recipient has failed to make a full disclosure of all irregularities, the Commissioners reserve the right to commence a criminal investigation with a view to prosecution.
- The term 'deliberate conduct' means that the recipient knew that an entry or entries included in a tax return and/or accounts were wrong but submitted it/them anyway, or that the recipient knew that a tax liability existed but chose not to tell HMRC at the right time.
- In the course of the COP 9 investigation, if the recipient makes materially false or misleading statements, or provides materially false documents, the Commissioners reserve the right to commence a criminal investigation into that conduct as a separate criminal offence.

If the Commissioners decide to investigate using the COP 9 procedure the taxpayer will be given a copy of the above statement by an authorised officer.

Under its published Criminal Investigation Policy (see www.gov.uk/government/publications/criminal-investigation/hmrc-criminal-investigation-policy), HMRC reserve complete discretion to conduct a criminal investigation in any case, with a view to prosecution by the Crown Prosecution Service ('CPS') in England and Wales or the appropriate prosecuting authority in Scotland and Northern Ireland. Examples of the kind of circumstances in which HMRC will generally consider commencing a criminal, rather than civil, investigation are, inter alia, cases involving organised or systematic fraud including conspiracy; cases where an individual holds a position of trust or responsibility; cases where materially false statements are made or materially false documents are provided in the course of a civil investigation; cases where deliberate concealment, deception, conspiracy or corruption is suspected; cases involving the use of false or forged documents; cases involving money laundering; cases where there is a link to suspected wider criminality; and repeated offences.

See *R v CIR (ex p Mead and Cook)* QB 1992, 65 TC 1 as regards HMRC discretion to seek monetary settlements or institute criminal proceedings. See *R v CIR (ex p Allen)* QB 1997, 69 TC 442 for an unsuccessful application for judicial review of a Revenue decision to take criminal proceedings. HMRC have an unrestricted power to conduct a prosecution in the Crown Court, there being no requirement for the consent of the Attorney-General (*R (oao Hunt) v Criminal Cases Review Commission* DC, [2000] STC 1110). See also **30.2** HMRC — ADMINISTRATION.

The Crown Prosecution Service is not precluded from instituting criminal proceedings in circumstances where HMRC has accepted a monetary settlement (*R v W and another* CA, [1998] STC 550). However, the Revenue in commenting on this case stated that the CPS will ordinarily bring proceedings that encompass tax evasion charges only where that evasion is incidental to allegations of non-fiscal criminal conduct (Revenue Tax Bulletin June 1998 pp 544, 545).

Statements made or documents produced by or on behalf of a taxpayer are admissible as evidence in proceedings against him notwithstanding that reliance on HMRC's practice above or on their policy for mitigating penalties (see **52.31** PENALTIES) may have induced him to make or produce them. [*TMA 1970, s 105*].

See generally HMRC Fraud Civil Investigation Manual.

Contractual disclosure facility

The contractual disclosure facility (CDF) commenced on 31 January 2012 is an opportunity offered to taxpayers to tell HMRC about any tax fraud in which they have been involved. See www.gov.uk/guidance/admitting-tax-fraud-the-contractual-disclosure-facility-cdf. HMRC write to taxpayers whom they suspect have committed a tax fraud; their letter will offer a CDF contract and will be accompanied by a copy of COP 9 (see above). Taxpayers have 60 days from date of receipt to either accept or formally reject the offer of a contract. If they accept, they must produce an Outline Disclosure within the same 60-day period; this should contain a brief description of the frauds committed, a formal admission of deliberately bringing about a loss of tax, details of any non-fraudulent irregularities and any proposals for a payment on account. If the Outline Disclosure is accepted, the taxpayer will be required to make progress towards the production of a Certificate of Full Disclosure.

Under the terms of the CDF contract the taxpayer will not be criminally investigated, with a view to prosecution, for matters covered by the Outline Disclosure. The customer's co-operation will have the potential to maximise reductions in penalties. If the taxpayer rejects the offer of a contract or makes no response, HMRC have the option of starting a criminal investigation, though in most cases they will pursue a civil investigation.

See also HMRC Fraud Civil Investigation Manual FCIM101000 where the CDF contract is offered before 30 June 2014 and FCIM200000 where it is offered on or after that date.

If a taxpayer wishes to own up to a fraud without waiting to be contacted by HMRC, he may complete form CDF1 (www.gov.uk/government/publications/voluntary-disclosure-contractual-disclosure-facility-cdf1) or use the digital disclosure service (see below); HMRC will then consider the taxpayer for a CDF contract.

Digital disclosure service

Taxpayers wishing to disclose unreturned or unpaid taxes (including capital gains tax and corporation tax) may do so online using HMRC's digital disclosure service. Disclosures may be made under any of HMRC's campaigns or otherwise. See www.gov.uk/government/publications/hm-revenue-and-customs-disclosure-service.

Simon's Taxes. See A6.1007–1014.

HMRC use of Police and Criminal Evidence Act 1984 powers

[34.14] HMRC are able to exercise certain powers under the *Police and Criminal Evidence Act 1984* when conducting direct tax criminal investigations. The powers involved include those concerning search warrants and arrest. Only HMRC officers authorised by the Commissioners for HMRC are able to exercise the powers. Similar powers are available to HMRC in Scotland and Northern Ireland.

As a result of the availability of the above police powers, the power to seek judicial authority to require the delivery of documents at **34.16** below is restricted to circumstances where the equivalent police power cannot be used because the material concerned is outside its scope.

[*Police and Criminal Evidence Act 1984, s 114; SI 2007 Nos 3166, 3175; SI 2015 No 1783*].

See HMRC Technical Note 'Criminal investigation powers and safeguards', 30 November 2007.

HMRC use of Proceeds of Crime Act 2002 powers

[34.15] With effect from 17 July 2013, HMRC are able to exercise certain powers under the *Proceeds of Crime Act 2002* directly when conducting direct tax criminal investigations. The powers involved are those for search and seizure of cash, production orders, search and seizure warrants, customer information orders and account monitoring orders. Previously these powers could be exercised by the police on behalf of HMRC.

[*Proceeds of Crime Act 2002, Pts 5, 8; FA 2013, s 224, Sch 48*].

Order for delivery of documents in serious tax fraud cases

[34.16] Under *TMA 1970, s 20BA, Sch 1AA*, introduced by *FA 2000, s 149, Sch 39*, HMRC may apply to the appropriate judicial authority (a Circuit judge in England and Wales, a sheriff in Scotland or a County Court judge in NI) for an order requiring any person who appears to have in his possession or power documents specified or described in the order to deliver them to an HMRC officer within ten working days after the day of service of the notice, or such longer or shorter period as may be specified in the order. The judicial authority must be satisfied, on information on oath given by an authorised HMRC officer, that there is reasonable ground for suspecting that an offence involving serious tax fraud has been or is about to be committed, and that the documents may be required as evidence in proceedings in respect of the offence. In Scotland, a single sheriff may make orders in respect of persons anywhere in Scotland as long as one of the orders relates to a person residing or having a place of business at an address in the sheriff's own sherriffdom. Orders may not be made in relation to items subject to legal privilege (as defined) unless they are held with the intention of furthering a criminal purpose. Failure to comply with an order is treated as contempt of court, and there are severe penalties for falsification of documents.

These provisions are restricted to circumstances where the equivalent power under the *Police and Criminal Evidence Act 1984* (see **34.14** above) cannot be used because the material concerned cannot be obtained using those powers.

Schedule 1AA lays down detailed requirements in relation to applications under these provisions, and these may be supplemented by regulations (see now *SI 2000 No 2875*). In particular, a person is entitled to at least five days' notice of intention to apply for such an order, and to appear and be heard at the application, unless the judicial authority is satisfied that this would seriously prejudice investigation of the offence. Until the application has been dismissed or abandoned, or an order made or complied with, any person given such notice must not conceal, destroy, alter or dispose of any document to which the order sought relates, or disclose information etc. likely to prejudice the investigation, except with the leave of the judicial authority or the written permission of the Commissioners for HMRC (or, before 18 April 2005, the Board of Inland Revenue). Professional legal advisers may, however, disclose such information etc. in giving legal advice to a client or in connection with legal proceedings, provided that it is not disclosed with a view to furthering a criminal purpose. Failure to comply with these requirements is treated as failure to comply with an order under these provisions. The procedural rules where documents are delivered in accordance with an order are as for

Search and seizure under *TMA 1970, s 20CC(3)–(9)*. The regulations include procedural rules for resolving any dispute between HMRC and a person against whom an order is made as to whether a document (or part thereof) is an item subject to legal privilege.

[*TMA 1970, s 20BA, Sch 1AA; Police and Criminal Evidence Act 1984, s 14B; FA 2000, s 149, Sch 39; SI 2007 No 3166*].

Data-gathering powers

[34.17] HMRC have a single cross-tax power to require by notice the provision of 'relevant data' from a data-holder falling within one of a list of specified categories. The power applies to all UK taxes and also to foreign taxes covered by the EU Directive for exchange of information (Directive 77/799/EEC) or by a tax information exchange agreement (see **31.2**(c) HMRC — CONFIDENTIALITY OF INFORMATION). It can be used both for the purposes of risk assessment and for obtaining third-party data in connection with specific tax checks and may be used to obtain personal data such as names and addresses of individuals. It cannot, however, generally be used to check the tax position of the data-holder to whom the notice is sent. '*Relevant data*' is data of a kind specified in regulations for each type of data-holder: see *SI 2012 No 847*. A data-holder notice under these provisions must specify the data to be provided. Only data which HMRC have reason to believe could have a bearing on periods ending within the last four years can be obtained.

A notice under these provisions can be given without the approval of the Tribunal, but where such approval is obtained by HMRC the data-holder has no right of appeal against the notice or a requirement in it. If approval is not sought by HMRC the data-holder can appeal against the notice or a requirement in it on the grounds that compliance would be unduly onerous, that the data-holder is not within the list of specified data-holders or that the data specified in the notice is not relevant data. No appeal can be made against a requirement to provide data forming part of the data-holder's statutory records (i.e. records required to be kept and preserved under any tax enactment). The procedures for appeals are the same as those for appeals against information notices under *FA 2008, Sch 36* (see **34.6** above).

Where approval is sought from the Tribunal, the application for approval must be made by, or with the agreement of, an authorised HMRC officer. The data-holder must normally have been told that the data are required and have been given a reasonable opportunity to make representations to HMRC, but is not entitled to be present at the hearing. The Tribunal must be given a summary of any representations made. Where the Tribunal is satisfied that informing the data-holder would prejudice any purpose for which the data is required, it can approve the giving of the notice without the data-holder having been informed.

The data required by a notice must be provided by the means and in the form reasonably specified in the notice. If the data has to be sent somewhere, it must be sent to the specified address within the period reasonably specified in the notice. If documents are to be made available for inspection, they must be so made available either at a place (other than one used solely as a dwelling) and time reasonably specified in the notice or at a place and time agreed between an HMRC officer and the data-holder. A notice requiring the provision of specified documents only requires their provision if they are in the data-holder's possession or power. An HMRC officer may take copies of, or make extracts from, documents provided and, if he thinks it reasonable to do so, may retain documents for a reasonable period. If a document is retained, the data-holder may request a copy of it if he reasonably requires it for any purpose.

[*FA 2011, s 86, Sch 23 paras 1–7, 28, 29, 45, 46, 65*].

Responsibility of company officers

Everything to be done by a company under the above provisions must be done by it through the '*proper officer*' (i.e. the secretary of a corporate body, except where a liquidator or administrator has been appointed when the latter is the proper officer, or the treasurer of a non-corporate body) or, except where a liquidator has been appointed, any authorised officer. The service of a notice on a company may be effected by serving it on the proper officer. [*TMA 1970, s 108; FA 2011, Sch 23 para 43(1)*].

Data-holders

The following is a list of the categories of data-holders who are subject to the above provisions. Note that further conditions apply in some cases. The provisions also apply to persons who previously fell within a category but no longer do so.

(1) An employer.
(2) A third party making payments to or in respect of another person's employees.
(3) An approved payroll giving agent (within *ITEPA 2003, s 714*).
(4) A person carrying on a business (as defined) in connection with which certain payments relating to services provided by persons other than employees or in respect of intellectual property rights are made or are likely to be made.
(5) A person by or through whom interest, building society share dividends, foreign dividends or alternative finance return are paid or credited.
(6) A person who is in receipt of money or value of or belonging to another.
(7) A person who has a contractual obligation to make payments to retailers in settlement of payment card transactions (a 'merchant acquirer').
(8) A person who provides services by which monetary value is stored electronically for the purpose of payments being made in respect of transactions to which the provider of the services is not a party (often known as a 'digital wallet').
(9) A person who provides services to enable or facilitate transactions between suppliers and customers (other than services solely enabling payments to be made) and receives information about such transactions in doing so (a 'business intermediary').

(10) A person who is the registered or inscribed holder of securities.
(11) A person who receives a payment derived from securities or would be entitled to do so if a payment were made.
(12) A person who receives a payment for the purchase by an unquoted company of its own shares (within *CTA 2010, s 1033*).
(13) A person who receives a chargeable payment within *CTA 2010, Pt 23 Ch 5* (company distributions: demergers).
(14) A person who makes a payment derived from securities that has been received from or is paid on behalf of another.
(15) A person by whom a payment out of public funds is made by way of grant or subsidy.
(16) A person by whom licences or approvals are issued or a local authority or statutory register is maintained.
(17) A lessee, an occupier of land, a person having the use of land and a person who, as agent, manages land or receives rent or other payments from land.
(18) A person who effects or is a party to securities transactions (as defined) wholly or partly on behalf of others.
(19) A person who, in the course of business, acts as registrar or administrator in respect of securities transactions.
(20) A person who makes a payment derived from securities to anyone other than the registered or inscribed holder.
(21) A person who makes a payment derived from bearer securities.
(22) A stamp duty reserve tax accountable person (within *SI 1986 No 1711*).
(23) The committee or other person or body managing a clearing house for any terminal market in commodities.
(24) An auctioneer.
(25) A person carrying on a business of dealing in, or of acting as an intermediary in dealings in, tangible movable property.
(26) A Lloyd's syndicate managing agent.
(27) An ISA plan manager or child trust fund account provider.
(28) A *Petroleum Act 1998* licence holder.
(29) The responsible person (within *Oil Taxation Act 1975, Pt 1*) for an oil field.
(30) A person involved in an insurance business.
(31) A person who makes arrangements for persons to enter into insurance contracts.
(32) A person concerned in a business which is not an insurance business but who has been involved in the entering into of an insurance contract providing cover for any matter associated with the business.
(33) A person involved in subjecting aggregate to exploitation in the UK or connected activities, making or receiving supplies of commodities subject to climate change levy or landfill disposal.
(34) A person who makes a settlement (within *ITTOIA 2005, s 620*), the trustees of a settlement, a beneficiary under a settlement and any other person to whom income is payable under a settlement.
(35) A charity.

(36) (From the date of Royal Assent to *F(No 2)A 2017* but in relation to relevant data with a bearing on any period whether before, on or after that date) a money service business, i.e. a business providing money transfer, cheque cashing and currency exchange services (other than a credit institution such as a bank or building society).

[*FA 2011, Sch 23 paras 8–27; FA 2013, s 228; FA 2016, s 176; F(No 2)A 2017, s 69*].

Penalties

For penalties for failure to comply with a data-holder notice and for the provision of inaccurate information or documents see **52.17** PENALTIES.

Previous provisions

The above provisions replace a great number of separate powers each applicable only to individual taxes. The provisions which are relevant to tax on chargeable gains are as follows.

- *TMA 1970, s 14* (return of lodgers etc. — see **58.24** RETURNS).
- *TMA 1970, s 25* (issuing houses, stockbrokers, auctioneers etc. — see **58.25** RETURNS).
- *TMA 1970, s 26* (nominee shareholders — see **58.25** RETURNS).
- *TMA 1970, s 27* (parties to a settlement — see **62.6** SETTLEMENTS).
- *TMA 1970, s 77I; FA 1973, Sch 15 para 2* (petroleum licence holders — see **49.19** OVERSEAS MATTERS.
- *FA 2008, Sch 36 para 34A* (involved third parties — see **34.4** above).

Computer records etc.

[34.18] The following applies to any tax provisions requiring a person to produce a document or cause a document to be produced, furnished or delivered, or requiring a person to permit HMRC to inspect a document, to make copies of or extracts from, or remove, a document (i.e. including the provisions at **34.4**, **34.10**, **34.11**, **34.12**, and **34.16**).

For the purposes of such provisions, a reference to a document is a reference to anything in which information of any description is recorded, and a reference to a copy of a document is to anything onto which information recorded in the document has been copied, by whatever means and whether directly or indirectly. In *R(oao Glenn & Co (Essex Ltd) v HMRC* QB, [2010] EWHC 1469 (Admin), 2010 STI 2119, a computer was held to fall within this provision.

Where a document has been, or may be, required to be produced, inspected etc. under any such provisions, a person authorised by the Commissioners for HMRC (previously the Board of Inland Revenue) can obtain access to any computer and associated apparatus or material used in connection with the document at any reasonable time in order to inspect it and check its operation. Reasonable assistance can be required from the person by whom or on whose behalf the computer has been so used or any person in charge of the computer etc. or otherwise concerned with its operation.

A penalty of £300 (£500 before 21 July 2008) applies for obstruction of such access or refusal to provide assistance.

[*FA 1988, s 127; FA 2008, s 114*].

Key points on HMRC investigatory powers

[34.19] Points to consider are as follows.

- HMRC has aligned its powers across the majority of taxes and duties since April 2009 to increase its powers in most cases. HMRC can now inspect businesses and the taxpayer/employer is required to cooperate or face a financial penalty. In cases where HMRC can demonstrate the taxpayer concealed, destroyed or disposed of information then the person can face imprisonment and/or a fine.
- The adviser needs to carefully review any information notice to ensure it is addressed to the correct person, the correct address, there is reason to suspect tax has been lost or overpaid, the time allowed to provide the information is sufficient and the information request is reasonable and relevant.
- The adviser should cooperate with HMRC as long it is clear the information request is correct and accurate. It is recommended advisors explain to clients that HMRC has a statutory power to request information.
- If at all possible, it is recommended that clients do not sign mandates for third parties. The adviser should use all available routes to gather the information needed first. Otherwise, the information request can be very damaging to the commercial and business relationship with the bank, for example.
- HMRC has to observe the Human Rights Act 1998 and the person's 'right to privacy'. This means minimising the damage and disruption that an enquiry can cause. HMRC cannot exchange information with other jurisdictions or departments outside of the legal gateways in place. HMRC does not need to inspect private dwellings and it is recommended that where possible the records are examined at a neutral venue such the adviser's offices.
- Requests for information created more than six years before the date of the notice need to be agreed with a senior officer within HMRC. These cases normally involve deliberate failure to report or return income or gains.
- Always seek legal professional advice straightaway if there is any suggestion or reference to criminal proceedings.
- Prevention is better than cure and advisers should attempt where possible to avoid HMRC using its formal powers due to the financial penalties and time constraints involved. HMRC perceives the need to use formal powers where there is a lack of cooperation on the client's part.

- Although some enquiries/requests for information are random, regard should be had to the significant volume of data currently released to HMRC via UK and overseas sources and warn clients to consider carefully whether they have accidentally omitted any information from their returns.

35

HMRC Statements of Practice

Introduction to HMRC Statements of Practice

[35.1] The following is a summary of those current Statements of Practice published by HMRC, which are referred to in this work.

Statements are divided into those originally published before 18 July 1978 (which are given a reference letter (according to the subject matter) and consecutive number, e.g. E11) and later Statements (which are numbered consecutively in each year, e.g. SP 5/02).

The full text of current statements of practice is published in an internet-only document on the gov.uk website (www.gov.uk). Copies of recently announced statements are also available (with the relevant press release) on the website. The full text of all current statements is reproduced in Tolley's Yellow Tax Handbook and Tolley's Tax Link.

See **30.5** HMRC — ADMINISTRATION for the Treasury's power, by order, to legislate statements of practice where they provide a 'concession' (as defined).

The Statements

[35.2]

A8	**Stock dividends.** The interpretation of *ICTA 1988, s 251(2)* is clarified. See **63.10** SHARES AND SECURITIES.
A13	**Completion of return forms by attorneys.** In cases of age and infirmity of the taxpayer HMRC will accept the signature of an attorney who has full knowledge of the taxpayer's affairs. See **58.4** RETURNS.
B1	**Treatment of VAT.** The position of partly exempt persons is considered. See **39.3** INTERACTION WITH OTHER TAXES.
D1	**Part disposals of land.** Where part of an estate is disposed of, HMRC will accept that that part can be treated as a separate asset and the total cost apportioned accordingly (i.e. on an alternative basis to the usual part disposal formula). See **41.8** LAND.
D3	**Company liquidations: shareholders' capital gains tax.** Special rules can be applied where a shareholder receives more than one distribution in the liquidation. See **8.10** ASSETS HELD ON 6 APRIL 1965 and **63.12** SHARES AND SECURITIES.
D4	**Short delay by owner-occupier in taking up residence.** The period of occupation of a house will, in certain circumstances, include one year prior to taking up residence. This statement was replaced by ESC D49 on 18 October 1994. See **53.7** PRIVATE RESIDENCES.

D6 **Replacement of business assets: time limit.** Where land is acquired under a compulsory purchase order and leased back to the vendor, HMRC will, under certain conditions, extend the time limit for replacement. See **41.12** LAND.

D7 **Treatment of VAT.** See **39.3** INTERACTION WITH OTHER TAXES.

D10 **Termination of interest in possession in part of settled property.** HMRC will agree with the trustees what assets are to be identified with the termination. See **62.16** SETTLEMENTS.

D11 **Partnership: assets owned by a partner.** Rollover relief may be available. See **59.3** ROLLOVER RELIEF.

D12 **Partnerships.** This statement sets out a number of points on the capital gains tax treatment of partnerships (including limited liability partnerships) and of dealings between partners. It was revised in October 2002 and September 2015. See **50** PARTNERSHIPS.

D18 **Value-shifting: *TCGA 1992, s 30, Sch 11 para 10(1)*.** These provisions do not apply when a farmer retires, leases the farm to his son, and sells the freehold, subject to the lease, to an outside investor. See **4.10** ANTI-AVOIDANCE.

D19 **Replacement of business assets in groups of companies.** To obtain rollover relief, HMRC do not insist that a company be a member of the group at the time of the transaction carried out by the other company. See **59.10** ROLLOVER RELIEF.

D21 **Time limit for an election for valuation on 6 April 1965 under *TCGA 1992, Sch 2 para 17*: company leaving a group: *TCGA 1992, s 179*.** See **29.7** GROUPS OF COMPANIES.

D23 **Overseas resident company.** The appropriate proportion of any overseas tax payable by a non-resident company is deductible in computing the gain chargeable on a UK participator under *TCGA 1992, s 13*. See **49.7** OVERSEAS MATTERS.

D24 **Initial repairs to property.** Such expense, including the cost of decorating, not allowable for Schedule A purposes, is regarded as allowable for capital gains tax purposes. See **16.11**(b) COMPUTATION OF GAINS AND LOSSES.

SP 1/79 **Partnerships: extension of SP D12 above.** The practice whereby the capitalised value of an annuity paid to a retired partner is not treated as consideration for the disposal of his share in the partnership assets in certain circumstances is extended to cases where a lump sum is paid in addition. See **50.12** PARTNERSHIPS.

SP 8/79 **Compensation for acquisition of property under compulsory powers.** Any compensation for temporary loss of profits is taxable under *Schedule D, Case I or II*. See **10.2** CAPITAL SUMS DERIVED FROM ASSETS.

SP 10/79 **Power for trustees to allow a beneficiary to occupy a dwelling-house.** Depending upon the circumstances, this may be treated as giving rise to an interest in possession. See **62.4** SETTLEMENTS.

SP 14/79	**Unquoted shares or securities held on 6 April 1965: computation of chargeable gains where there has been a reorganisation of share capital.** See **8.10** ASSETS HELD ON 6 APRIL **1965**.
SP 14/80	**Relief for owner-occupiers.** This statement explains the relief for owner-occupiers who let living accommodation in their homes. See **53.9, 53.14** PRIVATE RESIDENCES.
SP 8/81	**Rollover relief for replacement of business assets: trades carried on successively.** The Board's practice in deciding whether trades are carried on successively, how acquisitions in the interval between trades are to be regarded, and how this treatment is to be applied to groups of companies, is explained. See **59.5, 59.10** ROLLOVER RELIEF.
SP 1/84	**Trade unions: provident benefits** include legal expenses in connection with a member's accident or injury claim or unfair dismissal. This statement is considered obsolete by HMRC. See **25.63** EXEMPTIONS AND RELIEFS.
SP 6/84	**Leasing of mobile drilling rigs etc. by overseas residents.** HMRC indicate their practice. See **49.19** OVERSEAS MATTERS.
SP 7/84	**Exercise of a power of appointment or advancement over settled property.** HMRC indicate how they will decide whether a new settlement has been created. See **62.14** SETTLEMENTS.
SP 10/84	**Foreign bank accounts.** HMRC give their practice regarding direct transfers from one foreign bank account to another. See **25.5** EXEMPTIONS AND RELIEFS and **55.7** REMITTANCE BASIS.
SP 5/86	**Rollover relief for employees and office-holders.** In certain circumstances relief is available to such persons where the land or building owned is in general use in the trade carried on by the employer. See **59.4** ROLLOVER RELIEF.
SP 5/87	**Tax returns: use of substitute forms.** HMRC states its requirements. See **58.4** RETURNS.
SP 6/88	**Double taxation relief.** HMRC describe some situations where double taxation relief is available. See **21.8** DOUBLE TAX RELIEF.
SP 1/89	**Partnerships.** The practice concerning changes in partnership sharing ratios (see D12 above) is extended to cover the 1988 re-basing provisions. See **50.7** PARTNERSHIPS.
SP 4/89	**Company purchasing own shares.** HMRC's practice where a purchase gives rise to a distribution is explained. See **63.19** SHARES AND SECURITIES.
SP 5/89	**Capital gains re-basing and indexation: shares held at 31 March 1982.** A single holding treatment will apply if some shares were held on 31 March 1982 and the remainder are treated as held on that date. See **9.6** ASSETS HELD ON 31 MARCH **1982**.
SP 1/90	**Company residence.** The Revenue's approach to the determination of a company's residence is explained. See **57.33** RESIDENCE AND DOMICILE.

SP 2/90 **Company migration: notice and arrangements under *FA 1988, s 130*.** Guidance is given on the procedure, information and arrangements HMRC will require under the provision. See **49.18** OVERSEAS MATTERS.

SP 5/90 **Accountants' working papers.** HMRC's investigatory powers as regards the disclosure of accountants' working papers are explained. This statement has been subsumed into Compliance Handbook CH231200. See **34.11** HMRC INVESTIGATORY POWERS.

SP 8/90 **Loans to traders evidenced by qualifying corporate bonds.** Loss relief will still be available where the security concerned ceases to have any value because it is redeemed early. See **44.13** LOSSES.

SP 2/91 **Residence in the UK: visits extended because of exceptional circumstances.** In deciding a person's residence status, days spent in the UK because of exceptional circumstances beyond the person's control will be ignored in certain cases. Withdrawn with effect from 6 April 2009. See **57.29** RESIDENCE AND DOMICILE.

SP 7/91 **Double taxation: business profits: unilateral relief.** The practice as regards admission of foreign taxes for unilateral relief is revised. See **21.4** DOUBLE TAX RELIEF.

SP 8/91 **Discovery assessments** (pre-self-assessment). The Revenue practice as regards the making of further assessments following 'discovery' is explained.

SP 10/91 **Corporation tax: a major change in the nature or conduct of a trade or business.** HMRC set out some of the circumstances which may amount to a major change in the nature or conduct of a trade for the purposes of, *inter alia*, *TCGA 1992, Sch 7A* (restriction of set-off of pre-entry losses where a company joins a group).

SP 17/91 **Ordinary residence in the UK.** The practice regarding the commencement of ordinary residence where the period to be spent in the UK is less than three years is explained. Withdrawn with effect from 6 April 2009. See **57.30** RESIDENCE AND DOMICILE.

SP 4/92 **Capital gains tax re-basing elections.** HMRC describe the three kinds of disposal which will not be treated as the first relevant disposal for a re-basing election. See **9.3** ASSETS HELD ON 31 MARCH 1982.

SP 5/92 **Non-resident trusts.** HMRC give their views on a number of detailed matters in connection with: the residence of trustees; past trustees' liabilities; the settlor's right to repayment from the trustees; trusts created before 19 March 1991; transactions entered into at arm's length; close companies; transactions with wholly-owned companies; loans made to settlements; loans made by trustees; failure to exercise rights to reimbursement; administrative expenses; life tenants; indemnities and guarantees; variations; *ultra vires* payments; and intra-group transfers. See **48** OFFSHORE SETTLEMENTS.

SP 8/92 **Hold-over relief: valuation of assets.** The circumstances in which HMRC will require a valuation of assets in respect of which a claim to hold-over relief is made are described. See **36.2** HOLD-OVER RELIEFS.

SP 5/93 **Double taxation agreement with Czechoslovakia.** The Revenue clarified the position following the split of Czechoslovakia into separate Czech and Slovak republics. See **21.3** DOUBLE TAX RELIEF.

SP 13/93 **Compulsory acquisition of freehold by tenant.** HMRC will accept a rollover relief claim from a landlord whose tenant has exercised certain statutory rights to acquire the freehold reversion or extension of the lease. See **41.12** LAND.

SP 15/93 **Incidental costs of acquisition and disposal.** In certain cases, large companies may round these costs to the nearest £1,000. See **16.11** COMPUTATION OF GAINS AND LOSSES.

SP 4/94 **Enhanced stock dividends received by trustees of interest in possession trusts.** HMRC set out their view on tax treatment. See **63.10** SHARES AND SECURITIES.

SP 8/95 **Venture capital trusts: default terms in loan agreements.** Certain standard terms will be ignored in deciding whether a loan qualifies as a security. See **71.2** VENTURE CAPITAL TRUSTS.

SP 3/97 **Investment trusts investing in authorised unit trusts or open-ended investment companies.** HMRC express their views of the tax implications of such investment. Replaces SP 7/94 with effect from 18 July 1997. See **70.4** UNIT TRUSTS ETC.

SP 4/97 **Taxation of commissions, cashbacks and discounts.** No chargeable gain arises on receipt of a cashback. See **25.23** EXEMPTIONS AND RELIEFS. See Tolley's Income Tax for income tax consequences of the receipt of commissions, cashbacks and discounts.

SP 6/98 **EIS, reinvestment relief and venture capital trusts: loans to investors.** HMRC explain how they apply the rules which deny or withdraw the above reliefs where investors receive loans linked to their investments. Replaces SP 3/94. See **23.4** ENTERPRISE INVESTMENT SCHEME, **25.86** EXEMPTIONS AND RELIEFS and **71.7**(d) VENTURE CAPITAL TRUSTS.

SP 1/99 **Self-assessment enquiries.** Where an enquiry into a personal, partnership or trust return remains open pending agreement of a CGT valuation, HMRC will not use the open enquiry to raise new issues which they would not otherwise have been able to raise. See **58.10** RETURNS.

SP 2/99 **Authorised unit trusts, approved investment trusts and open-ended investment companies — monthly savings schemes.** A simplified method of calculating the chargeable gain arising on a disposal can be used as regards acquisitions in accounting years of funds ending before 6 April 1999 where savings commenced before 6 April 1998. Replaces SP 2/97 which itself replaced SP 3/89. See **70.3, 70.4, 70.8** UNIT TRUSTS ETC.

SP 1/00 **Corporate venturing scheme: applications for advance clearance.** HMRC give guidance to potential qualifying issuing companies seeking advance clearance under the scheme.

SP 3/00 **EIS, venture capital trusts, corporate venturing scheme and reinvestment relief: location of activity.** HMRC's interpretation of the requirement that qualifying trades for the purposes of the above reliefs must be carried on wholly or mainly in the UK. Replaces SP 7/98. See **18.7** CORPORATE VENTURING SCHEME, **23.8** ENTERPRISE INVESTMENT SCHEME, and **71.4** VENTURE CAPITAL TRUSTS.

SP 4/00 **Tonnage tax regime.** HMRC guidance on the practical operation of the regime. See **25.17** EXEMPTIONS AND RELIEFS.

SP 4/01 **Double taxation conventions with the former USSR and with newly independent states.** The position is updated, superseding SP 3/92 above. See **21.2** DOUBLE TAX RELIEF.

SP 5/01 **Corporation tax self-assessment: claims to loss relief, capital allowances and group relief made outside the normal time limit.** The circumstances in which HMRC will exercise their discretion with regard to such late claims are explained. See **58.19** RETURNS.

SP 1/02 **Corporation tax self-assessment enquiries.** Where an enquiry into a corporation tax return remains open pending agreement of a chargeable gains valuation, HMRC will not use the open enquiry to raise new issues which they would not otherwise have been able to raise. See **58.19** RETURNS.

SP 3/02 **Financial futures and options.** HMRC's views on the tax treatment of transactions in certain financial futures and options, with particular reference to whether such transactions are to be regarded as profits or losses of a trade or taxed under the chargeable gains rules. Replaces SP 14/91. See **7.7**, **7.8** ASSETS.

SP 5/02 **Exemption for substantial shareholdings of companies.** HMRC guidance on the application of the anti-avoidance rule at **66.7** SUBSTANTIAL SHAREHOLDINGS OF COMPANIES.

SP 2/04 **Allowable expenditure: expenses incurred by personal representatives and corporate trustees under TCGA 1992, s 38(1)(b).** For deaths after 5 April 2004, a revised scale of expenditure is allowable for costs of establishing title in computing gains or losses of personal representatives on the sale of assets in a deceased person's estate. See **19.10** DEATH.

SP 3/04 **Double taxation convention with the former Yugoslavia.** The position is updated, superseding SP 6/93 above. See **21.2** DOUBLE TAX RELIEF.

SP 1/06 **Self-assessment — finality and discovery.** HMRC set out their views on finality of self-assessments and discovery following the decision in *Veltema v Langham*. See **6.10** ASSESSMENTS.

SP 2/06 **Venture capital trusts, EIS and corporate venturing scheme: value of gross assets.** HMRC set out their approach in applying the 'gross assets requirement'. Replaces SP 2/00. See **18.6** CORPORATE VENTURING SCHEME, **23.5** ENTERPRISE INVESTMENT SCHEME, and **71.4** VENTURE CAPITAL TRUSTS.

SP 3/07 **Double taxation convention with the former Yugoslavia.** The position is updated, superseding SP 3/04. See **21.3** DOUBLE TAX RELIEF.

36

Hold-Over Reliefs

Introduction	**36.1**
Relief for gifts of business assets	**36.2**
Definitions	**36.3**
Nature of relief	**36.4**
Agricultural property	**36.5**
Settled property	**36.6**
Restrictions on, and clawback of, relief	**36.8**
Relief for gifts of business assets before 14 March 1989	**36.9**
Gifts on which inheritance tax is chargeable etc.	**36.10**
Restrictions on, and clawback of, relief	**36.11**
General relief for gifts from 1980 to 1989	**36.12**
Key points	**36.13**

Cross-references. See **9.11** ASSETS HELD ON 31 MARCH **1982** for 50% relief etc. on held-over gains relating to an asset acquired before 31 March 1982; **10.3**, **10.4** CAPITAL SUMS DERIVED FROM ASSETS for reliefs available where capital sums received as compensation are expended on restoration or replacement; **14.11** COMPANIES for the relief available on a scheme of reconstruction; **25** EXEMPTIONS AND RELIEFS generally; **25.86** EXEMPTIONS AND RELIEFS for reinvestment relief which could be used as an alternative to the reliefs in this chapter where a qualifying investment is made before 6 April 1998; **27.3** GIFTS for summary of special reliefs relating to gifts; **29.3** GROUPS OF COMPANIES for relief on disposals within a group; **37** INCORPORATION AND DISINCORPORATION RELIEFS; **41.9**, **41.11**, **41.12** LAND for reliefs available on small part disposals and compulsory purchase of land; **49.3** OVERSEAS MATTERS for transfer of UK branch or agency to UK resident company, **49.12** for transfers of assets to a non-UK resident company, **49.13** for transfer or division of business between companies in different EC member states and **49.14** for transfer or division of non-UK business between companies in different EC member states; **59** ROLLOVER RELIEF.

Simon's Taxes. See **C1.425–C1.428**, **C3.5**.

Introduction

[36.1] There are currently two separate hold-over reliefs which apply to:

(a) disposals by individuals or trustees of business assets where the disposal is not at arm's length (for example, gifts); and
(b) disposals by individuals or trustees in respect of which inheritance tax is chargeable (or would be but for certain exemptions).

The effect of the reliefs is to reduce or eliminate the chargeable gain on the disposal and to make a corresponding reduction in the acquisition cost of the transferee. Relief must be claimed, usually by way of a joint claim by both transferor or transferee. Relief is denied in certain circumstances, including where the transferee is not UK-resident nor ordinarily resident or is the trustees of a settlor-interested settlement. Relief already given is also clawed back in certain circumstances, including where the transferee subsequently emigrates. See **36.8** and **36.11** below.

The current restricted hold-over reliefs replaced wider reliefs in 1989. These superseded reliefs are described briefly at **36.9** and **36.12** below for their possible ongoing effect on acquisition costs.

Relief for gifts of business assets

[36.2] The hold-over relief described below applies where:

(a) an individual ('*the transferor*') makes a disposal not at arm's length (e.g. a gift) of an asset specified below, and
(b) a joint claim for relief is made by him and the transferee, or, where the transferee is a trustee of a settlement, by him alone.

[*TCGA 1992, s 165(1); FA 2015, Sch 7 para 23(2)*].

Note that the transferee need not be an individual and may, for example, be a company. See also **36.5** below re agricultural property and **36.6** below re settled property. The relief extends to non-resident CGT disposals (see **41.25** LAND) to a UK-resident transferee and to disposals of UK residential property interests to non-residents.

An asset is within (a) above if:

(i) it is, or is an interest in, an asset used for the purposes of a trade, profession or vocation carried on by the transferor, his 'personal company' or a member of a 'trading group' of which the 'holding company' is his personal company), or
(ii) it consists of shares or securities of a 'trading company', or of the holding company of a trading group, where *either* the shares etc. are neither listed on a recognised stock exchange (within *ITA 2007, s 1005* — see **63.30** SHARES AND SECURITIES) nor dealt in on the Unlisted Securities Market (now closed) *or* the trading company or holding company is the transferor's personal company.

[*TCGA 1992, s 165(2)*].

Hold-over relief does not apply on a disposal if:

- the disposal is a transfer of shares or securities and the transferee is a company;
- the gain arises by virtue of *TCGA 1992, s 116(10)(b)* (disposal of qualifying corporate bonds derived from shares giving rise to deferred gain, see **54.4** QUALIFYING CORPORATE BONDS); or
- hold-over relief is available (or would be if a claim were made) under *TCGA 1992, s 260* in **36.10** below for gifts on which inheritance tax is chargeable etc.

[*TCGA 1992, s 165(3)*].

See also the restriction and clawback provisions in **36.8** below.

Definitions

[36.3] For the purposes of **36.2** above, an individual's '*personal company*' is a company the voting rights in which are 'exercisable', as to not less than 5%, by that individual. ('*Exercisable*' means capable of being exercised, whether or not in fact exercised (*Hepworth v Smith* Ch D 1981, 54 TC 396).)

'*Trading group*', '*holding company*' and '*trading company*' have the following meanings. For the purposes of the definitions, the activities of group members are regarded as a single business, so that intra-group activities are disregarded.

A '*trading group*' is a 'group of companies' (see below), one or more of whose members carry on 'trading activities' and the activities of whose members, taken together, do not include to a 'substantial' extent activities other than trading activities. '*Trading activities*' means activities carried on by a member of the group, being activities that would fall within (A)–(D) below if these are interpreted by reference not only to that member but also to any other member of the group. A group member acquires a '*significant interest*' (see (D) below) if it acquires sufficient ordinary share capital in the other company to make that company a member of the same group as the acquiring company, or to give the acquiring company a qualifying shareholding in a 'joint venture company'. In determining whether a group of companies is a trading group, there is disregarded any 'qualifying shareholding' held by any member of the group in a 'joint venture company'. Each such member is regarded as carrying on a share of the joint venture company's activities (or, if the joint venture company is itself a holding company of a trading group, a share of that group's activities) proportionate to its percentage shareholding in that company. This does not apply if the joint venture company is itself a member of the group.

The views expressed in HMRC's Capital Gains Manual on the meaning of 'trading company' (see below) are also of relevance to 'trading groups', but intra-group activities are disregarded in applying the various tests (HMRC Capital Gains Manual CG17953f).

A '*group of companies*' means a company and its '51% subsidiary(ies)' (within *CTA 2010, Pt 24 Ch 3*).

A '*holding company*' is a company with one or more 51% subsidiaries.

A '*trading company*' is a company carrying on 'trading activities' whose activities do not include to a 'substantial' extent activities other than trading activities. '*Trading activities*' means 'activities' carried on by the company:

- (A) in the course of, or for the purposes of, a 'trade' being carried on by it; or
- (B) for the purposes of a trade that it is preparing to carry on; or
- (C) with a view to its acquiring or starting to carry on a trade; or
- (D) with a view to its acquiring a 'significant interest' in the share capital of another company that is itself a trading company or the holding company of a trading group and that is not already a member of the same group as the acquiring company (where applicable).

'*Activities*' is interpreted by HMRC to mean what a company does, and thus the expression in itself includes engaging in trading activities, making and holding investments, planning, holding meetings and so forth (HMRC Capital Gains Manual CG17953). Activities qualify under (C) or (D) above only if the acquisition is made, or the trade commenced, as soon as reasonably practicable in the circumstances. A company acquires a '*significant interest*' (see (D) above) if it acquires sufficient ordinary share capital in the other company to make that company its 51% subsidiary (within *CTA 2010, Pt 24 Ch 3*), or to give the acquiring company a qualifying shareholding in a joint venture company without making the two companies members of the same group. For further interpretation of (A)–(D) above, see HMRC Capital Gains Manual CG17953i–17953l.

In determining whether a company with a qualifying shareholding in a joint venture company is a trading company, any holding of shares by it in the joint venture company is disregarded. It is regarded as carrying on a share of the joint venture company's activities proportionate to its percentage shareholding in that company.

For the purposes of the above definitions (but not for the general purposes of the above relief — see below) '*trade*' means a trade, profession or vocation, as understood for income tax purposes, which is conducted on a commercial basis with a view to realisation of profits. The expression also expressly includes the commercial letting of FURNISHED HOLIDAY ACCOMMODATION (**26**), but other letting of furnished property is excluded (*Patel v Maidment* Sp C 2003, [2004] SSCD 41, Sp C 384).

A '*joint venture company*' is a company:

(I) which is a trading company or the holding company of a trading group, *and*

(II) at least 75% in aggregate of the ordinary share capital (within *ITA 2007, s 989*) of which is held by no more than five persons (counting shares held by different members of a group of companies as held by a single company).

A company has a '*qualifying shareholding*' in a joint venture company if:

- it holds 10% or more of the ordinary share capital of the joint venture company, *or*
- (where the company is a member of a group of companies) the company and the other members of the group between them hold 10% or more of that ordinary share capital.

In interpreting the above, HMRC take '*substantial*' to mean 'more than 20%'. Depending on the facts of the case, this measure may be applied to turnover, expenditure and/or time spent by officers and employees where one or more of these items relate partly to non-trading activities, and/or to non-trading assets as a proportion of all assets (either of which may possibly include intangible assets such as goodwill). The fact that a company has investment income does not necessarily bring the 20% test into play. If it can be shown that holding the investment is integral to the conduct of the trade or is a short-term lodgement of surplus funds held to meet demonstrable trading liabilities, the investment is unlikely to be seen as evidence of a non-trading purpose. An investment outside these categories still has the safety net of the 20% test. As regards *property* owned by the company but surplus to immediate business requirements, HMRC do not *necessarily* regard any of the following as indicating a non-trading purpose:

- letting part of the trading premises;
- letting properties no longer required for the trade and intended to be sold eventually;
- subletting property where it would be impractical or uneconomic to assign or surrender the lease;
- acquiring property, whether vacant or already let, with the provable intention of bringing it into use for the purpose of the trade.

In establishing 'purposes' under the old definition, only those reflected in the company's actual, or seriously contemplated, activities are to be taken into account and not, for example, myriad activities theoretically available to the company under wide powers conferred by its articles of association.

'*Trade*', '*profession*' and '*vocation*' generally have the same meanings as in the *Income Tax Acts* but any UK property business which consists of, or so far as it consist of, the commercial letting of FURNISHED HOLIDAY ACCOMMODATION (**26**) in the UK is treated as a trade for relief purposes. Similarly (and subject to what is said at **26.1** FURNISHED HOLIDAY ACCOMMODATION), any overseas property business which consists of, or so far as it consists of, the commercial letting of such accommodation in one or more EEA states is treated as a trade. In determining whether for these purposes a company is a trading company, a '*trade*' includes the occupation of woodlands managed on a commercial basis by the occupier with a view to profit.

[*TCGA 1992, ss 165(8)(9), 165A, 241(3)(3A), 241A(4)(5); FA 2011, Sch 14 para 14(3)*].

Nature of relief

[36.4] Where there is no actual consideration for the disposal (as opposed to a deemed MARKET VALUE (**45.1**) consideration under *TCGA 1992, s 17(1)*), or where an actual consideration does not exceed the allowable expenditure within *TCGA 1992, s 38* (see **16.11** COMPUTATION OF GAINS AND LOSSES) relating to the asset, the effect of a claim is that the gain otherwise chargeable on the transferor and the transferee's acquisition cost are each reduced by the 'held-over gain'.

The 'held-over gain' for this purpose is the gain otherwise chargeable (termed the '*unrelieved gain*') but subject to the reductions described below. Where actual consideration exceeds the allowable expenditure, the held-over gain is the unrelieved gain less that excess (see the *example* at **36.7** below) but again subject to the reductions below.

Where the disposal is a non-resident CGT disposal (see **41.25** LAND) to a UK-resident transferee, the 'held-over gain' is the NRCGT gain otherwise chargeable.

[*TCGA 1992, s 165(4)(6)(7)–(7C); FA 2015, Sch 7 para 23(3)*].

HMRC consider that where assets are transferred between divorcing spouses under the terms of certain court orders, the spouse to whom the assets are transferred does not give actual consideration for the above purposes. The court orders concerned are orders for ancillary relief under the *Matrimonial Causes Act 1973* or similar orders under the *Family Law (Scotland) Act 1985* and orders formally ratifying an agreement reached by the divorcing parties dealing with the transfer of assets. (HMRC Capital Gains Manual CG67192; Tax Bulletin August 2003 pp 1051, 1052).

There is nothing in the legislation to deny relief if consideration for the use of the asset passes between an individual and a company, e.g. under a lease or tenancy agreement. It is understood that HMRC will apply SP D11 (see **59** ROLLOVER RELIEF — REPLACEMENT OF BUSINESS ASSETS) *mutatis mutandis* for this hold-over relief as it applies to rollover relief (Tolley's Practical Tax Newsletter 1990 p 143). Partial claims are not permitted. Where, however, a single transaction involves the transfer of a number of separate assets (i.e. where a separate chargeable gain accrues on each asset), a claim is required for each asset and the parties are free to choose which assets are to be the subject of a claim. (HMRC Capital Gains Manual CG67180). In such circumstances, some gains can potentially be left in charge to be covered by annual exemptions or losses etc.

Where hold-over relief applies to a disposal the transferee may deduct for capital gains tax purposes on a subsequent disposal made by him any inheritance tax attributable to the value of the asset on the transfer to him which qualified for relief and which is either a chargeable transfer or a potentially exempt transfer which proves to be a chargeable transfer. The tax deductible may be varied on the subsequent death of the transferor within seven years or otherwise but it cannot in any circumstances give rise to an allowable loss on the subsequent disposal. [*TCGA 1992, s 165(10)(11)*]. See also **39.2** INTERACTION WITH OTHER TAXES.

Claims

Hold-over relief claims must be made on a standard claim form (which can be found attached to HMRC Helpsheet HS 295). As they are usually bilateral claims, they cannot be made in the self-assessment tax return itself and will fall within the provisions of *TMA 1970, Sch 1A* (claims not included in returns — see **13.3** CLAIMS). A unilateral claim by a settlor will usually form part of his tax return. (Revenue Tax Bulletin April 1997 pp 417, 418).

In most circumstances, HMRC will admit a hold-over relief claim without requiring a computation of the gain, which would involve ascertaining the market value of the asset at the date of the transfer. Transferor and transferee must jointly request this in the standard claim form and must provide, in particular, a calculation incorporating informally estimated valuations and a statement that the claimants are satisfied that the value of the asset exceeds the allowable expenditure plus any indexation allowance due. Once accepted by HMRC, a claim made on this basis cannot be withdrawn. In many cases, a formal valuation will never become necessary; in others valuation may still be deferred until a subsequent disposal of the asset by the transferee. This practice applies equally to valuations on dates other than the date of transfer, where these are relevant to the computation of the gain. Where the asset was held by the transferor on 31 March 1982, then unless the transferee has paid *some* consideration, it will normally be necessary to agree a 31 March 1982 valuation only when the transferee disposes of the asset. (HMRC Statement of Practice 8/92). The informal valuations referred to above need not be made by an expert and are non-binding. (Revenue Tax Bulletin April 1997 pp 417, 418).

Reductions in the held-over gain

If the qualifying asset disposed of was not used for the purposes of the trade, profession or vocation concerned throughout the period of its ownership by the transferor, the held-over gain is reduced by multiplying it by the fraction of which the denominator is the total period of ownership and the numerator the number of days in the period during which the asset was so used. (*Note.* In the determination of the period of ownership there is no exclusion of any period before 31 March 1982 as there is at **59.8** ROLLOVER RELIEF.) Where the qualifying asset disposed of is a building or structure part only of which has been used for the trade etc. concerned over all or a 'substantial' part of the period of its ownership, the held-over gain is reduced as is 'just and reasonable'. [*TCGA 1992, Sch 7 paras 4, 5(1), 6(1)*].

If the disposal of shares or securities of a company qualifies for relief and the company or group (as appropriate) then has 'chargeable assets' which are not 'business assets' and *either* at any time in the twelve months before the disposal the transferor could exercise 25% or more of the company's voting rights (as exercisable in general meeting) *or* the company is the personal company (see above) of an individual transferor at any time within that period of twelve months, the held-over gain is reduced by multiplying it by the fraction of which the denominator is the then market value of all of the company's or group's chargeable assets and the numerator is the then market value of the company's or group's chargeable business assets. In considering a group, a holding in the ordinary share capital of one group member by another is ignored, and if a 51% subsidiary is not wholly owned directly or indirectly by the holding company the values of its chargeable and business assets are reduced in proportion to the share capital owned; and for both purposes the expressions used are as in *ICTA 1988, s 838*. An asset is a '*business asset*' if it is or is an interest in an asset used for the purposes of a trade etc. carried on by the company or another group member, and an asset is a '*chargeable asset*' if a gain accruing on its disposal by the company or another group member would be a chargeable gain. [*TCGA 1992, Sch 7 paras 4, 7*].

Gifts of UK residential property interests to non-residents

A disposal of a UK residential property interest (see **41.29** LAND) on or after 6 April 2015 to a transferee who is not resident in the UK qualifies for relief. The full amount of the gain that would otherwise have been chargeable may be held over and no chargeable gain arises at the time of the disposal, although the amount of the gain that would have been chargeable but for the relief is not in this case deducted from the transferee's base cost. Instead, on a subsequent disposal by the transferee the whole or corresponding part of the held over gain is deemed to accrue at that time, in addition to any gain that actually accrues.

Relief for any inheritance tax payable on a disposal for which holdover relief has been claimed may be obtained by the transferee when he subsequently disposes of the asset. The actual chargeable gain accruing to the transferee on the disposal of the asset (and not the held over gain deemed to accrue at that time) is reduced by an amount equal to the lesser of the inheritance tax attributable to the value of the asset and the amount of the chargeable gain including the held-over gain.

[*TCGA 1992, s 167A; FA 2015, Sch 7 para 26*].

Agricultural property

[36.5] If an asset, or an interest in an asset:

(a) is 'agricultural property' within the inheritance tax provisions of *IHTA 1984, Pt V Ch II* and *either* qualifies for an inheritance tax reduction in value in relation to a chargeable transfer made simultaneously with the disposal *or* would so qualify if there were a chargeable transfer on the disposal *or* would so qualify but for *IHTA 1984, s 124A* (additional conditions for transfers within seven years before death of transferor) (assuming, where there is no chargeable transfer, that there were); but
(b) it fails to qualify for hold-over relief solely because the agricultural property is not used for the purposes of a trade etc. carried on as in **36.2**(i) above,

then, notwithstanding (b) above, hold-over relief is granted to the individual transferor. Hold-over relief is also granted to trustees (see under settled property below) where the agricultural property would not otherwise qualify for relief solely because it is not used for the purposes of a trade etc. carried on as in **36.6**(i) below. In these circumstances *TCGA 1992, Sch 7 para 4, para 5(1), para 6(1)* in **36.2** above do not apply. [*TCGA 1992, s 165(5), Sch 7 paras 1, 3, 5(2), 6(2)*]. Where development value over and above the agricultural value of the land is inherent in the property transferred, hold-over relief is available in respect of the whole of the gain, i.e. not just that part which reflects the land's agricultural value (Revenue Tax Bulletin November 1991 p 5).

Settled property

[36.6] If:

(a) trustees of a settlement make a non-arm's length disposal of an asset specified below, and
(b) a claim for relief under *TCGA 1992, s 165* is made by the trustees and the transferee or, if trustees are also the transferee, by the trustees making the disposal alone,

then, subject to *TCGA 1992, s 165(3)* (see **36.2** above) and the provisions in **36.8** below, hold-over relief given by *TCGA 1992, s 165(4)* (see **36.2** above) applies to the disposal.

An asset is within (a) above if:

(i) it is, or is an interest in, an asset used for the purposes of a trade, profession or vocation carried on by the trustees making the disposal or a beneficiary who had an interest in possession in the settled property immediately before the disposal; or

(ii) it consists of shares or securities of a trading company, or of the holding company of a trading group, where *either* the shares etc. are neither listed on a recognised stock exchange (see **63.30** SHARES AND SECURITIES) *or* not less than 25% of the voting rights as exercisable in general meeting are held by the trustees at the time of disposal.

Where hold-over relief is granted to trustees in this way, references to the trustees are substituted for references to the transferor in *TCGA 1992, s 165(4)(a)* above; and where hold-over relief is granted on a disposal deemed to occur by virtue of *TCGA 1992, s 71(1)* or *s 72(1)* (see **62.16–62.18** SETTLEMENTS and **36.8** below), no reduction in the held-over gain is made under *TCGA 1992, s 165(7)* in **36.2** above (reduction by excess of actual consideration over allowable expenditure). [*TCGA 1992, s 165(5), Sch 7 para* 2]. See also **36.5** above re agricultural property.

Example — partial consideration

[36.7]

Zoë owns a freehold property which she lets to the family trading company, Sphere Ltd, in which she and her father each own half the shares and voting rights. Zoë inherited the property in April 1990 at a probate value of £50,000, and since then the whole of the property has been used for the purposes of the company's trade. In November 2017, Zoë transfers the property to her boyfriend. Its market value at that time is £115,000. The intention is that he should give sufficient consideration to leave Zoë with a chargeable gain exactly equal to the annual exempt amount (there being no other disposals in 2017/18).

Actual consideration should be £61,300 as shown by the following computation

	£
Deemed consideration	115,000
Deduct: Cost	50,000
Unrelieved gain	65,000
Held-over gain (see below)	53,700
Chargeable gain covered by annual exempt amount	£11,300

Computation of held-over gain

	£	£
Unrelieved gain		65,000
Actual consideration	61,300	
Less allowable expenditure	50,000	11,300
Held-over gain		£53,700

Note to the example

(a) On a subsequent disposal of the property, the allowable expenditure would be £61,300 (deemed proceeds of £115,000 less held-over gain of £53,700).

Restrictions on, and clawback of, relief

[36.8] Hold-over relief under *TCGA 1992, s 165, Sch 7* is restricted or clawed back in the following circumstances.

Gifts to non-residents

Except where *TCGA 1992, s 167A* applies (see **36.4** above), relief is not to apply where the transferee is not resident in the UK. It also does not apply where the transferee is an individual or company which, though resident in the UK, is regarded as resident elsewhere by virtue of DOUBLE TAX RELIEF (**21.2**) arrangements such that it would not under those arrangements be taxable in the UK on a gain arising on a disposal of the asset immediately after its acquisition. [*TCGA 1992, s 166; FA 2013, Sch 46 paras 99, 112; FA 2015, Sch 7 para 24*].

Gifts to foreign-controlled companies

Except where *TCGA 1992, s 167A* applies (see **36.4** above), relief under *TCGA 1992, s 165(4)* is also denied where the transferee is a company which is controlled by a person who, or by persons each of whom, is not UK-resident and is connected (see **17** CONNECTED PERSONS) with the person making the disposal. In determining a person's residence status for this purpose, a person who either alone or with others controls a company by virtue of holding assets relating to that or any other company and who is UK-resident is regarded as not UK-resident if he is regarded under a double tax agreement as resident overseas in circumstances in which he would not be liable to a UK tax charge on a gain arising on a disposal of the assets. [*TCGA 1992, s 167; FA 2013, Sch 46 paras 100, 112; FA 2015, Sch 7 para 25*]. See *Foulser and another v MacDougall* CA, [2007] STC 973, in which a complex avoidance scheme failed because of the application of this provision. In the Ch D the taxpayers' contention that the application of *section 167* to their case was incompatible with the EC Treaty was rejected and this decision was upheld by the CA. In *Reeves v Revenue and Customs Commissioners* [2017] UKFTT 192 (TC), [2017] SFTD 765, [2017] SWTI 1123, R, who was non-UK resident, transferred a UK business to a new UK incorporated and resident company of which he was the sole shareholder. However, his wife was also not resident in the UK, and as an associate of R could be deemed to control the new company and so *TCGA 1992, s 167* applied, denying R holdover relief. R contended that a literal construction of *s 167* would produce an unjust result but the First-tier Tribunal dismissed the appeal, stating it was not 'abundantly sure' that this was against the intention of the legislation. The Tribunal also found that the legislation was not in breach of the *European Convention on Human Rights*, nor discriminatory for EU law purposes as R had been treated in the same way as a UK resident with a non-UK resident wife.

Gifts into dual resident trusts

Hold-over relief under *TCGA 1992, s 165* is not available where the transferees are trustees who are resident in the UK where, on a notional disposal of the asset by the trustees immediately after the disposal of it to them, the trustees would be regarded for double tax relief arrangements as resident overseas and as not liable to UK tax arising on the notional disposal. [*TCGA 1992, s 169; FA 2013, Sch 46 paras 102, 112*].

Emigration of transferee

Subject to the exceptions mentioned below, a gain held over under *TCGA 1992, s 165* (at a time, for disposals on or after 6 April 2015, when the transferee was a UK resident individual) will be clawed back if the individual transferee concerned ceases to be UK-resident. The clawback may be made within six years after the end of the tax year in which the disposal for which hold-over relief was claimed was made; otherwise (e.g. where trustees are the transferee) no time limit is specified. The charge, which is on a gain deemed to have accrued just prior to the cessation of UK residence, is reduced to the extent that the held-over gain has already been taken into account in a disposal by the transferee (e.g. on a part disposal). For the latter purpose, a disposal does not include a no gain/no loss disposal between married persons or civil partners (see **46.5** MARRIED PERSONS AND CIVIL PARTNERS) under *TCGA 1992, s 58*. If such a transfer occurs, a disposal by the acquiring spouse or civil partner is treated as made by the spouse or partner who originally acquired the asset to which the held-over gain related. If not paid within twelve months from the due date of payment, tax on the deemed gain assessed on the transferee can be assessed on the transferor within six years after the end of the tax year in which the disposal for which hold-over relief was claimed was made, although the transferor then has the right to recover any tax so paid from the transferee.

Where a deemed gain relating to a previously held-over gain has been assessed under the above, then on a subsequent disposal of the asset in question the allowable expenditure relating to it is not reduced by the held-over gain.

An exception to the above clawback applies where the disposal for which relief was claimed was made to an individual, and

(a) the reason for his becoming not resident in the UK is that he works in an employment or office, all of the duties of which are performed abroad, and
(b) he again becomes UK-resident within three years of ceasing to be so, and
(c) in the meantime, the asset which is the subject of the hold-over relief has not been subject to a disposal by him in connection with which the allowable expenditure attaching to the asset, if the individual had been UK-resident, would have been reduced by the held-over gain; for this purpose the same provisions as above for inter-spouse transfers apply.

Where (a) applies, and (b) and (c) *may* apply, no assessment under the main provisions outlined above will be made before the end of the three-year period.

A second exception is that, if the transferee so elects, a held-over gain does not accrue on the deemed disposal if the gain or loss would have been an NRCGT gain or loss on the assumption that the disposal was a non-resident CGT disposal (see **41.25** LAND). However, the NRCGT gain or loss that would have accrued on the deemed disposal is treated as accruing at the time of any subsequent disposal of the interest, in addition to any gain or loss which actually accrues.

[*TCGA 1992, ss 168, 168A; FA 2013, Sch 46 paras 101, 112; FA 2015, Sch 7 paras 27, 28*].

Clawback of relief on life tenant's death

The exemption otherwise available for gains arising on deemed disposals under *TCGA 1992, s 71(1)* or *s 72(1)(a)* on the death of a life tenant etc. (see **62.16–62.18** SETTLEMENTS) does not apply to an asset (or part asset) where a claim for hold-over relief was made under *TCGA 1992, s 165* in relation to an original disposal of that asset to the trustees. Any chargeable gain accruing to the trustees will, however, be restricted to the held-over gain (or corresponding part) on the original disposal of the asset. Where the life tenant's interest was in part only of the settled property, and that property is subject to a deemed disposal under *TCGA 1992, s 71(1)*, the clawback is proportional to the life tenant's interest. [*TCGA 1992, s 74*]. It seems to be possible for the trustees to claim hold-over relief under *TCGA 1992, s 165* (provided all the conditions are met) in respect of any gain arising from this clawback provision (Tolley's Practical Tax Newsletter 1983 p 142). Alternatively, if the termination of the life interest is a chargeable transfer for inheritance tax purposes, hold-over relief can be claimed under **36.10** below (HMRC Capital Gains Manual CG33552).

Limited liability partnerships (LLPs)

Where, when the transparency treatment afforded by *TCGA 1992, s 59A(1)* ceases to apply to an LLP (see **50.18** PARTNERSHIPS) (for example, by virtue of its going into liquidation), a member of the LLP holds an asset whose CGT acquisition cost is reduced by a gain held over under *TCGA 1992, s 165* on a disposal to a partnership, a chargeable gain equal to the amount of the reduction is treated as accruing to the member immediately before that time. [*TCGA 1992, s 169A*]. In the absence of such a rule, the held-over gain would have fallen out of charge as a result of the tax treatment of an LLP in liquidation.

Exemptions relating to substantial shareholdings of companies

Where a company disposes of an asset whose CGT acquisition cost is reduced by a gain previously held over under *TCGA 1992, s 165*, and, by virtue of the provisions of *TCGA 1992, Sch 7AC*, any gain on the disposal would otherwise be exempt, the held-over gain, or an appropriate proportion of it, is treated as accruing to the company at that time (see **66.21** SUBSTANTIAL SHAREHOLDINGS OF COMPANIES).

Gifts to settlor-interested settlements

Hold-over relief under *TCGA 1992, s 165* is not available in the case of a disposal (the '*relevant disposal*') to the trustees of a settlement if either:

(a) there is a 'settlor' who has an 'interest in the settlement' (or an 'arrangement' subsists under which such an interest will or may be acquired by a settlor) immediately after the making of the relevant disposal or at any time in the 'clawback period', or

(b) the following conditions are met:

- disregarding any hold-over relief, a chargeable gain would accrue to the transferor on the relevant disposal,
- in computing that gain, the allowable expenditure would be reduced in consequence, directly or indirectly, of a claim under *TCGA 1992, s 165* or *TCGA 1992, s 260* (see **36.10** below) in respect of an earlier disposal by an individual (whether or not to the transferor), and
- that individual has an interest in the settlement (or an arrangement subsists under which such an interest will or may be acquired by him) immediately after the making of the relevant disposal or at any time in the 'clawback period'.

Where neither of the above conditions are met immediately after the relevant disposal and relief under *s 165* is claimed (and the claim is not revoked), if either of the conditions are subsequently met at a time during the clawback period, then a chargeable gain is treated as accruing to the transferor at the first such time (the '*material time*') of an amount equal to the held-over gain under *s 165*. This does not apply if the transferor is an individual who has died before the material time. Where the relief is clawed back in this way, the chargeable gains and allowable losses of the trustees or of any person whose title to any property derives to any extent from them (whether directly or indirectly) are determined on the basis that *s 165* never applied to the relevant disposal. Any necessary adjustments can be made to give effect to these provisions, whether by assessment, discharge or repayment of tax or otherwise, notwithstanding any time limits for the making of such adjustments.

Definitions

For these purposes, a person is a '*settlor*' in relation to a settlement if he is an individual and the settled property consists of or includes property originating from him. Property originates from a settlor where he provides it directly or indirectly for the purposes of the settlement (including property provided by another person under reciprocal 'arrangements') and where property represents such property (or a part thereof) or accumulated income from such property. '*Arrangements*' include any scheme, agreement or understanding, whether or not legally enforceable.

A settlor has an '*interest in a settlement*' if:

(i) any property which may at any time be comprised in the settlement or any 'derived property' is, or will or may become, payable to or applicable for the benefit of the settlor or his spouse or civil partner in any circumstances whatsoever, or

(ii) the settlor, or his spouse or civil partner, enjoys a benefit deriving directly or indirectly from any property which is comprised in the settlement or any derived property.

At any time after 5 April 2006 (but see below), a settlor also has an interest in a settlement if:

(iii) any property which is or may at any time be comprised in the settlement or any derived property is, or will or may become, payable to or applicable for the benefit of a child of the settlor at any time when that child is a 'dependent child' of his, in any circumstances whatsoever, or

(iv) a dependent child of the settlor enjoys a benefit deriving directly or indirectly from any property which is comprised in the settlement or any derived property.

Where the relevant disposal is made before 6 April 2006, a settlement is not, however, treated as becoming settlor-interested during the clawback period by virtue of (iii) or (iv) above.

A '*dependent child*' of the settlor is, for this purpose, a child or stepchild under the age of 18 who is unmarried and does not have a civil partner.

References to the spouse or civil partner of the settlor in (i) and (ii) above do not include a spouse or civil partner from whom the settlor is separated under a court order, separation agreement or in circumstances such that the separation is likely to be permanent, or the widow, widower or surviving civil partner of the settlor. No account is taken of a term of the settlement relating to dependent children of the settlor at any time when he has no such children.

A settlor does not have an interest under (i) above if and so long as none of the property which may at any time be comprised in the settlement and no derived property can become applicable or payable as mentioned in (i) above except in the event of:

- in the case of a marriage settlement or civil partnership settlement, the death of both the parties to the marriage or partnership and all or any of the children of one or both of the parities to the marriage or partnership (for disposals before 5 December 2005, all or any of the children of the marriage); or
- the death of a child of the settlor who had become beneficially entitled to the property or any derived property at an age not exceeding 25.

For these purposes, '*derived property*' in relation to any property means income from that property or any property directly or indirectly representing proceeds of, or proceeds of income from, that property or income therefrom.

Exclusions

The above provisions do not apply to a disposal to trustees of a heritage maintenance settlement if they have elected or, for disposals in 2012/13 onwards, could have elected under *ITA 2007, s 508* (formerly *ICTA 1988, s 691(2)*) that income arising under the settlement or part of the settlement involved is not to be treated as income of the settlor for the tax year in which the disposal is made.

The above provisions also do not apply if, immediately after the making of the relevant disposal:

(A) for disposals on or after 8 April 2013 (subject to the transitional rule below), the settled property is held on trusts which secure that, during the lifetime of a 'disabled person';
   - if any of the property is applied for the benefit of a beneficiary it is applied for the benefit of the disabled person; and
   - either the disabled person is entitled to all the income (if any) arising from any of the property or that if any such income is applied for the benefit of a beneficiary, it is applied for the benefit of the disabled person.

(B) if one or more settlors has an interest in the settlement (disregarding any interest arising because of a spouse, civil partner or dependent child) or will or may acquire such an interest under subsisting arrangements, each such settlor is a disabled person and a beneficiary (or would be a beneficiary if he had the interest acquirable under the arrangements).

If the property is held on trusts of the kind described in *Trustee Act 1925, s 33* (protective trusts), the reference above to 'the lifetime of the disabled person' is to be interpreted as the period during which the property is held on trust for him.

For disposals before 8 April 2013 (and see the transitional rule below), condition (A) above was that the settled property had to be held on trusts securing that, during the lifetime of a disabled person:

- not less than half of the property which is applied, is applied for the benefit of the person concerned; and
- that person is entitled to not less than half of the income arising from the property, or no such income may be applied for the benefit of any other person, or no interest in possession subsists in the settled property.

For disposals on or after 8 April 2013 (subject to the transitional rule below), '*disabled person*' means either a person who by reason of mental disorder is incapable of administering his property or managing his affairs or a person in receipt of any one or more specified State benefits. A person is treated as being a disabled person for these purposes if he satisfies HMRC that he would be entitled to receive the State benefit in question were it not for his being resident outside the UK or in a care home, hospital or prison. A broadly similar definition applied for disposals before 8 April 2013.

For disposals on or after 8 April 2013 (subject to the transitional rule below), condition (A) above is not treated as not met by reason only of:

(I) the trustees' having powers that enable them to apply in any tax year otherwise than for the benefit of the disabled person amounts (whether consisting of income or capital or both) not exceeding the 'annual limit'; or

(II) the trustees' having the powers conferred by *Trustee Act 1925, s 32* (powers of advancement) (or its NI equivalent); or

(III) the trustees' having those powers but free from, or subject to a less restrictive limitation than, the limitation imposed by *Trustee Act 1925, s 32(1)(a)* (or its NI equivalent); or

(IV) the trustees' having powers to the like effect as the powers mentioned in (II) or (III).

The '*annual limit*' in (I) above is £3,000 or, if lower, 3% of the maximum value of the settled property during the tax year in question.

For disposals before 8 April 2013, condition (A) was not treated as not met by reason only of powers of advancement conferred on the trustees under *Trustee Act 1925, s 32* or *Trustee Act (Northern Ireland) 1958, s 33*. Where the income from the settled property is held for the benefit of a person on protective trusts, as under *Trustee Act 1925, s 33*, the reference in (A) above to the lifetime of a person is to be construed as a reference to the period during which the income is so held.

Transitional rule

The changes above which apply to disposals on or after 8 April 2013 do not prevent the exclusion from applying to settlements created before 8 April 2013 if the trusts have not been altered on or after that date or to settlements arising on or after 8 April 2013 under a will executed before, and unaltered in relation to the settlement on or after, that date. The changes also do not prevent the exclusion from applying to settlements arising on or after 8 April 2013 under a will executed or confirmed on or after that date if the provisions in it relating to the settlement are the same as those in a previous will made on or before that date. For this purpose, a will includes a codicil.

Information

Before 13 August 2009, an HMRC officer could require by notice a trustee, a beneficiary or a settlor (or the spouse or civil partner of a settlor or a person who has been the spouse or civil partner of a settlor at any time after the making of the relevant disposal) to give him such particulars as he thought necessary for the purposes of the above provisions within such time as he directed, not being less than 28 days. This power has been repealed as it is no longer considered necessary following the introduction of the general information powers in *FA 2008, Sch 36* (see **34** HMRC INVESTIGATORY POWERS).

[*TCGA 1992, ss 169B–169G; FA 2013, Sch 44 paras 12, 20; SI 2009 No 2035, Sch paras 30, 31*].

Miscellaneous

See also **27.4** GIFTS for the recovery by the trustees from the transferor of tax paid in respect of the deemed chargeable gain arising under the clawback provisions above and **51.5** PAYMENT OF TAX for payment of tax on such a gain by instalments.

Relief for gifts of business assets before 14 March 1989

[36.9] Hold-over relief was available where an individual ('*the transferor*') made a disposal before 14 March 1989 not at arm's length (e.g. a gift) to a person resident or ordinarily resident in the UK ('*the transferee*') of:

(a) an asset which was, or was an interest in, an asset which was used for the purposes of a trade, profession or vocation carried on by the transferor or by a company which was his 'family company' (as defined), or
(b) shares or securities of a 'trading company' (as defined) which was the transferor's family company.

The relief operated, as with other hold-over reliefs, by reducing the gain otherwise chargeable on the transferor and the transferee's acquisition cost by the held-over gain. Hold-over relief could also be claimed in certain circumstances where a trustee was deemed under *TCGA 1992, s 71(1)* (see **62.16** and **62.18** SETTLEMENTS) to have disposed of, and immediately reacquired, a business asset.

As a result of the availability of the general relief for gifts in **36.12** below, the rules relating specifically to gifts of business assets were of restricted application for gifts after 5 April 1980 and before 14 March 1989. None of the provisions in **36.8** above applied to the hold-over relief described above.

[*CGTA 1979, s 126, Sch 4*].

Gifts on which inheritance tax is chargeable etc.

[36.10] The hold-over relief described below is, subject to conditions, available if:

(a) an individual or trustees ('the transferor') make a disposal within (i)–(vii) below of an asset;
(b) the asset is acquired by an individual or trustees ('the transferee'); and
(c) a claim for relief is made by the transferor and transferee or, where trustees are the transferee, by the transferor alone.

The relief extends to non-resident CGT disposals (see **41.25** LAND) to a UK-resident transferee and to disposals of UK residential property interests to non-residents.

[*TCGA 1992, s 260(1); FA 2015, Sch 7 para 31(2)*].

A disposal is within (a) above if it is made otherwise than under a bargain at arm's length (e.g. a gift) and it:

(i) is a chargeable transfer within *IHTA 1984* (or would be but for annual exemptions under *IHTA 1984, s 19*) and is not a potentially exempt transfer within the meaning of *IHTA 1984*; or
(ii) is an exempt transfer by virtue of *IHTA 1984, s 24, s 27* or *s 30* (political parties, maintenance funds for historic buildings and designated property); or
(iii) is a disposition to which *IHTA 1984, s 57A* applies and by which the property disposed of becomes held on trusts referred to in *IHTA 1984, s 57A(1)(b)* (maintenance funds for historic buildings); or
(iv) by virtue of *IHTA 1984, s 71(4)* (accumulation and maintenance trusts where property settled before 22 March 2006) does not constitute an occasion on which tax is chargeable under that provision; or

(v) by virtue of *IHTA 1984, s 71B(2)* (trusts for bereaved minors) does not constitute an occasion on which tax is chargeable under that provision; or

(vi) by virtue of *IHTA 1984, s 71E(2)* (age 18 to 25 trusts) does not constitute an occasion on which tax is chargeable under that provision; or

(vii) by virtue of *IHTA 1984, s 78(1)* (works of art etc., see also **25.41** and **25.85** EXEMPTIONS AND RELIEFS) does not constitute an occasion on which tax is chargeable under *IHTA 1984, Pt III Ch III*; or

(viii) is a disposal of an asset comprised in a settlement where, as a result of the asset or part of it becoming comprised in another settlement, there is no charge, or a reduced charge, to inheritance tax by virtue of *IHTA 1984, Sch 4 para 9, para 16* or *para 17* (maintenance funds for historic buildings).

[*TCGA 1992, s 260(2)*].

The '*held-over gain*' on a disposal is the chargeable gain otherwise accruing and relief is given by deducting this amount from the gain otherwise accruing to the transferor and from the consideration otherwise regarded as being given by the transferee. [*TCGA 1992, s 260(3)(4)*].

Hold-over relief is reduced or eliminated to nil on a disposal where there is actual consideration (as opposed to any deemed MARKET VALUE (**45**) consideration) which exceeds the allowable expenditure under *TCGA 1992, s 38* (see **16.11** COMPUTATION OF GAINS AND LOSSES). Any such excess is deducted from the held-over gain, but no deduction is made of any such excess where *TCGA 1992, s 260(3)* above applies to a deemed disposal under *TCGA 1992, s 71(1)* or *s 72(1)* (see **62.16–62.18** SETTLEMENTS). [*TCGA 1992, s 260(5)*].

Where the disposal is a non-resident CGT disposal (see **41.25** LAND) to a UK-resident transferee, the 'held-over gain' is the NRCGT gain otherwise chargeable. [*TCGA 1992, s 260(6ZA)–(6ZC); FA 2015, Sch 7 para 31(3)*].

Hold-over relief does not apply to a disposal if it arises by virtue of *TCGA 1992, s 116(10)(b)* (disposal of qualifying corporate bonds derived from shares giving rise to deferred gain, see **54.4** QUALIFYING CORPORATE BONDS). [*TCGA 1992, s 260(6)*].

Where hold-over relief is claimed, or could have been claimed, on a transfer within (i) above, the transferee may deduct for capital gains tax purposes on a subsequent disposal made by him any inheritance tax attributable to the value of the asset on the transfer to him which qualified for hold-over relief. The tax deductible may be varied if the inheritance tax itself is varied but it cannot in any circumstances give rise to an allowable loss. [*TCGA 1992, s 260(7)(8)*]. See also **39.2** INTERACTION WITH OTHER TAXES.

Where a disposal is only partly within (i)–(vii) above, or is a disposal within (viii) above on which there is a reduced charge to inheritance tax, the foregoing provisions apply to an appropriate part of the disposal. [*TCGA 1992, s 260(10)*].

Partial claims are not permitted. Where, however, a single transaction involves the transfer of a number of separate assets (i.e. where a separate chargeable gain accrues on each asset), a claim is required for each asset and the parties are free to choose which assets are to be the subject of a claim. (HMRC Capital Gains Manual CG67180). In such circumstances, some gains can be left in charge to be covered by annual exemptions or losses etc.

See **53.13** PRIVATE RESIDENCES for the exclusion from relief under *TCGA 1992, s 223* where relief is claimed under the above provisions.

Gifts of UK residential property interests to non-residents

A disposal of a UK residential property interest (see **41.29** LAND) on or after 6 April 2015 to a transferee who is not resident in the UK qualifies for relief. The full amount of the gain that would otherwise have been chargeable may be held over and no chargeable gain arises at the time of the disposal, although the amount of the gain that would have been chargeable but for the relief is not in this case deducted from the transferee's base cost. Instead, on a subsequent disposal by the transferee the whole or corresponding part of the held over gain is deemed to accrue at that time, in addition to any gain that actually accrues.

Relief for any inheritance tax payable on a disposal for which holdover relief has been claimed may be obtained by the transferee when he subsequently disposes of the asset. The actual chargeable gain accruing to the transferee on the disposal of the asset (and not the held over gain deemed to accrue at that time) is reduced by an amount equal to the lesser of the inheritance tax attributable to the value of the asset and the amount of the chargeable gain including the held-over gain.

[*TCGA 1992, s 261ZA; FA 2015, Sch 7 para 33*].

Restrictions on, and clawback of, relief

[36.11] Hold-over relief under *TCGA 1992, s 260* is restricted or clawed back in the following circumstances.

Gifts to non-residents

Except where *TCGA 1992, s 261ZA* applies (see **36.10** above), relief is denied where the transferee is not UK-resident. Relief is also denied where the transferee is an individual who though UK-resident is regarded under a double tax agreement as resident overseas in circumstances where he would not be liable to a UK tax charge on a gain arising on a disposal of an asset immediately after its acquisition. [*TCGA 1992, s 261; FA 2013, Sch 46 paras 104, 112; FA 2015, Sch 7 para 32*].

Gifts into dual resident trusts

TCGA 1992, s 169 (see **36.8** above) operates, with appropriate modifications, for hold-over relief claimed under *TCGA 1992, s 260* in respect of gifts after 13 March 1989 as it does for hold-over relief under *TCGA 1992, s 165* in respect of gifts made after that date. [*TCGA 1992, s 169*].

Emigration of transferee

TCGA 1992, s 168 (see **36.8** above) operates, with appropriate modifications, for hold-over relief claimed under *TCGA 1992, s 260* as it does for hold-over relief under *TCGA 1992, s 165*. [*TCGA 1992, s 168*].

Clawback of relief on life tenant's death

TCGA 1992, s 74 (see **36.8** above) operates, with appropriate modifications, for hold-over relief claimed under *TCGA 1992, s 260* as it does for hold-over relief under *TCGA 1992, s 165*. [*TCGA 1992, s 74*].

Limited liability partnerships (LLPs)

Clawback under *TCGA 1992, s 169A* (see **36.8** above) applies in relation to hold-over relief under *TCGA 1992, s 260* as it does in relation to hold-over relief under *TCGA 1992, s 165*.

Gifts to settlor-interested settlements

TCGA 1992, ss 169B–169G (see **36.8** above) apply to hold-over relief under *TCGA 1992, s 260* as they apply to relief under *TCGA 1992, s 165*.

General relief for gifts from 1980 to 1989

[36.12] A general relief for gifts by individuals applied after 5 April 1980 and before 14 March 1989. It applied also for gifts by trustees after 5 April 1982.

The effect of the relief was that the gain otherwise chargeable (less any retirement relief (see **25.88** EXEMPTIONS AND RELIEFS)), and the transferee's acquisition cost, were each reduced by the '*held-over gain*', i.e. the gain otherwise chargeable (less any retirement relief) less any excess of actual consideration over the aggregate of allowable expenditure within *TCGA 1992, s 38* and any retirement relief.

In computing any chargeable gain accruing on the subsequent disposal of the asset, the transferee may deduct any inheritance tax (or capital transfer tax) attributable to the value of the asset on the original transfer, being either a chargeable transfer or a potentially exempt transfer which proves to be a chargeable transfer. The tax deductible may be varied on the subsequent death of the original transferor or otherwise but cannot create an allowable loss on the subsequent disposal. See also **39.2** INTERACTION WITH OTHER TAXES.

Clawback of relief on life tenant's death

TCGA 1992, s 74 (see **36.8** above) operated (and continues to operate after 13 March 1989) *mutatis mutandis* for hold-over relief claimed under the above provisions where the original gift to the trustees was after 5 April 1981 and before 14 March 1989 as it does to hold-over relief under *TCGA 1992, s 165* in respect of gifts made after 13 March 1989. See **9.11** ASSETS HELD ON 31 MARCH **1982** for the treatment by HMRC of the clawback in relevant cases occurring after 5 April 1988.

[*TCGA 1992, ss 67, 74; CGTA 1979, s 56A; FA 1980, s 79; FA 2013, Sch 46 para 81*].

Key points

[36.13] Points to consider are as follows.

- Hold-over relief under either *TCGA 1992, s 165* or *s 260* must be claimed on the form attached to the HMRC Helpsheet HS295. The time limit is four years after the end of the tax year in which the disposal took place.
- Gifts of business assets, such as the gift of a family company to the next generation, require careful planning. Where the family company is not a trading company then hold-over relief under *TCGA 1992, s 165* is unlikely to be available. The donor could consider a restructure of the company prior to the gift in order to meet the definition of a trading group and to qualify for hold-over relief.
- Where a donor is considering gifting agricultural property, he should determine whether holding on to such assets until they form part of the death estate is advantageous for tax purposes — agricultural property relief at 100% may be available on death, with a capital gains tax free uplift in base cost for the recipient.
- Transferors may wish to insure against a clawback of hold-over relief where they consider that this is a possibility. For example, gains held over may be clawed back where the transferee becomes non-resident in the UK within six years of the end of the year in which the disposal was made. Trustees who hold over gains on the distribution of capital to beneficiaries may wish to take reasonable precautions if they believe that a beneficiary may become non-resident within six years. Strictly the deemed gain is due for payment by the transferee (in this case, the beneficiary) but if the transferee cannot be located, the gain will be assessed on the transferor (the trustees). Depending on the circumstances, the trustees may wish to insure against such a claim.
- Hold-over relief under *TCGA 1992, s 260* is generally available where inheritance tax is immediately chargeable on a transfer. Before any gift is made, careful consideration of the effects of both taxes together is required. A client will be more interested in what a transaction will cost them in terms of tax, rather than which particular tax they are required to pay.
- Trustees of life interest settlements where there is an elderly or infirm life tenant should undertake sufficient planning where the trust holds assets upon which hold-over relief was claimed (either under *TCGA 1992, s 165* or *s 260*). This may include disposing of the assets over a number of tax years to utilise annual exempt amounts and avoid a clawback of the hold-over relief on the death of the life tenant. Keeping clear and accurate records is of utmost importance.
- Partially breaking the conditions for hold-over relief can enable a small gain to be realised that is covered by the annual exempt amount (hence low tax) whilst enabling a higher base cost to be

carried forward. This can be particularly useful if the recipient of the asset is likely to make an onwards sale in the next few years. Hold over relief can be restricted where:

- the consideration for the disposal exceeds the allowable cost;
- the asset has not been used wholly for the purposes of the trade during the entire period of ownership (but note that non-business use at the end of ownership can prevent any claim — see HMRC Capital Gains Manual CG66950);
- the assets transferred are shares and the company's chargeable assets include non business assets.

For example, a sole trader, Jack's only chargeable asset is goodwill worth £100,000 (nil base cost). If he sells the business to Chloe for £15,000 and claims hold-over relief, Jack will have a capital gain of £15,000 (less annual exempt amount) and Chloe will have a base cost of £15,000.

- Hold-over relief takes precedence over entrepreneurs' relief — if an entire gain is held-over, there is no relevant gain for entrepreneurs' relief purposes, but entrepreneurs' relief can be claimed on part of a gain that is not held over. If there is a risk that entrepreneurs' relief would not be available on a subsequent disposal, it may be better to claim that relief instead of hold-over relief and pay tax at 10% upfront.

37

Incorporation and Disincorporation Reliefs

Introduction	37.1
Transfer of business to a company — incorporation relief	37.2
Election to disapply incorporation relief	37.3
Disincorporation relief	37.4
Conditions for relief	37.4
Effect of relief	37.4
Claims	37.4
Key points	37.5

Cross-references. See 36 HOLD-OVER RELIEFS; 59 ROLLOVER RELIEF.

Simon's Taxes. See C3.4.

Introduction

[37.1] Incorporation relief is a form of rollover relief which applies where a person who is not a company transfers a business to a company as a going concern in exchange for shares issued by the company. The transfer must include the whole of the assets of the business (or the whole of those assets other than cash). The relief operates by reducing or eliminating the chargeable gain arising on the disposal and reducing the acquisition cost of the shares by a corresponding amount.

Where the conditions are satisfied, incorporation relief applies automatically without the need for a claim, but an election can be made to disapply it.

Disincorporation relief is also a form of rollover relief, and can be claimed where certain small companies transfer their business to shareholders who are individuals on or after 1 April 2013 and before 1 April 2018. Goodwill and land and buildings used in the business are treated as transferred to the shareholders at a reduced value for chargeable gains purposes (and, in the case of goodwill, for the purposes of the intangible assets regime) so that no corporation tax is payable by the company on the transfer of the assets. Shareholders to whom the assets are transferred inherit the reduced transfer values for the purpose of capital gains tax and must use them for any subsequent disposals.

Transfer of business to a company — incorporation relief

[37.2] Where a person who is not a company transfers to a company a business as a going concern, together with the *whole* of the assets of the business (or together with the whole of those assets other than cash) ('the old assets') and the transfer is made wholly or partly in exchange for shares issued by the company to the transferor ('the new assets'), the chargeable gain on the disposal of the old assets is deferred. This is done by reducing the amount otherwise chargeable, by the fraction A/B, where 'A' is the 'cost of the new assets' and 'B' is the value of the overall consideration received by the transferor in exchange for the business. An election can be made to disapply this treatment (see **37.3** below).

'*The cost of the new assets*' means the total allowable expenditure under *TCGA 1992, s 38(1)(a)* if the new assets were disposed of as a whole in circumstances giving rise to a chargeable gain. (See **16.11** COMPUTATION OF GAINS AND LOSSES.)

The total expenditure otherwise allowable on the new assets is reduced by the amount of the chargeable gain deferred, and if the new assets comprise different classes of share, the reduction is apportioned by reference to the market value of each class of share at the time of their acquisition by the transferor. Deferment on part of the gain on the old assets therefore remains until the new assets are disposed of.

[*TCGA 1992, s 162*].

Whether a business is transferred 'as a going concern' is determined by reference to the circumstances at the time of transfer. If the business continues without interruption after that time, relief will be available notwithstanding the existence of a planned move of the entire assets of the business from one place to another (*Gordon v CIR (and cross-appeal)* CS 1991, 64 TC 173). For HMRC's interpretation of 'business' and 'going concern', see HMRC Capital Gains Manual CG65710, 65715. In *Ramsay v HMRC* UT, [2013] STC 1764, an activity consisting of letting flats in a large house in Belfast was held to amount to a business for the purpose of incorporation relief. The Upper Tribunal held that the activity undertaken in respect of the property outweighed 'what might normally be expected to be carried out by a mere passive investor'. See also *Roelich v HMRC* FTT, [2014] UKFTT 579 (TC); 2014 STI 2891.

HMRC are prepared not to treat the assumption of business liabilities by the transferee company as consideration for the transfer; the relief is not precluded if some or all of the liabilities of the business are not taken over by the company. However, the assumption of *personal* liabilities, which includes tax liabilities pertaining to the unincorporated business, is treated as part of the consideration. (HMRC Extra-Statutory Concession D32 and see also HMRC Capital Gains Manual CG65745). (See **4.19** ANTI-AVOIDANCE for the charge arising where concessions involving deferral of gains are abused.)

If some of the assets are retained by the original owner, relief under *TCGA 1992, s 162* above is not available and liability to capital gains tax arises by reference to the market value of any chargeable assets transferred. Where *s 162* relief is not available, it is likely that a business asset hold-over relief claim under *TCGA 1992, s 165* (see **36.2** above) will prevail, provided that the transfer is by way of a non-arm's length bargain, including a transaction deemed to be such because it is between connected persons (see **4.12** ANTI-AVOIDANCE) (see HMRC Capital Gains Manual CG66973–66979).

Relief under *TCGA 1992, s 162* is available to individuals who are members of a partnership (even if one of the partners is a company) where the whole of the partnership business is transferred to a company. The relief is computed separately for each individual partner and is not precluded by virtue of any other partner receiving all or part of his consideration otherwise than in shares. HMRC consider that relief is not available where a partnership incorporates into an existing corporate partner. As the corporate partner already owns a share of the business assets, the whole of the business is not transferred (HMRC Capital Gains Manual CG65700).

For further commentary and examples, see HMRC Capital Gains Manual CG65700–65765.

Interaction with other reliefs

Subject to **37.3** below, incorporation relief under *TCGA 1992, s 162* is mandatory, although a claim for ROLLOVER RELIEF (**59**) takes precedence (HMRC Capital Gains Manual CG61560). Although *s 162* relief cannot be restricted so as to leave sufficient gains in charge to make use of the annual exempt amount or allowable losses, the same result can effectively be achieved by arranging for an appropriate part of the total consideration to be payable other than in the form of shares in the company, for example in cash or by way of amount left to the credit of the transferor on loan account, so that a sufficient chargeable gain arises.

Example

W has carried on an antiquarian bookselling business for many years. He decides to form an unquoted company, P Ltd, to carry on the business. He transfers, in May 2017, the whole of the business undertaking, assets and liabilities to P Ltd, in consideration for the issue of shares, plus an amount left outstanding on interest-free loan. W becomes a director of P Ltd. The business assets and liabilities transferred are valued as follows

		Value	Chargeable gain
	£	£	£
Freehold shop premises (acquired in 2000)		80,000	42,000
Goodwill		36,000	16,000
Fixtures and fittings		4,000	—
Trading stock		52,000	—
Debtors		18,000	—
		190,000	
Mortgage on shop	50,000		
Trade creditors	20,000	70,000	—
		£120,000	£58,000

The company issues 100,000 £1 ordinary shares, valued at par, to W in May 2017, and the amount left outstanding is £20,000. If W does not elect to disapply *TCGA 1992, s 162* treatment (see **37.3** below), the amount of the chargeable gain rolled over on transfer of the business is as follows.

$\frac{100{,}000}{120{,}000} \times £58{,}000$	£48,334

Of the chargeable gain, £9,666 (£58,000 – £48,334) remains taxable and is covered by the annual exempt amount.

The allowable cost of W's shares is £51,666 (£100,000 – £48,334).

Note to the example

(a) In the hands of the company, the goodwill will not qualify for the special treatment of intangible assets of companies introduced by *FA 2002*, because it was acquired from a related party and was created before 1 April 2002 (by virtue of the business having been carried on before that date). See **15.14** COMPANIES — CORPORATE FINANCE AND INTANGIBLES.

Simon's Taxes. See **C3.4**.

Election to disapply incorporation relief

[37.3] On a transfer (of a business) that is within **36.13** above, the transferor may make an election to the effect that incorporation relief should not apply. The election must be made by notice in writing to HMRC. The deadline for making it is normally the second anniversary of 31 January following the tax year in which the transfer takes place. If, however, by the end of the tax year following that in which the transfer takes place, the transferor has disposed of *all* the 'new assets' (see below), the deadline is brought forward by one year. For this purpose, a transfer within *TCGA 1992, s 58* (see **46.5** MARRIED PERSONS AND CIVIL PARTNERS) is not counted as a disposal, but a subsequent disposal by the recipient spouse or civil partner (other than a transfer back to the original spouse or partner) counts as a disposal by the original spouse or partner.

As in **37.2** above, the '*new assets*' are the shares received by the transferor in exchange for the business, but in this case the expression also includes any shares or debentures treated by virtue of *TCGA 1992, s 127* (reorganisations of share capital — see **63.2** SHARES AND SECURITIES) as the same asset as the shares received in exchange for the business. The reference to *s 127* includes that *section* as applied by any other chargeable gains enactment (see, for example, **63.5**, **63.7**, **63.8** SHARES AND SECURITIES).

Where, immediately before the transfer of the business, it was owned by two or more persons (e.g. by a partnership, including a Scottish partnership), each person has a separate right to make the election in respect of his own entitlement to incorporation relief under *TCGA 1992, s 162* and by reference to his own share of the 'new assets'.

[*TCGA 1992, s 162A*].

Disincorporation relief

[37.4] Disincorporation relief can be claimed where certain small companies transfer their business to shareholders who are individuals on or after 1 April 2013 and before 1 April 2018. Where the relief is claimed, goodwill and land and buildings used in the business are treated as transferred to the shareholders at a reduced value for chargeable gains purposes (and, in the case of goodwill, for the purposes of the intangible assets regime) so that no corporation tax is payable by the company on the transfer of the assets. Shareholders to whom the assets are transferred inherit the reduced transfer values for the purpose of capital gains tax and must use them for any subsequent disposals. In effect the gain that would have arisen to the company is deferred until the disposal of the assets by shareholders.

Where the business is transferred under a contract, the date of the transfer is the date the contract is made or, where the contract is conditional, the date on which the condition is satisfied. If the business is transferred under more than one contract, the date of the transfer is determined by reference to the contract under which the goodwill of the business is transferred.

See also HMRC Notice 'Disincorporation relief — HMRC guidance', 13 August 2013 and HMRC Capital Gains Manual CG65800 onwards.

Conditions for relief

The transfer of a business from a company to some or all of its shareholders qualifies for disincorporation relief if:

(a) the business is transferred as a going concern;
(b) the business is transferred together with all of the assets of the business (or all of the assets other than cash);
(c) the total 'market value' of the 'qualifying assets' of the business included in the transfer does not exceed £100,000;
(d) all of the shareholders to whom the business is transferred are individuals (including individuals acting as a member of a partnership other than a limited liability partnership); and
(e) each of those shareholders held shares in the company throughout the 12-month period ending on the date of the transfer.

Condition (d) above is satisfied if the transfer is to a nominee or bare trustee for individuals who are shareholders, and condition (e) above is satisfied if the shares are held by a nominee or bare trustee for an individual.

'*Qualifying assets*' are goodwill and interests in land not held as trading stock. '*Market value*' means the price which an asset might reasonably be expected to fetch on a sale in the open market.

[*FA 2013, ss 58, 59*].

Effect of relief

The disposal by the company and acquisition by the shareholders of any qualifying asset of the business included in the transfer is deemed to be for a consideration equal to the lower of:

(i) the total deductions allowable in computing the company's gain on the asset in question under the rules at **16.11** COMPUTATION OF GAINS AND LOSSES; and
(ii) the asset's market value.

Where the goodwill is dealt with in the company's hands under the intangible assets regime (see **15.14** COMPANIES—CORPORATE FINANCE AND INTANGIBLES), the acquisition by the shareholders is deemed to be for a consideration equal to the transfer value under that regime, as follows.

(A) If the goodwill has been written down under the regime, the transfer value is the lower of the tax written-down value immediately before the transfer and the market value.
(B) If the goodwill is shown in the balance sheet but has not been written down, the transfer value is the lower of the cost of the goodwill (i.e. the cost recognised under the intangible assets regime) and its market value.
(C) If neither (A) nor (B) above apply, the transfer value is nil.

[*TCGA 1992, ss 162B, 162C; CTA 2009, s 849A; FA 2013, s 61*].

Claims

A claim for disincorporation relief must be made jointly by the company and all of the shareholders to whom the business is transferred within the two years beginning with the date of the transfer. A claim is irrevocable. [*FA 2013, s 60*].

Key points

[37.5] Points to consider are as follows.

- Incorporation relief is automatic if the conditions are met (but a taxpayer can elect to disapply it). However it is quite easy to avoid wasting the annual exempt amount, for example by part of the consideration being paid in cash.
- Although it is often the case, the company to which the business is transferred does not have to be new. It can be an existing company.
- HMRC frequently challenge over optimistic valuations of goodwill. The post transaction valuation procedure (form CG34) enables a value to be agreed with HMRC. Where practical it is advantageous to make the transfer early in the tax year and immediately file a CG34 as this enables a value to be agreed prior to the tax return being filed.

38

Indexation

Introduction	38.1
Calculation of indexation allowance	38.2
Part disposals	38.3
Disposals on a no gain/no loss basis	38.4
Receipts affecting allowable expenditure	38.5
Reorganisation, reconstructions etc	38.6
Calls on shares	38.7
Options	38.8

Cross-references. See **8** ASSETS HELD ON 6 APRIL **1965**; **9** ASSETS HELD ON 31 MARCH **1982**; **16** COMPUTATION OF GAINS AND LOSSES; **41.14** LAND for concessionary treatment of indexation allowance on the merger of leases; **64** SHARES AND SECURITIES IDENTIFICATION RULES; **70.3**, **70.4**, **70.8** UNIT TRUSTS ETC. for HMRC practice in the case of unit trust units, investment trust shares and open-ended investment company shares acquired under monthly savings schemes.

Simon's Taxes. See C2.3.

Introduction to indexation

[38.1] Indexation allowance is intended to eliminate the effects of inflation from the calculation of chargeable gains. In effect the allowance increases the amount of allowable expenditure in line with inflation, so that only any real-terms gain is taxed. The allowance applies **for corporation tax purposes only**, having been abolished for capital gains tax purposes (i.e. for disposals by individuals, trustees and personal representatives) in computing gains made on disposals on or after 6 April 2008.

Calculation of indexation allowance

[38.2] For corporation tax purposes only, the gain (if any) arrived at by deducting an amount of allowable expenditure from the amount of consideration realised (see **16** COMPUTATION OF GAINS AND LOSSES), or deemed to be realised, on a disposal is termed an '*unindexed gain*'. In arriving at the chargeable gain, there is to be allowed against the unindexed gain an 'indexation allowance', which is the aggregate of the 'indexed rise' in each item of 'relevant allowable expenditure' (see below).

Indexation allowance is given *only* against an unindexed gain. If the disposal gives rise to a loss, no indexation allowance is given and if the indexation allowance equals or exceeds the unindexed gain on a disposal so as to extinguish it, the disposal is regarded as one on which, after taking account of the indexation allowance, neither a gain nor a loss accrues.

'*Relevant allowable expenditure*' is allowable expenditure within *TCGA 1992, s 38(1)(a)* and *s 38(1)(b)*, i.e. basically acquisition cost or value, taken for these purposes as incurred when the asset is acquired or provided, and expenditure on enhancement and on establishing, preserving and defending title and rights to the asset (see **16.11**(a)–(c) COMPUTATION OF GAINS AND LOSSES). Such expenditure being taken for these purposes as incurred when it becomes due and payable. Disposal costs are excluded. In determining relevant allowable expenditure, account is taken of any provision of any enactment which, for the purpose of computing gains, increases, excludes or reduces any item of expenditure, or provides for it to be written down.

The '*indexed rise*' in each item of relevant allowable expenditure is computed by multiplying that item by a figure (rounded to the nearest third decimal place) calculated by the formula:

$$\frac{RD - RI}{RI}$$

where:

RD = retail prices index for the month in which the disposal occurs or, if earlier and for capital gains tax (not corporation tax) purposes, April 1998; and

RI = retail prices index for March 1982 or the month in which the expenditure was incurred, whichever is the later.

If, in relation to any item of expenditure, RD in the formula is equal to, or less than, RI, there is no indexed rise for that item.

[*TCGA 1992, ss 53, 54, 288(1); ITA 2007, s 989*].

The above rules do not apply to 'section 104 holdings' (i.e. single asset pools) of shares or securities. Separate indexation provisions apply to such holding — see **64.4** SHARES AND SECURITIES — IDENTIFICATION RULES.

Special provisions apply to the calculation of indexation allowance in relation to disposals involving ASSETS HELD ON 31 MARCH **1982** (**9**).

The rules outlined above are subject to the special provisions in **38.3–38.8** below.

Indexation factors

The figure given by the above formula is commonly called the '*indexation factor*'. The consistent calculation of the indexation factor to more than three decimal places is generally accepted.

HMRC publishes the retail prices index and the associated indexation factors on its website. Yearly tables of indexation factors are contained in Tolley's Tax Data. The retail prices index is reproduced below.

Values of the retail prices index (RPI) for March 1982 and subsequent months are as follows.

	1982	1983	1984	1985	1986	1987	1988	1989	1990	1991
Jan	—	82.61	86.84	91.20	96.25	100.0	103.3	111.0	119.5	130.2
Feb	—	82.97	87.20	91.94	96.60	100.4	103.7	111.8	120.2	130.9
Mar	79.44	83.12	87.48	92.80	96.73	100.6	104.1	112.3	121.4	131.4
Apr	81.04	84.28	88.64	94.78	97.67	101.8	105.8	114.3	125.1	133.1
May	81.62	84.64	88.97	95.21	97.85	101.9	106.2	115.0	126.2	133.5
Jun	81.85	84.84	89.20	95.41	97.79	101.9	106.6	115.4	126.7	134.1
Jul	81.88	85.30	89.10	95.23	97.52	101.8	106.7	115.5	126.8	133.8
Aug	81.90	85.68	89.94	95.49	97.82	102.1	107.9	115.8	128.1	134.1
Sep	81.85	86.06	90.11	95.44	98.30	102.4	108.4	116.6	129.3	134.6
Oct	82.26	86.36	90.67	95.59	98.45	102.9	109.5	117.5	130.3	135.1
Nov	82.66	86.67	90.95	95.92	99.29	103.4	110.0	118.5	130.0	135.6
Dec	82.51	86.89	90.87	96.05	99.62	103.3	110.3	118.8	129.9	135.7

	1992	1993	1994	1995	1996	1997	1998	1999	2000	2001
Jan	135.6	137.9	141.3	146.0	150.2	154.4	159.5	163.4	166.6	171.1
Feb	136.3	138.8	142.1	146.9	150.9	155.0	160.3	163.7	167.5	172.0
Mar	136.7	139.3	142.5	147.5	151.5	155.4	160.8	164.1	168.4	172.2
Apr	138.8	140.6	144.2	149.0	152.6	156.3	162.6	165.2	170.1	173.1
May	139.3	141.1	144.7	149.6	152.9	156.9	163.5	165.6	170.7	174.2
Jun	139.3	141.0	144.7	149.8	153.0	157.5	163.4	165.6	171.1	174.4
July	138.8	140.7	144.0	149.1	152.4	157.5	163.0	165.1	170.5	173.3
Aug	138.9	141.3	144.7	149.9	153.1	158.5	163.7	165.5	170.5	174.0
Sep	139.4	141.9	145.0	150.6	153.8	159.3	164.4	166.2	171.7	174.6
Oct	139.9	141.8	145.2	149.8	153.8	159.5	164.5	166.5	171.6	174.3
Nov	139.7	141.6	145.3	149.8	153.9	159.6	164.4	166.7	172.1	173.6
Dec	139.2	141.9	146.0	150.7	154.4	160.0	164.4	167.3	172.2	173.4

	2002	2003	2004	2005	2006	2007	2008	2009	2010	2011
Jan	173.3	178.4	183.1	188.9	193.4	201.6	209.8	210.1	217.9	229.0
Feb	173.8	179.3	183.8	189.6	194.2	203.1	211.4	211.4	219.2	231.3
Mar	174.5	179.9	184.6	190.5	195.0	204.4	212.1	211.3	220.7	232.5
Apr	175.7	181.2	185.7	191.6	196.5	205.4	214.0	211.5	222.8	234.4
May	176.2	181.5	186.5	192.0	197.7	206.2	215.1	212.8	223.6	235.2
Jun	176.2	181.3	186.8	192.2	198.5	207.3	216.8	213.4	224.1	235.2
Jul	175.9	181.3	186.8	192.2	198.5	206.1	216.5	213.4	223.6	234.7
Aug	176.4	181.6	187.4	192.6	199.2	207.3	217.2	214.4	224.5	236.1
Sep	177.7	182.5	188.1	193.1	200.1	208.0	218.4	215.3	225.3	237.9
Oct	177.9	182.6	188.6	193.3	200.4	208.9	217.7	216.0	225.8	238.0
Nov	178.2	182.7	189.0	193.6	201.1	209.7	216.0	216.6	226.8	238.5
Dec	178.5	183.5	189.9	194.1	202.7	210.9	212.9	218.0	228.4	239.4

	2012	2013	2014	2015	2016	2017
Jan	238.0	245.8	252.6	255.4	258.80	265.5
Feb	239.9	247.6	254.2	256.7	260.00	268.4
Mar	240.8	248.7	254.8	257.1	261.1	269.3

	2012	2013	2014	2015	2016	2017
Apr	242.5	249.5	255.7	258.0	261.4	270.6
May	242.4	250.0	255.9	258.5	262.1	271.7
Jun	241.8	249.7	256.3	258.9	263.1	272.3
Jul	242.1	249.7	256.0	258.6	263.4	272.9
Aug	243.0	251.0	257.0	259.8	264.4	
Sep	244.2	251.9	257.6	259.6	264.9	
Oct	245.6	251.9	257.7	259.5	264.8	
Nov	245.6	252.1	257.1	259.8	265.5	
Dec	246.8	253.4	257.5	260.6	267.1	

Examples

(1) X Ltd acquired an asset in November 1985 for £28,000. It disposes of the asset on 11 August 2017 for £99,000. The retail prices index for November 1985 is 95.92 and for August 2017 it is 273.6 (assumed).

	£
Sale consideration	99,000
Cost of asset	28,000
Unindexed gain	71,000
Indexation allowance	
(273.6 – 95.92)/95.92 = 1.852	
1.852 × £28,000	51,856
Chargeable gain	£19,144

(2) Facts as in (1) above except that X Ltd receives consideration of £18,000.

	£
Sale consideration	18,000
Cost of asset	28,000
Allowable loss (no indexation allowance available)	£10,000

(3) Facts as in (1) above except that X Ltd received consideration of £40,000.

	£
Sale consideration	40,000
Cost of asset	28,000
Unindexed gain	£12,000

Indexation allowance is as in (1) above (£51,856) but as this exceeds the amount of the unindexed gain, the disposal gives rise neither to a gain nor to a loss.

Part disposals

[38.3] Where a disposal is a part disposal of an asset, apportionment of relevant allowable expenditure is to take place before computing the indexation allowance. The allowance is then only calculated for relevant allowable expenditure attributable to the part disposed of. [*TCGA 1992, s 56(1)*].

Example

X Ltd sells part of a plot of land on 18 January 2017 for £100,000. The then market value of the remaining part of the plot is £30,000. The cost, in September 1984, of the whole plot was £25,000. The retail prices index at September 1984 is 90.11 and for January 2017 it is 265.5.

	£
Allowable expenditure attributable to the part disposed of	
$\frac{100,000}{100,000 + 30,000} \times £25,000$	£19,231
Unindexed gain: £100,000 – £19,231	80,769
Indexation allowance	
(265.5 – 90.11)/90.11 = 1.946	
1.946 × £19,231	37,424
Chargeable gain	£43,345

Note to the example

(a) No indexation allowance is computed at this stage on the balance of expenditure to be carried forward of £5,769 (£25,000 – £19,231).

Disposals on a no gain/no loss basis

[38.4] On a 'no gain/no loss disposal' by a company, both the disposal consideration of the transferor and the corresponding acquisition consideration of the transferee are calculated for the purposes of *TCGA 1992* on the assumption that, on the disposal, an unindexed gain accrues to the transferor which is equal to the indexation allowance on that disposal, and so that after taking account of the indexation allowance the disposal is one on which neither a gain nor a loss accrues. This rule applied also to such disposals by individuals, trustees or personal representatives before 6 April 2008. Where the acquisition consideration for an asset was determined in this way, the amount of that consideration is not affected by the abolition of indexation allowance for capital gains tax purposes.

For the purposes of calculating indexation allowance under *TCGA 1992, ss 53, 54* (see **38.2** above), any enactment is disregarded to the extent to which it provides that, on a subsequent disposal of an asset by the transferee which was acquired by him on a no gain/no loss disposal as above, the transferor's acquisition of the asset is to be treated as the transferee's acquisition of it. [*TCGA 1992, ss 52A, 56(2)*]. For further applications of this provision, see **9.6** ASSETS HELD ON 31 MARCH **1982** and **64.4** SHARES AND SECURITIES — IDENTIFICATION RULES.

Where otherwise a loss would accrue on the disposal of an asset, and the sums allowable as a deduction in computing the loss would include an amount attributable to the application of the assumption contained in *TCGA 1992, s 56(2)* above on any no gain/no loss disposal, those sums are determined as if *TCGA 1992, s 56(2)* had not applied and the loss is reduced accordingly or, if those sums are then equal to or less than the consideration for the disposal, the disposal is to be one on which neither a gain nor a loss accrues. [*TCGA 1992, s 56(3)*].

For the purposes of *TCGA 1992, s 56(1)* (part disposals; see **38.3** above) and *TCGA 1992, s 56(2)(3)* above, a '*no gain/no loss disposal*' is one which, by virtue of any enactment other than *TCGA 1992, s 35(4)* (no gain/no loss disposal where the general re-basing rule of *TCGA 1992, s 35(1)(2)* would otherwise convert a gain into a loss and vice versa; see **9.2** ASSETS HELD ON 31 MARCH **1982**), *s 53(1)* (no gain/no loss disposal where indexation allowance equals or exceeds gain before indexation; see **38.2** above) or *s 56* itself, is treated as a disposal on which neither a gain nor a loss accrues. [*TCGA 1992, s 56(4)*]. For these purposes the definition is not therefore confined to those no gain/ no loss disposals mentioned in **9.6** ASSETS HELD ON 31 MARCH **1982**.

Receipts affecting allowable expenditure

[38.5] Where account is to be taken, in determining relevant allowable expenditure (see **38.2** above) of any provision which, for the purposes of computing gains, reduces such expenditure by reference to a '*relevant event*' (i.e. any event which is not treated as a capital gains tax disposal), the computation of the indexation allowance proceeds in three stages.

(i) The 'indexed rise' (see **38.2** above) is calculated for each item of expenditure ignoring the reduction.
(ii) The 'indexed rise' is calculated of a notional item of expenditure equal to the amount of the reduction, as if that notional amount had actually been incurred on the date of the 'relevant event'.
(iii) The figure calculated in (ii) above is deducted from that in (i) above.

[*TCGA 1992, s 57*]. Examples of such 'relevant events' are small part disposals of land as in **41.9** LAND and the sale of rights nil paid where the consideration received is small as in **63.2** SHARES AND SECURITIES.

Example

Z Ltd purchases a large area of land in April 1990 for £800,000. In June 1993, it sells a small part of that land at arm's length for £2,000. In August 2017, it sells all the remaining land for £4,500,000. The retail prices index for April 1990 is 125.1, for June 1993 it is 141.0 and for August 2017 is 273.6 (assumed).

	£	£

Sale consideration		4,500,000
Cost	800,000	
Small sale not treated as a disposal	2,000	798,000
Unindexed gain		£3,702,000
Indexation allowance on cost		£
(273.6 – 125.1)/125.1 = 1.187		
1.187 × £800,000		949,600
Indexation allowance on notional expenditure equal to small sale consideration		
(273.6 – 141.0)/141.0 = 0.940		
0.940 × £2,000		1,880
Reduced indexation allowance		£947,720
Chargeable gain = £(3,702,000 – 947,720)		£2,754,280

Reorganisation, reconstructions etc.

[38.6] In computing indexation allowance, any consideration given for 'the new holding' (treated under *TCGA 1992, s 127* as the same asset as 'the original shares' on a reorganisation or reduction of a company's share capital) is to be treated as an item of relevant allowable expenditure incurred when the consideration was, or was liable to be, given, i.e. not related back to the acquisition date of 'the original shares', as would normally be the case under *TCGA 1992, s 128(1)*.

'*Reorganisation*', the '*original shares*' and '*the new holding*' are as defined in *TCGA 1992, s 126(1)*. In addition the above provisions also apply where the treatment under *TCGA 1992, s 127* is adapted for a conversion of securities and for company reconstructions. See **63.2–63.8** SHARES AND SECURITIES. [*TCGA 1992, ss 131, 132(1), 135(3)*].

Example

In November 1989, Y Ltd purchases 5,000 shares in A plc for £3,500. In June 1991, it acquires, for £960, 1,000 further shares by way of a 1 for 5 rights issue. In August 2017, it sells all its holding for £15,000. The retail prices index for November 1989 is 118.5, for June 1991 it is 134.1 and for August 2017 it is 273.6 (assumed).

	£	£
Sale consideration		15,000
Original cost	3,500	
Cost of rights	960	
		4,460
Unindexed gain		£10,540
Indexation allowance on original cost		£
(273.6 – 118.5)/118.5 = 1.309		
1.309 × £3,500		4,582
Indexation allowance on cost of taking up rights		
(273.6 – 134.1)/134.1 = 1.040		
1.040 × £960		998
Total indexation allowance		£5,580
Chargeable gain = £(10,540 – 5,580)		£4,960

Note to the example

(a) Technically, the pooling provisions in **64.4** SHARES AND SECURITIES — IDENTIFICATION RULES apply, as the acquisition in November 1989 is a 'section 104 holding'. For practical purposes, where, as in this example, there is a single acquisition and disposal, the above computation gives essentially the same result.

Calls on shares

[38.7] Where the whole or part of the consideration for the issue of shares, securities or debentures is given after the period of twelve months beginning on the date of the issue of the shares etc., that consideration (or part) is treated as a separate item of expenditure for indexation purposes, incurred at the time it is given and not at the time at which the shares etc. were acquired or provided. [*TCGA 1992, s 113*]. Any calls paid within the twelve-month period are thus treated as incurred at the time the shares etc. were acquired or provided.

Options

[38.8] Where, on a disposal, relevant allowable expenditure includes both:

(a) the cost of acquiring an option binding the grantor to sell ('*the option consideration*'); and

(b) the cost of acquiring what was sold as a result of the exercise of the option ('*the sale consideration*'),

the option consideration and sale consideration are regarded as separate items of expenditure incurred when the option was acquired and when the sale took place respectively. An option binding the grantor both to sell and to buy is treated for these purposes as two separate options with one half of the consideration attributable to each. These provisions do not apply where those at **64.4** SHARES AND SECURITIES — IDENTIFICATION RULES (under 'Consideration for options') apply. [*TCGA 1992, s 145*].

As in **7.7** ASSETS, the reference above to an 'option' includes a reference to an option binding the grantor to grant a lease for a premium, or enter into any other transaction which is not a sale. [*TCGA 1992, ss 144(6), 145(3)*].

In the case of the grantee of a 'cash-settled' option (see **7.7** ASSETS), the cost of the option is treated as incurred when the option was acquired for the purposes of calculating any indexation allowance. [*TCGA 1992, s 144A(3)(c)*].

39

Interaction with Other Taxes

General and income tax	**39.1**
Inheritance tax	**39.2**
Value added tax	**39.3**

Cross-references. See **2** ANNUAL RATES AND EXEMPTIONS for rates applicable to gains for 2010/11 onwards by reference to income tax bands; **16** COMPUTATION OF GAINS AND LOSSES for acquisition and disposal consideration taken into account for capital gains tax purposes generally; **36.10** HOLD-OVER RELIEFS for relief given to gifts after 13 March 1989 on which inheritance tax is chargeable etc; **41.16–41.19** LAND for premiums on leases of land charged to income tax; **63** SHARES AND SECURITIES for interaction with income tax provisions; **69.2** UNDERWRITERS AT LLOYD'S for treatment of assets in premium trust funds.

General and income tax

[39.1] Any money or money's worth charged to income tax as income of, or taken into account as a receipt in computing income or profits or gains or losses of the person making the disposal is excluded from the consideration for the disposal of the asset for capital gains tax purposes. From 2017/18 onwards, there is also excluded any amount brought into account, by the person making the disposal, as a receipt under the cash basis for small businesses because the person ceases to use the asset in the trade (without disposing of it) or because there is an increase in the person's non-business use of the asset, these being deemed disposals for the purpose of the cash basis. This is the case provided such amounts have not already been excluded on a previous disposal of the asset. There are similar exclusions from 2017/18 onwards for such receipts brought into account under the cash basis for unincorporated property businesses. See Tolley's Income Tax for details of the cash basis.

However,

(a) this is not to be taken as excluding any money or money's worth:
   - taken into account in making a balancing charge for the purposes of capital allowances (other than assured tenancy allowances) (see *Hirsch v Crowthers Cloth Ltd* Ch D 1989, 62 TC 759); or
   - brought into account as the disposal value of plant or machinery for capital allowances purposes; or
   - brought into account as the disposal value of an asset representing qualifying expenditure under *CAA 2001, Pt 6* (research and development allowances);
   - taken into account in computing a return on which income tax is charged under *ITTOIA 2005, Pt 4 Ch 2A* (disguised interest); and

(b) the capitalised value of a rentcharge (as in the case where a rentcharge is exchanged for another asset), ground annual or feu duty, or of a right of any other description to income or to payments in the nature of income over a period, or to a series of payments in the nature of income may be taken into account for capital gains tax purposes.

Income or profits charged or chargeable to tax include amounts from which a sum representing income tax is required to be deducted.

Where, under *ITA 2007, s 759(6)* or *CTA 2010, s 821(3)(5)* (transactions in land before 5 July 2016 — see **41.4** LAND), the person charged to tax is a person other than the person by whom the gain was realised and the tax has been paid, then, for the purposes of the above provisions, the amount charged to tax is regarded as having been charged as the income of the person by whom the gain was realised.

Where, under *ITA 2007, s 517G(4)(6)* or *CTA 2010, s 356OG(4)(6)* (transactions in UK land on or after 5 July 2016 — see **41.6** LAND), an amount is charged to tax as income of a person other than the person by whom the gain was realised and the tax has been paid, then, for the purposes of the above provisions, the amount charged to tax is regarded as having been charged as the income of the person by whom the gain was realised.

Similarly, where, under *ITA 2007, s 777(5)* (sales of occupation income — see Tolley's Income Tax), the person charged to tax is a person other than the person ('A') for whom the capital amount was obtained or by whom the property or right was sold or realised and the tax has been paid, then, for the purposes of the above provisions, the amount charged to tax is regarded as having been charged as the income of A.

See also **16.10** COMPUTATION OF GAINS AND LOSSES for the exclusion from disposal consideration of certain amounts under finance leases where anti-avoidance provisions apply.

[*TCGA 1992, ss 37, 39, 52(2)(3)(5), Sch 8 para 5(6); TIOPA 2010, Sch 8 para 231; FA 2013, Sch 12; FA 2016, ss 77(7)(8), 79(8)(9); F(No 2)A 2017, s 16, Sch 2 paras 44, 64(1)*].

In *Drummond v HMRC* CA, [2009] STC 2206, an individual (D) contracted to purchase five life assurance policies for a stated consideration of £1,962,233. On the following day he asked the vendor to surrender the policies. The surrender value was £1,751,376. In his tax return, D claimed that the effect of this was that he had made an allowable loss of £1,962,233 for CGT purposes. HMRC rejected the claim and D appealed, contending that the effect of *TCGA 1992, s 37* was that the 'surrender value' could be excluded from the computation of the gain or loss on the disposal. The Ch D reviewed the evidence in detail, rejected this contention, and rejected D's claim. Norris J observed that for income tax purposes the surrender had given rise to a 'chargeable event gain' of £1,351; and that the transactions had cost D £210,857. He held that this £210,857 represented professional fees which had not been 'wholly and exclusively expended in the acquisition of the policies'. Accordingly, for CGT purposes, the disposal had produced a loss of £1,351, being the amount chargeable to income tax and the only amount which fell to be excluded from the consideration charged to CGT by virtue of *TCGA 1992, s 37*. The CA unanimously upheld this decision. Rimer LJ held that 'the interpretation of legislation involves more than black letter literalism. In a case such as the present, in which there is a question as to which of limbs (i) and (ii) applies, it is necessary to give the statute a purposive construction'. The purpose of *TCGA 1992, ss 37–39* was 'to prevent the double taxation that might otherwise arise from the circumstance that the disposal of an asset will or may give rise to a charge to income tax and also be a disposal for CGT purposes. ... It is not their purpose to enable the creation of an imaginary loss that the taxpayer can set against a real gain and so reduce a CGT liability'. This decision was followed in *Smith v HMRC* (Sp C 725), [2009] SSCD 132 and *Abbeyland Ltd v HMRC* FTT, [2013] SFTD 1212.

For income tax matters relating to know-how and patents (and which have a capital gains tax effect), see **7.4**, **7.5** ASSETS). See also **49.10** OVERSEAS MATTERS for offshore funds.

Expenditure

Expenditure which is deductible in computing profits or losses for income tax purposes (or would be so deductible if the asset were held as a fixed asset of a trade) is excluded from being allowable expenditure for capital gains tax purposes. For this purpose, where, under *ITA 2007, s 759(6)* or *CTA 2010, s 821(3)(5)* (transactions in land before 5 July 2016 — see **41.4** LAND), the person charged to tax is a person other than the person by whom the gain was realised and the tax has been paid, then, for the purposes of the above provisions, the amount charged to tax is regarded as having been charged as the income of the person by whom the gain was realised. Where, under *ITA 2007, s 517G(4)(6)* or *CTA 2010, s 356OG(4)(6)* (transactions in UK land on or after 5 July 2016 — see **41.6** LAND), an amount is charged to tax as income of a person other than the person by whom the gain was realised and the tax has been paid, then, for the purposes of the above provisions, the amount charged to tax is regarded as having been charged as the income of the person by whom the gain was realised. [*TCGA 1992, s 39(1)(2)(4); FA 2016, ss 76(8), 78(9)*]. See **16.13** COMPUTATION OF GAINS AND LOSSES.

Assessments etc.

Any assessment to income tax or decision on a claim under the *Income Tax Acts*, and any decision on an appeal in connection therewith, is conclusive for capital gains tax purposes where liability to tax depends on the provisions of the *Income Tax Acts*. [*TCGA 1992, s 284*]. Where *alternative* income tax and capital gains tax assessments are made in respect of the same transactions, the fact that the capital gains tax assessment becomes final does not preclude the income tax assessment taking effect instead (*Bye v Coren* CA 1986, 60 TC 116). See also *Lord Advocate v McKenna* CS 1989, 61 TC 688 and *CIR v Wilkinson* CA 1992, 65 TC 28.

Income or capital?

Whether the gain arising on the disposal of an asset is of income or capital nature has been tested in the courts on numerous occasions and the outcome is likely to be one of fact and degree. In particular, see **41.3** LAND for isolated and speculative transactions in land. 'No part of our law of taxation presents such almost insoluble conundrums as the decision whether a receipt or outgoing is capital or income for tax purposes' (Lord Upjohn in *Strick v Regent Oil Co Ltd* HL 1965, 43 TC 1 which see for a comprehensive review of the law). A widely used test is the 'enduring benefit' one given by Viscount Cave in *Atherton v British Insulated & Helsby Cables Ltd* HL 1925, 10 TC 155.

Inheritance tax

[39.2] A lifetime disposal which contains an element of gift may incur liability to inheritance tax (IHT) as well as capital gains tax. For the purposes of IHT, no account is taken of any capital gains tax borne by the transferor in determining the reduction in value in his estate. [*IHTA 1984, s 164*].

> *Example 1*
>
> A makes a gift of land, to a non-UK resident discretionary trustee, B, which is valued at £20,000 and on which there is a capital gains tax liability of £3,000. The value for IHT purposes (subject to grossing-up for the IHT payable) is £20,000 (i.e. the same as if A had sold the land and given the £20,000 proceeds to B).

Relief for CGT against IHT

Capital gains tax paid will be taken into account for IHT purposes in the following instances.

(a) If the transferor fails to pay all or part of the capital gains tax within twelve months of the due date, an assessment may be made on the donee (see **27.4** GIFTS) and the amount of such tax borne by the donee is treated as reducing the value transferred. There is a similar effect when the transfer is from a settlement but, after 8 March 1982, this only applies if the capital gains tax is borne by a person who becomes absolutely entitled to the settled property concerned. [*IHTA 1984, s 165(1)(2)*].

(b) Where a person sells, or is treated as having sold, national heritage property on the breach or termination of an undertaking (see **25.85** EXEMPTIONS AND RELIEFS) any capital gains tax payable is deductible in determining the value of the asset for IHT purposes. [*TCGA 1992, s 258(8)*].

> *Example 2*
>
> In *Example 1* above, if A fails to pay the £3,000 capital gains tax and it is borne by B, the value transferred by A is £17,000 for the purposes of IHT (again subject to grossing-up for the IHT payable).

Relief for IHT against CGT

Where hold-over relief is granted under:

(i) *TCGA 1992, s 165* in relation to gifts made after 13 March 1989 (see **36.2** HOLD-OVER RELIEFS),
(ii) *TCGA 1992, s 260* in relation to gifts after 13 March 1989 (see **36.10** HOLD-OVER RELIEFS), or
(iii) *FA 1980, s 79* in relation to gifts after 5 April 1980 and before 14 March 1989 (see **36.12** HOLD-OVER RELIEFS),

the transferee may deduct on a subsequent disposal any IHT attributable to the value of the asset on the original transfer (being either a chargeable transfer or a potentially exempt transfer which proves to be a chargeable transfer). The tax deductible may be varied on the subsequent death of the transferor or otherwise but it cannot in any circumstances create an allowable loss on the subsequent disposal. [*TCGA 1992, ss 67(1)–(3), 165(10)(11), 260(7)(8)*]. In the case of (ii) above, the same treatment applies if a hold-over relief claim *could have been made* (HMRC Capital Gains Manual CG67050).

There is no relief for IHT under (i) and (iii) above if hold-over relief is *not* claimed, so that even where the gain otherwise arising is negligible or covered by reliefs a hold-over relief claim may still be beneficial overall. A hold-over relief claim can be made even if an allowable loss arises on the original gift and so give rise to an IHT deduction on a subsequent disposal by the donee whilst not affecting the loss relief position of the donor. Where only part of the asset gifted is subsequently disposed of, HMRC accept that any IHT paid on the original gift can still be deducted in full on the part disposal (subject to the size of the gain arising) and there is no need to apportion IHT paid between the part disposed of and the part retained (Taxation 5 October 1989 pp 12, 14). There is no provision for indexation allowance to be calculated by reference to the IHT that can be deducted.

Valuation of assets

Valuations of assets made *at death* for the purpose of the application of an IHT charge on the value of a person's estate immediately before death are binding for capital gains tax purposes. [*TCGA 1992, s 274; IHTA 1984, s 168; FA 2008, Sch 4 para 8*]. See also Revenue Tax Bulletin April 1995 p 209. Therefore, quoted shares and securities are then valued using the IHT valuation (see **45.3** MARKET VALUE). In the case of land and quoted shares and securities, proceeds of certain post-death sales within a specified period may be substituted for values at date of death for IHT purposes. The value of related property (as defined for IHT purposes) may also be revised in the event of a post-death sale. If such substitutions/revisions are made for IHT purposes, they must be made for CGT purposes also (but see *Stonor and Another (Executors of Dickinson deceased) v CIR* (Sp C 288), [2001] SSCD 199 in which the executors failed in an attempt to use this rule to upgrade values of freehold properties for CGT purposes where there was no IHT liability). See Tolley's Inheritance Tax for details.

Value added tax

[39.3] If VAT is suffered on the purchase of an asset, but is available for set-off in full in the purchaser's VAT account (e.g. a capital asset purchased by a trader who is registered for VAT), then the cost of the asset for capital gains tax purposes is the cost exclusive of VAT. Where no VAT set-off is available, the cost is inclusive of VAT borne. On the disposal of an asset, VAT chargeable is disregarded in computing the disposal consideration for capital gains tax purposes (HMRC Statement of Practice D7).

A person whose output is partly exempt and partly taxable may set off only part of his VAT on inputs against his VAT on outputs. In such a case, although the computation of disposal proceeds is as above, it will be necessary to allocate the VAT ultimately suffered to the various expense payments made. Inspectors will be prepared to consider any reasonable arrangements made to carry out this apportionment. A taxable person making both taxable and exempt supplies may therefore treat as part of the capital gains tax cost of an asset the input tax that was not available for credit in respect of the acquisition (HMRC Statement of Practice B1).

The above practices should be read in the light of a Revenue Press Release of 20 March 1990 which mentioned that VAT on certain inputs (broadly land, buildings and computers with values above certain levels) after 31 March 1990 may require annual adjustment for a period of up to ten years after the input concerned under the VAT capital goods scheme. In certain circumstances a VAT adjustment may reduce the amount of expenditure on an asset qualifying for **59** ROLLOVER RELIEF. Where a VAT adjustment is made after a claim to rollover relief has been determined, HMRC will not normally seek to reopen the claim.

40

Investors' Relief

Introduction to investors' relief	**40.1**
Operation of investors' relief	**40.2**
Disposals by trustees	**40.3**
Previous disposal of shares in the holding	**40.4**
Lifetime limit on investors' relief	**40.5**
Claims for relief	**40.6**
Shares qualifying for investors' relief	**40.7**
Disqualification of shares where value received	**40.8**
Reorganisations	**40.9**
Election to disapply reorganisation provisions	**40.10**

Cross-references. See 24 ENTREPRENEURS' RELIEF.

Introduction to investors' relief

[40.1] Investors' relief can be claimed by individuals or trustees in respect of certain disposals on or after 6 April 2019 of qualifying ordinary shares in unlisted trading companies subscribed for on or after 17 March 2016. The relief is not available to companies.

The main features of the relief are as follows:

- The relief can be claimed by individuals or trustees who dispose of ordinary shares, or an interest in ordinary shares, in unlisted trading companies or unlisted holding companies of trading groups for which they have subscribed on or after 17 March 2016.
- Gains on disposals of qualifying shares are chargeable to capital gains tax at a rate of 10% (after deduction of any allowable losses).
- Relief is subject to a lifetime limit of £10 million.
- Claims must be made on or before the first anniversary of 31 January following the tax year of disposal.
- The investor must hold the shares throughout the period beginning with the date the share was issued and ending with the date of disposal. That period must be at least three years, or, where the share was issued before 6 April 2016, at least three years plus the period beginning with the date of issue and ending on 5 April 2016.
- Relief is not available if the investor or a connected person has been an officer or employee of the company or a connected company at any time in the share-holding period;
- Where there have been previous disposals from a holding of shares, special identification rules apply to determine what proportion of the shares subsequently disposed of are qualifying shares.

- Shares are disqualified from relief if the investor receives any value worth, broadly, more than £1,000 from the company at any time in the period beginning one year before, and ending immediately before the third anniversary of, the date on which the shares were issued.
- There are provisions to determine the qualifying status of shares held following a reorganisation of share capital, exchange of shares or scheme of reconstruction. Broadly, shares held following such an event take on the history of the original shares proportionally.
- The investor can make an election to disapply the reorganisation provisions so that a claim to investors' relief can be made if the new shares would not qualify for relief.

Operation of investors' relief

[40.2] A 'qualifying person' can make a claim for investors' relief on the disposal of, or the disposal of an 'interest' in, a 'holding', or part of a holding, of shares in a company if, immediately before the disposal, some or all of the shares are 'qualifying shares' (see 40.7 below). See 40.3 below for the further condition applicable to disposals by trustees. Subject to the lifetime limit at 40.5 below, the relief applies as follows.

Where a claim is made and all of the shares in the holding are qualifying shares, the gain on the disposal (after deduction of any allowable losses) is taxable at the rate of 10%.

If only some of the shares are qualifying shares, only a corresponding proportion of the gain (after deduction of any allowable losses) is taxable at the rate of 10%. The proportion is the number of qualifying shares treated as disposed of divided by the total number of shares disposed of. For this purpose, qualifying shares are treated as disposed of in priority to non-qualifying shares. See 40.4 below where there has been a previous disposal of shares from the holding.

A '*holding*' of shares means a holding which is treated as a single asset under *TCGA 1992, s 104(1)* (see 64.4 SHARES AND SECURITIES – IDENTIFICATION RULES). A '*qualifying person*' is an individual or the trustees of a settlement.

Disposal of an interest in shares

In relation to the disposal of an interest in a holding of shares, a '*holding*' means a number of shares in a company of the same class which were acquired in the same capacity either by the qualifying person solely or by the same two or more persons including the qualifying person. An '*interest*' in a holding means any interests of the qualifying person, in any of the shares in the holding, which are treated as a single asset under *TCGA 1992, s 104(1)*. An interest includes a part of an interest. References throughout this chapter to a holding of shares include a reference to the interest disposed of, and references to the disposal of all of part of a holding include a reference to a disposal by a qualifying person of an interest in the holding.

[*TCGA 1992, ss 169VC, 169VD, 169VJ, 169VY; FA 2016, Sch 14 para 2*].

Disposals by trustees

[40.3] Where the disposal is by the trustees of a settlement, investors' relief is not available unless there is at least one 'eligible beneficiary' in respect of the disposal. An individual is an '*eligible beneficiary*' if:

- he has an interest in possession (other than for a fixed term) in settled property that includes the holding of shares immediately before the disposal;
- he has had such an interest throughout the three years ending with the date of the disposal;
- he has not been a 'relevant employee' (see 40.7 below) in respect of the company at any time in the three-year period; and
- he has elected to be treated as an eligible beneficiary.

An election must be made to the trustees by the time of the claim for relief and can be withdrawn at any time until the claim is made.

[*TCGA 1992, s 169VH; FA 2016, Sch 14 para 2*].

If there is more than one person with an interest in possession in the settled property which includes the holding of shares immediately before the disposal, the trustees can only claim investors' relief in respect of the eligible beneficiary's share of the gain or, where there is more than one eligible beneficiary, on the aggregate of their shares. A person's share of a gain is the proportion of the gain equal to his interest in possession in the income from the holding of shares divided by all the interests in possession in that income. [*TCGA 1992, s 169VI; FA 2016, Sch 14 para 2*].

Previous disposal of shares in the holding

[40.4] Where, before a disposal in respect of which a claim to investors' relief is made, there have been one or more previous disposals of shares from the same holding, the following rules apply, where needed, to determine which shares are treated as having been previously disposed of (and therefore which shares are treated as in the holding immediately before the current disposal). The rules operate to preserve the maximum potential relief for future disposals.

Claim to investors' relief made in respect of previous disposal

Where a claim to investors' relief was made in respect of the previous disposal:

(a) all of the qualifying shares in the holding immediately before the previous disposal are treated as having been disposed of or, if less, so many of the qualifying shares as equals the total number of shares disposed of;

(b) if the number of qualifying shares in the holding immediately before the previous disposal was less than the total number of shares disposed of and excluded shares (broadly, shares which can never be qualifying shares: see 40.7 below) were in the holding at that time, then the excluded shares are also treated as having been disposed of, up to a maximum of the total number of shares in the disposal less those treated as having been disposed of in (a) above; and

(c) if the total number of shares treated as having been disposed of under (a) and (b) above is less than the total number of shares disposed of, so many of the potentially qualifying shares in the holding (i.e. shares which would be qualifying shares if they had been held by the qualifying person for sufficient time: see 40.7 below) as make up the difference are treated as having been disposed of (on a last in first out basis).

No claim made in respect of previous disposal

Where no claim to investors' relief was made in respect of the previous disposal, the identification order is altered so that:

(i) all of the excluded shares in the holding immediately before the previous disposal are treated as having been disposed of or, if less, so many of the excluded shares as equals the total number of shares disposed of;

(ii) if the number of excluded shares in the holding immediately before the previous disposal was less than the total number of shares disposed of and potentially qualifying shares were in the holding at that time, then the potentially qualifying shares are also treated as having been disposed of (on a last in first out basis), up to a maximum of the total number of shares in the disposal less those treated as having been disposed of in (i) above; and

(iii) if the total number of shares treated as having been disposed of under (i) and (ii) above is less than the total number of shares disposed of, so many of the qualifying shares in the holding as make up the difference are treated as having been disposed of.

[*TCGA 1992, ss 169VE–169VG; FA 2016, Sch 14 para 2*].

Lifetime limit on investors' relief

[40.5] Investors' relief is subject to a lifetime limit of £10 million, which applies as follows.

The amount to which relief would otherwise apply in respect of a disposal is added to any amounts to which relief applied in respect of earlier disposals. Where the total exceeds the limit, only so much (if any) of the amount to which relief would otherwise apply in respect of the current disposal as, together with the earlier amounts, does not exceed the limit qualifies for the 10% rate. Any part of the gain excluded by the application of this rule is chargeable at the normal rates of CGT.

The earlier disposals to be taken into account are:

(a) where the current disposal is made by an individual, earlier disposals made by him and earlier disposals by trustees in respect of which he is an eligible beneficiary; and

(b) where the current disposal is by trustees and an individual is an eligible beneficiary, earlier disposals by the trustees in respect of which that individual is an eligible beneficiary and earlier disposals made by that individual.

Where, in relation to an earlier disposal by trustees, there is more than one person with an interest in possession in the settled property, only the individual's share of the gain (see **40.3** above) is taken into account in (a) or (b) above.

[*TCGA 1992, ss 169VK, 169VL; FA 2016, Sch 14 para 2*].

Example 1

In May 2019, Sara sells her entire holding of shares in Watkins Ltd, an unlisted trading company, for £900,000. Sara subscribed for the shares in April 2016 for £200,000. She claims investors' relief in respect of the disposal. She has made no previous claim to the relief and makes no other disposals in 2019/20.

Sara's capital gains tax liability for 2019/20 is calculated as follows.

	£
Sale consideration	900,000
Less cost of shares	200,000
Chargeable gain	700,000
Annual exemption (assumed)	12,000
Gain chargeable to tax	£688,000
Capital gains tax payable (£688,000 × 10%)	£68,800

Example 2

In August 2020 Ms Moorer sells her entire shareholding in Alison Ltd, realising a gain of £10,050,000, which qualifies for investors' relief. Ms Moorer makes no other disposals in 2020/21 and has made no previous disposals qualifying for investors' relief. She is an additional rate income tax payer for 2020/21.

Ms Moorer's capital gains tax liability for 2020/21 is calculated as follows.

	£
Chargeable gain	10,050,000
Annual exemption (assumed)	12,000
Gain chargeable to tax	£10,038,000
Capital gains tax payable	
£10,000,000 × 10%	1,000,000
£38,000 × 20%	7,600
	£1,007,600

Note to the example

(a) The annual exemption of £12,000 is allocated against the part of the gain chargeable to tax at 20% as this gives the greater tax saving.

Claims for relief

[40.6] Investors' relief must be claimed on or before the first anniversary of the 31 January following the tax year in which the disposal is made. In the case of a disposal by trustees, the claim must be made jointly by the trustees and the eligible beneficiary or beneficiaries. [*TCGA 1992, s 169VM; FA 2016, Sch 14 para 2*].

Shares qualifying for investors' relief

[40.7] A share which is in a holding of shares is a '*qualifying share*' immediately before a disposal of all or part of the holding if:

(a) it was subscribed for (solely or jointly) by the individual or trustees making the disposal (the '*investor*');
(b) it was issued to the investor for consideration wholly in cash;
(c) it was fully paid up at the time it was issued;
(d) it was subscribed for, and issued, for genuine commercial reasons and not as part of 'arrangements' with a main purpose of securing a 'tax advantage' to any person;
(e) it was subscribed for, and issued, by way of a bargain at arm's length;
(f) the investor has held it continuously for the period beginning with its issue and ending with the disposal;
(g) it was issued on or after 17 March 2016;
(h) at the time it was issued, none of the shares or securities of the company were listed on a recognised stock exchange (see **63.30** SHARES AND SECURITIES);
(i) it was an 'ordinary share' when issued and immediately before the disposal;
(j) the company was a 'trading company' or the 'holding company of a trading group' when the share was issued and has been so throughout the share-holding period;
(k) neither the investor nor a connected person has been a 'relevant employee' (see below) in relation to the company at any time in the share-holding period; and
(l) the period beginning with the date the share was issued and ending with the date of disposal is at least three years, or, where the share was issued before 6 April 2016, at least three years plus the period beginning with the date of issue and ending on 5 April 2016.

A share is a '*potentially qualifying share*' if conditions (a) to (k) above are met but condition (l) above is not yet completed.

A share is an '*excluded share*' if it is neither a qualifying share nor a potentially qualifying share.

Where an individual (A) who has subscribed for shares transfers them to another individual (B) who is then living together with A as A's spouse or civil partner, B is treated as having subscribed for the shares and A's period of ownership is added to, and treated as part of, B's period of ownership.

In (d) above, '*arrangements*' and '*tax advantage*' have the same meaning as at **44.7** LOSSES.

In (i) above, '*ordinary shares*' means any shares forming part of the company's ordinary share capital within *ITA 2007, s 989*. In (j) above, '*trading company*' and '*holding company of a trading group*' have the same meaning as at **36.3** HOLD-OVER RELIEFS. A company is not, however, treated as ceasing to be a trading company or the holding company of a trading group only because of anything done as a result of the company or a subsidiary being in administration or receivership or of a resolution or order for winding-up. The entry into administration or receivership or the resolution or order and everything done as a result must be for genuine commercial reasons and not part of a scheme or arrangement a main purpose of which is tax avoidance.

In (k) above (and for the purposes of **40.3** above), a person who has at any time in the 'relevant period' been an officer or employee of the issuing company or a connected company is at that time a '*relevant employee*' in respect of the issuing company. An unremunerated director of the issuing company or a connected company is not, however, a relevant employee if neither he nor any person connected with him was connected with the issuing company or involved in carrying on any part of the trade, business or profession of the issuing company or a connected company at any time before the relevant period. A person who becomes an employee of the issuing company or a connected company within the relevant period, but not within its first 180 days, is not a relevant employee if there was, at the start of the relevant period, no 'reasonable prospect' of him becoming an employee within the relevant period and he is not a director at any time in that period. The '*relevant period*' for the purposes of (k) above is the share-holding period; for the purposes of **40.3** above it is the three-year period mentioned there. A company is a connected company if it is at any time in the relevant period connected with the issuing company There is a '*reasonable prospect*' of something if it is more likely than not.

An '*unremunerated director*' is a director who does not receive in the relevant period any 'disqualifying payment' from the issuing company or a 'related person' and who is not entitled to receive any such payment for that period or any part of it. A '*disqualifying payment*' is any payment other than:

- payment or reimbursement of travelling or other expenses wholly, exclusively and necessarily incurred in the performance of the director's duties;
- interest representing no more than a reasonable commercial return on money lent to the issuing company or a related person;
- a dividend or other distribution representing no more than a normal return on investment;
- a payment for the supply of goods not exceeding market value;
- payment of rent for any property occupied by the issuing company or a related person not exceeding a reasonable and commercial rent; or
- any necessary and reasonable remuneration for 'qualifying services' provided to the issuing company or a related person in the course of a trade or profession carried on wholly or partly in the UK which are taken into account in calculating the taxable profits of that trade or profession.

A '*related person*' is a connected company of which the person concerned is a director or any person connected with such a company or with the issuing company. '*Qualifying services*' are services which are not secretarial or managerial services or services of a kind provided by the person to whom they are provided.

[*TCGA 1992, ss 169VH, 169VU-169VY; FA 2016, Sch 14 para* 2].

Disqualification of shares where value received

[40.8] Shares which would otherwise be qualifying shares or potentially qualifying shares for the purposes of investors' relief are disqualified from relief and treated as excluded shares if the investor receives any value, other than 'insignificant value', from the company at any time in the '*period of restriction*', i.e. the period beginning one year before, and ending immediately before the third anniversary of, the date on which the shares were issued.

The provisions apply equally to value received from a person who is connected with the company at any time in the period of restriction and to value received by an '*associate*' (defined as in *CTA 2010, s 448*, but excluding a brother or sister) of the investor. References below to a payment or disposal to an investor include a payment or disposal to the person indirectly or to his order or for his benefit.

An investor '*receives value*' from the company if it:

(a) repays, redeems or repurchases any of its share capital or securities which are held by the investor, or makes any payment to him for giving up any right to any of the company's share capital or securities on its cancellation or extinguishment; or
(b) repays, in pursuance of any 'arrangements' for or in connection with the acquisition of the shares, any debt owed to him other than one incurred by the company on or after the date of issue of the shares and otherwise than in consideration of the extinguishment of a debt incurred before that date; or
(c) makes any payment to the investor for giving up his right to any debt on its extinguishment; or
(d) releases or waives any liability of the investor to the company (which it is deemed to have done if discharge of the liability is twelve months or more overdue) or discharges or undertakes to discharge any liability of his to a third person; or
(e) makes a loan or advance to him (defined as including any debt, other than an 'ordinary trade debt', either to the company or to a third person but assigned to the company) which has not been repaid in full before the issue of the shares; or
(f) provides a benefit or facility for him; or
(g) disposes of an asset to him for no consideration or for consideration less than market value; or
(h) acquires an asset from him for consideration exceeding market value; or
(i) makes any other payment to him other than a 'qualifying payment'.

Additionally, the investor '*receives value*' from the company if any person connected with the company purchases any shares or securities of the company from him, or pays him for giving up any right in relation to such shares or securities.

A debt or liability is not taken into account for these purposes if it would be discharged by the company making a qualifying payment. Similarly, any benefit or facility is excluded if, had a payment of equal value to the benefit or facility been made, that payment would have been a qualifying payment. A '*qualifying payment*' means:

- (i) payment by any company of reasonable remuneration for services as an officer or employee;
- (ii) payment or reimbursement by any company of travelling or other expenses wholly, exclusively and necessarily incurred by the investor to whom the payment is made in the performance of duties as an officer or employee;
- (iii) payment by any company of interest representing a reasonable commercial return on money lent to it;
- (iv) payment by any company of a dividend or other distribution not exceeding a normal return on any investment in its shares or securities;
- (v) payment for the supply of goods of not more than market value;
- (vi) payment for the acquisition of an asset not exceeding its market value;
- (vii) payment of rent by any company for a property occupied by it of no more than a reasonable and commercial amount;
- (viii) reasonable and necessary remuneration paid to any company for services rendered to it in the course of a trade or profession carried on wholly or partly in the UK and taken into account in calculating the taxable profits of the trade of profession; or
- (ix) payment to discharge an ordinary trade debt.

An '*ordinary trade debt*' means a debt for goods or services suppled in the ordinary course of a trade or business on normal credit terms of no more than six months.

The amount of value received by the investor is:

- where any of (a)–(c) above applies, the greater of the amount received by the investor and the market value of the share capital, securities or debt;
- where (d) above applies, the amount of the liability;
- where (e) above applies, the amount of the loan or advance not repaid before the shares are issued;
- where (f) above applies, the cost of providing the benefit or facility less any consideration given by the investor;
- where (g) or (h) above applies, the difference between market value and any consideration given;
- where (i) above applies, the amount of the payment;
- where a payment is made for purchase of, or for giving up rights in relation to, the company's shares or securities, the greater of the amount received by the investor and the market value of the shares or securities.

Insignificant value

An amount of '*insignificant value*' is an amount of value which does not exceed £1,000. If, at any time in the period beginning one year before the date of issue of the shares and ending with the date of issue, there are in existence arrangements (as broadly defined) providing for the investor (or an associate) to receive, or become entitled to receive, any value from the issuing company (or a connected person) at any time in the period of restriction, no amount of value received by the investor or associate is treated as an amount of insignificant value. References to an associate or person connected with the company include anyone who has such status at *any* time in the period of restriction.

There are provisions to aggregate a receipt of value, whether insignificant or not, with amounts of insignificant value received previously, and treating that aggregate, if it is not itself an amount of insignificant value, as an amount of value received at the time of the latest actual receipt.

Replacement value

The 'value received' provisions above (other than where (b) above applies) are disapplied if the person from whom the value was received (the '*original supplier*') receives, by way of a 'qualifying receipt', and whether before or after the original receipt of value, at least equivalent replacement value from the original recipient. A receipt is a '*qualifying receipt*' if it arises by reason of:

(A) any one, or any combination of, the following:
  - (i) a payment by the original recipient to the original supplier other than a payment within (1) to (6) below or a payment covered by (C) below;
  - (ii) the acquisition of an asset by the original recipient from the original supplier for consideration exceeding market value;
  - (iii) the disposal of an asset by the original recipient to the original supplier for no consideration or for consideration less than market value; or

(B) (where the original receipt of value falls within (d) above) an event having the effect of reversing the original event; or

(C) (where the original receipt of value arose from the purchase from the individual by a person connected with the company of shares or securities of the company or from a payment for giving up any right in relation to them) the repurchase by the original recipient of the shares or securities in question, or reacquisition of the right in question, for consideration not less than the original value.

The amount of replacement value is:

- in a case within (A) above, the amount of any such payment plus the difference between the market value of any such asset and the consideration received;
- in a case within (B) above, the same as the amount of the original value; and
- in a case within (C) above, the consideration received by the original supplier.

A receipt of replacement value is disregarded if it occurs before the start of the period of restriction or, if it is received after the original value, it is not received as soon after the original value was received as is reasonably practicable in the circumstances.

A receipt of replacement value is also disregarded if it has previously been set against a receipt of value to prevent any shares being treated as excluded shares.

The following payments are excluded from (A)(i) above:

(1) a reasonable (in relation to their market value) payment for any goods, services or facilities provided (in the course of trade or otherwise) by the original supplier;
(2) a payment of interest at no more than a reasonable commercial rate on money lent to the original recipient;
(3) a payment not exceeding a reasonable and commercial rent for property occupied by the original recipient;
(4) a payment not exceeding market value for the acquisition of an asset;
(5) a payment in discharge of an ordinary trade debt;
(6) a payment for any shares or securities in any company in circumstances not within (A)(ii) above.

Each reference in (1)–(3) above to the original supplier or recipient includes a reference to any person who at any time in the period of restriction is an associate of his or, in the case of the supplier, is connected with him.

[*TCGA 1992, Sch 7ZB; FA 2016, Sch 14 para 3*].

Reorganisations

[40.9] The following rules apply to determine the qualifying status for the purposes of investors' relief of shares held following a reorganisation within *TCGA 1992, s 126* (see **63.2** SHARES AND SECURITIES), exchange of shares or scheme of reconstruction.

For these purposes, a '*new holding*' means a holding that is the new holding for the purposes of the reorganisation provisions (see **63.2** SHARES AND SECURITIES) or, where that new holding consists of two or more actual holdings, any of those actual holdings. '*Original shares*' means the shares held by the qualifying person immediately before the reorganisation that were original shares (as in **63.2** SHARES AND SECURITIES) in relation to the reorganisation. '*Consideration*' has the same meaning as 'additional consideration' in **63.2** SHARES AND SECURITIES.

Reorganisation where no consideration given

Where a qualifying person disposes of shares which form all or part of a new holding following a reorganisation and that person did not give or become liable to give any consideration for any part of a new holding, the following assumption is made.

If a number of the original shares were subscribed for by the qualifying person, were issued on a particular date and were held continuously for a period ending immediately before the reorganisation, an appropriate number of shares in the new holding are treated as having been subscribed for and as having been issued on, and held continuously from, the same date as those original shares. The number of shares so treated is found by multiplying the total number of shares in the new holding immediately after the reorganisation by the number of original shares so subscribed for, issued and held divided by the total number of original shares.

The provisions in **40.4** above apply, where needed, to determine which shares are included in a holding immediately before a reorganisation.

[*TCGA 1992, ss 169VN, 169VO; FA 2016, Sch 14 para* 2].

Reorganisation where consideration given

The following applies where a qualifying person disposes of shares which form all or part of a new holding following a reorganisation and that person gave or became liable to give consideration for shares issued to him on the reorganisation and which, immediately after the reorganisation, were in a new holding. In determining the qualifying status of shares in that new holding, the date of issue of the shares issued for consideration is taken to be their actual date of issue (and not the date of issue of any of the original shares). In determining the qualifying status of any shares forming any part of the new holding for which consideration was not given, the same assumption is made as above for reorganisations where no consideration was given but by reference only to that part of the new holding. That assumption is also made for any other new holding for which the qualifying person did not give or become liable to give consideration.

[*TCGA 1992, s 169VP; FA 2016, Sch 14 para* 2].

Exchange of shares

Where *TCGA 1992, s 135* (see **63.5** SHARES AND SECURITIES) applies to an issue of shares in a company (company B) in exchange for shares in another company (company A), the reorganisation provisions above apply as if companies A and B were the same company and the exchange were a reorganisation of that company's share capital. [*TCGA 1992, s 169VQ; FA 2016, Sch 14 para* 2].

Scheme of reconstruction

Where *TCGA 1992, s 136* (see **63.7** SHARES AND SECURITIES) applies to an arrangement between a company (company A) and its shareholders (or a class of them) under which another company (company B) issues shares to those shareholders in exchange for shares in another company (company A) and the shareholders are treated as exchanging company A shares for the shares held by them as a result of the arrangement, the reorganisation provisions above apply as if companies A and B were the same company and the exchange were a reorganisation of that company's share capital. [*TCGA 1992, s 169VR; FA 2016, Sch 14 para* 2].

Conditions for being a qualifying share

On the disposal of a share which is in a new holding following an exchange of shares or deemed exchange under a scheme of reconstruction, the conditions at **40.7**(j) and (k) above are met if, and only if:

- they are met by the original share for the period beginning with the issue of the original share and ending with the exchange; and
- they are met by a share representing the original share for the period beginning with the exchange and ending with the disposal.

Where there has been more than one exchange before the disposal, this rule applies to each stage of the sequence and must be met (with the necessary modifications) in respect of all of them.

[*TCGA 1992, s 169VS; FA 2016, Sch 14 para 2*].

Election to disapply reorganisation provisions

[40.10] Where a reorganisation within *TCGA 1992, s 126* (see **63.2** SHARES AND SECURITIES) or an exchange of shares treated as such a reorganisation by *TCGA 1992, s 135* or *s 136* (see **63.5**, **63.7** SHARES AND SECURITIES) takes place and *TCGA 1992, s 127* would otherwise apply to treat the 'original shares' and the 'new holding' as the same asset (see **63.2** SHARES AND SECURITIES, an election can be made to disapply that section so that a claim for investors' relief can be claimed in respect of the disposal of the original shares. (Note that the disapplication of *s 127* takes effect only where a claim to investors' relief is made; without such a claim the election has no effect.)

An election must be made on or before the first anniversary of the 31 January following the tax year in which the reorganisation etc. takes place. Where the disposal arising from the reorganisation etc. is by trustees, the election must be made jointly by the trustees and the eligible beneficiary or beneficiaries.

Such an election may be beneficial where the original shares qualify for investors relief but the shares in the new holding following the reorganisation do not.

[*TCGA 1992, s 169VT; FA 2016, Sch 14 para 2*].

41

Land

Introduction	41.1
Interaction with tax on income	41.2
Isolated or speculative transactions	41.3
Transactions in land before 5 July 2016	41.4
Exemptions	41.5
Transactions in UK land on or after 5 July 2016	41.6
Land sold with right of reconveyance	41.7
Part disposals	41.8
Small part disposals	41.9
Compulsory purchase	41.10
Small part disposals	41.11
Rollover relief	41.12
Rollover relief for exchange of joint interests in land	41.13
Leases	41.14
Leases as wasting assets	41.15
Premiums for leases	41.16
Premiums taxed as receipts of property business	41.17
Sub-leases granted out of short leases	41.18
Allowances to payer for premiums paid	41.19
Restriction of allowable expenditure of payer of premium	41.20
Anti-avoidance provisions	41.21
New lease of land after assignment or surrender — proportion of capital sum received to be taxed as income in certain circumstances	41.22
Value shifting — adjustment of leasehold rights	41.23
Contingent liabilities	41.24
Non-resident CGT disposals of UK residential property	41.25
Liability to non-resident capital gains tax	41.26
Persons not chargeable	41.27
Meaning of disposal of UK residential property interest	41.29
Computation of gains and losses — main rules	41.30
Computation of gains and losses involving high value disposals of dwellings	41.31
Computation of gains and losses — further provisions	41.32
NRCGT groups	41.33
Key points	41.34

Cross-references. See **7.7** ASSETS for granting of options and **7.9** re milk quota; **8.6** ASSETS HELD ON 6 APRIL **1965** for land reflecting development value and **8.7–8.12** for other land held at that date; **10.2** CAPITAL SUMS DERIVED FROM ASSETS for treatment of statutory compensation received by tenants of land and **10.4** for buildings destroyed and replaced out of compensation; **16.12**(k) COMPUTATION OF GAINS AND LOSSES for the deduction as enhancement expenditure of betterment levy; **25.19** EXEMPTIONS AND RELIEFS for certain agricultural grants;

25.40 for woodlands, **25.53** for housing associations, **25.62** for self-build societies and **25.85** for disposal by gift of national heritage property; **44.11** LOSSES for buildings becoming of negligible value; **45.6** MARKET VALUE; **47** MINERAL ROYALTIES; **51.5** PAYMENT OF TAX for payment by instalments on gifts of land; **53** PRIVATE RESIDENCES with land attached; **59** ROLLOVER RELIEF — REPLACEMENT OF BUSINESS ASSETS for a claim on disposal of land occupied for trade purposes.

Simon's Taxes. See **C2.11**, **C2.12**.

Introduction

[41.1] The general principles of tax on chargeable gains apply to disposals of land, but there are also a number of special provisions in the legislation relating to land.

In the first instance it is necessary to determine whether a gain on an isolated transaction in land may be taxable as income rather than as a chargeable gain, either under general principles or under specific legislation. Even if a gain is not itself chargeable to tax as income, in certain circumstances, part of the consideration may be so chargeable as income and excluded from the consideration. For the interaction with tax on income generally see **41.2–41.7** below and see **41.17** and **41.22** below for such interaction in relation to leases.

Special provisions apply where a disposal of land is a part disposal. HMRC will accept an alternative basis for apportioning allowable expenditure and, where the part disposed of is small, the taxpayer can claim for the transfer not to be treated as a disposal and for the consideration to be deducted from the allowable expenditure. See **41.8**, **41.9** below.

A similar relief is available where a small part disposal occurs as a result of a compulsory purchase. For compulsory purchases generally, rollover relief can be claimed where the proceeds are reinvested in new land. See **41.10–41.12** below. Rollover relief can also be claimed on the exchange of joint interests in land (see **41.13** below).

There are a number of special provisions relating to leases of land, see **41.14–41.23** below. For contingent liabilities on the disposal of land, see **41.24** below.

This chapter also describes the CGT charge on disposals of UK residential property interest by non-residents — see **41.25** below.

Meaning of 'land'

The definition of 'land' for the purposes of *TCGA 1992* is not exclusive and may lead to difficulties of interpretation, especially where property derives its existence from the existence of the physical land. '*Land*' includes for such purposes, except where the context otherwise requires, messuages, tenements and hereditaments, houses and buildings of any tenure. [*TCGA 1992, s 288(1)*]. This is the original 1851 definition and should be compared with the current *Interpretation Act 1978* definition which is that '*land*' includes buildings and other structures, land covered with water, and any estate, interest, easement, servitude or right in or over land. That said, many provisions in *TCGA 1992* refer to 'land' as including any interest in or right over land or to an interest in an asset which can include land or buildings etc. (e.g. *TCGA 1992, s 152* (ROLLOVER RELIEF (**59**), although *TCGA 1992, s 155* treats buildings and the underlying land as separate) and *TCGA 1992, s 247* (**41.12** below)). Deciding whether property is an interest or right over land can thus depend on general legal principles and the surrounding facts. Milk quota does not constitute such an interest or right (see **7.9** ASSETS).

Interaction with tax on income

[41.2] In the first instance it is necessary to determine whether a gain on an isolated transaction in land may be taxable as income rather than as a chargeable gain. The following considerations are relevant.

(a) An isolated or speculative transaction may be liable to income tax rather than to capital gains tax as amounting to an adventure or concern in the nature of trade (see **41.3** below).
(b) Even where (a) above does not apply, capital gains from certain transactions in land may be treated as income (see **41.4** and **41.7** below).

Isolated or speculative transactions

[41.3] A line is drawn between realisations of property held as investment or as a residence and transactions amounting to an adventure or concern in the nature of a trade. Whether the surplus on the purchase and resale of land, otherwise than in the course of an established commercial enterprise, is derived from an adventure or concern in the nature of trade depends upon the facts.

Paragraph 116 of the Final Report of the Royal Commission on the Taxation of Profits and Income (1955 HMSO Cmd. 9474) lists six 'badges of trade':

(a) The subject matter of the realisation.
(b) The length of period of ownership.
(c) The frequency or number of similar transactions.
(d) Supplementary work on assets sold.
(e) Reason for the sale.
(f) Motive.

Other relevant factors may be the degree of organisation, whether the taxpayer is or has been associated with a recognised business dealing in similar assets and how the purchases were financed.

In *Leeming v Jones* HL 1930, 15 TC 333 an income tax assessment on the acquisitions and disposal of options over rubber estates was confirmed by Commissioners. The Crown had defended the assessment under both Schedule D, Case I and Case VI. In a Supplementary Case the Commissioners found there had been no concern in the nature of trade. The Court held there was no liability. Per Lawrence LJ 'in the case of an isolated transaction . . . there is really no middle course open. It is either an adventure in the nature of trade, or else it is simply a case of sale and resale of property.' See also *Pearn v Miller* KB 1927, 11 TC 610 and *Williams v Davies* below.

Property transactions by companies

Such transactions were held to be trading in *Californian Copper Syndicate v Harris CES 1904, 5 TC 159* (purchase of copper bearing land shortly afterwards resold); *Thew v South West Africa* Co CA 1924, 9 TC 141 (numerous sales of land acquired by concession for exploitation); *Cayzer, Irvine & Co v CIR* CS 1942, 24 TC 491 (exploitation of landed estate acquired by shipping company); *Emro Investments v Aller* and *Webb (Lance) Estates v Aller* Ch D 1954, 35 TC 305 (profits carried to capital reserve on numerous purchases and sales); *Orchard Parks v Pogson* Ch D 1964, 42 TC 442 (land compulsorily purchased after development plan dropped); *Parkstone Estates v Blair* Ch D 1966, 43 TC 246 (industrial estate developed — land disposed of by sub-leases for premiums); *Eames v Stepnell Properties Ltd* CA 1966, 43 TC 678 (sale of land acquired from associated company while resale being negotiated). See also *Bath & West Counties Property Trust Ltd v Thomas* Ch D 1977, 52 TC 20.

Realisations were held to be capital in *Hudson's Bay Co v Stevens* CA 1909, 5 TC 424 (numerous sales of land acquired under Royal Charter — contrast *South West Africa Co* above); *Tebrau (Johore) Rubber Syndicate v Farmer* CES 1910, 5 TC 658 (purchase and resale of rubber estates—contrast *Californian Copper* above); *Mamor Sendirian Berhad v Director-General of Inland Revenue* PC, [1985] STC 801 (sales of timber in the course of developing forest land into an oil palm plantation).

See also *Lim Foo Yong Sendirian Berhad v Comptroller-General of Inland Revenue* PC, [1986] STC 255 where it was held that a company may hold property on both trading and capital account and the fact that acquisitions and disposals have taken place on the former does not automatically determine for all time the company's intention in acquiring, holding and developing other property; and contrast *Richfield International Land and Investment Co Ltd v Inland Revenue Commissioner* PC, [1989] STC 820 where an initial finding that a property sale had been on trading account was upheld, such finding only being inferred from previous property sales which had either been taxed or accounted for as trading transactions.

In *Rand v Alberni Land Co Ltd* KB 1920, 7 TC 629 sales of land held in trust were held not to be trading but contrast *Alabama Coal etc. Co Ltd v Mylam* KB 1926, 11 TC 232; *Balgownie Land Trust v CIR* CS 1929, 14 TC 684; *St Aubyn Estates v Strick* KB 1932, 17 TC 412; *Tempest Estates Ltd v Walmsley* Ch D 1975, 51 TC 305.

Sales of property after a period of letting were held to be realisations of investments or not trading in *CIR v Hyndland Investment Co Ltd* CS 1929, 14 TC 694; *Glasgow Heritable Trust v CIR* CS 1954, 35 TC 196; *Lucy & Sunderland Ltd v Hunt* Ch D 1961, 40 TC 132 but were held to be trading in *Rellim Ltd v Vise* CA 1951, 32 TC 254 (notwithstanding that the company was previously admitted as an investment company); *CIR v Toll Property Co* CS 1952, 34 TC 13; *Forest Side Properties (Chingford) v Pearce* CA 1961, 39 TC 665. But sales by the liquidator of property owned by companies following the abandonment of a plan for their public flotation were held to be not trading in *Simmons v CIR* HL 1980, 53 TC 461 (reversing Commissioners' decision). In *Rosemoor Investments v Inspector of Taxes* (Sp C 320), [2002] SSCD 325, it was not open to the Commissioners to recharacterise as trading a complex transaction routed via an investment company subsidiary and structured to produce capital.

Property transactions by individuals and partnerships

Profits were held assessable as income in *Reynold's Exors v Bennett* KB 1943, 25 TC 401; *Broadbridge v Beattie* KB 1944, 26 TC 63; *Gray & Gillitt v Tiley* KB 1944, 26 TC 80; *Laver v Wilkinson* KB 1944, 26 TC 105; *Foulds v Clayton* Ch D 1953, 34 TC 382; *Kirkby v Hughes* Ch D 1992, 65 TC 532; *Lynch v Edmondson* (Sp C 164), [1998] SSCD 185 in all of which the taxpayers were or had been associated with building or estate development, and contrast *Williams v Davies* KB 1945, 26 TC 371 in which the taxpayers were closely associated with land development but a profit on transactions in undeveloped land belonging to their wives was held not assessable as income. The acquisition and resale of land for which planning permission had been or was obtained was held as trading in *Cooke v Haddock* Ch D 1960, 39 TC 64; *Turner v Last* Ch D 1965, 42 TC 517 and *Pilkington v Randall* CA 1966, 42 TC 662 (and cf. *Iswera v Ceylon Commr* PC 1965, 44 ATC 157), but contrast *Taylor v Good* CA 1974, 49 TC 277 (in which a house bought as a residence was found unsuitable and resold to a developer after obtaining planning permission) and *Kirkham v Williams* CA 1991, 64 TC 253 (in which a site was acquired principally as a capital asset to be used in the taxpayer's trade but which was later developed and sold), in both of which cases it was held that there had not been an adventure.

In *Burrell v Davis* Ch D 1948, 38 TC 307; *Johnston v Heath* Ch D 1970, 46 TC 463; *Reeves v Evans, Boyce & Northcott* Ch D 1971, 48 TC 495 and *Clark v Follett* Ch D 1973, 48 TC 677 the short period of ownership or other evidence showed an intention to purchase for resale at a profit and not for investment, and contrast *CIR v Reinhold* CS 1953, 34 TC 389, *Taylor v Good* above and *Marson v Morton* Ch D 1986, 59 TC 381. For other cases in which profits were held assessable as income see *Hudson v Wrightson* KB 1934, 26 TC 55, *MacMahon v CIR* CS 1951, 32 TC 311 and *Eckel v Board of Inland Revenue* PC 1989, 62 TC 331.

Transactions in land before 5 July 2016

[41.4] Certain gains on disposals of 'land' before 5 July 2016 are treated as income chargeable to income tax or corporation tax where:

(a) land (or any 'property deriving its value from land') is acquired with the sole or main object of realising a gain from disposing of it;
(b) land is held as trading stock; or
(c) land is developed with the sole or main object of realising a gain from disposing of it when developed.

The provisions are repealed for disposals on or after 5 July 2016 and are effectively replaced by those at **41.6** below.

Subject to the above, the provisions apply if all or any part of the land in question is in the UK and a gain of a capital nature is obtained (for himself or for 'another person') from the 'disposal' of the land or any part of it by the person acquiring, holding or developing it (or by CONNECTED PERSONS (17), or a person party to, or concerned in, any arrangement or scheme to realise the gain indirectly or by a series of transactions).

For this purpose, a gain is of a capital nature if it does not (apart from these provisions) fall to be included in any computation of income for tax purposes. Any number of transactions may be treated as a single arrangement or scheme if they have, or there is evidence of, a common purpose. '*Another person*' may include a partnership or partners in a partnership, the trustees of settled property and personal representatives and for this purpose these are regarded as persons distinct from the individuals or persons who are for the time being partners, trustees or personal representatives.

The gain from the disposal is, subject as below, treated for all tax purposes as income of the person realising the gain (or the person who transmitted to him, directly or indirectly, the opportunity of making that gain) assessable to income tax or to corporation tax on income for the chargeable period in which the gain is realised. See *Yuill v Wilson* HL 1980, 52 TC 674 and its sequel *Yuill v Fletcher* CA 1984, 58 TC 145, *Winterton v Edwards* Ch D 1979, 52 TC 655 and *Sugarwhite v Budd* CA 1988, 60 TC 679. Genuine commercial transactions, not entered into with tax avoidance in view, may be caught by the legislation. See *Page v Lowther and Another* CA 1983, 57 TC 199.

An amount treated as arising under these provisions to a non-UK resident is treated as being from a source in the UK only to the extent that the land to which the disposal relates is in the UK.

The above provisions apply subject to *ITTOIA 2005, Pt 5 Ch 5* (amounts treated as income of settlor) and to any other provision treating income as belonging to a particular person.

'*Land*' is as defined in *Interpretation Act 1978, Sch 1*. '*Property deriving its value from land*' includes any shareholding in a company, partnership interest, or interest in settled property, deriving its value, directly or indirectly, from land, and any option, consent or embargo affecting the disposition of land. But see 'Exemptions' below. Land is '*disposed of*' for the above purposes if, by any one or more transactions or by any arrangement or scheme (whether concerning the land or any property deriving its value therefrom), the property in, or control over, the land is effectively disposed of. For the date of disposal where instalments are involved see *Yuill v Fletcher* above. See also under 'General' below.

Exemptions

[41.5] The following provisions are repealed for disposals on or after 5 July 2016 and are effectively replaced by those at **41.6** below. Subject to this, exemptions from the provisions at **41.4** above are as follows:

(i) An individual's gain made from the sale, etc., of his residence exempted from capital gains tax under *TCGA 1992, ss 222–226* or which would be so exempt but for *TCGA 1992, s 224(3)* (acquired for purpose of making a gain, see **53.13** PRIVATE RESIDENCES).

(ii) A gain on the sale of shares in a company holding land as trading stock (or a company owning, directly or indirectly, 90% of the ordinary share capital of such a company) *provided that* the company disposes of the land by normal trade and makes all possible profit from it, and the share sale is not part of an arrangement or scheme to realise a land gain indirectly. This does not apply if the person obtaining the gain is only a party to, or concerned in, an arrangement or scheme to realise the gain indirectly or by a series of transactions. See *Chilcott v CIR* Ch D 1981, 55 TC 446.

(iii) If the liability arises solely under **41.4**(c) above, any part of the gain fairly attributable to a period before the intention was formed to develop the land.

Computation of gains

Gains are to be computed 'as is just and reasonable in the circumstances', taking into account the value of what is obtained for disposing of the land and allowing only for expenses attributable to the land disposed of. The following may be taken into account:

(A) if a leasehold interest is disposed of out of a freehold, the way in which the taxable trading profits of a person dealing in land are computed;

(B) any adjustment under *CTA 2009, s 136* or *ITTOIA 2005, s 158* for the amount of any lease premium treated as a receipt of a property business (see Tolley's Income Tax).

Any necessary apportionments of consideration, expenses etc. are to be made on a just and reasonable basis.

Where the computation of a gain in respect of the development of land (as under **41.4**(c) above) is made on the footing that the land or property was appropriated as trading stock, that land, etc., is also to be treated for chargeable gains purposes (under *TCGA 1992, s 161*; see **16.9** COMPUTATION OF GAINS AND LOSSES) as having been transferred to stock.

Trustees

Income treated as above as arising to trustees of a settlement is treated as being income chargeable at the trust rate of income tax.

Recovery of tax

Where tax under the above provisions is assessed on, and paid by, a person other than the one who actually realised the gain, the person paying the tax may recover it from the other party (for which purpose HMRC will, on request, supply a certificate of income in respect of which tax has been paid).

Clearance

The person who made or would make the gain may (if he considers that **41.4**(a) or (c) above may apply), submit to HMRC particulars of any completed or proposed transactions. If he does so, HMRC must, within 30 days of receiving those particulars, notify the taxpayer whether or not they are satisfied that liability under above does not arise. If HMRC are so satisfied no assessment can thereafter be made on that gain under the provisions above, provided that all material facts and considerations have been fully and accurately disclosed.

General

There are also provisions to prevent avoidance by the use of indirect means to transfer any property or right, or enhance or diminish its value, e.g., by sales at less, or more, than full consideration, assigning share capital or rights in a company or partnership or an interest in settled property, disposal on the winding-up of any company, partnership or trust etc. For ascertaining whether, and to what extent, the value of any property or right is derived from any other property or right, value may be traced through any number of companies, partnerships and trusts, at each stage attributing property held by the company etc. to its shareholders etc., 'in such manner as is appropriate to the circumstances'. Where the person liable is non-resident, HMRC may direct that any part of an amount taxable under these provisions on that person be paid under deduction of income tax at the basic rate (for the tax year of payment).

For the above purposes HMRC may require, under penalty, any person to supply them with any particulars thought necessary, including particulars of:

(I) transactions or arrangements in which he acts, or acted, on behalf of others, and
(II) transactions or arrangements which in the opinion of HMRC should be investigated, and
(III) what part, if any, he has taken, or is taking, in specified transactions or arrangements. (A *solicitor* who has merely acted as professional adviser is not treated as having taken part in a transaction or arrangement.)

A solicitor who has merely acted as professional adviser is not compelled to do more than state that he acted and give his client's name and address.

The transactions of which particulars are required need not be identified transactions (*Essex v CIR* CA 1980, 53 TC 720).

[*ITA 2007, ss 752–772; CTA 2010, ss 815–833, Sch 1 paras 240, 547; ICTA 1988, ss 776–778; TCGA 1992, s 161(5)(6); FA 2016, ss 77(4), 79(5), 81(1), 82(1); SI 2009 No 2859, Arts 2, 4*].

Transactions in UK land on or after 5 July 2016

[41.6] Measures introduced by *FA 2016* seek to ensure that the tax is charged on the full amount of profits from dealing in or developing land in the UK, regardless of whether the company is resident or non-resident in the UK. They generally have effect in relation to disposals on or after **5 July 2016**. In order to prevent forestalling, there is a targeted anti-avoidance rule that applies in relation to disposals on or after 16 March 2016, the day the measures were announced.

The provisions override the general territorial rule for trading income whereby the charge on profits arising to a non-UK resident individual or company normally depends on the extent to which the trade is carried on in the UK.

The provisions introduce specific income tax and corporation tax charges on profits from dealing in or developing UK land. The charge applies in specified circumstances to profits and gains of a capital nature arising when land is disposed of, and also to disposals of assets deriving their value from land in the UK. There is provision to ensure that the charge applies only to profits not otherwise chargeable to UK tax as income.

For the purposes of these provisions, where any property is disposed of under a contract, the time at which the disposal is made is the time the contract is made and not, if different, the time at which the property is conveyed or transferred. This effectively meant that the provisions did not have effect in relation to disposals made on or after 5 July 2016 under a pre-5 July 2016 contract. However, *F(No 2)A 2017* provides that all profits recognised in accounts drawn up (in accordance with generally accepted accounting practice) for a period of account beginning on or after 8 March 2017 are to be brought into charge regardless of when the contract was entered into. This also applies for periods of account straddling 8 March 2017, but only by reference to profits that would be so recognised if the period of account began on that date.

See Tolley's Income Tax and Tolley's Corporation Tax under Transactions in UK Land.

[*ITTOIA 2005, s 6B; ITA 2007, ss 517A–517U; CTA 2009, s 5B; CTA 2010, ss 356OA–356OT; FA 2016, ss 76(5), 77(1), 78(2), 79(1), 81(1), 82(1), 82(9); F(No 2)A 2017, s 39*].

Where a person is charged to income tax or corporation tax under the above provisions on the basis that a main purpose of developing the land was to realise a profit or gain from disposing of it once developed (i.e. where *ITA 2007, s 517B(7)* or *CTA 2010, s 356OB(7)* applies), that land is also to be treated for chargeable gains purposes (under *TCGA 1992, s 161*; see **16.9** COMPUTATION OF GAINS AND LOSSES) as having been transferred to stock. [*TCGA 1992, s 161(5)(6); FA 2016, ss 77(9), 79(10)*].

Land sold with right of reconveyance

[41.7] Where an interest in land is sold on terms requiring it to be subsequently reconveyed at a future date after the sale (or leased back one month or more after the sale) to the vendor, or a person connected with him, and the price at which the interest is sold exceeds that at which it is to be reconveyed (or, in the case of a lease-back, the value of the reversionary interest plus any premium for the lease), the excess less $^{1}/_{50}$th for each full year (minus one) between the sale and the date of the earliest possible reconveyance (or lease-back) is treated as a receipt of the vendor's property business. [*ITTOIA 2005, ss 284–286, 301, 302; CTA 2009, ss 224, 225, Sch 1 para 16; ICTA 1988, s 36; FA 2008, Sch 39 paras 17, 51, 52*].

Any amount (as adjusted under *ITTOIA 2005, ss 301, 302* or *CTA 2009, ss 238, 239*) brought into account as a receipt of a property business under these provisions is excluded from the consideration brought into account in the computation for capital gains purposes *except* in the denominator of the part disposal fraction (A/(A+B); see **16.5** COMPUTATION OF GAINS AND LOSSES). This does not apply where what is disposed of is the remainder of a lease or a sub-lease out of a lease the duration of which does not exceed 50 years. See **41.18** below for the alternative provisions which apply. [*TCGA 1992, Sch 8 paras 5(3)(4), 6(3); ITTOIA 2005, Sch 1 para 451(2); CTA 2009, Sch 1 para 388(2)(4)*].

Part disposals

[41.8] The general provisions for part disposals in *TCGA 1992, s 42* apply to disposals of land. See **16.5** COMPUTATION OF GAINS AND LOSSES. These require the use of the market value of the part retained. HMRC will, however, accept an alternative basis of calculation in the case of land.

Under this basis, the part disposed of will be treated as a separate asset and any fair and reasonable method of apportioning part of the total cost to it will be accepted — e.g. a reasonable valuation of that part at the acquisition date. Where the market value at 6 April 1965 is to be taken as the cost, a reasonable valuation of the part at that date will similarly be accepted.

The cost of the part disposed of will be deducted from the total cost of the estate (or the balance of total cost) to determine the cost of the remainder of the estate; thus the total of the separate amounts adopted for the parts will not exceed the total cost. The cost attributed to each part must also be realistic in itself and HMRC reserve the right to apply the general rule if not satisfied that apportionments are fair and reasonable. The taxpayer can always require that the general rule should be applied (except in cases already settled on the alternative basis). If he chooses the general rule it will normally be necessary to apply this rule to all subsequent disposals out of the estate; but where the general rule has been applied for a part disposal before the introduction of the alternative basis and it produced a result broadly the same as under the alternative basis, the alternative basis may be used for subsequent part disposals out of the estate.

So long as disposals out of an estate acquired before 6 April 1965 are dealt with on the alternative basis, each part disposal will carry a separate right to elect for acquisition at market value on 6 April 1965. Similarly, where part is sold with development value, the mandatory valuation at 6 April 1965 will apply only to that part. Even where the part is to be treated as acquired at market value on 6 April 1965, however, it will still be necessary to agree how much of the actual cost should be attributed to the part disposed of: first, to ensure that any allowable loss does not exceed the actual loss, and second, to produce a balance of total cost for subsequent disposals.

Adoption of the alternative basis is without prejudice to the treatment of small disposals set out in **41.9** below (HMRC Statement of Practice D1).

For provisions which apply to land held on 6 April 1965 generally, see **8.6–8.12** ASSETS HELD ON 6 APRIL **1965**. Although HMRC have yet to confirm it, it seems the above practice could be applied to land held on 31 March 1982 with suitable modifications. See generally, **9** ASSETS HELD ON 31 MARCH **1982**.

Small part disposals

[41.9] Where there is a transfer of land forming part only of a holding of land (or an estate or interest in land) and the amount or value of the consideration does not exceed one-fifth of the market value of the holding as it existed immediately before the disposal, the transferor may claim under *TCGA 1992, s 242(2)* that the transfer is not treated as a disposal. The consideration which would have been brought into account in the capital gains tax computation is then treated as a reduction of allowable expenditure in relation to any subsequent disposal of the remaining holding.

The consideration for the transfer or, if the transfer is not for full consideration, the market value of the land transferred, must not exceed a limit of £20,000. Where the transferor has made other disposals of land in the tax year, the total amount or value of the consideration for all such disposals of land (other than those within **41.11** below) must not exceed the limit.

The provisions do not apply to:

(a) transfers treated as giving rise to neither a gain nor a loss between spouses or civil partners (see **46.5** MARRIED PERSONS AND CIVIL PARTNERS) or between companies in the same group (see **29.2** GROUPS OF COMPANIES); or
(b) an estate or interest in land which is a wasting asset (e.g. a short lease under **41.15** below).

A claim for small part disposals must be made for the purposes of capital gains tax on or before the first anniversary of 31 January following the tax year in which the transfer is made. For corporation tax purposes, the claim must be made within two years after the end of the accounting period in which the transfer is made.

Where the allowable expenditure is less than the consideration for the part disposal (or is nil) the claim referred to above cannot be made but, if the recipient elects under *TCGA 1992, s 244(2)* and there is allowable expenditure, the consideration for the part disposal is reduced by the amount of the allowable expenditure. None of that expenditure is then allowable as a deduction in computing the gain accruing on the part disposal or any subsequent disposal.

[*TCGA 1992, ss 242, 244*].

Example

C owns land which cost £134,000 in May 1988. In February 1996, a small plot of land is exchanged with an adjoining landowner for another piece of land. The value placed on the transaction is £18,000. The value of the remaining estate excluding the new piece of land is estimated at £250,000. In March 2018, C sells the whole estate for £300,000. He makes no other disposals in 2017/18. The indexation factor for May 1988 to February 1996 is 0.421.

(i) No claim made under *TCGA 1992, s 242(2)*

		£	£
(a)	Disposal in February 1996		
	Disposal proceeds		18,000
	Allowable cost		
	$\dfrac{18{,}000}{18{,}000 + 250{,}000} \times £134{,}000$		9,000
	Unindexed gain		9,000
	Indexation allowance £9,000 × 0.421		3,789
	Chargeable gain 1995/96		£5,211
(b)	Disposal in March 2018		
	Disposal proceeds		300,000
	Allowable cost		
	Original land £(134,000 – 9,000)	125,000	
	Exchanged land	18,000	143,000
	Chargeable gain 2017/18		£157,000

(ii) Claim made under *TCGA 1992, s 242(2)*

		£	£
(a)	No disposal in February 1996		
	Allowable cost of original land		134,000
	Deduct disposal proceeds		18,000
	Adjusted allowable cost		£116,000
	Allowable cost of additional land		£18,000
		£	£
(b)	Disposal in March 2018		
	Disposal proceeds		300,000
	Allowable cost		
	Original land	116,000	
	Additional land	18,000	134,000
	Chargeable gain 2017/18		£166,000

Compulsory purchase

[41.10] The transfer of an interest in land to an 'authority exercising or having compulsory powers' (see **41.11** below) is a disposal for capital gains purposes.

If the land is acquired under a contract, the date of disposal is the time the contract is made (and not, if different, the time at which the asset is conveyed or transferred). If the contract is conditional, the date of disposal is the time when the condition is satisfied. See also **16.4** COMPUTATION OF GAINS AND LOSSES.

Otherwise, the disposal and acquisition are made at the time at which compensation for the acquisition is agreed or otherwise determined (any variation on appeal against the original determination being disregarded).

[*TCGA 1992, ss 28, 246*].

Relief is available for small part disposals (see **41.11** below). Rollover relief may be claimed in certain circumstances (see **41.12** below).

In addition, where land or an interest in or right over land is acquired and the acquisition is (or could have been) made under compulsory powers, then the existence of the compulsory powers and any statutory provision treating the purchase price, compensation or other consideration as exclusively paid in respect of the land itself is disregarded in considering whether, under *TCGA 1992, s 52(4)* (just and reasonable apportionments), the purchase price etc. should be apportioned on a just and reasonable basis and treated in part as a capital sum within *TCGA 1992, s 22(1)(a)* (whether as compensation for loss of goodwill, for disturbance or otherwise) or should be apportioned in any other way. [*TCGA 1992, s 245(1)*]. The effect of this is that, where it is just and reasonable, part of the proceeds may be treated as a capital sum derived from an asset. See **10.2**(a) CAPITAL SUMS DERIVED FROM ASSETS.

The receipt of severance compensation or compensation for injurious affection where part of a holding of land is or could have been compulsorily purchased is treated as a part disposal of the remaining land. [*TCGA 1992, s 245(2)*]. Where the conditions are satisfied, a claim for rollover relief may be made (see **41.12** below) in which case the consideration rolled over will include such compensation and there will be no deemed disposal of the remaining land. [*TCGA 1992, s 247(6)*].

Example

(i) Rollover not claimed

D owns freehold land purchased for £77,000 in 1978. Part of the land is made the subject of a compulsory purchase order. The compensation of £70,000 is agreed on 10 August 2017. The market value of the remaining land is £175,000. The value of the total freehold land at 31 March 1982 was £98,000.

		£
Disposal consideration		70,000
Market value 31.3.82		
	$£98{,}000 \times \frac{70{,}000}{70{,}000 + 175{,}000}$	28,000
Chargeable gain		£42,000

(ii) **Rollover claimed under *TCGA 1992, s 247***

If, in (i), D acquires new land costing, say, £80,000 in, say, December 2017, relief may be claimed as follows.

	£
Allowable cost of land compulsorily purchased	28,000
Actual consideration	70,000
Chargeable gain rolled over	£42,000
Allowable cost of new land (£80,000 – £42,000)	£38,000

Small part disposals

[41.11] Where a part of a holding of land (or an interest therein) is transferred to an 'authority exercising or having compulsory powers', the transferor may claim under *TCGA 1992, s 243(2)* that the transfer is not treated as a disposal, in which case the consideration which would have been brought into account is treated as a reduction of allowable expenditure in relation to any subsequent disposal of the remaining holding.

A claim must be made for the purposes of capital gains tax on or before the first anniversary of 31 January following the tax year in which the transfer is made. For corporation tax purposes the claim must be made within two years after the end of the accounting period in which the transfer is made.

[*TCGA 1992, s 243(2A)*].

A holding of land for these purposes comprises only the land in respect of which allowable expenditure would be apportioned under *TCGA 1992, s 42* if the transfer had been treated as a part disposal. The consideration for the transfer (or, if the transfer is not for full consideration, the market value of the land transferred) must be 'small' as compared with the market value of the holding immediately before the transfer. For this purpose, HMRC regard 'small' as meaning 5% or less but they also regard an amount of £3,000 or less as 'small', regardless of whether or not it would pass the 5% test (HMRC Capital Gains Manual CG57836, 72201; Revenue Tax Bulletin February 1997 p 397).

The transferor must not have taken any steps, by advertising or otherwise, to dispose of any part of the holding or to make his willingness to dispose of it known to anyone. The provisions do not apply to wasting interests in land (e.g. a short lease under **41.15** below) but subject to this any estate or interest in land is included as a holding.

Where the allowable expenditure is less than the consideration for the part disposal (or is nil) the claim referred to above cannot be made but, if the recipient elects under *TCGA 1992, s 244(2)* and there is allowable expenditure, the consideration for the part disposal is reduced by the amount of the allowable expenditure. For capital gains tax purposes, an election must be made on or before the first anniversary of the 31 January next following the tax year in which part disposal is made; and for corporation tax purposes it must be made within two years after the end of the accounting period in which the part disposal is made. None of that expenditure is then allowable as a deduction in computing the gain accruing on the part disposal or any subsequent disposal.

'*Authority exercising or having compulsory powers*' means, in relation to the land transferred, a person or body of persons acquiring it compulsorily or who has or have been, or could be, authorised to acquire it compulsorily for the purposes for which it is acquired, or for whom another person or body of persons has or have been, or could be, authorised so to acquire it.

[*TCGA 1992, ss 243, 244*].

Example

(i) No rollover relief claimed

T inherited land in June 1988 at a probate value of £290,000. Under a compulsory purchase order, a part of the land is acquired for highway improvements. Compensation of £32,000 and a further £10,000 for severance, neither sum including any amount in respect of loss of profits, is agreed on 14 May 2017. The value of the remaining land is £900,000. Prior to the compulsory purchase, the value of all the land had been £950,000.

	£
Total consideration for disposal (£32,000 + £10,000)	42,000
Deduct allowable cost $\frac{42,000}{42,000 + 900,000} \times £290,000$	12,930
Chargeable gain	£29,070

(ii) Rollover relief claimed under *TCGA 1992, s 243*

Total consideration for disposal is £42,000, less than 5% of the value of the estate before the disposal (£950,000). T may therefore claim that the consideration be deducted from the allowable cost of the estate.

Revised allowable cost (£290,000 – £42,000)	£248,000

Rollover relief

[41.12] ROLLOVER RELIEF (59) can be claimed by any landowner who disposes of land to an 'authority exercising or having compulsory powers' (see **41.11** above) where the landowner reinvests part or the whole of the proceeds in acquiring new land. Relief is not confined to land (or any interest in or right over land) which is used and occupied for the purposes of a trade.

Any land which is a dwelling-house or part of one and on which the whole or part of the gain on a subsequent disposal within six years would be covered by the exemptions for PRIVATE RESIDENCES (53) is excluded. Where any land is not so excluded at the time of its acquisition, but becomes so within six years, relief is withdrawn.

The effect of a claim (under *TCGA 1992, s 247(2)*) is to defer capital gains tax by deducting the otherwise chargeable gain on the original land from the acquisition cost of the newly acquired land. Relief is restricted where part only of the proceeds is reinvested in qualifying land. See **59.8** ROLLOVER RELIEF.

The following further matters should be noted.

(a) The landowner must not have taken any steps, by advertising or otherwise, to dispose of the old land or to make his willingness to dispose of it known. In practice, any event which occurred more than three years before the date of disposal is ignored. (CCAB Statements TR 476 and 477, May and June 1982 and HMRC Capital Gains Manual CG61900, 72202).

(b) The new land must be acquired in the period beginning twelve months before and ending three years after the disposal or such longer period as HMRC may allow e.g. where it has not been practical to acquire new land within the time limit.
New town corporations and similar authorities may purchase land for development and then grant the previous owner a lease or tenancy of the land until they are ready to commence building. Where land is so acquired under a compulsory purchase order or under the threat of such an order and is immediately leased back to the previous owner HMRC are prepared, so long as there is a clear continuing intention that the sale proceeds will be used to acquire assets qualifying for rollover relief, to extend the time limit to a date three years after the land ceases to be used by him for his trade. An assurance to this effect will be given in appropriate cases subject to the reservation that it would be necessary to raise a protective assessment on the gain arising if exceptionally the lease or tenancy continued so long as to extend beyond the statutory time limit for making assessments (HMRC Statement of Practice D6). See HMRC Capital Gains Manual CG60660.

(c) Where the new land is a depreciating asset, similar provisions apply as in **59.9** ROLLOVER RELIEF except that the gain is held over for ten years or until the new asset is disposed of, whichever is the sooner. For corporation tax purposes, and, for disposals before 6 April 2008, for capital gains tax purposes, a gain previously held over is never deemed to accrue in consequence of an event occurring after 5 April 1988 if the application of this provision would be directly attributable to the disposal of an asset before 1 April 1982.

(d) The normal treatment of severance compensation as a part disposal (see **41.10** above) is expressly excluded. Such compensation is treated as additional consideration for the old land.

(e) Claims under these provisions and under *TCGA 1992, s 243* (see **41.11** above) are mutually exclusive.

(f) Subject to all other conditions for the granting of relief being met, HMRC will accept a claim from a landlord whose leasehold tenant has exercised the following statutory rights:
  - his right under the *Leasehold Reform Act 1967* or the *Leasehold Reform, Housing and Urban Development Act 1993* to acquire the freehold reversion of a property or an extension of the lease,
  - his right to buy or to acquire the freehold or an extension of the lease under the *Housing Acts 1985* to *1996* (which covers the situation where a tenant's right to buy is preserved following a transfer of housing stock into the private sector) or the right to purchase tenanted property under the *Housing (Scotland) Act 1987*, or
  - the right of a crofting community body to purchase croft land under *Land Reform (Scotland) Act 2003, Pt 3*.

  (HMRC Statement of Practice 13/93; HMRC Tax Bulletin June 2005, pp 1212, 1213).

(g) ROLLOVER RELIEF (**59**) is available where there is a compulsory purchase from one group member and acquisition of land by another.

[*TCGA 1992, ss 247, 248, Sch 4 paras A1, 4(5); FA 2008, Sch 2 paras 74(2), 76*].

Provisional claims are permitted, in much the same way as for ROLLOVER RELIEF (**59.11**).

The claimant may make a declaration in his tax return for a tax year or company accounting period in which he has made a qualifying disposal of land that the whole or a specified part of the consideration will be invested, within the requisite time limits (see (b) above), in new land (or an interest in or right over land) and that the new land is not excluded by virtue of the availability of the private residence exemption (see above). As long as the declaration continues to have effect, the same consequences ensue as if both an acquisition and a valid rollover relief claim had been made. The declaration ceases to have effect on the day, and to the extent that, it is withdrawn or is superseded by a valid claim, if either occurs before the 'relevant day'. It otherwise ceases to have effect on the relevant day itself. On its ceasing to have effect, all necessary adjustments will be made to the claimant's tax position, even if they would otherwise be out of time.

The '*relevant day*' means:

- in relation to capital gains tax, the third anniversary of 31 January following the tax year of disposal, e.g. 31 January 2011 for disposals in 2006/07; and
- in relation to corporation tax, the fourth anniversary of the last day of the accounting period of disposal.

[*TCGA 1992, s 247A*].

To the extent that a provisional claim is withdrawn or lapses, interest on unpaid tax is chargeable as if no such claim had been made.

Rollover relief for exchange of joint interests in land

[41.13] A form of rollover relief is available for certain exchanges of joint interests in land. Relief is available, where a claim is made, if:

(a) a 'holding of land' or two or more separate holdings of land are held jointly;
(b) one of the owners (the 'taxpayer') disposes of an interest in the holding or one or more of the holdings to one or more of the co-owners;
(c) the consideration for the disposal is or includes an interest in a holding of land held jointly by the taxpayer and the co-owners concerned;
(d) as a result of the exchange, the taxpayer and each of the co-owners become the sole owner of part of the holding or of one or more of the holdings; and
(e) the interest acquired by the taxpayer is not an interest in 'excluded land'.

For this purpose, '*holding of land*' includes an estate or interest in a holding of land and is to be construed in accordance with *TCGA 1992, s 243(3)* (see **41.11** above). Land is held jointly if it is held as joint tenants or tenants in common (in Scotland as joint owners or owners in common; in NI as joint tenants, tenants in common or coparceners). Land is '*excluded land*' to the extent that it is a dwelling-house (or part of, or an interest in or right over, a dwelling-house) and, under *TCGA 1992, ss 222–226* (see **53** PRIVATE RESIDENCES), the whole or part of any gain on a disposal of it within six years after the exchange would be exempt. If land is not excluded land at the time of the exchange but subsequently, and within the following six years, becomes excluded land, rollover relief is withdrawn. See below for the relief available for exchanges of interests in private residences.

Spouses or civil partners living together are treated as if they were one person for this purpose, so that an exchange of interests which results in such a couple alone becoming joint owners of land will meet the above conditions.

Where a claim for relief is made, the taxpayer is normally treated as if the disposal consideration were reduced to the amount which would secure that neither a gain nor a loss accrues and the acquisition cost of the acquired interest were reduced by the amount of the reduction in the disposal consideration. If this rule applies to exclude a gain which is not all chargeable gain (as a result of the rules for ASSETS HELD ON 6 APRIL **1965** (**8**)), the amount of the reduction in the acquisition is restricted to the amount of the otherwise chargeable gain.

If, however, the disposal consideration is greater than the market value of the interest disposed of the above relief is not available. Partial relief is, however, available if the excess of the consideration over the market value is less than the gain on the disposal (whether or not the gain is all chargeable gain). In that event, the gain is treated as reduced to the amount of the excess (and if the gain is not all chargeable gain, the chargeable part is reduced proportionately). The acquisition cost of the acquired interest is then reduced by the amount by which the chargeable gain is reduced.

Where milk quota (see **7.9 ASSETS**) is associated with both the holding disposed of and the holding acquired, the above provisions apply equally to the quota disposed of and acquired.

[*TCGA 1992, ss 248A–248D; SI 2010 No 157, Art 8*].

Private residences

A similar rollover relief applies to the exchange of joint interests in private residences. The relief applies, on the making of a joint claim, where:

(i) interests in two or more dwelling-houses are held jointly (as above);
(ii) one of the owners (the 'taxpayer') disposes of an interest in one or more of the dwelling-houses to one or more of the co-owners;
(iii) the consideration for the disposal is or includes an interest in one of the other dwelling-houses;
(iv) as a result of the exchange, the dwelling-house in which the taxpayer acquires an interest becomes his only or main residence and each of the other dwelling-houses becomes the only or main residence of one (and only one) of the co-owners; and
(v) if each dwelling-house were disposed of immediately after the exchange, then under *TCGA 1992, ss 222, 223* (see **53.2–53.10 PRIVATE RESIDENCES**) no part of each gain would be a chargeable gain.

Spouses or civil partners living together are treated as if they were one person for this purpose, so that an exchange of interests which results in such a couple alone becoming joint owners of a dwelling-house will meet the above conditions.

Where the taxpayer and the co-owners make a joint claim, the taxpayer is treated as if the disposal consideration were reduced to the amount which would secure that neither a gain nor a loss accrues. The taxpayer's acquisition is treated as made at the time of the acquisition of the joint interest and at the original base cost at that time.

[*TCGA 1992, s 248E; SI 2010 No 157, Art 8*].

Leases

[41.14] For capital gains tax purposes, a '*lease*' in relation to land includes an underlease, sub-lease or any tenancy or licence, and any agreement for a lease, underlease, sub-lease or tenancy or licence. In the case of land outside the UK, any interest corresponding to a lease as so defined is included. '*Lessor*', '*lessee*' and '*rent*' are construed accordingly. [*TCGA 1992, s 240, Sch 8 para 10(1)*].

Where a leaseholder of land acquires a superior interest in that land (whether a superior lease or the freehold reversion) so that the first lease is extinguished, the two interests are merged within the meaning of *TCGA 1992, s 43* (assets derived from other assets). On a subsequent disposal the allowable expenditure relating to the merged interest will include the cost of the first lease, after exclusion, in the case of a lease with less than 50 years to run, of the part which was wasted under *TCGA 1992, Sch 8* to the date of the acquisition of the superior interest (see **41.15** below) and the cost of the superior interest. Where the superior interest is itself a lease with less than 50 years to run, the total of these two amounts will also be wasted under *TCGA 1992, Sch 8* down to the date of disposal. Strictly, indexation allowance, where applicable, should be calculated on the total of these two amounts by reference to the date of acquisition of the superior interest, but, by concession, indexation on the expenditure on the earlier, inferior lease, is calculated by reference to the date of its acquisition. (HMRC Extra-Statutory Concession D42).

Where a lease is surrendered on terms which include the release of the tenant from a liability under the lease to make good any dilapidations or from any other onerous liability, the value attributable to the release is consideration for the surrender (HMRC Capital Gains Manual CG71260).

Leases as wasting assets

[41.15] A lease of land is not a wasting asset until the time when its duration does not exceed 50 years. [*TCGA 1992, Sch 8 para 1(1)*].

Duration of a lease

For this purpose, the duration of a lease is to be decided by reference to the facts known or ascertainable at the time when the lease was acquired or created. In determining the duration, the following provisions apply.

(a) Where the terms of the lease include provision for the determination of the lease by notice given by the landlord, the lease is not to be treated as granted for a term longer than one ending at the earliest date on which it could be determined by notice given by the landlord.
(b) Where any of the terms of the lease or any other circumstances render it unlikely that the lease will continue beyond a date earlier than the expiration of the terms of the lease, the lease is not to be treated as having been granted for a longer term than one ending on that date. This applies in particular where the lease provides for rent to go up after a given date, or for the tenant's obligation to become more onerous after a given date, but includes provision for the determination of the lease on that date, by notice given by the tenant, and those provisions render it unlikely that the lease will continue beyond that date.
(c) Where the terms of the lease include provision for the extension of the lease beyond a given date by notice given by the tenant, the duration of the lease applies as if the term of the lease extended for as long as it could be extended by the tenant, but subject to any right of the landlord to determine the lease by notice.

[*TCGA 1992, Sch 8 para 8*].

A lease granted under *Landlord and Tenant Act 1954* to follow on from another is not a continuation of the old lease and is to be treated as having been acquired on the date it was granted (*Bayley v Rogers* Ch D 1980, 53 TC 420).

A similar view was taken in *Lewis v Walters* Ch D 1992, 64 TC 489 regarding the right of a tenant to be granted a lease under *Leasehold Reform Act 1967* to follow on from another and where it was also held that (c) above did not apply since such a right was not included in the terms of the original lease.

Where a lease is 'extended' by the surrender of an old lease and the grant of a new one for a longer term, a disposal of the old lease will in strictness occur, the consideration for it normally being the value, if any, of the new lease. By concession, a disposal is not treated as arising in these circumstances provided that:

- the parties are not connected and the transaction is at arm's length (or the parties *are* connected but the terms of the transaction are equivalent to those to be expected in an arm's length transaction between unconnected parties);
- the transaction is not part of or connected with a larger scheme or series of transactions;
- no capital sum is received by the lessee;
- the extent of the property in which the lessee has an interest is unchanged; and
- the terms of the leases remain the same except as regards the duration and amount of rent payable. For this purpose, trivial differences will be ignored.

(HMRC Extra-Statutory Concession D39). (See **4.19** ANTI-AVOIDANCE for the charge arising where concessions involving deferral of gains are abused.)

Computation where lease is a wasting asset

If a lease of land is a wasting asset, its original cost and any enhancement expenditure are not written off on a straight line basis (as would otherwise be required under *TCGA 1992, s 46*) but on a reducing basis as set out in the table below.

Table for depreciation of leases

Years	Percentage	Years	Percentage	Years	Percentage
50 (or more)	100.000	33	90.280	16	64.116
49	99.657	32	89.354	15	61.617
48	99.289	31	88.371	14	58.971
47	98.902	30	87.330	13	56.167
46	98.490	29	86.226	12	53.191
45	98.059	28	85.053	11	50.038
44	97.595	27	83.816	10	46.695
43	97.107	26	82.496	9	43.154
42	96.593	25	81.100	8	39.399
41	96.041	24	79.622	7	35.414
40	95.457	23	78.055	6	31.195
39	94.842	22	76.399	5	26.722
38	94.189	21	74.635	4	21.983
37	93.497	20	72.770	3	16.959
36	92.761	19	70.791	2	11.629
35	91.981	18	68.697	1	5.983
34	91.156	17	66.470	0	0

The fraction of the *original cost* which is not allowed is given by the fraction

$$\frac{P(1) - P(3)}{P(1)}$$

where

P(1) = the percentage derived from the table for the duration of the lease at acquisition
P(3) = the percentage derived from the table for the duration of the lease at the time of disposal

The fraction of any *enhancement expenditure* which is not allowed is given by the fraction

$$\frac{P(2) - P(3)}{P(2)}$$

where

P(2) = the percentage derived from the table for the duration of the lease at the time when the item of expenditure is first reflected in the nature of the lease
P(3) = as above

If the duration of the lease is not an exact number of years, the percentage is that for the whole number of years plus one twelfth of the difference between that and the percentage of the next higher number of years for each odd month, counting an odd 14 days or more as one month.

[*TCGA 1992, Sch 8 para 1(3)(4)*].

The provisions above apply even if the period of ownership of the lease exceeds 50 years. Accordingly, in such a case, any cost or enhancement expenditure incurred before the lease becomes a wasting asset is not reduced until the lease does become a wasting asset. [*TCGA 1992, Sch 8 para 1(5)*]. In these circumstances P(1) and P(2) will each be 100 in the fractions given above.

Example

X purchases a 30-year lease of business premises in 2011 for £250,000. In 2014, when 27 years of the lease remain, he spends £25,000 on improvements which are at once reflected in the value of the lease and continue to be so until he disposes of it with 24 years remaining in 2017. His allowable expenditure is reduced as follows:

Original cost (£250,000) × $\frac{(87.330 - 79.622)}{87.330}$	=	£22,066
Additional cost (£25,000) × $\frac{(83.816 - 79.622)}{83.816}$	=	£1,251

	£23,317
The total allowable expenditure is then (£275,000 – £23,317)	= £251,683

Exceptions

The above provisions do not apply in the following circumstances.

(i) If at the beginning of the period of ownership of a lease, it is subject to a *sub-lease not at a rackrent* and the value of the lease at the end of the sub-lease (estimated at the beginning of the period of ownership) exceeds the expenditure allowable in computing the gain accruing on the disposal of the lease (see **16.11**(a) COMPUTATION OF GAINS AND LOSSES), the lease is *not* a wasting asset until the end of the duration of the sub-lease. [*TCGA 1992, Sch 8 para 1(2)*].

(ii) Where the land, throughout the ownership of the person making the disposal, is used solely for the purposes of a trade, profession or vocation, and capital allowances have, or could have, been claimed in respect of its cost, or in respect of any enhancement expenditure. This also applies where the cost of land has otherwise qualified in full for any capital allowances. Where, however, the land disposed of has been used partly for non-business purposes, or has only partly qualified for capital allowances, the expenditure and consideration are apportioned and the restriction of allowable expenditure as above applies only to that portion of expenditure which has not qualified for capital allowances, or which relates to the period of non-business use. [*TCGA 1992, s 47, Sch 8 para 1(6)*].

Premiums for leases

[41.16] Where the payment of a 'premium' is required under a lease (or otherwise under the terms subject to which the lease is granted) there is a part disposal of the freehold or other interest out of which that lease is granted. [*TCGA 1992, Sch 8 para 2(1)*].

In the part disposal computation (which follows the normal rules in *TCGA 1992, s 42*, see **16.5** COMPUTATION OF GAINS AND LOSSES) the property which remains undisposed of includes a right to any rent or other payments (other than a premium) payable under the lease, and that right is valued at the time of the part disposal. [*TCGA 1992, Sch 8 para 2(2)*].

Meaning of 'premium'

'*Premium*' includes any like sum, whether payable to the intermediate or superior landlord and includes any sum (other than rent) paid on or in connection with the granting of a tenancy except when the other sufficient consideration for the payment can be shown to have been given. In Scotland, '*premium*' includes in particular a *grassum* payable to any landlord or intermediate landlord on the creation of a sub-lease. [*TCGA 1992, Sch 8 para 10(2)(3)*].

Capital sums treated as premiums

The legislation provides for other capital amounts payable under leases to be treated as if they were premiums. Where the landlord is a freeholder, or is a leaseholder and that lease has more than 50 years to run, and

(a) *under the terms of a lease*, a sum becomes payable by the tenant in lieu of the whole or part of the rent for any period ('commutation of rent'), or as consideration for the surrender of the lease, or
(b) a sum becomes payable by the tenant (otherwise than by way of rent) as consideration for the variation or waiver of any of the terms of the lease,

the lease is deemed to have required payment of a premium to the landlord (in addition to any actual premium) of the amount of that sum. This premium is treated as being due when the sum is payable by the tenant and as being in respect of, where (a) applies, the period in relation to which it is payable or, where (b) applies, the period from the time the variation or waiver takes effect to the time it ceases to have effect. The deemed receipt of the premium does not require a chargeable gain arising from the receipt of any other premium to be recomputed. Instead, it is regarded as a separate transaction effected at the time the premium is deemed to be due and as a part disposal (or further part disposal) of the freehold (or other asset out of which the lease is granted) or, in the case of a payment for surrender, as a disposal by the landlord of his interest in the lease.

Where a sum falls within (b) above and the transaction is not at arm's length and/or is entered into gratuitously, the amount actually payable is replaced in the tax computation by such sum as might have been required of the tenant in an arm's length transaction.

The rules are modified (but not where the payment is consideration for the surrender of a lease) if the landlord is himself a tenant under a lease with 50 years or less to run at the time the capital sum is paid. The premium is deemed to have been given by way of consideration for the grant of the part of the sub-lease covered by the period in respect of which the premium is treated as having been paid. It is *not* thereby treated as having been received at the time the sub-lease was granted; the date of disposal is determined under general principles — see **16.4** COMPUTATION OF GAINS AND LOSSES. See the worked example at HMRC Capital Gains Manual CG71371. As far as the sub-lessee is concerned, the payment is treated as allowable enhancement expenditure (see **16.11**(b) COMPUTATION OF GAINS AND LOSSES) incurred by him and attributable to the aforementioned part of the sub-lease.

[*TCGA 1992, Sch 8 para 3*].

See HMRC Capital Gains Manual CG71350–71371 for further commentary on the above and worked examples.

If a capital sum is paid by a tenant for commutation of rent and the terms of the lease do *not* provide for such a payment, the above rules do not apply. The transaction is treated as a part disposal within *TCGA 1992, s 22* (see **10.2** CAPITAL SUMS DERIVED FROM ASSETS). (HMRC Capital Gains Manual CG71351, 71372).

Reverse premiums

A reverse premium (as defined) is chargeable to income tax or corporation tax as a *revenue* receipt. See *CTA 2009, ss 96–100, 250; ITTOIA 2005, ss 99–106*, and Revenue Tax Bulletin April 1999 p 641, and see Tolley's Income Tax for full coverage.

General

In *Clarke v United Real (Moorgate) Ltd* Ch D 1987, 61 TC 353, the taxpayer company contracted for a freehold site which it owned to be developed by a third party. Subsequently it entered into an 'agreement for a lease' with another third party ('A') under which A agreed to reimburse the company's development costs and the company was to grant him a long lease of the developed site at a rent below market value, which was to be ascertained by reference to his reimbursement payments to the company. The granting of the lease was agreed to be a part disposal. The reimbursement payments were held to be a premium within *TCGA 1992, Sch 8 paras 2(1), 10(2),* because they were made to the company in its capacity as landlord, and not to meet an obligation incurred by the company on behalf of A.

Premiums taxed as receipts of property business

[41.17] Where a premium is received for a lease not exceeding 50 years and part of it is liable to tax as a receipt of a UK property business under *CTA 2009, ss 217–221* or *ITTOIA 2005, ss 277–281A*, that part is excluded from the computation for capital gains purposes *except* in the denominator of the part disposal fraction of A/(A+B) given by *TCGA 1992, s 42*. '*Premium*' includes a deemed premium under (a) or (b) in **41.16** above. [*TCGA 1992, Sch 8 para 5(1)(5); CTA 2009, Sch 1 para 388(2)*].

Where the terms of a lease impose an obligation on the tenant to carry out work on the premises concerned, an amount equal to the increase in value of the landlord's interest occasioned by the work is treated as a premium except insofar as the obligation relates to work which, had it been carried out by the landlord, would have been deductible as an expense of any property business carried on by the landlord. [*ITTOIA 2005, s 278; CTA 2009, s 218, Sch 1 para 16; ICTA 1988, s 34(2)(3)*]. For capital gains purposes the consequential effect is that the landlord is treated as incurring enhancement expenditure of that amount on the premises at the time of the grant of the lease. [*TCGA 1992, Sch 8 paras 7, 7A; CTA 2009, Sch 1 para 388(5)(6)*].

Example

X grants a 14-year lease of premises for a premium of £5,000 in 2017/18 and retains the freehold interest. The amount chargeable to income tax for that year is

	£
Premium	5,000
Deduct $\frac{14-1}{50} \times £5,000$	1,300

Chargeable to income tax	£3,700

If the allowable expenditure on the original unencumbered freehold (acquired in 2005) is £30,000 and the value of the reversion £47,000, the gain is computed as follows:

	£
Consideration received (i.e. the premium)	5,000
Deduct amount chargeable to income tax	3,700
	£1,300
Allowable expenditure attributable to the part disposal	
$\frac{1{,}300}{(5{,}000+47{,}000)} \times £30{,}000 =$	£750
Chargeable gain: £1,300 – £750 =	£550

Sub-leases granted out of short leases

[41.18] Where a sub-lease is granted out of a head-lease with less than 50 years to run, the normal part disposal rules do not apply. Instead, subject to below, a proportion of the cost and enhancement expenditure attributable to the lease is apportioned to the part disposed of as follows:

$$\frac{P(1) - P(3)}{P(2)}$$

where:

P(1) = the percentage derived from the table in **41.15** above for the duration of the lease at the date of granting the sub-lease
P(3) = the percentage for the duration of the lease at the date of termination of the sub-lease
P(2) = the percentage for the duration of the lease at the date of acquisition (for apportionment of cost) *or* the date when expenditure is first reflected in the nature of the lease (for apportionment of enhancement expenditure)

If the amount of the premium is less than what would be obtainable by way of premium for the sub-lease if the rent payable under the sub-lease were the same as the rent payable under the lease, the percentage attributable to the sub-lease as calculated above must be multiplied by the premium received over the premium so obtainable before being applied to cost or enhancement expenditure. [*TCGA 1992, Sch 8 para 4(1)(2)*].

Example

X purchases a 40-year lease of a flat in 2012 for £15,000. In 2017, he sub-lets the flat to Y for 20 years for a premium of £8,000. The premium obtainable on the basis of the rent paid under the head-lease is £10,000. X's original expenditure of £15,000 is apportioned as follows:

$$\frac{91.981 - 61.617}{95.457} = 0.3180908 \times \frac{8,000}{10,000} = 0.2544726$$

0.2544726 × £15,000 = £3,817

The expenditure attributable to the part disposal is therefore £3,817 as against £4,771 (£15,000 × 0.3180908) if the premium had been the maximum obtainable, £10,000.

Where the sub-lease is a sub-lease of part only of the land comprised in the lease, the cost and enhancement expenditure of the head-lease must be apportioned between the sub-lease and the remainder in proportion to their respective values. [*TCGA 1992, Sch 8 para 4(3)*].

Where a premium (including a deemed premium as in **41.17** above) is paid for the sub-lease, an amount of which is liable to tax as a receipt of a UK property business under *CTA 2009, ss 217–221* or *ITTOIA 2005, ss 277–281*, that amount is deducted from any *gain* accruing on the disposal for which the premium is consideration but not so as to convert the gain into a loss or to increase any loss. [*TCGA 1992, Sch 8 para 5(2)(5); CTA 2009, Sch 1 para 388(2)*]. Similar provisions apply where, under *CTA 2009, ss 224, 225* or *ITTOIA 2005, ss 284–286* (see **41.7** above) what is disposed of is the remainder of a lease or a sub-lease out of a lease the duration of which does not exceed 50 years. [*TCGA 1992, Sch 8 para 5(4)*].

Allowances to payer for premiums paid

[41.19] Where a premium paid on the grant of a lease falls to be included in computing the property business profits of the recipient (see **41.17** above and **41.21** below), or would have done but for exemption, the tenant is treated as incurring an expense of a revenue nature at a rate equivalent to the amount so included spread over the period to which it relates. Where the lease is sub-let, this expense is an allowable deduction in computing the property business profits of the intermediate landlord. [*ITTOIA 2005, s 292; CTA 2009, s 232, Sch 1 para 16; ICTA 1988, s 37(4)*]. If the sub-lease is granted for a premium, however, the deduction is restricted. See Tolley's Income Tax under Property Income for full details.

Where a person is treated in consequence of having granted a sub-lease as incurring revenue expenses under *ITTOIA 2005, s 292* or *CTA 2009, s 232*, the amount of any *loss* accruing for capital gains purposes to that person on the disposal by way of the grant of the sub-lease is reduced by the total amount of the expenses, but not so as to convert the loss into a gain. Any adjustment under *ITTOIA 2005, ss 301, 302* or *CTA 2009, ss 238, 239* (see **41.7** above) is taken into account. [*TCGA 1992, Sch 8 para 6(1)(3); CTA 2009, Sch 1 para 388(4)*].

Example

On 21 January 2011 C is granted a lease of a shop for 21 years for a rent and a premium of £12,800. On 21 January 2018 he grants a sub-lease for a period of 7 years for a premium of £1,000 and a rent equal to that payable under the terms of the head-lease. C is treated under *ITTOIA 2005, s 292* as incurring deductible expenses of £1,680. C's capital gains tax position is as follows.

	£	£
Premium received		1,000
Consideration given for lease	12,800	
Percentage applicable to lease of 21 years	74.635	
Percentage applicable to lease of 14 years	58.971	
Percentage applicable to lease of 7 years	35.414	
Amount allowable		
$\frac{58.971 - 35.414}{74.635} \times £12,800$		4,040
Loss		3,040
Deduct amount allowable in computing profits		1,680
Allowable loss		£1,360

Restriction of allowable expenditure of payer of premium

[41.20] Where a premium is paid for the acquisition of a short lease, and the person acquiring the lease uses the property for the purposes of his trade, profession or vocation, such that income tax or corporation tax relief under *CTA 2009, ss 62–67* or *ITTOIA 2005, ss 60–67* is available (see Tolley's Income Tax), then on a subsequent disposal of the lease, the allowable expenditure is reduced by the tax relief actually given. This reduction is made **before** the depreciation fraction at **41.15** above is applied, so that only the net expenditure is depreciated. (HMRC Capital Gains Manual CG71200–71202).

Anti-avoidance provisions

[41.21] Where a lease not exceeding 50 years granted at *less than market value* is assigned for a consideration exceeding any premium for which it was granted (or the consideration on any previous assignment) the excess, up to the limit of the amount of any premium, or additional premium, which the grantor forwent when granting the lease, is treated as a receipt of the assignor's property business to the same extent that an additional premium would have been so treated (see **41.17** above). [*ITTOIA 2005, s 282; CTA 2009, s 222, Sch 1 para 16; ICTA 1988, s 35*].

Any assessment to income or corporation tax under these provisions is not taken into account in any capital gains computation. [*TCGA 1992, Sch 8 para 6(2); CTA 2009, Sch 1 para 388(4)*]. There may, therefore, be a double charge to tax.

New lease of land after assignment or surrender — proportion of capital sum received to be taxed as income in certain circumstances

[41.22] The following applies where a lessee of land under a lease is entitled to one of a specified type of deduction for rent (i.e. a relevant deduction within *CTA 2010, s 860* or *ITA 2007, s 681BK*) and assigns or surrenders the lease. If the lease when so transferred or surrendered has no more than 50 years still to run and a new lease is granted to the lessee or a linked person for *15 years or less*, any increased rent payable, so far as it does not exceed a commercial rent, is allowable as a deduction from profits, but of the consideration received by the lessee for giving up the original lease (or undertaking to pay an increased rent) a proportion equivalent to one-fifteenth of that consideration multiplied by the number of years by which the term of the lease-back falls short of 16 years will be treated as an income receipt instead of a capital one.

Appropriate adjustment is made where the lease-back is of part only of the property previously leased.

For the above purposes the term of the new lease is deemed to end on any date whereafter the rent payable is reduced, or, if the lessor or lessee has power to end the lease or the lessee has power to vary its terms, on the earliest date on which the lease can be so ended or varied.

[*ITA 2007, ss 861B–861BM; CTA 2010, ss 849–862; FA 2012, Sch 16 para 228*].

Value shifting — adjustment of leasehold rights

[41.23] Where an owner of land (or of any other description of property) enters into a transaction whereby he becomes the lessee of that property (e.g. a sale and lease-back) and there is a subsequent adjustment of rights and liabilities under the lease (whether or not involving the grant of a new lease) which is on the whole favourable to the lessor, such an adjustment is a disposal by the lessee of an interest in the property. [*TCGA 1992, s 29(4)*]. See **4.8** ANTI-AVOIDANCE for full coverage.

Contingent liabilities

[41.24] In the first instance, no allowance is made in a capital gains tax computation for:

(a) in the case of a disposal by way of assigning a lease of land or other property, any liability remaining with, or assumed by, the person making the disposal which is contingent on a default in respect of liabilities thereby or subsequently assumed by the assignee under the terms and conditions of the lease; and

(b) any contingent liability of the person making the disposal in respect of any covenant for quiet enjoyment or other obligation assumed as vendor of land, or of any estate or interest in land, or as a lessor.

If it is subsequently shown to the satisfaction of the inspector that any such contingent liability has become enforceable, and is being or has been enforced, such adjustment is made as is required in consequence.

[*TCGA 1992, s 49(1)(a)(b), (2)(3)*].

The receipt of a contingently repayable deposit in return for the grant of an option to purchase land was valued subject to the contingency because on the facts the contingency was not within (b) above (*Randall v Plumb* Ch D 1974, 50 TC 392).

Non-resident CGT disposals of UK residential property

[41.25] For 2015/16 onwards, capital gains tax is extended to disposals of UK residential property by non-residents. The change means that CGT is now charged on the basis of where such a property is located rather than where the seller is located. The provisions apply to disposals on or after 6 April 2015. [*FA 2015, Sch 7 para 60*]. As a result of the provisions, changes have also been made to the main residence election rules (see **53.10** PRIVATE RESIDENCES) so that residences, wherever situated, may only qualify for main residence relief for a particular tax year, either as fact or by nomination, if a tax residency test and occupation test are met. It is therefore possible for properties subject to this non-resident CGT regime to qualify for main residence relief for tax years in which they meet these two tests.

The CGT charge can apply to non-resident individuals (including on disposals in the non-resident part of a split tax year), non-resident trustees, personal representatives of non-resident deceased persons, certain non-resident companies, and any such person who is a partner in a partnership.

The main features of the provisions are as follows.

- Capital gains tax is charged on gains ('*NRCGT gains*') accruing on a disposal of a UK residential property interest by a non-resident person.
- Tax is charged on the total amount of the NRCGT gains arising in a tax year after deduction of any allowable losses on disposals of UK residential property interests (whether or not NRCGT losses) of the same tax year, and any unused such losses brought forward from previous years.
- Gains and losses are calculated as for CGT (or corporation tax) purposes but there are special rules for property interests held on 5 April 2015. Unless an election is made, only the gain arising after that date is charged. Alternatively an election can be made for time apportionment or, particularly where a loss arises, for the whole of the gain to be charged.
- There are special provisions for calculating the gain or loss where the disposal is, or includes, a disposal chargeable under the provisions for high-value disposals of dwellings.
- Relief for losses arising on non-resident CGT disposals can generally only be obtained against NRCGT gains but an NRCGT loss arising to an individual in the overseas part of a tax year which is a split year can be deducted against general chargeable gains arising in the UK part of the year and unused NRCGT losses can be carried forward and set against general chargeable gains of a later tax year for which the taxpayer is resident in the UK (or operates through a UK permanent establishment or via a UK branch or agency).

- Companies are charged to capital gains tax (and not corporation tax) on the chargeable gains at 20%.
- Individuals are charged to capital gains tax at either 18% or 28% depending on the level of their taxable income. Trustees and personal representatives are charged at 28%. The annual exempt amount is available in the normal way.
- A person who makes a non-resident CGT disposal must, in most cases, make a special return reporting the disposal to HMRC within 30 days following the day of the completion of the disposal. See **58.20** RETURNS.
- Tax on NRCGT gains is generally due 30 days after completion of sale (i.e. on the date the return reporting the disposal is due), except where the person is registered for self-assessment, in which case payment may be made on the normal payment date for CGT, though the disposal must still be reported in a return within 30 days. See **51.3** PAYMENT OF TAX.
- Qualifying members of a group of companies may make an election to be treated as an NRCGT group. Disposals of UK residential property interests between members of the group are disregarded, and the charge to tax applies as if the members of the group were a single body.

The government has consulted on bringing NRCGT gains arising in companies within the scope of UK corporation tax, as part of a wider consultation which proposes bringing certain income received by non-resident companies into the UK corporation tax regime. The consultation closed in June 2017. See www.gov.uk/government/consultations/non-resident-companies-chargeable-to-income-tax-and-non-resident-capital-gains-tax.

Liability to non-resident capital gains tax

[41.26] Capital gains tax is charged on gains (‘*NRCGT gains*’) accruing on a disposal (a ‘*non-resident CGT disposal*’) of a UK residential property interest (see further **41.29** below) to which any of the following applies:

(a) in the case of a disposal by an individual, he is not resident in the UK in the tax year in which the gain accrues (or would accrue if there were a gain), or the gain accrues (or would have accrued) in the overseas part of a split tax year (see **57.18** RESIDENCE AND DOMICILE);
(b) in the case of a disposal by personal representatives, that the single and continuing body (as in **19.9** DEATH is not UK resident;
(c) in the case of a disposal by trustees, that the deemed single person (see **62.6** SETTLEMENTS) is not resident in the UK during any part of the tax year in question; and
(d) in any other case the person is not resident in the UK when the gain accrues (or would accrue if there were a gain).

In order to prevent double taxation the gain is not chargeable under these provisions if it is already chargeable under *TCGA 1992, s 10(1)* or *s 10B* (non-resident with UK branch or agency, or non-resident company with UK permanent establishment: see **49.3** OVERSEAS MATTERS) or under *ITA 2007, s 517C* or *CTA 2010, s 356OC* (profits and gains on disposals of UK land treated as trading income — see **41.6** above). Where the disposal is made by an individual in the overseas part of a split tax year, these provisions do not apply if the gain is already chargeable because *TCGA 1992, s 10(1)* would have applied if the individual had been non-resident for the year (see **1.2** INTRODUCTION).

The non-resident CGT rules take precedence over the temporary non-residence rules (see **49.5** OVERSEAS MATTERS) but the latter can apply to any part of the gain that is not within the non-resident CGT rules.

Tax is charged on the total amount of the NRCGT gains arising in the tax year (other than gains accruing to a member of an NRCGT group, as to which see **41.33** below) after deduction of any allowable losses on disposals of UK residential property interests (whether or not NRCGT losses — see below) of the same tax year, and any unused such losses brought forward from previous years (but not from a year before 1965/66). No other deductions can be made (except for an individual's NRCGT losses carried back from the tax year of death — see **19.7** DEATH).

Relief for losses ('*NRCGT losses*') arising on non-resident CGT disposals can only be obtained against NRCGT gains as above with the following exceptions:

- an NRCGT loss arising to an individual in the overseas part of a tax year which is a split year (see **57.18** RESIDENCE AND DOMICILE) can be deducted against general chargeable gains arising in the UK part of the year; and
- unused NRCGT losses can be carried forward and set against general chargeable gains of a later tax year for which the taxpayer is resident in the UK (or operates through a UK permanent establishment or via a UK branch or agency).

NRCGT losses cannot be carried back with the exception of those arising in the tax year of death. Relief for an NRCGT loss under the above provisions can be given only once and cannot be given if relief has or may be given for income tax or corporation tax purposes.

Companies are charged to capital gains tax (and not corporation tax) on the chargeable gains at 20%.

Individuals are charged to capital gains tax at either 18% or 28% depending on the level of their taxable income (see **2.2** ANNUAL RATES AND EXEMPTIONS). Trustees and personal representatives are charged at 28%. The annual exempt amount is available in the normal way (see **2.6** ANNUAL RATES AND EXEMPTIONS).

HMRC consider that where a person will also be charged to tax on the disposal in their country of residence, the UK tax charge still applies and relief for the UK tax paid may be available against any tax due in the country of residence. See HMRC 'Capital Gains Tax for non-UK residents: sales and disposals of UK residential property' FAQs Question 22, 18 March 2015.

For payment of tax on NRCGT gains see **51.3** PAYMENT OF TAX and for NRCGT returns see **58.20** RETURNS.

[*TCGA 1992, ss 2(2A)(2B), 4(3B), 14B, 14D, 14E; FA 2015, Sch 7 paras 3, 6, 11; FA 2016, s 77(6), Sch 11 para* 2].

Persons not chargeable

[41.27] The following are not chargeable to non-resident CGT under the above provisions if they make a claim to that effect.

(i) A diversely-held company, i.e. any company that is not a 'closely-held company'. A '*closely-held company*' is one which is under the control of five or fewer participators, or one where five or fewer 'participators' have or are entitled to acquire rights that would entitle them to the majority of assets available for distribution on winding up (excluding, if necessary, rights any person has as a loan creditor). The assets available for distribution among the participators include those to which they are entitled as participators in any other company which is itself a participator in the original company. '*Participator*' is as defined in *CTA 2010, s 454* but also includes a participator in any other company which has or is entitled to receive assets in the winding up of the original company. For the purpose of determining whether five or fewer participators possess or are entitled to acquire the necessary rights, no account is taken of a participator which is a company unless the company has or is entitled to acquire rights in a fiduciary or representative capacity.

A person (P) is treated as having '*control*' of a company (C) if P exercises, is able to exercise, or is entitled to acquire, direct or indirect control over C's affairs. It includes the possession of, or right to acquire:

- the greater part of the share capital or issued share capital of C; or
- the greater part of the voting power of C; or
- so much of the issued share capital of C as would give the right to receive the greater part of the company's income, were all that income distributed (disregarding any rights that P or any other person has as a loan creditor); or
- rights to the greater part of C's assets in a distribution on a winding-up or in any other circumstances.

If two or more persons together satisfy any of the above conditions, they are treated as having control of C. Any rights or powers which a person possesses on behalf of another person or may be required to exercise on that other person's direction or behalf are to be attributed to that other person. The rights of an 'associate' (including rights exercisable jointly by two or more associates) are taken into account to determine if a person (P) has control. An 'associate' is a relative of P (i.e. a spouse or civil partner, parent or remoter forebear, child or remoter issue, or brother or sister) and the trustees of a settlement of which P, or any relative of P (living or dead) is the settlor.

A company is not a closely-held company if it can only be regarded as such by including as one of its five or fewer participators either a company which is itself a diversely-held company, or a company which is a loan creditor, and which is itself a diversely-held company or a 'qualifying institutional investor'. A '*qualifying institutional investor*' is a widely-marketed unit trust scheme or open-ended investment company (or non-UK equivalent) (see below); a trustee or manager of a qualifying pension scheme; a company carrying on life assurance business; or a person not liable for income tax or corporation tax on the grounds of sovereign immunity. The Treasury may by regulations amend the definition of 'qualifying institutional investor'.

Any share or interest which either a qualifying institutional investor or a general partner of a limited partnership which is a collective investment scheme has as a participator in the company is automatically treated as a share held by more than five participators. There is an exception to this rule where the general partner is entitled to assets for distribution on a winding up of the company.

A 'divided company' is considered to be a closely-held company if the gain or loss on the non-resident GCT disposal is primarily or wholly attributable to a particular division of the company (as defined) and, if that division were a separate company, it would be closely-held. A company is a '*divided company*' if under the law under which it is formed, under its articles of association or other regulatory documents or under arrangements entered into by or in relation to it some or all of the assets are available primarily or only to meet particular liabilities of the company and some or all of the members and creditors of the company have rights primarily or only in relation to particular assets of the company.

(ii) A unit trust scheme, or open-ended investment company (or non-UK equivalent), which is 'widely-marketed' (see below) throughout the period from the date the scheme acquired the interest in land which is the subject of the non-resident CGT disposal to the date of disposal, or if shorter, throughout the period of five years ending on the date of disposal.

(iii) A unit trust scheme, or open-ended investment company (or non-UK equivalent), which has as an investor an offshore fund, open-ended investment company or authorised unit trust (the '*feeder fund*'), where the scheme and the feeder fund have the same manager, and the scheme is widely-marketed (see below), after taking account of scheme documents for the feeder fund and the intended investors of the feeder fund, throughout the shortest of: the period from the date the scheme acquired the interest in land which is the subject of the disposal to the date of disposal; the period of five years ending on the date of disposal; and the period from the date the feeder fund first became an investor to the date of disposal.

(iv) A company carrying on life assurance business if immediately before the disposal the interest in land which is the subject of the non-resident CGT disposal is held to provide benefits to policyholders in the course of that business.

A scheme is '*widely-marketed*' if the following conditions are met:

(a) the scheme produces documents available to investors and HMRC specifying the intended categories of investor, and undertaking that units will be widely available and marketed in accordance with (c) below;
(b) the specification of intended categories of investor, and any other terms governing participation, do not restrict investors to a limited number of specific persons or groups of connected persons, or deter a reasonable investor in one of the specified intended categories from investing in the scheme;
(c) units are marketed and made available sufficiently widely to reach, and in a manner appropriate to attract, the intended categories of investors, and a person within one of the categories can, upon request to the scheme manager, obtain information about it and acquire units in it. A scheme does not fail to meet this requirement because it has no capacity to receive additional investment unless the capacity is fixed by scheme documents and a pre-determined number of specific persons or specific groups of connected persons make investments which exhaust all or substantially all of the capacity.

Arrangements (as defined) one of the main purposes of which is to avoid the charge by virtue of being considered a diversely-held company or a widely-marketed scheme are disregarded for these purposes.

The claim for exemption must be made in the NRCGT return form which must be submitted 30 days from the date the property is conveyed (see **58.20** RETURNS).

[*TCGA 1992, ss 14F–14H, Sch C1; FA 2015, Sch 7 paras 11, 37*].

Meaning of disposal of UK residential property interest

[41.29] For the purposes of **41.25** onwards above, a '*disposal of a UK residential property interest*' is a disposal of an 'interest in UK land' which has, at any time in the period from acquisition or, if later, 6 April 2015 to the day before the date of disposal (the '*relevant period of ownership*'), consisted of or included a 'dwelling', or which subsists for the benefit of land that has consisted of or included a dwelling at any time in that period. Alternatively it is a disposal of an interest in UK land which subsists under a contract for an off-plan purchase, i.e. a contract for acquisition of land consisting of, or including, a building or part of a building that is to be constructed or adapted as a dwelling. In determining the period of ownership, where the interest disposed of results from interests which have been acquired at different times, the date of acquisition of the first interest is taken as the date on which all the interests were acquired. The grant of an option (defined as at **7.7** ASSETS) binding the grantor to sell an interest in UK land is treated for these purposes as the disposal of an interest in UK land.

An '*interest in UK land*' is an estate, interest, right or power in or over land in the UK, or the benefit of an obligation, restriction or condition affecting the value of such, but not including:

(a) any interest or right (other than a rentcharge, or in Scotland, a feu duty) held to secure payment of money or performance of any other obligation;
(b) a licence to use or occupy land; or
(c) in England, Wales or Northern Ireland, a tenancy at will or a manor.

A '*dwelling*' is a building (including a part of a building) which is used or suitable for use as a dwelling or is in the process of being constructed or adapted for such use. It includes gardens and grounds (and any building or structure in a garden or grounds). The following are excluded from being a dwelling:

(i) school residential accommodation;
(ii) residential accommodation for members of the armed forces;
(iii) homes or institutions providing residential accommodation for children;
(iv) homes or institutions providing residential accommodation with personal care for the elderly, the disabled, persons with drug or alcohol dependency or a mental disorder;
(v) hospitals and hospices;
(vi) prisons and similar establishments;
(vii) hotels, inns and similar establishments;
(viii) any other institution which is the sole or main residence of its residents; and
(ix) buildings occupied by students managed or controlled by their educational establishments (within *Housing Act 2004, Sch 14 para 4* or corresponding Scottish or NI provision).

In addition, a building which includes at least 15 bedrooms, is purpose-built or converted for occupation by students other than school pupils and is occupied by them for at least 165 days in a tax year is not a dwelling for that year.

Buildings which become temporarily unsuitable for use as a dwelling are generally treated as continuing to be such, but there are some exceptions. A building is not considered suitable for use as a dwelling if the temporary unsuitability resulted from damage to the building which was accidental, or otherwise outside the control of the person making the disposal and the period of temporary unsuitability was at least 90 days (whether or not within the relevant period of ownership but ending before the disposal). If this is the case any work done within that period is not treated as construction or adaption of the building for use as a dwelling. Any damage occurring during alterations to, or partial demolition of, a building which involved, or could be expected to involve, the building being unsuitable for use as a dwelling for at least 30 days is not considered accidental or otherwise outside the control of the person making the disposal for these purposes.

A building which has been demolished either to ground level or, in accordance with planning permission or development consent, to a single façade (double if on a corner) is regarded as having ceased to exist. Where a person disposes of an interest in UK land which contains or contained a building which has been suitable for use as a dwelling at any time in the relevant period of ownership, and that building has undergone complete or partial demolition or other works which result in it ceasing to exist or becoming unsuitable as a dwelling before the 'completion' of disposal then, provided the conditions below are met, the building is treated as being unsuitable as a dwelling throughout the period when the works were in progress, and any period ending immediately before that during which the building was, for reasons connected with the works, not used as a dwelling. The conditions are that:

- the works result in the building ceasing to exist or becoming unsuitable as a dwelling before the completion of the disposal; and
- any planning permission or development consent has been issued (even if retrospectively after completion of the disposal) and the works were carried out in accordance therewith.

If planning permission or development consent for the works was required but not granted (unless given subsequently), or it was contravened, the building is not treated as being unsuitable as a dwelling.

'*Completion*' occurs either at the time of disposal or when the interest is conveyed where the contract is completed by conveyance.

The Treasury may by regulations exclude any other interest or right from being treated as an interest in UK land and amend the definition of 'dwelling'.

[*TCGA 1992, Sch B1; FA 2015, Sch 7 para 36; FA 2016, Sch 11 para 4, Sch 12 para 4*].

Computation of gains and losses—main rules

[41.30] The normal CGT rules apply in calculating NRCGT gains and losses but, as only the part of the gain arising after 5 April 2015 is chargeable, there are special rules to calculate the chargeable amount. There are three methods for doing this and the default method (rebasing) will apply unless the taxpayer elects otherwise. The rules apply equally to the disposal of contracts for off-plan purchases (see **41.29** above) as if the interest were a dwelling throughout the period in which the taxpayer owned the interest.

For the computation of gains and losses involving relevant high value disposals see **41.31** below.

Interest held on 5 April 2015

Default method

The method applies where P held the interest disposed of on 5 April 2015. A calculation is made of the notional gain or loss which would arise on the disposal of the interest had the taxpayer acquired it at market value on 5 April 2015 (the '*notional post-April 2015 gain or loss*'). This notional gain or loss is then apportioned by the fraction:

$$\frac{RD}{TD}$$

where RD is the number of days in the period from 6 April 2015 to the day before the date of disposal (the 'post-commencement ownership period') on which the disposed of interest consisted wholly or partly of a dwelling (see **41.29** above); and
TD is the number of days in that period.

The resulting gain or loss is the NRCGT gain or NRCGT loss.

Where there are any days in the post-commencement ownership period on which the land disposed of consists partly but not exclusively of one or more dwellings (i.e. there is '*mixed use*') a just and reasonable apportionment should be made to calculate the gain or loss.

The gain or loss which is not a NRCGT gain or loss (the 'non-NRCGT gain or loss') is calculated using the following steps.

Step 1 — Calculate the notional gain or loss which would arise on 5 April 2015 if the interest had been disposed of at market value (the '*notional pre-April 2015 gain or loss*').

Step 2 — If there is a notional post-April 2015 gain on the disposal (see above) determine the amount of that gain remaining after deducting the NRCGT gain.

Step 3 — If there is a notional post-April 2015 loss on the disposal determine the amount of that loss remaining after deducting the NRCGT loss.

Step 4 — Find the sum of the gain or loss from Step 1 and any gain in Step 2, or any loss is Step 3, as the case may be.

The resulting gain or loss is the non-NRCGT gain or loss.

If the taxpayer is a company, notional post-April 2015 and pre-April 2015 gains and losses are computed as for corporation tax purposes (so that, for example, INDEXATION (**38**) allowance is taken into account in the calculation).

Note that rebasing to April 2015 under this method cannot apply to the sale of a UK residential property by a UK resident (for example, where a property acquired in a non-resident period before moving to the UK was sold after the individual had become UK-resident). (HMRC 'Capital Gains Tax for non-UK residents: sales and disposals of UK residential property' FAQs Question 20, 18 March 2015).

HMRC give the following example of a rebasing calculation involving main residence relief (see **53** PRIVATE RESIDENCES).

Example

Mr X purchased a property on 5 January 1990 for £70,000 with £2,200 costs. He used it as his main residence and it qualifies for main residence relief for the period 5 January 1990 to when he left the UK to retire abroad on 5 April 2010. An extension was added to the property on 1 September 2005 costing £20,000. The market value of the property at 5 April 2015 was £200,000. The property was sold for £270,000 (disposal costs £4,000), with exchange of contracts on 5 June 2020. Conveyance was completed on 15 June 2020. The property was let or available for let as a dwelling throughout the period 6 April 2010 to sale. The annual exempt amount is assumed to be unchanged from 2017/18.

	£
Disposal proceeds	270,000
Less: incidental costs	(4,000)
Net proceeds	266,000
Market value 5 April 2015	(200,000)
Gain over period from 6 April 2015	66,000

Mr X did not spend 90 nights in the property for any of the tax years from 6 April 2015 to disposal and so cannot consider nominating this property as his main residence for any the tax years between 6 April 2015 and 5 June 2020. Ownership from 6 April 2015 to 5 June 2020 is 62 months. Main residence relief is due for the last 18 months of ownership: 18/62 × £66,000 = £19,162. Lettings relief is also due and the lowest calculated figure is equal to the private residence relief of £19,162 (see **53.14** PRIVATE RESIDENCES).

	£
Gain	66,000
Main residence relief	(19,162)
Lettings relief	(19,162)
Net gain	27,676
Annual exempt amount	(11,300)
Taxable NRCGT gain 2020/21	£16,376

Time-apportionment method

If the taxpayer makes an election he can instead calculate the NRCGT gain or loss on the basis of straight-line time apportionment. Initially a calculation of the gain or loss is made under the normal CGT (or corporation tax) rules from the date of acquisition to the date of disposal. It is then necessary to apportion this to the post-commencement ownership period (see above) and the pre-commencement ownership period using the following fractions.

The post-commencement fraction is:

$$\frac{PCD}{TD}$$

where PCD is the number of days in the post-commencement ownership period, and

TD is the number of days in the period of ownership, which runs from the date of acquisition, or 31 March 1982 if later, to the day before the date of disposal.

The pre-commencement fraction is:

$$\frac{TD - PCD}{TD}$$

The post-commencement fraction is then the notional post-April 2015 gain or loss, and the pre-commencement fraction is the notional pre-April 2015 gain or loss. The notional post-April 2015 gain or loss is then apportioned by the fraction RD/TD (as under the default method above) to take account of the number of days in the post-commencement ownership period in which the interest consisted wholly or partly of a dwelling and the result is the NRCGT gain or loss. A just and reasonable apportionment should also be made where there is mixed use (see the default method above). Equally, the non-NRCGT gain or loss is calculated as under the default method but substituting the notional post-April 2015 gain or loss and the notional pre-April 2015 gain or loss as calculated under this method into the Steps 1–4 above.

Retrospective basis of computation

This method may be preferred where a loss accrues. Where the taxpayer so elects, the gains or losses are computed (as for CGT or corporation tax) on the basis of the position over the whole period of ownership. The gain or loss is then apportioned by the following fraction:

$$\frac{RD}{TD}$$

where RD is the number of days in the period from the date of acquisition, or 31 March 1982 if later, to the day before the date of disposal on which the disposed of interest consisted wholly or partly of a dwelling (see **41.29** above); and

TD is the number of days in that period.

The result is the NRCGT gain or loss which must be further apportioned if there is mixed use of the land as described in the default method above.

The non-NRCGT gain or loss is the unapportioned gain or loss less the NRCGT gain or loss as appropriate.

Making an election

An election for the time-apportionment or retrospective basis of computation can only be made in the self-assessment tax return for the tax year in which the disposal is made or in the non-resident CGT return for the disposal (or in an amendment to either type of return). Such an election is irrevocable. Where an election has been made by a company under *TCGA 1992, Sch 4ZZA para 5* (election to disapply transitional rules under the high value disposals of dwellings provisions — see **14.10** COMPANIES), the election is treated as if it were also an election for the retrospective basis under the non-resident CGT provisions. This rule applies even if the election was made before the non-resident CGT provisions came into force. Where an election under either set of provisions has been made in respect of the same asset, no further election under either set may be made.

Interest acquired after 5 April 2015

Where the interest disposed of was acquired after 5 April 2015, the NRCGT gain or loss is calculated using the retrospective basis of computation above.

Obtaining valuations

HMRC consider that it is optional whether a person obtains a professional valuation. Any valuation can be checked using form CG34 (see **58.5** RETURNS) but this process takes at least two months and it is necessary to report the disposal and pay the tax due within 30 days of the disposal being completed (see **58.20** RETURNS). If the valuation changes an amendment may be made to the NRCGT return. (HMRC 'Capital Gains Tax for non-UK residents: sales and disposals of UK residential property' FAQs Question 5, 18 March 2015).

Unascertainable consideration

The following rules apply where a person makes an NRCGT disposal and receives all or part of the consideration in the form of a right for future consideration which is unascertainable. If the person subsequently receives all or part of that consideration (the 'ascertained consideration') in a tax year for which he is not UK-resident, the consideration is not treated as accruing on the disposal of the right, and the amount by which it exceeds the original consideration relating to the right (if any) is instead treated as accruing on the original disposal. If the ascertainable consideration is less than the original consideration the latter is reduced. An NRCGT gain or loss will accrue accordingly at the time of receipt of the ascertained consideration.

For this purpose, a right is a right to unascertainable consideration only if it is a right to consideration the amount or value of which is unascertainable at the time the right is conferred on account of its being referable, in whole or part, to matters which are uncertain at that time because they have not yet occurred. Consideration is not regarded as unascertainable by reason only that the right to receive the whole or any part of it is postponed or contingent, but the amount or value, or the part of it in question, is taken into account in computing the gain on the disposal of the asset in question in accordance with *TCGA 1992, s 48* (see **16.13**(g) COMPUTATION OF GAINS AND LOSSES). Nor is it regarded as unascertainable by reason only that the right to receive it is postponed and may to any extent be satisfied by the receipt of property which some person has a right to select. A right is also not regarded as being a right to unascertainable consideration simply because either the amount or value of the consideration has not been fixed if the amount is to be fixed by reference to the value and the value is ascertainable or vice versa.

[*TCGA 1992, s 48A, Sch 4ZZB, paras 2–10, 21–23; FA 2015, Sch 7 paras 14, 39*].

Computation of gains and losses involving high value disposals of dwellings

[41.31] Where a non-resident CGT disposal by a company is, or involves, one or more high value disposals of dwellings within **14.10** COMPANIES the NRCGT gain or loss is the sum of the NRCGT gains or losses accruing on each such high value disposal calculated as outlined below. Where part only of the land disposed of is such a high value disposal, the remaining part of the land is treated for these purposes in the same way as if it formed part of the high value disposal. Where there are any days in the ownership period in question on which the land disposed of consists partly but not exclusively of one or more dwellings (i.e. there is '*mixed use*') a just and reasonable apportionment should be made to calculate the NRCGT gain or loss on the non-high value disposal. The provisions below apply equally to the disposal of contracts for off-plan purchases (see **41.29** above) as if the interest were a dwelling throughout the period in which the company owned the interest.

Assets held on 5 April 2015: no election to compute gains or losses on the basis of the position over the whole period of ownership, and no additional rebasing in 2016 required

Where the disposed of interest is held on 5 April 2015, no election is made under *TCGA 1992, Sch 4ZZA para 5* (election to disapply transitional rules under the high value disposals of dwellings provisions — see **14.10** COMPANIES or *TCGA 1992, Sch 4ZZB para 2(1)(b)* (for the retrospective basis of computation based on entire period of ownership (see **41.30** above)), and no rebasing is required for certain disposals after 5 April 2016 (see below), the NRCGT gain or loss is the proportion of the 'notional post-April 2015 gain or loss' (as for the default method in **41.30** above) which remains after applying the following fraction:

$$\frac{SD}{TD}$$

where SD is the number of days in the period from 6 April 2015 to the day before the date of disposal on which the interest disposed of consisted wholly or partly of a dwelling but which was not an ATED chargeable day (see **14.10** COMPANIES); and
TD is the total number of days in that period.

The corporation tax rules, such as indexation allowance, apply to the calculation of the notional post-April 2015 gain or loss.

The amount of the gain or loss which is neither ATED-related nor an NRCGT gain or loss in these circumstances is the balancing part of the gain or loss. This is the sum of the balancing part of the notional post-April 2015 gain or loss; the balancing part of the notional pre-April 2015 gain or loss (that which would have accrued on 5 April 2015 if the interest had been disposed of at market value on that date); and *TCGA 1992, Sch 4ZZA para 6A* applies (see **14.10** COMPANIES under 'Interaction with non-resident CGT disposals') the sum also includes the gain or loss which would have accrued on 5 April 2013 had the interest been disposed of at market value (the 'notional pre-April 2013 gain or loss'). For disposals before 26 November 2015, the notional pre-April 2013 gain or loss is included only where *TCGA 1992, Sch 4ZZA para 6A* applies (see **14.10** COMPANIES under 'Interaction with non-resident CGT disposals').

The balancing part of the notional post-April 2015 gain or loss is given by the fraction:

$$\frac{BD}{TD}$$

where BD is the number of days in the period from 6 April 2015 to the day before the date of disposal which are neither days on which the interest disposed of consisted wholly or partly of a dwelling but was not an ATED chargeable day nor ATED chargeable days, and
TD is the number of days in that period.

The balancing part of the notional pre-April 2015 gain or loss is given by the fraction:

$$\frac{NAD}{TD}$$

where NAD is the number of days in the period from the date of acquisition, or 6 April 2013 if later, to 5 April 2015 which are not ATED chargeable days, and
TD is the number of days in that period.

The corporation tax rules, such as indexation, apply to the calculation of the notional post-April 2015, pre-April 2015 and pre-April 2013 gains or losses.

Asset acquired after 5 April 2015, or election made, but no additional rebasing in 2016 required

Where an election is made under *TCGA 1992, Sch 4ZZA para 5* (election to disapply transitional rules under the high value disposals of dwellings provisions — see **14.10** COMPANIES or *TCGA 1992, Sch 4ZZB para 2(1)(b)* (for the retrospective basis of computation based on entire period of ownership (see **41.30** above), or where the company did not hold the interest throughout the period from 5 April 2015 to the date of disposal, the NRCGT gain or loss is the proportion of the gain or loss calculated under normal rules as remains after applying the following fraction:

$$\frac{SD}{TD}$$

where SD is the number of days in the period from date of acquisition, or 31 March 1982 if later, to the day before the date of disposal on which the interest disposed of consisted wholly or partly of a dwelling but which was not an ATED chargeable day, and
TD is the total number of days in that period.

The corporation tax rules, such as indexation allowance, apply to the calculation of the gain or loss.

The amount of the gain or loss which is neither ATED-related nor an NRCGT gain or loss in these circumstances is the balancing part of the gain or loss, i.e. the fraction of the gain or loss relating to the days in the period outlined above which are neither days on which the interest disposed of consisted wholly or partly of a dwelling but was not an ATED chargeable day nor ATED chargeable days.

Rebasing in 2016

The above provisions are overridden if the disposed of interest was held on 5 April 2016, the high value disposal falls within Case 3 in **14.10** COMPANIES and no election is made under *TCGA 1992, Sch 4ZZB para 2(1)(b)*. In this case the NRCGT gain or loss is the sum of a proportion of the 'notional post-April 2016 gain or loss' and a proportion of the 'notional pre-April 2016 gain or loss'. The proportion of the notional post-April 2016 gain or loss is that given by the fraction:

$$\frac{SD}{TD}$$

where SD is the number of days in the period from 6 April 2016 to the day before the date of disposal on which the interest disposed of consisted wholly or partly of a dwelling but which was not an ATED chargeable day, and
TD is the total number of days in that period.

The proportion of the notional pre-April 2016 gain or loss is that given by the fraction:

$$\frac{SD}{TD}$$

where SD is the number of days in the period from the date of acquisition, or 5 April 2015 if later, to 5 April 2016, on which the interest disposed of consisted wholly or partly of a dwelling but which was not an ATED chargeable day, and
TD is the total number of days in that period.

The 'notional post-April 2016 gain or loss' is the notional gain or loss on the disposal of the disposed of interest had the company acquired it at market value on 5 April 2016. The 'notional pre-April 2016 gain or loss' is that which would have accrued on 5 April 2016 if the interest had been disposed of at market value on that date, unless the company held the interest on 5 April 2015, in which case it is that which would have accrued on 5 April 2016 if P had disposed of it at market value, having acquired it for market value on 5 April 2015.

The corporation tax rules, such as indexation, apply to the calculation of the notional post-April 2016, pre-April 2016, and pre-April 2015 gains or losses.

The amount of the gain or loss which is neither ATED-related nor an NRCGT gain or loss in these circumstances is the balancing part of the gain or loss. This is the sum of the balancing part of the notional post-April 2016 gain or loss and the balancing part of the notional pre-April 2016 gain or loss, and if the company held the interest on 5 April 2015, the gain or loss which would have accrued on 5 April 2015 had the interest been disposed of at market value. The balancing parts are the fraction of the gains or losses relating to the days in the appropriate period (as outlined above) which are neither days on which the interest disposed of consisted wholly or partly of a dwelling but were not an ATED chargeable day nor ATED chargeable days.

[*TCGA 1992, Sch 4ZZB paras 11–23; FA 2015, Sch 7 para 39; FA 2016, s 90(2)(4)*].

Computation of gains and losses — further provisions

[41.32] The following further provisions apply.

Wasting assets

Any assumption for the purposes of **41.30** or **41.31** above that an interest was acquired on 5 April 2015 or 5 April 2016 is ignored when determining whether the interest is a WASTING ASSET (**72**). [*TCGA 1992, Sch 4ZZB para 24; FA 2015, Sch 7 para 39*].

Capital allowances

Where an assumption is to be made in a computation for the purposes of **41.30** or **41.31** above that an interest was acquired on 5 April 2015 or 5 April 2016 at market value, *TCGA 1992, s 41* (restriction of losses by reference to capital allowances: see **16.13** COMPUTATION OF GAINS AND LOSSES) and *TCGA 1992, s 47* (wasting assets qualifying for capital allowances: see **72.2** WASTING ASSETS) apply in relation to any capital or renewals allowance made in respect of the expenditure actually incurred in acquiring or providing the asset as if that allowance were made in respect of the expenditure treated as incurred on the deemed acquisition date. [*TCGA 1992, Sch 4ZZB para 25; FA 2015, Sch 7 para 39*].

NRCGT groups

[41.33] An election can be made by a group of companies (see **29.2** GROUPS OF COMPANIES) to pool NRCGT gains and losses. All members of the group which are 'qualifying members' must make the election. The '*qualifying members*' are all the members of the group which meet the qualifying conditions on the date the election specifies it is to have effect. The qualifying conditions are that the company is not UK-resident; it is a closely-held company (see **41.27** above); it is not carrying on life assurance business; it does not hold any 'chargeable residential assets'; and it does hold an asset the disposal of which would be a disposal of a UK residential property interest (see **41.29** above). A '*chargeable residential asset*' is a UK residential property interest the disposal of which would give rise to a non-resident CGT disposal but for the fact that it is chargeable under *TCGA 1992, s 10B* (non-resident company with UK permanent establishment: see **49.3** OVERSEAS MATTERS) or *ITA 2007, s 517C* or *CTA 2010, s 356OC(1)* (gains on certain disposals of UK land treated as trading profits — see **41.6** above).

The election, which is irrevocable, must be made within 30 days of the date it is specified to take effect.

The companies which make the election from an '*NRCGT group*'. As long as at least one of the companies which made the election continues to be a member of the group, and meet the qualifying conditions, then the NRCGT group continues to exist. A transfer by way of a non-resident CGT disposal between two members of the same NRCGT group is disregarded and the transferee company stands in the shoes of the transferor company. At any later disposal of the transferred property, the transferee company is treated as having acquired the property when the transferor company acquired it, and is also treated as having done everything that the previous owner did in relation to the property insofar as these are relevant to the computation of NRCGT gains and losses.

The NRCGT gains accruing in a tax year to the members of an NRCGT group are treated as accruing to a single body comprising all the companies which are a member of the group at any time during that tax year. Anything required or authorised to be done by this body for the purposes of *TCGA 1992* and *TMA 1970* is required or authorised to be done by all the members of the NRCGT group (including any companies which have subsequently become members), and they all have joint and several liability for the payment of tax and interest on unpaid tax. The NRCGT group may nominate (in writing) a company (the '*representative company*') to discharge the obligations of the other members to make returns, payments on account of tax liabilities or any other obligations arising to the NRCGT members. The nomination may be revoked, also in writing.

The single body is charged to CGT at 20% on the NRCGT gains accruing to any member of the group after deducting NRCGT losses accruing to any member ('*group losses*') for that tax year, any unused NRCGT losses brought forward for any member from previous years (but not from earlier than 2015/16), and any other losses brought forward which accrued to any member on the disposal of a UK residential property interest in a previous tax year (but not before 1965/66). No other deduction can be made. Group losses can only be deducted once and are only deductible from chargeable gains if they are not relievable under any other tax provision. Such losses can only be deducted in accordance with this provision.

Joining the group

If a group company is eligible to become a member of an NRCGT group by virtue of being a qualifying member it may elect to become a member. However any qualifying member which holds a UK residential asset for a 12-month period during which it is eligible to join the NRCGT group must elect to become a member of the group by the end of the 12-month period, otherwise it forfeits the right to do so. Another right to elect becomes available if the company no longer holds the whole or part of the asset but instead holds another UK residential asset. A 'UK residential asset' is an interest in UK land the disposal of which would be a disposal of a UK residential property interest.

Leaving the group

A company ceases to be a member of an NRCGT group if it ceases to be a member of the group of companies or ceases to meet the qualifying conditions. On ceasing to be a member of the NRCGT group the company is treated as having disposed of and immediately reacquired at market value any assets it holds the disposal of which would be a disposal of a UK residential property interest. A company does not cease to be a member of an NRCGT group simply because it can no longer be a member of the group of companies because another company ceases to exist. There is no deemed disposal and reacquisition where all companies cease to be members of the NRCGT group because an event causes the principal company of the group of companies to cease to be a closely-held company, or causes the head of a 'sub-group' of which they are members to cease to be a closely-held company or to become a member of another group. There is also no deemed disposal and reacquisition where a member of the NRCGT group ceases to be a member of the group of companies only because the principal company of that group becomes a member of another group. A '*sub-group*' is anything that would be a group as defined for chargeable gains purposes in the absence of the requirement for the principal company not to be 75% subsidiary of another company and the rule that a company can only be a member of one group; and the head of the sub-group is the company which is not a 75% subsidiary of any other member of the sub-group.

[*TCGA 1992, ss 4(3B)(b), 188A–188K; FA 2015, Sch 7 paras 6, 30; FA 2016, s 77(10)*].

Key points

[41.34] Points to consider are as follows:

- A gain on the disposal of land could be taxed as income if the transaction was an adventure in the nature of trade, or if the land was acquired or developed with the object of realising a gain.
- The joint ownership of land does not in itself constitute a partnership, and where there is not otherwise a partnership the share of a gain on disposal of a jointly owned investment property should simply be reported in the joint owners' self-assessment returns.
- Rollover relief is available for certain exchanges of joint interests in land. This can be a useful tool if joint owners want to go their separate ways.
- Lease termination payments can be structured so as to achieve a tax-free lease surrender receipt, a tax-deductible payment to exit an onerous lease, or a tax-free inducement to a new tenant.

- Where two individuals intend to enter into marriage or civil partnership, and one of them owns a property with a market value lower than the cost price, it may be possible to crystallise a loss by transferring an interest to the other individual prior to the marriage/civil partnership.
- In any transaction involving land, practitioners must always consider the possible impact of VAT and SDLT.
- HMRC have a toolkit 'capital gains tax for land and buildings' that considers the perceived risk areas such as access to historical data, date of disposal, valuations, qualifying expenditure and reliefs. Using the toolkit or an alternative checklist may help show that reasonable care has been taken. Showing reasonable care is important if the computation of the gain is subsequently challenged and found to be incorrect as it affects the penalty that can be charged.

42

Late Payment Interest and Penalties

Introduction to late payment interest and penalties	**42.1**
Late payment interest (the new regime)	**42.2**
Persons other than companies — the old regime	**42.3**
Tax becoming due where notice of appeal given	**42.4**
Tax becoming due after determination of an appeal by the courts	**42.5**
Surcharges on unpaid tax	**42.6**
Companies	**42.7**
Exchange restrictions and delayed remittances	**42.8**
Miscellaneous issues related to late payment interest	**42.9**
Late payment penalty	**42.10**

Cross-references. See **6** ASSESSMENTS; **51** PAYMENT OF TAX; **52** PENALTIES.

Introduction to late payment interest and penalties

[42.1] A new harmonised regime for interest is being introduced to apply to all of the taxes and duties administered by HMRC. In relation to interest on late payment of capital gains tax, the new regime is described at **42.2** below. For the purposes of income tax and capital gains tax self-assessment, it comes into force on **31 October 2011**. To the extent that the new regime is in force, it replaces the old regime described at **42.3** below. The new regime is expected to apply to corporation tax in future, but in the meantime the rules at **42.7** below continue to apply.

With effect from 6 April 2011 tax for 2010/11 and subsequent years capital gains tax which is paid more than 30 days late is subject to the penalty provisions at **42.10** below. Previously tax paid more than 28 days late was subject to surcharges — see **42.6** below. No surcharges apply to corporation tax, but the late payment penalty is to be extended to corporation tax in future.

The interest system mirrors that under which HMRC pay interest on overpaid tax (see **56** REPAYMENT INTEREST) but the rates of interest for overpaid tax are considerably lower.

Late payment interest (the new regime)

[42.2] A new harmonised regime for interest is being introduced to apply to all of the taxes and duties administered by HMRC. To the extent that the new regime is in force in relation to interest on capital gains tax payable, it replaces the rules described at **42.3** below.

For the purposes of any 'self-assessment amount' payable by any person to HMRC, the regime comes into force on 31 October 2011. A '*self-assessment amount*' means:

- any tax or other amount in relation to which, for any tax year, a personal, trustees' or partnership tax return falls to be made or a discovery assessment is made; and
- any penalties assessed in relation to that tax or amount.

Where interest is already accruing immediately prior to 31 October 2011 on a self-assessment amount, it accrues on and after that date under the new regime. Interest payable on or after 31 October 2011 on a self-assessment amount is known as '*late payment interest*'.

Late payment interest is payable without deduction of tax at source and is recoverable (as if it were tax) as a Crown debt. Interest is refundable to the extent that the tax concerned is subsequently discharged (and a tax repayment may be treated as a discharge for this purpose).

The rate of late payment interest is set by reference to the official bank rate set by the Bank of England Monetary Policy Committee; for details, see *SI 2011 No 2446, Reg 3*. Changes to the rate will be announced by HMRC News Release.

Rates of interest are:

2.75% p.a. from 23 August 2016
3.00% p.a. from 31 October 2011 to 22 August 2016

Period for which interest accrues

A payment of tax within these provisions carries interest at the late payment interest rate from the 'late payment interest start date' until the date on which payment is made. The '*late payment interest start date*' in respect of any amount is the date on which that amount becomes due and payable. (It matters not that it might be a non-business day.) However, see also below under Assessments and amendments to self-assessments.

A payment to HMRC may take the form of a set-off against an amount payable by HMRC, in which case the date on which the payment is made is the date from which the set-off takes effect. In general, for the date on which an amount is treated as paid to HMRC, see **51.10** PAYMENT OF TAX.

Assessments and amendments to self-assessments

A special rule applies to determine the late payment interest start date if:

(a) there is an amendment or correction to an assessment or self-assessment; or
(b) HMRC make an assessment in place of, or in addition to, an assessment made by a taxpayer; or
(c) HMRC make an assessment in place of an assessment that *ought to have been made* by a taxpayer.

In relation to any amount due and payable as a result of any of the above, the late payment interest start date is what it would have been if:

- the original assessment or self-assessment had been complete and accurate and had been made on the date (if any) by which it was required to be made; and

- accordingly, the amount had been due and payable as a result of that original assessment or self-assessment.

The above rule applies to any assessment or determination (however described) of any amount due and payable to HMRC. A case in which the taxpayer failed to give notice of chargeability to tax when required by law to do so (see **52.3** PENALTIES) falls within (c) above. Where the requirement arises after a notice to make a return was withdrawn (see **58.3** RETURNS), (c) above applies by reference to the assessment which the taxpayer would have been required to make had there been no withdrawal notice.

Tax postponed

If an amount of tax is postponed pending determination of an appeal against a capital gains tax assessment (see **51.17** PAYMENT OF TAX), this does not have the effect of deferring the late payment interest start date, which is the same as it would have been had there been no appeal.

Tax over-repaid

Where an assessment is raised to collect an amount of income tax previously over-repaid (see **51.31** PAYMENT OF TAX), the late payment interest start date in relation to that amount is 31 January following the tax year for which the assessment is made.

[*FA 2009, ss 101, 103, 104, Sch 53 paras 1, 2, 3–5, 15, 16; TMA 1970, s 69; FA 2013, Sch 51 para 7; SI 2011 Nos 701, 2401, 2446*].

Miscellaneous

See **42.10** below for penalties for late payment of capital gains tax.

See also **42.9** below.

Persons other than companies — the old regime

[42.3] For the purposes of income tax and capital gains tax self-assessment, the rules described below are superseded by those at **42.2** above on and after **31 October 2011**. Where interest is already accruing immediately prior to 31 October 2011 on a 'self-assessment amount' (as defined in **42.2** above), it will accrue on and after that date under the new regime.

Interest is charged by HMRC on late payments of capital gains tax, whether payable under a self-assessment or an assessment made by HMRC or as a result of an HMRC amendment to a self-assessment following an enquiry. (For details of interest charged on late payment of income tax, including interim payments, see Tolley's Income Tax.)

Interest at the rates listed below accrues from the 'relevant date' (even if a non-business day) to the date of payment. The '*relevant date*' is, with one statutory exception, 31 January following the year of assessment. The exception is that where the due date for payment of tax is deferred until three months after notice is given to deliver a self-assessment tax return (see **51.2**

PAYMENT OF TAX), the relevant date is identically deferred. Where the due date of payment is *later* than the relevant date, either under the circumstances in **51.2** PAYMENT OF TAX or because a successful application is made to postpone tax (see **51.17** PAYMENT OF TAX), this does *not* alter the relevant date for interest purposes.

[*TMA 1970, s 86(1)–(3); SI 2011 No 701, Art 5*].

In practice, where a self-assessment return is submitted by 31 October for calculation by HMRC of the tax due (see **58.6** RETURNS) and HMRC fail to notify the taxpayer of the tax due in time for the correct tax to be paid at the due date, any interest or surcharge arising in the period of delay attributable to HMRC will be waived (HMRC Self-Assessment Legal Framework Manual, SALF204). This is of no significance where returns are filed over the internet (see **58.4** RETURNS) as the tax due is automatically computed during the filing process. See **42.9** below for a point concerning personal representatives.

For the date on which payment of tax is treated as made, see **51.10** PAYMENT OF TAX.

Capital gains tax for 2009/10 and earlier years which is paid more than 28 days after the due date is also subject to a surcharge, with an additional surcharge where payment is more than six months late (see **42.6** below). See **42.10** below for penalties for late payment for 2010/11 onwards.

Rates of interest are:

3.00% p.a. from 29 September 2009 to 30 October 2011
2.50% p.a. from 24 March 2009 to 28 September 2009
3.50% p.a. from 27 January 2009 to 23 March 2009
4.50% p.a. from 6 January 2009 to 26 January 2009
5.50% p.a. from 6 December 2008 to 5 January 2009
6.50% p.a. from 6 November 2008 to 5 December 2008
7.50% p.a. from 6 January 2008 to 5 November 2008
8.50% p.a. from 6 August 2007 to 5 January 2008
7.50% p.a. from 6 September 2006 to 5 August 2007
6.50% p.a. from 6 September 2005 to 5 September 2006
7.50% p.a. from 6 September 2004 to 5 September 2005
6.50% p.a. from 6 December 2003 to 5 September 2004
5.50% p.a. from 6 August 2003 to 5 December 2003
6.50% p.a. from 6 November 2001 to 5 August 2003
7.50% p.a. from 6 May 2001 to 5 November 2001
8.50% p.a. from 6 February 2000 to 5 May 2001
7.50% p.a. from 6 March 1999 to 5 February 2000
8.50% p.a. from 6 January 1999 to 5 March 1999
9.50% p.a. from 6 August 1997 to 5 January 1999
8.50% p.a. from 31 January 1997 to 5 August 1997

Interest charges are calculated automatically and, however small, will appear on taxpayer statements of account under self-assessment. There is no minimum limit for charging interest. The rates are adjusted automatically by reference to changes in the official bank rate of the Bank of England, and are announced by HMRC Press Release. Before 12 August 2009, the rates were determined by reference to the average of base lending rates of certain clearing banks. See *SI 1989 No 1297, Reg 3*.

Interest is also chargeable at the above rates from 9 March 1998 on late payment of surcharges (see **42.6** below) and penalties (see **52.22** PENALTIES). [*TMA 1970, ss 59C(6), 103A; SI 1989 No 1297, Reg 3; SI 2011 No 701, Art 10*].

Interest is payable gross and recoverable, as if it were tax charged, as a Crown debt; it is *not deductible from profits or income*. [*ITTOIA 2005, ss 54, 272, 869; TMA 1970, ss 69, 90; SI 2009 No 56, Sch 1 paras 438, 442*]. It is refundable to the extent that the tax concerned is subsequently cancelled. [*TMA 1970, s 91*].

Tax becoming due where notice of appeal given

[42.4] The rules for determining the due and payable date where an assessment etc. is under appeal are explained at **51.17**, **51.18** PAYMENT OF TAX. For right of appeal, see **5.2** APPEALS. The giving of notice of appeal, whether or not accompanied by a postponement application, does not affect the date from which interest accrues, which remains as in **42.3** above. (A similar situation applies for corporation tax purposes.)

Tax becoming due after determination of an appeal by the courts

[42.5] The rules for determining the due and payable date where further tax is found to be chargeable on determination by the courts of an appeal against an assessment etc. are explained at **51.18** PAYMENT OF TAX. These rules do *not* affect the date from which interest accrues, which remains as in **42.3** above. (A similar situation applies for corporation tax.)

Surcharges on unpaid tax

[42.6] The provisions described below are replaced by a new penalty for failing to make payments on time at **42.10** below. The new penalty applies for CGT purposes with effect from 6 April 2011 to tax payable for 2010/11 and subsequent years.

For tax not subject to the new penalty, an initial surcharge is payable where an amount of CGT (and/or income tax), whether payable under a self-assessment or an assessment made by HMRC or as a result of an HMRC amendment to a self-assessment following an enquiry, remains unpaid more than 28 days after the due date for payment. The due date for payment of CGT is normally 31 January following the year of assessment, but see **51.2** PAYMENT OF TAX for exceptions (and note also the postponement rules at **51.17**, **51.18** PAYMENT OF TAX). The surcharge is equal to **5%** of the amount of tax unpaid. **An additional 5%** surcharge is payable on any of that tax which remains unpaid more than six months after the due date. Interest accrues on an unpaid surcharge with effect from the expiry of 30 days beginning with the date of the notice imposing the surcharge. An appeal may be made, within the same 30-day period, against the imposition of a surcharge as if it were an assessment to tax, and the surcharge may be set aside if it appears that, *throughout* the period from the due date until payment of the tax, the taxpayer had a 'reasonable excuse' for non-payment. Inability to pay the tax, i.e. due to insufficient funds, is not to be regarded as a reasonable excuse. The decision as to whether a taxpayer meets these criteria rests ultimately with the Tribunal. See also Revenue Tax Bulletin April 1998 pp 527–529.

There are provisions to prevent a double charge where tax has been taken into account in determining the tax-geared penalties of *TMA 1970, s 7* or *FA 2008, Sch 41* (see **52.3** PENALTIES), *TMA 1970, s 93(5)* (tax-geared penalty for failure to make return for income tax and capital gains tax; see **52.4** PENALTIES), *s 95* (incorrect return etc. for income tax or capital gains tax; now repealed), *s 95A* (incorrect return etc. for partnerships; now repealed) and *FA 2007, Sch 24* (errors in documents and assessments; see **52.8–52.10** PENALTIES). Any such tax will not be subject to a surcharge. HMRC have discretion to mitigate, or to stay or compound proceedings for recovery of, a surcharge and may also, after judgment, entirely remit the surcharge.

[*TMA 1970, s 59C; SI 2009 No 56, Sch 1 para 39; SI 2009 No 571, Sch; SI 2010 No 530; SI 2011 No 702, Art 5*].

Where the due date is 31 January, it is HMRC's view that surcharge can only be avoided by full payment of the tax on or before 28 February. HMRC's view was confirmed by *Thompson v Minzly* Ch D 2001, 74 TC 340. See **51.10** PAYMENT OF TAX for effective dates of payment.

In practice, where a self-assessment return is submitted by 31 October for calculation by HMRC of the tax due (see **58.6** RETURNS), the due date by reference to which any surcharge is triggered is delayed until 30 days after notification by HMRC of the amount due, where this occurs after 31 December following the tax year (ICAEW Technical Release TAX 9/94, June 1994).

No surcharge will be imposed where a taxpayer has entered into a 'Time to Pay' agreement (see **51.5** PAYMENT OF TAX), provided that the payment proposals lead to an acceptable agreement to defer the tax, and the taxpayer does not break the agreement. For this purpose, a taxpayer breaks an agreement if the tax is not paid by the agreed date or if a condition of the agreement is not complied with. If the taxpayer does break the agreement HMRC can serve a notice reinstating the surcharge. [*FA 2009, s 108*]. This provision applies to agreements made on or after 24 November 2008, but similar provisions applied previously by concession — see HMRC Self-Assessment Legal Framework Manual, SALF307.

Companies

[42.7] Corporation tax carries interest (under *TMA 1970, s 87A*) from the due and payable date (see **51.4** PAYMENT OF TAX), even if it is a non-business day, until payment. Where corporation tax assessed on a company may be assessed on other persons in certain circumstances, the due and payable date is that which refers to the company's liability. Corporation tax is to be brought within the late payment interest regime at **42.2** above (with special additional rules) at a future date.

The interest rate is determined by criteria contained in Treasury regulations made by statutory instrument; see *SI 1989 No 1297, Regs 3ZA, 3ZB.*

The rates of interest (such interest being deductible for tax purposes — see below) as regards corporation tax becoming due **on or after the normal due date** (nine months and one day after the end of the accounting period) are:

2.75% p.a. from 23 August 2016
3.00% p.a. from 29 September 2009 to 22 August 2016
2.50% p.a. from 24 March 2009 to 28 September 2009
3.50% p.a. from 27 January 2009 to 23 March 2009
4.50% p.a. from 6 January 2009 to 26 January 2009
5.50% p.a. from 6 December 2008 to 5 January 2009
6.50% p.a. from 6 November 2008 to 5 December 2008
7.50% p.a. from 6 January 2008 to 5 November 2008
8.50% p.a. from 6 August 2007 to 5 January 2008
7.50% p.a. from 6 September 2006 to 5 August 2007
6.50% p.a. from 6 September 2005 to 5 September 2006
7.50% p.a. from 6 September 2004 to 5 September 2005
6.50% p.a. from 6 December 2003 to 5 September 2004
5.50% p.a. from 6 August 2003 to 5 December 2003
6.50% p.a. from 6 November 2001 to 5 August 2003
7.50% p.a. from 6 May 2001 to 5 November 2001
8.50% p.a. previously

The rates for corporation tax payable by earlier **instalments,** under the quarterly accounting rules for large companies (see **51.4** PAYMENT OF TAX), are:

1.25% p.a. from 15 August 2016
1.50% p.a. from 16 March 2009 to 14 August 2016
2.00% p.a. from 16 February 2009 to 15 March 2009
2.50% p.a. from 19 January 2009 to 15 February 2009
3.00% p.a. from 15 December 2008 to 18 January 2009
4.00% p.a. from 17 November 2008 to 14 December 2008
5.50% p.a. from 20 October 2008 to 16 November 2008
6.00% p.a. from 21 April 2008 to 19 October 2008
6.25% p.a. from 18 February 2008 to 20 April 2008
6.50% p.a. from 17 December 2007 to 17 February 2008
6.75% p.a. from 16 July 2007 to 16 December 2007
6.50% p.a. from 21 May 2007 to 15 July 2007
6.25% p.a. from 22 January 2007 to 20 May 2007
6.00% p.a. from 20 November 2006 to 21 January 2007
5.75% p.a. from 14 August 2006 to 19 November 2006
5.50% p.a. from 15 August 2005 to 13 August 2006
5.75% p.a. from 16 August 2004 to 14 August 2005
5.50% p.a. from 21 June 2004 to 15 August 2004
5.25% p.a. from 17 May 2004 to 20 June 2004
5.00% p.a. from 16 February 2004 to 16 May 2004

4.75% from 17 November 2003 to 15 February 2004
4.50% p.a. from 21 July 2003 to 16 November 2003
4.75% p.a. from 17 February 2003 to 20 July 2003
5.00% p.a. from 19 November 2001 to 16 February 2003
5.50% p.a. from 15 October 2001 to 18 November 2001
5.75% p.a. from 1 October 2001 to 14 October 2001
6.00% p.a. from 13 August 2001 to 30 September 2001
6.25% p.a. from 21 May 2001 to 12 August 2001
6.50% p.a. from 16 April 2001 to 20 May 2001
6.75% p.a. from 19 February 2001 to 15 April 2001
7.00% p.a. from 20 April 2000 to 18 February 2001
8.00% p.a. from 21 February 2000 to 19 April 2000
7.75% p.a. from 24 January 2000 to 20 February 2000
7.50% p.a. from 15 November 1999 to 23 January 2000
7.25% p.a. from 20 September 1999 to 14 November 1999
7.00% p.a. from 21 June 1999 to 19 September 1999
7.25% p.a. from 19 April 1999 to 20 June 1999
7.50% p.a. from 15 February 1999 to 18 April 1999
8.00% p.a. from 18 January 1999 to 14 February 1999
8.25% p.a. from 7 January 1999 to 17 January 1999

The latter set of rates applies up to the earlier of the date of payment and the normal due date (whereafter the normal rates apply).

Interest on tax subsequently discharged is adjusted or repaid so as to secure that the total is as it would have been had the tax discharged never been charged. However, where surplus advance corporation tax of a later accounting period displaces mainstream corporation tax paid in respect of an earlier accounting period, or trading losses or non-trading deficits of a later accounting period are offset against profits of an earlier period, or there is a combination of such events, any such adjustment or repayment of interest is restricted. In considering an adjustment or repayment of interest, then, where relief for tax paid for an accounting period is given by way of repayment of tax, the amount repaid is, as far as possible, treated as if it were a discharge of the corporation tax charged for that period.

Interest is paid without deduction of income tax and is deductible in computing profits (as a non-trading debit under the loan relationship rules — see **15.2–15.6** COMPANIES — CORPORATE FINANCE AND INTANGIBLES and Tolley's Corporation Tax). It is recoverable (as if it were tax charged and due and payable under an assessment) as a Crown debt.

[*TMA 1970, ss 69, 87A, 90, 91(1A)(2A); FA 1989, s 178; SI 1998 No 3175, Reg 7; FA 2009, s 105(6)*].

Exchange restrictions and delayed remittances

[42.8] Where gains arising overseas cannot be remitted to the UK due to government action in the country of origin etc., and HMRC agree to defer collection of the tax, interest under **42.3** above ceases to run from the date on which HMRC were first in possession of information necessary to enable them to agree to deferment. If that date is three months or less from the due and payable date, no interest is payable. But where a demand is later made for payment of the deferred tax, interest (from the date of demand) is only chargeable if the tax is not paid within three months of that demand. [*TMA 1970, s 92*]. HMRC may defer collection indefinitely. See **49.6** OVERSEAS MATTERS for an alternative relief under *TCGA 1992, s 279*.

Miscellaneous issues related to late payment interest

Unreasonable delay by HMRC

[42.9] Where the taxpayer complains, HMRC may remit or reimburse any interest on unpaid tax incurred during a period of unreasonable delay by HMRC in dealing with his affairs (HMRC Code of Practice 1 (COP 1)).

Death of taxpayer

A special rule applies if a person chargeable to an amount of tax dies before the amount becomes due and payable and the executor or administrator is unable to pay the amount until he obtains probate or letters of administration (or, in Scotland, the executor is unable to pay the amount before he obtains confirmation). In relation to that amount, the late payment interest start date in **42.2** above is the *later* of:

- the date which would have been the late payment interest start date apart from this special rule; and
- the date falling 30 days after the date of grant of probate etc.

[*FA 2009, s 101, Sch 53 para 12; SI 2011 No 701*].

An identical rule applies, but by concession, to interest on overdue tax as in **42.3** above (HMRC ESC A17).

Disasters of national significance

No interest is chargeable on unpaid tax where HMRC agree that payment may be deferred by reason of circumstances arising from a disaster or emergency specified by order in a statutory instrument made for the purpose. This applies whether the agreement was made before or after the tax became due or the order was made.

The period for which interest does not arise is the period beginning with a date specified in the order or, if HMRC direct, a later date from which the agreement for deferred payment has effect and ending with the date on which that agreement ceases to apply or, if earlier, the date on which the order is revoked. For this purpose, the agreement for deferred payment ceases to have effect at the end of the period of deferment specified in the agreement or, if HMRC agree to extend (or further extend) that period, with the end of the extended period. If the agreement is for payment by instalments, the period of deferment in relation to each instalment ends with the date by which it is to be paid, but if an instalment is not paid by the agreed date (and HMRC do not agree to extend the period of deferment), the whole agreement is treated as ceasing to apply on that date.

If no agreement for deferred payment is made, but HMRC are satisfied that one could have been made, these provisions apply as if one had been made on terms which HMRC are satisfied would have been agreed in the circumstances.

Where these provisions apply, no liability to a surcharge (see **42.6** above) on the deferred amount arises during the deferment period.

The Treasury may make an order specifying a disaster or emergency for the purposes of these provisions only if they consider it to be of national significance.

These provisions take effect on 21 July 2008, but an order under the provisions may specify an earlier date.

[*FA 2008, s 135*].

The severe floods in the UK in June and July 2007 have been designated as a disaster within the above provisions. The date specified in the order is 1 June 2007. [*SI 2008 No 1936*].

Interest on judgment debts

With effect for periods beginning on or after 8 July 2015, the same rate of interest as under **42.2** above applies to interest payable to HMRC under *Judgments Act 1838, s 17* or under an order under *County Courts Act 1984, s 74* where the debt to which the interest relates arises from court proceedings relating to a tax matter. See *F(No 2)A 2015, s 52*. With effect from 15 September 2016, similar rules apply in Scotland and Northern Ireland. See *FA 2016, ss 170, 171*.

Late payment penalty

[42.10] A new unified penalty code for failure to make payments on time (the '*late payment penalty*') has been introduced across a range of taxes including capital gains tax and corporation tax. The code applies for capital gains tax purposes with effect from 6 April 2011 to tax payable for 2010/11 and subsequent years. The code does not yet apply for corporation tax purposes except for corporation tax due under an exit charge payment plan, with effect where the first day after the period of nine months beginning immediately after the accounting period in question falls on or after 11 December 2012. The penalty code is described below, but only to the extent that it relates to capital gains tax and corporation tax. For capital gains tax (and income tax) purposes, the late payment penalty replaces surcharges on unpaid tax (see **42.6** above).

A penalty is payable under the code if a taxpayer fails to make a payment of tax on or before the date specified in the table below. For the purposes of the following provisions, the 'penalty date' is the day after the table date.

	Tax to which payment relates	Amount of tax payable	Date after which penalty is incurred
1	CGT	Amount contained in taxpayer's self-assessment.	30 days after the due date. The due date is normally 31 January following the tax year in question but is deferred in certain cases where tax return is issued late by HMRC — see **51.2** PAYMENT OF TAX.
2	CGT	Amount contained in simple assessment.	30 days after the date the amount becomes due and payable — see **51.2** PAYMENT OF TAX.
3	Corporation tax	Amount shown in company tax return.	The filing date for the tax return for the accounting period for which the tax is due (see **58.19** RETURNS).
4	Corporation tax	Amount payable under quarterly accounting rules (see **51.4** PAYMENT OF TAX).	The filing date for the tax return for the accounting period for which the tax is due (see **58.19** RETURNS).
5	CGT and corporation tax	Amount payable under a determination of tax where no return is made on time.	CGT: 30 days after the date by which the amount would have been required to be paid if it had been shown in the return (i.e. the same date as for 1 above). Corporation tax: The filing date for the tax return for the accounting period for which the tax is due (see **58.19** RETURNS).
6	CGT	Amount payable where a determination of tax under *TMA 1970, s 28C* (see **58.15** RETURNS) is superseded by a self-assessment.	30 days after the date on which the amount would have been payable had it fallen within 1 above — see **58.15** RETURNS.
7	CGT	Amount payable in respect of tax under appeal but not postponed (or of tax ceasing to be postponed) or amount payable on determination of appeal.	30 days after the due date (see **51.17, 51.18** PAYMENT OF TAX).
8	CGT	Amount payable as a result of a correction or amendment of a self-assessment.	30 days after the due date (see **51.2** PAYMENT OF TAX).
9	CGT	Amount payable under an assessment other than a self-assessment.	30 days after the due date (which itself is 30 days after the date of the assessment).

10	CGT and corporation tax	Amount (not within 7–9 above) shown in an amendment or correction of a return.	30 days after the later of the due date and the date on which the amendment or correction is made.
11	CGT and corporation tax	Amount (not within 7–9 above) shown in an assessment or determination made by HMRC in circumstances other than where the taxpayer was required to make a return but failed to do so on time and that return, had it been made, would have shown an amount of tax payable.	30 days after the later of the due date and the date on which the assessment or determination is made.
12	Corporation tax	Amount payable under an exit charge payment plan (see **51.8** PAYMENT OF TAX).	The later of the first day after the 12-month period beginning immediately after the migration accounting period and the date on which the amount is payable under the plan.

If a failure is within more than one of the above categories, a penalty is payable in respect of each such category.

Amount of penalty

Where a failure to pay tax on or before the relevant specified date occurs, the taxpayer is liable to an initial penalty of 5% of the unpaid tax.

If any of the tax remains unpaid after the end of the five months beginning with the penalty date (three months where the tax is within 3 or 4 above), the taxpayer is liable to an additional penalty of 5% of the amount remaining unpaid at that time. A further additional penalty becomes due if any of the tax is unpaid after the end of the eleven months (nine months where the tax is within 3 or 4 above) beginning with the penalty date, again equal to 5% of the amount remaining unpaid.

Reduction in special circumstances

HMRC can reduce, stay or agree a compromise in relation to proceedings for a penalty if they think it right to do so because of special circumstances. Ability to pay and the fact that a potential loss of revenue from one taxpayer is balanced by a potential overpayment by another are not special circumstances for this purpose.

Suspension of penalty during time to pay agreement

A taxpayer is not liable to a penalty under the above provisions if, before the penalty arises, he makes a request to HMRC for the deferral of the tax concerned and HMRC agree (whether before or after the penalty date) to the deferral. See **51.5** PAYMENT OF TAX for 'time to pay' arrangements.

The taxpayer remains liable, however, for any penalty which arises after the end of the agreed deferral period. If the taxpayer breaks the agreement then he becomes liable to any penalty to which he would have been liable but for the agreement, provided that HMRC notify him to that effect. For this purpose, a taxpayer breaks an agreement if he fails to pay the tax when the deferral period ends or if he fails to comply with a condition forming part of the agreement.

Where a deferral agreement is varied, the above rules apply to the agreement as varied from the time of the variation.

Reasonable excuse

None of the above penalties are due in respect of a failure to make a payment if the taxpayer satisfies HMRC or, on appeal, the Tribunal, that there is a reasonable excuse for the failure. Insufficiency of funds is not a reasonable excuse for this purpose and neither is the taxpayer's reliance on another person to do anything, unless he took reasonable care to avoid the failure. If the taxpayer had a reasonable excuse, he is treated as continuing to have a reasonable excuse after the excuse has ceased if the failure is remedied without unreasonable delay.

Double jeopardy

No penalty arises for a failure or action in respect of which the taxpayer has been convicted of an offence.

Procedure

For the making of assessments to penalties under these provisions see **52.33** PENALTIES. For the right of appeal against such an assessment see **52.34** PENALTIES

[*FA 2009, Sch 56 paras 1–4, 9, 10, 16, 17; FA 2013, Sch 49 para 7, Sch 50 para 11; FA 2016, s 167, Sch 23 para 9; SI 2011 No 702, Art 3; SI 2011 No 703, Art 3*].

43

Life Insurance Policies and Deferred Annuities

Disposal of rights	43.1
Profits on assigned policies	43.2

Cross-reference. For the treatment of other kinds of insurance policy, see **25.10** EXEMPTIONS AND RELIEFS.

Disposal of rights

[43.1] A gain on the disposal of, or of an interest in, rights under a life insurance policy or contract for a deferred annuity is not a chargeable gain unless, in the case of a disposal of the rights, the rights or any interest in the rights, or, in the case of a disposal of an interest in the rights, the rights, the interest or any interest from which all or part of the interest directly or indirectly derives, have at any time been acquired by any person for 'actual consideration'.

For this purpose, '*actual consideration*' is consideration other than consideration deemed to be given under any provision relating to tax on chargeable gains. Amounts paid under the policy or contract by way of premiums or as lump sum consideration are not actual consideration. Actual consideration given for a disposal made by one spouse or civil partner to the other, an 'approved post-marriage disposal', an 'approved post-civil partnership disposal', or an intra-group transfer to which *TCGA 1992, s 171(1)* (see **29.3** GROUPS OF COMPANIES) applies, is treated as not being actual consideration. A disposal is an '*approved post-marriage disposal*' or an '*approved post-civil partnership disposal*' if it is one made in consequence of the dissolution or annulment of a marriage or civil partnership by one party to the marriage or partnership to the other, with the approval, agreement or authority of, or pursuant to an order of, a court (or other person or body) having jurisdiction under the law of any country or territory, where the rights or interest disposed of were held by the person making the disposal immediately before the marriage or partnership was dissolved or annulled. An '*interest*' in relation to any rights is an interest as co-owner of the rights, whether the rights are owned jointly or in common and whether or not the interests of the co-owners are equal.

Where an allowable loss would otherwise accrue on a disposal of, or of an interest in, the rights under a life insurance policy or contract for a deferred annuity but if *TCGA 1992, s 37* (exclusion from consideration of amounts charged to income tax — see **39.1** INTERACTION WITH OTHER TAXES) and *TCGA 1992, s 39* (exclusion from allowable expenditure of amounts deductible in computing profits or losses for income tax purposes — see 39.1 INTERACTION WITH OTHER TAXES) were disregarded there would be a loss of a smaller amount, that smaller amount is taken to be the loss on the disposal. Where, disregarding those provisions, either a gain or neither a gain nor a loss would accrue, the disposal is taken to be one on which neither a gain nor a loss accrue.

In the case of a life insurance policy, the receipt of the sum assured by the policy, the transfer of investments or other assets to the owner in accordance with the policy and the surrender of the policy are each treated as a disposal of the rights (or of all of the interests in the rights) under the policy. In the case of a contract for a deferred annuity, the receipt of the first instalment of the deferred annuity and the surrender of the rights under the contract are treated as a disposal of the rights (or of all the interests in the rights) under the contract. Where there is a disposal of (or of an interest in) the rights under a contract for a deferred annuity on receipt of the first instalment, the amount of the consideration for the disposal is deemed to be the aggregate of the amount or value of the first instalment and the then market value of the outstanding instalments (or, in the case of a disposal of an interest, such proportion of that aggregate as is just and reasonable), and no gain accruing on any subsequent disposal of the rights or any interest in them is a chargeable gain.

[*TCGA 1992, s 210*].

Where a policy-holder receives compensation for mis-selling of the policy, no chargeable gain arises in respect of that compensation provided that the exemption in *TCGA 1992, s 210(2)* above applies to the policy. In such circumstances, HMRC Extra-Statutory Concession D33 (see **7.2** ASSETS) applies (HMRC Capital Gains Manual CG69071).

Any transfer of investments or other assets to a policy-holder in accordance with a policy is deemed to be made at market value. [*TCGA 1992, s 204(3)(6)*].

Subject to the restriction noted above in relation to losses, in computing any chargeable gain or allowable loss under the above provisions, allowable expenditure will be:

(a) the base cost of the policy to the person to whom the gain accrues (this will be either market value or what that person paid for the policy), and
(b) any premiums paid by that person.

Profits on assigned policies

[43.2] *ITTOIA 2005, ss 461–546* provide for income tax to be charged on the profits arising on certain life policies and life annuity contracts. Before 26 June 1982, where such policies or contracts were assigned for money or money's worth, any profit subsequently arising was taken out of charge to income tax and was subject instead to capital gains tax. To counter the tax advantages previously gained by the use of such policies and contracts, any profit on policies etc. taken out after 25 June 1982 cease to escape the charge to income tax. The former provisions also cease to apply to policies etc. issued and assigned for money or money's worth before 26 June 1982 if, after 23 August 1982,

(i) the rights under the policy etc. are again assigned for money or money's worth; or
(ii) further capital is injected; or
(iii) subject to certain conditions, loans are taken against the security of the policy etc.

[*ICTA 1988, ss 540(3), 542(3), 544*].

For full details, see Tolley's Income Tax.

The equivalent corporation tax provisions in *ICTA 1988, Pt XIII Ch II* are, broadly, repealed for accounting periods beginning on or after 1 April 2008. [*FA 2008, Sch 14 paras 2, 16*]. For such accounting periods, 'investment life insurance contracts' (broadly, life insurance policies which have a surrender value, contracts for a purchased life annuity and capital redemption policies) held by a company which is not a life insurance company are treated as creditor relationships of the company. See *CTA 2009, ss 560–569*.

For full details, see Tolley's Corporation Tax.

44

Losses

Introduction to losses	**44.1**
Set-off of capital losses against chargeable gains	**44.2**
Computation of allowable loss	**44.3**
Notification of capital losses	**44.4**
Carry-back prohibited	**44.5**
Connected persons	**44.6**
Anti-avoidance	**44.7**
Interaction with annual exempt amount	**44.8**
Profit and losses of theatre backers (angels)	**44.9**
Special reliefs for losses	**44.10**
Assets of negligible value	**44.11**
Loans to traders	**44.12**
Loans to traders evidenced by qualifying corporate bonds becoming irrecoverable	**44.13**
Qualifying corporate bonds — reorganisations etc. thereof and relief under 42.13 above	**44.14**
Losses on shares in unlisted trading companies — individuals	**44.15**
Qualifying trading company	**44.16**
Losses on shares in unlisted trading companies — investment companies	**44.18**
Deferred unascertainable consideration — election for treatment of loss as accruing in earlier year	**44.19**
Restriction on losses — write-off of government investment	**44.20**
Set-off of trading losses etc. against chargeable gains	**44.21**
Key points concerning losses	**44.22**

Cross-references. See also **4.32–4.36** ANTI-AVOIDANCE for restrictions on the use of losses under the serial avoiders regime; **14.6** COMPANIES; **18.18**, **18.19** CORPORATE VENTURING SCHEME; **23.13** ENTERPRISE INVESTMENT SCHEME; **41.25** LAND; **55** REMITTANCE BASIS; **62.16**, **62.22** SETTLEMENTS; **66.3–66.5** SUBSTANTIAL SHAREHOLDINGS OF COMPANIES.

Simon's Taxes. See **C1.5**, **C3.7**.

Introduction to losses

[44.1] For capital gains tax purposes, allowable losses are calculated in the same way as chargeable gains. The basic rule is that losses incurred in a tax year are set off against gains of the same tax year, and to the extent that they cannot be so set off, are carried forward for set off against gains of subsequent years. Losses cannot, with two exceptions, be carried back to previous tax years. The exceptions are for certain losses on rights to deferred unascertainable consideration (see **44.19** below) and for losses carried back from the tax year of death (see **19.7** DEATH).

See **14.6** COMPANIES for losses incurred by companies. Relief for losses of a corporate body is restricted where any amount of an investment by the Government in the body is written off (see **44.20** below).

There are also a number of special rules giving rise to losses or providing for alternative reliefs as follows.

	Relief	Reference	Para
1	**Assets of negligible value.** Where an asset has become of negligible value, the owner may claim to crystallise a loss without disposing of the asset. Claim can be backdated up to two years before tax year of claim.	*TCGA 1992, s 24(1A)–(3)*	**44.11**
2	**Loan to trader.** Loss relief is available where a loan to a UK resident used wholly for the purposes of a trade etc. becomes irrecoverable. Claim can be backdated up to two years before tax year of claim. **Payment made under guarantee.** Relief also applies to a payment made by a guarantor of such a loan. Claim cannot be backdated.	*TCGA 1992, s 253*	**44.12**
3	**Loan to trader evidenced by QCB.** Loss relief is available where a 'qualifying loan' backed by a qualifying corporate bond made before 17 March 1998 becomes irrecoverable. Claim can be backdated up to two years before tax year of claim.	*TCGA 1992, s 254*	**44.13**
4	**Losses on shares in unlisted trading companies — individuals.** Income tax relief can be claimed by an individual for a capital loss on shares in a qualifying trading company for which he subscribed or for shares to which EIS income tax relief is attributable. The loss can be relieved against income of the tax year in which the loss is incurred and/or the preceding tax year.	*ITA 2007, ss 131–151*	**44.15**

5	**Losses on shares in unlisted trading companies — investment companies.** An investment company may claim relief against income for a loss on shares in a qualifying trading company for which it subscribed. Relief is given first against income of the accounting period of loss, with any unrelieved balance set off against income of the preceding twelve months.	*CTA 2010, ss 68–90*	44.18

The final relief described in this chapter is relief for trading losses which can in certain circumstances be set off against the chargeable gains of a person other than a company. See **44.21** below.

Set-off of capital losses against chargeable gains

[44.2] The charge to capital gains tax is on all chargeable gains accruing to the taxpayer in the tax year, less any 'allowable losses' (see **44.3** below) accruing to him in that year and, so far as not allowed as a deduction from chargeable gains accruing in any previous tax year, any allowable losses accruing to him in any previous year (but not earlier than 1965/66). This rule applies subject to the annual exempt amount (see **2.6** ANNUAL RATES AND EXEMPTIONS). See also **44.8** below for the interaction of the annual exempt amount with losses brought forward. [*TCGA 1992, s 2(2)*].

Losses are not deductible if, and so far as, other tax relief can be claimed in respect of them and may only be deducted once for capital gains tax purposes. They may not be deducted at all if already given relief for income tax (see **44.15** and **44.18** below regarding an election for capital losses arising on the disposal of certain shares in unquoted trading companies to be set off against general income). [*TCGA 1992, s 2(3)*].

Where it is necessary to determine from which chargeable gains a loss may be deducted or which losses are to be deducted from a chargeable gain, the losses may be used in the most beneficial way (see **2.2** ANNUAL RATES AND EXEMPTIONS).

For anti-avoidance provisions relating to allowable losses, see **44.7** below.

For provisions relating to losses of companies see **14.6** COMPANIES.

Set-off against attributed gains

A person's allowable losses, whether of the tax year under review or brought forward from previous years (or brought back from the year of death — see **19.7** DEATH), can be set off against attributed gains under *TCGA 1992, s 86* (charge on settlor of non-UK resident settlement in which he has an interest (see **48.5** OFFSHORE SETTLEMENTS)). Personal losses cannot be set off against gains treated under *TCGA 1992, s 87* or *s 89(2)* as accruing to a beneficiary of a non-UK resident settlement (see **48.14–48.20** OFFSHORE SETTLEMENTS).

Where any personal losses are to be set against two or more attributed gains from different settlements and those gains are insufficient to extinguish them fully, a proportion of those losses is deducted from each of those gains on a pro rata basis. This rule will affect the amount recoverable by the settlor from the trustees in respect of tax on the attributed gains (see **48.11** OFFSHORE SETTLEMENTS).

[*TCGA 1992, s 2(4)–(7); FA 2008, Sch 2 paras 2, 21, 24, 56(3)*].

Remittance basis

See **55.2** REMITTANCE BASIS.

Non-resident CGT losses

None of the above provisions apply to an NRCGT gains or to an allowable NRCGT loss. See **41.25** LAND for relief for NRCGT losses against NRCGT gains, for the limited circumstances in which such losses may be relieved against general chargeable gains and for relief for certain allowable losses which are not NRCGT losses against NRCGT gains. [*TCGA 1992, s 2(7B); FA 2015, Sch 7 para 3*].

Miscellaneous

Short-term losses which accrued before 1971/72 but which were not relieved under *Sch D, Case VII* may be brought forward against gains chargeable to capital gains tax. [*TCGA 1992, Sch 11 para 12*]. This is the only instance where losses incurred before 6 April 1965 can be carried forward.

A person may be able to enjoy the benefit of unutilised losses of trustees which have accrued to them in respect of property to which the person has become absolutely entitled. However, where a person becomes so entitled after 15 June 1999, the previously unfettered right to utilise such losses is significantly restricted. See **62.16** SETTLEMENTS. This facility to transfer losses does not apply as regards personal representatives and legatees (see **19.9** DEATH).

Computation of allowable loss

[44.3] Losses are computed as for gains (see **16** COMPUTATION OF GAINS AND LOSSES) except as in **44.21** below and where expressly provided otherwise (e.g. as in **38.2** INDEXATION).

Wherever an exemption is given so as to make a gain not a chargeable gain, that exemption applies similarly to losses so that they are not to be '*allowable losses*'.

[*TCGA 1992, s 16(1)(2); ICTA 1988, s 834(1); CTA 2010, s 1119*].

For anti-avoidance provisions relating to allowable losses, see **44.7** below and, for those applicable only for corporation tax purposes, see **14.6** COMPANIES.

Where a loss accrues on the disposal of an asset held on 6 April 1965 there are provisions (e.g. time apportionment), which may restrict the loss allowable (but these rules apply only for corporation tax purposes for disposals after

5 April 2008). See 8 ASSETS HELD ON 6 APRIL 1965. Similar observations may apply to disposals after 5 April 1988 of assets held on 31 March 1982. See 9 ASSETS HELD ON 31 MARCH 1982. See also 16.13(*j*) COMPUTATION OF GAINS AND LOSSES where an asset has qualified for capital allowances.

A loss accruing to a person in a tax year for which the residence condition at 1.2 INTRODUCTION is not met is not an allowable loss unless:

- if there had been a gain instead of a loss, he would have been chargeable under *TCGA 1992, s 2B* (high value disposals of dwellings — see **14.10** COMPANIES), *TCGA 1992, s 10* or *s 10B* (non-resident trading in the UK through permanent establishment or branch or agency — see **49.3** OVERSEAS MATTERS) or *TCGA 1992, s 14D* or *s 188D* (non-resident disposals of UK residential property interests — see **41.25** LAND) in respect of that gain; or
- it is a loss accruing to trustees in a tax year for which *CGTA 1979, s 17* or *TCGA 1992, s 87* (see **48** OFFSHORE SETTLEMENTS) applies to the settlement.

Where the tax year is a split year for an individual under the statutory residence test (see **57.18** RESIDENCE AND DOMICILE), this rule applies to any losses accruing during the overseas part of that year.

[*TCGA 1992, ss 16(3), 97(6); FA 2013, Sch 45 para 97, Sch 46 paras 78, 112; FA 2015, Sch 7 para 12*].

For the treatment of losses arising to an individual not domiciled in the UK but resident here in respect of the disposal of an asset overseas, see **55** REMITTANCE BASIS.

Example

On 30 April 2017 Q sells for £40,000 a part of the land which he owns. The market value of the remaining estate is £160,000. Q bought the land for £250,000 in March 1993.

	£
Disposal consideration	40,000
Allowable cost $\frac{40{,}000}{40{,}000 + 160{,}000} \times £250{,}000$	50,000
Allowable loss	£10,000

Notification of capital losses

[44.4] Under self-assessment, a capital loss is not an allowable loss unless its amount is quantified and notified to HMRC. Such a notice is subject to the provisions of *TMA 1970, s 42*, and to the enquiry regime (see **58.9** RETURNS, **13.3** CLAIMS), as if it were a claim for relief (see **13.2** CLAIMS). For capital gains tax purposes, losses must, if possible, be notified on the self-assessment tax return or in an amendment to it, or failing that may be notified separately in writing within the normal time limits for claims (see **13.5** CLAIMS [*TCGA 1992, s 16(2A)*]).

No notification time limit applies to capital losses arising in 1995/96 and earlier years or in company accounting periods ending before 1 July 1999. In *Tod v South Essex Motors (Basildon) Ltd* Ch D 1987, 60 TC 598, the absence of any statutory machinery before 1996/97 for claiming capital losses, other than to the extent that there were gains against which they could be set, meant that an agreement under *TMA 1970, s 54* (see **5.9** APPEALS) allied to the existence of a loss for a chargeable period did not preclude the Revenue from challenging its size or existence in a later chargeable period in which gains arose.

Order of set-off

Losses arising to individuals, trustees and personal representatives in the year 1996/97 and subsequent years are to be treated as utilised before losses arising in earlier years. Similarly, losses accruing to companies for accounting periods ending on or after 1 July 1999 will have preference to losses arising in accounting periods ending before that date. [*FA 1995, s 113(2)*].

Carry-back prohibited

[44.5] Losses may not normally be carried back against the gains of an earlier year. There are two exceptions to this rule. See **19.7** DEATH for carry-back of losses from the year of death and **44.19** below for the election to treat a loss on a right to unascertainable consideration as accruing in an earlier year.

Connected persons

[44.6] A loss on a disposal to a CONNECTED PERSON (**17**) is deductible only from chargeable gains arising on other disposals to that same person while he is still connected.

A disposal which settles capital and income wholly or primarily for educational, cultural or recreational purposes, the beneficiaries being ‘an association of persons’ most of whom are *not* connected persons, is not subject to this restriction on losses.

[*TCGA 1992, s 18(3)(4)*].

The restriction does not apply where a person becomes absolutely entitled as against the trustee to property in a settlement (see **62.16** SETTLEMENTS).

Where the disposal is of an option to enter into a transaction with the disposer, no loss accruing to a connected person who acquires the option is allowable unless it accrues on the disposal of the option at arm’s length to a person unconnected with the acquirer. [*TCGA 1992, s 18(5)*].

See **4.12** ANTI-AVOIDANCE for special market value provisions for disposals between connected persons.

Debts

A loss accruing on the disposal of a debt by a person making the disposal (the 'subsequent creditor') who acquired it from the 'original creditor' at a time when the original creditor or his personal representative or legatee was connected with the subsequent creditor, is not an allowable loss. Purchases through persons all of whom are connected with the subsequent creditor are also included as are acquisitions from the original creditor's personal representative or legatee. Where trustees of a settlement are the original creditor (or, for debts created before 6 April 2006, where the original creditor is a trustee and the debt, when created, is settled property), any loss accruing to the subsequent creditor is not allowable if he is connected with any person (or his personal representative or legatee) who becomes absolutely entitled to the debt on its ceasing to be settled property. [*TCGA 1992, s 251(4)(5)*].

HMRC takes the view that these provisions do not apply to debts on a security (HMRC Capital Gains Manual CG53451). For debts generally, see **25.5** EXEMPTIONS AND RELIEFS.

Anti-avoidance

[44.7] The following provisions apply to restrict losses in cases of avoidance.

Arrangements to secure tax advantage

An anti-avoidance provision applies so that a loss accruing on a disposal directly or indirectly in consequence of, or otherwise in connection with, any 'arrangements' the main purpose of which, or one of the main purposes of which, is to secure a 'tax advantage' is not an allowable loss. It does not matter whether the loss accrues at a time when there are no chargeable gains against which it could be set or whether the tax advantage would be secured for the person incurring the loss or another person.

'*Arrangements*' include any agreement, understanding, scheme, transaction or series of transactions, whether or not legally enforceable. '*Tax advantage*' means relief or increased relief from, or repayment or increased repayment of, capital gains tax, corporation tax or income tax or the avoidance or reduction of a charge or assessment to any of those taxes or the avoidance of a possible assessment to any of those taxes.

[*TCGA 1992, ss 8(2), 16A, 184D*].

HMRC have published guidance on the operation of the provision. In their view, interdependence of transactions or of the terms on which transactions take place is a strong indicator (although not a necessary condition) of the existence of an arrangement. If, on the facts, any participant in arrangements is found to have a main purpose of achieving a tax advantage, that is considered to be sufficient to demonstrate that one of the main purposes of the arrangements is the securing of a tax advantage. HMRC is likely to examine carefully any relevant case in which a normal commercial objective is lacking, or where commercial objectives are not being sought in a straightforward manner. Where there is more than one way of achieving a commercial objective and a course of action is chosen on commercial grounds, any incidental tax advantage is not relevant. However, where the tax advantage was material to the choice the anti-avoidance legislation may be in point, but HMRC have indicated that this is unlikely to be the case unless there is evidence of additional, complex or costly steps included solely for tax reasons. Using a marketed tax avoidance scheme will be taken as an indicator that securing a tax advantage was a main purpose of the arrangements.

The guidance also includes 14 examples demonstrating how HMRC think the provision operates in different circumstances.

(HMRC Guidance 'Avoidance through the creation and use of capital losses', 19 July 2007).

Miscellaneous

Where a deemed disposal arises under *TCGA 1992, s 29(2)* on the transfer of value between different shares or rights in a company by the person controlling it, no loss is allowable on such a disposal. See **4.8** ANTI-AVOIDANCE. Value-shifting to give a tax free benefit may result in losses being allowable only to such extent as is just and reasonable. See **4.11** ANTI-AVOIDANCE.

Where there are depreciatory transactions within a group of companies or where there is 'dividend stripping' by one company holding 10% or more of a class of shares in another company, any related loss is only allowable to the extent that it is just and reasonable. See **4.17**, **4.18** ANTI-AVOIDANCE.

A restriction of a loss accruing to a company which is a member of a group of companies may occur where the loss is wholly or partly referable to a time before it joined the group or the disposal of an asset which was held by another group member when that member company joined the group. See **29.18** GROUPS OF COMPANIES.

Trading losses effectively converted into allowable capital losses as in **44.21** below cannot be carried forward as a deduction against chargeable gains after the time the trade concerned ceases.

Interaction with annual exempt amount

[44.8] In giving relief for capital losses brought forward from earlier years (or carried back from a subsequent year in which the taxpayer dies — see **19.7** DEATH), such losses are deducted from the 'adjusted net gains' for the year only to the extent necessary to reduce those net gains to the amount of the annual exempt amount for the year, thus avoiding any wastage of losses brought forward (or back). Any balance of losses remains available to carry forward (or back). The '*adjusted net gains*' are, broadly, the chargeable gains for the year (including, where relevant, NRCGT gains under the non-resident CGT disposals of UK residential property interests rules — see **41.25** LAND) less current year allowable losses. See **2.6** ANNUAL RATES AND EXEMPTIONS for the detailed definition and for worked examples. [*TCGA 1992, s 3(5)–(5D); FA 2015, Sch 7 para 5*].

Profit and losses of theatre backers (angels)

[44.9] *Angels* are theatrical backers who invest in productions. An investment which occurs in the normal course of a backer's trade falls within the trading income rules (see Tolley's Income Tax). Special tax treatment applies to non-trading backers.

HMRC's view is that the profits of non-trading theatre angels are assessable as income whilst a loss forms an allowable loss for capital gains tax.

A '*profit*' for these purposes is the return the angel receives over and above the original investment. A '*loss*' arises where there is no further prospect of a return from the investment. The contract is viewed in normal circumstances as an asset for capital gains purposes (although most certainly this would have to be established on the facts of each case).

However, by concession HMRC will allow the profits and losses of non-trading theatre angels resident in the UK to be assessed and relieved accordingly under income tax rules. Where this treatment applies, any loss cannot also be treated as an allowable loss for capital gains tax purposes.

(HMRC Extra-Statutory Concession A94).

The concession is withdrawn with effect for all new productions from 1 April 2017. Productions using the concession before that date may continue to do so until 31 March 2019 if they have notified HMRC of their intention to do so. See www.gov.uk/government/publications/withdrawal-of-extra-statutory-concession-esc-a94-theatre-angels.

Special reliefs for losses

[44.10] There are a number of special rules giving rise to losses or providing for alternative reliefs and these are described at **44.11–44.19** below. See **44.1** above for a summary table.

Assets of negligible value

[44.11] Where the owner of an asset makes a 'negligible value' claim, he is treated as if he had sold, and immediately reacquired, the asset at the time of the claim or (subject to the following) at any earlier time specified in the claim for a consideration of an amount equal to the value specified in the claim.

An earlier time can be specified in the claim if the claimant owned the asset at that time, the asset had become of negligible value at that time and that time is not more than two years before the beginning of the tax year in which the claim is made or, for corporation tax, is on or after the first day of the earliest accounting period ending not more than two years before the time of the claim.

A negligible value claim can be made where either:

(a) the asset has become of negligible value while owned by the claimant; or
(b) the disposal by which the claimant acquired the asset was a no gain/no loss disposal at the time of which the asset was of negligible value and, between the time at which the asset became of negligible value and that disposal, any other disposal of the asset was a no gain/no loss disposal.

For the purposes of a negligible value claim, a building may be regarded as a separate asset from the land on which it stands, but where there is a deemed sale of a building, the land comprising the site of the building (including any land occupied for purposes ancillary to the use of the building) is likewise treated as if it was sold, and immediately reacquired, at its then market value.

[*TCGA 1992, s 24(1A)–(3)*].

'*Negligible value*' is not defined but is taken by HMRC to mean 'worth next to nothing' (HMRC Capital Gains Manual CG13125).

In *Director v Inspector of Taxes* (Sp C 161), [1998] SSCD 172, a negligible value claim was refused on the grounds that the shares in question had a nil acquisition cost by virtue of *TCGA 1992, s 17* (see **45.1** MARKET VALUE) and thus could not *become* of negligible value (but see (b) above). See also *Barker and others v HMRC* FTT 2011, [2012] SFTD 244 and *Dyer v HMRC* UT 2016, [2017] STC 189.

In *Drown & Leadley (JJ Leadley's Executors) v HMRC* UT [2017] UKUT 111 (TCC), an individual (L) subscribed for shares in two companies which subsequently became insolvent. In May 2010 L was killed in a motoring accident. His executors submitted claims for relief under *ITA 2007, s 131* (see **44.15** below) on the basis that the shares had become of negligible value by the date of L's death. HMRC accepted that the shares had become of negligible value but rejected the claims on the basis that any claim had to be made by the shareholder and could not be made posthumously by a shareholder's executors. The First-tier Tribunal allowed the executors' appeals, holding that 'there is nothing any of the relevant Acts that expressly provides that personal representatives can, or cannot, make claims in respect of the deceased's chargeability which the deceased could have made had he lived to file his return'. However, the Upper Tribunal reversed the decision, finding that there was no indication in the legislation that a negligible value claim could be taken as made at a time other than that at which it was submitted and *TCGA 1992, s 24* suggested that a claimant must still own the asset at the point such a claim is submitted in respect of it. A deceased person and his personal representatives could not equated; *TCGA 1992, s 62* provided that the personal representatives were deemed to acquire the assets of a deceased person on his death for a consideration equal to their market value without a disposal (see **19.2** DEATH). The personal representatives could not submit a negligible value claim.

For certain qualifying corporate bonds becoming of negligible value where evidencing a 'qualifying loan', see **44.13** below.

The backdating facility above cannot be used by a company to obtain relief for a loss that would otherwise be non-allowable under the provisions for SUBSTANTIAL SHAREHOLDINGS OF COMPANIES (see **66.19**).

For HMRC practice and procedure, see HMRC Capital Gains Manual CG13120–13150. HMRC offer their post-transaction valuation checking service (see **58.5** RETURNS) to taxpayers making negligible value claims. Form CG34 must be submitted at the same time or after the claim is made. Acceptance by HMRC of the value submitted does not mean that they necessarily accept that all the conditions for the claim are met or that any allowable loss arises. (HMRC Internet Statement 31 January 2006).

Quoted securities

HMRC have accepted that certain quoted securities have become of negligible value within the meaning of *TCGA 1992, s 24(2)*. For securities so accepted in recent years, see the HMRC website (at www.hmrc.gov.uk).

Example

In June 2017, John sells an asset, realising a chargeable gain of £26,500. In December 2017, John learns that his shareholding in Jones Ltd has become worthless. He acquired the shares in 1995 for their then market value of £15,000. John makes no other disposals in 2017/18.

If John makes a claim under *TCGA 1992, s 24* no later than 5 April 2020, then his capital gains tax liability for 2017/18 is as follows.

	£
Chargeable gain	26,500
Less allowable loss	15,000
	11,500
Less annual exempt amount	11,300
Gains chargeable to tax 2017/18	£200

Loans to traders

[44.12] The following reliefs are available for losses on loans to traders.

Relief for lender on loan becoming irrecoverable

Loss relief is available to the extent that any outstanding amount of the principal of a 'qualifying loan' made by the claimant after 11 April 1978 has become irrecoverable otherwise than under the express terms of the loan or related arrangements, or by reason of any act or omission by the lender (or, as appropriate, the guarantor of a loan claiming the relief below). The relief is available provided that, at the time of the claim, the claimant and borrower were neither spouses or civil partners living together nor companies in the same 'group' when the loan was made or at any subsequent time, and that the claimant has not assigned his right of recovery.

The loss is treated as accruing either when the claim under *TCGA 1992, s 253(3)* is made or, within limits (see below), at an earlier specified time. The amount of the loss cannot include any amount falling to be relieved by way of a debit under the loan relationship provisions in **15.2–15.7** COMPANIES — CORPORATE FINANCE AND INTANGIBLES.

[*TCGA 1992, s 253(3)(12)(14)(a)(aa), (15)*].

For cases in which the Revenue failed in contending that the loans became irrecoverable by reason of acts of the lender, see *Cann v Woods* (Sp C 183), [1999] SSCD 77, and *Crosby and Others (Crosby's Trustees) v Broadhurst* (Sp C 416), [2004] SSCD 348.

The allowable loss accrues at the time of the claim or at whatever earlier time is specified in the claim, so long as the amount claimed was also irrecoverable at that earlier time. For capital gains tax purposes, the time specified cannot be earlier than two years before the beginning of the tax year in which the claim is made. For corporation tax purposes, the time specified must fall on or after the first day of the earliest accounting period ending within the two years ending with the date of claim. [*TCGA 1992, s 253(3)(3A)*].

Relief is not available and nor is a clawback of relief made (see below) if the amount in question is taken into account for computing income for the purposes of income tax or corporation tax. [*TCGA 1992, s 253(10)*].

Qualifying loan

A '*qualifying loan*' is a loan to a UK resident borrower in the case of which the money lent is used by him wholly for the purposes of a trade, profession or vocation (not being a trade which consists of or includes the lending of money) carried on by him (and for this purpose money used by a borrower for setting up a trade which is subsequently carried on by him is treated as used for the purposes of that trade), and which is not a 'debt on a security'.

However, for guarantees see below, and for loans evidenced by securities which are qualifying corporate bonds, see **44.13** below.

The 'commercial letting' of 'furnished holiday accommodation' is treated as a trade. See **26** FURNISHED HOLIDAY ACCOMMODATION.

A '*debt on security*' is defined by reference to *TCGA 1992, s 132*, security therefore including any loan stock or similar security of any government or public or local authority in the UK or elsewhere, or of any company, and whether secured or unsecured. See further **25.5** EXEMPTIONS AND RELIEFS.

Where a company re-lends money to a 'trading company' in the same group, the original loan is treated as having been used by the first company as it is used by the second while the second remains a member of the group. For the purposes of these provisions, a group of companies is construed in accordance with **29.2** GROUPS OF COMPANIES. '*Trading company*' has the same meaning for this purpose as at **36.2** HOLD-OVER RELIEFS.

[*TCGA 1992, s 253(1)(2)(14)(b)(c); FA 2008, Sch 2 para 38*].

A loan was held not to be a qualifying loan in *Robson v Mitchell* CA, [2005] STC 893.

Relief for payment made under guarantee

The relief given above to a lender also applies (with the exception of the backdating facility) to a guarantor of a qualifying loan who makes a claim. The guarantor must have made a payment under the guarantee to the lender or a co-guarantor and he is treated as if an allowable loss of the amount of the payment had accrued to him when the payment was made. The guarantee must have been given after 11 April 1978. Relief is available even though the original loan is a 'debt on a security' (see above and **44.13** below).

Where loss relief is given, no allowable loss and no chargeable gain (otherwise than on a clawback of relief as below) will accrue on the disposal of rights consequent on the guarantor having made a payment (which may include a payment in respect of interest as well as principal) under the guarantee. Relief is reduced to the extent that any contribution is 'payable' to the claimant by any co-guarantor.

[*TCGA 1992, s 253(4)(11)(15)*].

Claims made on or after 1 April 2010 must be made not more than four years after the end of the tax year or accounting period in which the payment was made. For claims made before 1 April 2010, a capital gains tax claim had to be made on or before the fifth anniversary of 31 January following the tax year in which the payment was made; and in the case of corporation tax within six years after the end of the accounting period in which the payment was made. For capital gains tax purposes (but not for corporation tax purposes), these changes in time limits apply by reference to claims made before, or on or after, 1 April 2012 where the claim concerned relates to a tax year for which the taxpayer has not been given notice to make a return under *TMA 1970, s 8* or *s 8A* (see **58.3** RETURNS) or *s 12AA* (see **58.16** RETURNS) within one year of the end of the tax year (in effect, where the taxpayer is outside self-assessment). This rule does not, however, apply if for that year any gains which ought to have been assessed have not been assessed, or an assessment has become insufficient, or any relief given has become excessive. [*TCGA 1992, s 253(4A); FA 2008, s 113, Sch 39 para 29; SI 2009 No 403*].

'*Payable*' has its ordinary meaning, so that if under general legal principles the claimant could have made a recovery against one or more co-guarantors of part of a sum paid by him under a guarantee but chose not to do so, the relief given to him is reduced proportionately (*Leisureking Ltd v Cushing* Ch D 1992, 65 TC 400).

'*Guarantee*' covers the case where a person's property is charged as security for a qualifying loan. It does not include an indemnity, which creates a primary liability. A guarantee can apply to the repayment of an overdraft but not a hire purchase agreement. (CCAB Memorandum TR 308, 4 October 1978).

HMRC ignore voluntary payments, only those being made as a consequence of the formal calling in of a guarantee being covered by the relief. (Tolley's Practical Tax Newsletter 1987 p 147). The Revenue confirmed that a trading debt arising from the supply of stock to a trading company was considered capable of being treated as a qualifying loan as regards a guarantee made in respect of the debt. (Tolley's Practical Tax Newsletter 1988 p 40).

Clawback of relief

Where loss relief has been obtained by the person who made the loan or a guarantor of it, and all or part of the outstanding amount of, or of interest in respect of (in the case of a guarantor), the principal of the loan is recovered, a chargeable gain is deemed to accrue to him at the time of recovery equal to so much of the allowable loss (for which relief was claimed) as corresponds to the amount recovered. Where a claimant has obtained loss relief in respect of a payment under a guarantee and recovers the whole or any part of that payment, he will be treated as if there had accrued to him at that time a chargeable gain equal to so much of the allowable loss as corresponds to the amount recovered.

A similar treatment will apply to a company ('the second company') which recovers the whole or any part of the outstanding amount of the principal of a loan which has become irrecoverable in circumstances where a company ('the first company'), which made the loan originally and is in the same group as the second company when the loan was made or at any subsequent time, has obtained loss relief in respect of that loan becoming irrecoverable. Where the first company has obtained loss relief in relation to a payment made under a guarantee in respect of a loan which has become irrecoverable, a similar treatment of the second company applies if it recovers the whole or any part of the outstanding amount of, or of interest in respect of, the principal of the loan, or the whole or any part of the guarantee payment made by the first company. An amount is treated as recovered if money or money's worth is received in satisfaction of the right of recovery. If this right is assigned otherwise than at arm's length, its full market value at that time is deemed to have been received.

[*TCGA 1992, s 253(5)–(9)(13)*].

Loans to traders evidenced by qualifying corporate bonds becoming irrecoverable

[44.13] A loss incurred on a qualifying corporate bond is not an allowable loss (see **54.2** QUALIFYING CORPORATE BONDS). However, special provisions apply for capital gains tax purposes only if, at the time of a claim under *TCGA 1992, s 254* by a person who has made a 'qualifying loan' **before 17 March 1998,** one of the three conditions given below is fulfilled. The claimant is treated as if an allowable loss equal to the 'allowable amount' had accrued to him either at the time of the claim or, within limits (see below), at an earlier specified time. The provisions are **repealed** in relation to loans made after 16 March 1998.

A '*qualifying loan*' means a loan in the case of which:

(a) the borrower's debt is a debt on a security within *TCGA 1992, s 132* (see **44.12** above) which was issued after 14 March 1989, or issued before 15 March 1989 but held on 15 March 1989 by the person who made the loan,
(b) but for the borrower's debt being a debt on a security, the loan would be a qualifying loan within *TCGA 1992, s 253* (see **44.12** above), and
(c) the security is a **54** QUALIFYING CORPORATE BOND, other than a deeply discounted security (see **63.21** SHARES AND SECURITIES) and with certain other modifications (see *TCGA 1992, s 117(13)*), in particular so as to exclude building society permanent interest bearing shares.

The first condition is that:

(i) the value of the security has become negligible (but relief will still be available where the security ceases to have any value because it is redeemed early; HMRC Statement of Practice 8/90 and see (1) below for 'redemption date'),
(ii) the claimant has not assigned his right to recover any outstanding amount of the principal of the loan, and
(iii) the claimant and the borrower are not companies which have been in the same group (within *TCGA 1992, s 170*, see **29.2** GROUPS OF COMPANIES) at any time after the loan was made.

The second condition is that:

(1) the security's 'redemption date' (i.e. the latest date on which, under the terms under which the security was issued, the company or body which issued it can be required to redeem it) has passed,
(2) all the outstanding amount of the principal of the loan was irrecoverable (taking the facts existing on that date) or proved to be irrecoverable (taking the facts existing on a later date), and
(3) the requirements in (ii) and (iii) above are fulfilled.

The third condition is that:

(A) the security's redemption date (as at (1) above) has passed,
(B) sub-condition (2) of the second condition above was fulfilled on a similar basis as regards part (rather than the whole) of the outstanding principal of the loan, and
(C) the requirements in (ii) and (iii) above are fulfilled.

Where the first or second condition is fulfilled, '*the allowable amount*' is the lesser of the outstanding amount of the principal of the loan and the amount of the security's acquisition cost (i.e. the amount or value of the consideration in money or money's worth given, by or on behalf of the person who made the loan, wholly and exclusively for the acquisition of the security, together with the incidental costs to him of the acquisition). However, if any amount of the principal of the loan has been recovered the amount of the security's acquisition cost is for this purpose reduced (but not beyond nil) by the amount recovered. An amount is treated as recovered if money or money's worth is received in satisfaction of the right of recovery. If this right is assigned otherwise than at arm's length, its full market value at that time is deemed to have been received.

Where the third condition is fulfilled, then '*the allowable amount*' is an amount equal to the excess (if any) of the security's acquisition cost over the 'relevant amount' or nil (if there is no such excess). The '*relevant amount*' is the aggregate of the amount (if any) of the principal of the loan which has been recovered (as above) and the amount (if any) of the principal of the loan which has not been recovered but which is recoverable.

The allowable loss accrues at the time of the claim or at whatever earlier time is specified in the claim, so long as the relevant condition was also fulfilled at that earlier time. The time specified cannot be earlier than two years before the beginning of the tax year in which the claim is made.

Relief is not available and nor is a clawback of relief made (see below) if the amount in question is taken into account for computing income for the purposes of income tax or corporation tax. An amount is not treated as irrecoverable for the purposes of the relief if it becomes irrecoverable under the express terms of the loan or related arrangements, or by reason of any act or omission by the lender.

[*TCGA 1992, ss 254(1)–(8)(12), 255(1)(2)(4)(5)*].

Clawback of relief

Where the above relief has been given and the whole or any part of the 'relevant outstanding amount' is at any time recovered (as above) by the claimant, he is treated as if there had accrued to him at that time a chargeable gain equal to so much of the allowable loss as corresponds to the amount recovered. The '*relevant outstanding amount*' means, in a case where the first or second condition was fulfilled, the amount of the principal of the loan outstanding when the claim was allowed or, in a case where the third condition was fulfilled, the amount of the part (or the greater or greatest part) arrived at by the inspector under sub-condition (B) of the third condition above.

[*TCGA 1992, ss 254(9)–(11), 255(3)–(5)*].

Qualifying corporate bonds — reorganisations etc. thereof and relief under 44.13 *above*

[44.14] *TCGA 1992, s 116(10)(11)* deals with the situation where, on a reorganisation etc. of shares (which are not qualifying corporate bonds), such shares ('the old asset') are replaced by securities ('the new asset') which are qualifying corporate bonds (and thus exempt from capital gains tax). The broad effect is to defer the chargeable gain or allowable loss that would have accrued on a disposal of the old asset at its market value immediately before the reorganisation until such time as a part or the whole of the new asset is disposed of, at which time the corresponding part or the whole of the deferred gain or loss is deemed to accrue. See **54.4** QUALIFYING CORPORATE BONDS for full details.

In such a case and where the new asset is a qualifying corporate bond in respect of which an allowable loss is treated as accruing under *TCGA 1992, s 254(2)* in **44.13** above, and the loss is treated as so accruing at a time falling after the reorganisation but before any actual disposal of the new asset subsequent to the reorganisation, then, for the purposes of *TCGA 1992, s 116(10)(11)*, a disposal of the new asset is deemed to have occurred at (and only at) the time the loss is deemed to have accrued. This applies whatever the time the reorganisation occurs. [*TCGA 1992, s 116(15)*]. The effect is that the deferred gain or loss relating to the old asset will be deemed to accrue at the same time as the loss arising on a claim under *TCGA 1992, s 254(2)* above in respect of the new asset is deemed to accrue, and any later disposal of the new asset is ignored for the purposes of ascertaining when and in what amount the deferred gain or loss is treated as arising.

A concessional practice, contained in HMRC Extra-Statutory Concession D38, applies as follows. Where a person acquired corporate bonds in respect of shares and securities and those bonds became, or would fall to be treated as, qualifying corporate bonds by virtue only of *FA 1989, s 139* (extension of definition to include a wider range of sterling bonds; see **54.3** and **54.4** QUALIFYING CORPORATE BONDS), an allowable loss, computed in accordance with the rules in *TCGA 1992, s 116* (see **44.13** above), will accrue if:

(a) the qualifying corporate bonds were issued in respect of shares or other securities before 14 March 1989 and were still retained at that date by the person to whom they were issued;
(b) the bonds were acquired in a transaction within *TCGA 1992, s 116(10)(11)* (see above) and on disposal after 13 March 1989 fall to be treated as qualifying corporate bonds as a result of *FA 1989, s 139*;
(c) relief under *TCGA 1992, s 254* would have been available had the loan been a qualifying loan within *TCGA 1992, s 254(1)*;
(d) the taxpayer claiming the concessional relief agrees that if all or part of the amount relieved is subsequently recovered the relief will be clawed back in the same way as if *TCGA 1992, s 254* had applied, save that in all cases the chargeable gain will be treated as accruing to the claimant; and
(e) when this concession applies, any gain or loss on the original shares or securities will be treated as accruing at the same time as the loss on the bonds in accordance with *TCGA 1992, s 116(15)* (see above and also **54.4** QUALIFYING CORPORATE BONDS for an additional relief which may apply in such circumstances where the bonds are gifted to a charity).

Under the concession the allowable loss will be treated as arising when a claim is made but it will be treated as arising in an earlier tax year or accounting period provided the claim is made not later than two years after the end of that year or accounting period, all the conditions for relief are satisfied at the date of claim, and the relief would have been available at the end of the tax year or accounting period for which relief is claimed.

Losses on shares in unlisted trading companies — individuals

[44.15] See generally HMRC Venture Capital Schemes Manual VCM10010 *et seq.*, 70000 *et seq.*

An individual may claim relief from income tax, instead of from capital gains tax, for an allowable loss (as computed for capital gains tax purposes) on a disposal of 'qualifying shares'.

Relief is available only if:

- the disposal is at arm's length; or
- it is by way of a distribution on a winding-up; or
- the value of the shares has become negligible and a claim to that effect made under *TCGA 1992, s 24(2)* (see **44.11** above); or
- a deemed disposal occurs under *TCGA 1992, s 24(1)* (which deems the entire loss, destruction, dissipation or extinction of an asset to be a disposal — see **10.2** CAPITAL SUMS DERIVED FROM ASSETS).

Relief is not available where the shares are the subject of an exchange or arrangement within *TCGA 1992, ss 135* or *136* undertaken for tax avoidance purposes or other than for genuine commercial reasons so that a chargeable disposal under *TCGA 1992, s 137* arises. See **4.15** ANTI-AVOIDANCE.

Qualifying shares

'*Qualifying shares*' are ordinary shares or stock:

- in a 'qualifying trading company' (see **44.16** below) for which the individual 'subscribed'; or
- to which EIS income tax relief is attributable (see **23** ENTERPRISE INVESTMENT SCHEME).

For this purpose, an individual '*subscribes*' for shares if they are issued to him by the company in consideration of money or money's worth, or were transferred to him *inter vivos* by his spouse or civil partner who had similarly subscribed for them. The spouses or civil partners concerned must be living together (see **46.4** MARRIED PERSONS AND CIVIL PARTNERS) at the time of the transfer, and the shares are treated as issued to the transferee at the time they were issued to the transferor. Where an individual has subscribed for shares, he is treated as having subscribed for any bonus shares subsequently issued to him in respect of those shares provided that the bonus shares are in the same company, of the same class and carry the same rights as the original shares. The bonus shares are treated as issued at the time the original shares were issued.

Where, for shares subscribed for before 10 March 1981, the consideration was deemed equal to the market value under *CGTA 1979, s 19(3)*, the loss allowable on disposal cannot exceed what the loss would have been without applying that subsection. (For shares subscribed for after 9 March 1981, market value is not substituted where the consideration is less than market value.)

[*ITA 2007, ss 131, 135, 150, 151(1)*].

Shares issued to joint owners or nominees

HMRC accept that relief can be claimed by an individual even if the shares were subscribed for in joint names or through a nominee. In the case of qualifying shares to which EIS income tax relief is *not* attributable, HMRC previously did not accept that relief was available in such circumstances, but they published a change in practice on 12 October 2010. Claims relating to years ending before that date can be made in accordance with the revised practice where they are not out of time. (HMRC Brief 41/2010).

In *Murray-Hession v HMRC FTT*, [2016] UKFTT 612 (TC) the taxpayer was held to have subscribed for shares previously held by another person as nominee, agent or otherwise on his behalf.

Operation of and claims for relief

A loss may be claimed against income:

- of the tax year in which the loss is incurred; and/or
- of the tax year preceding that in which the loss is incurred.

If a claim is made in relation to both tax years, it must specify the year for which relief is to be given first. The loss is deducted in calculating net income for the specified tax year, and, if the claim relates to both tax years, any remaining part of the loss is then deducted in calculating net income for the other year.

Where, against income of the same year, claims are made both in respect of that year's loss and in respect of the following year's loss, the claim for the current year's loss takes precedence.

A claim for relief must be made in writing on or before the first anniversary of 31 January following the tax year *in which the loss is incurred.*

Relief under these provisions is given in priority to relief under *ITA 2007, s 64* (trading losses set against general income) and *ITA 2007, s 72* (further relief for trading losses to be set against general income in early years of a trade) for the same tax year.

To the extent that relief in respect of a loss is obtained under these provisions, the loss is not an allowable loss for capital gains tax purposes. Any part of the loss for which income tax relief is not given does, however, remain an allowable loss for capital gains tax purposes.

[*ITA 2007, ss 132, 133; TCGA 1992, s 125A(1)*].

Limits on relief

Where an individual claims relief under these provisions in respect of a loss on the disposal of qualifying shares which form part of a 'section 104 holding' (see **64** SHARES AND SECURITIES — IDENTIFICATION RULES) either at the time of disposal or at an earlier time, the relief is restricted to the sums that would have been allowable as deductions in computing the loss if the qualifying shares had not formed part of the holding.

Where the qualifying shares were acquired on the same day as other shares that are not capable of being qualifying shares (see below), such that, by virtue of *TCGA 1992, s 105(1)(a)* (see **64.2** SHARES AND SECURITIES — IDENTIFICATION RULES), all the shares are treated as acquired by a single transaction, the amount of relief is restricted to the sums that would have been allowable as deductions in computing the loss if the qualifying shares were treated as acquired by a single transaction and the other shares were not so treated.

Where the qualifying shares, taken as a single asset, and other shares or debentures in the same company which are not capable of being qualifying shares, also taken as a single asset, are treated for capital gains tax purposes as the same asset under *TCGA 1992, s 127* (see **63.2** SHARES AND SECURITIES), the amount of relief is restricted to the sums that would have been allowable as deductions in computing the loss if the qualifying shares and the other shares were not to be treated as the same asset.

For the above purposes, shares to which EIS income tax relief is not attributable are not capable of being qualifying shares at any time if they were acquired otherwise than by subscription, if condition (c) at **44.16** below was not met in relation to the issue of the shares or condition (d) at **44.16** below would not be met if the shares were disposed of at that time. Additionally, for the purposes only of the 'same asset' restriction above, shares to which EIS income tax relief is not attributable are not capable of being qualifying shares at any time if they are shares of a different class from the qualifying shares concerned.

[*ITA 2007, s 147; FA 2008, Sch 2 paras 98, 100*].

With effect for 2013/14 onwards there is a limit of the level of deduction than can be obtained in relation to certain income tax reliefs, including, subject to certain exceptions, share loss relief. The amount of relief is limited to the higher of £50,000 or 25% of the taxpayer's adjusted total income for the tax year [*ITA 2007, s 24A; FA 2013, Sch 3 paras 1, 3; FA 2014, Sch 11 para 5*].

Identification

The following provisions apply to identify whether a disposal of shares forming part of a mixed holding (i.e. a 'holding' of shares including shares that are not capable of being qualifying shares and other shares) is a disposal of qualifying shares and, if so, to which of any qualifying shares acquired at different times the disposal relates.

Except as noted below, the normal capital gains tax identification rules apply and where shares are thereby identified with the whole or any part of a section 104 holding, they are further identified with acquisitions on a last in/first out (LIFO) basis.

The above rules do not apply where the holding includes *any* of the following:

- shares in respect of which Business Expansion Scheme (BES) was given and was not withdrawn (see **25.22** EXEMPTIONS AND RELIEFS);
- shares to which Enterprise Investment Scheme (EIS) income tax relief is attributable (see **23** ENTERPRISE INVESTMENT SCHEME);
- shares to which EIS capital gains deferral relief is attributable (see **23.14** ENTERPRISE INVESTMENT SCHEME).

Instead, disposals are identified in accordance with the identification rules generally applicable to BES and EIS shares (first in/first out (FIFO), subject to certain special rules — see **23.13** ENTERPRISE INVESTMENT SCHEME, **25.22** EXEMPTIONS AND RELIEFS).

Where the above rules cannot identify the shares disposed of, the identification is to be made on a just and reasonable basis.

A '*holding*' of shares for the above purposes is any number of shares of the same class held by one individual in the same capacity, growing or diminishing as shares of that class are acquired or disposed of. Shares comprised in a 'new holding' following a reorganisation to which *TCGA 1992, s 127* applies are treated as having been acquired when the original shares were acquired. Any shares held or disposed of by a nominee or bare trustees for an individual are treated as held or disposed of by that individual.

[*ITA 2007, ss 148, 149; FA 2008, Sch 2 paras 99, 100*].

See the example at **44.17** below.

Anti-avoidance

Any claim to relief will bring in the provisions of *TCGA 1992, s 30* (value-shifting to give a tax-free benefit — see **4.10** ANTI-AVOIDANCE) so that the relief may be adjusted for any benefit conferred whether tax-free or not. [*TCGA 1992, s 125A(2)*].

Company reorganisations etc.

The following applies only to shares to which EIS income tax relief is not attributable. Where shares are disposed of and represent a new holding identifiable under *TCGA 1992, s 127* (see **63.2** SHARES AND SECURITIES) with 'old shares' after a reorganisation or reduction of share capital, relief is not available unless it could have been given if an allowable loss had arisen on the disposal of the old shares at arm's length at the reorganisation etc. had this legislation been in force. Where the reorganisation did not so qualify, but new consideration was given for the new shares, relief is limited to such of that new consideration as is an allowable deduction. '*New consideration*' is money or money's worth but excluding any surrender or alteration to the original shares or rights attached to them, and the application of assets of the company or distribution declared but not made out of the assets.

For new shares issued on or after 6 April 2007, the above does not apply where the share exchange provisions below apply.

[*ITA 2007, s 136*].

See HMRC Venture Capital Schemes Manual VCM75390.

Share exchanges

The following provisions apply in relation to shares to which EIS income tax relief is not attributable. Where, by means of an exchange of shares, all of the shares (the old shares) of a company (the old company) are acquired by a company (the new company) in which the only previously issued shares are subscriber shares, then, subject to the further conditions below being satisfied, the exchange is not regarded as involving a disposal of the old shares and an acquisition of the new company shares (the new shares). Where old shares held by an individual were subscribed for by him and EIS relief was not attributable to them, the new shares stand in the shoes of the old shares, e.g. as if they had been subscribed for and issued at the time the old shares were subscribed for and issued and as if any requirements under the above provisions met at any time before the exchange by the old company had been met at that time by the new company.

The further conditions are as follows.

(a) The shares must be issued after 5 April 1998.
(b) The consideration for the old shares must consist entirely of the issue of the new shares.
(c) The consideration for old shares of each description must consist entirely of new shares of the 'corresponding description'.
(d) New shares of each description must be issued to holders of old shares of the 'corresponding description' in respect of and in proportion to their holdings.
(e) For new shares issued on or after 6 April 2007, the exchange of shares is not treated for capital gains tax purposes as involving a disposal of the old shares or an acquisition of the new shares by virtue of *TCGA 1992, s 127*.

(f) For new shares issued before 6 April 2007, before the issue of the new shares, on the written application (for which see **4.15** ANTI-AVOIDANCE) of either the old or new company, HMRC must have notified to that company their satisfaction that the exchange:
   (i) is for genuine commercial reasons; and
   (ii) does not form part of a scheme or arrangements to which *TCGA 1992, s 137(1)* (see **4.15** ANTI-AVOIDANCE) applies.

   HMRC may, within 30 days of an application, request further particulars, which must then be supplied within 30 days of the request (or such longer period as they may allow in any particular case).

For these purposes, old and new shares are of a '*corresponding description*' if, assuming they were shares in the same company, they would be of the same class and carry the same rights.

References above to 'shares' (other than those to 'shares to which EIS income tax relief is not attributable' or 'subscriber shares') include references to 'securities'.

An exchange within these provisions, or arrangements for such an exchange, does not breach the control and independence requirement at **44.16** below.

[*ITA 2007, ss 145, 146*].

Qualifying trading company

[44.16] As regards shares issued after **5 April 1998**, a '*qualifying trading company*' is a company which:

(a) either (i) on the date of disposal meets the trading, control and independence, qualifying subsidiaries and (for shares issued on or after 17 March 2004) the property managing subsidiaries requirements below, or (ii) has ceased to meet any of those requirements within three years before that date and has not since that cessation been an 'excluded company', an '*investment company*' (i.e. a company whose business consists wholly or mainly in, and the principal part of whose income derives from, making investments, but excluding the holding company of a 'trading group') or a '*trading company*' (i.e. a company, other than an excluded company, whose business consists wholly or mainly of the carrying on of a trade or trades, or which is the holding company of a trading group); *and*
(b) either (i) has met each of the requirements in (a)(i) above for a continuous period of at least six years prior to the disposal (or prior to the cessation in (a)(ii) above, as the case may be), or (ii) has met each of those requirements for a shorter continuous period ending with the disposal or cessation and has not previously been an excluded company, an investment company or a trading company; *and*
(c) met the gross assets requirement below both immediately before and immediately after the issue of the shares and (for shares issued after 6 March 2001) met the unquoted status requirement below at the 'relevant time'; *and*

(d) has carried on its business wholly or mainly in the UK throughout the period ending with the date of disposal of the shares and beginning with the incorporation of the company, or, if later, one year before the date on which the shares were issued.

For shares issued before 7 March 2001, it was also a condition that the company be an 'unquoted' company (as defined for the purposes of the unquoted status requirement below) throughout that part of the period mentioned in (d) above that falls before 7 March 2001.

As regards shares issued **before 6 April 1998**, a '*qualifying trading company*' is a company none of whose shares have been listed on a recognised stock exchange at any time in the period ending with the date of disposal of the shares and beginning with the incorporation of the company, or, if later, one year before the date on which the shares were subscribed for, and which:

(1) either (i) is a trading company on the date of the disposal or (ii) has ceased to be a trading company within the previous three years and has not since that time been an investment company or an 'excluded company'; and
(2) either (i) has been a trading company for a continuous period of six years ending on the date of disposal of the shares or the time it ceased to be a trading company or (ii) if shorter, a continuous period ending on that date or that time and had not before the beginning of that period been an excluded company or an investment company; and
(3) has been resident in the UK since incorporation until the date of disposal.

Securities on the Alternative Investment Market ('AIM') are treated as unlisted for these purposes. (Revenue Press Release 20 February 1995).

An '*excluded company*' is a company which has a trade consisting mainly of dealing in land, in commodities or futures or in shares, securities or other financial instruments (as regards shares issued before 6 April 1998 — dealing in shares, securities, land, trades or commodity futures) or which is not carried on on a commercial basis with a reasonable expectation of profit, or a company which is the holding company of a group other than a trading group, or which is a building society (see **10** BUILDING SOCIETIES) or a registered society within *Co-operative and Community Benefit Societies Act 2014* or NI equivalent (previously, a registered industrial and provident society).

A '*trading group*' is a 'group' (i.e. a company and its 51% subsidiaries) the business of the members of which, taken together, consists wholly or mainly in the carrying on of a trade or trades (disregarding any trade carried on by a subsidiary which is an excluded company or, as regards shares issued before 6 April 1998, which is non-UK resident).

The six requirements referred to at (a) to (c) above are as follows.

The trading requirement

The company must either:

(i) exist wholly for the purpose of carrying on one or more 'qualifying trades' (see **23.9** ENTERPRISE INVESTMENT SCHEME) (disregarding purposes having no significant effect on the extent of its activities), or

(ii) be a '*parent company*' (i.e. a company that has one or more 'qualifying subsidiaries' (see **23.6** ENTERPRISE INVESTMENT SCHEME)) and the business of the '*group*' (i.e. the company and its qualifying subsidiaries) must not consist wholly or as to a substantial part in the carrying on of 'non-qualifying activities'.

Where the company intends that one or more other companies should become its qualifying subsidiaries with a view to their carrying on one or more qualifying trades, then, until any time after which the intention is abandoned, the company is treated as a parent company and those other companies are included in the group for the purposes of (ii) above. (This provision is made explicit in *ITA 2007* but reflects previous practice (see Change 42 listed in Annex 1 to the Explanatory Notes to *ITA 2007*).)

For the purpose of (ii) above, the business of the group means what would be the business of the group if the activities of the group companies taken together were regarded as one business. Activities are for this purpose disregarded to the extent that they consist in:

- holding shares in or securities of any of the company's subsidiaries,
- making loans to another group company,
- holding and managing property used by a group company for the purposes of a qualifying trade or trades carried on by any group company, or
- holding and managing property used by a group company for the purposes of research and development from which it is intended either that a qualifying trade to be carried on by a 'group company' will be derived or, for shares issued after 5 April 2007, a qualifying trade carried on or to be carried on by a group company will benefit. '*Group company*' includes, for this purpose, any existing or future company which will be a group company at any future time.

Activities are similarly disregarded to the extent that they consist, in the case of a subsidiary whose main purpose is the carrying on of qualifying trade(s) and whose other purposes have no significant effect on the extent of its activities (other than in relation to incidental matters), in activities not in pursuance of its main purpose.

'*Non-qualifying activities*' are:

- excluded activities within **23.9** ENTERPRISE INVESTMENT SCHEME, and
- non-trading activities (other than research and development (as defined)).

References in the definition of 'qualifying trade' and 'excluded activities' at **23.9** ENTERPRISE INVESTMENT SCHEME to 'period B' are to be taken for the above purposes to refer to the continuous period mentioned in (b) above.

For the ascertainment of the purposes for which a company exists, see HMRC Venture Capital Schemes Manual VCM13050.

A company ceases to meet the trading requirement if before the time that is relevant for the purposes of (a) above a resolution is passed or an order is made for the winding-up of the company or if the company is dissolved without winding-up. This does not, however, apply if the winding-up is for genuine commercial reasons and not part of a scheme a main purpose of which is tax avoidance and the company continues, during the winding-up, to be a trading company. (Note that the continuation of trading condition now applies in relation to shares issued after 5 April 2001 but did originally apply up to and including 20 March 2000, after which a drafting error inadvertently altered the law.) For shares issued after 20 March 2000, a company does not cease to meet the trading requirement by reason of anything done as a consequence of its being in administration or receivership (both as defined by *ITA 2007, s 252*), provided everything so done and the entry into administration or receivership are for genuine commercial (and not tax avoidance) reasons. For shares issued after 16 March 2004, these provisions are extended to refer also to the winding-up, dissolution, administration or receivership of any of the company's subsidiaries.

The control and independence requirement

Subject to the share exchange provisions at **50.14** above, the issuing company must not:

(I) control another company other than a qualifying subsidiary (see **23.6** ENTERPRISE INVESTMENT SCHEME) or, for shares issued before 21 March 2000, have a 51% subsidiary other than a qualifying subsidiary, 'control' being construed in accordance with *CTA 2010, ss 450, 451* and being considered with or without connected persons within *ITA 2007, s 993*,

(II) be a 51% subsidiary of another company or otherwise under the control of another company, 'control' being construed in accordance with *ITA 2007, s 995* (previously *ICTA 1988, s 840*) and again being considered with or without connected persons, or

(III) be capable of falling within (I) or (II) by virtue of any arrangements (as very broadly defined).

The qualifying subsidiaries requirement

The company must not have any subsidiaries other than qualifying subsidiaries (see **23.6** ENTERPRISE INVESTMENT SCHEME).

The property managing subsidiaries requirement

For shares issued on or after 17 March 2004, any 'property managing subsidiary' (see **23.5** ENTERPRISE INVESTMENT SCHEME) that the company has must be a 'qualifying 90% subsidiary' (see **23.7** ENTERPRISE INVESTMENT SCHEME).

The gross assets requirement

The value of the company's gross assets must not exceed £7 million immediately before the issue of the shares in respect of which relief is claimed and must not exceed £8 million immediately afterwards. In relation to shares issued before 6 April 2006, these limits were £15 million and £16 million respectively; the higher limits continue to apply in relation to shares issued after 5 April 2006 to a person who subscribed for them before 22 March 2006.

If the issuing company is a parent company, the gross assets test applies by reference to the aggregate gross assets of the company and all its qualifying subsidiaries (disregarding certain assets held by any such company which correspond to liabilities of another).

The general approach of HMRC to the gross assets requirement is that the value of a company's gross assets is the sum of the value of all of the balance sheet assets. Where accounts are actually drawn up to a date immediately before or after the issue, the balance sheet values are taken provided that they reflect usual accounting standards and the company's normal accounting practice, consistently applied. Where accounts are not drawn up to such a date, such values will be taken from the most recent balance sheet, updated as precisely as practicable on the basis of all the relevant information available to the company. Values so arrived at may need to be reviewed in the light of information contained in the accounts for the period in which the issue was made, and, if they were not available at the time of the issue, those for the preceding period, when they become available. The company's assets immediately before the issue do not include any advance payment received in respect of the issue. Where shares are issued partly paid, the right to the balance is an asset, and, notwithstanding the above, will be taken into account in valuing the assets immediately after the issue regardless of whether it is shown in the balance sheet. (HMRC SP 2/00).

The unquoted status requirement

For shares issued on or after 7 March 2001, the company must be 'unquoted' at the time (the '*relevant time*') at which the shares are issued and no arrangements must then exist for it to cease to be unquoted. If, at the time of issue, arrangements exist for the company to become a wholly-owned subsidiary of a new holding company by means of a share exchange within the provisions below, no arrangements must exist for the new company to cease to be unquoted. A company is '*unquoted*' if none of its shares etc. are listed on a recognised stock exchange or on a foreign exchange designated for the purpose, or dealt in on the Unlisted Securities Market (now closed) or outside the UK by such means as may be designated for the purpose. Securities on the Alternative Investment Market ('AIM') are treated as unquoted for these purposes. (Revenue Press Release 20 February 1995).

Treasury power to amend requirements

The Treasury may amend the above requirements by order.

[*ITA 2007, ss 134, 137–144, 151(1)(7); Co-operative and Community Benefit Societies Act 2014, Sch 4 para 105; FA 2014, Sch 39 para 10*].

Example

[44.17]

P subscribed for 3,000 £1 ordinary shares at par in W Ltd, a qualifying trading company, in June 1989. In September 1996, P acquired a further 2,200 shares at £3 per share from another shareholder. In December 2017, P sold 3,900 shares at 40p per share.

Establish 'section 104 holding' pool.

	Shares	Qualifying expenditure
		£
June 1989 subscription	3,000	3,000
September 1996 acquisition	2,200	6,600
	5,200	9,600
December 2017 disposal	(3,900)	(7,200)
Pool carried forward	1,300	£2,400

Step 1. Calculate the CGT loss in the normal way, as follows

	£
Disposal consideration 3,900 × £0.40	1,560
Allowable cost	7,200
Allowable loss	£5,640

Step 2. Applying a LIFO basis, identify the qualifying shares (1,700) and the non-qualifying shares (2,200) comprised in the disposal.

Step 3. Calculate the proportion of the loss attributable to the qualifying shares.

Loss referable to 1,700 qualifying shares $\frac{1,700}{3,900} \times £5,640$ £2,458

Step 4. Compare the loss in *Step 3* with the actual cost of the qualifying shares, *viz.*

Cost of 1,700 qualifying shares $\frac{1,700}{3,000} \times £3,000$ £1,700

The loss available against income is restricted to £1,700 (being lower than £2,458).

The loss not relieved against income remains an allowable loss for CGT purposes.

£5,640 – £1,700 = £3,940

Losses on shares in unlisted trading companies — investment companies

[44.18] Where an 'investment company' disposes of shares in a 'qualifying trading company' for which it has 'subscribed', and thereby incurs an allowable capital loss, it may claim relief for the loss against income instead of against chargeable gains.

The investment company must have been such on the date of the disposal and must either:

(a) have been an investment company for a continuous period of six years ending on that date; or
(b) have been an investment company for a shorter continuous period ending on that date, and must not have been, before the beginning of that period, a 'trading company' or an 'excluded company'.

It must also not have been 'associated' with, or have been a member of the same 'group' as, the qualifying trading company, at any time in the period beginning with the date of its (the investment company's) subscription for the shares, and ending with the date of disposal.

Relief is available only if:

- the disposal is at arm's length, or
- it is by way of a distribution on a winding-up, or
- the value of the shares has become negligible and a claim to that effect made under *TCGA 1992, s 24(2)* (see **44.11** above), or
- a deemed disposal occurs under *TCGA 1992, s 24(1)* (which deems the entire loss, destruction, dissipation or extinction of an asset to be a disposal — see **10.2** CAPITAL SUMS DERIVED FROM ASSETS).

Relief is not available where the shares are the subject of an exchange or arrangement within *TCGA 1992, ss 135* or *136* undertaken for tax avoidance purposes or other than for genuine commercial reasons so that a chargeable disposal under *TCGA 1992, s 137* arises. See **4.15** ANTI-AVOIDANCE.

For this purpose, '*qualifying trading company*', '*trading company*', '*excluded company*' and '*group*' are all defined as at **44.16** above. Companies are '*associated*' with each other if one controls the other, or both are under the control of the same person or persons. The general definitions of *CTA 2010, ss 450, 451* (meaning of 'control') apply for this purpose. See Tolley's Corporation Tax under Close Companies. A company 'subscribes' for shares in another company if they are issued to the company by the other company in consideration of money or money's worth. Any corresponding bonus shares subsequently issued to the company are treated as subscribed for on the date on which the original shares were subscribed for.

Operation of and claims for relief

A loss may be claimed against income of the accounting period in which it is incurred. Additionally, if the company was an investment company at that earlier time, it may claim to set off any balance of the loss remaining against income of the twelve months immediately preceding the accounting period in which the loss was incurred (income of the relevant accounting periods being time apportioned for this purpose where necessary).

Relief must be claimed within two years of the end of the accounting period in which the loss arises and is given before any deduction for charges on income, expenses of management or other deductions, except that a claim for a loss on a Corporate Venturing Scheme investment to be relieved against income does take priority (see **18.19** CORPORATE VENTURING SCHEME).

To the extent that relief in respect of a loss is obtained under these provisions, the loss is not an allowable capital loss. Any part of the loss for which income relief is not given does, however, remain an allowable capital loss.

Limits on relief

Where a company claims relief under these provisions for a loss on the disposal of shares which form part of a 'section 104 holding' or a '1982 holding' (i.e. holdings of shares which are pooled for chargeable gains purposes) either at the time of the disposal or an earlier time, the relief is restricted to the sums that would have been allowable as deductions in computing the loss if the qualifying shares had not formed part of the holding.

Where the qualifying shares were acquired on the same day as other shares that are not capable of being qualifying shares (see below), so that under *TCGA 1992, s 105(1)(a)* all the shares are treated as acquired by a single transaction, the amount of relief is restricted to the sums that would have been allowable as deductions in computing the loss if the qualifying shares and the other shares were not so treated.

Where the qualifying shares, taken as a single asset, and other shares or debentures in the same company which are not capable of being qualifying shares, also taken as a single asset, are treated for chargeable gains purposes as the same asset under *TCGA 1992, s 127*, the relief is restricted to the sums that would have been allowable as deductions in computing the loss if the qualifying shares and the other shares or debentures were not to be treated as the same asset.

For these purposes, shares are not capable of being qualifying shares at any time if they were not acquired by subscription, if condition (c) at **44.16** above is not met or if condition (d) at **44.16** above would not be met if the shares were disposed of at that time. Additionally, for the purposes only of the 'same asset' restriction above, shares are not capable of being qualifying shares at any time if they are shares of a different class from the qualifying shares concerned.

Identification

Where it is necessary to determine whether a disposal of shares forming part of a mixed 'holding' (i.e. a holding which includes both shares for which the company has subscribed and other shares) qualifies for relief under these provisions, disposals are to be identified with acquisitions on a last in/first out (LIFO) basis. This does not apply where the holding includes shares to which investment relief under the Corporate Venturing Scheme is attributable and which have been held continuously (see **18.19** CORPORATE VENTURING SCHEME) by the company; the identification rules at **18.16** CORPORATE VENTURING SCHEME (generally first in/first out) apply instead.

A '*holding*' of shares for these purposes is any number of shares of the same class held by one company in the same capacity, growing or diminishing as shares of that class are acquired or disposed of. Shares comprised in a 'new holding' following a reorganisation to which *TCGA 1992, s 127* applies are treated as having been acquired when the original shares were acquired. Any shares held or disposed of by a nominee or bare trustee for a company are treated as held or disposed of by the company.

Anti-avoidance

Any claim to relief will bring in the provisions of *TCGA 1992, s 30* (value-shifting to give a tax-free benefit — see **4.10** ANTI-AVOIDANCE) so that the relief may be adjusted for any benefit conferred whether tax-free or not.

Company reorganisations etc.

Where shares are disposed of and represent a new holding identifiable under *TCGA 1992, s 127* (see **63.2** SHARES AND SECURITIES) with 'old shares' after a reorganisation or reduction of share capital, relief under these provisions is not available unless it could have been given if an allowable loss had arisen on the disposal of the old shares at arm's length at the reorganisation etc. had this legislation been in force. Where the reorganisation did not so qualify, but new consideration was given for the new shares, relief is limited to such of that new consideration as is an allowable deduction. '*New consideration*' is money or money's worth but excluding any surrender or alteration to the original shares or rights attached thereto, and the application of assets of the company or distribution declared but not made out of the assets.

Share exchanges

Where, by means of an exchange of shares, all of the shares (the old shares) of a company (the old company) are acquired by a company (the new company) in which the only previously issued shares are subscriber shares, then, subject to the further conditions below being satisfied, the exchange is not regarded as involving a disposal of the old shares and an acquisition of the new company shares (the new shares). Where old shares held by a company were subscribed for by it, the new shares stand in the shoes of the old shares, e.g. as if they had been subscribed for and issued at the time the old shares were subscribed for and issued and as if any requirements under the above provisions met at any time before the exchange by the old company had been met at that time by the new company.

The further conditions are as follows.

(a) The shares must be issued after 5 April 1998.
(b) The consideration for the old shares must consist entirely of the issue of the new shares.
(c) The consideration for old shares of each description must consist entirely of new shares of the 'corresponding description'.
(d) New shares of each description must be issued to holders of old shares of the 'corresponding description' in respect of and in proportion to their holdings.
(e) For new shares issued on or after 6 April 2007, the exchange of shares is not treated for chargeable gains purposes as involving a disposal of the old shares or an acquisition of the new shares by virtue of *TCGA 1992, s 127*.
(f) For new shares issued before 6 April 2007, before the issue of the new shares, on the written application (for which see **4.15** ANTI-AVOIDANCE) of either the old or new company, HMRC must have notified to that company their satisfaction that the exchange:

(i) is for genuine commercial reasons; and
(ii) does not form part of a scheme or arrangements to which *TCGA 1992, s 137(1)* (see **4.15** ANTI-AVOIDANCE) applies.

HMRC may, within 30 days of an application, request further particulars, which must then be supplied within 30 days of the request (or such longer period as they may allow in any particular case).

For these purposes, old and new shares are of a '*corresponding description*' if, assuming they were shares in the same company, they would be of the same class and carry the same rights.

An exchange within these provisions, or arrangements for such an exchange, do not breach the control and independence requirement at **44.16** above.

[*CTA 2010, ss 68–90, Sch 2 paras 27–51; TCGA 1992, s 125A; Co-operative and Community Benefit Societies Act 2014, Sch 4 para 158; FA 2014, Sch 39 para 12; SI 2008 No 954, Art 10; SI 2009 No 2859, Art 2*].

Deferred unascertainable consideration — election for treatment of loss as accruing in earlier year

[44.19] Where a person within the charge to capital gains tax makes a disposal of a right to future unascertainable consideration (see below) acquired as consideration for the disposal of another asset, and a loss accrues, he may, subject to conditions, make an election for the loss to be treated as arising in the year in which that other asset was disposed of. Accordingly, where the election is made, the loss on disposal of the right can be carried back to be set against the gain arising on the disposal of the original asset. The detailed provisions are described below.

Conditions for making election

The election is available where a person (the '*taxpayer*') disposes of a right and the following conditions are satisfied.

(1) An allowable loss (the '*relevant loss*') accrues on the disposal.
(2) The tax year in which the relevant loss actually accrues (the '*year of the loss*') is one in which the taxpayer is chargeable to capital gains tax in respect of chargeable gains accruing to him in that year, or would be so chargeable (apart from the deduction of any allowable losses and the annual exempt amount) were there any such gains.
(3) The right was, in whole or part, acquired by the taxpayer as the whole or part of the consideration for a disposal (the '*original disposal*') by him of another asset (the '*original asset*').
(4) The original disposal was made in a tax year earlier than that in which the disposal of the right is made. Where the right was acquired as consideration for two or more disposals, this condition must be satisfied with respect to all those disposals.
(5) On the taxpayer's acquisition of the right, there was no corresponding disposal of it.
(6) The right is a 'right to unascertainable consideration' (see below).

(7) A chargeable gain accrued to the taxpayer, or would have so accrued but for the deferral provisions of *TCGA 1992, Sch 5B para 2(2)(a)* (see **23.15** ENTERPRISE INVESTMENT SCHEME) or *Sch 5C para 2(2)(a)* (see **71.12** VENTURE CAPITAL TRUSTS), on one or more of the following events:
   (a) the original disposal,
   (b) an earlier disposal of the original asset by the taxpayer in the tax year of the original disposal, or
   (c) a later disposal of the original asset by the taxpayer in a tax year earlier than the actual year of the disposal of the right.

   Where the right was acquired as consideration for two or more original disposals, any reference in (a) to (c) above to the original disposal should be read as a reference to any of the original disposals, any reference to the original asset as a reference to the original asset in relation to that original disposal, and any reference to the tax year of the original disposal should be construed accordingly.

(8) There is a tax year (an '*eligible year*'), which is earlier than the year of the loss but not earlier than 1992/93, in which a chargeable gain within (7) above accrued to the taxpayer and for which there remains a relevant amount on which capital gains tax is chargeable immediately before the election. Where the deferral provisions mentioned in (7) above applied to prevent a gain within (7) above from accruing, a tax year in which a chargeable gain is treated as accruing to the taxpayer in respect of that gain under *TCGA 1992, Sch 5B paras 4, 5* or *Sch 5C paras 4, 5* (chargeable events — see **23.15** ENTERPRISE INVESTMENT SCHEME and **71.12** VENTURE CAPITAL TRUSTS) will be an eligible year.

   For these purposes, a tax year is one for which there remains a relevant amount on which capital gains tax is chargeable immediately before an election if, immediately before the making of the election, there remains for that year an amount in respect of which the taxpayer is chargeable to capital gains tax, after taking account of any previous elections under these provisions, after excluding any gains attributed under *TCGA 1992, ss 87* or *89(2)* and, for 2002/03 and earlier years (other than any of the years 2000/01, 2001/02 and/or 2002/03 for which an election under *FA 2002, Sch 11 para 8* is made), gains attributed under *TCGA 1992, ss 77* or *86* (see **44.2** above), and on the assumption that no losses fall to be deducted in consequence of any election under these provisions which could be, but has not been, made.

For the above purposes, any question as to whether a chargeable gain or loss is one that accrues (or would accrue but for any particular provision) on a particular disposal or a disposal of any particular description, or the time at which, or year in which, any particular disposal takes place, is determined without regard to *TCGA 1992, s 10A* (gains and losses accruing during period of temporary non-residence treated as accruing in period of return — see **49.5** OVERSEAS MATTERS). This provision does not, however, affect the determination of any question as to the period in which, by virtue of *TCGA 1992, s 10A(2)*, the gain or loss is treated as accruing (apart from the effect of an election under these provisions), nor does it prevent a loss accruing during a period of temporary non-residence from being an allowable loss.

[*TCGA 1992, ss 279A, 279B(1)(7)(8); FA 2008, Sch 2 paras 40, 41, 56(2)(3); FA 2013, Sch 45 para 122*].

Effect of election

Where an election is made under the above provisions, the relevant loss is treated for capital gains tax purposes as if it were a loss accruing in the earliest tax year which is an eligible year.

Where that year is 2008/09 or a subsequent year, the amount of the relevant loss that can be deducted from chargeable gains of that year is limited to the amount (the '*first year limit*') of the chargeable gains accruing to the taxpayer in the year, excluding any amounts attributed to him under *TCGA 1992, ss 87* or *89(2)* (see **48.14** OFFSHORE SETTLEMENTS), and after deducting any amounts in respect of allowable losses. Account must be taken of any previous elections made under these provisions, but no account must be taken of the relevant loss.

Where the earliest eligible year is 2007/08 or an earlier year, the first year limit is found by taking the following steps.

Step 1.

Take the total amount of chargeable gains accruing to the taxpayer in the year.

Step 2.

Exclude from that amount any amounts attributed to the taxpayer under *TCGA 1992, ss 77, 86, 87* or *89(2)* (see **2.6** ANNUAL RATES AND EXEMPTIONS).

Step 3.

Deduct from the remaining amount any amounts in respect of allowable losses except for any losses falling to be set against gains attributed to the taxpayer under *TCGA 1992, ss 77* or *86* (see **44.2** above). Account must be taken of any previous elections made under these provisions, but no account must be taken of the relevant loss.

Where the earliest eligible year is one of the years 2003/04 to 2007/08 inclusive, or where it is a year in respect of which an election under *FA 2002, Sch 11 para 8* has been made, two further steps must be taken to arrive at the first year limit, as follows.

Step 4.

Add to the remaining amount every amount attributed to the taxpayer as a chargeable gain under *TCGA 1992, ss 77* or *86*.

Step 5.

Deduct any losses falling to be set against such attributed gains.

To the extent that the relevant loss exceeds the first year limit (and so is not utilised in the first eligible year), it may be carried forward for set-off against gains of later years. In the case of tax years falling between the first eligible year and the year of the loss, any remaining part of the relevant loss can only be deducted if the year is an eligible year. For such years, the amount of the loss which may be deducted is limited to the amount (the '*later year limit*') in respect of which the taxpayer would be chargeable to capital gains tax for the year:

- on the assumption that no part of the relevant loss, or any other loss in respect of which an election under these provisions could be made but which, immediately after the making of the election in question, has not been made, falls to be deducted from the gains for the year;
- taking account of any previous elections under these provisions; and
- and any gains from which the taxpayer's personal losses are not deductible (see **44.2** above).

[*TCGA 1992, s 279C; FA 2008, Sch 2 paras 43, 56(2)*].

Where the right in respect of which an election is made is an earn-out right within the meaning of *TCGA 1992, s 138A* (see **63.6** SHARES AND SECURITIES) conferred before 10 April 2003, no election can be made under that section for the right to be treated as a security, whether at the same time as the election under these provisions or subsequently. [*FA 2003, s 162(2)(4)*].

Meaning of 'right to unascertainable consideration'

A right is a '*right to unascertainable consideration*' if, and only if, it is a right to consideration the amount or value of which is unascertainable when the right is conferred because it is referable, in whole or part, to matters which are uncertain at that time because they have not yet occurred.

The amount or value of any consideration is not regarded as unascertainable by reason only:

(i) that the right to receive all or part of the consideration is postponed or contingent, to the extent that the consideration is brought into account in accordance with *TCGA 1992, s 48* (see **16.13**(g) COMPUTATION OF GAINS AND LOSSES) in the computation of a gain accruing to the taxpayer on the disposal of an asset;
(ii) in a case where the right to receive all or part of the consideration is postponed and may be to any extent satisfied by the receipt of alternative types of property, that some person has the right to select the property or type of property that is to be received; or
(iii) that either the amount or the value of the consideration has not been fixed, if either the amount will be fixed by reference to the value, and the value is ascertainable, or the value will be fixed by reference to the amount, and the amount is ascertainable.

An earn-out right treated as a security by virtue of *TCGA 1992, s 138A* (see **63.6** SHARES AND SECURITIES) is not regarded as a right to unascertainable consideration for the purposes of these provisions.

[*TCGA 1992, s 279B(2)–(6)*].

Making of election

An election under the above provisions is irrevocable and must be made by notice in writing to HMRC on or before the first anniversary of 31 January following the year of the loss. The notice must specify the following:

- the amount of the relevant loss,
- the right disposed of,
- the tax year of the right's disposal, and, if different, the year of the loss,
- the tax year in which the right was acquired,
- the original asset or assets,
- the eligible year in which the relevant loss is to be treated as accruing,
- the first year limit, and
- the amount to be deducted from gains of that year.

If any part of the relevant loss is to be carried forward to later eligible years, the notice must also specify each such year and the later year limit and amount to be deducted for each such year.

A separate notice is required for each loss in respect of which an election is being made. Where two or more elections are made on the same day, the notices must specify the order in which they are to be treated as made. [*TCGA 1992, s 279D*].

Example

Tanya owns 2,000 £1 ordinary shares in Be Good Ltd, for which she subscribed at par in January 1993. On 31 March 2011, she and the other shareholders in Be Good Ltd sold their shares to another company for £20 per share plus a further unquantified cash amount calculated by means of a formula relating to the future profits of Be Good Ltd. The value in March 2011 of the deferred consideration was estimated at £5.10 per share. Tanya makes no other disposals of chargeable assets in 2010/11. On 30 April 2017, Tanya receives a further £3.60 per share under the sale agreement.

Without an election under *TCGA 1992, s 279A*, Tanya's capital gains position is as follows.

2010/11		
	£	£
Disposal proceeds	40,000	
Value of rights	10,200	50,200
Cost of acquisition		2,000
Chargeable gain 2010/11		£48,200

2017/18	
Disposal of rights to deferred consideration	
Proceeds 2,000 × £3.60	7,200
Deemed cost of acquiring rights	10,200
Allowable loss 2017/18	£3,000

If Tanya makes an election under *TCGA 1992, s 279A* by 31 January 2020 the 2017/18 loss is treated as arising in 2010/11 and can be set off against the gain of that year as follows.

2010/11	
	£
Chargeable gain as above	48,200
Less Allowable loss	3,000
Taxable gains 2010/11 (subject to annual exempt amount)	£45,200

Restriction on losses — write-off of government investment

[44.20] Where any amount of an investment, by the Government, in a *company* other than an unincorporated association, is written off, an equal amount is to be set off against the body's tax 'losses', starting with losses available at the end of the accounting period ended before the write-off, and continuing for subsequent periods, until the investment is covered. The definition of '*losses*', for this purpose, includes, inter alia, unrelieved allowable losses under *TCGA 1992, s 8* (capital losses of companies). It should be noted, however, that the investment is only written off against capital losses as a last resort, i.e. after the extinction of other losses, unrelieved capital allowances, management expenses and charitable donations. The investment can also be written off against the losses of any member of the same 51% group. An investment is written off if the liability to repay any money lent is extinguished; if any shares subscribed for out of public funds are cancelled; or if 'commencing capital debts' (as defined) or 'public dividend capital' (as defined) is reduced otherwise than by being paid off or repaid. These provisions do not apply where the investment written off is replaced in some other form. [*CTA 2010, ss 92–96*]. See Tolley's Corporation Tax under Losses for further details.

Set-off of trading losses etc. against chargeable gains

[44.21] A person other than a company cannot normally set off his allowable losses for capital gains tax purposes against his income. A company, also, cannot normally set off its allowable losses for the purposes of corporation tax on chargeable gains against income but trading losses or management expenses of a company can, in certain cases, be set off against total profits, such profits including chargeable gains. See **14.3**, **14.6** COMPANIES. See, however, **44.15** and **44.18** above for the allowance of capital losses arising on the disposal of certain shares in unquoted trading companies against general income of *individuals* and *investment companies* respectively.

There are specific provisions enabling trading losses and certain other expenditure for income tax purposes to be set off against chargeable gains to the extent that they cannot be relieved against income (due to an insufficiency of income) for the tax year in question. These are described below.

Set-off of trading losses against chargeable gains of a person other than a company

Where trading losses arise so that relief is available under *ITA 2007, s 64* (set-off for income tax purposes of trading losses against general income — see Tolley's Income Tax under Losses) for a tax year and either a claim is made under that section or the person's total income for the year is either nil or does not include any income from which the loss can be deducted, a claim may also be made for the determination of the '*relevant amount*', which is so much of the trading loss as:

(a) is not deducted in calculating the claimant's net income for the year of claim, and
(b) has not already been relieved for any other year.

The claim is not deemed to be determined until the relevant amount for the year can no longer be varied, whether by the Tribunal (before 1 April 2009, the Commissioners) on appeal or on the order of any court.

The relevant amount, as finally determined, is to be treated for the purposes of capital gains tax as an allowable loss accruing to the claimant in the tax year, except that it cannot exceed the 'maximum amount'. Any such excess remains an income tax loss.

The tax years for which relief may be claimed under *ITA 2007, s 64* against income, and consequently under *TCGA 1992, s 261B* against gains, are the year in which the trading loss is incurred or the preceding year.

The '*maximum amount*' for this purpose is the amount on which the claimant would be chargeable to capital gains tax for the year, disregarding the annual exemption available under *TCGA 1992, s 3(1)* and the effect of this relief provision. Note that taper relief is abolished for gains accruing, or treated as accruing, in 2008/09 and subsequent years.

In computing the maximum amount, no account is taken of any event occurring after the determination of the relevant amount and in consequence of which the amount chargeable to capital gains tax is reduced by virtue of any capital gains tax legislation (e.g. a claim for rollover relief in a later year having the effect of reducing the amount chargeable for the year for which this relief provision is claimed; in such a case the allowable capital losses flowing from a claim under this provision would be displaced by the effect of the rollover claim but would be available for carry forward to subsequent years).

No amount treated as an allowable loss under this provision may be deducted from chargeable gains accruing in a tax year which begins after the claimant has ceased to carry on the trade in which the loss was sustained. For the purpose of applying this rule, any such losses brought forward are treated as set against gains in priority to genuine capital losses (HMRC Business Income Manual BIM85035).

A claim must be made on or before the first anniversary of the normal self-assessment filing date for the tax year in which the loss was made. Before 2007/08, strictly the claim had to form part of the claim under what is now *ITA 2007, s 64*. In practice, however, HMRC accepted separate claims where there was no income for the year against which the loss could be claimed (see Change 160 listed in Annex 1 to the Explanatory Notes to *ITA 2007*). They also accepted separate claims where (i) relief against general income had previously been claimed and a claim under these provisions could have been made, (ii) the separate claim was made within the time limits for the original claim, (iii) after the relief against general income there was a balance of unrelieved trading losses, and (iv) all other conditions for relief under these provisions were satisfied. (Revenue Tax Bulletin August 1993 p 87).

The above provisions apply also to employment losses relievable under *ITA 2007, s 128*.

[*ITA 2007, ss 71, 130; TCGA 1992, ss 261B, 261C; FA 1991, s 72; FA 2008, Sch 2 paras 39, 56(3); SI 2009 No 56, Sch 1 paras 182, 183*].

Anti-avoidance

For 2007/08 onwards, no relief under the above provisions can be obtained where the loss arises directly or indirectly from arrangements which have as a main purpose the avoiding of a tax liability by means of sideways income tax relief or relief under the above provisions. For arrangements entered into, broadly, before 21 October 2009, this applied only to individuals carrying on a trade in a non-active capacity. See *ITA 2007, ss 74ZA* and *74B* and Tolley's Income Tax under Losses for the detailed provisions.

Also for 2007/08 onwards, where an individual carries on a trade in a non-active capacity and the above prohibition on relief does not apply the total amount of sideways income tax relief against non-trade income and capital gains relief under the above provisions for a tax year is restricted to £25,000. See *ITA 2007, s 74A* and Tolley's Income Tax under Losses for the detailed provisions.

Example

M has carried on a trade for some years, preparing accounts to 30 June each year. For the year ended 30 June 2017 he makes a trading loss of £17,000. His taxable profit for 2016/17 is £5,000, and his other income for both 2016/17 and 2017/18 amounts to £2,000. He makes a capital gain of £14,000 and a capital loss of £1,000 for 2017/18 and has capital losses brought forward of £6,800. M makes claims for loss relief, against income of 2016/17 and income and gains of 2017/18, under *ITA 2007, s 64* and *TCGA 1992, s 261B*.

Calculation of 'relevant amount'	
	£
Trading loss — year ended 30.6.17	17,000
Relieved against other income for 2017/18	(2,000)
Relieved against income for 2016/17	(7,000)
Relevant amount	£8,000

Calculation of 'maximum amount'

		£
Gains for 2017/18		14,000
Deduct Losses for 2017/18		(1,000)
Unrelieved losses brought forward		(6,800)
Maximum amount		£6,200
Relief under *TCGA 1992, s 261B*		
	£	£
Gains for the year		14,000
Losses for the year	1,000	
Relief under *TCGA 1992, s 261B*	6,200	
		7,200
Gain (covered by annual exempt amount)		£6,800
Capital losses brought forward and carried forward		£6,800

Loss memorandum

	£
Trading loss	17,000
Claimed against income of 2017/18	(2,000)
Claimed against income of 2016/17	(7,000)
Claimed under *TCGA 1992, s 261B*	(6,200)
Unutilised loss	£1,800

Note to the example

(a) In this example, £4,500 of the capital gains tax annual exempt amount of £11,300 is wasted, but the brought forward capital losses are preserved for carry-forward against gains of future years. If M had *not* made the claim under *TCGA 1992, s 261B*, his net gains for the year of £13,000 would have been reduced to the annual exempt amount by deducting £1,700 of the losses brought forward. Only £5,100 of capital losses would remain available for carry-forward against future gains and a further £6,200 of trading losses would have been available for carry-forward against future trading profits. So the effect of the claim is to preserve capital losses at the expense of trading losses.

Set-off of post-cessation expenditure of a trade or property business against capital gains

Relief is available against both income and capital gains for individuals who incur qualifying business expenditure in connection with a trade, profession or property business which has ceased within seven years of its ceasing. Broadly, qualifying expenditure includes costs of remedying defective work or services rendered and damages in respect thereof, insurance premiums paid to insure against such costs and legal and other professional expenses incurred in connection therewith. Relief is also given for bad debts which prove to be bad or which are released in whole or in part, and for the costs of collecting debts which have been taken into account in the final accounts. The relief is reduced by accruals for costs in the final accounting period which remain unpaid. On a claim, the relief may be set against income and then against capital gains of the tax year in which the qualifying expenditure is incurred, otherwise it will have to be carried forward to be set only against any post-cessation receipts under *ITTOIA 2005, s 254*. Claims must be made within twelve months after the normal self-assessment filing date for the tax year in which the expenditure was incurred. A claim for relief cannot exceed the capital gains available, disregarding losses brought forward, the annual exemption and trading losses set against gains as above.

Relief under the above provisions is not available for a payment or event on or after 12 January 2012 (13 March 2012 for property businesses) which is made or occurs directly or indirectly in consequence of, or otherwise in connection with, 'tax avoidance arrangements' to which the taxpayer is a party. For this purpose, '*tax avoidance arrangements*' are arrangements the main purpose, or one of the main purposes, of which is to obtain a reduction in tax liability under the above provisions, and '*arrangements*' include any agreement, understanding, scheme transaction or series of transactions, whether or not legally enforceable. This restriction does not apply to payments made on or after 12 January 2012 (13 March 2012 for property businesses) if they are made under an unconditional obligation (as defined) in a contract made before that date.

For full details of the provisions see Tolley's Income Tax under Post-Cessation Receipts and Expenditure.

[*ITA 2007, ss 98A, 101, 126; TCGA 1992, ss 261D, 261E; FA 2012, s 9*].

Set-off of post-employment deductions against capital gains

Relief against income or capital gains is available to former employees who bear the costs of indemnity insurance or certain work-related uninsured liabilities relating to their former employment where such costs are incurred by them up to six years after the year in which the employment ended. On a claim, the relief may be set against income and then against capital gains of the tax year in which the qualifying expenditure is incurred, otherwise it will be lost. Claims made on or after 1 April 2010 must be made four years after the end of the tax year to which the claim relates. Previously, claims had to be made within five years after 31 January following the tax year to which the claim related. A claim for relief cannot exceed the capital gains available, disregarding losses brought forward, the annual exemption, trading losses and post-cessation expenditure set against gains as above. For full details of the provisions see Tolley's Income Tax under Employment Income. [*TCGA 1992, s 263ZA; ITEPA 2003, ss 555–564*].

Key points concerning losses

[44.22] Points to consider are as follows.

- Under self-assessment, a capital loss is not allowable unless it is quantified and notified to HMRC.

- A loss on a disposal carried out to secure a tax advantage is not allowable. In addition, the tax tribunals and courts now rarely rule in the taxpayer's favour in cases involving a loss arising from a scheme or arrangement where the taxpayer has suffered no economic loss.
- Relief for losses brought forward are more flexible than in year losses as they are offset to preserve the benefit of the annual exempt amount. Consideration should therefore be given to the timing of realising small gains potentially covered by the annual exempt amount and losses. Where beneficial and practical there may be an advantage to realising a small profit and loss in separate tax years.
- A loss on a disposal to a connected person can generally only be set against a gain on a disposal to that same person. This is often referred to as a 'clogged loss'.
- A settlor with an interest in a non-UK resident settlement (but not a beneficiary of such a settlement) can set personal losses against settlement gains attributed to them.
- Investment companies can claim relief for a loss on disposal of shares in a qualifying trading company for which they subscribed against income instead of gains. Similarly, individuals who subscribed for shares in an unquoted trading company can claim relief for a loss in respect of those shares against income. However, the conversion of a loan into shares in an attempt to obtain this relief will not succeed if the shares had already become of negligible value. At current personal tax rates, relief against income is normally more favourable.
- A penalty can be charged in respect of an overstated loss, even where this has not yet been utilised, so particular care should be taken with negligible value claims and other losses involving asset valuations.

45

Market Value

Introduction to market value	**45.1**
Chargeable intangible assets	**45.2**
Quoted shares and securities	**45.3**
Unquoted shares	**45.4**
Alternative investment market (AIM)	**45.5**
Land	**45.6**
Exchange control	**45.7**

Cross-references. See **4.12** and **4.13** ANTI-AVOIDANCE for anti-avoidance provisions which may override or amend the general rules given below; **5.4** APPEALS for appeals relating to market values; **8.2** ASSETS HELD ON 6 APRIL **1965** for valuation of quoted shares and securities held on 6 April 1965; **16.11** COMPUTATION OF GAINS AND LOSSES for allowable expenditure relating to acquisition of assets at market value; **19.5** DEATH for valuation at death; **44.11** LOSSES for loss relief where the market value of an asset has become negligible; **50** PARTNERSHIPS for further valuation rules which apply to partnership assets.

Introduction to market value

[45.1] Market value is the price which assets might reasonably fetch in the open market, sold individually, with no allowance being made for any reduction in market value arising out of the whole of the assets being placed on the market at one and the same time. This provision applies subject to special rules applying under *TCGA 1992, s 25A* (deemed disposals of plant or machinery on commencement or termination of long funding lease — see **7.6** ASSETS) and *TCGA 1992, s 41A* (restriction on loss on disposal of fixture used for leasing under long funding lease — see **16.13**(j) COMPUTATION OF GAINS AND LOSSES). [*TCGA 1992, s 272(1)(2)(6)*].

After 9 March 1981, acquisition and disposal are treated as being made at market value (subject to any other provision and the exception below) if the transaction is:

(a) not at arm's length (which includes, in particular, any transaction between connected persons — see **4.12** ANTI-AVOIDANCE), or
(b) by way of gift, or
(c) on a transfer into settlement by a settlor, or
(d) a distribution from a company in respect of shares in that company, or
(e) wholly or partly for a consideration that cannot be valued (see *Fielder v Vedlynn Ltd* Ch D 1992, 65 TC 145), or
(f) in connection with his own or another's loss of office or employment, diminution of emoluments (see *Whitehouse v Ellam* Ch D, [1995] STC 503), or in consideration for or recognition of his or another's services (in any office, employment or otherwise), past or future.

Exception

The market value provisions in (a)–(f) above do not apply to the *acquisition* of an asset if there is no corresponding disposal of it *and* there is no consideration in money or money's worth (or the consideration is of an amount or value lower than the market value of the asset).

[*TCGA 1992, s 17*].

An attempt by a taxpayer to substitute market value for actual price paid in a transaction between unconnected persons failed in *Bullivant Holdings Ltd v CIR* Ch D 1998, 71 TC 22. For the application of the market value rule to shares acquired by reason of employment, see **22.3, 22.5, 22.14, 22.23, 22.24, 22.25, 22.28** EMPLOYEE SHARE SCHEMES.

Special rules applied to disposals by 'excluded persons' after 9 March 1981 and before 6 April 1985. See the 2005/06 and earlier editions of this work.

Chargeable intangible assets

[45.2] Where, after 31 March 2002, there is a transfer of an intangible asset between 'related parties' (see below), at least one of which is a company, and the asset is a 'chargeable intangible asset' in the hands of the transferor or transferee (or both), the transfer is treated for *all* direct tax purposes (as regards both transferor and transferee) as being at 'market value'. For this purpose, the '*market value*' of an asset is the price it might reasonably be expected to fetch on a sale in the open market. An asset is a '*chargeable intangible asset*' if a gain on its realisation would give rise to a credit falling to be brought into account under the intangible assets regime summarised at **15.14** COMPANIES — CORPORATE FINANCE AND INTANGIBLES and covered in detail in Tolley's Corporation Tax under Intangible Assets.

There are a number of exceptions to the above rule, as follows.

(1) Where the consideration for the transfer falls to be adjusted under the transfer pricing rules in *TIOPA 2010, Pt 4* or, in certain circumstances, *would* fall to be so adjusted were it not for the fact that the consideration is an arm's length amount.

(2) Where the transfer is 'tax-neutral' under any provision of the intangible assets regime; this applies mainly in connection with intra-group transfers and certain transfers of a business.

(3) Where the asset is transferred to the company and a reduction is made under *TCGA 1992, s 165(4)(a)* (reduction of chargeable gain on gift of business asset — see **36.2** HOLD-OVER RELIEFS). In this case, for the purposes of the intangible assets regime, the transfer is treated as being at market value less the amount of the reduction.

(4) Where:
   - the asset is transferred from the company at less than its market value or to the company at more than market value;
   - the related party is not a company or, if it is a company, the asset is not a chargeable intangible asset in its hands; and

- the transfer gives rise (or would but for the above rule) to an amount to be taken into account in computing any person's income, profits or losses for tax purposes under *CTA 2010, Pt 23 Ch 2* (company distributions) or *ITEPA 2003, Pt 3* (earnings and benefits treated as employment income).

In this case, the market value rule above is disapplied only for the purposes of the computation mentioned above.

(5) Where the transfer would be tax-neutral on a transfer within a group but for the transferor having at any time held the asset wholly or partly for the purposes of a non-UK permanent establishment and having made an election under *CTA 2009, s 18A* (exemption for foreign permanent establishments — see **49.8** OVERSEAS MATTERS) and the transferor has not so held the asset during any part of the period of ownership for which the election has applied. In this case, the transfer is treated as being for the tax written-down value of the asset plus the amount which would be the 'foreign permanent establishments amount' if the transfer were at market value.

(6) Where the provisions at **37.4** INCORPORATION AND DISINCORPORATION RELIEFS apply.

For transfers on or after 25 November 2015, persons are treated as related parties (so that the market value rule above applies) where the transfer pricing 'participation condition' (see *TIOPA 2010, s 147*) is met between them. Transfers pursuant to an unconditional contractual obligation before that date are excluded.

[*CTA 2009, ss 844–849A; FA 2013, s 61(2); FA 2016, s 53*].

Parties are '*related parties*' in any of the following circumstances.

- Both are companies, and one has 'control' of, or holds a 'major interest' in, the other (as defined in *CTA 2009, ss 836, 837*).
- Both are companies, and both are under the 'control' of the same person (except, broadly, where that person is a state, a government or an international organisation).
- One is a close company (within the meaning given by *CTA 2010, ss 439–454*) and the other is, or is an 'associate' of, a 'participator' (both within *CTA 2009, s 841*) in that company.
- One is a close company and the other is, or is an associate of, a participator in a company that has control of, or holds a major interest in, that company.
- Both are companies within the same 'group' (as defined in *CTA 2009, ss 764–773*).

Parties are treated as related parties where they would be so treated under the above provisions but for any person (other than an individual) being the subject of 'insolvency arrangements'. For this purpose, '*insolvency arrangements*' include:

- arrangements under which a person acts as the liquidator, provisional liquidator, receiver, administrator or administrative receiver of a company or partnership;

- voluntary arrangements proposed or approved under *Insolvency Act 1986, Pt 1* (or NI equivalent); and
- equivalent arrangements under the law of any country or territory (whether made when the person is solvent or insolvent).

[*CTA 2009, ss 834, 835*].

Quoted shares and securities

[45.3] The market value of quoted shares and securities for capital gains tax purposes is determined as follows.

6 April 2015 onwards

The market value of shares, securities or strips which are included in the official UK list is:

- on any day the Stock Exchange is open, the lower of the two prices quoted in the Stock Exchange Daily Official List as the closing price for that day plus one-half of the difference between those prices; and
- on any day the Stock Exchange is closed, that value on the latest previous day on which it was open.

The above method of valuation does not apply for inheritance tax purposes but instead the method which was used for capital gains tax purposes before 6 April 2015 (see below) continues to apply. Where assets are valued to determine an inheritance tax charge *on death*, that value is also taken to be the market value on death for capital gains tax purposes under *TCGA 1992, s 274* (see **19.5** DEATH). Therefore, the value of quoted shares or securities for inheritance tax purposes (determined below) is also taken to apply for capital gains tax in such a scenario, even after 6 April 2015.

The above method of valuation does not apply for computing the value of shares or securities where special circumstances may affect the value.

The market value of securities or strips which are not included in the official UK list but are listed on a recognised foreign stock exchange is:

- on any day the exchange is open, the closing price shown in the exchange list for that day (or, if more than one price is shown, the lower of the two prices plus one-half of the difference between them; and
- on any day the exchange is closed, that value on the latest previous day on which it was open.

If securities are quoted in more than one foreign exchange list, then any foreign exchange list published for a foreign exchange which is regarded as the major exchange for such securities is to be used to determine the market value. If there is no such exchange, any foreign exchange list for an exchange in the territory in which the issuing company is resident is used in preference to any other such list. If a strip or a security exchanged for strips of that security is quoted in more than one foreign exchange list, any such list published for a foreign stock exchange in the territory of the issuing government is used in preference to any other such list and any such list published for a major exchange in that territory for such strips or securities is used in preference to any other such list.

[*TCGA 1992, s 272(3)(4); SI 2015 Nos 616, 635*].

Before 6 April 2015

Before 6 April 2015, the market value of shares and securities quoted in The Stock Exchange Daily Official List is the lesser of:

(a) the lower of the two prices quoted in The Stock Exchange Daily Official List for the relevant date, plus a quarter of the difference between those prices (*'the quarter-up rule'*); and
(b) the average of the highest and lowest prices for normal bargains recorded on that date, if any.

If the London trading floor is closed on the relevant date, the prices are to be taken by reference to the latest previous date or to the earliest subsequent date, whichever produces the lower figure.

The above method of valuation continues to apply for inheritance tax purposes after 6 April 2015.

The above method of valuation does not apply for computing the value of shares as at 6 April 1965 (see **8.2** ASSETS HELD ON 6 APRIL **1965**), nor where special circumstances may affect the value.

[*TCGA 1992, s 272(3)(4)(6), Sch 11 para 6(1)(2)(4), para 7(1)*].

See *Hinchcliffe v Crabtree* HL 1971, 47 TC 419.

Units in unit trusts

Units in unit trusts, subject to similar valuation rules at 6 April 1965 (as above), are valued at the lower of the two prices published by the managers on the relevant date or if no price is published at that time, on the latest date before the relevant date. [*TCGA 1992, s 272(5)(6), Sch 11 para 6(1)(3)*].

Simon's Taxes. See **C2.122.**

Unquoted shares

[45.4] Market value of unquoted shares is determined on the assumption that all information is available which a prudent prospective purchaser might reasonably require before purchase by private treaty at arm's length from a willing vendor. [*TCGA 1992, s 273*]. This counteracts *In re Lynall* HL 1971, 47 TC 375.

This provision applies to disposals after 5 July 1973 and valuations are made on the present basis in connection both with acquisition (even if before 6 July 1973, or 6 April 1965) and disposal. Otherwise, the chargeable gain on a part disposal before 6 July 1973 is not itself affected but it is re-computed on the present basis for the purpose of calculating the gain on a subsequent disposal after 5 July 1973. As regards deemed acquisitions on death after 30 March 1971 and before 6 July 1973, the present basis does not apply if the shares constituted a controlling holding and were valued on the assets basis for estate duty purposes. [*TCGA 1992, Sch 11 paras 3–5*].

In arriving at a valuation, unpublished information concerning the company's profits may be taken into account (*Caton's Administrators v Couch* (Sp C 6), [1995] SSCD 34; *Clark (Clark's Executor) v Green & CIR* (Sp C 5), [1995] SSCD 99).

Other cases concerning disputes as to the value of unquoted shares include *Hawkings-Byass v Sassen (and related appeals)* (Sp C 88), [1996] SSCD 319; *Denekamp v Pearce* Ch D 1998, 71 TC 213; *Billows v Hammond* (Sp C 252), [2000] SSCD 430; *Marks v Sherred* (Sp C 418), [2004] SSCD 362; *Shinebond Ltd v Carrol* (Sp C 522), [2006] SSCD 147; *Green v HMRC* FTT, [2014] UKFTT 396(TC); 2014 STI 2235; *Foulser v HMRC* FTT, [2015] UKFTT 220 (TC), 2015 STI 2537.

Simon's Taxes. See **C2.124**.

Alternative investment market (AIM)

[45.5] Companies not wishing to apply for a full listing have access to the Alternative Investment Market (AIM) launched on 19 June 1995. AIM replaced the existing Rule 4.2 (of the Stock Exchange) dealing facility, and transitional provisions were available to assist companies already under Rule 4.2 to migrate to the AIM at minimum cost. AIM companies are not treated as 'quoted' or 'listed' for those provisions of the Taxes Acts which use such terms in relation to securities. (HMRC Press Releases 20 February 1995, 28 November 2001).

Land

[45.6] Where, at a certain date, freehold land was subject to a tenancy by a company controlled by the freeholder, the valuation had to be of the reversion in the land expectant on the determination of the tenancy and not of the unencumbered freehold (*Henderson v Karmel's Exors* Ch D 1984, 58 TC 201).

Exchange control

[45.7] In relation to assets of a kind the sale of which was subject to restrictions imposed under the *Exchange Control Act 1947*, a determination of market value at any time before 13 December 1979 is subject to adjustment for the premium which would have been payable by a purchaser but not receivable by a seller. [*TCGA 1992, Sch 11 para 7(2)*].

46

Married Persons and Civil Partners

Introduction	**46.1**
Married persons	**46.2**
Civil partners	**46.3**
'Living together'	**46.4**
Transfers between spouses or civil partners	**46.5**

Cross-references. See 2 ANNUAL RATES AND EXEMPTIONS; 8.1 and 8.3 ASSETS HELD ON 6 APRIL 1965; 36 HOLD-OVER RELIEFS; 44.12 LOSSES for loss relief restrictions on qualifying loans between spouses; 53.2 and 53.7 PRIVATE RESIDENCES; 57 RESIDENCE AND DOMICILE for treatment of spouses.

Simon's Taxes. See C1.202.

Introduction

[46.1] Married persons and same-sex civil partners are treated for capital gains tax purposes as separate individuals, so that each has their own annual exempt amount and losses of one cannot be set against gains of the other. Where the partners are living together, however, transfers of assets between them are treated as made on a 'no gain/no loss' basis.

Married persons

[46.2] Spouses, whether or not 'living together' (see **46.4** below), are each treated as separate individuals so that:

(a) each spouse is assessed and charged by reference only to their own gains and circumstances (e.g. the rate of tax applicable);
(b) losses of one spouse are not deductible from the gains of the other; and
(c) each spouse has a separate right to the whole of the annual exempt amount available to individuals generally.

Where spouses have made a declaration under *ITA 2007, s 837* in respect of their individual beneficial interests in, and in the income from, jointly held property (see Tolley's Income Tax under Married Persons) and the declaration is still effective at the time of disposal of the property, there is a presumption that the declared split of interests is effective for capital gains tax purposes. Where there is no declaration which has effect at the time of disposal but it is clear that there is a particular split of ownership (e.g. a separate agreement may provide for the spouses' respective rights or that one spouse is merely a nominee and has no beneficial interest in the property) any gain on a disposal should be reported to HMRC on that basis. In other cases where the split of ownership is not clear HMRC will normally accept that the spouses hold the property in equal shares (Revenue Press Release 21 November 1990).

Transfers of assets between spouses living together are treated as made on a 'no gain/no loss basis' as in **46.5** below.

Where:

(i) the husband makes a claim under *TCGA 1992, s 279* (enforced delay in remitting gains from disposals of overseas assets, see **49.6** OVERSEAS MATTERS) in respect of gains accruing to the wife before 6 April 1990 (when gains of the wife were, with certain exceptions, assessed on the husband), and

(ii) under that provision the amount of the gains falls to be assessed as if it were an amount of gains accruing after 5 April 1990,

the assessment is to be made on the wife (or her personal representatives). [*TCGA 1992, s 279(7)*].

Gains accruing to one spouse as trustee or personal representative cannot affect the position of the other spouse. [*TCGA 1992, s 65(2)*].

Spouses living together may claim exemption in respect of only one main residence. See **53.2** PRIVATE RESIDENCES.

See **64.2** SHARES AND SECURITIES — IDENTIFICATION RULES as regards joint husband and wife shareholdings.

Civil partners

[46.3] Transfers of assets between civil partners who are living together are treated as made on a 'no gain/no loss basis' as in **46.5** below.

Civil partners living together may claim exemption in respect of only one main residence. See **53.2** PRIVATE RESIDENCES.

For this purpose a '*civil partnership*' is one which exists under or by virtue of the *Civil Partnerships Act 2004* and '*civil partner*' is to be construed accordingly. [*FA 2005, s 103*].

'Living together'

[46.4] Individuals who are married to, or are civil partners of, each other are treated as living together unless they are:

(a) separated under a court order or separation deed, or

(b) in fact separated in circumstances which render permanent separation likely.

[*ITA 2007, s 1011; TCGA 1992, s 288(3)*].

Both (a) and (b) above require the marriage or civil partnership to have broken down (HMRC Capital Gains Manual CG22073).

Transfers between spouses or civil partners

[46.5] Transfers of assets, in a tax year, between spouses or civil partners who are living together (see **46.4** above) in any part of that year are regarded as made on a 'no gain/no loss' basis. This treatment also applies to transfers between spouses or civil partners in the part of a year following the start of the marriage or civil partnership and in the whole of the year in which separation takes place, even though the spouses or civil partners may not be 'living together' at the time of transfer (but does not apply following a decree absolute). The no gain/no loss treatment does not apply to transfers (i) by way of *donatio mortis causa* (see **19.6** DEATH); (ii) to or from trading stock of either spouse or civil partner; or (iii) of exempt employee shareholder shares where any gain would be wholly exempt (see **22.26** EMPLOYEE SHARE SCHEMES). Where a transfer of employee shareholder shares would only be partly exempt as a result of the lifetime limit for gains on such shares, the transfer is treated as made for a consideration equal to the amount (not exceeding market value) which results in a gain of an amount equal to the balance of the lifetime limit. [*TCGA 1992, s 58; FA 2013, Sch 23 para 17; FA 2016, s 88(7)–(10)*].

The deemed consideration for a no gain/no loss transfer between spouses or civil partners is equal to the transferor's acquisition cost for CGT purposes, including any enhancement expenditure, plus indexation allowance if applicable (see **38** INDEXATION). The no gain/no loss rule cannot be disapplied, and any *actual* consideration given for the transfer is ignored. It should be noted that the transaction is still a disposal by the transferor spouse or partner and an acquisition by the transferee as at the date of transfer; the legislation does not operate by deeming no disposal to have taken place.

Where either spouse or civil partner is non-UK resident, but the definition at **46.4** above nevertheless treats them as 'living together', there is no authority for disapplying the no gain/no loss treatment even if the transfer results in an asset leaving the UK tax net (see HMRC Capital Gains Manual CG22300 and see *Gubay v Kington* HL 1984, 57 TC 601).

See **16.5** COMPUTATION OF GAINS AND LOSSES for part disposals between spouses or civil partners and **41.9** LAND for small part disposals of land.

Example 1

(A) No inter-spouse transfer

Paul and Heidi are a married couple. For 2017/18 Heidi's taxable income (after personal allowance) is £50,000 and Paul's is £15,000. On 4 July 2017, Heidi sells two paintings which she had acquired in June 1994 at a cost of £5,000 each. Net sale proceeds amount to £16,300 and £25,000. Neither spouse disposed of any other chargeable assets during 2017/18.

Chargeable gains — Heidi

	£
Net proceeds of painting 1	16,300
Cost	5,000
Chargeable gain	£11,300
Net proceeds of painting 2	25,000
Cost	5,000
Chargeable gain	£20,000

Total chargeable gains (£11,300 + £20,000)	31,300
Annual exempt amount	11,300
Taxable gains 2017/18	£20,000
Tax payable £20,000 × 20%	£4,000.00

(B) Inter-spouse transfer

The facts are as in (A) above except that in April 2017, Heidi gives painting 2 to Paul who then makes the sale on 4 July 2017.

Chargeable gains — Heidi

	£
Deemed consideration for painting 2 (April 2017) note (a)	5,000
Cost	5,000
Chargeable gain	Nil
Net proceeds of painting 1	16,300
Cost	5,000
Chargeable gain	£11,300
Total chargeable gains	11,300
Annual exempt amount	11,300
Taxable gains 2017/18	£Nil

Chargeable gain — Paul

	£
Net proceeds (4.7.17)	25,000
Cost (April 2017)	5,000
Chargeable gain	20,000
Annual exempt amount	11,300
Taxable gain	£8,700
Capital gains tax £8,700 × 10%	£870.00
Tax saving compared with (A) above (£4,000 – £870)	£3,130

Notes to the example

(a) The inter-spouse transfer is deemed to be for such consideration as to ensure that no gain or loss accrues.

(b) The fact that transfers of assets between husband and wife are no gain/no loss transfers enables savings to be made by ensuring that disposals are made by a spouse with an unused annual exempt amount or who pays CGT at only 10%.

(c) An inter-spouse transfer followed by a sale could be attacked by HMRC as an anti-avoidance device. To minimise the risk, there should be a clear time interval between the two transactions and no arrangements made to effect the ultimate sale until after the transfer. The gift should be outright with no strings attached and with no 'arrangement' for eventual proceeds to be passed to the transferor. See also **44.7** LOSSES for anti-avoidance provisions applying where there are arrangements to secure a tax advantage involving a loss. It is not clear whether HMRC would seek to apply the provisions where an asset is transferred between spouses and then sold at a loss so that the loss can be set against a gain of the transferee spouse (see *Taxation* Magazine 19 April 2007, pp. 428–431).

Example 2

In May 2021, Amy transfers shares with a market value of £90,000 to her husband Rory. The shares are exempt employee shareholder shares (see **22.26** EMPLOYEE SHARE SCHEMES) acquired by Amy in May 2016 for £15,000. The capital gains tax consequences of the transfer are as follows.

(i) No previous disposals of exempt employee shareholder shares

Exempt gain — Amy

	£
Deemed consideration (market value)	90,000
Cost	15,000
Exempt gain	£75,000
Lifetime limit remaining unused (£100,000 – £75,000)	£25,000

Rory is deemed to have acquired the shares at market value for £90,000.

(ii) Lifetime limit previously used up

Chargeable gain — Amy

	£
Deemed consideration (no gain/no loss)	15,000
Cost	15,000
Exempt gain	£Nil

Rory is deemed to have acquired the shares for £15,000.

(iii) £60,000 of lifetime limit previously used up

Balance of lifetime limit (£100,000 – £60,000)	£40,000

Chargeable gain — Amy

	£
Deemed consideration (amount resulting in gain equal to balance of lifetime limit)	55,000

Cost	15,000
Gain (exempt as equal to the balance of the lifetime limit)	£40,000

Rory is deemed to have acquired the shares for £55,000.

Transfers whilst spouses separated or treated as separated

In a case in which spouses, after several years of separation, were divorced and the court order (by consent) on the decree nisi provided for the transfer of certain property (which was not otherwise exempt) it was held that the property had been disposed of at the time of the decree nisi. As the divorce was not then absolute, the spouses were still connected persons and the consideration was to be taken as the market value. See **17.1** CONNECTED PERSONS and **45.1** MARKET VALUE and HMRC Capital Gains Manual CG22400–22505. The normal 'no gain/no loss' basis did not apply as the spouses were not living together. (*Aspden v Hildesley* Ch D 1981, 55 TC 609).

Unmarried couples

The no gain/no loss rule applies only to transfers between persons legally recognised as married or as civil partners under English or Scottish law. Polygamous marriages may be so recognised in limited circumstances (see HMRC Capital Gains Manual CG22070). The rule does not apply to a transfer to a so-called 'common-law' husband or wife. An unmarried couple or a couple who are not civil partners are not CONNECTED PERSONS (**17**) by reason of their relationship alone (though they may be for other reasons, for example if they are also business partners). However, a transfer of an asset between them is likely to be treated as taking place at MARKET VALUE (see **45.1**) unless made at arm's length in any case.

47

Mineral Royalties

Cross-reference. See **41** LAND.

[47.1] Where a person resident or ordinarily resident in the UK is entitled to receive mineral royalties before 6 April 2013 (1 April 2013 for corporation tax purposes) under a lease, licence or agreement conferring a right to win and work minerals in the UK or under a sale or conveyance of such minerals, only one-half of any such royalties receivable in any tax year or accounting period is treated as income for the purposes of income tax or for corporation tax on income. The other half of the royalties is treated as a chargeable gain to which no allowable expenditure attaches.

For this purpose, mineral royalties consist of so much of any rents, tolls, royalties or periodical payments as relates to the winning and working of minerals other than water, peat, topsoil, etc. In *Bute v HMRC* Ch D, [2009] STC 2138, a wayleave agreement was held to be within these provisions.

Regulations may be made by HMRC to facilitate these provisions. [*SI 1971 No 1035*]. They deal with apportionments of payments where they relate to other matters as well as mineral royalties.

The above provisions are repealed with effect for royalties which a person is entitled to receive on or after 6 April 2013 (1 April 2013 for corporation tax purposes).

Terminal losses

A 'terminal loss' which accrues on a 'relevant event' may (if the taxpayer so claims within four years of the event (six years for claims before 1 April 2010)) be carried back and set against chargeable gains accruing in the tax years or accounting periods falling wholly or partly within a period of 15 years before the relevant event, taking later years first. This relief applies only where the mineral lease concerned is entered into before 6 April 2013 (1 April 2013 for corporation tax purposes).

For capital gains tax purposes (but not for corporation tax purposes), the change in time limits for making a claim applies by reference to claims made before, or on or after, 1 April 2012 where the claim concerned relates to a tax year for which the taxpayer has not been given notice to make a return under *TMA 1970, s 8* or *s 8A* (see **58.3** RETURNS) or *s 12AA* (see **58.16** RETURNS) within one year of the end of the tax year (in effect, where the taxpayer is outside self-assessment). This rule does not, however, apply if for that year any gains which ought to have been assessed have not been assessed, or an assessment has become insufficient, or any relief given has become excessive.

A '*relevant event*' occurs on the expiry or termination of the mineral lease or the disposal (or deemed disposal under any provision) of the interest held in the land to which the lease relates ('*the relevant interest*'). The taxpayer must have been entitled to receive mineral royalties under the mineral lease and held the interest immediately before the relevant event.

A '*terminal loss*' is an allowable loss for chargeable gains purposes which arises:

(a) on the expiry or termination of the mineral lease, and on an additional claim within the same time limit as above, by which the taxpayer is treated as if he had disposed of and immediately re-acquired the relevant interest at its market value; or
(b) on the actual disposal (or any other deemed disposal under any provision) of the relevant interest.

Relief in any one tax year or accounting period is restricted to the chargeable gains previously assessed by reason of the treatment above in respect of the mineral lease in question, except that any unrelieved balance is treated as accruing at the date of the relevant event and as allowable against general gains. If no claim is made for the terminal loss to be treated as above, the whole of such loss is treated as accruing at the date of the relevant event and as an allowable loss against general gains. Repayments of tax are made as may be necessary.

[*TCGA 1992, ss 201–203; ICTA 1988, s 122(1)(5)–(7); ITTOIA 2005, ss 157, 319, 340–343; CTA 2009, ss 274–276; FA 2012, s 227, Sch 39 paras 43–47; SI 2009 No 403*].

Example

L Ltd, which prepares accounts to 31 December, is the holder of a lease of land acquired in 1999 for £66,000, when the lease had an unexpired term of 65 years. In January 2007, L Ltd grants a 10-year licence to a mining company to search for and exploit minerals beneath the land. The licence is granted for £60,000 plus a mineral royalty calculated on the basis of the value of any minerals won by the licensee. The market value of the retained land (exclusive of the mineral rights) is then £10,000. L Ltd receives mineral royalties as follows:

		£
Year ended	31 December 2007	12,000
	31 December 2008	19,000
	31 December 2009	29,000
	31 December 2010	38,000
	31 December 2011	17,000
	31 December 2012	10,000

On 2 January 2013, L Ltd relinquishes its rights under the lease and receives no consideration from the lessor.

(i) Chargeable gains 2008

		£
(a)	Disposal proceeds	60,000
	Allowable cost $\frac{60,000}{60,000 + 10,000} \times £66,000$	56,571
	Chargeable gain subject to indexation	£3,429

(b) ½ × £12,000	£6,000

(ii) Chargeable gains 2009 to 2013

	£
2008 ½ × £19,000	9,500
2009 ½ × £29,000	14,500
2010 ½ × £38,000	19,000
2011 ½ × £17,000	8,500
2012 ½ × £10,000	5,000

(iii) Loss 2014

Proceeds of disposal of lease	Nil
Allowable cost £66,000 – £56,571	9,429
Allowable loss	£9,429

(iv) The loss may be set off against the chargeable gains arising on the mineral royalties as follows

	£
2013 (whole)	5,000
2012 (part)	4,429
	£9,429

48

Offshore Settlements

Introduction to offshore settlements	**48.1**
Charge on trustees ceasing to be resident in the UK	**48.2**
Trustees both resident and non-resident in tax year	**48.3**
Disposal of settled interest	**48.4**
Charge on settlor with interest in settlement	**48.5**
Test whether settlor has an interest	**48.6**
Inclusion of grandchildren in list of defined persons	**48.7**
Exceptions to charge	**48.8**
Meaning of 'settlor'	**48.9**
Qualifying settlements	**48.10**
Right of recovery	**48.11**
HMRC information powers	**48.12**
Interaction with other provisions	**48.13**
Charge on beneficiary in respect of capital payments received from settlement	**48.14**
2008/09 and subsequent years	**48.15**
Dual resident settlements	**48.16**
Migrant settlements	**48.17**
Transfers between settlements	**48.18**
Payments by and to companies	**48.19**
HMRC information powers	**48.20**
Further charge on beneficiary in respect of capital payments received from settlement	**48.21**
Anti-avoidance — transfers of value by trustees linked with trustee borrowing	**48.22**
Transfers of value — attribution of gains to beneficiaries	**48.23**
Post-*FA 2008* provisions	**48.24**
Miscellaneous	**48.25**
Definitions	**48.26**
Computation of *Schedule 4B* trust gains	**48.27**
Increase in tax payable by beneficiary receiving capital payments	**48.28**
Information required to be returned in respect of settlements with a foreign element	**48.29**
Key points concerning offshore settlements	**48.30**

Cross-references. See **49.3** OVERSEAS MATTERS for non-UK residents trading in the UK through branch or agency or permanent establishment; **57** RESIDENCE AND DOMICILE for the determination of a person's residence, ordinary residence and domicile status; and **62** SETTLEMENTS for settlements generally and provisions relating to UK resident settlements.

Simon's Taxes. See **C4.4.**

Introduction to offshore settlements

[48.1] The provisions set out in this chapter apply generally to settlements whose trustees are, or become, not resident and not ordinarily resident in the United Kingdom or where the trustees are regarded for the purposes of **21** DOUBLE TAX RELIEF arrangements as resident outside the UK. Such trustees are not, in general, chargeable to capital gains tax (see **49.1** and **49.3** OVERSEAS MATTERS) but trustees becoming non-resident are subject to an 'exit charge', and charges arise in certain circumstances on settlors and beneficiaries of such offshore settlements. See also **48.22–48.28** for an anti-avoidance provision specific to offshore settlements and **48.29** for information required to be provided to HMRC in relation to such settlements.

Residence of trustees

The trustees of a settlement are treated as if they were a single person (distinct from the persons who may from time to time be trustees). [*TCGA 1992, s 69(1)*].

The deemed single person is treated as resident and, for 2012/13 and earlier years, ordinarily resident in the UK at any time when either all the trustees are resident in the UK or:

(a) at least one trustee is resident in the UK and at least one is not so resident; and
(b) a settlor of the settlement was resident or domiciled in the UK (or deemed domiciled in the UK — see below) at a time when he made the settlement (or was treated as making the settlement — see below) or, where the settlement arose on his death, immediately before his death. For 2012/13 and earlier years, this condition was also satisfied where a settlor was ordinarily resident in the UK at the relevant time.

For the circumstances in which a settlor makes a settlement or is treated as making a settlement, see **62.5** SETTLEMENTS. In the case of a transfer of property between two settlements to which *TCGA 1992, s 68B* (identification of settlor on transfer of property between settlements — see **62.5** SETTLEMENTS) applies, (b) above is satisfied in relation to the transferee settlement if a settlor of the transferred property satisfied the condition in relation to the transferor settlement before the transfer.

For 2013/14 onwards, an individual trustee who is resident in the UK for a tax year is treated as not UK-resident for these purposes if the year is a split year under the statutory residence test (see **57.18** RESIDENCE AND DOMICILE) and the individual begins or ceases to be a trustee during the year and is not a trustee during any part of the UK part of the year.

A trustee who is not resident in the UK (including an individual treated as not resident under the split year rule) is nevertheless treated for these purposes as if he were so resident at any time when he acts as trustee in the course of a business he carries on in the UK through a branch, agency or permanent establishment.

For 2013/14 onwards, a deemed person not treated as resident in the UK under the above provisions is treated as not resident in the UK. For 2012/13 and earlier years, a deemed person not treated as resident and ordinarily resident in the UK is treated as neither resident nor ordinarily resident in the UK.

For a settlement made on or after 6 April 2017, including on the death of a settlor on or after this date, (b) above is satisfied if the settlor is *deemed* domiciled in the UK (see **57.34** RESIDENCE AND DOMICILE) at the time of the settlement or, where the settlement arose on the settlor's death, immediately before his death.

[*TCGA 1992, s 69(2)–(2F); FA 2013, Sch 45 paras 102, 153(2), Sch 46 paras 82, 112; F(No 2)A 2017, Sch 8 para* 6].

For HMRC guidance on the application of the above rules to overseas trust companies, and in particular those owned by UK-based groups, see HMRC Guidance Note 3 August 2009.

See *Smallwood and another v HMRC* CA, [2010] STC 2045.

See also **57.29** and **57.30** RESIDENCE AND DOMICILE for the meaning of resident and ordinarily resident.

Most non-UK resident settlements are dealt with by HMRC Trusts & Estates, Non Resident Trusts, Ferrers House, PO Box 38, Castle Meadow Road, Nottingham NG2 1BB, telephone number 0300 123 1072.

Charge on trustees ceasing to be resident in the UK

[48.2] Where, at any time ('*the relevant time*'), trustees of a settlement become not resident (for 2012/13 and earlier years, neither resident nor ordinarily resident) in the UK (see **48.1** above), they are deemed for capital gains tax purposes to have disposed of 'the defined assets' immediately before the relevant time, and immediately to have reacquired them, at their market value at that time.

'*The defined assets*' are all assets constituting settled property of the settlement immediately before the relevant time. However, if immediately after the relevant time the trustees carry on a trade in the UK through a branch or agency, or, in the case of corporate trustees, through a permanent establishment, and any assets are situated in the UK and either used in or for the purposes of the trade or used or held for the purposes of the branch or agency or permanent establishment, those assets are not defined assets (see also **49.3** OVERSEAS MATTERS). In addition, assets are not defined assets if they are of a description specified in any DOUBLE TAX RELIEF (**21.2**) arrangements, and were the trustees to dispose of them immediately before the relevant time, the trustees would fall to be regarded for the purposes of those arrangements as not liable in the UK to tax on gains accruing to them on the disposal (but see below under Dual resident trustees).

TCGA 1992, s 152 (**59** ROLLOVER RELIEF) does not apply where the trustees have disposed of, or their interest in, 'the old assets' before the relevant time, and acquire 'the new assets', or their interest in them, after that time. However, this denial of relief does not apply to new assets if, at the time they are acquired, the trustees carry on a trade in the UK through a branch or agency or permanent establishment, and any new assets are situated in the UK and either used in or for the purposes of the trade or used or held for the purposes of the branch or agency or permanent establishment. '*The old assets*' and '*the new assets*' have the same meanings as in *TCGA 1992, s 152.*

[*TCGA 1992, s 80; FA 2013, Sch 46 paras 84, 112*].

If the trustees so elect, no gain or loss accrues on the deemed disposal if the gain or loss would have been an NRCGT gain or loss on the assumption that the disposal was a non-resident CGT disposal (see **41.25** LAND). However, the NRCGT gain or loss that would have accrued on the deemed disposal is treated as accruing at the time of any subsequent disposal of the interest, in addition to any gain or loss which actually accrues. [*TCGA 1992, s 80A; FA 2015, Sch 7 para 18*].

For HMRC's practice in this area, see HMRC Statement of Practice 5/92, paras 2 and 3. Revenue Tax Bulletin April 2001 p 840 illustrated a perceived method of circumventing the above rules, using the 30-day matching rule at **64.2** SHARES AND SECURITIES — IDENTIFICATION RULES; whilst the Revenue concluded that this method does not work, others may be far less certain.

The normal rules for assessment of trustees (see **6.6** ASSESSMENTS) are disapplied so that no assessment to CGT payable under *TCGA 1992, s 80* by the migrating trustees can be made on a person who ceased to be a trustee of the settlement before the relevant time and who shows that, when he did so cease, there was no proposal that the trustees might migrate. [*TCGA 1992, s 65(3)(4); FA 2013, Sch 46 para 80*].

Death of trustee — special rules

Special rules apply where *TCGA 1992, s 80* above applies as a result of the death of a trustee of the settlement, and within the period of six months beginning with the death, the trustees of the settlement become resident (for 2012/13 and earlier years, resident and ordinarily resident) in the UK. In such circumstances, *TCGA 1992, s 80* is to apply as if the defined assets were restricted to such assets (if any) as would, apart from this special rule, be defined assets and which either:

- are disposed of by the trustees in the period which begins with the death and ends when the trustees become resident (or resident and ordinarily resident) in the UK, or
- are of a description specified in any double tax relief arrangements; constitute settled property of the settlement immediately after the trustees become resident (or resident and ordinarily resident) in the UK; and, were the trustees to dispose of them at that time, the trustees would fall to be regarded for the purposes of the arrangements as not liable in the UK to tax on gains accruing to them on the disposal.

Further special rules apply where at any time the trustees of a settlement become resident (for 2012/13 and earlier years, resident and ordinarily resident) in the UK as a result of the death of a trustee of the settlement, and

TCGA 1992, s 80 above applies as regards the trustees of the settlement in circumstances where the relevant time (within the meaning of that provision) falls within the period of six months beginning with the death. In such circumstances, *TCGA 1992, s 80* is to apply as if the defined assets were restricted to such assets (if any) as would, apart from this special rule, be defined assets and which the trustees acquired in the period beginning with the death and ending with the relevant time as a result of a disposal in respect of which relief is given under *TCGA 1992, s 165* (hold-over relief for gifts of business assets; see **36.2** HOLD-OVER RELIEFS) or in relation to which *TCGA 1992, s 260(3)* (hold-over relief for gifts on which inheritance tax is chargeable etc; see **36.10** HOLD-OVER RELIEFS) applies.

[*TCGA 1992, s 81; FA 2013, Sch 46 paras 85, 112*].

Past trustees: liability for tax

Where *TCGA 1992, s 80* above applies to the trustees of a settlement ('*the migrating trustees*'), and any resulting capital gains tax which is payable by them is not paid within six months from the time when it became payable, HMRC may act as below.

HMRC may, at any time before the end of the period of three years beginning with the time when the amount of tax is finally determined, serve on any person who, at any time within the 'relevant period', was a trustee of the settlement (but not so as to include a person ceasing to be a trustee before the end of the relevant period who can show that at the time he ceased to be a trustee there was no proposal that the trustees might migrate), a notice requiring the payment of outstanding tax and interest within 30 days from the service of the notice. The notified amount can be recovered from the person concerned as if it were tax due and payable; and he may recover from the migrating trustees any amount paid by him. No tax relief is given on any such payment in computing taxable profits etc.

The '*relevant period*' is the period of twelve months ending with the relevant time. (Where the relevant time for the purposes of *TCGA 1992, s 80* above was within the period of twelve months beginning with 19 March 1991, the relevant period was restricted to the period beginning with that date and ending with that time.)

[*TCGA 1992, s 82; FA 2013, Sch 46 paras 86, 112*].

For HMRC's practice in this area, see HMRC Statement of Practice 5/92, paras 4–6.

Dual resident trustees

Charge on becoming dual resident

Where, at any time, the trustees of a settlement, while continuing to be resident (for 2012/13 and earlier years, resident and ordinarily resident) in the UK, become trustees who fall to be regarded for the purposes of any DOUBLE TAX RELIEF (**21.2**) arrangements as resident overseas and as not liable in the UK to tax on gains accruing on disposals of assets ('*relevant assets*') which constitute settled property of the settlement and fall within descriptions specified in the arrangements, they are deemed for capital gains tax purposes to have disposed of the relevant assets immediately before that time, and immediately to have reacquired them, at their market value at that time. [*TCGA 1992, s 83; FA 2013, Sch 46 paras 87, 112*].

Disapplication of rollover relief provision

TCGA 1992, s 152 (**59.2** ROLLOVER RELIEF) does not apply where:

- the new assets (as in **59.2** ROLLOVER RELIEF) are, or the interest in them is, acquired after 18 March 1991 by the trustees of a settlement;
- at the time of acquisition the trustees are resident (before 6 April 2013, resident and ordinarily resident) in the UK and fall to be regarded for the purposes of any double tax relief arrangements as resident overseas;
- the assets are of a description specified in the arrangements; and
- were the trustees to dispose of the assets immediately after the acquisition, the trustees would fall to be regarded for the purposes of the arrangements as not liable in the UK to tax on gains accruing to them on the disposal.

[*TCGA 1992, s 84; FA 2013, Sch 46 paras 89, 112*].

Trustees both resident and non-resident in tax year

[48.3] The following applies where a chargeable gain accrues to trustees of a settlement on a disposal of an asset in a tax year in which they are within the charge to capital gains tax but at a time when they are 'non-UK resident'.

Nothing in any **21** DOUBLE TAX RELIEF arrangements is to be read as preventing the trustees from being chargeable to capital gains tax (or as preventing a charge to tax arising, whether or not on the trustees) in respect of the gain.

For these purposes, trustees are within the charge to capital gains tax for a tax year if, during any part of the year they are resident (for 2012/13 and earlier years, both resident and ordinarily resident) in the UK and not 'treaty non-resident'. Trustees are '*non-UK resident*' at a particular time if they are then not resident (before 6 April 2013, neither resident nor ordinarily resident) in the UK or they are then resident (or resident and ordinarily resident) in the UK but are treaty non-resident.

Trustees are '*treaty non-resident*' if they fall to be regarded as resident in a territory outside the UK for the purposes of **21** DOUBLE TAX RELIEF arrangements. For the meaning of 'resident' and 'ordinarily resident' see **57** RESIDENCE AND DOMICILE.

[*TCGA 1992, ss 83A, 288(7B); FA 2013, Sch 46 paras 88, 112*].

Disposal of settled interest

[48.4] The exemption in *TCGA 1992, s 76(1)* (see **62.15** SETTLEMENTS) by virtue of which no chargeable gain accrues in certain circumstances on the disposal of an interest created by or arising under a settlement does not apply to such disposals in either of the following circumstances.

(a) At the time of disposal, the trustees are not resident (for 2012/13 and earlier years, neither resident nor ordinarily resident) in the UK (see **48.1** above) and the disposal is not one which arises on a person becoming absolutely entitled to settled property as against the trustees and accordingly treated under *TCGA 1992, s 76(2)* (see **62.15** SETTLEMENTS) as made in consideration of his obtaining the settled property. [*TCGA 1992, s 85(1); FA 2013, Sch 46 paras 90, 112*].

(b) Subject to the same exclusion as in (a) above, there has ever been a time when the trustees of the settlement were not resident (for 2012/13 and earlier years, neither resident nor ordinarily resident) in the UK or fell to be treated under a double tax agreement as resident in a territory outside the UK. Nor does the exemption apply if any property comprised in the settlement in question derives directly or indirectly from a settlement which is caught by this provision. [*TCGA 1992, s 76(1A)(1B)(3); FA 2013, Sch 46 paras 83, 112*].

Calculation of gain on disposal of interest after trustees becoming non-resident

Subject to the exceptions below, for the purpose only of calculating any chargeable gain accruing to a person on the disposal of an interest created by or arising under a settlement, where:

(i) *TCGA 1992, s 80* at **48.2** above (charge on trustees becoming non-resident) applies as regards the trustees of the settlement;

(ii) the disposal is made after the 'relevant time' (see **48.2** above) and the circumstances are such that the exemption for disposal of an interest in a settlement is prevented from applying by (a) above; and

(iii) the interest was created for his benefit, or he otherwise acquired it, before the relevant time,

he is treated as if he had disposed of the interest immediately before the relevant time, and immediately reacquired it, at its market value at that time.

This treatment does not apply where:

- *TCGA 1992, s 83* at **48.2** above (charge on trustees ceasing to be liable to UK tax under double tax relief arrangements) applied as regards the trustees in circumstances where 'the time concerned' (see **48.2** above) fell before the time when the interest was created for the benefit of the person disposing of it or when he otherwise acquired it; or
- the relevant time fell after 20 March 2000 and the settlement had 'relevant offshore gains' at that time.

A settlement has '*relevant offshore gains*' at any time if, were the tax year to end at that time, chargeable gains would be treated under *TCGA 1992, s 89(2)* (see **48.17** below) or *TCGA 1992, Sch 4C para 8* (see **48.23** below) as accruing in the following tax year to a beneficiary receiving a capital payment from the trustees in that year.

The above treatment is also disapplied where conditions (i)–(iii) above apply but, in addition, *TCGA 1992, s 83* at **48.2** above applied as regards the trustees in circumstances where 'the time concerned' (see **48.2** above) fell in the 'relevant period' (see below). In these circumstances, for the purposes only of calculating any chargeable gain accruing on the disposal of the interest, the person disposing of it is instead treated as if he had disposed of it immediately before the time concerned (where there is only one such time) or the earliest time concerned (where there is more than one because *TCGA 1992, s 83* applied more than once), and had immediately reacquired it, at its market value at that time. This treatment does not apply where the time concerned or, as the case may be, the earliest time concerned, fell after 20 March 2000 and the settlement had relevant offshore gains (as defined above) at that time.

For this purpose, the '*relevant period*' is the period which begins when the interest was created for the benefit of the person disposing of it or when he otherwise acquired it, and ends with the relevant time (within the meaning of *TCGA 1992, s 80* at **48.2** above).

[*TCGA 1992, s 85(2)–(11)*].

Charge on settlor with interest in settlement

[48.5] Where all the conditions listed below are fulfilled, chargeable gains of an amount equal to that referred to in (f) below are treated as accruing in a particular year of assessment to 'the settlor' (see **48.9** below) of a settlement such that they are treated as forming the highest part of the amount on which he is chargeable to capital gains tax for the year. Where the year is a split year under the statutory residence test for 2013/14 onwards (see **57.18** RESIDENCE AND DOMICILE), the gains are treated as accruing in the UK part of the year. See also **48.13** below.

The conditions are:

(a) the settlement is a 'qualifying settlement' (see **48.10** below) in a particular year of assessment;
(b) (for 2013/14 onwards) *either*:
  (i) there is not time in the year when the trustees are resident in the UK (see **48.1** above); or
  (ii) there is such a time but, whenever the trustees are resident in the UK during the year, they fall to be regarded for the purposes of any DOUBLE TAX RELIEF (**21.2**) arrangements as resident overseas;
(c) (for 2012/13 and earlier years) *either*:
  (i) the trustees are neither resident nor ordinarily resident in the UK during any part of the year (see **48.1** above); or
  (ii) the trustees are resident and ordinarily resident during any part of the year, but at any time of such residence and/or ordinary residence they fall to be regarded for the purposes of any DOUBLE TAX RELIEF (**21.2**) arrangements as resident overseas;
(d) the person who is the settlor in relation to the settlement is domiciled in the UK (or, from 2017/18 onwards, deemed domiciled in the UK — see **57.34** RESIDENCE AND DOMICILE) at some time in the year and is resident in the UK for the year (or, for 2012/13 and earlier years, either resident in the UK during any part of the year or ordinarily resident in the UK during the year) (and see **49.5** OVERSEAS MATTERS re 'temporary' non-residence);

(e) at any time during the year the settlor has an 'interest' (see **48.6** below) in the settlement;

(f) by virtue of disposals of any of the settled property 'originating' from the settlor (see **48.9** below), there is an amount on which the trustees would be chargeable to tax for the year under *TCGA 1992, s 2(2)* (i.e. an amount of chargeable gains less current and brought forward allowable losses — see **44.2** LOSSES) if the assumption as to residence below were made; and

(g) the provisions in **48.8** below do not preclude a charge.

Where the residence condition specified in (b)(i) or (c)(i) above applies, the assumption as to residence in (f) above is that the trustees are resident (or, where (c)(i) above applies, resident and ordinarily resident) in the UK throughout the year; and where the residence condition specified in (b)(ii) or (c)(ii) above applies, the assumption as to residence in (f) above is that the double tax relief arrangements do not apply.

Where the disposal in (f) above is a non-resident CGT disposal (see **41.25** LAND) any amount on which the trustees are chargeable as an NRCGT gain is not attributed to the settlor.

Carried interest gains (see **50.20** PARTNERSHIPS) which would otherwise be included in the amount mentioned in (f) above are disregarded (under *F(No 2)A 2017, s 32(3)* but for gains accruing both before and after the passing of that Act).

In arriving at the amount to be charged on the settlor for a particular year of assessment, the effects of *TCGA 1992, s 3* (annual exempt amount — see **62.8** and **62.9** SETTLEMENTS) are ignored. In addition, any deductions provided for by *TCGA 1992, s 2(2)* (current and brought forward allowable losses) are to be made in respect of disposals of any of the settled property originating from the settlor, and *TCGA 1992, s 16(3)* (losses of non-resident not to be allowable — see **49.3** OVERSEAS MATTERS) is to be assumed not to prevent losses accruing to trustees in one year of assessment from being allowed as a deduction from chargeable gains in a later year (so far as not previously set against gains).

Where trustees are participators in a company in respect of property which originates from the settlor, and under *TCGA 1992, s 13* (gains of non-resident close company assessable on shareholder — see **49.7** OVERSEAS MATTERS) gains or losses would be treated as accruing to the trustees in a particular year of assessment by virtue of so much of their interest as participators as arises from that property if the assumption as to residence in (f) above were made, the gains or losses are taken into account in arriving at the amount charged on the settlor as regards that year as if they had accrued by virtue of disposals of settled property originating from the settlor.

Where the trustees fall within the residence condition specified in (b)(i) above, further rules apply to arrive at the amount to be charged on the settlor as regards a particular year of assessment ('*the year concerned*'). If the conditions for the charge to apply are not fulfilled as regards the settlement in any year of assessment falling before the year concerned, no deductions are made for losses accruing before the year concerned. If those conditions are fulfilled as regards the settlement in any year or years of assessment falling before the year concerned, no deductions are made for losses accruing before that year (or the first of the years) so falling. However, these two prohibitions on deductions being made for losses are not to prevent deductions being made in respect of losses accruing in a year of assessment in which the conditions in (a) to (d) and (f) above are fulfilled as regards the settlement.

Where, as regards a particular year of assessment, there would otherwise be an amount to be charged on the settlor and the trustees fall within the residence condition specified in (b)(ii) above, the following assumptions and adjustments to the amount are made. It is to be assumed that references in the foregoing to settled property originating from the settlor were to such of it as constitutes 'protected assets' and that references in the foregoing to shares originating from the settlor were to such of them as constitute protected assets. The amount (if any) to be charged on the settlor is found on those assumptions, and if there is no amount found there is deemed to be no amount to be charged on the settlor, and if an amount is found on these assumptions it is compared with the amount which would otherwise be charged on the settlor, and the smaller of the two is taken to be the amount to be charged on the settlor.

Protected assets

Assets are '*protected assets*' if they are of a description specified in the double tax relief arrangements mentioned in connection with the residence condition specified in (b)(ii) above, and were the trustees to dispose of them at any 'relevant time', the trustees would fall to be regarded for the purposes of the arrangements as not liable in the UK to tax on gains accruing to them on the disposal. For this purpose, the alternative assumptions as to residence in (e) above are ignored, the '*relevant time*' is any time, in the year of assessment concerned, when the trustees fall to be regarded for the purposes of the arrangements as resident overseas, and if different assets are identified by reference to different relevant times, all of them are protected assets.

[*TCGA 1992, s 86(1)–(5), Sch 5 para 1; FA 2013, Sch 45 para 100, Sch 46 paras 91, 112; FA 2015, Sch 7 para 19; F(No 2)A 2017, s 32(3)(5), Sch 8 para 7*].

Test whether settlor has an interest

[48.6] A settlor has an interest in a settlement if:

(a) any property originating from the settlor ('*relevant property*') which is or may at any time be comprised in the settlement is, or will or may become, applicable for the benefit of or payable to a 'defined person' in any circumstances whatever;

(b) any income originating from the settlor ('*relevant income*') which arises or may arise under the settlement is, or will or may become, applicable for the benefit of or payable to a defined person in any circumstances whatever; or

(c) any defined person enjoys a benefit directly or indirectly from any relevant property which is comprised in the settlement or any relevant income arising under the settlement.

Each of the following is a '*defined person*':

- the settlor;
- the settlor's spouse;
- the settlor's civil partner;
- any child (which term includes stepchild) of the settlor or of the settlor's spouse or civil partner;
- the spouse or civil partner of any such child;
- any grandchild of the settlor or of the settlor's spouse or civil partner (see **48.7** below as regards the inclusion of grandchildren in the list of defined persons); ('*grandchild*' includes a child of a stepchild or a stepchild of a child or stepchild);
- the spouse or civil partner of any such grandchild (see **48.7** below as regards the inclusion of grandchildren and their spouses or civil partners in the list of defined persons);
- a company controlled by a person or persons mentioned in the foregoing (see **48.7** below as regards the inclusion of grandchildren and their spouses or civil partners in the fore-mentioned categories); ('*control*' is construed as in *CTA 2010, ss 450, 451* but for these purposes no rights or powers of (or attributed to) an associate or associates of a person are attributed to him under *CTA 2010, s 451(4)–(6)* if he is not a participator (within *CTA 2010, s 454*, but subject to restrictions on the definition of participator (see **48.9** below)) in the company);
- a company associated with any such company; ('*associated*' is construed as in *CTA 2010, s 449* but for these purposes where it falls to be decided whether a company is controlled by a person or persons, a similar relaxation to that for 'control' applies as above).

A settlor does not have an interest in a settlement at any time when none of the property or income concerned can become applicable or payable as mentioned above except in the event of:

- the bankruptcy of some person who is or may become beneficially entitled to that property or income;
- any assignment of or charge on the property or income being made or given by some such person;
- in the case of a marriage settlement or civil partnership settlement, the death of both parties to the marriage or civil partnership and of all or any of the children of one or both of the parties to the marriage or civil partnership (before 5 December, all or any of the children of the marriage); or
- the death under the age of 25 or some lower age of some person who would be beneficially entitled to the property or income on attaining that age.

He also does not have an interest in a settlement under (a) above at any time when some person is alive and under the age of 25 if during that person's life none of the property or income concerned can become applicable or payable as mentioned in (a) above except in the event of that person becoming bankrupt or assigning or charging his interest in the property or income concerned.

[*TCGA 1992, Sch 5 para 2*].

Inclusion of grandchildren in list of defined persons

[48.7] Grandchildren and their spouses or civil partners (and companies which they control or which are associated with such companies) are included in the list of defined persons in **48.6** above **in relation to disposals made on or after 17 March 1998**. Their inclusion applies as regards all disposals by settlements created on or after that date.

As regards settlements created before that date, post-16 March 1998 disposals (whether giving rise to gains or losses) to which the 'charge on settlor' provisions would not apply if the inclusion of grandchildren etc. to the list were disregarded are left out of account (i.e. are regarded as not falling within **48.5**(e) above) unless they are made in a tax year in which one of the following events occurs or in a subsequent tax year. (Where the tax year in question is 1997/98, only post-16 March 1998 events are taken into account.)

(a) Property or income is provided directly or indirectly for the purposes of the settlement (i.e. is added to the settlement) otherwise than under an arm's length transaction and otherwise than in pursuance of a liability incurred by any person before 17 March 1998. Property or income provided towards (and not beyond) an excess for a tax year of trust expenses (relating to administration and taxation) over trust income is ignored.
(b) The trustees cease to be UK resident (or, before 6 April 2013, become neither resident nor ordinarily resident in the UK) or begin to fall to be regarded under a double tax agreement as resident in a territory outside the UK.
(c) The terms of the settlement are varied so as to enable for the first time any one or more of the persons mentioned below to benefit from the settlement.
(d) Any one or more of the persons mentioned below does enjoy a benefit for the first time but would not have been capable of doing so by reference to the terms of the settlement as they stood immediately before 17 March 1998.

The persons mentioned in (c) and (d) above are: any grandchild (as in **48.6** above) of the settlor or of the settlor's spouse or civil partner, the spouse or civil partner of any such grandchild, a company controlled by any such grandchildren and/or their spouses or civil partners (with or without other defined persons — see **48.6** above) and a company associated with any such company. (For these purposes, '*control*' and '*associated*' are to be construed as in **48.6** above.)

[*TCGA 1992, Sch 5 para 2A; FA 2013, Sch 46 para 108(2)(4)*].

Exceptions to charge

[48.8] There is no charge on the settlor if he dies in the year.

There is also no charge on the settlor where **both** (a) and (b) below apply.

(a) The settlor has no interest in the settlement at any time in the year except for one (or, where they are satisfied by reference to the same person, for two or all) of the following reasons:
- property is, or will or may become, applicable for the benefit of or payable to a person, being the settlor's spouse or civil partner, any child (which term includes stepchild) or grandchild (defined as in **48.6** above, and see below for the addition of grandchildren to this list) of the settlor or of the settlor's spouse or civil partner, or the spouse or civil partner of any such child or grandchild;
- income is, or will or may become applicable for the benefit of or payable to such a person; or
- such a person enjoys a benefit from property or income.

(b) Either:
- the person referred to in (a) above dies in the year; or
- where the person referred to in (a) above is the settlor's spouse or civil partner or the spouse or civil partner of any child or grandchild of the settlor or of the settlor's spouse or civil partner, that person ceases to be married to, or to be a civil partner of, the settlor, the child or the grandchild concerned (as the case may be) during the year.

Again no charge arises on the settlor in the following circumstances:

(i) the settlor has no interest in the settlement at any time in the year except for the reason that there are two or more persons, each of whom is one of the following: the settlor's spouse or civil partner, any child (which term includes stepchild) or grandchild (defined as in **48.6** above, and see below for the addition of grandchildren to this list) of the settlor or of the settlor's spouse or civil partner, or the spouse or civil partner of any such child or grandchild and stands to gain for one or more of the following reasons:
- property is, or will or may become, applicable for his benefit or payable to him;
- the income is, or will or may become, applicable for his benefit or payable to him; or
- he enjoys a benefit from property or income, *and*

(ii) each of the persons referred to in (i) dies in the year.

References above to grandchildren apply only where the 'charge on settlor' provisions would otherwise apply by reference to grandchildren (see **48.6** and **48.7** above).

[*TCGA 1992, Sch 5 paras 3–5*].

Deemed domicile protection

From 2017/18, a UK resident settlor who is *deemed* domiciled in the UK (see **57.34** RESIDENCE AND DOMICILE) at some time in the year of the assessment, meets condition (d) in **48.5** above. However, protection provisions mean there is no charge on the settlor in a tax year ('*the particular year*') if all the following conditions are met:

(A) the particular year is 2017/18 or a later tax year;

(B) the settlor was not domiciled in the UK when the settlement was created, nor deemed domiciled in the UK at that time (for a settlement created on or after 6 April 2017);

(C) the settlor is not domiciled in the UK, nor deemed domiciled in the UK by virtue of being UK resident and born in the UK with a UK domicile of origin, at any time in the particular year; and

(D) the settlor, or the trustees of another settlement of which the settlor is the settlor or beneficiary, provides no property or income directly or indirectly for the purposes of the settlement, at a time during the period from 6 April 2017 (or, from the creation of the settlement, if later) to the end of the particular year when the settlor is domiciled or deemed domiciled in the UK.

Condition (C) above is narrowly-drawn in respect of deemed domicile such that a non-domiciled settlor who is deemed domiciled in the UK in the particular year by virtue of long-term residence *only* (see **57.34** RESIDENCE AND DOMICILE) is not excluded from this protection. However, the wider definition of deemed domicile is relevant to conditions (B) and (D) i.e. there is no exception from the charge for a settlor who was deemed domiciled in the UK by virtue of long-term residence when creating the settlement or when providing property or income to it.

Provision of property or income such that condition (D) is not met, '*taints*' the settlement (not a statutory term). If value is added to property in the settlement, this is also regarded for condition (D) as a direct provision of property for the purposes of the settlement, tainting the settlement. However, a settlement is not tainted by the provision of property or income where:

- property or income is provided under a transaction (other than a loan) on arm's length terms;
- property or income is provided (other than by way of a loan) without the intention to confer any gratuitous benefit;
- loans are made to the trustees on arm's length terms (here meaning interest is payable at least annually at the official rate or more), but see exception below;
- interest is paid to trustees under a loan made by them on arm's length terms (here meaning any interest payable is payable at no more than the official rate);
- a loan made by the trustees is repaid;
- property or income is paid pursuant to a liability incurred by any person before 6 April 2017; or
- the property or income constitutes a payment to cover the excess of taxation and administration expenses over settlement income.

In the case of a loan made to the trustees on arm's length terms by the settlor (or the trustees of a settlement of which the settlor is the settlor or a beneficiary), the loan *is* treated as provided (i.e. the settlement is tainted), if interest is not paid as required under the loan terms, or it is capitalised or if the loan is varied such that the terms become non-arm's length. The loan is treated as being provided at the time of the failure to pay interest, the interest capitalisation or the loan variation.

A settlor becoming deemed domiciled on a date (the '*deemed domicile date*') on or after 6 April 2017, may have made a loan to the trustees before this, or the trustees of a settlement of which the settlor is the settlor or a beneficiary may have made such a loan before the deemed domicile date. If the loan is not on arm's length terms and any outstanding amount of the loan on the deemed domicile date is payable or repayable on demand on or after that date, this outstanding amount is also treated as directly provided (i.e. taints the settlement) on the deemed domicile date. The exception to this is if the deemed domicile date is 6 April 2017 and either the loan is repaid (and all interest payable is paid) before 6 April 2018, or before 6 April 2018 the loan becomes a loan on arm's length terms and interest is paid as prescribed — effectively such that from 6 April 2017 it is on arm's length terms.

[*TCGA 1992, Sch 5 para 5A; F(No 2)A 2017, Sch 8 para 18*].

Meaning of 'settlor'

[48.9] For the purposes of these provisions, a person is a '*settlor*' in relation to a settlement if the settled property consists of or includes property originating from him. [*TCGA 1992, Sch 5 para 7*].

Meaning of 'originating'

References to property originating from a person are taken as references to property provided by that person, property representing property provided by that person, and so much of any property provided by that person and other property as, on a just apportionment, can be taken to represent property provided by that person. References to income originating from a person are taken as references to income from property originating from that person and income provided by that person.

Where a person who is a settlor in relation to a settlement makes reciprocal arrangements with another person for the provision of property or income, then the property or income provided by the other person under the arrangements is treated as provided by the settlor, but property or income provided by the settlor under the arrangements is treated as provided by the other person (and not by the settlor).

Where property is provided by a '*qualifying company*' (i.e. a company which is a close company within *CTA 2010, ss 439–454* or which would be a close company if it were resident in the UK) controlled (construed as in *CTA 2010, ss 450, 451* but with the same relaxation as in **48.6** above) by one person alone at the time it is provided, that person is taken to provide it. Where property is provided by a qualifying company controlled by two or more persons (taking each one separately) at the time it is provided, those persons are taken to provide the property in equal shares. Where property is provided by a qualifying company controlled by two or more persons (taking them together) at the time it is provided, the persons who are participators (construed as in *CTA 2010, s 454*) in the company at the time it is provided are taken to provide it in just proportions (save that where a person would otherwise be treated under this last provision as providing less than 5% of any property, he is not taken as providing any property). A beneficiary in the settlement is not to be regarded as a participator in the company solely by virtue of his status as beneficiary (prior to 6 April 2017 this was by concession — HMRC Extra-Statutory Concession D40).

References to property representing other property include references to property representing accumulated income from that other property. A person is treated as providing property or income if he provides it directly or indirectly.

[*TCGA 1992, Sch 5 para 8; SI 2017, No 495*].

See *Coombes v HMRC* Ch D 2007, [2008] STC 2984.

Qualifying settlements

[48.10] All settlements are '*qualifying settlements*' for the purposes of **48.5**(a) above except for certain settlements created before 19 March 1991.

A settlement created before 19 March 1991 which was not a qualifying settlement under the rules applicable for 1998/99 and earlier years, is not a qualifying settlement if it was a 'protected settlement' immediately after the beginning of 6 April 1999, it has not ceased to be a protected settlement and none of the four conditions set out below has been fulfilled. Such a settlement becomes a qualifying settlement with effect in and after any tax year in which either the settlement ceases to be a protected settlement or any of the four conditions becomes fulfilled.

A settlement is a '*protected settlement*' at any time if at that time the 'beneficiaries' are confined to persons falling within some or all of the following categories:

- children of a settlor or of a spouse or civil partner of a settlor who are under 18 either at that time or at the end of the immediately preceding tax year;
- unborn children of a settlor, of a spouse or civil partner of a settlor, or of a future spouse or civil partner of a settlor;
- future spouses or civil partners of any children or future children of a settlor, a spouse or civil partner of a settlor or any future spouse or civil partner of a settlor;
- a future spouse or civil partner of a settlor;
- persons who are not at that time defined persons (see **48.6** above) in relation to the settlement and by reference to any current settlor.

Despite the inclusion of grandchildren to the list of defined persons (see **48.7** above), HMRC do *not* regard the existence as beneficiaries of the settlor's (or his spouse's) grandchildren (of whatever age) as denying protected settlement status (Revenue Tax Bulletin December 1998 p 620).

The term 'children' includes stepchildren. For these purposes, a person is a '*beneficiary*' of a settlement if:

- there are any circumstances whatever in which:
  - (a) 'relevant property' which is, or may become, comprised in the settlement, or

(b) 'relevant income' which arises, or may arise, under the settlement,

is, or will or may become, applicable for his benefit or payable to him; or

- he enjoys a benefit directly or indirectly from any 'relevant property' comprised in, or 'relevant income' arising under, the settlement.

'*Relevant property*' and '*relevant income*' mean, respectively, property and income originating (see **48.9** above) from a settlor.

The **four conditions** referred to above are as follows.

- The first condition is that after 18 March 1991 property or income is provided directly or indirectly for the purposes of the settlement otherwise than under a transaction entered into at arm's length and otherwise than in pursuance of a liability incurred by any person before 19 March 1991. However, if the settlement's expenses relating to administration and taxation for a year of assessment exceed its income for the year, property or income provided towards meeting those expenses is ignored for the purposes of this condition if the value of the property or income so provided does not exceed the difference between the amount of those expenses and the amount of the settlement's income for the year. By concession, a repayable on demand loan which was made to a relevant trust on non-commercial terms before 19 March 1991 was not caught by this condition provided that, before 31 July 1992, it was either repaid in full with any outstanding interest or made subject to fully commercial terms (HMRC Extra-Statutory Concession D41 — this concession contained further detailed notes on the treatment of amounts paid where the loan was put on a commercial basis. See also Revenue Tax Bulletin August 1993 p 83).
- The second condition is that the trustees cease after 18 March 1991 to be resident in the UK (or, before 6 April 2013 but after 18 March 1991 become neither resident nor ordinarily resident in the UK), or the trustees, while continuing to be resident (and, before 6 April 2013, ordinarily resident) in the UK, become after 18 March 1991 trustees who fall to be regarded for the purposes of any double tax relief arrangements as resident overseas.
- The third condition is that after 18 March 1991 the terms of the settlement are varied so that a defined person (see **48.6** above) becomes for the first time a person who will or might benefit from the settlement.
- The fourth condition is that after 18 March 1991 a defined person enjoys a benefit from the settlement for the first time and the person concerned is not one who (looking only at the terms of the settlement immediately before 19 March 1991) would be capable of enjoying a benefit from the settlement on or after that date.

For the purposes of the third and fourth conditions above, grandchildren (as in **48.6** above) and their spouses (and companies which they control or which are associated with such companies) are not defined persons in relation to events before 17 March 1998 (see also **48.7** above).

[*TCGA 1992, Sch 5 para 9; FA 2013, Sch 46 para 108(3)(4)*].

For HMRC's practice in this area, see HMRC Statement of Practice 5/92, paras 11–37, Revenue Tax Bulletin August 1993 p 82 and April 1995 pp 204, 205, and ICAEW guidance note TAX 20/92, 14 December 1992, paras 7–23.

Right of recovery

[48.11] Where a charge is made on a settlor, any tax he pays as a result may be recovered by him from any person who is a trustee of the settlement. For this purpose, the settlor may require certificated proof from HMRC of the amount of the gains concerned and the amount of tax paid. [*TCGA 1992, Sch 5 para 6*].

For HMRC's practice in this area, see HMRC Statement of Practice 5/92, paras 7–10 and ICAEW guidance note TAX 20/92, 14 December 1992, paras 5, 6 and 24–26.

HMRC information powers

[48.12] Before 13 August 2009, HMRC could by notice require a trustee, beneficiary or settlor to provide, within a specified time limit of at least 28 days beginning with the day the notice was given, particulars they thought necessary for the purposes of these provisions. Penalties under *TMA 1970, s 98* applied for failure. This power has been repealed as it is no longer considered necessary following the introduction of the general information powers in *FA 2008, Sch 36* (see **34** HMRC INVESTIGATORY POWERS). [*TCGA 1992, Sch 5 para 10; SI 2009 No 2035, Sch para 35*].

Interaction with other provisions

[48.13] Where *TCGA 1992, s 87* (gains of overseas resident settlements chargeable on beneficiaries — see **48.14–48.20** below) applies to a settlement, any amounts chargeable on the settlor under the provisions in **48.5** above are deducted in arriving at the 'section 2(2) amount' (see **48.15** below). For 2007/08 and earlier years, such amounts are deducted from the 'trust gains for the year'. Such amounts are also deducted from the 'Schedule 4B trust gains' of *TCGA 1992, Sch 4C* (gains chargeable on beneficiaries accruing on transfer of value linked with borrowing by trustees of overseas resident settlement — see **48.23** below). [*TCGA 1992, s 87(3)(4), Sch 4C paras 3, 6*]. Where amounts chargeable on the settlor are so chargeable by virtue of *TCGA 1992, s 10A* (charge on temporary non-residents — see **49.5** OVERSEAS MATTERS), there are provisions (see below) to prevent a double tax charge where gains have been charged on beneficiaries.

Settlor temporarily non-resident

Where a charge on a settlor arises under the provisions in **48.5** above by virtue of the charge under *TCGA 1992, s 10A* (the charge on individuals temporarily non-resident in the UK — see **49.5** OVERSEAS MATTERS) in the year of his return to the UK, there is a limitation on the amount to be so charged. The provisions were rewritten by *FA 2013* to make them consistent with the statutory residence test (see **57.3** RESIDENCE AND DOMICILE) and income tax rules for temporary non-residence. The rewritten provisions apply where the 'year of departure' (see **49.5** OVERSEAS MATTERS) is 2013/14 or a later year. [*FA 2013, Sch 45 para 153(3)*]. For convenience the rewritten and previous provisions are described separately below.

These provisions interact with those of *TCGA 1992, s 87(4)(b)* (see **48.15** below) under which trust gains potentially chargeable on beneficiaries are reduced by amounts chargeable on settlors of the settlement.

Year of departure 2013/14 or subsequent year

The limitation applies if beneficiaries of the settlement are charged to tax under *TCGA 1992, s 87* or *s 89(2)* (see **48.14** below) or *TCGA 1992, Sch 4C* (see **48.23** below) for one or more tax years each of which is earlier than the year of return (i.e. the tax year which includes the 'period of return' (see **49.5** OVERSEAS MATTERS)) and the amounts charged to tax are in respect of 'matched capital payments' received by the beneficiaries.

A '*matched capital payment*' is a capital payment all of which is matched with the section 2(2) amount for the year of return under the matching rules at **48.15** below.

Where the beneficiaries were charged to tax under *TCGA 1992, s 87* or *s 89(2)*, the amount of the gains otherwise chargeable on the settlor under the provisions in **48.5** above by virtue of *TCGA 1992, s 10A* is reduced by:

- the sum of the amounts charged on the beneficiaries for tax years earlier than the year of return to the extent that the matched capital payments are matched with the section 2(2) amount for the year of return; or
- where the settlement property has at any time included property not originating from the settlor, only so much (if any) of that sum as, on a just and reasonable apportionment, is property referable to the settlor.

Where, with respect to the year of return, an amount remains to be treated under *TCGA 1992, s 10A* as accruing to any of the settlors after having made the reductions under the above provisions, the aggregate of those amounts (for all the settlors) are applied in reducing so much of the section 2(2) amount for the year as has not already been matched with a capital payment for any prior year (but not so as to reduce the section 2(2) amount below zero).

[*TCGA 1992, s 86A; FA 2013, Sch 45 para 120*].

Where the beneficiaries were charged to tax under *TCGA 1992, Sch 4C* (see **48.23** below), the provisions of *TCGA 1992, s 86A* above do not apply. Instead, the following applies. For transfers of value within *TCGA 1992, Sch 4B* (see **62.21** SETTLEMENTS) made on or after 6 April 2008, where an amount of chargeable gains for any year ('year A') which falls within the charge on the settlor under these provisions would fall to be attributed to the settlor for the year of return, the amount of the gains is reduced to the *section 2(2)* amount for year A that is in the *Schedule 4C* pool for the settlement after applying the charge on the beneficiaries under *Schedule 4C* for the year of return (if the *s 2(2)* amount is less than the amount of the gains).

[*TCGA 1992, Sch 4C paras 1, 12; FA 2013, Sch 45 para 123(1)–(4)*].

Year of departure 2012/13 or earlier year

The limitation applies if for any intervening year (i.e. any complete tax year between the 'year of departure' and the 'year of return' — see **49.5** OVERSEAS MATTERS), beneficiaries of the settlement were charged to tax in respect of any capital payments received by them from the settlement under *TCGA 1992, s 87* or *s 89(2)* (see **48.14** below) or *TCGA 1992, Sch 4C* (see **48.23** below).

Where the beneficiaries were charged to tax under *TCGA 1992, s 87* or *s 89(2)*, the limitation applies by reducing the amount falling within the charge on the settlor under these provisions for the intervening year (or years), and to be attributed to the settlor for the year of return, by the excess (if any) of the 'relevant chargeable amounts for the non-residence period' over the amount of the 'section 87 pool' at the end of the 'year of departure' (as defined in **49.5** OVERSEAS MATTERS).

The '*relevant chargeable amounts for the non-residence period*' is the aggregate of the amounts on which beneficiaries of the settlement are charged to capital gains tax in respect of any capital payments received by them from the settlement under *TCGA 1992, s 87* or *s 89(2)* for the intervening year or years.

The '*section 87 pool*' at the end of a year of assessment is the amount (if any), under that section, of 'the section 2(2) amount' (see **48.15** below) which are to be carried forward from that year to be included in the amount of the trust gains for the immediately following year of assessment. In calculating the above amounts, where the settlement property has at any time included property not originating from the settlor, only so much (if any) of any capital payment or amount of trust gains for the year carried forward as, on a just and reasonable apportionment, is properly referable to property originating from the settlor (see **48.9** above) is taken into account.

[*TCGA 1992, s 86A*].

Where the beneficiaries were charged to tax under *TCGA 1992, Sch 4C* (see **48.23** below), the provisions of *TCGA 1992, s 86A* above do not apply. Instead, the following applies. For transfers of value within *TCGA 1992, Sch 4B* (see **62.21** SETTLEMENTS) made on or after 6 April 2008, where an amount of chargeable gains for an intervening year which falls within the charge on the settlor under these provisions would fall to be attributed to the settlor for the year of return, the amount of the gains is reduced to the *section 2(2)* amount for the intervening year that is in the *Schedule 4C* pool for the settlement after applying the charge on the beneficiaries under *Schedule 4C* for the year of return (if the *s 2(2)* amount is less than the amount of the gains).

[*TCGA 1992, Sch 4C paras 1, 12*].

Charge on beneficiary in respect of capital payments received from settlement

[48.14] The following provisions apply to treat gains accruing to non-UK resident trustees of a settlement as the chargeable gains of beneficiaries who receive capital payments from them. The provisions are substantially rewritten for 2008/09 onwards to include detailed rules for matching gains with capital payments and the provisions as they apply for such years are covered at **48.15** below. For proposed future developments regarding non-resident beneficiaries see **48.15** below. For the provisions as they apply for earlier years see the 2011/12 or earlier edition.

Where the charge applies to a non-UK domiciled individual who uses the REMITTANCE BASIS (55), settlement gains attributed to him are taxed on that basis irrespective of the location of the asset concerned.

The provisions apply to a settlement for 2013/14 and any subsequent tax year if there is not time in that year when the 'trustees' are resident in the UK. The provisions apply to a settlement for 2012/13 or any earlier tax year if the trustees are neither resident nor ordinarily resident in the UK (see **48.1** above) during any part of the year.

[*TCGA 1992, s 87(1)(6); FA 2013, Sch 46 paras 92(2), 112*].

As regards capital payments received by UK charities as beneficiaries, see **11.3** CHARITIES.

For allowable expenditure on a subsequent disposal of an asset transferred to a beneficiary, see **45.1** MARKET VALUE.

See **48.23** below for the interaction of these provisions with those of *TCGA 1992, Sch 4C* (transfers of value linked with trustee borrowing: attribution of gains to beneficiaries).

Definitions

'*Settlor*' is defined as at **62.5** SETTLEMENTS. '*Settlement*' is defined as in *ITTOIA 2005, s 620* (see **41.28** CONNECTED PERSONS) and 'settled property' and references to property comprised in a settlement are construed accordingly. [*TCGA 1992, s 97(7)*].

In a case where a residuary legatee (who was domiciled, resident and ordinarily resident in the UK) settled the unadministered residue of the estate of a testator (who was domiciled, resident and ordinarily resident outside the UK) under a deed of family arrangement within *TCGA 1992, s 62(6)* (see **19.8** DEATH), it was held that the legatee was the settlor for the purposes of *TCGA 1992, s 87* (*Marshall v Kerr* HL 1994, 67 TC 56).

'*Trustee*' is specifically expressed to include, where a settlement would otherwise have no trustees, any person in whom the settled property or its management is vested. [*TCGA 1992, s 97(7A)*].

'*Beneficiary*' is not otherwise defined, but in any case where:

(1) a capital payment is received from the trustees of a settlement or is treated as so received by virtue of *TCGA 1992, s 96(1)* (see below under Payments by and to companies);
(2) it is received by a person, or treated as received by a person by virtue of *TCGA 1992, s 96(2)–(5)* (see below under Payments by and to companies);
(3) at the time it is received or treated as received, the person is not otherwise a beneficiary of the settlement; and

(4) certain exceptions do not apply;

then for the purposes of *TCGA 1992, ss 87–90* (for which see further below) and *TCGA 1992, Sch 4C* (see **48.23** below) the person is treated as a beneficiary of the settlement as regards events occurring on or after that time. The first exception is where a payment within (1) above is made in circumstances where it is treated (otherwise than under the provision in the last sentence) as received by a beneficiary. The second exception is where the trustees of the settlement concerned or trustees of any other settlement are beneficiaries of the settlement concerned. [*TCGA 1992, s 97(8)–(10)*].

Capital payments

These are any 'payments' which either are not chargeable to income tax on the 'recipient', or, in the case of a recipient not resident (for 2012/13 and earlier years, neither resident nor ordinarily resident) in the UK, are payments received otherwise than as income. A capital payment does not include a payment under a transaction entered into at arm's length. [*TCGA 1992, s 97(1); FA 2013, Sch 46 paras 95, 112*].

A beneficiary is regarded as having received a capital payment from the trustees where:

- the beneficiary receives the payment from them, whether directly or indirectly;
- the trustees, directly or indirectly, apply the payment in settlement of any of the beneficiary's debts, or it is otherwise paid or applied for his benefit; or
- a third party receives it at the beneficiary's direction.

[*TCGA 1992, s 97(5)*].

In *Bowring v HMRC* UT 2015, [2016] STC 816, a trust had realised gains on the disposal of assets and transferred the funds to a new trust. The application of the anti-avoidance provisions in *TCGA 1992, Sch 4B* (see **48.22** below) had been intentionally triggered by linking the transfer with trustee borrowings so that the provisions at **48.18** below were disapplied and the gains remained in the original trust. Capital payments were then made to the beneficiaries of the new trust. The Upper Tribunal rejected HMRC's contention that the new trust was a mere intermediary so that the above provisions applied. The capital payments had been made solely by the new trust.

'*Payment*' includes the transfer of an asset and the conferring of any other benefit. It also includes any occasion where settled property becomes property to which *TCGA 1992, s 60* applies (e.g. property held by nominees or on bare trusts for persons absolutely entitled). [*TCGA 1992, s 97(2)*]. A benefit treated (in whole or in part), under *ITA 2007, s 733* (transfer of assets abroad: liability of non-transferors on benefits received — see Tolley's Income Tax under Anti-Avoidance), as the recipient's income for a year of assessment *later* than the year of receipt, is not precluded from being treated as a capital payment in relation to any year *prior* to the year of assessment for which it is treated as income. It cannot, however, be treated as a capital payment in relation to the year for which it is treated as income, or in relation to any *subsequent* year. [*TCGA 1992, s 97(3)*].

The amount of capital payment made by way of loan, and of any other capital payment which is not an outright payment of money, is to be taken as the value of the benefit conferred by it. For capital payments in 2017/18 and subsequent years, the value of the benefit conferred is determined by the following rules where a capital payment is made by a loan or by making tangible moveable property or land available.

In the case of a loan to a person P, the value of the benefit conferred on P, for each tax year in which the loan is outstanding, is the amount (if any) by which the interest that would have been payable on the loan at the official rate exceeds the interest actually paid by P. Previously, case law had determined the value in a similar manner in the case of loans made by trustees repayable on demand (*Cooper v Billingham; Fisher v Edwards* CA 2001, 74 TC 139).

The value of the benefit conferred by a capital payment consisting of making tangible movable property (other than money) available, without any transfer of the property in it, to P is, for each tax year in which the benefit is conferred:

$$((CC \times R \times D)/Y) - T$$

where:

CC	=	the capital cost of the movable property, when it is first made available to P in the tax year, where that capital cost is the consideration given for the property by the person conferring the benefit (or, if greater, its market value when acquired by that person) plus any enhancement expenditure incurred on it by that person;
D	=	the number of days in the tax year on which the property is made available to P (the '*relevant period*');
R	=	the official rate of interest (or the average official rate) for the relevant period;
Y	=	the number of days in the tax year; and
T	=	the total paid by P in the tax year, to the person conferring the benefit, in respect of the property's availability to P, plus any other amounts paid by P for the repair, insurance, maintenance or storage of the property.

The value of the benefit conferred by a capital payment consisting of making land available for the use of P (without the person conferring the benefit transferring the whole of their interest in the land to P) is, for each tax year in which the benefit is conferred, the excess of:

- the land's 'rental value' for the period of the tax year during which it is made available to P over
- the total paid by P in the tax year, to the person conferring the benefit, in respect of the land's availability to P, plus any other amounts paid by P for the repair, insurance or maintenance of the land.

The '*rental value*' of the land is broadly its letting value in the open market on the assumption that the tenant pays all taxes, rates and charges usually paid by a tenant, and the landlord bears the cost of repairs, maintenance and insurance.

[*TCGA 1992, ss 97(4), 97A, 97B, 97C; F(No 2)A 2017, Sch 9 paras 1, 3*].

2008/09 and subsequent years

[48.15] Where **48.14** applies for 2008/09 or any subsequent year, chargeable gains are treated as accruing in the tax year concerned to a beneficiary of the settlement if he has received a capital payment from the trustees in that year or an earlier year and all or part of the payment is matched (as below) with the 'section 2(2) amount' for that year or any earlier year. The amount of the chargeable gains is equal to the capital payment or, if only part of the payment is matched, the matched part.

Where the year is a split year under the statutory residence test for 2013/14 onwards (see **57.18** RESIDENCE AND DOMICILE), the beneficiary is chargeable only on part of the amount on which he would otherwise be chargeable. The chargeable part is that attributable to the UK part of the year calculated by time apportionment.

For this purpose, the '*section 2(2) amount*' for a tax year for which the settlement is within *TCGA 1992, s 87* (i.e. where **48.14**(a) and, where relevant, (b) apply) is the amount which would have been chargeable on the trustees under *TCGA 1992, s 2(2)* (i.e. chargeable gains less current year and brought forward losses), had they been resident (for 2012/13 and earlier years, resident and ordinarily resident) in the UK in that year *less*, if *TCGA 1992, s 86* (offshore settlement where settlor has interest — see **48.5** above) applies to the settlement for the year, any chargeable gains for the year under that section. The section 2(2) amount for a tax year for which *s 87* does not apply is nil.

In determining the s 2(2) amount, where the amount on which the trustees would be chargeable accrues on a non-resident CGT disposal (see **41.25** LAND) any amount on which the trustees are in fact chargeable as an NRCGT gain is not chargeable on the beneficiary.

Carried interest gains (see **50.20** PARTNERSHIPS) which would otherwise be included in the s 2(2) amount are disregarded (under *F(No 2)A 2017, s 32(4)* but for gains accruing both before and after the passing of that Act).

[*TCGA 1992, s 87; FA 2013, Sch 45 para 101, Sch 46 paras 92, 112; FA 2015, Sch 7 para 20; F(No 2)A 2017, s 32(4)(5)*].

Transitional rules

Where *TCGA 1992, s 87* applied to a settlement for 2007/08 or any earlier year the following transitional provisions apply to deal with unmatched gains and payments and to ensure that no double taxation arises on already matched gains and payments.

- In order to apply the matching rules below for 2008/09 onwards, section 2(2) amounts for 2007/08 and earlier years must be calculated and matched with the total chargeable gains treated as accruing to beneficiaries under *TCGA 1992, ss 87* or *89(2)* (see **48.17** below) for those years. The total deemed gains are subtracted from the section 2(2) amount for each year, earliest first and working forward to 2007/08 on a year-by-year basis. If the trustees made a transfer of value before 6 April 2008 to which *TCGA 1992, Sch 4B* applied, this provision applies subject to just and reasonable modification on account of the application of *TCGA 1992, Sch 4C* (see **48.23** below) to the settlement. This provision does not apply if, before 6 April 2008, there was a transfer of settled property to or from the settlement to which *TCGA 1992, s 90* (see **48.18** below) applied: instead special matching provisions apply — see *FA 2008, Sch 7 para 121*. [*FA 2008, Sch 7 para 120*].

- Where chargeable gains have by reason of a capital payment been treated as accruing to a beneficiary in 2007/08 or an earlier year (whether under *TCGA 1992, ss 87* or *89(2)* or *Sch 4C para 8*), the capital payment is reduced to nil (or, where only part of a payment has resulted in such chargeable gains, reduced by that part). For this purpose, where more than one capital payment was taken into account in determining the amount of the gains, earlier payments are treated as matched with the gains before later ones. [*FA 2008, Sch 7 para 122*].

Matching rules

Capital payments are matched with section 2(2) amounts on a last-in first-out basis by applying the following steps for each year to which to which *TCGA 1992, s 87* applies to the settlement.

Step 1.

Find the section 2(2) amount for the year concerned.

Step 2.

Find the total capital payments received by beneficiaries from the trustees in the year.

Step 3.

Match the section 2(2) amount for the year as follows:

(i) where the total capital payments received in the year do not exceed the section 2(2) amount for the year, match the amount with each capital payment so received; or

(ii) otherwise, apportion the section 2(2) amount between each of those capital payments.

Step 4.

Where (i) above applies, reduce the section 2(2) amount for the tax year by the total amount of capital payments for the year and reduce those payments to nil. Where (ii) above applies, reduce the section 2(2) amount for the year to nil and reduce the amount of each capital payment by the matched proportion.

Step 5.

Start again at Step 1. In doing so, if the section 2(2) amount for the year has not been reduced to nil, at Step 2 substitute the capital payments received in the latest tax year which is before the last tax year for which Steps 1 to 4 have been undertaken. If the section 2(2) amount for the year has been reduced to nil, at Step 1 substitute the section 2(2) amount for the latest tax year which is before the last year for which Steps 1 to 4 have been undertaken and for which the section 2(2) amount is not nil.

If either all the capital payments received in the year or any earlier year or the section 2(2) amounts for the year and any earlier years have been reduced to nil there is no need to return to Step 1.

Reductions made in Step 4 above are then taken into account in applying the above Steps for any subsequent tax year.

[*TCGA 1992, s 87A*].

Non-UK domiciled beneficiaries

Chargeable gains treated as accruing under *TCGA 1992, s 87* to a non-UK domiciled individual in a tax year to which *ITA 2007, ss 809B, 809D* or *809E* (see **55.2** REMITTANCE BASIS) apply to him are 'foreign chargeable gains' within *TCGA 1992, s 12* (so that the gains are taxed on the remittance basis). This applies regardless of the location of the assets disposed of.

In determining whether gains are remitted to the UK (see **55.2** REMITTANCE BASIS), property or benefits are treated as deriving from the gains if the capital payment by reason of which the gains are treated as accruing consists of either the payment or transfer of the property or its becoming property to which *TCGA 1992, s 60* (property held by nominees and bare trustees — see **62.3** SETTLEMENTS) applies, or the conferring of the benefit.

[*TCGA 1992, s 87B; FA 2013, Sch 46 para 18*].

If chargeable gains are treated under the above provisions or *TCGA 1992, s 89(2)* (see **48.17** below) as accruing to an individual in a year in which he is not domiciled in the UK, he is not charged to capital gains tax on the gains to the extent that they accrue by reason of a capital payment received (or treated as received) by him before 6 April 2008 or by reason of the matching of a capital payment with the section 2(2) amount for 2007/08 or an earlier year.

Where an individual was resident or ordinarily resident in the UK in 2007/08 but was not UK domiciled in that year and he receives a capital payment from trustees on or after 12 March 2008 but before 6 April 2008, no account is taken of that payment for the purpose of matching settlement gains for 2008/09 or any subsequent year, provided that he is resident or ordinarily resident, but not domiciled in the UK, in the year in which the gains accrue.

[*FA 2008, Sch 7 paras 124, 125*].

Election for re-basing of gains attributed to non-domiciled beneficiaries

Where *s 87* applies to a settlement for 2008/09, the trustees can make an irrevocable election (on Form RBE1) the broad effect of which is to re-base the settlement assets to the market value at 6 April 2008 so that the element of any gains relating to the period before that date will not be chargeable when attributed to a non-UK domiciled beneficiary.

An election must be made in the way and form specified by HMRC and must be made on or before 31 January following the end of the first tax year (beginning with 2008/09) in which either a capital payment is received (or treated as received) by a UK-resident beneficiary of the settlement (or, where the settlement has a *Sch 4C* pool), by a UK-resident beneficiary of a relevant settlement (see **48.23** below) or the trustees transfer all or part of the settled property to another settlement and *TCGA 1992, s 90* (see **48.18** below) applies to the transfer.

The effect of the election is that where chargeable gains are treated under *s 87*, *s 89(2)* or *Sch 4C para 8* as accruing to an individual who is resident but not domiciled in the UK by virtue of the matching of a capital payment with a section 2(2) amount for 2008/09 or a subsequent year, the individual is only charged to capital gains tax on the 'relevant proportion' of the gains.

The '*relevant proportion*' for this purpose is equal to what would be the *s 2(2)* amount for the year if every 'relevant asset' had been sold immediately before 6 April 2008 and immediately reacquired at market value, divided by the actual section 2(2) amount for the year. An asset is a '*relevant asset*' if a chargeable gain or allowable loss accrues to the trustees in the year by reason of it, provided that it has been comprised in the settlement throughout the period from the beginning of 6 April 2008 to the time of the event giving rise to the gain or loss.

An asset is also a relevant asset if chargeable gains are treated as accruing to the trustees in the year under *TCGA 1992, s 13* (attribution of gains of overseas resident companies — see **49.7** OVERSEAS MATTERS) by reason of it, but only if the company realising the actual gains owned the asset throughout the period from the beginning of 6 April 2008 to the time of the event giving rise to the gains (the '*relevant period*') and, if it had disposed of the asset at any earlier time in that period, part of the gains would have been attributed to the trustees under *s 13*. Where the proportion of chargeable gains treated as accruing to the trustees under *s 13* is greater than the smallest proportion of gains that would have been attributable to the trustees on a disposal of the asset in the relevant period, only a proportion of the asset is a relevant asset. The proportion is the smallest proportion of gains divided by the relevant proportion.

For the above purposes, where a company disposes of an asset to another company in the same group such that *TCGA 1992, s 171* (see **29.3** GROUPS OF COMPANIES) applies, the transferee company is treated as having owned the asset throughout the period when the transferor company owned it. Where an asset is a relevant asset as a result of this rule, then for the purpose of calculating the relevant proportion, the gains are treated as accruing to the company which owned the asset at the beginning of 6 April 2008 and the proportion of those gains attributable to the trustees under *s 13* are treated as the proportion of the gains actually accruing that are so attributable.

An asset is also a relevant asset if chargeable gains or allowable losses accrue to the trustees (or are treated as so accruing under *s 13*) by reason of it, the value of the asset derives wholly from another asset and *TCGA 1992, s 43* (assets derived from other assets — see **16.5** COMPUTATION OF GAINS AND LOSSES) applies to the calculation of the gains or losses. Either the new asset or the original asset must have been comprised in the settlement throughout the period from the beginning of 6 April 2008 to the time of the event giving rise to the gains or losses or, where the gains or losses are treated as accruing under *s 13*, the company realising the actual gains or losses must have owned the asset throughout the period from the beginning of 6 April 2008 to the time of the event giving rise to the gains or losses and, if it had disposed of the asset at any earlier time in that period, part of the gains would have been attributed to the trustees under *s 13*.

[*FA 2008, Sch 7 para 126*].

Non-resident beneficiaries

A beneficiary would not be chargeable if he was neither resident nor ordinarily resident (despite being domiciled) in the UK for the tax year in question under the general rules of *TCGA 1992, s 2(1)* (see **49.1** OVERSEAS MATTERS). Thus, in respect of capital payments received by a beneficiary in these circumstances, whilst section 2(2) amounts are attributed to those capital payments, no charge to tax can be made in respect of them.

Draft legislation released on 26 January 2017 (www.gov.uk/government/publications/draft-legislation-deemed-domicile-income-tax-capital-gains-tax-and-inheritance-tax) covering deemed domicile rules for capital gains tax, included changes to the treatment of capital payments to non-resident beneficiaries. While much of the deemed domicile legislation (see **57.34** RESIDENCE AND DOMICILE) was subsequently enacted in *F(No 2)A 2017*, those provisions relating to such capital payments were deferred. Amended draft legislation was published on 13 September 2017 intended for inclusion in *Finance Bill 2017–2018* (see www.gov.uk/government/publications/offshore-trusts-anti-avoidance) and intended to have effect from 6 April 2018. These draft provisions disregard capital payments made to non-resident beneficiaries for the purposes of *TCGA 1992, ss 87, 87A* (i.e. s 2(2) amounts are not matched with such payments). The draft legislation also includes a charge on the settlor where the capital payment is to a close family member of the UK resident settlor and provisions in the case of certain onward gifts from the originally beneficiary to a UK resident. Capital payments to temporary non-residents and migrating beneficiaries, and capital payments in the year a settlement ends are covered separately.

Disregard of capital payments to non-UK companies

Capital payments are disregarded for the above purposes if received (or treated as received) from the trustee by a company which is not resident in the UK and which would be a close company if it were so resident. This does not apply where the payment is treated under *TCGA 1992, s 96(3)–(5)* (see **48.19** below) as received by another person. [*TCGA 1992, s 87C*].

Losses

Where a loss accrues to the trustees in a tax year for which these provisions apply or *CGTA 1979, s 17* applied, the loss is allowable against gains accruing to the trustees in any later year (1981/82 onwards) insofar as it has not previously been set against gains for the purpose of a computation under these provisions, those of *CGTA 1979, s 17* or otherwise. [*TCGA 1992, s 97(6)*].

The beneficiary's own losses, whether of the current tax year of assessment or brought forward from previous years, cannot be set off against gains treated as accruing to him as above. See **44.2** LOSSES.

Example

C, resident and domiciled in the UK, is the sole beneficiary of a discretionary settlement created by his father in 2003 and administered in the Cayman Islands. The trustees are all individuals resident in the Cayman Islands. The trustees make no gains or capital payments in 2013/14 or any earlier year, but make the following capital payments to C in 2014/15 onwards.

	£
2014/15	50,000
2015/16	60,000
2016/17	50,000
2017/18	70,000

In 2017/18, the trustees sell two settlement assets (shareholdings) realising a gain of £350,000 and a loss of £50,000. They make no other disposals in that year. C makes only one disposal in 2017/18, realising an allowable loss of £25,000, and pays income tax at the higher rate.

The settlement's 'section 2(2) amount' for 2017/18 is:

	£
Gain	350,000
Less Loss	50,000
Section 2(2) amount for 2017/18	£300,000

The *s 2(2)* amount is matched with the capital payments made to C on a last-in first-out basis as follows.

	£
Section 2(2) amount	300,000
2017/18 capital payment	70,000

	£
2016/17 capital payment	50,000
2015/16 capital payment	60,000
2014/15 capital payment	50,000
Unmatched amount carried forward	£70,000

C's liability to capital gains tax for 2017/18 is as follows.

	£
Matched section 2(2) amount (£70,000 + £50,000 + £60,000 + £50,000)	230,000
Less Annual exempt amount	11,300
Amount chargeable to capital gains tax 2017/18	£218,700
Capital gains tax (£218,700 × 20%)	£43,740

Note

(a) C's personal loss of £25,000 for 2017/18 cannot be relieved against gains chargeable under *TCGA 1991, s 87* — see **44.2** LOSSES.

Dual resident settlements

[48.16] *TCGA 1992, s 87* (see **48.14–48.15** above) also applies to a settlement if the trustees are resident (for 2012/13 and earlier years, resident and ordinarily resident) in the UK during any part of the year *and* at any time of such residence (and ordinary residence) they fall to be regarded for the purposes of a double tax agreement as resident overseas.

For 2008/09 and subsequent years, the '*section 2(2) amount*' (see **48.15** above) for a tax year for which *TCGA 1992, s 87* applies by virtue of this provision is the 'assumed chargeable amount' *less*, if *TCGA 1992, s 86* (offshore settlement where settlor has interest — see **48.5** above) applies to the settlement for the year, any chargeable gains for the year under that section.

The '*assumed chargeable amount*' in respect of a tax year is the lesser of: the amount on which the trustees would be chargeable to tax for the year under *TCGA 1992, s 2(2)* on the assumption that the double tax relief arrangements did not apply; and the amount on which, by virtue of disposals of protected assets, the trustees would be chargeable to tax for the year under *TCGA 1992, s 2(2)* on the assumption that those arrangements did not apply. Assets are '*protected assets*' if they are of a description specified in the double tax relief arrangements, and were the trustees to dispose of them at any 'relevant time', the trustees would fall to be regarded for the purposes of the arrangements as not liable in the UK to tax on gains accruing to them on the disposal. For the purposes of this definition of protected assets: the second assumption in the first sentence of this paragraph is ignored; '*the relevant time*' is any time, in the tax year concerned, when the trustees fall to be regarded for the purposes of the arrangements as resident overseas; and if different assets are identified by reference to different relevant times, all of them are protected assets. For the purposes of *TCGA 1992, s 87* as it applies by virtue of this provision, capital payments received before 6 April 1991 are disregarded.

[*TCGA 1992, s 88; FA 2013, Sch 46 paras 93, 112*].

Migrant settlements

[48.17] A capital payment (see **48.14** above) made to a beneficiary in a period of one or more tax years 'for each of which *TCGA 1992, s 87* (see **48.14** above) does not apply to the settlement (a '*resident period*') is disregarded provided that the payment is not anticipatory of a disposal by the trustees in a succeeding period of one or more tax years for which *TCGA 1992, s 87* applies to the settlement (a '*non-resident period*'). [*TCGA 1992, s 89(1)*].

The following applies where a resident period follows a non-resident period and for the last year of the non-resident period all capital payments received by beneficiaries in that year or any earlier year have been reduced to nil under the matching rules at **48.15** above. Chargeable gains are treated as accruing to a beneficiary in any tax year in the resident period if he receives a capital payment from the trustees in that year and all or part of the payment is matched with the section 2(2) amount for the last non-resident year or any earlier year.

TCGA 1992, s 87C (disregard of capital payments to non-UK companies — see **48.15** above) and *s 87B* (attributed chargeable gains treated as foreign chargeable gains — see **48.15** above) apply for the purposes of this provision as for the purposes of *TCGA 1992, s 87.*

[*TCGA 1992, s 89(1A)–(4)*].

Transfers between settlements

[48.18] There are provisions for the carry-over of unattributed gains under *TCGA 1992, s 87* or *s 89(2)* (apportioned where necessary), in cases where transfers of settled property are made from one settlement to another. If neither of the last mentioned provisions would otherwise apply to the transferee settlement for the year of transfer, *TCGA 1992, s 89(2)* is deemed to apply to it for that year and subsequent years. These provisions do not apply to a transfer to which *TCGA 1992, Sch 4B* (transfers of value by trustees linked with trustee borrowing — see **62.21** SETTLEMENTS) applies, or to any *s 2(2)* amount that is in a 'Schedule 4C pool' within **48.23** below. [*TCGA 1992, ss 90, 90A*].

Where an election has been made by the transferor trustees under *FA 2008, Sch 7 para 126* (gains attributed to non-UK domiciled beneficiaries: re-basing — see **48.15** above) there are provisions to ensure that, following the transfer, any non-UK domiciled beneficiary is charged to capital gains tax only on the post-5 April 2008 element of gains of a non-UK resident company in which the transferor trustees were participators (so that *TCGA 1992, s 13* applies — see **49.7** OVERSEAS MATTERS). [*FA 2008, Sch 7 para 127*].

Payments by and to companies

[48.19] By virtue of *TCGA 1992, s 96(1)*, where a capital payment is received from a 'qualifying company' which is 'controlled' by the trustees of a settlement at the time it is received, it is treated for the purposes of *TCGA 1992, s 87* (see **48.14–48.15** above) and *ss 88–90* above and *TCGA 1992, Sch 4C* (see **48.23** below) as received from the trustees.

A '*qualifying company*' is a close company within *CTA 2010, ss 439–454* or a company which would be a close company if it were UK resident. A company is '*controlled*' by the trustees of a settlement if it is 'controlled' by the trustees alone or by the trustees together with a person who (or persons each of whom) is a settlor in relation to the settlement or is connected (see **17 CONNECTED PERSONS**) with such a settlor. '*Control*' is to be construed in accordance with *CTA 2010, ss 450, 451* except that for this purpose no rights or powers of (or attributed to) an associate or associates of a person are attributed to him under *CTA 2010, s 451(4)–(6)* if he is not a participator (within *CTA 2010, s 454*) in the company. A beneficiary in the settlement is not to be regarded as a participator in the company solely by virtue of his status as beneficiary (prior to 6 April 2017 this was by concession — HMRC Extra-Statutory Concession D40).

By virtue of *TCGA 1992, s 96(2)–(5)*, where a capital payment is received from trustees of a settlement (or treated as so received under the foregoing) and it is received by a '*non-resident qualifying company*' (i.e. a company which is not resident in the UK and would be a close company if it were so resident), the following provisions apply for the purposes of *TCGA 1992, ss 87–90* and *TCGA 1992, Sch 4C* (see **48.23** below).

If the company is 'controlled' (construed as above) by one person alone at the time the payment is received, and that person is (or is deemed to be) then resident (before 6 April 2013, resident or ordinarily resident) in the UK, it is treated as a capital payment received by that person.

If the company is controlled by two or more persons (taking each one separately) at the time the payment is received, then: if one of them is (or is deemed to be) then resident (before 6 April 2013, resident or ordinarily resident) in the UK, it is treated as a capital payment received by that person; and if two or more persons are (or are deemed to be) then resident (or resident or ordinarily resident) in the UK ('*the residents*') it is treated as being as many equal capital payments as there are residents and each of them is treated as receiving one of the payments.

If the company is controlled by two or more persons (taking them together) at the time the payment is received, it is treated as being as many capital payments as there are participators in the company at the time it is received; and each such participator (whatever his residence or ordinary residence) is treated as receiving one of the payments, quantified on the basis of just and reasonable apportionment. But where a participator would otherwise be treated as receiving less than 5% of the payment actually received by the company, he is not treated as receiving anything by virtue of the foregoing.

For HMRC's practice in this area, see SP 5/92, paras 38–40.

For the above purposes, an *individual* is deemed to be resident in the UK at any time in any year of assessment for which he is not so resident if the year falls within a temporary period of non-residence for the purposes of the charge to capital gains tax on temporary non-residents (see **49.5** OVERSEAS MATTERS). Where the year of departure (see **49.5** OVERSEAS MATTERS) was before 2013/14 this rule applied to any year of assessment which was an intervening year for the purposes of that charge. Where it appears after the end of a year of assessment that the rule does apply to an individual and consequential adjustments are required to the amounts of tax chargeable on any person under the above provisions, no time limits for making any assessment or claim prevent the making of those adjustments (whether by assessment, amended assessment, tax repayment or otherwise).

[*TCGA 1992, s 96; FA 2013, Sch 45 paras 121, 153(3), Sch 46 paras 94, 112; SI 2017, No 495*].

HMRC information powers

[48.20] HMRC may, by notice in writing, require any person, within such time as it directs (not less than 28 days), to furnish them with such particulars as they think necessary for the purposes of *TCGA 1992, ss 87–90* and *TCGA 1992, Sch 4C* (see **48.23** below). The very wide information powers of *ITA 2007, ss 748(3)–(5), 749, 750*, suitably adapted, are also expressly stated to apply. [*TCGA 1992, s 98*].

Further charge on beneficiary in respect of capital payments received from settlement

[48.21] Further provisions apply where the provisions in **48.14–48.20** above for taxing beneficiaries of overseas resident settlements apply. They provide for an increased tax charge on the beneficiary in certain cases. The provisions are amended for 2008/09 onwards to take account of the changes made to *TCGA 1992, s 87* (see **48.14** above). In particular, the introduction of detailed matching rules (see **48.15** above) for the purposes of that section means that separate matching rules are no longer required for the purposes of the provisions below. The revised matching rules mean that capital payments are matched with gains on a last-in first-out basis rather than the previous first-in first-out basis.

For 2008/09 onwards, the provisions apply where:

(I) chargeable gains are treated under *TCGA 1992, s 87* or *s 89(2)* as accruing to a beneficiary as a result of the matching of all or part of a 'capital payment' (see **48.14** above) with the '*section 2(2) amount*' (see **48.15** above) for a tax year (the '*relevant tax year*');
(II) the beneficiary is charged to tax as a result of the matching; and
(III) the capital payment was made more than one year after the end of the relevant tax year.

Effect of provisions

Where the provisions apply, the tax payable by the beneficiary in respect of the payment is increased by the amount found below, except that it cannot be increased beyond the amount of the payment.

The amount is equal to the interest that would be yielded if an amount equal to the tax which would be otherwise payable by him in respect of the payment carried interest for the 'chargeable period' at the rate of 10% per annum. The percentage may be amended by Treasury Order.

The *'chargeable period'* is the period which begins with the later of 1 December in the tax year immediately after the relevant tax year and 1 December falling six years before 1 December in the tax year following that in which the capital payment is made, and ends with 30 November in the tax year following that in which the capital payment is made.

In arriving, for the above purposes, at the amount of CGT payable by the beneficiary in respect of the capital payment, that payment is deemed to form the lowest slice of the beneficiary's total gains (HMRC Helpsheet IR 301 p 1). Therefore, it may, for example, be reduced by the annual exemption.

[*TCGA 1992, s 91*].

Anti-avoidance — transfers of value by trustees linked with trustee borrowing

[48.22] See **62.21** SETTLEMENTS for provisions deeming chargeable gains to arise to trustees of a settlement where they make a 'transfer of value' (as defined). Where the trustees are not UK resident or they are treated as non-resident under double tax relief arrangements, the resulting gains are, in certain circumstances, chargeable either on the settlor (see **48.5** above) or on beneficiaries who receive capital payments under TCGA 1992, Sch 4C (see 48.23 below).

Transfers of value — attribution of gains to beneficiaries

[48.23] The provisions charging beneficiaries receiving capital payments from trustees in respect of gains within *TCGA 1992, Sch 4B* (see **48.22** above) have been twice substantially amended. The first amendments, by *FA 2003*, were to prevent the exploitation of the provisions for tax avoidance purposes. The avoidance schemes at which the amendments were aimed typically relied on the transferor settlement (see below) having realised gains but few, if any, assets. Such a scheme was held to be ineffective in *DP & Mrs B Herman v HMRC* (Sp C 609), [2007] SSCD 571. The *FA 2008* amendments were made to take account of the changes to *TCGA 1992, s 87* (see **48.14–48.15** above) and to bring non-UK domiciled beneficiaries within the scope of the provisions. The post-*FA 2008* provisions apply in respect of 'transfers of value' (within **62.21** SETTLEMENTS) made after 5 April 2008. Both the pre- and post-*FA 2003* provisions apply in respect of transfers of value made after 20 March 2000, but the latter broadly apply only where capital payments are made after 8 April 2003. The post-*FA 2008* provisions are described below.

Post-FA 2008 provisions

[48.24] The following provisions apply where the trustees of a 'settlement' (the '*transferor settlement*') make a 'transfer of value' to which *TCGA 1992, Sch 4B* (see **62.21** SETTLEMENTS) applies on or after 6 April 2008, whether or not any chargeable gain or allowable loss accrues in respect of the transfer under that Schedule. Where the provisions apply, *TCGA 1992, s 86A* (limitation on amount chargeable on temporarily non-resident settlor following transfer of value — see **48.13** above) and *ss 87–95* (the normal provisions attributing gains to beneficiaries receiving capital payments from offshore settlements — see **48.14–48.21** above) have effect subject to them. Accordingly,

- in computing the '*section 2(2) amount*' in accordance with *TCGA 1992, s 87*, no account is taken of any chargeable gains or allowable losses accruing by virtue of *TCGA 1992, Sch 4B* (except in computing the increase in that amount for the year in which the transfer is made (see below));
- for the purposes of *TCGA 1992, ss 87* and *89(2)*, no account is taken of any section 2(2) amount in a Schedule 4C pool (see below); and
- in computing the gains or losses accruing by virtue of *TCGA 1992, Sch 4B*, no account is taken of any chargeable gains or allowable losses to which *TCGA 1992, ss 87–89* apply.

Where the provisions apply, the transferor settlement's section 2(2) amount for the tax year in which the transfer of value is made is increased by the amount of the '*Sch 4B trust gains*' (see below) accruing on the transfer and any further transfers of value made in the year.

The transferor settlement is then treated as having a '*Schedule 4C pool*' containing the settlement's section 2(2) amounts that are outstanding at the end of that tax year.

Section 2(2) amount

The section 2(2) amount that is outstanding at the end of a tax year (the '*relevant year*') is calculated as follows.

Step 1.

Calculate the section 2(2) amounts for the relevant tax year and earlier years, as reduced under the matching rules of *TCGA 1992, s 87A* (see **48.15** above) as applied for those years. Where, in or before the relevant year, there has been a transfer of settled property to or from the trustees to which *TCGA 1992, s 90* (see **48.18** above) applies, the effect of that section must be taken into account.

Step 2.

Where, as a result of the matching of a section 2(2) amount for a tax year (the '*applicable year*') with a 'capital payment' (within *TCGA 1992, s 97(1)* — see **48.14** above), chargeable gains are treated as accruing in the relevant tax year under *TCGA 1992, s 87* or *s 89(2)* to a beneficiary who is not 'chargeable to tax' in that year, the amount found in Step 1 for the applicable year is increased by the amount of the gains.

In the event of a further transfer of value in a subsequent tax year, then, if the settlement has a Schedule 4C pool at the beginning of the tax year of that transfer (see below), the section 2(2) amounts in the pool are increased by the section 2(2) amounts that are outstanding at the end of that year and the section 2(2) amount in the pool for that year is increased (or further increased) by the Schedule 4B trust gains accruing on the transfer. If the settlement does not have a Schedule 4C pool at the beginning of the year a new pool is created. For these purposes, a settlement has a Schedule 4C pool until the end of the tax year in which all section 2(2) amounts in the pool have been reduced to nil under the matching rules below.

Effect of provisions

Chargeable gains are treated as accruing in a tax year to a beneficiary if he has received a capital payment from the trustees of a 'relevant settlement' in that year or an earlier year and all or part of the payment is matched (as below) with the section 2(2) amount in the Schedule 4C pool for that year or any earlier year. The amount of the chargeable gains is equal to the capital payment or, if only part of the payment is matched, the matched part.

TCGA 1992, s 87B (attributed gains: remittance basis — see **48.15** above) applies to gains treated as accruing under these provisions as it applies to gains accruing under *TCGA 1992, s 87*.

Matching rules

The matching rules in *TCGA 1992, s 87A* apply with modifications for the purposes of these provisions as follows. Capital payments received from the trustees of a relevant settlement are matched with section 2(2) amounts in the Schedule 4C pool on a last-in first-out basis by applying the following steps.

Step 1.

Find the section 2(2) amount in the Schedule 4C pool for the year concerned.

Step 2.

Find the total capital payments received from the trustees by beneficiaries who are chargeable to tax in the year.

Step 3.

Match the section 2(2) amount in the Schedule 4C pool for the year with:

(i) where the total capital payments found in Step 2 do not exceed the *s 2(2)* amount in the *Sch 4C* pool for the year, each such capital payment received; or
(ii) otherwise, apportion the section 2(2) amount in the Schedule 4C pool between each of those capital payments.

Step 4.

Where (i) above applies, reduce the section 2(2) amount in the Schedule 4C pool for the tax year by the total amount of capital payments found in Step 2 and reduce those payments to nil. Where (ii) above applies, reduce the section 2(2) amount in the Schedule 4C pool for the year to nil and reduce the amount of each capital payment by the matched proportion.

Step 5.

Start again at Step 1. In doing so, if the section 2(2) amount in the Schedule 4C pool for the year has not been reduced to nil, in Step 2 substitute the capital payments received in the latest tax year which is before the last tax year for which Steps 1 to 4 have been undertaken and which is a year in which capital payments (which have not been reduced to nil) were received by beneficiaries who were chargeable to tax in the year. If the section 2(2) amount in the Schedule 4C pool for the year has been reduced to nil, in Step 1 substitute the section 2(2) amount in the Schedule 4C pool for the latest tax year which is before the last year for which Steps 1 to 4 have been undertaken and for which the section 2(2) amount in the Schedule 4C pool is not nil.

If either all the capital payments received in the year or any earlier year or all section 2(2) amounts in the Schedule 4C pool have been reduced to nil there is no need to return to Step 1. Reductions made in Step 4 above are then taken into account in applying the above Steps for any subsequent tax year.

TCGA 1992, s 87A applies as above for a tax year before it applies for that year for the purposes of *TCGA 1992, s 87*.

Where a capital payment is, on or after 6 April 2008, matched with the gains in an existing Schedule 4C pool under the post-*FA 2003* provisions, it is reduced to nil for the purposes of the above provisions. Where only part of such a payment is so matched, the amount of the payment is reduced by that part. For this purpose, where more than one capital payment is taken into account in determining the amount of the gains treated as accruing, earlier payments are treated as matched with the gains before later ones.

Capital payments received before 21 March 2000 or before the tax year preceding that in which the transfer of value is made are disregarded. Also disregarded are capital payments received on or after 6 April 2008 by a non-UK resident company which would be a close company if it were so resident, provided that the payments are not treated as received by someone else under *TCGA 1992, s 96(3)–(5)* (see **48.19** above). See also below under 'Residence of trustees from whom capital payment received' for further circumstances in which capital payments are disregarded.

Attribution of gains to temporarily non-resident beneficiaries

Where, by virtue of *TCGA 1992, s 10A* (the charge on individuals temporarily non-resident in the UK — see **49.5** OVERSEAS MATTERS) an amount of gains would be treated as accruing to a beneficiary under *TCGA 1992, s 87* in the period of his return to the UK in respect of a capital payment made to him during the temporary period of non-residence (see **49.5** OVERSEAS MATTERS), so much of that capital payment as exceeds the amount of such gains (or any gains attributed to him under *TCGA 1992, s 89(2)*) is treated as a capital payment for the purposes of these provisions, made to the beneficiary in the period of return. For the purposes of the provisions at **48.28** below only, the deemed capital payment is treated as made at the time of the actual capital payment. Where the year of departure (see **49.5** OVERSEAS MATTERS) was 2012/13 or an earlier year, this provision applied to capital payments made in an intervening year (i.e. any complete tax year between the year of departure and the 'year of return').

Attribution of gains to non-UK domiciled beneficiaries

If chargeable gains are treated under the above provisions as accruing to an individual in a year in which he is not domiciled in the UK, he is not charged to capital gains tax on the gains to the extent that they accrue by reason of a capital payment received (or treated as received) by him before 6 April 2008 or by reason of the matching of a capital payment with the section 2(2) amount for 2007/08 or an earlier year.

Where an individual was resident or ordinarily resident in the UK in 2007/08 but was not UK domiciled in that year and he receives a capital payment from trustees on or after 12 March 2008 but before 6 April 2008, no account is taken of that payment for the purpose of the above provisions for 2008/09 or any subsequent year, provided that he is resident or ordinarily resident, but not domiciled in the UK, in that year.

Effect of settlement ceasing to exist after transfer of value

Where a settlement ceases to exist at any time after the trustees have made a transfer of value to which *TCGA 1992, Sch 4B* applies, the above provisions apply as if a tax year ended immediately before that time (and the Schedule 4C pool is calculated on that basis).

[*TCGA 1992, ss 85A, 87A, Sch 4C paras 1, 1A, 7B, 8, 8AA, 9, 12A, 13A; FA 2013, Sch 45 paras 123(5), 153(3)*].

Miscellaneous

[48.25] The following further provisions are relevant.

Payments by and to companies

See **48.14** above for the application of these provisions where capital payments are made by or to certain companies.

Residence of trustees from whom capital payment received

Subject to the following exception, it is immaterial for the purposes of the above provisions that the trustees of any relevant settlement are or have at any time been resident (and, before 6 April 2013, ordinarily resident) in the UK.

A capital payment received by a beneficiary of a settlement from the trustees in a tax year during the whole of which the trustees are resident and ordinarily resident in the UK is disregarded for the purposes of the above provisions if it was made before, but was not made in anticipation of, chargeable gains accruing under the provisions of *TCGA 1992, Sch 4B* or of a transfer of value being made to which those provisions apply. For these purposes, trustees are not regarded as resident (and, before 6 April 2013, ordinarily resident) in the UK at any time when they fall to be treated as resident outside the UK for the purposes of any double tax relief arrangements. [*TCGA 1992, Sch 4C paras 9(3), 10; FA 2013, Sch 46 paras 107(5)(6), 112*].

HMRC information powers

See **48.14** above for details of HMRC's information powers in relation to the above provisions.

Definitions

[48.26] '*Settlement*' is defined by the references in *ITTOIA 2005, s 620* — see **17.6** CONNECTED PERSONS.

The following are '*relevant settlements*' in relation to a *Sch 4C* pool:

- the '*transferor settlement*' (being the settlement the trustees of which made the transfer of value);
- any '*transferee settlement*' (i.e. any settlement of which the settled property includes property representing, directly or indirectly, the proceeds of the transfer of value); and
- where the trustees of a relevant settlement make a transfer of value to which *TCGA 1992, Sch 4B* applies or a transfer of settled property to which *TCGA 1992, s 90* applies (see **48.14** above under 'Transfers between settlements'), any transferee settlement in relation to that transfer.

Where the trustees of a settlement which is a relevant settlement in relation to a Schedule 4C pool make a transfer of value to which *TCGA 1992, Sch 4B* applies, any other settlement which is a relevant settlement in relation to that pool is also a relevant settlement in relation to the Schedule 4C pool arising from the further transfer.

A settlement is '*within TCGA 1992, s 87*' for a tax year if in that year the trustees are at no time resident or ordinarily resident in the UK or they fall to be regarded for the purpose of any **21** DOUBLE TAX RELIEF arrangements as resident outside the UK.

For the purpose of the post-*FA 2008* provisions, a beneficiary is '*chargeable to tax*' for 2013/14 or a later tax year if he meets the residence condition at **1.2** INTRODUCTION. A beneficiary is 'chargeable to tax' for 2012/13 or an earlier tax year if he is resident or ordinarily resident in the UK in that year.

'*Beneficiaries*' include:

- persons who have ceased to be beneficiaries by the time the chargeable gains accrue; and
- persons who were beneficiaries of the settlement before it ceased to exist (where this is the case),

but who were beneficiaries of the settlement at a time in a previous tax year when a capital payment was made to them. See **48.14** above for a further circumstance in which, by virtue of *TCGA 1992, s 97(8)–(10)*, a person is treated as a beneficiary.

[*TCGA 1992, s 97(7), Sch 4C paras 1, 1A(3), 8(4), 8A, 14; FA 2013, Sch 46 paras 107(2), 112*].

Computation of Schedule 4B trust gains

[48.27] The amount of the '*Schedule 4B trust gains*', which is to be computed for the above purposes in relation to each transfer of value, is given by

CA – SG – AL, where:

CA = the 'chargeable amount' (see below);

SG = the amount of any gains attributed to the settlor (within the meaning below); and

AL = the amount of any allowable losses that may be deducted as described below.

Chargeable amount

If the transfer of value is made in a tax year during which the trustees of the transferor settlement are at no time resident and ordinarily resident in the UK, the '*chargeable amount*' is the amount on which the trustees would have been chargeable to CGT by virtue of *TCGA 1992, Sch 4B* (i.e. the chargeable gains, net of allowable losses, on the disposals deemed to occur at the time of the transfer of value — see **62.21** SETTLEMENTS) if they had been resident (for 2012/13 and earlier years, resident and/or ordinarily resident) in the UK in the year and they had made the deemed disposals. Where any of the disposals included in this amount are non-resident CGT disposals (see **41.25** LAND) only any gain or loss accruing thereon which is not an NRCGT gain or loss is taken into account in the chargeable amount.

If the transfer of value is made in a tax year where the trustees of the transferor settlement are treated as resident outside the UK for the purposes of any double tax relief arrangements at a time when they are, in fact, UK-resident (and, for 2012/13 and earlier years, ordinarily resident), the chargeable amount is the lesser of:

- the amount on which the trustees would be chargeable to CGT by virtue of *TCGA 1992, Sch 4B* on the assumption that the double tax relief arrangements did not apply and the deemed disposals were made; and
- the amount on which the trustees would be so chargeable to CGT by virtue of disposals of 'protected assets' (as defined by *TCGA 1992, s 88(4)* — see **48.14** above under Dual resident settlements).

Gains attributed to the settlor means the amount of any chargeable gains arising by virtue of the transfer of value that:

(a) are treated as accruing to the settlor under *TCGA 1992, s 86(4)* (see **48.5** above), disregarding any losses arising otherwise than under *TCGA 1992, Sch 4B*, or

(b) where *TCGA 1992, s 10A* applies (charge on individuals temporarily non-resident in the UK — see **49.5** OVERSEAS MATTERS and also **48.13** above), are treated as accruing to the settlor in the year of his return to the UK.

Allowable losses

The allowable losses that may be deducted in arriving at the *Schedule 4B* trust gains in relation to a transfer of value by the trustees of a settlement are losses arising under *TCGA 1992, Sch 4B* in relation to other transfers of value by those trustees, and any such loss is deductible *only* in accordance with the following rules.

- The loss is deducted first from chargeable amounts arising from other transfers of value made in the same tax year.
- If there is more than one chargeable amount and the aggregate allowable losses is less than the aggregate chargeable amounts, each of the chargeable amounts is reduced proportionately.
- If in any tax year the aggregate allowable losses exceeds the aggregate chargeable amounts, the excess is carried forward to the following tax year and treated as if it were an allowable loss arising in relation to a transfer of value made in that following year.

Losses are deducted from chargeable amounts after any deduction for gains attributed to the settlor as above.

[*TCGA 1992, Sch 4C paras 3–7; FA 2013, Sch 46 paras 107(3)(4), 112; FA 2015, Sch 7 para 40*].

Increase in tax payable by beneficiary receiving capital payments

[48.28] The following provisions apply where:

(I) chargeable gains are treated under **48.23** above as accruing to a beneficiary as a result of the matching of all or part of a capital payment with the *s 2(2)* amount for a tax year (the '*relevant tax year*'); and
(II) the beneficiary is charged to tax as a result of the matching.

The tax payable by the beneficiary is increased by an amount equal to the interest that would be yielded if an amount equal to that tax carried interest for the 'chargeable period' at the rate specified in *TCGA 1992, s 91(3)* (i.e. 10% per annum — see **48.21** above), except that it cannot be increased beyond the amount of the payment.

The '*chargeable period*' is the period which:

(a) begins with the later of
    (i) 1 December in the tax year immediately after the relevant tax year, and
    (ii) 1 December falling 6 years before 1 December in the tax year following that in which the capital payment is made; and
(b) ends with 30 November in the tax year following that in which the capital payment is made.

For this purpose, the '*year of the gain*' is, in the case of a *Sch 4B* trust gain, the tax year in which the transfer of value took place, or, in the case of a *section 87/89* gain, the year in which it first forms part of the settlement's 'trust gains for the year' (see **48.14** above).

[*TCGA 1992, Sch 4C paras 8B(3), 13; FA 2008, Sch 7 paras 139, 145–147*].

Information required to be returned in respect of settlements with a foreign element

[48.29] There are extensive requirements for information relating to 'settlements with a foreign element' to be returned to HMRC within certain time limits *without a notice to make a return having to be given by HMRC.*

Penalties under *TMA 1970, s 98* apply for failure to comply although no failure will arise where information already has been returned or will be returned later under any other provision. In particular, the following requirements should be observed.

(a) Where property is transferred after 16 March 1998, otherwise than by way of an arm's length transaction or in pursuance of a liability incurred on or before that date, to a settlement created before 17 March 1998 which is non-UK resident at the time of transfer, a return of certain particulars must be made by the transferor within twelve months of the day ('the relevant day') of the transfer if he knows, or has reason to believe, the residence status of the settlement. (Before 17 March 1998, this requirement operated only in relation to transfers to settlements created before 19 March 1991.)

(b) Where a settlement is created at a time after 18 March 1991 which, at that time, is either non-UK resident or both UK resident and, under double tax relief arrangements, resident elsewhere, a return of certain particulars must be made by the settlor within twelve months of the day ('*the relevant day*') he first fulfils after 2 May 1994 the condition that he is UK domiciled and UK resident (or, before 6 April 2013, ordinarily resident), not having met that condition at the time of the settlement's creation. Similarly, where such a settlement is created after 2 May 1994, a return of certain particulars must be made by the settlor who meets the above condition (as extended to include deemed UK domicile for settlements created on or after 6 April 2017) at the time of the settlement's creation within *three months* of the day ('*the relevant day*') on which the settlement was created.

(c) Where a settlement becomes at any time ('*the relevant time*') after 2 May 1994 non-UK resident or, whilst continuing to be UK resident becomes at any time ('*the relevant time*') after 2 May 1994, under double tax relief arrangements, resident elsewhere, a return of certain particulars must be made by a person who was a trustee immediately before the relevant time within *twelve months* of the day ('*the relevant day*') when the relevant time falls.

[*TCGA 1992, s 98A, Sch 5A; FA 2013, Sch 46 para 109; F(No 2)A 2017, Sch 8 para 9*].

Key points concerning offshore settlements

[48.30] Points to consider are as follows.

- When determining the residence of the trustees, and where there are both resident and non-resident trustees, the residence, ordinary residence or domicile of the settlor at the time the settlement was made is the deciding factor in determining the residence of the trust. Practitioners should be aware of the effect of the death of a trustee on the residence of the trust and take suitable steps to prevent any undesirable outcomes.

- In practice, many offshore settlements that were created (or expatriated) when the tax rules were more favourable have subsequently become regarded as settlor-interested. This is because the definition of a settlor-interested trust now includes those trusts in which the settlor, his children or grandchildren (or the spouse or civil partners of those people) can benefit from the trust. For many family trusts with a UK resident and domiciled settlor, the children and grandchildren are the most likely beneficiaries of these types of settlements. The gains of these settlements are therefore assessed on the settlor under *TCGA 1992, s 86*.
- For offshore settlements holding assets that are pregnant with gains, the capital gains tax charge on the settlor if the trust were to be wound up may be prohibitive, particularly if the trust assets are distributed to a beneficiary other than the settlor.
- A charge on the beneficiary(ies) under *TCGA 1992, s 87* arises where capital payments are made from offshore settlements where *s 86* does not apply. In practice this may be for settlements where the settlor is deceased, or where the settlor was non-UK domiciled. For 2008/09 onwards, the *s 87* charge applies to non-UK domiciled beneficiaries (as well as to UK domiciled beneficiaries, as before).
- Many offshore family settlements no longer offer a tax advantage and clients may consider repatriation of these trusts to the UK. Repatriation prevents stockpiled gains from accruing further, but does not eliminate the pool of stockpiled gains, which will continue to be matched against capital payments to beneficiaries.
- The further charge on beneficiaries in receipt of capital payments (known as the supplementary charge) is calculated as 10% 'interest' per year for each of the years between the gains arising and the capital distribution (up to a maximum of six years). Where the capital gains tax rate is 20%, this means an effective maximum tax rate on capital distributions of 32% (20% tax plus the supplementary charge at 2% per year for six years). Where the lower rate of 10% capital gains tax applies, the maximum rate is reduced to 16%, making the cost of distributing capital to beneficiaries much more affordable. Trustees may wish to consider their distributions to take advantage of the lower rate where this is possible.
- Detailed records of the trust's gains history should be kept, as different capital gains tax rules may have applied in the past. Settlements created before 19 March 1991 which were not previously qualifying settlements (within the 'charge on settlor' provisions), became qualifying settlements with effect from 1999/2000.
- Trust gains and capital payments should be disclosed to HMRC using Form 50(FS).

49

Overseas Matters

Introduction to overseas matters	**49.1**
Individuals not domiciled in the UK disposing of overseas assets	**49.2**
Trading in the UK through permanent establishment or branch or agency	**49.3**
UK representatives of non-residents	**49.4**
Individuals temporarily non-resident in the UK	**49.5**
Year of departure 2013/14 or subsequent year	**49.5**
Year of departure before 2013/14	**49.5**
Relief for unremittable overseas gains	**49.6**
UK resident participator in overseas resident company	**49.7**
Exemption for profits of foreign permanent establishments of UK resident company	**49.8**
UK resident company having an interest in a controlled foreign company	**49.9**
Offshore funds	**49.10**
Current regime	**49.11**
UK resident company transferring assets to overseas resident company	**49.12**
Transfers, divisions and mergers within the European Union	**49.13**
Transfer or division of UK business between companies in different EC member states	**49.13**
Transfer or division of non-UK business between companies in different EC member states	**49.14**
European cross-border mergers	**49.15**
Transparent entities — disapplication of reliefs	**49.16**
Company ceasing to be UK resident etc.	**49.17**
Compliance	**49.18**
Exploration and exploitation rights to territorial sea-bed and continental shelf	**49.19**
European Economic Interest Groupings	**49.20**
Collection of tax	**49.21**
Tax collection agreement with Switzerland	**49.22**
Key points concerning overseas matters	**49.23**

Cross-references. See **7.3** ASSETS for location of assets; **14.15** COMPANIES for European Companies (SEs); **16.12** COMPUTATION OF GAINS AND LOSSES for acquisitions from persons neither resident nor ordinarily resident in the UK after 9 March 1981 and before 6 April 1985; **21** DOUBLE TAX RELIEF for relief which may be claimable and for double tax agreements which may override or amend statutory provisions; **36** HOLD-OVER RELIEFS for clawback of relief where transferee becomes before 19 March 1991 neither resident nor ordinarily resident in the UK; **45.1** MARKET VALUE for special market value rules which apply to disposals by persons neither resident nor ordinarily resident in the UK after 9 March 1981 and before 6 April 1985; **48** OFFSHORE SETTLEMENTS for provisions dealing with settlements whose trustees are, or become, neither resident nor ordinarily resident in the UK; **50.2** PARTNERSHIPS for partnerships controlled and managed abroad; **57** RESIDENCE AND DOMICILE for the determination of a person's residence, ordinary residence and domicile status; **62.6** SETTLEMENTS for the residence status of settlements; and **69.5** UNDERWRITERS AT LLOYD'S for overseas resident underwriters.

Simon's Taxes. See **C1.6, D4.811, D6.520–D6.536.**

Introduction to overseas matters

[49.1] There are special rules which apply where an individual is not domiciled in the UK but resident here, and where a person not resident in the UK trades etc. in the UK through a branch or agency or permanent establishment. See **49.2** and **49.3** below.

Gains on assets acquired by an individual whilst UK resident and disposed of during a period of temporary non-residence are charged in the tax year of his resuming UK residence — see **49.5** below.

Where a person's gains are taxed on the arising basis he may be unable to remit overseas gains to the UK. See **49.6** below for the special relief available in such circumstances.

Persons may also be assessed by reference to chargeable gains accruing to non-UK resident persons with whom they have certain specified relationships. See **49.7** below for circumstances where a UK resident is a participator in a closely-held overseas resident company; and see **48** OFFSHORE SETTLEMENTS where a UK domiciled individual is a beneficiary of an overseas resident settlement and where a UK domiciled settlor has an interest in an overseas resident settlement.

A UK resident company can make an election for profits arising from its foreign permanent establishments, including chargeable gains, to be exempt from corporation tax (and for losses from those permanent establishments to be excluded). See **49.8** below.

Where a UK resident company has an interest in a 'controlled foreign company' and where a UK resident has 'offshore income gains' arising out of certain interests in 'offshore funds', there may be a capital gains tax effect. See **49.9** and **49.10** below.

A special relief is available where a UK resident company transfers the assets of an overseas trading branch or agency to an overseas resident company in exchange for shares in that company. See **49.12** below.

See **49.13** below for the special relief claimable where a UK business is transferred or divided between companies in different EC member states and **49.14** for the claim and double taxation relief available where a non-UK business is transferred or divided between companies in different EC member states. See **49.15** below for relief on European cross-border mergers and **49.16** below for the disapplication of these reliefs where a transparent entity is involved.

There are 'exit charges' and provisions for the recovery of unpaid tax where a company ceases to be UK resident etc., is a dual resident company (before 30 November 1993) or is not resident in the UK. See **49.17** and **49.18** below. See also **48.2** OFFSHORE SETTLEMENTS for the 'exit charge' where trustees of a settlement cease to be UK-resident etc.

For exploration and exploitation rights to the UK territorial sea-bed, see **49.19** below.

For European Economic Interest Groupings, see **49.20** below.

For the collection of tax where an overseas element is involved, see **49.21** below.

Individuals not domiciled in the UK disposing of overseas assets

[49.2] Individuals not domiciled in the UK, but resident here, are liable on gains arising in the UK. Gains from disposals of assets abroad are in certain circumstances subject to the remittance basis. See **55** REMITTANCE BASIS.

Trading in the UK through a permanent establishment or a branch or agency

[49.3] There are separate rules for companies and other persons.

Persons other than companies

Subject to any exceptions in the legislation, a person is chargeable to capital gains tax in respect of chargeable gains accruing to him in a year of assessment if the residence condition at **1.2** INTRODUCTION is not met and the gains are made at a time when he is carrying on a trade, profession or vocation in the UK through a 'branch or agency', and is so chargeable on chargeable gains accruing on the disposal:

(a) of assets situated in the UK and used in or for the purposes of the trade, profession or vocation at or before the time when the gain accrued, or
(b) of assets situated in the UK and used or held for the purposes of the branch or agency at or before that time, or assets acquired for use by or for the purposes of the branch or agency.

The commercial letting of FURNISHED HOLIDAY ACCOMMODATION (**26.2**) in the UK, although treated as a trade for certain capital gains tax provisions, is not so treated for these purposes.

'*Branch or agency*' means, for *TCGA 1992, s 10* and capital gains tax provisions generally, any factorship, agency, receivership, branch or management. For consideration of this definition in relation to a partnership where two of the partners were resident outside the UK at the time of disposal of a partnership asset but the third partner was UK resident at that time, see *White v Carline* (Sp C 33), [1995] SSCD 186. See also *Puddu v Doleman* (Sp C 38), [1995] SSCD 236 (where a non-UK resident sole trader employed a supervisor to manage the UK trading activity) and *Willson v Hooker* Ch D 1995, 67 TC 585 (where a UK resident individual was held to be an agent of a non-UK resident company in relation to the company's purchase and subsequent sale of UK land, being transactions in which the individual was closely involved).

[*TCGA 1992, s 10(1)(2)(5)(6); FA 2013, Sch 46 paras 76, 112*].

Companies

Similar provisions to those above apply to non-resident companies, but with the substitution of the term 'permanent establishment' for 'branch or agency'. [*TCGA 1992, s 10B; FA 2012, Sch 16 para 73*].

For this purpose, and for chargeable gains purposes generally, a company has a '*permanent establishment*' in a territory if:

(i) it has a 'fixed place of business' there through which the business of the company is wholly or partly carried on; or
(ii) an agent (other than one of independent status acting in the ordinary course of his business) acting on behalf of the company has and habitually exercises there authority to do business on behalf of the company,

unless the activities carried on there are only of a 'preparatory or auxiliary character'. A '*fixed place of business*' includes a place of management, a branch, an office, a factory, a workshop, an installation or structure for the exploration of natural resources, a mine, an oil or gas well, a quarry or other place of extraction of natural resources, or a building, construction or installation project. Activities of a '*preparatory or auxiliary character*' include the use of facilities for the purpose of storage, display or delivery of goods or merchandise belonging to the company; the maintenance of a stock of goods or merchandise belonging to the company for the purpose of storage, display, delivery or processing by another person; or purchasing goods or merchandise, or collecting information, for the company. Where 'alternative finance return' within *CTA 2009, ss 511–513* (alternative finance arrangements; see Tolley's Corporation Tax) is paid to a non-UK resident company, the company is not regarded as having a permanent establishment in the UK merely by virtue of anything done for the purposes of the arrangements by the other party or any other person acting for the company. [*TCGA 1992, s 288(1); CTA 2010, ss 1141–1144*].

Deemed disposal on asset leaving UK

Where an asset ceases by virtue of becoming situated outside the UK to be a 'chargeable asset' (as below) in relation to a person, he is deemed to have disposed of the asset immediately before the time when the asset becomes situated outside the UK and immediately to have reacquired it, both such transactions being treated as made at market value. This does not apply where the asset becomes situated outside the UK contemporaneously with the person involved ceasing to carry on a trade, profession or vocation in the UK through a branch or agency or permanent establishment, or where the asset is an '*exploration or exploitation asset*' (i.e. an asset used in connection with 'exploration or exploitation activities' carried on in the UK or a 'designated area' as defined by *TCGA 1992, s 276* in **49.19** below; in this case comparable provisions apply). [*TCGA 1992, s 25(1)(2)(8)*].

Where an asset ceases to be a chargeable asset in relation to a person by virtue of his ceasing to carry on a trade, profession or vocation in the UK through a branch or agency or permanent establishment, he is deemed to have disposed of the asset immediately before the time when he ceased to carry on the trade, profession or vocation in the UK through the branch or agency or permanent establishment and immediately to have reacquired it, both such transactions being treated as made at market value. The deemed disposal and reacquisition does not apply to an asset which is a chargeable asset in relation to the person concerned at any time after he ceases to carry on the trade, profession or vocation in the UK through a branch or agency or permanent establishment and before the end of the chargeable period in which he does so. There is no deemed disposal and reacquisition on a transfer or division within *TCGA 1992, s 140A* of a UK business between companies in different EC member states (see **49.13** below).

There is no deemed disposal and reacquisition of an asset by reason of the transfer of the trade by a company to another company in circumstances such that the assets transferred are transferred at no gain/no loss by virtue of *TCGA 1992, s 139* or *s 171* (see, respectively, **14.11** COMPANIES and **29.3** GROUPS OF COMPANIES).

Unless an election is made (within two years of cessation in the case of a company), no gain or loss accrues on the deemed disposal if the gain or loss would have been an NRCGT gain or loss on the assumption that the disposal was a non-resident CGT disposal (see **41.25** LAND). However, the NRCGT gain or loss that would have accrued on the deemed disposal is treated as accruing at the time of any subsequent disposal of the interest, in addition to any gain or loss which actually accrues.

[*TCGA 1992, ss 25(3)–(6)(8), 25ZA, 140A(4)(b); FA 2015, Sch 7 para 13*].

For the purposes of *TCGA 1992, s 25* above, an asset is at any time a '*chargeable asset*' in relation to a person if, were it to be disposed of at that time, any chargeable gains accruing to him on the disposal either would be chargeable under *TCGA 1992, s 10(1)* or would form part of his chargeable profits for corporation tax purposes by virtue of *TCGA 1992, s 10B*. [*TCGA 1992, s 25(7)*].

Exit charge payment plans

See **51.8** PAYMENT OF TAX for the availability of exit charge payment plans under which a company can defer the payment of tax in respect of a number of exit charge provisions, including the above provisions.

Rollover relief

Rollover relief under *TCGA 1992, s 152* (see **59** ROLLOVER RELIEF) is not available if the old assets are 'chargeable assets' (having the same meaning as in *TCGA 1992, s 25* above) in relation to the person concerned at the time of disposal unless the new assets are chargeable assets in relation to him immediately after the time they are acquired.

References to acquisition of the new assets include references to acquisition of an interest in them or to entering into an unconditional contract for the acquisition of them.

Rollover relief will, however, apply, where the acquisition of the new assets takes place after the disposal of the old assets and immediately after the time of acquisition the person concerned is resident (before 6 April 2013, resident or ordinarily resident) in the UK, unless he is also then a 'dual resident' and the new assets are 'prescribed assets'. A '*dual resident*' is a person who is resident (before 6 April 2013, resident or ordinarily resident) in the UK and falls to be regarded under any DOUBLE TAX RELIEF (**21.2**) arrangements as resident overseas. A '*prescribed asset*', in relation to a dual resident, is one which under any double tax relief arrangements would not give rise to a UK tax charge on him in respect of a gain accruing to him on a disposal of it.

[*TCGA 1992, s 159; FA 2013, Sch 46 paras 98, 112*].

Rollover relief on a non-resident CGT disposal on or after 6 April 2015 (see **41.25** LAND) may only be claimed where the new assets are qualifying residential property interests (i.e. interests in UK land which consist of or include a dwelling) immediately after they are acquired. [*TCGA 1992, s 159A; FA 2015, Sch 7 para 22*].

Double tax agreements

No charge to tax under *TCGA 1992, s 10* or *s 10B* applies to a person who, by virtue of any relevant double tax agreement, is exempt from income tax or corporation tax for the particular period in respect of profits or gains from the permanent establishment or branch or agency. [*TCGA 1992, ss 10(4), 10B(3); TIOPA 2010, Sch 8 para 41*].

Losses

Losses accruing to a person in a year of assessment during no part of which he is resident in the UK are not allowable unless, under *TCGA 1992, s 10* or *TCGA 1992, s 10B* above, he would be chargeable in respect of a chargeable gain if there had been a gain instead of a loss on that occasion. [*TCGA 1992, s 16(3)*].

See **57.29** RESIDENCE AND DOMICILE for the exclusion of extra-statutory concession D2 in respect of the period from the cessation of UK residence to the end of the year of assessment.

UK representatives of non-residents

[49.4] Certain obligations and liabilities fall upon UK representatives of non-residents carrying on a trade in the UK through a branch or agency. Provided detailed conditions are satisfied, certain persons, e.g. casual agents, brokers, investment managers and persons acting in relation to alternative finance arrangements, are not treated as UK representatives for these purposes. Subject to this, a branch or agency in the UK through which a non-resident carries on (solely or in partnership) a trade, profession or vocation is his UK representative in relation to capital gains arising in connection with the branch or agency and chargeable under *TCGA 1992, s 10*. Where the non-resident ceases to carry on the trade etc. through the branch or agency, it continues to be his UK representative for tax purposes in relation to amounts arising during the period of the agency.

For corporation tax purposes a UK permanent establishment through which a non-resident company carries on a trade is its UK representative in relation to chargeable gains within *TCGA 1992, s 10B* arising in connection with the permanent establishment. Where the company ceases to carry on the trade through the permanent establishment, it continues to be the UK representative for tax purposes in relation to amounts arising during the period of trading. Subject to detailed conditions, certain brokers, investment managers and Lloyd's agents in relation to certain transactions are not regarded as UK representatives of non-resident companies.

A UK representative is regarded as a legal entity distinct from the non-resident.

As regards the taxation of any amounts in relation to which a non-UK resident has a UK representative, legislation making provision for, or in connection with, the assessment, collection and recovery of income tax, corporation tax and capital gains tax, and interest on tax, has effect as if the obligations and liabilities of the non-resident were *also* obligations and liabilities of the UK representative. Obligations and liabilities attaching to the non-resident because of a notice or document are not, however, obligations or liabilities of the UK representative unless the notice or document was also served on the representative. A UK representative is not treated as committing any criminal offence committed by the non-resident unless the representative actually committed the offence or consented to or connived in its commission.

[*TCGA 1992, ss 271A–271J; ITA 2007, ss 835C–835Y; CTA 2010, ss 969–972, 1145–1153*].

For the full provisions, see Tolley's Income Tax under Non-Residents and Tolley's Corporation Tax under Residence.

Individuals temporarily non-resident in the UK

[49.5] The following provisions apply to tax chargeable gains made by an individual during a period of temporary non-UK residence when UK residence resumes. The provisions were rewritten by *FA 2013* to make them consistent with the statutory residence test (see **57.3** RESIDENCE AND DOMICILE) and income tax rules for temporary non-residence. The rewritten provisions apply where the 'year of departure' is 2013/14 or a later year. [*FA 2013, Sch 45 para 153(3)*]. For convenience the rewritten and previous provisions are described separately below.

Year of departure 2013/14 or subsequent year

An individual who is 'temporarily non-resident' is chargeable to capital gains tax as if the following gains or losses were chargeable gains or losses accruing in the 'period of return'. The gains or losses are:

(a) gains or losses accruing to the individual during the 'temporary period of non-residence';
(b) chargeable gains that would be treated as accruing to the individual, or losses that would be allowable to the individual, under *TCGA 1992, s 13* (gains of non-resident companies attributed to members — see **49.7** below) in that period if the 'residence assumption' were made; and

(c) chargeable gains that would be treated under *TCGA 1992, s 86* (attribution of gains to settlors with an interest in non-resident or dual-resident settlements — see **48.5** OFFSHORE SETTLEMENTS) as accruing to the individual in a tax year wholly within the temporary period of non-residence if he had been UK-resident for that year.

Gains which are otherwise chargeable are excluded provided that a claim could not be made for exemption under any arrangements for DOUBLE TAX RELIEF (**21**). Losses which are otherwise allowable are similarly excluded. See below for other exclusions.

The 'residence assumption' is that the individual had been resident in the UK for the tax year in which the gain or loss accrued to the company or, if that year was a split year under the statutory residence test (see **57.18** RESIDENCE AND DOMICILE), that the gain or loss accrued to the company in the UK part of it.

Where (b) above applies, losses are calculated as follows. For each tax year wholly or partly in the temporary period of non-residence the amount of 'sum A' that does not exceed 'sum B' is calculated. The resulting amounts are then added together to arrive at the losses to be included. '*Sum A*' is the aggregate of the losses accruing to the non-resident company in the year which, under **49.7** below, would have been allowable to the individual if the residence assumption had been made. '*Sum B*' is the amount of the gains of the company (or another non-resident company) that would have been attributed to the individual if the residence assumption had been made.

Where (c) above applies, see **48.13** OFFSHORE SETTLEMENTS for details of the limitation on the amount to be brought into charge where beneficiaries of the settlement have been charged in respect of capital payments from the settlement.

If *ITA 2007, ss 809B, 809D* or *809E* (remittance basis for 2008/09 onwards — see **55.2**(a)–(c) REMITTANCE BASIS) apply for the year of return (i.e. the tax year which includes the period of return), any foreign chargeable gains (see **55.2** REMITTANCE BASIS) remitted to the UK in the temporary period of non-residence are treated as so remitted in the period of return. If the temporary period of non-residence began before 8 July 2015, the deemed domicile rules (see **57.34** RESIDENCE AND DOMICILE) do not apply in the year of return for these purposes i.e. the remittance basis claim may be made in the year of return of an individual who is not domiciled in the UK under general law even if the individual would otherwise be treated as deemed domiciled in the UK under *ITA 2007, s 835BA*. In such a case, where a claim is made in any tax year of return from 2017/18 to 2020/21 inclusive, the individual does not pay the remittance basis charge and does not lose the personal allowance or annual exempt amount in that tax year.

Where these provisions apply, any assessment to capital gains tax may be made for the year of departure at any time before the second anniversary of 31 January following the year of return.

Nothing in any DOUBLE TAX RELIEF (**21**) arrangements is to be read as preventing the taxpayer from being chargeable to capital gains tax under the above provisions.

[*TCGA 1992, ss 10A, 10AA(4)(5); FA 2013, Sch 45 para 119; F(No 2)A 2017, Sch 8 para 16*].

Temporary non-UK residence

An individual is regarded as '*temporarily non-resident in the UK*' if:

(i) he has 'sole UK residence' for a 'residence period' ('period A');
(ii) immediately following period A, one or more residence periods occur for which the individual does not have sole UK residence;
(iii) at least four of the seven tax years immediately preceding the 'year of departure' were either:
  – a tax year for which the individual had sole UK residence; or
  – a split year (see **57.18** RESIDENCE AND DOMICILE) that included a residence period for which the individual had sole UK residence; and
(iv) the '*temporary period of non-UK residence*', i.e. the period between the end of period A and the start of the next residence period for which the individual has sole UK residence, is five years or less.

A '*residence period*' is normally a tax year. However, when a tax year is a split year, the UK part and overseas parts of the split year are separate residence periods.

An individual has '*sole UK residence*' for a residence period consisting of an entire tax year if he is resident in the UK for that year and is not '*treaty non-resident*' at any time in that year. An individual has '*sole UK residence*' for a residence period consisting of the UK part of a split year if he is not treaty non-resident at any time in that part of the year.

An individual is '*treaty non-resident*' at any time if at the time he falls to be regarded under a double tax treaty as resident in a country outside the UK.

In (iii) above, the '*year of departure*' is the tax year that consists of or includes period A. The '*period of return*' is the first residence period after period A for which the individual again has sole UK residence.

Transitional rule

Although the definition of 'temporarily non-resident in the UK' applies where the year of departure is 2013/14 or a subsequent year, it may be necessary to consider the taxpayer's residence status in earlier years for the purposes of the test in (iii) above. In relation to such a tax year, the test at (iii) above is that at least four of the seven tax years immediately preceding the year of departure were tax years meeting the following conditions:

- the individual was resident in the UK for the year; and
- there was no time in the year when the individual was treaty non-resident.

Whether an individual was resident in the UK for a tax year before 2013/14 is to be determined in accordance with the rules in force before the statutory residence test was introduced.

[*FA 2013, Sch 45 paras 109–115, 156*].

Exclusions from the charge

The gains or losses treated as accruing in the period of return do not include a gain or loss on the disposal of an asset if it was acquired by the taxpayer in the temporary period of non-residence, provided that:

(A) the asset was not acquired by means of a 'relevant disposal' (see below) which is treated as having been a disposal on which neither a gain nor a loss accrued, by virtue of *TCGA 1992, s 58* (transfer between husband and wife — see **46.5** MARRIED PERSONS AND CIVIL PARTNERS), *TCGA 1992, s 73* (reversion of settled property to settlor on death of person entitled to interest in possession — see **62.18** SETTLEMENTS) or *TCGA 1992, s 258(4)* (gifts of national heritage property — see **25.85** EXEMPTIONS AND RELIEFS);

(B) that asset is not an interest created by or arising under a settlement; and

(C) the acquisition cost of the asset to the taxpayer does not fall, by reference to any 'relevant disposal' (see below), to be treated as reduced under any of the following provisions:
   - *TCGA 1992, s 23(4)(b)* or *(5)(b)* (rollover where the replacement asset is acquired after receipt of compensation or insurance money — see **10.4** CAPITAL SUMS DERIVED FROM ASSETS);
   - *TCGA 1992, s 152(1)(b)* (rollover relief (**59**) on business assets);
   - (in relation to relevant disposals made on or after 16 March 2005) *TCGA 1992, s 153(1)(b)* (rollover relief (**59**) on business assets where assets only partly replaced);
   - *TCGA 1992, s 162(3)(b)* (hold-over relief where shares are acquired on the disposal of a business to a company — see **37.2** INCORPORATION AND DISINCORPORATION RELIEFS);
   - *TCGA 1992, s 247(2)(b)* or *(3)(b)* (rollover relief where replacement land is acquired on the compulsory acquisition of other land — see **41.12** LAND).

For the purposes of (A) and (C) above, a '*relevant disposal*' is a disposal of an asset acquired by the person making the disposal at a time when that person was resident in the UK and was not treaty non-resident.

Note that this exclusion applies only to gains or losses arising on the disposal of assets and not to attributed gains under *TCGA 1992, ss 86, 87* (see **48.5**, **48.14** OFFSHORE SETTLEMENTS) or *TCGA 1992, s 13* (see **49.7** below).

Where a chargeable gain has accrued on the disposal of an asset which is not within (A)–(C) above, but the gain falls to be postponed by virtue of one of the following CGT deferral provisions and treated as accruing on the disposal of the whole or part of another asset which is within (A)–(C) above, the above exclusion from the charge does not apply. The said provisions are:

- *TCGA 1992, s 116(10)* or *(11)* (deferral of gain arising on a company reconstruction where the new asset is a qualifying corporate bond (see **54.4**));
- *TCGA 1992, s 134* (deferral of gain arising where gilts are acquired as compensation for compulsory acquisition of shares and securities (see **63.8**));

- *TCGA 1992, s 154(2)* or *(4)* (deferral of gain on a business asset where a depreciating asset is acquired as replacement — see **59.9** ROLLOVER RELIEF).

[*TCGA 1992, s 10AA(1)–(3); FA 2013, Sch 45 para 119*].

Year of departure before 2013/14

Conditions

The provisions apply where an individual leaves the UK before 6 April 2013 for a period of temporary residence outside the UK, and:

- four out of the seven years of assessment immediately preceding the 'year of departure' were years for which the individual satisfied 'the residence requirements', and
- there are fewer than five years of assessment (the '*intervening years*') falling between (and not including) the 'year of departure' and the 'year of return'.

For the purposes of these provisions, the '*year of departure*' means the last year of assessment before the year of return for which the taxpayer satisfied the 'residence requirements'. The '*year of return*' is any year of assessment for which the individual satisfies the 'residence requirements' and which immediately follows one or more years of assessment for which he did not satisfy those requirements.

An individual satisfies the '*residence requirements*' for a tax year if during any part of the year he is resident in the UK and not 'treaty non-resident' or if during the year he is ordinarily resident in the UK and not treaty non-resident. This definition applies where the year of departure is, or (on the assumption that the definition as amended had always had effect) would be, 2005/06 or a subsequent year and also applies where the year of departure is (or on the same assumption would be) 2004/05 if at a time in that year on or after 16 March 2005 the individual was resident or ordinarily resident in the UK and not treaty non-resident.

Previously, an individual satisfied the '*residence requirements*' for a tax year if that year was one during any part of which he was resident in the UK or during which he was ordinarily resident in the UK.

For the meaning of 'resident' and 'ordinarily resident' see **57** RESIDENCE AND DOMICILE. In determining whether an individual is resident in the UK for 2013/14 or a subsequent year, the statutory residence test (see **57.3** RESIDENCE AND DOMICILE) applies. An individual is '*treaty non-resident*' at any time if he falls at that time to be regarded for the purposes of DOUBLE TAX RELIEF (**21**) arrangements as resident in a territory outside the UK.

The charge

Where the above conditions apply, and subject to the exclusions below, the individual is chargeable to capital gains tax as if all the chargeable gains and losses which accrued to him in the intervening years were gains or losses accruing to him in the year of return. Any gains or losses accruing in the year of departure (whether accruing before or after the date of departure), and any gains or losses accruing in the year of return (whether accruing before or after the date of return) are chargeable to capital gains tax in the year of departure or return under general principles (*TCGA 1992, s 2(1)* — see **49.1** above). The treatment otherwise available under ESC D2 (whereby, subject to certain conditions, an individual is charged to capital gains tax in respect of gains accruing in a year in which his residence status changes only to the extent that the gains accrued from disposals made before his departure or, as the case may be, after his return) does not apply where the above conditions are satisfied. See **57.29** RESIDENCE AND DOMICILE.

The chargeable gains to be treated as accruing in the year of return include any chargeable gains which would have been treated as having accrued to him in any intervening year, if he had been resident in the UK throughout that year, under:

(i) *TCGA 1992, s 13* (gains of non-resident companies attributed to members — see **49.7** below); or
(ii) *TCGA 1992, s 86* (attribution of gains to settlors with an interest in non-resident or dual-resident settlements — see **48.5** OFFSHORE SETTLEMENTS).

Where (i) above applies, any losses accruing to the non-resident company in an intervening year which, under **49.7** below, would have been allowable to the individual if he had been UK-resident throughout that year are treated as accruing in the year of return but only to the extent that such losses do not exceed the amount of the gains of the company (or another non-resident company) attributed to the individual for that same year and similarly treated.

Where (ii) above applies, see **48.13** OFFSHORE SETTLEMENTS for details of the limitation on the amount to be brought into charge where beneficiaries of the settlement have been charged in respect of capital payments from the settlement.

Where a tax year is an intervening year only because the taxpayer is at some time in that year treaty non-resident, gains attributed to him under *TCGA 1992, ss 87 or 89(2)* (attribution of gains to beneficiaries of OFFSHORE SETTLEMENTS (**48.14–48.20**)) for that year are not chargeable in the year of return under these provisions. The year is treated as not being an intervening year for the purpose of attributing gains under (i) and (ii) above.

Where these provisions apply, any assessment to capital gains tax may be made for the year of departure at any time before the second anniversary of 31 January following the year of return.

Nothing in any DOUBLE TAX RELIEF (**21**) arrangements is to be read as preventing the taxpayer from being chargeable to capital gains tax under the above provisions in respect of gains other than those attributed under (i) and (ii) above.

If *ITA 2007, ss 809B, 809D* or *809E* (remittance basis for 2008/09 onwards — see **55.2**(a)–(c) REMITTANCE BASIS) apply for the year of return and the taxpayer is not domiciled in the UK in that year, any foreign chargeable gains (see **55.2** REMITTANCE BASIS) remitted to the UK in an intervening year are treated as so remitted in the year of return. (Note that this does not apply where *ITA 2008, s 809B* is deemed to apply to a year before 2008/09 for the purpose of the transitional provision in *FA 2008, Sch 7 para 84* — see **55.2** REMITTANCE BASIS.) If the year of departure is before 2013/14 and the year of return is 2017/18, the deemed domicile rules (see **57.34** RESIDENCE AND DOMICILE) do not apply in the year of return for the purpose of these rules i.e. the remittance basis claim may be made in the year of return (2017/18) of an individual who is not domiciled in the UK under general law even if the individual would otherwise be treated as deemed domiciled in the UK under *ITA 2007, s 835BA*. In such a case, the individual does not pay the remittance basis charge and does not lose the personal allowance and annual exempt amount, in 2017/18.

Exclusions from the charge

The gains or losses treated as accruing in the year of return do not include a gain or loss on the disposal of an asset in the intervening years if it was acquired by the taxpayer at a time either in the year of departure or in an intervening year when he was neither resident nor ordinarily resident in the UK or, where the amended definition of the residence requirements above applies, when he was resident or ordinarily resident in the UK but was treaty non-resident, provided that:

(a) the asset was not acquired by means of a 'relevant disposal' (see below) which is treated as having been a disposal on which neither a gain nor a loss accrued, by virtue of *TCGA 1992, s 58* (transfer between husband and wife — see **46.5** MARRIED PERSONS AND CIVIL PARTNERS), *TCGA 1992, s 73* (reversion of settled property to settlor on death of person entitled to interest in possession — see **62.18** SETTLEMENTS) or *TCGA 1992, s 258(4)* (gifts of national heritage property — see **25.85** EXEMPTIONS AND RELIEFS);
(b) that asset is not an interest created by or arising under a settlement; and
(c) the acquisition cost of the asset to the taxpayer does not fall, by reference to any 'relevant disposal' (see below), to be treated as reduced under any of the following provisions:
  - *TCGA 1992, s 23(4)(b)* or *(5)(b)* (rollover where the replacement asset is acquired after receipt of compensation or insurance money — see **10.4** CAPITAL SUMS DERIVED FROM ASSETS);
  - *TCGA 1992, s 152(1)(b)* (ROLLOVER RELIEF (**59**) on business assets);
  - (in relation to relevant disposals made on or after 16 March 2005) *TCGA 1992, s 153(1)(b)* (ROLLOVER RELIEF (**59**) on business assets where assets only partly replaced);
  - *TCGA 1992, s 162(3)(b)* (hold-over relief where shares are acquired on the disposal of a business to a company — see **37.2** INCORPORATION AND DISINCORPORATION RELIEFS);
  - *TCGA 1992, s 247(2)(b)* or *(3)(b)* (rollover relief where replacement land is acquired on the compulsory acquisition of other land — see **41.12** LAND).

For the purposes of (a) and (c) above, a '*relevant disposal*' is a disposal of an asset acquired by the person making the disposal at a time when that person was resident or ordinarily resident in the UK and was not treaty non-resident.

Where the acquisition by the person making the disposal was before 16 March 2005, the requirement was simply that the acquisition had to be made at a time when that person was resident or ordinarily resident in the UK.

Note that this exclusion does not apply to assets acquired within a non-resident trust to which the provisions of *TCGA 1992, ss 86, 87* (see **48.5**, **48.14** OFFSHORE SETTLEMENTS) apply or a non-resident company to which *TCGA 1992, s 13* (see **49.7** below) applies.

Where a chargeable gain has accrued on the disposal of an asset which is not within (a)–(c) above, but the gain falls to be postponed by virtue of one of the following CGT deferral provisions and treated as accruing on the disposal of the whole or part of another asset which *is* within (a)–(c) above, the above exclusion from the charge does not apply. The said provisions are:

- *TCGA 1992, s 116(10)* or *(11)* (deferral of gain arising on a company reconstruction where the new asset is a QUALIFYING CORPORATE BOND (see **54.4**));
- *TCGA 1992, s 134* (deferral of gain arising where gilts are acquired as compensation for compulsory acquisition of SHARES AND SECURITIES (see **63.8**));
- *TCGA 1992, s 154(2)* or *(4)* (deferral of gain on a business asset where a depreciating asset is acquired as replacement — see **59.9** ROLLOVER RELIEF).

Also excluded from the charge is any chargeable gain or allowable loss accruing to the taxpayer in an intervening year which is brought into account for that year under *TCGA 1992, ss 10, 16(3)* (non-residents carrying on a trade etc. in the UK through a branch or agency — see **49.3** above) or *TCGA 1992, s 14D* (non-resident CGT on disposals of UK residential property interests — see **41.25** LAND).

[*TCGA 1992, ss 10A, 288(7B); FA 2013, Sch 45 para 157; FA 2015, Sch 7 para 9; F(No 2)A 2017, Sch 8 para 15*].

Relief for unremittable overseas gains

[49.6] Where chargeable gains accrue from assets situated abroad and the taxpayer is unable with reasonable endeavour to transfer those gains to the UK due to the laws of the territory where the assets were situated at the time of disposal, or to the executive action of its government, or to the impossibility of obtaining foreign currency in that territory, he may claim under *TCGA 1992, s 279(1)* that they be left out of account.

Claims made on or after 1 April 2010 must be made no later than four years after the end of the tax year or accounting period in which the gains arose. Previously a claim for the purposes of capital gains tax had to be made no later than the fifth anniversary of 31 January following the year of assessment in which the gains arose; or in the case of corporation tax no more than six years after the end of the accounting period in which the gains arose. For capital gains tax purposes (but not for corporation tax purposes), the change in time limits for making claims applies by reference to claims made before, or on or after, 1 April 2012 where the claim concerned relates to a tax year for which the taxpayer has not been given notice to make a return under *TMA 1970, s 8* or *s 8A* (see **58.3** RETURNS) or *s 12AA* (see **58.16** RETURNS) within one year of the end of the tax year (in effect, where the taxpayer is outside self-assessment). This rule does not, however, apply if for that year any gains which ought to have been assessed have not been assessed, or an assessment has become insufficient, or any relief given has become excessive.

Where a claim is made, the gains are then treated as gains of the year, if any, in which the conditions cease to apply. The claim is open to personal representatives.

[*TCGA 1992, s 279(1)–(3)(5)(6)(8); SI 2009 No 403*].

These provisions cannot be relied upon as a defence against an assessment under *TCGA 1992, s 13* (see **49.7** below) if the taxpayer's inability to transfer the gain to the UK is owing to the company's failure to distribute the gain. Relief can only be given if the gain is represented by money, or money's worth, in the hands of the taxpayer (*Van Arkadie v Plunket*, Ch D 1982, 56 TC 310).

See **42.8** LATE PAYMENT INTEREST AND PENALTIES for an alternative relief given to interest on tax overdue, where collection of tax is deferred in similar circumstances.

Gains which are subject to payments made by the Export Credits Guarantee Department under statutory arrangements for export guarantees do not qualify for the relief above to the extent of such payments. [*TCGA 1992, s 279(4)*].

UK resident participator in overseas resident company

[49.7] The following provisions apply where chargeable gains accrue after 27 November 1995 to a company which is not resident in the UK but which would be a close company (within *CTA 2010, ss 439–454* — see Tolley's Corporation Tax under Close Companies) if it were so resident. The ECJ has held that the provisions contravene EU law — see *European Commission v United Kingdom* ECJ (C-112/14), [2015] STC 591.

Subject to the following, every person who at the time when the gain accrues to the company is resident in the UK and who is a participator (within *CTA 2010, s 454*) in the company, is treated for the purposes of capital gains tax (or corporation tax on chargeable gains) as if part of the chargeable gain had accrued to him. See below for the application of the remittance basis for non-domiciled individual participators.

Where the participator is an individual, the above provision does not apply if the tax year in which the gain accrues to the company is a split year under the statutory residence test for 2013/14 onwards (see **57.18** RESIDENCE AND DOMICILE) and the gain accrues in the overseas part of the year.

The amount of the gain accruing to the non-resident company is computed (where it is not the case) as if the company were within the charge to UK corporation tax on chargeable gains.

The part that is taken as accruing to the participator is equal to the proportion of the gain that corresponds to the extent of the participator's interest as a participator in the company. However, there is **no charge** on the participator where the aggregate amount otherwise falling to be apportioned to him and to persons connected (see **17** CONNECTED PERSONS) with him does not exceed **one-quarter** of the gain.

References to a person's interest as a participator in a company are references to the interest in the company which is represented by all the factors by reference to which he falls to be treated as such a participator. References to the extent of such an interest are references to the proportion of the interests as participators of all the participators in the company (including any who are not resident in the UK) which on a just and reasonable apportionment is represented by that interest.

Exclusions

These provisions do *not* apply in relation to:

- a gain accruing on the disposal of an asset used only for the purposes of a trade carried on by the company wholly outside the UK;
- a gain accruing on the disposal of an asset used only for the purposes of the part carried on outside the UK of a trade carried on by the company partly within and partly outside the UK;
- a gain on which the company is chargeable to UK tax by virtue of *TCGA 1992, s 10B* (trade carried on via UK permanent establishment — see **49.3** above); or
- a gain accruing on the disposal of an asset only used for the purposes of economically significant activities carried on by the company wholly or mainly outside the UK;
- a gain accruing on the disposal of an asset where it is shown that neither the disposal of an asset by the company, nor the acquisition or holding of the asset by the company, formed part of a scheme or arrangements where the main purpose or one of the main purposes was the avoidance of a capital gains tax charge;
- a gain accruing before 6 April 2012 on the disposal of foreign currency or of a debt within *TCGA 1992, s 252(1)* (see **25.5** EXEMPTIONS AND RELIEFS) which in either case is or represents money used for the purposes of a trade carried on by the company wholly outside the UK;
- an ATED-related gain on a high value disposal of a dwelling (see **14.10** COMPANIES);
- a gain on a non-resident disposal of a UK residential property interest (see **41.25** LAND); or
- carried interest gains (see **50.20** PARTNERSHIPS).

Relief where company makes a distribution

Where any amount of tax (i.e. capital gains tax or corporation tax on chargeable gains) is paid by a participator as a result of the charge above and an amount in respect of the gain charged is distributed (either by way of dividend or distribution of capital or on the dissolution of the company) within a specified period, that amount of tax (so far as neither reimbursed by the company nor applied as a deduction under the further provisions below) is applied for reducing or extinguishing any liability of his to income tax, capital gains tax or corporation tax in respect of the distribution. The specified period is whichever of the following ends earlier:

- the period ending three years after the end of the period of account of the non-resident company in which the gain accrued; or
- the period of four years beginning with the date the gain accrued.

Deduction for tax paid

Any tax paid by the participator resulting from the above treatment (so far as neither reimbursed by the company nor applied as above for reducing any liability to tax) is treated as allowable expenditure in the computation of the gain arising on his disposal of any asset representing his interest as a participator in the company (e.g. shares in the company by reference to which he is a participator). (This applies also to tax paid under *TCGA 1992, s 13* as it applied to gains accruing before 28 November 1995.)

In ascertaining for the purposes above the amount of capital gains tax or income tax chargeable on a participator for any year on or in respect of any chargeable gain or distribution, any distribution as is mentioned above which falls to be treated as his income for that year is regarded as forming the highest part of the income on which he is chargeable to tax for the year.

Losses

Any loss arising on the disposal of assets by a non-resident company which would be a close company if it were UK resident can be similarly treated as accruing to the participator concerned, but only insofar as it reduces or extinguishes gains apportioned to him under these provisions and treated as accruing in the same year of assessment. Losses can be set off against gains of the same company or different companies (HMRC Capital Gains Manual CG57295).

Non-resident company participator

If a person who is a participator in the company at the time when the chargeable gain accrues to the company is itself a company which is not resident in the UK but which would be a close company if it were resident in the UK, an amount equal to the amount which would otherwise have been apportioned as above out of the chargeable gain to the participating company's interest as a participator in the company to which the gain accrues is further apportioned among the participators in the participating company according to the extent of their respective interests as participators, and an amount is apportioned to them as above accordingly in relation to the amounts further apportioned, and so on through any number of companies.

Trustees and pension schemes

The persons treated by these provisions as if a part of a chargeable gain accruing to a company had accrued to them expressly include the trustees of a settlement who are participators in the company, or in any company amongst the participators in which the gain is apportioned as above, if when the gain accrues to the company the trustees are not resident in the UK. See further in **48** OFFSHORE SETTLEMENTS. For anti-avoidance provisions concerning the attribution of gains under these provisions to trustees of a UK-resident trust, see **62.23** SETTLEMENTS. An interest held by trustees (other than bare trustees) is treated as the beneficial interest in determining if and how the gain of the non-resident company should be attributed to participators; the interests of the beneficiaries are disregarded.

A gain accruing to a non-resident company is not attributed under these provisions to a pension scheme or superannuation fund which is exempt from capital gains tax on disposals of assets forming part of the scheme etc. (see **25.60** EXEMPTIONS AND RELIEFS) if it would otherwise be attributed only if such exempt assets were taken into account in determining the extent of the scheme's interest as a participator.

Payment of tax by company

If any tax payable by a participator as a result of a gain accruing to a non-resident company is paid by that company, or in a case where there are other intervening non-UK resident companies as above is paid by any such other company, the amount so paid is left out of account in relation to that person for income tax, capital gains tax and corporation tax purposes.

[*TCGA 1992, ss 13, 288(1); FA 2012, s 35(2)(6); FA 2013, Sch 45 paras 96, 153(2), Sch 46 paras 77, 112; FA 2015, Sch 7 para 10; SI 2009 No 56, Sch 1 para 178; F(No 2)A 2017, s 32(2)(5)*].

Double tax relief

The appropriate proportion of any overseas tax in respect of its gain which the company pays in its country of residence is deductible, by way of double tax relief, against UK capital gains tax payable by the participator. To the extent that the overseas tax cannot be relieved in this way, the deduction may be made in arriving at the amount of the gain chargeable on the participator. (HMRC Statement of Practice D23). HMRC has confirmed that where the overseas resident company is a subsidiary of a UK resident parent company and the relevant double taxation agreement has an article exempting residents of the overseas territory from a charge to UK capital gains tax, then such an article may prevent the imposition of a charge under the above provisions (CCAB Statement TR 500 March 1983).

Temporary non-residents

An individual who is 'temporarily' non-UK resident, such as to be within the charge to tax under *TCGA 1992, s 10A* on his return to the UK, is chargeable for the tax year of return on gains that would have been attributed to him under the above provisions had he remained UK-resident. See **49.5** above.

General

For the purposes of the above, the provisions at **29.3**, **29.4**, **29.7** GROUPS OF COMPANIES and *TCGA 1992, s 175(1)* at **59.10** ROLLOVER RELIEF apply, with appropriate modifications, in relation to non-UK resident companies which are members of a non-UK resident group of companies as they apply in relation to members of a CGT group as in **29.2** GROUPS OF COMPANIES. [*TCGA 1992, s 14*]. The provisions mentioned in *section 14* are so applied not only where the UK-resident participator or shareholder on whom gains fall to be assessed is subject to corporation tax on chargeable gains but also where he is within the charge to capital gains tax (Revenue Tax Bulletin May 1993 p 74).

The relief for unremittable overseas gains (see **49.6** above) is not a defence to an assessment under the above provisions. See also **49.9** below for a UK resident company having an interest in a 'controlled foreign company'.

Note that, because of the loan relationship rules, a gain arising to a company on disposal of a debt represented by a balance in a non-sterling bank account cannot be a chargeable gain so that the above provisions cannot apply to such a disposal (HMRC Notice 10 December 2009).

Non-UK domiciled individual participators

Gains accruing before 6 April 2008 cannot be attributed under the above provisions to individual participators who are not domiciled in the UK. Gains accruing on or after that date are attributed to such participators. Such a gain is a 'foreign chargeable gain' within *TCGA 1992, s 12* (and hence eligible to be taxed on the REMITTANCE BASIS (**55.2**)) only if the asset disposed of is situated outside the UK.

Where the remittance basis in fact applies to a gain attributed to an individual under the above provisions, in determining whether the gain is remitted to the UK, the consideration obtained by the company for the asset disposed of is treated as deriving from the attributed gain. Where the consideration was not at least equal to the market value of the asset (or, before 22 April 2009, was not equal to the market value), the asset itself is also treated as deriving from the gain.

Where the remittance basis applies to an attributed gain, when that gain is remitted to the UK so that a chargeable gain accrues, that chargeable gain cannot be reduced or extinguished by a loss accruing to the company and attributed to the individual under the above provisions.

[*TCGA 1992, s 14A*].

Exemption for profits of foreign permanent establishments of UK resident company

[49.8] UK-resident companies are normally chargeable to corporation tax on gains arising worldwide, with double tax relief usually available for any foreign tax paid. See **14.2** COMPANIES and **21** DOUBLE TAX RELIEF. Such a company can, however, make an election for profits arising from its foreign permanent establishments, including chargeable gains, to be exempt from corporation tax (and for losses from those permanent establishments to be excluded). Profits and losses are not left out of account if they are (for disposals of land on or after 5 July 2016), profits or losses of a company's trade of dealing in or developing UK land (within *CTA 2009, s 5B*) or would be such profits or losses if the company were non-UK resident. An election will apply to all accounting periods of the company beginning on or after the 'relevant day'. For this purpose, the 'relevant day' is the day on which, at the time of the election, the next or (for elections made on or after 1 January 2013) the first accounting period is expected to begin. If, in the event, an accounting period begins before and ends on or after the relevant day, then for corporation tax purposes that period is treated as two accounting periods, the first ending immediately before the relevant day and the second starting on that day. Profits and losses are to be apportioned to the two periods on a just and reasonable basis. An election can only be revoked by the company which made it before the relevant day, but it is revoked automatically where the company ceases to be UK resident on or after 1 January 2013. Otherwise the election is irrevocable.

With effect from 1 January 2013, an election can also be made by a non-UK resident company which expects to become UK resident. In such cases, the relevant day is the day on which the company becomes UK resident.

For each accounting period to which an election applies appropriate adjustments are made in calculating the company's total taxable profits to secure that profits and losses making up the 'foreign permanent establishments amount' are left out of account.

The '*foreign permanent establishments amount*' is the aggregate of the 'profits amount' for each territory outside the UK in which the company carries on, or has carried on, business through a permanent establishment, less the aggregate of the 'losses amount' for each such territory.

The calculation of the profits amount and losses amount differs depending on whether or not there is a double tax treaty between the territory and the UK which includes a provision (a '*non-discrimination provision*') that a permanent establishment of an enterprise of a contracting state is not to be taxed less favourably in the other state than an enterprise of that other state carrying on the same activities. Where there is such a treaty, the '*profits amount*' is the profits which would be taken to be attributable to the permanent establishment in ascertaining the amount of any credit relief for foreign tax (see **21.2**, **21.6** DOUBLE TAX RELIEF). The '*losses amount*' is calculated on the same basis. If an amount of credit relief does not depend on the profits taken to be attributable to the permanent establishment because, under the treaty, the foreign tax is not charged by reference to such profits, then only profits which would be taken to be attributable to the permanent establishment if the foreign tax were charged by reference to such profits are included in the profits amount (and only such losses are included in the losses amount).

Where there is no such treaty, the profits amount and losses amount are the amounts which would be taken to be so attributable to the permanent establishment if there were such a treaty and it was in the terms of the OECD model tax convention.

If a treaty does not include provisions for a credit to be allowed against tax computed by reference to the same profits as those by reference to which the tax was computed in the foreign territory concerned, it is assumed, for the above purposes, to do so.

Special rules apply to the calculation of the adjustments to the company's total taxable profits in relation to chargeable gains and gains taken into account in computing income, capital allowances, income from immovable property, profits and losses from investment business, payments subject to deduction of tax and certain employee share acquisitions. See below for the chargeable gains rules and see Tolley's Corporation Tax for the remaining rules.

[*CTA 2009, ss 18A, 18F, 18R, 18S; FA 2012, Sch 20 paras 3, 5, 55; FA 2016, ss 76(7), 81(1)*].

If, at any time in an accounting period to which an election applies, the company is a 'small company' then there is no profits amount or losses amount for that period for any permanent establishment in a territory which does not have a double tax treaty with a non-discrimination provision. A '*small company*' is a micro or small enterprise within the Annex to Commission Recommendation 2003/361/EC.

If the company is a close company (within *CTA 2010, s 439*) at any time during such an accounting period, so much of the company's profits which are derived from chargeable gains are not profits amounts or losses amounts. For accounting periods beginning on or after 1 January 2013 this exclusion does not apply to gains on the disposal of assets used only for the purposes of a trade carried on through the permanent establishment concerned or to gains on the disposal of foreign currency or a debt within *TCGA 1992, s 252(1)* (see **25.5** EXEMPTIONS AND RELIEFS) where the currency or debt is or represents money in use for the purposes of such a trade.

[*CTA 2009, ss 18P, 18S; FA 2012, Sch 20 paras 7, 55*].

Chargeable gains etc

The adjustments to be made under the above provisions include adjustments to remove the effect of any gains or losses relating to the disposal of assets taken into account in computing the foreign permanent establishments amount, so that, in appropriate cases, a gain may be increased to reflect a loss so taken into account or a loss increased to reflect a gain.

The profits to be taken into account in computing the 'profits amount' for a permanent establishment above include any gains in respect of immoveable property which has been used for the purposes of he business carried on through the permanent establishment, to an extent which is appropriate having regard to the extent which it has been so used. This also applies to the 'losses amount' and losses in respect of such property. Gains and losses which would be taken to be attributable to the permanent establishment for the purposes of ascertaining credit relief in respect of foreign tax payable before the election takes effect are excluded from the profits and losses amounts.

[*CTA 2009, s 18B*].

Where a company to which an election applies makes a no gain/no loss disposal (see **9.6** ASSETS HELD ON 31 MARCH **1982** but also including a disposal within *TCGA 1992, s 152* (ROLLOVER RELIEF (**59**)), the amount of the deemed consideration which results in that no gain/no loss, is to be arrived at after taking account of any adjustments under these provisions (so that the consideration includes the amount which would be the foreign permanent establishments amount attributable to the disposal for the accounting period in which it was made if the disposal were not a no gain/no loss disposal). [*TCGA 1992, s 276A*].

Pre-entry losses

Where losses have arisen in any of the company's foreign permanent establishments in the six-year period ending at the end of the accounting period in which the election is made and those losses have not been eliminated by profits from those establishments before the end of that period then the company will have an 'opening negative amount' and no adjustments can be made to the company's total taxable profits until that amount has been eliminated.

The '*opening negative amount*' is ascertained by calculating the foreign permanent establishments amount (excluding chargeable gains and allowable losses) for each accounting period ending less than six years before the end of the accounting period in which the election is made and for that accounting period. The earliest negative amount is carried forward to the next period where it is either increased by another negative amount or reduced or eliminated by a positive amount, but not so as to cause the result to be positive. This process continues through each accounting period and if there is a negative amount remaining after applying it to the last period, that amount is the opening negative amount. The period for which this process must be carried out is extended if there is a losses amount of more than £50 million in an accounting period beginning within the six-year period ending on 18 July 2011, if that period would not otherwise fall within the normal six-year period. Where the period is extended in this way, the process must be carried out for the period of the losses amount and each subsequent accounting period up to and including that in which the election is made.

In each subsequent accounting period (starting with the first to which the election applies) the total opening negative amount is then reduced by the aggregate of any profits amounts for the period. In the first accounting period in which that aggregate exceeds the remaining opening negative amount, adjustments can be made to the company's total taxable profits under the above provisions of an amount equal to the excess and the company can specify which profits are to be adjusted in its tax return for that period.

Alternatively, the company can elect for the opening negative amount to be streamed. If such an election is made then, in effect, the above provisions are applied separately to losses in a particular territory so that they do not delay the application of the exemption to other permanent establishments which would otherwise have no, or a shorter, transitional period. The election must be made at the same time as the exemption election and can only be revoked before the first accounting period to which the exemption election applies. It must specify the territories which are to be streamed. Where not all of the negative opening amount is streamed in this way, the residual amount must be eliminated against the residual profits amounts (i.e. for each accounting period, the total profits amount less the streamed profits amounts) in the same way.

Where a business carried on through a foreign permanent establishment is transferred to a connected company and the business has a 'transferred total opening negative amount', adjustments are made to ensure, broadly, that the above provisions apply to the same extent as they would have been had the business been carried on by the transferee throughout. Where the transferee makes an exemption election which takes effect after the transfer day and the accounting period of the transfer is to be taken into account in calculating its opening negative amount (as above), the transferred total opening negative amount is added to the foreign permanent establishments amount for that period, but only to the extent that it is attributable to the period by reference to which the opening negative amount is calculated. If the effect of this rule would be to exclude a losses amount of more than £50 million arising in an accounting period beginning within the six-year period ending on 18 July 2011 which would otherwise be taken into account as above, that amount is added to the foreign permanent establishments amount of the transferee for the accounting period of the transfer. If the transferee's exemption election took effect before the transfer, the transferred total opening negative amount is treated as the transferee's opening negative amount (in addition to any such actual amount). A separate streaming election can be made in respect of the transferred amount, which does not have to be made at the same time as the exemption election. The transferred total opening negative amount is disregarded in applying the above provisions to the transferor after the day on which the transfer takes place.

If the transferor has not made an election for exemption before the transfer day, the '*transferred total opening negative amount*' is the amount that would have been that company's opening negative amount if it had carried on no business other than the transferred business, there had been no transfer and the company had made an election which took effect from the day after the transfer day. If the transferor made an election which took effect before the transfer day, the transferred opening negative amount is the remaining part of the transferor's opening negative amount insofar as it is attributable to the transferred business.

[*CTA 2009, ss 18J–18O; FA 2011, Sch 13 paras 34, 35*].

Anti-diversion

Anti-avoidance provisions apply to prevent a company using the exemption to divert profits to a low tax territory. The provisions apply by excluding the diverted profits from the profits amount for the affected territory, but this does not apply to chargeable gains and allowable losses. See *CTA 2009, ss 18G–18ID* and Tolley's Corporation Tax for full details.

UK resident company having an interest in a controlled foreign company

[49.9] Legislation relating to controlled foreign companies ('CFC's') is contained in *TIOPA 2010, ss 371AA–371VJ* (added by *FA 2012, Sch 20*) and applies, broadly, for accounting periods beginning on or after 1 January 2013. There are no specific provisions relating to chargeable gains. However, the previous CFC regime, contained in *ICTA 1988, ss 747–756, Schs 24–26* (as amended) did include two such provisions. Those provisions are described below, together with a brief description of the regime generally. For full coverage of the CFC provisions see Tolley's Corporation Tax under Controlled Foreign Companies.

Under the pre-*FA 2012* regime, a '*CFC*' is a company which is:

(i) resident outside the UK for the purposes of the provisions;
(ii) 'controlled' by persons resident in the UK; and
(iii) subject to a 'lower level of taxation' in the territory in which it is 'resident'.

Where the provisions apply, a UK resident company which has an 'interest' in the CFC at any time in the accounting period is then liable to a sum as if it were corporation tax. Such sum is computed by multiplying the part of the 'chargeable profits' arising in an accounting period of the CFC that is proportionate to the interest held by the UK resident company and the 'appropriate rate' of UK corporation tax. *FA 2007* introduced provisions enabling a company to apply to HMRC for the chargeable profits of a CFC to be treated as reduced for this purpose to a specified amount (including nil) where the CFC has a business establishment in an 'EEA territory' (as defined) and undertakes genuine economic activities there.

The foregoing is subject to further detailed rules and exemptions. See Tolley's Corporation Tax for these and the definitions assigned to the terms given above. Rules specifically relating to corporation tax on chargeable gains are given below.

(a) **Gains on disposal of shares.** Relief may be claimed where:
  (i) an apportionment falls to be made in respect of a CFC's accounting period under the pre-*FA 2012* regime;
  (ii) a UK resident company (the '*claimant company*') disposes of shares, acquired before the end of that accounting period, in either the CFC or another company whose shares give rise to the claimant company's interest in the CFC; and
  (iii) chargeable profits of the CFC are apportioned to the claimant company, and a sum is accordingly chargeable on it as if it were corporation tax.

  Where a claim is made, in the computation of the chargeable gain accruing on the disposal in (ii) above, a deduction is allowed of the sum chargeable as in (iii) above, reduced to the proportion thereof that the average market value, in the period for which the apportionment falls to be made, of the interest in the CFC in respect of which the charge as in (iii) above arose bears to the average market value in that period of the shares disposed of. A sum chargeable as at (iii) above may only be relieved once in this way.

  Relief may, however, be restricted where, before the disposal, a dividend is paid by the CFC out of profits from which the chargeable profits in (iii) above derived. If either:
  (1) the effect of the payment of the dividend is to reduce the value of the shares disposed of as in (ii) above; or

(2) the claimant company obtains relief (see (b) below) in respect of a dividend paid on the shares disposed of as in (ii) above, by reference to sums including that referred to in (iii) above,

then relief is denied in respect of so much of the sum chargeable as corresponds to the part of the chargeable profits in (iii) above corresponding to the profits which the dividend represents.

Claims for relief must be made within three months of the later of the end of the accounting period in which the disposal occurs and the date the assessment in (iii) above becomes final and conclusive. Such claims are outside the main provisions governing claims under corporation tax self-assessment (included in returns or otherwise).

Identification of shares disposed of for this purpose is with those acquired earlier before those acquired later.

[*ICTA 1988, Sch 26 para 3; TIOPA 2010, Sch 8 para 35; FA 2012, Sch 20 para 14*].

(b) **Dividends from the CFC.** The total of assessments on UK resident companies under the provisions in respect of a CFC's chargeable profits (the '*gross attributed tax*') is treated as underlying tax for double taxation relief purposes (see Tolley's Corporation Tax under Double Taxation Relief) where a dividend is paid by the CFC wholly or partly out of profits from which those chargeable profits derive. The gross attributed tax is *not,* however, treated as increasing the amount of the dividend income in determining liability on that income.

If *TIOPA 2010, ss 36, 40, 41* or *42* act to limit the foreign tax credit by reference to the UK tax on the dividends concerned, the amount so debarred from relief, insofar as it does not exceed the foreign tax *other than* underlying tax attributable to the dividend, is set against the gross attributed tax chargeable on UK resident companies. On a claim by any of those companies, the tax so chargeable on it is reduced and, if appropriate, repaid.

Any condition for double tax relief under *TIOPA 2010, s 2(1)* (by agreement with other countries) or *s 8* (unilateral relief) (see **21** DOUBLE TAX RELIEF) requiring a particular degree of control of the company paying the dividend is treated as satisfied for these purposes.

Where the CFC dividend is paid out of unspecified profits, and any part of its chargeable profits is apportioned other than to UK resident companies, the gross attributed tax is attributed to the proportion of the chargeable profits apportioned to UK resident companies (the '*taxed profits*'). So much of the dividend as is received by, or by a 'successor in title' of, any such company is regarded as paid primarily out of the taxed profits. '*Successor in title*' for this purpose refers to a successor in respect of the whole or part of the interest in the CFC giving rise to a charge under these provisions.

If:

(i) relief has been allowed for the purposes of corporation tax on chargeable gains, on a disposal of shares, in respect of a sum chargeable under these provisions (see (a) above); and

(ii) that sum forms part of the gross attributed tax in relation to a dividend, as above; and

(iii) a person receiving the dividend in respect of the shares referred to in (i) above (the '*primary dividend*'), or any other dividend in respect of shares in a company resident outside the UK representing profits consisting directly or indirectly of or including the primary dividend, is entitled to relief by way of underlying tax (as above) by reference to the whole or part of the gross attributed tax,

then the relief available as in (iii) above is reduced or extinguished by deducting therefrom the amount allowed by way of relief as in (i) above.

[*ICTA 1988, Sch 26 paras 4–6; TIOPA 2010, Sch 8 para 35; FA 2012, Sch 20 para 14*].

Simon's Taxes. See **D4.377, D4.378.**

Offshore funds

[49.10] Since 1984, gains arising on disposals of certain investments in offshore funds have been chargeable to income tax rather than capital gains tax. Broadly, this applies to investments that accumulate income rather than distribute it. Without special rules the accumulated income would be reflected in the value on disposal and would be converted into a chargeable gain.

For full coverage, see Tolley's Income Tax and Tolley's Corporation Tax. To the extent that it relates to tax on chargeable gains, the new regime is described at **49.11** below.

Current regime

[49.11] The tax treatment of participants in a fund depends on whether or not the fund is a 'reporting fund'.

Meaning of offshore fund

For the purposes of the new tax regime, an '*offshore fund*' is one of the following:

(a) a 'mutual fund' constituted by a body corporate (other than a limited liability partnership) resident outside the UK;
(b) a mutual fund under which property is held on trust for the participants, where the trustees are not UK-resident; or
(c) a mutual fund constituted by other arrangements taking effect under the law of a territory outside the UK and creating co-ownership rights.

Note that *TCGA 1992, s 103A* below does not apply to funds within (a) above. Funds constituted by two or more persons carrying on a business in partnership are excluded from (c) above.

Broadly, '*mutual fund*' means arrangements whose purpose or effect is to enable the participants to participate in, or to receive profits or income from, the acquisition, holding, management or disposal of property without having day-to-day control of it. It is an additional condition that, under the terms of the fund, a reasonable investor would expect to be able to realise all or part of his investment on a basis calculated either by reference to the net asset value of the property or by reference to an index.

[*TIOPA 2010, ss 355–359*].

Tax treatment of funds

For chargeable gains purposes, an offshore fund which is neither constituted by a company nor by two or more persons carrying on a trade or business in partnership, nor a unit trust scheme is treated as if it were a company, and the rights of the participants were shares in the company. [*TCGA 1992, s 103A; SI 2011 No 1211, Regs 1, 44(2); SI 2013 No 1400, Reg 10*].

A fund which is treated as a company under the above provisions is treated as not resident (and, before 6 April 2013, not ordinarily resident) in the UK (if it would not otherwise be so) if it is an undertaking for collective investment in transferable securities authorised under Article 5 of EU Directive 2009/65/EC. [*TIOPA 2010, s 363A; FA 2013, Sch 46 para 146*].

Participants in non-reporting funds

Any fund that is not a reporting fund (for which see below) is a '*non-reporting fund*'. [*SI 2009 No 3001, Reg 4*]. A charge to income tax or corporation tax on income normally arises if a person disposes of an interest (i.e. an investment) in a non-reporting fund and an offshore income gain (as defined) arises on the disposal. [*SI 2009 No 3001, Regs 17, 18*]. The above charge to income tax may also arise if the interest disposed of is an interest in a reporting fund which has been a non-reporting fund at some time since the interest was acquired.

A single disposal may give rise to both an offshore income gain chargeable to tax as income and a chargeable gain. To avoid a double charge, the following apply in such circumstances in place of *TCGA 1992, s 37(1)* (deduction of consideration chargeable to tax on income).

(i) The amount of the offshore income gain is deducted from the sum which would otherwise constitute the amount or value of the consideration in the calculation of the capital gain. The offshore gain is not, however, to be deducted in calculating the figure 'A' in the A/(A + B) fraction under the rules relating to part disposal (see **16.5** COMPUTATION OF GAINS AND LOSSES).

(ii) Where the disposal forms part of a transfer within *TCGA 1992, s 162* (see **37.2** INCORPORATION AND DISINCORPORATION RELIEFS) the offshore income gain is taken into account to reduce 'B' in the A/B fraction determined under those provisions.

(iii) Where, by virtue of *TCGA 1992, s 103G* or *103H* (collective investment schemes; see **70.2** UNIT TRUSTS ETC.) or *s 135* or *136* (reorganisation of shares or securities etc. (see **63.5** and **63.7** SHARES AND SECURITIES respectively)), the transaction does not constitute a disposal for capital gains purposes, but does constitute a disposal for the purposes of the offshore fund provisions, the amount of any offshore income gain to which the disposal gives rise is treated as consideration for the 'new holding' (within *TCGA 1992, s 128* — see **63.2** SHARES AND SECURITIES).

(iv) Where, by virtue of *TCGA 1992, s 127* (see **63.2** SHARES AND SECURITIES) an exchange of interests of different classes in an offshore fund does not constitute a disposal for capital gains purposes, but does constitute a disposal of an interest in an offshore fund, the amount of any offshore income gain to which the disposal gives rise is treated as consideration for the new holding.

[*SI 2009 No 3001, Regs 44–47; SI 2013 No 1400, Reg 15*].

Interests in non-reporting funds are designated 'relevant securities' and amended identification rules apply. See **64.6** SHARES AND SECURITIES — IDENTIFICATION RULES.

Participants in reporting funds

A '*reporting fund*' is an offshore fund that has applied for and been approved by HMRC as a reporting fund. An existing offshore fund may apply to HMRC for reporting fund status, as may a fund that has yet to be established. [*SI 2009 No 3001, Regs 51, 55*]. A reporting fund must comply with various duties as to the preparation of accounts, the computation of its reportable income, the provision of information to HMRC and in particular, the provision of reports to participants. [*SI 2009 No 3001, Regs 57–93, 106, 107*]. Such reports must be made within six months of each 'reporting period' (as defined) and must include details of the amount distributed to participants per unit of interest in the fund in respect of the reporting period and of any excess of the reportable income per unit for the reporting period over the amount distributed. [*SI 2009 No 3001, Regs 90–93*]. Participants within the charge to income tax are then taxed on actual distributions from the fund plus their share of any such excess. For corporation tax purposes, the participant's share of the excess is exempt to the same extent as any actual distibutions. [*SI 2009 No 3001, Regs 94–98*].

A disposal by a participant of his interest in a reporting fund is a disposal of an asset for chargeable gains purposes. An amount equal to the 'accumulated undistributed income' is treated for chargeable gains purposes as part of the acquisition cost of the asset within *TCGA 1992, s 38(1)(a)* (see **16.11** COMPUTATION OF GAINS AND LOSSES). For this purpose, the '*accumulated undistributed income*' is the aggregate of the amounts in respect of undistributed income on which the participant has been charged to tax under the above provisions. The deemed expenditure is normally treated as incurred on the fund distribution date for the reporting period concerned (i.e. the date on which the fund report is issued or, if the report is not issued within six months after the reporting period, the last day of the reporting period). Where, however, the participant receives an amount in respect of his interest in the fund after the disposal and that amount is chargeable to income tax, that amount is treated as received immediately before the disposal. Where the amount of any distributions to the participant has been treated as reduced under *SI 2009 No 3001, Reg 94A* (equalisation amounts not treated as distributions) the acquisition cost is treated as reduced by the amount of the reduction. [*SI 2009 No 3001, Regs 94(4), 99; SI 2011 No 1211, Reg 13*].

Fund becoming or ceasing to be a non-reporting fund

If an offshore fund ceases to be a reporting fund and becomes a non-reporting fund, a participant may make an election to be treated for chargeable gains purposes:

- as disposing of an interest in the reporting fund at the end of that fund's final period of account; and
- as acquiring an interest in the non-reporting fund at the beginning of that fund's first period of account.

The deemed disposal and acquisition are treated as made for a consideration equal to the net asset value of the participant's interest in the fund at the end of the period of account for which the final reported income is reported to him. The election must be made by being included in a tax return for the tax year or accounting period which includes the final day of the reporting fund's final period of account, but cannot be made if a report has not been made available to the participant for that period. The normal purpose of an election would be to crystallise the gain accrued to date as a chargeable gain; any subsequent gain on actual disposal would be an offshore income gain chargeable to income tax.

[*SI 2009 No 3001, Reg 100*].

A similar election can be made by a participant in a non-reporting fund which becomes a reporting fund in order to crystallise the gain accrued to date as an offshore income gain, leaving any subsequent gain on actual disposal to be taxed within the chargeable gains regime: see *SI 2009 No 3001, Reg 48*.

Transparent funds

TCGA 1992, s 99B (accumulation units — see **70.3** UNIT TRUSTS AND OTHER INVESTMENT VEHICLES) applies for the purposes of computing the gain on a disposal by a participant of an interest in an offshore fund which is a 'transparent fund' but not a unit trust as if the fund were a unit trust, the participant were a unit holder and the interest in the fund were units in a unit trust (but not an authorised unit trust). For this purpose, a fund is a '*transparent fund*' if:

(1) in the case of investors who are UK resident individuals, any sums forming part of the fund's income are of such a nature that they are chargeable to tax under a provision listed in *ITTOIA 2005, s 830(2)* (relevant foreign income); or

(2) (1) above would apply if not for the fact that the income is derived from assets within the UK.

[*TCGA 1992, s 103B; SI 2009 No 3001, Reg 11; SI 2011 No 1211, Regs 1, 44(3)*].

Constant NAV funds

A '*constant NAV fund*' is an offshore fund whose net asset value (expressed in the currency in which units are issued) does not fluctuate by more than an insignificant amount throughout the fund's existence, as a result of the nature of the fund's assets, and the frequency with which it distributes its income. The reporting fund rules above are modified for such funds. If the value of such a fund's assets (expressed in the currency in which units are issued) does increase by more than an insignificant amount and the fund has not notified HMRC that it has ceased to be a constant NAV fund, a participant who subsequently disposes of his interest in the fund and who makes a chargeable gain on the disposal is treated as making an offshore income gain (chargeable to tax on income). [*SI 2009 No 3001, Regs 119–124*].

UK resident company transferring assets to overseas resident company

[49.12] The following deferral relief applies where a UK resident company carrying on a trade (which includes vocations, offices and employments) outside the UK through a permanent establishment transfers the whole or part of that trade together with its assets, or its assets other than cash, to a company not resident in the UK in exchange, wholly or partly, for shares (or shares and loan stock) in that company, so that thereafter it holds one quarter or more of the transferee company's ordinary share capital.

If the chargeable gains on the transfer exceed the allowable losses, a proportion of the resulting net chargeable gains relating to the shares (in the proportion that the market value of the shares at the time of the transfer bears to the market value of the whole consideration received) may be claimed by the transferor company as being deferred and not treated as arising until the happening of one of the following events.

(i) The transferor company disposes of all or any of the shares received. The 'appropriate proportion' of the deferred gain (insofar as not already charged under this specific provision or under (ii) below) is then treated as a chargeable gain arising at that time. This gain is in addition to any gain or loss actually arising on the disposal of the shares. The '*appropriate proportion*' is the proportion which the market value of the shares disposed of bears to the market value of the shares held immediately before the disposal. However, for corporation tax purposes, no addition to the consideration is made under this provision if its application would be directly attributable to the disposal of an asset before 1 April 1982.

(ii) The transferee company disposes, within six years of the transfer, of the whole or part of the assets on which chargeable gains were deferred. The gain chargeable (insofar as it has not already been charged under this provision, or under (i) above) is the proportion which the deferred gain on the assets disposed of bears to the total deferred gain on assets held immediately before the disposal.

The following disposals are disregarded.

- For the purposes of (i) above, intra-group transfers within *TCGA 1992, s 171* (see **29.3** GROUPS OF COMPANIES). A charge will arise when a subsequent group company makes a disposal outside the group.

- For the purposes of (i) above, securities transferred by a transferor as part of the process of a merger to which *TCGA 1992, s 140E* applies (see **49.15** below). In relation to a subsequent disposal of the shares or disposal by the transferee company of assets within (ii) above, the transferee is treated as if it were the transferor company.
- For the purposes of (i) above, securities transferred by a transferor company as part of the process of the transfer of a business to which **49.13** or **49.14** below applies. In relation to a subsequent disposal of the securities or disposal by the transferee company of assets within (ii) above, the transferee is treated as if it were the transferor company.
- For the purposes of (ii) above, intra-group transfers which would be within *TCGA 1992, s 171* if for those purposes a group included (without qualification) non-UK resident companies. A charge will arise when a subsequent group company makes a disposal outside the group.

A claim under *TCGA 1992, s 140C* (transfer or division of non-UK business between different EC member states; see **49.14** below) precludes a claim under the above.

[*TCGA 1992, s 140, Sch 4 paras A1, 4(5); SI 2007 No 3186, Sch 1 para 7, Sch 2 para 5*].

For interaction between (i) above and the exemptions relating to SUBSTANTIAL SHAREHOLDINGS OF COMPANIES, see **66.21**.

Transfers, divisions and mergers within the European Union

Transfer or division of UK business between companies in different EC member states

[49.13] The following reliefs apply to transfers or divisions of UK businesses between companies resident in different member states.

Transfer of UK business

A special relief may be claimed where a company resident in one EC member state transfers the whole or part of a business carried on by it in the UK to a company resident in another member state wholly in exchange for shares or debentures in the latter company, provided that the further conditions below are satisfied.

For transfers before 1 January 2007, the relief could only be claimed in respect of a transfer of a trade, and both the transferor and transferee had to be a body incorporated under the law of a member state.

A company is regarded as resident in a member state under the laws of which it is chargeable to tax because it is regarded as so resident (unless it is regarded under DOUBLE TAX RELIEF (**21.2**) arrangements entered into by the member state as resident in a territory not within any of the member states).

Division of UK business

The relief may also be claimed where a company resident in one EC member state transfers, on or after 1 January 2007, part of its business to one or more companies at least one of which is resident in another member state. The part of the transferor's business which is transferred must be carried on by the transferor in the UK and the transferor must continue to carry on a business after the transfer.

The transfer must be made in exchange for the issue of shares in or debentures of each transferee to the holders of shares in or debentures of the transferor, except where, and to the extent that, a transferee is prevented from meeting this requirement by reason only of *Companies Act 2006, s 658* (rule against limited company acquiring its own shares) or a corresponding provision in another member state.

The further conditions below must also be satisfied.

Further conditions

A claim for relief must be made by both the transferor and the transferee (or each of the transferees). The anti-avoidance provision below must not apply, and either:

- (i) if the transferee company is, or each of the transferee companies are, non-UK resident immediately after the transfer, any chargeable gain accruing to it, or them, on a disposal of the assets included in the transfer would form part of its, or their, corporation tax profits under *TCGA 1992, s 10(3)* or *s 10B*; or
- (ii) if it is, or they are, UK resident at that time, none of the assets included in the transfer is exempt from UK tax on disposal under double tax relief arrangements.

Effect of relief

Any assets included in the transfer are treated for the purposes of corporation tax on chargeable gains as transferred for a no gain/no loss consideration, and *TCGA 1992, s 25(3)* (deemed disposal by non-resident on ceasing to trade in the UK through a permanent establishment or a branch or agency, see **49.3** above) does not apply to the assets by reason of the transfer.

In the case of a division of a UK business, where the transfer is not made wholly in exchange for the issue of shares in or debentures of each transferee, neither *TCGA 1992, s 24* (deemed disposal where asset lost, destroyed or becoming of negligible value — see **16.4** COMPUTATION OF GAINS AND LOSSES and **44.11** LOSSES) nor *TCGA 1992, s 122* (capital distributions — see **63.11** SHARES AND SECURITIES) apply to the transfer.

Also in the case of a division of a UK business, where the transferor and transferee (or each of the transferees) are all resident in EU member states, but are not all resident in the same state, the transfer of assets is treated as if it were a scheme of reconstruction within *TCGA 1992, s 136* (see **63.7** SHARES AND SECURITIES) if it would not otherwise be so treated. Where *s 136* applies as a result of this provision, the anti-avoidance provision at *s 136(6)* does not apply (and neither does *s 137* (restrictions on company reconstructions — see **4.15** ANTI-AVOIDANCE)).

Anti-avoidance

The above provisions do not apply unless the transfer is effected for *bona fide* commercial reasons and not as part of a scheme or arrangement a main purpose of which is avoidance of income, corporation or capital gains taxes. Advance clearance may be obtained from HMRC on the application of the companies, to the same address and subject to the same conditions and appeal procedures as apply to clearances under *TCGA 1992, s 138* (see **4.15** ANTI-AVOIDANCE).

[*TCGA 1992, ss 140A, 140B, 140DA, 140L(2); FA 2007, s 110; SI 2007 No 3186, Sch 1 paras 2, 3, 6, Sch 3 para 1; SI 2011 No 1431*].

The above provisions were introduced to comply with *EEC Directive No 90/434/EEC*. The changes applying on or after 1 January 2007 were made to comply with *Directive No 2005/19/EC*.

See also **59.9** ROLLOVER RELIEF.

Transfer or division of non-UK business between companies in different EC member states

[49.14] The following reliefs apply to the transfer or division of a non-UK business between companies in different member states.

Transfer of non-UK business

Special provisions apply, on a claim, where a company resident in the UK transfers to a company resident in another member state the whole or part of a business carried on by the UK company immediately before the transfer through a permanent establishment in a member state other than the UK. The transfer must be wholly or partly in exchange for shares or debentures in the non-UK transferee company and the further conditions below must be satisfied.

For transfers before 1 January 2007, the provisions only applied in respect of a transfer of a trade, and both the transferor and transferee had to be a body incorporated under the law of a member state.

A company is not regarded as resident in the UK if it were regarded under any DOUBLE TAX RELIEF (**21.2**) arrangements to which the UK is a party as resident in a territory not within any of the member states. A company is regarded as resident in another member state under the laws of which it is chargeable to tax because it is regarded as so resident (unless it is regarded under a double tax relief arrangement entered into by the member state as resident in a territory not within any of the member states).

Division of non-UK business

The provisions may also apply where a company resident in the UK transfers, on or after 1 January 2007, part of its business to one or more companies at least one of which is resident in another member state other than the UK. The part of the transferor's business which is transferred must be carried on by the transferor immediately before the transfer in a member state other than the UK through a permanent establishment and the transferor must continue to carry on a business after the transfer.

The transfer must be made in exchange for the issue of shares in or debentures of each transferee to the holders of shares in or debentures of the transferor, except where, and to the extent that, a transferee is prevented from meeting this requirement by reason only of *Companies Act 2006, s 658* (rule against limited company acquiring its own shares) or a corresponding provision in another member state.

The further conditions below must also be satisfied.

Further conditions

The transfer must include all the UK company's assets used in the business or part (with the possible exception of cash) and the anti-avoidance provision below must be satisfied. The aggregate of the chargeable gains accruing to the UK company on the transfer must exceed the aggregate of the allowable losses so accruing.

The UK company must make a claim for the provisions to apply. No claim may, however, be made where a claim is made under *TCGA 1992, s 140* at **49.12** above in relation to the same transfer.

Effect of provisions

The transfer is treated as giving rise to a single chargeable gain of the excess of the aggregate of the chargeable gains accruing to the UK company on the transfer over the aggregate of the allowable losses so accruing.

In the case of a division of a non-UK business, where the transferor and transferee (or each of the transferees) are all resident in EU member states, but are not all resident in the same state, the transfer of assets is treated as if it were a scheme of reconstruction within *TCGA 1992, s 136* (see **63.7** SHARES AND SECURITIES) if it would not otherwise be so treated. Where *s 136* applies as a result of this provision, the anti-avoidance provision at *s 136(6)* does not apply (and neither does *s 137* (restrictions on company reconstructions — see **4.15** ANTI-AVOIDANCE)).

Anti-avoidance

The transfer must be effected for *bona fide* commercial reasons and not as part of a scheme or arrangement a main purpose of which is avoidance of income, corporation or capital gains taxes. Advance clearance may be obtained from HMRC on the application of the UK company, to the same address and subject to the same conditions and appeal procedures as apply to clearances under *TCGA 1992, s 138* (see **4.15** ANTI-AVOIDANCE).

[*TCGA 1992, ss 140C, 140D, 140DA, 140L; FA 2007, s 110; FA 2012, Sch 16 para 75; SI 2007 No 3186, Sch 1 paras 4–6; Sch 3 para 1; SI 2011 No 1431*].

The above provisions were introduced to comply with *EEC Directive No 90/434/EEC* (the 'Mergers Directive'). The changes applying on or after 1 January 2007 were made to comply with *Directive No 2005/19/EC*. See now the revised Mergers Directive *No 2009/133/EC*.

Double tax relief

Where the above provisions apply, where gains accruing to the UK company would have been chargeable to tax under the law of the member state in which the trade was carried on immediately before the transfer but for the Mergers Directive, the amount of tax is treated for double tax relief purposes as tax paid in that other member state. In calculating the amount of the tax so treated it is assumed that, so far as permitted under the law of the member state, any losses arising on the transfer are set against the gains, and that the UK company claims any available reliefs.

These provisions apply also where *TCGA 1992, s 140F* (European cross-border merger: assets not left within UK tax charge — see **49.15** below) applies.

[*TIOPA 2010, s 122; ICTA 1988, s 815A*].

European cross-border mergers

[49.15] The following provisions were originally introduced to facilitate the tax-neutral formation of SEs (see **14.15** COMPANIES) by merger, but have since been extended to apply also to the formation of SCEs (see **14.16** COMPANIES) by merger and other mergers of companies resident in different EU member states. Accordingly, the provisions apply to:

(a) the formation of an SE by the merger of two or more companies in accordance with *Council Regulation (EC) No 2157/2001, Arts 2(1), 17(2)*;
(b) the formation of an SCE on or after 18 August 2006 by the merger of two or more 'co-operative societies', at least one of which is a registered society within *Co-operative and Community Benefit Societies Act 2014* or NI equivalent (previously, a society registered under *Industrial and Provident Societies Act 1965*), in accordance with *Council Regulation (EC) No 1435/2003*;
(c) a merger on or after 1 January 2007 effected by the transfer by one or more companies or co-operative societies of all their assets and liabilities to a single existing company or co-operative society; and
(d) a merger on or after 1 January 2007 effected by the transfer by two or more companies of all their assets to a single new company (which is not an SE or SCE) in exchange for the issue by the transferee company of shares or debentures to each person holding shares in or debentures of a transferee company.

For the purposes of (b) and (c) above, a '*co-operative society*' is a registered society within *Co-operative and Community Benefit Societies Act 2014* or NI equivalent (previously, a society registered under the *Industrial and Provident Societies Act 1965*) or a similar society established under the law of a member state other than the UK.

Each of the merging companies or co-operative societies must be resident in a member state but they must not all be resident in the same state. A company resident in a member state for this purpose if it is within a charge to tax under the law of the State as being resident for that purpose and it is not regarded, for the purposes of any DOUBLE TAX RELIEF (**21**) arrangements to which the state is a party, as resident in a territory not within a member state.

Treatment of securities issued on merger

If it does not constitute or form part of a scheme of reconstruction within the meaning of *TCGA 1992, s 136* (see **63.7** SHARES AND SECURITIES), the merger is nevertheless treated as if it were a scheme of reconstruction for the purposes of that section, but the anti-avoidance provision at *section 136(6)* does not apply (and neither does *s 137* (restrictions on company reconstructions — see **4.15** ANTI-AVOIDANCE)). See, however, the anti-avoidance provision below.

Assets left within UK tax charge

If:

(i) *TCGA 1992, s 139* (reconstruction involving transfer of business — see **14.11** COMPANIES) does not apply to the merger;
(ii) where the merger is within (b) or (c) above, or is within (a) above and takes place on or after 18 August 2006, the transfer of assets and liabilities is made in exchange for the issue of shares in or debentures of the transferee to the holders of shares in or debentures of a transferor, except where, and to the extent that, the transferee is prevented from meeting this requirement by reason only of *Companies Act 2006, s 658* (rule against limited company acquiring its own shares) or a corresponding provision in another member state; and
(iii) where the merger is within (d) above, in the course of the merger each transferor ceases to exist without being in liquidation (within the meaning of *Insolvency Act 1986, s 247*),

then any 'qualifying transferred assets' are treated for chargeable gains purposes as acquired by the transferee (i.e. the SE, SCE or merged company) for a consideration resulting in neither gain nor loss for the transferor company or co-operative society.

For this purpose, an asset transferred to the transferee as part of the merger process is a '*qualifying transferred asset*' if:

- either the transferor was resident in the UK at the time of the transfer or any gain accruing on disposal of the asset immediately before that time would have been a chargeable gain forming part of the transferor's chargeable profits by virtue of *TCGA 1992, s 10B* (trade carried on via UK permanent establishment — see **49.3** above); and
- either the transferee is resident in the UK at the time of the transfer or any gain accruing to it on disposal of the asset immediately after the transfer would have been a chargeable gain forming part of its chargeable profits by virtue of *TCGA 1992, s 10B*.

Where the condition at (ii) above applies, but the transfer is not made wholly in exchange for the issue of shares in or debentures of each transferee, neither *TCGA 1992, s 24* (deemed disposal where asset lost, destroyed or becoming of negligible value — see **16.4** COMPUTATION OF GAINS AND LOSSES and **44.11** LOSSES) nor *TCGA 1992, s 122* (capital distributions — see **63.11** SHARES AND SECURITIES) apply to the transfer.

Assets not left within UK tax charge

If:

- in the course of the merger a company or co-operative society resident in the UK (company A) transfers to a company or co-operative society resident in another member state all the assets and liabilities relating to a business carried on by company A in a member state other than the UK through a permanent establishment;
- the aggregate chargeable gains accruing to company A on the transfer exceed the aggregate allowable losses;
- where the merger is within (b) or (c) above, or is within (a) above and takes place on or after 18 August 2006, the transfer of assets and liabilities is made in exchange for the issue of shares in or debentures of the transferee to the holders of shares in or debentures of a transferor, except where, and to the extent that, the transferee is prevented from meeting this requirement by reason only of *Companies Act 2006, s 658* or *Companies Act 1985, s 143* (rule against limited company acquiring its own shares) or a corresponding provision in another member state; and
- where the merger is within (c) or (d) above, in the course of the merger each transferor ceases to exist without being in liquidation (within *Insolvency Act 1986, s 247*),

the allowable losses are treated as set off against the chargeable gains and the transfer is treated as giving rise to a single chargeable gain equal to the excess. See **49.14** above for special double tax relief provisions applying where this provision applies.

Anti-avoidance

The above provisions do not apply if the merger is not effected for *bona fide* commercial reasons or if it forms part of a scheme or arrangements of which the main purpose, or one of the main purposes, is avoiding liability to UK tax. The advance clearance provisions of *TCGA 1992, s 138* (see **4.15** ANTI-AVOIDANCE) apply, with any necessary modifications, for this purpose as they apply for the purposes of *TCGA 1992, s 137*.

Subsidiary merging with parent

Where a merger is effected by the transfer by a company or all its assets and liabilities to a single company which holds the whole of its ordinary share capital and *TCGA 1992, s 139* does not apply, then, if, in the course of the merger, the transferor ceases to exist without being in liquidation, neither *TCGA 1992, s 24* nor *TCGA 1992, s 122* apply to the transfer. Note that this provision, so far as it applies to mergers relating to the formation of an SE, applies only to such mergers taking place on or after 18 August 2006.

[*TCGA 1992, ss 140E–140GA, 140L; FA 2007, s 110; Co-operative and Community Benefit Societies Act 2014, Sch 4 paras 47–49; FA 2014, Sch 39 paras 3–5; SI 2007 No 3186, Sch 2 para 2, Sch 3 para 1; SI 2008 No 1579, Sch 1 paras 3, 4; SI 2011 No 1431*].

Held-over gains

For the effect of a cross-border merger on various hold-over reliefs, see **49.12** above, **54.4** QUALIFYING CORPORATE BONDS and **59.9** ROLLOVER RELIEF.

Transparent entities — disapplication of reliefs

[49.16] The following provisions operate to disapply certain of the tax reliefs enacted to comply with the European Mergers Directive (see now EC Directive No *2009/133/EC*; previously *EEC Directive No 90/434/EEC*) where one of the parties to the transaction is a 'transparent entity'. In some cases, the disapplication of the reliefs is accompanied by a notional tax credit for the shareholder or interest holder in the transparent entity. The provisions apply in relation to mergers relating to the formation of an SE (see **14.15** COMPANIES) or SCE (see **14.16** COMPANIES) which take place on or after 18 August 2006, in relation to all other mergers which take place on or after 1 January 2007 and in relation to cross-border transfers of business which take place on or after 1 January 2007. [*SI 2007 No 3186, Reg 3(3); SI 2008 No 1579, Reg 4(2)*].

A '*transparent entity*' for this purpose is an entity resident in a member state other than the UK which is listed as a company in Part A of Annex I to the Mergers Directive but which does not have an 'ordinary share capital' (within *CTA 2010, s 1119*) and, if it were UK-resident, would not be capable of being a company within the meaning of *Companies Act 2006*.

Except where the context requires otherwise, a '*company*' is, for the purposes of the provisions, an entity listed as a company in the Annex to the Mergers Directive. A company is regarded as resident in another member state under the laws of which it is chargeable to tax because it is regarded as so resident (unless it is regarded under a double tax relief arrangement entered into by the member state as resident in a territory not within any of the member states).

[*TCGA 1992, s 140L; SI 2007 No 3186, Sch 3 para 1; SI 2008 No 1579, Sch 1 para 7; SI 2011 No 1431, Reg 2*].

Share exchanges

Where a company (company B) issues shares or debentures to a person in exchange for shares in or debentures of another company (company A) and either of the companies is a transparent entity, the share exchange provisions at *TCGA 1992, s 135* (see **63.5** SHARES AND SECURITIES) are disapplied.

Where the exchange otherwise meets the conditions for *TCGA 1992, s 135* to apply, any tax which would, but for the Mergers Directive, have been chargeable on a gain accruing to a holder of shares in or debentures of company A on the exchange under the law of a member state other than the UK is treated, for the purposes of DOUBLE TAX RELIEF (**21**), as if it had been so chargeable. This notional tax is calculated on the basis that, so far as permitted under the law of the relevant member state, losses arising on the exchange are set against gains arising from the exchange and that any relief available to company A under that law has been claimed.

[*TCGA 1992, s 140H; TIOPA 2010, Sch 8 para 44; SI 2007 No 3186, Sch 3 para 1; SI 2011 No 1431, Reg 2*].

Division of business or transfer of assets

Where:

- there is a transfer of a business, or part of a business, of a kind mentioned in *TCGA 1992, s 140A(1)* or *(1A)* (see **49.13** above) (or which would be of such a kind if the business or part transferred were carried on by the transferor in the UK and either **49.13**(i) or (ii) above were satisfied in relation to the transferee or each of the transferees), and
- either the transferor or transferee, or one of the transferees, is a transparent entity,

then, if the transferor is the transparent entity, neither *section 140A* nor *TCGA 1992, s 140DA* (transfer of assets treated as scheme of reconstruction — see **49.13** above) apply to the transfer. If a transferee is the transparent entity, *section 140DA* does not apply to the transfer to it.

Any tax which would, but for the Mergers Directive, have been chargeable on a 'transfer gain' under the law of a member state other than the UK is treated, for the purposes of DOUBLE TAX RELIEF (**21**), as if it had been so chargeable. This notional tax is calculated on the basis that, so far as permitted under the law of the relevant member state, losses arising on the transfer are set against gains arising from the transfer and that any relief available under that law has been claimed. A '*transfer gain*' for this purpose is a gain accruing to a transparent entity (or which would be treated as accruing to such an entity were it not transparent) by reason of the transfer of assets by the transparent entity to the transferee.

[*TCGA 1992, s 140I; TIOPA 2010, Sch 8 para 44; SI 2007 No 3186, Sch 3 para 1; SI 2008 No 1579, Sch 1 para 5*].

Cross-border merger

Where there is a merger of a kind within **49.15**(a)–(d) above which meets the conditions at **49.15**(i)–(iii) and one or more of the merging companies is a transparent entity:

- if the assets and liabilities of a transparent entity are transferred to another company on the merger, *TCGA 1992, s 140E* (assets left within charge to UK tax — see **49.15** above) and *TCGA 1992, s 140G* (treatment of securities issued on merger — see **49.15** above) do not apply; and
- if the assets and liabilities of one or more companies are transferred to a transparent entity on the merger, *TCGA 1992, s 140G* does not apply.

Any tax which would, but for the Mergers Directive, have been chargeable on a 'merger gain' under the law of a member state other than the UK is treated, for the purposes of DOUBLE TAX RELIEF (**21**), as if it had been so chargeable. This notional tax is calculated on the basis that, so far as permitted under the law of the relevant member state, losses arising on the merger are set against gains arising from the merger and that any relief available under that law has been claimed. A '*merger gain*' for this purpose is a gain accruing to a transparent entity (or which would be treated as accruing to such an entity were it not transparent) by reason of the transfer of assets by the transparent entity on the merger.

[*TCGA 1992, s 140J; TIOPA 2010, Sch 8 para 44; SI 2007 No 3186, Sch 3 para 1; SI 2008 No 1579, Sch 1 para 6*].

Taxation of transparent entity after merger or division

Where:

(i) a transparent entity (company A) is a transferee for the purposes of *TCGA 1992, s 140A(1A)* (division of UK business — see **49.13** above) or *TCGA 1992, s 140E* (cross-border merger: assets left within charge to UK tax — see **49.15** above);
(ii) a person ('X') with an interest in company A was or is also a shareholder or debenture holder of a company (company B);
(iii) X became entitled to an interest, or an increased interest, in company A in exchange for a disposal of shares in, or debenture of, company B on a merger to which *TCGA 1992, s 140E* applied or on a transfer to which *TCGA 1992, s 140(1A)* applied;
(iv) a chargeable gain accrued to X on the disposal of shares or debentures of company B;
(v) in calculating that gain account was taken of the value of an asset of company B; and
(vi) X makes a disposal of his interest in the asset,

then, in calculating the gain on the disposal in (vi) above, the amount allowed as the acquisition cost in relation to the interest, or proportion of the interest, which X acquired on the merger or transfer is the amount to be taken into account in computing the gain on the disposal of his shares in, or debentures of, company B.

References above to an interest in company A include an interest in the assets of, or shares in or debentures of, company A.

[*TCGA 1992, s 140K; SI 2007 No 3186, Sch 3 para 1*].

Company ceasing to be UK resident etc.

[49.17] If, at any time ('*the relevant time*'), a company ceases to be resident in the UK and does not cease to exist:

(a) it is deemed to dispose of immediately before the relevant time, and immediately reacquire, all its 'assets' at market value at that time; and
(b) ROLLOVER RELIEF (59) under *TCGA 1992, s 152* is not subsequently available by reference to disposals of old assets made before that time and acquisitions of new assets after that time.

If at any later time the company carries on a trade in the UK through a permanent establishment (as defined in **49.3** above), the foregoing does not apply:

(i) for (a) above, to any assets which, immediately after the relevant time; or

(ii) for (b) above, to any new assets which, after the relevant time,

are situated in the UK and are used in or for a trade, or are used or held for the permanent establishment. '*Assets*' include various assets and rights relating to exploration or exploitation activities in the UK or a designated area of the sea, within *TCGA 1992, s 276* in **49.19** below. [*TCGA 1992, s 185; FA 2012, Sch 16 para 78*].

If the deemed disposal described in (a) above includes any '*foreign assets*' (i.e. assets which are situated, and are used in or for a trade carried on, outside the UK), any charge to tax will be postponed, as described below, if:

(A) immediately after the relevant time the company was a '75% subsidiary' (see below) of a company ('*the principal company*') which was resident in the UK; and

(B) both companies elect in writing within two years after that time.

The excess of gains over losses arising on the foreign assets included in the deemed disposal is treated as a single chargeable gain not accruing to the company on the disposal. An equal amount ('*the postponed gain*') is instead treated as follows.

If within six years after the relevant time the company disposes of any assets (the '*relevant assets*') capital gains on which were taken into account in arriving at the postponed gain, a chargeable gain equal to the whole, or 'the appropriate proportion', of the postponed gain, so far as this has not already been treated as a chargeable gain under these provisions, is deemed to accrue to the principal company. '*The appropriate proportion*' is the proportion which the chargeable gain taken into account in arriving at the postponed gain in respect of the part of the relevant assets disposed of bears to the aggregate of the chargeable gains so taken into account in respect of the relevant assets held immediately before the time of the disposal.

If at any time:

(I) the company ceases to be a 75% subsidiary of the principal company on a disposal by the principal company of ordinary shares in it; or

(II) after the company otherwise ceases to be a 75% subsidiary, the principal company disposes of ordinary shares in it; or

(III) the principal company ceases to be resident in the UK,

a chargeable gain, equal to so much of the postponed gain as has not previously been charged under these provisions, is deemed to arise.

If any part of the postponed gain becomes chargeable, and the subsidiary has unrelieved capital losses, the companies can elect within two years for part or all of the losses to be set against the amount chargeable.

For the purposes of the above provisions a company is a '*75% subsidiary*' of another company if and so long as not less than 75% of its ordinary share capital is owned *directly* by that other company. [*TCGA 1992, s 187*].

Unless a company so elects (within two years after ceasing to be UK-resident), neither a gain nor a loss accrue on the deemed disposal if the gain or loss would have been an NRCGT gain or loss on the assumption that the disposal was a non-resident CGT disposal (see **41.25** LAND). However, the NRCGT gain or loss that would have accrued on the deemed disposal is treated as accruing at the time of any subsequent disposal of the interest, in addition to any gain or loss which actually accrues. [*TCGA 1992, s 187B; FA 2015, Sch 7 para 29*].

Exit charge payment plans

See **51.8** PAYMENT OF TAX for the availability of exit charge payment plans under which a company can defer the payment of tax in respect of a number of exit charge provisions, including the above provisions.

Compliance

[49.18] Before a company ceases to be resident in the UK, it must give HMRC:

(a) notice of its intention to cease to be resident, specifying the time when it intends to do so;
(b) a statement of the amount of tax which it considers payable for periods beginning before that time; and
(c) particulars of the arrangements which it proposes to make to secure the payment of that tax (which may include a proposal to enter into an exit charge payment plan (see **49.17** above).

Except to the extent that payment of that tax is to be secured by the company entering into an exit charge payment plan, the company must also make arrangements to secure the payment of the tax; and the arrangements must be approved by HMRC.

References to tax payable are not defined but include specified liabilities such as certain income tax payments, sub-contractors' deductions and amounts payable under *TMA 1970, s 77C* (territorial extension of charge of tax as in **49.19** below). Interest on unpaid tax is included in certain circumstances.

Any question as to the amount of tax payable is to be determined by the Tribunal (before 1 April 2009, the Special Commissioners). If any information provided by the company does not fully and accurately disclose all the material facts and considerations, any resulting approval is void.

A person who is, or is deemed to be, involved in a failure to comply with the foregoing provisions is liable to a penalty not exceeding the amount of unpaid tax for periods beginning before the failure occurred.

Any tax in respect of accounting periods beginning before the cessation of UK residence which is still unpaid six months after the time when it became payable can (see also **49.17** above), within three years of final determination of the tax due, be recovered from a person who is, or in the twelve months before the cessation of UK residence was, a member of the same group of companies (as in *TCGA 1992, s 170* (see **29.2** GROUPS OF COMPANIES) but substituting 51 per cent subsidiary for '75 per cent subsidiary') or a controlling director (as defined). Where the tax is subject to an exit charge payment plan, it can be recovered in this way within three years of the later of the first day after the twelve months following the migration accounting period and the date on which the tax is payable under the plan.

[*TMA 1970, ss 109B–109F; FA 1988, ss 130–132; TIOPA 2010, Sch 7 para 54; FA 2013, Sch 49 paras 4, 5; SI 2009 No 56, Sch 1 para 164*].

Guidance on the procedure to be followed under these provisions is given in HMRC Statement of Practice 2/90. In particular, notice under (a) above should be sent to HMRC, International Division (Company Migrations), Room 312, Melbourne House, Aldwych, London, WC2B 4LL.

Exploration and exploitation rights to territorial sea-bed and continental shelf

[49.19] Any gains accruing on the disposal of 'exploration or exploitation rights' are treated for the purposes of *TCGA 1992* as gains accruing on the disposal of assets situated in the UK. For this and all other purposes of the taxation of chargeable gains, the territorial sea of the UK is deemed to be part of the UK. (Under the *Territorial Sea Act 1987, s 1*, the breadth of the territorial sea adjacent to the UK is 12 nautical miles, a nautical mile being approximately 1,852 metres.)

Gains accruing on the disposal of 'exploration or exploitation assets' which are situated in a 'designated area', or 'unquoted shares' (i.e. not listed on a recognised stock exchange — see **63.30** SHARES AND SECURITIES) deriving their value or the greater part of their value directly or indirectly from exploration or exploitation assets situated in the UK or a designated area or from such assets and exploration or exploitation rights taken together, are treated for the purposes of *TCGA 1992* as gains accruing on the disposal of assets situated in the UK. Gains accruing to a person not resident in the UK on the disposal of such rights or of such assets (the latter including for this purpose unquoted shares of the description above) are treated for the same purposes as gains accruing on the disposal of assets used for the purposes of a trade carried on by that person in the UK through a branch or agency or, in the case of a non-resident company, through a permanent establishment (for which see **49.3** above).

If exploration or exploitation rights or exploration or exploitation assets (the latter including for this purpose unquoted shares of the description above) are disposed of by a company resident in an overseas territory to either a company resident in the same territory or a UK-resident company, or by one UK-resident company to another, the provisions at **29.3**, **29.4**, **29.7**, **29.10** GROUPS OF COMPANIES apply, with appropriate modifications.

Definitions

'*Exploration or exploitation rights*' means rights to assets to be produced by 'exploration or exploitation activities' or to interests in or to the benefit of such assets. '*Exploration or exploitation activities*' means activities carried on in connection with the exploration or exploitation of so much of the seabed and subsoil and their natural resources as is situated in the UK or a designated area.

References in the above to the disposal of exploration or exploitation rights include references to the disposal of shares deriving their value or the greater part of their value directly or indirectly from such rights, other than shares listed on a recognised stock exchange. '*Shares*' includes stock and any security as defined in *CTA 2010, s 1117(1)*. '*Designated area*' means an area designated by Order in Council under the *Continental Shelf Act 1964, s 1(7)*.

For the above purposes, an asset disposed of is an '*exploration or exploitation asset*' if either:

(a) it is not a mobile asset and it is being or has at some time (for disposals before 14 March 1989, being a time within the period of two years ending at the date of disposal) been used in connection with exploration or exploitation activities carried on in the UK or a designated area; or

(b) it is a mobile asset which has at some time (for disposals before 14 March 1989, being a time within the period of two years ending at the date of disposal) been used in connection with exploration or exploitation activities so carried on and is dedicated to an oil field in which the person making the disposal, or a person connected with him, is or has been a participator;

and expressions used in (a) and (b) above have the same meanings there as if those paragraphs were included in *Oil Taxation Act 1975, Pt I*.

[*TCGA 1992, s 276*].

Compliance

There are comprehensive information and enforcement powers in relation to tax assessed by virtue of *TCGA 1992, s 276* above. In particular, unpaid tax so assessed on an overseas resident person may be recovered together with interest thereon from the holder of a licence granted under *Petroleum Act 1998* in respect of chargeable gains accruing on the disposal of exploration or exploitation rights connected with activities authorised, or carried on in connection with activities authorised, by the licence. An overseas resident liable to charge and who HMRC are satisfied will meet his obligations under the *Taxes Acts* may apply for a certificate to be issued to the licence holder exempting him (subject to detailed conditions) from a charge on the default of the applicant. The information provisions are replaced with effect from 1 April 2012 by the new data-gathering power under *FA 2011, Sch 23*. See **34.17** HMRC INVESTIGATORY POWERS. [*TMA 1970, ss 77B–77K; FA 1973, s 38(2)(8), Sch 15; TIOPA 2010, Sch 7 paras 2–4; FA 2011, Sch 23 paras 51(2), 52, 65*].

Asset ceasing to be chargeable

Where an 'exploration or exploitation asset' (for this purpose, an asset used in connection with 'exploration or exploitation activities' carried on in the UK or a 'designated area', both expressions having the same meanings as in *TCGA 1992, s 276* above) ceases to be 'chargeable' in relation to a person by virtue of ceasing to be 'dedicated to an oil field' in which he, or a person connected with him, is or has been a 'participator' (these last two expressions having the same meanings as in *Oil Taxation Act 1975, Pt I*), he is deemed for all purposes of *TCGA 1992* to have disposed of the asset immediately before the time when it ceased to be so dedicated, and immediately to have reacquired it, at its market value at that time.

An asset is a '*chargeable*' asset at any time in relation to a person if, were it to be disposed of at that time, any chargeable gains accruing to him on the disposal would be brought into charge for capital gains tax or corporation tax by virtue of *TCGA 1992, s 10(1)* or *s 10(3)* or *s 10B* respectively.

Trade ceasing to be carried on through branch etc.

A similar deemed disposal and acquisition takes place where a person in respect of whom the residence condition for 2013/14 onwards at **1.2** INTRODUCTION is not met ceases to carry on a trade through a branch or agency, or, in the case of a non-resident company through a permanent establishment, in respect of any exploration or exploitation asset, other than a mobile asset, used in or for the purposes of the trade at or before the time of the deemed disposal. No such deemed disposal and reacquisition takes place if, immediately after the cessation of the trade carried on through the UK branch or agency, the asset is used in or for the purposes of exploration or exploitation activities carried on by him in the UK or a designated area. However, on a person ceasing after 13 March 1989 so to use the asset, there will be a deemed disposal and reacquisition.

For 2012/13 and earlier years, the above provision applied where a person was not resident or ordinarily resident in the UK.

[*TCGA 1992, s 199; FA 2013, Sch 46 paras 103, 112*].

As regards leasing of mobile drilling rigs and other assets by overseas resident companies, see HMRC Statement of Practice 6/84.

See also **57.36** RESIDENCE AND DOMICILE for the territorial extent of the UK.

European Economic Interest Groupings

[49.20] There are special provisions governing the tax treatment of European Economic Interest Groupings ('groupings'), wherever registered, within *EEC Council Regulation No 2137/85* dated 25 July 1985. For the purposes of charging tax in respect of chargeable gains and subject to exceptions as below, a grouping is regarded as acting as the agent of its members. Its activities are regarded for such purposes as those of its members acting jointly, each member being regarded as having a share of its property, rights and liabilities. Where the grouping carries on a trade or profession, the members are regarded for the purposes of tax on gains as carrying on that trade or profession in partnership. A person is regarded as acquiring or disposing of a share of the grouping's assets not only where there is an acquisition or disposal by it while he is a member but also where he becomes or ceases to be a member or there is a change in his share of its property. A member's share in a grouping's property, rights or liabilities is that determined under the contract establishing the grouping or, if there is no provision determining such shares, it will correspond to the profit share to which he is entitled under the provisions of the contract (or if the contract makes no such provision, members are regarded as having equal shares).

[*TCGA 1992, s 285A; CTA 2010, s 990*].

The EEC provision of 25 July 1985 mentioned above covers all groupings established within the European Economic Area on the coming into force of the European Economic Area Agreement on 1 January 1994 (Revenue Press Release 9 February 1994).

See also **58.23** RETURNS, and **52.6**, **52.7** PENALTIES as regards non-compliance.

Collection of tax

[49.21] Although tax is legally assessable by notice served abroad, there are difficulties in collection. The UK courts will not enforce the revenue laws of other countries, see *Government of India v Taylor (re Delhi Electric Supply & Traction Co. Ltd)* HL, [1955] AC 491 and *Brokaw v Seatrain UK Ltd*, CA, [1971] 2 All ER 98. See, however, **31.2**(c) **HMRC** — CONFIDENTIALITY OF INFORMATION for agreements for mutual assistance in the collection of taxes. See also **49.4** above for the assessment of UK resident agents of overseas resident traders and **49.18** above for arrangements required to secure payment of tax by a company ceasing to be UK resident or by a non-UK resident company. See also **48.2** OFFSHORE SETTLEMENTS for the arrangements where trustees become non-resident.

Tax collection agreement with Switzerland

[49.22] The UK Government entered into an agreement with Switzerland under which Swiss bank accounts of UK taxpayers were subject to a one-off deduction to settle unpaid UK tax liabilities and are subject to a withholding tax to satisfy ongoing liabilities. The legislation giving effect to the agreement (and subsequent amendments to it) in the UK is at *FA 2012, s 218, Sch 36*. The agreement took effect on 1 January 2013. The agreement is terminated on the coming into force of the automatic exchange of information agreement between Switzerland and the EU. That agreement provides for the exchange of account date from 2018.

Initial deduction

The initial deduction of between 21% and 41% of the funds in accounts held by individual UK taxpayers was taken from accounts in 2013 where the account was open on both 31 December 2010 and 31 May 2013. The deduction settled income tax, capital gains tax, inheritance tax and VAT liabilities in relation to the funds in the account. No deduction was applied if the taxpayer instructed the bank to disclose details of the account to HMRC. The effect was, in most cases, that amounts which suffered the deduction and on which the taxpayer should have paid tax, but which were untaxed, ceased to be liable to UK tax. In certain cases, however, the deduction was instead treated as a credit against UK tax, interest and penalties on the untaxed amount. Where the UK liability was removed, there are provisions to ensure that the taxpayer's liability to tax on other income or gains was what it would have been if the amounts no longer liable to UK tax had remained so liable. See *FA 2012, Sch 36 paras 2–12*.

Withholding tax

The withholding tax is applied from 2013 to income and gains arising on investments held by individual UK taxpayers in Swiss banks, the rates being close to the highest UK rates. For capital gains (as defined in the agreement), the rate is usually 27% (28% in certain cases). As with the initial deduction, the withholding tax does not apply if the taxpayer authorises the bank to disclose details to HMRC and pays any associated taxes in the UK. The effect of the withholding tax is that the taxpayer ceases to be liable to income tax or capital gains tax on the income or gain concerned, but the taxpayer can elect for the tax to be treated as a credit against income tax and/or capital gains tax. An election must be made in the tax return for the year concerned, and that return must include all of the income or gains in respect of which tax has been withheld. See *FA 2012, Sch 36 paras 13–19*.

Remittance basis

Where the taxpayer uses the remittance basis (55), foreign income or gains are treated as not remitted to the UK when money is brought to the UK pursuant to a transfer to HMRC in accordance with the agreement. If the money is transferred from a mixed fund, the bringing of it to the UK is treated as an offshore transfer (see 55.3 REMITTANCE BASIS). [*FA 2012, Sch 36 paras 26A, 26B; FA 2013, s 221*].

Key points concerning overseas matters

[49.23] Points to consider are as follows.

- A person is generally chargeable to capital gains tax on gains accruing in a year of assessment in which he is resident in the UK. Persons carrying on a trade in the UK through a branch or agency, and companies carrying on a trade in the UK through a permanent establishment, are also charged to tax on gains on disposal of trade-related assets situated in the UK.
- Non-UK domiciled individuals can elect for the remittance basis to apply to gains on disposal of assets situated abroad.
- Gains on assets acquired by an individual whilst UK resident and disposed of whilst not UK resident for less than five years will be charged in the tax year when UK residence is resumed.
- Gains of a company which is not resident in the UK, and which would be a close company if UK resident, can be charged on UK resident participators. The European Court has, however, found these provisions to contravene EU law.
- If a UK-resident settlement or company becomes non-resident, there is a deemed disposal and reacquisition of assets, which can give rise to an 'exit charge'.
- Where a gain is potentially taxable both in the UK and in another country, the terms of any double taxation agreement should always be consulted to determine which country has the taxing rights.

- The UK has entered into a number of tax information exchange agreements with other countries to help counter and prevent tax avoidance.

50

Partnerships

Introduction to partnerships	**50.1**
General rules	**50.2**
Partners' fractional shares	**50.3**
Transactions within the partnership	**50.4**
Contribution of assets to a partnership	**50.5**
Changes in sharing ratios	**50.6**
Re-basing to 1982 and indexation allowance (SP 1/89)	**50.7**
Application of reliefs	**50.9**
Accounting adjustments	**50.10**
Consideration outside the accounts	**50.11**
Annual payments to retired partners	**50.12**
Fractional shares acquired in stages	**50.13**
Partnership assets distributed in kind	**50.14**
Miscellaneous	**50.15**
Mergers	**50.15**
6 April 1965 and 31 March 1982 elections	**50.16**
Corporate partners	**50.17**
Limited liability partnerships	**50.18**
Alternative investment fund management partnerships	**50.19**
Carried interest arising to investment managers	**50.20**
Key points concerning partnerships	**50.22**

Cross-references. See **49.20** OVERSEAS MATTERS for European Economic Interest Groupings deemed to carry on a trade in partnership; **59** ROLLOVER RELIEF and **61** SELF-ASSESSMENT.

Simon's Taxes. See C3.2.

Introduction to partnerships

[50.1] A partnership is defined in *Partnership Act 1890, s 1* as 'the relation which subsists between persons carrying on a business in common with a view of profit'. This does not include purely capital transactions, e.g. the sale of a house by joint tenants.

An English partnership or firm is not a legal entity distinct from the partners themselves, but a collection of separate persons (which may be companies or individuals). In Scotland a firm is a legal person, but in general this does not affect the application of the *Taxes Acts*. A partnership cannot be a company for the purposes of *TCGA 1992*. [*TCGA 1992, s 288(1)*]. See **50.18** below as regards limited liability partnerships.

The taxation of partnership gains is based on a body of HMRC practice superimposed on the general capital gains rules. There are few specific references to partnerships in the capital gains legislation. For a useful codification of HMRC practice, reference should be made to HMRC Statements of Practice D12 (revised most recently in September 2015), 1/79 and 1/89 on which much of this chapter is based. The Statements of Practice are supplemented by the HMRC Capital Gains Manual at CG27000–28420.

Where a trade is carried on in partnership, tax is charged on each partner separately in respect of chargeable gains on the disposal of partnership assets. Each partner is treated as owning a fractional share of each asset. Consequently, a transfer of an asset to a partnership as a capital contribution by a partner is treated as a part disposal, and changes in sharing ratios result in the disposal or acquisition of a share in partnership assets by each partner as his share increases or decreases. A chargeable gain is likely to arise in such circumstances, however, only where assets have been revalued upwards in the partnership accounts or actual consideration is given for an increased share.

Special provisions apply to corporate partners and to limited liability partnerships.

For details of the requirement for partnership tax returns, see **58.16–58.18** RETURNS.

In 2016, HMRC consulted on a number of proposed changes to partnership taxation to provide clarity on areas where it considered the tax rules to be unclear or to produce inappropriate outcomes. HMRC published the summary of responses in March 2017. See www.gov.uk/government/consultations/partnership-taxation-proposals-to-clarify-tax-treatment. On 13 September 2017, draft legislation was published which includes a number of provisions relevant to income tax to be included in *Finance Bill 2017–2018*. See www.gov.uk/government/publications/partnership-taxation-proposals-to-clarify-tax-treatment and Tolley's Income Tax for details.

General rules

[50.2] Where two or more persons carry on a trade or business in partnership, tax is assessed and charged on them separately in respect of chargeable gains accruing to them on the disposal of any partnership assets. (The treatment of partnerships in Scotland as a legal person is ignored for this purpose.) Any partnership dealings are treated as dealings by the partners and not by the firm as such. [*TCGA 1992, s 59(1)(a)(b)*].

In general terms, it will be the residence and domicile circumstances of each partner (whether an individual or company) that will dictate the basis of charge on him. For example, an individual partner who is resident in the UK and domiciled there will be chargeable wherever partnership gains arise and whether remitted to the UK or not. An individual partner not resident in the UK would only be liable in respect of partnership assets under *TCGA 1992, s 10* (UK branch or agency; see **49.3** OVERSEAS MATTERS). However, it is specifically provided that, if, under a double tax agreement, any capital gains of a partnership which resides outside the UK or which carries on any trade, profession or business the control or management of which is situated outside the UK is relieved from tax in the UK, such relief is not to affect the liability of any UK resident partner's share of the capital gains. For this purpose, 'partner' includes any person entitled to a share of the partnership's capital gains. [*TCGA 1992, s 59(2)–(4)*].

Partners' fractional shares

[50.3] Each partner is regarded as owning a fractional share of each asset, which is calculated by reference to his asset-surplus-sharing ratio. Where no such ratio is specified, the share will follow the treatment in the accounts, subject to any external agreement. Failing that, regard will be had to the normal profit-sharing ratios. For appeals regarding apportionments of amounts etc., see 5 APPEALS and *White v Carline* (Sp C 33), [1995] SSCD 186.

The fraction is applied to the value of the total partnership interest in the asset disposed of, and no discount is allowed against market value for the size of an individual partner's share.

Expenditure on the acquisition of partnership assets will be allocated for capital gains tax purposes, in similar fashion to gains/losses, at the time of acquisition, subject to adjustment on any subsequent change in partnership sharing ratios.

(SP D12 (revised September 2015) introduction and sections 1, 2).

Examples

Each of the following partnerships disposes of its offices to outside parties at arm's length at a chargeable gain of £30,000. The gain is apportioned among the partners in the manner shown.

(a) *A & Co.* The partnership agreement states that each of the three partners shall be entitled to share equally in any surplus arising from assets disposed of by the partnership. Each partner is therefore treated as if he had made a gain of £10,000.

(b) *B & Co.* The three partners in B & Co have no formal agreement, but interest on capital contributed to the partnership is shown in the accounts at the same sum for each. The inference is that the capital has been equally contributed and can be equally withdrawn, so that the apportioned gain is £10,000 to each partner.

(c) *C & Co.* The three partners in C & Co, X, Y, and Z, have no formal agreement and the capital is shown in the accounts as a global sum. The profit-sharing ratio is 3:2:1, so that the apportioned gain is X–£15,000, Y–£10,000, and Z–£5,000.

A partner makes a disposal (or part disposal) of his fractional share of a partnership asset not only when the partnership disposes (or part disposes) of the asset as above but also when his share is extinguished (or reduced) for which see 50.6–50.11 below.

Transactions within the partnership

[50.4] Transactions within the partnership are not treated as made between CONNECTED PERSONS (17), provided they are pursuant to genuine commercial arrangements, unless the partners are otherwise connected. Market value will be substituted for actual consideration only if the consideration would have been different had the parties been at arm's length. Where market value is applied, the deemed disposal proceeds are treated in the same way as payments outside the accounts as in **50.11** below. (SP D12 (revised September 2015) sections 8.3, 8.4).

Contribution of assets to a partnership

[50.5] Where an asset is transferred to a partnership by means of a capital contribution by a partner, HMRC consider that the partner makes a part disposal of the asset equal to the fractional share that passes to the other partners. Where the market value rule does not apply, the consideration for the disposal is a proportion of the total consideration given by the partnership for the asset. The proportion is equal to the fractional share of the asset passing to the other partners. HMRC consider that a sum credited to the partner's capital account represents consideration for this purpose. Allowable costs are apportioned on a fractional basis as in **50.6** below.

(SP D12 (revised September 2015) section 5; HMRC Brief 3/2008).

Changes in sharing ratios

[50.6] Where changes occur in partnership sharing ratios (including partners joining or leaving the firm), each partner is treated as acquiring or disposing of part or the whole of a share in each of the partnership assets, insofar as his share increases or decreases.

Subject to (a) and (b) below, the disposal consideration of each chargeable asset is equal to the relevant fraction (i.e. the fractional share changing hands) of the current balance sheet value. In certain cases (where the partners' CGT base cost is equal to the balance sheet value), the disposal will be a *no gain/no loss disposal*. This is unlikely to be the case where, for example, the asset has been revalued in the partnership accounts, where a partner transferred the asset to the partnership for an amount that is not equivalent to the CGT base cost or where the partners' base costs were determined under *TCGA 1992, s 171* (see **29.3** GROUPS OF COMPANIES).

A partner whose share decreases will carry forward a smaller proportion of cost to set against any future disposal (including a disposal of one or more of the assets outside the partnership), and a partner whose share increases will carry forward a larger proportion of cost than before. An incoming partner will thereby take over a proportion of the cost of existing assets in accordance with his fractional entitlement. The *cost* of any part disposal under these provisions is calculated as a corresponding fraction of the total acquisition cost, and *not* by way of apportionment under *TCGA 1992, s 42* as in **16.5** COMPUTATION OF GAINS AND LOSSES.

(SP D12 section 4).

See the *example* at **50.8** below.

A different disposal consideration figure may have to be used in the following cases.

(a) Where a direct payment is made in connection with the change in sharing ratios (see **50.11** below).

(b) Where the change in sharing ratios results from a transaction made otherwise than at arm's length or made between CONNECTED PERSONS (17). The meaning of connected persons for these purposes is narrowed. See **50.4** above.

Re-basing to 1982 and indexation allowance (SP 1/89)

[50.7] HMRC have agreed that a disposal of a share of partnership assets which is treated under SP D12 section 4 above as on a no gain/no loss basis may be treated as if it were within the no gain/no loss provisions in **9.6** ASSETS HELD ON 31 MARCH **1982**. Such a disposal may also be treated as if it were a no gain/no loss disposal for the purposes of *TCGA 1992, s 36, Sch 4* (deferred charges — see **9.11** ASSETS HELD ON 31 MARCH **1982**).

Where such a disposal occurs, for capital gains tax (but not corporation tax) purposes, before 6 April 2008, the amount of the consideration is calculated on the assumption that an unindexed gain accrues to the transferor equal to the indexation allowance, so that after taking into account the indexation allowance due, neither a gain nor a loss accrues. Where under the above a partner is treated as having owned the asset on 31 March 1982 in relation to a disposal of all or part of his share of partnership assets, the indexation allowance on the disposal may be calculated as if he had acquired the share on 31 March 1982. A disposal of a share in a partnership asset (for capital gains tax (but not corporation tax) purposes, before 6 April 2008) which is treated under SP D12 section 4 above as on a no gain/no loss basis may be treated for the purposes of *TCGA 1992, s 55(5)(6)* as if it were a no gain/no loss disposal within those provisions (see **9.6** ASSETS HELD ON 31 MARCH **1982**). A special rule applies, however, where the share changed hands after 5 April 1985 (31 March 1985 in the case of an acquisition from a company) and before 6 April 1988: in these circumstances the indexation allowance is calculated by reference to the 31 March 1982 value *but* from the date of the last disposal of the share before 6 April 1988.

(HMRC Statement of Practice 1/89).

For disposals of an interest in partnership assets between partners after 5 April 2008 HMRC continue to accept that, for capital gains tax purposes, where the disposal is treated under SP D12 section 4 above as on a no gain/no loss basis it may be treated as if it were within the no gain/no loss provisions. On a disposal after 5 April 2008 of an interest previously transferred on a no gain/no loss basis (whether under this provision or SP 1/89), the allowable expenditure to be taken into account then includes the value of the asset at 31 March 1982 and any indexation allowance for the period from 31 March 1982 to the earlier of the month in which the person making the disposal acquired the asset and April 1998. (HMRC Brief 9/2009).

For indexation allowance in relation to no gain/no loss disposals generally, see **38.4** INDEXATION.

Note that, other than for companies, indexation allowance is abolished for disposals on or after 6 April 2008 and was previously frozen at its April 1998 level — see **38.2** INDEXATION. *TCGA 1992, s 36, Sch 4* applies only for corporation tax purposes for disposals on or after 6 April 2008, and for disposals on or after that date, re-basing to 31 March 1982 applies without exceptions for capital gains tax purposes (but not corporation tax purposes).

For further commentary, see HMRC Capital Gains Manual CG28300–28340.

Example

[50.8]

J and K have traded in partnership since 2001, sharing capital and income equally. The acquisition costs of the chargeable assets of the firm are as follows

	Cost
	£
Premises	60,000
Goodwill	10,000

The assets have not been revalued in the firm's balance sheet. On 1 June 2017, J and K admit L to the partnership, and the sharing ratio is J 35%, K 45% and L 20%.

J and K are regarded as disposing of part of their interest in the firm's assets to L as follows

	£
J	
Premises	
Deemed consideration	
£60,000 × (50% – 35%)	9,000
Allowable cost	9,000
Chargeable gain	—
Goodwill	
Deemed consideration	
£10,000 × (50% – 35%)	1,500
Allowable cost	1,500
Chargeable gain	—

	£
K	
Premises	
Deemed consideration	
£60,000 × (50% – 45%)	3,000
Allowable cost	3,000
Chargeable gain	—
Goodwill	
Deemed consideration	
£10,000 × (50% – 45%)	500
Allowable cost	500
Chargeable gain	—

The allowable costs of the three partners are now:

	Freehold land	Goodwill
	£	£
J	21,000	3,500
K	27,000	4,500
L (note (b))	12,000	2,000

Notes to the example

(a) The treatment illustrated above is taken from SP D12 section 4. Each partner's disposal consideration is equal to his share of current balance sheet value of the asset concerned, and each disposal treated as producing no gain and no loss.

(b) L's allowable costs comprise 20% of original cost.

Application of reliefs

[50.9] Where a partner is treated as making a disposal it may also qualify for HOLD-OVER RELIEFS (36), or ROLLOVER RELIEF (59). As regards a partner's acquisition, this may be used to cover a chargeable gain as in ROLLOVER RELIEF (59). A partner treated as disposing of a partnership asset (or share) can roll over any chargeable gain arising against an acquisition in another trade carried on, whether as sole trader or in another partnership trade, and *vice versa*. See 59.3 ROLLOVER RELIEF as regards assets owned personally by a partner and let to the partnership.

Accounting adjustments

[50.10] An upward revaluation of a partnership asset with the consequent credit to a partner's current or capital account does not give rise to a chargeable gain, but if after such a revaluation, a reduction occurs in a partner's sharing ratio (see 50.6 above), the disposal which he is thereby treated as making takes place at the increased value and may therefore give rise to a chargeable gain. Any acquisition is similarly treated.

Examples

(a) X, Y and Z are partners in D & Co and share both capital and income profits and losses in the ratio 3:2:1. X wishes to take a less active part in the business, and Z to devote more time to it. The asset-surplus-sharing ratio is amended to 2:2:2. X is treated as having disposed of a one-sixth interest in each chargeable asset belonging to the partnership for a consideration equal to one-sixth of their respective book values, and Z as having acquired that interest for the same consideration.

(b) The facts are as (a) above, save that before the ratio is altered, the partnership premises are written up in the books from £120,000 to £180,000. No charge arises on this occasion. On the change in sharing ratio, however, X is treated as having made a gain of £10,000 (one-sixth of the book gain) and this forms part of Z's acquisition cost on a future disposal.

A downward revaluation, even if following an upward revaluation, is similarly not treated as giving rise to an allowable loss, but a change in partnership shares following such a revaluation may do so.

(SP D12 (revised September 2015) section 6).

Consideration outside the accounts

[50.11] Where actual consideration is given in connection with an alteration in partnership sharing ratios (see **50.6** above), it is added to the consideration deemed to have been received under the rules in **50.6** and **50.10** above, and may therefore give rise to a chargeable gain or increased gain, the payer's acquisition cost being adjusted accordingly. Such an extraneous payment is often in respect of goodwill not included in the balance sheet. A payment is only deductible by the payer from a subsequent disposal (including a reduction in his share) of the asset, or on the payer's leaving the partnership. (SP D12 revised September 2015) section 7).

Example

D, E and F are partners in a firm of accountants who share all profits in the ratio 7:7:6. G is admitted as a partner in May 2017 and pays the other partners £10,000 for goodwill. The new partnership shares are D $^{3}/_{10}$, E $^{3}/_{10}$, F $^{1}/_{4}$ and G $^{3}/_{20}$. The book value of goodwill is £18,000, its cost on acquisition of the practice from the predecessor in 1993.

The partners are treated as having disposed of shares in goodwill as follows:

D	£	£
$^{7}/_{20} - ^{3}/_{10} = ^{1}/_{20}$		
Disposal consideration		
Notional $^{1}/_{20}$ × £18,000	900	
Actual $^{7}/_{20}$ × £10,000	3,500	
		4,400
Allowable cost $^{1}/_{20}$ × £18,000		900
Chargeable gain		£3,500

E		
$^7/_{20} - ^3/_{10} = ^1/_{20}$		
Disposal consideration (as for D)		4,400
Allowable cost (as for D)		900
Chargeable gain		£3,500
F		
$^6/_{20} - ^1/_4 = ^1/_{20}$		
Disposal consideration		
Notional $^1/_{20}$ × £18,000	900	
Actual $^6/_{20}$ × £10,000	3,000	
		3,900
Allowable cost		900
Chargeable gain		£3,000
G's allowable cost of his share of goodwill is therefore		
Actual consideration paid		10,000
Notional consideration paid $^3/_{20}$ × £18,000		2,700
		£12,700

Annual payments to retired partner

[50.12] To the extent that annual payments (whether under covenant or not) to a retired partner exceed an amount regarded as a reasonable recognition of the partner's past work for the firm, the capitalised value of the annuity is treated as consideration for the disposal of his partnership share (and as allowable expenditure by the remaining partners). If he had been a partner for at least ten years, the maximum 'reasonable' annuity is two-thirds of his average share of the partnership profits (before capital allowances or charges on income) in the best three of the last seven years in which he was required to devote substantially the whole of his time to the partnership. The ten-year period includes any period during which the partner was a member of another firm which has been merged with the existing firm. For periods less than ten years, the relevant fractions are as follows (instead of two-thirds).

Complete years	Fraction
1–5	$^1/_{60}$ for each year
6	$^8/_{60}$
7	$^{16}/_{60}$
8	$^{24}/_{60}$
9	$^{32}/_{60}$

This treatment applies to certain cases in which a lump sum is paid as well as the annuity. (SP D12 (revised September 2015) section 9). Where the aggregate of the annuity and one-ninth of the lump sum does not exceed the appropriate fraction of the retired partner's average share of the profits (as above), the capitalised value is not treated as consideration in his hands. The lump sum continues to be treated as consideration. (HMRC Statement of Practice 1/79).

Fractional shares acquired in stages

[50.13] Where a partner's fractional share in one or more partnership assets is built up in stages, i.e. acquired at different times as a result of different transactions, such acquisitions are pooled for capital gains tax purposes. A subsequent part disposal is then regarded as a part disposal of a single asset and the pooled acquisition cost is apportioned accordingly (as in **50.6** above). However, pooling does not apply to any part of the fractional share that was acquired before 6 April 1965; part disposals are to be identified with each such acquisition separately, on a first in/first out basis, in priority to the post-5 April 1965 pool (unless this produces an unreasonable result when applied to purely temporary changes in partners' shares, for example when a partner's departure and a replacement partner's admission are out of step by a few months). (SP D12 (revised September 2015) section 11).

Example

Q is a partner in a medical practice. The partnership's only chargeable asset is a freehold house used as a surgery. The cost of the house to the partnership was £3,600 in 1986 and it was revalued in the partnership accounts to £50,000 in 2002. Q was admitted to the partnership in June 1988 with a share of $^1/_6$ of all profits. As a result of partnership changes, Q's profit share altered as follows:

1992 $^1/_5$
2000 $^1/_4$
2005 $^3/_{10}$

For capital gains tax, Q's allowable cost of his share of the freehold house is calculated as follows:

	£
1988 $^1/_6$ × £3,600	600
1992 ($^1/_5$ – $^1/_6$) × £3,600	120
2000 ($^1/_4$ – $^1/_5$) × £3,600	180
2005 ($^3/_{10}$ – $^1/_4$) × £50,000	2,500
	£3,400

Note to the example

(a) On Q's acquisition of an increased share of the property in 2005 (subsequent to the revaluation in 1990), any partner with a reduced share will be treated as having made a disposal and thus a gain or loss (see **50.10** above).

Partnership assets distributed in kind

[50.14] The disposal of a partnership asset to one or more of the partners is treated as being made at market value which is apportioned among all the partners as in **50.6** above. Chargeable gains thus attributable to partners receiving no asset are taxed at the time of the disposal. Any gain notionally accruing to a receiving partner is treated as reducing his allowable expenditure on a subsequent disposal of the asset. The same principle applies where a loss arises. (SP D12 (revised September 2015) section 3).

Example

R, S and T are partners sharing all profits in the ratio 4:3:3. Farmland owned by the firm is transferred in November 2017 to T for future use by him as a market gardening enterprise separate from the partnership business. No payment is made by T to the other partners but a reduction is made in T's future share of income profits. The book value of the farmland is £50,000, its cost in 1993, but the present market value is £150,000.

		£
R		
Deemed disposal consideration	4/10 × £150,000	60,000
Allowable cost	4/10 × £50,000	20,000
Gain		£40,000
S		
Deemed disposal consideration	3/10 × £150,000	45,000
Allowable cost	3/10 × £50,000	15,000
Gain		£30,000
T		
Partnership share	3/10 × £50,000	15,000
Market value of R's share		60,000
Market value of S's share		45,000
Allowable cost of land for future disposal		£120,000

Miscellaneous

Mergers

[50.15] Mergers of existing partnerships are treated as in **50.6–50.11** above. If gains arise for reasons similar to **50.10** and **50.11** above, a continuing partner may claim ROLLOVER RELIEF (**59**) insofar as he disposes of his share of assets of the old firm and acquires a share in other assets of the new firm. (SP D12 (revised September 2015) section 10).

6 April 1965 and 31 March 1982 elections

[50.16] The election under *TCGA 1992, Sch 2 para 4* for quoted securities, whereby 6 April 1965 market value is substituted for acquisition cost and the securities form part of the '1982 holding' for identification purposes (see **8.3**, **8.4** ASSETS HELD ON 6 APRIL **1965**) is available separately to each partner as regards his share of partnership assets. Each partner's right to elect is distinct from his right to elect in respect of securities held by him in his personal capacity. The time limit for making the election in respect of a particular partner's share of partnership securities operates by reference to the earlier of the first relevant disposal by the partnership and the first post-19 March 1968 reduction of his share of partnership assets. (SP D12 (revised September 2015) section 12).

A universal re-basing election made under *TCGA 1992, s 35(5)* (see **9.3** ASSETS HELD ON 31 MARCH **1982**) by a person in one capacity does not cover disposals made by him in a different capacity. [*TCGA 1992, s 35(7); FA 2008, Sch 2 para 58(8)*]. HMRC have confirmed that an election for assets held privately will not apply to assets held in the capacity of partner, and *vice versa*. As regards partnership assets, the election is available separately to each partner in respect of his share. (Revenue Tax Bulletin November 1991 p 5).

Note that, for disposals on or after 6 April 2008, re-basing to 31 March 2008 applies automatically in all cases for capital gains tax purposes (but not for the purposes of corporation tax on chargeable gains). As a result, elections under *TCGA 1992, s 35(5)* and *Sch 2 para 4* have no effect for such disposals. See **9.2** ASSETS HELD ON 31 MARCH **1982**.

Corporate partners

[50.17] The above rules apply, with appropriate modifications, to company partners, but bearing in mind the differences listed at **14.2** COMPANIES between capital gains tax and corporation tax on chargeable gains. See also **15.3** COMPANIES — CORPORATE FINANCE AND INTANGIBLES.

Limited liability partnerships

[50.18] A limited liability partnership (LLP) is in law a body corporate (with legal personality separate from that of its members) incorporated under *Limited Liability Partnerships Act 2000*. [*LLPA 2000, s 1*]. But, for the purposes of income tax and corporation tax, a trade, profession or business carried on by an LLP with a view to profit is treated as if carried on instead by its members in partnership, and the property of the LLP is treated for those purposes as partnership property. [*ITTOIA 2005, s 863; CTA 2009, s 1273(1)*]. The essential feature of an LLP is that it combines the organisational flexibility and tax status of a partnership with limited liability for its members. LLPs are used mainly by professional partnerships.

Similarly, for the purposes of taxing chargeable gains, assets held by an LLP carrying on a trade or business with a view to profit are treated as held by its members as partners, and dealings by an LLP are treated as dealings by its members in partnership. As in **50.2** above, tax is assessed and charged on the members separately in respect of chargeable gains accruing to them on the disposal of LLP assets. [*TCGA 1992, s 59A(1)*].

All references to partnerships and partnership members in the legislation on taxation of chargeable gains are to be taken as including LLPs within *s 59A(1)* and members of such LLPs. [*TCGA 1992, s 59A(2)*]. Thus, the preceding paragraphs of this chapter generally apply as if an LLP were an ordinary partnership.

If an LLP *temporarily* ceases to carry on a trade or business with a view to profit, the treatment under *TCGA 1992, s 59A(1)* above continues. In the case of a permanent cessation, *s 59A(1)* treatment continues during an informal winding-up, provided the winding-up is not wholly or partly for tax avoidance reasons and is not unreasonably prolonged. *Section 59A(1)* treatment does, however, cease upon the appointment of a liquidator or (if earlier) the making of a winding-up order by the court (or upon the equivalent in each case under non-UK law). Neither the commencement of *s 59A(1)* treatment nor its ceasing to apply is to be taken as giving rise to the disposal of any assets by the LLP itself or by any of its members. During a liquidation period, an LLP is itself taxable (through its liquidator) on disposals of assets, under the normal corporate insolvency rules. Chargeable gains on assets disposed of in the liquidation period are taxed as if *s 59A(1)* tax treatment had never applied, and the only capital asset which a member then holds for tax purposes is his interest in the LLP. The proceeds of disposal of that interest is based on the amount of the liquidator's capital distributions (if any). In calculating the chargeable gain or allowable loss on that disposal, the member's interest is to be taken as acquired on the date he originally joined the LLP and by reference to the capital cost of his becoming a member. [*TCGA 1992, s 59A(3)–(6)*].

See **36.8, 36.11** HOLD-OVER RELIEFS, **59.3** ROLLOVER RELIEF for other implications.

Revenue Tax Bulletin December 2000 pp 801–805 set out the Revenue's views on matters concerning LLPs. In particular: the transfer of the business of an ordinary partnership to an LLP does not of itself constitute a disposal by the partners of their interests in the underlying assets and does not affect the availability of INDEXATION (**38**) allowance; the transfer from an ordinary partnership to an LLP of a partner's annuity rights and/or annuity obligations to former members or the agreement by an annuitant to the substitution (as payer) of the LLP for the old partnership is not regarded as a chargeable disposal, provided that the rights/terms remain substantially the same; HMRC Statement of Practice SP D12 (revised September 2015 and referred to throughout this chapter) applies equally to the members of an LLP for as long as it remains within *TCGA 1992, s 59A(1)*; the above treatment of an LLP in liquidation and of its members does not affect the tax treatment of pre-liquidation disposals, which will remain undisturbed.

Property investment LLPs

The normal exemptions for income and gains of pension funds, life insurance companies in respect of their pension business, and friendly societies in respect of their tax-exempt business do not apply where the income or gains accrue to the fund etc. in its capacity as a member of a 'property investment LLP'. See, for example, **25.60** EXEMPTIONS AND RELIEFS. A '*property investment LLP*' is an LLP whose business consists wholly or mainly in the making of investments in land and the principal part of whose income is derived therefrom. Whether or not an LLP is within this definition must be judged for each period of account separately. [*TCGA 1992, s 288(1); CTA 2010, s 1135*].

Alternative investment fund management partnerships

[50.19] For 2014/15 onwards, there are provisions under which members of an alternative investment fund management partnership can allocate certain profits to the partnership itself for income tax purposes rather than to individual or corporate partners. The profits concerned are certain amounts of 'variable remuneration' which partners cannot immediately access because of requirements of the Alternative Investment Fund Managers Directive (2011/61/EU), which will include remuneration which, if it vests in a partner, will vest in the form of instruments of the fund. See *ITTOIA 2005, ss 863H–863L*. The following applies where:

(1) under *ITTOIA 2005, s 863I* a partner in a partnership allocates to the partnership an amount of profit (the 'allocated profit') representing variable remuneration which, if it vests in the partner, will vest in the form of instruments;
(2) there is a disposal to the partner of instruments which are partnership assets of the partnership for the purposes of 50.2 above;
(3) by virtue of that disposal the variable remuneration vests in the partner; and
(4) where the disposal in (2) above is by a company which is a partner in the partnership, the company would, as such a partner, have been charged to tax on the allocated profit but for adjustments made under *CTA 2009, s 1264A(2)* or *ITTOIA 2005, s 850C(5)* (excess profit allocation to non-individual partners — see Tolley's Income Tax).

Both the persons making the disposal in (2) above and the partner are treated for capital gains purposes as if the instruments were acquired by the partner from those persons for a consideration equal to the allocated profit net of the income tax for which the partnership is liable under *ITTOIA 2005, s 863I* in respect of it.

[*TCGA 1992, ss 59B, 59C; FA 2014, Sch 17 paras 17, 21*].

Carried interest arising to investment managers

[50.20] Special provisions apply where an individual performs investment management services (as defined) directly or indirectly in respect of an '*investment scheme*' (either a 'collective investment scheme' or an investment trust) under 'arrangements' involving at least one partnership and 'carried interest' arises (see 50.21 below) to the individual under the arrangements on or after 8 July 2015. The provisions do not, however, apply if the carried interest arises in connection with the disposal of assets of a partnership or partnerships before that date.

For sums arising on or after 6 April 2016, a '*collective investment scheme*' includes arrangements which permit an external investor to participate in investments by the scheme without participating in the scheme itself and arrangements under which sums arise to an individual performing investment management services in respect of the scheme without those sums arising from the scheme itself. *Arrangements*' include any agreement, understanding, scheme, transaction or transactions, whether or not legally enforceable.

Where the carried interest arises in connection with the disposal of one or more assets of the partnership or partnerships, a chargeable gain equal to the amount of the carried interest less any permitted deductions (and no other such gain or loss) is deemed to accrue to the individual on the disposal at the time the carried interest arises. If the carried interest arises in any other circumstances, a chargeable gain equal to the amount of the carried interest less any permitted deductions is deemed to accrue to the individual at the time the carried interest arises. These provisions do not apply to the extent that the carried interest is brought into account in calculating the individual's profits of a trade, profession or vocation for any tax year or if it constitutes a 'co-investment' repayment of return. For sums arising on or after 6 April 2016, there are statutory provisions which in effect require certain 'income-based' carried interest to be brought into account in calculating the profits of the trade etc. and so to exclude it from the CGT charge. See *ITA 2007, ss 809FZA–809FZZ* and Tolley's Income Tax.

'*Permitted deductions*' means so much of the following amounts as is just and reasonable:

(a) any consideration given to the scheme by or on behalf of the individual wholly and exclusively for entering into the arrangements (but excluding consideration in respect of co-investments);
(b) any amount which constituted earnings of the individual under *ITEPA 2003, Pt 3 Ch 1* in respect of the individual entering into the arrangements (but excluding any earnings in respect of co-investments and any exempt income within *ITEPA 2003, s 8*); and
(c) any amount which, due to events occurring no later that the time the carried interest arises, counts as the individual's income under *ITEPA 2003, s 426* (restricted shares — see **22.13** EMPLOYEE SHARE SCHEMES), *s 438* (conversion of convertible shares — see **22.15** EMPLOYEE SHARE SCHEMES), *s 446U* (shares acquired for less than market value — see **22.8** EMPLOYEE SHARE SCHEMES), or *s 447* (receipt of benefit — see **22.12** EMPLOYEE SHARE SCHEMES) or under *ITEPA 2003, s 476* (by virtue of *s 477(3)(a)* — acquisition of shares under employment-related share option — see **22.6** EMPLOYEE SHARE SCHEMES) or under *FA 2005, s 21* (transitional charge on shares in spin-out companies) in respect of the individual's participation in the arrangements (but excluding amounts in respect of co-investments).

No other amount may be deducted from the carried interest in computing the deemed gain.

For this purpose, a '*co-investment*' is an investment made directly or indirectly in the scheme by the individual where there is no return on the investment which is not an arm's length return (as defined by *ITA 2007, s 809EZB(2)*).

Where the carried interest arises as a result of the individual's acquisition of a right to it from another person for consideration in money given by or on behalf of the individual, the deemed chargeable gain is reduced by the amount of the consideration provided that the individual makes a claim to that effect.

Foreign chargeable gains

A gain accruing under the above provisions when carried interest arises is a foreign chargeable gain for the purpose of the REMITTANCE BASIS (55.2) only to the extent that the individual performs the investment management services outside the UK.

Anti-avoidance

In determining whether the above provisions apply to an individual, any arrangements a main purpose of which is to secure that the provisions do not apply to the individual (or the individual and one or more other individuals) are disregarded.

Relief for double taxation

An individual who is charged to CGT under these provisions may make a claim for adjustments to the charge where either:

- the individual has paid tax (i.e. income tax or another tax) charged in relation to the carried interest, the tax has not been repaid, and the amount on which the tax is charged is not a permitted deduction within (b) or (c) above; or
- tax (income tax or another tax) charged on another person in relation to the carried interest has been paid by that person and not repaid.

On a claim, HMRC must make such of the adjustments claimed (if any) as are just and reasonable. The value of the adjustments must not exceed the lesser of the two tax charges. Adjustments may be made for any period regardless of any time limits. Where both tax charges arise in the same tax year HMRC accept that a claim can be made in the appropriate tax return without the need to pay both tax liabilities. HMRC consider that, where a sum comprises a series of items, relief must be given on an item by item basis (i.e. it will only be possible to set the other tax due on a particular component of the sum arising against the CGT due on that component, rather than the CGT due on the sum as a whole). This is the only approach which HMRC consider to be 'just and reasonable'. See Chapter 2 paras 45–47 of HMRC's guidance referred to below.

Where the individual has capital losses brought forward which would be automatically set-off against his chargeable gains including those on carried interest and he makes a claim under these provisions, he may elect to reduce the losses to be set-off by an amount up to that on which the other tax is charged.

Relief for external investors on disposal of partnership asset

Where a chargeable gain arises to an 'external investor' in an investment scheme on the disposal of one or more partnership assets and the investor makes a claim, the gain is reduced by any part of the sum invested by the investor which, on a just and reasonable basis, is referable to the asset or assets disposed of, less any amount deducted in computing the gains for acquisition consideration. This relief reverses the effect of 'base cost shift' for the investor (as the above provisions are intended to reverse its effect for the fund manager). Base cost shift can arise as a result of the operation of HMRC Statement of Practice D12 and involves the effective transfer to the fund manager of base cost (i.e. the allowable deduction in respect of acquisition consideration) of underlying investments held by a fund partnership which is derived from contributions made by investors. When calculating their chargeable gains investors would therefore be entitled to deduct a smaller amount of base cost than the amount they themselves actually contributed to the fund. See the Appendix to HMRC's guidance referred to below.

An '*external investor*' is a participator in the scheme other than an individual who performs investment management services directly or indirectly in relation to the scheme or a person through whom sums are to, or may, arise directly or indirectly to such an individual from the scheme under the arrangements.

[*TCGA 1992, ss 103KA, 103KC–103KF, 103KH(1); ITA 2007, ss 809EZA(6)(7), 809EZE(1); F(No 2)A 2015, s 43(1)(2); FA 2016, s 36(3)(5)*].

HMRC guidance

For HMRC guidance on the provisions see 'Investment managers: Capital Gains Tax treatment of carried interest (July 2015)', 20 July 2015, www.gov.uk/government/publications/investment-managers-capital-gains-tax-treatment-of-carried-interest-july-2015/investment-managers-capital-gains-tax-treatment-of-carried-interest-july-2015.

Previous rules

Before the above provisions took effect there were no specific legislative provisions dealing with carried interest. HMRC Statement of Practice D12 applied in the normal way (and could result in base cost shift as described above). See HMRC Company Tax Manual CTM36580 for a statement issued by the British Venture Capital Association in 1987 on how carried interest was to be treated.

Meaning of 'carried interest'

[50.21] '*Carried interest*' means a sum which arises to the individual under the arrangements by way of 'profit-related return'. A sum arises by way of '*profit-related return*' if under the arrangements:

- the sum can arise only if there are profits for a period on, or from the disposal of, the scheme investments or on particular scheme investments;
- the amount of the sum is variable, to a substantial extent, by reference to those profits; and
- returns to external investors are also determined by reference to those profits.

Where any part of the sum does not meet these conditions, that part is not to be regarded as arising by way of profit-related return. Where one or more sums arise to the individual under the arrangements by way of profit-related return in a tax year, but there was no significant risk that a sum of at least a certain amount would fail to arise, only the excess (if any) over that amount is carried interest. There are rules for determining how that amount is to be apportioned between the actual sums arising where more than one such sum arises in the tax year (see *ITA 2007, s 809EZC(7)(8)*). There are also rules for assessing the risk (see *ITA 2007, s 809EZC(4)–(6)*).

A sum is regarded as '*carried interest*', notwithstanding the above definition, if all, or substantially all, of the investments in the scheme made by the participants have been repaid to the participants, and each external investor has received a 'preferred return' on all, or substantially all, of his investments in the scheme. This also applies, with appropriate modification, where the scheme profits and preferred return are calculated on the basis of particular investments. '*Preferred return*' is an amount at least equivalent to compound interest on an investment at 6% per annum, with annual rests, for the whole of the period during which the investment was invested in the scheme.

Consideration received or receivable by an individual for the disposal, variation, loss or cancellation of a right to carried interest is treated as carried interest arising to that individual at the time of the disposal etc. This does not, however, apply to any extent that the consideration is a disguised fee within *ITA 2007, s 809EZA* (disguised investment management fees — see Tolley's Income Tax). It also does not apply to a variation occurring on or after 8 July 2015 and before 22 October 2015.

Carried interest '*arises*' to an individual if and only if it arises to him for the purposes of the disguised investment management fees provisions at *ITA 2007, ss 809EZA–809EZH*.

However, the following further provisions apply to carried interest arising on or after 22 October 2015 unless it arises in connection with the disposal of an asset or assets of a partnership or partnerships before that date. *Income Tax Act 2007, s 809EZDB* (which treats a sum as arising to the individual in certain cases where it arises to another person) does not apply in relation to a sum of carried interest arising to a company connected with the individual, or a person not connected with him, where the sum is 'deferred carried interest' in relation to him.

'*Deferred carried interest*' in relation to an individual is a sum of carried interest the provision of which to the individual or a connected person (other than, where relevant, the company to which the carried interest arises) is deferred (because, for example, further conditions need to be met) and it includes the individual's share, on a just and reasonable basis, of any carried interest the provision of which to the individual and one or more other persons, taken together, has been deferred. The sum is deemed to arise to the individual when it ceases to be deferred carried interest unless none of the enjoyment conditions below is met at that time and there is no reasonable likelihood that any of them will ever be met. The enjoyment conditions are:

(1) the sum, or part of it, is in fact calculated at some time to enure for the benefit of the individual or a connected person;
(2) the sum's ceasing to be deferred carried interest increases the value, either to the individual or a connected person, of any assets which they hold or which are held for their benefit;

(3) receives or is entitled to receive at any time any benefit provided or to be provided out of the sum or part of it;

(4) the individual or a connected person may become entitled to the beneficial enjoyment of the sum or part thereof if one or more powers are exercised or successively exercised (by anyone and with or without the consent of another person);

(5) the individual or a connected person can control directly or indirectly the application of the sum or part of it.

Where this provision applies because a sum arises to a company connected to the individual, in (1)–(5) above a connected person does not include that company.

In determining whether any of the above conditions is met regard must be had to the substantial result and effect of all relevant circumstances and all benefits which may at any time accrue to a person as a result of the sum ceasing to be deferred carried interest in relation to the individual must be taken into account (whatever their nature and whether or not there is a legal or equitable right to them).

Conditions (2), (3), and (4) above are not met if they would be met only because the individual holds shares or an interest in shares in a company. Conditions (1) and (5) are not met where the sum arises to a company connected with the individual and either the company includes the sum in it profits chargeable to corporation tax or the company is a controlled foreign company and the tax exemption in *TIOPA 2010, ss 371NA–371NE* applies for the accounting period in which the sum arises, or would be so apply if the company were a controlled foreign company. These provisions which prevent the conditions being met do not, however, apply where there are arrangements that have a main purpose of avoiding tax. This applies automatically where the sum is applied directly or indirectly as an investment in a collective investment scheme.

The disapplication of *ITA 2007, s 809EZDB* is ignored where the sum is applied directly or indirectly as an investment in a collective investment scheme and as a result, arrangements are deemed to be in place for the purposes of that section which have a main purpose of avoiding tax. The disapplication also does not apply where the deferral is not as a result of 'genuine commercial arrangements', or it is as a result of such arrangements but they have a main purpose of avoiding tax. '*Genuine commercial arrangements*' are arrangements involving the individual (alone or jointly with others performing investment management services) and external investors in the investment scheme.

[*TCGA 1992, ss 103KB, 103KG, 103KH(2); ITA 2007, ss 809EZC, 809EZD; F(No 2)A 2015, s 43(1)(3)(4)*].

Key points concerning partnerships

[50.22] Points to consider are as follows.

- A partnership is not treated as a separate entity for capital gains tax purposes. This also applies to a Limited Liability Partnership (LLP), except where it enters into a formal liquidation, when it is treated as a company.
- The legislation contains few specific rules in relation to partnership capital gains. HMRC's views on the application of the legislation to partnership matters are set out in Statements of Practice, the HMRC Capital Gains Tax Manual (CG27000–CG28420) and HMRC Briefs.
- Partners are treated as owning a share of each partnership asset, and are charged to tax separately on disposals. The market value of a partner's share is not discounted for the size of their partnership interest.
- For the purposes of transactions within a partnership, partners are not treated as connected simply because they are partners, so it is normally unnecessary to substitute market value for actual consideration.
- A partner who contributes an asset to a partnership makes a part-disposal of the share that passes to other partners. If a partnership asset is distributed to one or more partners, those who do not receive it are taxed on any gain at the time of distribution; for those who receive it, their base cost is reduced by the amount of any gain at the time of distribution.
- The revaluation of a partnership asset is not of itself an occasion of charge.
- Where there is a change in profit sharing ratios, a partner whose share increases or decreases is treated as acquiring or disposing of part or all of their share of each partnership asset.
- The incorporation of a partnership into an LLP does not of itself constitute a disposal by the partners of their interests in the old partnership's assets.
- A rolled-over or held-over gain in relation to any LLP assets crystallises if the LLP enters into formal liquidation.
- Transfers between partners who are spouses or civil partners are always treated as no gain/no loss disposals.
- Penalties for late filing of partnership tax returns are chargeable on each partner to whom the return relates. This can make the late filing of a partnership tax return very expensive. HMRC's free software for filing tax returns does not extend to partnerships. Paper returns should therefore be filed by 31 October or commercial software used to file online by 31 January following the end of the tax year.
- In normal circumstances a partner's personal tax return includes the amount that the partnership statement says is their share of the partnership profit or loss. However in exceptional circum-

stances where an individual partner does not agree with the profits allocated to them they can enter what they consider to be the correct amount. They must advise HMRC that they have done so by making an entry in the white space notes.

51

Payment of Tax

Introduction to payment of tax	**51.1**
Due date	**51.2**
Capital gains tax	**51.2**
Payments on account of CGT: non-resident disposals	**51.3**
Corporation tax (on chargeable gains)	**51.4**
Payment by instalments etc	**51.5**
'Time to pay' arrangements	**51.6**
Managed payment plans	**51.7**
Corporation tax exit charge payment plans	**51.8**
Methods of payment	**51.9**
Effective dates of payment	**51.10**
Certificates of tax deposit	**51.11**
Payment of tax in euros	**51.12**
Mandatory electronic payment	**51.13**
Fee for payment by specified methods	**51.14**
Overpayments of tax	**51.15**
Effect of making an appeal	**51.16**
Postponement of tax pending appeal	**51.17**
Payment of tax on determination of appeal	**51.18**
Collection and enforcement	**51.19**
Enforcement by deduction from accounts	**51.20**
Information notice	**51.21**
Hold notice	**51.22**
Deduction notice	**51.23**
Recovery of tax in respect of disposals by others	**51.24**
Recovery of tax from officers	**51.25**
Collection of unpaid tax from other members of the group and controlling directors	**51.26**
Recovery from shareholders	**51.27**
Cases in which HMRC do not pursue payment	**51.29**
Remission of tax in cases of HMRC delay	**51.29**
Reduced payments under 'equitable liability'	**51.30**
Over-repayments of tax	**51.31**
Recovery of foreign taxes etc	**51.32**
Key points concerning payment of tax	**51.33**

Cross-references. See **5** APPEALS; **6** ASSESSMENTS; **11.10** CHARITIES for gifts of tax repayments to charities via the tax return; **42** LATE PAYMENT INTEREST AND PENALTIES; **48.2** OFFSHORE SETTLEMENTS as regards the liability of migrating trustees of a settlement; **49.6** OVERSEAS MATTERS for relief for unremittable overseas gains and **49.18** for companies ceasing to be UK-resident and non-resident companies; **61** SELF-ASSESSMENT.

Introduction to payment of tax

[51.1] Both capital gains tax and corporation tax operate under a system of self-assessment in which it is the taxpayer's responsibility to calculate his liability and pay the tax by the due date (although for capital gains tax, HMRC will normally calculate the liability if the taxpayer does not wish to do so). The requirement to pay tax is not, therefore, dependent on the receipt of a demand from HMRC. Late payment will result in LATE PAYMENT INTEREST AND PENALTIES (42).

Capital gains tax is normally due on 31 January following the tax year. Corporation tax is due nine months and one day after the end of the accounting period, or, for large companies, by quarterly instalments. Tax may be paid by instalments where the disposal consideration is itself receivable in instalments or (capital gains tax only) where the disposal is by way of gift. Taxpayers can also negotiate with HMRC to enter into 'time to pay' arrangements or 'managed payment plans'.

Tax may be paid by any one of a number of methods but HMRC operate rules to determine the effective date for each method and they charge a fee for payment by certain methods.

Where a taxpayer has appealed against an assessment or amendment to a self-assessment and considers that he is overcharged to tax he may apply to HMRC for the tax to be postponed pending the determination of the appeal. This does not affect the date from which interest on unpaid tax runs. When the appeal is determined any postponed tax must be paid in accordance with the decision, even if a further appeal is made to the Upper Tribunal or court.

See **51.19** below for HMRC's collection and enforcement powers. In certain circumstances tax which is unpaid may be collected from a person other than the person who made the disposal giving rise to the liability. HMRC also have powers to re-assess any tax which has been wrongly repaid.

In two limited situations, HMRC will not seek to collect tax which is legally due. The situations are where the arrears result from HMRC's failure to make proper use of information supplied by the taxpayer and where the 'equitable liability' practice applies.

HMRC have powers to collect foreign taxes under the EU Mutual Assistance Recovery Directive or under tax enforcement agreements with other countries.

The Government announced that from April 2019 a payment on account of capital gains tax due on a disposal of residential property will have to be made within 30 days of completion. See Autumn Statement 2015, para 3.76. Draft legislation was due to be included in *Finance Bill 2017* but was omitted.

Due date

Capital gains tax

[51.2] Capital gains tax becomes due and payable as part of a taxpayer's self-assessment or under a simple assessment (see below). The normal due date for payment (or repayment) is 31 January following the tax year (so that, for example, capital gains tax for 2017/18 becomes due on 31 January 2019). Where the taxpayer gave notice of chargeability under *TMA 1970, s 7* (see **52.3** PENALTIES) within six months after the end of the tax year, but was not given notice under *TMA 1970, s 8* or *s 8A* (personal and trustee's return; see **58.3** RETURNS) until after 31 October following the tax year; in such a case, the due date is the last day of the three months beginning with the date of the said notice. Where a notice to file a return under *TMA 1970, s 8* or *s 8A* has been withdrawn (see **58.3** RETURNS) and a further such notice is subsequently given after 31 October following the tax year, the due date is the last day of the three months beginning with the date of the original withdrawn notice.

The amount of the payment so due is equal to the combined income tax (including certain Class 4 national insurance contributions treated as income tax) and capital gains tax liabilities contained in the self-assessment (see **58.6** RETURNS) less the aggregate of any payments on account (whether under *TMA 1970, s 59A, TMA 1970, s 59AA* (unless already repaid — see **51.3** below) or otherwise) and any income tax deducted at source. This means that, in effect, the capital gains tax payable is reduced by any income tax overpayment for the year. If the second total exceeds the first, a repayment will be made. For this purpose, income tax deducted at source does not include, where the taxpayer is a charity, any income tax already repaid on a claim in respect of gift aid payments or other exempt income.

Where an HMRC officer enquires into the return (see **58.9** RETURNS) and a repayment is otherwise due, the repayment is not required to be made until the enquiry is fully completed (see **58.12** RETURNS) although the officer may make a provisional repayment at his discretion. [*TMA 1970, s 59B; F(No 2)A 2017, Sch 15 paras 20, 44*]. Tax repayments arising from a partial closure notice (see **58.12** RETURNS) will not automatically be repaid, e.g. where tax is due in respect of other issues not covered by the partial closure notice (www.gov.uk/government/publications/tax-enquiries-closure-rules).

Simple assessments

In general, the due date for payment of the tax charged by a 'simple assessment' (see **6.9** ASSESSMENTS), net of any payments on account and income tax deducted at source, is 31 January following the tax year to which the assessment relates. However, where a person is given notice of the simple assessment after 31 October following the tax year to which it relates, the due date is deferred until the last day of the period of three months following the day on which the notice was given.

[*TMA 1970, s 59B(1)–(4A)(7)(8), s 59BA; FA 2012, Sch 15 paras 9, 17(3); FA 2013, Sch 51 para 5; FA 2015, Sch 7 para 52; FA 2016, s 167, Sch 23 para 8*].

Amendments and corrections

Where an amount of tax is payable (repayable) as a result of an amendment or correction to an individual's or trustees' self-assessment under any of (a)–(e) below, then, subject to the appeal and postponement provisions in, respectively, **5.2** APPEALS and **51.17** below, the due date for payment (repayment) is as stated below (if this is later than the date given under the general rules above). Note that these rules do *not* defer the date from which interest accrues, which is as in **42.2**, **42.3** LATE PAYMENT INTEREST AND PENALTIES (**56.2**, **56.3** REPAYMENT INTEREST).

(a) Taxpayer amendment to return as in **58.7** RETURNS: 30 days after the date of the taxpayer's notice of amendment.
(b) HMRC correction to return as in **58.7** RETURNS: 30 days after the date of the officer's notice of correction.
(c) Taxpayer amendment to return whilst enquiry in progress as in **58.13** RETURNS, where accepted by HMRC: tax payable 30 days after the date of a final or partial closure notice; tax repayable 30 days after the date of a final closure notice, regardless of whether or not a partial closure notice was previously given (see **58.12** RETURNS).
(d) HMRC amendment to return where amendment made by a final or partial closure notice on completion or part completion of an enquiry (see **58.12** RETURNS): 30 days after the date of the closure notice.
(e) HMRC amendment of self-assessment to prevent potential loss of tax to the Crown (see **58.13** RETURNS): 30 days after the date of the notice of amendment.

As regards amendments and corrections to partnership returns, (e) above is not relevant, and the equivalent date in each of (a)–(d) above as regards each partner is 30 days after the date of the officer's notice of consequential amendment to the partner's own tax return. The same applies in the case of a consequential amendment by virtue of an amendment of a partnership return on discovery (see **6.11** ASSESSMENTS).

[*TMA 1970, s 59B(5), Sch 3ZA; F(No 2)A 2017, Sch 15 paras 21, 44*].

Assessments other than self-assessments or simple assessments

Subject to the appeal and postponement provisions in **5.2** APPEALS and **51.17** below, the due date for payment of tax charged by assessment otherwise than by self-assessment or simple assessment, e.g. a discovery assessment under *TMA 1970, s 29* (see **6.10** ASSESSMENTS), is 30 days after the date of the assessment (but see also **42** LATE PAYMENT INTEREST AND PENALTIES). [*TMA 1970, s 59B(6); FA 2016, Sch 23 para 7*].

Small amounts outstanding

Note that statements of account (advisory statements issued to taxpayers notifying them of payments due and outstanding) are not routinely issued to taxpayers for amounts of less than £32, the amount instead being carried forward to the next statement, though this practice does not prevent interest accruing as normal (Revenue 'Working Together' Bulletin December 2001 p 5).

Payments on account of CGT: non-resident disposals

[51.3] Where a person is required to make an 'NRCGT return' containing an 'advance self-assessment' in relation to a tax year he must make a payment on account of his liability to capital gains tax for the tax year of an amount (the 'balancing amount') equal to the excess of the 'amount notionally chargeable' contained in the advance self-assessment over any previous such payments on account for the tax year. The payment is due on the filing date for the return (usually the 30th day following the day of the completion of the non-resident CGT disposal). If the amount notionally chargeable is less than the previous payments on account, the difference is repayable to the taxpayer on the filing date. In the case of an NRCGT group (see **41.33** LAND), the group is responsible for discharging the obligations to pay any balancing amount; such a payment is treated as a payment on account of the CGT liability of the group member which made the disposal.

If, in a repayment case, HMRC enquire into the return (see **58.21** RETURNS), the repayment does not have to be made before the enquiry is fully completed, but HMRC may make an earlier repayment on a provisional basis to the extent that they think fit.

Where an amount is payable on account (or repayable) as a result of an amendment or correction to an advance self-assessment under any of (a)–(d) below, the due date for payment (repayment) is as stated below (if this is later than the date given under the general rules above).

(a) Taxpayer amendment to return as in **58.20** RETURNS: 30 days after the date of the taxpayer's notice of amendment.
(b) HMRC correction to return as in **58.20** RETURNS: 30 days after the date of the officer's notice of correction.
(c) Taxpayer amendment to return while enquiry in progress as in **58.21** RETURNS, where accepted by HMRC: 30 days after the date of the closure notice (see **58.21** RETURNS).
(d) HMRC amendment to return where amendment made by closure notice following enquiry (see **58.21** RETURNS): 30 days after the date of the closure notice.

No payment on account is required, or repayment due, if the NRCGT return is not required to contain an advance self-assessment (i.e. where, broadly, the taxpayer is within self-assessment or has made an annual tax on enveloped dwellings return — see **58.20** RETURNS). The normal rules for payment of CGT apply instead.

For the meaning of 'NRCGT return', 'advance self-assessment' and 'amount notionally chargeable', and for the filing date for an NRCGT return, see **58.20** RETURNS.

[*TMA 1970, s 59AA, Sch 3ZA paras 1–3, 5; FA 2015, Sch 7 paras 51, 55; F(No 2)A 2017, Sch 15 paras 19, 44*].

Corporation tax (on chargeable gains)

[51.4] Subject to the rules outlined below for payment by 'large' companies by quarterly instalments, corporation tax (including that in respect of chargeable gains) for an accounting period is due and payable on the day following the expiry of nine months from the end of the period.

If the company subsequently has grounds for believing that a change in circumstances has rendered payment for a period excessive, it may, by notice to an officer of the Board stating the grounds and the amount it considers should be repaid, claim repayment of the excess. Such notice may not be given before the date on which the tax became (or would have become) due and payable as above, or after an assessment for the period has become final. If the company wishes to claim repayment at a time when an assessment for the period is under appeal, the company must apply to the Tribunal (before 1 April 2009, the Appeal Commissioners) for a determination of the amount to be repaid pending determination of the appeal. Such an application may be combined with an application for postponement of tax pending an appeal (see **51.17** below).

[*TMA 1970, ss 59D, 59DA; SI 2009 No 56, Sch 1 para 40*].

Quarterly accounting by large companies

'Large' companies pay corporation tax under a system of *quarterly accounting* (i.e. payment by instalments). [*TMA 1970, s 59E; FA 2012, Sch 20 para 12*].

'Large' companies are those with profits (including UK dividend income, other than intra-group dividends, plus tax credits for dividends received prior to 6 April 2016) exceeding £1,500,000 in an accounting period, divided by one plus the number of related 51% group companies (within *CTA 2010, s 279F*), if any, at the end of the preceding accounting period. For accounting periods ending before 1 April 2015, the £1,500,000 limit is divided by one plus the number of active associated companies in the accounting period if any. However, such a company is not treated as 'large' in respect of an accounting period if its total corporation tax liability for that period does not exceed £10,000, which might be the case if it would otherwise be large only by reference to the number of its related 51% group companies or associated companies or the level of its dividend income. A company is also exempt from payment by instalments for an accounting period if it was not 'large' in the 12 months preceding the accounting period and its profits for the accounting period do not exceed £10 million, divided by one plus the number of related 51% group companies (or, for accounting periods ending before 1 April 2015, active associated companies) as at the end of the preceding accounting period. Each of these monetary limits is proportionately reduced for accounting periods of less than 12 months.

The first instalment is due 6 months and 14 days into the accounting period and the last is due 3 months and 14 days after the end of the accounting period. Interim instalments are due at quarterly intervals. Except for accounting periods of less than 12 months, the amount of each instalment should be one quarter of the total liability (or, under the transitional provisions below, the total payable by instalments). Interest on tax underpaid by any instalment will run from the due date of that instalment. In cases of deliberate or reckless non-payment or underpayment, a penalty of up to twice the amount of interest may be charged. Subject to similar penalty for fraud or negligence, a company may claim repayment of tax paid by instalments if its circumstances change such that the total liability is likely to be less than previously calculated.

In the July 2015 budget it was announced that dates for payments of instalments by companies with profits exceeding £20 million are to be brought forward so that payments will be due in the third, sixth, ninth and twelfth months of each accounting period. The £20 million threshold will be reduced for companies which are members of one or more 51% groups (in the same way as the £1,500,000 threshold above is reduced). It was initially expected that this change would apply to accounting periods commencing on or after 1 April 2017 but it was announced in the 2016 budget that this will be delayed and will apply to accounting periods commencing on or after 1 April 2019. See www.gov.uk/government/publications/corporation-tax-payments-for-very-large-companies/corporation-tax-payments-for-very-large-companies.

See Revenue Tax Bulletins February 2000 pp 723–726 and April 2001 pp 831–836 for practical articles on the operation of the system. HMRC are given extensive powers to require information and records to ascertain reasons for non-payment of an instalment, the validity of a repayment claim or whether the amount of an instalment is consistent with the quality and quantity of information available as to the company's likely corporation tax liability. See below re HMRC guidance on use of their information and penalty powers.

[*SI 1998 No 3175; SI 2014 No 2409; F(No 2)A 2015, s 39*].

HMRC have published guidance outlining the way in which they will use their information and penalty powers under the above regulations; the information powers are not intended for routine use, and the majority of cases of late or inadequate payment will attract only an interest charge, not a penalty. A penalty will be sought in only the most serious cases involving flagrant abuse of the regulations. (Revenue Press Release 8 June 1999). Further guidance on 'acceptable' methods of estimating quarterly instalments has been published on HMRC's website (Revenue Internet Statement 28 June 2002).

Penalties are also chargeable for non-compliance with a notice to produce information, records etc. [*TMA 1970, s 98*].

Groups of companies

HMRC may enter into arrangements ('Group Payment Arrangements') with some or all of the members of a group of companies (defined to include all 51% subsidiaries) for one of them to discharge any liability of each of them for the accounting period to which the arrangements relate. [*TMA 1970, s 59F; TIOPA 2010, Sch 7 para 79; FA 2012, Sch 20 para 13*]. See Revenue Tax Bulletins April 1999 pp 647–650 and April 2001 pp 831–836.

There are also provisions to allow two companies within a group (as defined for group relief purposes under *CTA 2010, Pt 5*) to jointly give notice to HMRC that a 'tax refund relating to an accounting period' which falls to be made to one of them should be surrendered in whole or part to the other. The surrendering company is then treated as having received on the 'relevant date' a payment equal to the refund (or part), and the recipient company as having paid on that date corporation tax equal to the amount of the refund (or part). [*CTA 2010, ss 963–966; FA 1989, s 102*]. These provisions are designed to enable group members to rearrange their tax liabilities without suffering a disadvantage because of the higher rates for interest on unpaid tax as compared with those for interest on overpaid tax. See Tolley's Corporation Tax under Groups of Companies for full coverage of the provisions. For the interaction between these provisions and the Group Payment Arrangements referred to above, see Revenue Tax Bulletin April 2001 pp 834, 835.

Payment by instalments etc.

[51.5] Where the whole or part of the consideration for a disposal is receivable by instalments over a period exceeding 18 months, beginning not earlier than the date of disposal, the tax arising may at the option of the person making the disposal be paid by such instalments as HMRC allows, over a period not exceeding eight years (and ending not later than the time at which the last of the instalments of the consideration is payable). [*TCGA 1992, s 280*].

Example

Paul sells an asset on 31 March 2018 for £360,000. The consideration is to be paid by twelve annual instalments of £30,000 beginning on 31 March 2018. Paul originally purchased the asset for £13,700 in 1990 and his allowable costs of sale are £5,000. The gain is not an upper rate gain and does not qualify for entrepreneurs' relief and Paul has no other chargeable gains in 2017/18.

Paul's liability to capital gains tax for 2017/18 is as follows.

	£
Consideration	360,000
Less costs of sale	5,000
Acquisition cost	13,700
Chargeable gain 2017/18	341,300
Annual exempt amount	11,300
Gain chargeable to tax	£330,000
Capital gains tax payable (£330,000 × 20%)	£66,000

If Paul opts under *TCGA 1992, s 280* to pay the tax by instalments, the following payments will be due.

31 January 2019	£15,000
31 March 2019	£15,000
31 March 2020	£15,000
31 March 2021	£15,000
31 March 2022	£6,000

Notes to the example

(a) HMRC's practice is to ask for instalments of tax equal to half of each instalment of consideration until the total tax liability has been discharged. To the extent that instalments of consideration under the contract fall due on or before the normal due date for the payment of tax (31 January in the tax year following that in which the disposal occurred), the respective instalments of tax are payable on that normal due date. Where instalments of consideration fall due after that time, then the respective instalments of tax are payable on the dates when the taxpayer is contractually entitled to receive the consideration. (HMRC Capital Gains Manual CG14912).

(b) Interest on unpaid tax is charged on each instalment only if it is paid late and will run from the date when the instalment was due until the date of payment. (HMRC Self-Assessment Manual SAM80072).

(c) The instalment provisions do not apply to deferred consideration which is unquantified and contingent. See **10.2** CAPITAL SUMS DERIVED FROM ASSETS and **16.13** COMPUTATION OF GAINS AND LOSSES.

See HMRC Capital Gains Manual CG14910–14922.

Gifts of land or shares etc.

Subject to the conditions below, capital gains tax chargeable on a gift may, on election in writing, be paid by ten equal yearly instalments. The first instalment is due on the ordinary due date and the unpaid tax will attract interest on unpaid tax in the usual way and which will be payable with each instalment. The outstanding balance together with accrued interest may be paid at any time. The deferral of payment is available where the whole or any part of specified assets is disposed of by way of gift or is deemed to be disposed of by trustees under *TCGA 1992, s 71(1)* or *s 72(1)* (see **62.16–62.18** SETTLEMENTS) and the disposal is *either* one to which neither *TCGA 1992, s 165(4)* nor *s 260(3)* (see **36.2** and **36.10** HOLD-OVER RELIEFS) applies (or would apply if a claim was made) *or* one to which either of those sections does apply but on which the held-over gain only partly reduces the gain otherwise arising or is nil.

The assets specified for this purpose are: land or any interest or estate in land; any shares or securities of a company which, immediately before the disposal, gave control to the person making or deemed to be making the disposal; and any shares or securities of a company not falling within the foregoing and not listed on a recognised stock exchange (see **63.30** SHARES AND SECURITIES) nor dealt in on the Unlisted Securities Market (now closed).

Tax and any accrued interest is payable immediately if the disposal was by way of a gift to a person connected (see **17** CONNECTED PERSONS) with the donor or was deemed to be made under *TCGA 1992, s 71(1)* or *s 72(1)* and the assets are disposed of for a valuable consideration under a subsequent disposal (whether or not made by the original donee). Interest on unpaid tax is chargeable on each instalment as if no election to pay by instalments had been made. Instalments and interest may be paid at any time with the interest calculation adjusted accordingly.

These provisions apply in relation to a chargeable gain accruing under *TCGA 1992, s 169C(7)* (clawback of relief under *TCGA 1992, s 165* or *s 260* if settlement becomes settlor-interested — see **36.8** HOLD-OVER RELIEFS) as they apply to a gain accruing on a disposal if:

- the 'relevant disposal' (see **36.8** HOLD-OVER RELIEFS) in question was a disposal of the whole or part of any asset of a type specified above, and
- at the time that the chargeable gain is deemed to accrue, no part of the subject-matter of the relevant disposal has been disposed of for valuable consideration under a subsequent disposal (whether or not by the trustees to whom the relevant disposal was made).

Tax and accrued interest are payable immediately if any part of the subject-matter of the relevant disposal is disposed of for valuable consideration under a subsequent disposal (whether or not by the trustees to whom the relevant disposal was made).

[*TCGA 1992, s 281*].

Example

On 1 June 2017, Chris gives a parcel of land to his son Scott. The market value of the land on that date is £401,000. Chris purchased the land in 1990 for £199,700, and makes no other disposals in 2017/18. For the purposes of this example only, the rate of interest on unpaid capital gains tax is taken to be 4% throughout.

Chris's liability to capital gains tax for 2017/18 is as follows:

	£
Consideration	401,000
Less acquisition cost	199,700
Chargeable gain 2017/18	201,300
Annual exempt amount	11,300
Gain chargeable to tax	£190,000
Capital gains tax payable (£190,000 × 20%)	£38,000

If Chris elects under *TCGA 1992, s 281*, before 31 January 2019 to pay the tax by instalments, the following payments will be due.

	£	£
1st instalment due 31.1.19		3,800
2nd instalment due 31.1.20	3,800	
Interest 4% × £34,200	1,368	5,168
3rd instalment due 31.1.21	3,800	
Interest 4% × £30,400	1,216	5,016
4th instalment due 31.1.22	3,800	
Interest 4% × £26,600	1,064	4,864
5th instalment due 31.1.23	3,800	
Interest 4% × £22,800	912	4,712
6th instalment due 31.1.24	3,800	
Interest 4% × £19,000	760	4,560
7th instalment due 31.1.25	3,800	
Interest 4% × £15,200	608	4,408
8th instalment due 31.1.26	3,800	
Interest 4% × £11,400	456	4,256

	£	£
9th instalment due 31.1.27	3,800	
Interest 4% × £7,600	304	4,104
10th instalment due 31.1.28	3,800	
Interest 4% × £3,800	152	3,952
Total tax and interest		£44,840

Notes to the example

(a) An election under *TCGA 1992, s 281* may be made at any time before the tax becomes payable (HMRC Capital Gains Manual CG66530).

(b) Interest on unpaid tax is charged as if no election had been made. The interest on the unpaid portion of the tax is added to each instalment and must be paid accordingly.

For a summary of other reliefs available to disposals by way of gift etc., see **27.3** GIFTS.

'Time to pay' arrangements

[51.6] By concession, under a 'time to pay' arrangement, a taxpayer enters into a negotiated agreement with HMRC, which takes full account of his circumstances (e.g. illness, unemployment, unforeseen short-term business difficulties), and thereby commits to settle his tax liabilities by regular instalments. Clear reasons for allowing settlement over an extended period that runs beyond the due date must be established during negotiations and any such arrangement is normally subject to adequate provision being made to settle future liabilities on time. Interest on unpaid tax is chargeable in the normal way on the full amount unpaid at the due date and not just on overdue instalments. However, a late payment penalty or surcharge may be avoided where a 'time to pay' arrangement is in force (see **42.6, 42.10** LATE PAYMENT INTEREST AND PENALTIES). (HMRC Debt Management and Banking Manual DMBM800000 onwards). With effect from 3 August 2015, HMRC require all instalment payments under a 'time to pay' arrangement made on or after that date to be made by direct debit, unless the taxpayer is unable to set up a direct debit. (HMRC Notice 14 July 2015).

With effect from 1 April 2010, a business seeking a time to pay arrangement on a tax debt of £1 million or more must provide HMRC with an independent business review. This must be carried out by a qualified professional advisor and must be paid for by the business making the request. (HMRC Press Notice 29 March 2010).

HMRC has introduced a Business Payment Support Service (telephone 0300 200 3835) to facilitate the arrangement of 'time to pay' arrangements.

The Government has announced that 'time to pay' arrangements are available for those suffering cash flow difficulties as a result of the Greek financial crisis of 2015. A special dedicated helpline (telephone 0300 3308 100) has been set up to provide advice. (Written Ministerial Statement 12 August 2011).

Managed payment plans

[51.7] Under a managed payment plan, a taxpayer agrees with HMRC to pay income tax, capital gains tax or corporation tax (other than corporation tax payable under a group payment arrangement — see **51.4** above) by instalments which are 'balanced' equally before and after the normal due date. If the taxpayer then pays all of the instalments in accordance with the plan, he is treated as having paid the total amount on the due date, so that no interest or late payment surcharge or penalty will arise.

Where the taxpayer pays one or more of the instalments in accordance with the plan but then fails to pay one or more later instalments, the total of the instalments paid before the failure are treated as paid on the due date. Where the failure takes place before the due date, the taxpayer is, nevertheless, entitled to be paid any interest on the early payments made if he would have been so entitled but for the plan. Where, following a failure, the taxpayer makes payments after the due date, HMRC can notify him that any or all of those payments will not be liable to a late payment surcharge or penalty.

Instalments to be paid before the due date are '*balanced*' with instalments to be paid after it if the time value of each set of instalments is equal or approximately equal. HMRC can make regulations to determine when, for this purpose, two amounts are approximately equal. The time value of an instalment is calculated by multiplying it by the number of days before or after the due date it is to be paid.

The legislation providing for managed payment plans applies where the due date is after 21 July 2009 but HMRC have not yet implemented the scheme.

[*TMA 1970, ss 59G, 59H*].

Corporation tax exit charge payment plans

[51.8] *FA 2013* introduced a facility for a company which ceases to be resident in the UK to enter into an exit charge payment plan with HMRC to defer payment of the exit charges which arise under a number of corporation tax provisions, including the chargeable gains provisions. The facility can also be used by certain non-resident companies which cease to carry on all or part of a trade in the UK through a permanent establishment. The facility is intended to ensure that the UK's exit charges comply with EU law.

The legislation providing for payment plans applies for accounting periods ending on or after 10 March 2012. Where the deadline for applying for a plan would otherwise fall before 31 March 2013, the deadline is extended to that date.

[*FA 2013, Sch 49 para 8*].

Company ceasing to be UK-resident

An 'eligible company' which ceases to be resident in the UK can enter into an exit charge payment plan if it becomes resident in another European Economic Area (EEA) state and is liable to pay 'qualifying corporation tax' in respect of the 'migration accounting period'. The following further conditions must be satisfied:

(i) on ceasing to be UK-resident the company must carry on a business in an EEA state; and
(ii) on becoming resident in the other EEA state, the company must not be treated as resident in a non-EEA territory for the purposes of any double tax arrangements.

The company must apply to HMRC to enter into the plan before the end of the nine-month period following the migration accounting period and must include in the application all the required information (see below).

An '*eligible company*' is one that has a right to freedom of establishment under EU law or under the Agreement on the EEA. The '*migration accounting period*' is, if an accounting period comes to an end on the company ceasing to be UK-resident, that accounting period. In any other case, the migration accounting period is the accounting period during which the company ceases to be UK-resident.

A company is liable to pay '*qualifying corporation tax*' in respect of the migration accounting period if the corporation tax it is liable to pay for the period (CT1) is greater than the amount of corporation tax it would be liable to pay if any income, profits, gains, losses or debits arising only under the exit charge provisions listed below were ignored (CT2). The amount of the qualifying corporation tax is the difference between CT1 and CT2. The exit charge provisions are:

(a) *TCGA 1992, s 185* (deemed disposal of assets on company ceasing to be UK-resident; see **49.17** OVERSEAS MATTERS);
(b) *TCGA 1992, s 187(4)(c)* (postponed gains charged when principal company ceases to be UK-resident; see **49.17** OVERSEAS MATTERS);
(c) *CTA 2009, s 162* as applied by *CTA 2009, s 41(2)(b)* (valuation of trading stock on ceasing to be within the charge to corporation tax);
(d) *CTA 2009, s 333* (deemed assignment of loan relationships on company ceasing to be UK-resident);
(e) *CTA 2009, s 609* (deemed assignment of derivative contract rights and liabilities on company ceasing to be UK-resident);
(f) *CTA 2009, s 859(2)(a)* (deemed realisation of intangible fixed asset on it ceasing to be chargeable intangible asset when company ceases to be UK-resident);
(g) *CTA 2009, s 862(1)(c)* (postponed gains on intangible fixed assets charged when parent company ceases to be UK-resident).

For the purposes of these provisions, '*exit charge assets*' and '*exit charge liabilities*' are assets or liabilities in respect of which income, profits or gains arise in the migration accounting period under the exit charge provisions above. '*TCGA or trading stock exit charge assets*' are exit charge assets in respect of which income, profits or gains arise under (a)–(c) above, other than any intangible fixed assets excluded from the intangible assets regime by that regime's commencement rules (see **15.14** COMPANIES — CORPORATE FINANCE AND INTANGIBLES). '*Financial exit charge assets or liabilities*' are exit charge assets or liabilities in respect of which income, profits or gains arise under (d) or (e) above. '*Intangible exit charge assets*' means exit charge assets in respect of which income, profits or gains arise under (f) or (g) above together with intangible assets excluded from being TCGA or trading stock exit charge assets as above.

[*TMA 1970, s 59FA, Sch 3ZB paras 1–3; FA 2013, Sch 49 paras 2, 6*].

Non-UK resident company with UK permanent establishment

An eligible company (defined as above) which is not resident in the UK but carries on a trade there through a permanent establishment in an accounting period (the '*migration accounting period*') can enter into an exit charge payment plan if one or more 'PE qualifying events' occurs and the company is liable to pay 'qualifying corporation tax' in respect of the migration accounting period.

The company must apply to HMRC to enter into the plan before the end of the nine-month period following the migration accounting period and must include in the application all the required information (see below).

A '*PE qualifying event*' occurs in relation to an asset or liability of the company (a PE qualifying asset or liability) if:

- an event occurs which triggers a deemed disposal and reacquisition of the asset or liability, or a valuation of the asset, under one of the exit charge provisions listed below;
- the event occurs during the migration accounting period or causes that period to end; and
- at the time of the event, the company is not treated as resident in a non-EEA territory for the purposes of any double tax arrangements.

A company is liable to pay '*qualifying corporation tax*' in respect of the migration accounting period if the corporation tax it is liable to pay for the period (CT1) is greater than the amount of corporation tax it would be liable to pay if any income, profits, gains, losses or debits arising only under the exit charge provisions listed below were ignored (CT2). The amount of the qualifying corporation tax is the difference between CT1 and CT2. The exit charge provisions are:

(A) *TCGA 1992, s 25* (deemed disposal of assets leaving UK; see **49.3** OVERSEAS MATTERS);
(B) *CTA 2009, s 162* as applied by *CTA 2009, s 41(2)(b)* (valuation of trading stock on ceasing to be within the charge to corporation tax);
(C) *CTA 2009, s 334* (deemed assignment of loan relationship on company ceasing to hold relationship for UK permanent establishment);
(D) *CTA 2009, s 610* (deemed assignment of derivative contract rights and liabilities on company ceasing to hold contract for UK permanent establishment);
(E) *CTA 2009, s 859(2)(b)* (deemed realisation of intangible fixed asset on asset ceasing to be a chargeable intangible asset).

For the purposes of these provisions, '*exit charge assets*' and '*exit charge liabilities*' are PE qualifying assets or liabilities in respect of which income, profits or gains arise in the migration accounting period under the exit charge provisions above. '*TCGA or trading stock exit charge assets*' are exit charge assets in respect of which income, profits or gains arise under (A) or (B) above, other than any intangible fixed assets excluded from the intangible assets regime by that regime's commencement rules (see **15.14** COMPANIES — CORPORATE FINANCE AND INTANGIBLES). '*Financial exit charge assets or liabilities*' are exit charge assets or liabilities in respect of which income, profits or gains arise under (C) or (D) above. '*Intangible exit charge assets*' means exit charge assets in respect of which income, profits or gains arise under (E) above together with intangible assets excluded from being TCGA or trading stock exit charge assets as above.

[*TMA 1970, s 59FA, Sch 3ZB paras 4–6; FA 2013, Sch 49 paras 2, 6*].

Entering into a payment plan

An exit charge payment plan takes effect where the company agrees to pay, and HMRC agree to accept payment of, all or part of the qualifying corporation tax in accordance with the 'standard instalment method', the 'realisation method' or a combination of both. The company must also agree to pay interest on the tax as described below. The plan must specify the following:

(1) where the company ceases to be UK-resident, the date on which it so ceases and the EEA state in which the company has become resident;
(2) where the company has a UK permanent establishment, the EEA state in which it is resident and, if the PE qualifying event is the company ceasing to trade in the UK through a permanent establishment, the date of cessation;
(3) the amount of qualifying corporation tax which the company considers is payable for the migration accounting period;
(4) whether that tax is to be paid using the standard instalment method, the realisation method or a combination of both;
(5) if the tax is to be paid by a combination of the methods, the method to be used for each of the company's exit charge assets or liabilities and the amount of tax to be paid under each method.

Where tax attributable to an exit charge asset or liability is to be paid using the realisation method, the plan must also specify:

- each such asset or liability (so far as not already specified under (5) above) and the amount of tax attributable to it;
- requirements for ongoing provision of information to HMRC in relation to the asset or liability;
- in the case of a financial exit charge asset or liability the remaining term of which is less than ten years, the number of years in the remaining term (rounded up to the nearest whole year); and
- in the case of an intangible exit charge asset the remaining useful life of which is less than ten years, how many years of the useful life remain (rounded up to the nearest whole year).

The amount of tax attributable to each exit charge asset or liability for this purpose is the proportion of the tax postponed under the plan that the income, profits or gains arising in respect of that asset or liability under the exit charge concerned bears to the total income, profits or gains arising in respect of all the exit charges or liabilities under the exit charge provisions.

Where HMRC consider that entering into a plan would otherwise present a serious risk to collection of the tax, the plan may include provision for HMRC to take security for the tax. This would usually be in the form of a bank guarantee.

A payment plan is void if any information provided by the company does not fully and accurately disclose all facts and considerations material to HMRC's decision to enter into it.

[*TMA 1970, s 59FA, Sch 3ZB paras 7, 8, 10–12; FA 2013, Sch 49 paras 2, 6*].

Effect of payment plan

An exit charge payment plan does not prevent the tax included in it from becoming due and payable in the normal way, but HMRC may not seek payment otherwise than in accordance with the plan. HMRC may, however, make repayments of any amount of the tax paid, or amount paid on account of the tax, before the plan is entered into.

The tax deferred under the plan carries interest as if the plan had not been entered into. Each payment under the plan must include any interest on the tax.

A late payment penalty (see **42.10** LATE PAYMENT INTEREST AND PENALTIES) will only be payable if the company fails to make payments in accordance with the plan.

There is nothing to prevent a company paying any of the tax before the time it becomes payable under the plan.

[*TMA 1970, s 59FA, Sch 3ZB para 9; FA 2013, Sch 49 paras 2, 6*].

Standard instalment method

A payment plan may specify that the tax is to be paid under the standard instalment method only if:

- in the case of a company ceasing to be UK-resident, the company's ceasing to be so resident is not part of arrangements with a main purpose of deferring the payment of any of the qualifying corporation tax; or
- in the case of a company with a UK permanent establishment, none of the PE qualifying events are part of such arrangements.

Where the standard instalment method is used, the tax is payable in six equal instalments. The first instalment is due nine months and one day after the end of the migration accounting period. The remaining instalments are due on each of the first five anniversaries of that date.

Where the company becomes insolvent, enters administration or a liquidator is appointed, the balance of the tax is payable in full on the date on which the next instalment would otherwise be due. This applies also where the company becomes insolvent etc. under a corresponding law of an EEA state and where the company ceases to be resident in an EEA state without becoming resident in another EEA state.

[*TMA 1970, s 59FA, Sch 3ZB paras 10(5), 13; FA 2013, Sch 49 paras 2, 6*].

Realisation method

Where the realisation method is used for a TCGA or trading stock exit charge asset, the tax becomes payable on the occurrence of the first of the following events:

(I) the disposal or part disposal of the asset at any time after the company becomes non-UK resident or the PE qualifying event occurs;
(II) the tenth anniversary of the end of the migration accounting period;
(III) the company becoming insolvent or entering administration or liquidation under UK or a corresponding EEA state law; and
(IV) the company ceasing to be resident in an EEA state without becoming resident in another EEA state.

Where (I) or (II) apply, the tax is payable on the date of disposal or on the tenth anniversary. Where (III) or (IV) apply the tax is due nine months and one day after the end of the migration accounting period or, if that date has already passed, the next anniversary of that date.

Where part of an asset is disposed of after an event within (I) above, the tax attributable to it is apportioned on a just and reasonable basis.

Where the realisation method is used for a financial exit charge asset or liability or for an intangible exit charge asset, the tax is payable in ten equal annual instalments, unless the remaining term of the loan relationship or derivative contract, or the remaining useful life of the intangible asset, is specified in the plan as fewer than ten years. In the latter case, the number of instalments is the specified number. The first instalment is due nine months and one day after the end of the migration accounting period. The remaining instalments are due on each of the subsequent anniversaries of that date.

All of the outstanding tax attributable to an asset or liability is payable on the date the company ceases to be a party to the loan relationship or derivative contract or disposes of the intangible asset. All of the outstanding balance is also payable if an event within (III) or (IV) above occurs, the tax becoming due on the date of the next instalment.

Where there is a disposal of rights or liabilities under the loan relationship or derivative contract which amounts to a related transaction (within *CTA 2009, s 304* or *s 596*) but the company does not cease to be party to the relationship or contract, so much of the outstanding tax as is attributable, on a just and reasonable basis, to the transaction is payable immediately. The remainder of the outstanding tax continues to be payable by instalments under the plan. This rule applies also where there is a transaction which results in a reduction in the accounting value of an intangible exit charge asset but does not result in the asset ceasing to be recognised in the company's balance sheet. If the asset has no balance sheet value already, it is treated for this purpose only as if it did have such a value.

[*TMA 1970, s 59FA, Sch 3ZB paras 14–17; FA 2013, Sch 49 paras 2, 6*].

Methods of payment

[51.9] Capital gains tax and corporation tax can be paid by any one of a number of methods, including cheques, postal orders, electronic transfer or credit card. Each method has its own effective date of payment for the purposes of calculating any interest or surcharges. See **51.10** below. Capital gains tax may be paid by certificate of tax deposit. HMRC may charge a fee for accepting certain types of payment — see **51.14** below.

HMRC have the power to make regulations requiring electronic payment and they have used this power to require companies to make payments on or after 1 April 2011 electronically. See **51.13** below. With effect from 16 December 2011 electronic payments can be made using the Faster Payment Service (HMRC Notice 20 December 2011).

Effective dates of payment

[51.10] HMRC take the date of payment in respect of each payment method to be as follows.

- Cheques, cash, postal orders handed in at HMRC offices or received by post (except as below): the day of receipt by HMRC.
- Cheques, cash, postal orders received by post following a day when the office has been closed for whatever reason (including a weekend): the day the office was first closed.
- Electronic Funds Transfer — payment by BACS (transfer over two days) or CHAPS (same day transfer): one day prior to receipt by the Revenue.
- Bank Giro or Girobank: the date on which payment was made at the bank or Post Office.

(Revenue 'Working Together' Bulletin July 2000 p 3).

For the purposes of *TMA 1970* generally and also of the statutory provisions dealing specifically with repayment supplement (see **56.3** REPAYMENT INTEREST), it is provided by law that where any payment to HMRC is received by cheque and the cheque is paid on its first presentation to the bank on which it is drawn, the payment is treated as made on the date of receipt of the cheque by HMRC. [*TMA 1970, s 70A*]. This is subject to a power given to HMRC to make regulations providing for a payment by cheque to HMRC to be treated as made when the cheque clears. [*FA 2007, s 95*]. Where a company makes a payment on or after 1 April 2011 by cheque and that payment should have been made electronically under the provisions at **51.13** below, *TMA 1970, s 70A* is disapplied and the payment is treated as made on the second business day after the day HMRC receive the cheque. [*SI 2003 No 282, Reg 3A; SI 2009 No 3218, Sch para 10*].

Certificates of tax deposit

[51.11] Such certificates, which enable money to be set aside for payment of future tax liability, may be used in payment of capital gains tax (but not corporation tax). Interest is received on these certificates from the date of purchase until the date on which the tax in respect of which they are surrendered falls due. Certificates may also be encashed (with interest to the date of encashment) but a lower rate of interest is then paid. For further details, see Tolley's Income Tax.

Payment of tax in euros

[51.12] British businesses may, if they wish, pay tax in euros (the European single currency). The taxpayer will be credited with the sterling value actually received by HMRC after conversion at the prevailing rate. There is no facility for making tax repayments in euros. (Revenue Press Release 31 July 1998).

Mandatory electronic payment

[51.13] HMRC have wide powers to make regulations requiring payment by electronic means of any tax or duty for which they are responsible. [*FA 2003, ss 204, 205*].

Corporation tax after 31 March 2011

Companies are required to make the following payments by electronic means where the payment is made after 31 March 2011:

- corporation tax, including instalment payments;
- interest on overdue corporation tax; and
- any penalty (fixed or tax-related) under *FA 1998, Sch 18 paras 17, 18* for failure to deliver a company tax return (see **58.5** RETURNS).

See **51.10** above for cases in which such payments are nevertheless made by cheque.

[*SI 2003 No 282, Reg 3; SI 2009 No 3218*].

Fee for payment by specified methods

[51.14] HMRC charge a fee for payment of tax by certain payment methods.

Where a payment is made on or after 1 April 2016 using a credit card, the fee is the percentage of the payment given by the following table.

Personal credit cards	Rate %
Visa Personal	0.415
Mastercard Personal	0.386
Mastercard World Premium	0.374
Mastercard Signia Premium	0.606
Mastercard Elite Premium	0.606
Corporate credit cards	
Visa Business	1.508
Visa Corporate	1.744
Visa Purchasing	1.755
Mastercard Business	1.973
Mastercard Corporate	2.248
Mastercard Purchasing	2.406
Mastercard Fleet	2.134

Where a payment is made on or after 2 April 2012 and before 1 April 2016 using a credit card and the authorisation to make the payment is given by telephone, the fee is 1.5% of the payment. For such payments made on or after 14 December 2009 and before 2 April 2012 the fee is 1.25%; for such payments made on or after 13 August 2008 and before 14 December 2009, the fee is 0.91%.

Where a payment is made on or after 2 November 2015 and before 1 April 2016 using a credit card and the authorisation to make the payment is given via the internet, the fee is 1.5% of the payment. For such payments made on or after 1 April 2011 and before 2 November 2015, the fee is 1.4% of the payment; for such payments made on or after 9 December 2008 and before 1 April 2011, the fee is 1.25%.

[*FA 2008, s 136; SI 2008 Nos 1948, 2991; SI 2009 No 3073; SI 2011 No 711; SI 2012 No 689; SI 2015 No 1777; SI 2016 No 333*].

Overpayments of tax

[51.15] For an article on HMRC practice re allocations of overpayments under self-assessment, see Revenue Tax Bulletin June 1999 pp 673, 674.

Effect of making an appeal

[51.16] Where a taxpayer appeals against an HMRC decision he can also apply for any tax due to be postponed pending the determination of the appeal. See 51.17 below. Note that postponement does not affect the date from which interest on the tax will run should it become payable on determination of the appeal.

Where a party to an appeal makes a further appeal against a decision of the Tribunal any tax due in accordance with that decision is nevertheless payable. See 51.18 below.

Postponement of tax pending appeal

[51.17] The following applies in the case of APPEALS (5) against:

(a) a conclusion stated or amendment made by a final or partial closure notice on completion or part completion of an enquiry into a personal, trustee or partnership tax return (see **58.12**, **58.18** RETURNS);
(b) an HMRC amendment made by a final or partial closure notice on completion or part completion of an enquiry into a company tax return (see *FA 1998, Sch 18 para 34; F(No 2)A 2017, Sch 15 paras 30, 44*);
(c) an HMRC amendment to a self-assessment during enquiry to prevent potential loss of tax (see **58.13** RETURNS and, for companies, *FA 1998, Sch 18 para 30*); and
(d) an assessment other than a self-assessment.

In the absence of any application for postponement of tax as below, tax is due and payable as if there had been no appeal.

If the appellant has grounds for believing that he is overcharged to tax by the amendment or assessment or as a result of the conclusion stated (as the case may be), he (or his agent) may, by notice in writing, apply to HMRC for a determination by them of the amount of tax which should be postponed pending the determination of the appeal. The application must be made within 30 days of the 'specified date' and must state the amount believed to be overcharged and the grounds for that belief.

Where the taxpayer disagrees with HMRC's determination, he can refer the application to the Tribunal within 30 days from the date of the document notifying HMRC's decision.

The '*specified date*' is the date of issue of the notice of amendment or assessment or, in the case of an appeal within (a) above, the date of issue of the closure notice. The mount to be postponed is the amount in which it appears that there are reasonable grounds for believing that the taxpayer is overcharged.

If the taxpayer and HMRC come to an agreement as to the amount of tax to be postponed (if any), the agreement takes effect only if it is in writing or either the taxpayer or HMRC confirm it in writing.

On the determination of (or agreement on) the amount of tax to be postponed, the balance of tax not postponed (if any) becomes due and payable as if it had been charged by an amendment or assessment issued on the date of that determination or agreement (or on the date of notice of confirmation of the latter) and in respect of which there had been no appeal.

Application for postponement may be made outside the normal 30-day time limit if the appeal itself was made later or if there is a change in circumstances which gives grounds for belief that the appellant is overcharged by the amendment etc. In relation to the pre-self-assessment rules, the Revenue indicated that a 'change in circumstances' is not just a change of mind but a change in the circumstances in which the original decision not to apply for postponement was made. An example cited by the Revenue was where it has become apparent that further relief (e.g. loss or group relief) is due (CCAB Statement TR 477, 28 June 1982). A late application does not, however, defer the due date of any balance of tax not postponed.

If, after the determination of an amount of tax to be postponed and as a result of a change in the circumstances of the case, either the appellant or HMRC have grounds for believing that the amount postponed is excessive or insufficient, and the parties cannot agree on a revised determination, either party can apply to the Tribunal for a revised determination of the amount to be postponed. If, on this further determination or agreement, an amount of tax ceases to be postponed, that amount is treated as charged by an assessment issued on the date of the further determination (or on the date of notice of confirmation of the agreement) and in respect of which no appeal is pending. If, on the other hand, an amount of tax has been overpaid, that amount becomes repayable.

A postponement application is subject to the normal appeal provisions, but the decision of the Tribunal is final and conclusive (so that there can be no further appeal to the Upper Tribunal or Court of Appeal).

Tax which is subject to an accelerated payment notice cannot be postponed. Tax which is postponed and subsequently becomes subject to such a notice becomes due and payable. See **4.31** ANTI-AVOIDANCE.

[*TMA 1970, s 55(1)–(3)(3A)(4)–(8)(8B)–(8D)(10)(10A)(10B)(11); FA 2012, Sch 20 para 11; FA 2014, s 224(1); SI 2009 No 56, Sch 1 para 34*].

The giving of notice of appeal, whether or not accompanied by a postponement application, does *not* affect the date from which interest accrues.

Payment of tax on determination of appeal

[51.18] The following applies where tax is payable in accordance with the determination of an appeal within **51.17**(a)–(d) above and it is either tax postponed in accordance with **51.17** above or an addition to the tax charged by the amendment or assessment before appeal. Such tax becomes due and payable as if it were charged by an amendment or assessment issued on the date on which HMRC issued to the taxpayer a notice of the total amount payable in accordance with the determination and in respect of which there had been no appeal. Any tax found to be overpaid on determination of the appeal becomes repayable. [*TMA 1970, s 55(9); SI 2009 No 56, Sch 1 para 34*].

Tax is payable or repayable in accordance with a decision of the Tribunal even if a party appeals to the Upper Tribunal. If the amount charged in the assessment concerned is subsequently altered by the Upper Tribunal, any amount undercharged is due and payable at the end of the thirty days beginning with the date on which HMRC issue the appellant with a notice of the amount payable in accordance with the Upper Tribunal's decision. Any amount overpaid will be refunded along with such interest as may be allowed by the decision. This provision applies equally to any further appeal from a decision of the Upper Tribunal to the Courts. See **4.31** ANTI-AVOIDANCE for applications to the court or Tribunal by HMRC to disapply the requirement to repay tax where an accelerated payment notice is in force. [*TMA 1970, s 56; FA 2014, s 225(1); SI 2009 No 56, Sch 1 para 35*]. HMRC have announced that they will apply this provision consistently to all cases where the decision of the Tribunal or Court is made on or after 1 April 2010. Payment will not, however, be enforced pending further appeal where an agreement not to do so was made before 9 December 2009 or where to do so would drive the taxpayer into bankruptcy or liquidation. (HMRC Internet Statement, 11 March 2010).

Collection and enforcement

[51.19] From 6 April 2014, the procedure in *TCEA 2007, Sch 12* (taking control of goods) is used by HMRC in England and Wales to recover unpaid sums. In Scotland, HMRC can apply to the sheriff for a summary warrant authorising the recovery of unpaid sums. In Northern Ireland and, before 6 April 2014, in England and Wales, the Collector of Taxes may distrain. [*TMA 1970, ss 61–64; TCEA 2007, Sch 10 paras 32, 33; FA 2008, ss 127–129; SI 2009 No 3024; SI 2014 No 906*]. See also *Herbert Berry Associates Ltd v CIR* HL 1977, 52 TC 113.

Where an amount of CGT or corporation tax due is less than £2,000, the Collector may within one year after the due date take summary magistrates' court proceedings. HMRC may also recover tax by proceedings in the county court. [*TMA 1970, ss 65, 66; CRCA 2005, s 25(1A)(6); SI 1991 Nos 724, 1877*]. But for limitations in Scotland and NI see *TMA 1970, ss 65(4), 66(3)(4), 67*, and see *Mann v Cleaver* KB 1930, 15 TC 367.

Unpaid tax (and arrears) may also be recovered (with full costs) as a Crown debt in the High Court. [*TMA 1970, s 68*].

The amount of an assessment which has become final cannot be re-opened in proceedings to collect the tax (*CIR v Pearlberg* CA 1953, 34 TC 57; *CIR v Soul* CA 1976, 51 TC 86), and it is not open to the taxpayer to raise the defence that the Revenue acted *ultra vires* in raising the assessment (*CIR v Aken* CA 1990, 63 TC 395).

For whether unpaid tax is a business liability for commercial etc. purposes, see *Conway v Wingate* CA, [1952] 1 All ER 782; *Stevens v Britten* CA, [1954] 3 All ER 385; *R v Vaccari* CA, [1958] 1 All ER 468; *In re Hollebone's Agreement* CA, [1959] 2 All ER 152.

HMRC can apply to the High Court for a freezing order where there is a risk of the dissipation of assets to avoid compliance with an assessment in the period before the tax is due and payable: *HMRC v Ali* Ch D 2011, [2012] STC 42.

For the limited priority given to payment of corporation tax in a winding-up of a company, see **14.4** COMPANIES.

Amounts payable on account of CGT under the non-resident CGT disposals rules (see 50.2A above) are recoverable as if they were an amount of tax. [*TMA 1970, s 59AB; FA 2015, Sch 7 para 51*].

Set-off of amounts owed to taxpayer against amounts payable

On or after 21 July 2008, HMRC may set a sum payable by them to a person under any enactment and certain sums repayable by them to that person (a '*credit*') against any sum payable to them by that person (a '*debit*') under any enactment or under a contract settlement (see **6.8** ASSESSMENTS). The sums repayable by HMRC that can be credits for this purpose are sums paid by the taxpayer in connection with any liability (including any purported or anticipated liability) to make a payment to HMRC under any enactment or under a contract settlement. For this purpose, sums paid or payable include sums that have been or are to be credited.

This provision applies without prejudice to any other power of HMRC to set off amounts (in relation to indirect taxes and national insurance contributions) but is subject to any obligation of HMRC to set the credit against any other sum and extends only to England, Wales and Northern Ireland.

The above provisions cannot be used, where an insolvency procedure has been applied to a person, to set a 'post-insolvency credit' against a 'pre-insolvency debit'. For this purpose, a '*post-insolvency credit*' is a credit which became due after the insolvency procedure was applied and which relates to, or to matters occurring at, times after it was applied, and a '*pre-insolvency debit*' is a debit which arose before the insolvency procedure was applied or which arose after it was applied but relates to, or to matters occurring at, times before it was applied. An insolvency procedure is applied when a bankruptcy order or winding up order is made, an administrator is appointed, a taxpayer is put into administrative receivership, a company passes a resolution for voluntary winding up, a voluntary arrangement comes into force or a deed of arrangement takes effect. An insolvency procedure is not treated as being applied to a person if it is applied at a time when another insolvency procedure applies to that person or if it is applied immediately upon another insolvency procedure ceasing to apply.

[*FA 2008, ss 130, 131, 139; FA 2012, s 50(3)(a)*].

Set-off of amounts assigned by original creditor

Where there has been a 'transfer' on or after 25 June 2008 of a right to be paid a sum by HMRC, HMRC must set that sum against a sum payable to them by the original creditor if they would have had an obligation to do so under any enactment had the original creditor retained the right. If, but for the transfer, HMRC would have had the power under any enactment to set the sum against a sum payable to them by the original creditor, they may (but are not required to) do so. To the extent of any such set-off, the obligations of HMRC to the transferee creditor and the obligations of the original creditor are discharged. Where the right to be paid the transferred sum is dependent on a claim, these provisions apply only where such a claim is made.

In determining the amount of the sum to be paid, HMRC can make any reduction that they could have made but for the transfer, including a reduction arising from any defence to a claim for the sum.

A '*transfer*' for the above purposes includes a transfer by assignment, assignation or any other means but does not include a transfer by a direction under *ITA 2007, s 429* (giving through tax return (repealed with effect from 6 April 2012) — see **11.10** CHARITIES). Where there has been more than one transfer of a right, the original creditor is the person from whom the right was first transferred.

[*FA 2008, s 133; FA 2012, s 50(2)(c)*].

Recovery of debts through the PAYE system

For 2012/13 onwards, HMRC has the power to collect tax debts, including capital gains tax, through the PAYE system (where the taxpayer is an employee) by making adjustments to the taxpayer's tax code. For 2014/15 and earlier years, deductions of more than £3,000 in a single tax year require the consent of the taxpayer.

For 2015/16 onwards, the £3,000 limit is increased for unpaid self-assessment debts of taxpayers with a primary source of annual PAYE income of £30,000 or over. A graduated scale will applies so that a maximum of £17,000 can be coded out for a person with earnings over £90,000. The £3,000 limit continues to apply to self-assessment balancing payments.

[*ITEPA 2003, s 684; SI 2003 No 2682, Reg 14A; SI 2011 Nos 1583, 1584, 1585; SI 2014 Nos 2438, 2689*].

See Tolley's Income Tax for full coverage of PAYE.

Power to obtain details of debtors

HMRC can by notice in writing require certain third parties to provide the details of a person who owes HMRC a sum by or virtue of an enactment or under a contract settlement. The third parties concerned are companies, local authorities, local authority associations and also other persons if HMRC have reasonable grounds to believe that they have obtained the details in the course of carrying on a business. Charities, and others providing services on behalf of a charity, are excluded if the details were obtained in the course of providing services free of charge to the recipient. HMRC must have reasonable grounds to believe that the third party has the details required.

Where such a notice is given, the third party must provide the details within such time, by such means and in such form as is reasonably indicated in the notice. There is a right of appeal against a notice or a requirement in a notice on the ground that compliance would be unduly onerous. A penalty of £300 (or a sum specified by Treasury regulations) applies for failure to comply with a notice.

[*FA 2009, s 97, Sch 49*].

Enforcement by deduction from accounts

[51.20] With effect from 18 November 2015 HMRC have the power in England, Wales and Northern Ireland to enforce certain debts by direct recovery from the bank etc. account of the debtor. HMRC may issue a hold notice (see **51.22** below) to 'deposit-takers' effectively freezing the funds needed to pay the debt and giving the taxpayer and certain other interested parties an opportunity to object to HMRC against the issuing of the notice. If HMRC dismiss any objections there is a right of appeal to the county court. If there is no objection or appeal or if they are unsuccessful HMRC may issue a deduction notice (see **51.23** below) requiring the deposit-taker to deduct specified amounts from the taxpayer's accounts and pay them over to HMRC. Before issuing a hold notice HMRC may, but are not required to, issue an information notice (see **51.21** below) to ascertain which accounts are held by the taxpayer with a particular deposit-taker. All notices must be given in writing.

The power can be used to collect sums which are due and payable by a person to HMRC under or by virtue of an enactment or under a contract settlement where the following conditions are met:

(1) the sum is at least £1,000;
(2) the sum is an 'established debt' or is due under (or is the disputed tax specified in) an accelerated payment notice or partner payment notice (see **4.29** ANTI-AVOIDANCE onwards); and
(3) HMRC are satisfied that the taxpayer is aware that the sum is due and payable to them.

A sum is an '*established debt*' if there is no possibility that it, or any part of it, will cease to be due and payable to HMRC. This will be the case where there is no right of appeal, where the period for making an appeal has expired without an appeal having been made or where an appeal has been finally determined or withdrawn. Powers to grant permission to make a late appeal are disregarded for this purpose.

Before issuing an information notice or hold notice HMRC must consider whether, to the best of their knowledge, there are any matters as a result of which the taxpayer is, or may be, at a particular disadvantage in dealing with HMRC in relation to the unpaid sum. Any such matters must be taken into account in deciding whether or not to issue a notice. HMRC have published guidance on the factors which they consider to be relevant to deciding whether a person is at a particular disadvantage. The guidance sets out four indicators which HMRC will consider: a disability or long-term health condition; a temporary illness, physical or mental health condition; personal issues (such as redundancy, bereavement or trauma) and lower levels of literacy, numeracy and/or education. See www.gov.uk/government/publications/direct-recovery-of-debts-and-vulnerable-customers/direct-recovery-of-debts-vulnerable-customers.

A '*deposit-taker*' is, broadly, a person who may lawfully accept deposits in the UK in the course of a business. A deposit-taker is not liable for damages for anything done in good faith to comply with these provisions.

Joint accounts

References below to an account held by a person include a joint account held by that person and one or more others.

[*F(No 2)A 2015, s 51, Sch 8 paras 2, 5, 18, 22–24*].

Tax charged in a determination

Where HMRC are taking action under these provisions in respect of tax charged by a determination within **58.15** RETURNS (or a corporation tax determination, see **58.19** RETURNS) and the determination is superseded by a self-assessment, the action may be continued as if it were an action to recover so much of the tax charged by the self-assessment as is due and payable, has not been paid and does not exceed the amount charged in the determination. [*TMA 1970, s 28C(4A); FA 1998, Sch 18 para 40(5); F(No 2)A 2015, Sch 8 paras 25, 40*].

Regulations

The Treasury has wide powers to make regulations for supplementary provisions and to amend, revoke or repeal enactments in connection with these provisions. HMRC may make regulations to alter various amounts, thresholds and time limits, to exclude certain types of account or amount from the provisions and to prescribe the information which can be required by notices. [*F(No 2)A 2015, s 51, Sch 8 paras 19–21*].

Penalties

Penalties apply to deposit-takers for various failures to comply with the provisions and for disclosures likely to prejudice HMRC's ability to recover an unpaid sum using the provisions. See **52.28** PENALTIES.

Administrative costs

A deposit-taker may charge the account holder in respect of administrative costs incurred in complying with these provisions of up to £55. A charge may only be made if there is an agreement with the account holder or holders for such a charge. The deposit-taker must have made the final payment to HMRC in accordance with a deduction notice before the charge can be made. [*SI 2016 No 44*].

Information notice

[51.21] If it appears to HMRC that a person has failed to pay a sum meeting the above conditions and that the person holds one or more accounts with a deposit-taker, they may give the deposit-taker an information notice. Such a notice requires the deposit-taker to provide HMRC with the following information:

(1) the taxpayer's name and address, national insurance number, email addresses and phone numbers and, in respect of any joint accounts, the proportion of the balance to which the taxpayer is entitled; and

(2) for each account held by the taxpayer, any account number, roll number and sort code, the type of account (including whether it is a joint account), the account balance (in the currency in which it is held), whether, and what rate of, interest is payable, any minimum balance required to keep the account open, any contractual terms under which the taxpayer or any '*interested third parties*' (i.e. persons with a beneficial interest in an amount in the account) may suffer economic loss as a result of a hold notice or deduction notice, and, for each joint account holder, interested third party or person with power of attorney in respect of the account, the information specified in (1) above.

Information must be provided only if it is in the possession of, or immediately available to, the deposit-taker at the time the notice is given.

A notice must explain the time limit for complying with it and the penalties for non-compliance (see **52.28** PENALTIES). HMRC may issue a notice only for the purpose of determining whether to give the deposit-taker a hold notice (see below) in respect of the taxpayer concerned. The recipient of a notice must comply with it as soon as reasonably practicable and, in any event, within ten working days beginning with the day on which the notice was given.

[*F(No 2)A 2015, Sch 8 paras 3, 8(11); SI 2015 No 1986, Regs 2–4*].

Hold notice

[51.22] If it appears to HMRC that a person has failed to pay a sum meeting the conditions at **51.20** above and that the person holds one or more accounts with a deposit-taker, they may give the deposit-taker a hold notice. The notice must:

(a) specify the taxpayer's name and last known address;
(b) specify a 'specified amount';
(c) specify a 'safeguarded amount';
(d) set out any rules which are to decide the priority order to be used to determine the held amount for each account (see Step 3 below);
(e) explain the effects of the notice, the penalties for non-compliance and any provisions made by regulation excluding certain types of account and amounts from inclusion in a hold notice; and
(f) contain a statement about HMRC's compliance with the requirement to consider whether a taxpayer is at a particular disadvantage in dealing with HMRC (see above).

The notice may also specify any additional information which HMRC considers might assist the deposit-taker in identifying accounts. It may also exclude an account, type of account or specified amount from the notice.

In (b) above, the '*specified amount*' must not exceed what is left of the 'notified sum' after deducting the specified amounts in any other hold notices which relate to the same debts and which were either given on the same day to other deposit-takers or given on an earlier day to either the same or another deposit-taker. The specified amount of an earlier hold notice is not deducted if HMRC has received a notification from the deposit-taker that there are no affected accounts as a result of that notice (see further below). For this purpose, two hold notices relate to the same debts if at least one of the unpaid sums in respect of which they are issued is the same.

The '*safeguarded amount*' must, in general, be at least £5,000 but HMRC may specify a smaller amount (including nil) if they consider it appropriate to do so having regard to the value in sterling (determined in a manner prescribed by regulations) of any amounts in a non-sterling account which would be a 'relevant account' (see below) in relation to the notice if it were denominated in sterling. The safeguarded amount must be nil if HMRC has previously given a hold notice relating to the same debts and, within the 30 days ending with the date the current hold notice is given, HMRC have been notified that there is a held amount as a result of the earlier notice.

HMRC may not give more than one hold notice relating to the same debts to a single deposit-taker on the same day.

Effect of notice

A deposit-taker to whom a hold notice is given must, for each 'relevant account' determine whether or not there is a 'held amount' (greater than nil) for that account and if so must either:

(1) put in place arrangements to ensure that it does not do anything, or permit anything to be done, which would reduce the amount in the account below the held amount; or
(2) transfer an amount equal to the held amount into a specially-created 'suspense account' and put in place arrangements to ensure that it does not do anything, or permit anything to be done, which would reduce the amount in the suspense account below the held amount.

The deposit-taker must comply with these requirements as soon as reasonably practicable and, in any event, within five working days beginning with the day on which the notice is given and must maintain any arrangements made under (1) or (2) above until the notice ceases to be in force.

All accounts held by the taxpayer with the deposit-taker are '*relevant accounts*' unless they are not denominated in sterling or are suspense accounts or they have been excluded from the hold notice by HMRC or excluded from such notices generally by regulations. A relevant account is an '*affected account*' if as a result of the notice there is a held amount in relation to it.

A hold notice ceases to be in force when either HMRC cancel it or a deduction notice is given.

If the deposit-taker determines that there are one or more affected accounts it must give HMRC a notice setting out prescribed information about each account (and in the case of a joint account, about the other account holders) and the held amount for each account. The prescribed information is:

- the information within **51.21**(1) and (2) above;
- confirmation of which accounts are affected accounts;
- the date on which the deposit-taker complied with the requirements above;
- confirmation that the deposit-taker understands the penalties for making a disclosure likely to prejudice HMRC's ability to use these provisions to recover the unpaid tax (see **52.28** PENALTIES);
- the total of all held amounts;
- for each account, the amount not subject to action within (1) or (2) above; and
- a description of any economic loss suffered by an account holder or interested third party under any contractual term as a result of the hold notice.

Information must be provided only if it is the possession of, or immediately available to, the deposit-taker at the time the hold notice is given.

The notice must be given within five working days beginning with the day on which the deposit-taker complies with the hold notice. HMRC must then, as soon as reasonably practicable, give a copy of the hold notice to the taxpayer together with a notice which:

(A) specifies and states the amounts of the unpaid sums to which the hold notice relates;
(B) states the total of the unpaid amounts to which the notice relates; and
(C) states the 'notified sum' for the hold notice, i.e. the total in (B) above.

HMRC must also give a notice to any joint account holders other than the taxpayer and to any 'interested third parties' (see **51.21** above) in respect of whom information has been provided in the deposit-taker's notice. The notice must explain that a hold notice has been given in respect of the account concerned and explaining the effects of the notice and the objection and appeal provisions below.

Once it has complied with the hold notice, the deposit-taker may (but is not required to) notify the taxpayer, any joint account holders and any interested third parties stating that a hold notice has been received and the effect of the notice on the account concerned.

If the deposit-taker determines that there are no affected accounts as a result of the hold notice it must notify HMRC accordingly, including in the notice any information which it has taken into account to determine that there are no affected accounts. The notice must be given within five working days beginning with the day on which it makes the determination.

Held amounts

If there is only one relevant account, the '*held amount*' for that account is, if the 'available amount' exceeds the safeguarded amount, the excess up to the specified amount. If the available amount is not more than the safeguarded amount then the held amount is nil. If there is more than one relevant account, the held amount for each such account is found using the following steps:

Step 1. Determine the available amount for each relevant account.

Step 2. Add the available amounts together to determine the total of those amounts for all such accounts. If the total is no more than the safeguarded amount then the held amount for all of the accounts is nil.

Step 3. If the total in Step 2 is more than the safeguarded amount, the safeguarded amount is matched against the available amounts in the relevant accounts, taking the accounts in reverse priority order. The priority order is determined by the deposit-taker, but joint accounts must have a lower priority than other accounts and any rules included in the hold notice (see (d) above) must be followed. Note that it is the reverse of the priority order that is used in this Step.

Step 4. Match the specified amount against what remains of the available amounts by taking each account in priority order. The held amount for each account is then so much of the account balance as is so matched; if no part of an account balance is so matched, the held amount for that account is nil. Balances which are excluded from the effect of the hold notice by regulations are not matched.

The '*available amount*' is the amount standing to the credit of the account at the time the deposit-taker complies with the hold notice. In the case of a joint account, the available amount is restricted to the appropriate fraction of that amount, according to the number of account holders.

Cancellation or variation

HMRC may cancel or vary a hold notice by notifying the deposit-taker. Variation may take the form of cancelling the effect of the notice in relation to one or more accounts or in relation to part of the held amount for an account or accounts. HMRC must give a copy of the notice of cancellation or variation to the taxpayer and any other person HMRC consider is affected by it and who is a joint account holder or an interested third party.

On receipt of a notice the deposit-taker must cancel or adjust the arrangements made to comply with the hold notice as soon as reasonably practicable and, in any event, within five working days beginning with the day the notice of cancellation or variation was given.

Objections and appeals

The taxpayer, an interested third party or a joint account holder may notify HMRC of an objection to a hold notice on the grounds that:

(i) the debts have been wholly or partly paid;
(ii) at the time the hold notice was given there was no unpaid sum or the taxpayer did not hold an account with the deposit-taker;
(iii) the notice is causing or will cause exceptional hardship to the person making the objection or another person; or
(iv) there is an interested third party in relation to one or more of the affected accounts.

The objection notice must state the grounds of objection and must normally be made within 30 days beginning with the day on which a copy of the hold notice was given to the taxpayer. A joint account holder or independent third party who has received a notice from HMRC explaining that a hold notice has been issued may make an objection within 30 days beginning with the day on which that notice was given. HMRC may, however, agree to the making of a late objection and must do so if they are satisfied that there was reasonable excuse for not making the objection in time and that the person making the objection had sent a written request for agreement to the making of a late objection without unreasonable delay after the reasonable excuse ceased.

HMRC must consider any objections within 30 days of being given the objection notice. They must then decide whether to cancel or vary the hold notice (as above) or to dismiss the objection and must notify their decision to the taxpayer, any other person who objected and any other joint account holder or interested third party who HMRC consider to be affected. HMRC must also notify the deposit-taker if it has decided to cancel or vary the hold notice. A copy of HMRC's notice to the deposit-taker must be given to each of the persons to whom HMRC notified their decision.

The taxpayer, any joint account holder or any interested third party may appeal against HMRC's decision, but only on grounds within (i) to (iv) above. The appeal must state the grounds and must normally be made within 30 days beginning with the day on which the appellant was given notice of HMRC's decision. A joint account holder or independent third party who has not received a notice of HMRC's decision may appeal within 30 days beginning with the day on which the taxpayer was given notice of HMRC's decision. The appeal is to the county court which may cancel or vary the notice or dismiss the appeal.

Where an appeal is on the grounds of exceptional hardship (see (iii) above), the appellant may apply to the court to suspend the effect of the hold notice in full or in relation to a particular account or amount while the appeal is pending. Adequate security must be provided.

If the deposit-taker is served with a court order to cancel or vary the hold notice, it must make any necessary resulting arrangements as soon as reasonably practicable and, in any event, within five working days beginning with the day the order was given.

The normal provisions governing APPEALS (5) do not apply to objections or appeals under these provisions.

[*F(No 2)A 2015, Sch 8 paras 4, 6–12; SI 2015 No 1986, Regs 3, 5, 6*].

Deduction notice

[51.23] If it appears to HMRC that a person in respect of whom a hold notice given to a deposit-taker is in force has failed to pay a sum meeting the conditions at **51.20** above and that the person holds one or more accounts with the deposit-taker in respect of which there is a held amount relating to the unpaid sum, they may give the deposit-taker a deduction notice. The notice will specify one or more affected accounts (see **51.22** above) and require the deposit-taker to deduct and pay a 'qualifying amount' from each account to HMRC by the day specified in the notice. If a held amount for a particular account has been transferred to a suspense account (see **51.22** above), the deduction must be made from the suspense account. HMRC may amend or cancel the notice by notifying the deposit-taker.

A '*qualifying amount*' in an affected account is an amount not exceeding the held amount for that account. The total qualifying amounts specified in a deduction notice must not exceed the unpaid sum. The deposit-taker must not, while a deduction notice is in force, do anything or permit anything to be done that would reduce the amount in a specified account (or a suspense account) to fall below the amount required to make the deduction. A deduction notice must explain this provision and the penalties for non-compliance. A deduction notice comes into force when it is given to the deposit-taker and ceases to be in force when the deposit-taker is given a notice cancelling it or when the final required payment is made.

A deduction notice cannot be given in respect of an account unless the period for making an objection has passed and either no objections were made or any objections have been decided or withdrawn and, if objections were made and decided, unless the period for making an appeal has passed and any appeal or further appeal has been finally determined.

HMRC must give a copy of a deduction notice to the taxpayer and, for each account, must give a notice explaining that a notice has been given and its effect to any joint account holders other than the taxpayer and to any interested third parties about whom HMRC have sufficient information to do so. Similar copies and notices must be given where HMRC cancel or amend a deduction notice.

[*F(No 2)A 2015, Sch 8 para 13*].

Recovery of tax in respect of disposals by others

[51.24] There are instances in the legislation whereby HMRC can assess, and/or recover tax from, persons other than the person actually making the disposal which gives rise to the liability. This right usually follows from the non-payment of tax by the person originally assessed in respect of the chargeable disposal by him but may also arise because of specific legislation (e.g. UK-residents charged in respect of disposals made by certain overseas resident companies, see **49.7** OVERSEAS MATTERS). The person from whom tax is recovered is normally given a right of recovery from any person originally assessed.

The following table summarises the legislation relevant to tax on chargeable gains. See also **41.4** LAND.

Description	Legislation	Location
Recovery of tax from officers. Tax may be recovered from the treasurer of a company which is not a body corporate.	*TMA 1970, s 108(2)(3)*	51.25
Collection of unpaid tax from other members of the group and controlling directors. Where corporation tax in respect of a chargeable gain remains unpaid for six months it may be collected from certain group members or, if the gain arises to a UK permanent establishment, from a controlling director.	*TCGA 1992, s 190*	51.26
Recovery from shareholders. Where a person connected with a UK-resident company receives, in respect of shares in that company, a capital distribution which is not a reduction of capital but which is derived from a disposal of assets from which a chargeable gain accrues to the company, and the company does not pay the corporation tax for the period of the gain within six months, the recipient of the distribution may be required to pay a proportion of the corporation tax.	*TCGA 1992, s 198*	51.27

Description	Legislation	Location
Company reconstructions. Tax charged under the anti-avoidance provision restricting the application of the relief for company reconstructions which is not paid within six months can be recovered from any person holding the shares issued to the original chargeable person following an inter-spouse or intra-group transfer.	*TCGA 1992, s 138(4)*	**4.15** ANTI-AVOIDANCE
Children. For 2011/12 and earlier years, tax on disposals by children may in certain circumstances be assessed on or collected from parents, guardians or tutors etc.	*TMA 1970, ss 72, 73, 77*	**12.3, 12.4** CHILDREN
Reconstructions involving transfer of business. Tax charged under the anti-avoidance provision restricting the application of the relief for such reconstructions which is not paid within six months can be recovered from the acquiring company or from any person holding the assets following an intra-group transfer.	*TCGA 1992, s 139(6)(7)*	**14.11** COMPANIES
Gifts — recovery from donee. Where CGT on a gift is not paid within twelve months it may be recovered from the donee.	*TCGA 1992, s 282*	**27.4** GIFTS
Hold-over reliefs — emigration of transferee. Where tax arising on the clawback of hold-over relief when the transferee emigrates is not paid by the transferee within twelve months it may be recovered from the transferor.	*TCGA 1992, s 168(7)*	**36.8, 36.11** HOLD-OVER RELIEFS
Trustees becoming non-resident. Tax charged on trustees as a result of their becoming non-resident which is not paid within six months may be recovered from certain former trustees.	*TCGA 1992, s 82*	**48.2** OFFSHORE SETTLEMENTS
Company ceasing to be UK-resident. Tax in respect of accounting periods beginning before the cessation of UK residence which is not paid within six months can be recovered from a member of the same group or a controlling director.	*TMA 1970, s 109E*	**49.18** OVERSEAS MATTERS
Exploration or exploitation rights. unpaid tax assessed on an overseas resident person may be recovered from the holder of a licence granted under *Petroleum Act 1998* in respect of chargeable gains accruing on the disposal of such rights under the licence.	*TMA 1970, ss 77B–77E*	**49.19** OVERSEAS MATTERS
Recovery from beneficiary. Tax charged on trustees which is not paid within six months may be recovered from any beneficiary to whom the asset concerned or the proceeds from the disposal have been transferred.	*TCGA 1992, s 69(4)*	**62.10** SETTLEMENTS

Description	Legislation	Location
Change in company ownership. Unpaid corporation tax due from a company can be recovered from persons controlling the company, in certain circumstances where there has been a change of ownership.	*CTA 2010, ss 706–718*	Tolley's Corporation Tax
Non-UK resident companies. Unpaid corporation tax due from a non-UK resident company can be recovered from other companies within the same group, from any member of a consortium owning the company, or from any member of the same group as a member of that consortium.	*CTA 2010, ss 973–980*	Tolley's Corporation Tax

Recovery of tax from officers

[51.25] Tax which has fallen due may be recovered from the treasurer or acting treasurer (the 'proper officer') of a company which is not a body corporate or not incorporated under a UK enactment or by charter. That officer then has a right of reimbursement out of moneys coming into his hands on behalf of that company, and to be indemnified by the company for any balance. [*TMA 1970, s 108(2)(3); SI 2009 No 1890, Art 3*].

Collection of unpaid tax from other members of the group and controlling directors

[51.26] Where a chargeable gain accrues to a company (hereafter referred to as the taxpayer company) and either:

- that company is UK-resident at the time the gain accrues, or
- the gain is within the charge to corporation tax by virtue of *TCGA 1992, s 10B* (non-UK resident company trading in the UK through a permanent establishment — see **49.3** OVERSEAS MATTERS),

the following rules apply where all or part of the corporation tax assessed on the company for the relevant accounting period (i.e. the accounting period in which the gain accrues) remains unpaid six months after it became payable.

HMRC may serve on any of the following persons a notice requiring that person to pay, within 30 days, the unpaid tax or, if less, an amount equal to corporation tax on the chargeable gain at the appropriate rate.

(a) If the taxpayer company was a member of a 'group' at the time the gain accrued:
   - a company which was at that time the 'principal company of the group'; and
   - any other company which, in any part of the period of 12 months ending with that time, was a member of the group *and* owned the asset, or any part of the asset, disposed of (or, where that asset is an interest in, or a right over, another asset, owned either asset or any part of either asset).

(b) If the gain is within the charge to corporation tax by virtue of *TCGA 1992, s 10B*, any person who is, or has been during the 12 months ending with the time the gain accrued, a controlling director of the taxpayer company or of a company which has, or has had within that 12-month period, control over the taxpayer company.

For the purpose of (a) above, '*group*' and '*principal company of the group*' are construed as in **29.2** GROUPS OF COMPANIES but as if references there to 75% subsidiaries were references to 51% subsidiaries. For the purposes of (b) above and in determining whether a director is a controlling director, 'control' is construed in accordance with *CTA 2010, ss 450, 451*, and 'director' has the wide meaning given by *ITEPA 2003, s 67(1)(2)* and *CTA 2010, s 452(1)*.

The notice must state the amount of tax assessed, the original due date and the amount required from the person on whom it is served. It has effect, for the purposes of collection, interest and appeals, as if it were a notice of assessment on that person. The notice must be served within three years beginning with the date on which the liability of the taxpayer company for the relevant accounting period is finally determined. That date varies according to whether the unpaid tax is charged in a self-assessment (and, if so, whether there is an enquiry into the tax return in question), in a discovery assessment (and, if so, whether there is an appeal) or in consequence of a 'determination' (see Tolley's Corporation Tax under Self-Assessment). In the simplest case of a self-assessment and no enquiry, the liability is determined on the last date on which notice of enquiry could have been given.

A person paying an amount under these provisions may recover it from the taxpayer company, but such an amount is not deductible for any tax purpose.

[*TCGA 1992, s 190*].

Recovery from shareholders

[51.27] Where a person connected with a UK-resident company (see **17** CONNECTED PERSONS) receives, or becomes entitled to receive, in respect of shares in that company, a capital distribution within *TCGA 1992, s 122* (see **63.11** SHARES AND SECURITIES) which is not a reduction of capital but which constitutes, or is derived from, a disposal of assets from which a chargeable gain accrues to the company, and the company does not pay, within six months after the later of the due date and the date the assessment was made, the corporation tax due for the accounting period in which the gain accrued, the recipient of the distribution may be required to pay so much of that corporation tax as relates to chargeable gains but not exceeding the lesser of:

(i) part of that tax, at the rate in force when the gain accrued, proportionate to his share of the total distribution made by the company, and
(ii) the value of the distribution he received or became entitled to receive.

The recipient then has a right of recovery against the company, which extends to any interest on unpaid tax which he has paid on the outstanding tax. The assessment on the recipient must be made within two years after the later of the date the tax became due and payable by the company and the date the assessment was made on the company. These provisions do not affect any liability of the recipient in respect of any chargeable gain accruing to him as a result of the capital distribution. [*TCGA 1992, s 189*].

Cases in which HMRC do not pursue payment

[51.28] HMRC operate two practices under which they will not seek to collect tax which is due and payable.

Remission of tax in cases of HMRC delay

[51.29] Arrears of income tax or capital gains tax may be given up if they result from HMRC's failure to make proper and timely use of information supplied by:

- a taxpayer about his or her own income, gains or personal circumstances;
- an employer where the information affects a taxpayer's coding; or
- the Department for Work and Pensions about a taxpayer's State retirement, disability or widow's pension.

Tax will normally be given up only where the taxpayer could reasonably have believed that his or her tax affairs were in order; and

- was notified of the arrears more than twelve months after the end of the tax year in which HMRC received the information in question; or
- was notified of an over-repayment after the end of the tax year following the year in which the repayment was made.

In exceptional circumstances arrears of tax notified twelve months or less after the end of the relevant tax year may be given up if HMRC either failed more than once to make proper use of the facts they had been given about one source of income or allowed the arrears of tax to build up over two whole tax years in succession by failing to make proper and timely use of information they had been given.

(HMRC Extra-Statutory Concession A19).

A decision by HMRC not to apply this concession can only be challenged by way of judicial review (*Prince v HMRC* FTT, [2012] SFTD 786).

Under *TMA 1970*, unless a longer or shorter period is prescribed, no statutory claim for relief is allowed unless it is made on or before the fifth anniversary of 31 January following the tax year to which it relates. However, repayments of tax will be made in respect of claims made outside the statutory time limit where an overpayment of tax has arisen because of an error by HMRC or another Government Department, and where there is no dispute or doubt as to the facts (HMRC Extra-Statutory Concession B41).

Reduced payments under 'equitable liability'

[51.30] With effect for claims made on or after 1 April 2011 the relief below is replaced by the special relief at **13.7** CLAIMS.

An assessment not appealed against or for which a late appeal application is refused becomes final and conclusive and HMRC is able to take recovery proceedings accordingly for the full amount charged even though this may be in excess of the actual liability. Whilst there is no legal right to adjustment of the liability, where the taxpayer has exhausted all other possible remedies, HMRC may, depending on the circumstances, be prepared not to pursue its legal right to recover the full amount due where it would be unscrupulous to do so.

HMRC may be prepared to operate the practice of 'equitable liability' where, depending on the circumstances and in the light of all the evidence, it is clearly demonstrated that the liability assessed is greater than the amount which would have been charged had the returns etc. required been submitted at the proper time, and acceptable evidence (not an estimate) is provided of what the correct liability should have been. This treatment is conditional on the taxpayer's affairs being brought fully up to date and full payment of the reduced tax being made, and only most unusually will it be applied more than once in favour of the same taxpayer.

Under self-assessment, there is in most cases no need for HMRC to operate the above practice because of the ability of the taxpayer to displace an HMRC determination of tax liability by a self-assessment made within the later of the first anniversary of the date of determination and the fifth anniversary of the statutory filing date for the year of assessment concerned. Where exceptionally a determination can no longer be displaced and the conditions of the practice described above are fulfilled, HMRC will be prepared to consider extending its practice to meet this situation.

Cases are dealt with in HMRC's Enforcement and Insolvency Services in Worthing, Belfast and Edinburgh but local officers will be involved in considering the quantum of any claims for reduction in liability and the acceptability of the supporting evidence (HMRC Self-Assessment Claims Manual SACM12210; Revenue Tax Bulletin August 1995 p 245).

Over-repayments of tax

[51.31] If not otherwise assessable under *TMA 1970, s 29* (discovery assessments — see **6.10** ASSESSMENTS), capital gains tax repaid in error, or over-repaid, by HMRC may be assessed and recovered as if it were unpaid tax. For this purpose, a repayment includes an amount allowed by way of set-off. HMRC's right to assess under these provisions is subject to the same exceptions (modified as appropriate) as apply to discovery assessments. Excess repayment supplement (see **56.3** REPAYMENT INTEREST) may be similarly assessed or may be included in an assessment of over-repaid tax. The normal deadline for raising assessments is extended in the above cases to the later of:

- the end of the tax year following that in which the repayment was made, and
- in the event of an HMRC enquiry into a return, the day on which the enquiry is fully completed (see **58.12** RETURNS).

Comparable provisions apply for the purposes of corporation tax (and interest on overpaid corporation tax). The normal deadline for raising assessments is extended to the later of:

- the end of the accounting period following that in which the repayment was made, and
- in the event of an HMRC enquiry into a relevant company tax return, the end of the period of three months following the day on which the enquiry is completed (in accordance with *FA 1998, Sch 18 para 32*).

[*TMA 1970, s 30; FA 1998, s 117, Sch 18 paras 52, 53; F(No 2)A 2017, Sch 15 paras 16, 44*].

The exercise by HMRC of their discretion to raise an assessment under *TMA 1970, s 30* can be challenged only by way of judicial review (see **5.35** APPEALS) and not by appeal to the Appeal Commissioners (*Guthrie v Twickenham Film Studios Ltd* Ch D, [2002] STC 1374).

Recovery of foreign taxes etc.

[51.32] EU member states. Provision is made for the recovery in the UK of direct taxes (and interest and penalties) in respect of which a request for enforcement has been made in accordance with the Mutual Assistance Recovery Directive (now *Directive 2010/24/EU*, formerly *Directive 2008/55/EC* and *Directive 76/308/EEC*) by an authority in another EU member state. Disclosure of information by a UK tax authority (e.g. HMRC) for these purposes (or for the purposes of a request by the UK for enforcement elsewhere) is not generally precluded by any obligation of secrecy.

Broadly, the UK tax authority has the same powers it would have for a corresponding claim in the UK, in particular in relation to interest and penalties. Treasury regulations may make provision for procedural and supplementary matters (see now *SI 2004 No 674*). Regulations may also be made by the UK tax authority for the application, non-application or adaptation of the law applicable to corresponding UK claims.

No proceedings may be taken against a person under these provisions if he shows that proceedings relevant to the liability in question are pending (i.e. still subject to appeal), or are about to be instituted, before a competent body in the relevant member state. This does not apply to any steps which could be taken in similar circumstances in the case of a corresponding UK claim or if the foreign proceedings are not prosecuted or instituted with reasonable expedition. If a final decision on the foreign claim (i.e. one no longer appealable) (or a part of it) has been given in the taxpayer's favour by a competent body in the relevant member state, no proceedings may be taken under these provisions in relation to the claim (or part).

[*FA 2011, s 87, Sch 25; FA 2002, s 134, Sch 39; SI 2005 No 1479; SI 2008 No 2871; SI 2011 No 2931*].

Tax enforcement agreements

Provision is made for the Treasury to make regulations for the recovery in the UK of foreign taxes covered by a tax enforcement agreement with another country (see also **31.2**(c) HMRC — CONFIDENTIALITY OF INFORMATION). See now *SI 2007 No 3507*. [*FA 2006, s 175*].

Key points concerning payment of tax

[51.33] Points to consider are as follows.

- For individuals and trustees tax due on capital gains tax is usually payable by 31 January following the year of assessment (ending 5 April) in which the gains arise. Tax for 2016/17 is therefore payable by 31 January 2018.
- If HMRC was notified of chargeability by the taxpayer within six months of the end of the year of assessment but did not issue a tax return or a notice to complete one by the following 31 October then the tax becomes due three months after such a return or notice is issued.
- Penalties for failure to notify can normally be avoided if the tax is **paid** by a specific date; for income tax by the normal due date (31 January) and for corporation tax by the notification date (one year after the end of the accounting period).
- Penalties apply for late payment of capital gains tax. The penalty code does not yet apply for corporation tax purposes except to corporation tax due under an exit charge payment plan.
- Capital gains tax arising from an amendment to a self-assessment tax return (made after 1 January following the year of assessment) or from a discovery assessment is due and payable 30 days after the date of the amendment or assessment although interest will run from the normal due date.
- Capital gains tax is not taken into account in the calculation of self-assessment payments on account for a subsequent year.
- HMRC may be flexible regarding payments if a taxpayer is having difficulty and allow arrangements to pay by instalments. Penalties for late payment of tax can be suspended where the taxpayer agrees a time to pay arrangement, subject to meeting the terms of the arrangement.
- Tax can be paid by credit card but HMRC will charge a fee.
- For companies (who pay corporation tax on chargeable gains) the tax is paid along with the normal corporation tax and is generally due nine months and one day following the end of the accounting

period. Large companies must pay the tax in quarterly instalments. Payments of corporation tax must be made using an electronic means.

52

Penalties

Introduction to penalties	**52.1**
Reasonable excuse (general)	**52.2**
Notification of chargeability	**52.3**
Failure to deliver tax return on or before filing date	**52.4**
Company returns	**52.4**
Cross-tax penalty for failure to make returns	**52.5**
European Economic Interest Grouping returns	**52.6**
European Economic Interest Groupings — negligence or fraud in connection with return or accounts	**52.7**
Careless or deliberate errors in documents	**52.8**
Error in taxpayer's document attributable to another person	**52.9**
Failure to notify HMRC of error in assessment	**52.10**
Arrangements counteracted by the general anti-abuse rule	**52.11**
Penalty for offshore asset moves	**52.12**
Asset-based penalty for offshore inaccuracies and failures	**52.13**
Failure to correct offshore tax non-compliance	**52.14**
Failure to keep and preserve records	**52.15**
Penalties in respect of investigatory powers under *FA 2008, Sch 36*	**52.16**
Penalties in respect of data-gathering powers under *FA 2011, Sch 23*	**52.17**
Two or more tax-related penalties in respect of same tax	**52.18**
Dishonest conduct by tax agents	**52.19**
Enabling offshore tax evasion	**52.20**
Enablers of defeated tax avoidance	**52.21**
Interest on penalties	**52.22**
Special returns etc	**52.23**
Failure to disclose tax avoidance scheme	**52.24**
High-risk promoters of avoidance schemes	**52.25**
Failure to comply with follower notice	**52.26**
Failure to make accelerated payment	**52.27**
Penalties in respect of powers of enforcement by deduction from accounts	**52.28**
Penalties under the serial avoiders regime	**52.29**
Failure to comply with requirement to publish tax strategy	**52.30**
Mitigation of penalties	**52.31**
Other HMRC action where a penalty is chargeable	**52.32**
Procedure	**52.33**
Appeals	**52.34**
Proceedings before Tribunal	**52.35**
Proceedings before court	**52.36**
General matters	**52.37**
Time limits	**52.38**
Bankrupts	**52.39**
Liability under criminal law	**52.40**
Key points concerning penalties	**52.41**

Cross-references. See 42 LATE PAYMENT INTEREST AND PENALTIES; 49.18 OVERSEAS MATTERS for companies ceasing to be UK resident; 51 PAYMENT OF TAX; 58 RETURNS.

Simon's Taxes. See A6.340–A6.345.

Introduction to penalties

[52.1] Financial penalties can be charged or sought by HMRC for a substantial number of offences by taxpayers or their agents. The current penalties relevant to capital gains tax and corporation tax on chargeable gains are summarised in the table below and are described in detail in the paragraphs of this chapter or where indicated in the table.

Offence	Penalty	Para
1. Failure to notify chargeability to tax. Failure to comply with the obligation to notify chargeability to CGT within six months of tax year or to CT within one year of accounting period. *FA 2008, Sch 41.*	Deliberate and concealed failure: 100% of potential lost revenue. Deliberate but unconcealed failure: 70% of potential lost revenue. Any other case: 30% of potential lost revenue. A statutory reduction in the amount of the penalty is made for disclosure of a failure. HMRC can also reduce a penalty in special circumstances. Where the failure is linked to an offshore matter relating to certain categorised territories the amount of the penalty is increased.	52.3
2. Failure to deliver corporation tax return on time. *TMA 1970, s 7; FA 1998, Sch 18 paras 17, 18.*	(i) £100 if up to 3 months late (£500 if previous two returns also delivered late);	52.4
	(ii) £200 if over 3 months late (£1,000 if previous two returns also late);	
Failure continuing at later of final day for delivery of return and 18 months after return period	Further penalty of 10% of tax unpaid 18 months after return period (20% of tax unpaid at that date if return not made within 2 years of return period)	

Offence		Penalty	Para
3. Failure to make return on time (income tax and capital gains tax). *FA 2009, Sch 55*	(i)	initial penalty of £100.	52.5
	(ii)	if failure continues three months after penalty date and HMRC give notice, a further penalty of £10 per day for each day failure continues in 90-day period beginning with date specified in notice.	
	(iii)	if failure continues six months after penalty date, a further penalty of the greater of 5% of the tax liability and £300.	
To be extended to corporation tax returns from a date to be fixed.	(iv)	if failure continues twelve months after penalty date and the withholding of information is deliberate or concealed a further penalty of the greater of 100% of the tax liability and £300; if the withholding is deliberate and not concealed, the greater of 70% of the liability and £300; or otherwise, greater of 5% of the liability and £300.	
		A statutory reduction in the amount of the penalty is made for disclosure of a failure. HMRC can also reduce a penalty in special circumstances. Where the failure is linked to an offshore matter relating to certain categorised territories the amount of the penalty is increased.	
4. Failure to make payment of CGT on time. *FA 2009, Sch 56*	A 5% penalty applies if full amount not paid within 30 days of due date. If amount remains unpaid six months after due date a penalty of 5% applies; a further 5% penalty applies if amount is still unpaid after a further six months.		**42.10** LATE PAYMENT INTEREST AND PENALTIES

Offence	Penalty	Para
5. Error in taxpayer's document. Careless or deliberate error in document amounting to or leading to understatement of liability, overstatement or loss or false or inflated claim to repayment of tax. *FA 2007, Sch 24 para 1.*	Deliberate and concealed error: 100% of potential lost revenue. Deliberate but unconcealed error: 70% of potential lost revenue. Any other case: 30% of potential lost revenue. A statutory reduction in the amount of the penalty is made for disclosure of an error. HMRC can also reduce a penalty in special circumstances. Where the error is linked to an offshore matter relating to certain categorised territories the amount of the penalty is increased.	52.8
6. Error in taxpayer's document attributable to another person. Deliberately supplying false information to, or deliberately withholding information from, a person giving a document to HMRC resulting in document containing an inaccuracy amounting to or leading to understatement of liability, overstatement of loss or false or inflated claim to repayment of tax. *FA 2007, Sch 24 para 1A.*	100% of potential lost revenue subject to statutory reduction for disclosure or in special circumstances.	52.9
7. Failure to notify HMRC of error in assessment. Failure to take reasonable steps to notify HMRC of an under-assessment within the 30 days beginning with the date of the assessment. *FA 2007, Sch 24 para 2.*	30% of potential lost revenue subject to statutory reduction for disclosure or in special circumstances.	52.10
8. Arrangements counteracted under the GAAR. A person is liable to a penalty if HMRC counteract a tax advantage by making adjustments under the general anti-abuse rule ('GAAR'). *FA 2013, s 212A.*	60% of the counteracted advantage.	52.11

Offence	Penalty	Para
9. Offshore asset move where taxpayer becomes liable to another penalty under 1, 3 or 5 above. *FA 2015, Sch 21.*	50% of original penalty.	**52.12**
10. Asset-based penalty for offshore inaccuracies and failures. *FA 2016, Sch 22.*	Lower of (i) 10% of value of the asset, and (ii) the offshore potential lost revenue x 10, subject to statutory reduction for disclosure.	**52.13**
11. Failure to correct offshore tax non-compliance. *F(No 2)A 2017, Sch 18.*	200% of potential lost revenue subject to statutory reduction for disclosure or in special circumstances to minimum of 100% of potential lost revenue.	**52.14**
12. Failure to maintain records. Failure to keep and preserve appropriate records supporting personal and trustees' returns or partnership returns. *TMA 1970, s 12B.*	Up to £3,000	**52.15**
13. Failure to comply with HMRC investigatory powers. Failure to comply with an information notice within *FA 2008, Sch 36 Pt 1* or deliberately obstructing an HMRC officer in the course of an inspection of business premises under *FA 2008, Sch 36 Pt 2* which has been approved by the First-tier Tribunal. *FA 2008, Sch 36.*	(i) initial penalty of £300. (ii) if failure/obstruction continues, a further penalty up to £60 per day. (iii) if failure/obstruction continues after penalty under (i) imposed, a tax-related amount determined by the Upper Tribunal.	**52.16**
14. HMRC investigatory powers: inaccurate information and documents *FA 2008, Sch 36.*	Up to £3,000	**52.16**
15. HMRC data-gathering powers: failure to comply *FA 2011, Sch 23.*	(i) initial penalty of £300. (ii) if failure continues, a further penalty up to £60 per day. (iii) if failure continues for more than 30 days after penalty under (ii) imposed, a further daily penalty determined by the Upper Tribunal up to £1,000 per day.	**52.17**

Offence	Penalty		Para
16. HMRC data-gathering powers: inaccurate data *FA 2011, Sch 23.*	Up to £3,000		52.17
17. Dishonest conduct by tax agents *FA 2012, Sch 38 para 26.*	Up to £50,000 (minimum £5,000)		52.19
18. Tax agents: failure to comply with file access notice *FA 2012, Sch 38 paras 22, 23.*	(i)	Initial penalty of £300.	
	(ii)	If failure continues, a further penalty up to £60 per day.	52.19
19. Enabling offshore tax evasion. *FA 2016, s 162, Sch 20*	Higher of 100% of the potential lost revenue and £3,000. If the original tax non-compliance resulted in a penalty under *FA 2015, Sch 21* (see 9 above), higher of 50% of the potential lost revenue in respect of the original tax non-compliance and £3,000.		52.20
20. Enablers of defeated tax avoidance. *F(No 2)A 2017, s 65, Sch 16.*	The total amount or value of the consideration received or receivable by the enabler for anything done by him which enabled the arrangements.		52.21
21. Special returns etc. Failure to comply with a notice to deliver any return or other document, to furnish any particulars, to produce any document or record, to make anything available for inspection or give any certificate under specified provisions. *TMA 1970, s 98.*	Up to £300 (£3,000 in specified cases)		52.23
22. Failure to disclose tax avoidance scheme. Failure to comply with any of a number of requirements under the disclosure of tax avoidance schemes rules. *TMA 1970, s 98C.*	(i)	Initial penalty of £5,000.	52.24
	(ii)	continuing daily penalty of £600 (£5,000 in specified cases) after penalty in (i) has been imposed.	
	(iii)	Penalty of £100 for failure of party to notifiable arrangements to notify HMRC of scheme reference number. Increased to £500 for second failure in three-year period and £1,000 for third failure.	

Offence	Penalty		Para
23. High-risk promoters of avoidance schemes. Failure to comply with any of a number of requirements under the high-risk promoters of avoidance schemes rules. Provision of inaccurate information or documents in compliance with such a requirement. *FA 2014, Sch 35*.	Various		52.25
24. Failure to comply with a follower notice. [*FA 2014, s 208*].	Up to 50% of the value of the denied tax advantage or 20% in partnership cases.		52.26
25. Failure to make accelerated payment. [*FA 2014, s 226*].	A 5% penalty applies if full amount not paid by due date. If amount remains unpaid five months after due date a penalty of 5% applies; a further 5% penalty applies if amount is still unpaid after a further six months.		52.27
26. Powers of enforcement by deduction from accounts. [*F(No 2)A 2015, Sch 8*]. Various compliance failures or making disclosure likely to prejudice HMRC's ability to use the powers to recover the sum in question.	(i)	Initial penalty of £300.	52.28
	(ii)	If failure continues, a further penalty up to £60 per day.	
27. Penalties under the serial avoiders regime. [*FA 2016, Sch 18*]. Where a person suffers a defeat of an avoidance scheme used whilst in a warning period.	Penalty of 20% of the value of the counteracted advantage. If, before the relevant defeat is incurred, the person was liable to be given prior warning notices, the penalty is increased. It is increased to 40% where there has been a single prior warning notice, and to 60% where there has been more than one such notice.		52.29
28. Failure to comply with requirement to publish tax strategy. [*FA 2016, Sch 19*].	(i)	Initial penalty of £7,500.	52.30
	(ii)	If failure continues for six months, a further penalty of £7,500.	
	(iii)	If failure continues, a further penalty of £7,500 at the end of each subsequent month.	

For the procedure for charging penalties see **52.33** onwards below. See **52.40** below for potential liability under the criminal law.

Reasonable excuse (general)

[52.2] It is generally provided for the purposes of *TMA 1970* that a person is deemed not to have failed to do anything required to be done where there was a reasonable excuse for the failure and, if the excuse ceased, provided that the failure was remedied without unreasonable delay after the excuse had ceased. Similarly, a person is deemed not to have failed to do anything required to be done within a limited time if he did it within such further time as HMRC, or the Commissioners or officer concerned, may have allowed. [*TMA 1970, s 118(2); F(No 2)A 1987, s 94*]. Consideration of what constitutes a reasonable excuse was made in *R v Sevenoaks Commrs, ex p. Thorne*; *Thorne v Sevenoaks Commrs & CIR*, Ch D & QB 1989, 62 TC 341. See also *Rowland v HMRC* (Sp C 548), [2006] SSCD 536 in which it was held that reliance on a third party could, in principle, be a reasonable excuse.

There are separate 'reasonable excuse' let-outs as regards penalties for late returns (see **52.4**, **52.5** below), penalties for failure to comply with a duty under the high-risk promoter provisions (see **52.25** below), penalties for failure to make an accelerated payment (see **52.27** below) and penalties and surcharges for late payment of tax (see **42.6**, **42.10** LATE PAYMENT INTEREST AND PENALTIES).

Notification of chargeability

[52.3] Taxpayers who do not automatically receive tax returns for completion have an obligation to notify HMRC of their chargeability to capital gains tax or corporation tax within specified time limits. Penalties apply for failure to do so as described below.

Capital gains tax (and income tax)

A person chargeable to income tax or capital gains tax for a particular tax year who has not received a notice under *TMA 1970, s 8* (see **58.3** RETURNS) to deliver a return for that year of his income and chargeable gains has until 5 October following that tax year to notify HMRC that he is so chargeable. Where a person chargeable to income tax or capital gains tax has received such a notice, but the notice has subsequently been withdrawn (see **58.3** RETURNS), he must notify HMRC that he is chargeable within 30 days after the date on which the notice was withdrawn (or before 6 October if later).

A person is excepted from the requirement to notify HMRC if his total income is fully taxed at source or chargeable at a nil rate (see Tolley's Income Tax for the detailed provisions) *and* he has no chargeable gains for the year; in practice, this is taken to mean no chargeable gains in excess of the annual exempt amount — see HMRC Self Assessment Legal Framework Manual SALF210.

The above applies equally to 'relevant trustees' of settlements by reference to a notice under *TMA 1970, s 8A* (see **58.3** RETURNS) to deliver a tax return.

Where a 'simple assessment' is made for a tax year (see **6.9** ASSESSMENTS), the requirement to notify chargeability does not then apply for that year unless the person is chargeable on any income or gain that is not included in the simple assessment.

[*TMA 1970, s 7; FA 2013, Sch 51 para 2; FA 2016, Sch 23 para 2; SI 2009 No 511*].

The trustees of occupational pension schemes which have income or capital gains are also within these provisions (see Revenue Press Release 29 August 1997, Pension Schemes Office Update 30, 5 September 1997 and see generally Revenue Tax Bulletin February 1999 pp 628, 629).

Where the requirement to notify chargeability for a tax year would otherwise be triggered only by a non-resident CGT disposal giving rise to an NRCGT gain (see **41.25** LAND), that gain is disregarded for the above purposes so that notification is not required, provided that an NRCGT return which includes an advance self-assessment (see **58.20** RETURNS) for the disposal has been made within the time limit for notification above. [*TMA 1970, s 7A; FA 2015, Sch 7 para 42*].

Corporation tax

A company chargeable to corporation tax for a particular accounting period which has not received a notice to deliver a company tax return has twelve months after the end of the accounting period in which to notify HMRC that it is so chargeable.

[*FA 1998, s 117, Sch 18 para 2; SI 2009 No 511*].

See also **58.19** RETURNS for the requirement to give notice of coming within the charge to corporation tax within three months of the *beginning* of an accounting period.

Penalties for non-compliance with obligations to notify chargeability

Penalties for non-compliance with the above provisions are charged under a unified penalty code for failures relating to a range of taxes. The code is described below, but only to the extent that it relates to the above provisions.

A person is not liable to a penalty for a failure in respect of which he has been convicted of an offence.

Amount of penalty

The amount of the penalty depends on whether or not the failure is deliberate and is subject to reduction as detailed below. It also depends on which of four categories the failure falls in. The categories are as follows.

- **Category 0.** Not yet in operation — see below under Future developments.
- **Category 1.** Failures involving a 'domestic matter' or inaccuracies involving an 'offshore matter' where the territory concerned is a category 1 territory or the tax involved is neither income tax nor capital gains tax.

- **Category 2.** Failures involving an offshore matter or (for an obligation to notify arising in respect of 2016/17 or a subsequent tax year) an 'offshore transfer' where the territory involved is a category 2 territory and the tax is income tax or capital gains tax.
- **Category 3.** Failures involving an offshore matter or (for an obligation to notify arising in respect of 2016/17 or a subsequent tax year) an offshore transfer where the territory involved is a category 3 territory and the tax is income tax or capital gains tax.

If a failure is within more than one category it is treated as if it were separate failures, one in each of the categories concerned according to the matters it involves, and the 'potential lost revenue' (see below) is calculated separately for each deemed failure.

A failure involves an '*offshore matter*' if it results in potential lost revenue charged on, or by reference to, income arising from a source in, or assets (including sterling) held or situated in, a territory outside the UK, activities carried on wholly or mainly in such a territory or anything having effect as if it were such income, assets or activities.

A failure involves an *offshore transfer* if:

- it does not involve an offshore matter;
- it is deliberate (whether or not concealed) and results in a potential loss of revenue; and
- the proceeds of the disposal on (or by reference to which) the tax is charged (or any part of those proceeds):
  - are received in a territory outside the UK; or
  - are transferred to a territory outside the UK before the date by reference to which the potential lost revenue is to be calculated. The reference to the transfer of proceeds is to be read as including a reference to the transfer of any assets derived from or representing those proceeds.

Where more than one category of territory is involved in an offshore transfer, the level of penalty is to be determined by reference to the highest category of territory involved.

A failure involves a '*domestic matter*' if it does not involve an offshore matter or an offshore transfer. The classification of territories to categories 1, 2 or 3 is as follows.

- **Category 1:** Anguilla; Aruba; Australia; Belgium; Bulgaria; Canada; Cayman Islands; Cyprus; Czech Republic; Denmark (not including Faroe Islands and Greenland); Estonia; Finland; France; Germany; Greece; Guernsey; Hungary; Ireland; Isle of Man; Italy; Japan; Latvia; Liechtenstein (from 24 July 2013); Lithuania; Malta; Montserrat; Netherlands (not including Bonaire, Sint Eustatius and Saba); New Zealand (not including Tokelau); Norway; Poland; Portugal; Romania; Slovakia; Slovenia; South Korea; Spain; Sweden; Switzerland (from 24 July 2013); United States of America (not including overseas territories and possessions).
- **Category 2:** All territories (except the UK) not within categories 1 or 3.

- **Category 3:** Albania; Algeria; Andorra; Bonaire, Sint Eustatius and Saba; Brazil; Cameroon; Cape Verde; Colombia; Republic of the Congo; Cook Islands; Costa Rica; Curaçao; Cuba; Democratic People's Republic of Korea; Dominican Republic; Ecuador; El Salvador; Gabon; Guatemala; Honduras; Iran; Iraq; Jamaica; Kyrgyzstan; Lebanon; Macau; Marshall Islands; Federated States of Micronesia; Monaco; Nauru; Nicaragua; Niue; Palau; Panama; Paraguay; Peru; Seychelles; Sint Maarten; Suriname; Syria; Tokelau; Tonga; Trinidad and Tobago; United Arab Emirates; Uruguay. The following territories were originally in category 3 but moved to category 2 with effect from 24 July 2013: Antigua and Barbuda; Armenia; Bahrain; Barbados; Belize; Dominica; Grenada; Mauritius; Saint Kitts and Nevis; Saint Lucia; Saint Vincent and the Grenadines; San Marino.

The amount of the penalty (subject to the reductions below) is the percentage of the potential lost revenue found using the table below.

	Percentage of potential lost revenue		
Type of failure	*Category 1*	*Category 2*	*Category 3*
deliberate and concealed	100	150	200
deliberate but not concealed	70	105	140
any other	30	45	60

A deliberate and concealed failure occurs where the failure was deliberate and the taxpayer made arrangements to conceal the situation giving rise to the obligation. A deliberate but not concealed failure occurs where the failure was deliberate but the taxpayer did not make arrangements to conceal the situation giving rise to the obligation.

For income tax and capital gains tax purposes, the '*potential lost revenue*' is in most cases equal to the amount of tax payable for the year that, by reason of the failure, remains unpaid on 31 January following that year. Where an obligation to notify chargeability arises following the withdrawal of a notice to make a return (see **58.3** RETURNS), the '*potential lost revenue*' is the amount of tax that is, by reason of the failure to comply with the obligation:

(a) where the period for notification is extended to 30 days after the date of the withdrawal notification and that period ends after the 'relevant date', unpaid at the end of that period; or
(b) in any other case, unpaid on the relevant date.

The '*relevant date*' for this purpose is 31 January following the tax year or, where, after that date, HMRC refund a payment on account for the year, the day after the refund is issued.

For corporation tax purposes, the '*potential lost revenue*' is equal to the amount of tax payable for the accounting period that, by reason of the failure, remains unpaid twelve months after the end of the period. Tax payable is computed disregarding any deferred relief arising from the repayment of loans made to close company participators.

The fact that potential lost revenue may be balanced by a potential overpayment by another person is ignored, except to the extent that that person's tax liability is required or permitted to be adjusted by reference to the taxpayer's.

No penalty is due in relation to a failure that is not deliberate if the taxpayer satisfies HMRC or, on appeal, the Tribunal, that there is a reasonable excuse for the failure. Insufficiency of funds is not a reasonable excuse for this purpose and neither is the taxpayer's reliance on another person to do anything, unless he took reasonable care to avoid the failure. If the taxpayer had a reasonable excuse, he is treated as continuing to have a reasonable excuse after the excuse has ceased if the failure is remedied without unreasonable delay.

Reduction for disclosure — necessary disclosures

A reduction in a penalty will be given where the taxpayer discloses a failure to notify. The penalty will be reduced to a percentage which reflects the quality of the disclosure and the amount of the reduction will depend on whether the disclosure is 'prompted' or 'unprompted' and is subject to a minimum percentage (see tables below). A disclosure is '*unprompted*' if made when the taxpayer has no reason to believe HMRC have discovered or are about to discover the failure. In all other cases, disclosures are '*prompted*'.

In the case of a failure that involves a domestic matter, or in the case of a *non-deliberate* failure involving an offshore matter, a person is treated as making a disclosure for these purposes only if he tells HMRC about the failure, gives them reasonable help in quantifying the tax unpaid and allows them access to records for the purpose of checking how much tax is unpaid.

In the case of a *deliberate* failure (whether concealed or not) involving an *offshore matter* or any failure involving an *offshore transfer*, a person (P) will be treated as making a disclosure only if P tells HMRC about the failure, gives them reasonable help in quantifying the tax unpaid, and allows them access to records for the purpose of checking how much tax is unpaid. With effect on and after 1 April 2017, P must also tell HMRC if there is:

- any person who encouraged, assisted or otherwise facilitated the failure; and
- any asset situated or held outside the UK that is held on P's behalf by another person,

and must provide further specified details if either is the case.

Reduction for disclosure — domestic matters

The minimum percentage (i.e. the percentage below which a penalty may not be reduced) for each level of penalty in relation to domestic matters is as follows. Where relevant, the 'Case A' minimum applies where HMRC become aware of the failure less than twelve months after the time when the tax first becomes unpaid by reason of the failure; otherwise the 'Case B' minimum applies.

Standard percentage	Minimum percentage for prompted disclosure	Minimum percentage for unprompted disclosure
30	case A: 10 case B: 20	case A: 0 case B: 10
70	35	20
100	50	30

Reduction for disclosure — offshore matters

For a failure involving an offshore matter or offshore transfer, the penalty cannot be reduced below a minimum percentage shown in the table below. The minimum percentage shown in each case applies on or after 1 April 2017 and has effect in relation to 2016/17 onwards; the percentage shown in parentheses immediately after it is the one previously applicable. Where relevant, the 'Case A' minimum applies where HMRC become aware of the failure less than 12 months after the time when the tax first becomes unpaid by reason of the failure; otherwise the 'Case B' minimum applies.

Standard percentage	Minimum percentage for prompted disclosure	Minimum percentage for unprompted disclosure
30	case A: 10 (10) case B: 20 (20)	case A: 0 (0) case B: 10 (10)
45	case A: 15 (15) case B: 30 (30)	case A: 0 (0) case B: 15 (15)
60	case A: 20 (20) case B: 40 (40)	case A: 0 (0) case B: 20 (20)
70	45 (35)	30 (20)
100	60 (50)	40 (30)
105	62.5 (52.5)	40 (30)
140	80 (70)	50 (40)
150	85 (75)	55 (45)
200	110 (100)	70 (60)

Reduction in special circumstances

HMRC can also reduce, stay or agree a compromise in relation to proceedings for a penalty if they think it right to do so because of special circumstances. Ability to pay and the fact that a potential loss of revenue from one taxpayer is balanced by a potential overpayment by another are not special circumstances for this purpose.

Reduction for other penalty or surcharge

The amount of a penalty in respect of a failure is reduced by the amount of any other penalty or late payment surcharge (see **42.6** LATE PAYMENT INTEREST AND PENALTIES), the amount of which is determined by reference to the same tax liability. No reduction is made for a tax-related penalty within **52.16** below or for a penalty within **52.13**, **52.26** or **52.27** below.

No reduction is made for a penalty within **42.10** LATE PAYMENT INTEREST AND PENALTIES where the payment default relates to 2014/15 or a later year.

Agents

A person is liable to a penalty under the above provisions where the failure is by a person acting on his behalf. He is not, however, liable to a penalty in respect of anything done or omitted by his agent, if he satisfies HMRC or, on appeal, the tribunal, that he took reasonable care to avoid the failure.

Company officers

Where a company is liable to a penalty under the above provisions for a deliberate failure and the failure was attributable to a company 'officer', the officer is liable to pay such part (including all) of the penalty as HMRC specify by written notice. In relation to a body corporate other than a limited liability partnership, a director, shadow director, manager or secretary of the company is an '*officer*'; in relation to a limited liability partnership, a member is an '*officer*'; and in any other case, a director, manager, secretary or any other person managing or purporting to manage any of the company's affairs is an '*officer*'. The procedural provisions (see **52.33** onwards below) apply to a part of a penalty payable by a company officer as if it were itself a penalty.

Future developments

With effect on and after a day to be appointed by the Treasury, a new category (category 0) is to be introduced alongside categories 1 to 3 above. A category 0 territory will be a territory designated as such by Treasury order. The intention is that only territories that adopt automatic exchange of information under the Common Reporting Standard (see Tolley's Income Tax for details of international co-operation including the Common Reporting Standard) will be given category 0 status.

Category 0 will have the same penalty levels as the current category 1 (and all penalties for domestic matters and corporation tax will be moved to category 0). The current penalty levels for category 1 will be increased from 100%, 70% and 30% to 125%, 87.5% and 37.5% respectively. The penalty levels for categories 2 and 3 will remain the same. The new category 1 penalty levels can be reduced for unprompted disclosure to a minimum of 50%, 35% and 0% respectively and for prompted disclosure to a minimum of 72.5%, 53.75% and 12.5% respectively. If, however, HMRC do not become aware of the failure until 12 months or more after the time tax first becomes unpaid by reason of the failure, the 37.5% penalty cannot be reduced below 12.5% for unprompted disclosure and 25% for prompted disclosure.

[FA 2008, s 123, Sch 41 paras 1, 5–7, 11–15, 20–24; FA 2013, Sch 50 paras 13, 16(3), Sch 51 para 6; FA 2014, Sch 33 para 4; FA 2015, s 120, Sch 20 paras 9–13; FA 2016, s 163, Sch 21 paras 5–8, Sch 22 para 20(4); SI 2009 No 511; SI 2011 Nos 975, 976; SI 2013 No 1618; SI 2016 No 456, Art 4; SI 2017 Nos 259, 345].

See **52.12** below as regards a possible further penalty where assets are moved between overseas territories in order to prevent or delay the discovery of a potential loss of revenue giving rise to the above penalty.

Failure to deliver tax return on or before filing date

Company returns

[52.4] A company which fails to deliver a company tax return for an accounting period on or before the 'filing date' when required to do so by notice under *FA 1998, Sch 18 para 3* is liable to a flat-rate penalty of:

- £100, if the return is delivered within three months after the filing date; or
- £200, if the return is delivered more than three months after the filing date.

The '*filing date*' is the last day of whichever of the periods at **58.19**(a)–(c) RETURNS is the last to end (see *FA 1998, Sch 18 para 14*). In the straightforward case, it will be the last day of the twelve months following the accounting period in question.

For a third successive failure, the above amounts are increased to £500 and £1,000 respectively. Such a failure occurs where a company is within the charge to corporation tax throughout three successive accounting periods, is required to deliver a return for each such period, is liable to a flat-rate penalty in respect of each of the first two such periods, and is again liable in respect of the third such period.

The flat-rate penalty does not apply if the period for which the return is required (the 'return period') is one for which accounts are required under *Companies Act 2006* or *Companies Act 1985* (or NI equivalent) and the return is delivered to HMRC no later than the last day for delivery of the accounts to the Registrar of Companies.

If a failure to deliver a return continues beyond the 18 months following the end of the accounting period in question (or beyond the filing date if, exceptionally, it falls later than that), then, in addition to a flat-rate penalty, the company is liable to a tax-related penalty. This is equal to 10% of the 'unpaid tax', increasing to 20% if the return is still not delivered within two years after the end of the return period. The '*unpaid tax*' is so much of the tax payable for the accounting period in question as remains unpaid beyond the 18-month period referred to above (or beyond the filing date if later). Tax payable is computed for this purpose in accordance with *FA 1998, Sch 18 para 8* (but disregarding any deferred relief arising from the repayment of loans made to close company participators).

[*FA 1998, s 117, Sch 18 paras 17–19; SI 2008 No 954, Art 25(3)*].

Replacement of penalty

The above provisions are to be replaced by the new penalties at **52.5** below at a future date..

Cross-tax penalty for failure to make returns

[52.5] A unified penalty code for failure to make a return applies across a range of taxes including capital gains tax. The code was originally intended to be extended to corporation tax, but this has not yet happened. The penalties are described below, but only to the extent that they relate to capital gains tax and will relate to corporation tax.

Where a return is required under any of the provisions listed below, a penalty under the code is payable if the taxpayer fails to make or deliver the return to HMRC on or before the 'filing date'. For this purpose a requirement to make a return includes the requirement to deliver any accounts, statement or document which must be delivered with the return. The provisions are:

(a) *TMA 1970, s 8* (personal tax return — see **58.3** RETURNS);
(b) *TMA 1970, s 8A* (trustee's tax return — see **58.3** RETURNS);
(c) *TMA 1970, s 12ZB* (NRCGT return — see **58.20** RETURNS);
(d) *TMA 1970, s 12AA* (partnership tax return — see **58.16** RETURNS); and
(e) *FA 1998, Sch 18 para 3* (corporation tax return — see **58.19** RETURNS).

For returns within (a) and (b) above, the '*filing date*' is:

- if the return is a non-electronic return, 31 October following the tax year to which it relates or, if later, within three months beginning with the date of the notice;
- if the return is an electronic return, 31 January following the tax year to which it relates or, if later, within three months beginning with the date of the notice.

For returns within (e) above, the '*filing date*' is the last day of whichever of the periods at **58.19**(a)–(c) RETURNS is the last to end (see *FA 1998, Sch 18 para 14*). In the straightforward case, it will be the last day of the twelve months following the accounting period in question. See **58.16** RETURNS for the filing date for partnership returns.

If a failure to make a return falls within the terms of more than one of the following penalties, the taxpayer is liable to each of those penalties (subject to the overall limit for tax-geared penalties below). A taxpayer is not liable to a penalty for a failure or action in respect of which he has been convicted of an offence.

Where HMRC issue a notice withdrawing a notice to make a return within (a), (b) or (d) above (see **58.3, 58.16** RETURNS), the notice may also cancel a penalty under these provisions for failing to make a return.

Initial penalty

An initial penalty of £100 is payable for failure to make a return on or before the filing date.

Daily penalty

HMRC can impose a daily penalty where the taxpayer's failure to make the return continues after the end of three months beginning with the day after the filing date (the '*penalty date*').

The amount of the penalty is £10 for each day that the failure continues during the period of 90 days starting with a date specified by HMRC. HMRC must notify the taxpayer of the starting date, which date cannot be earlier than the end of the three-months beginning with the penalty date. The date can, however, be earlier than the date of the notice.

HMRC stated to Institute of Chartered Accountants in England and Wales (ICAEW) in July 2017, that it would use its discretion and not charge daily penalties in the case of (c) above in respect of late NRCGT returns. See ion.icaew.com/taxfaculty/b/weblog/posts/late-nrcgt-returns-hmrc-will-not-charge-daily-penalties. In *McGreevy v HMRC* FTT (TC 6109), [2017] UKFTT 690 (TC), the Tribunal found that the daily penalties in respect of a late NRCGT return had been incorrectly imposed (as there was no evidence that the decision to impose them had been made by an HMRC officer and HMRC had not notified the taxpayer of the start date) and also noted that HMRC had ceased to impose such penalties. In the case of the remaining tax-geared penalties (see below) in respect of this NRCGT return, the taxpayer was found to have a reasonable excuse for the delay as the Tribunal observed that the return was in the first year of operation and it had been reasonable for the taxpayer to think that she only needed to mention the gain on her self-assessment tax return. The Tribunal rejected HMRC's contention that the taxpayer had not taken reasonable care as she should have stayed up to date with legislation affecting her activities in the UK, finding that this obligation identified by HMRC had no source; it was not the law.

Tax-geared penalties

First tax-geared penalty

If the failure continues after the end of six months starting with the penalty date the taxpayer is liable to a penalty equal to the greater of £300 and 5% of any tax liability which would have been shown in the return.

For this purpose (and that of the second tax-geared penalty below), the tax liability which would have been shown in a return is the amount which, had a correct and complete return been delivered on the filing date, would have been shown to be due and payable in respect of the tax for the period concerned. If a penalty is assessed before the return is made, HMRC must determine the tax liability to the best of their information and belief. Then, when the return is subsequently made, the penalty must be re-assessed by reference to the amount of tax shown in the return to be due and payable (but subject to any amendments or corrections to the return). Any deferred relief arising from the repayment of loans made to close company participators is disregarded.

Second tax-geared penalty

A further tax-geared penalty is payable if the failure continues the end of twelve months starting with the penalty date. The amount of the penalty depends on whether or not, by failing to make the return, the taxpayer deliberately withholds information which would enable or assist HMRC to assess the tax liability.

If there is deliberate withholding of information, the amount of the penalty further depends on whether the withholding is concealed and on which of four categories the information falls within. The categories are as follows.

- **Category 0.** This category is not yet in operation — see below under Future developments.
- **Category 1.** Information involving a 'domestic matter' or involving an 'offshore matter' or (as regards returns for 2016/17 onwards) an 'offshore transfer' where the territory concerned is a category 1 territory or the tax involved is neither income tax nor capital gains tax.
- **Category 2.** Information involving an offshore matter or (as regards returns for 2016/17 onwards) an offshore transfer where the territory involved is a category 2 territory and the tax is income tax or capital gains tax.
- **Category 3.** Information involving an offshore matter or (as regards returns for 2016/17 onwards) an offshore transfer where the territory involved is a category 3 territory and the tax is income tax or capital gains tax.

If the information withheld is within more than one category, the failure is treated as if it were separate failures, one in each of the categories concerned and the tax liability which would be shown in the return is apportioned on a just and reasonable basis.

Information involves an '*offshore matter*' if the liability which would have been shown in the return includes a liability to tax charged on, or by reference to, income arising from a source in, or assets (including sterling) held or situated in, a territory outside the UK, activities carried on wholly or mainly in such a territory or anything having effect as if it were such income, assets or activities.

Information involves an '*offshore transfer*' if:

- it does not involve an offshore matter;
- it is information which would enable or assist HMRC to assess the taxpayer's liability to income tax;
- by failing to make the return, the taxpayer deliberately withholds the information (whether or not the withholding of the information is also concealed); and
- the proceeds of the disposal on (or by reference to which) the tax is charged (or any part of the proceeds):
  - are received in a territory outside the UK; or

– are transferred to a territory outside the UK before the date on which the taxpayer becomes liable to the second tax-geared penalty. The reference to the transfer of proceeds is to be read as including a reference to the transfer of any assets derived from or representing those proceeds.

Where more than one category of territory is involved in an offshore transfer, the level of penalty is to be determined by reference to the highest category of territory involved.

Information involves a '*domestic matter*' if it does not involve an offshore matter or an offshore transfer. The classification of territories to categories 1, 2 or 3 is as at **52.3** above.

The amount of the penalty is the greater of £300 and the percentage of the tax liability which would be shown in the return found using the table below.

	Percentage of tax liability		
	Category 1	*Category 2*	*Category 3*
deliberate and concealed withholding of information	100	150	200
deliberate but not concealed withholding of information	70	105	140
any other	5	5	5

For this purpose, the withholding of information by a taxpayer is concealed if the taxpayer makes arrangements to conceal that it has been withheld.

See **52.12** below as regards a possible further penalty where the second tax-geared penalty is chargeable and assets are moved between overseas territories in order to prevent or delay the discovery by HMRC of the loss of tax revenue.

Maximum tax-geared penalty

Where both the first and second tax-geared penalties are due in relation to the same tax liability, the total of those penalties cannot exceed the 100%, 150% or 200% limit as appropriate.

Partnerships

In the case of a partnership return, where the partner required to make the return or his successor (see **58.16** RETURNS) fails to make the return on or before the filing date, a penalty is payable by each person who was a partner at any time in the period for which the return is required.

Reasonable excuse

None of the above penalties are due in respect of a failure to make a return if the taxpayer satisfies HMRC or, on appeal, the Tribunal, that there is a reasonable excuse for the failure. Insufficiency of funds is not a reasonable excuse for this purpose and neither is the taxpayer's reliance on another person to do anything, unless he took reasonable care to avoid the failure. If the taxpayer had a reasonable excuse, he is treated as continuing to have a reasonable excuse after the excuse has ceased if the failure is remedied without unreasonable delay.

In *Hauser v HMRC* FTT 2015, [2016] SFTD 423 the taxpayer was held to have a reasonable excuse after submitting her return online even though HMRC did not receive the return owing to a glitch in the computer system.

In *Chartridge Developments Ltd v HMRC* FTT 2016, [2017] UKFTT 766 (TC), 2017 STI 332, the taxpayer had delegated the task of submitting a return to an employee who had failed to do so. The company was held not to have a reasonable excuse as there was no evidence that it had taken any steps to ensure that the return would be submitted on time or to check that it had in fact been submitted other than delegating the task to the employee.

Reduction for disclosure

A reduction in the second tax-geared penalty above will be given where the taxpayer discloses information which has been withheld by a failure to make a return. The penalty will be reduced to a percentage which reflects the quality of the disclosure (including its timing, nature and extent) and the amount of the reduction will depend on whether the disclosure is 'prompted' or 'unprompted' and is subject to a minimum percentage. In all cases the amount of the penalty cannot be reduced below £300.

For penalties involving a *domestic* matter, the minimum percentage (i.e. the percentage below which a penalty may not be reduced) is as follows.

Standard percentage	Minimum percentage for prompted disclosure	Minimum percentage for unprompted disclosure
70	35	20
100	50	30

In the case of information involving an *offshore matter* or *offshore transfer*, the minimum percentage shown in the table below in each case applies on and after 1 April 2017 and has effect in relation to 2016/17 onwards; the percentage shown in parentheses immediately after it is the one previously applicable.

Standard percentage	Minimum percentage for prompted disclosure	Minimum percentage for unprompted disclosure
70	45 (35)	30 (20)
100	60 (50)	40 (30)
105	62.5 (52.5)	40 (30)
140	80 (70)	50 (40)
150	85 (75)	55 (45)
200	110 (100)	70 (60)

In the case of a failure that involves a domestic matter, or a *non-deliberate* failure that involves an offshore matter, a person (P) is treated as making a disclosure for these purposes only if P tells HMRC about the information, gives them reasonable help in quantifying the tax unpaid by reason of the information having been withheld and allows them access to records for the purpose of checking how much tax is unpaid. In addition, in the case of a *deliberate* failure (whether concealed or not) involving an *offshore matter*, or in the case of any failure involving an *offshore transfer*, then with effect on and after 1 April 2017, P must also tell HMRC if there is:

- any person who encouraged, assisted or otherwise facilitated the withholding of the information; and
- any asset situated or held outside the UK that is held on P's behalf by another person,

and must provide further specified details if either is the case.

A disclosure is '*unprompted*' if made when the taxpayer has no reason to believe HMRC have discovered or are about to discover the information. In all other cases, disclosures are '*prompted*'.

Reduction in special circumstances

HMRC can also reduce, stay or agree a compromise in relation to proceedings for a penalty if they think it right to do so because of special circumstances. Ability to pay and the fact that a potential loss or revenue from one taxpayer is balanced by a potential overpayment by another are not special circumstances for this purpose.

Reduction for other penalty

The amount of a tax-geared penalty is reduced by the amount of any other penalty the amount of which is determined by reference to the same tax liability. No such reduction is made for another penalty under the above provisions (but see above for the maximum tax-geared penalty under these provisions), for a tax-related penalty for late payment of tax within **42.10** LATE PAYMENT INTEREST AND PENALTIES or for a penalty within **52.13**, **52.26** or **52.27** below.

Future developments

With effect on and after a day to be appointed by the Treasury, a new category (category 0) is to be introduced for the second tax-geared penalty alongside categories 1 to 3 above. A category 0 territory will be a territory designated as such by Treasury order. The intention is that only territories that adopt automatic exchange of information under the Common Reporting Standard (see Tolley's Income Tax for details of the Common Reporting Standard) will be given category 0 status. Category 0 will have the same penalty levels as the current category 1 (and all penalties for domestic matters will be moved to category 0). The higher current penalty levels for category 1 will be increased from 100% and 70% to 125% and 87.5% respectively, with the 5% level staying unchanged. Where both the first and second tax-geared penalties are due in relation to the same tax liability, the total of those penalties cannot exceed the new 125% limit. The penalty levels for categories 2 and 3 will remain the same. The new higher category 1 penalty levels can be reduced for unprompted disclosure to a minimum of 50% and 35% respectively and for prompted disclosure to a minimum of 72.5% and 53.75% respectively; the overriding minimum will continue to be £300.

[*FA 2009, s 106, Sch 55 paras 1–6AB, 14–17B, 23–27; FA 2013, Sch 50 paras 2–5, Sch 51 para 8; FA 2014, Sch 33 para 5; FA 2015, s 120, Sch 7 para 59, Sch 20 paras 14–19; FA 2016, 163, 169(6)(7), Sch 21 paras 9–12, Sch 22 para 20(5); SI 2011 No 702, Art 2; SI 2011 No 703, Art 2; SI 2011 Nos 975, 976; SI 2016 No 456, Art 5; SI 2017 Nos 259, 345*].

European Economic Interest Grouping returns

[52.6] For income tax and capital gains tax purposes, a failure by a European Economic Interest Grouping (see 49.20 OVERSEAS MATTERS) or a member thereof to deliver a return under *TMA 1970, s 12A* (see 58.23 RETURNS) for 1996/97 or a subsequent year (for corporation tax purposes, for accounting periods ending on or after 1 July 1999) is subject to a fixed penalty of £300 multiplied by the number of members of the grouping at the time of failure. For continuing failure, there is a further daily penalty of up to £60 multiplied by the number of members of the grouping at the end of the day on which the grouping or member is notified of a direction to impose such a penalty by the Tribunal (before 1 April 2009 the Appeal Commissioners) on an application by an HMRC officer, such daily penalty to start from the day after the taxpayer is so notified (but not for any day for which such a daily penalty has already been imposed). Neither the fixed nor the daily penalty can be imposed after the failure is remedied, and the aggregate of any fixed and daily penalties cannot exceed £100 if there is no income or chargeable gain to be included in the return. [*TMA 1970, s 98B(1)–(4); SI 2009 No 56, Sch 1 para 44*].

European Economic Interest Groupings — negligence or fraud in connection with return or accounts

[52.7] If a European Economic Interest Grouping (see 49.20 OVERSEAS MATTERS) or a member thereof fraudulently or negligently delivers an incorrect return, accounts or statement under *TMA 1970, s 12A* (see 58.23 RETURNS) or makes an incorrect declaration in such a return, the grouping or member is liable to a maximum penalty of £3,000 multiplied by the number of members of the grouping at the time of delivery. [*TMA 1970, s 98B(5)*]. Note that this provision is not replaced by those at 52.8 below.

Careless or deliberate errors in documents

[52.8] The following provisions apply to a wide range of documents relating to both direct and indirect taxes which may be given by a taxpayer to HMRC, including the following which are relevant for the purposes of capital gains tax and corporation tax on chargeable gains:

- a tax return under *TMA 1970, s 8* or *s 8A* (personal or trustees' return — see **58.3** RETURNS);
- a company tax return under *FA 1998, Sch 18 para 3* (see **58.19** RETURNS);
- a return, statement or declaration in connection with a claim for an allowance, deduction or relief;
- accounts in connection with ascertaining liability to tax;
- a partnership return;
- a statement or declaration in connection with a partnership return;
- accounts in connection with a partnership return;
- an NRCGT return under *TMA 1970, s 12ZB* (see **58.20** RETURNS); and
- any other document (other than one in respect of which a penalty is payable under *TMA 1970, s 98* — see **52.23** below) likely to be relied on by HMRC to determine, without further inquiry, a question about the taxpayer's liability to tax, his payments by way of or in connection with tax, other payments (such as penalties) by the taxpayer or repayments or any other kind of payment or credit to him.

A penalty is payable by a person who gives HMRC such a document if it contains a careless or deliberate inaccuracy which amounts to, or leads to, an understatement of his (or another person's) tax liability or a false or inflated statement of a 'loss' or claim to 'repayment of tax'. If there is more than one inaccuracy in the document a penalty is payable for each inaccuracy. See **52.9** for the penalty payable where an inaccuracy in a document is attributable to the supply of false information or the withholding of information by another person.

For this purpose, giving HMRC a document includes making a statement or declaration in a document and giving HMRC information in any form and by any method (including post, fax, email or telephone). A '*loss*' includes a charge, expense, deficit or any other amount which may be available for, or relied on to claim, a deduction or relief. '*Repayment of tax*' includes allowing a credit against tax and payment of a corporation tax credit (as defined).

A person is not liable to a penalty for an inaccuracy in respect of which he has been convicted of an offence.

See **52.12** below as regards a possible further penalty where assets are moved between overseas territories in order to prevent or delay the discovery of a potential loss of revenue (as in **55.7** below) giving rise to the above penalty.

Amount of penalty

The amount of the penalty depends on whether the inaccuracy is careless or deliberate and is subject to reduction as detailed below. For this purpose, an inaccuracy in a document which was neither careless nor deliberate is treated as careless if the taxpayer or a person acting on his behalf discovered the inaccuracy after giving HMRC the document but did not take reasonable steps to inform them. Reasonable steps to inform HMRC would, in their view, include consulting with an accountant or agent to discuss the position so that they can inform HMRC, or contacting HMRC directly to discuss the inaccuracy (HMRC Guidance Note, 1 April 2008).

The amount of the penalty also depends on which of four categories the inaccuracy falls in. The categories are as follows.

- **Category 0.** Not yet in operation — see below under Future developments.
- **Category 1.** Inaccuracies involving a 'domestic matter' or inaccuracies involving an 'offshore matter' where the territory concerned is a category 1 territory or the tax involved is neither income tax nor capital gains tax.
- **Category 2.** Inaccuracies involving an offshore matter or (for documents relating to 2016/17 onwards) an 'offshore transfer' where the territory involved is a category 2 territory and the tax is income tax or capital gains tax.
- **Category 3.** Inaccuracies involving an offshore matter or (for documents relating to 2016/17 onwards) an offshore transfer where the territory involved is a category 3 territory and the tax is income tax or capital gains tax.

If an inaccuracy is within more than one category it is treated as if it were separate inaccuracies, one in each of the categories concerned according to the matters it involves, and the 'potential lost revenue' (see below) is calculated separately for each deemed inaccuracy.

An inaccuracy involves an '*offshore matter*' if it results in potential lost revenue charged on, or by reference to, income arising from a source in, or assets (including sterling) held or situated in, a territory outside the UK, activities carried on wholly or mainly in such a territory or anything having effect as if it were such income, assets or activities.

An inaccuracy involves an *offshore transfer* if:

- it does not involve an offshore matter;
- it is deliberate (whether or not concealed) and results in a potential loss of revenue; and
- the proceeds of the disposal on (or by reference to) which the tax is charged (or any part of those proceeds):
  - is received in a territory outside the UK; or
  - is transferred to a territory outside the UK before the date when the document containing the inaccuracy is given to HMRC. The reference to the transfer of proceeds is to be read as including a reference to the transfer of any assets derived from or representing those proceeds.

Where more than one category of territory is involved in an offshore transfer, the level of penalty is to be determined by reference to the highest category of territory involved.

An inaccuracy involves a '*domestic matter*' if it does not involve an offshore matter or an offshore transfer. The classification of territories to categories 1, 2 or 3 is as at **52.3** above.

The amount of the penalty (subject to the reductions below) is the percentage of the potential lost revenue found using the table below.

Type of action	Percentage of potential lost revenue *Category 1*	*Category 2*	*Category 3*
careless	30	45	60
deliberate but not concealed	70	105	140
deliberate and concealed	100	150	200

Type of action

For this purpose, careless action occurs where the taxpayer or a person acting on his behalf failed to take reasonable care. HMRC consider that what constitutes 'reasonable care' has to be viewed in the light of each person's abilities and circumstances. They do not expect the same level of knowledge or expertise from an unrepresented self-employed individual as from a large multinational company. They expect a higher degree of care to be taken over large and complex matters than simple straightforward ones. In HMRC's view, it is reasonable to expect a person encountering a transaction or other event with which they are not familiar to take care to check the correct tax treatment or to seek suitable advice. (HMRC Brief 19/2008). In *Mariner v HMRC* FTT 2013; [2014] SFTD 504, a taxpayer who had relied on the professional advice of an accountant was held not to have been careless. Prior to the rules below coming into effect (where carelessness is then presumed), reliance on legal advice was disregarded in determining whether or not an inaccuracy was careless if the advice was given or procured by a monitored promoter (see **20.7** DISCLOSURE OF TAX AVOIDANCE SCHEMES onwards) and related to arrangements of which the monitored promoter was a promoter.

With effect in relation to documents given to HMRC on or after the date of Royal Assent to *F(No 2)A 2017* and for tax periods beginning on or after 6 April 2017 and ending on or after the date of Royal Assent, there is a presumption of carelessness where a document contains a non-deliberate inaccuracy as a result of its being submitted on the basis that particular 'avoidance arrangements' had an effect which in fact they did not have. The presumption is disapplied if the taxpayer satisfies HMRC or an Appeal Tribunal that he took reasonable care to avoid inaccuracy, but neither HMRC nor the Tribunal can take any account of any evidence of any reliance by the taxpayer on 'disqualified advice'.

Arrangements (as widely defined) are '*avoidance arrangements*' for this purpose if it would be reasonable to conclude that the obtaining of a tax advantage (also widely defined) was a main purpose of them. There is a let-out for arrangements which accord with established practice accepted by HMRC. Where arrangements are caught by specified anti-avoidance or anti-abuse legislation, they are automatically avoidance arrangements for this purpose, and the let-out does not apply.

'*Disqualified advice*' is defined in broadly similar terms as in **52.14** below. There is a limited exemption for certain advice received in connection with 'avoidance-related rules' (as in **4.36** ANTI-AVOIDANCE). The question of whether the taxpayer has taken reasonable steps to find out whether or not advice is disqualified, and believes it not to be so, is judged as at the time when the document containing the inaccuracy is given to HMRC. Where a document is given to HMRC by the personal representative of a deceased person, the disqualified advice rules are applied by reference both to the deceased and the personal representative.

See **14.19** COMPANIES for circumstances in which an error is treated as careless if made when a special measures notice is in force.

Deliberate but not concealed action occurs where the inaccuracy was deliberate but the taxpayer did not make arrangements to conceal it. Deliberate and concealed action occurs where the inaccuracy was deliberate and the taxpayer made arrangements to conceal it (for example, by submitting false evidence in support of an inaccurate figure).

Reduction for disclosure

A reduction in a penalty will be given where the taxpayer discloses an inaccuracy in a document. The penalty will be reduced to a percentage which reflects the quality of the disclosure and the amount of the reduction will depend on whether the disclosure is 'prompted' or 'unprompted' and is subject to a minimum percentage.

In the case of a failure involving a domestic matter, the minimum percentage (i.e. the percentage below which a penalty may not be reduced) for each level of penalty is as follows.

Standard percentage	Minimum percentage for prompted disclosure	Minimum percentage for unprompted disclosure
30	15	0
70	35	20
100	50	30

For an inaccuracy involving an *offshore matter* or *offshore transfer* the penalty cannot be reduced below a minimum percentage as shown below. The minimum percentage shown in the table in each case applies on and after 1 April 2017 and has effect in relation to 2016/17 onwards; the percentage shown in parentheses immediately after it is the one previously applicable.

Standard percentage	Minimum percentage for prompted disclosure	Minimum percentage for unprompted disclosure
30	15 (15)	0 (0)
45	22.5 (22.5)	0 (0)
60	30 (30)	0 (0)
70	45 (35)	30 (20)
100	60 (50)	40 (30)
105	62.5 (52.5)	40 (30)
140	80 (70)	50 (40)

150	85 (75)	55 (45)
200	110 (100)	70 (60)

A person (P) is treated as making a disclosure for these purposes only if P tells HMRC about the inaccuracy, gives them reasonable help in quantifying the inaccuracy and allows them access to records for the purpose of ensuring that the inaccuracy is fully corrected. In the case of a *deliberate* inaccuracy (whether concealed or not) that involves an *offshore matter*, or any inaccuracy involving an *offshore transfer*, with effect on and after 1 April 2017, P must also tell HMRC if there is:

- any person who encouraged, assisted or otherwise facilitated the inaccuracy etc.; and
- any asset situated or held outside the UK that is held on P's behalf by another person,

and must provide further specified details if either is the case.

A disclosure is '*unprompted*' if made when the taxpayer has no reason to believe HMRC have discovered or are about to discover the inaccuracy. In all other cases, disclosures are '*prompted*'.

Example 1

Alec, a trustee of a settlement, included a capital gain in the trust's tax return. The gain is the subject of a compliance check. During the check, Alec discloses that he has used the wrong acquisition value as there was a held-over gain on the transfer of the asset to the settlement. This is related to the subject under review and so is a prompted disclosure.

Example 2

Tessa is the subject of a compliance check into her employment expenses. There is no intention to expand the scope of the check. She discloses that she has not declared a capital gain. This is an unprompted disclosure.

Note to the examples

The above examples are based on the examples given by HMRC in their Compliance Handbook at CH82422. They therefore reflect HMRC's view of what constitutes a prompted or unprompted disclosure.

Reduction in special circumstances

HMRC can also reduce, stay or agree a compromise in relation to proceedings for a penalty if they think it right to do so because of special circumstances. Ability to pay and the fact that a potential loss of revenue from one taxpayer is balanced by a potential overpayment by another are not special circumstances for this purpose. It is expected that this power will be used only in rare cases (see Treasury Explanatory Notes to the 2007 Finance Bill). See *Roche v HMRC* FTT, [2012] UKFTT 333 (TC); 2012 STI 2364 in which the Tribunal granted a reduction due to special circumstances where the taxpayer was suffering stress at the time of completing her return. In *White v HMRC* FTT, [2012] UKFTT 364 (TC); 2012 STI 2502, special circumstances were held to apply in a case in which the taxpayer failed to include a redundancy payment in her return. She had received confusing information from her employer and had made genuine efforts to resolve the confusion. The Tribunal reduced the penalty by 60%. The Tribunal reduced a penalty to nil in *Usher and another v HMRC* FTT, [2016] UKFTT 50 (TC); 2016 STI 1410.

Reduction for other penalty or surcharge

The amount of a penalty in respect of a document relating to a particular tax year or accounting period is reduced by the amount of any other penalty or late payment surcharge (see **42.6** LATE PAYMENT INTEREST AND PENALTIES), the amount of which is determined by reference to the same tax liability. Where a penalty is imposed under these provisions and those at **52.9** below in respect of the same inaccuracy, the aggregate of the penalties cannot exceed 100% of the potential lost revenue for a Category 1 inaccuracy, 150% of the potential lost revenue for a Category 2 inaccuracy and 200% of the potential lost revenue for a Category 3 inaccuracy. No reduction is made for a tax-related penalty within **52.16** below or for a penalty within **52.13**, **52.26** or **52.27** below.

No reduction is made for a penalty within **42.10** LATE PAYMENT INTEREST AND PENALTIES where the payment default relates to 2014/15 or a later year.

Potential lost revenue

The '*potential lost revenue*' is the additional tax due or payable as a result of correcting the inaccuracy in the document. This includes any amount payable to HMRC having been previously repaid in error and any amount which would have been repayable by HMRC had the inaccuracy not been corrected. Relief under *CTA 2010, s 458* (close company loans) and group relief are ignored (but this does not prevent a penalty being charged for an inaccurate claim for relief). 'Tax' includes, for this purpose, amounts payable on account of CGT under *TMA 1970, s 59AA* (see **51.3** PAYMENT OF TAX).

Where the amount of potential lost revenue depends on the order in which inaccuracies are corrected, careless inaccuracies are taken to be corrected before deliberate inaccuracies, and deliberate but not concealed inaccuracies are taken to be corrected before deliberate and concealed inaccuracies. Where there are inaccuracies in one or more documents relating to a particular tax year or accounting period and those inaccuracies include both understatements and overstatements, the overstatements are taken into account in calculating the potential lost revenue and are set off against understatements in the order which reduces the level of penalties the least (i.e. against understatements not liable to a penalty first, then against careless understatements, and so on). The fact that potential lost revenue may be balanced by a potential overpayment by another person is also ignored.

Special rules apply where an inaccuracy leads to there being a wrongly recorded loss which has not been wholly used to reduce a tax liability. The potential lost revenue in respect of that part of the loss which has not been so used is restricted to 10% of the unused part. Where, however, there is no reasonable prospect of a loss being used to support a claim to reduce a tax liability (of any person) because of the taxpayer's circumstances or the nature of the loss, the potential lost revenue is nil.

Where an inaccuracy results in an amount of tax being declared later than it would have been (otherwise than because of a wrongly recorded loss), the potential lost revenue is 5% of the delayed tax for each year of delay (applied pro rata for periods of less than a year).

Suspension of penalty

HMRC can suspend all or part of a penalty for a careless inaccuracy. A notice in writing must be given to the taxpayer setting out what part of the penalty is to be suspended, the period of suspension (maximum two years) and the conditions of suspension with which the taxpayer must comply. The conditions can specify an action to be taken and a period within which it must be taken. A penalty can be suspended only if compliance with a condition of suspension will help the taxpayer to avoid further penalties under these provisions.

A suspended penalty will become payable:

- at the end of the suspension period, if the taxpayer does not satisfy HMRC that the conditions have been complied with; and
- if, during the suspension period, the taxpayer incurs another penalty under these provisions.

Otherwise, the penalty is cancelled at the end of the suspension period.

Agents

A person is liable to a penalty under the above provisions where a document containing a *careless* inaccuracy is given to HMRC on his behalf. He is not, however, liable to a penalty in respect of anything done or omitted by his agent, if he satisfies HMRC that he took reasonable care to avoid inaccuracy.

Company officers

Where a company is liable to a penalty under the above provisions for a deliberate inaccuracy and the inaccuracy was attributable to a company 'officer', the officer is liable to pay such part (including all) of the penalty as HMRC specify by written notice. In relation to a body corporate (other than a limited liability partnership), a director, shadow director, manager or secretary of the company is an '*officer*'; in relation to a limited liability partnership, a member is an '*officer*'; and in any other case, a director, manager, secretary or any other person managing or purporting to manage any of the company's affairs is an '*officer*'. The procedural provisions (see **52.33** onwards below) apply as if the part payable by the officer were itself a penalty.

Partnerships

Where a partner is liable to a penalty arising from an inaccuracy in, or in connection with, a partnership return, and the inaccuracy affects the amount of tax payable by another partner, that other partner is also liable to a penalty. The potential lost revenue is calculated separately for each partner by reference to the proportions of any tax liability that would be borne by each of them. The suspension provisions above are, however, applied jointly to the partners' penalties.

Powers to amend provisions

The Treasury may by order make any incidental, supplemental, consequential, transitional, transitory or saving provision in connection with these provisions and those at **52.9** and **52.10** below.

Future developments

With effect on and after a day to be appointed by the Treasury, a new category (category 0) is to be introduced alongside categories 1 to 3 above. A category 0 territory will be a territory designated as such by Treasury order. The intention is that only territories that adopt automatic exchange of information under the Common Reporting Standard will be given category 0 status.

Category 0 will have the same penalty levels as the current category 1 (and all penalties for domestic matters will be moved to category 0). The current penalty levels for category 1 will be increased from 30%, 70% and 100% to 37.5%, 87.5% and 125% respectively. The penalty levels for categories 2 and 3 will remain the same. The new category 1 penalty levels can be reduced for unprompted disclosure to a minimum of 0%, 35% and 50% respectively and for prompted disclosure to a minimum of 18.75%, 53.75% and 72.5% respectively.

Where penalties are imposed as described in this section and **52.9** below in respect of the same inaccuracy, the aggregate penalty cannot exceed 100% of the potential lost revenue for an inaccuracy in new category 0 or 125% of the potential lost revenue for an inaccuracy in amended category 1.

[*FA 2007, s 97, Sch 24 paras 1, 3–12, 14, 18–28; FA 2009, Sch 56 para 9A; FA 2012, s 219; FA 2013, Sch 50 paras 13, 16(3); FA 2014, s 276, Sch 33 para 3; FA 2015, s 120, Sch 7 para 56, Sch 20 paras 2–8; FA 2016, s 163, Sch 8 para 8, Sch 19 para 48, Sch 21 paras 1–4, Sch 22 para 20(3); F(No 2)A 2017, s 64; SI 2008 No 568; SI 2009 No 571, Art 2; SI 2011 Nos 975, 976; SI 2016 No 456, Art 3; SI 2017 Nos 259, 345*].

Error in taxpayer's document attributable to another person

[52.9] With effect from 1 April 2009, where a document (of a type listed at **52.8** above) given to HMRC contains an inaccuracy which amounts to, or leads to, an understatement of a tax liability or a false or inflated statement of a 'loss' or claim to 'repayment of tax', and the inaccuracy is attributable to a person deliberately supplying false information to the person giving the document to HMRC (whether directly or indirectly) or deliberately withholding information from that person, with the intention of the document containing the inaccuracy, a penalty is payable by the person supplying or withholding the information. See **52.8** above for the meaning of 'loss' and 'repayment of tax'.

The penalty is 100% of the potential lost revenue (defined as at **52.8** above, with the necessary modifications), subject to the same reductions that apply under the provisions at **52.8** above for special circumstances or disclosure.

Where a penalty is imposed under these provisions and those at **52.8** above in respect of the same inaccuracy, see **52.8** above for the maximum aggregate of the penalties.

A person is not liable to a penalty for an inaccuracy in respect of which he has been convicted of an offence.

[*FA 2007, Sch 24 paras 1A, 4, 4B, 5, 7–12, 21; FA 2016, Sch 22 para 20(3); SI 2009 No 571, Art 2*].

Failure to notify HMRC of error in assessment

[52.10] In relation to assessments for tax years or accounting periods beginning on or after 1 April 2008, a penalty is payable by a person if an assessment issued to him by HMRC understates his liability to tax and he or a person acting on his behalf has failed to take reasonable steps to notify HMRC of the under-assessment, within the 30 days beginning with the date of the assessment. With effect from 21 July 2009, this penalty applies also to determinations.

The penalty is 30% of the potential lost revenue (defined as at **52.8** above, with the necessary modifications), subject to the same reductions that apply under the provisions at **52.8** above for special circumstances or disclosure. HMRC must consider whether the taxpayer or a person acting on his behalf knew, or should have known, about the under-assessment and what steps would have been reasonable to take to notify HMRC.

A person is not liable to a penalty under this provision in respect of anything done or omitted by his agent, if he satisfies HMRC that he took reasonable care to avoid unreasonable failure to notify HMRC.

The amount of a penalty under this provision in respect of a document relating to a particular tax year or accounting period is reduced by the amount of any other penalty the amount of which is determined by reference to tax liability for the period (but see **52.8** above for exclusions from this rule)

A person is not liable to a penalty for a failure in respect of which he has been convicted of an offence.

[*FA 2007, s 97, Sch 24 paras 2, 4–12, 18, 21, 28; FA 2014, Sch 33 para 3; SI 2008 No 568*].

Arrangements counteracted by the general anti-abuse rule

[52.11] A person (P) is liable to a penalty if:

- a tax advantage arising from tax arrangements entered into on or after 15 September 2016 has been counteracted by the making of adjustments under the general anti-abuse rule ('GAAR'; see **4.3** ANTI-AVOIDANCE) following a referral to the GAAR Advisory Panel;
- a tax document has been given to HMRC on the basis that the tax advantage arises to P from the arrangements; and

- the document was given to HMRC by P or by another person and P knew, or ought to have known, that the document was given on the basis that the tax advantage arises to P from the arrangements.

The penalty is 60% of the 'value of the counteracted advantage'. For this purpose, a '*tax document*' means a return, claim or other document submitted in compliance (or purported compliance) with any provision of an Act.

The '*value of the counteracted advantage*' is the additional amount due or payable in respect of tax as a result of the counteraction. This includes any amount previously repaid by HMRC which is now payable, together with any amount which would be repayable by HMRC if the counteraction were not made and any consequential adjustments. If the counteraction affects P's liability to more than one tax, each of the taxes is considered together in determining the value of the counteracted advantage. Group relief and relief in connection with loans to participators (under *CTA 2010, s 458*) are ignored in the calculation of the additional amount. Where the tax advantage counteracted under the GAAR created or increased a 'loss', and the loss was used to reduce the amount of tax payable, the additional amount due or payable can be ascertained, and the penalty calculated, in the normal way. However, where the loss has not been wholly used in this way, the value of the counteracted advantage is deemed to be 10% of any part of the loss not so used. In the case of an aggregate loss recorded for a group of companies, group relief may be taken into account. The value of the counteracted advantage in respect of a loss is nil where there is no prospect of the loss being used to support a claim to reduce a tax liability (of any person). To the extent that the tax advantage is a deferral of tax, the value of the counteracted advantage is the lower of:

(a) 25% of the deferred tax for each year of deferral (or a proportionate amount for part years); and
(b) 100% of the deferred tax.

For these purposes, a '*loss*' includes a charge, expense, deficit or other amount which may be available for , or relied on to claim, a deduction or relief. A repayment of tax includes a reference to allowing a credit against tax or to a payment of certain corporation tax credits. Giving a document to HMRC includes communicating information in any form and by any method (post, fax, email, telephone or otherwise).

Interaction with other penalties

The following applies where more than one penalty arises in respect of the same amount, one of those penalties is a GAAR penalty, and one or more of the others is incurred under *FA 2007, Sch 24* (errors; see **52.8–52.10** above), *FA 2008, Sch 41* (failure to notify; see **52.3** above), *FA 2009, Sch 55* (failure to make return; see **52.5** above) or *FA 2016, Sch 18* (serial avoiders; see **52.29** below). The general rule is that the aggregate penalty must not exceed 100% of the amount in question or, if at least one of the penalties is a £300 penalty under *FA 2009, Sch 55*, £300 (if greater). Where the maximum penalty under one of the other provisions is more than 100% because of the rules for offshore matters and offshore transfers, the aggregate penalty must not exceed that higher maximum percentage. See **52.26** below for the maximum aggregate penalties where a GAAR penalty and a penalty under *FA 2014, s 212* (follower notices) is incurred in respect of the same tax.

[*FA 2013, s 212A, Sch 43C paras 1–4, 8; FA 2015, Sch 20 para 20; FA 2016, s 158(2)(3)(14)(15)*].

Penalty for offshore asset moves

[52.12] With effect for movements occurring after 26 March 2015, a penalty (the '*offshore asset moves penalty*') applies where assets are moved between overseas territories and a main purpose of that movement is to prevent or delay the discovery by HMRC of a potential loss of revenue that itself gives rise to one of the penalties listed below. The offshore asset moves penalty is intended to address a risk that assets will be moved from territories committed to exchanging information under the Organisation for Economic Co-operation and Development's Common Reporting Standard to other territories for the purpose of continuing to conceal past failures or actions for which other penalties are chargeable.

The offshore asset moves penalty applies where the person concerned (P) becomes liable to another penalty (the '*original penalty*') and this is either:

- the penalty for failure to notify chargeability in **52.3** above; or
- the second tax-geared late filing penalty in **52.5** above; or
- the penalty for careless or deliberate errors in documents in **52.8** above; or
- the penalty for failure to correct offshore tax non-compliance in **52.14** below.

However, the offshore asset moves penalty applies only where the original penalty is for a deliberate failure or action (regardless of whether or not it was concealed) and where the tax involved is income tax, capital gains tax or inheritance tax (or, for a penalty under **52.3**, income tax or capital gains tax). In the case of a penalty for failure to correct, the failure is deliberate if P was aware at any time during the RTC period (see **52.14** below) that at the end of 2016/17 he had offshore tax non-compliance to correct.

The offshore asset moves penalty is chargeable even if the liability for the original penalty first arose on or before 26 March 2015, except that it is not chargeable if, on or before that date, the failure was remedied (in the case of a penalty under **52.3** or **52.5**) and any tax unpaid as a result of the failure or inaccuracy has been assessed or determined.

The amount of the offshore asset moves penalty is 50% of the amount of the original penalty payable by P. Even though the original penalty may be determined by reference to a liability to tax, the offshore asset moves penalty is not.

For the offshore asset moves penalty to apply, there has to be a 'relevant offshore asset move' which occurs after the 'relevant time'. There is a '*relevant offshore asset move*' if, at a time when P is the beneficial owner of an 'asset' and without his ceasing entirely to be the beneficial owner of it:

- the asset ceases to be situated or held in a 'specified territory' and becomes situated or held in a non-specified territory; or
- the person who holds the asset ceases to be resident in a specified territory and becomes resident in a non-specified territory; or
- there is a change in the arrangements for the ownership of the asset.

Where P disposes of an asset and reinvests all or part of the proceeds in another, the original and new asset are to be treated as the same asset for the purposes of determining whether there is a relevant offshore asset move. '*Asset*' has the same meaning as for capital gains tax purposes (see **7.2** ASSETS) but also includes sterling. The question of whether or not a territory is a specified territory is to be determined as at the time one of these events occurs. A '*specified territory*' is a territory designated as such by the Treasury by means of statutory instrument (see *SI 2015 No 866*). The intention is that a territory will be so designated once it has committed to exchanging information under the Common Reporting Standard (Treasury Explanatory Notes to the first 2015 Finance Bill).

The '*relevant time*' for capital gains tax purposes is determined according to the nature of the original penalty as follows.

- Where the original penalty is a penalty for failure to notify chargeability, the relevant time is the beginning of the tax year to which the obligation to notify relates.
- Where the original penalty is a second tax-geared late filing penalty, the relevant time is the beginning of the tax year to which the return or document relates.
- Where the original penalty is a penalty for careless or deliberate errors in documents, the relevant time is the beginning of the tax year to which the document containing the inaccuracy relates.
- Where the original penalty is a penalty for failure to correct offshore tax non-compliance, the relevant time is the date of Royal Assent of *F(No 2)A 2017*.

[*FA 2015, Sch 21 paras 1–6, 9; F(No 2)A 2017, Sch 18 para 27; SI 2015 No 866*].

Asset-based penalty for offshore inaccuracies and failures

[52.13] Effective on and after 1 April 2017, an asset-based penalty is payable by a person where:

(a) one or more 'offshore tax penalties' have been imposed on a person in relation to 2016/17 or a subsequent tax year; and
(b) the potential lost revenue threshold is met in relation to that year.

Where the above conditions are met in relation to more than one tax year falling within the same 'investigation period', only one asset-based penalty is payable in that investigation period in relation to any given asset. This penalty is charged by reference to the tax year within the investigation period that has the highest 'offshore PLR' (see below under Potential lost revenue threshold).

In relation to a person (P), the first '*investigation period*' begins on the day on which the asset-based penalty regime comes into force and ends on 5 April in the last tax year before P is notified of an asset-based penalty in respect of an asset. Subsequent investigation periods begin on the day following the end of the previous investigation period and end on 5 April in the last tax year before P is notified of a subsequent asset-based penalty in respect of the asset. Different investigation periods may apply in relation to different assets. The investigation period rules do not apply where the offshore tax penalty is a penalty under *F(No 2)A 2017, Sch 18* (failure to correct offshore tax non-compliance). Where such a penalty is imposed, and (b) above is met, only one asset-based penalty is payable in relation to any given asset.

Meaning of 'offshore tax penalty'

For the purposes of (a) above and these provisions generally, an '*offshore tax penalty*' is any of the following:

- a penalty under *FA 2007, Sch 24 para 1* (errors in documents) imposed for deliberate action (whether or not concealed) where the inaccuracy for which the penalty is imposed involves an offshore matter or an offshore transfer (see **52.8** above);
- a penalty under *FA 2008, Sch 41 para 1* (failure to notify chargeability) imposed for deliberate failure (whether or not concealed) where the failure involves an offshore matter or an offshore transfer (see **52.3** above);
- a penalty under *FA 2009, Sch 55 para 6* (the second tax-geared late filing penalty) imposed for deliberate withholding of information (whether or not concealed) where the withholding of information involves an offshore matter or an offshore transfer (see **52.5** above); or
- a penalty under *F(No 2)A 2017, Sch 18* (failure to correct offshore tax non-compliance) where the person was aware at any time during the RTC period that at the end of 2016/17 he had offshore tax non-compliance to correct (see **52.14** below),

but only if the tax at stake is (or includes) a tax within the asset-based penalty regime, i.e. 'asset-based income tax', capital gains tax and, where applicable, inheritance tax. Capital gains tax payable by companies in respect of NRCGT gains (see **41.25** LAND) is excluded. Where the tax at stake includes any taxes other than those, the offshore tax penalty is the part of the penalty which relates to those taxes. '*Asset-based income tax*' is income tax that is charged under any of a significant number of charging provisions listed at *FA 2016, Sch 22 para 13(2)*; see also below under Identification and valuation of assets. Where the inaccuracy etc. for which a penalty is imposed also involves a domestic matter, the offshore tax penalty is only that part of the penalty that involves the offshore matter or offshore transfer; this is not relevant to a penalty for failure to correct.

For the purposes of (a) above, as regards income tax or capital gains tax, the tax year to which an offshore tax penalty relates is the tax year to which the document containing the inaccuracy, the obligation to notify chargeability, the late return or the offshore tax non-compliance relates.

Potential lost revenue threshold

For the purposes of (b) above, the potential lost revenue threshold is reached where the 'offshore PLR' in relation to a tax year exceeds £25,000. The '*offshore PLR*', in relation to a tax year, is the total of:

- the potential lost revenue (as in **52.3** and **52.8** above and **52.14** below); and
- the liability to tax (as in **52.5** above),

by reference to which all of the offshore tax penalties imposed in relation to the tax year are assessed. Where a penalty assessed relates to an offshore tax penalty and one or more other penalties (a '*combined penalty*'), only the potential lost revenue or liability to tax relating to the offshore tax penalty is taken into account in calculating the offshore PLR. Where necessary for the purposes of calculating the offshore PLR in such a case, income and gains relating to domestic matters are taken to have been taxed before income and gains relating to offshore matters and offshore transfers, and income and gains relating to taxes within the asset-based penalty regime are taken to have been taxed before income and gains relating to taxes outside the regime. Where it cannot otherwise be determined, the potential lost revenue or liability to tax relating to the offshore tax penalty is taken to be such share of the total potential lost revenue or liability to tax by reference to which the combined penalty was calculated as is just and reasonable. Where an offshore tax penalty or combined penalty relates to two or more taxes, including asset-based income tax and capital gains tax, then where necessary for the purposes of calculating the offshore PLR, income and gains relating to asset-based income tax are taken to have been taxed before income and gains relating to capital gains tax.

Amount of penalty

The penalty is the lower of (i) 10% of the value of the asset (see below) and (ii) the offshore PLR (see above) x 10.

HMRC must reduce the penalty where the taxpayer makes a disclosure of the inaccuracy or failure relating to the offshore tax penalty, provides HMRC with a reasonable valuation of the asset and provides HMRC with information or access to records that HMRC require for the purposes of valuing the asset. The reduction must reflect the quality of the disclosure, valuation and information provided (and for these purposes 'quality' includes timing, nature and extent). From 1 April 2017, the maximum amount by which a penalty can be reduced is 50% of the standard amount in a case involving only unprompted disclosures and 20% of the standard amount in a case involving prompted disclosures. A case involves only unprompted disclosures if all the offshore tax penalties to which the asset-based penalty relates were reduced on the basis of unprompted disclosures. A case involves prompted disclosures if any of the offshore tax penalties to which the asset-based penalty relates was reduced on the basis of a prompted disclosure.

HMRC may also reduce, stay, or agree a compromise in relation to proceedings for, an asset-based penalty because of special circumstances if they think it right to do so. Ability to pay and the fact that a potential loss of revenue from one taxpayer is balanced by a potential overpayment by another are not special circumstances for this purpose.

Identification and valuation of assets

Where the 'principal tax at stake' is capital gains tax, the asset is the asset which is the subject of the disposal by reference to which the capital gains tax to which the offshore tax penalty relates is charged. The value of the asset is taken to be the consideration for the disposal for capital gains tax purposes. Where the disposal is a part disposal of an asset, the asset-based penalty is calculated by reference to the full market value of the asset. The '*principal tax at stake*' is the tax to which the offshore tax penalty relates. If the offshore tax penalty relates to more than one tax, it is the tax which gives rise to the highest offshore PLR value, i.e. the potential lost revenue or liability to tax by reference to which the part of the penalty relating to each tax was assessed. An asset-based penalty may relate to more than one asset.

Where an asset-based penalty is chargeable in relation to an asset that is jointly held by the taxpayer (P) and another person (A), the value of the asset is the value of P's share of it. If P and A are living together in a marriage or civil partnership, the asset is taken to be jointly owned by them in equal shares, unless it appears to HMRC that this is not the case.

[*FA 2016, s 165, Sch 22 paras 1–11, 14, 19; F(No 2)A 2017, Sch 18 para 28; SI 2017 Nos 277, 334*]

Failure to correct offshore tax non-compliance

[52.14] A penalty is payable by a person who has 'offshore tax non-compliance' to correct at the end of 2016/17 and fails to correct it within the period 6 April 2017 to 30 September 2018 inclusive (known as the '*RTC period*'). [*F(No 2)A 2017, Sch 18 para 1*]. The penalty applies to income tax, capital gains tax and inheritance tax non-compliance; the coverage below focuses on its application to capital gains tax. The penalty does not apply to capital gains tax payable by companies in respect of NRCGT gains (see **41.26** LAND).

Meaning of offshore tax non-compliance

For this purpose, '*offshore tax non-compliance*' means 'tax non-compliance' which involves an 'offshore matter' or an 'offshore transfer', whether or not it also 'involves an onshore matter'. Any of the following is '*tax non-compliance*' for this purpose:

(a) failure to notify chargeability to capital gains tax by the required date (see **52.3** above);
(b) failure to deliver a tax return or other document (as listed in *F(No 2)A 2017, Sch 18 para 8(3)*) by the required date (see **52.5** above); and

(c) delivery of a return or other document (as listed in *F(No 2)A 2017, Sch 18 para 8(3)(4)*) containing an inaccuracy (whether or not careless or deliberate) amounting to, or leading to, an understatement of a tax liability or a false or inflated statement of a loss or claim to repayment of tax.

Tax non-compliance '*involves an onshore matter*' if and to the extent that it does not involve an offshore matter or an offshore transfer. The question of whether tax non-compliance involves an '*offshore matter*' is determined in the same way as for other penalties to which this is relevant. See **52.3**, **52.5** and **52.8** above. The determination is made by reference, in a case within (a) above, to the potential loss of revenue; in a case within (b) above, to the tax liability (if any) that would have been shown in the return etc.; and, in a case within (c) above, to the information that should have been given in the document.

Tax non-compliance involves an '*offshore transfer*' if it does not involve an offshore matter and:

- in a case within (a) or (b) above, the proceeds of the disposal on (or by reference to which) tax is charged (or any part of those proceeds) were received in a territory outside the UK or were transferred before 6 April 2017 to a territory outside the UK; and
- in a case within (c) above, the information that should have been given in the document relates to proceeds of disposal which were received in a territory outside the UK or were transferred before 6 April 2017 to a territory outside the UK.

In any of these cases, the reference to the transfer of proceeds is to be read as including a reference to the transfer of any assets derived from or representing those proceeds. '*Assets*' has the same meaning as for capital gains tax purposes (see *TCGA 1992, s 21(1)*) but also includes sterling.

It is an overriding condition that tax non-compliance can involve an offshore matter or offshore transfer only, in a case within (b) above, where a complete and accurate return etc. would have included information enabling or assisting HMRC to assess the person's tax liability; and, in a case within (c) above, if the inaccuracy relates to information that would have enabled or assisted HMRC to assess the person's liability.

[*F(No 2)A 2017, Sch 18 paras 7–12*].

When the rules apply

A person has offshore tax non-compliance to correct at the end of 2016/17 if:

- Conditions A and B below are met in respect of any offshore tax non-compliance committed before 6 April 2017 (the '*original offshore tax non-compliance*'); and
- Condition C below is met.

Condition A is that the original offshore tax non-compliance has not been fully corrected before the end of 2016/17. Condition B is that the original offshore tax non-compliance involved a potential loss of revenue when it was committed and that, in the case of partial correction before the end of 2016/17, the uncorrected part of that time involved a potential loss of revenue.

Condition C is that on 6 April 2017 HMRC would in law have been able to assess the taxpayer to the tax liability arising from the non-compliance if they had been aware at that time of the information missing as a result of the failure to correct. What is said below under Extension of period for assessment of offshore tax is disregarded for the purpose of applying Condition C.

[*F(No 2)A 2017, Sch 18 paras 3–6*].

Correcting offshore tax non-compliance

Offshore tax non-compliance can be corrected by giving HMRC the 'relevant information' by:

- in a case within (a) above, delivering a tax return;
- in a case within (b) above, delivering the requisite return or document;
- in a case within (c) above, amending the document or delivering a new document;
- using the digital disclosure service (see below) or any other service provided by HMRC as a means of correcting tax non-compliance;
- communicating it to an HMRC officer in the course of an enquiry; or
- using any other method agreed with an HMRC officer.

The '*relevant information*' is the information relating to offshore tax that, were it not for the non-compliance, would have enabled or assisted HMRC to calculate the offshore tax due.

[*F(No 2)A 2017, Sch 18 para 13*].

It is anticipated that in most cases the requirement to correct will be met via HMRC's Worldwide Disclosure Facility at www.gov.uk/guidance/worldwide-disclosure-facility-make-a-disclosure. The Facility is available to anyone disclosing a UK tax liability that relates wholly or partly to an offshore issue. See www.gov.uk/guidance/offshore-disclosure-facilities.

Amount of penalty

The penalty is **200%** of the 'offshore PLR' attributable to the offshore tax non-compliance remaining uncorrected when the RTC period ends. The '*offshore PLR*' is the potential loss of revenue (PLR) attributable to the offshore tax non-compliance in question, and is determined as follows:

- in a case within (a) above, it is calculated in similar matter as in **52.3** above and is thus usually the amount of tax payable that, by reason of the non-compliance, remains unpaid on 31 January following the tax year in question.
- In a case within (b) above, it is the tax liability that would have been shown as due or payable in a complete and accurate return delivered on the due date.
- In a case within (c) above, it is calculated in similar manner as in **52.8** above and is thus usually the additional tax due or payable as a result of correcting the inaccuracy in the document. *F(No 2)A 2017, Sch 18 para 15(3)* modifies the rules in **52.8** for this purpose; the principal modification is that where the amount of PLR depends on the order in

which inaccuracies are corrected, the PLR attributable to any offshore tax non-compliance constituted by any one of those inaccuracies is taken to be such amount as is just and reasonable.

Any 'combined tax non-compliance' is treated for these purposes as if it were two separate acts of tax non-compliance. '*Combined tax non-compliance*' is tax non-compliance that involves an offshore matter or an offshore transfer but also involves an onshore matter. The PLR attributable to the offshore tax non-compliance is to be taken to be such share of the total PLR as is just and reasonable.

Reductions

HMRC must reduce the penalty if the person liable discloses any of the following matters that is relevant to the non-compliance or its correction or to the assessment or enforcement of the offshore tax attributable to it: chargeability to tax (where the tax non-compliance is a failure to notify chargeability); a missing tax return; an inaccuracy in a document; a supply of false information or a withholding of information; or a failure to disclose an under-assessment. The reduction must reflect the quality of the disclosure (and for these purposes 'quality' includes timing, nature and extent) but the penalty cannot be reduced below 100% of the offshore PLR. A person discloses a matter for these purposes only by: telling HMRC about it; giving HMRC reasonable help in relation to it (for example by quantifying an inaccuracy in a document); informing HMRC of any person who acted as an enabler of the offshore tax non-compliance or the failure to correct it; and allowing HMRC access to records for any reasonable purpose connected with resolving the matter and to ensure that HMRC can identify all persons who may have acted as enablers. A person acts as an enabler of offshore tax non-compliance by another if he encourages, assists or otherwise facilitates the conduct constituting the non-compliance.

HMRC may also reduce, stay, or agree a compromise in relation to proceedings for, the penalty because of special circumstances if they think it right to do so. Ability to pay and the fact that a potential loss of revenue from one taxpayer is balanced by a potential overpayment by another are not special circumstances for this purpose.

Reasonable excuse

Liability to the above penalty does not arise in relation to a particular failure to correct any offshore tax non-compliance within the RTC period if the taxpayer (T) satisfies HMRC or, on appeal, the Appeal Tribunal, that there is a reasonable excuse for the failure. Insufficiency of funds is not a reasonable excuse for this purpose, unless attributable to events outside T's control, and nor is reliance on another person to do anything (unless T took reasonable care to avoid the failure) or reliance on 'disqualified' advice. A person with a reasonable excuse is treated as having continued to have it if the failure in question was remedied without unreasonable delay after the excuse ceased.

Advice is '*disqualified*' if it (i) was given to T by an interested person; or (ii) was given to T as a result of arrangements between an 'interested person' and the person who gave the advice; or (iii) was given by a person without the appropriate expertise; or (iv) did not take account of all T's individual circumstances (so far as relevant); or (v) was addressed to, or given to, a person other than T. However, the advice is not disqualified if, at the end of the RTC period, T has taken reasonable steps to find out whether or not the advice falls within any of (i)–(iv) and reasonably believes that it does not. An '*interested person*' is one who participated in 'relevant avoidance arrangements' or any transaction forming part of them, or one who, for consideration, facilitated T's entering into such avoidance arrangements. Avoidance arrangements are arrangements (as widely defined) in respect of which it would be reasonable to conclude that a main purpose is the obtaining of a tax advantage (also as widely defined). However, arrangements are not avoidance arrangements if they accord with established practice, and HMRC had, at the time the arrangements were entered into, indicated their acceptance of that practice. Where any offshore tax non-compliance arose originally because information was submitted to HMRC on the basis that particular avoidance arrangements had an effect which they did not have, those avoidance arrangements are '*relevant avoidance arrangements*' in relation to that non-compliance.

Double jeopardy

A person is not liable to the above penalty in respect of any conduct (or any failure to act) for which he has been convicted of an offence or for which he is liable to, and has been assessed to, a penalty under other provisions (provided the assessment has neither been successfully appealed against nor withdrawn). The reference here to a penalty under other provisions includes the second tax-geared late filing penalty but does not include any of the other late filing penalties in **52.5** above. Where a person is thus liable to both the above penalty and the *first* tax-geared late filing penalty in **52.5**, and the amount of the latter has been determined by reference to a liability to tax, the aggregate penalty must not exceed 200% of that liability to tax.

[*F(No 2)A 2017, Sch 18 paras 14–17, 23, 24*].

Extension of period for assessment of offshore tax

Where:

- at the end of 2016/17 a person has offshore tax non-compliance to correct; and
- the last day on which it would otherwise be lawful for HMRC to assess the person to any 'offshore tax' falls within the period 6 April 2017 to 4 April 2021 inclusive,

the period in which it is lawful for HMRC to assess the person to the offshore tax is extended so as to end with 5 April 2021. This would appear to enable offshore tax for any of the years 2013/14 to 2015/16 (as well as 2016/17) to be assessed at any time on or before 5 April 2021. '*Offshore tax*' is tax corresponding to the offshore PLR in respect of the offshore tax non-compliance in question.

[*F(No 2)A 2017, Sch 18 para 26*].

Power to publish details

The Commissioners for HMRC may in some circumstances publish information about an individual who incurs penalties under the above provisions — see **31.4** HMRC — CONFIDENTIALITY OF INFORMATION.

Failure to keep and preserve records

[52.15] The maximum penalty for non-compliance with *TMA 1970, s 12B* (records to be kept and preserved for the purposes of self-assessment tax returns — see **58.8** RETURNS) in relation to any tax year is £3,000. [*TMA 1970, s 12B(5)–(5B)*]. The same applies for companies under corporation tax self-assessment. [*FA 1998, s 117, Sch 18 para 23*].

A separate maximum £3,000 penalty applies in relation to records relating to a claim made otherwise than in a self-assessment tax return (see **13.3** CLAIMS). [*TMA 1970, Sch 1A para 2A(4)(5)*]. This also applies in relation to certain claims by companies under corporation tax self-assessment. [*FA 1998, s 117, Sch 18 paras 57(4), 58(3), 59*].

Penalties in respect of investigatory powers under FA 2008, Sch 36

[52.16] The penalties below apply to offences under the investigatory powers of *FA 2008, Sch 36.*

Failure to comply — fixed and daily penalties

Where a person fails to comply with an information notice within *FA 2008, Sch 36 Pt 1* (see **34.4 HMRC** INVESTIGATORY POWERS) he is liable to a fixed penalty of £300 and, for each subsequent day of continuing failure, a further penalty not exceeding £60. If the failure continues for more than 30 days beginning with the date on which notice of an assessment to a daily penalty is given, an HMRC officer may make an application to the Tribunal for an increased daily penalty. Such an application can only be made if the person concerned has been told that it may be made. If the Tribunal decides to impose an increased daily penalty, that penalty replaces the £60 daily penalty with effect for the day specified in HMRC's notice to the data-holder of the increased penalty and each subsequent day of continuing failure. Subject to a maximum of £1,000 per day the Tribunal, in determining the amount of the increased penalty, must have regard to the likely cost to the data-holder of complying with the notice and any benefits to the data-holder or anyone else of not the data-holder not complying.

For this purpose, failing to comply with a notice includes concealing, destroying or otherwise disposing of, or arranging for the concealment, destruction or disposal of, a document in breach of *FA 2008, Sch 36 paras 42, 43* (see **34.7 HMRC** INVESTIGATORY POWERS).

Where a person deliberately obstructs an HMRC officer in the course of an inspection of business premises under *FA 2008, Sch 36 Pt 2* (see **34.8 HMRC** INVESTIGATORY POWERS) which has been approved by the First-tier Tribunal he is liable to a fixed penalty of £300 and, for each subsequent day of continuing obstruction, a further penalty not exceeding £60.

No penalty is due where a person fails to do anything required to be done within a limited time period if he does it within such further time as an HMRC officer allows. A person is not liable to a penalty if he satisfies HMRC or (on appeal) the First-tier Tribunal that there is a reasonable excuse for the failure or obstruction. An insufficiency of funds is not a reasonable excuse for this purpose unless it is attributable to events outside the person's control. Where a person relies on another person to do anything, that is not a reasonable excuse unless the first person took reasonable care to avoid the failure or obstruction. Where a person has a reasonable excuse which ceases, he is treated as continuing to have a reasonable excuse if the failure is remedied or the obstruction stops without unreasonable delay.

The Treasury can make regulations amending the amounts of the above penalties.

[*FA 2008, s 108, Sch 36 paras 39–41, 44, 45, 49A, 49B; FA 2009, Sch 46 paras 13, 14, 16*].

Failure to comply — tax-related penalty

A tax-related penalty may be imposed by the Upper Tribunal where a person's failure or obstruction continues after a fixed penalty has been imposed under the above provisions. An HMRC officer must have reason to believe that the amount of tax that that person has paid, or is likely to pay is significantly less than it would otherwise have been as a result of the failure or obstruction, and the officer must make an application to the Upper Tribunal before the end of the twelve months beginning with the 'relevant date'. In deciding the amount of the penalty (if any), the Upper Tribunal must have regard to the amount of tax which has not been, or is likely not to be, paid by the person.

The '*relevant date*' is the date on which the person became liable to the penalty. Where, however, the penalty is for a failure relating to an information notice against which a person can appeal, the relevant date is the later of the end of the period in which notice of such appeal could have been given and, where an appeal is made, the date on which the appeal is determined or withdrawn.

A tax-related penalty is in addition to the fixed penalty and any daily penalties under the above provisions. No account is taken of a tax-related penalty for the purposes of **52.18** below and no reduction in a penalty charged under *FA 2007, Sch 24* (see **52.8–52.10** above) or *FA 2008, Sch 41* (see **52.3** above) is to be made in respect of a penalty under these provisions.

[*FA 2008, Sch 36 para 50*].

A penalty under these provisions was imposed by the Upper Tribunal in *HMRC v Tager* UT, [2015] STC 1687.

Inaccurate information or documents

A penalty not exceeding £3,000 applies if, in complying with an information notice, a person provides inaccurate information or produces a document that contains an inaccuracy. The penalty is due if the inaccuracy is careless (i.e. due to a failure to take reasonable care) or deliberate; or the person complying with the notice later discovers the inaccuracy and fails to take reasonable steps to inform HMRC; or knows of the inaccuracy at the time the information or document is provided but does not inform HMRC at that time. If the information or document contains more than one inaccuracy, a penalty is payable for each of them.

The Treasury can make regulations amending the amounts of the above penalties.

[*FA 2008, Sch 36 paras 40A, 41; FA 2009, Sch 46 paras 15, 16*].

A person is not liable to a penalty under any of the above provisions in respect of anything for which he has been convicted of an offence. [*FA 2008, Sch 36 para 52*].

Penalties in respect of data-gathering powers under FA 2011, Sch 23

[52.17] The penalties below apply to offences under the data-gathering powers of *FA 2011, Sch 23* (see **34.17 HMRC** INVESTIGATORY POWERS) which apply with effect from 1 April 2012.

Failure to comply

Where a person fails to comply with a data-holder notice he is liable to a fixed penalty of £300. If the failure continues after the data-holder has been notified of the assessment of the penalty he is liable, for each subsequent day of continuing failure, to a further penalty not exceeding £60. If the failure continues for more than 30 days beginning with the date on which notice of an assessment to a daily penalty is given, an HMRC officer may make an application to the Tribunal for an increased daily penalty. Such an application can only be made if the data-holder has been told that it may be made. If the Tribunal decides to impose an increased daily penalty, that penalty replaces the £60 daily penalty with effect for the day determined by the Tribunal and specified in HMRC's notice to the data-holder of the increased penalty and each subsequent day of continuing failure. Subject to a maximum of £1,000 per day the Tribunal, in determining the amount of the increased penalty, must have regard to the likely cost to the data-holder of complying with the notice and any benefits to the data-holder or anyone else of not the data-holder not complying.

For this purpose, failing to comply with a notice includes concealing, destroying or otherwise disposing of, or arranging for the concealment, destruction or disposal of, a 'material document'. A document is a '*material document*' if a data-holder notice has been given in respect of it or of data contained in it or if an HMRC officer has informed the data-holder that such a notice will be or is likely to be given. Once a notice has been complied with, the documents concerned are no longer material documents unless HMRC notify the data-holder in writing that the document must be preserved; in such circumstances the document continues to be a material document until HMRC's notification is withdrawn. If no data-holder notice is made within six months after the data-holder was last informed that a data-holder notice was to be made, any relevant documents cease to be material documents.

No penalty is due where a person fails to do anything required to be done within a limited time period if he does it within such further time as an HMRC officer allows. A person is not liable to a penalty if he satisfies HMRC or (on appeal) the First-tier Tribunal that there is a reasonable excuse for the failure. An insufficiency of funds is not a reasonable excuse for this purpose unless it is attributable to events outside the person's control. Where a person relies on another person to do anything, that is not a reasonable excuse unless the first person took reasonable care to avoid the failure. Where a person has a reasonable excuse which ceases, he is treated as continuing to have a reasonable excuse if the failure is remedied without unreasonable delay.

The Treasury can make regulations amending the amounts of the above penalties.

[*FA 2011, s 86, Sch 23 paras 30, 31, 33, 34, 38, 39, 41, 65; FA 2016, s 177(2)(3)*].

Inaccurate data

A penalty not exceeding £3,000 applies if, in complying with a data-holder notice, a person provides inaccurate data. The penalty is due if either the inaccuracy is due to a failure to take reasonable care or is deliberate, if the data-holder knows of the inaccuracy at the time the data is provided but does not inform HMRC at that time, or he later discovers the inaccuracy and fails to take reasonable steps to inform HMRC.

The Treasury can make regulations amending the amounts of the above penalty.

[*FA 2011, Sch 23 paras 32, 41, 65*].

A person is not liable to a penalty under any of the above provisions in respect of anything for which he has been convicted of an offence. [*FA 2011, Sch 23 para 42*].

Two or more tax-related penalties in respect of same tax

[52.18] Where two or more tax-related penalties are determined by reference to the same income tax, capital gains tax or corporation tax liability, the aggregate penalty is reduced to the greater or greatest of those separate penalties. Note that the penalties at **52.8**, **52.10**, **52.11**, **52.13** and **52.16** above and **52.26** and **52.29** below are not taken into account for the purposes of this provision (as they have their own equivalent provision). For defaults relating to 2014/15 onwards, penalties under **42.10** LATE PAYMENT INTEREST AND PENALTIES are also not taken into account for the purposes of this provision. [*TMA 1970, s 97A; FA 1998, s 117, Sch 18 para 90, Sch 19 para 3; FA 2007, Sch 24 para 12(3); FA 2008, Sch 36 para 50(6); FA 2009, Sch 56 para 9A; FA 2013, Sch 43C para 8(4), Sch 50 paras 13, 16(3); FA 2014, s 212(3); FA 2016, s 158(3), Sch 18 para 40(3), Sch 22 para 21*]. See **52.31** below for mitigation of penalties.

Dishonest conduct by tax agents

[52.19] The following penalties apply to offences relating to HMRC's powers in respect of dishonest conduct by tax agents (see **34.11 HMRC** INVESTIGATORY POWERS) which apply with effect from 1 April 2013. The Treasury has the power to amend the amounts of the penalties by statutory instrument — see *FA 2012, Sch 38 para 35*.

Penalties for dishonest conduct

An individual who engages in dishonest conduct (see **34.11 HMRC** INVESTIGATORY POWERS) is liable to a penalty of no less than £500 and no more than £50,000. Such a penalty can be charged only if the individual has been given a conduct notice (see **34.11 HMRC** INVESTIGATORY POWERS) and either the time allowed for appealing against the determination in the notice has expired without an appeal being made, any appeal which has been made has been withdrawn or the determination has been confirmed on appeal. For this purpose, a determination that is appealed is not considered to have been confirmed until the time allowed for any further appeal has expired or any further appeal has been withdrawn or determined.

In assessing the amount of the penalty regard must be had to whether the individual 'disclosed' the dishonest conduct, whether that disclosure was prompted or unprompted, the 'quality' of the disclosure and the quality of the individual's compliance with any file access notice (see **34.11 HMRC** INVESTIGATORY POWERS) connected with the dishonest conduct. An individual '*discloses*' dishonest conduct by telling HMRC about it, giving them reasonable help in identifying the clients concerned and the amount of lost tax revenue and allowing HMRC access to records for the purpose of ensuring the recovery of that revenue. A disclosure is unprompted if made when the individual has no reason to think that HMRC have discovered or are about to discover the dishonest conduct; otherwise a disclosure is prompted. '*Quality*' in relation to disclosure or compliance includes timing, nature and extent.

If HMRC intend to assess a penalty of £5,000, they may reduce the penalty below that amount (including to nil), stay the penalty or agree a compromise in relation to proceedings for the penalty, if they think it right to do so because of special circumstances. Such circumstances do not include ability to pay or the fact that a loss of tax revenue from a client is balanced by an overpayment by another person (whether or not a client).

[*FA 2012, s 223, Sch 38 paras 7(4), 26, 27, 29(2)(3)*].

Power to publish details of tax agents engaging in dishonest conduct

The Commissioners for HMRC may publish information about an individual who incurs a penalty under the above provisions: see **31.5 HMRC —** CONFIDENTIALITY OF INFORMATION.

Penalties for failure to comply with a file access notice

A person who fails to comply with a file access notice (see **34.11 HMRC INVESTIGATORY POWERS**) is liable to a penalty of £300. If the failure continues after notification of the penalty, the person is liable to a further penalty of up to £60 for each subsequent day on which the failure continues. No penalty is due, however, if the file access notice is complied with within such further time as HMRC have allowed.

Failing to comply with a file access notice also includes concealing, destroying or otherwise disposing of (or arranging for the concealment etc. of) a 'required document'. A '*required document*' is a document that a person is required to provide by a file access notice where either the notice has not been complied with or, if it has been complied with, he has been notified in writing by HMRC that he must continue to preserve the document (and the notification has not been withdrawn). A document is also a required document if at the time the person conceals it etc. HMRC have informed him that he will, or is likely to, be required to provide the document by a file access notice and no more than six months have passed since he was, or was last, so informed.

No penalty is due if the person otherwise liable to it satisfies HMRC (or, on appeal, the Tribunal) that there is a reasonable excuse for the failure to comply with the notice. An insufficiency of fund is not, however, a reasonable excuse unless attributable to event's outside the person's control. If the person relies on another person to do anything, that is not a reasonable excuse unless the first person took reasonable care to avoid the failure to comply with the notice. If a person had a reasonable excuse which has ceased, he is treated as continuing to have the excuse if the failure is remedied without unreasonable delay after the excuse ceased.

[*FA 2012, Sch 38 paras 22–25*].

Double jeopardy

A person is not liable to a penalty under any of the above provisions in respect of anything for which he has been convicted of an offence or in respect of anything for which he is personally liable to a penalty under *FA 2007, Sch 24* (see **52.8–52.9** above), *FA 2008, Sch 41* (see **52.3** above) or *FA 2009, Sch 55* (see **52.5** above). [*FA 2012, Sch 38 paras 33, 34*].

Enabling offshore tax evasion

[52.20] With effect for acts or omissions occurring on or after 1 January 2017, a penalty is payable by a person (P) who has 'enabled' another person (Q) to carry out offshore tax evasion or non-compliance if:

(a) P knew when his actions were carried out that they enabled, or were likely to enable, Q to carry out such evasion or non-compliance; and
(b) either:
   (i) Q has been convicted of one of the offences listed below and the conviction is final; or

(ii) Q has been found to be liable to one of the penalties listed below and either the penalty is final or a contract settlement with HMRC has been agreed under which HMRC undertake not to assess the penalty or to take proceedings to recover it.

For these purposes Q carries out offshore tax evasion or non-compliance by committing an offence within (1)–(3) below or engaging in conduct that makes him liable (if the applicable conditions are met) to a civil penalty within (A)–(D) below, where in either case the tax at stake is income tax, capital gains tax or inheritance tax. Nothing in (b) above affects the law of evidence as to the relevance of the conviction, penalty or contract settlement in proving that (a) above applies. For the purposes of these provisions, '*conduct*' includes a failure to act.

P has '*enabled*' Q to carry out offshore tax evasion or non-compliance if he has encouraged, assisted or otherwise facilitated such conduct. Where (b)(i) above applies, Q must have been convicted of the full offence and not, for example, an attempt. A conviction or a penalty becomes final when the time allowed for any appeal against it expires or, if later, when any appeal has been determined.

The offences referred to in (b)(i) above are:

(1) an offence of cheating the public revenue involving 'offshore activity';
(2) an offence under *TMA 1970, s 106A* (fraudulent evasion of income tax — see **52.40** below) involving offshore activity; and
(3) an offence under *TMA 1970, ss 106B, 106C* or *106D* (offences relating to offshore income, assets or activities — see **52.41** below).

The penalties referred to in (b)(ii) above are:

(A) a penalty under *FA 2007, Sch 24 para 1* (error in document — see **52.8** above) involving an offshore matter or offshore transfer (as defined at **52.8** above);
(B) a penalty under *FA 2008, Sch 41 para 1* (failure to notify — see **52.3** above) for a failure to notify chargeability involving offshore activity;
(C) a second tax-geared penalty under *FA 2009, Sch 55 para 6* (failure to make return — see **52.5** above) involving offshore activity; and
(D) a penalty under *FA 2015, Sch 21 para 1* (offshore asset moves — see **52.12** above).

It is immaterial that any offence or penalty may also relate to conduct by Q other than offshore tax evasion or non-compliance. Conduct involves '*offshore activity*' if it involves an 'offshore matter', an 'offshore transfer' or an 'offshore asset move'. '*Offshore matter*' and '*offshore transfer*' are defined as at **52.8** above and '*offshore asset move*' has the same meaning as at **52.12** above.

Amount of penalty

Except where (D) above applies, the amount of the penalty is the higher of 100% of the 'potential lost revenue' and £3,000.

Where (D) above applies, the amount of the penalty is the higher of 50% of the potential lost revenue in respect of the original tax non-compliance and £3,000. For this purpose, the potential lost revenue in respect of the original tax non-compliance is the potential lost revenue under *FA 2007, Sch 24* (see **52.8** above) or *FA 2008, Sch 41* (see **52.3** above) or the tax liability which would have been shown on the return (see **52.5** above) according to which provision the original penalty was incurred under.

Where (1), (2) or (3) above apply, the '*potential lost revenue*' is the same amount as the potential lost revenue applicable for the purposes of the corresponding civil penalty (determined as below). For offences within (1) or (2) above, the corresponding civil penalty is that to which Q is liable as a result of the offending conduct. For offences within (3) above, the corresponding civil penalty is *FA 2008, Sch 41* where the offence is under *TMA 1970, s 106B*; *FA 2009, Sch 55* where the offence is under *TMA 1970, s 106C*; and *FA 2007, Sch 24* where the offence is under *TMA 1970, s 106D*. The fact that Q has been prosecuted for the offending conduct is disregarded for this purpose.

Where (A) or (B) above apply, the '*potential lost revenue*' is the amount that is the potential lost revenue under *FA 2007, Sch 24* or *FA 2008, Sch 41*. Where (C) above applies, the '*potential lost revenue*' is the tax liability that would have been shown on the return.

Where any amount of potential lost revenue is only partly attributable to offshore tax evasion or non-compliance, a just and reasonable apportionment is made.

Reduction for disclosure

A reduction in the amount of a penalty will be given where P makes a disclosure to HMRC of a matter relating to an inaccuracy in a document, a supply of false information or a failure to disclose an under-assessment, a disclosure of P's enabling of Q's actions or a disclosure of any other information HMRC regard as assisting them in relation to the assessment of the penalty. A person is treated as making a disclosure of a matter for these purposes only if he tells HMRC about it, gives them reasonable help in relation to it and allows them access to records for any reasonable purpose connected with resolving it.

A reduction will also be given if P assists HMRC in any investigation leading to Q being charged with an offence or found liable to a penalty. A person is treated as assisting HMRC for this purpose only by assisting or encouraging Q to disclose all relevant facts to HMRC, allowing HMRC access to records or any other conduct which HMRC consider assists them in investigating Q.

The penalty will be reduced to an amount that reflects the quality of the disclosure or assistance (including its timing, nature and extent). The amount of the reduction will depend on whether the disclosure or assistance is 'prompted' or 'unprompted'. The penalty may not be reduced below the higher of 10% of the potential lost revenue and £1,000 for unprompted disclosure or assistance and not below the higher of 30% of the potential lost revenue and £3,000 for prompted disclosure or assistance. Disclosure or assistance is '*unprompted*' if made at a time when P has no reason to believe that HMRC have discovered or are about to discover Q's offshore tax evasion or non-compliance. In all other cases, disclosure or assistance is '*prompted*'.

Reduction in special circumstances

HMRC can also reduce, stay or agree a compromise in relation to proceedings for a penalty if they think it right to do so because of special circumstances. Ability to pay and the fact that a potential loss of revenue from one taxpayer is balanced by a potential overpayment by another are not special circumstances for this purpose.

Double jeopardy

A person is not liable to a penalty under these provisions in respect of conduct for which he has been convicted of an offence or has been assessed to another penalty.

[*FA 2016, s 162, Sch 20 paras 1–9, 15; SI 2016 No 1249*].

Information powers

The information and inspection powers of *FA 2008, Sch 36* (see **34.3** HMRC INVESTIGATORY POWERS) apply, with necessary modifications, for the purpose of checking the penalty position of a person whom an HMRC officer has reason to suspect may have enabled offshore tax evasion or non-compliance. The modifications include, in particular, that the exclusions from information notices for auditors and tax advisers (see **34.5** HMRC INVESTIGATORY POWERS) do not apply and that there is no tax-related penalty for failure to comply (see **52.16** above). [*FA 2016, Sch 20 paras 18–21*].

Publishing details of enablers

HMRC may publish information about a person who has been found to have incurred one or more penalties under these provisions (and has been assessed or entered into a contract settlement) if the total potential lost revenue exceeds £25,000 or if that person has been found to be liable to five or more such penalties in any five year period. Information cannot be published if the maximum reduction of the penalty has been given for disclosure or if the penalty has been reduced to nil or stayed as a result of special circumstances. The Treasury may vary the £25,000 threshold by statutory instrument.

Before publishing any information HMRC must notify the person and give an opportunity to make representations. No information may be published before the day on which the penalty becomes final or, where there is more than one penalty, before the latest day on which any of them becomes final. Information may not be published for the first time more than one year after that day. For this purpose, a penalty becomes final when no further appeal can be made, any appeal is finally determined or when a contract settlement is made.

The information which can be published is the person's name (including trading name, previous name or pseudonym), address, the nature of the person's business, the amount of the penalties and the periods or times to which they relate and any other information HMRC consider appropriate to make the person's identity clear. HMRC may publish the information in any way they think appropriate.

[*FA 2016, Sch 20 paras 22, 23*].

Enablers of defeated tax avoidance

[52.21] With effect for arrangements entered into on or after the date of Royal Assent to *F(No 2)A 2017*, a penalty is payable by a person who has 'enabled' 'abusive tax arrangements' entered into by another person (T) if T incurs a 'defeat' in respect of them. Any actions carried out by a person before the date of Royal Assent are disregarded in determining whether that person enabled arrangements. The penalty applies to a number of taxes, including corporation tax and capital gains tax.

Definitions

Arrangements are '*tax arrangements*' if, taking into account all the circumstances, it would be reasonable to conclude that the obtaining of a tax advantage was the main purpose, or one of the main purposes, of the arrangements. For this purpose, '*arrangements*' include any agreement, understanding, scheme, transaction or series of transactions, whether or not legally enforceable.

Tax arrangements are '*abusive*' if entering into them or carrying them out cannot reasonably be regarded as a reasonable course of action in relation to the tax provisions in question, having regard to all the circumstances. Those circumstances include:

- whether the substantive results of the arrangements are consistent with any express or implied principles on which the provisions are based and their policy objectives;
- whether the means of achieving the results of the arrangements involve one or more contrived or abnormal steps; and
- whether the arrangements are intended to exploit any shortcomings in the provisions.

Where the tax arrangements form part of other arrangements regard must be had to those other arrangements.

The legislation gives the following non-exhaustive examples of what might indicate that tax arrangements are abusive (assuming that the result was not anticipated when the relevant provisions were enacted).

- The arrangements result in taxable income, profits or gains significantly less than the economic amount.
- The arrangements result in a tax deduction or loss significantly greater than the economic amount.
- The arrangements result in a claim for repayment or crediting of tax, including foreign tax that has not been, and is unlikely to be, paid.

The legislation also gives an example of what might indicate that arrangements are not abusive; the arrangements accord with established practice accepted by HMRC.

A '*tax advantage*' includes relief or increased relief from tax, repayment or increased repayment of tax, receipt or advancement of receipt of a tax credit, avoidance or reduction of a charge or assessment to tax or a liability to pay tax, avoidance of a possible assessment to tax or liability to pay tax or of an obligation to deduct or account for tax, deferral of a payment of tax, and advancement of a repayment tax.

T incurs a '*defeat*' in respect of arrangements if T, or a person on his behalf, has given HMRC a document on the basis that a tax advantage arose from the arrangements and that tax advantage has been counteracted, with the counteraction having become final. The document must be of a kind list in *FA 2007, Sch 24 para 1* (penalty for errors in documents — see **52.8** above) or a document amending such a document. A tax advantage is counteracted for this purpose if adjustments have been made to T's tax position (by assessment, modification of an assessment or return, amendment or disallowance of a claim, payment or entering into a contract settlement) on the basis that all or part of the tax advantage does not arise. Counteraction is final when the adjustments and any amounts arising from them can no longer be varied.

T also incurs a '*defeat*' in respect of arrangements if HMRC have made an assessment which counteracts (i.e. prevents T from obtaining all or part of) a tax advantage which it is reasonable to assume T expected to obtain from the arrangements and the counteraction is final. A counteraction is final for this purpose when either a contract settlement which prevents T from obtaining all or part of the tax advantage is made or the assessment and any amounts arising from it can no longer be varied.

A person has '*enabled*' arrangements if he falls within any of the following categories. In the case of (a)–(c) or (e) below, the person must be acting in the course of a business carried on by him. Note that it is possible for there to be more than one enabler of particular arrangements.

(a) **A designer of the arrangements.** A person who was to any extent responsible for the design of the arrangements or a proposal implemented by them. Providing advice which is taken account of in the design of the arrangements does not make a person a designer of the arrangements unless either:
  (i) any of the advice suggested arrangements or an alteration of proposed arrangements (or a proposal for arrangements or an alternation of such a proposal) and it is reasonable to assume that the suggestion was made with a view to arrangements being designed so that a tax advantage or greater tax advantage might be expected to arise from them; or
  (ii) when the advice was given, the person providing it knew, or could reasonably be expected to know, that the advice would be taken account of in designing abusive tax arrangements or a proposal for such arrangements or that it was likely that the advice would be so taken account of.

  In (i) above, advice does not suggest anything which was put forward for consideration if the advice can be reasonably read as advising against it. 'Advice', for these purposes, includes giving an opinion.

(b) **A manager of the arrangements.** A person who was to any extent responsible for organising or managing the arrangements and who, when carrying out functions relating to such organising or managing, knew or could reasonably be expected to know that the arrangements were abusive tax arrangements. Facilitating T's withdrawal from the arrangements is not organising or managing the arrangements for this purpose if it is reasonable to assume that T's purpose in withdrawing is not to obtain a tax advantage.

(c) **A person who marketed the arrangements.** A person who made available for implementation by T a proposal subsequently implemented by the arrangements or who informed T or another person about a proposal subsequently implemented by the arrangements with a view to T entering into the arrangements or transactions forming part of them.

(d) **An enabling participant.** A person, other than T, who enters into the arrangements or a transaction forming part of them where, without that participation (or the participation of another person in the same capacity), the arrangements would not be expected to result in a tax advantage for T. The person must have known or have been reasonably expected to know, when entering into the arrangements or transaction, that what was being entered into was abusive tax arrangements or a transaction forming part of such arrangements.

(e) **A financial enabler.** A person who provided a financial product directly or indirectly to T or an enabling participant within (d) above where it is reasonable to assume that a purpose of T or the other participant in obtaining the product was to participate in the arrangements. The person must have known or have been reasonably expected to know, when providing the product, that a purpose of obtaining it was to participate in abusive tax arrangements. Financial products include loans, shares, derivative contracts, repos, stock-lending arrangements, alternative finance arrangements and contracts which would be required to be treated under generally accepted accounting practice as a loan, deposit or other financial asset or obligation. The Treasury may amend the list of financial products by statutory instrument.

T and, if T is a company, any member of the same group, cannot be treated as an enabler of the arrangements even if they fall within any of the above categories. Two companies are members of a group, for this purpose, if one is a 75% subsidiary of the other or both are 75% subsidiaries of a third company. The Treasury can add to the categories of enabler or provide that a person who would otherwise be an enabler is not to be treated as such in specified circumstances by statutory instruments.

Amount of penalty

The amount of the penalty for each enabler of the arrangements is the total amount or value of the consideration received or receivable by that person for anything done by him which enabled the arrangements. VAT and any consideration previously taken into account in calculating a penalty under these provisions are excluded. Consideration paid (or payable), under arrangements, to a person other than the enabler is treated for this purpose as paid (or payable) to the enabler. If consideration is attributable to more than one transaction it must be apportioned on a just and reasonable basis. Where consideration is given for what is in substance one bargain, the consideration must be treated as attributable to all elements of the bargain even if separate consideration is given for, or there are separate transactions in respect of, different elements.

Reduction and mitigation of penalty

The amount of the penalty is reduced by the amount of any other penalty incurred by, and assessed on, the enabler in respect of the same conduct.

HMRC have discretion to reduce a penalty, entirely remit a penalty or to stay or agree a compromise in respect of proceedings for the recovery of a penalty.

Assessment of penalty

For the general provisions relating to the assessment of a penalty under these provisions see **52.33** below. The decision to make an assessment must be taken by an HMRC officer designated by the Commissioners for HMRC for the purposes of these provisions (a '*designated HMRC officer*'). If HMRC do not have all the information needed to determine the amount of the consideration on which the penalty is based, they may make an assessment on the basis of a reasonable estimate, provided that they have taken all reasonable steps to obtain the information.

If a proposal for arrangements has been implemented more than once and all of the arrangements are substantially the same, HMRC cannot assess any penalty until more than 50% of the arrangements have incurred a defeat. Any person liable to a penalty may, however, request that an assessment be made sooner.

Notification of a penalty assessment must be accompanied by a report of the opinion of the GAAR Advisory Panel (see **4.3** ANTI-AVOIDANCE) on which HMRC relied in making the assessment (see below).

GAAR Advisory Panel opinion

A penalty assessment cannot be made unless either of the following applies.

(A) A 'GAAR final decision notice' has been given in relation to the arrangements or other 'equivalent' arrangements and a designated HMRC officer has considered the opinion of the GAAR Advisory Panel which was considered by HMRC in preparing that notice. If the final decision notice related to equivalent arrangements only, a designated HMRC officer must first give the person liable to the penalty a notice in writing explaining HMRC's view, specifying the arrangements concerned and describing the material characteristics of the equivalent arrangements. The notice must also include a report by HMRC of the opinion of the Panel and must explain the right of the person liable to the penalty to make representations. Representations as to why the arrangements under consideration are not equivalent to those considered by the Panel can be made in writing within 30 days beginning with the day the notice is given. HMRC may, on written request, extend the deadline (but are not required to do so). A penalty assessment cannot be made unless a notice has been given, the time allowed for representations has expired and the officer has considered any representations made.
A '*GAAR final decision notice*' is a notice of HMRC's final decision on whether arrangements are to be counteracted under the GAAR after considering the Panel's decision (see **4.4**(10) and **4.6** ANTI-AVOIDANCE).

Arrangements are '*equivalent*' to one another if they are substantially the same with regard to their results or intended results, the means of achieving those results and the characteristics making them abusive tax arrangements.

(B) A designated HMRC officer has referred the arrangements to the GAAR Advisory Panel. An assessment cannot be made until the officer has considered the opinion of the Panel. See below for the procedure for referring arrangements. If the officer considers that a person is liable to a penalty in relation to particular arrangements on the basis that the opinion of the Panel 'applies' to the arrangements but that person was not notified of the referral to the Panel, then before making an assessment the officer must give that person a notice in writing explaining HMRC's view and specifying the arrangements concerned. The notice must also include a report by HMRC of the opinion of the Panel and must explain the right to make representations. Representations as to why the opinion does not apply to the arrangements in question can be made in writing within 30 days beginning with the day the notice is given. HMRC may, on written request, extend the deadline (but are not required to do so). A penalty assessment cannot be made unless a notice has been given, the time allowed for representations has expired and the officer has considered any representations made.

An opinion of the Panel '*applies*' to the arrangements in respect of which the referral was made and any equivalent arrangements.

The procedure for referring arrangements to the Panel is as follows.

(1) A designated HMRC officer may make a referral if he considers that a person is liable to a penalty in respect of particular arrangements. A referral may not be made if a GAAR final decision notice has already been given in relation to the arrangements in question or equivalent arrangements. Before making a referral the officer must give a notice to each person who he then considers to be liable to a penalty in respect of the arrangements giving his view and explaining why he considers the arrangements to be abusive tax arrangements. The notice must also state that HMRC are considering making a referral and must explain the right to make representations. Representations can be made in writing within 45 days beginning with the day the notice is given. HMRC may, on written request, extend the deadline (but are not required to do so).

A referral is of the question whether the entering into and carrying out of the tax arrangements described in the 'referral statement' is a reasonable course of action in relation to the tax provisions concerned. The '*referral statement*' must accompany the referral and is a general statement of the material characteristics of the arrangements including a factual description of them, HMRC's view as to whether they accord with established practice, why HMRC consider that the tax advantage arises from abusive arrangements, any matters of which HMRC are aware that may suggest that their view is not correct and any other matters which HMRC consider to be required for the purposes of the Panel's functions.

(2) Where a designated HMRC officer decides whether to make a referral he must, as soon as reasonably practicable, give written notice of that decision to each person to whom a notice within (1) above was given.

(3) A referral must be accompanied by the referral statement, a declaration that, as far as HMRC are aware, nothing material has been omitted from the statement, a copy of each notice within (1) above and (4) below and of any representations received, together with any comments on the representations.

(4) At the same time as the referral is made, a designated HMRC officer must give each person to whom a notice within (1) above was given a written notice confirming that the referral has been made and including a copy of the referral statement and of any comments on representations made by that person. It must also explain the right to make representations to the Panel and the requirement to send a copy of any representations to HMRC.

(5) A person who has received a notice under (4) above has 21 days beginning with the day on which the notice was given to send written representations to the Panel about the notice in (1) above or any comments made by HMRC on representations made by him in response to that notice. The Panel may, on written request, extend the deadline (but are not required to do so). A copy of the representations must be sent to HMRC. If no representations had been made in response to the notice in (1) above, HMRC may provide the Panel with comments on the representations now made, and must send a copy of any such comments to the person to whom the notice was given.

(6) The Chair of the Panel must arrange for a sub-panel of three members to consider the referral. The sub-panel may invite any person to whom a notice was given under (1) above or the designated HMRC officer (or both) to supply further information within a specified time period. A copy of any information must be given to the designated HMRC officer or to each of the notice recipients.

(7) The sub-panel must produce an opinion notice stating their joint opinion as to whether or not the entering into and carrying out of the tax arrangements was a reasonable course of action in relation to the tax provisions concerned, having regard to the referral statement and the meaning of 'abusive'. An opinion notice may indicate that the sub-panel consider that it is not possible to reach a view on the information available. Alternatively, the sub-panel may produce two or three opinion notices which taken together state the opinions of all the members. An opinion notice must include the reasons for the opinion and is given to the designated HMRC officer.

In any court or tribunal proceedings in connection with a penalty under these provisions, any question as to whether the arrangements were abusive must be determined taking account of the Panel's opinion on which HMRC relied in assessing the penalty. The court or tribunal may also take into account any guidance, statements or other material (of HMRC, a government minister or anyone else) in the public domain when the arrangements were entered into and any evidence of established practice at that time.

[*F(No 2)A 2017, s 65, Sch 16 paras 1–19, 21, 23–36*].

Double jeopardy

A person is not liable to a penalty under these provisions in respect of conduct for which he has been convicted of an offence.

[*F(No 2)A 2017, Sch 16 para 52*].

Information powers

The information and inspection powers of *FA 2008, Sch 36* (see **34.3** HMRC INVESTIGATORY POWERS) apply, with necessary modifications, for the purpose of checking the penalty position of a person whom an HMRC officer has reason to suspect may be liable to a penalty under these provisions. [*F(No 2)A 2017, Sch 16 paras 40–43*].

Privileged communications

Where a person cannot provide information to demonstrate that he is not liable to a penalty because communications by a lawyer are subject to legal professional privilege (or in Scotland, protected from disclosure in legal proceedings on grounds of confidentiality of communication), that lawyer or another lawyer can make a declaration that the person is not liable to the penalty. Such a declaration must be treated by HMRC, a court or tribunal as conclusive evidence of the things stated in it unless HMRC, the court or tribunal is satisfied that it contains incorrect information. The Treasury may impose requirements as to the form and content of such declarations by statutory instrument. Lawyers, for this purpose, are barristers, advocates, solicitors and other legal representatives communications with whom may be subject to legal professional privilege (or Scottish equivalent). A penalty not exceeding £5,000 applies for carelessly or deliberately giving incorrect information in a declaration. A declaration can also be made, where relevant, in respect of such a penalty. An assessment to such a penalty must be made within the 12 months beginning with the date on which sufficient facts came to HMRC's knowledge to indicate that a penalty is due. Subject to this, the rules for making assessments and appeals are the same as for the main penalty under these provisions (see **52.33** and **52.34** below). [*F(No 2)A 2017, Sch 16 paras 44, 45*].

Publishing details of enablers

HMRC may publish information about a person who has been found to have incurred one or more penalties under these provisions (and has been assessed or entered into a contract settlement) if the total amount of the penalty or penalties exceeds £25,000 or if that person has been found to be liable to 50 or more other such penalties. Penalties and their amounts are only aggregated for this purpose if the 'entry dates' of the penalties fall within a period of 12 months. For this purpose, the '*entry date*' of a penalty is the date (or latest date) on which the arrangements or any agreement or transaction forming part of them was entered into by the person whose defeat resulted in the penalty arising. Penalties which have been reduced to nil or stayed are disregarded as are penalties by reference to which information has already been published and penalties where the arrangements concerned are related to other arrangements in respect of which a penalty has been charged and information published. Penalties are also disregarded if the arrangements are related to other arrangements and it is not the case that HMRC reasonably believe that defeats have been incurred in all of the related arrangements and that each penalty in relation to those arrangements has become final. Arrangements are related to each other if they implement the same proposal for tax arrangements and are substantially the same.

The Treasury may vary the £25,000 and 50 penalties thresholds by statutory instrument.

Before publishing any information HMRC must notify the person and give an opportunity to make representations. No information may be published before the day on which the penalty becomes final or, where there is more than one penalty, before the latest day on which any of them becomes final. Information may not be published for the first time more than one year after that day. For this purpose, a penalty becomes final when no further appeal can be made, any appeal is finally determined or when a contract settlement is made. Information cannot be republished or continue to be published after the 12 months beginning with the date of first publication.

The information which can be published is the person's name (including trading name, previous name or pseudonym), address, the nature of the person's business, the number and amount of the penalties and any other information HMRC consider appropriate to make the person's identity clear. HMRC may publish the information in any way they think appropriate.

[*F(No 2)A 2017, Sch 16 paras 46–51*].

Interest on penalties

[52.22] All of the above penalties (other than those under *FA 2008, Sch 41* (see **52.3** above) and those at **52.8**, **52.10**, **52.16**, **52.17**, **52.19** and **52.20** above) carry interest, calculated from the due date (broadly, 30 days after issue of a notice of determination by an HMRC officer — see **52.33** below, or immediately upon determination by the Tribunal or judgement of the High Court — see **52.35**, **52.36** below) to the date of payment. [*TMA 1970, s 103A; FA 1998, s 117, Sch 19 para 40; SI 1998 No 311*]. For income tax and capital gains tax, rates of interest on penalties are synonymous with those on late paid tax — see **42.3** LATE PAYMENT INTEREST AND PENALTIES.

See **42.2** LATE PAYMENT INTEREST AND PENALTIES for late payment interest on penalties charged on 'self-assessment amounts' accruing on or after 31 October 2011.

See also **52.25** below for interest on penalties under *FA 2014, Sch 35*.

Special returns etc.

[52.23] Failure to render any information or particulars or any return, certificate, statement or other document which is required, whether by notice or otherwise, under the provisions listed in *TMA 1970, s 98* is the subject of a maximum penalty of £300, plus £60 for each day the failure continues after that penalty is imposed (but not for any day for which such a daily penalty has already been imposed). For transactions before 1 July 2009, these penalties are increased by a factor of ten in the case of a failure under *ICTA 1988, s 765A* (movements of capital between residents of EC member states). The maximum penalty for an incorrect return etc. given fraudulently or negligently is £3,000. Penalties for failure to render information etc. required by notice cannot be imposed after the failure is rectified, and daily penalties can similarly not be imposed where the information etc. was required other than by notice. [*TMA 1970, s 98; FA 2009, Sch 17 paras 2, 13; SI 2009 No 2035, Sch para 8*].

Failure to allow access to computers renders a person liable to a maximum £300 penalty (£500 before 21 July 2008). [*FA 1988, s 127; FA 2008, s 114*].

Failure to disclose tax avoidance scheme

[52.24] Penalties are chargeable for failures to comply with the following requirements under the disclosure provisions at **20.2–20.5** DISCLOSURE OF TAX AVOIDANCE SCHEMES:

(a) duty of promoter to notify HMRC of notifiable proposals or arrangements (*FA 2004, s 308(1)(3)*);
(b) duty of taxpayer to notify where the promoter is not UK-resident (*FA 2004, s 309(1)*);
(c) duty of parties to arrangements to notify where there is no promoter (*FA 2004, s 310*);
(d) duty of promoter to notify parties of the scheme reference number (*FA 2004, s 312(2)*);
(e) (from 1 November 2008) duty of client to notify parties (and, from 26 March 2015, employees) of the reference number (*FA 2004, s 312A(2)(2A)*);
(f) (from 17 July 2013) duty of client to provide information to promoter (*FA 2004, s 312B*);
(g) (from 1 January 2011) duty of promoter to provide details of clients (*FA 2004, s 313ZA*);
(h) (from 17 July 2013) enquiry following disclosure of client details (*FA 2004, s 313ZB*);
(i) (from 19 July 2007) duty of promoter to respond to inquiry (*FA 2004, ss 313A, 313B*);
(j) (from 1 January 2011) duty of introducer to give details of person who have provided, or (from 26 March 2015) been provided with, information (*FA 2004, s 313C*);
(k) (from 17 July 2014) duty to provide further information requested by HMRC (*FA 2004, s 310A*);
(l) (from 26 March 2015) duty to provide updated information (*FA 2004, s 310C*);
(m) (from 26 March 2015) duty to provide additional information with reference number (*FA 2004, s 316A*); and
(n) (from 26 March 2015) duty or employer to notify HMRC of details of employees (*FA 2004, s 313ZC*).

An initial penalty of up to £5,000 can be determined by the First-tier Tribunal for any failure to comply with one of the above duties. With effect from 1 January 2011, however, where the failure relates to (a)–(c) or (k) above, the initial penalty is up to £600 per day during the period beginning with the day after that on which the time limit for complying with the requirement expires and ending with the earlier of the day on which the penalty is determined or the last day before the failure ceases. The amount of the daily penalty must be arrived at after taking account of all relevant considerations, including the desirability of deterring repeated failures and having regard to the amount of fees likely to be received by a promoter or the tax saving sought by the taxpayer. If the daily penalty appears to the Tribunal to be inappropriately low, it can be increased to an amount not exceeding £1 million. Where HMRC consider that a daily penalty has been determined to run from a date later than it should, they can commence proceedings for a redetermination of the penalty. This could happen where the failure was in response to an order under *FA 2004, s 306A* for a proposal or arrangements to be treated as notifiable (see **20.5** DISCLOSURE OF TAX AVOIDANCE SCHEMES), so that the initial time limit for compliance was ten days after the giving of the order. If it subsequently becomes clear that the proposal or arrangements were notifiable from the outset, the date by reference to which the penalty should have applied would be considerably earlier.

A further penalty or penalties of up to £600 applies for each day on which the failure continues after the initial penalty is imposed.

Higher maximum daily penalties of up to £5,000 apply where:

(i) an order has been made under *FA 2004, s 306A* (order by Tribunal to treat proposal or arrangements as notifiable); or
(ii) there is a failure to comply with an order made under *FA 2004, s 314A* (order by the Tribunal to make a disclosure).

In the case of (ii) above, however, the increased maximum only applies to days falling after the period of ten days beginning with the date of the order. This also applies to (i) above with effect from 1 January 2011.

Where an order is made under *FA 2004, s 314A* or, from 1 January 2011, *FA 2004, s 306A*, the person mentioned in the order cannot rely on doubt as to notifiability as a reasonable excuse after the period of ten days beginning with the date of the order and any delay in compliance after that time is unreasonable unless there is another excuse.

Parties to notifiable arrangements who fail to notify HMRC of the scheme reference number etc. are liable to a penalty of up to £5,000 in respect of each scheme to which the failure relates. The penalty is increased for a second failure, occurring within three years from the date on which the first failure began, to up to £7,500 in respect of each scheme to which the failure relates (whether or not the same as the scheme to which the first failure relates). Any further such failures occurring within three years from the date on which the previous failure began, result in a penalty of up to £10,000 in respect of each scheme to which the failure relates (whether or not the same as the schemes to which any of the previous failures relates). Before 26 March 2015, these were fixed penalties of £100, £500 and £1,000 respectively.

Where a person fails to comply with a duty within (b) above and the promoter is a 'monitored promoter' for the purposes of the high-risk promoter provisions at **20.7** DISCLOSURE OF TAX AVOIDANCE SCHEMES onwards or with a duty within (c) above where the arrangements concerned are arrangements of a monitored promoter, then legal advice which the person took into account is disregarded in determining whether he has a reasonable excuse if the advice was given or procured by that monitored promoter. In determining whether a monitored promoter has a reasonable excuse for a failure to comply with a duty within (a) to (j) above, reliance on legal advice is taken automatically not to be a reasonable excuse if either the advice was not based on a full and accurate description of the facts or the conclusions in the advice were unreasonable.

The Treasury has the power to amend the £5,000, £600 and £1 million limits above by statutory instrument.

[*TMA 1970, s 98C; FA 2013, s 223(4); FA 2014, ss 275, 284(5)–(11); FA 2015, Sch 17 paras 3, 8, 11, 13, 15, 18–20; SI 2004 No 1864, Reg 8B; SI 2007 Nos 3103, 3104; SI 2008 No 1935; SI 2010 No 2743; SI 2010 No 2928, Reg 4; SI 2010 No 3019; SI 2012 No 1836, Reg 16*].

High-risk promoters of avoidance schemes

[52.25] Penalties are chargeable for failure to comply with any duty imposed under the high-risk promoters of avoidance schemes provisions at **20.7–20.17** DISCLOSURE OF TAX AVOIDANCE SCHEMES. The maximum penalty for failure to comply with each duty is set out in the table below.

	Provision	Maximum penalty
1	Duty to notify clients of monitoring notice (*FA 2014, s 249(1)*)	£5,000
2	Duty to publicise monitoring notice (*FA 2014, s 249(3)*)	£1,000,000
3	Duty to include information in correspondence etc. (*FA 2014, s 249(10)*)	£1,000,000
4	Duty of promoter to notify client of reference number (*FA 2014, s 251*)	£5,000
5	Duty of others to notify clients and intermediaries of reference number (*FA 2014, s 252*)	£5,000
6	Duty to notify HMRC of reference number (*FA 2014, s 253*)	(a) £5,000 unless (b) or (c) apply;
		(b) £7,500 where the person has previously failed to comply with the duty once during the 36 months before the current failure;

		(c) £10,000 where the person has previously failed to comply with the duty two or more times during the 36 months before the current failure.
7	Duty to provide information or produce document (*FA 2014, s 255*)	£1,000,000
8	Ongoing duty to provide information or produce document (*FA 2014, s 257*)	£1,000,000
9	Duty of person dealing with non-resident promoter (*FA 2014, s 258*)	£1,000,000
10	Duty of monitored promoter to provide information about clients (*FA 2014, s 259*)	£5,000
11	Duty of intermediary to provide information about clients (*FA 2014, s 260*)	£5,000
12	Duty to provide information about clients following enquiry (*FA 2014, s 261*)	£10,000
13	Duty to provide information required to monitor conduct notice (*FA 2014, s 262*)	£5,000
14	Duty to provide information about address (*FA 2014, s 263*)	£5,000
15	Duty to provide information to promoter (*FA 2014, s 265*)	£5,000

For failures within 1, 4, 5, 10 or 11 above, the maximum penalty specified is a maximum which may be imposed on each person to whom the failure relates.

The amount of the penalty actually imposed must be arrived at after taking account of all relevant considerations, including the desirability of setting it at a level which appears appropriate for deterring the person on whom it is imposed, or other persons, from similar future failures. In particular, regard must be had, for penalties within 7 and 8 above, to the amount of fees received and, for penalties within 9 above imposed for a failure to comply with a duty within **20.13**(3) or (4) DISCLOSURE OF TAX AVOIDANCE SCHEMES, the tax advantage gained or sought.

If the failure to comply with a duty within 7–14 above continues after a penalty has been imposed, a further daily penalty not exceeding £600 or, where the initial maximum penalty was £1,000,000, £10,000 may be imposed for each day on which the failure continues after the day on which the initial penalty was imposed.

A failure to do anything required to be done within a limited time period does not give rise to a penalty under these provisions if the duty is complied with within such further time as HMRC or the Tribunal have allowed.

Reasonable excuse

No penalty arises under the above provisions if there is a reasonable excuse for the failure. Insufficiency of funds is not a reasonable excuse for this purpose unless attributable to events outside the control of the person who failed to comply with the duty, and neither is that person's reliance on another person to do anything, unless he took reasonable care to avoid the failure. If the person had a reasonable excuse, he is treated as continuing to have a reasonable excuse after the excuse has ceased if the failure is remedied without unreasonable delay. Reliance by a monitored promoter on legal advice is automatically taken not to constitute a reasonable excuse if either it was not based on a full and accurate description of the facts or the conclusions in the advice that the promoter relied on were unreasonable. Reliance on legal advice is also automatically taken not to constitute a reasonable excuse for failure to comply with a duty within 9 above if the advice was given or procured by the monitored promoter.

Inaccurate information and documents

Where a person provides inaccurate information or produces a document which contains an inaccuracy in complying with a duty within 7–14 above, the person is liable to a penalty if:

(a) the inaccuracy is careless or deliberate; or
(b) the person knows of the inaccuracy at the time of providing the information or producing the document but does not inform HMRC at that time; or
(c) the person subsequently discovers the inaccuracy and fails to take reasonable steps to inform HMRC.

In (a) above, an inaccuracy is careless if it is due to a failure by the person to take reasonable care. In determining whether or not a monitored promoter took reasonable care, reliance on legal advice is disregarded if either it was not based on a full and accurate description of the facts or the conclusions in the advice that the promoter relied on were unreasonable. Reliance on legal advice is disregarded in determining whether or not a person complying with a duty within 9 above took reasonable care if the advice was given or procured by the monitored promoter.

The maximum penalty is the same as the maximum penalty for failure to comply with the duty in question. If the information or document contains more than one inaccuracy, only one penalty is payable.

Interaction with other penalties etc.

A person is not liable to a penalty under these provisions for anything in respect of which he has been convicted of an offence.

A person is not liable to a penalty under the provisions at **52.8–52.10** and **52.24** above or under any other provision prescribed by statutory instrument by reason of any failure to include in any return or account a reference number required by *FA 2014, s 253* (see 6 above).

Procedure

Penalties under the above provisions are imposed by the Tribunal, using the procedure in **52.35** below. This does not apply, however, to daily penalties for continuing failure to comply with a duty where the maximum penalty is £600; such penalties are instead imposed by HMRC using the procedure at **52.33** below.

Interest on penalties

Interest on a penalty under the above provisions runs, at the rate applicable under *FA 1989, s 178*, from the date on which the penalty is determined until payment.

Power to change amount of penalties

The Treasury may, by statutory instrument, change the maximum penalties under the above provisions.

[*FA 2014, Sch 35 paras 1–5, 8–13*].

Failure to comply with follower notice

[52.26] Where a person who has been given a follower notice (see **4.25** ANTI-AVOIDANCE) fails to take the necessary corrective action before the specified time, that person is liable to a penalty of 50% of the value of the denied tax advantage. If, before the specified time, the person takes the necessary corrective action in respect only of part of the denied tax advantage, the penalty is 50% of the value of the remainder of the advantage. In the case of a partnership follower notice, each person who was a partner during the period for which the return in question was required is liable to the penalty, but the maximum is only 20% of the value of the advantage (or remainder). Each partner is only liable for a share of the penalty in proportion to the profit-sharing arrangements for the period or, if HMRC do not have sufficient information to make such an apportionment, as determined by HMRC.

The value of the denied tax advantage for this purpose is the additional amount of tax due or payable as a result of counteracting the advantage, including any amount payable having been erroneously repaid by HMRC and any amount which would have been repayable by HMRC if the advantage were not counteracted. Relief under *CTA 2010, s 458* (repayment of loan etc. by participator in a close company) and group relief are ignored (subject to the exception below).

Where the denied tax advantage resulted in a wrongly recorded loss which has been partly used to reduce the tax due or payable, the value of the denied advantage is increased by 10% of the part of the loss not so used. This rule applies both where the entire loss is attributable to the denied advantage and where only part of the loss is so attributable (but in the latter case, the rule applies only to that part). Where a denied advantage creates or increases an aggregate loss recorded for a group of companies group relief may be taken into account. To the extent that, because of its nature or the taxpayer's circumstances, there is no reasonable prospect of a loss resulting from a denied advantage being used to reduce a tax liability of any person, the value of the denied advantage is nil.

To the extent that the denied advantage is a deferral of tax (other than one resulting from a loss), the value of it is 25% of the amount of deferred tax for each year of deferral and a proportion of 25% for any separate period of deferral which is less than a year. The value cannot exceed 100% of the deferred tax.

HMRC may reduce the amount of a penalty to reflect the quality (including the timing, nature and extent) of any co-operation by the taxpayer. The maximum reduction is to 10% of the value of the denied advantage, or 4% in the case of a partnership notice. A taxpayer co-operates only if he does one or more of the following:

- providing HMRC with reasonable assistance in quantifying the tax advantage;
- counteracting the denied tax advantage;
- providing HMRC with information enabling corrective action to be taken by HMRC;
- providing HMRC with information enabling them to enter an agreement with the taxpayer for the purpose of counteracting the denied advantage; and
- allowing HMRC to access tax records to ensure that the denied advantage is fully counteracted.

Interaction with other penalties

Where a taxpayer incurs a penalty under the above provisions and a penalty under *FA 2007, Sch 24* (see **52.8–52.9** above), *FA 2008, Sch 41* (see **52.3** above), *FA 2009, Sch 55* (see **52.5** above), *FA 2013, s 212A* (see **52.11** above) or *FA 2016, Sch 18* (see **52.29** below) in respect of the same amount of tax, the aggregate of the penalties is restricted to a maximum of the highest percentage of the amount of tax chargeable under any of the provisions (subject to a minimum limit of 100%). Where one of the penalties is a penalty of £300 under *FA 2009, Sch 55*, the maximum aggregate penalty is £300 if that is greater.

[*FA 2014, ss 208(2), 209, 210, 212, Sch 30, Sch 31 paras 4(2), 5(2)–(6); FA 2016, s 158(11), Sch 18 para 60*].

Failure to make accelerated payment

[52.27] Where a person who has been given an accelerated payment notice or partner payment notice (see **4.29** ANTI-AVOIDANCE) fails to pay any amount of the accelerated payment within the time limit (see **4.31** ANTI-AVOIDANCE) an initial penalty of 5% of that amount is chargeable. If any amount is still unpaid at the end of the period of five months beginning with the day after the day on which the time limit expired (the '*penalty day*'), a further penalty of 5% of that amount is chargeable. A further 5% penalty applies to any amount remaining unpaid after the end of the eleven months beginning with the penalty day.

Reduction in special circumstances

HMRC can reduce, stay or agree a compromise in relation to proceedings for a penalty if they think it right to do so because of special circumstances. Ability to pay and the fact that a potential loss of revenue from one taxpayer is balanced by a potential overpayment by another are not special circumstances for this purpose.

Suspension of penalty during time to pay agreement

A taxpayer is not liable to a penalty under the above provisions if, before the penalty arises, he makes a request to HMRC for the deferral of the payment concerned and HMRC agree (whether before or after the penalty date) to the deferral. See **52.5** PAYMENT OF TAX for 'time to pay' arrangements.

The taxpayer remains liable, however, for any penalty which arises after the end of the agreed deferral period. If the taxpayer breaks the agreement then he becomes liable to any penalty to which he would have been liable but for the agreement, provided that HMRC notify him to that effect. For this purpose, a taxpayer breaks an agreement if he fails to pay the accelerated payment when the deferral period ends or if he fails to comply with a condition forming part of the agreement.

Where a deferral agreement is varied, the above rules apply to the agreement as varied from the time of the variation.

Reasonable excuse

None of the above penalties are due in respect of a failure to make a payment if the taxpayer satisfies HMRC or, on appeal, the Tribunal, that there is a reasonable excuse for the failure. Insufficiency of funds is not a reasonable excuse for this purpose and neither is the taxpayer's reliance on another person to do anything, unless he took reasonable care to avoid the failure. If the taxpayer had a reasonable excuse, he is treated as continuing to have a reasonable excuse after the excuse has ceased if the failure is remedied without unreasonable delay.

Double jeopardy

No penalty arises for a failure or action in respect of which the taxpayer has been convicted of an offence.

[*FA 2009, Sch 56 paras 9–10, 16, 17; FA 2014, s 226, Sch 32 para 7*].

Penalties in respect of powers of enforcement by deduction from accounts

[52.28] Under the powers of HMRC to enforce collection of unpaid tax by deduction from the taxpayer's account (see **51.20** PAYMENT OF TAX), a deposit-taker is liable to a penalty of £300 if it:

(a) fails to comply with an information notice;

(b) fails to comply with a hold notice or deduction notice;
(c) fails to comply with an obligation to notify HMRC of the effects of a hold notice;
(d) fails to comply with an obligation to cancel or modify the effect of a hold notice;
(e) fails to comply with an obligation to cancel or adjust arrangements to give effect to HMRC's decision about an objection to a hold notice; or
(f) after receiving an information or hold notice, makes a disclosure of information (other than the required notice) to the taxpayer or any other person which is likely to prejudice HMRC's ability to use their powers to deduct the unpaid tax.

If a failure within (a) to (e) above continues after the day on which notice of a penalty is given, the deposit-taker is liable to a further penalty or penalties of up to £60 per day on which the failure continues.

A failure to comply does not give rise to a penalty if the deposit-taker complies within such further time as HMRC allow. No penalty applies if the deposit-taker satisfies HMRC or the Tribunal that there is a reasonable excuse for the failure or disclosure. Relying on another person to do something is not, for this purpose, a reasonable excuse unless the deposit-taker took reasonable care to avoid the failure or disclosure. Where a reasonable excuse ceases, the deposit-taker is treated as continuing to have the excuse if the failure is remedied without unreasonable delay.

[*F(No 2)A 2015, Sch 8 para 14*].

Penalties under the serial avoiders regime

[52.29] A person is liable to a penalty if he incurs a relevant defeat (see **4.34** ANTI-AVOIDANCE) in relation to any arrangements which he has used whilst in a warning period (see **4.33** ANTI-AVOIDANCE). The time at which a person has 'used' arrangements is determined by *FA 2016, Sch 18 para 55* (see **4.36** ANTI-AVOIDANCE). The standard penalty is 20% of the 'value of the counteracted advantage'. If, before the relevant defeat is incurred, the person has been given (or become liable to be given) 'prior warning notices', the penalty is increased. It is increased to 40% where there has been a single prior warning notice, and to 60% where there has been more than one such notice. A '*prior warning notice*' is a warning notice in relation to the defeat of arrangements which the person has used in the warning period.

If a person incurs simultaneously two or more relevant defeats in relation to different arrangements, then for the purpose of determining the penalty those defeats are placed in order of value, the defeat of greatest value being deemed to be the first incurred; the value of a defeat is the value of the counteracted advantage. If a person has been given a single warning notice in relation to two or more relevant defeats, he is treated for penalty purposes as having been given a separate warning notice in relation to each defeat.

The Commissioners for HMRC have discretion to mitigate a penalty under these provisions, or stay or compound any proceedings for such a penalty. They may also, after judgment, further mitigate or entirely remit the penalty.

Value of the counteracted advantage

The '*value of the counteracted advantage*' is the additional amount of tax due or payable as a result of the counteraction or corrective action. To the extent that the counteracted advantage has resulted in a loss being wrongly recorded or increased but the counteracted loss has not been wholly used to reduce tax payable, the value of the counteracted advantage is increased by 10% of the part of the counteracted loss not so used. However, the value of a counteracted loss is nil if, due to the nature of the loss or the person's circumstances, there is no reasonable prospect of the loss ever being used to reduce the tax liability of any person. To the extent that the counteracted advantage is a deferral of tax, the value of the advantage is 25% of the amount of deferred tax for each year of the deferral, but not so as to exceed 100% of the total amount of deferred tax.

Interaction with other penalties

The amount of a penalty is to be reduced by any other penalty incurred by the person if the amount of that other penalty is determined by reference to the same tax liability. Other penalties do not for this purpose include the GAAR penalty at **52.11** above and the penalties at **52.26** and **52.27** above (follower notices and accelerated payments notices).

Reasonable excuse

A person is not liable to a penalty in respect of a relevant defeat if he satisfies HMRC or, on appeal, the Tribunal that he had a reasonable excuse for the failures or inaccuracies in question. In determining the rate of penalty an earlier warning notice is disregarded if it relates to a relevant defeat in respect of which the person had a reasonable excuse. Otherwise, the same comments apply regarding 'reasonable excuse' as in **4.36** ANTI-AVOIDANCE.

[*FA 2016, Sch 18 paras 30–35, 40, 42–44*].

Failure to comply with requirement to publish tax strategy

[52.30] A company or partnership is liable to a penalty if it is responsible for ensuring that a tax strategy is published as in **14.18** COMPANIES and either:

(i) there is a failure to publish the tax strategy; or
(ii) the tax strategy is published but the requirement for it to remain available to public view free of charge until the next year's strategy is published or (if no such strategy need be published) for at least one year, is not met.

The amount of the penalty is £7,500. Only one penalty can be charged where both (i) and (ii) above apply in respect of a tax strategy for a particular financial year.

A further penalty of £7,500 is chargeable where a failure within (i) above continues for six months and further penalties of £7,500 are chargeable at the end of each subsequent month of continued failure.

A company or partnership is not liable to a penalty for failure to do something within a limited period of time it is done within such further time as HMRC may have allowed.

The Treasury may, by regulations, adjust the £7,500 figure above for inflation.

Reasonable excuse

A company or partnership is not liable to a penalty if it satisfies HMRC or, on appeal, the Tribunal that it had a reasonable excuse for the failure in question. Reasonable excuse does not include insufficiency of funds (unless attributable to events outside the taxpayer's control) or reliance on another person to do anything (unless the taxpayer took reasonable care to avoid the failure or inaccuracy in question or, in the case of a UK group or UK sub-group, where the person relied on is another member of the group or sub-group). A company or partnership with a reasonable excuse is treated as having continued to have it if the failure or inaccuracy in question was remedied without unreasonable delay after the excuse ceased.

[*FA 2016, Sch 19 paras 18, 21, 24, 25, 27, 28, 32*].

Mitigation of penalties

[52.31] The Commissioners for HMRC may mitigate penalties before or after judgment. [*TMA 1970, s 102; FA 2013, Sch 43C para 10; FA 2016, s 157(3), Sch 18 para 44*]. This rule does not apply to penalties under *FA 2007, Sch 24* (see **52.8–52.9** above), *FA 2008, Sch 36* (see **52.16** above) and *Sch 41* (see **52.3** above), *FA 2009, Sch 55* (failure to make returns — see **52.5** above) and *Sch 56* (late payment penalty — see **42.10** LATE PAYMENT INTEREST AND PENALTIES), *FA 2012, Sch 38* (see **52.19** above), *FA 2014, s 208* (see **52.26** above) and *s 226* (see **52.27** above), *FA 2016, Sch 18 Pt 5* (see **52.29** above) and *FA 2016, Sch 22* (asset-based penalty for offshore inaccuracies and failures — see **52.13** above), *F(No 2)A 2017, Sch 16* (see **52.21** above) and *F(No 2)A 2017, Sch 18* (see **52.14** above), which include specific rules for the reduction of penalties in certain cases. [*TMA 1970, s 103ZA*; *FA 2012, Sch 38 para 49; FA 2014, Sch 33 para 2; FA 2016, s 158(10), Sch 18 para 59, Sch 22 para 20(1); F(No 2)A 2017, Sch 16 para 58, Sch 18 para 29(2)*]. A binding agreement by a taxpayer to pay an amount in composition cannot be repudiated afterwards by him or his personal representatives (*A-G v Johnstone* KB 1926, 10 TC 758; *A-G v Midland Bank Executor and Trustee Co Ltd* KB 1934, 19 TC 136; *CIR v Richards* KB 1950, 33 TC 1).

See also **52.2** above as regards *TMA 1970, s 118(2)* (reasonable excuse for failure etc.).

For the validity of tax amnesties, see *R v CIR (ex p. National Federation of Self-Employed and Small Businesses Ltd)* HL 1981, 55 TC 133.

Other HMRC action where a penalty is chargeable

[52.32] Where it is established that a penalty is chargeable HMRC may also take the following actions.

Certificates of full disclosure

HMRC may request that the taxpayer complete a certificate of full disclosure stating that complete disclosure has been made of, inter alia, all banking, savings and loan accounts, deposit receipts, building society accounts and accounts with other financial institutions; all investments including savings certificates and premium bonds and loans (whether interest-bearing or not); all other assets, including cash and life assurance policies, which the taxpayer now possesses, or has possessed, or in which he has or has had any interest or power to operate or control during the stated period; all gifts in any form, by the taxpayer to his spouse, domestic partner, children or other persons during the stated period; all sources of income and all income derived therefrom; and all facts bearing on liability to income tax, capital gains tax and other duties for the stated period. Great care must be exercised before signing such a certificate, since subsequent discovery of an omission could lead to heavy penalties including, in serious cases, criminal prosecution.

Managing deliberate defaulters programme

With effect from February 2011 HMRC have announced that they will closely monitor the tax affairs of individuals and businesses which have deliberately evaded tax for a period of two to five years. Monitoring may include:

- making announced or unannounced inspection visits to carry out pre-return checks of books and records;
- asking for certain records so that they can be checked;
- requiring that additional information or documents are submitted with tax returns;
- conducting in-depth compliance checks into all or any part of the taxpayer's affairs; and
- observing and recording the taxpayer's business activities (e.g. by making test purchases or inspecting supplier or customer records) and cross-checking details in the accounts.

(HMRC Press Notice 22 February 2011).

Procedure

[52.33] *Except* in the case of:

(a) penalties under *FA 2007, Sch 24*, *FA 2008, Schs 36, 41*, *FA 2009, Schs 55, 56*, *FA 2011, Sch 23*, *FA 2012, Sch 38*, *FA 2013, s 212A*, *FA 2015, Sch 21*, *F(No 2)A 2015, Sch 8*, *FA 2016, Schs 18, 19, 20* and *22*, *F(No 2)A 2017, Sch 16* and *F(No 2)A 2017, Sch 18* (see further below) ; or
(b) penalty proceedings instituted before the courts in cases of suspected fraud (see **52.36** below); or
(c) penalties under *TMA 1970, s 98(1)(i)* (£300 penalty for non-filing of returns etc. under the provisions listed in *TMA 1970, s 98* — see **52.23** above); or
(d) penalties under *TMA 1970, s 98C(1)(a)* (penalty of up to £5,000 for failure to disclose tax avoidance scheme — see **52.24** above); or

(e) penalties in respect of which application to the Commissioners is specifically required, as mentioned where relevant in the preceding paragraphs of this chapter (for example, the daily penalty for late income tax and capital gains tax returns as in **52.4** above); or
(f) penalties under *FA 2014, Sch 35* (see **52.25** above) other than daily penalties where the maximum amount is £600; or
(g) penalties under *FA 2014, s 208* and *s 226* (see further below),

an authorised HMRC officer may make a determination imposing a penalty under any tax provision and setting it at such amount as, in his opinion, is correct or appropriate.

The notice of determination must state the date of issue and the time within which an appeal can be made. It cannot be altered unless:

- there is an appeal (see **52.34** below); or
- an authorised HMRC officer discovers that the penalty is or has become insufficient (in which case he may make a further determination); or
- the penalty is an automatic or tax-related penalty under *TMA 1970, s 93* (late delivery of personal or trustees' tax returns — see **52.4** above) or arises under *TMA 1970, s 94(6)* or *FA 1998, Sch 18 para 18(2)* (tax-related penalty for late filing of company tax returns — see **52.4** above), and an authorised HMRC officer subsequently discovers that the amount of tax is or has become excessive (in which case it is to be revised accordingly).

A penalty under these provisions is due for payment 30 days after the issue of the notice of determination, and is treated as tax charged in an assessment which is due and payable. Before the date fixed for the implementation of the penalties at **52.8** and **52.10** above, a determination which could have been made on a person who has died can be made on his personal representatives, and is then payable out of his estate.

[*TMA 1970, ss 100, 100A, 103ZA; FA 2012, Sch 38 para 49; FA 2014, Sch 33 para 2, FA 2015, s 18; FA 2016, s 158(10), Sch 18 para 59, Sch 22 para 20(1); F(No 2)2017, Sch 16 para 58, Sch 18 para 29(2); SI 1994 No 1813*].

Penalties under *FA 2007, Sch 24* and *FA 2008, Sch 41*

Penalties under *FA 2007, Sch 24* (see **52.8–52.9** above) and *FA 2008, Sch 41* (see **52.3** above) are charged by HMRC assessment. The assessment is treated in the same way as an assessment to tax and can be enforced accordingly. It may also be combined with a tax assessment. The notice of assessment must state the accounting period or tax year in respect of which the penalty is assessed. Subject to the time limits below, HMRC can make a supplementary assessment if an existing assessment operates by reference to an underestimate of the 'potential lost revenue' (see **52.3** and **52.8** above).

Penalties must be paid before the end of the period of 30 days beginning with the day on which the notification of the penalty is issued.

An assessment of a penalty within **52.3** above must be made before the end of the twelve months beginning with the end of the 'appeal period' for the assessment of tax unpaid by reason of the failure or, where there is no such assessment, the date on which the amount of tax unpaid by reason of the failure is ascertained.

An assessment of a penalty within **52.8** or **52.9** above must be made before the end of the twelve months beginning with the end of the 'appeal period' for the decision correcting the inaccuracy or, where there is no assessment correcting it, the date on which the inaccuracy is corrected.

The '*appeal period*' is the period during which an appeal could be brought or during which an appeal that has been brought has not been determined or withdrawn.

An assessment of a penalty within **52.10** above must be made before the end of the twelve months beginning with the end of the appeal period for the tax assessment which corrected the understatement (or, if there is no such assessment, the date on which the understatement is corrected).

[*FA 2007, Sch 24 paras 13, 28; FA 2008, s 123, Sch 41 para 16; FA 2013, Sch 50 para 1*].

Penalties under *FA 2008, Sch 36*

Fixed and daily penalties (other than increased daily penalties imposed by the Tribunal) for failure to comply or obstruction and penalties for inaccuracies (see **52.16** above) are charged by HMRC assessment. The penalty can be enforced as if it were income tax charged in an assessment. An assessment to a fixed or daily penalty must be made within twelve months of the date on which the liability arose. Where, however, the penalty is for a failure relating to an information notice against which a person can appeal, the assessment must be made within twelve months of the later of the end of the period in which notice of such appeal could have been given and, where an appeal is made, the date on which the appeal is determined or withdrawn. An assessment to a penalty for an inaccuracy must be made within twelve months of HMRC first becoming aware of the inaccuracy and within six years of the person becoming liable to the penalty. The penalty must be paid within the 30-day period beginning with the date on which HMRC issue notification of the penalty assessment or, if an appeal against the penalty is made, within the 30-day period beginning with the date on which the appeal is determined or withdrawn.

A liability to an increased daily penalty imposed by the Tribunal or to a tax-related penalty is notified by HMRC to the person liable and may be enforced as if it were income tax charged in an assessment. It must be paid within the 30-day period beginning with the date on which the notification is issued.

[*FA 2008, Sch 36 paras 46, 49, 49B, 49C, 50(4), 51*].

Penalties under *FA 2009, Sch 55*

Penalties under *FA 2009, Sch 55* (failure to make return — see **52.5** above) are charged by HMRC assessment. The assessment is treated in the same way as an assessment to tax and can be enforced accordingly. It may also be combined with a tax assessment. The notice of assessment must state the period in respect of which the penalty is charged. Subject to the time limits below, HMRC can make a supplementary assessment if an existing assessment operates by reference to an underestimate of the tax liability. Similarly, for defaults relating to 2013/14 and earlier years, a replacement assessment can be made where an assessment operates by reference to an overestimate. For defaults relating to 2014/15 onwards, in such cases, the procedure is for HMRC to amend the existing assessment. Such an amendment does not affect when the penalty must be paid, and can be made even if the time limit for making the assessment has passed.

Penalties must be paid before the end of the period of 30 days beginning with the day on which the notification of the penalty is issued.

An assessment must be made on or before the later of:

(1) the last day of the two years beginning with the filing date; and
(2) the last day of the twelve months beginning with the end of the appeal period (as above) for the assessment of the tax liability which would have been shown in the return or, if no such return has been made, the date on which that liability is ascertained (or is ascertained to be nil).

These time limits do not, however, apply to a re-assessment of a tax-geared penalty following the submission of the late tax return (see **52.5** above).

[*FA 2009, Sch 55 paras 18, 19; FA 2013, Sch 50 paras 7, 8*].

Penalties under *FA 2009, Sch 56* and *FA 2014, s 226*

Penalties under *FA 2009, Sch 56* (late payment penalty — see **42.10** LATE PAYMENT INTEREST AND PENALTIES) are charged by HMRC assessment. The assessment is treated in the same way as an assessment to tax and can be enforced accordingly. It may also be combined with a tax assessment. The notice of assessment must state the period in respect of which the penalty is charged. Subject to the time limits below, HMRC can make a supplementary assessment if an existing assessment operates by reference to an underestimate of an amount of unpaid tax. Similarly, for defaults relating to 2013/14 and earlier years, a replacement assessment can be made where an assessment operates by reference to an overestimate. For defaults relating to 2014/15 onwards, in such cases, the procedure is for HMRC to amend the existing assessment. Such an amendment does not affect when the penalty must be paid, and can be made even if the time limit for making the assessment has passed.

Penalties must be paid before the end of the period of 30 days beginning with the day on which the notification of the penalty is issued.

An assessment must be made on or before the later of:

(1) the last date on which payment could have been made without incurring a penalty (i.e. the last day of the two years beginning with the date specified in the table at **42.10** LATE PAYMENT INTEREST AND PENALTIES); and

(2) the last day of the twelve months beginning with the end of the appeal period (as above) for the assessment of the tax in respect of which the penalty is assessed or, if no such assessment, the date on which that tax is ascertained.

These time limits do not, however, apply to a re-assessment of a tax-geared penalty following the payment of the tax.

[*FA 2009, Sch 56 paras 11, 12; FA 2013, Sch 50 paras 14, 16(3)*].

The above provisions apply, with any necessary modifications, to penalties under *FA 2014, s 226* (see **52.27** above). [*FA 2014, s 226(7)*].

Penalties under *FA 2011, Sch 23*

Fixed and daily penalties (other than an increased daily penalty imposed by the Tribunal before 15 September 2016) for failure to comply and penalties for inaccuracies (see **52.17** above) are charged by HMRC assessment. An increased daily penalty imposed by the Tribunal on or after 15 September 2016 is also charged by HMRC assessment and HMRC must notify the data-holder of the increased daily amount and the date from which it applies. The penalty can be enforced as if it were income tax charged in an assessment. An assessment to a fixed or daily penalty must be made within twelve months of the date on which the liability arose. Where, however, the penalty is for a failure relating to a data-holder notice against which a person can appeal, the assessment must be made within twelve months of the later of the end of the period in which notice of such appeal could have been given and, where an appeal is made, the date on which the appeal is determined or withdrawn (if that date is later than the date on which the liability arose). An assessment to a penalty for an inaccuracy must be made within twelve months of HMRC first becoming aware of the inaccuracy and within six years of the person becoming liable to the penalty. The penalty must be paid within the 30-day period beginning with the date on which HMRC issue notification of the penalty assessment or, if an appeal against the penalty is made, within the 30-day period beginning with the date on which the appeal is determined or withdrawn.

A liability to an increased daily penalty imposed by the Tribunal before 15 September 2016 is notified by HMRC to the person liable and may be enforced as if it were income tax charged in an assessment. It must be paid within the 30-day period beginning with the date on which the notification is issued.

[*FA 2011, Sch 23 paras 35, 38–40; FA 2016, s 177(2)–(4)*].

Penalties under *FA 2012, Sch 38*

Fixed and daily penalties under the dishonest conduct provisions at **52.19** above are charged by HMRC assessment. The penalty can be enforced as if it were income tax charged in an assessment. An assessment to a fixed or daily penalty under *FA 2012, Sch 38 paras 22, 23* (failure to comply with file access notice) must be made within twelve months of the date on which the liability arose. An assessment to a penalty under *FA 2012, Sch 38 para 26* (dishonest conduct) must be made within twelve months of the later of the first day on which HMRC may assess the penalty and 'day X'. If there is no loss of tax revenue as a result of the dishonest conduct, '*day X*' is the day on which HMRC ascertain that no tax revenue has been lost. If there is a loss of tax revenue, '*day X*' is the day immediately following the end of the 'appeal period' for the assessment or determination of the tax revenue lost (or the last such day) or, if there is no such assessment or determination, the day on which the amount of lost revenue is ascertained. The '*appeal period*' is the period during which an appeal could be brought or during which an appeal that has been brought has not been withdrawn or determined.

The penalty must be paid within the 30-day period beginning with the date on which HMRC issue notification of the penalty assessment or, if an appeal against the penalty is made, within the 30-day period beginning with the date on which the appeal is determined or withdrawn.

[*FA 2012, Sch 38 paras 29(1)(4), 30, 32*].

Penalties under *FA 2013, s 212A*

Penalties under *FA 2013, s 212A* (see **52.11** above) are charged by HMRC assessment. The assessment is treated in the same way as an assessment to tax and can be enforced accordingly. It may also be combined with a tax assessment. The notice of assessment must state the accounting period or tax year in respect of which the penalty is assessed. Subject to the time limits below, HMRC can make a supplementary assessment if an existing assessment operates by reference to an underestimate of the value of the counteracted advantage (see **52.11** above) and an assessment may be revised if it overestimates that value. Where, following the making of a penalty assessment, consequential adjustments are made (see **4.3** ANTI-AVOIDANCE under 'Effect of the GAAR'), HMRC must make any just and reasonable alterations to the penalty assessment to take account of those adjustments, and may do so regardless of any time limits which would otherwise prevent them.

An assessment to a penalty must be made within the twelve months beginning with the end of the appeal period for the assessment giving effect to the counteraction under the GAAR (see **4.3** ANTI-AVOIDANCE) or, if there is no such assessment, the twelve months beginning with the latest of the dates on which the counteraction becomes final. For this purpose, counteraction becomes final when the adjustments made, and any amounts resulting from them, can no longer be varied, on appeal or otherwise.

Penalties must be paid before the end of the period of 30 days beginning with the day on which the notification of the penalty is issued.

[*FA 2013, Sch 43C paras 5–7; FA 2016, s 158(3)*].

Penalties under *FA 2014, s 208*

Penalties under *FA 2014, s 208* (see **52.26** above) are charged by HMRC assessment. The assessment is treated in the same way as an assessment to tax and can be enforced accordingly. It may also be combined with a tax assessment. The notice of assessment must state the accounting period or tax year in respect of which the penalty is assessed. Subject to the time limits below, HMRC can make a supplementary assessment if an existing assessment operates by reference to an underestimate of the value of the denied tax advantage (see **52.26** above).

Penalties must be paid before the end of the period of 30 days beginning with the day on which the notification of the penalty is issued.

Where the follower notice (see **4.25** ANTI-AVOIDANCE) was given whilst an enquiry was in progress, an assessment of a penalty must be made before the end of the period of 90 days beginning with the day the enquiry is completed. Where the follower notice was given whilst an appeal was open, an assessment of a penalty must be made before the end of the period of 90 days beginning with the earliest of the day on which the taxpayer takes the necessary corrective action (see **4.27** ANTI-AVOIDANCE), the day on which a ruling is made on the appeal or further appeal which is a final ruling (see **4.25** ANTI-AVOIDANCE) and the day on which the appeal, or further appeal, is abandoned or otherwise disposed of before being finally determined.

[*FA 2014, ss 211, 213*].

Penalties under *FA 2015, Sch 21*

The offshore asset moves penalty at **52.12** above is charged by HMRC assessment. The penalty can be enforced as if it were an assessment to tax. The time within which an assessment must be made is the same as that allowed for the assessment of the 'original penalty' (see **52.12**) to which the offshore asset moves penalty is linked. If, after an offshore asset moves penalty is assessed, the amount of the original penalty changes (because HMRC either amend the assessment of it or make a supplementary assessment), HMRC must similarly amend the offshore asset moves assessment, or make a supplementary assessment, to ensure that it is based on the correct amount of the original penalty. The offshore asset moves penalty must be paid within the 30-day period beginning with the date on which HMRC issue the notice of assessment. [*FA 2015, Sch 21 paras 7, 9*].

Penalties under *F(No 2)A 2015, Sch 8*

Fixed and daily penalties under the enforcement of tax debts by deduction from accounts provisions at **52.28** above are charged by HMRC assessment. The penalty can be enforced as if it were income tax charged in an assessment. An assessment to a penalty within **52.28**(a) above must be made within 12 months beginning with the date on which the liability to the penalty arose. An assessment to a penalty within **52.28**(b)–(f) above must be made within 12 months beginning with the latest of the date on which the liability to the penalty arose, the end of the period in which an appeal against the hold notice could have been made and, if such an appeal is made, the date on which the appeal is finally determined or withdrawn.

The penalty must be paid within the 30-day period beginning with the date on which HMRC issue notification of the penalty assessment or, if an appeal against the penalty is made, within the 30-day period beginning with the date on which the appeal is finally determined or withdrawn.

[*F(No 2)A 2015, Sch 8 paras 15, 17*].

Penalties under FA 2016, Sch 18

Penalties under *FA 2016, Sch 18* (see **52.29** above) are charged by HMRC assessment. The assessment is treated in the same way as an assessment to tax and can be enforced accordingly. It may also be combined with a tax assessment. The notice of assessment must state the period in respect of which the penalty is assessed. HMRC can make a supplementary assessment if an earlier assessment underestimated the value of the counteracted advantage, and an assessment can be revised if it overestimated that value.

The penalty must be paid within the 30 days beginning with the date of issue of the notice of assessment.

The assessment itself must be made within the 12 months beginning with the date of the relevant defeat in question.

[*FA 2016, Sch 18 paras 38, 39*].

Penalties under FA 2016, Sch 19

Penalties under *FA 2016, Sch 19* (see **52.30** above) are charged by HMRC assessment. The penalty can be enforced as if it were corporation tax charged in an assessment.

The penalty must be paid within the 30 days beginning with the date of issue of the notice of assessment or, if an appeal is made, within the 30 days beginning with the day on which the appeal is determined or withdrawn.

The assessment itself must be made within the six months after the failure first comes to the attention of an HMRC officer and cannot be made more than six years after the end of the financial year to which the failure relates.

[*FA 2016, Sch 19 paras 29, 31*].

Penalties under *FA 2016, Sch 20*

Penalties under *FA 2016, Sch 20* (see **52.20** above) are charged by HMRC assessment. The assessment is treated in the same way as an assessment to tax and can be enforced accordingly. The notice of assessment must state the period in respect of which the penalty is assessed. Subject to the time limit below, HMRC can make a supplementary assessment if an existing assessment operates by reference to an underestimate of tax that would have been shown on a return. If an assessment is based on a liability to tax that would have been shown in a return and that liability is found by HMRC to have been excessive, HMRC may amend the assessment accordingly, and may do so after the normal time limit for making the assessment has expired. Such an amendment does not affect when the penalty must be paid.

An assessment must be made no more than two years after the fulfilment of the conditions at **52.20**(a) and (b) above first came to the attention of an HMRC officer.

Penalties must be paid before the end of the period of 30 days beginning with the day on which the notification of the penalty is issued.

[*FA 2016, Sch 20 paras 10, 11*].

Penalties under *FA 2016, Sch 22*

Penalties under *FA 2016, Sch 22* (asset-based penalty for offshore inaccuracies and failures — see **52.13** above) are charged by HMRC assessment. The assessment is treated in the same way as (and can be combined with) an assessment to tax and can be enforced accordingly. The notice of assessment must state the tax year in respect of which the penalty is assessed and the investigation period (see **52.13**) in which that tax year falls. An assessment must be made within the period allowed for making an assessment of the offshore tax penalty to which the asset-based penalty relates (or, where the asset-based penalty relates to more than one offshore tax penalty, within the latest of those periods). Penalties must be paid within the 30-day period beginning with the day on which the notice of assessment is issued. [*FA 2016, Sch 22 para 15*].

Penalties under *F(No 2)A 2017, Sch 16*

Penalties under *F(No 2)A 2017, Sch 16* (enabling defeated tax avoidance — see **52.21** above) are charged by HMRC assessment. The assessment is treated in the same way as an assessment to tax and can be enforced accordingly. Penalties must be paid within the 30-day period beginning with the day on which the notice of assessment is issued.

An assessment to a penalty may not be made after whichever of the following times applies:

(i) where a GAAR final decision notice has been given in relation to the arrangements in question (see **52.21**(A) above), the end of 12 months beginning with the date on which T incurs the defeat;
(ii) where a GAAR final decision notice has been given in relation to equivalent arrangements and HMRC have given a notice stating their view that it is relevant to the arrangements in question (see **52.21**(A) above), the end of 12 months beginning with the end of the time allowed for representations in respect of that notice;
(iii) where HMRC have made a referral to the GAAR Advisory Panel (see **52.21**(B) above) in respect of the arrangements in question and (iv) below does not apply, the end of 12 months beginning with the date on which the Panel's opinion is given;
(iv) where the taxpayer was not given a notice within **52.21**(1) above before the referral of arrangements to the GAAR Advisory Panel but HMRC have given a notice stating their view that its opinion applies to the arrangements in question (see **52.21**(B) above), the end of 12 months beginning with the end of the time allowed for representations in respect of that notice.

If HMRC cannot assess a penalty until more than 50% of arrangements which are substantially the same have incurred a defeat, the time limit is extended to the end of the 12 months beginning with the date on which the required percentage is reached. If, in such a case, a person requests assessment of the penalty before the percentage is reached, the assessment must be made before the end of the 12 months beginning with the date of the request. If a declaration that a person is not liable to a penalty has been made by a lawyer under the provisions for privileged communications and facts then come to HMRC's knowledge that in their opinion are sufficient to indicate that the declaration contained a material inaccuracy, the deadline for assessing the penalty is extended to the end of the 12 months beginning with the date on which the facts come to HMRC's knowledge.

[*F(No 2)A 2017, Sch 16 paras 19(1), 20, 22*].

Penalties under *F(No 2)A 2017, Sch 18*

Penalties under *F(No 2)A 2017, Sch 18* (failure to correct offshore tax non-compliance — see **52.14** above) are charged by HMRC assessment. The assessment is treated in the same way as an assessment to tax (and may be combined with an assessment to tax) and can be enforced accordingly. The notice of assessment must state the uncorrected offshore tax non-compliance to which the penalty relates and the tax year to which that non-compliance relates. Subject to the time limit below, HMRC can make a supplementary assessment if an existing assessment operates by reference to an underestimate of the tax liability. If an assessment is based on a tax liability found by HMRC to have been excessive, HMRC may amend the assessment accordingly, and may do so after the normal time limit for making the assessment has expired, but the amendment does not affect when the penalty must be paid. Penalties must be paid within the 30-day period beginning with the day on which the notice of assessment is issued.

Where the non-compliance is the delivery of a tax document containing an inaccuracy, the assessment must be made before the end of the 12 months beginning with the end of the 'appeal period' for the decision correcting the inaccuracy or, if there is no assessment to tax, the date on which the inaccuracy is corrected. In other cases, the assessment must be made before the end of the 12 months beginning with the end of the appeal period for the assessment of tax unpaid by reason of the non-compliance, or where there is no such assessment, the date on which the amount of tax unpaid by reason of the non-compliance is ascertained. The 'appeal period' is the period during which an appeal could be brought or during which an appeal that has been brought has not been determined or withdrawn.

[*F(No 2)A 2017, Sch 18 paras 18, 19*].

Appeals

[52.34] Subject to the following points, the general APPEALS (5) provisions apply to an appeal against a determination of a penalty as in **52.33** above.

TMA 1970, s 50(6)–(8) (see **5.20** APPEALS) do not apply. Instead (subject to below), on appeal the First-tier Tribunal can:

- in the case of a penalty which is required to be of a particular amount, set the determination aside, confirm it, or alter it to the correct amount; and

- in any other case, set the determination aside, confirm it if it seems appropriate, or reduce it (including to nil) or increase it as seems appropriate (but not beyond the permitted maximum).

Neither *TMA 1970, s 50(6)–(8)* nor the above apply on an appeal against a determination of an automatic late filing penalty for personal or partnership tax returns (see **52.4**, **51.5** above), where the 'reasonable excuse' let-out may have effect (see **52.4** above for the options open to the Tribunal in those cases).

In addition to the right to appeal to the Upper Tribunal on a point of law, the taxpayer can so appeal (with permission) against the amount of a penalty determined by the First-tier Tribunal.

[*TMA 1970, ss 100B, 103ZA; FA 2012, Sch 38 para 49; FA 2014, Sch 33 para 2, FA 2016, s 158(10), Sch 18 para 59, Sch 22 para 20(1); F(No 2)A 2017, Sch 16 para 58, Sch 18 para 29(2); SI 2009 No 571, Sch; SI 2009 No 56, Sch 1 para 45*].

Penalties under *FA 2007, Sch 24* and *FA 2008, Sch 41*

Assessments of penalties under *FA 2007, Sch 24* (see **52.8–52.9** above) and *FA 2008, Sch 41* (see **52.3** above) are subject to specific appeal provisions. An appeal can be made against an HMRC decision that a penalty is payable or against a decision as to the amount of a penalty. In relation to penalties within **52.8** above, an appeal can be made against a decision not to suspend a penalty or against conditions of suspension.

The powers of the Tribunal are restricted in certain cases, to where it thinks that HMRC's decision was flawed when considered in the light of principles applicable in proceedings for judicial review. The decisions concerned are as follows:

- a decision as to the extent to which the provisions for reduction of a penalty in special circumstances apply;
- a decision not to suspend a penalty; and
- a decision as to the conditions of suspension.

See **52.8** above for cases in which an appeal to the Tribunal for a reduction in a penalty by reason of special circumstances was successful.

Where the Tribunal orders HMRC to suspend a penalty, there is a further right of appeal against the provisions of HMRC's notice of suspension. [*FA 2007, Sch 24 paras 15–17; FA 2008, s 123, Sch 41 paras 17–19; SI 2009 No 56, Sch 1 paras 466, 467, 473*].

Penalties under *FA 2008, Sch 36*

Appeals can be brought to the First-tier Tribunal against an HMRC decision that a penalty other than a tax-related penalty (see **52.16** above) is payable or against a decision as to the amount of such a penalty. Notice of appeal must be given in writing within the 30-day period beginning with the date on which HMRC notification of the penalty assessment is issued, and must state the grounds of appeal. Subject to this, the general APPEALS (5) provisions apply as they apply to income tax assessments. [*FA 2008, Sch 36 paras 47, 48; FA 2009, Sch 46 paras 18, 19*].

Penalties under *FA 2009, Sch 55*

Assessments of penalties under *FA 2009, Sch 55* (failure to make return — see **52.5** above) are subject to specific appeal provisions. An appeal can be made against an HMRC decision that a penalty is payable or against a decision as to the amount of a penalty. An appeal is treated in the same way as an appeal against an assessment to the tax concerned (but not so as to require payment of the penalty before the appeal is determined).

The powers of the Tribunal on appeal are restricted in relation to HMRC's use of the provisions for reduction of a penalty because of special circumstances. The Tribunal may apply the special reduction provisions to an extent different from HMRC's decision only if it thinks that HMRC's decision was flawed when considered in the light of principles applicable in judicial review cases.

In partnership cases, an appeal can be brought only by the partner required to make the return or his successor. Such an appeal is treated as an appeal against every penalty payable by any partner in respect of the failure concerned. This provision was applied in *Dyson v HMRC* FTT [2015] SFTD 529, despite the Tribunal holding that it contravened the European Convention on Human Rights

[*FA 2009, Sch 55 paras 20–22, 25(4)(5)*].

Penalties under *FA 2009, Sch 56* and *FA 2014, s 226*

Assessments of penalties under *FA 2009, Sch 56* (late payment penalty— see **42.10** LATE PAYMENT INTEREST AND PENALTIES) are also subject to specific appeal provisions. An appeal can be made against an HMRC decision that a penalty is payable or against a decision as to the amount of a penalty. An appeal is treated in the same way as an appeal against an assessment to the tax concerned (but not so as to require payment of the penalty before the appeal is determined).

The powers of the Tribunal on appeal are restricted in relation to HMRC's use of the provisions for reduction of a penalty because of special circumstances. The Tribunal may apply the special reduction provisions to an extent different from HMRC's decision only if it thinks that HMRC's decision was flawed when considered in the light of principles applicable in judicial review cases.

[*FA 2009, Sch 56 paras 13–15*].

The above provisions apply, with any necessary modifications, to penalties under *FA 2014, s 226* (see **52.27** above). [*FA 2014, s 226(7)*].

Penalties under *FA 2011, Sch 23*

Appeals can be brought to the First-tier Tribunal against an HMRC decision that a penalty is payable or against a decision as to the amount of such a penalty. No such appeal could be made against an increased daily penalty imposed by the Tribunal before 15 September 2016 (see **52.17** above); and no appeal can be made against the amount of such a penalty imposed on or after that date. Notice of appeal must be given in writing within the 30-day period beginning with the date on which HMRC notification of the penalty assessment is issued, and must state the grounds of appeal. Subject to this, the general APPEALS (5) provisions apply as they apply to income tax assessments. [*FA 2011, Sch 23 paras 36, 37; FA 2016, s 177(5)*].

Penalties under *FA 2012, Sch 38*

Assessments of penalties under *FA 2012, Sch 38* (dishonest conduct by tax agents (see **52.19** above)) are also subject to specific appeal provisions. An appeal can be made against the imposition of a penalty under *FA 2012, Sch 38 paras 22, 23* (failure to comply with file access notice) or against the amount of a penalty under *FA 2012, Sch 38 paras 22, 23* or *FA 2012, Sch 38 para 26* (dishonest conduct). Notice of appeal must be given in writing within the 30-day period beginning with the date on which HMRC notification of the penalty assessment is issued, and must state the grounds of appeal.

If the appeal is against the imposition of a penalty and it goes to the Tribunal, the Tribunal may affirm or cancel HMRC's decision to impose. If the appeal is against the amount of a penalty and it goes to the Tribunal, the Tribunal may affirm the amount charged or substitute its own amount (but only an amount that HMRC could have chosen to charge). Subject to this, the general APPEALS (5) provisions apply as they apply to income tax assessments

The powers of the Tribunal on appeal are restricted in relation to HMRC's use of the provision for reduction of a penalty because of special circumstances. The Tribunal may apply the special reduction provisions to an extent different from HMRC's decision only if it thinks that HMRC's decision was flawed when considered in the light of principles applicable in judicial review cases.

[*FA 2012, Sch 38 para 31*].

Penalties under *FA 2013, s 212A*

Assessments of penalties under *FA 2013, s 212A* (counteraction under GAAR (see **52.11** above)) are also subject to specific appeal provisions. An appeal can be made against the imposition of a penalty or against the amount of a penalty. An appeal must be made within the 30-day period beginning with the date on which HMRC notification of the penalty assessment is issued. An appeal against the imposition of a penalty can only be made on the grounds that the arrangements concerned were not abusive or that there was no tax advantage to be counteracted (see **4.3** ANTI-AVOIDANCE). An appeal against the amount of a penalty can only be made on the grounds that the penalty is based on an overestimate of the counteracted advantage (see **52.11** above).

If the appeal is against the imposition of a penalty and it is heard by the Tribunal, the Tribunal may affirm or cancel HMRC's decision to impose the penalty. If the appeal is against the amount of a penalty and it is heard by the Tribunal, the Tribunal may affirm the amount charged or substitute its own amount (but only an amount that HMRC could have chosen to charge). Subject to this, the general APPEALS (5) provisions apply as they apply to assessments to the tax concerned, but not so as to require payment of the penalty before any appeal is determined.

[*FA 2013, Sch 43C para 9; FA 2016, s 158(3)*].

Penalties under *FA 2014, s 208*

Assessments of penalties under *FA 2014, s 208* (failure to comply with follower notice (see **52.26** above)) are also subject to specific appeal provisions. An appeal can be made against the imposition of a penalty or against the amount of a penalty. No appeal can be made, however, against the apportionment of a penalty between partners. An appeal must be made within the 30-day period beginning with the date on which HMRC notification of the penalty assessment is issued. An appeal against a penalty in respect of a partnership follower notice must be made by the representative partner or his successor.

The grounds on which an appeal can be made include in particular that the conditions for giving the follower notice at **4.26**(a), (b) or (d) ANTI-AVOIDANCE were not satisfied; that the judicial ruling is not relevant to the arrangements which are the subject of the notice; that the notice was given outside the time limit; and that it was reasonable in all the circumstances not to take the necessary corrective action (see **4.27** ANTI-AVOIDANCE).

If the appeal is against the imposition of a penalty and it is heard by the Tribunal, the Tribunal may affirm or cancel HMRC's decision to impose the penalty. If the appeal is against the amount of a penalty and it is heard by the Tribunal, the Tribunal may affirm the amount charged or substitute its own amount (but only an amount that HMRC could have chosen to charge). Subject to this, the general APPEALS (5) provisions apply as they apply to assessments to the tax concerned. The cancellation of HMRC's decision to impose a penalty on the grounds that it was reasonable not to take the corrective action does not affect the validity of the follower notice nor of any accelerated payment notice or partner payment notice (see **4.29** ANTI-AVOIDANCE) related to the follower notice.

[*FA 2014, s 214, Sch 31 para 5(7)–(10)*].

Penalties under *FA 2015, Sch 21*

An appeal may be made against a decision by HMRC to impose an offshore asset moves penalty (see **52.12** above). If the appeal goes to the Tribunal, the Tribunal may affirm or cancel HMRC's decision. Subject to this, the general APPEALS (5) provisions apply as they apply to capital gains tax assessments. [*FA 2015, Sch 21 paras 8, 9*].

Penalties under *F(No 2)A 2015, Sch 8*

An appeal can be made against the imposition of a penalty under *F(No 2)A 2015, Sch 8 para 14* (enforcement of tax debts by deduction from accounts) or against the amount of such a penalty. Notice of appeal must be given in writing within the 30-day period beginning with the date on which the HMRC notification of the penalty assessment is issued and must state the grounds of appeal.

If the appeal is against the imposition of a penalty, the Tribunal may affirm or cancel HMRC's decision to impose. If the appeal is against the amount of the penalty, the Tribunal may affirm the amount charged or substitute its own amount (but only an amount that HMRC had the power to charge). Subject to this, the general APPEALS (5) provisions apply as they apply to income tax assessments.

[*F(No 2)A 2015, Sch 8 para 16*].

Penalties under FA 2016, Sch 18

An appeal can be made against the imposition of a penalty under *FA 2016, Sch 18* (see **52.29** above) or against the amount of a penalty. It must be made within the 30 days beginning with the date of issue of the notice of assessment. The appeal is to be treated in the same way as an appeal against an assessment to the tax at stake (including in relation to making the appeal , HMRC review and determination by the Tribunal) but not so as to require payment before the appeal is determined. The Tribunal, on an appeal brought before it, may affirm HMRC's decision in relation to the penalty or may substitute for HMRC's decision another decision that HMRC has power to make.

[*FA 2016, Sch 18 para 41*].

Penalties under FA 2016, Sch 19

An appeal can be made against the imposition of a penalty under *FA 2016, Sch 19* (see **52.30** above). It must be made within the 30 days beginning with the date of issue of the notice of assessment. The appeal is to be treated in the same way as an appeal against an assessment to income tax but not so as to require payment before the appeal is determined. The Tribunal, on an appeal brought before it, may confirm or cancel HMRC's decision to impose the penalty. [*FA 2016, Sch 19 para 30*].

Penalties under *FA 2016, Sch 20*

An appeal can be made against the imposition of a penalty under *FA 2016, Sch 20* (enabling offshore tax evasion) or against the amount of such a penalty. An appeal is treated in the same way as an appeal against an assessment to the tax at stake (including in relation to making the appeal , HMRC review and determination by the Tribunal) but not so as to require payment before the appeal is determined.

If the appeal is against the imposition of a penalty, the Tribunal may affirm or cancel HMRC's decision to impose. If the appeal is against the amount of the penalty, the Tribunal may affirm the amount charged or substitute its own amount (but only an amount that HMRC had the power to charge). The Tribunal may substitute its own decision on any reduction for disclosure or assistance or for special circumstances only if it thinks that HMRC's decision was flawed in the light of the principles applicable to judicial review (see **5.35** APPEALS).

[*FA 2016, Sch 20 paras 12–14*].

Penalties under *FA 2016, Sch 22*

An appeal can be made against the imposition of a penalty under *FA 2016, Sch 22* (asset-based penalty for offshore inaccuracies and failures — see **52.13** above) or against the amount of such a penalty. An appeal is treated in the same way as an appeal against an assessment to the tax concerned but not so as to require payment before the appeal is determined. If the appeal is against the imposition of a penalty and it goes to the Tribunal, the Tribunal may affirm or cancel HMRC's decision to impose. If the appeal is against the amount of the penalty and it goes to the Tribunal, the Tribunal may affirm the amount charged or substitute its own amount (but only an amount that HMRC had the power to charge). The Tribunal has power to make a reduction for special circumstances to the same extent as HMRC, which may mean applying the same percentage reduction as HMRC but to a different starting point. It may make a reduction to a different extent to HMRC, but only if it thinks that HMRC's decision was flawed when considered in the light of the principles applicable in proceedings for judicial review. [*FA 2016, Sch 22 paras 16–18*].

Penalties under *F(No 2)A 2017, Sch 16*

An appeal can be made against the imposition of a penalty under *F(No 2)A 2017, Sch 16* (enabling defeated tax avoidance — see **52.21** above) or against the amount of such a penalty. An appeal is treated in the same way as an appeal against an assessment to the tax concerned but not so as to require payment before the appeal is determined. If the appeal is against the imposition of a penalty and it goes to the Tribunal, the Tribunal may affirm or cancel HMRC's decision to impose. If the appeal is against the amount of a penalty and it is heard by the Tribunal, the Tribunal may affirm the amount charged or substitute its own amount (but only an amount that HMRC could have chosen to charge). If the Tribunal substitutes its own amount, it must rely on the provision to mitigate the penalty to the same extent as HMRC, which may mean applying the same percentage reduction as HMRC but to a different starting point. It may make a reduction to a different extent to HMRC, but only if it thinks that HMRC's decision was flawed when considered in the light of the principles applicable in proceedings for judicial review. [*F(No 2)A 2017, Sch 16 paras 36–39*].

Penalties under *F(No 2)A 2017, Sch 18*

An appeal can be made against the imposition of a penalty under *F(No 2)A 2017, Sch 18* (failure to correct offshore tax non-compliance — see **52.14** above) or against the amount of such a penalty. An appeal is treated in the same way as an appeal against an assessment to the tax concerned but not so as to require payment before the appeal is determined. If the appeal is against the imposition of a penalty and it goes to the Tribunal, the Tribunal may affirm or cancel HMRC's decision to impose. If the appeal is against the amount of a penalty and it goes to the Tribunal, the Tribunal may affirm the amount charged or substitute its own amount (but only an amount that HMRC had the power to charge). The Tribunal has power to make a reduction for disclosure or special circumstances to the same extent as HMRC, which may mean applying the same percentage reduction as HMRC but to a different starting point. It may make a reduction to a different extent to HMRC, but only if it thinks that HMRC's decision was flawed when considered in the light of the principles applicable in proceedings for judicial review. [*F(No 2)A 2017, Sch 18 paras 20–22*].

Proceedings before Tribunal

[52.35] For a penalty within **52.33**(c) above or a penalty within **52.25** above (other than a daily penalty where the maximum amount is £600), an authorised HMRC officer can commence proceedings before the First-tier Tribunal. The taxpayer will be a party to the proceedings. In addition to the right to appeal to the Upper Tribunal on a point of law, the taxpayer can so appeal (with permission) against the amount of a penalty determined by the First-tier Tribunal. A similar right of appeal to the High Court (in Scotland, the Court of Session) applied before 1 April 2009. The Upper Tribunal (or court) can set the determination aside, confirm it if it seems appropriate, or reduce it (including to nil) or increase it as seems appropriate (but not beyond the permitted maximum). The penalty is treated as tax charged in an assessment and due and payable. [*TMA 1970, s 100C; SI 2009 No 56, Sch 1 para 46*].

Proceedings before court

[52.36] If the Commissioners for HMRC consider that liability for a penalty arises from fraud by any person, proceedings can be brought in the High Court (or Court of Session). If the court does not find fraud proved, it can nevertheless impose a penalty to which it considers the person liable. [*TMA 1970, s 100D*]. This rule does not apply to penalties under *FA 2007, Sch 24* (see **52.8–52.9** above), *FA 2008, Sch 36* (see **52.16** above) and *Sch 41* (see **52.3** above), *FA 2009, Sch 55* (failure to make returns — see **52.5** above) and *Sch 56*, *FA 2012, Sch 38* (see **52.19** above), *FA 2013, s 212A* (see **52.11** above), *FA 2014, s 208* (see **52.26** above) and *s 226* (see **52.27** above) and *FA 2016, Sch 18 Pt 5* (see **52.29** above), *FA 2016, Sch 22* (see **52.13** above), *F(No 2)A 2017, Sch 16* (see **52.21** above) and *F(No 2)A 2017, Sch 18* (see **52.14** above). [*TMA 1970, s 103ZA; FA 2012, Sch 38 para 49; FA 2014, Sch 33 para 2; FA 2016, s 158(10), Sch 18 para 59, Sch 22 para 20(1); F(No 2)A 2017, Sch 16 para 58, Sch 18 para 29(2)*].

General matters

[52.37] Non-receipt of notice of the hearing at which the Commissioners awarded penalties is not a ground of appeal to the courts (*Kenny v Wirral Commrs* Ch D 1974, 50 TC 405; *Campbell v Rochdale Commrs* Ch D 1975, 50 TC 411).

A mere denial of liability to penalties implies an intention by the taxpayer to set up a case in refutation, and details must be supplied (*CIR v Jackson* CA 1960, 39 TC 357).

For the validity of penalty proceedings while assessments remain open, see *A-G for Irish Free State v White* SC (RI) 1931, 38 TC 666 and *R v Havering Commrs (ex p. Knight)* CA 1973, 49 TC 161. For other procedural matters, see *Collins v Croydon Commrs* Ch D 1969, 45 TC 566; *Bales v Rochford Commrs* Ch D 1964, 42 TC 17; *Sparks v West Brixton Commrs* Ch D, [1977] STC 212; *Moschi v Kensington Commrs* Ch D 1979, 54 TC 403; and for other appeals against penalties for failure to make returns, see *Dunk v Havant Commrs* Ch D 1976, 51 TC 519; *Napier v Farnham Commrs* CA, [1978] TR 403; *Garnham v Haywards Heath Commrs* Ch D 1977, [1978] TR 303; *Cox v Poole Commrs and CIR (No 1)* Ch D 1987, 60 TC 445; *Montague v Hampstead Commrs & Others* Ch D 1989, 63 TC 145; *Cox v Poole Commrs (No 2)* Ch D 1989, 63 TC 277.

For variation etc. of penalties by the court, see *Dawes v Wallington Commrs* Ch D 1964, 42 TC 200; *Salmon v Havering Commrs* CA 1968, 45 TC 77; *Williams v Special Commrs* Ch D 1974, 49 TC 670; *Wells v Croydon Commrs* Ch D 1968, 47 ATC 356; *Taylor v Bethnal Green Commrs* Ch D 1976, [1977] STC 44; *Stableford v Liverpool Commrs* Ch D 1982, [1983] STC 162; *Sen v St. Anne, Westminster Commrs* Ch D, [1983] STC 415; *Jolley v Bolton Commrs* Ch D 1986, 65 TC 242; *Lear v Leek Commrs* Ch D 1986, 59 TC 247; *Walsh v Croydon Commrs* Ch D 1987, 60 TC 442; *Fox v Uxbridge Commrs & CIR* Ch D 2001, [2002] STC 455.

For the test used by the court in considering whether penalties are excessive, see *Brodt v Wells Commrs* Ch D 1987, 60 TC 436. Per Scott LJ, penalties awarded by different bodies of Commissioners 'should, in relation to similar cases, bear some resemblance to one another'.

Statements made or documents produced by or on behalf of a taxpayer are admissible evidence in proceedings against him, notwithstanding that reliance on the Board's practice in cases of full disclosure may have induced him to make or produce them. [*TMA 1970, s 105; FA 1989, ss 149(5), 168(1)(5)*].

Time limits

[52.38] The time within which a penalty (other than those noted below) can be determined, or proceedings can be commenced, depends on the penalty, as follows.

(a) If the penalty is ascertainable by reference to tax payable, the time is:
   (i) six years after the date the penalty was incurred, or
   (ii) (subject to below) a later time within three years after the final determination of the amount of tax.

(b) If the penalty arises under *TMA 1970, s 99* (assisting in preparation of incorrect return etc. — see **52.21** above) the time is twenty years after the date it was incurred.

(c) In any other case, the time is six years from the time when the penalty was, or began to be, incurred.

Where the person liable has died, and the determination falls to be made in relation to his personal representatives, the extension in (a)(ii) above does not apply if the tax is charged in an assessment made more than six years after 31 January following the chargeable period for which it is charged. This ceases to apply from a date to be appointed by the Treasury by statutory instrument.

[*TMA 1970, s 103; FA 2007, Sch 24 para 29(b); FA 2012, Sch 37 para 48; SI 2009 No 56, Sch 1 para 48*].

This rule does not apply to penalties under *FA 2007, Sch 24* (see **52.8–52.9** above), *FA 2008, Sch 36* (see **52.16** above) and *Sch 41* (see **52.3** above) and *FA 2009, Sch 55* (failure to make returns — see **52.5** above) and *Sch 56* (late payment penalty — see **42.10** LATE PAYMENT INTEREST AND PENALTIES), *FA 2012, Sch 38* (see **52.19** above), *FA 2013, s 212A* (see 51.12A above), *FA 2014, s 208* (see **52.26** above) and *s 226* (see **52.27** above), *FA 2015, Sch 21* (see **52.12** above), *F(No 2)A 2015, Sch 8* (see **52.28** above), *FA 2016, Sch 18* (see **52.29** above, *FA 2016, Sch 19* (see **52.30** above), *FA 2016, Sch 20* (see **52.20** above), *FA 2016, Sch 22* (see **52.13** above), *F(No 2)A 2017, Sch 16* (see **52.21** and **52.33** above) and *F(No 2)A 2017, Sch 18* (see **52.14** and **52.33** above). [*TMA 1970, s 103ZA; FA 2012, Sch 38 para 49; FA 2014, Sch 33 para 2; FA 2016, Sch 18 para 59, Sch 22 para 20(1); F(No 2)2017, Sch 16 para 58, Sch 18 para 29(2)*]. See instead **52.33** above.

Final determination of tax

Provisional agreement of the amount due subject to the inspector being satisfied later with statements of assets, etc. is not final determination (*Carco Accessories Ltd v CIR* CS 1985, 59 TC 45).

Bankrupts

[52.39] Penalties awarded after a bankruptcy are provable debts, but in practice HMRC does not proceed for penalties during a bankruptcy where there are other creditors. The trustee may agree to compromise any penalties awarded but the compromise must also be agreed by the bankrupt (*Re Hurren* Ch D 1982, 56 TC 494).

Liability under criminal law

[52.40] 'False statements to the prejudice of the Crown and public revenue' are criminal offences (*R v Hudson* CCA 1956, 36 TC 561). False statements in income tax returns, or for obtaining any allowance, reduction or repayment may involve liability to imprisonment for up to two years, under *Perjury Act 1911, s 5,* for 'knowingly and wilfully' making materially false statements or returns for tax purposes. Also, in Scotland, summary proceedings may be taken under *TMA 1970, s 107*.

Criminal prosecutions for tax fraud in England and Wales are conducted by the Crown Prosecution service. For HMRC practice in considering whether to accept a money settlement or institute criminal proceedings for fraud, see **34.13 HMRC** INVESTIGATORY POWERS.

Falsification etc. of documents which are required to be produced, as in **34.12, 34.16 HMRC** INVESTIGATORY POWERS, is a criminal offence punishable, on summary conviction, by a fine of the statutory maximum or, on indictment, by a fine or imprisonment for up to two years or both. [*TMA 1970, s 20BB; FA 2012, Sch 38 para 46*]. Similar punishments apply for the concealment, destruction or disposal of documents required to be produced as in **34.4, 34.11 HMRC** INVESTIGATORY POWERS. See **34.10** and **34.11**.

The fraudulent evasion of *income tax* (not capital gains tax or corporation tax) on behalf of oneself or another person is itself a criminal offence. [*TMA 1970, s 106A*].

Offshore evasion

With effect from a day to be appointed by the Treasury (which will be no earlier than 6 April 2017), a new criminal offence is introduced for failure to properly declare offshore income or chargeable gains as set out below. It applies only if a threshold limit is exceeded for any particular tax year. The threshold will be set by statutory instrument, but will not be less than £25,000. There is no requirement for the prosecution to prove intent to evade tax. The offence will not apply to failures and inaccuracies in respect of notices or returns relating to a tax year prior to that in which the appointed day falls.

The offence covers the following:

(a) failure to give timely notification of chargeability to tax (as in **52.3** above), where the tax in question is chargeable (wholly or partly) on offshore income, assets or activities and the threshold limit is exceeded (by which is meant that the total income tax and CGT chargeable for the tax year on offshore income, assets or activities exceeds the threshold);

(b) failure to file a personal tax return before the end of period during which the notice under *TMA 1970, s 8* to file the return can be withdrawn (see **58.3** RETURNS), where an accurate return would have disclosed liability to income tax or CGT (or both) chargeable for the tax year on offshore income, assets or activities and the threshold limit is exceeded (as in (a) above); and

(c) an inaccuracy in a personal tax return required by notice under *TMA 1970, s 8*, where (i) the return contains the inaccuracy at the end of the 'amendment period'; (ii) its correction would result in an increase in the income tax or CGT (or both) chargeable for the tax year on offshore income, assets or activities; and (iii) the amount of that increase exceeds the threshold limit. The '*amendment period*' is the period during which the taxpayer can amend the return (see **58.7** RETURNS).

References to tax being chargeable on offshore income, assets or activities include tax being chargeable by reference to offshore income, assets or activities.

A person guilty of an offence is liable, on summary conviction, to, in England and Wales, an unlimited fine and/or imprisonment for up to six months for offences committed before the coming into force of *Criminal Justice Act 2003, s 281(5)* and 51 weeks thereafter and, in Scotland and NI, a fine of up to level 5 on the standard scale and/or imprisonment for up to six months.

It is a defence for a person to prove that he had a reasonable excuse for failing to give the notice required in (a) or deliver the return in (b) or to prove that he took reasonable care to ensure that the return in (c) was accurate. Where a deadline is extended under *TMA 1970, s 118(2)*, the extension applies for the purposes of the deadlines relevant to (a)–(c) above. A person is not guilty of an offence if the capacity in which he is required to give the notice or file the return is as a relevant trustee of a settlement or as executor or administrator of a deceased person.

Regulations will stipulate that the offence will not apply in relation to offshore income, assets or activities reportable to HMRC in accordance with certain international arrangements such as the Common Reporting Standard (www.gov.uk/government/publications/tax-administration-criminal-offence-for-offshore-tax-evaders). Regulations may also include provision as to the calculation of the tax chargeable on offshore income, assets or activities.

Offshore income, assets or activities means income arising from a source in, assets situated or held in, or activities carried on wholly or mainly in, a territory outside the UK. 'Assets' has the meaning given in *TCGA 1992, s 21(1)* (see **7.2** ASSETS), but also includes sterling.

[*TMA 1970, ss 106B–106H; FA 2016, s 166*].

Failure to prevent facilitation of tax evasion

With effect from 30 September 2017, a company is guilty of an offence if an employee or agent of the company or any other person performing services for the company commits a 'UK tax evasion facilitation offence' or a 'foreign tax evasion facilitation offence' when acting in the capacity of employee, agent etc. In the case of a foreign tax evasion facilitation offence, the company must be UK incorporated, carry on a business in the UK and any conduct forming part of the facilitation offence must take place in the UK.

It is a defence for the company to prove either than, when the facilitation offence was committed, it had in place procedures designed to prevent employees etc., from committing facilitation offences which it was reasonable to expect it to have in place, or that it was not reasonable to expect the company to have such procedures in place. The Government has a statutory duty to publish guidance on such procedures.

A '*UK tax evasion facilitation offence*' is an offence under UK law consisting of:

(a) being knowingly concerned in, or in taking steps with a view to, the fraudulent evasion of tax by another person;
(b) aiding, abetting, counselling or procuring the commission of a 'UK tax evasion offence'; or
(c) being involved 'art and part' in the commission of an offence within (a) above.

Conduct within (a) above is not a UK tax evasion facilitation offence unless the other person has committed a UK tax evasion offence facilitated by that conduct. A 'UK tax evasion offence' is an offence of cheating the public revenue or an offence under UK law consisting of being knowingly concerned in, or in taking steps with a view to, the fraudulent evasion of tax. 'Tax' includes any UK tax or National Insurance contributions.

A '*foreign tax evasion facilitation offence*' is conduct which amounts to an offence under the law of a foreign country, relates to the commission by another person of a 'foreign tax evasion offence' under that country's law and would be a UK tax evasion facilitation offence if the foreign tax evasion offence were a UK tax evasion offence. A '*foreign tax evasion offence*' is conduct which amounts to an offence under the law of a foreign country, relates to a breach of a duty relating to a tax of that country and would be regarded by UK courts as amounting to being knowingly concerned in, or in taking steps with a view to, the fraudulent evasion of that tax.

A company guilty of an offence under these provisions is liable to a fine. The provisions apply equally to partnerships.

[*Criminal Finances Act 2017, ss 44–52, 58(5); SI 2017 No 739*].

Key points concerning penalties

[52.41] Points to consider are as follows.

- There are a number of reasons that HMRC can charge penalties and these apply across several taxes and not just capital gains tax. In general penalties are imposed for doing something wrong either in error or deliberately such as:
  - (a) Failure to notify chargeability.
  - (b) Late submission or errors in a tax return or other documents.
  - (c) Failure to keep records.
  - (d) Disclosing information.
  - (e) Failure to tell HMRC that an assessment or determination is insufficient.
  - (f) Late payment of tax.
- Practitioners should be aware that there can be a £3,000 penalty for assisting in or inducing the preparation or delivery of incorrect information, returns, accounts or other documents. In addition, *FA 2016* has introduced a penalty for enabling offshore tax evasion.
- Some penalties are fixed but others fall within a range (as a percentage of the tax involved). The seriousness and magnitude of the offence as well as the level of cooperation from the taxpayer will determine the level of the penalties imposed by HMRC. Where it can be shown that an inaccuracy in a return was made despite taking reasonable care no penalty may be charged. HMRC have issued various toolkits which focus on the errors HMRC officers find commonly occur. Using the toolkits does not supplant the taxpayer's obligation to ensure that their returns are complete and accord with the taxes act but their use, or use of an alternative checklist, may, depending on the precise facts, help support an argument that reasonable care was taken. The main toolkits currently in issue relevant to capital gains tax are:
  - Capital gains tax for land and buildings;
  - Capital gains tax for shares;
  - Capital v revenue expenditure;
  - Chargeable gains for companies;
  - Capital gains tax for trusts and estates.

- The penalty regimes also allow for a penalty to be set aside where the taxpayer had a reasonable excuse. Recent interesting quotes from Tribunals are:
  - 'An excuse is likely to be reasonable where the taxpayer acts in the same way as someone who seriously intends to honour their tax liabilities and obligations would act.' *B&J Shopfitting Services* TC390.
  - 'HMRC argues that a "reasonable excuse" must be some exceptional circumstance which prevented timeous filing. That, as a matter of law, is wrong. Parliament has provided the penalty will not be due if the appellant can show it has "reasonable excuse". If Parliament had intended to say that the penalty would not be due only in exceptional circumstances, it would have said so in those terms. The phrase "reasonable excuse" uses ordinary English words in every-day usage which must be given their plain and ordinary meaning.' *NA Dudley Electrical Contractors Ltd* TC1124.
- Where more than one tax geared penalty applies to the same tax the amount charged is usually limited to the larger of the separate penalties.
- When making a voluntary disclosure of an inaccuracy always consider whether the circumstances are such that the disclosure could be made under an HMRC's amnesty or agreement. HMRC are undertaking a rolling amnesty programme aimed at specific trade sectors e.g., electricians; doctors etc, and have a number of international agreements such as Liechtenstein. Some of the amnesties/agreements cover wide circumstances and may offer potentially lower fixed rates of penalty.
- There are often commercial reasons why accurate figures cannot be shown on a tax return, for example, admission of new partners to an existing partnership. Late filing penalties can normally be avoided by filing a return containing provisional or estimated figures and amending the return as soon as the actual figures become available. The estimate must be reasonable and clearly marked.

53

Private Residences

Introduction	53.1
Exemption generally	53.2
Dwelling-house	53.3
Main residence	53.4
The permitted area	53.5
Subsidiary buildings	53.6
Periods of ownership qualifying for exemption	53.7
Part-business use, changes of use etc	53.9
Election for main residence	53.10
Occupation under terms of settlement or by will or intestacy	53.11
Occupation by dependent relative	53.12
Exclusions from exemptions	53.13
Exemption for letting as residential accommodation	53.14
Key points	53.15

Cross-references. See **41** LAND generally; **22.20**, **22.34** EMPLOYEE SHARE SCHEMES for restriction on rollover relief arising from disposal of shares to, respectively, a tax-advantaged share incentive plan and, before 6 April 2001, an employee share ownership trust, where replacement asset is or becomes exempt as a private residence.

Simon's Taxes. See **C2.13**.

Introduction

[53.1] An exemption from capital gains tax applies on the disposal by an individual of a dwelling-house which has been his only or main residence. The exemption also extends to garden or grounds held for the individual's own occupation and enjoyment with that residence. The exemption is either total or fractional, depending on whether and to what extent the residence has been the only or main residence of the individual throughout his period of ownership (and for this purpose certain periods of absence from the property are ignored). For disposals on or after 6 April 2015 the relief is restricted when the residence is in a country where neither the person making the disposal nor their spouse or civil partner is tax resident.

An individual can only have one main residence at a time, and this applies also to an individual and spouse or civil partner so long as they are living together. Where an individual or couple has more than one residence an election may be made for one of the residences to be treated as the main residence. The election may subsequently be varied.

The exemption is extended to situations where a residence is occupied under the terms of a settlement or by will or intestacy and to occupation by a dependant relative which began before 6 April 1988.

A further exemption is available where partial relief under the above provisions is available and the residence has also been let as residential accommodation during part of the period of ownership. See **53.14** below.

Exemption generally

[53.2] Where a gain accrues to an individual so far as attributable to the disposal of, or of an interest in:

(a) a dwelling-house or part of a dwelling-house (see **53.3** below) which is, or has at any time in his period of ownership been, his only or main residence (see **53.4** below), or

(b) land which he has for his own occupation and enjoyment with that residence as its garden or grounds up to the 'permitted area' (see **53.5** below),

then either the whole or a fraction of the gain is exempt as below. [*TCGA 1992, s 222(1)*].

Any loss accruing is similarly treated as being wholly or partly a non-allowable loss. [*TCGA 1992, s 16(2)*].

Note that the exemption is *not* restricted to dwelling-houses situated in the UK.

In *Harte and another v HMRC* FTT, [2012] UKFTT 258 (TC); 2012 STI 2219, the taxpayer's occupation of a house for short periods of time whilst deciding whether to live in it permanently or to sell it was held not to amount to 'residence' for these purposes, so that the exemption could not be claimed. In *Moore v HMRC* FTT, [2013] UKFTT 433 (TC); 2013 STI 3371 the taxpayer's occupation of a house for several months after separating from his wife and before purchasing a house with his new partner, 'did not have any degree of permanence or expectation of continuity'. The taxpayer had never envisaged the house as a long-term home, so that his occupation of it did not constitute 'residence' for the purposes of the exemption. In *Gibson v HMRC* FTT, [2013] UKFTT 636 (TC) the taxpayer's camping on a site on which his previous dwelling-house had been situated during the building of a replacement house which he planned to sell was held not to be residence for the purposes of the exemption. In *Ive and another v HMRC* FTT, [2014] UKFTT 436 (TC); 2014 STI 2523, a couple's occupation of a flat for 25 days was held not to amount to residence.

In *Dutton-Forshaw v HMRC FTT*, [2015] UKFTT 478 (TC); 2016 STI 146, the taxpayer's occupation of a London flat for seven weeks was held to be 'residence' for the purposes of the exemption. It was clear that the taxpayer hoped to live in the flat on a continuous basis at the time he moved in but was aware that circumstances might arise which would require him to live elsewhere. In *TC06085: Stephen Bailey v Revenue and Customs Comrs* [2017] UKFTT 658 (TC), B occupied a property for two short periods of a few months each, moving out once because he could not secure a suitable mortgage and for the second time after deciding to sell due to health problems. The First-tier Tribunal found that each time he had moved into the property, he had intended it would be his home and so principal private residence relief should be due.

Spouses and civil partners

There can only be one main residence in the case of an individual and his spouse or civil partner living with him, so long as they are 'living together' (see **46.4** MARRIED PERSONS AND CIVIL PARTNERS). [*TCGA 1992, s 222(6)*]. As regards separation or divorce, see **53.7** below.

Total exemption

Total exemption (under *TCGA 1992, s 223(1)*) applies to a gain within *TCGA 1992, s 222(1)* above if the dwelling-house or part of a dwelling-house has been the individual's only or main residence throughout the period of ownership, or throughout the period of ownership except for all or any part of the last 18 months of that period (36 months for disposals before 6 April 2014). A 36-month final period continues to apply to certain disposals by disabled persons and long-term residents in a care home (see further below).

Fractional exemption

Fractional exemption (under *TCGA 1992, s 223(2)*) applies where total exemption does not apply to a gain within *TCGA 1992, s 222(1)*. The fraction of the gain that is exempt is given by:

(i) the length of the part or parts of the period of ownership during which the dwelling-house (or part) was the individual's only or main residence, but inclusive of the last 18 months of the period of ownership in any event (36 months for certain disposals by disabled persons and long-term residents in a care home (see below) and for all disposals before 6 April 2014), divided by;
(ii) the length of the period of ownership.

Disposals by disabled persons or persons in care homes

For disposals by an individual on or after 6 April 2014, the final period of ownership that qualifies for exemption even where the dwelling-house was not then the only or main residence is extended from 18 months to 36 months where, at the time of the disposal:

(1) the individual is a 'disabled person' or a 'long-term resident' in a 'care home' and does not have any other right in a private residence (see below); or
(2) the individual's spouse or civil partner is a disabled person or a long-term resident in a care home and neither the individual nor the spouse or civil partner has any other right in a private residence.

'*Disabled person*' is defined for this purpose at *FA 2005, Sch 1A*. An individual is a '*long-term resident*' in a care home at the time of a disposal if at that time he is resident there and has been resident, or can reasonably be expected to be resident there, for at least three months. A '*care home*' is an establishment providing accommodation together with nursing or personal care.

An individual has any other right in a private residence at the time of a disposal if:

- at that time either he owns or holds an interest in a dwelling-house, or part of one, other than that on which the gain in question arises or the trustees of a settlement own or hold such an interest and the individual is entitled to occupy that dwelling-house or part under the settlement's terms; and
- a gain on the disposal of that dwelling-house or interest (or of part of it) at that time would have qualified for exemption, or would have qualified if an election under **53.10** below had been made.

Period of ownership

In considering 'period of ownership' for the purposes of the total or fractional exemption (but *not* for determining for the purposes of *TCGA 1992, s 222(1)* above whether the dwelling-house (or part) has at any time in the period of ownership been the only or main residence), any period before 31 March 1982 (6 April 1965 for disposals before 6 April 1988) is ignored. For disposals on or after 6 April 2015 any period before that date is also excluded if the whole or part of the gain is an NRCGT gain (i.e. a gain on a non-resident disposal of an interest in UK residential property — see **41.25** LAND) unless an election for the retrospective basis of calculation is made (see **41.30** LAND).

See **53.7** below for certain periods of ownership that additionally qualify for the purposes of total and fractional exemption.

[*TCGA 1992, s 223(1)(2)(5)–(7A), s 225E; FA 2014, s 58; FA 2015, Sch 9 paras 4, 9, 10*].

Change in interest

Where the individual has had different interests at different times, the period of ownership is taken for the purposes of *TCGA 1992, ss 222–226* generally (i.e. all the provisions contained in this chapter) to begin from the first acquisition taken into account in arriving at the amount of the allowable expenditure deductible in the computation of the gain to which *TCGA 1992, s 222(1)* above applies. In the case of an individual living with his spouse or civil partner:

(A) if one disposes of, or of his interest in, the dwelling-house (or part) which is their only or main residence to the other, and in particular if it passes on death to the other as legatee, the other's period of ownership is treated as beginning with the beginning of the period of ownership of the one making the disposal, and

(B) if (A) above applies, but the dwelling-house (or part) was not the only or main residence of both throughout the period of ownership of the one making the disposal, account is taken of any part of that period during which it was his only or main residence as if it was also that of the other.

[*TCGA 1992, s 222(7); FA 2015, Sch 9 para 2*].

Apportionments

For the purposes of *TCGA 1992, ss 222–226*, apportionments of consideration are to be made wherever required, and, in particular, where a person disposes of a dwelling-house only part of which is his only or main residence. [*TCGA 1992, s 222(10)*].

See **53.9** to **53.14** below for provisions supplementary to the above.

TCGA 1992, s 222(10) seems to override *TCGA 1992, s 52(4)* (apportionments to be on just and reasonable basis; see **16.5** COMPUTATION OF GAINS AND LOSSES) so that, because of the absence of the 'just and reasonable' criterion, there may be an argument that a different basis of apportionment may apply, e.g. where the residence and the permitted area of land block access to other land outside the permitted area but sold together with the residence etc. it may fall that the value of the other land should reflect the situation as if the two areas were in separate ownership (*Taxation* 7 December 1995 p 256).

Dwelling-house

[53.3] An immobilised caravan with main services installed has been held to be a dwelling-house (*Makins v Elson* Ch D 1976, 51 TC 437) but one still on wheels and with no services installed was not so held (*Moore v Thompson* Ch D 1986, 61 TC 15).

A houseboat will often be an exempt asset in its own right (see **25.4** EXEMPTIONS AND RELIEFS regarding tangible movable wasting assets). If this is not the case, it may qualify as a dwelling-house if it is permanently located on a site and connected to all mains services. Such a houseboat *will* be regarded as a dwelling-house if it has been used as an immobile residence for a period of six months or more and has had its engines removed. Other cases will be considered on their merits. (HMRC Capital Gains Manual CG64328).

Green v CIR CS 1982, 56 TC 10 involved the disposal of a mansion (occupied by the taxpayer) and its two wings. The Commissioners' finding that the wings were not part of his dwelling-house was upheld.

In *Gibson v HMRC* FTT, [2013] UKFTT 636 (TC) the taxpayer knocked down an existing house and built a new house because it was cheaper than extending the house. The tribunal held that the two dwelling-houses could not be treated as the same dwelling-house for the purposes of the exemption.

Main residence

[53.4] Where a taxpayer has more than one residence, the question as to which is the main residence is a question of fact, subject to the making of an election as in **53.10** below.

See *Frost v Feltham* Ch D 1980, 55 TC 10 (which concerned mortgage interest relief for income tax purposes). See also HMRC Capital Gains Manual CG64545 for factors which HMRC will consider in deciding if a residence is a main residence in the absence of an election.

In *Regan and anor v Revenue and Customs Comrs (No 2)* TC 2247 [2012] UKFTT 570 (TC) the First Tier Tribunal held that when considering the facts of what constitutes a main residence it should be determined based on the quality of the occupation not the quantity of the occupation.

The permitted area

[53.5] The '*permitted area*' in **53.2**(b) above means an area (inclusive of the house itself) of 0.5 hectares (i.e. 5,980 sq. yards or 5,000 sq. metres) or larger area if required for the reasonable enjoyment of the whole or part of the dwelling-house as a residence having regards to its size and character.

Where part of the land occupied with a residence is and part is not within **53.2**(b) above, then (up to the permitted area) the part that is to be taken within **53.2**(b) is that part which would be most suitable for occupation and enjoyment with the residence if the remainder were separately occupied.

[*TCGA 1992, s 222(2)–(4)*].

In *Varty v Lynes* Ch D 1976, 51 TC 419, the taxpayer owned and occupied a house and garden (together comprising an area less than one acre, the latter being the then 'maximum' permitted area subject to an appeal Commissioners' determination). He sold the house and part of the garden in June 1971. In May 1972, he sold at a substantial profit the rest of the garden for which he had meanwhile obtained planning permission. An assessment on the gain accruing on the disposal of the remainder of the garden was upheld. The exemption provided by **53.2**(b) above related only to the actual moment of disposal of the land, and in relation to land formerly used as garden and grounds did not apply to a disposal subsequent to the disposal of the residence. HMRC apply this decision so that no relief is due on any sale of a garden taking place after a prior sale of the dwelling-house (Revenue Tax Bulletin August 1994 pp 148, 149 and see HMRC Capital Gains Manual CG64377–64385).

For a useful summary of the considerations made by HMRC in arriving at the 'permitted area' (and whether a subsidiary building forms part of the residence as a whole — see **53.6** below), see Revenue Tax Bulletin, February 1992, p 10. The Revenue made the point that land, other than that taken by the site of the dwelling-house, must be 'garden or grounds' at the time of sale if it is to be within the permitted area. In deciding whether an area of garden or grounds larger than 0.5 hectares is 'required for the reasonable enjoyment' of the dwelling-house as a residence, it considers the following words of Du Parcq J in the compulsory purchase case of *In Re Newhill Compulsory Purchase Order 1937, Payne's Application* KB 1937, [1938] 2 All ER 163 to be useful guidance:

> ' "Required", I think, in this Section does not mean merely that the occupiers of the house would like to have it, or that they would miss it if they lost it, or that anyone proposing to buy the house would think less of the house without it than he would if it was preserved to it. "Required" means, I suppose that without it there will be such a substantial deprivation of amenities or convenience that a real injury would be done to the property owner.'

In *Longson v Baker* Ch D 2000, 73 TC 415, in which a permitted area of 7.56 hectares was unsuccessfully claimed and in which the taxpayer stressed the equestrian aspect of the property, it was held that the reasonable enjoyment test is an objective one. It was not objectively *required*, in other words necessary, to keep horses at a house to enjoy it *as a residence*. An individual taxpayer may subjectively wish to do so but that was not the same thing.

In *Ritchie v Revenue and Customs Commissioners* [2017] UKFTT 449 (TC), [2017] All ER (D) 112 (Jun), the Ritchies' disposed of house and grounds on a site greater than 0.5 hectares. Having found that a large shed on the site was part of the dwelling house (see more about whether subsidiary buildings form part of a residence at **53.6** below), the First-tier Tribunal concluded that the approach path to the shed was part of the permitted area but not land lying on the other side. In deciding how to apportion the gain between the permitted and unpermitted areas, the Tribunal found that all of the land was of equal value to a developer.

It should be noted that HMRC considers that a separate disposal of part of the garden or grounds of a residence may be prima facie evidence that the part disposed of was not required for the reasonable enjoyment of the dwelling-house as a residence although this only becomes of relevance where the area of the garden or grounds exceeds 0.5 hectares. However, it accepts that there are two common circumstances where this inference may be incorrect. The first is where the owner of the land makes a disposal to a member of his family where he may be prepared to tolerate some curtailment of the reasonable enjoyment of the residence. The second is where financial necessity may force the owner to sell land which would be regarded as part of the most suitable area of garden or grounds to be included in the permitted area (HMRC Capital Gains Manual CG64832).

There is no requirement that the land occupied and used with the residence as garden or grounds at the time of disposal has to adjoin the land on which the dwelling-house stands. See *Wakeling v Pearce* (Sp C 32), [1995] SSCD 96 where the distance between the garden (which was disposed of) and the land including the dwelling-house (which was retained) was less than 10 metres. However, HMRC consider the facts of the case and the decision do not affect its interpretation of the underlying provisions and that it will be rare for exemption to be given to land (even if used as a garden) separated from the residence by other land which is not in the same ownership as the residence (see Revenue Tax Bulletin August 1995 p 239).

See *Taxation 5 January 1989, p 311* for a case where the Ombudsman considered the District Valuer to have been wrong in taking the view that the presence of a tennis court and swimming pool must be regarded as irrelevant in deciding what was the permitted area.

Subsidiary buildings

[53.6] The courts have considered whether a building which is separate from the main dwelling-house building can fall within the exemption a number of times.

A lodge built for occupation rent-free by a caretaker/gardener and his wife, the housekeeper, and separated from the main house by the width of a tennis court (around nine yards) with the total area of land involved being around 1.1 acres, was held to be within the exemption (*Batey v Wakefield* CA 1981, 55 TC 550). A residence for exemption purposes was declared to be a dwelling-house and all of those buildings which are part and parcel of the whole, where each part is appurtenant to and occupied for the purposes of the building occupied by the taxpayer. However, this is a question of fact and degree.

In *Markey v Sanders* Ch D 1987, 60 TC 245, a finding by Commissioners that a staff bungalow situated 130 metres away from the main dwelling-house and screened from it by a belt of trees, formed part of the taxpayer's residence was not accepted by the Court. It was held that *Batey v Wakefield* laid down two tests:

(1) the occupation of the building must increase the taxpayer's enjoyment of the main dwelling-house; and
(2) the building must be 'very closely adjacent to' the main dwelling-house.

Each of these was held to be a necessary, but not by itself sufficient, test and in the present case the first test was satisfied but not the second. The total area of land involved was around twelve acres.

However, *Markey v Sanders* was expressly not followed in *Williams v Merrylees* Ch D 1987, 60 TC 297, so that a finding by Commissioners that a lodge situated 200 metres from the main dwelling-house formed part of the taxpayer's residence during his occupation of the latter was upheld. The total area of the property was around four acres. In the latter case doubt was expressed whether the *Batey v Wakefield* decision did require the satisfaction of two distinct conditions and it was concluded that all the circumstances should be looked at to see whether there is 'an entity which could sensibly be described as being a dwelling-house though split up into different buildings performing different functions'.

The *Williams v Merrylees* decision was itself disapproved by the Court of Appeal in *Lewis v Rook* CA 1992, 64 TC 567. A finding by Commissioners that a gardener's cottage some 170 metres from the main dwelling-house formed part of the taxpayer's residence was initially upheld in the High Court, but was rejected in the Court of Appeal. The true test was declared to be whether the cottage was 'within the curtilage of, and appurtenant to [the main house], so as to be part of the entity which, together with [the main house], constituted the dwelling-house occupied by the taxpayer as her residence'.

The curtilage concept was derived from a non-tax case, *Methuen-Campbell v Walters* CA, [1979] QB 525 (and see also *Dyer v Dorset County Council* CA, [1989] QB 346), in which Buckley LJ stated that 'for one corporeal hereditament to fall within the curtilage of another, the former must be so intimately associated with the latter as to lead to the conclusion that the former in truth forms part and parcel of the latter'. The cottage in *Lewis v Rook* was not 'intimately associated' with the main house as it was some way off and separated from it by a large garden. The total area of land involved was around 10.5 acres and Balcombe LJ remarked that as

> 'the "permitted area" of garden and grounds which is exempt from capital gains tax is limited to one acre [now 0.5 hectares] or such larger area as the [Appeal] Commissioners may determine as required for the reasonable enjoyment of the dwelling-house as a residence, it does seem to me to be remarkable that a separate lodge or cottage which by any reasonable measurement must be outside the permitted area can nevertheless be part of the entity of the dwelling-house'.

HMRC consider that whether or not a particular building is within the curtilage of the main house is a matter of fact and degree. The building must be geographically close to the main house and be an integral part of it. However, as the necessary proximity required will vary in each case HMRC do not attempt to set a generally acceptable limit. Buildings within the curtilage of the main house will of necessity be 'appurtenant' to it. See HMRC Capital Gains Manual CG64245, 64255 for further discussion.

In *Honour v Norris* Ch D 1992, 64 TC 599, the taxpayer owned four separate, self-contained flats in a London square. Two of these were adjacent and were converted to form a single property, the other two being some way off and not adjacent to each other. Although the taxpayer and his wife had occasionally used the non-adjacent flats themselves, their main function was to provide sleeping accommodation for guests and a nanny. The Commissioners upheld the taxpayer's contention that one of the distant flats, which had been sold, was part of his main residence. However, the Revenue's appeal was upheld in the High Court, Vinelott J remarking that the proposition that the flat which had been sold formed part of the taxpayer's main residence was 'an affront to common sense'.

Periods of ownership qualifying for exemption

[53.7] For the purposes of the total or fractional exemption of a gain to which *TCGA 1992, s 222(1)* in **53.2** above applies the following apply.

(a) **Periods of absence.** A '*period of absence*' means a period during which the dwelling-house (or part) was not occupied by the individual as a residence. For disposals before 6 April 2015, it means a period during which the dwelling-house (or part) was not the individual's only or main residence and throughout which he had no residence or main residence eligible for relief under the provisions of *TCGA 1992, s 223* in **53.2** above. In applying the total or fractional exemption in **53.2** above (i.e. ignoring periods of ownership before 31 March 1982) and, for disposals on or after 6 April 2015, for the purposes of **53.10** below:
   (i) a period of absence not exceeding three years (or periods of absence which together did not exceed three years), and in addition,
   (ii) any period of absence throughout which the individual worked in an employment or office all the duties of which were performed outside the UK or lived with a spouse or civil partner who worked in such an office or employment, and in addition,
   (iii) any period of absence not exceeding four years (or periods of absence which together did not exceed four years) throughout which the individual was prevented from residing in the dwelling-house (or part) in consequence of the situation of his

place of work or in consequence of any condition imposed by his employer requiring him to reside elsewhere, being a condition reasonably imposed to secure the effective performance by the employee of his duties, and in addition,

(iv) any period of absence not exceeding four years (or periods of absence which together did not exceed four years) throughout which the individual lived with a spouse or civil partner to whom (iii) above applied for that period or periods,

is treated as if in that period of absence the dwelling-house (or part) was occupied by the individual as a residence (for disposals before 6 April 2015, as if in that period of absence the dwelling-house (or part) was the individual's only or main residence). This rule applies only where, before the period, there was a time when the dwelling-house (or part) was the individual's only or main residence and after the period, either:

(A) where any of (i)–(iv) above apply, there was a time when the dwelling-house (or part) was the individual's only or main residence;

(B) where any of (ii)–(iv) above apply, the individual was prevented from resuming residence in the dwelling-house because of the situation of his place of work or a condition imposed by the terms of his employment requiring him to reside elsewhere (the condition being reasonably imposed to secure the effective performance of the duties); or

(C) where any of (ii)–(iv) above apply, the individual lived with a spouse or civil partner to whom (B) above applied.

Where the period of ownership is deemed to begin on 6 April 2015 (because the gain is an NRCGT gain — see **53.2** above under 'Period of ownership'), then in establishing whether any of the above permitted periods of absence apply, the rule that the dwelling-house or part must have been occupied as the only or main residence at some time before the period of absence is determined ignoring times before 6 April 2015. However, pre-6 April 2015 periods can be used to satisfy the requirement if the individual so elects. An election must be made in the NRCGT return for the disposal (see **58.20** RETURNS) and specify the day before 6 April 2015 relied on in relation to the period of absence. The prior period of absence (i.e. that before 6 April 2015) is deducted from the amount of absence available for relief after 5 April 2015.

[*TCGA 1992, ss 223(3)–(3B)(7)(7B), 223A; FA 2015, Sch 9 paras 4, 5, 10; SI 2009 No 730, Arts 7, 8*].

Note that, for disposals before 6 April 2009, (iv) above, (B) and (C) above (and (ii) above to the extent that it applies to cases where it is the spouse or civil partner who works outside the UK) applied only by concession (HMRC Extra-Statutory Concessions D3, D4).

HMRC will view residence as a question of fact. A minimum period is not specified and HMRC do not attempt to impose one. They take the view that it is quality of occupation rather than length of occupation which determines whether a dwelling-house is its owner's residence. Miller J in *Moore v Thompson* Ch D 1986, 61 TC 15 commented that 'the Commissioners were alive to the fact that even occasional and short residence in a place can make that a residence; but the question was one of fact and degree' (Revenue Tax Bulletin, August 1994, p 149). In *Goodwin v Curtis* CA 1998, 70 TC 478, it was held that the nature, quality, length and circumstances of the taxpayer's 32-day occupation of a farmhouse was such that he had moved into it on a temporary basis and his occupation did not qualify as residence. *Dicta* of Viscount Cave in *Levene v CIR* (see **57.30** RESIDENCE AND DOMICILE) applied.

Where the periods of absence exceed the three or four years mentioned in (i) and (iii) above, it is only the excess which does not qualify for the exemption treatment (CCAB Statement TR 500, 10 March 1983).

The requirement that the period of absence is a period throughout which the individual has no residence or main residence eligible for relief under *TCGA 1992, s 223* may be difficult to meet in practice given the view (see commentary in **53.10** below) of HMRC that any residence in which the individual has a legal or equitable interest or, broadly before 17 October 1994, which the individual occupies under licence can constitute an individual's residence eligible for relief, albeit that it may only have a negligible capital value. However, HMRC will accept a main residence election as in **53.10** below nominating the residence from which the taxpayer is absent even though he is not using it as a residence. No other residence is then eligible for relief, so the requirement is satisfied. See HMRC Capital Gains Manual CG65047.

Example

T purchased a house on 1 August 1981 from which date it was used as her only residence until 10 February 1982 when she moved to France to live in rent-free accommodation provided by her employer whilst she carried out all the duties of the employment there. She returned from France on 4 August 1990 when she again occupied the house as her only residence. On 30 November 2011 she left the house empty and moved to live with her elderly father in a residence owned by him, intending to sell her own house. In the event, the house was not sold until 1 November 2017 when an otherwise chargeable gain of £72,000 was realised.

	£
Gain on sale	72,000
Deduct ((8y4m + 21y4m + 1y6m)/35y7m) × £72,000	63,063
Chargeable gain	£8,937

Notes to the example

(1) The period of ownership for the exemption calculation does not include any period before 31 March 1982.

(2) All of the period spent in France (ignoring the period before 31 March 1982) counts as a period of residence under (ii) above. It is assumed that the supply of accommodation to T in France was such that it was not eligible for relief under *TCGA 1992, s 223* (e.g. a licence; see 53.5 below for HMRC comment). None of the period from 30 November 2011 to 1 November 2017 can count as a period of residence under (i) above as there was not a time afterwards that the house was T's only or main residence. However, under *TCGA 1992, s 223(1)* the last 18 months of ownership

are exempt provided the house has at some time during the period of ownership (not restricted to periods after 31 March 1982) been the only or main residence.

(b) **Delay in taking up residence.** The treatment as the individual's only or main residence applies during the twelve months (or longer period up to a maximum of two years if a good reason can be shown) prior to taking up residence during which the dwelling-house was built, alterations etc. were made to it or the necessary steps were being taken to dispose of the individual's previous residence. (HMRC Extra-Statutory Concession D49 replacing Statement of Practice D4). The period will not be extended beyond twenty-four months. If the twelve-month or longer period allowed is exceeded, none of the period of ownership prior to taking up residence is treated as a period of residence. No main residence election (see **53.10** below) is required if the effect of this concession is to treat an individual as having two residences for a period since relief will be available for both residences for that period (HMRC Capital Gains Manual CG65009–65013).

In *Mr & Mrs AJ Henke v HMRC*, Sp C [2006] SSCD 561 (Sp C 550) a married couple purchased 2.66 acres of land in 1982, with planning permission for the construction of one house. In 1991 they began building a house on the land. The construction was completed in 1993, and the couple then moved into the house. When they subsequently sold part of the land, the couple contended that the whole of the gain should be treated as exempt under *TCGA 1992, s 222*. One of their arguments was that the period of ownership for the purposes of *TCGA 1992, s 223(1)* began in 1993 when the house was completed. The Special Commissioner found, however, that there was only one asset, the land, which by virtue of *TCGA 1992, s 288(1)* included any buildings on it. The period of ownership therefore began in 1982 and accordingly only fractional exemption was available under *TCGA 1992, s 223(2)*.

In *Higgins v Revenue and Customs Commissioners* [2017] UKFTT 236 (TC), [2017] SFTD 814, [2017] SWTI 1176 H entered into a contract in 2006 for the purchase of a flat off-plan. He did not have any right to occupy it until January 2010 when he completed the purchase, and the flat did not exist for most of the period before then. It was accepted that he occupied the flat as his principal residence from January 2010 until its sale in December 2011 and so some relief was available under *TCGA 1992, s 222* but the issue was the period of ownership. H contended that the ownership period began with legal completion of the purchase contract in January 2010. HMRC considered ownership to begin in 2006 being the date of acquisition under *TCGA 1992, s 28* (see **16.4** COMPUTATION OF GAINS AND LOSSES), such that only partial exemption was available, restricted to the period of occupation from January 2010 only. The First-tier Tribunal found that the deeming provisions of *s 28* did not apply in the context of determining the period of ownership of a dwelling and that the period of ownership here coincided with the period of occupation, giving full exemption.

(c) **Separation of married persons or civil partners.** Where an individual ceases to live with his or her spouse or civil partner and subsequently, as part of a divorce or separation settlement (within *TCGA 1992, s 225B(2)*), disposes of the home which had been their only or main residence, or an interest in it, to the other partner, the transferring partner may make a claim for the home to be regarded for the purposes of the exemption as continuing to be his or her only or main residence from the date occupation ceases until the date of transfer. Throughout this period, the home must have continued to be the other partner's only or main residence, and the transferring partner must not elect for another house to be treated as his or her main residence for any part of the period. [*TCGA 1992, s 225B; FA 2015, Sch 9 para 8; SI 2009 No 730, Art 9*]. Note that, for disposals before 6 April 2009, this provision applied only by concession (HMRC Extra-Statutory Concession D6). See also **46.5** MARRIED PERSONS AND CIVIL PARTNERS.

(d) **'Job-related' accommodation.** If at any time during an individual's period of ownership (as for *TCGA 1992, s 222(1)* in **53.2** above so that a period before 31 March 1982 is *not* ignored) of part or the whole of a dwelling-house he resides in 'job-related' living accommodation and he intends in due course to occupy the dwelling-house (or part) as his only or main residence, he is deemed at that time to occupy the dwelling-house (or part) as a residence for the purposes of *TCGA 1992, ss 222–226* (i.e. all the provisions contained in this chapter). Living accommodation is 'job-related' for these purposes if it is provided for a taxpayer by reason of his (or for his spouse or civil partner by reason of their) employment, in any of the following cases.

   (i) Where it is necessary for the proper performance of the duties of the employment that the employee should reside in that accommodation.

   (ii) Where the provision of such accommodation is customary and it is provided for the better performance of the duties of employment.

   (iii) Where there is a special threat to the employee's security, special security arrangements are in force, and the employee resides in the accommodation as part of those arrangements.

With certain exceptions, (i) and (ii) above do not apply to accommodation provided to its directors by a company (or associated company). In respect of residence after 5 April 1983, living accommodation is also job-related if either the person claiming the relief or his or her spouse or civil partner is carrying on a trade, profession or vocation on premises or other land provided by another person, under tenancy or otherwise, and is bound under an arm's length contract to live in those premises or on other premises provided. Relief is not given if the accommodation is provided, in whole or in part, by a company in which the borrower, or his or her spouse or civil partner, has a material interest (as defined) or by any person or persons with whom he or she carries on a business in partnership. [*TCGA 1992, s 222(8)(8A)–(8D)(9); SI 2012 No 736, Art 8*].

The above treatment still applies if the dwelling-house is disposed of without having been occupied by the individual (but subject to the test of intention to occupy being satisfied previously) or if the property has been let (see **53.14** below). It appears that the above provisions do not obviate the need to consider, subject to HMRC's views there mentioned, a main residence election as in **53.10** below.

(e) **Relocation of employees.** The exemption is extended to cases where an individual sells his home, or an interest in it, as a consequence of a change in his place of work or that of a 'co-owner' (i.e. another individual holding an interest in the home jointly or in common), if the change is required by the individual's or co-owner's employer. The disposal must be made under an agreement with the employer or a person operating under an agreement with the employer which must include a term entitling the individual to a share of any profit made on the subsequent disposal of the house or interest by the purchaser. If, within three years of the initial disposal, the individual receives such a profit share and that share would otherwise fall within *TCGA 1992, s 22* (CAPITAL SUMS DERIVED FROM ASSETS (**10**)), it is instead treated as a gain attributed to the individual's disposal of the home or interest, but accruing at the time the sum is received. The result is that the profit share will generally be exempt to the same extent as the home itself. [*TCGA 1992, s 225C; SI 2009 No 730, Art 10*]. Note that, for disposals before 6 April 2009, this provision applies only by concession (HMRC Extra-Statutory Concession D37). Where the provision does not apply, the receipt of the profit share cannot itself attract any private residence relief as it is not a disposal of an interest in a residence (HMRC Capital Gains Manual CG14970, 64611).

Non-qualifying tax years

[53.8] For disposals on or after 6 April 2015, the dwelling-house or part of a dwelling-house in **53.2**(a) above is not treated as being occupied as a residence by an individual at any time in his period of ownership which falls into a 'non-qualifying' tax year or non-qualifying 'partial tax year'. A non-qualifying tax year can be a tax year before 2015/16 only if the disposal is a non-resident CGT disposal (see **41.25** LAND).

The effect of this provision is that the property can neither be exempt as the individual's factual only or main residence, nor as their main residence by election (see **53.10** below), for a non-qualifying tax year. The rule applies to any property, wherever situated, and any gain attributable to the non-qualifying tax year(s) is chargeable to capital gains tax when the property is sold, at which date the owner may be resident or non-resident. In the latter case the charge will be under the non-resident CGT regime applying to interests in UK residential property (see **41.25** LAND).

A '*non-qualifying*' tax year is a tax year in the individual's period of ownership where neither the individual nor their spouse or civil partner is tax resident in the territory in which the dwelling house is situated, and the individual does not meet the day count test for that year. Where only part of the tax year falls into the period of ownership that part is a '*partial tax year*' and the day count test is applied to the partial tax year (see below). for this purpose, an individual is resident in a non-UK territory for a tax year if either he is liable to tax in the overseas territory, under its law relating to residency or domicile, for periods making up more than half of the year or he would be resident there under the UK statutory residence test (see 57.3 RESIDENCE AND DOMICILE) if the rules of the test were applied to that territory.

The exemption for periods of absence (see 53.7(a) above) can still apply for a non-qualifying tax year. The exemption for job-related accommodation (see 53.7(d) above) may also apply. However, the exemption provided for visiting forces under *TCGA 1992, s 11(1)(a)* is disregarded for these purposes (see 25.65 EXEMPTIONS AND RELIEFS).

Day count test

The day count test applies to any property that is occupied as a residence, wherever situated. The test is met if either the individual or his spouse or civil partner spends at least 90 days (prorated for a partial tax year, rounded up to the nearest whole day) in one or more houses which are situated in the same overseas territory, and which either the individual or his spouse or civil partner has an interest in. A day is spent at the house if the person is there at midnight or was there at some time on that day and the following day and had stayed overnight. The 90 days do not need to be consecutive, and days spent in different houses can be aggregated, but a day which both the individual and the spouse or civil partner spend at a house is not counted twice.

[*TCGA 1992, ss 222B, 222C; FA 2015, Sch 9 paras 3, 10*].

Part-business use, changes of use etc.

[53.9] If a gain accrues on the disposal of a dwelling-house or part of a dwelling-house part of which is used *exclusively* for the purposes of a trade or business, or of a profession or vocation, the gain is apportioned and *TCGA 1992, s 223* applied in relation to the part of the gain apportioned to the part which is not exclusively used for those purposes. [*TCGA 1992, s 224(1)*].

It will be noted that the apportionment required by *TCGA 1992, s 224(1)* applies only where part of the house is used *exclusively* for business purposes. A room used partly for business and partly for residential purposes does not give rise to any restriction. However, in determining exclusivity, occasional and very minor residential use of a business room, for example its use for the keeping of private possessions, is disregarded (HMRC Capital Gains Manual CG64663). An apportionment based on the number of rooms used respectively for business and residential purposes will often suffice in cases of relatively small business use. It may not produce a result acceptable to HMRC if the residential part of a mixed property is likely to have a disproportionately lower value than the business part, as is probable in the case of, for example, accommodation above a public house (see the worked example at HMRC Capital Gains Manual CG64674). An apportionment fraction already in use for income tax purposes is not necessarily appropriate for CGT purposes (HMRC Capital Gains Manual CG64663 and, as regards farmhouses, CG64680).

The legislation does not specifically address the question of part of a residence used for the purposes of an employment, though it is arguable that the reference in *TCGA 1992, s 224(1)* to a 'business' includes the business carried on by the individual's employer. In practice, HMRC do not require a restriction to be made for the use (exclusive or otherwise) for employment purposes of a small part of a residence, for example a room used as a study, and this remains the case even if an expenses allowance has been given against employment income. If, however, a 'substantial part' of the property is used exclusively in connection with the employment, they will insist on a restriction of the CGT exemption on the more general grounds that relief is available only for a dwelling-house (or part) which has been the individual's only or main *residence* (see **53.2** above). (HMRC Capital Gains Manual CG 64690).

If at any time in the period of ownership there is a change in what is occupied as the individual's residence, whether on account of a reconstruction or conversion of a building or for any other reason, or there have been changes as regards the use of part of the dwelling-house for the purpose of a trade etc. or for any other purpose, the relief given under *TCGA 1992, s 223* may be adjusted in such manner as is just and reasonable. [*TCGA 1992, s 224(2)*].

HMRC's approach in cases falling within *TCGA 1992, s 224(2)* is to deal with each case on its merits, and to require an adjustment which as far as possible reflects the extent to which, and the length of time over which, each part of the dwelling-house has been used as part of residence. It is not normally considered appropriate to take into account intervening market values when apportioning gains to different periods in such cases since *TCGA 1992, s 223* clearly provides for time apportionment as the appropriate method (Revenue Tax Bulletin August 1994 p 149). Where part of a residence has been used for part of the period of ownership for other (e.g. business) purposes, but has *at some time* during the period of ownership been used as part of the main residence, the last 36 months of ownership is an exempt period by virtue of the rule at **53.2**(i) above, and this applies regardless of actual use during those last 36 months (HMRC Capital Gains Manual CG64764, 64985).

ROLLOVER RELIEF (**59**) may be available in respect of any chargeable gain arising on the business portion of a dwelling-house if a new dwelling-house is acquired, part of which will also be used *exclusively* for the purposes of a trade etc. The rolled over gain will be set against the acquisition cost of the business part of the new property.

Letting the dwelling-house may restrict the exemption given by **53.2** and **53.7** above (subject to the relief at **53.14** below) but there is no restriction where a lodger lives as part of a family (but a restriction is applied if there are two or more lodgers — see HMRC Capital Gains Manual CG64702), sharing their living accommodation and taking meals with them (HMRC Statement of Practice 14/80). Participation in the 'rent a room' income tax relief scheme of *ITTOIA 2005, ss 784–802* will not normally lead to any capital gains tax liability (HL Written Answers, 27 January 1993, Vol 514 col 94).

Adult placement carers

For disposals on or after 9 December 2009, the occupation of part of a dwelling-house by a person under an 'adult placement scheme' is disregarded in determining the period during which the dwelling-house is the main residence of the individual making the disposal. For the purposes of the part-business use provisions above, the occupation of the part of the residence under the scheme is not regarded as the use of that part exclusively for the purposes of a trade etc. The effect of theses provisions is that no restriction on the amount of relief will be required in such cases.

An '*adult placement scheme*' is a scheme to which a registration requirement under *Care Standards Act 2000, s 11* applies and under which an individual agrees to provide care and support, including accommodation, to an adult. In Scotland this relief applies by reference to arrangements constituting an adult placement service (as defined). In Northern Ireland it applies by reference to arrangements made with an adult placement agency (as defined) for the provision of accommodation to an adult.

[*TCGA 1992, s 225D; F(No 3)A 2010, s 16(3)–(5)*].

Election for main residence

[53.10] So far as it is necessary to determine which of two or more residences is an individual's main residence for 'any period' (see below), the individual may conclude that question by written notice to an HMRC officer. The notice must be given within two years from the beginning of that period but the individual may vary that notice by a further written notice to an HMRC officer as respects any period beginning not earlier than two years before the giving of the further notice. [*TCGA 1992, s 222(5)*]. With effect from 6 April 2015, there is a separate, more restricted election available where a taxpayer disposes of a residence which is the subject of a non-resident CGT disposal (see **41.25** LAND) (referred to here as a 'section 222A election').

In the case of a husband and wife or of civil partners, there can only be one residence or main residence for both, so long as 'living together' (see **46.4** MARRIED PERSONS AND CIVIL PARTNERS) and, where a notice specifying the main residence affects both spouses or civil partners, it must be given by both. [*TCGA 1992, s 222(6)*]. If when a couple marry or register a civil partnership they each have a residence and they continue to use both, the two-year period for jointly nominating the main residence begins on the date of marriage or registration (HMRC Capital Gains Manual CG64525). See Revenue Tax Bulletin, August 1994, pp 149, 150 for further discussion on elections by married couples.

The nomination of a residence as the main residence has effect until the earlier of, if any, the date from which the original notice is varied and the date on which the taxpayer's combination of residences changes (such that a new nomination becomes possible) (HMRC Capital Gains Manual CG64497). In the absence of a nomination covering any particular period of time, the question of which is the main residence is decided on the facts. The main residence will not necessarily be the one at which the taxpayer spends most of his time, although it commonly will be; for other criteria taken into account by HMRC, see HMRC Capital Gains Manual CG64545.

It is worth noting that the choice is not between two or more properties but between two or more *residences*. A property never occupied by the taxpayer as a residence cannot enter the equation (see *Harte and another v HMRC* FTT, [2012] UKFTT 258 (TC); 2012 STI 2219). A nomination given more than two years after the *acquisition* of a property will not be late if made within two years after the property is first occupied as a residence (see further below).

The case of *Griffin v Craig-Harvey* Ch D 1993, 66 TC 396 upheld the Revenue's long-standing view (see HMRC Capital Gains Manual CG64495) that, broadly and subject to the following, initial notice nominating the main residence *must* be given within two years after the individual first begins to have two or more residences if it is to be effective. Notice(s) of variation can then be made subsequently but not so as to vary the nomination of the main residence more than two years before the giving of the further notice.

In the judgment in *Griffin v Craig-Harvey* the following hypothetical situations were put forward.

(1) The taxpayer owns two houses, each of which he occupies as a residence. More than two years have elapsed since he began to have two residences. He then begins to use a third house as a residence. A new two-year period begins to run at that time so that he can make an election as between all three residences during that two-year period.
(2) If on the same facts the taxpayer ceased, after acquiring a third residence, to use one of them as a residence a new period will begin at the time of cesser so that, again, he will have a period of two years during which he can elect between the remaining residences.
(3) The taxpayer owns two houses which he occupies as residences. The taxpayer conveys one of the houses to the trustees of the settlement under which he has a beneficial interest and the trustees have power which they exercise to permit him to continue to reside in the residence. A new two-year period begins at the time when he creates the settlement and again an election can be made (jointly by the taxpayer and the trustees; see **53.11** below) within the subsequent two years.
(4) The taxpayer has two residences, one owned by him and the other by the trustees of a settlement under which the trustees have power to permit the taxpayer to occupy it as a residence. No election is made during the two years following the inception of this state of affairs. If the trustees have and exercise a power to transfer the residence which they own to the taxpayer he can elect that that residence is to be his main residence at any time during the subsequent two years.

In commenting on these examples, Vinelott J said (1) and (2) 'do no more than illustrate the inevitable consequence of [*TCGA 1992, s 222(5)*], namely that it becomes necessary to determine which of two or more residences is an individual's main residence whenever there is a change in the number of properties which he occupies as a residence'. As regards the examples at (3) and (4) above, Vinelott J said they:

> 'seem to be altogether unsurprising consequences of the legislation. If [there is a transfer as in (3) and (4) above], the transfer of the house to the trustees or from the trustees to the taxpayer is a disposal giving rise to a charge to capital gains tax on any gain so far as not exempt under [*TCGA 1992, s 222*]. The position is the same as if he had bought the house from or sold it to a stranger'.

Where a *s 222(5)* nomination has been made, it does not cease to be effective at any time simply because at that time another residence is treated as not being occupied as a residence for tax year because it is a non-qualifying tax year (see **53.8** above). [*TCGA 1992, s 222(6A); FA 2015, Sch 9 para 2*].

Where the disposal is a non-resident CGT disposal a *s 222A* election can be made in the online NRCGT return which must be submitted within 30 days of completion of the disposal (see **58.20** RETURNS). While such an election can generally vary a previously made *s 222(5)* election, it cannot vary a previous election for a residence which has already been disposed of (in whole or in part). In addition a *s 222A* election cannot subsequently be varied, either under *TCGA 1992, s 222A* or *s 222(5)*.

This provision gives an opportunity for an election where a non-resident individual who has a main residence abroad retains a UK residential property which is sold while they are non-resident rather than re-occupied (for example, because their employer assigns them to a new location, rather than returning them to the UK). Note however that the election can only be made for years which are not non-qualifying tax years.

If a *s 222A* election affects the individual's spouse or civil partner who was living with them, and both the individual and the spouse or civil partner must submit an NRCGT return, an election by the individual is only effective in relation to a period when they were living together as spouses or civil partners if the spouse or civil partner also so elects. If they are not both required to submit a return, the election made by the individual is only effective for that period if it is accompanied by a written notice of agreement by the spouse or civil partner.

[*TCGA 1992, s 222A; FA 2015, Sch 9 para 3*].

HMRC takes the view that an election can only be valid where there is a legal or equitable interest (which includes all forms of ownership, from that of the sole owner of the fee simple absolute in possession to that of the co-owner of a minimal tenancy) in the residence. Job-related accommodation (see **53.7** above) may be occupied under either a service occupancy (i.e. under a licence) or a tenancy. (Revenue Tax Bulletin October 1994 p 167).

Where for any period an individual has, or is treated by the *Taxes Acts* as having, more than one residence but his interest in each of them, or in each of them except one, is such as to have no more than a negligible capital value on the open market (e.g. a weekly rented flat or accommodation provided by an employer), the two-year time limit laid down by *TCGA 1992, s 222(5)* for nominating one of those residences as the individual's main residence will be extended where the individual was unaware that such a nomination could be made. In such cases the nomination may be made within a reasonable time of the individual becoming aware of the possibility of so doing, and it will be regarded as effective from the date on which the individual first had more than one residence (HMRC Extra-Statutory Concession D21).

Example 1

S purchased the long lease of a London flat on 1 June 2009. He occupied the flat as his sole residence until 31 July 2011 when he acquired a property in Shropshire. Both properties were thereafter occupied as residences by S until the lease of the London flat was sold on 28 February 2018, realising an otherwise chargeable gain of £75,000. S is UK-resident throughout.

The possibilities open to S are:

(i) Election for London flat to be treated as main residence throughout

Exempt gain	£75,000

(ii) Election for Shropshire property to be treated as main residence from 31 July 2011 onwards

Exempt gain $£75{,}000 \times \frac{2y2m + 1y6m}{8y9m}$	£31,429

(iii) Election for London flat to be treated as main residence up to 31 August 2016, with election for the Shropshire property to be so treated thereafter

Exempt gain $£75{,}000 \times \frac{7y3m + 1y6m}{8y9m}$	£75,000

Note to the example

(a) The elections in (iii) are the most favourable, provided they could have been made by 31 July 2013 in respect of the London flat, and by 31 August 2018 in respect of the Shropshire property. Note that the last eighteen months' ownership of the London flat is an exempt period in any case (see **53.2** above). The advantage of (iii) over (i) is that the period of ownership 1 September 2016 to 28 February 2018 of the Shropshire property will be treated as a period of residence as regards any future disposal of that property.

Example 2

HMRC themselves gave the example of an individual with two residences, X and Y. He has long since nominated X as his main residence but on, say, 15 January 2018 he disposes of Y at a substantial gain. On, say, 1 March 2018, he gives notice of variation nominating Y as his main residence from, say, 1 March 2016. On 8 March 2018, he gives further notice of variation renominating X as his main residence from, say, 8 March 2016.

> The outcome is that Y has been the individual's main residence at some time during the period of ownership, albeit for only one week at the beginning of March 2016. This is enough to give the individual the benefit of the 'final 18 months' exemption at **53.2** above, so he has secured eighteen months' relief on Y at a cost of just one week's relief on X.
>
> (HMRC Capital Gains Manual CG64510).

Occupation under terms of settlement or by will or intestacy

[53.11] The provisions of *TCGA 1992, ss 222–224* (see **53.2–53.10** above) also apply in relation to a gain accruing to the trustees of a settlement on a disposal of settled property being an asset within *TCGA 1992, s 222(1)* (see **53.2** above) where, during the period of ownership of the trustees, the dwelling-house (or part) has been the only or main residence of a person entitled to occupy it under the terms of the settlement.

In the application of those provisions, references to the individual are taken as references to the trustees except in relation to the occupation of the dwelling-house, residence in a territory and meeting the day count test at **53.8** above. References to an individual being, or being the spouse or civil partner of, a disabled person or long-term resident in a care home are taken as references to the person entitled under the settlement so being. Any *s 222(5)* election for main residence treatment under **53.10** above is to be a joint notice by the trustees and the person entitled to occupy. Any *s 222A* election under **53.10** above given by the trustees must be accompanied by a written notification from the beneficiary agreeing to its terms. The trustees must make a claim for *s 223* to apply in this way.

[*TCGA 1992, ss 225, 225E(7); FA 2014, s 58(3); FA 2015, Sch 9 para 6*].

The exemption was held to apply in *Wagstaff v HMRC* FTT, [2014] UKFTT 43 (TC).

A person is 'entitled' to occupy if he does so by permission of the trustees of a discretionary trust of which he is a beneficiary (*Sansom v Peay* Ch D 1976, 52 TC 1). See **62.4 SETTLEMENTS** as to HMRC's views on whether an 'interest in possession' is created in such circumstances.

TCGA 1992, ss 222–224 (see **53.2–53.10** above) similarly apply in relation to a gain accruing to personal representatives on a disposal of an asset within *TCGA 1992, s 222(1)* (see **53.2** above) provided that:

(a) *immediately before and after* the deceased's death the dwelling-house (or part) was the only or main residence of one or more individuals, one or more of whom have a 'relevant entitlement'; and
(b) the aggregate relevant entitlements of those individuals account for at least 75% of the 'net proceeds of disposal' of the property.

For this purpose, '*relevant entitlement*' means an entitlement as legatee of the deceased to, or to an interest in possession in, the whole or any part of the net proceeds of disposal. The '*net proceeds of disposal*' are the disposal proceeds realised by the personal representatives less any incidental costs allowable as a deduction under *TCGA 1992, s 38(1)(c)* (see **16.11** COMPUTATION OF GAINS AND LOSSES) but on the assumption that none of the proceeds is needed to meet the liabilities of the estate, including any inheritance tax liability.

In the application of *ss 222–224*, references to the individual are taken as references to the personal representatives except in relation to the occupation of the dwelling-house (or part), residence in a territory and meeting the day count test at **53.8** above. Any *s 222(5)* election for main residence treatment under **53.10** above is to be a joint notice by the personal representatives and the individuals entitled to occupy. Any *s 222A* election under **53.10** above given by the personal representatives must be accompanied by a written notification from the individuals entitled to occupy agreeing to its terms.

The personal representatives must make a claim for *s 223* to apply in this way.

[*TCGA 1992, s 225A; FA 2015, Sch 9 para 7*].

Occupation by dependent relative

[53.12] If an individual so claims, relief as in **53.2–53.10** above is given to a gain accruing to him so far as attributable to the disposal of, or of an interest in, a dwelling-house (or part) which, on 5 April 1988 or at any earlier time in his period of ownership, was the *sole* residence of a 'dependent relative' of the individual, provided 'rent-free and without any other consideration'.

Such relief is given in respect of the dwelling-house and its garden and grounds as would be given under *TCGA 1992, ss 222–224* if the dwelling-house had been the individual's only or main residence in the period of residence by the dependent relative; and any such relief is to be in addition to any relief already available under those provisions. Not more than one dwelling-house (or part) may qualify for relief as the residence of a dependent relative at any one time. In the case of an individual and his spouse or civil partner living with him, no more than one dwelling-house may qualify as the residence of a dependent relative of the claimant or of the claimant's spouse or civil partner at any one time.

[*TCGA 1992, s 226(1)(2)(4)*].

If in a case within *TCGA 1992, s 226(1)* above the dwelling-house (or part) ceases, whether before 6 April 1988 or later, to be the sole residence (provided as mentioned above) of the dependent relative, any subsequent period of residence beginning after 5 April 1988 by that or any other dependent relative is disregarded for the purposes of the above relief. [*TCGA 1992, s 226(3)*]. If a dependent relative is obliged temporarily to live elsewhere (e.g. in a nursing home), the absence will not normally be treated as bringing this provision into play (ICAEW Statement TR 739, 13 February 1989).

The condition that the dwelling-house must have been provided 'rent-free and without any other consideration' will be regarded as satisfied where the dependent relative paid all or part of the occupier's rates or council tax and the cost of repairs to the dwelling-house attributable to normal wear and tear. In addition, the exemption will not be lost where the dependent relative made other payments in respect of the property either to the individual claiming the exemption or to a third party, provided that no net income was receivable by the individual, taking one year with another. For this purpose, the income receivable and allowable deductions will be computed in accordance with normal property business income tax rules, except that account will be taken of mortgage payments (including both income and capital elements) and of other payments made by the dependent relative as consideration for the provision of the property, whether such payments were made directly to the mortgagee or other recipient or indirectly via the individual (HMRC Extra-Statutory Concession D20).

Dependent relative

'*Dependent relative*' means, in relation to an individual:

(a) any 'relative' of the individual or of his spouse who is incapacitated by old age or infirmity from maintaining himself, or
(b) the mother of the individual or of his spouse who, whether or not incapacitated, is widowed, separated, or a single woman in consequence of dissolution or annulment of marriage.

[*TCGA 1992, s 226(5)(6)*].

This definition seems to exclude the mother of a child born out of wedlock (unless the mother either is incapacitated or has married subsequent to the child's birth and then become widowed etc.) but HMRC have confirmed that such persons will in practice be included (Tolley's Practical Tax Newsletter 1986 p 143). '*Relative*' is undefined but HMRC accept that the following are relatives: a blood relation; a person who, while under the age of 16 years was an adopted child of the claimant; the husband or wife (or widow or widower) of a blood relation; a stepbrother (or sister) and a stepson (or daughter) — whether a blood relation or not; a foster parent and a foster brother (or sister) where the foster parent had custody of and maintained the foster child at his or her own expense when the child was under the age of 16; and a blood relation of the claimant's deceased wife (or husband). (HMRC Capital Gains Manual CG65574).

Old age, according to HMRC, is reached at an age of 65 years in any case, and can be reached at an age greater than 54 years if the individual becomes, only because of age, not capable of working again 'in his own industry' (i.e. a man aged 57 years is not considered to have reached old age if he chooses not to work again or is unemployed because of a general lack of jobs). An individual is regarded as infirm if he is prevented by physical or mental illness from supporting himself by working. (HMRC Capital Gains Manual CG65575–65577).

Lettings exemption

Where a property qualifies for the main private residence exemption only by virtue of these provisions, HMRC accept that the residential lettings exemption at **53.14** below may be available. (HMRC Capital Gains Manual CG64716). Note that this represents a change of view by HMRC, who, before August 2007 took the opposite view that the exemption was not available in such circumstances. See HMRC Internet Statement 1 August 2007.

Exclusions from exemptions

[53.13] The following exclusions from the exemptions described in this chapter apply.

Dwelling-house acquired for profit

The exemptions given by *TCGA 1992, s 223* do not apply in relation to a gain if the acquisition of, or of the interest in, the dwelling-house (or part) was made wholly or partly for the purpose of realising a gain from the disposal of it, and do not apply in relation to a gain *so far as attributable to* any expenditure which was incurred after the beginning of the period of ownership and was incurred wholly or partly for the purpose of realising a gain from the disposal. [*TCGA 1992, s 224(3)*]. HMRC's practice is not to take into account expenditure incurred in obtaining planning permission or in removing restrictive covenants when considering whether to apply the second leg of *TCGA 1992, s 224(3)* (Revenue Tax Bulletin, August 1994, p 150).

The two most common applications of the second leg are:

- acquisition by a leaseholder of a superior interest in the property, and
- conversion of an undivided house into self-contained flats.

(HMRC Capital Gains Manual CG65243).

In *Jones v Wilcock* (Sp C 92), [1996] SSCD 389, a married couple incurred a loss on the sale of their house. They contended that the house had been purchased 'wholly or partly for the purpose of realising a gain'. However, from the facts of the case it was decided that the house was purchased to use as the couple's home.

Relief obtained under *TCGA 1992, s 260* on earlier disposal

Anti-avoidance provisions apply to prevent perceived exploitation of the interaction between the exemption for private residences and hold-over relief under *TCGA 1992, s 260* (see **36.10** HOLD-OVER RELIEFS). Subject to the transitional rules below, the provisions apply where:

- exemption under *s 223* would otherwise be available in relation to a gain (or part of a gain) accruing after 9 December 2003 to an individual or the trustees of a settlement on a disposal (the '*later disposal*'), and
- in computing the chargeable gain which would (apart from *s 223*) accrue on that disposal, the allowable expenditure falls to be reduced to any extent in consequence, directly or indirectly, of a claim or claims under *s 260* in respect of one or more earlier disposals (whether or not made to the person making the later disposal).

Where the claim to relief under *s 260* in respect of the earlier disposal (or, if there is more than one earlier disposal, any of them) is made on or before the making of the later disposal (or, in the case of trustees, on or before the making of a claim for relief under *s 223*), the exemption given by *TCGA 1992, s 223* does not apply in relation to the gain (or part of the gain) on the later disposal. Where the claim (or any of the claims) is made after the later disposal (or claim for relief under *s 223*), *s 223* is treated as never having applied to the gain (or part of the gain) on the later disposal and any adjustments required, whether by assessment, discharge or repayment of tax or otherwise, can be made notwithstanding any time limit for the making of adjustments.

Where a claim under *s 260* is revoked, it is treated for the purposes of these provisions as having never been made.

The above provisions do not apply to a later disposal made by the trustees of a settlement if they have elected for *ITA 2007, s 508* (certain income from heritage maintenance property not to be income of settlor — see Tolley's Income Tax) to apply in relation to each tax year in which there is a '*relevant earlier disposal*' (i.e. an earlier disposal in respect of which a claim under *s 260* is made).

Transitional provisions

The above provisions are modified where the relevant earlier disposal, or, if more than one, each of the relevant earlier disposals, is made before 10 December 2003. Total exemption (under *s 223(1)*) is excluded as above, but fractional exemption (under *s 223(2)*) can be obtained. In calculating the fractional exemption, the dwelling-house (or part thereof) in question is taken not to have been the individual's only or main residence at any time after 9 December 2003, and the period of ownership after that date is taken not to form part of the last 36 months of the period of ownership.

[*TCGA 1992, ss 226A, 226B*].

Exemption for letting as residential accommodation

[53.14] Where a gain to which *TCGA 1992, s 222* (see **53.2** above) applies accrues to an individual and the dwelling-house in question, or any part of it, is or has at any time in his 'period of ownership' been wholly or partly let (thus including any tenancy or licence or agreement for a lease, tenancy or licence; see *TCGA 1992, Sch 8 para 10*) by him as residential accommodation, the part of the gain, if any, which otherwise would be a chargeable gain by reason of the letting is exempt to the extent of the lower of:

(a) £40,000 (£20,000 for disposals before 19 March 1991); and
(b) the amount of the gain otherwise exempt under *TCGA 1992, s 222(1)–(3)* (see **53.2** and **53.7** above).

[*TCGA 1992, s 223(4)*].

'*Period of ownership*' does not include any period before 31 March 1982. [*TCGA 1992, s 223(7)*].

The maximum gain that can be relieved under these provisions is the gain arising by reason of the letting. In a simple case in which a dwelling-house has at all times either been used as the owner's only or main residence or been let as residential accommodation, the gain remaining after the main private residence relief can be taken to be the gain arising by reason of the letting. See also *Example 2* below.

Note that the exemption applies to gains arising both from a residential letting of the entire residence whilst the owner is not occupying the property and to a partial residential letting whilst the owner is in residence.

The length of a letting is not determinative and the words 'residential accommodation' do not limit the above relief to accommodation which is used by a tenant etc. as his home (*Owen v Elliott* CA 1990, 63 TC 319). (In this case the taxpayer let short- and long-term accommodation in private hotel premises which he also occupied different parts of at different times of the year as his main residence in such a way that every part of the premises had at some time in his period of ownership been his main residence and it was agreed that on a disposal of the premises one-third of the gain arising was exempt under *TCGA 1992, ss 222–224*. The CA held that the above relief was also available in respect of the remaining non-exempt gain but Leggatt LJ indicated that it would not be available 'to a taxpayer the whole or part of whose dwelling-house is exclusively used as an hotel or boarding house. It will apply only where a dwelling-house has at any time been used wholly or partly for that or a like purpose by a person whose only or main residence it is'.)

Whether the let accommodation is part of the owner's dwelling-house, or is itself a separate dwelling-house, will depend on the facts of particular cases. In HMRC's view, the relief will apply to the common case where the owner of a house, which was previously occupied as his or the family home, lets part as a flat or set of rooms without structural alteration, or with only minor adaptations. Whether or not the tenants have separate washing or cooking facilities will not affect the relief. Where a property, although part of the same building, forms a dwelling-house separate from that which is, or has been, the owner's dwelling-house, e.g. a fully self-contained flat with its own access from the road, relief will not be granted. (HMRC Statement of Practice 14/80).

Where husband and wife are joint owners, they are treated like any other joint owners for the purposes of this exemption, with the result that relief of up to £80,000 is potentially available to the couple. However, HMRC officers have instructions to investigate the fact of a property being in joint ownership of husband and wife where the tax is significant. (HMRC Capital Gains Manual CG64716, 64738).

The availability of the residential lettings exemption extends to gains accruing to trustees and qualifying for the main private residence exemption under *TCGA 1992, s 225* (see **53.11** above). (HMRC Capital Gains Manual CG64716).

Where a property qualifies for the main private residence exemption due only to its having been occupied by a dependent relative on or before 5 April 1988 (see **53.12** above), HMRC accept that the residential lettings exemption may be available. (HMRC Capital Gains Manual CG64716). Note that this represents a change of view by HMRC, who, before August 2007 took the opposite view that the exemption was not available in such circumstances. See HMRC Internet Statement 1 August 2007.

These provisions do not apply to restrict an allowable loss.

For the capital gains tax consequences of eligibility for 'rent a room' income tax relief, see **53.9** above.

For reliefs applicable to the commercial letting of furnished holiday accommodation in the UK, see **26** FURNISHED HOLIDAY ACCOMMODATION.

Example 1

P sold a house in Yorkshire on 1 July 2017 realising an otherwise chargeable gain of £50,540. The house was originally purchased by P on 1 April 1988 and was occupied as a residence until 30 June 1995 when P moved to another residence, letting the house as residential accommodation. He did not re-occupy the house prior to its sale. P is UK-resident throughout.

	£
Gain on sale	50,540
Deduct Exempt amount under main residence rules	
$\frac{7y3m + 1y6m}{29y3m} \times £50,540$	15,119
	35,421
Deduct Let property exemption (see note (1))	15,119
Net chargeable gain 2017/18	£20,302

Note to the example

(1) The gain attributable to the letting (£35,421) is exempt to the extent that it does not exceed the lesser of £40,000 and the gain otherwise exempt (£15,119 in this example).

Example 2

Q purchased a house in Sussex on 1 February 2005, moved in immediately and occupied it as his main residence until 31 January 2006. It was let as residential accommodation from 1 February 2006 to 31 January 2007, was then empty until 31 January 2010, was again let as residential accommodation until 31 January 2012 and was subsequently let as office accommodation until being sold on 31 January 2018 at an otherwise chargeable gain of £78,000. Q is UK-resident throughout.

			£
Gain on sale			78,000
Deduct Exempt amount under main residence rules			
$\frac{1y + \text{last } 18m}{13y} \times £78,000$			15,000
			63,000
Deduct Let property exemption:			
Lowest of:	main residence relief	£15,000	
	statutory limit	£40,000	
	gain attributable to residential letting*	£18,000	15,000
Chargeable gain 2017/18			£48,000

$$^{*}\frac{1y + 2y}{13y} \times £78,000 = £18,000$$

Key points

[53.15] Points to consider are as follows.

- Even if the property does not qualify as the only or main residence since 31 March 1982, such occupation before that date will provide for the last 18 months of ownership to be exempt.
- Where ownership is transferred between spouses or civil partners, whether the previous period of occupation and exemption profile is also transferred depends on whether the property was the only or main residence at the time of the transfer. This can give rise to planning opportunities:
  - (a) Say a wife owns a residence for many years that has always been let out but the couple move in and use it as their main residence. On a subsequent sale the let period will not be exempt (apart from 'lettings relief') even if the property is transferred to the husband prior to sale. However if the property is transferred to the husband before it becomes the couple's main residence, his period of ownership will start on the date of transfer rather than his wife's original acquisition date and so only the period between transfer and the occupation will not be exempt. The whole of the prior non-exempt period falls out of account.
  - (b) This rule can be disadvantageous as well. Where a property owned by one spouse prior to marriage and qualifying as a main residence, but is no longer their main residence, is transferred to the spouse who has never lived there, the acquiring spouse will lose the benefit of exempt periods including the final 18 months.
- Periods of absence — to gain the benefit of exempt periods of absence the property must be the only or main residence after the period of absence (unless employment elsewhere prevents occupation). The legislation does not prevent the subsequent period being the subject of an election (if it qualifies) to make it the only or main residence thus securing the extra exempt periods.
- When couples separate the marital home can continue to be the only or main residence of the departing spouse until it is disposed of even though that spouse no longer occupies the property.
- Where there is more than one residence an election in favour of one or other property can be beneficial. A two year window to make an election opens when there is a change in the combination of residences. Once made, an election can be varied outside this window but it should be noted that when the combination of residences again changes any existing election ceases to have effect.
- Private residence relief is not intended to relieve speculative gains or gains arising from development (**53.13**). Property owners normally expect a gain and are often willing to undertake a variety of activities to enhance a potential gain. Activities comparable to property development can create planning opportuni-

ties and pitfalls and considerable care is required. However, simply, obtaining planning permission for future alternations is often acceptable. (See CG65243).

- It is increasingly common for individuals to work from home. In such cases, a taxpayer may be keen to maximise the proportion of expenses allowable for income tax. If the fixed-rated deduction is not used, the normal method of apportionment for income tax is based upon floor space and time used, e.g. an outbuilding designated as an office makes up 30% of floor space and is so used 100% of the time. Where an area is used **exclusively** for business purposes, private residence relief is restricted. It is important when considering income tax claims to remembers the impact exclusive use will have on the capital gains tax exemption. If practical and possible, retaining a reasonable element of private use may in the long term be preferable.
- If a property was occupied by a 'dependent relative' before 6 April 1988 or by a beneficiary of a settlement then some period of exemption may apply.
- When a property has not been the main residence throughout the period of ownership, it has frequently been let. Lettings relief is a valuable extension to private residence relief. Where the property is jointly owned the maximum relief of £40,000 applies to each owner (including spouses and civil partners). However, watch out for the flies in the letting relief ointment:
  - Lettings relief only relates to 'the gain by reason of letting' — beware of large periods of ownership where the property was unoccupied or not the elected main residence. For example, Matt sold a property that he had owned for ten years making a gain of £100,000. He had lived in it as his main residence for the first year, used it as holiday home for the next six years and let it for the final three years. The gain qualifying for private residence relief is 4/10 (£40,000). The gain remaining after private residence relief is £60,000 but the gain by reason of letting is only 3 out of 10 years (3/10). The max lettings relief is therefore only £30,000.
  - Lettings relief is not available in respect of property let for trade or professional use (unless let as residential accommodation);
  - Lettings relief is not available where the property which is let forms a separate dwelling house (see **53.14** for HMRC view on a flat created without structural alteration or only minor adaptations).

54

Qualifying Corporate Bonds

Introduction	**54.1**
Exemption rules	**54.2**
Definitions	**54.3**
Reorganisation of share capital	**54.4**

Simon's Taxes. See **C2.820**, **C2.821**, **D6.110**, **D6.115**.

Introduction

[54.1] Gains on qualifying corporate bonds are exempt from tax on chargeable gains. This chapter describes the exemption and also the special provisions which apply to reorganisations of share capital where either the original shares or the new shares are qualifying corporate bonds.

The definition of a qualifying corporate bond is also given. Different rules apply for corporation tax and capital gains tax purposes. For corporation tax purposes, any asset representing a loan relationship of a company is a qualifying corporate bond. For capital gains tax, broadly, a qualifying corporate bond is a security on which the debt is a normal commercial loan and which is expressed in sterling with no provision for its conversion into, or redemption in, another currency. See **54.3** below for the detailed provisions.

See **44.13** LOSSES for allowable loss relief in respect of certain qualifying corporate bonds evidencing loans made before 17 March 1998 which become irrecoverable etc.

Exemption rules

[54.2] A gain on the disposal of a qualifying corporate bond (as defined in **54.3** below) is not a chargeable gain, and a loss is not an allowable loss. [*TCGA 1992, s 115(1)(a)*].

The same applies to disposals of options or contracts to acquire or dispose of qualifying corporate bonds (see **7.7**, **7.8** ASSETS).

See **54.4** below re share capital reorganisations involving qualifying corporate bonds.

Definitions

[54.3] Different definitions apply for the purposes of corporation tax and capital gains tax.

Corporation tax

For corporation tax purposes 'qualifying corporate bond' means *any* asset representing a loan relationship of a company (see **15.5** COMPANIES — CORPORATE FINANCE AND INTANGIBLES).

[*TCGA 1992, s 117(A1)*].

Capital gains tax

Definition of corporate bond

Before defining a 'qualifying corporate bond', it is first necessary to define a 'corporate bond'. Subject to the specific inclusion of certain securities within this definition (see below) and the exclusion of some (again, see below), a '*corporate bond*' is a 'security' which fulfils both the following conditions.

(a) The debt on the security represents, and has at all times represented, a 'normal commercial loan'.
'*Normal commercial loan*' is as would be defined by *CTA 2010, s 162* if, for *subsection (2)(a)–(c)* of that section, there were substituted the words 'corporate bonds (within the meaning of *TCGA 1992, s 117*)'. The broad effect of the modification is that securities can be treated as corporate bonds if they carry conversion rights into other corporate bonds but not if the conversion rights relate to securities other than corporate bonds. Securities carrying an indirect right of conversion into ordinary shares were held not to be corporate bonds in *Weston v Garnett* CA, [2005] STC 1134.

(b) The security is expressed in sterling and no provision is made for its conversion into, or redemption in, a currency other than sterling.
A security is *not* treated as expressed in sterling if the amount of sterling falls to be determined by reference to the value at any time of any other currency or asset. A provision for redemption in a currency other than sterling is disregarded provided the rate of exchange to be used is that prevailing at redemption.
Securities carrying an option for redemption in a foreign currency do not become corporate bonds when the option lapses (*Harding v HMRC* CA, [2008] STC 3499). In *Blumenthal v HMRC* FTT, [2012] SFTD 1264, however, the variation of the terms of securities to remove an option for redemption in a foreign currency was held to have the effect of converting the securities into corporate bonds. In *Trigg v HMRC* UT , [2016] STC 1310, bonds which were denominated in sterling but which had been issued with a provision for their conversion into euros if the UK were to adopt the euro were held not to be qualifying corporate bonds as a result of the provision.

[*TCGA 1992, s 117(1)(2)*].

'*Security*' includes any loan stock or similar security of any government or public or local authority in the UK or elsewhere, or of any company, and whether secured or unsecured. [*TCGA 1992, ss 117(1), 132(3)(b)*].

Inclusion of other securities within the definition of corporate bond

A deeply discounted security (within **63.21** SHARES AND SECURITIES) is a corporate bond (and is also a qualifying corporate bond — see below). [*TCGA 1992, s 117(2AA)*].

Save in relation to the application of this definition for the purposes of *TCGA 1992, s 254* (loss relief for irrecoverable loans made before 17 March 1998 to traders and evidenced by qualifying corporate bonds — see **44.13** LOSSES), 'corporate bond' also includes a share in a building society (within *Building Societies Act 1986*) which meets the condition in (b) above and which is a 'qualifying share' (i.e. a share which is either a 'permanent interest bearing share', as defined, or is of a description specified in Treasury regulations for this purpose). [*TCGA 1992, s 117(4)–(6)(11)(b), (12)(13); SI 1999 No 1953*].

'Corporate bond' also includes any debenture issued after 15 March 1993 which is not a 'security' as defined above but would fall to be treated as such under *TCGA 1992, s 251(6)* (see **25.5** EXEMPTIONS AND RELIEFS). This does not apply to debentures acquired by a person following a prior disposal of a qualifying corporate bond derived from shares giving rise to a deferred gain (where the general exemption in *TCGA 1992, s 115* has had effect in accordance with *TCGA 1992, s 116(10)(c)* — see **54.4** below). (This provision and *TCGA 1992, s 251(6)* prevent, in certain circumstances, the issue of a debenture which neither represents a debt on a security nor is a qualifying corporate bond.) [*TCGA 1992, s 117(6A)*].

An alternative finance arrangement which is an investment bond arrangement within *TCGA 1992, s 151N* (see **3.3** ALTERNATIVE FINANCE ARRANGEMENTS) is a 'corporate bond' if:

- the 'capital' is expressed in sterling;
- the arrangements do not include provision for the 'redemption payment' to be in a currency other than sterling;
- entitlement to the redemption payment is not capable of conversion into an entitlement to the issue of securities other than other such arrangements; and
- the 'additional payments' are not determined wholly or partly by reference to the value of the bond assets.

For this purpose, '*capital*', '*redemption payment*' and '*additional payments*' are all defined as at **3.3** ALTERNATIVE FINANCE ARRANGEMENTS.

[*TCGA 1992, ss 117(6D), 151T; TIOPA 2010, Sch 2 para 40, Sch 8 para 200*].

Securities excluded from being corporate bonds

An excluded indexed security (as defined by *ITTOIA 2005, s 433* and meaning broadly a security the amount payable on redemption of which is linked to the value of chargeable assets) issued after 5 April 1996 is not a corporate bond. An excluded indexed security issued before that date is a corporate bond only if it satisfies the general conditions above and if the question of whether or not it is a corporate bond arises only for the purposes of *TCGA 1992, s 116(10)* (reorganisation of share capital involving the issue of a qualifying corporate bond — see **54.4** below). [*TCGA 1992, s 117(6B)(6C)*].

Definition of qualifying corporate bond

A corporate bond:

(A) is a '*qualifying corporate bond*' if it is issued after 13 March 1984; and

(B) becomes a '*qualifying corporate bond*' if, having been issued before 14 March 1984, it is acquired by any person after 13 March 1984 unless

- (i) the acquisition is as the result of *any* disposal treated as a no gain/no loss transaction or a disposal where the consideration is reduced by an amount of held-over gain under *TCGA 1992, s 165* or *s 260* (see **36.2–36.12** HOLD-OVER RELIEFS); and
- (ii) the bond was not a qualifying corporate bond before the disposal.

[*TCGA 1992, s 117(7)(8)*].

See the example below.

Where a right to a security is comprised in a provisional letter of allotment or similar instrument, the security is not deemed to be issued until acceptance has been made. [*TCGA 1992, s 117(11)(a)*].

A security which is a corporate bond due to its being a deeply discounted security (see above) is a qualifying corporate bond whatever its date of issue. [*TCGA 1992, s 117(8A)*].

Example

B has the following transactions in 5% unsecured loan stock issued in 1983 by F Ltd.

		£
11.11.83	Purchase £2,000	1,800
10.7.89	Gift from wife £1,000 (original cost £800)	—
30.9.97	Purchase £2,000	2,100
5.6.17	Sale £4,000	(3,300)

Apart from the gift on 10.7.89, all acquisitions were arm's length purchases. B's wife acquired her £1,000 holding on 11.11.83. Indexation allowance of £266 arose on the transfer from wife to husband.

For the purposes of the accrued income scheme, the sale is without accrued interest and the rebate amount is £20. The stock is a corporate bond as defined by *TCGA 1992, s 117(1)* and therefore a 'relevant security'.

Under the rules for matching relevant securities in *TCGA 1992, s 106A* (see **64.2** SHARES AND SECURITIES — IDENTIFICATION RULES), the stock disposed of is identified with acquisitions as follows.

(i) Identify £2,000 with purchase on 30.9.97 (LIFO)

		£
Disposal consideration	$£3,300 \times \frac{2,000}{4,000}$	1,650
Add rebate amount	$£20 \times \frac{2,000}{4,000}$	10
		1,660
Allowable cost		2,100
Loss		£440

The loss is *not* allowable as the £2,000 stock purchased on 30.9.97 is a qualifying corporate bond (note (a)). [*TCGA 1992, s 115*].

(ii) Identify £1,000 with acquisition on 10.7.89

		£
Disposal consideration	$£3,300 \times \frac{1,000}{4,000}$	825
Add rebate amount	$£20 \times \frac{1,000}{4,000}$	5
		830
Allowable cost (including indexation to 10.7.89)		1,066
Allowable loss		£236

The loss is allowable as the stock acquired on 10.7.89 is not a qualifying corporate bond (note (b)).

(iii) Identify £1,000 with part of purchase on 11.11.83

		£
Disposal consideration	$£3,300 \times \frac{1,000}{4,000}$	825
Add rebate amount	$£20 \times \frac{1,000}{4,000}$	5
		830
Allowable cost	$£1,800 \times \frac{1,000}{4,000}$	900
Allowable loss		£70

The loss is allowable as the stock acquired on 11.11.83 is not a qualifying corporate bond (note (c)).

Notes to the example

(a) The acquisition on 30.9.97 is a qualifying corporate bond as it was acquired after 13 March 1984 otherwise than as a result of an excluded disposal.

(b) The acquisition on 10.7.89 was the result of an excluded disposal, being a no gain/no loss transfer between spouses where the first spouse had acquired the stock before 14 March 1984. It is therefore not a qualifying corporate bond.

(c) Securities acquired before 14 March 1984 cannot be qualifying corporate bonds in the hands of the person who so acquired them.

Reorganisation of share capital

[54.4] Special provisions apply to a transaction ('*relevant transaction*') where otherwise *TCGA 1992, ss 127–130* (share reorganisation rules for 'original shares' and 'new holding'; see **63.2** SHARES AND SECURITIES) would apply under any provision contained in *TCGA 1992, Pt IV Ch II* (reorganisation of share capital, conversion of securities etc.), and either the original shares would consist of or include a qualifying corporate bond and the new holding would not, or the original shares would not and the new holding would consist of or include such a bond.

The provisions apply equally to a conversion of securities effected other than by means of a transaction, for example in consequence of the terms of the security. Where the qualifying corporate bond would constitute the original shares it is referred to as '*the old asset*', the shares and securities constituting the new holding being referred to as '*the new asset*'. Where the qualifying corporate bond would constitute the new holding it is referred to as '*the new asset*', the shares and securities constituting the original shares being referred to as '*the old asset*'.

TCGA 1992, ss 127–130 do not apply to the relevant transaction so far as it relates to the old asset and the new asset. (HMRC has stated that where shares (or other chargeable securities) are exchanged, converted etc. for a new holding consisting partly of qualifying corporate bonds and partly of shares etc., then *TCGA 1992, ss 127–130* are only disapplied to the extent that the consideration takes the form of qualifying corporate bonds, any apportionment of the base cost of the original shares being on a just and reasonable basis under *TCGA 1992, s 52(4)* by reference to the respective market values at the time of exchange etc. of the shares etc. and qualifying corporate bonds received in exchange etc. (Revenue Tax Bulletin February 1993 p 57).

Where the qualifying corporate bond would constitute the old asset, the shares or securities which constitute the new asset are to be treated as being acquired on the date of the relevant transaction and for a consideration of the market value of the old asset immediately before the relevant transaction. Similar provisions apply where the qualifying corporate bond constitutes the new asset. Where a sum of money by way of consideration for the old asset is received, in addition to the new asset, that sum is to be deducted from the deemed market value consideration and where a sum of money is paid by way of consideration, in addition to the old asset, that sum is to be added to the deemed market value consideration. See also (ii) below.

Old asset consisting of qualifying corporate bond

Where the old asset consists of a qualifying corporate bond, then so far as it relates to the old and the new asset, the relevant transaction is to be treated as a disposal of the old asset and an acquisition of the new asset. [*TCGA 1992, s 116(9)*].

Other cases

In all other cases (e.g. where the new asset consists of a qualifying corporate bond) then so far as it relates to the old asset and to the new asset the relevant transaction is *not* to be treated as a disposal of the old asset but:

(a) the chargeable gain or allowable loss is calculated that would have accrued had the old asset been disposed of at the time of the relevant transaction at its market value immediately before that time, and

(b) subject to the exclusions below, the whole or a corresponding part of the calculated chargeable gain or allowable loss at (a) above is to be deemed to accrue on a subsequent disposal of the whole or part of the new asset. The exemption provided by **54.2** above applies only to the gain or loss that actually accrues on that disposal and not to the gain or loss that is deemed to accrue. [*TCGA 1992, s 116(10)*].

Exclusions

The following exclusions are made to the above provisions.

(i) The provisions in (b) above do not apply to disposals falling within: *TCGA 1992, s 58(1)* (see **46.5** MARRIED PERSONS AND CIVIL PARTNERS); *s 62(4)* (see **19.14** DEATH); *s 139* in respect of disposals after 13 March 1989 (see **14.11** COMPANIES); *s 140A* (see **49.13** OVERSEAS MATTERS); *s 140E* (see **49.15** OVERSEAS MATTERS); *s 171(1)* (see **29.3** GROUPS OF COMPANIES); or *s 172* (now repealed — see **49.3** OVERSEAS MATTERS). Where there is such a disposal (and without there having been a previous disposal other than such a disposal or a devolution on death) the person who has acquired the new asset is treated for the purposes of (b) above as if the new asset had been acquired by him at the same time and for the same consideration as it was acquired by the person making the disposal.

(ii) Where a chargeable gain arises under (a) above and part of the consideration for the old asset is received as money, a proportion of the chargeable gain is deemed to accrue at that time. The proportion is the ratio which the sum of money bears to the market value of the old asset immediately before the relevant transaction. On a later disposal of a part or the whole of the new asset, the proportion already deemed to have accrued is to be deducted from the gain accruing under (b) above. However, if the sum of money is 'small' in comparison with the market value of the old asset immediately before the relevant transaction, HMRC may direct that no chargeable gain accrues at that time. The money consideration is then deducted from allowable expenditure on any subsequent disposal (see **10.3** CAPITAL SUMS DERIVED FROM ASSETS).

For the purpose of the above, HMRC regard 'small' as meaning 5% or less (see HMRC Capital Gains Manual CG53857, 57836) and also regard an amount of £3,000 or less as 'small', regardless of whether or not it would pass the 5% test (Revenue Tax Bulletin February 1997 p 397).

(iii) The treatment at (a) and (b) above) is disapplied in certain circumstances (with the result that the transaction is treated as a disposal of the old asset and an acquisition of the new asset) where the old asset consists of shares or securities that have qualified for tax relief under the corporate venturing scheme or the community investment tax credit scheme. See **18.21** CORPORATE VENTURING SCHEME and Tolley's Income Tax under Community Investment Tax Relief. See also **66.14** SUBSTANTIAL SHAREHOLDINGS OF COMPANIES.

[*TCGA 1992, s 116(1)–(14)*].

In *Hancock v HMRC* CA, [2017] EWCA Civ 198, a married couple held the entire share capital of a company (B). In 2000 they sold the shares to another company (L), receiving loan notes as consideration. The terms of issue of the loan notes included a provision enabling the noteholders to require repayment in US dollars, which prevented the loan notes from constituting qualifying corporate bonds within *TCGA 1992, s 117*. The sale agreement also included provision for further consideration depending on the subsequent performance of B's business. In 2001 the couple received further loan notes under this provision. These further notes initially also included a provision enabling the noteholders to require repayment in US dollars, but that provision was removed by deeds of variation in 2002, with the result that these further notes did constitute qualifying corporate bonds. In May 2003 the couple exchanged both their QCB and non-QCB holdings of loan notes for further loan notes, which constituted qualifying corporate bonds, and which were redeemed in June 2003. HMRC issued assessments charging CGT under *TCGA 1992, s 116*. The couple appealed. They contended that there had been only one conversion so that the original gain (realised on the disposal of the shares) had been rolled into exempt qualifying corporate bonds. The Upper Tribunal found however that the overall structure of the provisions suggested that each conversion was a different transaction and that each original single asset or single security should be treated as the subject of a conversion. The Tribunal therefore concluded that the conversion of the first set of loan notes into the further loan notes was a conversion to which *s 116(1)* applied so that on their redemption, the frozen gain was realised, triggering a taxable gain calculated at the earlier point of the removal of the dollar redemption provision. The Court of Appeal upheld the decision that the transaction should be treated as two separate conversions so that the gain did not disappear. It noted that if Mr and Mrs H's argument were correct, transactions which include QCBs and non-QCBs on the input side and QCBs on the output side would be excluded from the operation of *s 116* as one 'side' must not include QCBs. The gain accrued on the non-QCBs would then escape CGT altogether, which the Court noted could not be the right reading of *s 116*. This result would not be possible if the conversions of QCBs and non-QCBs were treated separately and this was justified as a 'necessary adaptation'.

Miscellaneous

See also **66.20** SUBSTANTIAL SHAREHOLDINGS OF COMPANIES.

Where the new asset is a qualifying corporate bond which is subsequently gifted to a charity (within **11.7** CHARITIES), HMRC take the view that no deferred gain or loss will arise to the donor (or the charity) under (b) above (Revenue Tax Bulletin May 1992 p 21 and HMRC Capital Gains Manual CG66624).

A special rule has effect where, before 15 February 1999, there occurred a transaction (the original transaction) to which *TCGA 1992, ss 127–130* applied and the new holding consisted of or included something (the new asset) which becomes a 'deeply discounted security' (and thus a qualifying corporate bond — see **54.3** above) by virtue of the widening of the definition of that term to take further account of potential redemptions before maturity (see **63.21** SHARES AND SECURITIES). In relation to any disposal or part disposal of the new asset after 14 February 1999, there is deemed to have been a transaction subsequent to the original transaction whereby the holder of the new asset disposed of it and immediately re-acquired it. The re-acquired asset is deemed to consist of a qualifying corporate bond and the subsequent transaction is deemed to be one to which *TCGA 1992, s 116* applies, with the same consequences as in (a) and (b) above. The subsequent transaction is deemed to have occurred immediately after the original transaction, except that where the original transaction occurred before 5 April 1996 the subsequent transaction is deemed to have occurred on that date. [*FA 1999, s 66*].

See **22.33** EMPLOYEE SHARE SCHEMES for the interaction of the provisions above with those relating to certain disposals to employee share ownership trusts.

See **44.13** LOSSES for the interaction of the provisions above with the now repealed provisions relating to loss relief by reference to certain qualifying corporate bonds evidencing loans which become irrecoverable etc.

Example

D holds 5,000 £1 ordinary shares in H Ltd. He acquired the shares in April 2001 by subscription at par. On 1 August 2006, he accepted an offer for the shares from J plc. The terms of the offer were one 25p ordinary share of J plc and £10 J plc 10% unsecured loan stock (a qualifying corporate bond) for each H Ltd ordinary share. Both the shares and the loan stock are listed on the Stock Exchange. In December 2017, D sells £20,000 loan stock at its quoted price of £105 per cent.

The value of J plc ordinary shares at 1 August 2006 was £3.52 per share and the loan stock was £99.20 per cent.

The cost of the H Ltd shares must be apportioned between the J plc ordinary shares and loan stock.

	£
Value of J plc shares	
5,000 × £3.52	17,600
Value of J plc loan stock	
£50,000 × 99.2%	49,600

	£67,200
Allowable cost of J plc shares	
$\frac{17,600}{67,200} \times £5,000$	£1,310
Allowable cost of J plc loan stock	
$\frac{49,600}{67,200} \times £5,000$	£3,690

Chargeable gain on H Ltd shares attributable to J plc loan stock to date of exchange

	£
Deemed disposal consideration	49,600
Allowable cost	3,690
Deferred chargeable gain	£45,910
Deferred chargeable gain accruing on disposal of loan stock in December 2017	
Loan stock sold (nominal)	£20,000
Total holding of loan stock before disposal (nominal)	£50,000
Deferred chargeable gain accruing in 2017/18	
$\frac{20,000}{50,000} \times £45,910$	£18,364

Notes to the example

(a) The gain on the sale of J plc loan stock is exempt (as the stock is a qualifying corporate bond) except for that part which relates to the gain on the previous holding of H Ltd shares. [*TCGA 1992, ss 115, 116(10)*]. There will also be income tax consequences under the accrued income scheme.

(b) The qualifying corporate bond is treated as acquired at the date of the reorganisation, so even if the original shares had been held at 31 March 1982, re-basing would *not* apply on the subsequent disposal, after 5 April 1988, of the loan stock.

(c) The exchange of J plc ordinary shares for H Ltd shares is dealt with under *TCGA 1992, ss 127–130* (see **63.2** SHARES AND SECURITIES), and no gain or loss will arise until the J plc shares are disposed of.

55

Remittance Basis

Introduction to the remittance basis	55.1
2008/09 and subsequent years	55.2
Chargeable gains remitted to the UK	55.3
Property used to make qualifying investments	55.4
Charge for claiming the remittance basis	55.5
Foreign currency bank accounts	55.6
2007/08 and earlier years	55.8
Remittances generally	55.9
Key points concerning the remittance basis	55.10

Cross-references. See **7.3** ASSETS for the location of assets; **21.6** DOUBLE TAX RELIEF for relief available where remittance basis applies; **49.6** OVERSEAS MATTERS for relief available where overseas gains are unremittable to the UK; **57** RESIDENCE AND DOMICILE.

Simon's Taxes. See **C1.603**, **E6.324–E6.332**.

Introduction to the remittance basis

[55.1] UK residents are, subject to any DOUBLE TAX RELIEF (**21**), normally liable to capital gains tax on the whole of their worldwide chargeable gains arising in a tax year (the arising basis). The remittance basis is available to UK resident individuals who are not domiciled in the UK. From 2017/18, in most cases (but see **55.2** below) the individual must also not be deemed domiciled in the UK (see **57.34** RESIDENCE AND DOMICILE) for the remittance basis to apply. The remittance basis provides for foreign source chargeable gains to be charged to tax by reference to the extent to which they are remitted to, or received in, the UK.

Fundamental changes were made to the remittance basis by *FA 2008*, so that from 2008/09 a claim is required in most cases. The claim applies for income tax purposes also. An individual who claims the remittance basis loses entitlement to the annual exempt amount and, if he is a 'long-term UK resident', he is also liable to an additional tax charge (see **55.5** below). For 2011/12 and earlier years, HMRC operated a number of concessionary practices to simplify the effect of the remittance basis on foreign currency bank accounts, but there were also anti-avoidance provisions to prevent losses arising on such accounts where no economic loss was suffered. Such gains are exempt where made by individuals, trustees or personal representatives on or after 6 April 2012. See **55.2–55.7** below.

For the application of the remittance basis for 2007/08 and earlier years, see **55.8** below.

HMRC's views on the practical operation of the remittance basis are contained in HMRC Capital Gains Manual CG25300–25431.

2008/09 and subsequent years

[55.2] For 2008/09 onwards, chargeable gains ('*foreign chargeable gains*') arising to an individual in a tax year on the disposal of assets situated outside the UK are taxed on the remittance basis if he is resident in the UK for that year but not domiciled in the UK in that year and:

- (a) he makes a claim for the remittance basis to apply under *ITA 2007, s 809B*; or
- (b) his 'unremitted foreign income and gains' for the year are less than £2,000; or
- (c) he has no UK income or gains for the year other than taxed investment income (as defined) not exceeding £100, no relevant foreign income or gains are remitted to the UK in that year (see below) and either he is under 18 throughout the year or he has been UK resident in not more than six of the immediately preceding nine tax years.

For 2017/18 and subsequent tax years, the individual must also not be deemed domiciled in the UK in that tax year (see **57.34** RESIDENCE AND DOMICILE) in order to make a claim under (a) above, or for the automatic remittance basis treatment under (c) above to apply. The remittance basis *does* still apply automatically in the case of (b) above for an individual who is deemed domiciled in the UK, but who is not domiciled in the UK under general law.

Where the above applies, the remittance basis applies for the year concerned for both capital gains tax and income tax purposes. Where (a) above applies, the remittance basis is subject to the charge on nominated income or chargeable gains at **55.5** below. Where (b) or (c) above apply, the individual can notify HMRC in his tax return for that year that the remittance basis is not to apply.

If the tax year is a split year under the statutory residence test (see **57.18** RESIDENCE AND DOMICILE) foreign chargeable gains arising in the overseas part of the year are not taxed on the remittance basis regardless of the part of the year in which they are remitted; such gains are either exempt or chargeable under the provisions for temporary non-residents (see **49.5** OVERSEAS MATTERS).

In (b) above, an individual's '*unremitted foreign income and gains*' for a tax year are his 'foreign income and gains' for the year less so much of those income and gains as are remitted to the UK in that year. In (c) above, the foreign income and gains which must not be remitted to the UK in the year are any foreign income and gains for that year, for every other year for which (a), (b) or (c) above apply and every year before 2008/09 in which the taxpayer was UK resident but was not UK domiciled. An individual's '*foreign income and gains*' for a tax year are:

- (i) chargeable overseas earnings (within *ITEPA 2003, s 23*);
- (ii) non-UK general earnings within *ITEPA 2003, s 26(1)*;
- (iii) foreign securities income within *ITEPA 2003, s 41F* (previously *ITEPA 2003, s 41A*);

(iv) amounts chargeable as disguised remuneration under *ITEPA 2003, ss 554Z9(2)* or *553Z10(2)*;

(v) relevant foreign income within *ITTOIA 2005, s 830* (but for 2007/08 and earlier years, relevant foreign income is included only if the remittance basis applied to that income under *ITTOIA 2005, s 831, ICTA 1988, s 65(5)* or an earlier enactment); and

(vi) where he is not domiciled in the UK, foreign chargeable gains.

[*TCGA 1992, s 12(1)(1A)(4); ITA 2007, ss 809B–809E, 809Z7; FA 2012, Sch 12 paras 2, 5; FA 2013, Sch 45 para 152(2)–(4), Sch 46 paras 2–5, 17, 24; FA 2014, s 59; FA 2015, s 24(2); SI 2016 No 74; F(No 2)A 2017, Sch 8 para 14(2)(4)(6)*].

Chargeable gains treated as accruing to an individual under *TCGA 1992, s 87* in 2008/09 or a subsequent year are foreign chargeable gains regardless of the location of the assets disposed of. See **48.15** OFFSHORE SETTLEMENTS.

Effect of remittance basis

Chargeable gains are treated as accruing to the individual in any tax year in which any of the foreign chargeable gains are remitted to the UK. If the tax year is a split year under the statutory residence test (see **57.18** RESIDENCE AND DOMICILE) the gains are treated as accruing in the part of the year (i.e. the UK part of the year or the overseas part of the year) in which the gains are remitted. The amount of the gains treated as accruing is equal to the full amount of those gains remitted in the year or, in the case of a split year, that part of the year. [*TCGA 1992, s 12(2)–(3); FA 2013, Sch 45 para 95*]. Where the remittance basis applied for 2007/08 or an earlier year (see **55.8** below) and gains arising in any such year are not remitted to the UK before 6 April 2008, this provision applies to those gains for 2008/09 onwards as if the taxpayer had made a claim under (a) above for the year in which the gain arose. [*FA 2008, Sch 7 para 84*].

For the circumstances in which chargeable gains are treated as remitted to the UK, see **55.3** below.

Annual exempt amount

No annual exempt amount (see **2.6** ANNUAL RATES AND EXEMPTIONS) is available for a tax year in respect of which a claim for the remittance basis under (a) above has been made. [*TCGA 1992, s 3(1A)*].

Losses

An individual who is not domiciled in the UK who claims the remittance basis (see (a) above) for the first time can make an irrevocable election for the year concerned so that the following provisions apply in that and subsequent years. From 2017/18, the deemed domicile rules apply here (see **57.34** RESIDENCE AND DOMICILE). If no such election is made in respect of that year, losses accruing in that year and any subsequent year (other than one in which he is domiciled in the UK) on the disposal of assets situated outside the UK ('*foreign losses*') are not allowable losses.

If an individual has made such an election, but then later, in a tax year (from 2017/18 onwards) becomes domiciled in the UK (for example, by becoming deemed domiciled through long-term residence), the election no longer applies to that or subsequent tax years. However, from 2017/18, the election can also be made by an individual who is not domiciled in the UK, in the first tax year in which they claim the remittance basis following a period of UK domicile. Therefore, an individual whose previous election lapsed on becoming UK domiciled, is not prevented from making the election again once the conditions are met.

The election must be made within the normal time limit for CLAIMS (**13.5**). [*TCGA 1992, s 16ZA; F(No 2)A 2017, Sch 8 para 3*].

Gains remitted in tax year after year in which they accrue

Where an election has effect, allowable losses and the annual exempt amount (where available) cannot be set off against chargeable gains treated as accruing as a result of the remittance to the UK of foreign chargeable gains in a year subsequent to that in which they arose. (The gains may, however, already have been reduced by losses matched with them — see below.) [*TCGA 1992, s 16ZB; FA 2013, Sch 45 para 98; F(No 2)A 2017, Sch 8 para 4*].

Calculation of taxable amount for year to which remittance basis applies

Where an election has effect, the amount on which an individual who is not domiciled in the UK is charged to capital gains tax in respect of a year to which the remittance basis applies under (a)–(c) above is calculated as follows.

Step 1.

Allowable losses are deducted from chargeable gains (excluding gains attributed under *TCGA 1992, s 87* or *s 89(2)* (see **48.14** OFFSHORE SETTLEMENTS)) in the following order:

(I) foreign chargeable gains arising in the year and remitted to the UK in the year or, where the year is a split year under the statutory residence test (see **57.18** RESIDENCE AND DOMICILE), the UK part of the year;

(II) foreign chargeable gains arising in the year but either not remitted to the UK or, where the year is a split year, remitted to the UK in the overseas part of the year; and

(III) all other chargeable gains arising in the year (other than gains treated as accruing on the remittance to the UK of foreign chargeable gains arising in a previous year).

If the losses reduce but do not exhaust gains within (II) above, the losses are deducted from those gains in reverse chronological order (starting with the last gain to arise in the year). Where necessary, losses are deducted from gains arising on the same day on a pro rata basis.

Step 2.

Only the amounts deducted in Step 1 from gains within (I) and (III) above are deducted as allowable losses in calculating the amount on which the individual is chargeable to capital gains tax for the year.

Any losses deducted from gains under Step 1 above cannot be carried forward, but where a loss is deducted from a foreign chargeable gain within (II) above, the amount of that gain is reduced by the amount deducted (so that relief for the loss is effectively obtained if the gain is subsequently remitted to the UK).

[*TCGA 1992, ss 16ZC, 16ZD; FA 2013, Sch 45 para 99; F(No 2)A 2017, Sch 8 para 5*].

Example

Daanish is resident but not domiciled in the UK. He claims the remittance basis for the first time in 2016/17 and also claims that basis for 2017/18. He makes the following gains and losses.

	£
2016/17	
Foreign chargeable gain — remitted to the UK in 2017/18	£20,000
2017/18	
Foreign chargeable gain — remitted to the UK in 2017/18	£10,000
Foreign chargeable gain — not remitted to the UK	£12,000
Foreign loss	£27,000
UK chargeable gain	£25,000

If Daanish makes an election under *TCGA 1992, s 16ZA* for 2016/17, his chargeable gains computation for 2017/18 is as follows.

Allocation of allowable loss to gain

		£
(i)	2017/18 foreign gain remitted in 2017/18	10,000
(ii)	2017/18 foreign gain not remitted to UK	12,000
(iii)	2017/18 UK chargeable gain (part)	5,000
		£27,000

Chargeable gains 2017/18

2016/17 foreign gain remitted in 2017/18	20,000
2017/18 foreign gain remitted in 2017/18	10,000
UK chargeable gain	25,000
	55,000
Less allowable loss (£10,000 + £5,000)	15,000
Taxable gains	£40,000

Notes to the example

(a) Daanish is not entitled to the annual exempt amount for 2017/18 (or 2016/17).

(b) The part of the loss (£12,000) which is allocated against the foreign gain not remitted to the UK may be given effect by reducing that gain to nil if it is remitted to the UK in a subsequent year.

Chargeable gains remitted to the UK

[55.3] Subject to the exceptions below, an individual's chargeable gains are remitted to the UK in any of circumstances (a)–(c) below.

(a) Property (which may include money) is brought to, or received or used in, the UK by, or for the benefit of, a 'relevant person' or a service is provided in the UK to, or for the benefit of, a relevant person, and
   (i) the property, service or consideration for the service (as the case may be) is (wholly or in part) the gains; or
   (ii) the property, service or consideration derives from the gains and, in the case of property or consideration, is property of a relevant person or consideration given by a relevant person; or
   (iii) gains are used outside the UK (directly or indirectly) in respect of a 'relevant debt'; or
   (iv) anything deriving from the gains is used as mentioned in (iii) above.

   The references in (ii) and (iv) above to something 'deriving from the gains' are references to its so deriving wholly or in part and directly or indirectly.

(b) 'Qualifying property' of a 'gift recipient':
   (i) is brought to, or received or used in, the UK, and is enjoyed by a relevant person; or
   (ii) is consideration for a service that is enjoyed in the UK by a relevant person; or
   (iii) is used outside the UK (directly or indirectly) in respect of a relevant debt.

(c) Property of a person other than a relevant person (apart from qualifying property of a gift recipient as in (b) above):
   (i) is brought to, or received or used in, the UK, and is enjoyed by a relevant person; or
   (ii) is consideration for a service that is enjoyed in the UK by a relevant person; or
   (iii) is used outside the UK (directly or indirectly) in respect of a relevant debt,

   in circumstances where there is a 'connected operation'.

In (a)(iii), (b)(iii) and (c)(iii) above, 'in respect of a relevant debt' would appear to mean 'to satisfy, or partly satisfy, a relevant debt'. In addition, if property (including income or gains) is used to pay interest on a debt, it is regarded as used in respect of the debt. HMRC consider that foreign income and gains used as collateral for a loan are used in respect of the relevant debt, so there is a taxable remittance when the loan is brought to the UK. Where foreign income and gains are also used to pay interest on the debt or to repay the borrowed capital the income or gains are also used in respect of a relevant debt and are treated as a remittance. In such circumstances there are potentially two possible sources of a taxable remittance. For lands brought into or used in the UK before 4 August 2014 HMRC operated a concession under which collateral in commercial situations was not treated as a remittance if regular servicing payments were made, but this concession has been withdrawn. When the concession was originally withdrawn, HMRC intended to apply the statutory treatment to loans brought into or used in the UK before 4 August 2014 unless the taxpayer gave a written undertaking (subsequently honoured) by 31 December 2015 that the foreign income or gains security either had been, or would be replaced by non-foreign income or gains security before 5 April 2016, or the loan or part of the loan that was remitted to the UK either had been, or would be repaid before 5 April 2016. These transitional rules were, however, themselves withdrawn so that the concessional treatment continues to apply to loans brought into or used in the UK before 4 August 2014. See HMRC Residence, Domicile and Remittance Basis Manual RDRM33170, HMRC Notice 4 August 2014 and HMRC Brief 16/2015.

In a case where (b)(i) or (ii) or (c)(i) or (ii) above applies to the importation or use of property, the gains are taken to be remitted at the time the property or service is first enjoyed by a relevant person by virtue of that importation or use.

Enjoyment of property or a service by a relevant person is to be disregarded for the above purposes if it is minimal (i.e. the property or service is enjoyed virtually to the entire exclusion of all relevant persons); if the relevant person gives full consideration in money or money's worth for the enjoyment; or if the property or service is enjoyed by relevant persons in the same way (and on the same terms) that it may be enjoyed by the public (or a section of the public).

[*ITA 2007, ss 809L(1)–(6)(9)–(10), 809N(9), 809O(6)*].

In determining whether a remittance has been made in the case of a foreign chargeable gain on a disposal at undervalue (and if so, how much), the amount of the gain is taken to be the gain that would have arisen if the disposal had been at market value. [*ITA 2007, s 809T*].

If a foreign chargeable gain would otherwise be treated as remitted to the UK before it accrues, by virtue of anything done in relation to anything regarded as deriving from the gain, the remittance is instead treated as made at the time the gain accrues. [*ITA 2007, s 809U*].

The following are '*relevant persons*' for the above purposes: the individual; the spouse or civil partner of the individual; a child or grandchild (under 18) of any of the aforementioned; a close company in which any other person within this definition is a participator (as defined) or, after 21 April 2009, a company which is a 51% subsidiary (within *CTA 2010, Pt 24 Ch 3*) of such a company; a company which would be close if it were UK resident and in which any other person within this definition is a participator or, after 5 April 2010, a company which is a 51% subsidiary of such a company; the trustees of a settlement of which any other person within this definition is a beneficiary; and a body connected with such a settlement. For this purpose, a cohabiting couple are treated as husband and wife or, as the case may be, civil partners; a body is 'connected with' a settlement if the body falls within **17.2**(c) or (d) CONNECTED PERSONS as regards the settlement; in relation to a settlement that would otherwise have no trustees, a 'trustee' means any person in whom the settled property or its management is for the time being vested.

The question of whether a person whose property is dealt with as in (c) above is a relevant person is to be determined at the time the property is so dealt with.

In relation to an individual's income or chargeable gains for any year before 2008/09, only the individual himself is a relevant person.

[*ITA 2007, ss 809M, 809O(2); FA 2012, Sch 12 paras 13, 17*].

A '*relevant debt*' is a debt that relates (wholly or in part, and directly or indirectly) to property within (a) above; a service within (a) above; property dealt with as in (b)(i) or (c)(i) above; or a service falling within (b)(ii) or (c)(ii) above. Before 22 April 2009, a debt that relates to property or a service includes a debt for interest on money lent, where the lending relates to the property or service. [*ITA 2007, s 809L(7)(8)*].

A '*gift recipient*' is a person (other than a relevant person) to whom the individual makes a gift of money or property that is (or derives from) chargeable gains of the individual. The question of whether a person is a relevant person is determined by reference to the time of the gift; but if a person subsequently becomes a relevant person, he then ceases to be a gift recipient. A disposition of property at less than full consideration is a gift to the extent of the deficit. Property is considered to have been gifted even in a case where the disponor retains an interest in it or a right to benefit from it.

'*Qualifying property*' in (b) above, in relation to a gift recipient, means the property gifted or anything that derives from it (as widely defined). It also means any other property if it is dealt with as in (b)(i), (ii) or (iii) above by virtue of an operation effected with reference to, or to enable or facilitate, the gift of the property to the gift recipient.

In relation to an individual's income or chargeable gains for any year before 2008/09, the initial reference in the definition of 'gift recipient' above to a relevant person is to the individual, and the subsequent references are to be disregarded.

[*ITA 2007, s 809N(1)–(8)(10)*].

A '*connected operation*' in relation to property dealt with as mentioned in any of (c)(i)–(iii) above is an operation which is effected with reference to, or to enable or facilitate, a 'qualifying disposition'. A '*qualifying disposition*' is a disposition made by a relevant person to or for the benefit of the person whose property is dealt with as in (c) above, which is a disposition of money or other property that is, or derives from, chargeable gains of the individual. There is no qualifying disposition if the disposition represents, or is part of, the giving of full consideration for the fact that the property is so dealt with. In relation to an individual's income or chargeable gains for any year before 2008/09, only the individual is a relevant person for this purpose. [*ITA 2007, s 809O(1), (3)–(5), (7)*].

Determining the amount remitted to the UK

ITA 2007, s 809P provides rules to determine the amount remitted by reference to (a)–(c) above. In the most straightforward case, where the property, service or consideration for a service is the chargeable gains, or derives from them, the amount remitted is equal to the amount of the gains or (as the case may be) the amount of gains from which the property, service or consideration derives. If the gains, or anything deriving from them, are used outside the UK in respect of a relevant debt, the amount remitted is equal to the amount of gains used, or the amount from which what is used derives. In cases within (b) above, the amount remitted is, broadly, equal to the gains of which the property in question consists or consisted, or from which it derives or derived. In cases within (c) above, the amount remitted is equal to the gains which are the qualifying disposition or from which the qualifying disposition is derived.

In all cases involving a relevant debt, if the debt relates only partly to the property or service in question, the amount remitted is limited (if it would otherwise be greater) to the amount the debt would be if it related wholly to the property or service.

In all cases, where the amount remitted, together with amounts previously remitted, would otherwise exceed the amount of the gains, the amount remitted is limited to an amount equal to the amount of gains.

For property remitted after 21 April 2009, if the property remitted is part of a set only part of which is in the UK, the amount remitted is a just and reasonable portion of the amount that would have been remitted if the complete set had been brought to, or received or used in, the UK when the part was.

[*ITA 2007, s 809P*].

Transfers from mixed funds

Where money or other property is brought to, or received or used in, the UK by, or for the benefit of, a relevant person or a service is provided in the UK to, or for the benefit of, a relevant person (i.e. the first leg of (a) above), the property or the consideration for the service may be, or may derive from, a transfer from a 'mixed fund' (or part of it may), or a transfer from a mixed fund (or something deriving from such a transfer) may be used in respect of a relevant debt (as in (a)(iii) above). In such cases, there are rules to determine if the second leg of (a) above (i.e. any of (a)(i)–(iv)) applies and, if so, to determine the amount remitted.

A '*mixed fund*' means money or other property which immediately before the transfer consists of (or derives from) income or capital of more than one of the following nine categories, or for more than one tax year:

(A) employment income (other than income within (B) or (C) below or income subject to a foreign tax);
(B) amounts within **55.2**(i) or (ii) above, other than those subject to a foreign tax;
(C) amounts within **55.2**(iii) above, other than income subject to a foreign tax;
(D) relevant foreign income within *ITTOIA 2005, s 830*, other than income subject to a foreign tax;
(E) foreign chargeable gains, other than gains subject to a foreign tax;
(F) employment income subject to a foreign tax;
(G) 'relevant foreign income' subject to a foreign tax;
(H) foreign chargeable gains subject to a foreign tax; and
(I) any income or capital not within any of (A)–(H) above.

For this purpose, references to anything derived from income or capital within (I) above do not include income or gains within (A)–(H) above, or anything derived from such income or gains.

For each of categories (A)–(I), find the amount of income and capital for the 'relevant tax year' in the mixed fund immediately before the transfer in question. The '*relevant tax year*' is the tax year in which the transfer takes place. For the purpose of determining the composition of the mixed fund, property which derives (wholly or in part, and directly or indirectly) from an individual's income or capital for a tax year is treated as consisting of or containing that income or capital. Similarly, if a debt relating (wholly or partly, and directly or indirectly) to property is satisfied (wholly or partly) at any time by an individual's income or capital for a particular tax year, or by anything deriving from it, the property is to be treated from that time as consisting of or containing that income or capital if, and to the extent that, it is just and reasonable to do so. If an 'offshore transfer' is made from a mixed fund, it is to be regarded as containing the same proportion of each kind of income or capital as was contained in the fund before the transfer (except where the provisions for cleansing mixed funds apply, as described below). A transfer is an '*offshore transfer*' if these rules (i.e. the rules in *ITA 2007, s 809Q*) do not apply to it; a transfer is *treated as* an offshore transfer if, and to the extent that, these rules do not apply to it at the end of the tax year in which it is made and will not do so on the best estimate that can reasonably be made at that time. If the rules in *ITA 2007, s 809Q* apply to part of a transfer, they are to be applied before applying the offshore transfer rules to the rest of the transfer.

If the amount in category (A) does not exceed the amount of the transfer in question, regard the transfer as containing the income and gains in that category for the relevant tax year. Reduce the amount of the transfer by the amount in (A) and compare what remains with the amount in category (B). Continue by reference to each category, in the order in which they are listed, until the amount of the transfer is reduced to nil.

If, after going through all the categories, the amount of the transfer is still not fully matched, repeat the process by reference to income and capital of the preceding tax year, and so on until the amount of the transfer is fully matched.

If the amount in category (A) does exceed the amount of the transfer, regard the transfer as containing the appropriate proportion of each kind of income and gains in that category for the relevant tax year; similarly if the amount in subsequent category exceeds what remains of the amount of the transfer.

[*ITA 2007, ss 809Q, 809R; FA 2013, Sch 6 para 5*].

See also Tolley's Income Tax for special rules for income from mixed employments.

The mixed fund rules do not apply for the purposes of determining whether income or chargeable gains for any tax year before 2008/09 are remitted to the UK in 2008/09 or any subsequent year (or of determining the amount of any such income or chargeable gains so remitted). However, specific rules *do* apply in relation to the cleansing of mixed funds containing pre-6 April 2008 income or gains as described below. [*FA 2008, Sch 7 para 89; F(No 2)A 2017, Sch 8 para 46*].

If, by reason of an arrangement (as widely defined) a main purpose of which is to secure an 'income tax advantage' or a 'CGT advantage', a mixed fund would otherwise be regarded as containing income or capital within any of (F) to (J) above, the mixed fund should be treated as containing so much of such income or capital as is just and reasonable. For this purpose, an '*income tax advantage*' means a relief or increased relief from income tax, a repayment, or increased repayment of income tax, the avoidance or reduction of a charge or assessment to income tax or the avoidance of a possible assessment to income tax. '*CGT advantage*' is similarly defined. [*ITA 2007, s 809S*].

Cleansing of mixed funds

The deemed domicile rules introduced by *F(No 2)A 2017* (see **57.34** RESIDENCE AND DOMICILE) include a one-off opportunity for qualifying individuals to 'cleanse' mixed funds i.e. to separate such funds into their constituent parts. A '*qualifying individual*' is one who has used the remittance basis in any tax year from 2008/09 to 2016/17 inclusive, either by claim (*ITA 2007, s 809B*) or automatically (under *ITA 2007, s 809D* or *ITA 2007, s 809E*), and who was *not* born in the UK with a UK domicile of origin. If the prescribed conditions (below) are met, an offshore transfer made in either 2017/18 or 2018/19 is *not* regarded as containing a proportion of each kind of income or capital in the mixed fund before transfer. Instead the individual specifies the kind of income or capital, or the amounts and kinds of different income and capital, to be regarded as contained in the transfer, in a nomination. The amount specified for a kind of income or capital in such a nomination cannot exceed the amount of that kind which is in the mixed fund immediately before the transfer.

For this treatment to apply to an offshore transfer, the transfer must be a transfer of money made in 2017/18 or 2018/19, from a mixed fund (account A) to another account B and the qualifying individual must make the nomination for the treatment to apply. There cannot have been a previous nomination, in respect of a transfer from account A to account B.

The rules are extended to a transfer from a mixed fund (overseas account A) which contains income or chargeable gains for the tax year 2007/08 or earlier ('*pre-6 April 2008 income or chargeable gains*'), to another overseas account B. However, this requires specific provisions to determine the composition of such a mixed fund as the above mixed fund rules (*ITA 2007, ss 809Q–809R*) do not apply to pre-6 April 2008 amounts.

- **Transfer of money before 6 April 2008 from the mixed fund to another overseas account.** Calculate the total income and gains in the mixed fund immediately before transfer, and then the proportion of this which is income, and the proportion which is gains. If the transfer amount is less than the total income and gains, the transfer is treated as consisting of income and chargeable gains in these proportions. If the transfer amount exceeds the total income and gains, the transfer is treated as consisting of all the income and gains in the mixed fund prior to transfer, plus other capital in the mixed fund making up the balance.
- **Transfer of money before 6 April 2008 from another overseas account to the mixed fund, where there is insufficient evidence to determine the composition of the transfer.** Calculate the total income and gains in the other overseas account immediately before transfer, and then the proportion of this which is income, and the proportion which is gains.

The transfer consists of income and gains in these proportions. Where there is insufficient evidence to determine whether an amount in the other overseas account is income or gains, treat it as income.

[*F(No 2)A 2017, Sch 8 paras 44–46*].

Foreign chargeable gains where disposal not for full consideration

For the purposes of the above provisions, where foreign chargeable gains accrue on the disposal of an asset for consideration of less than the market value (before 22 April 2009, consideration other than the market value), the asset is treated as deriving from those chargeable gains. [*ITA 2007, s 809T*].

Property treated as not remitted to the UK

To the extent described below, money and other property brought into the UK are treated for tax purposes as not remitted to the UK.

- **Payment of the remittance basis charge.** Direct payments to HMRC from untaxed foreign income or gains in settlement of the charge in **55.5** below are not treated for tax purposes as remittances to the UK. This exemption applies only if the amount is paid in respect of the tax due for a tax year for which the remittance basis has been claimed and for which the charge applies. The exemption covers any number of direct payments up to the total amount of the charge. If any of the money is repaid by HMRC, for example because the taxpayer withdraws his claim, the exemption is to that extent deemed never to have applied. [*ITA 2007, s 809V; FA 2012, Sch 12 paras 4, 5*].
  To qualify for this exemption, the money must be sent direct from an overseas bank account to HMRC by way of a cheque drawn on the overseas bank account or a form of electronic transfer, and not via a UK bank account (Treasury Explanatory Notes to the 2008 Finance Bill).
  Where an individual is liable to the charge for a tax year (year A), any income tax self-assessment payments on account (see **61.2** SELF-ASSESSMENT) that are made for the following tax year (year B) will be at least partly based on that charge. If the individual does not claim the remittance basis for year B, and is thus not liable to the charge for that year, a repayment may be due from HMRC of all or part of the payments on account. If the payments on account were made out of untaxed foreign income or gains, that repayment constitutes a taxable remittance.
  An exemption applies in relation to payments on account made for 2012/13 (i.e. those due on 31 January and 31 July 2013) or any subsequent year. The 'relevant amount of income or gains' is treated as not remitted to the UK if money equal to that amount is taken offshore by 15 March in the tax year following year B or such later date as HMRC may allow on a claim by the individual. A claim may be made only if the individual has submitted a personal tax return for year B and reasonably expects to receive a tax repayment for that year; it must be made no later than 5 April in the tax year following year B.
  The '*relevant amount of income or gains*' is the lower of:
  - the amount brought to the UK by virtue of the making of the payments on account; and

  - the amount of the remittance basis charge for year A (see **55.5** below).

See **55.4** below as to what is meant by taking money offshore. Money that is thus taken offshore is treated as having the same composition of kinds of income and capital as the money used to make the payments on account.

[*ITA 2007, ss 809UA, 809Z9; FA 2013, s 21(3)–(5)*].

- **Property used to make qualifying investments.** Where, on or after 6 April 2012, a 'relevant event' occurs, and income or chargeable gains of an individual would otherwise be regarded as remitted to the UK by virtue of that event, the income or gains are treated as not remitted to the UK if the individual makes a claim under *ITA 2007, s 809VA*. See **55.4** below.
- **Consideration for certain services.** An exemption applies if:
  - gains would otherwise be treated as remitted to the UK because of (a) above;
  - the first leg of (a) is met because a service is provided in the UK;
  - the second leg of (a) is met because (a)(i) or (ii) applies to the consideration for that service; and
  - both Conditions A and B below are met.

  Where this exemption applies, income or gains are treated as not remitted to the UK.

  Condition A is that the service provided relates wholly or mainly to property situated outside the UK.

  Condition B is that the whole of the consideration for the service is given by way of payments to bank accounts held outside the UK by or on behalf of the person providing the service.

  The exemption does not apply if the service relates to the provision in the UK either of a benefit treated as deriving from the income under *ITA 2007, s 735* or a benefit treated under *TCGA 1992, s 87B* as deriving from the chargeable gains (see **48.15** OFFSHORE SETTLEMENTS).

  [*ITA 2007, s 809W*].

  Condition A would cover, for example, fees paid to a UK bank for managing an individual's overseas investments. It would also cover legal or brokerage fees in respect of offshore assets, such as legal fees on the sale of a foreign house. The term 'wholly or mainly' in Condition A is not statutorily defined, but will be taken to mean more than half. (Treasury Explanatory Notes to the 2008 Finance Bill).
- **Exempt property.** 'Exempt property' which is brought to, or received or used in, the UK, such that the first leg of (a) above applies, is treated as not remitted to the UK. The following are '*exempt property*' for this purpose.
  - Property which meets the 'public access rule'. This rule allows certain property to be imported into the UK, without giving rise to a tax charge on the remittance basis, if all the conditions set out below are met.

    The property must be a work of art, a collectors' item or an antique, within the meaning of *Council Directive 2006/112/EC* (and, in particular, *Annex IX* to that *Directive*). This condition is abolished on and after 6 April 2013 or, in the case of property already in the UK on that date, from the time it ceases to be in the UK or is lost or stolen.

The property must be available for public access (as defined) at an approved museum, gallery or similar establishment or in storage at, or in transit to or from, the establishment (or other commercial premises in the UK used by the establishment for storage) pending or following public access.

During the 'relevant period', the property must meet the above condition for no more than two years (or such longer period as HMRC may in a particular case allow). The '*relevant period*' is the period beginning with the importation of the property and ending when it next ceases to be in the UK, except that if the property is lost or stolen on or after 6 April 2013 the relevant period is suspended.

The property must attract a 'relevant VAT relief' (for which see *ITA 2007, s 809Z1*). This condition is abolished on and after 6 April 2013 or, in the case of property already in the UK on that date, from the time it ceases to be in the UK or is lost or stolen.

- Clothing, footwear, jewellery and watches which meet certain additional conditions.
- Property where the 'notional remitted amount' (as defined) is less than £1,000, or if the property meets certain conditions as to temporary importation or importation for repair.

For these purposes, 'property' does not include money (or specified items equivalent to money). Subject to the exceptions below, if property ceases to be exempt property at any time after it is brought to, or received or used in, the UK, it is treated as remitted to the UK at that time. Property ceases to be exempt property if it (or part of it) is sold (or otherwise converted into money or specified items equivalent to money) whilst in the UK. Property which is exempt by virtue of one or more of the 'public access rule', the 'personal use rule', the 'temporary importation rule' and the 'repair rule' also ceases to be exempt property if it ceases to meet the rule(s) relied upon whilst in the UK, provided it does not meet any of the remaining rules. Property which ceases to be exempt property as a result of ceasing to meet one of those rules is not, however, treated as remitted to the UK at that time if, no later than the time it ceases to be exempt property, it has been donated in circumstances within *FA 2012, Sch 14 para 1* (gifts to the nation — see **11.9** CHARITIES). In such a case the property continues to be treated as not remitted to the UK.

Property used to make qualifying investments. With effect where property ceases to be exempt property on or after 6 April 2012 and a claim for this relief is made, it is *not* treated as remitted to the UK at that time if the property is used by a relevant person (as above) to make a qualifying investment (as in **55.4** below) within the 45 days beginning with the day on which it ceased to be exempt property. The claim must be made (by the individual whose income or gains would otherwise be treated as remitted) no later than the first anniversary of 31 January following the tax year in which the property ceases to be exempt property. The relief also applies where the formerly exempt property is disposed of or otherwise converted into money and the disposal proceeds or the money are used to make the investment.

Where this relief has effect, the potentially chargeable event rules at **55.4** below if there is subsequently such an event in relation to the qualifying investment. If the investment is made using more than just the formerly exempt property, only the part made using that property is treated as the qualifying investment for the purposes of applying those rules.

In applying the mixed fund rules, the formerly exempt property (or thing into which it was converted) used to make the investment is treated as containing (or deriving from) an amount of each kind of income and gain mentioned in (A)–(H) above equal to the amount of that kind of income or gain contained in the property when it was brought to, or received or used in, the UK.

Sales of exempt property. The following has effect in relation to exempt property that is sold on or after 6 April 2012 (including property sold pursuant to a contract that is entered into before that date but does not become unconditional until on or after that date). If property ceases to be exempt property because the whole of it is sold whilst in the UK, it is *not* treated as remitted to the UK at that time if all the conditions listed at (1)–(6) below are met. This relief does not apply if the sale is made as part of, or as a result of, a tax avoidance scheme or arrangements.

(1) The sale is to a person other than a relevant person (as above).
(2) The sale is by way of a bargain made at arm's length.
(3) Once the sale is completed, no relevant person:
    - has any interest in the property;
    - is able or entitled to benefit from the property by virtue of any interest, right or arrangement; or
    - has any right to acquire any such interest, ability or entitlement.
(4) The whole of the disposal proceeds are 'released' (whether all at once or in instalments) on or before the first anniversary of 5 January following the tax year in which the property ceases to be exempt property.
(5) The whole of the disposal proceeds are taken offshore or used by a relevant person to make a qualifying investment (as in **55.4** below) within the 45 days beginning with the day on which the proceeds are 'released'. If the disposal proceeds are paid in instalments, the condition is that each instalment is taken offshore or used in that way within the 45 days beginning with the day on which the instalment is released. In both cases, there is an overriding deadline of the first anniversary of 5 January following the tax year in which the property ceases to be exempt property, if this falls within the 45 days normally permitted.
(6) If (5) above is satisfied wholly or partly by the making of a qualifying investment, a claim for relief must be made (by the individual whose income or gains would otherwise be treated as remitted) on or before the first anniversary of 31 January following the tax year in which the property is sold.

For the purposes of (5) and (6) above, proceeds or instalments are '*released*' on the day on which they first become available for use by or for the benefit of any relevant person. An officer of HMRC may (on the request of the individual whose income or gains would otherwise be treated as remitted) agree to extend any deadline within (5) above if circumstances are exceptional.

In applying the mixed fund rules, where this relief has effect, the disposal proceeds are treated as containing (or deriving from) an amount of each kind of income and gain mentioned in (A)–(H) above equal to the amount of that kind of income or gain contained in the exempt property when it was brought to, or received or used in, the UK. Also where this relief has effect and (5) above was satisfied by the making of a qualifying investment, the potentially chargeable event rules at **55.4** below apply if there is subsequently such an event in relation to the investment. If the investment is made using more than just the disposal proceeds, only the part made using those proceeds is treated as the qualifying investment for the purposes of applying those rules.

Where a chargeable gain (but not a loss) accrues to an individual on a sale of exempt property, and this relief applies to prevent the property being treated as remitted to the UK, the gain is treated for the purpose of applying the remittance basis as a foreign chargeable gain (see **55.2** and (E) above) and, for the purposes of **55.2**(c) above as not being part of the individual's UK income and gains. Where this rule applies, *ITA 2007, s 809U* (see above) is disregarded, and anything done in relation to any part of the disposal proceeds before the part is taken offshore or used to make a qualifying investment does not count as a remittance to the UK of any of the gain. This rule applies also to an individual to whom part of such a gain is apportioned under *TCGA 1992, s 13* (see **49.7** OVERSEAS MATTERS). The rule can, however, be disapplied by notice in writing to HMRC. Such a notice must be given on or before the first anniversary of the 31 January following the tax year in which the gain is made or, where the taxpayer is temporarily non-UK resident in that year (see **49.5** OVERSEAS MATTERS), the year of return. A notice is irrevocable after the expiry of the time limit for making it.

Property lost, stolen or destroyed. In relation to property lost, stolen or destroyed on or after 6 April 2013 whilst in the UK, the property cannot cease to be exempt property in the circumstances outlined above after it is lost, stolen and destroyed and (in the case of loss or theft followed by recovery) before it is 'recovered'. For this purpose, property is '*recovered*' on the day it becomes available to be used or enjoyed in the UK by or for the benefit of a relevant person (as above). Property ceases to be exempt property where a payment of compensation (whether under an insurance policy or otherwise) is 'released' in respect of exempt property that has been lost, stolen or destroyed on or after 6 April 2013. A compensation payment is '*released*' on the day on which it first becomes available for use in the UK by or for the benefit of any relevant person.

However, property is not treated as remitted to the UK by virtue of a release of compensation as above if the whole of the compensation payment is taken offshore or used by a relevant person to make a qualifying investment (as in **55.4** below) within the 45 days beginning with the day on which the payment is released. To the extent that this relief arises from the making of a qualifying investment, a claim for the relief must be made no later than the first anniversary of 31 January following the tax year in which the payment is released.

For the purposes of the mixed fund rules, the compensation payment is treated as containing (or deriving from) an amount of each kind of income and gain mentioned in (A)–(H) above equal to the amount of that kind of income or gain contained in the exempt property when it was brought to, or received or used in, the UK.

Where this relief has effect by virtue of the making of a qualifying investment, the rules at **55.4** below apply if there is subsequently a potentially chargeable event in relation to the investment. If the investment is made using more than just the compensation payment, only the part made using that payment is treated as the qualifying investment for the purposes of applying those rules.

[*ITA 2007, ss 809X–809Z5, 809Z10; FA 2012, Sch 12 paras 10, 17–19, Sch 14 para 35; FA 2013, Sch 7, Sch 46 para 23*].

- **Offshore mortgages.** In certain circumstances, relevant foreign income of an individual used outside the UK before 6 April 2028 to pay the interest on a debt is treated as not remitted to the UK. A similar exemption applies to interest on a subsequent replacement loan. [*FA 2008, Sch 7 para 90*].

Property used to make qualifying investments

[55.4] Where, on or after **6 April 2012**, a 'relevant event' occurs, and income or chargeable gains of an individual would otherwise be regarded as remitted to the UK by virtue of that event, the income or gains are treated as not remitted to the UK if the individual makes a claim under *ITA 2007, s 809VA* for the relief. A '*relevant event*' occurs if money or other property:

(a) is used by a relevant person (as in **55.3** above) to make a 'qualifying investment' (see below); or
(b) is brought to or received in the UK in order to be used by a relevant person for the purpose of making such an investment (but see below for 45-day time limit).

The relief (known as **business investment relief**) is equally available where income or gains would otherwise be treated under the exempt property rules at **55.3** above as remitted to the UK by virtue of the relevant event, e.g. because exempt property is sold to raise the capital for the investment. This applies where property ceases to be exempt property on or after 6 April 2012.

A claim for relief must be made no later than the first anniversary of 31 January following the tax year in which the income or gains would otherwise be regarded as remitted to the UK. No relief is available if the relevant event occurs, or the investment is made, as part of, or as a result of, a tax avoidance scheme or arrangement.

45-day rule

Relief by virtue of (b) above is available to the extent only that the investment is made within the period of 45 days beginning with the day on which the money etc. is brought to or received in the UK. If this requirement is only partly satisfied, the portion of the income or gains which attracts the relief is determined on a just and reasonable basis. Where money etc. is brought to the UK with the intention of making a qualifying investment but some or all of that money etc. is not invested within the 45-day limit, the income or gains thereby not qualifying for the relief are nevertheless treated as not remitted to the UK if and to the extent that the unused money etc. is taken offshore within the same 45-day period. Where only part of the unused amount is taken offshore within the time limit, the portion of the income or gains which attracts the relief is again determined on a just and reasonable basis.

[*ITA 2007, ss 809VA, 809VB, 809Z10; FA 2012, Sch 12 paras 7, 16, 17*].

Qualifying investments

For the above purposes, a person makes an investment if shares in, or securities of, a company are issued to him or acquired by him or if he makes a loan (whether secured or unsecured) to a company. Before 6 April 2017, shares and securities acquired by an investor, but not issued to him, did not count as investments for this purpose. In order to be a '*qualifying investment*', the investment must satisfy both conditions A and B below at the time it is made.

Where a loan agreement authorises a company to draw down amounts of a loan over time, entry into that loan agreement is not treated as the making of a loan for these purposes. Instead, a separate loan is treated as being made each time an amount is drawn down; each drawdown will thus be a separate investment.

Condition A

The company in which the investment is made (the '*target company*') must be an 'eligible trading company', an 'eligible stakeholder company', an 'eligible holding company' or, after 5 April 2017, an 'eligible hybrid company'.

A company is an '*eligible trading company*' if:

- it is a 'private limited company';
- it carries on one or more 'commercial trades' or is preparing to do so within the next five years (previously, before 6 April 2017, two years); and
- carrying on commercial trades is all or substantially all of what it does (or of what it is expected to do when it begins trading).

A company is a '*private limited company*' if none of its shares are listed on a recognised stock exchange; limited liability partnerships are not private limited companies.

A company is an '*eligible stakeholder company*' if:

- it is a 'private limited company' (as above);

- it exists wholly for the purpose of making investments (as defined above) in eligible trading companies (ignoring any minor or incidental purposes); and
- it holds one or more such investments or is preparing to do so within the next five years (previously, before 6 April 2017, two years).

A company is an '*eligible holding company*' if:

- it is a member of an 'eligible trading group' or of an 'eligible group' that is reasonably expected to become an eligible trading group within the next five years (previously, before 6 April 2017, two years); and
- an eligible trading company in the group is a 51% subsidiary of it. Where the eligible holding company owns the share capital of the eligible trading company indirectly, each intermediary company must also be a member of the group.

A company is an '*eligible hybrid company*' if:

- it is a 'private limited company' (as above), and neither an eligible trading company nor an eligible stakeholder company;
- it carries on one or more 'commercial trades' or is preparing to do so within the next five years;
- it holds one or more investments in eligible trading companies or is preparing to do so within the next five years; and
- the carrying on of commercial trades and the making of investments in eligible trading companies are all (or substantially all) of what it does (or of what it is reasonably expected to do once it begins operating).

For the above purposes, a group means a parent company and its 51% subsidiaries. A group is an '*eligible group*' if the parent company and each of its 51% subsidiaries are private limited companies. An eligible group is an '*eligible trading group*' if carrying on 'commercial trades' is all or substantially all of what the group does (taking the activities of its members as a whole).

A trade is a '*commercial trade*' if it is conducted on a commercial basis and with a view to the realisation of profits. For this purpose, a trade includes anything that is treated for corporation tax purposes as if it were a trade and also includes a business carried on for 'generating income from land' (as defined by *CTA 2009, s 207*). It includes the carrying on of research and development activities from which it is intended that a commercial trade will be derived or will benefit. A corporate partner in a partnership is not regarded for these purposes as carrying on a trade carried on by the partnership; this has statutory effect after 5 April 2017 but confirms a view previously applied in practice by HMRC.

Condition B

Condition B is that no relevant person (as in **55.3** above) has (directly or indirectly) obtained, or become entitled to obtain, any related benefit, and that no relevant person expects to obtain any such benefit. A benefit is related if it is directly or indirectly attributable to the making of the investment or if it is reasonable to assume that the benefit would not be available in the absence of the investment. A benefit includes the provision of anything which would not be provided to the relevant person in the ordinary course of business or would be provided on less favourable terms. It does not include the provision of anything to the relevant person in the normal course of business and on arm's length terms.

[*ITA 2007, ss 809VC–809VF, 809Z10; FA 2012, Sch 12 paras 7, 16, 17; F(No 2)A 2017, s 15(2)(3)(4)(8)*].

Potentially chargeable events

Where relief has been given as above, the occurrence of a 'potentially chargeable event' (PCE) may result in the 'affected income or gains' being treated as having been remitted to the UK. This can be avoided if appropriate steps are taken in mitigation but each step must be taken within a specified period of grace allowed for that step. In the absence of one or more mitigation steps, the remittance is deemed to take place immediately after the end of the appropriate grace period. The '*affected income or gains*' means such portion of the income or gains relieved as above as reflects the portion of the qualifying investment affected by the PCE. This will usually be the whole of the qualifying investment, but where the event is a part disposal it is the portion disposed of. Where there is a second or subsequent PCE in relation to a single investment, the relieved income or gains that may then be treated as remitted do not include any amounts treated as remitted or used in mitigation as a result of a previous PCE.

Where an investment is made which consists partly of funds which qualify for relief under the qualifying investment provisions and partly of other funds, the investment is treated as two separate investments for these purposes.

Meaning of 'potentially chargeable event'

Any of the following is a '*potentially chargeable event*':

- the target company (see above) is for the first time neither an eligible trading company nor an eligible stakeholder company nor an eligible holding company nor, after 5 April 2017, an eligible hybrid company;
- the relevant person who made the investment disposes of all or part of it;
- the extraction of value rule is breached (see below); or
- the five-year start-up rule (previously, before 6 April 2017, the two-year start-up rule) is breached (see below).

If consideration for a disposal is paid in instalments, the disposal is treated for these purposes as if it were separate disposals, one for each instalment and each giving rise to a separate PCE.

If a PCE occurs because of an 'insolvency step' taken for genuine commercial reasons, it will not be treated as a PCE. However, this does not prevent the receipt of value as a result of the insolvency step from being a PCE. Broadly, an '*insolvency step*' is taken if a company enters into administration or receivership, or is wound up or dissolved (or the overseas equivalent in each case).

Extraction of value rule

On and after 6 April 2017, the extraction of value rule is breached if the relevant person who made the investment or any other relevant person receives, or receives the benefit of, value in money or money's worth from any person in circumstances that are directly or indirectly attributable to the investment.

Before 6 April 2017, the extraction of value rule is breached if the relevant person who made the investment or any other relevant person receives, or receives the benefit of, value in money or money's worth from either an 'involved company' or from anyone else in circumstances which are attributable to the investment or to any other investment made by a relevant person in an involved company. Any of the following is an '*involved company*': the target company; (if the target company is an eligible stakeholder company) any eligible trading company in which it has made or intends to make an investment; (if the target company is an eligible holding company) any eligible trading company that is a 51% subsidiary of it; and any company that is connected with any such company (within **17** CONNECTED PERSONS).

At all times, the extraction of value rule is not breached if the value is received as a result of a disposal that is itself a PCE. Also, the rule is not breached merely because a relevant person receives value which is treated as income for tax purposes (or would be if the relevant person were liable to income tax or corporation tax), provided the value is paid or provided on arm's length terms and in the ordinary course of business; an example of such value would be director's remuneration.

Five-year start-up rule

The five-year start-up rule is breached if:

- immediately after the end of the five years beginning with the day on which the investment was made, the target company is not operational; or
- at any time after the end of that period, the target company ceases to be operational.

Before 6 April 2017, the above applied by reference to two years rather than five. In order to be operational, the target company must either be trading (i.e. carrying on a commercial trade), be a stakeholder in at least one eligible trading company which is trading, be a member of an eligible trading group and have at least one 51% subsidiary which is trading or, after 5 April 2017, be an eligible hybrid company which is trading or is a stakeholder in at least one eligible trading company which is trading.

Mitigation steps and periods of grace

If the PCE is a disposal, the appropriate mitigation step is to take the proceeds offshore or use them to make another qualifying investment (whether in the same or a different company). If the proceeds are themselves a qualifying investment (for example on a share for share exchange), the appropriate step is regarded as having been taken. Otherwise, the period of grace allowed to take the step is the 45 days beginning with the day on which the disposal proceeds first become available for use by, or for the benefit of, the investor or any other relevant person. See below for the meaning of disposal proceeds and for what is meant by taking proceeds offshore.

If the PCE is anything other than a disposal, the appropriate mitigation step is twofold, as follows. Firstly, the investor must dispose of the entire investment (or so much of it as he still holds when the PCE occurs). Secondly, he must take the proceeds of that disposal offshore or use them to make another qualifying investment. The period of grace allowed for the first leg of this mitigation step is the 90 days beginning (if the PCE is a breach of the extraction of value rule) with the day on which value is received or (in any other case) with the day on which a relevant person first became aware, or ought reasonably to have become aware, of the PCE. The period of grace allowed for the second leg is the 45 days beginning with the day on which the disposal proceeds first become available for use by, or for the benefit of, the investor or any other relevant person. If the first leg is not carried out within the 90 days allowed, it is immediately after the end of those 90 days that the affected income or gains is deemed to have been remitted to the UK.

After 5 April 2017, the above does not apply if the PCE is a breach of the five-year start-up rule by virtue of the target company ceasing to be operational after the end of the five-year period. Instead, the total period of grace allowed for carrying out both legs of the mitigation step is the two years beginning with the day on which the investor or any other relevant person first became aware, or ought reasonably to have become aware, of the PCE.

Where a breach of the extraction of value rule takes place in connection with the winding-up or dissolution of the target company, there is no need to dispose of the holding, and references to the disposal proceeds in these provisions are to the value received.

Applicable proceeds

In any case where proceeds need to be taken offshore or reinvested, the amount of proceeds to which this applies is the total disposal proceeds or, if less, so much of those proceeds as equals the sum originally invested (as defined). For this purpose, the sum originally invested is deemed to be reduced by so much of it as has, on previous occasions involving the same investment:

- been taken into account in determining the amount of income and gains treated as remitted after a PCE; or
- been taken offshore or reinvested as an appropriate mitigation step; or
- been used to purchase a certificate of tax deposit (see below under Retention of funds to meet CGT liabilities).

For example, in Year 1 an individual invests £3 million of foreign income in an eligible trading company. In Year 5, he sells half the holding for £2 million. The appropriate mitigation step is to take £2 million offshore or reinvest it. In Year 6, he sells the remaining holding for £3.5 million. The appropriate mitigation step is to take £1 million (£3 million less £2 million) offshore or reinvest it. In all, he has invested £3 million and realised £5.5 million; the amount he has been required to take offshore or reinvest is limited to £3 million.

Extension of grace periods

An officer of HMRC may agree in a particular case to extend the grace period allowed for an appropriate mitigation step:

- where the target company has ceased to be a private limited company by virtue of having some or all of its shares listed on a recognised stock exchange or has become a subsidiary of another company (the 'new company') which is a body corporate some or all of whose shares are (or are to be) so listed, and the investor is unable to comply with an appropriate mitigation step without breaching the terms of a 'lock-up agreement';
- where the investor is prevented from taking an appropriate mitigation step by a prohibition imposed by or under any enactment;
- where taking an appropriate mitigation step would breach the terms of a court order; or
- in exceptional circumstances (to be defined in HMRC published guidance).

A '*lock-up agreement*' is a contract entered into by the investor with one or more of the target company, the new company or professional advisors retained by the target or new company in relation to the listing of the shares, where the contract is directly related to the listing of the shares and imposes restrictions on the time or manner in which the investor may dispose of some or all of his holding in the target company or of any shares in the new company received by him in return for his holding in the target company.

The extension may be for a length of time that is indefinite but is capable of becoming definite by means identified in advance, such as the satisfaction of conditions.

Amounts reinvested

Where disposal proceeds are used to make another qualifying investment as part of appropriate mitigation steps, these provisions apply with the necessary modifications to the new investment as they applied to the original investment; for example, references to the sum originally invested are henceforth to the sum reinvested. Where the new investment is made in a greater sum than is required to satisfy the rules, it is treated as two separate investments, one of an amount equal to the minimum amount required to meet the rules and the other of an amount equal to the balance; the latter then falls outside these provisions.

A reinvestment of proceeds requires a further claim under *ITA 2007, s 809VA* (see above). This must be made no later than the first anniversary of 31 January following the tax year in which the reinvestment is made. If the claim is not made, the appropriate mitigation steps will not be regarded as having been taken.

Retention of funds to meet CGT liabilities

The legislation recognises that the disposal proceeds of a qualifying investment may have to be retained in the UK to meet a CGT liability on that disposal. It deals with this by enabling the amount otherwise required to be taken offshore or reinvested to be reduced by a set amount, provided the amount is used to purchase a certificate of tax deposit (CTD) (see **51.11** PAYMENT OF TAX) within the 45-day grace period allowed as above. It must be confirmed in writing to HMRC that the CTD purchased is intended to relate to *ITA 2007, s 809VK* and that the amount of the deposit is no greater than the 'shortfall'. The '*shortfall*' is the amount (if any) by which the actual disposal proceeds fall short of Amount Y, where Amount Y is the sum of the amount otherwise required to be taken offshore or reinvested and the amount resulting when the highest potential CGT rate is applied to the chargeable gain on the disposal. (The shortfall is calculated by reference to proceeds actually received even if the disposal was not made on arm's length terms.) The set amount can be anything up to the amount of the shortfall.

If the CTD is used to pay the individual's CGT liability for the tax year in which the disposal took place, this does not count as remitting to the UK the portion of the affected income or gains that is represented by the payment. If, however, any of the 'CTD conditions' is breached, the portion of the affected income or gains to the UK that is affected by the breach are treated as having been remitted to the UK immediately after the day on which the breach occurs. The '*CTD conditions*' are as follows.

- The CTD must not be used to pay any other tax liability.
- If any of the amount deposited is withdrawn by the depositor, the amount withdrawn must be taken offshore or invested in a qualifying company within the 45 days beginning on the date of withdrawal.
- Any part of the amount deposited that has been neither used to pay a tax liability nor withdrawn by the due date for payment of the said CGT liability must be withdrawn by the depositor and taken offshore or invested in a qualifying company within the 45 days beginning with that date.

Where an amount withdrawn is invested in a qualifying company, these provisions apply with the necessary modifications to the new investment as they applied to the original investment. Again, a further claim is required under *ITA 2007, s 809VA*.

Order of disposals

There are rules to determine the order in which disposals are treated as being made where there are multiple acquisitions and disposals in the same target company or group and also where both qualifying and non-qualifying investments have been made.

The first rule applies where income or gains of an individual are treated as not remitted to the UK as a result of more than one qualifying investment in either the same target company or the same eligible trading group or in both an eligible trading company and its eligible stakeholder company or, after 5 April 2017, its eligible hybrid company. The investments are treated as a single investment for the purpose of applying the PCE rules. A disposal of all or part of that deemed single investment affects it in the order in which the qualifying investments were made, i.e. first in, first out. It does not matter whether the investments in question are held by the same relevant person (as in **55.3** above) or different ones.

The second rule applies where income or gains of an individual are treated as not remitted to the UK as a result of one or more qualifying investments and a relevant person holds at least one non-qualifying investment in the same target company, the same eligible trading group or a 'related eligible company'. The investments are treated as a single investment for the purpose of applying the PCE rules. A disposal of all or part of that deemed single investment is taken to be a disposal from a qualifying investment until all the qualifying investments have been disposed of. It does not matter whether the investments in question are held by the same relevant person or different ones. Two companies are '*related eligible companies*' if one is an eligible trading company and the other is its eligible stakeholder company or, after 5 April 2017, its eligible hybrid company.

Meaning of disposal proceeds

For these purposes, in relation to a sale or any other disposal, the disposal proceeds are the amount of consideration for the disposal less any fees or other incidental costs deducted from the consideration before it is accounted for to the person making the disposal or to any relevant person (as in 55.3 above). If the consideration is provided in the form of property rather than money, the amount of the consideration is the market value of the property at the time of the disposal. If the disposal is not at arm's length, it is deemed to be made for a consideration equal to the market value of the thing being disposed of. A disposal made to another relevant person or to a person connected with a relevant person is always treated as made other than at arm's length.

Fees and other incidental costs are not deductible if payable by one relevant person to another except to the extent that they relate to a service actually provided by the recipient in connection with effecting the disposal and do not exceed what would normally be charged for that service on arm's length terms.

Taking proceeds etc. offshore or investing them

For the purposes of these provisions, things (e.g. disposal proceeds) are to be regarded as '*taken offshore*' if (and only if) they are taken outside the UK such that, on leaving the UK, they cease to be available to be used or enjoyed in the UK by, or for the benefit of, a relevant person (as in 55.3 above) or used or enjoyed in any other way that would count as remitting income or gains to the UK. If money needs to be taken offshore or invested in order to satisfy a statutory requirement, and it is paid temporarily into an account pending satisfaction of that requirement, the requirement is satisfied only if the money actually taken offshore or invested is taken from the same account. If the thing required to be taken offshore or invested is something in money's worth, the requirement can be satisfied either by taking the thing offshore or investing it or by taking offshore or investing money or other property of equivalent value. A requirement to take something offshore or invest it can be met by taking part of it offshore and investing the other part. If a disposal is deemed to be made at market value (see above under Meaning of disposal proceeds), the requirement can be satisfied by taking offshore or investing money or other property of a value equal to the amount of the deemed consideration less any deductible fees or other incidental costs.

Where, as above, a statutory requirement can be met by taking offshore or investing property of equivalent value, that property is treated as deriving from the thing required to be taken offshore or invested and as having the same composition of kinds of income and capital as that thing (see **55.3** above). Such property must not be exempt property (as in **55.3** above) or consideration for a disposal of exempt property, and it must not be consideration for the disposal of all or part of a qualifying investment.

[*ITA 2007, ss 809VG–809VP, 809Z8, 809Z9, 809Z10; FA 2012, Sch 12 paras 7, 16, 17; SI 2012 No 1898; F(No 2)A 2017, s 15(5)-(8)*].

Investments made from mixed funds

The following applies if, but for the above relief, income or gains would have been remitted to the UK by virtue of a relevant event and *ITA 2007, s 809Q* (transfers from mixed funds — see **55.3** above) would have applied in determining the amount that would have been so remitted. The relevant event counts as an offshore transfer for the purposes of *ITA 2007, s 809R(4)*. The investment holding is treated as containing a proportion of each of the kinds of income and capital in **55.3**(A)–(H) equal to the proportion of that kind of income or capital contained in the money or other property used to make the investment.

The following applies where, under the rules for potentially chargeable events above, money or other property is treated as not remitted to the UK because an amount is taken offshore, reinvested or used to purchase a certificate of tax deposit. The amount in question is treated, immediately after the step is taken, as containing the same proportion of each kind of income and capital contained in the investment holding.

The following applies where income and gains are treated as remitted to the UK because the appropriate mitigation steps were not taken within the grace period. The mixed fund rules at **55.3** above do not apply to determine the amounts remitted. The affected income and gains (see above) are so much of the 'fixed amount' of each kind of income or gain that would have been remitted to the UK by virtue of the relevant event as reflects the portion of the investment affected by the potentially chargeable event. The '*fixed amount*' is the amount of that kind of income or gain that the investment holding is treated as containing (as above).

The anti-avoidance rule at *ITA 2007, s 809S* (see **55.3** above) applies equally in relation to the above.

[*ITA 2007, s 809VO; FA 2012, Sch 12 paras 7, 17*].

Charge for claiming the remittance basis

[55.5] An individual who claims the remittance basis for 2008/09 or any subsequent tax year (see **55.2**(a) above) incurs an additional tax charge for that year if the following circumstances apply to him:

- he is 18 years of age or over in that tax year; and
- he meets the 'seven-year residence test' or, for 2012/13 and subsequent years only, the 'twelve-year residence test' or, for 2015/16 and 2016/17 only, the '17-year residence test'.

For 2015/16 and 2016/17, where the individual meets the 17-year test the charge is £90,000. For 2015/16 onwards, if the individual meets the 12-year test the charge is £60,000 and if he meets the seven-year test it is £30,000. For 2012/13 to 2014/15 inclusive, where the individual meets the 12-year test the charge is £50,000 and where the individual meets the seven-year test the charge is £30,000. For 2008/09 to 2011/12 inclusive, only the seven-year test existed and the charge was £30,000.

The '*seven-year residence test*' is met for a tax year if the individual does not meet the 12-year residence test but has been UK resident in at least seven of the nine tax years immediately preceding that year. These preceding years may include years prior to 2008/09.

The '*twelve-year residence test*' is met for a tax year if the individual does not meet the 17-year residence test (which applies in 2015/16 and 2016/17 only) but has been UK resident in at least 12 of the 14 tax years immediately preceding that year. These preceding years may include years prior to 2012/13 and indeed prior to 2008/09.

The '*17-year residence test*' applies to 2015/16 and 2016/17 only and is met for such a tax year if the individual has been UK resident in at least 17 of the 20 tax years immediately preceding that year. These preceding years may include years prior to 2015/16 and indeed prior to 2008/09. From 2017/18 onwards, the 17-year residence test is repealed; an individual who is not UK domiciled under general law but who has been UK resident for at least 15 of the 20 tax years immediately preceding a tax year, is deemed domiciled in the UK in that tax year (see **57.34** RESIDENCE AND DOMICILE),so can no longer claim the remittance basis (see **55.2** above), and therefore the remittance basis charge does not apply.

The charge is made on income and gains not remitted to the UK and is thus in addition to the tax charge on remitted income and gains. The individual can nominate the income and/or gains on which this charge is to be levied, and the remittance basis does not then apply to the nominated amount. For example, a taxpayer liable to the £30,000 charge could nominate a £107,143 chargeable gain on the disposal of a foreign residential property on which tax is then chargeable at 28%, giving a liability of £30,000. The point of nominating is that the nominated income and/or gains are not then charged to tax again if they are remitted in a later year. The nomination is made in the individual's claim within **55.2**(a) above, and the nominated amount must be part (or all) of his 'foreign income and gains' for the year (see **55.2** above). If the nominated amount is insufficient to increase the taxpayer's total income tax and CGT liability by the required amount (after taking into account all reliefs and deductions due, but ignoring any income tax charged under *ITA 2007, s 424* (Gift Aid)), he is treated for this purpose only as if he had nominated sufficient additional *income* to bring the tax increase up to that amount; this remains the case even if in reality he has insufficient income to nominate. Income *treated as* nominated does not count as nominated income for the purpose of the subsequent remittances rule below).

As the charge is a charge to tax (whether it be income tax or CGT), the normal self-assessment payment dates apply. It is also available to cover Gift Aid payments. The Treasury are of the view that it should be recognised as tax for the purposes of double tax agreements. If, however, insufficient income and gains are nominated, the income *treated as* nominated, and the tax on that income, does not qualify for double tax relief as it is not tax on specific income. (Treasury Explanatory Notes to the 2008 Finance Bill). The US Internal Revenue Service has ruled that the charge is a tax on income and that credit is allowed under US tax law (www.irs.gov/pub/irs-drop/rr-11-19.pdf).

[*ITA 2007, ss 809C, 809H; FA 2012, Sch 12 paras 2, 3, 5; FA 2015, s 24; F(No 2)A 2017, Sch 8 para 14(3)(5)*].

Direct payments to HMRC from untaxed foreign gains (or income) in settlement of the charge are not treated for tax purposes as remittances to the UK (see **55.3** above).

Nominated income and gains subsequently remitted

For the purpose of applying the exemption from charge of nominated income and gains if later remitted, nominated income and gains are treated as not remitted (even if, in fact, they have been) until all other previously unremitted foreign income and gains have been remitted. In considering the extent to which other previously unremitted foreign income and gains have been remitted, one takes into account income and gains arising in the tax year under review and all other years for 2008/09 onwards for which the remittance basis has applied to the individual (on a claim or otherwise).

'Nominated income and gains' means income and gains actually nominated and does not include income merely treated as nominated as above.

For 2012/13 onwards, the above treatment is disapplied (and the steps below do not need to be taken) if the cumulative total of nominated income and gains from each year that have been remitted in years up to and including the current year does not exceed £10.

Where nominated income and gains are, in fact, remitted in a tax year but are to be treated as above as having not been remitted, the following steps determine the income and gains that are to be treated as having been remitted instead.

Step 1.

Add the amount of nominated income and gains for the tax year and any earlier tax year which are remitted in the tax year to the amount of other foreign income and gains remitted in the tax year that has arisen in any year for 2008/09 onwards for which the remittance basis has applied to the individual.

Step 2.

Next, find the amount (if any) of the individual's foreign income and gains for the year (other than nominated income and gains) that fall within each of the following categories:

- amounts within **55.2**(i) or (ii) above other than those subject to a foreign tax;

- income within 55.2(iii) above other than income subject to a foreign tax;
- income within 55.2(iv) above other than income subject to a foreign tax;
- foreign chargeable gains, other than gains subject to a foreign tax;
- amounts within 55.2(i) or (ii) above subject to a foreign tax;
- income within 55.2(iii) above subject to a foreign tax;
- income within 55.2(iv) above subject to a foreign tax; and
- foreign chargeable gains subject to a foreign tax.

If the tax year is one to which the remittance basis does not apply, ignore this Step and Step 3 below.

Step 3.

Compare the total in Step 1 to each of the amounts in Step 2 in the order in which those amounts are listed.

If the first such amount does not exceed the total in Step 1, regard the total in Step 1 as containing the income and gains in that category. Reduce the total in Step 1 by the amount of that income and gains and compare what remains with the next of the amounts in Step 2 and so on.

If the first such amount does exceed the total in Step 1, regard the total in Step 1 as containing the appropriate proportion of each kind of income and gains in that category; similarly if the amount in any subsequent category exceeds what remains of the amount in Step 1.

Step 4.

If the total in Step 1 is still not fully matched, repeat Steps 2 and 3 by reference to income and gains of the 'appropriate tax year' that had not yet been remitted (or treated under these provisions as remitted) by the beginning of the tax year in question. The '*appropriate tax year*' is the latest of the preceding years (ignoring years before 2008/09) for which the remittance basis applied.

If the tax year in question is one to which the remittance basis does not apply, carry out this Step instead of Steps 2 and 3.

Step 5.

If the total in Step 1 is still not fully matched, repeat Steps 2 and 3 by reference to the next latest of the preceding years for which the remittance basis applied, and so on.

[*ITA 2007, ss 809I, 809J; FA 2012, Sch 12 paras 20, 21*].

Foreign currency bank accounts

Restriction of losses on disposal of amount in account

[55.6] For 2011/12 and earlier years, transactions involving amounts in foreign currency bank accounts potentially give rise to chargeable gains or allowable losses (see 25.5 EXEMPTIONS AND RELIEFS). Where the remittance basis is used it would in some circumstances be possible for an allowable loss to arise in circumstances where there was no economic loss. The following provisions apply to disallow such losses. They are repealed with effect for disposals on or after 6 April 2012 as they are no longer required following the introduction of exemption for transactions involving amounts in foreign currency bank accounts by individuals, trustees and personal representatives.

The provisions apply where an individual makes a disposal on or after 16 December 2009 and before 6 April 2012 of a foreign currency debt situated outside the UK which consists of a sum in a bank account and money or money's worth which is chargeable to income tax on the remittance basis is excluded from the consideration for the disposal under *TCGA 1992, s 37* (see **39.1** INTERACTION WITH OTHER TAXES) or would be but for these provisions. The amount so excluded is referred to below as the '*section 37 amount*'.

If the *s 37* amount constitutes the whole of the unreduced consideration (i.e. the consideration before exclusion of the *s 37* amount) the following applies:

(a) if the disposal is a part disposal (i.e. a transfer of only part of the balance in the account (and see **55.7** below)), in making the apportionment of the acquisition cost required by *TCGA 1992, s 42* (see **16.5** COMPUTATION OF GAINS AND LOSSES), amount A is taken to be the unreduced consideration; and
(b) any loss on the disposal is not an allowable loss.

If the *s 37* amount constitutes only part of the unreduced consideration, the disposal is treated as if it were two separate disposals, one of the proportion of the debt disposed of represented by the *s 37* amount ('*debt A*') and the other of the remainder of the debt disposed of ('*debt B*'). The consideration for each disposal (before any exclusion under *TCGA 1992, s 37*) is the *s 37* amount for debt A and the remainder of the unreduced consideration for debt B.

If the actual disposal is not a part disposal, the '*section 37* proportion' of the allowable expenditure within *TCGA 1992, s 38(1)((a)–(c)* (see **16.11** COMPUTATION OF GAINS AND LOSSES) is attributed to debt A and the remaining such expenditure to debt B. For this purpose, the '*section 37 proportion*' is the proportion of the unreduced consideration which constitutes the *s 37* amount.

If the actual disposal is a part disposal, the allowable expenditure is divided into the 'debt costs' (i.e. the allowable expenditure within *TCGA 1992, s 38(1)(a)(b)*) and the disposal costs, with different apportionment rules applying to each. The debt costs are apportioned between debt A, debt B and the remainder of the debt (i.e. the untransferred balance) in the proportions which those parts of the debt bear to each other. The *s 37* proportion (as above) of the disposal costs is attributed to debt A and the remainder to debt B.

Any loss on the deemed disposal of debt A is not an allowable loss.

[*TCGA 1992, s 252A, Sch 8A; FA 2012, s 35(5)(6)*].

HMRC practice

[55.7] As noted at 55.2, where an individual claims the remittance basis, no annual exempt amount is available for the year concerned. As a result, numerous small transactions involving foreign currency bank accounts could, before 6 April 2012, potentially give rise to chargeable gains (see **25.5** EXEMPTIONS AND RELIEFS). Such gains are exempt where made by individuals, trustees or personal representatives on or after 6 April 2012. HMRC have published the following guidance intended to simplify the calculation of such gains arising before that date.

Acquisition costs at 6 April 2008

The acquisition cost of a debt represented by a non-sterling account as at 6 April 2008 can, at the taxpayer's option, be calculated using the average exchange rate for the six years to April 2008 or, for accounts open for less than six years at that time, the average rate for the number of years for which the account was open (to the nearest year). HMRC have provided the following such average rates for US dollars and euros: £1 = US$0.560275917; and £1 = €0.68058106. (HMRC Notice 10 December 2009).

Part disposal rules

HMRC have confirmed that, for 2008/09 onwards, they consider that gains and losses on transfers of amounts from a foreign currency account should be calculated using the normal rules for part disposals (see **16.5** COMPUTATION OF GAINS AND LOSSES) and not the share matching rules (see **64.2** SHARES AND SECURITIES — IDENTIFICATION RULES). Although HMRC consider that this has always been the correct view, they will not insist on revisiting computations made for 2007/08 and earlier years using the share matching rules. (HMRC Notice 10 December 2009).

Aggregation of debits and credits

A net figure for deposits into and withdrawals from a foreign currency bank account may be computed for each calendar month or part month within a tax year to ease the task of computing gains and losses on numerous withdrawals. The net deposit or withdrawal thus computed is then converted to sterling at the average exchange rate for the month and the acquisition cost deducted using the part disposal rules. In the formula for apportioning the acquisition cost (see **16.5** COMPUTATION OF GAINS AND LOSSES), A is the total withdrawals for the month expressed in the foreign currency and B is the balance on the account at the start of the month plus the total deposits into the account in the month, both expressed in the foreign currency. If a taxpayer uses this method, he must use it for all accounts in the currency concerned for the whole of the tax year in question. (HMRC Capital Gains Manual CG78327). Note that this practice is not restricted to those using the remittance basis.

Accounts in one currency treated as one account

A taxpayer may treat all bank accounts in his name containing a particular foreign currency which are not situated in the UK (see **7.3**(l) ASSETS) as one account and so disregard direct transfers among such accounts which would otherwise constitute disposals and acquisitions. The practice, once adopted, must be applied to all future direct transfers among bank accounts in the taxpayer's name designated in that currency. This practice did not apply to non-domiciled individuals before 6 April 2008. (HMRC Statement of Practice 10/84; HMRC Guidance Note 28 January 2010).

Small remittances

Where the amount of net gains from transfers on overseas non-sterling bank accounts which an individual remits to the UK is less than £500 in any tax year in which the individual uses the remittance basis, those gains do not have to be reported on the individual's tax return. This practice applies for 2008/09 onwards. (HMRC Guidance Note 28 January 2010).

2007/08 and earlier years

[55.8] Subject to any relevant double taxation agreement, the remittance basis applies automatically for 2007/08 and earlier years to disposals by individuals resident but not domiciled in the UK of assets situated abroad (with no allowance for losses arising abroad). [*TCGA 1992, ss 12(1), 16(4)*]. There were also rules governing constructive remittances; these are superseded for 2008/09 onwards by the rules at **55.2** above.

HMRC practice appears to be to leave out of account remittances made out of the proceeds of disposals made whilst a non-UK domiciled individual was not resident in the UK and, subject to this, to treat a remittance as taxable to the extent given by the proportion which represents chargeable gain on normal disposal principles (see **16.11** COMPUTATION OF GAINS AND LOSSES for allowable expenditure and proceeds in foreign currency). This practice even seems to extend to the case where the taxpayer divides the proceeds of disposal but only makes remittances from that part which represents the original allowable expenditure and indexation allowance.

In an appeal to General Commissioners, the Revenue were successful in applying the provisions where the individual was at all material times resident in the UK but acquired a UK domicile between the realisation of the gains in question and the time, in a later year of assessment, when the proceeds of the gains were remitted to the UK (Taxation, 6 June 1991, p 257).

For the situation where an individual becomes, or ceases to be, resident in the UK, see **57.29** RESIDENCE AND DOMICILE.

Forward agreements

It is known that it was Revenue practice in the past to make 'forward tax agreements' with certain wealthy non-UK domiciled individuals, under which the individual would pay a set amount each year, agreed in advance, 'in full and final settlement' of his UK income tax and CGT liability. Such agreements have, however, been held to be illegal (*Fayed and Others v Advocate-General for Scotland (representing CIR)* SCS, [2002] STC 910).

Remittances generally

[55.9] By analogy with cases relating to income tax, a taxable remittance may include the repatriation of reinvested gains, provided those gains were made whilst the disposer was resident in the UK (*Scottish Provident Institution v Farmer* CS 1912, 6 TC 34 and *Kneen v Martin* CA 1934, 19 TC 33). Similarly, a remittance from a foreign bank account into which overseas gains have been paid may be assessable, depending on the circumstances, see *Walsh v Randall* KB 1940, 23 TC 55 (sterling draft on foreign bank received by UK resident drawer before handing to UK payee) and *Thomson v Moyse* HL 1960, 39 TC 291 (dollar cheques on US bank sold to the Bank of England held to be remitted) but cf. *Carter v Sharon* KB 1936, 20 TC 229 (drafts on foreign bank posted abroad by UK drawer for daughter's maintenance; held no remittance as, under relevant foreign law, gift to daughter complete on posting of draft).

In *Harmel v Wright* Ch D 1973, 49 TC 149 an amount received via two South African companies, ending as a loan from one of them, was held to be a remittance. An erroneous remittance by a bank, contrary to the customer's instructions, was held not liable in *Duke of Roxburghe's Exors v CIR* CS 1936, 20 TC 711.

In *Grimm v Newman & Another* CA, [2002] STC 1388 (a negligence case in which the Revenue were not a party), an absolute inter-spousal gift, perfected abroad, of overseas assets subsequently used to purchase a matrimonial home in the UK was held not to be a remittance.

The above decisions pre-dated the fundamental legislative changes made to the remittance basis for 2008/09 onwards.

Key points concerning the remittance basis

[55.10] Points to consider are as follows.

- The remittance basis can be claimed by non-domiciled UK residents and applies to foreign capital gains and income. It cannot be claimed for gains (or income) in isolation.
- The remittance basis can be claimed on a year by year basis.
- Claiming the remittance basis causes the loss of the capital gains tax annual exempt amount (and income tax personal allowances).
- Long-term residents (aged over 18) may need to pay the remittance basis charge. The level of charge depends upon the number of years the individual is resident; £30,000 for at least seven years; £60,000 for at least 12 years and (for 2015/16 and 2016/17 only) £90,000 for at least 17 years. The charge can be paid out of foreign gains without this being a remittance of those gains.
- The definition of a remittance is very wide and includes virtually anything where a 'relevant person' brings, receives or uses the gain in the UK. However when considering the remittance of gains that arose before 6 April 2008 the definition of a relevant person is restricted to the individual. There is a relief for remittances used for the purpose of making qualifying commercial investments.
- If an individual disposed of an asset, realising a foreign capital gain, before 6 April 2008 in a year for which the remittance basis applied, and remits that gain to the UK in 2016/17 that gain is

taxable in 2016/17. However if the proceeds of the disposal are gifted (offshore) to another person (including a spouse or civil partner) those proceeds can be brought to the UK tax free. It is important that the individual who realised the gain does not benefit from the funds remitted to the UK. The difficulty here is isolating the pre-2008 capital gains to enable the remittance. Especially where the mixed fund rules apply to post April 2009 funds

- Foreign capital losses cannot be remitted to the UK and are not allowable. However, a once and for all election can be made, so that foreign losses are allowable but the order in which all losses (including UK losses) must be utilised will generally mean that such an election will not be worthwhile.

56

Repayment Interest

Introduction	**56.1**
Repayment interest (the new regime)	**56.2**
Persons other than companies — the old regime	**56.3**
Companies	**56.4**
Miscellaneous	**56.5**

Cross-reference. See **51** PAYMENT OF TAX.

Introduction

[56.1] A new harmonised regime for interest is being introduced to apply to all of the taxes and duties administered by HMRC. In relation to interest on capital gains tax repaid by HMRC, the new regime is described at **56.2** below. For the purposes of income tax and capital gains tax self-assessment, it comes into force on **31 October 2011**. To the extent that the new regime is in force, it replaces the old regime described at **56.3** below. The new regime is expected to apply to corporation tax in future, but in the meantime the rules at **56.4** below continue to apply.

The repayment interest system mirrors that under which HMRC charge interest on late paid tax (see **42** LATE PAYMENT INTEREST AND PENALTIES) but the rates of interest for overpaid tax are considerably lower.

Repayment interest (the new regime)

[56.2] A new harmonised regime for interest is being introduced to apply to all of the taxes and duties administered by HMRC. To the extent that the new regime is in force (see below) in relation to interest on capital gains tax repaid by HMRC, it replaces the rules described at **56.3** below.

An amount carries interest only if it is payable by HMRC to any person under or by virtue of an enactment or if it is a repayment by HMRC of any sum that was paid in connection with any liability (including any purported or anticipated liability) to make a payment to HMRC under or by virtue of an enactment.

For the purposes of any 'self-assessment amount' payable by HMRC to any person, the regime comes into force on **31 October 2011**. A '*self-assessment amount*' means:

- any tax or other amount in relation to which, for any tax year, a personal, trustees' or partnership tax return falls to be made or a discovery assessment is made; and

- any penalties assessed in relation to that tax or amount.

Where interest is already accruing immediately prior to 31 October 2011 on a self-assessment amount, it accrues on and after that date under the new regime. Interest added to a repayment made on or after 31 October 2011 of a self-assessment amount is known as '*repayment interest*'.

Rates of repayment interest are significantly lower than those by reference to which late payment interest is charged (see **42.2** LATE PAYMENT INTEREST AND PENALTIES). The rates are set by reference to the official bank rate set by the Bank of England Monetary Policy Committee; for details, see *SI 2011 No 2446, Reg 4*. There is a minimum rate of repayment interest of 0.5%, so that some interest will be due even when the official rate would otherwise be too low. Changes to the rate of repayment interest will be announced by HMRC News Release.

Rates of interest are:

0.50% p.a. from 31 October 2011

Period for which interest accrues

A repayment within these provisions carries interest at the repayment interest rate from the 'repayment interest start date' until the date on which the repayment is made. The '*repayment interest start date*' is arrived at as set out below. It matters not that the repayment interest start date might be a non-business day.

- Where the repayment is of an amount which has been paid to HMRC, the repayment interest start date is the *later* of date A and date B, where:
  date A = the date on which the amount was paid to HMRC; and
  date B = the date on which payment of the amount to HMRC became due and payable to HMRC (where the amount was paid in connection with a liability to make a payment to HMRC).
- Where the repayment is of an amount which has not been paid to HMRC but is payable by them by virtue of a return having been filed or a claim having been made, the repayment interest start date is the *later* of date C and date D, where:
  date C = the date (if any) on which the return was required to be filed or the claim was required to be made; and
  date D = the date on which the return was in fact filed or the claim was in fact made.
- Where the repayment is the result of a loss relief claim affecting two or more years (see **13.2** CLAIMS), the repayment interest start date is 31 January following the *later* year in relation to the claim, i.e. on a claim to carry back a loss, the tax year in which the loss arises.

A repayment may take the form of a set-off against an amount owed to HMRC, in which case the date on which the repayment is made is the date from which the set-off takes effect.

As regards the date on which an amount is treated as paid to HMRC, see **51.10** PAYMENT OF TAX.

Supplementary

Repayment interest is not payable on an amount payable in consequence of an order or judgment of a court having power to allow interest on the amount.

[*FA 2009, ss 102, 103, 104, Sch 54 paras 1–5, 7; SI 2011 Nos 701, 2401, 2446*].

Persons other than companies — the old regime

[56.3] For the purposes of income tax and capital gains tax self-assessment, the rules described below are superseded by those at **56.2** above on and after **31 October 2011**. Where interest is already accruing immediately prior to 31 October 2011 on a 'self-assessment amount' (as defined in **56.2**), it will accrue on and after that date under the new regime.

A repayment by HMRC of capital gains tax paid by or on behalf of an individual (or trustees of a settlement or personal representatives of a deceased person) carries interest at the rate(s) listed below. The amount by which the repayment is so increased is known as a **repayment supplement.**

The interest runs from the date the tax is paid until the date on which the order for the repayment is issued by HMRC.

[*TCGA 1992, s 283(1)(2)(4); FA 2006, Sch 12 para 24; SI 2011 No 701, Art 5*].

A repayment supplement is not taxable in the hands of the recipient. [*ITTOIA 2005, s 749; ICTA 1988, s 824(8)*].

Rates of interest are:

0.50% p.a. from 29 September 2009
0.00% p.a. from 27 January 2009 to 28 September 2009
0.75% p.a. from 6 January 2009 to 26 January 2009
1.50% p.a. from 6 December 2008 to 5 January 2009
2.25% p.a. from 6 November 2008 to 5 December 2008
3.00% p.a. from 6 January 2008 to 5 November 2008
4.00% p.a. from 6 August 2007 to 5 January 2008
3.00% p.a. from 6 September 2006 to 5 August 2007
2.25% p.a. from 6 September 2005 to 5 September 2006
3.00% p.a. from 6 September 2004 to 5 September 2005
2.25% p.a. from 6 December 2003 to 5 September 2004
1.50% p.a. from 6 August 2003 to 5 December 2003
2.25% p.a. from 6 November 2001 to 5 August 2003
3.00% p.a. from 6 May 2001 to 5 November 2001
4.00% p.a. from 6 February 2000 to 5 May 2001
3.00% p.a. from 6 March 1999 to 5 February 2000
4.00% p.a. from 6 January 1999 to 5 March 1999
4.75% p.a. from 6 August 1997 to 5 January 1999
4.00% p.a. from 31 January 1997 to 5 August 1997

HMRC announced on 6 September 2005 that the interest rates that they had previously used for the period 6 May 2001 to 5 September 2005 were incorrect. The above rates are the corrected rates published on 6 September

2005. The incorrect rates used were higher than those above but HMRC did not attempt to recover any amounts overpaid. Where, however, a repayment was reviewed for other reasons, the correct amount of interest was calculated. (HMRC News Release 6 September 2005).

It will be noted that the rates are considerably lower than those by reference to which interest is charged on late paid tax (see **42.3** LATE PAYMENT INTEREST AND PENALTIES). The rates are adjusted automatically by reference to changes in the official bank rate of the Bank of England, and are announced by HMRC Press Release. Before 12 August 2009 the rates were determined by reference to the average of base lending rates of certain clearing banks. See *SI 1989 No 1297, Reg 3AB*.

There is no requirement that the taxpayer be resident in the UK or European Community.

Although repayment supplement runs from the date the tax was paid, even if this falls before the due date, HMRC have stated that they will not pay repayment supplement on any amount deliberately overpaid (Revenue Press Release 12 November 1996). This is intended to deter taxpayers from using HMRC as a source of tax-free interest. Where a payment of tax is not set against any liability and repayment is not claimed, the payment remains on record until the next liability arises, but no repayment supplement will be given. (Revenue Tax Bulletin June 1999 p 674). As regards the date on which payment is treated as made, see **51.10** PAYMENT OF TAX. Interest is not payable on repayments made by order or judgement of a court having power to allow interest (for which see **51.18** PAYMENT OF TAX). [*TCGA 1992, s 283(3)*].

Repayment supplement is added in similar fashion to any repayment of a penalty imposed under any provision of *TMA 1970* (see **52** PENALTIES) or of a surcharge imposed under *TMA 1970, s 59C* (see **42.6** INTEREST AND SURCHARGES ON UNPAID TAX). [*ICTA 1988, s 824*]. For full details of repayment supplement under *s 824*, see Tolley's Income Tax.

See **13.2** CLAIMS for special rule where a claim affects two or more years, e.g. a loss carry-back claim.

Companies

[56.4] Where a repayment of corporation tax falls to be made to a company for an accounting period ending on or after 1 July 1999 (self-assessment), the repayment carries interest (under *ICTA 1988, s 826*) from the 'material date' until the order for repayment is issued. Corporation tax is to be brought within the repayment interest regime at **56.2** above (with special additional rules) in future.

The '*material date*' is the later of the date the corporation tax was paid and the date on which it became (or would have become) due and payable, i.e. the day following the expiry of nine months from the end of the accounting period (see **51.4** PAYMENT OF TAX).

In the case of large companies which are required to make instalment payments under the quarterly accounting rules (see **51.4** PAYMENT OF TAX) a special rate applies to any excess instalment payments until nine months after the end of the accounting period concerned, and the normal rate applies after that time. The special rate also applies to payments made by a company outside the quarterly accounting regime before the day following the expiry of nine months after the end of the accounting period concerned. Such interest is payable from the date of payment until that day although not for periods before the first instalment date (or the date which would be the first instalment date were the company within the quarterly accounting regime).

The interest rates are determined by criteria contained in Treasury regulations made by statutory instrument, see *SI 1989 No 1297, Regs 3BA, 3BB.*

The rates of interest for amounts overpaid **on or after the normal due date** for payment of corporation tax (see above) are:

0.50% p.a. from 29 September 2009
0.00% p.a. from 27 January 2009 to 28 September 2009
1.00% p.a. from 6 January 2009 to 26 January 2009
2.00% p.a. from 6 December 2008 to 5 January 2009
3.00% p.a. from 6 November 2008 to 5 December 2008
4.00% p.a. from 6 January 2008 to 5 November 2008
5.00% p.a. from 6 August 2007 to 5 January 2008
4.00% p.a. from 6 September 2006 to 5 August 2007
3.00% p.a. from 6 September 2005 to 5 September 2006
4.00% p.a. from 6 September 2004 to 5 September 2005
3.00% p.a. from 6 December 2003 to 5 September 2004
2.00% p.a. from 6 August 2003 to 5 December 2003
3.00% p.a. from 6 November 2001 to 5 August 2003
4.00% p.a. from 6 May 2001 to 5 November 2001
5.00% p.a. previously

The rates for amounts overpaid **before the due date, for example under the quarterly accounting rules for large companies,** are:

0.50% p.a. from 21 September 2009
0.25% p.a. from 16 March 2009 to 20 September 2009
0.75% p.a. from 16 February 2009 to 15 March 2009
1.25% p.a. from 19 January 2009 to 15 February 2009
1.75% p.a. from 15 December 2008 to 18 January 2009
2.75% p.a. from 17 November 2008 to 14 December 2008
4.25% p.a. from 20 October 2008 to 16 November 2008
4.75% p.a. from 21 April 2008 to 19 October 2008
5.00% p.a. from 18 February 2008 to 20 April 2008
5.25% p.a. from 17 December 2007 to 17 February 2008
5.50% p.a. from 16 July 2007 to 16 December 2007
5.25% p.a. from 21 May 2007 to 15 July 2007
5.00% p.a. from 22 January 2007 to 20 May 2007
4.75% p.a. from 20 November 2006 to 21 January 2007
4.50% p.a. from 14 August 2006 to 19 November 2006
4.25% p.a. from 15 August 2005 to 13 August 2006
4.50% p.a. from 16 August 2004 to 14 August 2005
4.25% p.a. from 21 June 2004 to 15 August 2004
4.00% p.a. from 17 May 2004 to 20 June 2004
3.75% p.a. from 16 February 2004 to 16 May 2004

3.50% p.a. from 17 November 2003 to 15 February 2004
3.25% p.a. from 21 July 2003 to 16 November 2003
3.5% p.a. from 17 February 2003 to 20 July 2003
3.75% p.a. from 19 November 2001 to 16 February 2003
4.25% p.a. from 15 October 2001 to 18 November 2001
4.50% p.a. from 1 October 2001 to 14 October 2001
4.75% p.a. from 13 August 2001 to 30 September 2001
5.00% p.a. from 21 May 2001 to 12 August 2001
5.25% p.a. from 16 April 2001 to 20 May 2001
5.50% p.a. from 19 February 2001 to 15 April 2001
5.75% p.a. from 21 February 2000 to 18 February 2001
5.50% p.a. from 24 January 2000 to 20 February 2000
5.25% p.a. from 15 November 1999 to 23 January 2000
5.00% p.a. from 20 September 1999 to 14 November 1999
4.75% p.a. from 21 June 1999 to 19 September 1999
5.00% p.a. from 19 April 1999 to 20 June 1999
5.25% p.a. from 15 February 1999 to 18 April 1999
5.75% p.a. from 18 January 1999 to 14 February 1999
6.00% p.a. from 7 January 1999 to 17 January 1999

The latter set of rates applies up to the earlier of the date of repayment and the normal due date (whereafter the normal rates apply).

There are restrictions on the amount of the interest where surplus advance corporation tax of a later accounting period displaces mainstream corporation tax paid in respect of an earlier accounting period, or trading losses or non-trading deficits of a later accounting period are offset against profits of an earlier period or there is a combination of such events.

Interest is paid without deduction of income tax and is chargeable to corporation tax as a non-trading credit under the loan relationship rules (see **15.2–15.7** COMPANIES — CORPORATE FINANCE AND INTANGIBLES and Tolley's Corporation Tax). Corporation tax repayments are as far as possible treated as repayments of tax paid on a later date rather than an earlier date.

Interest on overpaid tax paid to a company which becomes recoverable because of a change in the company's assessed corporation tax liability and not because of HMRC error can be recovered without an assessment.

[*ICTA 1988, ss 826, 826A; FA 1989, ss 178, 179(1)(c)(ii), 180(6); SI 1989 No 1297; SI 1998 No 3175, Reg 8; FA 2009, s 105(6); SI 2009 No 2032*].

Miscellaneous

[56.5] See **51.31** PAYMENT OF TAX as regards assessment of repayment supplement or interest overpaid.

Unauthorised demands for tax

There is a general right to interest under *Supreme Court Act 1981, s 35A* in a case where the taxpayer submits to an unauthorised demand for tax, provided that the payment is not made voluntarily to close a transaction (*Woolwich Equitable Building Society v CIR* HL 1992, 65 TC 265).

Interest on judgment debts

With effect for periods beginning on or after 8 July 2015, a special rate of interest applies to interest payable by HMRC under *Judgments Act 1838, s 17* or under an order under *County Courts Act 1984, s 74* where the debt to which the interest relates arises from court proceedings relating to a tax matter. The annual rate is the Bank of England official rate plus 2%. See *F(No 2)A 2015, s 52*. With effect from 15 September 2016, similar rules apply in Scotland and Northern Ireland. See *FA 2016, ss 170, 171*.

57

Residence and Domicile

Introduction	**57.1**
HMRC administrative procedures	**57.2**
Statutory residence test for 2013/14 onwards	**57.3**
The automatic UK tests	**57.4**
The automatic overseas tests	**57.5**
Automatic tests — supplementary	**57.6**
The sufficient ties test	**57.11**
UK ties	**57.12**
Split year treatment	**57.18**
Transitional provisions	**57.28**
Residence for 2012/13 and earlier years	**57.29**
Ordinary residence	**57.30**
Visits abroad and claims to non-UK residence and to non-UK ordinary residence	**57.31**
Members of Parliament	**57.32**
Companies	**57.33**
Domicile and deemed domicile	**57.34**
Appeals	**57.35**
United Kingdom	**57.36**
Ireland	**57.37**
Key points	**57.38**

Cross-references. See **19.9** DEATH for residence etc. status of personal representatives; **21** DOUBLE TAX RELIEF for double tax agreements which may override or amend statutory provisions or HMRC practice for the purposes of such agreements; **48** OFFSHORE SETTLEMENTS; **49** OVERSEAS MATTERS; **50.2** PARTNERSHIPS for overseas resident partners and partnerships; and **62.6** SETTLEMENTS for residence etc. status of trustees.

Simon's Taxes. See C1.201, C1.6, E6.1, E6.3.

Introduction

[57.1] An individual is chargeable to capital gains tax on gains made in a tax year during any part of which he is resident in the UK or, for 2012/13 and earlier years, during which he is ordinarily resident in the UK. Individuals who are not domiciled in the UK can claim to use the remittance basis. This chapter looks at the meaning of 'residence', 'ordinary residence' and 'domicile'. It also considers the residence status of companies.

For 2013/14 and subsequent years, an individual's residence status is determined under the statutory residence test at **57.3** below onwards. The concept of ordinary residence is abolished for capital gains tax purposes with effect on and after 6 April 2013.

Previously, the legislation contained few specific directions about how to ascertain a person's 'residence' and 'ordinary residence' status in a particular tax year for general tax purposes and this was especially so of capital gains tax. Consequently, it was a body of case law that brought about the view that these terms were to be interpreted according to their normal meanings and that each case had to rest on its own facts and particular circumstances. HMRC have taken case decisions, *inter alia*, in formulating their own practice as to the determination of residence and ordinary residence (see **57.29–57.31** below for individuals for 2012/13 and earlier years and **57.33** for companies).

The term 'domicile' is governed by the general legal meaning such that each case rests on its own facts. However, from 2017/18 a 'deemed domicile' rule applies for income tax and capital gains tax purposes, with statutory definition. See **57.34** below.

For appeals relating to residence and domicile generally, see **57.35** below.

The extent of the UK for tax purposes is given in **57.36** below and special rules relating to residence status in connection with the double taxation agreement between the UK and Ireland are in **57.37** below.

HMRC administrative procedures

[57.2] Before 1 June 2010, individuals who came to the UK to take up employment were asked to complete Form P86 to enable their residence status to be considered. This form also included a section on domicile but this should no longer have been completed for arrivals after 5 April 2008. Before 25 March 2009, Form DOM1 was used to obtain the information necessary to the determination of domicile, but following the changes to the remittance basis for 2008/09 onwards the form has been withdrawn because the remittance basis now has to be claimed in most cases, requiring taxpayers to determine their own domicile status (HMRC Brief 17/09). On leaving the UK, a shortened form P85 (Form P85(S)) is used to enable any repayment to be claimed in straightforward cases. Otherwise, Form P85 is used.

Individuals who regard themselves as not resident or not domiciled in the UK are required to self-certify their status in the self-assessment tax return and to complete the 'NON-RESIDENCE ETC.' supplementary pages to the return. HMRC do not provide residence 'rulings' but will give specific advice in limited circumstances. HMRC queries on residence status and domicile aspects may be made as part of an enquiry into the self-assessment return or into an initial claim made outside the return (see **58.9** RETURNS, **13.3** CLAIMS). See Revenue Tax Bulletin June 1997 pp 425–427.

HMRC Guidance Note RDR1 describes HMRC's practice in relation to residence issues for 2013/14 onwards. It replaces HMRC Leaflet HMRC 6 which applied for 2009/10 to 2012/13.

Statutory residence test for 2013/14 onwards

[57.3] Statutory rules apply to determine whether an individual is resident or not resident in the UK for **2013/14** or any subsequent tax year. [*FA 2013, Sch 45 para 153(1)*]. These rules are known collectively as the '*statutory residence* *test*'. [*FA 2013, s 218, Sch 45*]. References in the rules to an individual are to one acting in any capacity, including as trustee or personal representative. [*FA 2013, Sch 45 para 145*]. The rules do not apply to determine whether an individual is resident or not resident in England, Wales, Scotland or Northern Ireland specifically (rather than in the UK as a whole). [*FA 2013, Sch 45 para 1(3)*]. Any reference in any capital gains tax enactment to an individual being resident (or not resident) in the UK is to be taken as a reference to his being resident (or not resident) in the UK in accordance with the statutory residence test. [*FA 2013, Sch 45 paras 2(1)(2), 145*].

Subject to the split year treatment at **57.18** below where there are certain changes of circumstances, an individual who, in accordance with the statutory residence test, is resident (or not resident) in the UK *for* a tax year is regarded as being UK resident (or not UK resident) at *all* times in that tax year. [*FA 2013, Sch 45 para 2(3)(4)*].

See **57.28** below for transitional provisions.

For HMRC guidance, with examples, on the statutory residence test see www.gov.uk/government/publications/rdr3–statutory-residence-test-srt.

The basic rule

Under the statutory residence test an individual (P) is resident in the UK for a tax year if for that year:

- the 'automatic residence test' is met; or
- the 'sufficient ties test' (see **57.11** below) is met.

If neither of those tests is met, P is not resident in the UK for that year.

[*FA 2013, Sch 45 paras 3, 4*].

Automatic residence test

The '*automatic residence test*' is met for a year if P meets at least one of the 'automatic UK tests' (see **57.4** below) and none of the 'automatic overseas tests' (see **57.4** below). [*FA 2013, Sch 45 para 5*].

The automatic UK tests

[57.4] There are four '*automatic UK tests*'. As stated in **57.3** above, an individual (P) need meet only one of them to pass the automatic residence test.

(1) The first automatic UK test is that P spends at least 183 days in the UK in the tax year in question (year X). See **57.7** below as regards days spent in the UK.

(2) The second automatic UK test is that:
   - P has a home (see **57.8** below) in the UK for at least part of year X;
   - P is present at that home (while it is a home of his) for at least some of the time on at least 30 days (whether consecutive or intermittent) in year X;
   - while it is a home of P's, there is at least 1 period of 91 consecutive days throughout which condition A or condition B (or a combination of those conditions) is met; and

- at least 30 days of that 91-day period fall within year X.

Condition A is that P has no home overseas. Condition B is that P does have 1 or more homes overseas but each of them is a home at which he is present for at least some of the time on fewer than 30 days (whether consecutive or intermittent) in year X.

If, in fact, P has more than 1 home in the UK, the test must be applied to each of those homes individually, but the test has to be met only in relation to at least 1 of them.

(3) The third automatic UK test is that:

- P works 'sufficient hours in the UK' (see **57.9** below), as assessed over a period of 365 days;
- there are no 'significant breaks' from UK work within that period;
- at least part of that period falls within year X;
- of the total number of days in that period when P does more than 3 hours' work, more than 75% of them are days when he does more than 3 hours' work in the UK; and
- at least 1 day in year X is a day on which P does more than 3 hours' work in the UK.

For these purposes there is a '*significant break*' from UK work if at least 31 days go by and not 1 of them is a day on which P does more than 3 hours' work in the UK (or would have done so but for being on annual leave, sick leave or parenting leave).

See **57.9** below as regards work generally.

The third automatic UK test does not apply to P if:

- at any time in year X he has a 'relevant job' on board a vehicle, aircraft or ship (see **57.10** below); and
- at least six of the trips that he makes in year X as part of that job are cross-border trips that begin or end in the UK (or both begin and end in the UK).

(4) The fourth automatic UK test is that:

(a) P dies in year X;

(b) for each of the previous three tax years, P was resident in the UK by virtue of meeting the automatic residence test;

(c) the tax year preceding year X would not be a split year (see **57.19** below) as regards P, even if he is non-UK resident for year X;

(d) when P died, his home (see **57.8** below) (or at least one of his homes if more than one) was in the UK; and

(e) if P had a home overseas during all or part of year X, P did not spend a sufficient amount of time there in year X.

In (b) above, the words 'by virtue of meeting the automatic residence test' do not apply where the previous year in question is 2012/13 or an earlier year, unless the election in **57.28** below is made in respect of that year. In (e) above, P spent a sufficient amount of time in year X at the overseas home if there were at least 30 days in the year when P was present there on that day for at least some of the time (no matter how short a time) or P was present there for at least some of the time (no matter how short a time) on each day of year X up to and including the day of P's death. There is no requirement for the 30 days to be consecutive, but P is only treated as present at a home if it is a home of P's at the time of his presence. If P had more than one overseas home each must be considered separately.

[*FA 2013, Sch 45 paras 6–10, 29(1), 145, 146, 154(5)*].

The automatic overseas tests

[57.5] There are five '*automatic overseas tests*'. As stated in 57.3 above, the automatic residence test is failed if an individual (P) meets at least one of the automatic overseas tests.

(1) The first automatic overseas test is that:
- P was resident in the UK for one or more of the three tax years preceding the tax year in question (year X);
- the number of days in year X that P spends in the UK is less than 16; and
- P does not die in year X.

(2) The second automatic overseas test is that:
- P was resident in the UK for none of the three tax years preceding year X; and
- the number of days in year X that P spends in the UK is less than 46.

(3) The third automatic overseas test is that:
- P works 'sufficient hours overseas' (see 57.9 below), as assessed over the course of year X;
- there are no 'significant breaks' from overseas work during year X;
- the number of days in year X on which P does more than 3 hours' work in the UK is less than 31; and
- the number of days spent by P in the UK in year X is less than 91 (disregarding any days *treated* as spent in the UK under the 'deeming rule' in 57.7 below).

For these purposes there is a '*significant break*' from overseas work if at least 31 days go by and not one of them is a day on which P does more than 3 hours' work overseas (or would have done so but for being on annual leave, sick leave or parenting leave).

See 57.9 below as regards work generally.

The third automatic overseas test does not apply to P if:
- at any time in year X he has a 'relevant job' on board a vehicle, aircraft or ship (see 57.10 below); and
- at least six of the trips that he makes in year X as part of that job are cross-border trips that begin or end in the UK (or both begin and end in the UK).

(4) The fourth automatic overseas test is that:
(a) P dies in year X;
(b) P was resident in the UK for neither of the two tax years preceding year X; and
(c) the number of days that P spends in the UK in year X is less than 46.

P also meets the condition in (b) above if he was not resident in the UK for the tax year preceding year X but the year before that was a split year as regards P because the circumstances fell within Case 1, Case 2 or Case 3 at **57.20–57.22** below.

(5) The fifth automatic overseas test is that:
- (a) P dies in year X;
- (b) P was resident in the UK for neither of the two tax years preceding year X because he met the third automatic overseas test for each of those years; and
- (c) P would meet the third automatic overseas test for year X if that test were assessed by reference to the period from the start of year X up to (but not including) the date of death.

In (b) above, the words 'because he met the third automatic overseas test for each of those years' do not apply where the preceding year in question is 2012/13 or an earlier year, unless the election in **57.28** below is made in respect of that year.

P also meets the condition in (b) above if he was not resident in the UK for the tax year preceding year X because he met the third automatic overseas test for that year but the year before that was a split year as regards P because the circumstances fell within Case 1 at **57.20** below. If that preceding year is 2012/13, the words 'because he met the third automatic overseas test for that year' do not apply unless the election in **57.28** below is made in respect of that year.

[*FA 2013, Sch 45 paras 11–16, 29(2), 145, 146, 154(5)*].

See **57.7** below as regards days spent in the UK.

Automatic tests — supplementary

[57.6] The following paragraphs (**57.7–57.10**) supplement, and provide definitions for the purposes of, the automatic UK and overseas tests at **57.4** and **57.5** above and these provisions generally.

Days spent in the UK

[57.7] Generally, if an individual (P) is present in the UK at the end of a day, that day counts as a day spent by P in the UK for the purposes of the statutory residence test. If, however, P arrives in the UK on one day and departs on the next, he is not treated as spending a day in the UK (despite his presence at the end of the day of arrival) if between arrival and departure he does not engage in activities that are to a substantial extent unrelated to his passage through the UK, i.e. he is merely a passenger in transit. Note that this precludes not only his engaging in activities relating to business or employment but also in many activities of a non-business nature such as spending time with family.

A day at the end of which P is present in the UK due only to exceptional circumstances beyond his control that prevent his leaving the UK does not count as a day spent by P in the UK. Exceptional circumstances include, for example, a sudden or life-threatening illness or injury and national or local emergencies such as war, civil unrest or natural disasters; in all cases it must be P's intention to leave the UK as soon as those circumstances permit. The maximum number of days in a tax year on which P can rely on this exclusion is limited to 60. Accordingly, once the number of days for which the exclusion applies reaches 60 (counting forward from the start of the tax year), any subsequent days, whether involving the same or different exceptional circumstances, will count as days spent by P in the UK.

For further information about how HMRC interpret the term 'exceptional circumstances' see HMRC guidance, Annex B.

The 'deeming rule'

If P is not present in the UK at the end of a day, that day does not count as a day spent by P in the UK, but this is subject to a rule known as the 'deeming rule'. The '*deeming rule*' applies if:

- P has at least three 'UK ties' (see **57.12** below) for a tax year (year X) (determined without reference to the deeming rule itself);
- P was resident in the UK for at least one of the three tax years preceding year X; and
- the number of days ('*visiting days*') in year X when P is present in the UK at some point in the day, but *not* at the end of it, is more than 30.

The deeming rule is that, once the number of visiting days in year X reaches 30 (counting forward from the start of the tax year), each subsequent visiting day in year X is treated as a day spent by P in the UK.

[*FA 2013, Sch 45 paras 22–24*].

An individual's home

[57.8] For the purposes of the statutory residence test, an individual's home could be a building or part of a building or, for example, a vehicle, vessel or structure of any kind. Whether, for a given building etc., there is sufficient degree of permanence or stability about an individual's arrangements there for it to count as his home (or one of his homes) depends on all the circumstances of the case. A place that an individual uses periodically as nothing more than a holiday home or temporary retreat (or similar) does not count as a home of his. A place can count as an individual's home whether or not he holds any estate or interest in it; but the mere fact that he still holds an estate or interest does not continue to make a place an individual's home once he has moved out. [*FA 2013, Sch 45 para 25*].

For further information about how HMRC interpret the term 'home' in the context of applying the statutory residence test see HMRC guidance, Annex A paras A1–A22.

Work

[57.9] For the purposes of the statutory residence test, an individual (P) is considered to be 'working' (or 'doing work') at any time when he is doing something either in performing the duties of an employment or in the course of a trade carried on by him (whether alone or in partnership). A voluntary post for which P has no contract of service does not count as an employment for these purposes. Throughout these provisions 'trade' includes a profession or vocation, anything treated as a trade for income tax purposes and the commercial occupation of woodlands. Whilst in most cases it will be obvious, *FA 2015, Sch 43 para 26(2), (3)* contain extra rules for determining whether something is being done in performing the duties of an employment or in the course of a trade etc.

Time spent *travelling* counts as time spent working:

- if the cost of the journey would, if incurred by P, be deductible in calculating his taxable earnings or, as the case may be, taxable profits (on the assumption that P is within the charge to income tax); or
- to the extent that P does something else during the journey that would itself count as work.

Time spent undertaking *training* counts as time spent working if:

- in the case of employment, the training is provided or paid for by the employer and is undertaken to help P in performing his duties; and
- in the case of a trade etc., the cost of the training is deductible in calculating taxable profits (on the assumption that P is within the charge to income tax).

[*FA 2013, Sch 45 paras 26, 145*].

Being on-call or stand-by may count as time spent working depending on the conditions of P's employment and the nature of his duties (HMRC guidance, para 3.18).

Location of work

Work is regarded as done where it is actually done, regardless of where the employment is held or the trade is carried on. However, work done by way of, or in the course of, travelling to or from the UK by air, sea or tunnel is assumed to be done overseas even during the part of the journey in or over the UK. For this purpose, the travelling begins when P boards the aircraft, ship or train that will take him to another country from the UK or vice versa and ends when he disembarks.

In the case of people with relevant jobs on board vehicles, aircraft or ships (see **57.10** below), the above is subject to **57.15** below.

[*FA 2013, Sch 45 para 27*].

Working sufficient hours

For the purposes of the third automatic UK test at **57.4**(3) above, P works '*sufficient hours in the UK*' if his weekly 'net UK hours' are at least 35.

P's total '*net UK hours*' are determined by identifying, for any given period of 365 days and including all employments held and trades carried on by him, the total number of hours that P works in the UK during that period. However, any hours that he works in the UK on 'disregarded days' are not to be included in this total. A '*disregarded day*' is a day on which P does more than three hours' work overseas (even if he also does work in the UK on the same day).

Similarly, for the purposes of the third automatic overseas test at 57.5(3) above, P works '*sufficient hours overseas*' if his weekly 'net overseas hours' are at least 35. P's total '*net overseas hours*' are determined by identifying, for year X and including all employments held and trades carried on by him, the total number of hours that P works overseas during that period. Any hours that he works overseas on 'disregarded days' are not to be included in the total. A '*disregarded day*' is a day on which P does more than three hours' work in the UK (even if he also does work overseas on the same day).

The reference period

P's weekly net UK hours is his total net UK hours divided by the number of weeks in the 'reference period'. The '*reference period*' is calculated by subtracting from 365 the total number of disregarded days as above and, if appropriate, reducing the total as described below. The number of weeks in the reference period is calculated by dividing the reference period by 7; the result is rounded down to the nearest whole number, unless it is less than 1 in which case it is rounded up to 1.

P's weekly net overseas hours are computed in similar fashion, except that if year X is a leap year the starting point in calculating the reference period is 366. Where 57.5(5)(c) is in point, the starting point is the number of days in the period from the start of year X up to (but not including) the date of P's death.

In all cases the reference period can be reduced to take account of:

(a) reasonable amounts of annual leave or parenting leave taken (having regard to, for example, the nature of the work and the country in which it is performed);
(b) reasonable sick leave taken; and
(c) any 'non-working days' 'embedded' within a block of leave for which a reduction is made under (a) or (b).

No such reduction can be made in respect of a disregarded day. If the total days for which a reduction is available under (a) or (b) is not a whole number, the number is rounded down (but the rounding is ignored for the purposes of (c)). A '*non-working day*' is any day on which P is not normally expected to work (according to his contract of employment or usual pattern of work) and does not in fact work. Non-working days are '*embedded*' within a block of leave only if there are at least three consecutive days of leave taken both before and after the non-working day (or series of non-working days) in question.

If there is a change of employment during the reference period, with a gap in between the two jobs, the reference period is reduced by the number of days in the gap. The reduction for any 1 gap is limited to 15 days; if there is more than 1 such gap, the maximum reduction for all the gaps is limited to 30 days.

[*FA 2013, Sch 45 paras 9(2), 14(3), 16(3), 28, 145, 146*].

Relevant job on board vehicle, aircraft or ship

[57.10] For the purposes of the statutory residence test, an individual (P) has a relevant job on board a vehicle, aircraft or ship if conditions A and B are both met. Condition A is that:

(a) P holds an employment, the duties of which consist of duties to be performed, or
(b) carries on a trade, the activities of which consist of work to be done or services to be provided,

on board a vehicle, aircraft or ship while it is travelling. The condition at (b) is met only if, in order to do the work or provide the services, P has to be present (in person) on board the vehicle etc. while it is travelling.

Condition B is that substantially all of the trips made in performing those duties or carrying on those activities are trips that involve crossing an international boundary (*'cross-border trips'*).

In determining whether conditions A and B are met, duties or activities of a purely incidental nature are ignored.

[*FA 2013, Sch 45 para 30*].

See also 57.15 below.

The sufficient ties test

[57.11] As stated in 57.3 above, the sufficient ties test is an alternative to the automatic residence test. The '*sufficient ties test*' is met by an individual (P) for the year in question (year X) if P meets none of the automatic UK tests (57.4 above) and none of the automatic overseas tests (57.5 above), but P has sufficient 'UK ties' (see 57.12 below) for the year. Whether P has sufficient UK ties for year X depends upon whether he was resident in the UK for any of the previous three tax years and the number of days he spends in the UK in year X. See the tables below, and note the modifications where death occurs in year X. See 57.7 above as regards days spent in the UK.

Sufficient UK ties tables

Where P was UK resident for at least 1 of the 3 tax years preceding year X

Days spent by P in the UK in year X	*Number of UK ties that are sufficient*
More than 15 but not more than 45	At least 4
More than 45 but not more than 90	At least 3
More than 90 but not more than 120	At least 2
More than 120	At least 1

Where P was UK resident for none of the 3 tax years preceding year X

Days spent by P in the UK in year X	*Number of UK ties that are sufficient*
More than 45 but not more than 90	4
More than 90 but not more than 120	At least 3
More than 120	At least 2

Modification of tables on death in year X

If P dies in year X, the first modification is that in the first table the top row of the first column reads 'not more than 45' instead of 'more than 15 but not more than 45'.

The second and final modification is that if the death occurs before 1 March in year X, both tables have effect as if each number of days quoted in the first column were reduced by the 'appropriate number'. The '*appropriate number*' is found by multiplying the number of days quoted, in each case, by A/12, where A = the number of 'whole months' in year X after the month in which P dies. A '*whole month*' means an entire calendar month, e.g. the month of January. If the appropriate number is not a whole number it is rounded down if the first figure after the decimal point is less than 5; otherwise it is rounded up. If P dies on, say, 17 December in year X, the number of whole months is 3. So, for example, in the top row of the first column of the second table, the figure of 45 is reduced by 11 (45 x 3/12) and the figure of 90 is reduced by 23. The top row then reads 'more than 34 but not more than 67', reflecting the fact that P is alive for approximately only three-quarters of the tax year.

[*FA 2013, Sch 45 paras 17–20, 145*].

UK ties

[57.12] If the individual (P) was resident in the UK for at least one of the three tax years preceding the tax year in question (year X), each of the following counts as a '*UK tie*' for the purposes of **57.11** above and these provisions in general:

(a) a 'family tie' (**57.13** below);
(b) an 'accommodation tie' (**57.14** below);
(c) a 'work tie' (**57.15** below);
(d) a '90-day tie' (**57.16** below); and
(e) a 'country tie' (**57.17** below).

If P was resident in the UK for none of the three tax years preceding year X, each of the types of tie listed at (a)–(d) above, but not (e) above, counts as a UK tie.

In order to have the requisite number of UK ties for year X, each of P's ties has to be of a different type.

[*FA 2013, Sch 45 para 31*].

Family ties

[57.13] For the purposes of 57.12(a) above, P has a '*family tie*' for year X if:

(a) in year X, a 'relevant relationship' exists at any time between P and another person; and
(b) that other person is resident in the UK for year X (see further below).

A '*relevant relationship*' exists at any time between P and another person if at that time:

- they are husband and wife or civil partners and are not separated (whether by court order, deed of separation or in circumstances where the separation is likely to be permanent);
- they are living together as if they were husband and wife or civil partners; or
- the other person is a child of P and is under 18. P does not have a family tie by virtue of this condition if he sees the child in the UK on fewer than 61 days in total in year X (or, where relevant, in the part of year X before the child's 18th birthday); a day counts as a day on which P sees the child if he sees the child in person for all or part of the day.

Whether 'other person' is UK resident

The following rules apply in determining whether a person is resident in the UK for year X for the purposes of (b) above (and only for those purposes).

A family tie based on the fact that a family member has, by the same token, a relevant relationship with P is to be disregarded in deciding whether that family member is someone who is resident in the UK for year X.

A family member who:

- is a child of P under 18,
- is in full-time education in the UK at any time in year X, and
- is resident in the UK for year X but would not be so resident if time spent in full-time education in the UK were disregarded,

is treated as being not resident in the UK for year X if the number of days that he spends in the UK in the part of year X outside term-time is less than 21. Half-term breaks, and any other breaks when teaching is not provided during a term, are considered to form part of term-time for these purposes.

[*FA 2013, Sch 45 paras 32, 33*].

For further information about how HMRC interpret the term 'family tie' see HMRC guidance, Annex C.

Accommodation ties

[57.14] For the purposes of 57.12(b) above, P has an '*accommodation tie*' for year X if:

(a) P has a place to live in the UK;

(b) that place is available to P during year X for a continuous period of at least 91 days (but see below); and

(c) P spends at least one night at that place in that year (but see below).

For the purposes of (a) above, P is considered to have a place to live in the UK if:

- P's home or at least one of his homes (if more than one) is in the UK; or
- P has a holiday home or temporary retreat (or similar) in the UK; or
- accommodation is otherwise available to P where he can live when in the UK. Accommodation may be regarded as available to P even if he holds no estate or interest in it and even if he has no legal right to occupy it.

See 57.8 above for what is meant by an individual's home.

For the purposes of (b) above, if there is a gap of fewer than 16 days between periods in year X when a particular place is available to P, that place is treated as continuing to be available to P during the gap.

For the purposes of (c) above, if the accommodation is the home of a 'close relative' of P, the condition is met only if P spends a total of at least 16 nights there in year X (as opposed to 1 night). For this purpose, a '*close relative*' means a parent or grandparent, a brother or sister, a child aged 18 or over or a grandchild aged 18 or over; it is irrelevant whether the relationship subsists by blood or half-blood or by virtue of marriage or civil partnership.

[*FA 2013, Sch 45 para 34*].

For further information about what HMRC consider to be an accommodation tie see HMRC guidance, Annex A paras A23–A42.

Work ties

[57.15] For the purposes of 57.12(c) above, P has a '*work tie*' for year X if he works in the UK for at least 40 days (whether continuously or intermittently) in year X. For these purposes, P works in the UK for a day if he does more than 3 hours' work in the UK on that day. See 57.9 above for what is meant by working.

Relevant job on board vehicle, aircraft or ship

If P has a relevant job on board a vehicle, aircraft or ship (see 57.10 above), he is assumed for the above purposes to do more than three hours' work in the UK on any day on which he starts a cross-border trip (as part of that job) that begins in the UK. He is assumed to do fewer than three hours' work in the UK on any day on which he completes a cross-border trip (as part of that job) that ends in the UK. Any day on which P both starts and completes a cross-border trip is treated as one on which he does more than three hours' work in the UK. In the case of a cross-border trip to or from the UK that is undertaken in stages, the day on which the trip begins or, as the case may be, ends is the day on which the stage of the trip that involves crossing the UK border begins or ends. Any day on which a stage of the trip is undertaken by P solely within the UK is to be counted, if it lasts for more than three hours, as a day on which P does more than three hours' work in the UK.

[*FA 2013, Sch 45 paras 35, 36*].

90-day ties

[57.16] For the purposes of **57.12**(d) above, P has a '*90-day tie*' for year X if P has spent more than 90 days in the UK in either or both of the 2 tax years preceding year X. [*FA 2013, Sch 45 para 37*].

Country ties

[57.17] For the purposes of **57.12**(e) above, P has a '*country tie*' for year X if the country in which P meets the 'midnight test' for the greatest number of days in year X is the UK. P meets the '*midnight test*' in a country for a day if he is present in that country at the end of that day. In the event that the greatest number of days is equal for two or more countries, P has a country tie for year X if one of those countries is the UK. [*FA 2013, Sch 45 para 38*].

Split year treatment

[57.18] The effect of a tax year being a split year is to relax the general rule in **57.3** above that treats individuals who are UK resident (or not resident) *for* a tax year as being UK resident (or not resident) at all times in that tax year. A split year is divided into a UK part and an overseas part as set out in each of **57.20–57.27** below. Split year treatment has effect in calculating liability to capital gains tax for 2013/14 or any subsequent year.

The effect of split year treatment on the various capital gains tax charging rules is covered throughout this work where relevant: see in particular **1.2** INTRODUCTION, **48.5** OFFSHORE SETTLEMENTS, **58.3** RETURNS.

See also the transitional provisions on split year treatment in **57.28** below.

Split year treatment does not apply to personal representatives, and applies to only a limited extent to trustees (see **48.1** OFFSHORE SETTLEMENTS). The existence of special charging rules for cases involving split years is not intended to affect any question as to whether an individual would fall to be regarded under a double tax treaty as UK resident.

[*FA 2013, Sch 45 paras 39–42, 153(2)*].

What is a split year?

[57.19] For the purposes of **57.18** above and the statutory residence test generally, a tax year (year X) is a '*split year*' as regards an individual (P) if he is resident in the UK for year X and the circumstances of the case fall within any of Cases 1–8 at **57.20–57.27** below. Cases 1–3 involve departure from the UK, and Cases 4–8 involve arrival in the UK. [*FA 2013, Sch 45 para 43*].

If the taxpayer falls within two or all of Cases 1–3, Case 1 takes priority over Cases 2 and 3, and Case 2 takes priority over Case 3. [*FA 2013, Sch 45 para 54*].

If the taxpayer falls within two or more of Cases 4–8 the following priority rules apply.

- If both Case 5 and Case 6 apply, Case 6 takes priority unless the 'split year date' for Case 5 is earlier than the split year date for Case 6, in which case, Case 5 takes priority.
- If Case 7 and Case 5 (but not Case 6) apply Case 7 takes priority unless the split year date for Case 5 is earlier than the split year date for Case 7, in which case, Case 5 takes priority.
- If two or all of Cases 4, 5 and 8 apply but neither Case 6 nor Case 7 apply, the Case with the earliest split year date has priority. If two or all of the Cases share the earliest split year date, those Cases take priority.

The '*split year date*' means the first day of the UK part of the year under the Case concerned.

[*FA 2013, Sch 45 para 55*].

Case 1

[57.20] The circumstances of a case fall within Case 1 if they are of the description below. The overseas part of the split year is the part beginning with the first day of the period mentioned in (2) below. If there is more than one such period, the overseas part of the split year is the part beginning with the first day of the longest of those periods. The UK part of the split year is the part that is not the overseas part.

(1) P was resident in the UK for the tax year preceding year X (whether or not that previous year was itself a split year).
(2) There is a period that:
   - begins with a day in year X on which P does more than three hours' work overseas;
   - ends with the last day of year X; and
   - satisfies the 'overseas work criteria'.

   There may be more than one such period.
(3) P is not resident in the UK for the tax year following year X, and this is because he meets the third automatic overseas test (see 57.5(3) above) for that following year.

For the purposes of (2) above, a period satisfies the '*overseas work criteria*' if:

- P works 'sufficient hours overseas', as assessed over that period;
- there are no 'significant breaks' from overseas work during that period (see 57.5(3) above);
- the number of days in that period on which P does more than three hours' work in the UK does not exceed the 'first permitted limit'; and
- the number of days in that period spent by P in the UK does not exceed the 'second permitted limit'. (Any days *treated* as spent in the UK under the 'deeming rule' in 57.7 above do not count for this purpose.)

The question of whether P works '*sufficient hours overseas*' is determined as in 57.9 above except that the starting point in calculating the reference period is the number of days in the period mentioned in (2) above. The maximum number of days by which the reference period may be reduced for multiple gaps between employments is equal to the 'first permitted limit' (instead of 30 as in 57.9).

The '*first permitted limit*' is 30 minus the 'appropriate number'; the '*second permitted limit*' is 90 minus the 'appropriate number'. The '*appropriate number*' is the product of:

$$A \times \frac{B}{12}$$

A = either 30 or 90, depending on whether one is calculating the first or second permitted limit; and

B = the number of whole months in the part of year X before the day on which begins the period mentioned in (2) above. A '*whole month*' means an entire calendar month, e.g. the month of January; the period from 6 April to 30 April inclusive also counts as a whole month.

If the appropriate number is not a whole number it is rounded down if the first figure after the decimal point is less than 5; otherwise it is rounded up.

[*FA 2013, Sch 45 paras 29(2), 44, 52–56, 145*].

Case 2

[57.21] The circumstances of a case fall within Case 2 if they are of the description below. The UK part of the split year is the part of the tax year ending immediately before the 'deemed departure day' in (4) below; the remainder of the tax year is the overseas part of the split year.

(1) P was resident in the UK for the tax year preceding year X (whether or not that previous year was itself a split year).

(2) P has a 'partner' whose circumstances fall within Case 1 at 57.20 above for year X or the previous tax year. '*Partner*' means a spouse or civil partner or a person with whom P is living as if they were husband and wife or civil partners.

(3) On a day in year X, P moves overseas in order to continue living with the partner while the partner is working overseas.

(4) In the part of year X beginning with the 'deemed departure day':
   - P either has no home (see 57.8 above) in the UK or has homes in both the UK and overseas but spends the greater part of the time living in the overseas home; and
   - the number of days that P spends in the UK does not exceed the 'permitted limit'. (See 57.7 above as regards days spent in the UK.)

(5) P is not resident in the UK for the tax year following year X.

If (2) above applies by reference to year X itself, the '*deemed departure day*' is the later of the day mentioned in (3) above and the first day of what is, for P's partner, the overseas part of the year (see 57.20 above). If (2) above applies by reference to the previous tax year, the '*deemed departure day*' is the day mentioned in (3) above.

The '*permitted limit*' is 90 minus the 'appropriate number. The '*appropriate number*' is the product of:

$$A \times \frac{B}{12}$$

A	=	90
B	=	the number of whole months in the part of year X before the deemed departure day. A '*whole month*' means an entire calendar month, e.g. the month of January; the period from 6 April to 30 April inclusive also counts as a whole month.

If the appropriate number is not a whole number it is rounded down if the first figure after the decimal point is less than 5; otherwise it is rounded up.

[*FA 2013, Sch 43 paras 45, 52–56, 145*].

Case 3

[57.22] The circumstances of a case fall within Case 3 if they are of the description below. The UK part of the split year is the part of the tax year ending immediately before the day mentioned in (2)(a) below; the remainder of the tax year is the overseas part of the split year.

(1) P was resident in the UK for the tax year preceding year X (whether or not that previous year was itself a split year).

(2) At the start of year X P had one or more homes (see **57.8** above) in the UK but:
   - (a) there comes a day in year X when P ceases to have any home in the UK; and
   - (b) from then on, P has no home in the UK for the rest of that tax year.

(3) In the part of year X beginning with the day mentioned in (2)(a) above, P spends fewer than 16 days in the UK. (See **57.7** above as regards days spent in the UK.)

(4) P is not resident in the UK for the tax year following year X.

(5) At the end of the period of six months beginning with the day mentioned in (2)(a) above, P has a 'sufficient link' with a country overseas.

For the purposes of (5) above, P has a '*sufficient link*' with a country overseas if (and only if):

- he is considered for tax purposes to be a resident of that country in accordance with its domestic laws; or
- he has been in that country at the end of each day of the six-month period mentioned in (5) above; or
- his only home is in that country or, if he has more than one home, they are all in that country.

[*FA 2013, Sch 45 paras 46, 52–56*].

Case 4

[57.23] The circumstances of a case fall within Case 4 if they are of the description below. The UK part of the split year is the part of the tax year beginning on the day mentioned in (2) below; the earlier part of the tax year is the overseas part of the split year.

(1) P was not resident in the UK for the tax year preceding year X.
(2) At the start of year X, P did not meet the 'only home test', but there comes a day in year X when he starts to meet that test and he then continues to meet it for the remainder of the tax year; or
The '*only home test*' is met if P has only one home (see **57.8** above) and it is in the UK or if P has more than one home and all of them are in the UK.
(3) For the part of year X before the day mentioned in (2) above, P does not have sufficient UK ties.

The sufficient ties test at **57.11** above applies for the purposes of (3) above, but with the following modifications:

- references to 'year X' are to be read as references to the part of year X in question (except that when applying the family ties test in **57.13** above, the residence of the 'other person' is still determined by reference to year X); and
- both tables have effect as if each number of days quoted in the first column were reduced by the 'appropriate number'.

For this purpose, the '*appropriate number*' is found by multiplying the number of days quoted, in each case, by $^{A}/_{12}$, where A = the number of 'whole months' in year X beginning with the day mentioned in (2) above. A '*whole month*' means an entire calendar month, e.g. the month of January. If the appropriate number is not a whole number it is rounded down if the first figure after the decimal point is less than 5; otherwise it is rounded up.

[*FA 2013, Sch 45 paras 47, 52–56, 145*].

Case 5

[57.24] The circumstances of a case fall within Case 5 if they are of the description below. The overseas part of the split year is the part before the period mentioned in (2) below begins. If there is more than one such period, the overseas part of the split year is the part before the first of those periods begins. The UK part of the split year is the part that is not the overseas part.

(1) P was not resident in the UK for the tax year preceding year X.
(2) There is at least one period of 365 days beginning in year X in respect of which all the following conditions are met:
    (a) the period begins with a day on which P does more than three hours' work in the UK;
    (b) in the part of year X before the period begins, P does not have sufficient UK ties;
    (c) P works 'sufficient hours in the UK' (see **57.9** above), as assessed over the period;

(d) there are no 'significant breaks' from UK work (see **57.4**(3) above) during that period; and
(e) of the total number of days in the period when P does more than three hours' work, at least 75% of them are days when he does more than three hours' work in the UK.

The sufficient ties test at **57.11** above applies for the purposes of (2)(b) above, but with the same modifications as in **57.23** above; the appropriate number is computed in the same way as in **57.23** but by reference to the number of whole months in year X beginning with the day on which the 365-day period in (2) begins.

[*FA 2013, Sch 45 paras 48, 52–56, 145*].

Case 6

[57.25] The circumstances of a case fall within Case 6 if they are of the description below. The overseas part of the split year is the part ending with the last day of that period. If there is more than one such period, the overseas part of the split year is the part ending with the last day of the longest of those periods. The UK part of the split year is the part that is not the overseas part.

(1) P was not resident in the UK for the tax year preceding year X, and this is because he met the third automatic overseas test (see **57.5**(3) above) for that preceding year.
(2) There is a period that:
   - begins with the first day of year X and ends in that year;
   - ends with a day on which P does more than three hours' work overseas; and
   - satisfies the 'overseas work criteria'.

   There may be more than one such period.
(3) P is resident in the UK for the tax year following year X (whether or not that following year is itself a split year).

In (2) above, '*overseas work criteria*' has the same meaning as in Case 1 at **57.20** above, except that, in computing the 'appropriate number', B = the number of whole months in the part of year X after the period in (2) ends.

[*FA 2013, Sch 45 paras 49, 52–56, 145*].

Case 7

[57.26] The circumstances of a case fall within Case 7 if they are of the description below. The UK part of the split year is the part of the tax year beginning with the 'deemed arrival day' in (4) below; the earlier part of the tax year is the overseas part of the split year.

(1) P was not resident in the UK for the tax year preceding year X.
(2) P has a 'partner' whose circumstances fall within Case 6 at **57.25** above for year X or the previous tax year. '*Partner*' means a spouse or civil partner or a person with whom P is living as if they were husband and wife or civil partners.
(3) On a day in year X, P moves to the UK in order to continue living with the partner on the partner's return or relocation to the UK.

(4) In the part of year X before the 'deemed arrival day':
- P either has no home (see **57.8** above) in the UK or has homes in both the UK and overseas but spends the greater part of the time living in the overseas home; and
- the number of days that P spends in the UK does not exceed the 'permitted limit'. (See **57.7** above as regards days spent in the UK.)

(5) P is resident in the UK for the tax year following year X (whether or not that following year is itself a split year).

If (2) above applies by reference to year X itself, the '*deemed arrival day*' is the later of the day mentioned in (3) above and the first day of what is, for P's partner, the UK part of the year (see **57.25** above). If (2) above applies by reference to the previous tax year, the '*deemed arrival day*' is the day mentioned in (3) above.

In (4) above, '*permitted limit*' is the same as in Case 2 at **57.21** above, except that, in computing the 'appropriate number', B = the number of whole months in the part of year X beginning with the deemed arrival day.

[*FA 2013, Sch 45 paras 50, 52–56, 145*].

Case 8

[57.27] The circumstances of a case fall within Case 8 if they are of the description below. The UK part of the split year is the part of the tax year beginning on the day mentioned in (2)(a) below; the earlier part of the tax year is the overseas part of the split year.

(1) P was not resident in the UK for the tax year preceding year X.

(2) At the start of year X, P had no home (see **57.8** above) in the UK, but:
  (a) there comes a day when, for the first time in that year, P does have a home in the UK; and
  (b) from then on, he continues to have a home in the UK for the remainder of year X and for the whole of the following tax year.

(3) For the part of year X before the day mentioned in (2)(a) above, P does not have sufficient UK ties.

(4) P is resident in the UK for the tax year following year X, and that following year is not a split year as regards P.

The sufficient ties test at **57.11** above applies for the purposes of (3) above, but with the same modifications as in **57.23** above; the appropriate number is computed in the same way as in **57.23** but by reference to the number of whole months in year X beginning with the day mentioned in (2)(a) above.

[*FA 2013, Sch 45 paras 51–56, 145*].

Transitional provisions

[57.28] There will be occasions where, in applying the statutory residence test for 2013/14, 2014/15 or 2015/16, it will be necessary to determine whether an individual was UK resident or non-UK resident for a tax year before 2013/14 (a '*pre-commencement year*'); for example, in ascertaining which of the sufficient ties tables at **57.11** above should be applied. Where this is the case, the question of residence for any pre-commencement year is to be determined in accordance with the rules in force before the statutory residence test was introduced, for which see **57.29** below. However, the individual can elect for the question to be determined in accordance with the statutory residence test instead. The election can be made in respect of any one or more pre-commencement years. (The making of an election does not alter an individual's actual residence status for the pre-commencement year or affect his tax liability for that year.) The election must be made by notice in writing to HMRC no later than the first anniversary of the end of year X (where year X is the year 2013/14, 2014/15 or 2015/16, whichever one is in point); the election is irrevocable. [*FA 2013, Sch 45 para 154(1)–(4)*].

Split year treatment

Where the year for which income tax liability is being calculated is 2013/14 or a subsequent year and it is necessary to determine whether a pre-commencement year was a split year (see **57.18** above), the determination is made in accordance with the non-statutory split year treatment at **57.29** below. [*FA 2013, Sch 45 para 155*].

Residence for 2012/13 and earlier years

[57.29] For tax years prior to the introduction of the statutory residence test at **57.3** above, the following applies to determine whether or not an individual is resident in the UK.

An individual can be resident for a particular tax year in one or more countries for tax purposes so that a claim not to be UK resident merely because of resident status in another country will usually fail. Unusually, an individual may be regarded as not resident in any country.

Subject to the above, an individual is resident in the UK for a tax year before 2013/14 if any one of the following applies.

(a) He is in the UK for some temporary purpose only and not with any view or intent to establish his residence in the UK and, for 2008/09 onwards, if, and only if, he spends (in total) at least 183 days in the UK. For 2007/08 and earlier years, the test was that the period (or the sum of the periods) for which the individual was resident (i.e. physically present) in the UK in the tax year exceeded six months. [*TCGA 1992, s 9(3); FA 2013, Sch 45 para 148(2)*].
The question whether for the purposes of this provision an individual is in the UK for some temporary purpose only and not with any view or intent to establish his residence in the UK is decided without regard to any living accommodation available in the UK for his use. [*TCGA 1992, s 9(4)*].
For 2008/09 onwards, a day is treated as spent in the UK only if the individual is present in the UK at the end of the day. Days on which he arrives in the UK are not, however, counted if he departs from the UK the next day and during the time between arrival and departure he does not engage in activities substantially unrelated to his passage through the UK. [*TCGA 1992, s 9(5)(6); FA 2013, Sch 45 para 148(2)*].

For 2007/08 and earlier years, the six months' rule was rigidly applied, even in cases of force majeure, and in border-line cases hours could strictly be significant. See *Wilkie v CIR* Ch D 1951, 32 TC 495 where 'six months' was held to mean six calendar months. In practice, however, HMRC regarded six months as 183 days and days of arrival and departure were normally ignored.

HMRC treat, *with no exceptions*, an individual as resident if he is in the UK for 183 days or more during the year. Otherwise, to be regarded by HMRC as UK resident for a tax year an individual would normally have to be physically present in the UK at some time in the tax year and would also depend on the circumstances. (Leaflet HMRC 6, para 2.2). See, for example, *Shepherd v HMRC* Ch D, [2006] STC 1821, in which an airline pilot who was in the UK for only 80 days in a tax year was nevertheless held to be resident in the UK for that year.

In *HMRC v Grace* CA 2009, [2009] STC 2707, the presence of the taxpayer, an airline pilot, in the UK in order to fulfil duties under a permanent (or at least indefinite) contract of employment was held to be not for a temporary purpose. This did not in itself mean, however, that the taxpayer's presence in the UK amounted to residence (and the case was remitted to the tribunal to assess his residence in the light of all other relevant factors — see *Grace v HMRC (No 2)* FTT, [2011] SFTD 669).

(b) He *visits the UK year after year* and the annual visits are for a substantial period or periods of time. HMRC would normally regard an average annual period or periods which amount to 91 days or more as substantial. Where, after four years, the individual's visits average 91 days or more per year, he is treated as resident from the beginning of the fifth year. However, he will be treated as resident from the beginning of the first year if it is clear at the time of his first visit that he intends to make such visits. Also, if the individual realises that he will make such visits before the beginning of the fifth year, he will be treated as resident from the beginning of the year in which that realisation is reached (Leaflet HMRC 6, para 7.5). For an example of the averaging calculation, see Leaflet HMRC 6, para 7.6.

Any days spent in the UK because of exceptional circumstances beyond the individual's control are excluded ,but this does not apply for the purposes of the 183-day rule in (a) above (HMRC Statement of Practice 2/91 and Leaflet HMRC 6, para 2.2).

In applying the 91-day test above, for 2008/09 onwards, HMRC apply the statutory rules in *TCGA 1992, s 9(5)(6)* (see (a) above) (Treasury Explanatory Notes to the 2008 Finance Bill). Previously, days of arrival in and departure from the UK were normally disregarded. In *Gaines-Cooper v HMRC* Ch D 2007, [2008] STC 1665, however, HMRC successfully argued before the Special Commissioners that, in the particular circumstances of the case, disregarding those days produced a distorted picture of the taxpayer's presence in the UK and therefore days of arrival and departure should not be disregarded. The Ch D upheld the Special Commissioners' decision. Following the decision in this case, HMRC indicated that they considered the 91-day test to apply only where the taxpayer had left the UK (which the appellant in that case had not). HMRC continued normally to disregard days of arrival and departure where they were satisfied that an individual had left the UK. (HMRC Brief 1/2007).

(c) He has left the UK for the purpose only of 'occasional residence' abroad having been at the time of leaving both resident and ordinarily resident in the UK (although the legislation is unclear whether the provisions apply equally to capital gains tax as well as income tax). This provision was enacted in slightly different terms before 2007/08 but the above represents HMRC's existing practice (see Change 123 listed in Annex 1 to the Explanatory Notes to *ITA 2007*). [*TCGA 1992, s 9(1); ITA 2007, s 829; ICTA 1988, s 334; FA 2013, Sch 45 paras 148(2), 152(6)*]. For a discussion of the meaning of 'occasional residence', see *Reed v Clark* Ch D 1985, 58 TC 528.

If an individual works full-time in a trade, profession or vocation of which no part is carried on in the UK, or in an office or employment the whole of the duties under which (apart from mere 'incidental' duties) are performed outside the UK, or in a combination of such activities, any living accommodation available in the UK for his use is disregarded in determining whether or not he is resident in the UK (although the legislation is unclear whether this provision applies equally to capital gains tax as well as income tax). [*TCGA 1992, s 9(1); ITA 2007, s 830; ICTA 1988, s 335; FA 2013, Sch 45 paras 148(2), 152(6)*]. As to whether duties are 'incidental', see *Robson v Dixon* Ch D 1972, 48 TC 527 where an airline pilot was employed abroad but occasionally landed in the UK where the family home was maintained. In that case, the UK duties were more than incidental. See also Leaflet HMRC 6, para 10.6. 'Full-time' employment, in an ordinary case involving a standard pattern of hours, requires an individual working hours clearly comparable with those in a typical UK working week. See Leaflet HMRC 6, sidenote to para 8.5 for this and for HMRC's interpretation of the requirement in less straightforward cases.

Change in residence status

In general, residence status in the UK for part of a year is taken to apply for a whole year (see *Neubergh v CIR* Ch D 1977, 52 TC 79 and *Gubay v Kington* HL 1984, 57 TC 601) and, for capital gains tax in particular, disposals are chargeable where they accrue to a person in a year of assessment *during any part of which* he is resident in the UK. [*TCGA 1992, s 2(1)*]. Concessional split year treatment for a year in which an individual's residence status changes is, however, available in the following circumstances.

- Where an individual comes to live in the UK and is treated as resident in the UK for any tax year from the date of arrival, he or she is charged to capital gains tax only in respect of chargeable gains from disposals made after arrival, provided that he or she has not been resident or ordinarily resident in the UK at any time during the five tax years immediately preceding the tax year in which he or she arrived in the UK.

- Where an individual leaves the UK and is treated on departure as not resident and not ordinarily resident in the UK, he or she is not charged to capital gains tax on gains from disposals made after the date of departure, provided that the individual was not resident and not ordinarily resident in the UK for the whole of at least four out of the seven tax years immediately preceding the tax year of departure.

(HMRC Extra-Statutory Concession D2).

The circumstances in which an individual will be treated by HMRC on departure as not resident and not ordinarily resident in the UK or on arrival as resident and ordinarily resident are those set out in HMRC Extra-Statutory Concession A11 (see Tolley's Income Tax).

ESC D2 does not apply to:

- any person in relation to gains accruing to him on the disposal of assets in the UK which, at any time between his departure and the end of the year, are used for a trade, profession or vocation carried on by him in the UK through a branch or agency, or are used for or acquired for use by or for such a branch or agency (see also **49.3** OVERSEAS MATTERS);
- trustees who commence or cease residence in the UK (see **48.2, 48.4** OFFSHORE SETTLEMENTS);
- a settlor who commences or ceases UK residence during a year in relation to gains of a settlement which are assessed on him; or
- a settlor on whom gains are taxed under *TCGA 1992, s 86, Sch 5* (see **48.5** OFFSHORE SETTLEMENTS).

As with all published extra-statutory concessions, ESC D2 will not be applied in cases where it would have been part of a tax avoidance arrangement (see **33** HMRC EXTRA-STATUTORY CONCESSIONS and *R v CIR (ex p. Fulford-Dobson)* QB 1987, 60 TC 168). In straightforward cases where the terms of a disposal are negotiated before emigration but the contract is not signed until after the date of departure from the UK, HMRC will not withhold the concession merely on the grounds that the disposal was arranged to take place after departure. On its own, a genuine postponement of the disposal is not regarded as an attempt to use the concession for tax avoidance, but where coupled with other arrangements it might be so regarded. (HMRC Capital Gains Manual CG25793).

For visits to the UK for educational purposes, see **57.30** below. For visits abroad generally, see **57.31** below.

Longer-term visitors to the UK

An individual is treated as resident throughout any period for which he comes to the UK for a purpose (such as employment) that will mean remaining (apart from holidays or short business trips) for at least two years. This will also apply if accommodation is owned or is acquired or taken on a lease of three years or more in the year of arrival. Otherwise, such visitors will be treated as ordinarily resident from the beginning of the tax year in which such accommodation is acquired or leased. (Leaflet HMRC 6, paras 7.4, 7.7.1–7.7.4).

Examples

(*Note*. The case law decisions below, which all predate 1993/94, should be read in the light of the enactment of *TCGA 1992, s 9(4)* mentioned in (a) and (c) above (no regard to be had for the purposes of *TCGA 1992, s 9(3)* to any living accommodation available in the UK for an individual's use).)

A resident of the Republic of Ireland making monthly visits here as director of a British company, having no place of abode here, but a permanent one in Ireland, was held to be resident and ordinarily resident (*Lysaght v CIR* HL 1928, 13 TC 511). However, compare *CIR v Combe* CS 1932, 17 TC 405. An officer succeeding to an Irish estate, intending to return there permanently but prevented by military duties in the UK, was held, on the facts, to be resident in both countries (*Inchiquin v CIR* CA 1948, 31 TC 125).

In *CIR v Brown* KB 1926, 11 TC 292, and *CIR v Zorab* KB 1926, 11 TC 289, it was held that retired Indian civil servants making periodical visits to, but having no business interests in, the UK, were not resident.

An American holding a lease of a shooting box in Scotland and spending two months there every year (*Cooper v Cadwalader CES* 1904, 5 TC 101), and a merchant physically present and carrying on business in Italy, but owning a house in the UK where he resided for less than six months (*Lloyd v Sulley CES* 1884, 2 TC 37) have both been held to be resident.

A Belgian who had at his disposal for the visits he paid here a house owned not by him but by a company which he controlled, so that it was in fact available whenever he chose to come, was held to be taxable as a resident (*Loewenstein v De Salis* KB 1926, 10 TC 424). But in *Withers v Wynyard* KB 1938, 21 TC 724, an actress (after 18 months abroad) performing in the UK and occupying for 3½ months in 1933/34 a leasehold flat (unable to be disposed of and sub-let when possible), was held not to be UK resident for that year.

A husband and wife who were not actually physically present during the year, although their children were in the UK, were held not to be UK resident (*Turnbull v Foster* CES 1904, 6 TC 206). In *Reed v Clark* Ch D 1985, 58 TC 528 the taxpayer had left the UK with the intention to remain abroad throughout a year of assessment and, in the event, did so remain abroad. He was held not to be resident in the UK for the year of absence since his purpose was not only of 'occasional residence' abroad (see (c) above).

The taxpayer's presence in the UK need not be voluntary, see *In re Mackenzie decd* Ch D 1940, 19 ATC 399 (taxpayer confined in a lunatic asylum).

Ordinary residence for 2012/13 and earlier years

[57.30] The concept of ordinary residence is **abolished** for capital gains tax purposes with effect **on and after 6 April 2013**.

The term 'ordinary residence' is not defined in the *Taxes Acts*. Broadly, it denotes greater permanence than the term 'residence' (see **57.29** above), and is equivalent to habitual residence; if an individual is resident year after year, he is ordinarily resident. An individual, whose home has been abroad, coming to the UK to live here permanently or intending to stay here for three years or more is treated as resident and ordinarily resident here from the date of his arrival (Leaflet HMRC 6, para 7.2). An individual may be resident in the UK under the 183-days rule of *TCGA 1992, s 9(3)* (see **57.29**(a) above) without becoming ordinarily resident. Equally, he may be ordinarily resident without being resident in a particular year, e.g. because he usually lives in the UK but is absent on an extended holiday throughout a tax year. (Leaflet HMRC 6, para 1.5.15).

An individual will be treated as ordinarily resident in the UK if he visits the UK regularly and his visits average 91 days or more per tax year (ignoring days spent in the UK for exceptional circumstances beyond his control, for example his own or family illness). Ordinary residence will commence from 6 April in the tax year of first arrival if the intention to make such visits to the UK for at least four tax years is clear on that first visit, or from 6 April in the fifth tax year after four years of such visits (unless the decision to make regular visits was made in an earlier tax year, in which case it applies from 6 April in that earlier year). (Leaflet HMRC 6, paras 3.2, 7.5, 7.6).

Longer term visitors — commencement of ordinary residence

If it is clear on arrival in the UK that the intention is to stay for at least three years (disregarding holidays and short business trips abroad), ordinary residence commences on arrival. An individual coming to the UK, but not intending to stay more than three years (and not buying or leasing for three years or more accommodation for use in the UK), is treated as ordinarily resident from the beginning of the tax year in which falls the third anniversary of arrival. (This is according to Leaflet HMRC 6, but SP 17/91 says 'from the beginning of the tax year after the third anniversary of arrival'.) If, before the beginning of that tax year, either there is a change in the individual's intention (i.e. to an intention to stay in the UK for three years or more in all) or accommodation for use in the UK is bought (or leased for three years or more), ordinary residence is treated as commencing at the beginning of the tax year in which either of those events happens. If an individual is treated as ordinarily resident solely because he has accommodation in the UK and he disposes of the accommodation and leaves the UK within three years of arrival, he will be treated as not ordinarily resident for the duration of his stay. (HMRC Statement of Practice 17/91 and Leaflet HMRC 6, paras 7.7–7.7.4).

Education

An individual who comes to the UK for a period of study or education which is not expected to exceed four years will be treated as not ordinarily resident provided that:

(i) he does not own or buy accommodation here, or acquire it on a lease of three years or more; or
(ii) on leaving the UK he will not be returning regularly for visits which average 91 days or more in each tax year.

(Leaflet HMRC 6, para 7.3).

Spouse accompanying employee working overseas

See **57.31**(b) below.

Averaging of visits to UK over a period

Where this applies in the above, see **57.29**(b) above for HMRC's practice in applying averaging treatment.

Case law

In *Reid v CIR* CS 1926, 10 TC 673, a British subject was held ordinarily resident in the UK although she had no fixed residence either here or abroad and was regularly absent abroad for 8½ months every year. She had here an address, family ties, bank account and furniture in store.

Levene v CIR HL 1928, 13 TC 486, was decided similarly (British subject abroad for health reasons since 1918, no fixed residence here since (or abroad until 1925), but having ties with this country and in the usual ordering of his life making habitual visits to the UK for 20 weeks yearly for definite purposes). The judgments in this case interpreted the meaning of 'ordinarily resident' by the following phrases: 'habitually resident', 'residence in a place with some degree of continuity' and 'according to the way a man's life is usually ordered'.

In *Peel v CIR* CS 1927, 13 TC 443, although the taxpayer had his business and house in Egypt, he was held ordinarily resident in the UK because he also had a house here, and spent an average of 139 days of each year in the UK.

In *Kinloch v CIR* KB 1929, 14 TC 736, a widow living mainly abroad with a son at school in the UK, who had won an appeal in previous years but continued regular annual visits, was held to be resident and ordinarily resident.

In *Elmhirst v CIR* KB 1937, 21 TC 381 the taxpayer was held to have been ordinarily resident although denying any intention at the time of becoming so.

See *Miesegaes v CIR* CA 1957, 37 TC 493 (minor at school here for five years, spending the occasional vacation with his father in Switzerland, held ordinarily resident).

In *R v Barnet London Borough Council, ex p. Nilish Shah* HL 1982, [1983] 1 All E R 226, a non-tax case, the words 'ordinarily resident' were held to refer to a man's abode in a particular place or country which he has adopted voluntarily and for settled purposes (i.e. with a sufficient degree of continuity) as part of the regular order of his life for the time being, whether of short or long duration.

In *Reed v Clark* Ch D 1985, 58 TC 528, ordinary residence was held to be the converse of 'occasional residence' (see **57.29**(d) above).

In *Tuczka v HMRC* UT, [2011] STC 1438, the taxpayer was held to be ordinarily resident in the UK from the second tax year of his stay in the UK despite his intention to return to Austria after a two to three year period. He had demonstrated that his purpose in living in the UK had become settled in that tax year and that pattern of living continued for several years. The commencement of his ordinary residence therefore had to be taken back to the earliest tax year in which that pattern could be shown.

In *Turberville v HMRC* FTT, [2010] UKFTT 69 (TC); 2010 STI 1619, the taxpayer's intention to leave the UK did not alter his ordinary residence status until the date of departure. The fact that it was clear that he would go did not affect the quality of his residence in the UK which was a continuation of his residence during the preceding four tax years. As the Tribunal could not apply a split-year treatment the taxpayer become not ordinarily resident for the tax year following departure from the UK.

In *Carey v HMRC* FTT, [2015] UKFTT 466 (TC); 2016 STI 144, the taxpayer was held to be ordinarily resident for the tax year following that in which he had left the UK for an initially temporary purpose. He did not become not ordinarily resident until, in the later tax year, he severed his work ties with the UK and realised a substantial economic interest in his UK employer.

See also the cases under 57.29 above.

Visits abroad and claims to non-UK residence and to non-UK ordinary residence

[57.31] The following applies for 2012/13 and earlier years (i.e. before the introduction of the statutory residence test at 57.3 above). Visits abroad during those years are broadly differentiated by HMRC as follows.

(a) **Visits abroad for short periods.** Short trips abroad, e.g. on holiday or business trips, do not alter the residence status of a person who usually lives in the UK (see (b) above) (Leaflet HMRC 6, para 8.1).
HMRC will not usually accept that *mobile workers*, i.e. those who live in the UK but make frequent and regular trips abroad in the course of their employment or business (e.g. lorry or coach drivers driving to and from the Continent and those working on cross-Channel transport), are anything other than resident and ordinarily resident in the UK (Revenue Tax Bulletin April 2001 pp 836–838).

(b) **Going abroad for full-time work under a contract of employment.** An individual (and accompanying spouse) leaving to work abroad full-time under a contract of employment is treated as non-UK resident provided that both the absence from the UK and the employment cover a complete tax year, and that any interim visits to the UK do not amount to either 183 days or more in any tax year or an average of 91 days or more per tax year (averaged over a maximum of four years (see Leaflet HMRC 6, para 8.3 for method of averaging), and ignoring days spent in the UK for exceptional circumstances beyond the person's control, for example own or family illness). Similar conditions apply to an individual leaving to work abroad full-time in a trade, profession or vocation. These conditions are applied separately in relation to the employee and the accompanying spouse, but must be satisfied by the employee for the concession to be available to the accompanying spouse. (Leaflet HMRC 6, paras 8.4–8.9). See *R (oao Davies & James) v HMRC* CA, [2010] STC 860, for discussion of the operation of this rule. See also *Hankinson v HMRC* FTT, [2009] UKFTT 384 (TC); 2010 STI 1368.

(c) **Permanent emigration for reasons other than a full-time service contract abroad.** An individual leaving the UK permanently is nevertheless treated as continuing to be UK resident if visits to the UK average 91 days or more per tax year (subject to exceptional circumstances). Some evidence will normally be required in support of a claim to have become non-resident (and not ordinarily resident), e.g. steps taken to acquire a permanent home abroad, and, if UK property is retained, a reason consistent with the stated aim of permanent residence abroad. If such evidence is satisfactory, UK residence (and ordinary residence) will be treated as ceasing on the day after departure from the UK. (Leaflet HMRC 6, para 8.2).

In *R (oao Gaines-Cooper) v HMRC* SC, [2011] STC 2249, the taxpayer failed to establish non-residence under this rule as he had not established 'a distinct break' from his social and family ties in the UK. See also *Shepherd v HMRC* (Sp C 484), [2005] SSCD 644, in which an airline pilot was held to have remained resident in the UK for a tax year in which he had been physically in the UK for only 80 days. See also *HMRC v Grace* CA 2009, [2009] STC 2707, *Karim v HMRC* FTT, [2009] UKFTT 368 (TC); 2010 STI 1289 and *Grace v HMRC (No 2)* FTT, [2011] SFTD 669, *Broom v HMRC FTT*, [2011] UKFTT 760 (TC); 2012 STI 39 and *Glyn v HMRC* UT 2015, [2016] STC 1020.

Members of Parliament

[57.32] For 2010/11 onwards, subject to some transitional provisions, a person who for any part of a tax year is a member of the House of Commons or, with certain exceptions, the House of Lords is treated for income tax and capital gains tax purposes as resident, domiciled and, before 2013/14, ordinarily resident in the UK for the whole of that tax year. [*Constitutional Reform and Governance Act 2010, ss 41, 42; FA 2013, Sch 46 para 147*].

Companies

[57.33] A company incorporated in the UK is regarded for corporation tax purposes as resident there, irrespective of any rule of law giving a different place of residence. [*TCGA 1992, s 286A; CTA 2009, s 14*].

A company which would otherwise be regarded as resident in the UK for corporation tax purposes, and is regarded for the purposes of any double tax relief arrangements as resident in a territory outside the UK and not resident in the UK (on the assumption that a claim for relief under those arrangements has been made and under the claim it falls to be decided whether the company is to be so regarded for the purposes of those arrangements), is treated for corporation tax purposes as resident outside the UK and not resident in the UK. This treatment applies whether the company would otherwise be regarded as resident in the UK for corporation tax purposes under the 'incorporation test' above, the test for SEs below or by virtue of some other rule of law (see below). [*TCGA 1992, s 286A; CTA 2009, s 18; FA 1994, s 249*].

For companies incorporated outside the UK there is no statutory definition of residence. The courts have determined that such a company resides where its real business is carried on, i.e. '*where its central management and control actually abide*'. This was the criterion applied to all companies prior to the introduction of the above provisions.

A company doing business abroad but controlled from the UK is therefore resident in the UK (subject to any overriding provisions contained in relevant double taxation agreements). In the following cases, the company was held to be managed and controlled from, and hence resident in, the UK:

- *Calcutta Jute Mills Co Ltd v Nicholson* Ex D 1876, 1 TC 83 (UK company operating abroad but directors and shareholders meeting in UK);
- *De Beers Consolidated Mines Ltd v Howe* HL 1906, 5 TC 198 (South African company operating there but important affairs controlled from UK where majority of directors resided);
- *New Zealand Shipping Co Ltd v Thew* HL 1922, 8 TC 208 (New Zealand company with New Zealand directors, but overall control lay with separate London board);
- *American Thread Co v Joyce* HL 1913, 6 TC 163 (UK company operating in USA with US directors in charge of current business, but overall control in London);
- *John Hood & Co Ltd v Magee* KB (I) 1918, 7 TC 327 (company registered in both UK and USA, with the only director resident in USA, but general meetings and material trading activities in UK);
- *Laerstate BV v HMRC* FTT, [2009] SFTD 551 (Netherlands company with policy, strategic and management matters decided in UK sby sole shareholder).

But in *A-G v Alexander* Ex D, [1874] 10 Ex 20, a foreign state bank with a UK branch was held resident abroad, notwithstanding that shareholders' meetings were held in London. See also *Wood v Holden* CA, [2006] STC 443 where a subsidiary company registered in the Netherlands with Netherland's directors was held to be non-resident. Even though the subsidiary was formed for a limited purpose as part of a plan devised purely for tax purposes of UK taxpayers, the board of directors in the Netherlands was independent. By contrast, in *TC06007: Development Securities (no 9) Ltd v Revenue and Customs Comrs* [2017] UKFTT 565 (TC), subsidiary companies in Jersey, again formed for a limited purpose as part of tax planning, were found to be UK resident. In this case, the companies' real business was to undertake the parent's plan which was the realisation of enhanced capital losses through the acquisition of assets at an overvalue under call option arrangements. It was therefore inherent to the uncommercial nature of the only decision of the subsidiaries' directors that they were simply implementing decisions taken by the UK parent. The subsidiaries were therefore UK resident.

HMRC's approach to applying the basic test of the place of central management and control is first to ascertain whether the directors in fact themselves exercise central management and control; if so, to determine where that central management and control is exercised (not necessarily where they meet); if not, to establish where and by whom it is exercised. The concept of the place of central management and control is directed at the highest level of control of the company's business, rather than the place where the main business operations are to be found. This must always be a question of fact in any particular case, but the place of directors' meetings will usually be of significance if they are the medium through which central management and control is exercised. If, however, central management and control is in reality exercised by, for example, a single individual, the company's residence will be where that individual exercises his powers. With regard to the particular problem of residence of a subsidiary, HMRC would not normally seek to impute to the subsidiary the residence of its parent unless the parent in effect usurps the functions of the Board of the subsidiary. Matters taken into account would include the extent to which the directors of the subsidiary take decisions on their own authority as to investment, production, marketing and procurement without reference to the parent (and see below).

In all cases, HMRC will seek to determine whether a major objective of the existence of any particular factors bearing on residence is the obtaining of tax benefits from residence or non-residence, and to establish the reality of the central management and control (HMRC Statement of Practice 1/90).

A company may be resident in more than one country. See *Swedish Central Railway Co Ltd v Thompson* HL 1925, 9 TC 342, and for an authoritative discussion of dual residence, *Union Corporation Ltd v CIR* HL 1953, 34 TC 207.

A company may have a domicile (see *Gasque v CIR* KB 1940, 23 TC 210), but it would seem from the *Union Corporation* case above that, for a company, ordinary residence and residence are synonymous. In the light of *CTA 2009, s 19* and *TCGA 1992, s 10B* it would seem, anyway, that ordinary residence is not relevant to the chargeable gains of companies.

European Companies (SEs) and European Co-operatives (SCEs)

An SE (a European Company — see **14.15** COMPANIES) which transfers its registered office to the UK on or after 1 April 2005 in accordance with *Council Regulation (EC) 2157/2001, Art 8* is regarded upon registration in the UK as resident in the UK for tax purposes. If a different place of residence is given by any rule of law, that place is not taken into account for tax purposes. Where this rule applies, the SE is not treated as ceasing to be UK-resident by reason only of the subsequent transfer from the UK of its registered office. The same rules apply also to an SCE (a European Co-operative — see **14.16** COMPANIES) which transfers its registered office to the UK on or after 18 August 2006 in accordance with *Council Regulation (EC) 1435/2003, Art 7*. [*TCGA 1992, s 286A; CTA 2009, ss 16, 17; SI 2007 No 3186, Sch 2 para 15*]. These provisions are subject to the double tax agreement provisions above.

Domicile and deemed domicile

[57.34] An individual may have only one domicile under general law at any given time, denoting the country or state considered his natural home. Domicile does not necessarily correspond with either residence or nationality and is essentially a question of fact (*Earl of Iveagh v Revenue Commissioners* SC (RI), [1930] IR 431).

Under rules introduced by *F(No 2)A 2017*, certain long-term residents and returning expatriates are *deemed* domiciled in the UK by statute (see further below) for specific purposes in relation to income tax and capital gains tax, even if they do not have a UK domicile under general law as described here.

Under general law, a *domicile of origin* is acquired at birth (normally that of the taxpayer's father, see below), but may be replaced by a *domicile of choice* (to be proved by subsequent conduct). A domicile of choice may be replaced by another domicile of choice (if the necessary proof is forthcoming), but if a domicile of choice is lost without another being acquired, the domicile of origin immediately revives (*Fielden v CIR* Ch D 1965, 42 TC 501).

It is normally more difficult to show the displacement of a domicile of origin than that of a domicile of choice. See *CIR v Bullock* CA 1976, 51 TC 522 where a taxpayer with a domicile of origin in Canada lived in England and intended to remain here during his wife's lifetime. He was held not to have acquired an English domicile of choice (the judgements in this case give a useful review of the law relating to domicile). In *Buswell v CIR* CA 1974, 49 TC 334, the taxpayer had a domicile of origin in South Africa. He came to England to school in 1928, and was called up into the British Army during the Second World War, serving in India. On his return, he signed a written declaration that he intended to remain permanently in the UK. In 1955, he took out a South African passport. In 1961, he married an English lady and their children were brought up in the UK, though registered as South African nationals. In 1968, he and his wife visited South Africa for the first time for 40 years and, with the intention of eventually settling there permanently, bought property there in which they spent three months in each year. He was held never to have abandoned his domicile of origin.

In *Re Clore (decd.) (No 2), Official Solicitor v Clore and Others* Ch D, [1984] STC 609, it was held that an English domicile of origin was never lost as, on the evidence, the taxpayer never formed a settled intention to reside permanently elsewhere. Contrast *Qureshi v Qureshi* Fam D, [1972] Fam D 173, and *In re Lawton* Ch D 1958, 37 ATC 216. Actual settlement abroad is necessary as well as intention; see *Plummer v CIR* Ch D 1987, 60 TC 452.

In *Steiner v CIR* CA 1973, 49 TC 13, a Jewish man who had acquired a German domicile of choice, but who fled to England in 1939 and obtained British naturalisation was held to have acquired an English domicile of choice. In *F and Another (Personal Representatives of F deceased) v CIR* 1999 (Sp C 219), [2000] SSCD 1, an Iranian who had obtained British naturalisation following the 1979 Islamic Revolution was held on the facts to have had a settled intention to return to Iran permanently and thus not to have abandoned his domicile of origin. See also *Moore's Executors v CIR* (Sp C 335), [2002] SSCD 463, *Surveyor v CIR* (Sp C 339), [2002] SSCD 501, *Johnson's Executors v HMRC* (Sp C 481), [2005] SSCD 614; *Gaines-Cooper v HMRC* Ch D 2007, [2008] STC 1665 and *TC06010: Henderson v Revenue and Customs Comrs* [2017] UKFTT 556 (TC).

In determining domicile for capital gains tax, relevant action taken by a person in connection with electoral rights is disregarded unless otherwise requested by the person whose liability is in question. Relevant action refers to prospective or actual registration as an overseas elector or use of such vote. [*FA 1996, s 200; TIOPA 2010, Sch 7 para 74*].

Married women

Up to 31 December 1973, a woman automatically acquired the domicile of her husband on marriage. From 1 January 1974 onwards, the domicile of a married woman is ascertained in the same way as any other individual capable of having an independent domicile, except that a woman already married on that date will retain her husband's domicile until it is changed by acquisition or revival of another domicile. [*Domicile and Matrimonial Proceedings Act 1973, ss 1, 17(5)*]. See *CIR v Duchess of Portland* Ch D 1981, 54 TC 648. But a woman who is a national of the USA and who married a man with UK domicile before 1974 will be treated (after 5 April 1976) in determining her domicile, as if the marriage had taken place in 1974. See Article 4(4) of the US/UK Double Tax Agreement and any similar provisions in double tax agreements with other countries. A widow retains her late husband's domicile unless she later acquires a domicile of choice (or reverts to a domicile of origin) (*In re Wallach* PDA 1949, [1950] 1 All ER 199).

Minors

The domicile of a minor follows that of a person on whom he is legally dependent (usually his father). Under *Domicile and Matrimonial Proceedings Act 1973, s 3* (which does not extend to Scotland), a person first becomes capable of having an independent domicile when he attains 16 (in Scotland, 14 for boys and 12 for girls) or marries under that age. Under *section 4* of that Act, where a child's father and mother are living apart, his domicile is that of his mother if he has his home with her and has no home with his father.

Deemed domicile

Rules of deemed domicile have been introduced under *F(No 2)A 2017* for specific income tax and capital gains tax purposes (such as the REMITTANCE BASIS IN **55.2**). An individual who is not domiciled in the UK under general law at a time in a tax year is treated as domiciled in the UK for certain capital gains tax provisions if either:

(A) the individual was born in the UK with a UK domicile of origin and is UK resident in that tax year; or

(B) the individual has been resident in the UK for at least 15 out of the last 20 tax years, immediately preceding that tax year (although this does not apply if the individual is not resident in the UK from 6 April 2017 onwards).

Capital gains tax re-basing: deemed domicile

An individual who is deemed domiciled under (B) above may re-base a foreign asset held on 5 April 2017 to its market value on that date, if he is a 'qualifying individual' and the asset is disposed of on or after 6 April 2017. The asset must not have been situated in the UK at any time from 16 March 2016 (or the date of acquisition by the individual, if later) to 5 April 2017 inclusive (the '*relevant period*'), but with some exceptions (see below). A '*qualifying individual*' is one who:

(a) has paid the remittance basis charge under *ITA 2007, s 809H* in a tax year prior to 2017/18 (see **55.5** REMITTANCE BASIS);

(b) is *not* an individual who was born in the UK and whose domicile of origin was in the UK;
(c) was *not* domiciled in the UK under general law at any time in a tax year from 2017/18 until the tax year of the disposal inclusive ('*relevant tax years*'); and
(d) was deemed domiciled under (B) above in each relevant tax year.

The re-basing is automatic on a disposal where the conditions are met. However, the conditions are tested for each disposal such that re-basing does not apply universally to all foreign assets held by an individual on 5 April 2017. An irrevocable election may be made in respect of a particular disposal for the re-basing *not* to apply. The claim must be made within four years of the end of the tax year of disposal.

Where *TCGA 1992, s 127* applies to a reorganisation such that an original holding of shares and a new holding are treated as a single asset (see **63.2** SHARES AND SECURITIES), neither holding must have been situated in the UK in the relevant period.

Re-basing applies where the conditions are met notwithstanding the nil gain nil loss treatment for disposals between spouses under *TCGA 1992, s 58(1)* (see **46.5** MARRIED PERSONS AND CIVIL PARTNERS).

A foreign asset brought into the UK before the end of the relevant period is still treated as being outside the UK (and so can benefit from re-basing) if it falls into one of the following exceptions.

(i) It meets the conditions of *ITA 2007, s 809Z(3)* being available for public access (as defined) at an approved museum, gallery or similar establishment or being in storage at, or in transit to or from, the establishment (or other commercial premises in the UK used by the establishment for storage) pending or following public access.
(ii) It meets the conditions of *ITA 2007, s 809Z3(3)* being under repair or restoration, or being in storage at, or in transit to or from, UK premises used for the repair or restoration (or other commercial premises in the UK used by the restorer for storage), pending or following repair or restoration.
(iii) It is brought into the UK with the sole or principal purpose of selling it.
(iv) It is clothing, footwear, jewellery or a watch for the personal use of the individual or their husband, wife or civil partner (or a child or grandchild of such a person if the child or grandchild is under 18 years old). For these purposes, couples living together as husband and wife or civil partners are treated as such.
(v) It is not treated as remitted as the notional remitted amount is less than £1,000 (under *ITA 2007, s 809X(5)(c)*).
(vi) It meets certain conditions as to temporary importation (under *ITA 2007, s 809Z4*).

[*F(No 2)A 2017, s 29, Sch 8 paras 41–42*].

Appeals

[57.35] For 2007/08 and earlier years, ordinary residence and domicile in relation to capital gains tax are determined by the Commissioners for HMRC. Before 1 April 2009, any appeal from a decision of the Commissioners or Board is to the Special Commissioners. The normal appeal time limit of thirty days from the receipt of written notice of the decision is extended to three months if the appeal concerns ordinary residence or domicile. [*TCGA 1992, s 9(2); ICTA 1988, s 207; ITEPA 2003, ss 42, 43; SI 2009 No 56, Sch 1 para 335*]. These provisions are repealed for 2008/09 onwards. Instead, for such years, disputes about ordinary residence and domicile are settled by appeal against the relevant assessment in the ordinary way as are other disputes regarding residence for all years. See generally, 5 APPEALS.

United Kingdom

[57.36] The United Kingdom for tax purposes comprises England, Scotland, Wales and Northern Ireland. The Channel Islands (Jersey, Guernsey, Alderney, Sark, Herm and Jethou) and the Isle of Man are excluded. Great Britain comprises England, Scotland and Wales only.

See 49.19 OVERSEAS MATTERS for the territorial extension of the UK in certain circumstances.

Ireland

[57.37] For double taxation relief purposes a person cannot be resident in both the UK and Ireland. The residence of an *individual* is first determined under normal tax rules relating to abode, domicile etc. If this results in him being technically resident in both States the question is decided by reference successively to permanent home, personal and economic ties, habitual abode, and nationality, and if necessary is decided by agreement between the States. A *company or body of persons* is deemed to be resident where its place of effective management is situated. [*SI 1976 Nos 2151, 2152*].

Key points

[57.38] Points to consider are as follows.

- Non-resident individuals are usually outside the scope of UK capital gains tax, except in the case of UK residential property (see 41.25 LAND).
- From 2013/14 a statutory residence test applies to determine an individual's residence status; prior to this, it depended on the particular circumstances. There have been a number of tax cases dealing with residence.
- Residence status depends on number of days and other facts. Detailed record keeping and supporting evidence is vital.

- It is possible to be resident in more than one country at the same time and reference then needs to be made to any double taxation agreements between the jurisdictions involved.
- Non-residents who are returning to the UK after an absence during which they were temporarily non-resident (see **49.5** OVERSEAS MATTERS) will be taxable on any gains arising during their absence on assets which they held before they left the UK.
- Individuals becoming resident in the UK for the first time or following a period of absence of more than five years should consider uplifting the base cost of shares and securities by means of a 'bed & breakfast' transaction. This is because the '30 day' rule does not apply to non-residents.
- A UK resident non-domiciled individual is entitled to claim the remittance basis of taxation. Such a claim means that non-UK gains are only taxable in the UK to the extent that they are remitted to the UK. One of the costs of claiming the remittance basis is, in most cases, the loss of the capital gains tax annual exempt amount.
- It is difficult for an individual to change their domicile but care needs to be taken when considering future intentions not to inadvertently acquire a domicile of choice in the UK. A long-term resident or an individual returning to the UK who was originally born in the UK with a UK domicile of origin, may become deemed domiciled.

58

Returns

Introduction to returns	**58.1**
Electronic filing of returns	**58.2**
Returns by individuals etc.	**58.3**
Annual tax returns	**58.3**
Form and delivery of returns	**58.4**
Post-transaction valuation checks	**58.5**
Self-assessments	**58.6**
Amendments of returns other than where enquiries made	**58.7**
Record-keeping	**58.8**
Enquiries into returns	**58.9**
Conduct of enquiry	**58.10**
Information powers	**58.11**
Completion or part completion of enquiry	**58.12**
Amendments of returns where enquiries made	**58.13**
Referral of questions during enquiry	**58.14**
Determination of tax where no return delivered	**58.15**
Partnership returns	**58.16**
Partnership statements	**58.17**
Enquiries into returns	**58.18**
Company tax returns	**58.19**
NRCGT returns	**58.20**
Enquiries into NRCGT returns	**58.21**
Determination of amount notionally chargeable where no NRCGT return made	**58.22**
Other returns	**58.23**
European Economic Interest Groupings	**58.23**
Hotels and boarding houses	**58.24**
Issuing houses, stockbrokers, auctioneers, nominee shareholders etc	**58.25**
Key points about returns	**58.26**

Cross-references. See 52 PENALTIES as regards late or incorrect returns; 52.3 PENALTIES as regards duty to notify chargeability to tax.

Introduction to returns

[58.1] Both capital gains tax and corporation tax are administered through a system of self-assessment under which the key document is the tax return. Individuals, partnerships, trustees, personal representatives and companies all have obligations to file returns of their income and gains where HMRC, by notice, require them to do so. Such returns must also include a self-assessment of the taxpayer's liability for the period concerned (although for taxpayers other than companies, this requirement need not be complied with if the return is made within specified time limits). In practice, where a return is filed electronically the tax due is automatically computed during the filing process. Failure to make a return will result in penalties and enable HMRC to make a determination of tax liability which can only be displaced by filing the return.

The obligations under self-assessment of individuals and others within the charge to capital gains tax are covered at **58.3–58.15** below, together with HMRC's powers to enquire into filed returns. For convenience, income tax obligations are also covered to some extent, but see Tolley's Income Tax for full coverage of those. Partnership obligations are covered at **58.16–58.18** below. For companies see **58.19** below.

As well as the powers to require self-assessment returns, HMRC can also require certain other types of return. To the extent that these are relevant to tax on chargeable gains, see **58.23** onwards below.

Making tax digital

The Government intends to abolish tax returns for individuals and for companies and replace them with digital tax accounts phased in over time. See generally www.gov.uk/government/publications/making-tax-digital. The implementation has been delayed and will initially relate to VAT compliance, but primary legislation for income tax is included in *F(No 2)A 2017, ss 60, 61, Sch 14* and draft secondary and tertiary legislation was published on 13 September 2017 for consultation. See www.gov.uk/government/consultations/making-tax-digital-reforms-affecting-businesses.

See also **6.9** ASSESSMENTS for simple assessment by HMRC of an individual's or trustee's income tax or capital gains tax liability for **2016/17** or a subsequent year without the taxpayer first being required to complete a self-assessment tax return on the basis of information already held by HMRC.

Electronic filing of returns

[58.2] Individuals and companies can file tax returns electronically via the online gateway on gov.uk.

Agents are authorised to file individual and company clients' tax returns over the internet subject to certain conditions (see **30.4** HMRC — ADMINISTRATION).

See also **30.4** HMRC — ADMINISTRATION for HMRC's powers to make regulations requiring electronic filing of information (including returns).

Corporation tax returns

With effect for returns for accounting periods ending after 31 March 2010 which are delivered on or after 1 April 2011, companies are *required* to file their tax returns online using a specified data format (known as iXBRL). This does not apply to companies which are subject to a winding-up order, or in administration or administrative receivership. A further exception applies where the use of electronic communications is contrary to the beliefs of a religious group of which all the company's directors are practising members (or, in the case of an unincorporated association, of which all the individuals in the association are practising members). [*SI 2003 No 282, Reg 3; SI 2009*

No 3218; SI 2010 No 2942]. Companies with less complex tax affairs are able to use HMRC's own filing software to do so. (HMRC News Release 20 August 2009). HMRC have published guidance on their approach to the transition filing using iXBRL. See HMRC Guidance Note 'Mandatory online filing of company tax returns: managing the transition', 9 February 2011.

Returns by individuals etc.

Annual tax returns

[58.3] For the purposes of establishing the amounts in which a person is chargeable to income tax and capital gains tax for a tax year, an officer of Revenue and Customs may by notice require that person to deliver a return (i.e. a self-assessment tax return) within the following time limits.

Returns must be delivered on or before 31 January following the tax year, except that returns which are not 'electronic returns' must be delivered on or before 31 October following the tax year. Where the notice to make a return is given on or after 1 August but before 1 November following the tax year the return must be delivered within three months beginning with the date of the notice or, in the case of an electronic return, on or before 31 January. Where notice is given after 31 October following the tax year, the return must be delivered within three months beginning with the date of the notice.

The return must contain such information and be accompanied by such accounts, statements and documents as may reasonably be required. The return must include a declaration that, to the best of the knowledge of the person making it, it is complete and correct. The information, accounts and statements required by the notice may differ in relation to different periods, or different sources of income, or different descriptions of person.

[*TMA 1970, s 8*].

An '*electronic return*' is a return delivered using HMRC's Self-Assessment Online service (see **58.2** above). (Revenue Directions under *SI 2003 No 282, Reg 3* and prescribing of electronic returns, 4 April 2008).

Similar provisions apply in relation to returns by trustees. [*TMA 1970, ss 8A, 12*].

See **52.4** PENALTIES as regards automatic and possible daily penalties for non-compliance (i.e. late returns).

Withdrawal of notice to make return

HMRC may withdraw a notice to an individual or trustee to make a return for 2014/15 or a subsequent year. The notice can be withdrawn within two years of the end of the tax year to which the notice relates or, in exceptional circumstances, within such extended period as HMRC may determine. HMRC were similarly able to withdraw notices for 2012/13 and 2013/14, but only where the individual or trustee requested HMRC to do so.Such a request could be made within two years of the end of the tax year to which the notice related or, in exceptional circumstances, within such extended period as HMRC agreed.

A notice may not be withdrawn if the taxpayer has already filed his return for the year or if HMRC have made a determination under the provisions at

58.15 below.

If HMRC withdraw a notice they do so by giving a withdrawal notice specifying the date on which the notice is withdrawn. Withdrawing a notice in this way does not prevent HMRC subsequently issuing a further notice for the same year.

A withdrawal notice may also cancel a penalty for failing to make a return (see **52.5** penalties).

[*TMA 1970, s 8B; FA 2009, Sch 55 para 17A; FA 2013, Sch 51 paras 3, 8, 9; FA 2016, s 169*].

Reporting limits

Where an individual's chargeable gains for a year do not exceed the annual exempt amount (see **2.6** ANNUAL RATES AND EXEMPTIONS) *and* the aggregate amount or value of the consideration for all disposals of chargeable assets other than those treated under *TCGA 1992, s 58* as giving rise to neither a gain nor a loss (see **46.5** MARRIED PERSONS AND CIVIL PARTNERS) does not exceed *four times* the annual exempt amount, a statement in the self-assessment tax return to that effect complies with the above obligations so far as they relate to chargeable gains (though not so as to prejudice HMRC's right to more detailed information). For this purpose, the amount of an individual's chargeable gains is, where allowable losses are to be deducted, the amount before the deduction of such losses. These reduced reporting requirements do not apply where *ITA 2007, s 809B* (claim for remittance basis (**55.2**(a))) or *TCGA 1992, s 16ZB* (certain gains charged on remittance basis) apply for the year.

Where the year is a split year under the statutory residence test for 2013/14 onwards (see **57.18** RESIDENCE AND DOMICILE), the above rules apply by reference to the UK part of the year only.

[*TCGA 1992, ss 3(6), 3A(1)–(3); FA 2008, Sch 2 paras 27, 56(3), Sch 7 paras 57, 81; FA 2013, Sch 45 paras 94, 153(2)*].

These provisions apply to personal representatives as they apply to individuals but only for the year of assessment in which the individual concerned dies and the next two tax years. [*TCGA 1992, ss 3(7), 3A(4)*]. Similar provisions apply to the trustees of settlements. The total gains limit applies by reference to reduced annual exempt amounts (see **62.8** SETTLEMENTS) where applicable, but the aggregate consideration limit is four times the annual exempt amount *for an individual*. [*TCGA 1992, ss 3(8), 3A(5), Sch 1 para 1(1)(5A), para 2(1)(3)(6A)*].

The above-mentioned statement should *not*, however, be made if a net capital loss has been incurred: a claim has to be made for such a loss to be allowable (see **44.4** LOSSES) and this requires full disclosure.

Acquisitions of chargeable assets

Before 13 August 2009, the notice under *TMA 1970, s 8* (or *s 8A* for trustees) could also require particulars of chargeable assets acquired in the tax year including the consideration given for them and possibly even details of the person from whom an asset was acquired. [*TMA 1970, s 12(2)(3)(5); SI 2009 No 2035, Sch para 2*]. In practice though, the standard self-assessment tax return did *not* ask for this information.

Informal procedure for personal representatives of deceased estates

In respect of income tax and capital gains tax liabilities arising during the administration period of a deceased estate, HMRC operate an informal procedure under which self-assessment tax returns are not required. HMRC will normally operate the procedure where the estate is not complex and the tax arising during the whole of the administration period is less than £10,000. Where this procedure is used, only a simple computation of the estate's liability need be submitted to HMRC, who in turn provide the personal representative with a payslip to enable payment of the tax due. Self-assessment returns are required in all cases not meeting the above conditions. For these purposes, HMRC consider an estate to be complex where there is a very high probate or confirmation value, generally in excess of £2.5 million, the administration of the estate is continuing and has entered the third tax year from the date of death, or the personal representatives have disposed of a chargeable asset and the sale proceeds exceed £250,000. (Revenue Tax Bulletin August 2003 p 1043).

See **58.7** below for amendments of returns and self-assessments. See **58.8** below for record-keeping requirements and **58.9** below for enquiries into returns. See **58.15** below for determination of tax liability where no return delivered.

Form and delivery of returns

[58.4] The power of the Commissioners for HMRC to prescribe the form of returns is given by *TMA 1970, s 113(1)*. The basic self-assessment tax return does not include a space to enter details of chargeable gains and allowable losses. These must be entered on supplementary pages, which form part of the return and which may come attached to it if the taxpayer has a history of making taxable gains and/or allowable losses but must otherwise (unless the return is to be made online) be downloaded from www.gov.uk/government/publications/self-assessment-capital-gains-summary-sa108 or ordered via the HMRC Orderline on 0300 2003610, along with any required Helpsheets (see **32.5** HMRC EXPLANATORY PUBLICATIONS). If the statement mentioned in **58.3** above under 'Reporting limits' can be made, it is made in the basic return, and the supplementary pages are not then required. Similarly, if the only gain arises from the disposal of the taxpayer's main residence and it is wholly exempt under the provisions in **53** PRIVATE RESIDENCES, a statement in the basic return to this effect is sufficient. Following submission of the return, HMRC have the power, under the enquiry provisions at **58.9** below, to require full details of gains and losses.

HMRC accept schedules which mimic the capital gains supplementary pages as an alternative to completion of the pages themselves. These may include computer generated schedules, but they must follow the *form* of the actual supplementary pages. (Revenue 'Working Together' Bulletin July 2000 p 4).

The capital gains supplementary pages do not include space to enter details of individual gains and losses, so that computations for each disposal must be submitted along with the pages. It is necessary in any case to indicate on the return that a valuation (for which see also **58.5** below) or an estimate had been used in calculating a gain or loss. The return also includes space for additional information to be entered.

Provisional figures

A return containing a provisional figure will be accepted provided that the figure is reasonable, taking account of all available information, and is clearly identified as such. An explanation should be given as to why the final figure is not available, all reasonable steps having been taken to obtain it, and when it is expected to be available (at which time it should be notified without unreasonable delay). The absence of such explanation and expected date will influence HMRC in selecting returns for enquiry (see **58.9** below). Pressures of work and complexity of tax affairs are not regarded as acceptable explanations. If the provisional figure is accepted but the final figure is not provided by the expected date, HMRC will take appropriate action to obtain it, which may mean opening an enquiry. See HMRC Tax Return Guide, Revenue Tax Bulletins October 1998 pp 593–596, December 1999 p 705, June 2001 p 848 and February 2002 p 916, and Revenue 'Working Together' Bulletin July 2000 p 5. Note that a provisional figure is different in concept to an estimate that is not intended to be superseded by a more accurate figure.

Where the replacement of a provisional figure by a final figure leads to a *decrease* in the self-assessment, and the time limit for making amendments (see **58.7** below) has passed, the amendment may be made by way of a claim for repayment of tax (see **13.7** CLAIMS) where the conditions for such relief are otherwise met. Where such replacement leads to an *increase* in the self-assessment, a discovery assessment (see **6.10** ASSESSMENTS) may be made to collect the additional tax due. (Revenue Tax Bulletin December 2000 p 817).

Signing of returns

Returns (or claims) may, in cases of physical inability to sign, be signed by an attorney acting under a general or enduring power. The attorney must have full knowledge of the taxpayer's affairs and a copy of the original power or a certified copy will need to be provided when the return (or claim) is first made. The attorney will need to be appointed under an enduring power registered with the Court of Protection (except in Scotland, where there is no such registration, and a signature of an attorney or curator bonis will be accepted) where he acts in the case of a mentally incapacitated person, for whom any receiver or committee appointed by the Court may also sign. These criteria apply similarly to any other declaration required for tax purposes. An attorney cannot sign in any case where the taxpayer is physically capable of signing, even if he is unavailable abroad. (HMRC Statement of Practice A13 and Revenue Tax Bulletin February 1993 p 51).

Although the above practice pre-dates self-assessment, HMRC have published further information in their Tax Bulletin, which confirms that the only exceptions to the personal signature requirement are where, due to his age, physical infirmity or mental incapacity, the taxpayer is unable to cope adequately with the management of his affairs or where his general health might suffer if he were troubled for a personal signature. In all other cases, HMRC expect the return to be signed personally and will reject the return as unsatisfactory, and send it back to whoever submitted it (taxpayer or agent), if it is not (see also **52.4** PENALTIES). In the case of a return submitted via the internet (see **58.2** above), the taxpayer's personal authentication (password and User ID) takes the place of his signature.

Where a return is filed electronically by an agent, the taxpayer must sign a copy before the electronic version is sent. (Revenue Tax Bulletin June 2001 pp 847, 848).

Substitute returns

HMRC have issued a Statement of Practice (HMRC SP 5/87) concerning the acceptability of facsimile and photocopied tax returns. Whenever such a substitute form is used, it is important to ensure that it bears the correct taxpayer's reference. HMRC do not accept computer generated substitute individual, partnership or trust returns (HMRC Internet Statement, 25 October 2007).

Post-transaction valuation checks

[58.5] Individuals, trustees and companies may submit asset valuations used in their capital gains tax calculations to HMRC for checking before they make their returns (**post-transaction valuation checks**). The service is free of charge, but valuations will be considered only *after* the relevant transaction has occurred. Full information about the transactions to which they relate together with any relevant tax computations must be submitted to HMRC with the valuations using Form CG34. The service extends to valuations of assets that are the subject of a negligible value claim (see **44.11** LOSSES).

Most forms CG34 for individuals and partnerships should be sent to HMRC P&CGT Compliance, SO970, Newcastle NE98 1ZZ. Taxpayers dealt with by Trust Offices should send the form to Trusts and Estates, Trusts SO842, Ferrers House, Castle Meadow, Nottingham NG2 1BB. Taxpayers dealt with by Specialist PT HMWU or Public Departments 1 should send the form to the relevant tax office. Companies should send the form to the office dealing with the company's affairs.

If HMRC agree the valuations they will not be challenged when the return is submitted unless information affecting the valuation was not provided. If HMRC disagree with the valuations they will suggest alternatives. HMRC should be allowed a minimum of two months to agree a valuation or suggest an alternative. The due date for filing the return cannot be deferred.

(Revenue Press Release 4 February 1997; HMRC Working Together Publication 38, November 2009).

Under the principles at **16.11**(d) COMPUTATION OF GAINS AND LOSSES, costs reasonably incurred in making a valuation or apportionment submitted for a post-transaction valuation check are deductible in arriving at the gain, but any costs incurred in making the submission or in subsequent negotiations cannot be so deducted (HMRC Capital Gains Manual CG15260, 16615).

See also 30.3 HMRC — ADMINISTRATION for procedures for non-statutory clearances.

Self-assessments

[58.6] Every return under *TMA 1970, s 8* or *s 8A* (see 58.3 above) must include, subject to the exception below, an assessment (a self-assessment) of the liability, based on the information in the return and taking into account all reliefs, allowances, tax credits, tax at source and tax repayments, of the person making the return to income tax and capital gains tax for the year of assessment. HMRC's Tax calculation summary notes, available online with the tax calculation summary pages at www.gov.uk/government/publications/self-assessment-tax-calculation-summary-sa110, are designed to assist in the calculation of the tax liability.

A person need not comply with this requirement if he makes and delivers his return on or before 31 October following the tax year or, where the notice to deliver a return is given after 31 August following the tax year, within two months beginning with the date of the notice. In such cases, HMRC will compute the tax due. For returns submitted outside these time limits, HMRC will calculate the tax and make the assessment if the taxpayer fails to do so, but will not guarantee to do so before the due date for payment of tax.

Assessments made as above by an HMRC officer are treated as self-assessments by the person making the return and as included in the return.

[*TMA 1970, ss 8, 8A, 9(1)–(3A)*].

The 31 October deadline is of no significance where returns are filed over the internet (see 58.4 above) as the tax due is automatically computed during the filing process.

Time limits

Subject to any provision allowing a longer period, a self-assessment contained in a return under *TMA 1970, s 8* or *s 8A* for 2012/13 or a later year cannot be made more than four years after the end of the tax year. Self-assessments for 2011/12 and earlier years cannot be made after 5 April 2017 (which is also the deadline for 2012/13, applying the four-year rule). This provision does not, however, prevent a person who has received a notice to make a return within the four-year period (or for 2012/13 and earlier years, before 6 April 2017) from making a return including a self-assessment within three months beginning with date of the notice where the three months expires after the end of the four-year period. Similarly, the provision does not prevent a person from making a self-assessment to supersede a determination under *TMA 1970, s 28C* (see **58.15** below) within the time limits at **58.15** below.

[*TMA 1970, s 34A; FA 2016, s 168(3)*].

Amendments of returns other than where enquiries made

[58.7] A person may by notice to an HMRC officer amend his return at any time within twelve months after the filing date (for this purpose treated as 31 January following the tax year or, where the notice to deliver the return is given after 31 October following the tax year, the end of the three-month period beginning with the date of the notice).

At any time within nine months after the delivery of a person's return, an HMRC officer may by notice to that person amend his return to correct obvious errors and omissions (whether of principle, arithmetical or otherwise). An HMRC officer may also correct anything else in the return that he has reason to believe is incorrect in the light of information available to him. Where the correction is required in consequence of an amendment by the taxpayer as above, the nine-month period begins immediately after the date of the taxpayer's amendment. The taxpayer has a legal right to reject an officer's correction, by notice within 30 days beginning with the date of the notice of correction. In practice HMRC will reverse a correction regardless of this 30-day limit, unless they are no longer empowered to do so, i.e. if all deadlines for corrections and amendments (by HMRC or taxpayer) have passed and the HMRC enquiry window (see **58.9** below) has closed (Revenue Tax Bulletin June 2001 pp 850, 851).

[*TMA 1970, ss 9(4)(6), 9ZA, 9ZB; FA 2008, s 119(1)(9)*].

For amendments to returns subject to an HMRC enquiry, see **58.12**, **58.13** below.

Record-keeping

[58.8] For capital gains tax and income tax, any person who may be required to make and deliver a personal or trustee tax return (see **58.3** above) for a tax year or a partnership tax return (see **58.16** below) for any period is required by law to keep all records necessary for the preparation of a complete and correct return *and* to preserve them until the end of the 'relevant day'. The 'relevant day' is initially:

(a) in the case of a person carrying on a trade (including for these purposes any letting of property), profession or business, whether alone or in partnership, the fifth anniversary of 31 January following the tax year or, for partnership returns, the sixth anniversary of the end of the period covered by the return;
(b) otherwise, the first anniversary of 31 January following the tax year; or
(c) (with effect from a date to be fixed by order) in either case, such earlier day as may be specified in writing by HMRC.

Where, as is normal, notice to deliver the return is given before the day given by whichever is the applicable of (a) and (b) above, the '*relevant day*' is the *later* of that day and whichever of the following applies:

(i) where HMRC enquiries are made into the return, the day on which the enquiries are fully completed (see **58.12** below);
(ii) where no such enquiries are made, the day on which HMRC no longer have power to enquire (see **58.9** below).

Where notice to deliver a return is given *after* the day given by whichever is the applicable of (a) and (b) above, (i) and (ii) above still apply to determine the relevant day but only in relation to such records as the taxpayer has in his possession at the time the notice is given.

HMRC have the power to make regulations specifying records which are required to be kept and preserved under these provisions and specifying that those records include specified supporting documents. Subject to this, in the case of a person within (a) above, the records to be preserved include records concerning business receipts and expenditure and, in the case of a trade involving dealing in goods, all sales and purchases of goods. All supporting documents (including accounts, books, deeds, contracts, vouchers and receipts) relating to such items must also be preserved.

Generally, copies of documents may be preserved instead of the originals and are admissible in evidence in proceedings before the Tribunal. (For computer records in particular, see HMRC Compliance Handbook CH13400.) Exceptions to this are vouchers, certificates etc. which show tax credits or deductions at source of UK or foreign tax, e.g. dividend vouchers, interest vouchers (including those issued by banks and building societies) and evidence of tax deducted from payments to sub-contractors under the construction industry tax deduction scheme, which must be preserved in their original form. The right to preserve copies of documents is subject to any conditions or further exceptions specified in writing by HMRC.

The maximum penalty for non-compliance in relation to any tax year or accounting period is £3,000. This does not apply to records only required for claims, elections or notices not included in the return, as there are separate record-keeping requirements (and a separate penalty) for those (see **13.3** CLAIMS) nor does it apply in respect of original dividend vouchers and interest certificates where HMRC are satisfied that other documentary evidence supplied to them proves any facts they reasonably require to be proved and which such vouchers etc. would have proved.

[*TMA 1970, s 12B; FA 2008, s 115, Sch 37 para 2; TIOPA 2010, Sch 8 para 3; F(No 2)A 2017, Sch 15 paras 9, 44; SI 2009 No 56, Sch 1 para 7; SI 2009 No 402; SI 2009 No 2035, Sch para 4*].

HMRC have given guidance as to the type of records to be kept. For capital gains tax, it is recommended that the following records be kept:

- contracts for the purchase, sale, lease or exchange of assets;
- documentation relating to assets acquired other than by purchase;
- details of assets gifted to others (including a trust);
- copies of valuations used in a computation of chargeable gains or losses;
- bills, invoices or other evidence of payment records such as bank statements and cheque stubs for costs claimed for the purchase, improvement or sale of assets;
- any correspondence with a purchaser or vendor leading up to the sale or acquisition of an asset;
- details supporting any apportionment (e.g. where home is partly let or partly used for business purposes).

(HMRC Pamphlet SA/BK4).

Enquiries into returns

[58.9] An HMRC officer may enquire into a personal or trustees' return, and anything (including any claim or election) contained (or required to be contained) in it. An enquiry can also extend to consideration by HMRC of whether to give the taxpayer a transfer pricing notice under *TIOPA 2010, s 168(1)* and whether to give the taxpayer a notice under *TIOPA 2010, s 81(2)* (schemes and arrangements designed to increase DOUBLE TAX RELIEF (**21.9**)).

Notice of enquiry

The officer must give notice that he intends to carry out an enquiry (notice of enquiry) within whichever of the following periods is appropriate:

(a) in the case of a return delivered on or before the filing date (i.e. the date on or before which the return must be delivered — see **58.3** above), the twelve months after the day on which the return was delivered;
(b) in the case of a return delivered after the filing date, the period ending with the 'quarter day' next following the first anniversary of the delivery date;
(c) in the case of a return amended by the taxpayer under **58.7** above, the period ending with the 'quarter day' next following the first anniversary of the date of amendment.

For these purposes, the '*quarter days*' are 31 January, 30 April etc. A return cannot be enquired into more than once, except in consequence of an amendment (or further amendment). If notice under (c) above is given at a time when the deadline in (a) or (b) above, as the case may be, has expired or after an enquiry into the return has been fully completed, the enquiry is limited to matters affected by the amendment. The same applies if a partial closure notice has been issued (see **58.12** below) in relation to the matters to which the amendment relates.

[*TMA 1970, s 9A; TIOPA 2010, Sch 8 paras 2, 107; F(No 2)A 2017, Sch 15 paras 2, 44*].

The 'giving' of notice under *TMA 1970, s 9A* is effected not when the notice is issued or posted but at the time it would be received in the ordinary course of post (generally taken to be four working days for second class mail) or, if proved, the time of actual receipt (*Holly and another v Inspector of Taxes* 1999 (Sp C 225), [2000] SSCD 50, and see also *Wing Hung Lai v Bale* (Sp C 203), [1999] SSCD 238). HMRC now accept this to be the case.

In *R (oao Spring Salmon and Seafood Ltd) v CIR* CS, [2004] STC 444 it was held that, under the corporation tax self-assessment enquiry powers of *FA 1998, Sch 18 para 24*, a notice of enquiry need not be in writing. Furthermore, it need not be sent to a company's registered office but is valid if sent to a company's place of business.

Conduct of enquiry

[58.10] HMRC have published an Enquiry Manual as part of their series of internal guidance manuals (see **32.2** HMRC EXPLANATORY PUBLICATIONS) and, as an extended introduction to the material on operational aspects of the enquiry regime covered in the manual, a special edition of their Tax Bulletin (Special Edition 2, August 1997). The following points are selected from the Bulletin.

- Early submission of a tax return will not increase the likelihood of selection for enquiry.
- HMRC do not have to give reasons for opening an enquiry — and they *will not do so* (but see further below).
- Enquiries may be full enquiries or 'aspect enquiries'. An aspect enquiry will fall short of an in-depth examination of the return (though it may develop into one), but will instead concentrate on one or more aspects of it.
- Greater emphasis than before is placed on examination of underlying records. HMRC will make an informal request for information before, if necessary, using their powers under *TMA 1970, s 19A* (see **58.11** below).
- Where penalties are being sought, HMRC will aim to conclude the enquiry by means of a contract settlement (see **6.8** ASSESSMENTS) rather than issue a final closure notice under *TMA 1970, s 28A* (see **58.12** below).

Where an enquiry remains open beyond the period during which notice of intention to enquire had to be given (see above) and solely because of an unagreed valuation for capital gains tax purposes, HMRC will not take advantage of the open enquiry to raise further enquiries into matters unrelated to the valuation or the CGT computation except in circumstances where a 'discovery' (see **6.10** ASSESSMENTS) could in any case have been made if the enquiry had been completed (HMRC Statement of Practice 1/99).

Information powers

[58.11] See **34.3–34.10** HMRC INVESTIGATORY POWERS for HMRC's powers to require the production of information and documents. See in particular **34.5** for the restriction on those powers where a return has been made.

Completion or part completion of enquiry

[58.12] An enquiry is completed when an officer of HMRC gives the taxpayer notice (a final closure notice) that he has completed his enquiries. As regards enquiries commenced on or after the date of Royal Assent to *F(No 2)A 2017*, or in progress on that date, an HMRC officer can issue a partial closure notice, which completes the enquiry insofar as it concerns the matters specified in the notice. The enquiry is not fully completed until a final closure notice has been issued to inform the taxpayer that the officer has completed his remaining enquiries. A partial or final closure notice takes effect when it is issued and must state the officer's conclusions and make the necessary amendments to the return to give effect to those conclusions or state that no amendment is required. An amendment made by a closure notice is in the nature of an assessment by HMRC (*R (on the application of Archer) v Revenue and Customs Commissioners* [2017] EWHC 296 (Admin), [2017] 3 All ER 524, [2017] 1 WLR 2066).

During the course of an enquiry, the taxpayer may apply to the Appeal Tribunal for a direction requiring HMRC to issue a partial or final closure notice within a specified period, such application to be heard and determined in a similar manner to an appeal. The Tribunal must give the direction unless satisfied that there are reasonable grounds for not issuing the partial or final closure notice within a specified period. [*TMA 1970, s 28A; FA 2015, Sch 7 para 44; F(No 2)A 2017, Sch 15 paras 12, 44*].

Guidance is given to HMRC officers as to when they might agree to an application to issue a closure notice without the need for a Tribunal hearing (HMRC Enquiry Manual EM1976, 1980). HMRC will make use of partial closure notices where the taxpayer's affairs are complex or where there is tax avoidance or large amounts of tax at risk; HMRC officers may issue a partial closure notice at their own discretion by agreement with the taxpayer (www.gov.uk/government/publications/tax-enquiries-closure-rules).

See **5.2** APPEALS for right of appeal against any conclusion stated or amendment made by a partial or final closure notice.

Where an enquiry is to be concluded by means of a contract settlement (see **6.8** ASSESSMENTS) HMRC do not normally issue a closure notice. A notice will be issued only if the taxpayer or agent insist. (HMRC Enquiry Manual EM6001).

Amendments of returns where enquiries made

[58.13] If a return is amended by the taxpayer under **58.7** above or in accordance with the requirements of a follower notice (see **4.27** ANTI-AVOIDANCE) while an enquiry is in progress in relation to any matter affected by the amendment, the amendment does not restrict the scope of the enquiry but may itself be taken into account in the enquiry. The amendment does not take effect to alter the tax payable until a partial closure notice is issued in relation to the matters to which the amendment relates or, if no such notice is issued, a final closure notice is issued. See **58.12** above for partial and final closure notices. The amendment may then be taken into account separately or, if the officer so states in the closure notice, in arriving at the amendments contained in that notice. It does not take effect if the officer concludes in the closure notice that the amendment is incorrect.

The above has effect where the enquiry begins on or after the date of Royal Assent to *F(No 2)A 2017* or is in progress on that date, and allows for the fact that such an enquiry may be partly completed by the issue of a partial closure notice. Previously, if a return was amended by the taxpayer while an enquiry into it was in progress, the amendment did not restrict the scope of the enquiry but could itself be taken into account in the enquiry. The amendment did not take effect to alter the tax payable until the enquiry was completed.

[*TMA 1970, s 9B; FA 2014, Sch 33 para 1; F(No 2)A 2017, Sch 15 paras 3, 44*].

If in his opinion there is otherwise likely to be a loss of tax in relation to any matter, an officer may amend a self-assessment contained in the return while an enquiry is still in progress in relation to that matter. If the enquiry is itself limited to an amendment to the return (see **58.9** above), the officer's power in this respect is limited accordingly. [*TMA 1970, s 9C; F(No 2)A 2017, Sch 15 paras 4, 44*].

Referral of questions during enquiry

[58.14] There are provisions as below to enable specific contentious points to be litigated while the enquiry is still open, instead of waiting until it is completed. Where the enquiry begins on or after the date of Royal Assent to *F(No 2)A 2017* or is in progress on that date, this applies while an enquiry is still open into any matter (allowing for the fact that such an enquiry may be partly completed by the issue of a partial closure notice as in **58.12** above).

At any time whilst the enquiry is in progress, any one or more questions arising out of it may be referred, jointly by the taxpayer and an HMRC officer, to the Appeal Tribunal for its determination. More than one notice of referral may be given in relation to the enquiry. Either party may withdraw a notice of referral. Until the questions referred have been finally determined (or the referral withdrawn), no final closure notice may be given or applied for in relation to the enquiry, and no partial closure notice relating to the question referred may be given or applied for.

The determination of the question(s) by the Tribunal is binding on both parties in the same way, and to the same extent, as a decision on a preliminary issue in an appeal. HMRC must take account of it in concluding their enquiry. Following completion of the enquiry, the question concerned may not be reopened on appeal except to the extent (if any) that it could have been reopened had it been determined on appeal following the enquiry rather than on referral during the enquiry.

[*TMA 1970, ss 28ZA–28ZE; SI 2009 No 56, Sch 1 paras 12–16; F(No 2)A 2017, Sch 15 paras 10, 11, 44*].

Determination of tax where no return delivered

[58.15] Where a notice has been given under *TMA 1970, s 8* or *s 8A* (notice requiring an individual or trustee to deliver a return — see **58.3** above) and the return is not delivered by the 'filing date', an HMRC officer may make a determination of the amounts of taxable income, capital gains and income tax payable which, to the best of his information and belief, he estimates for the tax year. The officer must serve notice of the determination on the person concerned. Tax is payable as if the determination were a self-assessment, with no right of appeal (see *Bartram v HMRC* UT, [2012] STC 2144). No determination may be made after the expiry of three years beginning with the filing date.

A determination is automatically superseded by any self-assessment made (whether by the taxpayer or HMRC), based on information contained in a return. Such self-assessment must be made within the three years beginning with the filing date or, if later, within twelve months beginning with the date of the determination. Any tax payable or repayable as a result of the supersession is deemed to have fallen due for payment or repayment on the normal due date, usually 31 January following the tax year (see **51.2** PAYMENT OF TAX). Any recovery proceedings commenced before the making of such a self-assessment may be continued in respect of so much of the tax charged by the self-assessment as is due and payable and has not been paid.

The '*filing date*' for these purposes is 31 January following the tax year or, where the notice to deliver the return is given after 31 October following the tax year, the end of the three-month period beginning with the date of the notice.

See also **51.20** PAYMENT OF TAX for the continuation of action under the provisions for enforcement of tax debts by deduction from accounts where a determination is superseded by a self-assessment.

[*TMA 1970, ss 28C, 59B(5A); F(No 2)A 2015, Sch 8 para 25*].

Partnership returns

[58.16] Any partner (including a company) may be required by notice to complete and deliver a return of the partnership profits (a partnership return) together with accounts, statements etc. The return must include the names, addresses and tax references of all persons (including companies) who were partners during the period specified in the notice and such other information as may reasonably be required by the notice, which may include information relating to disposals of partnership property and, before 13 August 2009, to acquisitions (see **58.3** above). The general requirements are similar to those for personal returns under *TMA 1970, s 8* (see **58.3** above). The notice will specify the period (the relevant period — normally a period of account of the partnership) to be covered by the return and the date by which the return should be delivered (the filing date — see below).

Where the partner responsible for dealing with the return ceases to be available, a successor may be nominated for this purpose by a majority of the persons (or their personal representatives) who were partners at any time in the period covered by the return. A nomination (or revocation of a nomination) does not have effect until notified to HMRC. Failing a nomination, a successor will be determined according to rules on the return form or will be nominated by HMRC.

Filing date — partnership including at least one individual

For returns for 2007/08 onwards, two different filing dates may be specified in the notice, depending on whether or not the return will be an 'electronic return' (see **58.3** above). For an electronic return, the filing date will be no earlier than 31 January following the tax year concerned (normally that in which the period of account ends); for non-electronic returns it will be no earlier than 31 October following the tax year. Where, however, the notice to make the return is given on or after 1 August but before 1 November following the tax year, the filing date must be at least three months after the date of the notice or, in the case of an electronic return, no earlier than 31 January. Where notice is given after 31 October following the tax year, the filing date must be at least three months after the date of the notice.

In *Fitzpatrick and Co Solicitors v HMRC* FTT, [2012] SFTD 816, a partnership return submitted as a PDF attached to the online personal returns of the partners was held to constitute an electronic return.

The filing date for a return for 2006/07 or an earlier year will be no earlier than 31 January following the tax year concerned or, if later, the last day of the three-month period beginning with the date of the notice.

Filing date — partnership including at least one company

Two different filing dates may be specified in the notice, depending on whether or not the return will be an electronic return. For an electronic return, the filing date will be no earlier than the first anniversary of the end of the relevant period; for non-electronic returns, it will be no earlier than nine months after the end of the relevant period. Where notice is given more than nine months after the end of the relevant period, the filing date must be at least three months after the date of the notice.

[*TMA 1970, s 12AA; SI 2009 No 2035, Sch para 3*].

See **52.5** PENALTIES re penalties for non-compliance. For the capital gains tax position as regards partnership transactions, see **50** PARTNERSHIPS.

Withdrawal of notice to make return

A partner who has received a notice to make a partnership return for 2012/13 or a subsequent year (or, where the partnership includes one or more companies, a return for a relevant period beginning on or after 6 April 2012) may request HMRC to withdraw the notice. Such a request can be made within the two years of the end of the tax year or relevant period to which the notice relates or, in exceptional circumstances, within such extended period as HMRC may agree. A partner cannot make such a request if he has already filed the return for the year.

If HMRC agree to withdraw the notice they do so by giving a withdrawal notice specifying the date on which the notice is withdrawn. Withdrawing a notice in this way does not prevent HMRC subsequently issuing a further notice for the same year or period.

A withdrawal notice may also cancel a penalty for failing to make a return (see **52.5** PENALTIES).

[*TMA 1970, s 12AAA; FA 2009, Sch 55 para 17B; FA 2013, Sch 51 paras 4, 8, 9*].

Partnership statements

[58.17] Each partnership return must include a statement (a partnership statement) showing, in respect of the period covered by the return and (if that period is not a single period of account) each period of account ending within that period:

- the amount of the partnership income or loss from each source;
- the amounts of tax deducted at source from or tax credits on partnership income;
- the amount of consideration for each disposal of partnership property,

and each partner's share of each of those amounts. [*TMA 1970, s 12AB(1)(5); ITA 2007, s 989*].

Where a company carries on a trade etc. in partnership the company tax return (see **58.19** below) for any period must include amounts in respect of the company's share of any income, loss, consideration, tax credit or charge stated in any relevant statement falling to be made by the partnership for a period which includes, or includes any part of, the period in respect of which the return is required. [*FA 1998, s 117, Sch 18 para 12*]. In the case of an individual carrying on a trade etc. in partnership, a return under *TMA 1970, s 8* (see **58.3** above) must include each amount, which according to any 'relevant partnership statement' is his share of any income, loss, tax, credit or charge for the period covered by the statement. A '*relevant partnership statement*' is a statement falling to be made, as respects the partnership, under the above provisions for a period which includes, or includes any part of, the year of assessment or its basis period. [*TMA 1970, s 8(1B)(1C)*].

Amendments to partnership returns

Provisions similar to those in **58.7** above apply as regards amendments and corrections to partnership returns. Where a partnership return is so amended or corrected (and the correction is not rejected by the taxpayer), the partners' returns will be amended by HMRC accordingly, by notice to each partner concerned. [*TMA 1970, ss 12AB(2)–(5), 12ABA, 12ABB; FA 2008, s 119(2)(9)*].

Enquiries into returns

[58.18] Provisions similar to those at **58.9** above apply as regards enquiries into a partnership return. The notice of enquiry may be given to a successor (as defined) of the person who made the return (see **58.16** above). The giving of such notice is deemed to include the giving of notice under *TMA 1970, s 9A* (see **58.9** above) (or, where applicable, the equivalent corporation tax provision of *FA 1998, Sch 18 para 24*) to each partner affected. [*TMA 1970, ss 12AC, 118(1)(3)*].

HMRC's power to call for documents at **58.11** above also applies here.

Similar provisions to those at **58.12–58.14** above apply in the case of an enquiry into a partnership return. However, there is no equivalent provision to *TMA 1970, s 9C* in **58.13** above (amendment by HMRC while enquiry in progress). Where a partnership return is amended under the relevant provisions in **58.12, 58.13** above, HMRC will, by notice, make any necessary consequential amendments to the partners' returns (including those of company partners). [*TMA 1970, ss 12AD, 28ZA–28ZE, 28B; SI 2009 No 56, Sch 1 paras 12–16, 18; F(No 2)A 2017, Sch 15 paras 7, 8, 10, 11, 13, 44*].

Company tax returns

[58.19] The following provisions apply to companies.

Notification of coming within charge to corporation tax

A company must give notice to HMRC of the beginning of its first accounting period and of the beginning of any subsequent accounting period that does not immediately follow the end of a previous accounting period (i.e. the first accounting period following a period of dormancy). The notice must be given in writing to an HMRC officer not later than three months after the beginning of the accounting period. It must state when the accounting period began and include the following information:

- the company's name, registered number, registered office and principal place of business;
- the nature of the business carried on;
- the date to which accounts are to be drawn up;
- the full name and home address of each of the directors;
- if the company has taken over a business, the name and address of that former business and the name and address of the person from whom it was acquired;
- the name of any parent company and its registered office; and
- if the company then has any PAYE obligations, the date on which those obligations first arose.

Penalties under *TMA 1970, s 98* (see **52.23** PENALTIES) applied for failure to meet this requirement, but a company which has a reasonable excuse for failing to give the required notice is not regarded as failing to comply until the excuse ceases and, after the excuse ceases, is not so regarded if the notice is given without unreasonable delay. The requirement does not apply to unincorporated associations or partnerships. [*FA 2004, s 55; SI 2004 No 2502*].

Note that *FA 2004, s 55* is removed from the list of provisions in respect of which a penalty can be charged under *TMA 1970, s 98* by *FA 2008, Sch 41 para 25* obligations arising on or after 1 April 2010. No replacement penalty provision has been enacted.

Notification of chargeability

A company chargeable to corporation tax for any accounting period which has neither made a return of its profits for that period nor received a notice requiring such a return (see below) must give notice of its chargeability to HMRC within 12 months after the end of that accounting period. [*TMA 1970, s 10(1); FA 1988, s 121; FA 1998, s 117, Sch 18 para 2*].

See **52.3** PENALTIES regarding failure to meet the requirement.

Self-assessment returns

If so required by notice, a company must make a return of such information, relevant to its corporation tax liabilities, as is required under the notice. Supporting accounts, statements and reports may also be required, although the accounts required of companies resident in the UK throughout the period to which the return relates (*'the return period'*), and required to prepare accounts under *Companies Act 2006* or *Companies Act 1985* (or NI equivalent) for any period consisting of or including the return period, are only those it is so required to prepare. Before 13 August 2009, a notice requiring a return could require details of chargeable assets acquired, with certain specified exceptions.

The return must include a declaration to the effect that, to the best of the knowledge of the person making it, it is correct and complete. *TMA 1970, s 108(1)* requires that person to be *'the proper officer of the company'* (i.e. the secretary of a corporate body, except where a liquidator (or, where a company enters administration on or after 15 September 2003, an administrator) has been appointed when the latter is the proper officer, or the treasurer of a non-corporate body) or, except where a liquidator has been appointed, any authorised person.

Similar self-assessment provisions as in **58.6**, **58.7** above apply, except that a company does not have the option of requiring HMRC to compute the tax liability.

[*FA 1998, s 117, Sch 18 paras 3, 7, 8, 11, 13, 15, 16; FA 2008, s 119(4)(9); TIOPA 2010, Sch 8 para 54(2); FA 2012, Sch 20 para 17(3); SI 2001 No 3629, Art 103; SI 2008 No 954, Art 25(2); SI 2009 No 2035, Sch para 37*].

The return must be made by the later of:

(a) twelve months after the end of the period to which it relates,
(b) twelve months after the end of the period for which the company makes up accounts (*'period of account'*) in which falls the last day of the accounting period to which it relates (except that periods of account in excess of 18 months are treated as ending after 18 months for this purpose), and
(c) three months after service of the notice requiring the return.

If the period specified by the notice for the making of a return (*'the specified period'*) is not an accounting period of the company, but the company is within the charge to corporation tax for some part of the specified period, the notice is to be taken as referring to all company accounting period(s) ending in or at the end of the specified period. If there is no such accounting period, but there is a part of the specified period which does not fall within an accounting period, the notice is to be treated as requiring a return for that part of the period. Otherwise, the notice is of no effect, and the company is not required to make any return pursuant to it. For the determination of a company's accounting period, see Tolley's Corporation Tax under Accounting Periods. See also **58.17** above where a company carries on a trade in partnership.

[*ICTA 1988, s 832(1); FA 1998, s 117, Sch 18 paras 5, 14; FA 2002, s 103(1)(6), s 141, Sch 40 Pt 3(16)*].

With effect for accounting periods ending after 31 March 2011 all companies are required to file their tax returns online using a specified data format (known as iXBRL). Companies with less complex tax affairs are able to use HMRC's own filing software to do so. (HMRC News Release 20 August 2009; HMRC Directions under *SI 2003 No 282, Regs 3* and *10*, 6 January 2010).

In the absence of a return, HMRC have power to determine the corporation tax liability. [*FA 1998, s 117, Sch 18 paras 36–40; FA 2008, Sch 39 paras 38–40*].

An enquiry regime analogous to that in **58.9–58.14** above applies to companies. Note that in addition to the matters mentioned at **58.9** above in respect of which an enquiry can be made, for corporation tax purposes an enquiry can also extend to consideration of whether to give the taxpayer a notice under *TIOPA 2010, s 232* or *s 249* (tax arbitrage see **4.20** ANTI-AVOIDANCE) or *TCGA 1992, s 184G* or *s 184H* (avoidance utilising losses — see **14.7** COMPANIES). [*FA 1998, Sch 18 paras 24–35; FA 2006, s 71(2); FA 2008, s 119(5)–(9), Sch 36 paras 88, 92(i); TIOPA 2010, Sch 8 para 321; F(No 2)A 2017, Sch 15 paras 24–28, 44; SI 2009 No 56, Sch 1 paras 254–262*].

Similar record-keeping requirements as in **58.8** above apply to companies under corporation tax self-assessment. A company must preserve its records for six years from the end of its return period (subject, from a date to be fixed by order, to HMRC specifying, in writing, an earlier date). [*FA 1998, s 117, Sch 18 paras 21–23; FA 2008, s 115, Sch 37 para 8; TIOPA 2010, Sch 8 para 54(3)(4); SI 2009 No 402*]. For an article on the record-keeping requirements for corporation tax purposes, see Revenue Tax Bulletin October 1998 pp 587–589.

Corporation tax self-assessment is covered in full in Tolley's Corporation Tax.

HMRC offer post-transaction (pre-return) valuation checks to companies (in relation to their chargeable gains) as they do to individuals (see **58.5** above).

Where an enquiry remains open beyond the period during which notice of intention to enquire had to be given and solely because of an unagreed valuation for chargeable gains purposes, HMRC will not take advantage of the open enquiry to raise further enquiries into matters unrelated to the valuation or the chargeable gains computation except in circumstances where a 'discovery' (see **6.10** ASSESSMENTS) could in any case have been made if the enquiry had been completed (HMRC Statement of Practice 1/02).

See **52.4** PENALTIES regarding non-compliance. See also **14.15** COMPANIES regarding the application of these provisions where a company ceases to be UK-resident in the course of the formation of an SE and where an SE becomes non-UK resident.

NRCGT returns

[58.20] Subject to below, where a non-resident CGT disposal is made (see **41.25** LAND), the person to whom any NRCGT gain on the disposal would accrue must make a return (an '*NRCGT return*') to HMRC in respect of the disposal on or before the 30th day following the day of the 'completion' of the disposal. Where the disposal is made by a member of an NRCGT group (see **41.33** LAND), the obligation to make the return falls on the members of the group (both those companies which were members of the NRCGT group at the time of the disposal and any companies which were members of the group at any previous time in the tax year in which the disposal is made). An NRCGT return must contain the information prescribed by HMRC and include a declaration by the person making it that it is to the best of that person's knowledge correct and complete. A return is not required for a transfer within an NRCGT group.

For this purpose, the '*completion*' of a disposal occurs at the time of the disposal or, where the disposal is under a contract completed by conveyance, at the time of that conveyance.

Only one return is required where the completion of two or more disposals occurs on the same date and any NRCGT gains arising from the disposals would be chargeable in the same tax year.

An online return can be completed at https://online.hmrc.gov.uk/shortforms/form/NRCGT_Return.

An NRCGT return must include an assessment (an '*advance self-assessment*') of the amount notionally chargeable (see below) at the filing date for the return and, if the taxpayer is required to make an NRCGT return in respect of a CGT disposal made earlier in the same tax year, the amount of any increase in the amount notionally chargeable for the year. The '*amount notionally chargeable*' at the filing date for a return is the amount of CGT which would be chargeable under *TCGA 1992, s 14D* or *s 188D* (see **41.26, 41.33** LAND respectively) for the tax year, as determined:

(i) on the assumption that no NRCGT gains or losses arise in that year on disposals the completion of which occurs after day of the completion of the disposal (or disposals) to which the return relates;
(ii) as if all allowable losses on disposals of assets in that year where the completion of the disposal occurs on or before the day of the completion of the disposal (or disposals) to which the return relates which can be deducted from NRCGT gains, and any other applicable reliefs or allowances, are so deducted; and
(iii) where the taxpayer is an individual, on the basis of a reasonable estimate of whether or not income tax will be chargeable for the year at the higher rate or dividend upper rate and, if not, how much of the basic rate band will be available in calculating the CGT liability.

The advance self-assessment must include particulars of any estimate within (iii) above. A reasonable estimate (i.e. one made on a fair and reasonable basis, having regard to the circumstances) is treated as not being inaccurate for the purposes of the penalty at **52.8** PENALTIES.

An NRCGT return does not need to include an advance self-assessment if:

(1) the taxpayer (or, where the taxpayer is the trustees of the settlement, any of the trustees) has been given a notice to deliver a self-assessment tax return under **58.3** above for the tax year in question or the preceding tax year (and the notice has not been withdrawn);
(2) where the taxpayer is a company, it has been given a notice to deliver a self-assessment return under **58.19** above which specifies a period including all or part of the tax year in question or the preceding tax year (and the notice has not been withdrawn); or

(3) where the taxpayer is a company, an annual tax on enveloped dwellings return has been delivered by the company (or a representative partner) for the chargeable period ending on 31 March in the preceding tax year.

The Treasury may by regulations prescribe further cases in which an advance self-assessment is not required.

Where a taxpayer is not required to notify HMRC of his chargeability to income tax or capital gains tax for a tax year (see **52.3** PENALTIES) because of the exclusion for cases where an NRCGT return including an advance self-assessment has been made, he is treated for tax purposes as having been required to make a self-assessment return under **58.3** above and the NRCGT return is then treated as that return (so that the normal provisions as to amendment, enquiries etc. apply). The return is treated as delivered on 31 January following the tax year or on an earlier date where a notice to that effect is given to HMRC by the taxpayer. Such notification must be made before 31 January following the tax year and must include a statement that the taxpayer considers the advance self-assessment to be an accurate self-assessment for the purposes of **58.6** above. The date on which the return is then treated as having been delivered is either the date the actual NRCGT return was delivered or, if later, the date on which notification was given. If the taxpayer makes a subsequent NRCGT return (i.e. a return for a disposal with a later date of completion) which relates to the tax year in question, that return is treated as amending the self-assessment treated as included in the original NRCGT return. Similar provisions apply to trustees.

With effect from 15 September 2016, an NRCGT return is not required (but the taxpayer may choose to make a return) where the disposal is a no gain/no loss disposal (see **9.6** ASSETS HELD ON **31** MARCH **1982**) or the grant of a lease at arm's length to an unconnected person for no premium. The Treasury may add or remove circumstances in which a return is not required by statutory instrument. Where the taxpayer chooses to make a return which is not required, there can be no penalty for failure to make a return within the time limit.

[*TMA 1970, ss 12ZA–12ZC, 12ZE–12ZI; FA 2015, Sch 7 para 43; FA 2016, s 91*].

See **52.5** PENALTIES for the penalty for failure to make a return and **52.8** PENALTIES for the penalty for errors in a return.

Options

Where the grant of an option binding the grantor to sell an interest in UK land is, on exercise, treated for CGT purposes as the same transaction as the sale (see **7.7** ASSETS) and both the grant and the transaction entered into by the grantor in fulfilment of his obligations under the option would be non-resident CGT disposals (if they were treated separately), the grantor must nevertheless make a return and any payment on account (see **51.3** PAYMENT OF TAX) in respect of the grant of the option. The consideration for the option is disregarded in calculating the amount of CGT notionally chargeable at the completion date of the deemed single transaction. [*TMA 1970, s 12ZD; FA 2015, Sch 7 para 43*].

Determination of residence status

Whether or not a disposal of a UK residential property interest is a non-resident CGT disposal so that an NRCGT return is required is determined as follows:

(a) The relevant residence condition at **41.26**(a)–(d) LAND is taken to be met if it is uncertain whether or not it will be met but it is reasonable to expect that it will be met.
(b) If it later becomes certain that the condition is not met, the disposal is treated as not being, and never having been, a non-resident CGT disposal (and any repayments or adjustments are made as necessary).
(c) If it is uncertain at the time of completion of a disposal whether the relevant residence condition at **41.26**(a)–(d) LAND is met but (a) above does not apply and it later becomes certain that the condition is met, the filing date for the NRCGT return is the 30th day following the day on which it becomes certain the condition is met.

[*TMA 1970, s 12ZJ; FA 2015, Sch 7 para 43*].

Amendments to an NRCGT return

A person may by notice to an HMRC officer amend an NRCGT return at any time within 12 months after the 31 January following the tax year.

At any time within nine months after the delivery of a person's NRCGT return, an HMRC officer may by notice to that person amend the return to correct obvious errors and omissions (whether of principle, arithmetical or otherwise) or anything else in the return that he has reason to believe is incorrect in the light of information available to him. Where the correction is required in consequence of an amendment by the taxpayer as above, the nine-month period begins immediately after the date of the taxpayer's amendment. The taxpayer has a legal right to reject an officer's correction, by notice within 30 days beginning with the date of the notice of correction.

[*TMA 1970, ss 12ZK, 12ZL; FA 2015, Sch 7 para 43*].

Enquiries into NRCGT returns

[58.21] An HMRC officer may enquire into an NRCGT return, and anything (including any claim or election) contained (or required to be contained) in it.

Notice of enquiry

The officer must give notice that he intends to carry out an enquiry (notice of enquiry) within whichever of the following periods is appropriate:

(a) in the case of a return delivered on or before 31 January following the tax year, the 12 months after the day on which the return was delivered;
(b) in the case of a return delivered after that date, the period ending with the 'quarter day' next following the first anniversary of the delivery date;
(c) in the case of a return amended under **58.20** above, the period ending with the 'quarter day' next following the first anniversary of the date of amendment.

For these purposes, the '*quarter days*' are 31 January, 30 April etc. A return cannot be enquired into more than once, except in consequence of an amendment (or further amendment). If notice under (c) above is given at a time when the deadline in (a) or (b) above, as the case may be, has expired or after an enquiry into the return has been fully completed, the enquiry is limited to matters affected by the amendment. The same applies if a partial closure notice has been issued (see **58.12** above) in relation to the matters to which the amendment relates.

[*TMA 1970, s 12ZM; FA 2015, Sch 7 para 43; F(No 2)A 2017, Sch 15 paras 5, 44*].

Information powers

HMRC's investigatory powers at **34.3–34.10** HMRC INVESTIGATORY POWERS can be used for the purposes of non-resident CGT. See in particular **34.5** for the restriction on those powers where an NRCGT return has been made.

Completion of enquiry

An enquiry is completed when an HMRC officer gives the taxpayer notice (a final closure notice) that he has completed his enquiries. As regards enquiries commenced on or after the date of Royal Assent to *F(No 2)A 2017*, or in progress on that date, an HMRC officer can issue a partial closure notice, which completes the enquiry insofar as it concerns the matters specified in the notice. The enquiry is not fully completed until a final closure notice has been issued to inform the taxpayer that the officer has completed his remaining enquiries. A partial or final closure notice takes effect when it is issued and must state the officer's conclusions and make the necessary amendments to the NRCGT return to give effect to those conclusions or state that no amendment is required.

During the course of an enquiry, the taxpayer may apply to the Appeal Tribunal for a direction requiring HMRC to issue a partial or final closure notice within a specified period, such application to be heard and determined in a similar manner to an appeal. The Tribunal must give the direction unless satisfied that there are reasonable grounds for not issuing the partial or final closure notice within a specified period. [*TMA 1970, s 28A; FA 2015, Sch 7 para 44; F(No 2)A 2017, Sch 15 paras 12, 44*].

See **5.2** APPEALS for right of appeal against any conclusion stated or amendment made by a partial or final closure notice.

Amendment of return during enquiry

If a return is amended by the taxpayer under **58.20** above while an enquiry is in progress in relation to any matter affected by the amendment, the amendment does not restrict the scope of the enquiry but may itself be taken into account in the enquiry. The amendment does not take effect to alter the amount notionally chargeable (see **58.20** above) until a partial closure notice is issued in relation to the matters to which the amendment relates or, if no such notice is issued, a final closure notice is issued. See **58.12** above for partial and final closure notices. The amendment may then be taken into account separately or, if the officer so states in the closure notice, in arriving at the amendments contained in that notice. It does not take effect if the officer concludes in the closure notice that the amendment is incorrect.

The above has effect where the enquiry begins on or after the date of Royal Assent to *F(No 2)A 2017* or is in progress on that date, and allows for the fact that such an enquiry may be partly completed by the issue of a partial closure notice. Previously, if a return was amended by the taxpayer while an enquiry into it was in progress, the amendment did not restrict the scope of the enquiry but could itself be taken into account in the enquiry. The amendment did not take effect to alter the amount notionally chargeable until the enquiry was completed.

[*TMA 1970, s 12ZN; FA 2015, Sch 7 para 43; F(No 2)A 2017, Sch 15 paras 6, 44*].

Determination of amount notionally chargeable where no NRCGT return made

[58.22] Where it appears to an HMRC officer that a person is required to make an NRCGT return containing an advance self-assessment (see 58.20 above) but no such return has been made by the filing date (i.e. the 30th day after the date of the completion of the disposal), the officer may make a determination, to the best of his information and belief, of the amount of CGT which should have been assessed in the return as the amount notionally chargeable (see 58.20 above). The officer must serve notice of the determination on the person concerned. Until it is superseded by an advance self-assessment in an NRCGT return, the determination is treated as if it were such an advance self-assessment and tax is payable accordingly. No determination may be made after the expiry of three years beginning with 31 January following the tax year.

A determination is automatically superseded by any advance self-assessment made based on information contained in an NRCGT return. Such advance self-assessment must be made within the three years beginning 31 January following the tax year or, if later, within 12 months beginning with the date of the determination. Any amount payable or repayable as a result of the supersession is deemed to have payable or repayable on or before the filing date. Any recovery proceedings commenced before the making of such an advance self-assessment may be continued in respect of so much of the amount charged by the advance self-assessment as is due and payable and has not been paid.

[*TMA 1970, ss 28G, 59AA(11)(12); FA 2015, Sch 7 para 45*].

Other returns

European Economic Interest Groupings

[58.23] A European Economic Interest Grouping (see 49.20 OVERSEAS MATTERS) registered in the UK or having an establishment there must make and deliver a return (through its manager or the individual representative of its manager) containing such information and accompanied by such accounts and statements as may be required by a notice given by the inspector. In the case of any other grouping, a return is required from any member of it resident in the UK, or, if none is, from any member. [*TMA 1970, s 12A*]. See **52.6** PENALTIES as regards non-compliance.

Hotels and boarding houses

[58.24] Certain details of all lodgers and persons resident in any dwelling-house, hostel, hotel, etc. must be given by the proprietor, if required by notice from the inspector given before 1 April 2012. [*TMA 1970, s 14; FA 2011, Sch 23 paras 51(2), 65*]. This provision is replaced with effect from 1 April 2012 by the new data-gathering power under *FA 2011, Sch 23*. See **34.17** HMRC INVESTIGATORY POWERS.

Issuing houses, stockbrokers, auctioneers, nominee shareholders etc.

[58.25] Certain details of assets dealt with from issuing houses, members of stock exchanges (but not jobbers or market makers), commodity clearing houses and auctioneers must be given together with a return of the parties to the transaction, if required by notice from the inspector given before 1 April 2012. [*TMA 1970, s 25; FA 2011, Sch 23 paras 51(2), 65*]. HMRC have published spreadsheet templates for making returns under this provision on their website (www.hmrc.gov.uk).

In respect of shares, securities and loan capital registered in the name of a person, that person must, if required by notice from the inspector issued before 1 April 2012 for the purpose of obtaining particulars of chargeable gains, state whether he is the beneficial owner thereof or otherwise provide the name and address of the persons on whose behalf he acts as nominee. [*TMA 1970, s 26; FA 2011, Sch 23 paras 51(2), 65*].

These provisions are replaced with effect from 1 April 2012 by the new data-gathering power under *FA 2011, Sch 23*. See **34.17** HMRC INVESTIGATORY POWERS.

Key points about returns

[58.26] Points to consider are as follows.

- The deadline for submitting self-assessment tax returns for individuals, partnerships and trustees is generally 31 January following the year of assessment for electronic returns or 31 October following the year of assessment for paper returns. These returns include details of income and allowances as well as capital gains.
- A company generally has twelve months after the end of its accounting period to submit a self-assessment return which would include any chargeable gains and allowable losses.

- The penalty regime for late filing of returns is being reformed across a range of taxes. The new rules have applied for income tax returns filed late since 2010/11. Although corresponding rules have been announced for corporation tax the commencement date has been delayed to enable corporate taxpayers to adjust to the requirements of iXBRL. Practitioners should ensure that they are familiar with the new rules which tend to apply higher automatic penalties. The new tax geared penalties are a percentage of tax due (tax payable) for a period, not tax outstanding.
- Capital gains only need reporting on a personal return if the chargeable gains (before losses) are less than the annual exempt amount and the proceeds for all disposals do not exceed four times that amount. For this purpose the following are not taken into account:
  (a) The disposal of exempt assets such as a principal private residence.
  (b) Transactions between spouses or civil partners.
- If the remittance basis of taxation is claimed the annual exempt amount is not generally available and so the above reporting limits do not apply. All disposals of chargeable assets must be disclosed.
- If there are net losses for the year a disclosure will be required whatever the level of proceeds.
- Returns can be amended within twelve months of the normal filing date and HMRC can raise an enquiry within twelve months of the date of delivery of a return if filed before the normal filing date. The enquiry window may be longer when the return is late.

59

Rollover Relief — Replacement of Business Assets

Introduction	**59.1**
Conditions for relief	**59.2**
Application of relief to particular traders	**59.3**
Qualifying assets	**59.4**
Other qualifying undertakings	**59.5**
Effect of relief	**59.6**
Interaction with other provisions	**59.7**
Partial relief	**59.8**
Depreciating assets	**59.9**
Groups of companies	**59.10**
Claims for relief	**59.11**
Key points	**59.12**

Cross-references. See **9.11** ASSETS HELD ON 31 MARCH **1982** for 50% relief on rolled over gains relating to an asset acquired before 31 March 1982; **22.32** EMPLOYEE SHARE SCHEMES for application of rollover relief in relation to certain disposals to employee share ownership trusts; **26.2** FURNISHED HOLIDAY ACCOMMODATION for application of rollover relief to such accommodation in the UK; **36** HOLD-OVER RELIEFS generally; **41.12** and **41.13** LAND for rollover relief on compulsory purchase of land and exchanges of joint interests in land (including milk and potato quotas in certain cases) respectively; **48.2** OFFSHORE SETTLEMENTS for disapplication of rollover relief where trustees cease to be UK-resident or liable to UK tax; **49.3**, **49.17** and **49.19** OVERSEAS MATTERS for restriction on rollover relief in certain cases.

Simon's Taxes. See C3.3.

Introduction

[59.1] Rollover relief enables traders and certain others (see **59.5** below) to defer chargeable gains on the disposal of qualifying assets used for business purposes where they invest the proceeds in other qualifying assets for use in the business. The replacement assets must normally be acquired within one year before or three years after the disposal of the old assets (see **59.2** below). The relief must be claimed (see **59.11** below).

There are nine classes of qualifying asset, including land, fixed plant and machinery and certain Lloyd's assets. Goodwill and certain agricultural and fishing quotas and payment entitlements are also qualifying assets for capital gains tax purposes, but following the introduction of the corporation tax intangible fixed assets regime (see **15.14** COMPANIES — CORPORATE FINANCE AND INTANGIBLES), these assets are not normally qualifying assets for corporation tax purposes. See **59.4** below.

The way in which relief is given depends on the nature of the new assets. If the new assets are not depreciating assets (see **59.9** below), the disposal consideration for the old assets is reduced to an amount which results in neither a gain nor a loss and the acquisition cost of the new assets is decreased by the amount of that reduction (see **59.6** below). If the new assets are depreciating assets, the gains on the old assets are not rolled over into the acquisition cost of the new assets but simply deferred until the earlier of the disposal of the new assets, their ceasing to be used for business purposes, or ten years after their acquisition (see **59.9** below). Partial relief is available in certain cases where the proceeds from the old assets are not fully reinvested or where the old assets were only partly used for business purposes or not used for business purposes for the whole of the period of ownership (see **59.8** below).

Groups of companies are able to claim rollover relief where the disposal is made by one group company and the acquisition by another. See **59.10** below.

Conditions for relief

[59.2] Rollover relief can be claimed where:

(a) a person carrying on a trade disposes of, or of his interest in, assets (the 'old assets') used, and used only, for the purposes of the trade throughout the period of ownership (excluding any period before 31 March 1982);

(b) he applies the consideration obtained for the disposal, within a specified period (see below), in acquiring other assets, or an interest in other assets (the 'new assets') which on the acquisition are taken into use, and used only, for the purposes of the trade; and

(c) the old assets and the new assets are within the classes of assets listed at **59.4** below.

[*TCGA 1992, s 152(1)(3)(9)*].

Partial relief is available in certain cases where the proceeds from the old assets are not fully reinvested or where the old assets were only partly used for business purposes or not used for business purposes for the whole of the period of ownership. See **59.8** below.

'*Trade*' has the same meaning as in the *Income Tax Acts*, but not so as to apply the provisions of the *Income Tax Acts* as to the circumstances in which, on a change in the persons carrying on a trade, a trade is to be regarded as discontinued, or as set up and commenced. [*TCGA 1992, s 158*]. '*Trade*' includes any venture in the nature of trade. [*ITA 2007, s 989*]. For discussion of the meaning of 'trade' for rollover relief purposes, see *CIR v Richmond and Jones (Re Loquitur Ltd)* Ch D 2003, 75 TC 77.

Commercial letting of 'furnished holiday accommodation' is treated as a trade for the purposes of the relief. See **26** FURNISHED HOLIDAY ACCOMMODATION. HMRC have indicated that both parties to a genuine share farming agreement may be considered to be carrying on a farming trade for taxation purposes (HMRC Business Income Manual BIM55075).

For the application of rollover relief to certain qualifying undertakings other than trades, see **59.5** below.

The old assets must actually be used for the trade in question. Any original intention for such use is ignored. Relief was refused, for example, where land was purchased on which it was proposed to build a factory for use in the taxpayer's trade but was sold without the factory being built (*Temperley v Visibell Ltd* Ch D 1973, 49 TC 129).

It is not normally necessary for the purposes of (b) above to establish a direct link between the actual disposal proceeds and their application: the taxpayer is simply required to reinvest an amount equal to the proceeds received (HMRC Capital Gains Manual CG60770). The Inland Revenue indicated in 1991 that there was no reason why in principle relief should not be available where the acquisition consideration is satisfied by the issue of shares by a company (Institute of Taxation TIR/11/91, 1991 STI 1097). They have also confirmed that relief is available where assets are exchanged (CCAB Statement TR 508 9 June 1983).

Use of new assets

Subject to the concession below, the new assets must be taken into trading use immediately on acquisition. Again any original intention to attempt at immediate use is ignored. See *Campbell Connelly & Co. Ltd v Barnett* CA 1993, 66 TC 380. On the authority of statements of Knox J in the Ch D in that case, HMRC consider that the time at which the asset must be taken into use is normally the time that any contracts are completed by conveyance or delivery and possession has been obtained. (HMRC Capital Gains Manual CG60830).

Where a new asset is not, on acquisition, immediately taken into trading use it will nevertheless qualify for relief by concession provided:

(i) the owner proposes to incur capital expenditure for the purpose of enhancing its value;
(ii) any work arising from such capital expenditure begins as soon as possible after acquisition, and is completed within a reasonable time;
(iii) on completion of the work the asset is taken into use for the purpose of the trade and for no other purpose; and
(iv) the asset is not let or used for any non-trading purpose in the period between acquisition and the time it is taken into use for the purposes of the trade.

Where a person acquires land with a building on it, or with the intention to construct a building on it, the land is treated as qualifying for the above concession provided that the building itself qualifies for relief whether under the above concession or otherwise and provided that the land is not let or used for any non-trading purpose between its acquisition and the time that both it and the building are taken into use for the purposes of the trade.

(HMRC Extra-Statutory Concession D24).

In *Steibelt v Paling* Ch D 1999, 71 TC 376, Sir Richard Scott V-C commented that on the facts of the case the taxpayer had failed to comply with condition (ii) above.

Tonnage tax regime

Rollover relief is not available to the extent that the new asset is used wholly and exclusively for the purposes of a shipping company's activities within the tonnage tax regime (see **25.17** EXEMPTIONS AND RELIEFS). If a new asset begins to be used for such purposes after rollover relief has been given, the rolled over gain becomes a chargeable gain, which is, however, deferred until the new asset is disposed of. [*FA 2000, Sch 22 para 67*].

Disposal and acquisition of same asset

Relief is not strictly available where there is a disposal and reacquisition of the same asset. By concession, however, where an asset is repurchased for purely commercial reasons after having been sold, HMRC will not object to a rollover relief claim on those grounds (HMRC Extra-Statutory Concession D16). This concessional treatment also applies to partnership changes which result in reacquisition of fractional shares in partnership assets. (HMRC Capital Gains Manual CG60820).

In *Watton v Tippett* CA 1997, 69 TC 491, a trader made a part disposal of some business premises and attempted unsuccessfully to roll over the gain against the previous acquisition of the part of those premises still retained. It was held that the premises had been acquired as, and until the part disposal continued to be, a single asset, and that the acquisition cost could not be divided between the part of the premises sold and the part retained and treated as having been given for two separate assets.

Proceeds used to enhance or acquire further interest in existing asset

Where the proceeds from the disposal of an old asset are used to enhance the value of other assets already held, the expenditure is treated for rollover relief purposes (and for the purposes of *TCGA 1992, Sch 4* (deferred charges on gains before 31 March 1982; see **9.11** ASSETS HELD ON 31 MARCH **1982**)) as incurred in acquiring other assets provided the other assets are used only for the purposes of the trade or, on completion of the enhancement work, the assets are immediately taken into use and used only for the purposes of the trade. (HMRC Extra-Statutory Concession D22). Similar treatment is given where a further interest is acquired in another asset which is already in use for the purposes of the trade (HMRC Extra-Statutory Concession D25).

Time limit for replacement of assets

The acquisition of the new assets must take place within one year before, or three years after, the disposal of the old assets or at such later or earlier time as HMRC allow by notice. It is sufficient if an unconditional contract for acquisition is entered into within the specified periods, but if, in such circumstances, relief is given on a provisional basis, any necessary adjustments can be made, without time limit, if the contract is not completed. [*TCGA 1992, s 152(3)(4)*].

HMRC's practice is to extend the above time limits where the trader can show that he had a firm intention to acquire new assets within the time limit but was prevented from doing so by circumstances outside his control and that he acted as soon as he reasonably could after ceasing to be so prevented (HMRC Capital Gains Manual CG60640). The non-exercise of HMRC's statutory discretion to extend the time limit may be challenged by judicial review but cannot be reviewed by the Appeal Commissioners (*Steibelt v Paling* Ch D 1999, 71 TC 376). Such a challenge was unsuccessful in *R (oao Barnett) v CIR* QB 2003, [2004] STC 763.

For corporation tax purposes, where the disposal occurs after 31 March 2002 and is of an asset within Classes 4 to 7 at **59.4** below, the acquisition of the new asset must be made before that date (and within twelve months before the disposal). [*FA 2002, s 84(1), Sch 29 para 132(1)*].

Taxpayer becoming non-resident before acquisition of new asset

HMRC accept that a rollover relief can be validly made where the taxpayer has become neither resident nor ordinarily resident in the UK before the acquisition of the new assets. (HMRC Capital Gains Manual CG60270). Note, however, the restrictions in **48.2** OFFSHORE SETTLEMENTS and **49.3**, **49.17** and **49.19** OVERSEAS MATTERS in certain cases.

Anti-avoidance

Relief is denied if the acquisition of the new assets was made wholly or partly for the purpose of realising a gain from their subsequent disposal. [*TCGA 1992, s 152(5)*]. See also **4.19** ANTI-AVOIDANCE for the charge arising where concessions involving deferral of gains are abused, including those relating to rollover relief.

Application of relief to particular traders

[59.3] Rollover relief applies as follows to certain types of trader.

Taxpayer with more than one trade

Rollover relief is available to a person who, either successively or at the same time, carries on two or more trades as if both or all of them were a single trade. [*TCGA 1992, s 152(8)*].

Where a trader ceases carrying on one trade and, within three years, commences carrying on another, HMRC will treat the trades as carried on 'successively'. If the disposal or acquisition takes place in the intervening period, relief will be restricted in respect of the period during which the assets disposed of were not used for trade purposes (see **59.8** below), and will be conditional on the replacement assets not being used or leased for any purpose prior to commencement of the new trade, and on their being taken into use for the purposes of the new trade on its commencement (HMRC Statement of Practice 8/81). In *Steibelt v Paling* Ch D 1999, 71 TC 376, a nine-year gap between trades meant that they could not be said to be carried on successively.

Trade carried on by individual's personal company

Where:

(i) the person disposing of the old assets and acquiring the new assets is an individual, and
(ii) the trade or trades in question are carried on not by that individual but by a company, which, both at the time of disposal and at the time of the acquisition referred to in (i) above, is his 'personal company',

then, for rollover relief purposes, references to the person carrying on the trade include a reference to that individual.

For this purpose, an individual's '*personal company*' is a company the voting rights in which are 'exercisable', as to not less than 5%, by that individual. ('*Exercisable*' means capable of being exercised, whether in fact exercised (*Hepworth v Smith* Ch D 1981, 54 TC 396).) See also *Boparan v HMRC* (Sp C 587), [2007] SSCD 297.

[*TCGA 1992, s 157*].

Assets must be disposed of and acquired by the individual for use by the same personal company and the provisions of *TCGA 1992, s 175(1)* (see **59.10** below) do not apply to treat all companies within a group as one taxable entity for this purpose. The payment of rent to the individual by the company concerned for the use of property will not debar relief under *TCGA 1992, s 157*. (HMRC Capital Gains Manual CG61250).

Partnerships

Relief is available to the owner of assets let to a trading or professional partnership of which he is a member, provided they are used for the purposes of the partnership's trade or profession (HMRC Statement of Practice D11). See also **50.9** PARTNERSHIPS as regards disposals by partners and **50.15** as regards mergers of partnerships and **59.10** below for partnerships involving a member of a group of companies.

Where land or other assets used for the purposes of a trade carried on in partnership are partitioned by the partners, the asset acquired is treated as a newly acquired asset provided the partnership is dissolved immediately thereafter (HMRC Extra-Statutory Concession D23).

Limited liability partnerships (LLPs)

Where a member of an LLP (see **50.18** PARTNERSHIPS) has rolled over a gain into an LLP asset and, at a later time but before any disposal of the asset, the transparency treatment afforded by *TCGA 1992, s 59A(1)* ceases to apply to the LLP (for example, by virtue of its going into liquidation), a chargeable gain equal to the amount rolled over is treated as accruing to the member immediately before that later time. Similarly, a postponed gain under **59.9** below (where the LLP asset is a depreciating asset) is brought back into charge immediately before that time. [*TCGA 1992, s 156A*]. In the absence of such a rule, the rolled over or postponed gain would have fallen out of charge as a result of the tax treatment of an LLP in liquidation.

Companies

For the application of the relief to groups of companies, see **59.10** below.

Rollover relief is not available where one company makes a disposal and an associated company makes an acquisition (*Joseph Carter & Sons Ltd v Baird; Wear Ironmongers & Sons Ltd v Baird* Ch D 1998, 72 TC 303).

Where a company ceases to be a member of a group such that a gain (a 'degrouping charge') arises under *TCGA 1992, s 179* (see **29.7** GROUPS OF COMPANIES) on a deemed sale and reacquisition of an asset, and the asset is a qualifying asset for rollover relief purposes, the company may claim rollover relief if it acquires a new qualifying asset. The rollover relief rules described in this chapter apply in modified form.

Intangible fixed assets

Following the introduction of the intangible assets regime in *FA 2002* (see **15.14** COMPANIES — CORPORATE FINANCE AND INTANGIBLES), the rollover relief provisions are amended for corporation tax purposes only.

- **Disposals.** A gain on the disposal on or after 1 April 2002 of an asset that is both an intangible fixed asset and within one of the classes of qualifying assets at **59.4** below may qualify for rollover relief only where the acquisition of the new asset occurs before that date (and within twelve months before the disposal). As a result, rollover relief normally ceases to be available for disposals of intangible fixed assets after 31 March 2003, whether or not the asset falls within the intangible assets regime. After that time, the acquisition of the new asset cannot be made both within twelve months prior to the disposal and before 1 April 2002. Disposals of intangible fixed assets (whether or not within one of the classes of qualifying assets) excluded from the intangible assets regime by virtue of its commencement rules do, however, qualify for relief under the intangible fixed assets rollover relief provisions (see now *CTA 2009, ss 898, 899*), which are modified for this purpose. Where relief is claimed in such a case, then in calculating the chargeable gain on the disposal of the asset, the consideration is treated as reduced by the amount available for relief. Note that intangible asset rollover relief is an entirely separate relief from the capital gains relief; for details of the relief see Tolley's Corporation Tax under Intangible Assets. A gain on a disposal on or after 1 April 2002 but before 1 April 2003 of an intangible fixed asset which is also within one of the classes of qualifying assets may potentially qualify for both capital gains rollover relief (where a new asset is acquired before 1 April 2002) and intangible asset rollover relief (where a 'new asset' is acquired on or after 1 April 2002) (provided in either case that all the appropriate conditions are met). Where this is the case, the company may claim relief under either set of provisions or partly under one and partly under the other.
- **Acquisitions.** Assets within Classes 4 to 7 and 9 at **59.4** below and acquired on or after 1 April 2002 are not qualifying assets for corporation tax purposes if they are 'chargeable intangible assets'. An asset is a '*chargeable intangible asset*' if a gain on its realisation would

give rise to a credit falling to be brought into account under the intangible assets regime. Because of a drafting error in *TCGA 1992, s 156ZB* (added by *CTA 2009*), it became in principle possible to claim rollover relief on or after 1 April 2009 on the disposal of a tangible asset where the proceeds were reinvested in a chargeable intangible asset. If such a claim were made, no adjustment could be required to be made to the acquisition cost of the intangible asset. The law has now been amended, with effect for claims made on or after 19 March 2014, to confirm that assets within Classes 4 to 7 and 9 at **59.4** below are not qualifying assets for corporation tax purposes if they are 'chargeable intangible assets'. In any cases where a claim to rollover relief was made on or after 1 April 2009 and before 20 March 2014, the written-down value of the intangible asset is treated as reduced on 19 March 2014 by the amount of the rollover relief given.

[*TCGA 1992, ss 156ZA, 156ZB; CTA 2009, s 870A; FA 2014, s 62*].

Qualifying assets

[59.4] Subject to the overriding requirement of use for the purposes of a trade (see **59.2** above), qualifying assets are divided into the classes listed below (the Treasury having power to specify additional classes or amend the existing classes). Further comment on certain classes is made after the list under relevant headings. Both the old and the new assets must fall within these classes though not necessarily within the same class.

For capital gains tax purposes, and for corporation tax purposes for acquisitions before 1 April 2002, the classes are as follows.

(1) Assets within (a) and (b) below.
  (a) Land, buildings (including parts thereof) and any permanent or semi-permanent structures in the nature of buildings, all such assets being occupied (as well as used) only for the purposes of the trade.
  (b) Fixed plant or machinery (see *Williams v Evans* 2 Ch D, 1982, 59 TC 509) which does not form part of a building or of a permanent or semi-permanent structure in the nature of a building.

(2) Ships, aircraft and hovercraft.

(3) Satellites, space stations and spacecraft (including launch vehicles).

(4) Goodwill.

(5) Assets within (a) and (b) below.
  (a) 'Milk quotas'; i.e. rights to sell dairy produce without liability to pay milk levy, or to deliver dairy produce without liability to pay a milk levy contribution (see also **7.9** ASSETS).
  (b) 'Potato quotas'; i.e. rights to produce potatoes without liability to pay more than the ordinary contribution to the Potato Marketing Board's fund.

(6) 'Ewe and suckler cow premium quotas', i.e. rights in respect of any ewes or suckler cows to receive payments by way of any subsidy entitlement to which is determined by reference to limits contained in a European Community instrument.

(7) Fish quota, i.e. an allocation of quota to catch fish stocks, which derives from the Total Allowable Catches set in pursuance of specified European Community instruments (see also below).

(a) Syndicate rights of an individual (i.e. non-corporate) underwriting member of Lloyd's (see **69.6** UNDERWRITERS AT LLOYD'S).

(b) Syndicate rights of an individual (i.e. non-corporate) underwriting member of Lloyd's held through a Members' Agent Pooling Arrangement (MAPA) and treated by *FA 1999, s 82* as a single asset (see **69.7** UNDERWRITERS AT LLOYD'S).

(a) Payment entitlements under the single payment scheme, i.e. the scheme of income support for farmers under Title III of EC Council Regulation 73/2009 (previously EC Council Regulation 1782/2003).

(b) Where the disposal of the old asset or acquisition of the new asset is on or after 20 December 2013, payment entitlements under the basic payment scheme, i.e. the scheme of income support for farmers under European Parliament and Council Regulation 1307/2013.

For corporation tax purposes, Classes 4 to 7 and 9 do not apply as regards the acquisition on or after 1 April 2002 of new assets that are 'chargeable intangible assets' for the purposes of the intangible fixed assets regime (see **59.3** above).

[*TCGA 1992, ss 155, 156ZB; FA 2012, s 37(1)(4); FA 2014, s 61; SI 1999 No 564; SI 2005 No 409*].

Land and buildings

Land and buildings are treated as separate assets for rollover relief purposes (HMRC Capital Gains Manual CG60970).

Where the trade is one of dealing in or developing land or of providing services for the occupier of land in which the trader has an interest, the trader's disposal of the land does not qualify for relief. However, this does not apply where a profit on the sale of any land held for the purposes of a trade of dealing in or developing land would not form part of the trading profits. [*TCGA 1992, s 156(1)–(3)*]. See also **26** FURNISHED HOLIDAY ACCOMMODATION.

A lessor of tied premises, within *CTA 2009, s 42* or *ITTOIA 2005, s 19*, is treated as occupying (as well as using) those premises for the purposes of the trade (to the extent that the conditions of *CTA 2009, s 42(1)* or *ITTOIA 2005, s 19(1)* are met in relation to the premises). [*TCGA 1992, s 156(4)*].

Where a building is rebuilt after having been destroyed by fire, gains on other assets may be rolled over into the cost of rebuilding (subject to any claim made under *TCGA 1992, s 23* in respect of insurance proceeds, see **10.3** and **10.4** CAPITAL SUMS DERIVED FROM ASSETS and CCAB Statement TR 508 9 June 1983).

In *Anderton v Lamb* Ch D 1980, 55 TC 1, it was held that houses occupied by farm employees were not occupied for the purposes of the business, and, therefore, were not qualifying assets. The taxpayer appealed to the CA where the appeal was stayed on agreed terms: see 1982 STI 179.

An assignment, for a capital sum, of the right to receive rental income for a fixed period (a 'rent factoring' transaction) was held to be a part disposal of the property in question, producing a chargeable gain, in this case eligible for rollover relief (*CIR v John Lewis Properties plc* CA, [2003] STC 117), but note that, under subsequent legislation, rent factoring receipts are now chargeable as income (see Tolley's Corporation Tax under Property Income).

Options over land

Provided relief would be due on the disposal of the underlying land which is the subject of the grant of an option, HMRC are prepared to ignore the separate disposal treatment of *TCGA 1992, s 144(1)* so that any gain arising on the grant of the option can be the subject of a rollover relief claim. HMRC point out that relief will only be obtained if the land continues to be occupied and used for the claimant's trade (Revenue Tax Bulletin, February 1992, p 13). For options generally, see **7.7** ASSETS.

Goodwill

See HMRC Capital Gains Manual CG68000–68330 for consideration of what constitutes goodwill. In *Balloon Promotions Ltd v Wilson* (Sp C 524) [2006] SSCD 167 the Special Commissioner questioned the applicability of HMRC's then approach to goodwill. HMRC have subsequently published their view on the implications of this case in HMRC Tax Bulletin June 2006 pp 1291, 1292 and rewritten their internal guidance accordingly. See also HMRC Guidance Note, 30 January 2009, which describes HMRC's approach to the apportionment of goodwill where a business is sold as a going concern and the assets sold include a 'trade related property' such as a public house, hotel, petrol station, restaurant or care home.

See also *Kirby v Thorn EMI plc* CA 1987, 60 TC 519, and *Mertrux Ltd v HMRC* CA, [2013] STC 2199.

Fish quota

These are amounts of various types of fish that are allocated by the EU to the UK and sub-allocated to UK fishermen according to rules prescribed by the Fisheries Departments. They are one of a number of items that may be involved in a disposal of a fishing vessel (and may be disposed of separately in certain circumstances). The vessel itself is a qualifying asset for rollover relief. A fishing vessel licence and a 'track record' (being the amount of particular stocks of fish caught in previous years) are separate chargeable assets; each is treated as constituting goodwill and thus eligible for rollover relief in its own right. Fish quota is also a separate chargeable asset but is not regarded as goodwill. However, prior to the addition of fish quota to the above classes of qualifying assets, the Revenue concession treated sales of fish quota as qualifying for rollover relief on a similar basis as a licence and track record. (Revenue Press Release 2 March 1999).

Single payment scheme

Payments under the single payment scheme ceased in 2014 and were replaced by payments under the basic payment scheme from 1 January 2015 (Treasury Explanatory Notes to the 2014 Finance Bill).

See generally HMRC Tax Bulletin, Special Edition June 2005.

Other qualifying undertakings

[59.5] Rollover relief applies with necessary modifications to the following activities as it applies to a trade.

(a) The discharge of the functions of a public authority.
(b) The occupation of woodlands where the woodlands are managed by the occupier on a commercial basis and with a view to the realisation of profits.
(c) A profession, vocation, office or employment.
(d) Such of the activities of a body of persons whose activities are carried on otherwise than for profit and are wholly or mainly directed to the protection or promotion of the interests of its members in the carrying on of their trade or profession as are so directed.
(e) The activities of an unincorporated association or other body chargeable to corporation tax, being a body not established for profit whose activities are wholly or mainly carried on otherwise than for profit, but in the case of assets within (1)(a) in **59.4** above only if they are both occupied and used by the body, and in the case of other assets only if they are used by the body.
(f) The activities of a company owned by an association or body within (e) above (the '*parent body*'), but in the case of assets within 1.(a) in **59.4** above only if they are both occupied and used by the parent body, and in the case of other assets only if they are used by the parent body. For this purpose, a parent body owns a company if it holds at least 90% of the ordinary share capital, is beneficially entitled at least 90% of the profits available for distribution to equity holders and would be so entitled on a winding up to at least 90% of the assets available for distribution to equity holders. Note that, for disposals before 6 April 2009, this activity qualifies only by concession (HMRC Extra-Statutory Concession D15).

'Profession', 'vocation', 'office' and 'employment' have the same meanings as in the Income Tax Acts.

[*TCGA 1992, s 158; SI 2009 No 730, Art 6*].

If land or a building is owned by an employee or office-holder but is made available to the employer for general use in his trade, the employee etc. may nonetheless satisfy the occupation test of *TCGA 1992, s 155* (see **59.4** above at (1)) provided the employer does not make any payment (or give other consideration) for his use of the property nor otherwise occupy it under a lease or tenancy. The qualifying use of assets by an employee etc. for the purposes of *TCGA 1992, s 152* (see **59.1** above) will include any use or operation of those assets by him, in the course of performing the duties of his employment or office, as directed by the employer (HMRC Statement of Practice 5/86). The practice may be compared with the relief available under *TCGA 1992, s 157* (see **59.3** above) where the trade is carried on by the individual's personal company, although in relation to SP 5/86 consideration passing or the existence of a lease or tenancy would deny relief.

Effect of relief

[59.6] Where the conditions at **59.2**(a)–(c) above are met and the taxpayer makes a claim (see **59.11** below), he is treated for capital gains purposes:

(a) as if the consideration for the disposal of, or of the interest in, the old assets were (if otherwise of a greater amount or value) of such an amount as would secure that on the disposal neither a gain nor a loss accrues to him, and

(b) as if the amount or value of the consideration for the acquisition of, or of the interest in, the new assets were reduced by the excess of the amount or value of the actual consideration for the disposal of, or of the interest in, the old assets over the amount of the consideration which he is treated as receiving under (a) above.

This treatment does not affect the treatment for capital gains purposes of the other party to the transaction involving the old assets, or of the other party to the transaction involving the new assets.

Where (a) above applies to exclude a gain which, in consequence of *TCGA 1992, Sch 2* (ASSETS HELD ON 6 APRIL **1965** (8)), is not all chargeable gain, the amount of the reduction to be made under (b) above is the amount of the chargeable gain, and not the whole amount of the gain.

[*TCGA 1992, s 152(1)(2)(9)*].

For partial relief where the proceeds from the old assets are not fully reinvested or where the old assets were only partly used for business purposes or not used for business purposes for the whole of the period of ownership, see **59.8** below. For the effect of the relief where the new assets are depreciating assets, see **59.9** below.

Example

L Ltd carries on a vehicle repair business. In December 2003 it sells a workshop for £90,000 net of costs. The workshop had cost £45,000 inclusive in April 1995. A new workshop is purchased for £144,000 (including incidental costs of acquisition) in January 2005 and is sold for £168,000 in January 2018.

Indexation factors:	April 1995 to December 2003	0.232
	January 2005 to January 2018 (estimated)	0.438

	£
Allowable cost of original workshop	45,000
Indexation allowance £45,000 × 0.232	10,440
	55,440

	£
Actual disposal consideration	90,000
Chargeable gain rolled over	£34,560
Cost of new workshop	144,000
Deduct amount rolled over	34,560
Deemed allowable cost	£109,440
Disposal consideration, replacement workshop	168,000
Allowable cost	109,440
Unindexed gain	58,560
Indexation allowance £109,440 × 0.438	47,935
Chargeable gain	£10,625

Interaction with other provisions

[59.7] Any provision which fixes the amount of consideration deemed to be given for the acquisition or disposal of assets is applied before operating the relief. [*TCGA 1992, s 152(10)*]. However, the relief is not affected by the fact that the new asset may have attracted a grant such as to reduce the expenditure allowable on a subsequent disposal — see **16.13**(c) COMPUTATATION OF GAINS AND LOSSES (*Wardhaugh v Penrith Rugby Union Football Club* Ch D 2002, 74 TC 499). The Revenue indicated that in its view gifts of assets are within *TCGA 1992, s 152(10)*. (Institute of Taxation TIR/11/91, 1991 STI 1097).

HMRC accept that rollover relief can be claimed where the disposal of the old assets is a deemed disposal, for example, under either *TCGA 1992, s 22* (see **10.2** CAPITAL SUMS DERIVED FROM ASSETS) or *TCGA 1992, s 161(1)* (asset appropriated from capital to trading stock — see **16.9** COMPUTATION OF GAINS AND LOSSES). They also accept that relief can be claimed where the acquisition of the new assets is a deemed acquisition. Relief is not, however, available where there is a deemed disposal and re-acquisition of the same asset. (HMRC Capital Gains Manual CG60790).

Although relief under *TCGA 1992, s 162* (transfer of a business to a company — see **37.2** INCORPORATION AND DISINCORPORATION RELIEFS) is mandatory (unless disapplied by election — see **37.3**), a valid claim for rollover relief takes precedence (HMRC Capital Gains Manual CG61560).

Partial relief

[59.8] Partial rollover relief is available in the following circumstances.

Disposal consideration not reinvested in full

Partial rollover relief is available where not all of the amount or value of the consideration received for the disposal of the old assets is applied in acquiring the new assets. Provided that the part of the disposal consideration not applied in acquiring the new assets is less than the amount of the gain (whether all chargeable gain or not) otherwise accruing on the disposal of the old assets, the claimant is treated for capital gains purposes:

(a) as if the gain accruing on the disposal of the old assets were reduced to the amount of the said part, and

(b) as if the amount or value of the consideration for the acquisition of the new assets were reduced by the amount by which the gain is reduced in (a) above.

If not all the gain is a chargeable gain, (a) above applies but with a proportionate reduction in the amount of the chargeable gain, and in (b) above the reduction in consideration is the amount by which the chargeable gain is proportionately reduced. Neither (a) nor (b) above affects the capital gains treatment of the other parties to the transactions involving the old and new assets. [*TCGA 1992, s 153*].

Only part of building or structure used for trade purposes. If, over the period of ownership (excluding any period before 31 March 1982) or any substantial part of the period of ownership, part of a building or structure is, and part is not, used for the purposes of a trade, rollover relief applies as if the part so used, with any land occupied for purposes ancillary to the occupation and use of that part of the building or structure, were a separate asset, and subject to any necessary apportionments of consideration for an acquisition or disposal of the building or structure and other land. [*TCGA 1992, s 152(6)(9)*].

See Revenue Tax Bulletin, October 1994, p 166 for further discussion on partial relief.

Where the taxpayer acquires an undivided share in the new asset which is only partly used for trade purposes, relief is limited to the proportion so used of the individual's undivided share of the asset (*Tod v Mudd* Ch D 1986, 60 TC 237).

Old assets not used for trade purposes throughout period of ownership

If the old assets were not used for the purposes of the trade throughout the period of ownership (excluding any period before 31 March 1982) rollover relief applies as if a part of the asset representing its use for the purposes of the trade having regard to the time and extent to which it was, and was not, used for those purposes, were a separate asset which had been wholly used for the purposes of the trade, and this treatment applies in relation to that part subject to any necessary apportionment of consideration for an acquisition or disposal of the asset. [*TCGA 1992, s 152(7)(9)*].

Apportionment

Without prejudice to *TCGA 1992, s 52(4)* (just and reasonable apportionments of consideration and expenditure; see **16.5** COMPUTATION OF GAINS AND LOSSES), where consideration is given for the acquisition or disposal of assets some or part of which are assets in relation to which a rollover relief claim applies, and some or part of which are not, the consideration is apportioned in such manner as is just and reasonable. [*TCGA 1992, s 152(11)*].

Examples

(a) In 1995, X purchased a factory for £40,000. It was used and occupied entirely for carrying on his trade until sold for £100,000 in October 2017. In the same month X bought another factory for £120,000 which was immediately used and occupied for carrying on a new trade carried on by him. He claimed rollover relief, computed as follows.

	£
Proceeds of sale of factory 1	100,000
Allowable expenditure on factory 1	40,000
Chargeable gain eligible to be rolled over	£60,000
Cost of factory 2	120,000
Rolled-over gain	60,000
Base cost for factory 2 on subsequent disposal	£60,000

(b) Facts as in (a) above, except factory 2 is bought for £90,000. The part of the £100,000 disposal consideration of factory 1 which is not applied in acquiring factory 2 is £10,000. This is less than the gain otherwise arising on the disposal of factory 1 (£60,000). The gain deemed to arise on the disposal of factory 1 is therefore £10,000. The gain so arising has therefore been reduced by £50,000, with the result that this amount is deducted from the £90,000 consideration given for factory 2, and so producing a base cost of £40,000 on a subsequent disposal.

(c) In September 2017, Y purchased a new factory for £100,000, having sold his old one in the same month for £52,000. The original factory had been bought in September 2007 for £20,000 but had only been used for his trade since September 2009. He claimed rollover relief. It is accepted that one-quarter of the new factory is not used for trade purposes.

	£
Proceeds of sale of old factory	52,000
Cost of old factory	20,000
Chargeable gain	£32,000

$$\frac{\text{Period of trading use of old asset}}{\text{Period of ownership}} = \frac{8\text{years}}{10\text{years}}$$

Gain on old asset eligible for relief	
£32,000 × $^8/_{10}$	£25,600
Cost of qualifying part of new factory	
($^3/_4$ × £100,000)	75,000
Rolled-over gain	25,600
Base cost of qualifying part of new factory	£49,400

The unrelieved gain of £6,400 (£32,000 – £25,600) is brought into charge on the disposal of the old factory. The base cost of the non-qualifying part of the new factory, treated as separate, is £25,000.

Depreciating assets

[59.9] Where rollover relief is claimed and the new asset is a 'depreciating asset', the gain on the disposal of the old asset is not deducted from the acquisition consideration of the new asset, but held over until ten years after the time of acquisition of the new asset, or until the new asset is disposed of, or until the new asset ceases to be used for the trade, whichever is the sooner. When the relevant event occurs, the held-over gain becomes chargeable as a capital gain. For corporation tax purposes and, for disposals before 6 April 2008, for capital gains tax purposes, however, the held-over gain is not brought into charge under this provision in consequence of an event after 5 April 1988 if its application would be directly attributable to the disposal of an asset before 1 April 1982. [*TCGA 1992, s 154(1)(2)(7), Sch 4 paras A1, 4(5)*].

If, however, not later than the time when the held-over gain would be brought into charge, a further asset is acquired which is not a depreciating asset, the trader may claim rollover relief as if it had been acquired within the time limits of *TCGA 1992, s 152(3)* for the application of the proceeds of the disposal of the old asset, the depreciating asset being effectively disregarded. The trader may claim relief if only part of the proceeds can be treated in this way, the balance remaining held over until crystallisation by virtue of one of the events specified. [*TCGA 1992, s 154(4)–(6)*].

A gain which has been held over under *TCGA 1992, s 154* will crystallise on a disposal even where the disposal concerned is within *TCGA 1992, s 162* (INCORPORATION AND DISINCORPORATION RELIEFS **37**) (Tolley's Practical Tax Newsletter 1985 p 139).

See **59.3** above for a special rule where the new asset is held by a limited liability partnership at the time of its going into liquidation.

Meaning of 'depreciating asset'

For the above purposes, an asset is a '*depreciating asset*' if, at the time of acquisition, it is a WASTING ASSET (**72**) or will become so within ten years beginning at that time.

A building constructed on leasehold land where the lease has less than 60 years to run at the time of construction is considered by HMRC to be a depreciating asset. This is despite the treatment of land and buildings as separate assets for rollover relief purposes (and contrary to the general rule for land as in **41.2** LAND).

If, as contemplated by *TCGA 1992, s 155*, an item of fixed plant or machinery has effectively become a part of a building or structure, it will be so treated for rollover relief purposes, with the result that such assets acquired for installation in a building etc. then held freehold or on a lease with more than 60 years to run will not be treated as depreciating assets. Subject to this, because an item of plant and machinery is always to be treated as being a wasting asset (see **72.2** WASTING ASSETS), it will also be treated as a depreciating asset. Deciding whether an item of fixed plant or machinery has become part of a building etc.

will normally be done by reference to the size and nature of the item in question, how it is attached to the building and whether damage to the fabric of the building would be caused if the item was removed (Revenue Tax Bulletin May 1993 p 73).

Milk quota (see **7.9** ASSETS) is not regarded by HMRC as a wasting asset (HMRC Capital Gains Manual CG77940).

Death of trader

By concession, where a held-over gain would otherwise be brought into charge on a cessation of trading use due to the trader's death before 6 April 2016, no charge to tax will arise (HMRC Extra-Statutory Concession D45).

Cross-border mergers

A transfer of the new asset or of shares in a company which holds the new asset as part of the process of a cross-border merger to which *TCGA 1992, s 140E* (European cross-border mergers: assets left within UK charge to tax — see **49.15** OVERSEAS MATTERS) applies does not bring the held-over gain into charge under the above provisions. In such circumstances, if the transferee holds the new asset it is treated as if it had claimed the rollover relief. If the transferee holds shares in the company which holds the new asset, *TCGA 1992, s 175* (see **59.10** below) applies as if the transferee's group were the same group as any group of which the company claiming the rollover relief was a member before the merger. [*TCGA 1992, s 154(2A)(2C); SI 2007 No 3186, Sch 2 para 6*].

Where, as part of the process of a cross-border merger to which *TCGA 1992, s 140E* applies, the transferee becomes a member of a group of which a company which has claimed rollover relief in respect of a wasting asset is a member, *TCGA 1992, s 175* (see **59.10** below) applies for the purposes of determining when the held-over gain is brought into charge as if the group of which the transferee is a member were the same group as the group of which the claimant was a member before the merger. [*TCGA 1992, s 154(2B)(2C); SI 2007 No 3186, Sch 2 para 6*].

The above cross-border merger provisions apply also to the transfer of an asset on or after 1 January 2007 in circumstances where *TCGA 1992, s 140A* (transfer or division of UK business between companies in different EC member states — see **49.13** OVERSEAS MATTERS) applies (with references to a merger being treated as references to the transfer). [*TCGA 1992, s 154(2D); SI 2007 No 3186, Sch 1 para 8*].

Example

In March 2013, a father and son partnership carrying on a car dealing trade sold a freehold showroom for £400,000 realising a chargeable gain (after indexation) of £190,000. On 30 June 2013, the firm purchased for £450,000 the remaining term of a lease due to expire on 30 June 2043 and used the premises as a new showroom. The whole of the gain on the old asset was held over under *TCGA 1992, s 154* on the acquisition of the new asset. In consequence of the father's decision to retire from the business and the resulting need to downsize the operation, the firm assigns the lease for £490,000 on 1 July 2017.

The chargeable gains to be apportioned between the two partners for 2017/18 are as follows

	£	£
Proceeds of assignment		490,000
Cost (see note (a))	450,000	
Deduct Wasted $\frac{87.330 - 82.496}{87.330} \times £450,000$	24,909	425,091
Chargeable gain 2017/18		£64,909
Held-over gain becoming chargeable under *TCGA 1992, s 154(2)(a)*		£190,000

Note to the example

(a) The gain is deferred as opposed to being rolled over and does not reduce the cost of the new asset.

Groups of companies

[59.10] Cross-reference.

For rollover relief purposes, all the trades carried on by members of a group of companies (within **29.2** GROUPS OF COMPANIES) are treated as a single trade. Any trade carried on by a non-UK resident company otherwise than in the UK through a permanent establishment or, for accounting periods beginning before 1 January 2003, through a branch or agency is, however, excluded. Acquisitions as a group member by a 'dual resident investing company' within *ICTA 1988, s 404* are excluded from this treatment. [*TCGA 1992, s 175(1)(1A)(2)*].

Where there is a disposal by a member of a group of companies and an acquisition by another member of the same group and both companies make a claim, then for rollover relief purposes, the companies are treated as if they were the same person. The following conditions must be met:

- either the company making the disposal is UK-resident at the time of disposal or the assets in question are 'chargeable assets' in relation to that company immediately before that time; and
- either the acquiring company is UK-resident at the time of acquisition or the assets are 'chargeable assets' in relation to that company immediately after that time.

For these purposes, an asset is a 'chargeable asset' in relation to a company at a particular time if, on a disposal by that company at that time, any gain would be a chargeable gain and would be within the charge to corporation tax by virtue of *TCGA 1992, s 10B* (non-UK resident company trading in the UK through a permanent establishment — see **49.3** OVERSEAS MATTERS.

Rollover relief is also available where a non-trading member of a group makes a disposal or acquisition of assets used only for trading purposes by other members of the same group.

However, rollover relief will not apply where there is an acquisition of new assets by a member of a group from another member of that group resulting from a disposal within the no gain/no loss provisions (see **9.6** ASSETS HELD ON 31 MARCH **1982**) or one where, under *TCGA 1992, ss 195B, 195C* or *195E* (oil licence swaps) the disposal gives rise to neither a gain nor a loss.

[*TCGA 1992, s 175(2A)–(2C)*].

Where the new asset is a depreciating asset, *TCGA 1992, s 154(2)* (see **59.9** above) applies where the company making the claim is a member of a group of companies as if all members of the group for the time being carrying on trades within these provisions (see above) were the same person (and, in accordance with *TCGA 1992, s 175(1)* above, as if all those trades were the same trade) and so that the gain accrues to the member of the group holding the asset concerned on the occurrence of the event mentioned in *TCGA 1992, s 154(2)* (i.e. the earlier of the disposal of the depreciating asset, cessation of its trading use or the expiry of ten years from its acquisition). [*TCGA 1992, s 175(3)*].

The disposing company must be a member of a group at the time of disposal, and the acquiring company must be a member of the same group at the time of acquisition, but HMRC does not insist that either company be a member of that group at the time of the transaction carried out by the other (HMRC Statement of Practice D19). Where this applies in a case where one member of a group makes the disposal and a second the acquisition, it may happen that the disposal takes place after the first company has ceased to trade, or the acquisition takes place before the second company commences trading. Relief will then be restricted in respect of the period during which the assets disposed of were not used for business purposes, and will be conditional on the replacement assets not being used or leased for any purpose prior to the second company's commencing trading, and being taken into use for the purposes of the trade on its commencement (HMRC Statement of Practice SP 8/81, and see also **59.8** above).

If a qualifying unincorporated association uses property owned by a company in which at least 90% of the shares are held by or on behalf of the association or its members, rollover relief can be claimed subject to the usual conditions. (HMRC Extra-Statutory Concession D15). (See **4.19** ANTI-AVOIDANCE for the charge arising where concessions involving deferral of gains are abused.)

See **41.12**(g) LAND above with regard to rollover relief in cases of compulsory purchase of land.

Claims for relief

[59.11] A claim for rollover relief relates to both a disposal and an acquisition of assets and so cannot be made until both have occurred (but see below re provisional claims under self-assessment).

Form of claim

A claim for relief must be made in writing and must specify:

- the identity of the claimant;

- the old assets which have been disposed of;
- the amount received for each of those assets;
- the date of disposal of each of those assets;
- the new assets which have been acquired;
- the date of acquisition of each of those assets or the dates on which unconditional contracts for the acquisition of each of those assets were entered into;
- the cost of each of those assets; and
- the amount of the proceeds from each of the old assets which has been used to acquire each new asset.

(HMRC Helpsheet HS 290).

Where the disposal is made by one group company and the acquisition made by another (see **59.10** above), a rollover relief claim must be made by both companies. [*TCGA 1992, s 175(2A)*].

Time limits for claims

As no time limit is specified, the general time limits in *TMA 1970, s 43* and *FA 1998, Sch 18 para 55* apply (see **13.5** CLAIMS). For rollover relief purposes, the period of time allowed for the making of a claim (four years (for claims made before 1 April 2010 (2012 in certain cases), six years for companies and approximately five years ten months for other persons)) begins with the later of:

- the end of the tax year or company accounting period in which the disposal takes place, and
- the end of the tax year or company accounting period in which the new assets are acquired.

A claim to relief is not prevented by the finality of an assessment on chargeable gains.

(HMRC Capital Gains Manual CG60600).

Provisional claims

It would be anomalous to require a taxpayer, who intends to roll over gains, to pay the tax on those gains under self-assessment and thus reduce the funds available to invest in the new assets. Provisional rollover relief claims are therefore possible as outlined below.

The claimant may make a declaration in his tax return for a tax year or company accounting period in which he has made a disposal of qualifying assets (see **59.4** above) that the whole or a specified part of the consideration will be invested, within the requisite time limits (see **59.2** above), in qualifying assets which on acquisition will be taken into use exclusively for the purposes of the trade. The form in HMRC Helpsheet HS 290 referred to above may be used by an individual for this purpose. As long as the declaration continues to have effect, the same consequences ensue as if both an acquisition and a valid rollover relief claim had been made. The declaration ceases to have effect on the day, and to the extent that, it is withdrawn or is superseded by a valid claim, if either occurs before the 'relevant day'. It otherwise ceases to have effect on the relevant day itself. On its ceasing to have effect, all necessary adjustments will be made to the claimant's tax position, even if they would otherwise be out of time.

The '*relevant day*' means:

- in relation to capital gains tax, the third anniversary of 31 January following the tax year of disposal, e.g. 31 January 2018 for disposals in 2013/14; and
- in relation to corporation tax, the fourth anniversary of the last day of the accounting period of disposal.

[*TCGA 1992, s 153A*].

To the extent that a provisional claim is withdrawn or lapses, interest on unpaid tax is chargeable as if no such claim had been made. There is nothing to prevent a valid claim subsequently being made if new assets are acquired either within the normal time limit or within such further time as may be allowed by HMRC (see **59.2** above).

Key points

[59.12] Points to consider are as follows.

- Rollover relief must be claimed.
- The replacement assets must normally be acquired within the period of one year before or three years after the disposal of the old assets, but HMRC can extend the limit if the taxpayer can show that an intention to do so was prevented by circumstances beyond his control, and that he acted as soon as he could thereafter. Where a taxpayer intends to reinvest (i.e. in years two or three) they can make a provisional claim to avoid the payment of the tax on the gain. See CG60700 for HMRC view on penalties in exceptional circumstances when provisional relief is withdrawn.
- It is the consideration (deemed or actual) that must be reinvested and not as in the case of EIS deferral relief the gain.
- Partial relief may be available where sale proceeds are not fully reinvested in replacement assets, or where the old assets were either only partly used for business purposes or were not so used for the whole of the period of ownership. It may be possible to use this to ensure the annual exemption is not wasted.
- Relief will generally be available where a UK-resident company in a group disposes of an asset and another UK-resident group company acquires a replacement asset.
- Spouses and civil partners are separate persons for roll over-relief. The case of *Tod v Mudd (1986)* demonstrates the apportionment for joint ownership of a new asset (plus its only partial business use.)

- Relief can be claimed on a deemed disposal of old assets or a deemed acquisition of replacement assets.
- Rollover relief takes precedence over entrepreneurs' relief — if an entire gain is rolled-over, there is no relevant gain for entrepreneurs' relief purposes, but entrepreneurs' relief can be claimed on part of a gain that is not rolled over. If it appeared that entrepreneurs' relief would not be available on disposal of the replacement asset, it may be better to claim that relief instead of rollover relief and pay tax at 10% upfront.
- Rolled over gains normally arise on the disposal of the replacement asset. However provided the conditions are met, this gain can also be rolled over. Rolled over gains normally escape capital gains tax on the death of the taxpayer. (Separate rules apply where the new assets are depreciating assets).

60

Seed Enterprise Investment Scheme

Introduction to the Seed Enterprise Investment Scheme	**60.1**
Conditions for income tax relief	**60.2**
Bare trustees and nominees	**60.3**
General requirements of Seed Enterprise Investment Scheme	**60.4**
The shares requirement	**60.5**
The 'purpose of the issue' requirement	**60.6**
The 'spending of the money raised' requirement	**60.7**
The 'no pre-arranged exits' requirement	**60.8**
The 'no tax avoidance' requirement	**60.9**
The 'no disqualifying arrangements' requirement	**60.10**
Qualifying investor	**60.11**
The 'no employee investors' requirement	**60.12**
The 'no substantial interest in the issuing company' requirement	**60.13**
The 'no related investment arrangements' requirement	**60.14**
The 'no linked loans' requirement	**60.15**
The 'no tax avoidance' requirement	**60.16**
Qualifying company	**60.17**
The trading requirement	**60.18**
The 'issuing company to carry on the qualifying business activity' requirement	**60.19**
The UK permanent establishment requirement	**60.20**
The financial health requirement	**60.21**
The 'unquoted status' requirement	**60.22**
The control and independence requirement	**60.23**
The 'no partnerships' requirement	**60.24**
The gross assets requirement	**60.25**
The 'number of employees' requirement	**60.26**
The 'no previous other risk capital scheme investments' requirement	**60.27**
The 'amount raised through the SEIS' requirement	**60.28**
The subsidiaries requirements	**60.29**
Qualifying business activity	**60.30**
New qualifying trade	**60.31**
Form of SEIS income tax relief	**60.32**
Attribution of relief to shares	**60.33**
Claims for relief	**60.34**
Reduction or withdrawal of income tax relief	**60.35**
Disposal of shares	**60.36**
Value received by investor	**60.37**
Acquisition of trade or trading assets	**60.38**
Acquisition of share capital	**60.39**
Relief subsequently found not to have been due	**60.40**
Married persons and civil partners	**60.41**
Issuing company acquired by new company	**60.42**
Capital gains tax	**60.43**

Reduction of relief where value received etc. 60.44
SEIS reinvestment relief 60.45

Introduction to the Seed Enterprise Investment Scheme

[60.1] *FA 2012, Sch 6* introduces a new tax-advantaged venture capital scheme, the Seed Enterprise Investment Scheme (SEIS), with effect in relation to shares issued to individuals **on or after 6 April 2012**. Originally the scheme was to end on 5 April 2017 but it has now been made permanent. [*ITA 2007, s 257A; FA 2012, Sch 6 paras 1, 23(1); FA 2014, s 54*]. The scheme is focused on smaller, early stage companies and runs alongside the pre-existing ENTERPRISE INVESTMENT SCHEME (**23**), to which it is has many similarities. The main features of the SEIS are as follows.

- Income tax relief is available for investment in small companies (i.e. those with 25 or fewer employees and assets of up to £200,000) that are carrying on, or preparing to carry on, a new qualifying business.
- The relief is available on share subscriptions of up to £100,000 per individual. Relief can be carried back to the preceding year (though not from 2012/13 to 2011/12).
- The maximum relief is 50% of the amount subscribed.
- The shares must be retained for at least three years.
- The scheme incorporates many of the requirements of the Enterprise Investment Scheme (EIS), for example the requirement that the investor have no more than a 30% stake in the investee company.
- Any one company may raise investment of up to £150,000 under the SEIS in any three-year period.
- Chargeable gains on disposals of SEIS shares are exempt from CGT provided the shares are held for the requisite three-year period.
- Chargeable gains realised from disposals of any assets are exempt from CGT if invested via the SEIS in the same year.

The relief applies to investments made on or after 6 April 2012.

This chapter concentrates on the capital gains tax reliefs but the conditions for income tax relief are included in detail at **60.2** onwards. For completeness, a brief summary of the income tax relief is also included at **60.32** — for full details see Tolley's Income Tax under Seed Enterprise Investment Scheme. See also HMRC Venture Capital Schemes Manual VCM30000 onwards for both income tax and CGT reliefs.

Conditions for income tax relief

[60.2] An individual investor is eligible for SEIS income tax relief in respect of an amount subscribed by him on his own behalf for an issue of shares in a company if:

- the shares are issued to the investor;
- the six general requirements at **60.4** below are met in respect of the shares;

- the investor is a 'qualifying investor' (see **60.11** below) in relation to the shares; and
- the company issuing the shares is a 'qualifying company' (see **60.17** below) in relation to the shares.

[*ITA 2007, s 257AA; FA 2012, Sch 6 paras 1, 23(1)*].

Bare trustees and nominees

[60.3] SEIS relief is available where shares which satisfy the requirement at 60.5(a) below are held on a bare trust for two or more beneficiaries as if each beneficiary had subscribed as an individual for all of those shares, and as if the amount subscribed by each was the total subscribed divided by the number of beneficiaries.

Shares subscribed for, issued to, held by or disposed of for an individual by a nominee are treated for the purposes of SEIS relief as subscribed for, issued to, held by or disposed of by the individual.

[*ITA 2007, s 257HE; FA 2012, Sch 6 paras 1, 23(1)*].

General requirements of Seed Enterprise Investment Scheme

[60.4] The six general requirements mentioned in **60.2** above are described at 60.5–60.10 below.

The shares requirement

[60.5] The shares must:

(a) be ordinary shares which do not, at any time during 'period B' below, carry (subject to below) any present or future preferential right to dividends or to assets on a winding-up or any present or future right to be redeemed; and

(b) unless they are bonus shares, be subscribed for wholly in cash and be fully paid up at the time of issue.

Shares are, however, permitted to carry a preferential right to dividends provided the amount and timing of the dividends do not depend on a decision of the company, the shareholder or any other person and provided the dividends are not cumulative.

Period B

'*Period B*' is the three-year period beginning with the issue of the shares.

[*ITA 2007, ss 257AC, 257CA; FA 2012, Sch 6 paras 1, 23(1)*].

The 'purpose of the issue' requirement

[60.6] The shares (other than any bonus shares) must be issued to raise money for the purposes of a 'qualifying business activity' (see **60.30** below) carried on, or to be carried on, by the issuing company or a 'qualifying 90% subsidiary' (see **60.29** below) of that company. [*ITA 2007, ss 257CB, 257HJ(1); FA 2012, Sch 6 paras 1, 23(1)*].

The 'spending of the money raised' requirement

[60.7] Before the end of period B (as in **60.5** above) all of the money raised by the issue of the shares (other than any of them which are bonus shares) must be spent for the purposes of the qualifying business activity (see **60.30** below) for which the money was raised. However, this requirement does not fail to be met merely because an amount of money which is not significant is spent for another purpose or remains unspent at the end of period B. The spending of money on the acquisition of shares or stock in a company does not of itself amount to spending it for the purposes of a qualifying business activity.

[*ITA 2007, ss 257CC, 257HJ(1); FA 2012, Sch 6 paras 1, 23(1)*].

The 'no pre-arranged exits' requirement

[60.8] The 'issuing arrangements' must not:

(a) provide for the eventual disposal by the investor of the shares in question or other shares or securities of the issuing company; or
(b) provide for the eventual cessation of a trade of the company or of a person connected with it; or
(c) provide for the eventual disposal of all, or a substantial amount (in terms of value) of, the assets of the company or of a person connected with it; or
(d) provide (by means of any insurance, indemnity, guarantee or otherwise) complete or partial protection for investors against what would otherwise be the risks attached to making the investment (disregarding any arrangements which merely protect the issuing company and/or its subsidiaries against normal business risks).

Arrangements with a view to the company becoming a wholly-owned subsidiary of a new holding company within the terms of *ITA 2007, s 257HB(1)* (see **60.42** below) are excluded from (a) above. For shares issued on or after 5 December 2016, arrangements with a view to shares in the company being exchanged for, or converted into, shares of a different class in that company, are also excluded from (a) above. Arrangements applicable only on an unanticipated winding-up of a company for genuine commercial reasons are excluded from (b) and (c) above.

'*Issuing arrangements*' means the arrangements under which the shares are issued to the individual or any arrangements made, before the shares were issued, in relation to or in connection with the issue. If, before the shares were issued, information on pre-arranged exits, i.e. information indicating the possibility of making during period B (as in **60.5** above) arrangements of the kind described in any of (a)–(d) above, was made available to prospective subscribers, the term also includes any arrangements made during period B. The term 'arrangements' is broadly defined.

[*ITA 2007, ss 257CD, 257HJ(1); FA 2012, Sch 6 paras 1, 23(1); F(No 2)A 2017, s 11(3)(4)*].

The 'no tax avoidance' requirement

[60.9] The shares must be issued for genuine commercial reasons and not as part of a scheme or arrangement a main purpose of which is the avoidance of tax. [*ITA 2007, s 257CE; FA 2012, Sch 6 paras 1, 23(1)*].

The 'no disqualifying arrangements' requirement

[60.10] The shares must not be issued, nor any money raised by the issue spent, in consequence or anticipation of, or otherwise in connection with, 'disqualifying arrangements'. Arrangements (as broadly defined) are '*disqualifying arrangements*' if they are entered into with the purpose of ensuring that any of the 'relevant tax reliefs' (see below) are available in respect of the issuing company's business (or, where applicable, that of its qualifying 90% subsidiary) and either or both of conditions A and B below are met. It is immaterial whether the issuing company is a party to the arrangements.

Condition A is that, as a result of the money raised by the issue of the shares being spent as required by **60.7** above, an amount representing the whole or most of the amount raised is, in the course of he arrangements, paid to (or for the benefit of) one or more parties to the arrangements or a person or persons connected with such a party (within **17** CONNECTED PERSONS). Condition B is that, in the absence of the arrangements, it would have been reasonable to expect that the whole or greater part of the component activities (as defined) of the qualifying business activity for which the issue of the shares raised money would have been carried on as part of another business by one or more parties to the arrangements or a person or persons connected with such a party.

The 'relevant tax reliefs' are those listed at **23.3** ENTERPRISE INVESTMENT SCHEME.

[*ITA 2007, ss 257CF, 257HJ(1); FA 2012, Sch 6 paras 1, 23(1); F(No 2)A 2017, Sch 1 paras 11(3), 16*].

Qualifying investor

[60.11] An individual is a '*qualifying investor*' in relation to shares if the requirements at **60.12–60.16** are met.

The 'no employee investors' requirement

[60.12] Neither the investor nor an associate (see below) of the investor may at any time during period B (as in **60.5** above) be an employee of the issuing company or of any 'qualifying subsidiary' (see **60.29** below) of that company. However, for this purpose a person is not to be treated as an employee of the issuing company etc. at any time when he is a director of the company.

Meaning of 'associate'

The SEIS provisions adopt the EIS definition of 'associate' in *ITA 2007, s 253*. An '*associate*' of any person is any 'relative' (i.e. spouse, civil partner, ancestor or linear descendant) of that person, the trustee(s) of any settlement in relation to which that person or any relative (living or dead) is or was a settlor and, where that person has an interest in any shares of obligations of a company which are subject to any trust or are part of a deceased estate, the trustee(s) of the settlement or the personal representatives of the deceased. For this purpose, 'settlor' is defined as in *ITA 2007, ss 467–473*.

[*ITA 2007, ss 257BA, 257HJ(1); FA 2012, Sch 6 paras 1, 23(1)*].

The 'no substantial interest in the issuing company' requirement

[60.13] The investor must not have a 'substantial interest' in the issuing company at any time during 'period A' below.

An individual has a '*substantial interest*' in a company if:

(a) he directly or indirectly possesses, or is entitled to acquire, more than 30% of the ordinary or issued share capital of, or more than 30% of the voting power in, the company or any 'subsidiary'; or
(b) he directly or indirectly possesses, or is entitled to acquire, such rights as would entitle him to more than 30% of the assets of the company or a subsidiary that are available for distribution to equity holders in, for example, a winding-up; or
(c) he has control (within *ITA 2007, s 995*) of the company or any subsidiary.

For these purposes a company (Y) is a '*subsidiary*' of another (Z) if Y is a 51% subsidiary of Z at any time in period A. For the purposes of (b), *CTA 2010, Pt 5 Ch 6* has effect, with appropriate modifications, to determine the persons who are equity holders of a company and the percentage of assets to which an individual would be entitled.

An individual is treated as entitled to acquire anything which he is entitled to acquire at a future date or will at a future date be entitled to acquire. Rights or powers of associates (see **60.12** above) are attributed to the individual.

An individual does *not* have a substantial interest in a company merely because one or more shares in the company are held by him, or by his associate, at a time when the company has not issued any shares other than subscriber shares and has not begun to carry on, or make preparations for carrying on, a trade or business.

Period A

'*Period A*' is the period beginning with the incorporation of the issuing company and ending immediately before the third anniversary of the issue of the shares.

[*ITA 2007, ss 257BB, 257BF, 257HJ(1); FA 2012, Sch 6 paras 1, 23(1)*].

The 'no related investment arrangements' requirement

[60.14] The investor must not subscribe for the shares as part of an arrangement (as broadly defined) which provides for another person to subscribe for shares in another company in which the investor, or any other individual who is party to the arrangement, has a 'substantial interest' (see **60.13** above). [*ITA 2007, ss 257BC, 257HJ(1); FA 2012, Sch 6 paras 1, 23(1)*].

The 'no linked loans' requirement

[60.15] No loan may be made by any person to the investor or to an associate (see **60.12** above) at any time in period A (as in **60.13** above) if it would not have been made, or would not have been made on the same terms, if the investor had not subscribed, or had not been proposing to subscribe, for the shares. The giving of credit to, or the assignment of a debt due from, the investor or associate is counted as a loan for these purposes. [*ITA 2007, s 257BD; FA 2012, Sch 6 paras 1, 23(1)*].

It seems likely that, in their interpretation of the above, HMRC will apply SP 6/98 which already covers the similar requirement under the EIS — see **23.4** ENTERPRISE INVESTMENT SCHEME.

The 'no tax avoidance' requirement

[60.16] The shares must be subscribed for by the investor for genuine commercial reasons and not as part of a scheme or arrangement a main purpose of which is the avoidance of tax. [*ITA 2007, s 257BE; FA 2012, Sch 6 paras 1, 23(1)*].

Qualifying company

[60.17] The issuing company is a '*qualifying company*' in relation to the shares if the requirements at **60.18–60.29** below are met.

The trading requirement

[60.18] The company must meet the 'trading requirement' throughout period B (as in **60.5** above). The '*trading requirement*' is that:

(a) the company exists wholly for the purpose of carrying on one or more new qualifying trades (see **60.31** below) (disregarding purposes having no significant effect on the extent of its activities); or

(b) the company is a '*parent company*' (i.e. a company with one or more 'qualifying subsidiaries' — see **60.29** below) and the business of the '*group*' (i.e. the company and its qualifying subsidiaries) does not consist wholly or as to a substantial part (i.e. broadly 20% — see HMRC Venture Capital Schemes Manual VCM3010) in the carrying on of 'non-qualifying activities'.

If period B begins after the incorporation of the company, the requirement must have been complied with since incorporation, apart from any interval between incorporation and commencement of business.

Where the company intends that one or more other companies should become its qualifying subsidiaries with a view to their carrying on one or more new qualifying trades, then, until any time after which the intention is abandoned, the company is treated as a parent company and those other companies are included in the group for the purposes of (b) above.

For the purpose of (b) above, the business of the group means what would be the business of the group if the activities of the group companies taken together were regarded as one business. Activities are for this purpose disregarded to the extent that they consist in:

(i) holding shares in or securities of any of the company's qualifying subsidiaries;
(ii) making loans to another group company;
(iii) holding and managing property used by a group company for the purposes of one or more qualifying trades (see **60.31** below) carried on by a group company; or
(iv) holding and managing property used by a group company for the purposes of research and development from which it is intended either that a qualifying trade to be carried on by a group company will be derived or that a qualifying trade carried on or to be carried on by a group company will benefit.

References in (iv) above to a group company include references to any existing or future company which will be a group company at any future time.

Activities are similarly disregarded to the extent that they consist, in the case of a subsidiary whose main purpose is the carrying on of qualifying trade(s) and whose other purposes have no significant effect on the extent of its activities (other than in relation to incidental matters), in activities not in pursuance of its main purpose.

Non-qualifying activities

'*Non-qualifying activities*' are:

- excluded activities within **23.9** ENTERPRISE INVESTMENT SCHEME; and
- non-trading activities (not including research and development — see **60.30** below).

Winding-up etc.

A company is not regarded as ceasing to meet the trading requirement merely because of anything done in consequence of the company or any of its subsidiaries being in administration or receivership (both as defined by *ITA 2007, s 252*) or because the company or any of its subsidiaries is wound up or otherwise dissolved. The entry into administration or receivership, winding-up or dissolution, and anything done as a consequence of the company concerned being in administration or receivership, must be for genuine commercial reasons and not part of a tax avoidance scheme or arrangements.

[*ITA 2007, ss 257DA, 257DB, 257HJ(1)(2); FA 2012, Sch 6 paras 1, 23(1)*].

The 'issuing company to carry on the qualifying business activity' requirement

[60.19] At no time in period B (as in **60.5** above) must any of the following be carried on by a person other than the issuing company or a 'qualifying 90% subsidiary' (see **60.29** below) of that company:

- the '*relevant new qualifying trade*', i.e. the 'new qualifying trade' (see **60.31** below) which is the subject of the qualifying business activity referred to in **60.6** above;
- '*relevant preparation work*', i.e. preparations to carry on a new qualifying trade where such preparations are the subject of that qualifying business activity (see **60.30**(a) below);

- research and development which is the subject of that qualifying business activity (see **60.30**(b) below); and
- any other preparations for the carrying on of the new qualifying trade.

Where relevant preparation work is carried on by the issuing company or a qualifying 90% subsidiary, the carrying on of the relevant new qualifying trade by a company other than the issuing company or a qualifying 90% subsidiary is disregarded for these purposes if it occurs before the issuing company (or subsidiary) carries on that trade.

The requirement is not regarded as failing to be met if, by reason only of a company being wound up or dissolved or being in administration or receivership (both as defined by *ITA 2007, s 252*), the relevant new qualifying trade ceases to be carried on in period B by the issuing company or a qualifying 90% subsidiary and is subsequently carried on in that period by a person who is not connected (within **17** CONNECTED PERSONS) with the issuing company at any time in period A (as in **60.13** above). This let-out applies only if the winding-up, dissolution or entry into administration or receivership (and everything done as a consequence of the company concerned being in administration or receivership) is for genuine commercial reasons and not part of a tax avoidance scheme or arrangements.

[*ITA 2007, ss 257DC, 257HJ(2); FA 2012, Sch 6 paras 1, 23(1)*].

The UK permanent establishment requirement

[60.20] Although the issuing company need not be UK resident, it must have a permanent establishment in the UK. The company must meet this requirement throughout period B (as in **60.5** above).

In determining whether or not a company has a permanent establishment in the UK, the same rules apply as for the identical requirement under the EIS — see **23.5** ENTERPRISE INVESTMENT SCHEME.

[*ITA 2007, ss 257DD, 257HJ(1); FA 2012, Sch 6 paras 1, 23(1)*].

The financial health requirement

[60.21] This requirement must be met at the beginning of period B (as in **60.5** above). The requirement is that the issuing company is not 'in difficulty'. A company is '*in difficulty*' if it is reasonable to assume that it would be regarded as a firm in difficulty for the purposes of the *EU Guidelines on State Aid for Rescuing and Restructuring Firms in Difficulty (2004/C 244/02)*. [*ITA 2007, s 257DE; FA 2012, Sch 6 paras 1, 23(1)*].

The 'unquoted status' requirement

[60.22] The issuing company must be 'unquoted' at the beginning of period B (as in **60.5** above), and no arrangements must then exist for it to cease to be unquoted. If, at the time of issue, arrangements exist for the company to become a wholly-owned subsidiary of a new holding company by means of a share exchange within **60.42** below, no arrangements must exist for the new company to cease to be unquoted. A company is '*unquoted*' if none of its shares etc. are listed on a recognised stock exchange or on a foreign exchange designated for the purpose, or dealt in outside the UK by such means as may be designated for the purpose.

[*ITA 2007, s 257DF; FA 2012, Sch 6 paras 1, 23(1)*].

The control and independence requirement

[60.23] The issuing company must not at any time in period A (ignoring any on-the-shelf period) (as in **60.13** above) either:

(a) control another company (other than a 'qualifying subsidiary' — see **60.29** below), 'control' being construed in accordance with *CTA 2010, ss 450, 451* and being considered with or without CONNECTED PERSONS (17); or

(b) (subject to **60.42** below) be under the control of another company, 'control' being construed in accordance with *ITA 2007, s 995* and again being considered with or without connected persons; or

(c) be capable of falling within (a) or (b) by virtue of any arrangements which are in existence for a company to control another (as broadly defined).

An on-the-shelf period is defined as a period during which the issuing company has not yet issued any shares other than subscriber shares and has not made preparations to begin carrying on a trade or business.

[*ITA 2007, ss 257DG, 257HJ(3); FA 2012, Sch 6 paras 1, 23(1)*].

The 'no partnerships' requirement

[60.24] Neither the issuing company nor any 'qualifying 90% subsidiary' (see **60.29** below) of that company may, at any time during period A (as in **60.13** above), be a member of a partnership. This includes a limited liability partnership and a foreign entity of similar nature to a partnership. [*ITA 2007, s 257DH; FA 2012, Sch 6 paras 1, 23(1)*].

The gross assets requirement

[60.25] The value of the issuing company's assets must not exceed £200,000 immediately before the issue of SEIS shares. If the issuing company is a parent company, the gross assets test applies by reference to the aggregate gross assets of the company and all its qualifying subsidiaries (disregarding certain assets held by any such company which correspond to liabilities of another). [*ITA 2007, ss 257DI, 257HJ(1); FA 2012, Sch 6 paras 1, 23(1)*].

For HMRC's approach to the gross assets requirement see HMRC Venture Capital Schemes Manual VCM34100.

The 'number of employees' requirement

[60.26] The issuing company must have fewer than the equivalent of 25 full-time employees when the SEIS shares are issued. If the company is a parent company, this rule applies by reference to the aggregate number of full-time employees of itself and its qualifying subsidiaries. To ascertain the equivalent number of full-time employees of a company, take the actual number of full-time employees and add to it a just and reasonable fraction for each employee who is not full-time. For this purpose, an 'employee' includes a director but does not include anyone on maternity or paternity leave or a student on vocational training. [*ITA 2007, ss 257DJ, 257HJ(1); FA 2012, Sch 6 paras 1, 23(1)*].

HMRC consider that a full-time employee is one whose standard working week (excluding lunch breaks and overtime) is at least 35 hours (HMRC Venture Capital Schemes Manual VCM34110).

The 'no previous other risk capital scheme investments' requirement

[60.27] This requirement is that:

- no EIS investment or VCT investment is or has been made in the issuing company on or before the day on which the SEIS shares are issued; and
- no EIS investment or VCT investment has been made on or before that day in a company which at the time the SEIS shares are issued is a 'qualifying subsidiary' (see **60.29** below) of the issuing company.

An EIS investment is made if the company issues shares (for which money has been subscribed) and provides a compliance statement under *ITA 2007, s 205* in respect of the shares. The investment is made when the shares are issued. A VCT investment is made if an investment (of any kind) in the company is made by a VCT (see **71** VENTURE CAPITAL TRUSTS). [*ITA 2007, s 257DK; FA 2012, Sch 6 paras 1, 23(1)*].

The 'amount raised through the SEIS' requirement

[60.28] The total amount of SEIS investments made in the issuing company, together with any other de minimis State aid received by the company, in the period of three years and one day ending on the date of the current issue must not exceed £150,000.

A SEIS investment is made if the company issues shares (for which money has been subscribed) and provides a compliance statement under **60.34** below in respect of them; the investment is made on the day the shares are issued. De minimis aid is defined by reference to Article 2 of Commission Regulation (EC) No 1998/2006; the amount of the aid is the amount of the grant or, if the aid is not in the form of a grant, the gross grant equivalent amount (within the meaning of that Regulation).

Where the current share issue would take the total amount of SEIS investments (plus de minimis aid) to more than £150,000, the requirement is treated as met in relation to an appropriate proportion of the shares in the issue (and in any other issue made on the same day). For example, if 200,000 shares are issued for £1 each and there has been no previous issue in the last three years (and no de minimis aid), 150,000 of the shares can be SEIS shares. Those shares and the remainder of the shares comprised in the issue are then treated as two separate issues for SEIS purposes.

[*ITA 2007, s 257DL; FA 2012, Sch 6 paras 1, 23(1)*].

The UK Government does not maintain a list of all State aids covered by the EU regulations on de minimis aid. If a company has received any small amounts of funding or support from a government measure (whether the UK Government or any other EU member state) and is not clear about whether that funding should be counted towards the SEIS limit, the company should seek clarification from the provider of the funds or the administrator of the scheme as to whether that funding is a de minimis State aid (HMRC Venture Capital Schemes Manual VCM34130).

The subsidiaries requirements

[60.29] At all times in period B (as in **60.5** above), any subsidiary of the issuing company must be a 'qualifying subsidiary' (see below). [*ITA 2007, s 257DM; FA 2012, Sch 6 paras 1, 23(1)*].

The company must not at any time in period B have a 'property managing subsidiary' which is not a 'qualifying 90% subsidiary' (see below) of the company. A '*property managing subsidiary*' is a subsidiary whose business consists wholly or mainly in the holding or managing of land or any 'property deriving its value from land'. For this purpose, '*property deriving its value from land*' includes any shareholding in a company, and any partnership interest or interest in settled property, which derives its value directly or indirectly from land and any option, consent or embargo affecting the disposition of land. [*ITA 2007, s 257DN; FA 2012, Sch 6 paras 1, 23(1)*].

Qualifying subsidiary and qualifying 90% subsidiary

Both '*qualifying subsidiary*' and '*qualifying 90% subsidiary*' have the same meanings as they do for EIS purposes. See respectively **23.6** and **23.7** ENTERPRISE INVESTMENT SCHEME. [*ITA 2007, s 257HJ(1); FA 2012, Sch 6 paras 1, 23(1)*].

Qualifying business activity

[60.30] Either of the following is a '*qualifying business activity*' in relation to the issuing company:

- (i) the carrying on of a 'new qualifying trade' (see **60.31** below) which, on the date of issue of the shares, the company or a 'qualifying 90% subsidiary' (see **60.29** above) is carrying on; or
- (ii) the activity of preparing to carry on such a trade which, on the date of issue of the shares, is intended to be carried on by the company or any such subsidiary and which is eventually carried on by the company or any such subsidiary; or
- (iii) the eventual carrying on of the trade mentioned in (ii) above; and

(b) the carrying on of 'research and development' which, on the date of issue of the shares, the company or a 'qualifying 90% subsidiary' is carrying on or which the company or any such subsidiary begins to carry on immediately afterwards, and from which it is intended on that date that a new qualifying trade which the company or any such subsidiary will carry on will be derived or will benefit.

For the purposes of (b) above, when research and development is begun to be carried on by a qualifying 90% subsidiary of the issuing company, any carrying on of the research and development by it before it became such a subsidiary is ignored. '*Research and development*' has the meaning given by *ITA 2007, s 1006*. References in (a) and (b) above to a qualifying 90% subsidiary include, in cases where the new qualifying trade is not carried on at the time of issue of the shares, references to any existing or future company which will be such a subsidiary at any future time.

[*ITA 2007, ss 257HG, 257HJ(1); FA 2012, Sch 6 paras 1, 23(1)*].

New qualifying trade

[60.31] '*Qualifying trade*' is defined as for EIS purposes — see **23.9** ENTERPRISE INVESTMENT SCHEME. A qualifying trade carried on by the issuing company or a 'qualifying 90% subsidiary' (see **60.29** above) of that company is a '*new qualifying trade*' if (and only if):

- the trade does not begin to be carried on (whether by the company concerned or any other person) before the period of two years ending immediately before the day on which the shares are issued; and
- at no time before the company concerned begins to carry on the trade was any other trade being carried on by the issuing company or by any company that was a 51% subsidiary of the issuing company at the time in question.

[*ITA 2007, s 257HF; FA 2012, Sch 6 paras 1, 23(1)*].

Form of SEIS income tax relief

[60.32] Subject to the carry-back facility described below, relief is given for the tax year in which the shares are issued. It is given by means of a reduction in what would otherwise be the individual's income tax liability (a '*tax reduction*') equal to tax at the SEIS rate for the year on the amount (or aggregate amounts) subscribed for shares in respect of which he is eligible for and claims SEIS relief. The SEIS rate is 50%. Investors can restrict their claim for SEIS relief to only some of the shares issued to them at any one time.

There is an upper limit of £100,000 on the amount of investment on which an individual may obtain relief in a tax year.

For the order in which tax reductions are given against an individual's tax liability see Tolley's Income Tax under Allowances and Tax Rates. A tax reduction must be restricted to the extent (if any) that it would otherwise exceed the individual's remaining income tax liability after making all prior reductions.

Carry-back

Where shares in respect of which an individual is eligible for SEIS relief are issued at any time in 2013/14 or any subsequent tax year, the individual may claim relief as if any number of shares up to the full number issued to him had been issued in the tax year preceding that in which they were actually issued. This carry-back is subject to the overriding rule that the total amount of investment on which relief can be obtained for any one year cannot exceed the annual maximum for that year.

[*ITA 2007, s 257AB; FA 2012, Sch 6 paras 1, 23(1)*].

Attribution of relief to shares

[60.33] Subject to any reduction or withdrawal of relief (see **60.35** *et seq.* below), where an individual's income tax liability is reduced for a tax year as in **60.32** above by reason of an issue or issues of shares made (or treated as made) in that year, the tax reduction is attributed to that issue or those issues (being apportioned in the latter case according to the amounts claimed for each issue). Issues of shares of the same class by a company to an individual on the same day are treated as a single issue for this purpose. A proportionate amount of the reduction attributed to an issue is attributed to each share in the issue in respect of which the claim was made and is adjusted correspondingly for any subsequent bonus issue of shares of the same class and carrying the same rights.

An issue to an individual part of which is treated as having been made in the preceding tax year (as in **60.32** above) is treated as two separate issues, one made on a day in the previous year.

Where relief attributable to an issue of shares falls to be withdrawn or reduced, the relief attributable to each of the shares in question is reduced to nil (if relief is withdrawn) or proportionately reduced (where relief is reduced).

[*ITA 2007, ss 257E, 257HI; FA 2012, Sch 6 paras 1, 23(1)*].

Claims for relief

[60.34] A claim for SEIS income tax relief is valid only if it is made no later than the fifth anniversary of 31 January following the tax year in which the shares are issued.

The claimant must have received, with the authority of HMRC, a compliance certificate from the issuing company before making the claim. The certificate must state that the requirements for relief, except in so far as they fall to be satisfied by the investor, are for the time being satisfied in relation to the shares in question.

Before issuing such a certificate, the company must supply to HMRC a compliance statement that the requirements for relief are satisfied for the time being and have been satisfied at all times since the shares were issued.

If a certificate or statement is made fraudulently or negligently, or a certificate was issued when it should not have been, the issuing company is liable to a fine of up to £3,000.

No application for postponement of tax pending appeal can be made on the ground that relief is due under these provisions unless a claim has been duly submitted.

[*ITA 2007, ss 257EA–257EG; FA 2012, Sch 6 paras 1, 23(1)*].

Reduction or withdrawal of relief

[60.35] The following provisions apply to reduce or withdraw SEIS income tax relief in certain circumstances. References to a reduction of relief include its reduction to nil, and references to the withdrawal of relief in respect of any shares are to the withdrawal of the relief attributable to those shares (see **60.33** above). Where no relief has yet been given, a reduction applies to reduce the amount which would otherwise be available for relief, and a withdrawal means the shares cease to be eligible for relief. [*ITA 2007, s 257HJ(4); FA 2012, Sch 6 paras 1, 23(1)*].

An assessment to income tax withdrawing or reducing SEIS relief is made for the tax year for which the relief was given.

Disposal of shares

[60.36] Where, before the end of period B (as in **60.5** above), the investor disposes of shares to which relief is attributable (see **60.33** above) or grants an option the exercise of which would bind him to sell the shares, then:

(a) if the disposal is at arm's length, relief attributable to those shares (see **60.33** above) is withdrawn or, if that relief is greater than an amount equal to tax at the SEIS rate (see **60.32** above) on the disposal consideration, is reduced by that amount; or
(b) if the disposal is not at arm's length, the relief is withdrawn.

Where the relief attributable to the shares is less than tax at the SEIS rate on the amount subscribed for the issue, the amount referred to in (a) above is correspondingly reduced. An issue to an individual part of which is treated as having been made in the preceding tax year (as in **60.32** above) is treated as two separate issues, one made on a day in the previous year. Where the relief attributable to the shares has been reduced (otherwise than as a result of an issue of bonus shares — see **60.33** above) before the relief was obtained, then in calculating the amount referred to in (a) above the relief attributable to the shares before that reduction is used.

A share exchange within *TCGA 1992, s 136* is treated as a disposal of shares for these purposes, as is a disposal of an interest or right in or over shares. If, at any time in period A (as in **60.13** above), a person grants the investor an option the exercise of which would bind the grantor to purchase any shares to which relief is attributable, the relief is withdrawn.

These provisions do not apply to a disposal of shares occurring as a result of the investor's death. See **60.41** below for transfers of shares between spouses or civil partners.

Identification rules

For the above purposes, disposals are identified with shares of the same class issued on an earlier day before shares issued on a later day, i.e. first in/first out (FIFO). Where shares within two or more of the categories listed below were acquired on the same day, any of those shares disposed of (applying the FIFO basis) are treated as disposed of in the order in which they are listed, as follows:

- shares to which no SEIS income tax relief is attributable;
- shares to which SEIS income tax relief, but not SEIS reinvestment relief (see **60.45** below), is attributable;
- shares to which both SEIS income tax relief and SEIS reinvestment relief are attributable.

Shares transferred between spouses or civil partners living together are treated as if they were acquired by the transferee spouse or partner on the day they were issued (see also **60.41** below). Shares comprised in a 'new holding' following a reorganisation to which *TCGA 1992, s 127* applies (see **63.2** SHARES AND SECURITIES) are treated as having been acquired when the original shares were acquired.

[*ITA 2007, ss 257FA–257FD, 257HA, 257HH; FA 2012, Sch 6 paras 1, 23(1)*].

Value received by investor

[60.37] If, at any time in period A (as in **60.13** above), the investor receives value (other than insignificant value) from the issuing company, any relief attributable to those shares (see **60.33** above), and not previously reduced in respect of the value received, is withdrawn or, if that relief exceeds an amount equal to tax at the SEIS rate on the value received, is reduced by that amount.

[*ITA 2007, ss 257FE–257FI, 257FM; FA 2012, Sch 6 paras 1, 23(1)*].

For full details of the provisions, see Tolley's Income Tax.

Acquisition of trade or trading assets

[60.38] Relief attributable (see **60.33** above) to any shares in a company held by an individual is withdrawn if:

(a) at any time in period A (as in **60.13** above), the company or any 'qualifying subsidiary' (see **60.29** below)
  - begins to carry on as its trade, business or profession (or as part of its trade etc.) a trade etc. previously carried on at any time in that period by someone other than the company or any qualifying subsidiary; or
  - acquires the whole or the greater part of the assets used for the purposes of a trade etc. previously so carried on; and

(b) the individual is a person or one of a group of persons:
  (i) who owned at any time in period A more than a half share in the trade etc. previously carried on, and also own or owned at any such time such a share in the trade etc. carried on by the company; or

(ii) control (within *CTA 2010, ss 450, 451*), or at any time in period A has controlled, the company, and also, at any such time, controlled another company which previously carried on the trade etc.

In determining, for the purposes of (b)(i) above, the ownership of a trade and, if appropriate, the shares owned by multiple owners, *CTA 2010, s 941(6)* and *s 942* apply. Interests, rights or powers of 'associates' (see **60.12** above) of a person are treated as those of that person.

[*ITA 2007, ss 257FP, 257HJ(3); FA 2012, Sch 6 paras 1, 23(1)*].

Acquisition of share capital

[60.39] Relief attributable (see **60.33** above) to any shares in a company held by an individual is withdrawn if:

- the company, at any time in period A (as in **60.13** above), comes to acquire all the issued share capital of another company, and
- the individual is a person, or one of a group of persons, who control (within *CTA 2010, ss 450, 451*) or has, at any time in period A, controlled the company and who also, at any such time, controlled the other company.

[*ITA 2007, ss 257FQ, 257HJ(3); FA 2012, Sch 6 paras 1, 23(1)*].

Relief subsequently found not to have been due

[60.40] Relief is withdrawn if it is subsequently found not to have been due. If relief is to be withdrawn on the ground that the issuing company is not a qualifying company (see **60.17** above) or that the purpose of the issue or spending of the money raised requirements at **60.6, 60.7** are not met:

- the issuing company must have given notice to that effect under *ITA 2007, s 257GF*; or
- an HMRC officer must have given notice to the issuing company of his opinion that the whole or part of the relief was not due because of the ground in question.

The issuing company may appeal against an HMRC notice as though it were refusal of a claim by the company.

[*ITA 2007, ss 257FR, 257GA; FA 2012, Sch 6 paras 1, 23(1)*].

Married persons and civil partners

[60.41] The provisions for withdrawal of relief on the disposal of shares in respect of which relief has been given (see **60.36** above) do not apply to transfers between spouses or civil partners living together. On any subsequent disposal or other event, the spouse or partner to whom the shares were so transferred is treated as if:

- he or she were the person who subscribed for the shares;

- the amount he or she subscribed for the shares were the same amount as subscribed by the transferor spouse or partner;
- his or her liability to income tax had been reduced in respect of the shares by the same amount, and for the same tax year, as applied on the subscription by the transferor spouse or partner; and
- that amount of SEIS income tax relief had continued to be attributable to the shares despite the transfer.

Where the amount of SEIS relief attributable to the shares had been reduced before the relief was obtained by the transferor spouse or partner, the transferee is treated as if his or her relief had been correspondingly reduced before it was obtained.

Any assessment for reducing or withdrawing relief is made on the transferee spouse or partner. The identification rules for disposals at **60.36** above apply to determine the extent (if any) to which shares to which relief is attributable are comprised in the transfer.

[*ITA 2007, ss 257FA(4), 257H, 257HA(1); FA 2012, Sch 6 paras 1, 23(1)*].

Issuing company acquired by new company

[60.42] Where a company (Company A) has issued shares under the SEIS (and has issued a compliance certificate — see **60.34** above) and subsequently, by means of an exchange of shares, all of its shares (the old shares) are acquired by a company (Company B) in which the only previously issued shares are subscriber shares, then, subject to the further conditions below being satisfied:

- the exchange is not regarded as involving a disposal of the old shares (and a consequent withdrawal of relief) and an acquisition of the Company B shares (the new shares); and
- SEIS relief attributable to the old shares is regarded as attributable instead to the new shares for which they are exchanged. For SEIS purposes generally, the new shares stand in the shoes of the old shares, e.g. as if they had been subscribed for and issued at the time the old shares were subscribed for and issued and as if anything done by or in relation to Company A had been done by or in relation to Company B.

The further conditions are as follows.

(a) The consideration for the old shares must consist entirely of the issue of the new shares.
(b) The consideration for old shares of each description must consist entirely of new shares of the 'corresponding description'.
(c) New shares of each description must be issued to holders of old shares of the 'corresponding description' in respect of and in proportion to their holdings.
(d) Before the issue of the new shares, on the written application (for which see **4.15** ANTI-AVOIDANCE) of either Company A or Company B, HMRC must have notified to that company their satisfaction that the exchange:
   - is for genuine commercial reasons; and

- does not form part of a scheme or arrangements designed to avoid liability to corporation tax or capital gains tax.

HMRC may, within 30 days of an application, request further particulars, which must then be supplied within 30 days of the request (or such longer period as they may allow in any particular case).

For the purposes of (b) and (c) above, old and new shares are of a '*corresponding description*' if, assuming they were shares in the same company, they would be of the same class and carry the same rights.

References above to 'shares' (other than those to 'shares issued under the SEIS' or 'subscriber shares') include references to securities.

An exchange within these provisions does not breach the control and independence requirement at **60.23** above.

[*ITA 2007, ss 257HB–257HD; TCGA 1992, s 138(2); FA 2012, Sch 6 paras 1, 23(1)*].

Capital gains tax

[60.43] See also **60.45** below for SEIS reinvestment relief.

Gains

Gains arising on the disposal by the investor, after the end of period A (as in **60.13** above), of shares on which SEIS income tax relief has been given are not chargeable gains. (There is no such exemption for shares disposed of before the end of period A, and any SEIS income tax relief given will be withdrawn — see **60.36** above.)

Where SEIS income tax relief was not given on the full amount subscribed for the shares (other than by reason of the income tax liability being insufficient to support the relief), the capital gains tax exemption is restricted to a proportion of the gain. Where this arises, it will usually be because the investor's SEIS subscriptions exceeded the annual maximum on which relief is available (see **60.32** above). The exempt gain is the proportion of the gain found by applying the multiple R/T where:

R = the actual income tax relief given (expressed in terms of the reduction in the tax liability); and
T = tax at the SEIS rate on the amount subscribed for the issue.

[*TCGA 1992, s 150E(2)(4)(5); FA 2012, Sch 6 paras 3, 23(1)*].

Losses

If a disposal of shares on which SEIS income tax relief has been given results in a capital loss, the loss is allowable *regardless* of whether the disposal occurs within or without period A (see above). However, in calculating the loss, or in ascertaining whether a loss has indeed arisen, the cost of the shares for CGT purposes is reduced by the amount of SEIS income tax relief attributable to the shares disposed of (expressed in terms of the reduction in the tax liability) to the extent that this has not been, or does not fall to be, withdrawn.

[*TCGA 1992, s 150E(1)(3); FA 2012, Sch 6 paras 3, 23(1)*].

Identification rules

The normal identification rules (see **64.2** SHARES AND SECURITIES — IDENTIFICATION RULES) are each disapplied as regards SEIS shares. Instead, the rules described at **60.36** above apply to match disposals with acquisitions of shares of the same class in the same company, and they apply where at least some of those shares have attracted SEIS income tax relief. [*TCGA 1992, s 150E(6)(7); FA 2012, Sch 6 paras 3, 23(1)*].

Rights issues

If, immediately following a rights issue, EIS relief is attributable either to the original holding or the rights shares, the share reorganisation rules of *TCGA 1992, ss 127–130* (see **63.2** SHARES AND SECURITIES) are disapplied, with the result that the rights shares are treated as a separate acquisition. [*TCGA 1992, s 150E(8); FA 2012, Sch 6 paras 3, 23(1)*].

Company reconstructions

If as part of a reconstruction, shares or debentures in another company are issued to an SEIS shareholder in exchange for SEIS shares to which income tax relief remains attributable, then the shares in the new company are not generally deemed to stand in the place of shares in the old company under *TCGA 1992, s 135* or *s 136* (see **63.5**, **63.7** SHARES AND SECURITIES) and there is thus a disposal of the shares in the old company. However, *section 135* or *136* does apply in the normal way if:

- the new holding consists of new ordinary shares issued after the end of period A (applied by reference to the original shares and the company which issued them) and carrying no present or future preferential rights to dividends or assets or right to redemption; and
- the company issuing the new shares has previously issued shares under the SEIS and has issued the appropriate compliance certificate (see **60.34** above) enabling investors to obtain relief on that earlier issue.

In addition, *TCGA 1992, s 135* is not disapplied in a case to which *ITA 2007, s 257HB* (see **60.42** above) applies. That provision is instead applied for CGT purposes also.

[*TCGA 1992, s 150E(9)–(11)(13); FA 2012, Sch 6 paras 3, 23(1)*].

Example 1

On 8 November 2013 P subscribes £130,000 for 65,000 shares in the SEIS company, S Ltd, and obtains the maximum SEIS income tax relief of £50,000 (£100,000 × 50%) for 2013/14. On 3 April 2018 he sells the entire holding for £240,000.

The chargeable gain arising is calculated as follows.

£

Disposal proceeds	240,000
Cost	130,000
Gain	110,000
Less TCGA 1992, s 150E(2)(4)(5) exemption	
$£110{,}000 \times \frac{50{,}000\ (R)}{65{,}000 (T)} =$	84,615
Chargeable gain 2017/18	£25,384

Note:

R = relief given (£100,000 × 50%) = £50,000

T = £130,000 × 50% = £65,000

Example 2

Assuming the facts otherwise remain the same as in *Example 1* above but that the shares are sold for £50,000 on 3 April 2018.

The allowable loss arising is calculated as follows.

	£	£
Disposal proceeds		50,000
Less Cost	130,000	
Less Income tax relief given (and not withdrawn)	50,000	80,000
Allowable loss 2017/18		£30,000

Example 3

The facts are otherwise as in *Example 2* above except that the shares are sold in an arm's length bargain on 3 April 2015, i.e. within three years after their issue.

Income tax relief given for 2013/14 is withdrawn as follows.

Relief attributable (£100,000 @ 50%)	£50,000 (1)
Consideration	
$£50{,}000 \times \frac{50{,}000\ (£100{,}000\ @\ 50\%)}{65{,}000\ (£130{,}000\ @\ 50\%)}$ @ 50%	£19,230 (2)

The amount at (1) is greater than that at (2), so income tax relief of £19,230 is withdrawn. [*ITA 2007, ss 257FA, 257FB*].

The relief not withdrawn is therefore £(50,000 – 19,230) =	£30,770

The allowable loss arising is calculated as follows.

	£	£
Disposal proceeds		50,000
Less Cost	130,000	
Less Income tax relief not withdrawn	30,770	99,230

Allowable loss 2014/15	£49,230

Reduction of relief where value received etc.

[60.44] Where a gain on disposal of SEIS shares would otherwise be exempt due to their having been held until after the end of period A (as in **60.13** above), a special rule applies if SEIS income tax relief has been, or falls to be, reduced (though not fully withdrawn) as a result of the investor receiving value from the company (see **60.37** above).

The CGT exemption applies only to so much of the gain as remains after deducting so much of it as is represented by the fraction $^{A}/_{B}$ where:

A = the reduction(s) made, as mentioned above, to the income tax relief given; and
B = the income tax relief given before applying such reductions.

Where the CGT exemption has already been restricted because EIS income tax relief was not given on the full amount subscribed for the shares (see **60.43** above), the fraction is applied to the part of the gain otherwise exempt and the deduction made from that part.

[*TCGA 1992, s 150F; FA 2012, Sch 6 paras 3, 23(1)*].

SEIS reinvestment relief

[60.45] A CGT exemption is available where:

- an individual realises a chargeable gain on a disposal at any time in 2012/13 or any subsequent year; and
- he is eligible for, and claims, SEIS income tax relief for the year in which the disposal is made in respect of an amount subscribed for an 'issue of shares' in a company made to him (or treated as made to him) in that year.

If the issue of shares or any corresponding bonus shares (i.e. shares issued other than for payment which are in the same company and class and carry the same rights as the SEIS shares) precedes the disposal, it is an additional condition that the individual continue to hold those shares at the time of the disposal. For this purpose, an '*issue of shares*' means an issue of shares in a company which are of the same class and are issued to the individual in one capacity and on the same day.

On a claim by the individual, a specified percentage of so much of the 'unused' acquisition cost of the SEIS shares as is specified in the claim and does not exceed so much of the chargeable gain as is 'unmatched' is set against the gain. To the extent that an amount is set against the gain, the gain ceases to be a chargeable gain. For this purpose, the acquisition cost is '*unused*' to the extent that it has not already been set against a gain either under these provisions or under EIS deferral relief (see **23.14** ENTERPRISE INVESTMENT SCHEME); and a gain is '*unmatched*' to the extent that the acquisition costs of other SEIS shares or EIS shares have not already been set against it. Where the year of disposal is 2012/13 the specified percentage is 100%; for subsequent years it is 50%.

The total amount that can be set against gains cannot exceed £100,000, i.e. the maximum amount on which SEIS income tax relief is available. Where the individual's SEIS income tax relief is restricted to £100,000 (see **60.32** above), the £100,000 limit is apportioned between share issues. If the amount of SEIS income tax relief attributable (see **60.33** above) to any of the shares has been reduced by any of the provisions at **60.35–60.40** above (otherwise than because of corresponding bonus shares being issued) before the income tax relief was obtained, the amount which can be set against gains under these provisions is correspondingly reduced. If both of these restrictions apply, the £100,000 limit restriction is applied first.

The chargeable gain eligible for relief is the gain after taking into account any mandatory reductions, and any other reliefs or elections claimed or made in computing the chargeable gain, but before the deduction of losses or the annual exemption (HMRC Venture Capital Schemes Manual VCM45010).

Claims

A claim for SEIS reinvestment relief must be made no later than five years after the 31 January following the tax year in which the shares are issued. Where SEIS shares issued in one tax year and treated as issued in the previous tax year as a result of a SEIS income tax relief carry-back claim (see **60.32** above), they will thereby qualify to be used in a reinvestment relief claim (HMRC Venture Capital Schemes Manual VCM45010) for the earlier year. This does not, however, affect the time limit for making a claim.

Attribution of relief to shares

A proportionate part of the expenditure set off against a chargeable gain is attributed to each of the SEIS shares concerned and the attribution is adjusted correspondingly for any subsequent issue of corresponding bonus shares.

Removal or reduction of relief

If SEIS income tax relief attributable (see **60.33** above) to shares is withdrawn (see **60.34** onwards above), any SEIS reinvestment relief attributable to those shares is also withdrawn. If SEIS income tax relief attributable to shares is reduced, any SEIS reinvestment relief attributable to those shares is reduced in the same proportion. In either case, a chargeable gain is then deemed to accrue to the individual in the tax year in which the shares were issued of an amount equal to the amount of reinvestment relief to be withdrawn or the amount by which reinvestment relief falls to be reduced.

The relevant date for the purposes of **42.3** LATE PAYMENT INTEREST AND PENALTIES is 31 January following the tax year in which the assessment of the chargeable gain is made.

Transfer to spouse or civil partner

Where shares to which SEIS income tax relief is attributable are transferred by the individual to whom they were issued ('A') to that individual's spouse or civil partner ('B') during their lives, then, if that relief was not withdrawn or reduced on that transfer (see **60.41** above), any chargeable gain arising to remove or reduce SEIS reinvestment relief attributable to the shares is treated as arising to B.

[*TCGA 1992, s 150G, Sch 5BB; FA 2012, Sch 6 paras 4, 5; FA 2013, s 57; FA 2014, s 55*].

Example

On 1 June 2017, X sells an asset for £365,000. The asset had cost X £240,000 in 2005. X makes no other disposals in 2017/18. On 1 February 2018, X acquires by subscription 50,000 shares in ABC Ltd at a total price of £100,000. X claims SEIS income tax relief in respect of the acquisition.

If X makes a claim under *TCGA 1992, Sch 5BB* then his CGT position for 2017/18 is as follows.

	£
Consideration	365,000
Less Acquisition cost	240,000
Gain	125,000
Less Reinvestment relief	50,000
Chargeable gain	75,000
Less annual exempt amount	11,300
Taxable gain 2017/18	£63,700

61

Self-Assessment

Introduction	**61.1**
Capital gains tax (and income tax)	**61.2**
Corporation tax	**61.3**

Simon's Taxes. See E1.2.

Introduction

[61.1] Both capital gains tax and corporation tax on chargeable gains are administered under a system of self-assessment. Capital gains tax is incorporated within the income tax self-assessment system which has effect generally for 1996/97 and subsequent tax years, although some aspects of the system came into effect earlier and some in 1997/98. A separate (but similar) system applies for corporation tax purposes for accounting periods ending on or after 1 July 1999.

The term 'self-assessment' refers to the system whereby the tax return for the year or accounting period includes the taxpayer's own assessment of the tax liability. Payment of tax is then due automatically, based on the self-assessment.

A summary of the capital gains tax/income tax system is given at **61.2** below, and that for corporation tax at **61.3** below. This chapter does not cover the special rules for non-resident disposals of UK residential property interests. See **41.25** LAND for a summary of those provisions and also **51.3** PAYMENT OF TAX and **58.20** RETURNS.

The Government intends to abolish the tax returns for millions of individuals through the phased introduction of digital tax accounts ('Making Tax Digital'). See **58.1** RETURNS.

Capital gains tax (and income tax)

[61.2] The main features of the self-assessment regime for individuals, personal representatives and trustees are summarised below. The detailed provisions are covered as indicated.

- A person chargeable to capital gains tax (and/or income tax) for a particular tax year who has not received a notice to deliver a return for that year has until 5 October following that year to notify HMRC that he is so chargeable (see **52.3** PENALTIES).
- HMRC may withdraw a notice to an individual or trustee to make a return for 2014/15 or a subsequent year. The notice must normally be withdrawn within two years of the end of the tax year to which the

notice relates. HMRC were similarly able to withdraw notices for 2012/13 and 2013/14, but only where the individual or trustee requested HMRC to do so. If HMRC withdraw a notice, they will issue a withdrawal notice and no return needs to be submitted. See **58.3** RETURNS.

- HMRC can instead make a 'simple assessment' of an individual's or trustee's income tax or capital gains tax liability for **2016/17** or a subsequent year without the taxpayer first being required to complete a self-assessment tax return. The simple assessment will be made on the basis of information already held by HMRC, whether it was received from the taxpayer or a third party.
- Returns of income and gains must normally be filed with HMRC by 31 January following the tax year, except that, for returns for 2007/08 onwards, the deadline is brought forward to 31 October following the tax year if the return is not delivered electronically via HMRC's Self-Assessment Online service (see **58.3** RETURNS). The return must, subject to the exception below, include a self-assessment of the tax liability, based on the information in the return, although in practice the tax due is computed automatically during the filing of an electronic return. Electronic returns must be filed by 30 December following the tax year if the taxpayer wishes unpaid tax (where this is less than £3,000) to be collected via his tax code.
- Taxpayers who are not filing their return electronically and who prefer not to compute their own liabilities do not have to do so providing they file their return by 31 October following the tax year (or, if later, within two months of the date of the notice to file the return) (see **58.6** RETURNS). In such cases, HMRC will compute the tax due and make an assessment accordingly. Such an assessment is treated as a self-assessment by the person making the return and as included in the return.
- A separate return has to be filed by a partnership (in addition to the returns of each of the partners). This must include a statement of the allocation of partnership income between the partners. See **58.16–58.18** RETURNS.
- Penalties are imposed for failure to notify and for late submission of returns, subject to appeal on the grounds of reasonable excuse (see **52.3**, **52.4** and **52.5** PENALTIES).
- Before making a return, a taxpayer can ask HMRC to check any valuations used for capital gains tax purposes in completing the return (see **58.5** RETURNS).
- Taxpayers may amend their return at any time within twelve months after the filing date (treated, for this purpose, as 31 January following the tax year in most cases). HMRC may amend a return to correct obvious errors, omissions or anything else which they have reason to believe is incorrect in the light of information available to them at any time within nine months after its delivery, but the taxpayer can reject such a correction within 30 days. See **58.7** RETURNS.
- HMRC are given broadly one year from the day the return is delivered to give notice of their intention to enquire into the return (see **58.9** RETURNS). A formal procedure is laid down for such enquiries (see

58.9–58.14 RETURNS). HMRC can also make use of their powers under *FA 2008, Sch 36* to carry out 'compliance checks' (see **34.3** HMRC INVESTIGATORY POWERS).

- If HMRC do not give an enquiry notice, the return becomes final and conclusive, subject to any claim for recovery of overpaid tax by the taxpayer (see **13.7** CLAIMS) or 'discovery' assessment by HMRC (see **6.10** ASSESSMENTS).
- In the event of non-submission of a return, HMRC are able to make a determination of the tax liability; there is no right of appeal but the determination may be superseded upon submission of the return (see **58.15** RETURNS).
- A self-assessment contained in a return under for 2012/13 or a later year cannot normally be made more than four years after the end of the tax year. Self-assessments for 2011/12 and earlier years cannot be made after 5 April 2017 (which is also the deadline for 2012/13, applying the four-year rule). See **58.6** RETURNS
- Income tax (on all sources of taxable income) for a tax year is payable by means of two interim payments of equal amounts, based normally on the liability for the previous tax year and due on 31 January in the tax year and the following 31 July. A final balancing payment is due on the following 31 January which is also the due date for capital gains tax liability (see **51.2** PAYMENT OF TAX). Interim payments are not required where substantially all of a taxpayer's income is subject to deduction of tax at source or where the amounts otherwise due are below de minimis limits. See Tolley's Income Tax for further coverage of interim payments.
- Interest on overdue payments runs from the due date to the date of payment (see **42.2**, **42.3** LATE PAYMENT INTEREST AND PENALTIES). Interest on tax overpaid normally runs from the date of payment to the date of repayment (see **56.2**, **56.3** REPAYMENT INTEREST); the rate of interest is lower than that on overdue tax.
- Late payment penalties apply where tax due is unpaid more than 30 days after the due date. The penalties replace the previous surcharge regime which applied where tax was unpaid more than 28 days after the due date. See **42.6**, **42.10** LATE PAYMENT INTEREST AND PENALTIES.
- There is a statutory requirement for taxpayers to keep records for the purpose of making returns and to preserve such records for specified periods (see **58.8** RETURNS).
- For the formal procedure applying to the making of claims, elections and notices see **13.2** CLAIMS.
- For appeals see **5.2** APPEALS.

See also HMRC Self Assessment Legal Framework Manual.

Corporation tax

[61.3] The main features of the corporation tax self-assessment regime are summarised below. The detailed provisions are covered as indicated and in Tolley's Corporation Tax.

- A company must notify HMRC of the beginning of its first accounting period (and of the beginning of any subsequent accounting period that does not immediately follow the end of a previous accounting period) within three months after the beginning of the period (see **58.19** RETURNS).
- A company chargeable to corporation tax for an accounting period which has neither made a return for that period nor received a notice to deliver a return must notify HMRC of its chargeability within twelve months after the end of that period (see **58.19** RETURNS).
- Returns of profits and gains must normally be filed with HMRC within twelve months after the end of the period to which they relate (see **58.19** RETURNS). The return must include a self-assessment of the tax liability, based on the information in the return. Returns must be filed online using a specified data format (iXBRL).
- Penalties are imposed for failure to notify chargeability and for late submission of returns, subject to appeal on the grounds of reasonable excuse (see **52.3** and **52.4** PENALTIES).
- Before making its return, a company can ask HMRC to check any valuations used for chargeable gains purposes in completing the return (see **58.19** RETURNS).
- Companies may amend their return at any time within twelve months after the filing date. HMRC may amend a return to correct obvious errors, omissions or anything else which they have reason to believe is incorrect in the light of information available to them at any time within nine months after its delivery. The company can reject such a correction by amending its return or, where the time limit for amendment has passed, by notice within three months.
- HMRC are given broadly one year from the day the return is delivered (for returns for accounting periods ending on or before 1 April 2008, one year from the filing date) to give notice of their intention to enquire into the return (see **58.19** RETURNS).
- If HMRC do not give such notice, the return becomes final and conclusive, subject to any claim for recovery of overpaid tax by the company (see **13.7** CLAIMS) or 'discovery' assessment by HMRC.
- In the event of non-submission of a return, HMRC are able to make a determination of the tax liability; there is no right of appeal but the determination may be superseded upon submission of the return (see **58.15** RETURNS).
- For companies other than 'large' companies, corporation tax (including that in respect of chargeable gains) for an accounting period is due and payable on the day following the expiry of nine months from the end of the period. Large companies pay corporation tax under a system of quarterly instalments. See **51.4** PAYMENT OF TAX.
- Interest on overdue payments runs from the due date to the date of payment (see **42.7** LATE PAYMENT INTEREST AND PENALTIES). A different rate of interest applies to unpaid instalments under the quarterly instalment rules from the due date to the earlier of the date of payment and the normal due date (i.e. the day following the expiry of nine months from the end of the accounting period). Interest on tax overpaid normally

runs from the date of payment to the date of repayment (see **56.4** REPAYMENT INTEREST); again, a different rate of interest applies up to the normal due date (whether or not the quarterly instalment rules apply).

- There is a statutory requirement for taxpayers to keep records for the purpose of making returns and to preserve such records for six years from the end of the return period (see **58.19** RETURNS).
- For the formal procedure applying to the making of claims, elections and notices see **13.4** CLAIMS.
- For appeals see **5.2** APPEALS.

See also **Simon's Taxes**. See **D1.13**.

62

Settlements

Introduction to settlements	**62.1**
Settlements: definitions	**62.2**
Meaning of 'settled property'	**62.3**
Interests in settled property	**62.4**
Meaning of 'settlor'	**62.5**
Liability of trustees, settlors and beneficiaries	**62.6**
Rates of tax	**62.7**
Annual exemptions	**62.8**
Settlements for the disabled etc.	**62.9**
Collection of unpaid tax from beneficiaries etc.	**62.10**
Relevant trustees	**62.11**
Sub-fund settlements	**62.12**
Trusts with vulnerable beneficiary	**62.13**
Disposals during the life-cycle of a settlement	**62.14**
Creation of a settlement	**62.14**
Disposal of an interest in settled property	**62.15**
Person becoming absolutely entitled to settled property	**62.16**
Termination of life interest in possession on death of person entitled: assets remaining settled property	**62.17**
Termination of life interest on death of person entitled — person becoming absolutely entitled	**62.18**
Anti-avoidance	**62.19**
Deemed disposal of underlying assets on certain disposals of interests in settled property	**62.20**
Transfers of value by trustees linked with trustee borrowing	**62.21**
Restriction on set-off of settlement losses	**62.22**
Attribution to trustees of gains of non-resident companies	**62.23**
Key points related to settlements	**62.24**

Cross-references. See **2** ANNUAL RATES AND EXEMPTIONS; **6.6** ASSESSMENTS for assessments on trustees; **11** CHARITIES; **12.2** CHILDREN for bare trustees for children; **19** DEATH for provisions relating to death and to personal representatives; **22.30** EMPLOYEE SHARE SCHEMES for certain transfers of shares to employee share ownership trusts; **25.86** EXEMPTIONS AND RELIEFS for reinvestment relief available on disposals by trustees where proceeds reinvested before 6 April 1998; **25.91** EXEMPTIONS AND RELIEFS for settlements for the benefit of employees; **27** GIFTS and **36** HOLD-OVER RELIEFS for disposals not at arm's length and the availability of hold-over reliefs generally; **48** OFFSHORE SETTLEMENTS for overseas resident settlements etc.; **53.11** PRIVATE RESIDENCES for reliefs applicable to trustees; **58.10** RETURNS for returns by trustees; **63.10** SHARES AND SECURITIES for stock dividends received by trustees; **72.7** WASTING ASSETS for the situation where a disposal of a life interest in settled property gives rise to a chargeable event.

Simon's Taxes. See C4.2–C4.6.

Introduction to settlements

[62.1] Trustees of a settlement are liable to capital gains tax on disposals of settled property, as if they were a single person. This chapter describes the liability of trustees and also that of settlors and beneficiaries of settlements. Special rules apply to certain trusts with vulnerable beneficiaries (see **62.13** below).

Also covered in this chapter are the disposals which may arise during the life-cycle of a settlement, from its creation to the termination of a life interest. There are a number of anti-avoidance provisions relevant to settlements and these are covered at **62.19** onwards below.

For the capital gains tax rules which apply where the trustees of a settlement are not resident in the UK see **48** OFFSHORE SETTLEMENTS.

Settlements: definitions

[62.2] The following definitions apply for the purposes of this chapter.

Meaning of 'settled property'

[62.3] '*Settled property*' means any property held in trust other than property held by 'nominees' or 'bare trustees' (see below). References in *TCGA 1992*, however expressed, to property comprised in a settlement are references to settled property. Property held by a trustee or assignee in bankruptcy or under a deed of arrangement (see below) is not settled property. Property under a unit trust scheme (as defined) is also excluded from being settled property. [*TCGA 1992, ss 66(4), 68, 99*]. See also **70.3** UNIT TRUSTS ETC.

Nominees and bare trustees

Where property is held by a person:

(i) as nominee for another or others; or
(ii) as trustee for a person (or persons) 'absolutely entitled' as against him,

capital gains tax is chargeable as if the property were held by that other person or persons and such property were not settled property.

A person is '*absolutely entitled*', for these purposes, if he has the exclusive right (subject only to satisfying any outstanding charge, lien or other right of the trustee to resort to the property for the payment of duty, tax, costs or other outgoings) to direct how that property shall be dealt with, or would have that right but for being an infant or under some other legal disability (e.g. a mentally handicapped person).

[*TCGA 1992, s 60*].

The disability must arise from the general law, and not from the wording of the trust deed (see *Tomlinson v Glyn's Exor and Trustee Co* Ltd CA 1969, 45 TC 600 where the trustees were held assessable to capital gains tax because the beneficiary's interest was contingent on his attaining majority, and could not be deemed to be vested in him). In *Booth v Ellard* CA 1980, 53 TC 393, several taxpayers by agreement transferred their shares in a company to trustees. The trusts were determinable by a majority of the beneficiaries (who were also the settlors), each beneficiary had a right of pre-emption over the others' shares, and the income was to be distributed in proportion to the number of shares to which each beneficiary was entitled (which corresponded with the number which he had settled). It was held that each beneficiary retained his interest in the same number of shares as he had settled (albeit not the identical shares). Despite the restraints, it was within the beneficiaries' collective power to terminate the trusts, and each beneficiary was therefore absolutely entitled as against the trustees. See also *Jenkins v Brown, Warrington v Brown and related appeals* Ch D, [1989] STC 577.

Kidson v Macdonald Ch D 1973, 49 TC 503 laid down that tenants in common of land held on trust for sale were jointly absolutely entitled. It is not necessary that particular assets to which the beneficiaries are entitled should be identifiable (*Stephenson v Barclays Bank Trust Co Ltd* Ch D 1974, 50 TC 374), but see *Cochrane's Exors v CIR* CS 1974, 49 TC 299 (entitlement to residue) and *Crowe v Appleby* CA 1975, 51 TC 457. See also *Newman v Pepper; Newman v Morgan* (Sp C 243), [2000] SSCD 345.

Trustees of bare trusts treated as such for tax purposes are not required to complete self-assessment tax returns or make tax payments, the 'beneficiaries' being liable to give details of the income and gains in their own tax returns. (Revenue Tax Bulletin February 1997 p 395). The trustees may, *if they wish*, make a self-assessment return of income, and account for basic or lower rate income tax thereon. Capital gains and capital losses *cannot* be included in any such return, these being the sole responsibility of the beneficiaries. (Revenue Tax Bulletin December 1997 pp 486, 487).

Insolvents' assets

Assets held by a trustee or assignee in bankruptcy or under a 'deed of arrangement' are treated as if still owned by the bankrupt or debtor (the trustee's acquisitions from, or disposals to, the bankrupt being disregarded) and as if the trustee's acts in relation to those assets were acts of the bankrupt. But tax on chargeable gains arising from such acts is assessable on, and payable by, the trustee, etc. '*Deed of arrangement*' means a deed to which the *Deeds of Arrangement Act 1914* (or any corresponding Act in Scotland or NI) applies. [*TCGA 1992, s 66(1)(5)*].

When the bankrupt etc. dies, the assets held by the trustee are deemed for the purposes of *TCGA 1992, s 62(1)* (see **19.2** DEATH) to have then been acquired by the trustee as if he were a personal representative. The provisions above do not then apply after death. But if the bankrupt is dead before the trustee is appointed, the provisions above also do not apply, the assets being regarded as held by the deceased's personal representative. [*TCGA 1992, s 66(2)–(4)*].

In re McMeekin QB (NI) 1973, 48 TC 725 it was held that capital gains tax is an administration cost of bankruptcy.

Interests in settled property

[62.4] Interests in settled property take a variety of forms as outlined below. Their treatment for capital gains tax purposes is given in **62.15** to **62.18** below. See **62.3** above as regards bare trusts.

Interests created by or arising under a settlement

These include, in particular, an annuity or life interest (see below), and the reversion to an annuity or life interest, but are otherwise not specifically defined. [*TCGA 1992, s 76*].

Life interests in relation to a settlement

The meaning of 'life interest' includes a right under the settlement to the income of, or the use or occupation of, settled property for the life of a person other than the person entitled to the right, or for lives. [*TCGA 1992, s 72(3)(a)*]. Any right which is contingent on the exercise of the discretion of the trustee or some other person is not a life interest. [*TCGA 1992, s 72(3)(b)*]. The ordinary meaning of 'life interest' (i.e. the right of a person to income etc. during his life) is also accepted as applying. Interests which are not primarily defined by reference to a life are not considered to be life interests, so that a beneficiary with an interest in possession (see below) in settled property which will come to an end on obtaining a specified age does not have a life interest (HMRC Extra-Statutory Concession D43). However, concessional treatment is available for such non-life interests which cease on the death of a beneficiary as in **62.17** and **62.18** below.

An annuity created by the settlement is included as a life interest if:

- (i) some or all of the settled property is appropriated by the trustees as a fund out of which the annuity is payable; and
- (ii) there is no right of recourse to settled property not so appropriated or to the income thereof.

While such an annuity is payable, and on the occasion of the death of the annuitant, the appropriated part of the settled property is treated as being settled property under a separate settlement. Annuities, other than those above, are not life interests notwithstanding that they are payable out of, or charged on, settled property or the income thereof. [*TCGA 1992, s 72(3)(c), (4)*]. However, where an annuity which is not a life interest is terminated by the death of the annuitant, certain provisions in **62.17** and **62.18** below apply as on the termination of a life interest by the death of the person entitled thereto.

Life interest in possession in all or part of settled property

The legislation gives no meaning to the term 'life interest in possession' although it seems regard must be made to the meaning of 'life interest' (as above) and to judicial interpretation of the term 'interest in possession'. Such interpretation arose in *Pearson and Others v CIR* HL, [1980] STC 318 where the point at issue was the meaning of the term 'interest in possession' as used in certain capital transfer tax legislation dealing with settled property. The majority opinions of the HL indicated the following.

(a) There must be a *present right to the present enjoyment* of something for there to be an interest in possession in settled property. So a person with an interest in possession will have an immediate right to trust income as it arises.

(b) If the trustees have *any power to withhold income* as it arises there is no interest in possession. There is a distinction between a power to terminate a present right to present enjoyment and a power which prevents a present right of present enjoyment arising. It follows that:

   (i) a power to accumulate income is sufficient to prevent a beneficiary from having an interest in possession. The position is the same if there is a trust to accumulate. Whether or not income is in fact accumulated is irrelevant;

   (ii) an overriding power of appointment which could be used to defeat the interest of a beneficiary does not prevent that interest from being in possession if it does not affect the right of the beneficiary to the income which has already arisen;

   (iii) the possibility of future defeasance of an interest does not prevent it from being in possession until the occurrence of the relevant event; and

   (iv) a power of revocation does not prevent an interest from being in possession until it is exercised.

(c) There is a distinction between trustees' *administrative powers,* such as those to pay duties, taxes etc., and their *dispositive powers* to dispose of the net income of the trust. The existence of the former does not prevent an interest from being in possession. Any interest in possession will be in the net income of the trust after deduction of administrative expenses.

(d) The fact that an interest in settled property is not in remainder or reversion or contingent does not automatically make it an interest in possession.

If, in exercise of their powers under the settlement, the trustees grant a beneficiary an exclusive or joint right to occupy a dwelling-house which forms part of the settled property with the intention of providing the beneficiary with a permanent home, HMRC regard this as creating an interest in possession, even if the right is revocable or for a limited period. A right granted for non-exclusive occupation or for full consideration is not so regarded (HMRC Statement of Practice 10/79). See **53.11** PRIVATE RESIDENCES for the exemption available on the disposal of a dwelling-house which has been occupied in the above circumstances.

Meaning of 'settlor'

[62.5] The following extended definition of 'settlor' applies for all capital gains purposes, unless the context otherwise requires. There are, however, also definitions for the purposes of particular provisions.

Subject to the above, a '*settlor*' of a settlement is the person, or any of the persons, who has made, or is treated as having made, the settlement. A person is a settlor of property which is settled property by reason of his having made the settlement or of an event which causes him to be treated as having made the settlement or which derives from such property (see below).

For these purposes, a person is treated as having made a settlement if he has, directly or indirectly, made or entered into the settlement. In particular, a person is so treated if he has provided, or undertaken to provide, property directly or indirectly for the purposes of the settlement. Where the settlement arises by will, intestacy or otherwise on a person's death, that person is treated as having made the settlement if the settled property, or property derived from it, is or includes property of which he was 'competent to dispose immediately before his death'. A person making or entering into a settlement in accordance with reciprocal 'arrangements' with another person is not treated as having made the settlement by reason only of those arrangements. Instead, the other person is treated as having made the settlement.

A settlor is treated as ceasing to be a settlor of a settlement if:

- no property of which he is a settlor remains in the settlement;
- he has not undertaken to provide property directly or indirectly for the purposes of the settlement in the future; and
- he has not made reciprocal arrangements with another person to enter into the settlement in the future.

For the purposes of these provisions, 'arrangements' include a scheme, agreement or understanding, whether or not legally enforceable. Property is derived from other property if it derives, directly or indirectly, wholly or partly, from that property or any part of it or from income from that property or any part of it. Property of which a person was '*competent to dispose immediately before his death*' is any property which (otherwise than in right of a power of appointment or of the testamentary power conferred by statute to dispose of entailed interests) he could, if of full age and capacity, have disposed of by his will, assuming that all the property was situated in England and, if he was not domiciled in the United Kingdom, that he was domiciled in England, and include references to his severable share in any property to which, immediately before his death, he was beneficially entitled as joint tenant.

[*TCGA 1992, ss 62(10), 68A*].

Transfers between settlements

Where there is a 'transfer of property' from the trustees of one settlement to the trustees of a second settlement otherwise than for full consideration or at arm's length, the settlor or settlors of the property so transferred are treated from the time of the transfer as settlors of the second settlement. If there is more than one settlor of the property transferred, each is treated in relation to the second settlement as the settlor of a proportionate part of the 'transferred property'.

There is a '*transfer of property*' for these purposes if there is a disposal of property by the trustees of one settlement and the acquisition by the trustees of the second settlement either of property disposed of by the trustees of the first settlement or property created by the disposal. References above and below to '*transferred property*' are to property acquired by the trustees of the second settlement on the disposal. Where a transfer of property is between trustees who are CONNECTED PERSONS (**17**) the transfer is not treated as being otherwise than at arm's length by reason of the connection.

If and to the extent that property disposed of by the trustees of the first settlement was provided for the purposes of that settlement or is derived from property so provided, the transferred property is treated from the time of the disposal as having been provided for the purposes of the second settlement by the person or persons who provided the property disposed of or the property from which it was derived (and hence those persons are treated as having made the second settlement). If there is more than one such person each of them is treated as having provided a proportionate part of the transferred property. This does not apply to a transfer of property:

- occurring by reason of the assignment or assignation by a beneficiary of the first settlement of an interest in that settlement to the trustees of the second settlement;
- occurring by reason only of the exercise of a general power of appointment; or
- resulting from a variation of a will or intestacy within the provisions below such that property of which the deceased person is a settlor is comprised in a settlement immediately before the variation and immediately afterwards the property, or property derived from it, becomes comprised in another settlement.

[*TCGA 1992, s 68B*].

Variation of will or intestacy

The following provisions apply where, within two years of a person's death, there is a variation in a disposition of property of which the deceased was competent to dispose to which *TCGA 1992, s 62(6)* (deeds of family arrangement etc. — see **19.8** DEATH) applies.

Where property becomes settled property as a result only of the variation, the following persons are treated as having made the settlement and as having provided property for the purposes of the settlement:

- a person who immediately before the variation was entitled absolutely as legatee to the property or property from which it derives, or who would have been so entitled but for being an infant or other person under a disability; and
- a person who would, but for the variation, have become absolutely entitled as legatee to the property or property from which it derives or who would have become so entitled but for being an infant or other person under a disability.

In determining for this purpose whether a person was, or would be entitled absolutely as legatee, property taken under a testamentary disposition or on an intestacy or partial intestacy includes any property appropriated by the personal representative in or towards satisfaction of a pecuniary legacy or any other interest or share in the property devolving.

Where property which would, but for the variation, have become comprised in an existing settlement (whether or not the deceased was the settlor) or a settlement arising on the death of the deceased person (by will, intestacy or otherwise) instead becomes comprised in another settlement as a result of the variation, the deceased person is treated as having made that other settlement. Unless that settlement arose on the deceased's death, he is treated as having made it immediately before his death.

Where property of which the deceased person is a settlor is comprised in a settlement immediately before the variation and immediately afterwards the property, or property derived from it, becomes comprised in another settlement, the deceased person is treated as having made that other settlement. Unless that settlement arose on the deceased's death, he is treated as having made it immediately before his death.

[*TCGA 1992, s 68C*].

Liability of trustees, settlors and beneficiaries

[62.6] Trustees of a settlement are liable to capital gains tax, under provisions relating to the tax generally, on disposals or deemed disposals of settled property (but subject, for 2007/08 and earlier years, to the charge on settlors with interests in settlements). The exempt amount for a tax year available to trustees is given in **62.8** and **62.9** below.

The trustees of a settlement are treated as if they were a single person (distinct from the persons who may from time to time be trustees). [*TCGA 1992, s 69(1)*]. For the residence etc. status of the deemed person, see **48.1** OFFSHORE SETTLEMENTS. See **62.12** below for the election available for the sub-fund of a settlement to be treated as a separate settlement.

Where an invalid appointment of trustees is made, the trustees of the settlement remain, for this purpose, the validly-appointed trustees, even if the latter believe that they have retired (see *Jasmine Trustees Ltd v Wells and Hind* Ch D, [2007] STC 660). Acts of the purported trustees are attributed to the actual trustees.

Special rules apply to overseas resident settlements etc. See **47** OFFSHORE SETTLEMENTS.

Where part of the property comprised in a settlement is vested in one trustee or set of trustees and part in another (and in particular settled land within the meaning of the *Settled Land Act 1925* is vested in the tenant for life and investments representing capital money are vested in the trustees of the settlement), all the trustees are treated as together constituting and, insofar as they act separately, as acting on behalf of a single body of trustees. [*TCGA 1992, s 69(3)*].

HMRC may by notice in writing given before 1 April 2012 require a person who is a 'party' to a settlement (within *ITTOIA 2005, s 620*) to provide within not less than 28 days information they think necessary for the purposes of *TCGA 1992*. [*TMA 1970, s 27; FA 2011, Sch 23 paras 51(2), 65*]. This provision is replaced with effect from 1 April 2012 by the new data-gathering power under *FA 2011, Sch 23*. See **34.17** HMRC INVESTIGATORY POWERS.

Rates of tax

[62.7] For 2016/17 and 2017/18 the rate of tax is 28% for upper rate gains (see **2.1** ANNUAL RATES AND EXEMPTIONS) and 20% for other gains, except for gains to which entrepreneurs' relief applies, in which case the rate is 10%. For 2011/12 to 2015/16, the rate of tax is 28% or, for gains to which entrepreneurs' relief applies, 10%. [*TCGA 1992, s 4(3); FA 2016, s 83(5)*].

Where trustees have gains chargeable at different rates, any allowable losses and annual exempt amount can be set against the gains in the most beneficial way. [*TCGA 1992, s 4B*].

Annual exemptions

[62.8] An annual exempt amount (sometimes known as an annual exemption) is allowed to trustees in the same way as it is to individuals, and the same rules apply as to the interaction between this amount and allowable losses. See **2.6** ANNUAL RATES AND EXEMPTIONS.

The level and availability of the exemption are subject to conditions. These are given below or, in the case of settlements for the disabled etc., in **62.9** below.

Settlements made before 7 June 1978

An outright exemption of *one-half* of the full annual exempt amount for individuals is available to trustees of such settlements. The exemption limit is thus £5,650 for 2017/18. Limits for earlier years are as follows.

2016/17	£5,550
2015/16	£5,550
2014/15	£5,500
2013/14	£5,450

Settlements made after 6 June 1978

The same exemption is available as for settlements made before 7 June 1978 above with the addition of special provisions for 'groups' of settlements. Where a settlement is one of two or more 'qualifying settlements' comprised in a group, the annual exempt amount is the amount given by dividing one-half of the full annual exempt amount for individuals (see above) by the number of settlements in the group. However, there is a minimum exemption per settlement of one-tenth of the full annual exempt amount for individuals. These provisions apply without regard to any sub-fund settlement elections (see **62.12** above), so that a principal settlement and its sub-fund settlements count as only one settlement for the purpose of dividing up the exempt amount. See also below regarding sub-fund settlements.

A '*qualifying settlement*' is any settlement made after 6 June 1978 and which is not a settlement for the disabled, etc. (see **62.9** below) or an 'excluded settlement' (see below). A '*group*' of settlements constitutes all those qualifying settlements with the same 'settlor'. Where, in consequence of this, a settlement is comprised in two or more groups because that settlement was made by two or more settlors, then, in determining the level of annual exempt amount available as above, it is deemed to be in the group comprised of the greatest number of settlements.

'*Settlor*' is as in **62.5** above.

'*Excluded settlements*' are any of the following:

(i) Settlements, the trustees of which are not for the whole or any part of the year of assessment resident in the UK (see **48.1** OFFSHORE SETTLEMENTS).
(ii) Settlements, the property in which is held solely for charitable purposes and cannot become applicable for other purposes. See also **11.2** CHARITIES.
(iii) Settlements, the property in which is held for the purposes of certain pension schemes and funds which are exempt from a charge on capital gains.

Before 13 August 2009, an HMRC officer could, by notice in writing, require any party to a settlement to provide, within a stipulated time (not less than 28 days), such information as the officer thought necessary for the application of the above provisions. This power has been repealed as it is no longer considered necessary following the introduction of the general information powers in *FA 2008, Sch 36* (see **34** HMRC INVESTIGATORY POWERS).

[*TCGA 1992, s 3(1)–(5D), Sch 1 paras A1, 2; FA 2012, s 34; FA 2013, Sch 46 paras 105, 112; FA 2014, ss 8, 9; FA 2015, Sch 7 paras 5, 35; SI 2010 No 923*].

Sub-fund settlements

Where a settlement has been divided for tax purposes into a principal settlement and one or more sub-fund settlements (see **62.12** above), the exempt amount available to the trustees of each deemed settlement is, initially, the amount that would be available to the trustees of the principal settlement under the provisions above or those at **62.9** below if no sub-fund settlement elections had been made. The amount available to each set of trustees is reduced, however, where the deemed settlements include two or more non-excluded settlements (i.e. settlements which are not excluded settlements (see above)). In such circumstances, the exempt amount available to each set of trustees is equal to the amount otherwise available divided by the number of non-excluded settlements. [*TCGA 1992, Sch 1 para 3*].

Settlements for the disabled etc.

[62.9] Subject to the 'grouping' provisions below the same annual exempt amount as for individuals (**£11,300** for 2017/18) (applied, in general, as for individuals: see **2.6** ANNUAL RATES AND EXEMPTIONS for this and for exemptions for earlier years) is available to trustees of such settlements if the following conditions are satisfied.

For 2013/14 and subsequent years (subject to the transitional rule below), the conditions are that, during the whole or part of the tax year concerned, the settled property is held on trusts which secure that, during the lifetime of a disabled person:

(i) if any of the property is applied for the benefit of a beneficiary it is applied for the benefit of the disabled person; and

(ii) either the disabled person is entitled to all the income (if any) arising from any of the property or that if any such income is applied for the benefit of a beneficiary, it is applied for the benefit of the disabled person.

For 2012/13 and earlier years, the conditions are that, during the whole or part of the tax year concerned, the settled property is held on trusts which secure that, during the lifetime of a disabled person:

(a) not less than half of the property which is applied, is applied for the benefit of the person concerned; and

(b) that person is entitled to not less than half of the income arising from the property, or no such income may be applied for the benefit of any other person.

For 2013/14 onwards (subject to the transitional rule below), '*disabled person*' means either a person who by reason of mental disorder is incapable of administering his property or managing his affairs or a person in receipt of any one or more specified State benefits. A person is treated as being a disabled person for these purposes if he satisfies HMRC that he would be entitled to receive the State benefit in question were it not for his being resident outside the UK or in a care home, hospital or prison. A broadly similar definition applied for 2012/13 and earlier years.

For 2013/14 onwards (subject to the transitional rule below), a trust is not disqualified from the relief by reason only of:

(I) the trustees' having powers that enable them to apply in any tax year otherwise than for the benefit of the disabled person amounts (whether consisting of income or capital or both) not exceeding the 'annual limit'; or

(II) the trustees' having the powers conferred by *Trustee Act 1925, s 32* (powers of advancement) (or its NI equivalent); or

(III) the trustees' having those powers but free from, or subject to a less restrictive limitation than, the limitation imposed by *Trustee Act 1925, s 32(1)(a)* (or its NI equivalent); or

(IV) the trustees' having powers to the like effect as the powers mentioned in (II) or (III).

The '*annual limit*' in (I) above is £3,000 or, if lower, 3% of the maximum value of the settled property during the tax year in question.

For 2012/13 and earlier years, powers of advancement conferred on the trustees under *Trustee Act 1925, s 32* or *Trustee Act (Northern Ireland) 1958, s 33* do not, as such, disqualify the trust from the relief, and requirements that income be applied for qualifying purposes 'during the lifetime' of a person are deemed satisfied if income is applied for such purposes, during a period where it is held for that person on protective trusts, as under *Trustee Act 1925, s 33*.

Transitional rule

The changes above which apply for 2013/14 onwards do not prevent the relief from applying to settlements created before 8 April 2013 if the trusts have not been altered on or after that date or to settlements arising on or after 8 April 2013 under a will executed before, and unaltered in relation to the settlement on or after, that date. The changes also do not prevent the relief from applying to settlements arising on or after 8 April 2013 under a will executed or confirmed on or after that date if the provisions in it relating to the settlement are the same as those in a previous will made on or before that date. For this purpose, a will includes a codicil.

Groups

Where a settlement is one of two or more 'qualifying settlements' made after 9 March 1981 comprised in a 'group', the annual exempt amount is the full annual exempt amount for individuals divided by the number of settlements in the 'group'. However, there is a minimum exemption of one-tenth of the full annual exempt amount. These provisions apply without regard to any sub-fund settlement elections (see **62.12** above), so that a principal settlement and its sub-fund settlements count as only one settlement for the purpose of dividing up the exempt amount. See also **62.8** above.

A '*qualifying settlement*' is any settlement for a disabled person, etc. within the provisions above made after 9 March 1981 and which is not an 'excluded settlement'. A '*group*' of settlements constitutes all those qualifying settlements with the same 'settlor'. Where in consequence of this, a settlement is comprised in two or more groups because that settlement was made by two or more settlors, then, in determining the level of annual exempt amount available as above, it is deemed to be in the group comprised of the greatest number of settlements.

'*Settlor*' and '*excluded settlement*' are as defined in **62.8** above in relation to other settlements made after 6 June 1978 and, before 13 August 2009, there were similar powers to call for information.

[*TCGA 1992, s 3(1)–(5D), Sch 1 paras A1, 1; FA 2012, s 34; FA 2013, Sch 44 paras 13, 20; FA 2014, s 8; FA 2015, Sch 7 paras 5, 35; SI 2010 No 923*].

Collection of unpaid tax from beneficiaries etc.

[62.10] If tax assessed on trustees in respect of a chargeable gain accruing to them is not paid within six months from the date when it becomes payable *and* before or after that date the asset in respect of which the gain accrued, or any part of the proceeds of sale of that asset, is transferred to a person who becomes absolutely entitled to it, or the proceeds etc., that person may be assessed and charged in the name of the trustees within two years from the time when the tax became payable. The tax chargeable is not to exceed the tax chargeable on an amount equal to the chargeable gain and, where only a part of the asset or of the proceeds was transferred, is not to exceed a proportionate part of that amount. [*TCGA 1992, s 69(4)*].

Relevant trustees

[62.11] For the purposes of the assessment and collection of tax on trust income and gains where there is more than one trustee, anything done by a 'relevant trustee' is regarded as done by all the relevant trustees, including the making of returns and self-assessment. Liability for penalties, interest or surcharge may be recovered (but only once) from any one or more of the relevant trustees other than one who was not a relevant trustee at the relevant time (as defined by *TMA 1970, s 107A(3)*). In relation to chargeable gains, the '*relevant trustees*' of a settlement are the persons who are trustees in the tax year in which the gains accrue and any persons who subsequently become trustees. [*TMA 1970, ss 7(2)(9), 8A(1)(5), 107A, 118(1); FA 2008, Sch 36 para 75; FA 2015, Sch 7 para 53; FA 2016, Sch 22 para 20(2); F(No 2)A 2017, Sch 18 para 29(3); SI 2009 No 571, Sch 1 para 4; SI 2010 No 530; SI 2011 No 701, Art 8*].

Chargeable gains which accrue to a settlement can be assessed on any relevant trustee (see **6.6** ASSESSMENTS).

Sub-fund settlements

[62.12] Trustees of a settlement (the '*principal settlement*') may make an irrevocable election under which a specified part (a '*sub-fund*') of the settled property is treated for capital gains tax purposes as a separate settlement, known as a '*sub-fund settlement*'. [*TCGA 1992, s 69A, Sch 4ZA paras 1, 13*].

The election applies also for income tax purposes (see *ITA 2007, s 477* and Tolley's Income Tax).

For an election to be made, the principal settlement must not be itself a sub-fund settlement, and the following conditions must be satisfied when the election is made and throughout the period (if any) beginning with the time the election is treated as taking effect (see below) and ending immediately before it is made.

(i) The sub-fund must not be the whole of the property comprised in the principal settlement.

(ii) On the assumption that the election had then taken effect, the sub-fund settlement would not include an 'interest' in any asset in which an interest was retained by the principal settlement. The provisions of *TCGA 1992, s 104* and *s 109* treating certain holdings of shares etc. as a single asset (see **64.2** shares and securities — identification rules) are ignored for this purpose. An '*interest*' in an asset means an interest as co-owner, whether the asset is owned jointly or in common and whether or not the interests of the co-owners are equal.

(iii) On the assumption that the election had then taken effect, nobody would be a beneficiary of both the sub-fund settlement and the principal settlement. A person is a beneficiary of a settlement for this purpose if any property which is or may at any time be comprised in the settlement, or any 'derived property', is or will or may be payable to him or applicable for his benefit in any circumstances whatsoever, or if he enjoys a benefit deriving directly or indirectly from any property comprised in the settlement or any derived property. '*Derived property*' means income from other property, property directly or indirectly representing proceeds of, or of income from, other property or income from property which is itself derived property.

A person is not treated as a beneficiary, however, if property comprised in the settlement or any derived property will or may become payable to him or applicable for his benefit by reason only of:

- his marrying or becoming a civil partner of a beneficiary;
- the death of a beneficiary;
- the exercise by the trustees of the principal settlement of a power of advancement within *Trustee Act 1925, s 32* (or Northern Ireland equivalent), a similar power conferred by the law of a jurisdiction other than England and Wales or Northern Ireland, or a power of advancement which is subject to the same restrictions as those specified in *Trustee Act 1925, s 32(1)(a)(c)* and which is conferred by either the instrument creating the settlement or another instrument made in accordance with the terms of the settlement; or
- the failure or determination of protective trusts within *Trustee Act 1925, s 33*.

[*TCGA 1992, Sch 4ZA paras 3–9; FA 2008, Sch 2 para 67*].

Making an election

An election, which is irrevocable, must be made by notice in writing to HMRC in such form as HMRC may require. The notice must specify the date on which the election is to be treated as having taken effect, which must not be later than the date on which it is made. The election must be made within one year after 31 January following the tax year in which the date on which it is to be treated as taking effect falls. An election must include:

- a declaration of consent by each trustee of the principal settlement;
- a statement by those trustees that the conditions for making an election are satisfied;
- such information as HMRC may require in relation to the principal settlement including, in particular, information relating to the trustees, the trusts, property comprised in the settlement, the settlors and the beneficiaries;
- a declaration by the trustees of the principal settlement that the information given in the election is correct to the best of their knowledge and belief; and
- such other declarations as HMRC may require.

A penalty under *TMA 1970, s 98* applies for fraudulently or negligently providing incorrect information in an election.

Where an election is made, HMRC had, before 13 August 2009, the power to require, by notice in writing, a person who is or has been a trustee, beneficiary or settlor of either the principal settlement or the sub-fund settlement to supply information for the purpose of determining whether the conditions for making an election are satisfied. The notice had to specify a period of not less than 60 days within which the information had to be supplied and was subject to a penalty under *TMA 1970, s 98* for failure to comply or fraudulently or negligently providing incorrect information. This power has been repealed as it is no longer considered necessary following the introduction of the general information powers in *FA 2008, Sch 36* (see **34** HMRC INVESTIGATORY POWERS).

[*TCGA 1992, s 283(1), Sch 4ZA paras 10–16; SI 2009 No 2035, Sch para 34*].

Consequences of an election

A sub-fund settlement election takes effect at the beginning of the day, not being before 6 April 2006, specified in the election. If there is a deemed disposal by the trustees of the principal settlement at the beginning of that day under the provisions below, the election is deemed to take effect on that day immediately after that disposal.

The sub-fund settlement is treated as having been created at the time the election takes effect. Each trustee of the trusts on which the property in the sub-fund settlement is held is treated as a trustee of the sub-fund settlement and, unless he is also a trustee of trusts on which property in the principal settlement is held, as ceasing to be a trustee of the principal settlement from the time the election takes effect. A trustee of the principal settlement is not treated as a trustee of the sub-fund settlement unless he is also a trustee of trusts on which property in that settlement is held.

The trustees of the sub-fund settlement are treated as becoming absolutely entitled to the property comprised in that settlement as against the trustees of the principal settlement at the time the election takes effect.

The taking effect of the election may trigger deemed disposals by the trustees of the principal settlement under:

(a) *TCGA 1992, s 71(1)* (person becoming absolutely entitled to settled property — see **62.16** below); and
(b) *TCGA 1992, s 80(2)* (see **48.2** OFFSHORE SETTLEMENTS) where the principal settlement becomes non-UK resident as a result of the trustees of the sub-fund settlement ceasing to be trustees of the principal settlement.

Such a deemed disposal is treated as being made at the beginning of the day on which the election takes effect. No deemed disposal of an asset is treated as being made by virtue of (b) above if there is a deemed disposal of the same asset by virtue of (a) above. Any assets acquired by the trustees of the sub-fund settlement in respect of which there is a deemed disposal are treated as acquired by them at the time the election takes effect.

If the trustees of the sub-fund settlement are treated as becoming absolutely entitled as above to money expressed in sterling they are treated as acquiring it at the time the election takes effect and the trustees of the principal settlement are treated as disposing of it at the beginning of the day on which the election takes effect.

In the case of non-resident settlements, if there is a deemed disposal of an asset within (a) above when the election takes effect, then for the purposes of the provisions charging beneficiaries to capital gains tax in respect of capital payments (see **48.14** OFFSHORE SETTLEMENTS) and the further charge on such beneficiaries (see **48.21** OFFSHORE SETTLEMENTS), the trustees of the principal settlement are treated as having transferred the asset to the sub-fund settlement trustees (so that the relevant provisions for transfers between settlements may apply). This applies also if there would have been such a deemed disposal at that time of money expressed in sterling if (a) above applied to such property.

[*TCGA 1992, Sch 4ZA paras 2, 17–22*].

HMRC accept that where the transaction creating the sub-fund settlement is a chargeable transfer for inheritance tax purposes and it takes place on the day the election takes effect, the deemed disposal will qualify for relief under *TCGA 1992, s 260* (see **36.10** HOLD-OVER RELIEFS). (HMRC Capital Gains Manual, CG33331).

Trusts with vulnerable beneficiary

[62.13] The trustees of a settlement may claim special tax treatment for a tax year if:

- in that year they hold property on 'qualifying trusts' for the benefit of a 'vulnerable person', and
- a 'vulnerable person election' has effect for all or part of that year in relation to those trusts and that person.

[*FA 2005, ss 23, 24, 45*].

The claim has effect for both income tax and capital gains tax purposes; for the income tax consequences see Tolley's Income Tax.

Definitions

A '*vulnerable person*' is a 'disabled person' or a 'relevant minor'.

For 2013/14 onwards, the meaning of '*disabled person*' is given by *FA 2005, Sch 1A*. It means either a person who by reason of mental disorder is incapable of administering his property or managing his affairs or a person in receipt of any one or more specified State benefits. A person is treated as being a disabled person for these purposes if he satisfies HMRC that he would be entitled to receive the State benefit in question were it not for his being resident outside the UK or in a care home, hospital or prison. A broadly similar definition applied for 2012/13 and earlier years under *FA 2005, s 38*.

A person under the age of 18 is a '*relevant minor*' if at least one of his parents has died.

Where property is held on trusts for the benefit of a disabled person, those trusts are '*qualifying trusts*' if they secure that, during the lifetime of the disabled person or until the termination of the trusts (if earlier) the following conditions are satisfied. The conditions are:

- that if any of the property is applied for the benefit of a beneficiary it is applied for the benefit of the disabled person; and
- either that the disabled person is entitled to all the income (if any) arising from any of the property or that if any such income is applied for the benefit of a beneficiary, it is applied for the benefit of the disabled person.

But, for 2013/14 onwards, the trusts are not to be treated as failing to secure that the above conditions are met by reason only of:

(a) the trustees' having powers that enable them to apply in any tax year otherwise than for the benefit of the disabled person amounts (whether consisting of income or capital or both) not exceeding the 'annual limit'; or
(b) the trustees' having the powers conferred by *Trustee Act 1925, s 32* (powers of advancement) (or its NI equivalent); or
(c) the trustees' having those powers but free from, or subject to a less restrictive limitation than, the limitation imposed by *Trustee Act 1925, s 32(1)(a)* (or its NI equivalent); or
(d) the trustees' having powers to the like effect as the powers mentioned in (b) or (c).

The '*annual limit*' in (a) above is £3,000 or, if lower, 3% of the maximum value of the settled property during the tax year in question.

For 2012/13 and earlier years, trusts are not to be treated as failing to secure that the above conditions are met by reason only of:

(i) a power of advancement conferred on the trustees by *Trustee Act 1925, s 32* (or its NI equivalent); or
(ii) a similar power of advancement conferred on the trustees by the law of a jurisdiction other than England and Wales or NI; or
(iii) a power of advancement conferred on the trustees by instrument and subject to similar restrictions as those in *Trustee Act 1925, s 32*.

If the property is held on trusts of the kind described in *Trustee Act 1925, s 33* (protective trusts), the reference above to 'the lifetime of the disabled person' is to be interpreted as the period during which the property is held on trust for him.

Where property is held on trusts for the benefit of a relevant minor, those trusts are '*qualifying trusts*' if they are:

(i) statutory trusts for the relevant minor under *Administration of Estates Act 1925, ss 46, 47(1)* (succession on intestacy and statutory trusts in favour of relatives of intestate);
(ii) trusts established under the will of a deceased parent of the relevant minor; or
(iii) trusts established under the Criminal Injuries Compensation Scheme (i.e. schemes established under *Criminal Injuries Compensation Act 1995*, arrangements made by the Secretary of State for compensation for criminal injuries in operation before the commencement of those schemes or the scheme established under the *Criminal Injuries (Northern Ireland) Order 2002 SI 2002 No 796*).

Trusts within (ii) or (iii) above must secure that:

- when the relevant minor reaches 18 he will become absolutely entitled to the property, any income arising from it, and any income that has arisen from property held on the trusts for his benefit which has been accumulated before that time;
- until the relevant minor reaches 18 (so long as he is living), any property applied for the benefit of a beneficiary is applied for his benefit; and
- until the relevant minor reaches 18 (so long as he is living), either the minor is entitled to all the income (if any) arising from any of the property or if any such income is applied for the benefit of a beneficiary, it is applied for the benefit of the minor.

But trusts are not to be regarded as failing to secure the meeting of these conditions by reason only of, for 2013/14 onwards, the trustees' having powers as in (a)–(d) above or, for 2012/13 and earlier years, powers of advancement being conferred on the trustees as in (i)–(iii) above.

For the purposes of these provisions, property held on trusts includes a part of an asset if that part (and any income arising from it) can be identified for the purpose of determining whether the trusts are qualifying trusts.

[*FA 2005, ss 23(7), 34–36, 38, 39, Sch 1A; FA 2013, Sch 44 paras 15–19; FA 2014, s 291*].

The above definitions apply in Scotland with certain modifications (see *FA 2005, s 42*).

Vulnerable person election

A '*vulnerable person election*' can be made jointly by the trustees and a beneficiary if the trusts are qualifying trusts and the beneficiary is a vulnerable person. The election is irrevocable and must be made by notice in writing to HMRC in such form as they may require. It must specify the date from which it will take effect and be made within twelve months of 31 January following the tax year in which that date falls or within such further time as HMRC may by notice allow. The notice of election must include a statement that the trusts are qualifying trusts, a declaration that all the information included is correct to the best of the knowledge and belief of the trustees and beneficiary, a declaration by the beneficiary that he authorises the trustees to make a claim under these provisions for any tax year as they consider appropriate, and any other information and declarations as HMRC may require.

An election is effective until the beneficiary ceases to be a vulnerable person or the trusts cease to be qualifying trusts or are terminated. Where the trustees become aware that one of these events has occurred, they must, subject to a penalty under *TMA 1970, s 98* for failure, notify HMRC that the election has ceased to have effect within 90 days beginning on the day on which they first became aware of the event.

Where property held on trusts in respect of which an election is in force is treated for tax purposes as comprised in a sub-fund settlement (see **62.12** above) and the election was not made by the trustees of that settlement, the election applies to those trusts as if it had been made by those trustees and the vulnerable person. This treatment does not relieve the trustees of the principal settlement (see **62.12** above) from their notification obligations under the above provisions in relation to matters arising before the sub-fund settlement election took effect.

HMRC have powers to require the trustees or the vulnerable person by notice in writing to provide any particulars that they may require to determine whether the requirements for an election were met at the time it was made or whether an event has occurred such that the election ceases to be effective. The notice must specify the time (at least 60 days) within which the information must be provided. If HMRC determine that the requirements were not so met or that such an event has occurred they may give notice in writing to the trustees and the vulnerable person that the election never had effect or, as appropriate, that it ceased to have effect from a specified date. This is subject to a right of appeal, which must be made within 30 days after the notice was given. The provisions above which treat an election as made by trustees of a sub-fund settlement do not prevent HMRC from issuing a notice to the trustees of the principal settlement in relation to matters arising before the sub-fund settlement election took effect.

[*FA 2005, ss 37, 40, 41(1), 43; SI 2009 No 56, Sch 1 para 445*].

Capital gains tax

The special capital gains tax treatment described below applies for a tax year if:

(1) chargeable gains (the '*qualifying trusts gains*') accrue in that year to the trustees of a settlement from the disposal of settled property (see **62.3** above) which is held on qualifying trusts for the benefit of a vulnerable person;
(2) the trustees would (apart from these provisions) be chargeable to capital gains tax in respect of those gains;
(3) the trustees are resident in the UK during any part of the year (see **62.6** above); and
(4) a claim for special tax treatment for the year is made by the trustees. (Note that a claim applies for income tax purposes also.)

The treatment does not apply for a tax year in which the vulnerable person dies.

The qualifying trusts gains in (1) above include attributed gains of non-resident companies within **49.7** OVERSEAS MATTERS.

[*FA 2005, s 30; FA 2013, Sch 45 para 151(3), Sch 46 para 133*].

UK resident vulnerable person

If the vulnerable person is UK resident for the tax year, then the trustees' liability to capital gains tax for the year is reduced by an amount equal to:

TQTG – (TLVA –TLVB)

where:

TQTG = the amount of capital gains tax to which the trustees would, apart from these provisions, be liable for the tax year in respect of qualifying trust gains;
TLVB = the total amount of capital gains tax to which the vulnerable person is liable for the tax year; and
TLVA = what TLVB would be if the qualifying trust gains accrued to the vulnerable person instead of the trustees, and no allowable losses were deducted from them.

[*FA 2005, ss 31, 41(2)(a); FA 2013, Sch 45 para 151(4)(6)*].

Example

Harry was born in 2002. In June 2008 both of his parents are killed in a road accident. Neither parent has made a will, so that a statutory trust is established for Harry under the intestacy rules of *Administration of Estates Act 1925, ss 46, 47(1)*. The trustees and Harry's guardian make a vulnerable person election (by 31 January 2012) to take effect on 6 April 2009. On 16 May 2017, the trustees sell an asset, realising a chargeable gain of £20,000. The trustees (who are resident in the UK throughout) make no other disposals in 2017/18. Harry is resident in the UK throughout the tax year and has no personal chargeable gains. If the gain had been taxable on Harry, CGT would have been payable at 10%.

If the trustees make a claim for special tax treatment under *FA 2005, s 24* for 2017/18, their capital gains tax liability is calculated as follows.

	£
Gain	20,000
Annual exempt amount	5,650
Taxable gain 2017/18	£14,350
CGT £14,350 × 20%	2,870.00
Less reduction under *FA 2005, s 31*	2,000.00
CGT payable by trustees	£870.00

The reduction under *FA 2005, s 31* is equal to:

TQTG – (TLVA – TLVB)

In this case, TQTG = £2,870.00 (as above), TLVB is nil, and TLVA is calculated as follows.

	£
Gain	20,000
Annual exempt amount	11,300
Taxable gain	£8,700
CGT £8,700 × 10% (TLVA)	£870.00
The reduction is therefore £2,870 – (£870 – Nil) =	£2,000.00

Non-resident vulnerable person

If the vulnerable person is not UK resident for the tax year, the trustees' liability to capital gains tax for the year is reduced by an amount equal to:

TQTG – (TLVC –TLVD)

where:

> TQTG = the amount of capital gains tax to which the trustees would, apart from these provisions, be liable for the tax year in respect of qualifying trust gains;
> TLVD = (for 2008/09 and subsequent years) the total amount of capital gains tax to which the vulnerable person would be liable for the tax year if his taxable amount for capital gains tax purposes (see **2.6** ANNUAL RATES AND EXEMPTIONS) for the tax year were equal to his 'deemed CGT taxable amount'; and
> TLVC = (for 2008/09 and subsequent years) what TLVD would be if his taxable amount for capital gains tax were equal to the aggregate of his deemed CGT taxable amount and the amount of the qualifying trust gains.

For 2007/08 and earlier years

> TLVD = the total amount of income tax and capital gains tax to which the vulnerable person would be liable for the tax year if his income for the tax year were equal to the sum of his 'actual income' and the 'trustees' specially taxed income' and his taxable amount for capital gains tax purposes (see **2.6** ANNUAL RATES AND EXEMPTIONS) for the tax year were equal to his 'deemed CGT taxable amount'; and
> TLVC = what TLVD would be if his taxable amount for capital gains tax included his 'notional section 77 gains' for the tax year.

For this purpose, the vulnerable person's '*actual income*' for a tax year is the income which would be assessable to income tax for the year on the assumption that he was resident and domiciled in the UK throughout the year. The '*trustees' specially taxed income*' for a tax year is the income of the trustees for the year from property held on qualifying trusts for the benefit of the vulnerable person in connection with which special income tax treatment applies by virtue of a claim under these provisions.

The vulnerable person's '*deemed CGT taxable amount*' for a tax year is the total of his taxable amount for the year calculated by reference only to 'actual gains' and 'actual losses' and his taxable amount calculated only by reference to 'assumed gains' and 'assumed losses'. Any claims or elections made in relation to any assumed gains are disregarded. In calculating the taxable amount by reference to assumed gains and assumed losses, no deduction is made for losses brought forward or, on the death of the vulnerable person, for losses carried back.

The '*actual gains*' are any chargeable gains accruing to the vulnerable person in respect of which he is chargeable to capital gains tax for the tax year. '*Actual losses*' are allowable losses, including losses brought forward. '*Assumed gains*' are any chargeable gains, other than actual gains, in respect of which the vulnerable person would be chargeable to capital gains tax on the assumption that:

(A) he is resident and domiciled in the UK throughout the tax year; and
(B) he has given a notice to HMRC quantifying the amount of any losses accruing in the tax year (see **44.4** LOSSES).

Note that assumption (A) above does not apply for the purposes of *TCGA 1992, s 10A* (temporary non-residents — see **49.5** OVERSEAS MATTERS).

'*Assumed losses*' are any allowable losses, other than actual losses, which would accrue to the vulnerable person for the tax year on the same assumptions as apply for calculating assumed gains. A vulnerable person's '*notional section 77 gains*' for a tax year are the chargeable gains that would be treated as accruing to him under *TCGA 1992, s 77* by virtue of the above provisions for UK resident beneficiaries on the same assumptions.

[*FA 2005, ss 32, 33, 41(2), Sch 1; FA 2013, Sch 45 para 151(5)(6)*].

For HMRC guidance on trusts with vulnerable beneficiaries, see HMRC Capital Gains Manual CG35500–35550.

Disposals during the life-cycle of a settlement

Creation of a settlement

[62.14] The provisions described at 62.14–62.18 apply to the various occasions during the life-cycle of a settlement when chargeable gains may arise.

A transfer into settlement, whether revocable or irrevocable, is a disposal of the entire property settled even if the transferor is a beneficiary or trustee of the settlement. [*TCGA 1992, s 70*]. The acquisition and disposal are treated as being made at MARKET VALUE (**45**) subject to the exclusion at **45.1** MARKET VALUE. HOLD-OVER RELIEFS (**36**) may be available in respect of chargeable gains that would otherwise arise to the settlor. The settlor of a settlement and the trustees of that settlement are CONNECTED PERSONS (**17**) and further rules may operate as to valuation and losses (in particular see **4.12** and **4.13** ANTI-AVOIDANCE, **45.1** MARKET VALUE and **44.6** LOSSES).

Example

In December 2017, C transfers to trustees of a settlement for the benefit of his disabled daughter 10,000 shares in W plc, a quoted company. The value of the gift is £85,000. C bought the shares in 1981 for £20,000 and their value at 31 March 1982 was £35,000.

	£
Deemed disposal consideration	85,000
Market value 31.3.82	35,000
Chargeable gain	£50,000
Trustees' allowable cost	£85,000

Note to the example

(a) If the transfer is a chargeable lifetime transfer for inheritance tax purposes, or would be one but for the annual inheritance tax exemption and C does not have an interest in the settlement within *TCGA 1992, s 169F* (see **36.8** HOLD-OVER RELIEFS), C could elect under *TCGA 1992, s 260* to hold the gain over against the trustees' base cost of the shares. The trustees do not join in any such election.

Exercise of power of appointment or advancement

For the consequences of the exercise of such a power see *Hoare Trustees v Gardner*; *Hart v Briscoe* Ch D 1977, 52 TC 53; *Chinn v Collins* HL 1980, 54 TC 311; *Roome v Edwards* HL 1981, 54 TC 359; *Eilbeck v Rawling* HL 1981, 54 TC 101; *Bond v Pickford* CA 1983, 57 TC 301; *Swires v Renton* Ch D 1991, 64 TC 315.

Following the decision in *Bond v Pickford* above, the Revenue issued Statement of Practice 7/84 to set out their views on the capital gains tax implications of the exercise of a power of appointment or advancement when continuing trusts are declared.

The Revenue stated in SP 7/84 that the judgments in *Roome v Edwards* emphasised that, in deciding whether or not a new settlement has been created by the exercise of a power of appointment or advancement, each case must be considered on its own facts, and by applying established legal doctrine to the facts in a practical and commonsense manner. The Court of Appeal judgments in *Bond v Pickford* explained that the consideration of the facts must include examination of the powers which the trustees purported to exercise, and the determination of the intention of the parties, viewed objectively.

HMRC consider it now clear that a deemed disposal under *TCGA 1992, s 71(1)* (see **62.16** below) cannot arise unless the power exercised by the trustees, or the instrument conferring the power, expressly or by necessary implication, confers on the trustees authority to remove assets from the original settlement by subjecting them to trusts of a different settlement. Such powers (which may be powers of advancement or appointment) were referred to by the Court of Appeal in *Bond v Pickford* as 'powers in the wider form'. HMRC consider that a deemed disposal will not arise when such powers are exercised and trusts are declared in circumstances such that:

(a) the appointment is revocable; or
(b) the trusts declared of the advanced or appointed funds are not exhaustive so that there exists a possibility at the time when the advancement or appointment is made that the funds covered by it will, on the occasion of some event, cease to be held upon such trusts and once again come to be held upon the original trusts of the settlement.

HMRC also consider it unlikely a deemed disposal will occur when trusts are declared following the exercise of such a power if the duties of trusteeship as regards the appointed assets fall to the trustees of the original settlement. This follows from the provision in *TCGA 1992, s 69(1)* that the trustees of a settlement form a single and continuing body (see **62.6** above).

In conclusion, HMRC accept that a power of appointment or advancement can be exercised over only a part of settled property and that the foregoing would apply to that part.

See *Begg-McBrearty v Stilwell* Ch D 1996, 68 TC 426 for interpretation of *Family Law Reform Act 1969*.

HMRC practice regarding validity of trust deeds for general and tax law purposes

New trust deeds (other than those for special types of trust such as unit trusts, charitable trusts and employee trusts) are not examined individually by HMRC for their validity under general law as well as tax law. HMRC normally rely on the information shown in returns etc. made by the settlors, trustees and beneficiaries and only seek further information where necessary, and only exceptionally will they ask to see deeds or other documents. Trustees are asked to supply information about themselves and the settlor and whether the trustees have power to accumulate income or to distribute it at their discretion (Revenue Press Release 19 December 1990).

Disposal of an interest in settled property

[62.15] Subject to the exclusions below for settlements which are, or have ever been, non-resident settlements, no chargeable gain accrues on the disposal of an interest created by or arising under a settlement (see **62.4** above) if the disposal was made:

(a) by the person for whose benefit the interest was created by the terms of the settlement; or

(b) by any other person except one who acquired, or derives his title from one who acquired, the interest for a consideration in money or money's worth, other than consideration consisting of another interest under the settlement.

Subject to the above, where a person who has acquired an interest in settled property becomes, as the holder of that interest, absolutely entitled (see **62.3** above) as against the trustee to any settled property, he is treated as disposing of the interest in consideration of obtaining the property so received (but without prejudice to any gain accruing to the trustee on the deemed disposal by the trustee under *TCGA 1992, s 71(1)* (see **62.16** below)).

[*TCGA 1992, s 76(1)(2)*].

Where the disposal of a life interest in settled property does give rise to a chargeable event, the interest may be treated as a wasting asset in certain circumstances. See **72.7** WASTING ASSETS.

See **62.20** below for anti-avoidance provisions deeming there to be, in specified circumstances, a disposal of underlying assets at the same time as an actual disposal of an interest in settled property for consideration.

Exclusion for non-resident settlements

The exemption above does not apply to disposals of interests in settlements which are, or have ever been, non-resident. See **48.4** OFFSHORE SETTLEMENTS.

Person becoming absolutely entitled to settled property

[62.16] Subject to the exception below, where a person becomes absolutely entitled to any settled property as against the trustee, all the assets forming part of the settled property to which he becomes so entitled are deemed to have been disposed of by the trustee and immediately reacquired by him in the capacity of bare trustee or nominee within *TCGA 1992, s 60(1)* (see **62.3** above) for a consideration equal to the market value of the assets. [*TCGA 1992, s 71(1)*].

See *Figg v Clarke* Ch D 1996, 68 TC 645 for interpretation of date of absolute entitlement. See also *McLaughlin v HMRC* FTT, [2012] SFTD 1003 for discussion of circumstances in which a person becomes absolutely entitled.

Where an interest in possession in part of settled property terminates (whether voluntarily or involuntarily) and the part can properly be identified with one or more specific assets, or where within a reasonable time, normally three months, of the termination, the trustees appropriate specific assets to give effect to the termination, HMRC will treat the deemed disposal and reacquisition as applying to those assets, and not to any part of the other assets comprised in the settlement. In particular, agreement will be made of lists of assets properly identifiable with the termination, and any such agreement will be regarded as binding on HMRC and the trustees (HMRC Statement of Practice D10).

Any resulting net chargeable gain is assessed on the trustee in the usual way (subject to a claim for HOLD-OVER RELIEFS (**36**).

Losses

Where a person (the beneficiary) becomes absolutely entitled to any settled property as against the trustee and a loss accrues to the trustee on the resulting deemed disposal under *TCGA 1992, s 71(1)* (see above) of an asset comprised in that property, then, subject to the restrictions below, the loss is treated as a loss accruing to the beneficiary instead of to the trustee.

Such treatment is mandatory, but applies only to the extent that the loss cannot be deducted from gains accruing to the trustee either on the deemed disposal of other assets on that occasion or on disposals made earlier in the same year of assessment, and for this purpose only such a loss is treated as deductible in priority to any other allowable losses accruing to the trustee in that year.

Where a loss is so treated as accruing to the beneficiary, it is allowable *only* against chargeable gains accruing to him on disposal by him of the same asset, i.e. the asset on the deemed disposal of which the loss occurred, or, where the asset is land, any asset which is 'derived' from it (as defined). The loss can be carried forward to subsequent years of assessment until such time as it has been fully allowed against such gains. Where there is such a gain, the loss in question is treated as deductible in priority to any other allowable losses accruing to the beneficiary in the year of assessment concerned and, where it is brought forward, is deductible as if it were a loss accruing in that year (see **44.2** LOSSES for set-off of losses generally). For a worked example, see Tolley's Tax Computations.

These provisions are equally applicable where it is another set of trustees who become absolutely entitled as against the trustees with the losses (HMRC Capital Gains Manual CG37209).

[*TCGA 1992, s 71(2)–(2D)*].

The position should be contrasted with that of allowable losses made by personal representatives as in **19.9** DEATH.

Where trust losses are transferable to a beneficiary as above, HMRC do not restrict those losses under *TCGA 1992, s 18(3)* (see **44.6** LOSSES) where the trustees and the person becoming absolutely entitled are CONNECTED PERSONS (**17**) (Revenue Tax Bulletin February 1993 p 57).

No loss is transferable to beneficiaries unless it has been notified by the trustees under the normal self-assessment rules at **44.4** LOSSES (HMRC Capital Gains Manual CG37210).

Miscellaneous

References in the above to the case where a person becomes absolutely entitled to settled property as against the trustee include references to the case where a person would become so entitled but for being an infant or other person under disability. [*TCGA 1992, s 71(3)*].

Where a person disposes of an asset held by another person as trustee to which he became absolutely entitled as against the trustee, any incidental expenditure incurred by that person or the trustee in relation to the transfer of the asset to him is allowable as a deduction in the computation of the gain arising on the disposal. [*TCGA 1992, s 64(1)*]. The expenditure incurred by the person concerned, but not that incurred by the trustees, may qualify for indexation allowance (HMRC Capital Gains Manual CG 31192).

Exception where a life interest is terminated by the death of the person entitled thereto

Where, as above, a person becomes absolutely entitled as against the trustee to assets forming part of settled property and that occasion is the termination of a life interest by the death of the person entitled to that interest then, where that interest meets certain conditions (and, subject to exceptions), *no* chargeable gain arises on the deemed disposal. See **62.18**(a) below for full details.

Termination of life interest in possession on death of person entitled — assets remaining settled property

[62.17] Where an interest in possession in all or part (see SP D10 in **62.16** above) of settled property is terminated on the death of the person entitled to it (e.g. a life tenant), the whole or a corresponding part of each of the assets forming part of the settled property and not at that time ceasing to be settled property is deemed to be disposed of and immediately reacquired by the trustee at that time for a consideration equal to the whole or a corresponding part of the market value of the asset. However, any gain arising on such a deemed disposal is not a chargeable gain. Where the deceased became entitled to the interest in possession on or after 22 March 2006, this applies only if:

(i) the deceased died under the age of 18 and, immediately before his death, *IHTA 1984, s 71D* (age 18 to 25 trusts) applies to the property in which the interest subsists; or

(ii) immediately before his death:

  (a) the interest in possession is an immediate post-death interest within *IHTA 1984, s 49A*;

  (b) the interest is a transitional serial interest within *IHTA 1984, s 49B*;

  (c) the interest is a disabled person's interest within *IHTA 1984, s 89B* (for deaths before 5 December 2013, within *IHTA 1984, s 89B(1)(c)(d)*); or

  (d) *IHTA 1984, s 71A* (trusts for bereaved minors) applies to the property in which the interest subsists.

[*TCGA 1992, s 72(1)–(1C); FA 2014, s 60(2)(a), (4)*].

(See the exception below as regards previously held-over gains.)

The above provisions also apply where the person entitled to an interest in possession in all or part of the settled property dies but the interest does not then terminate. Again, where the deceased became entitled to the interest in possession on or after 22 March 2006, this applies only if, immediately before his death, one of (ii)(a) to (c) above applies. [*TCGA 1992, s 72(2)(2A)*].

Annuities

The above provisions apply on the death of the person entitled to any annuity payable out of, or charged on, settled property or the income of settled property as it applies on the death of a person whose interest in possession in the whole or any part of settled property terminates on his death. Where, in the case of any entitlement to an annuity created by a settlement some of the settled property is appropriated by the trustees as a fund out of which the annuity is payable, and there is no right of recourse to, or to the income of, settled property not so appropriated, then without prejudice to *TCGA 1992, s 72(5)* below, the settled property so appropriated is, while the annuity is payable, and on the occasion of the death of the person entitled to the annuity, treated for the purposes of *TCGA 1992, s 72* as being settled property under a separate settlement. [*TCGA 1992, s 72(3)(4)*]. In the case where the annuity is not paid out of specified funds, HMRC treats the corresponding part (see above) of the assets forming the settled property as being given by the proportion which the amount of the annuity bears to the whole of the settlement income arising in the year prior to the date of death.

Part interests and income interests

For the purposes of the above provisions, an interest which is a right to part of the income of settled property is treated as such an interest in a corresponding part of the settled property. [*TCGA 1992, s 72(1)*].

If there is an interest in income in a part of settled property such that there is no right of recourse to, or to the income from, the remainder of the settled property, then the part of the settled property in which such interest subsists is similarly treated as being settled property under a separate settlement for so long as such an interest subsists. [*TCGA 1992, s 72(5)*].

Disabled person's interests

For deaths on or after 5 December 2013, disabled person's interests within *IHTA 1984, s 89B(1)(a)(b)* (which are treated as interests in possession for inheritance tax purposes) are treated as interests in possession for the purposes of the above provisions. [*TCGA 1992, s 72(6); FA 2014, s 60(2)(b), (4)*].

Exception where hold-over relief under *TCGA 1992, s 165* or *s 260* or *FA 1980, s 79* claimed previously

In certain circumstances where a claim has been made for hold-over relief in respect of the disposal of an asset to the trustee and, subsequently, the trustee is deemed to dispose of and immediately reacquire the asset so that under *TCGA 1992, s 72* above there would otherwise be no chargeable gain arising, it is specifically provided by *TCGA 1992, s 67* or *s 74* that a chargeable gain, restricted to the amount of the held-over gain, is to accrue to the trustee. See **36.8**, **36.11** and **36.12** HOLD-OVER RELIEFS.

Termination of life interest on death of person entitled — person becoming absolutely entitled

[62.18] The following applies on the termination of life interest where property leaves the trust.

(a) Where, under *TCGA 1992, s 71(1)* in **62.16** above, the assets forming part of any settled property are deemed to be disposed of and reacquired at market value by the trustee on the occasion when a person becomes, or would but for a disability become, absolutely entitled thereto as against the trustee, then, if that occasion is the death of a person entitled to an interest in possession in the settled property (e.g. the death of a life tenant):
   (i) no chargeable gain accrues on the deemed disposal; and
   (ii) if on the death the property reverts to the disponer (e.g. the original settlor), the disposal and reacquisition by the trustee is treated as taking place on a no gain/no loss basis, and if the acquisition by the trustee was at a time prior to 31 March 1982 (for disposals before 6 April 2008, prior to 6 April 1965), the reversion is related back to that date.

   In relation to a sub-fund settlement (see **62.12** above), (ii) above is treated as applying if the property does not revert to the trustees of the principal settlement (see **62.12** above) only because it becomes comprised in another sub-fund of the principal settlement in respect of which a sub-fund settlement election is in force.
(b) Where the interest is an interest in part (see SP D10 in **62.16** above) only of the settled property to which the person becomes absolutely entitled, (a)(i) above does not apply but although a chargeable gain will accordingly arise as under *TCGA 1992, s 71(1)* in **62.16** above it is reduced by a proportion corresponding to that represented by the part in which the interest subsisted. Any remaining chargeable gain may be the subject of a claim for one of the HOLD-OVER RELIEFS (**36**).

Where the deceased became entitled to the interest in possession on or after 22 March 2006, these provisions apply only if either **62.17**(i) or (ii) above applies.

[*TCGA 1992, s 73(1)(2)(2A); FA 2008, Sch 2 paras 61, 71*].

(See the exception below as regards previously held-over gains.)

Annuities

The above provisions apply on the death of the person entitled to any annuity payable out of, or charged on, settled property or the income of settled property as it applies on the death of a person whose interest in possession in the whole or any part of settled property terminates on his death. Where, in the case of any entitlement to an annuity created by a settlement some of the settled property is appropriated by the trustees as a fund out of which the annuity is payable, and there is no right of recourse to, or to the income of, settled property not so appropriated, then without prejudice to *TCGA 1992, s 72(5)* below, the settled property so appropriated is, while the annuity is payable, and on the occasion of the death of the person entitled to the annuity, treated for the purposes of *TCGA 1992, s 72* as being settled property under a separate settlement. [*TCGA 1992, ss 72(3)(4), 73(3)*]. In the case where the annuity is not paid out of specified funds, HMRC treats the 'proportion corresponding to that represented by the part in which the interest subsisted' (see (b) above) of the assets forming the settled property as being given by the proportion which the amount of the annuity bears to the whole of the settlement income arising in the year prior to the date of death.

Part interests and income interests

For the purposes of (a) and (b) above, an interest which is a right to part of the income of settled property is treated as such an interest in a corresponding part of the settled property. [*TCGA 1992, ss 72(1), 73(3)*].

If there is an interest in income in a part of settled property such that there is no right of recourse to, or to the income from, the remainder of the settled property, then the part of the settled property in which such interest subsists is similarly treated as being settled property under a separate settlement for so long as such an interest subsists. [*TCGA 1992, ss 72(5), 73(3)*].

Disabled person's interests

For deaths on or after 5 December 2013, disabled person's interests within *IHTA 1984, s 89B(1)(a)(b)* (which are treated as interests in possession for inheritance tax purposes) are treated as interests in possession for the purposes of the above provisions. [*TCGA 1992, ss 72(6), 73(3); FA 2014, s 60(3)(4)*].

Exception where hold-over relief under *TCGA 1992, s 165* or *s 260* or *FA 1980, s 79* claimed previously

In certain circumstances where a claim has been made for hold-over relief in respect of the disposal of an asset to the trustee and, subsequently, the trustee is deemed to dispose of and immediately reacquire the asset so that under

TCGA 1992, s 73 above there would otherwise be no chargeable gain arising, it is specifically provided by *TCGA 1992, s 67* or *s 74* that a chargeable gain, restricted to the amount of the held-over gain, is to accrue to the trustee. See **36.8**, **36.11** and **36.12** HOLD-OVER RELIEFS.

Anti-avoidance

[62.19] A number of anti-avoidance provisions apply specifically to settlements and these are described at **62.20–62.23** below.

Deemed disposal of underlying assets on certain disposals of interests in settled property

[62.20] Cross-reference. See **62.15** above for the general exemption from CGT on a disposal of an interest in settled property.

Deemed disposal

Where:

- a disposal of an 'interest in settled property' is made, or is effectively completed (see below under Time lapse before effective completion), after 20 March 2000,
- the disposal is 'for consideration', and
- specified conditions are present as detailed below (as to UK residence of trustees and settlor and as to settlor interest in the settlement),

the trustees of the settlement are deemed for all CGT purposes to have disposed of and immediately reacquired the underlying assets (see below) at market value. The deemed disposal takes place at the same time as the actual disposal of the interest in settled property. It is regarded as made under a bargain at arm's length (which effectively precludes a claim for the gain to be deferred as in **36.2** or **36.10** HOLD-OVER RELIEFS).

[*TCGA 1992, s 76A, Sch 4A paras 1, 4(1)(3), para 9*].

See below for modifications to the above where there is a time lapse before effective completion of the actual disposal.

Where the trustees have made an election under *ITA 2007, s 508* in respect of income arising from heritage maintenance property, no charge arises under these provisions in relation to the settlement for that year. [*TCGA 1992, Sch 4A para 14*].

For these purposes, an '*interest in settled property*' is any interest created by or arising under the settlement. This includes the right to enjoy any benefit arising from the exercise of a discretion or power by the trustees of a settlement or by any person in relation to a settlement. A disposal is '*for consideration*' if actual consideration is given or received by any person for, or in connection with, any transaction by which the disposal is effected. Consideration deemed to have been given under any CGT provision is disregarded for these purposes. Consideration in the form of another interest under the same settlement is also disregarded, as long as that interest has not previously been disposed of by any person for consideration. [*TCGA 1992, Sch 4A paras 2, 3*].

HMRC consider that consideration for these purposes does not include incidental costs, in particular reasonable fees charged by professional advisers for legal and tax advice as to the effects of the transaction or for drafting and executing the relevant paperwork. Where there are no payments other than in respect of such costs, the transaction does not fall within these provisions. (Revenue Tax Bulletin August 2003 p 1048).

Underlying assets

Where the interest disposed of is in the whole of the settled property, the deemed disposal is of each of the assets comprised in that property. Where the interest disposed of is in a specific fund or other defined part of the settled property, the deemed disposal is of each of the assets comprised in that fund or part. In either case, the deemed disposal is of the whole of each of the assets concerned, unless the interest disposed of is an interest in a specified fraction or amount of the income or capital, in which case the deemed disposal is of a corresponding part of each of the assets concerned. Where part only of an asset is comprised in a specific fund or other defined part of the settled property, that part of the asset is treated as a separate asset for the purposes of these provisions. [*TCGA 1992, Sch 4A para 8*].

See also below under Time lapse before effective completion.

Conditions

All the following conditions must be present for the disposal of underlying assets to be deemed to take place (and see also the modifications below under Time lapse before effective completion).

UK residence of trustees

The trustees must have been resident in the UK during any part of the tax year of disposal and not regarded under a double tax agreement as resident elsewhere.

UK residence of settlor

In the tax year of disposal or in any of the previous five tax years, a person who is a 'settlor' (see below) in relation to the settlement must have met the residence condition at **1.2** INTRODUCTION. Where the year of disposal or any of the previous tax years is 2012/13 or an earlier year, the test operates by reference to the requirement that a person who is a settler must have been either resident in the UK during all or part of the year or ordinarily resident in the UK during the year.

Settlor interest in the settlement

At some time during the 'relevant period', either:

- a person who is a 'settlor' in relation to the settlement must have had an interest in the settlement (see below); or
- the settlement must have comprised property derived, directly or indirectly, from another settlement in which a settlor had an interest at any time in the relevant period.

'*Settlor*' is defined for this purpose as in **48.9** OFFSHORE SETTLEMENTS, but excluding the provisions there relating to property provided by a qualifying company. The circumstances in which a settlor has an interest in a settlement are defined as for the purposes of the gifts to settlor-interested settlements provisions at **36.8** HOLD-OVER RELIEFS.

The '*relevant period*' is the period beginning two years before the beginning of the tax year of disposal and ending with the date of the disposal of the interest in settled property.

The above condition is treated as not present in a tax year in which the settlor dies or where:

- he has an interest in a settlement only because property is, or will or may become, payable to or applicable for the benefit of his spouse or civil partner *or* his spouse or civil partner enjoys a benefit from property, or for both such reasons, and his spouse or civil partner dies, or he and his spouse or civil partner cease to be married to or to be civil partners of each other, during the year; or
- he has an interest in a settlement only because property is, or will or may become, payable to or applicable for the benefit of a dependent child of his *or* a dependent child of his enjoys a benefit from property, or for both such reasons, and he ceases during the year to have (and does not in that year subsequently come to have) any such dependent children.

A '*dependent child*' of the settlor is, for this purpose, a child or stepchild under the age of 18 who is unmarried and does not have a civil partner.

[*TCGA 1992, Sch 4A para 4(2), paras 5–7, 12; FA 2008, Sch 2 paras 7, 21, 22; FA 2013, Sch 46 para 106*].

Prevention of double charge

Where there would be a deemed disposal as above and the actual disposal of the interest in settled property is not itself exempt by virtue of *TCGA 1992, s 76* (see **62.15** above), the following provisions apply to ensure that there is no double charge or double allowance of a loss.

- If both the deemed disposal and the actual disposal give rise to a chargeable gain (or in the case of the deemed disposal a net chargeable gain by reference to all the assets involved), the lower gain is disregarded.
- If both disposals give rise to an allowable loss (or net allowable loss), the lower loss is disregarded.
- If one disposal gives rise to a (net) chargeable gain and the other a (net) allowable loss, the loss is disregarded.
- If the actual disposal gives rise to neither a chargeable gain nor an allowable loss, any net chargeable gain on the deemed disposal is taken as accruing instead.

[*TCGA 1992, Sch 4A para 10*].

Trustees' right of recovery

Where tax becomes chargeable in respect of a deemed disposal as above and either it is chargeable on the trustees or it is chargeable on the settlor and recovered by him from the trustees, the trustees have the right to recover the tax from the person who made the actual disposal (i.e. of an interest in the settlement) giving rise to the deemed disposal. For this purpose, they may require an inspector to certify the gain and the tax paid.

[*TCGA 1992, Sch 4A para 11*].

Time lapse before effective completion

The above provisions are subject to the modifications below where there is a period between the beginning of the disposal of the interest in settled property and the effective completion of that disposal. For these purposes, the disposal begins when a contract is entered into or, where relevant, an option is granted. It is effectively completed when the person acquiring the interest becomes for all practical purposes unconditionally entitled to the whole of the intended subject matter of the disposal.

Where the beginning of the disposal and the effective completion take place in different tax years:

- the deemed disposal is treated as taking place in the tax year of effective completion;
- the conditions as to UK residence of trustees and settlor are treated as present if they are present by reference to either of those tax years or any intervening year;
- the '*relevant period*' for the purpose of the condition as to settlor interest in the settlement is the period beginning two years before the beginning of the first of those tax years (or beginning on 6 April 1999 if later) and ending with the effective completion.

If the identity or value of the underlying assets changes during the period between the beginning of the disposal and its effective completion, an asset is subject to the deemed disposal rules if it was comprised in the settled property (or specific fund or other defined part) at any time during that period, unless it was disposed of (and not reacquired) by the trustees during that period under a bargain at arm's length. The market value of an asset for the purposes of the deemed disposal is its highest market value at any time in that period.

[*TCGA 1992, Sch 4A para 13*].

HMRC have given examples of circumstances in which they would consider that the person acquiring the asset is for all practical purposes unconditionally entitled to the intended subject matter of the disposal (as above). These are where the buyer has the power to compel the trustees to transfer the property to him on giving due notice, and where the buyer has a right to enjoy the property now, but is not entitled to it until a particular contingency is fulfilled, and there is no real likelihood of its not being fulfilled. (Revenue Tax Bulletin August 2003 p 1049).

Transfers of value by trustees linked with trustee borrowing

[62.21] The following provisions were introduced to counter a particular avoidance scheme (known as the 'flip-flop' scheme), although they apply in any case where the conditions are met without regard to any avoidance motive. The scheme was considered in *Trennery v West* HL 2005, [2005] STC 214, [2005] UKHL 5.

See Revenue Tax Bulletin August 2003 pp 1048–1051, for HMRC's views on various terms used in the provisions.

Deemed disposal

Where:

- the trustees of a settlement make a 'transfer of value';
- the transfer is treated as 'linked with trustee borrowing'; and
- it takes place in a tax year in which the settlement is within *TCGA 1992, s 86* or *s 87* (see below),

the trustees are deemed for all CGT purposes to have disposed of and immediately reacquired the whole or a proportion (see below) of each of the 'chargeable assets' that continue to form part of the settled property immediately after the transfer ('*the remaining chargeable assets*').

The deemed disposal takes place at the time of the transfer of value and is treated as made under a bargain at arm's length and for a consideration equal to the whole or, as the case may be, a proportion of the market value of each asset. Where applicable, gains (less losses) on the deemed disposals are then chargeable on the settlor under *TCGA 1992, s 86* (see **48.5** OFFSHORE SETTLEMENTS) or on beneficiaries receiving capital payments under *TCGA 1992, Sch 4C* (see **48.22** OFFSHORE SETTLEMENTS).

The significance of the deemed disposal being treated as an arm's length disposal is that the provisions at **36.2** and **36.10** HOLD-OVER RELIEFS are thereby disapplied.

For these purposes, an asset is a '*chargeable asset*' if a gain on a disposal of the asset by the trustees at the time of the transfer of value would be a chargeable gain. A settlement is within *TCGA 1992, s 86* (see **48.5** OFFSHORE SETTLEMENTS) in a tax year if, assuming that there were net gains (after deducting losses) accruing to the trustees from disposals of any of the settled property originating from the settlor, chargeable gains would be treated as accruing to the settlor in that year under that section. A settlement is within *TCGA 1992, s 87* (see **48.14** OFFSHORE SETTLEMENTS) in a tax year if *section 87* applies to it in that year or chargeable gains (or for 2008/09 onwards, offshore income gains within **49.11**, **49.12** OVERSEAS MATTERS) would be treated under *TCGA 1992, s 89(2)* (see **48.17** OFFSHORE SETTLEMENTS) as accruing to a beneficiary who received a capital payment from the trustees in that year.

[*TCGA 1992, s 76B, Sch 4B paras 1, 3, 10; FA 2008, Sch 2 paras 8, 22, Sch 7 para 130*].

Transfer of value

Trustees of a settlement make a '*transfer of value*' if they:

- lend money or any other 'asset' to any person;

- 'transfer an asset' to any person and receive either no consideration or a consideration lower than the market value of the asset transferred; or
- issue a security of any description to any person and receive either no consideration or a consideration lower than the value of the security.

For the purposes of these provisions, an '*asset*' includes money expressed in sterling. References below to the value or market value of such an asset are to its amount. The '*transfer of an asset*' includes anything that is, or is treated as, a disposal of the asset for capital gains tax purposes, or would be if money expressed in sterling were an asset for capital gains tax purposes. Part disposals are not excluded. However, a transfer of an asset does not include a transfer of an asset that is itself created by the part disposal of another asset. For example, the grant of a leasehold interest in freehold land is for these purposes a transfer of the freehold (and not of the leasehold).

The transfer of value is treated as made at the time when the loan is made, the transfer is 'effectively completed' or the security is issued. A transfer is '*effectively completed*' at the point at which the person acquiring the asset becomes for practical purposes unconditionally entitled to the whole of the intended subject matter of the transfer.

The amount of value transferred is taken to be:

- in the case of a loan, the market value of the asset;
- in the case of a transfer of an asset:
  - (i) if any part of the value of the asset is 'attributable to trustee borrowing' (see below), the market value of the asset; or
  - (ii) if no part of the value of the asset is attributable to trustee borrowing, the market value of the asset reduced by any consideration received for it; and
- in the case of the issue of a security, the value of the security reduced by any consideration received for it.

For this purpose, the value of an asset is its value immediately before the time the transfer of value is treated as made, unless the asset does not exist before that time in which case its value immediately after that time is taken.

[*TCGA 1992, Sch 4B paras 2, 13*].

HMRC consider that a distribution made by the trustees of a discretionary trust which is income of the recipient for UK tax purposes is not a transfer of value for the purposes of these provisions. Likewise, where a beneficiary occupies property under rights arising as a consequence of the trust deed or the will, the Revenue consider that the occupation does not give rise to a transfer of value. They may not take this view where the rights arise as a consequence of the exercise of a power of appointment or advancement. 'Lending money' does not include putting money into a conventional current or deposit account at a bank or building society. (Revenue Tax Bulletin August 2003 pp 1049, 1050).

Transfer of value linked with trustee borrowing

Trustees of a settlement are treated as borrowing if:

- money or any other asset is lent to them; or

- an asset is transferred to them and, in connection with the transfer, the trustees assume a contractual obligation (whether absolute or conditional) to restore or transfer to any person that or any other asset.

References below to a '*loan obligation*' include any such obligation as is mentioned above.

The amount borrowed (the '*proceeds*' of the borrowing) is taken to be:

- in the case of a loan, the market value of the asset;
- in the case of a transfer, the market value of the asset reduced by any consideration received for it.

For this purpose, the market value of an asset is its market value immediately before the loan is made, or the transfer is effectively completed (see above under Transfer of value), unless the asset does not exist before that event in which case its market value immediately after that event is taken.

A transfer of value by trustees is treated as '*linked with trustee borrowing*' if at the time of the transfer there is 'outstanding trustee borrowing'. There is '*outstanding trustee borrowing*' at any time to the extent that:

- any loan obligation is outstanding, and
- there are proceeds of trustee borrowing that have not been either:
  - 'applied for normal trust purposes', or
  - taken into account under these provisions in relation to an earlier transfer of value which was treated as linked with trustee borrowing.

For the purposes of these provisions, the proceeds of trustee borrowing are '*applied for normal trust purposes*' if and only if:

(a) they are applied by the trustees in making a payment in respect of an 'ordinary trust asset' and the following conditions are met:
   (i) the payment is made under a transaction at arm's length or is not more than the payment that would be made if the transaction were at arm's length;
   (ii) the asset forms part of the settled property immediately after the transfer of value or, if it (or part of it) does not do so, the alternative condition described below is met; and
   (iii) the sum paid is allowable under *TCGA 1992, s 38* (see **16.11** and **16.13** COMPUTATION OF GAINS AND LOSSES) as a deduction in computing a gain accruing to the trustees on a disposal of the asset (or would be so allowable were it not for the application of *TCGA 1992, s 17*, see **45.1** MARKET VALUE, or *TCGA 1992, s 39*, see **16.13**(a) COMPUTATION OF GAINS AND LOSSES); or
(b) they are applied by the trustees in wholly or partly discharging a loan obligation, and the whole of the proceeds of the borrowing connected with that obligation (or all but an insignificant amount) have been applied by the trustees for normal trust purposes; or
(c) they are applied by the trustees in making payments to meet *bona fide* current expenses incurred by them in administering the settlement or any of the settled property.

The following are '*ordinary trust assets*':

(1) shares or securities (the latter as defined in *TCGA 1992, s 132* — see **63.8** SHARES AND SECURITIES);
(2) tangible property, whether movable or immovable, or a lease of such property;
(3) property not within (1) or (2) above which is used for the purposes of a trade, profession or vocation carried on by the trustees or by a beneficiary who has an interest in possession in the settled property; and
(4) any right in or over, or any interest in, property of a description within (2) or (3) above.

The alternative condition mentioned in (a)(ii) above in relation to an asset (or part of an asset) which no longer forms part of the settled property is that:

- the asset (or part) is treated as having been disposed of by virtue of *TCGA 1992, s 24(1)* (entire loss or destruction of an asset — see **10.2** CAPITAL SUMS DERIVED FROM ASSETS); or
- one or more ordinary trust assets which taken together directly or indirectly represent the asset (or part):
  - form part of the settled property immediately after the transfer of value; or
  - are treated as having been disposed of by virtue of *TCGA 1992, s 24(1)*.

Where there has been a part disposal of the asset, the main condition in (a)(ii) above and the alternative condition above may be applied in any combination in relation to the subject matter of the part disposal and what remains.

The Treasury has the power to make regulations to add to, amend or repeal any of the provisions defining the circumstances in which the proceeds of trustee borrowing are treated as applied for normal trust purposes.

[*TCGA 1992, Sch 4B paras 4–9*].

HMRC consider that 'borrowing' for these purposes includes borrowing from a company controlled by the trustees or their associates, and that outstanding trustee borrowing can include money borrowed before 21 March 2000. Genuine delay in payment of a bill, for example for repairs to trust property, is not borrowing for these purposes. A futures contract relating to commodities is not an ordinary trust asset. (Revenue Tax Bulletin August 2003 pp 1049, 1050). See this article also for HMRC's views on whether the proceeds of borrowing are applied for normal trust purposes.

Whether deemed disposal is of the whole or a proportion of the assets

If the amount of value transferred:

- is less than the amount of outstanding trustee borrowing immediately after the transfer of value; and
- is also less than the 'effective value' of the remaining chargeable assets,

the deemed disposal and reacquisition is of the proportion of each of the remaining chargeable assets given by:

$$\frac{VT}{EV}$$

where:

VT = the amount of value transferred; and
EV = the effective value of the remaining chargeable assets.

If the amount of value transferred:

- is not less than the amount of outstanding trustee borrowing immediately after the transfer of value; but
- is less than the effective value of the remaining chargeable assets,

the deemed disposal and reacquisition is of the proportion of each of the remaining chargeable assets given by:

$$\frac{TB}{EV}$$

where:

TB = the amount of outstanding trustee borrowing immediately after the transfer of value; and
EV = the effective value of the remaining chargeable assets.

In any other case the deemed disposal and reacquisition is of the whole of each of the remaining chargeable assets.

The '*effective value*' of the remaining chargeable assets is the aggregate market value of those assets immediately after the transfer of value, reduced by so much of that value as is attributable to trustee borrowing (see below).

[*TCGA 1992, Sch 4B para 11*].

Value attributable to trustee borrowing

The value of any asset is '*attributable to trustee borrowing*' to the extent that:

- the trustees have applied the proceeds of trustee borrowing in acquiring or enhancing the value of the asset; or
- the asset represents directly or indirectly an asset whose value was attributable to the trustees having so applied the proceeds of trustee borrowing.

Where the asset itself has been borrowed by trustees, in addition to any extent to which the value of the asset may be attributable to trustee borrowing by virtue of the above, the value of the asset is attributable to trustee borrowing to the extent that the proceeds of that borrowing have not been applied for normal trust purposes (see above).

For these purposes, an amount is treated as applied by the trustees in acquiring or enhancing the value of an asset if it is applied by them wholly and exclusively:

- as consideration in money or money's worth for the acquisition of the asset;
- for the purpose of enhancing the value of the asset in a way that is reflected in the state or nature of the asset;
- in establishing, preserving or defending their title to, or to a right over, the asset; or
- where the asset is a holding of shares or securities (the latter as defined in *TCGA 1992, s 132* — see **63.8** SHARES AND SECURITIES) that is treated as a single asset, by way of consideration in money or money's worth for additional shares or securities forming part of the same holding,

at a time when, and to the extent that, there is outstanding trustee borrowing.

[*TCGA 1992, Sch 4B para 12*].

Restriction on set-off of settlement losses

[62.22] Cross-reference. See **62.16** above for restrictions on transfer of settlement losses to beneficiary becoming absolutely entitled to settled property.

Where the circumstances set out below apply in relation to a chargeable gain accruing to the trustees of a settlement, no allowable losses accruing to the trustees (whether in the same tax year or brought forward from an earlier year) may be set against any part of that gain.

The circumstances are as follows.

- In computing the gain in question, the allowable expenditure would be greater if it were not for a claim having been made for gifts hold-over relief under *TCGA 1992, s 165* or *s 260* (see **36.2**, **36.10** HOLD-OVER RELIEFS) in respect of an earlier disposal (not necessarily of the same asset) to the trustees; and
- the person who made that earlier disposal, or a person connected with him (within *TCGA 1992, s 286* — see **17** CONNECTED PERSONS), has at any time acquired an 'interest in the settled property' (defined as in **62.20** above), or entered into an arrangement to acquire such an interest, as a result of which any person has at any time received (or become entitled to receive) any consideration.

[*TCGA 1992, s 79A*].

Attribution to trustees of gains of non-resident companies

[62.23] The following apply where the trustees of a settlement are participators (within *CTA 2010, s 454*) in a close company (within *CTA 2010, ss 439–454* — broadly a company under the control of five or fewer participators or of directors who are participators, see Tolley's Corporation Tax under Close Companies) or in a non-UK resident company which would otherwise be a close company.

Where, by reason of such participation by the trustees, any part of a chargeable gain accruing to a non-UK resident company falls to be attributed to them under *TCGA 1992, s 13* (see **49.7** OVERSEAS MATTERS), nothing in any double tax agreement (see **21.2** DOUBLE TAX RELIEF) is to be taken as averting the tax charge otherwise arising.

Where:

(a) a chargeable gain accrues to a non-UK resident company which would otherwise be a close company;
(b) all or part of the gain is attributed under *TCGA 1992, s 13* to a close company which, by reason of a double tax agreement, is not chargeable to corporation tax on the gain; and
(c) had that close company been a non-UK resident company, all or part of the chargeable gain would have been attributed to the trustees by reason of such participation as is mentioned above;

then, for the purposes of the provisions in **49.7** OVERSEAS MATTERS which enable a gain to be attributed through a chain of companies, the company in (b) above is treated as a non-UK resident company, with the result that the gain can be attributed to the trustees. This treatment also applies to any other company which, if it were non-UK resident, would have been part of the chain, such that all or part of the gain in question would have been attributed as in (c) above.

[*TCGA 1992, s 79B*].

Key points related to settlements

[62.24] Points to consider are as follows.

- In general, capital gains tax is calculated in the same way for trustees as it is for individuals. The highest rate of capital gains tax for trustees is 28%. With the current 45% rate of income tax for discretionary trusts, many trustees may be keen to move towards assets that are assessed to capital gains, rather than to income tax.
- The trustees' annual exempt amount (which is, in general, one half of the individual annual exempt amount) is further divided by the number of settlements created by the same settlor after 6 June 1978. Be aware that different restrictions apply to the capital gains tax annual exempt amount and the income tax standard rate band. For example, a father creates a settlement for the benefit of each of his four children when they are born, in 1977, 1979, 1981 and 1983. For income tax purposes there are four qualifying settlements, therefore each trust's standard rate band will be divided by four. For capital gains tax purposes, the earliest settlement is pre-6 June 1978 and it will therefore be eligible for the full trustees' annual exempt amount. The remaining three settlements form a qualifying group and will each receive one-third of the trustees' annual exempt amount.
- Additionally, if in the above example the child born in 1983 was disabled, then the capital gains tax annual exempt amount available to that trust would be one third of the full annual

exempt amount (the amount due to individuals), rather than half of this amount, being the amount due to trustees (in general). This would have no effect on the amounts due to the other two trusts in the qualifying group.

- The creation of a settlement (or subsequent transfer of assets into an existing settlement) is a chargeable event for capital gains tax purposes. The settlor of the assets is treated as having disposed of them at full market value, and the gain is calculated thereon. In many cases involving settlements, an immediate charge to inheritance tax arises on the same occasion, and in order to prevent a double taxation charge, gifts hold-over relief may be available — see **36** HOLD-OVER RELIEFS.
- In qualifying interest in possession trusts (interest in possession settlements created before 22 March 2006, or those created after that date which are classed as an immediate post-death interest, a transitional serial interest, a disabled person's interest or a trust for bereaved minors) the underlying assets of the trust are treated as those of the life tenant and the life tenant is absolutely entitled to the income generated by those assets. The life tenant does not usually have a right to the capital of the trust and therefore the gains are assessable on the trustees for capital gains tax purposes.

63

Shares and Securities

Introduction to shares and securities	63.1
Reorganisation of share capital	63.2
Bonus issues (aka scrip issues)	63.3
Rights issues	63.4
Exchange of securities for those in another company	63.5
Earn-out rights	63.6
Scheme of reconstruction involving issue of securities	63.7
Conversion of securities	63.8
Quoted option granted following reorganisation	63.9
Stock dividends (aka scrip dividends)	63.10
Capital distributions	63.11
Distributions in a liquidation: unquoted shares	63.12
Distributions of assets in specie in a liquidation	63.13
Disposal of shares to employee-ownership trust	63.14
Trading requirement	63.15
All-employee benefit requirement	63.16
Controlling interest requirement	63.17
Limited participation requirement	63.18
Company purchase of own shares (aka share buy-back)	63.19
Accrued income scheme	63.20
Deeply discounted securities	63.21
Depositary receipts	63.22
Close companies	63.23
Life assurance policies	63.24
Stock lending arrangements	63.25
Agreements for sale and repurchase of securities ('repos')	63.26
Building society and other de-mutualisations	63.27
Shareholders in Northern Rock plc and Bradford and Bingley plc	63.28
Members of Dairy Farmers of Britain	63.29
Recognised stock exchanges	63.30
Tax treatment of new types of security	63.31
Key points on shares and securities	63.32

Cross-references. See 4 ANTI-AVOIDANCE for certain provisions which apply to share disposals; 5.6 APPEALS for appeals regarding values of unquoted shares; 7.3 ASSETS for location of shares; 7.7 ASSETS for options to acquire shares; 8 ASSETS HELD ON 6 APRIL 1965; 9 ASSETS HELD ON 31 MARCH 1982; 14 COMPANIES; 15.2–15.6 COMPANIES — CORPORATE FINANCE AND INTANGIBLES; 25.5 EXEMPTIONS AND RELIEFS for meaning of 'debt on a security'; 25.22 EXEMPTIONS AND RELIEFS for business expansion scheme shares; 28 GOVERNMENT SECURITIES; 36 HOLD OVER RELIEFS for relief in respect of gifts of shares in certain cases and transfers to companies in exchange for shares; 45 LOSSES for reliefs available for losses arising from certain share disposals and for negligible value claims; 40 INVESTORS' RELIEF; 45 MARKET VALUE; 49 OVERSEAS MATTERS for shares in certain overseas resident companies and funds; 54 QUALIFYING CORPORATE BONDS; 59 ROLLOVER RELIEF — REPLACEMENT OF BUSINESS ASSETS for relief where shares etc. are held in certain companies; 70 UNIT TRUSTS ETC.; 71 VENTURE CAPITAL TRUSTS.

Simon's Taxes. See C2.7–C2.8, D6.1, D6.2, D6.6, D9.450, D9.524, D9.528, D9.10.

Introduction to shares and securities

[63.1] There are many complex tax rules dealing with capital gains on shares and securities. The main provisions are listed below and described in more detail in this chapter or as indicated. For further relevant provisions, see 63.19–63.30 below and the list of cross-references at the head of the chapter.

Identification rules

Because one batch of shares or securities of the same class in a company are (unless numbered) effectively indistinguishable from another batch, special rules are needed to match disposals with multiple acquisitions. There are different rules for capital gains tax purposes and for corporation tax purposes. See 64 SHARES AND SECURITIES — IDENTIFICATION RULES.

Reorganisation of share capital

Such reorganisations, including bonus and rights issues, are not normally treated as disposals. Instead, the 'new holding' is treated as the same asset, acquired at the same date, as the 'original shares'. See 63.2–63.4 below.

Exchanges, schemes of reconstruction, etc.

The share reorganisation provisions apply also to the exchange of securities for those in another company (for example, in the course of a takeover, grouping exercise or buy-out). See 63.5 below. Similarly, the provisions also apply to certain arrangements made as part of a scheme of reconstruction involving the issue of securities (such as a merger or division) and on the conversion of securities. See 63.7 and 63.8 below.

Stock dividends (aka scrip dividends)

See 63.10–63.13 below.

Capital distributions

A capital distribution, on liquidation or otherwise, is normally treated as a disposal of an interest in the shares. See 63.11 below.

Substantial shareholdings of companies

A corporation tax exemption is available for a disposal by a company of shares after 31 March 2002. The company making the disposal must have held a 'substantial shareholding' in the company whose shares are the subject of the disposal throughout a continuous twelve-month period beginning not more than six years (two years, for disposals prior to 1 April 2017) before the disposal. See 66 SUBSTANTIAL SHAREHOLDINGS OF COMPANIES.

Employee share schemes

For the CGT consequences where employees receive shares in their employing companies, see **22** EMPLOYEE SHARE SCHEMES.

Venture capital schemes

There are currently three schemes under which various tax reliefs are available for investment in shares of qualifying companies. Individuals can invest in such companies directly via the ENTERPRISE INVESTMENT SCHEME (**23**) or the SEED ENTERPRISE INVESTMENT SCHEME (**60**) or indirectly through VENTURE CAPITAL TRUSTS (**71**). Before 1 April 2010, companies could make direct investments using the CORPORATE VENTURING SCHEME (**18**).

Sale of controlling interest in company to employee-ownership trust

FA 2014 introduced a relief from capital gains tax which applies to a disposal on or after 6 April 2014 of certain shares in a trading company to the trustees of a settlement which operates for the benefit of all the employees of the company. The relief is available only if the settlement acquires a controlling interest in the company in the tax year of the disposal. See **63.14** below.

Reorganisation of share capital

[63.2] A 'reorganisation' does not normally constitute a disposal. Instead, the 'new holding' is treated as the same asset, acquired at the same date, as the 'original shares'.

For this purpose:

- '*original shares*' means shares held before, and concerned in, the reorganisation, and
- '*new holding*' means, in relation to any original shares, the shares in and debentures of the company which, following the reorganisation, represent the original shares, and any remaining original shares.

[*TCGA 1992, ss 126(1), 127*].

In certain cases involving ENTREPRENEURS' RELIEF (**24.12**), an election may be made for the reorganisation to be treated as an actual disposal and reacquisition.

Separate rules apply to a reorganisation of share capital involving qualifying corporate bonds. See **54.4** QUALIFYING CORPORATE BONDS.

See **63.9** below where a quoted option to subscribe for shares in a company is dealt in (on the stock exchange where it is quoted) within three months after (or such longer period after as may be allowed in written notice by HMRC) a reorganisation within these provisions.

Scope of provisions

A 'reorganisation' is defined as a '*reorganisation or reduction of a company's share capital*'. '*Reorganisation of a company's share capital*' includes the making of bonus and rights issues of shares or debentures in proportion to the original holdings (see **63.3** and **63.4** below), the reduction of share capital and the alteration of rights attaching to the original shares. '*Reduction of share capital*' does not include the paying off of redeemable share capital, and where shares in a company are redeemed by the company otherwise than by the issue of shares or debentures (with or without other consideration) and otherwise than in a liquidation, the shareholder is treated as disposing of the shares at the time of the redemption. [*TCGA 1992, s 126*].

In strictness, the alteration of rights attaching to shares is a reorganisation only where there is already more than one class of shares in issue. HMRC, however, accept that a reorganisation can occur where there is only one class of shares in issue. (HMRC Capital Gains Manual CG51780).

In *Dunstan v Young Austen Young Ltd* CA 1988, 61 TC 448, the Court of Appeal held that an increase in share capital can be a reorganisation even if it is not a conventional bonus or rights issue, 'provided that the new shares are acquired by existing shareholders because they are existing shareholders and in proportion to their existing beneficial holdings'. See also *Unilever (UK) Holdings Ltd v Smith* CA, 2002 STI 1806 and *Fletcher v HMRC* (Sp C 711), [2008] SSCD 1219.

HMRC will treat any subscription for shares under an 'open offer', which is equal to or less than the shareholder's minimum entitlement under the offer, as a share reorganisation. Any shares subscribed for in excess of the minimum entitlement will be treated as a separate acquisition. (An 'open offer' is where a company invites its shareholders to subscribe for shares subject to a minimum entitlement based on their existing holdings, and possibly enabling them to subscribe also for shares which other shareholders do not want.) (HMRC Capital Gains Manual CG51756).

No part of any acquisition of shares by existing shareholders under a 'vendor placing' can be treated as a share reorganisation. For this purpose, a '*vendor placing*' takes place where a company wishes to pay for the purchase of an asset by issuing its own shares and, with the vendors not wanting the shares, the company makes arrangements to sell the shares on the vendors' behalf to its existing shareholders. (HMRC Capital Gains Manual CG51763).

For HMRC's views on the treatment of rights to acquire shares in other companies, see HMRC Capital Gains Manual CG52065.

The share reorganisation provisions also apply to exchanges of securities for those in another company within **63.5** below, to schemes of reconstruction within **63.7** below and on the conversion of securities (see **63.8** below).

Consideration given by shareholder

Any additional consideration given by the shareholder at the time of reorganisation (e.g. as a subscription for a rights issue — see **63.4** below) is added to the cost of the original holding for the purpose of computing the unindexed gain on a subsequent disposal.

The surrender, cancellation or alteration of the original holding or the rights attached thereto, and any consideration met out of the assets of the company (e.g. on a bonus issue) or represented by a dividend or other distribution declared but not paid are not regarded as 'additional consideration'. Similarly, in the case of a reorganisation occurring after 9 March 1981, any consideration given, otherwise than by way of a bargain made at arm's length, for part or all of the new holding will be disregarded, to the extent that its amount or value exceeds the amount by which the market value of the new holding, immediately after the reorganisation, exceeds the market value of the original shares immediately before the reorganisation. (See also *CIR v Burmah Oil Co. Ltd* HL 1981, 54 TC 200.)

[*TCGA 1992, s 128(1)(2)*].

See **38.6** INDEXATION for the calculation of indexation allowance in respect of the additional consideration.

Consideration received by shareholder

Where, on a reorganisation, a person receives (or is deemed to receive), or becomes entitled to receive, any consideration, other than the new holding, for the disposal of an interest in the original shares, and in particular:

(i) where under *TCGA 1992, s 122* he is to be treated as if he had in consideration of a capital distribution disposed of an interest in the original shares (see **63.11** below and note the procedure where the amount of the capital distribution is small or exceeds the allowable expenditure attaching to the original shares), or

(ii) where he receives (or is deemed to receive) consideration from other shareholders in respect of a surrender of rights derived from the original shares,

he is treated as if the new holding resulted from his having for that consideration disposed of an interest (but without prejudice to the original shares and the new holding being treated in accordance with *TCGA 1992, s 127* above as the same asset). [*TCGA 1992, s 128(3)*].

Collective investment schemes

See **70.3** UNIT TRUSTS ETC. for the treatment (generally, and therefore for the purposes of the share reorganisation provisions) of an authorised unit trust as a company and the rights of unit holders as shares in that company. See **70.2** UNIT TRUSTS ETC. for the disapplication of the above provisions as regards collective investment schemes entitling participants to exchange rights in one part of a scheme property for rights in another.

Valuation of different classes of share on subsequent disposal

Where the new holding consists of more than one class of share, security, debenture, etc. none of which is quoted on a recognised stock exchange within three months of the reorganisation, the allowable acquisition cost is arrived at on the basis of the market value of the various classes at the date of a chargeable disposal of the new holding or part thereof. This also applies where consideration, other than the new holding, is received as in *TCGA 1992, s 128(3)* above. [*TCGA 1992, ss 128(4), 129*].

However, in the case of shares and securities any one class or more of which is or are listed on a recognised stock exchange (see **63.30** below) (or, in the case of unit trust rights, of which the prices were published daily by the managers) within three months after the reorganisation takes effect (or such longer time as HMRC may allow), the base value is determined *once and for all* by reference to the respective market value, on the first day on which the market values or prices of the shares are quoted or published (whether published before or after the actual reorganisation). The provisions apply also to the reorganisation of rights under unit trusts. See **70** UNIT TRUSTS AND OTHER INVESTMENT VEHICLES. A reorganisation which involves the allotment of holdings is deemed to take effect on the day following the day on which the right to renounce any allotment expires. [*TCGA 1992, ss 130, 288(1)*].

For the application of the indexation provisions to holdings of shares arising out of these rules, see **38.6** INDEXATION and **64.4, 64.5** SHARES AND SECURITIES — IDENTIFICATION RULES.

Assets held on 6 April 1965

See **8.5** and **8.10** ASSETS HELD ON 6 APRIL 1965 for certain situations that may still arise in relation to reorganisations.

Example

A Ltd, an unquoted company, was incorporated in 1996 with an authorised share capital of £50 million denominated into 500 million Ordinary Shares of 10p each, of which 300 million were issued at par on incorporation. In 2005, the directors decide to reorganise the company's share capital by issuing the balance of the authorised share capital in the form of a bonus issue of 200 million Ordinary Shares of 10p so that two such shares are issued for every three of such shares already held. The 500 million Ordinary Shares of 10p each in issue are then consolidated into 50 million New Ordinary Shares of £1 each. A rights issue is then made on the basis of one 7% Cumulative Preference Share of £1 issued at par for every five New Ordinary Shares of £1 already held.

X was issued 90,000 Ordinary Shares of 10p on incorporation and has held them continually since then. Assuming he takes up the rights issue, his new holding after the reorganisation is as follows.

	No. of shares	Par value	Cost
			£
Original holding: 10p Ords	90,000	10p	9,000
Bonus issue: 10p Ords	60,000	10p	Nil
	150,000		£9,000
Consolidation: 10p Ords to £1			
New Ords	15,000	£1	9,000
Rights issue: £1 Prefs	3,000	£1	3,000
Cost of complete new holding			£12,000

X disposes of 1,500 £1 Prefs in 2017 when each such share is worth £3 and each £1 New Ord is worth £1.80. The apportionment is as follows

		£
Total value of £1 Prefs: (£3 × 3,000)	=	9,000

Total value of £1 New Ords: (£1.80 × 15,000)	=	27,000
		£36,000
Proportional value of £1 Prefs × original cost		
$^9/_{36}$ × £12,000	=	£3,000
Allowable cost of 1,500 £1 Prefs (£3,000 × 2)	=	£1,500

Note

If X later disposes of the remainder (1,500) of the £1 Prefs when their value is £4 each and that of the £1 Ords is £2 each, the calculation will be made as follows:

		£
Total value of £1 Prefs: (£4 × 1,500)	=	6,000
Total value of £1 Ords: (£2 × 15,000)	=	30,000
		£36,000
Original cost (as reduced by previous disposal)	=	£10,500
Proportional value of £1 Prefs × original cost		
$^6/_{36}$ × £10,500	=	£1,750
Allowable cost of 1,500 £1 Prefs	=	£1,750

Bonus issues (aka scrip issues)

[63.3] A bonus issue is a reorganisation within **63.2** above, but see **63.10** below for stock dividends.

Where a company has acquired its own shares and holds them as treasury shares (see **63.19** below) a bonus issue in respect of shares of the same class can be a reorganisation whether or not bonus shares are issued in respect of the treasury shares (HMRC Capital Gains Manual CG51750).

In practice, where a bonus issue follows a repayment of share capital (e.g. under *CTA 2010, s 1022*), and is treated as income of the recipient, the amount of that income net of basic rate tax is treated as the acquisition cost of the new shares (HMRC Capital Gains Manual CG51825).

Example

X plc, a quoted company, makes a bonus issue in September 2017 of one preference share for every eight ordinary shares held. On first trading after issue, the preference shares were valued at £10 and the ordinary shares at £6.

Mr A had purchased 1,000 ordinary shares in December 2012 for £7,000. After the issue of preference shares, the allowable expenditure on a subsequent disposal of the ordinary and preference shares is computed as follows.

£

Initial value of preference shares (125 × £10)			1,250
Initial value of ordinary shares (1,000 × £6)			6,000
Total			£7,250
Allowable cost of 1,000 ordinary shares	$\frac{6,000}{7,250} \times 7,000$	=	£5,790
Allowable cost of 125 preference shares	$\frac{1,250}{7,250} \times 7,000$	=	£1,210

Rights issues

[63.4] A rights issue of shares or debentures in respect of shares already held in a company is a reorganisation within **63.2** above. A company cannot grant rights in respect of treasury shares, but this will not in itself prevent the rights issue being a reorganisation (HMRC Capital Gains Manual CG51750).

Disposal of rights

Where a person receives or becomes entitled to receive in respect of any shares in a company a provisional allotment of shares in or debentures of the company and he disposes of his rights, *TCGA 1992, s 122* applies as if the amount of consideration for the disposal were a capital distribution received by him from the company in respect of the first-mentioned shares, and as if he had, instead of disposing of the rights, disposed of an interest in those shares. This rule also applies to rights obtained in respect of any debentures of a company. [*TCGA 1992, s 123*].

See **63.11** below for *TCGA 1992, s 122* and note the procedure where the amount of the capital distribution is small or exceeds the allowable expenditure attaching to the original shares etc.

Example

W plc is a quoted company which in June 1992 made a rights issue of one £1 ordinary share for every eight £1 ordinary shares held, at £1.35 payable on allotment. V, who held 16,000 £1 ordinary shares purchased in May 1984 for £15,000, took up his entitlement in full, and was allotted 2,000 shares. In December 2017, he sells 6,000 of his shares for £30,000.

'Section 104 holding'	Shares	Qualifying expenditure £
May 1984 acquisition	16,000	15,000
June 1992 rights issue	2,000	2,700
	18,000	17,700
December 2017 disposal	(6,000)	(5,900)
Pool carried forward	12,000	£11,800

Calculation of chargeable gain		£
Disposal consideration		30,000
	Allowable cost $\frac{6,000}{18,000} \times £17,700$	5,900
Chargeable gain 2017/18		£24,100

Exchange of securities for those in another company

[63.5] The share reorganisation provisions at 63.2 above apply also where a company (company B) issues shares or debentures in exchange for the shares or debentures of another company (company A), provided that one of the following conditions is satisfied. The conditions are that:

- company B holds, or in consequence of the exchange will hold, more than 25% of company A's 'ordinary share capital';
- company B holds, or in consequence of the exchange will hold, more than 50% of the voting power in company A; or
- company B issues the shares etc. as the result of a general offer made to the members of company A (or any class of them) and the offer is initially made on a condition which, if satisfied, would give company B control of company A. (This covers abortive takeover bids which become unconditional, but which do not succeed.)

In applying the share reorganisation provisions, company A and company B are treated as if they were the same company. Following the exchange, therefore, the shares etc. in company B (which form the 'new holding' for the purposes of the reorganisation provisions) are treated, in the hands of the original holders of the exchanged company A shares etc., as the same asset, acquired at the same date, as the exchanged shares etc. (which form the 'original shares').

For this purpose, the '*ordinary share capital*' of a company is all its issued share capital (by whatever name called), other than shares carrying only a right to fixed rate dividends and no other right to participate in profits and also includes units in a unit trust and, in relation to a company with no share capital, interests in the company possessed by its members. In relation to such a company, references above to shares or debentures include any such interests. For HMRC's interpretation of 'ordinary share capital', see HMRC Brief 87/2009.

These provisions are subject to the anti-avoidance rule below.

[*TCGA 1992, s 135; CTA 2010, s 1119*].

The above provisions can apply in several different commercial situations, including straightforward takeovers, reverse takeovers, forming groups out of associated companies and buy-outs. See HMRC Capital Gains Manual CG52570. Where the conditions are satisfied, the provisions apply automatically, without claim.

See **70.2** UNIT TRUSTS ETC. for the application of the provisions as regards collective investment schemes entitling participants to exchange rights in one part of a scheme for rights in another.

For the tax consequences of a share exchange before 14 March 1988 within a group of companies, see *Westcott v Woolcombers Ltd* CA 1987, 60 TC 575 and *NAP Holdings UK Ltd v Whittles* HL 1994, 67 TC 166 at **29.3** GROUPS OF COMPANIES.

See **63.9** below where a quoted option to subscribe for shares in a company is dealt in (on the stock exchange where it is quoted) within three months after (or such longer period after as may be allowed in written notice by HMRC) an exchange within these provisions.

Treasury shares

Where company A has acquired its own shares and is holding them as treasury shares (see **63.19** below) at the time of the exchange, no issue of shares by Company B can be made in respect of the treasury shares. The treasury shares do not count as issued share capital in determining whether the conditions for the above treatment are met. A disposal of its treasury shares by Company B is treated as the company issuing those shares. (HMRC Capital Gains Manual CG52521).

Incidental costs of acquisition and disposal and warranty payments in respect of contingent liabilities

Any such costs or payments attributable to the new holding of shares or debentures are by concession treated as consideration given for that holding. In the case of warranty payments, relief under this concession and *TCGA 1992, s 49(1)(c)* (see **16.13** COMPUTATION OF GAINS AND LOSSES) will in total be restricted to what would have been allowed under *TCGA 1992, s 49(1)(c)* had *TCGA 1992, s 135* not applied (HMRC Extra-Statutory Concession D52).

Anti-avoidance

The above provisions do not apply unless the exchange is made for genuine commercial reasons and does not form part of a scheme or arrangements of which the main purpose, or one of the main purposes, is the avoidance of capital gains tax or corporation tax. In such cases, a chargeable disposal is treated as taking place except where a person to whom the new shares or debentures are issued owns (or he and persons connected with him together own) less than 5% of, or any class of, the shares or debentures of company A. There are provisions for advance clearance of an exchange by HMRC. [*TCGA 1992, ss 137, 138*].

For full coverage, see **4.15** ANTI-AVOIDANCE.

Where the provisions are disapplied, then under general principles the disposal proceeds will be the value in money's worth of the shares or debentures issued by the acquiring company or, if the transaction is not a bargain made at arm's length, the market value of the shares or debentures sold (if different).

Miscellaneous

TCGA 1992, s 135 is disapplied in certain circumstances (with the result that an exchange of securities is treated as a disposal of the original holding and an acquisition of a new holding) in relation to shares and securities that have qualified for tax relief under one of the various venture capital tax schemes or the community investment tax credit scheme. See **18.22** CORPORATE VENTURING SCHEME, **23.13**, **23.17** ENTERPRISE INVESTMENT SCHEME, **25.22** EXEMPTIONS AND RELIEFS (as regards the Business Expansion Scheme), **71.11** VENTURE CAPITAL TRUSTS and Tolley's Income Tax under Community Investment Tax Relief. See also **66.14** SUBSTANTIAL SHAREHOLDINGS OF COMPANIES.

HMRC have confirmed that it is possible for a Delaware Limited Liability Company that issues shares to be a party to share exchanges within *TCGA 1992, s 135* (Revenue Tax Bulletin February 2001 p 827).

> ***Example***
>
> Wendy buys 10,000 shares in Never Ltd for £20,000 in November 2002. Never Ltd is taken over by Ryan plc on 1 May 2017 and Wendy receives 4,000 shares in Ryan plc in exchange for her Never Ltd shares.
>
> Wendy is not treated as making a disposal of the Never Ltd shares on 1 May 2017. Instead her Ryan plc shares are treated as acquired in November 2002 at the same cost (£20,000) as her shares in Never Ltd.

Earn-out rights

[63.6] An agreement for the sale of shares in a company may include the right to receive deferred consideration which is itself unascertainable at the time of the agreement, usually because it depends on the future profit performance of the company. Such a right was held to be a separate asset in *Marren v Ingles* HL 1980, 54 TC 76 (see **10.2** CAPITAL SUMS DERIVED FROM ASSETS). In certain circumstances, where the right (known as the 'earn-out right') is a right to receive securities, the right itself is treated as a security so that the share exchange provisions at **63.5** above can apply. The subsequent issue of the actual securities in pursuance of the right is then treated as a conversion of securities within **63.8** below. Such treatment is mandatory, subject to the option to disapply it by election.

Detailed provisions

Where a person ('the seller') transfers securities (i.e. shares or debentures) of a company and, as all or part of the consideration for the transfer, has conferred upon him a right to receive securities ('the new securities') of another company ('the acquiring company'), the value or quantity of which is 'unascertainable' (see below) at that time, such right is known as an '*earn-out right*'. It is a further condition that the terms of the right are such that it cannot be discharged otherwise than by the issue of the new securities. Any right to receive cash and/or an ascertainable amount of securities as part of the total consideration does not fall within these provisions and must be distinguished from the earn-out right.

Provided that *TCGA 1992, s 135* (exchange of securities — see **63.5** above) would have applied if the earn-out right were an ascertainable amount of securities of the acquiring company, the right is treated for capital gains purposes as if it were itself a security of the acquiring company (so that *s 135* may apply). This treatment does not apply if the seller so elects.

An election is irrevocable and must be made by written notice to an HMRC officer by the first anniversary of 31 January following the tax year in which the earn-out right is conferred, or, where made by a company, within two years after the end of the accounting period in which the right is conferred. In *Adams v HMRC* FTT, [2009] SFTD 184, the making of a return on the basis that an election applied was held to amount to a valid election.

Where security treatment applies, it is then assumed, as regards the seller and any subsequent owner of the earn-out right, that:

(a) the earn-out right is a security within the definition in *TCGA 1992, s 132* (see **63.8** below);
(b) the notional security represented by the earn-out right is not a QUALIFYING CORPORATE BOND (**54**);
(c) all references in *TCGA 1992* to a debenture include references to such a notional security; and
(d) the eventual issue of actual securities in pursuance of the earn-out right constitutes a conversion of the right, insofar as it is discharged by the issue, into those securities (see **63.8** below re conversion of securities).

Where an earn-out right is treated as a notional security of a company as above and it is extinguished and replaced with a new right to be issued with securities of the same company, the value or quantity of which is 'unascertainable' (see below) at that time, the new right is treated for CGT purposes as if it were a security of the company, with the same consequences as above. The person on whom the new right is conferred may make an election to disapply this treatment. The time limits for election operate by reference to the tax year or accounting period in which the new right is conferred.

Meaning of 'unascertainable'

(1) The value or quantity of securities to be issued in pursuance of an earn-out right is unascertainable at a particular time if, and only if, it is made referable to matters relating to any business or assets of one or more 'relevant companies' and those matters are then uncertain on account of future business or future assets being included in the business or assets to which they relate. A '*relevant company*' is either the acquiring company or the acquired company or any company in the same group of companies as either of those. A group of companies is construed in accordance with **29.2** GROUPS OF COMPANIES.
(2) The value or quantity of securities to be issued in pursuance of an earn-out right is *not* to be taken as unascertainable merely by reason of any part of the consideration for the transaction being contingent or of any risk of its being irrecoverable. In such cases, *TCGA 1992, s 48* (consideration due after time of disposal — see **16.13** COMPUTATION OF GAINS AND LOSSES) applies in computing the gain.

(3) The existence of an option to choose between shares in and debentures of the acquiring company does not in itself render unascertainable the value or quantity of such securities. However, neither does such option prevent the above provisions from applying.

(4) If the value of securities to be issued in pursuance of an earn-out right is ascertainable and the quantity is to be fixed by reference thereto, or *vice versa*, this does not in itself render the value or quantity unascertainable.

[*TCGA 1992, s 138A*].

Note that an earn-out right treated as a security by virtue of *TCGA 1992, s 138A* is not regarded as a right to unascertainable consideration for the purposes of *TCGA 1992, ss 279A–279D* (loss on right to unascertainable consideration treated as accruing in earlier year — see **44.19** LOSSES). [*TCGA 1992, s 279B(6)*].

For HMRC's views on earn-outs, see HMRC Capital Gains Manual CG58000–58101.

Example

K owns 10,000 ordinary shares in M Ltd, which he acquired for £12,000 in December 2002. In July 2016, the whole of the issued share capital of M Ltd was acquired by P plc. Under the terms of the takeover, K receives £2 per share plus the right to further consideration up to a maximum of £1.50 per share depending on future profit performance. The initial consideration is receivable in cash, but the deferred consideration is to be satisfied by the issue of shares in P plc. In December 2017, K duly receives 2,000 ordinary shares valued at £6 per share in full settlement of his entitlement. The right to future consideration is valued at £1.40 per share in July 2016.

If K elects to disapply *TCGA 1992, s 138A* the position would be

2016/17

	£	£
Disposal proceeds 10,000 × £2	20,000	
Value of rights 10,000 × £1.40	14,000	34,000
Cost		12,000
Chargeable gain		£22,000

2017/18

	£
Disposal of rights to deferred consideration:	
Proceeds — 2,000 P plc shares @ £6	12,000
Deemed cost of acquiring rights	14,000
Allowable loss	£2,000
Cost for CGT purposes of 2,000 P plc shares	£12,000

Without an election, the position would be

2016/17

	£
Proceeds (cash) (as above)	20,000
Cost $£12{,}000 \times \dfrac{20{,}000}{20{,}000 + 14{,}000}$	7,059
Chargeable gain	£12,941
Cost of earn-out right for CGT purposes (£12,000 – £7,059)	£4,941

2017/18
The shares in P plc stand in the place of the earn-out right and will be regarded as having been acquired in December 2002 for £4,941. No further gain or loss arises until a disposal of the shares takes place.

Scheme of reconstruction involving issue of securities

[63.7] The share reorganisation provisions at **63.2** above apply also where certain arrangements between a company (company A) and its share- or debenture-holders (or any class of them) are entered into for the purposes of, or in connection with, a 'scheme of reconstruction'. Under the arrangement, another company (company B) must issue shares or debentures to those holders in respect of, or in proportion to (or as nearly as may be in proportion to), their original holdings, which latter are then retained, cancelled or otherwise extinguished.

In such a case, the holders are treated as exchanging their holdings in company A for the shares or debentures held by them as a consequence of the arrangement and the share reorganisation provisions apply as if company A and company B were the same company and the exchange were a reorganisation of its share capital. Any shares in or debentures of company A that are of a class involved in the scheme and that are retained are treated as if they had been cancelled and replaced by a new issue.

Where company A carries out an actual reorganisation of its share capital as a prelude to a scheme of reconstruction the above provisions apply to the position after the preliminary reorganisation has been carried out.

References above to shares or debentures being retained include their being retained in altered form, whether as a result of reduction, consolidation, division or otherwise. In relation to a company with no share capital, references to shares or debentures include any interests in the company possessed by its members.

[*TCGA 1992, s 136*].

See **63.9** below where a quoted option to subscribe for shares in a company is dealt in (on the stock exchange where it is quoted) within three months after (or such longer period after as may be allowed in written notice by HMRC) a scheme of reconstruction within these provisions.

Meaning of 'scheme of reconstruction'

A '*scheme of reconstruction*' is a scheme of merger, division or other restructuring that meets the following conditions.

(1) The scheme must involve the issue of 'ordinary share capital' of a company or companies (the '*successor company(ies)*') to holders of 'ordinary share capital' of another company (the '*original company*') (or, where relevant, to the holders of one or more particular classes of 'ordinary share capital' involved in the scheme). Where there is more than one original company involved in the scheme, the issue must be to holders of 'ordinary share capital' of (or of one or more particular classes of 'ordinary share capital' of) any of those companies. The scheme must *not* involve the issue of ordinary share capital of the successor company(ies) to anyone else. For this purpose a transfer of treasury shares (i.e. of the company's own shares acquired and held by it — see **63.19** below) is treated as an issue of shares (HMRC Capital Gains Manual CG52707a).

(2) Holders of a class of ordinary share capital (of the original company(ies)) involved in the scheme must each have the same proportionate entitlement to acquire ordinary share capital of the successor company(ies) (see example at HMRC Capital Gains Manual CG52707b). This does not apply to treasury shares because such shares are treated as if they had been cancelled (HMRC Capital Gains Manual CG52707b).

(3) Unless condition (4) below is satisfied, the effect of the restructuring must be that the business or substantially the whole of the business carried on by the original company is carried on either by a successor company which is not the original company or by two or more successor companies (which may include the original company). Where there is more than one original company, the effect must be that all or part of the business(es) carried on by one or more of the original companies is carried on by a different company *and* the whole or substantially the whole of the businesses carried on by the original companies is carried on:

  – by the successor company (which may be one of the original companies) where there is only one such company, or
  – by the successor companies (which may be the same as the original companies or include any of them) where there are two or more such companies.

  For the above purposes, the whole or substantially the whole of a business (or businesses) is carried on by two or more successor companies if, inter alia, the activities of those companies taken together embrace the whole or substantially the whole of that business (or those businesses). A business carried on by a company that is under the control (within *CTA 2010, s 1124*) of another company is treated as carried on by each of them. This enables a holding company with no business of its own to meet condition (3) by reference to the business of its subsidiary. See HMRC Capital Gains Manual CG52709 for the meaning of 'business' for these purposes.

For the purposes of this condition, there are disregarded any assets retained by an original company in order to make a capital distribution within *TCGA 1992, s 122* (see **63.11** below), for example to any significant minority of shareholders who indicated their unwillingness to maintain their investment in the business following the reconstruction.

(4) If condition (3) above is not satisfied, the scheme must be carried out in pursuance of a compromise or arrangement under *Companies Act 2006, Pt 26* (previously *Companies Act 1985, s 425*) (or NI or foreign equivalent) without involving any transfer of the business of the original company(ies).

For these purposes, '*ordinary share capital*' is as defined in **63.5** above, including the extension to units in a unit trust and, in relation to a company with no share capital, interests in the company possessed by its members.

Where any of the original companies 'reorganise' (within **63.2** above) their share capital as a prelude to a scheme of reconstruction, conditions (1) and (2) above apply to the position after the preliminary reorganisation has been carried out. For the purposes of those two conditions, there is disregarded any issue of shares in or debentures of any of the successor companies which is made after the latest date on which any of the successor companies issues shares or debentures:

- in consideration of the transfer of any business (or part of a business) under the scheme, or
- (where applicable) in pursuance of the compromise or arrangement mentioned in condition (4) above.

[*TCGA 1992, s 136(4), Sch 5AA; SI 2008 No 954, Art 17*].

For practical illustrations of schemes of reconstruction, including demergers, see HMRC Capital Gains Manual CG52720–52728.

Anti-avoidance

The same anti-avoidance rule applies as in **63.5** above [*TCGA 1992, s 136(6)*].

For full coverage see **4.15** ANTI-AVOIDANCE.

Incidental costs of acquisition and disposal and warranty payments in respect of contingent liabilities

Any such costs or payments attributable to the new holding of shares or debentures are by concession treated as consideration given for that holding. In the case of warranty payments, relief under this concession and *TCGA 1992, s 49(1)(c)* (see **16.13** COMPUTATION OF GAINS AND LOSSES) will in total be restricted to what would have been allowed under *TCGA 1992, s 49(1)(c)* had *TCGA 1992, s 136* not applied (HMRC Extra-Statutory Concession D52).

Miscellaneous

TCGA 1992, s 136 is disapplied in certain circumstances (with the result that a scheme of reconstruction is treated as a disposal of the original holding and an acquisition of a new holding) in relation to shares and securities that have qualified for tax relief under one of the various venture capital tax schemes or the community investment tax credit scheme. See **18.22** CORPORATE VENTURING SCHEME, **23.13**, **23.17** ENTERPRISE INVESTMENT SCHEME, **25.22** EXEMPTIONS AND RELIEFS (as regards the Business Expansion Scheme), **71.11** VENTURE CAPITAL TRUSTS and Tolley's Income Tax under Community Investment Tax Relief. See also **66.14** SUBSTANTIAL SHAREHOLDINGS OF COMPANIES.

Cross-border divisions and mergers

Certain transfers of assets on the division of a business between companies in different EC member states and certain transfers of assets and liabilities on cross-border mergers are treated as schemes of reconstruction. See **49.13–49.15** OVERSEAS MATTERS.

Example

N Ltd carries on a manufacturing and wholesaling business. In 1994, it was decided that the wholesaling business should be carried on by a separate company. Revenue clearance under *TCGA 1992, s 138* was obtained, and a company, R Ltd, was formed which, in consideration for the transfer to it by N Ltd of the latter's wholesaling undertaking, issued shares to the shareholders of N Ltd. Each holder of ordinary shares in N Ltd received one ordinary share in R Ltd for each N Ltd share he held. W, who purchased his 2,500 N shares for £10,000 in December 1991, received 2,500 R shares. None of the shares involved is quoted. In August 2017, W sells 1,500 of his N shares for £6 each, a total of £9,000, agreed to be their market value. The value of W's remaining N shares is also £6 per share, and the value of his R shares is £4.50 per share.

	£
Disposal consideration	9,000
Allowable cost $£10{,}000 \times \dfrac{9{,}000}{9{,}000 + (1{,}000 \times £6) + (2{,}500 \times £4.50)}$	3,429
Chargeable gain 2017/18	£5,571

Conversion of securities

[63.8] The share reorganisation provisions at **63.2** above apply also to the '*conversion of securities*', which phrase includes:

(a) a conversion of securities of a company into shares in that company;
(b) a conversion of a security which is not a qualifying corporate bond (QCB) (see **54** QUALIFYING CORPORATE BONDS) into a security of the same company which is a QCB;
(c) a conversion of a QCB into a security of the same company which is not a QCB;
(d) a conversion in lieu of redemption at the option of the holder of the securities; and
(e) any exchange of securities in pursuance of compulsory purchase powers.

Any of the above is a conversion of securities regardless of whether effected by a transaction or occurring as a result of the operation of the terms of any security or debenture.

'*Security*' includes any loan stock or similar security issued by national or local government or public authority in the UK or elsewhere, or by a company, and whether secured or unsecured. Certain company debentures are deemed under *TCGA 1992, s 251* to be securities for the purposes of that section (see **25.5** EXEMPTIONS AND RELIEFS). There are provisions to ensure that (b) and (c) above operate in relation to such debentures.

[*TCGA 1992, s 132*].

An amendment to the terms of loan notes which was intended to transform the notes into a QCB by removing the right to redeem them in dollars was held to be a conversion of the notes within the above provisions in *Klincke v HMRC* UT, [2010] STC 2032.

A premium in money (in addition to a new holding) on a conversion of securities is treated in virtually identical terms as under *TCGA 1992, s 122* for a capital distribution in **63.11** below. (It would appear that the case of *O&Rourke v Binks* CA 1992, 65 TC 165 mentioned therein applies equally to premiums on conversion within this provision as it does to capital distributions within *TCGA 1992, s 122*.) Similar rules as in *s 122* apply if the premium is 'small' (which is as defined in **63.11** below). [*TCGA 1992, s 133*].

See **63.9** below where a quoted option to subscribe for shares in a company is dealt in (on the stock exchange where it is quoted) within three months after (or such longer period after as may be allowed in written notice by HMRC) a conversion within these provisions.

Alternative rules apply to the conversion of securities of a company involving qualifying corporate bonds. See **54.4** QUALIFYING CORPORATE BONDS.

See also **70.2** UNIT TRUSTS ETC. for the disapplication of *TCGA 1992, s 132* as regards collective investment schemes entitling participants to exchange rights in one part of a scheme for rights in another.

Example

N bought £10,000 8% convertible loan stock in S plc, a quoted company, in June 1991. The cost was £9,800. In August 1995, N exercised his right to convert the loan stock into 'B' ordinary shares of the company, on the basis of 50 shares for £100 loan stock, and acquired 5,000 shares. In June 2017, N sells 3,000 of the shares for £10.00 each.

		£
Disposal consideration		30,000
	Cost $\frac{3,000}{5,000} \times £9,800$	5,880
Chargeable gain 2017/18		£24,120

Notes to the example

(a) The shares acquired on the conversion in 1995 stand in the shoes of the original loan stock. [*TCGA 1992, s 132*].

(b) The loan stock cannot be a corporate bond (and thus cannot be a qualifying corporate bond) as it is convertible into securities other than corporate bonds, i.e. into ordinary shares. [*CTA 2010, s 162; ICTA 1988, Sch 18 para 1(5); TCGA 1992, s 117(1)*].

Compensation stock

Instead of *TCGA 1992, s 132* above applying, where gilt-edged securities are issued on the compulsory acquisition of shares or securities the gain that would have accrued had the shares or securities been disposed of at their value at that time is not treated as arising until the gilt-edged securities are disposed of. However, for corporation tax purposes, where the gilt-edged securities received are disposed of after 5 April 1988 no gain arises under this provision if its application would be directly attributable to the disposal of an asset before 1 April 1982.

Disposals are, so far as possible, identified with gilts issued under the above provisions rather than with other gilts of the same kind and subject to this, with gilts issued at an earlier time rather than with those issued at a later time.

The deferment of the gain otherwise arising on the issue of the gilt-edged securities is extended to the recipient where their later disposal is within *TCGA 1992, s 58(1)* (spouses or civil partners), *s 62(4)* (legatee acquiring asset from personal representatives) and *s 171(1)* (groups of companies).

[*TCGA 1992, s 134, Sch 4 paras A1, 4(5); FA 2008, Sch 2 paras 74(2), 76*].

Euroconversion of securities

A 'small' cash payment received on a 'euroconversion' of a security, not involving a disposal of the security and therefore not within *TCGA 1992, s 132* (see above), is treated in virtually identical terms as a 'small' capital distribution under *TCGA 1992, s 122* (see **63.11** below). '*Euroconversion*' for these purposes refers to the redenomination into euros of a security expressed in the currency of an EU member state participating in the European single currency. [*TCGA 1992, s 133A*].

Quoted option granted following reorganisation

[63.9] If a quoted option (within *TCGA 1992, s 144(8)* — see **7.7** ASSETS) to subscribe for shares in a company is dealt in (on the stock exchange where it is quoted) within three months after (or such longer period after as may be allowed in written notice by HMRC) a reorganisation, reduction, conversion, exchange or scheme of reconstruction (within the provisions in **63.2–63.8** above) relating to the company granting the option, then:

(a) the option is regarded for those provisions as the shares which could be acquired following the reorganisation etc. by exercising the option; and
(b) the ordinary market value rules for quoted securities apply (see **45.3** MARKET VALUE).

[*TCGA 1992, s 147*].

Stock dividends (aka scrip dividends)

[63.10] Stock or 'scrip' dividends are issues of shares in lieu of a dividend and are treated for tax purposes as described below.

Issues of shares in lieu of dividend to individuals by non-UK resident companies are treated as bonus issues, and no allowance for capital gains tax purposes is made for the cash dividend forgone. Issues made by a UK resident company are subject to income tax (see Tolley's Income Tax under Savings and Investment Income).

An issue of shares by a UK resident company does not constitute a reorganisation but is treated in the hands of the recipient shareholder as a free-standing acquisition made at the time of the issue for a consideration equal to the 'cash equivalent of the share capital'. [*TCGA 1992, s 142*]. This rule applies also to stock dividends issued by a UK real estate investment trust ('REIT') or the parent company of a UK group REIT where the issue is attributed to the property rental business within the REIT regime (see **70.5** UNIT TRUSTS AND OTHER INVESTMENT VEHICLES). [*TCGA 1992, s 142A*].

The above provisions apply not only where the shares are issued as a consequence of an option to receive additional shares instead of a cash dividend but also where they are issued as a bonus issue in a case where the existing shares carry the right under the original terms of issue (or original terms as extended or varied) to receive bonus share capital of the same or a different class. [*ITTOIA 2005, s 410(1)*].

The '*cash equivalent of the share capital*' in the case of an issue of shares in lieu of dividend is the amount of the cash dividend alternative, except where the difference between that amount and the market value of the shares issued is 15% or more of the market value, in which case, the cash equivalent is the market value. In the case of a bonus issue of share capital, the cash equivalent is the market value of the shares issued. [*ITTOIA 2005, s 412*].

If two or more persons are entitled to the shares issued, those shares (and the appropriate amount in cash) are apportioned among them by reference to their interests in the shares at the date of issue. [*ITTOIA 2005, s 413(5)(6)*].

Settlements and personal representatives

The position above applies equally to personal representatives, to trustees of discretionary and accumulation trusts where the dividend would have been chargeable at the trust rate if received in cash, and to trustees of interest in possession trusts. [*TCGA 1992, s 142; ITTOIA 2005, s 410(2)–(4)*]. The trustees' acquisition cost of the original shareholding remains unaltered and the beneficiaries are regarded as acquiring the stock dividend shares as at the dividend date for the appropriate amount in cash. However, see SP 4/94 below re enhanced stock dividends.

The beneficiaries of a bare trust are treated in the same way as individuals, the trust being ignored for this purpose (HMRC Capital Gains Manual CG33810).

In the case of a discretionary or accumulation trust where the dividend would have been chargeable at the trust rate if received in cash, the appropriate amount in cash forms part of the trustees' allowable expenditure. Any subsequent distribution of the stock dividend shares to the beneficiaries is a part disposal at market value by the trustees, with the normal identification rules applying (see **64** SHARES AND SECURITIES — IDENTIFICATION RULES).

In the case of an *enhanced stock dividend*, i.e. one which is worth significantly more than the cash dividend forgone, there was some doubt as to whether the position for interest in possession trusts outlined above could apply, the point being that the stock dividend may under trust law be capital rather than income. It is up to the trustees to decide in the light of the trust deed whether the enhanced stock dividend should properly be regarded as income or as capital. The Revenue issued Statement of Practice 4/94 setting out their views. They are prepared to accept whichever of the three approaches listed below the trustees conclude that they should adopt, provided that their conclusion is supportable on the facts of the case.

- If the trustees treat the dividend as income, the beneficiary is chargeable to income tax under *ITTOIA 2005, s 410* and is treated as acquiring the shares for the 'appropriate amount in cash'. The issue is not treated as a reorganisation.
- If the trustees treat the dividend as capital, the issue is a reorganisation within *TCGA 1992, s 126* (see **63.2** above) and the trustees are not regarded as having made any payment for the shares.
- If the trustees treat the dividend as capital but pay compensation to a beneficiary in the form of shares for forgoing the cash dividend alternative, the transfer constitutes a part disposal of the new holding.

See HMRC Capital Gains Manual CG33810–33817 for a full discussion of the above.

Close companies

The appropriate amount in cash relating to shares issued in lieu of a dividend made by a UK resident company to a close company in accounting periods ending before 1 April 1989 was treated as part of its apportionable income for income tax purposes, and any income tax in respect of such income apportioned (but not paid) to a participator can be added to his allowable expenditure, for capital gains tax purposes, on a disposal of shares in the close company. The close company's allowable expenditure in respect of the shares was increased by the cash equivalent of the share capital. [*TCGA 1992, s 124; ICTA 1988, Sch 19 para 12*]. See further in **63.23** below. There is no addition to allowable expenditure of the shares held for later accounting periods or, for any accounting period, where the shares are held by a non-close company.

Example

D holds ordinary 20p shares in PLC, a quoted company. The company operates a scrip dividend policy whereby shareholders are given the option to take dividends in cash or in new fully-paid ordinary 20p shares, the option being exercisable separately in relation to each dividend. D purchased 2,000 shares for £1,500 in March 1980 and a further 3,000 shares for £8,100 in May 1992 and up until the end of 1997 he had always taken cash dividends. In January 1998, he opts for a scrip dividend and receives 25 shares instead of a cash dividend of £100. On 20 April 1998, he purchases a further 1,000 shares for £3,950. In July 1998, he opts for a scrip dividend of 44 shares instead of a cash dividend of £180. He opts for cash dividends thereafter. In May 2017, he sells 2,069 shares for £8,550 (ex div), leaving himself with a holding of 4,000.

In the case of both scrip dividends taken by D, the market value of the new shares is equivalent to the cash dividend forgone. The 'cash equivalent of the share capital' is thus the amount of that dividend. The market value at 31 March 1982 of 20p shares in PLC is 80p.

The 'section 104 holding' is as follows.

Section 104 **holding**

	Shares	Qualifying expenditure
		£
March 1980 acquisition	2,000	1,600
May 1992 acquisition	3,000	8,100
January 1998 scrip dividend	25	100
April 1998 acquisition	1,000	3,950
July 1998 scrip dividend	44	180
	6,069	13,930
May 2017 disposal	(2,069)	(4,749)
Pool carried forward	4,000	£9,181

	£
Proceeds	8,550
Cost £13,930 × 2,069/6,069	4,749
Chargeable gain 2017/18	£3,801

Capital distributions

[63.11] A capital distribution (other than of a new holding within 63.2 above) is treated as accruing to the shareholder from the disposal of an interest in the shares.

For this purpose, a '*capital distribution*' is any distribution, on liquidation or otherwise, in money or money's worth by a company to a shareholder, which is not treated as income for tax purposes.

The circumstances in which a distribution is treated as income for tax purposes include where a distribution to which the charge to corporation tax on income under *CTA 2009, Pt 9A* would apply were the distribution not exempt for the purposes of that Part.

[*TCGA 1992, s 122(1)(5)(6)*].

If the amount or value of the capital distribution is 'small' as compared with the value of the shares in respect of which it is made, the capital distribution shall not be treated as a disposal, in which case no immediate capital gains tax liability arises, but the proceeds are deducted from the acquisition cost of the shares on a subsequent disposal. [*TCGA 1992, s 122(2)*].

For this purpose, HMRC regard 'small' as meaning 5% or less and additionally regard an amount of £3,000 or less as 'small', regardless of whether or not it would pass the 5% test (see HMRC Capital Gains Manual CG57836 and Revenue Tax Bulletin February 1997 p 397).

Where the amount or value of the capital distribution exceeds any allowable expenditure on the shares, the taxpayer may elect to have *all* such expenditure set against the distribution with the balance of the distribution being treated as on a part disposal and the expenditure deducted not allowable on that or any subsequent disposal. [*TCGA 1992, s 122(4)*]. In *O'Rourke v Binks* CA 1992, 65 TC 165, it was held that the right to make the election under *TCGA 1992, s 122(4)* was constrained by the requirement of *TCGA 1992, s 122(2)* that the amount or value of the capital distribution be small as compared with the value of the shares in respect of which it was made.

Income tax charges under *ICTA 1988, s 186(3)* (approved profit sharing schemes — see **22.28** EMPLOYEE SHARE SCHEMES) are to be disregarded in determining whether a distribution is a capital distribution. [*TCGA 1992, s 238(2)(b)*].

Example 1

T holds 10,000 ordinary shares in a foreign company M SA. The shares were bought in April 1996 for £80,000. In February 2018, M SA has a capital reconstruction involving the cancellation of one-fifth of the existing ordinary shares in consideration of the repayment of £10 to each shareholder per share cancelled. T's holding is reduced to 8,000 shares, valued at £96,000.

	£
Disposal consideration (2,000 × £10)	20,000

Allowable cost	$\frac{20,000}{20,000 + 96,000} \times £80,000$	13,793
Chargeable gain 2017/18		£6,207
The allowable cost of the remaining shares is £80,000 – £13,793		£66,207

Example 2 (Sale of rights)

X is a shareholder in K Ltd, owning 2,500 £1 ordinary shares which were purchased for £7,000 in October 1996. K Ltd makes a rights issue, but X sells his rights, without taking them up, for £700 in August 2017. The ex-rights value of X's 2,500 shares at the date of sale is £14,500.

'Section 104 holding' of K Ltd £1 ordinary shares

	Shares	Qualifying expenditure £
October 1996 acquisition	2,500	7,000

HMRC cannot require the capital distribution to be treated as a disposal, as the £700 received for the rights does not exceed 5% of (£700 + £14,500) and in any case does not exceed £3,000. If the transaction is not treated as a disposal, the £700 is deducted from the acquisition cost of the shares leaving a balance of £6,300. If the transaction is treated as a disposal (possibly because X wishes to utilise part of his annual exempt amount), the computation is as follows

		£
Disposal proceeds		700
Allowable cost	$\frac{700}{700 + 14,500} \times £7,000$	322
Chargeable gain 2017/18		£378

The allowable cost of the shares is then reduced to £6,678 (£7,000 – £322).

Distributions in a liquidation: unquoted shares

[63.12] Instead of requiring a strict valuation of unquoted shares for the purposes of the part disposal arising on a distribution, HMRC are prepared to accept a reasonable estimate of the residual value of the shares if the liquidation is expected to be completed within two years of the first distribution. If the distribution takes longer, the valuations may be reopened. Where time apportionment (see **8.7** *et seq.* ASSETS HELD ON 6 APRIL 1965) applies, HMRC are prepared to calculate the gain on each distribution by applying the time apportionment fraction as at the date of the first distribution (HMRC Statement of Practice D3).

Distributions of assets in specie in a liquidation

[63.13] Where a company-owned asset, for example shares in a subsidiary, is distributed by the liquidator in specie to shareholders, *TCGA 1992, s 17* (see **45.1** MARKET VALUE) must be applied in determining the acquisition cost of an asset so received by a shareholder. For this purpose, each distribution to each shareholder is considered in isolation from the others. For example, if an asset is distributed equally to each of five shareholders, the acquisition cost for capital gains tax purposes of the part received by each (and also its disposal value from the point of view of the company) is the value of a 20% share, and not one-fifth of the value of a 100% share which may have produced a different (and almost certainly higher) figure. In a case in which the company is controlled by persons connected with each other, so that each such person is connected with the company (see **17.5** CONNECTED PERSONS), it is understood that the above nevertheless applies and that HMRC would not normally invoke the linked transactions provisions of *TCGA 1992, s 19* (see **4.13** ANTI-AVOIDANCE) so as to value each distribution as a percentage of the whole.

Disposal of shares to employee-ownership trust

[63.14] *FA 2014* introduced a relief from capital gains tax which applies to a disposal on or after 6 April 2014 of certain shares in a trading company to the trustees of a settlement which operates for the benefit of all the employees of the company. The relief is available only if the settlement acquires a controlling interest in the company in the tax year of the disposal. The person making the disposal must make a claim for the relief.

The requirements for relief are as follows:

(a) a person other than a company disposes of any 'ordinary share capital' of a company to the trustees of a settlement;
(b) the person making the disposal makes a claim for relief;
(c) the company meets the trading requirement at **63.15** below at the time of the disposal and continues to meet that requirement for the remainder of the tax year;
(d) the settlement meets the all-employee benefit requirement at **63.16** below at the time of the disposal and, for disposals on or after 26 June 2014, continues to meet that requirement for the remainder of the tax year;
(e) the settlement does not meet the controlling interest requirement at **63.17** below immediately before the tax year in which the disposal is made, but does meet it at the end of that year and, for disposals on or after 26 June 2014, if it meets the requirement before the end of that year (whether before or after the time of the disposal) it continues to meet it throughout the remainder of that year;

(f) the limited participation requirement at **63.18** below is met; and
(g) relief under these provisions does not apply to any 'related' disposal by the person making the disposal in question or a person connected with him in an earlier tax year.

For the purposes of (d) above as it applies to disposals on or after 26 June 2014, unless the settlement met the all-employee benefit requirement at the time of disposal on the basis that it was created before 10 December 2013 and satisfied the conditions at **63.16**(A), (B) below, that basis cannot be used to determine whether the settlement continues to meet the requirement. If the settlement initially met the requirement on that basis but subsequently meets the requirement on the basis of meeting the conditions at **63.16**(a)–(d) below, it cannot revert to meeting the requirement on the original basis.

'*Ordinary share capital*' means all issued share capital of a company except that carrying a fixed rate of dividend only. For the purposes of (g) above, a disposal in an earlier tax year is '*related*' to the disposal in question if both are of ordinary share capital of the same company or the earlier disposal is of ordinary share capital of a company which is, or was at the time of the earlier disposal, a member of the same group (see **63.15** below) as the company in question. In determining whether a person is connected with another, the provisions in **17 CONNECTED PERSONS** apply as if 'relative' included any aunt, uncle, niece or nephew.

Relief is also available where the trustees of a settlement (the 'acquiring settlement') become absolutely entitled to settled property consisting of ordinary share capital of a company as against the trustee of that settled property (the 'transferring trustee') so that a deemed disposal arises under *TCGA 1992, s 71(1)* (see **62.16 SETTLEMENTS**) and the conditions at (c)–(f) above are met. The transferring trustee must make a claim.

Effect of the relief

Where the above requirements are met, the disposal and the trustees' acquisition (or the deemed disposal and acquisition) are treated as made for a consideration resulting in no gain and no loss.

Disqualifying events

For disposals on or after 26 June 2014, if there is one or more 'disqualifying event' in the tax year following that in which the disposal is made, no claim for relief may be made on or after the day of the first such event, and, if a claim has been made before that day, the claim is treated as revoked and all affected chargeable gains and allowable losses of any person are recalculated as if the claim had never been made. A 'disqualifying event' occurs if and when:

(i) the company ceases to meet the trading requirement (see **63.15** below); or
(ii) the settlement ceases to meet the controlling interest requirement (see **63.17** below); or
(iii) the settlement ceases to meet the all-employee benefit requirement (see **63.16** below); or
(iv) the participation fraction exceeds 2/5 (see **63.18** below); or

(v) the trustees act in a way which the trusts, as required by the all-employee benefit requirement, do not permit.

For the purposes of (iii) above, unless the settlement met the all-employee benefit requirement at the time of acquisition on the basis that it was created before 10 December 2013 and satisfied the conditions at **63.16**(A), (B) below, that basis cannot be used to determine whether the settlement continues to meet the requirement. If the settlement initially met the requirement on that basis but subsequently meets the requirement on the basis of meeting the conditions at **63.13**(a)–(d) below, it cannot revert to meeting the requirement on the original basis.

Where the participator fraction exceeds two fifths for a period lasting no more than six months, any time in that period is ignored for the purposes of (iv) above if the fraction exceeded the limit because of events outside the reasonable control of the trustees.

Where relief is obtained under these provisions, the relief is effectively clawed back on the acquiring trustees on the first occasion after the tax year following the tax year of the disposal on which there is a disqualifying event. The trustees are treated as having disposed of and immediately reacquired any ordinary share capital of the company acquired in circumstances in which relief was obtained (and not previously disposed of and reacquired) at market value immediately before the event. For disposals before 26 June 2014 this provision applies simply on the first occasion on which there is a disqualifying event.

Claims

A claim for relief must include information to identify the settlement acquiring the share capital, the name of the company and its registered office address, the date of disposal and the number of shares disposed of or deemed to be disposed of.

Share identification

Shares held by trustees which are acquired or deemed to be acquired in circumstances in which the above relief applied (and which have not been subsequently disposed of and reacquired) are treated as of a different class to any other shares held by the trustees for the purposes of the share identification provisions (see **64** SHARES AND SECURITIES — IDENTIFICATION RULES). Where the trustees hold shares which would be of the same class but for this rule and they dispose of some, but not all, of them, they may determine what proportion of the shares disposed of are shares to which the above relief applied (up to the number of such shares held). This rule does not, however, apply to a disposal deemed to arise on the happening of a disqualifying event.

[*TCGA 1992, ss 104(4A), 236H, 236NA–236Q, 236S(1)(3); FA 2014, Sch 37 paras 1–3, 18*].

Trading requirement

[63.15] A company meets the trading requirement if it is either a '*trading company*' which is not a member of a group or the 'principal company' of a 'trading group'.

For this purpose a '*trading company*' is a company carrying on trading activities (i.e. activities carried on in the course of, or for the purposes of, a trade) and not carrying on any other activities to a substantial extent. A '*trade*' means one conducted on a commercial basis and with a view to the realisation of profits.

A '*trading group*' is a group one or more of whose members carry on trading group activities (i.e. activities carried on by a group member in the course of, or for the purposes of, a trade being carried on by any group member) and the activities of whose members, taken together, do not include to a substantial extent any activities which are not trading group activities.

In determining whether a company is a trading company or the principal company of a trading group, the activities of the group's members are treated as one business (so that intra-group activities are ignored) and a business carried on in partnership is treated as not being a trading activity or trading group activity.

'*Group*', membership of a group and '*principal company*' of a group are defined for these purposes in *TCGA 192, s 170* (see **29.2** GROUPS OF COMPANIES). Where applied to a company incorporated outside the UK, references to a group must be construed with any necessary modifications.

[*TCGA 1992, ss 236I, 236S(1)(2); FA 2014, Sch 37 paras 1, 2*].

All-employee benefit requirement

[63.16] A settlement meets the all-employee benefit requirement if the trusts of the settlement do not permit at any time:

(a) any settled property or income arising from it to be applied otherwise than for the benefit of all the 'eligible employees' on the same terms;
(b) the trustees to apply at any time any settled property or income arising from it by creating a trust or transferring property to the trustees of another settlement other than by an 'authorised transfer';
(c) the trustees to make loans to beneficiaries; and
(d) the trustees or any other person to amend the trusts so that they would not comply with any of (a)–(c) above.

In (a) above, employees and office-holders of the company or any group member are '*eligible employees*' unless:

(i) they are a participator in the company or a group member;
(ii) they are a participator in a close company which has made a disposition under which property became comprised in the settlement if that disposition would have been a transfer of value for inheritance tax purposes but for *IHTA 1984, ss 13, 13A* (dispositions by close company for benefit of employees or to employee-ownership trusts);
(iii) they have been a participator in a company within (i) or (ii) above at any time on or after the first day of the 10 years ending on later of the 10 December 2013 and the day on which any property first entered the settlement; or
(iv) they are connected (see **63.14** above) with any person within (i) to (iii) above.

A participator who is not beneficially entitled to (or to rights entitling him to acquire) 5% or more of (or of any class of the shares in) the company's capital and who on a winding-up would not be entitled to 5% of more of the assets is not, however, excluded from being an eligible employee by (i)-(iv) above. Where the company has ceased to meet the trading requirement or the trustees have ceased to hold any shares in the company, an individual who was an eligible employee at any time in the two years before that event continues to be an eligible employee. '*Close company*' and '*participator*' are defined for these purposes as in *IHTA 1984, s 102*. If the company is not a close company, 'participator' means a person who would be a participator by applying that definition if the company were close.

The condition in (a) above is not infringed by reason only that the trusts:

(1) permit the settled property or income from it to be applied as if the spouse, civil partner or dependant of a deceased eligible employee were themselves an eligible employee for up to a year after the death;
(2) prevent the settled property or income from it being applied for the benefit of employees who have not been eligible employees for a continuous period of up to twelve months;
(3) permit the trustees to comply with a written request by a person not to receive the benefit of any settled property or income from it; or
(4) prevent the settled property or income from it being applied for the benefit of all office-holders.

The condition in (a) above is also not infringed by reason only that the trusts also permit the settled property or income from it to be applied for charitable purposes. Subject to these exceptions, the condition in (a) above is infringed if the trusts permit the settled property or any income from it to be applied by reference to factors other than remuneration, length of service or hours worked. The condition is not infringed by reason only that the trusts permit the settled property or any income from it to be applied for the benefit of all the eligible employees by reference to those factors unless the terms of the trusts are such that some (but not all) eligible employees receive no benefits (other than where (2)–(4) above apply). Where settled property or income is applied by reference to more than one of those factors, each such factor must give rise to a separate entitlement to benefits and the total entitlement must be the sum of those separate entitlements.

In (b) above, an '*authorised transfer*' is a transfer of property which includes any ordinary share capital of a company which meets the trading requirement in **63.15** above to the trustees of a settlement which meets the controlling interest requirement in **63.17** below in relation to the company immediately after the transfer and meets the all-employee benefit requirement (ignoring the provisions below which deem that requirement to be met in certain cases).

Where a settlement would not otherwise meet the all-employee benefit requirement at any time it is treated as doing so at that time if it was created before 10 December 2013 and:

(A) on that date *IHTA 1984, s 86* (trusts for the benefit of employees) applied to the settled property, the trustees held a 'significant interest' in the company and the settlement did not otherwise meet the all-employee benefit requirement; and
(B) the trustees do not, during the twelve months ending with the time in question: apply any of the settled property or income from it otherwise than for the benefit of all eligible employees on the same terms; apply any of that property or income by creating a trust or by transferring property to the trustees of a settlement other than by an authorised transfer; or make loans to beneficiaries.

For the purposes of (A) above, the trustees held a 'significant interest' in the company on 10 December 2013 if on that date:

(I) they held 10% or more of the ordinary share capital of the company and had voting powers in the company which would yield 10% or more of the total available votes;
(II) they were entitled to 10% or more of the profits available for distribution to the company's equity holders;
(III) they would have been entitled, on a winding-up of the company, to 10% or more of the assets available for distribution to equity holders; and
(IV) there were no provisions in any agreement or instrument affecting the company's constitution or management or its shares or securities under which the conditions in (I)-(III) above could cease to be satisfied without the trustees' consent.

The provisions of *CTA 2010, ss 157–182* (group relief: equity holders and profits available for distribution) apply for the purposes of (I)–(IV) above. For the purposes of (II) above, trustees are treated as entitled to dividends on shares even if they are required or permitted by the trusts to waive their entitlement. In determining whether (IV) above applies, any provision of a mortgage or charge granted by the trustees to a third party to secure any debt and any agreement in respect of a loan made to the trustees by a third party are ignored if they confer an entitlement on the third party in the event of a default by the trustees. '*Third party*' for this purpose means a person other than the company, a group member, a person who is, or has at any time in the preceding twelve months been, a participator in the company or a group member, or a person connected with such a person.

The requirement in (B) above that the trustees must not apply property or income otherwise than for the benefit of all eligible employees on the same terms is treated as infringed or not infringed in the same circumstances as apply to the condition in (a) above. Anything done by the trustees before 10 December 2013 is ignored for the purposes of (B) above.

[*TCGA 1992, ss 236J–236L, 236R; FA 2014, Sch 37 paras 1–4(1)*].

Controlling interest requirement

[63.17] A settlement meets the controlling interest requirement if:

(a) the trustees hold more than 50% of the ordinary share capital of the company and have voting powers in the company which would yield a majority of the total available votes;
(b) they are entitled to more than 50% of the profits available for distribution to the company's equity holders;
(c) they would be entitled, on a winding-up of the company, to more than 50% of the assets available for distribution to equity holders; and
(d) there are no provisions in any agreement or instrument affecting the company's constitution or management or its shares or securities under which the conditions in (a)-(c) could cease to be satisfied without the trustees' consent.

The provisions of *CTA 2010, ss 157–182* (group relief: equity holders and profits available for distribution) apply for the purposes of (a)–(d) above. For the purposes of (b) above, trustees are treated as entitled to dividends on shares even if they are required or permitted by the trusts to waive their entitlement. In determining whether (d) above applies, any provision of a mortgage or charge granted by the trustees to a third party to secure any debt and any agreement in respect of a loan made to the trustees by a third party are ignored if they confer an entitlement on the third party in the event of a default by the trustees. '*Third party*' for this purpose means a person other than the company, a group member, a person who is, or has at any time in the preceding twelve months been, a participator in the company or a group member, or a person connected with such a person.

[*TCGA 1992, ss 236M, 236R; FA 2014, Sch 37 paras 1, 2*].

Limited participation requirement

[63.18] The limited participation requirement is met if:

(1) there was no time in the twelve months ending immediately after the disposal when the person making the disposal was a 'participator' in the company and the 'participator fraction' exceeded two fifths; and
(2) for disposals on or after 26 June 2014, the participator fraction does not exceed 2/5 at any time in the period beginning with that disposal and ending at the end of the tax year in which it occurs.

Where, however, the participator fraction exceeds two fifths for a period lasting no more than six months, any time in that period is ignored for the purposes of (1) and (2) above if the fraction exceeded the limit because of events outside the reasonable control of the trustees.

The '*participation fraction*' is NP/NE where:

NP is the sum of the number of persons who are both participators and employees or office-holders of the company and the number of other persons who are both connected with such persons and are also employees or office-holders of the company or a member of the group.

NE is the number of employees of the company or any member of the group.

Participators who are not beneficially entitled to, or to rights entitling them to acquire, 5% or more of, or of any class of, the company's share capital and who would be entitled to less than 5% of the company's assets on a winding-up are excluded in calculating the participation fraction.

'*Participator*' for the purposes of the above provisions is defined as in *CTA 2010, s 454*. If the company is not a close company, 'participator' means a person who would be a participator by applying that definition if the company were close.

[*TCGA 1992, s 236N; FA 2014, Sch 37 paras 1, 2*].

Company purchase of own shares (aka share buy-back)

[63.19] The *Companies (Acquisition of Own Shares) (Treasury Shares) Regulations 2003 SI 2003 No 1116* permit listed companies (including those listed on the Alternative Investment Market) to purchase *and hold* their own shares. Such shares, often referred to as 'treasury shares' can then be sold, transferred to an employee share scheme or cancelled.

Treasury shares

The following provisions ensure that for tax purposes own shares held without cancellation are treated as if cancelled, and as newly issued shares if they are subsequently sold.

Where a company acquires any of its shares, whether by purchase, bonus issue or otherwise, it is not treated for tax purposes as acquiring an asset. The company is not treated as a result of acquiring or holding the shares, or of being entered on its register of members in respect of any of them, as a member of itself. The company's issued share capital is treated as reduced by the nominal value of the shares acquired. Any shares not cancelled on acquisition are treated as cancelled, and any subsequent cancellation is disregarded (and is therefore not a disposal of an asset and does not give rise to an allowable loss). If the shares were issued to the company as bonus shares (i.e. share capital issued as paid up otherwise than by the receipt of new consideration within *CTA 2010, s 1115*) they are treated as if they had not been issued.

Where a company holds any treasury shares and it issues bonus shares in respect of those shares or any class of those shares, the above provisions do not prevent the existing shares being the company's 'holding' of shares for the purposes of the application of *TCGA 1992, s 126* (reorganisation of share capital — see **63.2** above) other than its application in modified form by virtue of any chargeable gains provision (see, for example, *TCGA 1992, s 192(2)* at **14.12** COMPANIES).

Where a company disposes of any of its treasury shares, the shares are not treated as having been disposed of by the company at the time of the disposal but are treated as having been issued as new shares by the company at that time. The person acquiring the shares is treated as having subscribed for them for an amount equal to any consideration payable for the disposal of the shares by the company. If that consideration does not exceed the nominal value of the shares, the share capital of the shares is treated for the purposes of *CTA 2010, Pt 23* (company distributions etc.) as being the amount of the consideration. If the consideration exceeds the nominal value, the shares are treated as issued at a premium equal to that excess.

The above provisions do not apply to a company purchasing its own shares if the price payable by the company is taken into account in computing its trading profits.

[*FA 2003, s 195*].

Treatment of vendor on company purchasing own shares

Any consideration given by a company for the redemption, repayment or purchase of its own shares (whether or not those shares are then held as treasury shares), *except* insofar as it represents repayment of share capital, is normally treated as a distribution, and hence as income in the hands of the recipient (see Tolley's Corporation Tax under Distributions). Such payments after 5 April 1982 in respect of shares in certain unquoted trading companies (or holding companies) are *not* treated as distributions, and thus give rise to liability to capital gains tax (or corporation tax on chargeable gains) on the recipient in the normal way. See Tolley's Corporation Tax under Purchase by a Company of its Own Shares for detailed conditions. [*CTA 2010, ss 1033–1048*].

HMRC have published guidance on some of the main tax issues that may arise where employees sell shares to their employer under arrangements facilitated by the *Companies Act 2006 (Amendment of Part 18) Regulations 2013, SI 2013/999*. See HMRC Notice, 'Purchase of own shares by non-quoted companies—tax implications for employees selling shares', 4 July 2013.

If the purchase of its own shares by a UK resident company gives rise to a distribution, and the shareholder receiving such a distribution is itself a company, HMRC's practice is to include the distribution in the consideration for the disposal of the shares for the purposes of the charge to corporation tax on chargeable gains. In HMRC's view the effect of *ICTA 1988, s 208* (now *CTA 2009, s 1285*) and *TCGA 1992, s 8(4)* is that the distribution does not suffer a tax charge as income within the terms of *TCGA 1992, s 37(1)* (see **39.1** INTERACTION WITH OTHER TAXES) (HMRC Statement of Practice 4/89). The legality of HMRC's practice in this respect was, however, rejected in *Strand Options and Futures Ltd v Vojak* CA 2003, [2004] STC 64. In that case, Carnwath LJ held that *ICTA 1988, s 208* should be construed as preventing the imposition of 'a tax which is directly charged on the dividends as such, rather than indirectly as part of the computation of a taxable amount'.

Example

Paul has 50 £1 shares in Tracy Ltd bought back by the company at £6 per share in August 2017. Paul had originally purchased the shares for £150 in July 1999, from a person who had subscribed from them at par. The buy back does not qualify for capital treatment.

Paul is treated as receiving a distribution from Tracy Ltd as follows.

	£
Disposal proceeds	300
Less nominal value	50
Dividend	£250

Paul has also made a capital disposal and the allowable loss is calculated as follows.

	£
Disposal proceeds	300
Less amount charged to income tax	250
	50
Less acquisition cost	150
Allowable loss	£100

Accrued income scheme

[63.20] The accrued income scheme provisions (see now *ITA 2007, ss 615–681*) apply, broadly, to transfers of any government, public authority or company loan stock. (See further **64.6** SHARES AND SECURITIES — IDENTIFICATION RULES.)

The accrued income scheme does not apply for the purposes of corporation tax. [*ICTA 1988, s 710(1A)*].

It also does not apply on a transfer to which *ITTOIA 2005, ss 427–460* apply (charge to or relief from tax on the profit or loss realised from the discount on a deeply discounted security — see **63.21** below).

If a transfer is with accrued interest, a payment (calculated under *ITA 2007, s 632* and broadly representing the accrued interest) is treated as made by the transferee to the transferor in the interest period in which the settlement day falls. If the transfer is without accrued interest, a payment (calculated under *ITA 2007, s 633* and broadly representing the interest accruing from the settlement day to the next interest payment day) is treated as made by the transferee to the transferor in the relevant interest period. Special rules apply to transfers with unrealised interest and of variable rate securities. For each kind of security transferred by or to a person in an interest period, the deemed payments are then used to calculate (under *ITA 2007, ss 628–631*) his accrued income profits or losses. Profits are chargeable to income tax and losses are carried forward as payments made in the next interest period.

Capital gains

Where there is a transfer within the accrued income provisions either with or without accrued interest, neither *TCGA 1992, s 37* nor *s 39* applies (see **39.1** INTERACTION WITH OTHER TAXES). Instead, where a transfer is with accrued interest, an amount equal to deemed payment under *ITA 2007, s 632* is excluded from the transferor's disposal consideration, and the same amount is excluded from the transferee's allowable expenditure when he makes a subsequent disposal. Where the transfer is without accrued interest, an amount equal to the deemed payment under *ITA 2007, s 633* is added to the transferor's disposal consideration, and the same amount is added to the transferee's allowable expenditure when he makes a subsequent disposal. Similar rules apply to transfers with unrealised interest and of variable rate securities and where there is a disposal (e.g. a deemed disposal) without there being a contemporaneous transfer within the scope of the accrued income provisions.

Where on a 'conversion' (being one within *TCGA 1992, s 132*; see **63.8** above) or an 'exchange' (being one which is not treated as a disposal: see generally **63.2** above) of securities, a payment is treated under the accrued income provisions as made to the transferor (or an accrued income profit is treated as accruing to him in respect of variable rate securities), an equal amount less any consideration received on the conversion or exchange (other than the new holding of securities) is treated for the purposes of *TCGA 1992* as consideration given on the conversion or exchange. Where the consideration received on the conversion or exchange (other than the new holding of securities) equals or exceeds an amount equal to the accrued amount, that consideration is treated for the purposes of *TCGA 1992* as reduced by that amount. If on a conversion or exchange of securities, a payment is treated under the accrued income provisions as made by the transferor, an equal amount is treated for the purposes of *TCGA 1992* as consideration received on the conversion or exchange.

[*TCGA 1992, s 119*].

See Tolley's Income Tax for full details of the accrued income scheme.

The above procedures will not be required for the purposes of computing a chargeable gain where the security is otherwise exempt. See **28** GOVERNMENT SECURITIES and **54** QUALIFYING CORPORATE BONDS.

Deeply discounted securities

[63.21] When a person transfers a 'deeply discounted security', or becomes entitled, as holder, to any payment on its redemption, he is chargeable to **income tax** on the excess of the amount payable on the transfer or redemption over the amount paid for its acquisition. In the event of a loss on a transfer or redemption of listed securities held on 26 March 2003 or strips of government securities, a claim may be made for relief against income of the tax year of transfer or redemption. There are anti-avoidance provisions denying loss relief in respect of strips of government securities where there is a scheme for the manipulation of the acquisition, sale or redemption price. The provisions are extended to prevent an allowable loss arising for capital gains tax purposes as a result of the making of a payment under such a scheme otherwise than in respect of the acquisition or disposal of a strip (see now *TCGA 1992, s 151C*). Similar provisions prevent an allowable loss arising for capital gains tax as a result of the making of a payment under a scheme for the manipulation of the acquisition, sale or redemption price of a 'corporate strip' (see below) acquired after 1 December 2004 (see now *TCGA 1992, s 151D*).

See Tolley's Income Tax for the detailed provisions. The provisions do **not** apply for corporation tax purposes.

Meaning of 'deeply discounted security'

A '*deeply discounted security*' is, except as excluded below, any security such that the amount payable on redemption (excluding interest) is or might be an amount involving a '*deep gain*', i.e. the issue price is less than the amount payable on redemption by 15% of that amount or, if less, by 1/2% per annum of that amount (counting months and part months as 1/12th of a year) to the redemption date. This comparison is made as at the time of issue of the security and assuming redemption in accordance with the terms of issue. 'Redemption' for these purposes referred originally to redemption on maturity or, if the holder of the security could opt for earlier redemption, the earliest occasion on which the holder might require redemption. In addition to redemption on maturity, possible earlier occasions on which a security might be redeemed must also be considered. The security will be a deeply discounted security if it would be such by reference to at least one such occasion. One need not take into account any occasion on which there may be a redemption other than at the option of the holder *unless* issuer and holder are connected or the obtaining of a tax advantage (as defined) is a main benefit that might be expected to accrue from the redemption provision. Additionally, where the holder has an option entitling him to redeem only on the occurrence of an 'event adversely affecting the holder' (as defined) or of a person's default *and* such entitlement is unlikely, judged at time of issue, to arise, the potential redemption is disregarded.

Gilt strips and strips of overseas government securities acquired after 26 March 2003 are always deeply discounted securities regardless of their issue terms. Strips of interest-bearing corporate securities ('*corporate strips*') acquired after 1 December 2004 are likewise always deeply discounted securities regardless of their issue terms.

Special rules apply to determine the issue price of (and the amount paid for the acquisition of) securities issued to a person in accordance with the terms of a 'qualifying earn-out right' (as defined). See Tolley's Income Tax for details.

The following are not deeply discounted securities:

(i) shares in a company;
(ii) gilt-edged securities (but see above concerning gilt strips and strips of overseas government securities);
(iii) excluded indexed securities (as defined);
(iv) life assurance policies;
(v) capital redemption policies; and
(vi) (with exceptions) securities issued under the same prospectus as other securities issued previously but not themselves deeply discounted securities.

Securities within (iii) and (vi) above may, however, be treated as deeply discounted securities in certain circumstances involving their being held by a person connected with the issuer. *ITA 2007, s 993* applies to determine whether persons are connected for the purposes of these provisions but without taking any account of the security under review or any security issued under the same prospectus.

[*ITTOIA 2005, ss 427–460; TCGA 1992, ss 151C, 151D; FA 2012, Sch 39 para 48*].

Avoidance of double charge

For the avoidance of a double charge, i.e. to both income tax and capital gains tax (and double relief for losses), any deeply discounted security, whatever its date of issue, is brought within the definition of a QUALIFYING CORPORATE BOND (**54**). [*TCGA 1992, s 117(2AA)(8A)*]. However, a deeply discounted security does not qualify for the relief at **44.13** LOSSES for irrecoverable pre-17 March 1998 loans on securities.

Depositary receipts

[63.22] Depositary receipts are used as substitute instruments indicating ownership of shares and securities and designed primarily to enable investors to hold and deal in shares of companies located outside the investor's country. They are issued by a bank or other financial institution (the depositary), with whom the share certificate is deposited. Where a depositary receipt is issued in the UK, HMRC's view is that its holder retains beneficial ownership of the underlying shares. This has the following results.

- A transfer of shares by a shareholder to a depositary in exchange for an issue of depositary receipts is not a disposal of the shares for CGT purposes.
- A disposal of the depositary receipts is a disposal of both the depositary receipts and the underlying shares. In practice, the value of depositary receipts will track the value of the underlying shares and to that extent HMRC regard the consideration for the disposal of the depositary receipts as consideration for the disposal of the shares.
- In a share exchange (see **63.5** above) or company reconstruction (see **63.7** above) in which shareholders have an option to receive depositary receipts instead of being issued with shares, HMRC accept that the shares are treated for the purpose of *TCGA 1992, s 135* as being issued to the shareholders.

Following the decision in the stamp duty reserve tax case of *HSBC Holdings and Bank of New York Mellon v HMRC* FTT, [2012] UKFTT 163 (TC), HMRC consider that, where a depositary receipt is issued outside the UK, the beneficial ownership of the underlying shares should be determined by reference to the law of the territory in which the depositary receipt was issued. If the beneficial ownership cannot be determined conclusively, HMRC will consider the holder of a depsoitary receipt as holding the beneficial interest in the underlying shares, with the same consequences as above. If the relevant law means that the holder of a depositary receipt is not the beneficial owner of the underlying shares, the consequences are as follows.

- A transfer of shares by a shareholder to a depositary in exchange for an issue of depositary receipts is a disposal of the shares for CGT purposes.
- A disposal of the depositary receipts is not a disposal of the underlying shares.
- In a share exchange (see 63.5 above) or company reconstruction (see 63.7 above) in which shareholders have an option to receive depositary receipts instead of being issued with shares, HMRC consider that *TCGA 1992, s 135* will not apply to shareholders taking depsoitary receipts as they will not have been issued with shares.
- Where a holder of depositary receipts converts them into the underlying shares there will be a disposal of the depositary receipts and an acquisition of the shares.

(HMRC Capital Gains Manual CG50240). See 7.3 ASSETS as regards location of shares held in depositary receipt form.

Close companies

[63.23] Income tax which has been charged on a participator as a result of an apportionment under *ICTA 1988, ss 423–430, Sch 19* (broadly only in relation to accounting periods ending before 1 April 1989) and paid by him in respect of income of a close company which has not subsequently been distributed (including stock dividends; see 63.10 above), may be deducted, pro rata, in computing a gain on the disposal of any of his shares in that company. Shares are identified on a first in, first out basis. [*TCGA 1992, s 124*].

Tax paid which is referable to gains of a non-resident company charged on a UK participator or shareholder under *TCGA 1992, s 13* (see 49.7 OVERSEAS MATTERS) is similarly deductible. See also 16.12 COMPUTATION OF GAINS AND LOSSES for an alternative concessional treatment.

Life assurance policies

[63.24] Investments or other assets transferred to a policy holder by an insurance company, in accordance with a life assurance policy, are deemed to be transferred at market value. [*TCGA 1992, s 204(3)(6)*].

Stock lending arrangements

[63.25] The following provisions apply in relation to 'stock lending arrangements'.

Definition

A '*stock lending arrangement*' is an arrangement between two persons ('the borrower' and 'the lender') under which:

(a) the lender transfers 'securities' to the borrower otherwise than by way of sale; and
(b) a requirement is imposed on the borrower to transfer those securities back to the lender otherwise than by way of sale.

Subject to the following provisions, the disposals and acquisitions made in pursuance of any stock lending arrangement *are disregarded* for the purposes of capital gains tax. [*TCGA 1992, s 263B(1)(2)*].

Disposals by the borrower

If the borrower under any stock lending arrangement disposes of any securities transferred to him under the arrangement such that that disposal is made otherwise than in the discharge of the requirement for the transfer of securities back to the lender, and that requirement, so far as it relates to the securities disposed of, has been or will be discharged by the transfer of securities other than those transferred to the borrower, any question relating to the acquisition of the securities disposed of shall be determined as if the securities disposed of were the securities with which that requirement (so far as relating to the securities disposed of) has been or will be discharged. [*TCGA 1992, s 263B(3)*].

Transfer back to the lender not taking place

The ensuing consequences will occur in the case of any stock lending arrangement, where it becomes apparent, at any time after the making of the transfer by the lender, that the requirement for the borrower to make a transfer back to the lender will not be complied with.

(i) The lender is deemed to have made a disposal at that time of the securities transferred to the borrower;
(ii) The borrower is deemed to have acquired them at that time; and
(iii) *TCGA 1992, s 263B(3)* (above) shall have effect in relation to any disposal before that time by the borrower of securities transferred to him by the lender as if the securities deemed to have been acquired by the borrower were to be used for discharging a requirement to transfer securities back to the lender.

The disposal in (i) above and acquisition in (ii) above are at market value.

This provision does not apply where the insolvency provisions below apply.

[*TCGA 1992, s 263B(4)*].

References, in relation to a person to whom securities are transferred, to the transfer of those securities back to another person are to be construed as if the cases where those securities are taken to be transferred back to that other person included any case where securities of the same description as those securities are transferred to that other person either:

(a) in accordance with a requirement to transfer securities of the same description; or
(b) in exercise of a power to substitute securities of the same description for the securities that are required to be transferred back.

[*TCGA 1992, s 263B(5)*].

Securities are not taken to be of the same description as other securities unless they are in the same quantities, give the same rights against the same persons and are of the same type and nominal value as the other securities. '*Securities*' means shares of any company resident in the United Kingdom (*UK shares*), securities of the Government of the United Kingdom, any public or local authority in the United Kingdom or of any company or other body resident in the United Kingdom (*UK securities*) or shares, stock or other securities issued by a government or public or local authority of a territory outside the United Kingdom or by any other body of persons not resident in the United Kingdom *(overseas securities)*. [*ICTA 1988, Sch 23A; TCGA 1992, s 263B(6)(7); CTA 2010, ss 806, 814*].

Provisions to ensure continuity of treatment for stock lending arrangements involving securities redenominated in euros following the introduction on 1 January 1999 of the European single currency in certain EU member states other than the UK are contained in *SI 1998 No 3177, Regs 20–23*.

Stock lending involving redemption

A transfer back to a person of securities transferred by him shall be taken to include references to the payment to him, in pursuance of an obligation arising on any person's becoming entitled to receive an amount in respect of the redemption of those securities, of an amount equal to the amount of the entitlement. Where, in pursuance of any such obligation, the lender under any stock lending arrangement is paid any amount in respect of the redemption of any securities to which the arrangement relates:

(A) that lender shall be deemed to have disposed, for that amount, of the securities in respect of whose redemption it is paid ('*the relevant lent securities*');

(B) the borrower shall not, in respect of the redemption, be taken to have made any disposal of the relevant lent securities; and

(C) *TCGA 1992, s 263B(3)* (see above) shall have effect in relation to disposals of any of the relevant lent securities made by the borrower before the redemption as if:
   - (i) the amount paid to the lender were an amount paid for the acquisition of securities, and
   - (ii) the securities acquired were to be used by the borrower for discharging a requirement under the arrangement to transfer the relevant lent securities back to the lender.

[*TCGA 1992, s 263C*].

Provisions to ensure continuity of treatment for stock lending arrangements involving securities redenominated in euros following the introduction on 1 January 1999 of the European single currency in certain EU member states other than the UK are contained in *SI 1998 No 3177, Regs 20–23*.

Insolvency of borrower

Subject to the commencement provisions below, the following applies where the borrower under a stock lending arrangement becomes 'insolvent' after the lender has transferred the securities and as a result, the buyer's requirement to make a transfer back to the lender will not be fully complied with.

If 'collateral' is used directly or indirectly to enable the lender to acquire replacement securities of the same description as those which will not be transferred back within 30 days beginning with the date of the insolvency, then, for chargeable gains purposes:

(i) the transfer of the original securities by the lender is not treated as a disposal (but see further below);
(ii) the borrower is treated as having acquired the securities which will not be transferred back at market value on the date of the insolvency; and
(iii) the lender's acquisition of the replacement securities is treated as if it were a transfer back of securities under the arrangement (and so is not treated as an acquisition).

If the number of replacement securities is less than the number of securities the buyer is treated as acquiring as in (ii) above, the lender is treated as disposing of the difference on the date of the insolvency. The consideration for the disposal is nil if all of the collateral is used to enable the lender to acquire the replacement securities. If not all of the collateral is used, the consideration is the difference between the market value on the date of the insolvency of the number of securities which could have been acquired using the collateral, and the market value on that date of the number of securities which were acquired. If the lender subsequently receives an amount in respect of the buyer's liability in respect of the securities treated as disposed of by the lender, that amount is treated as a chargeable gain of the lender at the time the amount is received.

For this purpose, the borrower becomes '*insolvent*' if a company or individual voluntary arrangement takes effect, if an administration application is made or a receiver or manager, or administrative receiver is appointed, on the commencement of a winding up, on the presentation of a bankruptcy petition, if a compromise or arrangement under *Companies Act 2006, Pt 26* takes effect, or a bank insolvency or administration order takes effect, or on the occurrence of a corresponding event under Scottish, NI or non-UK law. '*Collateral*' is an amount of money or property provided under the stock lending arrangement (or arrangements of which it forms part) which is payable to or made available for the benefit of the lender to secure the discharge of the requirement to transfer securities back to him.

These provisions apply where the borrower becomes insolvent after 23 November 2008. They also apply where the borrower becomes insolvent between 1 September 2008 and 23 November 2008 inclusive if the lender makes an election. Such an election must relate to all stock lending arrangements with the same lender and borrower and must be made by 31 January 2011 or, where the lender is a company, within two years after the end of the lender's accounting period in which 23 November 2008 falls.

[*TCGA 1992, s 263CA*].

Agreements for sale and repurchase of securities ('repos')

[63.26] There are special income tax and corporation tax provisions dealing with agreements for sale and repurchase of securities (commonly known as 'repos'). Such an agreement involves one party agreeing to sell securities (typically these would be corporate bonds, gilts or other Government securities or shares) to another, with a related agreement (either a forward contract or an option) to buy back the securities at an agreed date and price. Broadly, any difference between the sale and repurchase price is treated for the purposes of tax on income as interest, and the sale and repurchase are ignored for the purposes of tax on chargeable gains. Separate rules apply for corporation tax purposes, based on accounting principles. The pre-existing rules continue to apply for income tax and capital gains tax purposes. See Tolley's Income Tax and Tolley's Corporation Tax under Anti-Avoidance for the detailed income provisions. The chargeable gains provisions are detailed below.

Corporation tax on chargeable gains

Debtor repos

Where a company (the '*borrower*') has a 'debtor repo' and, having sold the securities under the repo arrangement to another party (the '*lender*'), is the only person with the right or obligation under the arrangement to repurchase those or similar securities, the sale and repurchase are ignored for the purposes of corporation tax on chargeable gains.

Where, however, at any time after the initial sale, it becomes apparent that the borrower will not make the repurchase or the accounting condition below ceases to be met, the borrower is treated for chargeable gains purposes as disposing of the securities at that time at market value. If the borrower does in fact subsequently make the repurchase this is not then ignored under the above provision.

The accounting condition mentioned above ceases to be met if, under generally accepted accounting practice, the borrower's accounts for any period after the one in which the 'advance' (i.e. the money or other asset received from the lender) is made do not record a financial liability in respect of the advance (except as a result of the subsequent purchase of the securities or similar securities).

For this purpose, a '*debtor repo*' is defined in *CTA 2009, s 548* as, broadly, a repo from the point of view of the company selling and repurchasing the securities. References above to the borrower include a partnership of which the borrower is a member.

[*FA 2007, s 47, Sch 13 para 6*].

Creditor repos

Similarly, where a company (the '*lender*') has a 'creditor repo' and, having bought the securities under the repo arrangement from another party (the '*borrower*'), is the only person with the right or obligation under the arrangement to sell those or similar securities, the purchase and sale under the arrangement are ignored for the purposes of corporation tax on chargeable gains.

Where, however, at any time after the initial sale, it becomes apparent that the lender will not make the sale under the agreement or the accounting condition below ceases to be met, the lender is treated for chargeable gains purposes as acquiring the securities at that time at market value. If the seller does in fact subsequently make the sale this is not then ignored under the above provision.

The accounting condition ceases to be met if, under generally accepted accounting practice, the lender's accounts for any period after the one in which the 'advance' (i.e. the money or other asset received by the lender) is made do not record a financial asset in respect of the advance (except as a result of the subsequent sale of the securities or similar securities).

For this purpose, a '*creditor repo*' is defined in *CTA 2009, s 543* as, broadly, a repo from the point of view of the company buying and then selling the securities. References above to the lender include a partnership of which the lender is a member.

[*FA 2007, s 47, Sch 13 para 11*].

Redemption arrangements

The above provisions apply with modifications in cases involving 'redemption arrangements'. For this purpose, a case involves '*redemption arrangements*' where arrangements, corresponding to those in repo cases, are made in relation to securities that are to be redeemed in the period after the sale, and a person, instead of having the right or obligation to buy back those or other securities, has a right or obligation in respect of the benefits that will result from the redemption. The definitions of 'debtor repo' and 'creditor repo' are modified to include such arrangements, and for chargeable gains purposes, the company selling the securities under the arrangement is treated as disposing of the securities when the redemption takes place, and the company buying the securities is treated as acquiring them at that time, for an amount equivalent to the redemption proceeds. [*FA 2007, Sch 13 para 15(6); SI 2007 No 2485, Regs 3, 4*].

Treasury power to amend provisions

The Treasury may, by regulations, modify the above provisions in relation to certain non-standard repos and cases involving redemption arrangements. This may include modification of *TCGA 1992* in relation to cases where, as a result of the regulations, an acquisition or disposal is excluded from those ignored for chargeable gains purposes under the above provisions. Regulations have been made in respect of redemption arrangements (see above) and non-standard repos involving the substitution of securities. [*FA 2007, Sch 13 para 15; SI 2007 No 2485*].

Capital gains tax

Where *ITA 2007, s 607(1)* applies to treat the price differential on sale and repurchase as an interest payment, the acquisition and disposal by the interim holder, and (except where the repurchaser is or may be different from the original owner) the disposal and acquisition (as repurchaser) by the original owner, are disregarded for chargeable gains purposes. For these purposes a repurchase arrangement is also deemed to exist where the repurchaser is connected to the original owner (see **17** CONNECTED PERSONS). Arrangements for repurchase include:

(a) requirement to buy back the securities by the agreement or related agreement;

(b) requirement to buy back the securities by exercise of an option under the agreement or related agreement; or
(c) exercise of an option to buy back the securities which was acquired under the agreement or related agreement.

References to buying back securities include the purchase of similar securities by the original owner or the repurchase of the original or similar securities by someone connected to the original owner. Simliar securities are defined as securities which:

(a) give the same rights against the same person to capital, distributions, interest and dividends; and
(b) the same remedies to enforce those rights.

This definition extends to situations where there may be differences in the total nominal value of the securities, the form in which they are held or the manner in which they can be transferred.

This does not, however, apply:

(a) if the agreement(s) in question are non-arm's length agreements, or if all the benefits or risks arising from fluctuations in the market value of the securities accrue to, or fall on, the interim holder; or
(b) in relation to any disposal or acquisition of QUALIFYING CORPORATE BONDS (**54**) where the securities disposed of by the original owner, or those acquired by him or another person as repurchaser, are not such bonds.

Where, however, at any time after the initial sale, it becomes apparent that the interim holder will not dispose of the securities to the repurchaser, he is treated for capital gains tax purposes as acquiring the securities at that time at market value. Similarly, where at any time it becomes apparent that the original owner will not acquire the securities as repurchaser, he is treated for capital gains tax purposes as disposing of the securities at that time at market value.

In a case involving 'redemption arrangements' (defined, broadly as above, at *ITA 2007, s 613(2)*), the original owner is treated as disposing of the securities when the redemption takes place, and the interim holder is treated as acquiring them at that time, for an amount equivalent to the redemption proceeds.

[*TCGA 1992, s 263A–263AA; FA 2013, Sch 12; SI 2007 No 2486, Regs 3, 4*].

Where *ITA 2007, s 607* applies but *TCGA 1992, s 263A* does not, the repurchase price is, as the case may be, either reduced by the excess of that price over the sale price or increased by the excess of the sale price over that price for chargeable gains purposes. [*TCGA 1992, s 261G*].

Where the repurchase price falls to be computed by reference to the provisions of *ITA 2007, s 604* (deemed increase in repurchase price: price differences under repos) and *TCGA 1992, s 263A* does not apply, the deemed increase in that price also has effect for chargeable gains purposes. For capital gains tax purposes, where *ITA 2007, s 604* applies, either there must be no difference for the purposes of *ITA 2007, s 607* between the sale and repurchase price as a result of the increase, or that section must not apply as a result of an exemption in *ITA 2007, s 608*. [*TCGA 1992, s 261F*].

Gain accruing to person paying manufactured dividend

The following provisions apply where a person resident in the UK, other than a company,

(a) disposes of 'UK shares' (as defined in *ITA 2007, s 566(2)*)
  (i) transferred to him as the interim holder under a repurchase agreement which is a 'repo' within *ITA 2007, Pt 11*,
  (ii) transferred to him as the borrower under a stock lending arrangement (as above), or
  (iii) under a 'short sale transaction' (i.e. a contract or other arrangements for the transfer of the equities which is neither a repurchase agreement nor a stock lending arrangement) to which he is a party; and

(b) pays a 'manufactured dividend' under that agreement, arrangement or transaction, which is representative of a dividend on those equities.

If a chargeable gain accrues to that person on the disposal, an allowable loss is treated as accruing to him on the same date, deductible only from that gain. The amount of the loss is the lowest of: the chargeable gain, the manufactured dividend and the dividend of which the manufactured dividend is representative. For manufactured dividends paid (or treated as paid) before 31 January 2008, the amount of the loss is the lesser of the chargeable gain and the 'adjusted amount'. For this purpose the '*adjusted amount*' is equal to the lesser of the manufactured dividend and the dividend of which the manufactured dividend is representative less so much of the manufactured dividend as is allowable as a deduction for income tax purposes under *ITA 2007, ss 574, 575*.

A 'manufactured dividend' is as defined in *ITA 2007, Pt 11 Ch 2*, and references above to a manufactured dividend being paid include deemed payment under *ITA 2007, s 602(1)* but do not include deemed payment under *ITA 2007, s 596(2)*. See Tolley's Income Tax under Anti-Avoidance.

[*TCGA 1992, s 263D; FA 2008, s 63, Sch 23 paras 11, 12*].

Treasury powers to amend provisions

The Treasury has powers to amend *TCGA 1992, ss 261F, 261G, 263A, 263D* above by regulations. [*TCGA 1992, ss 261H, 263F–263I*].

Building society and other de-mutualisations

[63.27] The following applies where there is a transfer of the whole of a building society's business to a successor company in accordance with the relevant provisions of the *Building Societies Act 1986*.

Statutory rules

Subject to the operation of *TCGA 1992, s 217(1)* (rights to acquire shares in successor company treated as valueless options, see 7.7(f) ASSETS), shares issued to members by the successor company, or disposed of to members by the society, are regarded as acquired for any new consideration given and as having at the time of acquisition a value equal to such new consideration (if any). Where shares are so issued or disposed of to trustees of a settlement on terms providing for their transfer to members for no new consideration:

(a) they are regarded as acquired by the trustees for no consideration;
(b) a member's interest in the shares is regarded as acquired for no consideration and as having no value at the time of acquisition;
(c) on the member becoming absolutely entitled to any shares, or where such entitlement would arise but for the member being an infant or otherwise under disability, the shares are treated as disposed of and reacquired by the trustees in a nominee capacity under *TCGA 1992, s 60(1)* and at a no gain/no loss price and *TCGA 1992, s 71* (see **62.16** SETTLEMENTS) does not then apply; and
(d) on the member disposing of his interest in the settled property, any gain is a chargeable gain and *TCGA 1992, s 76(1)* (see **62.15** SETTLEMENTS) does not then apply.

Any gain on the disposal by the society of shares in the successor company in connection with the transfer is not a chargeable gain. [*TCGA 1992, ss 216(1), 217(2)–(7)*].

The conferring of any benefit under the above or *TCGA 1992, s 217(1)* on a member of a society in connection with a transfer, or any payment in lieu of such a benefit, or any distribution in pursuance of *Building Societies Act 1986, s 100(2)(b)*, is not regarded as either the making of a distribution for corporation tax purposes or the payment of a dividend by the society. However, any such disregarded benefit etc. may be taken into account as a capital distribution as in **63.11** above. [*FA 1988, Sch 12 para 6*].

Practice

It become customary for building societies to offer their members cash bonuses or free shares as an inducement towards their voting in favour of de-mutualisation of the society, i.e. a takeover by a limited company or a unilateral conversion from mutual to corporate status. In *Foster v Williams; Horan v Williams* (Sp C 113), [1997] SSCD 112, concerning *cash payments* received by investors on the takeover of Cheltenham and Gloucester Building Society by Lloyds Bank plc in August 1995, a Special Commissioner, allowing the taxpayers' appeals, held that both share account and deposit account investors in the society had made a total disposal of their accounts, for which the consideration consisted of the opening balances on new accounts with the successor company plus the cash bonus payments. No chargeable gain arose on the disposal of a *deposit account*, this being the disposal of a debt (which was not a debt on a security) (see **25.5** EXEMPTIONS AND RELIEFS). On the disposal of a share account, a chargeable gain did arise, and the allowable expenditure was the amount of the closing credit balance on the account on the vesting day (plus INDEXATION (**38**) allowance, which could therefore reduce or eliminate the gain). The Revenue accepted the decision without further appeal and announced that it would also be applied to cash payments received as a result of the de-mutualisation of other building societies. (Revenue Press Release 27 March 1997 and Revenue Tax Bulletin April 1998 pp 517–523).

The treatment of *shares* issued to members on the de-mutualisation of a building society is governed by *TCGA 1992, s 217* (see above) and remains unchanged, the member realising no chargeable gain or allowable loss on receipt of the shares but, in the case of free shares, having no acquisition cost (and thus no indexation allowance) in computing the gain on a subsequent disposal. (Revenue Press Releases 21 March 1996, 27 March 1997 and Revenue Tax Bulletin April 1998 pp 517–523).

The Revenue Tax Bulletin article referred to above also comments on a number of specific points, *viz.* the treatment of multiple accounts (a separate calculation is required for each account in the case of cash bonuses; free shares acquired before 6 April 1998 are pooled), free shares sold immediately by successor company on investor's behalf (this is *not* equivalent to a cash bonus), statutory cash bonuses received by members ineligible to vote (treated like any other cash bonus), joint accounts (cash bonus/free shares treated as received/acquired equally between account holders), child, nominee and client accounts (cash bonus/free shares treated as received/acquired wholly by the beneficial owner of the account, i.e. the child etc.), partnership accounts (cash bonus/free shares treated as received/acquired by all the partners in accordance with their partnership sharing ratios), and accounts in the form of permanent interest bearing shares (PIBs) (cash bonuses are free of CGT as a PIB is a QUALIFYING CORPORATE BOND (55)).

There is also a detailed discussion in Tax Bulletin of the position, including that for inheritance tax, where an investor dies before de-mutualisation. Where death occurs after the de-mutualisation is announced and the entitlement to a cash bonus or free shares passes to the personal representatives/beneficiaries, the value of the right to receive the cash bonus or free shares may increase the value at death of a share account for both CGT and inheritance tax purposes (and see *Ward and others (Executors of Cook, deceased) v CIR* 1998 (Sp C 175), [1999] SSCD 1). A Table is provided to assist in valuations. The Bulletin also covers the position of a surviving holder of a joint account.

The CGT treatment of 'windfalls' received on the de-mutualisation of other organisations, e.g. insurance companies, sports clubs, depends on the facts of each particular case. The Tax Bulletin comments on the conversion of Norwich Union (where the position differs according to the date the free shares were unconditionally allotted to policy holders) and the takeover of Scottish Amicable, both in 1997.

(Revenue Tax Bulletin April 1998 pp 517–523).

The treatment of windfalls made to Scottish Widows policy holders is covered in Revenue 'Working Together' Bulletin August 2001 p 8.

Mergers of building societies

Cash payments on the merger of two building societies are chargeable to income tax (Revenue Press Release 21 March 1996).

Cashbacks

Cashbacks paid by banks and building societies as an inducement to purchase goods or services, e.g. to take out a mortgage, are not chargeable to capital gains tax (HMRC Statement of Practice 4/97). See **25.23** EXEMPTIONS AND RELIEFS.

Shareholders in Northern Rock plc and Bradford & Bingley plc

[63.28] HMRC have published guidance on the capital gains consequences of the transfer of Northern Rock plc into temporary national ownership in February 2008. They consider that the entire loss to each shareholder of his shares as a result of the transfer constitutes a disposal occurring on 22 February 2008. As no consideration was received for the shares, the disposal will normally give rise to a loss, except to the extent that the disposal includes free shares received when Northern Rock demutualised in 1997 (see **63.27** above).

Any payment made to a shareholder under the terms of the *Northern Rock plc Compensation Scheme Order 2008 SI 2008 No 718* will be chargeable under the provisions for capital sums derived from assets (9), the asset being the former shareholding.

(HMRC Brief 32/08).

Similar guidance has also been published in relation to the transfer of Bradford & Bingley plc into temporary national ownership in September 2008. HMRC consider that the entire loss to each shareholder of his shares as a result of the transfer constitutes a disposal occurring on 29 September 2008. As no consideration was received for the shares, the disposal will normally give rise to a loss, except to the extent that the disposal includes free shares received when Bradford & Bingley demutualised.

Any payment made to a shareholder under the terms of the *Bradford & Bingley plc Compensation Scheme Order 2008 SI 2008 No 3249* will be chargeable under the provisions for capital sums derived from assets (9), the asset being the former shareholding.

(HMRC Brief 16/09).

The above Briefs also provides guidance on the income tax consequences for shares and share options held by employees under employee share schemes.

Members of Dairy Farmers of Britain

[63.29] HMRC have published guidance on the capital gains consequences of the entry into receivership of Dairy Farmers of Britain on 3 June 2009. They consider that £5 Ordinary shares, 'B' shares and preference shares have become of negligible value so that members holding such shares can claim and allowable loss accordingly. Whether or not holders of 'A' Ordinary shares issued on 27 March 2009 can claim an allowable loss depends on the nature of the debt from which the shares were converted. No allowable loss arises in respect of member's loan stock. Limited allowable losses may arise in respect of member's liability loan or member's capital or investment account in specified circumstances. (HMRC Brief 5/10).

Recognised stock exchanges

[63.30] The expression '*recognised stock exchange*' means:

(i) the London Stock Exchange and any other market of a 'recognised investment exchange' which is designated as a recognised stock exchange by Order; and
(ii) any overseas stock exchange designated by Order.

A '*recognised investment exchange*' is, for this purpose, an exchange in relation to which a recognition order is in force under *Financial Services and Markets Act 2000, s 285*.

A list of designated overseas stock exchanges is available on the HMRC website (www.hmrc.gov.uk). A list of recognised stock exchanges also appears in **Simon's Taxes**, Binder 1, p TT-21. Certain exchanges have been designated as recognised stock exchanges for the purposes only of investment bond arrangements within **3.3** ALTERNATIVE FINANCE ARRANGEMENTS. See HMRC's Order, 20 July 2007.

Securities, shares or stock are listed on a recognised stock exchange if:

- they are admitted to trading on that exchange; and
- they are either included in the 'official UK list' (i.e. the official list within *Financial Services and Markets Act 2000, Pt 6*) or are officially listed, in a country outside the UK which has a recognised stock exchange, under provisions corresponding to those generally applicable in European Economic Area countries.

[*ITA 2007, s 1005; CTA 2010, s 1137; ICTA 1988, s 841; TCGA 1992, s 288(1)(5A)(5B)*].

Shares solely admitted to trading on the Alternative Investment Market are not included in the official UK list and are accordingly not listed on a recognised stock exchange. (HMRC Guidance Note 29 March 2007).

Tax treatment of new types of security

[63.31] The Treasury has the power to make regulations determining the tax treatment of new types of security created under any regulatory requirement imposed, or which appears to the Treasury to be likely to be imposed, by any EU legislation or enactment on authorised persons (within *Financial Services and Markets Act 2000, s 31*) or the parent undertakings of such persons. [*FA 2012, s 221; FA 2014, s 295*]. The power is intended, in particular, to deal with the tax consequences of the Basel III reform measures which take effect from 1 January 2013.

Key points on shares and securities

[63.32] Points to consider are as follows.

- The tax treatment of a reorganisation (as defined in *TCGA 1992, s 126*) is mandatory. You cannot elect out of the regime and HMRC cannot refuse to apply it. There is no motive test associated with this relief. See **63.2**.
- A rights issue is still a reorganisation even if some shareholders choose not to take up their entitlements. It is the initial allotment or allocation of shares that must be pro rata to the original shareholding, so the actual take-up of the offer doesn't matter. See **63.2**.
- It is important to keep records of the amounts paid and received for shares and of any reorganisations events, throughout your period of ownership. Otherwise, it can become difficult to compute any gains or losses on eventual disposal. See **63.2** onwards.
- The tax treatment of an exchange of securities or of a scheme of reconstruction as if they were a reorganisation is only mandatory so long as the appropriate motive tests are satisfied (genuine commercial reasons and not for the avoidance of capital gains tax of corporation tax). But if those conditions are satisfied, you cannot elect out of the regime (but for a very specific situation relating to entrepreneurs' relief) and HMRC cannot refuse to apply it. See **63.5** and **63.7**.
- While HMRC is mandatorily required to consider clearance applications (see **4.15**), it is your responsibility to ensure that the transactions you are intending to carry out will constitutes an exchange of securities reorganisation or a scheme of reconstruction, as defined as *TCGA 1992, Sch 5AA*. See **63.5** and **63.7**.
- The generic term 'earn-out right' can apply to any situation where an amount of consideration falls to be ascertained by reference to future events, it is not restricted to future profits of the business sold. Another common example is where the further consideration being predicated on low levels of customer turnover. See **63.6**.
- Earn outs normally give at least two different CGT disposals (the share sale and the part/final disposal of the earn out right). Historically, sellers have preferred to minimise the gain on the first disposal by giving a low value to the earn out right. However, where sellers have ample entrepreneurs' relief capacity (current limit £10 million) and with current low interest rates the opposite can be true. This is because only the first disposal normally qualifies for entrepreneurs' relief and the subsequent disposals are taxable at marginal CGT rates (usually 20%). Giving a high value to the earn out right gives a cash flow disadvantage in that tax is paid earlier but an 10% tax saving (20% – 10%). Also if the initial value of the earn out is overly optimistic the seller can claim to carry back the loss.

- In the *Strand Options and Futures* case, the Courts upheld the finding that the buy-back of the shares was a disposal and chargeable under *TCGA 1992, s 1*, without any need for the intervention of *s 122*. See **63.19**.
- HMRC have a toolkit 'capital gains tax for shares' that considers the perceived risk areas such as access to historical data, date of disposal, valuations, qualifying expenditure and reliefs. Using the toolkit or an alternative checklist may help show that reasonable care has been taken. Showing reasonable care is important if the computation of the gain is subsequently challenged and found to be incorrect as it affects the penalty that can be charged.

64

Shares and Securities — Identification Rules

Introduction	64.1
Capital gains tax — identification rules on or after 6 April 2008	64.2
Identification rules for shares and securities for corporation tax purposes	64.3
'Section 104 holdings' of securities	64.4
'1982 holding'	64.5
Relevant securities	64.6

Cross-references. See 38 INDEXATION; 63 SHARES AND SECURITIES.

Simon's Taxes. See C2.7–C2.8, D1.920–D1.922.

Introduction

[64.1] Because one batch of shares or securities of the same class in a company are (unless numbered) effectively indistinguishable from another batch, special rules ('identification rules') are needed to match disposals with multiple acquisitions. There are different rules for capital gains tax purposes and for corporation tax purposes.

Capital gains tax — disposals on or after 6 April 2008

Disposals of shares (and securities) on or after 6 April 2008 are to be identified with acquisitions by the same person of shares (and securities) of the same class in the same company in the following order:

(1) acquisitions on the same day as the disposal;
(2) acquisitions within 30 days after the day of disposal (thus countering 'bed and breakfasting');
(3) shares comprised in the 'section 104 holding' in **64.4** below; and
(4) if the shares disposed of are still not exhausted, shares acquired subsequent to the disposal (and beyond the above-mentioned 30-day period).

The detailed provisions are covered at **64.2** below.

Capital gains tax — disposals before 6 April 2008

In summary, disposals are to be identified with acquisitions in the following order.

(1) acquisitions on the same day as the disposal;

(2) acquisitions within 30 days after the day of disposal;
(3) previous acquisitions after 5 April 1998 on a last in/first out (LIFO) basis;
(4) shares acquired after 5 April 1982 and comprised in the pool at 5 April 1998 (i.e. the 'section 104 holding' in **64.4** below — previously known as the 'new holding');
(5) shares acquired before 6 April 1982 (the '1982 holding' in **64.5** below);
(6) shares acquired on or before 6 April 1965 on a LIFO basis;
(7) if the shares disposed of are still not exhausted, shares acquired subsequent to the disposal (and beyond the above-mentioned 30-day period).

For coverage of the detailed provisions see the 2011/12 or earlier edition.

Corporation tax

The rules applying for the purposes of corporation tax on chargeable gains are covered at **64.3** below. Those rules also applied for capital gains tax purposes pre-6 April 1998. In summary disposals are to be identified with acquisitions in the following order:

(1) acquisitions on the same day as the disposal;
(2) acquisitions in the previous nine days;
(3) shares acquired after 5 April 1982 and comprised in the 'section 104 holding' in **64.4** below;
(4) shares acquired before 6 April 1982 and comprised in the '1982 holding' in **64.5** below;
(5) shares acquired on or before 6 April 1965 on a LIFO basis;
(6) if the shares disposed of are still not exhausted, shares acquired subsequent to the disposal, taking the earliest acquisition first.

Capital gains tax — identification rules on or after 6 April 2008

[64.2] See **64.1** above for a summary of the capital gains tax identification rules for disposals on or after 6 April 2008 as detailed below. **The provisions described below do not apply for the purposes of corporation tax on chargeable gains.**

The identification rules detailed below apply to disposals on or after 6 April 2008 for the purposes of capital gains tax. They apply for the purpose of identifying a disposal of shares with an acquisition of shares etc. of the same class made by the person making the disposal and held by him in the same capacity as that in which he makes the disposal. For identification purposes, disposals are considered in the date order in which they take place. These rules override any identification purporting to be made by the disposal itself or by a transfer or delivery giving effect to it.

Shares etc. held by a person who acquired them as an employee of the company concerned or of anyone else and on terms which for the time being restrict his right to dispose of them (known as 'clogged shares') are treated as being of a different class from both:

- shares etc. held by him in the same company and acquired otherwise than as an employee; and
- shares etc. held by him in the same company which are not, or are no longer, subject to the same restrictions.

Upon the removal of restrictions, where the clogged shares form a separate section 104 holding (see below) that holding is merged with any such holding for shares of the same class in the same company which are not clogged. (HMRC Capital Gains Manual CG51580).

For disposals on or after 6 April 2014, shares held by trustees which are acquired or deemed to be acquired in circumstances in which the relief at **63.14** SHARES AND SECURITIES (disposals to employee-ownership trusts) applied (and which have not been subsequently disposed of and reacquired) are treated as of a different class to any other shares held by the trustees.

The rules below do not apply to shares (or securities) to which Enterprise Investment Scheme relief, venture capital trust scheme relief or community investment tax relief is attributable or to shares in respect of which relief has been given (and not withdrawn) under the Business Expansion Scheme (BES). Disposals of such shares retain their own identification rules — see **23.13**, **23.15**, **23.18** ENTERPRISE INVESTMENT SCHEME, **71.11**, **71.12** VENTURE CAPITAL TRUSTS, **25.22** EXEMPTIONS AND RELIEFS (as regards the BES) and Tolley's Income Tax under Community Investment Tax Relief. The rules also do not apply to assets to which income tax social investment relief is attributable — again such assets retain their own identification rules — see **65.45** SOCIAL INVESTMENT RELIEF.

Different rules apply to '*relevant securities*' (i.e. securities within the accrued income ('bondwashing') provisions, QUALIFYING CORPORATE BONDS (**54**) and securities which are, or have been, material interests in non-qualifying offshore funds or which are interests in a non-reporting offshore fund) and 'relevant EMI shares'. See below.

The rules below *do* apply to the matching of share transactions carried out during a period of non-UK residence (Revenue Tax Bulletin April 2001 p 839).

HMRC take the view that shares etc. held in the name of an individual are held in the same capacity as his or her portion of any shares of the same class in the same company which are held in the joint names of that individual and his or her spouse (Taxation 13 May 1999 p 170). See **46.2** MARRIED PERSONS AND CIVIL PARTNER re jointly held assets generally.

Application of rules to other assets

These identification rules apply not only to shares but to securities of a company but also to any other assets of such nature as to be dealt in without identifying the particular assets disposed of or acquired, e.g. units in a unit trust and milk quota, such assets being known as *fungible* assets. Shares and securities are treated as being of the same class only if they are, or would be, so treated by the practice of a recognised stock exchange (as defined by *ITA 2007, s 1005* — see **63.30** SHARES AND SECURITIES).

Identification rules

The rules apply **in the order set out below**, so that each rule is taken into account only to the extent that the shares disposed of are not exhausted by the preceding rule(s).

(1) **Same day rule.** Where two or more acquisitions of shares etc. of a particular class are made on the same day by the same person in the same capacity, they are treated as a single acquisition. The same applies to disposals. A disposal is then identified first and foremost and as far as possible with an acquisition made on the same day. In certain limited circumstances, an election is available for alternative treatment of same-day acquisitions by individuals (see below). Where some of the shares acquired are relevant EMI shares, they are treated as a single acquisition separate from the remainder of the shares (which are also treated as a single acquisition). The relevant EMI shares are then treated as disposed of after the remainder of the shares.

(2) **30-day rule.** If within the period of 30 days after a disposal, the person making it acquires shares of the same class, the disposal is identified with those acquisitions, taken in the order in which they occur within that period. Where the person acquires relevant EMI shares in the 30-day period, the disposal is matched with shares which are not relevant EMI shares first. This rule does not require shares to be identified with shares which the person making the disposal acquires at a time when he is neither resident nor ordinarily resident in the UK or when he is '*treaty non-resident*' (i.e. at a time when he falls to be regarded as resident in a territory outside the UK for the purposes of DOUBLE TAX RELIEF (**21**) arrangements). See also below under 'Bed and breakfasting'.

It is confirmed by HMRC Capital Gains Manual CG51560 that a disposal of rights attached to shares (see **63.4** SHARES AND SECURITIES) does not fall to be matched under the 30-day rule with a subsequent acquisition of shares of the same class but with no rights attached. Nor does a disposal of shares fall to be matched with shares of the same class subsequently acquired by a scrip or rights issue (as the reorganisation rules deem such shares to have been acquired at the same time as the original shares to which they attach — see below).

(3) **Section 104 holding.** The disposal is then identified with the 'section 104 holding' (if any), i.e. the single asset pool for shares, whenever acquired (see above and **64.4** below). Acquisitions matched under the same day or 30-day rules above do not form part of the section 104 holding.

(4) **Shares acquired subsequent to the disposal.** To the extent, if any, that the rules at (1)–(3) above have not exhausted the shares disposed of, the disposal is finally identified with shares acquired after the disposal (and after the expiry of the 30-day period in (2) above), taken in the order in which such acquisitions occur.

Same-day rule — election for alternative treatment

An election is available (under *TCGA 1992, s 105A*) to modify the application of the same-day rule at (1) above, as it relates to acquisitions, where:

(a) an individual acquires shares of the same class on the same day in the same capacity; and

(b) some, but not all, of those shares are acquired on the exercise of an option under an enterprise management incentive scheme (see **22.22** EMPLOYEE SHARE SCHEMES), or under a tax-advantaged employee share option scheme (see **22.24–22.27** EMPLOYEE SHARE SCHEMES) in circumstances such that no income tax charge arises.

Where the election is made:

(i) the shares in (b) above (the '*tax-advantaged-scheme shares*') and the balance of the shares in (a) above (the '*remainder shares*') are treated as *separate* acquisitions; and

(ii) any disposal falling to be matched (under the identification rules above) with the shares acquired on the day in question is matched with the remainder shares in priority to the tax-advantaged-scheme shares.

The election must be made by written notice to an HMRC officer on or before the first anniversary of 31 January following the tax year in which the individual first makes a disposal within (ii) above. It then has effect in relation to that disposal and all subsequent disposals within (ii) above. In determining, for these purposes, which is the first disposal, any capital distribution treated as a disposal by *TCGA 1992, s 122(1)* (see **63.11** SHARES AND SECURITIES) is disregarded, as is a receipt of consideration, on a capital reorganisation etc., treated as a disposal by virtue of any application of *TCGA 1992, s 128(3)* (see **63.2** SHARES AND SECURITIES).

Where the election is made, any 'clogged shares' (see above) acquired on the same day and in the same capacity as the shares in (a) above are automatically brought within the election from the time they cease to be treated as being of a different class from the shares in (a) above. Shares or securities received on a capital reorganisation etc. and treated by virtue of any application of *TCGA 1992, s 127* (see **63.2, 63.5, 63.7, 63.8** SHARES AND SECURITIES) as the same asset as the shares in (a) above are split proportionately between the tax-advantaged-scheme shares and the remainder shares and continue to be covered by the election.

The election cannot be made in respect of ordinary shares in VENTURE CAPITAL TRUSTS (**71**).

[*TCGA 1992, ss 104(4A), 105A(1)–(3)(5)(6), 105B; FA 2014, Sch 8 paras 122, 123, Sch 37 para 18*].

'Bed and breakfasting'

The 30-day rule at (2) above is designed to counter the previously common practice known as 'bed and breakfasting' whereby shares are sold and bought back the next day or very shortly afterwards, the purpose being to realise a gain by reference to historical cost. (The 30-day rule applies equally to disposals of 'relevant securities' (see **64.6** below).)

'Bed and breakfasting' remains feasible for couples where the disposal is by one partner and the acquisition is by the other. This is subject to the transaction not falling within the anti-avoidance provision at **44.7** LOSSES for losses arising from arrangements to secure a tax advantage.

It is confirmed by HMRC Capital Gains Manual CG51560 that a disposal of rights attached to shares (see **63.4** SHARES AND SECURITIES) does not fall to be matched under the 30-day rule with a subsequent acquisition of shares of the same class but with no rights attached. Nor does a disposal of shares fall to be matched with shares of the same class subsequently acquired by a scrip or rights issue (as the reorganisation rules deem such shares to have been acquired at the same time as the original shares to which they attach).

Scrips, rights issues etc.

For the purpose of applying the above identification rules, shares and securities acquired as a result of a reorganisation, e.g. a scrip or bonus issue or a rights issue, and treated under *TCGA 1992, s 127* (see **63.2** SHARES AND SECURITIES) as equating to shares already held are regarded as having been acquired at the time the original shares were acquired.

Relevant securities

The above identification order does not apply in relation to disposals of relevant securities (see above). Instead, disposals are identified in the following order.

(i) **30-day rule.** If within the period of 30 days after a disposal, the person making it acquires relevant securities of the same class, the disposal is identified with those acquisitions, taken in the order in which they occur within that period. This rule does not require securities to be identified with securities which the person making the disposal acquires at a time when he is not resident (before 6 April 2013, at a time when he is neither resident nor ordinarily resident) in the UK or when he is '*treaty non-resident*' (i.e. at a time when he falls to be regarded as resident in a territory outside the UK for the purposes of DOUBLE TAX RELIEF (**21**) arrangements).

(ii) **LIFO basis.** The disposal is then identified with acquisitions made at any time on a last in/first out (LIFO) basis.

Relevant EMI shares

Subject to the rules in (1) and (2) above, disposals of company shares are identified with relevant EMI shares before other shares, and with relevant EMI shares on a first in/first out basis. Relevant EMI shares cannot form part of a new or existing section 104 holding. Where an election is made under *FA 2013 Sch 23 para 6(3)* (see below), shares disposed of in 2012/13 are identified with shares which are not relevant EMI shares before those that are, and with relevant EMI shares on a last in/first out basis.

'*Relevant EMI shares*' are defined at **24.3** ENTREPRENEURS' RELIEF, broadly as shares acquired on or after 6 April 2012 by exercising a qualifying option within the enterprise management incentives scheme (see **22.22** EMPLOYEE SHARE SCHEMES). In certain cases an election must be made under *FA 2013 Sch 23 para 6(3)* for shares acquired in 2012/13 to be treated as relevant EMI shares.

[*TCGA 1992, ss 104, 105, 106A, 288(7B); FA 2013, Sch 24 paras 3–6; Sch 46 paras 97, 112; SI 2011 No 1211, Reg 44(4)*].

Deemed disposals and reacquisitions

Where under any capital gains tax legislation shares are deemed to be disposed of and immediately reacquired by the same person (see, for example, **44.11** LOSSES as regards negligible value claims), it is HMRC's view that neither the same day rule at (1) above nor the 30-day rule at (2) above require the deemed disposal to be matched with the deemed reacquisition (Revenue Tax Bulletin April 2001 pp 839, 840).

Example

Z, who is resident in the UK throughout, has the following acquisitions/disposals of ordinary 25p shares in MIB plc. MIB ordinary 25p shares were worth 210p per share at 31 March 1982. In 2017/18, Z made no disposals of chargeable assets other than as shown below.

Date	No. of shares bought/(sold)	Cost/(proceeds)
		£
1 May 1980	1,000	2,000
1 October 1983	2,000	4,500
1 December 1996	500	1,800
1 May 2017	(1,000)	(3,900)
25 May 2017	2,000	7,600
2 January 2018	(3,000)	(18,000)
Remaining holding	1,500	

The disposal on 1 May 2017 is matched with 1,000 of the shares acquired on 25 May 2017 (under the 30-day rule at (2) above). The resulting chargeable gain is as follows.

	£
Proceeds 1.5.17	3,900
Cost (£ 7,600 × 1,000/2,000)	3,800
Chargeable gain	£100

The disposal of 3,000 shares on 2 January 2018 is matched with 3,000 of the 4,500 forming the 'section 104 holding' (see (3) above) as follows.

	No. of shares	Qualifying expenditure
		£
Shares acquired 1 May 1980 (note (a))	1,000	2,100
Additional shares 1 October 1983	2,000	4,500
Additional shares 1 December 1996	500	1,800
Additional shares 25 May 2017	1,000	3,800
	4,500	12,200
Disposal 2 January 2018	(3,000)	(8,133)

	No. of shares	Qualifying expenditure
		£
Pool carried forward	1,500	£4,067

The chargeable gain is as follows.

	£
Proceeds 2.1.18	18,000
Cost (£12,200 × 3,000/4,500)	8,133
Chargeable gain	£9,867
Total chargeable gains 2017/18 £100 + £9.867	£9,967

Note to the example

(a) Re-basing to market value at 31 March 1982 applies automatically for capital gains tax purposes for disposals on or after 6 April 2008. Accordingly, the qualifying expenditure included in the section 104 holding in respect of the shares acquired on 1 May 1980 is the market value of those shares on 31 March 1982. See **64.4** below.

Identification rules for shares and securities for corporation tax purposes

[64.3] For disposals for corporation tax purposes on or after 1 April 1985 (referred to as the '*1985 date*') the identification rules for securities are as set out below. (These rules also applied for the purposes of capital gains tax, but by reference to a '1985 date' of 6 April 1985 and only before 6 April 1998.)

Special rules apply to the following.

(a) Shares to which Enterprise Investment Scheme relief or venture capital trust scheme relief is attributable, shares in respect of which relief has been given (and not withdrawn) under the Business Expansion Scheme (BES) and shares or securities held by companies to which investment relief under the corporate venturing scheme or community investment tax relief is attributable. Disposals of such shares retain their own identification rules — see **23.13**, **23.15**, **23.18** ENTERPRISE INVESTMENT SCHEME, **71.11**, **71.12** VENTURE CAPITAL TRUSTS, **25.22** EXEMPTIONS AND RELIEFS (as regards the BES), **18.16** CORPORATE VENTURING SCHEME and Tolley's Income Tax under Community Investment Tax Relief.

(b) '*Relevant securities*', i.e. securities within the accrued income ('bondwashing') provisions, QUALIFYING CORPORATE BONDS (**54**) and securities which are, or have been, material interests in non-qualifying offshore funds. See **64.6** below for further details.

For shares and securities not falling within (a) and (b) above and any other assets dealt in without identifying the particular assets disposed of or acquired, then, subject to the rules for:

(i) disposals on or before the day of acquisition (see below); and

(ii) acquisitions and disposals within a ten day period (see below),

securities disposed of are identified, in order of priority, with:

(A) securities acquired on or after the '1982 date' (see **64.4** below) and forming part of a 'section 104 holding' (see **64.4** below);
(B) securities forming part of a '*1982 holding*' (see **64.5** below); and then
(C) other securities on a 'last in, first out' basis. (Broadly, those held on 6 April 1965, see **8.4** and **8.9** ASSETS HELD ON 6 APRIL **1965** for quoted and unquoted securities respectively.)

Securities held by a person in one capacity cannot be identified with similar securities which he holds or can dispose of only in some other capacity (e.g. as a trustee).

[*TCGA 1992, ss 104(1)–(3), 107(1)(1A)(2)(7)–(9), 150(5), 150A(5)*].

Disposals and acquisitions on the same day

Securities disposed of on a particular day are matched with securities acquired on the same day by the same person in the same capacity and the pooling rules do not apply for this purpose. Where more securities are disposed of than are acquired, and the excess can neither be identified with previous acquisitions or a 'section 104 holding' (see **64.4** below), that excess is matched with a subsequent acquisition or acquisitions, taking the earliest first. [*TCGA 1992, s 105; FA 2006, s 72(2)(b)*].

Acquisitions and disposals within a ten-day period

Subject to the rules for disposals on or before the day of acquisition (see above) if, within a ten-day period, a number of securities are acquired which would otherwise increase or constitute a 'section 104 holding' (see **64.4** below) and subsequently a number of securities are disposed of, which would otherwise decrease or extinguish the same 'section 104 holding', then the securities disposed of are identified with those acquired and are not regarded as forming part of, or constituting, a 'section 104 holding'. If the number of securities acquired exceeds the number disposed of, the excess is regarded as forming part of, or constituting, a 'section 104 holding' and where securities were acquired at different times within the ten-day period, securities disposed of are first identified with those acquired at an earlier time (first in/first out). If the number of securities disposed of exceeds the number acquired, the excess is not identified under this rule. Any securities which are identified under this rule do not qualify for indexation allowance. [*TCGA 1992, s 107(3)–(6)*].

Example

B Ltd has the following transactions in 25p ordinary shares of H plc, a quoted company. At no time did B Ltd's holding amount to 2% of H plc's issued shares.

		Cost/(proceeds)
		£
6.6.78	Purchased 500 at £0.85	425

		Cost/(proceeds)
		£
3.11.81	Purchased 1,300 at £0.80	1,040
15.5.82	Purchased 1,000 at £1.02	1,020
8.9.82	Purchased 400 at £1.08	432
1.2.86	Purchased 1,200 at £1.14	1,368
29.7.87	Sold 2,000 at £1.30	(2,600)
8.6.90	Purchased 1,500 at £1.26	1,890
21.12.93	Received 1,000 from group company (cost £1,250, indexation to date £250)	1,500
10.4.17	Sold 3,900 at £4.00	(15,600)

The shares stood at £1.00 at 31.3.82.

Indexation factors	**March 1982 to April 2017**	2.406
	May 1982 to April 1985	0.161
	September 1982 to April 1985	0.158
	April 1985 to February 1986	0.019
	February 1986 to July 1987	0.054
	July 1987 to June 1990	0.245
	June 1990 to December 1993	0.120
	December 1993 to April 2017	0.907

Disposal on 10 April 2017

The 'section 104 holding' pool immediately prior to the disposal should be as follows

	Shares	Qualifying expenditure	Indexed pool
		£	£
15.5.82 acquisition	1,000	1,020	1,020
Indexation to April 1985 £1,020 × 0.161			164
8.9.82 acquisition	400	432	432
Indexation to April 1985 £432 × 0.158			68
Pool at 6.4.85	1,400	1,452	1,684
Indexed rise: April 1985 – Feb. 1986 £1,684 × 0.019			32
1.2.86 acquisition	1,200	1,368	1,368
	2,600	2,820	3,084
Indexed rise: February 1986 – July 1987 £3,084 × 0.054			167
	2,600	2,820	3,251
29.7.87 disposal	(2,000)	(2,169)	(2,501)
	600	651	750
Indexed rise: July 1987 – June 1990 £750 × 0.245			184
8.6.90 acquisition	1,500	1,890	1,890

	Shares	Qualifying expenditure	Indexed pool
		£	£
	2,100	2,541	2,824
Indexed rise: June 1990 – December 1993			
£2,824 × 0.120			339
21.12.93 acquisition	1,000	1,250	1,500
	3,100	3,791	4,663
Indexed rise: December 1993 – April 2017			
£4,663 × 0.907			4,229
	3,100	3,791	8,892

The '1982 holding' is as follows

	Shares	Allowable expenditure
		£
6.6.78 acquisition	500	425
3.11.81 acquisition	1,300	1,040
	1,800	1,465

(i) Identify 3,100 shares sold with 'section 104 holding'

	£
Disposal consideration 3,100 × £4.00	12,400
Allowable cost	3,791
Unindexed gain	8,609
Indexation allowance £8,892 – £3,791	5,101
Chargeable gain	£3,508

(ii) Identify 800 shares sold with '1982 holding'

	£	£
Disposal consideration 800 × £4.00	3,200	3,200
Cost $\frac{800}{1,800} \times £1,465$	651	
Market value 31.3.82 $\frac{800}{1,800} \times £1,800$		800
Unindexed gain	2,549	2,400
Indexation allowance £800 × 2.406	1,925	1,925
Gain after indexation	£624	£475
Chargeable gain		£475
Total chargeable gain 10 April 2017 (£3,508 + £475)		£3,983

'*Section 104* holdings' of securities

[64.4] Different provisions apply for the purposes of capital gains tax and corporation tax.

Capital gains tax

In relation to disposals on or after 6 April 2008, securities are pooled to form a 'section 104 holding' regardless of when they were acquired (subject to the rules at **64.2**(1)(2) above).

Corporation tax

Pooling applies to securities acquired on or after 1 April 1982.

Effect of pooling

Any securities of the same class to which pooling applied and held by the same person in the same capacity immediately before the '1985 date' (see **64.3** above) are pooled as a single asset which grows or diminishes as acquisitions and disposals are made on or after that date. Securities of the same class acquired for the first time on or after the '1985 date' are pooled as a single asset in the same way. This treatment has no effect on any market value that has to be ascertained.

Shares and securities of a company are not to be treated as being of the same class unless they are so treated by the practice of the Stock Exchange or would be so treated if dealt with on the Stock Exchange.

The single asset is referred to as the 'section 104 holding') and the part disposal rules apply on any disposal other than one of the whole holding.

A separate 'section 104 holding' applies in relation to any securities held by a person to whom they were issued as an employee of the company or of any other person on terms which restrict his rights to dispose of them, so long as those terms are in force (known as 'clogged shares'). While such a separate 'section 104 holding' exists the owner of it is treated as holding it in a different capacity to that in which he holds any other securities of the same class. Upon the removal of restrictions, two such separate 'section 104 holdings' merge. (HMRC Capital Gains Manual CG51580).

Indexation allowance

For corporation tax purposes, on any disposal from a 'section 104 holding' (other than the whole of it) the 'qualifying expenditure' and the 'indexed pool of expenditure' are apportioned between the part disposed of and the remainder in the same proportions as, under the normal capital gains tax rules for part disposals, the relevant allowable expenditure is apportioned (see **16.5** COMPUTATION OF GAINS AND LOSSES). The indexation allowance on the disposal is the amount by which the part of the indexed pool of expenditure apportioned to the part disposed of exceeds the equivalent part of the qualifying expenditure. On a disposal of the whole of the 'section 104 holding', the indexation allowance is the amount by which the indexed pool of expenditure at the time of disposal exceeds the qualifying expenditure at that time.

The '*qualifying expenditure*' is, at any time, the amount which would be the aggregate of the 'relevant allowable expenditure' in relation to a disposal of the whole of the holding at that time. See **38.2** INDEXATION for '*relevant allowable expenditure*'.

The '*indexed pool of expenditure*' in the case of a 'section 104 holding' in existence immediately before the '1985 date' comes into existence immediately before that date. It consists of the aggregate of the qualifying expenditure at that time and the indexation allowance which would have been available if all the securities in the holding were disposed of at that time on the assumption that the twelve-month qualifying period and restrictions on loss-making disposals (which applied before the '1985 date') had never applied. In the case of any other 'section 104 holding', the indexed pool of expenditure is created at the same time as the holding (or, if earlier, when any of the qualifying expenditure is incurred) and is equal, at that time, to the qualifying expenditure.

Where a disposal on or after 30 November 1993 to a person acquiring or adding to a 'section 104 holding' is treated under any enactment as one on which neither a gain nor a loss accrues to the person making the disposal, *TCGA 1992, s 56(2)* (general treatment on no gain/no loss disposal; see **38.4** INDEXATION) does not apply to the disposal (so that the amount of the consideration on the disposal is not calculated on the assumption that an unindexed gain of an amount equal to the indexation allowance accrues to the person making the disposal). However, an amount equal to the indexation allowance on the disposal is added to the indexed pool of expenditure for the holding acquired or, as the case may be, held by the person to whom the disposal is made, and in such a case where there is an addition to the indexed pool of a 'section 104 holding' already held, the addition is made after any increase required by (a) below.

Whenever there is an event, called an '*operative event*', which has the effect of increasing or reducing the qualifying expenditure, a change is made to the indexed pool of expenditure.

(a) The indexed pool of expenditure is increased by the 'indexed rise' since the last operative event or, if none, since the pool came into being. This is done before the calculation of the indexation allowance on a disposal
(b) If the operative event increases the qualifying expenditure, the indexed pool of expenditure is increased by the same amount.
(c) If there is a disposal resulting in a deduction in the qualifying expenditure, the indexed pool of expenditure is reduced in the same proportion. This is done after the calculation of the indexation allowance on the disposal.
(d) If the qualifying expenditure is reduced but there is no disposal, the indexed pool of expenditure is reduced by the same amount.

The '*indexed rise*' is the sum obtained by multiplying the value of the indexed pool of expenditure immediately before the operative event by a figure (expressed as a decimal but with no express requirement as to the number of decimal places to be calculated) calculated by the formula:

$$\frac{RE - RL}{RL}$$

where:

RE = the retail prices index for the month in which the operative event occurs; and
RL = the retail prices index for the month of the immediately preceding operative event or, if none, that in which the indexed pool of expenditure came into being.

If RE is equal to or less than RL, the indexed rise is nil.

See **38.2** INDEXATION for values of the retail price index for March 1982 and subsequent months.

Note

Reorganisations of shares do not normally constitute disposals or acquisitions but they may constitute an operative event as above; e.g. an issue of shares of the same class for payment under a rights issue would be an operative event as the qualifying expenditure is increased, but a bonus issue of shares of the same class would not be. Where the reorganisation involves shares of a different class this automatically gives rise to an operative event as the qualifying expenditure attributable to the 'section 104 holding' consisting of the original class of shares is decreased. An additional 'section 104 holding' is created as only shares of the same class can be pooled in the original 'section 104 holding'. The rules in **63.2** SHARES AND SECURITIES determine the proportions of qualifying expenditure to be attributed to holdings of shares following a reorganisation and these also apply to the indexed pool of expenditure.

Consideration for options

Where an increase in qualifying expenditure under (b) above is wholly or partly attributable to the cost of acquiring an option binding the grantor to sell, then the indexed pool of expenditure is additionally increased by a sum obtained by multiplying the consideration for the option by a figure (expressed as a decimal but without any clarification as to the number of decimal places to be calculated) calculated by the formula:

$$\frac{RO - RA}{RA}$$

where:

RO = the retail prices index for the month in which the option is exercised; and

RA = the retail prices index for the month in which the option was acquired, or March 1982 if later.

If RO is equal or less than RA, the indexed rise is nil.

[*TCGA 1992, ss 104(1)(3)–(6), 110, 114*].

Capital gains tax: no gain/no loss transfer before 6 April 2008

For disposals on or after 6 April 2008, where there were any additions to a 'section 104 holding' between 30 November 1993 and 5 April 2008 resulting from a no gain/no loss disposal, the amount of the original cost will not include any element of indexation (as the indexation element would, as described above, have been allocated to the indexed pool of expenditure) (Treasury Explanatory Notes to the 2008 Finance Bill). In such cases, the indexation allowance is lost, which differs from the position for other types of asset where *TCGA 1992, s 56(2)* (see **38.4** INDEXATION) applied to the no gain/no loss disposal. See, however, *Taxation* Magazine, 25 September 2008, pp. 340–342 for an argument that this only applies to no gain/no loss disposals before 6 April 1998, as later such disposals would not have resulted in an addition to a 'section 104 holding'.

Securities held on 31 March 1982

In relation to disposals on or after 6 April 2008, for capital gains tax purposes, a 'section 104 holding' can include or consist of securities held on 31 March 1982. Where this is the case, the re-basing provisions of *TCGA 1992, s 35(2)* (see **9.2** ASSETS HELD ON 31 MARCH **1982**) apply to any of the securities constituting or forming part of the section 104 holding which were held on 31 March 1982 by the person making the disposal. [*TCGA 1992, s 104(3A)*].

'1982 holding'

[64.5] For corporation tax purposes, the '1982 holding' comprises all shares of the same class in the same company acquired between 7 April 1965 and 5 April 1982 (31 March for companies) in so far as those shares have not been identified with disposals under current or previous identifiction rules. The pooled holding includes quoted securities held on 6 April 1965 where an election had been made that their actual cost be ignored and computations made by reference to their market value at 6 April 1965 only. See **8.3** and **8.4** ASSETS HELD ON 6 APRIL **1965**.

The 1982 holding is a single asset but one which cannot grow by the acquisition of additional securities of the same class. The relevant allowable expenditure attributable to it for capital gains tax purposes is the aggregate of that for the assets of which it is comprised.

Where securities forming part of a 1982 holding were acquired between 1 and 5 April 1982 inclusive, they are treated for the purposes of the re-basing rules of **9** ASSETS HELD ON 31 MARCH **1982**.

[*TCGA 1992, s 109; FA 2006, Sch 12 para 18*].

Relevant securities

[64.6] Separate rules apply for capital gains tax and for corporation tax purposes.

Capital gains tax

For disposals on or after 6 April 2008, see **64.2** above.

Corporation tax

The identification rules in **64.3** above do not apply to disposals of 'relevant securities'. Instead, the following rules apply.

'*Relevant securities*' are as follows.

(a) Qualifying corporate bonds.
(b) Securities within the accrued income ('bondwashing') scheme (other than those within (a) above). These comprise any loan stock or similar security of any government, public or local authority in the UK or elsewhere or any company or other body other than:
    (i) shares in a company (except qualifying shares in a building society);
    (ii) national savings and war savings certificates;
    (iii) certificates of deposit;
    (iv) any security which is redeemable, for which the amount payable on redemption exceeds the issue price and in respect of which no return other than the amount of that excess is payable; and
    (v) any deeply discounted security within **63.21** SHARES AND SECURITIES transferred or redeemed after 26 March 2003.
(c) Securities which are, or at any time have been, interests in a non-reporting offshore fund (before 1 December 2009, material interests in a non-qualifying offshore fund).

Relevant securities are not subject to pooling. The identification rules direct how disposals of such securities are to be identified with acquisitions of securities of the same class held by the same person in the same capacity. Where relevant securities were held on 6 April 1965, special rules apply. See **8.4** and **8.9** ASSETS HELD ON **6** APRIL **1965** for quoted and unquoted securities respectively.

The general rules are subject to special rules for 'contangos' (see below) and, in order of priority, are as follows.

(a) For identification purposes, disposals are to be taken in chronological order. The identification of relevant securities comprised in an earlier disposal therefore determine (by elimination) which securities can be comprised in a later disposal.
(b) Securities disposed of for transfer or delivery on a particular date (e.g. a stock exchange settlement date) or in a particular period (e.g. a stock exchange account) are not to be identified with securities acquired for transfer or delivery on a later date or in a later period. They must be identified with acquisitions of securities for transfer or delivery on or

before that date, or, in or before that period. However, subject to this, they have to be first identified with acquisitions for *transfer or delivery* on or after the contract disposal date. (The 'transfer or delivery', i.e. settlement, date is generally different from the contract date. See also *MacPherson v Hall* Ch D 1972, 48 TC 210.)

(c) Disposals are to be identified, on a 'first in, first out' basis, with acquisitions within the twelve months preceding the disposal. Otherwise, disposals are to be identified with acquisitions on a 'last in, first out' basis.

(d) Disposals are to be identified with acquisitions at different times on the same day in as nearly as may be equal proportions.

Contangos

Where, under arrangements designed to postpone the transfer or delivery of securities disposed of, a person by a *single bargain* acquires relevant securities for transfer or delivery on a particular date or in a particular period (the 'earlier date' or 'earlier period'), and disposes of them for transfer or delivery on a later date or in a later period, then the disposal and acquisition covered by the single bargain are matched. Any previous disposal which, apart from the above matching provisions, would have been identified with the acquisition under the contango arrangement must (subject to the general rule that disposals must be taken in chronological sequence) be identified with any 'available securities' acquired for transfer or delivery on the earlier date or in the earlier period. '*Available securities*' are securities which have not been matched under the above 'single bargain' rule, or under the general identification rules, with disposals for transfer or delivery on the earlier date or in the earlier period. Insofar as the previous disposal cannot be identified with 'available securities', the disposal is to be treated as being for transfer or delivery on the later date, or in the later period.

Where any of the securities within (c) or (d) above are disposed of on or after the '1985 date' and within a period of ten days beginning on the day on which the expenditure was incurred, no indexation allowance is due.

[*TCGA 1992, ss 54(2), 108; TIOPA 2010, Sch 8 para 164; SI 2009 No 3001, Reg 127*].

65

Social Investment Relief

Introduction	**65.1**
Social enterprises	**65.2**
Eligibility for income tax relief	**65.3**
Conditions relating to investor and investment	**65.4**
Types of investment permitted	**65.5**
Condition that amount invested must be paid over	**65.6**
The 'no pre-arranged exits' requirements	**65.7**
The 'no risk avoidance' requirement	**65.8**
The 'no linked loans' requirement	**65.9**
The 'existing investments' requirement	**65.10**
The 'no tax avoidance' requirement	**65.11**
The 'no disqualifying arrangements' requirement	**65.12**
Restrictions on being an employee, partner or paid director	**65.13**
The requirement not to be interested in capital etc.	**65.14**
The 'no collusion' requirement	**65.15**
Conditions relating to the social enterprise	**65.16**
The 'continuing to be a social enterprise' requirement	**65.17**
The 'maximum amount raised' requirement before 6 April 2017	**65.18**
The gross assets requirement	**65.19**
The 'unquoted status' requirement	**65.20**
The control and independence requirement	**65.21**
The subsidiaries requirements	**65.22**
The 'number of employees' requirement	**65.23**
The 'no partnerships' requirement	**65.24**
The 'financial health' requirement	**65.25**
The trading requirement	**65.26**
The 'purpose of the issue' requirement	**65.27**
The 'minimum period' requirements	**65.28**
The 'social enterprise to carry on the trade' requirement	**65.29**
Limits on amounts that may be invested	**65.30**
Qualifying trade	**65.31**
Qualifying subsidiaries	**65.32**
90% social subsidiaries	**65.33**
Form of income tax relief	**65.34**
Attribution of relief to investments	**65.35**
Claims to relief	**65.36**
Withdrawal or reduction of relief	**65.37**
Disposal of investment	**65.38**
Value received by investor	**65.39**
Repayments etc of share capital to other persons	**65.40**
Acquisition of trade or trading assets	**65.41**
Acquisition of share capital	**65.42**
Relief subsequently found not to have been due	**65.43**
Married persons and civil partners	**65.44**

Capital gains tax 65.45
Capital gains deferral relief 65.46

Introduction

[65.1] Income tax and capital gains tax reliefs are available to an individual making an eligible investment **on or after 6 April 2014** in a 'social enterprise' (see **65.2** below). See **65.3** below as to eligibility. The measure of the income tax relief ('*social investment relief*') is 30% of the amount invested, and this is deducted from the individual's income tax liability for the tax year in which the investment is made. The investment may be a subscription for shares or a 'qualifying debt investment' (see **65.3** below). There is a £1 million limit on the annual amount of investment per investor that can qualify for relief, but relief can be carried back to the previous tax year. There is also a maximum amount that a qualifying social enterprise can raise by such investment over a period of three years (see **65.18** below).

Chargeable gains accruing on or after 6 April 2014 and attributable to an increase in the value of an eligible investment are not liable to capital gains tax if the investment is held for a minimum period. Tax on chargeable gains on other assets can be deferred in certain circumstances where the individual invests in a social enterprise. See **65.45, 65.46** below.

Under current law, the reliefs will cease to be available for investments made after 5 April 2021. [*ITA 2007, s 257K(1)(5); FA 2014, Sch 11 para 1; F(No 2)A 2017, Sch 1 para 2*].

The relief is administered by HMRC's Small Company Enterprise Centre. For guidance on the relief see www.gov.uk/topic/business-tax/investment-schemes.

This chapter concentrates on the capital gains tax reliefs but the conditions for income tax relief are included in detail at **65.3** onwards. For completeness a brief summary of the income tax relief is also included at **65.34** — for full details see Tolley's Income Tax under Social Investment Tax Relief.

Meaning of Periods A and B

In these provisions, '*Period A*' is the period beginning with:

- the day on which the social enterprise is incorporated (if it is a body corporate) or established, or
- if later, the day which is one year before the date the investment is made,

and ending with the third anniversary of the date the investment is made.

'*Period B*' is the period beginning with the date the investment is made and ending with the third anniversary of that date.

[*ITA 2007, s 257KC; FA 2014, Sch 11 para 1*].

When is an investment made?

So far as the investment is in shares, the investment is made when the shares are issued to the investor by the social enterprise.

So far as it is in qualifying debt investments, the investment is made when the social enterprise issues the debenture or debentures to the investor; in a case where there is no such issuing, the investment is made when the debenture or debentures take effect between the social enterprise and the investor. If the investment is the second of multiple advances covered by the debenture(s) concerned, or a subsequent one of those advances, it is treated as made when the amount of that advance is fully advanced in cash, if that would give an earlier date than under the aforementioned rule.

[*ITA 2007, s 257KB; FA 2014, Sch 11 para 1*].

Confidentiality

HMRC's normal obligations of confidentiality neither prevent their disclosing to a social enterprise that relief has been given or claimed in respect of a particular number or proportion of any investments nor prevent disclosure, subject to safeguards, to the Regulator of Community Interest Companies for the purposes of the Regulator's functions. In the case of an accredited social impact contractor (see **65.2** below), those obligations do not prevent disclosure to a Minister of the Crown (or his delegate) for the purposes of his functions. [*ITA 2007, s 257SI; FA 2014, Sch 11 para 1*].

Social enterprises

[65.2] For the purposes of this chapter, '*social enterprise*' means:

(a) a '*community interest company*' (within *Companies (Audit, Investigations and Community Enterprise) Act 2004, Pt 2*);
(b) a 'community benefit society' (see below) that is not a charity;
(c) a charity (as in **11.2** CHARITIES);
(d) an 'accredited social impact contractor'; or
(e) any other body prescribed, or of a description prescribed, by Treasury order made by statutory instrument. There is provision to the effect that where a body is a social enterprise as a result of a Treasury order that has come into force, no subsequent Treasury order can undo that fact in respect of times before the subsequent order comes into force.

[*ITA 2007, s 257J(2)(3); FA 2014, Sch 11 para 1*].

Community benefit societies

A '*community benefit society*' is a body that:

- is registered as a community benefit society under *Co-operative and Community Benefit Societies Act 2014*, or
- is a society that, immediately before 1 August 2014, is registered or treated as registered under *Industrial and Provident Societies Act 1965* (or NI equivalent) and whose business is being, or is intended to be, conducted for the benefit of the community,

and is of a kind prescribed by *Reg 5* of *Community Benefit Societies (Restriction on Use of Assets) Regulations 2006* (*SI 2006 No 264*) (or NI equivalent) and whose rules include a rule in the terms set out in *Sch 1* of those

Regulations. *ITA 2007, s 257JB(5)–(7)* vary this definition to allow for times before *Co-operative and Community Benefit Societies Act 2014* comes into force. [*ITA 2007, s 257JB; FA 2014, Sch 11 para 1*].

Accredited social impact contractors

An '*accredited social impact contractor*' is a company limited by shares that is accredited under these provisions as a social impact contractor. Applications for accreditation must be made to a Minister of the Crown in a form and manner to be specified. A Minister is to accredit a company only if satisfied that (i) it has entered into a 'social impact contract'; (ii) it is established for the sole purpose of entering into and carrying out such a contract; and (iii) its activities in carrying out the contract will not consist wholly, or as to a substantial part, in 'excluded activities' (within **65.31** below), taking the 2017 changes to excluded activities as having come into force on 6 April 2017. If, subsequently, a Minister is satisfied that condition (ii) or (iii) has ceased to be met in relation to an accredited social impact contractor, he must withdraw the accreditation with effect from the time the condition ceased to be met or a later time.

The accreditation process is administered by the Minister for the Cabinet Office; for guidance see www.gov.uk/government/publications/social-investment-tax-relief-accreditation-for-sib-contractors. A company can appeal against a refusal to grant, or the withdrawal of, an accreditation.

A '*social impact contract*' is a contract that meets the following criteria.

(1) A 'contracting authority' within *SI 2006 No 5, Reg 3(1)* (which includes Minsters of the Crown, government departments, the Houses of Parliament, local authorities, fire and police authorities, etc.) must be a party to the contract.
(2) The contract must define the outcomes intended to be achieved.
(3) The Minister for the Cabinet Office must be satisfied that those outcomes have a social or environmental purpose (as defined) and satisfy the conditions specified in Part 2B of the Cabinet Office's guidance (see above).
(4) Where services are to be provided under the contract, the contract must distinguish between those services and the defined outcomes intended to arise from the services.
(5) The defined outcomes must be capable of being objectively measured, and the method of measurement must be set out in the contract.
(6) The progress towards achieving the defined outcome must be assessed at intervals which the Minister for the Cabinet Office is satisfied are appropriate. (Before 9 January 2016, the requirement was for the contract to provide for such assessment.)
(7) At least 60% of the total payments what could be made by the contracting authority to the company must be conditional on achieving defined outcomes which the Minister for the Cabinet Office is satisfied meet the criteria in (3) and (5) above.

An accreditation as a social impact contractor has effect for a period beginning with the day specified in the accreditation and of a length specified in, or determined in accordance with, the accreditation. The start date may be backdated but cannot be earlier than 6 April 2014. An accredited social impact contractor must notify the Minister of any change in name or address and of any changes to the social impact contract. It must also notify the Minister if any of the conditions or requirements of accreditation cease to be met. An annual report must be made to the Minister. The Minister has the power to require a social impact contractor to provide specified information by notice.

[*ITA 2007, ss 257JD–257JH; FA 2014, Sch 11 para 1; SI 2014 No 3066; SI 2015 No 2051*].

Social impact contracts (known as social impact bonds) are expected to be awarded by public sector bodies for the delivery of social outcomes; payment will be made according to outcomes agreed with the contractor and will be dependent on the desired social outcomes being achieved.

Special meaning of 'company'

In these provisions (except in the above definition of 'accredited social impact contractor') any reference to a company includes a charity that is a trust. [*ITA 2007, s 257JC; FA 2014, Sch 11 para 1*].

Eligibility for income tax relief

[65.3] In order for an individual to be eligible for income tax social investment relief on an investment in a social enterprise, a number of conditions must be met. See **65.4–65.15** below for conditions relating to the investor and the investment and **65.16–65.30** below for conditions relating to the social enterprise.

An investor is not eligible for social investment relief on an amount invested if:

- the investor has obtained in respect of that amount, or any part of it, community investment tax relief or relief under the ENTERPRISE INVESTMENT SCHEME (**23**) or the SEED ENTERPRISE INVESTMENT SCHEME (**60**); or
- that amount, or any part of it, has been set against a chargeable gain under the capital gains deferral provisions at **23.14** ENTERPRISE INVESTMENT SCHEME.

Nominees

The investment in the social enterprise must be made by the investor on his own behalf. However, investments made by, subscribed for, issued to, held by or disposed of for an individual by a nominee are treated for these purposes as made by, subscribed for, issued to, held by or disposed of by the individual.

[*ITA 2007, s 257K(1)–(3); FA 2014, Sch 11 para 1*].

Conditions relating to investor and investment

[65.4] The conditions relating to the investor and the investment are described at **65.5–65.15** below.

Types of investment permitted

[65.5] At all times during Period B (see **65.1** above) the investment in the social enterprise must be in the form of:

- shares that meet conditions A and B below and are issued to the investor by the social enterprise in return for the amount invested; or
- 'qualifying debt investments' of which the investor is the holder in return for his advancing the amount invested to the social enterprise.

Condition A is that the shares must carry neither of the following:

- a right to a return which (or any part of which) is a fixed amount; or is at a fixed rate; or is otherwise fixed by reference to the amount invested; or is fixed by reference to some other factor that is not contingent on successful financial performance by the social enterprise; and
- a right to a return at a rate greater than a reasonable commercial rate.

Condition B is that, for the purpose of determining the amounts due to holders of the shares on a winding-up of the social enterprise:

- those amounts rank after all debts of the social enterprise except any due to holders of qualifying debt investments in their capacity as such; and
- the shares do not rank above any other shares in the social enterprise (ignoring any debts postponed by rules under *Insolvency Act 1986, s 411* or any other enactment).

Shares acquired from another investor do not qualify.

Qualifying debt investments

'*Qualifying debt investments*' are any debentures of the social enterprise in respect of which the following conditions are met:

- neither the principal of the debt, nor any return on that principal, is charged on any assets;
- the rate of return on the principal is no greater than a reasonable commercial rate of return; and
- in the event of a winding-up of the social enterprise and so far as the law allows, any sums due in respect of the debt (whether principal or return):
  - are subordinated to all other debts of the social enterprise (ignoring any debts postponed by rules under *Insolvency Act 1986, s 411* or any other enactment) except sums due in the case of other unsecured debentures which rank equally;
  - rank equally, if there are shares in the social enterprise and they all rank equally among themselves, with amounts due to shareholders; and
  - rank equally, if there are shares in the social enterprise and they do not all rank equally, with amounts due to the holders of the lowest ranking shares.

For these purposes, 'debenture' includes any instrument creating or acknowledging indebtedness.

[*ITA 2007, s 257L; FA 2014, Sch 11 para 1*].

Condition that amount invested must be paid over

[65.6] So far as the investment is in shares, they must be subscribed for wholly in cash and fully paid-up at the time of issue. So far as the investment is in qualifying debt investments (see **65.5** above), the full amount of the advance covered by the debenture(s) must have been advanced wholly in cash by the time the investment is made. There must be no undertaking to pay cash to any person at a future time in respect of the acquisition of the shares or qualifying debt investments. [*ITA 2007, s 257LA; FA 2014, Sch 11 para 1*].

The 'no pre-arranged exits' requirements

[65.7] There must not at any time in Period B (see **65.1** above) exist any arrangements (as widely defined) for the investment to be redeemed, repaid, repurchased, exchanged or otherwise disposed of in that period. Except where the social enterprise is an accredited social impact contractor (see **65.2** above), the 'issuing arrangements' for the investment must not include:

(a) arrangements for, or with a view to, the cessation of any trade which is being, or is to be or may be, carried on by the social enterprise or a person connected with it (within **17 CONNECTED PERSONS**); or

(b) arrangements for the disposal of, or of a substantial amount (in terms of value) of, the assets of the social enterprise or of a person connected with it.

The '*issuing arrangements*' are the arrangements under which the investor makes the investment, but also include any arrangements made before, and in relation to or in connection with, the making of the investment by the investor. The arrangements referred to in (a) and (b) above do not include any arrangements applicable only on the winding-up of a company unless the issuing arrangements include arrangements for the company to be wound up or they are applicable otherwise than for genuine commercial reasons.

[*ITA 2007, ss 257LB, 257TE(1), 993; FA 2014, Sch 11 para 1*].

The 'no risk avoidance' requirement

[65.8] There must not at any time in Period B (see **65.1** above) exist any arrangements (as widely defined) a main purpose of which is (by means of any insurance, indemnity, guarantee, hedging of risk or otherwise) to provide partial or complete protection for the investor against what would otherwise be the risks attached to the investment. This does not include any arrangements which are confined to the provision for the social enterprise itself (and/or, where applicable, its subsidiaries) of any such protection against the risks arising in the ordinary course of carrying on business. [*ITA 2007, ss 257LC, 257TE(1); FA 2014, Sch 11 para 1*].

The 'no linked loans' requirement

[65.9] No loan may be made to the investor or to an 'associate' at any time in Period A (see **65.1** above) if it would not have been made, or would not have been made on the same terms, if the investor had not made the investment or had not been proposing to do so. The giving of credit to, or the assignment of a debt due from, the investor or associate is counted as a loan. [*ITA 2007, s 257LD; FA 2014, Sch 11 para 1*]. It is anticipated that HMRC SP 6/98 (see **23.4** ENTERPRISE INVESTMENT SCHEME) will be applied for this purpose.

Meaning of 'associate'

An '*associate*' of any person is any 'relative' (i.e. spouse, civil partner, ancestor or linear descendant) or partner of that person, the trustee(s) of any settlement in relation to which that person or any relative (living or dead) is or was a settlor and, where that person has an interest in any shares or obligations of a company which are subject to any trust or are part of a deceased estate, the trustee(s) of the settlement or the personal representatives of the deceased. [*ITA 2007, s 257TC; FA 2014, Sch 11 para 1*].

The 'existing investments' requirement

[65.10] This requirement applies to investments made on or after 6 April 2017. If, immediately before the investment is made, the investor holds any shares in or debentures of the social enterprise, or a company which is at that time its qualifying subsidiary (see **65.32** below), those shares or debentures must be 'risk finance investments' or (in the case of shares) 'permitted subscriber shares'.

A share or debenture is a '*risk finance investment*' for these purposes if:

- it is a share issued to the investor, or a debenture of which the investor is the holder in return for advancing an amount; and
- at any time, an SITR compliance statement (see **65.36** below), an EIS compliance statement (see **23.11** ENTERPRISE INVESTMENT SCHEME) or an SEIS compliance statement (see **60.34** SEED ENTERPRISE INVESTMENT SCHEME) is provided in respect of it or of shares or investments including it.

Subscriber shares are '*permitted subscriber shares*' for these purposes if:

- they were issued to the investor and have been continuously held by him ever since; or
- they were acquired by the investor at a time when the issuing company had issued no shares other than subscriber shares and had not begun to carry on, or make preparations for carrying on, any trade or business.

For these purposes 'debenture' includes any instrument creating or acknowledging indebtedness.

[*ITA 2007, s 257LDA; F(No 2)A 2017, Sch 1 paras 3, 14(1)*].

The 'no tax avoidance' requirement

[65.11] The investment must be made for genuine commercial reasons and not as part of any arrangements (as widely defined) a main purpose of which is the avoidance of tax. [*ITA 2007, ss 257LE, 257TE(1); FA 2014, Sch 11 para 1*].

The 'no disqualifying arrangements' requirement

[65.12] This requirement applies to investments made on or after 6 April 2017, but arrangements which include any transaction entered into before that date are excluded from being disqualifying arrangements. The investment must not be made, and money raised by the social enterprise from the making of the investment must not be employed, in consequence or anticipation of, or otherwise in connection with, 'disqualifying arrangements'. Arrangements are '*disqualifying arrangements*' if:

- a main purpose is to secure both that an activity is (or will be) carried on by the social enterprise (or its 90% social subsidiary — see **65.33** below) and that one or more of the 'relevant tax reliefs' are available in respect of the activity;
- the activity in question is the qualifying trade or activity in **65.27** below for the purposes of which the investment raised money; and
- one or both of Conditions A and B below are met. It is immaterial whether the social enterprise itself is a party to the arrangements.

Condition A is that, as a result of the money raised by the investment being employed as required by **65.28** below, an amount representing the whole or most of the amount raised is, in the course of the arrangements, paid to or for the benefit of one or more 'relevant persons'. Condition B is that, in the absence of the arrangements, it would have been reasonable to expect that the whole or greater part of the activities making up the qualifying trade or activity would have been carried on as part of another business by one or more 'relevant persons'.

A '*relevant person*' is one who is a party to the arrangements or a person connected with such a party (within **17** CONNECTED PERSONS). The '*relevant tax reliefs*' are those listed at **23.3** ENTERPRISE INVESTMENT SCHEME.

[*ITA 2007, s 257LEA; F(No 2)A 2017, Sch 1 paras 4, 14(3)(4)*].

Restrictions on being an employee, partner or paid director

[65.13] Neither the investor nor any individual who is an associate of his (see **65.9** above) can at any time in Period A (see **65.1** above) be:

(a) an employee of the social enterprise, or of a 'subsidiary' of the enterprise, or of a partner of the enterprise, or of a partner of a subsidiary of the enterprise;
(b) a partner of the enterprise or of a subsidiary of the enterprise;
(c) a trustee of the enterprise or of a subsidiary of the enterprise; or
(d) a 'remunerated' director of the enterprise or of a 'linked company'.

For these purposes, a '*subsidiary*' of the social enterprise means a company which at *any* time in Period A is a 51% subsidiary of the enterprise. In (d) above, 'director' does not include a trustee of a charity that is a trust. For the purposes of (d), a '*linked company*' means (i) a subsidiary of the enterprise or (ii) a company which is a partner of the enterprise or (iii) a company which is a partner of a subsidiary of the enterprise.

Meaning of 'remunerated'

For the purposes of (d) above, an individual who is a director of the social enterprise or of a linked company is '*remunerated*' if the individual (or a partnership of which he is a member):

- receives at any time in Period A a payment from a 'related person', or
- is entitled to receive a payment from a related person in respect of any time in Period A,

other than by way of:

(i) payment or reimbursement of travelling or other expenses wholly, exclusively and necessarily incurred by the individual in the performance of his duties as a director;
(ii) interest at no more than a commercial rate on money lent;
(iii) dividends etc. representing no more than a normal return on investment;
(iv) payment for supply of goods at no more than market value;
(v) rent at no more than a reasonable and commercial rent for property occupied by a related person; or
(vi) any necessary and reasonable remuneration for services rendered to a related person in the course of a trade or profession (other than secretarial or managerial services or of a kind provided by the person to whom they are rendered) which is taken into account in computing the profits of that trade or profession.

'*Related person*' means (i) the social enterprise, (ii) a person connected with the enterprise (within **17** CONNECTED PERSONS), (iii) a linked company (see above) of which the individual is a director, or (iv) a person connected with any such linked company.

If either of the following two conditions are met, there is also disregarded for the above purpose any other reasonable remuneration (including any benefit or facility) received by the individual, or to which he is entitled, for services rendered by him to the company (whether the social enterprise or a linked company) of which he is a director and rendered by him in his capacity as a director (or in his capacity as an employee where he is both director and employee). The first condition is that the investor made the investment, or previously made another investment meeting the requirements in **65.5** above, at a time (the '*qualifying time*') when:

- the above requirements and also those of **65.14** and **65.15** below would have been met even if each reference in those provisions to any time in Period A were a reference to any time before the qualifying time; and
- the investor had never been involved (whether on his own account or as a partner, director or employee) in carrying on the whole or any part of the trade, business or profession carried on by the social enterprise or by a subsidiary.

The second condition applies only where the first is not met and is that the investment is made before the third anniversary of the date when the investor last made an investment in the social enterprise which did meet the first condition.

Generally, an individual who is both a director and an employee of a company is treated for these purposes as a director and not an employee.

[*ITA 2007, ss 257LF, 993; FA 2014, Sch 11 para 1*].

The requirement not to be interested in capital etc.

[65.14] Neither the investor nor any individual who is an associate of his (see **65.9** above) must at any time in Period A (see **65.1** above):

- have 'control' of a 'related company'; or
- directly or indirectly possess or be entitled to acquire (whether he is so entitled at a future date or will at a future date be so entitled):
  - more than 30% of the ordinary share capital of a related company;
  - more than 30% of the loan capital of a related company; or
  - more than 30% of the voting power in a related company.

'*Related company*' means the social enterprise or any company which at *any* time in Period A is a 51% subsidiary of the enterprise.

There is to be disregarded any shares in a related company held by the individual, or by an associate of his, at a time when that company has not issued any shares other than subscriber shares and has not begun to carry on, or make preparations for carrying on, any trade or business. Loan capital includes any debt incurred by the company (i) for money borrowed, (ii) for capital assets acquired, (iii) for any right to income created in its favour, or (iv) for insufficient consideration, but it excludes any debt incurred for overdrawing a bank account in the ordinary course of the bank's business. Rights or powers of associates of an individual are attributed to the individual for the purposes of these provisions.

[*ITA 2007, s 257LG; FA 2014, Sch 11 para 1*].

Meaning of 'control'

'*Control*' is to be construed in accordance with *CTA 2010, ss 450, 451* but as if references there to a company included a charity that is a trust. A charity that is a trust has control of another person if the trustees (in their capacity as such) have (or any of them has) control of the person. A trustee of a charity who, alone or together with other trustees who are connected with him (within **17 CONNECTED PERSONS**), can exercise some or all of the powers of the trustees, is regarded as controlling the charity. A person who either alone or with others has the power to appoint or remove trustees of a charity, or to approve or direct the trustees' functions, is also regarded as controlling the charity. A regulator is to be treated as not having control of any company regulated by him. [*ITA 2007, s 257TD; FA 2014, Sch 11 para 1*].

The 'no collusion' requirement

[65.15] There must not at any time in Period A (see **65.1** above) be any arrangements (as widely defined):

(a) as part of which either the investor makes the investment or the investor (or an individual who is an associate of his — see **65.9** above) makes any other investment in the social enterprise;
(b) which provides for a person to make an investment in a company other than the social enterprise, where that person is not the individual who invests as in (a) above; and
(c) to which there is a party (whether or not the individual who invests as in (a) above) who is an individual in relation to whom not all of the requirements in **65.13** and **65.14** above would be met if (i) references in those provisions to the investor were references to that individual, and (ii) references in those provisions to the social enterprise were references to the company mentioned in (b) above.

[*ITA 2007, ss 257LH, 257TE(1); FA 2014, Sch 11 para 1*].

Conditions relating to the social enterprise

[65.16] The conditions mentioned at **65.3** above relating to the social enterprise are described at **65.17–65.30** below.

The 'continuing to be a social enterprise' requirement

[65.17] The social enterprise must be a social enterprise throughout Period B (see **65.1** above). [*ITA 2007, s 257M; FA 2014, Sch 11 para 1*].

The 'maximum amount raised' requirement before 6 April 2017

[65.18] This requirement applies in relation to investments made before 6 April 2017. See the replacement rules at **65.30** below as regards investments made on or after that date.

A limit is set on the amount of tax-advantaged investment which a social enterprise may receive in a rolling three-year period. This limit is imposed by the need to comply with EC regulations on de minimis State aid, which restrict such aid to an amount not exceeding 200,000 euros in any three-year period. The total amount invested in the social enterprise must not be more than the amount given by:

$$\left(\frac{€200,000 - M}{RCG + RSI}\right) - T$$

where

T = the total in euros of any 'scheme investments' made in the 'aid period';
M = the total in euros of any de minimis State aid, other than scheme investments, that is granted during the aid period to the social enterprise or to a 'qualifying subsidiary' (see **65.32** below) at a time when it is such a subsidiary;
RCG = the highest rate at which capital gains tax is charged in the aid period; and

RSI = the highest SI rate (see **65.34** below) in the aid period.

The '*aid period*' is the three years ending with the day on which the investment is made. In the case of that day itself, the aid period includes only the part of the day before the investment is made. For these purposes, a '*scheme investment*' is an investment in respect of which the social enterprise (at any time) provides a compliance statement (see **65.36** below). The rules in **65.1** above on when an investment is made apply with appropriate modifications to determine when scheme investments are made.

If the investment or any scheme investments are made, or any aid is granted, in sterling or any other currency that is not the euro, its amount is to be converted into euros at an appropriate spot rate of exchange for the date on which the investment is made or the aid is paid.

[*ITA 2007, ss 257MA, 257MB; FA 2014, Sch 11 para 1; F(No 2)A 2017, Sch 1 paras 6(2), 14(1)*].

The gross assets requirement

[65.19] If the social enterprise is a single company, the value of its gross assets must not exceed £15 million immediately before the investment is made and must not exceed £16 million immediately afterwards. If the social enterprise is a parent company, the gross assets test applies by reference to the aggregate gross assets of all the group members (disregarding certain assets held by any group company which correspond to liabilities of another). [*ITA 2007, s 257MC; FA 2014, Sch 11 para 1*]. HMRC SP 2/06 (see **23.5** ENTERPRISE INVESTMENT SCHEME) applies for this purpose.

The 'unquoted status' requirement

[65.20] At the beginning of Period B (see **65.1** above), the social enterprise must not be a quoted company, and no arrangements (as widely defined) must then exist for it to become a quoted company. Also, there must be no arrangements then in existence for the social enterprise to become a subsidiary of a company by virtue of a share exchange if arrangements have been made with a view to that company becoming a quoted company. A company is a quoted company if any of its shares etc. are listed on a recognised stock exchange or on a designated foreign exchange, or dealt in outside the UK by such means as may be designated. [*ITA 2007, ss 257MD, 257TE(1); FA 2014, Sch 11 para 1*].

The control and independence requirement

[65.21] The social enterprise must not at any time in Period B (see **65.1** above) either:

(a) control (whether on its own or together with any person connected with it — within **17** CONNECTED PERSONS) another company other than a 'qualifying subsidiary' (see **65.32** below); or
(b) be a 51% subsidiary of another company or otherwise be under the control of a company or under the control of a company and a person connected with that company; or

(c) be capable of falling within (a) or (b) above by virtue of any arrangements (as widely defined).

'*Control*' is construed as in **65.14** above.

[*ITA 2007, ss 257ME, 257TD, 257TE(1); FA 2014, Sch 11 para 1*].

The subsidiaries requirements

[65.22] At all times in Period B (see **65.1** above) any subsidiary of the social enterprise must be a 'qualifying subsidiary' (see **65.32** below). [*ITA 2007, s 257MF; FA 2014, Sch 11 para 1*].

The social enterprise must not at any time in Period B have a 'property managing subsidiary' which is not a '90% social subsidiary' (see **65.33** below) of the social enterprise. A '*property managing subsidiary*' is a subsidiary whose business consists wholly or mainly in the holding or managing of land or any property deriving its value (directly or indirectly) from land. [*ITA 2007, s 257MG; FA 2014, Sch 9 para 1*]. The legislation does not define what is meant by property deriving its value indirectly from land, but examples given by the explanatory notes are the enterprise having shareholdings in a company deriving its value from land, having any interest in settled property deriving its value from land, or having any option, consent or embargo affecting the disposition of land.

The 'number of employees' requirement

[65.23] If the social enterprise is a single company, it must have fewer than the equivalent of 250 full-time employees when the investment is made. In relation to investments made before 6 April 2017, this figure was 500. If the social enterprise is a parent company, this rule applies by reference to the aggregate number of full-time employees of itself and its 'qualifying subsidiaries' (see **65.32** below). To ascertain the equivalent number of full-time employees of a company, take the actual number of full-time employees and add to it a just and reasonable fraction for each employee who is not full-time. For this purpose, an 'employee' includes a director but does not include anyone on maternity or paternity leave or a student on vocational training. [*ITA 2007, s 257MH; FA 2014, Sch 11 para 1; F(No 2)A 2017, Sch 1 paras 7, 14(1)*].

The 'no partnerships' requirement

[65.24] At no time in Period B (see **65.1** above) can the social enterprise be a member of a partnership or can any '90% social subsidiary' (see **65.33** below) of the social enterprise be a member of a partnership. [*ITA 2007, s 257MI; FA 2014, Sch 11 para 1*].

The 'financial health' requirement

[65.25] This requirement applies in relation to investments made on or after 6 April 2017. The requirement must be met at the beginning of Period B (see **65.1** above) and is that the social enterprise is not 'in difficulty'. The social enterprise is '*in difficulty*' if it is reasonable to assume that it would be regarded as a firm in difficulty for the purposes of the *EU Guidelines on State Aid for Rescuing and Restructuring Firms in Difficulty (2004/C 244/02)*. [*ITA 2007, s 257MIA; F(No 2)A 2017, Sch 1 paras 8, 14(1)*].

The trading requirement

[65.26] Except where it is an accredited social impact contractor (see **65.2** above), the social enterprise must, throughout Period B (see **65.1** above), be:

(a) a charity; or
(b) a single company that is not a charity and whose business does not, if things done for incidental purposes are ignored, consist to any extent in the carrying-on of 'non-trade activities' and does not consist wholly, or as to a substantial part, in the carrying-on of 'excluded activities' (within **65.31** below); or
(c) a parent company that is not a charity, where the business of the group (i.e. the company and its qualifying subsidiaries) does not consist wholly, or as to a substantial part, in the carrying-on of 'non-qualifying activities'.

For the purposes of (b) above, '*non-trade activities*' are activities which are neither activities carried on in the course of a trade nor activities carried on in the course of preparing to carry on a trade. For the purposes of similar legislation elsewhere, a 'substantial part' (see (b) and (c) above) is generally taken to mean more than 20%.

If the social enterprise intends that one or more companies should become its qualifying subsidiaries with a view to their carrying on one or more qualifying trades, then, until any time after which the intention is abandoned, the social enterprise is treated as a parent company and those other companies are included in the group for the above purposes.

The business of the group means what would be the business of the group if the activities of the group companies taken together were regarded as one business. Activities are for this purpose disregarded to the extent that they consist in:

- holding shares in or securities of any of the parent company's subsidiaries;
- making loans to another group company; or
- holding and managing property used by a group company for the purposes of a qualifying trade or trades carried on by any group company.

Activities of a group company are also disregarded to the extent that they are activities carried on by a 'mainly trading subsidiary' otherwise than for its main purpose. A '*mainly trading subsidiary*' is a qualifying subsidiary which exists wholly for the purpose of carrying on one or more qualifying trades (disregarding purposes having no significant effect on the extent of its activities).

Non-qualifying activities

'*Non-qualifying activities*' are:

- excluded activities within **65.31** below; and
- activities, other than activities carried on by a charity, that are carried on otherwise than in the course of a trade.

[*ITA 2007, ss 257MJ, 257TE(1); FA 2014, Sch 11 para 1*].

Administration or receivership etc.

The social enterprise is not regarded as ceasing to meet the trading requirement merely because of anything done in consequence of the enterprise or any of its subsidiaries being in administration or receivership (both as defined by *ITA 2007, s 257TB*). The entry into administration or receivership, and everything done as a result of the company concerned being in administration or receivership, must be for genuine commercial reasons and not part of arrangements (as widely defined) of which a main purpose is tax avoidance.

The social enterprise ceases to meet the trading requirement if before the end of Period B (see **65.1** above) a resolution is passed, or an order is made, for the winding-up of the social enterprise or any of its subsidiaries or in the event of a dissolution without winding-up, but this does not apply if the winding-up or dissolution is for genuine commercial reasons, and is not part of arrangements of which a main purpose is tax avoidance.

[*ITA 2007, ss 257MK, 257TE(1); FA 2014, Sch 11 para 1*].

The 'purpose of the issue' requirement

[65.27] Except where it is an accredited social impact contractor (see **65.2** above), the social enterprise must be a party to the making of the investment (so far as not in bonus shares) in order to raise money for the carrying on (by the social enterprise or a '90% social subsidiary' — see **65.33** below) of:

- a 'qualifying trade' (see **65.31** below) which on the date the investment is made is carried on by the social enterprise or a 90% social subsidiary; or
- the activity of preparing to carry on a qualifying trade which is intended to be carried on by the social enterprise or a 90% social subsidiary and which is begun to be carried within two years after the date the investment is made. In determining when a qualifying trade is begun to be carried on by a 90% social subsidiary, any carrying on of the trade by it before it became such a subsidiary is disregarded.

[*ITA 2007, s 257ML; FA 2014, Sch 11 para 1*].

The 'minimum period' requirements

[65.28] Except where it is an accredited social impact contractor (see **65.2** above), all of the money raised by the social enterprise from the making of the investment must, no later than the end of 28 months beginning with the date the investment is made, be employed wholly for the purpose for which it was raised (as to which see **65.27** above). Employing money on the acquisition of shares or stock in a body does not of itself amount to employing the money for such purpose. In relation to investments made on or after 6 April 2017, employing money on the repayment of a loan does not amount to employing the money for such purpose. The requirement does not fail to be met merely because an amount of money which is not significant is employed for other purposes.

The chosen trade must have been carried on for a period of at least four months ending at or after the time the investment is made. The trade must have been carried on for those months by no person other than the social enterprise or a '90% social subsidiary' (see **65.33** below) of the enterprise. A trading period shorter than four months is permitted if this is by reason only of the winding-up or dissolution of any company or anything done as a consequence of a company being in administration or receivership, provided the winding-up etc. is for genuine commercial reasons and not part of arrangements (as widely defined) of which a main purpose is tax avoidance.

Where the social enterprise is an accredited social impact contractor, all of the money raised by it from the making of the investment must, no later than the end of 24 months beginning with the date the investment is made, be employed wholly for the carrying out of the social impact contract in question. Again, insignificant employment of money for other purposes is ignored.

[*ITA 2007, ss 257MM, 257TE(1); FA 2014, Sch 11 para 1; F(No 2)A 2017, Sch 1 paras 9, 14(1)*].

The 'social enterprise to carry on the trade' requirement

[65.29] Except where the social enterprise is an accredited social impact contractor (see **65.2** above), there must not be a time in Period B (see **65.1** above) when the chosen trade (or the preparation activity for the chosen trade) is carried on by a person who is neither the social enterprise nor a '90% social subsidiary' (see **65.33** below) of the enterprise.

Where preparation work is carried on in Period B by the social enterprise or a 90% social subsidiary, the carrying on of the chosen trade in that period by any other person is disregarded for these purposes if it occurs before the enterprise or a 90% social subsidiary carries on that trade.

The requirement is not regarded as failing to be met if, as a consequence a company being wound up or dissolved or being in administration or receivership (both as defined by *ITA 2007, s 257TB*), the chosen trade ceases to be carried on in Period B by the social enterprise or a 90% social subsidiary and is subsequently carried on by a person who is not connected (within **17 CONNECTED PERSONS**) with the enterprise at any time in Period A (see **65.1** above). This let-out applies only if the winding-up, dissolution or entry into administration or receivership (and everything done as a consequence of the company concerned being in administration or receivership) is for genuine commercial reasons and not part of arrangements (as widely defined) a main purpose of which is the avoidance of tax.

[*ITA 2007, ss 257MN, 257TE(1), 993; FA 2014, Sch 11 para 1*].

Limits on amounts that may be invested

[65.30] The following rules apply in relation to investments made on or after 6 April 2017 and supersede **65.18** above.

Where investment is made in first seven years

Where either:

(a) the investment is made before the end of the seven years beginning with the 'relevant first commercial sale'; or
(b) the investment is made later than that but a 'relevant investment' had been made in the social enterprise before the end of that seven-year period and some or all of the money raised by that relevant investment was employed for the purposes of the same qualifying trade or activity (see **65.27** above) for which the money raised by the current investment is employed,

the total amount of relevant investments made in the social enterprise on or before the date the investment is made must not exceed £1.5 million. In determining whether or not this investment limit has been reached, certain investments made other than in the social enterprise itself are taken into account. These include investments in 51% subsidiaries of the social enterprise, investments in companies that were previously 51% subsidiaries of the social enterprise, and investments in a trade prior to that trade being acquired by the social enterprise or a subsidiary (see *ITA 2007, s 257MNB*).

'*Relevant investments*' have the same meaning as in **23.3** ENTERPRISE INVESTMENT SCHEME (reading references there to a company as including any social enterprise). '*First commercial sale*' has the same meaning as in the EC's Guidelines on State aid to promote risk finance investments. The '*relevant first commercial sale*' is defined in *ITA 2007, s 175A(6)* (as modified by *ITA 2007, s 257MNA(4)*) by reference to the earliest date of any commercial sale made by (broadly) the social enterprise or a 51% subsidiary or any other person who has carried on any trade which is carried on by the social enterprise or a subsidiary. Definitions are suitably modified (by *ITA 2007, s 257MNA(6)*) where the social enterprise is an accredited social impact contractor (as in **65.2** above).

Other cases

Where the investment is made after the end of the seven-year period in (a) above and the condition in (b) above is *not* met, the £1.5 million limit applies as above but with the additional proviso that the amount invested in the social enterprise must not be more than the amount given by:

$$\left(\frac{€200,000 - M}{RCG + RSI}\right) - T$$

where

T = the total in euros of any relevant investments made in the social enterprise in the 'aid period';
M = the total in euros of any de minimis State aid, other than relevant investments, that is granted during the aid period to the social enterprise or to a 'qualifying subsidiary' (see **65.32** below) at a time when it is such a subsidiary;
RCG = the highest rate at which capital gains tax is charged in the aid period; and
RSI = the highest SI rate (see **65.34** below) in the aid period.

The '*aid period*' is the three years ending with the day on which the investment is made. In the case of that day itself, the aid period includes only the part of the day before the investment is made. If the investment or any scheme investments are made, or any aid is granted, in sterling or any other currency that is not the euro, its amount is to be converted into euros at an appropriate spot rate of exchange for the date on which the investment is made or the aid is paid.

[*ITA 2007, ss 257MNA–257MNE; F(No 2)A 2017, Sch 1 paras 6(3), 14(1)(2)*].

Qualifying trade

[65.31] A trade is a '*qualifying trade*' if it is conducted on a commercial basis with a view to the realisation of profits and it does not, at any time in Period B (see **65.1** above), consist to a substantial extent in the carrying on of 'excluded activities'. For these purposes, 'trade' does not include a venture in the nature of trade. '*Excluded activities*' are:

(a) dealing in land, commodities or futures, or in shares, securities or other financial instruments;
(b) banking, insurance, money lending, debt factoring, hire-purchase financing or other financial activities;
(c) (in relation to investments made on or after 6 April 2017) leasing (including letting ships on charter or other assets on hire);
(d) (in relation to investments made on or after 6 April 2017) receiving royalties or licence fees;
(e) (in relation to investments made on or after 6 April 2017) operating or managing nursing homes or residential care homes (both as defined) or managing property used as such;
(f) (in relation to investments made on or after 6 April 2017) generating electricity, exporting electricity or making electricity generating capacity available;
(g) (in relation to investments made on or after 6 April 2017) generating heat;
(h) (in relation to investments made on or after 6 April 2017) generating any form of energy not within (f) or (g);
(i) (in relation to investments made on or after 6 April 2017) producing gas or fuel;
(j) 'property development';

(k) fishery and aquaculture production activities (defined by reference to relevant EU State aid rules);
(l) primary production of agriculture products (which includes both livestock and crops and the production of alcohol from plants and fruit);
(m) (in relation to investments made before 6 April 2017) subsidised generation or export of electricity;
(n) road freight transport for hire or reward; and
(o) providing services or facilities for a business in (a)–(n) which is carried on by another person (other than a parent company), where one person has a 'controlling interest' in both businesses.

In relation to the enterprise investment scheme, HMRC regard as 'substantial' for similar purposes a part of a trade which consists of 20% or more of total activities, judged by any reasonable measure (normally turnover or capital employed), and it seems likely that the same interpretation will apply for the above purposes.

As regards (b) above, the activity of lending money to a social enterprise was not an excluded activity in relation to investment before 6 April 2017.

Exclusion (e) above applies only if the person carrying on the activity has an estate or interest (e.g. a lease) in the property concerned or occupies that property.

For the purposes of (f) and (m) above, electricity is exported if it is exported onto a distribution or transmission system.

'*Property development*' in (j) above means the development of land by a company, which has (or has had at any time) an 'interest in the land' (as defined), with the sole or main object of realising a gain from the disposal of an interest in the developed land.

The exclusion in (m) above referred to the generation or export of electricity in respect of which the company received a feed-in tariff under a UK Government scheme to encourage small-scale low-carbon generation of electricity or a financial incentive granted under a similar overseas scheme.

As regards (o) above, a person has a '*controlling interest*' in a business carried on by a company if (i) he 'controls' (see **65.14** above) the company; or (ii) the company is a close company and he or an 'associate' (see **65.9** above) is a director of the company and the owner of, or able to control, more than 30% of its ordinary share capital; or (iii) at least half the business could, under *CTA 2010, s 942*, be regarded as belonging to him for the purposes of *CTA 2010, s 941* (company reconstructions without change of ownership). In any other case a person has a controlling interest in a business if the person is entitled to at least half of the assets used for, or of the income arising from, the business. In any case, the rights and powers of a person's associates are attributed to him for these purposes.

The Treasury has power to amend the list of excluded activities by statutory instrument. Where any such amendment results in activities ceasing to be excluded, it may have retrospective effect (but not from a date before 6 April 2015).

[*ITA 2007, ss 257MP–257MQA, 257MR–257MT, 257MW; FA 2014, Sch 11 para 1; FA 2015, Sch 6 paras 1, 13, 14; F(No 2)A 2017, Sch 1 paras 10, 12, 15*].

Qualifying subsidiaries

[65.32] In order to be a '*qualifying subsidiary*' a subsidiary must be a '51% subsidiary' (within *CTA 2010, Pt 24 Ch 3*) of the parent, and no person other than the parent or another of its subsidiaries may have 'control' (see **65.14** above) of the subsidiary. No arrangements (as widely defined) may exist by virtue of which either of these conditions would cease to be met.

The above conditions are not regarded as ceasing to be met by reason only of the subsidiary or any other company being wound up or dissolved or by reason only of anything done as a consequence of any such company being in administration or receivership (both as defined by *ITA 2007, s 257TB*), provided the winding-up, dissolution, entry into administration or receivership or anything done as a consequence of its being in administration or receivership is for genuine commercial reasons and is not part of arrangements a main purpose of which is the avoidance of tax. Also, the above conditions are not regarded as ceasing to be met by reason only of arrangements being in existence for the disposal of the interest in the subsidiary held by the parent (or, as the case may be, by another of its subsidiaries) if the disposal is to be for genuine commercial reasons and is not to be part of arrangements a main purpose of which is the avoidance of tax.

[*ITA 2007, ss 257MU, 257TE(1); FA 2014, Sch 11 para 1*].

90% social subsidiaries

[65.33] A company ('*the subsidiary*') is a '*90% social subsidiary*' of another company ('*the parent*') if:

- the subsidiary is a social enterprise;
- the parent possesses at least 90% of both the issued share capital of, and the voting power in, the subsidiary;
- the parent would be beneficially entitled to at least 90% of the assets of the subsidiary available for distribution to equity holders on a winding-up or in any other circumstances;
- the parent is beneficially entitled to at least 90% of any profits of the subsidiary available for distribution to equity holders;
- no person other than the parent has control (see **65.14** above) of the subsidiary; and
- no arrangements (as widely defined) exist by virtue of which any of the above conditions would cease to be met.

For the above purposes, *CTA 2010, Pt 5 Ch 6* applies, with appropriate modifications, to determine the persons who are equity holders and the percentage of assets available to them. Similar let-outs apply as in **65.32** above where a company is wound up or dissolved or enters into administration or receivership or where arrangements exist for the disposal of the interest in the subsidiary.

A company ('company A') which is a subsidiary of another company ('company B') is a 90% social subsidiary of a third company ('company C') if:

- company A is a 90% social subsidiary of company B, and company B is a '100% social subsidiary' of company C; or
- company A is a 100% social subsidiary of company B, and company B is a 90% social subsidiary of company C.

For this purpose, no account is to be taken of any control company C may have of company A, and '*100% social subsidiary*' is defined similarly to '90% social subsidiary' but substituting '100%' for '90%'.

[*ITA 2007, s 257MV; FA 2014, Sch 11 para 1*].

Form of income tax relief

[65.34] Where an individual who is eligible for income tax social investment relief (see **65.3** above) makes a claim for relief, he is entitled to a reduction in his income tax liability for the year in which the investment is made. The claim may be for all or part of the amount invested. The reduction is equal to 30% (the '*SI rate*') of the amount on which relief is claimed for the year, subject to a maximum relief for any year of 30% of £1 million.

For the order in which tax reductions are given against an individual's tax liability see Tolley's Income Tax under Allowances and Tax Rates. A tax reduction must be restricted to the extent (if any) that it would otherwise exceed the individual's remaining income tax liability after making all prior reductions.

As to *when* an investment is made, see **65.1** above.

Carry-back of relief

A claim for income tax social investment relief may be made as if all or part of the amount eligible for relief had been invested in the tax year preceding that in which the investment was, in fact, made. This carry-back is subject to the overriding rule that the total amount of investment on which relief can be obtained for any one year cannot exceed the maximum referred to above. The first year to which relief can be carried back is 2014/15, i.e. where the investment is made in 2015/16.

[*ITA 2007, s 257JA; FA 2014, Sch 11 para 1*].

Attribution of relief to investments

[65.35] Subject to any withdrawal or reduction of relief (see **65.37** onwards below), where an individual's income tax liability is reduced for a tax year as in **65.34** above by reason of one or more 'distinct investments' made (or treated as made) in that year, the tax reduction is attributed to that investment or those investments (being apportioned in the latter case according to the amounts claimed by the investor in respect of each of those investments). A '*distinct investment*' is an investment, made on a single day, in:

(a) a single share or a single 'qualifying debt investment' (see **65.5** above); or

(b) two or more shares, or two or more qualifying debt investments, where the shares or qualifying debt investments are in the same social enterprise and of the same class.

A proportionate amount of the tax reduction attributed to a distinct investment within (b) above is attributed to each of the shares, or qualifying debt investments, concerned. An investment of which part is treated as having been made in the preceding tax year (as in **65.34** above) is treated for these purposes as two separate investments, one made on a day in the preceding year. If bonus shares (in the same company, of the same class, and carrying the same rights) are issued to an investor in respect of any shares to which relief is attributed, the bonus shares are treated as if they had been issued to the investor on the same day as the original shares, and the tax reduction attributed to the original shares is then apportioned between the increased number of shares now held.

[*ITA 2007, s 257N; FA 2014, Sch 11 para 1*].

Claims to relief

[65.36] A claim for relief must be made not earlier than the end of the four-month minimum period at **65.28** above, and not later than the fifth anniversary of 31 January following the tax year in which the investment is made (or, in the case of a carry-back claim as in **65.34** above, in which it is treated as made). The four-month minimum does not apply where the social enterprise is an accredited social impact contractor (see **65.2** above).

The claimant must have received a compliance certificate from the social enterprise before making the claim. The certificate must state that the requirements for relief, except in so far as they fall to be satisfied by the investor, are for the time being fulfilled in relation to the investment. A certificate may not be issued without the authority of an HMRC officer. Where a notice under *ITA 2007, s 257SF* (information to be provided by social enterprise etc. — see Tolley's Income Tax) has been given to HMRC, a compliance certificate must not be issued unless the authority is given or renewed after receipt of the notice. For appeal purposes, an HMRC officer's refusal to authorise a certificate is treated as a decision disallowing a claim by the social enterprise.

Before issuing such a certificate, the social enterprise must supply to HMRC a compliance statement that those requirements are fulfilled for the time being and have been fulfilled at all times since the investment was made. The statement must contain such information as HMRC may reasonably require, and a declaration that it is correct to the best of the social enterprise's knowledge and belief. The statement must be provided to HMRC within two years after the end of the tax year in which the investment was made (or, if the four-month minimum period at **65.28** below ends in a subsequent tax year, within two years after the end of that four-month period). The statement cannot be provided to HMRC before the four-month minimum period (where applicable) expires.

References above to requirements being fulfilled for the time being are, in the case of requirements that cannot be fulfilled until a future date, references to nothing having occurred to prevent their being fulfilled.

If a certificate or statement is made fraudulently or negligently, or a certificate is issued despite being prohibited (as above), the social enterprise is liable to a penalty of up to £3,000.

No application for postponement of tax pending appeal can be made on the ground that relief is due under these provisions unless a claim has been duly submitted.

[*ITA 2007, ss 257P–257PE; FA 2014, Sch 11 para 1*].

Withdrawal or reduction of relief

[65.37] The following provisions apply to withdraw or reduce income tax social investment relief in certain circumstances. References to a reduction of relief include its reduction to nil, and references to the withdrawal of relief in respect of an investment are to the withdrawal of the relief attributable to that investment (see **65.35** above). Where no relief has yet been given, a reduction applies to reduce the amount which would otherwise be available for relief, and a withdrawal means the investment ceases to be eligible for relief.

For the procedure for withdrawing or reducing relief see Tolley's Income Tax.

Disposal of investment

[65.38] The rules below apply where the investor disposes of the whole or part of an investment to which income tax social enterprise relief is attributable (see **65.35** above) before the end of Period B (see **65.1** above). Reference to a 'disposal', in relation to any shares or other investments, includes a disposal of an interest or right in or over them.

If the disposal is at arm's length, the relief attributable to the investment is normally withdrawn. However, if that relief exceeds an amount equal to tax at the SI rate (see **65.34** above), for the tax year for which the relief was obtained, on the disposal consideration, the relief is instead reduced by that amount. If the disposal is not at arm's length, the relief is always withdrawn.

Where the relief attributable to the investment is less than tax at the SI rate on the amount on which relief is claimed, the amount referred to in (a) above is correspondingly reduced. Where the relief attributable has been reduced (otherwise than as a result of an issue of bonus shares — see **65.35** above) before the relief was obtained, then in calculating the amount referred to in (a) above, the gross relief attributable to the investment before that reduction is used.

If the investor grants an option the exercise of which would bind him to sell the whole or part of the investment, the grant of the option is treated for the above purposes as a disposal. Relief is also withdrawn where, during Period A (see **65.1** above), an option is granted to the investor, the exercise of which would bind the grantor to purchase the whole or part of the investment; where applicable. there are rules for identifying the part of an investment to which an option relates.

These provisions do not apply to a disposal occurring as a result of the investor's death. See **65.44** below for transfers of shares between spouses or civil partners.

[*ITA 2007, ss 257R–257RC, 257TE; FA 2014, Sch 11 para 1*].

Identification rules

For the above purposes, disposals are identified with investments of the same class made on an earlier day before those made on a later day (i.e. first in/first out (FIFO)). Investments made on the same day are treated as disposed of in the following order:

(i) firstly, investments to which neither social investment income tax relief nor social investment capital gains deferral relief (see **65.46** below) is attributable;
(ii) next, those to which capital gains deferral relief, but not income tax relief, is attributable;
(iii) next, those to which income tax relief, but not capital gains deferral relief, is attributable; and
(iv) finally, any to which both income tax relief and capital gains deferral relief are attributable.

Any investment within (iii) or (iv) above which is treated as issued on an earlier day by virtue of the carry-back provisions at **65.34** above is to be treated as disposed of before any other investment within the same category. Investments transferred between spouses or civil partners living together are treated as if they were acquired by the transferee spouse or partner on the day they were made (see also **65.44** below). Shares comprised in a 'new holding' following a reorganisation to which *TCGA 1992, s 127* applies (see **63.2** SHARES AND SECURITIES) are treated as having been acquired when the original shares were acquired.

[*ITA 2007, s 257TA; FA 2014, Sch 11 para 1*].

Value received by investor

[65.39] If the investor receives value (other than an insignificant receipt) from the social enterprise at any time in Period A (see **65.1** above), any income tax social investment relief given in respect of the investment is normally withdrawn. However, if that relief exceeds an amount equal to tax at the SI rate (see **65.34** above), for the tax year for which the relief was given, on the value received, the relief is instead reduced by that amount.

[*ITA 2007, ss 257Q–257QI; FA 2014, Sch 11 para 1*].

For full details of the provisions see Tolley's Income Tax.

Repayments etc. of share capital to other persons

[65.40] If social investment relief is attributable (see **65.35** above) to the whole or any part of an investment and, at any time in Period A (see **65.1** above), the social enterprise or any 'subsidiary':

(a) repays, redeems or repurchases any of its share capital which belongs to any member other than:
   (i) the investor; or
   (ii) a person whose relief is thereby withdrawn or reduced by virtue of **65.38** or **65.39**(a) above; or
(b) makes any payment to any such member for giving up his right to any of the share capital of the social enterprise or subsidiary on its cancellation or extinguishment,

the relief is normally withdrawn. If, however, the relief exceeds an amount equal to tax at the SI rate (see **65.34** above), for the tax year for which the relief was obtained, on the sum received by the member, the relief is instead reduced by that amount. There is an exception for insignificant payments.

[*ITA 2007, ss 257QJ–257QP; FA 2014, Sch 11 para 1*].

For full details of the provisions see Tolley's Income Tax.

Acquisition of trade or trading assets

[65.41] Income tax social enterprise relief attributable to an investment (see 65.5 above) is withdrawn if, at any time in Period A (see **65.1** above), the social enterprise or any qualifying subsidiary (see **65.32** above), begins to carry on as its trade, business or profession (or part), a trade etc. (or part) previously carried on at any time in that period otherwise than by the social enterprise or a qualifying subsidiary, or acquires the whole or the greater part of the assets used for a trade etc. previously so carried on, and the investor is a person who, or one of a group of persons who together, either:

(a) owned at any time in Period A more than a half share in the trade etc. previously carried on, and also own or owned at any such time such a share in the trade etc. carried on by the social enterprise; or
(b) 'control' (see **65.14** above), or at any time in Period A have controlled, the social enterprise, and also, at any such time, controlled another company which previously carried on the trade etc.

In determining, for the purposes of (a) above, the ownership of a trade and, if appropriate, the shares owned by multiple owners, *CTA 2010, s 941(6)* and *s 942* apply. For those purposes, interests etc. of 'associates' (see **65.9** above) are taken into account.

There are special rules relating to shares held by certain directors of, or of a partner of, the social enterprise or any subsidiary.

[*ITA 2007, s 257QQ; FA 2014, Sch 11 para 1*].

Acquisition of share capital

[65.42] Income tax social enterprise relief attributable to an investment (see 65.35 above) is withdrawn if:

- the social enterprise, at any time in Period A (see **65.1** above), comes to acquire all the issued share capital of another company; and

- the investor is a person, or one of a group of persons, who control (see **65.14** above) or has, at any time in Period A, controlled the social enterprise and who also, at any such time, controlled the other company.

There are special rules relating to investments held by certain directors of, or of a partner of, the social enterprise or any subsidiary.

[*ITA 2007, s 257QR; FA 2014, Sch 11 para 1*].

Relief subsequently found not to have been due

[65.43] Income tax social investment relief is withdrawn if it is subsequently found not to have been due. Relief cannot be withdrawn on the ground that the conditions at **65.16–65.30** above relating to the social enterprise are not met unless:

(a) the social enterprise has given notice under the social investment relief information provisions (see Tolley's Income Tax); or
(b) an HMRC officer has given notice to the social enterprise of his opinion that the whole or part of the relief was not due because of the ground in question.

The social enterprise may appeal against an HMRC notice as in (b) above as though it were the refusal of a claim.

[*ITA 2007, ss 257QS, 257SA; FA 2014, Sch 11 para 1*].

Married persons and civil partners

[65.44] The provisions for withdrawal of relief on the disposal of investments to which income tax social investment relief is attributable (see **65.37** above) do not apply to transfers between spouses or civil partners living together. On any subsequent disposal or other event, the spouse or partner to whom the investment was transferred is treated as if:

- he or she were the person who made the investment;
- his or her liability to income tax had been reduced in respect of the investment by the same amount, and for the same tax year, as applied on the making of the investment by the transferor spouse or partner; and
- that amount of social investment relief had continued to be attributable to the investment despite the transfer.

Where the amount of relief attributable to the investment had been reduced before the relief was obtained by the transferor spouse or partner, the transferee is treated as if his or her relief had been correspondingly reduced before it was obtained.

Any assessment for withdrawing or reducing relief is made on the transferee spouse or partner. The identification rules for disposals at **65.38** above apply to determine the extent (if any) to which investments to which relief is attributable are comprised in the transfer.

[*ITA 2007, ss 257R(1)(d), 257T, 257TA(1); FA 2014, Sch 11 para 1*].

Capital gains tax

[65.45] See also **65.46** below for deferral relief.

In determining the gain or loss on a disposal of an asset to which any income tax social enterprise income tax relief is attributable (see **65.35** above):

(a) if a loss would otherwise arise, the consideration the individual is treated as having given for the asset is treated as reduced by the amount of the relief;
(b) if the disposal is after the end of the three years beginning with the day the individual acquired the asset, and a gain would otherwise arise, the gain is not a chargeable gain (although this does not prevent a loss arising in these circumstances from being an allowable loss).

Where social enterprise income tax relief was not given on the full amount invested (other than by reason of the income tax liability being insufficient to support the relief), the capital gains tax exemption in (b) above is restricted to a proportion of the gain. This will usually be because the individual's social enterprise investments exceeded the annual maximum on which relief is available (see **65.34** above). The exempt gain is the proportion of the gain found by applying the multiple A/B where:

A = the income tax relief given; and
B = tax at the SI rate (see **65.34** above), for the tax year for which the relief was obtained, on the amount invested in the asset.

Where, because of (b) above, a gain (or part of a gain) on a disposal would not be a chargeable gain, but the income tax relief on the asset disposed of is reduced on account of value received from the company by the claimant or by other persons (see **65.39**, **65.40** above) before the disposal, then a corresponding proportion of the gain is chargeable. This rule applies after applying any restriction on the exemption where the maximum income tax relief was not originally obtained.

[*TCGA 1992, ss 255B–255D; FA 2014, Sch 12 para 2*].

Identification rules

The normal identification rules (see **64.2** SHARES AND SECURITIES — IDENTIFICATION RULES) are each disapplied as regards assets to which income tax social investment relief is attributable. Instead, the rules described at **65.38** above apply to match disposals with acquisitions of shares of the same class in the same company, and they apply where at least some of those shares have attracted SEIS income tax relief. [*TCGA 1992, s 255B(4)(6); FA 2014, Sch 12 para 2*].

Reorganisations of share capital

Where income tax social investment relief has been given on some shares in a particular company but not others and there is a reorganisation within the meaning of *TCGA 1992, s 126*, then *TCGA 1992, s 127* (see **63.2** SHARES AND

SECURITIES) applies separately as regards the shares attracting and not attracting relief so that, in each case, the new shares will stand in the place of the old shares. A distinction is also made, as regards shares attracting income tax relief, between those (if any) to which deferral relief (see **65.46** below) is attributable and those to which it is not, and the separate treatment described above also applies to each of those two categories.

Rights issues

If, immediately following a rights issue, EIS relief is attributable either to the original holding or the rights shares, the share reorganisation rules of *TCGA 1992, ss 127–130* (see **63.2** SHARES AND SECURITIES) are disapplied, with the result that the rights shares are treated as a separate acquisition.

[*TCGA 1992, s 255E(1)–(4); FA 2014, Sch 12 para 2*].

Company reconstructions

If as part of a reconstruction, shares or debentures in another company are issued to a shareholder in exchange for shares to which income tax social investment relief remains attributable, then the shares in the new company are not generally deemed to stand in the place of shares in the old company under *TCGA 1992, s 135* or *s 136* (see **63.5**, **63.7** SHARES AND SECURITIES) and there is thus a disposal of the shares in the old company. However, *section 135* or *136* does apply in the normal way if:

- the new holding consists of new ordinary shares issued after the end of the three years beginning with the day the individual acquired the original shares and which meet conditions A and B at **65.5** above; and
- the company issuing the new shares has previously issued shares eligible for income tax social investment relief and has issued the appropriate compliance certificate (see **65.33** above) enabling investors to obtain relief on that issue.

[*TCGA 1992, s 255E(5)–(7); FA 2014, Sch 12 para 2*].

Capital gains deferral relief

[65.46] If an amount equal to the amount of a chargeable gain is invested in a social enterprise within a specified time then the individual making the gain and the investment may claim for the gain be treated as accruing when the investment is disposed of and not at an earlier time.

This deferral relief applies where:

(a) a chargeable gain accrues to an individual on the disposal of any asset or on the occurrence of a chargeable event within (3) or (4) below or an aggregate chargeable gain is deemed to arise as in **24.8** ENTREPRENEURS' RELIEF (but only to the extent that the deemed gain would not be chargeable to capital gains tax at the 10% rate);
(b) the individual makes an investment on his own behalf in a social enterprise on which he is eligible for social investment income tax relief;
(c) the gain accrues on or after 6 April 2014 and before 6 April 2019;

(d) the individual is UK resident both when the gain accrues and when he makes the investment; and
(e) the investment is made during the three years beginning with the day the gain accrues or during the twelve months immediately preceding that day.

Deferral relief also applies if:

(i) a gain accrues as a result of a chargeable event within (1)–(3) below;
(ii) the chargeable event is the disposal to a social enterprise of shares in or debentures of the enterprise or the cancellation, extinguishment, redemption or repayment by a social enterprise of its shares or debentures;
(iii) as part of the chargeable event or in connection with it, and in place of the shares or debentures, the investor acquires one or more assets from the social enterprise, being shares in or debentures of the enterprise and the investor suffers no detriment in return for the acquisition of those shares or debentures (other than ceasing to hold the original shares or debentures);
(iv) but for **65.6** above (consideration for acquisition to be wholly in cash and fully-paid) the investor would be eligible for social investment income tax relief in respect of consideration given for the assets thus acquired; and
(v) conditions (c) to (e) above are met by reference to the above-mentioned acquisition.

For the purposes of (i)–(v) above, 'debenture' includes any instrument creating or acknowledging indebtedness.

Where (a)–(e) above apply, the investor may make a claim for the chargeable gain to be reduced by the amount invested or by a smaller amount specified in the claim. Where (i)–(v) above apply, the investor may make a claim for the gain to be reduced to the extent specified in the claim. The reduction may not be more than the original gain or, if the gain has already been reduced under these provisions or as a result of a claim for deferral relief under the ENTERPRISE INVESTMENT SCHEME (**23.14**) or the SEED ENTERPRISE INVESTMENT SCHEME (**60.45**), the reduced gain.

The total of all such reductions claimed for any tax year cannot exceed £1 million.

Claims

Subject to what is said at **13.2** CLAIMS regarding claims being included in a self-assessment tax return if possible, there is no statutory form in which a claim *must* be made. The provisions for income tax relief claims (see **65.36** above) are applied, with modifications, to deferral relief claims. Thus, a deferral relief claim cannot be made earlier than the end of the four-month minimum period referred to at **65.36** above and cannot be made later than the fifth anniversary of 31 January following the tax year in which the shares were issued. A claim cannot be made until, with the authority of HMRC, the company has furnished the individual with a compliance certificate to the effect that, from its point of view, the conditions for deferral relief are satisfied.

Attribution of relief to assets

Relief is attributable to the asset or assets acquired as in (b) or (iii) above. Relief ceases to be attributable to any particular asset (or any part of an asset) when a chargeable event (see below) occurs in relation to it or the person holding it dies.

Deferred gain becoming chargeable

The deferred gain will become chargeable when any of the chargeable events listed below occurs (without any chargeable event having previously occurred) in relation to the '*social holding*' (i.e. the assets acquired as in (b) or (iii) above). If a chargeable event occurs in relation to part only of the social holding (without any chargeable event having previously occurred in relation to that part) only a proportion of the deferred gain becomes chargeable. The proportion is found by attributing a proportionate part of the deferred gain (as reduced by any previous application of this rule) to each part of the social holding held immediately before the chargeable event by the investor or by a person who has acquired it from the investor on a transfer between spouses or civil partners within *TCGA 1992, s 58*.

A chargeable event occurs in relation to an asset forming the whole or any part of the social holding if (after the acquisition of the holding):

(1) the investor disposes of the asset otherwise than by a transfer between spouses or civil partners within *TCGA 1992, s 58*;
(2) the asset is disposed of, otherwise than by a disposal to the investor, by a person who acquired it by a transfer between spouses or civil partners within *TCGA 1992, s 58*;
(3) the asset is cancelled, extinguished, redeemed or repaid; or
(4) any of the eligibility conditions for income tax social enterprise relief (see **65.4–65.29** above) fails to be met.

For this purpose, references above to an asset include a part of an asset.

Where the chargeable event is within (1) or (2) above, the deferred gain is treated as accruing to the person making the disposal. Where (3) or (4) above apply, the gain is treated as accruing to the person who held the asset, or part, when the chargeable event occurs.

Nothing which occurs at or after the time of the investor's death or the death of a person who acquired the whole or part of a social holding by a transfer between spouses or civil partners within *TCGA 1992, s 58* is a chargeable event.

Identification rules

In determining whether any assets of a particular class disposed of are assets to which deferral relief is attributable, the normal identification rules (see **64.2** SHARES AND SECURITIES — IDENTIFICATION RULES) are disapplied and, instead, the same rules as in **65.38** above apply (broadly, first in/first out but with special rules where shares acquired on the same day fall into different specified categories).

Where at the time of the chargeable event, any asset that formed the whole or part of the social holding is regarded under capital gains tax legislation as represented by assets which consist of or include assets other than that asset, the deferred gain attributable to that asset is to be apportioned between those other assets on a just and reasonable basis. As between different assets regarded as representing the same asset, the identification of those assets follows the same identification rules as above. For this purpose, the deferred gain attributable to an asset is found by attributing a proportionate part of the gain to each asset forming the whole or part of the social holding held, immediately before the chargeable event, by the investor or a person who acquired any part of the social holding from the investor by a transfer between spouses or civil partners within *TCGA 1992, s 58*.

[*TCGA 1992, s 255A, Sch 8B; FA 2014, Sch 12 paras 2, 3*].

66

Substantial Shareholdings of Companies

Introduction	**66.1**
Minor definitions	**66.2**
The exemptions	**66.3**
Exemption for shares	**66.3**
Exemption for assets related to shares	**66.4**
Exemption where main conditions previously met	**66.5**
Exemption: qualifying institutional investors	**66.6**
Anti-avoidance	**66.7**
'Substantial shareholding' requirement	**66.8**
Meaning of substantial shareholding	**66.8**
Holding period	**66.9**
Requirements to be met by investing company — disposals prior to April 2017	**66.10**
Requirements relating to investee company	**66.12**
Share reorganisations etc	**66.14**
Effect of earlier company reconstruction etc.	**66.15**
Effect of earlier demerger	**66.16**
Treatment of holdings in joint venture companies (JVCs)	**66.17**
Consequential rules	**66.18**
Degrouping charge	**66.18**
Negligible value claims	**66.19**
Reorganisation involving qualifying corporate bond	**66.20**
Held-over gains on gifts of business assets	**66.21**
FOREX matching regulations	**66.22**
Miscellaneous	**66.23**
Key points	**66.25**

Simon's Taxes. See **D1.10**.

Introduction

[66.1] A gain on a disposal by a company of shares is exempt (and a loss is not allowable) where, throughout a continuous twelve-month period beginning not more than six years before the disposal (not more than two years before, for disposals prior to 1 April 2017), the company (the '*investing company*') held a 'substantial shareholding' (broadly and usually, at least a **10%** interest) in the company (the '*investee company*') whose shares are the subject of the disposal. The exemption extends to assets related to shares (as in **66.4** below).

The investee company must be a trading company or the holding company of a trading group (or subgroup), and, for disposals prior to 1 April 2017 only, the investing company must be a trading company or a member of a trading group. Shares held by members of a worldwide group are aggregated in determining whether a company holds a substantial shareholding.

As indicated above, a number of changes are made to the conditions which must be met for the substantial shareholdings exemption to apply, with effect for disposals on or after 1 April 2017. The changes include a specific exemption (see **66.6** below) which applies where the investee company is not a trading company but the *investing company* is owned by qualifying institutional investors (as defined). In such a case a full or partial exemption may apply depending on the level of ownership by such investors, and the substantial shareholding condition may be met if the investing company's shareholding is below a 10% interest but cost more than £20 million (see **66.8**).

[*TCGA 1992, s 192A, Sch 7AC; FA 2002, s 44(1)–(3), Sch 8 para 1; F(No 2)A 2017, ss 27, 28*].

For HMRC's own coverage of these provisions, see HMRC Capital Gains Manual CG53000–53240. For clearance applications see **30.3** HMRC — ADMINISTRATION, and, before April 2008, HMRC Brief 41/2007.

The exemptions are of no application to a disposal the gain (or loss) on which would, by virtue of some other enactment, not be a chargeable gain (or an allowable loss). Neither do they apply to a disposal which, by virtue of any chargeable gains enactment, is a no gain/no loss disposal. [*TCGA 1992, Sch 7AC para 6(1); FA 2012, Sch 16 para 88(2)*].

Minor definitions

[66.2] For the purposes of these provisions, a '*company*' is as defined at **29.2** GROUPS OF COMPANIES. A '*group of companies*' is also as defined at **29.2** but as if each reference there to '75%' were a reference to '51%'. Thus, subject to the detailed rules there, a '*group*' comprises a company and its effective '51% subsidiaries' (within *CTA 2010, Pt 24 Ch 3*), and may include non-UK resident companies. A '*holding company*' of a group is the principal company of the group (within the meaning given in **29.2**). A '*subgroup*' is a number of companies that *would* form a group were it not for the fact that one of them (the '*holding company*' of the subgroup) is itself a 51% subsidiary. [*TCGA 1992, Sch 7AC para 26; Co-operative and Community Benefit Societies Act 2014, Sch 4 para 53; FA 2014, Sch 39 para 7*].

The exemptions

Exemption for shares

[66.3] A gain accruing to a company (the '*investing company*') on a disposal of shares (or an interest in shares — see **66.24** below) in another company (the '*investee company*') is not a chargeable gain if:

(a) the investing company held a 'substantial shareholding' (see **66.8** below) in the investee company throughout any continuous period of twelve months beginning not more than **six** years prior to the disposal (12 months beginning not more than **two** years prior to the disposal, for disposals prior to 1 April 2017) (see **66.9** below);

(b) the investing company meets the requirements at **66.10** below for disposals prior to 1 April 2017 only; and

(c) the requirements at **66.12** below are met in relation to the investee company.

See also the anti-avoidance rule at **66.7** below.

[*TCGA 1992, Sch 7AC paras 1, 7, 28; F(No 2)A 2017, s 27(2)(3)(6)*].

By virtue of *TCGA 1992, s 16(2)* (see **25.2** EXEMPTIONS AND RELIEFS), a loss on a disposal is not an allowable loss if a gain on that disposal would not have been a chargeable gain.

The nature of the condition at (a) above is such that part disposals out of a once-substantial shareholding can continue to attract the exemption for up to five years (one year for disposals prior to 1 April 2017) after the shareholding has ceased to be substantial.

Note that the exemption is available even where the shares disposed of are not the shares that meet the substantial shareholding requirement at (a) above. If (a) above is met in relation to ordinary shares (and (b) and (c) above are also met as necessary), a disposal of a holding of, say, fixed-rate preference shares in the investee company will qualify for the exemption, irrespective of the size and duration of that holding (HMRC Capital Gains Manual CG53155).

The exemption is automatic and does not require the making of a claim.

A disposal of shares qualified in full for the exemption in *Williamson Tea Holdings Ltd v HMRC* FTT, [2010] SFTD 1101 even though part of the consideration was given in return for the taxpayer company entering into a non-competition agreement.

Example

Martin Ltd is a trading company with 20,000 issued shares. In 2009, 3,000 of the shares are acquired by Steve Ltd. Steve Ltd then sells 1,200 of the shares on 31 July 2012, 800 of the shares on 30 June 2017 and the remaining 1,000 shares on 31 August 2017. Steve Ltd meets the requirements for an investing company as necessary for the first disposal. The exemption applies as follows.

Disposal on 31 July 2012

Steve Ltd has held at least 10% of the ordinary share capital throughout the period from acquisition in 2009 to disposal on 31 July 2012. The exemption applies.

Disposal on 30 June 2017

Steve Ltd holds only 9% of the shares in Martin Ltd on 30 June 2017. There is, however, a twelve month period beginning within the six years immediately before the disposal throughout which it held at least 10% of the shares. That is the period 1 August 2011 to 31 July 2012. The exemption applies.

Disposal on 31 August 2017

Steve Ltd holds only 5% of the shares in Martin Ltd on 31 August 2017. In the six years prior to that date (i.e. 1 September 2011 to 31 August 2017), Steve Ltd held at least 10% of the shares only in the period 1 September 2011 to 31 July 2012. As this period is less than twelve months, the exemption does not apply.

Exemption for assets related to shares

[66.4] A gain accruing to a company (Company A) on a disposal of an asset 'related to shares' in another company (Company B) is not a chargeable gain (and a loss is not an allowable loss) if:

- at the time of the disposal, Company A holds shares (or an interest in shares — see **66.24** below) in Company B; and
- any gain on a disposal at that time of those shares (or that interest) would be exempt under **66.3** above (disregarding *TCGA 1992, Sch 7AC para 6(1)* at **66.1** above).

This exemption also applies where:

- the shares etc. are held not by Company A itself but by another member of a group of companies (see **66.2** above) of which Company A is a member; and
- any gain on a disposal at that time of those shares etc., on the assumption that they were held by Company A, would be exempt under **66.3** above (disregarding *TCGA 1992, Sch 7AC para 6(1)* at **66.1** above).

Where assets of a company are vested in a liquidator, the above applies as if they were vested in the company and as if the acts of the liquidator were the acts of the company (disposals by the company to the liquidator, and vice versa, being disregarded).

See also the anti-avoidance rule at **66.7** below.

[*TCGA 1992, Sch 7AC paras 2, 6(2)*].

The exemption is automatic and does not require the making of a claim.

For this purpose, an asset is '*related to shares*' in a company if it is:

(a) an option to acquire or dispose of shares (or an interest in shares — see **66.24** below) in that company; or
(b) (broadly) a security that is convertible or exchangeable into shares (or an interest in shares) in that company, or into an option within (a) above, or into another security within this definition; or
(c) an option to acquire or dispose of a security within (b) above (or an interest in any such security); or
(d) an interest in, or option over, any option or security within (a)–(c) above; or
(e) an interest in, or option over, any interest or option within (d) above (or an interest in, or option over, any interest or option within this sub-paragraph).

As regards (b) above, a convertible or exchangeable security is not an asset related to shares if when the conversion etc. rights were granted there was no more than a negligible likelihood that they would be exercised to any significant extent. Therefore, it is not possible to bring a security within the scope of the exemption by attaching some spurious or extremely remote rights to convertibility in the event of some unlikely occurrence (HMRC Capital Gains Manual CG53010).

Note that certain securities, options etc. are outside the scope of corporation tax on chargeable gains, and thus outside the exemptions in this chapter, due to their falling within the special rules for loan relationships, derivative contracts etc. (see HMRC Capital Gains Manual CG53010).

An '*interest*' in a security or option has a similar meaning to an 'interest in shares' at **66.24** below.

[*TCGA 1992, Sch 7AC para 30*].

Exemption where main conditions previously met

[66.5] A further possibility of exemption is provided where either of the exemptions at **66.3** or **66.4** above does not apply because some of the conditions were not satisfied at the time of the disposal even though they *had been* satisfied at a time in the two years immediately preceding the disposal.

A gain accruing to a company (Company A) on a disposal of shares (or an interest in shares — see **66.24** below), or an asset related to shares (see **66.4** above), in another company (Company B) is not a chargeable gain (and a loss is not an allowable loss) if the conditions at **66.3** or **66.4** above, whichever is relevant, are not fully met (with the result that a chargeable gain or allowable loss would otherwise arise on the disposal) *but all* of the following conditions *are* met.

(a) At the time of disposal, Company A had held a 'substantial shareholding' (see **66.8** below) in Company B throughout any continuous period of twelve months beginning not more than six years (two years, for disposals prior to 1 April 2017) prior to the disposal (see also **66.9** below).
(b) At the time of disposal, either Company A is UK-resident or any chargeable gain accruing to it on the disposal would form part of its corporation tax profits by virtue of *TCGA 1992, s 10B* (trade carried on via UK permanent establishment — see **49.3** OVERSEAS MATTERS).
(c) There was a time within the two years ending with the disposal (the '*relevant period*') when a gain on a hypothetical disposal by:
   - Company A, or
   - a company that at any time in the relevant period was a member of the same group (see **66.2** above) as Company A,

   being a disposal of shares (or an interest in shares) in Company B that the disposing company then held, would have been exempt under **66.3** above (disregarding *TCGA 1992, Sch 7AC para 6(1)* at **66.1** above, and see also below).

(d) If, at the time of disposal, the requirements at **66.12** below as to the investee company are not met in relation to Company B, there was a time within the relevant period (as defined at (c) above) when Company B was controlled by:
- Company A; or
- Company A together with any persons connected with it (within *TCGA 1992, s 286* — see **17** CONNECTED PERSONS); or
- a company that at any time in the relevant period was a member of the same group (see **66.2** above) as Company A; or
- any such company together with persons connected with it.

'Control' is to be construed in accordance with *CTA 2010, ss 450, 451*.

In the case of disposals prior to 1 April 2017 only, if the exemption at **66.3** or **66.4** above is not available for the sole reason that the investing company fails to meet the requirement at **66.10**(b) below (as to its status immediately after the time of the disposal), this further possibility of exemption is available only if the failure is due to the actual or imminent winding-up or dissolution of the investing company (provided that, in a case where this is imminent, it actually takes place as soon as is reasonably practicable in the circumstances).

For the purpose only of determining the 'relevant period' for the purposes of (c) or (d) above, the time of disposal is taken as the time the contract is made, notwithstanding that the contract may be conditional. In determining whether the gain on the hypothetical disposal in (c) above would have attracted the exemption at **66.3** above, the requirements at **66.12**(b) below as to the status of the investee company immediately after the time of disposal are taken to be satisfied. For disposals prior to 1 April 2017, the requirements at **66.10**(b) below as to the status of the investing company immediately after the time of disposal are also taken to be satisfied.

See also the anti-avoidance rule at **66.7** below.

[*TCGA 1992, s 288(1), Sch 7AC para 3(1)–(4)(7)(8), para 6(2); F(No 2)A 2017, s 27(2)(6)*].

Thus, for example, where the investee company ceases to trade on being put into liquidation, so that it can no longer meet the requirements at **66.12** below, disposals by the investing company (including capital distributions — see **63.11** SHARES AND SECURITIES) can continue to attract the exemption for a further two years.

It should be noted, however, that the above exemption also contains an anti-avoidance element in that if, for example, the investee company's trade is transferred elsewhere (within a group, for instance) and the conditions above are all met, a loss on a disposal by the investing company within the two years following the transfer will not be an allowable loss.

A further anti-avoidance measure applies as follows to prevent the exemption from applying where value has been transferred into the investee company within the said two-year period. Where the above exemption would otherwise apply but:

(i) immediately before the disposal by Company A, Company B holds an asset; and

(ii) the allowable expenditure attributable to that asset has been reduced by a claim for gifts hold-over relief under *TCGA 1992, s 165* (see **36.2** HOLD-OVER RELIEFS) on an earlier disposal of the asset within the relevant period (as defined above),

a gain on the disposal by Company A does not attract the exemption *but* a loss on the disposal is not an allowable loss. (Where assets of Company B are vested in a liquidator, (i) above applies as if they were vested in the company.)

[*TCGA 1992, Sch 7AC para 3(5)(6)*].

The exemption is automatic and does not require the making of a claim.

Exemption: qualifying institutional investors

[66.6] For disposals on or after 1 April 2017, a full or partial exemption (see below) applies in respect of a gain accruing to an investing company on the disposal of shares in an investee company, if the *investing company* is fully or partially owned by 'qualifying institutional investors' and if:

(a) the investing company held a substantial shareholding (as modified — see **66.8** below) in the investee company throughout a period of 12 months beginning not more than six years prior to the disposal (the substantial shareholder requirement);
(b) the investee company does *not* meet the requirements at **66.12** below; and
(c) the investing company is not a 'disqualified listed company'.

Certain bodies would usually be exempt from tax in their own right, if they had owned the shares in a non-trading investee company directly. This exemption gives relief where such shares are held indirectly by a 'qualifying institutional investor' through an investing company. Specifically, a *'qualifying institutional investor'* is defined as any of the following persons (regulations may amend this list):

(a) the trustee or manager of a registered pension scheme (not an investment-regulated scheme as defined in *FA 2004, Sch 29A*) or an overseas pension scheme as per *FA 2004, Part 4*;
(b) a company carrying on life assurance business under *FA 2012, s 56*, where immediately before the disposal, the company's shareholding in the investing company is part of the company's long-term business fixed capital as defined by *FA 2012, s 137*;
(c) a person not liable for corporation tax or income tax because of sovereign immunity (sovereign wealth funds etc);
(d) a charity;
(e) an investment trust;
(f) an authorised investment fund under *SI 2006 No 964* meeting the genuine diversity of ownership condition;
(g) the trustees of an exempt unauthorised unit trust meeting the genuine diversity of ownership condition (*SI 2006 No 964*).

A '*disqualified listed company*' is a company with any ordinary share capital listed on a recognised stock exchange, which is not a qualifying institutional investor itself, and which is not a qualifying UK REIT. A qualifying UK REIT for these purposes is a UK REIT as per *CTA 2010, Part 12* which is not treated as a close company because it is controlled by or on behalf of the Crown (*CTA 2010, s 443*), or is a close company only because it has an institutional investor as a participator. The list of institutional investors is not the same as, although similar to, that above for qualifying institutional investors and is given by *CTA 2010, s 528(4A)*.

In determining the proportion of the investing company's ordinary shares owned by qualifying institutional investors, both direct and indirect holdings are taken into account in accordance with the rules set out in *CTA 2010, ss 1155–1157*, but with modifications. It is not possible to trace ownership through a disqualified listed company but it is possible to trace ownership through an exempt unauthorised unit trust (as per *SI 2013 No 2819*), which is treated as a body corporate for these purposes. For these purposes, under a repurchase agreement or stock lending arrangements (see **66.9** below), the original owner of the shares is regarded as owning them. Shares held by a partnership are treated as being owned by each partner in accordance with that partner's proportionate interest in the shares.

Amount of the exemption

The exemption applies in full i.e. no chargeable gain or allowable loss accrues to an investing company on the disposal of shares in an investee company, if qualifying institutional investors own 80% or more of the ordinary share capital of the *investing* company immediately before the disposal.

If qualifying institutional investors own at least 25% but less than 80% of the ordinary share capital of the investing company immediately before the disposal, the amount of the chargeable gain or loss is reduced by the percentage owned by such investors. For example, if two qualifying institutional investors together hold 75% of the investing company, the latter's gain on disposing of a holding in the investee company is reduced by 75% i.e. the investing company pays tax on only 25% of the gain. A similar rule applies to reduce allowable losses.

[*TCGA 1992, Sch 7AC paras 3A, 3B, 30A, 31; F(No 2)A 2017, s 28(2)(5)(7)*].

Anti-avoidance

[66.7] None of the exemptions in **66.3–66.6** above are available where:

(a) an 'untaxed' gain accrues to an investing company (Company A) on a disposal of shares (or an interest in shares — see **66.24** below), or an asset related to shares (see **66.4** above), in another company (Company B); and

(b) before the accrual of that gain, either:
   - Company A acquired control of Company B, or the same person(s) acquired control of both companies; or
   - there was a 'significant change of trading activities affecting Company B' at a time when it was controlled by Company A or when both companies were controlled by the same person(s);

and these circumstances occur in pursuance of arrangements (as very widely defined) from which the sole or main benefit that could be expected is that the gain would be exempt under any of **66.3–66.6** above.

For the above purposes:

(i) a gain is '*untaxed*' if it (or all but an insubstantial part of it) represents profits that have not been brought into account (in the UK or elsewhere and including profits apportioned to a UK resident company under the controlled foreign company rules — see **49.9** OVERSEAS MATTERS) for the purposes of tax on profits for a period ending on or before the date of the disposal; 'profits' means income or gains (including unrealised income or gains);

(ii) 'control' is to be construed in accordance with *CTA 2010, ss 450, 451*; and

(iii) there is a '*significant change of trading activities affecting Company B*' if:
- there is a 'major change in the nature or conduct of a trade' carried on by Company B or a 51% subsidiary of Company B; or
- there is a major change in the scale of the activities of a trade carried on by Company B or a 51% subsidiary; or
- Company B or a 51% subsidiary begins to carry on a trade.

By virtue of *CTA 2010, s 673*, a '*major change in the nature or conduct of a trade*' includes a major change in the type of property dealt in or services or facilities provided, or in customers, outlets or markets. Some of the circumstances which may amount to a major change are set out in HMRC Statement of Practice 10/91 (covered at **29.29** GROUPS OF COMPANIES).

[*TCGA 1992, s 288(1), Sch 7AC para 5*].

HMRC expect cases where this anti-avoidance rule is in point to be unusual and infrequent. It is a question of fact as to whether a gain wholly (or wholly but for an insubstantial part of it — interpreted by them as 20% or less) represents untaxed profits; this involves looking at how the consideration obtained for the disposal by Company A is derived from assets held directly or indirectly by Company B. Profits are not 'untaxed' if they are simply covered by a specific relief or if they represent dividends which are themselves paid out of taxed profits. If a gain represents both taxed and untaxed profits, it should be taken as first representing taxed profits, with only the balance representing untaxed profits. See HMRC Statement of Practice SP 5/02, 29 October 2002.

'Substantial shareholding' requirement

Meaning of substantial shareholding

[66.8] A company holds a '*substantial shareholding*' in another company if it holds shares (or interests in shares — see **66.24** below) in that company by virtue of which:

- it holds at least 10% of the company's ordinary share capital;
- it is beneficially entitled to at least 10% of the profits available for distribution to equity holders of the company; and

- it would be beneficially entitled on a winding-up to at least 10% of the assets of the company available for distribution to equity holders.

CTA 2010, Pt 5 Ch 6 applies, with suitable modifications, to define an 'equity holder' and to determine the profits or assets available for distribution.

[*TCGA 1992, Sch 7AC para 8; SI 2010 No 2902*].

Additionally, for disposals on or after 1 April 2017, where qualifying institutional investors own at least 25% of the ordinary share capital of the investing company (see **66.6** above), the investing company also holds a 'substantial shareholding' if it holds ordinary shares (or interests in ordinary shares) in the investee company that cost it at least £20 million (in one or over several acquisitions), whether representing a 10% interest or not. The shares (or any other shares in the investee company) must give the investing company beneficial entitlement to a percentage of profits and assets on a winding up at least equal to that percentage of ordinary shares held by the investing company, although this condition is treated as met if a shortfall is insignificant. This alternative way to satisfy the substantial shareholding condition is not restricted to the exemption at **66.6** above but can apply in respect of the other exemptions of *TCGA 1992, Sch 7AC*, but only where the investing company is owned at least 25% by qualifying institutional investors.

[*TCGA 1992, Sch 7AC para 8A; F(No 2)A 2017, s 28(3)(7)*].

For the purposes of deciding whether the 'substantial shareholding' test is satisfied, holdings of shares (and interests in shares) by members of the same group of companies (which may be a worldwide group — see **66.2** above) are aggregated. [*TCGA 1992, Sch 7AC para 9(1)*].

Where assets of the investing company, or of a member of the same group as the investing company, are vested in a liquidator, they are treated for the purposes of the substantial shareholding requirement (and those of **66.15**, **66.16** below) as if they were vested in the company and as if the acts of the liquidator were the acts of the company (disposals by the company to the liquidator, and vice versa, being disregarded). [*TCGA 1992, Sch 7AC para 16*].

Special rules apply in relation to assets held for the purposes of long-term insurance business where the investing company is an insurance company, or in certain cases a 51% subsidiary of an insurance company, or a member of the same group as an insurance company. [*TCGA 1992, Sch 7AC paras 9(2), 17; FA 2012, Sch 16 para 88*].

Holding period

[66.9] As stated at **66.3**(a) above, the investing company must have held a substantial shareholding in the investee company throughout a continuous period of twelve months beginning not more than six years prior to the disposal (two years, for disposals prior to 1 April 2017). Shares are treated as having been held for such a period if, for example, they were acquired at any time on 15 June 2016 and sold at any time on 14 June 2017; they do not have to be held on the anniversary of the acquisition (HMRC Capital Gains Manual CG53008). The following special rules apply.

No gain/no loss transfers

Where the investing company acquired any shares from another company by means of a no gain/no loss transfer, i.e. under any chargeable gains enactment that states that a disposal is to be treated as made for such consideration that no gain or loss accrues, the period during which it is treated as holding those shares is extended to include the period during which the previous owner held them. The period is further extended back through any series of no gain/no loss transfers by which the shares arrived in the hands of the present owner. The present owner is treated as having had the same entitlements, to shares and to any rights enjoyed by virtue of holding shares, as the company or companies by which they were held at any earlier time in the extended period. These include any entitlements etc. arising from the aggregation rule for groups of companies in **66.8** above. These rules also cover interests in shares (see **66.24** below), and the extension also covers any period during which the asset held by any of the previous companies concerned in the no gain/no loss series consisted of shares (or an interest in shares) from which the current shares (or interest) are 'derived'.

For the above purposes, any transfer falling within **29.3**(xii) GROUPS OF COMPANIES (intra-group share exchanges), and which would otherwise have been a no gain/no loss transfer within *TCGA 1992, s 171*, is treated as if it had been a no gain/no loss transfer. For disposals on or after 1 April 2017, a transfer between non-UK resident group companies even where the shares are not chargeable assets of the transferor company immediately before transfer or of the transferee company immediately after transfer, but which would otherwise have been a no gain/no loss transfer within *TCGA 1992, s 171*, is treated as a no gain/no loss transfer.

Shares (or interests in shares) are '*derived*' from other shares (or interests) only where:

- a company becomes co-owner of shares previously owned by it alone, or vice versa;
- a company's interest in shares as co-owner changes (but co-ownership continues);
- a shareholding is treated by virtue of *TCGA 1992, s 127* (including its application by virtue of another enactment — see, for example, **63.2**, **63.5**, **63.7**) as the same asset as another shareholding; or
- there is a sequence of two or more of the above occurrences.

[*TCGA 1992, Sch 7AC para 10; F(No 2)A 2017, s 27(4)(6)*].

> ***Example***
>
> X Ltd has a wholly-owned subsidiary, Y Ltd. On 1 April 2016 X Ltd buys 20% of the ordinary share capital of Z Ltd. On 1 March 2017 X Ltd transfers its Z Ltd shares to Y Ltd. On 30 September 2017 Y Ltd sells the shares.
>
> The transfer of the Z Ltd shares on 1 March 2017 is a no gain/no loss transfer under *TCGA 1992, s 171* (see **29.3** GROUPS OF COMPANIES). In determining whether, therefore, the substantial shareholding exemption applies to Y Ltd's sale of the

Z Ltd shares on 30 September 2017, Y Ltd is treated as holding the shares throughout the period 1 April 2016 to 30 September 2017.

Deemed disposals and reacquisitions

Where, under any corporation tax enactment, shares have been deemed to be disposed of and immediately reacquired by a company, the company is regarded as not having held the shares during any part of the holding period falling before the deemed disposal and reacquisition. This rule extends to interests in shares (see **66.24** below) and to shares (or interests) from which the current shares (or interest) are 'derived' (as above). [*TCGA 1992, Sch 7AC para 11*].

Sale and repurchase agreements (repos)

Where the company that holds shares transfers them under a repo (as defined), such that, by virtue of *FA 2007, Sch 13 para 6* or *TCGA 1992, s 263A* (see **63.26** SHARES AND SECURITIES), the disposal falls to be disregarded, it is similarly disregarded for the purposes of the provisions in this chapter. Thus, during the period covered by the repo, the ownership of the shares, and the entitlement to any rights attached to them, rests with the original owner and not the interim holder. If, at any time during that period, the original owner, or a member of the same group (see **66.2** above) as the original owner, becomes the *actual* holder of any of the shares transferred (or any shares directly or indirectly representing them), this rule ceases to have effect at that time in relation to the shares concerned.

[*TCGA 1992, Sch 7AC para 12*].

Stock lending arrangements

Rules identical to those above for repos apply where shares are transferred under a stock lending arrangement (as defined), such that, by virtue of *TCGA 1992, s 263B(2)* (see **63.25** SHARES AND SECURITIES), the disposal falls to be disregarded. [*TCGA 1992, Sch 7AC para 13*].

Transfer of trading assets within a group

The period in which the investing company is treated as holding a substantial shareholding in the investee company is extended if the following conditions are met:

(1) immediately before the disposal the investing company holds a substantial shareholding in the investee company;
(2) an asset which, at the time of the disposal, is being used for the purposes of a trade carried on by the investee company was transferred to it by the investing company or another company;
(3) at the time of the transfer company the investee company, the investing company and, where relevant, the company transferring the asset were all members of the same group (as in **66.2** above); and
(4) the asset was previously used by a member of the group, other than the investee company, for the purposes of a trade carried on by it at a time when it was such a member.

Where these conditions are satisfied, the investing company is treated as having held the substantial shareholding at any time during the twelve months ending with the time of disposal when the asset was used as in (b) above if it did not otherwise hold a substantial shareholding at that time.

For disposals on or after 1 April 2014, 'trade' in (2) and (4) includes oil and gas exploration and appraisal (within *CTA 2010, s 1134*).

[*TCGA 1992, Sch 7AC para 15A; FA 2014, s 72*].

Requirements to be met by investing company — disposals prior to April 2017

[66.10] The conditions for the exemption at **66.3** above are modified for disposals on or after 1 April 2017; in particular, there are no requirements to be met by the investing company. For disposals prior to 1 April 2017 only, the requirements to be met by the investing company for the purposes of the exemption at **66.3** above are that:

(a) it must have been a sole 'trading company' (see **66.11** below) or a member of a 'qualifying group' (see below) throughout the period:
  - beginning with the start of the latest twelve-month period (within the two years prior to disposal) for which the substantial shareholding requirement (see **66.3**(a) above) was met; and
  - ending with the time of the disposal; and

(b) it must be a sole 'trading company' or a member of a 'qualifying group' immediately after the time of the disposal.

A '*qualifying group*' is a 'trading group' (see **66.11** below) or a group that would be a trading group if the activities of any group member not established for profit were disregarded to the extent that they are carried on otherwise than for profit. In determining whether a company is established for profit, any object or power which is merely incidental to the company's main objects is to be ignored.

The requirement at (a) above is met if the company was a sole trading company for part of the said period and a member of a qualifying group for the rest of it.

Where the disposal is made under a contract and, by virtue of *TCGA 1992, s 28* (see **16.4** COMPUTATION OF GAINS AND LOSSES), the time of disposal for tax purposes precedes the conveyance or transfer of the asset disposed of, the requirements at both (a) and (b) above must be met by reference to the time of conveyance or transfer as well the time of the disposal.

The requirement at (a) above is treated as met if, at the time of the disposal (and, where relevant, the time of the conveyance or transfer):

- the investing company is a member of a group (as in **66.2** above); and
- the requirement is not met by that company but would have been met by another group member if, immediately before the disposal, the subject matter of the disposal had been transferred to that member under the no gain/no loss provisions of *TCGA 1992, s 171* (see **29.3** GROUPS OF COMPANIES) and that member had then made the disposal.

[*TCGA 1992, Sch 7AC para 18; F(No 2)A 2017, s 27(2)(6)*].

[66.11] For the purposes of this chapter, a '*trading company*' is a company whose activities do not include to a 'substantial' extent activities other than 'trading activities'. A '*trading group*' is a group (as in **66.2** above), one or more of whose members carry on 'trading activities' and the activities of whose members, taken together, do not include to a 'substantial' extent activities other than 'trading activities'. '*Substantial*', in this connection, is taken by HMRC to mean 'more than 20%' (Revenue Tax Bulletin December 2002 p 985). Depending on the facts of the case, this measure may be applied to turnover, expenditure and/or time spent by officers and employees where one or more of these items relate partly to non-trading activities, and/or to non-trading assets as a proportion of all assets (either of which may possibly include intangible assets such as goodwill). The fact that a company has investment income does not necessarily bring the 20% test into play. If it can be shown that holding the investment is integral to the conduct of the trade or is a short-term lodgement of surplus funds held to meet demonstrable trading liabilities, the investment is unlikely to be seen as evidence of a non-trading purpose. An investment outside these categories still has the safety net of the 20% test. As regards *property* owned by the company but surplus to immediate business requirements, HMRC do not *necessarily* regard any of the following as indicating a non-trading purpose:

- letting part of the trading premises;
- letting properties no longer required for the trade and intended to be sold eventually;
- subletting property where it would be impractical or uneconomic to assign or surrender the lease;
- acquiring property, whether vacant or already let, with the provable intention of bringing it into use for the purpose of the trade.

In relation to a single company, '*trading activities*' means 'activities' carried on by the company:

(a) in the course of, or for the purposes of, a 'trade' being carried on by it; or
(b) for the purposes of a 'trade' that it is preparing to carry on; or
(c) with a view to its acquiring or starting to carry on a trade; or
(d) with a view to its acquiring a 'significant interest' in the share capital of another company that is itself a trading company or the holding company (as in **66.2** above) of a trading group or 'trading subgroup' (see **66.13** below) and that is not already a member of the same group as the acquiring company.

'*Activities*' is interpreted by HMRC to mean what a company does, and thus the expression in itself includes engaging in trading activities, making and holding investments, planning, holding meetings and so forth (Revenue Tax Bulletin December 2002 p 984). '*Trade*' means any trade, profession or vocation conducted on a commercial basis with a view to profit. It also comprises the commercial letting of FURNISHED HOLIDAY ACCOMMODATION (**26**). Activities qualify under (c) or (d) above only if the acquisition is made, or the trade commenced, as soon as is reasonably practicable in the circumstances. A company acquires a '*significant interest*' (see (d) above) if it acquires sufficient ordinary share capital in the other company to make that company its 51% subsidiary (within *CTA 2010, Pt 24 Ch 3*), or to give the acquiring company a qualifying shareholding in a joint venture company (see **66.17** below) without making the two companies members of the same group.

In relation to a group, '*trading activities*' means activities carried on by a member of the group, being activities that would fall within (a)–(d) above if these are interpreted by reference not only to that member but also to any other member of the group. The activities of group members are regarded as a single business, so that intra-group activities are disregarded. A group member acquires a '*significant interest*' (see (d) above) if it acquires sufficient ordinary share capital in the other company to make that company a member of the same group as the acquiring company, or to give the acquiring company a qualifying shareholding in a joint venture company.

[*TCGA 1992, Sch 7AC paras 20, 21, 26(4), 27*].

Many of the expressions used above are considered further in Revenue Tax Bulletin December 2002 pp 982–987. Before 19 July 2006, a company could ask its tax district to give a view on its status for the above purposes, but any opinion expressed was subject to revision to the extent that it related to a time for which the full facts were not yet available.

See **66.17** below as regards the treatment of holdings in joint venture companies.

Requirements relating to investee company

[66.12] The requirements to be met in relation to the investee company for the purposes of the exemption at **66.3** above are that:

(a) it must have been a 'qualifying company' (see below) throughout the period:
  - beginning with the start of the latest twelve-month period for which the substantial shareholding requirement (see **66.3**(a) above) was met; and
  - ending with the time of the disposal; and

(b) it must be a 'qualifying company' immediately after the time of the disposal, in the case of disposals prior to 1 April 2017 and in certain limited circumstances (see below) for disposals on or after that date.

A '*qualifying company*' is a 'trading company' (see **66.11** above) or the holding company (as in **66.2** above) of a 'trading group' (see **66.11** above) or 'trading subgroup' (see **66.13** below).

Where the conditions at **66.9**(2)–(4) above (transfer of trading asset within a group) are satisfied in relation to a disposal, then, for the purposes of (a) above, the investee company is treated as having been a trading company at any time during the twelve months ending with the disposal when the asset concerned was used as in **66.9**(2) above.

In the case of disposals on or after 1 April 2017, the requirement at (b) above needs to be met only if the disposal is to a person connected with the investing company, or if the substantial shareholding holding period at **66.9** above is met because of the transfer of trading assets within the group as described in **66.9** above. For these purposes *CTA 2010, s 1122* applies for the meaning of 'connected persons'. In other circumstances for disposals on or after 1 April 2017, the investee company does not need to be a qualifying company immediately after the disposal.

Where the disposal is made under a contract and, by virtue of *TCGA 1992, s 28* (see **16.4** COMPUTATION OF GAINS AND LOSSES), the time of disposal for tax purposes precedes the conveyance or transfer of the asset disposed of, the requirements at both (a) and (b), where necessary, above must be met by reference to the time of the conveyance or transfer as well as the time of the disposal.

[*TCGA 1992, Sch 7AC para 19; F(No 2)A 2017, s 27(5)(6)*].

[66.13] For the purposes of this chapter, a '*trading subgroup*' is a subgroup (as in **66.2** above), one or more of whose members carry on 'trading activities' and the activities of whose members, taken together, do not include to a 'substantial' extent (see **66.11** above) activities other than 'trading activities'. '*Trading activities*' are defined in relation to a subgroup as they are in relation to a group (for which see **66.11** above), with the appropriate modifications; the activities of subgroup members are regarded as a single business, so that intra-subgroup activities are disregarded, but this does not extend to activities between a member of the subgroup and a company that is a member of the main group but not the subgroup (Revenue Tax Bulletin December 2002 p 983).

[*TCGA 1992, Sch 7AC para 22*].

It is worth noting that it is possible to have a trading subgroup within an otherwise non-trading group. See **66.17** below as regards the treatment of holdings in joint venture companies.

Share reorganisations etc.

[66.14] Without the special rules below, the exemptions at **66.3–66.6** above would be of no relevance to any of the following events (in relation to shares held by the investing company in the investee company).

(a) A reorganisation of share capital, company take-over/reconstruction or conversion of securities which, by virtue of *TCGA 1992, s 127*, does not constitute a disposal (see **63.2**, **63.5**, **63.7**, **63.8** SHARES AND SECURITIES), the 'new holding' standing in the shoes of the original shares.

(b) An event which would have been within (a) above but for the fact that the 'new asset' consists of a qualifying corporate bond and which, by virtue of *TCGA 1992, s 116(10)*, is not treated as a disposal (see **54.4** QUALIFYING CORPORATE BONDS).

(c) A tax-exempt distribution on a demerger which, by virtue of *TCGA 1992, s 192* (see **14.12** COMPANIES), does not constitute a capital distribution within **63.11** SHARES AND SECURITIES).

To the extent that a gain would thereby be exempt (or a loss non-allowable) under **66.3–66.6** above, the enactment mentioned in (a), (b) or (c) above, whichever is relevant, is disapplied, so that an event in (a) or (b) is treated as a disposal, a distribution in (c) is treated as a capital distribution and the new shares or securities are normally treated as acquired at market value. This disapplication does not, however, have effect if the result would be a withdrawal or reduction (under *FA 2000, Sch 15 para 46*) of investment relief under the CORPORATE VENTURING SCHEME (**18.10**). Where it does have effect, the provisions at **18.23** CORPORATE VENTURING SCHEME, where relevant, are modified accordingly.

[*TCGA 1992, Sch 7AC para 4*].

HMRC have provided illustrations of how these and related provisions operate in two different types of intra-group transaction and also in relation to a share exchange outside a group in CG53170a.

Effect of earlier company reconstruction etc.

[66.15] The following applies where:

(a) shares held by the investing company in the investee company were acquired as a result of either:
    (i) an exchange of securities within *TCGA 1992, s 135* (see **63.5** SHARES AND SECURITIES); or
    (ii) a scheme of reconstruction within *TCGA 1992, s 136* (see **63.7** SHARES AND SECURITIES); and
(b) *TCGA 1992, s 127* (see **63.2** SHARES AND SECURITIES) applied, such that the event was not treated as a disposal and the 'new holding' stood in the shoes of the original shares; and
(c) *TCGA 1992, s 127* did not fall to be disapplied by **66.14** above (because, for example, the conditions for the exemptions at **66.3–66.6** above were not satisfied or the event took place before 1 April 2002).

The question of whether, at any time *before* the event in (a)(i) or (ii) above, the substantial shareholding requirement at **66.8** above was met, or the requirements relating to the investee company at **66.12** above were met, is determined by reference to the shares held by the investing company at that time. This rule can apply more than once, i.e. where there has been more than one event within (a)(i) or (ii) above, and it can apply in combination with the rule at **66.16** below where there have been one or more transfers within that paragraph as well as one or more events within (a)(i) or (ii) above.

[*TCGA 1992, Sch 7AC paras 14, 25*].

Example

On 1 October 2016 Prosser Ltd acquires 40% of the ordinary share capital of Cooper Ltd. On 30 April 2017 Cooper Ltd is acquired by Oyster Ltd, Prosser Ltd receiving Oyster Ltd shares in exchange for its Cooper Ltd shares. As a result, Prosser Ltd holds 12% of the ordinary share capital of company Y.

> The substantial shareholding exemption is not available at the time of the share exchange because Prosser Ltd did not hold the Cooper Ltd shares for at least twelve months. Instead *TCGA 1992, s 127* applies so that there is no disposal and no acquisition and the Oyster Ltd shares are treated as the same asset as the Cooper Ltd shares.
>
> If on 30 September 2017 Prosser Ltd sells its shares in Oyster Ltd, the period over which the substantial shareholding requirement and the investee company requirements must be satisfied for exemption to apply is 1 October 2016 to 30 September 2017. The tests must be determined by reference to the Cooper Ltd shares in the period 1 October 2016 to 30 April 2017 and by reference to the Oyster Ltd shares from 30 April 2017 to 30 September 2017.

Effect of earlier demerger

[66.16] The following applies where:

- shares held by the investing company in the investee company were acquired as a result of a transfer by a parent company of shares in its subsidiary; and
- the demerger provisions of *TCGA 1992, s 192* applied (see **14.12** COMPANIES), such that the transfer was not treated as a capital distribution and the transferred shares in the subsidiary fell to be treated as received as a result of a reorganisation of share capital and thus (by virtue of *TCGA 1992, s 127*) as standing in the shoes of the shares previously held in the parent company.

The question of whether, at any time *before* the transfer, the substantial shareholding requirement at **66.8** above was met, or the requirements relating to the investee company at **66.12** above were met, is determined by reference to the shares held by the investing company at that time. This rule can apply more than once, i.e. where there has been more than one such transfer, and it can apply in combination with the rule at **66.15** above where there have been one or more events within that paragraph as well as one or more transfers within this paragraph.

[*TCGA 1992, Sch 7AC paras 15, 25*].

Treatment of holdings in joint venture companies (JVCs)

[66.17] For the following purposes, a company is a '*joint venture company*' (JVC) if (and only if):

(i) it is a 'trading company' (see **66.11** above) or the holding company (as in **66.2** above) of a 'trading group' (see **66.11** above) or 'trading subgroup' (see **66.13** below); *and*

(ii) there are five or fewer persons who between them hold **75% or more** of its ordinary share capital (within *CTA 2010, s 1119*) (counting members of a group of companies, as in **66.2** above, as if they were a single company).

The following provisions apply only where a company has a 'qualifying shareholding' in a JVC. A company has a '*qualifying shareholding*' in a JVC if (and only if):

(a) it is a sole company (i.e. not a member of a group) and it holds shares, or an interest in shares (see **66.24** below), in the JVC by virtue of which it holds **10% or more** of the JVC's ordinary share capital, or
(b) it is a member of a group, the group members between them hold 10% or more of the ordinary share capital of the JVC *and* the company itself holds part of that ordinary share capital.

Where the above conditions are satisfied, definitions of 'trading company', 'trading group' and 'trading subgroup' have effect with the modifications in (1)–(3) below. Where the JVC is itself a 'holding company' (as in **66.2** above), the references in (1), (2) and (3) below to its activities are to the activities (other than intra-group activities) of the JVC and its '51% subsidiaries' (within *CTA 2010, Pt 24 Ch 3*). Each reference below to a holding of shares in a JVC includes securities of the JVC or an interest in shares in, or securities of, the JVC.

(1) In determining whether a company with a qualifying shareholding in a JVC is a 'trading company' (see **66.11** above), its holding of shares in the JVC is disregarded. It is treated as carrying on a share of the JVC's activities proportionate to its percentage shareholding in the JVC. This does not apply if the company and the JVC are members of the same group of companies.
(2) In determining whether a group, of which a company with a qualifying shareholding in a JVC is a member or is the holding company, is a 'trading group' (see **66.11** above), there is disregarded any holding of shares in the JVC by any member of the group which has a qualifying shareholding in the JVC. Each such member is treated as carrying on a share of the JVC's activities proportionate to its percentage shareholding in the JVC. This does not apply if the JVC is itself a member of the group.
(3) In determining whether a company with a qualifying shareholding in a JVC is the holding company of a 'trading subgroup' (see **66.13** above), there is disregarded any holding of shares in the JVC by the company and by any of its 51% subsidiaries which itself has a qualifying shareholding in the JVC. The company and each such subsidiary is treated as carrying on a share of the JVC's activities proportionate to its percentage shareholding in the JVC. This does not apply if the JVC is a member of the same group as the company.

[*TCGA 1992, Sch 7AC paras 23, 24, 26(4)*].

HMRC consider that where a group has an interest in a joint enterprise not falling within the above definition of a 'joint venture company' it is not necessarily the case that that interest must be treated as a non-trading activity. Whether it represents part of the group's overall trading activities will be a question of fact and will depend on the circumstances of the case. Similar considerations apply to an interest in an entity that does not have issued share capital. (HMRC Brief 29/2011, 2 August 2011).

Consequential rules

Degrouping charge

[66.18] See **29.9** GROUPS OF COMPANIES for interaction between the exemptions in this chapter and the charge where a company ceases to be a member of a 75% group of companies and has had an asset transferred to it by another group member within the preceding six years.

Negligible value claims

[66.19] Where:

- a company makes a negligible value claim under *TCGA 1992, s 24(2)* (see **44.11** LOSSES) in respect of an asset; and
- by virtue of the provisions in this chapter, a loss on a disposal of that asset at the time of the claim would not be an allowable loss,

the consequent deemed disposal and reacquisition is regarded as taking place at the time of the claim and cannot be backdated to an earlier time. Thus, in these circumstances, a negligible value claim cannot result in an allowable loss. [*TCGA 1992, Sch 7AC para 33*].

Reorganisation involving qualifying corporate bond

[66.20] Where, on a reorganisation of share capital, the 'new asset' consists of a qualifying corporate bond (see **54.4** QUALIFYING CORPORATE BONDS), the exemptions in this chapter do not apply to or affect the chargeable gain or allowable loss deemed to accrue under *TCGA 1992, s 116(10)(b)* on a subsequent disposal of the whole or part of the new asset. This does not apply if the 'reorganisation' was, in fact, a deemed disposal and reacquisition within *FA 1996, s 92(7)* (asset ceasing to be a 'convertible security' but continuing to be a creditor relationship of the company — see **15.7**(i) COMPANIES — CORPORATE FINANCE AND INTANGIBLES). [*TCGA 1992, Sch 7AC para 34; SI 2010 No 614, Art 2*].

Note that the above is of no application where the reorganisation has itself been treated as an exempt disposal by virtue of **66.14** above.

Held-over gains on gifts of business assets

[66.21] Where:

(a) a company disposes of an asset;
(b) the allowable expenditure attributable to that asset would have been greater were it not for a claim for gifts hold-over relief under *TCGA 1992, s 165* (see **36.2** HOLD-OVER RELIEFS) having been made in respect of an earlier disposal; and
(c) by virtue of the provisions in this chapter, any gain on the disposal in (a) above would not be a chargeable gain,

the amount of the held-over gain is treated as a gain accruing to the company at the time of the disposal in (a) above and as being a gain which is outside the exemptions in this chapter. If the disposal in (a) above is a part disposal, only an appropriate proportion of the held-over gain becomes chargeable on that occasion. [*TCGA 1992, Sch 7AC para 37*].

FOREX matching regulations

[66.22] No gain or loss is treated as arising under the provisions for matching of foreign exchange differences on foreign currency assets with loan relationships or derivative contracts on a disposal on which any gain would be exempt under the provisions in this chapter — see **15.3** COMPANIES — CORPORATE FINANCE AND INTANGIBLES.

Miscellaneous

[66.23] The question of whether an asset is a chargeable asset for the purposes of corporation tax on chargeable gains generally is to be determined without regard to the availability, or potential availability, of the exemptions covered in this chapter, and references throughout this book to 'chargeable assets' should be read accordingly. [*TCGA 1992, Sch 7AC para 32*].

[66.24] For the purposes of this chapter, an '*interest in shares*' is an interest as a co-owner of shares (whether they be owned jointly or in common and whether the interests of the co-owners are equal or disparate). [*TCGA 1992, Sch 7AC para 29*].

Key points

[66.25] Points to consider are as follows.

- If the conditions are satisfied for the exemption to apply, a gain is exempt even on shares that have only been held for a short time. For example, a trading company holds 10% of the shares in another trading company for the requisite period, then acquires the other 90% of the shares. A few days later, 50% of the shares are sold as a gain. The whole gain is exempt, even though the majority of the shares had only been held for a few days. See **66.3**.
- Where the conditions for exemption have previously been met, and a disposal would be at a loss, it may be worth considering whether the disposal can be delayed by just over 2 years, in order to get outside the scope of *TCGA 1992, Sch 7AC para 3*. See **66.5**.
- The liquidation scenario in **66.5** appears to be interpreted by HMRC as meaning that the exemption is available to the disposal by a holding company of its last trading subsidiary (or sub-group), so long as the holding company will then be wound up. This does not accord with the wording of the legislation and some care needs to be taken before relying on HMRC's interpretation. See **66.5**.
- The anti-avoidance rule at *TCGA 1992, Sch 7AC para 5* is of limited scope and is rarely applicable in practice. See **66.7**.
- The words 'by virtue of' in the 10% substantial shareholding requirement can be crucial. If a company owns 100% of the shares of a subsidiary as well as, say, a convertible loan note of

that subsidiary, it could be that all the assets of the subsidiary would pass to the parent under the terms of the loan note, not the share capital. In that case, the parent is not beneficially entitled to the assets of the subsidiary by virtue of its substantial shareholding and the test is failed. See **66.8**.

- The mere holding of cash, for example, the consideration of a disposal of a subsidiary, is not generally considered by HMRC to be an activity. Therefore, it is unlikely that holding cash will constitute a non-trading activity. See **66.11**.
- It is important to remember that the 20% test of substantial, in the context of substantial non-trading activity, is only HMRC's opinion and will not necessarily be upheld by the Tribunals or the Courts. Equally, HMRC does not consider the 20% to be a safe harbour, either. Even if the various measures do not exceed 20% non-trading activity, it is possible that a more holistic view of the position would suggest that a company does not qualify as trading. See **66.11**.
- It is recommended that you review the case law on trading activities in cases of doubt. See **66.10–66.13**.
- In many cases, HMRC will disregard transactions or arrangements between a sub-group and the vendor group where these are being unwound as part of the disposal. For example, a sub-group might contain a company that holds the group's trading properties, and that non-trading activity might exceed 20% of the activities of the sub-group as a whole. If those arrangements are unwound as part of the disposal – say, the properties are sold to the vendor group before the disposal – HMRC will not consider the rental income to taint the trading status of the target sub-group. See **66.13**.

67

Time Limits — Fixed Dates

Introduction	**67.1**
Time limits of one year or less	**67.2**
One-year ten-month (approx.) time limits (and equivalent two-year time limits for companies)	**67.3**
Two-year time limits	**67.4**
Two-year ten-month (approx.) time limits	**67.5**
Three-year time limits	**67.6**
Three-year ten-month (approx.) time limits	**67.7**
Four-year time limits	**67.8**
Other action before 6 April 2018	**67.9**

Cross-references. See also **13.5** CLAIMS; **68** TIME LIMITS — MISCELLANEOUS.

Introduction to time limits: fixed dates

[67.1] This chapter lists fixed date time limits (for capital gains tax) falling in the **twelve months to 30 September 2018**. It also notes time limits for corporation tax on chargeable gains where these are dependent upon the company's accounting date (see also Tolley's Corporation Tax).

Exercise of HMRC discretion

The legislation dealing with certain claims and elections allows the time limit to be extended at the discretion of the Commissioners of HMRC but where this is not the case the Commissioners may make an extension by exercising its collection and management powers. Cases in which they would do so are limited but there would be a presumption in favour of admitting a late claim where there had been a relevant error on the part of HMRC, and the claim is made shortly after the error has been drawn to the taxpayer's attention; where the taxpayer has given clear notice of his intention to claim, but before the time limit expires he has not completed any statutory requirement or specified the claim in sufficient detail; or where the reason for the delay in making the claim was clearly beyond the taxpayer's control (e.g. because he – or in the case of a company the only individual who had the relevant information and experience – was seriously ill and there was no-one else who could reasonably be expected to stand in his shoes). The same stance seems to be taken as regards the withdrawal of elections that are stated to be irrevocable. Claims that have not become final may be withdrawn (even after the time for making a claim has expired), and the same applies to elections that are not irrevocable. (HMRC Capital Gains Manual CG13800–13850).

Time limits of one year or less

[67.2] Time limits of one year or less are as follows:

(a) **5 October 2017** for action in respect of **2016/17.**
Chargeability to tax. A person chargeable to CGT for a tax year must, unless he has received a tax return for completion, notify HMRC, within six months after the end of that year, that he is so chargeable. See **52.3** PENALTIES.

(b) **31 October 2017** for action in respect of **2016/17.**
Self-assessment. Tax returns other than electronic returns must be delivered on or before 31 October following the tax year to which it relates. See **58.3** RETURNS.

(c) **Nine months from end of company accounting period.**
Payment of tax. Payment of corporation tax in respect of chargeable gains is normally required by the day following the expiry of nine months from the end of the accounting period if interest on unpaid tax is to be avoided. ('Large' companies must pay by instalments.) See **51.4** PAYMENT OF TAX.

(d) **31 January 2018** for action in respect of **2016/17.**
   (i) *Returns.* A person other than a company who has received a self-assessment tax return for completion and is filing electronically must generally do so on or before 31 January following the tax year to which it relates. See **58.3** RETURNS.
   (ii) *Payment of tax.* CGT is normally due on or before 31 January following the year of assessment. See **51.2** PAYMENT OF TAX.

(e) **5 April 2018** for action in respect of **2016/17.**
   (i) *Claims following late assessments.* A claim (including a supplementary claim) which could not have been allowed but for the making of an assessment to CGT after the tax year to which it relates or the making of an HMRC amendment to a self-assessment issued as part of an enquiry closure notice (see **58.12** RETURNS), may be made at any time before the end of the tax year following that in which the assessment or amendment was made. See **13.5** CLAIMS.
   (ii) *Claims following discovery assessments.* Where a discovery assessment is made otherwise than to make good a loss of tax brought about carelessly or deliberately, a relevant claim, election etc. can be made, revoked or varied within a year after the end of the tax year (or company accounting period) in which the assessment was made. The provisions apply also to an HMRC amendment to a self-assessment issued as part of an enquiry closure notice (see **58.12** RETURNS). See **13.5** CLAIMS.
   (iii) *Tax over-repaid.* This (and any associated excess repayment supplement) may be recovered by the end of the tax year (or company accounting period) following that in which the repayment was made, where the normal time limit for assessment has expired. This deadline is extended in the event of an HMRC enquiry into a self-assessment tax return. See **51.31** PAYMENT OF TAX.

(iv) *Capital payments made by an overseas resident settlement.* Broadly, trustees of overseas resident settlements must distribute capital gains no later than the end of the tax year following that in which the gains arose if a supplementary CGT charge under *TCGA 1992, s 91* on UK resident beneficiaries is to be avoided. See **48.21** OFFSHORE SETTLEMENTS for the detailed rules.

(f) **Twelve months from end of company accounting period.**

(i) *Chargeability to tax.* A company chargeable to corporation tax for an accounting period must, unless it has received notice to file a return for that period, notify HMRC, within twelve months after the end of that period, that it is so chargeable. See **58.19** RETURNS.

(ii) *Corporation tax returns.* A company must generally comply with a notice to make a corporation tax return within twelve months of the end of the relevant accounting period or, if later, within three months of service of the notice. See **58.19** RETURNS.

One-year ten-month (approx.) time limits (and equivalent two-year time limits for companies)

[67.3] That is, for CGT, action in respect of **2015/16** must be taken on or before **31 January 2018** (and for the purposes of corporation tax on chargeable gains, where applicable, action must be taken within two years after the end of the accounting period in question).

(a) **Quoted shares and securities held on 6 April 1965: companies only.** Election for adoption of 6 April 1965 values for quoted securities (within either of the two categories) that were held on that date, where the first relevant disposal since 19 March 1968 took place during a particular company accounting period must be made within two years after the end of that accounting period. With respect to disposals after 31 March 1985 the foregoing is to be read as if '31 March 1985' were substituted for '19 March 1968'. See **8.3** ASSETS HELD ON 6 APRIL **1965**. An election is only relevant if the rules for ASSETS HELD ON 31 MARCH **1982** (**9**) do not apply.

(b) **Miscellaneous disposals of assets held on 6 April 1965: companies only.** Election for adoption of 6 April 1965 value of miscellaneous assets (apart from quoted investments and UK land disposed of for a consideration including development value) disposed of must be made within two years after the end of the company accounting period in which the disposal was made. See **8.8** ASSETS HELD ON 6 APRIL **1965**. An election is only relevant if the rules for ASSETS HELD ON 31 MARCH **1982** (**9**) do not apply.

(c) **Assets held on, and gains arising before, 31 March 1982: companies only.** The latest time for making an irrevocable election for universal re-basing at 31 March 1982 is two years after the end of the company accounting period in which 'the first relevant disposal' occurs. See **9.3** ASSETS HELD ON 31 MARCH **1982**. A claim for 50% relief in taxing deferred charges on gains before 31 March 1982 must be made within two years after the end of the company accounting period in which the disposal or deferred gain in question occurs or accrues. See **9.11** ASSETS HELD ON 31 MARCH **1982.**

(d) **Loss relief for subscribing individual shareholders.** A claim for a loss arising in a tax year on a disposal of qualifying unlisted shares by a subscriber to be set against his income of that year or the preceding year must be made on or before the first anniversary of 31 January following the year in which the loss is incurred. See **44.15** LOSSES.

(e) **Furnished holiday accommodation.** A claim for 'averaging' of let periods of holiday accommodation must be made on or before the first anniversary of 31 January following the relevant tax year (or within two years after the end of the relevant company accounting period). See **26.1** FURNISHED HOLIDAY ACCOMMODATION.

(f) **Loss on right to unascertainable consideration.** An election to treat a loss arising on disposal of a right to unascertainable consideration as accruing in an earlier year, enabling the loss to be set against the gain on the disposal in respect of which the right was acquired must be made on or before the first anniversary of 31 January following the actual tax year of the loss. See **44.19** LOSSES.

(g) **Relief for trading losses to be set against chargeable gains of a person other than a company.** A claim to set off a trading loss against chargeable gains of the same or the preceding tax year must be made on or before the first anniversary of 31 January following the tax year in which the loss is incurred. See **44.21** LOSSES.

(h) **Relief for post-cessation expenditure of a trade to be set against chargeable gains of a person other than a company.** A claim to set off excess post-cessation expenditure of a trade against chargeable gains, which can be made only in conjunction with a claim under *ITA 2007, s 96* against income, must be made on or before the first anniversary of 31 January following the tax year in which the expenditure is incurred. See **44.21** LOSSES.

(i) **Amendment of tax return.** A person other than a company has up to twelve months after the filing date (for this purpose normally treated as 31 January following the tax year) to notify an amendment to his tax return. See **58.7** RETURNS.

(j) **Appropriation of asset to trading stock.** An election may be made to treat the transfer as, effectively, taking place at cost instead of market value. See **16.9** COMPUTATION OF GAINS AND LOSSES.

(k) **Small part disposals of land (claim for disposal not to be treated as such).** See **41.9** and **41.11** LAND.

(l) **Earn-out rights.** An election for a right to receive securities of unascertainable value acquired in consideration for a transfer of securities not to be treated as a security itself for chargeable gains purposes must be made on or before the first anniversary of 31 January following the tax year in which the earn-out right is conferred (or within two years of the end of the accounting period in which it is conferred). See **63.6** SHARES AND SECURITIES.

(m) **Incorporation relief.** An election to disapply incorporation relief under *TCGA 1992, s 162* on a transfer of a business to a company must be made on or before the first anniversary of 31 January following the tax year in which the transfer takes place. This applies only if *all* the shares etc. received in exchange for the business transferred are disposed of by the end of the tax year following that in which the transfer takes place; in other cases, an extra one year is given to make the election (see **67.5** below). See **37.3** INCORPORATION AND DISINCORPORATION RELIEFS.

(n) **Same-day acquisitions of shares.** With regard to shares acquired by an individual on the same day, an election may be made to treat certain shares acquired under employee share options as acquired separately from other shares for the purpose of identifying the shares comprised in any subsequent part disposal. The election must be made on or before the first anniversary of 31 January following the tax year in which falls the first disposal falling to be matched with acquisitions on the day in question. See **64.2** SHARES AND SECURITIES — IDENTIFICATION RULES.

(o) **Trusts with vulnerable beneficiaries.** A vulnerable person election allowing claims to be made for special income tax and capital gains tax treatment must be made on or before the first anniversary of 31 January following the tax year in which the election is to take effect. See **62.13** SETTLEMENTS.

(p) **Sub-fund settlements.** An election by trustees of a settlement under which a specified part of the settled property is treated for capital gains tax purposes as a separate settlement must be made on or before the first anniversary of 31 January following the tax year in which the election is to take effect. See **62.12** SETTLEMENTS.

(q) **Entrepreneurs' relief.** Entrepreneurs' relief must be claimed on or before the first anniversary of 31 January following the tax year in which the qualifying business disposal is made. See **24.6** ENTREPRENEURS' RELIEF.

Two-year time limits

[67.4] That is, for CGT, where applicable, action in respect of **2015/16** must be taken not later than **5 April 2018** (and for the purposes of corporation tax on chargeable gains, action must be taken within two years after the end of the accounting period in question).

(a) **Relief for assets of negligible value, loans to traders becoming irrecoverable and loans to traders evidenced by qualifying corporate bonds.** Broadly, a claim to this effect may be made within two years after the end of the tax year (or company accounting period) in which the relevant date falls. See **44.11, 44.12, 44.13** LOSSES. (The last-mentioned relief is abolished for loans made after 16 March 1998 — see **44.13** LOSSES.)

(b) **Loss relief for subscribing investment companies.** A claim for a loss arising on a disposal of qualifying unlisted shares by a subscribing investment company to be set against income must be made within two years after the end of the accounting period in which the loss is incurred. See **44.18** LOSSES.

(c) **Loss relief for companies investing under the Corporate Venturing Scheme.** A claim for a loss arising on a disposal of shares to which corporate venturing scheme investment relief is attributable to be set against income must be made within two years after the end of the accounting period in which the loss is incurred. See **18.19** CORPORATE VENTURING SCHEME.

(d) **Amendment of company tax return.** A company has up to twelve months after the filing date (which itself is normally twelve months after the end of the relevant accounting period) to notify an amendment to its tax return. [*FA 1998, Sch 18 para 15*].

Two-year ten-month (approx.) time limits

[67.5] Therefore, action in respect of **2014/15** must be taken on or before **31 January 2018.**

Incorporation relief

An election to disapply incorporation relief under *TCGA 1992, s 162* on a transfer of a business to a company must be made on or before the second anniversary of 31 January following the tax year in which the transfer takes place. If, however, *all* the shares etc. received in exchange for the business transferred are disposed of by the end of the tax year following that in which the transfer takes place, the deadline is brought forward by one year as in 67.3(n) above. See **37.3** INCORPORATION AND DISINCORPORATION RELIEFS.

Three-year time limits

[67.6] Therefore, action in respect of **2014/15** must be taken by **5 April 2018.**

Charities

Where property ceases to be held on charitable trusts in circumstances giving rise to a deemed disposal by the trustees, an assessment on the cumulative gains must be made within three years after the end of the tax year in which the cessation occurred. See **11.3** CHARITIES.

Three-year ten-month (approx.) time limits

[67.7] Therefore, action in respect of **2013/14** must be taken on or before **31 January 2018.**

Rollover relief — provisional claims

If not superseded by an actual claim or withdrawn, a provisional claim for rollover relief on replacement of business assets for capital gains tax (not corporation tax) purposes lapses on the third anniversary of 31 January following the tax year in which the disposal occurred. (This does not in itself prevent an actual claim being made at a later date.) See **59.11** ROLLOVER RELIEF.

Four-year time limits

[67.8] That is, for CGT, where applicable, action in respect of **2013/14** must be taken by **5 April 2018**.

The more important of these time limits are as follows.

(a) **Deceased persons.** Assessments on gains arising or accruing before death must be made on the deceased's personal representatives within four years following the tax year in which death occurred. See **6.13**.
(b) **Recovery of overpaid tax.** See **13.7** CLAIMS.
(c) **Raising assessments** other than where loss of tax brought about carelessly or deliberately. See **6.13** ASSESSMENTS.
(d) **Claim against double assessment** where the same person has been assessed 'for the same cause' in the same year. See **6.4** ASSESSMENTS.
(e) **Relief against double taxation.** See **21** DOUBLE TAX RELIEF.
(f) **Relief for unremittable overseas gains.** See **49.6** OVERSEAS MATTERS.
(g) **Disposals by way of gift etc. (election for tax to be paid by instalments).** See **51.5** PAYMENT OF TAX.
(h) **Capital distributions in respect of shares etc.** Where allowable expenditure on shares etc. is less than the amount of a capital distribution, the taxpayer may make an election to set off all that expenditure against the distribution. See **63.11** SHARES AND SECURITIES.
(i) **Extension of private residence exemption to a residence occupied by a dependent relative on or before 5 April 1988.** See **53.12** PRIVATE RESIDENCES.
(j) **Hold-over relief** for gifts of business assets and assets on which inheritance tax is chargeable etc. See **36.2–36.11** HOLD-OVER RELIEFS.
(k) **Rollover relief.** See **59.11** ROLLOVER RELIEF and note that the period for claiming relief starts with the later of the end of the tax year or company accounting period in which the disposal takes place and the end of the tax year or company accounting period in which the new assets are acquired.
(l) **Relief on compulsory acquisition of land.** See **41.12** LAND and note also that proceeds must not be invested in land which would be exempt from CGT under the private residence rules on a disposal of it within six years of acquisition.
(m) **EIS deferral relief.** See **23.18** ENTERPRISE INVESTMENT SCHEME and note that the period for claiming relief starts with the later of the end of the year of assessment in which the gain accrues and the end of the year of assessment in which the qualifying investment (i.e. a subscription for EIS shares) is acquired.
(n) **Relief for post-employment deductions to be set against chargeable gains.** A claim can be made only in conjunction with a claim under *ITEPA 2003, ss 555–564* against income. See **44.21** LOSSES.
(o) **Notification of capital losses.** See **44.4** LOSSES.

Other action before 6 April 2018

Tax-loss selling

[67.9] Appropriate disposals should be made if it is desired to realise capital losses to set off against chargeable gains in 2017/18. See **44** LOSSES.

Use of annual exempt amount

Action should be taken so as to utilise the CGT annual exempt amount for 2017/18. See **2.6** ANNUAL RATES AND EXEMPTIONS.

Bed and breakfasting of shares and securities

'Bed and breakfasting' of shares and securities, i.e. the sale and subsequent repurchase of shares etc. where the seller and buyer are *not* the same person, e.g. disposal by one spouse, repurchase by the other. See **64.2** SHARES AND SECURITIES — IDENTIFICATION RULES.

68

Time Limits — Miscellaneous

Introduction	68.1
Time limits of one year or less	68.2
Two-year time limits	68.3
Three-year time limits	68.4
Six-year time limits	68.5

Cross-reference. See **67** TIME LIMITS — FIXED DATES (in particular, the section at **67.1** dealing with HMRC's practice regarding late claims and elections which apply equally here).

Introduction

[68.1] Time limits which operate otherwise than by reference to the end of a tax year or company accounting period are set out in this chapter.

Time limits of one year or less

[68.2] Time limits of one year or less are as follows:

(a) **Thirty days:**

(i) For appeals against assessments, HMRC amendments to self-assessment tax returns and claims made outside returns, and HMRC conclusions on completion of enquiry, notice of appeal must be lodged within thirty days. See **5.3** APPEALS, **13.3** CLAIMS. For postponement of tax, see **42.2**, **42.4** LATE PAYMENT INTEREST AND PENALTIES, **51** PAYMENT OF TAX.

(ii) Rejections of HMRC corrections to self-assessment tax returns must be made within thirty days after the notice of correction. See **58.7** RETURNS.

(iii) A notice specifying the apportionment of a reduction in tax liability involving more than one period or person, in certain discovery cases, must be given within thirty days of HMRC issuing a notice apportioning it. See **13.5** CLAIMS.

(iv) Where HMRC offer to review a decision under appeal, the taxpayer has thirty days beginning with the date of the document notifying him of the offer to notify HMRC of acceptance of it. Alternatively, the appellant can, within the same thirty-day period, notify the appeal to the Tribunal for it to decide the matter in question. See **5.6** APPEALS.

(v) Following an HMRC review of a decision under appeal, the taxpayer can notify the appeal to the Tribunal. This must normally be done within the period of thirty days beginning with the date of the document notifying the conclusions of the review. Where, however, HMRC have failed to notify the conclusions within the required period, the time limit is extended to thirty days after the date of the document notifying the appellant that the review is to be treated as if concluded on the basis of HMRC's original opinion. See **5.6** APPEALS.

(vi) Where a non-resident disposal of an interest in UK residential property is made (see **41.25** LAND), the person to whom any NRCGT gain on the disposal would accrue must make a return (an '*NRCGT return*') to HMRC in respect of the disposal on or before the 30th day following the day of the 'completion' of the disposal. See **58.20** RETURNS.

(b) **One month:**

(i) If the First-tier Tribunal gives permission to appeal to the Upper Tribunal (or the Upper Tribunal gives permission (see (ii) below) but directs that the application for permission should not be treated as a notice of appeal) an appellant can appeal to the Upper Tribunal by providing a notice of appeal, to be received by the Tribunal within one month after the notice giving permission to appeal was sent. See **5.27** APPEALS.

(ii) Applications to the Upper Tribunal for permission to appeal against a decision of the First-tier Tribunal must be received no later than one month after the date on which the First-tier Tribunal sent the notice refusing permission to appeal (see (d) below). See **5.27** APPEALS.

(iii) Applications to the Upper Tribunal for permission to appeal to the Court of Appeal etc. must be received by the Tribunal within one month after the date it sent written reasons for the decision. See **5.32** APPEALS.

(c) **Fifty six days:**

An application to the First-tier Tribunal for permission to appeal against its decision must be received by the Tribunal no later than fifty six days after the date it sent full reasons for the decision. See **5.22** APPEALS.

(d) **Ninety-two days:**

The grant of an option under the Enterprise Management Incentives scheme must be notified to HMRC within ninety-two days after the option is granted. See **22.22** EMPLOYEE SHARE SCHEMES.

(e) **Three months:**

(i) Applications for judicial review must be made within three months of the date when the grounds for application arose. See **5.35** APPEALS.

(ii) Certain particulars of a settlement with a foreign element etc. must be supplied within three months of the creation of it. See **48.29** OFFSHORE SETTLEMENTS.

(f) **Six months:**
In respect of the form of rollover relief available on a disposal of shares to a tax-advantaged share incentive plan, the disposal consideration must be used to acquire replacement assets within six months (or longer period in certain cases) of the disposal. See **22.18, 22.30** EMPLOYEE SHARE SCHEMES.

(g) **Twelve months:**
   (i) To qualify for rollover relief an acquisition must be made twelve months before the associated disposal (or three years after). See **59.2** ROLLOVER RELIEF. This applies also to the general relief for compulsory acquisition of land (see **41.12** LAND).
   (ii) Where, within twelve months of receipt, a capital sum, received as compensation is applied in replacing an asset lost or destroyed, a claim may be made for the deemed disposal arising on the loss etc. to be treated as made for a 'no gain, no loss' consideration. See **10.4** CAPITAL SUMS DERIVED FROM ASSETS.
   (iii) Certain particulars of a settlement with a foreign element etc. must be supplied within twelve months of certain events. See **48.29** OFFSHORE SETTLEMENTS.
   (iv) Acquisition of EIS shares must, for the purpose of EIS capital gains deferral relief, take place within twelve months before the disposal or other chargeable event giving rise to the gain to be deferred (or three years after). See **23.15** ENTERPRISE INVESTMENT SCHEME.
   (v) Social investment must, for the purpose of social investment capital gains deferral relief, be made within twelve months before the disposal or other chargeable event giving rise to the gain to be deferred (or three years after). See **65.46** SOCIAL INVESTMENT RELIEF.

Two-year time limits

[68.3] Two-year time limits are as follows:

(a) **Only or main residence.** The election by individuals with more than one private residence must be made within two years after the acquisition of the second residence. Subsequent notice of variation must be given within two years after the date from which it is to take effect. See **53.10** PRIVATE RESIDENCES.

(b) **Family arrangements and disclaimers after death** must be made within two years of the death. See **19.8** DEATH.

(c) **Unpaid corporation tax — certain capital distributions and reconstructions.** In a case where unpaid corporation tax falls to be recovered from a shareholder in receipt of a capital distribution, notice of liability must be served within two years after the later of the date on which the assessment was made on the company and the date on which the tax became due and payable. See **51.27** PAYMENT OF TAX. Similar rules apply in a case where unpaid corporation tax falls to be recovered from a third party following a scheme of reconstruction involving the transfer of a company's business to another company. See **14.11** COMPANIES.

(d) **Know-how.** A joint election for know-how not to be treated as goodwill must be made within two years of the disposal. See **7.4** ASSETS.

(e) **Company ceasing to be UK resident etc. — postponement of charge on deemed disposal.** Subject to certain conditions an election may be made by the company concerned and the principal company within two years of the cessation of UK residence etc. so that postponement is obtained. If any part of the postponed gain becomes chargeable on the principal company, it and the company concerned can elect within two years of the time the gain becomes chargeable that any unrelieved capital losses of the company be set against the gain. See **49.17** OVERSEAS MATTERS.

(f) **Share Incentive Plan: rollover relief.** In respect of the form of rollover relief available on a disposal of shares, other than by a company, to the trustees of an approved share incentive plan, the relief must be claimed within the two years beginning with the acquisition of the replacement assets. See **22.19** EMPLOYEE SHARE SCHEMES.

(g) **Disincorporation relief.** A claim for relief must be made jointly by the company and all of the shareholders to whom the business is transferred within two years beginning with the date of the transfer. See **37.5** INCORPORATION AND DISINCORPORATION RELIEFS.

Three-year time limits

[68.4] Three-year time limits are as follows:

(a) **Rollover relief** is only available if the acquisition is made within three years after the disposal (or twelve months before). See **59.2** ROLLOVER RELIEF. This applies also to the general relief for compulsory acquisition of land (see **41.12** LAND).

(b) **Acquisition of EIS shares** must, for the purpose of EIS capital gains deferral relief, take place within three years after the disposal or other chargeable event giving rise to the gain to be deferred (or twelve months before). See **23.15** ENTERPRISE INVESTMENT SCHEME.

(c) A gain deferred by means of **EIS capital gains deferral relief** becomes chargeable if the investor becomes neither resident nor ordinarily resident in the UK within the period ending immediately before the third anniversary of the issue date or, if later, the third anniversary of the date of commencement of the qualifying trade (except in certain cases of temporary working abroad). See **23.15** ENTERPRISE INVESTMENT SCHEME.

(d) **Unpaid corporation tax — groups and non-resident companies.** The principal company of the group (and other group members in certain circumstances) or a controlling director of a non-UK resident company trading in the UK through a permanent establishment (previously a branch or agency) can be held liable for unpaid corporation tax on a chargeable gain accruing to a group company or to the non-resident company in question. Notice of liability must be served within three years beginning with the date on which the liability of the defaulting company is finally determined. See **51.26** PAYMENT OF TAX and see also **68.3**(e) above and (j) below.

(e) **Unpaid corporation tax — company ceasing to be UK-resident.** Any tax due by a company ceasing to be UK resident and not paid within six months of becoming payable can, within three years of the amount being finally determined, be recovered from a person who is, or was in the twelve months before residence ceased, a member of the same group or a controlling director. See **49.18** OVERSEAS MATTERS.

(f) **Distribution of gains by overseas companies.** Capital gains tax or corporation tax on chargeable gains paid by a participator on part of a gain which is apportioned to him can be used to offset income tax, capital gains tax or corporation tax in respect of the distribution if the gain is distributed within three years after the end of the period of account of the non-resident company in which it accrued or within four years beginning with the date it accrued, whichever gives the earlier date. See **49.7** OVERSEAS MATTERS.

(g) Social investment must, for the purpose of social investment capital gains deferral relief, be made within three years after the disposal or other chargeable event giving rise to the gain to be deferred (or twelve months before). See **65.46** SOCIAL INVESTMENT RELIEF.

Six-year time limits

[68.5] Six-year time limits are as follows:

(a) **Intra-group transfers: company ceasing to be a member of a group.** If a company leaves a group within six years of the transfer to it of a capital asset by another member of the group, it will be liable to a degrouping charge. See **29.7** GROUPS OF COMPANIES. Similar provisions apply where the company which acquired such an asset becomes an investment trust or venture capital trust. See **29.11**, **29.12** GROUPS OF COMPANIES.

(b) **Company ceasing to be UK resident etc. — postponement of charge on deemed disposal.** If within six years after the cessation of residence etc. the company disposes of assets held at that time, the whole or the appropriate part of the postponed gain (insofar as not already so treated) is deemed to accrue to the principal company. See **49.17** OVERSEAS MATTERS.

69

Underwriters at Lloyd's

Introduction	**69.1**
Individuals	**69.2**
Trust funds	**69.2**
Corporate underwriters	**69.3**
Scottish limited partnerships and limited liability partnerships	**69.4**
Overseas residents	**69.5**
Transactions in syndicate capacity	**69.6**
Members' Agent Pooling Arrangements	**69.7**
Conversion to underwriting through successor company	**69.8**

Introduction to underwriters at Lloyd's

[69.1] This chapter describes the special chargeable gains provisions which apply to Lloyd's underwriters, whether individual, corporate or partnership. In particular, it looks at the various trust funds held by members: the premiums trust fund, the ancillary trust fund and the special reserve fund.

Members are able to buy and sell syndicate capacity, i.e. the right to underwrite on a particular syndicate, which is a chargeable asset for CGT purposes. The CGT consequences are described at **69.6** and **69.7** below. See **69.8** below for reliefs available on conversion to underwriting through a successor company.

Individuals

Trust funds

[69.2] Trust funds held by an underwriting member of Lloyd's are classified as to '*premium trust funds*' (defined by reference to the Insurance Prudential Sourcebook (previously the Lloyd's Sourcebook), part of the FSA Handbook, made by the Financial Services Authority under *Financial Services and Markets Act 2000*), 'special reserve funds' (see below) and 'ancillary trust funds'. An '*ancillary trust fund*', in relation to the member, does not include his premium trust fund or special reserve fund but otherwise means any trust fund required or authorised by Lloyd's rules, or required by a members' agent of his.

Premium trust funds

In general terms, disposals of assets in a Lloyd's member's premium trust fund are now only taken into account for income tax purposes, consideration relating to acquisitions and disposals of those assets being left out of account for CGT purposes.

Gains from ancillary trust funds

Gains arising from the disposals of assets forming part of an ancillary trust fund are charged in the normal way to CGT (and losses are treated as allowable capital losses) on a fiscal year basis. See **69.8** below for rollover relief on disposal of ancillary trust fund assets to a successor company.

Entitlement of member

A member is treated for CGT purposes as absolutely entitled as against the trustees to the assets forming part of any of his premium trust fund or ancillary trust funds. Money deposits required to be paid out of a premium trust fund under overseas regulatory arrangements are still deemed to form part of the fund. Both such funds are therefore not 'settled property' as in **62.3** SETTLEMENTS.

[*FA 1993, ss 171, 172, 174(1), 176, 184; FA 1994, s 228, Sch 21 para 1(1)(3)(a), paras 2, 3, 8, Sch 26 Pt V; SI 2001 No 3629, Arts 79, 82; SI 2006 No 3273*].

Special reserve funds

A '*special reserve fund*' is a fund authorised by *FA 1993, s 175(1)*. The member is treated for CGT purposes as absolutely entitled as against the trustees to the assets forming part of his fund but the transfer by the member of an asset to the trustees is a chargeable event for CGT purposes. Profits and losses arising from assets forming part of the fund are excluded for all CGT (and income tax) purposes. [*FA 1993, s 175, Sch 20 para 8, para 9(1); FA 1994, s 228, Sch 21 para 13; SI 1999 No 3308, Reg 4*].

On cessation of underwriting, whether on death or otherwise, the amount of a member's special reserve fund, so far as not required as cover for cash calls and syndicate losses, must be paid over to him. Where an asset is transferred by the trustees to the member or his personal representatives or assigns, whether on cessation or otherwise, the asset is treated as acquired by the member etc.:

- in a case where the asset was held by the trustees at the end of the 'penultimate underwriting year', at the end of that year at its market value at that time;
- in a case where it was acquired by the trustees after the end of the 'penultimate underwriting year', at the date on which, and for the consideration for which, it was acquired by the trustees; and
- in a case where it was both acquired by the trustees and transferred to the member etc. before the end of the 'penultimate underwriting year', at the date of transfer at its market value at that time.

The '*penultimate underwriting year*' is the underwriting year corresponding to the year of assessment immediately preceding the member's final year of assessment.

[*FA 1993, s 175, Sch 20 para 11(4)(5); FA 1994, s 228, Sch 21 para 15(2)(3); SI 1995 No 353, Reg 8; SI 1999 No 3308, Reg 6(5)*].

Corporate underwriters

[69.3] The provisions at 69.2 above apply, with necessary modifications, to corporate members of Lloyd's except that there is no provision for a corporate member to set up a special reserve fund. [*FA 1994, ss 219–227B, 229, 230*].

Scottish limited partnerships and limited liability partnerships

[69.4] Regulations provide for the tax treatment of profits or losses arising to the partners of a Scottish limited partnership or a limited liability partnership from its business as a Lloyd's underwriting member. They apply to accounting periods of Scottish limited partnerships ending on or after 1 December 1997 and to accounting periods of limited liability partnerships ending on or after 14 February 2006. See *SI 1997 No 2681* as amended by *SI 2006 No 111*.

Overseas residents

[69.5] Where a capital gains tax treatment, rather than an income tax, or corporation tax charging income, treatment, would apply to assets held as part of an individual underwriter's or corporate underwriter's trust funds, then if the individual or company is neither resident nor, in the case of an individual, ordinarily resident in the UK, he or the company is still liable to capital gains tax or corporation tax on chargeable gains on such assets which are situate in the UK. See **7.3** ASSETS and **49.3** OVERSEAS MATTERS. For this purpose, investments comprised in the Lloyd's American and Canadian Trust Funds are regarded as not situate in the UK. Investments held in the Lloyd's Sterling Trust Fund are situate in the UK, except for non-UK equities. The double taxation arrangements between the UK and the relevant countries should be consulted, as well as the relevant domestic legislation of the overseas countries concerned. For overseas matters generally and for the determination of residence and domicile, see **50** OVERSEAS MATTERS and **57** RESIDENCE AND DOMICILE.

Transactions in syndicate capacity

[69.6] A Lloyd's member can participate in a particular underwriting syndicate only to the extent that he possesses the relevant rights to do so. A member is permitted to realise all or part of his rights in any particular syndicate (his syndicate capacity) by offering them for sale at one of the periodical syndicate capacity auctions or by entering into a bilateral agreement with a purchaser. Each member's right to participate in each syndicate of which he is a member is therefore a marketable asset. For capital gains tax purposes any gain arising on disposal is a chargeable gain. For corporation tax purposes gains are dealt with under the intangible assets regime (see **15.14** COMPANIES — CORPORATE FINANCE AND INTANGIBLES) and are consequently removed from the charge to corporation tax on chargeable gains. In exceptional cases, transactions in syndicate capacity may be sufficiently frequent so as to constitute a trade of dealing, in which case income tax may apply in the case of an individual. The date of disposal in the case of an auction is normally the day after it takes place. Allowable costs of disposal include tendering and auction expenses. HMRC do not accept that rights in syndicates had any acquisition value for CGT purposes prior to the 1995 Account. The allowable expenditure on the disposal of rights acquired subsequently by purchase will be their acquisition cost plus any incidental expenditure. As regards a new syndicate set up for the 1996 Account onwards, the allowable expenditure is normally the price paid to the managing agent by the member to join that syndicate. The initial Lloyd's admission fee is also an allowable expense, which may be relieved once the member has resigned.

'Bespoke' capacity is the term given to rights held by a member in his own name. Bespoke capacity must be kept separate from MAPA (Members' Agent Pooling Arrangement) capacity, for which see **69.7** below.

As regards acquisitions and disposals of syndicate rights by non-corporate members, such rights are a qualifying asset for the purposes of ROLLOVER RELIEF (**59**) on replacement of business assets. [*TCGA 1992, s 155*].

Current HMRC practice is to treat all a member's bespoke capacity in one syndicate as a single asset. Further acquisitions are treated as enhancement expenditure, part disposals are dealt with under the normal rules at **16.5** COMPUTATION OF GAINS AND LOSSES. (Lloyd's Market Bulletin TAX/HAB/In/Y2122, 6 September 1999).

Conversion to corporate status

The transfer of syndicate capacity by an individual member to a corporate vehicle, whether by gift or in exchange for shares, is a disposal for CGT purposes. See **69.8** below for rollover relief on transfer of syndicate capacity in exchange for shares. Alternatively, where the necessary conditions are satisfied, the reliefs at **36.2** HOLD-OVER RELIEFS and **37** INCORPORATION AND DISINCORPORATION RELIEFS are available. (Lloyd's Market Bulletin TAX/HAB/In/Y2122, 6 September 1999).

Example

Justin acquired a £1m line on Syndicate X for £60,000 on 30 April 2015. He acquired a further £250,000 line on the same Syndicate for £20,000 on 1 June 2016. The £1.25m line is a single asset for CGT purposes costing £80,000. On 1 May 2017, Justin sells a £500,000 line for £50,000. The remaining £750,000 line is therefore worth £75,000. Incidental costs of acquisition and disposal are ignored for the purposes of this example. Justin makes no other disposals in 2017/18.

	£
Proceeds	50,000
Deduct Cost:	
$£80{,}000 \times \frac{50{,}000}{50{,}000 + 75{,}000} =$	32,000
Chargeable gain (subject to annual exempt amount)	£18,000

Members' Agent Pooling Arrangements

[69.7] A Members' Agent Pooling Arrangement (MAPA), in relation to a member, is an arrangement under which:

- a 'members' agent' arranges for the member's participation in Lloyd's syndicates,
- the member must participate in each syndicate to which the arrangement relates, and
- the extent of his participation is determined by the members' agent or in accordance with a formula provided for in the arrangement.

A '*members' agent*' is a person registered as such at Lloyd's and acting as such for the member concerned. [*FA 1999, s 83(1)(2)*].

MAPAs have been in existence since 1994 and allow a member access to a wide range of syndicates. It is understood that most individual members underwrite wholly or partly through a MAPA rather than solely through rights (capacity) held directly in individual syndicates. In the absence of special rules, there could be numerous transactions each year which should strictly count as a CGT disposal. For example, whenever a new participant joins a MAPA, the total syndicate rights held in the MAPA have to be re-divided between all participants, so that each existing participant will have disposed of a fraction of his capacity to the new participant. Sales of rights by the MAPA and changes in the syndicates in which it partakes likewise give rise to CGT disposals by its participants. There are, therefore, special provisions to avoid such complexities. They do not apply to corporate members of Lloyd's. The provisions do apply, with appropriate modification, to Scottish limited partnerships which are Lloyd's members (see **69.4** above).

The provisions apply where an individual (i.e. non-corporate) Lloyd's member has entered into a MAPA, and apply for the purpose of determining any CGT liabilities of his that may arise from transactions effected in pursuance of the MAPA. They apply in relation to any MAPA entered into on or after 6 April 1999 and also to any MAPA entered into earlier and still in existence on that date (see also below). Under these provisions, the syndicate rights held by the member under the MAPA are treated as a single asset acquired by him at the time of his entering into the MAPA. The member's initial acquisition cost is the amount paid by him on joining the MAPA. Any other amount paid by him under the MAPA is treated as allowable enhancement expenditure on the single asset. A disposal (or, as the case may be, a part disposal) of the single asset occurs *only* when an amount is paid to the member, the disposal proceeds being equal to that amount, or, by virtue of *TCGA 1992, s 24(1)* (see **10.2** CAPITAL SUMS DERIVED FROM ASSETS), where the asset is entirely extinguished.

If the MAPA was entered into before 6 April 1999, the time of acquisition is taken to be the earliest time that the member acquired any of the syndicate rights still held by him through the MAPA immediately before 6 April 1999, the initial acquisition cost is the amount paid for such of those rights as were acquired at that earlier time, and the amount paid for any additional rights acquired between that time and 6 April 1999 (and still held) qualifies as enhancement expenditure. The incidental costs of rights acquired before 6 April 1999 (and still held) are taken to be the incidental costs of acquiring the single asset.

References above to the payment of any amount include payments in money's worth, in which case the member's expenditure or disposal proceeds, as the case may be, is equivalent to the market value of the money's worth at the time of payment. This covers, for example, the transfer by a member into a MAPA of syndicate rights which he previously owned directly, and *vice versa*. On the other side of the coin, a transfer of rights by a member into a MAPA constitutes a disposal by him of those rights at market value, and similarly a transfer of rights from a MAPA to a member constitutes an acquisition by him at market value.

[*FA 1999, ss 82, 83*].

Note that where a member has two or more MAPAs, each is treated as a *separate* single asset.

As regards acquisitions and disposals of syndicate rights held through a MAPA and treated as a single asset as above, such rights are a qualifying asset for the purposes of ROLLOVER RELIEF (59) on replacement of business assets. [*TCGA 1992, s 155*]. It is thought that additions on or after 6 April 1999 to a MAPA held on and before that date (which fall to be treated as expenditure on enhancing the single asset — see above) would qualify for rollover relief by virtue of ESC D22 which allows gains to be rolled over against enhancement expenditure in appropriate circumstances (see **59.2** ROLLOVER RELIEF).

Conversion to underwriting through successor company

[69.8] Where an individual Lloyd's underwriter converts to underwriting through a company under Lloyd's rules, two reliefs are available to defer charges to CGT on certain assets transferred to the company. To qualify for the reliefs the following conditions must be met.

(a) The member must give (and not withdraw) notice of his resignation from membership of Lloyd's in accordance with the rules or practice of Lloyd's, and in accordance with those rules must not undertake any new insurance business at Lloyd's after the end of his '*last underwriting year*' (i.e. the underwriting year in which, or at the end of which, he ceases to be an underwriting member and becomes a non-underwriting member).

(b) All of the member's 'outstanding syndicate capacity' must be disposed of by the member under a 'conversion arrangement' to a 'successor company' with effect from the beginning of the underwriting year next following the member's last underwriting year. For this purpose, a member's '*outstanding syndicate capacity*' consists of any of his syndicate capacity (see **69.6** above) which is not disposed of to a person other than a 'successor member' (as defined by the rules or practice of Lloyd's) at or before the end of his last underwriting year and which does not cease to exist with effect from the end of that year. A '*conversion arrangement*' is one made under the rules or practice of Lloyd's. A '*successor company*' is a corporate member (within *FA 1994, Pt IV Ch V*) which is a successor member.

(c) Immediately before the disposal of outstanding syndicate capacity, the member must control (within *CTA 2010, ss 450, 451*) the successor company and beneficially own more than 50% of its ordinary share capital (as defined in *ITA 2007, s 989*).

(d) The disposal of outstanding syndicate capacity must be made in consideration only of the issue to the member of shares in the successor company.

(e) The successor company must start to carry on its underwriting business (as in *FA 1994, Pt IV Ch V*) in the underwriting year next following the member's last underwriting year.

For the purposes of these provisions, shares comprised in a letter of allotment are treated as issued unless the rights to the shares conferred by it remains provisional until accepted, and there has been no such acceptance.

Where a member has made a claim for one or more of the reliefs below and subsequently withdraws his notice of resignation from membership of Lloyd's, he must, subject to penalties for fraudulent or negligent failure, give notice in writing of such withdrawal to an HMRC officer within six months from the date of the withdrawal. All necessary adjustments can be made, whether by assessment, discharge or repayment of tax or otherwise, as a result of the withdrawal of the notice of resignation notwithstanding any time limits for making such adjustments.

[*FA 1993, s 179B, Sch 20A paras 1, 5, 9–11*].

Rollover relief on disposal of outstanding syndicate capacity

If, on the disposal of outstanding syndicate capacity in (b) above, the aggregate chargeable gains exceed the aggregate allowable losses and the member makes a claim to an HMRC officer, the amount of that excess is reduced for CGT purposes by 'the amount of the rolled-over gain'. For this purpose 'the amount of the rolled-over gain' is the lesser of the amount of the excess and the aggregate of any amounts which would be allowable as a deduction under *TCGA 1992, s 38(1)(a)* (cost of acquisition — see **16.11** COMPUTATION OF GAINS AND LOSSES) if the 'issued shares' were disposed of as a whole by the member in circumstances giving rise to a chargeable gain. (The '*issued shares*' are the shares in the successor company issued to the member in consideration for the disposal of outstanding syndicate capacity.)

The amount of the rolled-over gain is apportioned between the issued shares as a whole. If the issued shares are not all of the same class, the apportionment is made in accordance with their market values at the time of acquisition by the member. On a disposal by the member of an issued share (or any asset directly or indirectly derived from any issued share), the amount allowable as a deduction in computing the chargeable gain under *TCGA 1992, s 38(1)(a)* (cost of acquisition — see **16.11** COMPUTATION OF GAINS AND LOSSES) is reduced by the amount of the rolled-over gain apportioned to the share. In the case of a derived asset, the reduction is restricted to an appropriate proportion of the apportioned amount.

[*FA 1993, Sch 20A para 3*].

Rollover relief on disposal of assets of ancillary trust fund

Rollover relief is also available if at the time of, or after, the disposal of outstanding syndicate capacity in (b) above, assets forming some or all of the member's ancillary trust fund (ATF) are withdrawn from the fund and disposed of by him to the successor company without unreasonable delay in consideration solely of the issue to him of shares (the '*issued shares*') in that company. The member must make a claim to an HMRC officer for relief to apply, and must control the successor company and beneficially own more than 50% of its ordinary share capital throughout the period beginning with the outstanding syndicate capacity disposal and ending with the disposal of the ATF assets. Relief is not available if the member could have made a claim for rollover relief on the disposal of the outstanding syndicate capacity but has not done so. If such a claim has been made but is subsequently revoked, it is treated for this purpose as never having been made. Note that the relief is available only for the first qualifying disposal of ATF assets after 5 April 2004. Although the disposal of ATF assets must be made after 5 April 2004, it is not necessary for the disposal of the outstanding syndicate capacity to have been made after that date.

Where relief is available the excess of the aggregate chargeable gains on the disposal of the ATF assets over the aggregate allowable losses is reduced for CGT purposes by 'the amount of the rolled-over gain'.

For this purpose '*the amount of the rolled-over gain*' is the lesser of the amount of the excess (reduced, for this purpose only, in certain circumstances as indicated below) and the aggregate of any amounts which would be allowable as a deduction under *TCGA 1992, s 38(1)(a)* (cost of acquisition — see **16.11** COMPUTATION OF GAINS AND LOSSES) if the issued shares were disposed of as a whole by the member in circumstances giving rise to a chargeable gain. The excess is reduced where, immediately before the disposal of the ATF assets, the market value of those assets exceeds 120% of 'the amount of the ATF assets required' (100% for ATF disposals before 16 June 2016). The reduction is made by multiplying the excess by the amount of ATF assets required and dividing by the market value of the ATF assets disposed of immediately before the disposal. For this purpose, '*the amount of the ATF assets required*' is, for ATF disposals on or after 16 June 2016, the percentage of the amount of the security required to be provided by the successor in respect of its underwriting business in the underwriting year in which the disposal is made which is equal to the percentage of the ordinary share capital of the company beneficially owned by the member immediately before the disposal. For ATF disposals before 16 June 2016, the amount of the ATF assets required is the lesser of:

- the amount of security required to be provided by the member in respect of his underwriting business in his last underwriting year, and
- the amount of security required to be provided by the successor company in respect of its underwriting business in its first underwriting year.

The amount of the rolled-over gain is apportioned between the issued shares as a whole. If the issued shares are not all of the same class, the apportionment is made in accordance with their market values at the time of acquisition by the member. On a disposal by the member of an issued share (or any asset directly or indirectly derived from any issued share), the amount allowable as a deduction in computing the chargeable gain under *TCGA 1992, s 38(1)(a)* (cost of acquisition — see **16.11** COMPUTATION OF GAINS AND LOSSES) is reduced by the amount of the rolled-over gain apportioned to the share. In the case of a derived asset, the reduction is restricted to an appropriate proportion of the apportioned amount.

[*FA 1993, Sch 20A paras 4, 11(2); SI 2016 No 597, Regs 1, 4*].

Conversion of partnership to underwriting through successor company

Provisions similar to those above apply to the conversion of a partnership to underwriting through a successor company where conditions broadly equivalent to those at (a)–(e) above are met. Rollover relief on the disposal of outstanding syndicate capacity is available for such disposals on or after 19 December 2014. Rollover relief on the disposal of assets of the partnership's ancillary trust fund is available for disposals of such assets on or after that date (even if the disposal of syndicate capacity is made before that date). [*FA 1993, s 179B, Sch 20A paras 5A–5D, 9A, 11; SI 2014 No 3133; SI 2016 No 597, Regs 1, 6–8*].

70

Unit Trusts and Other Investment Vehicles

Introduction to unit trusts and other investment vehicles	**70.1**
Collective investment schemes: exchanges, mergers and schemes of reconstruction	**70.2**
Authorised unit trusts	**70.3**
Investment trusts	**70.4**
Real estate investment trusts	**70.5**
Unauthorised unit trusts	**70.6**
Unit trusts for exempt unit holders	**70.7**
Open-ended investment companies	**70.8**
Qualified investor schemes	**70.9**
Funds investing in non-reporting offshore funds	**70.10**
Authorised contractual schemes	**70.11**
Court investment funds	**70.12**
Investment clubs	**70.13**
Venture capital trusts	**70.14**

Cross-references. See **8.2** ASSETS HELD ON 6 APRIL **1965** and **45.3** MARKET VALUE for valuation of units in unit trusts; **14.11** COMPANIES for transfers of businesses to authorised unit trusts and investment trusts; **29.3** GROUPS OF COMPANIES for intra-group disposals of assets by authorised unit trusts and investment trusts; **50.20** PARTNERSHIPS for carried interest arising to investment managers; **71.1** VENTURE CAPITAL TRUSTS.

Simon's Taxes. See D7.11, D7.339, D8.1.

Introduction to unit trusts and other investment vehicles

[70.1] This chapter describes capital gains provisions which are specific to various kinds of investment vehicles. Where those provisions form part of a wider scheme for the taxation of a type of entity, that scheme is also summarised to give context to the capital gains provisions.

A '*collective investment scheme*' is an arrangement with respect to property of any description, including money, the purpose or effect of which is to enable persons taking part in the arrangements (whether by becoming owners of all or part of the property or otherwise) to participate in or receive profits or income arising from the acquisition, holding, management or disposal of the property or sums paid out of such profits or income. [*TCGA 1992, s 288(1); Financial Services and Markets Act 2000, s 235; SI 2006 No 964, Reg 109(2)*]. The object of such a scheme is to enable a large number of investors to pool their money by investing in a professionally managed fund of investments, thus spreading risk. The most common forms of collective investment schemes are unit trusts (see **70.3** below) and open-ended investment companies (see **70.8** below). (HMRC Company Taxation Manual CT48105).

Collective investment schemes: exchanges, mergers and schemes of reconstruction

[70.2] The following provisions apply to a collective investment scheme which is an authorised contractual scheme which is a co-ownership scheme (see **70.11** below), a unit trust scheme or an offshore fund for disposals on or after 8 June 2013. For the purposes of the provisions, 'unit' includes shares in a company.

For the purposes of the tax treatment of the participants, the reorganisation of share capital provisions of *TCGA 1992, ss 126–138A* (see **63.2–63.8** SHARES AND SECURITIES) are disapplied in general although the exchange of securities provisions of *TCGA 1992, ss 135–138A* (see **63.5** SHARES AND SECURITIES) may apply if Company A or Company B is not a collective investment scheme of a type listed above.

Notwithstanding the above, the share reorganisation provisions of *TCGA 1992, ss 127–131* apply with necessary adaptations as if the scheme were a company and the event in question were a reorganisation of its share capital where:

(1) there is an exchange of units for other units in the same scheme of substantially the same value where the property subject to the scheme and the participants' rights are substantially the same immediately before and after the event;
(2) there is a reorganisation in the units in a scheme in which all the participants, or all the participants holding a particular class of units, exchange all their units for other units in the same scheme;
(3) units in a scheme are issued in exchange for units in another scheme under a general offer made to participants in that other scheme (or a class of them) where the offer is made in the first instance on a condition that, if satisfied, would result in the property of the first scheme including units in the second scheme giving rights to more than 50% of its capital and income;
(4) under an arrangement, participants in a scheme exchange units for units of substantially the same value in another scheme and as a result 85% or more of the property in that other scheme is units in the first scheme;
(5) under a scheme of reconstruction (as defined) an arrangement is entered into by all the participants in a scheme (or all the participants holding any class of those units) under which units in a successor scheme or feeder fund (as defined) are issued to those participants in respect of and in proportion to their units in the original scheme and the units in the original scheme are either retained, cancelled or otherwise extinguished; or
(6) under a scheme of reconstruction units in a scheme are issued to participants in another scheme in exchange for and in proportion to their existing units in accordance with *SI 2011 No 1613, Reg 12(1)(b)*.

Events within (3)–(6) above must be effected for bona fide commercial reasons unless the participant in question holds no more than 5% of the units in the scheme following the event.

[*TCGA 1992, ss 103E–103K, Sch 5AZA; SI 2013 No 1400, Regs 1, 11, 13*].

For disposals before 8 June 2013, if under a collective investment scheme, contributions to it and profits arising from it are pooled in relation to separate parts of the property in the scheme and the participants are entitled to exchange rights in one part for rights in another, then *TCGA 1992, s 127* (reorganisation etc. of shares etc.) is not to prevent the exchange constituting a disposal and acquisition for capital gains tax purposes. For this purpose *TCGA 1992, s 127* includes a reference to that provision as applied by *TCGA 1992, s 132* (conversion of securities) but does not include a reference to that provision as applied by *TCGA 1992, s 135* (exchange of securities for those in another company) or *s 136* (scheme of reconstruction); see **63.2**, **63.5**, **63.7** and **63.8** SHARES AND SECURITIES. [*TCGA 1992, s 102; SI 2013 No 1400, Regs 1, 9*].

Authorised unit trusts

[70.3] These are 'unit trust schemes' in respect of which an order under *Financial Services and Markets Act 2000, s 243* is in force. A '*unit trust scheme*' is a collective investment scheme under which the property is held on trust for the participants, but the Treasury may by regulation provide for any scheme of a specified description not to be treated as a unit trust scheme for capital gains purposes. Certain limited partnership schemes and employee share schemes have been excepted from treatment as unit trust schemes for such purposes. [*CTA 2010, s 616; TCGA 1992, s 99(2)(3); ICTA 1988, s 468(6); Financial Services and Markets Act 2000, s 237(1), Sch 20 para 4(3); TIOPA 2010, Sch 8 para 199; SI 1988 No 266; SI 2000 No 2550; SI 2001 No 3629, Arts 62(1), 116*].

For capital gains purposes, any unit trust scheme is treated as if the scheme were a company and the rights of the unit holders were shares in the company, and in the case of an authorised unit trust as if the company were resident and, before 6 April 2013, ordinarily resident in the UK. [*TCGA 1992, s 99(1); FA 2013, Sch 46 paras 96, 112*]. A unit trust scheme other than an authorised unit trust is not within the charge to corporation tax so that the trustees are assessable to capital gains tax unless there is exemption under **70.7** below (HMRC Capital Gains Manual CG41351).

Gains realised by authorised unit trusts (including umbrella schemes, see below) are not chargeable gains. [*TCGA 1992, s 100(1)*].

Monthly savings schemes

An individual acquiring units in authorised unit trusts under a monthly savings scheme could opt for a simplified arrangement for computing any chargeable gains arising. To do so, he had to make a written request to his tax office within specified time limits. The arrangement had to cover all an individual's monthly schemes in the same unit trust. Under the arrangement, the individual was treated in most cases as having made a single annual investment in the seventh month of the trust's accounting year. This would be made up of savings plus reinvested income less any small withdrawals in the year concerned. Following the freezing of indexation allowance to April 1998 (see **38.2** INDEXATION), the arrangement is withdrawn in all cases where savings commenced after 5 April 1998 and in other cases for acquisitions in any accounting year of a trust ending after 5 April 1999. (HMRC Statement of Practice SP 2/99). (This Statement of Practice updates SP 2/97 which itself replaced SP 3/89).

Accumulation units

No distributions are made to holders of accumulation units. Instead the net amount that would normally be distributed is automatically reinvested in the fund. No new units are issued but the value of the existing holding of units is increased. Where the notional distribution is charged to income tax as income of the unit holder (or would be but for a relief) or is taken into account as a receipt in calculating the profits, gains or losses of the unit holder for income tax purposes, it is treated as allowable expenditure for CGT purposes. Where the trust is an authorised unit trust, the deemed expenditure is treated as having been incurred on the 'distribution date' for the 'distribution period' in respect of which the amount is reinvested. In the case of any other unit trust scheme, the expenditure is deemed to be incurred on the date on which the notional distribution is reinvested. For this purpose, a '*distribution period*' is a period by reference to which the total amount available for distribution to unit holders is ascertained, and the '*distribution date*' for a distribution period is the date specified under the terms of the trust for any distribution for that period or, if no such date is specified, the last day of the period. [*ICTA 1988, s 468H(3)(4); TCGA 1992, s 99B; SI 2006 No 964, Regs 15(2)(4), 89; SI 2010 No 294, Reg 7*]. Note that this provision applies only to disposals on or after 16 March 2005: previously, however, the Revenue operated a broadly similar practice (see HMRC Capital Gains Manual CG57707).

Umbrella schemes

An '*umbrella scheme*' is collective investment scheme which is an authorised unit trust or, for disposals on or after 8 June 2013, an authorised contractual scheme which is a co-ownership scheme or an offshore fund which has arrangements for separate pooling of investors' contributions and the profits or income out of which payments are to be made to them, and under which investors can exchange rights in one pool for rights in another. [*TCGA 1992, s 99A(1); FA 2004, s 118(3); SI 2013 No 1400, Reg 8*].

Each sub-fund of the umbrella scheme is treated for capital gains purposes as being itself a collective investment scheme of the same type as the umbrella scheme as a whole and the umbrella scheme as a whole is treated as not being a collective investment scheme of that form or any other form (so that the provisions at **70.2** above do not apply to it). Any person who has rights in a particular sub-fund is treated as a unit holder in the deemed collective investment scheme consisting of that sub-fund. These provisions do not prevent gains or losses accruing to an umbrella scheme which is a unit trust scheme (but not an authorised unit trust) being regarded as gains or losses of the umbrella scheme as a whole. They also do not prevent gains of an umbrella scheme being regarded as the gains and losses of an authorised unit trust for the purposes of *TCGA 1992, s 100(1)* above and *TCGA 1992, s 139(4)* (reconstructions involving transfer of business — exclusion of transfers to authorised unit trusts etc. (see **14.11** COMPANIES)). [*TCGA 1992, s 99A(2)–(4); SI 2013 No 1400, Reg 8*].

Investment trusts

[70.4] See 70.5 below for real estate investment trusts.

Gains realised by investment trusts are not chargeable gains. [*TCGA 1992, s 100(1)*].

Definition of 'investment trust'

A new definition of an investment trust was introduced by *FA 2011* and applies to accounting periods beginning on or after 1 January 2012.

A company is an investment trust for an accounting period if it fulfils the following conditions.

(1) Throughout the period substantially all of its business consists of investing its funds in shares, land or other assets with the aim of spreading investment risk and giving its members the benefit of the results of the management of its funds.
(2) Throughout the period the shares making up the ordinary share capital or, if there are such shares of more than one class, those of each class, are admitted to trading on a regulated market (within the meaning of Directive 2004/39/EC).
(3) Throughout the period the company is neither a venture capital trust (see **71** VENTURE CAPITAL TRUSTS) nor a company UK real estate investment trust (see **70.5** below).
(4) The company is approved for the period by HMRC.

The Treasury has the power to make regulations amending condition (2) above or treating conditions (1) and (2) as satisfied in specified cases. Regulations may also be made specifying the circumstances in which a company can be approved and the process by which approval can be given, refused or withdrawn.

'*Shares*' includes stock.

'*Ordinary share capital*' means all the issued share capital (by whatever name called) of a company, other than that which produces a fixed rate of dividend and is non-participating. For HMRC's interpretation of 'ordinary share capital', see HMRC Brief 54/2007.

[*CTA 2010, ss 1119, 1158, 1159; SI 2011 No 2977*].

See HMRC Statement of Practice 2/99 (as in **70.3** above) re monthly savings schemes, which applied to investment trusts as it did to authorised unit trusts.

Real estate investment trusts

[70.5] For accounting periods beginning on or after 1 January 2007, companies meeting the necessary conditions (see below) can elect to become real estate investment trusts. The 'property rental business' (as defined, and including both UK and overseas property) of such a trust is ring-fenced and treated as if it were a separate business carried on by a separate company. Profits and gains arising in respect of the business (including, for accounting periods beginning on or after 17 July 2013, dividends from other UK real estate investment trusts) are generally exempt from corporation tax (although a tax charge may arise in certain tax avoidance cases or where a company fails to meet certain debt funding requirements or where it pays a dividend to a person with a 10% or more interest in the company). Profits of the company which are not from the tax-exempt business are chargeable to corporation tax at the main rate (currently 23%). To the extent that dividends paid by the company derive from ring-fenced profits and gains they are taxed in the hands of the recipient as property income rather than as distributions. Companies who entered the regime before 17 July 2012 had to pay an entry charge. Companies may exit the regime at any time by notice, and may be required to do so by HMRC notice where they repeatedly fail to meet certain conditions. Exit from the regime is automatic where one or more of conditions (1), (2), (5) or (6) below cease to be met. The provisions apply in modified form to enable real estate investment trusts to participate in joint ventures and for groups of companies to become group real estate investment trusts. [*CTA 2010, ss 518–609; FA 2012, Sch 4, Sch 16 para 219; FA 2013, Sch 19; SI 2006 Nos 2864–2867; SI 2007 Nos 3425, 3536, 3540; SI 2009 No 1482; SI 2009 No 2859, Art 3; SI 2014 No 518*]. For full coverage of the provisions see Tolley's Corporation Tax.

Conditions

A company may make an election to become a real estate investment trust only if it meets the following conditions.

(1) It is resident in the UK and not resident in another place for the tax purposes of that other place.
(2) It is not an open-ended investment company (see **70.8** below).

For the special tax regime to apply for an accounting period, the company must, subject to the exceptions noted below, meet the above conditions and the following conditions throughout the period.

(3) The shares forming its ordinary share capital are admitted to trading (for accounting periods beginning before 17 July 2012, listed) on a recognised stock exchange (see **63.30** SHARES AND SECURITIES).
(4) It is not a close company (defined, subject to certain modifications, as in *CTA 2010, s 439*) or is a close company only by virtue of having an institutional investor (as defined — for accounting periods beginning before 17 July 2012, restricted to a limited partnership which is a collective investment scheme (see **70.2** above)) as a participator.
(5) Each share issued by the company either forms part of the company's ordinary share capital or is a non-voting restricted preference share (as defined).

(6) The company is not a party to any loans under which the creditor is entitled to interest which varies according to the results of the company's business (except where the interest increases on the results deteriorating or decreases on their improving), which depends on the value of the company's assets or which exceeds a reasonable commercial return or under which the creditor is entitled on repayment to an amount greater than the amount lent or an amount reasonably comparable with the amount that would generally be repayable under the terms of securities listed on a recognised stock exchange.

(7) (For accounting periods beginning on or after 17 July 2012) either the shares forming its ordinary share capital are included in the official UK or qualifying overseas list or shares forming part of its ordinary share capital are traded on a recognised stock exchange.

The property rental business of the company must also meet the following conditions for the accounting period.

(i) Throughout the accounting period, the property rental business involves at least three properties.

(ii) Throughout the accounting period, no one property represents more than 40% of the total value (under international accounting standards) of the properties 'involved' in the property rental business.

(iii) Subject to certain exceptions, at least 90% of the profits of the property rental business and, for accounting periods beginning on or after 17 July 2013, all of those profits which are '*UK REIT investment profits*' (i.e. distributions from other UK real estate investment trusts) are distributed by way of dividend (either a cash dividend or a stock dividend), normally before the tax return filing date for the accounting period.

(iv) At least 75% of the company's total profits (as defined) for the accounting period arise from the property rental business.

(v) At the beginning of the accounting period, at least 75% of the company's assets by value are involved in the property rental business or, for accounting periods beginning on or after 17 July 2012, consist of cash or, for accounting periods beginning on or after 17 July 2013, shares in the principal company of a group UK real estate investment trust or in another company UK real estate investment trust.

Where a company's election to become a real estate investment trust specifies a date for entry into the regime on or after 17 July 2012, condition (4) does not have to be met in the period of three years beginning with the specified date. Where the three-year period ends during an accounting period, condition (4) only has to be met throughout the part of the accounting period falling outside the three-year period. For such companies, condition (7) is treated as met in relation to the first three accounting periods if at the end of the third accounting period the shares forming its ordinary share capital are included in the official UK or qualifying overseas list or if, during the three accounting periods, shares forming part of its ordinary share capital are traded on a recognised stock exchange.

References above to property which is '*involved*' in a business are references to an estate, interest or right by the exploitation of which the business is conducted.

Minor or inadvertent breaches of conditions (3), (4), (7) and (i) to (v) above may be ignored or give rise to a charge to tax instead of requiring the company to leave the regime in certain circumstances. See *CTA 2010, ss 561–569*.

[*CTA 2010, ss 523–531, 549A, 561–569; FA 2012, Sch 4 paras 2–4, 7–18, 21–27, 29–32; FA 2013, Sch 19 paras 2–4, 7; SI 2006 No 2864, Regs 2–9; SI 2014 No 518*].

Capital gains

On entry into the regime the company's accounting period is deemed to come to an end, and a new one begins. 'Assets' held by the company which immediately before entry into the regime are involved (as above) in the property rental business are treated for corporation tax purposes as sold immediately before, and reacquired immediately after, entry at market value. Any gain arising on the deemed sale is not a chargeable gain (and a loss is not an allowable loss). [*CTA 2010, s 536*].

A gain accruing to the company on the disposal of an asset which was used wholly and exclusively for the purposes of the property rental business is not a chargeable gain and a loss is not an allowable loss (but see below where the disposal is in the course of non-exempt trade). Likewise, a gain accruing on disposal of an asset, which was so used but for an aggregate period of less than one year in which it was partly used for the purposes of the property rental business and partly used for the purposes of '*residual business*' of the company (i.e. any business other than the property rental business), is not a chargeable gain (and a loss is not an allowable loss). Where the aggregate period of mixed use is one year or more, any gain or loss is apportioned and any part reasonably attributable to the property rental business, having regard to the extent of and the length of the periods of use for the different purposes, is not a chargeable gain or allowable loss. Corporation tax on the non-exempt part of a gain is chargeable at the main rate (currently 28%).

Where an asset which has been used wholly and exclusively for the purposes of the property rental business begins to be used (otherwise than by being disposed of in the course of trade), wholly and exclusively for other purposes, it is treated as disposed of and immediately reacquired at that time at market value. Any gain is not a chargeable gain (and a loss is not an allowable loss).

Where an asset which has been used wholly and exclusively for the purposes of the property rental business is disposed of in the course of trade for the purposes of residual business of the company, the disposal is treated as made in the course of that business (so that the gain is brought into account as part of the business's trading profits) and any deemed disposal and reacquisition on entry into the regime is disregarded. Where the asset was held at the time of entry and the company had to pay the entry charge, the company may claim repayment of part of that charge. This provision applies in particular where a property has been developed since acquisition, the cost of that development exceeds 30% of the fair value (under international accounting standards) of the property at the time of entry into the regime or of acquisition, whichever is later, and the company disposes of the property within three years of completion of the development. For disposals on or after 17 July 2012, this provisions does not apply if the disposal is by a company which is a member of a group real estate investment trust to another member.

Where an asset which has been used wholly and exclusively for the purposes of residual business of the company begins to be used wholly and exclusively for the purposes of the rental property business, it is treated as disposed of by the residual business and immediately reacquired by the property rental business at market value. Any gain arising is a chargeable gain, and any loss an allowable loss.

There are special provisions to ensure continuity of treatment on the demerger of a tax-exempt business. The provisions apply where an asset is disposed of by a company's property rental business to a 75% subsidiary (S) of the company and the company disposes of its interest in S to another company (P). P must give notice to HMRC on the date it acquires the interest in S that the group of which S is now a member will enter the real estate investment trust regime from the start of a specified accounting period beginning within six months of the disposal and it must in fact so enter the regime. P may give such a notice even if it does not expect conditions (3) to (6) above to be met throughout the specified accounting period.

Where these conditions are met, the provisions above dealing with the transfer of assets out of the property rental business do not apply to the disposal of the asset and there is no deemed disposal and re-acquisition of the asset by S on entry of its group into the regime (and therefore no entry charge, where applicable, in respect of it). This does not apply, however, if conditions (3), (5) and (6) above (or, where the exception to condition (4) noted above does not apply, conditions (3) to (6) above) are not met by the end of the six-month period beginning with the disposal of the asset.

Similar provisions apply where a company leaves a group real estate investment trust.

[*CTA 2010, ss 535, 555–560; FA 2012, Sch 4 paras 5, 6, 13, 35–37, 43, 44*].

On exit from the regime, any assets involved in the property rental business immediately before exit are treated as being disposed of immediately before exit and reacquired immediately afterwards at market value. The above provisions then apply to determine whether, and to what extent, the gain is a chargeable gain or the loss is an allowable loss.

If a company which has chosen to leave the regime, having been within it for a continuous period of less than ten years, disposes of an asset which was involved in the property rental business within two years of exit, its liability to corporation tax is determined disregarding any deemed disposals of the asset on exit from the regime, on transfer out of the property rental business and, where a gain arose, on entry to the regime. Where a company is forced, by HMRC notice or automatically, to leave the regime within ten years of entry, HMRC may direct (subject to appeal) that the above provisions and corporation tax provisions generally will apply with specified modifications.

[*CTA 2010, ss 579–582*].

For the purposes of the above provisions, an '*asset*' includes part of an asset and an interest in, or right in relation to, an asset. References to assets used in a business include references to assets acquired for the purposes of the business and not in use in another business, assets available for use in the business and assets which are in any other way held in respect of, or associated or connected with, the business. Deemed disposals and reacquisitions of assets have effect for the purposes of all subsequent disposals, real or deemed, except where indicated above. [*CTA 2010, ss 602, 608*].

Unauthorised unit trusts

[70.6] *FA 2013, s 217* gave the Treasury power to introduce regulations (see now *SI 2013 No 2819*) revising the tax treatment of the trustees and unit holders of unauthorised unit trusts (UUTs), i.e. unit trust schemes not within 70.3 above.

The regulations enable an eligible UUT to apply to HMRC for approval as an exempt UUT, and provide for the taxation of exempt UUTs and their investors. They also provide for the tax treatment of non-exempt UUTs and their investors. The provisions relating to applications for approval have effect on and after 1 November 2013, but otherwise the provisions have effect on and after 6 April 2014.

A UUT is an exempt UUT for a period of account if its trustees are UK resident, all of its unit holders are 'eligible investors', it is approved by HMRC and it is not treated by regulations as not being a unit trust scheme for the purposes of the definition of 'unauthorised unit trust' in *ITA 2001, s 989*. Otherwise a UUT is a non-exempt UUT. A UUT is not, however, a non-exempt UUT if at all times in the period beginning with 24 May 2012 and ending with 5 April 2014 the UUT had at least one unit holder which was, and at least one unit holder which was not, an eligible investor. Once a UUT has been approved, the approval has effect for the period of account specified in the application and all subsequent periods, unless it is withdrawn by HMRC as a result of the failure of the UUT to satisfy the continuing requirements for approval.

A unit holder is an '*eligible investor*' if any gain on a disposal of its units would be wholly exempt from CGT or corporation tax (otherwise than by reason of residence) or if it holds all of its units pending disposal in the capacity of manager of the UUT.

Gains of an exempt UUT are not chargeable gains. The trustees of a non-exempt UUT are treated for tax purposes as if they were a UK resident company and the rights of the unit holders were shares in the company.

[*SI 2013 No 2819, Regs 1–10, 27, 28, 32; SI 2014 No 585*].

For HMRC's technical note on the new rules see www.hmrc.gov.uk/drafts/uu t-tech-note.pdf.

Unit trusts for exempt unit holders

[70.7] The following exemption is repealed on the introduction of the provisions at **70.6** above (and is effectively replaced by the exemption for exempt UUTs). Previously, it applied whenever the gains accrued, but was of practical importance only in relation to unit trust schemes which were not authorised unit trusts (see **70.3** above).

Subject to the above, if, for any reason other than non-residence, none of the holders of units in a unit trust scheme would be liable to capital gains tax (or to corporation tax on chargeable gains) on a disposal of units, gains accruing to the trust itself are not chargeable gains. In determining whether this rule applies, no account is taken of any units in a scheme which, having been disposed of by a unit holder, are held by the managers of the scheme, in their capacity as managers, pending disposal. No account is taken of the possibility of a corporation tax charge on income in respect of a gain accruing to an insurance company (within *FA 2012, s 65* (previously *ICTA 1988, s 431*)) or an incorporated or registered friendly society (within *FA 2012, s 172* (previously *ICTA 1988, s 466(2)*)).

[*TCGA 1992, s 100(2)–(2B); FA 2012, Sch 16 para 74, Sch 18 para 15; SI 2013 No 2819, Reg 34*].

Open-ended investment companies

[70.8] An '*open-ended investment company*' (OEIC) is a collective investment scheme under which the investments belong beneficially to, and are managed on behalf of, a body corporate having as its purpose the spreading of investment risk and giving its members the benefit of the results of management of those funds which is incorporated in the United Kingdom. [*CTA 2010, s 613; ICTA 1988, s 468(10) treated as inserted by SI 1997 No 1154, Reg 10(4), s 468A(2); TCGA 1992, s 99(2)(c) treated as inserted by SI 1997 No 1154, Reg 20; s 288(1); Financial Services and Markets Act 2000, s 236; F(No 2)A 2005, s 16; SI 2001 No 3629, Art 166; SI 2006 No 964, Regs 4, 109(2)*]. It is a form of retail investment fund which can be set up in the UK from 1997.

An OEIC is constituted as a company, with directors, and issues shares rather than units as with a unit trust. The Treasury are given power by *FA 1995, s 152* and *F(No 2)A 2005, s 17* to make the regulations necessary to establish a tax regime for UK incorporated OEICs (see now *SI 2006 No 964*). The regime is broadly equivalent to that which applies to authorised unit trusts and their investors. See Tolley's Corporation Tax for information concerning dividend and interest distributions.

OEICs are chargeable to corporation tax at a rate equal to the basic rate of income tax (before 6 April 2008, the savings rate). [*CTA 2010, s 614; ICTA 1988, ss 468(1A), 468A; FA 2008, Sch 1 paras 41, 42, 65; SI 1997 No 1154, Reg 5*].

Gains accruing to an OEIC are not chargeable gains. [*TCGA 1992, s 100(1) as modified by SI 1997 No 1154, Reg 5; SI 1997 No 1715, Reg 4; SI 2006 No 964, Reg 100*].

Investors incur chargeable gains and allowable losses in the normal way on disposals of shares. Where shares of a given class consist of both smaller and larger denomination shares, and a person owns both, the shares are treated for CGT purposes as being securities of the same class. [*SI 1997 No 1154, Reg 24; SI 2006 No 964, Reg 76*].

For disposals before 8 June 2013, the individual sub-funds of an umbrella company are treated as being separate OEICs in their own right and the umbrella company treated as if it were not a company. (An umbrella company is an OEIC whose investments are pooled separately in sub-funds, usually having different investment objectives, and whose shareholders are entitled to exchange their rights in one sub-fund for rights in another.) [*ICTA 1988, ss 468(11), 468A(3)(4); TCGA 1992, s 99AA treated as inserted by SI 2006 No 964, Reg 106; SI 1997 No 1154, Reg 10(4); SI 2013 No 1400, Reg 14*].

For disposals on or after 6 April 2006 (1 April 2006 for companies), the provisions at **70.3** above, dealing with accumulation units of unit trusts, apply equally to accumulation shares in an OEIC (i.e. shares in respect of which income is credited periodically to the capital part of the scheme property of the OEIC). [*SI 2006 No 964, Reg 103*].

See HMRC Statement of Practice SP 2/99 (as in **70.3** above) re monthly savings schemes, which applied to OEICs as it did to authorised unit trusts.

Authorised unit trusts are able to convert to, or merge with, OEICs without the incurring of any significant direct tax charges. [*SI 1997 No 1154, Regs 25–27; SI 2006 No 964, Regs 78–85*].

As far as investors are concerned, the exchange of units in an authorised unit trust for shares in an OEIC is subject to the normal rules for reconstructions (see **63.7** SHARES AND SECURITIES) so that the new shares will normally stand in the shoes of the old units and have the same acquisition date and cost for CGT purposes. (Revenue Press Release 7 April 1997, para 6).

Property AIFs

With effect from 6 April 2008, an OEIC meeting strict conditions can elect to become a property AIF. The regime is broadly similar to that for real estate investment trusts (see **70.5** above), but applies in relation to both property rental business and investments in real estate investment trusts and foreign equivalents. On entry or exit from the regime, the OEIC is deemed to dispose of and immediately re-acquire certain assets at market value, but any gains arising on such deemed sales are not chargeable gains (and losses are not allowable losses).

For disposals on or after 1 August 2012, where a fund which is not a property AIF converts, or intends to convert, to being a property AIF, *TCGA 192, ss 127–131* (reorganisation of share capital — see **63.7** SHARES AND SECURITIES) generally apply to the disposal and acquisition of units in the fund as part of the process of it becoming a property AIF. Also for disposals on or after that date, *TCGA 192, ss 127–131* generally apply to the exchange of units in a dedicated property AIF feeder fund (as defined) for units in the AIF (and vice versa). The application of *TCGA 192, ss 127–131* is in both cases subject to the anti-avoidance provision in *TCGA 1992, s 137* (see **4.15** ANTI-AVOIDANCE).

[*SI 2006 No 964, Regs 69A–69Z41; SI 2008 No 705, Regs 1, 5; SI 2008 No 3159, Regs 18–27; SI 2010 No 294, Regs 16, 17; SI 2011 No 2192, Reg 7; SI 2012 No 1783*].

For full coverage of the provisions see Tolley's Corporation Tax.

Qualified investor schemes

[70.9] A '*qualified investor scheme*' (QIS) is a fund (either an open-ended investment company or a unit trust), authorised by the Financial Conduct Authority, in which a statement that the fund is a qualified investor scheme is included in the instrument constituting the scheme. [*SI 2006 No 964, Regs 14B(4), 53(3)*; *SI 2008 No 3159, Regs 11, 17*]. Only institutional and certain sophisticated investors are eligible to participate in such schemes, which can be set up from 2004.

A QIS is treated for tax purposes in the same way as any other open-ended investment company or authorised unit trust provided that it meets a 'genuine diversity of ownership condition'. This rule applies to QISs established on or after 1 January 2009 and to existing QISs with effect on and after that date. QISs authorised before 1 January 2009 are, however, automatically deemed to satisfy the condition for the period beginning on that date and ending on the date on which the scheme's first accounting period beginning on or after that date ends.

Where the genuine diversity of ownership condition is not satisfied for an accounting period of the scheme, the QIS is treated for tax purposes as if it were a close investment holding company within *CTA 2010, s 34* (see Tolley's Corporation Tax).

[*SI 2006 No 964, Reg 14B; SI 2008 No 3159, Regs 1, 11, 30; SI 2009 No 2036, Reg 8; SI 2010 No 294, Reg 6*].

Previously, QISs were automatically treated in the same way as any other open-ended investment company or authorised unit trust, but large investors were subject to the substantial holdings regime below.

A QIS meets the 'genuine diversity of ownership condition' for an accounting period if:

(a) the scheme documents contain a statement that units in the scheme will be widely available, specify the intended categories of investor and that the scheme manager must market and make available the units in accordance with (c) below;
(b) neither the specification of intended investor categories, nor any other terms or conditions of investing in the scheme have the effect of either limiting investors to a limited number of specified persons or specified groups of connected persons (within *ITA 2007, ss 993, 994*), or of deterring any reasonable investor within the intended categories from investing in the scheme;
(c) units in the scheme are marketed and made available sufficiently widely to reach the intended categories of investors and in a way appropriate to attract those categories; and

(d) before 1 September 2009, any person within one of the specified categories of intended investor can, on request to the scheme manager, obtain information about the scheme and acquire units in it.

Conditions (c) and (d) above are treated as met even where the scheme has no current capacity to receive additional investments, unless the capacity to receive investments is fixed and a pre-determined number of specified persons or groups of connected persons make investments which collectively exhaust all, or substantially all, of that capacity.

A QIS also meets the genuine diversity of ownership condition if an investor in the scheme is a unit trust and the conditions at (a) to (d) above are met after taking into account investors in the unit trust. Both the QIS and the unit trust must have the same manager (or proposed manager). With effect from 1 September 2009, this applies only if the scheme is a property AIF (see **70.8** above).

[*SI 2006 No 964, Regs 9A, 14C; SI 2008 No 3159, Reg 11; SI 2009 No 2036, Regs 6, 9*].

There are procedures under which a QIS may obtain clearance from HMRC that it satisfies the genuine diversity of ownership condition. See *SI 2006 No 964, Regs 9B, 14D*.

Substantial holding rule

Prior to the introduction of the genuine diversity of ownership condition above, a special tax regime applied to participants with a 'substantial holding' in a QIS. The regime operated with effect from 6 April 2006 (1 April 2006 for companies), broadly as follows. The participant was required to ascertain the market value of his holding at specified measuring dates. The difference in value compared to the previous measuring date was then calculated, and the aggregate of those differences for a tax year or accounting period was taken. Where the aggregate was a positive amount, that amount was charged to tax under *ITTOA 2005, Pt 5 Ch 8* or under *Sch D, Case VI* (and a negative amount was an income loss). As increases in the value of a holding were taxed under the regime as income, no chargeable gain arose on disposals of all or part of the holding. A gain would arise at the time of the disposal, however, in respect of any increase in the value of the holding (or part) before entry into the regime. See below for full details.

The regime is brought to an end on the introduction of the genuine diversity of ownership rules above with effect on and after 1 January 2009, by treating 31 December 2008 as a final measuring date.

The regime did not apply to participants which were charities, registered pension schemes, insurance companies (where the holding was held as an asset of its long-term insurance fund), friendly societies, persons in whose hands any profit on a sale of units in the QIS would be trading income, and other QISs.

For these purposes, a holding in a QIS is a '*substantial holding*' if the participant, either alone or together with associates (within *ICTA 1988, s 417*) or connected persons (within *ICTA 1988, s 839* — see **17** CONNECTED PERSONS), owns (otherwise than as a nominee or bare trustee) units which represent rights to 10% or more of the net asset value of the fund.

[*SI 2006 No 964, Regs 53–69; SI 2008 No 3159, Regs 17, 31*].

See Tolley's Income Tax for full details of the regime.

Capital gains

On the 'first measuring date' in relation to a substantial holding in a QIS, the participant had to calculate the chargeable gain or loss that would have accrued on a disposal of the holding at market value at that time.

The general rule is that the '*first measuring date*' in relation to a substantial holding was the first date on which a participant owns the substantial holding. Where the participant owned a substantial holding on 6 April 2006 (1 April 2006 for companies) that date is the first measuring date (but if the participant ceased to own a substantial holding by the measuring date first occurring after 30 June 2006 that holding did not enter the special tax regime and 1 or 6 April 2006 was not the first measuring date). Special rules applied where a participant acquired a substantial holding within the period of twelve months beginning with the date of issue of the first prospectus of a new QIS or came to own a substantial holding in a QIS otherwise than as a result of acquiring units in it.

The gain calculated as above was not immediately chargeable (or the loss immediately allowable), but it became chargeable (or allowable) on disposal of all or part of the substantial holding before 1 January 2009. In the case of a disposal of part only of the holding, a corresponding part of the gain or loss was treated as accruing. On disposal of the whole of the holding, the whole gain or loss was treated as accruing or, where there was a previous part disposal, the remaining part of the gain or loss was treated as accruing.

The participant was treated as making the actual disposal of the whole or part of the substantial holding for such consideration as secured that neither a gain nor a loss accrues. This did not affect the acquisition cost of the person acquiring the holding.

Where the disposal would fall within one of the provisions listed below, the gain or loss calculated at the first measuring date was not deemed to accrue on the disposal. Instead, the transferee's holding in the QIS was treated as a substantial holding from the time of the disposal, and the gain or loss (or part thereof) was treated as accruing to the transferee on a disposal by him of all (or part) of the substantial holding. The provisions concerned are:

- *TCGA 1992, s 58(1)* (transfers between spouses or civil partners — see **46.5** MARRIED PERSONS AND CIVIL PARTNERS);
- *TCGA 1992, s 62(4)* (acquisition as legatee — see **19.14** DEATH);
- *TCGA 1992, s 139* (company reconstructions involving transfer of business — see **14.11** COMPANIES);
- *TCGA 1992, s 140A* (transfer or division of UK business between companies in different EC member states — see **49.13** OVERSEAS MATTERS);
- *TCGA 1992, s 140E* (European cross-border merger leaving assets within UK tax charge — see **49.15** OVERSEAS MATTERS); and
- *TCGA 1992, s 171(1)* (intra-group transfers — see **29.3** GROUPS OF COMPANIES).

TCGA 1992, s 127 (reorganisation of share capital — see **63.2** SHARES AND SECURITIES) and *TCGA 1992, s 116(10)* (reorganisations involving QUALIFYING CORPORATE BONDS (**54.4**)) did not apply to a substantial holding in a QIS. A transaction which would otherwise have fallen within either of those provisions was treated as involving a disposal and subsequent acquisition of the holding. The acquisition was treated as made at the market value of the holding immediately before the acquisition.

[*SI 2006 No 964, Regs 60–69; SI 2008 No 3159, Reg 17*].

Funds investing in non-reporting offshore funds

[70.10] Special rules apply to authorised investment funds (either unit trusts or open-ended investment companies) which invest in non-reporting offshore funds (see **49.11** OVERSEAS MATTERS). Such funds are known as 'FINROFs'. The rules came into effect on 6 March 2010 but apply to funds which meet the 'investment condition' below on that date with effect from 6 July 2010 (and such funds are treated as first meeting the condition on the latter date). The detailed provisions are described in Tolley's Income Tax and Corporation Tax but a brief summary together with the chargeable gains effects are given below.

The rules apply automatically to a fund which meets the investment condition but can also apply by election. The '*investment condition*' is that the total amount invested by the fund in non-reporting offshore funds or in other FINROFs is more than 50% (20% for accounting periods ending before 6 March 2011) of the gross asset value of the fund. The rules apply from the date that the condition is first met or the date specified in the election. Where a fund ceases to meet the investment condition, the fund manager may, subject to certain conditions, elect for the fund to cease to be a FINROF. The rules nevertheless continue to apply to participants in the fund unless they elect to be treated as disposing of, and immediately reacquiring, their units at market value on the date the fund ceases to be a FINROF.

A gain on a disposal of a unit in a FINROF is charged to tax as income. This applies also where the fund has previously been a FINROF and the investor has not made the election for deemed disposal. Broadly, such gains are calculated using the rules for chargeable gains (but, for corporation tax purposes, without any deduction of indexation allowance).

[*SI 2006 No 964, Regs 85A, 85D, 85G, 85M, 85Z1, 85Z9, 85Z11; SI 2010 No 294, Regs 21, 25; SI 2011 No 244, Regs 1, 5, 6, 8*].

Capital gains

On entry into the FINROF regime, a participant in the fund may elect to be treated for chargeable gains purposes as disposing of all his units and immediately acquiring units in the FINROF for a consideration equal to their market value. An election must be made by inclusion in the tax return for the tax year or accounting period in which the fund enters the regime. [*SI 2006 No 964, Reg 85L; SI 2010 No 294, Reg 21*].

Where a disposal gives rise to an income gain under the above rules and is also a disposal for chargeable gains purposes, then, in computing the chargeable gain, the income gain is deducted from the disposal consideration (and *TCGA*

1992, s 37(1) (deduction of consideration chargeable to tax on income — see **39.1** INTERACTION WITH OTHER TAXES) does not apply). Where the disposal is a part disposal (see **16.5** COMPUTATION OF GAINS AND LOSSES), the deduction is not made in calculating the formula for apportioning the allowable expenditure. The deduction is, however, made in calculating the disposal consideration for the purposes of applying the fraction A/B where incorporation relief under *TCGA 1992, s 162* (see **37.2** INCORPORATION AND DISINCORPORATION RELIEFS) applies to the disposal. Where an income gain arises because *TCGA 1992, s 135* or *s 136* (exchange of securities and schemes of reconstruction — see **63.5, 63.7** SHARES AND SECURITIES) are disapplied for the purposes of determining whether such gains arise, then, for chargeable gains purposes, the income gain is treated as if it were given by the person making the exchange as consideration for the new holding (within *TCGA 1992, s 128* — see **63.2** SHARES AND SECURITIES). [*SI 2006 No 964, Regs 85Z5–85Z8; SI 2010 No 294, Reg 21*].

Authorised contractual schemes

[70.11] An '*authorised contractual scheme*' is a type of collective investment scheme authorised by the Financial Conduct Authority. It may take the form of either a co-ownership scheme or a partnership scheme (as defined). [*Financial Services and Markets Act 2000, s 235A*]. Such schemes are broadly transparent for tax purposes, i.e. the scheme itself incurs no tax liability. This means that its investors are treated as if they had invested directly in the underlying assets of the scheme and are subject to personal taxation accordingly.

A participant's interests in the property subject to an authorised contractual scheme which is a co-ownership scheme and which is not a 'relevant offshore fund' are disregarded for capital gains purposes. Instead, units in the scheme are treated as assets for those purposes. In computing the gain or loss arising on disposal of a unit, the rules for accumulation units at **70.3** above apply as if the unit were a unit in a unit trust scheme (but not an authorised unit trust) and the participant were a unit holder. An offshore fund is a 'relevant offshore fund' if it is not constituted by a company or a partnership and it is not a unit trust scheme. [*TCGA 1992, s 103D; SI 2013 No 1400, Reg 3*].

See also **70.3** above as regards umbrella schemes.

Court investment funds

[70.12] These are common investment funds established under *Administration of Justice Act 1982, s 42*. The Accountant General is deemed to hold the funds (together with other funds in court) as nominee or bare trustee as in **62.3** SETTLEMENTS. [*TCGA 1992, ss 61, 100(3)*].

Gains realised by court investment funds are not chargeable gains. [*TCGA 1992, s 100(1)*].

Investment clubs

[70.13] An investment club is a group of people who join together to invest, primarily in the stock market. Each club will have its own rules, which will, *inter alia*, determine each member's proportionate entitlement to the club's investments, which will change frequently as capital is invested and withdrawn. Members share income, gains and losses according to their entitlement and are personally responsible for declaring the income etc. and personally liable for tax thereon. There are two ways in which members can return their shares of gains (and income) in a particular tax year:

- in accordance with a standard form of agreement (available from HMRC) whereby the secretary or other responsible officer makes a return of the gains based on less detailed computations than are statutorily required; or
- in accordance with strict statutory requirements, which, in addition to requiring gains (and income) to be returned by individual members, may also involve special returns being made by the treasurer and the person in whose name the club investments are held.

(HMRC Capital Gains Manual CG20600–20660).

Venture capital trusts

[70.14] Chargeable gains of venture capital trusts are not chargeable gains. See 71.10 VENTURE CAPITAL TRUSTS below.

71

Venture Capital Trusts

Introduction	**71.1**
Conditions for approval	**71.2**
Supplementary provisions	**71.3**
Qualifying holdings	**71.4**
Supplementary provisions	**71.5**
Income tax reliefs	**71.6**
Relief in respect of investments	**71.7**
Withdrawal of relief on investment	**71.8**
Relief on dividends	**71.9**
Capital gains tax reliefs	**71.10**
Relief on disposal	**71.11**
Deferral relief on reinvestment	**71.12**
Key points	**71.13**

Simon's Taxes. See **C3.11**.

Introduction

[71.1] The venture capital trust ('VCT') scheme described in this chapter is intended to encourage individuals to invest in unquoted trading companies through such trusts.

The scheme provides for a 30% income tax relief on investment in shares issued by an approved trust. The relief is withdrawn if the investor disposes of the shares within five years or the VCT loses its approval within that period. Dividends from a VCT are, subject to annual subscription limits, exempt from income tax. Gains made by a VCT are not chargeable gains and neither are gains made by investors in VCT shares (again subject to annual subscription limits). For shares issued before 6 April 2004 there was also a chargeable gains deferral relief for reinvestments in VCT shares; this is described at **71.12** below because deferred gains continue to be brought back into charge on the happening of certain chargeable events.

A VCT must meet strict conditions in order to receive approval, including conditions dealing with the nature and extent of its investments in unquoted trading companies. See **71.2–71.5** below.

The Treasury has wide powers to make regulations governing all aspects of the reliefs applicable to venture capital trust investments, and for the requirements as regards returns, records and provision of information by the trust. [*ITA 2007, ss 272, 284; FA 2014, Sch 10 para 5(2)*]. See now *SI 1995 No 1979*.

See generally HMRC Venture Capital Schemes Manual VCM2010–2070, 50000 *et seq*.

State aid information

With effect from 15 September 2016, HMRC may give a VCT a notice requiring it to provide specified information for the purpose of complying with EU state aid obligations. See *FA 2016, ss 180–182, Sch 24*.

Conditions for approval

[71.2] A '*venture capital trust*' ('VCT') is a company approved for this purpose by HMRC. Close companies (see Tolley's Corporation Tax under Close Companies) are excluded. The time from which an approval takes effect is specified in the approval, and may not be earlier than the time the application for approval was made. [*ITA 2007, ss 259, 283*].

Except as detailed further below, approval may not be given unless HMRC are satisfied that the following six conditions are met in relation to the most recent complete accounting period of the company and will be met in relation to the accounting period current at the time of the application for approval.

The listing condition

The company's ordinary shares (or each class thereof) must be admitted to trading on a regulated market (within Article 4.1(14) of the Directive of the European Parliament and of the Council on markets in financial instruments (2004/39/EC)) throughout those accounting periods. For accounting periods ending before 6 April 2011, the requirement was for the shares to be listed in the official UK list (within *Financial Services and Markets Act 2000, Pt 6*) or, before 19 July 2007, the Official List of the Stock Exchange.

The nature of income condition

The company's income (as defined) must be derived wholly or mainly from shares or 'securities'.

'*Securities*' for these purposes are deemed to include liabilities in respect of certain loans not repayable within five years, and any stocks or securities relating to which are not re-purchasable or redeemable within five years of issue. Provided that the loan is made on normal commercial terms, HMRC will not regard a standard event of default clause in the loan agreement as disqualifying a loan from being a security for this purpose. If, however, the clause entitled the lender (or a third party) to exercise any action which would cause the borrower to default, the clause would not be regarded as 'standard'. (HMRC SP 8/95).

The income retention condition

An amount greater than 15% of its income (as defined) from shares and securities must not be retained by the company.

This condition does not apply for an accounting period if the amount the company would be required to distribute is less than £10,000 (proportionately reduced for periods of less than twelve months), or if the company is required by law to retain income in excess of the 15% limit. The latter exclusion only applies, however, if the aggregate of the excess of retentions over those required by law and any distribution is less than £10,000 (proportionately reduced for periods of less then twelve months).

The 15% holding limit condition

No 'holding' in any company other than a VCT (or a company which could be a VCT but for the listing condition above) may represent more than 15% of the value of the company's investments at any time in those periods.

For this purpose, and that of the 70% qualifying holdings condition below, 'the company's investments' include (if it would not otherwise include) money in the company's possession and any sum owed to the company over which the company has 'account-holder's rights', i.e. the right to require payment either to the company or at its direction. Anything to which the company is not beneficially entitled is excluded (though, for this purpose, a company *is* beneficially entitled to sums subscribed for shares issued by it and anything representing such sums).

If this condition was met when a holding in a company was acquired, it is treated as continuing to be met until any more shares or securities of the company are acquired (otherwise than for no consideration).

'*Holding*' means the shares or securities of whatever class or classes held in any one company. Where, in connection with a 'scheme of reconstruction' (within *TCGA 1992, s 136*), a company issues shares or securities to persons holding shares or securities in another in respect of, and in proportion to (or as nearly as may be in proportion to) such holdings, without the recipients becoming liable for any consideration, the old and the new holdings are treated as the same. Holdings in companies which are members of a group (i.e. a company and its 51% subsidiaries), whether or not including the company whose holdings they are ('company A'), are treated as holdings in a single company if they are not excluded from the 15% holding limit condition. If company A is a member of a group, money owed to it by another group member is treated as a security and, as such, as part of its holding in that other group member.

See **71.3** below for the value of the company's investments.

The 70% qualifying holdings condition

Throughout the accounting periods at least 70% by value of the company's investments must be represented by shares or securities in 'qualifying holdings' (see **71.4** below).

This condition is relaxed where a VCT makes a disposal of a holding of shares or securities which was part of its qualifying holdings throughout the preceding six months provided that the consideration for the disposal is not wholly '*new qualifying holdings*' (i.e. shares or securities which, on transfer to the VCT, form part of its qualifying holdings). In such a case, the company is treated for the purposes of determining whether this condition is, has been or will be met:

(i) as continuing to hold the holding or, where the consideration consists partly of new qualifying holdings, part of the holding (see further below) for six months; and

(ii) as if the value of its investments in that period were reduced (but not below the value of its qualifying holdings) by any monetary consideration for the disposal.

The value of the holding or part in the six months following disposal is treated as being equal to its value immediately before the disposal. For this purpose, the part of the holding that the VCT is treated as continuing to hold is the proportion of the holding equal to:

$$\frac{TC - NQH}{TC}$$

where:

TC = the market value of the total consideration for the disposal, and

NQH = the market value of the new qualifying holdings.

This relaxation of the condition does not apply at any time in respect of shares or securities acquired with money raised on a second or subsequent issue of VCT shares the use of which is at that time ignored under the provisions below. The relaxation also does not apply to disposals between two companies during a merger within (1) or (2) below.

On a second and subsequent issue of shares by an approved VCT, this condition and the 70% eligible shares condition below do not have to be met, in relation to the money raised by the further issue, in the accounting period of the further issue or any later accounting period ending no more than three years after the making of the further issue. However, *SI 2004 No 2199, Reg 14* limits the operation of this rule by stipulating that the money raised by the further issue must be for the purposes of acquiring additional investments which do fulfil the conditions. Where any of that money (or assets derived therefrom) is used for another purpose, then from a time immediately before that use the whole of the money raised by the issue is deemed to be included in the company's investments in applying the percentage tests in the two conditions. If any of the money is used by the VCT to buy back its own shares, this stipulation is treated, in particular, as not fulfilled if HMRC regard the purchase as not insignificant in relation to the issued ordinary share capital of the VCT or if it is made as a result of a general offer to members. If the money is raised by a successor VCT (in a merger) and used to buy shares in the merging companies, the stipulation is treated, in particular, as not fulfilled if the money so used exceeds the least of three specified limits.

See the 15% holding limit condition above for the meaning of 'the company's investments' and see below for the value of investments.

The 70% eligible shares condition

At least 70% (30% for accounting periods ending before 6 April 2011) of the company's qualifying holdings (by value) must be represented throughout the accounting periods by holdings of '*eligible shares*', i.e. ordinary shares which do not carry any present or future preferential right to dividends or to assets on a winding up or any present or future right to redemption.

For accounting periods ending on or after 6 April 2011, a preferential right to dividends prevents ordinary shares from being eligible shares only if the amount payable under the rights or the date or dates of payment depend to any extent on the decision of the company, the holder of the share or any other person or if the amount of any dividends payable at any time under the right include any amount which was payable at an earlier time but unpaid.

The above two changes which apply for accounting periods ending on or after 6 April 2011 do not apply in relation to shares or securities issued before that date nor to shares or securities issued on or after that date but acquired by the company by means of investing money raised by the issue before that date of shares or securities (or money derived from the investment of such money raised).

See the 70% qualifying holdings condition above where a VCT makes a second or subsequent issue of shares and see below for the value of investments.

The non-qualifying investments condition

This condition has effect in relation to investments made on or after 6 April 2016. The condition is that the company has not made and will not make, in the accounting periods, an investment which does not form part of its qualifying holdings and does not come under any of the following descriptions:

(A) shares or units in an alternative investment fund which may be repurchased or redeemed on seven days' notice given by the investor; or
(B) shares or units in a UCITS (an undertaking for collective investment in transferable securities) which may be repurchased or redeemed on seven days' notice given by the investor; or
(C) ordinary shares or securities which are acquired by the company on a regulated market; or
(D) money in the investor's possession; or
(E) a sum owed to the investor over which the investor has the right to require payment, either to the investor or at the investor's direction, on no more than seven days' notice given by the investor.

The investment limits condition

This condition has effect in relation to investments made on or after 17 July 2012. However, the fact that an investment may already have been made by someone before that date does not prevent its being a 'relevant investment' as defined below. The condition is that the company has not made, and will not make, in the accounting periods, an investment which breaches the permitted investment limits.

In relation to investments made on or after 18 November 2015, an investment breaches the permitted investment limits if:

(i) the 'total annual investment' in the investee company exceeds £5 million;
(ii) the 'total investment' in the investee company at the date the current investment is made (the '*investment date*' exceeds £12 million or, if the company is a 'knowledge-intensive company' (see **71.4** below) at the investment date, £20 million; or

(iii) the total investment in the investee company at any time during the five-year post-investment period exceeds the limits in (ii) above *and* the company effectively acquires a company or trade after it receives the investment in question. This mirrors the 'maximum risk finance investments in five-year post-investment period' requirement at **71.4** below, which is described there in more detail, and the 'five-year post-investment period' is defined in similar manner.

In (i) above, the '*total annual investment*' in the investee company comprises the investment under review (the '*current investment*') and the total amount of other relevant investments made in the investee company by all investors in the 12 months ending with the day on which the current investment was made. The following also count towards the total annual investment:

- any investment in the said 12-month period in a 51% subsidiary (within *CTA 2010, Pt 24 Ch 3*) of the investee company (including any made before it became a 51% subsidiary but not any made after it last ceased to be one);
- any investment made in any company to the extent that the money raised by the investment has been employed for the purposes of a trade (as widely defined) carried on by another company that has at any time in the said 12-month period been a 51% subsidiary of the investee company (disregarding any money so employed after it last ceased to be such a subsidiary); and
- any other investment made in any company to the extent that the money raised has been employed for the purposes of a trade (as widely defined), and within that 12-month period, but after the investment was made, the trade (or a part of it) was transferred to the investee company, a 51% subsidiary or a partnership of which the investee company or a 51% subsidiary is a member.

In (ii) above, the '*total investment*' in the investee company is defined similarly to 'total annual investment' but disregarding references to a 12-month period and instead taking into account all times before the investment date. In (iii) above, 'total investment' also has a similar meaning but taking into account all times before the time in the five-year post-investment period when (iii) above is being tested.

In relation to investments made before 18 November 2015, only (i) above applied. The total annual investment in the investee company comprised the investment under review and the total amount of other relevant investments made in the investee company by all investors in the 12 months ending with the day on which the current investment was made.

For the purpose of the conditions for approval of a VCT, a '*relevant investment*' is made in a company if and when:

- an investment (of any kind) in the company is made by a VCT;
- the company issues shares (for which money has been subscribed) in respect of which it provides a compliance statement under **23.11** ENTERPRISE INVESTMENT SCHEME or **60.34** SEED ENTERPRISE INVESTMENT SCHEME;

- (in relation to investments made on or after 18 November 2015) an investment is made in the company and (at any time) the company provides a compliance statement under **65.36** SOCIAL INVESTMENT RELIEF in respect of it; *ITA 2007, s 257KB* (see **65.1** SOCIAL INVESTMENT RELIEF) applies in determining when such an investment is made; or
- any other investment is made in the company which is aid received by it pursuant to a measure approved by the EC as compatible with Article 107 of the Treaty on the Functioning of the European Union in accordance with the principles laid down in the EC's Guidelines on State aid to promote risk finance investment (previously the Community Guidelines on Risk Capital Investments in Small and Medium-sized Enterprises).

Investments within (A)–(C) above (under the non-qualifying investments condition) made by a company on or after 18 November 2015, and within (D) or (E) above made by a company on or after 6 April 2016, are disregarded for the purpose of the investment limits condition

The permitted maximum age condition

This condition has effect in relation to investments made on or after 18 November 2015. The condition is that the company has not made and will not make an investment, in the accounting periods, in a company which breaches the permitted maximum age limit. An investment breaches the limit if it is made after the 'initial investing period' and none of the conditions set out below is met. The '*initial investing period*' is the seven years beginning with the 'relevant first commercial sale' (ten years where the investee company is a 'knowledge-intensive company' (see **71.4** below) when the current investment is made).The conditions are that:

- a 'relevant investment' (as under the investment limits condition above) was made in the investee company before the end of the initial investing period, and some or all of the money raised by that investment was employed for the purposes of the same activities as the money raised by the current investment;
- the amount of the current investment plus the total amount of any other relevant investments made in the investee company in a period of 30 consecutive days which includes the date of the current investment date is at least 50% of the annual turnover of the investee company averaged over five years (see *ITA 2007, s 280C(8)–(9)*), and the money raised by those investments is employed for the purpose of 'entering a new product or geographical market' (as defined in the General Block Exemption Regulation (Commission Regulation (EU) No 651/2014); or
- the condition immediately above or the equivalent condition for EIS investments (see **23** ENTERPRISE INVESTMENT SCHEME) was previously met in relation to one or more relevant investments in the investee company, and some or all of the money raised by those investments was employed for the purposes of the same activities as the money raised by the current investment.

'*First commercial sale*' has the same meaning as in the EC's Guidelines on State aid to promote risk finance investments. The '*relevant first commercial sale*' is defined in *ITA 2007, s 280C(7)* by reference to the earliest date of any commercial sale made by (broadly) the investee company or a 51% subsidiary or any other person who has carried on any trade which is carried on by the company or a subsidiary.

Investments made by a company within (A)–(C) above (under the non-qualifying investments condition), and within (D) or (E) above made by a company on or after 6 April 2016, are disregarded for the purpose of the permitted maximum age condition.

See **71.5** below as regards modification of the permitted maximum age condition on and after 6 April 2017 in the event of certain company restructuring.

The no business acquisition condition

This condition has effect in relation to investments made on or after 18 November 2015. The condition is that the company has not made and will not make an investment, in the accounting periods, in a company which breaches the prohibition on business acquisitions. An investment breaches the prohibition if any of the money raised by it is employed (whether on its own or with other money) on the acquisition (directly or indirectly) of: an interest in another company such that a company becomes a 51% subsidiary of the investee company; a further interest in a 51% subsidiary of the investee company; a trade (as widely defined); or goodwill or other intangible assets employed for the purposes of a trade.

Investments made by a company within (A)–(C) above (under the non-qualifying investments condition), and within (D) or (E) above made by a company on or after 6 April 2016, are disregarded for the purpose of the no business acquisition condition.

[*ITA 2007, ss 274, 276, 277, 280, 280A–280D, 285; FA 2012, Sch 8 paras 2, 3, 18; F(No 2)A 2015, Sch 6 paras 3–5, 23(1)(4); FA 2016, ss 29(3)(6), 30, 31; SI 2009 No 2860, Art 5; SI 2011 No 662*].

Alternative conditions

Where any of the above conditions are not met, approval may nevertheless be given where HMRC are satisfied as to the meeting of those conditions (and in some cases other conditions imposed by regulations) in certain future accounting periods. [*ITA 2007, s 275; F(No 3)A 2010, Sch 2 para 2(3)*].

Supplementary provisions

[71.3] The following supplementary provisions apply to determine whether a company meets the conditions for approval.

Value of investments

The value of any investment for the purposes of the 15% holding limit condition, the 70% qualifying holdings condition and the 70% eligible shares condition at **71.2** above is the value when the investment was acquired, except that where it is added to by a further holding of an investment of the same description (otherwise than for no consideration), or a payment is made in discharge of any obligation attached to it which increases its value, it is the value immediately after the most recent such addition or payment.

For this purpose, where, in connection with a 'scheme of reconstruction' (within *TCGA 1992, s 136*), a company issues shares or securities to persons holding shares or securities in another in respect of, and in proportion to (or as nearly as may be in proportion to) such holdings, without the recipients becoming liable for any consideration, the old and the new holdings are treated as the same.

Where:

(i) shares or securities in a company are exchanged for corresponding shares and securities in a new holding company; or
(ii) a VCT exercises conversion rights in respect of certain convertible shares and securities,

then, subject to detailed conditions (see *ITA 2007, ss 326–329*), the value of the new shares is taken to be the same as the value of the old shares when they were last valued for these purposes.

Where, under a company reorganisation or other arrangement:

- a VCT exchanges a qualifying holding for other shares or securities (with or without other consideration); and
- the exchange is for genuine commercial reasons and not part of a tax avoidance scheme or arrangements,

regulations provide a formula which values the new shares or securities by reference to the proportion of the value of the old shares or securities that the market value of the new shares or securities bears to the total consideration receivable. If no other consideration is receivable, the value of the new is identical to that of the old. The provisions extend to new shares or securities received in pursuance of an earn-out right (see **63.6** SHARES AND SECURITIES) conferred in exchange for a qualifying holding, in which case an election is available (under *Reg 10*) to modify the formula by effectively disregarding the earn-out right itself.

[*ITA 2007, ss 278, 279; SI 2002 No 2661*].

Withdrawal of approval

Approval may be withdrawn where there are reasonable grounds for believing that:

(A) the conditions for approval were not satisfied at the time the approval was given; or
(B) a condition that HMRC were satisfied would be met has not been or will not be met; or
(C) in either the most recent complete accounting period or the current one, one of the six conditions at **71.2** above has failed or will fail to be met (unless the failure was allowed for as above); or

(D) where, in relation to a second or further issue by an approved VCT, the 70% qualifying holdings condition and the 70% eligible shares condition at **71.2** above do not have to be met in the period of issue or certain following accounting periods (see above), one of the six conditions will fail to be met in the first period for which those two conditions must be met; or

(E) any other conditions prescribed by regulations have not been met in relation to, or to part of, an accounting period for which the 70% qualifying holdings condition and the 70% eligible shares condition above do not have to be met; or

(F) (for shares issued on or after 6 April 2014) the VCT has issued shares and, before the end of the three years beginning at the end of the accounting period in which the shares were issued, it has:
- made a payment to all or any of its shareholders of an amount representing a repayment of its share capital, whether that payment was made out of a reserve arising from a reduction of share capital or otherwise, or
- where the shares were issued at a premium, made a payment to all or any of its shareholders of an amount representing that premium or any part of it, whether that payment was made out of a share premium reserve or otherwise, or
- used an amount which represents its share capital or an amount by which that share capital has been diminished or, where the shares were issued at a premium, that premium (or any part of it), to pay up new shares to be allotted to all or any of its shareholders,

and has done so other than for the purpose of redeeming or repurchasing any of the issued shares. A distribution of assets counts as a payment unless it is made in connection with the winding-up of the VCT.

For the purposes of (F) above, a VCT's share capital does not include any shares issued before 1 April 2014.

The withdrawal is effective from the time the company is notified of it, except that:

(1) where approval is given on HMRC's being satisfied as to the meeting of the relevant conditions in future accounting periods, and is withdrawn before all of the six conditions have been satisfied in relation to either a complete twelve-month accounting period or successive complete accounting periods constituting a continuous period of twelve months or more, the approval is deemed never to have been given; and

(2) for the purposes of relief for capital gains accruing to a VCT under *TCGA 1992, s 100* (see **71.10** below), withdrawal may be effective from an earlier date, but not before the start of the accounting period in which the failure occurred (or is expected to occur).

An assessment consequent on the withdrawal of approval may, where otherwise out of time, be made within three years from the time notice of the withdrawal was given.

For the detailed requirements as regards granting and refusal (and withdrawal) of approval, and appeals procedures, see *SI 1995 No 1979, Pt II*.

[*ITA 2007, ss 281, 282; FA 2014, Sch 10 para 3*].

With effect from 1 September 2008, regulations enable a VCT to apply to HMRC for a determination that they will not exercise, for a certain period, their power to withdraw approval by reason of a specified breach, including a future breach, of the above conditions. Broadly, the breach must be the result of circumstances outside the VCT's control and the VCT must have taken all reasonable measures to continue to meet the conditions. The breach must be rectified within a reasonable period. [*SI 1995 No 1979, Regs 8A–8J; SI 2008 No 1893, Reg 9*].

Mergers

Regulations enable two or more merging VCTs to retain VCT status and provide for investors in the merged VCTs who continue as investors in the 'successor company' not to lose their tax reliefs. This treatment can apply to two types of merger:

(1) where shares in one of the merging companies (company A) are issued to members of the other merging company or companies in exchange for their shares in that other company or by way of consideration for a transfer to company A of the whole or part of the business of that other company;
(2) where shares in a company (company B) which is not one of the merging companies are issued to members of the merging companies in exchange for their shares in those companies or as consideration for a transfer to company B of the whole or part of the businesses of those companies.

Company A or, as appropriate, company B is the '*successor company*'.

For the regulations to apply, a merging company or the successor company must apply to HMRC for approval, and approval must be granted before the merger takes place. For the procedure for obtaining approval see *SI 2004 No 2199, Reg 10*. HMRC will not approve the merger unless they are satisfied that strict conditions are met, including that the merger is for genuine commercial reasons and not part of a scheme or arrangements with a tax avoidance purpose. For the detailed conditions, see *SI 2004 No 2199, Reg 9(3)*.

Consequences of approval

Where approval is obtained, the following apply:

- income tax investment relief within **71.7** below cannot be obtained in respect of any shares issued to effect the merger by the successor company, and such shares are ignored in determining whether the 'permitted maximum' at **71.9** below has been exceeded;
- the nature of income, income retention, 70% qualifying holdings, 70% eligible shares and 15% holding limit conditions at **71.2** above, and the provisions at **71.4** below apply to the successor company:
  (i) as if the property of the merging companies were vested in the successor company (so that transfers between a merging company and the successor company are disregarded);

(ii) disregarding, in the hands of the successor company, any assets consisting in rights against, or shares or securities of, another company which is a merging company; and

(iii) disregarding, in the hands of the successor company, the use of any money which, in the hands of another company which is a merging company, would have been disregarded under *ITA 2007, s 280(2)* (use of money raised by further issue of shares to be ignored for certain periods for the purposes of the 70% qualifying holdings and 70% eligible shares conditions), for the same periods as are mentioned in that provision;

- a disposal by a merging company to the successor company after the merger of an asset held by the merging company immediately before, or in the period during which, the merger takes place is not prevented by *TCGA 1992, s 171(2)(cc)* (see **29.3**(via) GROUPS OF COMPANIES) from being treated as at no gain/no loss;
- for the purposes of the income tax reliefs at **71.7–71.9** below:

(i) any share for share exchange or share for business transfer is not treated as a disposal of the 'old shares' (i.e. the shares for which the shares issued to effect the merger (the '*new shares*') were issued or, in the case of a share for business transfer, the shares in respect of which the new shares were issued);

(ii) any other act (including the giving of relief) carried out, of failure to act, in relation to the old shares is treated as carried out, or omitted, in relation to the corresponding new shares; and

(iii) references to the company in which the old shares were held are to be read as references to the successor company;

- for the purposes of capital gains tax relief on disposal at **71.11** below, if the successor company is not otherwise a VCT at the time the shares issued to effect the merger are acquired but is a VCT at the time of a subsequent disposal of the shares, it is treated as a VCT at and from the time of acquisition;
- where any of the qualifying holding requirements at **71.4** below (other than the qualifying subsidiaries requirement) were satisfied to any extent or for any period in relation to an investment held by a merging company immediately before the merger, they are treated as satisfied to the same extent or for the same period when held by the successor company, as if the two companies were the same company;
- for the purposes of the 15% holding limit condition at **71.2** above and the qualifying subsidiaries requirement at **71.4** below, the period in which the merger takes place is disregarded and if as a result of the merger that test or requirement is no longer met, it is treated as met for a period of one year;
- for the purposes of the 70% qualifying holdings, 70% eligible shares and 15% holding limit conditionse and the proportion of eligible shares requirement at **71.4** below, the value of investments in the hands of the successor company immediately after the merger is taken to be their value when last valued before the merger in accordance with the rules governing those conditions and that requirement, unless there has been a transaction other than the merger as a result of which the investments would fall to be revalued; and

- where provisional approval of a merging company other than the successor company is withdrawn following the merger, the withdrawal takes effect from the time the company is notified of it (and the approval is not deemed never to have been given).

[*ITA 2007, ss 321–325; FA 2014, Sch 10 para 4; SI 2004 No 2199, Regs 1, 9–13*].

Winding-up

Regulations enable a VCT to retain its VCT status during a 'prescribed winding-up period', thereby enabling investors' reliefs to continue for that period.

A VCT-in-liquidation can obtain this treatment if either it has been approved as a VCT continuously for at least three years ending with the commencement of the winding-up or, where the winding-up is by court order, it is approved as a VCT immediately before the commencement. The winding-up must be for genuine commercial reasons and not part of tax avoidance arrangements and the VCT-in-liquidation must notify HMRC of the commencement. A VCT-in-liquidation which has been at any time a merger company (see above) without being a successor company does not qualify. The '*prescribed winding-up period*' for these purposes is the three years beginning with the commencement of the winding-up, but if the winding-up ends, the company ceases to be wound up or is dissolved, the period comes to an end with the earliest of those events.

Where the VCT-in-liquidation fulfils the above requirements, the following apply.

(I) For the purposes of the income tax relief on investments (see **71.7** below), the commencement of the winding-up does not affect the status of the VCT-in-liquidation as a VCT (i.e. the commencement itself is not treated as an event leading to the withdrawal of approval and the provisions for withdrawal of relief at **71.8** below are not triggered by it).

(II) Gains accruing to the VCT-in-liquidation during the prescribed winding-up period on disposal of assets acquired before the commencement of the winding-up are not chargeable gains (and losses are not allowable losses).

(III) Capital gains tax relief on disposal of VCT shares (see **71.11** below) is available (provided that the other conditions for that relief are met) for disposals in the prescribed winding-up period as if the VCT-in-liquidation were a VCT. If, at the end of that period the VCT-in-liquidation still exists and the conditions for approval as a VCT (see above) are not then fulfilled, approval is treated, for the purposes of that relief, as withdrawn at that time (with the consequences described at **71.10** below).

[*ITA 2007, ss 314–320, 324, 325; SI 2004 No 2199, Regs 1–7; SI 2011 No 660*].

Qualifying holdings

[71.4] A VCT's holding of shares or securities in a company is comprised in its '*qualifying holdings*' at any time if

- the requirements below are satisfied at that time in relation to the company and the shares or securities;
- the shares or securities were first issued to the VCT, and have been held by it ever since; and
- (for the purpose of determining whether shares or securities issued on or after 18 November 2015 are to be regarded as comprised in a VCT's qualifying holdings) the shares or securities were first issued by the company in order to raise money for the purposes of promoting the growth and development of the company or, where the company is a parent company, the group.

Where any of the maximum qualifying investment, use of money raised or relevant company to carry on the relevant qualifying activity requirements would be met as to only part of the money raised by the issue, and the holding is not otherwise capable of being treated as separate holdings, it is treated as two separate holdings, one from which that part of the money was raised, the other from which the rest was raised, with the value being apportioned accordingly to each holding. In the case of the use of money raised requirement, this does not require an insignificant amount applied for non-trade purposes to be treated as a separate holding.

[*ITA 2007, ss 286, 293(7); FA 2012, Sch 6 para 15, Sch 8 para 4; F(No 2)A 2015, Sch 6 paras 6, 23(2)(3)*].

The UK permanent establishment requirement

For shares or securities issued on or after 6 April 2011, the company must have a 'permanent establishment' in the UK at all times from the issue of the holding to the time in question.

For this purpose, a company has a '*permanent establishment*' in the UK if, and only if, either:

- it has a 'fixed place of business' there through which its business is wholly or partly carried on; or
- an agent (other than one of independent status acting in the ordinary course of his business) acting on its behalf has, and habitually exercises there, authority to enter into contracts on the company's behalf,

unless the activities carried on in the UK are of a 'preparatory or auxiliary character'. The Treasury can amend this definition by regulations.

A '*fixed place of business*' includes a place of management, a branch, office, factory or workshop, a mine, oil or gas well, quarry or other place of natural resource extraction and a building site, construction or installation project. Activities of a '*preparatory or auxiliary character*' include the use of facilities for the purpose of storage, display or delivery of goods or merchandise belonging to the company; the maintenance of a stock of goods or merchandise belonging to the company for the purpose of storage, display, delivery or processing by another person; or purchasing goods or merchandise, or collecting information, for the company.

A company is not treated as having a permanent establishment in the UK by reason of its controlling a company resident there or a company carrying on business there (whether or not through a permanent establishment).

[*ITA 2007, ss 286A, 302A; SI 2011 No 662*].

The financial health requirement

For shares or securities issued on or after 6 April 2011, the company must not be 'in difficulty' at the time of issue of the holding. For this purpose, a company is 'in difficulty' if it is reasonable to assume that it would be so regarded under the Community Guidelines on State Aid for Rescuing and Restructuring Firms in Difficulty (2004/C244/02).

[*ITA 2007, s 286B; SI 2011 No 662*].

The maximum qualifying investment requirement

For the purpose of determining whether shares or securities issued on or after 6 April 2012 are to be regarded as comprised in a VCT's qualifying holdings, this requirement applies only if:

- at the time of issue the company or any of its qualifying subsidiaries (see the qualifying subsidiaries requirement below) was a member of a partnership or a party to a joint venture;
- the qualifying trade in below was at that time being carried on, or to be carried on, by that partnership or joint venture; and
- the other partners or parties to the joint venture include at least one other company.

Previously this was a general requirement. The requirement is that the holding in question must not, when it was issued, have represented an investment in excess of the 'maximum qualifying investment' for the period from six months before the issue in question (or, if earlier, the beginning of the tax year of the issue) to the time of the issue. For this purpose, the maximum qualifying investment for a period is exceeded so far as the aggregate amount of money raised in that period by the issue to the VCT during that period of shares or securities of the company exceeds £1 million. Where this limit is exceeded, the shares or securities which represent the excess are treated as not being part of the holding concerned (so that £1 million can be included as a qualifying holding) and the money raised by those shares or securities is ignored for the purpose of any subsequent application of this requirement. Disposals are treated as far as possible as eliminating any such excess.

Where the conditions above are met, whether in relation to shares or securities issued on or after 6 April 2012 or previously, the £1 million limit is reduced by dividing it by the number of companies (including the company in question) which are members of the partnership or joint venture.

[*ITA 2007, s 287; FA 2012, Sch 8 paras 5, 19(1)*].

The no guaranteed loan requirement

The holding in question must not include any securities (as defined in **71.2** above) relating to a guaranteed loan. A security relates to a guaranteed loan if there are arrangements entitling the VCT to receive anything (directly or indirectly) from a 'third party' in the event of a failure by any person to comply with the terms of the security or the loan to which it relates. It is immaterial whether or not the arrangements apply in all such cases. '*Third party*' means any person other than the investee company itself and, if it is a parent company that meets the trading requirement below, its subsidiaries. This condition applies for accounting periods (of the VCT) ending after 1 July 1997, but does not apply in the case of shares or securities acquired by the VCT by means of investing money raised by the issue by it before 2 July 1997 of shares or securities (or money derived from the investment of any such money raised). [*ITA 2007, s 288*].

The proportion of eligible shares requirement

At least 10% (by value) of the VCT's *total* holding of shares in and securities of the company must consist of 'eligible shares' (as defined for the purposes of the 70% eligible shares condition at **71.2** above — broadly, ordinary, non-preferential, shares). For this purpose, the value of shares etc. at any time is taken to be their value immediately after the most recent of the events listed below, except that it cannot thereby be taken to be less than the amount of consideration given by the VCT for the shares etc. The said events are as set out below.

- The acquisition of the shares etc. by the VCT.
- The acquisition by the VCT (other than for no consideration) of any other shares etc. in the same company which are of the same description as those already held.
- The making of any payment in discharge (or part discharge) of any obligation attached to the shares etc. in a case where such discharge increases the value of the shares etc.

This requirement applies for accounting periods (of the VCT) ending after 1 July 1997, but, if necessary in order to satisfy the requirement, one may disregard shares and securities acquired by the VCT by means of investing money raised by the issue by it before 2 July 1997 of shares or securities (or money derived from the investment of any such money raised).

[*ITA 2007, s 289*].

The trading requirement

The company must either:

(a) exist wholly for the purpose of carrying on one or more 'qualifying trades' (disregarding any purpose having no significant effect on the extent of its activities); or

(b) be a '*parent company*' (i.e. a company that has one or more 'qualifying subsidiaries' — see the qualifying subsidiaries requirement below) and the business of the '*group*' (i.e. the company and its qualifying subsidiaries) must not consist wholly or as to a substantial part (i.e. broadly 20% — see HMRC Venture Capital Schemes Manual VCM3010) in the carrying on of 'non-qualifying activities'.

Where the company intends that one or more other companies should become its qualifying subsidiaries with a view to their carrying on one or more qualifying trades, then, until any time after which the intention is abandoned, the company is treated as a parent company and those other companies are included in the group for the purposes of (b) above.

For the purpose of (b) above, the business of the group means what would be the business of the group if the activities of the group companies taken together were regarded as one business. Activities are for this purpose disregarded to the extent that they consist in:

(i) holding shares in or securities of any of the company's subsidiaries;
(ii) making loans to another group company;
(iii) holding and managing property used by a group company for the purposes of a qualifying trade or trades carried on by any group company; or
(iv) holding and managing property used by a group company for the purposes of research and development from which it is intended either that a qualifying trade to be carried on by a group company will be derived or a qualifying trade carried on or to be carried on by a group company will benefit.

References in (iv) above to a group company include references to any existing or future company which will be a group company at any future time.

Activities are similarly disregarded to the extent that they consist, in the case of a subsidiary whose main purpose is the carrying on of qualifying trade(s) and whose other purposes have no significant effect on the extent of its activities (other than in relation to incidental matters), in activities not in pursuance of its main purpose.

'*Non-qualifying activities*' are:

(I) activities within **23.9**(a)–(c), (e)–(q) ENTERPRISE INVESTMENT SCHEME (other than those within **23.9**(e) which do not result in a trade being excluded from being a qualifying trade); and
(II) non-trading activities.

[*ITA 2007, ss 290, 332*].

A company does not cease to meet this requirement by reason only of anything done as a consequence of its being in administration or receivership (both as defined — see *ITA 2007, s 331*), provided everything so done and the making of the relevant order are for genuine commercial (and not tax avoidance) reasons. [*ITA 2007, s 292*].

Qualifying trade

A trade is a '*qualifying trade*' if it is conducted on a commercial basis with a view to the realisation of profits and it does not, at any time in the period since the issue of the shares to the VCT consist to a substantial extent in the carrying on of 'excluded activities'. For these purposes, 'trade' (except in relation to the trade mentioned in (t) below) does not include a venture in the nature of trade. '*Excluded activities*' are:

(a) dealing in land, commodities or futures, or in shares, securities or other financial instruments;
(b) dealing in goods otherwise than in an ordinary trade of wholesale or retail distribution (see below);
(c) banking, insurance or any other financial activities;
(d) leasing or letting or receiving royalties or licence fees;
(e) providing legal or accountancy services;
(f) 'property development';
(g) farming or market gardening;
(h) holding, managing or occupying woodlands, any other forestry activities or timber production;
(i) shipbuilding (defined by reference to relevant EU State aid rules);
(j) producing coal or steel (both defined by reference to relevant EU State aid rules and including the extraction of coal);
(k) operating or managing hotels or comparable establishments (i.e. guest houses, hostels and other establishments whose main purpose is to offer overnight accommodation with or without catering) or property used as such;
(l) operating or managing nursing homes or residential care homes (both as defined) or property used as such;
(m) (in relation to shares or securities issued to the VCT on or after 6 April 2016) generating or exporting electricity or making electricity generating capacity available;
(n) (in relation to shares or securities issued to the VCT on or after 6 April 2016) generating heat;
(o) (in relation to shares or securities issued to the VCT on or after 6 April 2016) generating any form of energy not within (m) or (n);
(p) (in relation to shares or securities issued to the VCT on or after 6 April 2016) producing gas or fuel;
(q) (in relation to shares or securities issued to the VCT before 6 April 2016) the subsidised generation or export of electricity;
(r) (in relation to shares or securities issued to the VCT before 6 April 2016) the subsidised generation of heat or subsidised production of gas or fuel;
(s) (in relation to shares or securities issued to the VCT on or after 30 November 2015 and before 6 April 2016) making reserve electricity generating capacity available (or using such capacity to generate electricity); and
(t) providing services or facilities for any business consisting of activities within any of (a) to (s) and carried on by another person (other than a parent company), where one person has a 'controlling interest' in both that business and the business carried on by the provider.

HMRC regard as 'substantial' for the above purposes a part of a trade which consists of 20% or more of total activities, judged by any reasonable measure (normally turnover or capital employed) (HMRC Venture Capital Schemes Manual VCM3010). As regards (a) above, dealing in land includes cases where steps are taken, before selling the land, to make it more attractive to a purchaser; such steps might include the refurbishment of existing buildings (HMRC Venture Capital Schemes Manual VCM3020).

As regards (b), (d)–(g), (k), (l), (q) and (r) above, see the comments in **23.9** ENTERPRISE INVESTMENT SCHEME on the corresponding exclusions there. As regards (t) above, the question of whether a person has a '*controlling interest*' in a business is determined in a similar manner as in **23.9**; for this purpose, '*control*' is determined in accordance with *CTA 2010, ss 450, 451* but with certain modifications.

[*ITA 2007, ss 300(1)(4), 303–307, 307A–307C, 308, 309, 309A, 309B, 310, 313(4)–(7), Sch 2 paras 81–85; FA 2012, Sch 8 paras 11–13, 22; FA 2014, s 56(5)–(7)(9); FA 2015, Sch 6 paras 6–9, 11, 12, 14; F(No 2)A 2015, s 27(2)(4); FA 2016, s 28(2)(4)(6)*].

'Research and development' from which it is intended that a qualifying trade either will be derived or will benefit is treated as the carrying on of a qualifying trade. Preparing to carry on such research and development does not, however, count as preparing to carry on a trade. '*Research and development*' has the meaning given by *ITA 2007, s 1006*.

[*ITA 2007, s 300(2)(3), Sch 2 para 78*].

The carrying on of a qualifying activity requirement

In relation to shares or securities issued to the VCT **after 16 March 2004**, a 'qualifying company' (whether or not the same such company at all times) must, when the shares were issued to the VCT and at all times since, have been carrying on one of the following two '*qualifying activities*':

(A) carrying on a 'qualifying trade' (see the trading requirement above); or
(B) preparing to carry on a qualifying trade.

The condition in (B) above is, however, relevant only for a period of two years after the issue of the shares, by which time the intended trade must have been commenced by a 'qualifying company', and ceases to be relevant at any time within those two years after the intention is abandoned.

For shares or securities issued before 6 April 2011, the qualifying trade in (A) above must be carried on 'wholly or mainly in the UK' (see the trading requirement above) and, where (B) above applies, it must have been the intention, at the time the shares were issued, for the qualifying trade to be carried on wholly or mainly in the UK.

For these purposes, '*qualifying company*' means the issuing company itself or any 'qualifying 90% subsidiary' of that company. (In determining the time at which a qualifying trade begins to be carried on by a 'qualifying 90% subsidiary', any carrying on of the trade by it before it became such a subsidiary is disregarded.) For the purposes of (B) above only, a qualifying 90% subsidiary includes any existing or future company which will be a qualifying 90% subsidiary at any future time.

A company (the subsidiary) is a '*qualifying 90% subsidiary*' of the issuing company at any time when:

- the issuing company possesses at least 90% of both the issued share capital of, and the voting power in, the subsidiary;

- the issuing company would be beneficially entitled to at least 90% of the assets of the subsidiary available for distribution to equity holders on a winding-up or in any other circumstances;
- the issuing company is beneficially entitled to at least 90% of any profits of the subsidiary available for distribution to equity holders;
- no person other than the issuing company has control (within *ITA 2007, s 995* — see **41.28** CONNECTED PERSONS) of the subsidiary; and
- no arrangements exist by virtue of which any of the above conditions would cease to be met.

For the above purposes, *CTA 2010, Pt 5 Ch 6* applies, with appropriate modifications, to determine the persons who are equity holders and the percentage of assets available to them. A subsidiary does not cease to be a qualifying 90% subsidiary by reason only of it or any other company having commenced winding up or by reason only of anything done as a consequence of any such company being in administration or receivership, provided the winding-up, entry into administration or receivership (both as defined) or anything done as a consequence of its being in administration or receivership is for genuine commercial reasons and is not part of a tax avoidance scheme or arrangements. Also, the listed conditions are not regarded as ceasing to be satisfied by reason only of arrangements being in existence for the disposal of the issuing company's interest in the subsidiary if the disposal is to be for genuine commercial reasons and is not to be part of a tax avoidance scheme or arrangements.

On or after 6 April 2007, a company (company A) is also a qualifying 90% subsidiary of the issuing company if:

- company A would be a qualifying 90% subsidiary of another company (company B) if that company were the issuing company and company B is a 'qualifying 100% subsidiary' of the issuing company; or
- company A is a qualifying 100% subsidiary of company B and company B is a qualifying 90% subsidiary of the issuing company.

No account is taken for this purpose of any control the issuing company may have of company A. The definition of a qualifying 90% subsidiary is used to define a '*qualifying 100% subsidiary*', replacing the references in that definition to 'at least 90%' with references to '100%'.

In relation to shares or securities issued to the VCT **on or before 16 March 2004**, the issuing company or a 'relevant qualifying subsidiary' must, when the shares were issued to the VCT and at all times since, have been either:

- carrying on a qualifying trade wholly or mainly in the UK; or
- preparing to carry on a qualifying trade which, at the time the shares were issued, it intended to carry on wholly or mainly in the UK;

but the second of these conditions is relevant only for a period of two years after the issue of the shares, by which time the trade must have commenced as intended, and ceases to be relevant at any time within those two years after the intention is abandoned. For this purpose, a '*relevant qualifying subsidiary*' is, broadly, a company which is 90% owned by the issuing company (or by a subsidiary of the issuing company) and which otherwise satisfies the conditions of *ICTA 1988, Sch 28B para 10* (as amended prior to *FA 2004*).

[*ITA 2007, ss 291, 301; SI 2011 No 662*].

A company does not cease to meet this requirement by reason only of anything done as a consequence of its being in administration or receivership (both as defined), provided everything so done and the making of the relevant order are for genuine commercial (and not tax avoidance) reasons. [*ITA 2007, s 292*].

The maximum amount raised annually through risk finance investment requirement

The total amount of 'relevant investments' (see below) made in the issuing company in the 12 months ending with the date of issue to the VCT must not exceed £5 million (£2 million for the purpose of determining whether shares or securities issued before 6 April 2012 are to be regarded as comprised in a VCT's qualifying holdings). The following also count towards this limit:

(1) any relevant investment in a 51% subsidiary (within *CTA 2010, Pt 24 Ch 3*) of the issuing company (including any made before it became a 51% subsidiary but not any made after it last ceased to be one);
(2) any relevant investment made in any company to the extent that the money raised by the investment has been employed for the purposes of a trade (as widely defined) carried on by another company that has at any time in the said 12-month period been a 51% subsidiary of the issuing company (disregarding any money so employed after it last ceased to be such a subsidiary); and
(3) any other relevant investment made in any company to the extent that the money raised has been employed for the purposes of a trade (as widely defined), and within that 12-month period, but after the investment was made, the trade (or a part of it) was transferred to the issuing company, a 51% subsidiary or a partnership of which the issuing company or a 51% subsidiary is a member (but disregarding trades transferred after a 51% subsidiary in question last ceased to be such a subsidiary).

For the purpose of determining whether shares or securities issued before 18 November 2015 were to be regarded as comprised in a VCT's qualifying holdings, (1)–(3) above did not apply but investments made in any company that was a subsidiary of the issuing company at any time in the said 12-month period counted towards the limit (regardless of whether or not it was a subsidiary when the investment was made).

[*ITA 2007, s 292A(1)–(2B)(7); FA 2012, Sch 8 paras 6, 19(1), 20; F(No 2)A 2015, Sch 6 paras 7, 23(3)(4); SI 2012 No 1901*].

Relevant investments

For the purposes of the VCT qualifying holding requirements, '*relevant investments*' comprise:

(a) investments (of any kind) made by a VCT;
(b) money subscribed for shares issued by the investee company under the ENTERPRISE INVESTMENT SCHEME (EIS) (**23**) or the SEED ENTERPRISE INVESTMENT SCHEME (SEIS) (**60**);

(c) (for the purpose of determining whether shares or securities issued on or after 18 November 2015 are to be regarded as comprised in a VCT's qualifying holdings) investments made under the SOCIAL INVESTMENT RELIEF (**65**) scheme; and

(d) (for the purpose of determining whether shares or securities issued on or after 6 April 2012 are to be regarded as comprised in a VCT's qualifying holdings) any other investment made in the company which is aid received by it pursuant to a measure approved by the EC as compatible with Article 107 of the Treaty on the Functioning of the European Union in accordance with the principles laid down in the EC's Guidelines on State aid to promote risk finance investment (previously the Community Guidelines on Risk Capital Investments in Small and Medium-sized Enterprises).

As regards (b) above, shares are treated as having been issued under the EIS or SEIS if at any time the investee company provides an EIS compliance statement (see **23.11** ENTERPRISE INVESTMENT SCHEME) or SEIS equivalent (see **60.34** SEED ENTERPRISE INVESTMENT SCHEME) in respect of those shares; an investment is regarded as made when the shares are issued. As regards (c) above, an investment is treated as made under the social investment relief scheme if at any time the investee company provides a compliance statement as in **65.36** SOCIAL INVESTMENT RELIEF; *ITA 2007, s 257KB* (see **65.1** SOCIAL INVESTMENT RELIEF) applies in determining when such an investment is made. If the provision of a compliance statement causes this requirement not to be met, the requirement is treated as having been met from the time the shares in question were issued to the VCT to the time the compliance statement was provided.

[*ITA 2007, s 292A(3)–(6); FA 2012, Sch 6 paras 16, 24(2), Sch 8 paras 6, 19(1), 20; F(No 2)A 2015, Sch 6 paras 7, 23(3)(4)*].

The maximum risk finance investments when holding is issued requirement

The following applies for the purpose of determining whether shares or securities issued on or after 18 November 2015 are to be regarded as comprised in a VCT's qualifying holdings. The total amount of 'relevant investments' (see above) made in the issuing company on or before investment date (i.e. the date the holding in question is issued) must not exceed £12 million or, if the company is a 'knowledge-intensive company' (see below) at the investment date, £20 million. Relevant investments of the kind in (a)–(c) above also count towards these limits, but disregarding references there to a 12-month period and instead taking into account all times before the investment date. If at any time the company provides a compliance statement under **23.11** ENTERPRISE INVESTMENT SCHEME, **60.34** SEED ENTERPRISE INVESTMENT SCHEME or **65.36** SOCIAL INVESTMENT RELIEF and this requirement ceases to be met as a result, it is nevertheless treated as having been met throughout the period from the investment date until the provision of the compliance statement. [*ITA 2007, s 292AA; F(No 2)A 2015, Sch 6 paras 8, 23(3)(4)*].

Knowledge-intensive companies

A '*knowledge-intensive company*' is broadly a company whose costs of research and development or innovation are at least 15% of its operating costs in at least one of the years comprising the 'relevant three-year period' or at least 10% of its operating costs in each of those years, and which meets at least one of the two conditions below. The '*relevant three-year period*' is normally the three years ending immediately before the beginning of the last accounts filing period. However, if the last accounts filing period ends more than 12 months before the applicable time, the relevant three-year period is the three years ending 12 months before the applicable time. The applicable time is the date on which the matter of whether a company is a knowledge-intensive company falls to be judged. (If the applicable time falls on or after 18 November 2015 and before 6 April 2016, a company may make an election under *FA 2016, s 30* the effect of which is that the relevant three-year period is in any case the three years ending 12 months before the applicable time.) A company's operating costs are defined by reference to the items recognised as expenses in its profit and loss account. The conditions to be met are that:

- the company has created, is creating or is intending to create, intellectual property (the '*innovation condition*'); or
- the company's full-time employees with a relevant Masters or higher degree who are engaged in research and development or innovation comprise at least 20% of the total of its full-time employees (the '*skilled employee condition*').

In order to meet the innovation condition, the company must be engaged in intellectual property creation at the applicable time, and it must be reasonable to assume that, within ten years after that time, the exploitation of its intellectual property, or business which results from new or improved products, processes or services utilising its intellectual property, will form the greater part of its business. A company is engaged in intellectual property creation if intellectual property is being created by the company, or has been created by it within the previous three years; or the company is taking (or preparing to take) steps in order that intellectual property will be created by it; or the company demonstrates via an independent expert's report that it is reasonable to assume it will create intellectual property in the foreseeable future. Intellectual property is taken into account only if the whole or greater part (in terms of value) of it is created by the company and it is created in circumstances in which the right to exploit it vests in the company (whether alone or jointly with others).

If the company is a parent company, the above rules are appropriately modified to also take account of its 'qualifying subsidiaries' (see below).

[*ITA 2007, ss 313(5), 331A; F(No 2)A 2015, Sch 6 paras 15, 20; FA 2016, ss 29(5)(6), 30*].

The maximum risk finance investments in five-year post-investment period requirement

The following applies for the purpose of determining whether shares or securities issued on or after 18 November 2015 are to be regarded as comprised in a VCT's qualifying holdings. This is a requirement which is tested only during a '*five-year post-investment period*', i.e. the period of five years beginning the day after the date the holding in question is issued (the '*investment date*'), and only if the company effectively acquires a company or trade after it receives the investment in question. The requirement is that at any time in the five-year post-investment period the total of the relevant investments (see above) so far made must not exceed £12 million or, if the company is a 'knowledge-intensive company' (see above) at the investment date, £20 million. Without this requirement, the investment limits above could be sidestepped where the acquired company or trade had already benefited from earlier relevant investments. Relevant investments of the kind in (a)–(c) above also count towards these limits, but disregarding references there to a 12-month period and instead taking into account all times before the time in the five-year post-investment period when the requirement is being tested. The requirement applies where:

- a company becomes a 51% subsidiary of the issuing company at a time during the five-year post-investment period;
- all or part of the money raised by the issue of the holding in question is employed for the purposes of a relevant qualifying activity consisting (wholly or partly) of a trade (as widely defined) carried on by that company; and
- the trade (or a part of it) was carried on by that company before that time.

The requirement also applies where all or part of the money raised by the issue of the holding in question is employed for the purposes of a relevant qualifying activity consisting (wholly or partly) of a trade (as widely defined) which, during the five-year post-investment period, is transferred as in (3) above.

Similar provision applies as in the 'maximum risk finance investments when holding is issued' requirement above if at any time the company provides a compliance statement under one of the other venture capital schemes or the social investment relief scheme and this requirement ceases to be met as a result. It is nevertheless treated as having been met throughout the period from the investment date until the provision of the compliance statement.

[*ITA 2007, s 292AB; F(No 2)A 2015, Sch 6 paras 8, 23(3)(4)*].

The spending of money raised by SEIS investment requirement

The following applied for the purpose of determining whether shares or securities issued before 6 April 2015 were to be regarded as comprised in a VCT's qualifying holdings. If a SEIS investment had been made in the company, at least 70% of the money raised by that investment had to have been spent as mentioned in **60.7** SEED ENTERPRISE INVESTMENT SCHEME before the issue of the holding in question to the VCT. A SEIS investment is made if the company issues shares for cash subscription and provides a compliance statement under *ITA 2007, s 257ED* in respect of them. [*ITA 2007, s 292B; FA 2012, Sch 6 paras 17, 23(2); F(No 2)A 2015, Sch 6 paras 9, 23(2)*].

The use of the money raised requirement

The money raised by the issue of shares to the VCT must be employed *wholly* (disregarding insignificant amounts) for the purposes of the 'relevant qualifying activity'. For shares issued after 21 April 2009, this requirement must be met only where at least two years have passed since the issue (or the date of commencement of the qualifying trade where this is later than the date of issue).

For shares issued before 22 April 2009, this requirement is treated as satisfied at any time within twelve months after the issue (or commencement of the qualifying trade) if at least 80% of that money has been, or is intended to be, so employed. At any time within the following twelve months, the requirement is treated as satisfied if at least 80% of that money *has been* so employed. These rules apply for the purpose of determining whether any shares or securities are, as at any time after 6 March 2001, to be regarded as comprised in the qualifying holdings of the VCT. Previously, the requirement was treated as satisfied at any time within the first twelve-month period if *all* the money was intended to be so employed, and no special treatment applied in the following twelve months.

For this purpose, a qualifying activity is a '*relevant qualifying activity*' if it was a qualifying activity at the time the shares were issued or if it is a qualifying trade and preparing to carry it on was a qualifying activity at that time.

Employing money on the acquisition of shares in a company does not of itself amount to employing it for the purposes of a relevant qualifying activity. This applies on and after 6 April 2012 except that it did not originally have effect in relation to an investment made by a VCT of 'protected money'. For this purpose, '*protected money*' is (i) money raised by the issue before 6 April 2012 of shares in or securities of the VCT and (ii) money derived from the investment of money so raised. However, for the purpose of determining whether shares or securities issued on or after 18 November 2015 are to be regarded as comprised in a VCT's qualifying holdings, the protected money let-out no longer applies. Additionally, for that same purpose, employing money on the acquisition of any of the following does not amount to employing it for the purposes of a relevant qualifying activity: an interest in another company such that a company becomes a 51% subsidiary of the issuing company; a further interest in a 51% subsidiary of the issuing company; a trade (as widely defined); and goodwill or other intangible assets employed for the purposes of a trade.

[*ITA 2007, s 293; FA 2012, Sch 8 paras 7, 21; F(No 2)A 2015, Sch 6 paras 10, 21, 23(3)*].

In relation to buy-outs (and in particular management buy-outs), HMRC will usually accept that where a company is formed to acquire a trade, and the funds raised from the VCT are applied to that purchase, the requirement that the funds be employed for the purposes of the trade is satisfied. Where the company is formed to acquire another company and its trade, or a holding company and its trading subsidiaries, this represents an investment rather than employment for the purposes of the trade. However, HMRC will usually accept that the requirement is satisfied if the trade of the company, or all the activities of the holding company and its subsidiaries, are hived up to the acquiring company as soon as possible after the acquisition. In the case of a holding company and its subsidiaries, to the extent that the trades are not hived up, the holding cannot be a qualifying holding. (Revenue Tax Bulletin August 1995 pp 243, 244).

The relevant company to carry on the relevant qualifying activity requirement

In relation to shares or securities issued to the VCT **after 16 March 2004**, at all times after the issue of the holding the relevant qualifying activity by reference to which the use of money raised requirement is satisfied must not be carried on by any person other than the issuing company or a 'qualifying 90% subsidiary' (see the carrying on of a qualifying activity requirement above) of that company.

This requirement is not treated as not met merely because the trade in question is carried on by a person other than the issuing company or a qualifying subsidiary at any time after the issue of the shares and before the issuing company or a qualifying 90% subsidiary carries on the trade. The carrying on of the trade by a partnership of which the issuing company or a qualifying 90% subsidiary is a member, or by a joint venture to which any such company is a party, is permitted.

The requirement is also not regarded as failing to be met if, by reason only of a company being wound up or dissolved or being in administration or receivership (both as defined), the qualifying trade ceases to be carried on by the issuing company' or a qualifying 90% subsidiary and is subsequently carried on by a person who has not been connected (within *ITA 2007, s 993* – see **17** CONNECTED PERSONS – but with the modifications to the meaning of 'control' that apply for the purposes of the control and independence requirement below) with the issuing company at any time in the period beginning one year before the shares were issued. This let-out applies only if the winding-up, dissolution or entry into administration or receivership (and everything done as a consequence of the company being in administration or receivership) is for genuine commercial reasons and not part of a tax avoidance scheme or arrangements.

In relation to shares or securities issued to the VCT **on or before 16 March 2004**, where the company is a 'parent company' within (b) above, the '*trader company*' (i.e. the company carrying on (or preparing to carry on) the required qualifying trade) must either:

- satisfy the requirements in (a) above; or
- be a company in relation to which those requirements would be satisfied if activities within (i) to (iv) above, or consisting of a subsidiary making loans to its parent, were disregarded; or
- be a 'relevant qualifying subsidiary' which either:
  (1) exists wholly for the purpose of carrying on activities within (iii) or (iv) above (disregarding purposes capable of having no significant effect (other than in relation to incidental matters) on the extent of its activities); or
  (2) has no corporation tax profits and no part of its business consists in the making of investments.

  A '*relevant qualifying subsidiary*' is, broadly, a company which is 90% owned by the investee company (or by a subsidiary of that company) and which otherwise satisfies the conditions of *ICTA 1988, Sch 28B para 10* (as amended prior to *FA 2004*).

[*ITA 2007, s 294*].

The 'permitted company age' requirement

The following applies for the purpose of determining whether shares or securities issued on or after 18 November 2015 are to be regarded as comprised in a VCT's qualifying holdings. If the holding in question is issued after the 'initial investing period', one of three conditions must be met. These are that:

(a) a 'relevant investment' (see above) was made in the issuing company before the end of the initial investing period, and some or all of the money raised by that investment was employed for the purposes of the same qualifying activity as that for which the money raised by the current issue is employed;

(b) the total amount of relevant investments made in the issuing company in a period of 30 consecutive days which includes the date of issue of the holding in question is at least 50% of the annual turnover of the company averaged over five years (see *ITA 2007, s 294A(7)–(8)*), and the money raised by those investments is employed for the purpose of 'entering a new product or geographical market' (as defined in the General Block Exemption Regulation (Commission Regulation (EU) No 651/2014); or

(c) the condition in (b) or the equivalent condition for EIS investments (see **23** ENTERPRISE INVESTMENT SCHEME) was previously met in relation to one or more relevant investments in the issuing company, and some or all of the money raised by those investments was employed for the purposes of the same qualifying activity as that for which the money raised by the current issue is employed.

The '*initial investing period*' is the seven years beginning with the 'relevant first commercial sale' (ten years where the issuing company is a 'knowledge-intensive company' (see above) when the holding in question is issued). '*First commercial sale*' has the same meaning as in the EC's Guidelines on State aid to promote risk finance investments. The '*relevant first commercial sale*' is defined in *ITA 2007, s 294A(6)* by reference to the earliest date of any commercial sale made by (broadly) the company or a 51% subsidiary or any other person who has carried on any trade which is carried on by the company or a subsidiary.

See **71.5** below as regards modification of the permitted company age requirement on and after 6 April 2017 in the event of certain company restructuring.

[*ITA 2007, s 294A; F(No 2)A 2015, Sch 6 paras 11, 23(3)(4); FA 2016, ss 29(4)(6), 30*].

The unquoted status requirement

The issuing company must be an '*unquoted company*' (whether or not UK resident), i.e. none of its shares, stocks, debentures or other securities must be:

- listed on a recognised stock exchange, or a designated exchange outside the UK; or

- dealt in on the Unlisted Securities Market, or outside the UK by such means as may be designated for the purpose by order.

Securities on the Alternative Investment Market ('AIM') are treated as unquoted for these purposes. (Revenue Press Release 20 February 1995).

If the company ceases to be an unquoted company at a time when its shares are comprised in the qualifying holdings of the VCT, this requirement is treated as continuing to be met, in relation to shares or securities acquired before that time, for the following five years.

[*ITA 2007, s 295*].

The control and independence requirement

The company must not 'control' (with or without 'connected persons') any company other than a 'qualifying subsidiary' (see the qualifying subsidiaries requirement below), nor must another company (or another company and a person connected with it) control it. Neither must arrangements be in existence by virtue of which such control could arise. For these purposes, '*control*' is as under *CTA 2010, ss 450, 451*, except that possession of, or entitlement to acquire, fixed-rate preference shares (as defined) of the company which do not, for the time being, carry voting rights is disregarded, as are possession of, or entitlement to acquire, rights as a loan creditor of the company and rights to dividends carried by shares in the company which are eligible shares held by the investing company. '*Connected persons*' are as under *ITA 2007, s 993* (see **17** CONNECTED PERSONS) except that the definition of 'control' therein is similarly modified. [*ITA 2007, ss 296, 313(4)–(8)*].

For the application of the control and independence requirement to co-investors in a company, and in particular the question of whether co-investors are connected by virtue of their acting together to secure or exercise control of the company, see Revenue Tax Bulletin October 1997 pp 471, 472.

The gross assets requirement

The value of the company's gross assets or, where the company is a parent company, the value of the 'group assets', must not have exceeded £15 million immediately before the issue or £16 million immediately thereafter. For the purpose of determining whether shares or securities issued before 6 April 2012 are to be regarded as part of a VCT's qualifying holdings, these figures are £7 million and £8 million respectively.

'*Group assets*' are the gross assets of each of the members of the group, disregarding assets consisting in rights against, or shares in or securities of, another member of the group.

[*ITA 2007, s 297; FA 2012, Sch 8 paras 8, 20; SI 2012 No 1901*].

The general approach of HMRC is that the value of a company's gross assets is the sum of the value of all the balance sheet assets. Where accounts are actually drawn up to a date immediately before or after the issue, the balance sheet values are taken provided that they reflect usual accounting standards and the company's normal accounting practice, consistently applied. Where accounts are not drawn up to such a date, such values will be taken from the most recent balance sheet, updated as precisely as practicable on the basis of all the relevant information available to the company. Values so arrived at may need to be reviewed in the light of information contained in the accounts for the period in which the issue was made, and, if they were not available at the time of the issue, those for the preceding period, when they become available. The company's assets immediately before the issue do not include any advance payment received in respect of the issue. Where shares are issued partly paid, the right to the balance is an asset, and, notwithstanding the above, will be taken into account in valuing the assets immediately after the issue regardless of whether it is stated in the balance sheet. (HMRC SP 2/06).

The number of employees requirement

The 'full-time equivalent employee number' for the issuing company must be less than 250 at the time the holding is issued. For the purpose of determining whether shares or securities issued before 6 April 2012 are to be regarded as part of a VCT's qualifying holdings, the limit is 50. For the purpose of determining whether shares or securities issued on or after 18 November 2015 are so to be regarded, the limit of 250 is doubled to 500 if the company is a 'knowledge-intensive company' (see above) at the time the holding in question is issued. If the company is a parent company, the sum of the full-time equivalent employee numbers for it and each of its qualifying subsidiaries must be less than the applicable limit at the time the holding issued.

A company's '*full-time equivalent employee number*' is the number of its full-time employees plus, for each employee who is not full-time, a just and reasonable fraction. Directors count as employees for this purpose, but employees on maternity or paternity leave and students on vocational training are excluded.

[*ITA 2007, s 297A; FA 2012, Sch 8 paras 9, 20; F(No 2)A 2015, Sch 6 paras 12, 23(3); SI 2012 No 1901*].

HMRC consider that a full-time employee is one whose standard working week (excluding lunch breaks and overtime) is at least 35 hours (HMRC Venture Capital Schemes Manual VCM15105).

The proportion of skilled employees requirement

The following applies for the purpose of determining whether shares or securities issued on or after 18 November 2015 are to be regarded as comprised in a VCT's qualifying holdings. There is a requirement, where the conditions below are met, that at all times in the period of three years beginning with the issue of the holding in question the company's full-time employees with a relevant Masters or higher degree who are engaged in research and development or innovation must comprise at least 20% of the total of its full-time employees. The conditions are that:

- one or more of the requirements in the 'maximum risk finance investments when holding is issued' requirement, (the 'permitted company age' requirement) and the 'number of employees' requirement is or are met only by reason of the company being a knowledge-intensive company at the time the holding in question was issued; and

- the innovation condition in the definition of 'knowledge-intensive company' above was not met by the company at that time.

If the company is a parent company, the above is appropriately modified to also take account of the company's 'qualifying subsidiaries' (see below). The requirement is not treated as failing to be met at a time when the company, by virtue of *ITA 2007, s 292* (companies in administration or receivership), is not regarded as having ceased to meet the trading requirement.

[*ITA 2007, s 297B; F(No 2)A 2015, Sch 6 paras 13, 23(3)(4)*].

The qualifying subsidiaries requirement

Any subsidiary that the issuing company has must be a 'qualifying subsidiary'.

A subsidiary is a '*qualifying subsidiary*' of the issuing company if the following conditions are satisfied in relation to that subsidiary and every other subsidiary of the issuing company.

In relation to shares or securities issued to the VCT **after 16 March 2004**, the subsidiary must be a **51%** subsidiary (see *CTA 2010, Pt 24 Ch 3*) of the issuing company and no person other than the issuing company or another of its subsidiaries may have control (within *ITA 2007, s 995* — see **41.28** CONNECTED PERSONS) of the subsidiary. Furthermore, no arrangements may exist by virtue of which either of these conditions would cease to be satisfied. The conditions are not regarded as ceasing to be satisfied by reason only of the subsidiary or any other company being in the process of being wound up or by reason only of anything done as a consequence of its being in administration or receivership, provided the winding-up, entry into administration or receivership or anything done as a consequence of its being in administration or receivership is for genuine commercial reasons and is not part of a tax avoidance scheme or arrangements.

In relation to shares or securities issued to the VCT **on or before 16 March 2004**, the issuing company, or another of its subsidiaries, must possess at least **75%** of the issued share capital of, and the voting power in, the subsidiary, and be beneficially entitled to at least **75%** of the assets available for distribution to equity holders on a winding-up etc. (see *ICTA 1988, Sch 18 paras 1, 3*) and of the profits available for distribution to equity holders. No other person may have control (within *ITA 2007, s 995* — see **41.28** CONNECTED PERSONS) of the subsidiary. Furthermore, no arrangements may exist by virtue of which any of these conditions could cease to be satisfied. A subsidiary does not fail these conditions by reason only of the fact that it is being wound up, provided that the winding-up is for *bona fide* commercial reasons and not part of a tax avoidance scheme or arrangements.

The conditions above are not regarded as ceasing to be satisfied by reason only of arrangements being in existence for the disposal of the interest in the subsidiary held by the issuing company (or, as the case may be, by another of its subsidiaries) if the disposal is to be for genuine commercial reasons and is not to be part of a tax avoidance scheme or arrangements.

[*ITA 2007, ss 298, 302, 989*].

The property managing subsidiaries requirement

In relation to shares or securities issued to the VCT **after 16 March 2004**, the company must not have a 'property managing subsidiary' which is not a 'qualifying 90% subsidiary' (see the carrying on of a qualifying activity requirement above) of the company. A '*property managing subsidiary*' is a subsidiary whose business consists wholly or mainly in the holding or managing of 'land' or any 'property deriving its value from land' (as defined). [*ITA 2007, s 299*].

The no disqualifying arrangements requirement

This requirement has effect for the purpose of determining whether shares or securities issued on or after 6 April 2012 are to be regarded as comprised in a VCT's qualifying holdings, and has that effect regardless of when the disqualifying arrangements were entered into. The requirement is that the holding in question must not have been issued, nor any money raised by the issue employed, in consequence or anticipation of, or otherwise in connection with, 'disqualifying arrangements'. Arrangements (as broadly defined) are '*disqualifying arrangements*' if a main purpose of them is to ensure that any of the 'relevant tax reliefs' are available in respect of the issuing company's business and either or both of conditions A and B below are met. It is immaterial whether the issuing company is a party to the arrangements.

Condition A is that, as a result of the money raised by the issue of the shares to the VCT being employed as required by the 'use of the money raised' requirement, an amount representing the whole or most of the amount raised is, in the course of the arrangements, paid to (or for the benefit of) one or more parties to the arrangements or a person or persons connected with such a party (within **17** CONNECTED PERSONS). Condition B is that, in the absence of the arrangements, it would have been reasonable to expect that the whole or greater part of the component activities (as defined) of the relevant qualifying activity would have been carried on as part of another by one or more parties to the arrangements or a person or persons connected with such a party.

The '*relevant tax reliefs*' are those listed at **23.3** ENTERPRISE INVESTMENT SCHEME. The addition of SOCIAL INVESTMENT RELIEF (**65**) to that list has effect for the purpose of determining whether shares or securities issued on or after 6 April 2017 are to be regarded as compromised in a VCT's qualifying holdings, but not so as to apply to arrangements involving transactions entered into before that date.

[*ITA 2007, ss 299A, 313(5); FA 2012, Sch 8 paras 10, 16, 19; F(No 2)A 2017, Sch 1 paras 11(4), 16(2)*].

Information powers

If an officer of HMRC has reason to believe that shares or securities have been issued to a VCT in consequence of, or otherwise in connection with, disqualifying arrangements, he may by notice require persons concerned to supply information within a specified time (at least 60 days). The penalty provisions of *TMA 1970, s 98* apply for failure to comply. [*ITA 2007, s 312A; FA 2012, Sch 8 paras 15, 19*].

Supplementary provisions

Winding up of the issuing company

[71.5] Where the company is being wound up, none of the requirements listed at **71.4** above are regarded on that account as not being satisfied provided that they would be met apart from the winding up, and that the winding up is for genuine commercial reasons and is not part of a scheme or arrangement a main purpose of which is the avoidance of tax. [*ITA 2007, s 312*].

Restructuring

Where shares or securities in a company are exchanged for corresponding shares and securities in a new parent company, then subject to detailed conditions, including HMRC approval, to the extent that (on and after 18 November 2015) any of the conditions, and (at any time) any of the requirements listed below were satisfied in relation to the old shares, it will generally be taken to be satisfied in relation to the new shares. The consideration for the old shares must consist wholly of the issue of shares in the new company. Certain deemed securities (see **71.2** above) which are not thus acquired by the new company may be disregarded where these provisions would otherwise be prevented from applying.

The said conditions are the investment limits condition, the permitted maximum age condition and the no business acquisition condition at **71.2** above.

The requirements to which the above provision applies are:

- the maximum qualifying investment requirement;
- the proportion of eligible shares requirement;
- the trading requirement;
- the carrying on of a qualifying activity requirement;
- the use of money raised requirement;
- the relevant company to carry on the relevant qualifying activity requirement;
- the control and independence requirement;
- the gross assets requirement;
- the number of employees requirement;
- (with effect on and after 8 November 2015) the maximum amount raised annually through risk finance investments requirement;
- (with effect on and after 8 November 2015) the maximum risk finance investments when holding is issued requirement;
- (with effect on and after 8 November 2015) the maximum risk finance investments in five-year post-investment period requirement;
- (with effect on and after 8 November 2015) the permitted company age requirement; and
- (with effect on and after 8 November 2015) the proportion of skilled employees requirement.

Legislation introduced in 2017 enables a new parent company (as above) which has acquired a company that has previously received funding from a VCT, to use the funding history of the acquired company when considering if follow-on funding is admissible to fund the continuing activities of that acquired company. The legislation achieves this by effectively treating relevant investments made in the acquired company before the restructuring, and before the end of the initial investing period, as having been made in the new company. This is relevant to the permitted maximum age condition at **71.2** above, in which case it has effect in relation to investments made on or after 6 April 2017, and the permitted company age requirement at **71.4** above, in which case it has effect in relation to shares or securities issued to a VCT on or after that date.

[*ITA 2007, ss 326–328; F(No 2)A 2015, Sch 6 paras 16–18; F(No 2)A 2017, s 12*].

Conversion of shares

Where a VCT exercises conversion rights in respect of certain convertible shares and securities, then subject to detailed conditions, for the purposes of the requirements listed below, the conversion is treated as an exchange of new shares for old shares to which the restructuring provisions above apply. The requirements are:

- the maximum qualifying investment requirement;
- the proportion of eligible shares requirement;
- the carrying on of a qualifying activity requirement;
- the use of money raised requirement;
- the relevant company to carry on the relevant qualifying activity requirement; and
- the gross assets requirement.

[*ITA 2007, s 329*].

Reorganisations etc.

Where, under a company reorganisation or other arrangement:

- a VCT exchanges a qualifying holding for other shares or securities (with or without other consideration); and
- the exchange is for genuine commercial reasons and not part of a tax avoidance scheme or arrangements,

the new shares or securities may be treated as being qualifying holdings for a specified period even if some or all of the requirements at **71.4** above are not otherwise satisfied. Regulations specify the circumstances in which, and conditions subject to which, they apply and which requirements are to be treated as met. Where the new shares or securities are those of a different company than before and they do not meet any one or more of the above requirements (disregarding the maximum qualifying investment requirement and the use of the money raised requirement), those requirements are treated as met for, broadly, three years in the case of shares or five years in the case of securities, reduced in either case to, broadly, two years where the company is not, or ceases to be, an unquoted company as in the unquoted status requirement above. A formula is provided for valuing the new shares or securities for the purposes of the proportion of eligible shares requirement above. The provisions extend to new shares or securities received in pursuance of an earn-out right (see **63.6** SHARES AND SECURITIES) conferred in exchange for a qualifying holding, in which case an election is available (under *Reg 10*) to modify the said valuation formula by effectively disregarding the earn-out right itself. [*ITA 2007, s 330; SI 2002 No 2661*].

F(No 2)A 2017 gives the Treasury power to make regulations covering cases where, on an exchange of *non-qualifying* shares or securities that is for genuine commercial reasons and not part of a tax avoidance scheme (i.e. the exchange meets the second condition above), a VCT receives other non-qualifying shares or securities. For context, see the non-qualifying investments condition in **71.2** above and note that this has effect only in relation to investments made on or after 6 April 2016. The regulations may, inter alia, make provision as to when the new shares or securities are to be regarded as having been acquired. [*ITA 2007, s 330; F(No 2)A 2017, s 13*].

Investments transferred from VCT-in-liquidation

Regulations enable certain investments comprised in the qualifying holdings of a VCT-in-liquidation (VCT1) which are transferred by it during its prescribed winding-up period (see **71.2** above under 'Winding-up') to another VCT (VCT2) to be treated as comprised in the qualifying holdings of VCT2. Where any of the qualifying holding requirements (see **71.4** above) which are listed below have been satisfied to any extent or for any period in relation to the investment when held by VCT1 (whether before or after the commencement of its winding-up), they are treated as satisfied to the same extent or for the same period in relation to the investment when held by VCT2. The requirements are:

- that the shares or securities concerned were first issued to the VCT-in-liquidation and have been held by it ever since;
- the maximum qualifying investment requirement;
- the use of money raised requirement; and
- the gross assets requirement.

This treatment applies where:

- VCT1 commences winding-up after 16 April 2002;
- the winding-up is for bona fide commercial reasons and not part of tax avoidance arrangements;
- VCT1 has made all reasonable endeavours to sell the shares or securities at or as near as possible to their market value but has been unable to do so;
- the transfer to VCT2 is by way of a bargain made at arm's length or at not less than market value; and
- the value of all shares or securities transferred by VCT1 to other VCTs in its prescribed winding-up period does not exceed 7.5% of the aggregate value of its investments at the commencement of the winding-up. For this purpose, the value of VCT1's investments at the commencement of the winding-up are taken to be those used in its statement of affairs, or, where this does not provide a value for an investment, its market value at that time.

[*ITA 2007, ss 317–320, 324, 325; SI 2004 No 2199, Regs 1(2), 8; SI 2011 No 660*].

Informal clearance

Enquiries from companies as to whether they meet the conditions for investment by a venture capital trust should be directed to HMRC's Small Company Enterprise Centre.

Income tax reliefs

[71.6] Relief from income tax is granted in respect of both investments in VCTs and dividends from such trusts. See also **71.2** above as regards mergers and winding-up of VCTs.

Nominees

For shares issued on or after 17 July 2014, for the purposes of the income tax reliefs, shares subscribed for, issued to, held by or disposed of for an individual by a nominee are treated as subscribed for, issued to, held by or disposed of by the individual. [*ITA 2007, s 330A; FA 2014, Sch 10 para 5(1)*].

Relief in respect of investments

[71.7] Subject to the conditions described below, an individual may claim relief for a tax year for the amount (or aggregate amounts) subscribed by him on his own behalf for 'eligible shares' issued to him in a year of assessment by a VCT (or VCTs) for raising money. There is a limit of **£200,000** on the relief which may be claimed for any year of assessment.

'*Eligible shares*' means new ordinary shares in a VCT which, throughout the five years following issue, carry no present or future preferential right to dividends or to assets on a winding up and no present or future right to redemption.

Relief is given by a reduction (a '*tax reduction*') in what would otherwise be the individual's income tax liability for the tax year by 30% of the amount eligible for relief.

Investors may restrict a claim to relief in respect of a tax year to only some of the shares issued to them. For the order in which tax reductions are given against an individual's tax liability, see Tolley's Income Tax under Allowances and Tax Rates. A tax reduction must be restricted to the extent (if any) that it would otherwise exceed the individual's remaining income tax liability after making all prior reductions.

An individual is **not** entitled to relief where:

(a) he was under 18 years of age at the time of issue of the shares;
(b) circumstances have arisen which, had the relief already been given, would have resulted in the withdrawal or reduction of the relief (see **71.8** below);
(c) the shares were issued or subscribed for other than for genuine commercial purposes or as part of a scheme or arrangement a main purpose of which was the avoidance of tax;

(d) a loan is made to the individual (or to an 'associate') by any person at any time in the period beginning with the incorporation of the VCT (or, if later, two years before the date of issue of the shares) and ending five years after the date of issue of the shares, and the loan would not have been made, or would not have been made on the same terms, if he had not subscribed, or had not been proposing to subscribe, for the shares. For HMRC's views on 'loan-linked' investments, see HMRC Statement of Practice 6/98. The granting of credit to, or the assignment of a debt due from, the individual or associate is counted as a loan for these purposes; or

(e) the shares were treated as issued by virtue of *FA 2003, s 195(8)* (company disposing of treasury shares — see **63.19** SHARES AND SECURITIES). Where a venture capital trust issues eligible shares to an individual in such circumstances it must give notice to the individual stating that he is not eligible for relief, and a copy of the notice must be sent to an HMRC officer within three months after the issue of the shares.

For the purposes of (d) above, an '*associate*' of any person is any 'relative' (i.e. spouse, civil partner, ancestor or linear descendant) of that person, the trustee(s) of any settlement in relation to which that person or any relative (living or dead) is or was a settler and, where that person has an interest in any shares of obligations of a company which are subject to any trust or are part of a deceased estate, the trustee(s) of the settlement or the personal representatives of the deceased. For this purpose, 'settlor' is defined as in *ITA 2007, ss 467–473*.

Investment relief applies to shares issued before 6 April 2025 but this date may be amended by the Treasury via statutory instrument.

[*ITA 2007, ss 261–264, 265, 271(4), 273, 332; F(No 2)A 2015, Sch 6 para 2*].

An individual or nominee subscribing for eligible shares may obtain from the VCT a certificate giving details of the subscription and certifying that certain conditions for relief are satisfied. [*SI 1995 No 1979, Reg 9; SI 2014 No 1929*].

Linked sales

For claims made by reference to shares issued on or after 6 April 2014, relief is restricted if an individual subscribes for shares in a VCT and makes at least one 'linked' sale of other shares. The amount subscribed is treated as reduced by the total consideration given for the linked sales. If a sale is linked in relation to more than one subscription, the consideration for it is applied to reduce subscriptions in the order in which they are made. A sale of shares is '*linked*' if:

- the shares sold are in the VCT or in a company which is (or later becomes) a successor or predecessor of the VCT as a result of a merger or restructuring; and
- either
  - the circumstances are such that the purchase of the shares from the individual is conditional upon his making the subscription or *vice versa*; or

- the subscription and the sale are within six months of each other (irrespective of which is first).

The above does not apply if, or to the extent that, the subscription is the result of the individual's electing to reinvest dividends on his VCT shares in acquiring further shares in the VCT.

[*ITA 2007, s 264A; FA 2014, Sch 10 para 2*].

Example

On 1 August 2017, A Ventura, who is UK resident but not a Scottish taxpayer and whose salary is £60,000 p.a. from UK employment, subscribes for 50,000 eligible £1 shares issued at par to raise money by VCT plc, an approved venture capital trust. On 1 March 2018 he purchases a further 190,000 £1 shares in VCT plc for £170,000 on the open market. The trust makes no distribution in 2017/18. Mr Ventura's other income for 2017/18 consists of dividends of £18,000.

Mr Ventura's income tax computation for 2017/18 is as follows.

	£
Earnings from UK employment	60,000.00
Dividends	18,000.00
Total income	78,000.00
Deduct personal allowance	11,500.00
Taxable income	£66,500.00
Tax payable:	£
33,500 @ 20%	6,700.00
15,000 @ 40%	6,000.00
5,000 @ 0%	0.00
13,000 @ 32.5%	4,225.00
	16,925.00
Deduct Relief in respect of investment in VCT plc:	
Lower of 30% of £50,000 subscribed and £16,925	15,000.00
Net tax payable (subject to PAYE deductions from salary)	£1,925.00

Withdrawal of relief on investment

Disposal of investment

[71.8] Where an individual disposes of eligible shares, in respect of which relief has been claimed as under 71.7 above, within five years of their issue and other than to a spouse or civil partner when they are living together (see below), then:

(a) if the disposal is otherwise than at arm's length, relief given by reference to those shares is withdrawn;
(b) if the disposal is at arm's length, the relief given by reference to those shares is reduced by an amount equivalent to 30% of the consideration received for the disposal or is withdrawn if the relief exceeds that amount.

For the above purposes, disposals of eligible shares in a VCT are identified with those acquired earlier rather than later. As between eligible shares acquired on the same day, shares by reference to which relief has been given are treated as disposed of after any other eligible shares.

Relief is **not** withdrawn where the disposal is by one spouse or civil partner to the other at a time when they are living together. However, on any subsequent disposal the spouse or partner to whom the shares were transferred is treated as if he or she were the person who subscribed for the shares, as if the shares had been issued to him or her at the time they were issued to the transferor spouse or partner, and as if his or her liability to income tax had been reduced by reference to those shares by the same amount, and for the same tax year, as applied on the subscription by the transferor spouse or partner. Any assessment for reducing or withdrawing relief is made on the transferee spouse or partner.

[*ITA 2007, ss 266, 267*].

Withdrawal of approval

Where approval of a company as a VCT is withdrawn (but not treated as never having been given) (see **71.2** above), relief given by reference to eligible shares in the VCT is withdrawn as if on a non-arm's length disposal immediately before the withdrawal of approval. See **71.2**(I) above for the position where a VCT enters liquidation. [*ITA 2007, s 268*].

Relief subsequently found not to have been due

Relief which is subsequently found not to have been due is withdrawn. [*ITA 2007, s 269*].

Assessments withdrawing or reducing relief

Such assessments are made for the tax year for which the relief was given. No such assessment is, however, to be made by reason of an event occurring after the death of the person to whom the shares were issued. An assessment made on or after 6 April 2014 can be made at any time not more than six years after the tax year for which the relief was given. [*ITA 2007, s 270; FA 2014, Sch 10 para 1*].

Information

Particulars of all events leading to the reduction or withdrawal of relief must be notified to HMRC by the person to whom the relief was given within 60 days of his coming to know of the event.

Before 13 August 2009, where HMRC had reason to believe that a notice so required has not been given, they could require that person to furnish them, within a specified time not being less than 60 days, with such information relating to the event as they reasonably required. This power has been repealed as it is no longer considered necessary following the introduction of the general information powers in *FA 2008, Sch 36* (see **34**).

The requirements of secrecy do not prevent HMRC disclosing to a VCT that relief has been given or claimed by reference to a particular number or proportion of its shares.

Penalties under *TMA 1970, s 98* apply for failure to comply with these requirements.

[*ITA 2007, s 271(1)–(3)(5); SI 2009 No 2035, Sch para 47*].

Example

On 1 August 2018, A Ventura in the *Example* at **71.7** above, who since 2017/18 has neither acquired nor disposed of any shares in VCT plc, gives 30,000 shares to his son. On 1 March 2020 he disposes of the remaining 210,000 shares for £195,000. The relief given in **71.7** above is withdrawn as follows.

Disposal on 1 August 2018

The shares disposed of are identified with 30,000 of those subscribed for, and, since the disposal was not at arm's length, the relief given on those shares is fully withdrawn.

Relief withdrawn 30,000/50,000 × £15,000 =	£9,000

Disposal on 1 March 2020

The balance of £6,000 of the relief originally given was in respect of 20,000 of the shares disposed of. The disposal consideration for those 20,000 shares is

$$195{,}000 \times \frac{20{,}000}{210{,}000} = \quad £18{,}571$$

The relief withdrawn is the lesser of the relief originally given and 30% of the consideration received, i.e.

30% of £18,571 = £5,571.	
Relief withdrawn is therefore	£5,571
The 2017/18 income tax assessment is therefore	£14,571

Relief on dividends

[71.9] A 'VCT dividend' to which a 'qualifying investor' is beneficially entitled is not treated as income for income tax purposes. Tax credits are not, however, repayable.

A '*qualifying investor*' is an individual aged 18 or over who is beneficially entitled to the dividend either as the holder of the shares or through a nominee (including the trustees of a bare trust).

A '*VCT dividend*' is a dividend (including a capital dividend) in respect of ordinary shares in a company which is a VCT which were acquired at a time when it was a VCT by the recipient of the dividend, and which were not shares acquired in excess of the 'permitted maximum' for the year of assessment. Shares must also have been acquired for *bona fide* commercial purposes and not as part of a tax avoidance scheme or arrangements. A VCT dividend does not include any dividend paid in respect of profits or gains of any accounting period ending when the company was not a VCT.

Shares are acquired in excess of the '*permitted maximum*' for a year where the aggregate of the market values of ordinary shares acquired in VCTs by the individual or his nominee(s) in that year exceeds £200,000, disregarding shares acquired other than for *bona fide* commercial reasons or as part of a scheme or arrangement a main purpose of which is the avoidance of tax. Shares acquired later in the year are identified as representing the excess before those acquired earlier, and in relation to same-day acquisition of different shares, a proportionate part of each description of share is treated as representing any excess arising on that day. Shares acquired at a time when a company was not a VCT are for these purposes treated as disposed of before other shares in the VCT. Otherwise, disposals are identified with earlier acquisitions before later ones, except that as between shares acquired on the same day, shares acquired in excess of the permitted maximum are treated as disposed of before any other shares. There are provisions for effectively disregarding acquisitions arising out of share exchanges where, for capital gains purposes, the new shares are treated as the same assets as the old.

[*ITTOIA 2005, ss 709–712; SI 1995 No 1979, Reg 10; SI 1999 No 819, Reg 4*].

Capital gains tax reliefs

[71.10] The capital gains of a VCT are not chargeable gains. [*TCGA 1992, s 100(1)*].

In addition, individual investors in VCTs are entitled to relief on disposal of VCT shares (see **71.11** below). An additional relief was previously available by deferral of chargeable gains on re-investment in VCT share issues before 6 April 2004 (see **71.12** below).

Various provisions of *TCGA 1992* which are superseded for these purposes by specific provisions (as below) are disapplied or applied separately to parts of holdings which do not fall within the reliefs.

See also **71.2** above for the effect on the reliefs where a VCT enters liquidation or there is a merger of VCTs.

Withdrawal of approval

Where approval of a company as a VCT is withdrawn (but not treated as never having been given) (see **71.2** above), shares which (apart from the withdrawal) would be eligible for the relief on disposal (see **71.11** below) are treated as disposed of at their market value at the time of the withdrawal. For the purposes of the relief on disposal, the disposal is treated as taking place while the company is still a VCT, but the re-acquisition is treated as taking place immediately after it ceases to be so. [*TCGA 1992, s 151B(6)(7)*].

Relief on disposal

[71.11] A gain or loss accruing to an individual on a 'qualifying disposal' of ordinary shares in a company which was a VCT throughout his period of ownership is not a chargeable gain or an allowable loss.

A disposal is a '*qualifying disposal*' if:

(a) the individual is 18 years of age or more at the time of the disposal;
(b) the shares were not acquired in excess of the 'permitted maximum' for any year of assessment; and
(c) the shares were acquired for *bona fide* commercial purposes and not as part of a scheme or arrangement a main purpose of which was the avoidance of tax.

The identification of those shares which were acquired in excess of the '*permitted maximum*' is as under **71.9** above, i.e. where the aggregate of the market values of ordinary shares acquired in VCTs by the individual or his nominee(s) in that year exceeds £200,000, disregarding shares acquired other than for *bona fide* commercial reasons or as part of a scheme or arrangement a main purpose of which is the avoidance of tax. Shares acquired later in the year are identified as representing the excess before those acquired earlier, and in relation to same-day acquisition of different shares, a proportionate part of each description of share is treated as representing any excess arising on that day. Shares acquired at a time when a company was not a VCT are for these purposes treated as disposed of before other shares in the VCT. Otherwise, disposals are identified with earlier acquisitions before later ones, except that as between shares acquired on the same day, shares acquired in excess of the permitted maximum are treated as disposed of before any other shares. See the examples at HMRC Venture Capital Schemes Manual VCM52060, 52080, 52090.

The normal rules for the pooling of shares and identification of disposals in *TCGA 1992, ss 104, 105, 106A, 107* (see **64.2, 64.3** SHARES AND SECURITIES — IDENTIFICATION RULES) are disapplied in respect of shares which are eligible for the above relief.

There are provisions (see below) for effectively disregarding acquisitions arising out of share exchanges where, for capital gains purposes, the new shares are treated as the same assets as the old.

Where an individual holds ordinary shares in a VCT which fall into more than one of the following groups:

(1) shares eligible for relief on disposal (as above) and by reference to which he has obtained or is entitled to claim relief under the provisions in **71.7** above (income tax relief on investments);
(2) shares eligible for relief on disposal but by reference to which he has not obtained or will be unable to claim relief under the provisions in **71.7** above;

(3) shares by reference to which he has obtained or is entitled to claim relief under the provisions in **71.7** above but which are not eligible for relief on disposal;

(4) shares not within (1)–(3) above,

then, if there is a reorganisation under *TCGA 1992, s 126*, the provisions in *TCGA 1992, s 127* (equation of original shares with new holding) (see **63.2** SHARES AND SECURITIES above) will apply separately to each group of shares (if any) in order that they continue to be kept within their respective groups.

Where an individual holds ordinary shares in a company ('the existing holding') and there is, by virtue of an allotment for payment within *TCGA 1992, s 126(2)(a)* (e.g. a rights issue), a reorganisation affecting the existing holding immediately following which the shares or allotted holding are shares falling within (1)–(3) above, the provisions in *TCGA 1992, ss 127–130* will not apply in relation to that existing holding. The effect is that the rights issue will be treated as an acquisition.

Where a holding consists of shares falling within (1) or (2) above and it is exchanged or is deemed to be exchanged for a second holding which does not consist of ordinary shares in a VCT, then the provisions in *TCGA 1992, ss 135, 136* will not apply (see **63.5** and **63.7** SHARES AND SECURITIES above). The effect is that there will be or deemed to be a disposal and acquisition.

[*TCGA 1992, ss 151A, 151B*].

See **71.10** above as regards relief on withdrawal of approval of the VCT.

Example

On the disposals in the *Example* at **71.8** above, a chargeable gain or allowable loss arises only on the disposal of the shares acquired in excess of the permitted maximum for 2017/18. The shares in VCT plc were acquired in 2017/18 for £220,000, so that there is a £20,000 excess over the permitted maximum. The 50,000 shares first acquired for £50,000 are first identified, so that shares representing the excess are two-seventeenths of the 190,000 shares subsequently acquired for £170,000 on 1 March 2018, i.e. 22,353 of those shares. The disposal identified with those shares is a corresponding proportion of the 210,000 shares disposed of for a consideration of £195,000 on 1 March 2020.

Mr Ventura's capital gains tax computation for 2019/20 is as follows.

Disposal consideration for 22,353 shares:

	$£195{,}000 \times \frac{22{,}353}{210{,}000} =$	£20,756
Deduct Cost:		
	$£170{,}000 \times \frac{22{,}353}{190{,}000} =$	£20,000
Chargeable gain		£756

Deferral relief on reinvestment

[71.12] The relief described below is **abolished** for shares issued on or after 6 April 2004.

TCGA 1992, Sch 5C applies where:

(a) a chargeable gain accrues to an individual after 5 April 1995
- on the disposal by him of any asset; or
- on the occurrence of a chargeable event under these provisions or the similar provisions governing reinvestment into EIS shares (see **23.15** ENTERPRISE INVESTMENT SCHEME);

(b) the individual makes a 'qualifying investment' before 6 April 2004; and

(c) the individual is UK resident or ordinarily resident both when the chargeable gain accrues to him and when he makes the 'qualifying investment', and is not, at the latter time, regarded as resident outside the UK for the purposes of any double taxation arrangements the effect of which would be that he would not be liable to tax on a gain arising on a disposal, immediately after their acquisition, of the shares comprising the 'qualifying investment', disregarding the exemption under *TCGA 1992, s 151A(1)* (see **71.11** above).

A '*qualifying investment*' is a subscription for shares in a company which is a VCT, by reference to which income tax investment relief is obtained under **71.7** above, within twelve months (extendible by HMRC) before or after the time of the accrual of the chargeable gain in question, and, if before, provided that the shares are still held at that time. The shares are not deemed to be issued by reason only of a letter of allotment.

Broadly, the detailed provisions below allow a claim for the chargeable gain to be rolled over into the VCT shares, and for the gain to become chargeable on certain events in relation to those shares (including, in particular, on their disposal).

Postponement of original gain

Where a chargeable gain would otherwise accrue to an individual ('the investor') and he acquires a qualifying investment, a claim can be made by him to defer the whole or part of that gain against a corresponding amount of his qualifying investment up to the amount of the gain, or for an amount so claimed, whichever is the smaller. The gain eligible for deferral is the gain after all available reliefs other than taper relief (HMRC Venture Capital Schemes Manual VCM53020). The amount of qualifying investment available for set-off is restricted to the amount on which income tax investment relief has been given under **71.7** above (maximum **£100,000** per tax year), less any amount already utilised against other gains. If income tax investment relief is restricted because the investor's income tax liability is insufficient to fully absorb the relief, deferral relief is still available on the full amount of the investment that would otherwise have qualified for the income tax relief. It is, however, necessary for *some* income tax investment relief to have been given; no deferral relief is available if the investor's income tax liability is nil without taking account of income tax investment relief. (HMRC Venture Capital Schemes Manual VCM53030).

Subject to what is said at **13.2** CLAIMS re claims being included in a self-assessment tax return if possible, there is no statutory form in which a claim must be made. The deferral claim must be made by the fifth anniversary of 31 January following the 'relevant tax year'. The '*relevant tax year*' is the tax year in which the *later* of the following events occurred:

- the gain to be deferred arose;
- the VCT shares were issued.

Chargeable event

The original gain deferred through the making of the above claim will subsequently crystallise if one of the following circumstances arise:

(A) the investor disposes of the shares in his qualifying investment ('the relevant shares') otherwise than under *TCGA 1992, s 58* (a transfer between spouses or civil partners);

(B) the relevant shares are disposed of by the spouse or civil partner of the investor (otherwise than by a transfer back to him), the spouse or partner having first acquired them from the investor under *TCGA 1992, s 58*;

(C) where shares falling within **71.11**(3) above are exchanged or treated as exchanged for any non-VCT holdings and under *TCGA 1992, s 135* or *TCGA 1992, s 136* (see **63.5** and **63.7** SHARES AND SECURITIES above) there is a requirement (or, but for *TCGA 1992, s 116* (see **54** QUALIFYING CORPORATE BONDS above) there would be a requirement) for those holdings to be regarded as the same assets as those shares;

(D) the investor becomes neither resident nor ordinarily resident in the UK whilst holding the relevant shares and within three years of the making of the qualifying investment (five years as regards shares issued before 6 April 2000);

(E) an individual who acquired the relevant shares through a transfer under *TCGA 1992, s 58* becomes neither resident nor ordinarily resident in the UK whilst holding those shares and within period referred to in (D) above;

(F) the company in which the relevant shares are held has its approval as a VCT withdrawn (in a case in which approval is not treated as never having been given) (see **71.2** above);

(G) the relief given under **71.7** above by reference to relevant shares is withdrawn or reduced in circumstances not falling within (A)–(F) above;

(H) the 'prescribed winding-up period' of a VCT-in-liquidation comes to an end, the VCT-in-liquidation then still being in existence (see **71.2** above).

In the case of (D) or (E) above, the original gain will not crystallise where the individual concerned became neither resident nor ordinarily resident in the UK through temporarily working abroad and he again becomes UK resident or ordinarily resident in the UK within three years of that event, without having disposed of any of the relevant shares in the meantime. An assessment will be issued by HMRC when it is clear that the individual will not regain UK resident status within the three-year period.

There is no crystallisation of the original gain where an event within (A)–(H) above occurs at or after the time of death of the investor or a person to whom the relevant shares were transferred under *TCGA 1992, s 58*.

Without prejudice to the following provisions in a case falling within (F) (or (H)) above, any reference above to a disposal excludes a reference to the disposal deemed to occur on the withdrawal of approval (or the deemed withdrawal at the end of the prescribed winding-up period (see **71.2** above) within **71.10** above.

Crystallisation of original gain

Where a chargeable event mentioned in (A)–(H) above relating to relevant shares occurs for the first time in connection with those shares, a chargeable gain is deemed to accrue at that time equal to so much of the expenditure on those shares which was set against the original gain.

Identification of shares

In determining whether any shares to which a chargeable gain relates are shares the expenditure on which has been set against the whole or part of any gain, disposals of shares are identified with those subscribed for earlier rather than later, and as between shares in a company acquired on the same day, those the expenditure on which has been set against a gain are treated as disposed of after any other shares in that company. The normal rules at **64.2** SHARES AND SECURITIES — IDENTIFICATION RULES are disapplied (regardless of whether or not the shares are eligible for CGT relief under **71.11** above). For a practical illustration, see the *Example* below and, for a more complex example, HMRC Venture Capital Schemes Manual VCM53170.

Assets

Where at the time of a chargeable event relevant shares are regarded as represented by assets which consist of or include assets other than relevant shares, the expenditure on those shares is apportioned between those assets on a just and reasonable basis. As between different assets regarded as representing the same relevant shares, the identification of those assets will be determined on a similar basis to the identification of shares.

Persons assessable

The chargeable gain is treated as accruing, as the case may be:

(i) to the individual who makes the disposal;
(ii) to the individual who holds the shares in question at the time of the exchange or deemed exchange;
(iii) to the individual who becomes non-UK resident etc.;
(iv) to the individual who holds the shares in question when the withdrawal of the approval takes effect;
(v) to the individual who holds the shares in question immediately following the end of the VCT-in-liquidation's prescribed winding-up period; or

(vi) to the individual who holds the shares in question when the circumstances arise in respect of which the relief is withdrawn or reduced.

A chargeable gain is computed separately for the investor without reference to any shares held at the time of the chargeable event by a recipient to the investor from a *TCGA 1992, s 58* transfer.

[*TCGA 1992, Sch 5C; SI 2004 No 2199, Reg 7; SI 2005 No 3229, Reg 128*].

The above relief is abolished for shares issued on or after 6 April 2004.

Example

On 1 August 2003, Mr Truman subscribes for 50,000 eligible £1 shares issued at par to raise money by VCT2 plc, an approved venture capital trust. On 1 March 2004 he purchases a further 90,000 £1 shares in VCT2 plc for £70,000 on the open market. Mr Truman sells a painting on 1 November 2003, realising a chargeable gain of £26,900.

In addition to the relief against income tax he receives, he also claims deferral of the gain against his subscription for shares in VCT2 plc up to an amount of £19,000, leaving £7,900 to be covered by his annual exemption.

On 1 August 2005, Mr Truman, who since 2003/04 has neither acquired nor disposed of any shares in VCT2 plc, gives 30,000 shares to his son. On 1 March 2006 he disposes of the remaining 110,000 shares for £95,000. The gain of £19,000 deferred on the disposal of the painting crystallises and forms part of his gains for 2005/06 as follows.

1 August 2005 disposal

The 30,000 shares disposed of on 1 August 2005 are initially identified on a first in/first out basis with the 50,000 shares subscribed for on 1 August 2003. Of those 50,000 shares acquired on the same day, deferral relief is attributable to 19,000 shares (acquired for £19,000, the amount of the deferred gain). The disposal is matched firstly with the shares to which no deferral relief is attributable, i.e. 31,000 shares. [*TCGA 1992, Sch 5C para 4(3); FA 1995, Sch 16*]. The disposal therefore includes none of the 19,000 shares to which deferral relief is attributable. See also HMRC Venture Capital Schemes Manual VCM68320.

1 March 2006 disposal

This disposal of 110,000 shares is firstly identified on a first in/first out basis with the remaining 20,000 of the shares subscribed for on 1 August 2003. Of those 20,000 shares acquired on the same day, deferral relief is attributable to 19,000 shares. The disposal is matched firstly with the shares to which no deferral relief is attributable, i.e. 1,000 shares, and then with the 19,000 shares to which deferral relief is attributable. The disposal includes all of the 19,000 shares to which deferral relief is attributable. Therefore, the whole of the £19,000 deferred gain is brought into charge on 1 March 2006.

The above interpretation of the rules for identifying disposals of VCT shares to which deferral relief is attributable is HMRC's interpretation at Venture Capital

Schemes Manual VCM68320. Where, as in this example, part disposals are involved, they act to the taxpayer's advantage (although in this example both part disposals are in the same tax year in any case). Note the contrast between the application of these rules and those for EIS deferral relief illustrated in the example at **23.15** ENTERPRISE INVESTMENT SCHEME.

NB: any taper relief available is disregarded for the purposes of this example.

Key points

[71.13] Points to consider are as follows.

- An investment in shares in a VCT provides for two types of tax relief:
  - (a) income tax relief, including tax free dividends, and
  - (b) exemption from capital gains tax.

  For shares issued before 6 April 2004 there was also the possibility of deferring some other capital gain. Where shares are disposed of any gain that had been deferred (before 6 April 2004) will be revived as though it was a gain arising at the date of disposal of the VCT shares.
- VCT income tax relief can be claimed via the self-assessment tax return or separately. If the VCT certificate is available early enough relief can be included in a PAYE code.
- The tax relief is only available in respect of VCT shares subscribed for within the annual limit which is currently £200,000.
- Where income tax relief is withdrawn or reduced it is done by means of an assessment issued by HMRC. It cannot be recovered through the self-assessment tax return although the liability will be added to the Statement of Account.

72

Wasting Assets

Introduction	72.1
Basic rule	72.2
Options and futures contracts	72.3
Leases of property other than land	72.4
Premiums for leases	72.5
Sub-leases granted out of short leases	72.6
Life interests	72.7
Key points	72.8

Cross-references. See **7.6** ASSETS for plant or machinery lease under a long finance lease; **25.4** EXEMPTIONS AND RELIEFS for tangible movable assets generally and **25.11** for private passenger motor vehicles; **41.14–41.23** LAND for leases of land which are wasting assets; and **59.9** ROLLOVER RELIEF for the relief available where assets are, or will within ten years, become wasting assets.

Simon's Taxes. See C2.9.

Introduction

[72.1] A wasting asset is, broadly, an asset with a predictable life of no more than fifty years. There are rules which apply to reduce the amount of the allowable expenditure on the disposal of such an asset. The original cost and any subsequent enhancement expenditure are in most cases treated as diminishing evenly day by day over the asset's life. Different rules apply to leases of land which are wasting assets, for which see **41.14–41.23** LAND, and there is an exclusion where the asset qualified for capital allowances. The detailed provisions are at **72.2** below. See also **25.4** EXEMPTIONS AND RELIEFS for the exemption for tangible movable assets (chattels) which are wasting assets.

This chapter also looks at three specific types of wasting assets: options and futures contracts, leases of property other than land and life interests.

Basic rule

[72.2] Subject to the following, where an asset disposed of is a 'wasting asset':

(a) the original cost, etc. (see **16.11** COMPUTATION OF GAINS AND LOSSES) less predictable residual value, is treated as diminishing evenly day by day over the asset's life, and
(b) additional expenditure (see **16.11** COMPUTATION OF GAINS AND LOSSES) is similarly treated as diminishing evenly over the remaining life of the asset as from the date the expenditure was first reflected in the state or nature of the asset

and only so much of the original cost and additional expenditure as, on the above basis, remains at the date of disposal is then deductible. If additional expenditure under (b) above creates or increases a residual value, then the new residual value is taken into account in (a) above. [*TCGA 1992, s 46*].

A '*wasting asset*' is an asset with a predictable 'life' not exceeding 50 years and, in relation to tangible movable property, '*life*' means 'useful life', having regard to the purpose for which the tangible assets were acquired or provided by the person making the disposal. However, plant and machinery are always regarded as having a predictable life of less than 50 years and that life is to be based on normal usage. Freehold land is never a wasting asset, whatever its nature and whatever the nature of the building or works on it. The predictable life and predictable residual value, if not immediately ascertainable by the nature of the asset, are to be taken on a disposal as they were known or ascertainable at the time when the asset was acquired by the person making the disposal. [*TCGA 1992, s 44*].

Milk quota (see **7.9** ASSETS) is not regarded by HMRC as a wasting asset (HMRC Capital Gains Manual CG77940).

A painting which was informally loaned to a company for display to the paying public as part of its trade was held to be plant and therefore a wasting asset in *Executors of Lord Howard of Henderskelfe v HMRC* CA, [2014] STC 1100. See now, however, **25.4** EXEMPTIONS AND RELIEFS for the denial of exemption under *TCGA 1992, s 45* for assets which are wasting assets only because of use in the trade etc. of a person other than the owner.

Assets qualifying for capital allowances

No restriction of allowable expenditure as above occurs where an asset, throughout the ownership of the person making the disposal, is used solely for the purposes of a trade, profession or vocation, and capital allowances have, or could have, been claimed in respect of its cost, or in respect of any enhancement expenditure. This also applies where an asset has otherwise qualified in full for any capital allowances. Where, however, the asset disposed of has been used partly for non-business purposes, or has only partly qualified for capital allowances, the expenditure and consideration are apportioned and the restrictions imposed above applied to that portion of expenditure which has not qualified for capital allowances, or which relates to the period of non-business use. [*TCGA 1992, s 47*].

Chattels

Tangible movable assets (chattels) which are wasting assets are exempt subject to certain conditions. See **25.4** EXEMPTIONS AND RELIEFS. Chattels such as antique clocks and certain motor vehicles may be 'machinery' and thus exempt subject to those conditions (which broadly correspond to those of *TCGA 1992, s 47* above). See Revenue Tax Bulletin, October 1994, pp 166, 167 for HMRC's meaning of machinery.

Example

V bought an aircraft on 31 May 2012 at a cost of £90,000 for use in his air charter business. It has been agreed that V's non-business use of the aircraft amounts to one-tenth, on a flying hours basis, and capital allowances and running costs have accordingly been restricted for income tax purposes. On 1 February 2018, V sells the aircraft for £185,000. The aircraft is agreed as having a useful life of 20 years at the date it was acquired.

	£	£
Amount qualifying for capital allowances		
Relevant portion of disposal consideration		
9/10 × £185,000		166,500
Relevant portion of acquisition cost 9/10 × £90,000		81,000
Chargeable gain 2017/18		£85,500
Amount not qualifying for capital allowances		
Relevant portion of disposal consideration		
1/10 × £185,000		18,500
Relevant portion of acquisition cost		
1/10 × £90,000	9,000	
Deduct wasted $£9{,}000 \times \dfrac{5y8m}{20y}$	2,550	6,450
Gain		£12,050
The whole of the £12,050 is exempt.		
The total chargeable gain is therefore		£85,500

Options and futures contracts

[72.3] For capital gains tax purposes, options are generally treated as wasting assets and are subject to the rules outlined in 72.2 above. However, there are specific statutory exceptions to this and these, together with further rules relating to options generally, are covered in 7.7 ASSETS. For employee share options, see 22 EMPLOYEE SHARE SCHEMES. See 25.60 EXEMPTIONS AND RELIEFS for options held by pension schemes.

See 7.8 ASSETS for certain commodity and financial futures which are excepted from wasting asset treatment.

For corporation tax purposes, options and futures contracts fall within the derivatives contracts regime — see 15.8–15.13 COMPANIES — CORPORATE FINANCE AND INTANGIBLES.

Leases of property other than land

[72.4] In accordance with the definition of a wasting asset given in 72.2 above a 'lease of property other than land' may be or become a wasting asset. Such a lease which is a wasting asset is subject to the rules in 72.2 above, and in particular those regarding allowable expenditure. This treatment should be compared with leases of land which are wasting assets where, instead of allowable expenditure being written off at a uniform rate, a special basis is used (see **41.15** LAND). Despite this, the legislation regarding leases of property other than land is mainly by direct reference to that covering leases of land with 'necessary modifications'. [*TCGA 1992, ss 44, 46, 47, 240, Sch 8 para 9(1)*].

A '*lease of property other than land*' means any kind of agreement or arrangement under which payments are made for the use of, or otherwise in respect of, property and '*lessor*', '*lessee*' and '*rent*' are construed accordingly. [*TCGA 1992, Sch 8 para 10(1)(b)*].

Duration of a lease

The duration of a lease is to be decided by reference to the facts known or ascertainable at the time when the lease was acquired or created. In determining the duration, the following provisions apply.

(a) Where the terms of the lease include provision for the determination of the lease by notice given by the lessor, the lease is not to be treated as granted for a term longer than one ending at the earliest date on which it could be determined by notice given by the lessor.
(b) Where any of the terms of the lease or any other circumstances rendered it unlikely that the lease will continue beyond a date earlier than the expiration of the terms of the lease, the lease is not to be treated as having been granted for a longer term than one ending on that date. This applies in particular where the lease provides for rent to go up after a given date, or for the lessee's obligation to become more onerous after a given date, but includes provision for the determination of the lease on that date, by notice given by the lessee, and those provisions render it unlikely that the lease will continue beyond that date.
(c) Where the terms of the lease include provision for the extension of the lease beyond a given date by notice given by the lessee, the duration of the lease applies as if the term of the lease extended for as long as it could be extended by the lessee, but subject to any right of the lessor to determine the lease by notice.
(d) In the case of a lease of an asset which itself is a wasting asset and also movable property, the lease is assumed to terminate not later than the end of the life of the wasting asset.

[*TCGA 1992, Sch 8 paras 8, 9(3)*].

Premiums for leases

[72.5] Where the payment of a 'premium' is required under a lease (or otherwise under the terms subject to which the lease is granted) there is a part disposal of the asset or other interest out of which that lease is granted.

In the part disposal computation (which follows the normal rules in *TCGA 1992, s 42*, see **16.5** COMPUTATION OF GAINS AND LOSSES) the property which remains undisposed of includes a right to any rent or other payments (other than a premium) payable under the lease, and that right is valued at the time of the part disposal. [*TCGA 1992, Sch 8 para 2*].

'*Premium*' includes any like sum, whether payable to the intermediate or superior lessor and includes any sum (other than rent) paid on or in connection with the granting of a lease except in so far as the other sufficient consideration for the payment is shown to have been given. Other capital sums payable by a tenant may fall to be treated as premiums (see **41.16** LAND).

Where by reference to any capital sum within the meaning of *ITA 2007, s 681DM* (assets leased to traders and others) any amount of that capital sum is charged to income tax then that amount is deducted from the consideration for capital gains tax purposes but not so as to convert a gain into a loss or increase a loss. [*TCGA 1992, Sch 8 para 9(2); TIOPA 2010, Sch 8 para 244*].

Sub-leases granted out of short leases

[72.6] Where a sub-lease is granted out of a head-lease with less than 50 years to run, the normal part disposal rules do not apply. Instead, subject to below, a proportion of the cost and enhancement expenditure attributable to the lease is apportioned to the part disposed of as follows:

$$\frac{P(1)}{P(2)}$$

where:

P(1) = the duration of the sub-lease
P(2) = the duration of the lease at the date of acquisition (for apportionment of cost) or the duration of the lease at the date when expenditure is first reflected in the nature of the lease (for apportionment of enhancement expenditure).

If the amount of the premium is less than what would be obtainable by way of premium for the sub-lease if the rent payable under the sub-lease were the same as the rent payable under the lease, the percentage attributable to the sub-lease as calculated above must be multiplied by the premium received over the premium so obtainable before being applied to cost or enhancement expenditure. [*TCGA 1992, Sch 8 para 4(1)(2)*].

Example

P purchases a 40-year lease of a non-wasting asset (other than land) in 2012 for £15,000. In 2017 he grants a sub-lease of the asset to Q for 20 years for a premium of £8,000. Had the rent under head-lease and sub-lease been the same the premium would have been £10,000. The expenditure attributable to the part disposal of the sub-lease is given by:

$$£15{,}000 \times \frac{20}{40} \times \frac{8{,}000}{10{,}000} = 0.4 \times £15{,}000 = £6{,}000$$

Where the sub-lease is a sub-lease of part only of the asset comprised in the lease, the cost and enhancement expenditure of the head-lease must be apportioned between the sub-lease and the remainder in proportion to their respective values. [*TCGA 1992, Sch 8 para 4(3)*].

Life interests

[72.7] Life interests in settled property above are treated as wasting assets when the expectation of life of the life tenant is 50 years or less. The predictable life of life tenants and annuities is ascertained from actuarial tables which have HMRC approval. [*TCGA 1992, s 44(1)(d)*]. See **62.15** SETTLEMENTS for the disposal of interests in settled property generally.

Example

N is a beneficiary under a settlement. On 30 June 2003, when her actuarially estimated life expectancy was 40 years, she sold her life interest to an unrelated individual, R, for £50,000. N dies on 31 December 2017, and the life interest is extinguished.

R will have an allowable loss for 2017/18 as follows

	£	£
Disposal consideration on death of N		Nil
Allowable cost	50,000	
Deduct wasted $\frac{14y6m}{40y} \times £50,000$	18,125	
		31,875
Allowable loss		£31,875

Note to the example

(a) The amount of the cost wasted is computed by reference to the predictable life, not the actual life, of the wasting asset.

Key points

[72.8] Points to consider are as follows.

- Wasting assets are, broadly, assets with a predictable life of no more than 50 years.
- For most assets, the base cost, less predictable residual value, and additional expenditure, are treated as diminishing evenly over their life, except where they are used in a trade or profession and are eligible for capital allowances.
- There are special rules for chattels, options and futures contracts, leases of land and life interests.

- Care should be taken to identify where there is a wasting asset as the gain is impacted and the tax can be a surprise to the owner. This is particularly the case with lease transactions.

73

Finance Acts 2017 — Summary of CGT Provisions

[73.1] The following is a brief summary of the main provisions of the *Finance Act 2017* and *Finance (No 2) Act 2017* that are concerned with, or impinge upon, capital gains tax (CGT) and/or corporation tax on chargeable gains. For an exhaustive list of current *Finance Act* provisions covered in Tolley's Capital Gains Tax, see 75 TABLE OF STATUTES.

Finance Act 2017

(Royal Assent 27 April 2017)

ss 12–14	**Employee shareholder shares.** The income tax and capital gains tax reliefs attached to the issue of shares in consideration of an employee shareholder agreement are abolished with effect where the agreement is entered into on or after 1 December 2016 (or, in limited circumstances, 2 December 2016). See **22.26** EMPLOYEE SHARE SCHEMES.
s 24	**Special compliance regime for high-risk promoters.** With effect from 8 March 2017, this section seeks to ensure that promoters of tax avoidance schemes cannot circumvent the regime by reorganising their business so that they either share control of a promoter business or put a person or persons between themselves and the promoter business. See **20.11** DISCLOSURE OF TAX AVOIDANCE SCHEMES.

Finance (No 2) Act 2017

The date of Royal Assent to *F(No 2)A 2017* is not yet known at time of going to press. It is expected to be in November 2017. Once Royal Assent has been given, the date should be available at https://services.parliament.uk/bills/2017-19/finance.html.

s 11	**Enterprise Investment Scheme (EIS) and Seed Enterprise Investment Scheme (SEIS).** In relation to shares issued on or after 5 December 2016, the EIS and SEIS requirements are amended to allow companies that issue shares with rights to a future conversion into, or future exchange for, shares of another class in that company to qualify for relief. See **23.3** ENTERPRISE INVESTMENT SCHEME and **60.8** SEED ENTERPRISE INVESTMENT SCHEME.

s 12 **Venture Capital Trusts (VCTs): restructuring of investee company.** In relation to investments made by VCTs on or after 6 April 2017, a new parent company which has acquired a company that has previously received funding from a VCT may use the funding history of that acquired company when considering if follow-on funding is permitted. See **71.5** VENTURE CAPITAL TRUSTS.

s 13 **VCTs: reorganisation of investee company.** This gives the Treasury power to make regulations covering cases where, on an exchange of non-qualifying shares or securities, a VCT receives other non-qualifying shares or securities. See **71.5** VENTURE CAPITAL TRUSTS.

s 14, Sch 1 **Social Investment Tax Relief (SITR).** A number of changes are made to the SITR scheme with effect for investments made on or after 6 April 2017. These include an increase in the amount that newer social enterprises may raise from investors under the scheme. They also include provisions to better target the scheme on higher risk activities and to deter abuse. See **65.1, 65.2, 65.10, 65.12, 65.18, 65.23, 65.25, 65.28, 65.30, 65.31**SOCIAL INVESTMENT RELIEF.

s 15 **Remittance basis: business investment relief.** A number of changes are introduced from 6 April 2017 to the business investment relief rules whereby relief from taxation of remittances may be claimed if a qualifying investment is made. The changes expand the types of business in which investment can be made, seek to ensure that anti-avoidance aspects do not discourage genuine investment and provide clarification. See **55.4** REMITTANCE BASIS.

s 16 Sch 2 **Trades and property businesses: cash basis.** With effect for 2017/18 onwards, changes are made to the rules for calculating gains when capital expenditure has been allowed under the cash basis, including in relation to property businesses. See **16.13** COMPUTATION OF GAINS AND LOSSES, **25.2** EXEMPTIONS AND RELIEFS and **39.1** INTERACTION WITH OTHER TAXES.

s 26 **Chargeable gains: elections in respect of assets appropriated to trading stock.** The provisions which enable an election to be made where assets are appropriated to trading stock so that no chargeable gain or allowable loss arises are amended so that an election can no longer be made if an allowable loss arises. The change applies to appropriations on or after 8 March 2017. See **16.9** COMPUTATIONS OF GAINS AND LOSSES and **29.23** GROUPS OF COMPANIES.

s 27 **Substantial shareholding exemption.** For disposals on or after 1 April 2017, the condition that the investing company must be a trading company or part of a trading group is removed and the condition that the investment must have been held for at least a continuous period of 12 months in the two years preceding the sale will be extended to a continuous period of 12 months in the six years preceding the sale.
See **66.1, 66.3, 66.5, 66.9, 66.10, 66.12** SUBSTANTIAL SHAREHOLDINGS OF COMPANIES.

s 28 **Substantial shareholding exemption: institutional investors.** For disposals on or after 1 April 2017, an exemption applies where the investee company is not a trading company if the investing company is owned by qualifying institutional investors (as defined). Full exemption will apply if at least 80% of the ordinary share capital is owned by such investors. Proportionate exemption will apply where between 25% and 80% is owned by such investors. In addition, where at least 25% is owned by qualifying institutional investors, the substantial shareholding condition may be met if the investing company's shareholding is below 10% of the ordinary share capital of the investee company but cost more than £20m. See **66.1, 66.6, 66.8** SUBSTANTIAL SHAREHOLDINGS OF COMPANIES.

s 29, Sch 8 **Deemed domicile.** With effect on or after 6 April 2017, individuals resident but not domiciled in the UK in any tax year are deemed to be domiciled in the UK for most income tax and capital gains tax purposes if they are UK born and have a UK domicile of origin or they have been UK resident for at least 15 of the 20 preceding tax years. See **57.34** RESIDENCE AND DOMICILE, **48.1, 48.5, 48.8, 48.29** OFFSHORE SETTLEMENTS, and **55.1, 55.2, 55.3, 55.5** REMITTANCE BASIS.

s 31, Sch 9 **Settlements: value of benefits conferred by certain capital payments.** With effect in relation to capital payments received in 2017/18 onwards, a means is given of determining the value of a benefit provided to a person where the capital payment involves a loan or the making available of tangible moveable property or land. See **48.14** OFFSHORE SETTLEMENTS.

s 32 **Exemption from attribution of carried interest gains.** Provisions exempt gains representing carried interest from various charges in respect of trusts, regardless of when the gains are treated as accruing. See **48.5, 48.15** OFFSHORE SETTLEMENTS and **49.7** OVERSEAS MATTERS.

s 39 **Transactions in UK land.** The provisions introduced in 2016 did not have effect in relation to disposals made on or after 5 July 2016 under a pre-5 July 2016 contract. All profits recognised in accounts on or after 8 March 2017 must now be brought into charge regardless of when the contract was entered into. See **41.6** LAND.

s 63, Sch 15	**Enquiries: partial closure notices.** As regards enquiries into returns commenced on or after the date of Royal Assent, or in progress on that date, an HMRC officer can issue a partial closure notice, which completes an enquiry insofar as it concerns the matters specified in the notice. See **58.12** RETURNS.
s 64	**Errors in documents.** With effect in relation to documents for tax periods beginning on or after 6 April 2017 and ending on or after the date of Royal Assent there is a presumption of carelessness where a document contains an inaccuracy as a result of its being submitted on the basis that particular avoidance arrangements had an effect which in fact they did not have. See **52.8** PENALTIES.
s 65, Sch 16	**Penalties for enablers of defeated tax avoidance.** With effect for arrangements entered into on or after the date of Royal Assent, a penalty is payable by a person who has enabled abusive tax arrangements entered into by another person that are defeated. See **52.21** PENALTIES.
s 67, Sch 18	**Failure to correct offshore tax non-compliance.** A penalty is payable by a person who has offshore tax non-compliance to correct at the end of 2016/17 and fails to correct it within the period 6 April 2017 to 30 September 2018 inclusive. See **52.14** PENALTIES.
s 69	**Data-gathering powers.** From the date of Royal Assent, money service businesses are added to the categories of data-holder who are subject to HMRC data-gathering powers. See **34.17** HMRC INVESTIGATORY POWERS.

74

Tax Case Digest

[74.1] Cases referred to in this chapter are cross-referenced to the relevant paragraph of this edition.

Statutory references marked with an asterisk (*) are to legislation which has replaced that involved in the case summarised.

Aberdeen Construction Group Ltd v CIR

Loan waiver condition of sale of shares – 'debt on a security'

See **16.2, 25.5**

A company sold its shares in a subsidiary for £250,000, a condition of the sale being that it waived repayment of unsecured loans of £500,000 it had made to the subsidiary. It was assessed on its gain from the sale of the shares with no allowance for the £500,000. The HL rejected the company's contentions that the loan was a 'debt on a security' within *TCGA 1992, s 251(1)** or that *TCGA 1992, s 43** applied, but held that the waiver of the loan was part of the consideration for the £250,000. The appeal was remitted to the Commissioners to make an appropriate apportionment under *TCGA 1992, s 52(4)**. *Aberdeen Construction Group Ltd v CIR* HL 1978, 52 TC 281; [1978] STC 127; [1978] 2 WLR 648; [1978] 1 All ER 962.

Allison v Murray

Insurance premium paid as part of trust variation

See **16.11**

A settlement in Scots form was varied by agreement on 3 March 1965 on terms whereby 60% of the trust fund, less £10,000, became absolutely vested in Mrs M who was required at her own expense to effect a single-premium policy in favour of the trustees against the event of her predeceasing Mrs W. In the event, Mrs W died on 1 March 1966, survived by Mrs M. Mrs M's husband was assessed for 1966/67 on the gain on the sale by the trustees of investments appropriated to Mrs M by reference to their market value at 6 April 1965. The assessment was upheld and a deduction refused for the insurance premium as not falling within *TCGA 1992, s 38(1)(a) or (b)**. Certain other contentions by the husband (who conducted his appeal in person) were rejected. *Allison v Murray* Ch D 1975, 51 TC 57; [1975] STC 524; [1975] 1 WLR 1578; [1975] 3 All ER 561.

Anders Utkilens Rederi AS v OY Lovisa Stevedoring Co AB

Compromise agreement for sale of defendant's property – whether a part disposal

See **16.5**

A Norwegian company obtained judgement against another company for a liquidated sum. The defendant company appealed, but a compromise agreement was reached whereby the defendant's premises, plant and machinery were to be sold and the proceeds divided between the parties. The defendant subsequently went into voluntary liquidation, and the property was sold a year later. The Ch D held that the compromise agreement effected a part disposal of the property by the defendant to the plaintiff, and that each party subsequently disposed of its interest then held to the ultimate purchaser. *Anders Utkilens Rederi AS v OY Lovisa Stevedoring Co AB & Another* Ch D 1984, [1985] STC 301; [1985] 2 All ER 669.

Aspden v Hildesley

Transfer of assets under Court Order on divorce

See **17.1**, **46.5**

The taxpayer and his wife had jointly owned certain property, not the private residence of either. They had been separated since 1970 and were divorced by decree nisi on 12 February 1976. The Court Order (by consent) provided, inter alia, for the taxpayer's half share of the property to be transferred to his wife, while she undertook to give an irrevocable order to her personal representatives that, should she die before 10 December 1984 and before her husband, a sum equal to half the equity in the property was to be paid to him out of her estate. The taxpayer was assessed on the footing that he had disposed of his share in the property on 12 February 1976, and that by virtue of *CGTA 1979, s 19(3)(a)** and *TCGA 1992, ss 18, 286** the consideration was to be taken as the market value. The Ch D upheld the assessment, reversing the decision of the Commissioners. On the facts, the taxpayer's interest in the property was transferred at the time of the decree nisi, the consent order being an unconditional contract for the transfer. As the decree was not then absolute, the parties were still married and *CGTA 1979, s 19(3)(a)** applied by virtue of *TCGA 1992, s 18(2)*, s 286(2)*. Aspden v Hildesley* Ch D 1981, 55 TC 609; [1982] STC 206; [1982] 1 WLR 264; [1982] 2 All ER 53. (Note. *CGTA 1979, s 19(3)* was repealed by *FA 1981* and replaced by what is now *TCGA 1992, s 17*.)

Atkinson v Dancer

Retirement relief

See **24.3**

A taxpayer farmed 89 acres and sold nine of them. He was assessed and claimed retirement relief, contending that the sale was a disposal of part of his business. The Ch D, reversing the Commissioners' decision, held that no relief was due, applying *McGregor v Adcock*. *Atkinson v Dancer* Ch D 1988, 61 TC 598; [1988] STC 758. (Note. Retirement relief is abolished for disposals after 5 April 2003 (see **25.88** EXEMPTIONS AND RELIEFS), but this case remains relevant to ENTREPRENEURS' RELIEF (**24.3**).)

Barrett v Powell

Retirement relief – surrender of agricultural tenancy by farmer – continuation of farming under temporary licence

See **24.3**

In March 1990 a tenant farmer received £120,000 from his landlord as compensation for surrendering his agricultural tenancy. He was allowed to continue to farm the land in question, under a temporary licence, until September 1991. The Revenue assessed the compensation to capital gains tax for 1989/90. The farmer appealed, contending that the payment of compensation qualified for retirement relief. The Ch D rejected this contention and upheld the assessment. On the evidence, the payment was made for the disposal of an asset, but was not made for the disposal of the whole or part of the farmer's business, since he had been able to continue farming the land in question for two summers under the temporary licence. *Jarmin v Rawlings* distinguished. *Barrett v Powell* Ch D 1998, 70 TC 432; [1998] STC 283. (Note. Retirement relief is abolished for disposals after 5 April 2003 (see **25.88** EXEMPTIONS AND RELIEFS), but this case remains relevant to ENTREPRENEURS' RELIEF (**24.3**).)

Batey v Wakefield

Bungalow separated from main residence – whether part of dwelling-house

See **53.6**

A taxpayer owned a house in Marlborough, built on 1.1 acres of land, but lived with his family in a London flat during the working week, returning to the house at weekends. He had elected under *TCGA 1992, s 222(5)** for the house to be treated as his main residence. Following a number of local burglaries, he had a bungalow built on the land, physically separate from the house and with separate road access. He arranged for the bungalow to be occupied by a farm labourer who acted as caretaker. In 1974 the taxpayer began living in the house on a full-time basis and, no longer needing a caretaker, sold the bungalow with 0.2 acres of land. The Revenue assessed the resulting gain to CGT and he appealed, contending that the bungalow had formed part of his dwelling-house and was exempt under *TCGA 1992, s 222**. The General Commissioners allowed his appeal, finding that the bungalow had been built for the purpose of providing services for the benefit of the main house, and holding that the occupation by the caretaker amounted to occupation by the taxpayer as part of his residence. The CA upheld the Commissioners' decision as one of fact, holding that they were entitled to conclude that the bungalow was part of the taxpayer's residence. *Batey v Wakefield* CA 1981, 55 TC 550; [1981] STC 521; [1982] 1 All ER 61. (Note. *Dicta* of Fox LJ were subsequently disapproved by the CA in *Lewis v Rook* below.)

Bayley v Rogers

Sale of new lease – whether a continuation of old lease

See **41.15**

A taxpayer's 14-year lease of his business premises expired in December 1974 and, following proceedings under the *Landlord and Tenant Act 1954*, he was granted a new lease. He disposed of the new lease in 1976 and was assessed on the gain on the footing that the new lease was a separate asset from the old. He appealed, contending that the new lease was a continuation of the old and that the straightline basis over the period from 1960 should be used by virtue of *TCGA 1992, Sch 2 para 16**. The Ch D, reversing the Commissioners' decision, held that the two leases were separate assets, and the second lease was not derived from the first within the meaning of *TCGA 1992, s 43**. *Bayley v Rogers* Ch D 1980, 53 TC 420; [1980] STC 544.

Baylis v Gregory

Avoidance Schemes

See **4.2**, **5.7**, **6.2**

The managing director of a company (PGI) controlled the company through his own and trustee shareholdings. Another company, C, entered into negotiations to acquire PGI, and the taxpayer and his associates set up a Manx company to exchange their shares in PGI with shares in the Manx company. However, C ended the negotiations. Nevertheless the share exchange was proceeded with and completed in March 1974. No further steps were taken to sell PGI until May 1975 when a third company, H, became interested in it. Eventually, the Manx company sold the PGI shares to H. The Special Commissioners allowed the taxpayer's appeals and their decision was upheld by the Ch D, the CA, and the HL. The transactions were not a 'pre-ordained series of transactions'. (The case was heard with *Craven v White*, in the CA and HL.) *Baylis v Gregory* HL 1988, 62 TC 1; [1988] STC 476; [1988] 3 WLR 423; [1988] 3 All ER 495.

Begg-McBrearty v Stilwell

Exercise of power of appointment in favour of grandchildren of settlor – whether grandchildren acquiring an interest in possession at age of 18 or 21

See **62.14**

In 1975 the trustees of a settlement made in 1959 exercised their power of appointment in favour of the settlor's three grandchildren, and thereafter held the trust fund contingently for the grandchildren contingently on their reaching the age of 21.

The eldest grandchild became 21 in 1990, and thus became absolutely entitled to a one-third share of the settled property. The Revenue issued a 1990/91 assessment on one of the trustees, charging CGT on the deemed disposal to the grandchild in accordance with *TCGA, s 71**. The trustee appealed, contending that the gain should be held over by virtue of *TCGA, s 260(2)(d)**. The Ch D upheld the assessment. The disposal could not be held over under *TCGA, s 260(2)(d)** because the grandchild had become entitled to an interest in possession in her share of the settled property in 1987, when she reached the age of 18. Before the exercise of the power of appointment, the grandchild had had only a revocable interest in the trust property. Her relevant interest arose from the power of appointment. Since this had been exercised in 1975, it fell within the provisions of Family Law Reform Act 1969 (which had reduced the age of majority to 18 with effect from 1 January 1970), even though the original settlement had been made before the date on which that act took effect. *Begg-McBrearty v Stilwell* Ch D 1996, 68 TC 426; [1996] STC 413; [1996] 1 WLR 951; [1996] 4 All ER 205.

Bentley v Pike

Rate of exchange where gain realised abroad

See **16.11**

Under German law, the taxpayer's wife and her sister became equally entitled to real property in Germany under the intestacy of their father, resident and domiciled abroad. The father died on 31 October 1967. Following the issue of the German equivalent of Letters of Administration, the sisters were entered in the German Land Registry in July 1972 as tenants in common of the property. The property was sold in July 1973, the sisters receiving their shares of the net proceeds in Deutschmarks. The Ch D upheld the Commissioners' decision that the taxpayer had been correctly assessed on his wife's gain taken as the difference between the Deutschmark value of her share of the property at her father's death, converted into sterling at the then ruling exchange rate, and the Deutschmarks she received on the sale, converted into sterling at the rate ruling at the date of sale. The taxpayer's contentions that the date of acquisition was the date his wife was entered in the Land Registry, and that the gain was the difference between the two Deutschmark figures converted at the rate at the time of disposal, were rejected. On the evidence, under German law, his wife became absolutely entitled on her father's death. This was the date of acquisition by virtue of *TCGA 1992, s 62(1)(a)**. The unit of account for assessment was sterling and the market value of the deemed acquisition on the death must be arrived at using the exchange rate at the time. *Bentley v Pike* Ch D 1981, 53 TC 590; [1981] STC 360.

Billows v Hammond

Value of unquoted shares

See **45.4**

In December 1986 the controlling director of a company gave most of his shares in the company to his two children. The Revenue issued an estimated CGT assessment, and the director appealed, contending that the shares had no value at the time of the transfer. The Special Commissioner rejected this contention and upheld the assessment in principle, holding on the evidence that the shares transferred had an open market value of £195 each. *Billows v Hammond* (Sp C 252), [2000] SSCD 430. (Note. The director had failed to notify the gift on his tax return and the Commissioner held that this constituted 'negligent conduct' within *TMA 1970, s 36*. In separate proceedings, the CA had previously held that the company's accounts were unreliable.)

Bond v Pickford

Power of Appointment

See **62.14**

In 1972 the trustees of a discretionary settlement, which had been established in 1961, executed two deeds to allocate part of the settled property. The allocated funds continued to be held by the trustees of the main settlement and were subject to the administrative powers of that settlement. The trustees were assessed on the basis that there had been a deemed disposal under *TCGA 1992, s 71(1)**. The Special Commissioners allowed their appeal and this decision was upheld by the Ch D and the CA. Applying dicta of Wilberforce J in *Roome v Edwards*, it would not be natural for a person with knowledge of the legal context of 'settlement', and applying that knowledge in a practical and commonsense manner to the facts, to say that separate settlements had been made by the allocations. There is a distinction between powers to alter the trusts of a settlement expressly or by necessary implication authorising the trustees to remove assets altogether from the original settlement (without rendering any person absolutely entitled to them), and powers which do not confer on the trustees such authority. The relevant powers here were of the latter type. *Bond v Pickford* CA 1983, 57 TC 301; [1983] STC 517.

Booth v Ellard

Shares transferred to trustees under pooling agreement – whether a disposal

See **62.3**

Twelve shareholders in a company entered into an agreement under which their shares were transferred to trustees. This was done so that they and their families could retain effective control of the company if its shares were dealt with on the Stock Exchange. The agreement was for 15 years but subject to determination by shareholders who, between them, held a specified proportion of the shares transferred. The broad effect of the agreement was that the shares were pooled. The participants received the trust income proportionate to the shares they transferred and they were able to direct the trustees how to exercise the votes attaching to the shares or decide should there be a rights issue, etc. Provisions ensured that the shares would remain in the family should a participant die or wish to sell. CGT assessments were made on the footing that the agreement was a settlement of the shares. The CA allowed on appeal by one of the shareholders, reversing the decision of the Commissioners. The shareholders collectively had power to end the trust, and although their interests in their shares were subject to restraints, they did not lose their beneficial interests. They were absolutely entitled to their shares as against the trustees, within *TCGA 1992, s 60(1)**; hence the transfer to the trustees was not a chargeable disposal. *Booth v Ellard* CA 1980, 53 TC 393; [1980] STC 555; [1980] 1 WLR 1443; [1980] 3 All ER 569.

Bullivant Holdings Ltd v CIR

Acquisition of shares – whether TCGA 1992, s 17 applicable*

See **45.1**

A company (B) acquired two 25% shareholdings in a publishing company, from different vendors, for a total of £25,000. It subsequently lodged a claim that *TCGA 1992, s 17** should be treated as applying to the acquisitions, so that its acquisition cost should be treated as market value rather than as £25,000. The Revenue rejected the claim and the Special Commissioner dismissed B's appeal. On the evidence, the shares had been acquired at arm's length and the consideration of £25,000 appeared to be 'a full and fair price'. Accordingly, *TCGA 1992, s 17** did not apply. The Ch D upheld this decision. *Bullivant Holdings Ltd v CIR* Ch D 1998, 71 TC 22; [1998] STC 905.

Burca v Parkinson

Beneficial ownership of asset

See **16.3**

The controlling director of a publishing company sold his shareholding in 1988. In his tax return, he only accounted for tax on part of the consideration which he had received. Subsequently the Revenue issued assessments charging CGT on the balance of the gain. The director appealed, contending that he had passed 60% of the shares to his parents in 1987. The Special Commissioner reviewed the evidence, rejected this contention, and upheld the assessments, finding that although the director had borrowed money from his parents, there was 'no evidence . . . of the taxpayer completing (either in writing or orally) a declaration of trust in favour of his parents or of his agreeing to hold shares for them as nominee'. The director appealed to the Ch D, which upheld the Commissioner's decision. *Burca v Parkinson* Ch D 2001, 74 TC 125; [2001] STC 1298.

Burman v Hedges & Butler Ltd

Avoidance scheme – whether TCGA 1992, s 171 (transfers within a group) applicable*

See **29.7**

A company (H) owned the share capital of B Ltd and was itself wholly owned by BC Ltd. BC Ltd agreed, subject to contract, to sell B Ltd to S Ltd, an unconnected company. To avoid the chargeable gain of about £½m which would have arisen on a direct sale, the following scheme was carried out. V Ltd was formed with capital of 76 £1 participating preference shares held by the taxpayer and 24 £1 ordinary shares held by S Ltd. Z Ltd was formed with share capital owned by V Ltd. Z Ltd bought the shares in B Ltd out of a loan to it by S Ltd. V Ltd then went into liquidation, the liquidator transferring its shares in Z Ltd to S Ltd as the ordinary shareholder of V Ltd. H was assessed on the basis that it had sold the shares in B Ltd to S Ltd. The Commissioners discharged the assessment, rejecting the Revenue's contention that V Ltd and Z Ltd had acted throughout as nominees or agents for S Ltd, and holding that the sale from H to Z Ltd was within *TCGA 1992, s 171**. Their decision was upheld by the Ch D. *Burman v Hedges & Butler Ltd* Ch D 1978, 52 TC 501; [1979] STC 136; [1979] 1 WLR 160.

Burman v Westminster Press Ltd

Wasting assets – whether TCGA 1992, s 45(2)(b) applicable where capital allowances withdrawn*

See **25.4**

In 1973 a company (W), which published regional newspapers, agreed to purchase a printing press. The purchase price was paid by instalments beginning in 1973 and ending in 1977. The press was not delivered until 1976, by which time it was surplus to W's requirements. It was never used in W's trade and was kept in storage until 1978 when it was sold to a Dutch company at a profit of more than £650,000. W had been given first-year allowances on the instalments of the purchase price, but these were subsequently withdrawn under *FA 1971, s 41(2)*. The Revenue included the profit on the sale of the press in a CT assessment on W. W appealed, contending that the press was a wasting asset within *TCGA 1992, s 45** and had not qualified in full for a capital allowance within the meaning of *TCGA 1992, s 45(2)(b)**, so that the gain was exempt under *TCGA 1992, s 45(1)**. The Special Commissioner allowed W's appeal and the Ch D upheld this decision. The expenditure on the press had not fulfilled the necessary conditions to attract a capital allowance, so that *TCGA 1992, s 45(2)(b)** did not apply. *Burman v Westminster Press Ltd* Ch D 1987, 60 TC 418; [1987] STC 669.

Campbell Connelly & Co Ltd v Barnett

Rollover relief – whether new premises used for trading purposes 'on' acquisition

See **59.2**

A music publishing company (C) sold its trading premises in 1984, and moved into the premises of its parent company. In January 1986, it purchased the freehold of another property, but was unable to obtain vacant possession because the property was occupied by lessees. In September 1986, C's parent company purchased the leasehold interest. C then moved into the property and began using it for trading purposes. C claimed rollover relief in respect of the gain on the sale of its previous premises. The Revenue refused to allow relief, considering that the premises had not been taken into trade use 'on the acquisition', as required by *TCGA 1992, s 152(1)**, and that the acquisition into which the gain could have been rolled over was the purchase of the leasehold interest, which had been carried out by the parent and not by C. The General Commissioners dismissed the company's appeal and the Ch D and CA upheld their decision. The premises had not been used for the purposes of C's trade on the acquisition of the freehold, and neither could the acquisitions of the freehold and leasehold interests by different legal persons be regarded as one transaction. Accordingly, relief was not due. *Campbell Connelly & Co Ltd v Barnett* CA 1993, 66 TC 380; [1994] STC 50. (Note. *TCGA 1992, s 152* has subsequently been amended by *FA 1995, s 48*.)

Cann v Woods

Irrecoverable loans to company – whether TCGA 1992, s 253(12) applicable

See **44.12**

In 1988 a wealthy investor (C) purchased a majority shareholding in a company (BG) which had four subsidiaries. The group was suffering financial difficulties. From 1989 to 1992 C made loans of more than £2,000,000 to one of BG's subsidiaries (B). However, B continued to suffer financial problems. In March 1994 BG sold its shareholding in B to another company (GD), and a week later B sold its net assets to GD. GD did not take over B's overdraft or the loans from C. C claimed relief under *TCGA 1992, s 253(3)* for his loans to B. The Revenue rejected the claim, considering that *TCGA 1992, s 253(12)* applied, on the basis that the loans had become irrecoverable as a result of an 'act . . . by the lender', namely the sale of B's shares and assets. C appealed, contending that the loans had become irrecoverable as a result of the commercial situation. The Special Commissioner accepted this contention and allowed the appeal. When C had first invested in B, he believed that it had commercial potential. However, he could not be expected to fund B indefinitely. By February 1994 B had become insolvent and C's loans had become irrecoverable. Such 'acts' as took place at the end of March played no part in their becoming irrecoverable at or before the end of February. Accordingly C was entitled to relief. (The Special Commissioner also rejected, as not supported by the evidence, an alternative contention by the Revenue that the loans had not been recoverable when they had been made and thus could not have 'become irrecoverable'.) *Cann v Woods* (Sp C 183), [1999] SSCD 77.

Capcount Trading v Evans

Computation of loss on asset purchased and sold in foreign currency

See **16.11**

Bentley v Pike (see above) was applied in this subsequent case where a company had made a loss on the disposal of shares in a Canadian company. The shares had been purchased and sold for Canadian dollars, and the Revenue computed the resulting loss by translating the dollar purchase price and the dollar sale price into sterling at the spot rates prevailing at, respectively, the date of purchase and the date of sale, and deducting the sterling equivalent of the sale price from the sterling equivalent of the purchase price. The company appealed, contending that the loss should be computed by deducting the dollar sale price from the dollar cost, and translating the resulting sum into sterling at the spot rate prevailing at the date of disposal. The Special Commissioner rejected this contention and dismissed the company's appeal. The CA upheld the Commissioner's decision. For the purpose of tax on capital gains, foreign currency was not money but was an asset. Therefore, when the company acquired the Canadian shares for Canadian dollars, it gave a consideration in money's worth which fell to be valued in sterling at that time. *Pattison v Marine Midland Ltd* distinguished. *Capcount Trading v Evans* CA 1992, 65 TC 545; [1993] STC 11; [1993] All ER 125.

Caton's Administrators v Couch

Costs of appealing against valuation of unquoted shares – whether 'incidental costs of disposal'

See **16.11**

In a share valuation case, the administrators of a deceased's estate contended that the costs of their appeal qualified as incidental costs of disposal. The Ch D rejected this contention and the CA dismissed the administrators' appeal. Morritt LJ held that, although the costs of an initial valuation were deductible, *TCGA** did not permit a liability to tax to be diminished (or even extinguished) by contesting it. If such expenses were to be treated as deductible, there would be a positive deterrent to reaching a sensible agreement as to the quantum of the liability. Applying *Smith's Potato Estates Ltd v Bolland*, there was a distinction between the costs of producing accounts from which to compute profits and the conduct of a tax controversy with the Revenue. The costs and expenses which a taxpayer might deduct under *TCGA 1992, s 38(2)(b)** were limited to those incurred in complying with the requirements of *TMA 1970, s 12* [and presumably *TMA 1970, s 8* under self-assessment from 1996/97], and did not extend to costs incurred in contesting the tax liability arising from a disposal. *Caton's Administrators v Couch* CA 1997, 70 TC 10; [1997] STC 970.

Chaloner v Pellipar Investments Ltd

*Development agreement providing for 'money's worth' in the form of site works – whether within TCGA 1992, s 22**

See **16.4**

Under a development agreement made in 1987, a company received 'money's worth' in the form of site works. The works were not completed until 1991. The Revenue considered that the effect of *TCGA 1992, s 28** was that the consideration was assessable in the company's accounting period ending June 1988, by reference to the date of the contract. The company appealed, contending that the consideration was a capital sum derived from an asset, within *TCGA 1992, s 22**, so that it was not assessable until the period in which it was received. The Special Commissioner allowed the company's appeal but the Ch D reversed this decision, holding that, since the benefit to the company of the development of the site represented consideration for a lease rather than a licence, it did not fall within *TCGA 1992, s 22(1)(d)*. *Chaloner v Pellipar Investments Ltd* Ch D 1996, 68 TC 238; [1996] STC 234.

Chaney v Watkis

Deductible money liability replaced by non-monetary obligation – whether money's worth and deductible

See **16.11**

The taxpayer had owned a house, occupied by his mother-in-law Mrs W as a protected tenant. He was offered £7,200 for the house subject to the tenancy but refused it. Subsequently he agreed with Mrs W that, if she would vacate the house, he would compensate her by paying her half the difference between the tenanted value and the actual sale price. The house was sold in 1981 for £26,000, but prior to completion he agreed with Mrs W that he would provide her with rent-free accommodation for life if in return she released him from his obligation to pay her £9,400 under their previous agreement. In the event she came to live in an extension to his own residence built for some £25,000. The appeal was against an assessment on the gain from the disposal of the house with no deduction for the £9,400. The Ch D allowed the appeal (reversing the decision of the Commissioners). It was common ground that, had the £9,400 been paid, it would have been deductible under *TCGA 1992, s 38(1)(b)**. The obligation to pay this sum was replaced by an obligation capable of being valued in money terms, despite the domestic nature of the agreement, which, applying *Oram v Johnson*, gave rise to an allowable deduction. The case was remitted to the Commissioners to determine the appeal in accordance with the judgment. *Chaney v Watkis* Ch D 1985, 58 TC 707; [1986] STC 89.

Chinn v Collins

Whether shares sold held under non-resident settlement

See **62.14**

Under a 1960 settlement, shares in L Ltd, a public quoted company, were held on discretionary trusts. A scheme was subsequently carried out to mitigate the incidence of CGT. The existing (resident) trustees were replaced by non-resident trustees and on 28 October 1969 the following transactions were effected. With the settlor's permission, 184,500 of the shares held by the trustees were appointed to each of two brothers, discretionary beneficiaries under the trust, contingently on their surviving three days; each brother assigned his contingent interest to a Jersey company for £352,705; that company contracted to sell each brother 184,500 shares in L Ltd for £355,162 (their then market value), the contract to be completed on 1 November. The brothers survived the three days. The upshot was that they had acquired the shares for their full price, the cost being financed by their disposal of their contingent interests (exempt under *TCGA 1992, s 76(1)**). The brothers were assessed on the basis that *FA 1965, s 42(2)* applied. Their appeals against the assessments were dismissed by the HL. The scheme was an arrangement within the definition of 'settlement' in *FA 1965, s 42(7)*. Although, following *CIR v Plummer*, a settlement must include an element of bounty, there was here an act of bounty in favour of the sons. The settlor's bounty was incomplete when he divested himself of the shares settled. *Chinn v Collins*; *Chinn v Hochstrasser* HL 1980, 54 TC 311; [1981] STC 1; [1981] 2 WLR 14; [1981] 1 All ER 189.

CIR v Beveridge

*Share exchange on takeover – application of TCGA 1992, Sch 2 para 19**

See **8.10**

In a case in which the issue was the application of *TCGA 1992, Sch 2 para 19**, the relevant shares were originally ordinary shares in S Ltd, a private company, acquired before 6 April 1965, exchanged for ordinary shares in L Ltd in 1967 on a takeover, and disposed of in 1974. There had been a substantial fall in the value of the shares between 1967 and 1974. The assessment was on the basis that *TCGA 1992, Sch 2 para 19(3)** applied. The taxpayer appealed, contending that it did not apply, because the shares in S Ltd were subject to a restriction on transfer to which those in L Ltd were not subject, and consequently not of the same class. The Commissioners allowed his appeal and the CS upheld their decision. The CS also held that *TCGA 1992, Sch 2 para 19(3)** was inapplicable as 'reorganisation of a company's share capital' cannot be construed to cover an amalgamation of two companies. *CIR v Beveridge* CS 1979, 53 TC 178; [1979] STC 592. (Note. See also SP 14/79.)

CIR v Burmah Oil Co

Avoidance Schemes

See **4.2, 63.2**

A company (H), which was a member of a group, was dormant but owned stock with a market value substantially less than its acquisition cost. Its parent company (B) carried out a series of transactions including a capital reorganisation and the loan of £160 million to H via another company in the same group. At the end of these transactions, B held the stock previously held by H, which had been put into liquidation. B claimed that it had made a loss of £160 million on the disposal of its shareholding in H. The HL rejected the claim (reversing the decision of the CS). The whole and only purpose of the scheme had been the avoidance of tax. Applying *WT Ramsay Ltd*, the transactions had 'no commercial purpose apart from the avoidance of a liability to tax', and should be disregarded. *CIR v Burmah Oil Co Ltd* HL 1981, 54 TC 200; [1982] STC 30.

CIR v Chubb's Trustee

Expenses of terminating trust

See **16.11**

Under a marriage settlement, a fund was settled on the wife for life with remainder to the issue of the marriage. The husband had died before the relevant period and the only child was a married daughter with infant children. Arrangements were made under which the trust was terminated and the trust fund vested absolutely in the widow and the daughter. In an appeal against the resultant assessment made under *TCGA 1992, s 71(1)**, the trustee claimed to deduct the cost of legal expenses (including fees to counsel for advice), stamp duty and other expenses as necessarily incurred to bring about the chargeable occasion under *TCGA 1992, s 71(1)**. The Commissioners allowed the deduction and the CS upheld their decision. *CIR v Chubb's Trustee* CS 1971, 47 TC 353.

CIR v John Lewis Properties plc

Assignment of rentals for five-year period – whether income within Schedule A or capital

See **16.5, 59.4**

In 1995 a property-holding company assigned to a bank its right to receive rental income for a five-year period, in return for a lump sum payment (a type of transaction generally known as rent factoring). The Revenue issued a corporation tax assessment on the basis that the payment was income chargeable under Schedule A. The company appealed, contending that the payment was a capital receipt for the part disposal of its interests in the properties (so that it was entitled to rollover relief). The Special Commissioner accepted this contention and allowed the appeal, and the CA upheld this decision. Applying *dicta* of Dixon J in the Australian case of *Hallstroms Property Ltd v Federal Commissioner of Taxation* CA(A) 1946, 72 CLR 634, the question of whether the money was received as capital or income 'depends on what the expenditure is calculated to effect from a practical and business point of view, rather than upon the juristic classification of the legal rights, if any, secured, employed or exhausted in the process'. Dyson LJ held that 'the payment made by the bank was one of capital. The sum was substantial, it was a single payment for the once and for all disposal by (J) of six years' rents, which resulted in a diminution in the value of its reversionary interests.' He observed that 'if J had granted the bank six-year leases at nominal rents, the premiums payable would have been capital payments . . . the differences between such a transaction and the one which they in fact entered into are not sufficiently significant that they should lead to a different fiscal result'. *CIR v John Lewis Properties plc* CA 2002, [2003] STC 117. (*Notes.* (1) With effect for transactions after 20 March 2000, rent factoring receipts are taxable as income under Schedule A — see Tolley's Corporation Tax under Property Income. (2) The Revenue's further submission that, if not chargeable as income, the full proceeds should be taken into account for corporation tax on chargeable gains, without the deduction of any acquisition cost, was rejected by the Special Commissioner; the disposal was a part disposal within *TCGA 1992, s 42*).

CIR v Montgomery

Sale of rights to insurance recoveries

See **10.2**

Property was extensively damaged by fire with the result that the owners (trustees of a will trust) became entitled to insurance recoveries of £75,192. The owners assigned their rights under the policies to G in consideration of £75,192 and were assessed on the resultant gain. The taxpayers' contention that there was no chargeable gain was upheld. The £75,192 was derived from the sale of the rights under the policies and no more and *TCGA 1992, s 22** was confined to cases where no asset was acquired by the person paying the capital sum. *CIR v Montgomery* Ch D 1974, 49 TC 679; [1975] STC 182; [1975] 1 All ER 664. (Note. The law was amended for disposals after 19 December 1974. See now *TCGA 1992, s 225*. *Dicta* of Walton J were disapproved by the HL in *Marren v Ingles*.)

CIR v Richards' Executors

Expenses of obtaining confirmation (probate)

See **19.10, 16.11**

The executors of a deceased person were assessed on their gains from disposals of investments forming part of the estate. On appeal, the Commissioners allowed their claim for the deduction for a proportionate amount of the fees paid to solicitors for valuing the estate, paying the estate duty, obtaining confirmation, etc. and for commission paid to them for their work done in disposing of the investments. The HL upheld this decision. *CIR v Richards' Executors* HL 1971, 46 TC 626; [1971] 1 WLR 571; [1971] 1 All ER 785.

Clark (Clark's Executor) v Green & CIR

*Valuation of unquoted shares – TCGA 1992, s 273(3)**

See **45.4**

A taxpayer held a 3.16% shareholding in a substantial unquoted company. She died in September 1987. The company's accounts for the year ending 31 August 1987 (which had not been published at the time of the taxpayer's death) showed pre-tax profits of £2,350,000. In April 1988 all the issued share capital of the company was sold. The Revenue issued a CGT assessment on the basis that the value of the shares at the time of the taxpayer's death was 30p each. (This valuation was computed by applying a gross price/earnings ratio of 12 to the earnings per share, and discounting it by 65% for unmarketability, leaving a net price/earnings ratio of 4.2.) Her executor appealed, contending that the shares should be valued at 18p each, since the Revenue's valuation took account of unpublished information concerning the company's profits which should have been ignored. The Special Commissioner dismissed the appeal and upheld the Revenue's valuation, holding that the effect of *TCGA 1992, s 273(3)** was that the unpublished information concerning the company's profits should be taken into account, and that the Revenue's valuation had been made on a reasonable basis. The Commissioner observed that *TCGA 1992, s 273** (which derived from *FA 1973, s 51*) had been enacted to overturn the decision in Lynall. Although the shareholding was a small minority holding, the hypothetical purchaser was 'considering an investment of something in the region of £100,000 –

£169,000'. The Commissioner also considered that the Revenue's valuation was 'if anything, rather low', and noted that the valuation was significantly less than the valuation of shares in the same company in *Caton's Administrators v Couch* (Sp C 6), [1995] SSCD 34, but observed that 'the difference between the two valuations reflects the difference in the size of the shareholdings which, in turn, reflects the amount of information assumed to be available'. (The valuation in *Caton's Administrators v Couch* was based on the assumption that the prospective purchaser would know that the company's entire share capital was likely to be sold in the near future, which was not the case here since the shareholding here was significantly smaller.) *Clark (Clark's Executor) v Green & CIR* (Sp C 5), [1995] SSCD 99.

Clarke v United Real (Moorgate) Ltd

Grant of lease of freehold property after development – whether reimbursement of development expenditure a premium within TCGA 1992, *Sch 8 para 2(1), para 10(2)*

See **41.16**

M, a company carrying on property investment and development, agreed in 1978 with contractors for the development of a freehold site it owned. In 1979 it signed an 'agreement for a lease' with another company, N, under which N agreed to reimburse M's expenditure on the development, on completion of which M was to grant N a long lease of the property at a rent below the market value, the formula for which was directly related to N's payments in reimbursement of M's development expenditure. The Ch D, reversing the decision of the Special Commissioner, held that the reimbursement of the expenditure was a premium within *TCGA 1992, Sch 8 para 2(1), para 10(2)**. M's contention that it had been reimbursed the expenditure in its capacity of property developer, and not in its capacity of landlord, was rejected. M developed the site for itself and not for N, which was not a party to the development contracts. *Clarke v United Real (Moorgate) Ltd* Ch D 1987, 61 TC 353; [1988] STC 273.

Cleveleys Investment Trust Co v CIR (No 1)

Advance for payment of shares – incorporeal rights

See **25.5**

C, an investment company, advanced £25,000 to F Ltd, which undertook to reconstruct its share capital, allotting a 51% holding to C. The £25,000 was to be used to acquire the shares. F Ltd accepted a bill of exchange for £25,000 drawn on it by C. F Ltd went into voluntary liquidation before its capital had been reconstructed and the £25,000 was not recovered. The CS held that the advance of £25,000 was part of a composite single transaction conferring incorporeal rights on C — see *TCGA 1992, s 21(1)(a)** — and its loss was an allowable loss. *Cleveleys Investment Trust Co v CIR (No 1)* CS 1971, 47 TC 300.

Cleveleys Investment Trust Co v CIR (No 2)

Guarantee payment – whether chargeable asset acquired

See **16.11**

An investment company guaranteed the bank overdraft of another company and paid £27,351 in pursuance of the guarantee. It contended that in so doing it had acquired the bank's rights as a creditor of the other company, that these rights were an asset for CGT purposes the value of which had become negligible within *TCGA 1992, s 24(2)**, and that accordingly it had an allowable loss of £27,351. The CS rejected this contention. The company's acquisition of the bank's worthless claim was an incident of its discharge of its obligation to the bank. *Cleveleys Investment Trust Co v CIR (No 2)* CS 1975, 51 TC 26; [1975] STC 457.

Coates v Arndale Properties Ltd

Avoidance scheme – whether TCGA 1992, s 173(1) applicable*

See **4.2**, **29.4**

Three companies, members of the same group, entered into transactions, not disputed to be genuine, but admittedly to secure expected favourable tax consequences. One company, SPI, had acquired and developed at a cost of £5,313,822 property the market value of which had fallen by March 1973 to £3,100,000. On 30 March 1973 it assigned the property to a property dealing company, A, for a consideration of £3,090,000. On the same day, A assigned the property for £3,100,000 to an investment company, APT. No cash passed, the matter being dealt with by book entries. A then purported to make an election under *TCGA 1992, s 161(3)**; the consequence would be that, by virtue of *TCGA 1992, s 171(1)**, the transfer from SPI to A would give rise to no loss or gain for CGT purposes, and in computing A's Case I profits it could treat the cost of the property as its market value plus the CGT loss which would have accrued under *TCGA 1992, s 161(1)** if the election had not been made. The Revenue assessed A under Case I on the footing that the election was invalid, contending that A had not acquired the property as trading stock within the meaning of *TCGA 1992, s 173(1)**. The HL upheld the assessment, holding that A never did decide to acquire, and never did acquire, the lease as trading stock. The transfer of the lease from SPI to A and from A to APT was procured with the object of obtaining group relief without in fact changing the lease from a capital asset to a trading asset. A lent its name to the transaction but it did not trade and never had any intention of trading with the lease. In these circumstances it was unnecessary to consider the principles enunciated in *CIR v Burmah Oil Co* and *Furniss v Dawson* or the dividend-stripping cases which had been considered in the courts below. *Coates v Arndale Properties Ltd* HL 1984, 59 TC 516; [1984] STC 637; [1984] 1 WLR 1328; [1985] 1 All ER 15.

Cooper v Billingham; Fisher v Edwards

Trustees making demand loans to settlor – whether any 'capital payments' within TCGA 1992, s 87(4)

See **48.14**

In 1987 a UK resident (C) established a settlement, the trustees of which were resident in Switzerland and the Cayman Islands. The trustees made a number of interest-free loans, repayable on demand, to C. The Revenue issued CGT assessments on the basis that C should be treated as having received capital payments, within *TCGA 1992, s 87(4)*, from the trustees of the settlement, the amount of such payments being the interest that would have been payable had the loans from the trustees been made on a commercial basis. C appealed, contending that, while there had been a nominal payment of capital when each initial loan was made, there was no further capital payment while that loan remained outstanding. The Ch D rejected this contention and upheld the assessments. Lloyd J held that, when the trustees had made a loan which was repayable on demand, they conferred a benefit on C 'by leaving the loan outstanding for any period, even for a single day'. The effect of *TCGA 1992, s 97* was that the benefits were to be treated as capital payments for the purposes of *TCGA 1992, s 87(4)*. The CA unanimously dismissed C's appeal against this decision. Applying *dicta* of Viscount Simon LC in *Nokes v Doncaster Amalgamated Collieries* HL, [1940] AC 1014; [1940] 3 All ER 549, 'if the choice is between two interpretations, the narrower of which would fail to achieve the manifest purpose of the legislation, we should avoid a construction which would reduce the legislation to futility and should rather accept the bolder construction based on the view that Parliament would legislate only for the purpose of bringing about an effective result'. Robert Walker LJ held that 'the whole scheme of the legislation requires the court to see what benefit a beneficiary actually receives, in cash or in kind, otherwise than as income or under an arm's length transaction. Any pre-existing beneficial interest belonging to the beneficiary is irrelevant.' *Cooper v Billingham; Fisher v Edwards* CA 2001, 74 TC 139; [2001] STC 1177.

Cottle v Coldicott

Sale of milk quota – whether part of cost of land deductible from gain

See 7.9

A farmer owned 56.68 acres of land and was entitled to 120,000 litres of milk quota. In September 1991, he sold 60,000 litres of milk quota to a company. On the same day, but under separate agreements, he granted the company a tenancy of 10.39 acres of his land for a ten-month period, and the company appointed him as its agent to enter into occupation of that part of the land. The land subject to the tenancy was not to be used for milk production, this short-term let being necessary to ensure a permanent and effective transfer of the milk quota, since milk quota could not be used or sold without the land to which it was attached. The Revenue issued a CGT assessment on the gain. The farmer appealed, contending that the sale of the milk quota should be treated as a part disposal of his land, so that part of the acquisition cost of the land should be allowed as a deduction and that on this basis he had made a capital loss rather than a capital gain. The Special Commissioners rejected this contention and rejected the farmer's appeal. The milk quota was a separate asset from the land. Although milk quota corresponded to a holding of land, it did not 'correspond to any particular parcel of land in that holding'. Milk quota did not derive from the occupier's land, but was 'an advantage derived from the context of the common organisation of the market in milk'. Milk quota was a valuable asset, and those holding it had the right (subject to restrictions laid down in EC law) to dispose of it for profit. *Dicta* of the European Court of Justice in *R v Ministry of Agriculture, Fisheries and Food (ex p. Bostock),* CJEC [1994] 1 ECR 955 applied. The sale of the milk quota was not a part disposal of the farmer's land within *TCGA 1992, s 21(2)(b)**, and was not a capital sum derived from the land within *TCGA 1992, s 22(1)**. Since the value of the quota did not derive from the holding, *TCGA 1992, s 43** did not apply. *Cottle v Coldicott* (Sp C 40), [1995] SSCD 239.

Craven v White

Anti-avoidance

See 4.2

Three members of a family owned all the shares in a UK company (Q), which owned a number of shops. From 1973 they conducted negotiations with various other companies with a view to selling Q or merging it with a similar business. In July 1976, at a time when they were negotiating with two unconnected companies, they exchanged their shares for shares in an Isle of Man company (M). Nineteen days later M sold the shares in Q to one of the two companies with which negotiations had been in progress at the time of the share exchange. The sale proceeds were paid by M to the shareholders over a period of five years. The Revenue issued CGT assessments for 1976/77 on the basis that, applying the Ramsay principle, the disposal of the shares to M and their subsequent sale by M should be treated as a single composite transaction and that the transfer of the shares to M was a fiscal nullity. The Special Commissioners reduced the assessments, holding that the transfer could not be treated as a fiscal nullity but that the shareholders were assessable on the amounts they had received from M at the time of receipt. The Revenue's appeals against this decision were dismissed by the Ch D, the CA, and (by a 3–2 majority) the HL. In giving the leading judgement for the majority, Lord Oliver indicated the limitations of the principle adopted in *CIR v Ramsay*, as defined by Lord Brightman in *Furniss v Dawson*. The principle in question — that the Commissioners are not bound to consider individually each step in a composite transaction intended to be carried through as a whole — applied only where there was a 'pre-ordained series of transactions' or 'one single composite transaction' and where steps were inserted which had no commercial purpose apart from the avoidance of a liability to tax. Although the decision in *Furniss v Dawson* extended the *Ramsay* principle, by applying it to a linear transaction as opposed to a circular self-cancelling one, it did no more than apply that principle to different events. It did not lay down any proposition that a transaction entered into with the motive of minimising tax was to be ignored or struck down. In the *Ramsay* case, Lord Wilberforce had emphasised the continuing validity and application of the principle enunciated by Lord Tomlin in *CIR v Duke of Westminster*. Lord Fraser had echoed this view, as had Lord Bridge in *Furniss v Dawson*. (The speech of Lord Roskill in that case, which implied the contrary, did not appear to represent the view of the majority.) The criteria by reference to which the Ramsay principle applied were not logically capable of expansion so as to apply to any similar case except one in which, when the intermediate transaction or transactions took place, the end result which in fact occurred was so certain of fulfilment that it was intellectually and practically possible to conclude that there had indeed taken place one single and indivisible process. For the principle to apply, the intermediate steps had to serve no purpose other than that of saving tax; all stages of the composite transaction had to be pre-ordained with a degree of certainty with the taxpayer having control over the end result at the time when the intermediate steps were taken; and there should be no interruption between the intermediate transaction and the disposal to the ultimate purchaser. In this case, however, the transactions that the Crown sought to reconstruct into a single direct disposal were not contemporaneous. Nor were they pre-ordained since, at the time of the share exchange, it was not certain what the ultimate destination of the property would be. Lord Jauncey considered that 'a step in a linear transaction which has no business purpose apart from the avoidance or deferment of tax liability will be treated as forming part of a pre-ordained series of transactions or of a composite transaction if it was taken at a time when negotiations or arrangements for the carrying through as a continuous process of a subsequent transaction which actually takes place had reached a stage when there was no real likelihood that such subsequent transaction would not take place and if thereafter such negotiations or arrangements were carried through to completion without genuine interruption'. Lord Oliver concurred with this definition. *Craven v White* HL 1988, 62 TC 1; [1988] STC 476; [1988] 3 WLR 423; [1988] 3 All ER 495.

Davenport v Chilver

*Compensation for confiscation of asset – application of TCGA 1992, s 22(1)**

See **7.2**

In 1940 the USSR nationalised private property in Latvia. Following the *Foreign Compensation (USSR) Order 1969 (SI 1969 No 735)*, a woman who was resident in the UK made a claim in respect of such property in Latvia, some of which she had held in her own right and some of which had been held by her mother. In 1972/73 she received a payment in respect of the claim. She appealed against a CGT assessment on the payment. The Ch D held that the compensation for the loss of the assets she had held was within *TCGA 1992, s 22(1)(a)**, and that the compensation for the assets her mother had held was within *TCGA 1992, s 21(a)**. The case was remitted to the Special Commissioner for figures to be determined. *Davenport v Chilver* Ch D 1983, 57 TC 661; [1983] STC 426; [1983] 3 WLR 481. (Note. See now *TCGA 1992, s 17*.)

Davis v Henderson

Statutory compensation for disturbance on surrender of agricultural lease

See **10.2**

Davis v Powell (see below) was applied in a subsequent case in which a farmer had surrendered an agricultural tenancy to his landlord under an agreement providing for payment of £455,180 as compensation for disturbance under *Agricultural Holdings Act 1986, s 60*, and £520,000 as additional compensation. The Revenue issued an assessment charging CGT on both payments. The farmer appealed, accepting that the £520,000 was chargeable to CGT but contending that the £455,180 was not taxable. The Special Commissioners accepted this contention and allowed the appeal, holding that the payment was statutory compensation under *Agricultural Holdings Act 1986*, and was therefore not taxable. The Commissioners held that 'the notice to quit need not necessarily be the sole or proximate cause of the termination of a tenancy: it may be sufficient for the notice to quit to be one of a number of links in a chain of causal events'. The Revenue's contention that the tenancy had been terminated by agreement was rejected. *Davis v Henderson* (Sp C 46), [1995] SSCD 308.

Davis v Powell

Statutory compensation for disturbance on surrender of agricultural lease

See **10.2**

A farmer surrendered to the Milton Keynes Development Corporation part of land he leased, receiving compensation of £5,971 from the Corporation. Included in this was £591 equal to one year's rent and representing compensation for disturbance under *Agricultural Holdings Act 1948, s 34*. The Ch D held that no gain could be made out of a sum of money given to compensate for loss or expense which was unavoidably incurred after the lease has gone and the £591 was not a capital sum 'derived from' the lease or 'received in return for . . . surrender of rights' (*TCGA 1992, s 22(1)**) and not liable to capital gains tax. (There was no dispute as to the tax treatment of the balance of the £5,971.) *Davis v Powell* Ch D 1976, 51 TC 492; [1977] STC 32; [1977] 1 WLR 258; [1977] 1 All ER 471.

De Rothschild v Lawrenson

*Interaction of TCGA 1992, s 77 and 87(2)**

In 1989 the trustees of two non-resident settlements, which had been established in 1982 by a UK resident, sold the trust funds and resolved to pay the whole amount realised to the settlor. The Revenue raised an assessment on the settlor under *TCGA 1992, s 87(2)**, charging CGT on the amount on which the trustees would have been chargeable to tax if they had been resident or ordinarily resident in the UK. The settlor appealed, contending that the effect of *TCGA 1992, s 77** was that the gains of the settlements were not to be treated as accruing to the trustees and that the assessment should be reduced to nil. The Special Commissioners dismissed his appeal and the Ch D upheld their decision. *TCGA 1992, s 77** did not apply, since it dealt with cases where trustees were in fact chargeable to tax on realised gains. In a case within *TCGA 1992, s 87(2)**, gains were to be computed on the amount on which the trustees would have been chargeable to tax if they had been resident or ordinarily resident in the UK. That provision did not make the trustees themselves chargeable to tax, and the gains so computed were to be treated as chargeable gains accruing to the beneficiary. *De Rothschild v Lawrenson* CA 1995, 67 TC 300; [1995] STC 623.

Director v Inspector of Taxes

*Relief under TCGA 1992, s 24(2) (assets of negligible value)**

See **44.11**

An individual (D) was allotted 30,000 £1 shares in a company, in consideration of future services to the company. Shortly after being allotted these shares, he was appointed a director of the company. The company's liabilities exceeded its assets, and it subsequently became insolvent. After correspondence, the Revenue accepted for Schedule E purposes that the shares had a nil market value at the time of their allotment. Three years later, D submitted a claim for relief under *TCGA 1992, s 24(2)* in respect of the shares. The Revenue rejected this claim and the Special Commissioner dismissed D's appeal. Under *TCGA 1992, s 17*, the shares were deemed to have been acquired for a consideration equal to their market value, which was clearly nil. Since the shares had a market value of nil when they were acquired, they were not capable of becoming of negligible value, within *section 24(2)*. (The Commissioner observed that D had 'sought both to have his cake and to eat it'.) *Director v Inspector of Taxes* (Sp C 161), [1998] SSCD 172.

Drummond v Austin Brown

Statutory compensation for disturbance on termination of tenancy of business premises

See **10.2**

Davis v Powell was followed in a case in which the taxpayer had for many years carried on practice as a solicitor in premises leased to him by a bank. The bank required the premises for the purposes of its own business and gave him notice under *Part II* of the *Landlord and Tenant Act 1954* that it would oppose a renewal of his lease. He did not oppose the notice and his tenancy was terminated from 1 April 1978. He received compensation of £31,384 under *Landlord and Tenant Act 1954, s 37*. The Revenue assessed him on this sum for 1977/78 on the footing that it was a capital sum derived from an asset within *TCGA 1992, s 22**. His appeal was allowed by the Special Commissioners, and the Ch D and CA upheld their decision. The right to the compensation was a statutory one. There was no entitlement to it under the lease and it was therefore not derived from the lease. Nor was it, as the Revenue contended, for the loss of an asset. The lease had expired, but it was never 'lost'. *Drummond v Austin Brown* CA 1984, 58 TC 67; [1984] STC 321; [1984] 3 WLR 381; [1984] 2 All ER 699.

Dunlop International AG v Pardoe

*Principal group company becoming non-resident – application of TCGA 1992, s 179**

See **29.7**

In May 1978, D, which had been the principal member of a group of companies, became non-resident. The Revenue issued an assessment on the basis that *TCGA 1992, s 179** applied, so that D was deemed to have sold and immediately re-acquired shares in a subsidiary company, which it had acquired from another group member in March 1978. The Special Commissioners upheld the assessment, observing that the change of residence 'was an appropriate point at which to bring to an end the deferral of any gain or loss'. The Ch D and the CA dismissed D's appeal against this decision. Chadwick LJ observed that the object of *section 179** was 'to prevent the transferee company from taking the asset out of the group in circumstances in which the gain will not crystallise on a subsequent disposal — because there will be no subsequent disposal'. *Dunlop International AG v Pardoe* CA 1999, 72 TC 71.

Dunstan v Young Austen Young Ltd

Whether issue of new shares not acquired at arm's length constituted a capital reorganisation

See **4.2**, **63.2**

The taxpayer company (Y) carried on business as a mechanical engineering contractor. In 1977 it acquired for £16,100 the 1,000 issued £1 shares of a company (J) in the same line of business. Shortly afterwards it joined a large group; one of the shares in J was registered in the name of a fellow-subsidiary (T), the remainder being registered in its own name. J was not trading profitably. By March 1979 it had incurred debts of £200,911 to other companies in the group, mainly to Y, and it was decided to sell it. An arm's length purchaser was found, and J issued a further 200,000 £1 shares on 12 June 1979. These were allotted to Y for £200,000 cash, which was promptly repaid to Y to clear its indebtedness. On 29 June an agreement was completed between Y, T and the purchaser for the sale of the 201,000 shares for £38,000. The appeal was against an assessment for the year to September 1979. The profits were agreed at nil and the substantive issue was whether Y had incurred a capital loss on its disposal of the shares in J and, if so, of what amount. It was common ground that Y acquired the additional 200,000 shares 'otherwise than by a bargain made at arm's length' and by virtue of *CGTA 1979, s 19(3)** the consideration for them should be taken to be their market value, which the Special Commissioner found to be nil 'or so near to it as to make no matter'. However, Y contended that the issue of the further 200,000 shares constituted a reorganisation of J's capital within *TCGA 1992, ss 126, 128**, with the consequence that the new shares would not be treated as a separate acquisition and that the £200,000 would be treated as having been given for the original 1,000 shares, making their cost £216,100 and the loss £178,100. This contention was upheld by the CA, reversing the decision of the Ch D and restoring that of the Special Commissioner. Properly construed, the phrase 'reorganisation of a company's share capital' in *TCGA 1992, s 126** included an increase in a company's share capital and the allotment of the new shares to its parent company for cash. *Dunstan v Young Austen Young Ltd,* CA 1988, 61 TC 448; [1989] STC 69. (Note. *CGTA 1979, s 19(3)* was repealed by *FA 1981*. See now *TCGA 1992, s 128(2)* as regards reorganisations on or after 10 March 1981.)

Eastham v Leigh London & Provincial Properties Ltd

Date of acquisition

See **16.4**

On 22 June 1962, a company agreed with the owners of land to erect on the land a building to be leased, on completion, to the company for 125 years from 24 June 1962. The building was completed and the lease granted in May 1964. On 28 July 1965, the company disposed of the lease at a large gain which was assessed on the basis that the acquisition and disposal of the lease took place within three years and *FA 1965, s 82(2)(3)* (interim charge of tax) applied. The company contended that the lease was acquired under the 1962 agreement. The Revenue contended that the 1962 agreement comprised two contracts, a building agreement and an agreement for a lease, the latter being a conditional contract within the meaning of *FA 1962, Sch 9 para 1* (compare *TCGA 1992, s 28(2)*), or alternatively, that there was a single but conditional contract. The CA held that the 1962 agreement was a single and absolute contract. *Eastham v Leigh London & Provincial Properties Ltd* CA 1971, 46 TC 687; [1971] Ch 871; [1971] 2 All ER 811.

Eilbeck v Rawling

Anti-avoidance – scheme of arrangement

See **4.2, 62.14**

A taxpayer made a chargeable gain of £355,094 in 1974/75 as to which there was no dispute. Later in the same year he entered into a chain of transactions with the object of creating a commensurate allowable loss, at a cost to him of only £370 apart from the fees, etc. paid for the scheme, which was an 'off the peg' avoidance device obtained from a Jersey company. The central feature of the scheme involved his acquiring reversionary interests in two trust funds, one held by Jersey trustees and the other by Gibraltar trustees. Under a special power of appointment, the Gibraltar trustees advanced £315,000 to the Jersey trustees to be held on the trusts of the Jersey settlement. The taxpayer then sold both reversionary interests, making a gain on the sale of his interest under the Jersey settlement (claimed to be exempt under *TCGA*

*1992, s 76(1)**) and a matching loss of £312,470 on the sale of his interest under the Gibraltar settlement (claimed as an allowable loss). The CA refused the claim on the ground, inter alia, that the exercise of the power of appointment did not take the £315,000 outside the Gibraltar settlement; hence the sale of his reversionary interest in the £315,000 was a part sale of his interest under the Gibraltar settlement. The taxpayer appealed to the HL. The appeal was considered with W T Ramsay Ltd, and dismissed for the same general reason that, on the facts, the scheme was to be looked at as a composite transaction under which there was neither gain nor loss apart from the £370. Furthermore, the HL upheld the CA decision that the sale of the reversionary interest in the £315,000 was a sale of part of the taxpayer's reversionary interest in the Gibraltar settlement. *Eilbeck v Rawling* HL 1981, 54 TC 101; [1981] STC 174; [1981] 2 WLR 449; [1981] 1 All ER 865. (Note. The device would also now be caught by the value shifting provisions of *TCGA 1992, s 30*.)

Emmerson v Computer Time International Ltd

Assignment of lease – whether arrears of rent deductible

See **16.13**

A company discontinued its trade and went into voluntary liquidation. It owed rent in respect of its business premises, held under leases with several years to run but which could not be assigned without the landlord's consent. The landlord gave his consent subject to payment of the arrears. The liquidator accordingly sold the leases for £93,135 and paid the landlord the arrears of rent including £6,131 for the period of liquidation after trading had ceased. The company claimed to deduct the £6,131 in arriving at the gain on the disposal of the leases on the ground that it was a payment to enhance the value of the leases or a capital payment for the right to assign them. The CA rejected the claim. The £6,131 was in discharge of the company's obligations under its lease and not within *TCGA 1992, s 38(1)(b)**. Further, even if it were within that provision, deduction would be precluded by *TCGA 1992, s 39(2)**. *Emmerson v Computer Time International Ltd* CA 1977, 50 TC 628; [1977] STC 170; [1977] 1 WLR 734; [1977] 2 All ER 545.

EV Booth (Holdings) Ltd v Buckwell

Sale of shares accompanied by waiver of debt – amount of consideration

See **16.5**

A company entered into an agreement under which it sold shares in a subsidiary for £35,000 and, in addition, accepted £20,969 in full satisfaction of a debt of £55,839 owed to it by the subsidiary. The debt was not a 'debt on a security'. The Ch D held that there were two disposals and that the consideration for the disposal of the shares was the £35,000. *Aberdeen Construction Group Ltd v CIR* distinguished. *EV Booth (Holdings) Ltd v Buckwell* Ch D 1980, 53 TC 425; [1980] STC 578.

Fielder v Vedlynn Ltd

Consideration for sale of companies with tax losses – whether to include sums payable under guarantees by reference to amount of losses

See **45.1**

In December 1977 a company (V) sold shares in eight subsidiary companies to an unconnected company (M). The subsidiary companies had incurred capital losses which had not been quantified at the date of the sale. The shares were sold for their market value of £19,529, but under the agreement M provided a guarantee that each of the eight companies should pay V an amount equal to 7.5% of their allowable capital losses. In December 1979 the losses in question were agreed at £19.5 million, and the amounts in question were paid to V by the subsidiaries. The Revenue issued a CGT assessment on V for the period ending 31 December 1977, including the amount received by V from the subsidiaries as part of the consideration for the sale of the shares. V appealed, contending that the consideration should be restricted to the £19,529 which was agreed to be the market value of the companies in December 1977. The Special Commissioner allowed V's appeal and the Ch D upheld this decision. The guarantees were terms of the sale agreements, and no additional monetary value could or should be placed on them. Further, even if they were to be regarded as part of the consideration, they were incapable of valuation within the meaning of *FA 1965, s 22(4)*. *Fielder v Vedlynn Ltd* Ch D 1992, 65 TC 145; [1992] STC 553. (Note. *FA 1965, s 22(4)* became *CGTA, s 19(3)*, which was repealed by *FA 1981, s 90* with effect from 10 March 1981 and replaced by what is now *TCGA 1992, s 17*.)

Figg v Clarke

'Absolutely entitled as against the trustee' (TCGA 1992, s 60) – Date on which beneficiaries absolutely entitled

See **62.16**

In 1963 the trustees of a settlement made an appointment whereby certain investments and income should be held 'upon trust for such of the children (of the settlor) now living or hereafter to be born . . . as shall attain the age of 21'. In 1964 the settlor was paralysed in an accident, leaving no realistic possibility that he could beget any more children. The settlor's youngest child became 21 in 1976 and the settlor died in 1990. The Special Commissioner held that the children became absolutely entitled as against the trustees in 1990 (rather than 1976). The Ch D upheld this decision. Blackburne J held that the court could not have regard to the impossibility of a person having children in the future. *Figg v Clarke* Ch D 1996, 68 TC 645; [1997] STC 247.

Fisher v Edwards

See *Cooper v Billingham* above.

Floor v Davis

*Arrangements to reduce liability – interpretation of TCGA 1992, s 29(2)**

See **4.8, 41.28**

It had been arranged that, subject to contract, the share capital of a company (IDM) would be sold (at a substantial profit to the shareholders) to another company (KDI). F and his two sons-in-law, who together controlled IDM, carried out a scheme under which the following transactions took place shortly after each other. They transferred their IDM shares to FNW, a company set up for the purpose, for preferred shares in FNW; FNW sold the IDM shares to KDI for cash; a Cayman Islands company, D, acquired a relatively insignificant holding of preferred shares in FNW; following a rights issue open to all preferred shareholders but accepted only by D, D became the sole ordinary shareholder in FNW; FNW went into liquidation and because of the differing rights attached to the two classes of shares, D, as the ordinary shareholder, became entitled to six-sevenths of the assets of FNW. The upshot was that the greater part of the proceeds of sale of the IDM shares reached D. The CA held (Eveleigh LJ dissenting), that F had disposed of his IDM shares to FNW (and not, as contended by the Revenue, to KDI) with the consequence that under *TCGA 1992, s 135** his FNW shares were treated as the IDM shares he originally held. However, the CA unanimously held that value had passed out of the FNW shares within the meaning of *TCGA 1992, s 29(2)** and F was assessable accordingly, on the grounds that (i) 'person' in *TCGA 1992, s 29(2)** includes the plural by virtue of *Interpretation Act 1889, s 1(1)(b)* and the definition of 'control' (see *TCGA 1992, s 288(1)**) and (ii) F and his sons-in-law had exercised their control, notwithstanding that two of them had not voted on the resolution to wind up FNW. The HL rejected F's appeal on this point. (The Revenue's contention that F had disposed of the shares to KDI was therefore not argued in the HL. See now as to this *Furniss v Dawson*, in which the dissenting judgement of Eveleigh LJ, who upheld the Revenue's contention that the shares had been disposed of to KDI, was approved.) *Floor v Davis* HL 1979, 52 TC 609; [1979] STC 379; [1979] 2 WLR 830; [1979] 2 All ER 677. (Notes. (1) The relevant transactions took place in 1969. See now for value-shifting transactions after 13 March 1989, *TCGA 1992, ss 30–34*. (2) The *Interpretation Act 1889* has since been repealed. See now *Interpretation Act 1978, s 6(c)*.)

Foster v Williams; Horan v Williams

Cash bonuses received on takeover of building society

See **63.27**

A building society transferred its business to a banking company. Shareholders and depositors were paid lump sums of £500 and percentage bonus payments calculated by reference to the balance on their accounts. Two shareholders appealed against CGT assessments, contending that they had made a complete disposal of their existing assets and that there was no chargeable gain. The Special Commissioner accepted this contention and allowed the appeals in principle, holding that there had been a total disposal of the relevant assets. With regard to the share accounts, the amount of the credit balance on each account was allowable expenditure within *TCGA 1992, s 38*. With regard to the deposit accounts, the effect of *TCGA 1992, s 251* was that there was no chargeable gain. Since payments were made to shareholders and depositors alike, none of the expenditure could be attributed to the shareholders' equity rights. *Foster v Williams*; *Horan v Williams* (Sp C 113), [1997] SSCD 112.

Fulford-Dobson, ex p., R v Inspector of Taxes

Gift by wife to husband about to become non-resident – application of ESC D2

See **57.29**

On 18 August 1980 an individual (F) entered into a contract of employment in Germany. He was required to begin work on 15 September and he left the UK for this purpose on 29 August 1980. From that date he became resident in Germany, having previously been resident and ordinarily resident in the UK. Acting on professional advice, and admittedly to take advantage of Revenue Extra-Statutory Concession D2, his wife transferred to him on that date a farm which she had inherited in 1977 and had been considering selling in 1980. The farm was in fact sold by auction on 17 September. The Revenue assessed F to CGT for 1980/81 on the gain on the sale. He applied for judicial review to quash the assessment, contending that the Revenue should have applied Revenue Extra-Statutory Concession D2. The QB rejected this contention and dismissed the application, holding that the Revenue had been entitled to refuse to apply the concession. It was clearly stated inside the front cover of Revenue Pamphlet IR1, listing the extra-statutory concessions in operation, that a 'concession will not be given in any case where an attempt is made to use it for tax avoidance'. *R v Inspector of Taxes (ex p. Fulford-Dobson),* QB 1987, 60 TC 168; [1987] STC 344; [1987] 3 WLR 277.

Furniss v Dawson

Anti-avoidance

See **4.2**, **64.3**

The shareholders in two family companies wished to dispose of their shares, and found an unconnected company (W) willing to acquire the shares at an agreed price. Before disposing of the shares, they exchanged them for shares in a Manx company which in turn sold them to W. The Revenue issued assessments on the basis that the shares should be treated as having been disposed of directly to W, since the interposition of the Manx company had been designed solely to take advantage of the law then in force with regard to company reconstructions and amalgamations. The HL unanimously upheld the assessments (reversing the decision of the CA). Applying *WT Ramsay Ltd*, the transactions should be regarded as a single composite transaction. Lord Bridge of Harwich observed that 'the distinction between form and substance . . . can usefully be drawn in determining the tax consequences of composite transactions'. Lord Brightman held that the *Ramsay* principle applied in cases where there was a 'pre-ordained series of transactions; or . . . one single composite transaction' and steps were 'inserted which have no commercial (business) purpose apart from the avoidance of a liability to tax — not "no business effect". If these two ingredients exist, the inserted steps are to be disregarded for fiscal purposes. The court must look at the end result.' *Furniss v Dawson* HL 1984, 55 TC 324; [1984] STC 153; [1984] 2 WLR 226; [1984] 1 All ER 530. (Notes. (1) See also *TCGA 1992, s 137*. (2) Although the decision was unanimous, there was implicit disagreement as to the continuing validity of the Duke of Westminster principle. Lords Bridge and Scarman indicated that the principle still applied, but Lord Roskill specifically refrained from endorsing the Westminster decision. For subsequent developments, see the judgement of Lord Templeman in *Ensign Tankers (Leasing) Ltd v Stokes*, and that of Lord Keith in *Countess Fitzwilliam v CIR*.)

Garner v Pounds Shipowners & Shipbreakers Ltd (and related appeal)

Grant of option to purchase land – treatment of payment for release of restrictive covenants

See **7.7, 16.11, 16.13**

A company (P) granted an option to purchase freehold land which was subject to certain restrictive covenants. P undertook to use its best endeavours to obtain the release of the covenants but the exercise of the option was not dependent on their release. The purchaser paid £399,750 for the option, this amount being held by P's solicitors as stakeholders pending the release of the covenants. P subsequently paid £90,000 to obtain the release of the covenants. The option was not, in fact, exercised. The Revenue issued an assessment charging tax on the consideration of £399,750 without allowing a deduction for the £90,000. The HL unanimously dismissed P's appeal and upheld the assessment. Lord Jauncey held that 'no payment by the company to a third party can alter the value of the cash sum of £399,750 paid by (the purchaser) in terms of the agreement as a consideration for the disposal, i.e. the grant of the option'. *Randall v Plumb* distinguished. Furthermore, the £90,000 was not allowable expenditure within *TCGA 1992, s 38**. The implementation of the obligation to obtain the release of the covenants was 'not a prerequisite of the option being exercised'. Accordingly, the expenditure was not 'wholly and exclusively incurred by (P) in providing' the option. Additionally, 'the expenditure referred to in *s 38(1)** must be expenditure which is extraneous to the asset rather than part of it'. On a sale of the land itself, there would be strong grounds for claiming the £90,000 as allowable expenditure, as the value of the land would have been enhanced by removal of the restrictive covenants. *Garner v Pounds Shipowners & Shipbreakers Ltd (and related appeal)* HL 2000, 72 TC 561; [2000] STC 420.

Golding v Kaufman

Amount received for release of put option

See 7.7

An employee of an investment company owned 25% of the shares of that company. He entered into an agreement with the company under which he could require the company to purchase his shareholding. In 1969 the company paid him £5,000 to relinquish his rights under this agreement. The Revenue included the £5,000 in a CGT assessment on him for 1968/69. He appealed, contending that, by virtue of *FA 1965,*

Sch 7 para 14(3), there had been no disposal of any asset. The Special Commissioners allowed his appeal but the Ch D reversed their decision and restored the assessment. A sum paid to a person who had the right to call on another person to buy property from him (a put option) was a capital sum derived from an asset. *FA 1965, Sch 7 para 14(3)* provided that the exercise of a put option would not be treated as a disposal for the purpose of creating allowable losses, but it did not exempt a gain made from such a transaction. *Golding v Kaufman* Ch D 1985, 58 TC 296; [1985] STC 152. (Note. *FA 1965, Sch 7 para 14(3)* was modified by *FA 1971*. See now *TCGA 1992, s 144(3)(4)*.)

Goodbrand v Loffland Bros North Sea Inc

Deferred consideration (TCGA 1992, s 48) – Exchange rate fluctuations – whether TCGA 1992, s 48 applicable*

See **16.13**

In 1985 a company (L) sold various assets under a lease-purchase agreement for $38,610,000. The Revenue issued an assessment on the basis that the sterling equivalent of the disposal proceeds, at the then exchange rate, was £33,313,000. As a result of subsequent fluctuations in the exchange rate, L only received £23,853,000. It claimed relief under *TCGA 1992, s 48** for the balance of £9,500,000. The Ch D upheld the Revenue's rejection of the claim, and the CA dismissed the company's appeal, holding that the 'consideration . . . brought into account' was the contractual consideration, rather than its sterling equivalent. The tax computation merely involved a valuation exercise, rather than an actual conversion of dollars into sterling. L had anticipated receiving $38,610,000 and had received that amount. The exchange loss of £9,500,000 was not irrecoverable consideration within the meaning of *TCGA 1992, s 48**. *Goodbrand v Loffland Bros North Sea Inc* CA 1998, 71 TC 57; [1998] STC 930.

Goodwin v Curtis

Private residence exemption (TCGA 1992, ss 222–225) – Farmhouse inhabited by claimant for only 32 days – whether eligible for relief under TCGA 1992, s 222.*

See **53.7**

In 1983 a company had exchanged contracts for the purchase of a farm, which included a nine-bedroomed farmhouse. It agreed that, following completion of the purchase, it would sell the farmhouse to one of its directors (G). The company did not complete the purchase of the farmhouse until 7 March 1985, and the sale to G was completed on 1 April 1985. G, who was in the process of separating from his wife, had already instructed estate agents with regard to the sale of the farmhouse, but moved into it immediately. On 3 April 1985 G completed the purchase of a small cottage, and on 11 April 1985 he advertised the farmhouse for sale. He continued to live in the farmhouse until 3 May 1985, when he completed the sale of the farmhouse and moved into the cottage. He appealed against a CGT assessment, contending that the gain on the sale of the farmhouse was eligible for relief under *TCGA 1992, s 222**. The General Commissioners rejected this contention, finding that G had not intended to occupy the farmhouse as his permanent residence, and holding that the gain did not qualify for relief. The CA upheld their decision. G had only lived in the farmhouse for 32 days, and the Commissioners had been entitled to find that he had not intended to occupy it as his permanent residence. *Dicta* of Viscount Cave in *Levene v CIR* applied. *Goodwin v Curtis* CA 1998, 70 TC 478; [1998] STC 475.

Gordon v CIR

Whether business transferred as a going concern

See **37.2**

A farmer entered into an agreement with his wife to farm an estate in partnership.

Five days later the partnership agreed to transfer its business to an unlimited company which the farmer and his wife had formed in the previous month. The Revenue issued a capital gains tax assessment charging tax on the transfer of the business to the company. The farmer appealed, contending that the business had been transferred as a going concern, so that rollover relief was available. The Special Commissioner dismissed his appeal, finding that, although the 'whole assets of the business' had been transferred, the farmer had intended that the company should sell the estate to an outside purchaser, and that the company had not taken over the business until contracts for the sale of the estate had been exchanged. Accordingly, the business had not been transferred as a going concern, since 'its end was too clearly and too closely in sight'. The CS allowed the farmer's appeal against this decision. Although contracts for the sale of the estate to an outside purchaser had been exchanged by the time when the company took over the farming of the estate, no such sale had been agreed at the time when the partnership had agreed to transfer the estate to the company. Accordingly, the company could have continued to operate the business if it had so wished. Furthermore, the company subsequently continued to farm an estate elsewhere, using machinery and cattle transferred to it from the partnership. Lord Hope held that 'a planned move of the entire assets of a business from one place to another is not inconsistent with the continuation of its trade'. On the facts found by the Commissioner, the only reasonable conclusion was that the company had received the whole assets of the business as a going concern. *Robroyston Brickworks Ltd* applied. *Gordon v CIR* CS 1991, 64 TC 173; [1991] STC 174.

Green v CIR

Whether wing of mansion part of residence – whether TCGA 1992, s 224(2) applicable*

See 53.3

In 1975 a taxpayer sold a mansion house and grounds which he had acquired in 1971. The building comprised a central block with 33 rooms, and two wings connected to it by corridors. Some work of reconstruction and redecoration had been carried out, during which the taxpayer and various members of his family and others had occupied parts of the central block, while a flat had been made in one of the wings for a gardener. The taxpayer claimed that the whole of the gain was within the private residence exemption. The General Commissioners held that the two wings were not part of the residence and that the gain on their sale was not within the relief. As regards the main block, they applied *TCGA 1992, s 224(2)**, adjusting the relief in respect of a 'change in what is occupied as the individual's residence', and allowed relief on one-third of the gain. The CS held that there was no factual material before the Commissioners which entitled them to adjust the relief under *TCGA 1992, s 224(2)**. Accordingly, the whole of the gain on the sale of the central block and grounds was exempt. Applying *Batey v Wakefield*, whether the wings were part of the residence was a matter of degree for the Commissioners, and their decision was not inconsistent with the evidence. Accordingly, the appeal failed as regards the gain on the sale of the wings. *Green v CIR* CS 1982, 56 TC 10; [1982] STC 485.

Griffin v Citibank Investments Ltd

Whether gain from certain transactions in financial options taxable as chargeable gain or as income

See 7.7

The Revenue contended that two options, purchased by the taxpayer company from the same fellow group company, intended to have effect together, and undoubtedly financial options within *TCGA 1992, s 144(8)(c)(i)* when considered separately, should be regarded as a single composite transaction that was not a financial option but a loan, the 'gain' on which should be taxed as income under Schedule D, Case III.

The taxpayer company had unused capital losses and had wished to receive funds in the form of capital gains. In allowing the company's appeal, the Special Commissioners held that, even if the options were a single composite transaction (which in their judgement was not the case), to re-characterise them as a loan would be to disregard the legal form and nature of the transactions and to go behind them to some supposed underlying substance. This was not possible in the absence of artificial steps as in *Ramsay* (see **4.2** ANTI-AVOIDANCE). The Ch D upheld this decision. On the evidence, the Commissioners were entitled to conclude that the options were not to be regarded as a single composite transaction. *Citibank Investments Ltd v Griffin* Ch D 2000, 73 TC 352; [2000] STC 1010

Griffin v Craig-Harvey

Main residence relief

See **53.10**

A taxpayer, who owned a house in Stockwell, acquired a house in Winchester on 12 August 1985. On 9 July 1986 he sold his house in Stockwell and bought another house in Clapham. On 21 January 1988 he submitted a notice under *TCGA 1992, s 222(5)** declaring that the house in Winchester should be treated as his main residence. On 26 January 1989 he sold that house, realising a capital gain of around £225,000. The inspector issued a CGT assessment on the basis that 11/41 of the gain was chargeable, considering that the period from August 1985 to June 1986 was not covered by the notice submitted in January 1988, since that notice was for the purpose of determining whether the Winchester house or the Clapham house should be treated as the taxpayer's main residence, and any notice determining whether the Stockwell house or the Winchester house had been the taxpayer's main residence would have had to have been lodged within two years of the taxpayer's acquisition of the Winchester house in August 1985. The taxpayer appealed, contending that the notice should be treated as effective from January 1986, so that only 5/41 of the gain was chargeable. The Ch D upheld the assessment (reversing the Special Commissioner's decision). The two-year period of *TCGA 1992, s 222(5)(a)* began to run from the time when it first became necessary to determine which of two specific residences should be treated as a taxpayer's main residence. The taxpayer had made no election covering the period when he owned a house in Stockwell as well as the house in Winchester. The election which he had made in January 1988 was an election between his house in Clapham and the house in Winchester. Since he had not acquired the house in Clapham until July 1986, the notice could not cover any period before that time. (Vinelott J observed that *TCGA 1992, s 222(5)** derived from *FA 1965*, and that during the relevant Parliamentary debates the Financial Secretary had stated that the intention of the clause was so that a taxpayer could 'exercise a choice within two years from the time when he acquires the second house'.) *Griffin v Craig-Harvey* Ch D 1993, 66 TC 396; [1994] STC 54.

Gubay v Kington

*Gift by resident husband to non-resident wife – application of TCGA 1992, s 58(1)**

See **46.5**, **57.29**

The taxpayer's wife took up residence in the Isle of Man on 4 April 1972. The taxpayer remained resident and ordinarily resident in the UK until October 1972, but meanwhile he visited his wife and lived with her in the Isle of Man most weekends. In July 1972 he gave his wife some valuable shares. He appealed against a 1972/73 assessment on him in respect of the resultant gain. The HL allowed his appeal (Lord Scarman dissenting), holding that the combined effect of *ICTA 1988, s 282* and *TCGA 1992, s 58(1)** was that no CGT was payable on the gift of the shares. *Gubay v Kington* HL 1984, 57 TC 601; [1984] STC 99; [1984] 1 WLR 163; [1984] 1 All ER 513.

Hart v Briscoe and Others

TCGA 1992, s 71(1) – 'absolutely entitled' – whether beneficial entitlement required*

See **62.14**

Two cases concerning *TCGA 1992, s 71(1)** were heard together. In *Hart v Briscoe*, trustees, acting under a 1955 settlement, declared that the whole of the settled property should be held on the trusts of a 1972 settlement, made for the purpose by the same settlor with the same trustees. In *Hoare Trustees,* trustees used a power of advancement in a settlement to declare trusts of assets advanced. It was held in both that the 'new' trustees had become absolutely entitled to settled property as against the old. 'Absolutely entitled' in *TCGA 1992, s 71(1)** does not imply beneficial ownership but whether an advancement is a continuance of the existing trust or a new trust is a question of fact and degree. *Hart v Briscoe and Others* Ch D 1977, 52 TC 53; [1978] STC 89; [1978] 2 WLR 832; [1978] 1 All ER 791. (See now *Roome v Edwards* and HMRC Statement of Practice SP 9/81.)

Hawkings-Byass v Sassen

Valuation of unquoted shares

See **45.4**

In three appeals heard together, members of the same family disposed of shares in an unquoted Cayman Islands company which was the holding company of a trading group concerned principally with the production and sale of sherry. Under the company's Articles of Association, the company could refuse to register the transfer of shares to anyone who was not a member of the two families which had originally formed the company (and the disposals were to members of the other family in question). The valuation of the shares at 31 March 1982 was disputed. The Special Commissioners reviewed the evidence in detail, holding that in the particular circumstances, it was not appropriate to value the shares on an earnings basis or on a dividend basis, but that the company should be valued on an assets basis and on a turnover basis to arrive at a notional quoted value which should be uplifted by a 'control premium' of 30% to arrive at an entirety value of £46,000,000. The shares should then be valued on the basis that the two smaller shareholdings (comprising 11.09% and 9.09% of the total shares respectively) could have been acquired with a bid of two-thirds of their 'entirety value' (i.e. at £256 each) and that, for the largest shareholding (comprising 18.16% of the share capital), a 20% premium should be added to this (arriving at a value of £307 each). *Hawkings-Byass v Sassen (and related appeals)* (Sp C 88), [1996] SSCD 319.

Henderson v Karmel's Executors

Election for 6 April 1965 valuation – whether land subject to a tenancy

See **45.6**

In 1975 a married woman (K) sold land which she had held for many years. From 1961 to 1972 it had been farmed by a company which she controlled, and from then until the sale she had farmed it in partnership. The company had originally paid an annual rental of £2,000, but this was waived in 1966. The Revenue issued a CGT assessment to the executors of K's husband, charging tax on the disposal. The executors appealed, contending that the land should be valued on the basis of vacant possession of the land at 6 April 1965. The Ch D rejected this contention and upheld the assessment (reversing the decision of the General Commissioners). On the evidence, at 6 April 1965 the land had clearly been subject to a tenancy. *Henderson v Karmel's Executors* Ch D 1984, 58 TC 201; [1984] STC 572.

Hinchcliffe v Crabtree

Value of quoted shares while secret takeover negotiations in progress

See **8.2**, **45.3**

A taxpayer was liable on his gain from the disposal during 1965/66 of certain quoted shares in a manufacturing company of which he was a joint managing director. The question at issue was their market value at 6 April 1965. At that date, takeover negotiations were in progress but had not been made public and the Commissioners accepted evidence that, had they been public, the quoted price at that date would have been substantially higher than the actual quoted price. The HL held that the mere fact that directors of a company possessed information which if made public would affect the quoted prices of its shares was not a special circumstance. (There was no evidence of impropriety in withholding the relevant information.) *Hinchcliffe v Crabtree* HL 1971, 47 TC 419; [1972] AC 725; [1971] 3 All ER 967.

Hirsch v Crowthers Cloth Ltd

*Machinery and plant – exclusion of amounts taken into account in computing balancing charge – TCGA 1992, s 37**

See **39.1**

In 1980 a company sold for £715,967 looms which it had purchased for £545,930. The sale gave rise to a balancing charge under *CAA 1990, s 24**. The company appealed against a CGT assessment on the overall gain of £170,037, contending that, by virtue of *TCGA 1992, s 37(1)**, the acquisition cost of the looms should be excluded from the disposal consideration, since it had been taken into account in computing the balancing charge. The Ch D, reversing the Commissioner's decision, held that the acquisition cost was not to be excluded from the disposal consideration. Although *TCGA 1992, s 37(2)**, which specifically excluded from the scope of *TCGA 1992, s 37(1)** amounts taken into account in making a balancing charge under *CAA 1968*, had subsequently been amended by *FA 1980* to refer also to amounts taken into account under *FA 1971*, this was merely making explicit what was already implicit in *TCGA 1992, s 37(1)**. Where legislation was ambiguously worded, it was necessary to have regard to the context and scheme of the Act under consideration, and to strive to find an interpretation which avoided injustice or absurdity. The words 'taken into account' in *TCGA 1992, s 37(1)** should be read as referring to sums which had to be brought directly into the computation. The purpose of the limitation of the disposal value to the cost of acquisition was to avoid double taxation of any profit on disposal. It would be paradoxical to find that the cost of acquisition was itself to be deducted from the disposal consideration, thereby ensuring that the gain escaped altogether the charge to tax. *Hirsch v Crowthers Cloth Ltd* Ch D 1989, 62 TC 759; [1990] STC 174.

HMRC v Morrison

Payment to settle court proceedings—whether within TCGA 1992, s 49(1)(c)

See **16.13**

In 2000 a public company (G) acquired the share capital of another public company (P). P's chairman (M) had owned a substantial shareholding in P, and following the takeover, he received consideration valued at more than £33,000,000. In 2002 M transferred much of this consideration (shares and loan notes) into a trust, giving rise to a CGT liability. Meanwhile G had formed the opinion that a profit forecast which M had provided during the takeover negotiations had been misleading. G began court proceedings against M, alleging fraudulent misrepresentation and seeking damages of £132,000,000. In 2006 M and G agreed an out-of-court settlement under which M paid G £12,000,000 plus legal costs of £5,668,648. M claimed that these sums should be deducted from his CGT liability for 2002/03. HMRC rejected the claim and M appealed, contending that the payments related to a 'contingent liability in respect of a warranty or representation made on a disposal', within *TCGA 1992, s 49(1)(c)*, and were deductible under *section 49(2)*. The First-tier Tribunal allowed the appeal in part, and both sides appealed to the Upper Tribunal, which allowed HMRC's appeal and dismissed M's cross-appeal. Lord Glennie held that 'what the court has to assess in the case of a contingent liability in respect of a warranty or representation made on a disposal by way of sale is whether the liability is directly related to the value of the consideration received by the taxpayer on the disposal of the property'. On the facts here, M's liability arising from the representations he had made in his capacity as P's chairman was 'wholly distinct from the consideration received by him for his shares'. Neither the payment of £12,000,000, nor the associated legal costs, qualified as a 'contingent liability' within *section 49*. *HMRC v Morrison* UT, [2013] UKUT 497 (TCC); [2014] STC 574. (Note. The First-tier Tribunal decision had been anonymised. The Upper Tribunal rejected an application for its hearing of the appeals to take place in private. Lord Glennie held that 'the court will not depart from the principle of open justice simply to save one or other party from embarrassment'.)

HMRC v Smallwood

Losses on disposal of units in enterprise zone unit trust – whether TCGA 1992, s 41(2) applicable.

See **16.13**

In 1989 an individual (S) invested £10,000 in an enterprise zone unit trust. The trustees used the funds to acquire land and buildings, and claimed capital allowances. S was credited with some of these allowances under *Income Tax (Definition of Unit Trusts Schemes) Regulations 1988 (SI 1988 No 267)*. Subsequently, the property was disposed of and S received distributions, which were treated for CGT purposes as part disposals of S's units. S claimed that these disposals gave rise to allowable losses. The Revenue rejected the claim on the basis that the effect of *TCGA 1992, s 41(2)* was that S's allowable expenditure had to be restricted by the capital allowances. S appealed, contending that *section 41(2)* did not apply because it was the trustees' expenditure, rather than his expenditure, which gave rise to capital allowances. The Special Commissioner accepted this contention and allowed S's appeal, holding that 'once the step has been taken of treating the unit trust as a company and the rights of the unitholders as shares in that company, then for CGT purposes . . . the computation of gains on disposals of units must be treated in the same way as the computation of gains on disposals of shares'. Accordingly, the expression 'any expenditure to the extent to which any capital allowance . . . has been or may be made in respect of it' in *TCGA 1992, s 41(2)* had to be construed as 'referring to expenditure comprised in the consideration given wholly and exclusively for the acquisition of the relevant asset, i.e. the £10,000 given by (S) for his units. Capital allowances were not given in respect of that expenditure. Thus *section 41(2)* does not apply.' The CA unanimously upheld this decision. Lawrence Collins LJ held that the effect of *TCGA 1992, s 99* was 'that there are two levels of capital gains tax. First, gains made by the trustee in respect of trust assets are taxed as if they were gains of a company (except that the tax paid would not be corporation tax but capital gains tax). Any tax on these gains is assessed on the trustee. Second, each unit holder is treated on a disposal of his units as if they were shares in a company, his gains or losses on units being taxed as if they were gains or losses on shares.' *HMRC v Smallwood* CA, [2007] STC 1237; [2007] EWCA Civ 462.

Honour v Norris

Whether self-contained flat formed part of dwelling-house

See **53.6**

The owner of four separate flats, located in separate buildings in the same square within 95 yards of each other, sold one of them, which had been used to provide occasional bedroom accommodation for his children and guests and, on rare occasions, sleeping accommodation for him and his wife. He appealed against an assessment on the gain, claiming relief under *TCGA 1992, s 222**. (The square contained 32 houses, most of which were divided into flats.) The Ch D rejected the claim and upheld the assessment (reversing the decision of the Commissioners). The flat was a separate dwelling-house, which could not be regarded as part of a common entity with the flat in which the owner and his wife lived. The fact that the owner had sometimes used it to accommodate his children or guests did not make it a part of his private residence. *Honour v Norris* Ch D 1992, 64 TC 599; [1992] STC 304.

Innocent v Whaddon Estates Ltd

*Transfers within a group – construction of TCGA 1992, s 171(2)**

See **29.3**

In 1961 the taxpayer company received, on the liquidation of a subsidiary, a capital distribution of shares in a public quoted company which at the time had a market value of 13s 4d each. The value fell to 6s 3d by Budget Day 1965, although this still exceeded their cost to the subsidiary. The company made various sales of the shares and appealed against assessments on the gains arrived at by treating the consideration for the shares as 6s 3d each. The Ch D upheld the assessments, rejecting the company's contention that the cost should be taken as 13s 4d each. The reference in *TCGA 1992, s 171(2)** to *TCGA 1992, s 122** applied to its disposal of its shares in the subsidiary, but not to the shares it acquired on the liquidation. *Innocent v Whaddon Estates Ltd* Ch D 1981, 55 TC 476; [1982] STC 115.

Jarmin v Rawlings

Retirement relief

See **24.3**

A farmer owned 64 acres with a milking parlour and yard, and had a dairy herd of 34 animals. In October 1988 he sold the parlour and yard, and during the next three months he sold 14 of the animals. He transferred most of the remaining animals to a farm three miles away which belonged to his wife. He ceased dairy farming and used his land for rearing and finishing store cattle, although he retained and leased the milk quota, with a view to enhancing the value of the land on an eventual sale. The Revenue issued an assessment charging CGT on the sale of the parlour and yard. He appealed, claiming retirement relief. The Revenue rejected his claim on the grounds that he had only sold assets of his business, rather than a part of his business. The Commissioners allowed his appeal, holding that the dairy farming had been 'a separate and distinguishable part of the taxpayer's business', that he had sold a part of his business and that the sale qualified for retirement relief. The Ch D upheld the Commissioners' decision. Knox J held that the Commissioners were entitled to find that the dairy farming was a separate business from the rearing and finishing of store cattle, and that 'the sale by auction and completion of that sale of the milking parlour and yard, coupled with the cessation at completion of all milking operations for the taxpayer's benefit, amounted to a disposal by him of his dairy farming business'. *Jarmin v Rawlings* Ch D 1994, 67 TC 130; [1994] STC 1005. (Note. Retirement relief is abolished for disposals after 5 April 2003 (see **25.88** EXEMPTIONS AND RELIEFS), but this case remains relevant to ENTREPRENEURS' RELIEF (**24.3**).)

Jerome v Kelly

Date of disposal/identity of disponor

See **16.4**

In April 1987 a married couple signed a contract to dispose of three plots of land. The sale of the first plot was not completed until 1990, and the sale of the final plot was not completed until 1992. Meanwhile, in 1989, the couple had assigned half of their beneficial interests in the land to the trustee of two Bermudan settlements which they had created. The Revenue issued a CGT assessment on the basis that the effect of *TCGA 1992, s 28** was that the couple had disposed of the whole of their interests in the land in 1987/88 (the year the contract was made). The husband (J) appealed, contending that the disposal in 1987/88 should be treated as being limited to the half of the beneficial interests which they still held when the sales were completed, and should not be treated as also covering the half of the beneficial interests which they had assigned in 1989. The HL accepted this contention and allowed the appeal. Lord Hoffmann observed that the draftsman responsible for (*TCGA 1992, s 28(1)**) 'did not think about what should happen in the situation which has arisen in this case'. He held that it would be wrong 'to attribute to Parliament an intention to impose a liability to tax upon a person who would not be treated as having made a disposal under the carefully constructed scheme for taxing the disposals of assets held on trust'. (*TCGA 1992, s 28(1)**) should be treated as 'concerned solely with fixing the time of disposal by a person whose identity is to be ascertained by other means. It follows that the disposal under the conveyance to the purchasers was made by the Bermudan trustees and not by (Mr and Mrs J).' Lord Walker of Gestingthorpe observed that 'the contingent way in which (*TCGA 1992, s 28(1)**) operates creates an obvious problem for a taxpayer who has entered into a contract to sell an asset, with completion postponed until a later tax year. Should he assume that the contract will be duly completed and, on that assumption, return a chargeable gain accruing on the date of the contract? The Revenue acknowledge that this is a flaw in the capital gains tax legislation. Good legislative practice requires that a taxpayer should not be left in doubt as to whether or not he has incurred a tax charge.' *Jerome v Kelly* HL, [2004] STC 887; [2004] UKHL 25; [2004] All ER(D) 168(May).

Johnson v Edwards

*Application of TCGA 1992, s 28(1)**

See **16.4**

In a case where the facts were complex, the owner of certain shares agreed on 25 February 1965 to sell them. The date of completion was fixed as 31 January 1970, but in fact completion did not take place until 1971/72. The Revenue assessed the resulting gain in 1971/72 and the taxpayer appealed, contending that, by virtue of *TCGA 1992, s 28(1)**, the date of disposal was 25 February 1965. The Ch D dismissed his appeal, holding that the words 'where an asset is disposed of under a contract' in *TCGA 1992, s 28* apply to a disposal after 5 April 1971 under a contract entered into after that date, but not to a disposal after that date under a contract entered into before that date. *Johnson v Edwards* Ch D 1981, 54 TC 488; [1981] STC 660.

Johnston Publishing (North) Ltd v HMRC

Interpretation of TCGA 1992, s 179(2)

See **29.7**

A company (G) was a member of a group, the ultimate parent company being M. In 1997 G acquired a newly-incorporated company (H). On the same day H made a large rights issue of shares to G. Another company in the M group (P) sold its shares in certain subsidiary companies to H. The effect of *TCGA 1992, s 171* was that this was treated for tax purposes as producing no gain or loss to P. However, because H and P did not by themselves form a group, they did not fall within the definition of 'associated companies' in *TCGA 1992, s 179(10)*. Following this sale, P paid a dividend to its immediate parent company (R) within a group election under *ICTA 1988, s 247*. Following the payment of this dividend, R sold its shares in P to H. Again, the effect of *TCGA 1992, s 171* was that this was treated for tax purposes as producing no gain or loss to R. In 1998 G sold its shares in H to an outside purchaser (Y). H and its subsidiaries (including P) then ceased to be a member of the M group. The Revenue issued an assessment on H, charging tax under *TCGA 1992, s 179* in respect of the subsidiaries which it had acquired from P when both companies were members of the M group. H appealed, contending that since H and P had been associated when they both left the M group, the effect of *section 179(2)* was that no tax was due. The Special Commissioner rejected this contention and upheld the assessment in principle, holding that the exemption under *section 179(2)* only applied where both companies were associated, within *section 179(10)(a)*, at the time of the intra-group transfer. In this case, H and P had been associated within *section 179(10)(a)* when they left the group in 1998, but had not been associated within *section 179(10)(a)* at the time of the intra-group transfer in 1997. Accordingly they did not qualify for exemption and tax remained due. The CA dismissed H's appeal (by a 2–1 majority, Toulson LJ dissenting). Sir John Chadwick observed that the object of the legislation was 'to prevent the transferee from taking the asset out of the group without crystallising the gain (and the liability to tax) which would have arisen (had the transferor and transferee not been members of the same group) at the time that the transferee acquired the asset'. Tuckey LJ held that the word 'associated' was included in s 179(2) 'as part of the test to be applied as at the time of the acquisition', and was 'addressing the question whether the companies in question were associated as at the time of the acquisition'. *Johnston Publishing (North) Ltd v HMRC*, CA [2008] EWCA Civ 858; [2008] All ER (D) 311 (Jul); [2008] STC 3116.

Jones v Wilcock

Loss on sale of property – whether TCGA, s 224(3) applicable

See **53.13**

In 1988 an accountant and his wife purchased a house for more than £120,000. They subsequently incurred considerable expenditure on improvements, but, following a general fall in house prices, sold the house for £97,000 in 1993. The husband had other capital gains in the year of disposal, and claimed that the loss on the house should be set against such gains. The Revenue rejected the claim, on the basis that the house had been the couple's private residence, so that the effect of *TCGA 1992, s 16, s 223(1)* was that the loss was not allowable. The husband appealed, contending that the house had been purchased 'wholly or partly for the purpose of realising a gain', within *TCGA 1992, s 224(3)*, so that *TCGA 1992, s 223* did not apply. The Special Commissioner rejected this contention and dismissed the appeal. On the evidence, the couple's purpose in buying the house was to use it as their home. Their hope that they would be able to make a profit on its eventual sale 'was not a purpose within *TCGA 1992, s 224(3)*'. *Jones v Wilcock* (Sp C 92), [1996] SSCD 389.

Joseph Carter & Sons Ltd v Baird; Wear Ironmongers & Sons Ltd v Baird

Companies claiming rollover relief in respect of land purchased by associated company

See **59.3**

Two associated companies (C and W) disposed of some land in Sunderland. Their controlling director purchased a farm in France, and transferred its ownership to a French company, the shares in which were owned by C and W. C and W claimed rollover relief. The Revenue rejected the claim on the grounds that neither the land in Sunderland, nor the farm in France, had been used for the purpose of the trades of C and W, and that the disposals and acquisition had not been by the same person, as required by *TCGA 1992, s 152**. The Commissioners dismissed the companies' appeals and the Ch D upheld their decision. *Joseph Carter & Sons Ltd v Baird*; *Wear Ironmongers & Sons Ltd v Baird* Ch D 1998, 72 TC 303; [1999] STC 120.

Kirby v Thorn EMI plc

Whether consideration for a non-competition covenant a capital sum derived from an asset

See 7.2, 10.2

A holding company (T) held the shares of M. In December 1977 an elaborate agreement between T, M and an American corporation (G) was completed, under which T procured the sale to G of three subsidiaries of M, engaged mainly in the repairing of electrical motors and generators, with the benefit of a covenant by T under which broadly it undertook that it and its subsidiaries would not engage in a competing business in the UK before 1983. The consideration was $1.73m of which $.575m (then equivalent to £315,934) was apportioned to the covenant. The CA accepted this contention, holding that the sum received in respect of the covenant gave rise to a chargeable gain (reversing the decisions of the Special Commissioners and the Ch D). The Revenue's contention that, by the covenant, T conferred rights on G, and the asset thus created had been disposed of by T to G, was rejected by the Commissioners, the Ch D and the CA. However, an alternative Revenue contention, not advanced in the Ch D, was that if a pre-existing asset was needed for the tax to apply to it, the goodwill of T was such an asset, of which it made a part disposal by the covenant, or from which it derived a capital sum. The CA accepted this contention, holding that the disputed amount was a capital sum derived from T's goodwill. Since the extent and valuation of this goodwill had not been canvassed before the Commissioners, Nicholls LJ considered that the case should be remitted to them, to reconsider the company's appeal in the light of his judgement. (Subsequently the Court agreed that there should be no such remitter and that both the Commissioners' determination and the judgement of the Ch D should be varied in specified terms set out in a schedule of 'terms of compromise'.) *Kirby v Thorn EMI plc* CA 1987, 60 TC 519; [1987] STC 621; 1988 STI 90; [1988] 1 WLR 445; [1988] 2 All ER 947.

Larner v Warrington

*Assets of negligible value – whether dissipated within TCGA 1992, s 24(1)**

See 5.14

The taxpayer made a substantial gain on the disposal of shares in M Ltd in 1973/74. Shortly after the disposal, he and his wife invested in two companies, the shares in which had become of negligible value by 5 April 1974. He was assessed on his 1973/74 gain in 1978 and appealed against the assessment, claiming relief under *TCGA 1992, s 24(2)** for 1973/74. The General Commissioners heard the appeal in July 1979 and allowed the taxpayer's claim in principle, adjourning the appeal for the value of the shares in M Ltd to be agreed. The appeal was restored for hearing in February 1984. In the interval *Williams v Bullivant* had been decided in the Ch D, and the Commissioners permitted the Revenue to raise the new argument that the notional loss provided for by *TCGA 1992, s 24(2)** took place not earlier than the making of the claim in 1978/79. The Commissioners accepted this, and determined the assessment accordingly. The taxpayer appealed to the Ch D, where he appeared in person and contended that the Commissioners should not have permitted their 1979 decision in his favour to be reopened. Further, since the shares in the companies in which he and his wife had invested had lost their value by April 1974, they had by then been dissipated within *TCGA 1992, s 24(1)**. Both contentions were rejected. There had been no final decision on any matter raised at the July 1979 hearing, as the value of the M Ltd shares was unsettled. The taxpayer had not been prejudiced, for if the final decision had been in his favour, the Revenue could, and no doubt would, have appealed to the Ch D. The relevant assets remained in existence, although they had become valueless, and loss in value as distinct from the loss, destruction, dissipation or extinction of an asset falls under *TCGA 1992, s 24(2)** and not under TCGA 1992, s 24(1)*. *Larner v Warrington* Ch D 1985, 58 TC 557; [1985] STC 442.

Lee v Jewitt

Legal costs relating to partnership dispute – whether within TCGA 1992, s 38(1)(b)

See **16.11**

In 1981 an accountancy partnership admitted three new partners. The new partners paid a total of £150,000 to the original partners. In the relevant agreements, 20% of this was attributed to goodwill. Following disagreements, the new partners took legal proceedings, seeking a dissolution of the partnership and the repayment of the £75,000 paid to one of the original partners (L). L incurred legal costs of some £13,000 in defending the proceedings. The Ch D ordered that the partnership should be dissolved, but rejected the claim for repayment. The Revenue issued a 1981/82 CGT assessment on L in respect of the partial disposal of the partnership goodwill. L appealed, contending that the legal costs should be allowed as a deduction. The Special Commissioner accepted this contention and allowed the appeal. In his view, there was clear evidence that the taxpayer was defending his title to the goodwill, for what the new partners were alleging was that the goodwill had turned out not to have existed at the time of their admittance. *Lee v Jewitt* (Sp C 257), [2000] SSCD 517.

Leisureking Ltd v Cushing

Loss relief for payment made under guarantee

See **44.12**

In 1985 a company (L), and ten companies in the same group, entered into a composite joint and several guarantee with a bank whereby the liabilities to the bank of each of the companies were guaranteed by all the other ten companies as co-guarantors. In 1988 the bank sought repayment of liabilities incurred by two of the associated companies, which were no longer solvent. L made a payment of £2,115,000 to the bank, and did not seek to recover any contributions from its co-guarantors. L claimed relief for the payment under *TCGA 1992, s 253(4)**. The Revenue considered that the relief should be restricted to take account of the fact that the liability was shared between L and the other companies which had acted as guarantors. The Special Commissioner found on the evidence that only three of the co-guarantors remained solvent at the time when L had made the payment in question, and held that L was entitled to relief in respect of one-third of the payment. The Ch D dismissed L's appeal against this decision. The amount of the relief had to be restricted to take account of potential contributions from the co-guarantors. (Chadwick J also observed that the Commissioner had apparently been wrong to disregard any possibility of recovery from a liquidation of the eight co-guarantors which were no longer solvent, but declined to remit the matter to the Commissioner to reconsider this point, since the Revenue had not appealed against the decision.) *Leisureking Ltd v Cushing* Ch D 1992, 65 TC 400; [1993] STC 46.

Lewis v Rook

See **53.6**

In 1968 a taxpayer purchased a large house, ten acres of land, and two cottages. In 1979 she sold one of the cottages, which was 190 yards from her house and had been occupied by a gardener. The Revenue issued an assessment on the gain and she appealed, contending that *TCGA 1992, s 222** applied. The Commissioners allowed her appeal but the CA reversed this decision and restored the assessment. Applying the non-tax cases of *Methuen Campbell v Walters* [1979] 1 QB 525 and *Dyer v Dorset County Council* [1989] QB 346, the true test was whether the cottage was within the curtilage of, and appurtenant to, the main property, so as to be part of the entity which, together with the main property, constituted the dwelling-house occupied by the taxpayer as her main residence. This was not the case here, where the cottage was some way from the main building and separated by a large garden. *Lewis v Rook* CA 1992, 64 TC 567, [1992] STC 171; [1992] 1 WLR 662.

Lewis v Walters

Whether lease a wasting asset

See **41.15**

On the death of their mother in 1982, a brother and sister inherited the freehold interest in a house. The house was subject to a lease, for a term of 99 years from 1904, in favour of their father. He died in 1985 and the brother and sister then acquired the lease as his executors. Neither of them lived in the house, and in 1987 they sold the freehold and leasehold interests to the same purchaser. The Revenue issued a CGT assessment in which the value of the house was apportioned between the leasehold and freehold interests. In the assessment the lease was treated as a wasting asset, so that its value at the date of acquisition was written down in accordance with *TCGA 1992, Sch 8**. The executors appealed, contending that, by virtue of *Leasehold Reform Act 1967*, the lease should not be treated as a wasting asset. Their appeal was dismissed by the General Commissioners and the Ch D. The lease as granted did not contain any express term providing for its extension beyond 2003. The rights conferred by the *Leasehold Reform Act* did not constitute a provision 'for the extension of the lease beyond a given date' within the meaning of *TCGA 1992, Sch 8 para 8(5)**. Furthermore, the executors' father had not given notice of any desire to extend the lease and the executors had no power to extend the lease either in their capacity as executors or as the heirs of his estate. Accordingly, the lease was a wasting asset and the assessment had been computed on the correct basis. *Lewis v Walters* Ch D 1992, 64 TC 489; [1992] STC 97.

Longson v Baker

Private residence exemption – area required for reasonable enjoyment

See **53.5**

An individual (L) separated from his wife in 1990 and moved out of the matrimonial home, which was a farmhouse including stables and 7.56 hectares of land. L and his family kept horses at the farm and had erected a further building for use as a riding school. In 1995 the couple divorced, and L disposed of his beneficial interest in the property to his former wife. The Revenue issued a CGT assessment on the basis that only 1.054 hectares qualified for private residence relief within *TCGA 1992, s 222(3)*. (It was accepted that L was entitled to relief by virtue of ESC D6, although he had not lived in the property since 1990.) L appealed against the assessment, contending that all 7.56 hectares had been 'required for the reasonable enjoyment of the dwelling-house'. The Special Commissioner rejected this contention and dismissed the appeal, holding that 'it cannot be correct that the dwelling-house . . . *requires* an area of land amounting to 7.56 hectares in order to ensure its reasonable enjoyment as a residence, having regard to its size and character.' While it may have been 'desirable or convenient' for L to have such an area, it was not *required* for the reasonable enjoyment of the dwelling-house. *In Re Newhill Compulsory Purchase Order* applied; *Green v CIR* distinguished. The Ch D upheld this decision as one of fact. Evans-Lombe J held that *section 222(3)* imposed an objective test. It is not objectively required, i.e. necessary, to keep horses at a house to enjoy it as a residence. An individual taxpayer may subjectively wish to do so but that is not the same thing. *Longson v Baker* Ch D 2000, 73 TC 415; [2001] STC 6.

In re Lynall

Value of unquoted shares while public flotation under consideration

See **45.4**

In an estate duty case the question at issue was the price which certain unquoted shares 'would fetch if sold in the open market at the time of the death of the deceased'. (*FA 1894, s 7(5)*. Compare *TCGA 1992, s 272(1)*.) At the time of the death, the directors were considering public flotation and favourable confidential reports had been made to them for that purpose by a firm of accountants and a firm of stockbrokers. The HL held, *inter alia*, that although no general rule could be laid down as to the information a hypothetical purchaser in an open market may be deemed to have, the board could not be deemed to disclose confidential information which, if published prematurely, might prejudice the company's interests, including reports on the possibility of a public issue. *In re Lynall* HL 1971, 47 TC 375; [1972] AC 680; [1971] 3 All ER 904. (Note. See now *FA 1973, s 51*, re-enacted as *TCGA 1992, s 273*, as to disposals after 5 July 1973. The substantive decision here is therefore now of limited application, but the judgements include a useful review of estate duty cases dealing with the valuation of unquoted shares. See also *Battle v CIR* and *CIR v Crossman*, and the 1995 cases of *Caton's Administrators v Couch* and *Clark (Clark's Executor) v CIR*.)

Lyon v Pettigrew

Consideration for disposal paid in instalments

See **16.4**

In 1979/80 a taxi-cab proprietor contracted to sell some of his cabs together with their licences. Under the contract for each, the purchase price was £6,000, payable in instalments of £40 over 150 weeks. The contract provided that the licence would not be transferred until 'payment of all monies hereunder'. The Revenue issued an assessment on the basis that the cabs had been disposed of in 1979/80. The proprietor appealed, contending that the sales had been conditional within *TCGA 1992, s 28(2)**, so that the disposal had not taken place until the date on which the final instalment was paid. The Commissioners allowed his appeal but the Ch D reversed their decision and restored the assessment. By virtue of the *Town Police Clauses Act 1847*, it was not possible to sever the licences from the taxicabs. The contracts as a whole were not conditional, and the full amount of the consideration was chargeable in 1979/80. *Eastham v Leigh London & Provincial Properties Ltd* applied. *Lyon v Pettigrew*, Ch D 1985, 58 TC 452; [1985] STC 369.

McGregor v Adcock

Sale of part of land by farmer

See **24.3**

A taxpayer, aged 70, had farmed 35 acres for over 10 years. He sold some 5 acres for which outline planning permission had been obtained. He was assessed on the large resulting gain and claimed retirement relief. The Ch D, reversing the decision of the Commissioners, held that no relief was due. The only reasonable conclusion on the facts was that there had been a sale of an asset of the business and not of part of the business. *McGregor v Adcock* Ch D 1977, 51 TC 692; [1977] STC 206; [1977] 1 WLR 864; [1977] 3 All ER 65. (Note. Retirement relief is abolished for disposals after 5 April 2003 (see **25.88** EXEMPTIONS AND RELIEFS), but this case remains relevant to ENTREPRENEURS' RELIEF (**24.3**).)

MacPherson v Hall

Identification of shares disposed of

See **64.6**

The rules for the identification of securities, etc. disposed of, introduced by *FA 1982, ss 88, 89*, are similar to those which had been in force for Sch D, Case VII (abolished from 6 April 1971). In a Case VII appeal, the taxpayer sold 6,000 shares of a company on the London Stock Exchange on 14 September 1964, the delivery date being 14 October. He had bought 6,000 shares of the same company some months previously and he also bought 6,000 on 11 September, the delivery date for which was 22 September. The Ch D held that under the legislation in force (the wording of *TCGA 1992, s 108(4)(b)* is identical) the shares disposed of should be identified with those acquired on 11 September, resulting in a loss of £20. (It was unsuccessfully contended for the taxpayer that the provision applied only to shares acquired on or after the date of disposal and that the shares sold should have been matched with those first purchased, producing a loss of £3,702.) *MacPherson v Hall* Ch D 1972, 48 TC 210.

Magnavox Electronics Co Ltd (in liquidation) v Hall

Anti-avoidance

See **4.2**

In September 1978 a company (M) exchanged contracts for the sale of a factory to another company (J) for £1,400,000. Completion was arranged for February 1979, but for financial reasons J was unable to complete the purchase, and forfeited its deposit. Meanwhile, M had gone into voluntary liquidation in December 1978. The liquidator did not rescind the contract of sale, but arranged for M to acquire an 'off-the-shelf' company (S), to which it assigned its beneficial interest under the contract on 6 July 1979. Three days later certain variations in the contract were agreed, including a reduction of the purchase price to £1,150,000 and a new completion date of 9 October 1979. On the same day S exchanged contracts with a fourth company (B) for the sale of the factory on terms practically identical with those in the original contract as varied. B duly completed. The Revenue issued an assessment on the basis that the disposal had taken place after M had gone into liquidation. M appealed, contending that the disposal had taken place in September 1978 (so that trading losses of that accounting period could be set against the gain). The Special Commissioners dismissed M's appeal, and the Ch D and CA upheld their decision. The disposal to B was not under the 1978 contract, but under a new contract made in July 1979. Furthermore, the interposition of S was part of an artificial avoidance scheme which could be disregarded, applying *Furniss v Dawson*. *Magnavox Electronics Co Ltd (in liquidation) v Hall*, CA 1986, 59 TC 610; [1986] STC 561.

Makins v Elson

Whether caravan a dwelling-house

See **53.3**

A taxpayer purchased land on which to build a house on which construction had commenced. Meanwhile, he lived with his family in a wheeled caravan jacked up and resting on bricks on the land, with water, electricity and telephone installed. Before completing the house, he sold the site, with the caravan, and was assessed on the resultant gain. The Ch D held that the caravan was a dwelling-house for the relevant period and that the gain was within the private residence exemption. *Makins v Elson* Ch D 1976, 51 TC 437; [1977] STC 46; [1977] 1 WLR 221; [1977] 1 All ER 572.

Mannion v Johnston

Retirement relief

See **24.3**

A taxpayer who farmed 78 acres sold 17 of them in April 1984 and a further 18 acres in December 1984. He was assessed and claimed retirement relief, contending that the sales were a disposal of part of his business. The Ch D, reversing the Commissioners' decision, held that no relief was due, applying *McGregor v Adcock*. Each of the two dispositions had to be considered separately and the changes caused by each one were merely limited changes of scale. *Mannion v Johnston* Ch D 1988, 61 TC 598; [1988] STC 758. (Notes. (1) The case was heard in the Ch D with *Atkinson v Dancer*. (2) Retirement relief is abolished for disposals after 5 April 2003 (see **25.88** EXEMPTIONS AND RELIEFS), but this case remains relevant to ENTREPRENEURS' RELIEF (**24.3**).)

Mansworth v Jelley

Acquisition of shares under share option scheme – application of TCGA 1992, s 17

See **7.7**, **22.6**, **22.22**

An employee (J) was granted options to acquire shares in his employer's parent company. He was not resident in the UK at the time he was granted these options, but subsequently became UK-resident, exercised the options, and then sold the shares. The Revenue issued CGT assessments on the basis that the base value of the shares was the sum of the price paid for the shares on the exercise of the options and the market value of the options when they were originally granted (which was treated as nil). J appealed, contending that the base value of the shares was their market value when the options were exercised. The Special Commissioner accepted this contention and allowed the appeal, and the Ch D and CA upheld this decision. Chadwick LJ held that the acquisition of the shares was clearly 'an incident of the taxpayer's employment', and was therefore within *TCGA 1992, s 17(1)(b)**. Accordingly, in the CGT computation, the cost of acquisition was 'the market value of the underlying asset', i.e. the shares, at the time when the options were exercised. *Mansworth v Jelley* CA 2002, 75 TC 1; [2003] STC 53.

Markey v Sanders

Private residence exemption

See **53.6**

In 1951, the taxpayer's mother purchased a small country estate of 4 acres with a main house and outbuildings reached by a 130 metre drive from the main entrance gates. In 1963, this was sold to the taxpayer, who had earlier (in 1956) acquired adjoining land of nearly 9 acres. In 1965, the taxpayer built a three-bedroom bungalow by the entrance gates, with a quarter-acre garden, which was occupied rent-free by a gardener and housekeeper. The bungalow was not separately rated. In September 1980, the whole estate, including the bungalow, was sold to a single purchaser. The issue in the appeal was whether the gain on the sale of the bungalow was within the private residence exemption. Walton J, reversing the Commissioners' decision and applying *Batey v Wakefield* held that it was not. Batey decided that 'residence' need not mean a single building, and a relevant fact there was that the bungalow was 'very closely adjacent' to the main residence. 'Very closely adjacent' is an imprecise test; he preferred to ask whether the relevant group of buildings, looked on as a whole, could be fairly regarded as a single dwelling-house used as the taxpayer's main residence. Here the only reasonable conclusion from the facts was that the bungalow was not part of the taxpayer's residence. *Markey v Sanders* Ch D 1987, 60 TC 245; [1987] STC 256; [1987] 1 WLR 864.

Marren v Ingles

*Deferred sale consideration – application of TCGA 1992, s 22(1)**

See **7.2**, **10.2**, **25.5**, **63.6**

Under an agreement of 15 September 1970, shares in a private company were sold for an immediate payment of £750 per share plus a further amount to be calculated by reference to the quoted price of shares representing them on the first dealing day following a proposed flotation of the company. In the event, the relevant dealing day was 5 December 1972 and the further consideration was agreed at £2,825 per share. It was common ground that, in arriving at the gain on the disposal of the shares, the £750 and the value at 15 September 1970 of the contingent right to further consideration were to be taken into account. A 1972/73 assessment was issued on the basis that the right to receive the further consideration, being a chose in action, was an asset from which a capital sum was derived on 5 December 1972; that there was a deemed disposal under *TCGA 1992, s 22(1)**; and that this right was not a debt within *TCGA 1992, s 251(1)**. The HL upheld the assessment. *Dicta* of Walton J in *CIR v Montgomery* on which the taxpayer relied, were disapproved. *Marren v Ingles* HL 1980, 54 TC 76; [1980] STC 500; [1980] 1 WLR 983; [1980] 3 All ER 95. See now *TCGA 1992, s 138A* at **63.6** SHARES AND SECURITIES.

Marshall v Kerr

Whether TCGA 1992, s 62(6) applicable to non-resident settlement established by a UK-resident beneficiary of a non-resident testator*

See **19.8**, **48.14**

K's father-in-law (B) died in 1977, resident and ordinarily resident in Jersey. Half of B's personal estate was bequeathed to K's wife, who was a UK resident. By a deed of family arrangement in 1978 she settled her share of the estate on Jersey trustees, to be held on discretionary trusts for herself and her family. The administration of the estate was not completed until 1979 and the assets were at no time vested in K's wife. Between 1981 and 1985 the settlement trustees made capital payments to K's wife. The Revenue issued assessments under *TCGA 1992, ss 87–98**. K appealed, contending that, by virtue of *TCGA 1992, s 62(6)**, B should be deemed to be the settlor of the trusts, so that, since he had been neither resident or ordinarily resident in the UK, there was no CGT liability. The HL upheld the assessments (restoring the decision of the Ch D which had reversed that of the Special Commissioner). The arrangement did not settle any specific assets comprised in the estate, but settled the legatee's half-share in the residuary estate, which had not by then been constituted. The property settled by the legatee constituted a separate chose in action. Where a legatee varied her entitlement under a will by means of a family arrangement, the making of the variation was deemed not to be a disposal in itself. However, *TCGA 1992, s 62(6)** did not have the further effect of treating the assets vested in the legatee as acquired from the deceased at the date of death. Accordingly, the legatee was the settlor of the arrangement for the purposes of *TCGA 1992, s 87**. *Marshall v Kerr* HL 1994, 67 TC 56; [1994] STC 638; [1994] 3 WLR 299; [1994] 2 All ER 106.

Marson v Marriage

Deferred sale consideration – whether TCGA 1992, s 48 applicable*

See **10.2**, **16.13**, **25.5**

A taxpayer agreed on 31 March 1965 to sell to a development company 47 acres of land with development possibilities. The consideration was £47,040 payable immediately with future payments of £7,500 for each acre developed and provision for compensation to the taxpayer should the land be compulsorily purchased from the company. In the event, the company developed the land in 1975 and paid £348,250 to the taxpayer in settlement of the agreement. He was assessed to CGT for 1975/76 on the basis that the £348,250 was a taxable receipt. The Ch D upheld the assessment, following *Marren v Ingles* and holding that the provision for compensation should the land be compulsorily purchased meant that the future consideration was not ascertainable at 31 March 1965. (The taxpayer had contended that, by virtue of *TCGA 1992, s 48**, the consideration could have been brought into account at that date.) *Marson v Marriage* Ch D 1979, 54 TC 59; [1980] STC 177.

Mashiter v Pearmain

Land value

See **8.6**

A taxpayer sold land in 1976 for consideration exceeding its current use value. The land had been acquired by gift in 1960, and the Revenue issued an assessment computed on the basis that the land should be treated as having been sold on 6 April 1965 and re-acquired at its market value on that date. The taxpayer appealed, contending that the gain should be time-apportioned over the whole period from 1960 to 1976. The CA rejected this contention and upheld the assessment. *Mashiter v Pearmain,* CA 1984, 58 TC 334; [1985] STC 165.

Moore v Thompson

Whether a caravan a dwelling house

See **53.3**

Makins v Elson was distinguished in a subsequent case where the General Commissioners held that a caravan installed in a small farm while the farmhouse was being renovated was not within the exemption of *TCGA 1992, s 222**, and the Ch D upheld their decision. The caravan was disposed of when the farmhouse was sold. The farmhouse was never occupied by the taxpayer, and the evidence was that she had never used the caravan as a permanent residence. *Moore v Thompson* Ch D 1986, 61 TC 15; [1986] STC 170.

Morgan v Gibson

Land reflecting development value

See **8.6**

In 1948 a taxpayer acquired an interest in land which had an agreed value of £15,545. In 1984 the land was sold to the British Airports Authority for £160,000, with the condition that, should the Authority obtain planning permission within 30 years, a further sum of up to £350,000 would be payable. The Revenue issued an assessment on the basis that the consideration received on disposal included development value and that therefore *TCGA 1992, Sch 2 para 9** applied. The taxpayer appealed, contending that the conditions of *TCGA 1992, Sch 2 para 9(1)(b)** were not satisfied, and that the assessment should be computed on a straight-line apportionment basis. The Ch D rejected this contention and upheld the assessment (reversing the General Commissioners' decision). There was a clear finding of fact that the sale price included an element of 'hope value', which was equivalent to anticipated development value. That being so, the provisions of *TCGA 1992, Sch 2 para 9** had to be applied. *Morgan v Gibson* Ch D 1989, 61 TC 654; [1989] STC 568.

Newman v Pepper; Newman v Morgan

*Date of disposal – Assets held as nominee for other persons – TCGA 1992, s 60**

See **62.3**

In 1982 a landowner (N) conveyed an area of farmland to his two sons as trustees. Two days later he and his sons granted a building company (W) an option to purchase most of the land. Under the option agreement, W covenanted to 'use all reasonable endeavours' to obtain the inclusion of the land 'in any relevant local plan or planning policy document for the area as land suitable for residential development'. In 1985 W assigned the benefit of the option to two other companies (M and C). Later that year the local council granted outline planning permission for residential development on 11.3 hectares of land. M and C subsequently exercised the option in respect of those 11.3 hectares, and paid more than £700,000 to N and his children in accordance with the agreement. In 1986 N and his sons released C from some of its obligations under the option agreement in return for a payment of £175,000. The Revenue issued CGT assessments on N's sons, against which they appealed. The Special Commissioners dismissed their appeals, holding that the date of disposal for CGT purposes was the date on which the option was exercised, and that, applying *Marren v Ingles* (see above), the value of the right to receive further consideration must be added to the cash actually received on the disposal. The effect of *TCGA 1992, s 60** was that N's sons were chargeable to CGT. *Newman v Pepper; Newman v Morgan* (Sp C 243), [2000] SSCD 345. (*Notes*. (1) The appellants appeared in person. (2) Appeals against assessments under *ICTA 1988, s 776* were also dismissed. (3) The Commissioners also found that N and his sons had submitted a hold-over election under *FA 1980, s 79* (see **36.12** HOLD-OVER RELIEFS), rejecting a contention by one of N's sons that their signatures had been forged.)

O'Brien v Benson's Hosiery (Holdings) Ltd

Payment from employee for release from service agreement

See **7.2**

A company, on acquiring the shares of another, entered into a seven-year service agreement with B, the sales director of the other company. After two years in which B carried out his duties with conspicuous success, he was released from the agreement on paying £50,000 to the first company, which was assessed on the £50,000 as a chargeable gain. The HL upheld the assessment (reversing the CA decision). The rights, although not assignable, could be turned to account in the hands of the employer and were an asset within the general scheme of the legislation. The concept of market value is introduced for certain purposes; it cannot be deduced from this that all assets within CGT must have a market value. *O'Brien v Benson's Hosiery (Holdings) Ltd* HL 1979, 53 TC 241; [1979] STC 735; [1979] 3 WLR 572; [1979] 3 All ER 652.

O'Rourke v Binks

*Capital distribution – TCGA 1992, s 122**

See **63.8, 63.11**

The taxpayer held a large number of shares in a company (C). The total allowable expenditure on any disposal of those shares was £214,000. Under a merger agreement between C and a public company, he exchanged his shares for 840,000 shares in the public company and 75,000 shares in a subsidiary company (the market value of these being £246,000). The transfer to the taxpayer of the shares in the subsidiary company was treated as a capital distribution and thus as a partial disposal of his shares in C. The Revenue issued a CGT assessment in which the total allowable expenditure was apportioned in accordance with *TCGA 1992, s 42**. The taxpayer appealed, contending that, since the total allowable expenditure was less than the value of the shares in the subsidiary, he was entitled to elect that the amount of the distribution should be reduced by the total allowable expenditure, in accordance with *TCGA 1992, s 122(4)**. The Special Commissioner allowed the appeal but the CA reversed this decision and restored the assessment. The words of *TCGA 1992, s 122(4)** were ambiguous, and in the circumstances the court should give effect to the presumed intention of the legislature by inserting words into the subsection. The taxpayer could not make an election under *TCGA 1992, s 122(4)** unless the distribution was 'small', within *TCGA 1992, s 122(2)**. The capital distribution here (which amounted to

15.58% of the total expenditure) was not small for the purposes of *TCGA 1992, s 122(2)**. *O'Rourke v Binks* CA 1992, 65 TC 165; [1992] STC 703.

Owen v Elliott

*Private residence partly used as guest house – relief under TCGA 1992, s 223(4)**

See **53.14**

A taxpayer and his wife had carried on a private guest house business from premises they owned and lived in. They had occupied different parts of the premises at different times of the year in such a way that every part of the premises had, at some time during their period of ownership, constituted their main residence. When the property was sold it was agreed that one-third of the gain was exempt under *TCGA 1992, s 222** and *s 223(2)**. The taxpayer appealed against an assessment on the gain, contending that further relief was due under *TCGA 1992, s 223(4)**. The CA allowed his appeal (reversing the decision of the Ch D). The phrase 'let by him as residential accommodation' in *TCGA 1992, s 223(4)** did not, directly or by association, mean premises let which were likely to be occupied as a home. It referred to living accommodation as distinct, for example, from office accommodation. The lettings undertaken by the taxpayer were within the words 'residential accommodation'. *Owen v Elliott* CA 1990, 63 TC 319; [1990] STC 469; [1990] 3 WLR 133.

Pepper v Daffurn

Retirement relief

See **24.3**

A farmer had owned 113 acres of land, on which he had reared and grazed cattle, for several years. He gradually ceased to rear cattle, and sold 83 acres in 1986. In 1987 he obtained planning permission in respect of a covered cattle yard comprising 0.6 acres, which he sold in 1988. Thereafter his only activity was cattle grazing. The Revenue issued a CGT assessment on the sale of the cattle yard, and the farmer appealed, contending that he was entitled to retirement relief. The Ch D upheld the assessment (reversing the decision of the General Commissioners). On the evidence, the farmer had changed the nature of his activities from rearing cattle to grazing them in preparation for the sale of the yard. Following this change, the yard was no longer necessary to the farmer's business, so that its sale did not constitute a disposal of a part of that business. *Pepper v Daffurn* Ch D 1993, 66 TC 68; [1993] STC 466. (Note. Retirement relief is abolished for disposals after 5 April 2003 (see **25.88** EXEMPTIONS AND RELIEFS), but this case remains relevant to ENTREPRENEURS' RELIEF (**24.3**).)

Powlson v Welbeck Securities Ltd

Surrender of an option

See **7.7**, **16.4**

In 1961 a company acquired an option to participate in a property development. In 1971 it began proceedings to enforce its option, but these were settled by consent in 1974, the company receiving £2,000,000 in return for agreeing to 'release and abandon' the option. The Revenue assessed the amount as a chargeable gain and the company appealed, contending that, by virtue of *TCGA 1992, s 144(4)**, the surrender of the option did not constitute the disposal of an asset. The CA dismissed the company's appeal, holding that *TCGA 1992, s 144(3)** constituted an exception to the operation of *TCGA 1992, s 24(1)** but did not confer any exemption from the chargeable disposal which arose under *TCGA 1992, s 22(1)** when the company received a capital sum for the surrender of the option. *Powlson v Welbeck Securities Ltd* CA 1987, 60 TC 269; [1987] STC 468.

Prest v Bettinson

Residuary legatees of estate subject to annuities include charities – whether charitable exemption applies

See **11.8**

Under a will the residuary estate was held on the usual trusts for sale and conversion for the benefit of five institutions, equally and absolutely, subject to certain annuities. The income was more than sufficient to cover the annuities and no annuity fund was set up. Assets of the estate were sold, so permitting capital distributions to the residuary legatees, and the gains were assessed on the trustee. Four of the residuary legatees were charities, and the trustee contended that four-fifths of the gains accrued to charities and were exempted by *TCGA 1992, s 256(1)**. The Ch D rejected this contention and upheld the assessment. *Prest v Bettinson* Ch D 1980, 53 TC 437; [1980] STC 607.

Purves v Harrison

Sale of premises nine months before sale of business – whether sale of premises qualifying for retirement relief

See **24.3**

The proprietor of a coach and a minibus service wished to retire. In March 1990 he sold his business premises. However, the purchaser granted him a licence to continue to occupy the premises, and he continued to carry on the business until December 1990, when he sold it to the same purchaser. He claimed retirement relief in respect of the sale of the business, including the premises. The Revenue accepted the claim in respect of the business sold in December 1990, but rejected the claim in respect of the earlier sale of the premises. The Ch D upheld the Revenue's ruling. Blackburne J held that the sales could not be treated as a single transaction. The sale of the premises in March could not be treated as part of the sale of the business in December. *Purves v Harrison* Ch D 2000, 73 TC 390; [2001] STC 267. (Note. Retirement relief is abolished for disposals after 5 April 2003 (see **25.88** EXEMPTIONS AND RELIEFS), but this case remains relevant to ENTREPRENEURS' RELIEF (**24.3**).)

Quinn v Cooper

Indexation allowance – Business Expansion Scheme – TCGA 1992, s 150

See **25.22**

An individual (C) had purchased a number of shares which entitled him to relief under the Business Expansion Scheme. He subsequently sold the shares at a loss. The Revenue issued CGT assessments on the basis that the effect of *TCGA 1992, s 150(3)** was that indexation allowance only applied to the sale proceeds of the shares. C appealed, contending that the effect of *TCGA 1992, s 53* and *s 150* was that indexation allowance should be applied to the original purchase price of the shares. The Ch D rejected this contention and upheld the assessments (reversing the decision of the Special Commissioner). Lightman J held that, having regard to the interrelationship of the relevant statutory provisions, indexation should only be applied to the cost as reduced by *section 150(3)*. *Quinn v Cooper* Ch D 1998, 71 TC 44; [1998] STC 772.

W T Ramsay Ltd v CIR

Artificial avoidance scheme – whether a nullity for tax purposes

See **4.2**, **25.5**

A company, having made a substantial gain on the sale of a farm, carried out a number of share and loan transactions with the object of creating a large allowable loss at little cost to itself. The loss emerged as one of about £175,000 on shares it subscribed for in a company formed for the scheme, the success of which depended on its establishing that a loan to the same company, sold at a profit of about £173,000, was not a debt on a security within *TCGA 1992, s 251(1)**. The acceptance of the offer of the loan was given orally, but evidenced by a statutory declaration (vide *Statutory Declarations Act 1835*) by a director of the borrowing company. The CA held that the loan, being evidenced by the statutory declaration, which represented a marketable security, was a debt on a security. The scheme therefore failed. The company appealed to the HL, where the appeal was considered with that in *Eilbeck v Rawling* and in both cases the Revenue advanced the new argument that the scheme should be treated as a fiscal nullity producing neither loss nor gain (other than a loss of £370 in *Eilbeck v Rawling*). The HL accepted this approach. Lord Wilberforce held that although the Duke of Westminster principle prevented a court from looking behind a genuine document or transaction to some supposed underlying substance, it did not compel the court to view a document or transaction in blinkers, isolated from its context. A finding that a document or transaction is genuine does not preclude the Commissioners from considering whether, on the facts, what is in issue is a composite transaction or a number of independent transactions. The Commissioners are not 'bound to consider individually each separate step in a composite transaction intended to be carried through as a whole'. The question of whether what is in issue is a composite transaction or a number of independent transactions is a matter of law, reviewable by the courts. Such an approach does not introduce a new principle when dealing with legal avoidance, but applies existing legislation to new and sophisticated legal devices; 'while the techniques of tax avoidance progress, the courts are not obliged to stand still'. Turning to the facts here, it was clear that the scheme was for tax avoidance with no commercial justification, and that it was the intention to proceed through all its stages to completion once set in motion. It would therefore be wrong to consider one step in isolation. The true view was that, regarding the scheme as a whole, there was neither gain nor loss. The company's appeal was dismissed. Furthermore, although this ended the appeal, the CA had been correct in holding that the relevant debt was a 'debt on a security'. *W T Ramsay Ltd v CIR* HL 1981, 54 TC 101; [1981] STC 174; [1981] 2 WLR 449; [1981] 1 All ER 865.

Randall v Plumb

Option payment contingently repayable

See 7.7, **41.24**

The owner of some land granted a gravel company an option to purchase the land for £100,000. He received £25,000 for the option. The agreement included a proviso that he would repay the £25,000 to the company if, after ten years, the company had not obtained planning permission to extract sand and gravel from the land. The Revenue assessed the £25,000 to CGT for the year in which the option was granted. The Ch D allowed his appeal against the assessment, holding that the consideration should not be the full amount of the £25,000, but that the £25,000 should be brought in at a valuation taking the contingency into account. *Randall v Plumb* Ch D 1974, 50 TC 392; [1975] STC 191; [1975] 1 All ER 734.

Rank Xerox Ltd v Lane

*Annual payments under covenant – TCGA 1992, s 237(c)**

See **5.22, 25.3**

R surrendered to X its licence from X to make use of the 'xerographic' process in certain areas in return for a 'royalty' of 5% of certain sales by X in those areas. The relevant agreements to pay the 'royalties' were made under seal. Subsequently, R distributed the 'royalty' rights in specie to its shareholders, who in turn surrendered them to X for a consideration. R was assessed to corporation tax on its gain from the disposal and appealed, contending that the 'royalties' were annual payments due under a covenant within *TCGA 1992, s 237(c)**. The HL rejected this contention and upheld the assessment. 'Covenant' here must be construed in its context and annual payments under a covenant are payments made gratuitously, the promise to pay them being enforceable only because of the form in which it was given, i.e. (in England) given under seal. Here the payments were for consideration and the presence of a seal on the relevant agreement added nothing to the obligation to pay them. *Rank Xerox Ltd v Lane* HL 1979, 53 TC 185; [1979] STC 740; [1979] 3 WLR 594; [1979] 3 All ER 657.

Reed v Nova Securities Ltd

Acquisition 'as trading stock' commercial justification

See **4.2**, **29.4**

The taxpayer company (N) had traded in shares and securities since 1955. In March 1973 it was acquired by the well-known Littlewoods group. On 17 August 1973 Littlewoods sold to it shares owned by Littlewoods in, and debts owing to Littlewoods by, certain foreign companies. The sale price for the assets was £30,000, their market value, but their capital gains cost to Littlewoods was nearly £4m. When offering the assets to N, Littlewoods' Board said that about £55,000 would be received in part repayment of the debts and N had received a payment of £35,447 in 1979. They were not part of Littlewoods' trading stock. N purported to make an election under *TCGA 1992, s 161(3)** in respect of the assets acquired, and the issue in the appeal was whether they were trading stock, as defined in *ICTA 1988, s 100(2)** (see *TCGA 1992, s 288**). The General Commissioners found that they were and their decision was upheld by the Ch D and the CA. The HL unanimously upheld the decision as regards the debts but reversed it as regards the shares. The Commissioners had determined the appeal on the basis of an agreed statement of facts, without recourse to oral evidence, and no reasonable body of Commissioners could have concluded that the company had acquired the shares as trading stock; its acquisition of shares that had no value was without commercial justification. *Reed v Nova Securities Ltd* HL 1985, 59 TC 516; [1985] STC 124; [1985] 1 WLR 193; [1985] 1 All ER 686.

Roome v Edwards

Exercise of power of appointment or advancement

See **62.14**

Under a 1944 marriage settlement (as varied), the trust fund, worth some £912,000, was held on trust for the wife for life with remainder to the husband for life with remainder to two daughters (born in 1948 and 1951) absolutely in equal shares. In March 1972 the beneficiaries assigned their respective interests to two Cayman Islands companies for sums totalling £868,000. The trustees were replaced by Cayman Islands trustees and in 1972/73 one of the companies assigned its interests to the other which, as a consequence, became absolutely entitled to the trust fund as against the trustees. In 1955, pursuant to powers in the 1944 settlement, investments in the fund worth some £13,000 had been appointed in trust for the elder daughter absolutely on attaining 25. There had been no relevant transaction regarding the 1955 fund, which had been administered separately from the 1944 fund and the trustees of which were UK residents. The substantial gain which arose under *TCGA 1992, s 71(1)** as a result of the transactions relating to the 1944 fund was assessed on the trustees of the 1955 fund on the footing that under *TCGA 1992, s 69(3)** the two sets of trustees fell to be treated as a single body of which the UK members could be assessed under *TCGA 1992, s 65(1)**. The HL upheld the assessment, reversing the decisions of the Ch D and CA. Whether a particular set of facts amounts to a settlement should be approached by asking what a person, with knowledge of the legal context of the word under established doctrine and applying this knowledge in a practical and commonsense manner to the facts under examination, would conclude. Here the intention throughout was to treat the 1955 fund as being held on the trusts of the 1944 settlement as added to and varied by the 1955 appointment. Further, the words 'accruing to the trustees of a settlement' in *TCGA 1992, s 65(1)** are to be read in the light of the situation created by *TCGA 1992, s 69(1)(3)**. *TCGA 1992, s 69(3)** is not restricted to cases where property vested in two sets of trustees is held on identical trusts. *Roome and Another v Edwards* HL 1981, 54 TC 359; [1981] STC 96; [1981] 2 WLR 268; [1981] 1 All ER 736. (For HMRC practice following this decision, see HMRC Statement of Practice 7/84.)

Sansom v Peay

Occupation of residence under discretionary trust

See **53.11**

The trustees of a discretionary trust permitted certain beneficiaries (as they were enabled to do under the trust) to occupy as their residence a house subject to the trust. The house was exchanged and it was held that the resultant gain was exempt under *TCGA 1992, s 225**. The Ch D rejected the Revenue's contention that the beneficiaries were not 'entitled' to occupy the house, because they had no absolute right under the trust. While the beneficiaries were in occupation with the trustees' permission they were entitled to occupy it. *Sansom & Another v Peay* Ch D 1976, 52 TC 1; [1976] STC 494; [1976] 1 WLR 1073; [1976] 3 All ER 375.

Schofield v HMRC

Attempt to establish CGT loss by transaction involving option

See **4.2**

In 2002/03 an individual (S) realised a substantial capital gain on the disposal of some loan notes. However, in his tax return, he claimed that he had made a loss of more than £11,000,000 on the disposal of a 'put' option. He had purchased the option on 7 February 2003, along with a corresponding 'call' option, and disposed of it on 4 April 2003. (He disposed of the 'call' option on 7 April 2003, by which time he had become resident in Spain, so that the gain on this disposal was outside the scope of UK CGT.) HMRC rejected the claim and S appealed. The First-Tier Tribunal dismissed his appeal, holding on the evidence that the options 'were inextricably linked with each other to form a continuous process which could be viewed commercially as a single or composite transaction'. The transactions had no commercial purpose, and their sole aim was to avoid tax. The Upper Tribunal and the CA unanimously upheld this decision, applying the principles laid down by Lord Fraser in *WT Ramsay Ltd v CIR*. Sir Andrew Morritt held that 'the relevant transaction was the four options together and such a transaction does not constitute a disposal' within *TCGA 1992, ss 1, 2*. Hallett LJ held that 'the relevant transaction here is plainly the scheme as a whole: namely a series of interdependent and linked transactions, with a guaranteed outcome. Under the scheme as a whole, the options were created merely to be destroyed. They were self cancelling. Thus, for capital gains purposes, there was no asset and no disposal. There was no real loss and certainly no loss to which the TCGA applies. There is in truth no significant difference between this scheme and the scheme in Ramsay, other than the nature of the "asset".' *HP Schofield v HMRC* CA, [2012] STC 2019.

Shepherd v Lyntress

Applicability of Ramsay principle where subsidiary company acquired with accumulated tax losses

See **4.2**

A major public company (N) had acquired shares in companies that had appreciated in value. It decided to acquire companies which had accumulated tax losses so that the gains on the holdings could be realised and the accrued losses could be set off against them. Accordingly, in 1979 N acquired the issued share capital of L, a company claiming to have £4m of accumulated tax losses available for set-off. In 1980 N sold part of its holding of appreciated assets to L, and a few days later L realised the gains by disposing of the assets on the Stock Exchange. The Revenue raised assessments on N on the basis that the Ramsay principle applied, and that the sale of the assets by N to L was to be ignored for fiscal purposes, so that the transactions would fall to be treated as disposals on the Stock Exchange by N, and on L on the basis that, again applying the *Ramsay* principle, the losses incurred within the company's former group were not available against gains accruing to a company outside that group. The Special Commissioners reduced the assessment on L, rejecting the Revenue's contention that the accumulated losses were not available for set-off. However, they upheld the assessment on N. Both sides appealed to the Ch D. Vinelott J allowed N's appeal and upheld the Commissioners' decision with regard to the assessment on L. On the facts, the Commissioners were clearly correct in rejecting the Revenue's contention that L's losses were not available for set-off. The real question in the case was whether the Commissioners were justified in concluding that the transfer and sale of the assets were part of a single composite transaction. Following *Craven v White*, this could not be held to be the case here, because no arrangements to sell the shares on the Stock Exchange had been made at the time when they were transferred from N to L. It was therefore impossible to conclude that the transfer of the shares to L, and their subsequent sale by L, was a single composite transaction within the *Ramsay* principle. L had an allowable loss at the time when its share capital was acquired by N. That loss remained an allowable loss after N had acquired L's share capital, and the gains which were realised when the transferred assets were sold on the Stock Exchange were gains realised by L at a time when it was a member of the same group of companies as N. *Shepherd v Lyntress Ltd*; *News International plc v Shepherd* Ch D 1989, 62 TC 495; [1989] STC 617. (Note. See now *TCGA 1992, Sch 7A*, introduced by *FA 1993, s 88*.)

Smith v Schofield

Indexation allowance – interaction with time-apportionment

See **8.7**

A taxpayer had acquired two chattels in 1952. She sold them in 1987. Her chargeable gain fell to be time-apportioned in accordance with *TCGA 1992, Sch 2 para 16(2)**. The Revenue deducted the indexation allowance from the unindexed gain before time-apportionment. She appealed, contending that the indexation allowance should be deducted only from the amount of the post-1965 gain. The HL rejected this contention and upheld the assessment (reversing the decision of the CA and restoring that of the Ch D). The issue had to be determined by construing the relevant statutory provisions against the underlying philosophy of the legislation, rather than by detailed consideration of hypothetical examples producing apparently anomalous results. The effect of the legislation was that the indexation allowance had to be applied to the gross gain before time-apportionment, and could not be set only against that part of the gain apportioned to the period after 6 April 1965. *Smith v Schofield* HL 1993, 65 TC 669; [1993] STC 268; [1993] 1 WLR 398.

Spectros International plc v Madden

Consideration for sale of company with substantial debt to bank

See **16.8**

A company (S) owned a number of subsidiary companies, one of which operated a liquid chromatography business. Another company (B) wished to purchase this business. S wished to structure the sale in such a way as to minimise its tax liability. In July 1986 one of S's wholly-owned subsidiary companies (H) declared a cash dividend of $20,000,000. It was offered an overdraft facility of this amount by a bank, the overdraft being secured by a deposit of that amount by S (so that, on payment of the dividend, the $20,000,000 effectively travelled in a circle). In September 1986 S sold a number of its subsidiary companies, including H, to B, and agreed not to compete with B in the liquid chromatography business. The agreement provided that B should pay $23,000,000 in total, of which $20,000,000 should be paid to the bank to clear the loan to H, and that $1,000 of the $23,000,000 related to the common stock of H. S appealed against an estimated assessment, contending that the consideration which it had received for the sale of H was only $1,000. The Special Commissioners rejected this contention and dismissed the appeal, holding that the effect of the agreement was that the consideration paid for the common stock of H was $20,001,000, since S 'could and did direct how that sum should be applied'. (The Commissioners noted that neither S nor the Revenue contended that the $20,000,000 should be apportioned between the assets of the liquid chromatography business.) The Ch D upheld the Commissioners' decision. Lightman J observed that, if the parties had intended that the sale of the common stock should be for $1,000, it would have been very simple to say so. Where a holding company sold a solvent subsidiary and the purchaser agreed to discharge a debt owed by that subsidiary, the amount of the debt would not necessarily constitute consideration for the shares in the subsidiary. However, in the case under appeal, the parties had specifically agreed that the amount of the debt should be allocated to the purchase price. Accordingly, on the wording of the specific agreements, the consideration for the common stock was $20,001,000. *Spectros International plc v Madden* Ch D 1996, 70 TC 349; [1997] STC 114.

Stanton v Drayton Commercial Investment Co Ltd

*Consideration satisfied by issue of shares – definition of 'value' in TCGA 1992, s 38(1)(a)**

See **16.11**

In September 1972 a company (D) agreed to acquire investments from an insurance company for £3,937,632, to be paid by means of 2,461,226 shares in D at their issue price of 160p per share. The agreement was conditional on permission being obtained for the shares to be dealt in on the Stock Exchange. The agreement became unconditional on 11 October, when the shares were issued. On 12 October, when they were first quoted on the Stock Exchange, their middle market price was 125p per share. Subsequently D sold some of the investments it had acquired from the insurance company. The Revenue issued an assessment on the gains, in which the cost of the investments was computed on the basis that the shares in D should be valued at 125p each. D appealed, contending that the shares should be valued at 160p each. The CA allowed D's appeal and the HL upheld this decision. There had been an honest arm's length agreement in which the shares had been valued at 160p, and there was no reason for going behind this agreed value. Market value was only relevant where no agreed value was available. *Stanton v Drayton Commercial Investment Co Ltd* HL 1982, 55 TC 286; [1982] STC 585; [1982] 3 WLR 214; [1982] 2 All ER 942.

Steibelt v Paling

Rollover relief – extension of three-year time limit for replacing assets; whether trades carried on successively; application of ESC D24

See **59.2, 59.3**

A publican sold his business in October 1986 for approximately £130,000 realising a chargeable gain of approximately £52,000. In February 1988 he purchased a barge for £20,000, which he intended to convert into a wine bar and restaurant. Between December 1989 and November 1994 he incurred enhancement expenditure of approximately £160,000 on the barge. He eventually began to trade from it in August 1995. He claimed rollover relief in respect of the 1986 gain. The Ch D rejected the claim (reversing the General Commissioners' decision). Sir Richard Scott V-C held that whilst the Revenue's decision not to exercise their statutory discretion to extend the three-year time limit laid down by *TCGA 1992, s 152(3)* might be challenged by judicial review, it was not reviewable by the Commissioners. In any case, the two trades, separated by a gap of nine years, could not be said to be carried on 'successively' as required by *TCGA 1992, s 152(8)*. In addition, the terms of ESC D24 (assets not brought immediately into trading use) were not satisfied. *Steibelt v Paling* Ch D 1999, 71 TC 376; [1999] STC 594.

Stephenson v Barclays Bank Trust Co Ltd

Trust fund subject to annuities – whether beneficiaries absolutely entitled

See **62.3**

Under a will, a fund was held in trust for such of the testator's grandchildren who should attain 21 years, subject to the payment of annuities to three daughters during widowhood. There were two grandchildren, both of whom had attained 21 before the relevant year. Under a deed of family arrangement entered into in 1968/69, a fund was appropriated for the annuities and a sum advanced to the grandchildren to purchase further income for the daughters with the intent that the balance of the trust fund, comprising mainly shares, should be transferred forthwith to the grandchildren. The trustees were assessed for 1968/69 on the footing of a notional disposal under *TCGA 1992, s 71(1)**, the grandchildren having become 'absolutely entitled as against' the trustees when the deed of family arrangement was entered into. The assessment was upheld. The trustees' contentions that the annuities were 'outgoings' within *TCGA 1992, s 60(2)** (with the result that the grandchildren became absolutely entitled when the younger attained 21) were rejected. *Kidson v Macdonald* followed as regards the construction of 'jointly' in *TCGA 1992, s 60(1)**. *Stephenson v Barclays Bank Trust Co Ltd* Ch D 1974, 50 TC 374; [1975] STC 151; [1975] 1 WLR 882; [1975] 1 All ER 625.

Strand Options and Futures Ltd v Vojak

Company purchasing own shares from another company – whether chargeable gain of vendor – whether excluded by ICTA 1988, s 208 or TCGA 1992, s 37

See **63.19**

In September 1995, a company (C) purchased 89,700 of its own shares from another company (S). The payment for the shares fell to be treated as a distribution. The Revenue applied SP 4/89 and thus took the view that the distribution should be included in the consideration for the disposal of the shares for the purposes of charging corporation tax on chargeable gains. S appealed, contending that the effect of *ICTA 1988, s 208* was that the consideration should not be treated as chargeable to corporation tax. The Special Commissioners rejected this contention and dismissed the appeal, holding that *ICTA 1988, s 208* did not provide 'a complete exemption', but simply exempted the consideration from Schedule F. The CA unanimously upheld the Commissioners' decision. Carnwath LJ held that *section 208* should be construed as preventing the imposition of 'a tax which is directly charged on the dividends as such, rather than indirectly as part of the computation of a taxable amount'. *Strand Options & Futures Ltd v Vojak*, CA, [2003] EWCA Civ 1457; [2003] All ER(D) 358(Oct).

Strange v Openshaw

Grant of option to purchase land – whether a part disposal

See **7.7**

Four brothers owned some agricultural land and their mother owned some adjoining land. They granted a company an option, exercisable within 10 years, to purchase the land on prescribed terms. (In the event, the option was not exercised.)

The company paid £125,000 for the option, and the Revenue issued assessments on the brothers charging CGT on the amount each received. They appealed, contending that, by virtue of *TCGA 1992, s 144(2)**, no assessment should be raised until the option was exercised or abandoned. The Commissioners rejected this contention, holding that there had been a part disposal. Both sides appealed. The Ch D allowed the Revenue's cross-appeal and upheld the assessments, holding that *TCGA 1992, s 144** was not intended to supersede *TCGA 1992, s 21**, but provided how the chargeable gain on the grant of an option was to be computed. Accordingly, the whole amount of the option price, less the costs of granting it, was a chargeable gain under the general provisions of *TCGA 1992, s 144(1)**. The part disposal rules were not applicable to the grant of an option. *Strange v Openshaw (and related appeals)* Ch D 1983, 57 TC 544; [1983] STC 416.

Swires v Renton

Exercise of power of appointment – whether a deemed disposal

See **62.14**

The trustees of a settlement executed a deed of appointment by which the trust fund was divided into two parts. One part of the fund was appointed to the settlor's daughter. The second part was placed on trust, the income to be paid to the daughter for life. It was accepted that the absolute appointment to the daughter gave rise to a deemed disposal of that part of the trust fund under *TCGA 1992, s 71(1)**, and CGT was assessed and paid accordingly. The inspector took the view that there had also been a deemed disposal of the second part of the fund, and issued a further CGT assessment on the grounds that a new and separate settlement of the appointed fund had been created. The principal trustee appealed, contending that the exercise of the power of appointment had not created a new settlement of the fund and had not amounted to a deemed disposal under *TCGA 1992, s 71(1)**. The Special Commissioner allowed the trustee's appeal and the Ch D upheld this decision. On the evidence, the assets of the appointed fund remained subject to the trusts of the original settlement as varied by the deed of appointment, and had not become subject to the trusts of a new settlement. Accordingly, the trustees' exercise of the power of appointment had not amounted to a deemed disposal under *TCGA 1992, s 71(1)**. *Swires v Renton* Ch D 1991, 64 TC 315; [1991] STC 490.

Tarmac Roadstone Holdings Ltd v Williams

Dollar floating rate notes – whether debts 'on a security'

See **25.5**

In July 1986 a US company issued its UK parent company twelve loan notes of $5,000,000 each. The notes could only be transferred with the prior consent of the issuing company, which could be refused without any reason being given, and the issuing company could redeem them at any time. They were redeemed at par in December 1987. Because of the fall in value of the dollar, the UK company made a loss of more than £6,000,000. It claimed that this loss should be allowed against its chargeable gains. The Revenue rejected the claim, considering that the effect of *TCGA 1992, s 251(1)** was that there was no chargeable gain or allowable loss. The company appealed, contending that the loans were debts 'on a security', so that the loss was allowable. The Special Commissioners rejected this contention and dismissed the appeal. The distinguishing feature of a debt on a security was that it is 'in the nature of an investment which can be dealt in as such'. The loan notes in this case were not in the nature of investments, since they could only be transferred with the prior consent of the issuing company and that company could redeem them at any time. *Aberdeen Group Construction Ltd v CIR* and *dicta* in *WT Ramsay Ltd v CIR* applied. *Tarmac Roadstone Holdings Ltd v Williams* (Sp C 95), [1996] SSCD 409.

Taylor Clark International Ltd v Lewis

Loan to overseas subsidiary secured on property – whether a 'debt on a security'

See **25.5**

In 1984 a company gave a promissory note for $15,193,000, repayable on demand, to a US subsidiary. The loan in question was repaid in two stages, in 1986 and 1992. Because of the fall in value of the dollar, the company made a loss on the loan. The company appealed against an assessment for its accounting period ending in 1992, contending that the loan was a 'debt on a security' and that the loss could be set against its chargeable gains. The Special Commissioners dismissed the appeal, holding that the loan was not a 'debt on a security', and the CA upheld their decision. The fact that a debt was secured did not necessarily mean that it qualified as a 'debt on a security'. On the evidence, the debt here was not a marketable security in any realistic sense. *Aberdeen Group Construction Ltd v CIR*, and *dicta* in *WT Ramsay Ltd v CIR*, applied. *Taylor Clark International Ltd v Lewis* CA 1998, 71 TC 226; [1998] STC 1259.

Thompson v Salah

Sale coupled with mortgage to purchaser

See **16.4**

A taxpayer's wife, having received an offer of £20,000 for land she owned, effected the sale by mortgaging the land to the purchaser for £20,000 and conveying the fee simple the next day in consideration of a release from her obligation to repay the £20,000. The taxpayer was assessed under Sch D, Case VII on the basis that the land had been sold for £20,000. He appealed, contending that the actual conveyance was for the equity of redemption of a nil market value. The Ch D held that the two transactions together constituted a conveyance on sale of the property free of the legal charge. *Thompson v Salah* Ch D 1971, 47 TC 559; [1972] 1 All ER 530.

Tod v Mudd

Quantum of relief where new asset used partly for business and partly owned by taxpayer as tenant in common

See **59.8**

The taxpayer sold a business asset (part of the goodwill of his practice as accountant) for a chargeable gain of £155,688 in April 1982. On 1 June 1982 he and his wife entered into partnership to carry on business as hoteliers at a house being purchased in their joint names. The business was to be carried on in the part of the premises 'attributable to the share provided by' the taxpayer. The total cost of the property with the furniture and fittings and expenses was £209,093, and it was common ground that 75% of this cost (i.e. £156,820) was provided by the taxpayer, and that the premises were used as to 75% for business purposes. The property was transferred to the husband and wife upon trust as to 75% for the taxpayer and 25% for his wife as tenants in common. In an appeal against an assessment on the gain of £155,688 the issue was the taxpayer's entitlement to rollover relief. The Ch D held that since the taxpayer and his wife, as tenants in common, were entitled to an interest in every part of the property, the relief was 75% of the taxpayer's contribution to the cost (i.e. £117,615, being 75% of £156,820) and not £156,820 as contended by the taxpayer. *Tod v Mudd* Ch D 1986, 60 TC 237; [1987] STC 141.

Trennery v West

Whether settlor benefiting from 'derived property' – TCGA 1992, s 77

See **62.21**

A company director (T) held 10,000 shares in an unquoted company. He executed a scheme designed to 'avoid and reduce' the CGT liability on his disposal of these shares.

Under the scheme, on 4 April 1995 he transferred 8,000 shares to a settlement which he had executed a few days earlier, and in which he was a beneficiary. On the same day the trustees borrowed cash, using the shares as security, and advanced the cash to a second settlement, in which T had an interest. On 5 April 1995 the trustees of the first settlement executed a deed of exclusion, excluding T and his wife from being beneficiaries of the first settlement, leaving other beneficiaries (their children) with an interest in possession. On 13 April 1995 the trustees of the first settlement sold the shares. The Revenue issued a CGT assessment for 1995/96, on the basis that T had benefited from 'derived property', within *TCGA 1992, s 77*. The HL unanimously upheld the assessment. Lord Millett observed that the purpose of *section 77* was 'to prevent taxpayers from obtaining the benefit of the lower rate of tax by transferring assets pregnant with capital gains into a settlement in which they retain an interest before procuring the trustees to dispose of them'. The effect of *section 77(2)* was that T was to be regarded as having had an interest in the first settlement during 1995/96. The trust funds of the second settlement, and the income paid to T, were 'derived property' within *section 77(8)*. Lord Millett also observed that 'the fact that the settlor obtained his right to income under the trusts of the second settlement is immaterial if the income represented the income of the proceeds of property comprised in the first settlement'. *Trennery v West (and related appeals) (aka Tee v HM Inspector of Taxes)*, HL 2005, [2005] STC 214, [2005] UKHL 5. (*Note*. See now *TCGA 1992, Sch 4B* at **62.21** SETTLEMENTS designed to counter the scheme used in this case.)

Underwood v HMRC

Attempt to establish CGT loss by transaction involving option—whether effective

See **16.3**

In 1990 an individual (U) purchased some land for £1,400,000. In April 1993 he contracted to sell the land to a company (R) for £400,000. On the same day R gave him an option to repurchase the land for £400,000 plus 10% of any subsequent increase in its value. In November 1994 R contracted to sell the land to U for £420,000. On the same day U contracted to sell the property to a company (B) which he controlled. U appealed against CGT assessments for 1993/94 and 1994/95, contending that the April 1993 transactions had resulted in a CGT loss which could be set against gains he had made on the disposal of certain shares. The Special Commissioners, the Ch D and the CA unanimously rejected this contention and dismissed his appeal. Lawrence Collins LJ held that 'there was no event which resulted in a disposal of the property by (U) to (R) under the 1993 contract or an acquisition by (R) of the property under that contract'. This was not a 'bed and breakfast' transaction in which 'the owner of the asset disposes of it and then re-acquires it' since, on the evidence, the beneficial interest in the property had never been transferred to R. *Underwood v HMRC* CA 2008, [2009] STC 239; [2008] EWCA 1423.

Unilever (UK) Holdings Ltd v Smith

Shares held on 6 April 1965 – whether subsequent Scheme of Arrangement a 'reorganisation'

See **8.10, 63.2**

A company (U) had acquired all the ordinary shares in a subsidiary company (B) before 6 April 1965. On 29 April 1965 B's share capital was the subject of a Scheme of Arrangement which involved the cancellation of all its preference shares, leaving only the ordinary shares. Before the Scheme of Arrangement, U had held 62% of the voting rights in B; after the Scheme, it held 100% of the voting rights. The issued ordinary share capital had not, however, increased. U sold its ordinary shares in B, at a loss, in 1992. It sought to set this loss against a subsequent gain, and contended that the shares should be treated as having been acquired at market value on 29 April

1965, on the basis that they had been concerned in a 'reorganisation' on that date within *TCGA 1992, s 126** with the result that *TCGA 1992, Sch 2 para 19(2)* applied. The Revenue rejected the claim on the basis that the ordinary shares had not been concerned in a 'reorganisation', so that the loss should be computed on a straight-line time apportionment basis. The Special Commissioners dismissed the company's appeal and the Ch D and CA upheld this decision. Jonathan Parker LJ held that the cancellation of the preference shares did not amount to a 'reorganisation', since it did not 'alter the rights attaching either to the ordinary shares or to the preference shares'. *Unilever (UK) Holdings Ltd v Smith* CA, 2002 STI 1806.

Van Arkadie v Plunket

*Foreign assets – delayed remittances – effect of TCGA 1992, s 279**

See **49.6**

A UK resident (P) owned one-third of the share capital of a Rhodesian company, which would have been a close company if it had been resident in the UK. The company made gains on the sale of assets outside the UK. Under *TCGA 1992, s 13**, part of the gains were treated as accruing to P, although the company did not make any distributions. Regulations imposed by the de facto Rhodesian government (which had made a unilateral declaration of independence from the UK) prohibited the company from paying dividends to shareholders resident in the UK. P claimed relief under *TCGA 1992, s 279**. The Ch D held that the relief was not due (reversing the General Commissioners' decision). *TCGA 1992, s 279** applied only where a gain was represented by money or money's worth in the hands of the taxpayer. P could not receive the money because the company had not made any distributions, so that *TCGA 1992, s 279** did not apply. *Van Arkadie v Plunket* Ch D 1982, 56 TC 310; [1983] STC 54.

Varty v Lynes

Part of garden retained on sale of house and subsequently sold

See **53.5**

A taxpayer owned and occupied a house and garden (of less than one acre). He sold the house and part of the garden in June 1971. In May 1972, he sold at a substantial profit the rest of the garden for which he had meanwhile obtained planning permission. The Ch D upheld an assessment on the gain, rejecting the taxpayer's contention that it was exempted by *TCGA 1992, s 222**. *TCGA 1992, s 222(1)(b)** related only to the actual moment of disposal of the land and *TCGA 1992, s 222(2)** did not extend to a subsequent disposal. *Varty v Lynes* Ch D 1976, 51 TC 419; [1976] STC 508; [1976] 1 WLR 1091; [1976] 3 All ER 447.

Wardhaugh v Penrith Rugby Union Football Club

Non-effect of TCGA 1992, s 50 on quantum of rollover relief

See **16.13, 59.2**

In 1995 a rugby club sold some land for £315,105, resulting in a chargeable gain of £204,165. The club used the proceeds of the land to build a new clubhouse. The clubhouse cost £600,459. The club received a grant of £409,000 from the Sports Council (which was accepted as a 'public authority' within *TCGA 1992, s 50*). The club claimed rollover relief under *TCGA 1992, s 152* in respect of the total cost of the new clubhouse. The Revenue ruled that the effect of *TCGA 1992, s 50* on rollover relief was that the consideration given for the acquisition of the new clubhouse was the net amount of £191,459 after deducting the Sports Council grant and that, consequently, not all of the proceeds of the land had been reinvested in the new asset. The General Commissioners allowed the club's appeal, holding that the only computation of a gain which *section 50* would affect would be the computation on a subsequent disposal of the clubhouse. The Ch D upheld this decision. Ferris J held that there was nothing in *section 152* which required *section 50* to be applied before giving effect to rollover relief, and 'no words in *section 50* itself which are capable of producing this result'. *Wardhaugh v Penrith Rugby Union Football Club* Ch D 2002, 74 TC 499; [2002] STC 776.

Wase v Bourke

Retirement relief – sale of milk quota following cessation of dairy farming

See **24.3**

In March 1988 a dairy farmer sold his entire herd. In February 1989, having reached the age of 60, he sold his milk quota. He appealed against a CGT assessment on the gain, contending that he was entitled to retirement relief on the basis that the sale of the milk quota was 'a disposal of the whole or part of a business'. The Ch D held that retirement relief was not due, since the milk quota was simply an asset and that its disposal was not the disposal of part of a business. The relevant business activity had ceased in March 1988 when the herd was sold. The subsequent disposal of another asset did not amount to the disposal of part of the business. *Atkinson v Dancer* applied; *Jarmin v Rawlings* distinguished. *Wase v Bourke* Ch D 1995, 68 TC 109; [1996] STC 18. (Note. Retirement relief is abolished for disposals after 5 April 2003 (see **25.88** EXEMPTIONS AND RELIEFS), but this case remains relevant to ENTREPRENEURS' RELIEF (**24.3**).)

Watton v Tippett

Rollover relief (TCGA 1992, ss 152–162) – purchase of single property followed by sale of part of property

See **59.2**

In 1988 a trader purchased some business premises. In 1989 he sold part of the premises at a profit. The Revenue issued a CGT assessment and he appealed, contending that he was entitled to treat the proceeds of sale as having been used in acquiring the balance of the premises, so that he was entitled to rollover relief under *TCGA 1992, s 152**. The CA rejected this contention and upheld the assessment. The disposal had been a part disposal of the original asset. The consideration which the trader had paid for the premises could not be divided and treated as partly attributable to the part of the premises which he subsequently sold and as partly attributable to the part which he retained. The premises had been acquired 'as a single asset and for an unapportioned consideration', and continued to constitute a single asset until the part disposal. *Watton v Tippett* CA 1997, 69 TC 491; [1997] STC 893.

Whitaker v Cameron

*Election for 6 April 1965 valuation – construction of TCGA 1992, Sch 2 para 17(1)(2)**

See **8.8**

A taxpayer disposed in 1973 of land he had acquired in 1957; his appeal was against an assessment on the gain made on the time apportionment basis. The market value at 6 April 1965 was slightly above the disposal figure, but there had been no timeous application for a 6 April 1965 valuation under *TCGA 1992, Sch 2 para 17(1)**, and an extension of the time limit had been refused. If there had been a timeous application there would have been a no loss/no gain situation as a result of *Sch 2 para 17(2)**, and the taxpayer contended that it was unnecessary to make a 6 April 1965 valuation election where it would produce a no loss/no gain result. The Ch D rejected the contention. The two sub-paragraphs are closely bound up and *Sch 2 para 17(2)** has effect only if there has been an election under *Sch 2 para 17(1)**. *Whitaker v Cameron* Ch D 1982, 56 TC 97; [1982] STC 665.

Whittles v Uniholdings Ltd (No 3)

Company borrowing US dollars and entering forward contract to purchase sufficient dollars to repay loan – whether transactions to be taxed separately

See **16.11**

In May 1982 a company borrowed some US dollars to finance an investment (the rate of interest on the dollar loan being less than the company could have obtained on a sterling loan). It simultaneously entered into a forward contract to purchase sufficient dollars to repay the loan when it matured some ten months later. During the intervening ten months the pound sterling depreciated substantially against the dollar. The Revenue treated the two transactions as separate, with the result that the company had made a loss on the dollar loan which was not allowable for CGT purposes, and had made a chargeable gain on the disposal of its rights under the forward contract. The CA upheld the Revenue's contentions (reversing the decision of the Special Commissioner). Nourse LJ held that the loan and the forward contract had to be considered separately. The fact that the subject matter of the forward contract was currency did not mean that the company had acquired a 'debt' within *TCGA 1992, s 251*. The forward contract was in substance no different from any contract for the sale of real or personal property with a deferred date for completion. In the absence of any specific provision to the contrary, it would be wrong in principle to value the acquisition cost of an asset on any date other than the actual date of acquisition. The cost of acquiring the US dollars had to be valued at May 1982 and their cost to the company was the value of its promise to repay them in March 1983, together with interest during that period. *Whittles v Uniholdings Ltd (No 3)* CA, [1996] STC 914.

Williams v Evans

Relief claimed on movable machinery

See **59.4**

A civil engineering partnership sold some earth-moving vehicles at a profit and reinvested the proceeds in two similar machines. They appealed against a CGT assessment on the gain, claiming roll over relief. The Ch D dismissed their appeals. *TCGA 1992, s 155 (Class 1, Head B)** confined the relief to fixed plant and fixed machinery. The relief did not extend to movable machinery. *Williams v Evans & related appeals* Ch D 1982, 59 TC 509; [1982] STC 498; [1982] 1 WLR 972.

Williams v Merrylees

Private residence exemption

See **53.6**

A taxpayer bought in 1956 a small estate in Sussex comprising a main house with 4 acres of garden and land and a lodge at the entrance of the estate, about 200 metres from the main house. The house became his main residence and the lodge was occupied by Mr and Mrs L whom he employed as caretaker/gardener and domestic help respectively. The house and lodge were rated together. Mrs L died in 1969. In 1976 the taxpayer sold the main house and estate apart from the lodge and a garden of less than an acre, and went to live in Cornwall in a house he had previously bought as a holiday home. He retained the lodge and allowed Mr L to live in it, in case he and his wife did not like their Cornwall house and decided to return to Sussex and live in the lodge. Mr L died in 1979 and the taxpayer then sold the lodge to the purchaser of the main house. The Commissioners held that the gain on the sale of the lodge was within the private residence exemption, finding as a matter of fact that from 1956 to 1976 the lodge had been part of the taxpayer's only or main residence and within the curtilage of the property and appurtenant to the main house. Vinelott J, after reviewing *Batey v Wakefield* and *Markey v Sanders*, considered that the test was whether there is an entity which can be sensibly described as being a dwelling-house although split up into different buildings performing different functions. The propinquity of the buildings is a relevant factor but should not be considered in isolation. Here, after considerable hesitation, he felt that it would be wrong for him to interfere with the Commissioners' decision as one inconsistent with the facts. *Williams v Merrylees* Ch D 1987, 60 TC 297; [1987] STC 445; [1987] 1 WLR 1511.

Willson v Hooker

*Sale of land – whether UK resident assessable as agent for Isle of Man company – TMA 1970, s 78**

See **49.3**

An Isle of Man company realised a gain from the purchase and sale of land in Wales. The Revenue assessed the gain on an individual (W) who was resident in the UK, considering that he was acting as an agent of the company, within *TMA 1970, s 78*. The General Commissioners upheld the assessment and W appealed, contending that he was not assessable because he was not carrying on a 'regular agency', within *TMA 1970, s 82*. The Ch D rejected this contention and dismissed W's appeal, holding on the evidence that W 'was the person through whom all the transactions of (the company) in the United Kingdom were carried out during the relevant period'. *Willson v Hooker* Ch D 1995, 67 TC 585; [1995] STC 1142.

Young v Phillips

Location of letters of allotment

See 7.3

Two brothers resident and ordinarily resident in the UK, but domiciled in South Africa, owned equally the ordinary shares of three associated UK companies, each with substantial sums to the credit of its profit and loss account. On professional advice, during 1978/79 they implemented a pre-arranged scheme with the aim of 'exporting' the shares outside the UK (and so taking them outside the scope of capital transfer tax) without incurring any CGT liability. In brief, each company created new preferred ordinary shares, ranking pari passu with the existing ordinary shares save for priority in a capital repayment on a winding up; capitalised the amounts credited to profit and loss; appropriated these amounts to the taxpayers and used them in paying up, in full, new preferred ordinary shares issued to them, in respect of which the company issued to them renounceable letters of allotment. Shortly afterwards two Channel Island companies, set up for the purpose, issued to the taxpayers shares at a premium of £1,364,216 and resolved to buy from them (by now directors of the Channel Island companies) their preferred ordinary shares in the UK companies for £1,364,216. The taxpayers then went to Sark with their letters of allotment and the scheme was completed by, inter alia, letters of renunciation in favour of the Channel Island companies. CGT assessments were made on the basis that there had been a disposal of assets situated in the UK. The Special Commissioners dismissed the taxpayers' appeals, and the Ch D upheld their decision. Nicholls J held that there had been a disposal of rights against the UK companies, and that these were situated in the UK irrespective of where the letters of allotment happened to be. Further, even had he held that there had been a disposal of assets outside the UK, *W T Ramsay Ltd* and *Furniss v Dawson*, would have applied, and he would have accepted an alternative Revenue contention that *TCGA 1992, s 29(2)** applied, the relieving provisions of *TCGA 1992, ss 127, 135** being curtailed by *TCGA 1992, s 137(1)** because one of the main purposes of the issuing of the shares in the UK companies was the avoidance of liability to tax. *Young and Another v Phillips* Ch D 1984, 58 TC 232; [1984] STC 520.

Zim Properties Ltd v Proctor

Amount received as part of out-of-court settlement – whether derived from an asset

See **7.2, 10.2**

In July 1973 a company (Z) contracted to sell three properties. The date of completion was fixed for 12 July 1974. However, the sale of the properties was not completed, because the original conveyance to one of them had been lost and Z was unable to provide proof of ownership. The purchaser refused to complete and successfully sued Z for the return of its deposit. Z issued a writ against its solicitors, claiming damages of more than £100,000. Following negotiations, Z agreed to accept payment of £69,000 in two instalments, in settlement of its claim. The Revenue included the amount of the first instalment as a chargeable gain in a CT assessment. Z appealed, contending that the gain was not chargeable since it had not been derived from an asset. The Special Commissioners held that the amount was a capital sum derived from Z's right against its solicitors, and that it was acquired for the purposes of *CGTA 1979, s 19(3)* otherwise than by way of an arm's length agreement, so that its market value was deductible. The Ch D upheld this decision (against which both sides had appealed) and referred the case back to the Commissioners for figures to be agreed. *O'Brien v Benson's Hosiery (Holdings) Ltd* applied. *Zim Properties Ltd v Proctor (and cross-appeal)* Ch D 1984, 58 TC 371; [1985] STC 90. (Notes. (1) See now ESC D33. (2) *CGTA 1979, s 19(3)* was subsequently repealed; see now *TCGA 1992, s 17*.)

75 Table of Statutes

1890 Partnership Act ... 50.1
1911 Perjury Act ... 52.40
1914 Deeds of Arrangement Act ... 62.3
1925 Administration of Estates Act
s 46 ... 62.13
47(1) ... 62.13
1925 Settled Land Act ... 62.6
1925 Trustee Act ... 62.9
s 32 ... 36.8; 62.12; 62.13
33 ... 62.12
1934 Petroleum (Production) Act ... 49.19
1939 National Loans Act ... 25.15
1942 Finance Act
s 47 ... 28.2
1945 Bretton Woods Agreement Act ... 25.54
1947 Exchange Control Act ... 16.12; 45.7
1948 Agricultural Holdings Act ... 10.2
1950 Foreign Compensation Act ... 10.2
1954 Charitable Trusts (Validation) Act ... 11.2
1954 Landlord and Tenant Act ... 41.15
Pt II (ss 23–46) ... 10.2
1955 International Finance Corporation Act ... 25.54
1958 Recreational Charities Act ... 11.2
1958 Trustee Act (Northern Ireland) ... 62.9
s 33 ... 36.8
1959 Chevening Estate Act ... 25.49
1960 Charities Act ... 11.4
1960 International Development Association Act ... 25.54
1964 Continental Shelf Act ... 49.19
1964 Diplomatic Privileges Act ... 25.50
1964 Petroleum (Production) Act (Northern Ireland) ... 9.4; 59.4
1965 Finance Act
s 44(2) ... 19.5
1965 Industrial and Provident Society Act ... 49.15
1967 Agriculture Act ... 25.19
1967 Leasehold Reform Act ... 41.12; 41.15
1968 International Organisations Act ... 25.54
1968 National Loans Act ... 25.15
1968 Theft Act ... 20.9
1969 Family Law Reform Act ... 62.14
1969 Finance Act
s 58 ... 31.2
1970 Income and Corporation Taxes Act
s 248 ... 14.5
267 ... 14.11
331–337 ... 25.51
1970 Taxes Management Act
s 1 ... 30.1
(1) ... 30.1
7 ... 6.14; 42.6; 51.2; 52.3
(2) ... 62.11
(9) ... 62.11
7A ... 52.3
8 .. 6.10; 6.12; 13.5; 21.7; 34.5; 44.12; 47.1; 49.6; 51.2; 52.3; 52.5; 52.8; 58.2; 58.3; 58.6; 58.15; 58.16; 58.17
(1B), (1C) ... 58.17
8A ... 6.10; 6.12; 13.5; 21.7; 34.5; 44.12; 47.1; 49.6; 51.2; 52.3; 52.5; 52.8; 58.2; 58.3; 58.6; 58.15
(1) ... 62.11
(5) ... 62.11
8B ... 58.3
9(1)–(3A) ... 58.6
(4) ... 58.7
(6) ... 58.7
9ZA, 9ZB ... 58.7
9A ... 4.25; 34.5; 58.9; 58.18
9B, 9C ... 58.13
10 ... 52.3; 58.19
11 ... 41.4; 51.18
12 ... 58.3
(2) ... 58.3; 58.19
(3) ... 58.3; 58.19
(5) ... 58.3
12ZA ... 58.20
12ZB ... 52.5; 52.8; 58.20
12ZC–12ZL ... 58.20
12ZM, 12ZN ... 58.21
12A ... 52.6; 52.7; 58.23
12AA ... 4.37; 13.5; 21.7; 34.5; 44.12; 47.1; 49.6; 52.5; 58.16; 58.2
12AB ... 58.17
12ABA ... 58.17
12ABB ... 58.17
12AC ... 4.25; 34.5; 58.18
12AD ... 58.18
12B ... 52.15; 58.8
(5)–(5B) ... 52.15
14 ... 34.17; 58.24
19A ... 58.10
20A ... 34.12
20B ... 34.12

1970 Taxes Management Act – *cont.*
s 20BA 34.16
20BB 23.13; 34.12; 52.40
20CC(3)–(9) 34.16
20D 34.12
25, 26 .... 34.17; 58.25
27 .... 34.17; 62.6
28 .... 49.7
28ZA–28ZE 58.14; 58.18
28A 58.10; 58.12
28B 58.18
28C 6.3; 13.7; 42.10; 58.15
(4A) 51.20
28G 58.22
28H–28J 6.9
29 .... 6.10; 51.2; 51.31
(1) 6.2
(6) 6.5; 21.9
(7) 21.9
29A 6.12; 6.13
30 .... 51.31
30A 6.2
(1)–(3) 6.2
(4) 6.5
(5) 6.2
30B 6.11
31(1), (2) 5.2
31AA 6.9
31A 5.3
32 .... 6.4
33 .... 13.7
34 .... 6.13
(2) 6.13; 6.15
(3) 6.13
34A 58.6
36(1) 6.14
(1A), (1B) 6.14
(3) 6.14; 6.15; 13.5
(3A) 6.14; 6.15
40 .... 6.4; 6.15
(1) 6.13
(2) 6.15
(3) 6.13; 6.15
42 .... 13.2; 13.4; 44.4
(7) 13.2
(11) 13.3
43 .... 59.11
(1) 13.5
(2), (3) 13.5
43A–43C 13.5
46(2) 5.36
47C 5.11
48 .... 5.2
49 .... 5.3
49A 5.5
49B, 49C 5.6
49D 5.8
49E, 49G 5.7
49H 5.6
49I 5.5
50 .... 5.36

1970 Taxes Management Act – *cont.*
s 50(6)–(8) 5.20; 52.34
(9)–(11) 5.20
54 .... 5.9; 44.4
(4), (5) 5.3
55 .... 51.17
(8B)–(8D) 4.31; 51.17
(9) 51.18
56 .... 5.23
(4)–(6) 4.31
56A(8), (9) 51.18
59A 51.2
59AA 51.3; 52.8
(11), (12) 58.22
59AB 51.19
59B 51.2
(1)–(4) 51.2
(4A) 51.2
(5A) 58.15
(6) 51.2
(7), (8) 51.2
59BA 51.2
59C 5.15; 42.6; 56.3
(6) 42.3
59D, 59DA 51.4
59E, 59F 51.4
59FA 51.8
59G, 59H 51.7
Pt VI (ss 60–70) 29.3
s 61–68 .... 51.19
69 .... 42.2; 42.3; 42.7
70A 51.10
71 .... 6.7
72 .... 12.3
73 .... 12.4
74, 75 .... 6.7
77 .... 6.7; 12.3; 12.4
77B 49.19
77C 49.18
77D–77H 49.19
77I 34.17; 49.19
77J, 77K 49.19
86 .... 42.3
(1), (2) 42.3
(3) 42.3
87A 42.7
88 .... 42.3
90 .... 42.3; 42.7
91 .... 42.3
(1A), (1B) 42.7
(2A) 42.7
92 .... 42.8
93 .... 52.33
(5) 42.6
94 .... 52.4; 52.33
(6) 52.33
95 .... 42.6
95A 42.6
97A 52.18

1970 Taxes Management Act – *cont.*
s 98 ... 18.9; 22.36; 34.12; 48.12; 48.29; 51.4; 52.3; 52.8; 52.23; 58.19; 62.12; 62.13; 71.4; 71.8
(1) ... 52.33
98B(1) ... 52.6
(2A)–(4) ... 52.6
(5) ... 52.7
98C ... 52.24
99 ... 34.1; 34.12; 52.38
100 ... 52.33
100A ... 52.33
100B ... 52.34
100C ... 52.35
100D ... 52.36
102 ... 52.31
103 ... 52.38
103A ... 42.3
103ZA 52.31; 52.33; 52.34; 52.36; 52.38
105 ... 52.37
106A ... 20.9; 52.40
106B–106H ... 52.40
107 ... 20.9; 52.40
107A ... 62.11
108 ... 34.3; 34.11; 34.17
(1) ... 58.19
(2), (3) ... 51.25
109(3A)–(5) ... 42.7
109B–109F ... 49.19
113(1) ... 58.4
114(1) ... 6.2
115A ... 58.2
118 ... 12.3
(1) ... 58.18
(2) ... 13.7; 52.2; 52.31
(3) ... 58.18
(5) ... 6.14
Sch 1AA ... 34.16
1A ... 4.3; 13.3; 13.4; 36.4
para 2A(4), (5) ... 52.15
5 ... 4.25
Sch 1AB ... 13.7
1B ... 13.4; 19.7
para 2 ... 13.2; 19.7
Sch 3ZA ... 51.2
paras 1–3, 5 ... 51.3
Sch 3ZB
para 1–9 ... 51.8
10(5) ... 51.8
11, 12 ... 51.8
14–17 ... 51.8
Sch 3A ... 58.2

1971 Finance Act
Sch 14
Pt V ... 19.5

1971 Town and Country Planning Act ... 10.2

1972 European Communities Act ... 25.54

1973 Domicile and Matrimonial Proceedings Act ... 57.34

1973 Finance Act
s 38(2) ... 49.19
(8) ... 49.19
Sch 15 ... 49.19

1973 Matrimonial Causes Act ... 10.2; 36.4

1973 Social Security Act ... 31.2

1974 Friendly Societies Act ... 25.51

1975 OECD Support Fund Act ... 7.3

1975 Oil Taxation Act ... 49.19

1978 Finance Act
s 77 ... 31.2

1978 Interpretation Act ... 41.1; 41.4

1979 Capital Gains Tax Act
s 17 ... 44.3
19(3) ... 44.15
32(5), (6) ... 16.12
56A ... 36.12
126 ... 36.8; 36.9
148 ... 9.6
Sch 4 ... 36.9
6
para 2(2) ... 19.5

1979 Customs and Excise Management Act
s 50 ... 20.9
167, 168 ... 20.9
170 ... 20.9
170B ... 20.9

1980 Finance Act
s 79 ..... 4.10; 9.11; 36.12; 39.2; 62.17; 62.18

1980 Limitation Act
s 32(1) ... 13.8
35 ... 13.8

1981 British Telecommunications Act ... 51.27

1981 Finance Act
s 78 ... 9.11
80(3) ... 16.12
88(2)–(7) ... 62.15
90(2) ... 16.12

1981 Supreme Court Act
s 31, 31A ... 5.35

1982 Administration of Justice Act ... 70.12

1982 Finance Act
s 82 ... 9.11
148 ... 9.6; 25.79; 38.4

1984 Finance Act
s 66(3) ... 16.12

1984 Friendly Societies Act ... 25.51

1984 Inheritance Tax Act
s 13 ... 25.91; 63.16

1984 Inheritance Tax Act – *cont.*
s 13A 63.16
19 .... 36.10
24 .... 25.70; 36.10
27 .... 36.10
28 .... 25.91
30 .... 36.10
(1) 25.85
31 .... 25.41; 25.85
32 .... 25.85
35A 25.85
49A, 49B 62.17
57A 36.10
71(4) 36.10
71B(2) 36.10
71C, 71D 62.17
71E(2) 36.10
78(1) 36.10
86 .... 25.91; 63.16
89B(1) 62.17
102 .... 63.16
124A 36.5
164 .... 39.2
165(1), (2) 39.2
168 .... 39.2
230(3) 11.9
Sch 3 ... 11.7; 11.8; 25.41; 25.76; 25.85; 27.2
4
para 9 .... 36.10
16, 17 .... 36.10
1984 Police and Criminal Evidence Act 34.1
s 12, 13 .... 34.5; 34.11; 34.12
14 .... 34.14
14B 34.16
1984 Telecommunications Act 14.11
1985 Companies Act ... 29.2; 52.4; 58.19
s 117 .... 18.14
135 .... 4.17
143 .... 49.15
245C 31.2
425 .... 63.7
1985 Family Law (Scotland) Act 36.4
1985 Finance Act
s 68(4)(5) 9.6
1985 Housing Act 41.12
1985 Transport Act 9.6; 14.11
1985 Trustee Savings Banks Act 9.6; 14.11
1986 Agriculture Act
s 13 .... 7.9
1986 Agricultural Holdings Act
s 60 .... 10.2
64 .... 10.2
1986 Airports Act 14.11
1986 Building Societies Act 7.7; 14.11; 54.3; 63.27
1986 Financial Services Act 70.4
1986 Gas Act 14.11
1986 Insolvency Act 14.4
s 247 .... 49.15
411 .... 65.5
1987 Housing (Scotland) Act 41.12
1987 Reverter of Sites Act 11.3
1987 Territorial Sea Act 49.19
1988 Arms Control and Disarmament (Privileges and Immunities) Act 25.50
1988 Housing Act 25.53
1988 Income and Corporation Taxes Act
s 56(3) 11.4
65(5) 55.2
85B 22.17
95 .... 15.5
109A 67.3
122 .... 47.1
122(1) 47.1
(5)–(7) 47.1
128 .... 7.8
130 .... 44.16
135 .... 22.24
138 .... 22.12
140A 22.14
140B, 140C 22.14
140D 22.15
162 .... 22.14
168(8), (9) 51.26
185 .... 22.27
(7) 22.27
186 .... 22.28
187 .... 22.27; 22.28
192(1) 57.37
201AA 67.8
207 .... 57.35
208 .... 63.11; 63.19
209(2) 4.14
(4) 4.14; 69.2
254 .... 63.19
334 .... 57.29
338 .... 14.5
Pt X, Ch IV (ss 402–413) 51.4
s 404 .... 29.3; 59.10
416 .... 18.7; 51.26
417 .... 70.9
(1) 62.20
(3) 23.4
(4) 23.4
(5) 51.26
(6) 51.26
423–426 .... 63.23
427 .... 63.23
428–430 .... 63.23
431 .... 70.7

1988 Income and Corporation Taxes Act – *cont.*
s 452(1) 69.2
459 .... 25.51
461 .... 25.51
461A 29.3
462 .... 25.51
463 .... 25.51
464, 465 .... 25.51
466 .... 25.51
(2) 70.7
468(1A) 70.8
(10), (11) 70.8
468A 11.4; 70.8
468H(3), (4) 70.3
486(8) 9.6; 14.11
(9) 14.11
508A 25.30
513 .... 14.11
519A 11.7
540(3) 43.2
542(3) 43.2
544 .... 43.2
558(4) 31.2
573 35
574 .... 23.13; 25.22; 35
575 .... 23.13; 35
576 .... 23.13; 44.16
660B 25.30
660G(2) 48.14; 48.23
685G 62.12
691(2) 36.8
703(1) 4.14
710(1A) 63.20
711–728 .... 8.4
730A(1) 20.2
747 .... 49.9
(3) 4.20
748–751 .... 49.9
751A 6.10
752–756 .... 49.9
765 .... 57.33
(1) 49.17; 49.18
765A 52.23
767A 34.5; 51.26; 51.27
767AA 34.5; 51.26; 51.27
767B, 767C 51.26; 51.27
769 .... 34.5
790 .... 49.9
815A(3) 49.14
824 .... 56.3
(8) 56.3
826 .... 56.4
826A 56.4
832(1) 62.7
833(2) 2.6
834(1) 44.3
838 .... 66.1
(1) 29.2
839 .... 20.2; 11.10
840 .... 23.5; 23.6; 44.16; 70.7

1988 Income and Corporation Taxes Act – *cont.*
s 840A 20.3
841 .... 63.30
842 .... 29.11
Sch 9 .... 22.27; 22.28
para 3 .... 22.28
9 .... 22.30
15 .... 22.24
Sch 10 .... 22.28
18 .... 4.20; 29.2
para 1(5) 63.8
Sch 19 .... 63.23
para 12 .... 63.10
Sch 24 .... 49.9
25 .... 49.9
26 .... 49.9
para 3–6 .... 49.9

1988 Finance Act
s 121 .... 52.3; 58.18
127 .... 34.18; 52.23
130–132 .... 49.18
Sch 12
para 6 .... 63.27
Sch 14
Pt VIII 58.10

1989 Electricity Act 14.11; 25.13

1989 Finance Act
s 67, 68 .... 22.29
69 .... 22.29; 22.30; 22.31
70–74 .... 22.29
102 .... 51.4
139 .... 44.14
149(5) 52.37
157 .... 42.4
159(1) 52.2
(3), (4) 52.2
168(1) 52.37
(5) 52.37
178 .... 42.7; 56.4
179(1) 56.4
(4) 56.4
180(6) 56.4
182, 182A 31.6
Sch 5 .... 22.29; 22.30; 22.36
para 7 .... 22.29

1989 Law of Property (Miscellaneous Provisions) Act 16.4

1989 Water Act 14.11

1990 Capital Allowances Act
s 121 .... 9.4

1990 Finance Act
Sch 12 .... 14.11
para 2(1) 9.6

1990 Law Reform (Miscellaneous Provisions) (Scotland) Act 11.2; 31.2

1992 Charities Act 11.2

1992 Employment Rights Act
s 205A(1) 22.26

1992 Finance (No 2) Act
s 24 .... 29.2
44 .... 49.13
45 .... 49.14
46(1) 9.6
(2) 9.6
(4) 49.12
50 .... 49.14
51(3) 31.6
56 .... 9.6; 25.50
77 .... 9.6
Sch 6
para 5 .... 29.2
10 .... 29.2
Sch 17
para 5 .... 9.6

1992 Friendly Societies Act
.... 25.51; 29.2

1992 Social Security Administration Act
.... 31.2

1992 Social Security Contributions and Benefits Act 62.9
s 64 .... 36.8; 62.13
67 .... 62.13
71 .... 36.8; 62.13
72 .... 62.13
Sch 1
para 3A, 3B 22.6; 22.13; 22.15

1992 Taxation of Chargeable Gains Act
s 1 .... 1.2
2(1) 1.2; 49.5; 57.29
(2) 2.6; 44.2; 48.5; 48.13; 48.15
(2A), (2B) 41.26
(3) 44.2
(4), (5) 44.2
(6), (7) 44.2
(7A) 14.10
(7B) 44.2
2A 25.93
2B 14.10; 44.3
2C–2F 14.10
3 .... 2.6; 48.5
(1) 2.6; 44.21; 62.8; 62.9
(1A) 55.2
(2)–(4) 2.6; 62.8; 62.9
(5) 2.6; 44.8; 62.8; 62.9
(5A)–(5D) 2.6; 44.8
(6) 58.3
(7) 2.6; 19.9; 58.3
(7A) 19.9
(8) 58.3
3A 58.3
4 .... 2.1; 2.2; 62.7
(1) 62.7
(1AA) 62.7
(3) 2.3; 62.7
(3A) 14.10
(3B) 41.26; 41.33

1992 Taxation of Chargeable Gains Act – *cont.*
s 4(10), (11) 2.1
4A 2.1; 2.2
4B 2.1; 2.2; 2.3; 62.7
4BA 2.1
8 .... 44.20
(1) 14.3; 14.6; 29.20
(2) 14.6; 44.7
(3) 14.2
(4) 14.2; 63.19
(5) 14.2
(6) 14.4
9 .... 57.29
(2) 57.35
(3), (4) 57.29; 57.30
10 .... 1.2; 14.11; 41.26; 44.3; 44.19; 49.4; 49.5; 50.2; 51.26
(1) 22.24; 49.3; 49.18
(2) 49.3
(3) 49.3; 49.13; 49.18; 49.19
(4)–(6) 49.3
10A 44.2; 48.13; 48.24; 48.27; 49.5; 49.7; 62.13
(2) 44.19
(3) 22.30
10AA(1)–(5) 49.5
10B 14.2; 14.11; 14.15; 18.20; 22.30; 29.3; 29.19; 41.26; 41.33; 44.3; 49.4; 49.7; 49.13; 49.15; 49.19; 51.26; 66.5
(3) 49.3
11(1) 25.65; 53.8
(2)–(4) 25.50
12 .... 48.15; 55.2
(1) 55.8
(1A) 55.2
13 .... 9.3; 29.7; 48.5; 48.15; 48.18; 49.5; 49.6; 49.7; 62.23; 63.23
14 .... 49.7
14A 49.7
14B 1.2; 41.26
14D 1.2; 41.26; 44.3; 58.20
14E 41.26
14F–14H 41.27
15 .... 16.2
16(1) 44.3
(2) 25.2; 44.3; 53.2; 66.3
(2A) 24.8; 44.4
(3) 44.3; 48.5; 49.3; 49.5
(4) 44.3; 55.8
16ZA 55.2
16ZB 2.6; 58.3
16ZC, 16ZD 55.2
16A 44.7
17 .... 8.6; 16.11; 19.5; 22.5; 22.14; 22.24; 22.25; 45.1; 62.21; 63.13
(1) 7.7; 15.11; 22.3; 27.1; 36.3
18 .... 4.12
(1), (2) 4.12
(3) 44.6; 50.17; 62.16

1992 Taxation of Chargeable Gains Act – *cont.*

s 18(4), (5) 44.6
(6), (7) 4.12; 7.7
(8) 4.12
19 .... 4.13; 19.5; 63.13
20 .... 4.13
21 .... 7.7
(1) 7.2; 52.14
(2) 16.5
22 .... 10.2; 41.16; 59.7
(1) 7.9; 10.4; 41.10
(2) 16.4
23 .... 59.4
(1) 10.3
(2) 9.8; 10.3
(3) 10.3
(4) 9.11; 10.2; 10.4
(b) 49.5
(5) 9.11; 10.2; 10.4
(b) 49.5
(6) 10.3; 10.4
(8) 10.3; 10.4
24 .... 49.13; 49.15
(1) . 10.2; 16.4; 18.10; 18.19; 44.11; 44.15; 44.18; 62.21; 69.7
(1A) 42.6
(2) 4.17; 18.10; 18.19; 44.11; 44.15; 44.18; 66.19
(3) 10.2; 44.11
25 .... 49.3; 51.8
(3) 49.13
25A 7.6; 45.1
26 .... 15.6; 16.3
26A 16.7
27 .... 16.4
28 .... 16.4; 25.1; 41.10; 53.7; 66.10; 66.12
(1) 16.4
(2) 7.7
29(1) 4.8
(2) 4.8; 4.11; 44.7
(3) 4.8
(4) 4.8; 41.23
(5) 4.8
29A(3)–(5) 45.2
30 .... 4.10; 4.11; 18.19; 44.15; 44.18
(1) 4.10
(2) 4.10
(3)–(7) 4.10
(9) 4.10
31 .... 4.10; 4.11
31A 4.10
32 .... 4.10
33 .... 4.10
34 .... 4.10
35 .... 9.2; 9.3; 9.6; 9.7; 9.9; 19.5
(1) 8.3; 9.2; 9.3; 9.6; 9.8; 9.10; 38.4
(2) 8.3; 9.2; 9.3; 9.6; 9.8; 9.10; 38.4; 64.4

1992 Taxation of Chargeable Gains Act – *cont.*

s 35(2A) 9.2
(3) 9.2; 9.3; 9.6; 38.4; 50.7
(4) 9.2; 9.6; 38.4
(5) 8.3: 9.3; 9.6; 13.5; 50.16
(6) 9.3
(7) 9.3; 50.16
(8) 9.3
(9) 8.1
(10) 9.6
35A 9.6
36 .... 9.11; 50.7
37 .... 15.10; 16.10; 22.7; 22.9; 39.1; 43.1; 55.6; 63.20
(1) 49.11; 50.17; 63.19; 70.10
37A 16.10
38 .... 14.5; 14.12; 16.2; 36.4; 36.10; 36.12; 62.21
(1) 7.7; 9.6; 16.11; 22.6; 22.8; 22.22; 22.25; 37.2; 38.2; 49.11; 53.11; 55.6; 69.8
(2) 16.11
(3) 16.13
(4) 16.11; 16.13
39 .... 15.10; 25.19; 43.1; 62.21; 63.20
(1) 16.13; 25.22; 39.1; 50.17
(2) 16.13; 25.22; 39.1
(3) 25.22
(4) 39.1
40 .... 14.5
41 .... 8.11; 9.7; 16.5; 16.13; 25.19
(1)–(7) 16.13
41A 16.13; 45.1
42 .. 7.9; 9.8; 16.5; 41.8; 41.11; 41.16; 41.17; 50.6; 55.6; 72.5
(2) 25.86
43 .... 9.9; 9.11; 16.5; 29.19; 48.15
44 .... 72.2; 72.4
(1)(d) 72.7
45 .... 25.4; 25.19
46 .... 7.8; 41.15; 72.2; 72.4
47 . 8.11; 9.7; 25.19; 41.15; 72.2; 72.4
47A, 47B 25.19
48 .... 16.13; 63.6
48A 41.30
49 .... 16.13; 29.13
(1) 41.24; 63.5; 63.7
(2), (3) 41.24
50 .... 16.13
51(1) 25.21
(2) 25.25
52(1) 16.2
(2), (3) 39.1
(4) 7.9; 16.5; 41.10; 53.2; 54.4; 59.8
(5) 39.1
52A 9.6; 38.4
53 .... 9.6; 38.2; 38.4
(1) 38.4
(3) 16.13

1992 Taxation of Chargeable Gains Act – *cont.*

s 54 .... 38.2; 38.4
(2) 64.6
55 .... 9.2
(1) 9.2; 9.3; 9.6; 9.7; 9.9
(2) 9.2; 9.3; 9.9
(3) 9.7
(4) 9.9
(5), (6) 9.6; 50.7
(7) 9.6
(8) 9.6
(9)–(11) 9.6
56(1) 16.5; 38.3; 38.4
(2) 9.6; 38.4
(3) 38.4
(4) 38.4
57 .... 38.5
57A 14.10
57C 2.1
58 . 9.6; 23.15; 25.22; 36.8; 37.2; 38.4; 46.5; 49.5; 65.46; 71.12
(1) .. 4.15; 16.5; 25.22; 54.4; 57.34; 63.8; 70.9
(2) 22.26
59(2)–(4) 50.2
59A(1) 36.8; 50.18; 59.3
(2)–(6) 50.18
59B, 59C 50.22
60 .... 12.2; 25.44; 48.15; 62.3
(1) 62.16; 63.27
61 .... 70.12
62 .... 19.5; 44.11
(1) 19.2
(2), (2A) 19.7
(3) 19.9
(4) 19.8; 19.14; 54.4; 63.8; 70.9
(4A) 19.14
(5) 19.6
(6) 19.8; 48.14
(7)–(9) 19.8
(10) 19.2; 62.5
63 .... 19.3
63A 19.4
64(1) 16.12; 19.14; 62.16
(2), (3) 19.6; 19.14
65(1) 6.6; 19.9
(2) 6.6; 19.9; 46.2
(3) 48.2
(4) 6.6; 19.9; 48.2
66(1)–(5) 62.3
67 .... 36.12; 62.4; 62.15
(1)–(3) 39.2
(4)–(6) 9.11
68 .... 62.3
68A–68C 62.5
69(1) 48.1; 62.6; 62.8
(2) 48.1
(2A)–(2F) 48.1
(3) 62.6
(4) 62.10

1992 Taxation of Chargeable Gains Act – *cont.*

s 69A 62.12
70 .... 62.14
71 .... 11.8; 16.11; 19.5; 25.91; 63.27
(1) .. 36.6; 36.8; 36.9; 36.10; 62.12; 62.14; 62.15; 62.16; 62.18; 63.14
(2)–(2D) 62.16
(3) 62.16
72(1) .. 36.6; 36.8; 36.10; 62.17; 62.18
(1A)–(2A) 62.17
(3), (4) 62.4; 62.18
(5)(6) 62.17; 62.18
73 .... 9.6; 49.5; 62.18
(1) 62.18
(2), (3) 62.18
74 ... 36.8; 36.11; 36.12; 62.17; 62.18
75 .... 62.17; 62.18
76 .... 62.4; 62.20
(1) 48.4; 62.15; 63.27
(1A), (1B) 48.4
(2) 48.4; 62.15
(3) 48.4
76A 62.20
76B 62.21
77 ... 25.86; 44.19; 48.5; 48.14; 62.13
(1) 21.10
78 .... 48.5; 48.23
79 .... 48.5; 48.23
79A 62.22
79B 62.23
80 .... 6.6; 48.2; 48.4
(2) 62.12
80A 48.2
81, 82 .... 48.2
83 .... 48.2; 48.4
83A 48.3
84 .... 48.2
85 .... 48.4
85A 48.24
(2) 48.14
86 . 2.6; 9.3; 44.2; 44.19; 48.15; 48.16; 49.5; 57.2; 62.21
(1) 48.5
(2), (3) 48.5
(4) 48.5; 48.27
(4ZA) 48.5
(5) 48.5
86A 48.13; 48.24
87 ... 2.6; 9.3; 11.3; 16.12; 19.7; 44.3; 44.19; 48.13; 48.14; 48.15; 48.16; 48.17; 48.18; 48.19; 48.20; 48.21; 48.24; 48.26; 49.5; 55.2; 62.21
(1) 48.14
(2) 48.13; 48.14; 48.15; 48.16; 48.17; 48.18; 48.19; 48.20; 48.21
(3) 48.13; 48.14
(4) 48.16; 48.23
(b) 48.13
(5) 48.16; 48.23
(6) 48.14

1992 Taxation of Chargeable Gains Act – *cont.*

s 87A ... 48.15
87B ... 48.15; 48.17
87C ... 48.15; 48.17
88 ... 48.16; 48.23
(4) ... 48.27
89 ... 48.16
(2) ... 2.6; 19.7; 44.2; 44.19; 48.4; 48.13; 48.14; 48.15; 48.16; 48.17; 48.18; 48.19; 48.20; 48.21; 48.23; 49.5; 55.2; 62.21
90 ... 48.15; 48.18; 48.24; 48.26
90A ... 48.18; 48.24
91 ... 48.21; 48.24; 67.2
(3) ... 48.28
92–95 ... 48.24
96 ... 35; 48.14; 48.15; 48.19; 48.24
97(1) ... 48.14; 48.26
(2)–(5) ... 48.14
(6) ... 44.3; 48.14; 48.15
(7) ... 48.14; 48.26
(7A) ... 48.14
(8)–(10) ... 48.14; 48.26
97A–97C ... 48.14
98 ... 48.20
98A ... 48.29
99 ... 62.3; 63.2
(1) ... 70.3
(2) ... 70.3; 70.8
(3) ... 70.3
99A ... 70.3
(3) ... 14.11; 25.60
99AA ... 70.8
99B ... 49.11; 70.3
100(1) .. 70.3; 70.4; 70.8; 70.12; 71.10
(2) ... 14.11; 70.7
(2A), (2B) ... 70.7
(3) ... 70.12
100A ... 14.10
101 ... 14.11
101A ... 29.11
101B ... 14.11
101C ... 29.12
102 ... 70.2
103A, 103B ... 49.11
103D ... 70.11
103E, 103F ... 70.2
103G, 103H ... 49.11; 70.2
103I–103K ... 70.2
103KA ... 50.20
(2) ... 2.1
103KB ... 50.21
103KC–103KF ... 50.20
103KBG ... 50.21
103KH(1) ... 50.20
(2) ... 50.21
104 ... 62.12; 64.2; 71.11
(1) ... 64.3; 64.4
(2) ... 64.3
(3) ... 8.4; 64.3; 64.4

1992 Taxation of Chargeable Gains Act – *cont.*

s 104(3A) ... 64.4
(4) ... 64.4
(4A) ... 63.14
(5), (6) ... 64.4
105 ... 8.4; 64.2; 64.3; 71.11
(1) ... 44.15
105A(4) ... 23.13; 23.15
(7), (8) ... 23.13; 23.15
106A ... 8.4; 54.3; 64.2; 71.11
107 ... 8.4; 71.11
(1), (1A) ... 64.3
(2)–(9) ... 64.3
108 ... 8.4; 64.6
(1) ... 54.3
109 ... 62.12; 64.5
(4), (5) ... 8.3
110 ... 64.4
113 ... 38.7
114 ... 64.4
115 ... 54.3; 54.4
(1) ... 7.7; 7.8; 28.1; 54.2
(2), (3) ... 7.8
116 ... 15.5; 15.6; 18.21; 25.86; 29.17; 29.21; 44.14; 54.4; 71.12
(1)–(9) ... 54.4
(10) ... 9.11; 15.6; 22.33; 24.12; 25.86; 29.19; 36.2; 36.10; 44.14; 49.5; 54.3; 54.4; 66.14; 66.20; 70.9
(11) ... 9.11; 44.14; 49.5; 54.4
(12) ... 54.4
(13)–(14) ... 54.4
(15) ... 44.14; 54.4
(16) ... 54.4
116A ... 15.5
116B ... 15.6
117 ... 54.3
(1) ... 63.8
(2AA) ... 63.22
(8A) ... 63.22
(13) ... 44.13
119 ... 63.20
119A ... 7.7; 22.6; 22.8; 22.12; 22.13; 22.15; 22.16; 22.22
(7) ... 22.2
119B . 22.6; 22.8; 22.12; 22.13; 22.15; 22.16
120 ... 7.7
(1) ... 22.22
(2) ... 22.6; 22.8; 22.14; 22.22; 22.25; 22.27
(3) ... 22.8
(4) ... 22.6; 22.22
(5A) ... 22.14
(6) ... 22.25; 22.27
(7) ... 22.2
(8) ... 22.2; 22.14
(9) ... 22.6
121 ... 25.15

1992 Taxation of Chargeable Gains Act – *cont.*
s 122 .... 4.14; 10.2; 14.12; 22.22; 24.3; 24.4; 29.4; 49.13; 49.15; 63.2; 63.4; 63.7; 63.8
(1) 63.11
(2) 63.11
(4) 9.8; 63.11
(5) 63.11
123 .... 63.4
124 .... 16.12; 63.10; 63.23
125 .... 4.14; 16.12
125A 4.10; 44.15; 44.18
Pt IV, Ch II (ss 126–140) 54.4
s 126 ... 8.5; 14.12; 18.21; 23.13; 24.12; 25.22; 40.9; 40.10;63.10; 63.19; 70.2; 71.11
(1) 38.6; 63.2
(2) 25.22; 63.2; 71.11
(3) 63.2
127 ... 8.5; 14.12; 18.16; 18.21; 22.22; 23.13; 24.12; 25.22; 25.86; 29.3; 29.7; 29.17; 37.2; 38.6; 40.10;44.15; 44.18; 49.11; 54.4; 57.34; 60.36; 63.2; 66.9; 66.16; 66.16; 66.16; 70.2; 70.9; 71.11
128 .... 14.12; 18.21; 22.22; 23.13; 25.22; 29.17; 49.11; 54.4; 63.6; 70.2; 71.11
(1) 38.6; 63.2
(2) 63.2
(3) 63.2
(4) 63.2
129, 130 .. 14.12; 18.21; 22.22; 23.13; 25.22; 29.17; 54.4; 63.2; 70.2; 71.11
131 .... 29.17; 38.6; 64.6
132 .... 4.10; 25.5; 44.12; 44.13; 49.3; 62.21; 63.6; 63.8; 63.20; 70.2
(1) 38.6
(3) 25.5; 54.3
133 .... 63.8; 70.2
(4) 9.8
133A 63.8; 70.2
134 .... 9.11; 49.5; 63.8; 70.2
135 . 4.15; 18.22; 18.23; 23.13; 24.12; 25.5; 25.22; 29.3; 40.9; 40.10; 44.15; 44.18; 49.11; 49.16; 60.43; 63.5; 63.6; 66.15; 70.2; 70.10; 71.11; 71.12
(1) 63.5
(2) 63.7
(3) 38.6; 63.5; 63.7
136 . 4.15; 14.11; 14.15; 18.19; 18.22; 23.13; 24.12; 25.5; 25.22; 40.9; 40.10; 44.15; 44.18; 49.11; 49.13; 49.14; 49.15; 60.36; 60.43; 63.7; 66.15; 70.2; 70.10; 71.11; 71.12
(1) 25.5
(2) 63.7
(4) 63.7

1992 Taxation of Chargeable Gains Act – *cont.*
s 136(6) 63.7
137 ... 4.15; 14.15; 25.5; 44.15; 44.18; 49.13; 49.14; 49.15; 63.5; 63.7; 70.2
(1) 25.5
138 . 4.15; 14.15; 49.13; 49.14; 49.15; 60.42; 63.5; 63.7
(1) 4.15; 14.11
(2)–(5) 51.27
138A 44.19; 63.6; 70.2
139 .... 4.16; 9.6; 14.11; 14.15; 15.14; 29.17; 38.4; 49.3; 49.15; 54.4; 70.9
(4) 14.11; 70.3
(5) 4.15; 14.11
140 .... 9.11; 29.17; 49.12; 49.14
(4), (5) 9.11
140A ... 4.18; 9.6; 15.14; 29.7; 29.17; 49.3; 49.12; 49.13; 54.4; 70.9
(4) 49.3
140B 4.15; 14.11; 49.13
140C 29.7; 49.14
(8) 49.12
140D 4.15; 14.11; 49.14
140DA 49.13; 49.14; 49.16
140E .. 9.6; 15.14; 29.7; 29.17; 49.12; 49.15; 49.16; 54.4; 59.9; 70.9
140F 49.14; 49.15
140G 49.15; 49.16; 63.7
140H–140L 49.16
142, 142A 63.10
143 .... 7.7; 7.8;
(1), (2) 7.7; 7.8
(3), (4) 7.8
(5)....................... 7.7; 7.8
(6) 7.8
(7), (8) 7.8
144 .... 7.8
(1) 7.7; 59.4
(2) 7.7; 15.11
(3) 7.7; 22.6
(4) 7.7; 22.7
(5) 7.7
(6) 7.7; 38.8
(7) 16.6
(8) 7.7; 63.9
(9) 7.7
144ZA 7.7; 22.6; 22.22
144ZB–144ZD 7.7
144A 7.8
(1)–(3) 7.7; 7.8; 38.8
(4), (5) 7.7
145 .... 38.8
146 .... 7.7
147 .... 63.9
148 .... 7.7
148A–148C 7.8
149 .... 7.7
149A 7.7; 22.3
149AA 22.13; 22.15

1992 Taxation of Chargeable Gains Act – *cont.*
s 149AB ... 22.16
149B ... 22.14
149C ... 22.37
150 ... 25.22
(5) ... 64.3
150A ... 23.13; 23.15; 23.17; 23.18
(5) ... 23.13; 64.3
150B ... 23.13
150C ... 23.15; 23.18
150E ... 60.43
150F ... 60.44
150G ... 60.45
151 ... 25.30
151A ... 71.11
(1) ... 71.12
151B ... 71.10; 71.11
151C, 151D ... 63.21
151E ... 15.3
151J, 151K ... 3.2
151N ... 3.2; 54.3
151O–151R ... 3.2
151S(3) ... 3.2
151U–151W ... 3.2
151X ... 3.2
151Y ... 3.3
152 ... 9.11; 16.5; 16.13; 22.31; 22.32; 29.17; 41.1; 48.2; 49.3; 59.2; 59.5; 59.6, 59.8
(1) ... 59.3; 59.6
(b) ... 49.5
(2) ... 59.6
(3) ... 59.2; 59.6
(4), (5) ... 59.2
(6), (7) ... 59.8
(9) ... 59.2; 59.6; 59.8
(10) ... 59.7
(11) ... 59.8
153 ... 16.5; 22.31; 22.32; 29.17; 59.8
(1)(b) ... 49.5
153A ... 22.31; 22.32; 59.11
154 ... 16.5; 22.31; 22.32; 59.9
(2) ... 9.11; 35; 49.5; 59.10
(3) ... 22.31
(4) ... 9.11; 49.5
155 ... 16.5; 22.31; 22.32; 41.1; 59.4; 59.5; 59.9; 69.6; 69.7
156 ... 16.5; 22.31; 22.32; 59.4
156ZA ... 59.3
156ZB ... 59.3; 59.4
156A ... 59.3
157 ... 16.5; 22.31; 22.32; 59.3; 59.5
158 ... 16.5; 22.31; 22.32; 59.2; 59.5
159 ... 29.2; 49.3
161 ... 29.4; 41.4
(1) ... 15.12; 16.9; 59.7
(2) ... 16.9
(3) ... 15.12; 16.9; 29.23
(3A) ... 16.9
(4) ... 16.9

1992 Taxation of Chargeable Gains Act – *cont.*
s 161(5) ... 41.4; 41.6
(6) ... 41.6
162 ... 9.11; 37.2; 37.3; 59.7; 59.9; 70.10
(3)(b) ... 49.5
162A ... 37.2
162B, 162C ... 37.4
164A, 164B ... 25.86
164F ... 23.15; 24.10; 25.86
164FA ... 23.15; 24.10; 25.86
164FF, 164FG ... 25.86
164G ... 25.86
164I, 164J ... 25.86
164L, 164N ... 25.86
165 ... 9.11; 27.4; 36.6; 36.7; 36.8; 36.11; 37.2; 39.2; 48.2; 54.3; 62.17; 62.18; 62.22; 66.5; 66.21
(1), (2) ... 36.2
(3) ... 36.2; 36.6
(4) ... 36.4; 36.6; 36.8; 45.2
(5) ... 36.5; 36.6
(6) ... 36.4
(7) ... 36.4; 36.6
(8), (9) ... 36.3
(10), (11) ... 36.4; 39.2
165A ... 24.3; 36.3
166, 167 ... 36.8
167A ... 36.4
168 ... 9.11; 36.8; 36.11; 36.12
168A ... 36.8
169 ... 36.11; 36.12
169A ... 36.8; 36.11
169B ... 36.8; 36.11
169C ... 36.8; 36.11
(7) ... 27.4
169D–169E ... 36.8; 36.11
169F ... 36.8; 36.11; 62.14
169G ... 36.8; 36.11
169H(2) ... 24.2
169I ... 24.3
169J ... 24.4
169K ... 24.5
169L ... 24.7
169LA ... 24.7
169M(1)–(3) ... 24.6
(4) ... 24.8
169N ... 24.8
169O ... 24.9
169P ... 24.10
169Q, 169R ... 24.12
169S(1) ... 24.2
(2)–(4) ... 24.3; 24.4
(5) ... 24.3; 24.4; 24.10
169SA ... 24.3
169T–169V ... 24.11
169VC ... 40.2
169VD ... 40.2
169VE–169VG ... 40.4
169VH ... 40.3; 40.7

1992 Taxation of Chargeable Gains Act – *cont.*
s 169VJ 40.2
169VK 40.5
169VL 40.5
169VM 40.6
169VN–169VS 40.9
169VT 40.10
169VU–169VX 40.7
169VY 40.2; 40.7
170 .... 4.11; 9.6; 29.2; 44.13; 49.3
(1) 29.2
(2) 29.2; 49.3
(3), (4) 29.2
(4A) 29.2
(5)–(8) 29.2
(9) 29.2; 49.3
(10) 29.2; 29.16; 29.19
(10A) 29.2; 29.16; 29.19
(11) 29.2
(12)–(14) 29.2
171 .. 4.10; 4.18; 9.5; 9.6; 29.3; 29.11; 29.12; 29.13; 29.19; 36.8; 38.4; 48.15; 49.3; 49.12; 66.10; 66.10
(1) .. 4.14; 4.15; 14.11; 16.5; 43.1; 54.4; 70.9
(2) 71.3
171A 29.13
171B 29.13
172 .... 4.18; 9.6; 36.8; 54.4
173 .... 29.4
174(4), (5) 8.1
175 .... 59.10
(1) 49.7; 59.3
(2A) 59.11
176 .... 4.17; 4.18
177 .... 4.18
177A 29.18
179 .... 4.10; 14.11; 14.12; 29.7; 29.8; 29.9; 29.10; 59.3
(1)–(2D) 29.7
(3) 9.11; 29.7
(4) 29.7
(5)–(8) 29.7; 29.8; 29.9
(9)–(13) 29.7
179ZA 29.8
181 .... 29.10
184A(1), (2) 29.16
(3) 29.17
(4), (5) 29.16
184B(1), (2) 29.16
(3) 29.17
(4), (5) 29.16
184C 29.16
184D 14.7; 29.16; 44.7
184E, 184F 29.17
184G 6.10; 58.19
(1) 14.8
(2) 14.7; 14.8
(3), (4) 14.8
(5) 14.7; 14.8

1992 Taxation of Chargeable Gains Act – *cont.*
s 184G(6) 14.7
(7) 14.8
(8), (9) 14.7
(10) 14.7; 14.8
184H 6.10; 58.19
(1) 14.9
(2) 14.7; 14.9
(3) 14.9
(4) 14.7; 14.9
(5) 14.9
(6) 14.7
(7) 14.9
(8), (9) 14.7
(10) 14.7; 14.9
(11) 14.9
185 .... 51.8
187 .... 29.17
(4)(c) 51.8
188A–188C 41.33
188D 41.33; 44.3; 58.20
188E–188K 41.33
189 .... 51.27
190 .... 51.26
192 .... 14.12; 66.14; 66.16
(2) 63.19
192A 66.1
194, 195 .... 1.2
195B, 195C 1.2; 9.2; 9.6; 59.10
195E 1.2; 9.2; 9.6; 59.10
196–198I 1.2
199 .... 49.19
201–203 .... 47.1
204(1), (2) 25.10
(3) 25.10; 43.1; 63.24
(4) 25.10; 63.24
(5) 25.3
(6) 43.1; 63.24
(7), (8) 25.3; 25.10
(9) 25.3
(10) 25.10
205 .... 16.13
210 .... 43.1
211 .... 9.6
212 .... 29.19
213 .... 29.19
215 .... 9.6; 14.11
216 .... 9.6; 14.11
(1) 7.7; 63.27
217 .... 63.27
(1) 7.7; 63.27
(2)–(5) 63.27
(6) 25.58; 63.27
(7) 63.27
217A 9.6; 25.51
217B, 217C 25.51
218 .... 9.6; 25.53
219 .... 9.6; 25.53; 25.62
220 .... 9.6; 25.53
221 .... 9.6; 25.77

1992 Taxation of Chargeable Gains Act – *cont.*

s 222 ..... 26.2; 41.4; 41.13; 53.2; 53.7; 53.10; 53.11; 53.12; 53.13; 53.14
(1) 22.34; 53.2; 53.7; 53.11; 53.14
(2), (3) 53.5; 53.14
(4) 53.5
(5) 53.10
(6) 53.2; 53.10
(6A) 53.10
(7) 53.2
(8), (9) 53.7
(10) 53.2
222A 53.10
222B, 222C 53.8
223 .... 36.10; 41.4; 41.13; 53.2; 53.3; 53.4; 53.5; 53.6; 53.7; 53.9; 53.11; 53.12; 53.13; 53.14
(1), (2) 53.2; 53.7; 53.13
(3)–(3B) 53.7
(4) 53.14
(5), (6) 53.2
(7) 53.2; 53.7; 53.14
(7B) 53.7
223A 53.7
224 .... 41.4; 41.13; 53.2; 53.7; 53.11; 53.14
(1), (2) 53.9
(3) 41.4; 53.13
225 .... 41.4; 41.13; 53.2; 53.7; 53.11; 53.14
225A 53.11
225B, 225C 53.7
225D 53.9
225E 53.2; 53.11
226 .... 41.4; 41.13; 53.2; 53.7
(1)–(6) 53.12
226A, 226B 53.13
227, 228 .... 22.30
229(1) 22.30; 22.31; 22.32; 22.33; 22.34; 22.35; 22.36
(2) 22.30
(3) 22.30; 22.31; 22.32; 22.33; 22.34; 22.35; 22.36
(4), (5) 22.30
230 .... 22.34
231 .... 22.35
232 .... 22.31; 22.32; 22.33; 22.36
233 .... 22.32; 22.36
234 .... 22.33; 22.36
235 .... 22.36
236(1), (2) 22.31; 22.32
(3), (4) 22.33
236A 22.18
236B–236G 22.26
236H 63.14
236I 63.16
236J–236L 63.16
236M 63.17
236N 63.18

1992 Taxation of Chargeable Gains Act – *cont.*

s 236NA–236Q 63.14
236R 63.16; 63.17
236S 63.16
237 .... 25.3
237A 22.4
238(2) 63.11
238A 22.17
239(1) 25.91
(2) 25.91
(3) 4.14
(4)–(8) 25.91
239ZA 25.91
239A 25.60
239B 25.60
240 .... 41.14; 72.4
241(1), (2) 26.1
(3) 24.2; 26.2; 36.3
(3A) 24.2; 36.3
(4)–(6) 26.2
(7) 26.1
(8) 26.2
241A 26.1; 26.2; 36.3
242 .... 41.9
243 .... 41.11; 41.12
(2) 41.11
(2A) 41.11
(3) 41.13
244 .... 9.8; 41.9; 41.11
(2) 41.9; 41.11
245(1), (2) 41.10
246 .... 41.10
247 .... 9.11; 41.1; 41.10; 41.12
(2) 41.12
(b) 49.5
(3)(b) 49.5
(6) 41.10
247A 41.12
248 .... 41.12
(3) 9.11
248A–248E 41.13
249 .... 25.19
250 .... 25.40
251 .... 25.5; 63.8
(1)–(3) 25.5
(4) 44.6
(5) 25.5; 44.6
(5A) 25.5
(6) 24.3; 25.5; 54.3
(7), (8) 25.5
252 .... 25.5
(1) 49.7; 49.8
253 .... 44.12; 44.13
(1)–(3A) 44.12
(4), (4A) 44.12
(5)–(15) 44.12
254 .... 44.13; 44.14; 54.3
(1), (2) 44.13; 44.14
(3)–(5) 44.13
(6) 44.13

1992 Taxation of Chargeable Gains Act – *cont.*

s 254(7)–(12) 44.13
255(1)–(5) 44.13
255A 65.46
255B–255E 65.45
256 ..... 11.4
(1) 11.3
(2) 11.3
256A, 256B 11.4
257 ..... 11.4; 11.7; 11.8; 11.11
(1) 11.7
(2) 9.6; 11.4; 11.7
(2A)–(2C) 11.7
(3) 9.6; 11.8
(4) 11.7
257A 11.11
258(1A) 11.9
(2) 25.41
(3) 25.85
(4) 9.6; 25.84; 49.5
(5)–(7) 25.85
(8), (8A) 25.85; 39.2
(9) 25.85
259 ..... 25.53
(2) 9.6
260 ..... 27.4; 36.2; 36.8; 36.11; 39.2; 53.2; 53.13; 54.3; 62.12; 62.14; 62.17; 62.18; 62.22
(1), (2) 36.10
(3) 36.10; 48.2
(4) 36.10
(6) 36.10
(6ZA)–(6ZC) 36.10
(7) 36.10; 39.2
(8) 36.10; 39.2
(9), (10) 36.10
261 ..... 36.11
261ZA 36.10
261A 7.4
261B 20.4; 20.13; 44.21
261C–261E 44.21
261F–261H 63.26
262 ..... 4.13; 25.4
263 ..... 25.11
263AZA 25.13
263ZA 44.21
263A 63.26; 66.9
263B 63.25
(2) 66.9
263C 63.25
263CA 63.25
263D 63.26
263E 4.21
263F–263I 63.26
264 ..... 9.6; 25.70; 38.4
265, 266 ..... 7.3
267 ..... 14.11
(2) 9.6
268 ..... 25.6
268A 10.2; 25.14

1992 Taxation of Chargeable Gains Act – *cont.*

s 268B 10.2
269 ..... 25.5; 25.8
270 ..... 25.49
271(1) 25.43; 25.49; 25.50; 25.57; 25.60; 70.3
(1ZA), (1ZB) 25.43
(1A), (1B) 25.60
(3) 25.55
(4) 25.15
(5) 25.54
(6) 25.45; 25.61
(7) 25.45; 25.52; 25.58; 25.59
(7A)–(8) 25.46
(10)–(12) 25.60
271A–271J 49.4
272(1), (2) 45.1
(3)–(6) 45.3
273 ..... 45.4
274 ..... 19.5; 39.2; 45.3
275–275C 7.3
276 ..... 49.3; 49.17; 49.19
276A 49.8
277 ..... 21.2; 21.3; 21.4; 21.6; 21.7; 22.24; 31.2
(1)–(1C) 21.10
278 ..... 21.5
279 ..... 42.8; 46.2; 49.6
(1) 49.6
(2) 49.6
(3)–(6) 49.6
(7) 46.2
(8) 49.6
279A 44.19
279B 44.19
(6) 63.6
279C 44.19
279D 44.19
280 ..... 7.9
282 ..... 27.4
283 ..... 56.3
284 ..... 39.1
284A, 284B 4.19
285 ..... 45.3
285A 49.20
286 ..... 17; 22.31; 23.17; 62.22; 66.5
286A 57.33
287 ..... 45.3
288(1) .. 1.1; 14.2; 16.9; 22.30; 25.60; 38.2; 41.1; 49.3; 49.7; 50.1; 53.7; 62.12; 63.2; 63.30; 66.5; 66.7; 70.1; 70.8
(1ZA) 1.1
(1A) 22.6
(2) 2.6
(3) 46.4
(3A) 9.6
(5) 54.3
(5A), (5B) 63.30
(6), (7) 7.7

1992 Taxation of Chargeable Gains Act – *cont.*

s 288(7B) 48.3; 49.5; 64.2
(8) 28.2
Sch A1 .... 25.93
B1 .... 41.29
BA1 .... 2.1
1
para 1.................... 58.3; 62.9
2.................... 58.3; 62.8
3.......................... 62.8
Sch 2 .... 8.1; 9.2; 59.6
para 1.......................... 8.2
2(1).......................... 8.2
(2), (3).................... 8.4
3.................... 8.3; 8.4
4.................... 8.3; 50.16
(1), (2).................... 8.3
(3)–(7).................... 8.4
(8)–(13).................... 8.3
5.......................... 8.3
6.......................... 8.5
8.......................... 8.3
9–15.......................... 8.6
11.......................... 8.3
16.................... 8.7; 9.10
(7), (8).................... 8.10
(10).................... 53.2
17(1).......................... 8.8
(2).................... 8.8; 9.2
(3)–(5).................... 8.8
18.......................... 8.9
19.......................... 8.10
20.......................... 8.11
21.......................... 8.12
23.......................... 10.4
Sch 3
para 1.......................... 9.6
1A.......................... 9.6
2.......................... 9.5
3.......................... 9.7
4.......................... 9.8
5.......................... 9.9
6.......................... 9.10
7.......................... 9.4
8.......................... 9.5
9.......................... 9.5
Sch 4 .... 9.11; 50.7; 59.2
para A1...... 9.11; 49.12; 59.9; 63.8
3.......................... 9.11
4.......................... 9.11
(5).... 41.12; 49.12; 59.9; 63.8
Sch 4ZZA 14.10
4ZZB 14.10
paras 2–10.................... 41.30
para 11–20.................... 41.31
21–23.............. 41.30; 41.31
24, 25.................... 41.32
Sch 4ZZC 2.1
4ZA 62.12
4A 62.20

1992 Taxation of Chargeable Gains Act – *cont.*

Sch 4B 48.13; 48.16; 48.23; 48.24; 48.25; 48.26; 48.27; 62.21
4C 48.14; 48.16; 48.19; 48.20; 48.22; 62.21
para 1........... 48.13; 48.24; 48.26
(2).......................... 48.14
1A.................. 48.24; 48.26
2.......................... 48.23
3.................. 48.13; 48.27
4, 5.......................... 48.27
6.................. 48.13; 48.27
7.......................... 48.27
7B.......................... 48.24
8.................. 48.24; 48.26
(3).......................... 48.4
8AA.......................... 48.24
8A.......................... 48.26
9.................. 48.24; 48.25
10.......................... 48.25
12.......................... 48.13
12A.......................... 48.24
13.......................... 48.28
13A.......................... 48.24
14.......................... 48.26
Sch 5 .... 37; 57.29
para 1.......................... 48.5
2.......................... 48.6
2A.......................... 48.7
3–5.......................... 48.8
6.......................... 48.11
7, 8.......................... 48.9
9.......................... 48.10
10.......................... 48.12
Sch 5A 48.29
5AZA 70.2
5AA 14.11; 63.7
5B 23.14; 23.15; 23.16; 23.17; 23.18
para 1.......................... 23.15
2.................. 23.15; 44.19
3.......................... 23.15
4, 5.................. 23.15; 44.19
6.......................... 23.15
7–15.......................... 23.17
16.................. 23.12; 23.17
17.......................... 23.16
18.......................... 23.17
19.......... 23.14; 23.15; 23.17
Sch 5BB 60.45
5C 36.10; 71.10; 71.12
para 2(2).......................... 44.19
4, 5.......................... 44.19
Sch 7 . 36.2; 36.3; 36.4; 36.5; 36.6; 36.7; 36.8
7ZA 24.3
7ZB 40.8
7A .. 29.18; 29.19; 29.20; 29.23; 38
para 1........... 29.18; 29.19; 29.21
(8).......................... 29.19

1992 Taxation of Chargeable Gains Act – *cont.*
para 6 .... 29.20
7 .... 29.21
8 .... 29.22
9 .... 29.19
10–12 .... 29.23
Sch 7AC 16.9; 36.8; 66.1
para 1 .... 66.3
2 .... 15.10; 66.4
3 .... 66.5
3A, 3B 66.6
4 .... 66.14
5 .... 66.7
6(1) 66.1; 66.4; 66.5
(2) 66.4; 66.5
7 .... 66.3
8–9 .... 66.8
10–13 .... 66.9
14 .... 66.15
15 .... 66.16
15A 66.9
16, 17 .... 66.8
18 .... 66.10
19 .... 66.12
20, 21 .... 66.11
22 .... 66.13
23, 24 .... 66.17
25 .... 66.16; 66.16
26 .... 66.2
(4) 66.11; 66.17
27 .... 66.11
28 .... 66.3
29 .... 66.24
30 .... 66.4
30A, 31 .... 66.6
32 .... 66.23
33 .... 66.19
34 .... 66.20
36 .... 16.9
37 .... 66.21
38 .... 29.9
Sch 7C 22.18
para 1–4 .... 22.18
5 .... 22.19
6 .... 22.20
7 .... 22.21
8 .... 22.18
Sch 7D
para 2–5 .... 22.17
7, 8 .... 22.17
10 .... 22.24
12, 13 .... 22.25
14–16 .... 22.22
Sch 8 .... 41.14
para 1(1)–(6) 41.15
2(1), (2) 41.16; 72.5
3 .... 41.16
4 .... 72.6
(1)–(3) 41.18; 72.6
5(1) 41.17

1992 Taxation of Chargeable Gains Act – *cont.*
para 5(2) 41.18
(3) 41.7
(4) 41.7; 41.18
(5) 41.17; 41.18
(6) 39.1
6(1) 41.19
(2) 41.21
(3) 41.7; 41.19
7 .... 41.17
7A 41.17
8 .... 41.15; 72.4
9(1) 72.4
(2) 72.5
(3) 72.4
10 .... 53.14
(1) 41.14; 72.4
(2), (3) 41.16
Sch 8B 65.46
9 .... 28.2
10
para 2 .... 49.7
Sch 11
para 3–5 .... 45.4
6 .... 8.2
(1)–(4) 45.3
7(1) 45.3
(2) 45.7
8 .... 19.5
11 .... 16.5
12 .... 14.6; 44.2
13, 14 .... 16.12
16(4) 54.3
Sch 12 .... 25.79

1993 Charities Act 11.4; 31.2

1993 Finance Act
s 92–92E 14.14
120 .... 13.5; 52.3
165 .... 14.14
171–176 .... 69.2
179B 69.8
180, 181 .... 69.2
184 .... 69.2
Sch 14
para 1 .... 52.3
10 .... 56.4
Sch 20
para 8, 9 .... 69.2
11 .... 69.2
14 .... 69.2
Sch 20A 69.8

1993 Leasehold Reform, Housing and Urban Development Act 41.12

1994 Coal Industry Act 9.6

1994 Finance Act
s 93(11) 29.14
94 .... 29.18
186 .... 58.18

1994 Finance Act – *cont.*
s 188 .... 58.12
196 .... 51.4; 58.18
219–227B 69.3
229, 230 .... 69.3
249 .... 36.8; 49.18; 57.33
252, 253 .... 9.6
Sch 15
para 29 .... 25.22
Sch 19
para 2 .... 58.23
Sch 24 .... 14.11
25 .... 14.11
26
Pt V 69.2
1994 Trade Marks Act
Sch 5 .... 7.3
1994 Value Added Tax Act
.... 6.2
s 72 .... 20.9
1995 Agricultural Tenancies Act
s 16 .... 10.2
1995 Criminal Injuries Compensation Act
.... 62.13
1995 Finance Act
s 47 .... 25.86
66 .... 23.13
67 .... 23.14
72 .... 36.10
(2) 71.10
125(1) 50.2
(3) 50.2
(5) 50.2
143 .... 69.2
152 .... 70.8
154 .... 25.40
Sch 6
para 36 .... 26.2
Sch 13
para 1–3 .... 36.10
4 .... 23.14
Sch 17
para 7 .... 11.4
1996 Broadcasting Act 9.6
1996 Finance Act
s 92(7) 66.20
94A 15.4
104 .... 25.5
105(1) 25.5
148 .... 25.60
200 .... 57.34
202 .... 28.2
Sch 14
para 62 .... 44.13
64 .... 25.5
Sch 15
para 7 .... 44.13
Sch 17 .... 13.2
19
para 4 .... 58.12
1996 Finance Act – *cont.*
Sch 20
para 22 .... 23.11
39 .... 49.14
54 .... 23.13
Sch 21
para 7 .... 23.11
35 .... 9.3
36 .... 16.9
43 .... 9.11
Sch 39
para 4 .... 44.11
Sch 40
para 8 .... 28.2
1996 Housing Act 41.12
1997 Finance Act
s 110 .... 31.2
1997 Plant Varieties Act 15.15
1998 Finance Act
s 31 .... 52.3
50 .... 22.14
117 .... 6.10; 6.13; 6.15; 51.31; 52.3; 52.4; 52.15; 52.16; 52.17; 52.18; 58.17; 58.19
120 .... 62.7
121(3) 26.2; 66.21
(4) 26.2; 44.2; 44.8; 49.6; 49.7
122(4) 49.7
125(1) 64.4
(3), (4) 38.2
(5) 38.2
141 .... 25.86
Sch 3
para 2 .... 52.3
4 .... 42.7
Sch 13
para 37 .... 25.22
39 .... 25.22
41, 42 .... 25.22
Sch 18 .... 14.15
para 2 .... 6.14; 52.3; 58.19
3 .... 34.5; 52.4; 52.5; 52.8
4–7 .... 58.19
8 .... 18.3; 52.3; 52.4; 58.19
9, 10 .... 13.4
11 .... 58.19
12 .... 58.17
13 .... 58.19
14 .... 52.4; 52.5; 58.19
15 .... 58.19; 67.4
16 .... 58.19
17 .... 51.13; 52.4
18 .... 51.13; 52.4; 52.33
19 .... 52.4
21, 22 .... 58.19
23 .... 52.15; 58.19
24 .... 4.25; 34.5; 58.9; 58.18; 58.19
25–28 .... 58.19
29 .... 58.19

1998 Finance Act – *cont.*
para 30 .... 51.17; 58.19
(3) 5.2; 5.3
(4) 5.3
31 .... 58.19
32 .... 51.31; 58.19
33 .... 58.19
34 .... 51.17; 58.19
(3) 5.2; 5.3
(4) 5.3
35 .... 58.19
paras 36, 37 .... 6.3; 13.7; 58.19
38, 39 .... 58.19
para 40 .... 51.20; 58.19
41, 42 .... 6.10
43, 44 .... 6.10; 14.7
45 .... 6.10
46(3) 6.13; 6.14; 6.15
47(1) 6.2
(2) 6.5
48(1) 5.2
(2) 5.3
49 .... 5.2
51 .... 13.7
51A–51G 13.7
52, 53 .... 51.31
54 .... 13.4
55 .... 13.5; 59.11
56 .... 13.4
57–59 .... 13.4; 13.6; 52.15
60 .... 13.4
61–64 .... 13.5
65 .... 6.14; 6.15; 13.5
87A–87C 14.15
90 .... 52.18
92(2) 5.3
97 .... 6.3
Sch 19
para 1 .... 52.3
4 .... 58.17
17 .... 6.13
18 .... 6.15
28 .... 51.17
29 .... 51.4
37 .... 52.18
Sch 21
para 8 .... 26.2
Sch 25 .... 25.85
27
para 32 .... 25.86
1998 Government of Wales Act
.... 25.53; 25.62
1998 Petroleum Act 9.4; 59.4
1999 Finance Act
s 66 .... 54.4
82 .... 69.7
83 .... 69.7
132 .... 30.4
133 .... 30.4

2000 Finance Act
s 54 .... 22.30
63(1) 18.1
(4) 18.1
82 .... 25.17
98 .... 51.26
143 .... 30.4
144 .... 52.40
149 .... 34.16
Sch 15
para 1 .... 18.1
2, 3 .... 18.2
4–13 .... 18.5
14 .... 18.5
15–24 .... 18.6
25–33 .... 18.7
34–38 .... 18.8
39 .... 18.3
40, 41 .... 18.4
42 .... 23.3; 71.4
43, 44 .... 18.4
45 .... 18.3
46 .... 18.10; 66.14
47, 48 .... 18.11
49, 50 .... 18.12
51–53 .... 18.11
54, 55 .... 18.13
56–58 .... 18.14
59 .... 18.15
60–66 .... 18.9
67–72 .... 18.19
73–79 .... 18.20
80 .... 18.21; 18.23
81 .... 18.21
82 .... 18.22
83–87 .... 18.23
93 .... 18.16
94 .... 18.18
96 .... 18.10; 18.22
97 .... 18.19
99 .... 18.5; 18.6; 18.12; 18.13
101 .... 18.5; 18.6
102(1) 18.5; 18.6; 18.7; 18.8; 18.11; 18.14
(3) 18.5; 18.6; 18.13
(4) 18.4; 18.6
(5) 18.12; 18.13
(8) 18.2
Sch 16
para 1 .... 18.9
2 .... 23.12
4 .... 23.17
Sch 22 .... 25.17
para 67 .... 59.2
Sch 23 .... 15.14
28 .... 51.26
29
para 9(3) 51.26
(4) 51.26
33 .... 22.30
Sch 38 .... 30.4

2000 Finance Act – *cont.*
Sch 39 ... 34.16
2000 Financial Services and Markets Act ... 7.7; 7.8; 15.15; 31.2; 45.3; 63.30; 69.2; 71.2
s 235 ... 70.1
236 ... 70.8
237 ... 11.4; 70.3
243 ... 70.3
285 ... 63.30
2000 Limited Liability Partnerships Act ... 50.18
2001 Anti-terrorism, Crime and Security Act ... 31.2
2001 Capital Allowances Act
s 63(2) ... 11.11
67 ... 14.14
Pt 2, Ch 6A (ss 70F–70YJ) ... 16.13
s 70G–70U ... 7.6
70YI(2) ... 7.6
394 ... 9.4
Pt 6 (ss 437–451) ... 39.1
s 462 ... 7.4
Sch 2
para 47 ... 7.4
78 ... 16.13
2001 Housing (Scotland) Act ... 11.11; 25.53; 25.62
2002 Finance Act
s 44 ... 26.2
(1) ... 66.1
(2) ... 66.1
(3) ... 66.1
(5) ... 29.7
48 ... 44.21
84(1) ... 59.2
98 ... 11.10
103(1) ... 15.15; 58.19
(2) ... 15.15
(3) ... 16.9
(6) ... 58.19
134 ... 51.32
135, 136 ... 30.4
141 ... 58.19
Sch 8
para 1 ... 66.1
3 ... 26.2
Sch 9
para 4 ... 71.2
(2) ... 25.22
5(7) ... 14.11; 29.3
(12) ... 25.5
Sch 11
para 8 ... 44.19
Sch 26 ... 20.2; 7.7; 7.8
27
para 14 ... 7.7; 7.8
Sch 28
para 1 ... 15.8
2002 Finance Act – *cont.*
para 4, 5 ... 15.13
7 ... 15.13
Sch 29 ... 7.2
para 1 ... 15.14
2–4 ... 15.15
88 ... 14.11
132(1) ... 59.2
Sch 39 ... 51.32
40
para 14 ... 70.4
16 ... 16.9; 58.19
2002 Proceeds of Crime Act
Pt 3 (ss 92–155) ... 31.2
5 (ss 240–316) ... 31.2; 34.15
s 240 ... 25.33
266 ... 25.33
276 ... 25.33
289 ... 25.33
298 ... 25.33
316 ... 25.33
Pt 6 (ss 317–326) ... 30.9
s 317 ... 30.9
320 ... 30.9
323 ... 30.9
326 ... 30.9
Pt 8 (ss 341–416) ... 34.15
s 436 ... 31.2
439 ... 31.2
448 ... 25.33
Sch 10
para 2, 3 ... 25.33
2002 Tax Credits Act ... 31.2
2003 Finance Act
s 44 ... 3.5
117 ... 3.5
141 ... 22.29
142 ... 22.29
148 ... 49.3
149(4) ... 49.3
(6) ... 49.3
155 ... 22.30
157 ... 43.1
159 ... 19.9;
162 ... 44.19
163(3) ... 48.14
195 ... 63.19
197(1)–(5) ... 31.2
204, 205 ... 51.13
Sch 21
para 1–8 ... 22.17
Sch 23 ... 22.29
27 ... 22.30
2003 Income Tax (Earnings and Pensions) Act
s 8 ... 22.13; 22.15; 50.20
15 ... 22.24
21 ... 22.24; 22.28
23 ... 55.2
26(1) ... 55.2

2003 Income Tax (Earnings and Pensions) Act – *cont.*
s 28 .... 25.30
41A .. 22.6; 22.8; 22.12; 22.13; 22.15; 22.16
41F, 41H 22.6; 22.8; 22.12; 22.13; 22.15; 22.16
42, 43 .... 57.35
67(1), (2) 51.26
192–197 .... 22.8; 22.14
198–200 .... 22.9
226A–226D 22.26
419 .... 22.6; 22.8; 22.9; 22.10; 22.11; 22.13; 22.15
420 .... 22.2
(8) 22.6
421 ... 22.6; 22.9; 22.10; 22.11; 22.12; 22.13; 22.15
421A .. 22.6; 22.9; 22.10; 22.13; 22.15
421B .. 22.2; 22.6; 22.8; 22.10; 22.11; 22.12; 22.13; 22.15
(6), (7) . 22.6; 22.13; 22.15; 22.16
421C 22.8; 22.10; 22.11; 22.12; 22.13; 22.15
421D .. 22.2; 22.6; 22.8; 22.10; 22.11; 22.12; 22.13; 22.15
421E(1) 22.12; 22.13; 22.15
(1A), (1B) 22.12; 22.13
(2) 22.8; 22.10; 22.11
(3)–(5) 22.8; 22.10; 22.11; 22.12; 22.13; 22.15
421F–421H 22.8; 22.10; 22.11; 22.12; 22.13; 22.15
421I 22.10; 22.13; 22.15
422–425 .... 22.13; 22.14
426 .... 22.13; 22.14; 50.20
427 .... 22.13; 22.14
428–432 .... 22.13; 22.14
434(1) 22.2
435–437 .... 22.15
438 .... 22.15; 50.20
439–446 .... 22.15
446A–446J 22.10
446K–446P 22.11
446Q–446T 22.8
446U 22.8; 50.20
446V, 446W 22.8
446X–446Z 22.9
447 .... 22.12; 50.20
448 .... 22.12
449, 450 .... 22.12; 22.16
451, 452 .... 22.16
453–456 .... 22.12
470(1) 22.2
471–173 .... 22.6
474 .... 7.7; 22.3; 22.6
475 .... 22.6
476 .... 22.6; 22.7; 22.8; 22.14; 22.22; 22.24; 50.20
477–484 .... 22.6
485 .... 22.6

2003 Income Tax (Earnings and Pensions) Act – *cont.*
s 487 .... 22.6
(1) 22.2
488–515 .... 22.17
516 .... 22.24
(4) 22.2
517–520 .... 22.24
521 .... 22.25
(4) 22.2
522–526 .... 22.25
527 .... 22.22
(4) 24.3
528–532 .... 22.22
533 .... 22.22; 24.3
534 .... 22.22
(1) 24.3
535–541 .... 22.22
542, 544 .... 22.37
548(1) 22.2
553Z10(2) 55.2
554Z9(2) 55.2
555–564 .... 44.21; 67.8
684 .... 51.19
701, 702 .... 22.17
714 .... 34.17
718 .... 22.6
721(1) 22.6; 22.13
Sch 2 .... 22.17
para 5(1).............................. 22.17
25–31.............................. 22.18
32.............................. 22.17; 22.18
33.............................. 22.18
77.............................. 22.17
96.............................. 22.17
Sch 3 .... 22.24
para 32.............................. 22.24
Sch 4 .... 22.25
5 .... 22.22; 24.3
para 58.............................. 22.2
Sch 6
para 18.............................. 22.14
143.............................. 58.2
210(5).............................. 22.14
(10).............................. 22.14
Sch 7
para 28, 29.............................. 22.8
30, 31.............................. 22.9
44–48.............................. 22.14
54.............................. 22.12
61A.............................. 22.9
62–67.............................. 22.6
86.............................. 22.17

2003 Land Reform (Scotland) Act
.... 41.12

2004 Child Trust Funds Act
s 13 .... 25.24

2004 Civil Partnerships Act
.... 46.3

2004 Companies (Audit, Investigation and Community Enterprise) Act ... 65.2
s 11 ... 31.2

2004 Energy Act
Sch 9
para 3 ... 9.6
18 ... 9.6
29 ... 9.6
32 ... 9.6

2004 Finance Act
s 55 ... 58.19
92 ... 11.10
Pt 4 (ss 149–284) ... 66.6
s 150(2) ... 25.60
306 ... 20.2
306A ... 20.5
307 ... 20.3
308 ... 4.34; 20.3; 20.9; 20.10; 52.24
309, 310 ... 4.34; 20.3; 6.14; 20.9; 20.10; 52.24
310A ... 20.3; 52.24
310B ... 20.3
310C ... 20.3; 52.24
311 ... 20.4
312 ... 20.4; 52.24
(6) ... 4.30
312A ... 52.24
312B ... 52.24
313 ... 20.4; 6.14
313ZA ... 20.3; 52.24
313ZB ... 20.3; 52.24
313ZC ... 20.3; 52.24
313A, 313B ... 20.5; 52.24
313C ... 20.3; 52.24
314 ... 20.2
314A ... 20.5; 52.24
315 ... 52.24
316 ... 20.3
316A ... 20.4; 52.24
316B ... 20.5
316C, 316D ... 20.6
317A ... 20.2
318(1) ... 20.2
319 ... 20.2
(3), (4) ... 20.3
320 ... 13.8
321 ... 13.8
Sch 10
para 77 ... 14.14
Sch 12
para 16 ... 58.19
Sch 21
para 7 ... 27.4
Sch 29A ... 66.6

2004 Housing Act
Sch 16 para 4 ... 41.29

2005 Commissioners for Revenue and Customs Act
s 3 ... 31.1

2005 Commissioners for Revenue and Customs Act – *cont.*
s 5 ... 6.2; 6.4; 21.7
7 ... 6.2; 21.7; 29.3
16A ... 30.7
17 ... 31.1
18 ... 31.1
19 ... 31.6
21 ... 31.2
25 ... 51.19
30 ... 20.9
34–42 ... 29.3; 30.1
Sch 2
para 18 ... 31.2
Sch 3 ... 30.1
4
para 12 ... 30.1
39 ... 31.6
68 ... 6.2

2005 Finance Act
s 20 ... 22.16
21 ... 22.16; 50.20
22 ... 22.16
(2) ... 22.12
(4) ... 22.12
23, 24 ... 62.13
30 ... 62.13
31 ... 62.13
32–43 ... 62.13
45 ... 62.13
102 ... 25.60
103 ... 46.3
Sch 1 ... 62.13
1A ... 62.13
4
para 6 ... 44.21
48 ... 22.22
Sch 5 ... 21.9

2005 Finance (No 2) Act
s 17 ... 70.8
46 ... 25.59
51 ... 63.7
62 ... 29.2
Sch 6
para 9 ... 15.8; 66.5
10 ... 66.5

2005 Income Tax (Trading and Other Income) Act
Pt 2, Ch 2 (ss 5–23) ... 16.9
s 6B ... 41.6
19 ... 59.4
25A ... 25.19
54 ... 42.3
60–67 ... 41.20
96A(3) ... 25.20
99–106 ... 41.16
109 ... 11.11
157 ... 47.1
158 ... 41.4
192–195 ... 7.4

2005 Income Tax (Trading and Other Income) Act – *cont.*
s 254 .... 44.21
272 .... 42.3
277–281 .... 41.17
282 .... 41.21
284–286 .... 41.7
292, 293 .... 41.19
301, 302 .... 41.7; 41.19
307E(12) 25.20
319 .... 47.1
323–326 .... 26.1
340–343 .... 47.1
Pt 4, Ch 2A (ss 381A–381E) 39.1
s 392–396 .... 22.17
399 .... 11.10
400 .... 11.10
405–408 .... 22.17
410 .... 63.10
412, 413 .... 63.10
414 .... 11.10
421 .... 11.10
427–432 .... 63.20; 63.21
433 .... 54.3; 63.20; 63.21
434–460 .... 63.20; 63.21
461–464 .... 43.2
465 .... 2.1; 2.2; 43.2
466–529 .... 43.2
530 .... 11.10; 43.2
531–534 .... 43.2
535 .... 2.1; 2.2; 43.2
536 .... 43.2
(1) 2.1; 2.2; 43.2
537 .... 2.1; 2.2; 43.2
538 .... 43.2
539 .... 2.1; 2.2; 43.2
540–546 .... 43.2
551 .... 7.7
552 .... 7.7
(2) 11.4
553, 554 .... 7.7
583–586 .... 7.4
620 .... 48.26; 62.6; 62.8
628 .... 11.11
656(3) 11.10
657(4) 11.10
669(1), (2) 2.1; 2.2
680(3), (4) 11.10
685A 11.10
694–701 .... 25.30
709–712 .... 71.9
731 .... 20.2
749 .... 56.3
756A 25.14
770 .... 22.17
778 .... 30.4
779 .... 7.7; 7.8
784–802 .... 53.9
830 .... 49.11; 55.2; 55.3
831 .... 55.2

2005 Income Tax (Trading and Other Income) Act – *cont.*
s 863 .... 50.18
863H–863L 50.22
869 .... 42.3

2005 Railways Act
Sch 10
para 5 .... 9.6
16 .... 9.6

2005 Serious Organised Crime and Police Act
s 34 .... 31.2

2006 Charities Act
s 2 .... 11.1

2006 Climate Change and Sustainable Energy Act 25.13

2006 Companies Act 63.7
s 1(1) 29.2
390 .... 14.17
442 .... 14.17
641 .... 4.17
658 .... 49.13; 49.14; 49.15
1161, 1162 .... 20.13; 34.3
Sch 7 .... 20.13; 34.3

2006 Finance Act
s 54 .... 11.5
64(8) 25.14
(10)–(12) 25.14
65–68 .... 25.56
71(2) 58.19
(4) 14.7
72(2) 8.4
173 .... 31.2
175 .... 51.32
Sch 5
para 24 .... 31.2
Sch 13
para 25 17

2006 Fraud Act
s 1 .... 20.9

2007 Finance Act
s 95 .... 51.10
(6) 51.13
97 .... 52.8; 52.10
107 .... 13.8
110 .... 14.16; 49.13; 49.14; 49.15
Sch 13 .... 20.2; 63.26
para 5 .... 15.5
6 .... 66.9
10 .... 15.5
Sch 24 .... 5.16; 52.16; 52.19; 52.31; 52.33; 52.34; 52.36; 52.38
para 1 .... 31.3; 52.8
1A 31.3; 52.9
2 .... 52.10
3 .... 52.8
4 .... 52.8; 52.9; 52.10
4B 52.9
5 .... 52.8; 52.9; 52.10

2007 Finance Act – *cont.*
para 6 .... 52.8; 52.10
7–11 .... 52.8; 52.9; 52.10
12 .... 52.8; 52.10; 52.18
13 .... 52.33
14 .... 52.8
15–17 .... 52.34
18 .... 52.8; 52.10
19 .... 52.8
20 .... 52.8; 52.10
21 .... 52.8; 52.9
22–27 .... 52.8
28 .... 52.8; 52.10; 52.33; 52.38
29 .... 52.33

2007 Income Tax Act
s 23 .... 2.1; 11.10
24 .... 4.36
24A 44.15
64 .... 44.16; 44.21
71 .... 44.16; 44.21
79ZA–79B 44.21
96 .... 11.4; 67.3
101 .... 44.21
125 .... 11.4
126 .... 44.21
128, 130 .... 44.21
131–133 .... 44.15
134 .... 44.16
135, 136 .... 44.15
137–144 .... 44.16
145–150 .... 44.15
151 .... 44.15; 44.16
157(1) 23.2
(2), (3) 23.10
158 .... 23.10
159(2) 23.4; 23.13
(3) 23.3; 23.5
(4) 23.5
163–171 .... 23.4
173–178A 23.3
179 .... 23.8
180A–183 .... 23.5
184 .... 23.5
(3) 18.6
185–188 .... 23.5
189 .... 23.9
190 .... 23.7
191 .... 23.6
191A 23.5
192–199 .... 23.9
200 .... 23.9
201 .... 23.10
202, 203 .... 23.11
205 .... 23.3; 60.27; 71.2; 71.4
209 .... 23.12
210 .... 23.12; 23.13
211, 212 .... 23.12
213 .... 23.12; 23.13
214–223 .... 23.12
224 .... 23.12; 23.13; 23.17
225–230 .... 23.12; 23.17

2007 Income Tax Act – *cont.*
s 231 .... 23.17
232, 233 .... 23.12
234, 236 .... 23.12
241 .... 23.12
245 .... 23.12
246 .... 23.12; 23.13
247 .... 23.5; 23.12; 23.13; 23.17
(1)(3A) 23.3
248, 249 .... 23.5; 23.12; 23.17
250 .... 23.2
251(1), (2) 23.2
(3) 23.10
252 ... 23.5; 23.7; 44.16; 60.18; 60.19
252A 23.3
253 .... 23.4; 23.9; 60.12
254 .... 23.12
255 .... 23.10
256 .... 23.3; 23.4; 23.13
256A 23.12
257(1) 23.3; 23.5; 23.8
(3) 23.5; 23.9; 23.12
(4) 23.12
(5) 23.3; 23.13
257A 60.1
257AA 60.2
257AB 60.32
257AC 60.5
257BA 60.12
257BB 60.13
257BC 60.14
257BD 60.15
257BE 60.16
257BF 60.13
257CA 60.5
257CB 60.6
257CC 60.7
257CD 60.8
257CE 60.9
257CF 60.10
257DA, 257DB 60.18
257DC 60.19
257DD 60.20
257DE 60.21
257DF 60.22
257DG 60.23
257DH 60.24
257DI 60.25
257DJ 60.26
257DK 60.27
257DL 60.28
257DM, 257DN 60.29
257E 60.33
257EA–257EC 60.34
257ED 23.3; 60.34; 71.4
257EE–257EG 60.34
257FA 60.36
(4) 60.41
257FB–257FD 60.36
257FE–257FI 60.37
257FM 60.37

2007 Income Tax Act – *cont.*
s 257FP 60.38
257FQ 60.39
257FR 60.40
257GA 60.40
257GF 60.40
257H 60.41
257HA 60.36
(1) 60.41
257HB 60.42; 60.43
(1) 60.8
257HC, 257HD 60.42
257HE 60.3
257HF 60.31
257HG 60.30
257HH 60.36
257HI 60.33
257HJ(1) 60.6; 60.7; 60.8; 60.10; 60.12; 60.13; 60.14; 60.18; 60.20; 60.25; 60.26; 60.29; 60.30
(2) 60.18; 60.19
(3) 60.23; 60.38; 60.39
(4) 60.35
257J(2)(3) 65.2
257JA 65.34
257JB–257JH 65.2
257K(1) 65.1; 65.3
(2)(3) 65.3
(5) 65.1
257KB 65.1
257KC 65.1
257L 65.5
257LA 65.6
257LB 65.7
257LC 65.8
257LD 65.9
257LDA 65.9
257LE 65.11
257LEA 65.11
257LF 65.13
257LG 65.14
257LH 65.15
257M 65.17
257MA, 257MB 65.18
257MC 65.19
257MD 65.20
257ME 65.21
257MF, 257MG 65.22
257MH 65.23
257MI 65.24
257MIA 65.25
257MJ, 257MK 65.26
257ML 65.27
257MM 65.28
257MN 65.29
257MNA(4) 65.30
(6) 65.30
257MNB-MNE 65.30
257MP–257MQA 65.31
257MR–257MT 65.31

2007 Income Tax Act – *cont.*
s 257MU 65.32
257MV 65.33
257MW 65.31
257N 65.35
257P–257PE 65.36
257Q–257QI 65.39
257QJ–257QP 65.40
257QQ 65.41
257QR 65.42
257QS 65.43
257R 65.38; 65.44
257RA–257RC 65.38
257SA 65.43
257SF 65.36
257SI 65.1
257T 65.44
257TA 65.38; 65.44
257TB 65.29; 65.29; 65.32
257TC 65.9
257TD 65.14; 65.21
257TE 65.38
(1) 65.7; 65.8; 65.11; 65.15; 65.20; 65.21; 65.29; 65.32; 65.29; 65.32
259 .... 71.2
261–265 .... 71.7
266–270 .... 71.8
271(1)–(3) 71.8
(4) 71.7
(5) 71.8
272 .... 71.1
273 .... 71.7
274–277 .... 71.2
278, 279 .... 71.3
280–283 .... 71.2
284 .... 71.1; 71.2
285 .... 71.2
286–301 .... 71.4
302A 71.4
303–310 .... 71.4
311, 312 .... 71.5
312A 71.4
313(4) 71.4
(7) 71.4
314–316 .... 71.2
317–320 .... 71.2; 71.5
321–323 .... 71.2
324, 325 .... 71.2; 71.5
326–329 .... 71.3; 71.5
330 .... 71.5
330A 71.6
332 .... 71.4; 71.7
414–416 .... 11.10
417 .... 11.10; 11.11
418–428 .... 11.10
429 .... 51.19
430 .... 11.10
431 .... 11.4; 11.8
432–446 .... 11.7
453 .... 11.10

2007 Income Tax Act – *cont.*
s 457–459 .... 11.10
467–473 .... 23.4; 23.9; 60.13
477 .... 62.12
508 .... 36.8; 53.13; 62.20
517A, 517B 41.6
517C 41.6; 41.26; 41.33
517D–517U 41.6
520 .... 11.10
524–537 .... 11.4
539–548 .... 11.4
549–557 .... 11.5
558–564 .... 11.4
564A7 .... 11.5
564T 22.2
566(2) 63.26
574, 575 .... 63.26
596(2) 63.26
602(1) 63.26
604 .... 63.26
607, 608 .... 63.26
613(2) 63.26
614B–614CD 16.10
615–681 .... 63.20
681DM 72.5
683 .... 55.3
701 .... 4.15; 14.11
705 .... 4.25
733 .... 48.14
748–750 .... 48.20
752–755 .... 41.4
756 .... 41.4
757, 758 .... 41.4
759 .... 41.4
(6) 39.1
760–772 .... 41.4
777(5) 39.1
809AAZA, 809AAZB 4.23
809AZA–809AZF 4.22
809B 48.15; 49.5; 55.2; 55.3; 58.3
809BZA–809BZS 4.21
809C 55.2; 55.5
809D 48.15; 49.5; 55.2; 55.3
809DZA, 809DZB 4.24
809E 48.15; 49.5; 55.2; 55.3
809EZA 50.20; 50.21
809EZB 50.20; 50.21
809EZC, 809EZD 50.21
809EZE 50.20; 50.21
809EZF–809EZH 50.21
809FZA–809FZZ 50.20
809H 55.5; 57.34
809I 55.5
809J 55.2; 55.5
809L–809W 55.3
809X 55.3
(5)(c) 57.34
809Y 55.3
809Z 55.3
(3) 57.34
809Z1, 809Z2 .... 55.3

2007 Income Tax Act – *cont.*
s 809Z3 .... 55.3
(3) 57.34
809Z4, 809Z5 .... 55.3; 57.34
809UA 55.3
809VA 55.3
809VB–809VP 55.4
809Y 55.3
809YF 55.3
809Z7 .... 55.2
809Z8 .... 55.4
809Z9 .... 55.3; 55.4
809Z10 .... 55.3; 55.4
809ZA–809ZR 11.11
829 .... 57.29
833 .... 25.65
835BA 49.5
835C–835Y 49.4
837 .... 46.2
841 .... 25.50
970(2), (3) 31.2
986(3) 11.4
989 . 2.6; 23.6; 24.3; 36.2; 38.2; 58.17; 59.2; 69.8; 71.4
991 .... 11.4
993 . 11.5; 11.11; 16; 22.2; 23.4; 23.5; 23.9; 23.12; 44.16; 63.21; 65.29; 65.41; 71.4
995 .... 22.18; 23.4; 23.5; 23.7; 44.16; 60.13; 60.24; 71.4
999, 1000 .... 34.3
1005 .... 11.4; 22.18; 36.2
1006 .... 60.30; 71.4
1011 .... 46.4
1016 .... 11.4
1025 .... 11.10

2007 Serious Crime Act
s 85 .... 31.2
Sch 8
para 93 .... 30.9
96 .... 30.9
132 .... 31.2

2007 Tribunals, Courts and Enforcement Act
s 3 .... 5.11
11 .... 5.22
12 .... 5.31
13 .... 5.32; 5.34
14 .... 5.34
25 .... 5.13; 5.26
29(4) 5.24
Sch 10
para 32, 33 .... 51.19

2008 Crossrail Act 14.11

2008 Dormant Bank and Building Society Accounts Act 16.3

2008 Finance Act
s 63 .... 63.26
114 .... 34.18; 52.23
115 .... 58.8; 58.19

2008 Finance Act – *cont.*
s 116 .... 20.2; 20.3; 20.4
118 .... 6.10; 6.11; 6.14; 6.15; 13.7
119(1) 58.7
(2) 58.17
(4)–(8) 58.19
(9) 58.7; 58.17
123 .... 52.33; 52.34
127–131 .... 51.19
133 .... 51.19
135 .... 42.9
136 .... 51.14
139 .... 51.19
160 .... 30.5
Sch 2
para 2.......................... 44.2
7.......................... 62.20
8.......................... 62.21
10.......................... 48.5
21.................. 44.2; 62.20
22.......... 48.5; 62.20; 62.21
24.......................... 44.2
26.................. 4.19; 44.8
27.......................... 58.3
30.......................... 48.5
38.......................... 44.12
39.......................... 44.21
40.......................... 44.19
41.................. 44.19; 70.8
42.......................... 70.8
43.......................... 44.19
44.......................... 2.6
48.......................... 48.23
56..... 44.2; 44.8; 44.19; 44.21; 58.3
58.......................... 50.16
61.......................... 62.18
65.......................... 70.8
67.......................... 62.12
68.......................... 29.23
71.......................... 62.18
73.......................... 9.11
74........... 41.12; 59.9; 63.8
76........... 41.12; 59.9; 63.8
98–100...................... 44.15
Sch 3
para 7.......................... 24.12
para 8.......................... 24.10
Sch 4
para 8.......................... 39.2
Sch 7
para 57.......................... 58.3
81.......................... 58.3
84.......................... 55.2
87–89...................... 55.3
90.......................... 55.3
107.......................... 48.4
120–122.................... 48.15
124, 125.................. 48.15
126.............. 48.15; 48.16
127.......................... 48.18

2008 Finance Act – *cont.*
para 130........................ 62.21
139........................ 48.28
145........................ 48.28
146........................ 48.28
147........................ 48.28
Sch 11
paras 12, 13.................... 71.4
Sch 13 .... 43.2
14
para 2.......................... 43.2
16.......................... 43.2
Sch 18 .... 25.51
23
para 11, 12.................... 63.26
Sch 36 . 34.1; 36.8; 48.12; 52.21; 52.33; 52.36; 52.38; 62.8; 62.12; 71.8
paras 1, 2................ 20.9; 34.4
para 3, 4...................... 34.4
5, 5A................ 20.9; 34.4
6–9........................ 34.4
10–12...................... 34.8
12A........................ 34.9
13, 14...................... 34.8
15, 16.............. 34.4; 34.8
17.......................... 34.8
18–27...................... 34.5
28.......................... 34.8
29–33...................... 34.6
34A.......... 34.4; 34.6; 34.17
35....... 34.3; 34.4; 34.5; 34.6
36.............. 34.4; 34.5; 34.6
37.................. 34.5; 34.6
38–41...................... 52.16
42, 43.............. 34.7; 52.16
44, 45...................... 52.16
46.......................... 52.33
47, 48...................... 52.34
49.......................... 52.33
49A........................ 52.16
49B.............. 52.16; 52.33
49C........................ 52.33
50.......... 52.16; 52.18; 52.33
51.......................... 52.33
52.......................... 52.16
53–55...................... 34.10
56.......................... 34.3
58.................. 34.3; 34.8
59–60...................... 34.3
61.......................... 34.6
63, 64...................... 34.3
68.......................... 34.12
69–70...................... 34.12
71.......................... 6.10
75.......................... 62.11
88.......................... 58.19
92.......................... 58.19
Sch 37
para 8.......................... 58.19
Sch 38
para 2–5........................ 20.2

2008 Finance Act – *cont.*
Sch 39
para 2 .... 58.15
30 .... 44.12
38–40 .... 58.19
Sch 41 .... 52.16; 52.19; 52.22; 52.31; 52.33; 52.34; 52.36; 52.38
para 1 .... 31.3; 52.3
5–7 .... 52.3
11–15 .... 52.3
16 .... 52.33
17–19 .... 52.34
20–24 .... 52.3
25 .... 58.19
Sch 43
para 1 .... 51.19
12 .... 51.19
2008 Housing and Regeneration Act
Sch 7 .... 9.6
2009 Corporation Tax Act
s 4 .... 14.2
5B 41.6; 49.8
8 .... 14.3
14 .... 57.33
16–18 .... 57.33
18A 9.6; 21.6; 49.8
18B 49.8
18F–18P 49.8
18S 49.8
19 .... 14.2; 57.33
42 .... 59.4
62–67 .... 41.20
96–100 .... 41.16
108 .... 11.11
136 .... 41.5
162 .... 51.8
176–179 .... 7.4
207 .... 55.4
217–221 .... 41.17; 41.18
222 .... 41.21
224, 225 .... 41.7; 41.18
232 .... 41.19
238, 239 .... 41.7; 41.19
250 .... 41.16
265–268 .... 26.1
274–276 .... 47.1
295–301 .... 15.3
302, 303 .... 15.5
304 .... 51.8
305 .... 15.5
306–312 .... 15.3
313 .... 15.3
(6) 15.5
314 .... 15.3
315–318 .... 15.3; 15.4
319–328H 15.3
333, 334 .... 51.8
415–417 .... 15.4
466 .... 15.6
478–486 .... 15.3

2009 Corporation Tax Act – *cont.*
s 486A–486E 4.20; 15.3
486F, 486G 4.22
487–489 .... 15.5
490 .... 15.5; 15.6
491–497 .... 15.5
501 .... 11.5; 15.5
503, 504 .... 15.5
505, 506 .... 15.5
507 .... 15.5
511–513 .... 49.3
521 .... 3.1
521A–521F 4.20; 15.6
523 .... 4.20
543 .... 63.26
546(2) 15.5
548 .... 63.26
551(2) 15.5
560–569 .... 15.5; 43.2
571, 572 .... 15.8
574 .... 15.8
576–586 .... 15.9
589–591 .... 15.9
592 .... 15.9; 15.10
593 .... 15.12
596 .... 51.8
606 .... 15.8
609, 610 .... 51.8
613–615 .... 15.4
622(4) 15.12
624–638 .... 15.8
639–650 .... 15.10
652–658 .... 15.11
659 .... 15.10
661, 662 .... 15.12
663, 664 .... 15.10
665, 666 .... 15.11
667–673 .... 15.10
674–698 .... 15.8
701 .... 15.9
703 .... 15.12
712, 713 .... 15.15
715 .... 15.15
764–773 .... 45.2
800–816A 15.15
831 .... 4.15; 14.11
834–837 .... 45.2
841 .... 45.2
844–849 .... 45.2
849A 37.4
858 .... 15.14
859(2)(a), (b) 51.8
861(1)(c) 51.8
870A 59.3
880–888 .... 15.14
898 .... 59.3
899 .... 15.14; 59.3
900 .... 15.14
908–910 .... 7.4
931H 4.11
931S 4.11

2009 Corporation Tax Act – *cont.*
s 981 .... 7.7; 7.8
983–998 .... 22.17
1006–1038 .... 22.29
1219 .... 14.6
1225 .... 14.6
1264A 50.22
1273(1) 50.18
1285 .... 63.11; 63.19
1287 .... 30.4
Sch 2
para 64 .... 15.4
2009 Finance Act
s 25 .... 30.2
93 .... 14.17
94 .... 20.9; 31.3
97 .... 51.19
101 .... 42.2; 42.9
102 .... 56.2
103, 104 .... 42.2; 56.2
105(6) 42.7; 56.4
106 .... 52.5
108 .... 42.7
Sch 17
para 2 .... 52.23
13 .... 52.23
Sch 46 .... 14.17
paras 13–16 .... 52.16
para 18, 19 .... 52.34
Sch 49 .... 51.19
53 .... 42.2
para 12 .... 42.9
Sch 54 .... 56.2
55 .... 52.19; 52.31; 52.34; 52.36; 52.38
para 1–6AB 52.5
14–17 .... 52.5
17A 52.5
17B 52.5; 58.3; 58.16
18, 19 .... 52.33
20–22 .... 52.34
23, 24 .... 52.5
25 .... 52.34; 52.5
26, 27 .... 52.5
Sch 56
para 1–4 .... 42.10
9 .... 42.10; 52.27
9A 52.8; 52.18; 52.27
10 .... 42.10; 52.27
11, 12 .... 52.33
13–15 .... 52.34
16, 17 .... 42.10; 52.27
Sch 61 .... 3.5
2010 Constitutional Reform and Governance Act
s 41, 42 .... 57.32
2010 Corporation Tax Act
s 5–16 .... 14.14
17(4) 14.14
34 .... 70.9

2010 Corporation Tax Act – *cont.*
s 37 .... 14.6
68, 69 .... 44.18
70 .... 18.19; 44.18
71–90 .... 44.18
92–96 .... 44.20
138–142 .... 29.7
157–161 .... 63.17
162 .... 54.3; 63.17
163–182 .... 63.17
187 .... 4.20
191–198 .... 11.5
200 .... 11.5; 11.11
203 .... 11.5
330(1) 4.20
356OA, 356OB 41.6
356OC 41.6; 41.26; 41.33
356OD–356OT 41.6
439 .... 4.14; 8.12; 25.91; 45.2; 48.9; 48.19; 49.7; 62.23
443 .... 66.6
448 .... 40.8
450, 451 . 4.14; 8.12; 18.5; 18.6; 23.5; 23.9; 23.12; 25.91; 29.7; 29.16; 44.16; 44.18; 45.2; 48.6; 48.9; 48.19; 49.7; 51.26; 60.23; 60.38; 60.39; 62.23; 65.14; 66.5; 66.7; 69.8; 71.4
452–454 .... 4.14; 8.12; 25.89; 45.2; 48.9; 48.19; 49.7; 62.23
458 .... 52.8; 52.11; 52.26
469, 470 .... 25.61
471 .... 11.10
478–489 .... 11.4
492–501 .... 11.4
502–510 .... 11.5
511–517 .... 11.4
Pt 12 (ss 518–609) 66.6
s 518–534 .... 70.5
535 .... 29.7; 70.5
536–609 .... 70.5
613 .... 11.4; 70.8
615 .... 11.4
616 .... 70.3
643–646 .... 25.53
650–657 .... 25.62
658–661C 11.12
661D 11.10
665–671 .... 11.12
710 .... 34.5
713 .... 34.5
748 .... 4.15; 14.11
750 .... 4.25
752–757 .... 4.22
757A, 757B 4.23
758–776 .... 4.21
779A, 779B 4.24
806, 814 .... 63.25
815–818 .... 41.5
819 .... 41.5
820 .... 41.5

2010 Corporation Tax Act – *cont.*
s 821 .... 41.5
(3) 39.1
(5) 39.1
822–833 .... 41.5
849–862 .... 41.5
899–929 .... 16.10
939A–939I 11.11
941 .... 23.12; 60.38; 65.31; 65.41
942 .... 23.12; 60.38; 65.31
963–966 .... 51.4
969–972 .... 49.4
990 .... 49.20
991, 993 .... 25.77
1009(3) 20.3
1022 .... 63.3
1033 .... 34.17; 63.19
1034–1043 .... 63.19
1044, 1045 .... 4.15; 14.11; 63.19
1046–1048 .... 63.19
1073–1090 .... 14.12
1091, 1092 .... 4.15; 14.11; 14.12
1093–1099 .... 14.12
1115 .... 63.19
1117(1) 49.19
1119 ... 29.2; 44.3; 49.16; 63.5; 66.17; 70.4
1120 .... 20.3
1122 ...... 4.20; 11.11; 17; 18.5; 18.6; 18.11; 18.13; 21.6; 21.9
1124 .... 18.6; 63.7
1132 .... 18.7
1135 .... 50.18
1137 .... 63.30
1138 .... 18.7; 25.61
1139 .... 4.23
1141–1144 .... 49.3
1145–1153 .... 49.4
1154 .... 29.2
1157 .... 66.6
1158 .... 29.3; 66.6; 70.4
1159 .... 70.4
1173 .... 11.4
Sch 2
para 27–51 .... 44.18
70 .... 11.4
73–76 .... 11.5
77 .... 11.4

2010 Criminal Justice and Licensing (Scotland) Act
s 49(1) 20.9

2010 Finance Act
Sch 6
para 1–7 .... 11.2

2010 Taxation (International and Other Provisions) Act
s 2 .... 21.2; 22.30; 49.9
3–7 .... 21.2
8, 9 .... 21.4
11 .... 21.4

2010 Taxation (International and Other Provisions) Act – *cont.*
s 18 .... 21.6
19 .... 21.7
26 .... 21.2
28 .... 21.4
30 .... 21.4
31(2) 21.5
32–35 .... 21.6
36 .... 49.9
40–42 .... 21.6; 49.9
80 .... 21.7
81 .... 21.9
(2) 6.10; 58.9
82–95 .... 21.9
113–115 .... 21.5
126–129 .... 31.2
137–145 .... 21.10
147 .... 15.14; 45.2
(3) 3.2
(5) 3.2
168(1) 58.9
232 .... 4.20; 58.19
233–248 .... 4.20
249 .... 4.20; 58.19
250–259 .... 4.20
355–359 .... 49.11
363A 49.11
366 .... 3.1
371AA–371VJ 49.9
Sch 2
para 21 .... 22.2
30, 31 .... 3.2
34 .... 3.2
36–39 .... 3.2
40 .... 54.3
41–43 .... 3.4
44 .... 3.2
45 .... 3.3
Sch 3
para 7 .... 16.10
Sch 6
para 13 .... 11.4
Sch 7
para 2–4 .... 49.19
31 .... 5.2
54 .... 49.18
74 .... 57.34
79 .... 51.4
95 .... 52.40
108 .... 14.15
Sch 8
para 2 .... 11.4
3 .... 58.8
5 .... 6.10
6 .... 13.5
8 .... 11.4
47 .... 22.30
54 .... 18.3; 58.19
56 .... 25.17
91 .... 15.3

2010 Taxation (International and Other Provisions) Act – *cont.*
para 119 ... 25.17
164 ... 64.6
172 ... 15.5
199 ... 70.3
200 ... 54.3
204 ... 22.2
229 ... 3.5
231 ... 39.1
244 ... 72.5
321 ... 6.10; 58.19
Sch 9
para 13 ... 21.4
2011 Charities Act
s 2, 3 ... 11.2
5 ... 11.2
10 ... 11.2
29 ... 11.2
54–59 ... 11.1
Sch 7
para 143 ... 11.2
2011 Finance Act
s 27 ... 11.5; 11.11
31 ... 29.7
40 ... 25.30
48 ... 49.8
86 ... 34.17; 52.16; 52.17
87 ... 51.32
Sch 3
para 1–3 ... 11.11
13, 14 ... 11.5
24, 25 ... 11.5
27 ... 11.5; 11.11
28 ... 11.11
29, 30 ... 11.5
31 ... 11.11
Sch 13
para 62 ... 21.6
7 ... 15.15
31 ... 49.8
34, 35 ... 49.8
Sch 23 ... 52.1
para 1–29 ... 34.17
30–34 ... 52.17
35 ... 52.33
36, 37 ... 52.34
38, 39 ... 52.17; 52.33
40 ... 52.33
41 ... 52.17
43 ... 34.17
45, 46 ... 34.17
51 ... 49.19; 58.24; 58.25; 62.6
52 ... 49.19
65 .. 34.17; 49.19; 52.17; 58.24; 58.25; 62.6
2011 Finance Act – *cont.*
Sch 25 ... 51.32
2011 Localism Act
Sch 24
para 6 ... 9.6; 25.83
2012 Financial Services Act
Sch 12 para 20 ... 31.2
2012 Finance Act
s 9 ... 44.21
34 ... 2.6; 62.8; 62.9
35 ... 25.5; 49.7; 55.6
36 ... 70.1
37 ... 59.4
50 ... 51.19
52 ... 11.12
56 ... 66.6
(3) ... 25.10
65 ... 70.7
137 ... 66.6
150–164 ... 25.51
165 ... 29.3; 25.51
166–171 ... 25.51
172 ... 70.7; 25.51
173–179 ... 25.51
181 ... 29.13
218 ... 49.22
219 ... 52.8
221 ... 63.31
222(1) ... 12.3; 12.4; 13.2
(3) ... 12.1
(5) ... 12.3; 12.4
223 ... 34.12
224(2), (3) ... 34.4
(4) ... 34.6
(7) ... 34.4
227 ... 25.77; 47.1
Sch 4 ... 70.5
6
para 1 ... 60.1; 60.2; 60.3; 60.5; 60.6; 60.7; 60.8; 60.9; 60.10; 60.12; 60.13; 60.14; 60.15; 60.16; 60.17; 60.18; 60.19; 60.20; 60.21; 60.22; 60.23; 60.24; 60.25; 60.26; 60.27; 60.28; 60.29; 60.30; 60.31; 60.32; 60.33; 60.34; 60.35; 60.36; 60.37; 60.38; 60.39; 60.40; 60.41; 60.42
3 ... 60.43; 60.44
4, 5 ... 60.45
10 ... 23.4
15, 16 ... 71.4
17 ... 23.14; 71.4
19 ... 23.13; 23.14
20 ... 23.14
21 ... 23.15

2012 Finance Act – *cont.*
para 23.. 60.1; 60.2; 60.3; 60.5; 60.6; 60.7; 60.8; 60.9; 60.10; 60.12; 60.13; 60.14; 60.15; 60.16; 60.17; 60.18; 60.19; 60.20; 60.21; 60.22; 60.23; 60.24; 60.25; 60.26; 60.27; 60.28; 60.29; 60.30; 60.31; 60.32; 60.33; 60.34; 60.35; 60.36; 60.37; 60.38; 60.39; 60.40; 60.41; 60.42; 60.43; 60.44; 71.4
Sch 7
para 2, 3 .... 23.10
4 .... 23.4
6–9 .... 23.3
10 .... 23.8
11, 12 .... 23.5
13 .... 23.3; 23.9
14, 15 .... 23.9
16 .... 23.9
17 .... 23.12
20 .... 23.10
21.. 23.3; 23.5; 23.6; 23.7; 23.8
22 .... 23.4; 23.10
23 .... 23.3; 23.5
24 .... 23.9
25 .... 23.3; 23.5; 23.6; 23.7
27, 28 .... 23.13
29 .... 23.15
30–32 .... 23.17
33 .... 23.15
34 .... 23.13; 23.17
35 .... 23.17
Sch 8
para 2, 3 .... 71.2
4–13 .... 71.4
15, 16 .... 71.4
18 .... 71.2
19–22 .... 71.4
Sch 12
para 2, 3 .... 55.5
4 .... 55.3
5 .... 55.3; 55.5
7 .... 55.4
10 .... 55.3
13 .... 55.3
16 .... 55.4
17 .... 55.3; 55.4
18, 19 .... 55.3
20, 21 .... 55.5
Sch 13
para 33 .... 4.21
38 .... 4.21
42, 43 .... 4.21
Sch 14 .... 11.9
para 1 .... 55.3
35 .... 55.3
Sch 15
para 6 .... 11.10
9 .... 51.2

2012 Finance Act – *cont.*
para 11 .... 13.2
14, 15 .... 13.4
17 .... 13.2; 13.4; 51.2
Sch 16
para 73 .... 49.3
74 .... 70.7
75 .... 49.14
78 .... 49.17
79 .... 25.10
88 .... 66.1; 66.8
147 .... 15.3
162 .... 15.3
167 .... 15.9
174–177 .... 15.15
185 .... 22.17
219 .... 70.5
228 .... 41.22
Sch 18 .... 25.51
para 15 .... 70.7
16 .... 29.3
Sch 19 .... 25.51
20
para 3 .... 49.8
5, 7 .... 49.8
11 .... 51.17
13 .... 51.4
14 .... 49.9
17 .... 58.19
18–20 .... 25.17
26, 27 .... 15.3
28 .... 15.6
49, 50 .... 15.6
55 .... 49.8
Sch 36
para 2–19 .... 49.22
25 .... 31.2
26A, 26B 49.22
68–70 .... 34.12
Sch 37
para 5 .... 25.65
Sch 38 ...... 52.31; 52.33; 52.34; 52.36; 52.38
para 2–6 .... 34.11
7 .... 34.11; 52.19
8–21 .... 34.11
22, 23 ...... 52.19; 52.33; 52.34
24, 25 .... 52.19
26 .... 52.19; 52.33; 52.34
27 .... 52.19
28 .... 31.5
29 .... 52.19; 52.33
30 .... 52.33
31 .... 52.34
32 .... 52.33
33–35 .... 52.19
36–43 .... 34.11
45 .... 34.12
46 .... 34.12; 52.39
47 .... 34.12
48 .... 52.38

2012 Finance Act – *cont.*
para 49... 52.31; 52.33; 52.34; 52.36
Sch 39
para 15, 16 .... 25.77
17 .... 9.6
18 .... 25.77
43–47 .... 47.1
49 .... 25.19
2013 Crime and Courts Act
Sch 8
paras 108, 122 .... 30.9
2013 Finance Act 4.41; 22.22
s 21 .... 55.3
41 .... 15.11
57 .... 60.45
58–60 .... 37.4
61 .... 37.4
(2) 45.2
66 .... 14.14
105(3) 14.10
132 .... 14.10
206 .... 4.3
209 .... 4.3
(9) 4.6
209A–209F 4.5
210(6) 4.3
211 .... 4.3
212A 52.1; 52.11; 52.26; 52.33; 52.34
213 .... 13.2
214(1) 4.3
(3) 4.6
215 .... 4.3
217 .... 70.6
218 .... 57.3
221 .... 49.22
223(2) 20.4
(3) 20.3
(4) 52.24
224 .... 34.15
228 .... 34.17
231(1) 13.7
(3) 13.7
(5) 13.7
232(1) 13.7
(3), (4) 13.7
Sch 2
paras 2–6 .... 22.17
7–13 .... 22.24
14, 15 .... 22.25
33–38 .... 22.17
39–43 .... 22.24
para 44 .... 22.25
Sch 3
paras 1, 2 .... 44.15
Sch 4 paras 45, 56 .... 25.19
6 para 5 .... 55.3
7 .... 55.3
12 .... 39.1; 63.26
18 para 9 .... 15.15
19 .... 70.5

2013 Finance Act – *cont.*
Sch 21
paras 1–10 .... 11.12
Sch 23
paras 1–3 .... 22.26
17 .... 46.5
18, 20 .... 22.26
para 38 .... 22.26
Sch 24
para 1 .... 24.3
paras 3, 4 .... 64.2
5, 6 .... 24.3; 64.2
Sch 25
paras 3–5 .... 14.10
9, 10 .... 14.10
16, 20 .... 14.10
Sch 28 .... 7.8
43 .... 4.4
43A 4.6
43B 4.6
43C
paras 1–4 .... 52.11
para 5–7 .... 52.33
8 .... 52.11; 52.18
9 .... 52.34
10 .... 52.31
Sch 44
para 12 .... 36.8
13 .... 62.9
15–19 .... 62.13
20 .... 36.8; 62.9
Sch 45
para 1(3) 57.3
2(1)–(4) 57.3
3–5 .... 57.3
9(2) 57.9
11–13 .... 57.5
14 .... 57.5
(3) 57.9
15 .... 57.5
16 .... 57.5
(3) 57.9
17–20 .... 57.11
22–24 .... 57.6
25 .... 57.7
26(2) 57.9
27 .... 57.9
28 .... 57.9
29(2) 57.5; 57.20
30 .... 57.10
31 .... 57.12
32, 33 .... 57.13
34 .... 57.14
35, 36 .... 57.15
37 .... 57.16
38 .... 57.17
39–42 .... 57.18
43 .... 57.19
44 .... 57.20
45 .... 57.21
46 .... 57.22

2013 Finance Act – *cont.*
para 47 ..... 57.23
48 ..... 57.24
49 ..... 57.25
50 ..... 57.26
51 ..... 57.27
52–56 ..... 57.20; 57.21; 57.22; 57.23; 57.24; 57.25; 57.26; 57.27
66 ..... 22.8; 22.9; 22.10; 22.11; 22.12; 22.13
67 ..... 22.6
93 ..... 1.2
(3) 2.6
94 ..... 58.3
95 ..... 55.2
96 ..... 49.7
97 ..... 44.3
98, 99 ..... 55.2
100 ..... 48.5
102 ..... 48.1
109–115 ..... 49.5
119 ..... 49.5
120 ..... 48.13
121 ..... 48.19
122 ..... 44.19
123(1)–(4) 48.13
(5) 48.24
145 ..... 57.3; 57.5; 57.9; 57.11; 57.20; 57.21; 57.23; 57.24; 57.25; 57.26; 57.27
146 ..... 57.5; 57.9
148(2) 57.29
151(3)–(6) 62.13
152(2)–(4) 55.2
(6) 57.29
153(1) 57.3
(2) 1.2; 48.1; 49.7; 57.18; 58.3
(3) 48.13; 48.19; 48.24; 49.5
154(1)–(4) 57.28
(5) 57.5
155 ..... 57.28
156 ..... 49.5
157 ..... 49.5
Sch 46
para 2–5 ..... 55.2
17 ..... 55.2
18 ..... 48.15
23 ..... 55.3
24 ..... 55.2
75 ..... 1.2
76 ..... 49.3
77 ..... 49.7
78 ..... 44.3
80 ..... 48.2
81 ..... 36.12
83 ..... 48.4
84–87 ..... 48.2
88 ..... 48.1; 48.3

2013 Finance Act – *cont.*
para 89 ..... 48.2
90 ..... 48.4
91 ..... 48.5
92 ..... 48.15
(2) 48.14
93 ..... 48.16
94 ..... 48.19
95 ..... 48.14
97 ..... 64.2
98 ..... 49.3
99–101 ..... 36.8
103 ..... 49.19
104 ..... 36.11
105 ..... 62.8
106 ..... 62.20
107(2) 48.26
(3) 48.27
(5), (6) 48.25
109 ..... 48.29
108(2) 48.7
(3) 48.10
(4) 48.7; 48.10
110 ..... 23.15
111 ..... 22.18
112 ..... 1.2; 36.8; 36.11; 44.3; 48.1; 48.2; 48.3; 48.4; 48.5; 48.14; 48.15; 48.16; 48.19; 48.25; 48.26; 48.27; 49.3; 49.7; 62.8; 64.2
117 ..... 13.3
133 ..... 62.13
138 ..... 15.14
146 ..... 49.11
147 ..... 57.32
Sch 48 ..... 34.15
49
para 2 ..... 51.8
4, 5 ..... 49.18
6 ..... 51.8
7 ..... 42.10
8 ..... 51.8
Sch 50
para 1 ..... 52.33
2–5 ..... 52.5
8 ..... 52.33
11 ..... 42.10
13 ..... 52.3; 52.8; 52.18
14 ..... 52.33
16(3) 52.3; 52.8; 52.18; 52.33
Sch 49
51
para 2 ..... 52.3
3 ..... 58.3; 58.16
5 ..... 51.2
6 ..... 52.3
7 ..... 42.2
8 ..... 52.5; 58.3; 58.16
9 ..... 52.5

2014 Co-operative and Community Benefit Societies Act 14.11; 14.16; 65.2

2014 Co-operative and Community Benefit Societies Act – *cont.*
Sch 4
para 6 .... 23.9
paras 47–49 .... 49.15
50 .... 29.2
53 .... 66.2
105 .... 44.16
158 .... 44.16
168 .... 29.2

2014 Finance Act
s 8 .... 2.6; 62.8; 62.9
9 .... 2.6; 62.8
49, 50 .... 22.17
54 .... 60.1
55 .... 60.45
56 .... 23.9; 71.4
58 .... 53.2; 53.11
59 .... 55.2
60 .... 62.17; 62.18
61 .... 59.4
62 .... 59.3
63(1) 14.8
(2) 14.9
(3) 14.8; 14.9
72 .... 66.9
109, 110 .... 14.10
200 .... 4.25; 4.29
201–203 .... 4.25
204 .... 4.26
205 .... 4.25
206, 207 .... 4.26
208 . 4.27; 52.26; 52.31; 52.33; 52.34; 52.36; 52.38
209, 210 .... 52.26
211 .... 52.33
212 .... 52.11; 52.18; 52.26
213 .... 52.33
214 .... 4.31; 52.34
216 .... 4.28
217 .... 4.26
219 .... 4.30
220 .... 4.30; 4.31
221, 222 .... 4.30
223 .... 4.31
224 .... 4.31; 51.17
225 .... 4.31; 51.18
226 ...... 52.27; 52.31; 52.33; 52.34; 52.36; 52.38
227 .... 4.30; 6.14
232 .... 4.25; 4.29
234–236 .... 20.8
237–241 .... 20.11
242–247 .... 20.12
248 .... 20.13; 20.15
249 .... 20.13; 52.25
250 .... 20.13
251–253 .... 20.13; 52.25
254 .... 20.8
255 .... 20.13; 20.15; 20.16; 52.25
(1) 5.23

2014 Finance Act – *cont.*
s 256 .... 20.13
257 .... 20.13; 20.15; 52.25
258–261 .... 20.13; 52.25
262 .... 20.11; 52.25
263 .... 20.13; 20.14; 20.15; 52.25
264 .... 20.14
265 .... 20.13; 20.14; 52.25
266–273 .... 20.14
275 .... 52.24
276 .... 52.8
278–280 .... 20.16
281A 20.7
283 .... 20.7; 20.8; 20.13
284 .... 20.3; 52.24
291 .... 62.13
292 .... 21.6
299 .... 13.8
Sch 4
para 01 .... 15.15
52 .... 14.11
Sch 8
paras 1–33 .... 22.17
para 34 .... 22.17; 22.18
35 .... 22.17
36–38 .... 22.17; 22.18
39–46 .... 22.17
47 .... 22.13; 22.17
48–50 .... 22.13; 22.17
51 .... 22.13; 22.17; 22.22
52–88 .... 22.13; 22.17
89 .... 22.13; 22.17; 22.18
90–96 .... 22.13; 22.17
97–123 .... 22.24
122, 123 .... 64.2
124 .... 22.17; 22.24
125–131 .... 22.24
132 .... 22.13; 22.24
133, 134 .... 22.6; 22.24
135–157 .... 22.24
158–183 .... 22.25
184 .... 22.17; 22.25
185–215 .... 22.25
194–197 .... 22.6
216–225 .... 22.22
Sch 9
para 8 .... 22.8; 22.10–22.13
paras 9–11 .... 22.13
12 .... 22.11; 22.13
14, 15 .... 22.6
22 .... 22.22
23 .... 22.3; 22.6; 22.8; 22.13; 22.15; 22.16
24 .... 22.6; 22.8; 22.13; 22.15; 22.16
25 .... 7.7
27 .... 22.13; 22.15
35 .... 22.2; 22.8; 22.10; 22.13
36 .... 22.13
37 .... 22.8
43–46 .... 22.3

2014 Finance Act – *cont.*
paras 47–50 ... 7.7; 22.6; 22.8; 22.13; 22.15; 22.16
Sch 10
para 1 ... 71.8
paras 2 ... 71.7
3, 4 ... 71.3
5 ... 71.1; 71.6
Sch 11
para 1 ... 65.1–65.3; 65.5–65.17; 65.17–65.36; 65.38–65.44
5 ... 44.15
11 ... 11.10
Sch 12
para 2 ... 65.45; 65.46
3 ... 65.46
Sch 17
paras 17, 21 ... 50.22
para 23 ... 4.22
24 ... 4.23
25 ... 4.24
27 ... 4.22
28 ... 4.23
29 ... 4.24
Sch 30 ... 52.26
31
para 2 ... 4.26
3 ... 4.26
4 ... 4.27; 52.26
5 ... 52.26; 52.33
Sch 32
para 1 ... 4.30
2, 3 ... 4.30
4 ... 4.30; 4.31
5 ... 4.30
6 ... 4.31
7 ... 52.27
8 ... 4.30
Sch 33
para 1 ... 58.13
2 ... 52.33; 52.34; 52.36; 52.38
3 ... 52.8; 52.10
4 ... 52.3
5 ... 52.5
Sch 34
paras 1–12 ... 20.9
para 13 ... 20.11
13A–13D ... 20.11
14 ... 20.9; 20.11
Sch 34A
paras 1–16 ... 20.10
para 17–19 ... 20.10; 20.11
20–23 ... 20.11
24–31 ... 20.10
Sch 35 ... 52.22; 52.33
paras 1–5 ... 52.25
para 6, 7 ... 20.15
8, 9 ... 52.25
10 ... 52.25; 52.33
8–13 ... 52.25
Sch 36

2014 Finance Act – *cont.*
Sch 36 – *cont.*
paras 1–3 ... 20.17
para 4 ... 20.11
4A ... 20.10
5 ... 20.11
6 ... 20.12
7–13 ... 20.17
14 ... 20.13
15–18 ... 20.17
19 ... 20.8
20–21 ... 20.8; 20.11
Sch 37
paras 1, 2 ... 63.14; 63.15; 63.16; 63.17; 63.18
para 3 ... 63.14; 63.16
4 ... 63.16
18 ... 63.14; 64.2
19 ... 22.17
20 ... 22.24
21 ... 22.25
22 ... 22.22
Sch 38 para 15 ... 2.2
39
para 1 ... 14.11
3–5 ... 49.15
6 ... 29.2
7 ... 66.2
10 ... 44.16
12 ... 44.18
13 ... 29.2

2014 Wales Act
s 9(13), (14) ... 2.1

2015 Finance Act
s 4 ... 2.2
20 ... 11.10
24 ... 55.2; 55.5
40 ... 25.4
41 ... 24.5
42 ... 24.7
43 ... 24.3
44 ... 24.11
120 ... 52.3; 52.5; 52.8
122 ... 14.18
123 ... 11.2
Sch 6
para 1 ... 65.31
2–5 ... 23.9
6–9 ... 71.4
10 ... 23.9
11 ... 71.4
12 ... 23.9; 71.4
13 ... 65.7
14 ... 23.9; 65.7; 71.4
Sch 7
para 2 ... 1.2
3 ... 41.26; 44.2
4 ... 14.10
5 ... 44.8; 62.8; 62.9
6 ... 41.26; 41.33

2015 Finance Act – *cont.*
para 7 .... 2.2; 2.3
8 .... 14.6
11 .... 1.2; 41.26; 41.27
12 .... 44.3
14 .... 41.30
15 .... 2.6; 14.10
17 .... 19.7
18 .... 48.2
19 .... 48.5
20 .... 48.15
21 .... 14.11
23 .... 36.2; 36.4
24, 25 .... 36.8
26 .... 36.4
27, 28 .... 36.8
30 .... 41.33
31 .... 36.10
33 .... 36.10
35 .... 62.8; 62.9
36 .... 41.29
37 .... 41.27
38 .... 14.10
39 .... 41.30; 41.31; 41.32
40 .... 48.27
42 .... 52.3
43 .... 58.20; 58.21
44 .... 58.12; 58.21
45 .... 58.22
46 .... 6.10
47 .... 6.12
48 .... 6.13
49 .... 13.2
51 .... 51.3; 51.19
52 .... 51.2
55 .... 51.3
56 .... 52.8
57 .... 34.5
59 .... 52.5
60 .... 1.2; 41.25
Sch 8 .... 14.10
9
para 2 .... 53.2; 53.10
3 .... 53.8; 53.10
4 .... 53.2; 53.7
5 .... 53.7
6, 7 .... 53.11
8 .... 53.7
9 .... 53.2
10 .... 53.2; 53.7; 53.8
Sch 17
paras 1, 2 .... 20.3
para 3 .... 52.24
4–7 .... 20.4
8 .... 52.24
9, 10 .... 20.3
11 .... 52.24
12 .... 20.3
13 .... 52.24
14 .... 20.4
15 .... 52.24

2015 Finance Act – *cont.*
para 16 .... 20.5
17 .... 20.6
18 .... 52.24
19 .... 20.3; 52.24
20 .... 20.4; 52.24
21 .... 20.6
Sch 18
para 12 .... 4.29
Sch 19
para 2 .... 20.11
4 .... 20.11
5 .... 20.8; 20.11
6, 7 .... 20.9
8 .... 20.9; 20.11
9 .... 20.8–20.11
Sch 20
paras 2–8 .... 52.8
para 9–13 .... 52.3
14–19 .... 52.5
20 .... 52.11
Sch 21
paras 1–6 .... 52.12
para 7 .... 52.33
8 .... 52.34
9 .... 52.12; 52.33; 52.34

2015 Finance (No 2) Act
s 6 .... 2.2
7 .... 14.3
27 .... 23.9; 71.4
28 .... 23.9
33 .... 15.15
39 .... 51.4
43(1) 50.20; 50.21
(2) 50.20
(3)(4) 50.21
34(13) 14.14
51 .... 51.20
52 .... 42.9; 56.5
Sch 5
para 2 .... 23.2
4, 5 .... 23.4
paras 7–12 .... 23.3
para 13 .... 23.5
15 .... 23.12
17 .... 23.3
19 .... 23.3
21 .... 23.3
22 .... 23.12
23 .... 23.3; 23.4; 23.5
Sch 6
para 2 .... 71.7
paras 3–5 .... 71.2
6–13 .... 71.4
para 15 .... 71.4
paras 16–18 .... 71.5
para 20 .... 71.4
21 .... 71.4
23 .... 71.2; 71.4
Sch 7
paras 3, 4 .... 15.3

2015 Finance (No 2) Act – *cont.*
para 7 .... 15.5
20 .... 15.3
21 .... 15.3
54 .... 15.3
55 .... 15.5
57 .... 15.6
paras 81–84 .... 15.11
85, 86 .... 15.10
para 98 .... 15.3
Sch 8
para 2 .... 51.20
3 .... 51.21
4 .... 51.22
5 .... 51.20
paras 6, 7 .... 51.22
para 8 .... 51.21; 51.22
paras 9–12 .... 51.22
para 13 .... 51.23
14 .... 52.28
15 .... 52.33
16 .... 52.34
17 .... 52.33
paras 18–24 .... 51.20
para 25 .... 51.20; 58.15
40 .... 51.20

2016 Finance Act
s 2 .... 2.1
27 .... 25.30
(3) 19.14
28(1) 23.9
(2) 71.4
(3) 23.9
(4) 71.4
(5) 23.9
(6) 71.4
29(1), (2) 23.3
(3) 71.2
(4), (5) 71.4
(6) 23.3; 71.2; 71.4
30 .... 23.3; 71.2; 71.4
31 .... 71.2
36(3), (5) 50.20
45 .... 14.3
52 .... 15.14
53 .... 45.2
55 .... 29.22
73(3) 16.13
76(5) 41.6
(7) 49.8
(8) 14.2
77(1) 41.6
(4) 41.5
(6) 41.26
(7), (8) 39.1
(9) 41.6
78(2) 41.6
79(1) 41.6
(5) 41.5
(8), (9) 39.1
(10) 41.6

2016 Finance Act – *cont.*
s 81(1) 41.5; 41.6; 49.8
82(1) 41.5; 41.6
83(1)–(4) 2.1
(5) 2.3; 2 6;2.7
(6)–(14) 2.1
(17)–(19) 2.1
84 .... 24.5
85 .... 24.7
88(2) 22.26
(3)–(6) 22.26
(8), (9) 46.5
(10) 22.26; 46.5
90(1) 14.10
(2) 41.31
(3) 14.10
(4) 41.31
91 .... 58.20
156 .... 4.5
157(2), (3) 4.6
(4)–(6) 4.3
(8) 4.3
(10) 4.6
(11) 4.4
(18)–(20) 4.30
(26)–(28) 4.30
(29) 20.9
(30) 4.4; 4.6
158(2) 52.11
(3) 52.11; 52.18; 52.31; 52.33; 52.34
(4) 4.3; 4.6
(8), (9) 4.4
(10) 52.31; 52.33; 52.34; 52.36
(11) 52.26
(14) 52.11
(15) 4.3; 4.4; 52.11
160(2) 20.10; 20.11
(3) 20.10
(4) 20.12
(5), (6) 20.11
(7) 20.7
(8) 20.8
(9) 20.7; 20.8
(11) 20.10
(12)–(16) 20.17
(20)–(25) 20.10
161(2) 14.18
(3) 14.19
162 .... 52.20
163 .... 52.3; 52.5; 52.8
164 .... 31.3
165 .... 52.13
166 .... 52.40
167 .... 5.2; 5.3; 6.9; 42.10; 51.2
168(2) 6.13
(3) 58.6
169 .... 58.3
(6), (7) 52.5
ss 170, 171 .... 42.9; 56.5
s 173 .... 11.10

2016 Finance Act – *cont.*
s 176 .... 34.17
177(2), (3) 52.17; 52.33
(4) 52.33
(5) 52.33
ss 180–182 .... 23.1; 71.1
Sch 8
para 8 .... 52.8
9 .... 15.15
Sch 10
para 2 .... 6.10
4 .... 6.10
15 .... 4.20
22 .... 4.20
24 .... 4.20
Sch 11
para 2 .... 41.26
4 .... 41.29
5 .... 2.1
Sch 12
para 3 .... 24.3
4 .... 41.29
5 .... 24.3
Sch 13 .... 23.1
14
para 2 .... 40.2–40.7; 40.9; 40.10
3 .... 40.8
Sch 18 .... 52.1; 52.26
paras 2, 3 .... 4.33
para 7 .... 4.32
8 .... 4.34
9 .... 4.35
10 .... 4.34
11–14 .... 4.34
17 .... 4.35
18 .... 4.40
19–29 .... 4.36
30–35 .... 52.29
38, 39 .... 52.33
40 .... 52.18; 52.29
41 .... 52.34
42, 43 .... 52.29
44 .... 52.29; 52.31
45, 46 .... 4.38
47, 48 .... 4.33
49–53 .... 4.37
54 .... 4.34
55 .... 4.36
58 .... 4.37
59 .. 52.31; 52.33; 52.34; 52.36; 52.38
60 .... 52.26
63–65 .... 4.32
Sch 19 .... 52.1
para 1–17 .... 14.18
18 .... 52.30
19, 20 .... 14.18
21 .... 52.30
22, 23 .... 14.18
24 .... 52.30
25 .... 14.18; 52.30

2016 Finance Act – *cont.*
para 27, 28 .... 52.30
29 .... 52.33
30 .... 52.34
31 .... 52.33
32 .... 52.30
35–53 .... 14.19
48 .... 52.8
Sch 20
para 1–9 .... 52.20
10, 11 .... 52.33
12–14 .... 52.34
15 .... 52.20
18–23 .... 52.20
Sch 21
para 1–4 .... 52.8
5–8 .... 52.3
9–12 .... 52.5
Sch 22
para 15 .... 52.33
16–18 .... 52.34
20 .... 52.3; 52.5; 52.8; 52.9; 52.31; 52.33; 52.34; 52.36; 52.38
21 .... 52.18
Sch 23
para 1 .... 52.13
2 .... 52.3; 52.13
3–11 .... 52.13
14 .... 52.13
19 .... 52.13
Sch 23
para 3 .... 6.9
4 .... 5.2
5 .... 5.3
6 .... 6.9
7, 8 .... 51.2
9 .... 42.10
Sch 24 .... 23.1; 71.1

2016 Scotland Act
s 15(4) 2.1

2017 Finance Act
s 12–14 .... 22.26
24 .... 20.11
44–52 .... 52.40

2017 Finance (No 2) Act 34.5
s 11(2) 23.3
(3) 60.8
(4) 23.3; 60.8
12, 13 .... 71.5
14(3) 55.5
(5) 55.5
15(2)–(8) 55.4
16 .... 16.13; 39.1
18 .... 14.6
20 .... 15.3
26 .... 29.23
(2) 16.9
(4) 16.9
27 .... 66.1

2017 Finance (No 2) Act – *cont.*
s 27(2) 66.3; 66.5; 66.10
(3) 66.3
(4) 66.9
(5) 66.13
(6) .. 66.3; 66.5; 66.10; 66.10; 66.13
28 .... 66.1
(2) 66.6
(3) 66.8
(5) 66.6
(7) 66.6; 66.8
29 .... 57.34
32(2) 49.7
(3) 48.5
(4) 48.15
(5) 48.5; 48.15; 49.7
39 .... 41.6
64 .... 52.8
65 .... 52.21
69 .... 34.17
82(9) 41.6
Sch 1
para 2.............. 65.1
3.............. 65.9
4.............. 65.11
6(2).............. 65.18
(3).............. 65.29
7.............. 65.23
8.............. 65.25
9.............. 65.28
10.............. 65.31
11(2).............. 23.3
(3).............. 60.10
(4).............. 71.4
(16).............. 60.10
12.............. 65.31
14(1). 65.9; 65.18; 65.23; 65.28; 65.28; 65.29
(2).............. 65.29
(3), (4).............. 65.11
15.............. 65.31
16.............. 23.3
(2).............. 71.4
Sch 2
para 44.............. 39.1
45.............. 16.13
46, 47.............. 25.20
64(1).............. 16.13; 39.1
Sch 4
para 6.............. 14.6
11.............. 14.6
Sch 5 .... 15.3
8
para 3–5.............. 55.2
6.............. 48.1
7.............. 48.5
8.............. 7.3
9.............. 48.29
14(2).............. 55.5
(4).............. 55.2
(6).............. 55.2

2017 Finance (No 2) Act – *cont.*
para 15.............. 49.5
16.............. 49.5
18.............. 48.8
41–42.............. 57.34
44–46.............. 55.3
Sch 9
para 1.............. 48.14
3.............. 48.14
Sch 15
para 2.............. 58.9
3, 4.............. 58.13
5.............. 58.21
6.............. 58.21
7, 8.............. 58.18
9.............. 58.8
10, 11.............. 58.14; 58.18
12.............. 58.12; 58.21
13.............. 58.18
14.............. 6.10
15.............. 6.12
16.............. 51.31
17.............. 6.11
18.............. 5.2
19.............. 51.3
(1).............. 52.33
20.............. 51.2
21.............. 51.2
22.............. 14.7; 52.33
24–28.............. 58.19
30.............. 5.2; 51.17
31, 32.............. 6.10
38, 39.............. 21.9
41, 42.............. 4.20
44... 4.20; 5.2; 6.10; 6.11; 6.12; 14.7; 21.9; 51.2; 51.3; 51.17; 51.31;58.8; 58.9; 58.13; 58.14; 58.18; 58.19; 58.21
Sch 16
para 1–19.............. 52.21
21.............. 52.21
23–26.............. 52.21
36–39.............. 52.34
40–43.............. 52.21
44, 45.............. 52.21
46–51.............. 52.21
52.............. 52.21
58.. 52.31; 52.33; 52.34; 52.36; 52.38
61.............. 20.9
Sch 18
para 1.............. 52.14
3–6.............. 52.14
7.............. 52.14
8(3), (4).............. 52.14
9–12.............. 52.14
13.............. 52.14
14, 15.............. 52.14
15(3).............. 52.14
16.17.............. 52.14
18, 19.............. 52.33

2017 Finance (No 2) Act – *cont.*
para 20–22 .... 52.34
23.24 .... 52.14
26 .... 52.14
27 .... 52.12
28 .... 52.13
29(2) 52.31; 52.33; 52.34; 52.36; 52.38
(3) 62.11
para 30, 31 .... 31.4
Sch 24
para 1 .... 52.21

2017 Savings (Government Contributions) Act
s 1 .... 25.30
3 .... 25.30
Sch 1 .... 25.30

76 Table of Statutory Instruments

Note. Statutory Instruments (SIs) referred to at 21.3, 21.10 DOUBLE TAX RELIEF are not listed below. Also not listed are those SIs which do no more than confirm indexed rises in tax rates and allowances as announced in the Budget or which alter the rates of interest on overpaid and unpaid tax, though these are referred to in the text where appropriate.

The list below is in date order.

1955 No 1954 International Finance Corporation Order 1955 .... 25.54

1960 No 1383 International Development Association Order 1960 .... 25.54

1967 No 149 Capital Gains Tax Regulations 1967 .... 5.4

1971 No 1035 Mineral Royalties (Tax) Regulations 1971 .... 47.1

1984 No 1836 Finance Act 1984 (Commencement No 2) Order 1984 .... 5.6

1986 No 1925 Insolvency Rules 1986 .... 14.4

1988 No 266 Capital Gains Tax (Definition of Unit Trust Scheme) Regulations 1988 .... 70.3

1989 No 1297 Taxes (Interest Rate) Regulations 1989 ..... 42.3; 42.7; 56.3; 56.4

1991 No 724 High Court and County Courts Jurisdiction Order 1991 .... 51.19

1991 No 1877 County Court Appeals Order 1991 .... 51.19

1992 No 572 IT (Stock Lending) (Amendment) Regulations 1992 .... 63.25

1992 No 3066 Corporation Tax Acts (Provisions for Payment of Tax and Returns), (Appointed Days) Order 1992 .... 14.11

1993 No 950 Capital Gains Tax (Gilt-edged Securities) Order 1993 .... 28.2

1994 No 87 Finance Act 1989, Section 152, (Appointed Day) Order 1994 .... 51.19

1994 No 236 Distraint by Collectors (Fees, Costs and Charges) Regulations 1994 .... 51.19

1994 No 1813 General and Special Commissioners (Amendment of Enactments) Regulations 1994 .... 52.33; 52.34

1994 No 2656 Capital Gains Tax (Gilt-edged Securities) Order 1994 .... 28.2

1995 No 353 Lloyd's Underwriters (Special Reserve Funds) Regulations 1995 .... 69.2

1995 No 1185 Lloyd's Underwriters (Special Reserve Funds) (Amendment) Regulations 1995 .... 69.2

1995 No 1979 Venture Capital Trust Regulations 1995 ..... 71.1; 71.2; 71.7; 71.9

1995 No 2151 Distraint by Collectors (Fees, Costs and Charges) (Amendment) Regulations 1995 .... 51.19

1995 No 3219 IT (Stock Lending) (Amendment No 2) Regulations 1995 .... 63.25

1996 No 1031 Capital Gains Tax (Gilt-edged Securities) Order 1996 .... 28.2

1996 No 2325 Housing Act 1996 (Consequential Provisions) Order 1996 .... 25.53; 25.62

1997 No 57 Electronic Lodgement of Tax Returns Order 1997 .... 58.2

1997 No 1154 Open-ended Investment Companies (Tax) Regulations 1997 .... 11.4; 70.8

1997 No 1715 Open-ended Investment Companies (Tax) (Amendment) Regulations 1997 .... 70.8

1997 No 2681 Lloyd's Underwriters (Scottish Limited Partnerships) (Tax) Regulations 1997 .... 69.4

1998 No 310 Taxes (Interest Rate) (Amendment) Regulations 1998 .... 42.3

1998 No 311 Finance Act 1989, Section 178(1), (Appointed Day) Order 1998 .... 42.3; 52.22

1998 No 1870 Individual Savings Account Regulations 1998 .... 25.30

1998 No 1871 Individual Savings Account (Insurance Companies) Regulations 1998 .... 25.30

1998 No 2244 Government of Wales Act 1998 (Commencement No 1) Order 1998 .... 25.53; 25.62

1998 No 3132 Civil Procedure Rules 1998 .... 5.34

1998 No 3174 Individual Savings Account (Amendment) Regulations 1998 .... 25.30

1998 No 3175 Corporation Tax (Instalment Payments) Regulations 1998 .... 42.7; 56.4

1998 No 3177 European Single Currency (Taxes) Regulations 1998 ..... 7.2; 7.7; 25.5; 49.1; 63.25

1999 No 527 Social Security Contributions (Transfer of Functions, etc) Act 1999 (Commencement No 1 and Transitional Provisions) Order 1999 .... 31.6

1999 No 564 Finance Act 1993, Section 86(2), (Fish Quota) Order 1999 .... 59.4

1999 No 1953 Capital Gains Tax (Definition of Permanent Interest Bearing Share) Regulations 1999 .... 54.3

1999 No 2975 Corporation Tax (Simplified Arrangements for Group Relief) Regulations 1999 .... 58.19

1999 No 3292 Special Commissioners (Jurisdiction and Procedure) (Amendment) Regulations 1999 .... 5.20

1999 No 3294 Special Commissioners (Amendment of the Taxes Management Act 1970) Regulations 1999 .... 5.26

1999 No 3308 Lloyd's Underwriters (Special Reserve Funds) Regulations 1999 .... 69.2

2000 No 945 Income Tax (Electronic Communications) Regulations 2000 .... 58.4

2000 No 2074 Donations to Charity by Individuals (Appropriate Declarations) Regulations 2000 .... 11.10

2000 No 2550 Capital Gains Tax (Definition of Unit Trust Scheme) (Amendment) Regulations 2000 .... 70.3

2001 No 56 Income Tax (Electronic Communications) (Incentive Payments) Regulations 2001 .... 30.4

2001 No 544 Financial Services and Markets Act 2000 (Regulated Activities) Order 2001 .... 7.7; 7.8

2001 No 916 Access to Justice Act 1999 (Commencement No 7, Transitional Provisions and Savings) Order 2001 .... 5.16

2001 No 1081 Income Tax (Electronic Communications) (Miscellaneous Amendments) Regulations 2001 .... 30.4

2001 No 1122 Capital Gains Tax (Gilt-edged Securities) Order 2001 .... 28.2

2001 No 1304 General Commissioners of Income Tax (Costs) Regulations 2001 .... 5.16

2001 No 3629 Financial Services and Markets Act 2000 (Consequential Amendments) (Taxes) Order 2001 .... 11.5; 45.3; 49.3; 58.19; 69.2; 70.8

2001 No 3799 Enterprise Management Incentives (Gross Asset Requirement) Order 2001 .... 22.22

2002 No 1967 Corporation Tax (Finance Leasing of Intangible Assets) Regulations 2002 .... 15.15

2002 No 1970 Exchange Gains and Losses (Bringing into Account Gains or Losses) Regulations 2002 .... 15.3

2002 No 2661 Venture Capital Trust (Exchange of Shares and Securities) Regulations 2002 .... 71.3; 71.5

2002 No 2849 Capital Gains Tax (Gilt-edged Securities) Order 2002 .... 28.2

2002 No 2976 General Commissioners and Special Commissioners (Jurisdiction and Procedure) (Amendment) Regulations 2002 .... 5.13; 5.20

2002 No 3036 Tax Credits (Administrative Arrangements) Regulations 2002 .... 31.2

2003 No 120 Proceeds of Crime Act 2002 (Commencement No 4, Transitional Provisions and Savings) Order 2003 .... 31.2

2003 No 282 Income and Corporation Taxes (Electronic Communications) Regulations 2003 .... 30.4

2003 No 1116 Companies (Acquisition of Own Shares) (Treasury Shares) Regulations 2003 .... 63.19

2003 No 1997 Finance Act 2003, Schedule 22, Paragraph 3(1) (Appointed Day) Order 2003 .... 22.6; 22.13

2003 No 2093 Enterprise Act 2002 (Commencement No. 4 and Transitional Provisions and Savings) Order 2003 .... 5.13

2003 No 2682 Income Tax (Pay As You Earn) Regulations 2003 .... 51.19

2004 No 438 Capital Gains Tax (Gilt-Edged Securities) Order 2004 .... 28.2

2004 No 674 Recovery of Duties and Taxes Etc. Due in Other Member States (Corresponding UK Claims, Procedure and Supplementary) Regulations 2004 .... 51.32

2004 No 1450 Child Trust Funds Regulations 2004
reg 24–38 .... 25.24

2004 No 1864 Tax Avoidance Schemes (Information) Regulations 2004 .... 20.2; 20.3; 20.4; 20.5; 52.24

2004 No 1865 Tax Avoidance Schemes (Promoters and Prescribed Circumstances) Regulations 2004 .... 20.3

2004 No 1945 Finance Act 2004, Section 85, (Commencement) Order 2004 .... 22.13; 22.15

2004 No 2199 Venture Capital Trust (winding up and Mergers) (Tax) Regulations 2004 .... 71.2; 71.5; 71.12

2004 No 2502 Corporation Tax (Notice of Coming within Charge — Information) Regulations 2004 .... 58.19

2004 No 2738 Financial Services and Markets Act (Stakeholder Products) Regulations 2004
reg 4–6 .... 25.30

2004 No 3256 Loan Relationships and Derivative Contracts (Disregard and Bringing into Account of Profits and Losses) Regulations 2004
reg 3, 5 .... 15.3

2005 No 276 Capital Gains Tax (Gilt-Edged Securities) Order 2005 .... 28.2

2005 No 409 Finance Act 1993, Section 86(2), (Single Payment Scheme) Order 2005 .... 59.4

2005 No 699 Companies (Defective Accounts) (Authorised Person) Order 2005 .... 31.2

2005 No 1449 Tonnage Tax (Further Opportunity for Election) Order 2005 .... 25.17

2005 No 1479 Recovery of Taxes Etc. Due in Other Member States (Amendment of Section 134 of the Finance Act 2002) Regulations 2005 .... 51.32

2005 No 1907 Pension Protection Fund (Tax) (2005–06) Regulations 2005 .... 25.60

2005 No 2790 Donations to Charity by Individuals (Appropriate Declarations) (Amendment) Regulations 2005 .... 11.10

2005 No 3229 Tax and Civil Partnerships Regulations 2005
reg 104 .... 11.10
119 .... 22.34
124(a) 8.3
130 .... 44.12

2005 No 3349 Child Trust Funds (Amendment No 3) Regulations 2005 .... 25.24

2006 No 111 Lloyd's Underwriters (Scottish Limited Partnerships) (Tax) (Amendment) Regulations 69.4

2006 No 184 Taxation of Chargeable Gains (Gilt-edged Securities) Order 2006 .... 28.2

2006 No 264 Community Benefit Societies (Restriction on Use of Assets) Regulations 2006 .... 65.3

2006 No 333 Tonnage Tax (Exception of Financial Year 2006) Order 2006 .... 25.17

2006 No 378 Serious Organised Crime and Police Act 2005 (Commencement No 5 and Transitional and Transitory Provisions and Savings) Order 2006 .... 31.2

2006 No 575 Pension Protection Fund (Tax) Regulations 2006 .... 25.60

2006 No 959 Income Tax (Trading and Other Income) Act 2005 (Consequential Amendments) Order 2006
art 3 .... 7.7; 16.9

2006 No 964 Authorised Investment Funds (Tax) Regulations 2006
reg 4 .... 70.8
15 .... 70.3
53–69 .... 70.9
69A–69Z41 .... 70.8
76 .... 70.8

2006 No 964 Authorised Investment Funds (Tax) Regulations 2006 – *cont.*
reg 78–85 .... 70.8
85A 70.10
85D 70.10
85G 70.10
85M 70.10
85Z1 .... 70.10
85Z5–85Z9 .... 70.10
85Z11 .... 70.10
89 .... 70.3
90 .... 15.5
94(7) 11.4
95 .... 15.5
96A 15.5
100 .... 70.8
103 .... 70.8
106 .... 70.8
107 .... 29.2
109 .... 70.1; 70.8

2006 No 1543 Tax Avoidance Schemes (Prescribed Descriptions of Arrangements) Regulations 2006 .... 20.2

2006 No 1544 Tax Avoidance Schemes (Information) (Amendment) Regulations 2006
reg 4 .... 20.2; 20.3; 20.4
6 .... 20.2; 20.3; 20.4

2006 No 2865 Real Estate Investment Trusts (Financial Statements of Group Real Estate Investment Trusts) Regulations 2006 .... 70.5

2006 No 2866 Real Estate Investment Trusts (Joint Ventures) Regulations 2006 .... 70.5

2006 No 2867 Real Estate Investment Trusts (Assessment and Recovery of Tax) Regulations 2006 .... 70.5

2006 No 3170 Taxation of Chargeable Gains (Gilt-edged Securities) (No.2) Order 2006 .... 28.2

2006 No 3194 Individual Savings Accounts (Amendment) Regulations 2006 .... 25.30

2006 No 3195 Child Trust Funds (Amendment No 3) Regulations 2006 .... 25.24

2006 No 3269 Finance Act 2002, Schedule 26, (Parts 2 and 9) (Amendment) Order 2006
art 1(3) 15.9
3–8 .... 15.9
10, 11 .... 15.12
12–15 .... 15.10
17–19 .... 15.10
21–23 .... 15.11

2006 No 3273 Lloyd's Sourcebook (Finance Act 1993 and Finance Act 1994) – *cont.*
(Amendment) Order 2006 .... 69.2

2007 No 850 Tonnage Tax (Exception of Financial Year 2007) Order 2007 .... 25.17

2007 No 1050 Corporation Tax (Taxation of Films) (Transitional Provisions) Regulations 2007
reg 8 .... 15.15

2007 No 1820 Income Tax Act 2007 (Amendment) (No 2) Order 2007 ..... 23.4; 23.5; 23.6; 23.7; 23.8; 23.9

2007 No 2119 Individual Savings Account (Amendment) Regulations 2007 .... 25.30

2007 No 2126 International Mutual Administrative Assistance in Tax Matters Order 2007 .... 31.2

2007 No 2130 Employment Income (Meaning of Securities) Order 2007 .... 22.2

2007 No 2134 Friendly Societies (Modification of the Corporation Tax Acts) (Amendment) Regulations 2007 .... 25.51

2007 No 2153 Tax Avoidance Schemes (Information) (Amendment) Regulations 2007 .... 20.5

2007 No 2484 Sale and Repurchase of Securities (Amendment of Instruments) Order 2007 .... 20.2

2007 No 2485 Sale and Repurchase of Securities (Modification of Schedule 13 to the Finance Act 2007) Regulations 2007 .... 63.26

2007 No 2486 Sale and Repurchase of Securities (Modification of Enactments) Regulations 2007 .... 63.26

2007 No 3103 Tax Avoidance Schemes (Information) (Amendment) (No 2) Regulations 2007 .... 52.24

2007 No 3104 Tax Avoidance Schemes (Penalty) Regulations 2007 .... 52.24

2007 No 3166 Finance Act 2007 (Sections 82 to 84 and Schedule 23) (Commencement) Order 2007 .... 34.14; 34.16

2007 No 3175 Police and Criminal Evidence Act 1984 (Application to Revenue and Customs) Order 2007 .... 34.14

2007 No 3186 Corporation Tax (Implementation of the Mergers Directive) Regulations 2007
reg 3(3) 49.16
Sch 1
para 2, 3 .... 49.13
4, 5 .... 49.14
6 .... 49.13; 49.14
7 .... 49.12
8 .... 59.9
9 .... 29.7
24 .... 15.14
Sch 2
para 2 .... 49.15
5 .... 49.12
6 .... 59.9
7 .... 29.7
15 .... 57.33
Sch 3
para 1 .... 49.16
2007 No 3425 Real Estate Investment Trusts (Joint Venture Groups) Regulations 2007 .... 70.5
2007 No 3426 Scientific Research Organisations Regulations 2007 .... 25.61
2007 No 3431 Loan Relationships and Derivative Contracts (Disregard and Bringing into Account of Profits and Losses) (Amendment No. 2) Regulations 2007 .... 15.3
2007 No 3507 Recovery of Foreign Taxes Regulations 2007 .... 51.32
2007 No 3536 Real Estate Investment Trusts (Financial Statements of Group Real Estate Investment Trusts) (Amendment) Regulations 2007 .... 70.5
2007 No 3540 Real Estate Investment Trusts (Breach of Conditions) (Amendment) Regulations 2007 .... 70.5
2007 No 3612 General Commissioners and Special Commissioners (Jurisdiction and Procedure) (Amendment) Regulations 2007
reg 5 .... 5.12; 5.13
2008 No 568 Finance Act 2007, Schedule 24 (Commencement and Transitional Provisions) Order 2008 .... 52.8; 52.10
2008 No 704 Individual Savings Account (Amendment) Regulations 2008 .... 25.30
2008 No 705 Authorised Investment Funds (Tax) (Amendment) Regulations 2008 .... 70.8
2008 No 706 Income Tax (Limits for Enterprise Management Incentives) Order 2008 .... 22.22
2008 No 755 Serious Crime Act 2007 (Commencement No. 2 and Transitional and Transitory Provisions and Savings) Order 2008 .... 30.9; 31.2
2008 No 954 Companies Act 2006 (Consequential Amendments) (Taxes and National Insurance) Order 2008
art 10 .... 44.18
17 .... 63.7
25 .... 52.4; 58.19
26 .... 18.14
39 .... 23.11
2008 No 1579 Corporation Tax (Implementation of the Mergers Directive) Regulations 2008
reg 4(2) 49.16
Sch 1
para 3, 4 .... 49.15
5–7 .... 49.15
2008 No 1588 Taxation of Chargeable Gains (Gilt-edged Securities) Order 2008 .... 28.2
2008 No 1934 Individual Savings Account (Amendment No. 2) Regulations 2008 .... 25.30
2008 No 1935 Finance Act 2008, Schedule 38, (Appointed Day) Order 2008 .... 20.4; 52.24
2008 No 1936 Finance Act 2008 Section 135 (Disaster or Emergency) Order 2008 .... 42.9
2008 No 1942 Friendly Societies (Transfers of Other Business) (Modification of the Corporation Tax Acts) Regulations 2008 .... 25.51
2008 No 1947 Tax Avoidance Schemes (Information) (Amendment) Regulations 2008 .... 20.4
2008 No 1948 Taxes (Fees for Payment by Telephone) Regulations 2008 .... 51.14
2008 No 2684 First-tier Tribunal and Upper Tribunal (Chambers) Order 2008
art 2 .... 5.11
5A 5.11
2008 No 2698 Tribunal Procedure (Upper Tribunal) Rules 2008
r 1 .... 5.33
2, 3 .... 5.11
5, 6 .... 5.25
7, 8 .... 5.26
9 .... 5.25
11, 12 .... 5.25
15, 16 .... 5.30

2008 No 2698 Tribunal Procedure (Upper Tribunal) Rules 2008 – *cont.*
r 17 .... 5.25
21, 22 .... 5.27
23–25 .... 5.28
26A 5.29
34–38 .... 5.30
39, 40 .... 5.31
44–46 .... 5.32
2008 No 2834 Appeals from the Upper Tribunal to the Court of Appeal Order 2008 .... 5.32; 5.34
2008 No 2871 Recovery of Taxes etc Due in Other Member States (Amendment of Section 134 of the Finance Act 2002) Regulations 2008 .... 51.32
2008 No 2991 Taxes (Fees for Payment by Internet) Regulations 2008 .... 51.14
2008 No 3002 Housing and Regeneration Act 2008 (Consequential Provisions) Order 2008 .... 9.6
2008 No 3159 Authorised Investment Funds (Tax) (Amendment No. 3) Regulations 2008
reg 1 .... 70.9
11 .... 70.9
17 .... 70.9
18–27 .... 70.8
30, 31 .... 70.9
2008 No 3165 Finance Act 2008, Section 31 (Specified Tax Year) Order 2008 .... 23.10
2009 No 23 Income Tax Act 2007 (Amendment) Order 2009
art 3 .... 11.4
2009 No 56 Transfer of Tribunal Functions and Revenue and Customs Appeals Order 2009
art 31 .... 5.20
Sch 1
para 7 .... 58.8
11 .... 34.12
12–16 .... 58.14; 58.18
17 .... 58.12
18 .... 58.18
19 .... 5.2
28 .... 5.2
29 .... 5.3
30 .... 5.5; 5.6; 5.7; 5.8
33 .... 5.9
34 .... 51.17; 51.18
35 .... 5.23; 51.18
39 .... 42.6
40 .... 51.4
43 .... 9.6
44 .... 52.6
45 .... 52.34
46 .... 52.35
2009 No 56 Transfer of Tribunal Functions and Revenue and Customs Appeals Order 2009 – *cont.*
Sch 1 – *cont.*
para 48 .... 52.38
53–58 .... 13.3
60–62 .... 58.2
109 .... 25.85
144–146 .... 25.51
147 .... 11.5
164 .... 49.18
178 .... 49.7
179 .... 4.15
182, 183 .... 44.21
254–256 .... 58.19
257 .... 5.2; 58.19
258–262 .... 58.19
333 .... 30.9
335 .... 57.35
438, 442 .... 42.3
445 .... 62.13
447–449 .... 70.5
453 .... 11.5
466, 467 .... 52.34
471 .. 34.4; 34.5; 34.6; 34.8; 34.10
473 .... 52.34
477 .... 21.10
703, 704 .... 11.5
Sch 2
para 3–5 .... 5.4
2009 No 196 First-tier Tribunal and Upper Tribunal (Chambers) (Amendment) Order 2009 .... 5.11
2009 No 273 Tribunal Procedure (First-tier Tribunal) (Tax Chamber) Rules 2009
r 2, 3 .... 5.11
5, 6 .... 5.12
7, 8 .... 5.13
9 .... 5.12
10 .... 5.24
11, 12 .... 5.12
15 .... 5.19
17–19 .... 5.12
20 .... 5.8
21 .... 5.12
23 .... 5.14; 5.18
24 .... 5.16
25 .... 5.15; 5.17
26 .... 5.15
27 .... 5.17
28 .... 5.18
29–33 .... 5.19
34, 35 .... 5.20
37, 38 .... 5.21
39–41 .... 5.22
2009 No 274 Tribunal Procedure (Amendment) Rules 2009
r 7 .... 5.33
16 .... 5.29
20, 21 .... 5.31

2009 No 402 Finance Act 2008, Schedule 37 (Appointed Day) Order 2009 .... 13.3; 58.8; 58.19

2009 No 403 Finance Act 2008, Schedule 39 (Appointed Day, Transitional Provision and Savings) Order 2009 .... 6.10; 6.11; 6.13; 13.5; 21.7; 44.12; 47.1; 49.6; 58.15

2009 No 404 Finance Act 2008, Schedule 36 (Appointed Day and Savings) Order 2009 .... 34.3; 34.4; 34.8

2009 No 405 Finance Act 2008, Section 119 (Appointed Day) Order 2009 .... 58.7

2009 No 511 Finance Act 2008, Schedule 41 (Appointed Day and Transitional Provisions) Order 2009 .... 52.3

2009 No 571 Finance Act 2008, Schedule 40 (Appointed Day, Transitional Provisions and Consequential Amendments) Order 2009
art 2 .... 52.8; 52.9
Schedule 39.1; 52.34; 62.11

2009 No 611 Tax Avoidance Schemes (Information) (Amendment) Regulations 2009
reg 4 .... 20.4

2009 No 730 Enactment of Extra-Statutory Concessions Order 2009
art 4 .... 44.11
5 .... 4.14
6 .... 59.5
7–10 .... 53.7
11 .... 25.91
12 .... 25.41

2009 No 1029 Substantial Donor Transactions (Variation of Threshold Limits) Regulations 2009
reg 2 .... 11.5

2009 No 1482 Real Estate Investment Trusts (Amendment of Schedule 16 to the Finance Act 2006) Regulations 2009 .... 70.5

2009 No 1550 Individual Savings Account (Amendment) Regulations 2009 .... 25.30

2009 No 1890 Companies Act 2006 (Consequential Amendments) (Taxes and National Insurance) Order 2009
art 3 .... 20.2; 29.2; 51.25
4 .... 25.91
8 .... 5.11
9 .... 4.17

2009 No 1916 Information Notice: Resolution of Disputes as to Privileged Communications Regulations 2009 .... 34.5

2009 No 1975 Tribunal Procedure (Amendment No 2) Rules 2009
r 15, 16 .... 5.27
17, 18 .... 5.28
19 .... 5.29
21 .... 5.31
29 .... 5.30

2009 No 2032 Taxes and Duties (Interest Rate) (Amendment) Regulations 2009 .... 56.4

2009 No 2033 Tax Avoidance Schemes (Prescribed Descriptions of Arrangements) (Amendment) Regulations 2009 .... 20.2

2009 No 2035 Finance Act 2009, Schedule 47 (Consequential Amendments) Order 2009
Schedule
para 2 .... 58.3
3 .... 58.16
4 .... 58.8
6 .... 49.7
8 .... 52.23
9 .... 13.3
30, 31 .... 36.8
32 .... 22.36
33 .... 62.8; 62.9
34 .... 62.12
35 .... 48.11
37 .... 58.19
47 .... 71.8

2009 No 2036 Authorised Investment Funds (Tax) (Amendment) Regulations 2009
reg 8 .... 70.9

2009 No 2568 Alternative Finance Arrangements (Amendment) Order 2009 .... 16.14

2009 No 2859 Income Tax Act 2007 (Amendment) (No 2) Order 2009
art 2 .... 41.5; 44.18
3 .... 70.5
4 .... 11.10; 41.5

2009 No 2860 Corporation Tax Act 2009 (Amendment) Order 2009
art 4 .... 16.14
5 .... 71.2

2009 No 2971 Mutual Societies (Transfers of Business) (Tax) Regulations 2009 .... 14.11

2009 No 3001 Offshore Funds (Tax) Regulations 2009 .... 49.11
reg 31 .... 11.4
126 .... 11.4; 11.7
127 .... 64.6
131 .... 15.5

2009 No 3024 Finance Act 2008, Section 128 and Part 2 of Schedule 43 (Appointed Day, Transitional Provision and Savings) Order2009 .... 51.19
2009 No 3054 Finance Act 2009, Section 96 and Schedule 48 (Appointed Day, Savings and Consequential Amendments) Order 2009 ..... 34.3; 34.4; 34.5; 34.6; 34.8; 34.9
2009 No 3073 Taxes, etc. (Fees for Payment by Telephone) Regulations 2009 .... 51.14
2009 No 3218 Income and Corporation Taxes (Electronic Communications) (Amendment) Regulations 2009 .... 51.10; 51.13; 58.2
2009 No 3227 Northern Rock plc (Tax Consequences) Regulations 2009
reg 3 .... 9.6
2010 No 40 First-tier Tribunal and Upper Tribunal (Chambers) (Amendment) Order 2010
r 16 .... 5.12
2010 No 157 Enactment of Extra-Statutory Concessions Order 2010 .... 30.5
art 7 .... 9.6
8 .... 41.13
9 .... 10.2
2010 No 294 Authorised Investment Funds (Tax) (Amendment) Regulations 2010
reg 6 .... 70.9
7 .... 70.3
16, 17 .... 70.8
21 .... 70.10
25 .... 70.10
2010 No 530 Finance Act 2008 (Penalties for Errors and Failure to Notify etc) (Consequential Amendments) Order 2010 .... 42.6; 62.11
2010 No 574 Finance Act 2009, Section 94 (Appointed Day) Order 2010 .... 31.3
2010 No 588 Income Tax Act 2007 (Amendment) Order 2010 .... 31.2
2010 No 614 Corporation Tax Act 2009 (Amendment) Order 2010 .... 66.20
2010 No 670 Finance Act 2009, Paragraph 12(2)(b) of Schedule 22 (Appointed Day) Order 2010 .... 49.11
2010 No 809 Exchange Gains and Losses (Bringing into Account Gains or Losses) (Amendment) Regulations 2010 .... 15.3
2010 No 1894 Child Trust Funds (Amendment No 3) Regulations 2010 .... 25.24
2010 No 1904 Taxes (Definition of Charity) (Relevant Territories) Regulations 2010 .... 11.2; 11.12
2010 No 2655 First-tier Tribunal and Upper Tribunal (Chambers) Order 2010 .... 5.11
2010 No 2743 Tax Avoidance Schemes (Penalty) (Amendment) Regulations 2010 .... 52.24
2010 No 2834 Tax Avoidance Schemes (Prescribed Descriptions of Arrangements) (Amendment) Regulations 2010 .... 20.2
2010 No 2902 Corporation Tax Act 2010 (Amendment) Order 2010 .... 29.2; 66.8
2010 No 2928 Tax Avoidance Schemes (Information) (Amendment) (No.2) Regulations 2010 .... 20.3; 52.24
2010 No 2942 Income and Corporation Taxes (Electronic Communications) (Amendment) Regulations 2010 .... 58.2
2010 No 2975 Individual Savings Account (Amendment No 2) Regulations 2010 .... 25.30
2010 No 3019 Finance Act 2010, Schedule 17 (Appointed Day) Order 2010 .... 20.3; 52.24
2011 No 23 Finance Act 2008, Section 39(7) (Commencement) Order 2011 .... 16.7
2011 No 37 Mutual Societies (Transfers of Business) (Tax) (Amendment) Regulations 2011 .... 14.11
2011 No 171 Tax Avoidance Schemes (Information) (Amendment) Regulations 2011 .... 20.3
2011 No 244 Authorised Investment Funds (Tax) (Amendment) Regulations 2011 .... 70.10
2011 No 660 Venture Capital Trust (Winding up and Mergers) (Tax) (Amendment) Regulations 2011 .... 71.3; 71.5
2011 No 662 Finance (No 3) Act 2010, Schedule 2 (Appointed Day) Order 2011 .... 23.5; 71.2; 71.4
2011 No 698 Loan Relationships and Derivative Contracts (Disregard and Bringing into Account of Profits and Losses) (Amendment) Regulations 2011 .... 15.3

2011 No 701 Finance Act 2009, Sections 101 to 103 (Income Tax Self Assessment) (Appointed Days and Transitional and Consequential Provisions) Order 2011 ..... 42.2; 42.3; 56.2; 56.3; 62.11

2011 No 702 Finance Act 2009, Schedules 55 and 56 (Income Tax Self Assessment and Pension Schemes) (Appointed Days and Consequential and Savings Provisions) Order 2011 ... 42.6; 42.10; 52.5

2011 No 703 Finance (No 3) Act 2010, Schedules 10 and 11 (Income Tax Self Assessment and Pension Schemes) (Appointed Days) Order 2011 .... 42.10; 52.5

2011 No 711 Taxes, etc (Fees for Payment by Internet) Regulations 2011 .... 51.14

2011 No 975 Finance Act 2010, Schedule 10 (Appointed Days and Transitional Provisions) Order 2011 ..... 52.3; 52.5; 52.8

2011 No 976 Penalties, Offshore Income etc (Designation of Territories) Order 2011 .... 52.3; 52.5; 52.8

2011 No 1037 Enactment of Extra-Statutory Concessions Order 2011 .... 13.7

2011 No 1079 International Mutual Administrative Assistance in Tax Matters Order 2011 .... 31.2

2011 No 1211 Offshore Funds (Tax) (Amendment) Order 2011 .... 49.11; 64.2

2011 No 1295 Taxation of Chargeable Gains (Gilt-edged Securities) Order 2011 .... 28.2

2011 No 1431 Corporation Tax (Implementation of the Mergers Directive) Regulations 2011 .... 49.13; 49.14; 49.15; 49.16

2011 No 1502 Taxation of Equitable Life (Payments) Order 2011 .... 25.25

2011 No 1583 Finance Act 2009 (Consequential Amendments) Order 2011 .... 51.19

2011 No 1584 Income Tax (Pay As You Earn) (Amendment) (No.3) Regulations 2011 .... 51.19

2011 No 1585 Income Tax (Earnings and Pensions) Act 2003 (Section 684(3A)) Order 2011 .... 51.19

2011 No 1613 Undertakings for Collective Investment in Transferable Securities Regulations 2011 .... 70.2

2011 No 1780 Individual Savings Account (Amendment No. 2) Regulations 2011 .... 25.30

2011 No 2192 Authorised Investment Funds (Tax) (Amendment No. 2) Regulations 2011 .... 70.8

2011 No 2401 Finance Act 2009, Section 103 (Appointed Day) Order 2011 .... 42.2; 56.2

2011 No 2446 Taxes and Duties, etc (Interest Rate) Regulations 2011 .... 42.2; 56.2

2011 No 2447 Child Trust Funds (Amendment No. 3) Regulations 2011 .... 25.24

2011 No 2459 Finance Act 2011, Section 42 (Appointed Day) Order 2011 .... 23.10

2011 No 2912 Loan Relationships and Derivative Contracts (Disregard and Bringing into Account of Profits and Losses) (Amendment No. 2) Regulations 2011 .... 15.3

2011 No 2931 MARD Regulations 2011 .... 51.32

2011 No 2977 Finance Act 2011, Section 49(6) (Appointed Day) Order 2011 .... 70.4

2012 No 519 Authorised Investment Funds (Tax) (Amendment) Regulations 2012 .... 15.5

2012 No 689 Taxes, etc. (Fees for Payment by Telephone) Regulations 2012 .... 51.14

2012 No 736 Finance Act 2010, Schedule 6, Part 2 (Commencement) Order 2012 .... 11.2; 53.7

2012 No 847 Data-gathering Powers (Relevant Data) Regulations 2012 .... 34.17

2012 No 1360 Income Tax (Limits for Enterprise Management Incentives) Order 2012 .... 22.22

2012 No 1709 British Waterways Board (Tax Consequences) Order 2012 .... 9.6

2012 No 1783 Authorised Investment Funds (Tax) (Amendment) Regulations 2012 .... 70.8

2012 No 1836 Tax Avoidance Schemes (Information) Regulations 2012 .... 20.3; 20.4; 52.24
- reg 8A 20.4
  - 13A, 13B 20.3

2012 No 1843 Taxation of Chargeable Gains (Gilt-edged Securities) Order 2012 .... 22.2

2012 No 1870 Child Trust Funds (Amendment) Regulations 2012 ... 25.24
2012 No 1871 Individual Savings Account (Amendment) (No. 2) Regulations 2012 ... 25.30
2012 No 1896 Finance Act 2012 (Enterprise Investment Scheme) (Appointed Day) Order 2012 ... 23.3; 23.5; 23.15
2012 No 1898 Business Investment Relief Regulations 2012 ... 55.4
2012 No 1901 Finance Act 2012 (Venture Capital Trusts) (Appointed Day) Order 2012 ... 71.4
2012 No 3008 Friendly Societies (Modifications of the Tax Acts) Regulations 2012 ... 25.51
2013 No 13 Taxation of Chargeable Gains (Gilt-edged Securities) Order 2013 ... 7.8
2013 No 279 Finance Act 2012, Schedule 38 (Tax Agents: Dishonest Conduct) (Appointed Day and Savings) Order 2013 ... 31.5; 34.11
2013 No 477 Tribunal Procedure (Amendment) Rules 2013
r 1 ... 5.12; 5.14; 5.20; 5.22; 5.24; 5.25; 5.31; 5.33
34 ... 5.14
35–38 ... 5.24
39 ... 5.12
41 ... 5.14
42 ... 5.20
43 ... 5.22
50–53 ... 5.33
54 ... 5.25
56 ... 5.31
2013 No 587 Finance Act 2012, Schedule 14 (Appointed Day) Order 2013 ... 11.9
2013 No 662 Capital Gains Tax (Annual Exempt Amount) Order 2013 ... 2.2
2013 No 999 Companies Act 2006 (Amendment of Part 18) Regulations 2013 ... 63.19
2013 No 1400 Collective Investment Schemes (Tax Transparent Funds, Exchanges, Mergers and Schemes of Reconstruction) Regulations 2013
r 1 ... 70.2
3 ... 70.11
8 ... 70.3
9 ... 70.2
10 ... 49.11
11 ... 70.2
13 ... 70.2
2013 No 1400 Collective Investment Schemes (Tax Transparent Funds, Exchanges, Mergers and Schemes of Reconstruction) Regulations 2013 – *cont.*
r 14 ... 70.8
15 ... 49.11
2013 No 1618 Penalties, Offshore Income etc (Designation of Territories) (Amendment) Order 2013 ... 52.3
2013 No 1744 Child Trust Funds (Amendment No 2) Regulations 2013 ... 25.24
2013 No 1755 Finance Act 2013, Schedule 23 (Employee Shareholder Shares) (Appointed Day) Order 2013 ... 22.26
2013 No 1815 Finance Act 2013, Section 66 (Appointed Day) Order 2013 ... 14.14
2013 No 1843 Exchange Gains and Losses (Bringing into Account Gains or Losses) (Amendment) Regulations 2013 ... 15.3
2013 No 2592 Tax Avoidance Schemes (Information) (Amendment, etc) Regulations 2013
reg 16 ... 20.4
20 ... 20.3
2013 No 2595 Tax Avoidance Schemes (Prescribed Descriptions of Arrangements) (Amendment) Regulations 2013 ... 20.2
2013 No 2819 Unauthorised Unit Trusts (Tax) Regulations 2013 ... 70.6; 70.7
2013 No 2983 Taxation of Chargeable Gains (Gilt-edged Securities) (No 2) Order 2013 ... 28.2
2013 No 3218 Corporation Tax Act 2009, Section 582 (Contract for Differences) (Amendment) Order 2013 ... 15.9
2014 No 518 Real Estate Investment Trust (Amendments to the Corporation Tax Act 2010 and Consequential Amendments) Regulations 2014 ... 70.5
2014 No 585 Unauthorised Unit Trusts (Tax) (Amendment) Regulations 2014 ... 70.6
2014 No 649 Child Trust Funds (Amendment) Regulations 2014 ... 25.24
2014 No 654 Individual Savings Account (Amendment) Regulations 2014 ... 25.30

2014 No 834 Public Bodies (Merger of the Director of Public Prosecutions and the Director of Revenue and Customs Prosecutions) Order 2014 .... 31.2

2014 No 1120 Taxation of Chargeable Gains (Gilt-edged Securities) Order 2014 .... 28.2

2014 No 1450 Individual Savings Account (Amendment No. 2) Regulations 2014 .... 25.30

2014 No 1453 Child Trust Funds (Amendment No. 2) Regulations 2014 .... 25.24

2014 No 1807 Taxes (Definition of Charity) (Relevant Territories) (Amendment) Regulations 2014 .... 11.2; 11.12

2014 No 2409 Corporation Tax (Instalment Payments) (Amendment) Regulations 2014 .... 51.4

2014 No 2438 Income Tax (Earnings and Pensions) Act 2003 (Section 684(3A)) Order 2014 .... 51.19

2014 No 2461 Finance Act 2014, Schedule 37, Paragraph 22 (Commencement) Order 2014 .... 22.22

2014 No 2689 Income Tax (Pay As You Earn) (Amendment No. 4) Regulations 2014 .... 51.19

2014 No 3066 Tax Relief for Social Investments (Accreditation of Social Impact Contractor) Regulations 2014 .... 65.2

2014 No 3133 Lloyd's Underwriters (Conversion of Partnerships to Underwriting through Successor Companies) (Tax) Regulations 2014 .... 69.8

2014 No 3188 Loan Relationships and Derivative Contracts (Disregard and Bringing into Account of Profits and Losses) (Amendment) Regulations 2014 .... 15.3

2014 No 3325 Changes in Accounting Standards (Loan Relationships and Derivative Contracts) Regulations 2014 .... 15.3

2015 No 130 Promoters of Tax Avoidance Schemes (Prescribed Circumstances under Section 235) Regulations 2015 .... 20.8

2015 No 131 Finance Act 2014 (Schedule 34 Prescribed Matters) Regulations 2015 .... 20.9

2015 No 549 Finance Act 2014 (High Risk Promoters Prescribed Information) Regulations 2015 .... 20.13; 20.14

2015 No 616 Market Value of Shares, Securities and Strips Regulations 2015 .... 45.3

2015 No 635 Finance Act 2007, Schedule 26, Paragraphs 4 and 5 (Valuation of Shares) (Appointed Day) Order 2015 .... 45.3

2015 No 725 Community Amateur Sports Clubs Regulations 2015 .... 11.12

2015 No 866 Offshore Asset Moves Penalty (Specified Territories) Regulations 2015 .... 52.12

2015 No 869 Individual Savings Account (Amendment No. 2) Regulations 2015 .... 25.30

2015 No 876 Child Trust Funds (Amendment No. 2) Regulations 2015 .... 25.24

2015 No 941 Individual Savings Account (Amendment No. 3) Regulations 2015 .... 25.30

2015 No 945 Tax Avoidance Schemes (Promoters and Prescribed Circumstances) (Amendment) Regulations 2015 .... 20.3; 20.5

2015 No 948 Tax Avoidance Schemes (Information) (Amendment) Regulations 2015 .... 20.3; 20.4

2015 No 1370 Individual Savings Account (Amendment No. 4) Regulations 2015 .... 25.30

2015 No 1371 Child Trust Funds (Amendment No. 3) Regulations 2015 .... 25.24

2015 No 1540 Housing and Regeneration Transfer Schemes (Tax Consequences) Regulations 2015 .... 9.6

2015 No 1777 Taxes, etc. (Fees for Payment by Internet) (Amendment) Regulations 2015 .... 51.4

2015 No 1783 Police and Criminal Evidence Act 1984 (Application to Revenue and Customs) Order 2015 .... 34.14

2015 No 1790 Taxation of Chargeable Gains (Gilt-edged Securities) Order 2015 .... 28.2

2015 No 1960 Exchange Gains and Losses (Bringing into Account Gains or Losses) (Amendment) Regulations 2015 .... 15.3

2015 No 1961 Loan Relationships and Derivative Contracts (Disregard and Bringing into Account of Profits and Losses) (Amendment) Regulations 2015 .... 15.3

2015 No 1986 Enforcement by Deduction from Accounts (Prescribed Information) Regulations 2015 .... 51.21; 51.22

2015 No 2051 Tax Relief for Social Investments (Accreditation of Social Impact Contractor) (Amendment) Regulations 2015 .... 65.2

2016 No 16 Individual Savings Account (Amendment) Regulations 2016 .... 25.30

2016 No 44 Enforcement by Deduction from Accounts (Imposition of Charges by Deposit-takers) Regulations 2016 .... 51.20

2016 No 74 Finance Act 2014, Schedule 9 (Consequential Amendment) Regulations 2016 .... 55.2

2016 No 99 Tax Avoidance Schemes (Prescribed Descriptions of Arrangements) (Amendment) Regulations 2016 .... 20.2

2016 No 333 Fees for Payment of Taxes, etc. by Credit Card Regulations 2016 .... 51.14

2016 No 364 Individual Savings Account (Amendment No. 2) Regulations 2016 .... 25.30

2016 No 456 Finance Act 2015, Schedule 20 (Appointed Days) Order 2016 .... 52.3; 52.5; 52.8

2016 No 597 Lloyd's Underwriters (Roll-over Relief on Disposal of Assets of Ancillary Trust Fund) (Tax) Regulations 2016 .... 69.8

2016 No 1010 Finance Act 2015, Section 20(2) and (3) and the Finance Act 2016, Section 173(1) (Appointed Days) Regulations 2016 .... 11.10

2016 No 1161 Scotland Act 2016 (Commencement No 2) Regulations 2016 .... 2.1

2016 No 1195 Donations to Charity (Gift Aid Declarations) Regulations 2016 .... 11.10

2016 No 1249 Finance Act 2016, Section 162(1) and Schedule 20 (Appointed Day) Regulations 2016 .... 52.20

2017 No 10 Taxation of Chargeable Gains (Gilt-edged Securities) Order 2017 .... 28.2

2017 No 185 Child Trust Funds (Amendment) Regulations 2017 .... 25.24

2017 No 186 Individual Savings Account (Amendment) Regulations 2017 .... 25.30

2017 No 259 Finance Act 2016, Schedule 21 (Appointed Days) Regulations 2017 .... 52.3; 52.6; 52.8

2017 No 261 Finance Act 2016, Section 164 (Appointed Day) Regulations 2017 .... 31.3

2017 No 277 Finance Act 2016, Schedule 22 (Appointed Days) Regulations 2017 .... 52.13

2017 No 345 Penalties Relating to Offshore Matters and Offshore Transfers (Additional Information) Regulations 2017 .... 52.3; 52.6; 52.8

2017 No 495 Enactment of Extra-Statutory Concessions Order 2017 .... 48.9; 48.19

2017 No 739 Criminal Finances Act 2017 (Commencement No 1) Regulations 2017 .... 52.40

77 Table of Cases

A

A v HMRC 5.19
FTT: [2012] UKFTT 541 (TC); [2012] SFTD 1257.
A-G v Alexander 57.33
Ex D 1874: (1874) LR 10 Ex 20.
A-G for Irish Free State v White 52.37
SC(I) 1931: (1931) 38 TC 666.
A-G v Johnstone 52.31
KB 1926: 10 TC 758.
A-G v Midland Bank Executor and Trustee Co Ltd 52.31
KB 1934: 19 TC 136.
PC 2000: [2000] 3 WLR 869.
Abbeyland Ltd v HMRC 39.1
FTT 2013: [2013] UKFTT 287 (TC); [2013] SFTD 1212.
Aberdeen Construction Group Ltd v CIR 16.2; 25.5; 74.1
HL 1978: 52 TC 281; [1978] STC 127, 52 TC 281.
Adams v HMRC 63.6
FTT: [2009] UKFTT 80 (TC); [2009] SFTD 184.
Alabama Coal, Iron, Land and Colonization Co Ltd v Mylam 41.3
KB 1926: 11 TC 232.
Allen v Farquharson Bros & Co 5.36
KB 1932: 17 TC 59.
Allison v Murray 16.11; 74.1
Ch D 1975: 51 TC 57; [1975] STC 524.
American Thread Co v Joyce 57.33
HL 1913: 6 TC 163.
Ames v HMRC 23.13
FTT: [2015] UKFTT 337 (TC); 2015 STI 3041.
Anders Utkilens Rederi A/S v O/Y Lovisa Stevedoring Co AB 16.5; 74.1
Ch D 1984: [1985] STC 301.
Anderson v CIR 5.20
CS 1933: 18 TC 320.
Anderson v HMRC 6.10
FTT 2017: [2016] UKFTT 335(TC); [2017] SFTD 100.
Anderson and another v HMRC 6.10
FTT: [2009] UKFTT 258 (TC); 2009 STI 2938.
Anderton v Lamb 59.4
Ch D 1980: 55 TC 1; [1981] STC 43.
Atherton v British Insulated and Helsby Cables Ltd 39.1
HL 1925: 10 TC 155.
Archer-Shee v Baker 5.34
CA 1928: 15 TC 1.
Ardmore Construction Ltd v HMRC 5.19
FTT 2014: [2014] UKFTT 453 (TC); 2014 STI 2585.
Aspden v Hildesley 17.1; 46.5; 74.1
Ch D 1981: 55 TC 609; [1982] STC 206.
Aspin v Estill 5.20; 52.21
CA 1987: 60 TC 549; [1987] STC 723.
Atkinson v Dancer 24.3
Ch D 1988: 61 TC 598; [1988] STC 758.

B

Bailey (Stephen) v Revenue and Customs Comrs 53.2
FTT 2017: (TC06085) [2017] UKFTT 658 (TC).
Bales v Rochford Commrs & CIR 52.37
Ch D 1964: 42 TC 17; 43 ATC 273.
Balgownie Land Trust v CIR 41.3
CS 1929: 14 TC 684.
Balloon Promotions Ltd v Wilson 59.4
(Sp C 524), [2006] SSCD 167.
Bank voor Handel en Scheepvaart NV v Administrator of Hungarian Property 25.49
HL 1954: 35 TC 311; [1954] AC 584; [1954] 1 All ER 969; [1954] 2 WLR 867
Barclays Mercantile Business Finance Ltd v Mawson 4.2
HL 2004: 76 TC 446; [2005] STC 1.
Barker and Another v HMRC 44.11
FTT: [2011] UKFTT 645 (TC); [2012] SFTD 244.
Barrett v Powell 24.3;, 74.1
Ch D 1998: 70 TC 432; [1998] STC 283.
Bartram v HMRC 58.15
UT: [2012] UKUT 184 (TCC); [2012] STC 2144.
Bastionspark LLP and others v HMRC 5.24
UT: [2016] STC 2549.
Batey v Wakefield 41.15; 53.6; 74.1
CA 1981: 55 TC 550; [1981] STC 521.
Bath and West Counties Property Trust Ltd v Thomas 4.2; 41.3; 74.1
Ch D 1977: 52 TC 20; [1978] STC 30.
Battle Baptist Church v CIR and Woodham 11.10
(Sp C 23), [1995] SSCD 176.
Bayley v Rogers 41.15; 74.1
Ch D 1980: 53 TC 420; [1980] STC 544.
Baylis v Gregory 4.2; 6.2; 74.1
HL 1988: 62 TC 1; [1988] STC 476.
Beach v Willesden Commrs 5.2; 5.3
Ch D 1981: 55 TC 663; [1982] STC 157.
Beckwith v HMRC 34.6
FTT: [2012] UKFTT 181 (TC); 2012 STI 1842.
Begg-MacBrearty v Stilwell 62.14; 74.1
Ch D 1996: 68 TC 426; [1996] STC 413.
Behague v HMRC 34.5
FTT: [2013] UKFTT 596 (TC); 2013 STI 3577.
Bentley v Pike 16.11; 74.1
Ch D 1981: 53 TC 590; [1981] STC 360.
Billows v Hammond 45.4; 74.1
(Sp C 252), [2000] SSCD 430.
Blackburn v HMRC 23.15; 23.17
CA 2008: [2008] EWCA Civ 1454; [2009] STC 188.
Blackwell v HMRC 16.11
UT 2015: [2016] STC 598.
Blumenthal v HMRC 54.3
FTT: [2012] UKFTT 497 (TC); [2012] SFTD 1264.
Boarland v Madras Electric Supply Corporation Ltd 25.49
HL 1955: 35 TC 612; [1955] AC 667; [1955] 1 All ER 753.
Bolands Ltd v CIR 5.34
SC(I) 1925: 4 ATC 526.
Bond v Pickford 62.14; 74.1
CA 1983: 57 TC 301; [1983] STC 517.
Bookey v Edwards 5.20
Ch D 1981: 55 TC 486; [1982] STC 135.
Booth v Ellard 62.3; 74.1
CA 1980: 53 TC 393; [1980] STC 555.
Boparan v HMRC 59.3

(Sp C 587), [2007] STC (SCD) 297.
Bowring v HMRC 48.14
UT 2015: [2015] UKUT 550 (TCC); [2016] STC 816.
Bradshaw v Blunden (No 2) 5.34
Ch D 1960: 39 TC 73.
Brady v Group Lotus Car Companies plc 5.20; 5.34
CA 1987: 60 TC 359; [1987] STC 635.
British Telecommunications plc v HMRC 10.2
(Sp C 535), [2006] SSCD 347.
Broadbridge v Beattie 41.3
KB 1944: 26 TC 63.
Brodt v Wells Commrs 52.37
Ch D 1987: 60 TC 436; [1987] STC 207.
Brokaw v Seatrain UK Ltd 49.21
CA 1971: [1971] 2 All ER 98; [1971] 2 WLR 791; 50 ATC 95.
Broom v HMRC [2011] UKFTT 760 (TC), [2012] SWTI 39 .... 5.13
FTT: [2011] UKFTT 760 (TC); 2012 STI 39.
Brown v Richardson 26.1
(Sp C 129), [1997] SSCD 233.
Brown's Trustees v Hay 31.1
CS 1897: 3 TC 598.
Bullivant Holdings Ltd v CIR 45.1; 74.1
Ch D 1998: 71 TC 22; [1998] STC 905
Burca v Parkinson 16.3; 74.1
Ch D 2001: 74 TC 125; [2001] STC 1298.
Burman v Westminster Press Ltd , ... 25.4; 74.1
Ch D 1987: 60 TC 418; [1987] STC 669.
Burrell & Others v Davis 41.3
Ch D 1948: 38 TC 307.
Burt v HMRC 16.4
(Sp C 684), [2008] SSCD 814.
Businessman v Inspector of Taxes [2003] STC (SCD) 403, SCD 54.3
Sp C: [2003] SSCD 403.
Buswell v CIR 57.34
CA 1974: 49 TC 334; [1974] STC 266.
Bute v HMRC 47.1
CS 2009: [2009] CSIH 42; 80 TC 1; [2009] STC 2138.
Buxton & Others v Public Trustee & Others 11.2; 29.4
Ch D 1962: 41 TC 235.
Bye v Coren 39.2
CA 1986: 60 TC 116; [1986] STC 393.

C

Cain v Schofield 5.20
Ch D 1953: 34 TC 362.
Calcutta Jute Mills Co Ltd v Nicholson 57.33
Ex D 1876: 1 TC 83.
Californian Copper Syndicate Ltd v Harris 41.3
CES 1904: 5 TC 159.
Cameron v HMRC 11.2
FTT: [2010] UKFTT 104 (TC); [2010] SFTD 664.
Campbell v Rochdale Commrs& CIR 52.37
Ch D 1975: 50 TC 411; [1975] STC 311.
Campbell Connelly & Co Ltd v Barnett 59.2; 74.1
CA 1993: 66 TC 380; [1994] STC 50.
Cann v Woods 44.12; 74.1
(Sp C 183), [1999] SSCD 77.
Cannon Industries Ltd v Edwards 5.34
Ch D 1965: 42 TC 625.

Capcount Trading v Evans 16.11; 74.1
CA 1992: 65 TC 545; [1993] STC 11.
Capital Air Services Ltd v HMRC 5.18; 5.24
UT: [2011] STC 617.
Carco Accessories Ltd v CIR 52.38
CS 1985: 59 TC 45; [1985] STC 518.
Carey v HMRC 52.5
FTT 2015: [2015] UKFTT 682 (TC); 2016 STI 144.
Carter v Sharon 55.9
KB 1936: 20 TC 229.
Carver v HMRC 24.3
FTT 2015: [2015] UKFTT 168 (TC); [2015] SFTD 573.
Carvill v CIR 5.35
Ch D 2002: [2002] EWHC 1488 (Ch); [2002] STC 1167.
Cash and Carry v Inspector of Taxes , SCD 45.3
(Sp C 148), [1998] SSCD 46.
Castledine v HMRC 24.3
FTT: [2016] SFTD 484.
Caton's Administrators v Couch 16.11, 45.4, 74.1
CA 1997: 70 TC 10; [1997] STC 970
Cayzer, Irvine & Co Ltd v CIR 41.3
CS 1942: 24 TC 491.
Cenlon Finance Co Ltd v Ellwood 57.30
HL 1962: 40 TC 176.
Chaloner v Pellipar Investments Ltd 16.4, 74.1
Ch D 1996: 68 TC 238; [1996] STC 234.
Chaney v Watkis 16.11; 74.1
Ch D 1985: 58 TC 707; [1986] STC 89.
Charlton v HMRC 6.10
UT: [2013] STC 866.
Chartridge Developments Ltd v HMRC 52.5
FTT 2016: [2017] UKFTT 766 (TC); 2017 STI 332.
Chilcott v CIR 41.4
Ch D 1981: 55 TC 446; [1982] STC 1.
Chinn v Collins 62.14; 74.1
HL 1980: 54 TC 311; [1981] STC 1.
CIR v Aken 51.19
CA 1990: 63 TC 395; [1990] STC 497.
CIR v Beveridge 8.10; 74.1
CS 1979: 53 TC 178; [1979] STC 592.
CIR v Bowater Property Developments Ltd 4.2
HL 1988: 62 TC 1; [1988] STC 476.
CIR v Brebner 4.15
HL 1967: 43 TC 705.
CIR v Brown 57.29
KB 1926: 11 TC 292.
CIR v Bullock 57.34
CA 1976: 51 TC 522; [1976] STC 409
CIR v Burmah Oil Co Ltd 4.2; 63.2; 74.1
HL 1981: 54 TC 200; [1982] STC 30.
CIR v Chubb's Trustee 16.11; 74.1
CS 1971: 47 TC 353.
CIR v Combe 57.29
CS 1932: 17 TC 405.
CIR v Duchess of Portland 57.34
Ch D 1981: 54 TC 648; [1982] STC 149.
CIR v Glasgow (City) Police Athletic Association 11.2
HL 1953: 34 TC 76.
CIR v Glasgow Heritable Trust Ltd 41.3
CS 1954: 35 TC 196.
CIR v Goodwin 4.15

HL 1976: 50 TC 583; [1976] STC 28.
CIR v Gull 11.2
KB 1937: 21 TC 374.
CIR v Hyndland Investment Co Ltd 41.3
CS 1929: 14 TC 694.
CIR v Jackson 52.37
CA 1960: 39 TC 357.
CIR v John Lewis Properties plc 16.5; 59.4; 74.1
CA 2002: [2002] EWCA Civ 1869; 75 TC 131; [2003] STC 117.
CIR v Montgomery 10.2; 74.1
Ch D 1974: 49 TC 679; [1975] STC 182.
CIR v National Federation of Self Employed and Small Businesses 5.35; 30.2; 52.15
HL 1981: 55 TC 133; [1981] STC 260.
CIR v Nuttall 6.8
CA 1989: 63 TC 148; [1990] STC 194.
CIR v Pearlberg 41.3
CA 1953: 34 TC 57.
CIR v Plummer 17.6
HL 1979: 54 TC 1; [1979] STC 793.
CIR v Reinhold 41.3
CS 1953: 34 TC 389; 32 ATC 10.
CIR v Richards 52.31
KB 1950: 33 TC 1.
CIR v Richards' Exors 16.11; 19.10; 74.1
HL 1971: 45 TC 626.
CIR v Richmond and Jones (Re Loquitar Ltd) 59.2
Ch D 2003: [2003] EWHC 999 (Ch); 75 TC 77; [2003] STC 1394.
CIR v Scottish Provident Institution 4.2
HL 2004: [2004] UKHL 52; 76 TC 538; [2005] STC 15.
CIR v Soul 51.19
CA 1976: 51 TC 86.
CIR v Toll Property Co Ltd 41.3
CS 1952: 34 TC 13; 31 ATC 322.
CIR v West 5.9
CA 1991: 64 TC 196; [1991] STC 357.
CIR v Wilkinson 39.1
CA 1992: 65 TC 28; [1992] STC 454.
CIR v Woollen 6.8
CA 1992: 65 TC 229; [1992] STC 944.
CIR v Zorab 57.29
KB 1926: 11 TC 289; 6 ATC 68.
Clark v CIR 4.15
Ch D 1978: 52 TC 482; [1978] STC 614.
Clark v Follett 41.3
Ch D 1973: 48 TC 677; [1973] STC 240
Clark v Green 45.4; 74.1
(Sp C 5), [1995] SSCD 99.
Clark v HMRC 13.7
FTT: [2015] UKFTT 324 (TC); 2015 STI 2660.
Clarke v United Real (Moorgate) Ltd 41.16; 74.1
Ch D 1987: 61 TC 353; [1988] STC 273
Cleveleys Investment Trust Co v CIR (No 1) 25.5; 74.1
CS 1971: 47 TC 300.
Cleveley's Investment Trust Co v CIR (No 2) 16.11; 74.1
CS 1975: 51 TC 26; [1975] STC 457.
Clunes v Revenue and Customs Comrs 5.19
FTT 2017: TC5692 [2017] UKFTT 204 (TC), [2017] SWTI 1070.
Coates v Arndale Properties Ltd 4.2; 29.4; 74.1
HL 1984: 59 TC 516; [1984] STC 637.
Cochrane v CIR 62.3
CS 1974: 49 TC 299; [1974] STC 335.

Coll v HMRC 4.15
UT: [2010] UKUT 114 (TCC); [2010] STC 1849.
Collins v Croydon Commrs & CIR(1969) 52.37
Ch D 1969: 45 TC 566; 48 ATC 119.
Collins v HMRC 4.2
(Sp C 675), [2008] SSCD 718.
Collins v HMRC 16.8
Ch D 2009: [2009] EWHC 284 (Ch); 79 TC 524; [2009] STC 1077.
Consolidated Goldfields plc v CIR 5.34
Ch D 1990: 63 TC 333; [1990] STC 357.
Conway v Wingate 51.19
CA 1952: [1952] 1 All ER 782; 31 ATC 148.
Cook v Billings 23.4
CA 2000: [2001] STC 16.
Cooke v Haddock 41.3
Ch D 1960: 39 TC 64;, 39 ATC 244.
Cooper v Billingham 48.14; 74.1
CA 2001: [2001] EWCA Civ 1041; 74 TC 139; [2001] STC 1177
Cooper v Cadwalader 55.3
CES 1904: 5 TC 101.
Corbally-Stourton v HMRC 6.10
(Sp C 692), [2008] SSCD 907.
Cotter v HMRC 13.3
SC 2013: [2013] UKSC 69; [2013] STC 2480.
Cottle v Coldicott 7.9, 74.1
(Sp C 40), [1995] SSCD 239.
Cox v Poole Commrs and CIR 52.37
Ch D 1987: 60 TC 445; [1988] STC 66.
Cox v Poole Commrs and CIR (No 2) [1990] STC 122n, ... 52.37
Ch D 1989: 63 TC 277
Coy v Kime 5.20
Ch D 1986: 59 TC 447; [1987] STC 114.
Craven v White 4.2, 74.1
HL 1988: 62 TC 1; [1988] STC 476.
Crosby and Others (Crosby's Trustees) v Broadhurst 44.12
(Sp C 416), [2004] SSCD 348.
Crowe v Appleby 62.3
Ch D 1975: 51 TC 457; [1976] STC 301.
Crusader v HMRC 16.8
(Sp C 640), [2008] SSCD 281.
Currie v HMRC 13.7
FTT 2014: [2015] SFTD 51; [2014] UKFTT 882 (TC).
Cutmore v Leach 5.20
Ch D 1981: 55 TC 602; [1982] STC 61.

D

D (MR) v Revenue and Customs Comrs 5.19
FTT 2017: (TC05575) [2017] UKFTT 850 (TC).
Davenport v Chilver 7.2; 74.1
Ch D 1983: 57 TC 661; [1983] STC 426.
Davis v Henderson 10.2; 74.1
(Sp C 46), [1995] SSCD 308.
Davis v Powell 10.2; 74.1
Ch D 1976: 51 TC 492; [1977] STC 32.
Dawes v Wallington Commrs & CIR 52.37
Ch D 1964: 42 TC 200; [1965] 1 WLR 323.
Day v Williams 57.33
CA 1969: 46 TC 59, 48 ATC 422.
De Beers Consolidated Mines Ltd v Howe 57.33

HL 1906: 5 TC 198; [1906] AC 455.
Delbourgo v Field 5.9
CA 1978: 52 TC 225; [1978] STC 234.
Denekamp v Pearce 5.34; 45.4
Ch D 1998: 71 TC 213; [1998] STC 1120.
Development Securities (no 9) Ltd v Revenue and Customs Comrs 57.33; 57.34
FTT 2017: (TC06007) [2017] UKFTT 565 (TC).
Director v Inspector of Taxes 44.11; 74.1
(Sp C 161), [1998] SSCD 172.
Domain Dynamics (Holdings) Ltd v HMRC 23.15
(Sp C 701), [2008] SSCD 1136.
Donnelly v Platten 5.20
CA (NI) 1980: [1981] STC 504.
Dreyfus (Camille and Henry) Foundation Inc v CIR 11.2
HL 1955: 36 TC 126; [1955] 3 WLR 451.
Drown and Leadley (JJ Leadley's Executors) v HMRC 44.11
FTT: [2014] UKFTT 892 (TC); 2014 STI 3707.
Drummond v Austin Brown 10.2, 74.1
CA 1984: 58 TC 67; [1984] STC 321.
Drummond v HMRC 39.1
CA 2009: [2009] EWCA Civ 608; 79 TC 793; [2009] STC 2206.
Duffield v Elwes 19.6
Ch D 1827: 1 Bligh's Reports (New Series) 497.
Duke of Westminster v CIR 4.2
HL 1935: 19 TC 490; [1936] AC 1.
Dunk v Havant Commrs 52.37
Ch D 1976: 51 TC 519; [1976] STC 460.
Dunlop International AG v Pardoe 29.7; 74.1
CA 1999: 72 TC 71; [1999] STC 909.
Dunstan v Young Austen Young Ltd 4.2; 63.2; 74.1
CA 1988: 61 TC 448; [1989] STC 69.
Dutton-Forshaw v HMRC 52.5
FTT 2015: [2015] UKFTT 478 (TC); 2016 STI 146.
Dyer v Dorset County Council 53.6
CA 1989: [1989] QB 346; [1988] 3 WLR 213.
Dyer v HMRC 44.11
UT 2016: [2017] STC 189.
Dyson v HMRC 5.2; 52.34
FTT: [2015] SFTD 529.

E

Eames v Stepnell Properties Ltd 41.3
CA 1966: 43 TC 678; [1967] 1 WLR 593: 45 ATC 65.
Earl of Iveagh v Revenue Commrs 41.3; 57.34
SC(I) 1930: [1930] IR 431; 1 ITC 316.
Earthshine Ltd v HMRC 5.24
FTT 2010: [2010] UKFTT 314 (TC); 2010 STI 2621.
Easinghall Ltd v HMRC 6.10
UT: [2016] UKUT 105 (TCC); [2016] STC 1476.
East Allenheads Estate Ltd v HMRC 23.15
FTT: [2015] SFTD 908.
Eastham v Leigh London and Provincial Properties Ltd 16.4; 74.1
CA 1971: 46 TC 687; [1971] Ch 871; [1971] 1 All ER 87; [1970] 3 WLR 848.
Eclipse Film Partners No 35 LLP v HMRC 5.24
CA 2014: [2014] UKUT EWCA Civ 184; 2014 STI 742.
Edwards v Bairstow & Harrison 5.34
HL 1955: 36 TC 207; [1956] AC 14; [1955] 3 All ER 48; [1955] 3 WLR 410.
Eilbeck v Rawling 4.2; 62.14; 74.1
HL 1981: 54 TC 101; [1981] STC 174.

Eke v Knight 5.20
CA 1977: 51 TC 121; [1977] STC 198.
Emmerson v Computer Time International Ltd 16.3; 74.1
CA 197750 TC 628; [1977] STC 170.
Emro Investments Ltd v Aller 41.3
Ch D 1954: 35 TC 305; 33 ATC 277;
Ensign Tankers (Leasing) Ltd v Stokes 4.2
HL 1992: 64 TC 617; [1992] STC 226.
Essex and Others v CIR 41.4
CA 1980: 53 TC 720; [1980] STC 378.
EU Commission v United Kingdom 49.7
ECJ: (C-112/14); 2014 STI 3297.
EV Booth (Holdings) Ltd v Buckwell 16.5; 74.1
Ch D 1980: 53 TC 425; [1980] STC 578.
Executors of Lord Howard of Henderskelfe v HMRC 72.2
CA 2014: [2014] STC 1100.
Executors of Connell v HMRC 4.2
FTT 2016: [2016] UKFTT 154 (TC); 2016 STI 1802.
Explainaway Ltd v HMRC 4.2
UT 2012: [2012] UKUT 362 (TCC);, [2012] STC 2525.

F

F (personal representatives of F, decd) v CIR 57.34
(Sp C 219), [2000] SSCD) 1.
Fayed and Others v Advocate General for Scotland (representing the CIR), ... 30.2; 55.8
SCS 2002: 77 TC 273; [2002] STC 910.
Trustees of the F D Fenston Will Trusts v HMRC 16.11
(Sp C 589), [2007] SSCD 316.
Fielden v CIR 57.34
Ch D 1965: 42 TC 501.
Fielder v Vedlynn Ltd 45.1; 74.1
Ch D 1992: 65 TC 145; [1992] STC 553.
Figg v Clarke 62.16;, 74.1
Ch D 1996: 68 TC 645; [1997] STC 247.
Fitzleet Estates Ltd v Cherry 5.34
HL 1977: 51 TC 708; [1977] STC 397.
Fitzpatrick v CIR 5.34
CS 1990: [1991] STC 34.
Fitzpatrick & Co Solicitors v HMRC 58.16
FTT 2012: [2012] UKFTT 238 (TC); [2012] SFTD 816.
Fitzwilliam (Countess) and Others v CIR 4.2; 17.6
HL 1993: 67 TC 614; [1993] STC 502.
Five Oaks Properties v HMRC 29.19
(Sp C 563), [2006] SSCD 769.
Fletcher v Harvey 5.19
CA 1990: 63 TC 539; [1990] STC 711.
Fletcher v HMRC 63.2
(Sp C 711), [2008] SSCD 1219.
Flix Innovations Ltd v HMRC 23.3
UT: [2016] STC 2206.
Floor v Davis 4.8; 41.28; 74.1
HL 1979: 52 TC 609; [1979] STC 379.
Forest Side Properties (Chingford) Ltd v Pearce 5.13; 41.3
CA 1960: 39 TC 665.
Forth Investments Ltd v CIR 5.19
Ch D 1976: 50 TC 617; [1976] STC 399.
Forthright (Wales) Ltd v Davies 23.3
Ch D 2004: 76 TC 134; [2004] STC 875.
Foster v Williams, SCD 63.27; 74.1

(Sp C 113), [1997] SSCD 112.
Foulds v Clayton 41.3
Ch D 1953: 34 TC 382.
Foulser v Macdougall 36.8
CA 2007: [2007] EWCA Civ 8; [2007] STC 973.
Foulser v HMRC 5.13
UT 2013: [2013] STC 917; [2013] UKUT 38 (TCC).
Foulser v HMRC 5.9
FTT 2014: [2014] UKFTT 483 (TC); 2014 STI 2764.
Foulser v HMRC 45.4
FTT 2015: [2015] UKFTT 220 (TC); 2015 STI 2537.
4Cast Ltd v Mitchell 23.3
(Sp C 455), [2005] SSCD 287.
Fox v Rothwell 5.9
(Sp C 50), [1995] SSCD 336.
Fox v Stirk 53.9
CA 1970: [1970] 2 QB 463; [1970] 3 All ER 7; [1970] 3 WLR 147.
Fox v Uxbridge Commrs & CIR 52.37
Ch D 2001: 75 TC 42; [2002] STC 455.
Foxton v HMRC 7.9
(Sp C 485), [2005] SSCD 661.
Frost v Feltham 53.4
Ch D 1980: 55 TC 10; [1981] STC 115.
Frowd v Whalley 5.34
Ch D 1965: 42 TC 599.
Fulford v Hyslop , 99 LJ Ch 80, 142 LT 185 .... 13.1
Ch D 1929: [1930] 1 Ch 71; 8 ATC 588.
Fullarton and Others v CIR 16.2
(Sp C 2004: [2004] SSCD 207.
Furniss v Dawson 4.2; 29.3; 64.3; 74.1
HL 1984: 55 TC 324;[1984] STC 153.

G

G C Trading Ltd v HMRC 23.3
(Sp C 630), [2008] SSCD 178.
Gaines-Cooper v HMRC 57.29; 57.34
Ch D 2007: [2007] EWHC 2617 (Ch); 81 TC 61; [2008] STC 1665.
Garner v Pounds Shipowners and Shipbreakers Ltd 7.7; 16.11; 16.13; 74.1
HL 2000: 72 TC 561; [2000] STC 420.
Garnham v Haywards Heath Commrs 52.37
Ch D 1977: [1978] TR 303.
Gasque v CIR 57.33
KB 1940: 23 TC 210; [1940] 2 KB 80.
George Wimpey International Ltd v Rolfe 21.6
Ch D 1989: 62 TC 597; [1989] STC 609.
Gibson v HMRC 53.2; 53.3
FTT 2013: [2013] UKFTT 636 (TC).
Gibson v Stroud Commrs and Morgan 5.9; 5.14
Ch D 1989: 61 TC 645; [1989] STC 421.
Glyn v HMRC 57.31
UT 2015: [2016] STC 1020.
Gold Nuts Ltd v HMRC 34.4
FTT: [2016] SFTD 371.
Golding v Kaufman 7.7; 74.1
Ch D 1985: 58 TC 296; [1985] STC 152.
Goodbrand v Loffland Bros North Sea Inc 16.13; 74.1
CA 1998: 71 TC 57; [1998] STC 930.
Goodwin v Curtis 53.7; 74.1
CA 1998: 70 TC 478; [1998] STC 475.

Gordon v CIR 37.2; 74.1
CS 1991: 64 TC 173; [1991] STC 174.
Government of India v Taylor 49.21
HL 1955: [1955] AC 491; [1955] 2 WLR 303; 34 ATC 10.
Grace v HMRC 57.29; 57.31
FTT 2011: [2011] UKFTT 36 (TC); [2011] SFTD 669.
Gray v CIR 19.5
CA 1994: [1994] STC 360.
Gray & Gillitt v Tiley 41.3
KB 1944: 26 TC 80.
Green v CIR 53.3; 74.1
CS 1982: 56 TC 10; [1982] STC 485.
Green v HMRC 45.4
FTT: [2014] UKFTT 396 (TC); 2014 STI 2235.
Griffin v Citibank Investments Ltd 7.7; 74.1
Ch D 2000: 73 TC 352; [2000] STC 1010.
Griffin v Craig-Harvey 53.10; 74.1
Ch D 1993: 66 TC 396; [1994] STC 54.
Grimm v Newman 55.9
CA 2002: [2002] EWCA Civ 1621; [2002] STC 1388.
Gubay v Kington 46.5; 57.29; 74.1
HL 1984: 57 TC 601; [1984] STC 99.
Guthrie v Twickenham Film Studios Ltd 51.31
Ch D 2002: [2002] EWHC 1936 (Ch); 74 TC 733; [2002] STC 1374.
Gwyther v Boslymon Quarries Ltd 5.34
KB 1950: [1950] 2 KB 59; 29 ATC 1.

H

H v H 38.2
Fam D 1980: 52 TC 454.
Hallamshire Industrial Finance Trust Ltd v CIR 6.2
Ch D 1978: 53 TC 631; [1979] STC 237.
Hamilton v CIR 5.19
CS 1930: 61 TC 28.
Hancock v CIR , SCD 6.10
(Sp C 213), [1999] SSCD 287.
Hancock v HMRC 54.4
UT 2016: [2016] UKUT 81 (TCC); [2016] STC1433.
Hankinson v HMRC 6.10; 57.31
CA 2011: [2011] EWCA Civ 1566;81 TC 424; [2012] STC 485.
Harding v HMRC 54.3
CA 2008: [2008] EWCA Civ 1164; 79 TC 885; [2008] STC 3499.
Hardy v HMRC 13.7
UT: [2016] UKUT 349 (TCC), [2016] STI 2592.
Hargreaves (Joseph) Ltd, in re 31.1
CA 1900; 4 TC 173.
Harmel v Wright 55.9
Ch D 1973: 49 TC 149; [1974] STC 88.
Hart v Briscoe 62.14; 74.1
Ch D 1977: 52 TC 53; [1978] STC 89.
Harte v HMRC 53.2; 53.10
FTT 2012: [2012] UKFTT 258 (TC); 2012 STI 2219.
Harvey's Jersey Cream Ltd v HMRC 23.15
FTT 2013: [2014] SFTD 599; [2013] UKFTT 663 (TC).
Hauser v HMRC 52.5
FTT 2015: [2015] UKFTT 682 (TC); [2016] SFTD 423.
Hawkings-Byass v Sassen 45.4; 74.1
(Sp C 88), [1996] SSCD 319.
Hawkins v Fuller 5.19

Ch D 1982: 56 TC 49; [1982] STC 468.
Haythornthwaite (T) & Sons Ltd v Kelly 5.20
CA 1927: 11 TC 657.
Henderson v Karmel's Exors 45.6; 74.1
Ch D 1984: 58 TC 201; [1984] STC 572.
Henderson v Revenue and Customs Comrs 57.34
FTT 2017: (TC06010) [2017] UKFTT 556 (TC).
Henke v HMRC 53.7
(Sp C 550), [2006] SSCD 561.
Hepworth v Smith 36.3, 59.3, 74.1
Ch D 1981: 54 TC 396; [1981] STC 354.
Herbert Berry Associates Ltd v CIR 51.19
HL 1977: 52 TC 113.
Herman v HMRC 48.23
(Sp C 609: [2007] SSCD 571.
Higgins v Revenue and Customs Comrs 53.7
FTT 2017: [2017] UKFTT 236 (TC), [2017] SFTD 814, [2017] SWTI 1176.
Hill Samuel Investments Ltd v HMRC 21.6
(Sp C 738), [2009] SSCD 315.
Hinchcliffe v Crabtree 8.2; 45.3; 74.1
HL 1971: 47 TC 419; [1971] 3 WLR 821.
Hirsch v Crowthers Cloth Ltd 39.1; 74.1
Ch D 1989: 62 TC 759; [1990] STC 174.
Hirst v HMRC 24.3
FTT 2014: [2014] UKFTT 924 (TC); 2015 STI 135.
Hitch and Others v Stone 4.2
CA 2001:[2001] EWCA Civ 63; [2001] STC 214.
HMRC v Ali 51.9
Ch D 2011: [2011] EWHC 880 (Ch); [2012] STC 42.
HMRC v Grace 57.29; 57.31
CA 2009: [2009] EWCA Civ 1082; [2009] STC 2707.
HMRC v McCarthy and Stone (Developments) Ltd 5.28
UT 2014: [2014] STC 973.
HMRC v Morrison 16.13
SCS 2015: [2015] STC 659.
HMRC v Prizedome Ltd 29.19
CA 2009: [2009] EWCA Civ 177; [2009] STC 980.
HMRC v Tager 52.16
UT: [2015] STC 1687.
Hoare Trustees v Gardner 62.14
Ch D 1977: 52 TC 53; [1978] STC 89.
Hollebone's Agreement, Re 51.19
CA 1959: [1959] 1 WLR 536; 38 ATC 142.
Holly v Inspector of Taxes 58.9
(Sp C 225), [2000] SSCD 50.
Honig v Sarsfield 6.13
CA 1986: 59 TC 337; [1986] STC 246.
Honour v Norris 53.6; 74.1
Ch D 1992: 64 TC 599; [1992] STC 304
Hood (John) & Co Ltd v Magee 57.33
KB (I) 1918: 7 TC 327.
Hood Barrs v CIR (No 3) 5.34
CA 1960: 39 TC 209.
Horan v Williams 63.27; 74.1
(Sp C 113), [1997] SSCD 112.
HSBC Holdings plc v HMRC 63.22
FTT 2012: [2012] UKFTT 163 (TC); [2012] SFTD 913.
HSBC Life (UK) Ltd v Stubbs 15.5
(Sp C 295), [2002] SSCD 9.
Hudson v Wrightson 41.3
KB 1934: 26 TC 55.

Hudson's Bay Co v Stevens 41.3
CA 1909: 5 TC 424.
Hurren, Re 52.39
Ch D 1982: 56 TC 494; [1982] STC 850.

I

Inchiquin (Lord) v CIR 57.29
CA 1948: 31 TC 125.
Innocent v Whaddon Estates Ltd 29.3; 74.1
Ch D 1981: 55 TC 476; [1982] STC 115.
Iswera v Ceylon Commisioner of Inland Revenue 41.3
PC 1965: [1965] 1 WLR 663; 44 ATC 157.
Ive and another v HMRC 45.4
FTT: [2014] UKFTT 436 (TC); 2014 STI 2523.

J

Jackson's Trustees v Lord Advocate 11.2
CS 1926: 10 TC 460.
Jarmin v Rawlings 24.3; 74.1
Ch D 1994: 67 TC 130; [1994] STC 1005.
Jasmine Trustees Ltd v Wells & Hind 62.6
Ch D 2007: [2007] EWHC 38 (Ch); [2007] STC 660.
Jeffries v Stevens 5.34
Ch D 1982: 56 TC 134; [1982] STC 639.
Jerome v Kelly 16.4; 74.1
HL 2004: [2004] UKHL 25; 76 TC 147; [2004] STC 887.
Johnson v Edwards 16.4; 74.1
Ch D 1981: 54 TC 488; [1981] STC 660.
Johnston v Heath 41.3
Ch D 1970: 46 TC 463; 49 ATC 187.
Johnston Publishing (North) Ltd v HMRC 29.7; 74.1
CA 2008: [2008] EWCA Civ 858; [2008] STC 3116.
Jolley v Bolton Commrs 52.37
Ch D 1986: 65 TC 242; [1986] STC 414.
Jones v Wilcock , SCD 53.13, 74.1
(Sp C 92), [1996] SSCD 389.
Jordan v HMRC 34.6
UT 2015: [2015] STC 2314.
Joseph Carter & Sons Ltd v Baird 59.3; 74.1
Ch D 1998: 72 TC 303; [1999] STC 120.

K

Karim v HMRC 57.31
FTT 2009: [2009] UKFTT 368 (TC); 2010 STI 1289.
Kellogg Brown & Root Holdings (UK) Ltd v HMRC 17.4
CA 2010: [2010] EWCA Civ 118; [2010] STC 925.
Kelsall v Investment Chartwork Ltd 5.20
Ch D 1993: 65 TC 750; [1994] STC 33.
Kenny v Wirral Commrs & CIR 52.37
Ch D 1974: 50 TC 405; [1975] STC 61.
Kerrison (Adrian) v Revenue and Cutoms Comrs 4.10
FTT 2017: (TC05800) [2017] UKFTT 322 (TC).
Khan v Edwards 5.19
Ch D 1977: 53 TC 597.

Kidson v MacDonald & Another 62.3
Ch D 1973: 49 TC 503; [1974] STC 54.
Kinloch v CIR 57.30
KB 1929: 14 TC 736; 8 ATC 469.
Kirby v Thorn EMI plc 7.2; 10.2; 59.4; 74.1
CA 1987: 60 TC 519; [1987] STC 621.
Kirkby v Hughes 41.3
Ch D 1992: 65 TC 532; [1993] STC 76.
Kirkham v Williams 41.3
CA 1991: 64 TC 253; [1991] STC 342.
Klincke v HMRC 63.8
UT 2010: [2010] UKUT 230 (TCC); [2010] STC 2032.
Kneen v Martin 55.9
CA 1934: [1935] 1 KB 499; 19 TC 33; 13 ATC 454.

L

Lack v Doggett 5.34
CA 1970: 46 TC 497.
Laerstate BV v HMRC 57.33
FTT 2009: [2009] UKFTT 209 (TC); [2009] SFTD 551.
Land Securities plc v Revenue and Customs Comrs 4.10
FTT 2011: [2011] UKFTT 599 (TC), 81 TC 843, [2012] SFTD 215, [2011] SWTI 3000; affd on other grounds [2013] UKUT 124 (TCC), [2013] STC 1043, 81 TC 843, [2013] SWTI 1493, [2013] All ER (D) 244 (Mar).
Lang v Rice 10.2
CA (NI) 1983: 57 TC 80; [1984] STC 172.
Lansdowne Partners Ltd Partnership v HMRC 6.10
CA 2011: [2011] EWCA Civ 1578; 81 TC 318; [2012] STC 544.
Larner v Warrington 6.10
Ch D 1985: 58 TC 557; [1985] STC 442.
Laver & Laver v Wilkinson 41.3
KB 1944: 26 TC 105; 23 ATC 244.
Lawton, Re 57.34
Ch D 1958: 37 ATC 216.
Lear v Leek Commrs 52.37
Ch D 1993: 59 TC 247; [1986] STC 542.
Lee v Jewitt 16.11, 74.1
(Sp C 257), [2000] SSCD 517.
Leeming v Jones 41.3
HL 1930: 15 TC 333; 9 ATC 134.
Leiserach v CIR 5.19
CA 1963: 42 TC 1; 42 ATC 431.
Leisureking Ltd v Cushing 44.12; 74.1
Ch D 1992: 65 TC 400; [1993] STC 46
Les Croupiers Casino Club v Pattinson 5.20
CA 1987: 60 TC 196; [1987] STC 594.
Lewis v Rook 41.15; 53.6; 74.1
CA 1992: 64 TC 567; [1992] STC 171.
Lewis v Walters 25.5; 41.15; 74.1
Ch D 1992: 64 TC 489; [1992] STC 97.
Lim Foo Yong Sdn Bhd v Comptroller-General of Inland Revenue (Malaysia) 41.3
PC 1986: [1986] STC 255.
Lloyd v Sulley 57.29
CES 1884: 2 TC 37.
Longson v Baker 53.5; 74.1
Ch D 2000: 73 TC 415; [2001] STC 6.
Lonrho plc v Fayed and Others (No 4) 31.1
CA 1993: 66 TC 220; [1994] STC 153.
Lord Advocate v McKenna 39.1

CS 1989: 61 TC 688; [1989] STC 485.
Lord v Tustain; Lord v Chapple 71.4
Ch D 1993: 65 TC 761; [1993] STC 755.
Lowenstein v De Salis 57.29
KB 1926: 10 TC 424.
Lucy & Sunderland Ltd v Hunt 41.3
Ch D 1961: 40 TC 132; 40 ATC 446.
Lynall, In Re 45.4; 74.1
HL 1971: 47 TC 375; 50 ATC 347.
Lynch v Edmondson 41.3
(Sp C 164), [1998] SSCD 185.
Lyon v Pettigrew 16.4; 74.1
Ch D 1985: 58 TC 452; [1985] STC 369.
Lysaght v CIR 57.29
HL 1928: 13 TC 511; 7 ATC 69.

M

McEwan v Martin 6.10
Ch D 2005: [2005] EWHC 714 (Ch); [2005] STC 993.
McGregor v Adcock 24.3; 74.1
Ch D 1977: 51 TC 692; [1977] STC 206.
Mackenzie, dec'd, Re 57.29
Ch D 1940: [1941] Ch 69; [1940] 4 All ER 310.
McGreevy v Revenue and Customs Comrs 52.5
FTT 2017: (TC 6109) [2017] UKFTT 690 (TC).
McKerron (R & D) Ltd v CIR 5.19
CS 1979: 52 TC 28; [1979] STC 815.
McLaughlin v HMRC 62.16
FTT 2012: [2012] UKFTT 174 (TC); [2012] SFTD 1003.
McMeekin, Re 62.3
QB (NI) 1973: 48 TC 725; [1974] STC 429.
MacNiven v Westmoreland Investments Ltd 4.2; 5.9
HL 2001: [2001] UKHL 6; 73 TC 1; [2001] STC 237.
Macpherson v Hall 64.6; 74.1
Ch D 1972: 48 TC 210.
McQuillan and another v HMRC 24.3
FTT: [2016] UKFTT 305 (TC); 2016 STI 2227.
Magnavox Electronics Co Ltd v Hall 4.2; 74.1
CA 1986: 59 TC 610; [1986] STC 561.
Makins v Elson 53.3, 74.1
Ch D 1976: 51 TC 437; [1977] STC 46.
Mamor Sdn Bhd v Director General of Inland Revenue (Malaysia) 41.3
PC 1985: [1985] STC 801.
Manchester Corporationn v Sugden 5.36
CA 1903: 4 TC 595.
Mann v Cleaver 51.19
KB 1930: 15 TC 367.
Mannion v Johnston 24.3; 74.1
Ch D 1988: 61 TC 598; [1988] STC 758.
Mansworth v Jelley 7.7; 22.6; 22.22; 74.1
CA 2002: [2002] EWCA Civ 1829; 75 TC 1; [2003] STC 53.
Mariner v HMRC 52.8
FTT 2013: [2014] SFTD 504.
Markey v Sanders 53.6; 74.1
Ch D 1987: 60 TC 245; [1987] STC 256.
Marks v Sherred 45.4
(Sp C 418), [2004] SSCD 362.
Marren v Ingles 7.2;10.2; 25.5; 74.1
HL 1980: 54 TC 76; [1980] STC 500.

Marriott v Lane 19.8; 24.3; 48.14; 74.1
Ch D 1996: 69 TC 157; [1996] STC 704.
Marshall v Kerr 10.2; 16.13; 19.8; 25.5; 48.14; 74.1
HL 1994: 67 TC 56; [1994] STC 638.
Marson v Marriage 10.2; 16.13; 24.3; 25.5; 74.1
Ch D 1979: 54 TC 59; [1980] STC 177.
Marson v Morton 41.3
Ch D 1986: 59 TC 381; [1986] STC 463.
Mashiter v Pearmain 8.6; 51.9; 74.1
CA 1984: 58 TC 334;[1985] STC 165.
Matrix-Securities Ltd v CIR 30.2
HL 1994: 66 TC 587; [1994] STC 272.
Mayes v HMRC 4.2
CA 2011: [2011] EWCA Civ 407; 81 TC 247; [2011] STC 1269.
Mertrux Ltd v HMRC 59.4
CA 2013: [2013] EWCA Civ 821; [2013] STC 2199.
Metallgesellschaft Ltd & Others v CIR 13.8
CJEC 2001: [2001] STC 452.
Methuen-Campbell v Walters 53.6
CA 1979: [1979] QB 525; [1979] 1 All ER 606; [1979] 2 WLR 113.
Miesegaes v CIR 57.30
CA 1957: 37 TC 493; 36 ATC 201.
Milnes v J Bean Group Ltd 5.34
Ch D 1975: 50 TC 675; [1975] STC 487.
Moll v CIR 5.23
CS 1955: 36 TC 384.
Monro v HMRC 13.8
CA 2008: [2008] EWCA Civ 306; 79 TC 579; [2008] STC 1815.
Montague v Hampstead Commrs & Othersn 52.37
Ch D 1989: 63 TC 145; [1989] STC 818.
Moodie v CIR & Sinnett 4.2
HL 1993: 65 TC 610; [1993] STC 188.
Moore v Austin 5.34; 39.1
Ch D 1985: 59 TC 110; [1985] STC 673.
Moore v HMRC 53.2
FTT 2013: [2013] UKFTT 433 (TC); 2013 STI 3371.
Moore v Thompson 53.3; 53.7; 74.1
Ch D 1986: 61 TC 15; [1986] STC 170.
Moore's Executors v CIR 57.34
(Sp C 335), [2002] SSCD 463.
Morgan v Gibson 8.6; 74.1
Ch D 1989: 61 TC 654; [1989] STC 568.
Moschi v Kensington Commrs 52.37
Ch D 1979: 54 TC 403; [1980] STC 1.
Muir v CIR 5.34
CA 1966: 43 TC 367; [1966] 1 WLR 251.
Murray-Hession v HMRC 44.15
FTT: [2016] UKFTT 612 (TC).

N

N Ltd v Inspector of Taxes 29.4
(Sp C 90). [1996] SSCD 346.
NAP Holdings UK Ltd v Whittles 63.5
HL 1994: 67 TC 166; [1994] STC 979.
Napier v Farnham Commrs 52.37
CA 1978: [1978] TR 403.
National Westminster Bank plc v CIR 23.3; 25.22
HL 1994: 67 TC 1; [1994] STC 580.
Neubergh v CIR 57.29

Ch D 1977: 52 TC 79; [1978] STC 181.
New Angel Court Ltd v Adam 29.4
CA 2004: [2004] EWCA Civ 242; 76 TC 9; [2004] STC 779.
New Zealand Commissioner of Inland Revenue v Challenge Corpn Ltd 4.2
PC 1986: [1986] STC 548.
New Zealand Shipping Co Ltd v Thew 57.33
HL 1922: 8 TC 208.
Newhill Compulsory Purchase Order, In, Re, Payne's Application 53.5
KB 1937: [1938] 2 All ER 163.
Newman v Pepper; Newman v Morgan , SCD 62.3; 74.1
(Sp C 243), [2000] SSCD 345.
News International plc v Shepherd 4.2; 74.1
Ch D 1989: 62 TC 495; [1989] STC 617.
Noble v Wilkinson 5.19
Ch D 1958: 38 TC 135; 37 ATC 307.

O

O'Brien v Benson's Hosiery (Holdings) Ltd 7.2; 74.1
HL 1979: 53 TC 241; [1979] STC 735.
O'Donnell (James) v Revenue and Customs Comrs 16.11
FTT 2017: (TC05821) [2017] UKFTT 347 (TC).
O'Rourke v Binks 63.8; 63.11; 74.1
CA 1992: 65 TC 165; [1992] STC 703.
Official Solicitor v Clore and Others Re. Clore (dec'd) (No 2) 57.34
Ch D 1984: [1984] STC 609.
Optos plc v HMRC 23.3
(Sp C 560), [2006] SSCD 687.
Orchard Parks Ltd v Pogson 41.3; 53.14; 74.1
Ch D 1964: 42 TC 442; 43 ATC 344.
Owen v Elliott 53.14; 74.1
CA 1990: 63 TC 319; [1990] STC 469.
Owton Fens Properties Ltd v Redden (Inspector of Taxes) 5.2
Ch D 1984: [1984] STC 618, 58 TC 218, [1985] LS Gaz R 124.

P

Page v Lowther 41.4
CA 1983: 57 TC 199; [1983] STC 799.
Parkstone Estates Ltd v Blair 41.3
Ch D 1966: 43 TC 246; 45 ATC 42.
Patel v Maidment 36.3
(Sp C 384), [2004] SSCD 41.
Pattullo v HMRC 6.10
UT: [2016] STC 2043.
Peel v CIR 57.30
CS 1927: 13 TC 443.
Pennine Raceway Ltd v Kirklees Metropolitan Borough Council 10.2
CA 1988: [1989] STC 122.
Pepper v Daffurn , ... 24.3; 59.7; 74.1
Ch D 1993: 66 TC 68; [1993] STC 466.
Pepper v Hart 5.34
HL 1992: 65 TC 421; [1992] STC 898.
Petch v Gurney 5.34
CA 1994: 66 TC 473; [1994] STC 689.
Philips v HMRC 5.2
FTT 2009: [2009] UKFTT 335 (TC); [2010] SFTD 332.
Pierson v Belcher 5.20

Ch D 1959: 38 TC 387.
Pigott v Staines Investments Co Ltd 4.2
Ch D 1995: 68 TC 342; [1995] STC 114.
Pilkington v Randall 41.3
CA 1966: 42 TC 662; 45 ATC 32.
Plummer v CIR 57.34
Ch D 1987: 60 TC 452; [1987] STC 698.
Potts v CIR 5.19
Ch D 1982: 56 TC 25; [1982] STC 611.
Powlson v Welbeck Securities Ltd 7.7; 16.4; 74.1
CA 1987: 60 TC 269; [1987] STC 468.
Prest v Bettinson 11.8; 74.1
Ch D 1980: 53 TC 437; [1980] STC 607.
R v CIR, ex p Preston 30.2
HL 1985: 59 TC 1; [1985] STC 282.
Prince v HMRC 51.29
FTT 2012: [2012] UKFTT 157 (TC); [2012] SFTD 786.
Pritchard v Purves 10.2
(Sp C 47), [1995] SSCD 316.
Property Dealing Co v Inspector of Taxes 29.4
(Sp C 360), [2003] SSCD 233.
Puddu v Doleman 11.2; 49.3
(Sp C 38), [1995] SSCD 236
Purchase v Tesco Stores Ltd 29.22, 49.3
Ch D 1984:58 TC 46; [1984] STC 304.
Purves v Harrison 24.3, 74.1
Ch D 2000: 73 TC 390; [2001] STC 267.

Q

Quinn v Cooper 25.22, 74.1
Ch D 1998: 71 TC 44; [1998] STC 772.
Qureshi v Qureshi 57.34
Fam D 1972: [1972] Fam D 173; [1971] 1 All ER 325; [1971] 2 WLR 518.

R

R v A-G (ex p. ICI plc) 30.2
CA 1986: 60 TC 1.
R v Barnet London Borough Council (ex p. Shah) 57.30
HL 1982: [1983] 2 AC 309; [1983] 1 All ER 226; [1983] 2 WLR 16.
R v Brentford Commrs (ex p. Chan) 5.35
QB 1985: 57 TC 651; [1986] STC 65.
R v Brixton Commrs 5.14
KB 1912: 6 TC 195.
R v CIR (ex p. Commerzbank AG) 56.4
CJEC: [1993] STC 605.
R v CIR (ex p. Davis Frankel & Mead) 34.12
QB 2000: 73 T 185; [2000] STC 595.
R v CIR (ex p Goldberg) 5.35
QB 1988: 61 TC 403; [1988] STC 524.
R v CIR (ex p. J Rothschild Holdings plc) 5.35; 31.1
CA 1987: 61 TC 178; [1987] STC 163.
R v CIR (ex p. Mead & Cook) 30.2
QB 1992: 65 TC 1; [1992] STC 482.
R v CIR (ex p. MFK Underwriting Agents Ltd) 30.2
QB 1989: 62 TC 607; [1989] STC 873.
R v CIR (ex p. Opman International UK) 63.8; 63.11; 74.1

QB 1985: 59 TC 352; [1986] STC 18.
R v CIR (ex p. S G Warburg & Co Ltd 5.35
QB 1994: 68 TC 300; [1994] STC 518.
R v CIR (ex p. Woolwich Equitable Building Society) 13.8
HL 1990: 63 TC 589.
R v Criminal Cases Review Commission (ex p.Hunt) 30.2
QB 2000: 73 TC 406; [2000] STC 1110.
R v Great Yarmouth General Commrs (ex p. Amis) 5.34
QB 1960: 39 TC 148; 40 ATC 42.
R v Hastings and Bexhill Commrs and CIR (ex p. Goodacre) 5.3
QB 1994: 67 TC 126; [1994] STC 799.
R v Havering Commrs (ex p. Knight) 52.37
CA 1973: 49 TC 161; [1973] STC 564.
R v HMIT (ex p. Brumfield) 5.35; 30.2
QB 1988: 61 TC 589; [1989] STC 151.
R v HMIT (ex p. Fulford-Dobson) 5.35; 30.2; 57.29; 74.1
QB 1987: 60 TC 168; [1987] STC 344.
R v HMIT (ex p. Kissane) 5.35
QB 1986: [1986] STC 152.
R v Hood Barrs 5.19
CA 1943: [1943] 1 KB 455; [1943] 1 All ER 665.
R v Hudson 52.40
CCA 1956: 36 TC 561; 35 ATC 63.
R v Newmarket Commrs (ex p. Huxley) 12.1
CA 1916: 7 TC 49.
R v North London General Commrs (ex p. Nii-Amaa) 5.35
QB 1999: 72 TC 634; [1999] STC 644.
R v O'Brien (ex p. Lissner) 5.19
QB 1984: 1984 STI 710.
R v Special Commr (ex p. Moschi) 5.19
CA 1981: [1981] STC 465.
R v Special Commr (ex p. Napier) 5.35
CA 1988: 61 TC 206; [1988] STC 573.
R v Special Commr (ex p. Stipplechoice Ltd) 5.35
CA 1985: [1985] STC 248.
R v Special Commr (ex p. Stipplechoice Ltd) (No 3) 5.35
QB 1988: 61 TC 391; [1989] STC 93.
R v Special Commrs (ex p. Elmhirst) 5.3
CA 1935: 20 TC 381.
R v Special Commrs (ex p. Emery) 5.35
QB 1980: 53 TC 555; [1980] STC 549.
R v Special Commrs (ex p. Esslemont) 5.35
CA 1984: 1984 STI 312.
R v Special Commrs (ex p. Morey) 5.35
CA 1972: 49 TC 71.
R v Special Commrs (in re Fletcher) 5.19
CA 1894: 3 TC 289.
R v Special Commrs (ex p. Magill) 5.3
QB (NI) 1979: 53 TC 135; [1981] STC 479.
R v Tavistock Commrs (ex p. Adams) 5.19
QB 1969: 46 TC 154; 48 ATC 406.
R v Tavistock Commrs (ex p. Worth & Another) 5.35
QB 1985: 59 TC 116; [1985] STC 564.
R v Vaccari 51.19
CCA 1958: [1958] 1 All ER 468; [1958] 1 WLR 297.
R v W 34.13
CA 1998: [1998] STC 550.
R v Walton Commrs (ex p. Wilson) 5.35
CA 1983: [1983] STC 464.
R v Wokingham Commrs (ex p. Heron) 5.14
QB 1984: 1984 STI 710.

R (oao Barnett) v CIR 59.2
QB 2003: [2003] EWHC 2581 (Admin); 75 TC 796; [2004] STC 763.
R (oao Browallia Cal Ltd) v CIR 5.3
QB 2003: [2003] EWHC 2779 (Admin); 75 TC 686; [2004] STC 296.
R (oao Carvill) v CIR 5.35
Ch D 2002: [2002] EWHC 1488 (Ch); [2002] STC 1167
R (oao Cook) v General Commrs of Income Tax 5.3
QB 2007: [2007] EWHC 167 (Admin); [2007] STC 499.
R (oao Cook) v General Commrs of Income Tax (No 2) 5.3
QB 2009: [2009] EWHC 590 (Admin); [2009] STC 1212.
R (oao Derrin Brothers Properties Ltd) v HMRC 5.35
CA 2016: [2016] EWCA Civ 15; 2016 STI 209.
R (oao Devine) v CIR 23.15
QB 2003: 75 TC 679.
R (oao Gaines-Cooper) v HMRC 57.31
SC 2011: [2011] UKSC 47; 81 TC 134; [2011] STC 2249.
R (oao Glenn & Co (Essex) Ltd) v HMRC 34.18
QB 2010: [2010] EWHC 1469 (Admin); [2010] STC 2386.
R (oao Graham and others) v HMRC 4.29
QB 2016: [2016] EWHC 1197 (Admin); [2017] STC 1.
R (oao Hely-Hutchinson) v HMRC 22.6
QB 2015: [2016] STC 962.
R (oao Higgs) v HMRC 6.13
UT: [2015] UKUT 92 (TCC); [2015] STC 1600.
R (oao HMRC) v Berkshire General Commrs 6.8
QB 2007: [2007] EWHC 871 (Admin); [2008] STC 1494.
R(oao Ingenious Media Holding plc) v HMRC 31.1
SC: [2016] STC 2306.
R (oao Pattullo) v HMRC 6.10
CS 2009: [2009] CSOH 137; [2010] STC 107.
R (oao Prudential plc) v Special Commr 34.5
CA 2010: [2010] EWCA Civ 1094; [2010] STC 2802.
R (oao Spring Salmon and Seafood Ltd) v CIR 58.9
CS 2004: 76 TC 609; [2004] STC 444.
R (oao Walapu) v HMRC 4.29
QB 2016: [2016] EWHC 658 (Admin); [2016] STC1682.
R (oao Archer) v Revenue and Customs Comrs 58.12
QB 2017: [2017] EWHC 296 (Admin), [2017] 3 All ER 524, [2017] 1 WLR 2066, [2017] STC 1037, [2017] SWTI 328, [2017] All ER (D) 166 (Feb).
Raftopoulou v HMRC 13.7
UT 2015: [2015] UKUT 579 (TCC); [2015] STC 656.
Ramsay v HMRC 37.2
UT 2013: [2013] STC 1764.
Rand v Alberni Land Co Ltd 41.3
KB 1920: 7 TC 629.
Randall v Plumb 7.7; 41.24; 74.1
Ch D 1974: 50 TC 392; [1975] STC 191.
Rank Xerox Ltd v Lane 25.3; 74.1
HL 1979: 53 TC 185; [1979] STC 740.
Reed v Clark 57.29, 57.30
Ch D 1985: 58 TC 528; [1985] STC 323.
Reed v Nova Securities Ltd 4.2; 29.4; 74.1
HL 1985: 59 TC 516; [1985] STC 124.
Reeves v Evans, Boyce and Northcolt Syndicate 41.3
Ch D 1971: 48 TC 495; 50 ATC 487.
Reeves v Revenue and Customs Comrs 36.8
FTT 2017: [2017] UKFTT 192 (TC), [2017] SFTD 765, [2017] SWTI 1123.
Regent Oil Co Ltd v Strick 39.1; 53.4
HL 1965: 43 TC 1; 44 ATC 264.
Reid v CIR 57.30
CS 1926: 10 TC 673; 5 ATC 357.

Rellim Ltd v Vise ... 41.3
CA 1951: 32 TC 254; 30 ATC 105.
Revenue and Customs Comrs v Banerjee ... 5.19
Ch D 2009: [2009] EWHC 1229 (Ch), [2009] 3 All ER 930n, [2009] STC 1930, 80 TC 625, [2009] EMLR 450, [2009] All ER (D) 204 (Jun).
Revenue and Customs Comrs v Hutchinson ... 22.6, 22.39
CA 2017: [2017] EWCA Civ 1075, [2017] STC 2048.
Revenue and Customs Comrs v McQuillan ... 24.3
UT 2017: [2017] UKUT 344 (TCC), [2017] SWTI 1972, [2017] All ER (D) 34 (Sep).
Reynolds's Exors v Bennett ... 41.3; 57.34
KB 1943: 25 TC 401.
Richards v HMRC ... 21.3
UT 2011: [2011] UKUT 440 (TCC); [2012] STC 174.
Richart v Bass Holdings Ltd ... 5.9; 6.2; 41.3
QB 1992: 65 TC 495; [1993] STC 122.
Richfield International Land & Investment Co Ltd v CIR ... 41.3
PC 1989: [1989] STC 820.
Ritchie v Revenue and Customs Commissioners ... 5.13; 53.5
FTT 2017: [2017] UKFTT 449 (TC), [2017] All ER (D) 112 (Jun).
Robson v Mitchell ... 44.12
CA 2005: [2005] EWCA Civ 585; [2005] STC 893.
Roche v HMRC ... 52.8
FTT 2012: [2012] UKFTT 333 (TC); 2012 STI 2364.
Roelich v HMRC ... 37.2
FTT 2014: [2014] UKFTT 579 (TC); 2012 STI 2891.
Roome v Edwards ... 62.14; 74.1
HL 1981: 54 TC 359; [1981] STC 96.
Rose v Humbles ... 5.19
CA 1971: 48 TC 103; 50 ATC 373.
Rose, Re, Rose v CIR ... 53.6
CA 1952: [1952] Ch 499; 31 ATC 138.
Rosemoor Investments v Inspector of Taxes ... 41.3
(Sp C 320), [2002] SSCD 325.
Rosette Franks (King Street) Ltd v Dick ... 5.20
Ch D 1955: 36 TC 100.
Rowland v HMRC ... 52.2
(Sp C 548), [2006] SSCD 536.
Roxburghe's (Duke of) Executors v CIR ... 55.9
CS 1936: 20 TC 711.
Royal Antediluvian Order of Buffaloes v Owens ... 41.3
KB 1927: 13 TC 176.
Rushden Heel Co Ltd v Keene ... 5.36
HL 1948: 30 TC 298; 27 ATC 141.

S

St Aubyn Estates Ltd v Strick ... 41.3
KB 1932: 17 TC 412; 12 ATC 31.
St Dunstan's v Major ... 11.10; 11.12
(Sp C 127), [1997] SSCD 212.
Sainsbury (J) plc v O'Connor ... 29.2
CA 1991: 64 TC 208; [1991] STC 318.
Salmon v Havering Commrs ... 52.37
CA 1968: 45 TC 77; 47 ATC 367.
Sanderson v HMRC ... 6.10
CA 2016: [2016] EWCA Civ 19; 2016 STI 237.
Sansom & Another v Peay ... 53.11; 74.1
Ch D 1976: 52 TC 1; [1976] STC 494.
Schofield v HMRC ... 4.2, 74.1
CA 2012: [2012] EWCA Civ 927; [2012] STC 2019.

Schuldenfrei v Hilton 5.9
CA 1999: 72 TC 167; [1999] STC 821.
Scott v HMRC 13.7
FTT 2015: [2015] UKFTT 420 (TC).
Scottish Provident Institution v Farmer 55.9
CS 1912: 6 TC 34.
Segesta Ltd v HMRC 23.17
UT 2012: [2012] UKUT 176 (TCC); [2012] STC 1847.
Sen v St Anne, Westminster Commrs 52.37
Ch D 1983: [1983] STC 415.
Shaw v Kay 31.1
CS 1904: 5 TC 74.
Shepherd v HMRC 57.2, 57.31
Ch D 2006: [2006] EWHC 1512 (Ch); 78 TC 389; [2006] STC 1821.
Shepherd v Lyntress Ltd 4.2; 74.1
Ch D 1989: 62 TC 495; [1989] STC 617.
Shinebond Ltd v Carrol 45.4
(Sp C 522), [2006] SSCD 147.
Simmons (as liquidator of Lionel Simmons Properties Ltd) v CIR 41.3
HL 1980: 53 TC 461; [1980] STC 350.
Skye Inns Ltd v HMRC 23.3
FTT 2009: [2009] UKFTT 366 (TC); 2010 STI 799.
Slaney v Kean 5.34
Ch D 1969: 45 TC 415.
Slater v Richardson and Bottoms Ltd 5.20
Ch D 1979: 53 TC 155; [1979] STC 630.
Smallwood and another v HMRC 16.13; 74.1
CA 2007: [2007] EWCA Civ 462; 78 TC 560; [2007] STC 1237.
Smallwood and another v HMRC 48.1
CA 2010: [2010] EWCA Civ 778; 80 TC 536; [2010] STC 2045.
Smith v HMRC 39.1
(Sp C 725), [2009] SSCD 132.
Smith v Schofield 8.7; 74.1
HL 1993: 65 TC 669; [1993] STC 268.
Smith's Potato Estates Ltd v Bolland 5.36
HL 1948: 30 TC 267; 27 ATC 131.
Snell v HMRC 4.15
Ch D 2007: [2006] EWHC 3350 (Ch); 78 TC 294; [2007] STC 1279.
Soul v Irving & Another 31.1
CA 1963: 41 TC 517; 42 ATC 424.
Sparks v West Brixton Commrs 52.37
Ch D 1977: [1977] STC 212.
Special Commrs v Pemsel 11.2
HL 1891: 3 TC 53.
Spectros International plc v Madden 16.8; 74.1
Ch D 1996: 70 TC 349; [1997] STC 114.
Spofforth and Prince v Golder 5.36
KB 1945: 26 TC 310.
SRI International v HMRC 5.21
FTT 2010: [2010] UKFTT 193 (TC); [2010] SFTD 873.
Stableford v Liverpool Commrs 52.37
Ch D 1982: [1983] STC 162.
Standard Chartered Bank Ltd v CIR 7.3
Ch D 1978: [1978] STC 272.
Stanton v Drayton Commercial Investment Co Ltd 16.11; 74.1
HL 1982: 55 TC 286; [1982] STC 585.
Steele v EVC International NV 41.28
CA 1996: 69 TC 88; [1996] STC 785.
Steibelt v Paling 59.2; 59.3; 74.1
Ch D 1999: 71 TC 376; [1999] STC 594.
Steiner v CIR 57.34

CA 1973: 49 TC 13; [1973] STC 547.
Stephenson v Barclays Bank Trust Co Ltd 62.3; 74.1
Ch D 1974: 50 TC 374; [1975] STC 151.
Stephenson v Waller 5.20
KB 1927: 13 TC 318.
Stevens v Britten , 98 Sol Jo 748, CA 51.19
CA 1954: [1954] 3 All ER 385; [1954] 1 WLR 1340.
Stoke-on-Trent City Council v Wood Mitchell & Co Ltd 10.2
CA 1978: [1979] STC 197.
Stoneleigh Products Ltd v Dodd 5.20
CA 1948: 30 TC 1.
Stonor and Another (Executors of Dickinson deceased) v CIR 19.5; 39.2
(Sp C 288), [2001] SSCD 199.
Strand Options and Futures Ltd v Vojak 63.19; 74.1
CA 2003: [2003] EWCA Civ 1457; ,76 TC 220; [2004] STC 64.
Strange v Openshaw 7.7, 74.1
Ch D 1983: 57 TC 544; [1983] STC 416.
Sugarwhite v Budd 41.4
CA 1988: 60 TC 679; [1988] STC 533.
Surveyor v CIR 57.34
(Sp C 339), [2002] SSCD 501.
Swedish Central Rly Co Ltd v Thompson 57.33
HL 1925: 9 TC 342; 4 ATC 163.
Swires v Renton 62.14; 74.1
Ch D 1991: 64 TC 315; [1991] STC 490.
Sword Services Ltd and others v HMRC 4.29
QB 2016: [2016] EWHC 1473 (Admin); 2016 STI 1799.

T

T & E Homes Ltd v Robinson 51.18
CA 1979: 52 TC 567; [1979] STC 351.
Talib v Waterson 5.20
Ch D 1980: [1980] STC 563.
Tarmac Roadstone Holdings Ltd v Williams 25.5; 74.1
(Sp C 95), [1996] SSCD 409.
Taylor v Bethnal Green Commrs and CIR 52.37
Ch D 1976: [1977] STC 44.
Taylor v Good 41.3
CA 1974: 49 TC 277; [1974] STC 148.
Taylor v HMRC 23.4
UT 2010: [2010] UKUT 417 (TCC); [2011] STC 126.
Taylor Clark International Ltd v Lewis 25.5; 57.30; 74.1
CA 1998: 71 TC 226; [1998] STC 1259.
Tebrau (Johore) Rubber Syndicate Ltd v Farmer 41.3
CES 1910: 5 TC 658.
Tempest Estates Ltd v Walmsley 41.3
Ch D 1975: 51 TC 305; [1976] STC 10
Test Claimants in the FII Group Litigation v HMRC 13.8
CJEU 2013: 2014 STI 246.
Thew v South West Africa Co Ltd 41.3
CA 1924: 9 TC 141.
Thompson v Hart 23.3
Ch D 2000: 72 TC 543; [2000] STC 381.
Thompson v Minzly 42.6
Ch D 2001: 74 TC 340; [2002] STC 450.
Thompson v Salah 16.4; 74.1
Ch D 1971: 47 TC 559; 50 ATC 415.
Thomson v Moyse 55.9
HL 1960: 39 TC 291; 39 ATC 322.

Thorne v Sevenoaks Commrs and Another 5.19; 52.2
CA & QB: 62 TC 341; [1989] STC 560.
Tod v Mudd , 60 TC 237 .... 59.8; 74.1
Ch D 1986: 60 TC 237; [1987] STC 141.
Tod v South Essex Motors (Basildon) Ltd 5.9; 44.4
Ch D 1987: 60 TC 598; [1988] STC 392.
Tomlinson v Glyns Exor and Trustee Co Ltd 62.3
CA 1969: 45 TC 600; 47 ATC 447.
Toshoku Finance UK plc, Re (Kahn and another v CIR) 14.4
HL 2002: [2002] UKHL 6; [2002] STC 368.
Tower Mcashback LLP v HMRC 4.2; 5.19
SC 2011: [2011] UKSC 19; 80 TC 641; [2011] STC 1143
Trennery v West 62.21; 74.1
HL 2005: [2005] UKHL 5; [2005] STC 214.
Trigg v HMRC 54.3
UT 2016: [2016] STC 1310.
Trustees of the Bessie Taube Discretionary Settlement Trust v HMRC 4.2
FTT 2010: [2010] UKFTT 473 (TC); [2011] SFTD 153.
Trustees of the Eyretel Unapproved Pension Scheme v HMRC 4.2
(Sp C 718), [2009] SSCD 17.
Trustees of the F D Fenston Will Trusts v HMRC 16.11
(Sp C 589), [2007] SSCD 316.
Trustees of the Morrison 2002 Maintenance Trust and others v HMRC 4.2; 7.7
FTT: [2016] UK FTT 250 (TC); [2016] SFTD 894.
Tuczka v HMRC 57.30
UT 2011: [2011] UKUT 113 (TCC); [2011] STC 1438.
Turberville v HMRC 57.30
FTT 2010: [2010] UKFTT 69 (TC); 2010 STI 1619.
Turnbull v Foster 57.29
CES 1904: 6 TC 206.
Turner v Last 41.3
Ch D 1965: 42 TC 517; 44 ATC 234.

U

Underwood v HMRC 16.3; 17.1
CA 2009: [2008] EWCA Civ 1423; 79 TC 631; [2009] STC 239.
Unilever (UK) Holdings Ltd v Smith 8.10; 63.2; 74.1
CA 2002: [2002] EWCA Civ 1787;76 TC 300; [2003] STC 15.
Union Corporation Ltd v CIR 57.33
HL 1953: [1953] 2 WLR 615; 34 TC 207.
United Kingdom v European Commission 13.8
CJEU (C-640/13): 2015 STI 52.
United Kingdom v European Commission 49.7
CJEU (C-112/14): [2015] STC591.
Usher v HMRC 52.8
FTT: [2016] UKFTT 50 (TC); 2016 STI 1410.

V

Van Arkadie v Plunket 49.6; 74.1
Ch D 1982: 56 TC 310; [1983] STC 54.
Vandervell Trustees Ltd v White 5.34
HL 1970: 46 TC 341.
Varty v Lynes 53.5, 74.1
Ch D 1976: 51 TC 419; [1976] STC 508.
Veltema v Langham 6.10
CA 2004: [2004] EWCA Civ 193; [2004] STC 544.

Vernon & Sons Ltd Employees Fund v CIR 11.2
Ch D 1956: 36 TC 484; [1956] 1 WLR 1169.
Vestey's (Lord) Exors v CIR 17.1
HL 1949: 31 TC 1; [1949] 1 All ER 1108.

W

W T Ramsay Ltd v CIR 4.2; 25.5; 74.1
HL 1981: 54 TC 101; [1981] STC 174.
Wagstaff v HMRC 53.11
FTT 2014: [2014] UKFTGT 43 (TC).
Wakeling v Pearce 53.5; 62.4
(Sp C 32), [1995] SSCD 96.
Wall v Cooper 5.20
CA 1929: 14 TC 552.
Wallach dec'd, in re 57.34
PDA 1949: [1950] 1 All ER 199; 28 ATC 486.
Walsh v Croydon Commrs 52.37
Ch D 1987: 60 TC 442; [1987] STC 456.
Walsh v Randall 55.9
KB 1940: 23 TC 55.
Ward v CIR , SCD 63.27
(Sp C 175), [1999] SSCD 1.
Wardhaugh v Penrith Rugby Union Football Club 16.13; 59.7; 74.1
Ch D 2002: 74 TC 499; [2002] STC 776.
Waring dec'd, re, Westminster Bank Ltd v Burton-Butler and Others 5.34
Ch D 1948: [1948] Ch 221; [1948] 1 All ER 257.
Warrington v Brown 41.13; 62.3
Ch D 1989: 62 TC 226; [1989] STC 577.
Wase v Bourke 24.3; 74.1
Ch D 1995: 68 TC 109; [1996] STC 18.
Watson v Samson Bros 5.34
Ch D 1959: 38 TC 346.
Watton v Tippett 59.2, 74.1
CA 1997: 69 TC 491; [1997] STC 893.
Wear Ironmongers Ltd v Baird 59.3; 74.1
Ch D 1998: 72 TC 303; [1999] STC 120.
Webb (Lance) Estates Ltd v Aller 41.3
Ch D 1954: 35 TC 305.
Wells v Croydon Commrs 52.37
Ch D 1968: 47 ATC 356.
Westcott v Woolcombers Ltd 63.5
CA 1987: 60 TC 575; [1987] STC 600.
Weston v Garnett 54.3
CA 2005: [2005] EWCA Civ 742; 77 TC 650; [2005] STC 1134.
Whitaker v Cameron 8.8; 74.1
Ch D 1982: 56 TC 97; [1982] STC 665.
White v Carline 49.3; 50.3
(Sp C 33), [1995] SSCD 186.
White v HMRC 52.8
FTT: [2012] UKFTT 364 (TC); 2012 STI 2502.
Whittles v Uniholdings Ltd 5.34
Ch D 1993: [1993] STC 671.
Whittles v Uniholdings Ltd (No 2) 5.34
Ch D 1993: [1993] STC 767.
Whittles v Uniholdings Ltd (No 3) 16.11; 74.1
CA 1996: 68 TC 528: [1996] STC 914.
Wicker v Fraser 5.19
Ch D 1982: 55 TC 641; [1982] STC 505.
Wilkie v CIR 57.29

Ch D 1951: 32 TC 495; [1952] Ch 153; [1952] 1 All ER 92.
Williams v Davies 41.3
KB 1945: 26 TC 371.
Williams v Evans (and related appeals) 59.3; 59.4; 74.1
Ch D 1982: 59 TC 509; [1982] STC 498.
Williams v Merrylees 53.6; 74.1
Ch D 1987: 60 TC 297; [1987] STC 445.
Williams v Singer 25.5
HL 1920: 7 TC 387.
Williams v Special Commrs & CIR 52.37
Ch D 1974: 49 TC 670; [1975] STC 167.
Wiliamson Tea Holdings Ltd v HMRC 66.3
FTT 2010: [2010] UKFTT 301 (TC); [2010] SFTD 1101.
Willis v Peeters Picture Frames Ltd 29.22
CA (NI) 1982: 56 TC 436.
Willson v Hooker 49.3; 74.1
Ch D 1995: 67 TC 585; [1995] STC 1142.
Winans v A-G (No 2) 7.3
HL 1909: [1910] AC 27.
Wing Hung Lai v Bale 58.9
(Sp C 203); [1999] SSCD 238.
Winterton v Edwards 41.4
Ch D 1979: 52 TC 655; [1980] STC 206.
Withers v Wynyard 57.29
KB 1938: 21 TC 724.
Wood v Holden 57.33
CA 2006: [2006] EWCA Civ 26; 78 TC 1; [2006] STC 443.
Woolwich Equitable Building Society v CIR 13.8; 56.5
HL 1992: 65 TC 265; [1990] STC 682.
Worthing Rugby Football Club Trustees v CIR 14.2
Ch D 1985: 60 TC 482; [1987] STC 273.
Wright v HMRC (No 3) 63.6
FTT 2009: [2009] UKFTT 227 (TC); [2009] SFTD 748.

Y

Yates v GCA International Ltd 21.4; 21.6
Ch D 1991: 64 TC 37; [1991] STC 157.
Young and Another v Phillips 7.3; 74.1
Ch D 1984: 58 TC 232; [1984] STC 520
Yuill v Fletcher 41.4
CA 1984: 58 TC 145; [1984] STC 401.
Yuill v Wilson 41.4
HL 1980: 52 TC 674; [1980] STC 460.

Z

Zim Properties Ltd v Procter 7.2; 10.2; 74.1
Ch D 1984: 58 TC 371; [1985] STC 90.

78 Index

This index is referenced to chapter and paragraph number.

NUMERIC

15% holding limit condition
venture capital trusts, 71.2
51% subsidiaries, effective, 29.2, 29.7
70% qualifying holdings condition
venture capital trusts, 71.2
75% subsidiaries, 29.2, 29.7
90-day ties
statutory residence tests, 57.16
90% social subsidiaries
social investment relief, 65.33

A

Abroad, *see* Overseas matters; Overseas residents
Absolutely entitled
settlements, 62.3, 62.16, 62.18
Abusive arrangements
tax avoidance, 52.21
Accelerated payment notices, 4.29–4.31
partnerships, 4.30
penalties for failure to make, 52.27
Accommodation
see also Furnished holiday accommodation, Main residence; Private residences; Residential property
available in UK, residence, 57.29
job-related, 53.7
ties, statutory residence tests, 57.14
Account managers, ISAs, 25.30
Accountants' working papers
investigatory powers, 34.2, 34.11
Accounting
derivative contract conditions, 15.9
large companies, 14.17
partnership adjustments, 50.10
Accredited social impact contractors, 65.2
Accrued income scheme, 8.4, 63.20
Accumulation units
authorised unit trusts, 70.3
Acquisitions
costs, shares and securities, 63.5
disposal, without corresponding, 45.1
own shares, of, 63.19
overseas residents, from, 16.12
stock, appropriations from, 16.9
Addresses
HMRC International Division, 49.18
HMRC Trusts & Estates, Non-Residents Trusts, 48.1
HMRC website, 32.1, 32.6
Small Company Enterprise Centre, 71.1
Adjudicators
complaints against HMRC, 30.8
Adjusted net gains, 2.6
Administration of estates on death, 19.9–19.13
Administration of HMRC, *see* HMRC
Admissible taxes, 21.4
Admission rights, charities, 11.11
ADR (alternative dispute resolution), 5.10, 5.11
Adult placement carers
private residences, 53.9
Advancement powers, 62.14
Age
permitted maximum, enterprise investment scheme requirement, 23.3
Agencies in UK
trading through, 49.3
Agents
agreements by, 5.9
assessments, copies of, for, 6.2
diplomatic agents, 25.50
electronic filing of returns, 30.4, 58.2, 58.4

Agents – *cont.*
information to, 60.4
Agreement to forgo corporation tax reliefs
HMRC and, 30.2
Agricultural grants
exempt gains and transactions, 25.19
Agricultural property
hold-over relief, 36.5
AIM (Alternative Investment Market), 45.5
Aircraft
location, 7.3
relevant jobs on board, statutory residence tests, 57.10, 57.15
rollover relief, 59.4
All-employee benefit requirement
employee ownership trusts, 63.16
Allowable expenditure, 16.11–16.12
Allowable losses, 44.3
Alternative dispute resolution (ADR), 5.10, 5.11
Alternative finance arrangements, 3.1
anti-avoidance, 3.5
CGT consequences of, 3.2
diminishing shared ownership arrangements, 3.2, 3.3
investment bond arrangements, 3.2, 3.4, 3.5
purchase and resale arrangements, 3.2
qualifying corporate bonds, 54.3
Alternative investment fund management partnerships, 50.19
Alternative Investment Market (AIM), 45.5
Amounts invested
social investment relief investor and investment condition, 65.6
Ancillary trust funds
Lloyd's underwriters, 69.2
Angels (theatre backers), losses, 44.9
Annual exempt amounts, 2.6
deduction, 2.1
key points, 2.7
losses, interaction with, 44.8
personal representatives, 2.3, 19.9
remittance basis, 55.2
settlements, 62.8, 62.9
use of, time limits, 67.9
Annual information notices
serial avoiders regime, 4.35
Annual payments
exempt assets, 25.3
Annual rates and exemptions, *see* Annual exempt amounts; Rates of tax
Annual tax on enveloped dwellings (ATED), 14.10
Annuities
deferred, 43.1–43.2
exempt assets, 25.3
life interests, 62.4
life interests, not as, 62.18
pension scheme, exempt assets, 25.3
retired partners, to, 50.12
Anti-avoidance, 4.1
accelerated payment notices, 4.29–4.31
alternative finance arrangements, 3.5
capital losses, 14.6–14.9
carried interest arising to investment managers, 50.20
case law, 4.2
charities, *see* Charities
close company assets transferred at undervalue, 4.14
companies
losses, 14.6–14.9
reconstructions and amalgamations, 4.15, 14.11
concessions, abuse of, 4.19
connected persons, 4.12, 4.14
courts, approach of, 4.2
depreciatory transactions, 4.17
disclosure of avoidance schemes, *see* Disclosure of tax avoidance schemes
disposals
assets through partnerships, 4.24
income streams through partnerships, 4.23
excluded persons, by, 45.1
dividend stripping, 4.18
double tax relief, 21.9
employee share schemes, 22.10–22.11
enterprise investment scheme, 23.17
factoring of income receipts, 4.21
follower notices, 4.25–4.28
foreign permanent establishments of UK resident companies, 49.8
general anti-abuse rule, *see* General anti-abuse rule
groups of companies, 4.17, 29.14–29.23
high-risk promoters, *see* Disclosure of tax avoidance schemes
income receipts, factoring of, 4.21

Anti-avoidance, – *cont.*
income streams
disposal through partnerships, 4.23
transfer of, 4.22
key points, 4.41
land, 41.4
leases, 41.21
legislation summary, 4.7
losses, 14.6–14.9, 44.6, 44.7, 44.21
market value, 45.1
mergers of UK businesses within EU, 49.13–49.15
offshore settlements, 48.22–48.28
overseas resident companies, UK participators in, 49.7
rollover relief, 59.2
sale and lease-back, 4.8
serial avoiders regime, *see* Serial avoiders regime
series of transactions, 4.14
settlements, 62.19–62.23
shams, meaning, 4.2
shares and securities, 63.5, 63.7
tax arbitrage, 4.20
transfers of income streams, 4.22
transfers of UK businesses within EU, 49.13, 49.14
value shifting, 4.8–4.11, 41.23

Appeals
see also Assessments
after 31 March 2009, 5.5
alternative dispute resolution, 5.10
claims, 13.3
costs, 5.18, 5.24, 5.33, 5.36
Court of Appeal, 5.34
determinations of, tax becoming due after, 42.5
domicile, 57.35
file access notices, 34.11
First-tier Tribunal, *see* First-tier Tribunal
high-risk promoters tax avoidance disclosure regime, 20.14
HMRC reviews, 5.6–5.7
information notices, against, 34.6
introduction to, 5.1
judicial reviews, 5.35
judicial rulings, against, 4.28
key points, 5.37
late, 5.3
making, 5.3
market value, determination of, 5.4
ordinary residence, 57.35
payment of tax pending further, 5.23
penalties, against, 52.34
postponement of tax pending, 51.17

Appeals – *cont.*
residence, 57.35
reviews by HMRC, 5.6–5.7
rights, 5.2
serial avoiders regime, 4.36
settlements by agreement, 5.9
third parties, joinder of, 5.4
time limits, 68.2
assessments, 5.3
domicile, 57.35
ordinary residence, 57.35
residence, 57.35
Tribunals, *see* First-tier Tribunal; Upper Tribunal
withdrawing, 5.3

Applicable proceeds
remittance basis, 55.4

Appointment, power of, 62.4, 62.14

Apportionment, 16.2, 16.5, 16.8, 16.10–16.12, 63.23
rollover relief, 59.8

Approved charitable investments, 11.4

Approved profit sharing schemes (APSS), 22.28

Arbitrage, tax, 4.20

Arising basis, 21.6

Armed forces
visiting, exempt organisations, 25.65

Arrangement, deeds of, 62.3

Arrears of tax
official error, due to, remission of, 51.29

Art works
exempt gains and transactions, 25.41

Asbestos compensation settlements
exempt organisations, 25.43

Assessable persons reliefs
venture capital trusts, 71.12

Assessments, 6.1
see also Appeals; Self-assessment
alteration of, 6.5
alternative, 39.1
construction of references to, 6.3
contents, 6.2
date, 6.13
deceased persons, 6.15
discovery, 6.10–6.11
double, 6.4
finality, 6.5
Lloyd's underwriters basis of, 69.2
making, 6.2
non-corporate bodies, 6.7
non-resident disposals, discovery determinations, 6.12
partnerships, 50.2

Assessments, – *cont.*
penalties for failure to notify errors in, 52.10
personal representatives, 6.6, 6.7, 6.13, 6.15, 19.9, 67.7
simple, 6.9
time limits, 6.13–6.15, 13.5, 67.8
trustees, 6.6, 62.11
years of, 1.1
Asset-based penalties
offshore inaccuracies, 52.13
Assets, 7.1
see also Trading assets; Wasting assets
Bitcoin, 7.12
bookmakers' pitches, 7.10
business, *see* Business assets
capital sums derived from assets, *see* Capital sums
close companies transferring at undervalue, 4.14
commodity futures, 7.8
compensation for loss of, 10.2
co-owners' interests, location, 7.3
cryptocurrencies, 7.12
depreciating, 59.9
derived from other assets, 9.9, 16.5
destruction, 10.2
deemed disposal claims, time limits, 68.2
disposals, 7.2, 16.2
assets through partnerships, 4.24
miscellaneous, time limits, 67.3
series of transactions, 4.14
value shifting, 4.8–4.11
distributions in specie in liquidations, 63.13
domain names, 7.11
exempt, 25.2–25.17
financial futures, 7.8
futures contracts, 7.8
gifts
charities, to, 11.7–11.9
hold-over relief
time limits, 67.8
gross
corporate venturing schemes requirement, 18.6
enterprise investment scheme requirement, 23.5
venture capital trusts, 71.4
held on 6 April 1965, 8.1
capital allowances, 8.11
close companies, assets transferred to, 8.12
development value, land reflecting, 8.6
Assets, – *cont.*
held on 6 April 1965, – *cont.*
disproportionately small original expenditure, 8.7
elections for value, 8.3, 8.8
fractional shares acquired in stages, partnerships, 50.13
Government securities, 8.4
groups of companies, 8.1, 8.3
identification rules for quoted securities, 8.4–8.5
key points, 8.13
land reflecting development value, 8.6
part disposal, time apportionment, 8.10
partnerships, 50.7, 50.16
quoted securities, 8.2–8.5
reorganisation following partial election, 8.5
reorganisation of share capital, time apportionment, 8.10
restrictions, time apportionment, 8.10
share capital reorganisation, time apportionment, 8.10
time apportionment, 8.7–8.10
time limits, 67.3
unit trusts, 8.2–8.5
unquoted securities, 8.9
held on 31 March 1982
assets derived from other assets, 9.9
automatic re-basing for CGT, 9.1
capital allowances, 9.7
deferred charges on gains before 31 March 1982, 9.11
election for 31 March 1982 re-basing, 9.3
general re-basing rule, 9.2
indexation allowance, 9.2, 9.3, 9.6
key points, 9.12
no gain/no loss disposals, 9.6
part disposals, 9.8
partnerships, 50.7–50.8, 50.16
re-basing, 9.1–9.5
share pools, 64.5
share valuations, 9.2, 9.6
valuations, 9.2, 9.6
image rights, 7.13
intangible, *see* Intangible assets of companies; Intangible fixed assets
interests of co-owners, location, 7.3
location, 7.3
loss, 10.2
deemed disposal claims, time limits, 68.2
meaning, 7.2
milk quotas, *see* Milk quotas

Assets, – *cont.*
miscellaneous disposals, time limits, 67.3
negligible value, 44.11
relief for, time limits, 67.4
new, rollover relief, 59.2
options, 7.7
overseas, 49.2, 49.6
partnerships, *see* Partnerships
plant or machinery used for long funding leases, 7.6
protected, settlors, offshore settlements, 48.5
recovery under Proceeds of Crime Act, exemptions and reliefs, 25.33
replacement, employee share ownership trusts, 22.31
restoration of, 10.3
rights, subject to, 4.8, 4.12, 7.2
seed enterprise investment scheme acquisition, 60.38
sets of, 25.4
single payment scheme payment entitlement, 7.14, 59.4
situs, 7.3
trades, used for and taxed on cash basis, 25.20
trading stock, appropriated to, elections
chargeable gains, Finance Acts 2017
summary, 73.1
transfers between civil partners, 9.6, 46.3, 46.5
transfers between married persons, 9.6, 46.2, 46.5
transfers between unmarried couples, 46.5
transfers to life assurance policy holders, 63.24
UK resident companies transferring to overseas resident companies, 49.12
undervalue transfers by close companies, 4.14
Assets Recovery Agency, 31.2
Assigned life insurance policies
profits on, 43.2
Assignees in bankruptcy, 62.3
Assignment of leases
new leases after, 41.22
Associated disposals
entrepreneurs' relief, 24.5, 24.10
Associated donations to charities, 11.11
Associated persons
serial avoiders regime, 4.33
ATED (annual tax on enveloped dwellings), 14.10
Attorney, powers of, 58.4
Auctioneers, returns by, 58.25
Auditors, papers of, 34.5
AUT, *see* Authorised unit trusts
Authorised contractual schemes, 70.11
Authorised investment funds (AIF), 70.10
Property (PAIF), 70.8
Authorised unit trusts (AUT), 70.3
loan relationships, 15.5
Authorities exercising or having compulsory powers, 41.11–41.12
Automatic overseas tests, 57.5
Automatic residence tests, 57.3–57.10
Automatic UK tests, 57.4
Averaging
furnished holiday accommodation, 26.1
holiday accommodation, 26.1

B

Banks
debts owed by not in sterling, 7.3, 25.5
dormant accounts, 16.7
foreign currency accounts, 7.3, 25.5, 55.6
Bankruptcy, 52.39, 62.3
Bare trustees, 12.2, 60.3, 62.3
exemptions and reliefs, 25.44
seed enterprise investment scheme, 60.3
Bare trusts
enterprise investment scheme shares held on, 23.2
Basic cases, First-tier Tribunal, 5.16
Basic payment scheme, 59.4
Bearer shares and securities, 7.3
Bed and breakfasting, 64.2, 67.9
Beneficial interests declarations
married persons, 46.2
Beneficial ownership, companies, 29.2
Beneficiaries, *see* Offshore settlements; Settled Property; Settlements
BES, *see* Business expansion scheme
Bespoke capacity
Lloyd's underwriters, 69.6
Betterment levy, 47.1
Betting winnings
exempt gains and transactions, 25.21

Bitcoin, 7.12
Boarding houses, returns by, 58.24
Boats, 25.4, 53.3
Bonds, *see* Investment bonds; Qualifying corporate bonds
Bondwashing, 64.2, 64.3, 64.6
Bonus issues
identification rules, 64.2
share capital reorganisations, 63.3
Bookmakers' pitches, 7.10
Borrowing
trustees, *see* Trustees
Bradford and Bingley plc, shareholders in, 63.28
Branches in UK
non-UK residents trading through, 49.3
British films certification
information disclosures by HMRC, 31.2
British Museum
exempt organisations, 25.45
Building societies
cashbacks, 63.27
exempt gains and transactions, 25.23
dormant accounts, 16.7
conversions, 63.27
de-mutualisation, 7.7, 14.11, 63.27
groups of companies, 29.2
mergers, 63.27
permanent interest bearing shares, 7.7, 15.5, 54.3
shares in, option rights over, 7.7
takeovers, 63.27
Buildings
see also Land
destroyed, 10.4
negligible value, 44.11
rollover relief, 59.4
subsidiary, private residences, 53.6
valuations held at 31 March 1982, 9.2
Business activities
qualifying
enterprise investment scheme, 23.5, 23.8
seed enterprise investment scheme, 60.30
Business assets
see also Rollover relief
compulsory purchase, 10.2
destroyed and replaced, 10.2
gifts
furnished holiday accommodation, 26.2
hold-over reliefs, 36.2–36.9, 36.12, 67.8
reliefs and deferrals, 25.75
material disposals, entrepreneurs' relief, 24.3, 24.5
Business assets – *cont.*
reinvestment in shares, *see* Reinvestment relief
replacement, *see* Rollover relief
retirement relief, *see* Retirement relief
transfers to companies, 25.94
trust disposals, entrepreneurs' relief, 24.4, 24.9
Business expansion scheme (BES)
exempt gains and transactions, 25.22
indexation, 25.22, 64.3
Business premises
HMRC inspection of, 34.8
Businesses
transfers to companies, 25.94
use of private residences, 53.9

C

CAB, *see* Criminal Assets Bureau, Ireland
Cable systems, 10.2
Call options
corporate venturing schemes, 18.15
enterprise investment scheme, 23.17
Capital
see also Share capital
interest charged to, 14.5
requirement not to be interested in, social investment relief investor and investment condition, 65.14
Capital allowances
assets held on 6 April 1965, 8.11
assets held on 31 March 1982, 9.7
ATED-related gains and losses and, 14.10
balancing charges, 39.1
chattels, 25.4
disposal values, 39.1
losses on assets, 16.13
motor cars, 25.11
NRCGT disposals, computation of gains and losses, 41.32
part disposals, 16.5
wasting assets, and, 72.2
Capital contributions by shareholders, 16.11
Capital distributions
corporation tax unpaid, time limits, 68.3
liquidation, in, 63.11–63.13
meaning, 63.11
payment of tax by recipients, 51.27
reliefs and deferrals, 25.67
shares, in respect of, time limits, 67.8

Capital gains companies, acquisition of, 29.15–29.17

Capital losses
anti-avoidance, 14.6–14.9
companies, acquisition of, 29.15–29.23
notification of, time limits, 67.8

Capital payments
overseas resident settlements, by, time limits, 67.2
overseas resident settlements, from, 48.14–48.21, 48.23–48.28
value of benefits conferred by, Finance Acts 2017 summary, 73.1

Capital sums
derived from assets, 10.1
compensation, assets lost and replaced out of, 10.4
compulsory purchase, 10.2
destruction of assets, 10.2
disposal, 7.2, 10.2
foreign assets, compensation for deprivation of, 10.2
general rule, 10.2
loss of assets, 10.2
replacement, applied in, 10.4
restoration, applied in, 10.3
small, 10.3
treated as lease premiums, 41.16

Car number plates, 25.11

Caravans as private residences, 53.3

Care and management powers, HMRC, 30.2

Care homes
residents in, private residences, 53.2

Carers
adult placement, private residences, 53.9

Carried interest, 2.1
arising to investment managers 50.20–50.21
exemption from attribution of gains, Finance Acts 2017 summary, 73.1
meaning, 50.21
settlors' gains, offshore settlements, 48.5

Carry-back of gift aid relief, 11.10

Cars, 25.11

CASC, *see* Community amateur sports clubs

Case management
First-tier Tribunal, 5.12
Upper Tribunal, 5.25

Cash
forfeiture, Proceeds of Crime Act, 25.33

Cash basis
Finance Acts 2017 summary, 73.1
trade assets used for and taxed on cash basis, 25.20

Cashbacks
exempt gains and transactions, 25.23, 63.27

Cash-settled options, 7.7, 38.8

CDF (Contractual disclosure facility), 34.13

Central banks
exempt organisations, 25.46

Certificates of full disclosure, 52.32

Certificates of tax deposit, 51.11

Certification of British films
information disclosures by HMRC, 31.2

Cessation of UK residence
companies, 49.17–49.18
settlements, 48.2

CFC (controlled foreign companies), 49.9

Channel Islands, meaning, 57.36

Charge to tax, 1.2–1.3

Chargeability
notification of, 52.3, 58.19
time limits, 67.2

Chargeable events
venture capital trusts, 71.12

Chargeable gains
assets appropriated to trading stock, elections
Finance Acts 2017 summary, 73.1
charities' exemption from tax on, 11.3–11.5
companies, *see* Companies
computation subject to special withholding tax, 21.10
derivative contracts basis of taxation, *see* Derivative contracts
foreign, remittance basis, 55.3
loan relationships, 15.6–15.7
post-employment deductions set against, time limits for relief for, 67.8

Charities, 11.1
admission rights, 11.11
anti-avoidance
payments to substantial donors, 11.5
tainted donations, 11.11
approved charitable investments, 11.4
approved charitable loans, 11.4
associated donations, tainted donations, 11.11
carry-back of gift aid relief, 11.10
charitable purposes condition, 11.2
companies, relief for
gifts of pre-eminent property to the nation, 11.9
connected persons, tainted donations, 11.11
declarations, gift aid, 11.10
definition, 11.2

Charities, – *cont.*
donations to, reliefs for, 11.6, 25.76
gifts of assets, 11.7
gifts of assets out of settlements, 11.8
gifts of pre-eminent property to the nation, 11.9
donors of gift aid donations, 11.10
excluded settlements, 62.8
exemption from tax on chargeable gains, 11.3
payments to substantial donors, 11.5
restriction, 11.4
exemptions and reliefs, 25.47
expenditure, 11.4
financial advantages, tainted donations, 11.11
gains, 25.47
gift aid donations, 11.10
tainted donations, 11.11
gifts to, 25.76
qualifying corporate bonds, of, 54.4
housing providers, tainted donations, 11.11
individuals, relief for
gift aid donations, 11.10
gifts of pre-eminent property to the nation, 11.9
intermediaries, gift aid, 11.10
jurisdiction condition, 11.2
limits on donor benefits, 11.10
linked persons, tainted donations, 11.11
management condition, 11.2
miscellaneous transactions, 11.4
non-charitable expenditure, 11.4, 11.5
pre-eminent property, 11.9
qualifying charity-owned companies, tainted donations, 11.11
qualifying gift aid donations, 11.10
qualifying gifts of pre-eminent property to the nation, 11.9
registration condition, 11.2
reliefs and deferrals, 25.76
substantial donors, 11.5
time limits, 67.6
Charter, HMRC, 30.7
Chattels
see also Tangible movable property
exempt assets, 25.4
wasting assets as, 25.4, 72.2
Chevening Estate trusts
exempt organisations, 25.49
Child trust funds
exempt gains and transactions, 25.24
Children, 12.1
bare trustees, 12.2
Children, – *cont.*
child trust funds, 25.24
default, 12.4
domicile, 57.34
guardians, 12.3
junior ISAs, 25.30
nominees, 12.2
Choice, domicile of, 57.34
Civil partners, 46.1
see also Private residences
assets held on 31 March 1982, 9.6
connected persons, 17.1
domicile, 57.34
living together, 46.4
main residence exemption, 46.3
no gain/no loss transfers, 46.5
private residences, 53.2, 53.7
reliefs and deferrals, 25.84
residence, 57.13–57.15, 57.22, 57.26
seed enterprise investment scheme, 60.41
separation, 46.4, 53.7
transfers of assets between, 46.3, 46.5
indexation, 9.6
re-basing, 9.6
Claims, 13.1
appeals, 13.3
assessments, extended time limits for, 13.5
charge for, remittance basis, 55.5
companies, by, 13.4
contract settlements, 13.7
corporate venturing scheme investment relief, 18.4
discovery assessments, 13.5, 13.7, 67.2
disincorporation relief, 37.4, 73.1
double assessment, against, time limits, 67.8
double tax relief, 21.7
enquiry amendments, 13.5
enterprise investment scheme income tax relief, 23.11
entrepreneurs' relief, 24.6
errors by Government department, 13.5
errors or mistakes, 13.8
hold-over reliefs, 36.4
investors' relief, 40.6
key points, 13.9
late assessments, following, time limits, 67.2
losses, 44.4
mistakes of law, 13.8
non-UK residence, to, 2012/13 and earlier, 57.31
overpaid tax recovery, 13.7
partnerships, 13.2, 13.7
recovery of tax overpaid, 13.7

Claims, – *cont.*
remittance basis, 55.5
returns, outside, 13.3
rollover relief, 59.11
seed enterprise investment scheme, 60.34
self-assessment, 13.2–13.4
social investment relief, 65.36
special relief, 13.7
tax overpaid, recovery of, 13.7
time limits, 13.3, 13.5, 44.11
two or more years, involving, 13.2
Cleansing of mixed funds
remittance basis, 55.3
Clearances
capital losses, 14.7
company reconstructions, 4.15, 14.11
informal, venture capital trusts, 71.5
non-statutory, HMRC and, 30.3
tax arbitrage, 4.20
transfer or division of UK business between companies in different EC member states, 49.13
transfer or division of non-UK business between companies in different EC member states, 49.14
Clients
disclosure of tax avoidance schemes details, 20.3
Close companies
assets transferred at undervalue by, 4.14
assets transferred to, time apportionment, 8.12
connected persons, 17.6
income tax paid by participators, 16.12
overseas, disposals by, 49.7
stock dividends, 63.10
Closure notices
enquiries into returns, 58.12
Codes of Practice, HMRC, 30.7
Collection of tax, 49.21–49.22, 51.19–51.26, 51.24
Collective investment schemes, 70.1, 70.2
see also Authorised contractual schemes; Authorised unit trusts; Open-ended investment companies; Unit trusts
Commercial letting of UK furnished holiday accommodation, 26.1–26.3
Commercial loans, 54.3
normal, 54.3
Commissioners for Revenue and Customs, *see* HMRC
Commodities, 25.4
futures, 7.8
Communications, privileged, 52.21
Community amateur sports clubs (CASC)
exemptions and reliefs, 25.48
gift aid donations, 11.10, 11.12
income condition, 11.12
location condition, 11.12
management condition, 11.12
registered clubs, 11.12
tainted donations, 11.11
tax exemptions, 11.12
Community benefit societies, 65.2
Companies
see also Close companies; Corporation tax; Groups of companies; Shares and securities
acquisition of own shares, 63.19
anti-avoidance, *see* Anti-avoidance
assessments, 6.2
business transfers to, incorporation relief, 37.2–37.3
capital payments received by, 48.14–48.20
ceasing to be UK resident, 49.17–49.18
central management and control location, 57.33
charge to tax, 1.2
chargeable gains
ATED-related, 14.10
loan relationships, 15.6–15.7
connected persons, 17.4, 17.5
control
connected persons, 17.6
value shifting, 4.8–4.11
controlled foreign, 49.9
corporate finance, *See* Derivative contracts; Loan relationships
creditor relationships, 15.5
shares treated as, 15.6
cross-border mergers, 49.15
debtor relationships, 15.5
definition, 14.2, 29.2
demergers, 14.12
derivative contracts, *see* Derivative contracts
divisions of non-UK business between companies in different EC states, 49.14
divisions of UK business between companies in different EC states, 49.13
dual resident, *see* Dual resident companies
dual resident investing companies, 29.3
dwellings, high value disposals, 14.10
European, *see* Societas Europaea

Companies – *cont.*
European Co-operative, *see* Societas Co-operative Europaea
European Union, transfers or divisions within, 49.13, 49.14
fraudulent or negligent conduct, 6.15
gifts of pre-eminent property to the nation, relief for, 11.9
government investments written off, 44.20
high value disposals of dwellings, 14.10
incorporation, places of, 57.33
intangible assets, *see* Intangible assets of companies
interest
charged to capital, 14.5
overpaid tax, on, 56.4
unpaid tax, on, 42.7
key points, 14.20
liquidation, 14.4
loan relationships, *see* Loan relationships
losses, 14.6
anti-avoidance, 14.6–14.9, 44.7
capital, 14.6–14.9
interest on overpaid and unpaid tax, 42.7, 56.4
substantial shareholdings exclusion, 66.3
trading, 14.6
unlisted trading, 23.13, 44.15, 44.18
meaning, 14.2, 29.2
mergers, cross-border, 49.15
notification of coming within charge to corporation tax, 58.19
offshore settlements, payments by and to, 48.19
overseas resident, *see* Overseas residents
own shares, purchase of, 63.19
partners, as, 50.17
payment of tax, 51.4
penalties, failure to deliver returns, 52.4
permanent establishments in UK, 49.3
persons controlling, connected persons, 17.5
privatisation, 14.11
property transactions, 41.3
purchase of own shares, 63.19
qualifying
enterprise investment scheme, 23.5
seed enterprise investment scheme, 60.17–60.29
reconstructions, *see* Reconstructions
related, high-risk promoters tax avoidance disclosure regime, 20.11
reliefs and deferrals, 25.68
reorganisations *see* Share capital

Companies – *cont.*
research institution spin-out, 22.16
residence, 57.33
returns of profits by, 58.19
self-assessment, 51.4, 58.19, 61.3
shareholders, recovery of tax from, 51.27
Societas Co-operative Europaea, *see* Societas Co-operative Europaea
Societas Europaea, *see* Societas Europaea
substantial shareholdings of, *see* Substantial shareholdings of companies
takeovers, 4.16
tax accounting arrangements, 14.17
tax returns, amendment of, time limits, 67.4
trading, unlisted, losses, 44.15, 44.18
transfers of non-UK business between companies in different EC states, 49.14
transfers of UK business between companies in different EC states, 49.13
unincorporated, 51.25
unlisted, capital loss on disposal treated as trading, 44.15, 44.18
value shifting, 4.8–4.11
winding-up, expenses in, 14.4
Company share option plans (CSOP), 22.25
Compensation
asbestos settlements, exempt organisations, 25.43
assets, for, 7.2, 10.4
capital sums received as, reliefs and deferrals, 25.72
exempt gains and transactions, 25.25
foreign asset, loss of, 10.2
foreign governments, from, exemptions and reliefs, 25.27
milk quota, 7.9
Proceeds of Crime Act payments, 25.33
Compensation stock
shares and securities, 63.8
Complaints, HMRC, *see* HMRC
Compliance
certificates, corporate venturing schemes, 18.4
disclosure of tax avoidance schemes, 20.5
statements, corporate venturing schemes, 18.4, 18.8
Compulsory purchase of land, *see* Land
Computation of gains and losses, 16.1
allowable expenditure, 16.2, 16.5–16.6, 16.11–16.12
allowable losses, 44.3
ATED-related, 14.10

Computation of gains and losses, – *cont.*
basic, 16.2
capital losses, 14.6
capital sums derived from assets, 10.3
compensation for assets, 10.4
consideration, 16.8
disposals
date of, 10.2
meaning, 16.3
deferred annuities, 43.1
depreciatory transaction in group, 4.17
expenditure
allowable, 16.2, 16.5–16.6, 16.11–16.12
non-allowable, 16.13
finance leases, 16.10
gains, 16.2, 38.2
indexation allowance, 38.2–38.8
indexed gains, 16.2, 38.2
interaction with other taxes, 39.1–39.3
key points, 16.14
life assurance policies, 43.1
losses, 14.6, 38.2, 44.1–44.22
market value, 45.1
negligible value, asset of, 44.11
non-allowable expenditure, 16.13
NRCGT disposals of UK residential property, *see* NRCGT disposals of UK residential property
part disposals, *See* Part disposals
rights, sums derived from, 10.2
series of transactions between connected persons, 4.14
settled property
beneficiaries becoming absolutely entitled, 62.16
disposal of interests in, 62.15
settlements, transfer into, 62.14
special measures regime, 14.19
special withholding tax, subject to, 21.10
stock, appropriations to and from, 16.9
tax strategies publication, 14.18
time of disposal, 10.2
unindexed gains, 16.2, 38.2
Computers, access by HMRC, 34.18
Concessions
see also Extra-Statutory Concessions
abuse, 4.19
HMRC and, 30.5
Conditional interests
employee share schemes, 22.14
Conduct notices
high-risk promoters tax avoidance disclosure regime, 20.11
tax agents, dishonest conduct by, 34.11
Confidentiality
disclosure of tax avoidance schemes, 20.2
information, of, HMRC, 31.1–31.6
Confirmation notices
unco-operative large businesses, 14.19
Confiscation of foreign property, 10.2
Connected persons
anti-avoidance, 4.12, 4.13
civil partners, 17.1
close companies, 17.6
companies, 17.4
persons controlling, 17.5
expressions used to define, 17.6
individuals, 17.1
losses, 44.6
married persons, 17.1
meaning, 17.1–17.5
partners, 17.3, 50.4
relatives, 17.1, 17.6
series of transactions, 4.14
settlements, 17.6
tainted donations to charities, 11.11
transactions between, 4.12, 44.6
trustees of settlements, 17.2
Consent orders
First-tier Tribunal, 5.20
Upper Tribunal, 5.31
Consideration
deductions allowed against, 16.11
deemed, no gain/no loss transfers between spouses or civil partners, 46.5
deferred, 16.13
deferred unascertainable, loss on right to, 44.19
disposal, on, 16.8
outside accounts, partnerships, 50.11
partial, hold-over reliefs example, 36.7
tax payments by instalments, 51.5
unascertainable, *see* Unascertainable consideration
Constant NAV funds, 49.11
Constituency associations
reliefs and deferrals, 25.70
Contangos, 64.6
Continental shelf
exploration and exploitation rights, 49.19
Contingent liabilities, 16.12
warranty payments in respect of, shares and securities, 63.5, 63.7
Continuing to be a social enterprise
social enterprise requirement, 65.17
Contract settlements
claims, 13.7
Contracts
date of disposal under, 16.4

Contracts – *cont.*
futures, 7.8
qualifying corporate bonds, 7.8
Contracts for differences, 15.9
deemed, 15.10
Contractual disclosure facility (CDF), 34.13
Control
companies, *see* Companies
enterprise investment scheme requirement, 23.5
high-risk promoters tax avoidance disclosure regime, 20.11
social enterprise condition, 65.21
venture capital trusts, 71.4
Controlled foreign companies (CFC), 49.9
Controlling interest requirement
employee ownership trusts, 63.17
Conversions of building societies, 63.27
Conversions of securities
share capital reorganisations, 63.8
Convertible shares
employee share schemes, 22.15
Co-owners' interests, location, 7.3
Copyright, 7.3
Corporate bonds *see* Qualifying corporate bonds
Corporate debt, 15.2
see also Loan relationships
Corporate partners, 50.17
Corporate trustees
administration of estates on death, 19.12–19.13
Corporate underwriters at Lloyd's, 69.3, 69.6, 69.8
Corporate venturing schemes (CVS)
allowable losses, 18.17
computation, 18.18
set-off against income, 18.19
call options, 18.15
chargeable gains, 18.17, 18.20
company restructuring, 18.21–18.23
compliance certificates, 18.4
compliance statements, 18.4, 18.8
deferral relief, 18.20
disposals, 18.10, 18.17, 18.20
financial activities, 18.5
funded trades, 18.4
gross assets requirement, 18.6
holding companies, new, 18.23
identification rules, 18.16
independence requirement, 18.6
individual-owners requirement, 18.6
introduction, 18.1
investment relief
claims for, 18.4
Corporate venturing schemes (CVS) – *cont.*
investment relief – *cont.*
eligibility, 18.2
form of, 18.3
general requirements, 18.8
qualification periods, 18.2
reduction of, 18.9–18.15
time limits, 18.4
withdrawal of, 18.9–18.15
joint ventures requirement, 18.6
key points, 18.24
loss relief for investing companies, time limits, 67.4
maximum annual amounts raised, 18.8
money raised, use of, 18.8
'no control' requirement, 18.5
'no reciprocal arrangements' requirement, 18.5
'no tax avoidance' requirement, 18.5
non-financial activities requirement, 18.5
non-financial trades, 18.5
non-financial trading groups, 18.5
number of employees requirement, 18.6
ordinary share capital, 18.5
partnerships requirement, 18.6
pre-arranged exits not permitted, 18.8
property managing subsidiaries requirement, 18.6
put options, 18.15
qualifying investing companies, 18.5
qualifying issuing companies, 18.6
qualifying periods, 18.2
qualifying subsidiaries requirement, 18.6
qualifying trades, 18.7
reconstructions, 18.21–18.23
relevant investments, 18.8
relevant preference shares, 18.5
reliefs and deferrals, 25.71
shares
being a chargeable asset requirement, 18.5
disposals, 18.10
general requirements, 18.8
rights issues, 18.21
subsidiary companies, issuing companies becoming, 18.23
tax avoidance motives not permitted, 18.8
time limits
deferral relief, 18.20
investment relief, 18.4
loss against income, 18.19
trading activities requirement, 18.6
unquoted status requirement, 18.6
value received, 18.11–18.14

Corporation tax, 14.2
- assessments, 6.2–6.5, 6.10, 6.13, 6.14
- chargeable gains
  - computation, 14.2
  - rate of tax, 14.3
- claims, 13.4
- coming within charge, notification of, 58.19
- interest
  - rates, 42.7
  - unpaid tax, on, 42.7
- payment
  - chargeable gains, on, 51.4
  - exit charge payment plans, 51.8
- re-basing of assets held on 31 March 1982, 9.1
- reduction
  - gifts of pre-eminent property to the nation, 11.9
- repos, chargeable gains of, 63.26
- returns, 58.2
  - time limits, 67.2
- self-assessment, 61.3
  - payment of tax, 51.4
  - tax returns, 58.19
- tainted donations, 11.11
- unpaid
  - capital distributions and reconstructions, time limits, 68.3
  - companies ceasing to be UK-resident, time limits, 68.4
  - groups, time limits, 68.4
  - interest on, 42.7
  - non-resident companies, time limits, 68.4

Costs
- First-tier Tribunal, 5.18, 5.24
- Upper Tribunal, 5.33

Country ties
- statutory residence tests, 57.17

Court
- anti-avoidance approach of, 4.2
- appeals to, 5.34
- foreign tax laws not enforceable by, 49.21
- interest awarded by, 51.18
- proceedings, penalties, 52.36

Court investment funds, 70.12

Covenants, 25.3

Credit cards
- payment fees on payment of tax, 51.14

Creditor relationships, 15.5
- shares treated as, 15.6

Creditor repos, 63.26

Criminal Assets Bureau (CAB), Ireland
- information disclosures by HMRC to, 31.2

Criminal investigations
- information disclosures by HMRC, 31.2

Criminal penalties, 34.13, 52.40

Cross-border mergers
- European, 49.15
  - transparent entities, disapplication of relief, 49.16
- rollover relief, 59.9
- shares and securities, 63.7

Cross-tax penalties
- failure to make returns, 52.5

Crown, the
- exempt organisations, 25.49

Cryptocurrencies, 7.12

Crystallisation of gain reliefs
- venture capital trusts, 71.12

CSOP (Company share option plans), 22.25

Currencies, *see* Foreign currencies

Curtilage of private residences, 53.6

CVS, *see* Corporate venturing scheme

D

Daily penalties, 52.5, 52.16

Dairy Farmers of Britain, 63.29

Damage to assets, 7.2, 10.2

Damages
- exempt gains and transactions, 25.25

Data-gathering powers, HMRC, 34.17
- Finance Acts 2017 summary, 73.1
- penalties failure to comply with, 52.17

Data-holder notices, 34.17

Date of disposal, 10.2, 16.4

Day count test
- private residences, 53.8

Days spent in the UK
- statutory residence tests, 57.7

Death
- *see also* Personal representatives
- administration of estates, 19.9–19.13
- corporate trustees, 19.12–19.13
- deeds of family arrangement etc, 19.8
- disclaimers, 19.8
- donatio mortis causa, 19.6
- enterprise investment scheme investors, 23.15

Death – *cont.*
family arrangements and disclaimers after, time limits, 68.3
fraudulent or negligent conduct, 6.15
general provisions, 19.2–19.6
key points, 19.15
late payment interest and penalties, 42.9
legatees, 19.14
life tenants, hold-over relief, 36.8, 36.11, 36.12
losses, carry-back, 19.7
Northern Ireland, 19.4
NRCGT losses, 19.7
penalties, time limits for, 52.38
Scotland, 19.3
time limits, 67.8
traders, rollover relief, 59.9
valuations, 19.5, 39.2
variation of dispositions, 19.8
Debentures
location, 7.3
qualifying corporate bonds, 54.3
Debtor repos, 63.26
Debtors
HMRC powers to obtain details of, 51.19
relationships, 15.5
Debts
exempt assets, 25.5
location, 7.3
losses, 44.6
security, on, 25.5, 44.12, 44.13
Deceased persons, *see* Death
Declarations
gift aid, 11.10
married persons' individual beneficial interests, 46.2
Decorations for valour, 25.6
Deduction notices
payment of tax, 51.23
Deduction of tax from accounts, 51.20–51.23
Deduction powers
penalties enforcement by, 52.28
Deduction schemes, tax arbitrage, 4.20
Deeds of arrangement, 62.3
Deeds of family arrangement on death, 19.8
Deeds of variation on death, 19.8
Deemed consideration
no gain/no loss transfers between spouses or civil partners, 46.5
Deemed contracts for differences, 15.10
Deemed disposal
companies ceasing to be UK resident, postponement of charge on
time limits, 68.3, 68.5
Deemed domicile, *see* Domicile
Deemed options, 15.11
Deeming rule
statutory residence tests, 57.7
Deeply discounted securities, 54.3, 54.4, 63.21
indexation, 64.3, 64.6
Default
children, 12.4
HMRC publication of details of defaulters, 31.3
managing deliberate defaulters, 52.32
NRCGT disposals, computation of gains and losses, method, 41.30
Default paper cases
First-tier Tribunal, 5.15
Defeat notices
high-risk promoters tax avoidance disclosure regime, 20.10
Defeated tax avoidance enablers
penalties, 52.21
Defeats
relevant, high-risk promoters tax avoidance disclosure regime, 20.10
Deferral reliefs
see also Reliefs and deferrals
corporate venturing scheme, 18.20
enterprise investment scheme, 23.14–23.18
reinvestment on, venture capital trusts, 71.12
social investment, 65.46
UK resident companies transferring assets to overseas resident companies, 49.12
venture capital trusts, 71.12
Deferred annuities, 43.1–43.2
Deferred charges on gains before 31 March 1982, 9.11
Deferred gains
entrepreneurs' relief, 24.11
Degrouping charges, *see* Groups of companies
Delaware Limited Liability Companies, 29.2, 63.5
Delayed remittances
late payment interest and penalties, 42.8

Delays
complaints against HMRC and, 30.6
late payment of interest and, 42.9
repayment of interest and, 42.9
Deliberate defaulters, managing, 52.32
Demergers, 14.12
Dependency, domicile of, 57.34
Dependent relatives' residence, 53.12
Depositary receipts, 63.22
Deposits
contingently repayable for land, 41.24
forfeited, 16.6
Depreciating assets, 59.9
Depreciatory transactions
groups of companies, 4.17
Deregistration of pension schemes, 25.60
Derivative contracts, 15.1, 15.8
accounting conditions, 15.9
assets subject of euroconversion, 7.7
charge to tax, 15.8
chargeable gains basis of taxation, 15.10
rules with potential consequences, 15.12
transitional provisions with, 15.13
contracts becoming or ceasing to be, 15.12
contracts for differences, 15.9
deemed, 15.10
definition, 15.9
disposal, 15.10
embedded, 15.4, 15.9, 15.10
securities with, issuers of, 15.11
equity instruments, 15.11
excluded contracts, 15.9
futures, 15.9
hybrid, 15.9
losses, carry back, 15.10
options, 15.9
deemed, 15.11
terminal exercise of, 15.10
property-based total return swaps, 15.10
transitional, 15.13
Design rights, 7.3
Designers of defeated tax avoidance
penalties, 52.21
Destruction of assets, 10.2
Determinations
late payment interest and penalties, tax becoming due after, 42.5
non-resident CGT disposals, 6.12, 58.22
payment of tax, on, 42.5
returns not delivered, 58.15
time limits, tax payable on, 42.5
Devaluation of sterling in 1967, 16.12
Devolution
income tax, 2.1
Differences, contracts for, *see* Contracts for differences
Digital currencies, 7.12
Digital disclosure service
serious tax fraud, HMRC, 34.13
Digital reporting and record-keeping
Finance Acts 2017 summary, 73.1
Digital tax accounts, 58.1
Diminishing shared ownership arrangements, 3.2, 3.3
Diplomatic agents
exempt organisations, 25.50
Direct recovery of tax from accounts, 51.20–51.23
Director of Public Prosecutions (DPP)
information disclosures by HMRC to, 31.2
Directors
paid, restrictions on being, social investment relief investor and investment condition, 65.13
Disabled persons
private residences, 53.2
settlements for, 62.9
Disasters of national significance
agreement for deferred payments, 42.9
Disclaimer of deceaseds' dispositions, 19.8
Disclosure of tax avoidance schemes (DOTAS), 20.1, 20.2–20.5
disclosure regime
arrangements requiring disclosure, 20.2
client details, 20.3
compliance, 20.5
confidentiality in cases involving a promoter, 20.2
confidentiality in cases not involving a promoter, 20.2
employee details provided by clients, 20.3
employment income provided through third parties, 20.2
financial products, 20.2
hallmarks, 20.2
HMRC further information requests, 20.3
information publication by HMRC, 20.6
introducers' disclosures, 20.3
leasing arrangements, 20.2
legal professional privilege, 20.2
loss schemes, 20.2
meaning of promoters, 20.3
non-UK promoters, 20.3
notifiable arrangements, 20.2
orders to disclose by HMRC, 20.5

Disclosure of tax avoidance schemes (DOTAS), – *cont.*
disclosure regime – *cont.*
parties not involving promoters, 20.3
persons required to make disclosures, 20.3
pre-disclosure enquiries, 20.5
premium fee, 20.2
promoters' disclosures, 20.3
prescribed arrangements, 20.2
reference numbers, 20.4
standardised tax products, 20.2
supplementary information, 20.5
update information provision, 20.3
voluntary disclosures, 20.5
high-risk promoters regime, 20.7
appeals, 20.14
conduct notices, 20.11
control, 20.11
defeat notices, 20.10
definitions, 20.8
documents, concealing, destroying or disposing of, 20.15
information provision, 20.11, 20.13–20.14
monitoring notices, 20.12–20.13
offences and penalties, 20.16
partnerships, 20.11, 20.17
reference numbers, 20.13
related companies and partnerships, 20.11
stop notices, 20.9
offences, 20.16
partnerships, 20.17
penalties, 20.16, 52.25
relevant defeats, 20.10
tax advisers, 20.14
threshold conditions, 20.9
voluntary disclosures, 20.14
key points, 20.18
penalties for failure, 52.24
serial avoiders regime, 4.34–4.35, 4.37
Discounted securities, 63.21
Discovery assessments, 6.10–6.11
claims, following, 13.7
Dishonest conduct by tax agents, 31.5, 34.11, 52.19
Disincorporation relief, 37.4
time limits, 68.3
Disposals
alternative finance arrangements, 3.1–3.5
assets, *see* Assets
associated, entrepreneurs' relief, 24.5, 24.10
business assets, *see* Business assets
Disposals – *cont.*
capital sums derived from assets, 10.2
compensation for assets, 10.4
corporate venturing schemes, 18.10, 18.17, 18.20
costs, shares and securities, 63.5
date of, 10.2, 16.4
deferred annuities, 43.1
depreciatory transaction in groups of companies, 4.17
derivative contracts, 15.10
enterprise investment scheme shares, 23.12
excluded, assets held on 31 March 1982, 9.4
excluded persons, 45.1
first relevant, 8.3, 9.3
gains, 16.2, 38.2
gift, by way of, time limits, 67.8
high value, *see* High value disposals
income streams through partnerships, 4.23
indexation allowance, 38.3–38.4
indexed gains, 16.2, 38.2
interaction with other taxes, 39.1–39.3
interests in settled property, of, 48.4, 62.15, 62.20, 62.21
investments, venture capital trusts, reliefs, 71.8
life assurance policies, 43.1
losses, 38.2, 44.1–44.22
market value, at, 45.1
meaning, 16.3
negligible value, assets of, 44.11
no gain/no loss, *see* No gain/no loss disposals
offshore settlements interests, 48.4
order of and meaning of proceeds, remittance basis, 55.4
part disposals, *see* Part disposals
reacquisitions of same assets and, rollover relief, 59.2
rights, sums derived from, 10.2
seed enterprise investment scheme shares, 60.36
series of transactions between connected persons, 4.14
settled property
beneficiaries becoming absolutely entitled, 62.16
disposal of interests in, 62.15
settlements, transfer into, 62.14
social investments, 65.38
stock, appropriations to and from, 16.9
time of, 10.2, 16.4
unindexed gains, 16.2, 38.2
venture capital trusts, 71.11

Distributions
see also Dividends
assets in specie in liquidations, 63.13
capital, *see* Capital distributions
gains by overseas companies, time limits, 68.4
relief, venture capital trusts, 71.9
Dividends
see also Distributions
manufactured, 63.26
stripping, 4.18
venture capital trusts and, 71.9
Divisions
cross-border, shares and securities, 63.7
Divorce, 46.5, 53.7
Docks, *see* Harbour reorganisation schemes
Documents
barristers, 34.5
concealing, destroying or disposing of
high-risk promoters tax avoidance disclosure regime, 20.15
delivery orders, HMRC, 34.16
errors in
Finance Acts 2017 summary, 73.1
penalties for, 52.8, 52.9
preservation of, 52.15, 58.8
production of, 34.4–34.7, 34.10, 34.11–34.16, 52.23
Domain names, 7.11
Domicile
appeals, 57.35
choice, of, 57.34
civil partners, 57.34
deemed, 48.1, 48.5, 48.8, 55.3, 57.34
Finance Acts 2017 summary, 73.1
dependency, of, 57.34
general law, 57.34
HMRC administrative procedures, 57.2
key points, 57.38
Members of Parliament, 57.32
origin, of, 57.34
persons with domicile abroad
forward tax agreements, 30.2, 55.8
losses, 44.3
overseas assets, 49.2
remittance basis, 55.1–55.10
Donatio mortis causa, 19.6
Donations to charities, *see* Charities
Dormant accounts, 16.7
DOTAS, *see* Disclosure of tax avoidance schemes
Double assessments, 6.4
Double tax relief
agreements, 21.2–21.3
Double tax relief – *cont.*
anti-avoidance, 21.9
arising basis, 21.6
arrangements to increase relief, 21.9
claims, 21.7
deduction, relief by, 21.5
employee share options, 22.38
HMRC practice, 21.8
key points, 21.11
limit, 21.6
minimisation of foreign tax, 21.6
remittance basis, 21.6
schemes to increase relief, 21.9
special withholding tax, 21.10
tax information exchange agreements, 31.2
time limits, 67.8
transfers of trades within EC, 49.14
unilateral relief, 21.4
DPP, see Director of Public Prosecutions
Dual residence
offshore settlements, 48.2, 48.16
Dual resident companies
ceasing to be UK resident, 14.13, 49.17–49.18
gift of business assets to, 36.8
intra-group transfers, 29.3
reconstructions of, 14.11
Dual resident investing companies, 29.3
Dual resident settlements, 48.16
Dual resident trustees, 48.2
hold-over reliefs, restriction on, 36.8, 36.11, 36.12
Dwelling houses
see Private residences
exempt assets, 25.7
Dwellings, high value disposals, 14.10

E

E-filing
HMRC and, 30.4
returns and, 58.2
form and delivery, 58.4
Earn-outs, 63.6, 63.21
time limits, 67.3

Education, visits to UK for, 57.30
EEIG, *see* European Economic Interest Groupings
Effective 51% subsidiaries, 29.2, 29.7
EIS, *see* Enterprise investment scheme
Elections
assets appropriated to trading stock
chargeable gains, Finance Acts 2017 summary, 73.1
main residence, 53.10
NRCGT disposals, computation of gains and losses, 41.30, 41.31
re-basing gains, offshore settlements, 48.15
sub-fund settlements, 62.12
Electronic communications
HMRC and, 30.4
returns and, 58.2
form and delivery, 58.4
Electronic lodgement, 58.2
Eligible shares
venture capital trusts, 71.7
Embedded derivatives, *see* Derivative contracts
Emergencies of national significance
agreement for deferred payments, 42.9
EMI, *see* Enterprise management incentives
Emigration
residence, 2012/13 and earlier, 57.31
Employee ownership trusts, disposal of shares to, 63.14
all-employee benefit requirement, 63.16
controlling interest requirement, 63.17
limited participation requirement, 63.18
trading requirement, 63.15
Employee share ownership trusts, 22.29
HMRC information powers, 22.36
rollover relief on disposals to, 22.30
dwelling-houses, 22.34
enterprise investment scheme, 22.35
qualifying corporate bonds, 22.33
replacement assets, 22.31
replacement property, 22.32
shares qualifying for EIS relief, 22.35
Employee share schemes, 22.1
anti-avoidance, 22.10–22.11
approved profit sharing schemes, 22.28
company share option plans, 22.25
conditional interests, 22.14
convertible shares, 22.15
double tax relief, 22.38
employee share ownership trusts, *see* Employee share ownership trusts
employee shareholder shares, 22.26
enterprise management incentives, *see* Enterprise management incentives
Employee share schemes, – *cont.*
executive share option schemes, 22.27
forfeiture, risk of, 22.14
key points, 22.39
market values
artificially depressed, 22.10
artificially enhanced, 22.11
shares acquired for less than, 22.8
shares disposed of for more than, 22.9
not tax-advantaged, 22.5–22.7
post acquisition benefits, 22.12
priority allocations in public share offers, 22.37
profit sharing schemes, 22.28
public offers, 22.37
research institution spin-out companies, 22.16
restricted shares, 22.13
same-day identification rule, 64.2
SAYE share options, 22.24
share incentive plans, *see* Share incentive plans
share options, *see* Share options
shares, extended meaning of, 22.2
Employee shareholder shares, 22.26
Finance Acts 2017 summary, 73.1
Employees
benefit settlements, reliefs and deferrals, 25.91
details, disclosure of tax avoidance schemes, 20.3
number of
corporate venturing schemes requirement, 18.6
enterprise investment scheme requirement, 23.5
social enterprise condition, 65.23
venture capital trusts, 71.4
private residences of, 53.7
relocation of, 53.7
restrictions on being, social investment relief investor and investment condition, 65.13
rollover relief, 59.5
settlements for benefit of, 25.91
Employment
private residences use for, 53.9
residence, 57.29
Employment income
provided through third parties, disclosure of tax avoidance schemes, 20.2
Enablers of defeated tax avoidance
penalties, 52.21, 37.1

England, meaning, 57.36
Enhancement expenditure,
Enforcement by deduction of tax from accounts, 51.20–51.23
Enquiries into returns, *see* Returns
Enterprise investment scheme (EIS), 23.1
see also Seed enterprise investment scheme
anti-avoidance, 23.17
bare trusts, shares held on, 23.2
call options, 23.17
capital gains/losses, 23.13
claims, 23.11, 23.15, 23.18
company reconstructions, 23.13
control and independence requirement, 23.5
death of investors, 23.15
deferral of gains, 23.14–23.18
deferral relief, time limits, 67.8, 68.2, 68.4
employee share ownership trusts, 22.35
entrepreneurs' relief transitional relief for, 24.11
exemption, capital gains, 23.13
exemptions and reliefs, 25.26
existing shareholdings requirement, 23.4
Finance Acts 2017 summary, 73.1
financial health requirement, 23.5
gains, 25.26
general requirements, 23.3
gross assets requirement, 23.5
income tax relief
claims for, 23.11
conditions for, 23.2
form of, 23.10
reduction where value received, 23.13
restriction or withdrawal of, 23.12
information to HMRC, 23.17
interaction IT and CGT, 23.13
investment-linked loans, 23.17
issuing company to carry on the qualifying business activity requirement, 23.5
key points, 23.19
knowledge-intensive companies, 23.3
losses on unlisted shares, 44.15
maximum amount raised annually through risk finance investments requirement, 23.3
maximum risk finance investments at the issue date requirement, 23.3
maximum risk finance investments during period B requirement, 23.3
minimum period requirement, 23.3
no connection with the issuing company requirement, 23.4
no disqualifying arrangements requirement, 23.3, 23.17
Enterprise investment scheme (EIS), – *cont.*
no linked loans requirement, 23.4
no pre-arranged exits requirement, 23.3, 23.17
no tax avoidance requirement, 23.3, 23.4
nominees, shares held by, 23.2
number of employees requirement, 23.5
permitted maximum age requirement, 23.3
property managing subsidiaries requirement, 23.5
purpose of the issue requirement, 23.3
put options, 23.17
qualifying 90% subsidiaries, 23.7
qualifying business activities, 23.8
qualifying companies, 23.5
qualifying investors, 23.4
qualifying subsidiaries, 23.6
qualifying trades, 23.9
reconstructions, 23.17
reinvestment relief, 23.14–23.18
relevant investments, 23.3
reliefs and deferrals, 25.73
share capital
acquisition, 23.12
reorganisations, 23.13, 23.17
share incentive plans, 22.21
shares
acquisitions, time limits, 68.4
disposal, 23.12
reinvestment into, 23.16–23.18
requirement, 23.3
rights issues, 23.13
spending of money raised by SEIS investment requirement, 23.3
trades or trading assets acquisition, 23.12
trading requirement, 23.5
trustees, 23.16
UK permanent establishment requirement, 23.5
unlisted trading companies, losses on shares in, 44.15
unquoted status requirement, 23.5
use of money raised requirement, 23.3
value received by investors from EIS company, 23.17
value received by other persons from EIS company, 23.17
venture capital trusts interaction with, 71.12
Enterprise management incentives (EMI), 22.22
entrepreneurs' relief, 24.3
option grants, time limits, 68.2

Entertainers, non-UK resident
information disclosures by HMRC to, 31.2
Entrepreneurs' relief, 25.74
amount of, 24.8
assets qualifying, 24.7
associated disposals, 24.5, 24.10
claims, 24.6
deferred gains, 24.11
enterprise investment scheme, transitional relief for, 24.11
furnished holiday accommodation, 26.2
goodwill, 24.7
introduction, 24.1
key points, 24.13
lifetime limits, 24.8
material disposals of business assets, 24.3, 24.5
partnerships, 24.3
qualifying business disposals, 24.2
reliefs and deferrals, 25.74
reorganisations, 24.12
restrictions on, 24.9–24.10
shares and securities, 24.3
time limits, 67.3
trust business assets disposals, 24.4, 24.9
venture capital trusts, transitional relief for, 24.11
Equitable Life payments
exempt gains and transactions, 25.25
Equitable liability, HMRC, 51.30
Equity instruments, 15.11
Error or mistake relief, 13.8
Errors
careless or deliberate in documents, penalties, 52.8
documents, in, Finance Acts 2017 summary, 73.1
HMRC, by, 30.6, 42.9, 51.29
ESC, *see* Extra-Statutory Concessions, HMRC
Estates
death on, administration of, 19.9–19.13
EU member states, *see* European Union member states
Euro
debts, 25.5
derivatives, 7.7
holding of, 7.2
payment in, 51.12
securities, redenomination into, 63.8
European Companies, *see* Societas Europaea
European Co-operatives, *see* Societas Co-operative Europaea
European Economic Interest Groupings (EEIG), 49.20, 52.6, 52.7, 58.23
European Union member states
cross-border mergers, 49.15
tax liabilities in, 51.32
transfers of businesses between, 49.13, 49.14
transparent entities, disapplication of reliefs, 49.16
Evidence
First-tier Tribunal, 5.19
Upper Tribunal, 5.30
Ewe premium quotas, 59.4
Exchange control, 45.7
Exchange gains and losses, *see* Foreign exchange
Exchange restrictions
late payment interest and penalties, 42.8
Exchanges of securities
share capital reorganisations, 63.5–63.6
Excluded derivative contracts, 15.9
Excluded persons, 45.1
Excluded settlements, 62.8
Excuse, reasonable, *see* Reasonable excuse
Executive share option schemes, 22.27
Exempt amounts for the year, *see* Annual exempt amounts
Exempt organisations
venture capital trusts, 25.64
Exempt unit holders, unit trusts for, 70.7
Exemptions and reliefs, 25.1
see also Reliefs and deferrals
agricultural grants, 25.19
annual exempt amounts, 2.3, 62.8, 62.9
annual payments, 25.3
annuities, 25.3
art, works of, 25.41
asbestos compensation settlements, 25.43
assets, exempt, 25.2–25.17
assets held on 31 March 1982, 9.3, 9.6
bare trustees, 25.44
betting winnings, 25.21
bonds, qualifying corporate, 54.1–54.4
British Museum, 25.45
business expansion scheme, 25.22
cars, 25.11
cashbacks, 25.23, 63.27
central banks, 25.46

Exemptions and reliefs, – *cont.*
charities, 25.47
donations to, 11.6–11.9
exemption from tax on chargeable gains, 11.3–11.5
chattels, 25.4
Chevening Estate trusts, 25.49
child trust funds, 25.24
commodities, 25.4
community amateur sports clubs, 11.12, 25.48
compensation
foreign governments, from, 25.27
personal, 25.25
spent on restoration, 10.3, 10.4
corporate bonds, 54.1–54.4
covenants, 25.3
Crown, The, 25.49
currency, 25.8
damages, personal, 25.25
debts, 25.5
debts on security, 25.5
decorations for valour or gallantry, 25.6
deferred charges, 9.11
diplomatic agents, 25.50
disincorporation relief, 37.4, 73.1
enterprise investment scheme, 25.26
Equitable Life payments, 25.25
exempt assets, 25.2–25.17
exempt gains, 25.18–25.41
exempt individuals, 25.42–25.65
exempt organisations, 25.42–25.65
exempt persons, 25.42–25.65
exempt transactions, 25.18–25.41
foreign currency, 25.8
friendly societies, 25.51
gains, exempt, 25.18–25.41
gallantry, decorations for, 25.6
gifts, hold-over reliefs, *see* Hold-over reliefs
government grants, agricultural, 25.19
government securities, *see* Government securities
grants, agricultural, 25.19
health service bodies, 25.55
Help to Buy ISAs, 25.30
Historic Buildings and Monuments Commission for England, 25.52
hold-over reliefs, *see* Hold-over reliefs
housing associations, 25.53
incorporation relief, 37.1–37.5
indexation, 38
individual savings accounts, 25.30
individuals, exempt, 25.42–25.65
insurance policies, 25.10, 43.1

Exemptions and reliefs, – *cont.*
international organisations, 25.54
investment trusts, 25.64, 70.4
junior ISAs, 25.30
legatees, 25.31
life assurance policies, 43.1
Lifetime ISAs, 25.30
Lloyd's underwriters' special reserve funds, 25.37
loans, 25.5, 44.12–44.14
local authorities, 25.55
London Olympic Games, 25.56
losses, 44.1–44.19
lottery winnings, 25.21
mis-sold pensions, 25.60
motor cars, 25.11
national debt, 25.57
National Heritage Memorial Fund, 25.58
National Radiological Protection Board, 25.59
Natural History Museum, 25.45
nominees, 25.44
non-approved pension schemes, 25.60
occupational pension schemes, 25.60
open-ended investment companies, 25.64, 70.8
organisations, exempt, 25.42–25.65
overseas residents, 48
pension schemes, 25.60
personal equity plans (PEP), 25.32
persons, exempt, 25.42–25.65
private residences, 53.1–53.15
prize winnings, 25.21
qualifying corporate bonds, 54.1–54.4
contracts, 7.8
loans evidenced by, 44.13, 44.14
options, 7.7
recovery of assets under Proceeds of Crime Act, 25.33
reliefs and deferrals, 25.66–25.96
renewables obligations certificates, 25.13
replacement of business assets, *see* Rollover relief
residences, private, 53.1–53.15
retirement annuity schemes, 25.60
rights to receive interest on deposits
victims of Nazi persecution, 25.14
rollover relief, *see* Rollover relief
savings accounts, 25.15
savings certificates, 25.15
savings schemes, 25.15
seed enterprise investment scheme, 25.34, 25.90
scientific research associations, 25.61
securities, government, 15.5, 28.1–28.2

Exemptions and reliefs, – *cont.*
self-build societies, 25.62
sets of assets, 25.4
settled property, 25.35, 62.16, 62.17
settlements, 25.16, 62.15
for employees, 25.91
shares
business expansion scheme, 25.22
gifts of, *see* Hold-over reliefs
individual savings accounts, 25.30
reinvestment in, 25.86
unlisted trading companies, in, 44.15, 44.18
ships, 25.17
short rotation coppice, 25.40
social investment relief, 25.36
special reliefs, losses, *see* Losses
substantial shareholdings of companies, *see* Substantial shareholdings of companies
superannuation funds, 25.3
tangible movable property, 25.4
trade, assets used for and taxed on cash basis, 25.20
trade unions, 25.63
transactions, exempt, 25.18–25.41
trusts, *see* settlements *above*
unit trusts, 25.64
unremittable gains, 49.6
valour, decorations for, 25.6
venture capital trusts, 25.39, 25.64
visiting forces, 25.65
wasting assets, 25.4
winnings, 25.21
woodlands, 25.40
works of art, 25.41
Existing investments requirement
social investment relief investor and investment condition, 65.10
Existing shareholdings requirement
enterprise investment scheme, 23.4
Exit charges
offshore settlements, 48.1
payment plans, 49.3, 49.17, 51.8
Expenditure
administration of deceased's estate, 19.10–19.11
allowable, 16.11–16.13
apportionment, 16.5
capital allowances, assets subject to, 8.11, 9.7
charities, 11.4
consideration, 16.11
deeply discounted securities, 63.21
deferred annuities, 43.1
Expenditure – *cont.*
deposits forfeited, 16.6
enhancement, 16.11
foreign tax, 21.5
forfeited deposits, 16.6
incidental costs, 16.11
income tax paid by close company participator, 16.12
inheritance tax, 39.2
interaction with other taxes, 39.1–39.3
interest charged to capital by companies, 14.5
land, 39.1–39.3
life assurance policies, 43.1
non-allowable expenditure, 16.13
offshore funds, 49.10–49.11
overseas ordinarily resident person, acquisition from, 16.12
overseas resident, acquisition from, 16.12
overseas tax, 21.5
part disposal, 16.5
personal representatives' expenses, 16.12, 19.10–19.11, 19.14
scrip dividends, 63.10
stock dividends, 63.10
title, expenditure concerning, 16.11
value added tax, 39.3
wasting assets treatment, 72.2
Exploration and exploitation rights to territorial sea-bed and continental shelf, 49.19
Extended time limits,
assessments 6.14–6.15
Extra-Statutory Concessions (ESC), HMRC, 33.1
abuse of, 4.19
failure to apply, 30.2, 57.29
list, 33.2
power to give statutory effect to, 30.5
Extraction of value rule
remittance basis, 55.4

F

Factoring of income receipts, 4.21
Fair values
loan relationships, 15.5
Families
deeds of family arrangement, 19.8
ties, statutory residence tests, 57.13
Farming
ewe premium quotas, 59.4
foot and mouth outbreak, 25.85

Farming – *cont.*
milk quotas, *see* Milk quotas
potato quotas, 59.4
single payment scheme payment entitlement, 7.14
suckler cow premium quotas, 59.4
FCA, *see* Financial Conduct Authority
File access notices, 34.11
penalties for failure to comply, 52.19
Finance Acts 2017
summary of provisions, 73.1
Financial activities
corporate venturing schemes, 18.5
Financial advantages
tainted donations to charities, 11.11
Financial Conduct Authority (FCA)
information disclosures by HMRC to, 31.2
Financial enablers of defeated tax avoidance
penalties, 52.21
Financial health
enterprise investment scheme requirement, 23.5
social enterprise condition, 65.25
venture capital trusts requirement, 71.4
Financial options, 7.7
Financial products
disclosure of tax avoidance schemes, 20.2
Financial Reporting Review Panel (FRRP)
information disclosures by HMRC to, 31.2
Finance leases, 16.10
FINROF (funds investing in non-reporting offshore funds), 70.10
First relevant disposal, 8.3, 9.3
First-tier Tribunal
appeals against decisions, 5.22, 5.27
appeals to, 5.8
basic cases, 5.16
case law, 5.20
case management, 5.12
categorisation of cases, 5.14
complex cases, 5.18
composition, 5.11
consent orders, 5.20
costs, 5.18, 5.24
decisions, 5.20–5.22
default paper cases, 5.15
evidence, 5.19
failure to attend, 5.19
hearings, 5.19
mistakes in decisions, correction, 5.21
First-tier Tribunal – *cont.*
objective, 5.11
onus of proof, 5.20
organisation of, 5.11
payment of tax pending further appeal, 5.23
penalties proceedings, 52.35
representation, 5.12
rules, failure to comply, 5.13
setting aside decisions, 5.21
standard cases, 5.17
starting proceedings, 5.12
striking out cases, 5.13
submissions, 5.19
transfer to Upper Tribunal, 5.18
withdrawal from cases, 5.12
witnesses, 5.19
Fish quota, 59.4
Five-year start-up rule
remittance basis, 55.4
Fixed interest securities, 8.3
Fixed penalties, 52.16
Fixed plant and machinery, 59.4, 59.9
Floods in 2014, taxpayers affected by, 30.2
Follower notices, 4.25–4.28
penalties for failure to comply, 52.26
Foot and mouth outbreak
national heritage property, 25.85
Foreign chargeable gains
remittance basis, 55.3
Foreign currencies
accounts in, 14.14
bank accounts, 7.3, 25.5, 55.6, 55.7
exchange, *See* Foreign exchange
exempt assets, 25.8
hedging instruments, 15.3
Foreign exchange (FOREX)
gains and losses, 15.3, 16.11
loan relationships and, 15.3, 25.8
Foreign tax, 16.12, 21.1–21.11, 51.32
FOREX, *see* **Foreign exchange**
Forfeited deposits, 16.6
Forfeiture of rights, 10.2
Fractional shares, partners, 50.3, 50.6, 50.13
Franchises, location, 7.3
Fraud
serious tax fraud, *see* HMRC
Freehold reversion of land, 41.12
Friendly societies
exempt organisations, 25.51

FRRP, *see* Financial Reporting Review Panel
Full-time working activities overseas, 57.29
Funded trades
corporate venturing schemes, 18.4
Funds investing in non-reporting offshore funds (FINROF), 70.10
Fungible assets
intangible asset regime for companies, 15.14, 15.15
milk quota, 7.9
Furnished holiday accommodation, 26.1–26.3
time limits, 67.3
Further charge
offshore settlements, 48.21
Futures, 15.9
contracts 25.60
non-UK, location, 7.3
wasting assets, 72.3
Futures exchange, recognised, 7.7

G

GAAR, *see* General anti-abuse rule
Gains
see also Computation of gains and losses
adjusted net, 2.6
art works, 25.41
betting winnings, 25.21
business expansion scheme, 25.22
buying, groups of companies, 29.15–29.17
carried interest, settlors, offshore settlements, 48.5
cashbacks, 25.23, 63.27
chargeable, *see* Chargeable gains
charities, 25.47
child trust funds, 25.24
compensation from foreign governments, 25.27
corporate venturing schemes, chargeable, 18.17, 18.20
deferral, enterprise investment scheme, 23.14–23.18
deferred charges on before 31 March 1982, 9.11
deferred, entrepreneurs' relief, 24.11
derivative contracts chargeable gains consequences, 15.10–15.12
disposals, 16.2, 38.2
distribution by overseas companies, time limits, 68.4
enterprise investment scheme, 25.26
foreign exchange, 15.3, 16.11

Gains – *cont.*
groups of companies
Help to Buy ISAs, 25.30
indexed, computation, 16.2, 38.2
individual savings accounts, 25.30
junior ISAs, 25.30
Lloyd's underwriters' special reserve funds, 25.37
losses set-off against, 44.2, 48.13
lottery winnings, 25.21
management expenses set against, 14.6
national purposes, gifts for, 25.41
net adjusted, 2.6
non-resident disposals of UK residential property
ATED-related gains or losses, interaction with, 14.10
overseas, 25.95
overseas residents companies
attribution of gains to UK settlements, 62.23
pension schemes, 25.60
pre-entry, groups, 29.15–29.17
prize winnings, 25.21
remittance basis, 55.2, 55.3, 55.5
residential property, 2.1
seed enterprise investment scheme, 25.34, 25.90
settled property, 25.35
settlements, non-resident companies, 62.23
social investment relief, 25.36
substantial shareholdings, 25.38
time apportionment
assets held on 31 March 1982, pre-6 April 1965 gains and losses, 9.10
time limits
deferred charges on gains before 31 March 1982, 9.11
delayed remittance of overseas gains, 49.6
individuals' trading losses set off against gains, 44.21
overseas companies, distribution of gains, 49.7
overseas gains, delayed remittance, 49.6
trading losses set off against non-corporate persons' gains, 44.21
trading losses, relief for against, 14.6, 44.21
unindexed, computation, 16.2, 38.2
unremittable, 25.95, 42.8, 49.6
upper rate, 2.1
venture capital trusts, 25.39
winnings, 25.21

Gallantry awards, 25.6
General anti-abuse rule (GAAR), 4.3
  Advisory Panel, 52.21
  equivalent arrangements, counteraction of, 4.6
  final decision notices, 52.21
  penalties, 52.11
  procedure, 4.4
  provisional counteraction notices, 4.5
Gift aid donations, 11.10
  community amateur sports clubs, 11.10, 11.12
  tainted, 11.11
Gifts
  see also Assets; Hold-over reliefs
  agricultural property, 36.5
  business assets, of, 25.75, 36.2–36.9
  charities, to
    assets, 11.7–11.9
    reliefs and deferrals, 25.76
  date of disposal, 16.4, 27.1
  disposals by way of, time limits, 67.8
  general relief, 36.12
  holdover relief, 25.75, 25.78
  inheritance tax, chargeable on, 36.10–36.11
  inheritance tax, deduction for, on subsequent disposal, 39.2
  key points, 27.5
  market values, 27.1, 45.1
  payment of tax by instalments, 51.5
  reliefs and deferrals, 25.75, 25.76, 25.78
  tax, recovery from donees, 27.4
Gilt-edged securities, *see* Government securities
Goodwill
  corporation tax regime, 15.14, 15.15
  entrepreneurs' relief, 24.7
  groups of companies, 4.17
  know-how, 7.4
  location, 7.3
  partnerships, 50.8, 50.11
  rollover relief, 59.4
Government debt, 15.2
Government grants
  agricultural, 25.19
Government securities
  contracts for, 7.8
  exempt, 28.2
  exempt assets, 25.9
  exemption rules, 7.7, 7.8, 28.1
  held on 6 April 1965, 8.4
  options for, 7.7
Grace periods
  remittance basis, 55.4
Grandchildren
  settlors, offshore settlements, 48.7
Grants, government
  agricultural, 25.19
Great Britain, meaning, 57.36
Gross assets requirement
  corporate venturing schemes, 18.6
  enterprise investment scheme, 23.5
  social enterprise condition, 65.19
  venture capital trusts, 71.4
Groups of companies
  see also Subsidiaries
  amalgamation, 14.11
  anti-avoidance provisions, 4.17, 29.14–29.23
  assets held on 6 April 1965, 8.1, 8.3
  assets held on 31 March 1982, 9.5, 9.6
  capital gain buying, 29.15–29.17
  capital loss buying, 29.15–29.23
  collection of tax, 51.26
  definitions, 29.2
  degrouping charges
    charge to tax, 29.7
    clawback of relief, 29.6
    deferral, 29.8
    exemptions, 29.9–29.10
    investment trusts, companies becoming, 29.11
    merger exemptions, 29.10
    substantial shareholdings exemptions, 29.9
    venture capital trusts, companies becoming, 29.12
  depreciatory transaction, 4.17
  dividend stripping, 4.18
  elections to transfer gains or losses, 29.13
  gains
    buying, 29.15–29.17
    elections to transfer, 29.13
  intra-group transfers, 29.3,
    clawback of relief, 29.6
    deemed, 29.13
    indexation, 9.6, 38.4
    main rules, 29.3
    re-basing, 9.6
  key points, 29.24
  leaving companies *see* degrouping charges *above*
  losses
    buying, 29.15–29.23
    elections to transfer, 29.13
  meaning, 29.2
  mergers, 29.10
  nationalised industries, 29.2

Groups of companies – *cont.*
non-financial trading, corporate venturing schemes, 18.5
NRCGT groups of companies, 41.33
payment of tax, 51.4
pre-entry gains, 29.15–29.17
pre-entry losses, 29.15–29.23
rollover relief, 59.10
serial avoiders regime, 4.38
substantial shareholdings exemption, *see* Substantial shareholdings of companies
tax refunds in, 51.4
trading stock of one company, 29.4
unpaid tax of other members, 51.26
value shifting, 4.8–4.11
venture capital trusts, 29.12
Guaranteed returns
transactions involving, derivative contracts, 15.9, 15.13
Guarantees of loans, 44.12
Guardians, 12.3
Guns, 25.4

H

Harbour reorganisation schemes, 25.77
Hallmarks of tax avoidance schemes, 20.2
Health Departments
information disclosures by HMRC to, 31.2
Health service bodies
exempt organisations, 25.55
Hearings
First-tier Tribunal, 5.19
Upper Tribunal, 5.30
Help to Buy ISAs
exempt gains and transactions, 25.30
Helpsheets, HMRC, 32.5
Her Majesty's Revenue and Customs, *see* HMRC
High-risk promoters
Special compliance regime, Finance Acts 2017 summary, 73.1
High value disposals
dwellings, 14.10
NRCGT disposals, computation of gains and losses, 41.31
Hire purchase, 16.4
Historic Buildings and Monuments Commission for England
exemptions and reliefs, 25.52
HMRC
Adjudicator, 30.8
administration, 30.1–30.9
administrative procedures
domicile, 57.2
agreement to forgo corporation tax reliefs, 30.2
Briefs, 32.4
care and management powers, 30.2
Charter, 30.7
codes of practice, 30.7
Commissioners for HMRC, 30.1
care and management powers, 30.2
complaints
Adjudicator, 30.8
delays by HMRC, 30.6
HMRC Charter, 30.7
mistakes by HMRC, 30.6
concessions, 30.5
confidentiality of information, 31.1
criminal offence of disclosure of tax information, 31.6
offshore tax non-compliance, persons failing to correct, publication of details of, 31.4
organisations to which information may be disclosed, 31.2
tax agents, publication of details of, 31.5
tax defaulters, publication of details of, 31.3
delays, 30.6, 42.9, 51.29
disclosure of tax avoidance schemes
further information requests, 20.3
information publication, 20.6
orders to disclose, 20.5
double tax relief practice, 21.8
electronic communications, 30.4
enablers of defeated tax avoidance, publication of details, 52.21
enterprise investment scheme information to, 23.17
equitable liability, 51.30
explanatory leaflets, 32.1
Extra-Statutory Concessions, *see* Extra-Statutory Concessions
information
see also information and inspection powers *below*
confidentiality, *see* confidentiality of information *above*
powers, employee share ownership trusts, 22.36
information and inspection powers, 34.3
appeals, 34.6

HMRC – *cont.*
information and inspection powers, – *cont.*
concealing, destroying or disposing of documents, 34.7
information and documents, 34.4–34.7
inspection of business premises, 34.8
inspection of other premises, 34.9
offences, 34.10
offshore settlements, 48.12, 48.20, 48.29
penalties, 34.10, 52.16
restrictions, 34.5
settlors, offshore settlements, 48.12
guidance manuals, 32.2
Helpsheets, 32.5
investigatory powers
computer records, 34.18
data-gathering, 34.17
debtors, power to obtain details of, 51.19
documents, power to call for, 34.4
information and inspection powers, *see* information and inspection powers *above*
introduction, 34.1
key points, 34.19
Police and Criminal Evidence Act, under, 34.14
Proceeds of Crime Act 2002, under, 34.15
serious tax fraud, *see* serious tax fraud *below*
self-assessment enquiries, 34.2, 58.9–58.14
tax agents, power to obtain files of, 34.11
mandatory e-filing, 30.4
mistakes, 30.6, 42.9, 51.29
non-statutory clearances, 30.3
online toolkits, 32.6
powers
care and management, 30.2
debtors' details, obtaining, 51.19
information, employee share ownership trusts, 22.36
information and inspection, *see* information and inspection powers *above*
investigatory, *see* investigatory powers *above*
statutory effect to concessions, giving, 30.5
publication of information, *see* confidentiality of information *above*
reviews, 5.6–5.7

HMRC – *cont.*
serious tax fraud
contractual disclosure facility (CDF), 34.13
digital disclosure service, 34.13
document delivery order, 34.16
Police and Criminal Evidence Act powers, 34.14
policy, 34.13
Proceeds of Crime Act powers, 34.15
Statements of Practice, 35.1–35.2
Tax Bulletin, 32.3
toolkits, 32.6
website, 32.6
Hold notices
payment of tax, 51.22
Hold-over reliefs
agricultural property, 36.5
assets on which inheritance tax is chargeable, gifts of, time limits, 67.8
business assets, 36.2–36.9, 67.8
claims, 36.4
clawback, 36.11
definitions, 36.3
general relief before 1989, 36.12
gifts, 25.75, 25.78
inheritance tax chargeable, 36.10–36.11
key points, 36.13
limited liability partnerships, 36.8, 36.11
nature of, 36.4
partial consideration example, 36.7
private residences and, 53.13
restrictions on, 36.11
settled property, 36.6
settlements, 36.6, 62.17, 62.18
settlor interested, gifts to, 36.8, 36.11
substantial shareholdings exemption, interaction with, 36.8
time limits 67.8
transfer of business to company, 37.2
Holding companies
new corporate venturing schemes, 18.23
Holdings
qualifying, venture capital trusts, 71.4, 71.5
Holiday accommodation, furnished, 26.1–26.3
Hops Marketing Board
reliefs and deferrals, 25.79
Hotels, returns by, 58.24
Houseboats, 25.4, 53.3
Houses, *see* Private residences
Housing associations
exempt organisations, 25.53

Housing providers
tainted donations, 11.11
Hovercraft, 59.4
Husbands and wives, *see* Married persons
Hybrid derivative contracts, 15.9
Hybrid entities
tax arbitrage, 4.20

I

Identification of shares reliefs
venture capital trusts, 71.12
Identification rules
see also Shares and securities
assets held on 6 April 1965
land reflecting development value, 8.6
miscellaneous assets, 8.7
quoted securities, 8.4–8.5
unquoted securities, 8.9
fungible assets, 7.9,
partnership fractional shares, 50.13
Image rights, 7.13
Immovable property, location, 7.3
Inadmissible taxes, 21.4
Incidental costs, 16.11
Income
conversion to capital, 14.7–14.9
employment, from, *see* Employment income
nominated, remittance basis, 55.5
receipts, factoring of, 4.21
streams
disposal through partnerships, 4.23
transfer of, 4.22
Income condition
community amateur sports clubs, 11.12
Income retention condition
venture capital trusts, 71.2
Income tax
credits, 21.8
devolution, 2.1
enterprise investment scheme relief, *see* Enterprise investment scheme
interaction with, 39.1, 41.17,44.21
land, 41.2–41.7
paid by close company participators, 16.12, 63.23
self-assessment, 61.2
social investment relief, *see* Social investment relief
Incorporation relief, 25.94, 37.1
election to disapply, 37.3
key points, 37.5
Incorporation relief, – *cont.*
time limits, 67.3, 67.5
transfer of business to a company, 37.2
Indemnities, 16.13
Independence
corporate venturing schemes requirement, 18.6
enterprise investment scheme requirement, 23.5
social enterprise condition, 65.21
venture capital trusts, 71.4
Indexation
abolition of for CGT, 38.1
allowance, 38.1–38.8
annual exempt amounts, 2.6
assets held on 6 April 1965
land reflecting development value, 8.6
other assets, 8.7
quoted securities, 8.2–8.3
assets held on 31 March 1982, 9.3, 9.6
bondwashing, 64.3, 64.6
business expansion scheme, 25.22, 64.3
calls on shares, 38.7
contangos, 64.6
deep discount securities, 64.3, 64.6
disposals during 1982–1985 period, 38.4, 38.5
freezing of, 38.2
general, 38.2
government securities, 64.6
identification rules, 64.4
indexation factor, 38.2
indexed pool of expenditure, 64.3, 64.4
indexed rise, 38.2, 64.3, 64.4
losses, 38.2
no gain/no loss disposals, 38.2, 38.4
offshore funds, 64.3, 64.6
operative events, 64.3, 64.4
options, 38.8
consideration for, 64.4
part disposals, 16.5, 38.3, 38.5
partnerships, 50.7–50.8
qualifying corporate bonds, 64.6
qualifying expenditure, 64.4
receipts affecting allowable expenditure, 38.5
relevant allowable expenditure, 38.2
relevant events, 38.5
relevant securities, 64.3, 64.6
reorganisations, etc, 38.6
retail prices index (RPI), 38.2
rolled-up, 9.6
sale of rights, 38.5
section 104 holdings, 64.2, 64.3, 64.4

Indexation – *cont.*
securities
1982 holding, 64.5
new holdings, 64.4
section 104 holdings, 64.2, 64.3, 64.4
shares, calls, 38.7
table, 38.2
time apportionment, 8.7
unindexed gain, 38.2
unit trusts, 70.3
Individual beneficial interests declarations
married persons, 46.2
Individual owners requirement
corporate venturing schemes, 18.6
Individual savings accounts (ISA)
exempt gains and transactions, 25.30
Individual underwriters at Lloyd's, 69.2
Individuals
exempt, 25.42–25.65
homes, statutory residence tests, 57.8
property transactions, 41.3
Industrial and provident societies, 9.6, 14.11
Information
confidentiality of, HMRC, *see* HMRC
disclosure of tax avoidance schemes, 20.3, 20.5, 20.6
high-risk promoters tax avoidance disclosure regime, 20.11, 20.13–20.14
publication
HMRC, by, *see* HMRC: confidentiality of information
unco-operative large businesses, 14.19
Information and inspection powers, HMRC, *see* HMRC
Information notices
HMRC investigatory powers, 34.4–34.6, 34.10, 51.21
partnerships, 4.37
payment of tax, 51.21
serial avoiders regime, 4.35
Inheritance tax, 19.5, 36.10–36.11, 39.2
Insolvency, 14.4, 52.39, 62.3
stock lending borrowers, of, 63.25
Instalments, payment of tax by, 51.5
large companies, 51.4
Insurance policies
exempt assets, 25.10
Intangible assets of companies, 15.14, 15.15
see also Intangible fixed assets
excluded assets, 15.15
fungible assets, 15.14
goodwill, 15.14
'intangible fixed asset, meaning of', 15.15
rollover relief, 59.3, 59.4
Intangible assets of companies, – *cont.*
transfers between related parties, 45.2
Intangible fixed assets, 15.1, 15.14
see also Intangible assets of companies
assets excluded, 15.15
definition, 15.15
goodwill, 15.15
intellectual property, *see* Intellectual property
key points, 15.16
know-how, 7.4
location, 7.3
milk quota, 7.9
patents, 7.5
Intellectual property
assets, treatment as, 7.4–7.5
corporation tax regime, 15.14, 15.15
Interaction with other taxes
betterment levy, 47.1
income tax, 2.2, 39.1, 41.17
inheritance tax, 39.2
value added tax, 39.3
Interest
carried, *see* Carried interest
charged to capital, 14.5, 16.12
corporation tax unpaid, on, 42.7
judgment debts, on, 42.9, 56.5
overpaid tax, on *see* Repayment interest
rate contracts, 15.9
repayment interest, *see* Repayment interest
unpaid tax, on, *see* Late payment interest and penalties
returns economically equivalent to, 15.6
Interests
see also Life interests
beneficial, married persons' declarations, 46.2
co-owners of assets, location, 7.3
conditional, employee share schemes, 22.14
settled property, in, 62.4
disposals, 48.4, 62.15, 62.20, 62.21
settlements, created by or arising under, 62.4
settlors, offshore settlements, 48.6
Intermediaries
gift aid, 11.10
International organisations
exempt organisations, 25.54
Internet
corporation tax service, 30.4
domain names, 7.11
HMRC website, 32.6
payment of tax via, 30.4
returns, filing of, 30.4, 58.4, 58.6

Intestacy
private residences occupation by, 53.11
Intra-group transfers, *see* Groups of companies
Introducers' disclosures
disclosure of tax avoidance schemes, 20.3
Investigatory powers, HMRC, *see* HMRC
Investment amounts
limits, social enterprise condition, 65.30
Investment bonds
alternative finance arrangements, 3.2, 3.4, 3.5
Investment clubs, 70.13
Investment companies
subscribing, loss relief for, time limits, 67.4
Investment contracts
life insurance, 15.5
Investment funds
alternative investment fund management partnerships, 50.19
Investment in ISAs
exempt gains and transactions, 25.30
Investment limits condition
venture capital trusts, 71.2
Investment-linked loans
enterprise investment scheme, 23.17
Investment managers
carried interest, 50.20
Investment reliefs
corporate venturing scheme, *See* Corporate venturing scheme
venture capital trusts, 71.7
Investment trusts
companies becoming, 29.11
definition, 70.4
exempt organisations, 25.64
exemptions and reliefs, 25.64
reconstructions and transfers, 14.11
real estate, 70.5
Investments
approved charitable, 11.4
charitable, 11.4
mixed funds, made from, remittance basis, 55.4
qualifying, venture capital trusts, 71.12
relevant
corporate venturing schemes, 18.8
enterprise investment scheme, 23.3
Investors
claims, 40.6
disqualification of shares, 40.8
lifetime limits, 40.5
Investors – *cont.*
qualifying
enterprise investment scheme, 23.4
seed enterprise investment scheme, 60.11–60.16
qualifying shares, 40.7
seed enterprise investment scheme value received by, 60.37
trustees, disposal by, 40.3
value received, 40.8, 65.39
Investors' relief
election to disapply reorganisation, 40.10
introduction to, 40.1
operation of, 40.2
previous disposal of shares, 40.4
reorganisations, 40.9, 40.10
Ireland, 57.37
ISA, *see* Individual savings accounts
Isle of Man, meaning, 57.36
Issuing companies
seed enterprise investment scheme, of, acquired by new companies, 60.42
Issuing houses, returns by, 58.25

J

Job-related accommodation, 53.7
Joint ventures
companies, substantial shareholdings exemption, 66.17
corporate venturing schemes requirement, 18.6
Judgment debts
interest on, 42.9, 56.5
location, 7.3
Judicial reviews, 5.35
application time limits, 68.2
Judicial rulings
appeals against, 4.28
Junior ISAs
exempt gains and transactions, 25.30
Jurisdiction condition, charities, 11.2

K

Know-how, 7.4
time limits, 68.3

Knowledge-intensive companies
enterprise investment scheme, 23.3

L

Land
see also Buildings; Property
anti-avoidance, 41.4
capital gains taxed as income, 41.4
compulsory purchase, 41.10
capital sums derived from assets, 10.2
reliefs and deferrals, 25.81
rollover relief, 41.12
small part disposals, 41.11
time limits, 67.8
contingent liabilities, 41.24
definition of, 41.1, 41.4
development value at 6 April 1965, 8.6
exchange of joint interests in, 41.13
freehold reversion, 45.6
income tax interaction, 41.2–41.7
introduction, 41.1
investment bond arrangements, 3.5
isolated transactions, 41.3
joint interests in, exchange of, 41.13
leases, *see* Leases
market value, 45.6
national heritage property, 25.85
non-resident CGT disposals of UK residential property, *see* Non-resident CGT disposals of UK residential property
options
contingently repayable deposits for, 41.24
rollover relief, 59.4
part disposals, 41.8
indexation, 38.5
reliefs and deferrals, 25.82
small, 41.9, 41.11, 67.3
private residences, appropriate to, 53.2
reconveyance, sales with right of, 41.7
rollover relief, 41.12, 59.4
exchange of joint interests, 41.13
sales
reconveyance, with right of, 41.7
speculative transactions, 41.3
tenanted, 45.6
trade, adventure or concern in nature of, 41.3
transactions
before 5 July 2016, 41.4
Finance Acts 2017 summary, 73.1

Land – *cont.*
transactions – *cont.*
isolated, 41.3
property, 41.3
on or after 5 July 2016, 41.6
speculative, 41.3
UK land, transactions in, 41.6
UK residential property, non-resident CGT disposals of, *see* Non-resident CGT disposals of UK residential property
valuations
freehold reversion, 45.6
held at 31 March 1982, 9.2
tenanted, 45.6
Large businesses
special measures regime, 14.19
tax strategies publication, 14.18
Late payment interest and penalties, 42.1
see also Payment of tax
agreements for deferred payment, 42.9
appeals, determinations of, tax becoming due after, 42.5
contract settlements, 6.8
companies, 42.7
death of taxpayers, 42.9
delay by HMRC, 42.9
delayed remittances, 42.8
determinations, tax becoming due after, 42.5
disasters of national significance, 42.9
exchange restrictions, 42.8
judgment debts, 42.9
late payment penalties, 42.10
new regime, 42.2
old regime, 42.3–42.5
persons other than companies, 42.3–42.5
surcharges, 42.6
Launch vehicles, 59.4
Leases
duration, wasting assets, 72.4
finance, 16.10
long funding, plant or machinery, 7.6
land
see also Assets held on 6 April 1965; Land
anti-avoidance, 41.21
assignment, new leases after, 41.22
capital sums treated as premiums, 41.16
compulsory purchase, following, 41.12
contingent liabilities, 41.24
duration, 41.15
extensions to, 41.15
freehold reversion of, 41.12
income tax, 41.17
meaning, 41.14

Leases – *cont.*
land – *cont.*
new leases after assignment, 41.22
new leases after surrender, 41.22
premiums, 41.16–41.21
release of onerous liability on surrender, 41.14
sale and lease-back, 4.8, 41.22
sub-leases, 41.18
surrender, new leases after, 41.22
surrender, release of onerous liabilities on, 41.14
tenanted, 45.6
value shifting, 4.8, 41.23
wasting assets, 41.15
premiums, wasting assets, 72.5
sub-leases, 41.18
granted out of short leases, wasting assets, 72.6
wasting assets, *see* Wasting assets
Leasing
disclosure of tax avoidance schemes, 20.2
Legal professional privilege
disclosure of tax avoidance schemes, 20.2
penalties and, 52.21
Legatees, 16.12, 19.14, 25.31
Letting of main residences, 53.14
Liabilities contingent at disposal, 16.13
Life insurance policies
assets transferred, 63.24
assigned, profits on, 43.2
disposal of rights, 43.1
losses, restriction on, 43.1
policy holders, asset transfers to, 63.24
Life interests
relation to settlements, in, 62.4
wasting assets, 72.7
Life tenants
see also Settlements
death, hold-over relief, 36.8, 36.11, 36.12
Lifetime ISAs
exemptions and reliefs, 25.30
Lifetime limits
entrepreneurs' relief, 24.8
investors' relief, 40.5
Limited liability partnerships (LLP)
exempt organisations, 25.60
hold-over reliefs, 36.8, 36.11
legal status, 50.18
property investment LLPs, 50.18
rollover relief, 59.3
Limited participation requirement
employee ownership trusts, 63.18
Linked persons
tainted donations to charities, 11.11
Linked transactions, 4.14
Liquidations
distributions in, 63.11–63.13
expenses, 14.4
venture capital trusts, 71.3, 71.5
Listing condition
venture capital trusts, 71.2
Living together
civil partners, 46.4
married persons, *see* Married persons
unmarried couples, 46.5
Lloyd's underwriters, *see* Underwriters at Lloyd's
LLP, *see* Limited liability partnerships
Loan relationships, 15.1–15.2
authorised unit trusts, 15.5
capital gains, 15.7
chargeable gains, 15.6–15.7
creditor relationships, 15.5
shares treated as, 15.6
debtor relationships, 15.5
definition, 15.5
embedded derivatives, 15.4
fair values, 15.5
foreign exchange gains and losses, 15.3
key points, 15.16
offshore funds, 15.5
open-ended investment companies, 15.5
qualifying investments test, 15.5
shares treated as, 15.6
summary of provisions, 15.3
Loans
approved charitable, 11.4
exempt assets, 25.5
guarantees of, 44.12
investment-linked, *see* Investment-linked loans
no linked loans enterprise investment scheme requirement, 23.4
normal commercial, 54.3
qualifying corporate bonds, evidenced by, 44.13, 44.14
relationships, *see* Loan relationships
securities, of, 63.25
traders, to, 67.4
Local authorities
exempt organisations, 25.55
information disclosures by HMRC to, 31.2
Local constituency associations
reliefs and deferrals, 25.70
Localism Act 2011 transfers
reliefs and deferrals, 25.83

Location condition
community amateur sports clubs, 11.12
Location of assets, 7.3
Lodges as private residences, 53.6
Loss schemes
disclosure of tax avoidance schemes, 20.2
Losses
see also Computation of gains and losses
allowable, computation, 44.3
angels (theatre backers), 44.9
annual exempt amount, 44.8
anti-avoidance, 14.6–14.9, 44.6, 44.7, 44.21
beneficiaries of settlements, transfer to, 62.16
brought forward
annual exempt amounts, interaction with, 2.6, 44.8
business expansion scheme, 25.22
capital, *see* Capital losses
capital allowances, assets qualifying for, 8.11, 9.7
carried back, 2.6, 44.5
death, on, 19.7
claims, 44.4
companies, *see* Companies
computation, 44.3
connected persons, 44.6
corporate venturing scheme investments, 18.17–18.19
death, 19.7
deduction, 2.1
deferred annuities, 43.1
deferred unascertainable consideration, 44.19
depreciatory transactions in groups of companies, 4.17
derivative contracts, carry back, 15.10
enterprise investment scheme, 23.13
exempt assets, 25.2
government investments in companies, 44.20
groups of companies, 29.15
guarantees of loans, 44.12
income losses set off against gains, 44.21
indexation allowance allowed/denied, 38.2
individual savings accounts, 25.30
individuals' trading losses set off against gains, 44.21
introduction, 44.1
key points, 44.22
life insurance policies, 43.1
loans to traders, 44.12–44.14
management expenses, relief for against gains, 14.6

Losses – *cont.*
mineral lease, 47.1
negligible value, assets of, 44.11
non-domiciled persons, 44.3
notification of, 44.4
order of set-off, 44.4
personal representatives, 19.7, 19.9
persons other than companies, 44.21
pre-entry
foreign permanent establishments of UK resident companies, 49.8
groups of companies, 29.15–29.23
qualifying corporate bonds evidencing loans, 44.13
qualifying trading companies, 44.16–44.18
reliefs
see also special reliefs *below*
income, against, 44.15, 44.18
subscribing individual shareholders, for, time limits, 67.3
remittance basis, 44.3, 55.2, 55.6
restrictions on set-off, 44.2
beneficiaries of offshore settlements, 48.15
settlements, 62.16, 62.22
settlors with interest in settlement, 48.13
returns, 44.4
self-assessment, under, 44.4
set-off against gains, 44.2, 44.4
settled property, person becoming absolutely entitled, 62.16
settlements, *see* Settlements
settlor gains, set-off against, 44.2, 48.13
short-term, 44.2
special reliefs, 44.1, 44.10
deferred unascertainable consideration, 44.19
loans to traders, 44.12
loans to traders evidenced by qualifying corporate bonds, 44.13–44.14
losses on shares in unlisted trading companies, individuals, 44.15–44.17
losses on shares in unlisted trading companies, investment companies, 44.18
negligible value, assets of, 44.11
stock, compensation for, 10.2
tangible movable property, 25.4
tax advantages, arrangements to secure, 44.7
temporary non-residence, 49.5
terminal, mineral royalties
theatre backers (angels), 44.9

Losses – *cont.*
trading, relief for against gains, 14.6, 44.21
unlisted trading companies, 23.13, 44.15–44.18
value shifting, 4.8–4.11
Lottery winnings
exempt gains and transactions, 25.21

M

Machinery, *see* Plant and machinery
Main residences, 53.2, 53.4
see also Private residences
election for, 53.10
exemption
civil partners, 46.3
married persons, 46.2
time limits, 68.3
Management condition
charities, 11.2
community amateur sports clubs, 11.12
Managers of defeated tax avoidance
penalties, 52.21
Manufactured dividends
gain arising to payer of, 63.26
Managed payment plans
payment of tax, 51.7
Management expenses set against gains, 14.6
MAPA (members' agent pooling arrangements), *see* Underwriters at Lloyd's
Market values
acquisitions of shares for less than, 22.8
Alternative Investment Market, 45.5
appeals, 5.4
artificially enhanced, 22.11
artificially depressed, 22.10
assets held on 31 March 1982, 9.2, 9.6
disposals of shares for more than, 22.9
employee share schemes, 22.8–22.11
exchange control, 45.7
gifts, 27.1, 45.1
intangible assets of companies, 45.2
meaning, 45.1
options and, 7.7, 22.6, 22.22
shares
quoted, 45.3
unquoted, 45.4
transactions treated as at, 45.1
Marketers of defeated tax avoidance
penalties, 52.21
Married persons, 46.1
see also Connected persons; Private residences
assets held on 31 March 1982, 9.6
connected persons, 17.1
declarations of individual beneficial interests, 46.2
divorce, 17.1, 46.5, 53.7
domicile, 57.34
living together, 46.4
main residence exemption, 46.2
no gain/no loss transfers, 46.5
private residences, 53.2, 53.7, 53.14
reliefs and deferrals, 25.84
residence, 57.13–57.15, 57.22, 57.26, 57.29, 57.31, 57.34
seed enterprise investment scheme, 60.41
separate treatment, 46.2
separation, 46.4, 53.7
share identification rules, 64.2
spouses accompanying, residence, 2012/13 and earlier, 57.31
transfers of assets between, 46.2, 46.5
indexation, 9.6
re-basing, 9.6
'Maximum amount raised'
social enterprise condition, 65.18
venture capital trusts, 71.4
Maximum qualifying investment requirement
venture capital trusts, 71.4
Members' agent pooling arrangements (MAPA), *see* Underwriters at Lloyd's
Members of Parliament (MPs)
residence and domicile, 57.32
Mentally disabled persons, settlements for, 62.9
Mergers
building societies, 63.27
businesses within EU, 49.13–49.14
cross-border
European cross-border, 49.15
rollover relief, 59.9
shares and securities, 63.7
exemptions, degrouping charges, 29.10
partnerships, 50.15
venture capital trusts, 71.3
Migrant settlements, 48.17
Milk Marque shares, 7.9
Milk quotas, 7.9, 41.13, 59.4
Mineral royalties, 47.1
Minimum period requirement
enterprise investment scheme, 23.3
social enterprise condition, 65.28
Miscellaneous transactions
charities, 11.4

Mistakes
HMRC, by, 30.6
law, of, 13.8
Mitigation
remittance basis, 55.4
serial avoiders regime, 4.36
Mixed funds
cleansing of, remittance basis, 55.3
investments made from, remittance basis, 55.4
transfers from, remittance basis, 55.3
Mobile workers
residence, 2012/13 and earlier, 57.31
Money debts, 15.5
Money raised
corporate venturing schemes, 18.8
enterprise investment scheme requirement, 23.3
seed enterprise investment scheme, 23.3, 60.7
venture capital trusts, 71.4
Monitoring notices
high-risk promoters tax avoidance disclosure regime, 20.12–20.13
Monthly savings schemes
authorised unit trusts, 70.3
investment trusts, 70.4
open-ended investment companies, 70.8
Mortgages
not a disposal, 16.2
rights or restrictions under, 4.12
Motor vehicles
exempt assets, 25.4, 25.11
Movable property, *see* Tangible movable property
MPs, *see* Members of Parliament
Mutual businesses, *see* Building societies

N

National Crime Agency (NCA), 30.9
information disclosures by HMRC to, 31.2
National Crime Squad
information disclosures by HMRC to, 31.2
National Criminal Intelligence Service
information disclosures by HMRC to, 31.2
National debt
exempt organisations, 25.57
National Heritage Memorial Fund
exemptions and reliefs, 25.58
National heritage property
reliefs and deferrals, 25.85
National purposes, gifts for
exempt gains and transactions, 25.41
National Radiological Protection Board
exemptions and reliefs, 25.59
Natural History Museum
exempt organisations, 25.45
Nature of income condition
venture capital trusts, 71.2
Nazi persecution, victims of
rights to receive interest on deposits, 25.14
NCA, *see* National Crime Agency
Neglect,
penalties, 52.7
Negligible value quoted securities, 44.11
No collusion requirement
social investment relief investor and investment condition, 65.15
No connection with issuing company
enterprise investment scheme requirement, 23.4
No control requirement
corporate venturing schemes, 18.5
No disqualifying arrangements
enterprise investment scheme requirement, 23.3, 23.17
seed enterprise investment scheme, 60.10
social investment relief investor and investment condition, 65.12
venture capital trusts, 71.4
No gain/no loss disposals, 9.6
indexation allowance, 38.4
No gain/no loss transfers
civil partners, 46.5
married persons, 46.5
No guaranteed loan requirement
venture capital trusts, 71.4
No linked loans
enterprise investment scheme requirement, 23.4
social investment relief investor and investment condition, 65.9
No partnerships requirement
social enterprise condition, 65.24
No reciprocal arrangements requirement
corporate venturing schemes, 18.5
No pre-arranged exits
seed enterprise investment scheme, 60.8
social investment relief investor and investment condition, 65.7
No risk avoidance requirement
social investment relief investor and investment condition, 65.8

No tax avoidance requirement
corporate venturing schemes, 18.5
seed enterprise investment scheme, 60.9
social investment relief investor and investment condition, 65.11
Nominated income
remittance basis, 55.5
Nominees, 62.3
children, 12.2
enterprise investment scheme shares held by, 23.2
exempt organisations, 25.44
returns by, 58.25
seed enterprise investment scheme, 60.3
Non-charitable expenditure
charities, 11.4, 11.5
Non-corporate bodies
assessment, 6.7
Non-financial activities requirement
corporate venturing schemes, 18.5
Non-financial trades
corporate venturing schemes, 18.5
Non-financial trading groups
corporate venturing schemes, 18.5
Non-qualifying tax years
private residences, 53.8
Non-reporting offshore funds, 49.11
funds investing in, 70.10
Non-residence, temporary, 49.5
Non-resident beneficiaries
offshore settlements, 48.15
Non-resident CGT disposals of UK residential property, 41.25
ATED-related gains or losses, interaction with, 14.10
computation of gains and losses, 41.30
capital allowances, 41.32
default method, 41.30
elections, 41.30, 41.31
high value disposals, 41.31
rebasing, 41.31
retrospective basis, 41.30
time-apportionment method, 41.30
unascertainable consideration, 41.30
valuations, obtaining, 41.30
wasting assets, 41.32
disposals of UK residential property interests, 41.29
groups of companies, 41.33
high-value disposals, 41.31
key points, 41.34
liability to tax, 41.26
Non-resident CGT disposals of UK residential property, – *cont.*
losses, death and, 19.7
NRCGT groups of companies, 41.33
NRCGT losses, death and, 19.7
payment on account, 51.3
persons not chargeable, 41.27
residence status determination, 58.20
returns, 58.20–58.22
UK residential property interests, 41.29
Non-residents, *see* Overseas residents
Non-statutory clearances, HMRC, and, 30.3
Non-UK domiciled beneficiaries
offshore settlements, 48.15
Non-UK options, location, 7.3
Non-UK ordinary residence, 57.31
Non-UK promoters
disclosure of tax avoidance schemes, 20.3
Non-UK residence, 57.31
Non-UK resident entertainers and sportsmen
information disclosures by HMRC to, 31.2
Normal commercial loans, 54.3
Northern Ireland
death, 19.4
meaning, 57.36
Northern Rock plc, shareholders in, 63.28
Notices
accelerated payment, *see* Accelerated payment notices
closure, *see* Closure notices
conduct, *see* Conduct notices
confirmation, *see* Confirmation notices
data-holder, 34.17
deduction, *see* Deduction notices
defeat, *see* Defeat notices
enquiries into returns, 58.9, 58.21
file access, 34.11
follower, *see* Follower notices
hold, *see* Hold notices
information, *see* Information notices
monitoring notices, *see* Monitoring notices
partial closure notices, *see* Partial closure notices
partnerships information, 4.37
provisional counteraction, 4.5
restriction of reliefs, 4.36
stop, *see* Stop notices
tax arbitrage, 4.20
warning, *see* Warning notices

Notifiable arrangements
disclosure of tax avoidance schemes, 20.2
Notification of coming within charge to corporation tax, 58.19
Notification of chargeability, 52.3, 58.19
NRCGT disposals of UK residential property, *see* Non-resident CGT disposals of UK residential property
Number of employees, *see* Employees
Number plates, personalised, 25.11

O

Occupational pension schemes
exempt organisations, 25.60
Occupational Pensions Board
information disclosures by HMRC to, 31.2
OEIC, *see* Open-ended investment companies
Offences, *see* Penalties
Officers of unincorporated companies
recovery of tax from, 51.25
Offshore asset moves
penalties, 52.12
Offshore funds, 49.10–49.11
funds investing in, 70.10
loan relationships, 15.5
Offshore settlements
anti-avoidance, 48.22–48.28
beneficiaries, charge on
companies, payments by and to, 48.19
conditions, 48.14–48.15
dual resident settlements, 48.16
further charge, 48.21
HMRC information powers, 48.20
losses, set-off, 48.14
main rules, 48.14–48.15
migrant settlements, 48.17
non-resident beneficiaries, 48.15
non-UK domiciled beneficiaries, 48.15
re-basing gains election, 48.15
section 2(2) amounts, 48.15
transfers between settlements, 48.18
trustee borrowing, 48.23–48.28
capital payments 48.14–48.21, 48.23–48.28
definition, 48.14
cessation of UK-residence, 48.2
deemed domicile, 48.1, 48.5, 48.8
disposal of interest in, 48.4
dual residence, 48.2, 48.16
exit charges, 48.1
HMRC information powers, 48.12, 48.29
Offshore settlements – *cont.*
introduction, 48.1
key points, 48.30
residence status, 48.1
settled interests, disposal of, 48.4
settlors, charge on, *see* Settlors
trustees
borrowing, 48.22
residence, 48.1
resident and non-resident in same year, 48.3
UK-residence, cessation of, 48.2, 48.3
Offshore tax non-compliance
failure to correct, Finance Acts 2017 summary, 73.1
penalties for failure to correct, 52.14
Olympic Games
exempt organisations, 25.56
Onus of proof
First-tier Tribunal, 5.20
Open-ended investment companies (OEIC), 70.8
exempt organisations, 25.64
loan relationships, 15.5
Options
see also Share options
call, *see* Call options
contracts 25.60
deemed, 15.11
indexation, 38.8, 64.4
land, contingently repayable deposits, 41.24
market value rule, and, 7.7
non-UK, location, 7.3
put, *see* Put options
qualifying corporate bonds, 7.7
terminal exercise of, 15.10
wasting assets, 72.3
Ordinary residence, 57.1, 57.30
appeals, 57.35
non-UK, 57.31
Origin, domicile of, 57.34
Overpaid tax, 51.15
see also Repayment interest
recovery of, 13.7, 67.8
Overseas gains, 25.95
Overseas matters
see also Domicile; Double tax relief; Euro; Foreign currencies; Foreign exchange; Offshore settlements; Offshore funds; Overseas residents; Residence
collection of tax, 49.21–49.22, 51.32
company ceasing to be UK resident etc., 49.17–49.18

Overseas matters – *cont.*
continental shelf, exploration and exploitation rights, 49.19
controlled foreign companies, 49.9
cross-border mergers, 49.15
transparent entities, 49.16
divisions of businesses within EU, 49.13–49.14
European cross-border mergers, 49.15
transparent entities, 49.16
exemptions for foreign permanent establishment profits 49.8
foreign assets, compensation for deprivation of, 10.2
foreign permanent establishment profits of companies, 49.8
individuals not domiciled, 49.2
key points, 49.23
mergers of businesses within EU, 49.13–49.14
partnerships controlled abroad, 50.2
Switzerland, tax collection agreement with, 49.22
temporary non-residence, 49.5
territorial sea-bed, exploration and exploitation rights, 49.19
transfers of businesses within EU, 49.13–49.14
unremittable gains, 42.8, 49.6
Overseas residents, 49.1
see also Domicile; Offshore settlements; Overseas matters; Residence
acquisition from, 16.12
companies
asset re-basing elections at 31 March 1982, 9.3
attribution of gains to UK settlements, 62.23
dual resident, *see* Dual resident companies
payment of tax by, 49.21
transfer of assets by UK resident companies to, 14.13, 49.12
UK participators in, 49.7
Lloyd's underwriters, 69.5
losses, 44.2
settlements, 48.1
share identification rules, 64.2
temporary non-residence, 49.5
trading in UK, 49.3
trustees, 48.1
UK branches or agencies, trading through, 49.3
UK representatives of, 49.4
underwriters, 69.5
Own shares, purchase of, 63.19

P

Paid directors
restrictions on being, social investment relief investor and investment condition, 65.13
PAIF (Property Authorised Investment Funds), 70.8
Part disposals, 16.5
assets held on 31 March 1982, 9.8
indexation, 9.6, 38.3
land, *see* Land
remittance basis rules, 55.7
Partial closure notices
enquiries into returns, 58.12
Finance Acts 2017 summary, 73.1
Partners, *see* Civil partners; Partnerships
Partnerships
accelerated payment notices, 4.30
accounting adjustments, 50.10
alternative investment fund management, 50.19
annuity payments to retired partners, 50.12
assessment on individuals, 50.2
assets
disposed of through, 4.24
distributed in kind, 50.14
held on 6 April 1965, 50.13, 50.16
held on 31 March 1982, 50.7–50.8, 50.16
revaluations, 50.10
business transferred to companies, 37.2–37.3
carried interest arising to investment managers, 50.20–50.21
claims, 13.2, 13.7
consideration outside accounts, 50.11
contribution of assets to, 50.5
controlled abroad, 50.2
corporate partners, 50.17
corporate venturing schemes requirement, 18.6
definition, 50.1
discovery, 6.11
entrepreneurs' relief, 24.3
follower notices, 4.26
fractional shares, 50.3, 50.6, 50.13
goodwill, 50.8, 50.11
high-risk promoters tax avoidance disclosure regime, 20.11, 20.17

Partnerships – *cont.*
income streams disposed of through, 4.23
indexation allowance, 50.7–50.8
information notices, 4.37
key points, 50.22
limited liability, *see* Limited liability partnerships
mergers, 50.15
partners
assessment on individuals, 50.2
corporate, 50.17
connected persons, 17.3, 50.4
fractional shares, 50.3, 50.6, 50.13
restrictions on being, social investment relief investor and investment condition, 65.13
retired, annuity payments to, 50.12
transactions between, 50.4
penalties for failure to make returns, 52.5
property transactions, 41.3
re-basing to 1982, 50.7–50.8, 50.16
related, high-risk promoters tax avoidance disclosure regime, 20.11
returns
amendments to, 58.17
enquiries into, 58.18
filing dates, 58.16
partnership statements, 58.17
rollover relief, 50.9, 59.3
Scottish, 50.1, 69.4
serial avoiders regime, 4.37
sharing ratios, changing, 50.6
statements, 6.11, 58.17
tax strategies publication, 14.18
transactions between partners, 50.4
Patents
location, 7.3
sale, 7.5
PAYE, recovery of debts through, 51.19
Payment of tax, 51.1
see also Self-assessment
accelerated payment notices, 4.29–4.31
capital gains tax, 51.2
certificates of tax deposit, 51.11
collection, 49.21–49.22, 51.19–51.26, 51.24
companies, 49.21, 51.4
corporation tax
chargeable gains, on, 51.4
exit charge payment plans, 51.8
credit card payment fees, 51.14
dates of payment, 51.10
debtors, power to obtain details of, 51.19
deduction notices, 51.23
determinations, on, 42.5, 51.18
Payment of tax, – *cont.*
due date
capital gains tax, 51.2
corporation tax, 51.4
instalments, 51.5
electronic funds transfer, 51.10
electronic, mandatory, 51.13
enforcement by deduction from accounts, 51.20–51.23
equitable liability, 51.30
EU member states, due in, 51.32
euros, in, 51.12
fees for payment by specified methods, 51.14
groups of companies, 51.4, 51.26
hold notices, 51.22
information notices, 51.21
instalments, 51.5
large companies, 51.4
internet, via, 30.4
key points, 51.33
late, *see* Late payment interest and penalties
managed payment plans, 51.7
methods, 51.9–51.15
monthly payments, 51.5
officers of unincorporated companies, recovery from, 51.25
overpayments, 51.15
over-repayments, 51.31
PAYE system, recovery of debts through, 51.19
payment on account of non-resident CGT, 51.3
pending further appeal, 5.23
postponement pending appeals, 51.17
quarterly accounting by large companies, 51.4
remission, 51.29
self-assessment, under, 51.2, 51.4
set-off of amounts owed to taxpayers against amounts payable, 51.19
settlements going offshore, 48.2
simple assessments, under, 51.2
tax enforcement agreements, 51.32
tax refunds in groups, 51.4
third parties, recovery from, 51.24
time limits, 67.2
'time to pay' arrangements, 51.6
unauthorised demands, 56.5
Penalties
accelerated payments, failure to make, 52.27
appeals, 52.34

Penalties – *cont.*
assessments, errors in, failure to notify, 52.10
asset-based for offshore inaccuracies, 52.13
bankrupts, 52.39
careless errors, 52.8
chargeability, notification of, 52.3
court proceedings, 52.36
criminal liability, 34.13, 52.40
cross-tax, failure to make returns, 52.5
daily, 52.5, 52.16
data-gathering powers under, failure to comply with, 52.17
data-holder notices, 34.17
deceased persons, time limit, 52.38
defeated tax avoidance enablers, 52.21
deliberate defaulters, managing, 52.32
deliberate errors, 52.8
dishonest conduct by tax agents, 52.19
documents, errors in, 52.8, 52.9
enabling of offshore evasion, 52.20
enforcement by deduction powers, 52.28
errors attributable to other persons, 52.9
evasion
failure to prevent facilitation of, 52.40
offshore, *see* offshore evasion *below*
file access notices, 34.11
failure to comply, 52.19
First-tier Tribunal proceedings, 52.35
fixed, 52.16
follower notices, failure to comply with, 52.26
general anti-abuse rule, 52.11
high-risk promoters of avoidance schemes, 20.16, 52.25
HMRC information and inspection powers, 34.10
initial, 52.5
interest on, 52.22
introduction to, 52.1
investigatory powers, failure to comply with, 52.16
key points, 52.41
late payment, *see* Late payment interest and penalties
mitigation of, 52.31
notification of chargeability, 52.3
offshore asset moves, 52.12
offshore evasion
criminal offence, 52.40
enabling, 52.20
offshore inaccuracies, asset-based penalties, 52.13

Penalties – *cont.*
offshore tax non-compliance
failure to correct, 52.14
publication of details of persons failing to correct, 31.4
other HMRC action, 52.32
partnerships, failure to make returns, 52.5
procedure, 52.33–52.37
proceedings, 52.35–52.37
prosecution, 34.13, 52.40
publication of details of defaulters, 31.3
reasonable excuse, 52.2, 52.5
records, failure to keep and preserve, 52.15
returns, failure to make
returns, incorrect
cross-tax, 52.5
companies, 52.8
EEIGs, 52.7
individuals, 52.8
partnerships, 52.8
returns, late delivery of
companies, 52.4
EEIGs, 52.6
returns, special, 52.23
serial avoiders, 4.39, 52.29
tax agents, dishonest conduct by, 52.19
tax avoidance schemes, failure to disclose, 52.24
tax-related, 52.2, 52.16, 52.18
tax strategy requirement, failure to comply with, 52.30
time limits, 52.38
Tribunal proceedings, 52.35
two or more tax-related, 52.18
unco-operative large businesses, 14.19
Upper Tribunal proceedings, 52.35
Pension funds and schemes
chargeability, notification of, 52.3
deregistration, 25.60
excluded settlements, 62.8
exempt organisations, 25.60
gains, 25.60
Pension Protection Fund 25.60
Pension schemes, *see* Pension funds and schemes
PEP (personal equity plans), 25.32
Permanent establishments
foreign, exemption for foreign profits of UK resident companies, 49.8
non-UK companies trading in UK through, 49.3
trading abroad through, 49.12
UK, enterprise investment scheme requirement, 23.5

Permanent establishments – *cont.*
venture capital trusts, 71.4
Permanent interest bearing shares (PIBS), 7.7, 15.5, 54.3
Permitted areas
private residences, 53.2, 53.5
Permitted maximum
venture capital trusts, 71.11
Permitted maximum age
enterprise investment scheme requirement, 23.3
Personal companies, 36.3, 59.3
Personal equity plans (PEP), 25.32
Personal pension schemes
exempt organisations, 25.60
Personal representatives
see also Death
administration of estates, 19.9–19.11
annual exemption, 19.9
assessments, 6.6, 6.13, 6.15, 19.9
informal procedures for, 58.3
interest on unpaid tax, 42.9
key points, 19.15
penalties referable to deceased, 52.38
rate of tax, 2.3
scrip dividends, 63.10
Personalised number plates, 25.11
PFI (Private Finance Initiative), 16.13
PIBS (permanent interest bearing shares), 7.7, 15.5, 54.3
Plant and machinery
fixed, rollover relief, 59.4, 59.9
long funding leases, 7.6
wasting assets, 25.4, 72.2
Police
information disclosures by HMRC to, 31.2
Police and Criminal Evidence Act
HMRC powers, serious tax fraud, 34.14
Pooling of shares, 8.3, 64.2, 64.3–64.5
Post-employment deductions
chargeable gains, set against, time limits for relief for, 67.8
Post-transaction valuations, 58.5, 58.19
Postponement of original gain
venture capital trusts, 71.12
Postponement of tax, 42.4, 51.17
Potato quotas, 59.4
Potentially chargeable events
remittance basis, 55.4
Powers of attorney, 58.4
Powers of HMRC, *see* HMRC
PRA. *see* Prudential Regulation Authority
Pre-disclosure enquiries
disclosure of tax avoidance schemes, 20.5
Pre-eminent property
gifts to the nation, 11.9
Pre-entry gains, groups, 29.15–29.17
Pre-entry losses, *see* Losses
Preference shares, 8.3
relevant, corporate venturing schemes, 18.5
Premises
HMRC inspection of, 34.8–34.9
Premium fees
disclosure of tax avoidance schemes, 20.2
Premium trust funds, 69.2
Premiums on leases, 41.16–41.21, 72.5
Prescribed arrangements
disclosure of tax avoidance schemes, 20.2
Principal company of group, 29.2
Priority allocations in public share offers, 22.37
Private Finance Initiative (PFI), 16.13
Private hotels, 53.14
Private residences, 53.1
see also Accommodation; Main residences, Residential property
absences from, 53.7
adult placement carers, 53.9
alterations to, 53.7
business use of, 53.9
caravans as, 53.3
care homes, residents in, 53.2
civil partners, 53.2, 53.7
compulsory purchase of land, 41.12
curtilage of, 53.6
day count test, 53.8
dependent relatives, occupied by, time limits, 67.8
disabled persons, 53.2
dependent relatives, for, 53.12
election for main residence, 53.10
employee share ownership trusts, 22.34
employment, use for, 53.9
exchange of joint interests, 41.13
exclusions from exemption, 53.13
exemption, 53.1–53.15
high value disposals of dwellings by companies, 14.10
hold-over relief and, 53.13
houseboats as, 25.4, 53.3
intestacy, 53.11
job-related accommodation, 53.7
joint interests, exchange of, 41.13
key points, 53.15
land appropriate to, 53.2
lettings, 53.12, 53.14
lodges, 53.6
non-qualifying tax years, 53.8

Private residences, – *cont.*
non-UK residential property interest, 2.1
only residence, time limits, 68.3
partial exemption, 53.2–53.10
permitted areas, 53.2, 53.5
profit, acquisition for, 53.13
rent a room income tax relief, 53.9
residential accommodation, 53.14
settlement beneficiaries, of, 53.11
share incentive plans, 22.20
spouses, 53.2, 53.7, 53.14
subsidiary buildings, 53.6
will trusts, 53.11
Privatisations, 14.11
Privileged communications, 52.21
Prize winnings
exempt gains and transactions, 25.21
Proceeds
applicable, remittance basis, 55.4
order of and meaning of, remittance basis, 55.4
Proceeds of Crime Act
Assets Recovery Agency, 31.2
cash forfeiture, 25.33
compensating payments, 25.33
criminal conduct, 30.9
HMRC powers, serious tax fraud, 34.15
recovery of assets, 25.33
Revenue confidentiality, 31.2
transfer of HMRC functions to National Crime Agency, 30.9
Professional privilege, 34.5
Profit sharing schemes, approved, 22.28
Profits
assigned life insurance policies, on, 43.2
private residences acquisition for, 53.13
Promoters
disclosure of tax avoidance schemes, 20.3
high-risk, *see* Disclosure of tax avoidance schemes
Proof, onus of, *see* Onus of proof
Property
see also Buildings; Land; Private residences; Residential property; Tangible movable property
company transactions, 41.3
individuals, transactions by, 41.3
partnerships, transactions by, 41.3
replacement, employee share ownership trusts, 22.32
settled, exemptions and reliefs, 25.35
transactions, 41.3
treated as not remitted to UK, remittance basis, 55.3
Property Authorised Investment Funds (PAIF), 70.8
Property-based total return swaps, 15.10
Property businesses
cash basis, Finance Acts 2017 summary, 73.1
Property investment LLPs, 50.18
Property managing subsidiaries
corporate venturing schemes requirement, 18.6
enterprise investment scheme requirement, 23.5
venture capital trusts, 71.4
Proportion of eligible shares requirement
venture capital trusts, 71.4
Prosecuting authorities
information disclosures by HMRC to, 31.2
Prosecution, 34.13, 52.40
Protected assets
settlors, offshore settlements, 48.5
Protected settlements
settlors, offshore settlements, 48.10
Provisional counteraction notices, 4.5
Prudential Regulation Authority (PRA)
information disclosures by HMRC to, 31.2
Public offers, 22.37
Publication of information by HMRC, *see* HMRC: confidentiality of information
Purchase of own shares, 63.19
Purpose of issue
enterprise investment scheme requirement, 23.3
social enterprise condition, 65.27
Put options
corporate venturing schemes, 18.15
enterprise investment scheme, 23.17

Q

QCB, *see* Qualifying corporate bonds
Qualified investor schemes (QIS), 70.9
Qualifying 90% subsidiaries
enterprise investment scheme, 23.7
Qualifying activities
venture capital trusts relevant company carrying on, 71.4
Qualifying business activities
enterprise investment scheme, 23.5, 23.8
seed enterprise investment scheme, 60.30
Qualifying business disposals
entrepreneurs' relief, 24.2

Qualifying charity-owned companies
tainted donations, 11.11
Qualifying companies
enterprise investment scheme, 23.5
seed enterprise investment scheme, 60.17–60.29
Qualifying corporate bonds (QCB), 54.1
alternative finance arrangements, 54.3
building society shares, 54.3
charities, gifted to, 54.4
companies, held by, 15.7, 54.3
contracts for, 7.8
debentures, 54.3
deeply discounted securities, 54.3, 54.4
definition, 54.3
employee share ownership trusts, 22.33
excluded securities, 54.3, 54.4
exempt assets, 25.12
exemption, 7.7, 7.8, 54.2
indexation, 64.6
loans evidenced by, 44.13, 44.14
options for, 7.7
reorganisations, 44.14, 54.4
Qualifying disposals
venture capital trusts, 71.11
Qualifying gift aid donations, 11.10
Qualifying gifts of pre-eminent property to the nation, 11.9
Qualifying holdings
venture capital trusts, 71.4, 71.5
Qualifying institutional investors
substantial shareholdings of companies exemptions, 66.6
Qualifying investing companies
corporate venturing schemes, 18.5
Qualifying investments
loan relationships test, 15.5
remittance basis, 55.4
venture capital trusts, 71.12
Qualifying investors
enterprise investment scheme, 23.4
seed enterprise investment scheme, 60.11–60.16
Qualifying issuing companies
corporate venturing schemes, 18.6
Qualifying periods
corporate venturing schemes, 18.2
Qualifying settlements, 62.8, 62.9
settlors, offshore settlements, 48.10
Qualifying shares
investors' relief, 40.7
Qualifying subsidiaries
corporate venturing schemes, 18.6
enterprise investment scheme, 23.6
social investment relief, 65.32
Qualifying subsidiaries – *cont.*
venture capital trusts, 71.4
Qualifying trades
corporate venturing schemes, 18.7
enterprise investment scheme, 23.9
seed enterprise investment scheme, 60.31
social investment relief, 65.31
venture capital trusts, 71.4
Qualifying trading companies
losses, 44.16–44.18
Quarterly accounting by large companies, 51.4
Quoted options, 7.7, 63.9
Quoted securities
assets held on 6 April 1965, 8.2–8.5
negligible value, 44.11
Quoted shares
market values, 45.3
time limits, 67.3

R

Rates of tax
companies, 2.5, 14.3
individuals, 2.1, 2.2
personal representatives, 2.3
settlements, 62.7
Real estate investment trusts, 70.5
Reasonable excuse, 42.6
penalties, 52.2, 52.5
serial avoiders regime, 4.36
Re-basing
assets held on 31 March 1982, 9.1–9.5
deemed domicile, 57.34
gains election, offshore settlements, 48.15
intra-group transfers, 9.6
NRCGT disposals, computation of gains and losses, 41.31
partnerships, 50.7–50.8, 50.16
time limits, 9.3, 9.11
transfers of assets between civil partners, 9.6
transfers of assets between married persons, 9.6
Receipts cases, tax arbitrage, 4.20
Receivers, assessment of, 6.7
Reclaim funds, 16.7
Recognised futures exchanges, 7.7
Recognised stock exchanges, 7.7, 63.30
Reconstructions, 63.7
anti-avoidance, 4.15, 4.16
corporate venturing schemes, 18.21–18.23
corporation tax unpaid, time limits, 68.3

Reconstructions, – *cont.*
demergers, 14.12
enterprise investment scheme, 23.13, 23.17
issues of securities, involving, 63.7
reliefs and deferrals, 25.69
transfers of business, 14.11
venture capital trusts, 14.11
Reconveyance, right of, 41.7
Records, 13.3, 52.15, 58.8, 73.1
Recovery of debts from accounts, 51.20–51.22
Reference numbers
disclosure of tax avoidance schemes, 20.4
high-risk promoters tax avoidance disclosure regime, 20.13
Reference periods
statutory residence tests, 57.9
Registered designs, location, 7.3
Registered pension schemes
exempt organisations, 25.60
Registration condition, charities, 11.2
Reinvested amounts
remittance basis, 55.4
Reinvestment relief
enterprise investment scheme, deferral relief, 23.14–23.18
reliefs and deferrals, 25.86
seed enterprise investment scheme, 60.45
venture capital trust deferral relief, 71.12
Related companies and partnerships
high-risk promoters tax avoidance disclosure regime, 20.11
Relatives
connected persons, 17.1, 17.6
dependent, 53.12
Relevant defeats
serial avoiders regime, 4.32–4.34
Relevant investments
corporate venturing schemes, 18.8
enterprise investment scheme, 23.3
venture capital trusts, 71.4
Relevant preference shares
corporate venturing schemes, 18.5
Relevant securities, 64.2, 64.3, 64.6
Relevant tax advantages
serial avoiders regime, 4.35
Relevant trustees, 62.11
Reliefs
see also Double tax relief; Exemptions and reliefs; Hold-over reliefs; Reinvestment relief; Reliefs and deferrals; Retirement relief; Rollover relief
error or mistake, 13.8

Reliefs – *cont.*
post-cessation expenditure of trades, time limits, 67.3
restriction, serial avoiders regime, 4.36
taper, 25.93
Reliefs and deferrals, 25.66
business assets, gifts of, 25.75
capital distributions, 25.67
charities, gifts to, 25.76
civil partners, 25.84
companies, 25.68
compensation, capital sums received as, 25.72
constituency associations, 25.70
corporate venturing schemes, 25.71
employees, settlements for benefit of, 25.91
enterprise investment scheme, 25.73
entrepreneurs' relief, 25.74
gifts, 25.75, 25.78
harbour reorganisation schemes, 25.77
Hops Marketing Board, 25.79
incorporation relief, 25.94
land
compulsory purchase, 25.81
part disposals, 25.82
local constituency associations, 25.70
Localism Act 2011 transfers, 25.83
married persons, 25.84
national heritage property, 25.85
reinvestment relief, 25.86
retirement relief, 25.88
seed enterprise investment scheme, 25.90
social investment relief, 25.92
taper relief, 25.93
venture capital trusts, 25.96
Remission of tax, 51.29
Remittance basis
2007/08 and earlier years
forward tax agreements, 30.2, 55.8
remittances, 55.9
2008/09 and subsequent years, 55.2
annual exempt amounts, 55.2
applicable proceeds, 55.4
charge for claiming, 55.5
chargeable gains remitted to the UK, 55.3
cleansing of mixed funds, 55.3
disposals, order of and meaning of proceeds, 55.4
effect of remittance basis, 55.2
extraction of value rule, 55.4
five-year start-up rule, 55.4
foreign chargeable gains, 55.3

Remittance basis – *cont.*
2008/09 and subsequent years, – *cont.*
foreign currency bank accounts, 55.6, 55.7
gains remitted, 55.2
grace periods, 55.4
investments made from mixed funds, 55.4
losses, 55.2, 55.6
mitigation steps, 55.4
nominated income and gains remitted, 55.5
part disposal rules, 55.7
potentially chargeable events, 55.4
property treated as not remitted to UK, 55.3
property used to make qualifying investment, 55.4
qualifying investments, 55.4
reinvested amounts, 55.4
retention of funds to meet CGT liabilities, 55.4
small remittances, 55.7
taxable amounts calculation, 55.2
transfers from mixed funds, 55.3
business investment relief, Finance Acts 2017 summary, 73.1
double tax relief, 21.6
introduction 55.1
key points, 55.10
tax collection agreement with Switzerland, 49.22
Remittances
delayed, late payment interest and penalties, 42.8
remittance basis, *see* Remittance basis
Renewables obligations certificates
exempt assets, 25.13
Rent a room income tax relief, 53.9
Reorganisations of share capital, *see* Share capital
Repayment interest, 56.1
see also Payment of tax
claims, 13.2
companies, 56.4
excess, recovery of, 51.31
judgment debts, 56.5
losses, carry-back on death, 19.7
new regime, 56.2
old regime, 56.3
persons other than companies, 56.3
unauthorised demands for tax, 56.5
Repayment supplement, 13.2, 51.15, 51.31, 56.3
carry-back to earlier year, 19.7
Reporting offshore funds, 49.11
Repos, 63.26
Research institution spin-out companies, 22.16
Reserve funds
special, Lloyd's underwriters, 69.2
Residence, 57.1
see also Domicile; Ordinary residence; Overseas residents
appeals, 57.35
available accommodation in UK, 57.29
change during year, 57.29
civil partners, 57.13–57.15, 57.22, 57.26
claims to non-UK, 2012/13 and earlier, 57.31
companies
ceasing to be UK resident, 49.17–49.18, 68.3
central management and control location, 57.33
group companies, 29.2
incorporation, places of, 57.33
emigration, 2012/13 and earlier, 57.31
employment, 57.29
group companies, 29.2
HMRC administrative procedures, 57.2
Ireland, 57.37
key points, 57.38
married persons, 57.13–57.15, 57.22, 57.26, 57.29, 57.31, 57.34
Members of Parliament, 57.32
mobile workers, 2012/13 and earlier, 57.31
non-UK, 57.31
self-assessment, 57.2
settlements, 48.1
cessation of UK, 48.2
trustees resident and non-resident in same year, 48.3
spouses accompanying, 2012/13 and earlier, 57.31
status
determination, non-resident CGT disposals of UK residential property, 58.20
venture capital trusts, 71.12
statutory residence tests
90-day ties, 57.16
accommodation ties, 57.14
automatic overseas tests, 57.5
automatic residence tests, 57.3–57.10
automatic UK tests, 57.4
basic rule, 57.3
country ties, 57.17
days spent in the UK, 57.7

Residence, – *cont.*
statutory residence tests – *cont.*
deeming rule, 57.7
family ties, 57.13
individuals' homes, 57.8
introduction, 57.3
location of work, 57.9
reference periods, 57.9
relevant jobs on board vehicles, aircraft or ships, 57.10, 57.15
split year treatment, 57.18–57.27
sufficiency of hours, 57.9
sufficient ties tests, 57.11–57.17
transitional provisions, 57.28
UK ties, 57.12–57.17
work, 57.9
work ties, 57.15
temporary non-residence, 49.5
United Kingdom, meaning, 57.36
visits abroad, 2012/13 and earlier, 57.31
Residential letting, 53.14
Residential property
see also Accommodation; Private residences
gains, 2.1
NRCGT disposals, *see* Non-resident CGT disposals of UK residential property
Restitution of tax payment,
mistakes of law, 13.8
Restoration of assets, 10.3
Restricted periods
serial avoiders regime, 4.36
Restricted shares
employee share schemes, 22.13
Restriction of reliefs notices, 4.36
Restructuring
venture capital trusts, 71.5
Retail prices index (RPI), 38.2
Retention of funds to meet CGT liabilities
remittance basis, 55.4
Retirement annuity scheme
see also Pension funds and schemes
exempt organisations, 25.60
Retirement relief
see also Hold-over reliefs
Lloyd's underwriters, 69.6
reliefs and deferrals, 25.88
Retrospective basis
NRCGT disposals, computation of gains and losses, 41.30
Returns
see also Penalties
amendment, time limits, 67.3
auctioneers, 58.25
boarding houses, 58.24
Returns – *cont.*
chargeability, notification of, 52.3
companies, 58.19
company tax returns, 58.19
corporation tax, 58.2
determinations in absence of, 58.15, 58.19
digital tax accounts, 58.1
discovery, HMRC powers of, 6.10–6.11
EEIGs, 58.23
electronic delivery of, 30.4, 58.2, 58.4
electronic lodgement of, 58.2
enquiries into
amendments arising from, 58.13
closure notices, 58.12
companies, 58.19
completion, 58.12, 58.21
conduct of, 58.10
notices of, 58.9, 58.21
NRCGT, 58.21
partial closure notices, 58.12
partial completion, 58.12
partnerships, 58.18
referral of questions during, 58.14
time limits, 58.9
hotels, 58.24
internet filing of, 30.4, 58.4, 58.6
issuing houses, 58.25
key points, 58.26
nominee shareholders, 58.25
NRCGT returns, 58.20
determinations in absence of, 58.22
enquiries into, 58.21
partnership tax returns, *see* Partnerships
personal representatives
informal procedures, 58.3
personal tax returns
amendment of, 58.7
attorney, powers of, 58.4
content, 58.3, 58.4
correction of, 58.7
delivery of, 58.4
electronic filing, 30.4, 58.2, 58.4
filing date, 58.3
form of, 58.4
provisional figures, 58.4
reporting limits, 58.3
self-assessments, 58.6, 58.7
post-transaction valuations, 58.5, 58.19
reasonable excuse, 52.2
record-keeping, 58.8
stockbrokers, 58.25
time limits, 67.2, 67.3
trustee tax returns, 58.3

Returns economically equivalent to interest, 15.6
Revaluations
partnership assets, 50.10
Reverse premiums, 41.16
Rights
assets subject to, 4.8, 4.12, 7.2
creation of, 16.5
deferred unascertainable consideration, to, losses, 44.19
forfeiture of, 10.2
Rights issues, *see* Shares and securities
Risk finance investments
enterprise investment scheme requirement, 23.3
Rolled-up indexation, 9.6
Rollover relief, 59.1
acquisitions, time limits, 68.2
anti-avoidance, 59.2
apportionment, 59.8
assets qualifying for, 59.4
associated companies, 59.3
basic payment scheme, 59.4
business transferred to company, 37.1–37.5
claims, 59.11
compulsory purchase of land, 41.12
concessions, abuse of, 4.19
cross-border mergers, 59.9
death of traders, 59.9
depreciating assets, 59.9
disposals and reacquisitions of same assets, 59.2
effect of, 59.6
enhancement of assets, 59.2
employees, 59.5
employee share ownership trusts, disposals to, *see* Employee share ownership trusts
furnished holiday accommodation, 26.2
groups of companies, 59.10
intangible assets of companies, 59.3, 59.4
interaction with other provisions, 59.7
key points, 59.12
land, *see* Land
limited liability partnerships, 59.3
Lloyd's underwriters on conversion to corporate, 69.8
new assets, 59.2
non-UK residents 48.2, 49.3
offshore settlements, 48.2
options over land, 59.4
part disposal, 16.5
partial relief, 59.8
partnerships, 50.9, 59.3
Rollover relief, – *cont.*
personal companies, 59.3
provisional claims, 59.11
qualifying assets, 59.4
qualifying undertakings, 59.5
replacement of business assets, 25.89
share incentive plans
disposals to, 22.18–22.21
time limits, 68.3
ships, 59.4
tax-advantaged share incentive plans, disposal of shares to, time limits, 68.2
time limits, 67.7, 67.8, 68.2–68.4
claims, for, 59.11
replacement, for, 59.2
tonnage tax, 59.3
underwriters, conversion to corporate, 69.8
wasting assets, 59.9
Royalties
mineral, 47.1
RPI (Retail prices index), 38.2

S

Sale and lease-back, 4.8, 41.22
Sale of land, 41.7
Sale of rights, 38.6, 63.4, 63.11
Satellites, 59.4
Savings accounts
exempt assets, 25.15
Savings certificates
exempt assets, 25.15
Savings schemes
exempt assets, 25.15
SAYE share options, 22.24
SCE, *see* Societas Co-operative Europaea
Scientific research associations
exempt organisations, 25.61
Scotland
death, 19.3
meaning, 57.36
partnerships, 50.1, 69.4
Scottish taxpayers, 2.1
Scrip dividends, 63.10
Scrip issues, 63.3
identification rules, 64.2
SE, *see* Societas Europaea
Sea-bed
territorial, exploration and exploitation rights, 49.19

Security, debts on, 25.5
Securities, *see* Government securities; Qualifying corporate bonds; Shares and securities
Seed enterprise investment scheme (SEIS)
acquisition of share capital, 60.39
acquisition of trade or trading assets, 60.38
attribution of relief to shares, 60.33
bare trustees, 60.3
capital gains tax, 60.43
reduction of relief, 60.44
reinvestment relief, 60.45
civil partners, 60.41
claims for relief, 60.34
conditions for income tax relief, 60.2
bare trustees, 60.3
nominees, 60.3
disposal of shares, 60.36
exemptions and reliefs, 25.34, 25.90
Finance Acts 2017 summary, 73.1
form of relief, 60.32–60.33
gains, 25.34, 25.90
general requirements
introduction, 60.4
'no disqualifying arrangements', 60.10
'no pre-arranged exits', 60.8
'no tax avoidance', 60.9
'purpose of the issue', 60.6
shares, 60.5
'spending of the money raised', 23.3, 60.7
income tax relief
claims, 60.34
conditions, 60.2–60.3
form, 60.32–60.33
general requirements, 60.4–60.10
new qualifying trades, 60.31
qualifying business activities, 60.30
qualifying companies, 60.17–60.29
qualifying investors, 60.11–60.16
reduction or withdrawal, 60.35–60.40
introduction, 60.1
issuing companies acquired by new companies, 60.42
married persons, 60.41
new qualifying trades, 60.31
'no disqualifying arrangements', 60.10
'no pre-arranged exits', 60.8
'no tax avoidance', 60.9
nominees, 60.3
'purpose of the issue', 60.6
qualifying business activity, 60.30
qualifying companies, 60.17–60.29
qualifying investors, 60.11–60.16
Seed enterprise investment scheme (SEIS) – *cont.*
reduction of relief, 60.35–60.40
reinvestment relief, 60.45
reliefs and deferrals, 25.90
share capital acquisition, 60.39
shares requirement, 60.5
'spending of the money raised', 60.7
trades acquisition, 60.38
trading assets acquisition, 60.38
value received by investors, 60.37
venture capital trusts spending of money raised by, 71.4
withdrawal of relief, 60.35–60.40
SEIS, *see* Seed enterprise investment scheme
Self-assessment
see also Assessments; Returns
agents, information to, 60.4
appeals, 5.1
assessments, 6.1
capital gains tax, 61.2
claims, 13.2–13.4
corporation tax, *see* Corporation tax
determinations, 58.15
income tax, 61.2
introduction, 61.1
payment of tax, 51.2, 51.4
residence, 57.2
settlements, 62.11
time limits, 58.6, 67.2
trustees, 62.11
Self-build societies
exempt organisations, 25.62
Separation
married persons and civil partners, 46.4, 53.7
Serial avoiders regime, 4.32
annual information notices, 4.35
appeals, 4.36
associated persons, 4.33
DOTAS arrangements, 4.34–4.35, 4.37
groups of companies, 4.38
information notices, 4.35
mitigation, 4.36
partnerships, 4.37
penalties, 4.39, 52.29
reasonable excuse, 4.36
relevant defeats, 4.32–4.34
relevant tax advantages, 4.35
restricted periods, 4.36
restriction of reliefs, 4.36
taxpayer details, publishing, 4.40
warning notices, 4.33

Series of transactions, 4.14
Serious tax fraud, *see* HMRC
Set of assets, 25.4
Settled property
see also Settlements
beneficiaries becoming absolutely entitled, 62.16
trustees' expenses, 16.12
death of life tenants, 62.16–62.18
definitions, 62.3
disposal of interests in, 48.4, 62.15
deemed, 62.20, 62.21
exemptions and reliefs, 25.35
gains, 25.35
hold-over relief, 36.6
interests in, 62.4
deemed disposals, 62.20, 62.21
disposals, 48.4, 62.15
meaning, 62.3
Settlements
see also Contract settlements; Offshore settlements; Settled property; Settlors; Trustees
absolutely entitled persons, 62.3, 62.16, 62.18
advancement, power of, 62.14
annual exempt amounts, 62.8, 62.9
annuities, 62.17, 62.18
anti-avoidance, 62.19–62.23
appointment, power of, 62.14
assets out of, gifts to charities, 11.8
bare trustees, 25.44, 62.3
beneficiaries, 16.12, 62.16
liabilities, 62.6
non-resident, offshore settlements, 48.15
non-UK domiciled, offshore settlements, 48.15
private residences, of, 53.11
recovery of tax from, 62.10
vulnerable, 62.13
benefit of employees, for, 25.91
business assets disposals, 24.4, 24.9
charitable, .8
connected persons, 17.6
contingent interest, .4
creation, 62.14
death of life tenants, 62.16–62.18
deed creating, validity of, 62.14
definitions, 62.2–62.3
disabled persons, settlements for, 62.9
disposal of interest, 62.15
dual residence, 36.8, 36.11, 36.12, 48.16
dwelling-houses, right to occupy, 53.11, 62.4
Settlements – *cont.*
enterprise investment scheme deferral relief, 23.16
employees benefit, for, 25.91
excluded settlements, 62.8
exemptions, 25.16, 62.15
foreign elements, time limits, 68.2
groups of, 62.8, 62.9
hold-over relief, 36.6, 62.17, 62.18
interests created by or arising under, 62.4
interests in, 62.4
absolutely entitled, person becoming, 62.16
disposal, 62.15
part, 62.17, 62.18
termination, 62.17, 62.18
interests in possession, 62.4–62.18
introduction, 62.1
key points, 62.24
land, tenants in common, 62.3
life interests, 62.4–62.18
loss, taken over by beneficiaries, 62.16
losses, 62.8
disabled persons, settlements for, 62.9
restrictions on set-off, 62.16, 62.20
transfer to beneficiaries, 62.16
mentally disabled persons, settlements for, 62.9
new settlement, whether created, 62.14
nominees, 62.3
non-resident companies, gains of, 62.23
ordinary residence, 48.5, 48.16, 48.19
overseas resident etc., 48
private residence, 53.11
qualifying, 62.8, 62.9
rates of tax, 62.7
recovery of tax from beneficiaries, 62.10
residence, 48.1
residue of estate, 62.3
scrip dividends, 63.10
self-assessment, 62.11
settlor interested, gifts to, 36.8, 36.11
settlors, charge on,
offshore settlements, 2.6, 44.2, 48.5–48.13, 48.22
sub-fund settlements, 62.8, 62.12
transfers into, 62.14
transfers of value, 62.21
trust for sale, land, 62.3
unpaid tax, collection from beneficiaries, 62.10
validation of deeds of, 62.14
value of benefits conferred by certain capital payments
Finance Acts 2017 summary, 73.1

Settlements – *cont.*
vulnerable beneficiaries, 62.13, 67.3
Settlors
charge on, offshore settlements, 48.22
carried interest gains, 48.5
commencement, 48.10
conditions, 48.5
deemed domicile, 48.1, 48.5, 48.8
definitions, 48.9
exceptions, 48.8
grandchildren, 48.7
HMRC information powers, 48.12
interaction with other provisions, 48.13
losses, set-off, 44.2, 48.13
protected assets, 48.5
protected settlements, 48.10
qualifying settlements, 48.10
recovery, right of, 48.11
settlors' interests, 48.6
temporary non-residence of settlors, 44.2, 48.13
trustee borrowing, 48.22
definition, 48.14
interests, offshore settlements, 48.6
meaning, 62.5
temporary non-residence, 48.13
Shams, meaning, 4.2
Share capital
see also Shares and securities
acquisition
enterprise investment scheme, 23.12
social investment relief, 65.42
distributions, 63.11–63.13
introduction, 63.1
ordinary, corporate venturing schemes, 18.5
reorganisations, 63.2
bonus issues, 63.3
conversion of securities, 63.8
corporate venturing scheme, 18.21–18.23
enterprise investment scheme, 23.13, 23.17
entrepreneurs' relief, 24.3, 24.12
exchanges of securities, 63.5–63.6
indexation, 38.6, 64.4
investors' relief, 40.9, 40.10
qualifying corporate bonds, 24.12, 44.14, 54.4
quoted options granted following, 63.9
reconstructions involving issues of securities, 63.7
reliefs and deferrals, 25.87
rights issues, 63.4
shares held on 6 April 1965, 8.5, 8.10
Share capital – *cont.*
reorganisations, – *cont.*
venture capital trusts, 71.11
repayments to other persons, social investment relief, 65.40
seed enterprise investment scheme, 60.39
time apportionment restrictions, 8.10
Share incentive plans (SIP), 22.17
rollover relief on disposals to, 22.18
dwelling-houses, 22.20
enterprise investment scheme shares, 22.21
form of, 22.19
time limits, 68.3
Share options
approved, 22.22, 22.27
company share option plans, 22.25
consideration for grant, 22.3
double tax relief, 22.38
employee shareholder shares, 22.26
enterprise management incentives, 22.22
executive share option schemes, 22.27
release and replacement, 22.4
same-day identification rule, 64.2
SAYE, 22.24
unapproved, 22.5–22.7
Shared ownership arrangements, diminishing, 3.2, 3.3
Shareholders
recovery of tax from, 51.27
Shareholdings
existing, enterprise investment scheme requirement, 23.4
substantial, *see* Substantial shareholdings of companies
Shares and securities
see also Employee share schemes; Share capital
acquisitions
costs, 63.5
same-day, time limits, 67.3
anti-avoidance, 63.5, 63.7
bearer shares location, 7.3
'bed and breakfasting', 64.2, 64.3, 67.9
bonus issues, 63.3
Bradford and Bingley plc, shareholders in, 63.28
building societies
de-mutualisations, 63.27
shares in, 7.7, 15.5, 54.3
shares in successor companies, 63.27
business expansion scheme, 25.22
calls on, 38.7
close companies
apportionment of income, 63.23

Shares and securities – *cont.*
close companies – *cont.*
stock dividend, 63.10
companies purchasing own shares, 63.19
company disposals, 4.11
compensation stock, 63.8
consideration in shares, 16.11
conversion of securities, 63.8
conversion of, venture capital trusts, 71.5
convertible shares, *see* Convertible shares
corporate bonds, 54.3
corporate venturing schemes shares, *see* Corporate venturing schemes
creditor relationships, shares treated as, 15.6
debts on, 25.5, 44.12–44.14
deeply discounted securities, 54.3, 54.4, 63.21
demergers, 14.12
depositary receipts, 63.22
depreciatory transactions in groups of companies, 4.17
discounted securities, 63.21
disposal costs, 63.5
disposals by companies, 4.11
disqualification, investors' relief, 40.8
divisions, cross-border, 63.7
earn-outs, 63.6
embedded derivatives, with, issuers of, 15.11
employee-ownership trusts, disposal to, 63.14–63.18
enterprise investment scheme, *see* Enterprise investment scheme
euroconversion of securities, 63.8
European cross-border mergers, issued on, 49.15
exchange of securities, 49.16, 63.5
extended meaning of shares, employee share schemes, 22.2
identification rules, 8.2–8.3
1982 holdings, 64.3, 64.5
assets held on 6 April 1965, 8.2–8.3
bed and breakfasting, 64.2, 64.3, 67.9
business expansion scheme shares, 25.22
capital gains tax rules, 64.1, 64.2
contangos, 64.6
corporate venturing scheme shares, 18.16
corporation tax rules, 64.3–64.6
deemed disposals, 64.2
employee shares, 64.2, 64.4
enterprise investment scheme shares, 23.13, 23.15, 23.18

Shares and securities – *cont.*
identification rules, – *cont.*
enterprise management incentive shares, 22.22
indexation allowance, 64.3, 64.4
pooling, 64.2–64.4
relevant securities, 64.2, 64.3, 64.6
reorganisations, equation with original shares, 63.2
section 104 holdings, 64.2, 64.3, 64.4
scrip dividends, 63.10
stock dividends, 63.10
unlisted traded companies, 44.15, 44.18
venture capital trust shares, 71.8, 71.11, 71.12
individual savings accounts, 25.30
introduction, 63.1
investors' relief, 40.1–40.10
key points, 63.32
life assurance policies, 63.24
liquidations, *see* Liquidations
loan relationship, treated as, 15.6
loans of securities, 63.25
location, 7.3
losses on, 44.15, 44.18
market value, 45.3–45.5
mergers, cross-border, 63.7
Milk Marque shares, 7.9
negligible value, 44.11
new types of securities, 63.31
no gain/no loss disposals, 9.6
Northern Rock plc, shareholders in, 63.28
offshore funds, 49.10–49.11
options, 7.7
own shares, purchase of, 63.19
pooling shares, venture capital trusts, 71.11
preference shares, corporate venturing schemes, 18.5
public offers, 22.37
purchase of own shares, 63.19
qualifying corporate bonds, *see* Qualifying corporate bonds
qualifying investors' relief, 40.7
quoted options, 63.9
reconstructions, 4.15, 4.16, 14.11, 63.7
reinvestment relief, 25.86
reorganisation of share capital, *see* Share capital
repos 63.26
restricted shares, 22.13
rights issues
corporate venturing schemes, 18.21
enterprise investment scheme shares, 23.13

Shares and securities – *cont.*
rights issues – *cont.*
enterprise management incentives, 22.22
identification rules, 64.2
share capital reorganisations, 63.4
sale of rights, 38.5, 63.4, 63.11
sale and repurchase, 63.26
securities, new types of, 63.31
seed enterprise investment scheme, 60.5
attribution of relief to, 60.33
disposals, 60.36
scrip dividends, 63.10
scrip issues, 63.3
stock dividends, 63.10
stock lending, 63.25
subscriptions to,
business expansion scheme, 25.22
losses on, 44.15, 44.18
substantial shareholdings, *see* Substantial shareholdings of companies
takeovers, 4.15, 4.16, 14.11, 63.5
building societies, 63.27
treasury shares, 63.5
unlisted companies
distributions in liquidations, 63.12, 63.13
held at 6 April 1965, 8.7, 8.9
losses on, 44.15
market value, 45.4
valuations, 9.6
value shifting, 4.8–4.11
warranty payments in respect of contingent liabilities, 63.5, 63.7
Ships
exempt assets, 25.17
location, 7.3
relevant jobs on board, statutory residence tests, 57.10, 57.15
rollover relief, 59.4
tonnage tax, 25.17, 59.2
Short rotation coppice
exemptions and reliefs, 25.40
Short-term capital gains, 44.2
Short-term capital losses, 14.6, 44.2
Simple assessments, 6.9
payment of tax under, 51.2
Single payment scheme, 7.14
rollover relief, 59.4
SIP, *see* Share incentive plans
SITR, *see* Social investment tax relief
Situs of assets, 7.3
Small remittances
remittance basis, 55.7
Social contracts, 65.2
Social investment relief, 25.36, 25.92, 65.1
capital gains tax relief, 65.45
capital gains tax deferral relief, 65.46
civil partners, 65.44
deferral relief, 65.46, 68.2, 68.4
exempt assets 25.36
income tax relief
attribution of, 65.35
claims, 65.36
investor and investment conditions, 65.4–65.15
social enterprise conditions, 65.16–65.29
eligibility, 65.3
form of, 65.34
reduction of, 65.37–65.43
withdrawal of, 65.37–65.43
married persons, 65.44
qualifying subsidiaries, 65.32
90% subsidiaries, 65.33
qualifying trades, 65.31
reliefs and benefits, 25.92
social enterprises, 65.2
Social investment tax relief (SITR)
Finance Acts 2017 summary, 73.1
Social Security Departments
information disclosures by HMRC to, 31.2
Societas Co-operative Europaea (SCE), 14.16
mergers to form, 49.15
residence, 57.33
Societas Europaea (SE), 14.15
residence, 57.33
mergers to form, 49.15
Sovereigns, 25.4
Spacecraft/stations, 59.4
Special measures regime (large businesses), 14.19
Special reliefs, 13.7
losses, *see* Losses
Special reserve funds
Lloyd's underwriters, 69.2
Special withholding tax
double tax relief for, 21.10
Split year treatment
statutory residence tests, 57.18–57.27
Sportsmen, non-UK resident
information disclosures by HMRC to, 31.2
Spouses, *see* Married persons
Standard cases, First-tier Tribunal, 5.17
Standardised tax products
disclosure of tax avoidance schemes, 20.2

Statements of Practice, HMRC, 35.1–35.2
Statutory residence tests, *see* Residence
Sterling
accounts not in, 14.14
currency other than, 7.2, 25.5, 25.8
debt owed by banks not in, 7.3, 25.5
Stock, *see* Shares and securities; Trading stock
Stock dividends, 63.10
Stock exchanges, recognised, 7.7, 8.2, 63.30
Stock lending, 63.25
Stockbrokers, returns by, 58.25
Stop notices
high-risk promoters tax avoidance disclosure regime, 20.9
Striking out cases
First-tier Tribunal, 5.13
Upper Tribunal, 5.26
Switzerland, tax collection agreement with, 49.22
Sub-fund settlements, 62.12
annual exemptions, 62.8
time limits, 67.3
Sub-leases, *see* Leases
Subsidiaries
see also Groups of companies
75%, 29.2, 29.7
effective 51%, 29.2, 29.7
issuing companies becoming, corporate venturing schemes, 18.23
property managing, enterprise investment scheme requirement, 23.5
qualifying
corporate venturing schemes requirement, 18.6
enterprise investment scheme, 23.6
social investment relief, 65.32
venture capital trusts, 71.4
qualifying 90%, enterprise investment scheme, 23.7
social enterprise condition, 65.22
Subsidiary buildings
private residences, 53.6
Substantial donors
charities' payments to, 11.5
Substantial holding rule
qualified investor schemes, 70.9
Substantial shareholdings of companies, 66.1
anti-avoidance, 66.7
definitions, 66.2
exemptions, 25.38
assets related to shares, 66.4
degrouping charges, 29.9
Substantial shareholdings of companies, – *cont.*
exemptions, – *cont.*
Finance Acts 2017 summary, 73.1
main conditions previously met, 66.5
qualifying institutional investors, 66.6
shares, 66.3
FOREX matching rules, 66.22
furnished holiday accommodation, 26.2
hold-over relief, interaction with, 36.8, 66.21
investee company conditions, 66.13, 66.13
investing company conditions, 66.11, 66.11
joint venture companies, 66.17
miscellaneous, 66.24, 66.24
negligible value assets, 66.19
reorganisations etc., 66.14–66.16
involving qualifying corporate bond, 66.20
'substantial shareholding', meaning of, 66.8
holding period, 66.9
Suckler cow premium quotas, 59.4
Sufficiency of hours
statutory residence tests, 57.9
Sufficient ties tests, 57.11–57.17
Superannuation funds, 25.3
Surcharges, 42.6, 42.9
Surrender of leases
new leases after, 41.22
Surrender of rights, 10.2
Swaps
property-based total return, 15.10
Syndicate capacity, *see* Underwriters at Lloyd's

T

Tainted donations, 11.11
Takeovers, 14.11, 63.5
anti-avoidance, 4.15
building societies, 63.27
Tangible movable property
see also Chattels
exemption, 25.4
location, 7.3
losses, 25.4
Taper relief, 25.93
Tax accountants
see also Tax agents

Tax accountants – *cont.*
documents to be produced by, 34.12
Tax accounting arrangements of large companies, 14.17
Tax advantages
losses, arrangements to secure, 44.7
relevant, serial avoiders regime, 4.35
Tax advisers
client communications of, 34.5
high-risk promoters tax avoidance disclosure regime, 20.14
Tax agents
dishonest conduct by, 31.5, 34.11, 52.19
working papers, investigatory powers, 34.2, 34.11
Tax arbitrage notices, 4.20
Tax avoidance
see also Anti-avoidance
abusive arrangements, 52.21
courts' approach, 4.2
defeated, enablers of, penalties, 52.21
disclosure of schemes, *see* Disclosure of tax avoidance schemes
not permitted requirements
corporate venturing schemes, 18.8
enterprise investment scheme, 23.3, 23.4
Tax Bulletin, HMRC, 32.3
Tax Case Digest, 74.1
Tax credits
income tax and capital gains tax, 21.8
Tax deposit certificates, 51.11
Tax enforcement agreements, 51.32
Tax evasion
failure to prevent facilitation of, penalties, 52.40
offshore
criminal offence, 52.40
enabling, 52.20
Tax information
disclosure, criminal offence of, 31.6
exchange agreements, 31.2
Taxable amounts, 2.6
Tax defaulters
publication of details, 31.3
Tax losses
selling, time limits, 67.9
Tax mitigation
courts' approach, 4.2
Tax over-repaid
time limits, 67.2
Tax-related penalties, 52.2, 52.16, 52.18
Tax strategy publication by large businesses, 14.18
penalties for failure to comply, 52.30
Taxable amounts
calculation, remittance basis, 55.2
Taxpayers
publishing details, serial avoiders regime, 4.40
Taxpayer's Charter, 30.7
Temporary non-residence, 49.5
Tenant farmers, milk quota, 7.9
Terminal losses
mineral royalties
Territorial sea-bed
exploration and exploitation rights, 49.19
Theatre backers (angels)
losses, 44.9
Third parties
employment income provided through, disclosure of tax avoidance schemes, 20.2
joinder in appeals, 5.4
recovery of tax from, 51.24
Threshold conditions
high-risk promoters tax avoidance disclosure regime, 20.9
Time apportionment
assets held on 6 April 1965, valuation, 8.7
assets held on 31 March 1982, pre-6 April 1965 gains and losses, 9.10
NRCGT disposals, computation of gains and losses, 41.30
Time limits, 67.1, 68.1
annual exempt amounts, use of, 67.9
appeals, *See* Appeals
assessments, raising of, 6.13–6.15
assets held on 31 March 1982, re-basing elections, 9.3, 9.11
assets of negligible value, claim, 44.11
claims, 13.5
bed and breakfasting, 67.9
capital gains tax, payment, 51.2
chargeability to tax, notification of, 52.3, 58.19
claims, 13.3, 13.5, 44.11
coming within charge to corporation tax, notification of, 58.19
companies ceasing to be UK resident, 49.17
compulsory acquisition of land, relief, 41.12
controlled foreign company reliefs, 49.9
corporate venturing scheme, *see* Corporate venturing scheme
corporation tax, payments, 51.4
correction of returns, 58.7
death
disclaimer after, 19.8

Time limits, – *cont.*
death – *cont.*
family arrangement after, election, 19.8
deceased persons, assessment, 6.13, 6.15
deferred charges on gains before 31 March 1982, 9.11
delayed remittance of overseas gains, 49.6
determinations, tax payable on, 42.5
domicile, appeal, 57.35
enquiries into returns, 58.9
enterprise investment scheme
deferral relief, 23.15, 23.18
income tax relief, 23.11
error or mistake claims, 13.8
fixed dates, 67.1–67.9
four-year, 67.8
fraudulent conduct, 6.15
furnished holiday accommodation, averaging, 26.1
group companies, liabilities after leaving groups, 51.26
guarantees of qualifying loans to traders, losses on, 44.12
HMRC discretion, 67.1
holiday accommodation, averaging, 26.1
incorporation relief, disapplication of, 37.3
individuals' trading losses set off against gains, 44.21
instalments, payment of tax by, 51.5
judicial reviews, 5.35
land
compulsory acquisition, relief, 41.12
part disposals, 41.9
late assessments, claims following, 13.5
Lloyd's underwriters for claims, 69.2
loss relief
corporate venturing scheme, 18.19
guarantees of qualifying loans to traders, 44.12
negligible value assets, 44.11
pre-entry losses, groups, 29.20
qualifying loans to traders, 44.12–44.13
qualifying shares in subscribing investment companies, 44.18
qualifying shares in unlisted trading companies, 44.15
settlor gains, against, 44.2
trading losses set off against non-corporate persons' gains, 44.21
negligent conduct, 6.15
negligible value assets, claim, 44.11
one year or less, 67.2, 68.2
one year ten-month, 67.3
ordinary residence, appeal, 57.35
over-repaid tax, recovery, 51.31

Time limits, – *cont.*
overseas companies, distribution of gains, 49.7
overseas gains, delayed remittance, 49.6
payment of tax
capital gains tax, 51.2
companies, 51.4
corporation tax, 51.4
instalments, by, 51.5
persons other than companies, 51.5
personal representatives, assessments on, 67.7
penalty proceedings, 52.38
post-cessation expenditure, 44.21
post-employment deductions, 44.21
postponement of tax, 42.4
pre-entry losses, groups, 29.20
private residence relief, election for main residence, 53.10
qualifying loans to traders, losses on, 44.12, 44.13
qualifying shares
subscribing in investment company, loss relief, 44.18
unlisted trading companies, loss relief, 44.15
quoted shares, election for 6 April 1965 values, 8.3
re-basing at 31 March 1982, 9.3
residence, appeal, 57.35
returns
companies, 58.19
individuals, 58.3
partnerships, 58.16
rollover relief, *see* Rollover relief
self-assessment, 58.6
shares
qualifying, loss relief, 44.15, 44.18
quoted, election for 6 April 1965, values, 8.3
same day acquisitions of, 64.2
six-year, 68.5
tax-loss selling, 67.9
tax over-repaid, recovery, 51.31
three-year, 67.6, 68.4
three-year ten-month, 67.7
trading losses set off against non-corporate persons' gains, 44.21
trading stock, appropriation to, at cost, 16.9
two year, 67.3, 67.4, 68.3
two year ten-month, 67.5
unpaid corporation tax, recovery from third parties, 14.11, 51.26, 51.27
venture capital trust deferral relief, 71.12

Time of disposal, 10.2, 16.4
'Time to pay' arrangements, 51.6, 51.8
Tonnage tax
exempt assets, 25.17
rollover relief, 59.2, 59.3
Trademarks
location, 7.3
Trade unions
exempt organisations, 25.63
Traded options, 7.7
Traders
loans, to, 67.4
Trades
acquisition of, social investment relief, 65.41
assets used for and taxed on cash basis, 25.20
carrying on, social enterprise condition, 65.29
cash basis, Finance Acts 2017 summary, 73.1
enterprise investment scheme acquisition, 23.12
land transactions in nature of, 41.3
qualifying
enterprise investment scheme, 23.9
seed enterprise investment scheme, 60.31
social investment relief, 65.31
venture capital trusts, 71.4
seed enterprise investment scheme acquisition, 60.38
Trading
employee ownership trusts requirement, 63.15
enterprise investment scheme requirement, 23.5
social enterprise condition, 65.26
venture capital trusts requirement, 71.4
Trading activities
requirement, corporate venturing schemes, 18.6
Trading assets
acquisition of, social investment relief, 65.41
enterprise investment scheme acquisition, 23.12
Trading losses
companies, 14.6
individuals, 44.21
relief for, time limits, 67.3
Trading stock
appropriations to and from, 16.9
Trading stock – *cont.*
appropriations to and from, – *cont.*
elections, Finance Acts 2017 summary, 73.1
time limits, 67.3
intra-group transfers, 29.4
losses, compensation for, 10.2
Transfers of businesses to companies
incorporation relief, *see* Incorporation relief
Transfers of value
settlements, 62.21
Transparent entities
disapplication of Mergers Directive reliefs, 49.16
Transparent funds, 49.11
Treasury shares, 63.5
Tribunals, *see* First-tier tribunal; Upper tribunal
Trust for sale, 62.3
Trust funds
Lloyd's underwriters, 69.2, 69.8
Trustees
see also Offshore settlements; Settled property; Settlements
annual exemption, 62.8, 62.9
assessment, 6.6, 62.11
bare, 12.2, 25.44, 62.3
borrowing
offshore settlements, 48.22, 48.23–48.28
settled property, 62.21
connected persons, 17.2
corporate, administration of estates on death, 19.12–19.13
disposal by, investors' relief, 40.3
dual residence, 48.2, 48.16
hold-over reliefs, restriction on, 36.8, 36.11, 36.12
enterprise investment scheme deferral relief, 23.16
overseas residents, 36.8, 36.10, 48.2–48.3
rates of tax, 62.7
relevant, 62.11
residence, 48.1
resident and non-resident in same year, 48.3
returns by, 58.3
self-assessment, 62.11
single person, treated as, 48.1, 62.6
Trusts, *see* Settlements

U

UK Film Council
information disclosures by HMRC to, 31.2
UK ties
statutory residence tests, 57.12–57.17
Umbrella schemes/companies,
authorised unit trusts, 70.3
open-ended investment companies, 70.8
Unapproved share options, 22.5
assignment, release or abandonment, 22.7
exercise, 22.6
Unascertainable consideration
loss on right to. time limits, 67.3
NRCGT disposals, computation of gains and losses, 41.30
Unauthorised unit trusts, 70.6
Unco-operative large businesses, 14.19
Underwriters at Lloyd's
ancillary trust funds, 69.2
assessment, basis of, 69.2
bespoke capacity, 69.6
corporate, 69.3
conversion to, 69.6, 69.8
individual, 69.2
members' agent pooling arrangements (MAPAs)
CGT treatment, 69.7
rollover relief, 59.4, 69.7
overseas residents, 69.5
premium trust funds, 69.2
retirement relief, 69.6
rollover relief on conversion to corporate, 69.8
Scottish limited partnerships, 69.4
special reserve funds, 25.37, 69.2
syndicate capacity
members' agent pooling arrangements, 69.7
rollover relief, 59.4, 69.8
transactions in, 15.15, 69.6
time limits for claims etc., 69.2
trust funds, 69.2, 69.8
Unilateral relief, 21.4
Unincorporated companies
recovery of tax from officers, 51.25
Unindexed gains, 38.2
Unit trusts
accumulation units, 70.3
authorised, 70.3
exempt organisations, 25.64
exempt unit holders, for, 70.7
exemptions and reliefs, 25.64
held on 6 April 1965, 8.2–8.4
Unit trusts – *cont.*
monthly savings schemes, 70.3
umbrella schemes, 70.3
unauthorised, 70.6
United Kingdom
definition, 57.36
Unlisted securities
see also Unquoted securities
losses on, 44.15–44.18
Unmarried couples
transfers between, 46.5
Unpaid tax, *see* Late payment interest and penalties
Unquoted securities
see also Unlisted securities
distributions in liquidations, 63.12, 63.13
held at 6 April 1965, 8.7
identification rules, 8.9
market values, 45.4
valuations at 31 March 1982, 9.2, 9.6
Unquoted status
corporate venturing schemes requirement, 18.6
enterprise investment scheme requirement, 23.5
social enterprise condition, 65.20
venture capital trusts, 71.4
Unremittable overseas gains, 25.95, 49.6
relief for, time limits, 67.8
Upper rate gains, 2.1
Upper Tribunal
appeals, 5.8
decisions of First-tier Tribunal, against, 5.27, 5.28
decisions of Upper Tribunal, against, 5.32
case management, 5.25
cases transferred or referred from First-tier Tribunal, 5.29
composition, 5.11
consent orders, 5.31
costs, 5.33
decisions, 5.31–5.32
evidence, 5.30
failure to attend, 5.30
hearings, 5.30
mistakes in decisions, correction, 5.31
objective, 5.11
organisation of, 5.11
penalties proceedings, 52.35
representation, 5.25
rules, failure to comply, 5.26
setting aside decisions, 5.31
striking out cases, 5.26
transfer from First-tier Tribunal, 5.18

Upper Tribunal – *cont.*
withdrawal from cases, 5.25
witnesses, 5.30

V

Valour
decorations for, 25.6
Valuations
buildings held at 31 March 1982, 9.2
death 19.5, 39.2
freehold reversion, 45.6
hold-over relief, 36.4
land held at 31 March 1982, 9.2
market value, 45.1–45.7
NRCGT disposals, computation of gains and losses, obtaining, 41.30
post-transaction, 58.5, 58.19
reorganised share capital, 63.2
shares as consideration, 16.11
shares held at 31 March 1982, 9.2, 9.6
Value
extraction of, remittance basis rule, 55.4
investments, venture capital trusts, 71.3
received
investors, by,
investors' relief, 40.8
corporate venturing schemes, 18.11–18.13, 18.14
enterprise investment scheme, 23.17
seed enterprise investment scheme, 60.37
social investment relief, 65.39
shifting, 4.8–4.11, 41.23
transfers, *see* Transfers of value
Value added tax
interaction with other taxes, 39.3
Variation, deeds of, 19.8
VCT, *see* Venture capital trusts
Vehicles
relevant jobs on board, statutory residence tests, 57.10, 57.15
Venture capital trusts (VCT), 71.1
15% holding limit condition, 71.2
70% qualifying holdings condition, 71.2
approval
conditions, 71.2, 71.3
withdrawal, *see* withdrawal of approval *below*
carrying on qualifying activity requirement, 71.4
chargeable events, 71.12
conditions, 71.2

Venture capital trusts (VCT), – *cont.*
control and independence, 71.4
conversion of shares, 71.5
crystallisation of original gain, 71.12
deferral relief on reinvestment, 71.12
definition, 71.2
disposals, 71.11
distribution relief, 71.9
dividends and, 71.9
eligible shares, 71.7
enterprise investment scheme interaction with, 71.12
entrepreneurs' relief transitional relief for, 24.11
exemptions and reliefs, 25.39, 25.64
Finance Acts 2017 summary, 73.1
financial health requirement, 71.4
gains, 25.39
gross assets, 71.4
group companies becoming, 29.12
income retention condition, 71.2
informal clearance, 71.5
introduction, 71.1
investments
limits condition, 71.2
transferred from VCT-in-liquidation, 71.5
key points, 71.13
liquidation, investments transferred from VCT in, 71.5
listing condition, 71.2
maximum amount raised annually, 71.4
maximum qualifying investment requirement, 71.4
mergers, 71.3
nature of income condition, 71.2
no disqualifying arrangements, 71.4
no guaranteed loan requirement, 71.4
number of employees, 71.4
permanent establishment requirement, 71.4
permitted maximum, 71.11
postponement of original gain, 71.12
property managing subsidiaries, 71.4
proportion of eligible shares requirement, 71.4
qualifying disposals, 71.11
qualifying holdings, 71.4, 71.5
qualifying investments, 71.12
qualifying subsidiaries, 71.4
qualifying trades, 71.4
relevant company carrying on qualifying activities, 71.4
reliefs against capital gains tax, 71.10
assessable persons, 71.12

Venture capital trusts (VCT), – *cont.*
reliefs against capital gains tax, – *cont.*
chargeable event, 71.12
crystallisation of gain, 71.12
disposal, 71.11
identification of shares, 71.12
postponement of original gain, 71.12
reinvestment, 71.12
withdrawal, 71.10
reliefs against income tax
disposal of investments, 71.8
dividends, on, 71.9
introduction, 71.6
investments, 71.7
withdrawal, 71.8
reliefs and deferrals, 25.96
reconstructions, 14.11
reinvestment, 71.12
relevant investments, 71.4
reorganisations, 71.11
requirements, 71.4
residence status of claimants, 71.12
restructuring, 71.5
share identification, 71.8, 71.12
share pooling, 71.11
spending of money raised by SEIS, 71.4
supplementary provisions, 71.3
trading requirement, 71.4
unquoted status, 71.4
use of money raised, 71.4
value of investments, 71.3
winding up
generally, 71.3
issuing company, 71.5
withdrawal of approval, 71.3
capital gains tax relief, 71.10
income tax relief, 71.8
withdrawal of income tax relief, 71.8
Visiting forces
exempt organisations, 25.65
Visits abroad
residence 2012/13 and earlier, 57.31
Voluntary disclosures
tax avoidance schemes, 20.5, 20.14
Voluntary winding-up, 14.4
Vulnerable beneficiary settlements, 62.13

W

Wales
meaning, 57.36
taxpayers, 2.1
Warning notices
serial avoiders regime, 4.33
unco-operative large businesses, 14.19
Warranties, 16.13
shares and securities contingent liabilities, 63.5, 63.7
Wasting assets
ATED-related gains and losses and, 14.10
basic rule, 72.2
capital allowances, and, 72.2
chattels, as, 25.4, 72.2
expenditure, treatment, 72.2
futures, 72.3
introduction, 72.1
key points, 72.8
leases
land, 41.15
other than land, 72.4–72.6
leases of property other than land
duration, 72.4
generally, 72.4
premiums, 72.5
sub-leases granted out of short leases, 72.6
'life', 72.2
life interests, 72.7
machinery, 25.4, 72.2
meaning, 72.1
NRCGT disposals, computation of gains and losses, 41.32
options, 72.3
premiums for leases, 72.5
qualifying for capital allowances, 72.2
rollover relief, 59.9
types, 72.1
'useful life', 72.2
Wives, *see* Married persons
Will trusts
private residences, 53.11
Winding-up, *see* Liquidation
Wine, 25.4
Winnings
exempt gains and transactions, 25.21
Withdrawal reliefs
venture capital trusts, 71.8, 71.10
Withholding tax
tax collection agreement with Switzerland, 49.22
Witnesses
First-tier Tribunal, 5.19
Upper Tribunal, 5.30
Woodlands
exempt gains and transactions, 25.40
Work
location, statutory residence tests, 57.9

Work – *cont.*
statutory residence tests, 57.9
ties, statutory residence tests, 57.15
Works of art
exempt gains and transactions, 25.41

Y

Years of assessment, 1.1